THE CAMBRIDGE
BIOGRAPHICAL DICTIONARY

THE CAMBRIDGE
BIOGRAPHICAL
DICTIONARY

Edited by
DAVID CRYSTAL

CAMBRIDGE
UNIVERSITY PRESS

Published by the Press Syndicate of the University of Cambridge
The Pitt Building, Trumpington Street, Cambridge CB2 1RP
40 West 20th Street, New York, NY 10011–4211, USA
10 Stamford Road, Oakleigh, Melbourne 3166, Australia

© Cambridge University Press 1996

First published 1996

Typeset by Technical Applications Group, Cambridge University Press
Printed in Great Britain at the University Press, Cambridge

A catalogue record for this book is available from the British Library

Library of Congress cataloguing in publication data

The Cambridge biographical dictionary / edited by David Crystal
p.   cm.
ISBN 0-521-56780-7 (pbk.)
1. Biography–Dictionaries. I. Crystal, David, 1941–
CT103.C25 1996
920'.003–dc20 [B] 95-40299 CIP

ISBN 0 521 56780 7 paperback

Contents

Editor
David Crystal

Editorial Administration
Hilary Crystal

Editorial Assistant
Ann Rowlands

Database Compilation
Tony McNicholl
Esther Pritchard

The name 'Biographical Dictionary' has been used in many different ways. In some works, it permits an extended and discursive treatment of people's lives, much in the manner of an encyclopedia, extending to several columns of print. In the present book, the term is being used much more narrowly, as befits a 'concise' work. Entries are given a succinct treatment, identifying a 'core' of information which in some ways resembles the compressed approach to word meaning found in lexicography. The aim has been to anticipate the chief biographical questions which people ask, and to provide the briefest of answers. Most entries, as a consequence, are no more than 50 words.

Treatment

What is the equivalent of a dictionary entry, when applied to people? The entries in *The Cambridge Biographical Dictionary* contain the following core points:

• The **headword** consists of the person's full name, along with any titles, nicknames, changes of name, or other information about status.

• We give the **pronunciation** of the person's surname (and occasionally first name) where this is not readily deducible from the spelling.

• We give a person's **year of birth** and, where relevant, **year of death**. In some cases, only an approximate time-period can be given.

• We give a person's **place of birth** – a town or city, and the country in which it is located. (For details of these conventions, see p. vii.)

• We give the person's **nationality**, where this cannot be deduced from the birthplace. In particular, we always specify the country when we are identifying rulers, politicians, and statesmen or stateswomen (i.e. those who have held ministerial office).

• We give an indication of the person's chief **occupation** or **claim to fame**. Often this involves showing a kinship with other people listed in the book, and bold type is used to identify important relatives or associates. Many of these can be followed up through the system of cross references at the end of an entry.

• We give a short statement summarizing the person's **chief achievement** or illustrating his/her **area of expertise**, focusing on facts rather than evaluations. In most cases, the entry is restricted to a single explanatory sentence, indicating why the person is included in the book – though of course in many instances (such as major historical rulers) it is not possible to be quite so succinct.

• The entry sometimes contains **dictionary information**. For example, if a person's name has entered the language as a whole (e.g. by being given to a bird or geographical location), this information is included.

• If an entry refers to another person who is included in the book, this information is shown using a **cross-reference** at the end of the entry.

Coverage

There are over 15,000 personalities included in *The Cambridge Biographical Dictionary*. The entries all derive from its parent volume, *The Cambridge Biographical Encyclopedia*, plus a few recent additions, and thus the same general features of coverage are to be found:

• There has been a particular effort to ensure **internationalism** of coverage, especially in relation to the leading English-speaking countries.

• In addition to the expected coverage of major historical figures, we have paid proportionately more attention to **20th-century** personalities, especially in such areas as television, cinema, science, and popular music.

• We have tried to make progress in **resolving imbalances** in the genre, by increasing the coverage of women, African-Americans, the Aboriginal and Maori peoples, and other groups who have traditionally received less than their fair share of attention.

In common with the other books in the Cambridge family, I welcome feedback from readers which will enable the editorial team to improve its coverage or treatment in future editions.

DAVID CRYSTAL

How to use The Cambridge Biographical Dictionary

Headwords

• The order of entries follows the English alphabet, ignoring capital letters, accents, diacritics, or apostrophes.

• The ordering is letter by letter, ignoring all spaces between the words of compound names, eg **Lebrun, Albert** precedes **Le Brun, Charles**, which precedes **Le Carré, John**, which precedes **Lecky, William**.

• We list rulers chronologically, ordering them by country if their titles are the same, eg **William I** (of England) precedes **William I** (of Germany). Names of non-British rulers, saints, etc are Anglicized, with a cross-reference used in cases where a foreign name is widely known, eg **Wilhelm I >> William I** (of Germany).

• When many people have the same name (eg **John**), we list them in the order rulers, saints, popes, others. Rulers with an identifying country or byname (eg **John of Austria**, **John the Baptist**) appear after single-element names, following the letter-by-letter order of the constituent words (eg **John of Trevisa** precedes **John the Baptist**). People with compound names (eg **John Paul I**) follow all instances of single-element names. The aim of this system is to ensure that all Johns, for example, are grouped together, which means that there are occasional exceptions to the letter-by-letter convention (eg **John the Baptist** precedes **Johnson**).

• Parts of a person's name that are not generally used are enclosed in parentheses, eg **Disney, Walt(er Elias)**, **Wells, H(erbert) G(eorge)**. Parenthesized elements are ignored in deciding alphabetical sequence, eg **Smith, (Robert) Harvey** precedes **Smith, Henry**.

Spelling Conventions

• All surnames beginning with **St** are located under the spelling **Saint**.

• All surnames beginning with **Mac**, **Mc**, or **M'** are listed in order of the next letter, eg **McBey, James** precedes **MacBride, Maud**, which precedes **McBride, Willie John**, which precedes **MacBryde, Robert**.

• We transliterate names in non-Roman alphabets, and add a cross-reference in cases where confusion could arise because more than one transliteration system exists. Letter symbols from other languages which do not appear in the English alphabet (such as Polish ł) are given their nearest English equivalents. Chinese names are given in pin-yin. In the case of Arabic, we have not transliterated the alif and ain symbols. No accent is shown on French capital letters.

Entry conventions

• Birth places are usually cited with reference to the location of the present-day town and country, eg towns formerly in Prussia are now identified in Germany. Exceptions include those locations where there is no clear modern equivalent, such as towns in ancient Greece which no longer exist. In some cases, to avoid ambiguity, both former and present-day locations are given.

• If a birthplace is a capital city, the name of the country is not given (this includes the chief cities of the divisions of the UK: London, Cardiff, Edinburgh, and Belfast). If the birthplace is in England and Wales, it is followed by the name of the county only; if in Scotland, by the name of the region; if in Northern Ireland, by the name of the district; if in Australia, by the name of the state; if in Canada, by the name of the province; and if in the USA, by the name of the state, except in the case of New York City, using the abbreviations listed later. In all other cases, the name of a country always follows the name of a town. We also add Scotland after the regions Borders and Central, in view of the widespread use of these names in other geographical contexts.

• Bold-face type is used within an entry to identify an important relative, or to identify someone of special professional significance, such as a partner or collaborator.

Cross-references

• Cross-references are always to headwords in the dictionary, with a distinguishing parenthesis if required, eg **Charles I** (of England). We do not include personal titles (eg Baron) in the cross-reference, and we give a distinguishing first name or initial if there are several entries with the same surname, eg **>> Johnson, Lyndon B**. The cross-references selected are those which provide the most relevant further perspective to an entry. Other people mentioned in the text may also have entries in the dictionary.

• All cross-references are preceded by the symbol >>, and listed in alphabetical order. Where cross-references share a common element, they are conflated, being separated by /, eg **Catherine de'/ Cosimo de' / Lorenzo de' Medici.**

Pronunciation Guide

• We give a pronunciation whenever it is unpredictable from the spelling, or where there is a possibility that a reader might choose the wrong form. In foreign names, we give the foreign pronunciation, unless there is a well-known English version. In a few cases, where both forms are current, we give both.

• Bold type is used to show stressed or strongly accented syllables, eg **Xerxes** [**zerk**seez]. We do not usually show the stress in languages (such as French, Chinese, Japanese) which have a very different rhythmical system to English, and where it would be misleading to identify one of the syllables as most prominent. We make an exception in cases where there is a widely used or predictable English pronunciation, as in French names beginning with **la**, eg [la**toor**].

• No distinctive symbol is given to show an unstressed English vowel, as in the first and last [a] vowels of **Balenciaga** [balenthi**ah**ga].

• The symbol [(r)] is used to mark cases where an r in the spelling may or may not be pronounced, depending on the accent, eg **Barbarossa** [bah(r)ba**ro**sa]. Speakers who do not pronounce [r] in these places (such as those using Received Pronunciation in Britain) should ignore this symbol; those who do pronounce [r] (such as most Americans) should pay attention to it. This symbol is not used when the transcription of a sound already contains an [r] symbol, in such cases as [er], [eer], and [air].

SYMBOL	SOUND	SYMBOL	SOUND
a	**ha**t	ng	si**ng**
ah	**fa**ther	o	**ho**t
air	h**air**	oh	s**ou**l
aw	s**aw**	oo	s**oo**n
ay	s**ay**	ow	c**ow**
b	**b**ig	oy	b**oy**
ch	**ch**ip	p	**p**in
d	**d**ig	r	**r**ed
e	s**e**t	s	**s**et
ee	s**ee**	sh	**sh**ip
er	b**ir**d	t	**t**in
f	**f**ish	th	**th**in
g	**g**o	th	**th**is
h	**h**at	u	p**u**t
i	s**i**t	uh	c**u**p
iy	l**ie**	v	**v**an
j	**j**et	w	**w**ill
k	**k**it	y	**y**es
l	**l**ip	z	**z**oo
m	**m**an	zh	lei**s**ure
n	**n**ip		

NON-ENGLISH SOUNDS

ã	French n**an**tes
hl	Welsh **ll**an
ĩ	French S**ain**t
õ	French b**on**
kh	Scots lo**ch**, German i**ch**
oe	French s**oeu**r, German m**ö**glich
ü	French t**u**, German m**ü**de

Abbreviations

This listing contains all the abbreviations used in this book where the meaning is not explained within an individual entry. When a date appears in parentheses, the month is abbreviated to the first three letters, eg (3 Jan 1888).

AD	Anno Domini	ICI	Imperial Chemical Industries
BAFTA	British Academy of Film and Television Arts	IRA	Irish Republican Army
		Is	Islands
BBC	British Broadcasting Corporation	Ital	Italian
BC	Before Christ	ITN	Independent Television News
c.	circa (used with dates)	Jr	Junior
-c	century	KGB	*Komitet Gossudarstvennoi Bezopas-nosti* (Committee of State Security)
C	central		
CBS	Columbia Broadcasting System	km	kilometre(s)
CERN	*Conseil Européen pour la Recherche Nucleaire* (European Council for Nuclear Research)	L	Lake
		Lat	Latin
Chin	Chinese	lb	pound(s)
CIA	Central Intelligence Agency	LP	long-playing (record)
CIO	Congress of Industrial Organizations	Ltd	Limited
Co	Company	m	metre(s)
Co	County	MCC	Marylebone Cricket Club
d.	died	MD	Doctor of Medicine
Dan	Danish	MEP	Member of the European Parliament
DNA	deoxyribonucleic acid	MGM	Metro-Goldwyn-Mayer
DOS	Disk Operating System	mi	mile(s)
DSO	Distinguished Service Order	min	minute(s)
E	east(ern)	Mme	Madame
EC	European Community	MP	Member of Parliament
edn	edition	Mt	Mount
EDVAC	Electronic Discrete Variable Automatic Computer	Mts	Mountains
		N	north(ern)
EEC	European Economic Community	NASA	National Aeronautics and Space Administration
eg	*exempli gratia* (for example)		
EMI	Electrical and Musical Industries	NATO	North Atlantic Treaty Organization
ENIAC	Electronic Numerical Integrator and Calculator	NBA	National Basketball Association
		NBC	National Broadcasting Company
EOKA	National Organization of Cypriot Fighters (translation)	NE	northeast(ern)
		No	number
FA	Football Association	p	page
FBI	Federal Bureau of Investigation	PGA	Professional Golfers Association
fl.	flourished	PLO	Palestine Liberation Organization
Fr	French	R	River
ft	foot/feet	RAF	Royal Air Force
Ger	German	Rev	Reverend
h	hour	RNA	ribonucleic acid
ha	hectare	S	south(ern)
Heb	Hebrew	SAS	Scandinavian Airlines System
HMS	Her/His Majesty's Service/Ship	SE	southeast(ern)
hp	horsepower	SI	*Système Internationale* (International System)
I	Island		
IBM	International Business Machines	Snr	Senior

SS	(i) Saints, (ii) steamship, (iii) *Schutzstaffel* (Nazi elite guard)
St(s)	Saint(s)
SW	southwest(ern)
trans	translated/translation (of title)
TUC	Trades Union Congress
TV	television
UK	United Kingdom
UN	United Nations
UNESCO	United Nations Educational, Scientific and Cultural Organization
UNICEF	United Nations Children's Fund (formerly, United Nations International Children's Emergency Fund)
UNIVAC	Universal Automatic Computer
US(A)	United States (of America)
USS	United States Ship
USSR	Union of Soviet Socialist Republics
v.	versus
VC	Victoria Cross
vol(s)	volume(s)
W	west(ern)
WBA	World Boxing Association
WBC	World Boxing Council

STATES OF THE USA

AK	Alaska
AL	Alabama
AR	Arkansas
AZ	Arizona
CA	California
CO	Colorado
CT	Connecticut
DC	District of Columbia
DE	Delaware
FL	Florida
GA	Georgia
HI	Hawaii
IA	Iowa
ID	Idaho
IL	Illinois
IN	Indiana
KS	Kansas
KY	Kentucky
LA	Louisiana
MA	Massachusetts
MD	Maryland
ME	Maine
MI	Michigan
MN	Minnesota
MO	Missouri
MS	Mississippi
MT	Montana
NC	North Carolina
ND	North Dakota
NE	Nebraska
NH	New Hampshire
NJ	New Jersey
NM	New Mexico
NV	Nevada
NY	New York
OH	Ohio
OK	Oklahoma
OR	Oregon
PA	Pennsylvania
RI	Rhode Island
SC	South Carolina
SD	South Dakota
TN	Tennessee
TX	Texas
UT	Utah
VA	Virginia
VT	Vermont
WA	Washington
WI	Wisconsin
WV	West Virginia
WY	Wyoming

Aakjaer, Jeppe [awkyayr] (1866–1930) Writer, born in Aakjaer, Denmark. A leader of the 'Jutland movement' in Danish literature, his works include the novel *Children of Wrath* (trans, 1904) and the poem *Songs of the Rye* (trans, 1906).

Aalto, (Hugo Henrik) Alvar [awltoh] (1898–1976) Architect and furniture designer, born in Kuortane, Finland. The father of Modernism in Scandinavia, his style was based on irregular forms and the imaginative use of natural materials, as in the Finlandia concert hall, Helsinki.

Aaltonen, Wäinö (Valdemar) [ahltonen] (1894–1966) Sculptor, born in St Mårtens, Finland. His best-known works include a bust of Sibelius and a statue of Olympic runner Paavo Nurmi.

Aaron [airon] (15th–13th-c BC) Biblical patriarch, the elder brother of Moses. He and his sons were ordained as priests after the construction of the Ark of the Covenant, and he was confirmed as hereditary high priest by the miracle of his rod blossoming into an almond tree (hence various plants nicknamed 'Aaron's Rod'). >> Moses

Aaron, Hank [airon], popular name of **Henry Lewis Aaron**, nickname **Hammerin' Hank** (1934–) Baseball player, born in Mobile, AL. He set almost every batting record in his 23-season career with the Milwaukee Braves, Atlanta Braves, and Milwaukee Brewers, retiring in 1976 with a total of 755 home runs.

Aasen, Ivar (Andreas) [awsen] (1813–96) Philologist, born in Sunmøre, Norway. He created the 'national language' called *Landsmål*, which achieved recognition alongside the official Dano-Norwegian *Riksmål* ('language of the realm') in 1885.

Abakanowicz, Magdalena [abakanovich] (1930–) Artist, born in Falenty, near Warsaw. In the 1960s she achieved international recognition with her monumental abstract woven fibre installations called 'Abakans'.

Abalkin, Leonid Ivanovitch [abalkin] (1930–) Russian economist. He was a member of the former Supreme Soviet with responsibility for economic affairs, and his published works centre on the theoretical problems of political economy under socialism.

Abarbanel, Isaac ben Jehudah [abah(r)banel] (1437–1508) Jewish writer, born in Lisbon, whose works comprise commentaries on the Bible and philosophical treatises. His eldest son, **Juda Leon** (c.1460–1535), a doctor and philosopher, wrote *Philosophy of Love* (trans, 1535).

Abati, Niccolo dell' >> **Abbate, Niccolo dell'**

Abbado, Claudio [abahdoh] (1933–) Musical conductor, born in Milan, Italy. He was conductor and director of La Scala, Milan (1968–86), and principal conductor of the London Symphony Orchestra (1979–87) and of the Berlin Philharmonic Orchestra (from 1989).

Abbas I [abas], known as **Abbas the Great** (1571–1629) Shah of Persia (1585–1628), who won back lost territory from the Uzbeks, Ottomans, and the Great Mughal. His reign marked a peak of Persian artistic achievement.

Abbas (c.566–c.652) Ancestor of the Abbasid dynasty of the Islamic empire who ruled as caliphs of Baghdad (750–1258). Uncle of Mohammed, he was at first hostile to him, but ultimately became the chief promoter of Islam. >> Mohammed

Abbas, Ferhat [abas] (1899–1985) Algerian nationalist leader, born in Taher, Algeria. He joined the Front de Libération Nationale (FLN) and founded (1958) the Provisional Government of the Algerian Republic. After independence (1962) he became president of the National Constituent Assembly, but fell out of favour and was exiled.

Abbas Hilmi Pasha [abas hilmee] (1874–1943) The last khedive of Egypt (1892–1914), the son of Tewik Pasha. He resisted British influence, and sided with Turkey in 1914, and was deposed when the British made Egypt a protectorate. >> Tewfik Pasha

Abbas Pasha [abas pasha] (1813–54) Khedive of Egypt from 1848. A grandson of Mehemet Ali, he supported his grandfather's Syrian war, but later hindered the progress made under him, notably by blocking the construction of the Suez Canal. >> Mehemet Ali

Abbate, Niccolo dell' [abahtay], also spelled **Abati** (c.1512–71) Painter, born in Modena, Italy. He executed frescoes for the palace of Fontainebleau, Paris, few of which are extant.

Abbe, Cleveland [ahbuh] (1838–1916) Meteorologist, born in New York City. He wrote on the atmosphere and on climate, and introduced the US system of Standard Time.

Abbe, Ernst [ahbuh] (1840–1905) Physicist, born in Eisenach, Germany. Professor at the University of Jena, he designed high quality microscope lenses, and became a partner in the optical company of Carl Zeiss. >> Zeiss

Abbey, Edwin Austin (1852–1911) Painter, born in Philadelphia, PA. His work includes the panels of *The Quest of the Holy Grail* in Boston Public Library, and illustrations of the works of Shakespeare and Robert Herrick.

Abbot, C(harles) G(reely) (1872–1973) Astrophysicist, born in Wilton, NH. As director of the Astrophysical Observatory at the Smithsonian Institution (1907–44), he studied solar radiation, and later devised an apparatus for converting solar energy to power.

Abbot, George (1562–1633) Calvinist clergyman, born in Guildford, Surrey. He was Dean of Winchester (1600) and three times Vice-Chancellor of Oxford University (1600–5).

Abbott, Diane (Julie) (1953–) British Labour politician, born in London. After working in local government, she was elected to parliament in 1987, and became the first black woman MP.

Abbott, George (1887–95) Director, producer, and playwright, born in Forestville, NY. He established himself with *The Fall Guy* in 1925. He wrote or co-wrote numerous plays and musicals, notably *The Pajama Game* (1954), and won six Tony awards for his work as a director.

Abbott, Jacob (1803–79) Clergyman, born in Hallowell, ME, the father of Lyman Abbott. He founded Mount Vernon School for Girls in Boston (1829), and wrote *The Young Christian* (1832). >> Abbott, Lyman

Abbott, Lyman (1835–1922) Congregational clergyman and editor, born in Roxbury, MA. He edited a new periodical, *The Illustrated Christian Weekly* (1870–6), then joined Henry Ward Beecher at the *Christian Union*, replacing him as editor in 1881. >> Beecher, Henry Ward

Abbott and Costello Comedy film partners: **Bud Abbott**, originally **William A Abbott** (1896–1974), born in Asbury Park, NJ, and **Lou Costello**, originally **Louis Francis Cristillo** (1908–59), born in Paterson, NJ. They teamed up as a comedy double act, Costello playing the clown and Abbott his straight man, and made many successful comedy films, beginning with *Buck Privates* (1941).

Abd-ar-Rahman I [abderrahman] (731–88) Umayyad emir. He conquered most of Muslim Spain and founded the emirate of al-Andlus (756), with its capital at Córdoba.

Abd-ar-Rahman III [abderrahman] (891–961) Emir of Córdoba, who ruled from 912 and proclaimed himself caliph in 929. Under him the Umayyad emirate reached the peak of its power, extending its boundaries in successful campaigns against the Fatimids and the kings of Leon and Navarre.

Abd-el-Kader [abdulkader] (1807–83) Algerian hero, born in Mascara, Algiers. Elected emir by the tribes of Oran, he waged a long struggle against the French (1832–47) but was eventually crushed. A later crusade was defeated at Isly in 1844.

Abd-el-Krim [abdulkrim], nickname **the Wolf of the Rif Mountains** (1882–1963) Berber chief, born in Ajdir, Morocco. He led revolts in 1921 and 1924 against Spain and France, surrendered before their combined forces in 1926, and was exiled to Réunion, but later amnestied (1947).

Abdias >> **Obadiah**

Abd-ul-Hamid II [abdulhamid], nickname **The Great Assassin** (1842–1918) The last sultan of Turkey (1876–1909). He promulgated the first Ottoman constitution in 1876, but his cruel suppression of revolts in the Balkans led to wars with Russia (1877–8) and the Armenian massacres (1894–6), and he was deposed and exiled.

Abdul-Jabbar, Kareem [abdul jaber], originally **Lewis Ferdinand Alcindor**, known as **Lew Alcindor** (1947–) Basketball player, born in New York City. A 7 ft 2 in/2 m 5 cm centre, he spent most of his career with the Los Angeles Lakers, playing more National Basketball League games (1560) than any other player, and scoring more points, 38 387.

Abdullah, Sheikh Mohammed [abdula], nickname **The Lion of Kashmir** (1905–82) Kashmiri statesman, born in Soura, near Srinagar, Kashmir, India. A Muslim, he spearheaded the struggle for constitutional government against the (Hindu) Maharajah of Kashmir, and was imprisoned (1931, 1953–68), but in 1975 became chief minister.

Abdullah (ibn Hussein) [abdula ibn husayn] (1882–1951) First king of Jordan (1946–51), the grandfather of King Hussein. Emir of the British mandated territory of Transjordan in 1921, he became king when the mandate ended in 1946, but was assassinated. >> **Hussein**

Abd-ul-Medjid [abdulmejid] (1823–61) Sultan of Turkey from 1839. He continued the Westernizing reforms of Mahmut II (1785–1839) and in 1854 secured an alliance with Britain and France to resist Russian demands, thus precipitating the Crimea War (1854–6).

Abdul Rahman (Putra Alhaj), Tunku [abdul rahman] (1903–90) The first prime minister of Malaya (1957–63) and Malaysia (1963–70), born in Alor Star, Kedah, Malaya. In 1945 he founded the United Malay's National Organization, and as prime minister negotiated the formation of the Federation of Malaysia.

Abe, Kobo [ahbay] (1924–93) Writer, born in Tokyo. His predominant theme of alienation was explored in a series of works, his novels including *Inter Ice Age Four* (1971), *The Woman in the Dunes* (1965), and *Secret Rendezvous* (1980).

à Becket, Thomas >> **Becket, Thomas à**

Abegg, Richard [abeg] (1869–1910) Chemist, born in Gdańsk, Poland. His 'rule of eight' (1904) concerning the electric basis of linkages between atoms was an important stage in the development of modern valency theory.

Abel, Sir Frederick (Augustus) [aybel] (1827–1902) Scientist, born in London. A chemist in the war department (1854–88), he devised the *Abel tester* for determining the flash-point of petroleum. He was also the inventor (with Dewar) of cordite. >> **Dewar**

Abel [aybel] Biblical character, the brother of Cain and sec-

ond son of Adam and Eve. He is described as a shepherd, whose offering God accepts; but he was then murdered by Cain. >> **Adam and Eve**; **Cain**

Abel, John Jacob [aybel] (1857–1938) Biochemist, born in Cleveland, OH. In 1914 he showed that blood contains amino acids - a finding which led the way towards dialysis in the treatment of kidney disease. In 1926 he first crystallized insulin and showed it to be a protein.

Abel, Karl Friedrich [ahbel] (1725–87) Musician, born in Köthen, Germany. A noted composer of symphonies, and a virtuoso on the viola da gamba, he became chamber musician to Queen Charlotte of England, and promoted a series of London concerts with J C Bach. >> **Bach, J C**

Abel, Niels Henrik [ahbel] (1802–29) Mathematician, born in Finnøy, Norway. He developed the concept of elliptic functions independently of Jacobi, and the theory of Abelian integrals and functions became a central theme of later 19th-c analysis. >> **Jacobi, Carl Gustav**

Abelard, Peter [abelah(r)d] (1079–1142) Theologian, born near Nantes, France. A lecturer at Notre-Dame, he secretly married Héloïse, the 17-year-old niece of the canon Fulbert. Opposition to their marriage led Héloïse to enter a convent and Abelard to become a monk. He founded a monastic school, for many years defending his teaching against charges of heresy.

Abeles, Sir (Emil Herbert) Peter [ayblz] (1924–) Industrialist, born in Budapest. In 1949 he went to Sydney, where he founded Alltrans, which in 1967 merged with Thomas Nationwide Transport (TNT). In 1979, TNT and Rupert Murdoch's News Limited took control of Ansett Airlines, and he became joint managing director until 1992. >> **Murdoch, Rupert**

Abell, Kjeld [ahbel] (1901–61) Playwright, born in Denmark. Known for his innovative stage designs and effects, his plays include *The Melody That Got Lost* (trans, 1935) and *Silkeborg* (1946).

Abelson, Phillip H(auge) [ayblson] (1913–) Physical chemist, born in Tacoma, WA. In 1940 he helped discover neptunium, and from 1941 was involved in the atomic bomb project, developing diffusion methods for obtaining enriched uranium-235.

Abercrombie, Lascelles [aberkrombee] (1881–1938) Poet and critic, born in Ashton-upon-Mersey, Greater Manchester. His works include *The Idea of Great Poetry* (1925) and *Principles of Literary Criticism* (1932).

Abercrombie, Sir (Leslie) Patrick [aberkrombee] (1879–1957) British architect and pioneer of town planning in Britain, the brother of Lascelles Abercrombie. His major work was the replanning of London, as in the *Greater London Plan* (1944). >> **Abercrombie, Lascelles**

Abercromby, Sir Ralph [aberkrombee] (1734–1801) Soldier and hero of the Napoleonic Wars, born in Menstrie, Central, Scotland. He served in Europe in the Seven Years' War (1756–63), and led the successful amphibious operation against the French at Aboukir Bay (1801), but died in action.

Aberdare, Henry Austin Bruce, Baron [aberdair] (1815–95) British statesman, born in Duffryn, Mid Glamorgan. He became a Liberal MP (1837), and was home secretary under Gladstone (1873–4). >> **Gladstone**

Aberdeen, George Hamilton Gordon, 4th Earl of (1784–1860) British prime minister (1852–5), born in Edinburgh. He was foreign secretary (1828–30, 1841–6), then resigned over the repeal of the corn-laws. In 1852 he became prime minister of a popular coalition government, but vacillating policy during the Crimean War led to his resignation.

Aberhart, William [aberhah(r)t], nickname **Bible Bill** (1878–1943) Canadian politician, born in Huron Co, Ontario, Canada. In 1935 he formed his own Social Credit Party, and was provincial premier (1935–43). Founder of the Calgary Prophetic Bible Institute (1918), his evangelical style of public-speaking gave him his nickname.

Abernathy, Ralph D(avid) [abernathee] (1926–90) Baptist clergyman and civil rights activist, born in Linden, AL. A leading confidante of Martin Luther King, Jr, he was pastor of the West Hunter Street Baptist Church in Atlanta, GA (1961–90), and became King's chosen successor as head of the Southern Christian Leadership Conference (1968–77). >> King, Martin Luther

Abernethy, John [abernethee] (1764–1831) Surgeon, born in London. He was full surgeon to St Bartholomew's Hospital (1815–29), where he became known for his eccentric lectures and rudeness of manners.

Abington, Fanny, *née* **Frances Barton** (1737–1815) Actress, born in London. Her first stage appearance was at the Haymarket in 1755. Extremely versatile, she excelled in the parts of Shakespeare's heroines and in a variety of comedy roles.

Abney, Sir William (de Wiveleslie) [abnee] (1844–1920) Chemist and educationist, born in Derby, Derbyshire. Adviser (1903) to the Board of Education, he was noted for his research in photographic chemistry and colour photography.

Abraham, Abram, or **Ibrahiz** (after 2000 BC) Biblical character revered as the ancestor of Israel and of several other nations. According to Genesis he migrated with his family to the 'Promised Land' of Canaan, and lived to be 175 years old. At 100 years of age he is said to have had a son, Isaac, by his previously barren wife, Sarah (*Gen* 21). In Judaism, Isaac was seen as the fulfilment of the divine promises, although Abraham was ordered by God to sacrifice his heir at Moriah as a test of faith (*Gen* 22). He is traditionally regarded as the father of Judaism, Christianity, and Islam. >> Isaac; Ishmael; Sarah

Abraham, Sir Edward (Penley) (1913–) Biochemist, born in Southampton, Hampshire. He became professor of chemical pathology at Oxford (1964–80), and played a major role in early studies of the penicillins, especially of the cephalosporin antibiotics.

Abraham, William, nickname **Mabon** (1842–1922) Trade unionist and politician, born in Cwmavon, Gwent. A leading figure in the miners' union in South Wales, he became MP for the Rhondda district (1885–1920), devoting himself to mining legislation.

Abrahams, Peter (1919–) Novelist, born in Vrededorp, South Africa. Much of his work, produced in exile, dealt with the political struggles of black people, such as *Mine Boy* (1946), *This Island Now* (1966), and *The View from Coyaba* (1985).

Abrams, Creighton Williams [aybramz] (1914–74) US army general, born in Springfield, MA. He commanded a tank battalion in World War 2, served in the Korean War (1950–3), and commanded US forces in Vietnam (1968–72).

Absalom [absalom] (11th-c BC) Biblical character, the third son of King David of Israel in the Old Testament. He rebelled against his father and drove him from Jerusalem, but was killed by Joab. >> David

Absalon or **Axel** [absalon] (1128–1201) Danish clergyman and statesman, the founder of the city of Copenhagen. As chief minister to **Valdemar I** (1131–82) he led an army against the Wends in 1169, and extended Danish territories in the Baltic.

Abse, Dannie [absee] (1923–) Writer and physician, born in Cardiff. His literary output includes several volumes of poetry, the novel *Ash on a Young Man's Sleeve* (1954), and the autobiographical *A Strong Dose of Myself* (1983).

Abu al-Faraj [aboo alfaraj], also known as **Bar-Hebraeus** (1226–86) Syrian historian, born in Armenia. A master of Syriac, Arabic, and Greek, he was also learned in philosophy, theology, and medicine, and as Bishop of Aleppo

became an important figure among Monophysite Christians.

Abu al-Faraj al-Isfahani [aboo alfaraj alisfahahnee] (897–967) Arabic scholar and literary historian, born in Baghdad. His work, *Al-Aghani*, is a treasury of Arabic song and poetry.

Abu al-Hassan ibn al Haytham >> **Alhazen**

Abu-Bakr or **Abu-Bekr** [aboo baker] (c.573–634) Muslim caliph, born in Mecca, the father of Mohammed's wife, Aïshah. He became the prophet's most trusted follower, succeeded him as the first caliph (632), and began the compilation of the Koran. During his short reign he put down a revolt and initiated conquests. >> Aïshah; Mohammed

Abu Mashar >> **Albumazar**

Abu Nasr al-Farabi >> **al-Farabi, Mohammed**

Abu Nuwas [aboo noowas] (c.760–c.815) Poet of the Abbasid period. He was popular at the Baghdad court, and figures in the *Arabian Nights*. >> Abbas

Abu Tammam, Habib ibn Aus [aboo tamam] (807–c.850) Poet and literary historian, born near Damascus, Syria. He discovered a private library of desert poetry at Hamadhan, and from this compiled an anthology of early Arab poetry, the *Hamasu*.

Abzug, Bella [abzug], *née* **Savitzky**, nickname **Battling Bella** (1920–) Feminist, lawyer, and politician, born in New York City. A leading peace campaigner, she founded Women Strike for Peace (1961) and the National Women's Political Caucus. Winning a seat in Congress (1971), she championed welfare issues.

Accum, Friedrich [akuhm] (1769–1838) Chemist, born in Buckeburg, Germany. In 1793 he came to London, where he pioneered the introduction of gas lighting.

Achard, Franz (Karl) [ashah(r)] (1753–1821) Chemist, born in Berlin. Following Marggraf's discovery of sugar in beet, he perfected a process for its extraction, and in 1801 opened the first beet sugar factory, in Silesia. >> Marggraf

Achebe, Chinua [achaybay], originally **Albert Chinualumogo** (1930–) Novelist, born in Ogidi, Nigeria. Four novels written between 1958 (*Things Fall Apart*) and 1966 (*A Man of the People*) describe the tensions of pre- and postcolonial Nigerian society. After a period in politics and education, he wrote *Anthills of the Savannah* (1987). Heralded as a fresh voice in African literature, he has also written short stories, poetry, essays, and children's books.

Achenbach, Andreas [akhenbakh] (1815–1910) Painter, born in Kassel, Germany. His paintings of the North Sea coasts of Europe were influential in Germany, and he came to be regarded as the father of 19th-c German landscape painting.

Acheson, Dean (Gooderham) [achesn] (1893–1971) US secretary of state (1949–53) born in Middletown, CT. In the Truman administration he formulated the Truman Doctrine (1947), helped to establish the Marshall Plan (1947), and promoted the formation of NATO (1949). >> Truman

Acheson, Edward Goodrich [acheson] (1856–1931) Chemist, born in Washington, PA. In 1891 he developed the manufacture of silicon carbide (carborundum), and in 1896 devised a way of making lubricants based on colloidal graphite.

Ackerley, Joseph (Randolf) [akerlee] (1896–1967) Writer, born in Herne Hill, Kent. His works include *My Dog Tulip* (1956) and his only novel, *We Think the World of You* (1960).

Ackermann, Rudolph [akerman] (1764–1834) Art publisher, born in Saxony, Germany. He is said to have introduced lithography as a fine art into England, and in 1795 opened a print shop in London.

Ackroyd, Peter (1949–) Writer, born in London. He is

known chiefly for his biographical studies of Pound, T S Eliot, and Dickens, and for his fiction, including *The Last Days of Oscar Wilde* (1983), *Hawksmoor* (1985), and *First Light* (1989).

Acland, Sir Richard (Thomas Dyke) [akland] (1906–90) British politician. He broke with the Liberals to found, with J B Priestley, the Common Wealth Party (1942). He became a Labour MP in 1945, but resigned in 1955 over Labour support for Britain's nuclear defence policy. >> Priestley, J B

Aconzio, Jacopo [akontsioh], Lat **Jacobus Acontius** (c.1500–66) Engineer, courtier, and writer, born in Trent, Italy. He repudiated Roman Catholicism and went to England, where he wrote *Stratagemata Satanae* (1565), advocating toleration.

Acton (of Aldenham), John Emerich Edward Dalberg Acton, Baron (1834–1902) Historian, born in Naples, Italy, the grandson of Sir John Acton. A leading Liberal Roman Catholic in England, he opposed the doctrine of papal infallibility. He was founder editor of the *Cambridge Modern History.* >> Acton, Sir John

Acton, Sir John (Francis Edward) (1736–1811) British naval officer in the service of Tuscany and Naples, born in Besançon, France. He became prime minister of Naples under Ferdinand IV (reigned 1759–1806).

Adair, John [adair] (c.1655–?1722) Scots surveyor and cartographer. He did notable work in mapping Scotland, and in 1703 published *Description of the Sea-Coast and Islands of Scotland.*

Adair, John (Eric) [adair] (1934–) British leadership-development consultant. His action-centred leadership model states that a leader has to ensure that needs are met in three related areas – getting the task done, maintaining the team, and establishing the personal requirements of its members.

Adair, Red [adair], popular name of **Paul Adair** (1915–) Fire-fighting specialist, born in Houston, TX. Called in as a troubleshooter to deal with major oil fires, he attended the disaster on the Piper Alpha oil rig in the North Sea (1988), and the fires in Kuwait at the end of the Gulf War (1991).

Adalbert, St [adalbert] (?–981), feast day 20 June. Benedictine missionary. In 961 he was sent by Emperor Otto I at the request of St Olga, Princess of Kiev, to convert the Russians. He became the first Bishop of Magdeburg in 968. >> Olga; Otto I

Adalbert, St [adalbert], known as **the Apostle of the Prussians** (956–97), feast day 23 April. Missionary priest, born in Bohemia. The first native Bishop of Prague (982), he carried the Gospel to the Hungarians, the Poles, and then the Prussians, who murdered him. He was canonized in 999.

Adalbert [adalbert] (c.1000–72) German archbishop. In 1043 he became Archbishop of Bremen and Hamburg, and as papal legate to the North (1053) carried Christianity to the Wends.

Adam, Adolphe (Charles) [adã] (1803–56) Composer, born in Paris. The son of the pianist **Louis Adam** (1758–1848), he is chiefly remembered for the ballet *Giselle* (1841).

Adam, Auguste Villiers de L'Isle >> **Villiers de L'Isle Adam, (Philippe) Auguste (Mathias)**

Adam, James >> **Adam, Robert**

Adam, Juliette [adã], *née* **Lamber** (1836–1936) Writer, born in Verberie, France. Her salon became renowned for the gathering of wits, artists, and politicians. In 1879 she founded the *Nouvelle Revue*, and later published her *Mémoires* (1895–1905).

Adam, Louis >> **Adam, Adolphe-Charles**

Adam, Paul (Auguste Marie) [adã] (1862–1920) Writer, born in Paris. His novels include *Chair Molle* (1885) and *La*

Force (1899), and he co-founded *Symboliste* and other French literary periodicals.

Adam, Robert (1728–92) Architect, born in Kirkcaldy, Fife. He established a practice in London in 1758, where he and his brother **James Adam** (1730–94) transformed the prevailing Palladian fashion in architecture by a series of romantically elegant variations on diverse classical originals, as in Home House, Portland Square, London. They also designed furniture and fittings.

Adam and Eve Biblical characters described in the Book of Genesis as the first man and woman created by God. Traditions describe their life in the garden of Eden, their disobedience and banishment, and the birth of their sons Cain, Abel, and Seth. Their fall into sin is portrayed as a temptation by the serpent. >> Abel; Cain

Adam de la Halle >> **Halle, Adam de la**

Adam of Bremen (?–c.1085) Ecclesiastical historian. He compiled a history of the Archbishopric of Hamburg (completed c.1075), the most important source of the history, geography, and politics of N Europe for the 8–11th-c.

Adamic, Louis [adamich] (1899–1951) Writer, born in Blato, Croatia. He became a US citizen in 1918, and began writing short stories in the early 1920s. His works include *Laughing in the Jungle* (1932) and *Dinner at the White House* (1946).

Adamnan, St [adamnan] (c.625–704), feast day 23 September. Monk, born in Co Donegal, Ireland. He joined the Columbian brotherhood of Iona and was chosen abbot in 679. His works include a revealing life of St Columba.

Adamov, Arthur [adahmof] (1908–70) Playwright, born in Kislovodsk, Russia. His early absurdist plays, such as *The Invasion* (trans, 1950), present the dislocations of a meaningless world. Later plays, such as *The Politics of Waste* (trans, 1967), show a transition to commitment.

Adams, Abigail, *née* **Smith** (1744–1818) Letter writer, born in Weymouth, MA. Her correspondence with her husband, John Adams (later US president), is valued as a contemporary source of social history during the early days of the republic. >> Adams, John

Adams, Ansel (Easton) (1902–84) Photographer, born in San Francisco, CA. Famous for his landscapes of W USA, he was an influential writer on photographic image quality, and was one of the founders of the f/64 Group (1932). >> Weston, Edward

Adams, Brooks (1848–1927) Geopolitical historian, born in Quincy, MA, the son of Charles Francis Adams. An impassioned racialist and prophet of American doom, his major work was *The Law of Civilization and Decay* (1896). >> Adams, Charles Francis

Adams, Charles Francis (1807–86) Diplomat and writer, born in Boston, MA, the son of John Quincy Adams. During the Civil War he was minister to Britain (1861–8), and in 1871–2 was one of the US arbitrators on the *Alabama* claims. >> Adams, John / John Quincy

Adams, Gerry, popular name of **Gerald Adams** (1948–) Northern Ireland politician, born in Belfast. In 1978 he became vice-president of Sinn Féin and later its president. He was elected to the UK parliament in 1983, but declined to take up his seat at Westminster. In 1994 he achieved national prominence as the chief contact with the IRA during the events leading to the IRA ceasefire.

Adams, Harriet S >> **Stratemeyer, Edward L**

Adams, Henry (Brooks) (1838–1918) Historian, born in Boston, MA, the son of Charles Francis Adams. Important works include *History of the United States during the Administrations of Jefferson and Madison* (9 vols, 1870–7), and a classic autobiography, *The Education of Henry Adams* (1907; Pulitzer, 1919). >> Adams, Charles Francis

Adams, Herbert Baxter (1850–1901) Historian, born in Shutesbury, MA. Appointed professor of history at the newly-formed Johns Hopkins University in 1876, his major work was the *Life and Writings of Jared Sparks* (1893).

Adams, John (1735-1826) US statesman and second president (1797-1801), born in Braintree (now Quincy), MA. Of strongly colonial sympathies, he led the protest against the Stamp Act (1765), and was 'the colossus of the debate' on the Declaration of Independence. He became the first US vice-president under Washington (1789); they were re-elected in 1792, and in 1796 Adams was chosen president by the Federalists. >> Adams, Abigail; Washington, George

Adams, John, alias **Alexander Smith** (c.1760-1829) British seaman, a ringleader in the mutiny on the *Bounty* in 1789. With other mutineers he founded a colony on Pitcairn I, and when eventually discovered (1809) he was the sole European survivor. >> Bligh

Adams, Sir John (1920-84) British nuclear physicist. He was a founder member of the Centre Européan pour la Recherche Nucléare (CERN) at Geneva, where he developed the 25 GeV proton synchroton (1954) and the 450 GeV super-proton-synchroton (1969-76). He was twice director-general at CERN.

Adams, John Bodkin (1899-1983) British doctor. A general practitioner in Eastbourne, he was tried and acquitted in 1957 for the murder of a patient, Edith Alice Morrell. While some believed he had killed for personal gain, others have argued that he practised a form of euthanasia.

Adams, John Couch (1819-92) Astronomer, born in Laneast, Cornwall. In 1845 he and Leverrier independently predicted the existence of Neptune by analyzing irregularities in the motion of Uranus. >> Leverrier

Adams, John Quincy (1767-1848) US statesman and sixth president (1825-9), born in Quincy, MA, the son of John and Abigail Adams. As secretary of state under Monroe, he negotiated with Spain the treaty for the acquisition of Florida, and was alleged to be the real author of the Monroe Doctrine. He was a noted promoter of anti-slavery views. >> Adams, John / Louisa; Monroe, James

Adams, Louisa (Catherine), *née* **Johnson** (1775-1852) US first lady (1825-9), born in London. In 1797 she married John Quincy Adams, and her many letters provide a revealing glimpse of her world. >> Adams, John Quincy

Adams, Richard (George) (1920-   ) Novelist, born in Berkshire. He came to prominence with his first novel, *Watership Down* (1972). Later novels include *Shardik* (1974) and *The Bureaucrats* (1985).

Adams, Roger (1889-1971) Chemist, born in Boston, MA. A founder of organic chemistry, he was influential in changing the emphasis of chemistry education in the USA from pure research towards a meshing of academic and industrial needs.

Adams, Samuel (1722-1803) American politician, born in Boston, MA, a cousin of President John Adams. He organized opposition to the Stamp Act (1765), was the chief agitator at the Boston Tea Party (1773), and was one of the signatories of the Declaration of Independence (1776). >> Adams, John

Adams, Walter (Sydney) (1876-1956) Astronomer, born in Antioch, Syria, of missionary parents. He joined the new Mt Wilson observatory in California (1904), where his pioneering work on stellar spectra led to the discovery of a spectroscopic method of measuring the velocities and distances of stars.

Adams, Will(iam) (1564-1620) Navigator, born in Gillingham, Kent. The first Englishman to visit Japan (1600), he was cast into prison as a pirate, but was freed after building two ships for Shogun Ieyasu, receiving a pension and the rank of samurai. >> Tokugawa

Adams, William (Bridges) (1797-1872) Engineer, born in Madeley, Staffordshire. He built some of the first steam rail-cars, and in 1847 patented the fish-plate which is now universally used for jointing rails.

Adamson, Joy (Friedericke Victoria), *née* **Gessner** (1910-80) Naturalist and writer, born in Austria. Living in Kenya with her third husband, British game warden **George Adamson** (1906-89), she is known for her series of books about the lioness Elsa, such as *Born Free* (1960) and *Elsa and Her Cubs* (1965). She was murdered in her home by tribesmen.

Adamson, Robert (1821-48) Chemist and photographic pioneer, born in Scotland. In 1843 he helped David Hill apply the calotype process of making photographic prints on silver chloride paper, producing some 2500 calotypes in all. >> Hill, David

Adanson, Michel [adãsõ] (1727-1806) Botanist, born in Aix-en-Provence, France. He was the first to develop a classification of plants into natural orders, before Linnaeus. The baobab genus of African trees, *Adansonia*, is named after him. >> Linnaeus

Addams, Charles Samuel (1912-88) Cartoonist, born in Westfield, NJ. A contributor to *The New Yorker* from 1935, he is known for the ghoulish group which was immortalized on television in the 1960s as *The Addams Family*.

Addams, Jane (1860-1935) Social reformer and feminist, born in Cedarville, IL. In 1899 she founded Hull House, Chicago, where she worked to secure social justice. In 1911 she founded the National Federation of Settlements, and was president of the Women's International League for Peace and Freedom (1919-35). She shared the Nobel Peace Prize in 1931. >> Kelley, Florence; Lathrop

Addington, Henry >> **Sidmouth, 1st Viscount**

Addinsell, Richard [adinsel] (1904-77) Composer, born in Oxford, Oxfordshire. He composed much film music, including the popular *Warsaw Concerto* for the film *Dangerous Moonlight* (1941).

Addison, Christopher, 1st Viscount (1869-1951) British statesman, born in Hogsthorpe, Lincolnshire. A Liberal MP, he became minister of munitions (1916), and Britain's first minister of health (1919). He resigned in 1921 and joined the Labour Party, becoming minister of agriculture in 1929.

Addison, Joseph (1672-1719) Essayist and politician, born in Milston, Wiltshire. He became an MP in 1708, while building a literary career with regular contributions to the *Tatler*, started by Richard Steele (1709), and the *Spectator* which they co-founded in 1711. In 1717 he was made secretary of state, but resigned through failing health. >> Steele, Richard

Addison, Thomas (1793-1860) Physician, born in Longbenton, Northumberland. His chief research was on the disease of the suprarenal capsules now known as *Addison's disease*, and into pernicious anaemia, *Addisonian anaemia*.

Adela, Princess [adayla] (c.1062-1137) Princess of England, the youngest daughter of William the Conqueror. In 1080 she married Stephen, Count of Blois, and had nine children. Her third son, Stephen, became King of England in her lifetime. >> Stephen; William I (of England)

Adelaide, Queen (1792-1849) British queen consort, the eldest daughter of George, Duke of Saxe-Coburg-Meiningen. In 1818 she married William, Duke of Clarence, who succeeded his brother, George IV, to the throne as William IV (1830-7). Their two children died in infancy. >> William IV

Adelaide, St, Ger **Adelheid** (931-99), feast day 16 December. Holy Roman Empress (from 962), a daughter of Rudolf II of Burgundy. After the death of her first husband, Lothair of Italy, she married Otto I of Germany (951), and exercised great influence as regent for her grandson **Otto III** (991-6). >> Otto I

Adenauer, Konrad [adenower] (1876-1967) German statesman, born in Cologne, Germany. He was president of the Prussian State Council (1920-33), and became the first chancellor of the Federal Republic of Germany (1949-63). His policy was to rebuild West Germany and establish closer post-war links with other European nations, with the ultimate aim of reunifying Germany.

Ader, Clément [adair] (1841-1926) Engineer and aviation pioneer, born in Muret, France. In 1890 he built a steam-powered bat-winged aeroplane, the *Eole*, which made the first powered take-off in history, but flew for only 50 m.

Adler, Alfred (1870-1937) Psychiatrist, born in Vienna. His *Study of Organ Inferiority and its Psychical Compensation* (trans, 1907) aroused great controversy, and led to one of the early schisms in psychoanalysis. His main contributions include the concept of the inferiority complex and his special treatment of neurosis as the exploitation of shock.

Adler, Larry, popular name of **Lawrence Cecil Adler** (1914-) Musician, born in Baltimore, MD. A self-taught virtuoso on the harmonica, he became a soloist with some of the world's leading symphony orchestras, and wrote music for several films, including *Genevieve* (1954).

Adler, Mortimer J(erome) (1902-) Philosopher and writer, born in New York City. He popularized the great ideas of Western civilization in such works as *Great Books of the Western World* (54 vols, 1954, revised 1990).

Adorno, Theodor (Wiesengrund) [adaw(r)noh] (1903-69) Social philosopher and musicologist, born in Frankfurt, Germany. A member of the movement known as the 'Frankfurt School', his philosophy is most fully presented in *Negative Dialects* (1966). His writings on music, mass-culture, and art include *Philosophy of Modern Music* (trans, 1949) and *Mahler* (1960).

Adrian IV, also **Hadrian,** originally **Nicholas Breakspear** (c.1100-59) The only Englishman to become pope (1154-9), born in Abbots Langley, Hertfordshire. He is said to have issued a controversial bull granting Ireland to Henry II. >> Henry II (of England)

Adrian VI, originally **Adrian Dedel** (1459-1523) The only Dutch pope (1522-3), born in Utrecht, The Netherlands. He attacked the sale of indulgences which had prompted Luther's first revolt. >> Luther

Adrian, Edgar Douglas, 1st Baron Adrian (1889-1977) Neurophysiologist, born in London. A founder of modern neurophysiology, he studied electrical impulses in the nervous system, and shared the 1932 Nobel Prize for Physiology or Medicine for his work on the function of neurones.

Æ >> **Russell, George William**

Ælfric [alfrik, alfrich], also known as **Ælfric Grammaticus** ('The Grammarian') (c.955-c.1020) Clergyman and writer, known for his use of the Anglo-Saxon vernacular. The first Abbot of Eynsham, his writings include a collection of homilies, a book of *Lives of the Saints*, a Latin-English glossary, and a Latin *Colloquy*.

Aelian, in full **Claudius Aelianus** (c.170-c.235) Greek rhetorician, born in Praeneste, near Rome. His works include *Historical Miscellanies* and *On the Characteristics of Animals* (trans titles).

Aelred of Rievaulx >> **Ailred of Rievaulx**

Aertsen, Pieter [airtsen] (1508/9-79) Painter, born in Amsterdam. The first of a family dynasty of painters, he is best known for paintings of everyday life and contemporary domestic interiors, often with religious reference.

Aeschines [eeskineez] (c.390 BC-?) Orator, second only to Demosthenes, born in Athens. Prominent in Athenian politics 348-330 BC, his advocacy of peace with Macedon brought him into bitter conflict with Demosthenes. Of his speeches, only three survive. >> Demosthenes

Aeschylus [eeskilus] (c.525-c.456 BC) Playwright, known as 'the father of Greek tragedy', born in Eleusis, near Athens. Of some 60 plays ascribed to him, only seven are extant, including the trilogy of the *Oresteia* (458): *Agamemnon, Choephori,* and *Eumenides.*

Aesop [eesop] (?6th-c BC) Legendary Greek fabulist, supposedly of Phrygia. The fables, anecdotes which use animals to make a moral point, were popularized by the Roman poet Phaedrus in the 1st-c AD, and rewritten by La Fontaine in 1668. >> La Fontaine; Phaedrus

Æthel- (Anglo-Saxon name) >> **Athel-, Ethel-**

Aëtius, Flavius [ayeetius] (c.390-454) Roman general, born in Moesia. He effectively ruled the Western Empire for Valentinian III (reigned 425-55), his main victory being the defeat of Attila the Hun at Châlons in 451. >> Attila

Afonso I >> **Alfonso I**

Africanus, Sextus Julius [afrikahnus] (c.160-c.240) Traveller and historian, born in Libya. He wrote *Chronologia*, a history of the world from the creation to AD 221.

Aga Khan III [ahga kahn], in full **Aga Sultan Sir Mohammed Shah** (1877-1957) Imam of the Ismaili sect of Muslims from 1885, born in Karachi, Pakistan. He worked for the British cause in both World Wars, and in 1937 was president of the League of Nations Assembly.

Aga Khan IV, Karim [ahga kahn] (1936-) Imam of the Ismaili sect of Muslims (from 1957), born in Geneva, the grandson of Aga Khan III. He married an English woman, Sarah Croker Poole, in 1969. >> Aga Khan III

Agassiz, Alexander (Emmanuel Rodolphe) [agasee] (1835-1910) Oceanographer, born in Neuchâtel, Switzerland, the son of Louis Agassiz. He became curator (1873-85) of Harvard's Museum of Comparative Zoology, founded by his father, made numerous oceanographic zoological expeditions, and refuted Darwin's ideas on atoll formation. >> Agassiz, Louis; Darwin, Charles

Agassiz, Jean Louis Rodolphe [agasee] (1807-73) Naturalist, born in Motier, Switzerland, the father of Alexander Agassiz. His *Studies of Glaciers* (trans, 1840) indicated the existence of ice ages in N Europe and the USA. In 1859 he founded a Museum of Comparative Zoology at Harvard, to which he gave his collections. >> Agassiz, Alexander

Agate, James (Evershed) [agayt] (1877-1947) Critic and writer, born in Manchester. He became drama critic for the *Sunday Times* (1923), and also wrote essays, novels, and an autobiography.

Agatha, St (?-251), feast day 5 February. Christian martyr from Catania, Sicily, who is said to have rejected the love of the Prefect Quintilianus, and suffered a cruel martyrdom in 251. She is the patron saint of Catania and of bell-founders, and is invoked against fire and lightning.

Agathocles [agathokleez] (361-289 BC) Tyrant of Syracuse, Sicily, from 317 BC. He fought the Carthaginians and invaded Tunisia, styling himself King of Sicily c.304 BC.

Agee, James [ayjee] (1909-55) Writer, born in Knoxville, TN. He is best known for *Let Us Now Praise Famous Men* (1941), in collaboration with photographer Walker Evans. His only novel was *A Death in the Family* (1957, Pulitzer). >> Evans, Walker

Agenbegyan, Abel (1932-) Economist, born in Tbilisi, Georgia. Personal economics adviser to Gorbachev, he helped develop the economic models which the Soviet government began to apply in the late 1980s. >> Gorbachev

Agesilaus [ajeesilayus] (444-360 BC) King of Sparta (399-360 BC). Initially a successful defender of Spartan interests, he ultimately brought about her downfall by precipitating the disastrous Battle of Leuctra against Thebes (371 BC).

Agnelli, Giovanni [agnelee] (1866-1945) Manufacturer, born in Piedmont, Italy. In 1899 he founded the Fiat automobile company (Fabbrica Italiana Automobili Torini).

Agnes, St (4th-c), feast day 21 January. Christian martyr, born in Rome. She is thought to have been killed c.304 when 13, during the persecutions of Diocletian, and is honoured as the patron saint of virgins. >> Diocletian

Agnes of Assisi, St (1197–1253) Christian saint, born in Assisi, Italy. She was the younger sister of St Clare, with whom she co-founded the order of the Poor Ladies of San Damiano in 1211. >> Clare, St

Agnesi, Maria Gaetana [anyayzee] (1718–99) Mathematician and scholar, born in Milan, Italy. A child prodigy, her mathematical textbook *Istituzioni analitiche* (1784) became famous throughout Italy. A curve, the *witch of Agnesi*, is named after her.

Agnew, Spiro T(heodore) [agnyoo] (1918–) US Republican vice-president (1969–73), born in Baltimore, MD. Nixon's running-mate in the 1968 election, he resigned in 1973, after an investigation into alleged tax violations. >> Nixon

Agnon, Shmuel Yosef, originally **Shmuel Josef Czaczkes** (1888–1970) Novelist, born in Buczacz, Poland. He wrote an epic trilogy of novels on Eastern Jewry in the early 20th-c, and in 1966 became the first Israeli to receive the Nobel Prize for Literature.

Agostini, Giacomo [agosteenee] (1944–) Motor-cyclist, born in Lovere, Italy. He won a record 15 world titles between 1966 and 1975, including the 500 cc title a record eight times (1966–72, 1975). He also won 10 Isle of Man TT Races (1966–75).

Agostino (di Duccio) [agosteenoh] (1418–81) Sculptor, born in Florence, Italy. His best work is the relief decoration for the Tempio Malatestiano church at Rimini.

Agoult, Marie de Flavigny, comtesse d' (Countess of) [agoo], pseudonym **Daniel Stern** (1805–76) Writer and socialite, born in Frankfurt, Germany. She held a famous salon in Paris, and wrote on numerous subjects. In 1827 she married Comte d'Agoult, but left him in 1834 for Liszt. >> Liszt

Agricola, Georgius [agrikola], Latin name of **Georg Bauer** (1494–1555) Mineralogist, born in Glauchau, Germany. He made the first scientific classification of minerals, and wrote *De re metallica* (1556) on the arts of mining and smelting.

Agricola, Gnaeus Julius [agrikola] (40–93) Roman statesman and soldier, born in Fréjus (Forum Julii). Rome's most successful governor in Britain (78–84), his fleet circumnavigated the coast, discovering Britain to be an island.

Agricola, Johann [agrikola], originally **Schneider** or **Schnitter**, also called **Magister Islebius** (1492–1566) Protestant reformer, born in Eisleben, Germany. He was sent to Frankfurt by Luther in 1525 to institute Protestant worship there, but later opposed him in the great Antinomian controversy. >> Luther

Agricola, Rudolphus [agrikola], originally **Roelof Huysmann** (1443–85) Humanist, born near Groningen, The Netherlands. He was the foremost scholar of the Renaissance 'new learning' in Germany; his writings greatly influenced Erasmus. >> Erasmus

Agrippa >> Herod Agrippa I and II

Agrippa, Marcus Vipsanius [agripa] (c.63–12 BC) Roman general and statesman. The right-hand man of Octavian (later, Emperor Augustus), he defeated Mark Antony at Actium in 31 BC. Through his marriage with Augustus' daughter, Julia, he gave Rome the Emperors Gaius (Caligula) and Nero. >> Antonius; Augustus; Julia

Agrippa von Nettesheim, Henricus Cornelius [agripa fon netes-hiym] (1486–1535) Occultist philosopher, born in Cologne, Germany. His major work was a treatise on magic, *On occult philosophy* (trans, 1510).

Agrippina [agripeena], known as **Agrippina the Elder** (c.14 BC–AD 33) Roman noblewoman, the grand-daughter of Emperor Augustus. She married Germanicus Caesar and was mother of Caligula and Agrippina (the Younger). After the suspicious death of Germanicus (AD 29), Emperor Tiberius banished her to the island of Pandateria, where she died of starvation. >> Agrippina (the Younger); Augustus; Caligula; Tiberius

Agrippina [agripeena], known as **Agrippina the Younger** (15–59) Roman noblewoman, the daughter of Agrippina (the Elder) and Germanicus, and mother of Emperor Nero. In 54 she ruthlessly engineered Nero's succession to the throne by poisoning his rivals and, supposedly, Emperor Claudius, her third husband. Jealous of her influence, Nero had her murdered. >> Agrippina (the Elder); Claudius; Nero

Aguesseau, Henri François d' [agesoh] (1668–1751) Jurist, born in Limoges, France. He was advocate general and attorney general to the Parlement of Paris, and between 1717 and 1750 was three times Chancellor of France under Louis XV. >> Louis XV

Aguinaldo, Emilio [agwinaldoh] (1870–1964) Filipino revolutionary, born near Cavite, Philippines. He led the rising against Spain in the Philippines (1896–8), then against the USA (1899–1901), but after capture took the oath of allegiance to America.

Ahab [ayhab] (9th-c BC) King of Israel (c.873–c.852 BC), the son of Omri. His reign was marked by battles against Syria, and a religious crisis when his wife Jezebel introduced worship of the Phoenician god, Baal, thus arousing the hostility of the prophet Elijah. >> Elijah; Jezebel

Ahidjo, Ahmadou [a-heejoh] (1924–89) Cameroonian president (1960–82), born in Garoua, Cameroon. Made prime minister in 1958, he led his country to independence in 1960, and was its first president.

Ahmad Shah Durani [ahmad shah jurahnee] (1724–73) Founder and first monarch of Afghanistan, a chieftain of the Abdali tribe. Elected king of the Afghan provinces in 1745, he established his capital at Kandahar, and in 1761 defeated the Marathas at the Battle of Panipat.

Ahmed Arabi [ahmed arabee], also known as **Arabi Pasha** (1839–1911) Egyptian soldier and nationalist leader. He led a rebellion against the khedive Tewfik Pasha in 1881, but the British intervened to protect their interests in the Suez Canal, and he was defeated at Tel-el-Kebir (1882). >> Tewfik Pasha

Ahmose I [ahmohs] (16th-c BC) Egyptian pharoah (ruled c.1570–1546 BC). He founded the 18th dynasty, drove the Hyksos from Egypt, and established control over Nubia.

Ahmose II [ahmohs] (6th-c BC) Egyptian pharoah (ruled 570–26 BC). A major achievement of his prosperous reign was the building of the temple of Isis at Memphis.

Aidan, St [aydn], known as the **Apostle of Northumbria** (?–651), feast day 31 August. A monk from the Celtic monastery on the island of Iona, born in Ireland. In 635 he founded the Northumbrian Church in England, becoming its first bishop and establishing the monastery at Lindisfarne. >> Oswald, St

Aiken, Conrad (Potter) [ayken] (1889–1973) Writer, born in Savannah, GA. His works include *Selected Poems* (1930, Pulitzer) and the autobiographical novel *Ushant* (1952).

Aiken, Howard (Hathaway) [ayken] (1900–73) Mathematician and computer engineer, born in Hoboken, NJ. He built the Automatic Sequence-Controlled Calculator, or Harvard Mark I, the world's first program-controlled calculator (1943). Mark II was built in 1947.

Ailey, Alvin [aylee] (1931–89) Dancer and choreographer, born in Rogers, TX. In 1958 he formed the Alvin Ailey American Dance Theater, a multi-racial modern dance ensemble.

Ailian, Dai (1916–) Dancer and choreographer, born in Trinidad. Working in China from 1940, she was instrumental in introducing the principles and study of Western ballet, and in 1959 co-founded the Central Ballet of China.

Ailly, Pierre d' [ayee], Lat **Petrus de Alliaco** (1350–1420) Theologian and philosopher, born in Compiègne, France. Appointed a cardinal in 1411, he was prominent in the election of Pope Martin V (1417), an event which ended the Great Schism.

Ailred of Rievaulx, St [aylred, reevoh], also **Aelred** or **Ethelred** (1109–66), feast days 12 January, 3 March. Chronicler, born in Hexham, Northumberland. A Cistercian monk at Rievaulx Abbey, he wrote an account of the battle at Northallerton (1138) between David I of Scotland and Stephen of England. >> David I; Stephen

Ainsworth, William Harrison [aynzwerth] (1805–82) Historical novelist, born in Manchester. He is best remembered for popularizing the story of Dick Turpin in *Rookwood* (1834) and the legend of Herne the Hunter in *Windsor Castle* (1843).

Ai Qing [iy ching] (1910–   ) Poet, born in Jinhua Co, China. He was an active propagandist for Communist-controlled literature, but in 1957 he was accused of revisionism, and in 1959 was exiled to Zinjiang. He began to publish again in 1978.

Airy, Sir George (Biddell) [airee] (1801–92) Astronomer and geophysicist, born in Alnwick, Northumberland. Greenwich Mean Time, measured using a telescope positioned in his observatory, became Britain's legal time in 1880. He held the position of astronomer royal (1835–81).

Aïshah or **Ayeshah** [aeesha] (c.613–78) The favourite of the nine wives of the prophet Mohammed, and daughter of Abu-Bakr. On Mohammed's death, she resisted Ali, the prophet's son-in-law, and secured the caliphate for her father. She opposed Ali again in 656, but was defeated and exiled. >> Abu-Bakr; Ali; Mohammed

Aitken, Sir John (William) Max(well) [aytken] (1910–85) Newspaper publisher, born in Montreal, Quebec, Canada, the son of Lord Beaverbrook. He joined his father in running Beaverbrook Newspapers (the *Daily Express* and the *Sunday Express*), and later became a leading ocean-racing skipper. >> Beaverbrook

Aitken, Robert Grant [aytken] (1864–1951) Astronomer, born in Jackson, CA. Director (1930–5) at Lick Observatory, CA, his discovery of more than 3000 double stars gained him the gold medal of the Royal Astronomical Society in 1932.

Akahito, Yamabe no [akaheetoh] (8th-c) Japanese poet. He is one of the 'twin stars' (with Hitomaro) of the great anthology of classical Japanese poetry known as the *Manyoshu* (Collection of a Myriad Leaves).

Akbar the Great [akber], in full **Jalal ud-Din Muhammad Akbar** (1542–1605) Mughal Emperor of India, born in Umarkot, Sind, India. He assumed power in 1560 and within a few years had gained control of the whole of India N of the Vindhya Mts. He promoted economic reforms, encouraged science and the arts, and pursued a tolerant religious policy. >> Jahangir

Akeley, Carl (Ethan) (1864–1926) and **Mary Lee Akeley** [ayklee] *née* **Jobe** Naturalists and explorers, born in Clarendon, NY and Tappan, OH, respectively. Carl Akeley worked as a taxidermist, perfecting new techniques for making large habitat groups of wild animals. His wife won international recognition for her conservation work in Africa.

à Kempis, Thomas >> Kempis, Thomas à

Aken, Jerome van >> Bosch, Hieronymus

Akenside, Mark [aykensiyd] (1721–70) Poet and physician, born in Newcastle upon Tyne, Tyne and Wear. His best-known work is *The Pleasures of Imagination* (1744). His haughty and pedantic manner was caricatured in Tobias Smollett's *Adventures of Peregrine Pickle* (1757).

Akhenaton [akenaton], also **Akh(e)naten** or **Amenhotep (Amenophis) IV** [amenhohtep] (14th-c BC) Egyptian king of the 18th dynasty. He renounced the old gods and intro-duced a monotheistic solar cult of the sun-disc (Aton). One of his wives was Nefertiti. >> Nefertiti; Tutankhamen

Akhmatova, Anna [akhmahtofa], pseudonym of **Anna Andreeyevna Gorenko** (1889–1966) Poet, born in Odessa, Ukraine. In 1910 she married Nicholas Gumilev, and with him started the Neoclassicist Acmeist movement. Her work was banned between 1922 and 1940, and again in 1946, but she was 'rehabilitated' in the 1950s. >> Gumilev

Akiba ben Joseph [akeeba ben johzef], also spelled **Akiva** (c.50–135) Rabbi and teacher in Palestine. He founded a rabbinical school at Jaffa, and was instrumental in reshaping the Mishnah. He supported the unsuccessful revolt of bar Kokhba, and was put to death by the Romans. >> bar Kokhba

Akihito [akiheetoh] (1933–   ) Emperor of Japan (1989–   ), the eldest son of Emperor Hirohito, born in Tokyo. In 1959 he became the first crown prince to marry a commoner, **Michiko Shoda** (1934–   ). They have three children. >> Showa Tenno

Akins, Zöe [aykinz] (1886–1958) Playwright, born in Humansville, MO. Her works include the dramatization of Edith Wharton's *The Old Maid* (1935, Pulitzer) and *The Greeks Had a Word for It* (1930).

Akiva ben Joseph >> Akiba ben Joseph

Aksakov, Sergei Timofeyevitch [aksahkof] (1791–1859) Novelist, born in Ufa, Russia. After a meeting with Gogol, his house became the centre of a Gogol cult. His works include *The Blizzard* (trans, 1834) and *Chronicles of a Russian Family* (trans, 1846–56).

Alacoque, St Marguerite Marie [alakok] (1647–90), feast day 17 October. French nun at Paray-le-Monial, and a member of the Visitation Order. The founder of the devotion to the Sacred Heart, she was canonized in 1920.

Alaia, Azzedine [aliya] Fashion designer, born in Tunis. He gave his first show in New York City (1982), and became known for his black leather-studded gauntlets, little black dresses, and use of zippers.

Alain-Fournier, Henri [ali foornyay], pseudonym of **Henri-Alban Fournier** (1886–1914) Writer, born in Sologne, France. He was killed at St Rémy in World War I, leaving a few short stories, and a novel *The Lost Domain* (trans, 1913), now considered a modern classic.

Alamán, Lucas [alaman] (1792–1853) Mexican statesman and historian, born in Guanajuanto, Mexico. An influential Conservative, he was chief minister (1829–32) under Bustamante, and founded the National Museum.

Alanbrooke (of Brookeborough), Alan Francis Brooke, 1st Viscount [alanbruk] (1883–1963) British field marshal, born in Bagnères-de-Bigorre, France. In World War 2 he commanded the 2nd corps of the British Expeditionary Force (1939–40), covering the evacuation from Dunkirk. He became Chief of the Imperial General Staff (1941–6), and was principal strategic adviser to Churchill. >> Churchill, Sir Winston

Alarcón (y Ariza), Pedro Antonio de [alah(r)hon] (1833–91) Writer, born in Guadix, Spain. He is best known for his novel *The Three-Cornered Hat* (trans, 1874) on which Manuel de Falla's ballet was based.

Alarcón (y Mendoza), Juan Ruiz de [alah(r)hon ee mendohtha] (c.1580–1639) Playwright, born in Taxco, Mexico. Now recognized as a leading playwright of the Golden Age of Spanish drama, among his character comedies is *The Suspect Truth* (trans, c.1619), the model for Corneille's *Le Menteur*. >> Corneille, Pierre

Alaric I [alarik] (c.370–410) King of the Visigoths from 395, the first Germanic conqueror of Rome, born in Dacia. He laid siege to Rome in 410, an event which marked the beginning of the decline of the Western Roman Empire. >> Honorius, Flavius; Stilicho

Alaric II [alarik] (450–507) King of the Visigoths (485–507), who reigned over Gaul S of the Loire, and over most of Spain. In 506 he issued a code of laws known as the Breviary of Alaric. An Arian Christian, he was killed by Clovis, King of the Franks. >> Clovis

Alas (y Ureña), Leopoldo [alas], pseudonym **Clarín** (1852–1901) Writer, lawyer, and critic, born in Zamora, Spain. He is best known for the short stories entitled *Moral Stories* (trans, 1895), and his novel *The Regent's Wife* (trans, 1885).

Alba, Duke of >> **Alva**

Alban, St [awlbn] (3rd-c), feast day 17 or 20 June. Roman soldier, venerated as the first British Christian martyr. When living in Verulamium (now St Albans), he was scourged and beheaded for protecting a Christian priest who had converted him.

Albani, Francesco [albahnee] (1578–1660) Painter of the Bolognese school, born in Bologna, Italy. He painted about 45 altarpieces, but most of his work depicts mythological or pastoral subjects.

al-Banna, Hassan [albana] (1906–49) Islamic fundamentalist, born in Mahmudiya, near Cairo. In 1928 he founded in Egypt the Society of Muslim Brothers. In 1948 the Egyptian prime minister was killed by a Brotherhood member, and in 1949 al-Banna was himself murdered.

Albany, Louisa Maximilienne Caroline, Countess of [awlbanee] (1752–1824) Wife of Charles Edward Stuart ('Bonnie Prince Charlie'). In 1772 she married the ageing Prince Charles in Florence, but the marriage was dissolved in 1784. >> Alfieri; Stuart, Charles

Albee, Edward (Franklin) [awlbee, albee] (1928–) Playwright, born near Washington, DC. His major works include *The Zoo Story* (1958), *The American Dream* (1960), and *Who's Afraid of Virginia Woolf?* (1962; filmed 1966). *A Delicate Balance* (1966) and *Seascape* (1975) won Pulitzer Prizes.

Albéniz, Isaac (Manuel Francisco) [albenith] (1860–1909) Composer and pianist, born in Camprodón, Spain. He became known for his picturesque piano works based on Spanish folk music, notably *Iberia* (1906–9).

Alberoni, Giulio [alberohnee] (1664–1752) Spanish statesman and cardinal, born in Firenzuola, Italy. As prime minister, he developed Spain's resources, but his aggressive foreign policy resulted in the destruction of the Spanish fleet. Dismissed in 1719, he returned to Italy.

Albers, Josef (1888–1976) Painter and designer, born in Bottrop, Germany. In 1933 he fled Nazi Germany to the USA. Interested chiefly in colour relationships, from 1950 he produced a series of abstract canvases, 'Homage to the Square'.

Albert, known as **the Bear** (c.1100–70) Count of Ballenstédt from 1123. He was the founder of the House of Ascania, which ruled in Brandenburg for 200 years.

Albert, known as **Albert the Bold** (1443–1500) Duke of Saxony, the son of Frederick the Gentle. He ruled jointly (1464–85) with his brother Ernest until, by the Treaty of Leipzig, they shared their inheritance and established the *Albertine* and *Ernestine* family lines.

Albert (1490–1568) Last grand master of the Teutonic Order (from 1511) and first duke of Prussia. He embraced the Reformation, and declared himself duke on the advice of Martin Luther. >> Luther

Albert, Prince, in full **Francis Albert Augustus Charles Emmanuel, Prince of Saxe-Coburg-Gotha** (1819–61) Prince Consort of Queen Victoria, born at Schloss Rosenau, near Coburg, Germany. In 1840 he married his cousin, an infatuated Queen Victoria, and became her chief adviser, first as Consort (1842), then as Prince Consort (1857). His death from typhoid occasioned a long period of seclusion by his widow, and the Albert Memorial was erected to his memory in 1871. >> Victoria

Albert I (1875–1934) King of the Belgians (1909–34), born in Brussels. At the outbreak of World War I, he led the Belgian army in a heroic resistance against German demands, and commanded the Belgian and French army in the final offensive on the Belgian coast in 1918.

Albert, Carl (Bert) (1908–) US politician, born in North McAlester, OK. A Democratic representative (1947–77), and majority leader (from 1962), he ensured the passage of President Johnson's Great Society legislation. >> Johnson, Lyndon B

Albert, Eugen (Francis Charles) d' [albair] (1864–1932) Pianist and composer, born in Glasgow, Strathclyde. Among his many works are several operas, notably *Tiefland* (1903).

Albert, Heinrich [albert] (1604–51) Composer, born in Lobenstein, Germany. He did much to develop *Lieder*, and composed many airs, songs, chorales, and hymn tunes.

Alberti, Domenico [albairtee] (c.1710–40) Composer, born in Venice, Italy. He is remembered as the inventor of the *Alberti bass*, common in 18th-c keyboard music.

Alberti, Leon Battista [albairtee] (1404–72) Architect, born in Genoa, Italy. His designs include the churches of S Francesco in Rimini and S Maria Novella in Florence. He was also skilled as a musician, painter, poet, and philosopher.

Albertus Magnus, St, Graf von (Count of) **Bollstädt,** known as **Doctor Universalis** ('Universal Doctor') (c.1200–80), feast day 15 November. Philosopher, bishop, and doctor of the Church, born in Lauingen, Germany. A Dominican, he helped to bring together theology and Aristotelianism, and had several famous pupils, notably Thomas Aquinas. He was canonized in 1931. >> Aquinas; Aristotle

Albin, Eleazar (?–1759) English naturalist and watercolourist, who published the first book on British birds with coloured plates. His works include *The History of Insects* (1720) and *A Natural History of British Birds* (3 vols, 1731–8).

Albinoni, Tomasso (Giovanni) [albinohnee] (1671–1751) Composer, born in Venice, Italy. He wrote 48 operas, and was one of the first to write concertos for solo violin.

Albinus >> **Alcuin**

Alboin [alboyn] (?–574) King of the Lombards in Pannonia from 561. He fought the Ostrogoths, and in 568 invaded Italy, making his capital at Pavia.

Albrechtsberger, Johann Georg [albrekhtsberger] (1736–1809) Composer and musical theorist, born in Klosterneuburg, Austria. He became court organist at Vienna and chapel master of St Stephen's. Hummel and Beethoven were among his pupils. >> Beethoven; Hummel

Albright, Ivan (Le Lorraine) (1897–1983) Painter, born in North Harvey, IL. During World War 1 he served as a medical draughtsman, where his observations of surgical operations influenced his later style, known as 'Magic Realism'.

Albright, W(illiam) F(oxwell) (1891–1971) Archaeologist and biblical scholar, born in Coquimbo, Chile, of US missionary parents. He became director of the American School of Oriental Research in Jerusalem (1921–9, 1933–6), and excavated many notable sites in Palestine.

Albumazar or **Abu-Mashar** [albumazah(r)] (787–885) Astronomer and astrologer, born in Balkh, Afghanistan. He lived mainly in Baghdad, where he was the leading astrologer of his day.

Albuquerque, Affonso d' [albookerkay], known as **Affonso the Great** (1453–1515) Portuguese viceroy of the Indies, born near Lisbon. He landed on the Malabar coast of India in 1502, conquered Goa (1510), and established the basis of the Portuguese East Indies.

Alcaeus [alseeus] (c.620–c.580 BC) Greek lyric poet, who lived at Mytilene on the island of Lesbos. He was the inventor of the *Alcaic* four-lined stanza; only fragments remain of his odes.

Alcamenes [al**kam**eneez] (5th-c BC) Greek sculptor, the pupil and rival of Phidias. A Roman copy of his 'Aphrodite' is in the Louvre. >> Phidias

Alciatus, Andrea Alciato [al**chah**tus] (1492–1550) Jurist, born in Milan, Italy. He was one of the leaders of legal humanism, and a correspondent of More and Erasmus. >> Erasmus; More, Thomas

Alcibiades [alsi**biy**adeez] (c.450–404 BC) Athenian statesman and general. A leader against the Spartans in the Peloponnesian War, he then sided with them against Athens, intrigued further with the Athenians and Persians, and was assassinated while in exile.

Alcindor, Lew >> **Abdul-Jabbar, Kareem**

Alcmaeon [alk**mee**on], (of Croton) (6th-c BC) Greek physician and philosopher from Croton, Italy. The first recorded anatomist, he was a pioneer of embryology through anatomical dissection.

Alcman (fl.620 BC) Greek lyric poet, probably born in Sardis, Lydia. The first to write erotic poetry, he composed in Doric dialect many songs, bridal hymns, and verses in praise of love and wine.

Alcock, Sir John William (1892–1919) Aviator, born in Manchester. On 14 June 1919, with Arthur Whitten Brown, he became the first to fly the Atlantic. The non-stop trip, from Newfoundland to Ireland, was made in a Vickers-Vimy biplane, and took 16 h 27 min. >> Brown, Arthur

Alcott, (Amos) Bronson [**awl**kot] (1799–1888) Teacher and philosopher, born near Wolcott, CT, the father of Louisa May Alcott. A member of the New England Transcendentalists, he was highly regarded as an educationist. >> Alcott, Louisa M

Alcott, Louisa M(ay) (1832–88) Writer, born in Germantown, PA. She achieved success with the children's classic, *Little Women* (1868), followed by *Good Wives* (1869), *An Old-Fashioned Girl* (1870), *Little Men* (1871), and *Jo's Boys* (1886). >> Alcott, Bronson

Alcuin [**alk**win], originally **Ealhwine**, Lat **Albinus** (c.737–804) Scholar, born in York, North Yorkshire. He joined Charlemagne's court at Aix-la-Chapelle (781) which, through his influence, became a school of culture for the Frankish empire, and inspired the Carolingian Renaissance. >> Charlemagne

Alda, Alan [**awl**da] (1936–) Actor, director, and writer, born in New York City. He is best known for the award-winning television series *M*A*S*H* (1972–83). His acerbic sense of humour is evident in such films as *Sweet Liberty* (1985) and *A New Life* (1988).

Alder, Kurt [**al**der] (1902–58) Organic chemist, born in Chorzow, Poland. With Otto Diels he discovered the Diels-Alder diene reaction (1928), valuable in organic synthesis. They shared the Nobel Prize for Chemistry in 1950. >> Diels

Aldhelm, St [**ald**helm], also spelled **Ealdhelm** (c.640–709), feast day 25 May. Anglo-Saxon scholar and clergyman. The first Abbot of Malmesbury (c.675), his works include treatises, letters, and verses, and he also built several churches and monasteries.

Aldington, Richard [**awl**dingtn], originally **Edward Godfree** (1892–1962) Writer, born in Hampshire. In 1913 he became editor of *The Egoist*, the Imagist periodical, and his works include the novel *Death of a Hero* (1929), biographies, and poetry. He married Hilda Doolittle in 1913 (divorced, 1937). >> Doolittle, Hilda

Aldiss, Brian (Wilson) [**awl**dis] (1925–) Writer, born in Dereham, Norfolk. Best known as a writer of science fiction, his novels include *Hothouse* (1962) and *The Saliva Tree* (1966). Other works include histories of science fiction and edited collections of short stories.

Aldred or **Ealdred** [**al**dred], also found as **Alred (?–1069)** Anglo-Saxon clergyman. He became Archbishop of York in 1060, crowned William I, and was the first English bishop to visit Jerusalem. >> William I (of England)

Aldrich, Nelson W(ilmarth) (1841–1915) US politician, born in Foster, RI. He served in the US Senate (1881–1911), and gained control of the Senate for the Republicans on domestic issues.

Aldrich, Thomas Bailey (1836–1907) Writer, born in Portsmouth, NH. His most successful work was an autobiographical novel, *The Story of a Bad Boy* (1870). He also wrote short stories and books of poetry.

Aldrin, Buzz [**awl**drin], popular name of **Edwin Eugene Aldrin** (1930–) Astronaut, born in Montclair, NJ. During the Gemini 12 Mission in 1966 he set a world record by walking in space for 5 h 37 min. He was the second man to set foot on the Moon in the Apollo 11 mission in 1969. >> Armstrong, Neil; Collins, Michael

Aldrovandi, Ulisse [aldro**van**dee, ool**ee**say] (1522–1605) Naturalist, born in Bologna, Italy. A professor at the University of Bologna, he established its botanical garden in 1567, and published many illustrated books on birds, fishes, and insects.

Aldus Manutius [**al**dus ma**noo**tius], Latin name of **Aldo Manucci** or **Manuzio** (c.1450–1515) Scholar and printer, born in Bassiano, Italy. He founded the Aldine Press, which produced the first printed editions of Greek and Roman classics, and was the first to use italics on a large scale. >> Campagnola, Giulio; Francia

Aleardi or **Aleardo, conte di** (Count of) [alee**ah**(r)**dee**] (1812–78) Italian patriot and poet, born in Verona, Italy. He took part in the rising against Austria in 1848, and entered the Italian parliament in 1866. He also wrote popular patriotic lyrics.

Aleichem, Sholem [a**lay**khem], also spelled **Sholom** or **Shalom**, pseudonym of **Solomon J Rabinowitz** (1859–1916) Writer, born in Pereyaslev, Ukraine. The pogroms of 1905 drove him to the USA, where he worked as a playwright for the Yiddish theatre in New York City. The musical *Fiddler on the Roof* is based on his stories.

Aleixandre, Vicente [alayk**sahn**dray] (1898–1984) Poet, born in Seville, Spain. He became established with a volume of collected poems in 1937, and he received the Nobel Prize for Literature in 1977.

Alekhine, Alexander Alexandrovich [ale**keen**] (1892–1946) Chess player, born in Moscow. He defeated Capablanca in 1927 to win the world championship, and held the title almost unbroken for nearly 20 years (1927–35, 1937–46). >> Capablanca

Alemán, Mateo [ale**man**] (1547–c.1614) Novelist, born in Seville, Spain. His most successful work was the picaresque novel, *The Spanish Rogue* (trans, 1599).

Alembert, Jean le Rond d' [al**abair**] (1717–83) Philosopher and mathematician, born in Paris. Until 1758 he was Diderot's principal collaborator on the *Encyclopédie*, of which he was the scientific editor, and wrote the *Discours préliminaire*, proclaiming the philosophy of the French Enlightenment. >> Diderot

Alessi, Galeazzo [a**lee**see] (1512–72) Architect, born in Perugia, Italy. He was known throughout Europe for his designs of palaces and churches in Genoa and elsewhere.

Alexander I (of Russia) (1777–1825) Tsar of Russia (1801–25), born in St Petersburg, the grandson of Catherine the Great. In 1805 Russia joined the coalition against Napoleon, but was forced to conclude the Treaty of Tilsit (1807) with France. When Napoleon broke the treaty by invading Russia in 1812, Alexander pursued the French back to Paris. A political reactionary and mystic in his later years, his mysterious death at Taganrog caused a succession crisis. >> Catherine the Great; Napoleon I

Alexander I (of Scotland) (c.1077–1124) King of Scots, the fifth son of Malcolm Canmore and Queen Margaret. In 1107 he succeeded to that part of the kingdom N of the Forth. He married Sibilla, daughter of Henry I of England. >> Henry I; Margaret (of Scotland) St

Alexander I (of Yugoslavia) (1888–1934) King of the Serbs, Croats, and Slovenes (1921–9), then King of Yugoslavia (1929–34), born in Cetinje, Yugoslavia, the second son of Peter I. He tried to unify Yugoslavia, but was assassinated. >> Peter I (of Serbia)

Alexander II (of Russia), known as **Alexander the Liberator** (1818–81) Tsar of Russia from 1855, born in St Petersburg, Russia, the son of Nicholas I. A determined reformer, the great achievement of his reign was the emancipation of the serfs in 1861 (hence his byname). Despite his liberal views, his government was harshly intolerant of peasant unrest, and he was assassinated. >> Nicholas I (of Russia)

Alexander II (of Scotland) (1198–1249) King of Scots (1214–49), born in Haddington, Lothian, the son of William I. He allied with the English barons against King John, later concluding a peace treaty with Henry III (1217), and marrying Henry's sister, Joan (1221).

Alexander III (of Russia) (1845–94) Tsar of Russia (1881–94), born in St Petersburg, Russia, the younger son of Alexander II. He consolidated Russia's hold on C Asia to the frontier of Afghanistan, provoking a crisis with Britain (1885). >> Alexander II (of Russia)

Alexander III (of Scotland) (1241–86) King of Scots (1249–86), the son of Alexander II. In 1251 he married **Margaret** (1240–75), the daughter of Henry III of England. After defeating Haakon IV of Norway at Largs (1263), he annexed the Hebrides and the Isle of Man. >> Alexander II (of Scotland)

Alexander III, originally **Orlando Bandinelli** (c.1105–81) Pope (1159–81), born in Siena, Italy. He was engaged in a struggle with Emperor Frederick I Barbarossa, who refused to recognize him, setting up antipopes until compelled to sign the Treaty of Venice in 1177. >> Frederick I

Alexander VI, originally **Rodrigo Borgia** (1431–1503) Pope (1492–1503), born in Játiva, Spain, the father of Cesare and Lucretia Borgia. He endeavoured to break the power of the Italian princes and to gain their possessions for his own family. During his pontificate, he apportioned the New World between Spain and Portugal. >> Borgia, Cesare / Lucretia

Alexander, Bill, popular name of **William Alexander** (1948–) Stage director, born in Hunstanton, Norfolk. He joined the Royal Shakespeare Company in 1977, and later became associate director there.

Alexander, Cecil Frances, *née* **Humphreys** (1818–95) Poet and hymn writer, born in Co Wicklow, Ireland. In 1848 she published *Hymns for Little Children*, which included such popular items as 'All Things Bright and Beautiful' and 'Once in Royal David's City'.

Alexander, Franz (Gabriel) (1891–1964) Psychoanalyst, born in Budapest. From 1932 he lived in the USA, where he founded the Chicago Institute for Psychoanalysis. His work on psychosomatic disorders was influential.

Alexander, Grover (Cleveland) (1887–1950) Baseball player, born in Elba, NE. A pitcher, he played for the Philadelphia Phillies (1911–17), Chicago Cubs (1918–26), and St Louis Cardinals (1926–9), sharing a record of 373 wins. >> Mathewson

Alexander, Jean (1925–) Actress, born in Liverpool, Merseyside. Between 1964 and 1987 she became a household name as the character Hilda Ogden in television's *Coronation Street*, for which she received a Best Performance Award in 1984.

Alexander, Samuel (1859–1938) Philosopher, born in Sydney, New South Wales, Australia. His growing concern for the situation of European Jewry led him to introduce Chaim Weizmann to Arthur James Balfour - a meeting

which led to the Balfour Declaration (1917). >> Balfour, Arthur; Weizmann

Alexander of Battenberg >> **Battenberg, Alexander of**

Alexander of Hales, known as **Doctor Irrefragabilis** ('Irrefutable Doctor') (c.1170–1245) English theologian and philosopher, born in Hales, Gloucestershire. A Franciscan, he is known chiefly from the major work ascribed to him, the *Summa theologica*.

Alexander (of Tunis), Sir Harold (Rupert Leofric George) Alexander, 1st Earl (1891–1969) British soldier, born in London. He served in Burma (1942), became commander-in-chief Middle East (1942–3) achieving a historic victory in his North African campaign, and was supreme allied commander in the Mediterranean.

Alexander of Tralles [**tra**leez] (6th-c) Greek physician, born in Tralles. He wrote a major work on pathology, the *Twelve Books on Medicine*, which was current for several centuries in Latin, Greek, and Arabic.

Alexander the Great (356–323 BC) King of Macedonia (336–323 BC), born at Pella, the son of Philip II. After crushing all opposition at home, he conquered Achaemenid Persia, defeating Darius III, taking Babylon, Persepolis, and other major cities, and founding the city of Alexandria. In India his exhausted army mutinied, and he died during the return journey. >> Philip II (of Macedon)

Alexander Nevski, St, also spelled **Nevsky** (c.1218–63), feast day 30 August or 23 November. Russian hero, prince of Novgorod, born in Vladimir, Russia. He received his surname from his victory over the Swedes on the R Neva in 1240, later defeating the Teutonic Knights in 1242. He was canonized by the Russian Orthodox Church in 1547.

Alexander Severus [se**ve**rus] (205–35) Roman emperor (221–35), the cousin and adopted son of Heliogabalus, whom he succeeded. Although successful against the Sassanid Ardashir I, he was a weak ruler and was murdered by mutinous troops. >> Ardashir I; Heliogabalus

Alexanderson, Ernst F(rederick) W(erner) (1878–1975) Electrical engineer and inventor, born in Uppsala, Sweden. Among his inventions were the *Alexanderson alternator* for transoceanic communication, a complete television system (1930), and a colour television receiver (1955).

Alexandra, Princess, the Hon Lady Ogilvy (1936–) Daughter of George, Duke of Kent, and Princess Marina of Greece. In 1963 she married Sir **Angus James Bruce Ogilvy** (1928–). They have a son, **James Robert Bruce** (1964–), who married Julia Rawlinson, and a daughter, **Marina Victoria Alexandra** (1966–). Marina married Paul Mowatt and they have a daughter, **Zenouska May** (1990–), and a son, **Christian Alexander** (1993–).

Alexandra, Queen (1844–1925) Consort of King Edward VII of Great Britain, the eldest daughter of King Christian IX of Denmark. She became known for her charity work, and in 1902 founded the Imperial (now Royal) Military Nursing Service. >> Edward VII

Alexandra Feodorovna [**fyod**orovna] (1872–1918) German princess, and Empress of Russia upon her marriage with Nicholas II (1894), born in Darmstadt, Germany. She came under the influence of Rasputin, and meddled disastrously in politics. She was later imprisoned with her husband and children at Yekaterinburg, where they were shot by Bolshevik revolutionaries. >> Nicholas II; Rasputin

Alexandrov, Pavel Sergeyevich [alek**sahn**drof] (1896–1982) Mathematician, born in Bogorodsk, Russia. The leader of the Soviet school of topologists, he developed many methods of combinatorial topology.

Alexey I Mihailovitch [alek**say**, mi**hiy**lovitch] (1629–76) Second Romanov tsar of Russia (1645–76). He waged war against Poland (1645–67), regaining Smolensk and Kiev.

By his second wife he was the father of Peter I. >> Peter I (of Russia)

Alexeyev, Mikhail Vasilevich [aleksayef] (1857–1918) Russian soldier. In World War I he was Chief of the Imperial General Staff (1915), directing the retreat from Warsaw. After the Revolution in 1917 he organized the volunteer army against the Bolsheviks.

Alexis [aleksis], in full **Alexey Petrovitch** (1690–1718) Prince, born in Moscow, the eldest son of Peter I. Having opposed the tsar's reforms, he was excluded from the succession, and died in prison. His son became tsar as Peter II (reigned 1727–30). >> Peter I (of Russia)

Alexius I Comnenus [komneenus] (1048–1118) Byzantine emperor (1081–1118), the founder of the Comnenian dynasty, born in Istanbul. He defeated the invading Normans of Sicily under Guiscard (1081–2) and aimed to re-establish Byzantine rule in Asia Minor, but his empire was invaded during the First Crusade (1096–1100). >> Guiscard

al-Farabi, Mohammed [al farahbee], also known as **Abu Nasr**, **Alfarabius**, and **Avennasar** (c.870–950) Islamic philosopher, born in Farab, Turkey. He published a utopian political philosophy, *The Perfect City*, much influenced by Plato's *Republic*, and came to be regarded as the first Islamic Neoplatonist. >> Plato

Alfieri, Vittorio, conte di (Count) [alfyayree] (1749–1803) Writer, a precursor of the Risorgimento, born in Asti, Italy. Among his best-known plays are *Cleopatra* (1775) and the tragedy *Saul*. His mistress was the Countess of Albany. >> Albany, Countess of

Alfonsín (Foulkes), Raul [alfonseen] (1927–) Argentinian president (1983–9), born in Chascomús, Argentina. He was responsible for bringing several leading military figures to trial for human rights abuses, and in 1986 was co-recipient of the Council of Europe's human rights prize.

Alfonso I or **Alfonso Henriques**, also spelled **Afonso** (c.1110–85) The earliest king of Portugal, born in Guimarães, Portugal. Wresting power from his mother in 1128, he defeated the Moors at Ourique (1139), and proclaimed himself king, taking Lisbon in 1147.

Alfonso III, known as **Alfonso the Great** (?–910) King of León, Asturias, and Galicia (866–910). He gained many victories over the Moors, and extended his territory to Portugal and Old Castile.

Alfonso X, nicknames **Alfonso the Astronomer** or **Alfonso the Wise** (1221–84) King of León and Castile (1252–84), born in Burgos, Spain. He captured Cadiz and Algarve from the Moors, thus uniting Murcia with Castile. He founded a Castilian national literature, and instituted a famous code of laws.

Alfonso XII (1857–85) King of Spain (1874–85), the son of Isabella II. In 1876 he suppressed the Carlists and drafted a new constitution. In 1879 he married **Maria Christina** (1858–1929), the daughter of Archduke Charles Ferdinand of Austria. >> Carlos, Don

Alfonso XIII (1886–1941) King of Spain (1886–1931), the posthumous son of Alfonso XII. In 1906 he married princess Ena, grand-daughter of Queen Victoria. After Spain voted for a republic (1931), he refused to abdicate, and died in exile. >> Alfonso XII

Alfred, known as **Alfred the Great** (849–99) King of Wessex (from 871), born in Wantage, Berkshire, the fifth son of King Ethelwulf. He inflicted on the Danes their first major reverse, at Edington (878), reorganized his forces into a standing army, built a navy, and established fortifications. He revived religion and learning, and provided his successors with the means to reconquer the Danelaw. The famous story of his being scolded by a peasant woman for letting her cakes burn is first recorded in the 11th-c.

Alfvén, Hannes (Olof Gösta) [alfen] (1908–) Theoret-

ical physicist, born in Norrköping, Sweden. In 1942 he predicted the existence of waves in plasmas (*Alfén waves*), and shared the Nobel Prize for Physics in 1970.

Alfvén, Hugo Emil [alfen] (1872–1960) Composer and violinist, born in Stockholm. His best-known piece is *Midsummer Vigil* (trans, 1904), better known as the *Swedish Rhapsody*. Other works include five symphonies and a ballet.

Algardi, Alessandro [algah(r)dee] (1598–1654) Sculptor, born in Bologna, Italy. His chief work is a large marble relief in St Peter's, Rome, showing Pope Leo I restraining Attila from marching on the city.

Algazel, Abu Mohammed al- >> **Ghazali, Abu Hamid Mohammed al-**

Alger, Horatio [aljer] (1832–99) Writer and clergyman, born in Revere, MA. He wrote boys' adventure stories on poor-boy-makes-good themes, such as *Ragged Dick* (1867) and *From Canal Boy to President* (1881).

Algren, Nelson (1909–81) Novelist, born in Detroit, MI. He was a leading member of the Chicago School of Realism. His works include *Somebody in Boots* (1935) and *The Man with the Golden Arm* (1949).

Alhazen [alhazen], Arabic **Abu al-Hassan ibn al Haytham** (c.965–1039) Mathematician and physicist, born in Basra, Iraq. He did notable work in physical optics, his best-known book being the *Treasury of Optics* (first published in Latin in 1270).

Ali (?–661) Fourth caliph (656–61), the cousin of Mohammed, whose daughter, Fatima, he married. He encountered much opposition during his reign and was assassinated in the mosque at Kufa. He is held by Shiah Muslims to be the only true successor to the phrophet. >> Fatima; Mohammed

Ali, (Chaudri) Mohamad (1905–80) Pakistani prime minister (1955–6), born in Jullundur, India. He became the first secretary-general of the Pakistan government (1947), finance minister (1951), and prime minister.

Ali, Muhammad, originally **Cassius (Marcellus) Clay, Jr** (1942–) Boxer, born in Louisville, KY. He won the world heavyweight title in 1964, defeating Sonny Liston. At that time he joined the Black Muslims and adopted the name Muhammad Ali. In 1971 he was beaten by Joe Frazier, but beat him in 1974. In 1978 he was beaten by Leon Spinks, but regained the title later that year - the first man to win the world heavyweight title three times. His flamboyant style made him a legend.

Alia, Ramiz [alia] (1925–) Albanian president (1985–92), born in Shkoder, Albania. He held various posts in the ruling Communist Party of Labour of Albania (APL), and on Hoxha's death (1985) took over as APL leader. >> Hoxha

Ali Bey [alee bay] (1728–73) Egyptian ruler, a slave from the Caucasus who rose to be chief of the Mamluks. He declared himself sultan (1768) and established an administration independent of Ottoman overlordship.

Alice Maud Mary, Princess (1843–78) British princess, the second daughter of Queen Victoria. In 1862 she married **Prince Louis of Hesse-Darmstadt** (1837–92). They had four daughters: the eldest became the mother of Louis, Earl Mountbatten; the youngest, Alexandra, married Nicholas II of Russia. >> Alexandra Feodorovna; Mountbatten (of Burma)

Ali Pasha, known as **the Lion of Janina** (1741–1822) Turkish leader. An Albanian brigand, he became Pasha of Trikala in 1787, of Janina (in Greece) in 1788, and Governor of Rumili in 1803. He was deposed in 1820 and put to death.

al-Khwarizmi, (Abu Ja'far Muhammad ibn Musa) [alchwarizmee] (c.800–c.850) Arab scholar, who wrote in Baghdad on astronomy, geography, and mathematics. The word *algebra* is derived from the title of his book on the subject.

al-Kindi [alkindee] (c.800–c.870) Arab philosopher, born in Kufa, Iraq. He was one of the first to spread Greek thought in the Arab world and synthesize it with Islamic doctrine.

Allais, Maurice [alay] (1911–) Economist amd engineer, born in Paris. He studied the reformulation of market equilibrium and efficiency, and the structural links between growth and inflation, and was awarded the Nobel Prize for Economics in 1988.

Allan, David (1744–96) Genre and portrait painter, known as the 'Scottish Hogarth', born in Alloa, Central, Scotland. He painted portraits in London (1777–80), and illustrated Allan Ramsay's *Gentle Shepherd*. >> Hogarth

Allan, Sir Hugh (1810–82) Shipowner, born in Saltcoats, Strathclyde. He settled in Canada (1826), where his shipbuilding company prospered, and he founded the Allan Line of steamers.

Allan, Sir William (1782–1850) Historical painter, born in Edinburgh. He spent several years in Russia and Turkey, painting scenes of Russian life. In 1841 he was appointed Queen's Limner (painter) in Scotland.

Allardice, Robert >> Barclay-Allardice, Robert

Allbutt, Sir Thomas (Clifford) (1836–1925) Physician, born in Dewsbury, West Yorkshire. He introduced the short clinical thermometer (1867), and wrote especially on the heart and on the history of medicine.

Allen, Edgar >> Doisy, Edward

Allen, Ethan (1738–89) American soldier, born in Litchfield, CT. He pursued independence for the Green Mountain area (now Vermont), and distinguished himself by the capture of Fort Ticonderoga. He later published the deist tract known as *Ethan Allen's Bible*.

Allen, Florence (Ellinwood) (1884–1966) Judge and feminist, born in Salt Lake City, UT. The first woman to sit on a general federal bench and the first on a court of last resort, she published the autobiographical *To Do Justly* in 1965.

Allen, George (1832–1907) Publisher and engraver, born in Newark, Nottinghamshire. He started a business in Fleet Street, London, which ultimately became the house of Allen and Unwin.

Allen, Sir George Oswald Browning, known as **Gubby Allen** (1902–89) Cricketer, born in Sydney, New South Wales, Australia. He played for England in 25 Tests, and is the only player to have taken all 10 wickets in an innings at Lord's (1929).

Allen, Sir Harry Brookes (1854–1926) Pathologist, born in Geelong, Victoria, Australia. In 1890 he persuaded the General Medical Council in London to recognize Melbourne medical degrees, pioneering the wider recognition of colonial academic qualifications.

Allen, James Van >> Van Allen, James

Allen, Paula Gunn (1939–) Writer, born in Cubero, NM. Of mixed Laguna Pueblo, Sioux, and Chicano parentage, she has been associated with the Native American Studies programme at the University of California, Berkeley.

Allen, Ralph, known as **the Man of Bath** (?1694–1764) English philanthropist. A deputy postmaster at Bath, Avon, he made a fortune by improving postal routes in England.

Allen, Red, originally **Henry Allen, Jr** (1908–67) Jazz trumpeter and singer, born in Algiers, LA. He performed with King Oliver's band in Chicago (1927), then with Fletcher Henderson (1932–4) and Louis Armstrong (1937–40), and in 1959 made a celebrated debut in Europe. >> Armstrong, Louis; Henderson, Fletcher; Oliver, King

Allen, Steve, originally **Stephen Valentine Patrick William Allen** (1921–) Entertainer, born in New York City. He successfully pioneered the first late-evening talk show, *The Tonight Show* (1953), for CBS. He composed many hit songs, notably 'This Could Be the Start of Something Big' and 'Impossible'.

Allen, Walter (Ernest) (1911–) Novelist and critic, born in Birmingham, West Midlands. Among his novels are *Innocence is Drowned* (1938) and *Dead Man Over All* (1950). Critical works include *The English Novel* (1954).

Allen, William (1532–94) Clergyman, born in Rossall, Lancashire. An exile in Flanders from 1561, in 1568 he founded the English college at Douai to train missionary priests for the reconversion of England. He became a cardinal in 1587.

Allen, William (Hervey) (1889–1949) Writer, born in Pittsburg, PA. He published his World War I diary, *Towards the Flame*, in 1926. His best-known novel is *Anthony Adverse* (1933).

Allen, Woody, originally **Allen Stewart Konigsberg** (1935–) Film actor and director, born in New York City. His major films, exploring the themes of mortality, sexual inadequacy, show-business nostalgia, psychoanalysis, and urban living, include *Annie Hall* (1977), *Manhattan* (1979), *Hannah and Her Sisters* (1986, Oscar), and *Husbands and Wives* (1992).

Allenby, Edmund Henry Hynman Allenby, 1st Viscount (1861–1936) British soldier, born in Brackenhurst, Nottinghamshire. In World War 1 he commanded the Third Army in France (1915–17), then the expeditionary force against the Turks, capturing Jerusalem (1917), and routing the Egyptians at Megiddo (1918).

Allende (Gossens), Salvador [ayenday] (1908–73) Chilean president (1970–3), born in Valparaíso. He helped found the Chilean Socialist Party (1933), and was elected president as leader of a left-wing coalition (1970). He was overthrown by a military junta, and died in the fighting.

Allende, Isabel [ayenday] (1942–) Novelist, born in Lima, Peru, the niece of Salvador Allende. In exile after the overthrow of Allende's government (1973), her experiences led to her first novel, *The House of the Spirits* (1985). >> Allende, Salvador

Alley, Rewi (1897–1987) Writer and teacher, born in Springfield, Canterbury, New Zealand. He settled in China in 1927, where he promoted the concept of industrial co-operative education through such projects as the *Gung Ho* ('work together') scheme.

Alleyn, Edward [alen] (1566–1626) Actor, born in London, the stepson-in-law of Philip Henslowe. He was associated with the Admiral's Men, and formed a partnership with Henslowe to run the Bear Garden and build the Fortune Theatre. >> Henslowe

Allgood, Sara (1883–1950) Actress, born in Dublin. At the Abbey Theatre she became noted for her performances in Sean O'Casey's plays, then settled in Hollywood (1940) and appeared in many films, such as *Jane Eyre* (1943).

Alliaco, Petrus de >> Ailly, Pierre d'

Allingham, Margery [alinguhm] (1904–66) Detective-story writer, born in London. The creator of the fictional detective Albert Campion, her novels include *Flowers for the Judge* (1936) and *The China Governess* (1963).

Allingham, William (1824–89) Poet, born in Ballyshannon, Co Donegal, Ireland. His works include *Day and Night Songs* (1854) and *Irish Songs and Poems* (1887).

Allitt, Beverley [alit] (1969–) British convicted murderer, dubbed the UK's first female serial killer. A nurse by profession, she was convicted in 1993 of the murder of four children in her care and of the attempted murder of three others.

Allori, Alessandro [alawree] (1535–1607) Florentine mannerist painter, adopted and trained by Bronzino. Both he and his son, **Cristofano** (1577–1621), were portrait painters at the Medici court, and executed religious works for the churches of Florence. >> Bronzino

Allsopp, Samuel [awlsop] (1780–1838) British philanthropist, a member of the brewing firm of Allsopp & Sons, Burton-on-Trent. The development of the firm was largely due to his youngest son **Henry** (1811–87).

Allston, Washington [awlston] (1779–1843) Artist and

writer, born in Waccamaw, SC. The earliest US Romantic painter, he produced large canvases, particularly of religious scenes, such as 'Belshazzar's Feast' and 'The Flood'.

Almack, William (?–1781) British clubman, of either Yorkshire or Scottish origin. He opened fashionable gaming clubs in London, notably the Almack's Assembly Rooms in King Street (1765).

Almagro, Diego de [al**mag**roh] (c.1475–1538) Conquistador, born in Almagro, Spain. He accompanied Pizarro on the first expedition against the Incas (1524–8), and later invaded Chile (1535–6). A dispute with Pizarro led to civil war between the Spaniards, and although Almagro was victorious at Cuzco (1537), he was later defeated and executed. >> Pizarro, Francisco

Alma-Tadema, Sir Lawrence [alma **tad**ema] (1836–1912) Painter, born in Dronrijp, The Netherlands. He specialized in Classical subjects from Greek, Roman, and Egyptian antiquity, as in 'The Roses of Heliogabalus' (1896).

Almeida, Brites de [al**may**da] (fl.1385) Legendary Portuguese heroine, born in Aljubarrota, Portugal. Supposedly a baker, during the war between John I and the King of Cadiz she led her townspeople against the Spanish and killed seven of them with her baker's shovel (c.1385).

Almeida, Francisco de [al**may**da] (c.1450–1510) Portuguese soldier, born near Lisbon. He was appointed the first viceroy of the Portuguese Indies (1505–9).

Almeida-Garrett, João Baptista da Silva Leitão [al**may**da ga**ret**] (1799–1854) Writer and politician, born in Oporto, Portugal. A pioneer of the Romantic movement and of modern Portuguese drama, his works include the historical play *Gil Vicente* (1838) and the epic *Camões* (1825).

Almirante, Giorgio [almi**ran**tay] (?1915–88) Leader of Italy's neo-Fascist Party, born near Parma, Italy. He helped to found the neo-Fascist movement after the war, becoming national secretary of the party (1969–87).

Almquist or **Almqvist, Carl Jonas Love** [**alm**kwist] (1793–1866) Writer, born in Stockholm. Most of his prolific literary output is included in a 14-volume series, *The Book of the Briar Rose* (trans, 1832–51).

Alonso, Alicia [a**lon**soh], originally **Alicia de la Caridad del Cobre Martínez Hoyo** (1921–) Dancer and choreographer, born in Havana. In 1948 she formed the Alicia Alonso Company, which became a national ballet company for Cuba.

Alonso, Dámaso [a**lon**soh] (1898–1990) Poet and philologist, born in Madrid. He established his reputation as an authority on Góngora y Argote. His best-known poetic work is *Children of Wrath* (trans, 1944). >> Góngora

Aloysius, St >> Gonzaga, Luigi

Alp-Arslan (Turk 'hero-lion') (1030–72) Seljuk sultan, who succeeded his uncle Tügrül Beg in 1062. He devoted his energies to extending the frontiers of the Seljuk empire.

Alpher, Ralph (Asher) (1921–) Physicist, born in Washington, DC. In 1948 he helped to devise a theory of the processes emitting energy in the early life of the universe, which has become part of the 'big bang' model of the universe. >> Bethe; Gamow

Alphonsus Liguori, St >> Liguori, St Alfonso Maria de'

Alpini, Prospero [al**pee**nee], Lat **Prosper Alpinus** (1553–1616) Botanist and physician, born in Marostica, Italy. While working in Egypt he studied many wild and cultivated botanical species, and brought the coffee plant and the banana to European attention.

Alred >> Aldred

Alston, Richard [**awl**ston] (1948–) Choreographer and director, born in Stoughton, West Sussex. In 1972 he co-founded Strider, the forerunner of the contemporary dance company Second Stride (1982), and later became artistic director of the Rambert Dance Company (1986–92).

Altdorfer, Albrecht [**alt**daw(r)fer] (c.1480–1538) Painter, engraver, and architect, born in Regensburg, Germany. A leading member of the Danube School of German painting, his major works depict biblical and historical subjects. He was also a pioneer of copperplate etching.

Alter, David (1807–81) Physicist, born in Westmoreland, PA. One of the earliest investigators of the spectrum, he pioneered the use of the spectroscope in determining the chemical constitution of a gas or vaporized solid.

Altgeld, John Peter (1847–1902) US politician and social reformer, born in Nassau, Germany. As a judge of the supreme court in Illinois (1886–91), he is remembered chiefly for his pardon of three anarchists convicted of complicity in the 1886 Chicago Haymarket Riots.

Althusser, Louis [alt-hüser] (1918–90) Political philosopher, born in Algiers. He wrote influential works on Marxist theory, including *Lenin and Philosophy* (trans, 1969). In 1980 he murdered his wife, and was confined in an asylum until his death.

Altichiero [alti**kyay**roh] (c.1330–c.1395) Painter and possible founder of the Veronese School, born near Verona, Italy. He worked in Verona, then moved to Padua, where his frescoes are in the Basilica of San Antonio (painted 1372–9) and the Oratory of San Giorgio (1377–84).

Altizer, Thomas J(onathan) J(ackson) [**al**tiyzer] (1927–) Theologian, born in Cambridge, MA. A proponent of the 1960s 'Death of God' theology, his writings include *The Gospel of Christian Atheism* (1966).

Altman, Sidney (1939–) Biochemist, born in Montreal, Canada. He made a breakthrough in the understanding of genetic processes by showing that the RNA molecule could rearrange itself, and shared the Nobel Prize for Chemistry in 1989. >> Cech, Thomas

Altman, Benjamin (1840–1913) Businessman and art collector, born in New York City. In 1906 he founded B Altman & Co, which became one of the country's most stylish department stores. He bequeathed his art collection to the Metropolitan Museum.

Altman, Robert (1925–) Film director, born in Kansas City, MO. He gained instant recognition for *M*A*S*H* (1970), and went on to direct and/or produce a series of highly individualistic films, such as *Nashville* (1975) and *The Player* (1991).

Altounyan, Roger Edward Collingwood [al**toon**yan] (1922–87) Physician and medical pioneer, born in Syria. He developed the drug sodium cromoglycate to combat asthma, and designed the Spinhaler device used to inhale it. He and his sisters were the real-life models of the children in Ransome's *Swallows and Amazons*. >> Ransome

Alva or **Alba, Ferdinand Alvarez de Toledo, duque d'** (Duke of) (1507–82) Spanish general and statesman, born in Piedratita, Spain. He was sent by Philip II to quell the revolt of the Netherlands (1567), where he established the ruthless Council of Blood. He defeated William of Orange, but Holland and Zeeland later destroyed his fleet, and he was recalled in 1573. >> Philip II (of Spain); William I (of the Netherlands)

Alvarado, Pedro de [alva**raht** hoh] (c.1485–1541) Conquistador, born in Badajoz, Spain. During the conquest of Mexico (1519–21) he accompanied Cortés, who later sent him on an expedition to Guatemala (1523–7), and he was made Governor of Guatemala in 1529. >> Cortés

Alvarez, José [al**vareth**] (1768–1827) Spanish sculptor of the Classical school. He was employed by Napoleon to decorate the Quirinal Palace, and in 1816 became court sculptor to Ferdinand VII in Madrid.

Alvarez, Luis W(alter) [al**vah**rez] (1911–88) Physicist, born in San Francisco. In 1947 he built the first proton linear accelerator, and later developed the bubble-chamber. He was awarded the Nobel Prize for Physics in 1968.

Alvarez Quintero [alvareth keentayroh] Playwrights and brothers: **Serafín Alvarez Quintero** (1871–1938) and **Joaquín Alvarez Quintero** (1873–1944), born in Utrera, Spain. They were the joint authors of numerous modern Spanish plays, all displaying a characteristic gaiety and sentiment, such as *Fortunato* (1928).

Alypius [alipius] (fl.c.360 BC) Greek writer on music. His surviving work, published in 1652, consists of a list of symbols for the notation of the Greek modes and scales.

Alzheimer, Alois [altshiymer] (1864–1915) Psychiatrist and neuropathologist, born in Marktbreit, Germany. He made a full clinical and pathological description (1907) of pre-senile dementia (*Alzheimer's disease*).

Amadeus >> **Hoffmann, E T W**

Amado, Jorge [amahdoo] (1912–) Novelist, born in Ferradas, Brazil. Brought up on a cacao plantation in NE Brazil, his early writing focussed on the poor social conditions of the workers, as seen in *The Violent Land* (trans, 1944).

Amagatsu, Yushio [amagatsoo] (1948–) Choreographer and dancer, born in Yokosuka, Japan. He became artistic director of the *butoh* dance-theatre troupe Sankai Juku, formed in 1975 and based partly in Paris.

Amanullah Khan [amanula kahn] (1892–1960) Ruler of Afghanistan (1919–29), born in Paghman, Afghanistan. After war with Britain (1919–22), he established Afghan independence (1922), assuming the title of king in 1926. His zeal for reforms provoked rebellion, and he was forced into exile.

Amarasimha (probably 6th-c) Sanskrit lexicographer. He wrote the *Amara-kosha*, a dictionary of synonyms in verse.

Amati, Andrea [amahtee] (c.1520–80) Violin-maker, the founder member of a famous family of violin-makers from Cremona, Italy. His grandson **Nicolò** (1596–1684), was the master of Guarnieri and Stradivari. >> Guarnieri; Stradivari

Ambartsumian, Viktor Amazaspovich (1908–) Astrophysicist, born in Armenia. He developed theories regarding young star clusters, and devised a method for computing the mass ejected from nova stars.

Ambedkar, Bhimrao Ramji [ambedker] (1893–1956) Indian politician, born near Bombay, India. He became a member of the Bombay Legislative Assembly and leader of 60 million Untouchables, and as minister of law (1947) was the principal author of the Indian Constitution.

Ambler, Eric (1909–) Writer, born in London. He specialized in the writing of spy thrillers, such as *Epitaph for a Spy* (1938) and *The Mask of Dimitrios* (1939).

Amboise, Georges d' [ämbwahz] (1460–1510) Clergyman and French statesman, born in Chaumont-sur-Loire, France. He became cardinal and prime minister under Louis XII (1498), and effected the Treaty of Blois (1505) which allied France and Spain. >> Louis XII

Ambrose, St (c.339–97), feast day 7 December. Roman clergyman, born in Trier, Germany. He is remembered for his preaching, literary works, and hymns. He also made improvements in the liturgy, notably the *Ambrosian ritual* and *Ambrosian chant*.

Amenhotep II [ahmenhohtep] (15th-c BC) King of Egypt in the 18th Dynasty (1450–1525 BC), the son of Thuthmose III. He fought successful campaigns in Palestine and on the Euphrates. >> Thuthmose

Amenhotep III [amenhohtep] (c.1411–1379 BC) King of Egypt (1417–1379 BC), the son of Thuthmose IV. In a reign of spectacular magnificence, he built the capital city of Thebes, and its finest monuments.

Amenhotep IV >> **Akhenaton**

Amery, L(eopold Charles Maurice) S(tennett) (1873–1955) British statesman, born in Gorakhpur, India. He served as secretary of state for India and Burma in Churchill's wartime administration.

Amery, John [aymeree] (1912–45) British pro-Nazi adventurer, the son of L S Amery. Recruited by the Nazis in France, he began pro-Hitler activities with broadcasts from Berlin in 1942. He was captured by Italian partisans in 1945, and hanged in London. >> Amery, L S

Ames, Joseph [aymz] (1689–1759) Bibliographer and antiquarian, born in Yarmouth, Isle of Wight. He compiled *Typographical Antiquities* (1749), the foundation of English bibliography.

Ames, William [aymz], Lat **Amesius** (1576–1633) Puritan theologian, born in Ipswich, Suffolk. He became a professor of theology in Holland, and is celebrated for his exposition of Calvinist doctrine.

Amherst, Jeffrey, 1st Baron Amherst (1717–97) British soldier, born in Sevenoaks, Kent. He commanded an expedition against the French in Canada, capturing Louisburg (1758) and Montreal (1760), and became Governor-General of British North America (1760–3).

Amherst (of Arakan), William Pitt, 1st Earl (1773–1857) Colonialist, born in Bath, Avon, the nephew and adopted son of Jeffrey, Baron Amherst. He was a successful Governor-General of India (1823–28). >> Amherst, Jeffrey

Amichai, Yehuda [amichiy] (1924–) Poet, born in Würzburg, Germany. In 1936 he went with his family to Palestine. His works include (trans titles) *Now in the Turmoil* (1968) and *Amen* (1978).

Amici, Giovanni Battista [ameechee] (1786–1868) Optician, astronomer, and natural philosopher, born in Modena, Italy. He constructed optical instruments, and in 1827 produced the dioptric, achromatic microscope that bears his name.

Amiel, Henri Frédéric [amyel] (1821–81) Philosopher and writer, born in Geneva. His fame rests on his diaries, written from 1847 onwards, and published posthumously as *Journal in time* (1883).

Amies, Sir (Edwin) Hardy [aymeez] (1909–) Couturier, and dressmaker by appointment to Queen Elizabeth II. Known for his tailored suits for women, he founded his own fashion house in 1946, and started designing for men in 1959.

Amin (Dada), Idi [ameen] (c.1925–) Ugandan soldier and dictator, born in Koboko. He staged a coup deposing Obote, and established a military dictatorship (1971–9). Throughout his rule there were many reports of atrocities, making his regime internationally infamous. Deposed by exiled Ugandans with the help of the Tanzanian army in 1979, he fled abroad. >> Obote

Amiot, Jacques >> **Amyot, Jacques**

Amis, Sir Kingsley [aymis] (1922–) Novelist and poet, born in London. He achieved success with his first novel, *Lucky Jim* (1954). Later books include *Jake's Thing* (1978), *The Old Devils* (1986, Booker), and *The Russian Girl* (1992). >> Amis, Martin

Amis, Martin [aymis] (1949–) Novelist and journalist, the son of Kingsley Amis. His works include the novels *The Rachel Papers* (1973) and *Time's Arrow* (1991), and a collection of short stories, *Einstein's Monsters* (1986). >> Amis, Kingsley

Amiss, Dennis (Leslie) [aymis] (1943–) Cricketer, born in Birmingham, West Midlands. He played for Warwickshire, and made 50 appearances in Test matches for England, scoring 11 centuries.

Amman, Jakob (c.1645–c.1730) Swiss Mennonite bishop whose followers founded the Amish sect in the 1690s. Their members still practise an exclusively rural and simple lifestyle in parts of the USA and Canada.

Ammanati, Bartolommeo [amanahtee] (1511–92)

Architect and sculptor, born in Settignano, Italy. Working in the late Renaissance style his designs include the ducal palace at Lucca, and the Ponte Santa Trinità (now destroyed) in Florence.

Ammann, Othmar Hermann (1879–1965) Structural engineer, born in Schaffhausen, Switzerland. He designed some of America's greatest suspension bridges, such as the Golden Gate Bridge in San Francisco (1937) and the Verrazano Narrows Bridge in New York (1965).

Ammianus Marcellinus [amiahnus mah(r)seleenus] (c.330–90) Roman historian, born of Greek parents in Antioch. He wrote a history of the Roman Empire from AD 98 in 31 books, of which only the last 18 are extant.

Ammonius [amohnius], known as **Ammonius Saccas** (c.160–242) Greek philosopher. He was the founder of Neoplatonic philosophy, and the teacher of Plotinus, Origen, and Longinus, but left no writings. >> Longinus; Origen; Plotinus

Amontons, Guillaume [amõtõ] (1663–1705) Physicist, born in Paris. His chief discovery was that equal changes in the temperature of a fixed volume of air result in equal variations in pressure.

Amory, Derick Heathcoat, 1st Viscount Amory [aymoree] (1899–1981) British statesman, born in Tiverton, Devon. He became a Conservative MP in 1945, and after several ministerial positions served as Chancellor of the Exchequer (1958–60).

Amory, Thomas [aymoree] (c.1691–1788) English writer and eccentric. He is best known for his *Life of John Buncle* (2 vols, 1756–66).

Amos [aymos] (835–765 BC) Old Testament prophet, the earliest prophet in the Bible to have a book named after him. He denounced the iniquities of the N kingdom of Israel.

Ampère, André Marie [ãpair] (1775–1836) Mathematician and physicist, born in Lyon, France. He laid the foundations of the science of electrodynamics. His name was given to the basic SI unit of electric current.

Amr ibn al-As [amribnalas] (?–664) Arab soldier, who joined the prophet Mohammed in c.629. He took part in the conquest of Palestine (638) and of Egypt (639), and was the first Muslim governor of Egypt (642–44). >> Mohammed

Amsberg, Claus-Georg von >> Beatrix

Amundsen, Roald (Engelbregt Gravning) [amundsen] (1872–1928) Explorer, born in Borge, Norway. His Antarctic expedition of 1910 reached the Pole in December 1911, one month ahead of Scott. In 1926 he flew the airship *Norge* across the North Pole, but was lost on a later expedition. >> Scott, R F

Amyot or **Amiot, Jacques** [amyoh] (1513–93) Humanist, born in Melun, France. He translated many Classical texts, notably his French version of Plutarch's *Lives*, which was the basis of North's English translation. >> North, Thomas; Plutarch

Anacreon [anakreeon] (c.570–c.475 BC) Greek lyric poet, born in Teos, modern Turkey. He was famous for his satires and elegant love poetry, of which only fragments remain.

Anand, Mulk Raj [anand] (1905–) Novelist, critic, and man of letters, born in Peshawar, modern Pakistan. His novels include *Untouchable* (1935) and *The Village* (1939), depicting life in the poverty-stricken Punjab.

Ananda [ananda] (5th–6th-c BC) The cousin and favourite pupil of the Buddha. Noted for his devotion to the Buddha, and a skilled interpreter of his teachings, he was instrumental in establishing an order for women disciples. >> Buddha

Anastasia [anastahzia], in full **Grand Duchess Anastasia Nikolaievna Romanova** (1901–18?) Youngest daughter of Tsar Nicholas II of Russia, born near St Petersburg, Russia. Although she is believed to have been executed by the Bolsheviks at Yekaterinburg in 1918, several women later claimed to be Anastasia, notably 'Anna Anderson' Manahan, who died in 1984. >> Nicholas II

Anatoli, Alexander >> **Kuznetsov, Alexander Vasilievich**

Anaxagoras [anaksagoras] (c.500–428 BC) Greek philosopher, born in Clazomenae. He taught in Athens, where his pupils included Pericles and Euripides. His scientific speculations led to prosecution for impiety, and he was banished. >> Euripides; Pericles

Anaximander [anakzimander] (c.611–547 BC) Greek philosopher, born in Miletus, the successor and perhaps pupil of Thales. He was the first thinker to develop a systematic philosophical view of the universe and Earth's place in it. >> Thales

Anaximenes [anakzimeneez] (?–c.500 BC) Greek philosopher, born in Miletus. He held air to be the primary form of matter from which all things, such as water, earth, and stone, were formed.

Ancre, Baron de Lussigny, marquis d' [ãkruh], originally **Concino Concini** (?–1617) Adventurer, born in Florence, Italy. He entered the French court in 1600, and became the chief favourite of the queen-regent, Marie de' Medici. He was assassinated during a rebellion. >> Marie de' Medici

Ancus Marcius [angkus mah(r)sius] (7th-c BC) Traditionally, the fourth king of Rome. He is said to have conquered the neighbouring Latin tribes, and settled them on the Aventine.

Anders, Władysław (1892–1970) Polish soldier, born in Blonie, Poland. He commanded the Polish forces in the Middle East and Italy in World War 2. Deprived of his nationality by the Polish Communist government (1946), he became a leading figure in the Free Polish community in Britain.

Andersen, Hans Christian (1805–75) Writer, born in Odense, Denmark. His works include collections of poems (1831–2), travel books, novels, and plays, but he is mainly remembered for his fairy-tales for children, such as *The Tin Soldier*, *The Tinderbox*, and *The Ugly Duckling*.

Anderson, Carl (David) (1905–91) Physicist, born in New York City. He discovered the positron (1932), worked on gamma and cosmic rays, and confirmed the existence of mesons (now muons). He shared the Nobel Prize for Physics in 1936.

Anderson, Elizabeth Garrett, née **Garrett** (1836–1917) Physician, the first English woman doctor, born in London. She faced difficulty qualifying as a doctor because of opposition to the admission of women, finally receiving an MD degree from the University of Paris in 1870.

Anderson, Gerry (1929–) British creator of puppet-character programmes for television. Among his best-known adventure series are *Fireball XL-5* (1961), *Thunderbirds* (1964–6), *Captain Scarlett and the Mysterons* (1967), and *Terrahawks* (1983–4).

Anderson, John (1726–96) Scientist, born in Roseneath, Strathclyde. Professor of oriental languages at Glasgow, and then of natural philosophy, he bequeathed all he had to found Anderson's College in Glasgow.

Anderson, John (1893–1962) Philosopher, born in Scotland. He was professor of philosophy at Sydney from 1927, and can be regarded as the founder and main exponent of an Australian school of philosophy.

Anderson, Sir John >> **Waverley, Viscount**

Anderson, Dame Judith, originally **Frances Margaret Anderson** (1898–1992) Actress, born in Adelaide, South Australia. She became noted as a classical actress during the 1930s, and in 1984 a Broadway theatre was named in her honour.

Anderson, Sir Kenneth (Arthur Noel) (1891–1959) British soldier, born in India. He served in France (1914–16) and Palestine (1917–18), and in World War 2

commanded the 1st British Army in North Africa, capturing Tunis (1943).

Anderson, Lindsay (Gordon) (1923–94) British stage and film director, born in Bangalore, India. He began with short documentary films, such as *Thursday's Children* (1955, Oscar), and became a leading proponent of the Free Cinema critical movement, his feature films including *This Sporting Life* (1963) and *O Lucky Man!* (1973).

Anderson, Marian (1902–1993) Contralto concert and opera singer, born in Philadelphia, PA. In 1955 she became the first African-American singer to appear at the New York Metropolitan Opera.

Anderson, Maxwell (1888–1959) Playwright, born in Atlantic, PA. His works, some of which are in blank verse, include *Elizabeth the Queen* (1930) and *Both Your Houses* (1933, Pulitzer), and he wrote the screenplay of Remarque's *All Quiet on the Western Front* (1930). >> Remarque

Anderson, Philip W(arren) (1923–) Physicist, born in Indianapolis, IN. He worked on the electronic structure of magnetic and disordered systems, and shared the Nobel Prize for Physics in 1977. >> Mott, Nevill F; Van Vleck

Anderson, Sherwood (1876–1941) Writer, born in Camden, OH. His best-known work is the collection of short stories, *Winesburg, Ohio* (1919).

Anderson, Thomas (1819–74) Organist chemist, born in Scotland. He became professor of chemistry at Glasgow, and is remembered for his discovery of pyridine.

Anderson, Willa >> Muir, Edwin

Andersson, Bibi, popular name of **Birgitta Andersson** (1935–) Actress, born in Stockholm. She is best known for her roles in Ingmar Bergman films, such as *The Seventh Seal* (1956) and *Persona* (1966). >> Bergman, Ingmar

Andersson, Dan(iel) (1888–1920) Poet and novelist, born in Skattlösbergget, Sweden. His poems about traditional charcoal-burners in *Kolarhistorier* (1914) and *Kolvakterens Visor* (1915) turned them into national folk-figures.

Andersson, Johan Gunnar (1874–1960) Archaeologist, born in Knista, Sweden. He was the first to identify prehistoric pottery in China (1921), and his excavations in caves near Peking (1921–6) discovered fossils of *Homo erectus* (Peking Man).

Anderton, Sir (Cyril) James (1932–) British police officer. As chief constable of the Greater Manchester Police Force (1976–91), he became known for his outspoken and sometimes controversial opinions.

Andrássy, Gyula, Gróf (Count) [ondrahshee] (1823–90) Statesman and prime minister (1867–71), born in Košice, Czech Republic (formerly Kassa, Hungary). He was prominent in the struggle for independence (1848–9), and when the Dual Monarchy was formed, he became prime minister of Hungary (1871–9).

Andre, Carl [ondray] (1935–) Sculptor, born in Massachusetts. He is best known for his minimalist sculptures of the 1960s, first in wood, and later with mass-produced materials.

André, John [ondray] (1751–80) British soldier, born in London. He joined the army in Canada (1774), and when Benedict Arnold obtained the command of West Point in 1780, André was chosen to arrange its betrayal. He was later captured and hanged.

Andreä, Johann Valentin [andraye] (1586–1654) Theologian, born near Tübingen, Germany. Long regarded as the founder or restorer of the Rosicrucians, he wrote *Chymische Hochzeit Christiani Rosenkreuz* (1616).

Andrea da Firenza [andraya da firentsa], originally **Andrea Bonaiuti** (fl.c.1343–77) Florentine painter. His most famous work is the monumental fresco cycle in the Spanish Chapel of the Dominican Church of S Maria Novella in Florence, painted c.1366–8.

Andreev, Leonid Nikolayevich >> **Andreyev, Leonid Nikolayevich**

Andretti, Mario (Gabriele) [andretee] (1940–) Motor racing driver, born in Montona, Italy. During his Formula One career (1968–82) he won 16 Grand Prix. In 1978 he won the racing drivers' world championship, and was twice winner (1969, 1981) of the Indianapolis 500.

Andrew (Albert Christian Edward), Duke of York (1960–) British prince, the second son of Queen Elizabeth II. In 1986 he married **Sarah (Margaret Ferguson** (1959–), and was made Duke of York. They have two children, **Princess Beatrice Elizabeth Mary** (1988–) and **Princess Eugenie Victoria Helena** (1990–) The couple separated in 1992. >> Elizabeth II

Andrew, St (d.60), feast day 30 November. One of the 12 apostles, the brother of Simon Peter. He preached the Gospel in Asia Minor and Scythia, and was crucified in Achaia. He is the patron saint of Scotland and of Russia. >> Peter, St

Andrew, Agnellus (Matthew) (1908–87) Roman Catholic bishop and broadcaster, born near Glasgow, Strathclyde. He worked in UK television as an adviser and commentator, and was founder-director of the National Catholic Radio and TV Centre (1955–80).

Andrewes, Lancelot (1555–1626) Anglican clergyman and scholar, born in Barking, Essex. A powerful preacher and defender of Anglican doctrines, he became Bishop of Chichester (1605), Ely (1609), and Winchester (1618).

Andrews, Eamon (1922–87) Broadcaster, born in Dublin. He began as a sports commentator in Ireland in 1939, and became well known as the host of several BBC television series, such as *What's My Line?* (1951–63, 1984–7) and *This is Your Life* (1955–87).

Andrews, Frank M(axwell) (1884–1943) US air force officer, born in Nashville, TN. In World War 2 he was head of the US Caribbean Defense Command (1941–2), the Middle East Command (1942–3), and commander of the US forces in Europe.

Andrews, Julie, originally **Julia Elizabeth Wells** (1935–) Singer and actress, born in Walton-on-Thames, Surrey. Her film debut was in the musical *Mary Poppins* (1964, Oscar), later films including *The Sound of Music* (1965) and *Victor/Victoria* (1982).

Andrews, Roy Chapman (1884–1960) Naturalist and explorer, born in Beloit, WI. Director of the American Museum of Natural History (1935–42), he is best known for his discovery, in Mongolia, of fossil dinosaur eggs.

Andrews, Thomas (1813–85) Physical chemist, born in Belfast. He is noted for his discovery of the critical temperature of gases, above which they cannot be liquefied, however great the pressure applied.

Andreyev, Leonid Nikolayevich [andrayef], also spelled **Andreev** (1871–1919) Writer and artist, born in Orel, Russia. Many of his works have been translated into English, such as *The Red Laugh* (1905) and *The Seven That Were Hanged* (1908).

Andrianov, Nikolay [andriahnof] (1952–) Gymnast, born in Vladimir, Russia. He won 15 Olympic medals (7 gold) between 1972 and 1980, and 12 world championship medals, including the overall individual title in 1978.

Andrić, Ivo [andrich] (1892–1975) Yugoslav diplomat and writer, born near Travnik, Bosnia and Herzegovina. His chief works, *The Bridge on the Drina* and *Bosnian Story* (both trans, 1945), earned him the 1961 Nobel Prize for Literature, and the nickname 'the Yugoslav Tolstoy'.

Andronicus [andronikus], known as **Cyrrhestes** (1st-c BC) Greek architect, born in Cyrrhus. He constructed the Tower of the Winds at Athens, known in the Middle Ages as the Lantern of Demosthenes.

Andronicus, Livius >> **Livius Andronicus**

Andronicus of Rhodes [andronikus] (fl.70–50 BC) Greek philosopher. He lived in Rome in Cicero's time, and edited the writings of Aristotle. >> Aristotle; Cicero

Andropov, Yuri Vladimirovich [andropof] (1914–84) General secretary of the Soviet Communist Party (1982–4) and president of the USSR (1983–4), born in Nagutskaya, Russia. He was head of the KGB (1967–72), and became president following the death of Brezhnev, but died soon after taking office. >> Brezhnev

Aneirin or **Aneurin** [aniyrin] (fl.6th–7th-c) Welsh court poet. His principal work, the *Gododdin*, celebrates the British heroes who were annihilated by the Saxons in the battle of Cattraeth c.600.

Anfinsen, Christian B(oehmer) (1916–) Biochemist, born in Monessen, PA. His chief work was on the sequence of amino acids which make up the enzyme ribonuclease, for which he shared the Nobel Prize for Chemistry in 1972.

Angas, George Fife (1789–1879) Shipowner, born in Newcastle upon Tyne, Tyne and Wear. Regarded as a founder of South Australia, he was appointed commissioner for the formation of the colony in 1834.

Angeles, Victoria de los [anjeles] (1923–) Lyric soprano, born in Barcelona, Spain. She achieved international recognition as both a concert and an operatic singer, noted for her 19th-c Italian roles and for her performances of Spanish songs.

Angelico, Fra [anjelikoh], originally **Guido di Pietro**, monastic name **Giovanni da Fiesole** (c.1400–55) Early Renaissance painter, born in Vicchio, Italy. He entered the Dominican monastery at Fiesole in 1407. His most important frescoes are those in the Convent of S Marco (now a museum) in Florence, and in the Vatican chapel of Nicholas V in Rome.

Angélique, Mère >> Arnauld, Angélique / Jacqueline-Marie-Angélique

Angell, Sir Norman [aynjl], originally **Ralph Norman Angell-Lane** (1872–1967) Writer and pacifist, born in Holbeach, Lincolnshire. He wrote *The Great Illusion* (1910) and *The Great Illusion, 1933* (1933), and was awarded the Nobel Peace Prize in 1933.

Angelou, Maya [anjeloo] (1928–) Writer, singer, and dancer, born in St Louis, MO. In the 1960s she was involved in African-American civil rights, then spent several years in Ghana as editor of *African Review*. She received success with her autobiographical *I Know Why the Caged Bird Sings* (1970).

Angiolieri, Cecco [anjohlyayree] (c.1260–c.1312) Poet, born in Siena, Italy. Nothing is known of his life except from his sonnets, which reveal a cynical, sardonic character. He attacked Dante in three poems. >> Dante

Anglesey, Henry William Paget, 1st Marquess of [angglsee] (1768–1854) British field marshal, born in London. He served in Flanders (1794), Holland (1799), and the Peninsular War (1808). For his services at Waterloo, where he lost a leg, he was made Marquess of Anglesey.

Angleton, James (Jesus) (1917–87) Public official, born in Boise, ID. As director of counter-intelligence at the CIA (1954–74), he came to distrust everyone, even within the CIA itself, and was eventually forced to resign.

Angliss, Sir William Charles (1865–1957) Businessman, born in Dudley, Worcestershire. He emigrated to Australia in 1884 and opened a butcher's shop in Melbourne. When sold in 1934, it had become the largest meat exporter in Australia.

Angoulême, Louis Antoine de Bourbon, duc d' (Duke of) [ãgoolem] (1775–1844) French soldier and aristocrat, the eldest son of Charles X of France. He fled from France after the revolution in 1789, and in 1799 married his cousin, Marie Thérèse (1778–1851), the only daughter of Louis XVI. After the July revolution in 1830, he accompanied his father into exile. >> Charles X

Ångström, Anders (Jonas) [angstruhm, **awng**stroem] (1814–74) Physicist, born in Lödgö, Sweden. He studied heat, magnetism, and spectroscopy, and the unit for measuring wavelengths of light is named after him.

Animuccia, Giovanni [animoo**chia**] (c.1500–71) Composer, born in Florence, Italy. He was influenced by St Philip Neri, for whose oratory he composed the *Laudi* - semidramatic religious pieces in popular style from which oratorio developed. >> Neri

An Lushan [an looshan], also spelled **An Lu-shan** (?–757) Chinese general under the Tang dynasty in China (618–907), of Turkish origin. He overthrew the crown, and established the short-lived Yan dynasty (755–7). Yang Guifei, mistress to Emperor Xuanzong, adopted him as her son. He rebelled in 755, forcing the emperor to flee, and Yang was executed. He made himself emperor (755), but was murdered by his own son. >> Xuanzong

Anna Amalia [a**mah**lia] (1739–1807) Duchess of Saxe-Weimar. Widowed in 1758, she acted as regent (1758–75) for her infant son, Charles Augustus, and became a notable patron of German literature.

Anna Comnena [kom**nay**na] (1083–1148) Byzantine princess and historian, the daughter of Alexius I Comnenus. After failing to gain the imperial crown for her husband, she took up literature, and eventually wrote the *Alexiad*, a Byzantine social history for the period 1069–1118. >> Alexius I

Anna Ivanovna [i**vah**novna] (1693–1740) Tsarina of Russia from 1730, the younger daughter of Ivan V and niece of Peter the Great. After the death of Peter II (1715–30), she ruled as an autocrat, along with her German favourite **Ernst Johann Biron** (1690–1772). >> Peter I (of Russia)

Annas [anas] (1st-c) Israel's high priest, appointed in AD 6 and deposed by the Romans in 15, but still described later by this title in the New Testament. He apparently questioned Jesus after his arrest (*John* 18) and Peter after his detention (*Acts* 4). >> Jesus Christ; Peter, St

Anne (1665–1714) Queen of Great Britain and Ireland (1702–14), born in London, the second daughter of James II. In 1683 she married Prince George of Denmark (1653–1708), bearing him 17 children, but only William, Duke of Gloucester (1689–1700) survived infancy. During much of her life she was greatly influenced by her close friend and confidante, Sarah Churchill, the future Duchess of Marlborough. In 1701 Anne signed the Act of Settlement designating the Hanoverian descendants of James I as her successors. >> Churchill, Sarah; James II (of England)

Anne (Elizabeth Alice Louise), Princess (1950–) British Princess Royal, the only daughter of Queen Elizabeth II and Prince Philip, born in London. She married **Mark Anthony Peter Phillips** (1948–), in 1973 (divorced, 1992). Their children are: **Peter Mark Andrew** (1977–) and **Zara Anne Elizabeth** (1981–). She married **Timothy Laurence** (1952–) in 1992. >> Elizabeth II; Phillips, Mark

Anne, St (fl.1st-c BC–1st-c AD), feast day 26 July. Wife of **St Joachim**, and mother of the Virgin Mary, first mentioned in the *Protevangelium* of James, in the 2nd-c. She is the patron saint of carpenters. >> Mary (mother of Jesus)

Anne of Austria (1601–66) Queen of France, the eldest daughter of Philip III of Spain and wife of Louis XIII of France. She became regent (1643–51) for her infant son, the future Louis XIV, and wielded power with Cardinal Mazarin as prime minister. >> Louis XIII / XIV; Mazarin

Anne of Bohemia (1366–94) Queen of England, the first wife of Richard II. The daughter of Emperor Charles IV (reigned 1355–78), she married Richard in 1382. >> Richard II

Anne of Brittany (1476–1514) Duchess of Brittany and twice queen of France. She fought to maintain Breton independence, but in 1491 was forced to marry Charles VIII of France (reigned 1483–98). In 1499, she married his successor, Louis XII. >> Louis XII

Anne of Cleves (1515–57) German princess, the fourth queen of Henry VIII (Jan 1540). Of plain appearance, she was chosen for purely political reasons after the death of Jane Seymour. The marriage was annulled by parliament six months later, and she remained in England until her death. >> Henry VIII; Seymour, Jane

Anne of Denmark (1574–1619) Danish princess, and queen of Scotland and England. In 1589 she married James VI of Scotland, the future James I of England. >> James I (of England)

Anne Boleyn >> **Boleyn, Anne**

Annenberg, Walter (Hubert) (1908–) Publisher and philanthropist, born in Milwaukee, WI. After inheriting a communications empire, he founded *Seventeen* magazine (1944) and *TV Guide* (1953), and purchased *The Philadelphia Daily News* (1957). He donated his large art collection to the Metropolitan Museum of Art.

Annigoni, Pietro [anigohnee] (1910–88) Painter, born in Milan, Italy. He employed the technical methods of the old masters, his most usual medium being tempera. His work includes portraits of Queen Elizabeth II and President Kennedy.

Anno, Mitsumasu [anoh] (1926–) Children's writer and illustrator, born in Tsuwano, Japan. He is renowned for his visual puzzles, such as *Topsy-Turvies: Pictures to Stretch the Imagination* (1970).

Annunzio, Gabriele d' >> **d'Annunzio, Gabriele**

Anouilh, Jean (Marie Lucien Pierre) [onwee] (1910–87) Playwright, born in Bordeaux, France. He was influenced by the Neoclassical fashion inspired by Giraudoux, his many plays including *Antigone* (1944), *Becket* (1959), and *The Trousers* (trans, 1978). >> Giraudoux

Anquetil, Jacques [äketeel] (1934–87) Racing cyclist, born in Normandy, France. The first man to win the Tour de France five times (1957, 1961–4), he also won the Grand Prix des Nations a record nine times (between 1953 and 1965).

Anschütz, Ottomar [anshüts] (1846–1907) Photographer, born in Yugoslavia. A pioneer of instantaneous photography, he was one of the first to make a series of pictures of moving animals and people.

Anselm, St (1033–1109), feast day 21 April. Theologian and philosopher, born in Aosta, Italy. Appointed Archbishop of Canterbury (1093), he was often in conflict with William II and Henry I. The main figure in early scholastic philosophy, he devised the ontological proof for the existence of God. He may have been canonized as early as 1163. >> William II (of England)

Ansermet, Ernest (Alexandre) [ansermay] (1883–1969) Conductor and musical theorist, born in Vevey, Switzerland. He was conductor of Diaghilev's Russian Ballet (1915–23), and founded the Orchestre de la Suisse Romande (1918), remaining conductor there until 1967. >> Diaghilev

Ansett, Sir Reginald (Myles) (1909–81) Pioneer of passenger flight, born in Inglewood, Victoria, Australia. He opened a regular air service to Melbourne in 1936, which became the largest private transport system in the S hemisphere.

Ansgar or **Anskar, St,** Ger **St Scharies,** known as **the Apostle of the North** (801–65), feast day 3 February. Frankish clergyman and missionary to Scandinavia, born in Picardy, France. A Benedictine monk, he was sent to preach the Gospel in Denmark (826), and built the first church in Sweden. He is the patron saint of Scandinavia.

Anson, George Anson, Baron (1697–1762) English naval commander, born at Shugborough Park, Staffordshire. In 1740 he sailed from England, circumnavigating the globe in three years and nine months.

Anstey, Christopher [anstee] (1724–1805) Writer, born in Brinkley, Cambridgeshire. He is best known for the *New Bath Guide* (1766), an epistolary novel in verse.

Anstey, F [anstee], pseudonym of **Thomas Anstey Guthrie** (1856–1934) Writer, born in London. A whimsical humorist, on the staff of *Punch* (1887–1930), his works include *Vice Versa* (1882) and *The Brass Bottle* (1900).

Antar, in full **l'Antarah Ibn Shaddād Al-Absi** (6th-c) Arab poet and warrior, born near Medina, Saudi Arabia. The author of one of the seven Golden Odes of Arabic literature, and the subject of the 10th-c *Romance of Antar*, he is regarded as the model of Bedouin heroism and chivalry.

Antenor [antaynaw(r)] (6th-c BC) Athenian sculptor. He is known to have executed bronze statues of 'Harmodius' and 'Aristogiton', and a statue of a maiden in the Acropolis.

Antheil, George [antiyl] (1900–59) Composer, born in Trenton, NJ. His works include the *Jazz Symphony* (1925), the opera *Transatlantic* (1930), and the controversial *Ballet Mécanique* (1926), written for 10 pianos and a variety of eccentric percussion instruments.

Anthony, St >> **Antony, St**

Anthony, C L >> **Smith, Dodie**

Anthony, Susan B(rownell) (1820–1906) Social reformer and women's suffrage leader, born in Adams, MA. In 1869 she co-founded the National American Woman Suffrage Association, and became its president in 1892. >> Stanton

Antigonus I [antigonus], known as **Cyclops** or **Monophthalmos** (Gr 'One-eyed') (382–301 BC) Macedonian soldier, one of the generals of Alexander the Great. On Antipater's death (319 BC) he waged incessant wars to become master of all Asia Minor and Syria, and assumed the title of king (306 BC), but was slain at Ipsus in Phrygia. >> Alexander the Great; Antipater (of Macedon)

Antigonus II [antigonus], known as **Gonatas** (c.319–239 BC) King of Macedon, who came to the throne in 276 BC. Pyrrhus of Epirus overran Macedonia in 274 BC, but Antigonus recovered his kingdom and consolidated it despite incessant wars. >> Pyrrhus

Antill, John Henry (1904–86) Composer, born in Ashfield, New South Wales, Australia. His major work, *Corroboree* (1944), blends Aboriginal and western themes. Other compositions include operas and choral works, ballet suites, and a symphony.

Antiochus I [antiohkus], known as **Antiochus Soter** (Gr 'Saviour') (324–261 BC) Seleucid king of Syria (281–261 BC), the son and successor of Seleucus I. He received his nickname for his victory over the Gallic invaders of Asia Minor. >> Seleucus I

Antiochus II [antiyokus], known as **Antiochus Theos** ('God') (286–247 BC) Seleucid king of Syria, the son and successor of Antiochus I. He married Berenice, the daughter of Ptolemy II, exiling his first wife, Laodice, and her children; but after his death, Laodice's son, Selecus II, succeeded the throne. >> Antiochus I; Ptolemy II

Antiochus III [antiohkus], known as **Antiochus the Great** (c.242–187 BC) Seleucid king of Syria (223–187 BC), the grandson of Antiochus II. He restored Seleucid prestige in the East (209–204 BC), and gained Palestine and Coele Syria (198 BC), but was defeated by the Romans at Thermopylae (191 BC) and Magnesia (190 BC). >> Antiochus II

Antiochus IV [antiyokus], known as **Antiochus Epiphanes** (c.215–163 BC) Seleucid king of Syria (175–163 BC), the son of Antiochus III. He conquered much of Egypt, and twice took Jerusalem, provoking the Jews to a successful insurrection under Mattathias and his sons, the Maccabees. >> Antiochus III

Antipater [antipater] (of Macedon) (398–319 BC) Macedonian general. He was highly trusted by Philip II of Macedon and also by Alexander the Great, who made him regent in Macedonia (334 BC). >> Alexander the Great; Philip II (of Macedon)

Antipater [antipater] (of Idumaea) (?–43 BC) The father of

Herod the Great, who laid the foundations of his family's ascendancy in Judaea in Roman times. Julius Caesar made him procurator of Judaea in 47 BC. >> Caesar; Herod

Antipater [antipater] (?–4 BC) Judaean prince, the son of Herod the Great by his first wife. He conspired against his half-brothers and had them executed, then plotted against his father, and was himself executed five days before Herod died. >> Herod

Antiphon [antifon] (5th-c BC) Greek philosopher and Sophist, generally distinguished from Antiphon the orator. Two works, *On Truth* and *On Concord*, survive in fragmentary form.

Antisthenes [antistheneez] (c.445–c.365 BC) Greek philosopher, thought to be co-founder, with his pupil Diogenes, of the Cynic school. He was a disciple of Gorgias, and later a close friend of Socrates. >> Diogenes of Sinhope; Gorgias; Socrates

Antoine, André [ătwahn] (1858–1943) Actor-manager, born in Limoges, France. He founded the Théâtre Libre (1887), and was director of the Odéon (from 1906).

Antonelli, Giacomo [antonelee] (1806–76) Clergyman, born in Sonnino, Italy. Pius IX appointed him cardinal-deacon (1847), premier and minister of foreign affairs (1848), and foreign secretary (1850). >> Pius IX

Antonello da Messina [antoneloh da meseena] (c.1430–79) Painter, born in Messina, Italy. He was an accomplished master of oil painting, and helped to popularize the medium, his work influencing Giovanni Bellini's portraits. >> Bellini, Giovanni

Antonescu, Ion [antoneskoo] (1882–1946) Romanian general and dictator for the Nazis in World War 2, born in Pitesti, Romania. He became chief-of-staff in 1937, and in 1940 assumed dictatorial powers, forcing the abdication of Carol II. He was overthrown in 1944 and later executed for war crimes. >> Carol II

Antoninus, M Aurelius >> **Aurelius**

Antoninus Pius [antoniynus piyus], originally **Titus Aurelius Fulvus** (AD 86–161) Roman emperor (138–161), born in Lanuvium. The adopted son of Emperor Hadrian, he extended the empire, and in Britain built the Antonine Wall between the Forth and Clyde rivers. >> Hadrian

Antonioni, Michelangelo [antoniohnee] (1912–) Film director, born in Ferrara, Italy. He made several documentaries (1945–50) before turning to feature films, and gained an international reputation with *L'avventura* (1959). Later films include *La notte* (1961) and *Blow-up* (1966).

Antonius, Marcus [antohnius] or **Mark Antony** (c.83–30 BC) Roman statesman and soldier. After Caesar's assassination, his speeches caused the flight of the conspirators from Rome, and left him with almost absolute power. He formed a triumvirate with Octavian and Lepidus to share the Roman world, defeating Brutus and Cassius at Philippi (42 BC). He then met and was captivated by Queen Cleopatra, whom he followed to Egypt (41 BC). In 40 BC a new division of the Roman world gave Antony the East, and he married Augustus's sister Octavia. His renewed liaison with Cleopatra provided Octavian with reasons to arouse the Roman people against him. Defeat at Actium (31 BC) followed, and Antony and Cleopatra both committed suicide. >> Augustus; Caesar; Cleopatra VII

Antonov, Oleg Konstantinovich [antonof] (1906–84) Soviet aircraft designer, born in Troitskoe, Russia. He wrote over 50 books on aircraft design, and his name lives on in the AN-225 six-engined super heavylift aircraft shown at the Paris Airshow in 1989.

Antony or **Anthony, St,** known as **Antony the Great,** also called **Antony of Egypt** (c.251–356), feast day 17 January. Religious hermit, the father of Christian monasticism, born in Koman, Upper Egypt. He spent 20 years in the desert, where he withstood a famous series of temptations, and in 305 founded a monastery near Memphis -

one of the earliest attempts to instruct people in the monastic way of life.

Antony or **Anthony of Padua, St** (1195–1231), feast day 13 June. Monk, born in Lisbon. In 1220 he entered the Franciscan order, and became known for his preaching. Canonized in 1232, he is the patron saint of Portugal, lost property, and the lower animals.

Anville, Jean Baptiste Bourguignon d' [ăveel] (1697–1782) Geographer and map-maker, born in Paris. He improved the standards of ancient and mediaeval map-making, and became the first geographer to the King of France.

Anzengruber, Ludwig [antsengrüber] (1839–89) Writer, born in Vienna. Among his best-known works are the play *The Pastor of Kirchfeld* (trans, 1870) and the novel *The Sternstein Farm* (trans, 1885).

Anzilotti, Dionisio [antsilotee] (1867–1950) Jurist, born in Pistoia, Italy. A founder of the positive school of international law, he became a judge of the Permanent Court of International Justice (1921–30), and also its president (1928–30).

Aouita, Said [aweeta] (1960–) Athlete, born in Rabat, Morocco. A middle- and long-distance track athlete, he set world records at 1500 m and 5000 m in 1985, later broke world records at 2 mi and 2000 m, and was the 1984 Olympic and 1987 World 5000 m champion.

Apelles [apeleez] (4th-c BC) Greek painter, probably born in Colophon, Asia Minor. He is said to have accompanied Alexander the Great on his expedition to Asia. None of his work has survived. >> Alexander the Great

Apgar, Virginia (1909–1974) Physician and anesthesiologist, born in Westfield, NJ. Best known for pioneering work in anesthesia relating to childbirth, in 1952 she developed the *Apgar Score* to evaluate newborns.

Apollinaire, Guillaume [apolinair, giyom], pseudonym of **Wilhelm Apollinaris de Kostrowitzki** (1880–1918) Poet and art critic, born in Rome, Italy. A leader of the Parisian movement rejecting poetic traditions in outlook, rhythm, and language, he coined the term *surrealist*. His work is expressed chiefly in *The Spirits* (trans, 1913) and *Calligrammes* (1918).

Apollinaris the Younger [apolinahris] (c.310–c.390) Syrian clergyman, the son of Apollinaris the Elder. He became Bishop of Laodicea (360), and upheld a doctrine (*Apollinarianism*) condemned by the Council of Constantinople (381) as denying the true human nature of Christ.

Apollodoros or **Apollodorus** [apolodorus] (5th-c BC) Athenian painter. He is said to have introduced the technique of *chiaroscuro* (light and shade).

Apollodoros or **Apollodorus** [apolodoros] (2nd-c BC) Athenian scholar. He wrote works on mythology and etymology, and is best known for his verse *Chronicle* of Greek history from the fall of Troy.

Apollodoros or **Apollodorus** [apolodoros] (2nd-c) Greek architect, who designed Trajan's column in Rome. He was executed in AD 129 for his fearless criticism of Emperor Hadrian's design for a temple.

Apollonius [apolohnius], known as **Dyskolos** ('Bad-tempered') (2nd-c) Greek grammarian, the first to reduce Greek syntax to a system. Only four of his many works on grammar survive.

Apollonius of Perga [apolohnius], known as **the Great Geometer** (280–210 BC) Greek mathematician, born in Perga, Anatolia. He was the author of the definitive ancient work on conic sections which laid the modern foundations on the subject.

Apollonius of Tyana [apolohnius] (c.3–c.97) Greek philosopher and seer, born in Tyana, Cappadocia. A zealous neo-Pythagorean teacher, he was hailed as a sage and worker of miracles.

Apollonius [apolohnius], known as **Apollonius Rhodius** (3rd-c BC) Greek scholar, born in Alexandria, Egypt, but long resident in Rhodes. He wrote many works on grammar, and an epic poem about the quest for the Golden Fleece, the *Argonautica*.

Appel, Karel Christian (1921–) Painter, born in Amsterdam. He became one of an influential group of Dutch, Belgian, and Danish Expressionists known as 'Cobra', his work relating to American abstract Expressionism.

Appert, Nicolas François [apair] (1752–1841) Chef and inventor, born in Châlons-sur-Marne, France. In 1795 he began experiments aimed at preserving food in hermetically sealed containers, and in 1812 established the world's first commercial food-canning business.

Appia, Adolphe [apia] (1862–1928) Scene designer and theatrical producer, born in Geneva, Switzerland. One of the first to introduce simple planes instead of rich stage settings, he pioneered the symbolic use of lighting, particularly in opera.

Appian of Alexandria [apian], Gr **Appianos** (2nd-c) Roman historian and lawyer, born in Alexandria, Egypt. He compiled 24 books of Roman conquests down to Vespasian, written in Greek, of which nine survive complete.

Appleton, Sir Edward (Victor) (1892–1965) Physicist, born in Bradford, West Yorkshire. He discovered the existence of a layer of electrically charged particles in the upper atmosphere (the *Appleton layer*), which plays an essential part in long-distance radio communication. He received the Nobel Prize for Physics in 1947.

Apponyi, Albert Georg, Gróf (Count) [oponyuh] (1846–1933) Hungarian statesman, born in Vienna. Leader of the moderate Opposition which became the National Party (1891), in 1899 he went over to the Liberal Government Party, and served as President of the Diet (1901–3).

Apraxin, Fyodor Matveyevich, Graf (Count) [apraksin] (1671–1728) Russian naval commander, known as the 'father of the Russian navy'. In the service of Peter the Great from 1682, he built up the navy into a powerful fighting force, and in the Great Northern War (1700–21) he routed the Swedish fleet (1713). >> Peter I (of Russia)

Apuleius, Lucius [apulayus] (2nd-c) Roman writer, born in Madaura, Numidia. His best-known work is the romance *Metamorphoses*, or *The Golden Ass*, a satire on the vices of the age.

Aquaviva, Claudius [akwaveeva] (1543–1615) Clergyman, born in Naples, Italy. Appointed fifth general of the Jesuit order in 1581, his book *The Reason and Establishment of Studies* (trans, 1586), laid the basis for later Jesuit education.

Aquila [akwila], known as **Ponticus** ('from Pontus') (2nd-c) Translator of the Old Testament into Greek, a native of Sinope. He is said to have been first a pagan, then a Christian, and finally a Jew.

Aquinas, St Thomas [akwiynas], known as **Doctor Angelicus** ('angelic doctor') (1225–74), feast day 7 March. Scholastic philosopher and theologian, born near Aquino, Italy. He entered the Dominican order, and became widely known as a teacher. He was the first among 13th-c metaphysicians to stress the importance of sense perception and the experimental foundation of human knowledge. His best-known works are two encyclopedic syntheses: the *Summa contra Gentiles* (1259–64) and the incomplete *Summa theologiae* (1266–73), which includes the famous 'five ways' or proofs of the existence of God. He was canonized in 1323.

Aquino, Cory [akeenoh], popular name of **(Maria) Corazon Aquino**, *née* **Cojuangco** (1933–) Philippines president (1986–92), born in Tarlac province. In 1956 she married **Benigno Aquino** (1932–83), the chief political opponent to

Ferdinand Marcos. The couple lived in exile in the USA until 1983, when Benigno returned to the Philippines and was assassinated. She took up her husband's cause, leading a non-violent 'people's power' movement which brought the overthrow of Marcos. >> Marcos

Arabi Pasha >> **Ahmed Arabi**

Arafat, Yasser [arafat], originally **Mohammed Abed Ar'ouf Arafat** (1929–) Palestinian president, born in Jerusalem. In 1959 he co-founded the Fatah resistance group, which in 1969 took control of the Palestine Liberation Organization. After the 1988 declaration of Palestinian statehood he was elected president, negotiating international recognition of Palestine in 1993.

Arago, (Dominique) François (Jean) [aragoh] (1786–1853) Scientist and statesman, born in Estagel, France. His scientific achievements were mainly in the fields of astronomy, magnetism, and optics. He took a prominent part in the July Revolution of 1830, and in 1848 entered the provisional government.

Aragon, Louis [aragõ] (1897–1982) Political activist and writer, born in Paris. A member of the Surrealist group, he co-founded the journal *Littérature* with André Breton in 1919. After converting to communism (1930), he wrote a series of social-realistic novels, *Le Réel* (1933–51). >> Breton, André

Araki, Sadao [arakee] (1877–1966) Japanese soldier and politician. An ultra-nationalist, he was a leader of the right-wing *Kodaha* ('Imperial Way') faction of the army. After World War 2 he was sentenced to life imprisonment, but released in 1965.

Aram, Eugene (1704–59) Scholar and murderer, born in Ramsgill, North Yorkshire. A philologist, he postulated the relationship between Celtic and Indo-European tongues. In 1745 he was tried for murder and acquitted, but later re-tried, and hanged at York.

Aranda, Pedro Pablo Abarca y Bolea, conde de (Count of) (1718–99) Spanish statesman and general, born in Siétamo, Spain. He was made prime minister in 1766, with the task of restoring order after risings. Prime minister again in 1792, he antagonized Godoy, and was forced to retire. >> Godoy

Arany, János [awrony] (1817–82) Poet, born in Nagy-Szalonta, Hungary. With **Sandor Petöfi** (1823–49) he was a leader of the popular national school, and is regarded a major Hungarian poet. His chief work is the *Toldi* trilogy (1847–54).

Arason, Jón [arason] (c.1484–1550) Icelandic national hero and clergyman, the last Roman Catholic bishop in Iceland, born in Eyjafjörður, Iceland. He fiercely resisted the imposition of Lutheranism from Denmark by the crown, was declared an outlaw, and eventually beheaded.

Arbarbanel >> **Abarbanel, Isaac ben Jehudah**

Arber, Agnes [ah(r)ber], *née* **Robertson** (1879–1960) Botanist and philosopher, born in London. Her works include the botanical *Herbals, Their Origin and Evolution* (1912) and the philosophical *The Manifold and the One* (1957).

Arber, Werner [ah(r)ber] (1929–) Microbiologist, born in Gränichen, Switzerland. He proposed that bacteria defend themselves against attack by viruses, using selective enzymes to cut the DNA chain of the infecting virus. He shared the Nobel Prize for Physiology or Medicine in 1978.

Arblay, Madame d' >> **Burney, Fanny**

Arbus, Diane [ah(r)buhs], *née* **Nemerov** (1923–71) Photographer, born in New York City. She sought to portray people 'without their masks', achieving fame in the 1960s with her ironic studies of social poses and the deprived classes.

Arbuthnot, John [ah(r)buhthnot] (1667–1735) Physician and writer, born in Inverbervie, Grampian. Settling in London, he became physician to Queen Anne (1705). His literary works include the satirical *The History of John Bull* (1712) and contributions to the *Memoirs of Martinus Scriblerus* (1741).

Arc, Joan of >> Joan of Arc, St

Arcadius [ah(r)**kay**dius] (377–408) Roman Emperor, born in Spain. On the death of his father, Emperor Theodosius (395), he received the E half of the Roman Empire, the W half falling to his brother Honorius. A weak ruler, he was dominated by his wife, **Eudoxia** (?–404). >> Honorius, Flavius; Theodosius

Arcaro, Eddie [ah(r)**ka**roh], popular name of **George Edward Arcaro** (1916–) Jockey, born in Cincinnati, OH. He won the Kentucky Derby five times, and was winner (1941, 1948) of the horse-racing triple crown (the Kentucky Derby, Preakness Stakes, and Belmont Stakes).

Arcesilaus [ah(r)sesi**lay**us] (c.316–c.241 BC) Greek philosopher, born in Pitane, Aeolia. He became the sixth head of the 'Old Academy' founded by Plato, and under his leadership the school became known as the 'Middle Academy'. >> Plato

Arch, Joseph (1826–1919) Preacher and reformer, born in Barford, Warwickshire. A farm labourer, he became a Primitive Methodist preacher, and went on to found the National Agricultural Labourers' Union in 1872.

Archelaus [ah(r)ke**lay**us] (1st-c) Ethnarch of Judaea, the son of Herod the Great, who succeeded his father in AD 1. After a nine-year reign, he was deposed by Emperor Augustus for his tyranny, and banished. >> Augustus; Herod

Archelaus [ah(r)ke**lay**us] (5th-c BC) Greek philosopher and cosmologist. He is reputed to have been the pupil of Anaxagoras and the teacher of Socrates. >> Anaxagoras; Socrates

Archer, Fred(erick) (1857–86) Jockey, born in Cheltenham, Gloucestershire. During his career he rode 2748 winners, including the Derby five times. His record of 246 winners in one season (1885) stood until beaten by Gordon Richards in 1933. >> Richards, Gordon

Archer (of Weston-Super-Mare), Jeffrey (Howard) Archer, Baron (1940–) Writer and politician. He became a Conservative MP (1969–74), but resigned following bankruptcy. He began writing fiction, and his many best-selling novels include *First Among Equals* (1984) and *As the Crow Flies* (1991).

Archer, Robyn (1948–) Singer and actress, born in Adelaide, South Australia. Particularly associated with the German cabaret songs of Weill, Eisler, and Dessau, her shows *A Star is Torn* (1979) and *The Pack of Women* (1981) both became successful books and recordings.

Archer, Thomas (1668–1743) Baroque architect, born in Tanworth, Warwickshire. His works include the churches of St John, Westminster (1714) and St Paul, Deptford (1712), and Roehampton House in Surrey.

Archilochus of Paros [ah(r)**ki**lokus] (760–670 BC) Greek poet from the island of Paros, regarded as the first of the lyric poets, and renowned for his vituperative satire. Only fragments of his work survive.

Archimedes [ah(r)ki**mee**deez] (c.287–212 BC) Greek scientist, born in Syracuse. He studied the theory of mechanics and hydrostatics, proving that a body plunged in a fluid becomes lighter by an amount equal to the weight of the fluid it displaces (*Archimedes' principle*) - a discovery which in popular tradition is remembered by his uttering *eureka* ('I have found it'). He was the first to evaluate areas and volumes of solids systematically, and gave a good approximation to π.

Archipenko, Alexander Porfirievich [ah(r)chi**peng**koh] (1887–1964) Sculptor and painter, born in Kiev, Ukraine. Influenced by Cubism, he became famous for his combinations of sculpture and painting, as in 'Medrano II' (1914).

Arcimboldo, Giuseppe [ah(r)chim**bohl**doh], also spelled **Arcimboldi** (c.1530–93) Painter, born in Milan, Italy. In Prague he became court painter to the Habsburgs, known for his fantastic heads composed of fragmented landscape, animals, flowers, and other objects, all brightly coloured and highly detailed.

Ardashir I [ah(r)da**sheer**] (c.211–42) King of Persia (224–42), founder of the Persian dynasty of the Sassanids. He overthrew Ardavan, the last of the Parthian kings (AD c.226), and murdered Darius III, but was defeated by Alexander Severus in 233.

Arden, Elizabeth, originally **Florence Nightingale Graham** (1878–1966) Beautician and businesswoman, born in Woodbridge, Ontario, Canada. She opened a beauty salon in New York City in 1910, producing cosmetics on a large scale, and developed a worldwide chain of salons.

Arden, John (1930–) Playwright, born in Barnsley, South Yorkshire. His works, which include *Sergeant Musgrave's Dance* (1959) and *The Workhouse Donkey* (1963), often experiment with dramatic form and theatrical technique.

Arendt, Hannah [arent] (1906–75) Philosopher and political theorist, born in Hanover, Germany. She went to the USA in 1940 as a refugee from the Nazis. Active in various Jewish organizations, her books include *Origins of Totalitarianism* (1951) and *The Life of the Mind* (1978).

Arensky, Anton Stepanovich [a**ren**skee] (1861–1906) Composer, born in Novgorod, Russia. From 1895 he conducted the court choir at St Petersburg, and his compositions include five operas and two symphonies.

Aretaeus [are**tee**us] (2nd-c) Greek physician of Cappadocia, considered to rank next to Hippocrates. The first four books of his great work on medicine treat of the causes and symptoms of diseases; the other four, of the cures. >> Hippocrates

Aretino, Pietro [are**tee**noh] (1492–1557) Poet, born in Arezzo, Italy. He became known throughout Europe for his literary attacks on well-known figures. At Rome he secured the favour of Pope Leo X, which he later lost by writing 16 salacious *Lewd Sonnets* (trans, 1524). >> Leo X

Argand, Aimé [ah(r)**gã**] (1755–1803) Physicist and chemist, born in Geneva, Switzerland. In Holland (1784), he invented the *Argand burner*, the first scientifically designed oil lamp, later used in lighthouses.

Argand, Jean-Robert [ah(r)**gã**] (1768–1822) Mathematician, born in Geneva, Switzerland. After him is named the *Argand diagram*, in which complex numbers are represented by points in the plane.

Argelander, Friedrich Wilhelm August [ah(r)ge**lan**der] (1799–1875) Astronomer, born in Memel, Germany. Between 1852 and 1861 he plotted the position of all stars of the N hemisphere above the ninth magnitude.

Argensola [ah(r)khen**sohl**a] Poets and brothers: **Bartolomé Leonardo de Argensola** (1562–1631) and **Lupercio de Argensola** (1559–1613), born in Barbastro, Spain. Their poems led them to be styled the 'Spanish Horaces', but they were also official historians of Aragon. >> Horace

Argenson, René Louis, marquis d' [ah(r)**zhã**sõ] (1694–1757) French statesman, born in Paris. Councillor to the Parlement of Paris (1716), and foreign minister under Louis XV (1744–7), his journal is an important contemporary source of information.

Argentina, La, popular name of **Antonia Mercé** (1890–1936) Dancer, born in Buenos Aires. She became a dancer with the Madrid Opera at age 11, and later devoted herself to Spanish dance, for which she became internationally renowned.

Argyll, Archibald Campbell, 5th Earl of [ah(r)**giyl**] (1530–73) Scottish Protestant, a follower of Mary, Queen of Scots, and involved in the assassination of Darnley. He later supported James VI and I and became Lord High Chancellor of Scotland (1572). >> Darnley; James I (of England); Mary, Queen of Scots

Argyll, Archibald Campbell, Marquess and 8th Earl of [ah(r)**giyl**] (1607–61) Scottish political leader. He supported parliament in the English Civil War, forming a Scottish government under Cromwell. After Charles I's execution (1649), he accepted Charles II's claim as king, but later submitted to Cromwell again. After the Restoration he was executed. >> Charles I / II (of England); Cromwell, Oliver

Argyll, Archibald Campbell, 9th Earl of [ah(r)**giyl**] (1629–85) Scottish royalist, born in Dalkeith, Lothian. In 1681 he opposed the Test Act, and was sentenced to death, but escaped to Holland. On his return he conspired with Monmouth to overthrow the king (1685), but was executed. >> Monmouth

Argyll, John Campbell, 2nd Duke of [ah(r)**giyl**] (1678–1743) Scottish Unionist, one of the strongest supporters of the Act of Union of 1707, born in Petersham, Greater London. He commanded the Hanoverian forces during the Jacobite rising in Scotland (1715–16).

Aribau, Bonaventura Carles [ari**bah**oo] (1798–1862) Economist and writer, born in Barcelona, Spain. He was appointed director of the Mint and of the Spanish Treasury (1847). His poem *Ode to the Fatherland* (trans, 1832) had a great influence on contemporary Catalan writers.

Ariosto, Ludovico [ari**o**stoh] (1474–1533) Poet, born in Reggio nell'Emilia, Italy. In the service of Cardinal d'Este at Ferrara, he produced his great poem, *Orlando furioso* (1516), the Roland epic that forms a continuation of Boiardo's *Orlando innamorato*. >> Boiardo; Roland

Aristarchus of Samos [arist**ah**(r)kos], also spelled **Aristarchos** (c.310–230 BC) Alexandrian astronomer who seems to have anticipated Copernicus, maintaining that the Earth moves round the Sun. Only one of his works has survived. >> Copernicus

Aristarchus of Samothrace [arist**ah**(r)**kos**] (c.215–145 BC) Alexandrian grammarian and critic, best known for his edition of Homer. He was in charge of the Library of Alexandria for over 30 years. >> Homer

Aristides [arist**iy**deez], known as **Aristides the Just** (c.530–c.468 BC) Athenian soldier and statesman. During the Greek–Persian Wars he commanded at Marathon (490 BC), Salamis (480 BC), and Plataea (479 BC). His greatest achievement was the organization of the Delian League after the defeat of the Persians.

Aristides [arist**iy**deez] (2nd-c) Greek Christian apologist. He wrote an *Apology for the Christian Faith*, mentioned by Eusebius and Jerome, which came to light in the late 19th-c. >> Eusebius of Caesarea; Jerome, St

Aristippus [arist**ip**us] (4th-c BC) Greek philosopher, born in Cyrene, Africa. A pupil of Socrates, he founded the influential Cyrenaic school of hedonism, whose main doctrine was that pleasure was the highest good. >> Socrates

Aristogeiton >> **Harmodius**

Aristophanes [arist**o**faneez] (c.448–c.388 BC) Greek playwright. He is said to have written 54 plays, but only 11 are extant. His works fall into three periods: to the first (up to c.425 BC), belong *The Acharnians*, *The Knights*, *The Clouds*, the *Wasps*, and *Peace*; to the second (up to 406 BC), *The Birds*, *Lysistrata*, *Thesmophoriazusae*, and *Frogs*; to the third (up to c.388 BC), *The Ecclesiazusae* and *The Plutus*.

Aristotle [arist**o**tl] (384–322 BC) Greek philosopher, scientist, and physician, born in Stagira, Macedonia. Associated with Plato's Academy for 20 years, in 335 BC he opened his own school (the Lyceum). He wrote the first systematic treatises on logic; made major contributions to the study of natural change, psychology, and biology;

and wrote some of the most influential philosophical works in the history of thought, notably his *Metaphysics*, *Nicomachean Ethics*, *Politics*, *Rhetoric*, and *Poetics*. >> Plato

Arius [**ah**rius] (Gr **Areios**) (c.250–336) Founder of Arianism, born in Libya. He claimed (c.319) that, in the doctrine of the Trinity, the Son was not co-equal with or co-eternal with the Father, but only the first and highest of all finite beings, created out of nothing by an act of God's free will. He won some support, but was excommunicated in 321.

Arkwright, Sir Richard (1732–92) Inventor of mechanical cotton-spinning, born in Preston, Lancashire. In 1768 he set up his celebrated spinning-frame in Preston, but popular opinion believed that his inventions threatened jobs, and in 1779 his mill was destroyed by a mob.

Arlen, Michael [**ah**(r)len], originally **Dikran Kouyoumdjian** (1895–1956) Novelist, born in Ruschuk, Bulgaria. He made his reputation with *Piracy* (1922), *The Green Hat* (1924), and several short-story collections.

Arlington, Henry Bennet, 1st Earl of (1618–85) English statesman, born in Arlington, Greater London. He was secretary of state (1662–74) under Charles II, and one of the king's Cabal ministry. In 1674 he was unsuccessfully impeached for popery and self-aggrandizement, later serving as Lord Chamberlain. >> Charles II (of England)

Arliss, George, originally **Augustus George Andrews** (1868–1946) Actor, born in London. He went to the USA in 1901, where he became known for his film representations of famous historical characters, notably in *Disraeli* (1929, Oscar).

Arlott, (Leslie Thomas) John (1914–91) Writer, journalist, and broadcaster, born in Basingstoke, Hampshire. He became a popular cricket commentator for BBC radio and television. His many books on cricket include *How to Watch Cricket* (1949, 1983) and *Arlott on Cricket* (1984).

Armani, Giorgio [ah(r)**mah**nee] (1935–) Fashion designer, born in Piacenza, Italy. He became a designer for Nino Cerruti (1930–) in 1961, before setting up his own company in 1975, designing first for men, then also for women.

Armfelt, Gustaf Mauritz (1757–1814) Swedish soldier and statesman, born near Turku, Finland. He served Gustav III in the war against Russia (1790), and was later Gustav IV's army commander in Pomerania against Napoleon (1805–7). >> Gustav III / IV; Napoleon I

Arminius [ah(r)**min**ius] (?–19) Chief of the German Cherusci. An officer in the Roman army, he acquired Roman citizenship, but in AD 9 allied with other German tribes to defeat the Romans. He was murdered by his own kinsmen.

Arminius, Jacobus [ah(r)**min**ius], Lat name of **Jakob Hermandszoon** (1560–1609) Protestant theologian, born in Oudewater, The Netherlands. Opposed to the Calvinistic doctrine of predestination, his teaching was formalized in the 'Remonstrance' of 1610.

Armitage, Edward (1817–96) Painter, born in London. Professor at the Royal Academy schools from 1875, his works were chiefly of historical and biblical subjects.

Armitage, Karole (1954–) Dancer and choreographer, born in Madison, WI. Trained in classical ballet, she danced in Switzerland and New York, then began a choreographic career, creating pieces for the Paris Opéra Ballet.

Armitage, Kenneth (1916–) Sculptor, born in Leeds, West Yorkshire. His bronzes are usually of semi-abstract figures, united into a group by stylized clothing.

Armour, Tommy, popular name of **Thomas Dickson Armour** (1895–1968) Golfer, born in Edinburgh. He emigrated to the USA in 1925, winning the US Open (1927) and the British Open (1931). He later became a teaching professional.

Armour, Jean >> **Burns, Robert**

Armstead, Henry Hugh (1828–1905) Sculptor, born in London. His best-known works are reliefs and bronze statues for the Albert Memorial, the fountain at King's College, Cambridge, and the reredos at Westminster Abbey.

Armstrong, Edwin H(oward) (1890–1954) Electrical engineer and inventor, born in New York City. He devised the superheterodyne radio receiver and perfected the frequency-modulation system of radio transmission.

Armstrong, Gillian (May) (1952–) Film director, born in Melbourne, Victoria, Australia. Her films often focus on the problems facing independent women, such as *My Brilliant Career* (1979) and *The Last Days of Chez Nous* (1991).

Armstrong, Henry, originally **Henry Jackson,** nickname **Hammerin' Hank** (1912–88) Boxer, born in Columbus, MS. He is the only man to have held three world titles at different weights simultaneously - featherweight (1937), welterweight, and lightweight (both 1938).

Armstrong, Henry Edward (1848–1937) Chemist, born in London. His major contribution was in chemical education, where he pioneered the heuristic method.

Armstrong, Johnnie (?–1529/30) Celebrated Scottish Border freebooter and cattle-rustler ('reiver'). He became the hero of many Border ballads.

Armstrong, Louis, nickname **Satchmo** (1898/1900–71) Jazz trumpeter and singer, born in New Orleans, LA. After joining King Oliver's band (1922), his melodic inventiveness established the central role of the improvising soloist in jazz, especially in a series of recordings known as the 'Hot Fives' and 'Hot Sevens' (1925–8). Film appearances include *Pennies from Heaven* (1936) and *High Society* (1956). >> Oliver, King

Armstrong, Neil (Alden) (1930–) Astronaut, born in Wapakoneta, OH. As commander of the Apollo 11 moon-landing mission, he became the first man to set foot on the Moon, on 20 July, 1969. >> Aldrin; Collins, Michael

Armstrong (of Ilminster), Robert, Baron (1927–) British civil servant. Under Margaret Thatcher he was secretary to the cabinet and head of the home civil service. He gained notoriety when he gave evidence in the 'Spycatcher' case in Australia (1987), admitting he had sometimes been 'economical with the truth'. >> Thatcher

Armstrong, William (16th-c) 'Kinmont Willie' of the Border ballad of that name, a Dumfriesshire moss-trooper. He was rescued in 1596 by Walter Scott from Carlisle Castle.

Armstrong, William George, Baron (1810–1900) Inventor and industrialist, born in Newcastle upon Tyne, Tyne and Wear. He produced an improved hydraulic engine (1840), the hydraulic crane (1845), and the Armstrong breech-loading gun.

Armstrong-Jones, Antony >> Snowdon

Armstrong-Jones, Lady Sarah >> Margaret, Princess

Arnarson, Ingólfur (late 9th-c) Viking from Hördaland, Norway. He was honoured as the first settler of Iceland in AD 874, and his descendants held the hereditary post of supreme chieftain of the Icelandic parliament (*Althing*) after its foundation in 930.

Arnason, Jón, known as **the Grimm of Iceland** (1819–88) Collector of folk-tales, born in Iceland. He collected and published Icelandic tales (1862–4), translated as *Legends of Iceland* by Eiríkur Magnússon (1864–6). >> Grimm

Arnaud, Arsène >> Claretie, Jules

Arnaud, Yvonne (Germaine) [ah(r)noh] (1892–1958) Actress, born in Bordeaux, France. She appeared in many musicals and farces on the British stage, and made several cinema adaptations of her stage successes, such as *Mon Oncle* (1958). A theatre at Guildford was opened in her honour in 1965.

Arnauld, Angélique [ah(r)noh], known as **Mère Angélique de Saint Jean** (1624–84) French Jansenist religious,

the niece of Antoine Arnauld. She became abbess of the convent of Port-Royal des Champs in Paris in 1678. During the persecution of the Port-Royalists she was known for her heroic courage. >> Arnauld, Antoine

Arnauld, Antoine [ah(r)noh], known as **the Great Arnauld** (1612–94) French philosopher, lawyer, mathematician, and priest. He became head of the Jansenist movement and collaborated on the work known as the *Port Royal Logic* (1662).

Arnauld, Jacqueline-Marie-Angélique [ah(r)noh], known as **Mère Angélique** (1591–1661) French Jansenist, the sister of Antoine Arnauld. She became abbess of Port-Royal in 1602 at the age of 11, and ultimately reformed the convent through severe discipline. >> Arnauld, Antoine

Arndt, Ernst Moritz [ah(r)nt] (1769–1860) Poet and German patriot, born in the island of Rügen (then Swedish). In his *Spirit of the Times* (trans, 1806) he boldly attacked Napoleon and had to take refuge in Stockholm (1806–9).

Arne, Thomas (Augustine) (1710–78) Composer, born in London. As composer to the Drury Lane Theatre, he composed famous settings of Shakespearean songs. His operas include *Rosamond* (1733), but his best-known work is 'Rule, Britannia'.

Arnheim, Rudolf [ah(r)nhiym] (1904–) Art theorist and psychologist, born in Berlin. He is most noted as a pioneering theorist of the psychology of the arts, in such works as *Art as Visual Perception* (1954).

Arnim, Achim von, originally **Karl Joachim Friedrich Ludwig von Arnim** (1781–1831) Writer of fantastic but original romances, born in Berlin. He published many volumes of tales and novels, including the folk-song collection *Des Knaben Wunderhorn*. His wife Bettina (1785–1859), was as a girl infatuated with Goethe, and afterwards published a *Correspondence* with him, as well as 10 volumes of tales and essays. >> Goethe

Arnim, Jürgen, Freiherr (Baron) **von** (1891–1971) German soldier, born of an old Silesian military family. He served in both World Wars, and succeeded Rommel in command of Army Group Africa. In 1943 he surrendered his troops to the Allies, and was interned. >> Rommel

Arno, Peter, originally **Curtis Arnoux Peters** (1904–68) Cartoonist, born in New York City. He was one of the first contributors to the *New Yorker* magazine, from 1925, with satirical drawings of New York cafe society.

Arnobius the Elder [ah(r)nohbius] (?–330) A teacher of rhetoric in Sicca, Numidia (Africa). He became a Christian c.300, and wrote a vigorous defence of Christianity, *Adversus nationes*.

Arnold, Aberhard (1883–1935) Founder of the Bruderhof movement in Nazi Germany, born in Breslau, Poland. A convinced pacifist associated with the Student Christian Movement, a selection of his writings, *God's Revolution*, was published in 1984.

Arnold, Benedict (1741–1801) American soldier and turncoat, born in Norwich, CT. In the War of Independence he fought with distinction in the colonial forces, but later conspired with John André to betray West Point. When André was captured, Arnold fled to the British lines, where he was given a command. >> André, John

Arnold, Sir Edwin (1832–1904) Poet and journalist, born in Gravesend, Kent. In 1856 he became principal of Deccan College, Poona. His best-known work is *The Light of Asia* (1879), on Buddhism.

Arnold, Henry Harley, popular name **Hap Arnold** (1886–1950) US air force officer, born in Gladwyne, PA. He became commanding general of the US Army Air Corps in 1938, chief of US Army Air Forces in 1941, and the first general of the independent US Air Force in 1947.

Arnold, Joseph (1782–1818) Botanist, born in Beccles, Suffolk. He accompanied Sir Thomas Stamford Raffles as naturalist to Sumatra, and discovered the largest flower known, *Rafflesia arnoldi*. >> Raffles

Arnold, Sir Malcolm (Henry) (1921–) Composer, born in Northampton, Northamptonshire. His works include nine symphonies, 18 concertos, ballets, operas, and film music, notably *Bridge over the River Kwai* (1957, Oscar).

Arnold, Matthew (1822–88) Poet and critic, born in Laleham, Middlesex, the eldest son of Dr Arnold of Rugby. An inspector of schools (1851–86) and professor of poetry at Oxford (1857–67), he also wrote several works of criticism, such as *Culture and Anarchy* (1869), and books on religious themes. >> Arnold, Thomas; Ward, Mary Augusta

Arnold, Mary Augusta >> Ward, Mary Augusta

Arnold, Samuel (1740–1802) Composer, born in London. He is best remembered for his valuable collection of cathedral music (1790) and his 36-volume edition of Handel (1786–97).

Arnold, Thomas (1795–1842) Teacher and scholar, born in East Cowes, Isle of Wight, the father of Matthew Arnold and Mary Augusta Ward. As headmaster of Rugby School from 1828, he instituted many reforms, graphically described in *Tom Brown's Schooldays* (1857). >> Arnold, Matthew; Hughes, Thomas; Ward, Mary Augusta

Arnold of Brescia [breshia] (c.1100–55) Clergyman and politician, born in Brescia, Italy. His criticism of the wealth and power of the Church led to his banishment from Italy in 1139. An insurrection against the papal government drew him to Rome (1143), where he was condemned for heresy, and hanged.

Arnolfo di Cambio [ah(r)**nol**foh dee **kam**bioh] (c.1245–1302) Italian sculptor and architect, the designer of Florence Cathedral. A pupil of Nicola Pisano, his work also includes the pulpit at Siena, and the wall-tomb of Cardinal de Braye at Orvieto. >> Pisano, Nicola

Arnon, Daniel I(srael) (1910–) Plant physiologist, born in Warsaw. Working at the University of California, Berkeley (1936–78), in 1954 he published results of the first photosynthetic process outside the living cell.

Arp, Jean or **Hans** (1887–1966) Sculptor, born in Strasbourg, France. He was one of the founders of the Dada movement in Zürich in 1916, becoming a major influence on organic abstract sculpture, based on natural forms.

Árpád [**ah(r)**pad] (?–907) The national hero of Hungary. A Magyar chieftain in the Caucasus, he led the Magyars from the Black Sea (c.896) and occupied modern Hungary. He founded the Árpád royal dynasty of Hungary, from St Stephen (997) to 1301.

Arrabal, Fernando [ara**bal**] (1932–) Playwright and novelist, born in Melilla, Spanish Morocco. His first play, *Picnic on the Battlefield* (trans, 1958), established him in the tradition of the Theatre of the Absurd.

Arrau, Claudio [arow] (1903–91) Pianist, born in Chillán, Chile. He is renowned as an interpreter of the 19th-c solo repertory. His musical thoughts were collected in *Conversations with Arrau* by Joseph Horowitz (1982).

Arrhenius, Svante (August) [ar**ay**nius] (1859–1927) Scientist, born near Uppsala, Sweden. He became professor of physics at Stockholm in 1895, and did valuable work on the dissociation theory of electrolysis. He was awarded the Nobel Prize for Chemistry in 1903.

Arriaga, Juan Crisóstomo [aria**hga**] (1806–26) Composer, born in Bilbao, Spain. A child prodigy, his first opera *The Happy Slaves* (trans title) was produced in 1820. Although only 19 when he died, his compositions show remarkable maturity, and include three string quartets and a symphony.

Arrian [arian], Lat **Flavius Arrianus** (c.95–180) Greek historian, a native of Nicomedia in Bithynia. An officer in the Roman army, he was appointed prefect of Cappadocia in 136. His chief work is a history of the campaigns of Alexander the Great, which has survived almost entire.

Arrol, Sir William (1839–1913) Engineer, born in Houston, Strathclyde. He founded his own engineering firm, which constructed the second Tay Railway Bridge (1882–7), the Forth Railway Bridge (1883–90), and Tower Bridge in London (1886–94).

Arrow, Kenneth J(oseph) (1921–) Economist, born in New York City. His primary field was the study of collective choice based on uncertainty and risk. He shared the Nobel Prize for Economics in 1972.

Arrowsmith, Aaron (1750–1823) Cartographer, born in Winston, Durham. By 1790 he had established a successful map-making business in London. His nephew **John Arrowsmith** (1790–1873), was also an eminent cartographer.

Arsinoë [ah(r)**sin**ohee] (316–270 BC) Macedonian princess, the daughter of Ptolemy I. She married first (c.300 BC) Lysimachus, King of Thrace, then Ptolemy Ceraunus, and finally (c.276 BC) her own brother, Ptolemy II Philadelphus. Several cities were named after her. >> Lysimachus; Ptolemy I / II

Arsonval, (Jacques-)Arsène d' [ah(r)sõval] (1851–1940) Physicist, born in Borie, France. He invented the reflecting galvanometer named after him, and experimented with high-frequency oscillating current for electromedical purposes.

Artaud, Antonin [ah(r)toh] (1896–1948) Playwright, actor, director, and theorist of the Surrealist movement, born in Marseille, France. As the creator of what has been termed the Theatre of Cruelty, his influence on post-war theatre was profound.

Artaxerxes I [ah(r)ta**zerk**seez], known as **Longimanus** ('long-handed') (5th-c BC) King of Persia (464–425 BC), the second son of Xerxes I. In a long and peaceful reign, he sanctioned the Jewish religion in Jerusalem, and appointed Nehemiah as Governor of Judea in 445. >> Nehemiah; Xerxes I

Artedi, Peter [ah(r)**tay**dee] (1705–35) Swedish ichthyologist and botanist, known as 'the father of ichthyology'. He wrote *Ichthyologia* (1738), a systematic study of fishes. The classification of animals and plants in his work inspired Linnaeus. >> Linnaeus

Artemisia I [ah(r)te**miz**ia] (5th-c BC) Ruler of Halicarnassus and the neighbouring islands. She accompanied Xerxes in his expedition against Greece, and distinguished herself at Salamis (480 BC). >> Xerxes

Artemisia II [ah(r)te**miz**ia] (?–c.350 BC) Sister and wife of Mausolus, ruler of Caria. She succeeded him on his death (c.353–352 BC), and erected a mausoleum at Halicarnassus to his memory, one of the seven wonders of the ancient world.

Artevelde, Jacob van [**ah(r)**tevelduh] (c.1295–1345) Flemish statesman, born in Ghent, Belgium. Elected Captain of Ghent in 1338, he ruled like an autocrat. In 1345 he proposed that Edward the Black Prince should be made Count of Flanders, but was assassinated in an ensuing riot.

Arthur (?6th-c) A semi-legendary king of the Britons. He is said to have fought the pagan invaders (5th–6th-c AD) in a series of battles, starting with a victory at 'Mount Baden' (?516) and ending with defeat and death at 'Camlan' (537), after which he was buried at Glastonbury. His story became interwoven with legends of the Round Table of Camelot and the Holy Grail.

Arthur, Chester A(lan) (1830–86) US lawyer and 21st president (1881–5), born in Fairfield, VT. A Republican Party leader, he was made US vice-president under Garfield in 1881, and president after Garfield's assassination. >> Garfield

Arthur, Sir George (1784–1854) British diplomat, born near Plymouth, Devonshire. He was Governor of British Honduras (1814–22), Van Diemen's Land (1823–36), Upper Canada (1837–41), and Bombay (1842–6).

Arthur, Prince (1187–?1203) Duke of Brittany, and claimant to the throne of England as grandson of Henry II, after the death of Richard I (1199). It was popularly believed that Richard's brother, King John, had Arthur captured and murdered. >> Henry II (of England); John

Arthur, Prince (1486–1502) The eldest son of Henry VII, born in Winchester, Hampshire. When an infant, a marriage was arranged with Catherine of Aragon to provide an alliance between England and Spain. The wedding took place in 1501, but Arthur, a sickly youth, died soon after. >> Catherine of Aragon; Henry VII

Artigas, José Gervasio [ah(r)teegas] (1764–1850) National hero of Uruguay, born in Montevideo. The most important local patriot leader in the wars of independence against Spain, he spent the last 30 years of his life in exile.

Artin, Emil (1898–1962) Mathematician, born in Vienna. From Hamburg he emigrated to the USA in 1937, where he worked mainly in algebraic number theory and class field theory.

Artzybashev, Mikhail Petrovich [ah(r)tsibahshef] (1878–1927) Writer, born in Kharkov province, Ukraine. He gained an international reputation with his liberalist novel, *Sanin* (1907). His son **Boris** (1899–1965), went to the USA in 1919, where he illustrated books and wrote children's stories.

Arundel, Thomas [aruhndl] (1353–1414) English clergyman and statesman, the third son of Robert FitzAlan, Earl of Arundel. He became Chancellor of England (1386) and Archbishop of Canterbury (1396). Banished by Richard II in 1397, he returned with Henry IV, whom he crowned in 1399. >> Henry IV (of England); Richard II

Arup, Sir Ove (Nyquist) [aruhp] (1895–1988) Civil engineer, born of Danish parents in Newcastle upon Tyne. His structural designs include Coventry Cathedral, St Catherine's College, Oxford, and the Sydney Opera House.

Asad, Hafez al- [asad] (1928–) Syrian general and president (1971–), born in Qardaha, Syria. A member of the minority Alawi sect, he instigated a coup in 1970, becoming prime minister and then president.

Asam Architects and decorators: **Cosmas Damian Asam** (1686–1739) and **Egid Quirin Asam** (1692–1750), born in Bavaria, sons of the fresco painter **Hans Georg Asam** (1649–1711). They worked together on church interiors.

Asbjörnsen, Peter Christian [asbyoe(r)nsen] (1812–85) Folklorist, born in Oslo. He collected popular poetry and folklore, and with **Jörgen Moe** (1813–82), Bishop of Christiansand, published a famous collection of Norwegian folk tales.

Asbury, Francis (1745–1816) Clergyman, born in Handsworth, Staffordshire. Sent in 1771 as a Methodist missionary to America, he founded the Methodist Episcopal Church, and in 1785 was the first to assume the title of bishop.

Asch, Sholem (1880–1957) Writer, born in Kutno, Poland. He emigrated to America in 1914. His novels and short stories, most of them originally in Yiddish, include *The Nazarene* (1939) and *Moses* (1951).

Ascham, Roger [asham] (1515–68) Humanist, born in Kirby Wiske, North Yorkshire. Tutor to both Mary I and Elizabeth I, his main works were *Toxophilus* (1545), a treatise in defence of archery, and *The Scholemaster* (1570).

Asclepiades [asklepiyadeez] (1st-c BC) Greek physician, born in Pruss, Bithynia. He settled in Rome, where his introduction of Greek medical ideas proved influential.

Ascoli, Graziadio Isaia [askohlee] (1829–1907) Philologist, born in Görz, Italy. The founder-editor of *Archivio glottologico italiano* (1873), he is known mainly for his work on Italian dialectology.

Ashari, al- [ashahree] (873/4–935/6) Islamic theologian and philosopher, born in Basra, Iraq. His major work is *Maqalat*, which defends the idea of God's omnipotence and reaffirms traditional interpretations of religious authority within Islam.

Ashbee, Charles Robert (1863–1942) Designer, architect, and writer, born in Isleworth, Greater London. He was founder-director of the Guild of Handicraft (1888–1908) in London's East End, which attempted to put into practice the ideals of the Arts and Crafts movement.

Ashbery, John (Lawrence) (1927–) Poet, born in New York City. Recognized as the major postmodern poet of his generation, his volumes include *The Tennis Court Oath* (1962), *Self-Portrait in a Convex Mirror* (1975, Pulitzer), and *Flow Chart* (1991).

Ashby (of Brandon), Eric, Baron (1904–92) Botanist and educator, born in London. He became Vice-Chancellor of Cambridge University (1967–9), and chaired the Royal Commission on Environmental Pollution (1970–3).

Ashcroft, Dame Peggy, originally **Edith Margaret Emily Ashcroft** (1907–91) Actress, born in Croydon, Greater London. Her notable stage roles included Juliet (1935), Cleopatra (1935), and Hedda Gabler (1954). Among her films were *The Thirty-nine Steps* (1935) and *A Passage to India* (1984, Oscar).

Ashdown, Paddy, popular name of **Jeremy John Durham Ashdown** (1941–) British politician, born in India. Elected to parliament in 1983, he acted as a Liberal Party spokesman on trade and industry, and became leader of the Social and Liberal Democratic Party in 1988.

Ashe, Arthur (Robert) (1943–93) Tennis player, born in Richmond, VA. He turned professional in 1969, and took the Wimbledon singles title in 1975. He retired in 1980, the first male African-American tennis player to have achieved world ranking.

Ashkenazy, Vladimir [ashkenahzee] (1937–) Pianist and conductor, born in Nizhni Novgorod, Russia. After earning an international reputation as a concert pianist, he turned increasingly to conducting, since 1987 directing the Royal Philharmonic Orchestra.

Ashley, Laura, née **Mountney** (1925–85) Fashion designer, born in Merthyr Tydfil, Mid Glamorgan. In 1949 she started a business designing and producing furnishing materials, later developing this into an international chain of boutiques selling clothes, furnishing fabrics, and wallpapers.

Ashley, Lord >> **Shaftesbury, Earl of**

Ashmole, Elias (1617–92) Antiquary, born in Lichfield, Staffordshire. In 1677 he presented to the University of Oxford a fine collection of rarities, thus founding the *Ashmolean Museum* (built in 1682).

Ashmun, Jehudi (1794–1828) Philanthropist, born in Champlain, NY. He was the founder in 1822 of the colony of Liberia for liberated slaves on the W coast of Africa.

Ashton, Sir Frederick (William Mallandaine) (1906–88) British dancer and choreographer, born in Guayaquil, Ecuador. He became co-director of Sadler's Wells (later the Royal Ballet) (1952–63), then director (1963–70).

Ashton, Sir John William, known as **Will Ashton** (1881–1963) Painter, born in York, North Yorkshire. He established a reputation as a landscape artist, especially for his French and Mediterranean subjects, and was a leading opponent of modern trends in painting.

Ashton, Julian (Rossi) (1851–1942) Painter and teacher, born in Alderstone, Surrey. In 1878 he emigrated to Australia, founded the Sydney Art School (1896), and worked strenuously for the recognition of Australian artists.

Ashton, Winifred >> **Dane, Clemence**

Ashurbanipal >> **Assurbanipal**

Asimov, Isaac [azimov] (1920–92) Novelist, critic, and popular scientist, born in Petrovichi, Russia. His family emigrated to the USA in 1923. Best known for his science-fiction writing, his works include the short-story collection *I, Robot* (1950), and the novels known as *The Foundation Trilogy* (1953).

Asinius >> **Pollio**

Aske, Robert (?-1537) English rebel leader, a Yorkshire attorney at Gray's Inn. He headed the Catholic rising known as the Pilgrimage of Grace in protest at Henry VIII's dissolution of the monasteries, and was hanged in York for treason. >> Henry VIII

Askew, Anne (1521-46) Protestant martyr, born near Grimsby, Humberside. Early embracing the Reformed doctrines, in 1545 she was arrested on a charge of heresy, tortured, and burned at Smithfield.

Askey, Arthur, nickname **Big-hearted Arthur** (1900-82) Comedian, born in Liverpool, Merseyside. He achieved national recognition on radio with *Band Wagon* (from 1938). He used his smallness of stature (1.6 m/5 ft 2 in) to comic advantage, and his twangy pronunciation of 'I thank you!' became a catchphrase.

Aśoka or **Ashoka** [ashohka] (3rd-c BC) King of India (c.264-238 BC), the last ruler of the Mauryan dynasty. He renounced armed conquest and became a convert to Buddhism, which subsequently spread throughout India and beyond.

Aspasia [aspayzha] (5th-c BC) Mistress of Pericles, born in Miletus, Anatolia. Intellectual and vivacious, she was lampooned in Greek satire, but was held in high regard by Socrates and his followers. >> Pericles; Socrates

Aspdin, Joseph (1779-1855) Bricklayer and inventor, born in Leeds, West Yorkshire. A stonemason by trade, in 1824 he patented *Portland cement*, manufactured from clay and limestone.

Aspel, Michael (Terence) (1933-) British broadcaster and writer. He worked as a television newsreader (1960-8), later becoming known as host of *Aspel and Company* (from 1984) and as presenter of *This is Your Life* (from 1988).

Aspinall, Sir John (Audley Frederick) [aspinawl] (1851-1937) Mechanical engineer, born in Liverpool, Merseyside. He designed many locomotives, and in 1904 completed one of the first main-line railway electrification schemes in Britain, from Liverpool to Southport.

Asplund, Erik Gunnar (1885-1940) Architect, born in Stockholm. He designed the Stockholm City Library (1924-7), and many buildings for the 1930 Stockholm Exhibition.

Asquith, Herbert Henry Asquith, 1st Earl of Oxford (1852-1928) British prime minister (1908-16), born in Morley, West Yorkshire. A Liberal MP, he rose to be home secretary (1892-5), Chancellor of the Exchequer (1905-8), and prime minister. His office was notable for the Parliament Act (1911), suffragette troubles, the declaration of war (1914), and the Sinn Féin rebellion (1916).

Assad, Hafez al- >> **Asad, Hafez al-**

Asselyn, Jan [aslin] (1610-52) Painter, born in Amsterdam. He became a successful painter of Italianate landscapes which depicted imaginary Arcadian vistas inspired by the Roman countryside.

Asser [aser] (850-?909) Welsh scholar, bishop, and counsellor to Alfred the Great. Enlisted into the royal service, he was made Bishop of Sherborne sometime before 900. He is best known for his unfinished Latin biography of Alfred. >> Alfred

Asser, Tobias (Michael Carel) [aser] (1838-1913) Jurist, born in Amsterdam. In 1911 he shared the Nobel Peace Prize with **Alfred Fried** (1864-1921) for his work in creating the Permanent Court of Arbitration at the Hague Peace Conference of 1899.

Assisi, Francis of, St >> **Francis of Assisi, St**

Assurbanipal or **Ashurbanipal** [asoorbanipal] (7th-c BC)

King of Assyria (668-627 BC), the son of Esarhaddon. A patron of the arts, he founded at Nineveh the first organized library in the ancient Middle East. >> Esarhaddon

Astaire, Fred [astair], originally **Frederick Austerlitz** (1899-1987) Actor and dancer, born in Omaha, NE. With partner Ginger Rogers, he revolutionized the film musical with his original tap-dance routines in such films as *Top Hat* (1935). Later turning to straight acting, he received an Oscar nomination for *The Towering Inferno* (1974). >> Rogers, Ginger

Astbury, John, known as **Astbury of Shelton** (1688-1743) Potter, probably born in Staffordshire. He established a factory in Shelton, Staffordshire, where he developed a type of earthenware pottery known as *Astbury ware*.

Astbury, William Thomas (1889-1961) X-ray crystallographer, born in Longton, Staffordshire. Using X-ray diffraction photographs, his pioneering studies on protein fibres laid the basis for much later work. With Florence Bell in 1938 he offered the first hypothetical structure for DNA.

Astley, Philip (1742-1814) Theatrical manager and equestrian, born in Newcastle-under-Lyme, Staffordshire. In London he started a circus at Lambeth (1770), built Astley's Amphitheatre (1798), and established amphitheatres throughout Europe.

Astley, Thea (1925-) Novelist and short-story writer, born in Brisbane, Queensland, Australia. She has won the Miles Franklin Award three times, her novels including *The Slow Natives* (1965) and *The Acolyte* (1972).

Aston, Francis (William) (1877-1945) Physicist, born in Birmingham, West Midlands. He invented the mass spectrograph in 1919, for which he was awarded the Nobel Prize for Chemistry in 1922. The *Aston dark space* in electronic discharges is named after him.

Astor, (Roberta) Brooke, née **Russell** (?1902-) Socialite, philanthropist, and writer, born in Portsmouth, NH. Left a fortune by her third husband, Vincent Astor, she donated several million dollars each year to civic and social projects in New York City.

Astor, John Jacob (1763-1848) Businessman, founder of the Astor family, born in Waldorf, Germany. In 1784 he went to the USA, where he founded the America Fur Co, and rose to become one of the country's most powerful financiers.

Astor, John Jacob (1864-1912) US financier, a great-grandson of John Jacob Astor, the fur trader. He served in the Spanish-American War, and built part of the Waldorf Astoria hotel in New York. He was drowned in the *Titanic* disaster.

Astor, Mary, originally **Lucille Langhanke** (1906-87) Film actress, born in Quincy, IL. She became established as a beautiful innocent in such historical dramas as *Beau Brummell* (1924). Later films include *The Great Lie* (1941, Oscar) and *Return to Peyton Place* (1961).

Astor, Nancy (Witcher) Astor, Viscountess, née **Langhorne** (1879-1964) British politician, born in Danville, VA, USA. Wife of Waldorf Astor, she succeeded him as Conservative MP for Plymouth and became the first woman to take a seat in the House of Commons (1919-45). >> Astor, William Waldorf

Astor, William Waldorf Astor, 1st Viscount (1848-1919) Newspaper proprietor, born in New York City, a great-grandson of John Jacob Astor, the fur trader. He emigrated to Britain in 1892, bought the *Pall Mall Gazette* and *Pall Mall Magazine*, and in 1911 bought *The Observer*.

Astor, (William) Waldorf Astor, 2nd Viscount (1879-1952) British politician, born in New York City, the son of William Waldorf Astor. Elected MP for Plymouth (1910), he passed to the House of Lords (1919), and his wife, Nancy Astor, succeeded him in the lower house. He was proprietor of *The Observer*. >> Astor, Nancy

Astor (of Hever), John Jacob Astor, Baron (1886–1971) Newspaper proprietor, born in New York City, the son of William Waldorf Astor. He became an MP in 1922, and chairman of the Times Publishing Company after the death of Lord Northcliffe. >> Astor, 1st Viscount

Astorga, Emanuele, Baron d' [astaw(r)ga] (c.1680–1757) Composer, born in Agosta, Italy. He composed numerous chamber cantatas and some operas, but is best known for his *Stabat Mater* (1707).

Astruc, Jean [astrük] (1684–1766) Physician and biblical scholar, medical consultant to Louis XV, born in Sauve, France. His work on Moses laid the foundations for modern criticism of the Pentateuch.

Asturias, Miguel Angel [astoorias] (1899–1974) Writer, born in Guatemala City. His novels include *Mr President* (trans, 1946) and *The Mulatta and Mr Fly* (trans, 1963). He received the Nobel Prize for Literature in 1967.

Atahualpa [atawalpa] (?–1533) Last Inca ruler of Peru. On his father's death he received the kingdom of Quito, and in 1532 seized Peru from his brother, Huascar. He was later captured by invading Spaniards under Pizarro, and executed. >> Pizarro, Francisco

Atanasoff, John (Vincent) [atanasof] (1903–95) Physicist and computer pioneer, born in Hamilton, NY. In 1942, with **Clifford Berry** (1918–63), he built an electronic calculating machine - the ABC (Atanasoff-Berry Computer) - one of the first calculating devices using vacuum tubes.

Atatürk [ataterk], originally **Mustafa Kemal** (1881–1938) Turkish army officer, politician, and president of Turkey (1923–38), born in Salonika, Greece. After a nationalist rebellion, he became virtual dictator, and launched a social and political revolution introducing Western fashions, the emancipation of women, educational reform, and the replacement of Arabic script with the Latin alphabet. In 1935 he assumed the surname Atatürk ('Father of the Turks').

Athanaric [athanarik] (?–381) Prince of the W Goths, who fought three campaigns against the Roman Emperor Valens (ruled 364–78). He was defeated in 369, and driven out by the Huns from the N of the Danube.

Athanasius, St [athanayzius] (c.296–373), feast day 2 May. Christian theologian and prelate, born in Alexandria. He led the opposition to the doctrines of the heretic Arius, and his teaching was supported after his death at the Council of Constantinople (381). The *Athanasian Creed* was little heard of until the 7th-c. >> Arius

Atheling >> Edgar the Ætheling

Athelstan or **Æthelstan** [athelstan] (c.895–939) Anglo-Saxon king, the son of Edward the Elder, whom he succeeded as King of Wessex and Mercia in 924. He successfully invaded Northumbria, thus establishing himself as effectively the first King of all England in 927. >> Edward (the Elder)

Athenaeus [atheneeus] (2nd-c) Greek writer, born in Naucratis, Egypt. He wrote *Deipnosophistae* (Banquet of the Learned), a collection of anecdotes and excerpts from ancient authors reproduced as dinner-table conversations.

Athenais >> Eudocia

Atherton, Gertrude (Franklin), *née* **Horn** (1857–1948) Novelist, born in San Francisco, CA. Her best-known books are *The Conqueror* (1902), a fictional biography of Alexander Hamilton, and *Black Oxen* (1923).

Atholl, Katherine Marjory Murray, Duchess of [athol], *née* **Russell** (1874–1960) Conservative politician, born in Banff, Grampian. She became an MP (1923), and was the first Conservative woman minister as parliamentary secretary to the Board of Education (1924–9). Her writing includes the best-selling *Searchlight on Spain* (1938).

Atiyah, Sir Michael (Francis) [ateeah] (1929–) Mathematician, born in London. He has worked on algebraic

geometry, algebraic topology, and the mathematics of quantum field theory, where he has been particularly concerned with bridging the gap between mathematicians and physicists.

Atkin (of Aberdovey), James Richard Atkin, Baron (1867–1944) Judge, born in Brisbane, Queensland, Australia. In the Court of Appeal (1919–28) and the House of Lords (1928–44), he delivered notable opinions in many leading cases, and made important contributions to legal education.

Atkinson, Thomas (Wittlam) (1799–1861) Architect and travel-writer, born in Cawthorne, South Yorkshire. He travelled in Asiatic Russia (1848–53) with his wife Lucy, painting and keeping journals which formed the basis of several works on that region.

Atkinson, Rowan (1955–) British comic actor and writer, born in Newcastle upon Tyne, Tyne and Wear. His shows include *The Nerd* (1984) and *The Sneeze* (1988). On television he has starred in *Not the Nine O'Clock News* (1979–82), *Blackadder* (1983–9), and as *Mr Bean*.

Atlas, Charles, originally **Angelo Siciliano** (1893–1972) Body-builder, born in Acri, Italy. He settled in the USA, and became popularly known as 'America's Most Perfectly Developed Man'.

Attenborough, Sir David (Frederick) [atenbruh] (1926–) Naturalist and broadcaster, born in London, the brother of Richard Attenborough. He joined the BBC in 1952, and became director of programmes (1969–72). He is known for his documentary series on wildlife in its natural habitat, such as *Zoo Quest* (1954–64), *Life on Earth* (1979), and *The Living Planet* (1984). >> Attenborough, Richard

Attenborough, Sir Richard (Samuel), Baron [atenbruh] (1923–) Film actor, producer, and director, born in Cambridge, Cambridgeshire, the brother of David Attenborough. He became well known following his role in *Brighton Rock* (1947). Major successes as a director include *Oh, What a Lovely War!* (1969), *Gandhi* (1982, 8 Oscars), *Cry Freedom* (1987), and *Chaplin* (1993). >> Attenborough, David

Atterbury, Francis (1663–1732) Anglican clergyman and controversialist, born in Milton, Buckinghamshire. In 1722 he was committed to the Tower for complicity in an attempt to restore the Stuarts, deprived of his offices, and exiled.

Atticus, Titus Pomponius [atikus] (109–32 BC) Intellectual, businessman, and writer, born in Rome. He acquired the surname Atticus because of his long sojourn in Athens (85–65 BC) to avoid the Civil War.

Attila [atila], known as **the Scourge of God** (c.406–53) King of the Huns (434–53). His dominion extended from the Rhine to the frontiers of China. He defeated Emperor Theodosius II (ruled 408–50), and in 451 invaded Gaul, but was routed by Aëtius and Theodoric I on the Catalaunian Plains. >> Aëtius; Theodoric I

Attlee, Clem, popular name of **Clement Richard Attlee, 1st Earl Attlee** (1883–1967) British Labour prime minister (1945–51), born in London. He served as dominions secretary (1942–3) and deputy prime minister (1942–5) in Churchill's War Cabinet. As prime minister, he carried through a vigorous programme of nationalization, and introduced the National Health Service.

Attwell, Mabel Lucie (1879–1964) Artist and writer, born in London. She was noted for her 'cherubic' child studies, with which she illustrated her own and other stories for children.

Atwood, Margaret (Eleanor) (1939–) Writer and critic, born in Ottawa, Ontario, Canada. Best known as a novelist, her works include *Lady Oracle* (1976), *The Handmaid's Tale* (1985; filmed 1990), and *Cat's Eye* (1988).

Auber, Daniel-François-Esprit [ohbair] (1782–1871) Composer of operas, born in Caen, France. His best-known works are *La Muette de Portici*, or *Masaniello* (1828), and *Fra Diavolo* (1830).

Aubert, Marie Henriette Suzanne [ohbair], known as **Mother Aubert** (1835–1926) Catholic nun and religious founder, born in Lyon, France. She went to New Zealand in 1860 as a missionary among the Maori people, and in 1892 founded a religious order, the Daughters of Our Lady of Compassion.

Aubert, Pierre [ohbair] (1927–) Swiss statesman, born in La Chaux-de-Fonds, Switzerland. He became vice-president of Switzerland in 1982, then president in 1983 and again in 1987.

Aublet, Jean Baptiste (Christophe Fusée) [ohblay] (1720–78) Botanist and humanist, born in Salon, France. He undertook botanical studies in Mauritius, the French West Indies, and French Guiana, founding forest botany in tropical America. He was also the first secular slavery abolitionist.

Aubrey, John [awbree] (1626–97) Antiquary and folklorist, born in Easton Percy, Wiltshire. One of the first collectors of English folklore, he wrote *Miscellanies* (1696), but most of his prolific output was published after his death. His best-known work is *Letters by Eminent Persons* (1813), better known as *Brief Lives*.

Aubusson, Pierre d' [ohbüsö] (1423–1503) French soldier and clergyman, and Grand Master of the Knights Hospitallers (from 1476), born in Monteil-au-Vicomte, France. His great achievement was the defence of Rhodes (1480) against the Turks.

Auchinleck, Sir Claude John Eyre [okhinlek] (1884–1981) British soldier. His regrouping of the 8th Army on El Alamein paved the way for ultimate victory, but at the time he was made a scapegoat for the retreat, and replaced in 1942.

Auchinloss, Louis Stanton, pseudonym **Andrew Lee** (1917–) Writer and critic, born in Lawrence, NY. His first novel, *The Indifferent Children* (1947), appeared under his pseudonym, but later books carried his own name, such as *The Embezzler* (1966).

Auden, W(ystan) H(ugh) [awden] (1907–73) Writer, born in York, North Yorkshire. His first volume of verse placed him in the forefront of a group of poets of left-wing sympathies. In 1939 he emigrated to New York, becoming a US citizen. His conversion to Anglicanism became evident in a more reflective style of writing, seen in *Homage to Clio* (1960) and *City Without Walls* (1969).

Audley (of Walden), Thomas Audley, Baron [awdlee] (1488–1544) English nobleman, born in Earls Colne, Essex. Active in furthering Henry VIII's designs, he profited from ecclesiastical confiscations, and became Lord Chancellor in 1532.

Audouin, Jean Victor [ohdwi̇̄] (1797–1841) Entomologist and naturalist, born in Paris. He was co-author of the *Dictionnaire classique d'histoire naturelle* (1822). *Audouin's gull* was named after him.

Audrey, St >> **Etheldreda, St**

Audubon, John James [awduhbon] (1785–1851) Ornithologist and bird artist, born in Les Cayes, Haiti. He went to the USA in 1804, where he built up a vast collection of bird illustrations, as shown in *The Birds of America* (1827–38). The National Audubon Society was founded in his honour in 1866.

Auenbrugger, Leopold [owenbruger] (1722–1809) Physician, born in Graz, Austria. He was the first to use percussion (tapping parts of the body and using the sound to aid diagnosis) in medical practice.

Auer, Carl, Freiherr (Baron) **von Welsbach** [ower] (1858–1929) Chemist, born in Vienna. He invented the incandescent gas mantle, the osmium lamp, and discovered the cerium-iron alloy known as *Auer metal* or mischmetal, now used as flints in petrol lighters.

Auerbach, Berthold [owerbakh], originally **Moses Baruch Auerbacher** (1812–82) Novelist, born in Nordstetten, Germany. He is best known for *Black Forest Village Stories* (trans, 1843). Other works include a novel based on the life of Spinoza (1837). >> Spinoza

Auerbach, Frank [owerbak] (1931–) Artist, born in Germany. He came to Britain in 1939. His oil paintings include portraits, and familiar views of Primrose Hill and Camden Town in London.

Auerbach, Red [owerbak], popular name of **Arnold Jacob Auerbach** (1917–) Basketball coach, born in New York City. As coach of the Boston Celtics (1950–66), his teams won nine national basketball Association championships, eight of them consecutively (1959–66). He retired in 1966 to become the team's general manager.

Augereau, Pierre François Charles, duc de (Duke of) **Castiglione** [ohzheroh] (1757–1816) French soldier, born in Paris. He served under Napoleon in Italy, where he fought with distinction at Lodi and Castiglione (1796). He was promoted marshal in 1804 and created Duke of Castiglione in 1808. >> Napoleon I

Augier, (Guillaume Victor) Emile [ohzhiay] (1820–89) Playwright, born in Valence, France. His *Théâtre complet* (7 vols, 1890) includes several social comedies, such as *Les Fourchambault* (1878).

August, Bille [owgust] (1948–) Film director and photographer, born in Denmark. His film *Pelle the Conqueror* (trans, 1987) was awarded the Golden Palm in Cannes in 1988, and in 1989 won an Oscar in the Best Foreign Language Film category.

Augustine, St [awguhstin], also known as **Augustine of Canterbury** (?–604), feast day 26/27 May. Clergyman, the first Archbishop of Canterbury, born probably in Rome. He was prior of a Benedictine monastery at Rome, when in 596 Pope Gregory I sent him with 40 other monks to convert the Anglo-Saxons to Christianity. He was made Bishop of the English in 597. >> Gregory I; Mellitus

Augustine, St [awguhstin], originally **Aurelius Augustinus**, also known as **Augustine of Hippo** (354–430), feast day 28 August. The greatest of the Latin Fathers, born in Tagaste, Numidia (modern Algeria). He became a Christian (387), then a priest (391), and was appointed Bishop of Hippo (396). A formidable antagonist to the heretical schools in the Donatist and Pelagian controversies, he wrote a famous autobiography, *Confessions* (397) and a vindication of the Christian Church, *De Civitate Dei* (413–26).

Augustulus, Romulus [awgustyulus], nickname of **Flavius Momyllus Romulus Augustus** (5th-c) Last emperor of the W half of the old Roman Empire (ruled 475–476). His father, Orestes, conferred the throne on him while he was still a child. After Orestes was killed, he was forced to retire to Naples.

Augustus, (Gaius Julius Caesar Octavianus) (63 BC–AD 14) Founder of the Roman Empire, the great nephew of Julius Caesar. On Caesar's assassination (44 BC), he raised an army and defeated Antony. When Antony returned from Gaul in force later that year with Lepidus, Octavian made a deal with his former enemies, joining them in a triumvirate, and taking Africa, Sardinia, and Sicily as his province. A later redivision of power gave him the entire western half of the Roman world, and Antony the eastern. In 31 BC, the Battle of Actium made Octavian victorious as sole ruler. >> Antonius; Caesar; Lepidus; Livia

Augustus II, known as **Augustus the Strong** (1670–1733) King of Poland (1697–1706, 1710–33), and elector of Saxony, born in Dresden, Germany. In alliance with Russia and Denmark, he invaded Livonia (1699), but was defeated by Charles XII of Sweden, and deposed. After the defeat of the Swedes at Poltava (1709), he recovered the Polish throne. >> Charles XII

Aulén, Gustaf Emmanuel Hildebrand [owlen]

(1879-1977) Lutheran theologian and church music composer, born in Ljungby, Sweden. Professor of systematic theology at Lund (1913-33) and Bishop of Strängnaumäs (1933-52), he was a leader of the Scandinavian school of theology.

Aumale, Henri-Eugène-Philippe-Louis d'Orléans, duc d' (Duke of) [ohmal] (1822-97) French soldier, born in Paris, the fourth son of Louis-Philippe. After an army career, at the revolution of 1848 he retired to England, and wrote *Histoire des princes de Condé* (1869-97). >> Louis-Philippe

Aungerville or **de Bury, Richard** [awnggervill] (1287-1345) Clergyman, born in Bury St Edmunds, Suffolk. He was a Benedictine monk at Durham and became bishop there. His chief work, *Philobyblon*, describes the state of learning in England and France.

Aung San Suu Kyi, Daw [owng san soo kyee] (1945-) Political leader, born in Yangon, Myanmar (formerly Rangoon, Burma), the daughter of the assassinated General Aung San, the father of Burmese independence. When the military took power, she co-founded the National League for Democracy, and was arrested in 1989. Still under house arrest, she was awarded the Nobel Peace Prize in 1991. She was released in July 1995.

Aurangzeb or **Aurungzib** [awrangzeb] ('ornament of the throne'), kingly title **Alamgir** (1618-1707) Last of the Mughal emperors of India (1658-1707), born at Dhod, Malwa, the third son of Emperor Shah Jahan. He struggled for power with his brothers, finally putting them to death. During his long reign, the empire remained prosperous, but he alienated the Hindus, warred with the Marathas, and died a fugitive. >> Shah Jahan

Aurelian [awreelian], in full **Lucius Domitius Aurelianus** (c.215-75) Roman emperor, born in Dacia or Pannonia. In a brief but brilliant reign, he restored army discipline and domestic order, and was successful against tribes throughout Europe. He was awarded the title 'Restorer of the World'.

Aurelius [awreelius], in full **Caesar Marcus Aurelius Antoninus Augustus**, originally **Marcus Annius Verus** (121-80) Roman emperor (161-80), born in Rome. The adopted son of Antoninus Pius, he ruled with him from 146. His reign saw constant warfare, and he personally directed operations on the Danube frontier for almost a decade. >> Antoninus Pius

Auric, Georges [ohrik] (1899-1983) Composer, born in Lodève, France. One of *Les Six*, his compositions ranged from full orchestral pieces to songs and film scores, such as *Passport to Pimlico* (1949) and *Moulin Rouge* (1952).

Auriol, Jacqueline [ohreeol] (1917-) French aviator, the daughter-in-law of Vincent Auriol. She broke the women's jet speed record in 1955 by flying at 715 mph (1150 kph) in a French *Mystère*. >> Auriol, Vincent

Auriol, Vincent [ohreeol] (1884-1966) French statesman, born in Revel, France. A socialist politician, he became president of the two constituent assemblies of 1946, and the first president of the Fourth Republic (1947-54).

Aurobindo, Sri [owrobindoh gohsay], originally **Aurobindo Ghose** (1872-1950) Philosopher, poet, and mystic, born in Calcutta, India. Renouncing nationalism and politics for yoga and Hindu philosophy, he founded an ashram at Pondicherry in 1910.

Aurungzeb(e) >> **Aurangzeb**

Ausonius, Decimus Magnus [awsohnius] (c.309-92) Latin poet, born in Burdigala (Bordeaux), France. His works include epigrams, poems, epistles in verse and prose, and idylls.

Austen, Jane (1775-1817) Novelist, born in Steventon, Hampshire. Of her six great novels, the first four were published anonymously during her lifetime: *Sense and Sensibility* (1811), *Pride and Prejudice* (1813), *Mansfield Park* (1814), *Emma* (1815); *Persuasion* and *Northanger Abbey* (both 1818).

Austen, Winifred (1876-1964) Wildlife artist, born in Ramsgate, Kent. She illustrated Patrick Chalmers' *Birds Ashore and Aforeshore* (1935), and painted postcards under the signature 'Spink'.

Austerlitz, Frederick >> **Astaire, Fred**

Austin, Alfred (1835-1913) Poet, born in Leeds, West Yorkshire. His works include *The Season: a Satire* (1861), *The Human Tragedy* (1862), and an autobiography (1911). He became Poet Laureate in 1896.

Austin, John (1790-1859) Jurist, born in Creeting Mill, Suffolk. His *Province of Jurisprudence Determined*, defining the sphere of ethics and law, came to revolutionize English views on the subject.

Austin, J(ohn) L(angshaw) (1911-60) Philosopher, born in Lancaster, Lancashire. A leading figure in the Oxford Philosophy movement, he pioneered the analysis of speech acts through his examination of ordinary linguistic usage, as seen in *How to Do Things with Words* (1962).

Austin, Robert Sargent (1895-1973) British etcher. Most of his life was spent refining the traditional art of line engraving. His mature work (1930-40) includes some of the finest prints of the period.

Austin, Stephen Fuller (1793-1836) Founder of the state of Texas, born in Austinville, VA. In 1822 he founded a colony on the Brazos R, and became leader of the movement for Texan independence.

Austin (of Longbridge), Herbert Austin, Baron (1866-1941) Car manufacturer, born in Little Missenden, Buckinghamshire. In 1895 he produced his first car, the Wolseley, and in 1905 opened his own works near Birmingham, producing an enormous output which included the popular 'Baby' Austin 7 (1921).

Austral, Florence [awstral], originally **Florence Wilson** (1894-1968) Soprano, born in Richmond, Victoria, Australia. She joined the Berlin State Opera as principal in 1930. After 1945 she taught in Australia until her retirement in 1959.

Avedon, Richard [avedon] (1923-) Photographer, born in New York City. A fashion photographer for *Harper's Bazaar* (1945-65), he became known for his stark portraits of celebrities in unusual poses, and published his work in *Observations* (1959).

Avennasar >> **al-Farabi, Mohammed**

Aventinus [aventiynus], Latin name of **Johannes Thurmayr** (1477-1534) Humanist scholar and historian, born in Abensberg, Bavaria, Germany. Known as the 'Bavarian Herodotos', he taught Greek and mathematics at Cracow, and wrote a history of Bavaria. >> Herodotos

Avenzoar [avenzoher], Arabic **Ibn Zohr** (c.1072-1162) Arab physician, born in Seville. Considered the greatest clinician in the western caliphate, he published influential medical works describing such conditions as kidney stones and pericarditis.

Averroës [averoheez], Latin form of **Ibn Rushd** (1126-98) The most famous of the mediaeval Islamic philosophers, born in Córdoba, Spain. His extensive commentaries on Aristotle's works offered a partial synthesis between Greek and Arabic philosophical traditions, and were influential in the Middle Ages. >> Aristotle

Avery, Milton (Clark) [ayveree] (1893-1965) Painter, born in Altmar, NY. An experimental artist, he produced figurative works, Expressionist style seascapes, drypoints, and a series of monotypes.

Avery, Oswald (Theodore) [ayveree] (1877-1955) Bacteriologist, born in Halifax, Nova Scotia, Canada. In 1944 he showed that genetic transformation in bacteria can be caused by DNA, a key result in the development of molecular biology.

Avery, Sewell (Lee) [ayveree] (1874-1960) Corporate executive, born in Saginaw, MI. In 1901 he joined the United States Gypsum Co, which as president (1905-37) and chairman (until 1951) he developed into a major international building materials manufacturer.

Avery, Tex [**ay**veree], originally **Frederick Bean** (1908–80) Film cartoon director, born in Texas. He created Daffy Duck, Droopy, and Screwy Squirrel, and developed Bugs Bunny in *A Wild Hare* (1940). He later joined Hanna–Barbera for the television series *The Flintstones* (1979).

Avicebron [avise**bron**], Arabic **Solomon ibn Gabirol** (c.1020–c.1070) Poet and philosopher of the Jewish 'Golden Age', born in Málaga, Spain. His great work, *Fountain of Life*, a dialogue on the nature of matter and the soul, was influential among later Christian scholastics.

Avicenna [avi**se**na], Arabic **Ibn Sina** (980–1037) Philosopher and physician, born near Bokhara, Kazakastan. One of the main interpreters of Aristotle to the Islamic world, he wrote over 200 works on science, religion, and philosophy. His textbook, *Canon of Medicine*, became a standard work. >> Aristotle

Avison, Charles [**ay**vison] (c.1709–70) Composer, born in Newcastle upon Tyne, Tyne and Wear. Also known as a critic, he wrote an *Essay on Musical Expression* (1752).

Avogadro, Amedeo [avoh**gad**roh] (1776–1856) Scientist, born in Turin, Italy. In 1811 he formulated the hypothesis, known as *Avogadro's law*, that equal volumes of gases contain equal numbers of molecules, when at the same temperature and pressure.

Avon, 1st Earl of >> Eden, Sir Anthony

Axel >> Absalon

Axelrod, Julius [**ak**selrod] (1912–) Pharmacologist, born in New York City. He discovered the substance which inhibits neural impulses, laying the basis for significant advances in neurophysiology, and shared the Nobel Prize for Physiology or Medicine in 1970.

Ayckbourn, Alan [**ayk**baw(r)n] (1939–) Playwright, born in London. The first of many West End successes was *Relatively Speaking* (1967), and he was quickly established as a master of farce. Among his best-known plays are *Absurd Person Singular* (1973), *The Norman Conquests* (1974), and *Joking Apart* (1979). Later plays include *Woman in Mind* (1986) and *Invisible Friends* (1991).

Ayer, Sir A(lfred) J(ules) [air] (1910–89) Philosopher, born in London. His book *Language, Truth and Logic* (1936) was hailed as a lucid exposition of logical positivism. Later works include *The Problem of Knowledge* (1956) and *The Central Questions of Philosophy* (1972).

Ayers, Sir Henry [airz] (1821–97) Politician, born in Portsea, Hampshire. He emigrated to South Australia (1841), and was premier several times. *Ayers Rock* was named after him in 1873.

Ayeshah >> Aïshah

Aylmer, Sir Felix (Edward) [**ayl**mer], originally Aylmer-Jones (1889–1979) British actor. At the Birmingham Repertory he became known as a highly versatile character actor. He also served as union president of British Actors' Equity (1949–69).

Aylmer, John [**ayl**mer] (1521–94) Clergyman, born in Norfolk. He was tutor to Lady Jane Grey, and during the reign of Mary I was forced to flee from persecution, later becoming Bishop of London in 1577. >> Grey, Lady Jane; Mary I

Aylward, Gladys [**ayl**werd] (1902–70) Missionary in China, born in London. She arrived in China in 1930, and helped found an inn at Yangcheng. From there, in 1938, she trekked across the mountains leading over 100 children to safety when the war with Japan threatened the area. The story was recounted in the film *The Inn of the Sixth Happiness* (1958).

Ayrton, Michael [**air**ton] (1920–75) Painter, sculptor, and art critic, born in London. His early paintings belong to the English neo-Romantic movement. Inspired by the legend of the minotaur, he constructed a maze of brick and stone in the Catskill Mountains, NY.

Ayton, Sir Robert [**ay**ton] (1570–1638) Poet and courtier, born in Kinaldie, near St Andrews, Fife. A courtier of James I in London, he wrote lyrics in English and Latin, and is credited with the prototype of the song 'Auld Lang Syne'. >> James I (of England)

Aytoun, William Edmonstoune [**ay**toon] (1818–65) Poet and humorist, born in Edinburgh. In 1836 he began a lifelong connection with *Blackwood's Magazine*, to which he contributed parodies and burlesque reviews.

Ayub Khan, Mohammad [ayub **kahn**] (1907–74) Pakistani soldier and president (1958–69), born in Hazara, India. He became president after a bloodless army coup, and established a stable economy and political autocracy, but was forced to relinquish power after widespread civil disorder.

Azaña (y Díaz), Manuel [a**than**ya] (1880–1940) Spanish president (1936–9), born in Alcalá de Henares, Spain. He became war minister (1931), prime minister (1931–3), then leader of the Republican Left (1936). He was elected president of the Second Republic, but was forced into exile by Franco. >> Franco

Azariah, Vedanayakam Samuel (1874–1945) Clergyman and first Indian bishop of the Anglican Church of India, Burma, and Ceylon, born in Vellalanvillai, Madras, India. He was appointed Bishop of Dornakal, Andhra Pradesh in 1912.

Azeglio, Massimo Taparelli, marchese d' (Marquess of) [a**zel**yoh] (1798–1866) Italian statesman, painter, and writer, born in Turin, Italy, a son-in-law of Manzoni. He took a leading part in the Risorgimento and the 1848 revolution, and became prime minister of Sardinia (1848–52). >> Manzoni

Azikiwe, Nnamdi [azee**kee**way] (1904–) Nigerian president (1963–6), born in Zungeri, Nigeria. He was prime minister of the E region (1954–9), Governor-General of Nigeria (1960–3), and first president of the Nigerian Republic, but his office was suspended during the military uprising of 1966.

Azorín [atho**rin**], pseudonym of **José Martínez Ruiz** (1874–1967) Novelist and critic, born in Monóvar, Spain. His novels include *Don Juan* (1922) and *Dona Inés* (1925).

B

Baade, (Wilhelm Heinrich) Walter [bahduh] (1893–1960) Astronomer, born in Schröttinghausen, Germany. He moved to the USA in 1931, working at the Mt Wilson (1931–58) and Palomar (1948–58) Observatories. His work gave new estimates for the age and size of the universe.

Baader, Andreas [bahder] (1943–77) Anarchist and terrorist, born in Munich, Germany. In 1968 he formed with Ulrike Meinhof the Red Army Faction, who carried out a series of terrorist outrages during the early 1970s. He was captured, sentenced to life imprisonment in 1977, and committed suicide. >> Meinhof

Baader, Franz Xaver von [bahder] (1765–1841) Roman Catholic theologian and mystical philosopher, born in Munich, Germany. A follower of Böhme, he opposed Kant by maintaining that the true ethical end is not obedience to a moral law, but a realization of the divine life. >> Böhme; Kant

Baal-Shem-Tov, originally **Israel ben Eliezer**, also known by his acronym, **Besht** (c.1699–1760) Jewish teacher and healer in Poland, born in Ukraine. He founded the Jewish spiritual movement of Hasidism c.1750.

Babangida, Ibrahim [babanggeeda] (1941–) Nigerian soldier, and president (1985–93), born in Minna, Nigeria. In 1985 he led a coup against President Buhari, and assumed the presidency, but stood down following controversy over election results, leaving the military regime in power.

Babar or **Babur**, (Arabic 'tiger'), originally Zahir-ud-din Muhammad (1483–1530) First Mughal Emperor of India, born in Fergana, C Asia. He invaded India and won a decisive victory at Panipat in 1526. A distinguished soldier, he was also a cultured man with interests in architecture, music, and literature.

Babbage, Charles (1791–1871) Mathematician and pioneer computer scientist, born in Walworth, London. He worked on the theory of logarithms, and built a calculating machine, the forerunner of the computer. His assistant was Byron's daughter, Augusta Ada, Lady Lovelace. >> Lovelace, Augusta Ada

Babbitt, Irving (1865–1933) Critic and writer, born in Dayton, OH. He was a leader of the 'new selective humanism' which flourished in America in the 1920s. His books include *Literature and the American College* (1908).

Babbitt, Isaac (1799–1862) Goldsmith, born in Taunton, MA. He manufactured the first Britannia metal tableware (1824) and invented an alloy, now called *Babbitt metal* (1839), which is still used in some metal bearings to reduce friction.

Babbitt, Milton (1916–) Composer and theorist, born in Philadelphia, PA. He was a leading proponent of total serialism, and composed many works for the electronic synthesizer.

Babcock, Harold (Delos) (1882–1968) Physicist, born in Edgerton, WI. He measured the magnetic field of the star 78 Virginis, which provided a link between electromagnetic and relativity theories. With his son **Horace Welcome Babcock** (1912–), he invented the solar magnetograph in 1951.

Babcock, Stephen (Moulton) (1843–1931) Agricultural chemist and originator of scientific dairying, born near Bridgewater, NY. He devised the *Babcock test* for measuring fat in milk, which much improved the quality of dairy produce.

Bab-ed-Din [babuhdin], (Arabic 'gateway of righteousness'), popular name of **Mirza Ali Mohammed** (1819–50) Religious leader, born in Iran. In 1844 he declared himself the Bab ('Gateway') to the prophesied 12th Imam, then claimed to be the Imam himself. He was imprisoned in 1847, and later executed.

Babel, Isaac (Emmanuilovich) [babel] (1894–?1941) Writer, born in the Jewish ghetto of Odessa, Ukraine. He wrote stories of the Jews in Odessa in *Odessa Tales* (trans, 1916), and stories of war in *Red Cavalry* (trans, 1926). Exiled to Siberia in the mid-1930s, he died in a concentration camp.

Babeuf, François-Noël [baboef], originally **Gracchus Babeuf** (1760–97) Political agitator, born in St Quentin, France. During the Revolution he conspired to destroy the Directory and establish an extreme communistic system. When this was discovered, he was guillotined.

Babilée, Jean [babeelay], originally Jean Gutman (1923–) Dancer and choreographer, born in Paris. He became a noted member of the Ballets de Champs-Elysées and Ballets de Paris, and later formed his own company.

Babinet, Jacques [babeenay] (1794–1872) Physicist, born in Lusignan, France. He standardized light measurement by using the red cadmium line's wavelength as the standard for the angstrom unit. *Babinet's principle* asserts that similar diffraction patterns are produced by two complementary screens.

Babington, Antony (1561–86) Conspirator, born in Dethick, Derbyshire. In 1586 he was induced to lead a conspiracy to murder Queen Elizabeth I and release Queen Mary of Scotland (the Babington Plot). The plan was discovered, and he was executed. >> Elizabeth I; Walsingham, Francis

Babinski, Joseph (François Felix) [babinskee] (1857–1932) Neurologist, born in Paris. He is known for his description of a foot reflex which is symptomatic of upper motor neurone disease. Independently of **Alfred Fröhlich** (1871–1953), a Viennese pharmacologist, he investigated an endocrinal disorder, now known as *Babinski–Fröhlich disease*.

Babits, Mihály [bahbeech] (1883–1941) Poet of the 20th-c literary renaissance, born in Szekszárd, Hungary. He was also a novelist, and a translator of Dante, Shakespeare, and the Greek classics.

Babrius [babrius] (2nd-c) Greek writer of fables. He collected Aesopic fables, which he turned into popular verse. These had almost all been lost, until 123 of them were discovered at Mt Athos, Greece, in 1841. >> Aesop

Babson, Roger (Ward) (1875–1967) Statistician, business forecaster, and writer, born in Gloucester, MA. He set up the Business Statistical Organization Inc (1904), the Babson Institute (1919), and founded Webber College, FL to train women for business (1927).

Babur >> Babar

Baby Doc >> Duvalier, Jean-Claude

Bacall, Lauren [bakawl], originally **Betty Joan Perske** (1924–) Actress, born in New York City. Her first leading role was in *To Have and Have Not* (1944), opposite Humphrey Bogart, whom she subsequently married. Other well-known films include *The Big Sleep* (1946), *Key Largo* (1948), and *The Shootist* (1976). >> Bogart

Bacchylides [bakilideez] (5th-c BC) Greek lyric poet, the nephew of Simonides of Ceos, and a contemporary of Pindar in Hiero's court at Syracuse. Fragments of his Epinician Odes were discovered in 1896. >> Pindar; Simonides of Ceos

Bacciochi, Maria Anna Elisa [bakiokee], *née* Bona-parte (1777–1820) Eldest of the sisters of Napoleon, born in Ajaccio, Corsica. She married Felice Bacciochi, was created a princess by her brother (1805), and became Grand Duchess of Tuscany (1809).

Baccio della Porta >> Bartolommeo, Fra

Bach, C(arl) P(hilipp) E(manuel), known as **the Berlin Bach** or **the Hamburg Bach** (1714–88) Composer, born in Weimar, Germany, the second surviving son of Johann Sebastian Bach. He published *The True Art of Clavier Playing* (1753), the first methodical treatment of the subject, introduced the sonata form, and composed numerous concertos, keyboard sonatas, church music, and chamber music. >> Bach, J S

Bach, Edward (1880–1936) British medical microbiologist. He developed a system of herbal remedies prepared from 38 different species of flowers. *Bach flower remedies* are especially used for disharmonies of the personality and emotional state.

Bach, J(ohann) C(hristian), known as **the London Bach** or **the English Bach** (1735–82) Composer, born in Leipzig, Germany, the youngest son of Johann Sebastian Bach. His works include two Masses, a requiem, a 'Te Deum', and operas. In 1762 he was appointed composer to the London Italian opera, and became musician to Queen Charlotte. >> Bach, C P E / J S

Bach, J(ohann) C(hristoph) F(riedrich), known as **the Bückeburg Bach** (1732–95) Composer, born in Leipzig, Germany, the ninth son of J S Bach. In 1750 he became chapel master at Bückeburg. He was an industrious but undistinguished church composer. >> Bach, J S

Bach, Johann Sebastian (1685–1750) Composer, one of the world's greatest musicians, born in Eisenach, Germany. In 1711 he became chapel master to Prince Leopold of Anhalt-Cöthen, where he wrote mainly instrumental music, including the 'Brandenburg' Concertos (1721) and *The Well-tempered Clavier* (1722). In 1723 he was appointed cantor of the Thomasschule in Leipzig, where his works included c.300 church cantatas, the *St Matthew Passion* (1727), and the *Mass in B Minor*. The most outstanding member of the celebrated Bach family, his main achievement was his development of polyphony. >> Bach, C P E / J C / J C F / W F

Bach, W(ilhelm) F(riedemann), known as **the Halle Bach** (1710–84) Composer, born in Weimar, Germany, the eldest and most gifted son of J S Bach. The greatest organ player of his time, he held posts at Dresden (1733) and Halle (1747). >> Bach, J S

Bachelard, Gaston [bashuhlah(r)] (1884–1962) Philosopher, born in Bar-sur-Aube, France. His range of interests brought together the history of science, psychoanalysis, and literary criticism, in such works as *La Psychoanalyse du feu* (1937).

Bacher, Ali [bakher] (1942–   ) Cricketer and sports administrator, born in Roodepoort, Transvaal, South Africa. He captained Transvaal and South Africa, was instrumental in organizing the 'rebel' tours to South Africa in the 1980s, and later became a key figure in the new non-racial administrative structures.

Bachman, John [bakman] (1790–1874) Clergyman and naturalist, born in Rhinebeck, NY. He is remembered as co-author, with John James Audubon, of *The Viviparous Quadrupeds of North America* (1845–9). >> Audubon

Bachofen, Johann Jakob [bahkhohfen] (1815–87) Jurist and historian, born in Basel, Switzerland. Professor of Roman law at Basel from 1841, he is known for his work on the theory of matriarchy, *Das Mutterrecht* (1841).

Baciccia [bacheechia], popular name of **Giovanni Battista Gaulli** (1639–1709) Painter, born in Genoa, Italy. He is best known for his Baroque illusionistic ceiling frescoes, such as the ceiling of the Jesuit Church of the Gusí in Rome.

Back, Sir George (1796–1878) Arctic explorer, born in Stockport, Cheshire. He sailed with Sir John Franklin on polar expeditions (1818–22, 1825–7), and between 1833–5 went in search of explorer Sir John Ross. >> Franklin, John; Ross, John

Backhuysen or **Bakhuizen, Ludolf** [bakhoysen] (1631–1708) Dutch marine painter, born in Emden, Germany. He is best known for his 'Rough Sea at the Mouth of the Maas' (Louvre) and several seascapes in London, Amsterdam, and The Hague.

Bacon, Francis, Viscount St Albans (1561–1626) Philosopher and statesman, born in London, the younger son of Sir Nicholas Bacon. He became attorney general (1613), privy counsellor (1616), Lord Keeper (1617), and Lord Chancellor (1618). His philosophy is best studied in *The Advancement of Learning* (1605) and *Novum Organum* (1620), where his stress on inductive methods influenced later scientific investigation. >> Bacon, Nicholas

Bacon, Francis (1909–92) Artist, born in Dublin. In England from 1928, he treated religious subjects in a highly individual surrealist manner, and is best known for his 'Three Studies for Figures at the base of a Crucifixion' (1945).

Bacon, Francis Thomas (1904–92) British engineer. He proposed the use of hydrogen-oxygen fuel cells in submarines, but his designs were first put to practical use in space to provide power, heat, and clean drinking water on board US spacecraft.

Bacon, Henry (1866–1924) Architect, born in New York City. He is best remembered for his last work, the Lincoln Memorial in Washington, DC.

Bacon, John >> Baconthorpe, John

Bacon, John (1740–99) Sculptor, born in London. His works include the monuments to William Pitt the Elder in Westminster Abbey and the Guildhall, and the statue of Dr Johnson in St Paul's.

Bacon, Nathaniel (c.1642–76) American colonial leader, born in Suffolk, England. He emigrated to Virginia in 1673, and began raids against the Indians. The English governor declared him a rebel in 1676, but Bacon died suddenly after the capture of Jamestown, and the rebellion ended.

Bacon, Sir Nicholas (1510–79) English statesman, born in Drinkstone, Suffolk, the father of Francis Bacon. Under Elizabeth I, he was made Lord Keeper of the Great Seal. A staunch anti-Catholic, he was an implacable enemy of Mary, Queen of Scots. >> Bacon, Francis

Bacon, Roger, known as **Doctor Mirabilis** ('Wonderful Doctor') (c.1220–92) Philosopher and scientist, probably born in Ilchester, Somerset. In 1247 he devoted himself to experimental science, and for Pope Clement IV he compiled his *Great Work* (trans. 1266–7). He became a Franciscan, but in 1277 his writings were condemned, and he was imprisoned.

Baconthorpe or **Bacon, John**, known as **Doctor Resolutus** ('Resolute Doctor') (c.1290–c.1346) Philosopher and theologian, born in Baconsthorpe, Norfolk, the grandnephew of Roger Bacon. He wrote commentaries on the Arab philosopher Averroës. >> Averroës; Bacon, Roger

Badarayana The name applied to an unknown Indian philosopher, the reputed author of the *Vedanta Sutra*. He is sometimes identified with the 5th-c sage Vyasa, who is traditionally credited with compiling the *Mahabharata*.

Baden-Powell, Robert Stephenson Smyth Baden-Powell, Baron [baydn powel] (1857–1941) British general, born in London. He won fame during the Boer War as the defender of Mafeking (1899–1900). In 1908 he founded the Boy Scout movement, and in 1910, with his sister **Agnes** (1858–1945), the Girl Guides.

Bader, Sir Douglas (Robert Stuart) [bahder] (1910–82)

Wartime aviator, born in London. He lost both legs in a flying accident in 1931, but overcame his disability and returned to the RAF in 1939, commanding the first Canadian Fighter Squadron. Captured in 1941, his example of fortitude and heroism became legendary.

Badoglio, Pietro [bah**dol**yoh] (1871–1956) Italian soldier and prime minister (1943–4), born in Grazzano Monferrato, Italy. On Italy's entry into World War 2 in 1940 he was made commander-in-chief, but later resigned. After Mussolini's downfall he became prime minister, forming a non-fascist government, and negotiated an armistice. >> Mussolini

Baeck, Leo [bek] (1873–1956) Jewish religious leader, born in Lissa, Germany. He was rabbi in Berlin (1912–42), and the political leader of German Jewry when the Nazis came to power. He was imprisoned in the Theresienstadt concentration camp (1942–5).

Baedeker, Karl [**bay**deker] (1801–59) Publisher, born in Essen, Germany. He started his own publishing business at Koblenz in 1827, and is best known for the guidebooks which still bear his name.

Baekeland, Leo (Hendrik) [**bayk**land] (1863–1944) Chemist, born in Ghent, Belgium. In 1889 he emigrated to the USA where he invented photographic printing paper usable with artificial light, discovered the first synthetic phenolic resin (*Bakelite*), and was a founder of the plastics industry.

Baer, Karl Ernst von [bair] (1792–1876) Naturalist, and pioneer in embryology, born in Piep, Estonia. He discovered the mammalian egg in the ovary, and the notochord, and formulated the 'biogenetic law' that in embryonic development general characters appear before special ones.

Baeyer, Johann (Friedrich Wilhelm Adolf) von [**bay**er] (1835–1917) Organic chemist, born in Berlin. Professor of chemistry at Munich (1875–1915), he is known for his synthesis of the dye indigo and his work on the mechanism of photosynthesis. He was awarded the Nobel Prize for Chemistry in 1905.

Baez, Joan [biyez] (1941–) Folksinger, born in New York City. During the revival of traditional folk music in the 1960s, she became popular with young audiences for her songs and political views in support of civil rights, peace, and other causes.

Baffin, William (c.1584–1622) Navigator, probably born in London. He was pilot in several expeditions in search of the Northwest Passage (1612–16), during which they found Baffin Bay (1615) and Lancaster, Smith, and Jones Sounds (1616).

Bagehot, Walter [**baj**uht] (1826–77) Economist and journalist, born in Langport, Somerset. In 1860 he succeeded his father-in-law, James Wilson (1805–60), as editor of the *Economist*. His *English Constitution* (1867) is still considered a standard work.

Bagford, John (1650–1716) Antiquary, born in London. He made a scrapbook collection of English broadside ditties and verses in 64 volumes, known as *The Bagford Ballads*.

Bagley, Sarah (fl.1835–47) Labour leader, of whose early life nothing is known. Active in the mills of Lowell, MA, she led 'turn-outs' (strikes) and organized the Female Labor Reform Association.

Baha-Allah [bah**hah**ula], (Arabic 'glory of God'), originally **Mirza Huseyn Ali** (1817–92) Religious leader, born in Teheran. In 1863 he proclaimed himself as the prophet that Bab-ed-Din had foretold, and became the leader of the new Baha'i faith. >> Bab-ed-Din

Bahr, Hermann (1863–1934) Writer and critic, born in Linz, Austria. He took a leading part in the Naturalism and Expressionism of the Habsburg empire period, publishing social novels and comedies.

Baïf, Jean Antoine de [bah**eef**] (1532–89) French poet, born in Venice, Italy. He was a member of the *Pléiade*, and wrote *Les amours de Méline* (1552), among other works.

Baikie, William Balfour [**bay**kee] (1825–64) Explorer, naturalist, and linguist, born in Kirkwall, Orkney Is. During his first Niger expedition (1854), he penetrated 400 km/250 mi farther than any previous traveller. He later translated parts of the Bible and prayer book into Hausa.

Bailey, David (Royston) (1938–) Photographer, born in London. Initially a fashion photographer, he became known for his portraits expressing the spirit of the 1960s, and for outstanding nude studies.

Bailey, Sir Donald (Coleman) (1901–85) Engineer, born in Rotherham, South Yorkshire. During World War 2 he designed the prefabricated, mobile, rapidly-erected *Bailey bridge*.

Bailey, Francis Lee (1933–) US criminal lawyer. As an attorney, his famous cases include his defence of the Boston Strangler, Albert Desalvo, and of the kidnapped heiress, Patty Hearst. >> Desalvo; Hearst, Patty

Bailey, James Anthony >> Barnum, P T

Bailey, Liberty Hyde (1858–1954) Horticulturalist and botanist, born in South Haven, MI. He founded the Bailey Hortorium of New York State College (1920), edited such works as the *Standard Cyclopedia of Horticulture* (1914–17), and coined the term *cultivar*.

Bailey, Nathan or **Nathaniel** (?–1742) English lexicographer. He compiled *An Universal Etymological English Dictionary* (1721, supplement 1727), used by Dr Johnson as the basis of his own dictionary. >> Johnson, Samuel

Bailey, Trevor, nickname **Barnacle Bailey** (1923–) Cricketer, writer, and sports broadcaster, born in Westcliff-on-Sea, Essex. An Essex all-rounder, during his Test career he played in 61 matches, made over 2200 runs, and took 132 wickets.

Baillie, Lady Grizel [**bay**lee], née **Hume** (1665–1746) Poet, born in Borders, Scotland, the daughter of the Scottish Covenanter **Sir Patrick Hume** (1641–1724). She protected him during his refuge in Polwarth Church in 1684, and also aided the Covenanting scholar, Robert Baillie of Jerviswood, whose son she married in 1692. >> Baillie, Robert

Baillie, Dame Isobel [**bay**lee] (1895–1983) Soprano, born in Hawick, Borders, Scotland. She won immediate success in her opening season in London in 1923, and came to be regarded as one of this century's leading oratorio singers.

Baillie, John [**bay**lee] (1886–1960) Theologian, born in Gairloch, Highland. After World War 1 he taught in the USA before returning to Scotland, where he became a key contributor to mid-century religious, social, and intellectual life.

Baillie, Matthew [**bay**lee] (1761–1823) Physician and anatomist, born in Shotts, Strathclyde. He studied anatomy under his uncle William Hunter, and took over his anatomy school in London in 1783, writing the first treatise in English on morbid anatomy (1793). >> Hunter, William

Baillie (of Jerviswood), Robert [**bay**lee] (1634–84) Presbyterian conspirator, a native of Lanarkshire, Strathclyde. He joined Monmouth's supporters in London, and on the discovery of the alleged Rye House Plot (1683) he was tried and hanged. >> Monmouth

Baillieu, William Lawrence [**bay**lyoo] (1859–1936) Businessman, born in Queenscliff, Victoria, Australia. He became a member of the Legislative Council of Victoria (1901–22), and co-founded the Melbourne newspaper *The Herald*.

Bailly, Jean Sylvain [bah**yee**] (1736–93) Astronomer and politician, born in Paris. His chief work was *History of Astronomy* (trans, 1775–87). He became president of the National Assembly during the Revolution (1789), but lost popularity and was guillotined.

Baily, Edward Hodges (1788–1867) Sculptor, born in Bristol, Avon. He executed many of the well-known London statues, including that of Lord Nelson in Trafalgar Square.

Baily, Francis (1774–1844) Astronomer, born in Newbury, Berkshire. He detected the phenomenon known as *Baily's beads* during an eclipse of the Sun in 1836.

Bain, Alexander [bayn] (1818–1903) Empirical philosopher and psychologist, born in Aberdeen, Grampian. His psychology was firmly based on physiology, and he sought to explain mind through a physical theory of the association of ideas.

Bainton, Edgar Leslie (1880–1956) Composer, teacher, and conductor, born in London. In 1938 he was appointed director of the Conservatory of Music, Sydney, New South Wales. A prolific composer, he wrote three operas, chamber music, songs, and piano pieces.

Bainton, Roland (1894–1984) Congregational minister and Reformation scholar, born in Ilkeston, Derbyshire. Taken to Canada in 1898, he later taught Church history at Yale Divinity School (1920–62), and became a leading scholar of the Protestant Reformation in America.

Baird, John Logie (1888–1946) Television pioneer, born in Helensburgh, Strathclyde. In 1926 he gave the first demonstration of a television image. His 30-line mechanically scanned system was experimentally broadcast by the BBC in 1929; and during 1936, transmissions of his improved 240-line system alternated with the rival Marconi-EMI 405-line electronic system, which was adopted in 1937.

Baird, Spencer Fullerton (1823–87) Naturalist, born in Reading, PA. He published *Catalogue of North American Mammals* (1857) and *Catalogue of North American Birds* (1858). *Baird's sandpiper* and *Baird's sparrow* are named in his honour.

Bairnsfather, (Charles) Bruce (1888–1959) Cartoonist, born in Murree, India. He became famous for his World War 1 cartoons featuring the character 'Old Bill'. In World War 2, he was an official cartoonist attached to the US army in Europe.

Bajazet >> Bayezit I

Ba Jin, pseudonym of **Li Feigan** (1904–) Writer, born in Chengdu, Sichuan, China. His major trilogy (*Family*, 1931, *Spring*, 1938, and *Autumn*, 1940) attacked the traditional family system, and was immensely popular with the younger generation.

Baker, Sir Benjamin (1840–1907) Civil engineer, born in Keyford, Somerset. In 1861 he began a long association with engineer John Fowler, and together they constructed the London Metropolitan Railway, Victoria Station, and the Forth Rail Bridge (opened 1890). >> Fowler, John

Baker, George, known as **Father Divine** (?1877–1965) Evangelist, born near Savannah, GA. He launched the Peace Mission movement in 1919, and gained a large following among African-Americans in New York and Philadelphia.

Baker, Sir Herbert (1862–1946) Architect, born in Kent. He designed Groote Schuur, near Cape Town, for Cecil Rhodes, and (with Edwin Lutyens) New Delhi in India. Other buildings include the new Bank of England and South Africa House in London. >> Lutyens

Baker, James A(ddison), III (1930–) US secretary of state (1989–92), born in Houston, TX. He served President Reagan as White House chief-of-staff (1981–5) and secretary of the Treasury (1985–8) before resigning to manage George Bush's campaign. Bush named him as secretary of state, and in 1992 he became chief-of-staff, running Bush's re-election campaign. >> Bush, George; Reagan

Baker, Dame Janet (Abbott) (1933–) Mezzo-soprano, born in Hatfield, South Yorkshire. She has had an extensive operatic career, especially in early Italian opera and the works of Benjamin Britten, and is also a noted interpreter of Mahler and Elgar. >> Britten

Baker, Josephine, originally **Freda Josephine McDonald** (1906–75) Dancer and entertainer, born in St Louis, MO. Hired to appear in an all-black act at the Folies Bergère, she became an instant success, and as the epitome of *le jazz hot*, remained the toast of France for five decades, gaining an international status.

Baker, Kenneth (Wilfred) (1934–) British statesman. He rose to become secretary of state for the environment (1985) and for education (1986), and was later appointed chairman of the Conservative Party (1989–90) and home secretary (1990–2).

Baker, Norma Jean >> Monroe, Marilyn

Baker, Sir Samuel (White) (1821–93) Explorer, born in London. In 1860 he began the exploration of the Nile sources, and reached the inland sea into which the Nile flows (1864), naming it Albert Nyanza (now L Mobutu Sese Seko).

Baker, Snowy, popular name of **Reginald Leslie Baker** (1884–1953) Athlete, born in Sydney, New South Wales, Australia. He became a swimming champion, played rugby union for his state, and won the Australian middleweight and heavyweight boxing titles in one night.

Baker, Richard (Douglas James) (1925–) Broadcaster and author, born in London. He joined the BBC as an announcer in 1950, and became known as a television newsreader (1954–82), and as a commentator on major state occasions.

Bakewell, Joan (Dawson) (1933–) Broadcaster and writer, born in Stockport, Greater Manchester. She became known for her BBC television series, such as *Late Night Line Up* (1965–72) and *Heart of the Matter* (1988–).

Bakewell, Robert (1725–95) Agriculturist, born in Dishley, Leicestershire. He established the Leicester breed of sheep and Dishley breed of longhorn cattle, and improved the management of sheep, cattle, and draught horses.

Bakhuizen, Ludolfr >> Backhuysen, Ludolf

Bakst, Léon [bahkst], originally **Lev Samoilovich Rosenberg** (1866–1924) Painter, born in St Petersburg, Russia. In 1908 he went to Paris, where he was associated with Diaghilev from the beginnings of the Russian ballet, designing the decor and costumes for numerous productions (1909–21). >> Diaghilev

Bakunin, Mikhail Aleksandrovich [bakoonin] (1814–76) Anarchist, born near Moscow. He took part in the German revolutionary movement (1848–9), and was sent to Siberia (1855), but escaped. He opposed Marx in the Communist International in 1868, and was expelled at the Hague Congress in 1872. >> Marx

Balaguer, Joaquín (Vidella) [balagair] (1907–) Dominican Republic president (1960–2, 1966–78, 1986–), born in Villa Bisonó, Dominican Republic. He served under dictator Rafael Trujillo (president, 1930–60), after whose assassination he fled to the USA. He returned in 1965 and regained power.

Balakirev, Mili Alekseyevich [balakiryef] (1837–1910) Composer, born in Nizhni Novgorod, Russia. He became leader of the national Russian school of music, and founded the Petersburg Free School of Music in 1862.

Balanchine, George [baluhncheen], originally **Georgi Melitonovich Balanchivadze** (1904–83) Ballet dancer and choreographer, born in St Petersburg, Russia. After a period in the Russian Ballet in Paris, he opened the School of American Ballet in New York City (1934), and became director of the New York City Ballet (1948). >> Diaghilev

Balard, Antoine Jérôme [balah(r)] (1802–76) Chemist, born in Montpelier, France. Professor at the Sorbonne and Collège de France, he discovered bromine (1826), hypochlorous acid, and chlorine monoxide.

Balassa or **Balassi, Bálint** [baw lawshaw] (1554–94) Hungarian knight, adventurer, and lyric poet, born in Kékkö. His poetry was inspired by military heroism, love, and religion, and he also experimented in drama.

Balbo, Cesare, conte (Count) [bal boh] (1789–1853) Italian statesman and writer, born in Turin, Italy. He was a prime minister in the first Piedmontese constitutional ministry. In 1839 he published a biography of Dante.

Balbo, Italo [bal boh] (1896–1940) Italian politician and aviator, born in Ferrara, Italy. A leader of the March on Rome, he was the first minister of aviation in Italy. He was killed when his plane was brought down at Tobruk (1940).

Balboa, Vasco Núñez de [bal boh a] (1475–1519) Explorer, born in Jerez de los Caballeros, Spain. In 1511 he joined the expedition to Darién, and founded a colony there, becoming the first European to see the Pacific Ocean (1513). He was executed after a quarrel with the governor of Darién.

Balbuena, Bernardo de [bal bway na] (1568–1627) Poet and clergyman, born in Valdepeñas, Spain. He settled in Central America, and became Bishop of Puerto Rico in 1620. His main work was an epic on the national hero, Bernardo del Capio (1624).

Balch, Emily Greene (1867–1961) Social reformer and pacifist, born in Jamaica Plain, MA. An active pacifist, she helped establish the Women's International League for Peace and Freedom in 1919, and shared the Nobel Peace Prize in 1946.

Balchen, Bernt (1899–1973) Aviator and Arctic explorer, born in Tveit Topdal, Norway. He was chief pilot to Byrd's first Antarctic expedition (1928–30) and to Ellsworth's Antarctic expedition (1932–5). >> Byrd, Richard; Ellsworth

Balchin, Nigel (Marlin) (1908–70) Novelist, born in Wiltshire. Trained as an industrial psychologist, he worked for the Army Council during World War 2, which led to his best-known novel, *The Small Back Room* (1943).

Balcon, Sir Michael (Elias) (1896–1977) Film producer, born in Birmingham, West Midlands. Following success with *The Thirty-Nine Steps* (1935), he made a string of successful films at Ealing Studios, including *Whisky Galore* (1948) and *The Lavender Hill Mob* (1951).

Baldinucci, Filippo [baldi noo chee] (1624–96) Art historian, born in Florence, Italy. He was entrusted by Cardinal Leopoldo Medici with the arrangement of the Medici collection.

Baldovinetti, Alesso [baldovi net ee] (c.1425–99) Painter, born in Florence, Italy. He produced frescoes, noted for their landscape backgrounds, and also worked with mosaics and stained glass.

Baldung or **Grien, Hans** (c.1476–1545) Painter and engraver, born in Weiersheim, Germany. The late Gothic style of his mature works can be seen in the quasi-Expressionist effects of 'Death and the Maiden' (Basel).

Baldwin I (1172–c.1205) Emperor of Constantinople, born in Valenciennes, France. He was a leader of the fourth Crusade, and in 1204 was crowned the first Latin emperor of Constantinople. Defeated in 1205, he died in captivity.

Baldwin (?–1190) Clergyman, born in Exeter, Devon. He became Bishop of Worcester in 1180, and Archbishop of Canterbury in 1184. He toured Wales preaching the Crusades, and himself died on a Crusade.

Baldwin, James (Arthur) (1924–87) Writer, born in Harlem, New York City. A civil rights activist, his novels include *Go Tell it on the Mountain* (1954) and *Just Above My Head* (1979).

Baldwin, James (Mark) (1861–1934) Psychologist, born in Columbia, SC. A specialist in child psychology and social psychology, he was the founder-editor of the *Psychological Review* (1894–1909).

Baldwin, Matthias (William) (1795–1866) Locomotive engineer and industrialist, born in Elizabethtown, NJ. His first locomotive, *Old Ironsides*, was completed in 1832, and the Baldwin Locomotive Works built over 1000 engines by 1861.

Baldwin, Robert (1804–58) Canadian statesman, born in Toronto (formerly York), Ontario, Canada. With **Louis Hippolyte Lafontaine** (1807–64) he became joint prime minister of the united province of Canada (1842–3, 1848–51).

Baldwin (of Bewdley), Stanley Baldwin, 1st Earl (1867–1947) British Conservative prime minister (1923–4, 1924–9, 1935–7), born in Bewdley, Worcestershire. He was President of the Board of Trade (1921–2) and Chancellor of the Exchequer (1922–3). He resigned as premier after criticism of his apparent failure to recognize the threat from Nazi Germany.

Bale, John (1495–1563) Cleric and playwright, born in Cove, Suffolk. He became a Protestant in 1533, and outraged Catholics with his polemical writings. His drama *King John* is considered the first English historical play.

Balenciaga, Cristóbal [balenthi ah ga] (1895–1972) Fashion designer, born in Guetaria, Spain. He left Spain for Paris as a result of the Spanish Civil War, where he produced clothes noted for their dramatic simplicity and elegance.

Balewa, Sir Abubakar Tafawa [ba lay wa] (1912–66) Nigerian statesman and first federal prime minister (1957–66), born in Bauchi, Nigeria. He was minister of works (1952–3) and of transport (1953–7), then became premier. He was assassinated in the military uprising of 1966.

Balfe, Michael William [balf] (1808–70) Composer, born in Dublin. In 1846 he was appointed conductor of the London Italian Opera. He wrote numerous operas, operettas, and other works, notably *The Bohemian Girl* (1843).

Balfour, Arthur James Balfour, 1st Earl [bal fer] (1848–1930) British Conservative prime minister (1902–5), born in Whittinghame, Lothian. He was chief secretary for Ireland (1887), and as foreign secretary (1916–19) was responsible for the *Balfour Declaration* (1917) on Palestine.

Balfour, Francis (Maitland) (1851–82) Embryologist, born in Edinburgh, the brother of Arthur Balfour. He published *Treatise on Comparative Embryology* (1880), and became the first professor of animal morphology at Cambridge in 1882. >> Balfour, Arthur James

Balfour, George (1872–1941) Electrical engineer, born in Portsmouth, Hampshire. In 1909, with Andrew Beatty, he founded Balfour Beatty Ltd, which built and operated town tramway systems, the first major hydro-electric schemes in Scotland, and pioneered the National Grid in the 1930s.

Bálint >> **Balassa**

Ball, C(harles) Olin (1893–1970) Food technologist, born in Abilene, KS. Working for the American Can Co in Illinois and New York (1922–41), his many patents included the basic heat-cool-fill canning method (1936) and processes for canning milk (1938–9).

Ball, John (?–1381) English rebel. An excommunicated priest, he was executed as one of the leaders in the Peasants' Revolt of 1381, led by Wat Tyler. >> Tyler, Wat

Ball, John (1818–89) Botanist and alpinist, born in Dublin. A Liberal MP and colonial under-secretary (1855–7), he was the first president of the Alpine Club (1857) and author of the *Alpine Guide* (1863–8).

Ball, Lucille (Désirée) (1911–89) Comedienne, born in Celaron, NY. She became one of television's best-loved characters in *I Love Lucy* (1951–5), *The Lucy Show* (1962–8), and *Here's Lucy* (1968–73). With husband Desi Arnaz, she became a successful production executive.

Ball, Murray Hone (1939–) Cartoonist, born in

Fielding, New Zealand. He is known for his comic strips, *Bruce the Barbarian*, *Stanley the Palaeolithic Hero*, and *Footrot Flats*.

Balla, Giacomo (1871–1958) Artist, born in Turin, Italy. He was one of the founders of Futurism and a signatory to the 1910 Futurist Manifesto.

Ballantyne Printers and brothers: **James Ballantyne** (1772–1833) and **John Ballantyne** (1774–1821), born in Kelso, Borders, Scotland. Walter Scott became a secret partner in the Edinburgh firm of John Ballantyne & Co (1808), but by 1826 the firm was bankrupt. >> Scott, Walter

Ballantyne, John >> **Bellenden, John**

Ballantyne, R(obert) M(ichael) (1825–94) Writer of boys' books, born in Edinburgh, a nephew of James and John Ballantyne. His early stories recounted his experiences in Canada, such as *The Young Fur Traders* (1856), but he is best known for *The Coral Island* (1858). >> Ballantyne, James

Ballard, J(ames) G(raham) (1930–) Writer, born in Shanghai, China. Among his works are the science-fiction novel *The Drowned World* (1962), the autobiographical novel *Empire of the Sun* (1984; filmed, 1987), and its sequel *The Kindness of Women* (1991).

Ballesteros, Sevvy [ba-yestairos], popular name of **Severiano Ballesteros** (1957–) Golfer, born in Pedrena, Spain. His successes include the British Open (1979, 1984, 1988), the US Masters (1980, 1983), and the World Matchplay (1981–2, 1984–5, 1991).

Ballou, Hosea [baloo] (1771–1852) Clergyman, born in Richmond, NH. Originally a Baptist minister, he was the chief founder of the Universalist Church, from 1817 working as a pastor in Boston.

Balmain, Pierre (Alexandre Claudius) [balmĩ] (1914–1982) Fashion designer, born in St Jean-de-Maurienne, France. He opened his own house in 1945. Famous for elegant simplicity, his designs included evening dresses, tailored suits, sportswear, and stoles.

Balmer, Johann Jakob [balmer] (1825–98) Physicist, born in Lausanne, Switzerland. The *Balmer series* is the atomic spectrum of hydrogen in the visible and near ultraviolet regions of the spectrum.

Balmont, Konstantin Dmitryevitch (1867–1943) Poet, translator, and essayist, born in Gumische, Russia. A leading Russian Symbolist, the exoticism in his work was a consequence of his extensive travels during periodic exiles.

Balnaves, Henry [balnavis] (c.1512–79) Protestant reformer, born in Kirkcaldy, Fife. He was imprisoned with John Knox in Blackness Castle, and when this was captured by the French (1547), he was sent to Rouen prison, where he wrote *The Confession of Faith* (1548). >> Knox, John

Balthasar, Hans Urs von [baltazah(r)] (1905–88) Catholic theologian, born in Lucerne, Switzerland. He drew inspiration for his theology from the mystic **Adrienne von Speyr** (1902–67), with whom he formed a secular institute after leaving the Jesuits.

Balthus, in full **Count Balthasar Klossowski de Rola** (1908–) Artist, born in Paris. He is chiefly known for works depicting interiors with adolescent girls, painted in a highly distinctive naturalistic style with a hint of Surrealism.

Baltimore, David (1938–) Microbiologist, born in New York City. In 1970 he discovered the reverse transcriptase enzyme which can transcribe DNA into RNA. For his research into the connection between viruses and cancer, he shared the 1975 Nobel Prize for Physiology or Medicine.

Baltimore, George Calvert, Baron (c.1580–1632) English statesman and colonialist, born in Kiplin, North

Yorkshire. He was secretary of state (1619–25), then declared himself a Catholic and resigned his office. He planned to found a province in America, and applied for a charter in what is now Maryland.

Balzac, Honoré de (1799–1850) Novelist, born in Tours, France. His chief work was *The Human Comedy* (trans, 1827–47), a complete picture of modern civilization, which includes such masterpieces as (trans titles) *Father Goriot*, *Lost Illusions*, and *The Peasants*.

Bambaataa (1958–) Record producer, arranger, and disc jockey, born in New York City. He developed the style of music known as 'rap', and his record *Planet Rock* (1982) was a major influence on both sides of the Atlantic.

Banach, Stefan [bahnahkh] (1892–1945) Mathematician, born in Krakow, Poland. He is regarded as one of the founders of functional analysis, and founded an important school of Polish mathematicians.

Ban Chao [ban chow], also spelled **Pan Ch'ao** (32–102) Chinese military leader and administrator, who first established Chinese control over Turkestan. He became (AD 91) protector of the Western Regions and conquered the whole of W Turkestan for the Han dynasty.

Bancroft, Edward (1744–1821) Secret agent and inventor, born in Westfield, MA. During the American Revolution, he worked in England as a double agent. He later made discoveries in textile dyes manufacturing.

Bancroft, George (1800–91) Historian and Democratic statesman, born in Worcester, MA. His major work was a *History of the United States* (10 vols, 1834–40, 1852–74). He was secretary to the navy (1845–6) and established the Naval Academy at Annapolis.

Bancroft, Hubert Howe (1832–1918) Historian, born in Granville, OH. His main work was the 39-volume *History of the Pacific States of America* (1875–90).

Bancroft, Richard (1544–1610) Anglican clergyman, born in Farnworth, Lancashire. He succeeded Whitgift as Archbishop of Canterbury in 1604, and assisted in re-establishing episcopacy in Scotland. >> Whitgift

Bancroft, Sir Squire (1841–1926) Actor-manager, born in London. In 1867 he married actress **Marie Wilton** (1840–1921), with whom he launched a series of successful comedies at the Prince of Wales's Theatre in London (1865–80).

Banda, Hastings (Kamuzu) (c.1906–) Malawi prime minister (1963–6) and first president (1966–), born in Kasungu, Malawi (formerly Nyasaland). Made life president in 1971, his autocratic rule brought defeat in the 1994 elections.

Bandaranaike, Sirimavo (Ratwatte Dias) [bandaraniykuh], née **Ratwatte** (1916–) Sri Lankan (Ceylonese) prime minister (1960–5, 1970–7), born in Ratnapura, Sri Lanka. After the assassination of her husband, S W R D Bandaranaike (1959), she led the Sri Lanka Freedom Party and became the world's first woman prime minister. >> Bandaranaike, S W R D

Bandaranaike, S(olomon) W(est) R(idgeway) D(ias) [bandaraniykay] (1899–1959) Sri Lankan (Ceylonese) prime minister (1956–9), born in Colombo. In 1951 he organized the Sri Lanka Freedom Party, and became prime minister on a policy of nationalization and neutralism. He was assassinated by a Buddhist monk, and succeeded by his wife. >> Bandaranaike, Sirimavo

Bandeira (Filho), Manuel (Carneiro de Sousa) [bandaira] (1886–1968) Poet, born in Recife, Brazil. His first books of poetry, *Destruction of the Hours* (trans, 1917) and *Carnival* (trans, 1919), identified him with the contemporary Modernist movement.

Bandelier, Adolph (Francis Alphonse) [bandeleer] (1840–1914) Archaeologist and anthropologist, born in Bern, Switzerland. He pioneered the study of the pre-Columbian Indian cultures of SW USA, Peru, and Bolivia

(1880-1903). Bandelier National Monument, a gorge near Santa Fe, New Mexico, was established in his memory in 1916.

Bandello, Matteo [bandeloh] (c.1485-1561) Cleric and writer of tales, born in Castelnuovo, Italy. Settling in France, he became Bishop of Agen in 1550. His 214 tales (1554-73) were used as source material by Shakespeare and others.

Bandiera Revolutionaries and brothers: **Attilio Bandiera** (1810-44) and **Emilio Bandiera** (1819-44) [bandyaira], born in Venice, Italy. As lieutenants in the Austrian navy, they attempted a rising in Naples against Austrian rule in favour of Italian independence, but were betrayed and shot at Cosenza.

Bandinelli, Baccio [bandinelee] (c.1493-1560) Sculptor, born in Florence, Italy. A rival of Michelangelo, he is best known for the bas-reliefs in Florence Cathedral. >> Michelangelo

Banerjea, Sir Surendranath [banerjee] (1848-1925) Indian politician and journalist, born in Calcutta, India. A fervent nationalist, he founded the Calcutta Indian Association in 1876 and was editor of *The Bengali* newspaper (1879-1921).

Banerjee, Satyendranath [banerjee] (1897-) Artist, born in West Bengal, India. He became a protégé of Rabindranath Tagore, and a teacher at the Calcutta College of Arts. >> Tagore

Bang, Bernhard (Lauritz Frederik) (1848-1932) Veterinary surgeon, born in Sorø, Denmark. He became professor of veterinary surgery at Copenhagen in 1880, and is remembered for his work on bovine brucellosis, known as *Bang's disease*.

Ban Gu [ban goo], also spelled **Pan Ku** (AD 32-92) Chinese historian, the brother of Ban Chao. His *History of the Former Han* (Han Shu) was begun in AD 54, and completed by Ban Gu's sister Ban Zhao. >> Ban Chao

Banim Novelists and brothers: **John Banim** (1798-1842) and **Michael Banim** (1796-1874), born in Kilkenny, Ireland. They collaborated in such novels as *Tales of the O'Hara Family* (1826), a faithful portrayal of humble Irish folk.

Bani-Sadr, Abolhassan [banee sadr] (1935-) Iranian politician, and first president of the Islamic Republic of Iran (1980-1). An important figure in the Iranian Revolution (1978-9), he was elected president, but was dismissed by Ayatollah Khomeini, and fled to France. >> Khomeini

Bankhead, Tallulah (1903-68) Actress, born in Huntsville, AL. Noted for her stage performances, her best film appearance was in *Lifeboat* (1944).

Banks, Don (1923-80) Composer, born in Melbourne, Victoria, Australia. His compositions include horn and violin concertos, a trilogy for orchestra, *An Australian Entertainment* (1979), and many film and TV scores.

Banks, Gordon (1937-) Footballer, born in Sheffield, South Yorkshire. He played in goal for Chesterfield, Leicester City, and Stoke City, and gave memorable performances in the 1966 and 1970 World Cup competitions, retiring in 1972.

Banks, Sir Joseph (1743-1820) Botanist, born in London. He accompanied Cook's expedition round the world in the *Endeavour* (1768-71). President of the Royal Society (1778-1819), he became an important patron of science. >> Cook, James

Banks, Nathaniel P(rentiss) (1816-94) US politician and soldier, born in Waltham, MA. He was Speaker of the House of Representatives (1856) and Governor of Massachusetts (1857, 1859, 1861). In the Civil War he commanded on the Potomac, and took Fort Hudson in 1863.

Banna, al- >> **al-Banna, Hassan**

Bannatyne, George (1545-1608) Antiquary, born in

Edinburgh. He acquired a 800-page manuscript of 15-16th-c Scottish poetry, known as the *Bannatyne Manuscript*. The Bannatyne Club was founded in his honour in 1823.

Banneker, Benjamin [baneker] (1731-1806) Astronomer and mathematician, born near Baltimore, MD, the son of a slave father and freed black mother. A farmer, he devoted his spare time to applied sciences, and published an almanac (1792-1802). In 1791 Jefferson hired him to help lay out the new capital and the District of Columbia. >> Jefferson, Thomas

Bannerman, Helen Brodie, *née* **Boog Watson** (1826-1946) Children's writer and illustrator, born in Edinburgh. She spent much of her life in India, where she wrote and illustrated the children's classic, *The Story of Little Black Sambo* (1899).

Bannister, Edward (Mitchell) (1828-1901) Painter, born in St Andrews, New Brunswick, Canada. A prominent black painter in his day, his landscapes were influenced by the naturalistic Barbizon style.

Bannister, Sir Roger (Gilbert) (1929-) Athlete and neurologist, born in Harrow, Greater London. He was the first man to run the mile in under 4 minutes (3 min 59·4 s), at Oxford (6 May 1954).

Banting, Sir Frederick Grant (1891-1941) Physiologist, born in Alliston, Ontario, Canada. In 1922, with J J R Macleod, he discovered the hormone insulin, used in the control of diabetes. They were jointly awarded the Nobel Prize for Physiology or Medicine in 1923. >> Best, Charles H; Macleod, J J R

Banville, (Etienne Claude Jean Baptiste) Théodore (Faullain) de [bãveel] (1823-91) Poet and playwright, born in Moulins, France. He was named 'King of Rhymes' for his skill in handling the difficult mediaeval ballades and rondels. His *Gringoire* (1866) holds an established place in French repertory.

Bao Dai [bow diy], (Vietnamese 'keeper of greatness'), originally **Nguyen Vinh Thuy** (1913-) Indo-Chinese ruler, born in Hué, Vietnam. He ruled as Emperor of Annam (1932-45), but renounced his hereditary title. In Saigon (1949) he became chief of the State of Vietnam within the French Union, but was deposed in 1955.

Baptist, John the >> **John the Baptist, St**

Bär, Karl Ernst von >> **Baer, Karl Ernst von**

Bara, Theda, *née* **Theodosia Goodman**, nickname **the Vamp** (1890-1955) Film actress, born in Cincinnati, OH. She became an overnight star in the film *A Fool There Was* (1915). Her nickname was gained through portrayals of exotic 'man-hungry' women, and the offscreen image she cultivated.

Barabbas [barabas] (1st-c) Political rebel and murderer (Mark 15, Luke 23). He was arrested but apparently released by popular acclaim in preference to Pilate's offer to release Jesus of Nazareth. >> Jesus Christ

Baraka, Imamu Amiri, originally **Le Roi Jones** (1934-) Writer and political activist, born in Newark, NJ. He became a Muslim and changed his name in 1967. His works include poetry, such as *Reggae or Not!* (1982), plays, short stories, and essays.

Bárány, Robert [baranyuh] (1876-1936) Physician and otologist, born in Vienna. He pioneered the study of the balancing apparatus of the inner ear, and was awarded the Nobel Prize for Physiology or Medicine in 1914.

Barba, Eugenio (1936-) Italian theatre director. He founded Odin Teatret, an experimental theatre company, and in 1979 established the International School of Theatre Anthropology.

Barbara, St (?-c.200), feast day 4 December. Christian virgin martyr, the patron saint of artillerymen. According to legend, her father immured her in a tower to discourage suitors. On discovering that she had become a Christian, he beheaded her and was instantly struck by lightning.

Barbarelli, Giorgio >> **Giorgione**

Barbari, Jacopo de' (c.1475–c.1516) Venetian painter and engraver. From 1510 he was court painter at Brussels, and is chiefly noted for his engravings, mainly of mythological figures.

Barbarossa, Frederick I >> **Frederick I**

Barbarossa [bah(r)barosa], ('Redbeard'), nickname of **Khair-ed-Din** (?–1546) Barbary pirate, born in Mitilini, Greece. He captured Algiers (1529) and was made admiral of the Ottoman fleet (1533). He defeated the Holy Roman Emperor, Charles V, at Preveza in 1538. >> Charles V (emperor)

Barbauld, Anna Letitia [bah(r)bawld], née **Aikin** (1743–1825) Writer, born in Kibworth-Harcourt, Leicestershire. Her best work includes *Early Lessons for Children*, and with her brother she began the well-known series *Evenings at Home* in 1792.

Barber, Samuel (1910–81) Composer, born in West Chester, PA. His early music includes the popular *Adagio for Strings*. Later works lay more emphasis on chromaticism and dissonance, and include the ballet *Medea* (1946) and the opera *Vanessa* (1958, Pulitzer).

Barbera, Joseph (Roland) >> **Hanna-Barbera**

Barbie, Klaus, known as **the Butcher of Lyon** (1913–91) Nazi leader, born in Bad Godesberg, Germany. Working for the Gestapo, he was responsible for sending thousands of people to Auschwitz. He later fled to South America but was extradited to France in 1983, and sentenced to life imprisonment.

Barbirolli, Sir John (Giovanni Battista) [bah(r)birolee] (1899–1970) Conductor and cellist, born in London. He was conductor (1943–58) of the Hallé Orchestra, later becoming its principal conductor (1959–68). In 1939 he married the oboist **Evelyn Rothwell** (1911–   ).

Barbon, Praise-God >> **Barebone, Praise-God**

Barbour, John [bah(r)ber] (c.1320–95) Poet, clergyman, and scholar, probably born in Aberdeen, Grampian, known as 'the father of Scottish poetry and history'. His national epic, *The Brus* (1370s), is a narrative poem on the life of King Robert I. >> Bruce, Robert

Barbusse, Henri [bah(r)büs] (1873–1935) Novelist, born in Asnières, France. A noted pacifist, his novels include *Under Fire* (trans, 1916) and *The Knife between the Teeth* (trans, 1921).

Barca, Pedro Calderón de la >> **Calderón de la Barca, Pedro**

Barclay, Alexander (c.1475–1552) Poet and writer, probably born in Scotland. His famous poem, *The Shyp of Folys of the Worlde* (1509), is part-translation, part-imitation of the German *Das Narrenschiff* (1494, The Ship of Fools) by Brant. >> Brant, Sebastian

Barclay, John (1582–1621) Writer, born in Pont-à-Mousson, France. He wrote, mostly in Latin, politico-satirical novels directed against the Jesuits, such as *Euphormio* (1603) and *Argenis* (1621).

Barclay, Robert (1648–90) Quaker, born in Gordonstoun, Grampian. He published many tracts in defence of Quakerism, notably *Apology for the True Christian Divinity* (1678). He became one of the proprietors of East New Jersey in 1682.

Barclay, Robert (1843–1913) British banker, who oversaw the merger of 20 banks to form Barclay & Co Ltd in 1896. In 1917 the name was changed to Barclay's Bank Ltd.

Barclay, William (1907–78) Theologian, religious writer, and broadcaster, born in Wick, Highland. He is remembered for his many popular writings and broadcasts, such as *A New Testament Wordbook* (1955) and the *Daily Study Bible*.

Barclay-Allardice, Robert, known as **Captain Barclay** (1779–1854) Scottish soldier and sportsman. He is celebrated for walking 1000 mi in 1000 consecutive hours, a feat performed at Newmarket from June to July 1809.

Barclay de Tolly, Mikhail Bogdanovich, Knaz (Prince) [bah(r)kliy duh tolyuh] (1761–1818) Russian field marshal, born in Luhda-Grosshof, Livonia (modern Estonia and Latvia). He served in Turkey, Sweden, and Poland, losing an arm at Eylau (1807). Defeated by Napoleon at Smolensk (1812), he later took part in the invasion of France.

Bar-Daisan >> **Bardesanes**

Bardeen, John [bah(r)deen] (1908–91) Physicist, the first person to receive two Nobel Prizes for Physics, born in Madison, WI. In 1947 he helped to develop the point contact transistor, for which he shared the Nobel Prize in 1956. His second prize (1972) was shared for his work on the first satisfactory theory of superconductivity. >> Brattain; Cooper; Schrieffer; Shockley

Bardesanes [bah(r)desahneez], also called **Bar-Daisan** (154–222) Syrian Christian theologian and poet, born in Urfa, Turkey. Known as 'the last of the Gnostics', he wrote *Dialogue of Destiny* and many hymns.

Bardot, Brigitte [bah(r)doh], originally **Camille Javal** (1934–   ) Film actress, born in Paris. The film *And God Created Woman* (trans, 1956), directed by husband Roger Vadim, established her international reputation as a sex kitten. Later films include *The Truth* (trans, 1960) and *If Don Juan Were a Woman* (trans, 1973). >> Vadim

Barebone or **Barbon, Praise-God** (c.1596–1679) Leather merchant and controversial Anabaptist preacher, born in London. He was nominated by Oliver Cromwell to sit in the Short Parliament of 1653, nicknamed after him the Barebone's Parliament. He was imprisoned in the Tower (1661–2).

Barenboim, Daniel [barenboym] (1942–   ) Pianist and conductor, born in Buenos Aires, Argentina. A noted exponent of Mozart and Beethoven, he gained his reputation as pianist/conductor with the English Chamber Orchestra. He was married to the cellist Jacqueline du Pré (1967–87). >> du Pré

Barents, Willem [baruhnts], also spelled **Barentz** (?–1597) Dutch navigator. He piloted several Dutch expeditions in search of the Northeast Passage, and died off Novaya Zemlya. The *Barents Sea* was named after him.

Barère (de Vieuzac), Bertrand [barair] (1755–1841) Revolutionary and regicide, born in Tarbes, France. Originally a moderate, he joined Robespierre as a member of the Committee of Public Safety. He was later imprisoned (1794), but escaped into exile, returning to Paris under an amnesty (1830). >> Robespierre

Barham, Richard (Harris), pseudonym **Thomas Ingoldsby** (1788–1845) Humorist, born in Canterbury, Kent. In 1837 he began his series of burlesque metrical tales collected under the title of *The Ingoldsby Legends* (3 vols, 1840–7).

Bar-Hebraeus >> **Abu al-Faraj**

Barke, James (1905–58) Novelist, born in Torwoodlee, Borders. He is best known for his devoted research on Robert Burns, producing a five-volume cycle of novels (1946–54) and an edition of *Poems and Songs of Robert Burns* (1955). >> Burns, Robert

Barker, Sir Ernest (1874–1960) Political scientist, born in Cheshire. His works include *Reflections on Government* (1942) and *Principles of Social and Political Theory* (1951).

Barker, George Granville (1913–   ) Writer, born in Loughton, Essex. A major work is *The True Confession of George Barker* (1950). He has also published essays, plays, scripts, and novels, and his *Collected Poems* appeared in 1987.

Barker, Harley Granville >> **Granville-Barker, Harley**

Barker, Howard (1946–   ) Playwright, born in London. His many works include *Cheek* (produced 1970), *The Power of the Dog* (1984), and *The Possibilities* (1988).

Barker, Ronnie, popular name of **Ronald William George Barker** (1929–   ) Comic actor, born in Bedford,

Bedfordshire. His many radio and television appearances include *Porridge* (1974–7; filmed 1979), *Open All Hours* (1976, 1981–5) and, in partnership with Ronnie Corbett, *The Two Ronnies* (1971–87). >> Corbett, Ronnie

Barkhausen, Heinrich Georg [bah(r)khowzen] (1881–1956) Physicist, born in Bremen, Germany. In 1919 he discovered that the magnetization of iron proceeds in discrete steps and devised a loudspeaker system to render this discontinuity audible (the *Barkhausen effect*).

Barkla, Charles Glover [bah(r)kla] (1877–1944) Physicist, born in Widnes, Lancashire. He conducted notable research into X-rays and other short-wave emissions, and was awarded the Nobel Prize for Physics in 1917.

Barkley, Alben W(illiam) [bah(r)klee] (1877–1956) US vice-president (1949–53) and legislator, born in Lowes, KY. In 1949, under Harry Truman, he was the oldest vice-president to take office. >> Truman

bar Kokhba, Simon [kokhba], also spelled **bar Kochba** (?–135) Jewish leader in Palestine. From 132, with the rabbi Akiba ben Joseph, he led a rebellion of Jews in Judaea against the Roman Emperor Hadrian, but was defeated and killed at the Battle of Bethar. >> Akiba ben Joseph; Hadrian

Barlach, Ernst [bah(r)lak] (1870–1938) Expressionist sculptor, playwright, and poet, born in Wedel, Germany. Although best known as a sculptor in wood, his greatest achievement was the bronze 'Angel of Death' war memorial at Güstrow Cathedral, later removed by Hitler.

Barlow, Joel (1754–1812) Poet and politician, born in Redding, CT. His best-known work is the mock-heroic poem, 'Hasty Pudding' (1796). He became US consul at Algiers and ambassador to France in 1811.

Barlow, Peter (1776–1862) Physicist, born in Norwich, Norfolk. His *New Mathematical Tables* (1814) were reprinted as late as 1947 as *Barlow's Tables*. The *Barlow lens* is an achromatic lens used as an astronomical eyepiece and in photography.

Barnard, Christiaan (Neethling) (1922–) Surgeon, born in Beaufort West, South Africa. At Groote Schuur Hospital he performed the first successful human heart transplant (1967), though the patient, Louis Washkansky, died of double pneumonia 18 days later. Later transplants proved to be increasingly successful.

Barnard, Edward (Emerson) (1857–1923) Astronomer, born in Nashville, TN. With Max Wolf, he was the first to appreciate the nature of 'black nebulae'. In 1916 he discovered the star which has the greatest known motion relative to other stars (*Barnard's star*). >> Wolf, Max

Barnard, Marjorie Faith, pseudonym **M Barnard Eldershaw** (1897–1987) Novelist, historian, and biographer, born in Sydney, New South Wales, Australia. She wrote many books with **Flora Sydney Patricia Eldershaw** (1897–1956) under their joint pseudonym. Best known are *A House is Built* (1929) and *Tomorrow and Tomorrow* (1947).

Barnardo, Thomas John [bah(r)nah(r)doh] (1845–1905) Doctor and philanthropist, born in Dublin. In London in 1867 he founded the East End Mission for destitute children in Stepney, and a number of homes in Greater London, which came to be known as the *Dr Barnardo's Homes*.

Barnato, Barney [bah(r)nahtoh], originally **Barnett Isaacs** (1852–97) Financier and speculator, born in London. In 1873 he went to Kimberley, South Africa, made a fortune in diamonds, and engineered the Kaffir boom in mining stocks of 1895.

Barnave, Antoine (Pierre Joseph Marie) [bah(r)nahv] (1761–93) French revolutionary, born in Grenoble, France. He brought back the royal family from their abortive flight to Varennes (1791), but subsequently developed royalist sympathies, and was guillotined.

Barnes, Djuna (1892–1982) Writer and illustrator, born in Cornwall-on-Hudson, NY. She wrote short stories, poems, novels, and plays. Her best-known work is the novel *Nightwood* (1936).

Barnes, Ernest William (1874–1953) Anglican clergyman, born in Birmingham, West Midlands. He became Bishop of Birmingham in 1924. His modernist and pacifist views involved him in continued controversy within the Church of England.

Barnes, Peter (1931–) Playwright and screenwriter, born in London. Works include *The Ruling Class* (1968), *The Bewitched* (1974), and *Red Noses* (1985).

Barnes, Thomas (1785–1841) Editor and journalist, born in London. He became dramatic critic of *The Times* in 1809, and editor in 1817, a post which he held for 24 years.

Barnes, William (1801–86) Pastoral poet, born in Sturminster Newton, Dorset. His three volumes of poetry were collected as *Poems of Rural Life in the Dorset Dialect* (1879). He also wrote several philological works.

Barnett, Samuel A(ugustus) (1844–1913) Anglican clergyman and social reformer, born in Bristol, Avon. Sympathetic to the plight of the London poor, he founded Toynbee Hall in Whitechapel in 1884, and advocated many reform measures. >> Toynbee

Barneveldt, Jan van Olden [bah(r)nevelt] (1547–1619) Dutch statesman and lawyer, born in Amersfoort, The Netherlands. As adviser to Prince Maurice, he opposed his warlike schemes and concluded a truce with Spain in 1609. Suspected of treason, he was executed. >> Maurice (Prince of Orange)

Barnum, P(hineas) T(aylor) (1810–91) Showman, born in Bethel, CT. He ran a museum in New York City, introducing freak shows, and sponsored the famous dwarf 'General Tom Thumb' (Charles Stratton). In 1881 he joined with his rival **James Anthony Bailey** (1847–1906) to found the Barnum and Bailey circus. >> Stratton

Barocci or **Baroccio, Federigo** [barochee] (c.1528–1612) Painter, born in Urbino, Italy. His fluent pictorial style had considerable influence on Rubens and his school. His 'Madonna del Popolo' is in the Uffizi Gallery, Florence. >> Rubens

Baroja (y Nessi), Pío [baroha] (1872–1956) Writer, born in San Sebastián, Spain. His book of short stories, *Sombre Lives* (trans, 1900), was the first of more than 70 volumes of novels and essays, many with a Basque setting.

Baronius, Caesar [baronius], originally **Cesare Baronio** (1538–1607) Church historian, born in Sora, Italy. A pupil of St Philip Neri, he became superior of the Oratory in 1593. He wrote the first critical Church history, the *Annales Ecclesiastici* (1588–1607). >> Neri

Barr, Alfred H (1902–81) US museum director. As director of the Museum of Modern Art in New York City (1929–43), he staged several controversial exhibitions.

Barras, Paul François Jean Nicolas, comte de (Count of) [bara] (1755–1829) French revolutionary, born in Foxemphoux, France. An original member of the Jacobin Club, and a regicide, he played the chief part in the overthrow of Robespierre, and became virtual dictator. One of the five members of the Directory in 1795, he was overthrown by Napoleon in 1799. >> Napoleon I; Robespierre

Barrault, Jean-Louis [baroh] (1910–94) Actor and producer, born in Le Vesinet, France. With his actress wife **Madeleine Renaud** (1903–), he founded his own theatre company, le Troupe Marigny. His films include *The Children of Paradise* (trans, 1945), *La Ronde* (1950), and *The Longest Day* (1962).

Barre, Raymond (1924–) French prime minister (1976–81), born in St Denis, Réunion. He was minister of foreign trade under Giscard d'Estaing, and became prime minister after the resignation of Chirac. >> Chirac; Giscard d'Estaing

Barré, (Mohammed) Siad [ba**ray**] (1919–95) Somali soldier and president (1969–91). He joined the army as a colonel in 1960, and became president after a military coup. Towards the end of his rule, the country broke up into warring factions, and he was deposed.

Barrès, (Auguste) Maurice [bares] (1862–1923) Politician and novelist, born in Charmes-sur-Moselle, France. He wrote a trilogy on his own self-analysis *Le Culte du Moi* (1888–91), and a nationalistic trilogy that included *L'Appel du Soldat* (1906).

Barrie, Sir J(ames) M(atthew) (1860–1937) Novelist and playwright, born in Kirriemuir, Tayside. Chiefly remembered for *Peter Pan* (1904), other notable plays include *The Admirable Crichton* (1902) and *Dear Brutus* (1917).

Barrington, George, originally **George Waldron** (1755–1804) Writer and adventurer, born in Maynooth, Co Kildare, Ireland. In 1790 he was transported to Botany Bay as a criminal. Set free in 1792, he became high constable of Parramatta, New South Wales, and wrote historical works on Australia.

Barrington, Sir Jonah (1760–1834) Judge and politician, born in Abbeyleix, Co Laois, Ireland. After a troubled career in Ireland, he settled in France, and wrote *The Rise and Fall of the Irish Nation* (1833) and *Personal Sketches of his own Time* (3 vols, 1827–32).

Barrington, Ken(neth Frank) (1930–81) Cricketer, born in Reading, Berkshire. During his career he played in 82 Tests, making a total of 6806 runs, including 20 centuries.

Barron, James (1768–1851) Naval officer, probably born in Norfolk, VA. He commanded the USS *Chesapeake* in its disastrous fight with the British *Leopold* (1807), for which he was court-martialled. Convinced that Stephen Decatur was blocking his career, he killed him in a duel in 1820. >> Decatur

Barros, João de (1496–1570) Historian, born in Viseu, Portugal. He is known for *Decades* (1552–1615), a history of the Portuguese in the East Indies, which earned him the title of the 'Portuguese Livy'.

Barrow, Clyde >> **Bonnie and Clyde**

Barrow, Errol Walton (1920–87) Barbadian politician and prime minister (1961–76, 1986–7), born in Barbados. He co-founded the Democratic Labour Party, which won the elections following independence in 1961, and he became the first prime minister.

Barrow, Isaac (1630–77) Mathematician and divine, born in London. He was the first Lucasian professor of mathematics at Cambridge (1663), but resigned (1669) to make way for Isaac Newton. He founded the library of Trinity College, Cambridge, where he became Master in 1673. >> Newton, Isaac

Barrow, Sir John (1764–1848) Naval administrator, born in Dragley Beck, Lancashire. Attached to the Admiralty (1804–45), he promoted Arctic expeditions. *Barrow Strait* and *Point Barrow* in the Arctic, and *Cape Barrow* in the Antarctic, were named in his honour, as was the northern duck, *Barrow's goldeneye*.

Barr Smith, Robert (1824–1915) Pastoralist and woolbroking pioneer, born in Lochwinnoch, Strathclyde. He settled in South Australia in 1854, and partnered Thomas Elder to form Elder, Smith & Co, which became one of the world's largest wool-brokers. >> Elder, Thomas

Barry, comtesse du >> **du Barry, comtesse**

Barry, Sir Charles (1795–1860) Architect, born in London. His best-known design is the new Palace of Westminster (Houses of Parliament, 1840–70), completed after his death by his son **Edward Middleton Barry** (1830–80). Another son **Sir John Wolfe-Barry** (1836–1918), was engineer of the Tower Bridge and Barry Docks.

Barry, James (1741–1806) Historical painter, born in Cork, Co Cork, Ireland. In 1782 he was appointed professor of painting at the Royal Academy. His best-known works are

'Adam and Eve' (1771) and 'Venus Rising from the Waves' (1772).

Barry, John (1745–1803) US naval officer, born in Co Wexford, Ireland. He commanded the USS *Lexington* and *Effingham* (1776–8), became the senior captain in the navy (1794), and commanded all US ships in the West Indies (1798–9).

Barrymore, Ethel, originally **Ethel Blythe** (1879–1959) Actress, born in Philadelphia, PA, the sister of Lionel and John Barrymore. She scored a great London stage success in *The Bells* (1897–8). Notable films include *None But the Lonely Heart* (1944, Oscar). >> Barrymore, John / Lionel

Barrymore, John, originally **John Blythe**, known as **the Great Profile** (1882–1942) Actor, born in Philadelphia, PA, the younger brother of Ethel and Lionel Barrymore. Known for his Shakespearean roles, notably *Hamlet* (1922), he also appeared in many films, such as *Grand Hotel* (1932). His classical nose and distinguished features won him his nickname. >> Barrymore, Ethel / Lionel

Barrymore, Lionel, originally **Lionel Blythe** (1878–1954) Actor, born in Philadelphia, PA, the elder brother of Ethel and John Barrymore. His many film roles include *Free Soul* (1931, Oscar) and *Duel in the Sun* (1947). Although wheelchair-bound in his later years, he scored a great success as Dr Gillespie in the original *Dr Kildare* film series. >> Barrymore, Ethel / John

Barstow, Stan(ley) (1928–) Novelist, born in Horbury, West Yorkshire. He achieved instant success with his first novel, *A Kind of Loving* (1960). Later works include *A Brother's Tale* (1980) and *Just you Wait and See* (1986).

Bart, Lionel (1930–) Composer and lyricist, born in London. His successful musicals include *Lock Up Your Daughters* (1959), *Oliver* (1960), *Blitz!* (1962), and *Maggie May* (1964).

Barth, Heinrich [bah(r)t] (1821–65) Explorer, born in Hamburg, Germany. In 1849 he was appointed by the British government to join a mission to C Africa to supress slavery. He later continued his explorations alone, travelling nearly 12 000 mi.

Barth or **Bart, Jean** [bah(r)t] (1650–1702) Privateer, born in Dunkirk, France. He joined the French navy, and in 1694, against a superior Dutch fleet, recaptured a convoy of 96 ships and brought them to Dunkirk.

Barth, John (Simmons) (1930–) Novelist and short-story writer, born in Cambridge, MD. His novels include *The Floating Opera* (1956), *Giles Goat-Boy* (1966), and *The Last Voyage of Somebody the Sailor* (1991).

Barth, Karl [bah(r)t] (1886–1968) Theologian, born in Basel, Switzerland. He played a leading role in the German Confessing Church and the Barmen Declaration (1934). Dismissed from his chair at Bonn for refusing to take an unconditional oath of allegiance to Hitler, he became professor at Basel (1935–62). The major exponent of Reformed theology, his many works include the monumental *Church Dogmatics* (trans, 1932–67).

Barthélemy Saint-Hilaire, Jules [bah(r)taylemee sãti-lair] (1805–95) French statesman and scholar, born in Paris. He co-founded the journal *Le Bons Sens* (1830), and translated Aristotle (35 vols, 1833–95). He was foreign minister (1880–1).

Barthelme, Donald (1931–89) Novelist and short-story writer, born in Philadelphia, PA. Associated with the avant-garde movement of the 1960s, his novels include *Snow White* (1967), *The Dead Father* (1975), and *Paradise* (1986).

Barthes, Roland (Gérard) [bah(r)t] (1915–80) Teacher, critic, and writer on semiology and structuralism, born in Cherbourg, France. His collection of essays *Writing Degree Zero* (trans, 1953) established him as France's leading critic of Modernist literature.

Bartholdi, (Frédéric) Auguste [bah(r)**thol**dee], Fr [bah(r)toldee] (1834–1904) Sculptor, born in Colmar,

France. He specialized in enormous monuments, such as the bronze Statue of Liberty in New York harbour, unveiled in 1886.

Bartholin, Thomas >> **Rudbeck, Olof**

Bartholomé, Paul Albert [bah(r)tolomay] (1848–1928) Sculptor, born in Thiverval, France. He is best known for the group of statuary 'Aux morts' (1895), and for the monument to Rousseau in the Panthéon.

Bartholomew, John George (1860–1920) Cartographer, born in Edinburgh. Best known for his system of layer colouring of contours, his works include *Physical Atlas of the World* (2 vols, 1889–1911).

Bart, Jean >> **Barth, Jean**

Bartlett, Sir Frederic (Charles) (1886–1969) Psychologist, born in Stow-on-the-Wold, Gloucestershire. The first professor of experimental psychology at Cambridge (1931–52), he is known for his pioneering cognitive approach to human memory.

Bartlett, John (1820–1905) Publisher and bookseller, born in Plymouth, MA. For many years he owned the University Book Store at Harvard (1849–63). He is best known as the compiler of *Bartlett's Familiar Quotations* (1855).

Bartlett, Josiah (1729–95) Physician and US governor, born in Amesbury, MA. A member of the Continental Congress (1775–6, 1778–9), he signed the Declaration of Independence, became chief justice of the state superior court (1788–90), and was New Hampshire's first governor (1790–4).

Bartók, Béla [**bah(r)**tok] (1881–1945) Composer, born in Nagyszentmiklós, Hungary. His compositions were greatly influenced by Hungarian and Balkan folk music. In 1939 he settled in the USA, where his many works include the opera *Duke Bluebeard's Castle* and the ballet *The Wooden Prince*.

Bartolommeo, Fra [bah(r)tolo**may**oh], originally **Baccio della Porta** (1472–1517) Painter, leading artist of the High Renaissance, born near Florence, Italy. He worked in Venice (1507), then in Florence (c.1509–12). His work is distinguished by controlled composition, delicate drawing, and the use of colour.

Bartolozzi, Francesco [bah(r)to**lot**see] (1727–1815) Engraver, born in Florence, Italy. He settled in London to become engraver to George III. His prints include line engravings and stippled works, printed in brown and red, called *Bartolozzi red*.

Bartolus [bah(r)**toh**lus], Latin name of **Bartolo di Sassoferrato** (c.1314–57) Jurist and judge, born in Venatura, Italy. He was leader of the school of commentators on Roman law who sought to derive principles of general application for solving contemporary problems. He was also a founder of international private law.

Barton, Clara, popular name of **Clarissa Harlowe Barton** (1821–1912) Founder of the American Red Cross, born in Oxford, MA. After working for the International Red Cross in Europe, she established the US branch of the Red Cross in 1881, becoming its first president (1881–1904).

Barton, Sir Derek (Harold Richard) (1918–) Organic chemist, born in Gravesend, Kent. He introduced conformational analysis as a method for studying the shape of organic molecules and the effect of shape on reactivity, and shared the Nobel Prize for Chemistry in 1969.

Barton, Sir Edmund (1849–1920) Australian statesman and jurist, born in Sydney, New South Wales, Australia. Leader of the Federation movement from 1896, he became the first prime minister of the Australian Commonwealth (1901–3).

Barton, Elizabeth, known as **the Maid of Kent** or **the Nun of Kent** (?1506–34) Prophet, born in Kent. A domestic servant, she began to have trances and make prophetic utterances against the authorities. She denounced Henry VIII's marriage to Anne Boleyn, was charged with treason, and hanged at Tyburn. >> **Henry VIII**

Barton, Gordon Page (1929–) Transport entrepreneur and Australian politician, born in Surabaya, Java. He developed the international Ipec and Skypac freight and courier network, becoming its managing director in 1962. He formed the Liberal Reform Group, which later became the Australia Party.

Barton, John (1928–) Stage director, born in London. In 1960 he joined the Royal Shakespeare Company at Stratford-upon-Avon. He wrote and directed *The Hollow Crown* (1961), and is the author of *Playing Shakespeare* (1984).

Bartram, John (1699–1777) Botanist, born near Darby, PA. He built up an unrivalled collection of North American plants. His son **William** (1739–1823), was also a naturalist.

Baruch [**ba**rukh] (7th–6th-c BC) Biblical character, described as the companion and secretary of the prophet Jeremiah (*Jer* 36). His name became attached to several Jewish works of much later date.

Baruch, Bernard (Mannes) (1870–1965) Financier and US statesman, born in Camden, SC. A powerful political influence, he was known as 'the adviser of presidents' and also of Churchill in World War 2. >> **Churchill, Sir Winston**

Bary, Heinrich Anton de >> **de Bary, Heinrich Anton**

Baryshnikov, Mikhail Nikolaievich [ba**rish**nikof] (1948–) Dancer, born in Riga, Latvia. In 1974 he defected to the West while on tour in Canada, joining the American Theater Ballet, where he later became artistic director (1980). >> **Balanchine; Kirkland**

Basaldella, Mirko [basal**de**la] (1910–1969) Sculptor and painter, born in Udine, Italy. He is best known for the bronze memorial doors he designed for the Ardeatine caves near Rome.

Baselitz, Georg [**ba**selitz] (1938–) Avant-garde artist, born in Deutschbaselitz, Germany. Known for his violent subject-matter and 'wild Expressionist' style, his forte is painting figures, trees, and other objects upside down.

Basevi, George [ba**say**vee] (1794–1845) Architect, born in London. His Neoclassical designs include the Fitzwilliam Museum in Cambridge and part of London's Belgravia. He also designed country mansions and Gothic churches.

Basho, Matsuo (1644–94) Poet, born in Ueno (Iga), Japan. Becoming master of the haiku, he started his own school. Influenced by Zen Buddhism, he journeyed extensively, and composed his celebrated book of travels *The Narrow Road to the Deep North* (trans, 1689).

Basie, Count [**bay**see], popular name of **William Basie** (1904–84) Jazz pianist, and bandleader, born in Red Bank, NJ. He joined the Benny Moten band in 1929, forming his own band in 1935 which became the Count Basie Orchestra. Nearly 50 years as a bandleader, his most popular compositions include 'One O'Clock Jump' and 'Jumpin' at the Woodside'.

Basil, St, known as **Basil the Great** (c.329–79), feast day 1 Jan (E), 2 Jan (W). One of the greatest of the Greek fathers, born in Caesarea, Cappadocia, the brother of Gregory of Nyssa. A fierce opponent of Arianism, he improved monastic standards and wrote many seminal works. >> **Gregory of Nyssa**

Basil, Wassili de >> **de Basil, Colonel Wassili**

Basil I, known as **Basil the Macedonian** (c.812–886) Byzantine emperor (867–86), born in Thrace, who founded the Macedonian dynasty. He formulated the Greek legal code, in a text known as the *Basilica*.

Basilides [basi**lid**eez] (2nd-c) Gnostic philosopher, who founded a sect in Alexandria which blended Christian thought with elements from Zoroaster, Indian philosophy, and magic. His disciples, *Basilidians*, were active into the 4th-c. >> **Zoroaster**

Basil II, known as **Basil Bulgaroctonus** ('slayer of the Bulgars') (c.958–1025) Byzantine emperor, who came to the throne as sole ruler in 976. His 15-year war against the Bulgarians culminated in the victory in the Belasica Mountains which earned him his surname.

Basilius, John >> **Bessarion, John**

Baskerville, John (1706–75) Printer, born in Wolverley, Worcestershire. In c.1750 he began experiments in letter founding, and produced the types named after him. In 1758 he became printer to Cambridge University.

Baskin, Leonard (1922–) Graphic artist and sculptor, born in New Brunswick, NJ. Among his etchings, woodblocks, and graphics are 'Man of Peace' (1952) and 'Angel of Death' (1959). In 1990 he began his major work, the Franklin D Roosevelt Memorial, for Washington, DC.

Basov, Nikolai Gennadiyevich [basof] (1922–) Physicist, born in St Petersburg, Russia. He developed the maser in 1955, for which he shared the 1964 Nobel Prize for Physics. In 1958 he invented the laser. >> **Prokhorov**

Bass, George [bas] (1771–1803) Naval surgeon, born in Aswarby, Lincolnshire. With Matthew Flinders he explored (1795–1800) the strait between Tasmania and Australia that bears his name. >> **Flinders**

Bass, Michael Thomas [bas] (1799–1884) Brewer, born in Burton-on-Trent, Staffordshire. He expanded the family business (founded by his grandfather William Bass, in 1777). His son **Michael Arthur Bass** (1837–1909) became Baron Burton in 1886.

Bassani, Giorgio [basahnee] (1916–) Novelist and poet, born in Bologna, Italy. His work, beginning with *Five Stories of Ferrara* (trans, 1956), chronicles the suffering of the Italian Jews under Fascism.

Bassano, Jacopo da [basahnoh], also known as **Giacomo da Ponte** (c.1510–92) Founder of genre painting in Europe, born in Bassano, Italy. His best works include the altarpiece of the Nativity at Bassano, 'Calvary' (c.1538), and 'Pastoral' (c.1565–70).

Bassi, Agostino Maria [basee] (1773–1856) Biologist and pioneer bacteriologist, born in Lodi, Italy. As early as 1835 he showed that a disease of silkworms (muscardine) was fungal and contagious, and proposed that many other diseases are transmitted by micro-organisms.

Bassompierre, François de [basôpyair] (1579–1646) French soldier and statesman, born in Harouel, France. Implicated in an unsuccessful plot to overthrow Cardinal Richelieu, he was imprisoned in the Bastille (1631–43). His *Memoirs* are an important source of contemporary history. >> **Richelieu**

Bastian, Adolf [bastian] (1826–1905) Ethnologist, born in Bremen, Germany. He is best known for his theory that variations in folk cultures could be traced back to the effects of local geographical conditions on a basic set of elementary ideas common to mankind.

Bastian, Henry (Charlton) (1837–1915) Biologist and physician, born in Truro, Cornwall. He championed the doctrine of spontaneous generation, and became one of the founders of British neurology through his work on aphasia.

Bastien-Lepage, Jules [bastyî luhpahzh] (1848–84) Painter, born in Damvillers, France. He painted genre rustic scenes, such as 'The Hayfield' (1878, Louvre), and portraits, such as those of Sarah Bernhardt and the Prince of Wales (later Edward VII).

Bastos, Augustos Roa (1917–) Paraguayan novelist, living in exile since 1947. Journalist, screenwriter, and academic, his masterpiece is *I the Supreme* (trans, 1947).

Bata, Tomas (1876–1932) Industrialist, born in Zlin, Czech Republic. He built up the largest leather factory in Europe which, in 1928, was producing 75 000 pairs of shoes a day.

Batchelor, Joy (1914–) Animated-cartoon producer, born in Watford, Hertfordshire. In 1941 she married John Halas, to form the Halas–Batchelor animation unit. They made the first British feature-length cartoon, *Handling Ships* in 1945. >> **Halas, John**

Bateman, H(enry) M(ayo) (1887–1970) Cartoonist, born in Sutton Forest, New South Wales, Australia. Brought up in England, he is best known for his drawings of embarrassing 'The Man Who...' situations, such as *The Guardsman Who Dropped His Rifle*.

Bates, H(erbert) E(rnest) (1905–74) Writer, born in Rushden, Northamptonshire. A noted exponent of the short-story, his best-known works are *Fair Stood the Wind for France* (1944), *The Jacaranda Tree* (1949), and *The Darling Buds of May* (1958), which became a popular UK television series.

Bates, H(enry) W(alter) (1825–92) Naturalist and traveller, born in Leicester, Leicestershire. He explored the Amazon valley (1848–59), returning with 8000 species of hitherto unknown insects. In 1861 his description of mimicry in animals (*Batesian mimicry*) contributed to the theory of natural selection.

Bates, Alan, originally **Arthur Bates** (1934–) Actor, born in Allestree, Derbyshire. His films include *The Entertainer* (1960), *A Kind of Loving* (1962), and *Women in Love* (1969), and the television production of *An Englishman Abroad* (1982, BAFTA).

Bates, Daisy May, *née* **O'Dwyer** (1863–1951) Anthropologist, born in Tipperary, Ireland. From 1899 she spent most of her life in Australia where she studied Aboriginal life and customs, and worked for Aboriginal welfare.

Bates, William (1860–1931) US ophthalmologist, whose book *Better Eyesight Without Glasses* (1919) explained poor sight as a disturbance of normal mind–body co-ordination. He developed exercises to improve the communication between eyes and brain.

Bateson, William (1861–1926) Geneticist, born in Whitby, North Yorkshire. He produced the first translation of Mendel's heredity studies in 1900, and named the science of genetics. >> **Mendel**

Bateson, Gregory (1904–80) Anthropologist, born in Grantchester, Cambridgeshire, the son of biologist William Bateson. With Margaret Mead he was involved with the culture-and-personality movement, seen in *Balinese Character* (1942). >> **Bateson, William; Mead, Margaret**

Bath, Henry Frederick Thynne, 6th Marquess of (1905–92) Stately home operator, born in Longleat House, Wiltshire. He caused a sensation by opening the house to the paying public as a tourist attraction in 1949. Wild animals were introduced to the estate grounds in the 1960s, creating the first safari park.

Batista (y Zaldívar), Fulgencio [bateesta] (1901–73) Cuban soldier and dictator, born in Oriente province, Cuba. Elected president (1940–4), he fostered a major programme of social and economic reform. In 1952 he overthrew President Socorras, and ruled as dictator until the coup by Castro (1959). >> **Castro**

Batoni or **Battoni, Pompeo Girolamo** [batohnee] (1708–87) Painter, born in Lucca, Italy. He is best known for his portraits, but he also painted religious, mythological, and historical works.

Batten, Jean (1909–82) Pioneer aviator, born in Rotorua, New Zealand. In 1934, in a Gypsy Moth, she broke Amy Johnson's record for the solo flight from England to Australia, and became the first woman to complete the return journey. >> **Johnson, Amy**

Battenberg, Prince Alexander of (1820–93) First prince of Bulgaria (1879–86), born in Verona, Italy, the uncle of Earl Mountbatten. He was overpowered in his palace by pro-Russian army conspirators, and forced to abdicate. >> **Mountbatten, Prince Louis Alexander**

Battenberg, Prince Louis Alexander of >> **Mountbatten, Prince Louis Alexander**

Batuta, ibn >> **Ibn Battutah**

Baudelaire, Charles (Pierre) [bohduhlair] (1821–67) Symbolist poet, born in Paris. His masterpiece is a collection of poems, *Les Fleurs du mal* (1857), for which he was prosecuted for impropriety in 1864. Later works include *Les Paradis artificiels* (1860) and *Petits Poèmes en prose* (1869).

Baudouin I [bohdwï] (1930–93) King of the Belgians (1951–93), born at Stuyvenberg Castle, near Brussels, the elder son of Leopold III. He succeeded to the throne on the abdication of his father, and in 1960 married the Spanish Doña Fabiola de Mora y Aragón. >> Leopold III

Baudry, Paul Jacques Aimé [bohdree] (1828–86) Painter, born in La Roche-sur-Yon, France. He is chiefly known for the 30 large panels, illustrative of music and dancing, executed for the foyer of the Paris Opera (1866–76).

Bauer, Georg >> **Agricola, Georgius**

Bauhin, Caspar or **Gaspard** (1560–1624) Botanist and physician, born in Basel, Switzerland. He compiled an influential medical textbook, *Microcosmographia* (trans, 1605), and his *Illustrated Exposition of Plants* (1623) introduced a system of binomial nomenclature by genus and species. >> Linnaeus

Baum, Vicki [bowm], originally **Vicki Hedvig** (1888–1960) Novelist, born in Vienna. Her works include *Grand Hotel* (1930), *Headless Angel* (1948), *The Mustard Seed* (1953), and several short stories and plays. She emigrated to the USA in 1931.

Baumé, Antoine [bohmay] (1728–1804) Chemist, born in Senlis, France. He invented the hydrometer named after him, and the *Baumé scale* of measurement for use with a hydrometer.

Baumeister, Willi [bowmiyster] (1889–1955) Painter, born in Stuttgart, Germany. His interest in prehistoric archaeology is reflected in such works as 'African Histories' and his illustrations for the 'Epic of Gilgamesh' (1942–53).

Baumer, Gertrude [bowmer] (1873–1954) Leader of the German feminist movement, born in Hohenlimburg, Germany. She became president of the League of German Women's Associations (1910–19), edited the newspaper *Die Frau* (1893–1944), and after World War 2 founded the Christian Social Union.

Baumgarten, Alexander Gottlieb [bowmgah(r)tn] (1714–62) Philosopher of the school of Christian von Wolff, born in Berlin. His main works were *Metaphysica* (1739) and *Aesthetica* (1750–58), a treatise which helped establish the modern term *aesthetics*. >> Wolff, Christian

Baur, Ferdinand Christian [bowr] (1792–1860) Theologian and New Testament critic, born in Schmiden, Germany. He founded the 'Tübingen School' of theology, the first to use strict historical research methods in the study of early Christianity.

Bausch, Pina [bowsh], popular name of **Philippine Bausch** (1940–) Choreographer and dancer, born in Solingen, Germany. In 1973 she became ballet director of the Wuppertal Dance Theatre, and later founded her own company, where her expressionist productions were highly influential.

Bawden, Nina (Mary) (1925–) Writer, born in London. Her novels for adults include *Who Calls the Tune* (1953) and *Circles of Deceit* (1987; televised 1990). She has also written adventure stories for children, notably *Carrie's War* (1973).

Bax, Sir Arnold (Edward Trevor), pseudonym **Dermot O'Byrne** (1883–1953) Composer, born in London. He wrote seven symphonies (1921–39), tone poems, such as *In the Faery Hills* (1909) and *Tintagel* (1917), chamber music, and piano concertos. In 1942 he was made Master of the King's (from 1952 Queen's) Musick.

Baxendale, Leo (1930–) Strip cartoonist, born in Lancashire. His work for the *Beano* comic began with *Little Plum* (1953), followed by *Minnie the Minx* (1953) and *The Bash Street Kids*, and he later designed the new weekly comic *Wham* (1964).

Baxter, George (1804–67) Engraver and print maker, born in Lewes, Sussex, the son of John Baxter. He developed a method of printing in oil colours, a process patented in 1835. >> Baxter, John

Baxter, James Keir (1926–72) Poet, playwright, and critic, born near Dunedin, New Zealand. His conversion to Roman Catholicism (1958) is reflected in his later poetry, such as *In Fires of No Return* (1958) and *Autumn Testament* (1972).

Baxter, John (1781–1858) Printer, the first to use an ink-roller, born in Surrey. He published the illustrated *Baxter's Bible* and the first book of cricket rules. >> Baxter, George

Baxter, Richard (1615–91) Nonconformist clergyman, born in Rowton, Shropshire. At the Restoration he was appointed a royal chaplain, but in 1662 the Act of Uniformity drove him out of the Church of England. He was frequently persecuted for his views.

Bayard, Pierre du Terrail, chevalier de [bayah(r)] (c.1476–1524) French soldier, known as 'the knight without fear and without reproach', born in the Château Bayard, near Grenoble, France. He served Louis XII with legendary bravery, and gained for Francis I a notable victory at Marignano in 1515. >> Francis I; Louis XII

Bayazid I >> **Bayezit I**

Bayer, Johann (1572–1625) Astronomer, born in Rhain, Germany. His *Uranometria* (1603) depicts the positions of many stars in addition to those given by Tycho Brahe. He introduced the method of identifying the brighter stars in a constellation through the use of Greek letters. >> Brahe

Bayes, Thomas (1702–61) Mathematician and clergyman, born in London. He is chiefly remembered for an essay (1763) which introduced the study of statistical inference. He was also one of the first six Nonconformist ministers to be publicly ordained in England.

Bayezit I [bajazet], also spelled **Bajazet** or **Bayazid**, nickname **Yildrim** ('Thunderbolt') (c.1354–1403) Sultan of the Ottoman Empire (1389–1402). He conquered many parts of the Balkans, most of Asia Minor, and defeated Sigismund of Hungary (1396) at Constantinople. In 1402 he was defeated near Ankara by Timur, in whose camp he died. >> Sigismund (Emperor); Timur

Bayle, Pierre (1647–1706) Protestant philosopher and critic, born in Carlat, France. In 1696 he completed his major work, the *Dictionnaire historique et critique*, which was influential in the 18th-c Enlightenment.

Baylis, Lilian Mary (1874–1937) Theatrical manager, born in London. She became manager of the first Old Vic company in 1912, and in 1931 acquired Sadler's Wells Theatre for the exclusive presentation of opera and ballet.

Bayliss, Sir William Maddock (1860–1924) Physiologist, born in Wolverhampton, Staffordshire. With Starling he did experimental work on the cardiovascular system, and discovered secretin, the first known hormone. >> Starling

Baylor, Elgin (Gay) (1934–) Basketball player, born in Washington, DC. He spent his playing career with the Minneapolis (later Los Angeles) Lakers (1958–72), and went on to coach with the New Orleans Jazz before returning to Los Angeles as an executive with the Clippers.

Bazaine, Achille (François) [bazen] (1811–88) French marshal, born in Versailles, France. In the Franco-Prussian War (1870–1), he became trapped, and surrendered after a siege of 54 days. For this he was court-martialled and imprisoned (1873), but later escaped to Spain.

Bazaine, Jean René [bazen] (1904–75) Painter, born in Paris. His style developed through Cubism to abstract art. He produced a number of tapestry designs as well as stained glass and mosaics.

Bazalgette, Sir Joseph William [bazaljet] (1819–91) Engineer, born in Enfield, Greater London. He constructed London's drainage system and the Thames embankment, and was a notable pioneer of public health engineering.

Bazin, René [bazí] (1853–1932) Novelist, born in Angers, France. His novels depicted the life of peasant folk in the French provinces, such as *Les Oberlé* (1901).

Baziotes, William [baziohteez] (1912–63) Painter, born in Pittsburgh, PA. In the 1940s he was one of a number of American painters whose art developed from European Surrealism. His dream-like images often contain suggestions of animal forms.

Beach, Amy (Marcy), née **Cheney** (1867–1944) Composer and pianist, born in Henniker, NH. Her *Gaelic Symphony* (1896) and piano concerto (1900) were the first such works by an American woman.

Beach, Sylvia Woodbridge (1887–1962) Bookseller and publisher, born in Baltimore, MD. She opened the Shakespeare and Co bookstore in Paris in 1919, which became an avant-garde publishing house, and in 1922 published the first edition of James Joyce's *Ulysses*.

Beachcomber >> Morton, John Cameron

Beaconsfield, Earl of >> Disraeli, Benjamin

Beadle, George (Wells) (1903–89) Biochemical geneticist, born in Wahoo, NE. In association with Tatum, he developed the idea that specific genes control the production of specific enzymes. They shared the Nobel Prize for Physiology or Medicine in 1958 with Lederberg. >> Lederberg; Tatum, Edward L

Beaglehole, John Cawte (1901–71) Writer and historian, born in Wellington, New Zealand. His life's work was his edition of *The Journals of Captain James Cook on his Voyages of Discovery* (1955–67), associated with which was *The Endeavour Journal of Sir Joseph Banks* (1962).

Beale, Dorothea (1831–1906) Pioneer of women's education, born in London. In 1885 she founded St Hilda's College, Cheltenham, as the first English training college for women teachers. She later became a suffragette.

Beale, Mary, née **Cradock** (1632–99) Painter, born in Barrow, Suffolk. Very little is known of her work before c.1670, but her commissions included several portraits of clerics.

Beamon, Bob, popular name of **Robert Beamon** (1946–) Athlete, born in New York City. A long jumper, he smashed the world record at the 1968 Olympic Games in Mexico City with a jump of 8·9 m/29 ft 2 in - 55 cm/21 in further than the previous record.

Bean, Alan L(aVern) (1932–) Astronaut, born in Wheeler, TX. He was a crew member of the historic Apollo 12 Moon-walk mission, and commander of the second crew to occupy the orbiting Skylab 3.

Bean, Charles Edwin Woodrow (1879–1968) Journalist and war historian, born in Bathurst, New South Wales, Australia. His major work was the 12-volume *Official History of Australia in the War of 1914–18* (1921–39), writing six of the volumes himself and editing the others.

Beard, Charles A(ustin) (1874–1948) Historian, born in Knightstown, IN. His best-known book is *An Economic Interpretation of the Constitution of the United States* (1913). His wife collaborated on many of his works. >> Beard, Mary Ritter

Beard, Dan(iel Carter), nickname **Uncle Dan** (1850–1941) Illustrator and youth leader, born in Cincinnati, OH. He wrote many books on handicrafts, and organized the Sons of Daniel Boone (1905) and the Boy Pioneers of America (1909). As National Scout Commissioner (1910–41), he was known as 'Uncle Dan' to a generation of American boys.

Beard, Mary Ritter (1876–1958) Feminist and historian, born in Indianapolis, IN. In 1910 she became a member of the Woman Suffrage movement, then worked for the Congressional Union (1913–17). With her husband she

wrote several works on American history. >> Beard, Charles Austin

Beardsley, Aubrey (Vincent) [beerdzlee] (1872–98) Illustrator, born in Brighton, East Sussex. He became known through his posters and illustrations for literary works such as *Morte d'Arthur* (1893). With Wilde he is regarded as leader of the 'Decadents' of the 1890s. >> Wilde, Oscar

Beaton, Sir Cecil (Walter Hardy) (1904–80) Photographer and designer, born in London. Known as a photographer of high-society celebrities, including royalty, he later designed scenery and costumes for stage and film productions including *My Fair Lady* and *Gigi*.

Beaton or **Bethune, David** (1494–1546) Scottish statesman and Roman Catholic cardinal, born in Balfour, Fife. On James V's death he unlawfully appointed himself a regent of the kingdom during the minority of Mary, Queen of Scots. He was assassinated for his persecution of Protestant conspirators. >> Mary, Queen of Scots

Beaton or **Bethune, James** (1470–1539) Scottish clergyman and statesman, the uncle of Cardinal David Beaton. He became Archbishop of Glasgow in 1509, and of St Andrews in 1522. An opponent of the Reformation, he initiated the persecution of Protestants. >> Beaton, David

Beatrix, in full **Beatrix Wilhelmina Armgard** (1938–) Queen of The Netherlands (1980–), born in Soestdijk, The Netherlands, the eldest daughter of Queen Juliana and Prince Bernhard Leopold. In 1966 she married West German diplomat **Claus-Georg Wilhelm Otto Friedrich Gerd von Amsberg** (1926–). They have three sons.

Beattie, James (1735–1803) Poet and essayist, born in Laurencekirk, Grampian. He is chiefly remembered for his long poem, *The Minstrel* (1771–74), a forerunner of Romanticism.

Beatty, David Beatty, 1st Earl (1871–1936) Naval commander, born in Nantwich, Cheshire. He sank the *Blücher* (1915), fought in the Battle of Jutland (1916), and succeeded Lord Jellicoe as commander-in-chief of the Grand Fleet. >> Jellicoe

Beatty, Warren, originally **Henry Warren Beaty** (1937–) Actor and film-maker, born in Richmond, VA, the younger brother of actress Shirley MacLaine. Film appearances include *Splendor in the Grass* (1961), *Bonnie and Clyde* (1967), *Reds* (1981), which earned him an Oscar for Best Director, and *Dick Tracy* (1990). >> MacLaine

Beauchamp, Pierre [bohshã] (1636–1705) Dancer and choreographer, born in Versailles, France. Director of the Académie Royale de Danse in 1671, some credit him with the invention of classical ballet's five positions.

Beaufort, Sir Francis [bohfert] (1774–1857) Naval officer, born in Navan, Co Meath, Ireland. As hydrographer to the British navy (1829–55), he devised the *Beaufort scale* of wind force.

Beaufort, Henry [bohfert] (1377–1447) English clergyman, the second illegitimate son of John of Gaunt and his mistress Catherine Swynford, and half-brother of Henry IV. He was chancellor three times (1403–4, 1413–17, 1424–6), and in 1426 was made a cardinal. During the 1430s he controlled the government of the young King Henry VI. >> Henry VI; John of Gaunt

Beaufort, Lady Margaret, Countess of Richmond [bohfert] (1443–1509) Daughter of John Beaufort, 1st Duke of Somerset, and mother of King Henry VII. She married Edmund Tudor, Earl of Richmond in 1455. A descendent of John of Gaunt, she acquired the Lancastrian claim to the English crown, through which her son Henry ascended the throne. >> Henry VII

Beauharnais, Alexandre, vicomte de (Viscount of) [bohah(r)nay] (1760–94) French soldier, born in Martinique. In 1779 he married Joséphine, afterwards wife of Napoleon. He became president of the Constituent Assembly in Paris (1791), but was arrested as an aristocratic 'suspect' and guillotined. >> Joséphine; Napoleon I

Beauharnais, Eugène Rose de [bohah(r)nay] (1781-1824) French soldier, the son of Alexandre de Beauharnais and Joséphine. He was made a prince of France (1805), married Princess Amelia Augusta of Bavaria (1806), was formally adopted by Napoleon, and made heir apparent to the throne of Italy. >> Napoleon I

Beauharnais, Hortense Eugénie Cécile [bohah(r)nay] (1783-1837) Queen of Holland, born in Paris, the daughter of Alexandre, Vicomte de Beauharnais. In 1802 she married Napoleon's brother Louis, King of Holland. The youngest of their three children became Napoleon III. >> Napoleon III

Beaumarchais, Pierre Augustin Caron de [bohmah(r)shay], originally **Pierre Augustin Caron** (1732-99) Comic playwright, born in Paris. He is best known for his two satirical comedies, *The Barber of Seville* (trans, 1775) and *The Marriage of Figaro* (trans, 1784).

Beaumont, Francis [bohmont] (c.1584-1616) Playwright, born in Gracedieu, Leicestershire. He wrote many plays with John Fletcher, such as *The Maid's Tragedy*. Attributed solely to Beaumont is *The Woman Hater* (1607), and he had the major share in *The Knight of the Burning Pestle* (1609). >> Fletcher, John

Beaumont, William [bohmont] (1795-1853) Army surgeon, born in Lebanon, CT. In 1822 he treated and later observed a patient who had received a gunshot wound that left a permanent opening in his stomach. This formed the basis of his pioneering study (1833) on the physiology of digestion.

Beauregard, P(ierre) G(ustave) T(outant) [bohregah(r)d] (1818-93) Confederate soldier, born near New Orleans, LA. He commanded at Charleston, SC, fought at Bull Run (1861), was defeated at Shiloh (1862), and defeated Butler at Drewry's Bluff (1864). >> Butler, Benjamin F

Beaurepaire, Sir Francis Joseph Edmund [bohrepair] (1891-1956) Freestyle swimmer, born in Melbourne, Victoria, Australia. He was a prominent figure in the Olympics of 1908-1924, and in 1910 set four world records.

Beauvoir, Simone de >> de Beauvoir, Simone

Beaverbrook (of Beaverbrook and of Cherkley), (William) Max(well) Aitken, Baron (1879-1964) Newspaper magnate and British politician, born in Maple, Ontario. In 1916 he took over the *Daily Express*, founded the *Sunday Express* (1921), and bought the *Evening Standard* (1929). During World War 2, he was made minister of supply (1941-2) and Lord Privy Seal (1943-5).

Bebel, Ferdinand August [baybel] (1840-1913) Socialist, born in Cologne, Germany. He became a leader of the German Social Democrat movement, and its chief spokesman in the Reichstag.

Beccafumi, Domenico [bekafoomee], originally **Domenico di Pace** (c.1486-1551) Painter, born in Siena, Italy. His paintings are usually regarded as an early manifestation of post-Renaissance Mannerism. Much of his best work remains in the Pinacoteca, Siena.

Beccaria, Cesare, marchese de (Marquess of) [bekahria] (1738-94) Jurist and philosopher, born in Milan, Italy. His influential *On Crimes and Punishments* (trans, 1764) denounced capital punishment and torture, and advocated the prevention of crime by education.

Becher, Johann Joachim [bekher] (1635-82) Chemist, born in Speyer, Germany. He worked on minerals, and his *Physica subterranea* (1669) was the first attempt to bring physics and chemistry into close relation.

Bechet, Sidney [beshay, beshay] (1897-1959) Jazz musician, born in New Orleans, LA. He took up the soprano saxophone, and became the first significant saxophone voice in jazz. In 1940 he was prominent in the traditional jazz revival, and later settled in Paris.

Bechstein, Karl [bekstiyn], Ger [bekhshtiyn] (1826-1900) Piano manufacturer, born in Gotha, Germany. He founded his famous factory in Berlin in 1856.

Beck, Aaron T(emkin) (1921-) Psychiatrist, born in Rhode Island. He introduced cognitive therapy as a treatment approach for neurotic disorders, particularly depression.

Beck, Julian (1925-85) Actor, producer, and director, born in New York City. With **Judith Malina** (1926-) he co-founded the Living Theater, and became known for his experimental and improvisatory approach.

Beckenbauer, Franz [bekenbower], nickname **the Kaiser** (1945-) Footballer, born in Munich, Germany. He led West Germany to success in the European Nations Cup (1972) and the World Cup (1974). Voted European Footballer of the Year in 1972, he retired in 1983, and became manager of Germany in 1986.

Becker, Boris [beker] (1967-) Tennis player, born in Leiman, Germany. The youngest winner of the men's singles at Wimbledon (17 years 227 days) in 1985, he retained the title in 1986 and 1989, and in 1992 won the Association of Tennis Professionals World Title.

Becker, Carl (Lotus) [beker] (1873-1945) Historian, born near Waterloo, IA. *The Heavenly City of the Eighteenth Century Philosophers* (1932), was the best presentation of Enlightenment ideas in his day.

Becker, Gary (Stanley) (1930-) Economist, born in Pottstown, PA. A member of the 'Chicago school' of economics, he applied microeconomic analysis to areas hitherto considered noneconomic, such as the family, and was awarded the Nobel Prize for Economics in 1992.

Becket, St Thomas à (1118-70), feast day 29 December. Saint and martyr, born in London. In 1155 he became Chancellor, the first Englishman since the Conquest to hold high office. When created Archbishop of Canterbury (1162), he resigned the chancellorship, and came into conflict with Henry II's aims to keep the clergy in subordination to the state. Henry's rashly-voiced wish to be rid of 'this turbulent priest' led to Becket's murder in Canterbury Cathedral (29 Dec 1170) by four of the king's knights. He was canonized in 1173. >> Henry II

Beckett, Sir Edmund >> Grimthorpe, Edward Beckett

Beckett, Samuel (Barclay) (1906-89) Writer and playwright, born in Dublin. He settled in France in 1937. Writing first in English, he later wrote in French, notably the novels *Molloy* (1951) and *Malone Dies* (trans, 1951) and the plays *Waiting for Godot* (trans, 1954) and *End Game* (trans, 1956). He was awarded the 1969 Nobel Prize for Literature.

Beckett, Walter >> Boyd, Martin

Beckford, William Thomas (1760-1844) Writer and art collector, born in Fonthill, Wiltshire. He is best known for his Gothic novel *Vathek* (1787). In 1796 he built a Gothic palace, Fonthill Abbey, designed by James Wyatt. >> Wyatt, James

Beckmann, Ernst Otto (1853-1923) Organic chemist, born in Solingen, Germany. He invented apparatus for the determination of freezing and boiling points, and devised the *Beckmann thermometer*.

Beckmann, Max (1884-1950) Expressionist painter and engraver, born in Leipzig, Germany. Forced to flee from the Nazis, he emigrated to the USA in 1947. In addition to his painting, he executed many self-portraits in various graphic media.

Becquerel, (Antoine) Henri [bekerel] (1852-1908) Physicist, born in Paris. He discovered the *Becquerel rays* emitted from the uranium salts in pitchblende, which led to the isolation of radium, and shared the Nobel Prize for Physics with the Curies in 1903. >> Curie, Marie

46

Beddoes, Thomas (1760–1808) Physician and writer, born in Shifnal, Shropshire. From 1798 to 1801 he developed at Clifton, Avon, a 'pneumatic institute' for the cure of diseases by the inhalation of gases, with assistant Humphry Davy. >> Davy, Humphry

Beddoes, Thomas Lovell (1803–49) Poet, born in Clifton, Avon, the eldest son of Thomas Beddoes. His works include The Bride's Tragedy (1822) and the Gothic-Romantic drama Death's Jest-book (1850). >> Beddoes, Thomas

Bede or **Baeda, St**, known as **the Venerable Bede** (c.673–735), feast day 25 May. Anglo-Saxon scholar, theologian, and historian, born near Monkwearmouth, Durham. His greatest work was the Latin Ecclesiastical History of the English People (trans, 731), the single most valuable source for early English history. He was canonized in 1899.

Bedford, David (1949–) Distance athlete, born in London. In 1972 he set the 10 000 m world record of 27 min 30·8 s. After retiring from competition he became an athletics promoter.

Bedford, John of Lancaster, Duke of (1389–1435) English prince, the third son of Henry IV. He became Guardian of England, and Regent of France during the minority of his nephew, Henry VI. In the Hundred Years' War he defeated the French in several battles, had Joan of Arc burned at the stake, and crowned Henry VI King of France in Paris. >> Henry VI; Joan of Arc

Bedford, 13th Duke of >> **Russell, John Robert**

Bédier, (Charles Marie) Joseph [baydyay] (1864–1938) Scholar and mediaevalist, born in Paris. His major work Les Légendes épiques (1908–13), developed a theory of the origin of the great cycles of romance.

Bednorz, (Johannes) Georg [bednaw(r)ts] (1950–) Physicist, born in Germany. With Karl Müller he found materials which showed superconductivity at higher temperatures than the near-absolute zero level previously observed, and they shared the Nobel Prize for Physics in 1987. >> Müller, Karl

Bedser, Alec (Victor) (1918–) Cricketer, born in Reading, Berkshire. With his twin brother, **Eric** (1918–), he was in the Surrey side that won seven consecutive county championships in the 1950s. A leading bowler, he took 236 wickets in 51 Tests.

Bee or **Bega, St** (7th-c) Irish princess, who took the veil from St Aidan. She founded the nunnery of St Bees in Cumberland. >> Aidan, St

Beebe, (Charles) William (1877–1962) Naturalist and explorer, born in Brooklyn, New York City. He explored ocean depths down to almost 1000 m in a bathysphere in 1934.

Beecham, Sir Thomas (1879–1961) Conductor and impresario, born in St Helens, Lancashire. Principal conductor (1932) at Covent Garden, and founder of the Royal Philharmonic Orchestra (1946), he was noted for his candid views on musical matters, his 'Lollipop' encores, and his after-concert speeches.

Beecher, Catharine Esther (1800–78) Educator and writer, born in East Hampton, NY, the daughter of Lyman Beecher. She founded the American Women's Education Association in 1852. With her sister, Harriet Beecher Stowe, she produced the influential The American Woman's Home (1869). >> Beecher, Lyman; Stowe, Harriet Beecher

Beecher, Henry Ward (1813–87) Congregationalist preacher, born in Litchfield, CT, the son of Lyman Beecher. In 1847 he became a pastor in New York City, defending temperance and denouncing slavery. During the Civil War, his church raised a volunteer regiment, but he later advocated reconciliation. >> Beecher, Lyman

Beecher, Lyman (1775–1863) Presbyterian minister and revivalist, born in New Haven, CT. In Cincinnati he became head of the newly founded Lane Theological Seminary (1832–59), where his evangelical zeal led to years of strife with more conservative Presbyterians. >> Beecher, Catharine / Henry Ward; Stowe, Harriet Beecher

Beecher Stowe, Harriet >> **Stowe, Harriet Beecher**

Beeching, Richard, Baron (1913–85) Engineer and administrator, born in Maidstone, Kent. As chairman of the British Railways Board (1963–5), he became known for the Beeching Plan, which substantially contracted the UK rail network.

Beene, Geoffrey (1927–) Fashion designer, born in Haynesville, LA. He opened his own New York company in 1962. His high-quality, ready-to-wear clothing for women and men brought him eight Coty Awards.

Beer, Gavin de >> **de Beer, Sir Gavin**

Beerbohm, Sir (Henry) Max(imilian) [beerbohm], nickname **the Incomparable Max** (1872–1956) Writer and caricaturist, born in London, the half-brother of Sir Herbert Beerbohm Tree. His best-known work was his only novel, Zuleika Dobson (1911), a parody of Oxford undergraduate life. >> Tree, Herbert Beerbohm

Beerbohm Tree, Herbert >> **Tree, Herbert Beerbohm**

Beethoven, Ludwig van [baytohvn] (1770–1827) Composer, born in Bonn, Germany. His music is usually divided into three periods. The first (1792–1802) includes the first two symphonies, the first six quartets, and the 'Pathétique' and 'Moonlight' sonatas. The second (1803–12) begins with the 'Eroica' symphony (1803), and includes his next five symphonies, the 'Kreutzer' sonata (1803), the Violin Concerto, and the 'Archduke' trio (1811). The third begins in 1813, and includes the Mass, the 'Choral' symphony (1823), and the last five quartets. His career was marred by deafness, which began in 1801 and was total by the early 1820s.

Beeton, Isabella Mary, née **Mayson**, known as **Mrs Beeton** (1836–65) British writer on cookery. Her Book of Household Management (1859–60), covering cookery and other branches of domestic science, made her name a household word.

Bega, St >> **Bee, St**

Beggarstaff, J and W >> **Nicholson, William Newzam Prior**

Begin, Menachem (Wolfovitch) [baygin] (1913–92) Israeli prime minister (1977–83), born in Brest-Litovsk, Belarus. In 1973 he led the nationalist Likud Front, forming a coalition government in 1977. For his role in the Middle East peace process, he shared the 1978 Nobel Peace Prize with President Sadat of Egypt. >> Sadat

Behaim, Martin [bayhiym] (1449–1507) Navigator and geographer, born in Nuremberg, Germany. He was associated with Portuguese discoveries along the African coast, and in Nuremberg (1490) constructed the oldest extant terrestrial globe. A Moon crater is named after him.

Beham, Hans Sebald [bayham] (1500–50) Painter and engraver, born in Nuremberg, Germany. One of Albrecht Dürer's seven followers known as the 'Little Masters', he produced woodcuts and copper engravings as book illustrations. >> Dürer

Behan, Brendan (Francis) [beean] (1923–64) Writer, born in Dublin. Twice imprisoned for IRA activities, and a famous alcoholic, his work includes the plays The Quare Fellow (1956; filmed 1962) and The Hostage (1958), and an autobiographical novel, Borstal Boy (1958).

Behan, Dominic [beean] (1928–89) Novelist and folklorist, born in Dublin, the brother of Brendan Behan. He adapted old airs and poems into contemporary Irish Republican material, notably in The Patriot Game. >> Behan, Brendan

Behn, Aphra [ben], née **Amis** (1640–89) Writer and adventurer, born in Wye, Kent. Considered the first professional woman author in England, she wrote many

Restoration plays, such as *The Rover* (1678). Her novel *Oroonoko* (1688), was based on her childhood experiences in Suriname.

Behrens, Peter [bairenz] (1868–1940) Architect and designer, born in Hamburg, Germany. As artistic adviser (1907) to Rathenau at the AEG electrical company in Berlin, he designed a turbine assembly works of glass and steel, a landmark in industrial architecture. >> Rathenau

Behring, Emil (Adolf) von [bayring] (1854–1917) Bacteriologist and pioneer in immunology, born in Hansdorf, Germany. He discovered diphtheria and tetanus antitoxins, and was awarded the first Nobel Prize for Physiology or Medicine in 1901.

Behrman, S(amuel) N(athaniel) [bairman] (1893–1973) Playwright, screenwriter, and journalist, born in Worcester, MA. His best-known play was *The Second Man* (1927), for which he was tagged the 'American Noel Coward'. >> Coward

Beiderbecke, Bix [biyderbek], popular name of **Leon Bismarck Beiderbecke** (1903–31) Cornettist, born in Davenport, IA. During his short career he became one of the most celebrated jazz performers of the 1920s. Ravaged by alcoholism, he died at the age of 28.

Beilby, Sir George Thomas [beelbee] (1850–1924) Industrial chemist, born in Edinburgh. He improved the method of shale oil distillation, and invented a manufacturing process for synthesizing alkaline cyanides.

Beilstein, Friedrich Konrad [bilstiyn] (1838–1906) Organic chemist, born in St Petersburg, Russia. His *Handbook of Organic Chemistry* (1881) formed a substantially complete catalogue of organic compounds.

Béjart, Maurice [bayzhah(r)], originally **Maurice Jean Berger** (1927–) Choreographer, born in Marseille, France. In 1954 he founded his own company in Brussels, developing a popular expressionistic form of modern ballet. In 1988 the company moved to Lausanne, Switzerland.

Beke, Charles Tilstone (1800–74) Explorer and biblical critic, born in London. A scholar of ancient history, he is best known for his *Origins of the Bible* (trans, 1834). He later explored the course of the Blue Nile and the region at the head of the Red Sea.

Békésy, Georg von [baykezee] (1899–1972) Physiologist, born in Budapest. He studied the human ear and how it transmits sounds to the brain, and was awarded the Nobel Prize for Physiology or Medicine in 1961.

Bekhterev, Vladimir Mikhailovich [byekterof] (1857–1927) Neuropathologist, born in Viatka province, Russia. He developed a theory of conditioned reflexes, independently of Pavlov, and founded the Psychoneurological Institute in St Petersburg. >> Pavlov

Bel, Joseph Achille Le >> **Le Bel, Joseph Achille**

Belasco, David [belaskoh] (1853–1931) Producer and playwright, born in San Francisco, CA. He built a theatre in New York City in 1906, and his experiments with visual effects greatly influenced standards of theatrical production.

Belcher, Sir Edward (1799–1877) British naval commander, born in Halifax, Nova Scotia, Canada. He explored the W coast of America (1836–42), later commanding a fruitless expedition to search for Sir John Franklin (1852). >> Franklin, John

Bel Geddes, Norman [bel gedis] (1893–1958) Industrial and theatrical designer, born in Adrian, MI. His designs for Broadway plays, notably *The Miracle* (1923), and his film sets marked him as an innovator in modern stage lighting. He was also a pioneer of streamlining in industrial design.

Belidor, Bernard Forest de [belidaw(r)] (1698–1761) Engineer, born in Catalonia, Spain. A professor of artillery, he wrote influential handbooks on military and civil engineering.

Belisarius [belisairius] (505–65) Byzantine general under Emperor Justinian, born in Germania, Illyria. He twice defeated the Persians (530, 542), defended Constantinople (532, 559), and repelled the Vandals in Africa (533–4) and the Ostrogoths in Italy (535–40). >> Justinian

Bell, Acton >> **Brontë**

Bell, Alexander Graham (1847–1922) Educationist and inventor, born in Edinburgh, the son of Alexander Melville Bell. He invented the articulating telephone, sending the first intelligible message to his laboratory assistant in 1875, and formed the Bell Telephone Company in 1877. >> Bell, Alexander Melville

Bell, Alexander Melville (1819–1905) Educationist, born in Edinburgh, the father of Alexander Graham Bell. He moved to Canada in 1870, then settled in Washington, DC. A teacher of elocution, he published *Visible Speech* (1867), a system showing the position of the vocal organs for each sound. >> Bell, Alexander Graham

Bell, Andrew (1753–1832) Educationist, founder of the 'Madras System' of education, born in St Andrews, Fife. In 1789 he became superintendent of the Madras military orphanage, India, where he introduced the monitorial system.

Bell, Sir Charles (1774–1842) Anatomist and surgeon, born in Edinburgh. He distinguished between the sensory and motor nervous system, and worked on the functions of the spinal nerves. *Bell's palsy* is named after him.

Bell, Currer >> **Brontë**

Bell, Ellis >> **Brontë**

Bell, George Kennedy Allen (1883–1958) Clergyman, born on Hayling I, Hampshire. He was Bishop of Chichester (1929–58), and a strong supporter of the ecumenical movement. During World War 2 he worked towards peace with Germany and condemned the policy of saturation bombing.

Bell, Gertrude (Margaret Lowthian) (1868–1926) Archaeologist and traveller, born at Washington Hall, Durham. She became oriental secretary to the British High Commission in Iraq, and first director of antiquities there.

Bell, Henry (1767–1830) Engineer and pioneer of steam navigation, born in Linlithgow, Lothian. In 1812 he successfully launched the 30-ton *Comet* on the Clyde, the first passenger-carrying steam-boat in European waters.

Bell, John (1811–1895) Sculptor, born in Hopton, Suffolk. His works include the Guards' Memorial (1858) in Waterloo Place, and the American group in the Hyde Park Albert Memorial (1873).

Bell, John Stewart (1928–90) Physicist, born in Belfast. He joined CERN in Geneva in 1960, where he developed the equations known as *Bell's inequalities*, predicting how measurements made on one proton would affect measurements on another.

Bell, Lawrence (Dale) (1894–1956) Aircraft designer and constructor, born in Mentone, IN. In 1935 he formed the Bell Aircraft Corporation, which produced the first US jet-propelled aircraft (1942), and the first rocket-propelled aeroplane, the Bell X-1 (1947), the first manned aircraft to exceed the speed of sound.

Bell, Patrick (1799–1869) Clergyman and inventor, born in Auchterhouse, Tayside. He developed a prototype of a mechanical reaper in 1827, the potential of which was only realized in the USA by Cyrus McCormick and others. >> McCormick

Bell, Robert Anning (1863–1933) Artist, born in London. A painter, designer, illustrator, and decorator, he executed mosaics in the Houses of Parliament and Westminster Cathedral.

Bell, Thomas (1792–1800) Naturalist, born in Poole, Dorset. His *British Stalk-eyed Crustacea* (1853) remains a standard work on British crabs and lobsters.

Bell, Vanessa, *née* **Stephen** (1879–1961) Painter and decorative designer, born in London, the elder sister of Virginia Woolf. A contributor to Roger Fry's Omega Workshops (1913–19), she exhibited with the London Group from 1920. >> Fry, Roger; Woolf, Virginia

Bella, Stefano della (1610–64) Engraver, born in Florence, Italy. His engravings were in the manner of Jacques Callot, and consisted of battle-pieces, landscapes, and animal and masque designs. >> Callot

Bellamy, David (James) (1933–) British botanist, writer, and broadcaster. He is widely known for his television programmes on the natural environment, such as *Bellamy's Britain* (1975) and *Bellamy's Birds' Eye View* (1988). He established the Conservation Foundation in 1988.

Bellamy, Edward (1850–98) Novelist, born in Chicopee Falls, MA. He achieved immense popularity with his Utopian romance *Looking Backward* (1888), a work which predicted a new social order and influenced economic thinking in the USA and Europe.

Bellany, John (1942–) Painter and etcher, born in Port Seton, Lothian. He is one of the generation of Scots who, in the 1970s, adopted an expressive form of Realism inspired by Leger and by German art. >> Leger

Bellarmine, St Robert [bel**ermin**], originally **Roberto Francesco Romolo Bellarmino** (1542–1621), feast day 17 May. Jesuit theologian, born in Montepulciano, Italy. He became a cardinal in 1599, and worked in the Vatican from 1605 until his death. The chief defender of the Church in the 16th-c, he was canonized in 1930.

Bellay, Joachim du [be**lay**] (1522–60) Poet and prose writer, born in Lire, France. A leading member of the *Pléiade*, he wrote the group's manifesto (1549), advocating the rejection of mediaeval linguistic traditions and a return to Classical models. >> Ronsard

Bell Burnell, Susan Jocelyn, *née* **Bell** (1943–) Radio astronomer, born in York, North Yorkshire. In 1967, working with Antony Hewish, she discovered an unusually regular signal, shown to be bursts of radio energy at a constant interval of just over a second - the first pulsar. >> Gold; Hewish

Belleau, Rémy [be**loh**] (1528–77) Poet, born in Nogent le Rotrou, France. A member of the *Pléiade*, he published in 1556 a translation of Anacreon that was at first believed to be an original imitation. >> Anacreon

Belle-Isle, Charles Louis Fouquet, duc de (Duke of) [bel eel] (1684–1761) French statesman and soldier, born in Villefranche, France. He became a Marshal of France (1741), served in the War of the Austrian Succession (1740–8), and was minister of war (1758–60) during the Seven Years' War.

Bellenden or **Ballantyne, John** (?–1587) Scottish ecclesiastic and writer. His translations (1533) of Boece's *Historia Gentis Scotorum*, and of the first five books of Livy, are vigorous specimens of early Scottish prose.

Bellingham, John >> **Perceval, Spencer**

Bellingshausen, Fabian Gottlieb Benjamin von [bel-ings-howzn] (1778–1852) Explorer, born in Ösel, Estonia. In 1819–21 he led an Antarctic expedition as far south as 70°, and gave his name to the *Bellingshausen Sea*.

Bellini, Gentile [be**lee**nee] (c.1429–1507) Painter, born in Venice, Italy, the son of Jacopo Bellini and brother of Giovanni Bellini. He is known for his portrait of Sultan Muhammad II in Constantinople (c.1480) and for his scenes of Venice. >> Bellini, Giovanni / Jacopo

Bellini, Giovanni [be**lee**nee] (c.1430–1516) Painter, born in Venice, Italy, the son of Jacopo Bellini and brother of Gentile Bellini. The leading Venetian painter of his time, almost all his pictures are religious, his innovations of light and colour becoming the hallmark of Venetian art. >> Bellini, Gentile / Jacopo

Bellini, Jacopo [be**lee**nee] (c.1400–70) Painter, born in Venice, Italy, the father of Gentile Bellini and Giovanni Bellini. He painted a wide range of subjects, but only a few Madonnas and drawings remain. >> Bellini, Gentile / Giovanni

Bellini, Vincenzo [be**lee**nee] (1801–35) Operatic composer, born in Catania, Italy. His best-known works are *La Sonnambula* (1831) and *Norma* (1832). He influenced several later operatic composers, including Wagner. >> Wagner, Richard

Bellman, Carl Michael (1740–95) Poet and writer of popular songs, born in Stockholm. His most important collections of songs are the *Epistles of Fredman* (trans, 1790) and the *Songs of Fredman* (trans, 1791).

Bello, Andrés [bayoh] (1781–1865) Writer and polymath, born in Caracas. His writings embrace language, law, education, history, philosophy, poetry, drama, and science.

Belloc, (Joseph) Hilaire (Pierre) [bel**ok**] (1870–1953) Writer, born in St Cloud, near Paris. A British Liberal MP (1906–10), he left politics and continued as a writer, producing travel books, historical studies, religious works, and nonsensical verse for children, such as *Cautionary Tales* (1907). He was a leading Roman Catholic of his day.

Bellotto, Bernardo [belo**toh**] (1720–80) Painter, born in Venice, Italy, the nephew of Antonio Canaletto. His views of European cities are renowned for their realism, and his paintings of Warsaw were used after World War 2 in the restoration of the city. >> Canaletto

Bellow, Saul (1915–) Writer, born in Lachine, Quebec, Canada. His novels include *The Dangling Man* (1944), *Henderson the Rain-King* (1959), *Herzog* (1964), and *Humboldt's Gift* (1975, Pulitzer). He was awarded the Nobel Prize for Literature in 1976.

Bellows, George (Wesley) (1882–1925) Painter and lithographer, born in Columbus, OH. A leading figure in the movement known as The Eight, his best-known work is 'Dempsey and Firpo' (1924).

Belmont, Alva (Erskine Smith Vanderbilt), *née* **Smith** (1853–1933) Social reformer, born in Mobile, AL. She entered the New York social elite through marriage (1875, divorced 1895) to **William Kissam Vanderbilt** (1849–1920). She became president of the National Woman's Party (1921–33).

Belon, Pierre [bel**ô**] (1517–64) Naturalist, born near Le Mans, France. He wrote valuable treatises on trees, herbs, birds, and fishes, and was one of the first to establish the homologies between the skeletons of different vertebrates.

Belshazzar [bel**sha**zer], Gr **Balt[h]asar** (?–539 BC) Ruler of Babylon (550–539 BC). In the Book of Daniel, mysterious writing appears on the wall of his palace which Daniel interprets as predicting the fall of the empire. He died during the capture of Babylon.

Bely, Andrey [be**lee**], pseudonym of **Boris Nikolayevich Bugayev** (1880–1934) Writer, born in Moscow. A leading Symbolist, his works include the collected poems *The Northern Symphony* (trans, 1902), the novel *St Petersburg* (trans, 1913–14), and the autobiographical *Kotik Letayev* (1922).

Belzoni, Giovanni Battista [belt**zoh**nee] (1778–1823) Explorer and antiquity-hunter, born in Padua, Italy. In Egypt (1815), Mehemet Ali commissioned him to construct hydraulic machinery. He removed many objects from royal tombs, including the colossal bust of Rameses II at Thebes, which he sent to the British Museum. >> Mehemet Ali

Bembo, Pietro [**bem**boh] (1470–1547) Poet and scholar, born in Venice, Italy. He wrote a treatise on Italian prose (1525), and much influenced the study of Italian grammar. He became a cardinal in 1539.

Bemelmans, Ludwig [**bem**elmanz] (1898–1962) Writer and illustrator, born in Merano, Italy. He became known for his children's books, such as *Madeline* (1939), which he also illustrated.

Benacerraf, Baruj (1920–) Immunologist, born in Caracas. His research led to the discovery of immune-response genes that regulate immunology in organ transplants, for which he shared the Nobel Prize for Physiology or Medicine in 1960.

Benaud, Richie [benoh], popular name of **Richard Benaud** (1930–) Cricketer, broadcaster, and international sports consultant, born in Penrith, New South Wales, Australia. An all-rounder, he played in 63 Test matches for Australia (captain in 28), scored 2201 Test runs, and took 248 wickets.

Benavente y Martínez, Jacinto [benaventay ee mah(r)-teeneth] (1866–1954) Playwright, born in Madrid. His numerous plays include several satirical society comedies, notably *The Bonds of Interest* (trans, 1907).

Ben Bella, (Mohammed) Ahmed [ben bela] (1918–) A key figure in the Algerian War of Independence against France, and Algeria's first prime minister (1962–3) and president (1963–5), born in Maghnia, Algeria. Deposed as president in 1965, he was imprisoned until 1980, and went into voluntary exile until 1990.

Benbow, John (1653–1702) English naval commander, born in Shrewsbury, Shropshire. His main engagements were in the War of the League of Augsburg (1689–97) and the War of the Spanish Succession (1701–13). He died from wounds received fighting the French in the West Indies.

Bench, Johnny (Lee) (1947–) Baseball player, born in Oklahoma City, OK. Playing in the National League with the Cincinnati Reds, he was the outstanding catcher of the 1970s, and hit over 200 home runs.

Benchley, Robert (Charles) (1889–1945) Writer, born in Worcester, MA. A drama critic for *Life* and *The New Yorker*, collections of his humorous sketches include *From Bed to Worse* (1934).

Bender, Charles Albert, known as **Chief Bender** (1884–1954) Baseball player, born in Crow Wing Co, MN. A Chippewa Indian, he won 210 games during his 16-year career as a pitcher (1903–25), mostly with the Philadelphia Athletics.

Bendix, Vincent (1882–1945) Inventor, born in Moline, IL. In 1907 he founded the Bendix Co of Chicago, mass-producing automobiles, and pioneering the starter drive in 1913. He later formed Bendix Helicopters.

Benedek, Ludwig von (1804–81) Austrian soldier, born in Oedenburg, Hungary. He fought in Galicia (1846), Italy (1847), Hungary (1849), and commanded at Solferino (1859), but was defeated at Sadowa (1866).

Beneden, Eduard van [beneden] (1846–1910) Cytologist, born in Liège, Belgium. In 1887 he demonstrated the constancy of the number of chromosomes in the cells of an organism, decreasing during maturation and restored at fertilization.

Benedict XV, originally **Giacomo della Chiesa** (1854–1922) Pope (1914–22), born in Pegli, Sardinia, Italy. He became cardinal in 1914, and succeeded Pius X the same year. He made repeated efforts to end World War 1, and organized war relief on a munificent scale.

Benedict of Nursia, St (c.480–c.547), feast day 11 July. The founder of Western monasticism, born in Nursia, Italy. At Subiaco he founded 12 small monastic communities, and his *Regula monachorum* (c.515) became the common rule of all Western monasticism (**the Benedictine rule**). He was declared the patron saint of all Europe by Pope Paul VI in 1964.

Benedict, Ruth, née **Fulton** (1887–1948) Anthropologist, born in New York City. She became a leading member of the culture-and-personality movement in American anthropology of the 1930s and 1940s. Her best-known work is *Patterns of Culture* (1934).

Benedict Biscop, St [bishop] (c.628–c.689), feast day 12 January. Anglo-Saxon clergyman. In 674 he founded a monastery at Wearmouth, endowing it richly with books, and in 682 founded a sister monastery at Jarrow. One of his pupils was the Venerable Bede. >> Bede

Benediktsson, Einar (1864–1940) Poet and entrepreneur, born near Reykjavík. A fervent nationalist, he spent many years touring Europe seeking capital (unsuccessfully) for ambitious industrial schemes in Iceland. He wrote ornate poetry reflecting the skaldic tradition.

Beneš, Edvard [benesh] (1884–1948) Czech statesman and president (1935–8, 1939–45 in exile, 1946–8), born in Kožlany, Czech Republic. In 1935 he succeeded Masaryk as president, but resigned in 1938, setting up a government in exile. Re-elected in 1945, he resigned after the Communist coup of 1948. >> Masaryk, Tomeš

Benesh, Rudolph (1916–75) and **Benesh, Joan** (1920–) [benesh], née **Rothwell** Dance notators, husband and wife, born in London and Liverpool, Merseyside, respectively. Their dance notation system, Choreology (1955), is now used to document all important Royal Ballet productions. They opened their own institute in 1962.

Benét, Stephen (Vincent) [binay] (1898–1943) Writer, born in Bethlehem, PA. He is best known for his long narrative poem on the Civil War, 'John Brown's Body' (1929, Pulitzer). >> Benét, William

Benét, William (Rose) [binay] (1886–1950) Writer, born in Fort Hamilton, NY, the brother of Stephen Benét. He is chiefly known as a poet, his collections of poems including *Merchants from Cathay* (1913) and *The Stairway of Surprise* (1947). >> Benét, Stephen

Benfey, Theodor [benfiy] (1809–81) Philologist, born near Göttingen, Germany. His works include the *Lexicon of Greek Roots* (1839–42) and the *Sanskrit-English Dictionary* (1866).

Ben-Gurion, David [ben gurion], originally **David Gruen** (1886–1973) Israeli statesman and prime minister (1948–53, 1955–63), born in Plonsk, Poland. In 1930 he became leader of the Mapai (Labour) Party, in 1948 the first ruling party in the state of Israel. After his retirement, he came to symbolize the Israeli state.

Benjamin, Judah P(hilip) (1811–84) Lawyer, born in St Thomas, Virgin Is. He joined Jefferson Davis's cabinet as attorney general in 1861. After Davis's capture (1865) he escaped to England, where he wrote a legal classic, *The Sale of Personal Property* (1868). >> Davis, Jefferson

Benjamin of Tudela (?–1173) Rabbi, born in Navarre, Spain. From 1159 to 1173 he journeyed extensively, and was the first European traveller to describe the Far East.

Benn, Anthony (Neil) Wedgwood, known as **Tony Benn** (1925–) British statesman, born in London, the son of Viscount Stansgate. He became a Labour MP (1950–60), but was debarred from the House of Commons on succeeding to his father's title. He renounced his title, was re-elected (1963), and went on to hold several ministerial posts. >> Stansgate

Benn, Gottfried (1886–1956) Poet and physician, born in Mansfeld, Germany. He began writing Expressionist verse on pessimistic themes, such as *Morgue* (1912). His later work was more versatile, and he became highly regarded in Germany after World War 2.

Bennet, Henry >> **Arlington, Earl of**

Bennett, Alan (1934–) Playwright, actor, and director, born in Leeds, West Yorkshire. His many plays include *Forty Years On* (1968) and *Single Spies* (1988). He has also written much for television, including *An Englishman Abroad* (1983) and a series of monologues, *Talking Heads* (1987).

Bennett, (Enoch) Arnold (1867–1931) Novelist, born near Hanley, Staffordshire. Among his many novels are *Anna of the Five Towns* (1902), *The Old Wives' Tale* (1908), and the *Clayhanger* series, all of which reflect life in the Potteries. His *Journals* were published posthumously.

Bennett, Floyd (1890-1928) Aviator, born near Warrensburg, NY. He accompanied Richard Byrd on the Macmillan expedition to Greenland in 1925, and in 1926 piloted Byrd on the first aeroplane flight over the North Pole. >> Byrd, Richard

Bennett, James Gordon (1795-1872) Journalist, born in Keith, Grampian, the father of James Gordon Bennett. In 1819 he emigrated to America, where he founded the *New York Herald* in 1835, editing it until 1867. >> Bennett, James Gordon (1841-1918)

Bennett, James Gordon (1841-1918) Journalist, born in New York City, the son and successor of James Gordon Bennett. In 1870 he sent Stanley to find Livingstone, and helped finance Livingstone's Congo journey (1874-8). >> Bennett, James Gordon (1795-1872); Livingstone

Bennett, Michael, originally **Michael Bennet Difiglia** (1943-87) Dancer, choreographer, director, and producer, born in Buffalo, NY. He choreographed many Broadway shows, such as *Promises, Promises* (1968), *Company* (1970), and the popular masterpiece *A Chorus Line* (1975).

Bennett, Richard Bedford Bennett, 1st Viscount (1870-1947) Canadian prime minister (1930-5), born in New Brunswick, Canada. He convened the Empire Economic Conference in Ottawa in 1932, out of which came a system of empire trade preference known as the Ottawa Agreements.

Bennett, Richard Rodney (1936-) Composer, born in Broadstairs, Kent. Well known for his music for films, such as *Murder on the Orient Express* (1973), he has also composed operas, orchestral works, chamber music, experimental works, and jazz pieces.

Bennett, Willard Harrison (1903-87) Physicist and inventor, born in Findlay, OH. His radio frequency mass spectrometer, a device that measured the mass of atoms, first went into space in 1957 aboard the Russian satellite Sputnik.

Bennett, William J(ohn) (1943-) US Federal official, born in Brooklyn, NY. Outspoken and controversial, he served as secretary of education (1985-8) promoting a conservative agenda, and as President Bush's 'drug tzar' (1989-91) co-ordinated the campaign against drugs.

Bennett, Sir William Sterndale (1816-75) Pianist and composer, born in Sheffield, South Yorkshire. His compositions include piano pieces, songs, and the cantatas *The May Queen* (1858) and *The Women of Samaria* (1867).

Benny, Jack, originally **Benjamin Kubelsky** (1894-1974) Comedian, born in Waukegan, IL. A child prodigy violinist, he went on to Broadway success, later earning his own radio series and television show, *The Jack Benny Show* (1950-65).

Benoît de Sainte-Maure [benwah] (12th-c) Poet, born in either Sainte-Maure near Poitiers, or Sainte-More near Tours, France. His vast *The Romance of Troy* (trans title), was a source book to many later writers, notably Boccaccio. >> Boccaccio

Benozzo di Lese >> **Gozzoli, Benozzo**

Benson, Sir Frank (Robert) (1858-1939) Actor-manager, born in Alresford, Hampshire. He was knighted by King George V on the stage of Drury Lane during a Shakespeare tercentenary matinee in 1916. The company he formed was the forerunner of the Royal Shakespeare Company.

Benson, Frank (Weston) (1862-1951) Artist, born in Salem, MA. He painted women and children, created sensitive etchings and wash drawings of wild fowl, and produced a series of murals for the Library of Congress.

Bentham, George (1800-84) Botanist, born in Stoke, Devon, the son of Samuel Bentham. He compiled, with Joseph Hooker, the great *Genera Plantarum* (3 vols, 1862-83). >> Bentham, Samuel; Hooker, Joseph

Bentham, Jeremy (1748-1832) Philosopher, jurist, and social reformer, born in London. He propounded utilitarianism in such works as *Introduction to the Principles of Morals and Legislation* (1789), arguing that the proper objective of all conduct and legislation is 'the greatest happiness of the greatest number'. >> Bentham, Samuel

Bentham, Sir Samuel (1757-1831) Inventor and naval architect, born in London, the brother of Jeremy Bentham and father of George Bentham. For many years he worked to build up Britain's naval strength during the Napoleonic Wars, and introduced reforms in the Admiralty dockyards. >> Bentham, George / Jeremy

Bentinck, Lord (William) George (Frederick Cavendish) (1802-48) British politician, born at Welbeck Abbey, Nottinghamshire. He formed a separate Conservative parliamentary group with Lord Stanley (1834), and led the Tory Opposition to Peel's introduction of free trade measures. >> Derby, 14th Earl; Peel

Bentinck, William, 1st Earl of Portland (1649-1709) English soldier and courtier, born in Holland. A lifelong friend of William III, he was entrusted with the secrets of his foreign policy, and after the revolution was rewarded with a peerage. >> William III

Bentinck, William Henry Cavendish, 3rd Duke of Portland (1738-1809) British prime minister (1783, 1807-9), born in Bulstrode, Buckinghamshire. He was also home secretary under Pitt, with charge of Irish affairs (1794-1801). >> Pitt (the Younger)

Bentinck, Lord William (Henry Cavendish) (1774-1839) British soldier and Governor-General of India (1828-35), born in Bulstrode, Buckinghamshire. As Governor of Madras (1803-7), his prohibition of sepoy beards and turbans caused the massacre at Vellore (1806), and he was recalled. Later, as governor-general, he introduced many educational reforms.

Bentine, Michael [benteen] (1921-) Comedy performer, born in Watford, Hertfordshire. An early member of *The Goons* radio series (1950-2), he later starred in his own television shows, notably *It's a Square World* (1960-4).

Bentley, E(dmund) C(lerihew) (1875-1956) Journalist and novelist, born in London. Chiefly remembered for the detective novel *Trent's Last Case* (1913), he also gave his name to a type of humorous verse-form known as the *clerihew*.

Bentley, Richard (1662-1742) Classical scholar, born in Oulton, West Yorkshire. He established an international reputation over his dispute with Charles Boyle, 4th Earl of Orrery (1697-9), in which he proved that the so-called *Epistles of Phalaris* were spurious.

Benton, Thomas Hart, known as **Old Bullion** (1782-1858) US statesman, born near Hillsborough, NC. A Missouri senator (1820-51), and chief Democratic spokesman in the Senate, he received his nickname from his opposition to paper currency.

Bentsen, Lloyd Millard, Jr (1921-) US statesman, born in Mission, TX. He was vice-presidential running-mate to Dukakis in the Democrats' 1988 presidential challenge, and in 1993 became secretary of the treasury in Clinton's administration. >> Clinton, Bill; Dukakis

Bentzon, Niels Viggo (1919-) Danish composer and pianist. His compositions include opera, symphonies, ballets, piano concertos, and chamber music.

Benvenuto Tisi >> **Garofalo, Benvenuto do**

Benz, Karl (Friedrich) (1844-1929) Engineer and car manufacturer, born in Karlsruhe, Germany. He developed a two-stroke engine in 1879, and completed his first car in 1885.

Benzer, Seymour (1921-) Geneticist, born in New York City. He first showed that genes can be split and then recombined, and related genes as chemical entities to their observed behaviour in biological systems.

Ben-Zvi, Itzhak [ben tsvee] (1884-1963) Israeli president (1952-63), born in Poltava, Ukraine. He migrated to Palestine in 1907, became a prominent Zionist, and helped found the Jewish Labour Party.

Bérain, Jean (the Elder) [bayrĩ] (c.1637-1711) Artist, born in Lorraine, France. The leading designer of stage scenery, costumes, fêtes, and displays at the court of Louis XIV, his work heralded the lighter Rococo style of the early 18th-c.

Béranger, Pierre Jean de [bayrãzhay] (1780-1857) Poet, born in Paris. His lyrics, coloured by his politics, led to spells of imprisonment in 1821 and 1828, but their vivacity, satire, and wit endeared him to the masses.

Bérard, Christian [bayrah(r)] (1902-49) French painter and designer. His fame rests mainly on his stage decor, especially for the productions of Molière by Barrault. >> Barrault

Berberian, Cathy >> **Berio, Luciano**

Berceo, Gonzalo de [berthayoh] (c.1180-c.1246) The earliest known Castilian poet, born in Berceo, Spain. He wrote over 13 000 verses on devotional subjects, notably a Life of St Oria, but his poems were not discovered and published until the late 18th-c.

Berchem, Claes Pietersz(oon) [berkhem], also called **Nicolaes Pieterszoon Berghem** (1620-83) Dutch landscape painter, born in Haarlem, The Netherlands. Also known for his pastoral scenes, his work is represented in most European collections.

Berchet, Giovanni [berket] (1783-1851) Poet, born in Milan, Italy. In 1816 he published a pamphlet which became a manifesto of the Romantic movement in Italy. His best-known work is *Il trovatore*.

Berdyayev, Nikolai Alexandrovich [berdyayef] (1874-1948) Religious philosopher, born in Kiev, Ukraine. A professor at Moscow, his unorthodox spiritual and libertarian ideals led to his dismissal in 1922. He moved to Berlin to found an Academy of the Philosophy of Religion, which later transferred to Clamart, near Paris.

Berengar of Tours [berãgah(r), toor] (c.999-1088) Scholastic theologian, born probably in Tours, France. An opponent of the doctrine of transubstantiation, he was excommunicated by Pope Leo IX in 1050.

Berenice [berenees] (1st-c) The daughter of Herod Agrippa I. Four times married, she became the mistress of Flavius Titus, son of Emperor Vespasian. She is the heroine of Racine's tragedy. >> Herod Agrippa I; Vespasian

Berenson, Bernard or **Bernhard** [berenson] (1865-1959) Art critic, born in Vilnius, Lithuania. A leading authority on Italian Renaissance art, he bequeathed his Italian villa and art collection to Harvard University, which developed it as the Center for Italian Renaissance Culture.

Beresford, Bruce (1940-) Film director, born in Sydney, New South Wales, Australia. He won the Austalian Film Institute's Best Director award for *Don's Party* (1976) and *Breaker Morant* (1979). Later films include *Driving Miss Daisy* (1989, Oscar) and *Black Robe* (1991).

Beresford, Charles William de la Poer Beresford, Baron (1846-1919) Naval commander, born in Philipstown, Co Offally, Ireland. He was a Lord of the Admiralty (1886-8), and commanded the Mediterranean Fleet (1905-7) and Channel Fleet (1907-9).

Beresford, William Carr Beresford, 1st Viscount (1768-1854) British soldier, the illegitimate son of the first Marquess of Waterford. He commanded the Portuguese army in the Peninsular War (1808-14), and in the Wellington administration (1828-30) was Master-General of the Ordnance.

Berg, Alban (1885-1935) Composer, born in Vienna. He studied under Schoenberg, and applied the 12-note system to a deeply traditional style. He is best known for his opera *Wozzeck* (1925), his violin concerto, and the *Lyric Suite* for string quartet. >> Schoenberg

Berg, Patty, popular name of **Patricia Jane Berg** (1918-) Golfer, born in Minneapolis, MN. She won 57 tournaments during her career, including 15 majors.

Berg, Paul (1926-) Molecular biologist, born in New York City. He devised a method for introducing 'foreign' genes into bacteria, so causing the bacteria to produce proteins determined by the new gene - a method of great value in synthesizing insulin and interferon. He shared the Nobel Prize for Chemistry in 1980.

Berganza, Teresa [berganza] (1935-) Mezzo-soprano, born in Madrid. Specially noted for Mozart and Rossini roles, she has performed internationally in concert and opera.

Berger, Hans (1873-1941) Psychiatrist, born in Neuses bei Coburg, Germany. He became professor of psychiatry at Jena University (1919), and is known for his invention of the electroencephalograph (1929).

Berger, John (Peter) (1926-) Writer and art critic, born in London. His Marxism and artistic background are ever present in his novels, which include *A Painter of Our Time* (1958), *Corker's Freedom* (1964), and *G* (1972, Booker).

Bergerac, Savinien Cyrano de >> **Cyrano de Bergerac, Savinien**

Berggrav, Eivind (1884-1959) Lutheran bishop, born in Stavanger, Norway. Primate of the Norwegian Church (1937-50), he led the Church's opposition to the Quisling government, and was imprisoned (1941-5). A strong ecumenist, he was president of the World Council of Churches (1950-4).

Berghem, Nicolaes Pieterszoon >> **Berchem, Claes Pietersz**

Bergius, Friedrich [bergius] (1884-1949) Organic chemist, born in Goldschmieden, Germany. He researched coal hydrogenation for the production of motor fuels, and the hydrolysis of wood to sugar, for which he shared the Nobel Prize for Chemistry in 1931.

Bergman, Hjalmar (Fredrik Elgérus) (1883-1931) Writer, born in Örebro, Sweden. His best-known works are the satirical novel *God's Orchid* (trans, 1919) and a comedy *The Swedenhielm Family* (trans, 1925).

Bergman, (Ernst) Ingmar (1918-) Film director and writer, born in Uppsala, Sweden. His films became something of a cult for art-cinema audiences, such as (trans titles) *The Seventh Seal* (1956), *Wild Strawberries* (1957), *Through a Glass Darkly* (1961, Oscar), and *Autumn Sonata* (1978). Later films include *Fanny and Alexander* (1982, Oscar).

Bergman, Ingrid (1915-82) Film actress, born in Stockholm. Her early film successes included *Casablanca* (1942) and *Gaslight* (1944, Oscar), and she later won Oscars for *Anastasia* (1956) and *Murder on the Orient Express* (1974).

Bergson, Henri (Louis) [bergsõ] (1859-1941) Philosopher and writer, born in Paris. He popularized the idea of a 'creative impulse' at the heart of evolution, rather than a deterministic natural selection, as seen in *Creative Evolution* (1907). He was awarded the Nobel Prize for Literature in 1927.

Bergström, Sune Karl [bairgstroem] (1916-) Biochemist, born in Stockholm. He isolated and purified prostaglandins, for which he shared the Nobel Prize for Physiology or Medicine in 1982.

Beria, Lavrenti Pavlovich [beria] (1899-1953) Soviet secret police chief, born in Mercheuli, Georgia. As minister for internal affairs (1938), he served as vice-president of the State Committee for Defence during World War 2, and actively purged Stalin's opponents. On Stalin's death (1953), he attempted to seize power, but was executed. >> Stalin

Berigan, Bunny, originally **Roland Bernhart** (1908-42) Swing trumpeter and crooner, born in Hilbert, WI. During his short career he performed with Goodman

(1935-6) and Dorsey (1937, 1949), then led his own band. He had a major hit with 'I Can't Get Started With You'. >> Dorsey, Tommy; Goodman, Benny

Bering, Vitus (Jonassen) [bayring], also spelled **Behring** (1681-1741) Navigator, born in Horsens, Denmark. In 1728 and 1741 he sailed towards the American continent, finally sighting Alaska, but was wrecked on Avatcha (now *Bering I*), where he died. *Bering Sea* and *Bering Strait* are named after him.

Berio, Luciano [berioh] (1925-) Composer and teacher of music, born in Oneglia, Italy. He married (1950-66) the US soprano **Cathy Berberian** (1925-83), for whom he wrote several works. He is particularly interested in combining live and pre-recorded sound, and using tapes and electronic music.

Berkeley, Busby [berklee], originally **William Berkeley Enos** (1895-1976) Choreographer and director, born in Los Angeles, CA. He became one of the cinema's most innovative choreographers, noted for his mobile camerawork and kaleidoscopic routines involving spectacular multitudes of chorus girls, in such films as *Forty Second Street* (1933).

Berkeley, George [bah(r)klee] (1685-1753) Anglican bishop and philosopher, born at Dysert Castle, Kilkenny, Ireland. He expounded his idealistic philosophy ('to be is to be perceived or a perceiver') in *Essay towards a New Theory of Vision* (1709) and later works.

Berkeley, Sir Lennox (Randall Francis) [bah(r)klee] (1903-89) Composer, born in Boars Hill, Oxfordshire. His works include the operas *Nelson* (1953) and *Ruth* (1956), and several orchestral pieces. >> Berkeley, Michael

Berkeley, Michael (Fitzhardinge) [bah(r)klee] (1948-) British composer, the son of Lennox Berkeley. Well known for his introductions to music on radio and television, his compositions include orchestral and choral works, including the oratorio *Or Shall We Die?* (1983). >> Berkeley, Lennox

Berkoff, Steven [berkof] (1937-) Playwright, actor, and director, born in London. He founded the London Theatre Group, for whom he directed his own adaptations from the classics. His own plays include *Greek* (1979) and *West* (1983).

Berkowitz, David [berkohvits] (c.1953-) Convicted US murderer, who dubbed himself 'Son of Sam' in a note to the New York Police Department. He terrorized the city for a year (1976-7), preying on courting couples and lone women. Following his capture he received a prison sentence of 365 years.

Berlage, Hendrick Petrus [berlaguh] (1856-1934) Architect and town planner, born in Amsterdam. He designed the Amsterdam Bourse (1903) in a neo-Romanesque style, but was later influenced by Frank Lloyd Wright, and was largely responsible for the spread of his theories in The Netherlands. >> Wright, Frank Lloyd

Berle, A(dolf) A(ugustus) [berl] (1895-1971) Lawyer, economist, and public official, born in Boston, MA. He was part of Franklin D Roosevelt's 1932 presidential campaign, and served as an assistant secretary of state (1938-44). He wrote several important works on business organization and on Latin America. >> Roosevelt, Franklin D

Berle, Milton [berl], originally **Milton Berlinger**, nickname **Mr Television** (1908-) Entertainer, born in New York City. From childhood he appeared in vaudeville and silent films, and later was nationally popular on US television (1940-66).

Berlichingen, Götz von >> Götz von Berlichingen

Berlin, Irving [berlin], originally **Israel Baline** (1888-1989) Composer who helped to launch 20th-c American popular music, born in Temun, Russia. Taken to the USA as a child, his 'Alexander's Ragtime Band' became an international hit in 1911. The 1940s saw him at the peak of his career, with the hit musicals *Annie Get Your Gun* (1946) and *Call Me Madam* (1950).

Berlin, Sir Isaiah (1909-) Philosopher and historian of ideas, born in Riga, Latvia. His family emigrated to England in 1920, and most of his academic career has been at Oxford. His defence of philosophical liberalism and pluralism is seen in several works, such as *Two Concepts of Liberty* (1959).

Berliner, Emile [berliner] (1851-1929) Inventor, born in Hanover, Germany. In the USA from 1870, he patented several improvements to Alexander Graham Bell's telephone, demonstrated the flat disc gramophone record, and invented the first acoustic tiles. >> Bell, Alexander Graham

Berlinguer, Enrico [bairlinggair] (1922-84) Italian politician, born in Sussari, Sardinia. He was committed to making the Italian Communist Party a major force in Italian politics, and became secretary-general in 1972. His vision of 'Eurocommunism' had a lasting impact.

Berlioz, (Louis-)Hector [berliohz] (1803-69) Composer, born in Côte-Saint-André, France. His works include the *Symphonie Fantastique* (1830), the symphonies *Harold en Italie* (1834) and *Roméo et Juliette* (1839), the cantata *La Damnation de Faust* (1846), and the operas *Les Troyens* (1856-8) and *Béatrice et Bénédict* (1860-2).

Berlitz, Charles (Frambach) (1914-) Languages educationist, born in New York City. He is the grandson of **Maximilian Delphinus Berlitz**, who founded the Berlitz School in 1878 as a German emigré to the USA.

Bernadette of Lourdes, St, originally **Marie Bernarde Soubirous** (1844-79), feast day 18 February or 16 April. Visionary, born in Lourdes, France, the daughter of a miller. She claimed in 1858 to have received 18 apparitions of the Blessed Virgin at the Massabielle Rock, which has since become a notable place of pilgrimage. She became a nun with the Sisters of Charity at Nevers, and was canonized in 1933.

Bernadotte, Folke, Greve (Count) [bernadot] (1895-1948) Humanitarian and diplomat, born in Stockholm. Appointed by the UN to mediate in Palestine, he produced a partition plan, but was assassinated by Jewish terrorists in Jerusalem.

Bernadotte, Jean >> Charles XIV

Bernal, John Desmond [bernal] (1901-71) Crystallographer, born in Nenagh, Co Tipperary, Ireland. He developed modern crystallography and was a founder of molecular biology, pioneering work on the structure of water.

Bernanos, Georges [bairnanos] (1888-1948) Writer, born in Paris. A Catholic polemicist, he attacked indifference and was preoccupied with problems of sin and grace. His books include *The Diary of a Country Priest* (trans, 1936).

Bernard, Claude [bairnah(r)] (1813-78) Physiologist, born near Villefranche, France. He made several discoveries on the role of the pancreas and liver, changes in temperature of the blood, and the sympathetic nerves.

Bernard, Emile [bairnah(r)] (1868-1941) Painter and writer, born in Lille, France. In Paris he joined the Group Synthétiste (1889), and launched a magazine, *La Rénovation esthétique* (1890). He is credited with founding the so-called Cloisonnist style.

Bernard of Clairvaux, St [klairvoh], known as **the Mellifluous Doctor** (1090-1153), feast day 20 August. Theologian and reformer, born in Fontaines, France. The first abbot of the newly-founded monastery of Clairvaux (1115), he founded over 70 monasteries. He was canonized in 1174. The monks of his reformed branch of the Cistercians are often called *Bernardines*.

Bernard of Menthon, St [matô], known as **the Apostle of**

the Alps (923–1008), feast day 28 May or 15 June. Clergyman, born in Savoy, Italy. As archdeacon of Aosta he founded the hospices in the two Alpine passes that bear his name. *St Bernard dogs* are also named after him. He was canonized in 1115.

Bernard of Morval or **Morlaix** (12th-c) Benedictine monk of Cluny in Burgundy, France. He wrote the long Latin poem, *De contemptu mundi*, partly translated by John Mason Neale into hymns, among them 'Jerusalem the Golden'. >> Neale

Bernardino >> **Pinturicchio**

Bernardino of Siena, St [bernah(r)**dee**noh, **syay**na] (1380–1444), feast day 20 May. Franciscan monk, born in Massa di Carrara, Italy. He was appointed Franciscan vicar-general for Italy (1438), and became famous by his rigid restoration of the rule. He was canonized in 1450.

Bernays, Edward L [ber**nayz**] (1891–95) Public relations executive, born in Vienna, the nephew of Sigmund Freud. Brought to the USA as a child, in 1919 he founded the country's first public relations firm. >> Freud, Sigmund

Berners, Gerald Hugh Tyrwhitt-Wilson, 14th Baron (1883–1950) Composer, born in Bridgnorth, Shropshire. His early works appeared under the name of Gerald Tyrwhitt, and include an orchestral fugue and several ballets, notably *The Triumph of Neptune* and *Wedding Bouquet*.

Berners, John Bourchier, 2nd Baron (c.1467–1533) Writer and soldier, born probably in Oxford, Oxfordshire. He became captain deputy of Calais in 1520, where he translated the works of Froissart and others.

Bernhard, Duke of Weimar [bern**hah**(r)t] (1604–39) Protestant general, born in Weimar, Germany. He served Gustav II of Sweden, after whose death he took chief command. He lost at Nördlingen (1634), and was abandoned by the Swedes, but later won victories at Rheinfelden and Breisach (1638). >> Gustav II

Bernhard Leopold [bern**hah**(r)t] (1911–) Prince of The Netherlands, born in Jena, Germany, the son of Prince Bernhard Casimir of Lippe. In 1937 he married Juliana, daughter of Wilhelmina, Queen of The Netherlands; they have four daughters. >> Juliana

Bernhardt, Sarah [bern**hah**(r)t], originally **Henriette Rosine Bernard** (1844–1923) Actress, born in Paris. Her most famous roles included the title role in *Phèdre* (1877) and as Marguerite in *La Dame aux camélias* (1844). A legendary figure, she founded the Théâtre Sarah Bernhardt in 1899.

Berni or **Bernia, Francesco** [bair**nee**] (c.1497–1535) Poet, born in Lamporecchio, Tuscany. He recast Boiardo's *Orlando innamorato* (1542), and played a large part in establishing Italian as a literary language. >> Boiardo

Bernini, Gian Lorenzo [ber**nee**nee] (1598–1680) Baroque sculptor, architect, and painter, born in Naples, Italy, the son of a sculptor, **Pietro Bernini** (1562–1629). He decorated the apse of St Peter's with the so-called 'Chair of Peter', and designed the colonnade in front of the cathedral.

Bernoulli, Daniel [ber**noo**lee] (1700–82) Mathematician, born in Groningen, The Netherlands, the son of Johann Bernoulli. He worked on trigonometric series, mechanics, vibrating systems, and hydrodynamics, and solved a differential equation now known as *Bernoulli's equation*. >> Bernoulli, Johann

Bernoulli, Jakob or **Jacques** [ber**noo**lee] (1655–1705) Mathematician, born in Basel, Switzerland, the brother of Johann Bernoulli. He investigated several topics in mathematics, and in 1690 applied Leibniz's differential calculus to a problem in geometry, first using the term *integral*. >> Bernoulli, Johann; Leibniz

Bernoulli, Johann or **Jean** [ber**noo**lee] (1667–1748) Mathematician, born in Basel, Switzerland, the brother of Jakob Bernoulli, and father of Daniel Bernoulli. He

wrote on differential equations, finding the length and area of curves, isochronous curves, and curves of quickest descent. >> Bernoulli, Daniel / Jakob

Bernstein, Carl [**bern**stiyn] (1944–) Journalist and writer, born in Washington, DC. With **Bob Woodward** (1943–) he unmasked the Watergate cover-up, winning for the *Washington Post* the 1973 Pulitzer Prize for public service. Together they wrote *All the President's Men* (1974; filmed 1976) and *The Final Days* (1976). >> Nixon

Bernstein, Eduard [**bern**shtiyn] (1850–1932) Socialist leader, born in Berlin. An associate of Engels, he was an advocate of revisionism, an evolutionary parliamentary form of Marxism, and was periodically a member of the Reichstag from 1902 to 1928. >> Engels

Bernstein, Leonard [**bern**stiyn] (1918–90) Conductor, pianist, and composer, born in Lawrence, MA. His compositions include three symphonies, a Mass, a ballet, and many choral works and songs, but he became most widely known for his two musicals, *On the Town* (1944) and *West Side Story* (1957).

Berosus or **Berossus** [be**roh**sus] (fl.c.260 BC) A priest of Babylon, who wrote in Greek three books of Babylonian –Chaldean history. Only a few fragments have been preserved.

Berra, Yogi, popular name of **Lawrence Peter Berra** (1925–) Baseball player and coach, born in St Louis, MO. He played with the New York Yankees (1946–63), including 14 World Series (a record), and set the record for most home runs by a catcher in the American League (313). He went on to manage and coach the Yankees, the New York Mets, and the Houston Astros.

Berri, Nabih (1939–) Lebanese soldier and statesman, born in Freetown, Sierra Leone. In 1978 he became leader of Amal ('Hope'), the main Shiite military force in Lebanon during the country's civil wars. He joined the Lebanese government in 1984 as minister of justice.

Berrigan, Daniel J(oseph) (1921–) Catholic radical, born in Virginia, MN, the brother of Philip Berrigan. Ordained a Jesuit in 1952, he became involved in anti-war protest, and in 1968–9 served 18 months in prison. He later won recognition as a poet. >> Berrigan, Philip

Berrigan, Philip F(rancis) (1923–) Catholic priest and activist, born in Two Harbors, MN, the brother of Daniel Berrigan. He was convicted with his brother in 1968 for destroying draft records. He married Elizabeth McAlister in 1969, and in 1973 they founded Jonah House - a community committed to a nonviolent approach to fighting the arms race. >> Berrigan, Daniel

Berruguete, Alonso [be**rooget**] (c.1489–1561) Painter and sculptor, born near Valladolid, Spain, the son of Pedro Berruguete. The major Spanish sculptor of the 16th-c, he encouraged the introduction of the Italian Mannerist style into Spain. >> Berruguete, Pedro

Berruguete, Pedro [be**rooget**] (c.1450–1504) Painter, born near Valladolid, Spain, the father of Alonso Berruguete. Considered the first truly Renaissance painter in Spain, his later work can be seen in the cathedrals of Toledo and Avila. >> Berruguete, Alonso

Berry, Charles Ferdinand, duc de (Duke of) (1778–1820) Aristocrat, born in Versailles, France, the second son of Charles X. In 1816 he married **Caroline Ferdinande Louise** (1798–1870), the daughter of Francis, later King of the Two Sicilies. He was assassinated by a Bonapartist fanatic. >> Charles X

Berry, Chuck, popular name of **Charles Edward Anderson Berry** (1926–) Rock singer and songwriter, born in St Louis, MO. His successes include 'Rock And Roll Music' (1957), 'Johnny B Goode' (1958), and 'My Ding A Ling' (1972).

Berry, James Gomer >> **Kemsley, James Gomer Berry**

Berryman, John (1914–72) Writer and academic, born in McAlester, OK. He is known chiefly as a poet, notably from

Homage to Mistress Bradstreet (1956) and the long sequence of 'Dream Songs' (begun in 1955), a development of the 'confessional' manner.

Bert, Paul [bair] (1833–86) Physiologist and French republican statesman, born in Auxerre, France. He did pioneering work in studying blood gases, the toxic effects of oxygen at high pressure, and anaesthetics.

Berthelot, (Pierre Eugène) Marcellin [bairteloh] (1827–1907) Chemist and French statesman, born in Paris. He helped to found the study of thermochemistry, and synthesized many fundamental organic compounds. He also served as foreign minister (1895–6).

Berthelot, Sabin [bairtuhloh] (1794–1880) Naturalist, born in Marseilles, France. In 1820 he went to the Canaries, where he became an expert botanist, and was later appointed French consul there (1847). *Berthelot's pipit* was named in his honour.

Berthier, Louis Alexandre [bairtyay] (1753–1815) French general, the first marshal of the French empire, born in Versailles, France. He became chief-of-staff to Napoleon, who made him Prince of Neuchâftel and Wagram. >> Napoleon I

Berthollet, Claude Louis, comte (Count) [bairtolay] (1748–1822) Chemist, born in Talloires, France. He aided Lavoisier in his researches on gunpowder and in forming the new chemical nomenclature, and did much original work in inorganic chemistry. >> Lavoisier

Bertillon, Alphonse [berteeyō] (1853–1914) Police officer, born in Paris. As chief of the identification bureau in Paris, in 1882 he devised a system of identifying criminals by anthropometric measurements.

Bertoia, Harry [bairtoya], originally **Enrico Bertoia** (1915–78) Sculptor and designer, born in San Lorenzo, Italy. He emigrated to the USA in 1930, where he became known for his early Cubist-influenced silver coffee and tea services and for his furniture, particularly the *Bertoia chair* (1952).

Bertolucci, Bernardo [bertohloochee] (1940–) Film director, born in Parma, Italy. His films include *Last Tango in Paris* (trans, 1972), *1900* (trans, 1976), *The Last Emperor* (1987, 9 Oscars), and *The Sheltering Sky* (1990).

Bertrand, Henri Gratien, comte (Count) [bairtrã] (1773–1844) French general, born in Châteauroux, France. He shared the Napoleon's banishment to both Elba and St Helena, his diary giving a detailed account of the emperor's life in exile. >> Napoleon I

Bérulle, Pierre de [bayrül] (1575–1629) Clergyman, born near Troyes, France. A leader of the Catholic reaction against Calvinism, he founded the French Congregation of the Oratory in 1611. He was made a cardinal in 1627.

Berwald, Franz (Adolf) [bairvalt] (1796–1868) Composer, born in Stockholm. The outstanding Swedish composer of the 19th-c, he is best known for his four symphonies (1842–5).

Berwick, James Fitzjames, 1st Duke of (1670–1734) Marshal of France, born in Moulins, France, the illegitimate son of James II (of England). He became marshal of France (1706), and in the War of the Spanish Succession (1701–14) established the throne of Philip V by defeating the English at Almansa (1707). >> James II (of England); Philip V

Berzelius, Jöns Jakob, Baron [berzaylius] (1779–1848) Chemist, born near Linköping, Sweden. His accurate determination of atomic weights established the laws of combination and Dalton's atomic theory. He also discovered the elements selenium, thorium, and cerium. >> Dalton, John

Besant, Annie [beznt], *née* **Wood** (1847–1933) Theosophist, born in London, the sister-in-law of Sir Walter Besant. A close associate of Bradlaugh, she was an ardent proponent of birth control and socialism. In 1889, after meeting Madame Blavatsky, she developed an interest in theosophy, and later went to live in India. >> Besant, Walter; Blavatsky; Bradlaugh

Besant, Sir Walter [beznt] (1836–1901) Novelist and social reformer, born in Portsmouth, Hampshire, the brother-in-law of Annie Besant. His novels, advocating social reform, resulted in the People's Palace (1887) for popular recreation, built in the east end of London. >> Besant, Annie

Besht >> **Baal-Shem-Tov**

Bessarion or **Basilius, John** [besarion] (1403–72) Byzantine theologian, born in Trebizond, Turkey. He was one of the earliest scholars to transplant Greek literature and philosophy into the West. He effected a union between the Greek and Roman Churches, after which he joined the Roman Church, and was made a cardinal.

Bessel, Friedrich Wilhelm (1784–1846) Mathematician and astronomer, born in Minden, Germany. He catalogued stars, investigated Kepler's problem of heliocentricity, and systematized the mathematical functions involved, which now bear his name. >> Kepler

Bessemer, Sir Henry [besemer] (1813–98) Inventor and engineer, born in Charlton, Hertfordshire. He originated over 100 inventions, but is best known for the *Bessemer process*, whereby molten pig-iron can be turned directly into steel by blowing air through it in a tilting converter.

Bessmertnova, Natalia [besmairtnova] (1941–) Ballerina, born in Moscow. A member of the Bolshoi Ballet company, she has figured significantly in works devised by her husband Yuri Grigorovich, particularly *Ivan the Terrible* (1975). >> Grigorovich

Besson, Jacques [besō] (c.1535–c.1575) Mathematician, engineer and inventor, born in Grenoble, France. He is remembered for his *Théâtre des Instruments Mathématiques et Méchaniques* (1578), which included designs for a wide range of instruments and machines.

Best, Charles H(erbert) (1899–1978) Physiologist, born in West Pembroke, ME. Associated with Banting and Macleod in their joint discovery of insulin (1922), he also discovered the vitamin choline and the enzyme histaminase, and introduced the use of the anti-coagulant, heparin. >> Banting; Macleod, J J R

Best, George (1946–) Footballer, born in Belfast. He was the leading scorer for Manchester United (1967–8), European and English Footballer of the Year in 1968, and played for Northern Ireland 37 times. His tempestuous lifestyle hastened his retirement.

Bethe, Hans (Albrecht) [baytuh] (1906–) Physicist, born in Strasbourg, France (then Germany). In 1939 he proposed the first detailed theory for the generation of energy by stars, and later (with Alpher and Gamow) a theory of the origin of chemical elements during the early development of the universe. He was awarded the 1967 Nobel Prize for Physics. >> Alpher; Gamow

Bethlen, Gábor, Ger **Gabriel Bethlen** (1580–1629) King of Hungary (1620–1). Elected Prince of Transylvania (1613), he invaded Hungary (1619) and declared himself king (1620). Although he soon relinquished this claim, he obtained religious freedom for Hungarian Protestants.

Bethmann-Hollweg, Theobald (Theodor Friedrich Alfred) von [baytman holvayk] (1856–1921) German statesman, born in Hohenfinow, Germany. He became imperial chancellor in 1909, and played an important role in the events leading to war in 1914.

Bethune, David >> **Beaton, David**

Bethune, Norman (1899–1939) Surgeon, born in Gravenhurst, Ontario, Canada. He worked as a surgeon in the Spanish Civil War (1936–7), and was in China during the Japanese war (1938–9), where he became a national hero.

Betjeman, Sir John [**bech**uhman] (1906–84) Writer and broadcaster, born in London. He became especially known for his light verse, as seen in his *Collected Poems* (1958) and verse autobiography, *Summoned by Bells* (1960). He became Poet Laureate in 1972.

Bettelheim, Bruno [**bet**lhiym] (1903–90) Psychologist, born in Vienna. He was appointed director of the Sonia Shankman Orthogenic School in 1944, becoming internationally renowned for his work with autistic children.

Betti, Ugo (1892–1953) Writer, born in Camerino, Italy. He is best known for his 26 plays, notably *The Landlady* (trans, 1929), his collections of verse, and his short stories, which often focus on issues of social justice.

Beust, Friedrich Ferdinand, Graf von (Count of) [boyst] (1809–86) Austrian statesman, born in Dresden, Germany. As imperial chancellor (1867–71), his chief achievement was the reconciliation of Hungary to Austria.

Beuys, Joseph [boys] (1921–86) Avant-garde artist, born in Krefeld, Germany. He became known for his 'assemblages' of bits and pieces of rubbish, and for his multimedia 'happenings'. A prominent political activist, he was a founder of the Green Party in Germany.

Bevan, Aneurin, known as **Nye Bevan** (1897–1960) British statesman, born in Tredegar, Gwent. As Labour minister of health (1945–51), he introduced the National Health Service (1948). 'Bevanism' was a left-wing movement to make the Labour Party more socialist and less 'reformist'. >> Lee, Jennie

Bevan, Brian, nickname **the Galloping Ghost** (1924–91) Rugby league player, born in Sydney, New South Wales, Australia. A wing-threequarter, he scored a record 796 tries in 18 seasons (1945–64), playing for Blackpool Borough and Warrington.

Bevan, Edward (John) (1856–1921) Industrial chemist, born in Birkenhead, Merseyside. In 1892, with Charles Cross, he patented the viscose process of rayon manufacture. >> Cross, Charles

Beveridge, William Henry Beveridge, Baron (1879–1963) Economist, born in Rangpur, Bengal, India. He is best known as the author of the *Report on Social Insurance and Allied Services* (The Beveridge Report, 1942), which helped to create the welfare state.

Bevin, Ernest (1881–1951) British statesman, born in Winsford, Somerset. He built up the National Transport and General Workers' Union, and was its general secretary (1921–40). In 1940 he became minister of labour and national service in Churchill's coalition government, and in the Labour government was foreign secretary (1945–51). >> Churchill, Sir Winston

Bewick, Thomas [**byoo**ik] (1753–1828) Wood engraver, born in Ovingham, Northumberland. Among his best works are the woodcuts for the *History of British Birds* (1797–1804). *Bewick's swan* was named in his honour.

Beyle, Marie-Henri >> **Stendhal**

Beza, Theodore [bayza], Fr **Bèze, Théodore de** (1519–1605) Religious reformer, born in Vézelay, France. With Calvin, in Geneva, he founded the academy (1559), becoming its first rector. On Calvin's death (1564), he became leader of the Genevese Church. >> Calvin, John

Bhartrihari [bah(r)tri**hah**ree] (7th-c) Hindu poet and philosopher. He was the author of three *satakas* ('centuries') of stanzas on practical conduct, love, and renunciation of the world, and an influential Sanskrit grammar.

Bhasa [**bah**sa] (3rd-c) Earliest known Sanskrit playwright. He was the author of plays on religious and legendary themes, some of which were discovered only in 1912.

Bhave, Vinoba [**bah**vay] (1895–1982) Land reformer, born in Gagode, Gujarat, India. In 1951 he began a walking mission throughout India to persuade landlords to give land to the peasants, and became the most notable spiritual figure in India after Gandhi's death. >> Gandhi

Bhindranwale, Sant Jarnail Singh [**bin**dranwahlay] (1947–84) Indian politician and former Sikh extremist leader. He campaigned for a separate state of 'Khalistan' during the early 1980s. After taking refuge with his followers in the Golden Temple complex at Amritsar, he was killed by the Indian Security Forces.

Bhumibol Adulyadej [poomee**pol** adoo**lyah**day] (1927–) King of Thailand, born in Cambridge, MA. He became King Rama VI in 1946 after the assassination of his elder brother, and married Queen Sirikit in 1950.

Bhutto, Benazir [**boot**oh] (1953–) Pakistani prime minister (1988–91, 1993–), born in Karachi, the daughter of Zulfikar Ali Bhutto. Joint leader in exile of the Opposition Pakistan People's Party, she returned to Pakistan in 1980, launched a nationwide campaign for 'open elections', and became prime minister. Unsuccessful in the 1991 election, she then faced charges of misconduct, but won a further election in 1993. >> Bhutto, Zulfikar Ali

Bhutto, Zulfikar Ali [**boot**oh] (1928–79) Pakistani statesman, president (1971–3) and prime minister (1973–7), born in Larkana, Sind. He founded the Pakistan People's Party (1967), and became president after the secession of E Pakistan (1971). Ousted in a military coup led by General Zia ul-Haq, he was tried for corruption and murder, and executed. >> Bhutto, Benazir; Zia ul-Haq

Biandrata, Giorgio >> **Blandrata, Giorgio**

Bias [**biy**as] (6th-c BC) Native of Priene in Ionia, famous for his pithy sayings. He was one of the 'Seven Wise Men' of Greece.

Bichat, (Marie-François) Xavier [beesha] (1771–1802) Physician, born in Thoirette, France. He was the first to simplify anatomy and physiology by reducing the complex structures of the organs to their elementary tissues.

Bickerdyke, Mary Ann, *née* **Ball**, known as **Mother Bickerdyke** (1817–1901) Nurse and humanitarian, born in Knox Co, OH. During the Civil War (1861–5) she became famous for her work as a nurse in the hospitals at the Union army base at Cairo, IL, and also in battle and behind the lines.

Bickford, William (1774–1834) Inventor, born near Camborne, Cornwall. Distressed by the accidents caused by premature detonation of explosive charges in mines, he combined gunpowder and flax yarn to develop a reliable slow-burning fuse (1831).

Bidault, Georges (Augustin) [beedoh] (1899–1983) French prime minister (1946, 1949–50, 1958), born in Paris. Leader of the Movement Républicaine Populaire, he opposed de Gaulle over the Algerian War, was charged with plotting against the state, and exiled (1962–8). >> de Gaulle

Bidder, George Parker, nickname **The Calculating Boy** (1806–78) Engineer and mathematician, born in Moretonhampstead, Devon. He invented the railway swing bridge, and designed the Royal Victoria Docks, which were opened in 1856.

Biddle, John (1615–62) Preacher, the founder of English Unitarianism, born in Wotton-under-Edge, Gloucestershire. In 1645 he was imprisoned for rejecting in his preaching the deity of the Holy Ghost, and was banished to the Scilly Is (1655–8). Arrested again in 1662, he died in jail.

Biddle, Nicholas (1750–78) US naval officer, born in Philadelphia, PA. One of the first five captains commissioned by Congress (1775), he participated in the capture of New Providence I, Bahamas (1776).

Biela, Wilhelm von [**bay**la] (1782–1856) Austrian army officer and astronomer. In 1826 he observed the periodic comet named after him, although it had already been seen in 1772.

Bienville, Jean Baptiste le Moyne, sieur de (Lord of) [byanveel] (1680–1768) Explorer and governor, born in Montreal, Quebec, Canada. The Governor of French

Louisiana (1701–13, 1717–14, 1733–43), he founded Mobile, AL (1710) and New Orleans, LA (1718).

Bierce, Ambrose (Gwinett) [beers] (1842–?1914) Journalist and writer, born in Meigs Co, OH. He wrote collections of sardonically humorous tales, such as *The Fiend's Delight* (1872) and *The Devil's Dictionary* (1906).

Bierstadt, Albert [beershtat] (1830–1902) Painter, born near Düsseldorf, Germany. In New York City he became associated with the Hudson River School, painting Romantic panoramic landscapes, particularly of the Rocky Mts.

Biffen, (William) John (1930–) British politician. Chief secretary to the Treasury in 1979, he became a successful Leader of the Commons, but lost his cabinet seat after the 1987 general election.

Biffen, Sir Rowland Harry (1874–1949) Botanist and geneticist, born in Cheltenham, Gloucestershire. Using Mendelian genetic principles, he pioneered the breeding of hybrid rust-resistant strains of wheat. >> Mendel

Bigelow, Erastus (Brigham) [bigeloh] (1814–79) Inventor, born in West Boylston, MA. He invented looms for various kinds of material, a carpet loom, and a machine for making knotted counterpanes. He founded the Massachusetts Institute of Technology in 1861.

Biggers, Earl (Derr) (1884–1933) Novelist, born in Warren, OH. He created the famous character Charlie Chan in his series of detective novels, starting with *The House without a Key* (1925).

Biggs, Ronald (1929–) Member of the gang who perpetrated the Great Train Robbery in 1963. One of the first to be arrested for the robbery, he escaped from Wandsworth Prison in 1965, eventually settling in Brazil, where he continues to attract press publicity.

Bigi, Francesco di Cristofano >> **Franciabigio**

Bihzad, Ustad Kamal al-Din [beezad] (c.1440–?) Painter and calligrapher, born in Herat, Afghanistan. The most famous Persian painter of the late 15th-c, he was called 'the Marvel of the Age'.

Bikila, Abebe [bikeela] (1932–73) Ethiopian marathon runner. Virtually unknown, and running in bare feet, he won the marathon at the 1960 Olympics in Rome, setting a new world record and becoming the first black African to win a gold medal.

Biko, Stephen (Bantu) [beekoh], known as **Steve Biko** (1946–77) South African black activist, born in King William's Town. The founder of the Black Consciousness Movement, in 1973 he was served with a banning order severely restricting his movements, and died in police custody, allegedly as a result of beatings. He was the subject of the film *Cry Freedom* (1987).

Bill, Max (1908–94) Swiss politican, artist and teacher, born in Winterthur, Switzerland. Working as a painter, sculptor, designer, and architect, he developed the essential Bauhaus principles of co-operative design along purely functionalist lines.

Billinger, Richard (1893–1965) Poet, born in St Marienkirchen, Austria. He was the author of collections of lyrics, as well as novels coloured by peasant life in Upper Austria.

Billings, Josh, originally **Henry Wheeler Shaw** (1818–85) Writer, born in Lanesboro, MA. He relied heavily on deliberate misspelling, as in the 'Essa on the Muel' (Essay on the Mule), which launched his writing career.

Billings, William (1746–1800) Composer, born in Boston, MA. One of the earliest professional musicians in the Colonies, he founded a singing class in Stoughton, MA (1774) and the first church choir.

Billroth, (Christian Albert) Theodor [bilroht] (1829–94) Surgeon, born in Bergen, Austria. A pioneer of modern abdominal surgery, he performed the first successful excision of the larynx (1874) and the first resection of the intestine (1881).

Billy the Kid >> **Bonney, William H, Jr**

Bindoff, Stanley Thomas, known as **Tom Bindoff** (1908–80) Historian, born in Brighton, West Sussex. His best-known work is *Tudor England* (1950), which (under the 'Pelican' imprint) launched the first academic paperback history series.

Binet, Alfred [beenay] (1857–1911) Psychologist, the founder of intelligence tests, born in Nice, France. In 1905 with Théodore Simon, he expanded his first tests to measure relative intelligence among deprived children (the *Binet–Simon* tests).

Binford, Lewis (Roberts) (1930–) US archaeologist, pioneer of the anthropologically-oriented 'processual' school of archaeology ('New Archaeology'). His works include *In Pursuit of the Past* (1983).

Bing, Sir Rudolf (1902–) Opera administrator, born in Vienna. He became manager of the opera at Glyndebourne (1935–49), co-founder and director (1947–9) of the Edinburgh Festival, and general manager of the Metropolitan Opera, New York City (1950–72).

Bingham, Hiram [bingham] (1875–1956) Explorer and politician, born in Honolulu, Hawaii, the son of an American missionary. He explored Latin America during the early 1920s, and discovered the Inca ruins of Machu Picchu (1911). He later became Republican senator for Connecticut (1924–32).

Bingham, Millicent [bingham], *née* **Todd** (1880–1968) Geographer and writer, born in Washington, DC. In 1920 she married Walter Van Dyke Bingham, and on a family-owned island in Maine, they allowed the Audubon Society to establish the first camp for adult conservation leaders in 1936.

Binyon, (Robert) Laurence (1869–1943) Poet and art critic, born in Lancaster, Lancashire. Keeper of Oriental prints and paintings at the British Museum (1913–33), his *Collected Poems* appeared in 1931. Extracts from his 'For the Fallen' adorn war memorials throughout the British Commonwealth.

Biondi, Matt(hew) [byondee] (1965–) Swimmer, born in Morego, CA. At the 1986 world championships he won a record seven medals, including three golds, and at the 1988 Olympics won seven medals, including five golds.

Biot, Jean Baptiste [beeoh] (1774–1862) Physicist and astronomer, born in Paris. He established the fundamental laws of the rotation of the plane of polarization of light by optically active substances, and in 1820 collaborated with Savart to show the relationship between an electric current and the magnetic field it produces (the *Biot–Savart law*). >> Savart

Birch, A(rthur) J(ohn) (1915–) Chemist, born in Sydney, New South Wales, Australia. At Oxford, with Robert Robinson, he was instrumental in the development of the oral contraceptive pill, and in 1948 he made the first synthetic male sex hormone. >> Robinson, Robert

Birch, (Louis) Charles (1918–) Biologist, eco-philosopher, and radical theologian, born in Melbourne, Victoria, Australia. Much of his work shows his concern for the philosophical and theological implications of science. In 1990 he won the Templeton Prize for Progress in Religion.

Bird, Robert Montgomery (1806–54) Writer, born in Newcastle, DE. His works include the popular tragedy *The Gladiator* (1831), and the novels *Calavar, a Mexican Romance* (1834) and *Nick of the Woods* (1837).

Bird, Vere Cornwall (1910–) Prime minister of Antigua and Barbuda (1981–94). In the pre-independence period he was also chief minister (1960–7) and premier (1967–71, 1976–81).

Birdseye, Clarence (1886–1956) Businessman and inventor, born in New York City. He is best known for developing a process for freezing food in small packages suitable for retailing, and became president of Birdseye Frosted Foods (1930–4).

Birdwood, William Riddell (1865–1951) Australian military leader, born in Kirkee, India. In 1914 he was put in command of the contingents arriving in Egypt for the Dardanelles offensive. He planned the landing at Gallipoli, and later took his troops to the Western Front.

Birendra, Bir Bikram Shah Dev [birendra] (1945–) King of Nepal from 1972, the son of King Mahendra, born in Kathmandu. He married Queen Aishwarya Rajya Laxmi Devi Rana in 1970, and has two sons and one daughter. He was forced to concede much of his power in 1990.

Birgitta, St >> Bridget, Brigit, or Birgitta (of Sweden), St

Biringuccio, Vannoccio (Vincenzio Agustino Luca) [biringoochio] (1480–1539) Metallurgical engineer, born in Siena, Italy. His *De la pirotechnia* (1540) was the earliest printed work covering the whole of mining and metallurgy as well as other important industrial processes.

Birkbeck, George (1776–1841) Physician and educationist, born in Settle, North Yorkshire. He was the founder and first president of the London Mechanics' or Birkbeck Institute (1824), now Birkbeck College, part of London University.

Birkeland, Kristian [beerkuhlahnd] (1867–1917) Physicist, born in Oslo. He demonstrated the electromagnetic nature of the aurora borealis, and in 1903 developed a method for obtaining nitrogen from the air.

Birkenhead, Frederick Edwin Smith, 1st Earl of (1872–1930) British statesman and lawyer, born in Birkenhead, Merseyside. A brilliant orator, he became attorney general (1915–19), Lord Chancellor (1919–22), and secretary of state for India (1924–8).

Birkett (of Ulverston), William Norman Birkett, Baron (1883–1962) Lawyer and politician, born in Ulverston, Cumbria. He earned a brilliant reputation as counsel in notable murder trials, and figured prominently in the Nuremberg Trials (1945–6).

Birkhoff, George (David) [berkof] (1884–1944) Mathematician, born in Overisel, MI. His main research was in the theory of dynamical systems, where he extended the work of Poincaré, and in the development of ergodic theory. >> Poincaré

Birley, Eric (1906–) Historian and archaeologist, born in Manchester. He joined the staff at Durham University in 1931, where he became professor of Romano–British history and archaeology (1956–71).

Birney, (Alfred) Earle (1904–) Writer and teacher, born in Calgary, Alberta, Canada. Award-winning works include his collections of poetry *David and Other Poems* (1942) and *Now is Time* (1945), and the novel *Turvey* (1949).

Birney, James (Gillespie) (1792–1857) Anti-slavery leader, born in Dernville, KY. He published the *Philanthropist* (1836), and stood as the anti-slavery presidential candidate in 1840 and 1844 (on behalf of the Liberty Party).

Biró, Ladislao José [biro] (1899–1985) Hungarian inventor. Realizing the advantage of quick-drying ink, in 1940 he went to Argentina with his ideas for developing a ballpoint pen, which eventually became a great success (the *biro*).

Biron, Ernst Johann >> Anna Ivanovna

Birrell, Augustine (1850–1933) British statesman and writer, born near Liverpool, Merseyside. He became chief secretary for Ireland (1907–16), resigning after the Easter Rising of 1916.

Birt, John (1944–) Broadcasting executive, born in Liverpool, Merseyside. He joined Granada Television (1968), moving to London Weekend Television (1971) as producer of *The Frost Programme*. In 1987 he was appointed

deputy director of the BBC, becoming director-general in 1993.

Birtwistle, Sir Harrison (1934–) Composer, born in Accrington, Lancashire. Among his later works are the operas *Punch and Judy* (1966–7), *The Masque of Orpheus* (1973–84), and *Gawain* (1990). In 1993 he became composer in residence to the London Philharmonic Orchestra at the South Bank Centre.

Biscop, Benedict >> Benedict Biscop, St

Bishop, Elizabeth (1911–79) Poet, born in Worcester, MA. Her first two collections, *North and South* (1946) and *A Cold Spring* (1955), received the Pulitzer Prize in 1955.

Bishop, Sir Henry Rowley (1786–1855) Composer, born in London. Few of his many works have survived, though some songs from them have remained popular, including 'Home, Sweet Home'.

Bishop, J(ohn) Michael (1936–) Virologist, born in York, PA. He and colleague **Harold E Varmus** (1939–) received the 1989 Nobel Prize for Physiology or Medicine for demonstrating that external agents, such as viruses or mutagens, may transform a cell's normal genes into cancer-generating oncogenes.

Bishop, John Peale (1892–1944) Writer, born in Charles Town, WV. He was managing editor of *Vanity Fair* after World War 1, but joined the exodus of US literati to Paris in 1922. *Collected Poems* was published in 1948.

Bishop, William Avery (1894–1956) Airman, born in Owen Sound, Ontario, Canada. He became the most successful Allied 'ace' of World War 1, and was awarded the VC in 1917. He was director of the Royal Canadian Air Force throughout World War 2.

Bismarck, Otto Eduard Leopold, Fürst von (Prince of) (1815–98) The first chancellor of the German Empire (1871–90), born in Schönhausen, Germany. Appointed prime minister in 1862, he was made a count in 1866, and created a prince and chancellor of the new German Empire. After the Peace of Frankfurt (1871), his policies aimed at consolidating the young Empire. In 1879, to counteract Russia and France, he formed the Austro-German Treaty of Alliance. Called the 'Iron Chancellor', he resigned the chancellorship in 1890, disapproving of Emperor William II's policy. >> William II (Emperor)

Bissell, Melville (Reuben) (1843–89) Inventor, born in Hartwick, NY. After opening a crockery business, he went on to amass a fortune through industry and real estate, successfully marketing the carpet sweeper (1876).

Biya, Paul [beeya] (1933–) Cameroonian president (1982–) and prime minister (1975–82, 1991–), born in Muomeka'a, Cameroon. Despite an attempt to overthrow him, he was re-elected as president in 1988 with more than 98% of the popular vote.

Bizet, Georges [beezay], originally **Alexandre César Léopold Bizet** (1838–75) Composer, born in Paris. His incidental music to Daudet's play *L'Arlésienne* (1872) was remarkably popular, and survives in the form of two orchestral suites. His masterpiece was the opera *Carmen* (1875). >> Daudet, Alphonse

Bjelke-Petersen, Sir Joh(annes) [byelk] (1911–) Australian statesman, born in Dannevirk, New Zealand. Premier of Queensland (1968–87), he was a vocal supporter of states' rights, controlling a strongly right-wing government. His wife, **Flo(rence) Bjelke-Petersen** (1920–), became deputy leader of the National Party in the Senate (1985–93).

Bjerknes, Jakob (Aall Bonnevie) [byerknes] (1897–1975) Meteorologist, born in Stockholm, the son of Norwegian physicist Vilhelm Bjerknes. With his father he formulated the theory of cyclones on which modern weather-forecasting is based. >> Bjerknes, Vilhelm

Bjerknes, Vilhelm F(riman) K(oren) [byerknes] (1862–1951) Physicist and meteorologist, born in Oslo, Norway.

A pioneer of weather-forecasting, he studied the large-scale dynamics of air masses, and with his son Jacob and others developed the theory of fronts. >> Bjerknes, Jacob

Björling, Jussi [byerling], originally **Johan Jonaton Björling** (1911–60) Tenor, born in Stora Tuna, Sweden. Although his repertoire was mainly Italian he sang rarely in Italy, but became a favourite in the USA, especially at the Metropolitan Opera, New York City.

Bjørnson, Bjørnstjerne (Martinius) [byernsn] (1832–1910) Writer and Norwegian statesman, born in Kvikne, Norway. Norway's national poet, his 'Yes, We Love This Land of Ours' (trans, 1870) became the national anthem. He was awarded the Nobel Prize for Literature in 1903.

Bjornson, Maria [byaw(r)nsn] (1949–) Stage designer, born in Paris. She has designed sets and costumes for drama and opera in many British theatres, notably for the Royal Shakespeare Company, and for the productions of Andrew Lloyd Webber's *The Phantom of the Opera* (1986) and *Aspects of Love* (1989).

Bjørnsson, Sveinn [byernsn] (1881–1952) Icelandic statesman and president (1944–52), born in Copenhagen. During the German occupation of Denmark he was elected Regent of Iceland, and when the republic was declared in 1944 he became president.

Blache, Paul Vidal de la >> Vidal de la Blache, Paul

Black, Conrad Moffat (1944–) London-based financier, born in Montreal, Canada. He achieved control of the Argus Corporation in Canada, becoming chairman in 1979 and chief executive in 1985. He bought many newspapers in Canada and the USA, and London's *Daily Telegraph* (1985).

Black, Eugene Robert (1898–1992) Banker, and president of the World Bank (1949–62), born in Atlanta, GA. He was instrumental in altering the emphasis of the Bank from post-World War 2 reconstruction to providing loans for economic development, particularly to the Third World.

Black, Hugo (La Fayette) (1886–1971) Judge, born in Clay Co, AL. Appointed to the Supreme Court in 1937, he held that the Fourteenth Amendment made the Bill of Rights generally applicable to the states, and that the First Amendment's guarantees of freedoms were absolute.

Black, Sir James (1924–) Pharmacologist, born in Uddingston, Scotland. His work led to the discovery of beta-blockers (1964) and the introduction of cimetidine in the treatment of stomach ulcers (1972). He shared the Nobel Prize for Physiology or Medicine in 1988.

Black, Joseph (1728–99) Chemist, born in Bordeaux, France. He evolved the theory of 'latent heat', as well as the theory of specific heats.

Black, Sir Misha (1910–77) British designer and writer on design, born in Baku, Russia. He designed the famous pre-1940 cafes for Kardomah, and after World War 2 worked for British Rail, London Transport, and the P & O line.

Black, Shirley Temple >> Temple, Shirley

Blackburn, Helen (1842–1903) Social reformer, born in Knightstown, Co Kerry, Ireland. She moved to London (1859), and became secretary of the National Society for Women's Suffrage (1874–95).

Blackburn, Robert (1885–1955) Aircraft designer, born in Leeds, West Yorkshire. He designed his first plane in 1910, and founded the Blackburn Aircraft Co in 1914 to build military biplanes.

Blacket, Edmund Thomas (1817–83) Architect, born in London. He became government architect for New South Wales, Australia (1849), returning to private practice (1854) to design the new University of New South Wales, and cathedrals in Sydney and Perth.

Blackett, Patrick M(aynard) S(tuart) Blackett, Baron (1897–1974) Physicist, born in London. He was the first to photograph nuclear collisions involving transmutation (1925), and independently of Carl Anderson discovered the positron (1932). He pioneered research on cosmic radiation, for which he was awarded the Nobel Prize for Physics in 1948. >> Anderson, Carl

Black Hawk (1767–1838) Chief of the Sauk and Fox Indians, born in Virginia Colony. Opposed to the removal west of his tribe, he fought against the USA (1831–2), and was defeated at Bad Axe River in Wisconsin.

Blackman, Frederick Frost (1866–1947) Botanist, born in London. Based at the Cambridge Botany School (1891–1936), he is renowned for his fundamental research on the respiration of plants, and on the limiting factors affecting their growth.

Blackmore, R(ichard) D(oddridge) (1825–1900) Writer, born in Longworth, Berkshire. After publishing several collections of poetry, he wrote 15 novels, mostly with a Devonshire background, of which *Lorna Doone* (1869) is his masterpiece.

Blackmun, Harry (Andrew) (1908–) Jurist, born in Nashville, IL. Appointed to the Supreme Court (1970–94), he was an effective influence in moderating the views of his more conservative colleagues.

Black Prince >> Edward the Black Prince

Blackstone, Harry, originally **Harry Boughton** (1885–1965) Magician, born in Chicago, IL. He enjoyed his greatest success touring with a full evening magic show (1920–50), his act featuring elaborate 'magic' effects and skilful sleight-of-hand and card tricks.

Blackstone, Sir William (1723–80) Jurist, born in London. He became solicitor general to the queen (1763) and a judge of the court of common pleas (1770–80). *Commentaries on the Laws of England* (1765–69) became the most influential exposition of English law.

Blackwell, Sir Basil (Henry) (1889–1984) Publisher and bookseller, born in Oxford, Oxfordshire, the son of **Benjamin Henry Blackwell**, who founded the famous Oxford bookshop in 1846. He founded the Shakespeare Head Press in 1921.

Blackwell, Elizabeth (1821–1910) Physician and feminist, born in Bristol, Avon, the sister of Emily Blackwell. Her family emigrated to the USA in 1832, where she became the first woman to receive a degree in medicine (1849), and pioneered medical education for women. From 1869 she lived in England, founding the London School of Medicine for Women. >> Blackwell, Emily

Blackwell, Emily (1826–1910) Doctor, born in Bristol, Avon, the sister of Elizabeth Blackwell. Her family emigrated to the USA in 1832, where she was the first woman doctor to undertake major surgery on a considerable scale. She became dean and professor of obstetrics and diseases of women at the Women's Medical College (1869–99). >> Blackwell, Elizabeth

Blackwood, Algernon Henry (1869–1951) Writer, born in Shooters Hill, Kent. His works reflect his taste for the occult, notably in such short-story collections as *Tongues of Fire* (1924) and *Tales of the Uncanny and Supernatural* (1949).

Blackwood, William (1776–1834) Publisher, born in Edinburgh. He became a bookseller in Edinburgh in 1804, and in 1817 started *Blackwood's Magazine*.

Blaine, James G(illespie) (1830–93) Journalist and statesman, born in West Brownsville, PA. He became speaker of the US House of Representatives (1869–75). Between 1876 and 1892 he was defeated four times in the Republican nominations for the presidency.

Blainey, Geoffrey Norman (1930–) Social historian, born in Melbourne, Victoria, Australia. He reached a wide popular audience through his books, notably the trilogy *A Vision of Australian History* (1966–80), and his television programme *The Blainey View*.

Blair, Tony, popular name of **Anthony Charles Lynton Blair** (1953–) British politician, born in Edinburgh. An MP from 1983, he became shadow secretary of state for energy (1988), employment (1989), and home affairs (1992), and was elected leader of the Labour Party in 1994.

Blair, Eric Arthur >> Orwell, George

Blair, Harold (1924–76) Tenor, born near Cherbourg, Queensland, Australia. He was the first Aborigine to gain a Diploma in Music (1949). He later worked for the South Australian Department of Aboriginal Affairs, before becoming a music teacher in Victoria.

Blair, Robert (1699–1746) Poet and preacher, born in Edinburgh. He is best known as the author of *The Grave* (1743), a blank-verse poem which heralded the 'church-yard school' of poetry.

Blaise or **Blasius, St** (?–c.316), feast day 3 February. Armenian clergyman and martyr, born in Sebastia, Cappadocia. Made Bishop of Sebastia, he is said to have suffered martyrdom during a period of persecution. Patron saint of woolcombers, he is invoked against throat trouble and cattle disease.

Blake, Eugene (Carson) (1906–85) Presbyterian clergyman and ecumenist, born in St Louis, MO. He became Stated Clerk of the Presbyterian Church, USA, and was appointed general secretary of the World Council of Churches (1967–72).

Blake, Nicholas >> Day-Lewis, Cecil

Blake, Peter (1932–) Artist, born in Dartford, Kent. During the mid-1950s, he became a pioneer of the Pop Art movement in Britain. His most widely known work is the cover design for the Beatles' LP *Sergeant Pepper's Lonely Hearts Club Band* (1967).

Blake, Robert (1599–1657) English admiral, born in Bridgwater, Somerset. In 1649 he blockaded Lisbon, and in 1652–3 routed the Dutch in several battles. His greatest victory was against the Spanish at Santa Cruz, but he died on the return journey to England.

Blake, William (1757–1827) Poet, painter, engraver, and mystic, born in London. His first book of poems, the *Poetical Sketches* (1783), was followed by *Songs of Innocence* (1789) and *Songs of Experience* (1794), which express his belief in the freedom of the imagination. These ideas found their fullest expression in his prophetic poems, especially *Jerusalem* (1804–20). His finest artistic work is to be found in the 21 *Illustrations to the Book of Job* (1826).

Blakemore, Colin (Brian) (1944–) British physiologist. He is director of the Centre for Cognitive Neuroscience (1989) and associate director of the Centre in Brain and Behaviour (1991). In 1988 he presented the BBC TV series *The Mind Machine*.

Blakeslee, Albert (Francis) (1874–1954) Botanist and geneticist, born in Geneseo, NY. From 1915 he was plant geneticist at the Carnegie Institute laboratories on Long Island, NY (director, 1936), and became world-famous for his genetic research into plants.

Blakey, Art [blaykee], popular name of **Arthur Blakey**, also known as **Abdulla Ibn Buhaina** (1919–90) Jazz drummer and bandleader, born in Pittsburgh, PA. He became a leading exponent of the attacking 'hard bop' style, and from 1954 led groups under the name of the Jazz Messengers, which introduced many outstanding young players.

Blalock, Alfred [blaylok] (1899–1964) Surgeon, born in Culloden, GA. He pioneered the surgical treatment of various congenital defects of the heart, and performed the first 'blue baby' operation with the paediatrician Helen Taussig. >> Taussig

Blamey, Sir Thomas Albert [blaymee] (1884–1951) Australian field marshal, born in Wagga Wagga, New South Wales, Australia. At the outbreak of World War 2 he commanded the Australian Imperial Forces in the Middle East. He led Allied land forces in Australia (1942), and received the Japanese surrender in 1945.

Blampied, Edmund (1886–1966) Artist, born in Jersey, Channel Is. He is best known for his etchings which depict everyday farming life, in particular horses and peasants.

Blanc, (Jean Joseph Charles) Louis [blã] (1811–82) French statesman and historian, born in Madrid. His chief work on socialism was *The Organisation of Labour* (trans, 1840). On the fall of the empire, he was elected to the National Assembly (1871) and Chamber of Deputies (1876).

Blanchard, Jean Pierre François [blãshah(r)] (1753–1809) Balloonist, and inventor of the parachute, born in Les Andelys, France. With Jeffries he was the first to cross the English Channel by balloon, from Dover to Calais, in 1785. He was killed during practice parachute jumps from a balloon. >> Jeffries, John

Blanchflower, Danny, popular name of **Robert Dennio Blanchflower** (1926–93) Footballer, born in Belfast. He was a member of the Northern Ireland side which reached the World Cup quarter finals in 1958. Transferring from Aston Villa to Tottenham Hotspur, he masterminded the London club's double success in the League and the FA Cup (1960–1).

Blanda, (George) Frederick (1927–) Player of American football, born in Youngwood, PA. He holds the record for the most points (2002) in any National Football League career. He played for the Chicago Bears (1949), the American Football League Houston Oilers (1960), and Oakland Raiders (1967).

Blandrata or **Biandrata, Giorgio** [blandrahta] (c.1515–88) Physician and theologian, born in Saluzzo, Italy, the founder of Unitarianism in Poland and Transylvania. In Geneva in 1556, he joined a Calvinist congregation, but in 1558 Calvin's displeasure at his anti-Trinitarianism drove him to Poland. >> Calvin, John

Blankers-Koen, Fanny [kern], popular name of **Francina Blankers-Koen** (1918–) Athlete, born in Amsterdam. She dominated women's events in the London Olympics of 1948, winning four gold medals: the 100 m and 200 m, the 80 m hurdles, and the 4 x 100 m relay.

Blanqui, (Louis) Auguste [blãkee] (1805–81) Revolutionary, born in Puget-Théniers, France. He built up a network of secret societies committed to violent revolution. He was arrested on the eve of the Paris Commune, but was elected president (1871). His followers were known as *Blanquists*.

Blasco Ibáñez, Vicente [blaskoh eevahnyeth] (1867–1928) Novelist, born in Valencia, Spain. He is best known for *The Four Horsemen of the Apocalypse* (trans, 1916), which vividly portrays World War 1.

Blashford-Snell, Colonel John (1936–) Explorer and youth leader, born in Hereford, Herefordshire and Worcestershire. He participated in over 40 expeditions, and led the Blue Nile (1968), British Trans-Americas (1972), and Zaire River (1975/84) projects.

Blasis, Carlo [blasees] (1797–1878) Dancer, choreographer, and teacher, born in Naples, Italy. He wrote noted treatises on the codification of ballet technique (1820, 1840, 1857), and is regarded as the most important ballet teacher of the 19th-c.

Blasius, St >> Blaise, St

Blass, Bill, popular name of **William Ralph Blass** (1922–) Fashion designer, born in Fort Wayne, IN. The winner of eight Coty Awards, he created high-priced, beautifully cut and tailored women's wear notable for its inventive combinations of patterns and textures.

Blatch, Harriet (Eaton Stanton), *née* **Stanton** (1856–1940) Suffrage leader, born in Seneca Falls, NY. She founded the Equality League of Self-Supporting Women (1907), and in 1908 founded the Women's Political Union.

Blavatsky, Helena Petrovna [blavatskee], *née* **Hahn**, known as **Madame Blavatsky** (1831–91) Theosophist, born in Yekaterinoslav, Ukraine. She went to the USA in 1873, and with Olcott founded the Theosophical Society in New York City in 1875, later carrying on her work in India. >> Besant, Annie; Olcott

Bleasdale, Alan [bleezdayl] (1946–) Playwright, born in Liverpool, Merseyside. His successful television series include the award-winning *The Boys from the Blackstuff* (1982), followed by *The Monocled Mutineer* (1986) and *GBH* (1991).

Blériot, Louis [blayryoh] (1872–1936) Airman, born in Cambrai, France. He made the first flight across the English Channel from Baraques to Dover, on 25 July 1909, in a small 24-hp monoplane.

Blessington, Marguerite Gardiner, Countess of (1789–1849) Writer and socialite, born near Clonmel, Co Tipperary, Ireland. She held a salon at her Kensington mansion, where she wrote sketches of London life, and formed a relationship with Comte d'Orsay (1801–57).

Bleuler, Eugen [bloyler] (1857–1939) Psychiatrist, born in Zollikon, Switzerland. He carried out research on epilepsy, then turned to psychiatry, and in 1911 published a study on what he called *schizophrenia*. Jung was one of his pupils. >> Jung

Blicher, Steen Steensen [bleeker] (1782–1848) Writer, born near Viborg, Denmark. His home province of Jutland forms the background of much of his work, notably in his collection of poetry, *The Migratory Birds* (trans, 1838), and his books of short stories.

Bligh, William [bliy] (c.1754–c.1817) Naval officer, born in Plymouth, Devon. In 1787 he was sent as commander of HMS *Bounty* to Tahiti. On the return voyage, the men mutinied under his harsh treatment, and in April 1789, he and 18 others were cast adrift in an open boat without charts. In June they arrived in Timor, having sailed 3618 miles. >> Christian, Fletcher

Bliss, Sir Arthur (Edward Drummond) (1891–1975) Composer, born in London. In 1953 he became Master of the Queen's Musick. His works include the ballet *Checkmate* (1937), the opera *The Olympians* (1949), chamber music, and works for piano and violin.

Blitzstein, Marc [blitstiyn] (1905–64) Composer, born in Philadelphia, PA. In the 1930s he began to write pieces with explicit social themes for the musical theatre, his most successful work being the adaptation of the Brecht/Weill *Threepenny Opera* (1954). >> Brecht; Weill

Blixen, Karen, Baroness, pseudonym **Isak Dinesen**, *née* **Karen Christence Dinesen** (1885–1962) Writer and story-teller, born in Rungsted, Denmark. She married her cousin, Baron Bror Blixen Finecke, and lived for a time in Kenya. Her works include *Seven Gothic Tales* (1934) and *Out of Africa* (1937).

Bloch, Ernest [blokh] (1880–1959) Composer, born in Geneva, Switzerland. A US citizen from 1924, his works include the *Israel* symphony (1912–16), the 'epic rhapsody' *America* (1926), and the Hebrew *Sacred Service* (1930–3).

Bloch, Felix [blokh] (1905–83) Physicist, born in Zürich, Switzerland. He left Europe for the USA in 1933, and later shared the 1952 Nobel Prize for Physics for work on nuclear magnetic resonance.

Bloch, Konrad (Emil) [blokh] (1912–) Biochemist, born in Neisse, Germany. He emigrated to the USA in 1936, and shared the 1964 Nobel Prize for Physiology or Medicine for work on the mechanism of cholesterol and fatty acid metabolism.

Bloch, Marc [blokh] (1886–1944) Historian, born in Lyon, France. He joined the Resistance in 1943, and was captured and shot by the Germans. His work has been extensively translated since his death.

Bloch, Martin [blokh] (1883–1954) Expressionist painter, born in Neisse, Germany. He came to England in 1934,

where he opened a school of painting with Roy de Maistre.

Block, Alexander >> **Blok, Alexander Alexandrovich**

Bloembergen, Nicolas [bloombergen] (1920–) Physicist, born in Dordrecht, The Netherlands. Working in the USA from 1946, he introduced a modification to Townes's early design of the maser, enabling it to work continuously. He shared the Nobel Prize for Physics in 1981. >> Townes

Blok, Alexander Alexandrovich (1880–1921) Poet, born in St Petersburg, Russia. His first book of poems, *Songs about the Lady Fair* (1904), was influenced by the mysticism of Soloviev. He welcomed the 1917 revolution, which greatly influenced his later work. >> Soloviev

Blomdahl, Karl-Birger (1916–68) Composer, born in Stockholm. Much inspired by Hindemith, his compositions include symphonies, concertos, operas, and electronic music. >> Hindemith

Blondel or **Blondel de Nesle** [blôdel] (12th-c) French minstrel. According to legend he accompanied Richard I to Palestine on the Crusades, and located him when imprisoned in the Austrian castle of Dürrenstein (1193) by means of the song they had jointly composed. >> Richard I

Blondin, Charles [blôdi], originally **Jean François Gravelet** (1824–97) Acrobat and tightrope-walker, born in Hesdin, France. In 1859 he crossed Niagara Falls on a tightrope, and later repeated the feat with variations (eg blindfolded, on stilts).

Blood, Thomas, known as **Captain Blood** (c.1618–80) Irish adventurer, known for his activities during the English Civil War and Restoration. His most famous exploit was his attempt to steal the crown jewels from the Tower of London (1671). He was captured, but pardoned by King Charles. >> Charles II (of England)

Bloom, Claire (1931–) Actress, born in London. A noted Shakespearean actress, she is also known for her film roles, such as *Limelight* (1952) and *Look Back in Anger* (1959). Her television work includes *Brideshead Revisited* (1981) and *Shadowlands* (1985, BAFTA).

Bloom, Ursula, pseudonym of **Mrs Gower Robinson** (1892–1984) Writer, born in Chelmsford, Essex. Her novels are mainly historical romances, such as *Pavilion* (1951) and *The First Elizabeth* (1953). Most of her plays were written for radio.

Bloomer, Amelia, *née* **Jenks** (1818–94) Champion of women's rights and dress reform, born in Homer, NY. She founded and edited the feminist paper *The Lily* (1849–55). In her pursuit of dress equality she wore her own version of trousers for women, which came to be called *bloomers*.

Bloomfield, Leonard (1887–1949) Linguist, born in Chicago, IL. He played a major part in making linguistics an independent scientific discipline, developing a behaviourist approach in *Language* (1933), and motivating a *Bloomfieldian* school which was influential until the 1950s.

Bloomfield, Robert (1766–1823) Poet, born in Honington, Suffolk. A shoemaker's apprentice, he wrote *The Farmer's Boy* (1800), followed by *Rural Tales* (1802) and *Wild Flowers* (1806).

Bloom, Harold (1930–) Literary critic, born in New York City. His books include *The Anxiety of Influence* (1973), *The Book of J* (1990), and *The Western Canon* (1994) - a controversial recommended short-list of 26 great authors.

Bloor, Ella, *née* **Reeve**, known as **Mother Bloor** (1862–1951) Radical and feminist, born on Staten Island, New York City. After two unsuccessful marriages, she became a political activist. She joined the Socialist Party in 1901, and in 1919 was one of the founders of the American Communist Party.

Blount, Charles, 8th Lord Mountjoy, Earl of Devonshire [bluhnt] (1563–1606) English soldier, and conqueror of Ireland. In 1600 he commanded against the rebellion of Hugh O'Neill, Earl of Tyrone, winning a decisive victory at Kinsale (1601). He became Lord Lieutenant of Ireland, and was given an earldom by James I. >> O'Neill, Hugh

Blow, John (c.1649–1708) Composer, born in Newark, Nottinghamshire. He is known for his vast output of anthems and church services, and also for his masque, *Venus and Adonis*(1687), performed before Charles II.

Blow, Susan Elizabeth (1843–1916) Educationist, born in St Louis, MO. She opened the first US public kindergarten in St Louis (1873), and a training school for kindergarten teachers (1874). The movement grew rapidly, leading to the formation of an International Union.

Blücher, Gebhard Leberecht von, Fürst von (Prince of) **Wahlstadt** [bloocher, blooker], nickname **Marshal Forward** (1742–1819) Prussian field marshal, born in Rostock, Germany. In 1813 he took chief command in Silesia, defeated Napoleon at Leipzig, and entered Paris in 1814. In 1815 he completed Wellington's victory at Waterloo by his timely appearance on the field. >> Napoleon I; Wellington

Blue, Lionel (1930–) British rabbi and broadcaster. He is well known for his humorous and off-beat comments on life, both on radio and in such books as *A Taste of Heaven* (1977) and *Blue Horizons*(1989).

Blum, Léon [blum] (1872–1950) French statesman and prime minister (1936–7, 1938, 1946–7), born in Paris. A Socialist Party leader, he led 'popular front' governments in 1936 and 1938. After World War 2 he was elected prime minister of the six-week caretaker government.

Blum, René [blum] (1878–1942) Impresario and critic, born in Paris. He became administrator of the Ballet Russes after Diaghilev's death in 1929, renaming it the Ballet Russes de Monte Carlo. He died in Auschwitz. >> Diaghilev

Blumberg, Baruch S(amuel) (1925–) Biochemist, born in New York City. He discovered the 'Australia antigen' that led to the development of a vaccine against hepatitis B, and shared the Nobel Prize for Physiology or Medicine in 1976.

Blume, Judy [bloom] (1938–) Writer of teenage fiction, born in New Jersey. Her third book, *Are You There, God? It's Me, Margaret* (1970), brought her acclaim for her candid approach to puberty and for her natural style, but attempts were made to restrict its circulation.

Blume, Peter [bloom] (1906–) Painter, born in Smorgon, Belarus. From 1911 he worked in Italy, later becoming an intermittent artist in residence at the American Academy of Rome (1956–73). His most famous work is 'The Eternal City' (1934–7), a denunciation of Fascism in Italy.

Blumenbach, Johann Friedrich [bloomenbahkh] (1752–1840) Anthropologist, born in Gotha, Germany. By his study of comparative skull measurements, he established a quantitative basis for racial classification.

Blunden, Edmund (Charles) (1896–1974) Poet and critic, born in Yalding, Kent. A lover of the English countryside, he is essentially a nature poet, as is evident in *Pastorals* (1916), but his prose work *Undertones of War* (1928) is widely considered his best.

Blunt, (Sir) Anthony (Frederick) (1907–83) Art historian and Soviet spy, born in Bournemouth, Hampshire. At Cambridge he supplied Burgess with names of likely recruits to the Communist cause and, during his war service in British Intelligence, passed on information to the Russian government. In 1964, after the defection of Philby, he confessed in return for immunity, and his role was made public only in 1979. >> Burgess, Guy; Maclean, Donald; Philby

Blunt, Wilfrid Scawen (1840–1922) Poet and traveller, born in Petworth, West Sussex. He travelled in the Near and Middle East, and was imprisoned in 1888 for activity in the Irish Land League. He wrote political verse and love poems.

Bly, Nellie, pseudonym of **Elizabeth Seaman**, *née* **Cochrane** (c.1865–1922) Journalist, born in Cochrane Mills, PA. As a reporter for the *New York World* she won renown for many stories, such as her exposé of conditions in an asylum on New York City's Blackwell's Island, where she posed as an inmate.

Bly, Robert (1926–) Poet, critic, translator, and editor, born in Madison, MN. His collections include *Silence in the Snowy Fields* (1962) and *Talking All Morning* (1980).

Blyth, Chay, popular name of **Charles Blyth** (1940–) British yachtsman, the first to sail single-handed 'the hard way' round the world. He rowed the Atlantic from W to E with John Ridgeway (1966), before making his epic voyage westward around the globe (1970–1). >> Ridgeway, John

Blyth, Edward (1810–73) Naturalist and zoologist, born in London. He was curator of the museum of the Asiatic Society in Bengal (1841–62). Several birds are named after him, including a kingfisher, pipit, and warbler.

Blythe, Ethel / John / Lionel >> **Barrymore, Ethel / John / Lionel**

Blyton, Enid (Mary) (1897–1968) Children's writer, born in London. In the late 1930s she began writing her many children's stories featuring such characters as Noddy, the Famous Five, and the Secret Seven. She published over 600 books, but in the 1980s her work was criticized in some quarters for racism, sexism, and snobbishness.

Boadicea >> **Boudicca**

Boal, Augusto [bohal] (1931–) Brazilian theatre director, playwright, and theorist. His revolutionary models of political theatre-making have gained an international reputation, especially through his book *Theatre of the Oppressed* (trans, 1975).

Boas, Franz [bohas] (1858–1942) Anthropologist, born in Minden, Germany. He emigrated to the USA in 1886, and became the dominant figure in establishing modern anthropology in the USA, as seen in his collection of papers, *Race, Language and Culture* (1940).

Bocage, Manoel Barbosa du [bookahzhuh] (1765–1805) Lyric poet, born in Setúbal, Portugal. In Lisbon (1790) he joined the literary coterie *Nova Arcadia*. He was essentially a Romantic, but his sonnets are Classical in form.

Boccaccio, Giovanni [bokahchioh] (1313–75) Writer and scholar, born in Tuscany or Paris. In 1358 he completed his great collection of tales, the *Decameron*, begun some 10 years before. He selected the plots of his stories from current popular fiction, and was a great influence on Chaucer, Shakespeare, and others.

Boccherini, Luigi (Rodolfo) [bokereenee] (1743–1805) Composer, born in Lucca, Italy. He was a cellist and prolific composer at the courts in Madrid and Prussia, best known for his chamber music, cello concertos, and sonatas.

Boccioni, Umberto [bochohnee] (1882–1916) Artist and sculptor, born in Reggio di Calabria, Italy. He was the most original artist of the Futurist school, and its principal theorist.

Bock, Fedor von (1880–1945) German soldier, born in Kostrzyn, Poland. He commanded the German armies which invaded Austria (1938), Poland (1939), and the Lower Somme, France (1940). Promoted to field marshal (1940), he successfully invaded Russia (1941), but was dismissed for failing to capture Moscow (1942).

Böcklin, Arnold [boekli] (1827–1901) Painter, born in Basel, Switzerland. His work, mainly of mythological subjects, combined Classical themes with dark Romantic landscapes, characteristic of 19th-c German painting.

Bode, Johann Elert [bohduh] (1747–1826) Astronomer,

born in Hamburg, Germany. He became director of the Berlin Observatory. The arithmetical relation he observed between the distances of the planets from the Sun is called *Bode's law*.

Bodenheim, Maxwell [**boh**denhiym], originally Bodenheimer (1893–1954) Writer, born in Hemanville, MS. He published *Minna and Myself* (1918), the first of 11 volumes of poetry. His novels, such as *Replenishing Jessica* (1925), were considered cynical and indecent. He and his third wife were murdered in Greenwich Village.

Bodenstein, Andreas Rudolf >> **Carlstadt**

Bodhidharma [bodhi**dah(r)**ma] (6th-c) Monk and founder of the Ch'an (or Zen) sect of Buddhism, born near Madras, India. He argued that merit applying to salvation could not be accumulated through good deeds, and taught meditation as the means of return to Buddha's spiritual precepts. >> Buddha

Bodichon, Barbara, *née* **Leigh Smith** (1827–90) Advocate of women's rights, born in London. She wrote *Women at Work* (1857), co-founded the feminist magazine *The Englishwoman's Journal* (1858), and was a founder of the college for women that became Girton College, Cambridge.

Bodin, Jean [bohdí] (1530–96) Political philosopher, born in Angers, France. His major work was *The Six Bookes of a Commonweale, 1606* (trans, 1576), which argued for a limited form of monarchy.

Bodley, Sir Thomas (1545–1613) Scholar and diplomat, born in Exeter, Devon. A lecturer in Greek at Oxford (1564), in 1587 he married a wealthy widow, then spent huge sums extending the university library, which was renamed the Bodleian Library and opened in 1602.

Bodmer, Johann Georg (1786–1864) Inventor, born in Zürich, Switzerland. A mechanical engineer, his many inventions reflected the wide range of his interests in textile machinery, machine tools, screw propellers, armaments, steam engines, furnaces, boilers, and locomotives.

Bodoni, Giambattista [bo**doh**nee] (1740–1813) Printer, born in Saluzzo, Italy. In 1790 he designed a modern typeface still widely used today. His press in Parma published elegant editions of the classics.

Boë, Franz de la >> **Sylvius, Franciscus**

Boece or **Boethius, Hector** [boys], also spelled **Boyis** (c.1465–c.1536) Historian, born in Dundee, Tayside. He became principal of the newly founded university of Aberdeen, and is best known for his popular *The History and Chronicles of Scotland* (trans, 1526), largely based on legendary sources.

Boehm or **Böhm, Theobald** [boem] (1794–1881) Flautist and inventor, born in Munich, Germany. In 1828 he opened a flute factory in Munich, and in 1847 produced the model on which the modern flute is based, using a key mechanism which later influenced the development of the clarinet.

Boehme, Jakob >> **Böhme, Jakob**

Boeing, William E(dward) [**boh**ing] (1881–1956) Aircraft manufacturer, born in Detroit, MI. He formed the Pacific Aero Products Co in 1916 to build seaplanes. Renamed the Boeing Airplane Co in 1917, it became the largest manufacturer of military and civilian aircraft in the world.

Boerhaave, Hermann [boor**hah**vuh] (1668–1738) Physician and botanist, born in Voorhout, The Netherlands. His fame chiefly rests on his *Medical Principles* (trans, 1708), *Aphorisms on the Recognition and Treatment of Diseases* (trans, 1709), and *Elements of Chemistry* (trans, 1724).

Boesak, Allan (Aubrey) [**bu**sak] (1945–) Clergyman, born in Kakamas, South Africa. An outspoken opponent of apartheid, he became president of the alliance of Black Reformed Christians in South Africa (1981), and of the World Alliance of Reformed Churches (1982).

Boesky, Ivan [**bes**kee] (1937–) Financier, born in Detroit,

MI. He formed his own securities firm in 1975, and pioneered the junk-bond market, but admitted to insider trading charges in 1986. Fined $100 million, he served time in prison before being paroled in 1990.

Boethius, Anicius Manlius Severinus [boh**ee**thius] (c.AD 480–524) Roman philosopher and statesman, born of a patrician Roman family. He wrote commentaries on Aristotle and Porphyry that became standard textbooks in the Middle Ages. Chief minister to the Gothic king Theodoric, he fell from favour, was imprisoned at Pavia, and executed. During his imprisonment he wrote (trans) *The Consolation of Philosophy*.

Boethius, Hector >> **Boece, Hector**

Boëx, Joseph and **Séraphin** >> **Rosny**

Boff, Leonardo (1938–) Franciscan liberation theologian, born in Concordia, Brazil. His best-known work, *Jesus-Christ Liberator* (1972), offers hope and justice for the oppressed rather than religious support of the *status quo* in Church and society.

Bogan, Louise [**boh**gan] (1897–1970) Poet and writer, born in Livermore Falls, MA. She was an influential critic, as in *Achievement in American Poetry 1900–1950* (1951), and a noted lyrical poet, as in *The Blue Estuaries* (1968).

Bogarde, Dirk [**boh**gah(r)d], originally **Derek Niven van den Bogaerde** (1921–) Actor and writer, born in London. His first film roles were mostly in light comedy, such as *Doctor in the House* (1954), but more challenging parts followed in such films as *The Servant* (1963) and *Death in Venice* (1971).

Bogardus, James (1800–74) Inventor, born in Catskill, NY. His many varied inventions include a method of engraving postage stamps (1839) which was adopted by the British government. He also erected the first cast-iron building in the USA.

Bogart, Humphrey (DeForest) [**boh**gah(r)t] (1899–1957) Film actor, born in New York City. Many of his performances have become classics, notably in *The Maltese Falcon* (1941) and *Casablanca* (1942). Later films include *The Big Sleep* (1946), *The African Queen* (1951, Oscar), and *The Caine Mutiny* (1954). >> Bacall

Bogdanov, Michael [bog**dah**nov] (1938–) Stage director, born in London. He has directed several major productions for the Royal Shakespeare Company and the National Theatre, and in 1986 became co-founder and artistic director of the touring English Shakespeare Company.

Bogdanovich, Peter [bog**dan**ovich] (1939–) Film director, born in Kingston, NY. His second film, *The Last Picture Show* (1971), depicting social change in a 1950s Texas town, received critical acclaim, though the sequel, *Texasville* (1990), was less successful.

Bogorad, Lawrence [**bo**gorad] (1921–) Plant physiologist, born in Tashkent, Uzbekistan. He lived in the USA from 1923. A pioneer in the study of chloroplasts, in the 1960s he worked on accessory plant pigments and the genetics of chloroplast formation.

Bohemond I [**boh**imond] (c.1056–1111) Prince of Antioch (1099–1111), the eldest son of Robert Guiscard. He led his father's army against Alexius I Comnenus (1081–5), but was defeated. In the first Crusade (1096), he was prominent in the capture of Antioch (1098), where he established himself as prince. >> Guiscard; Alexius

Böhm, Karl [boem] (1894–1981) Conductor, born in Graz, Austria. Remembered chiefly for his Mozart performances, he also conducted premieres of operas by Richard Strauss. >> Strauss, Richard

Böhm, Theobald >> **Boehm, Theobald**

Böhme or **Böhme, Jakob** [boe**muh**] (1575–1624) Theosophist and mystic, born in Altseidenberg, Germany. His meditations upon God, Man, and Nature in *Aurora* (1612) were condemned by the ecclesiastical authorities, and he suffered much persecution.

Bohr, Aage (Niels) [baw(r)] (1922–   ) Physicist, born in Copenhagen, the son of Niels Bohr. With Mottelson, he secured experimental evidence for the support of Rainwater's collective model of the atomic nucleus, and shared the Nobel Prize for Physics with them in 1975. >> Bohr, Niels; Mottelson; Rainwater

Bohr, Niels (Henrik David) [baw(r)] (1885–1962) Physicist, born in Copenhagen. He greatly extended the theory of atomic structure when he explained the spectrum of hydrogen by means of an atomic model and the quantum theory (1913). He founded the Institute of Theoretical Physics at Copenhagen, and was awarded the Nobel Prize for Physics in 1922. >> Bohr, Aage

Boiardo, Matteo Maria, conte di (Count of) **Scandiano** [boyah(r)doh] (c.1441–94) Poet, born in Scandiano, Italy. His fame rests on the unfinished *Orlando Innamorato* (1486), a long narrative poem about Roland, the greatest of Charlemagne's legendary heroes. >> Roland

Boieldieu, François Adrien [bwaeldyoe] (1775–1834) Composer, born in Rouen, France. His opera *The Caliph of Baghdad* (trans, 1800) brought him acclaim, and was followed by two masterpieces, *Jean de Paris* (1812) and *The White Lady* (trans, 1825).

Boileau(-Despréaux), Nicolas [bwahloh] (1636–1711) Poet and critic, born in Paris. His *Art of Poetry* (trans, 1674) expressing the classical principles for the writing of poetry, was highly influential in France and England.

Bois, Guy Péne du >> du Bois, Guy Péne

Bois, W E B Du >> Du Bois, W E B

Boisbaudran, Paul Emile Lecoq de [bwahbohdrã] (1838–1912) Physical chemist, born in Cognac, France. A founder of spectroscopy, he discovered gallium, samarium, and dysprosium.

Bois-Reymond, Emil du [bwah raymõ] (1818–96) Physiologist, the discoverer of neuroelectricity, born in Berlin. He became professor of physiology at Berlin in 1855, where he investigated the physiology of muscles and nerves, and demonstrated electricity in animals.

Boito, Arrigo [boheetoh] (1842–1918) Composer and poet, born in Padua, Italy. His first important work was the opera *Mefistofele* (1868), which later grew in popularity. He wrote libretti, including those for Verdi's *Otello* and *Falstaff*.

Bo Juyi [boe jooyee], also spelled **Po Chü-i** (772–846) Poet, government official, and governor of Hangzhou, born in Hsingcheng, Shensi Province, China. He was probably the first poet to be printed (c.810), and his vernacular poetry and prose affords insight into the life of Tang period scholar-gentry.

Bok, Edward (William) (1863–1930) Editor, born in Den Helder, The Netherlands. Emigrating to the USA as a child, he became editor of the *Brooklyn Magazine* at 19, and later of *The Ladies' Home Journal* (1889–1919). His several books include an acclaimed autobiography, *The Americanization of Edward Bok* (1920, Pulitzer).

Bokassa, Eddine Ahmed [bohkasa], originally **Jean Bédel Bokassa** (1921–   ) Central African Republic soldier, president (1966–79), and emperor (1977–9), born in Bobangui, Central African Republic. Following a coup (1965), he made himself life-president, and was crowned emperor as Bokassa I. He ran a dictatorial regime and in 1979 was himself ousted and went into exile. In 1988 he returned for trial and was found guilty, but his death sentence was commuted.

Bol, Ferdinand (c.1616–1680) Dutch painter who studied under Rembrandt in the 1630s. Working in Amsterdam, he painted in a style so close to his master's that some of his portraits have been mistaken for Rembrandt's. >> Rembrandt

Boldrewood, Rolf, pseudonym of **Thomas Alexander Browne** (1826–1915) Novelist, born in London. His family emigrated to Australia in 1830. His novels depict life at the cattle stations and diggings, and include *Robbery under Arms* (1888) and *Babes in the Bush* (1900).

Bolet, Jorge [bohlay] (1914–90) Pianist, born in Havana. He is renowned for his interpretation of Liszt, and of the German, Spanish, and Russian Romantics.

Boleyn, Anne [bolin], also spelled **Bullen** (c.1507–36) English queen, the second wife of Henry VIII (1533–6). She secretly married Henry, and was declared his legal wife; but his passion for her rapidly cooled. It was not revived by the birth (1533) of a princess (later Elizabeth I), still less by that of a stillborn son (1536). She was charged with treason and beheaded. >> Elizabeth I; Henry VIII

Bolger, James Brendan [boljer] (1935–   ) New Zealand prime minister (1990–   ), born in Opunake, New Zealand. A farmer, he entered parliament in 1972 for the National Party, and became Leader of the Opposition in 1986.

Bolingbroke >> Henry IV (of England)

Bolingbroke, Henry St John, 1st Viscount (1678–1751) English statesman and writer, born in London. He became secretary for war (1704), foreign secretary (1710), and joint leader of the Tory Party. On Queen Anne's death (1714), his Jacobite sympathies forced him to flee to France.

Bolívar, Simón [boleevah(r), bolivah(r)], known as **the Liberator** (1783–1830) The national hero of Venezuela, Colombia, Ecuador, Peru, and Bolivia, born in Caracas. He played the most prominent part in the wars of independence, and in 1819 proclaimed the vast Republic of Colombia, becoming its president.

Bolkiah, Hassanal [bolkia] (1946–   ) Sultan of Brunei (1967–   ), and prime minister since independence (1984). As head of an oil- and gas-rich state, he is reputed to be the richest individual in the world.

Böll, Heinrich (Theodor) [boel] (1917–85) Writer, born in Cologne, Germany. His work includes the trilogy *Acquainted with the Night* (trans, 1953), and *The Lost Honour of Katharina Blum* (trans, 1974). He was awarded the Nobel Prize for Literature in 1972.

Bolm, Adolph (1884–1951) Dancer, choreographer, and teacher, born in St Petersburg, Russia. A member of Anna Pavlova's first tours (1908–9) and Diaghilev's Ballets Russes, he remained in the USA after the 1916 tour. >> Diaghilev; Pavlova

Bologna, Giovanni da [bolonya], also called Giambologna (1529–1608) Sculptor and architect, born in Douai, France. He executed much sculptural work in Florence for the Medici, including the 'Flying Mercury' (1564) and the 'Rape of the Sabines' (1580).

Bolt, Robert (1924–95) Playwright, born in Manchester. He achieved success with *A Man for All Seasons* (1960). His screenplays include *Lawrence of Arabia* (1962), *Dr Zhivago* (1965), and *The Mission* (1986).

Boltwood, Bertram (Borden) (1870–1927) Radiochemist, born in Amherst, MA. He discovered the radioactive element ionium, and introduced lead:uranium ratios as a method for dating rocks (1907).

Boltzmann, Ludwig (Eduard) [boltsman] (1844–1906) Physicist, born in Vienna. He worked on the kinetic theory of gases, and helped to develop the science of statistical mechanics. *Boltzmann's law*, the principle of the equipartition of energy, and the *Boltzmann constant*, used in the study of gases, are named after him.

Bolyai, János (1802–60) Mathematician, born in Cluj, Romania. After attempting to prove Euclid's parallel postulate, he realized that it was possible to have a consistent system of geometry in which this postulate did not hold, and so became one of the founders of non-Euclidean geometry. >> Euclid

Bolzano, Bernhard [bolzahnoh] (1781–1848) Catholic theologian, philosopher, and mathematician, born in Prague. A professor of the philosophy of religion, he was deprived of his chair in 1819 for nonconformity. He was a pioneer of the theory of functions of a real variable, and of the mathematical concept of the infinite.

Bombard, Alain Louis [bombah(r)] (1924–) Physician and marine biologist, born in Paris. In 1952 he crossed the Atlantic alone in his rubber dinghy *L'Hérétique* to prove his claim that castaways could sustain life on a diet of fish and plankton.

Bomberg, David (1890–1957) Painter, born in Birmingham, West Midlands. A founder member of the London Group (1913), the influence of continental avant-garde artists is clear in such large compositions as 'The Mud Bath' and 'In the Hold' (1913–14).

Bombois, Camille [bōbwah] (1883–1970) Primitive painter, born in Venarey-les-Laumes, France. After working in a travelling circus, his painting became known in the 1920s, his themes including landscapes, and pictures of wrestlers and acrobats.

Bonaparte, (Maria Annunciata) Caroline [bohnapah(r)t] (1782–1839) Queen of Naples (1808–15), born in Ajaccio, Corsica, the youngest sister of Napoleon I. She married Joachim Murat in 1800, and brought a brilliant court life to the Neapolitan palaces of Caserta and Portici. >> Murat; Napoleon I

Bonaparte, Charles Joseph [bohnapah(r)t] (1851–1921) Lawyer and reformer, born in Baltimore, MD, the great-nephew of Napoleon I. In 1881 he founded the Civil Service Reform Association of Maryland and the National Civil Service Reform League, and later became secretary of the navy (1905) and attorney general (1906–9). >> Napoleon I

Bonaparte, Charles Louis Napoleon >> **Napoleon III**

Bonaparte, (Marie-Anne) Elisa [bohnapah(r)t] (1777–1820) Grand Duchess of Tuscany, born in Ajaccio, Corsica, the eldest surviving sister of Napoleon. As Duchess of Lucca from 1805, she managed the economy so well that in 1809 Napoleon sent her to Tuscany, where she revived the Pitti Palace. >> Napoleon I

Bonaparte, François Charles Joseph >> **Napoleon II**

Bonaparte, Jérôme [bohnapah(r)t] (1784–1860) Youngest brother of Napoleon, born in Ajaccio, Corsica. He served in the war against Prussia, ruled Westphalia (1807–14), and fought at Waterloo. His nephew Napoleon III created him a marshal of France in 1850. >> Napoleon I / III

Bonaparte, Joseph [bohnapah(r)t] (1768–1844) The eldest brother of Napoleon I, born in Corte, Corsica. He was made ruler of the Two Sicilies (1805), Naples (1806), and Spain (1808), but after defeat at Vitoria (1813) he abdicated. >> Napoleon I

Bonaparte, Louis [bohnapah(r)t] (1778–1846) The third surviving brother of Napoleon I, born in Ajaccio, Corsica. He married Napoleon's step-daughter, Hortense Beauharnais (1802), and ruled Holland as King Lodewijk I (1806–10). He was the father of Napoleon III. >> Beauharnais, Hortense; Napoleon III

Bonaparte, Lucien [bohnapah(r)t] (1775–1840) The second surviving brother of Napoleon I, born in Ajaccio, Corsica. He denounced his brother's policy towards the court of Rome, and was forced to leave Italy in 1810. >> Napoleon I

Bonaparte, Napoleon [bohnapah(r)t] >> **Napoleon I**

Bonaparte, Napoleon Joseph Charles Paul [bohnapah(r)t] (1822–91) French politican, born in Trieste, Italy, the son of Jérôme Bonaparte. In 1851 he was named as successor to Napoleon III, but after the fall of the empire he lived in England until 1872, and was exiled in 1886. >> Bonaparte, Jérôme

Bonaparte, (Marie-) Pauline [bohnapah(r)t] (1780–1825) Sister of Napoleon I, born in Ajaccio, Corsica. She married

General Leclerc (1797), after whose death she married Prince Camillo Borghese (1803). >> Napoleon I

Bonaventure or **Bonaventura, St** [bonavencher], known as **Doctor Seraphicus** ('Seraphic Doctor'), originally **Giovanni di Fidanza** (c.1221–74), feast day 15 July. Theologian, born near Orvieto, Italy. He became a Franciscan (1243), general of his order (1257), and Cardinal Bishop of Albano (1273). He was canonized in 1482.

Bond, Alan (1938–) Businessman, born in London. He emigrated in 1951 to Australia, where he developed the Bond Corporation. After the fall of his empire in the late 1980s he was convicted for dishonest business dealings with a merchant bank, but later acquitted.

Bond, Edward (1934–) Playwright and director, born in London. His early plays, such as *Saved* (1965), were notorious for their use of violence to portray contemporary society. Later plays include *Lear* (1971) and *Olly's Prison* (1991).

Bond, (Thomas) Michael (1926–) Writer of children's stories, born in Berkshire. He created the character of Paddington Bear (1958), who has since featured in many books, as well as in a television cartoon series.

Bondfield, Margaret Grace (1873–1953) Trade unionist and Labour stateswoman, born in Chard, Somerset. She became chairman of the TUC in 1923 and as minister of labour (1929–31) was the first woman to be a British cabinet minister.

Bondi, Sir Hermann (1919–) Mathematical physicist and astronomer, born in Vienna. He became director-general of the European Space Research Organisation (1967–71), and was one of the originators of the steady-state theory of the universe.

Bone, Henry (1755–1834) Enamel painter, born in Truro, Cornwall. In London he enamelled watches and fans, and made enamel portraits, brooches, and other ornaments.

Bone, Sir Muirhead (1876–1953) Artist, born in Glasgow, Strathclyde. During a long career he made over 500 etchings, drypoints, and lithographs, besides many thousands of drawings and watercolours.

Boner, Ulrich [boner] (c.1300–49) Swiss writer of fables. A Dominican friar in Bern from 1324, his *Edelstein*, a collection of fables and jokes, was one of the first German books printed, in 1461.

Bong, Richard (Ira) (1920–45) Aviator, born in Superior, WI. The greatest US fighter ace of World War 2, he shot down 40 Japanese aircraft in three combat tours in the Southwest Pacific (1942–4).

Bongo, Omar, originally **Albert-Bernard Bongo** (1935–) Gabonese president (1967–), born in Lewai, Gabon. In 1968 he created a one-party state based on the Gabonese Democratic Party, and in 1973 announced his conversion to Islam, adopting the name Omar.

Bonham-Carter (of Yarnbury), Mark Raymond Bonham-Carter, Baron [bonam] (1922–94) Administrator, the son of Violet Bonham-Carter. His posts included director of the Royal Opera House (1958–82), first chairman of the Race Relations Board (1966–70), and chairman of the Community Relations Commission (1971–7). >> Bonham-Carter, Violet

Bonham-Carter, Lady Violet, Baroness Asquith of Yarnbury [bonam] (1887–1969) English Liberal politician and publicist, the daughter of H H Asquith by his first marriage. In 1915 she married Sir Maurice Bonham-Carter (d.1960). >> Asquith; Bonham-Carter, Mark

Bonhoeffer, Dietrich [bonhoefer] (1906–45) Lutheran pastor and theologian, and opponent of Nazism, born in Breslau, Germany. Deeply involved in the German resistance movement, he was arrested (1943), imprisoned, and hanged.

Boniface, St [bonifas], originally **Wynfrith**, known as **the Apostle of Germany** (c.680–c.754), feast day 5 June. Anglo-

Saxon Benedictine missionary, born in Wessex, England. He set out in 718 to preach the Gospel to German tribes, and became Primate of Germany in 732. He was killed at Dokkum by heathens.

Boniface, St (970–1009) >> **Bruno, St**

Boniface VIII [bonifas], originally **Benedetto Caetani** (c.1235–1303) Pope (1294–1303), born in Anagni, Italy. He tried to reassert papal superiority over temporal powers, particularly those of England and France. A period of captivity by the French led to the papacy taking up residence at Avignon.

Bonington, Sir Chris(tian John Storey) (1934–) Mountaineer, born in London. He was a member of the first British team that conquered the N face of the Eiger (1962), and later climbed Annapurna South Face (1970) and Everest (1972, 1975 SW face).

Bonington, Richard Parkes (1802–28) Painter, born near Nottingham, Nottinghamshire. In France from c.1817, he excelled in light effects, as seen in his landscapes and seascapes in oils and watercolours.

Bonnard, Abel [bonah(r)] (1883–1968) Poet, novelist, and essayist, born in Poitiers, France. He won the national poetry prize with his first collection of poems, *Les Familiers* (1906), and took up the psychological novel with *Life and Love* (trans, 1913).

Bonnard, Pierre [bonah(r)] (1867–1947) Painter and lithographer, born in Paris. He joined the group called *Les Nabis*, which included Denis and Vuillard, with whom he formed the Intimist group. >> **Denis, Maurice; Vuillard**

Bonner, Edmund (c.1500–69) English clergyman and bishop. He became Bishop of London (1540), but was imprisoned (1549–53) for refusing to recognize royal supremacy during the minority of Edward VI. He was restored to office under Mary I, but imprisoned under Elizabeth I. >> **Edward VI; Elizabeth I; Mary I**

Bonner, James (Frederick) (1910–) Molecular biologist, born in Ansley, NE. Early research on ribosomes led to major contributions to studies of messenger RNA.

Bonner, Neville Thomas (1922–) Australian politician, born in Tweed Heads, New South Wales, Australia. He became the first Aboriginal member of the Australian parliament in 1971, and in 1972 was elected Liberal representative for Queensland.

Bonner, Yelena (1923–) Civil rights campaigner, born in Moscow. She married Andrei Sakharov (1971), resigned from the Soviet Communist Party (1972), and went on with her husband to lead the Soviet dissident movement. >> **Sakharov**

Bonnet, Charles (Etienne) [bonay] (1720–93) Naturalist and philosopher, born in Geneva, Switzerland. He is known for his discovery of parthenogenesis, and for his 'catastrophic' theory of evolution.

Bonney, William H, Jr, known as **Billy the Kid**, originally (?)**Henry McCarty** (1859–81) Bandit and gunfighter, born in New York City. A killer from the age of 12, he achieved legendary notoriety for his robberies in the SW. He was finally tracked down and shot by Sheriff Pat Garrett. >> **Garrett, Pat**

Bonnie and Clyde Notorious robbery partners: **Clyde Barrow** (1909–34), born in Telico, TX, and **Bonnie Parker** (1911–34), born in Rowena, TX. The pair met in 1932. With their gang, they committed a number of robberies and murders. They were shot dead at a police road-block in Louisiana.

Bonnie Prince Charlie >> **Stuart, Charles**

Bono, Edward de >> **de Bono, Edward**

Bono, Emilio de >> **de Bono, Emilio**

Bononcini or **Buononcini, Giovanni (Maria)** [bononcheenee] (1642–78) Composer, born near Modena, Italy. He published much chamber and vocal music, together with an influential treatise, the *Musico prattico*. His sons

Giovanni Battista Bononcini (1670–1755) and **Marc Antonio Bononcini** (1675–1726) were also notable composers.

Bony, Jean [bonee] (1908–) Architectural historian, born in Le Mans, France. His publications include *The English Decorated Style* (1979) and *French Gothic Architecture of the 12th and 13th Centuries* (1983).

Boole, George (1815–64) Mathematician and logician, born in Lincoln, Lincolnshire. He is best known for his *Mathematical Analysis of Logic* (1847) and *Laws of Thought* (1854), employing mathematical symbolism to express logical processes (*Boolean algebra*).

Boone, Daniel (c.1734–1820) Legendary pioneer, born in Berks Co, PA. He made a trail through the Cumberland Gap (1767) and became one of the first to explore Kentucky (1769–73). Twice captured by Indians, he repeatedly repelled Indian attacks on his stockade fort, now Boonesboro.

Boorman, John (1933–) Film director, born in Shepperton, Surrey. His films include *Catch Us if You Can* (1965), *Deliverance* (1972), and *Hope and Glory* (1987).

Boorstin, Daniel J(oseph) (1914–) Writer, lawyer, academic, and librarian, born in Atlanta, GA. His major works include *The Americans* trilogy (1958, 1965, 1973) and *The Discoverers* (1983).

Boot, Harry >> **Randall, John**

Boot, Sir Jesse, Baron Trent (1850–1931) Drug manufacturer, born in Nottingham, Nottinghamshire. In 1877 he opened his first chemist's shop in Nottingham, and by 1900 had built up the largest pharmaceutical retail trade in the world.

Booth, Charles (1840–1916) Shipowner, statistician, and social reformer, born in Liverpool, Merseyside. He spent 18 years preparing his great *Life and Labour of the People in London* (17 vols, 1902), the prototype of the modern social survey.

Booth, Edwin (Thomas) (1833–93) Actor, born in Harford County, MD, the brother of John Wilkes Booth. He was best known for his Shakespearean roles, notably *Hamlet* (1864), which he produced in New York City for a record run. >> **Booth, John Wilkes**

Booth, Hubert Cecil (1871–1955) British engineer. In 1900 he demonstrated the principle of cleaning carpets by suction, and in 1901 patented an electrically powered machine called a 'vacuum cleaner'.

Booth, John Wilkes (1839–65) Assassin, born near Bel Air, MD, the brother of Edwin Thomas Booth. He became an actor and was popular in the South. In 1865 he joined a conspiracy to avenge the defeat of the Confederates, and shot President Lincoln at Ford's Theatre, Washington, DC. He fled to Virginia, but was tracked down and shot. >> **Booth, Edwin; Lincoln**

Booth, William (1829–1912) Founder and 'general' of the Salvation Army, born in Nottingham, Nottinghamshire. In 1865 he founded the Army (so named in 1878) on military lines with mission work in London's East End. His wife, **Catherine Booth** (1829–90), was fully associated with him, and his first son **Bramwell Booth** (1856–1929) and daughters **Kate Booth** (1859–1955) and **Evangeline Booth** (1865–1950) succeeded him in the work.

Boothby (of Buchan and Rattray Head), Sir Robert (John Graham) Boothby, Baron (1900–86) Politician, born in Edinburgh. He served as Conservative MP for East Aberdeenshire (1924–58), was parliamentary private secretary to Winston Churchill (1926–9), and became well known as a commentator on public affairs on radio and TV.

Boothe, Clare >> **Luce, Clare Boothe**

Bopp, Franz (1791–1867) Philologist, born in Mainz, Germany. His greatest work is *A Comparative Grammar of Sanskrit, Zend, Greek, Latin, Lithuanian, Old Slavonic, Gothic and German* (trans, 6 vols, 1833–52).

Bór, General >> **Komorowski, Tadeusz**

Bora, Katherine von (1499–1552) German nun. Having adopted Lutheran doctrines, she ran away from the Cistercian convent of Nimptschen in 1523, and married Martin Luther in 1525. >> Luther

Borah, William E(dgar) (1865–1940) US politician, born in Fairfield, IL. Elected Republican senator for Idaho in 1906, he advocated disarmament, and was instrumental in blocking the United States' entry into the League of Nations.

Bordeaux, Henri [baw(r)doh] (1870–1963) Writer, born in Thonon, France. His novels are concerned with the defence of family life, often with a Savoy background, such as *Les Roquevillard* (1906) and *La Maison* (1913).

Borden, Lizzie (Andrew) (1860–1927) Alleged murderess, born in Fall River, MA. In one of the most sensational murder trials in US history, she was accused of murdering her father and step-mother with an axe in 1892, but was acquitted.

Borden, Sir Robert (Laird) (1854–1937) Canadian prime minister (1911–20), born in Grand Pré, Nova Scotia, Canada. He became leader of the Conservative Party (1901), and overthrew the Liberal government over the issue of reciprocity with the USA.

Border, Allan (Robert) (1955–) Cricketer, born in Sydney, New South Wales, Australia. Australia's most prolific batsman, he is the highest run-scorer in the history of Test cricket, retiring in 1994 with a record 11 174 runs.

Bordet, Jules (Jean Baptiste Vincent) [baw(r)day] (1870–1961) Physiologist, born in Soignies, Belgium. His discoveries include the immunity factors in blood serum, alexine, and the microbe responsible for whooping cough. He was awarded the Nobel Prize for Physiology or Medicine in 1919.

Bordone, Paris [baw(r)dohnay] (1500–71) Painter of the Venetian school, born in Treviso, Italy. His most celebrated work is 'Fisherman presenting the Ring of St Mark to the Doge' (1540).

Borel, (Félix Edouard Justin) Emile [borel] (1871–1956) Mathematician and French statesman, born in Saint Affrique, France. His mathematical work was mainly in analysis, measure theory, and probability. He was appointed minister for the navy (1925–40).

Boreman, Arthur I(ngram) (1823–96) US Republican governor and senator, born in Waynesburg, PA. He led the Wheeling Convention (1861) to establish a pro-union government in West Virginia, becoming the first governor (1863–9) of the new state.

Borg, Björn (Rune) (1956–) Tennis player, born in Södertälje, Sweden. He became Wimbledon singles champion five times (1976–80), a modern-day record, losing to McEnroe in the 1981 final. He also won the French singles title six times, and was the World Championship Tennis singles champion in 1976. >> McEnroe

Borge, Victor [baw(r)guh] (1909–) Entertainer and pianist, born in Denmark. Since 1940 he has worked in the USA for radio, television, and theatre, best known for his comedy sketches combining music and narrative.

Borges, Jorge Luis [baw(r)khes] (1899–1986) Writer, born in Buenos Aires. From 1918 he lived in Spain, where he joined the avant-garde Ultraist literary group, returning to Argentina in 1921. From 1941 he wrote mainly short stories, including *Fictions* (trans, 1945) and *The Aleph* (trans, 1949).

Borgia, Cesare [baw(r)ja] (c.1476–1507) Italian soldier, probably born in Rome, the illegitimate son of Cardinal Rodrigo Borgia (later Pope Alexander VI). In 1499 he became captain-general of the papal army, and fought to establish his own kingdom in central Italy. >> Alexander VI; Borgia, Lucrezia

Borgia, Lucrezia [baw(r)ja] (1480–1519) Noblewoman,

born in Rome, the illegitimate daughter of Cardinal Rodrigo Borgia (later Pope Alexander VI). In 1501 she married her third husband, **Alfonso** (1486–1534), son of the Duke of Este, and lived with him at Ferrara, where she established a brilliant court of artists and men of letters. >> Alexander VI; Borgia, Cesare

Borgia, Rodrigo >> **Alexander VI**

Borglum, (John) Gutzon (de la Mothe) [baw(r)gluhm] (1867–1941) Sculptor, born in St Charles, ID. He won renown for his colossal works, such as the Mt Rushmore National Memorial, hewn out of the mountainside (1939), and the head of Lincoln in the US Capitol Rotunda.

Bork, Robert H(eron) (1927–) Legal scholar and judge, born in Pittsburg, PA. He became US solicitor general (1971–7), and was nominated to the Supreme Court in 1987, but his conservative views led to his being rejected in a controversial US Senate vote.

Borlaug, Norman (Ernest) [baw(r)log] (1914–) Agricultural scientist, born in Cresco, IA. He developed strains of grain that greatly increased crop production, notably the tripling of Mexico's wheat yields, and made possible the 'green revolution'. He was awarded the Nobel Peace Prize in 1970.

Borman, Frank (1928–) Astronaut, born in Gary, IN. He was crew member of two historic missions: the Gemini 7 space endurance flight (1965) and the first manned flight around the Moon in Apollo 8 (1968).

Bormann, Martin (1900–?45) Nazi politician, born in Halberstadt, Germany. One of Hitler's closest advisers, he became *Reichsminister* (1941) after Hess's flight to Scotland, and was with Hitler to the last, though his own fate is uncertain. >> Hitler

Born, Max (1882–1970) Physicist, born in Breslau, Germany (now Wrocsaw, Poland). Professor of natural philosophy at Edinburgh (1936–53), in 1954 he shared the Nobel Prize for Physics with Walter Bothe for work in the field of quantum physics. >> Bothe

Borodin, Alexander Porfiryevich [borodeen] (1833–87) Composer and scientist, born in St Petersburg, Russia. His compositions include the unfinished opera, *Prince Igor*, three symphonies, and the symphonic sketch *In the Steppes of Central Asia*.

Borotra, Jean, nickname **the Bounding Basque** (1898–1994) Tennis player, born in Arbonne, near Biarritz, France. Among several achievements, he won the men's singles title at Wimbledon in 1924, and continued to compete in veterans' events until he was almost 80.

Borovansky, Edouard [borovanskee] (1902–59) Dancer, choreographer, and ballet director, born in Přerov, Czech Republic. A soloist in the Ballet Russe de Monte Carlo (1932–9), he stayed on in Melbourne during an Australian tour, opening a ballet school with his wife in 1940, which later became the Borovansky Ballet.

Borromeo, St Charles [boromayoh] (1538–84), feast day 4 November. Cardinal and archbishop, born in Arona, Italy. He did much to bring the Council of Trent (1545–63) to a successful conclusion, and in 1578 founded the community later known as the Oblates of St Ambrose. He was canonized in 1610.

Borromini, Francesco [boromeenee], originally **Francesco Castello** (1599–1667) Baroque architect and sculptor, born in Bissone, Italy. He spent all his working life in Rome, where his chief designs include the S Carlo alle Quattro Fontane (1641) and the oratorio of S Philippo Neri (1650).

Borrow, George (Henry) (1803–81) Writer and traveller, born in East Dereham, Norfolk. From 1825 to 1832 he wandered in England, sometimes in gypsy company, as described in *Lavengro* (1851) and *The Romany Rye* (1857). As agent of the Bible Society he visited many European countries.

Boru >> Brian

Borzov, Valeri [baw(r)zof] (1949–) Athlete, born in Sambor, Ukraine. At the 1972 Olympic Games in Munich he won both the 100 m and 200 m sprints, beating the Americans in what had become their monopoly events.

Bosch, Carl [bosh] (1874–1940) Chemist, born in Cologne, Germany, the brother-in-law of Fritz Haber. He shared the Nobel Prize for Chemistry in 1931 for the development of chemical high-pressure methods, notably the *Haber–Bosch process*, by which hydrogen is obtained from water gas and superheated steam. >> Haber

Bosch, Hieronymus, originally **Jerome van Aken** (c.1450–1516) Painter, born in 's Hertogenbosch, The Netherlands. Noted for his allegorical pictures displaying macabre devils, freaks, and monsters, his best-known works include 'The Garden of Earthly Delights' (Prado) and 'The Temptation of St Anthony' (Lisbon).

Bose, Sir Jagadis Chandra [bohs] (1858–1937) Physicist and botanist, born in Mymensingh, India. Founder of the Bose Research Institute in Calcutta (1917–37), he was known for his study of electric waves, and for his experiments demonstrating the sensitivity and growth of plants.

Bose, Subhas Chandra [bohs], known as **Netaji** ('Respected Leader') (c.1897–?1945) Indian Nationalist leader, born in Cuttack, Orissa, India. Frequently imprisoned, he became president of the All-India Congress (1938–9). Commander-in-chief of the Japanese-sponsored Indian National Army, he was reported killed in Formosa.

Bosman, Herman Charles (1905–51) Short-story writer, essayist, and novelist, born in Kuils River, near Cape Town, South Africa. He wrote short stories about rural Afrikaners, the prison memoir, *Cold Stone Jug* (1949), and two novels.

Bossuet, Jacques Bénigne [bosway] (1627–1704) Catholic churchman and pulpit orator, born in Dijon, France. As Bishop of Meaux (1681) he took a leading part in the Gallican controversy, asserting the king's independence from Rome in secular matters.

Boston, Ralph (1939–) Athlete, born in Laurel, MS. A leading long-jumper of the 1960s, he established an unusual treble by winning the gold medal at the 1960 Rome Olympics, a silver at Tokyo in 1964, and a bronze at Mexico City in 1968.

Boston Strangler >> Desalvo, Albert

Boswell, James (1740–95) Man of letters, born in Edinburgh. He met Dr Johnson in 1763, and took him on a journey to the Hebrides. The success of *Journal of a Tour to the Hebrides* (1785) led him to plan his masterpiece, the *Life of Samuel Johnson* (1791). >> Johnson, Samuel

Bosworth, Joseph (1789–1876) Philologist, born in Derbyshire. He compiled *An Anglo-Saxon Dictionary* (1838), and in 1867 gave £10 000 to endow a chair of Anglo-Saxon at Cambridge.

Both, Andries (c.1612–41) Painter, born in Utrecht, The Netherlands, the brother of Jan Both. Traditionally he was thought to have painted the figures in Jan's landscapes, but is now recognized as the author of genre scenes more akin to the work of Brouwer. >> Both, Jan; Brouwer

Both, Jan [bot] (c.1618–52) Painter, born in Utrecht, The Netherlands, the brother of Andries Both. He lived in Italy (1638–41), where he painted picturesque views of the Roman countryside. >> Both, Andries

Botha, Louis [bohta] (1862–1919) South African soldier, statesman, and prime minister (1910–19), born in Greytown, Natal, South Africa. In 1907 he became prime minister of the Transvaal colony under the new constitution, and in 1910 the first premier of the Union of South Africa.

Botha, P(ieter) W(illem) [bohta] (1916–) South African statesman, prime minister (1978–84), and first state president (1984–9), born in Paul Roux, Orange Free State, South Africa. He attempted to introduce constitutional reforms, involving limited power-sharing with non-whites, but this led to a right-wing defection in 1982 from his ruling National Party.

Botha, Roelof Frederik [bohta], known as **Pik Botha** (1932–) South African politician. He served as foreign minister under P W Botha and F W de Klerk, and in 1994 was appointed minister for minerals and energy in President Mandela's first cabinet. >> Botha, P W; de Klerk; Mandela, Nelson

Botham, Ian (Terence) [bohtham] (1955–) Cricketer, born in Heswall, Cheshire. An all-rounder, he played for England in 102 Test matches, scored 5200 runs, took 383 wickets, and held 120 catches. He retired from first class-cricket in 1993.

Bothe, Walther (Wilhelm Georg) [bohtuh] (1891–1957) Physicist, born in Oranienburg, Germany. For his work on the development of coincidence technique in counting processes, he shared the Nobel Prize for Physics in 1954.

Bothwell, James Hepburn, 4th Earl of (c.1535–78) Third husband of Mary, Queen of Scots. He was held responsible for the abduction and murder of Mary's second husband, Lord Darnley (1567). He was made Duke of Orkney, then married Mary, but fled to Denmark after her surrender to rebel forces. >> Darnley; Mary, Queen of Scots

Botolph, St, feast day 17 June. (?–c.680) Saxon abbot. He founded a monastery in 654 in Icanhoe (Ox Island), usually identified as Boston ('Botolph's Stone') in Lincolnshire.

Bottesini, Giovanni [boteseenee] (1821–89) Musician, born in Crema, Italy. A master of the double bass, he was also successful as a conductor and composer, and his works include symphonies, overtures, and several operas.

Botticelli, Sandro [botichelee], originally **Alessandro Filipepi** (1445–1510) Painter, born in Florence, Italy. He produced mostly religious works, but is best known for his mythological subjects, notably 'Spring' (c.1477) and the 'Birth of Venus' (c.1485), both in the Uffizi.

Bottomley, Gordon (1874–1948) Poet and playwright, born in Keighley, West Yorkshire. He is best remembered for his *Poems of Thirty Years* (1925) and his collections of plays, including *King Lear's Wife and Other Plays* (1920).

Botvinnik, Mikhail Moiseyevich [botveenik] (1911–95) Chess player, world champion (1948–57, 1958–60, 1961–3), born in St Petersburg, Russia. He won the 1948 tournament following the death of Alekhine. After regaining his title twice, he lost in 1963 to Petrosian. >> Alekhine; Petrosian

Boucher, François [booshay] (1703–70) Painter, born in Paris. He is recognized as a leading exponent of the Rococo style in painting, known for his mythological and pastoral scenes, his female nudes, and his portraits of Madame de Pompadour.

Boucher (de Crèvecoeur) de Perthes, Jacques [booshay duh pairt] (1788–1868) Archaeologist, born in Rethel, France. From 1837 in the Somme valley he discovered flint hand axes and the bones of extinct animals, from which he drew conclusions about the great antiquity of the human race.

Boucicault, Dion [booseekolt, -koh], originally **Dionysius Lardner Boursiquot** (1820–90) Playwright, actor, and theatre manager, born in Dublin. A versatile theatrical personality, he wrote or adapted some 130 plays. He went to America in 1853, where he worked to pass the first American Copyright Law of 1856.

Boudicca [boodika, boodika], also known as **Boadicea** (1st-c AD) British warrior-queen, wife of Prasutagus, king of the Iceni. Her army took Londinium and Verulamium, and put to death as many as 70 000 Romans. Defeated in battle by Suetonius Paulinus, she took poison.

Boudin, (Louis) Eugène [boodĩ] (1824–98) Painter, born in Honfleur, France. A precursor of Impressionism, he is noted for his seascapes, such as 'On the Beach of Deauville' (1869).

Bougainville, Louis Antoine, comte de (Count of) [booganveel] (1729–1811) Navigator, born in Paris. He led the first French circumnavigation of the world (1766–9), described in *A Voyage Round the World* (trans, 1771). The largest of the Solomon Is is named after him, as is the plant *bougainvillea*.

Boughton, Rutland (1878–1960) Composer, born in Aylesbury, Buckinghamshire. He founded the Glastonbury Festival (1914–26). His works include the opera *The Immortal Hour* (1913), a choral drama *Bethlehem* (1915), and other stage, choral, and instrumental works.

Bouguer, Pierre [boohgair] (1698–1758) Physicist, born in Le Croisie, France. His views on the intensity of light laid the foundation of photometry, and in 1748 he invented the heliometer.

Bouillon, Godfrey of >> **Godfrey of Bouillon**

Boulanger, Georges (Ernest Jean Marie) [boolãzhay] (1837–91) French soldier and statesman, born in Rennes, France. In 1886 he became minister of war, introduced reforms, and became a popular national figure. He lost office in 1887, demanded a revision of the constitution, and was forced to flee the country.

Boulanger, Nadia [boolãzhay] (1887–1979) Composer and teacher of music, born in Paris. She wrote many vocal and instrumental works, and was also a noted organist and conductor.

Boule, (Pierre) Marcellin [bool] (1861–1942) Palaeontologist, born in Montsalvy, France. He worked on the geology of the mountains of C France, and on human fossils, making the first complete reconstruction of a Neanderthal skeleton.

Boulez, Pierre [boolez] (1925–) Conductor and composer, born in Montbrison, France. He was conductor of the BBC Symphony Orchestra (1971–5) and of the New York Philharmonic (1971–7), and in 1977 took up a post at the Pompidou Centre in Paris.

Boulle, André Charles >> **Buhl, André Charles**

Boullée, Etienne-Louis [boolay] (1728–99) Architect, born in Paris. An important figure in the development of Neoclassicism in France, his visionary designs include a colossal spherical monument to Isaac Newton (1784).

Boult, Sir Adrian (Cedric) [bohlt] (1889–1983) Conductor, born in Chester, Cheshire. He became musical director of the BBC, conductor of the newly formed BBC Symphony Orchestra, and conductor-in-chief of the London Philharmonic Orchestra until 1957.

Boulton, Matthew [bohltn] (1728–1809) Engineer, born in Birmingham, West Midlands. He opened a manufacturing works at Birmingham in 1762, entered into partnership with Watt, and established a firm manufacturing steam engines. >> **Watt, James**

Boumédienne, Houari [boomaydyen], originally **Mohammed Boukharrouba** (1927–78) Algerian soldier and president (1965–78), born in Guelma, Algeria. When Algeria gained independence in 1962, he became minister of national defence. In 1965 he led a military coup against President Ben Bella and established an Islamic socialist government. >> **Ben Bella**

Bourbon, Charles de [boorbõ], known as **Constable de Bourbon** (1490–1527) French soldier and statesman. For his bravery at Marignano (1515) he was made Constable of France; but losing the favour of Francis I he concluded a private alliance with Emperor Charles V and Henry VIII of England. >> **Francis I**

Bourchier, Thomas [boorshyay] (c.1404–1486) English statesman and clergyman, an important figure during the Wars of the Roses. He became Archbishop of Canterbury (1454) and a cardinal (1473), and also Lord Chancellor (1455–6).

Bourdelle, (Emile) Antoine [boordel] (1861–1929) Sculptor and painter, born in Montauban, France. His style found inspiration in Greek art. He illustrated a number of books, and his teaching was influential.

Bourdon, Eugène [boordõ] (1808–84) Inventor and industrialist, born in Paris. In 1849 he patented a device which is still used today for measuring the pressure of steam and many other fluids, the *Bourdon gauge*.

Bourgeois, Jeanne >> **Mistinguett**

Bourget, Paul (Charles Joseph) [boorzhay] (1852–1935) Writer, born in Amiens, France. His novels include *L'Irréparable* (1884) and *Un Divorce* (1904). In later years he became better known for his critical works.

Bourguiba, Habib (ibn Ali) [boorgeeba] (1903–) Tunisian prime minister (1956–7) and president (1957–87), born in Monastir, Tunisia. In 1983–4 Islamic fundamentalists instigated riots, rendering his policies ineffective, and he was deposed in 1987.

Bourignon, Antoinette [booreenyõ] (1616–80) Religious mystic, born in Lille, France. Believing herself called to restore the pure spirit of the Gospel, she entered a convent, gathering many followers. *Bourignonism* became prevalent in Scotland c.1720–c.1889.

Bourke-White, Margaret [berk], originally **Margaret White** (1906–71) Photo-journalist, born in New York City. As staff photographer and associate editor on *Life* magazine, she covered World War 2, and was the first woman photographer to be attached to the US armed forces.

Bourne, Francis Alphonsus [baw(r)n] (1861–1935) Prelate, born in London. Cardinal Archbishop of Westminster, he is remembered for his zeal for education, and for his organization of the International Eucharistic Congress in 1908.

Bourne, Hugh [baw(r)n] (1772–1852) Preacher, born in Fordhays, Staffordshire. Opposition to his large open-air meetings led to a split with the Wesleyans in 1808. He formed a new group, adopting the title of Primitive Methodists (or 'Ranters') in 1810.

Bournonville, August [boornõveel] (1805–79) Dancer and choreographer, born in Copenhagen. From 1828 he worked with the Royal Danish Ballet as a dancer and (from 1830) as director.

Boussingault, Jean-Baptiste (Joseph) [boosĩgoh] (1802–87) Agricultural chemist, born in Paris. He demonstrated that plants absorb nitrogen from the soil, and showed that carbon is assimilated by plants from the carbon dioxide of the atmosphere.

Boutros Ghali, Boutros [galee] (1922–) Egyptian diplomat. He took office as the sixth secretary-general of the United Nations in 1992.

Bouts, Dierick [bowts], also spelled **Dirk**, or **Thierry** (c.1415–75) Painter, born in Haarlem, The Netherlands. He produced austere religious paintings with rich and gem-like colour, his best-known work being 'The Last Supper' (Louvain).

Boveri, Theodor Heinrich [bõveree] (1862–1915) Biologist and pioneer of cytology, born in Bamberg, Germany. His studies showed that normal development requires an appropriate number of chromosomes for the species, and that chromosome deficiency leads to abnormality.

Bovet, Daniel [bohvay] (1907–92) Pharmacologist, born in Neuchâtel, Switzerland. He developed the first antihistamine drug and the first synthetic muscle-relaxants, for which he was awarded the Nobel Prize for Physiology or Medicine in 1957.

Bow, Clara [boh] (1905–65) Film actress, born in New York

City. After winning a beauty contest at 17, she went on to Hollywood stardom in silent films, becoming popularly known as 'the It Girl'.

Bowditch, Henry (Pickering) (1840–1911) Physiologist, born in Boston, MA. He produced important experimental work on cardiac contraction, on the innervation of the heart, and on the reflexes.

Bowditch, Nathaniel (1773–1838) Astronomer and mathematician, born in Salem, MA. He greatly contributed to the *New American Practical Navigator* (1802), the 'seaman's bible', and provided a translation and commentary of Laplace's *Celestial Mechanics* (1829–39). >> Laplace

Bowdler, Thomas [bowdler] (1754–1825) Doctor and man of letters, born in Ashley, Somerset. He is immortalized as the editor of *The Family Shakespeare* (10 vols, 1818), in which 'those words and expressions are omitted which cannot with propriety be read aloud in a family'. *Bowdlerizing* has since become a synonym for prudish expurgation.

Bowen, Elizabeth (Dorothea Cole) (1899–1973) Writer, born in Dublin. Her works include collections of short stories, and the novels *The Death of the Heart* (1938) and *The Heat of the Day* (1949).

Bowen, Norman L(evi) (1887–1956) Geologist, born in Kingston, Ontario, Canada. He was a pioneer in the field of experimental petrology, particularly the study of silicates and igneous rocks.

Bowes-Lyon, Elizabeth >> **Elizabeth** (Queen Mother)

Bowie, David [bowee], originally **David Robert Jones** (1947–) Rock singer, born in London. His albums include *The Rise and Fall of Ziggy Stardust and the Spiders from Mars* (1972) and *Heroes* (1977). He has also acted in films, including *The Man Who Fell to Earth* (1976) and *Labyrinth* (1986).

Bowie, Jim [booee, bohee], popular name of **James Bowie** (c.1796–1836) US pioneer, born in Logan Co, KY. As a colonel in the Texan army, he was killed at the Battle of the Alamo. He may have been the inventor of the curved dagger or sheath-knife named after him.

Bowlby, (Edward) John (Mostyn) [bohlbee] (1907–90) British psychiatrist. He is best known for his work on the effects of maternal deprivation upon the mental health and emotional development of children.

Bowles, Paul (Frederick) [bohlz] (1910–) Writer and composer, born in New York City. His novels include *The Sheltering Sky* (1949) and *Up Above the World* (1966). He was also a translator and music critic.

Bowles, William Lisle [bohlz] (1762–1850) Clergyman and poet, born in King's Sutton, Northamptonshire. A forerunner of the Romantic movement in English poetry, he is known for *Fourteen Sonnets, Written Chiefly on Picturesque Spots During a Journey* (1789).

Bowman, Isaiah (1878–1950) Geographer, born in Waterloo, Ontario, Canada. He was director of the American Geographical Society (1915–35), and was appointed chief territorial specialist at the Versailles Peace Conference.

Bowman, Sir William (1816–92) Physician and ophthalmic surgeon, born in Nantwich, Cheshire. With **Richard B Todd** (1809–60) he published *Physiological Anatomy and Physiology of Man* (1845–56), and was noted for his work on the mechanism of kidney function.

Bowyer, William (1699–1777) Printer and Classical scholar. In 1722 he went into partnership with his father, **William Bowyer** (1663–1737), and in 1767 was nominated printer to the Houses of Parliament.

Boyce, William (1710–79) Composer, born in London. He composed choral and orchestral music, including the song 'Hearts of Oak', the serenata of *Solomon* (1743), and a valuable collection of *Cathedral Music* (1760).

Boycott, Charles Cunningham (1832–97) British soldier, born in Burgh St Peter, Norfolk. As a land agent, he was one of the first victims in 1880 of Parnell's system of social excommunication. His name is the source of the word 'boycott' in English.

Boycott, Geoffrey (1940–) Cricketer and broadcaster, born in Fitzwilliam, West Yorkshire. In 1981 he overtook Sobers' world record of 8032 Test runs, and in 108 Tests for England scored 8114 runs. Captain of Yorkshire (1971–8), he retired from first-class cricket in 1986. >> Sobers

Boyd, Anne (1946–) Composer and flautist, born in Sydney, New South Wales, Australia. Her interest in the ethnic music of Australia, Japan, and Java is reflected in such compositions as *As I Crossed the Bridge of Dreams* and her children's opera, *The Little Mermaid*.

Boyd, Arthur Merric (1862–1940) Painter, born in Opoho, New Zealand. He arrived in Australia in 1886, and became particularly known for his watercolours. >> Boyd, Martin / Merric

Boyd, Arthur Merric Bloomfield (1920–) Painter, sculptor, and potter, born in Murrumbeena, Victoria, Australia, the younger son of Merric Boyd. He worked for several years in Murrumbeena at the pottery established by his father. >> Boyd, Guy Martin / Merric

Boyd, Benjamin (c.1796–1851) Australian colonist, born at Merton Hall, near Newton Stewart, Dumfries and Galloway. He arrived in Hobson's Bay in 1842, and became one of the most powerful squatters in SE New South Wales. He left in 1849 to join the Gold Rush in California.

Boyd, Guy Martin (à Beckett) (1923–) Sculptor, born in Murrumbeena, Victoria, Australia, the elder son of Merric Boyd. His commissions include mural reliefs for Tullamarine (Melbourne) and Kingsford Smith (Sydney) airports. >> Boyd, Arthur Merric Bloomfield / Merric

Boyd, Martin (à Beckett), pseudonyms **Martin Mills** and **Walter Beckett** (1893–1972) Writer and poet, born in Lucerne, Switzerland, the younger son of Arthur Merric Boyd. His novels include *The Cardboard Crown* (1952) and *When Blackbirds Sing* (1962). >> Boyd, Arthur Merric / Merric

Boyd, (William) Merric (1888–1959) Ceramic artist, born in St Kilda, Victoria, Australia, the elder son of Arthur Merric Boyd. In the early 1920s he founded a famous studio at Murrumbeena, outside Melbourne, where he experimented with new ceramic techniques. >> Boyd, Arthur Merric / Arthur Merric Bloomfield / Guy

Boyd, Robin Gerard Penleigh (1919–71) Architect, critic, and writer, born in Melbourne, Victoria, Australia. His critical work, as seen in *The Great Australian Dream* (1972), much influenced the direction of Australian architecture.

Boyd, William (Clouser) (1903–) Biochemist, born in Dearborn, MS. His book *Genetics and the Races of Man* (1950), presented evidence for the existence of 13 human races, distinguishable by blood type.

Boyd Orr (of Brechin Mearns), John Boyd Orr, Baron (1880–1971) Nutritionist, born in Kilmaurs, Strathclyde. He became the first director of the UN Food and Agriculture Organization (1945–8), and for his efforts in improving the world food situation he received the Nobel Peace Prize in 1949.

Boye, Karin (Maria) (1900–41) Poet and novelist, born in Göteborg, Sweden. She became a leader of the Socialist *Clarté* movement, and founder editor of the poetry magazine *Spektrum* (1931).

Boyer, Charles [boyay] (1899–1978) Actor, born in Figeac, France. A star of the French stage and cinema, he settled in Hollywood in 1934, and was known as the screen's 'greatest lover' from such romantic roles as *Mayerling* (1936) and *Algiers* (1938).

Boyer, Herbert (Wayne) [boyer] (1936–) Biochemist, born in Pittsburgh, PA. In collaboration with **Stanley Cohen** (1935–), he successfully spliced a gene from a plasmid of one organism into the plasmid of another (1973), the technique becoming the foundation of genetic engineering.

Boyer, Jean Pierre [boyay] (1776–1850) Haitian politician, mulatto-born in Port-au-Prince. He established an independent republic, but his partiality towards the mulattos made the pure negroes rise in 1843, and he was forced to flee.

Boyer, Sir Richard (James Fildes) [boyer] (1891–1961) Broadcasting administrator, born in Taree, New South Wales, Australia. Chairman of the independent Australian Broadcasting Company (from 1945), the ABC Lectures were renamed the *Boyer Lectures* after his death.

Boyis, Hector >> Boece, Hector

Boyle, Robert (1627–91) Chemist and natural philosopher, born at Lismore Castle, Co Waterford, Ireland. He carried out experiments on air, vacuum, combustion, and respiration, and in 1662 arrived at *Boyle's law*, which states that the pressure and volume of gas are inversely proportional.

Boyle (of Handsworth), Sir Edward (Charles Gurney) Boyle, Baron (1923–81) British Conservative statesman and educational administrator. He became minister of education (1962–4), and also Vice-Chancellor of Leeds University (1970–81).

Boyle, Jimmy, popular name of **James Boyle** (1944–) Convicted murderer, born in the Gorbals, Glasgow, Strathclyde. In 1973 he participated in a prison rehabilitation programme, wrote his autobiography, *A Sense of Freedom* (1977), and after his release became Scotland's most celebrated reformed criminal.

Boyle, Kay (1902–92) Writer, born in St Paul, MN. She is particularly known for her volumes of short stories, such as *The Smoking Mountain* (1951).

Boys, Sir Charles Vernon (1855–1944) Physicist, born in Wing, Leicestershire. His many inventions include an improved torsion balance, the radiomicrometer, and a calorimeter.

Brabazon (of Tara), John Theodore Cuthbert Moore-Brabazon, Baron (1884–1964) British statesman and aviator, the first holder of a flying licence. He became private parliamentary secretary to Churchill at the War Office, minister of transport (1940), and minister of aircraft production (1941).

Brabham, Jack [brabuhm], popular name of **Sir John Arthur Brabham** (1926–) Motor-racing driver, born in Sydney, New South Wales, Australia. He became Australia's first world champion in 1959, repeating his success in 1960 and 1966.

Brace, Charles Loring (1826–90) Philanthropist and social reformer, born in Litchfield, CT. He founded the Children's Aid Society in 1853, and pioneered philanthropic methods based on self-help.

Bracegirdle, Anne (c.1663–1748) English actress. She was renowned for her beauty, and for her performances (1688–1707) in the plays of Congreve, to whom she is believed to have been married. >> Congreve, William

Bracken, Thomas (1843–98) Poet and journalist, born in Co Monaghan, Ireland. He settled in Dunedin, New Zealand, in 1869, and came to be regarded as the local equivalent of Tennyson or Longfellow, writing the words of the national anthem, 'God Defend New Zealand!'. >> Longfellow; Tennyson

Bradbury, Malcolm (1932–) Writer and critic, born in Sheffield, West Yorkshire. His novels include *Eating People is Wrong* (1959), *Stepping Westward* (1965), *The History Man* (1975, also a television series), and *Rates of Exchange* (1982).

Bradbury, Ray(mond Douglas) (1920–) Writer of science fiction, born in Waukegan, IL. Primarily a short-story writer, his best known stories are *The Day It Rained Forever*, *R Is for Rocket*, and those collected as *The Martian*

Chronicles (1950; filmed 1966). His novels include *Fahrenheit 451* (1953).

Braddock, Edward (1695–1755) British general, born in Perthshire, Tayside. Appointed commander of British troops in North America (1754), he was sent to expel the French from Fort Duquesne (now Pittsburgh), but was defeated and mortally wounded in the battle.

Braddock, James J(oseph), nickname **the Cinderella Man** (1905–74) Boxer, born in New York City. After an unpromising start, he he defeated Max Baer (1909–59) on points for the world heavyweight title in 1935 - a comeback that earned him his nickname.

Braddon, Russell Reading (1921–) Writer, born in Sydney, New South Wales, Australia. He wrote several popular novels, but is best known for his biographies, such as *Cheshire VC* (1954) and *Joan Sutherland* (1962).

Braden, Bernard (1916–93) Radio and television presenter, born in Canada. In England from 1949, he joined the BBC, presenting radio shows such as *Breakfast with Braden*, often with his wife, Barbara Kelly (married 1942), and TV series such as *On the Braden Beat*.

Bradfield, John Job Crew (1867–1943) Civil engineer and designer, born in Sandgate, Queensland, Australia. His designs include the bridge across Sydney Harbour and Sydney's underground electric railway system.

Bradford, William (1590–1657) Colonist, born in Austerfield, Nottinghamshire. In 1620 he joined the Pilgrim Fathers' expedition to the New World, sailing on the *Mayflower*, and in 1621 was elected governor of Plymouth Colony.

Bradlaugh, Charles [bradlaw] (1833–91) Social reformer and free-thinker, born in London. In 1880 he became MP for Northampton but, as an unbeliever, refused to take the parliamentary oath, and was expelled and re-elected regularly until 1886, when he was admitted.

Bradlee, Benjamin (Crowninshield) (1921–) Journalist and writer, born in Boston, MA. He became editor of the *Washington Post* in 1965, and encouraged the investigative journalism which reached its peak in the Watergate scandal. >> Nixon

Bradley, A(ndrew) C(ecil) (1851–1935) Critic, born in Cheltenham, Gloucestershire, the brother of F H Bradley. He became professor of poetry at Oxford (1901–6), and is remembered for his magisterial *Shakespearean Tragedy* (1904). >> Bradley, F H

Bradley, F(rancis) H(erbert) (1846–1924) Philosopher, born in Clapham, Surrey, the brother of A C Bradley. A leading figure in the British idealist movement of the period, his works include *Principles of Logic* (1883) and *Appearance and Reality* (1893). >> Bradley, A C

Bradley, Henry (1845–1923) British philologist and lexicographer. In 1886 he became joint editor of the *Oxford English Dictionary* with Murray, and senior editor in 1915. >> Murray, James

Bradley, Omar N(elson) (1893–1981) US general, born in Clark, MO. In World War 2, he commanded in Tunisia and Sicily, and in 1944 led the US invading armies through France and Germany.

Bradley, James (1693–1762) Astronomer, born in Sherborne, Gloucestershire. He published his discovery of the aberration of light in 1729, providing the first observational proof of the Copernican hypothesis.

Bradman, Sir Don(ald George) (1908–) Cricketer, born in Cootamundra, New South Wales, Australia. He played for Australia (1928–48), and was captain from 1936. His batting records include the highest score (452 not out), and an average of Test matches of 9994 runs per innings.

Bradshaw, George (1801–53) Printer, born in Salford, Greater Manchester. He became a Manchester mapmaker, but is best known for the series of railway guides (*Bradshaws*) which he originated in 1839.

Bradshaw, John (1602–59) Judge, born near Stockport, Cheshire. President at the trial of Charles I (1649), he later became permanent president of the Council of State and Chancellor of the Duchy of Lancaster. >> Charles I (of England)

Bradstreet, Anne, *née* **Dudley** (1612–72) Puritan poet, born probably in Northampton, Northamptonshire. She emigrated with her husband to Massachusetts in 1630, and is acknowledged as the first poet of note in British America.

Brady, Ian (1938–) Convicted murderer, born in Glasgow, Strathclyde. He and his lover **Myra Hindley** (1942–) were described as the 'Moors Murderers' because they buried most of their victims on Saddleworth Moor in the Pennines.

Brady, James Buchanan, nickname **Diamond Jim Brady** (1856–1917) Financier, born in New York City. In 1888 he was employed as the only agent in the USA for the Fox Pressed Steel Car Truck Co of England, accumulating a large fortune.

Brady, Matthew (1799–1826) Bushranger, born in Manchester. Transported to Australia in 1820, he escaped from a penal colony in Van Diemen's Land (now Tasmania), and terrorized the island until he was captured and hanged.

Brady, Matthew (1823–96) Photographer, born near Lake George, NY. He operated a portrait studio in New York City, but gave it up to take on a major project recording the American Civil War with the Union armies.

Bragg, Braxton (1817–76) US general, born in Warrenton, NC. A Confederate commander, he fought in several great battles of the Civil War, notably at Chickamauga.

Bragg, Sir (William) Lawrence (1890–1971) Physicist, born in Adelaide, South Australia, the son of Sir William Bragg. Father and son shared the 1915 Nobel Prize for Physics for their work on X-ray crystallography. >> Bragg, William

Bragg, Mabel Caroline, pseudonym **Watty Piper** (1870–1945) Writer and educator, born in Milford, MA. She became well known for her children's books, notably *The Little Engine That Could* (1945).

Bragg, Melvyn (1939–) Writer, and broadcaster, born in Wigton, Cumbria. His novels include *For Want of a Nail* (1965) and *A Time to Dance* (1990). He has presented ITV's *The South Bank Show* since 1978, and BBC Radio 4's *Start the Week* since 1988.

Bragg, Sir William (Henry) (1862–1942) Physicist, born in Wigton, Cumbria. With his son, William Lawrence Bragg, he founded X-ray crystallography. They were awarded a joint Nobel Prize for Physics in 1915, the only father–son partnership to share this honour. >> Bragg, Lawrence

Brahe, Tycho [brahhoe, tiykoh] (1546–1601) Astronomer, born in Knudstrup, Sweden. In 1573 he discovered serious errors in the astronomical tables, and rectified this by observing the stars and planets with unprecedented positional accuracy.

Brahms, Johannes (1833–97) Composer, born in Hamburg, Germany. He earned his living as a pianist until 1853, when he was able to concentrate on composition. Major works include four symphonies, two piano concertos, a violin concerto, chamber and piano music, and many songs. His greatest choral work is the *German Requiem* (first performed complete in 1869).

Braid, James (?1795–1860) Surgeon and hypnotist, born in Rylawhouse, Fife. He spent much of his working life investigating the phenomena associated with what he called *neurohypnotism* (later *hypnotism*). >> Mesmer, Franz Anton

Braid, James (1870–1950) Golfer, born in Earlsferry, Fife. He won the Open championship five times (1901–10), four

News of the World matchplay championships (1903–11), and the French Championship (1910).

Braille, Louis [brayl] (1809–52) Educationist, born in Coupvray, France. Blind from the age of three, in 1829 he devised a system of raised-point writing which the blind could both read and write.

Brailsford, Henry Noel (1873–1958) Socialist writer and political journalist, born in Yorkshire. He joined the Independent Labour Party in 1907 and edited its weekly publication, *The New Leader* (1922–6).

Brain, Dennis (1921–57) Horn player, born in London. He studied under his father **Aubrey Brain** (1893–1955) at the Royal Academy of Music, then worked with the Royal Philharmonic and Philharmonia Orchestras as chief horn player.

Braine, John (Gerard) (1922–86) Writer, born in Bradford, West Yorkshire. The theme of aggressive ambition and determination to break through social barriers identified him with the 'Angry Young Men' of the 1950s. His novels include *Room at the Top* (1957) and *The Vodi* (1959).

Brainerd, David (1718–47) Presbyterian missionary, born in Haddam, CT. He worked among the American Indians from 1742, and his *Journal* was published posthumously in 1749.

Braithwaite, Edward Kamau (1930–) Poet and academic historian, born in Bridgetown, Barbados. His chief work is contained in *The Arrivants: a New World Trilogy* (1973).

Braithwaite, R(ichard) B(evin) (1900–90) Philosopher, born in Banbury, Oxfordshire. He is best known for his theories in the philosophy of science, and the study of moral and religious philosophy, particularly the application of mathematical game theory.

Bramah, Joseph [brama] (1748–1814) Inventor, born in Stainborough, South Yorkshire. His numerous inventions include a safety lock, a hydraulic press (1795), and a machine for printing bank-notes (1806), and he was one of the first to propose the application of the screw-propeller.

Bramante, Donato [bramantay], originally **Donato di Pascuccio d'Antonio** (c.1444–1514) High Renaissance architect, born near Urbino, Italy. His designs included the new Basilica of St Peter's (1505–6), the Palazzo dei Tribunale (1508), and the Palazzo Caprini (1514).

Branagh, Kenneth (Charles) [brana] (1960–) Actor and director, born in Belfast. He joined the Royal Shakespeare Company (1984), co-founded the Renaissance Theatre Company (1987), and starred in several films, such as *Henry V* (1989) and *Much Ado About Nothing* (1993), both of which he directed. He married Emma Thompson in 1989. >> Thompson, Emma

Brancusi, Constantin [brankoozee] (1876–1957) Sculptor, born in Pestisani, Romania. In 1904 he settled in Paris. His works include the 'Sleeping Muse' (1910), the first of many characteristic, highly polished egg-shaped carvings.

Brand, Stewart (1938–) Editor and writer, born in Rockford, IL. He became the founding editor of the counterculture *The Whole Earth Catalogue* series (1968–71), and later editor-in-chief of *The Whole Earth Software Catalogue* (1983–5).

Brandeis, Louis (Dembitz) [brandiys] (1856–1941) Judge, born in Louisville, KY. His opinions on issues of governmental power and legal procedure rank him as a major legal theoretician, and he became the first Jewish member of the Supreme Court (1916–39).

Brando, Marlon (1924–) Film and stage actor, born in Omaha, NE. His many films include *Mutiny on the Bounty* (1962) and *Last Tango in Paris* (1972). An Oscar winner for *On the Waterfront* (1954) and *The Godfather* (1972), he refused the latter honour in protest at the film industry's treatment of American Indians.

Brandreth, Gyles (Daubeney) (1948–   ) British writer, broadcaster, and politician. Long interested in word games and the eccentricities of language, he is best known for his television series, such as *Chatterbox* (1977–8) and *Catchword* (1986). He became an MP in 1992.

Brandt, Bill [brant], popular name of **William Brandt** (1904–83) Photographer, born in London. He made a series of striking social records contrasting the rich and the poor during the 1930s, portrayed life in London during the Blitz, and later became known for his treatment of the nude.

Brandt, Willy [brant], originally **Karl Herbert Frahm** (1913–92) West German chancellor (1969–74), born in Lübeck, Germany. He became mayor of West Berlin (1957–66), and in 1966 led the Social Democratic Party into a coalition government with the Christian Democrats. He was awarded the Nobel Prize for Peace in 1971.

Brangwyn, Sir Frank (1867–1956) Artist, born in Bruges, Belgium. He excelled in many media, but was best known for his murals, such as his 'British Empire Panels' (1925, Swansea Guildhall). In 1936 a Brangwyn Museum was opened in Bruges.

Branner, H(ans) C(hristian) (1903–66) Writer, born in Ordrup, Denmark. His works include the psychological novels (trans titles) *Toys* (1936) and *Nobody Knows the Night* (1955), and the plays *The Riding Master* (1949) and *Brethren* (1952).

Brant, Sebastian (1458–1521) Poet and humanist, born in Strassburg, Germany. He is best known for his allegory *Das Narrenschiff* (1494), a satire on the follies and vices of his times, translated into English as *The Shyp of Folys*. >> Barclay, Alexander

Branting, Karl Hjalmar (1860–1925) Swedish prime minister (1920, 1921–3, 1924–5), born in Stockholm. He was co-founder of the Social Democratic Party in 1889, becoming its leader from 1907. In 1921 he shared the Nobel Peace Prize for his work in international diplomacy.

Brant, Joseph, Mohawk name **Thayendanegea** (1742–1807) Mohawk Indian chief, and brother-in-law of the Irish fur trader, Sir William Johnson. In the American War of Independence (1775–83) he commanded the Mohawks on the British side. He later became a Christian and founded the first Episcopal Church in Upper Canada. >> Johnson, William

Brantôme, Pierre de Bourdeille, seigneur de (Lord of) (c.1530–1614) French soldier and writer, born in Périgord, France. In 1565 he went to Malta to assist the Knights of St John against the sultan, and later became chamberlain to Charles IX and Henry III (of France), fighting against the Huguenots. >> Charles IX; Henry III (of France)

Braque, Georges [brak] (1882–1963) Painter, born in Argenteuil, France. He was one of the founders of classical Cubism, and worked with Picasso (1908–14). His paintings, mainly of still-life, include 'The Port of La Ciotat' (1907) and 'The Black Birds' (1957). >> Picasso

Brasher, Chris(topher William) [braysher] (1928–   ) British writer, broadcaster, and athlete. In the 1956 Olympic Games he won the gold medal for the 3000 m steeplechase. He later became a BBC reporter and (1969–72) head of BBC general features.

Brassaï [brasaee], professional name of **Gyula Halasz** (1899–1984) Painter and photographer, born in Brasso, Hungary. Working in Paris from 1923, he recorded the underworld and nightlife of the city throughout the 1930s, causing a sensation with his first collection, *Paris by Night* (trans, 1933).

Brassey, Thomas (1805–70) Engineer, born in Buerton, Cheshire. In 1836 he settled in London as a railway contractor, and soon extended his operations to all parts of the world.

Bratby, John (1928–92) Artist and writer, born in London. A leading protagonist of English 'New Realism' in the mid-1950s, he was associated with the 'kitchen sink' school. His novels include *Breakdown* (1960), which he also illustrated.

Brattain, Walter H(ouser) (1902–87) US physicist, born in Amoy, China, where his father was a teacher. In 1929 he joined Bell Telephone Laboratories, researching the surface properties of semiconductors. He helped to develop the point-contact transistor, and shared the Nobel Prize for Physics in 1956. >> Bardeen; Shockley

Braudel, Fernand [brohdel] (1902–85) Historian, born in Lorraine, France. He wrote, from memory, his great work *The Mediterranean and the Mediterranean World at the Time of Philip II* (trans) in a German prison camp during World War 2 (published in 1949).

Brauer, Adrian >> Brouwer, Adriaen

Braun, Eva [brown] (1910–45) Mistress of Adolf Hitler, born in Munich, Germany. She is said to have married him before they committed suicide together in the air-raid shelter of the Chancellery during the fall of Berlin. >> Hitler

Braun, (Karl) Ferdinand [brown] (1850–1918) Physicist, born in Fulda, Germany. In 1909 he shared the Nobel Prize for Physics for his work on wireless telegraphy and cathode rays.

Braun, Wernher von [brown] (1912–77) Rocket pioneer, born in Wirsitz, Germany. In 1936 he directed a rocket research station at Peenemünde, but refused to co-operate over the V-2 project. He became a US citizen, and in 1958 was responsible for launching the first US artificial Earth satellite, Explorer 1.

Brazil, Angela (1868–1947) Writer of girls' school stories, born in Preston, Lancashire. She produced over 50 school novels, from *The Fortunes of Philippa* (1906) to *The School of the Loch* (1946).

Brazza, Pierre Savorgnan de (1852–1905) Explorer, born in Rio de Janeiro, Brazil. He became a French citizen in 1874, and in 1878 explored Africa N of the Congo, where he secured vast grants of land for France, and founded Brazzaville.

Breakspear, Nicholas >> Adrian IV

Bréal, Michel [brayal] (1832–1915) Comparative philologist and mythologist, born in Rhenish Bavaria. In 1866 he became professor of comparative grammar at the Collège de France, founding the science of semantics.

Bream, Julian (Alexander) [breem] (1933–   ) Guitarist and lutenist, born in London. He formed the Julian Bream Consort in 1961, specializing in early ensemble music.

Breasley, Scobie, popular name of **Arthur Edward Breasley** (1914–   ) Jockey and trainer, born in Wagga Wagga, New South Wales, Australia. He came to Britain in 1950, and became champion jockey in 1957, 1961, 1962, and 1963.

Breasted, James Henry [brestid] (1865–1935) Archaeologist and historian, the founder of American Egyptology, born in Rockford, IL. His five-volume *Ancient Records of Egypt* (1906) transcribed every hieroglyphic inscription then known.

Brecht, (Eugene) Bertolt (Friedrich) [brekht] (1898–1956) Playwright and theatre director, born in Augsburg, Germany. Popularity came with *The Threepenny Opera* (trans, 1928). After leaving Nazi Germany, his major plays include (trans titles) *Mother Courage and her Children* (1938) and *The Caucasian Chalk Circle* (1945). In East Berlin from 1948, his work with the Berliner Ensemble established him as a major influence on 20th-c theatre. >> Weigel, Helene; Weill

Breckenridge, Sophonisba Preston (1866–1948) Social worker and educator, born in Lexington, KY. Known for her studies exposing slum conditions, she founded (1927) the *Social Service Review*, which she edited until her death.

Breckinridge, John C(abell) (1821–75) Vice-president of the USA (1857–61), born near Lexington, KY. He served under Buchanan, and in 1860 was the pro-slavery candidate for the presidency, but was defeated by Lincoln. He was secretary of war in Jefferson Davis's cabinet. >> Buchanan, James; Davis, Jefferson

Breitmann, Hans >> **Leland, Charles**

Brenan, Gerald (1894–1987) Travel writer and novelist, born in Malta. He settled in Spain where he wrote his best-known works, *The Spanish Labyrinth* (1943) and *South from Granada* (1957).

Brendan, St, known as **the Navigator** (484–577), feast day 16 May. Abbot and traveller, born in Tralee, Ireland. He is traditionally regarded as the founder of the monastery of Clonfert in Co Galway (561). The Latin *Navigation of St Brendan* (c.1050) recounts his legendary voyage to a land of saints.

Brendel, Alfred (1931–) Pianist, born in Wiesenberg, Czech Republic. He is especially known for his interpretations of Mozart, Beethoven, Schubert, Liszt, and Schoenberg.

Brennan, Christopher (John) (1870–1932) Poet and critic, born in Sydney, New South Wales, Australia. Much influenced by French Symbolist poetry, he published few volumes, the best of which (such as *XXI Poems: Towards the Source*, 1897) were written before 1900.

Brennan, William J(oseph), Jr (1906–) Judge, born in Newark, NJ. Appointed to the US Supreme Court (1956–90), he is remembered for judgments which reflect his concern to balance individual rights with the interests of the community as a whole.

Brenner, Sydney (1927–) Molecular biologist, born in Germiston, South Africa. He worked at Cambridge from 1957 on the information code of DNA, and in the 1970s moved to detailed studies of the relationship between genetic structure and the nervous system.

Brentano, Clemens von [brentahnoh] (1778–1842) Writer, born in Ehrenbreitstein, Germany, the uncle of Franz and Lujo Brentano. A founder of the Heidelberg Romantic school, he wrote poems, plays, and short stories, and co-edited *Des Knaben Wunderhorn* (1805–8), a collection of folk songs. >> Arnim, Achim von; Brentano, Franz / Lujo

Brentano, Franz [brentahnoh] (1838–1917) Psychologist and philosopher, born in Marienberg, Germany, the brother of Lujo Brentano. In his most important work, *Psychology from an Empirical Standpoint* (trans, 1874), he developed the doctrine of 'intentionality'. >> Brentano, Lujo

Brentano, Heinrich von [brentahnoh] (1904–64) German statesman, born in Offenbach, Germany. A founder of the Christian Democratic Party, he entered politics in 1945, was prominent in drafting the Constitution, and became foreign minister (1955–61).

Brentano, Lujo [brentahnoh], popular name of **Ludwig Josef Brentano** (1844–1931) Political economist, born in Aschaffenburg, Germany, the brother of Franz Brentano. Professor of political theory at several universities in Europe (1871–1931), and a prominent pacifist, he was awarded the Nobel Peace Prize in 1927. >> Brentano, Franz

Brent-Dyer, Elinor Mary (1894–1969) Writer of the 'Chalet School' girls' stories, born in South Shields, Tyne and Wear. Her fourth book, *The School at the Chalet*, established her famous series in 1925.

Brenton, Howard (1942–) Playwright, born in Portsmouth, Hampshire. His plays include *The Romans in Britain* (1980) and *The Genius* (1983), as well as several collaborations with David Hare. >> Hare, David

Brenz, Johann [brents] (1499–1570) Lutheran reformer, born in Weil, Germany. He was co-author of the Württemberg Confession of Faith, and his Catechism (1551) stands next to Luther's in Protestant Germany.

Bresson, Robert [bresõ] (1907–) Film director, born in Bromont-Lamothe, France. His production of (trans titles) *Diary of a Country Priest* (1951) earned international acclaim, subsequently repeated with *A Man Escaped* (1956) and *The Trial of Joan of Arc* (1962).

Breton, André [bruhtõ] (1896–1966) Writer, born in Tinchebray, France. In 1916 he joined the Dadaist group, and in 1922 became a founder of the Surrealist movement. His works include a novel, *Nadja* (1928), and collected poems (1948).

Breton, Nicholas [bretn] (c.1545–c.1626) Poet, born in London. A prolific writer, his best-known poem is 'The Passionate Shepheard' (1604). His prose *Wits Trenchmour* (1597) is a fishing idyll on which Walton drew for *The Compleat Angler*. >> Walton, Izaak

Breuer, Marcel (Lajos) [broyer] (1902–81) Architect and designer, born in Pécs, Hungary. His architectural projects included the UNESCO building in Paris. His classic furniture designs, including possibly the first tubular steel chair, made him a significant figure in the 'Modern Movement'. >> Gropius; Nervi

Breughel >> **Brueghel**

Breuil, Henri (Edouard Prosper) [broey] (1877–1961) Archaeologist, born in Mortain, France. He was responsible for the discovery of the decorated caves at Les Combarelles and Font de Gaume in the Dordogne (1901), and his work marked the beginning of the study of Palaeolithic art.

Brewer, Ebenezer Cobham (1810–97) Clergyman and writer, born in London. He studied law, then became a London schoolmaster. His most enduring work is the *Dictionary of Phrase and Fable* (1870).

Brewster, Sir David (1781–1868) Physicist, born in Jedburgh, Borders. In 1816 he invented the kaleidoscope, and in 1818 was awarded the Rumford gold and silver medals for his discoveries on the polarization of light.

Breytenbach, Breyten [braytinbokh] (1939–) Painter and writer, born in Bonnievale, South Africa. Working in France (1960–75), he was arrested on his return to South Africa, and imprisoned for nine years for 'terrorism'.

Brezhnev, Leonid Ilich [brezhnyef] (1906–82) Russian statesman, general secretary of the Soviet Communist Party (1964–82), and president of the Supreme Soviet (1977–82), born in Kamenskoye, Ukraine. He was the first to hold simultaneously the position of general secretary and president.

Brian [breean], known as **Brian Boroimhe** or **Boru** ('Brian of the Tribute') (c.926–1014) King of Ireland (1002–14). He became chief of D l Cais (976), made himself King of Leinster (984), and his rule was later acknowledged over the whole of Ireland. He was killed after defeating the Vikings at Clontarf.

Brian, (William) Havergal (1876–1972) Composer, and writer on music, born in Dresden, Staffordshire. He wrote 32 symphonies, a huge setting of Shelley's *Prometheus Unbound*, a violin concerto, and five operas, including *The Tigers* (1916–19) and *Faust* (1955–6).

Briand, Aristide [breeã] (1862–1932) French prime minister (1909–11, 1913, 1915–17, 1921–2, 1925–6, 1929), born in Nantes, France. A socialist, he was 11 times elected French premier, and acted as foreign minister (1925–32), helping to conclude the *Kellogg–Briand Pact* (1928). He shared the 1926 Nobel Peace Prize. >> Kellogg, Frank B

Brickhill, Paul (Chester Jerome) (1916–91) Writer, born in Sydney, New South Wales, Australia. He served with the Royal Australian Air Force during World War 2, and for two years was a prisoner-of-war in Stalag Luft III, Germany. He described his escape from the camp in *The Great Escape* (1951); other books include *The Dam Busters* (1951) and *Reach for the Sky* (1954).

Bride, St >> **Bridget, Brigid,** or **Bride, St**

Bridger, James (1804–81) Fur trader scout and 'mountain man', born in Richmond, VA. He established Fort Bridger in Wyoming (1843), found Bridger's Pass (1849), and guided a federal force in its campaign against the Mormons (1857–8).

Bridges, Robert (Seymour) (1844–1930) Poet, born in Walmer, Kent. He wrote three volumes of graceful lyrics (1873, 1879, 1880), plays, literary criticism, and other works, and became poet laureate in 1913.

Bridges, (Henry) Styles (1898–1961) US state governor, born in West Pembroke, ME. He was Republican governor of New Hampshire (1935–7), served in the US Senate (1937–61), and was chairman of the appropriations committee.

Bridget, Brigid, or **Bride, St** (453–523), feast day 1 February. Abbess, said to be the daughter of an Ulster prince. She entered a convent at Meath, later founding four monasteries for women, notably at Kildare. She is the patron saint of Leinster.

Bridget, Brigit, or **Birgitta (of Sweden), St** (c.1302–73), feast day 23 July or 8 October. Visionary, born in Finsta, Sweden. She was mistress of the Swedish royal household who, after the death of her husband, founded a monastery which gave rise to the *Bridgettines*. She was canonized in 1391. Her daughter, **St Katarina of Sweden** (1335–81), was canonized in 1489.

Bridgman, Laura (Dewey) (1829–89) Blind deaf-mute, born in Hanover, NH. Dr Samuel Howe educated her at the Perkins institution, where she later became a skilful teacher of blind deaf-mutes. >> Howe, Samuel

Bridgman, P(ercy) W(illiams) (1882–1961) Physicist, born in Cambridge, MA. He was awarded the Nobel Prize for Physics in 1946 for his work on high-pressure physics and thermodynamics.

Bridie, James, pseudonym of **Osborne Henry Mavor** (1888–1951) Playwright, born in Glasgow, Strathclyde. His plays include *The Anatomist* (1931) and *Dr Angelus* (1947), and he played a leading part in the foundation of the Glasgow Citizen's Theatre.

Bridport, Lord >> **Hood, Alexander**

Brierley, Sir Ronald (Alfred) [briyerlee] (1937–) Businessman, born in Wellington, New Zealand. In 1961 he founded Brierley Investments Ltd, becoming its chairman (1961–89) and president (1989–), and built the firm into a major international operation.

Briers, Richard (David) (1934–) Actor, born in Croydon, Surrey. He has played many major theatre roles, but is probably better known for such television series as *The Good Life* and *Ever Decreasing Circles*.

Briggs, Barry (1934–) Speedway rider, born in Christchurch, New Zealand. He appeared in a record 17 consecutive world championship finals (1954–70), winning the title in 1957–8, 1964, and 1966.

Briggs, Henry (1561–1630) Mathematician, born in Warley Wood, West Yorkshire. He proposed the use of the base 10 for logarithms, and published logarithmic and trigonometric tables to 14 decimal places.

Briggs, Raymond (Redvers) (1934–) Children's illustrator and writer, born in London. His books include *Mother Goose Treasury* (1966) and *Father Christmas* (1973), both of which were awarded the Kate Greenaway Medal. Later works include *The Snowman* (1978; animated film, 1982) and *When the Wind Blows* (1982; animated film, 1987).

Brigham Young >> **Young, Brigham**

Bright, John (1811–89) Radical British statesman and orator, born in Rochdale, Lancashire. In 1839 he became a leading member of the Anti Corn-Law League. As an MP, he was closely associated with the Reform Act of 1867, and became President of the Board of Trade (1868–70).

Bright, Richard (1789–1858) Physician, born in Bristol, Avon. He made many important medical observations, and gave his name to *Bright's disease* of the kidneys.

Brigid, St >> **Bridget, Brigid,** or **Bride, St**

Brigit, St >> **Bridget, Brigit,** or **Birgitta (of Sweden), St**

Brillat-Savarin, (Jean) Anthelme [breeyah savarī] (1755–1826) French politician, gastronome, and writer, born in Belley, France. His *The Physiology of Taste* (trans, 1825), a witty compendium of the art of dining, has been repeatedly republished.

Brindley, James (1716–72) Engineer and canal builder, born in Thornsett, Derbyshire. In 1759 the 3rd Duke of Bridgewater employed him to build the canal between Worsley and Manchester, completed in 1772. >> Egerton

Brinell, Johan August [brinel] (1849–1925) Engineer and metallurgist, born in Bringetofta, Sweden. He invented the *Brinell machine* for measuring the hardness of alloys and metals.

Brink, André (1935–) Writer, critic, and translator, born in Vrede, South Africa. An Afrikaner dissident, his seventh novel - translated as *Looking on Darkness* (1974) - was banned, and brought him to international attention.

Brisbane, Albert (1809–90) Social reformer, born in Batavia, NY. In his early years, he adopted the social philosophy of Charles Fourier, later publishing a major work, *General Introduction to Social Theory* (1876). >> Fourier, Charles

Brisbane, Sir Thomas Makdougall (1773–1860) British soldier and astronomer, born in Largs, Strathclyde. He became Governor of New South Wales (1821–5). Brisbane, the capital of Queensland, was named after him.

Brissot (de Warville), Jacques Pierre [breesoh] (1754–93) French revolutionary politician, born near Chartres, France. Representative for Paris in the National Assembly, he became the leader of the Girondins (or 'Brissotins'). In the Convention his moderation made him suspect, and he was guillotined.

Bristow, Eric, nickname **the Crafty Cockney** (1957–) Darts player, born in London. He was world professional champion a record five times (1980–81, 1984–6), and also won the World Masters (1977, 1979, 1981, 1983–4) and the World Cup individual (1983, 1985).

Britannicus, in full **Claudius Tiberius Britannicus Caesar** (41–55 AD) The son of the emperor Claudius and Messalina. Claudius's fourth wife, Agrippina the Younger, caused her husband to adopt her son Nero, and treat Britannicus as an imbecile; and Nero, after his accession, had his step-brother poisoned. >> Agrippina (the Younger); Claudius; Nero

Brittain, Vera (Mary) [britn] (1893–1970) Writer, born in Newcastle-under-Lyme, Staffordshire. She served as a nurse in World War 1, recording her experiences in *Testament of Youth* (1933). Her daughter is Shirley Williams. >> Williams, Shirley

Brittan, Sir Leon (1939–) British Conservative statesman, born in London. He became home secretary (1983–5) and trade and industry secretary (1985–6), but resigned in 1986, and became a vice-president of the European Commission in 1989.

Britten, (of Aldeburgh), (Edward) Benjamin Britten, Baron (1913–76) Composer, born in Lowestoft, Suffolk. His works were largely vocal and choral, major works including the operas *Peter Grimes* (1945), *Billy Budd* (1951), and *Gloriana* (1953).

Broad, Charlie Dunbar (1887–1971) Philosopher, born in London. He became professor of moral philosophy in Cambridge (1933–53), but also had a strong interest in parapsychology, and was president of the Society for Psychical Research.

Broadbent, Donald (Eric) (1926–93) British psychologist. A major figure in postwar experimental psychology, he was the most influential British psychologist in the movement to import ideas from communication theory and cybernetics into cognitive psychology.

Broadwood, John (1732–1812) Piano manufacturer, born in Cockburnspath, Borders, Scotland. He married the daughter of harpsichord-maker, Burkhardt Tschudi (1702–73), and founded with him the great London pianoforte house (1770).

Broca, Paul (Pierre) [brohka] (1824–80) Surgeon and anthropologist, born in Sainte-Foy-le-Grande, France. He was the first to locate the motor speech centre in the brain, and was also a major influence on the development of physical anthropology in France.

Broch, Hermann [brokh] (1886–1951) Writer, born in Vienna. When the Nazis invaded Austria in 1938 he was imprisoned, but his release was obtained and he emigrated to America in 1940. His philosophical novels include (trans titles) *The Death of Virgil* (1945) and *The Sleepwalkers* (3 vols, 1931–2).

Brockhaus, Friedrich Arnold [brokhows] (1772–1823) Publisher, born in Dortmund, Germany. He founded the firm of Brockhaus in Leipzig and published the famous dictionary begun by R G Lömbel, *Konversations-Lexikon* (1796–1811).

Brockhurst, Gerald Leslie (1891–1979) Artist and etcher, born in Birmingham, West Midlands. Influenced by the early Italian Renaissance painters, his etchings and lithographs are almost entirely concerned with the themes of young womanhood and portraiture.

Brockway, (Archibald) Fenner, Baron (1888–1988) British politician, a founder of the Campaign for Nuclear Disarmament, born in Calcutta. He joined the Independent Labour Party, became a militant pacifist, and was twice elected to parliament (1929–31, 1950–64).

Brod, Max (1884–1968) Writer, born in Prague. He became a Zionist and emigrated to Palestine in 1939. Although best known as the editor and biographer of Franz Kafka, he was a prolific writer in his own right. >> Kafka

Brodsky, Joseph (1940–96) Poet, born in St Petersburg, Russia, of Jewish parents. He was socially exiled, went to the USA, and was naturalized in 1977. Collections include (trans titles) *A Halt in the Wilderness* (1970) and *To Urania* (1984). He was awarded the Nobel Prize for Literature in 1987.

Brogan, Sir Denis (William) (1900–74) Historian, born in Rutherglen, Strathclyde. Professor of political science at Cambridge (1939), he is chiefly known for his work on historical and modern America.

Broglie, (Louis César Victor) Maurice, 6ᵉ duc de (6th Duke of) [broy, broglee] (1875–1960) Physicist, born in Paris. He founded a laboratory at Paris, where he made many contributions to the study of X-ray spectra.

Broglie, Louis (Victor Pierre Raymond), 7ᵉ duc de (7th Duke of) [broy, broglee] (1892–1987) Physicist, born in Dieppe, France. In 1929 he was awarded the Nobel Prize for Physics for his pioneer work on the wave nature of the electron (*de Broglie waves*).

Brome, Richard [broom] (?–c.1652) Jacobean playwright, of whom little is known except that he had once been servant to Ben Jonson. He wrote as many as 24 popular plays, notably *The Northern Lass* and *The Jovial Crew*. >> Jonson

Bromfield, Louis (1896–1956) Writer, born in Mansfield, OH. He moved to France in 1923, where he wrote highly acclaimed novels, such as *Early Autumn* (1926, Pulitzer) and *Until the Day Break* (1942).

Brongniart, Alexandre [brongniah(r)] (1770–1847) Naturalist and geologist, born in Paris. Professor at the Sorbonne and Museum of Natural History, he introduced the term *Jurassic* for the limestones and clays of the Cotswolds. His son **Adolphe Théodore Brongniart** (1801–76) was a noted botanist.

Bronhill, June, originally **June Gough** (1927–) Soprano, born in Broken Hill, New South Wales, Australia. In London she gained immediate success at Sadler's Wells (1954), and later took the lead in *Lucia di Lammermoor* at Covent Garden (1959).

Brønsted, Johannes Nicolaus [breonsted] (1879–1947) Physical chemist, born in Varde, Denmark. He is known for the *Brønsted–Lowry definition* (independently introduced in 1923 by British chemist Thomas Martin Lowry), which defines an acid as a substance with a tendency to lose a proton, and a base as a substance that tends to gain a proton.

Bronstein, Lev Davidovich >> **Trotsky, Leon**

Brontë [brontee], originally **Brunty** or **Prunty** Three literary sisters, **Anne** (1820–49), **Charlotte** (1816–55), and **Emily** (1818–48), born in Thornton, West Yorkshire. The family moved to Haworth (1820), where the children began to write, collaborating under a pseudonym on a collection of *Poems by Currer, Ellis and Acton Bell* (1846). Anne wrote two novels: *Agnes Grey* (1845) and *The Tenant of Wildfell Hall* (1848). Charlotte is best known for her masterpiece, *Jane Eyre* (1847), as well as *Shirley* (1849), *Villette* (1853), and *Emma* (unfinished at her death). Emily is known for her poetry, and for *Wuthering Heights* (1847).

Bronzino, il [bronzeenoh], originally **Agnolo di Cosimo di Mariano** (1503–72) Mannerist painter, born in Monticelli, Italy. He decorated the chapel of the Palazzo Vecchio in Florence, and his portraits include most of the Medici family, as well as Dante, Boccaccio, and Petrarch.

Brook, Peter (Stephen Paul) (1925–) Theatre and film director, born in London. In 1962 he joined the Royal Shakespeare Company in Stratford, his productions including *King Lear* (1962) and *A Midsummer Night's Dream* (1970). Among his films are *Lord of the Flies* (1962) and an adaptation of *The Mahabharata* (1989).

Brooke, Sir Basil Stanlake >> **Brookeborough, Basil Stanlake Brooke**

Brooke, (Bernard) Jocelyn (1908–66) Writer, poet, and amateur botanist, born in Kent. Following the success of *The Military Orchid* (1948), he wrote the other parts of the autobiographical trilogy (known subsequently as *The Orchid Trilogy*), *A Mine of Serpents* (1949) and *The Goose Cathedral* (1950).

Brooke, Lord >> **Greville, Fulke**

Brooke, Rupert (Chawner) (1887–1915) Poet, born in Rugby, Warwickshire. He died a commissioned officer on Skyros on his way to the Dardanelles, and was buried there. His *Poems* appeared in 1911, and *1914 and Other Poems* after his death.

Brookeborough, Basil Stanlake Brooke, 1st Viscount (1888–1973) Prime minister of Northern Ireland (1943–63), born in Fermanagh. He was minister of agriculture (1933) and of commerce (1941–5), and as premier was a staunch supporter of union with Great Britain.

Brookes, Sir Norman (Everard) (1877–1968) Tennis player, born in Melbourne, Victoria, Australia. In 1905 he won the all-comers' singles title at Wimbledon, and returned in 1906 to win the singles, doubles, and mixed doubles titles.

Brookner, Anita (1928–) Writer and art historian, born in London. An authority on 18th-c painting, her novels include *Hôtel du Lac* (1984, Booker), *Family and Friends* (1985), and *A Friend from England* (1987).

Brooks, Gwendolyn (Elizabeth) (1917–) Poet, born in Topeka, KS. Her verse narrative, *Annie Allen* (1949), won the first Pulitzer Prize awarded to an African-American woman (1950).

Brooks, Mel, originally **Melvin Kaminsky** (1926–) Film actor and director, born in New York City. He is known for his zany comedies satirizing established movie styles, among them *Blazing Saddles* (1974) and *Silent Movie* (1976).

Broom, Robert (1866–1951) Palaeontologist, born in Paisley, Strathclyde. In 1947 he found a partial skeleton of the hominid *Australopithecus*, including the pelvis, which proved that it had walked upright about 1–2 million years ago.

Broome, David (1940–) Show jumper, born in Cardiff. He won the World Championship on *Beethoven* (1970), was three times European champion, on *Sunsalve* (1961) and *Mister Softee* (1967, 1969), and was the individual bronze medallist at the 1960 and 1968 Olympics.

Broonzy, Big Bill, popular name of **William Lee Conley Broonzy** (1893–1958) Blues singer, composer, and musician, born in Scott, MS. He was one of the most eclectic stylists among the great blues performers, encompassing American folk-song and jazz as well as rural and urban blues.

Brophy, Brigid (Antonia) (1929–) Writer and critic, born in London. Her novels include *Hackenfeller's Ape* (1953) and *In Transit* (1970), and her non-fiction titles *Black Ship to Hell* (1962).

Brosse, Salomon de (1565–1626) Architect to Marie de Médicis, born in Verneuil, France. He designed the Luxembourg Palace in Paris (1615–20), and Louis XIII's hunting lodge (1624–6), the nucleus of Versailles. >> Marie de Médicis

Brothers, Richard (1757–1824) British religious fanatic, born in Newfoundland, Canada. In 1793 he claimed to be the 'nephew of the Almighty', apostle of a new religion, the Anglo-Israelites. He prophesied the destruction of the monarchy, and was sent to Newgate (1795), and later to an asylum.

Brougham, Henry Peter, Baron Brougham and Vaux [broom] (1778–1868) Jurist and politician, born in Edinburgh. He entered parliament in 1810, became Lord Chancellor (1830–4), and assisted in carrying the Reform Bill.

Broughton, William Grant [brawtn] (1788–1853) First Anglican bishop of Sydney, born in London. He arrived in Sydney in 1829, and became Bishop of Australia in 1836, later restyled Bishop of Sydney and Metropolitan of Australia.

Brouwer or **Brauer, Adriaen** [brower] (c.1605–38) Painter, born in Oudenarde, Belgium. His favourite subjects were scenes from tavern life, country merrymakings, card players, and roisterers generally.

Brouwer, Luitzen Egbertus Jan [brower] (1881–1966) Mathematician, born in Overschie, The Netherlands. He founded the intuitionist school of mathematical logic, and made fundamental advances in topology, proving the invariance of dimension, and the fixed point theorem named after him.

Brower, David (Ross) [brower] (1912–) Conservationist, born in Berkeley, CA. He was executive director of the Sierra Club (1952–69), becoming known as a militant environmentalist, and later formed the John Muir Institute and Friends of the Earth. >> Muir, John

Brown, Sir Arthur Whitten (1886–1948) Aviator, born in Glasgow, Strathclyde. As navigator with Alcock he made the first non-stop crossing of the Atlantic in a Vickers-Vimy biplane on 14 June 1919. >> Alcock

Brown, Capability >> Brown, Lancelot

Brown, Charles Brockden (1771–1810) Novelist, born in Philadelphia, PA. The first professional American writer, *Wieland* (1798) and *Jane Talbot* (1804) are among his Gothic Romances.

Brown, Edmund G(erald), known as **Pat Brown** (1905–) US state governor, born in San Francisco, CA. He became California's Democratic attorney general (1950–8) and as governor (1959–67) expanded the state university system.

Brown, Ford Madox (1821–93) British historical painter, born in Calais, France. Among his major works are

'Manfred on the Jungfrau' (1841) and 'Chaucer Reciting his Poetry' (1851), and he also produced designs for furniture and stained glass.

Brown, George (Alfred) >> George-Brown, Baron

Brown, George Douglas, pseudonym **George Douglas** (1869–1902) Writer, born in Ochiltree, Strathclyde. He is best known for *The House with the Green Shutters* (1901), written under his pseudonym.

Brown, (James) Gordon (1951–) Labour politician, born in Glasgow, Strathclyde. He became Opposition chief secretary to the Treasury (1987–9), Opposition trade and industry secretary (1989–92), and Shadow Chancellor (1992–).

Brown, Herbert (Charles), originally **Herbert Brovarnik** (1912–) Chemist, born in London. He shared the Nobel Prize for Chemistry in 1979 for his work in introducing boron compounds as important reagents in synthesis. >> Wittig

Brown, James (1928–) Pop singer, songwriter, and producer, born in Barnwell, SC. Mixing Gospel and blues roots, by 1962 he had become America's leading rhythm and blues star, his hit records including 'Out Of Sight' and 'America Is My Home'.

Brown, Jim, popular name of **James Nathaniel Brown** (1936–) Player of American football, born in St Simon Island, GA. He had nine outstanding years with the Cleveland Browns in the National League (1957–66), during which he led the league eight times in rushing.

Brown, John (c.1735–88) Physician, born in Bunkle parish, Borders, Scotland. His 'Brunonian' system of medicine divided all diseases into the sthenic, depending on an excess of excitement, and the asthenic; the former to be removed by debilitating medicines, and the latter by stimulants.

Brown, John (1800–59) Militant abolitionist, born in Torrington, CT. In 1859 he led a raid on the US Armory at Harper's Ferry in Virginia, trying to launch a slave insurrection, but the raid failed, and he was hanged. The song 'John Brown's Body' commemorates the raid.

Brown, Lancelot, known as **Capability Brown** (1715–83) Landscape gardener, born in Kirkharle, Northumberland. He established a purely English style of garden design, using simple artifices to produce natural effects, such as those at Blenheim and Kew.

Brown, Michael (Stuart) (1941–) Molecular geneticist, born in New York City. He worked on cholesterol metabolism with Goldstein, leading to the discovery of low-density or LDL receptors, for which they received the Nobel Prize for Physiology or Medicine in 1985. >> Goldstein, Joseph

Brown, Robert (1773–1858) Botanist, born in Montrose, Tayside. Naturalist on Flinders's coastal survey of Australia (1801–5), he brought back nearly 4000 species of plants. He was the first to recognize the nucleus as the basis of a cell, and also discovered the *Brownian movement* of fine particles in a liquid. >> Flinders

Brown, Trisha (1936–) Choreographer, born in Aberdeen, WA. She is known for her original 'equipment pieces', where dancers were rigged in block and tackle harness to allow them to walk in vertical directions.

Browne, Charles Farrar, pseudonym **Artemus Ward** (1834–67) Humorist, born in Waterford, ME. He wrote for the *Cleveland Plain Dealer* a description of an imaginary travelling menagerie, followed by a series of comic letters marked by puns, grotesque spelling, and satire.

Browne, Hablot Knight, pseudonym **Phiz** (1815–82) Illustrator, born in London. He is best known for his illustrations of works by Dickens, beginning with *The Pickwick Papers* (1836). >> Dickens

Browne, Robert (c.1550–1633) Clergyman, founder of the *Brownists*, born in Tolethorpe, Leicestershire. In the 1580s he formed a Church on congregational principles at Norwich, but later became reconciled to the Anglican Church.

Browne, Sir Thomas (1605–82) Writer and physician, born in London. His greatest work is the *Religio medici* (c.1635), a confession of faith revealing a deep insight into the mysteries of the spiritual life.

Browne, Thomas Alexander >> Boldrewood, Rolf

Browne, Tom (1870–1910) Strip cartoonist, illustrator, and painter, born in Nottingham, Nottinghamshire. He created *Weary Willie and Tired Tim*, and drew the front pages of several children's comics.

Browning, Elizabeth Barrett, *née* **Barrett** (1806–61) Poet, born in Durham, Co Durham. She seriously injured her spine in a riding accident (c.1821), and was long an invalid. In 1845 she met Robert Browning, with whom she eloped in 1846. Her best-known work is *Sonnets from the Portuguese* (1850). >> Browning, Robert

Browning, John Moses (1855–1926) Gunsmith and inventor, born in Ogden, UT. His inventions include a breech-loading single-shot rifle (1879), an automatic pistol (1911), a machine gun (1917), and an automatic rifle (1918).

Browning, Robert (1812–89) Poet, born in London. *Bells and Pomegranates* (1841–6) included several of his best-known lyrics, such as 'How they Brought the Good News from Ghent to Aix'. In 1846 he married Elizabeth Barrett, and they settled in Florence, where their son **Robert Barrett Browning** (1849–1912) the sculptor, was born. After his wife's death (1861) he wrote his masterpiece, *The Ring and the Book* (1869). >> Browning, Elizabeth

Brownlee, John (1900–69) Baritone, born in Geelong, Victoria, Australia. He was a regular soloist with the Paris Opéra until 1936, a founding soloist with the Glyndebourne Festival Opera, and appeared regularly with the Metropolitan Opera, New York City (1937–58).

Brownson, Orestes (Augustus) (1803–76) Clergyman and writer, born in Stockbridge, VT. In 1844 he became a Roman Catholic, founded and edited *Brownson's Quarterly Review* (1844–65, and 1872 onwards), and wrote many books.

Broz, Josip >> Tito

Brubeck, Dave, popular name of **David Warren Brubeck** (1920–) Pianist, composer, and bandleader, born in Concord, CA. He formed the Dave Brubeck Quartet in 1951, and went on to make many popular recordings, such as *Time Out* (1958), featuring 'Take Five' and 'Blue Rondo à la Turk'.

Bruce, Christopher (1945–) Dancer and choreographer, born in Leicester. In 1985 he became associate choreographer of English National Ballet, and then resident choreographer at Houston Ballet.

Bruce, Sir David (1855–1931) Microbiologist and physician, born in Australia. As an officer in the Royal Army Medical Corps (1883–1919), he identified the bacterium that causes the cattle disease *brucellosis* and undulant fever in humans, named *Brucella* (1887).

Bruce, David K(irkpatrick) E(ste) (1898–1977) US statesman and diplomat, born in Baltimore, MD. As director of the economic co-operation mission (1948–9) he administered the Marshall Plan in France, and was later ambassador to France and NATO. >> Marshall, George C

Bruce, James, nickname **the Abyssinian** (1730–94) Explorer, born in Larbert, Central, Scotland. In 1768 he journeyed to Abyssinia, and in 1770 reached the source of the Blue Nile.

Bruce, Lenny, originally **Leonard Alfred Schneider** (1925–66) Satirical comedian, born in New York City. The satire and 'black' humour of his largely improvised act often flouted the conventions of respectability. He was imprisoned for obscenity (1961), and refused permission to enter Britain (1963).

Bruce, Robert, 4th Lord of Annandale (?–1245) Scottish nobleman. He married Isabel, the second daughter of David, Earl of Huntingdon and Chester, brother of King William the Lion, and thus founded the royal house of Bruce.

Bruce, Robert (1274–1329) King of Scots (1306–29) as Robert I, and hero of the Scottish War of Independence. As Earl of Carrick, he joined the Scottish revolt under Wallace, and in 1306 was crowned king at Scone. He defeated the English at the Battle of Bannockburn (1314), and sporadic war with England continued until the Treaty of Northampton (1328), which recognized the independence of Scotland.

Bruce (of Melbourne), Stanley Melbourne Bruce, 1st Viscount (1883–1967) Australian prime minister (1923–9), born in Melbourne, Victoria, Australia. He represented Australia in the League of Nations Assembly, and later served as high commissioner in London (1933–45).

Bruch, Max [brukh] (1838–1920) Composer, born in Cologne, Germany. He is best known for his Violin Concerto in G minor, the *Kol nidrei* variations, and the *Scottish Fantasy*.

Bruckner, Anton [brukner] (1824–96) Composer and organist, born in Ansfelden, Austria. His fame chiefly rests on his nine symphonies (the last unfinished), but he also wrote four Masses, several smaller sacred pieces, and many choral works.

Brudenell, James Thomas >> Cardigan, James Thomas Brudenell

Brueghel, Pieter, also spelled **Bruegel** or **Breughel** [broygl], known as **the Elder** (c.1520–69) Flemish painter, probably born in the village of Brueghel, near Breda. He settled in Brussels, where he painted his genre pictures of peasant life, such as the 'Peasant Dance' (c.1568). His eldest son, **Pieter Brueghel the Younger** (c.1564–1637), is known as 'Hell' Brueghel, because of his paintings of devils, hags, and robbers. His younger son, **Jan Brueghel** (1568–1625), known as 'Velvet' Brueghel, painted still-life, landscapes, and religious subjects.

Brugmann, Karl (1849–1919) Philologist, born in Wiesbaden, Germany. He wrote a *Comparative Grammar of the Indo-Germanic Languages* (trans, 1886–3), and was a leading exponent of the Neogrammarian school, stressing the fixity of sound laws.

Brugsch, Heinrich Karl (1827–94) Egyptologist, born in Berlin. He was director of the School of Egyptology in Cairo (1870–90), helped to decipher demotic script, and published a hieroglyphic–demotic dictionary (1867–82).

Bruhn, Erik [broon], originally **Belton Evers** (1928–86) Dancer and ballet director, born in Copenhagen. An exponent of the Bournonville style, he was the director of the Royal Swedish Ballet (1967–72) and artistic director of the National Ballet of Canada (1983–6).

Brumby, Colin James (1933–) Composer and teacher, born in Melbourne, Victoria, Australia. His works include two operas, operettas for younger audiences, a symphony (1982), concertos, choral works, film scores, and chamber music.

Brumel, Valeri Nikolayevich (1942–) Athlete, born in Razvedki, Russia. He won the Olympic gold medal in the high jump at Tokyo in 1964, and between 1960 and 1963 raised the world record to 2·28 m.

Brummell, George Bryan, known as **Beau Brummell** (1778–1840) Dandy, born in London. A leader of early 19th-c fashion, he became a close friend and protégé of the prince regent (the future George IV), but after a quarrel, gambling debts forced him to flee to France (1816).

Brun, Charles Le >> Le Brun, Charles

Bruna, Dick [broona] (1927–) Dutch artist and writer, creator of a highly successful series of picture books for young children. Favourite characters include Miffy the rabbit and the small dog Snuffy.

Brundage, Avery (1887–1975) International athletics administrator, born in Detroit, MI. He served as president of the US Olympic Association (1929–53) and as president of the International Olympic Committee (1952–72).

Brundtland, Gro Harlem [**brunt**land] (1939–) First woman prime minister of Norway (1981, 1986–9, 1990–), born in Oslo. She was appointed environment minister (1974–9) and became leader of the Labour Party group. In 1987 she chaired the World Commission on Environment and Development which produced the report *Our Common Future*.

Brunel, Isambard Kingdom [broo**nel**] (1806–59) Engineer, born in Portsmouth, Hampshire, the son of Marc Brunel. He designed the *Great Western* (1837), the first steamship built to cross the Atlantic, the *Great Britain* (1843), the first ocean screw-steamer, and the *Great Eastern* (1853–8), then the largest vessel ever built. >> Brunel, Marc

Brunel, Sir Marc Isambard [broo**nel**] (1769–1849) Engineer and inventor, born in Hacqueville, France. He solved many of the problems of underwater tunnelling, and his main achievement was the 460 m/503 yd Thames Tunnel from Rotherhithe to Wapping (1825–43). >> Brunel, Isambard Kingdom

Brunelleschi, Filippo [broonel**es**kee] (1377–1446) Architect, goldsmith, and sculptor, born in Florence, Italy. The first great Renaissance architect, his chief work is the dome of the cathedral (1420–61) in Florence.

Bruner, Jerome (Seymour) [**broo**ner] (1915–) Psychologist, born in New York City. His humanities programme 'Man: a Course of Study' (1966) has been called a landmark in curriculum development. He is also well known for his work in child development.

Brüning, Heinrich (1885–1970) German chancellor (1930–2), born in Münster, Germany. Leader of the Catholic Centre Party from 1929, he was forced to resign by the Nazis. He left Germany in 1934, and took up academic posts in the USA.

Brunne, Robert of >> **Mannyng, Robert**

Brunner, (Heinrich) Emil (1889–1966) Reformed theologian, born in Winterthur, Switzerland. His reputation outside the European mainland was established by the translations of *The Mediator* (1927) and *The Divine Imperative* (1932).

Bruno, St (925–65), feast day 11 October. Clergyman, born in Cologne, Germany, the brother of Otto I, the Great. He was made imperial chancellor in 940, and became Archbishop of Cologne in 953. >> Otto I

Bruno, St, also known as **Boniface** (970–1009), feast day 19 June. Missionary, born in Querfurt, Germany. He worked as a missionary bishop in Poland, Hungary, and the Ukraine, but was killed in Prussia.

Bruno of Cologne, St (c.1030–1101), feast day 6 October. Clergyman, born in Cologne, Germany. In 1084 he withdrew to the mountains of Chartreuse, near Grenoble, where he founded the austere Carthusian order on the site of the present Grande Chartreuse.

Bruno, Giordano, originally **Filippo Bruno**, nickname **Il Nolano** (1548–1600) Philosopher and scientist, born in Nola, Italy. He travelled widely, propounding an extreme pantheistic philosophy. His championship of Copernicus brought him into conflict with the Inquisition, and after a 7-year trial he was burned at the stake. >> Copernicus

Brunoff, Jean de (1899–1937) and **Laurent de Brunoff** (1925–) [**broon**of] Illustrators, father and son, creators of Babar the Elephant, hero of a series of picture books. Drawn originally by Jean, Babar first appeared in 1931.

Brusilov, Alexey [**bru**silof] (1856–1926) Soldier, born in Tbilisi, Georgia. In World War 1 he distinguished himself in the successful *Brusilov Offensive* against the Austrians in 1916, and became chief-of-staff in 1917.

Brustein, Robert [broostiyn] (1927–) Drama critic, teacher, and director, born in New York City. In 1966 he founded the Yale Repertory Theater, and later became director of the American Repertory Theater, which took up residence at Harvard in 1980.

Brutus, Lucius Junius [broo**tus**] (fl.500 BC) Legendary Roman hero. When popular indignation was roused at the rape of Lucretia by Sextus, the son of the Etruscan king, Brutus drove the royal family from Rome (509 BC), founded the republic, and was elected to the first consulship >> Lucretia

Brutus, Marcus Junius [broo**tus**] (c.85–42 BC) Roman politician. When the civil war broke out, he submitted to Caesar, and was appointed Governor of Cisalpine Gaul. Cassius persuaded him to join the conspiracy against Caesar (44 BC), but he killed himself after the defeat at Philippi. >> Caesar; Cassius

Bruyère, Jean de la >> **La Bruyère, Jean de**

Bryan, William (Jennings) (1860–1925) Lawyer and US politician, born in Salem, IL. As Democratic candidate for the presidency, he was crushingly defeated by McKinley in 1896 and 1900, and by Taft in 1908. He was appointed secretary of state by Woodrow Wilson (1913–15). >> McKinley; Taft, William Howard; Wilson, Woodrow

Bryant, Bear, popular name of **Paul William Bryant** (1913–83) Coach of American football, born in Kingsland, AR. A coach from 1945, he broke the all-time career victories record in 1981 with 315 victories (not broken until 1985).

Bryant, William Cullen (1794–1878) Poet and journalist, born in Cummington, MA. He achieved fame as a poet with 'Thanatopsis' (1817), after which he turned to regular newspaper contributions in prose and verse, becoming co-owner and editor of the New York *Evening Post* in 1829.

Bryden, Bill, popular name of **William Bryden** (1942–) Stage director and playwright, born in Greenock, Strathclyde. Associate director of the Royal Lyceum Theatre, Edinburgh (1971–4), his productions included two of his own plays, *Willie Rough* (1972) and *Benny Lynch* (1974).

Bryussov, Valery Yakovlevich [**bryu**sof] (1873–1924) Poet, critic, and translator, born in Moscow. He was one of the leaders of the Russian Symbolist movement which looked to France for its inspiration, and he translated many of the major Modernist writers in Europe.

Brzezinski, Zbigniew [bzhe**zin**skee] (1928–) Academic and politician, born in Poland. He settled in the USA and took US citizenship in 1958, becoming national security adviser to President Carter (1977–80), and the chief architect of a tough human rights policy directed against the Soviet Union. >> Carter, Jimmy

Buber, Martin [**boo**ber] (1878–1965) Jewish theologian and philosopher, born in Vienna. He taught comparative religion at Frankfurt (1923–33), then fled to Palestine to escape the Nazis. He is best known for his religious philosophy, expounded in *I and Thou* (trans, 1923).

Bucer or **Butzer, Martin** [**but**ser] (1491–1551) Protestant reformer, born in Schlettstadt, Germany. At the Diet of Augsburg he declined to subscribe to the proposed Confession of Faith, and afterwards drew up the *Confessio tetrapolitana* (1530).

Buchan, Alexander [**buh**kn] (1829–1907) Meteorologist, born in Kinnesswood, Tayside. He postulated the *Buchan spells* theory, that the British climate is subject to successive warm and cold spells falling approximately between certain dates each year.

Buchan, Elspeth [**buh**kn], *née* **Simpson** (1738–91) Scottish religious, the wife of a potter. In 1784 she founded a fanatical sect in Irvine, the *Buchanites*, announcing herself to her 46 followers as the Woman of Revelations xii.

Buchan, John, Baron Tweedsmuir [buhkn] (1875–1940) Writer and statesman, born in Perth, Tayside. An MP (1927–35) and Governor-General of Canada, he wrote many fast-moving adventure stories, such as *Prester John* (1910) and *The Thirty-nine Steps* (1915).

Buchanan, George [byookanan] (c.1506–82) Scholar and humanist, born near Killearn, Central, Scotland. In 1561 he was appointed tutor to Mary, Queen of Scots, and later to the four-year-old King James VI of Scotland (1570–8). His main works include a 20-volume history of Scotland. >> James I (of England)

Buchanan, James [byookanan] (1791–1868) Fifteenth president of the USA (1857–61), born in Stony Batter, PA. A Democrat, he became secretary of state in 1845, and as president was strongly pro-slavery.

Buchanan, James M(cGill) [byookanan] (1919–   ) Economist, born in Murfreesboro, TN. He became director of the Center for Public Choice in 1969, and was awarded the Nobel Prize for Economics in 1986 for his work on the theories of public choice.

Buchanan, Ken(neth) [byookanan] (1945–   ) Boxer, born in Edinburgh. For almost 10 years he was one of the world's leading lightweight boxers, being British champion (1968–71, 1973–4), European champion (1974–5), and World Boxing Association lightweight champion (1970–2).

Buchman, Frank (Nathan Daniel) [buhkman] (1878–1961) Evangelist, born in Pennsburg, PA. In 1921, believing that there was an imminent danger of the collapse of civilization, he founded at Oxford the 'Group Movement', later known as 'Moral Rearmament'.

Büchner, Eduard [bükhner] (1860–1917) Chemist, born in Munich, Germany, the brother of Hans Büchner. He was awarded the Nobel Prize for Chemistry in 1907 for demonstrating that alcoholic fermentation is due not to physiological but to chemical processes in the yeast. >> Büchner, Hans

Büchner, Georg [bükhner] (1813–37) Playwright and pioneer of Expressionist theatre, born in Goddelau, Germany. His best-known works are the poetical dramas *The Death of Danton* (trans, 1835) and *Woyzeck* (1837).

Büchner, Hans [bükhner] (1850–1902) Bacteriologist, born in Munich, Germany, the brother of Eduard Büchner. Director of the Hygienisches Institut from 1894, he discovered that blood serum contains protective substances against infection. >> Büchner, Eduard

Buck, Frank (1884–1950) Big-game hunter and collector, born in Gainesville, TX. From 1911 he led several expeditions to capture wild animals for zoos and circuses, writing about his experiences in such books as *Bring 'Em Back Alive* (1930).

Buck, Sir Peter (Henry), originally **Te Rangi Hiroa** (1879–1951) Maori scholar and writer, born in Urenui, New Zealand. He was an MP (1909–14), served in World War 1, then became an anthropologist and museum director in Hawaii.

Buck, Pearl S(ydenstricker), pseudonym **John Sedges** (1892–1973) Novelist, born in Hillsboro, WV. She lived in China from infancy. Her novel *The Good Earth* (1931; filmed 1937) earned her the Pulitzer Prize, and in 1938 she was awarded the Nobel Prize for Literature.

Buckingham, George Villiers, 1st Duke of [buhkingam] (1592–1628) English statesman and court favourite, born in Brooksby, Leicestershire. He arranged the marriage of Prince Charles to Henrietta Maria of France. The abortive expedition against Cadiz (1625) exposed him to impeachment by the Commons, and only a dissolution rescued him. >> Charles I (of England)

Buckingham, George Villiers, 2nd Duke of [buhking-

am] (1628–87) English statesman, born in London. A member of the Cabal of Charles II, he was instrumental in Clarendon's downfall (1667), but lost power to Arlington, and was dismissed in 1674 for alleged Catholic sympathies. >> Arlington; Charles II (of England); Clarendon, 1st Earl of

Buckle, George Earle (1854–1935) Journalist, born in Bath, Avon. He was editor of *The Times* (1884–1912), and edited six volumes of Queen Victoria's *Letters* (1926–32).

Buckley, William, nickname **the Wild White Man** (1780–1856) Convict, born near Macclesfield, Cheshire. In 1802 he was transported to Australia for stealing, but escaped from Port Phillip and lived with a native tribe for 32 years before being found by an expedition.

Buckley, William F(rank), Jr (1925–   ) Writer, born in New York City. He founded the conservative journal *National Review* (1955), and wrote books on contemporary politics, as well as several spy novels.

Buckminster Fuller, Richard >> Fuller, Buckminster

Buckner, Simon B(olivar), Jr (1886–1945) US general, born in Munfordville, KY. He commanded the 10th army in the Central Pacific command, and in April 1945 led the invasion of Okinawa, where he was killed in action.

Budaeus, Guglielmus [budayus], Latin name of **Guillaume Budé** (1467–1540) Scholar, born in Paris. As royal librarian he founded the collection which later became the Bibliothèque Nationale.

Budd, Zola, married name **Pieterse** (1966–   ) Athlete, born in Bloemfontein, South Africa. She set a world record time for the 5000 m while still a South African citizen, then obtained British citizenship, and competed in the 1984 Olympic Games. She retired in 1988, but returned to international running when South Africa was re-admitted to international sports in 1992.

Buddha ('the enlightened one') (c.563–c.483 BC) The title of **Prince Gautama Siddhartha**, the founder of Buddhism, born the son of the rajah of the Sakya tribe ruling in Kapilavastu, Nepal. When about 30 years old he left the luxuries of the court, his wife, and all earthly ambitions for the life of an ascetic; after six years of austerity and mortification he saw in the contemplative life the perfect way to self-enlightenment. The goal is *Nirvana*, the absorption of the self into the infinite. For the next 40 years he taught, gaining many disciples, and died at the age of about 80 in Kusinagara, Oudh. His teaching is summarized in the *Four Noble Truths*.

Buddhaghosa [budagohsa] (5th-c) Buddhist scholar, born near Buddh Gaya, or Ghosa, India. He studied the Buddhist texts in Ceylon, and is best known for the *Visuddhimagga* (The Path of Purity), a compendium of Buddhist doctrines.

Budé, Guillaume >> Budaeus, Guglielmus

Budenny, Simeon Mikhailovich [boodenee] (1883–1973) Russian soldier, born in Kozyurin, Russia. After the revolution he became a Bolshevik, defeating the Whites in the Battles of Tsaritsyn (1918–19). In 1941 he commanded the SW sector against the Germans, but was relieved after a disaster at Kiev.

Budge, (John) Don(ald) (1915–   ) Tennis player, born in Oakland, CA. In 1938 he became the first player to win all four Grand Slam events in the same year, and won all three titles at Wimbledon in 1937 and 1938.

Bueno, Maria (Ester Audion) [bwaynoh] (1939–   ) Tennis player, born in São Paulo, Brazil. She won the Wimbledon singles title in 1959, 1960, and 1964, and the doubles title five times with the American Darlene Hard (1936–   ).

Buffalo Bill >> Cody, William F

Buffet, Bernard [bufay] (1928–   ) Painter, born in Paris. He made his name in the early 1950s with his murky, almost monochromatic, still-lifes and interiors, which seemed to catch the mood ('existential alienation') of postwar Paris. In 1973 a Buffet Museum was established in Japan.

Buffon, Georges-Louis Leclerc, comte de (Count of) [bufō] (1707–88) Naturalist, born in Montbard, France. In 1739 he was made director of the Jardin du Roi, and formed the design of his *Natural History* (trans, 1749–67), which foreshadowed the theory of evolution.

Bugatti, Ettore (Arco Isidoro) [boogatee] (1881–1947) Car manufacturer, born in Milan, Italy. He began designing cars in 1899, and set up his works in Strasbourg in 1907. His racing cars won international fame in the 1930s.

Buhl or **Boulle, André Charles** [bool] (1642–1732) Cabinetmaker, born in Paris. He introduced *boullework*, a style of decorating furniture by inlaying metals, shells, and pearls on ebony - a technique carried on by his sons.

Bujones, Fernando [boohohnes] (1955–) Dancer, born in Miami, FL. In 1972 he joined the American Ballet Theater, becoming principal in 1974, the same year that he won the gold medal in Varna, Yugoslavia.

Bukharin, Nikolay Ivanovich [bookharin] (1888–1938) Russian revolutionary and political theorist, born in Moscow. A leader of the October Revolution (1917), he supported Lenin's New Economic Policy and opposed Stalin's collectivization campaign. He was arrested in Stalin's Great Purge, and shot. >> Lenin; Stalin

Bukowski, Charles [bookofskee] (1920–94) Writer, born in Andernach, Germany. A cult figure who did not achieve popular success, his works include four novels, several collections of short stories, and many volumes of verse.

Bulfinch, Charles (1763–1844) Architect, born in Boston, MA. America's first native-born architect, he sought to make Boston a US model of Classical elegance. He succeeded Latrobe as architect of the US Capitol (1817–30). >> Latrobe

Bulgakov, Mikhail Afanasievich [bulgakof] (1891–1940) Writer, born in Kiev, Ukraine. His major novels include *The White Guard* (trans, 1925) and *The Master and Margarita* (trans, 1938). Several of his works were withdrawn, and re-emerged only in the 1960s.

Bulgakov, Sergey Nikolayevich [bulgakof] (1871–1944) Philosopher, economist, and Orthodox theologian, born in Livny, Russia. Expelled from Russia (1923), he moved to the Orthodox Theological Academy in Paris (1925–44), where he expounded Sophiology, the view that *sophia* (the Divine Wisdom) mediates between God and the world.

Bulganin, Nikolay Alexandrovich [bulgahnin] (1895–1975) Soviet statesman and prime minister (1955–8), born in Nizhni Novgorod (formerly, Gorky), Russia. He became premier after Malenkov resigned (1955), with Khrushchev wielding real power. 'B and K' travelled extensively abroad, conducting propaganda through lengthy letters to Western statesmen. >> Khrushchev; Malenkov

Bull, John (c.1562–1628) Musician, born in Somerset. A Catholic, he fled abroad in 1613 to escape persecution, and became organist of Antwerp Cathedral. He was one of the founders of contrapuntal keyboard music, and has been credited with composing the air 'God Save the King'.

Bullard, Sir Edward (Crisp) (1907–80) Geophysicist, born in Norwich, Norfolk. He made the first satisfactory measurements of geothermal heat-flow through the oceanic crust, and helped to develop the theory of continental drift.

Bullen, Anne >> Boleyn, Anne

Buller, Sir Redvers (Henry) (1839–1908) British soldier, born in Crediton, Devon. He was chief-of-staff in the 1st Boer War (1881), and commander-in-chief in the 2nd Boer War (1899–1900), when he raised the siege of Ladysmith (1900).

Bullinger, Heinrich [bulingger] (1504–75) Religious reformer, born in Bremgarten, Switzerland. A disciple of Zwingli, he succeeded him in 1531 as leader of the reformed party in Switzerland, and drew up the Helvetic Confessions of 1536 and 1566. >> Zwingli

Bullock, Alan (Louis Charles) Bullock, Baron (1914–) British historian. He was chairman of the Committee on Reading and Other Uses of the English Language (1972–4), the 'Bullock Report', and the author of numerous works on 20th-c Europe, including studies of Hitler, Bevin, and Stalin.

Bülow, Bernhard (Heinrich Martin Karl), Fürst von (Prince of) [büloh] (1849–1929) German chancellor (1900–9), born in Flottbeck, Germany. As foreign secretary (1897) he operated an aggressive foreign policy.

Bülow, Hans (Guido), Freiherr von (Baron) [büloh] (1830–94) Pianist and conductor, born in Dresden, Germany. In 1857 he married Liszt's daughter, Cosima, but she left him for Wagner in 1869, and thereafter he became an opponent of Wagner and his School. >> Liszt; Wagner, Richard

Bultmann, Rudolf (Karl) (1884–1976) Lutheran theologian and New Testament scholar, born in Wiefelstede, Germany. An early exponent of form criticism, he is best known for his influential programme (1941) to 'demythologize' the New Testament and interpret it existentially, employing the categories of the earlier work of Heidegger. >> Heidegger

Bulwer-Lytton, Edward George Earle >> Lytton, Edward George Earle Bulwer-Lytton

Bulwer-Lytton, Robert >> Lytton, Robert Bulwer-Lytton

Bunau-Varilla, Philippe Jean [bünoh vareeya] (1859–1940) Engineer, born in Paris. The chief organizer of the Panama Canal project, he became Panamanian minister to the USA and negotiated the *Hay–Bunau-Varilla Treaty* (1903), giving the USA control of the Canal Zone.

Bunche, Ralph (Johnson) [buhnch] (1904–71) US diplomat, born in Detroit, MI. He directed the UN Trusteeship department (1947–54), and became UN mediator in Palestine, where he arranged a cease-fire. He was awarded the Nobel Peace Prize in 1950.

Buncho, Tani (1773–1840) Painter, born in Edo (modern Tokyo). He attempted a synthesis of various schools and Chinese works with European techniques. A prolific painter, he excelled in landscapes, and also illustrated books.

Bundy, McGeorge (1919–) US government administrator, born in Boston, MA. He is remembered for his major role in foreign policy decisions during the Kennedy and Johnson administrations, notably in the Vietnam War. >> Johnson, Lyndon B; Kennedy, John F

Bundy, Ted (1954–89) US convicted murderer. He was a law student who is believed to have killed at least 36 females, both adults and children. Convicted in 1979, he was executed in Florida after a string of unsuccessful appeals.

Bunin, Ivan Alexeyevich [boonin] (1870–1953) Writer, born in Voronezh, Russia. His best-known work is *The Gentleman from San Francisco* (trans, 1922). He was the first Russian to receive the Nobel Prize for Literature (1933).

Bunny, Rupert (Charles Wulsten) (1864–1947) Artist, born in St Kilda, Victoria, Australia. He moved to Paris where his work was influenced more by Classical mythology than by the prevailing Impressionist school.

Bunsen, Robert Wilhelm (1811–99) Chemist and physicist, born in Göttingen, Germany. He shared with Kirchhoff the discovery of spectrum analysis (1859), and among the inventions from his laboratory are the *Bunsen burner* and the grease-spot actinometer. >> Kirchhoff

Bunting, Basil (1900–85) Poet, born in Scotswood, Northumberland. After some years in Paris, he returned to Britain and established his reputation with *Briggflatts* (1966), a semi-autobiographical poem rooted in the north-east.

Buñuel, Luis [buhn**wel**] (1900–83) Film director, born in Calanda, Spain. His first films were a sensation with their Surrealistic, macabre approach: *An Andalusian Dog* (trans, 1928) and *The Golden Age* (trans, 1930). Later films include *Viridiana* (1961), *The Discreet Charm of the Bourgeoisie* (1972), and *That Obscure Object of Desire* (1977).

Bunyan, John (1628–88) Writer, born in Elstow, Bedfordshire. In 1653 he joined a Christian fellowship, and in 1660 was arrested and spent 12 years in Bedford county gaol, where he wrote *Grace Abounding* (1666). Briefly released, he was reimprisoned for six months, and there wrote the first part of his allegorical work *The Pilgrim's Progress* (1678). The second part was published in 1684.

Buonaparte >> Bonaparte

Buonarroti >> Michelangelo

Buoninsegna, Duccio di >> Duccio di Buoninsegna

Buononcini, Giovanni >> Bononcini, Giovanni

Burbage, Richard [**ber**bij] (c.1569–1619) Actor, born in London. He was the leading performer with Shakespeare's company from 1594, and the first creator on stage of many of Shakespeare's greatest roles, including Hamlet, Othello, and Lear. >> Shakespeare, William

Burbank, Luther (1849–1926) Horticulturalist, born in Lancaster, MA. He developed the *Burbank potato* on a farm near Lunenberg, MA, and in 1875 moved to Santa Rosa, CA, where he bred over 800 new strains of fruits and flowers.

Burchfield, Charles (Ephraim) (1893–1967) Painter, born in Ashtabula Harbor, OH. He depicted nature and urban America, and was known especially for his commissioned paintings of railroads and mines in the late 1930s.

Burchfield, Robert (William) (1923–) Scholar and lexicographer, born in Wanganui, New Zealand. In 1957 he was appointed editor of a new *Supplement to the Oxford English Dictionary* (4 vols, 1972–86).

Burchleigh, Baron >> Cecil, William

Burckhardt, Jacob (Christopher) [**berk**hah(r)t] (1818–97) Historian, born in Basel, Switzerland. Professor of history at Basel University (1858–93), he is known for his works on the Italian Renaissance and on Greek civilization.

Burdett-Coutts, Angela Georgina Burdett-Coutts, Baroness [**ber**det **koots**] (1814–1906) Philanthropist, born in London, the grand-daughter of Thomas Coutts. Inheriting her grandfather's fortune in 1837, she used it to establish a shelter for fallen women, build model homes, and endow churches and colonial bishoprics. >> Coutts, Thomas

Buren, Martin Van >> Van Buren, Martin

Bürger, Gottfried August (1747–94) Lyric poet and writer of ballads, born in Molmerswende, Germany. Associated with a group of Göttingen poets, his ballad *Lenore* (1773) had a major effect on the development of Romanticism in Europe.

Burger, Warren E(arl) (1907–95) Judge, born in St Paul, MN. He became judge of the US Court of Appeals for the District of Columbia in 1955, and was appointed chief justice of the US Supreme Court in 1969.

Burges, William [**ber**jiz] (1827–81) Architect and designer, born in London. He employed a strong mediaeval element in both his architecture and furniture. His projects include the reconstructed Cardiff Castle (1868–81) and Castell Coch (1876–81).

Burgess, Anthony, pseudonym of **John Anthony Burgess Wilson** (1917–93) Writer and critic, born in Manchester. His novels include *A Clockwork Orange* (1962), *Malayan*

Trilogy (1965), and *Earthly Powers* (1980). Other works include critical studies, film scripts, and musical compositions.

Burgess, (Frank) Gelett (1866–1951) Writer and humorist, born in Boston, MA. He is known for publishing *The Lark* (1895–7), a humorous magazine, which carried his famous quatrain, 'The Purple Cow'.

Burgess, Guy (Francis de Moncy) (1910–63) British traitor, born in Devonport, Devon. He studied at Cambridge, where he became a communist, and was recruited as a Soviet agent in the 1930s. He was a member of the Foreign Office, and second secretary under Philby in Washington in 1950. Recalled in 1951 for 'serious misconduct', he and Maclean disappeared, re-emerging in the Soviet Union in 1956. >> Maclean, Donald; Philby

Burgh, Hubert de [ber] (?–1243) English statesman. He was the patriotic justiciar of England (1215–32), but is now chiefly remembered as the jailer of Prince Arthur. >> Arthur, Prince

Burghley or **Burghleigh, Lord >> Cecil, William**

Burgoyne, John, nickname **Gentleman Johnnie** (1722–92) British general and playwright, born in Sutton, Bedfordshire. In 1777 he was sent to America to lead an expedition from Canada, taking Ticonderoga, but surrendered at Saratoga. His best-known work was his comedy, *The Heiress* (1786).

Buridan, Jean [booreedã] (c.1300–c.1358) Scholastic philosopher, probably born in Béthune, France. He gave his name to the famous problem of decision-making called *Buridan's ass,* where an ass faced with two equidistant and equally desirable bales of hay starves to death because there are no grounds for preferring one rather than the other.

Burke, Edmund (1729–97) British statesman and political philosopher, born in Dublin. He became secretary for Ireland, and entered parliament in 1765. His *Reflections on the French Revolution* (1790) was influential throughout Europe.

Burke, John (1787–1848) Genealogist, born in Co Tipperary, Ireland. He was the compiler of *Burke's Peerage* - the first dictionary of baronets and peers in alphabetical order, published in 1826.

Burke, Martha Jane >> Calamity Jane

Burke, Robert O'Hara (1820–61) Explorer of Australia, born in St Clerans, Co Galway, Ireland. As leader of the Burke and Wills expedition (1860), he was one of the first white men to cross the Australian continent from S to N, but both he and Wills died of starvation on the return journey. >> Wills, William John

Burke, Thomas (1886–1945) Writer, born in London. The author of many popular books, he is best known for *Limehouse Nights* (1916).

Burke, Thomas Henry (1829–82) British politician. Permanent Irish under-secretary from 1868, he was murdered with Lord Frederick Cavendish in Phoenix Park, Dublin. >> Cavendish, Spencer Compton

Burke, William (1792–1829) Murderer, born in Orrery, Ireland. With his partner, **William Hare** (c.1790–c.1860), born in Londonderry, he carried out a series of infamous murders in Edinburgh in the 1820s, with the aim of supplying dissection subjects to an anatomist. Hare turned king's evidence, and died a beggar in London; Burke was hanged.

Burleigh, Henry Thacker [**ber**lee] (1866–1949) Baritone, composer, and arranger, born in Erie, PA. He composed many songs and ballads, and was noted for his arrangements of black spirituals such as 'Deep River' (1916).

Burleigh, Lord >> Cecil, William

Burlington, Richard Boyle, 3rd Earl of (1694–1753) Architect and patron of the arts, born in London. He was responsible for fostering the Palladian style in England,

which was to govern English building for half a century.
>> Palladio

Burne-Jones, Sir Edward Coley (1833–98) Painter and designer, born in Birmingham, West Midlands. Inspired by the early Italian Renaissance, he chose subjects drawn from the Arthurian romances and Greek myths. He also designed stained glass and tapestries, and illustrated several books.

Burnet, Sir (Frank) Macfarlane [bernet] (1899–1985) Physician and virologist, born in Traralgon, Victoria, Australia. He became a world authority on viral diseases, and shared the 1960 Nobel Prize for Physiology or Medicine for research on immunological intolerance in relation to skin and organ grafting.

Burnett, Frances (Eliza), *née* **Hodgson** (1849–1924) Writer, born in Manchester. In 1865 her family emigrated to Tennessee. She wrote several plays and over 40 novels, notably *Little Lord Fauntleroy* (1886) and *The Secret Garden* (1909).

Burnett, James >> Monboddo, Lord

Burney, Charles (1726–1814) Musicologist, born in Shrewsbury, Shropshire, the father of Fanny Burney. He travelled in Europe (1770–2) to collect material for his *General History of Music* (1776–89), long considered a standard work. >> Burney, Fanny

Burney, Fanny, popular name of **Frances Burney**, married name **Madame d'Arblay** (1752–1840) Writer and diarist, born in King's Lynn, Norfolk. Her first and best novel, *Evelina*, was published anonymously in 1778. Her *Letters and Diaries* (1846) show her skill in reporting events of her time.

Burnham, Daniel H(udson) [bernuhm] (1846–1912) Architect and leader of the Chicago School, born in Henderson, NY. His pioneering designs into urban planning in Chicago were widely influential, and he also designed the Selfridge Building in London (1908).

Burnham, (Linden) Forbes (Sampson) [bernuhm] (1923–85) Guyanese prime minister (1964–80), born in Kitty, Guyana. In 1957 he founded the Socialist People's National Congress, and led his country to independence in 1966.

Burnham, Harry Webster Lawson, 1st Viscount [bernuhm] (1862–1933) British statesman, born in London. He is chiefly known as chairman of the committees which inquired into the salaries of teachers and which recommended the *Burnham Scales*.

Burns, Tex >> L'Amour, Louis

Burns, Arthur F(rank) (1904–87) Economist, born in Stanislau, Austria. He came to the USA at the age of 10. A leading expert on business cycles, he served as an economic adviser to presidents Eisenhower and Nixon, and was chairman of the Federal Reserve (1970–8). >> Eisenhower; Nixon

Burns, Robert (1759–96) Scotland's national poet, born in Alloway, Strathclyde. The Kilmarnock edition of his poems (1786) brought him great acclaim, followed by the famous epistolary flirtations with 'Clarinda' (Agnes Maclehose). Among his best-known poems are The Jolly Beggars' (1785) and 'Tam o' Shanter' (1790). In 1788 he married **Jean Armour** (1767–1834). >> Maclehose

Burnside, Ambrose Everett (1824–81) Union general in the US Civil War, born in Liberty, IN. Repulsed at Fredericksburg (1862), he held Knoxville (1863), and served under Grant at the Battles of the Wilderness and Cold Harbor (1864). He lent his name to a style of side whiskers, later known as *sideburns*.

Burnside, William (1852–1927) Mathematician, born in London. He worked in mathematical physics, complex function theory, differential geometry, probability theory, and notably in group theory.

Burr, Aaron (1756–1836) US Republican vice-president

(1800–4). born in Newark, NJ. In 1804 he killed his political rival, Alexander Hamilton, in a duel, and fled. He then prepared to raise a force to conquer Texas and establish a republic, was tried for treason (1807), and acquitted. >> Hamilton, Alexander

Burra, Edward (1905–76) Artist, born in London. Well known as a colourist, his Surrealist paintings of figures against exotic (often Spanish) backgrounds are invariably in watercolour, as in 'Soldiers' (1942).

Burrell, Sir William (1861–1958) Ship-owner and art collector, born in Glasgow, Strathclyde. He entered the family business, and gradually accumulated a collection of works of art from around the world, which he gave to the city of Glasgow.

Burritt, Elihu, nickname **the Learned Blacksmith** (1810–79) Pacifist, born in New Britain, CT. He worked as a blacksmith but devoted all his leisure to mathematics and languages. Through his publications and travels he became known as an 'apostle of peace'.

Burroughs, Edgar Rice [buhrohz] (1875–1950) Writer, born in Chicago, IL. He made his name with the 'Tarzan' stories, beginning with 'Tarzan of the Apes' (1914).

Burroughs, John [buhrohz] (1837–1921) Naturalist and writer, born in Roxbury, NY. The John Burroughs Memorial Association was established in his memory, to encourage writing in natural history.

Burroughs, William Seward [buhrohz] (1855–98) Inventor, born in Auburn, NY. He developed a mechanical calculating machine in 1885, and a commercially successful adding machine in 1892. His grandson was William S Burroughs. >> Burroughs, William S

Burroughs, William S(eward) [buhrohz] (1914–) Writer, born in St Louis, MO. His novels *Naked Lunch* (1959) and *The Soft Machine* (1961) established him as a spokesman of the Beat movement of the late 1950s. His later work, much concerned with innovations in the novel form, includes *The Wild Boys* (1971).

Burrows, William (Ward) (1758–1805) American marine officer, born in Charleston, SC. A Revolutionary War veteran, he returned to service in 1798 when President Adams appointed him to oversee the early development of the newly formed Marine Corps. >> Adams, John

Burt, Sir Cyril (Lodowic) (1883–1971) Psychologist, born in London. He was largely responsible for the theory and practice of intelligence and aptitude tests. In the 1980s, the validity of some of his findings was called into question.

Burton, Decimus (1800–81) Architect, born in London. He planned the Regent's Park colosseum, the new layout of Hyde Park, and the triumphal arch at Hyde Park Corner.

Burton, Michael Arthur, Lord >> Bass, Michael Thomas

Burton, Sir Richard (Francis) (1821–90) Explorer, born in Torquay, Devon. In 1856 he set out with Speke on the journey which led to the discovery of L Tanganyika (1858). **Lady Burton**, *née* **Isabel Arundell** (1831–96), burned her husband's journals after his death.

Burton, Richard, originally **Richard Walter Jenkins** (1925–84) Stage and film actor, born in Pontrhydfen, West Glamorgan. His early films include *The Robe* (1953), for which he received one of his six Oscar nominations. His romance with Elizabeth Taylor during the making of *Cleopatra* (1962) and their eventual marriage (1964–74, 1975–6) projected them both into the 'superstar' category. Among his later films were *Beckett* (1964), *Equus* (1977), and *1984* (released after his death). >> Taylor, Elizabeth (Rosemond)

Burton, Robert (1577–1640) Writer, born in Lindley, Leicestershire. His great work was the *Anatomy of Melancholy* (1621), a learned miscellany on the ideas of his time.

Bury, J(ohn) B(agnell) [beree] (1861–1927) Historian and Classical scholar, born in Co Monaghan, Ireland. He wrote a monumental *History of the Later Roman Empire* (1889), and other major histories of Greece and Rome.

Busby, Sir Matt(hew) (1909–94) Footballer and football manager, born in Bellshill, Strathclyde. After playing with Manchester City and Liverpool, he became manager of Manchester United in 1945. Severely injured when his team was involved in an air crash at Munich (1958), he rebuilt the side to achieve European Cup success in 1968.

Busch, Adolf (1891–1952) Violinist, born in Siegan, Germany. In 1919 he formed the Busch Quartet and Busch Trio, with his brother **Hermann** (1897–1975) as cellist and his son-in-law Rudolf Serkin as pianist. Another brother, **Fritz** (1890–1951), was a conductor and noted Mozartian. >> Serkin

Busch, Wilhelm (1832–1908) Cartoonist and writer, born near Hanover, Germany. He worked as an illustrator for the *Fliegende Blätter* (1859–71), and wrote satirical verse-stories with his own illustrations, such as *Max und Moritz* (1865).

Bush, Alan (Dudley) (1900–) Composer and pianist, born in London. An active communist, he founded the Workers' Music Association in 1936. His works include four operas, four symphonies, concertos for violin and piano, choral works, chamber works, and songs.

Bush, George (Herbert Walker) (1924–) US statesman and 41st president (1989–93), born in Milton, MA. In 1980 he campaigned for the Republican nomination, but lost to Reagan, later becoming his vice-president. In 1988 he won the nomination, and defeated Michael Dukakis in the election. He lost to Bill Clinton in 1992. >> Clinton; Reagan

Bush, Vannevar (1890–1974) Electrical engineer and inventor, born in Everett, MA. From 1925 he worked on the development of mechanical, electro-mechanical, and electronic calculating machines or analogue computers.

Bushnell, David (1742?–1824) Inventor and physician, born in Saybrook, CT. He built the first US submarine, *Bushnell's turtle*, which was tried unsuccessfully against British ships.

Bushnell, Horace (1802–76) Congregational minister and theologian, born in Bantam, CT. He was influential among US Protestant theologians with his emphasis on bringing religion into harmony with human experience and nature.

Bushnell, Nolan (1943–) Inventor of the video game, born in Clearfield, UT. When the first microprocessor chip became available (1971), he set up his own company, Atari, and devised a simple tennis game, 'Pong' (1973), which could be linked to a TV set.

Busoni, Ferruccio (Benvenuto) [busohnee] (1866–1924) Pianist and composer, born in Empoli, Italy. An infant prodigy, in 1889 he became professor of the pianoforte at Helsinki. His works include a piano concerto, and the opera *Doktor Faust*.

Buss, Frances Mary (1827–94) British pioneer in women's education. At the age of 23 she founded the North London Collegiate School for Ladies, and became its head (1850–94) - the first woman to call herself a headmistress.

Bustamente, Sir (William) Alexander [bustamentay], originally **William Alexander Clarke** (1884–1977) Jamaican prime minister (1962–7), born near Kingston. In 1943 he founded the Jamaica Labour Party, and became premier in 1962, when Jamaica achieved independence.

Butcher, Rosemary (1947–) Choreographer, born in Bristol, Avon. She often works in conjunction with other artists, as in the fast-moving *Flying Lines* (1985).

Bute, John Stuart, 3rd Earl of (1713–92) British prime minister (1762–3), born in Edinburgh. He became a favourite of George III, who made him a principal secretary of state (1761). His government was highly unpopular, supporting the supremacy of the royal prerogative, and he was forced to resign. >> George III

Butenandt, Adolf Friedrich Johann [bootuhnant] (1903–) Biochemist, born in Bremerhaven-Lehe, Germany. He isolated oestrone from pregnancy urine (1929), and isolated the male hormone androsterone (1931). He shared the Nobel Prize for Chemistry in 1939, but was forbidden to accept it by the Nazi regime.

Buthelezi, Mangosuthu Gatsha [bootuhlayzee], known as **Chief Buthelezi** (1928–) Zulu leader and politician, born in KwaZulu Natal, South Africa. The founder-president of the Zulu-based movement, Inkatha, in 1994 he was appointed minister for home affairs in President Mandela's first cabinet. >> Mandela, Nelson

Butler, Alban (1710–73) Hagiographer and Roman Catholic priest, born in Appletree, Northamptonshire. His great work, the *Lives of the Saints* (1756–59), makes no distinction between fact and fiction.

Butler, Benjamin F(ranklin) (1818–93) Lawyer, general, and congressman, born in Deerfield, NH. A Democrat, he was elected to Congress in 1866, and became prominent in the efforts for the reconstruction of the Southern states and the impeachment of President Andrew Johnson. >> Johnson, Andrew

Butler, Lady Eleanor (1745–1829) Recluse, born in Dublin. In 1779 she and her friend Sarah Ponsonby (1755–1831) resolved to live in seclusion, and settled in Plasnewydd, in the vale of Llangollen. They became famous throughout Europe as the 'Maids of Llangollen' or 'Ladies of the Vale'.

Butler, Joseph (1692–1752) Moral philosopher and divine, born in Wantage, Berkshire. His major work, *The Analogy of Religion* (1736), argued that objections against revealed religion may also be levelled against the whole constitution of nature.

Butler, Josephine Elizabeth, *née* Gray (1828–1906) Social reformer, born in Milfield, Northumberland. She promoted women's education and successfully crusaded against licensed brothels and the white-slave traffic.

Butler, Nicholas (Murray) (1862–1947) Educationist, born in Elizabeth, NJ. He became president of the Carnegie Endowment for International Peace (1925–45), and shared the Nobel Peace Prize in 1931.

Butler, Reg(inald Cotterell) (1913–81) Sculptor, born in Buntingford, Hertfordshire. He was one of the leading exponents of 'linear' constructions in wrought iron, but in his later years turned to a more realistic style.

Butler, R(ichard) A(usten), Baron Butler, known as **Rab Butler** (1902–82) British statesman, born in Attock Serai, India. As minister of education (1941–5), he introduced the Education Act of 1944. Later posts included Chancellor of the Exchequer (1951), home secretary (1957), and deputy prime minister (1962). He narrowly lost the premiership to Douglas-Home in 1963, and was foreign secretary (1963–4) in his administration. >> Home

Butler, Samuel (1612–80) Satirist, baptized at Strensham, Worcestershire. His great poetic work, *Hudibras*, a burlesque satire on Puritanism, appeared in three parts (1663, 1664, 1678).

Butler, Samuel (1835–1902) Writer, painter, and musician, born at Langar Rectory, Nottinghamshire. He is known for his Utopian satire, *Erewhon* (1872), and for his autobiographical novel *The Way of All Flesh* (1903).

Butlerov, Alexander Mikhailovich [butlayrof] (1828–86) Organic chemist, born in Chistopol, Russia. In 1864 he correctly predicted the existence of tertiary alcohols, and was the first to introduce the idea of isomeric molecules existing in chemical equilibrium (tautomerism).

Butlin, Billy, popular name of **Sir William (Edmund) Butlin** (1899–1980) Holiday camp promoter, born in South Africa. In Britain, he opened his first camp at Skegness in 1936, followed by others at Clacton and Filey, and several more camps and hotels after World War 2.

Butor, Michel (Marie François) [bütaw(r)] (1926–) Writer and critic, born in Lille, France. One of the popular writers of the *roman nouveau* ('new novel'), his works include *Passing Time* (trans, 1959) and the non-fiction *Mobile* (1962).

Butt, Dame Clara (1872–1936) Contralto singer, born in Southwick, West Sussex. She became known for her performances in oratorios. Elgar's *Sea Pictures* were especially composed for her. >> Elgar

Butterfield, Sir Herbert (1900–79) Historian, born in Yorkshire. He won recognition as a diplomatic historian with *The Peace-Tactics of Napoleon 1806–8* (1929). *The Origins of Modern Science* (1949) inaugurated the worldwide development of the history of science.

Butterfield, William (1814–1900) Architect, born in London. Associated with the Oxford Movement, he was a leading exponent of the Gothic Revival. His designs include Keble College, Oxford, and St Augustine's College, Canterbury.

Butterley, Nigel Henry (1935–) Composer and pianist, born in Sydney, New South Wales, Australia. His works include *In the Head the Fire* (1966, Italia Prize), a two-act opera, *Lawrence Hargrave Flying Alone* (1987), and a major orchestral work *From Sorrowing Earth* (1992).

Button, Dick, popular name of **Richard Button** (1929–) Ice skater, born in Englewood, NJ. He was five times world champion (1948–52), and gold medal winner in the 1948 and 1952 Olympics.

Buttrose, Ita (Clare) (1942–) Journalist, publisher, and broadcaster, born in Sydney, New South Wales, Australia. In 1981 she joined News Limited as editor-in-chief of the *Sunday Telegraph*, in 1988 became editor of that paper's opposition, *The Sun Herald*, and by 1989 had started her own magazine, *Ita*.

Butzer, Martin >> **Bucer, Martin**

Buxtehude, Diderik or **Dietrich** [buksteehooduh] (1637–1707) Organist and composer, born in Oldesloe or Helsingborg, Sweden (formerly in Denmark). In 1668 he was appointed organist at the Marienkirche, Lübeck, where he began the famous *Abendmusiken* - Advent evening concerts of his own sacred music and organ works.

Buys Ballot, Christoph H(endrick) D(iederick) [biyz balot] (1817–90) Meteorologist, born in Kloetinge, The Netherlands. He was the inventor of the aeroklinoscope and of a system of weather signals. In 1857 he stated the law of wind direction in relation to atmospheric pressure (*Buys Ballot's law*).

BV >> **Thomson, James** (1834–82)

Byars, Betsy (Cromer) [biyerz] (1928–) Children's novelist, born in Charlotte, NC. Her novels include *The Summer of the Swans* (1970) and *Goodbye, Chicken Little* (1979).

Byatt, A(ntonia) S(usan), *née* **Drabble** (1936–) Writer and critic, the sister of Margaret Drabble. Her novels include *Virgin in the Garden* (1978), *Still-Life* (1985), and *Possession* (1990, Booker). >> Drabble

Bygraves, Max (Walter) (1922–) Entertainer, born in Rotherhithe, Greater London. A professional entertainer since 1946, his catchphrase, 'I wanna tell you a story', is also the title of his autobiography (1976).

Byng, George, 1st Viscount Torrington (1663–1733) English sailor, born in Wrotham, Kent. In 1708 he defeated the French fleet of James Stuart, the Pretender, and in 1718 destroyed the Spanish fleet off Messina. >> Stuart, Prince James

Byng (of Vimy), Julian Hedworth George Byng, 1st Viscount (1862–1935) British general, born in Wrotham Park, Middlesex. He commanded the 9th Army Corps in Gallipoli (1915), the Canadian Army Corps (1916–17), and the 3rd Army (1917–18).

Byrd, Harry (Flood) (1887–1966) US politician, born in West Virginia, the brother of Richard E Byrd. Senator for Virginia (1933–65), he became chairman of the US Senate Finance Committee, noted for his extreme conservatism and support for segregation. >> Byrd, Richard E

Byrd, Richard E(velyn) (1888–1957) Aviator, explorer, and rear-admiral, born in Winchester, VA, the brother of Harry Byrd. He was navigator on the first aeroplane flight over the North Pole (9 May 1926), and later flew over the South Pole (28–29 Nov 1929). >> Byrd, Harry

Byrd, William (1543–1623) Composer, probably born in Lincoln, Lincolnshire. Organist at Lincoln Cathedral and (with Tallis) at the Chapel Royal, he wrote music for both the Catholic and the Anglican services, as well as madrigals, songs, keyboard pieces, and music for strings. >> Tallis

Byrd, William (1674–1744) Tobacco planter, colonial official, and diarist, born in Virginia Colony. In 1737 he founded the town of Richmond, VA, and in 1743 became president of the Council of State.

Byrne, Donn, pseudonym of **Brian Oswald Donn-Byrne** (1889–1928) Novelist and short-story writer, born in New York City. His works include *Messer Marco Polo* (1921) and *Hangman's House* (1926).

Byrne, John (1940–) Playwright and stage designer, born in Paisley, Strathclyde. His plays include *The Slab Boys* (1978), *Cuttin' A Rug* (1980), and *Still Life* (1983), and he also wrote the highly acclaimed TV series *Tutti Frutti* (1987).

Byrnes, James F(rancis) (1879–1972) US public official and Supreme Court justice, born in Charleston, SC. Appointed to the Supreme Court in 1941, he stepped down to head the Office of Economic Stabilization (1942) and the Office of War Mobilization (1943). Under Truman he became secretary of state (1945–7).

Byrns, Joseph (Wellington) (1869–1936) US state representative, born in Cedar Hill, TN. He became a Democratic member of the US House of Representatives (1909–36), in 1933 successfully guiding 'New Deal' legislation through the House.

Byron (of Rochdale), George (Gordon) Byron, 6th Baron, known as **Lord Byron** (1788–1824) Poet, born in London. The popular *Childe Harold's Pilgrimage* (1812) gave to Europe the concept of the 'Byronic hero'; later works include *Don Juan* (1819–24). He actively helped the Italian revolutionaries, and in 1823 joined the Greek insurgents who had risen against the Turks, but died of a fever at Missolonghi. >> Lovelace, Augusta Ada

Byron, Robert (1905–41) Writer on travel and architecture, Byzantinist, and aesthete, born in Wiltshire. He is best remembered for his travelogues, such as *The Road to Oxiana* (1937).

C

Caballé, Montserrat [kabayay] (1933–) Soprano, born in Barcelona, Spain. She earned an international reputation, especially in operas by Donizetti and Verdi.

Cabell, James (Branch) [kabl] (1879–1958) Writer and critic, born in Richmond, VA. He made his name with his novel *Jurgen* (1919), the best known of a sequence of 18 novels, collectively called *Biography of Michael*, set in the imaginary mediaeval kingdom of Poictesme.

Cabet, Etienne [kabay] (1788–1856) Reformer and communist, born in Dijon, France. He set out his social doctrine in *Voyage en Icarie* (1840), describing a communistic utopia, and in 1849 led a group to Texas to found a utopian settlement called Icaria on the Red R.

Cable, George W(ashington) (1844–1925) Writer, born in New Orleans, LA. In 1884 he went to New England, and made his reputation with his Creole sketches in *Scribner's Magazine*.

Cabot, John [kabot], Ital **Giovanni Caboto** (1425–c.1500) Navigator, born possibly in Genoa, who discovered the mainland of North America. He settled in Bristol c.1490, and set sail in 1497 with two ships, accompanied by his three sons, sighting Cape Breton I and Nova Scotia. >> Cabot, Sebastian

Cabot, John M(oors) [kabot] (1901–81) US diplomat, born in Cambridge, MA. Assistant secretary of state for Inter-American Affairs (1953–4), his books include *Towards Our Common American Destiny (1955)*.

Cabot, Sebastian [kabot] (1474–1557) Explorer and navigator, born in Venice or Bristol, the son of John Cabot. He accompanied his father to the American coast, then served Ferdinand V of Spain as a cartographer (1512). He later explored the coast of South America (1526). >> Cabot, John

Cabral or **Cabrera, Pedro Alvarez** [kabral] (c.1467–c.1520) Explorer, born in Belmonte, Portugal. In 1500 he sailed from Lisbon for the East Indies, but was carried to Brazil, which he claimed on behalf of Portugal. He then made for India, but was forced to land at Mozambique, and provided the first description of that country.

Cabrera, Pedro Alvarez >> **Cabral, Pedro Alvarez**

Cabrera Infante, Guillermo [kabraira infantay] (1929–) Writer, born in Gibara, Cuba. He emigrated to England in 1966. Film critic, journalist, and translator, he is known chiefly for his fiction, notably *Three Sad Tigers* (trans, 1967) and *Infante's Inferno* (trans, 1979).

Cabrini, St Francesca Xavier [kabreenee] (1850–1917), feast day 13 November. Nun, born near Lodi, Italy. She founded the Missionary Sisters of the Sacred Heart (1886), emigrated to the USA in 1889, and became renowned for her social and charitable work. Canonized in 1946, she was the first US saint.

Caccini, Giulio [kacheenee] (c.1550–1618) Composer and singer, born in Rome. With Jacopo Peri he paved the way for opera by setting to music the drama *Euridice* (1602). >> Peri

Cadbury, George (1839–1922) Businessman, born in Birmingham, West Midlands, the son of John Cadbury. In partnership with his brother **Richard Cadbury** (1835–99), he expanded his father's cocoa and chocolate business, and established for the workers the model village of Bournville (1879).

Cadbury, Henry (Joel) (1883–1974) Quaker scholar, born in Philadelphia, PA. He held a chair in divinity (1934–54) at Harvard, and was active in the work of the American Friends Service Committee.

Cadbury, John (1801–89) Quaker businessman, the son of **Richard Tapper Cadbury**, who had settled in Birmingham in 1794. He founded the cocoa and chocolate business of Cadburys. >> Cadbury, George

Cade, Jack [kayd] (?–1450) Irish leader of the insurrection of 1450 against Henry VI. Assuming the title of Captain of Kent, he marched on London with a great number of followers, and entered the city. A promise of pardon sowed dissension among the insurgents, and he was killed. >> Henry VI

Cadell, Francis (Campbell Boileau) [kadl] (1883–1937) Painter, born in Edinburgh. In 1912 he founded the Society of Eight. One of the 'Scottish Colourists', he painted vivid landscapes, interiors, and still-lifes.

Cadillac, Antoine Laumet de la Mothe, sieur de (Lord of) [kadlak], Fr [kadayak] (1658–1730) French soldier and colonialist, born in Gascony, France. He went to America in 1683, and founded the settlement which became the city of Detroit. In 1711 he was appointed Governor of Louisiana, but returned to France in 1716.

Cadmus, Paul [kadmuhs] (1904–) Painter, born in New York City. A provocative artist who combines wit and social protest, his best-known paintings are 'The Fleet's In' (1934) and 'Fantasia on a Theme by Dr S' (1946).

Cadwaladr [kadwolader] (?–1172) Prince of Gwynedd, Wales. He conquered much of Wales with his older brother Owain until he was expelled by him (1143). Cadwaladr later fled to England, where Henry II restored him to his lands after the conquest of Wales (1158). >> Henry II (of England)

Cadwallon [kadwalon] (?–634) Pagan king of Gwynedd, Wales (from c.625). With Penda, the Mercian king, he invaded the Christian kingdom of Northumbria in 633 and slew King Edwin at Heathfield, near Doncaster. He was killed by King Oswald at Heavenfield, near Hexham. >> Edwin; Oswald, St

Caedmon [kadmon] (?–c.680) The first English poet of known name. Bede reports that, unlearned till mature in years, Caedmon became aware in a semi-miraculous way that he was called to exercise the gift of religious poetry. He became a monk at Whitby. >> Bede

Caesalpinus >> **Cesalpino, Andrea**

Caesar, in full **Gaius Julius Caesar** (c.101–44 BC) Roman politician, a member of the Julii, an aristocratic Roman family. His military genius, as displayed in the Gallic Wars (58–51 BC), enabled Rome to extend her empire to the Atlantic seaboard, but his ruthless ambition led to the breakdown of the Republican system of government at home. In 60 BC he joined with Pompey and Crassus (the First Triumvirate) to protect his interests in the state, and in 49 BC, to avoid being humbled by his enemies at Rome, led his army across the R Rubicon into Italy, plunging the state into civil war. Victory over the Pompeian forces (48–45 BC) left him in sole control, and he took the title 'Dictator for Life' in 44 BC. He was murdered by Republican-minded Romans under the leadership of Brutus and Cassius. >> Brutus, Marcus Junius; Cassius; Crassus, Marcus Licinius; Pompey the Great

Cage, John (1912–92) Composer, born in Los Angeles, CA. He was associated with ultra-Modernism, and variously experimented with the 'prepared piano', unorthodox musical notation, 'aleatory' (chance-dependent) music, and silence as an art form.

Cagliostro, Alessandro, conte di (Count of) [kalyohstroh], originally **Giuseppe Balsamo** (1743–95)

Adventurer and charlatan, born in Palermo, Italy. He married Lorenza Feliciani, and from 1771 they visited Europe as Count and Countess Cagliostro. Successful as physician, philosopher, alchemist, and necromancer, he ran a lively business in his 'elixir of immortal youth', but was imprisoned in 1789.

Cagney, James (1899–1986) Film actor, born in New York City. His film performance as the gangster in *The Public Enemy* (1931) brought him stardom. Later films include *Angels with Dirty Faces* (1938) and *Yankee Doodle Dandy* (1942, Oscar).

Caiaphas [kiyafas] (1st-c) Son-in-law of Annas, eventually appointed by the Romans to be his successor as high priest of Israel (c.18–36). In the New Testament he interrogated Jesus after his arrest (*Matt* 26) and Peter after his detention in Jerusalem (*Acts* 4). >> Annas; Jesus Christ

Caiger-Smith, Alan [kayger] (1930–) British potter. He established the Aldermaston Pottery (1955), producing tin-glazed earthenware with free hand brushwork and, occasionally, rich lustres.

Caillaux, Joseph (Marie Auguste) [kiyoh] (1863–1944) Financier and prime minister of France (1911–12), born in Le Mans, France. He was overthrown for showing too conciliatory an attitude towards Germany. In 1914, his second wife shot Gaston Calmette, editor of *Figaro*, who had launched a campaign against him; after a famous trial, she was acquitted.

Cailletet, Louis Paul [kiytay] (1832–1913) Ironmaster, born in Châtillon-sur-Seine, France. While engaged in research on the liquefaction of gases (1877), he liquefied hydrogen, nitrogen, oxygen, and air for the first time by compression, cooling, and sudden expansion.

Cain [kayn] Biblical character, the eldest son of Adam and Eve. He is portrayed (*Gen* 4) as a farmer whose offering to God was rejected, in contrast to that of his herdsman brother, Abel. This led to his murder of Abel, and Cain's punishment of being banished to a nomadic life. >> Abel; Adam and Eve

Cain, James M(allahan) [kayn] (1892–1977) Writer, born in Annapolis, MD. His novels include *The Postman Always Rings Twice* (1934), *Double Indemnity* (1943), and *The Butterfly* (1947). Several of his stories were made into films.

Caine, Michael [kayn], originally **Maurice Micklewhite** (1933–) Film actor, born in London. His many films include *Zulu* (1963), *The Ipcress File* (1965), *Educating Rita* (1983), and *Hannah and Her Sisters* (1986, Oscar).

Cairns, Sir Hugh William Bell (1896–1952) Surgeon, born in Port Pirie, South Australia. During World War 2 he was adviser on head injuries to the British Ministry of Health, and neurosurgeon to the army.

Cairoli, Charlie [kiyrohlee] (1910–80) Circus clown, born in France. He came to Britain in 1938, and was for 39 years a star attraction of the Blackpool Tower Circus.

Caitanya [kiytahnya] (c.1486–1533) Hindu mystic, born in Nadia, Bengal. Following conversion in 1510, he spent the latter part of his life in Puri, inspiring disciples with his emphasis on joy and love of Krishna, and the place of singing and dancing in worship.

Caius, John [keez] (1510–73) Physician and scholar, born in Norwich, Norfolk. President of the College of Physicians nine times, he was physician to Edward VI, Mary I, and Queen Elizabeth I. In 1559 he became the first Master of Gonville and Caius College, Cambridge.

Cajetan [kajetan], Ital **Gaetano**, originally **Thomas de Vio** (c.1469–1534) Clergyman and theologian, born in Gaeta, Italy. He became General of the Dominicans (1508), cardinal (1517), and legate to Hungary (1523). In 1518 he sought to induce Luther to recant at Augsburg. >> Luther

Calamity Jane, popular name of **Martha Jane Burke**, *née* **Cannary** (c.1852–1903) Frontierswoman, born in Princeton, MO. She became a living legend for her skill at riding

and shooting, and teamed up with US marshal **Wild Bill Hickock** (1847–76). She is said to have threatened 'calamity' for any man who tried to court her, but in 1885 she married.

Calas, Jean [kalahs] (1698–1762) Huguenot merchant, born in Lacabarède, France. In 1761 he was accused of murdering his eldest son (a suicide) in order to prevent him becoming a Roman Catholic. He was found guilty, and executed. Voltaire led a campaign which resulted in parliament declaring him innocent (1765). >> Voltaire

Caldara, Antonio [kaldahra] (1670–1736) Composer, born in Venice, Italy. His choral works provide outstanding examples of the polyphonic style. He also wrote many operas and oratorios, and some trio-sonatas in the style of Corelli. >> Corelli, Arcangelo

Caldecott, Randolph [kawldikot] (1846–86) Artist and illustrator, born in Chester, Cheshire. He illustrated Washington Irving's *Old Christmas* (1876) and numerous children's books, such as Aesop's Fables (1883). The *Caldecott Medal* has been awarded annually since 1938 to the best US artist-illustrator of children's books.

Calder, Alexander (Stirling) [kawlder] (1898–1976) Artist and pioneer of kinetic art, born in Philadelphia, PA. He specialized in abstract hanging wire mobiles, which he began to make in 1934.

Calder, (Peter) Ritchie, Baron Ritchie-Calder of Balmashannar [kawlder] (1906–82) Journalist and educationist, born in Forfar, Tayside. Specializing in the spread of scientific knowledge to lay readers, his books include *Living with the Atom* (1962) and *The Evolution of the Machine* (1968).

Calderón de la Barca, Pedro [kolduhron duh la bah(r)ka] (1600–81) Playwright, born in Madrid. In 1635 he was appointed to the court of Philip IV, where he wrote plays, masques, and operas for the court, the Church, and the public theatres. He became a priest in 1651, and wrote many religious plays.

Caldwell, Erskine [kawldwel] (1903–87) Writer, born in White Oak, GA. His best-known novel is *Tobacco Road* (1932). Other books include *God's Little Acre* (1933), *Love and Money* (1954), and *Close to Home* (1962).

Caldwell, Sarah [kawldwel] (1924–) Opera director and conductor, born in Maryville, MO. She formed her own opera company in Boston in 1958, especially noted for its productions of modern works.

Caletti-Bruni, Francesco >> Cavalli, Francesco

Calgacus [kalgakus] (1st-c) Caledonian chieftain in N Britain. He was leader of the tribes defeated by Agricola at the Battle of Mons Graupius. >> Agricola

Calhoun, John C(aldwell) [kalhoon] (1782–1850) US statesman, born in Abbeville County, SC. In 1817 he joined Monroe's cabinet as secretary of war, and was vice-president under John Quincy Adams and Jackson. In 1832 he entered the US Senate, becoming a leader of the states-rights movement. >> Adams, John Quincy; Jackson, Andrew; Monroe, James

Caliari, Paolo >> Veronese

Caligula [kaligyula], nickname of **Gaius Julius Caesar Germanicus** (12–41) Roman emperor (37–41), the youngest son of Germanicus and Agrippina, born in Antium. Brought up in an army camp, he was nicknamed Caligula from his little soldier's boots (*caligae*). Extravagant, autocratic, vicious, and mentally unstable, he wreaked havoc with the finances of the state, and terrorized those around him, until he was assassinated. >> Agrippina (the Elder); Germanicus

Calisher, Hortense (1911–) Writer, born in New York City. Her novels include *The New Yorkers* (1969), *Queenie* (1971), and *The Bobby-Soxer* (1986).

Calixtus [kalikstus], originally **Callisen Georg** (1586–1656) Lutheran theologian, born in Medelbye, Germany. He was declared guilty of heresy for statements which seemed favourable to Catholic dogmas, and for others which approached too near to the Calvinistic standpoint.

Calkins, (Earnest) Elmo (1868-1964) Advertising executive and writer, born in Geneseo, IL. He became founding president of Calkins and Holden, New York City (1902-31), and co-authored with Ralph Holden the first advertising textbook, *Modern Advertising* (1905).

Callaghan (of Cardiff), (Leonard) James Callaghan, Baron [kalahan], known as **Jim Callaghan** (1912–) British statesman and prime minister (1976-9), born in Portsmouth, Hampshire. He was Chancellor of the Exchequer (1964-7), home secretary (1967-70), and foreign secretary (1974-6), and became prime minister on Harold Wilson's resignation. >> Wilson, Harold

Callaghan, Morley (Edward) [kalahan] (1903–) Writer, born in Toronto, Ontario, Canada. His novels include *Strange Fugitive* (1928), *The Many Colored Coat* (1960), and *A Time for Judas* (1983).

Callas, Maria (Meneghini) [kalas], originally **Maria Kalogeropoulos** (1923-77) Operatic soprano, born in New York City of Greek parents. She sang with great authority in all the most exacting soprano roles, excelling in the intricate *bel canto* style of pre-Verdian Italian opera.

Callendar, Hugh Longbourne (1863-1930) Physicist, born in Hatherop, Gloucestershire. He devised a constant-pressure air thermometer which could measure up to 450°C, and also an accurate platinum resistance thermometer.

Calles, Plutarco Elias [kayes] (1877-1945) Mexican political leader and president of Mexico (1924-8), born in Guaymas, Mexico. He became secretary of the interior (1920-4), then president. In 1929 he founded the National Revolutionary Party, but was defeated by Cárdenas, and exiled to the USA (1936-41). >> Cárdenas

Callicrates >> **Ictinos**

Callimachus [kalimakus] (5th-c BC) Greek sculptor, working in Athens in the late 5th-c BC. Vitruvius says he invented the architectural Corinthian capital. >> Vitruvius

Callimachus [kalimakus] (299-210 BC) Greek poet, grammarian, and critic, born in Cyrene, Libya. He became head and cataloguer of the Alexandrian Library.

Callistratus [kalistratus] (4th-c BC) Athenian orator and statesman. In 366 BC he allowed the Thebans to occupy Oropus, and was prosecuted, but defended himself successfully in a brilliant speech. Prosecuted again in 361 for his Spartan sympathies, he was executed.

Callot, Jacques [kayoh] (c.1592-1635) Etcher and engraver, born in Nancy, France. Louis XIII invited him to Paris, where he executed etchings of the siege of La Rochelle, and made some 1600 realistic engravings of 17th-c society.

Callow, Simon (1949–) Actor, director, and writer, born in London. An actor at the Bristol Old Vic and the National Theatre, he has also directed new plays in fringe theatres, and published an autobiography, *Being An Actor* (1984).

Calloway, Cab(ell) (1907-94) Jazz musician, born in Rochester, NY. A versatile song and dance man, he led a succession of outstanding big bands (1928-53). He was featured in the 1979 movie *The Blues Brothers*.

Calman, Mel (1931-94) British cartoonist and writer. A regular cartoonist for several British national newspapers from 1957, he joined *The Times* in 1979.

Calmette, (Léon Charles) Albert [kalmet] (1863-1933) Bacteriologist, born in Nice, France. He is best known for the vaccine BCG (*Bacille Calmette-Guérin*), for inoculation against tuberculosis, which he jointly developed with **Dr Camille Guérin** (1872-1961).

Calvert, Frederick Crace (1819-73) Chemist, born in London. A consulting chemist in Manchester, he was largely instrumental in introducing carbolic acid as a disinfectant.

Calvert, George >> **Baltimore, George Calvert**

Calvi, Robert [kalvee], originally **Gian Roberto Calvini** (1920-82) Banker and financier, born in Milan, Italy. Chairman of Banco Ambrosiano, a 1978 report by the Bank of Italy on alleged illegal dealings led in 1981 to his imprisonment and release pending an appeal. His body was found hanging under Blackfriars Bridge in London, and the repercussions of the case (in which there were alleged links with the Vatican and the Mafia) continued well after his death.

Calvin, John (1509-64) Protestant reformer, born in Noyon, France. At Basel he issued his influential *Institutes of the Christian Religion* (trans, 1536), and at Geneva was persuaded by Farel to help with the reformation. The reformers proclaimed a Protestant Confession of Faith, but the Libertines party rose against this and Calvin and Farel were expelled (1538). In 1541 he was recalled, and by 1555 his authority was confirmed into an absolute supremacy. He left a double legacy to Protestantism by systematizing its doctrine and organizing its ecclesiastical discipline. >> Farel

Calvin, Melvin (1911–) Chemist, born in St Paul, MN. He is best known for his research into the role of chlorophyll in photosynthesis, for which he received the Nobel Prize for Chemistry in 1961.

Calvino, Italo [kalveenoh] (1923-85) Writer, essayist, and journalist, born in Santiago de las Vegas, Cuba, of Italian parents. His novels include (trans titles) *The Path to the Nest of Spiders* (1947), describing resistance against Fascism, and the experimental *If On a Winter's Night a Traveller* (1979).

Cam or **Cão** (15th-c) Portuguese explorer. In 1482 he discovered the mouth of the Congo. His voyages along the West African coast later enabled Bartholomew Diaz to find the sea route to the Indian Ocean around the Cape. >> Diaz, Bartholomew

Camara, Helder (Pessoa) [kamara] (1909–) Roman Catholic theologian and clergyman, born in Fortaleza, Brazil. Archbishop of Olinda and Recife (1964-84), he has been a champion of the poor and of non-violent social change in Brazil.

Camargo, Maria Anna de [kamah(r)goh] (1710-70) Dancer, born in Brussels. She won European fame for her performances at the Paris Opera, and is said to have been responsible for the shortening of the traditional ballet skirt which allowed more complicated steps to be seen.

Cambacérès, Jean Jacques Régis de [kābasayres] (1753-1824) Lawyer, born in Montpellier, France. He became arch-chancellor of the French Empire (1804), and Duke of Parma (1808). As Napoleon's chief legal adviser, his civil code formed the basis of the *Code Napoléon*. >> Napoleon I

Cambio, Arnolfo di >> **Arnolfo di Cambio**

Cambon, Joseph [kābō] (1756-1820) Financier and revolutionary, born in Montpellier, France. As head of the committee on finance (1793-95), he produced the 'Great Book of the Public Debt' in an attempt to stabilize the finances. He was banished as a regicide in 1815. >> Louis XVI

Cambrensis, Giraldus >> **Giraldus Cambrensis**

Cambridge, Ada (1844-1926) Writer and poet, born in St Germans, Norfolk. She settled in Melbourne, Australia, where her writing addressed the role of women in society. Her novels include *A Marked Man* (1890) and *Materfamilias* (1898).

Cambyses II [kambiyseez], Persian **Kambujiya** (?-522 BC) King of the Medes and Persians, who succeeded his father, Cyrus II, in 529 BC. He put his brother Smerdis to death, and in 527 or 525 BC conquered Egypt. >> Cyrus II

Camden, William (1551-1623) Antiquarian and historian, born in London. He compiled a pioneering topographical survey of the British Isles in Latin, *Britannia* (1586). The *Camden Society* (founded 1838) was named after him.

Camerarius, Joachim [kamerairius] (1500–74) Classical scholar and Lutheran theologian, born in Bamberg, Germany. He embraced the Reformation at Wittenberg in 1521, and helped to formulate the Augsburg Confession of 1530. >> Melanchthon

Camerarius, Rudolf Jakob [kamerairius] (1665–1721) Botanist, born in Tübingen, Germany. He showed by experiment in 1694 that plants can reproduce sexually, and identified the stamens and carpels as the male and female sexual apparatus, respectively.

Cameron, James (Mark) (1911–85) Journalist, born in London. He became known as a roving reporter on war, poverty, and injustice, renowned for his integrity, dry wit, and concise summaries. He also wrote and presented many television programmes, including *Cameron Country*.

Cameron, Julia Margaret, née **Pattle** (1815–79) British photographer, born in Calcutta, India. In 1838 she married an Indian jurist **Charles Hay Cameron** (1795–1880), and moved to England in 1848. An outstanding amateur photographer in the 1860s, her close-up portraits of Victorian celebrities received acclaim.

Cameron, Verney Lovett (1844–94) Explorer, born in Radipole, Dorset. In 1872 he was appointed to command an African E coast expedition to relieve David Livingstone, but met Livingstone's followers bearing his remains to the coast. He was the first European to cross Africa from coast to coast. >> Livingstone

Camillus, Marcus Furius [kamilus] (447–365 BC) Roman patrician who first appears as censor in 403 BC. He was five times made dictator, and in 390 BC, according to legend, is said to have driven the Gauls from Rome.

Camm, Sir Sydney (1893–1966) Aircraft designer, born in Windsor, Berkshire. He joined the Hawker Engineering Co in 1923, and became their chief designer, producing the Hurricane, the piston-engined Tornado, Typhoon, and Tempest, the jet-engined Sea Hawk and Hunter, and the jump-jet Harrier.

Camoens or **Camões, Luís de** [kamohenz] (1524–80) Poet, born in Lisbon. He went to India (1553) and was shipwrecked while returning to Goa (1558), losing everything except his major poem, *Os Luciados* (The Lusiads, or Lusitanians). Published in 1572, it has come to be regarded as the Portuguese national epic.

Camp, Walter (Chauncy) (1859–1925) Player of American football, born in New Britain, CT, the 'father of American football'. He helped to shape American football rules, introducing the 11-man side, the concept of 'downs' and 'yards gained', and the creation of a new points-scoring system.

Campagnola, Domenico [kampanyohla] (c.1490–c.1564) Painter, born in Padua, Italy. He is known for his religious frescoes in Padua, as well as for his masterly engravings and line drawings.

Campagnola, Giulio [kampanyohla] (1482–c.1515) Engraver, born in Padua, Italy. He designed type for Aldus Manutius, and produced fine engravings after Mantegna, Bellini, and Giorgione. >> Aldus Manutius

Campanella, Tommaso [kampanela] (1568–1639) Philosopher, born in Stilo, Italy. He was arrested in 1599 for heresy and conspiracy against Spanish rule, and was not finally released until 1626. From prison he wrote his utopian work, *City of the Sun* (trans, c.1601).

Campbell, Alexander (1788–1866) Leader of the 'Disciples of Christ', otherwise known as *Campbellites*, born near Ballymena, Antrim. He emigrated to the USA with his father in 1809, in 1813 succeeding him as pastor of an independent Church at Brush Run, PA.

Campbell, Sir Colin, Baron Clyde (1792–1863) British field marshal, born in Glasgow, Strathclyde. In the Crimean War he commanded the Highland Brigade in a campaign which included the renowned repulse

of the Russians by the 'thin red line' at Balaclava. During the Indian Mutiny he effected the final relief of Lucknow.

Campbell, Donald (Malcolm) (1921–67) Speed-record contestant, born in Horley, Surrey, the son of Sir Malcolm Campbell. In 1964 he set a water-speed record of 276·33 mph on L Dumbleyung, and a land-speed record of 403·1 mph at L Eyre salt flats, both in Australia. He was killed when his *Bluebird* turbo-jet hydroplane crashed on Coniston Water in England. >> Campbell, Malcolm

Campbell, John W(ood), Jr, pseudonym **Don A Stuart** (1910–71) Science-fiction writer, born in Newark, NJ. His novels include *When the Atoms Failed* (1930) and *Twilight* (1934), and he has come to be regarded as the father of modern science-fiction.

Campbell, Kim (Avril Phaedra Douglas) (1947–) Canada's first woman prime minister (1993), born in British Columbia, Canada. She served as minister of justice and defence in Mulroney's cabinet, became leader of the party and prime minister in spring 1993, but disastrously lost the general election some months later. >> Mulroney, Brian

Campbell, Sir Malcolm (1885–1948) Speed-record contestant, born in Chislehurst, Kent. He held land and water speed records from 1927 onwards, and in 1935 achieved 301·1292 mph at Bonneville Salt Flats, UT. In 1939 he achieved his fastest speed on water with 141·74 mph. >> Campbell, Donald

Campbell, Mrs Patrick, née **Beatrice Stella Tanner** (1865–1940) Actress, born in London. She went on the stage in 1888, and leapt to fame in *The Second Mrs Tanqueray* (1893). She played Eliza in Shaw's *Pygmalion* (1914), and formed a long friendship with the author. >> Shaw, George Bernard

Campbell, Reginald John (1867–1956) Clergyman, born in London. A Congregational minister, in 1907 he startled the evangelical world by his exposition of an 'advanced' *New Theology*. He became an Anglican in 1916.

Campbell, (Ignatius) Roy (Dunnachie) (1901–57) Poet and journalist, born in Durban, South Africa. His books of poetry include *The Flaming Terrapin* (1924), *The Wayzgoose* (1928), and *Flowering Rifle* (1939).

Campbell, William Wallace (1862–1938) Astronomer, born in Hancock Co, OH. Director of the Lick Observatory in California (1901–30), he is best known for his work on the radial velocity of stars.

Campbell-Bannerman, Sir Henry (1836–1908) British statesman and prime minister (1905–8), born in Glasgow, Strathclyde. He was chief secretary for Ireland (1884), war secretary (1886, 1892–5), and Liberal leader (1899). His popularity united the Liberal Party.

Campen, Jacob van [kampen] (1595–1657) Architect and painter, born in Haarlem, The Netherlands. He built the first completely Classical building in Holland. His masterpiece was the Mauritshuis, The Hague (1633).

Campendonck, Heinrich [kampendongk] (1889–1957) Expressionist painter, born in Krefeld, Germany. He was a member of the *Blaue Reiter* group founded by Marc and Kandinsky. >> Kandinsky; Marc

Campese, David (Ian) [kampeezee], nickname **Campo** (1962–) Rugby union player, born near Queanbeyan, New South Wales, Australia. One of the fastest wingers in international rugby, he was the star of Australia's 1991 World Cup victory.

Campi, Bernardino [kampee] (1522–c.1592) Italian artist, the son of a goldsmith, and possibly a kinsman of the painter and architect **Antonio Campi** (1536–c.1591). He imitated Titian with such success that it has been difficult to distinguish the copies from the originals. >> Titian

Campi, Giulio [kampee] (c.1502–72) Architect and painter, born in Cremona, Italy. He founded the Cremonese school of painting, to which his brothers **Vincenzo Campi** (1539–91) and **Antonio Campi** (1536–c.1591) also belonged.

Campin, Robert [kămpǐn] (c.1378–1444) Artist, born in Tournai, France. He was called **the Master of Flémalle** from his paintings of Flémelle Abbey near Liège.

Campion, Edmund, St (1540–81), feast day 1 December. The first of the English Jesuit martyrs, born in London. Fearing arrest, he escaped to Bohemia in 1573, but was recalled in 1580 for a Jesuit mission to England. After circulating his *Ten Reasons* (trans, 1581) against Anglicanism, he was tortured and hanged. He was canonized in 1970.

Campion, Jane (1954–) Film director, born in Waikanae, New Zealand. Her films include *Peel* (1984, Cannes Palme d'Or, best short film), her first feature *Sweetie* (1989), and *The Piano* (1993, shared Cannes Palme d'Or).

Campion, Thomas (1567–1620) Physician, poet, and composer, born in Witham, Essex. As well as poetry in Latin and English he left several books of 'ayres' for voice and lute.

Campoli, Alfredo [kampohlee] (1906–91) Violinist, born in Rome. He went to London in 1911, and during the 1930s became head of his salon orchestra.

Camus, Albert [kahmü] (1913–1960) French existentialist writer, born in Mondovi, Algeria. He earned an international reputation with his nihilistic novel, *The Outsider* (trans, 1942). Later novels include (trans titles) *The Plague* (1947) and *The Fall* (1956), and he also wrote plays and several political works. He received the Nobel Prize for Literature in 1957.

Canaletto [kanaletoh], originally **Giovanni Antonio Canal** (1697–1768) Painter, born in Venice, Italy. He painted a renowned series of views in Venice, and in England (1746–56) his views of London and elsewhere proved extremely popular.

Canaris, Wilhelm [kanahris] (1887–1945) Naval commander, born in Aplerbeck, Germany. He became admiral of the German navy and chief of the *Abwehr*, the military intelligence service of the high command of the armed forces. Associated with the 1944 bomb plot against Hitler, he was hanged. >> Hitler

Candela, (Outeriño) Felix [kandela] (1910–) Architect and engineer, born in Madrid. One of the world's foremost designers of slender reinforced concrete hyperbolic paraboloid shell roofs, his creations have included the Sports Palace for the Olympic Games in Mexico City (1968).

Candolle, Augustin Pyrame de [kãdol] (1778–1841) Botanist, born in Geneva, Switzerland. By 1813 he had developed a general scheme of plant taxonomy which was to dominate plant classification for 50 years.

Canetti, Elias [kanetee] (1905–94) Writer, born in Rustschuck, Bulgaria. He lived in England from 1938. His interest in crowd psychology produced two important works: the novel *The Tower of Babel* (trans, 1936) and the study *Crowds and Power* (trans, 1960). He was awarded the Nobel Prize for Literature in 1981.

Cange, seigneur du >> **du Cange, Charles du Fresne**

Caniff, Milt(on Arthur) (1907–88) Strip cartoonist, born in Hillsboro, OH. He created his first daily strip, *Dickie Dare*, in 1933, then joined the *New York Daily News* to create *Terry and the Pirates* (1934), later replacing this with the series *Steve Canyon* (1947–88).

Canmore, Malcolm >> **Malcolm III**

Canning, George (1770–1827) British statesman, born in London. Nominated Governor-General of India (1822), he was set to leave when Castlereagh's suicide saw him installed as foreign secretary. He was the first to recognize the free states of Spanish America, contended earnestly for Catholic Emancipation, and prepared the way for a repeal of the Corn Laws. In 1827 he formed an

administration with the aid of the Whigs, but died the same year. >> Castlereagh

Cannizzaro, Stanislao [kaneedzahroh] (1826–1910) Chemist, born in Palermo, Italy. He co-ordinated organic and inorganic chemistry, and discovered the reaction named after him.

Cannon, Annie Jump (1863–1941) Astronomer, born in Dover, DE. She reorganized the classification of stars in terms of surface temperature, and catalogued over 225 000 stars brighter than 9th or 10th magnitude.

Cannon, W(alter) B(radford) (1871–1945) Physiologist, born in Prairie du Chien, WI. He is known for his use of X-rays in the study of the alimentary tract, and for his work on hormones and nerve transmission. He also developed the concept of a constant internal physiological environment (*homoeostasis*).

Cano, Alonso [kahnoh] (1601–67) Painter, sculptor, and architect, born in Granada, Spain. In 1639 he was appointed court painter and architect, and designed the facade of Coranada Cathedral (c.1664).

Cano, Juan Sebastian del [kahnoh] (?–1526) The first man to circumnavigate the globe, born in Guetaria, Spain. In 1519 he sailed with Magellan in command of the *Concepción*, and after Magellan's death navigated the *Victoria* home to Spain. >> Magellan

Canova, Antonio [kanohva] (1757–1822) Sculptor, born in Possagno, Italy. He is regarded as the founder of a new Neoclassicist school. His best-known works are the tombs of popes Clement XIII, and XIV, and several statues of Napoleon.

Cantelupe, St Thomas de or **St Thomas of Hereford** [kanteloop] (c.1218–1282), feast day 3 October. Clergyman, born in Hambleden, Buckinghamshire. He supported the barons against Henry III, and became Chancellor of England (1264–5). In 1275 he was made Bishop of Hereford, and after his death his shrine became highly revered. He was canonized in 1320.

Canth, Minna, *née* **Ulrika Vilhelmina Johnsson** (1844–97) Playwright and feminist, born in Tampere, Finland. A powerful exponent of the Realist school, her best-known plays are *A Working-class Wife* (trans, 1885) and *Children of Misfortune* (trans, 1888).

Canton, John (1718–72) Physicist, born in Stroud, Gloucestershire. He invented an electroscope and an electrometer, originated experiments in induction, was the first to make powerful artificial magnets, and in 1762 demonstrated the compressibility of water.

Cantor, Eddie, originally **Edward Israel Iskowitz** (1892–1964) Entertainer, born in New York City. He became a touring vaudeville artiste and starred in Broadway reviews, notably *Kid Boots* (1923–6). He later hosted successful shows on radio and television.

Cantor, Georg (Ferdinand Ludwig Philipp) (1845–1918) Mathematician, born in St Petersburg, Russia. He worked out a highly original arithmetic of the infinite which resulted in a theory of infinite sets of different sizes, adding a new and important branch to mathematics.

Canute or **Cnut**, sometimes known as **the Great** (c.995–1035) King of England (from 1016), Denmark (from 1019), and Norway (from 1028), the younger son of Sweyn Forkbeard. He defeated Edmund Ironside at Assandun (1016), secured Mercia and Northumbria, and became King of all England after Edmund's death. The story of his failure to make the tide recede was invented by a 12th-c historian. >> Edmund II; Sweyn

Cao Xuequin [chow shwechin], also spelled **Ts'ao Hsüeh-ch'in** (1715–63) Writer, born into a family who had grown rich as directors of the Nanjing Imperial Textile Works. The family wealth was later squandered, and he recorded his memories in (trans title) *Dream of the Red Chamber*, important for its realistic detail of upper-class family life in the early 18th-c.

Cao Yu [chow yoo], pseudonym of **Wan Jiabao** (1910–) Playwright, born in Tianjin, China. His best-known work (trans title), *Thunderstorm*, was staged in 1935; other major plays include *Metamorphosis* (1940) and *Family* (1941).

Capa, Robert, originally **Andrei Friedmann** (1913–54) Photojournalist, born in Budapest. He recorded the Spanish Civil War (1935–7), covered China under the Japanese attacks of 1938, and reported World War 2 in Europe. He was killed in the Indo-China fighting which preceded the war in Vietnam.

Capablanca, José Raúl [kapablangka] (1888–1942) Chess player, born in Havana. In 1921 he won the world championship, defeating Lasker without losing a game. His defeat by Alekhine in 1927 was a major surprise, and despite further tournament successes he never regained his title. >> Alekhine; Lasker, Emanuel

Čapek, Josef [chapek] (1887–1945) Writer and painter, born in Schwadonitz, Czech Republic, the elder brother of Karel Čapek. His early literary works, written in collaboration with his brother, include the allegorical *The Insect Play* (trans, 1921). >> Čapek, Karel

Čapek, Karel [chapek] (1890–1938) Writer, born in Schwadonitz, Czech Republic, the brother of Josef Čapek. His best-known work is his play *R.U.R.* (Rossum's Universal Robots), produced in 1921, showing mechanization rampant. With his brother he wrote *The Insect Play* (trans, 1921). >> Čapek, Josef

Capell, Edward (1713–81) Scholar, born near Bury St Edmunds, Suffolk. He published an edition of Shakespeare (10 vols, 1768) based on the Folio and Quarto texts, and a full commentary, *Notes and Various Readings to Shakespeare* (3 vols, 1783).

Capella, Martianus Mineus Felix [kapela] (fl.480) North African scholar and writer. His *Satiricon*, a kind of encyclopaedia, highly esteemed during the Middle Ages, is a medley of prose and verse, full of curious learning.

Capet, Hugo or **Hugh** [kapet] (c.938–96) King of France, founder of the third Frankish royal dynasty (the Capetians), which ruled France until 1328. Son of Hugh the Great, he was elected king and crowned at Noyon (987).

Capgrave, John (1393–1464) Chronicler, theologian, and provincial of the Augustine Friars in England, born in Lynn, Norfolk. His works include Bible commentaries, sermons, and a Chronicle of England.

Capito or **Köpfel, Wolfgang Fabricius** [kapeetoh] (1478–1541) Religious reformer, born in Hagenau, Alsace. He entered the Benedictine order, and approved of Luther's action, but did not declare for the Reformation until later, when he became a Protestant leader in Strasbourg. >> Luther

Capone, Al [kapohn], popular name of **Alphonse Capone** (1899–1947) Gangster, born in New York City. He achieved worldwide notoriety as a racketeer during the prohibition era in Chicago. In 1931 he was sentenced to 10 years' imprisonment for tax evasion, but was released on health grounds in 1939.

Capote, Truman [kapohtee], pseudonym of **Truman Streckfus Persons** (1924–84) Writer, born in New Orleans, LA. His novels include *Breakfast at Tiffany's* (1958; filmed 1961) and *In Cold Blood* (1966), described as a 'nonfiction novel' because of the way he tells of actual events in novelistic form.

Capp, Al, originally **Alfred Gerald Caplin** (1909–79) Strip cartoonist, born in New Haven, CT. He joined Associated Press, where he introduced hill-billy characters and developed the successful *L'il Abner* (1934).

Capra, Frank (1897–1991) Film director, born in Palermo, Italy. Among his best-known films are *Mr Deeds Goes to Town* (1936, Oscar), *You Can't Take It with You* (1938, Oscar), and *Arsenic and Old Lace* (1942).

Caprivi, Georg Leo, Graf von (Count of) [kapreevee] (1831–99) German soldier and political leader, chancellor of Prussia (1890–4), born in Berlin. On Bismarck's fall in 1890, he became imperial chancellor and Prussian prime minister.

Caracalla or **Caracallus** [karakala], popular name of **Marcus Aurelius Severus Antoninus Augustus**, originally **Septimius Bassianus** (188–217) Roman emperor, born in Lugdunum (Lyon, modern France), the son of the emperor Septimius Severus. In 211 he became joint emperor with his brother Publius Septimius Antoninius Geta, whom he soon murdered, but was himself assassinated. >> Severus

Caractacus [karaktakus], **Caratacus**, or **Caradoc** (1st-c AD) A chief of the Catuvellauni, the son of Cunobelinus. He fought against the Romans in the years following the Claudian conquest (43). Taken to Rome (51), he was exhibited in triumph, and pardoned by Claudius. >> Claudius

Caran d'Ache [karã dash], pseudonym of **Emmanuel Poiré** (1858–1909) Caricaturist, born in Moscow. He moved to Paris, where he became a pioneer in the development of the French comic strip. His pseudonym came from the Russian word for 'pencil'.

Caratacus >> **Caractacus**

Carausius, Marcus Aurelius [karowsius] (c.245–293) Army officer, born in Menapia (modern Belgium). He set himself up in Britain as emperor (c.287), and ruled there until his murder by one of his officers.

Caravaggio [karavajioh], originally **Michelangelo Merisi** (1573–1610) Baroque painter, born in Caravaggio, Italy, whence his nickname. His works include altarpieces and religious paintings, notably several of St Matthew (1599–1603) and 'Christ at Emmaus' (c.1602–3).

Caravaggio, Polidoro Caldara da [karavajioh] (c.1492–1543) Painter, born in Caravaggio, Italy. He aided Raphael in his Vatican frescoes. His 'Christ Bearing the Cross' is in Naples. >> Raphael

Cardan, Jerome [kah(r)dan, kah(r)dahnoh], Ital **Geronimo Cardano**, Lat **Hieronymus Cardanus** (1501–76) Mathematician and physician, born in Pavia, Italy. His *Great Art* (trans, 1545) was influential in the development of algebra, giving the first published algebraic solution of cubic and quartic equations.

Cardano, Girolamo >> **Cardan, Jerome**

Carden, Joan Maralyn (1937–) Operatic and concert soprano, born in Melbourne, Victoria, Australia. She won the Dame Joan Hammond Award for Outstanding Service to Opera in Australia in 1987.

Cárdenas, Lázaro [kah(r)t henas] (1895–1970) Mexican soldier and president of the Mexican Republic (1934–40), born in Jiquilpan, Mexico. He wrested control of the government from President Calles and instituted a broad programme of social and economic reforms, thus ensuring Mexico's stability. >> Calles

Cardew, Michael (1901–82) British potter. After working in the Cotswolds and Cornwall, in 1942 he took over the Achimota College in Ghana, and started his own stoneware pottery at Vumé on the Volta.

Cardigan, James Thomas Brudenell, 7th Earl of (1797–1868) British general, born in Hambleden, Buckinghamshire. He commanded a cavalry brigade in the Crimea, and led the fatal charge of the Light Brigade at Balaclava (25 Oct 1854). The woollen jacket known as a *cardigan* is named after him.

Cardin, Pierre [kah(r)dï] (1922–) French fashion designer, born in Venice, Italy. He went to Paris in 1944, where he worked on costume design, notably for Cocteau's film *Beauty and the Beast* (1947). He opened his own house in 1953, producing fashion for both women and men. >> Cocteau

Cardozo, Benjamin (Nathan) [kah(r)**doh**zoh] (1870–1938) Judge, born in New York City. He sat on the bench of the New York Court of Appeals (1913–32) and in the US Supreme Court (1932–8), becoming known for his views on congressional power, control of inter-state commerce, and states' rights.

Carew, Thomas [ka**roo**] (1595–1639) Poet, born in West Wickham, Kent. A friend of Jonson and Donne, he wrote polished lyrics in the Cavalier tradition, and a masque *Coelum britannicum* (1634) which was performed at court. >> Donne; Jonson

Carey, George Leonard [**kair**ee] (1935–) Anglican clergyman, born in London. He was appointed Bishop of Bath and Wells in 1987 and Archbishop of Canterbury in 1991.

Carey, Henry C(harles) [**kair**ee] (1793–1879) Political economist, born in Philadelphia, PA. Originally a zealous free-trader, he came to regard free trade as an ideal, but impossible in the existing state of US industry.

Carey, Peter [**kair**ee] (1943–) Writer, born in Bacchus Marsh, Victoria, Australia. His books include *Bliss* (1981), *Oscar and Lucinda* (1988, Booker), and *The Tax Inspector* (1991).

Carey, William [**kair**ee] (1761–1834) Missionary and orientalist, born in Paulerspury, Northamptonshire. In 1793 he and John Thomas were chosen as the first Baptist missionaries to India, where he founded the Serampur mission (1799).

Carissimi, Giacomo [ka**ree**simee] (1605–74) Composer, born in Marino, Italy. He did much to develop the sacred cantata, and his works include the oratorio *Jephthah* (trans, 1650).

Carl XVI Gustaf (1946–) King of Sweden since 1973, born in Stockholm. In 1976 he married Silvia Sommerlath, and they have three children: **Victoria** (1977–), **Carl Philip** (1979–), and **Madeleine** (1982–). >> Silvia

Carle, Eric (1929–) Picture book artist, born in Germany. Using a distinctive collage technique, he has written and illustrated several children's books, including *The Very Hungry Caterpillar* (1970).

Carleton, Guy, Baron Dorchester (1724–1808) British soldier, born in Strabane, Northern Ireland. Governor of Quebec (1775–7, 1786–9, 1793–6), he defeated the Americans under Benedict Arnold on L Champlain in 1776. >> Arnold, Benedict

Carlile, Richard (1790–1843) Journalist and radical reformer, born in Ashburton, Devon. He sold the prohibited radical weekly *Black Dwarf* throughout London in 1817, and was imprisoned several times for his publications.

Carlile, Wilson (1847–1942) Anglican clergyman, born in London. In 1882 he founded the Church Army, and was made a prebendary of St Paul's in 1906.

Carlos, Don (1788–1855) Spanish pretender to the throne, the second son of Charles IV of Spain, born in Madrid. In 1833 he asserted his claim to the throne - a claim reasserted by his son, **Don Carlos** (1818–61), and by the latter's nephew, **Don Carlos** (1848–1909). *Carlist* risings occurred during 1834–9 and 1872–6.

Carlson, Carolyn (1943–) Dancer and choreographer, born in California. She created a piece for the Paris Opera Ballet in 1973 which was so well-received that a special post was invented for her. From 1980 she directed her own troupe at Venice's Teatro Fenice, but later returned to Paris.

Carlson, Chester (Floyd) (1906–68) Physicist, born in Seattle, WA. By 1938 he had devised a basic system of electrostatic copying on plain paper, resulting in the xerographic method which is now widely used.

Carlsson, Ingvar (Costa) (1934–) Swedish statesman and prime minister (1986–91). He became deputy to Olof Palme in 1982, and succeeded him as prime minister after Palme's assassination in 1986. >> Palme

Carlstadt or **Karlstadt** [**kah(r)l**shtat], originally **Andreas Rudolf Bodenstein** (?–1541) German reformer, born prior to 1483 in Carlstadt, Bavaria. In 1517 he joined Luther, but later opposed him on the question of the Eucharist. Accused of participation in the Peasants' War, he fled to Switzerland. >> Luther

Carlucci, Frank (Charles) [kah(r)**loo**chee] (1930–) US statesman, born in Scranton, PA. He served as US ambassador to Portugal, deputy director of the CIA, National Security Adviser (1968), and defence secretary (1987), supporting Soviet-US arms reduction initiatives.

Carlyle, Jane Baillie, née **Welsh** (1801–66) Diarist, born in Haddington, Lothian, the wife of Thomas Carlyle. After her death, he edited her letters and diaries, which show her to have been one of the most accomplished women of her time. >> Carlyle, Thomas

Carlyle, Thomas (1795–1881) Man of letters, born in Ecclefechan, Dumfries and Galloway. His best-known works are *Sartor Resartus* (1833–4), and studies on the French Revolution (3 vols, 1837) and on Frederick the Great (1858–65). >> Carlyle, Jane Baillie

Carmen Sylva, pseudonym of **Elizabeth, Queen of Romania** (1843–1916) The daughter of Prince Hermann of Wied Neuwied, who married the future King Carol I of Romania in 1869. After 1874 she began writing, and under her pseudonym published *Pilgrim Sorrow* (trans, 1882) and many other works. >> Carol I

Carmichael, Hoagy, popular name of **Howard Hoagland Carmichael** (1899–1981) Jazz pianist and composer, born in Bloomington, IN. Several of his many compositions became classics, such as 'Stardust' (1927) and 'In the Cool Cool Cool of the Evening' (1951, Oscar).

Carmichael, Stokely (1941–) Radical activist, born in Trinidad. In the USA from 1952, he popularized the phrase 'black power', and as a Black Panther came to symbolize black violence to many whites. He later favoured forging alliances with radical whites, which led to his resignation from the Panthers in 1968.

Carnap, Rudolf (1891–1970) Philosopher, born in Wuppertal, Germany. One of the leaders of the Vienna Circle of logical positivists, his writings include *The Logical Construction of the World* (trans, 1928) and *Meaning and Necessity* (1947).

Carnarvon, George Edward Stanhope Molyneux Herbert, 5th Earl of [kah(r)**nah(r)**von] (1866–1923) Amateur Egyptologist, born at Highclere Castle, Berkshire. From 1907 he sponsored Carter's excavations of royal tombs at Thebes, which discovered Tutankhamen's tomb. >> Carter, Howard; Tutankhamen

Carné, Marcel [kah(r)**nay**] (1909–) Film director, born in Paris. From 1931–49 he collaborated with Prévert in a series of productions, including (trans titles) *Port of Shadows* (1938), *Daybreak* (1939), and *Children of Paradise* (1944). >> Prévert

Carneades [kah(r)**nee**adeez] (c.214–129 BC) Greek philosopher, born in Cyrene. He became head of the Academy, which under his very different, sceptical direction became known as the 'New Academy'.

Carnegie, Andrew [kah(r)**nay**gee, or **kar**negee] (1835–1919) Industrialist and philanthropist, born in Dunfermline, Fife. His family emigrated to Pittsburgh, PA (1848), and by 1901 he had become a multimillionare. He gave generously to libraries and other public institutions, and several buildings are named after him.

Carnegie, Dale [kah(r)**nay**gee, or **kar**negee], originally **Dale Carnegey** (1888–1955) Lecturer on public speaking, born in Maryville, MO. His theories on public speaking and self-esteem were published in highly successful books, notably *How to Win Friends and Influence People* (1936).

Carnot, Lazare (Nicolas Marguerite) [kah(r)noh] (1753–1823) French statesman, known as 'the organizer of victory' during the Revolutionary Wars, born in Nolay, France. He was one of the Directors (1795), became minister of war (1800), and during the Hundred Days was minister of the interior.

Carnot, (Nicholas Léonard) Sadi [kah(r)noh] (1796–1832) Scientist, born in Paris. He spent much of his life investigating the design of steam engines, and his findings were the foundation of the science of thermodynamics.

Caro, Sir Anthony [kahroh] (1924–) Sculptor, born in London. His work is abstract, typically large pieces of metal welded together and painted in primary colours.

Carol I (1839–1914) The first king of Romania, born in Hohenzollern-Sigmaringen. He became king in 1881, and during his reign promoted economic development and military expansion, brutally crushing a peasant rebellion in 1907. >> Carmen Sylva

Carol II (1893–1953) King of Romania (1930–40), born in Sinaia, Romania. He renounced his right of succession (1925) because of a love affair, and went into exile. He returned through a coup in 1930, but was forced to abdicate in 1940 in favour of his son. >> Michael

Caroline of Ansbach, Wilhelmina (1683–1737) Queen of George II of Great Britain, born in Ansbach, Germany, the daughter of a German prince. She exercised a strong influence over her husband, and was a leading supporter of his chief minister, Robert Walpole. >> George II; Walpole, Robert

Caroline of Brunswick, Amelia Elizabeth (1768–1821) Wife of George IV of the Great Britain, born in Brunswick, Germany. She married the Prince of Wales in 1795, but once king (1820) he requested that she renounce the title of queen and live abroad. She refused, and was not permitted entry to the coronation in 1821. >> Charlotte, Princess; George IV

Carossa, Hans [karosa] (1878–1956) Writer and physician, born in Tölz, Germany. He became prominent with his autobiographical *A Childhood* (trans, 1922). Other works include a diary of his observations during World War 1, and many novels.

Carothers, Wallace (Hume) [karuht herz] (1896–1937) Industrial chemist, born in Burlington, IA. Working for the Du Pont Company at Wilmington, he produced the first successful synthetic rubber, neoprene, and followed this with nylon.

Carpaccio, Vittore [kah(r)pachioh] (c.1460–c.1525) Painter, born in Venice, Italy. His work includes the nine subjects from the life of St Ursula (1490–5), and his masterpiece, 'The Presentation in the Temple' (1510), executed for San Giobbe.

Carpenter, Mary (1807–77) Educationist and reformer, born in Exeter, Devon, the sister of William Carpenter. She opened a girls' school in Bristol in 1829, later founding a ragged school there, and several reformatories for girls. >> Carpenter, William

Carpenter, William Benjamin (1813–85) Biologist, born in Exeter, Devon, the brother of Mary Carpenter. He took part in a deep sea exploration expedition (1868–71), and carried out research on the Foraminifera. >> Carpenter, Mary

Carpentier, Alejo (1904–80) Writer, born in Havana. His numerous books (trans titles) include *The Kingdom of this World* (1949) and *The Lost Steps* (1953).

Carpini, John of Plano [kah(r)peenee], Ital **Giovanni da Pian del Carpini** (c.1182–c.1253) Franciscan monk and traveller, born in Umbria, Italy. He headed a mission sent by Pope Innocent IV to the Emperor of the Mongols, travelling from Lyon (April 1245) to the Karakoram Mts (July 1246). He returned in 1247, and wrote an account of his travels.

Carpocrates of Alexandria [kah(r)pokrateez] (2nd-c) Greek religious leader. He founded the gnostic sect of *Carpocratians*, who sought through contemplation the union of the individual soul with God.

Carr, Emily (1871–1945) Painter and writer, raised in Victoria, British Columbia, Canada. Her original work began at age 57, when she travelled E to meet members of the Group of Seven. After 1932 nature themes replaced the native themes of her early work.

Carr, Emma Perry (1880–1972) Chemist and educator, born in Holmesville, OH. She made significant contributions to the analysis of organic molecules with ultraviolet absorption spectroscopy.

Carrà, Carlo [kara] (1881–1966) Painter, born in Quargnento, Italy. He adopted a Futurist style, then in 1917 became influenced by the 'metaphysical painting' movement.

Carracci [karahchee] A family of painters, born in Bologna, Italy. The most famous was **Annibale Carracci** (1560–1609), who with his brother, **Agostino Carracci** (1557–1602), painted the gallery of the Farnese Palace, Rome. With their cousin, **Ludovico Carracci** (1555–1619), they founded an influential academy of painting in Bologna (1582).

Carranza, Venustiano >> Villa, Pancho

Carr-Boyd, Ann Kirsten (1938–) Composer, teacher, and music historian, born in Sydney, New South Wales, Australia. A leading authority on Aboriginal and early Australian music, her compositions include *Symphony in Three Movements* (1964) and *Australian Baroque* (1984).

Carré, John Le >> Le Carré, John

Carrel, Alexis (1873–1944) Biologist, born in Ste Foy-lès-Lyon, France. He discovered a method of suturing bloodvessels which made it possible to replace arteries, and was awarded the Nobel Prize for Physiology or Medicine in 1912.

Carreño de Miranda, Juan [karenyoh day miranda] (1614–85) Painter, born in Avilés, Spain. Assistant and successor of Velasquez at the Spanish court, he painted religious pictures and frescoes, as well as portraits. >> Velasquez

Carreras, José Maria [karairas] (1946–) Lyric tenor, born in Barcelona, Spain. He made his debut at Covent Garden and at the Metropolitan Opera in 1974. After severe illness in the mid-1980s, he returned to the stage.

Carrére, John Merven >> Hastings, Thomas

Carrier, Jean Baptiste [karyay] (1756–94) French revolutionary, born in Yolet, France. At Nantes in 1793 he massacred 16 000 Vendéan and other prisoners, chiefly by drowning them in the R Loire. After the fall of Robespierre he was tried and guillotined. >> Robespierre

Carrier, Willis (Haviland) (1876–1950) Engineer and inventor, born in Angola, NY. In 1915 he formed the Carrier Engineering Corporation, and in 1939 invented a practical air-conditioning system for skyscrapers.

Carriera, Rosalba [karyaira] (1675–1757) Painter, born in Venice, Italy. She was famed for her portraits and miniatures, some of them in pastel, especially on ivory. She moved to Paris in 1720, where she received many famous commissions.

Carrière, Eugène [karyair] (1849–1906) Artist, born in Gournay-sur-Marne, France. He lived and worked in Paris, specializing in domestic groups and portraits.

Carrington, Peter (Alexander Rupert) Carrington, 6th Baron (1919–) British statesman, born in London. He became secretary of state for defence (1970–4), Conservative Party chairman (1972–4), and foreign secretary (1979–82), but resigned over the Argentinian invasion of the Falkland Is, and later became secretary-general of NATO (1984–8).

Carroll, Charles (1737–1832) US statesman, born in Annapolis, MD, the cousin of John Carroll. He served in the

Continental Congress (1776–8), and was the first senator from Maryland to the US Senate (1789–92). >> Carroll, John

Carroll, James (1854–1907) Physician, born in Woolwich, Greater London. Serving as a US army surgeon, in association with Walter Reed, he did valuable research on yellow fever. >> Reed, Walter

Carroll, John (1735–1815) First US Roman Catholic bishop, born in Upper Marlboro, MD, the cousin of Charles Carroll. Appointed archbishop in 1808, he brought in European missionaries, started three seminaries, and cofounded (1789) a college that became Georgetown University. >> Carroll, Charles

Carroll, Lewis, pseudonym of **Charles Lutwidge Dodgson** (1832–98) Writer, born in Daresbury, Cheshire. His nursery tale *Alice's Adventures in Wonderland* (1865), and its sequel *Through the Looking-Glass* (1872), quickly became classics. He also wrote much humorous verse, such as 'The Hunting of the Snark' (1876).

Carruthers, Jimmy [karuht herz] (1929–90) Boxer, born in Paddington, New South Wales, Australia. He became world bantamweight champion in 1952, then retired at the age of 25.

Carson, Johnny, popular name of **John William Carson** (1925–) Television personality and businessman, born in Corning, IA. He starred in *The Johnny Carson Show* (1955–6), after which he hosted the hugely popular *The Tonight Show* (1962–92).

Carson, Kit, popular name of **Christopher Carson** (1809–68) Frontiersman, born in Madison Co, KY. He acted as guide in John Frémont's explorations (1842), was Indian agent in New Mexico (1853), and fought for the Union in the Civil War. Several places are named after him. >> Frémont

Carson, Rachel (Louise) (1907–64) Naturalist and publicist, born in Springdale, PA. In 1962 her *Silent Spring* directed much public attention to the problems caused by agricultural pesticides, and she became a pioneer in the conservationist movement of the 1960s.

Carson, Willie, popular name of **William Fisher Hunter Carson** (1942–) Jockey, born in Stirling, Central, Scotland. In 1972 he became the first Scotsman to be champion jockey, winning his first Classic on *High Top* in the 2000 Guineas. He was the 1979 Derby winner on *Troy*, and won again on *Henbit* in 1980.

Carstairs, John Paddy, originally **John Keys** (1914–70) Writer, film director, and artist. His best-known novel is *Love and Ella Rafferty* (1947). He also painted light-hearted landscapes in various media.

Carstens, Asmus Jakob (1754–98) Painter, born near Schleswig, Denmark. His 'Fall of the Angels' gained him a professorship in the Academy of Art in Berlin (1790). He lived in Rome from 1792, working on Classical themes.

Cartan, Elie (Joseph) [kah(r)tã] (1869–1951) Mathematician, born in Dolomieu, France. He founded the subject of analysis on differentiable manifolds, and discovered the theory of spinors, the method of moving frames, and the exterior differential calculus. His son, **Henri-(Paul) Cartan** (1904–) was also a mathematician, known for his work in the theory of analytic functions.

Carte, Richard D'Oyly >> **D'Oyly Carte, Richard**

Carter, Angela (1940–92) Writer, born in Eastbourne, East Sussex. Her novels and short stories are characterized by feminist themes and fantasy narratives; they include *The Magic Toyshop* (1967), *Nights at the Circus* (1984), and *Wise Children* (1991).

Carter, Benny, popular name of **Bennet Lester Carter** (1907–) Alto saxophonist, born in New York City. An outstanding writer of big band arrangements, he composed for the Henderson and Goodman orchestras, among others, and was influential in the development of British jazz. >> Goodman, Benny; Henderson, Fletcher

Carter, Elliott Cook, Jr (1908–) Composer, born in New York City. His works include two symphonies, four concertos, and several sonatas. In 1960 his second string quartet won a Pulitzer Prize.

Carter, Howard (1874–1939) Archaeologist, born in Swaffham, Norfolk. Under the patronage of George Herbert, Earl of Carnarvon, his discoveries included the tombs of Hatshepsut (1907) and Tutankhamen (1922). >> Carnarvon; Hatshepsut; Tutankhamen

Carter, Jimmy, popular name of **James (Earl) Carter** (1924–) US statesman and 39th president (1977–81), born in Plains, GA. In 1976 he won the Democratic presidential nomination, and defeated Gerald Ford. He arranged the peace treaty between Egypt and Israel (1979), and was much concerned with human rights at home and abroad. His administration ended in difficulties over the taking of US hostages in Iran and the Soviet invasion of Afghanistan, and he was defeated by Reagan in 1980. He has since been much involved in international diplomacy. >> Ford, Gerald R; Reagan

Carteret, John, 1st Earl Granville [kah(r)tuhret] (1690–1763) British chief minister (1742–4), born in London. He became secretary of state (1721) and Lord-Lieutenant of Ireland (1724–9). As Earl Granville, he was driven from power by the Pelhams (1744) because of his pro-Hanoverian policies. >> Pelham, Henry

Carteret, Philip [kah(r)tuhret] (?–1796) English navigator, who commanded the *Swallow* in Samuel Wallis's expedition round the world (1766). He discovered Pitcairn I and other small islands (one of the Solomons bears his name) and returned to England in 1769. >> Wallis, Samuel

Cartier, Sir Georges Etienne [kah(r)tyay] (1814–73) Canadian prime minister (1858–62), born in Antoine, Quebec, Canada. He became attorney general for Lower Canada in 1856, was joint prime minister with Sir John A Macdonald, and then prime minister. >> Macdonald, John A

Cartier, Jacques [ka(r)tyay] (1491–1557) Navigator, born in St-Malo, France. He made three voyages of exploration to North America (1534–42), surveying the coast of Canada and the St Lawrence R.

Cartier-Bresson, Henri [ka(r)tyay bresõ] (1908–) Photographer, born in Paris. He worked only in black-and-white, concerned exclusively with illustrating contemporary life. In the mid-1970s he gave up photography, and returned to his earlier interests of painting and drawing.

Cartimandua [kah(r)timandyooa] (1st-c AD) Pro-Roman queen of the Yorkshire Brigantes. She protected the N borders of the Roman province of Britain after the conquest (43) until overthrown by her ex-husband, the anti-Roman Venutius. >> Caractacus

Cartland, (Mary) Barbara (Hamilton) (1901–) Popular romantic novelist, born in Edgbaston, West Midlands. Since her first novel, *Jigsaw* (1923), she has written over 600 books, mostly romantic novels but also biographies, books on food, health, and beauty, and several volumes of autobiography.

Cartwright, Edmund (1743–1823) Inventor of the power loom (1785–90), born in Marnham, Nottinghamshire. Attempts to use the loom met with fierce opposition, and it was not until the 19th-c that it came into practical use. >> Cartwright, John

Cartwright, John (1740–1824) Political reformer, born in Marnham, Nottinghamshire, the elder brother of Edmund Cartwright. He advocated many political and social reforms, such as annual parliaments, the ballot, and manhood suffrage. >> Cartwright, Edmund

Cartwright, Peter (1785–1872) Methodist preacher of the US frontier, born in Amherst Co, VA. Ordained in Kentucky in 1806, he moved to Illinois in 1823. He wrote his autobiography (1856) and *The Backwoods Preacher* (1869).

Caruso, Enrico [ka**roo**zoh] (1873-1921) Operatic tenor, born in Naples, Italy. He made his debut in Naples in 1894. The extraordinary power of his voice, combined with his acting ability, won him worldwide recognition.

Carver, George Washington (c.1864-1943) Scientist, born near Diamond Grove, MO. He was born into an African-American slave family, and received little formal education in his early years. He became renowned for his research into agricultural problems and synthetic products, and was an influential teacher and humanitarian.

Carver, John (c.1575-1621) Colonist in America, born in Nottinghamshire or Derbyshire. He emigrated to Holland in 1609, later joining the *Mayflower* expedition in 1620. He was elected first governor of the colony at New Plymouth, MA.

Carver, Raymond (1939-88) Poet and short-story writer, born in Clatskanie, OR. His collections include *Will You Please Be Quiet, Please?* (1976) and *Cathedral* (1983).

Carver, Richard Michael Power Carver, Baron (1915-) British soldier, born in Surrey. In World War 2 he served with distinction in North Africa (1941-3), Italy (1943) and Normandy (1944). He later became chief of the general staff (1971-3) and of the defence staff (1973-6).

Carver, Robert (c.1490-c.1567) Composer, canon of Scone, who was attached to the Chapel Royal of Scotland. Five of his Masses have survived.

Cary, John [**kair**ee] (c.1754-1835) English cartographer. He produced the *New and Correct English Atlas* (1787) and the *New Universal Atlas* (1808), and in 1794 undertook a road survey of England and Wales.

Cary, (Arthur) Joyce (Lunel) [**kair**ee] (1888-1957) Writer, born in Londonderry, Northern Ireland. His best-known work is his trilogy, *Herself Surprised* (1940), *To be a Pilgrim* (1942), and *The Horse's Mouth* (1944). >> Cary, Tristram

Cary, Tristram [**kair**ee] (1925-) Composer and teacher, born in Oxford, Oxfordshire, the son of Joyce Cary. He pioneered the development of electronic music, and composed widely for films, theatre, radio, and television. >> Cary, Joyce

Casals, Pablo [ka**sals**], Catalan **Pau** (1876-1973) Cellist, conductor, and composer, born in Vendrell, Spain. In 1919 he founded the Barcelona Orchestra, which he conducted until he left Spain in 1936, and in 1950 founded an annual festival of classical chamber music in Prades, France.

Casanova (de Seingalt), Giacomo Girolomo [kasa-**noh**va] (1725-98) Adventurer, born in Venice, Italy. Alchemist, cabalist, and spy, he visited Europe, mixed with the best society, and had always to 'vanish' after a brief period of felicity. His main work is his autobiography, in which he emerges as one of the world's great lovers.

Casas, Las Bartolomé de >> **Las Casas, Bartolomé de**

Casella, Alfredo [ka**se**la] (1883-1947) Composer and musician, born in Turin, Italy. His work includes three operas, two symphonies, and concertos for cello, violin, and organ, as well as chamber music, piano pieces, and songs.

Casement, (Sir) Roger (David) [**kays**ment] (1864-1916) British consular official, born in Dun Laoghaire (formerly Kingstown), Co Dublin, Ireland. In 1916 he was arrested on landing in Ireland from a German submarine to head the Sinn Féin rebellion, and hanged for high treason in London. His controversial 'Black Diaries' were suppressed but published in 1959.

Casey, Richard Gardiner Casey, Baron (1890-1976) Australian statesman, born in Melbourne, Victoria, Australia. He became first Australian minister to the USA (1940), minister of state in the Middle East (1942), and minister for external affairs (1951).

Casey, William J(oseph) (1913-87) Lawyer and government official, born in New York City. As President Reagan's director of the Central Intelligence Agency (1981-7), he was known for extremely aggressive policies towards Communists.

Cash, Johnny, nickname **the Man in Black** (1932-) Country music singer, songwriter, and guitarist, born in Kingsland, AR. He signed for Sun Records in 1955, and early songs included 'Cry, Cry, Cry' and 'I Walk The Line'.

Cash, Martin (1810-77) Bushranger, born in Enniscorthy, Co Wexford, Ireland. Transported to Australia for attempted murder (1827), he escaped from prison (1837), and was captured after shooting a constable (1843). His death sentence was commuted to life imprisonment on Norfolk I, where he became a model prisoner, and was pardoned in 1853.

Casimir, Hendrik [**ka**zimeer] (1909-) Physicist, born in The Hague, The Netherlands. In 1934 he helped to devise a general theory of superconductivity which was later extended by Bardeen and others. >> Bardeen

Čáslavská, Vera [ka**slav**ska] (1942-) Gymnast, born in Prague. She won 22 Olympic, world, and European titles, including three Olympic gold medals in 1964, and four in 1968.

Caslon, William [**kaz**lon] (1692-1766) Type-founder, born in Cradley, Worcestershire. His 'old face' *Caslon types* were extensively used in Europe and the USA until the end of the 18th-c.

Casorati, Felice [kazo**rah**tee] (1886-1963) Painter, born in Novara, Italy. He was one of the exponents of Italian Neoclassicism, and is noted for his series of portraits of women.

Cass, Lewis (1782-1866) US statesman, born in Exeter, NH. He became secretary of war (1831-6) and secretary of state (1857-60), and twice failed in a bid for the presidency.

Cassander [ka**san**der] (c.358-297 BC) Ruler of Macedon after the death of his father Antipater in 319 BC, and its king from 305 BC. In the power struggle after Alexander's death (323 BC), he murdered Alexander's mother, widow, and son. >> Antipater (of Macedon)

Cassatt, Mary [ka**sat**] (1844-1926) Impressionist painter, born in Allegheny, PA. She worked mainly in France, where she was renowned for her etching and drypoint studies of domestic scenes.

Cassel, (Karl) Gustav (1866-1945) Economist, born in Stockholm. Professor at Stockholm from 1904, he became known as a world authority on monetary problems.

Cassell, John (1817-65) British publisher. He went to London and in 1850 turned to writing and publishing educational books and magazines for the working classes (*Cassell's Magazine*, 1852).

Cassian, St John (?360-c.435), feast day 23 July. Monk and theologian, born in Dobruja, Romania. He instituted several monasteries in the S of France, including the Abbey of St Victor at Massilia (Marseilles), which served as a model for many in Gaul and Spain.

Cassidy, Butch, originally **Robert LeRoy Parker** (1866-?1909) Outlaw, born in Beaver, UT. He joined the infamous Wild Bunch and was partner with the Sundance Kid. They roamed America, robbing banks, trains, and mine stations, until they were trapped and killed. >> Sundance Kid

Cassin, René [ka**see**] (1887-1976) Jurist and French statesman, born in Bayonne, France. During World War 2 he was principal legal adviser in negotiations with the British government. He played a leading part in the establishment of UNESCO, and was awarded the Nobel Peace Prize in 1968.

Cassini, Giovanni Domenico [ka**see**nee], also known as **Jean Dominique Cassini** (1625-1712) Astronomer, born in Perinaldo, Italy. In 1669 he became the first director of the observatory at Paris. *Cassini's division* (the gap between two of Saturn's rings) is named after him, and *Cassini's laws*, describing the rotation of the Moon, were formulated in 1693.

Cassini, Oleg [kaseenee] (1913–) Fashion designer, born in Paris. He established his own New York City firm in 1950. His trademarks included provocative sheaths, cocktail dresses, and the widely copied 'Jackie Kennedy' look.

Cassiodorus (Flavius Magnus Aurelius) [kasiohdawrus] (c.490–c.580) Roman writer and monk, born in Scylaceum (Squillace), Calabria. He was secretary to the Ostrogothic king, Theodoric, after whose death (526) he became chief minister to Queen Amalasontha. >> Theodoric

Cassirer, Ernst [kaseerer] (1874–1945) Neo-Kantian philosopher, born in Wroclaw, Poland. His best-known work, *The Philosophy of Symbolic Forms* (trans, 1923–9), analyses the symbolic functions underlying all human thought, language, and culture.

Cassius [kasius], in full **Gaius Cassius Longinus** (?–42 BC) Roman soldier and politician. Despite gaining polical advancement through Caesar, he played a leading part in the conspiracy to murder him (44 BC). He raised an army in Syria and marched against the Triumverate, but was defeated at Philippi (42 BC) and committed suicide. >> Caesar

Cassius, Dio(n) >> **Dio Cassius**

Cassivellaunus [kasivelawnus] (1st-c BC) British chief of the Catavellauni, a British tribe living in the area of modern Hertfordshire. He led the British resistance to Julius Caesar on his second invasion, 54 BC. >> Caesar

Casson, Sir Hugh (Maxwell) [kasn] (1910–) British architect. He directed the architecture of the Festival of Britain (1948), and was president of the Royal Academy (1976–84).

Casson, Sir Lewis [kasn] (1875–1969) Actor-manager and producer, born in Birkenhead, Merseyside. He is known especially for his productions of Shakespeare and Shaw. He married Sybil Thorndike in 1908. >> Thorndike, Sybil

Castagno, Andrea del [kastanyoh], originally **Andrea di Bartolo de Simone** (c.1421–57) Painter, born in Castagno, Italy. His celebrated 'Last Supper', painted for S Apollonia, is now in the Castagno Museum, as are his series of 'Famous Men and Women'.

Castelnau, Noel Marie Joseph Edouard, vicomte de (Viscount of) **Curières de** [kastelnoh] (1851–1944) French soldier, born in Aveyron, France. As commander of all French armies in France, he directed the Champagne offensive (1915), and became Joffre's chief-of-staff. >> Joffre

Castelnuovo-Tedesco, Mario [kastelnwohvoh tedeskoh] (1895–1968) Composer, born in Florence, Italy. He produced operas, orchestral and instrumental works, but is probably best known for his songs, especially his complete series of the lyrics from Shakespeare's plays.

Castelo Branco, Camilo, visconde de (Viscount of) **Correia Botelho** [kasteloo brangkoo] (1825–90) Writer, born in Lisbon. His works include such Gothic romances as *The Mysteries of Lisbon* (trans, 1854), *Revenge* (trans, 1858), and his best-known book, *Fatal Love* (trans, 1862).

Castigliano, (Carlo) Alberto [kasteelyahnoh] (1847–84) Civil engineer, born in Asti, Italy. He is noted for his two theorems of 1873 and 1875, which represented a great advance on the methods of classical theory of structures, especially in their application to statically indeterminate systems.

Castiglione, Baldassare, conte di (Count of) **Novilara** [kasteelyohnay] (1478–1529) Writer and diplomat, born near Mantua, Italy. His chief work, *Il cortegiano* (1528, The Courtier), is a manual for courtiers.

Castilho, Antonio Feliciano, Viscount [kasteelyoh]

(1800–75) Poet, blind from childhood, born in Lisbon. *Letters from Echo and Narcissus* (trans, 1821) and *Love and Melancholy* (trans, 1828) inaugurated the Portuguese Romantic movement.

Castle, Barbara (Anne), *née* **Betts** (1911–) British stateswoman, born in Bradford, West Yorkshire. She held a number of posts under Labour, including minister of transport (1965–8), secretary of state for employment and productivity (1968–70), and minister of health and social security (1974–8). She later became a MEP.

Castle, Vernon (1887–1918) and **Irene Castle** (1893–1969) English champion ballroom dancers, husband and wife. He was originally **Vernon Blythe**, born in Norwich, Norfolk. She was **Irene Foote**, from New Rochelle, NY. Married in 1911, they became the leading exhibition ballroom dancers of the period.

Castle, William (Ernest) (1867–1962) Biologist, born in Ohio. At Harvard he became professor of genetics (1908–36), and conducted research in the field of heredity and natural selection.

Castlereagh, Robert Stewart, Viscount [kaslray] (1769–1822) British statesman, born in Dublin. His major achievements date from 1812 when, as foreign secretary, he was at the heart of the coalition against Napoleon (1813–14). He represented England at Chaumont and Vienna (1814–15), Paris (1815), and Aix-la-Chapelle (1818), advocating 'Congress diplomacy' to avoid further warfare.

Castner, Hamilton (Young) (1859–99) Analytical chemist, born in New York City. He came to Britain in 1886, and invented a new process for the isolation of sodium from brine by electrolysis.

Castriota, George >> **Skanderbeg**

Castro (Ruz), Fidel (1927–) Cuban revolutionary, prime minister (1959–), and president (1976–), born near Birán, Cuba. In 1958 he mounted a successful attack against Batista, and as premier proclaimed a Marxist-Leninist programme. His overthrow of US economic dominance was balanced by his dependence on Russian aid. >> Batista

Catchpole, Margaret (1762–1819) Australian pioneer, born near Ipswich, Suffolk. A servant to the Cobbold family, she was convicted of stealing, and transported to New South Wales in 1801. Her letters provide a valuable account of early 19th-c life in the new colony. >> Cobbold

Catesby, Robert [kaytsbee] (1573–1605) Chief conspirator in the Gunpowder Plot, born in Lapworth, Warwickshire. A Catholic, he had suffered much as a recusant, and was shot dead while resisting arrest after the failure of the plot (1605). >> Fawkes

Cather, Willa (Sibert) [kat her] (1876–1947) Writer, born near Winchester, VA. Her novels include a trilogy, the third of which, *My Antonia* (1918), is generally regarded as her best book. Other novels include *One of Ours* (1922, Pulitzer).

Catherine I (1684–1727) Tsarina of Russia (1725–7), who succeeded her husband Peter I, the Great. The tsar married her in 1712, and in 1722 nominated her as his successor, having her crowned empress in 1724. >> Peter I (of Russia)

Catherine II, known as **Catherine the Great**, originally **Princess Sophie Friederike Auguste von Anhalt-Zerbst** (1729–96) Empress of Russia (1762–96), born in Szczecin (Stettin), Poland. In 1745 she was married to the heir to the Russian throne (later Peter III, r.1761–2) and succeeded him after a palace coup. She carried out an energetic foreign policy, extended the Russian Empire S to the Black Sea after the Russo–Turkish Wars (1774, 1792), and brought about the three partitions of Poland. Despite pretensions to enlightened ideas, her domestic policies achieved little for most Russians, and in 1774 she had to suppress a popular rebellion led by Pugachev. Her private life was dominated by a long series of lovers, notably Potemkin. >> Paul; Potemkin; Pugachev

Catherine, St (?–307), feast day 25 November. Traditionally, a virgin of royal descent in Alexandria. She publicly confessed the Gospel at a sacrificial feast appointed by Emperor Maximinus, and was beheaded after being tortured on a spiked wheel (later known as a *catherine wheel*).

Catherine de' Medici [**may**deechee] (1519–89) Queen of France, wife of Henry II, and regent (1560–74), born in Florence. During the minority of her sons, Francis II (1559–60) and Charles IX (1560–3), she assumed political influence which she retained as queen mother until 1588.

Catherine of Aragon [**a**ragon] (1485–1536) Queen of England, the first wife of Henry VIII (1509–33), born in Alcalá de Henares, Spain, the fourth daughter of Ferdinand and Isabella of Spain. She was first married in 1501 to Arthur (1486–1502), the son of Henry VII. Soon widowed, in 1509 she married her brother-in-law Henry, and bore him five children, but only the Princess Mary survived. Henry divorced her in 1533, and she retired to a religious life. >> Henry VIII

Catherine of Braganza [bra**gan**za] (1638–1705) Wife of Charles II of England, born in Vila Viçosa, Portugal, the daughter of King John IV of Portugal. She was married to Charles in 1662 as part of an alliance between England and Portugal, but failed to produce an heir. >> Charles II (of England)

Catherine of Valois [valwah] (1401–37) Queen of England, the wife of Henry V, and the youngest daughter of Charles VI of France. She married Henry in 1420, and in 1421 gave birth to a son, the future Henry VI. After Henry's death (1422), she secretly married Owen Tudor; their eldest son, Edmund, Earl of Richmond, was the father of Henry VII. >> Henry V

Catherine of Siena, St [syay**na**], originally **Caterina Benincasa** (1347–80), feast day 29 April. Nun and mystic, born in Siena, Italy. A Dominican, she prevailed on Pope Gregory XI to return the papacy from Avignon to Rome. Christ's stigmata was said to be imprinted on her body. She was canonized in 1461, and is the patron saint of Italy.

Catherwood, Frederick >> **Stephens, John Lloyd**

Catiline [**kat**ilyn], in full **Lucius Sergius Catilina** (c.108–62 BC) An impoverished Roman politician who tried to exploit the economic unrest of Rome in the 60s BC for his own political ends. His conspiracy against the state was foiled by Cicero in 63 BC, and he was killed in battle. >> Cicero

Catlin, George (1796–1872) Artist and writer, born in Wilkes-Barre, PA. During 1832–40 he studied the Indians of the Far West, painting pictures illustrative of life and manners.

Cato, Marcus Porcius [**kay**toh], known as **Cato the Elder** or **Cato the Censor** (234–149 BC) Roman statesman, orator, and man of letters, born in Tusculum, Latium. He became censor (184 BC) and was thereafter known by this name. He was so impressed by the power of the Carthaginians that he ended every speech in the Senate with the words: 'Carthage must be destroyed'.

Cato, Marcus Porcius [**kay**toh], known as **Cato the Younger** or **Cato Uticensis** (95–46 BC) Roman statesman, the great-grandson of Cato the Censor. A supporter of Pompey in the Civil War, after Pharsalus (48 BC) he escaped to Africa. On hearing of Caesar's victory at Thapsus (46 BC), he killed himself. >> Cato (the Elder); Pompey

Catroux, Georges [katroo] (1877–1969) French general and diplomat, born in Limoges, France. He was Governor-General of Indo-China (1939–40), commanded the Free French forces in Syria and the Near East (1940–1), and became Governor-General of Algeria in 1943.

Catt, Carrie Chapman, *née* **Lane** (1859–1947) Reformer and pacifist, born in Ripon, WI. As president of the National American Woman Suffrage Association (1900–4, 1915–47), she helped to bring about the 19th Amendment (1920), thus securing the vote for women.

Cattell, Raymond B(ernard) [ka**tel**] (1905–) Psychologist, born in Staffordshire. He is best known for his application of the statistical techniques of factor analysis to the study of personality differences.

Cattermole, George (1800–68) Watercolour painter and book illustrator, born in Dickleborough, Norfolk. He was known for his antiquarian and architectural paintings, and for his illustrations of Sir Walter Scott's 'Waverley Novels'.

Catullus, Gaius Valerius [ka**tuh**lus] (c.84–c.54 BC) Lyric poet, born in Verona, Italy. He settled in Rome (c.62 BC), where he met 'Lesbia' whom he addressed in his verses. His extant works comprise 116 pieces, many of them extremely brief.

Cauchy, Augustin Louis, Baron [koh**shee**] (1789–1857) Mathematician, born in Paris. He is primarily remembered as the founder of the theory of functions of a complex variable. In algebra he gave a definitive account of the theory of determinants, and developed the ideas of group theory.

Cavaco Silva, Anibal [ka**va**soh **seel**va] (1939–) Portuguese prime minister (1985–), born in Loulé, Portugal. In 1985 he became leader of the Social Democratic Party, and as prime minister led Portugal into the European Community in 1985.

Cavafy, Constantine [ka**va**fee], pseudonym of **Konstantine Petrou Kavafis** (1863–1933) Poet, born in Alexandria, Egypt, of a Greek family. His first book was privately published when he was 41, and reissued five years later with additional poems. He published no further work during his lifetime, but in recent years he has come to be regarded as a major modern Greek poet.

Cavalcanti, Alberto [kaval**kan**tee], originally **Alberto de Almeida-Cavalcanti** (1897–1982) Film director and producer, born in Rio de Janeiro, Brazil. He began his career in Britain, producing some notable films for Ealing Studios, including *Champagne Charlie* (1944) and *Nicholas Nickleby* (1947). He was a leading figure in the revival of Brazilian cinema.

Cavalcanti, Guido [kaval**kan**tee] (c.1230–1300) Poet, born in Florence, Italy. He was a friend of Dante, and wrote about 50 poems in the 'new style' of the period. A member of the Papal Party (the Guelphs), he married the daughter of the leader of the rival Imperial Party (the Ghibellines), and was banished.

Cavalieri, (Francesco) Bonaventura [kaval**yay**ree] (1598–1647) Mathematician, born in Milan, Italy. His 'method of indivisibles' began a new era in geometry and paved the way for the introduction of integral calculus.

Cavalieri, Emilio de' [kaval**yay**ree] (c.1550–1602) Composer, born in Rome. He lived mainly at the Florentine court of the Medici, where he was inspector general of arts. His dramatic works were forerunners of opera and oratorio.

Cavalli, (Pier) Francesco [ka**va**lee], originally **Francesco Caletti-Bruni** (1602–76) Composer, who assumed the name of his patron, born in Crema, Italy. He was organist and chapel master of St Mark's in Venice, and also an opera and church composer.

Cavallini, Pietro [kava**lee**nee] (c.1250–c.1330) Painter and artist in mosaic, born in Rome. His best-known work is the series of mosaics in the Church of Santa Maria at Trastevere, Rome.

Cavell, Edith [ka**vel**] (1865–1915) Nurse, born in Swardeston, Norfolk. Matron of the Berkendael Medical Institute, Brussels, she tended friend and foe alike in

1914–15, but was executed by the Germans for helping fugitives to escape capture.

Cavendish >> **Jones, Henry**

Cavendish, Henry (1731–1810) Physicist and chemist, born in Nice, France. In 1760 he studied the 'inflammable air', now known as hydrogen gas, and later ascertained that water resulted from the union of two gases.

Cavendish, Spencer Compton, 8th Duke of Devonshire, known as the **Marquess of Hartington** (1858–91) (1833–1908) British statesman, born in Lower Holker, Lancashire. In 1875 he became Leader of the Liberal Opposition, later serving as secretary of state for India (1880–2) and as war secretary (1882–5). He led the breakaway from the Liberal Party, becoming head of the Liberal Unionists from 1886. His younger brother, **Lord Frederick Cavendish** (1836–82), was appointed chief secretary for Ireland, but was murdered by 'Irish Invincibles' in Phoenix Park.

Cavendish, Sir Thomas (c.1555–c.1592) Circumnavigator of the globe, born near Ipswich, Suffolk. He joined Sir Richard Grenville's expedition to Virginia (1585). In 1586 he sailed for the Pacific, returning by the Cape of Good Hope to England in 1588. >> **Grenville, Richard**

Cavendish, William, Duke of Newcastle (1592–1676) English soldier and patron of the arts. He supported Charles I in the Civil War, and was general of all forces north of the Trent. A noted patron of poets and playwrights, he was himself the author of several plays. >> **Charles I (of England)**

Caventou, Joseph (Bienaimé) [kavãtoo] (1795–1877) Chemist, born in St Omer, France. In 1817, together with Pelletier, he introduced the term *chlorophyll*. They also discovered quinine (1820), strychnine, brucine, and cinchonine. >> **Pelletier**

Cavour, Camillo Benso, conte di (Count of) [kavoor] (1810–61) Piedmontese prime minister (1852–9), who brought about the unification of Italy (1861), born in Turin, Italy. As premier, he brought the Italian question before the Congress of Paris, and in 1860 secretly encouraged the expedition of Garibaldi.

Cawley, Yvonne (Fay), *née* **Goolagong** (1951–) Tennis player, born in Barellan, New South Wales, Australia, of Aboriginal descent. She won the Wimbledon singles title in 1971 and 1981, and the Australian Open four times.

Caxton, William (c.1422–c.1491) The first English printer, born possibly in Tenterden, Kent. In Cologne he probably learned the art of printing (1471–2), and printed the first book in English, *The Recuyell of the Historyes of Troye* (1473–4). He set up his wooden press at Westminster, producing the first books printed in England.

Cayley, Arthur [kaylee] (1821–95) Mathematician, born in Richmond, Surrey. He originated the theory of invariants and covariants, and worked on the theories of matrices and analytical geometry, and on theoretical astronomy.

Cayley, Sir George [kaylee] (1771–1857) Pioneer of aviation, born in Scarborough, North Yorkshire. In 1808 he constructed and flew a glider, probably the first heavier-than-air machine, and made the first successful man-carrying glider in 1853.

Cazaly, Roy [kazaylee] (1893–1963) Australian Rules footballer, born in Melbourne, Victoria, Australia. He played for St Kilda (1913–20), and transferred to South Melbourne (1921) before moving to Tasmania.

Ceadda, St >> **Chad, St**

Ceauşescu, Nicolae [chowsheskoo] (1918–1989) Romanian president (1967–89), born in Scorniceşti, Romania. As general secretary of the Romanian Communist Party, he made Romania increasingly independent of the USSR. In 1989 he was deposed when the army joined a popular revolt against his repressive government.

Following a trial by military tribunal, he and his wife, Elena, were shot.

Cecchetti, Enrico [cheketee] (1850–1928) Dancer, teacher, and choreographer, born in Milan, Italy. He settled in Russia in 1887, and later became ballet master of Diaghilev's Ballet Russes. >> **Diaghilev**

Cech, Thomas R [chek] (1947–) Biochemist, born in Chicago, IL. He showed that RNA could have an independent catalytic function aiding a chemical reaction without being consumed or changed, and he shared the Nobel Prize for Chemistry in 1989. >> **Altman**

Cecil, Lord (Edward Christian) David (Gascoyne) [sesil] (1902–86) Literary critic, born in London. He is known chiefly as a literary biographer, in such works as *Sir Walter Scott* (1933), *Jane Austen* (1935), and *Thomas Hardy* (1943).

Cecil (of Chelwood), Robert Cecil, 1st Viscount [sesil] (1864–1958) British statesman, born in London, the son of Robert Cecil (3rd Marquess of Salisbury). He became president of the League of Nations Union (1923–45), and was awarded the Nobel Peace Prize in 1937.

Cecil, Robert (Arthur Talbot Gascoyne), 3rd Marquess of Salisbury [sesil] (1830–1903) British statesman and prime minister (1885–6, 1886–92, 1895–1902), born in Hatfield, Hertfordshire. He was Conservative prime minister on three occasions, much of the time serving as his own foreign secretary. >> **Cecil, Robert, 1st Viscount**

Cecil, Robert (Arthur James Gascoyne), 5th Marquess of Salisbury [sesil] (1893–1972) British statesman, born in Hatfield, Hertfordshire. In the Churchill government of 1951 he became secretary of state for commonwealth relations and Lord President of the Council, but resigned in 1957. >> **Churchill, Winston**

Cecil, William, 1st Baron Burghley or **Burghleigh** [sesil] (1520–98) English statesmen, born in Bourn, Lincolnshire. In 1558 Elizabeth appointed him chief secretary of state, and for the next 40 years he was the chief architect of Elizabethan greatness, influencing her pro-Protestant foreign policy, securing the execution of Mary, Queen of Scots, and preparing for the Spanish Armada. In 1572 he became Lord High Treasurer, an office he held until his death.

Cecilia, St (2nd-c or 3rd-c), feast day 22 November. Christian martyr, and patron saint of music. According to tradition, she was compelled to marry despite a vow of celibacy, but her husband respected her vow, and she converted him to Christianity. They were both put to death.

Cela, Camilo José [thela] (1916–) Writer, born in La Coruña, Spain. The range of his work is vast and varied, but he is best known for *The Hive* (trans, 1951). He was awarded the Nobel Prize for Literature in 1989.

Celestine V, St, originally **Pietro di Morrone** (c.1215–96), feast day 19 May. Pope, born in S Italy. He reluctantly became pope in 1294, and resigned his office after five months - the first pope to abdicate. He founded the *Celestines*, and was canonized in 1313.

Céline, Louis-Ferdinand [sayleen], pseudonym of **Louis-Ferdinand Destouches** (1894–1961) Writer, born in Paris. His reputation is based on the two autobiographical novels he wrote during the 1930s: *Journey to the End of the Night* (trans, 1932) and *Death by Instalments* (trans, 1936).

Cellini, Benvenuto [cheleenee] (1500–71) Goldsmith, sculptor, engraver, and writer, born in Florence, Italy. His best work includes the gold saltcellar made for Francis I of France, and his bronze 'Perseus'. At the siege of Rome (1527) he killed the Constable de Bourbon. >> **Bourbon**

Celsius, Anders [selsius] (1701–44) Astronomer, born in Uppsala, Sweden. He devised the centigrade scale (*Celsius scale*) of temperature in 1742.

Celsus, Aulus Cornelius [selsus] (1st-c) Roman writer. He compiled an encyclopedia, the only extant portion of the work being the *De Medicina*, one of the first medical works to be printed (1478).

Cenci, Beatrice [**chen**chee] (1577–99) Noblewoman, born in Rome. Her father, Count Francesco Cenci, conceived an incestuous passion for her, and with her stepmother and her brother, she plotted his murder in 1598. The three were arrested and beheaded.

Cendrars, Blaise [sădrah(r)], pseudonym of **Frédéric Louis Sauser** (1887–1961) Writer, poet, and traveller, born in Chaux-de-Fonds, Switzerland. His works include the poem *Easter in New York* (trans, 1912) and the novel *Antarctic Fugue (trans, 1927–29)*.

Cenni di Peppi >> Cimabue

Centlivre, Susannah [sentl**ee**ver], née **Freeman** (c.1667–c.1723) Playwright, probably born in Holbeach, Lincolnshire. Her works include the tragedy *The Perjured Husband* (1700), and the comedy *Love at a Venture* (1706).

Centlivres, Albert van de Sandt [sentl**ee**ver] (1887–1966) Judge, born in Cape Town, South Africa. He became a judge of the Cape provincial division of the Supreme Court of South Africa (1935) and chief justice (1950–7). He played a substantial part in restoring Roman–Dutch law in South Africa.

Cerdic [**chair**dik] (?–534) Saxon leader who invaded Britain, landing in Hampshire with his son Cynric in 495. By 500 he had created the kingdom of Wessex for himself, and founded the West Saxon royal dynasty.

Cerinthus [se**rin**thus] (c.100) Jewish Gnostic heretic, born in Alexandria. He is said to have lived in Ephesus contemporaneously with the aged apostle John. >> John, St

Cernan, Eugene (Andrew) [**ser**nan] (1934–) Astronaut, born in Chicago, IL. He was a crew member of several historic missions - Gemini 9 (1966), Apollo 10 (1969), and Apollo 17 (1972) - and was involved in the Apollo–Soyuz Test Project in 1975.

Cerutty, Percy Wells [se**ruh**tee] (1895-1975) Athletics coach and trainer, born in Prahan, Victoria, Australia. He pioneered such concepts as training over sand dunes and the idea of the 'pain barrier'.

Cervantes (Saavedra), Miguel de [ser**van**teez], Span [thair**van**tes] (1547–1616) Writer of *Don Quixote*, born in Alcalá de Henares, Spain. Tradition maintains that he wrote *Don Quixote* (1605) in prison at Argamasilla in La Mancha. He produced the second part in 1615, after writing many plays and short novels.

Césaire, Aimé (Fernand) [sayzair] (1913–) Writer and Martinique politician, born in Basse-Pointe, Martinique. His works include the influential *Notebook of a Return to my Native Land* (trans, 1947), and several poems and plays.

Cesalpino, Andrea [chezal**pee**noh], Latin **Caesalpinus** (1519–1603) Botanist, anatomist, physician, and physiologist, born in Arezzo, Italy. He was the author of *De plantis* (1583), the first textbook establishing botany as a scientific subject.

Cesari, Giuseppe [**chay**zaree], known as **Il Cavaliere d'Arpino** (the Cavalier of Arpino) (c.1568–c.1640) Painter, born in Arpino, Italy. Honoured by five popes, he is best known for the frescoes in the Capitol at Rome.

Céspedes, Pablo de [**thays**pe̲t̲ hayz] (1538–1608) Painter, born in Córdoba, Spain. In 1577 he established a school of art in Córdoba. His works include the 'Last Supper' in Córdoba cathedral.

Cessna, Clyde (Vernon) [**ses**na] (1879–1954) Aviator, born in Hawthorne, LA. He designed a monoplane with the innovatory cantilever wing (1917), and with Victor Roos produced Cessna–Roos aircraft. He later founded the Cessna Aircraft Co, mass-producing modern, multipurpose planes.

Cetewayo or **Cetshwayo** [kete**way**oh] (c.1826–84) Ruler of Zululand from 1873, born near Eshowe, South Africa. In

1879 he defeated the British at Isandhlwana, but was himself defeated at Ulundi.

Cetti, Francesco [**che**tee] (1726–78) Jesuit and naturalist, born in Mannheim, Germany. He was a distinguished naturalist as well as a theologian and philosopher. The bird *Cetti's warbler* was named after him.

Ceulen, Ludolph van [**koe**len] (1540–1610) Mathematician, born in Hildesheim, Germany. He devoted himself to finding the value of π and finally worked it out to 35 decimal places (*Ludolph's number*).

Ceva, Giovanni [**chay**va] (?1647–1734) Geometer, born in Milan, Italy. He gave his name to a theorem on concurrent lines through the vertices of a triangle.

Cézanne, Paul [sayzan] (1839–1906) Postimpressionist painter, born in Aix-en-Provence, France. He abandoned his early sombre Expressionism for the study of nature, using his characteristic glowing colours. After 1886 he constructed pictures from a rhythmic series of coloured planes, thus becoming the forerunner of Cubism. Among his best-known paintings are 'L'Estaque' (c.1888) and 'The Card Players' (1890–2).

Chaban-Delmas, Jacques (-Pierre-Michel) [shabǎdelmas], originally **Jacques Delmas** (1915–) French prime minister (1969–72), born in Paris. A leading left-wing figure, he held a series of Cabinet posts before becoming President of the National Assembly (1958–69, 1978–81), and premier under Pompidou. >> Pompidou

Chabaneau, François [shabanoh] (1754–1842) Chemist, born in Nontron, France. He became professor of mineralogy, physics, and chemistry at Madrid, where he carried out the research on platinum which resulted in an ingot of malleable platinum (1783).

Chabrier, (Alexis) Emmanuel [shabreeyay] (1841-94) Composer, born in Ambert, France. He wrote operas, piano works, and songs, but his best-known pieces were inspired by the folk music of Spain, notably his orchestral rhapsody *España* (1883).

Chabrol, Claude [shabrol] (1930–) Film critic and director, born in Paris. Identified with the French *Nouvelle Vague*, his most widely-known films are dramas of abnormality in the provincial bourgeoisie, notably (trans titles) *The Butcher* (1970), *Red Wedding* (1973), and *Inspector Lavardin* (1986).

Chad, St, Old English **Ceadda** (?–672), feast day 2 March. Anglo-Saxon clergyman, born in Northumbria. He became Bishop of York in 666, and later Bishop of Mercia.

Chadli, Benjedid [**chad**lee] (1929–) Algerian soldier and president (1978–92), born in Sebaa, Algeria. He succeeded Boumédienne as secretary-general of the National Liberation Front and as president, but was forced to resign by the army in 1992. >> Boumédienne

Chadwick, Sir James (1891–1974) Physicist, born in Manchester. He discovered the neutron, for which he received the Nobel Prize for Physics in 1935. He led the UK's work on the atomic bomb in World War 2.

Chadwick, Lynn (Russell) (1914–) Sculptor, born in London. He began making mobiles (c.1946), then roughfinished solid metal sculptures. In 1956 he won the International Sculpture Prize at the Venice Biennale.

Chadwick, Roy (1893–1947) Aeronautical engineer, born in Farnworth, Greater Manchester. During World War 1 he designed many famous aeroplanes, including the Avro 504 trainer, and in World War 2 produced the Manchester and Lancaster heavy bombers.

Chagall, Marc [sha**gal**] (1887–1985) Artist, born in Vitebsk, Belarus. During World War 2 he moved to the USA. He illustrated several books, but is best known for his Surrealist paintings of animals, objects, and people from his life, dreams, and Russian folklore.

Chagas, Carlos Ribeiro Justiniano [**shah**gas] (1879–1934) Physician and microbiologist, born in Oliveira,

Brazil. He worked on malaria prevention, and during a field mission he first described a disease caused by a trypanosome, since named after him (*Chagas' disease*).

Chaikin, Joseph [chíykin] (1935–) Actor and theatre director, born in New York City. He performed with the Living Theater, and in 1963 founded The Open Theater, producing such original works as *America Hurrah* (1965).

Chain, Sir Ernst Boris [chayn] (1906–79) Biochemist, born in Berlin. Working in Britain, he was a key figure in the successful isolation of penicillin, and shared the Nobel Prize for Physiology or Medicine in 1945. >> Fleming, Alexander; Florey

Chaliapin, Fyodor Ivanovich [shalyapeen] (1873–1938) Bass singer, born in Kazan, Russia. Also talented as an actor, he sang in opera at Tiflis (1892), Moscow (1896), and London (1913). He left Russia after the Revolution.

Challender, Stuart (1947–91) Conductor, born in Hobart, Tasmania, Australia. In 1980 he was appointed resident conductor of the Australian Opera, and in 1987 became chief conductor and artistic director of the Sydney Symphony Orchestra.

Challoner, Richard [chaloner] (1691–1781) Roman Catholic clergyman and writer, born in Lewes, East Sussex. His best-known works are the prayer book, *The Garden of the Soul* (1740), and his revision of the Douai version of the Bible (5 vols, 1750).

Chalmers, James (1782–1853) Bookseller and inventor, born in Arbroath, Tayside. A bookseller and newspaper publisher in Dundee, he advocated faster mail services in 1825, and invented adhesive postage stamps.

Chalmers, Thomas (1780–1847) Theologian and reformer, born in Anstruther, Fife. In the Disruption of 1843 he led 470 ministers out of the Established Church of Scotland to found the Free Church of Scotland.

Chamberlain, Sir (Joseph) Austen (1863–1937) British statesman, born in Birmingham, West Midlands, the eldest son of Joseph Chamberlain. He was Chancellor of the Exchequer (1903–6, 1919–21), secretary for India (1915–17), foreign secretary (1924–9), and First Lord of the Admiralty (1931). He shared the 1925 Nobel Peace Prize for negotiating the Locarno Pact. >> Chamberlain, Joseph

Chamberlain, Joseph (1836–1914) British statesman, born in London. From 1889 he was leader of the Liberal Unionists, and in the coalition government of 1895 was secretary for the Colonies, resigning in 1903. >> Chamberlain, Austen / Neville

Chamberlain, Lindy (Alice Lynne) (1948–) Mother of the 'dingo baby', born in Whakatane, New Zealand. She was accused of murder after her nine-week-old daughter disappeared at Ayers Rock in 1980. Married to pastor Michael Chamberlain (tried with her), she claimed the baby was taken by a dingo. She was found guilty and gaoled, but released in 1986 when a baby's jacket was found near the rock.

Chamberlain, (Arthur) Neville (1869–1940) British Conservative prime minister (1937–40), born in Birmingham, West Midlands, the son of Joseph Chamberlain. He became Chancellor of the Exchequer (1923–4, 1931–7) and minister for health (1923, 1924–9, 1931). As prime minister, he advocated 'appeasement' of Italy and Germany, returning from Munich with his claim to have found 'peace for our time' (1938). >> Chamberlain, Joseph

Chamberlain, Owen (1920–) Physicist, born in San Francisco, CA. In 1959 he shared the Nobel Prize for Physics with Segrè for research on the antiproton. >> Segrè

Chamberlain, Wilt(on) Norman, nickname **Wilt the Stilt** (1936–) Basketball player, born in Philadelphia, PA. Height 1·85 m/7 ft 1 in, he played for the Philadelphia 76ers, and was seven times the National Basketball Association leading scorer (1960–6). During his career (1960–73) he scored 31 419 points.

Chamberlin, Edward Hastings (1899–1967) Economist, born in La Couner, WA. His *Theory of Monopolistic Competition* (1933) is regarded as one of the most influential books of 20th-c economics.

Chamberlin, Thomas (Chrowder) (1843–1928) Geologist, born in Mattoon, IL. Professor of geology at Chicago (1892–1918), his best-known work was in connection with the fundamental geology of the Solar System.

Chambers, Sir E(dmund) K(erchever) (1866–1954) Scholar and literary critic, born in Berkshire. His books include *The Elizabethan Stage* (1923) and *William Shakespeare* (1930).

Chambers, Ephraim (c.1680–1740) Encyclopedist, born in Kendal, Cumbria. He conceived the idea of a *Cyclopaedia, or Universal Dictionary of Arts and Sciences* (2 vols, 1728). A French translation inspired Diderot's *Encyclopédie.* >> Diderot

Chambers, John Graham (1843–83) Sportsman and journalist, born in Llanelli, Dyfed. He founded the Amateur Athletic Club in 1866, and drew up the rules for amateur athletic competitions. In 1867 he formulated the rules for boxing. >> Queensberry

Chambers, R(aymond) W(ilson) (1874–1942) British scholar and literary critic. His works include studies of *Widsith* and *Beowulf*, and an influential essay on *The Continuity of English Prose* (1932).

Chambers, Robert (1802–71) Publisher and writer, born in Peebles, Borders, Scotland, the brother of William Chambers. He began as a bookseller in Edinburgh (1818), and contributed regularly to *Chambers's Edinburgh Journal.* >> Chambers, William

Chambers, Whittaker, originally **Jay Vivian Chambers** (1910–61) Journalist, writer, and Soviet agent, born in Philadelphia, PA. He became an agent of Soviet intelligence, but later turned anti-Communist. In 1948 he testified that Alger Hiss had given him classified materials; this brought about a libel suit by Hiss, who was found guilty. >> Hiss, Alger

Chambers, Sir William (1726–96) Architect, born in Göteborg, Sweden. A leading architect in the Palladian style, his works include Somerset House (1776) and the pagoda in Kew Gardens.

Chambers, William (1800–83) Publisher and writer, born in Peebles, Borders, Scotland. In 1832 he started *Chambers's Edinburgh Journal*, and with his brother, Robert Chambers, founded the printing and publishing firm of W & R Chambers. >> Chambers, Robert

Chamfort, Sébastien Roch Nicolas [shãfaw(r)] (c.1741–94) Writer, born in Clermont, France. He joined the literary circles of Paris, and was known for his tales, dramas, and maxims.

Chamisso, Adelbert von [shameesoh], originally **Louis Charles Adelaide Chamisso de Boncourt** (1781–1838) Poet and biologist, born in Champagne, France. In Geneva he joined the literary circle of Madame de Staël, and is best known for his fairy tale *Peter Schlemihl* (1813). In 1819 he discovered in certain animals what he called 'alternation of generations'.

Champaigne, Philippe de [shãpen] (1602–74) Painter of portraits and religious subjects, born in Brussels. In 1621 he was appointed painter to Marie de Médicis in Paris, and his works include a triple portrait of Cardinal Richelieu. >> Marie de Médicis

Champlain, Samuel de [shãplĩ] (1567–1635) Governor of Canada, born in Brouage, France. He travelled to Canada (1603), explored the E coast (1604–7), and founded Quebec (1608), becoming governor there (1633). L Champlain is named after him.

Champollion, Jean François [shãpolyõ] (1790–1832)

Founder of Egyptology, born in Figeac, France. He is best known for his use of the Rosetta Stone to decipher Egyptian hieroglyphics (1822-4).

Chance, Britton (1913-) Biophysicist and biochemist, born in Wilkes-Barre, PA. In 1943 he demonstrated the existence of the complex formed between an enzyme and its substrate. He also invented automatic control systems and optical instruments.

Chancellor, Richard (?-1556) English seaman, chosen in 1553 as 'pilot-general' of Sir Hugh Willoughby's expedition in search of a Northeast Passage to India. After a storm separated the ships, he proceeded alone into the White Sea, and travelled overland to Moscow.

Chandler, Happy, popular name of **Albert Benjamin Chandler** (1898-1991) Public official and baseball commissioner, born in Corydon, KY. He served as a Democratic US senator (1939-45), and became baseball's second commissioner (1945-51).

Chandler, Raymond (Thornton) (1888-1959) Writer, born in Chicago, IL. His 'private-eye' novels include *The Big Sleep* (1939) and *Farewell, My Lovely* (1940), several of which were filmed. He is the creator of the detective antihero, Philip Marlowe.

Chandos, Oliver Lyttelton Chandos, 1st Viscount [chandos] (1893-1972) English Conservative statesman and industrialist. In the 1950s he was much involved in the plans for constitutional reform in many of the African colonies. He left politics to return to business in 1954.

Chandragupta II [chandragupta], also known as **Vikramaditya** (Sanskrit 'sun of valour') (4th-c) Indian emperor (c.380-c.415), the third of the imperial Guptas of N India. During his reign, art, architecture, and sculpture flourished, and the cultural development of ancient India reached its climax.

Chandrasekhar, Subrahmanyan [chandrasayker] (1910-) Astrophysicist, born in Lahore, Pakistan (formerly, India). Working in the USA, he studied stellar evolution, showing that the final fate of a star depends on its mass (the *Chandrasekhar limit*). He was awarded the Nobel Prize for Physics in 1983.

Chanel, Coco [shanel], popular name of **Gabrielle Chanel** (?1883-1971) Fashion designer, born in Saumur, France. She revolutionized women's fashions during the 1920s, her designs including the 'chemise' dress and the collarless cardigan jacket.

Chaney, Lon [chaynee], originally **Alonso Chaney** (1883-1930) Film actor, born in Colorado Springs, CO. He was famous for spine-chilling deformed villains and other horrific parts, as in *The Hunchback of Notre Dame* (1923). His son, **Lon Chaney, Jr** (1907-73), also acted in horror films.

Chang, M(in)-C(hueh) (1909-91) Reproductive biologist, born in Taiyuan, China. Working in the USA from 1945, he collaborated with Gregory Pincus and John Rock on the creation of an oral contraceptive for women ('the pill'). >> Pincus

Chang Kuo-t'ao >> Zhang Guotao

Channing, William (Ellery) (1780-1842) Clergyman and writer, born in Newport, RI. Ordained in 1803, he became the leader of the Unitarians, and was widely known for his essays.

Chaplin, Charlie, popular name of **Sir Charles Spencer Chaplin** (1889-1977) Film actor and director, born in London. He went to Hollywood in 1914, and in his early silent comedies he adopted the bowler hat, out-turned feet, moustache, and walking-cane which became his hallmark, as in *The Kid* and *The Gold Rush*. His first sound film was *The Great Dictator* (1940). In *Limelight* (1952) he acted, produced, directed, and composed the music.

Chapman, George (c.1559-1634) Writer, born near Hitchin, Hertfordshire. Best known for his translations of Homer, he collaborated in the composition of *Eastward Ho* (1605), and in 1607 appeared *Bussy d'Ambois*, which had a sequel in 1613.

Chapman, Mark (David) (c.1955-) US convicted murderer. He shot and killed former Beatles member John Lennon in Manhattan (8 Dec 1980). Found guilty of murder, he was sentenced to life imprisonment.

Chapman, Sydney (1888-1970) Applied mathematician and geophysicist, born in Eccles, Lancashire. Working in the USA from 1954, he made a major contribution to the kinetic theory of gases, and developed the theory of thermal diffusion.

Chappe, Claude [shap] (1763-1805) Engineer and inventor, born in Brulon, France. In 1793 he developed a hand-operated semaphore system, operating in towers built on high ground, which was copied throughout Europe.

Chappell, Greg(ory Stephen) (1948-) Cricketer, born in Unley, South Australia, the brother of Ian Chappell. He played 88 times for his country (1970-84), 48 as captain, and scored 24 Test centuries. >> Chappell, Ian

Chappell, Ian (Michael) (1943-) Cricketer, born in Unley, South Australia, the brother of Greg Chappell. He played 75 times for Australia (1976-80), scoring over 5000 runs and 14 Test centuries. >> Chappell, Greg

Chappell, William (1809-88) British antiquary, a member of a great London music publishing house. His *Collection of National English Airs* (2 vols, 1838-40) grew into *Popular Music of the Olden Time* (2 vols, 1855-9).

Charcot, Jean Baptiste (Etienne Auguste) [shah(r)koh] (1867-1936) Explorer, born in Neuilly, France, the son of Jean Martin Charcot. He commanded two Antarctic expeditions in the *Français* (1903-5) and *Pourquoi Pas?* (1908-1910). >> Charcot, Jean

Charcot, Jean Martin [shah(r)koh] (1825-93) Pathologist, one of the founders of neurology, born in Paris. He investigated chronic and nervous diseases, and made hypnotism a scientific study. The way joints deteriorate in some types of disease was named after him (*Charcot's joint*).

Chardin, Jean Baptiste Siméon [shah(r)dĩ] (1699-1779) Painter, born in Paris. He emerged as a genre painter, and produced many pictures of peasant life and domestic scenes, notably 'Bénédicité' (1740).

Chardin, Pierre Teilhard de >> **Teilhard de Chardin, Pierre**

Chardonne, Jacques [shah(r)don], pseudonym of **Jacques Boutelleau** (1884-1968) Writer, born in Barbezieux, France. He wrote domestic novels mainly set in his native Charente, among them *Claire* (1931) and *Romanesques* (1937).

Chardonnet, (Louis Marie) Hilaire Berignaud, comte de (Count of) [shah(r)donay] (1839-1924) Chemist, born in Besançon, France. By 1878 he was working on artificial fibres, and became a pioneer of the artificial-silk (rayon) industry.

Chargaff, Erwin [chah(r)gaf] (1905-) Biochemist, born in Czernowitz, Czech Republic. His work on the ratio of bases present in DNA (the *Chargaff rules*) provided a fundamental contribution to the double helix structure for DNA.

Charlemagne or **Charles the Great** [shah(r)luhmayn] (742-814) King of the Franks (771-814), and emperor of the West (800-14), the eldest son of Pepin the Short. He defeated the Saxons (772-804) and the Lombards (773-4), and took control of most of Christian W Europe. He later consolidated his vast empire, promoting Christianity, education, agriculture, the arts, manufacture, and commerce, and the period has become known as the *Carolingian Renaissance*. >> Pepin III

Charles I, (of Austria-Hungary) (1887-1922) Emperor of Austria (1916-18, as **Karl I**) and king of Hungary (1916-19, as **Kàroly IV**), born at Persenbeug Castle, Austria. The last of the Habsburg emperors, he became heir presumptive on the assassination (1914) of his uncle, Archduke Francis Ferdinand. In 1919 he was deposed and exiled.

Charles I (of England) (1600–49) King of Britain and Ireland (1625–49), born in Dunfermline, Fife, the second son of James I. He married the French princess, Henrietta Maria, thus disturbing the nation, for she was permitted the free exercise of the Catholic religion. He warred with France (1627–9), and in 1630 made peace with Spain, but his continuing need for money led to unpopular economic policies, and his attempt to anglicize the Scottish Church brought active resistance (1639). In 1642 he entered into the Civil War, was annihilated at Naseby (14 Jun 1645), and surrendered at Newark (1646). After a second Civil War (1646–8), he came to trial at Westminster, where his dignified refusal to plead was interpreted as a confession of guilt. He was beheaded at Whitehall. >> Cromwell, Oliver; Henrietta Maria

Charles II (of England) (1630–85) King of Britain and Ireland (1660–85), born in London, the son of Charles I. On his father's execution (1649), he assumed the title of king, and was crowned at Scone (1651). Leading poorly organized forces into England, he was defeated at Worcester (1651), and lived in exile until an impoverished England summoned him back as king (1660). In 1662 he entered into a childless marriage with the Portuguese princess, Catherine of Braganza. His war with Holland (1665–7) was unpopular, and led to the dismissal of Lord Clarendon (1667), who was replaced by a group of ministers (the Cabal). >> Catherine of Braganza; Charles I (of England); Clarendon, 1st Earl

Charles II (of Spain) (1661–1700) King of Spain (1665–1700), the last ruler of the Spanish Habsburg dynasty, born in Madrid. He bequeathed the entire Spanish Habsburg inheritance to Louis XIV's grandson, Philip of Anjou, in 1700. >> Philip V

Charles IV (of Spain) (1748–1819) King of Spain (1788–1808), born in Portici, Italy, the son of Charles III. His government was dominated by his wife, **Maria Luisa** (1751–1819) and her favourite, Manuel de Godoy. Nelson destroyed his fleet at Trafalgar, and in 1808 he abdicated. >> Godoy; Napoleon I; Nelson

Charles V (of France), known as **Charles the Wise** (1338–80) King of France, born in Vincennes, France. He came to the throne in 1364, and in a series of victories regained most of the territory lost to the English in the Hundred Years' War.

Charles V (Emperor) (1500–58) Holy Roman Emperor (1519–56), born in Ghent, Belgium. His rivalry with Francis I of France dominated W European affairs, and there was almost constant warfare between them. The defeat of Francis in 1525 led to the formation of the Holy League against Charles by Pope Clement VII, Henry VIII, Francis, and the Venetians. At the Diet of Augsburg (1530) he confirmed the 1521 Edict of Worms, which had condemned Luther, and in 1538 the pope, Francis, and Charles agreed to a truce. Charles's league with the pope drove the Protestants to rebellion, resulting in his defeat by Maurice of Saxony in 1552. >> Clement VII; Francis I; Philip II (of Spain)

Charles VI (of France), known as **Charles the Foolish** (1368–1422) King of France, born in Paris, who came to the throne as a young boy in 1380. He was defeated by Henry V at the Battle of Agincourt in 1415. >> Henry V

Charles VII (of France), known as **Charles the Victorious** (1403–61) King of France (1422–61), born in Paris. At his accession, the N of the country was in English hands, but after the siege of Orléans (1429) the English gradually lost nearly all they had gained in France. >> Joan of Arc

Charles IX (of France) (1550–74) King of France (1560–74),

the second son of Henry II and Catherine de' Medici, born in St Germain-en-Laye, France. Dominated by his mother, she drove him to authorize the massacre of Huguenots on St Bartholomew's Day (1572). >> Henry II (of France)

Charles X (of France) (1757–1836) The last Bourbon king of France (1824–30), born at Versailles, France. In 1814 he succeeded his brother Louis XVIII, but his repressive rule led to revolution, and his abdication and exile. >> Louis XVIII

Charles XII (of Sweden) (1682–1718) King of Sweden (1697–1718), born in Stockholm, the son of Charles XI. He attacked Denmark (1699), defeated the Russians at Narva (1700), dethroned Augustus II of Poland (1704), then invaded Russia again (1707), but was defeated at Poltava (1709). He later attacked Norway, but was killed at the siege of Halden. >> Augustus II

Charles XIV (of Sweden), originally **Jean Baptiste Jules Bernadotte** (1763–1844) King of Sweden (1818–44), born a lawyer's son in Pau, France. He became marshal in the French army in 1804, fought in several Napoleonic campaigns (1805–9), and was elected heir to the throne of Sweden (1810). He then refused to comply with Napoleon's demands, fought against him at Leipzig (1813), and was rewarded with the Kingdom of Norway. >> Napoleon I

Charles (Philip Arthur George), Prince of Wales (1948–) Eldest son of Queen Elizabeth II and Prince Philip, Duke of Edinburgh, and heir apparent to the throne, born at Buckingham Palace, London. He was given the title of Prince of Wales in 1958, and invested at Caernarfon (1969). He served in the RAF and Royal Navy, (1971–6), and in 1981 married **Lady Diana Frances Spencer**. They have two sons: **Prince William Arthur Philip Louis** (1982–) and **Prince Henry Charles Albert David** (1984–). The couple separated in 1992. >> Elizabeth II; Edinburgh; Spencer, Diana

Charles, (Mary) Eugenia (1919–) Dominican prime minister (1980–), born in Pointe Michel, Dominica. In 1970 she co-founded and led the centrist Dominica Freedom Party, and became the Caribbean's first female prime minister.

Charles, Jacques Alexandre César [shah(r)l] (1746–1823) Physicist, born in Beaugency, France. He made the first manned ascent by hydrogen balloon, reaching 3000 m/9800 ft in 1783, and formulated *Charles's law*, which relates the volume of a gas at constant pressure to its temperature.

Charles, Ray, originally **Ray Charles Robinson** (1930–) Singer and pianist, born in Albany, GA. Blind from childhood, he became influenced by jazz and blues, and developed an original blend of music identified as 'soul'.

Charles, Robert (1936–) Golfer, born in Carterton, New Zealand. In 1963 he became the only left-handed golfer to win the British Open championship, and also won five US Tour events.

Charles d'Orléans >> **Orléans, Charles**

Charles the Great >> **Charlemagne**

Charles Edward Stuart >> **Stuart, Charles Edward**

Charles Martel [mah(r)**tel**] (Old French, 'the hammer') (c.688–741) Mayor of the palace for the last Merovingian kings of the Franks, and the undisputed head of the Carolingian family by 723. He conducted many campaigns against the Frisians and Saxons, and halted Muslim expansion in W Europe at the Battle of Poitiers (732). >> Pepin III

Charlevoix, Pierre François Xavier de [shah(r)lvwah] (1682–1761) Jesuit explorer of North America, born in St Quentin, France. In 1720 he was sent to find a route to W Canada, travelling up the St Lawrence River, across the Great Lakes, and reaching New Orleans and the Gulf of Mexico.

Charlotte (Augusta), Princess (1796–1817) Princess of Great Britain and Ireland, the only daughter of George IV and Caroline of Brunswick. In 1816 she married the future King Leopold I of the Belgians, but died in childbirth the following year. >> George IV; Leopold I (of Belgium)

Charlotte Sophia of Mecklenburg-Strelitz (1744–1818) Queen of Great Britain and Ireland, the wife of George III. She married George in 1761, and bore him 15 children. Their eldest son was the future George IV. >> George III / IV

Charlton, Bobby, popular name of **Sir Robert Charlton** (1937–) Footballer, born in Ashington, Northumberland, the brother of Jack Charlton. He played for Manchester United throughout his career (1954–73). He won 106 caps for England, scoring a record 49 goals. >> Charlton, Jack

Charlton, Jack, popular name of **John Charlton** (1935–) Footballer, born in Ashington, Northumberland, the brother of Bobby Charlton. He played for Leeds United (1965–75), and was capped for England late in his career. In 1986 he was appointed manager of the Republic of Ireland team, taking them to the last stages of the World Cup in 1990 and 1994. >> Charlton, Bobby

Charney, Jule Gregory (1917–81) Meteorologist, born in San Francisco, CA. He helped pioneer the first computer-generated weather forecast, which resulted in daily predictions of gross climate and weather patterns.

Charnley, Sir John (1911–82) Orthopaedic surgeon, born in Bury, Lancashire. In the 1950s and 1960s he played a key role in both the technology and the surgical techniques of hip replacements.

Charonton, Enguerrand >> Quarton, Enguerrand

Charpentier, Gustave [shah(r)pätyay] (1860–1956) Composer, born in Dieuze, France. He wrote dramatic and choral works, and composed both the music and libretti for the operas *Louise* (1900) and *Julien* (1913).

Charrenton, Enguerrand >> Quarton, Enguerrand

Charteris, Leslie [chah(r)teris], originally **Leslie Charles Bowyer Yin** (1907–93) Crime-story writer, born in Singapore. He became a US citizen in 1941, and is especially known as the creator of Simon Templar, 'the Saint'.

Chartier, Alain [shah(r)tyay] (c.1385–c.1435) Writer, born in Bayeux, France. His works include *Book of the Four Ladies* (trans, 1415–16), *Quadrilogue invectif* (1422), and the allegorical poem *La Belle Dame sans merci* (1424).

Chase, James Hadley, pseudonym of **René Raymond** (1906–85) Novelist, born in London. He started the vogue for tough realism in gangster stories in the UK with his *No Orchids for Miss Blandish* (1939).

Chase, Mary Ellen (1887–1973) Writer, born in Blue Hill, ME. Her autobiographies and novels revealed a passion for her native Maine, notably *Mary Peters* (1934) and *Silas Crockett* (1935).

Chase, Salmon P(ortland) (1808–73) Jurist and statesman, born in Cornish, NH. He became Secretary of the Treasury (1861–4), after which he was appointed Chief Justice of the USA (1864), and presided at the trial of President Andrew Johnson (1868). >> Johnson, Andrew

Chase, Samuel (1741–1811) Jurist, born in Princess Anne, MD. A member of the Supreme Court from 1796, in 1804 he was impeached for his partisan hostility to political offenders, but was acquitted.

Chase, William Merritt (1849–1916) Painter, born in Franklin, IN. He painted landscapes, portraits, and still-lifes, gaining a reputation as a teacher.

Chasles, Michel [shahl] (1793–1880) Mathematician, born in Epernon, France. Professor of geometry at the Sorbonne (1846), he greatly developed synthetic projective geometry by means of cross-ratio and homographies without the use of co-ordinates.

Chataway, Chris(topher John) (1931–) Athlete and statesman, born in London. A member of the Olympic team (1952, 1956), he set a new world record time in the 5000 m. In 1959 he became a Conservative MP, and was minister for posts and telecommunications (1970–2) and for industrial development (1972–4).

Chateaubriand, François Auguste René, vicomte de (Viscount of) [shatohbreeä] (1768–1848) French politician and writer, born in St Malo, France. His major works include *Atala* (1801), *The Genius of Christianity* (trans, 1802), and a celebrated autobiography, *Memoirs from Beyond the Tomb* (not published as a whole until 1902).

Châtelet-Lomont, Gabrielle Emilie le Tonnelier de Breteuil, Marquise du (Marchioness of) [shatlay lohmõ] (1706–49) Scholar and writer, born in Paris. Her chief work was the translation into French of Newton's *Principia mathematica*, posthumously published in 1759.

Chatelier, Henry le [shatlyay] (1850–1936) Chemist, born in Paris. In 1888 he discovered the law of reaction governing the effect of pressure and temperature on equilibrium.

Chatham, 1st Earl of >> Pitt, William, 1st Earl of Chatham

Chatterjee, Bankim Chandra (1838–94) Writer, born in Katalpura, Bengal. His works included *Durges Nandini* (1864) and *Anandamath* (1882), a novel of the Sannyasi rebellion of 1772.

Chatterton, Thomas (1752–70) Poet, born in Bristol, Avon. His poems, purporting to be by Thomas Rowley, a 15th-c monk, were denounced as forgeries, and the debate over their authenticity raged for 80 years.

Chatwin, Bruce (1940–89) Writer and traveller, born in Sheffield, South Yorkshire. He wrote books which combine fiction, anthropology, philosophy, and travel, such as *In Patagonia* (1977, Hawthornden) and *Utz* (1988).

Chaucer, Geoffrey (c.1343–1400) Poet, probably born in London. Travelling extensively abroad on the king's service, he also held royal posts at home, including that of Comptroller of the Petty Customs (1382). His early writings, such as *Troilus and Criseyde*, were greatly influenced by Italian authors, notably Boccaccio. His later period includes his most famous work, the unfinished *Canterbury Tales*. Chaucer was the first great poet of the English nation; and in the Middle Ages he stands supreme. >> Boccaccio

Chauliac, Guy de [shohliak] (c.1300–68) Surgeon, born in Chauliac, France. He wrote *Chirurgia magna* (1363), which was translated into French over a century later and used as a manual by generations of doctors.

Chaussée, Pierre Claude Nivelle de La >> La Chaussée, Pierre Claude Nivelle de

Chavannes, Puvis de >> Puvis de Chavannes, Pierre

Chávez, Carlos [chahvays] (1899–1978) Composer, born in Mexico City. His works are influenced by Mexican folk music, and include ballets, symphonies, and concertos. He formed the Mexican Symphony Orchestra in 1928.

Chavez, Cesar (Estrada) [shavez, shahvez] (1927–93) Labour leader, born in Yuma, AZ. In 1962 he started the National Farm Workers Association, from 1966 the United Farm Workers of America, and was its president until his death.

Chayefsky, Paddy [chiyefskee], originally **Sidney Chayefsky** (1923–81) Stage and television playwright, born in New York City, NY. Best known for *Marty* (1953) and *The Bachelor Party* (1954), he received three Oscars for his film writing.

Chebyshev, Pafnuty Lvovich [chebishof] (1821–94) Mathematician, born in Okatovo, Russia. He made important contributions to the theory of the distribution of prime numbers, and his theory of approximation to functions by polynomials has become important in modern computing.

Cheever, John (1912–82) Short-story writer and novelist, born in Quincy, MA. His books include *The Wapshot Chronicle* (1957), its sequel *The Wapshot Scandal* (1964), and *The Stories of John Cheever* (1979, Pulitzer).

Che Guevara >> Guevara, Che

Cheke, Sir John [cheek] (1514–57) Humanist and scholar, born in Cambridge, Cambridgeshire. He adopted the doctrines of the Reformation, and became the first Regius professor of Greek at Cambridge (1540). After the accession of Mary I he was imprisoned (1553–4), and forced to recant his Protestantism.

Chekhov, Anton (Pavlovitch) [chekof] (1860–1904) Playwright and master of the short story, born in Taganrog, Ukraine. His early full-length plays were failures, but when *The Seagull* (trans, 1896) was revived in 1898 it was a great success. He then wrote his masterpieces: (trans titles) *Uncle Vanya* (1900), *The Three Sisters* (1901), and *The Cherry Orchard* (1904).

Chelcicky, Petz [chelchitskee] (c.1390–1460) Reformer and theologian, probably born in Chelčice, Bohemia. A radical follower of the Hussites, he founded the sect which became the Moravian Brethren.

Chelmsford, Frederick John Napier Thesiger, 1st Viscount and 3rd Baron (1868–1933) Colonial administrator, born in London. As Viceroy of India (1916–21), he helped increase the number of Indians taking part in government. He became First Lord of the Admiralty in 1924.

Chemnitz, Martin [kemnits] (1522–86) Lutheran theologian, born in Treuenbrietzen, Germany. He worked to unite the Lutheran Church (split after Luther's death), and was primarily responsible for the Formula of Concord (1577). >> Luther

Chen Yi (1901–72) Chinese Communist leader, born in Lochih, Szechwan. Created Marshal of the People's Republic in 1955, he became foreign minister in 1958, but was dropped from the Politburo during the Cultural Revolution in 1969.

Chen Duxiu [chen dooshoo], also spelled **Ch'en Tu-hsiu** (1879–1942) One of the founders of the Chinese Communist Party (1921). He saw Marxism as a vehicle for modernization, and established Communist cells in several cities. Expelled from the Party (1930) and imprisoned (1932–7), he left politics and turned to writing.

Chénier, André (Marie) de [shaynyay] (1762–94) Poet, born in Istanbul, the son of the French consul-general. He was sent to France as a child. Alarmed by the excesses of the Revolution, he offended Robespierre by pamphlets, and was guillotined. >> Robespierre

Chennault, Claire (Lee) [shenawlt] (1890–1958) Aviator, born in Commerce, TX. He went to work for the Chinese Nationalists in 1937, recruiting US pilots for operations against the Japanese. His 'Flying Tigers' became the most publicized flying unit of World War 2.

Chen Ning Yang >> Yang, Chen Ning

Cheops [keeops], Greek form of **Khufu** (26th-c BC) King of Memphis in Egypt, second ruler of the fourth dynasty. He is famous as the builder of the Great Pyramid.

Cherenkov, Pavel (Alexeyevich) [cherengkof] (1904–90) Physicist, born in Novaya Chigla, Russia. In 1934 he noted the emission of blue light from water and other transparent media when atomic particles, moving at a speed greater than that of light in that medium, are passed through it (the *Cherenkov effect*).

Cherkassky, Shura (Alexander Isaakovich) [cherkaskee] (1911–) Pianist, born in Odessa, Ukraine. In America from 1922, he excelled in the Romantic repertoire, touring and recording widely.

Chermayeff, Serge [chermiyef] (1900–) Architect and designer, born in the Caucasus. His early design work was for interiors, including studios for Broadcasting House, London (1931). In 1940 he emigrated to the USA.

Chernenko, Konstantin Ustinovich [chernyengko] (1911–85) Soviet president (1984–5), born in Bolshaya Tes, Russia. Regarded as a conservative, he was a rival of Andropov in the Communist Party leadership contest of 1982, and became party general secretary and head of state after Andropov's death. >> Andropov

Cherubini, (Maria) Luigi (Carlo Zenobio Salvatore) [kerubeenee] (1760–1842) Composer, born in Florence, Italy. His best-known opera is *The Water-Carrier* (trans, 1880). In 1822 he became director of the Paris Conservatoire.

Cherwell, Frederick Alexander Lindemann, 1st Viscount [chah(r)wel] (1886–1957) Scientist, born in Baden-Baden, Germany. In 1914 he became director of the Experimental Physics Station at Farnborough, where he evolved the mathematical theory of aircraft spin. He was appointed scientific adviser to Churchill in 1940. >> Churchill, Sir Winston

Cheshire (of Woodhall), (Geoffrey) Leonard Cheshire, Baron (1917–92) British bomber pilot and philanthropist. He was an official British observer of the atomic bomb over Nagasaki in 1945. The experience determined him to establish co-operative communities for ex-servicemen, from which grew the Cheshire Homes for the Disabled. >> Ryder, Sue

Chesney, Francis Rawdon [cheznee] (1789–1872) Soldier and explorer, born in Annalong, Co Down. In 1829 he surveyed the Isthmus of Suez, providing data later used in the construction of the Suez Canal, and after 1831 explored a route to India by rail and sea via Syria and the Euphrates.

Chesnius >> Duchesne, André

Chesnut, Mary, Boykin, *née* **Miller** (1823–86) Diarist, born near Camden, SC. She married James Chesnut, who joined the Confederate army during the Civil War, leaving his wife to write a journal of life on the Southern home-front, *A Diary from Dixie* (1905).

Chesnutt, Charles W(addell) (1858–1932) Writer, born in Cleveland, OH. The son of emancipated blacks, he wrote works on the theme of social injustice, such as *The Goophered Grapevine* (1887), the first published work by a black novelist.

Chessman, Caryl (Whittier), nickname **The Red Light Bandit** (1921–60) Convict and writer, born in St Joseph, MI. Sentenced to death in 1948, he was granted eight stays of execution over a 12-year period before sentence was carried out. He wrote best-selling books against capital punishment, such as *Cell 2455 Death Row* (1956).

Chesterfield, Philip Dormer Stanhope, 4th Earl of (1694–1773) English statesman, orator, and man of letters, born in London. A bitter antagonist of Robert Walpole, he joined the Pelham ministry (1744), and became Irish lord-lieutenant (1745) and a principal secretary of state (1746–8). >> Pelham, Thomas; Walpole, Robert

Chesterton, G(ilbert) K(eith) (1874–1936) Critic and writer, born in London. He wrote articles, poetry, and critical studies, gaining popularity with the amiable detective-priest introduced in *The Innocence of Father Brown* (1911). He became a Catholic in 1922, and thereafter wrote mainly on religious topics.

Chetham, Humphrey [chetm] (1580–1653) Merchant and philanthropist, born in Manchester. A cloth manufacturer in Manchester, he founded Chetham Hospital and a public library in the city.

Chettle, Henry [chetl] (?–c.1607) Playwright and pamphleteer, born in London. He wrote a picaresque romance, *Piers Plainnes Seven Yeres Prentiship* (1595), and plays for Philip Henslowe's Rose Theatre, notably *The Tragedy of Hoffman* (1602). >> Henslowe

Chevalier, Albert [shevalyey] (1861–1923) Entertainer,

born in London. He appeared as an actor at the old Prince of Wales' Theatre in 1877, and in 1891 became a music-hall singer, immortalizing such songs as 'My Old Dutch' and 'Knocked 'em in the Old Kent Road'.

Chevalier, Maurice [shevalyay] (1888–1972) Film and vaudeville actor, born in Paris. He became known for his individual, straw-hatted, *bon-viveur* personality and his distinctive French accent, in such films as *The Innocents of Paris* (1929) and *Gigi* (1958).

Chevallier, Gabriel [shevalyay] (1895–1969) Novelist, born in Lyon, France. He won wide acclaim with *Clochemerle* (1934), an earthy satire on petty bureaucracy. Other books include *Clarisse Vernon* (1933) and *Clochemerle Babylone* (1954).

Chevreul, Michel Eugène [shevroei] (1786–1889) Chemist, born in Angers, France. His best-known work was on animal fats, soap-making, candle-making, waxes, and natural dyes.

Chevrolet, Louis [shevrohlay] (1878–1941) Automobile designer and racing driver, born in La Chaux de Fonds, Switzerland. He emigrated to the USA in 1900, and became a motor-racing driver, founding in 1911 with William Crapo Durant (1861–1947) the Chevrolet Motor Co.

Ch'i Pai-shih [chee piyshee], also known as **Ch'i Huang** (1863–1957) Artist, born in Hsiang T'an, China. Sometimes called 'China's Picasso', his art is deeply rooted in folk tradition. He painted birds, flowers, fruit, landscapes, and subjects from daily life.

Chiang Ch'ing >> Jiang Qing
Chiang Ching-kuo >> Jiang Jingguo
Chiang Kai-shek >> Jiang Jieshi

Chiarelli, Luigi [kyarelee] (1884–1947) Playwright, born in Trani, Italy. His great success was *The Mask and the Face* (trans, 1916), a farcical comedy which has been often translated.

Chichele, Henry [chichlay] (c.1362–c.1443) English clergyman and diplomat. In 1414 he became Archbishop of Canterbury. He was the founder of two colleges at Oxford in 1437: St John's and All Souls.

Chichester, Sir Francis (Charles) [chichester] (1901–72) Pioneer air navigator, adventurer, and yachtsman, born in Barnstaple, Devon. In 1953 he took up ocean sailing, winning the first solo transatlantic yacht race (1960) in *Gipsy Moth III*, sailing from Plymouth to New York in 40 days. He also made a solo circumnavigation of the world (1966–7) in *Gipsy Moth IV*.

Chifley, Joseph Benedict (1885–1951) Australian Labour prime minister (1945–9), born in Bathurst, New South Wales, Australia. He became defence minister in 1929, and as premier expanded social services and reformed the banking system.

Chikatilo, Andrei [chikateeloh] (1938–94) Russian convicted murderer. He was convicted and sentenced to death in Russia in 1992 for a series of murders committed over a 12-year period, believed to be the world's worst serial-killing case.

Child, Charles M(anning) (1869–1954) Developmental biologist, born in Ypsilanti, MI. He studied the origin and development of the invertebrate nervous system, and is best known for his 'gradient theory' of regeneration (1911).

Child, Francis James (1825–96) Philologist, born in Boston, MA. His scholarly contributions include his edition of Spenser's *Poetical Works* (1855), for many years the authoritative text, and pioneered a comparative approach to folklore in *English and Scottish Popular Ballads* (10 vols, 1883–98).

Childe, (Vere) Gordon [chyld] (1892–1957) Archaeologist, born in Sydney, New South Wales, Australia. His early books, notably *The Dawn of European Civilisation* (1925) and *The Most Ancient Near East* (1928), established

him as the most influential archaeological theorist of his generation.

Childers, (Robert) Erskine [childerz] (1870–1922) Irish nationalist and writer, born in London. He joined the Irish Republican Army, and was active in the Civil War, but was captured and executed. His son **Erskine Hamilton Childers** (1905–74) was president of Ireland (1973–4).

Childs, Lucinda (1940–) Dancer and choreographer, born in New York City. As a founder member of the experimental Judson Dance Theatre (1962–4), she developed a minimalist style of choreography, often incorporating dialogue.

Chipp, Don(ald) Leslie (1925–) Australian politician, born in Melbourne, Victoria, Australia. He founded the Australian Democrats in 1977, a centrist group, and served as their parliamentary leader from 1977 until 1986, when he retired.

Chippendale, Thomas (1718–79) Furniture-maker and designer, baptised at Otley, West Yorkshire. He set up a workshop in London in 1754, and became famous for his Neoclassical furniture. *The Gentleman and Cabinet-maker's Director* (1754) was the first comprehensive trade catalogue of its kind.

Chirac, Jacques (René) [shirak] (1932–) French prime minister (1974–6) and president (1995–). Appointed prime minister by Giscard d'Estaing, he resigned over differences with him, and broke away to lead the Gaullist Party. He was unsuccessful in the 1981 and 1988 presidential elections, but won in 1995. >> Giscard d'Estaing

Chirico, Giorgio de [kireekoh] (1888–1978) Artist, born in Volo, Greece. About 1910 he began to produce a series of dreamlike pictures which had considerable influence on the Surrealists. His style after 1915 is often called 'metaphysical painting'.

Chisholm, Caroline [chizm] (1808–77) Social worker and philanthropist, born near Northampton, Northamptonshire. In 1838 she settled in Windsor, New South Wales, established an office to provide shelter for new arrivals in the colony, and set up the Family Colonization Loan Society.

Chisholm, Erik [chizm] (1904–65) Composer, born in Glasgow, Strathclyde. In 1945 he was appointed professor of music at Cape Town. His works include two symphonies, concertos for piano and violin, other orchestral music, and operas.

Chissano, Joaquim (Alberto) [chisahnoh] (1939–) Mozambique prime minister (1974–75) and president (1986–), born in Chibuto, Mozambique. When internal self-government was granted in 1974 he was appointed prime minister. He then served under Machel as foreign minister, and succeeded him as president. >> Machel

Chisum, John Simpson [chizm] (1824–84) Cattleman, born in Hardeman Co, TN, 'the cattle king of America'. He entered the cattle business in 1854, later moving his ranching operations to New Mexico, where he settled in 1873.

Chittenden, Russell H(enry) (1856–1943) Biochemist and educator, born in New Haven, CT. He made pioneering studies in the enzymatic digestion of proteins and starch, isolated glycogen ('animal starch') in 1875, and advocated a low-protein diet for humans.

Chladni, Ernst (Florens Friedrich) [kladnee] (1756–1827) Physicist, born in Wittenberg, Germany. The founder of the science of acoustics, he invented the euphonium. His study of the vibration of solid bodies resulted in the patterns known as *Chladni figures*.

Chlodovech or **Chlodwig >> Clovis I**

Choiseul(-Amboise), Etienne François, duc de (Duke of) [shwazoei] (1719–85) Minister of Louis XV, born in Lorraine, France. He arranged the alliance between France and Austria against Frederick the Great (1756), and as foreign minister (1758) obtained good terms for France at the end of the Seven Years' War (1763). >> Louis XV

Chomsky, (Avram) Noam (1928-) Linguist and political activist, born in Philadelphia, PA. His *Syntactic Structures* (1957) introduced a new theory of language called transformational generative grammar. Opposed to the Vietnam War, he became involved in the radical movement, as seen in *American Power and the New Mandarins* (1969).

Chopin, Frédéric (François) [shohpī] (1810-49) Composer and pianist, born in Zelazowa Wola, Poland. His works for the piano include 50 mazurkas, 27 études, 25 préludes, 19 nocturnes, 13 waltzes, 12 polonaises, four ballades, three impromptus, three sonatas, two piano concertos, and a funeral march. He lived with the novelist George Sand between 1838 and 1847. >> Sand

Chopin, Kate [shohpin], *née* **Katherine O'Flaherty** (1851-1904) Writer, born in St Louis, MO. Her realistic novel of sexual passion, *The Awakening* (1899), caused a furore, and was harshly condemned by the public, but she has since been acclaimed for her concerns about the freedom of women.

Chorley, Richard John (1927-) Geomorphologist, born in Minehead, Somerset. He became a leader in the group which challenged traditional geography and led to the British phase of the so-called 'quantitative revolution'.

Chou En-lai >> Zhou Enlai

Chrétien, (Joseph Jacques) Jean [kraytyen] (1934-) Canadian prime minister (1993-), born in Shawinigan, Quebec, Canada. After serving under Pearson and Trudeau, he became leader of the Liberal Party in 1990, and prime minister when his party won the 1993 general election. >> Pearson, Lester B; Trudeau

Chrétien de Troyes [kraytyī duh trwah] (?-c.1183) Mediaeval poet, born in Troyes, France. His best-known works are the metrical Arthurian romances, such as *Lancelot* and *Perceval*, which introduce all the ingredients of Celtic legend, and add the theme of the Holy Grail.

Christaller, Walter [kristaler] (1893-1969) Geographer, born in Berneck, Germany. He originated 'central place theory' (1933), which has found practical application as a planning tool in North America and The Netherlands.

Christensen, Willam [kristensen], originally **William Farr Christensen** (1904-89) Dancer and choreographer, born in Brigham City, UT. With his brothers, **Harold** (1904-89) and **Lew** (1909-84), he founded the San Francisco Ballet Company in 1937.

Christian X (1870-1947) King of Denmark (1912-47), born in Charlottenlund, Denmark. During 1940-5, he attracted great acclaim by remaining in Denmark and seeking to save the country from the harshest effects of German occupation.

Christian, Charlie, popular name of **Charles Christian** (1916-42) Jazz guitarist, born in Dallas, TX. He joined bandleader Benny Goodman in 1939, playing mainly with the Goodman sextet, and pioneering the use of the amplified guitar as a solo instrument. >> Goodman, Benny

Christian, Fletcher (18th-c) Seaman and ringleader of the mutiny on the *Bounty* (1789), born in Cockermouth, Cumbria. After the mutiny, he settled on Pitcairn I, where his descendants were found in 1808. >> Bligh

Christie, John (1882-1962) Opera patron, born in Eggesford, Devon. In the 1930s he built a small theatre on his country estate in Sussex, now internationally known as Glyndebourne Opera.

Christie, Dame Agatha (Mary Clarissa), *née* **Miller** (1890-1976) Writer, born in Torquay, Devon. She wrote more than 70 detective novels featuring the Belgian detective, Hercule Poirot, or the enquiring village lady, Miss Marple. Several of her stories have become popular films, such as *Murder on the Orient Express* (1974) and *Death on the Nile* (1978).

Christie, James (1730-1803) Auctioneer, born in London. He founded his well-known London firm in 1766. One of his sons, **James** (1773-1831), was also an auctioneer.

Christie, John Reginald Halliday (1898-1953) Murderer, born in Yorkshire. He was hanged at London for the murder of his wife, and confessed to killing six other women, including the wife of Timothy John Evans (hanged for the murder in 1950). Evans was granted a free pardon in 1966.

Christie, Julie (1940-) British actress, born in Chukua, Assam. Her many films include *Billy Liar* (1963), *Darling* (1965, Oscar), *The Go-Between* (1971), and *Power* (1985).

Christie, Linford (1960-) Sprinter, born in Jamaica. In 1993 he held the World, Olympic, Commonwealth, and European Cup titles for the 100 m, achieving 9·87 seconds at the world championships (a European record).

Christina (1626-89) Queen of Sweden (1632-54), born in Stockholm, the daughter and successor of Gustav II Adolf. In 1644 she negotiated the Peace of Westphalia, bringing to an end the Thirty Years War (1648). In 1654 she abdicated, became a Catholic, and went to Rome where she founded the Accademia dell'Arcadia. >> Gustav II

Christine de Pisan [peezan] (c.1363-c.1431) Poet, born in Venice, Italy. Brought up in Paris, in 1378 she married Etienne Castel (d.1389). Left with three children and no money, she began writing, and produced works in both prose and verse, including *The City of Ladies* (trans, 1405).

Christo, originally **Christo Javacheff** (1935-) Avant-garde artist, born in Gabrovo, Bulgaria. In 1964 he settled in New York City. His huge outdoor sculptures, which include wrapping objects (trees, cars, buildings) in canvas or plastic sheeting, have continued to arouse controversy.

Christoff, Boris (1914-93) Bass-baritone, born in Plovdiv, Bulgaria. He sang at La Scala in Milan in 1947, at Covent Garden in 1949, and in the USA from 1956.

Christophe, Henry [kristof] (1767-1829) Haitian revolutionary, born a slave on the island of Grenada. He joined the black insurgents on Haiti against the French (1790), and was appointed president (1807) and proclaimed king (1811). His rule led to an insurrection, and he shot himself.

Christopher, St (3rd-c), feast day 25 July. Syrian Christian martyr, traditionally a man of gigantic stature who carried the Christ-child across a river. He is said to have suffered martyrdom under Emperor Decius (reigned 249-251), and is the patron saint of wayfarers and motorists.

Christopher, Warren M(inor) (1925-) Lawyer and government official, born in Scranton, ND. As deputy secretary of state (1977-81), in 1989-91 he led successful US negotiations for the release of 52 hostages held in Iran, and was appointed secretary of state in 1993.

Christophersen, Henning [kristofersen] (1939-) Danish statesman, born in Copenhagen. He was leader of the Danish Liberal Party (1978), minister of foreign affairs (1978-9), and minister of finance and deputy prime minister (1982-4). He became a member of the EC Commission in 1984.

Christus, Petrus [kristus] (c.1420-c.1473) Painter, born in Baerle, Brabant, who became a master in Bruges in 1444. It is thought that he was an important source for the transmission of the Eyckian technique to Italian painters, notably Antonello da Messina. >> Antonello da Messina; Eyck, Jan van

Christy, Edwin P(earce) [kristee] (1815-62) Entertainer, born in Philadelphia, PA, the originator of the Christy Minstrels show. He gained success with his 'black-face' minstrelsy, taking his show to New York City and London. >> Foster, Stephen

Chrysander, Friedrich [krisander] (1826–1901) Musical historian, the biographer and editor of Handel, born in Lübtheen, Germany. He founded the Handel Society in 1856. >> Handel

Chrysippus [kriysipus] (c.280–c.206 BC) Stoic philosopher, born in Soli, Cilicia. He went to Athens and became the third and greatest head of the Stoa. He wrote over 700 works, of which only fragments remain.

Chrysler, Walter (Percy) [kriyzler] (1875–1940) Automobile manufacturer, born in Wamego, KS. He introduced the 'Plymouth' motor car and designed the first high compression engine.

Chrysostom, St John [krisostom] (c.347–407), feast day 13 September. Church Father, born in Antioch. Made Archbishop of Constantinople (398), his reproof of vices moved the Empress Eudoxia to have him banished (403).

Chu, Steven (1948–) Physicist, born in St Louis, MO. He has made major contributions to laser spectroscopy, the analysis of positronium atoms, and studies of gaseous sodium at temperatures approaching absolute zero.

Chubb, Charles (1772–1846) British locksmith. He patented improvements in 'detector' locks, originally (1818) patented by his brother, Jeremiah Chubb, of Portsea.

Chulalongkorn, Phra Paramindr Maha (1853–1910) King of Siam (1868–1910, as **Rama V**), born in Bangkok. He abolished slavery, proclaimed liberty of conscience, and introduced modern buildings, transport systems, and communications. His father, Mongkut (Rama IV), was the model for the film *The King and I* (1956).

Chun Doo-Hwan (1931–) South Korean soldier and president (1980–8), born in Taegu, South Korea. He took control following a coup in 1979, heading the newly formed Democratic Justice Party. Popular opposition to his authoritarian regime forced his retirement.

Chung, Kyung-Wha (1948–) Violinist, born in Seoul. She moved to New York City in 1960 and appeared with the New York Philharmonic. Her sister **Myung-Wha Chung** (1944–) is a cellist, and her brother **Myung-Whung Chung** (1953–) was appointed music director of the new Bastille Opera, Paris, in 1989.

Church, Frederick (Edwin) (1826–1900) Painter, born in Hartford, CT. Considered a member of the Hudson River School, his panoramic scenes reveal his dramatic use of lighting and naturalistic details, as seen in 'Niagara' (1857).

Church, Sir Richard (1785–1873) Soldier, born in Cork, Co Cork, Ireland. He served in the Greek War of Independence (1821–32), led the revolution in Greece (1843), and was promoted general (1854), having earned the nickname 'Liberator of Greece'.

Church, Richard Thomas (1893–1972) Writer, born in London. He made his name first as a poet, but is also known for his novels, such as *The Porch* (1937).

Churcher, Betty, popular name of **Elizabeth Ann Churcher** (1931–) Arts administrator, born in Brisbane, Queensland, Australia. She wrote the award-winning book *Understanding Art* (1974), and later became director of the Australian National Gallery (1990–).

Churchill, Arabella (1648–1730) English aristocrat, the elder sister of John Churchill, 1st Duke of Marlborough. In 1665 she became the mistress of the Duke of York (the future James II), by whom she had four children. >> James II (of England); Marlborough

Churchill, Caryl (1938–) Playwright, born in London. Her most successful work has been *Serious Money* (1987), satirizing the world of City financial brokers. Other plays include *Cloud Nine* (1979), *Top Girls* (1982), and *Mad Forest* (1990).

Churchill, Charles (1731–64) Satirical poet, born in London. He achieved fame with his *Rosciad* (1761), a fierce attack on contemporary actors. Other works include *The Prophecy of Famine* (1763) and *The Candidate* (1764).

Churchill, John >> **Marlborough, John Churchill**

Churchill, Randolph (Frederick Edward Spencer) (1911–68) Journalist, born in London, the son of Sir Winston Churchill. A forthright commentator on current affairs, he wrote *The Rise and Fall of Sir Anthony Eden* (1959), and published a biography of his father (2 vols, 1966–67). >> Churchill, Sir Winston

Churchill, Lord Randolph (Henry Spencer) (1849–95) British statesman, born in Blenheim Palace, Oxfordshire, the father of Winston Churchill. In 1880 he led a guerrilla band of Conservatives known as the 'Fourth Party'. He became secretary for India (1885–6), and was briefly Chancellor of the Exchequer. >> Churchill, Sir Winston

Churchill, Sarah, *née* **Jennings** (1660–1744) English aristocrat, the wife of John Churchill, 1st Duke of Marlborough. In 1673 she entered the service of the Duke of York (the future James II), and befriended his daughter, Anne. After Anne became queen, Sarah dominated the Whig ministry, but was later supplanted by a new favourite, Mrs Masham. >> Anne; Marlborough; Masham

Churchill, Winston (1871–1947) Historical novelist, born in St Louis, MO. His works include *Richard Carvel* (1899), *The Crisis* (1901), and *The Crossing* (1904).

Churchill, Sir Winston (Leonard Spencer) (1874–1965) British prime minister (1940–5, 1951–5), born in Blenheim Palace, Oxfordshire. Initially a Conservative MP (1900), he joined the Liberals in 1904, and was colonial under-secretary (1905), President of the Board of Trade (1908), home secretary (1910), and First Lord of the Admiralty (1911). After World War 1 he was secretary of state for war and air (1919–21), and Chancellor of the Exchequer (1924–9). In 1929 he returned to the Conservative fold, and on Chamberlain's defeat (May 1940) formed a coalition government, leading Britain through World War 2 with great oratory and steely resolution. Defeated in the July 1945 election, he was prime minister again in 1951, and after 1955 remained a venerated backbencher. He was awarded the Nobel Prize for Literature in 1953. His widow, Clementine Ogilvy Hozier, whom he had married in 1908, was made a life peer in 1965 for her indefatigable charitable work (Baroness Spencer-Churchill of Chartwell). >> Chamberlain, Neville

Churchward, George Jackson (1857–1933) Locomotive engineer, born in Stoke Gabriel, Devon. He was chief mechanical engineer of the Great Western Railway (1902–21), and his designs included the 4-6-0 'Star' series introduced in 1906.

Churriguera, Don José [chureegayra] (1650–1725) Architect, born in Salamanca, Spain. He developed the extravagant style known as *Churrigueresque*, and his designs included Salamanca Cathedral. His brothers **Joaquin** (1674–1720) and **Alberto** (1676–1750) were also architects.

Chu-ta >> **Zhu Da**

Chu-teh >> **Zhu De**

Chuter-Ede, Baron >> **Ede, James Chuter**

Ciano, Galeazzo, conte di (Count) **Cortellazzo** [chyah-noh] (1903–44) Italian politician, born in Livorno, Italy, the son-in-law of Mussolini. Minister of propaganda (1935) and of foreign affairs (1936–43), from 1942 he opposed Mussolini's alliance with Germany, and was shot for participating in his deposition (1943). >> Mussolini

Cibber, Colley [siber] (1671–1757) Actor and playwright, born in London. He spent most of his career at the Theatre Royal in Drury Lane. In 1696, his first comedy, *Love's Last Shift*, established his fame both as a dramatist and actor.

Cibber, Mrs [siber], *née* **Susannah Maria Arne** (1714–66) Actress and singer, born in London, the sister of the composer Thomas Arne. A contralto, she made her stage debut in 1733, and the next year married **Theophilus Cibber** (1703–58). She later turned to drama, playing opposite David Garrick at Drury Lane. >> Arne; Cibber, Colley; Garrick

Ciccone, Madonna Louise >> **Madonna**

Cicero, Marcus Tullius [siseroh], also known in English as **Tully** (106–43 BC) Roman orator, statesman, and man of letters, born in Arpinum, Latium. He foiled Catiline's revolutionary plot, and was exiled when Clodius became tribune in 58 BC. Recalled by the people, he lost the esteem of both Caesar's and Pompey's factions by vacillating between the two. Living in retirement (46–44 BC), he wrote his chief works on rhetoric and philosophy. In 43 BC he delivered his famous speeches against Antony, the so-called 'Philippics', and was murdered by Antony's soldiers. >> Antonius; Caesar; Catiline; Pompey

Cid, El [sid], Span [theed], popular name of **Rodrigo** or **Ruy Díaz de Vivar** (c.1043–99) Spanish hero, born in Burgos, Spain. He became known as the *Cid* (from the Moorish *Sidi*, 'lord'). His great achievement was the capture of Valencia in 1094.

Cidenas [sidaynas] (4th-c BC) Babylonian astronomer, the head of an astronomical school at Sippra. He discovered the precession of the equinoxes.

Cierva, Juan de la [thyairva] (1895–1936) Aeronautical engineer, born in Murcia, Spain. Among his many aircraft designs was the autogiro, a plane with a freely rotating rotor providing lift, which flew successfully in 1923.

Cilea, Francesco [cheelia] (1866–1950) Operatic composer, born in Palmi, Italy. He wrote several operas, of which the best known is *Adriana Lecouvreur* (1902).

Cilento, Lady Phyllis Dorothy [silentoh], *née* **McGlew** (1894–1987) Medical practitioner, writer, and broadcaster, born in Sydney, New South Wales, Australia. Her life's work was devoted to family planning, childbirth education, and nutrition. She married Raphael West Cilento in 1920. >> Cilento, Raphael West

Cilento, Sir Raphael West [silentoh] (1893–1985) Medical administrator, born in Jamestown, South Australia. He became director of public health in New Guinea (1924–8), and director-general of health and medical services for Queensland (1934–45). >> Cilento, Phyllis Dorothy

Cimabue [cheemabooay], originally **Cenni di Peppi** (c.1240–c.1302) Painter, born in Florence, Italy. Adopting traditional Byzantine forms at first, he turned to nature, inspiring the naturalism of his great pupil, Giotto. He executed several important frescoes in the Church of St Francis at Assisi. >> Giotto

Cimarosa, Domenico [cheemarohsa] (1749–1801) Composer of operas, born in Aversa, Italy. He was chapel master at Vienna (1791), where his comic opera *The Secret Marriage* (trans, 1792) was a great success. He also wrote church and chamber music.

Cimon [siymon] (?–449 BC) Athenian commander, the son of Miltiades. He defeated the Persian forces at the R Eurymedon (c.469 BC), but his opposition to democracy at home and support for Sparta abroad brought him into conflict with Pericles, and he was ostracized in 461 BC. >> Miltiades; Pericles

Cincinnatus, Lucius Quinctius [sinsinahtus] (5th-c BC) Roman statesman, farmer, and folk hero. Called from the plough to rescue the Roman army which had been trapped by the Aequi (458 BC), he voluntarily returned to his farm when the crisis was over.

Cineas [sinias] (?–270 BC) Greek politician from Thessaly. The friend and minister of Pyrrhus, the King of Epirus, he was said to be the most eloquent man of his time. >> Pyrrhus

Cinna, Lucius Cornelius [sina] (?–84 BC) Prominent

Roman politician of the turbulent 80s BC. Driven from Rome and illegally deposed while consul in 87 BC, he recaptured the city, and was all-powerful there until his murder in 84 BC. >> Marius, Gaius

Cipriani, Giambattista [chipriahnee] (1727–85) Historical painter, born in Florence, Italy. In 1755 he came to London, where his graceful drawings, engraved by Bartolozzi, gained great popularity. >> Bartolozzi

Cisneros, Henry (Gabriel) [siznairohs, seesnayrohs] (1947–) Mayor and cabinet official, born in San Antonio, TX. As mayor of his native city (1982–90) he gained a national reptutation for being a progressive, and in 1992 he became secretary of housing and urban affairs.

Citrine (of Wembley), Walter McLennan Citrine, Baron [sitreen] (1887–1983) Trade union leader, born in Liverpool, Merseyside. He was general secretary of the Trades Union Congress (1926–46) and president of the International Federation of Trades Unions (1928–45).

Citroën, André Gustave [sitrohen] (1878–1935) Engineer and motor manufacturer, born in Paris. After World War 1 he began to manufacture low-priced small cars, but became bankrupt in 1934 and lost control of the company which still bears his name.

Civitali, Matteo [chivitahlee] (1435–1501) Architect and sculptor, born in Lucca, Italy. His best work is in the cathedral at Lucca.

Ci-Xi or **Tz'u-hsi** [tsoe shee], **Xiaogin** or **Hsiao-ch'en**, family name **Yehonala**, known as **the Empress Dowager** (1835–1908) Chinese consort of the Xianfeng emperor (1851–62), born in Beijing. She bore the emperor his only son, who succeeded as the T'ung Chih emperor when only five, and over whom she kept control up to his death (1875). She ensured the succession of another minor, as the Guangxu emperor, and continued to assert control, taking China into war against the treaty powers in 1900. >> Zai Tian

Cixous, Hélène [seeshoo] (1937–) Academic and feminist, born in Algiers. She moved to France in 1955, and became a teacher. Her work is mostly concerned with the relationship between psychoanalysis and language, especially in its significance for women.

Claiborne, Craig [klaybaw(r)n] (1920–) Chef and writer, born in Sunflower, MS. As food editor of the *New York Times* (1957), his restaurant reviews set a new standard for food reporting. His cookbooks include the best-selling *New York Times Cook Book* (1961).

Clair, René, pseudonym of **René Chomette** (1898–1981) Film producer, born in Paris. His major works include *Under the Roofs of Paris* (trans, 1930), *The Ghost Goes West* (1935), and *It Happened Tomorrow* (1944).

Claparède, Edouard [klapared] (1873–1940) Psychologist and educationist, born in Geneva, Switzerland. In 1912 he founded the J J Rousseau Institute for the study of educational science. An exponent of functionalism, he pioneered studies in problem-solving and sleep.

Clapeyron, Bénoît Paul Emile [klapayrõ] (1799–1864) Civil engineer, born in Paris. He was the first to make use of the expansive action of steam in the cylinder of a locomotive, and also developed the 'theorem of three moments', relating to the analysis of beams.

Clapperton, Hugh (1788–1827) Explorer, born in Annan, Dumfries and Galloway. In 1821 he was sent with Dixon Denham to discover the source of the Niger, returning to England in 1825 as the first European to have entered N Nigeria. >> Denham, Dixon

Clare of Assisi, St (1194–1253), feast day 11 August. Abbess, born of a noble family in Assisi, Italy. In 1215 she founded with St Francis the order of Franciscan nuns known as the Poor Clares. She was canonized in 1255, and in 1958 was designated patron saint of television.

Clare, John (1793-1864) Poet, born in Helpston, Cambridgeshire. His works include *Poems Descriptive of Rural Life* (1820). He spent the last 23 years of his life in an asylum, where he wrote some of his best poetry.

Clarence, George, Duke of (1449-78) The third son of Richard, Duke of York, and brother of Edward IV and Richard III, born in Dublin. In 1469 he married **Isabella**, the daughter of Richard Neville, Earl of Warwick. In 1478 he was impeached by his brothers for treason, and secretly executed. >> Edward IV; Richard III; Warwick, Richard Neville; York, Richard, 3rd Duke of

Clarendon, Edward Hyde, 1st Earl of (1609-74) English statesman and historian, born near Salisbury, Wiltshire. He became High Chancellor in 1658, but fell victim to a court cabal, was impeached for high treason, and left the country for France. His major work is the *History of the Rebellion in England* (3 vols, 1704-7). >> Charles I (of England)

Clarendon, George William Frederick Villiers, 4th Earl of (1800-70) British statesman, born in London. As secretary of state for foreign affairs (1853), he incurred the responsibility for the Crimean War, and temporarily lost office, becoming foreign secretary again under Russell (1865-6) and Gladstone (1868-70). >> Gladstone, W E; Russell, John

Claretie, Jules [klaruhtee], originally **Arsène Arnaud** (1840-1913) Writer, born in Limoges, France. A leading critic, political writer, and popular novelist, he made a hit with his Revolution plays, *Les Muscadins* (1874), *Le Régiment de Champagne* (1877), and *Les Mirabeau* (1878).

Clarín >> Alas, Leopoldo

Clark, Charles Manning Hope (1915-91) Historian and writer, born in Burwood, New South Wales, Australia. His six-volume *History of Australia* (1962-88) did much to popularize the study of Australian history in schools and colleges.

Clark, George Rogers (1752-1818) Surveyor and soldier, born near Charlottesville, VA. At the outset of the Revolution he commanded the Kentucky militia, and is chiefly known for his epic campaign ending in the 'Night of the Long Knives' at Fort Sackville, Vincennes, IN (1779).

Clark, (John) Grahame Douglas (1907-95) Archaeologist, born in Shortlands, Kent. His *Archaeology and Society* (1939) and *World Prehistory* (1961, 1977) pioneered the use of the archaeological record to document the economic and social life of prehistoric communities.

Clark, Jim, popular name of **James Clark** (1936-68) Motor-racing driver, born in Kilmany, Fife. He joined the Lotus team (1960), and became World Champion Racing Driver (1963, 1965), winning 25 Grands Prix. He was killed during a Formula Two race in Hockenheim, Germany.

Clark, Joe, popular name of **(Charles) Joseph Clark** (1939-) Canadian prime minister (1979-80), born in High River, Alberta, Canada. Leader of the Progressive Conservative Party (1976), he became Canada's youngest ever prime minister, but lost the 1980 general election, and was deposed as party leader in 1983.

Clark, Josiah Latimer (1822-98) Electrical engineer, born in Great Marlow, Buckinghamshire. In 1854 he patented a pneumatic delivery tube, and contributed to the development of submarine cables.

Clark, Kenneth (Mackenzie) Clark, Baron (1903-83) Art historian, born in London. A specialist on Leonardo da Vinci, he wrote many popular books on his subject, and became widely known through his television series *Civilisation* (1969). >> Leonardo da Vinci

Clark, Mark (Wayne) (1896-1984) US general, born in Maddison Barracks, NY, of a military family. He was deputy commander under Eisenhower for the invasion of North Africa, and commander of the 5th Army at the Salerno landing (1943). He later led the US 6th Army in the Far East (1947-9) and commanded UN forces in Korea (1952-3). >> Eisenhower

Clark, Michael (1962-) Dancer and choreographer, born in Aberdeen, Grampian. He performed with the Royal Ballet and Ballet Rambert, starting his own company in 1984.

Clark, Ramsey (William) (1927-) Attorney general and political activist, born in Dallas, TX. He was attorney general (1967-9) during the anti-Vietnam War years. Twice an unsuccessful candidate for the US Senate, he later returned to public prominence as an outspoken critic of two Republican administrations.

Clark, Robert Sterling (1877-1956) and **Francine Clary Clark** (1876-1960) Art collectors, husband and wife, born in New York City and in France, respectively. An heir to the Singer sewing machine fortune, they settled in Williamstown, MA, where they built up a collection of paintings, and established the Sterling and Francine Clark Art Institute (1955). >> Singer, Isaac (Merritt)

Clark, Sir Wilfrid (Edward Le Gros) (1895-1971) Anatomist, born in Hemel Hempstead, Hertfordshire. Distinguished for his work on the anatomy of primates and especially the brain, he helped expose the 'Piltdown Man' hoax of the 1950s. >> Dawson, Charles

Clark, William (1770-1838) Explorer, born in Caroline Co, VA. He became joint leader with Meriwether Lewis of the successful transcontinental expedition to the Pacific coast and back (1804-6). >> Lewis, Meriwether

Clarke, Arthur C(harles) (1917-) Writer of science fiction, born in Minehead, Somerset. A prolific writer, he is especially known for *2001: a Space Odyssey* (1968), which became a highly successful film, and the sequels, *2010: Space Odyssey II* (1982; filmed 1984) and *2062: Odyssey III* (1988). >> Kubrick

Clarke, Austin (1896-1974) Writer, born in Dublin. *The Vengeance of Fionn*, the first of 18 books of verse, appeared in 1917, and his *Collected Poems* were published in 1974. He was also a novelist and verse dramatist.

Clarke, Charles Cowden (1787-1877) Shakespearean scholar, born in Enfield, Greater London. With his wife **Mary Victoria Novello** (1809-98), he published an annotated edition of Shakespeare (1869) and *The Shakespeare Key* (1879).

Clarke, David Leonard (1937-76) Archaeologist, born in Kent. His teaching and writing, particularly in *Analytical Archaeology* (1967), transformed European archaeology in the 1970s.

Clarke, Edith (1883-1959) Electrical engineer, born in Howard Co, MD. Working for General Electric (1922-45), she developed a calculating device that predicted the electrical behaviour of large power systems.

Clarke, Frank (Wigglesworth) (1847-1931) Geologist, born in Boston, MA. Chief chemist to the US Geological Survey (1883-1925), he was the first to calculate the chemical composition of the Earth's crust.

Clarke, Sir Fred(erick) (1880-1952) Educationist, born in Witney, Oxfordshire. Director of the Institute of Education, London (1936-45), his most influential work was *Education and Social Change* (1940).

Clarke, Gillian (1937-) Poet, born in Cardiff. Chair of the Welsh Academy since 1987, her collections of poetry include *Letting in the Rumour* (1989).

Clarke, James Freeman (1810-88) Minister and theologian, born in Hanover, NH. In 1841 he founded the Unitarian Church of the Disciples at Boston.

Clarke, Jeremiah (c.1674-1707) Composer, probably born in London. The real composer of the Trumpet Voluntary long attributed to Purcell, he wrote operas, theatre music, choral works, and music for harpsichord.

Clarke, Kenneth (Harry) (1940-) British Conservative statesman. He became secretary of state for health (1988), home secretary (1992), and Chancellor of the Exchequer (1993).

Clarke, Marcus (Andrew Hislop) (1846–81) Novelist, born in London. He emigrated to Australia at the age of 18. His best-known work is a story of the convict settlements, *For the Term of his Natural Life* (1874).

Clarke, Martha (1944–) Dancer and choreographer, born in Maryland. In 1972 she became one of the first female members of Pilobolus, a collectively-run dance-theatre ensemble, and later helped to form the trio Crowsnest.

Clarke, Ron(ald William) (1937–) Athlete, born in Melbourne, Victoria, Australia. At one time he simultaneously held six world records at various distances, but failed to win a medal in the 10 000 m in the Mexico City Olympics in 1968, being badly affected by the altitude.

Clarke, Samuel (1675–1729) Philosopher and theologian, born in Norwich, Norfolk. His Boyle Lectures of 1704–5 contained his 'Demonstration of the Being and Attributes of God' and expounded a 'mathematical' proof of God's existence.

Clarke, Thomas James (1858–1916) Irish nationalist, born in Hurst Castle, Isle of Wight. He was arrested for revolutionary activity (1883), and sentenced to life imprisonment, but later released (1898). For his involvement in the Easter Rising of 1916, he was court-martialled and shot.

Claude, Albert [klohd, klawd] (1898–1983) Cell biologist, born in Longlier, Belgium. He introduced the use of the centrifuge to separate the components of cells for analysis, and in 1942 was the first to use an electron microscope in biological research. He shared the Nobel Prize for Physiology or Medicine in 1974. >> Palade

Claude, Georges [klohd] (1870–1960) Chemist and physicist, born in Paris. He is noted for his work on gases, and is credited with the invention of neon lighting for signs (1910).

Claudel, Camille [klohdel] (1864–1943) Sculptor, born in La Fère-en-Tardenois, France, the sister of the poet Paul Claudel. She was the student, model, and mistress of Rodin. After breaking with him in 1898, she continued to sculpt, and achieved great renown. >> Claudel, Paul; Rodin

Claudel, Paul [klohdel] (1868–1955) Writer, born in Villeneuve-sur-Fère, France. A convert to Catholicism, his poetry, such as *Five Great Odes* (trans, 1910), and his plays, such as *The Annunciation to Mary* (trans, 1912), are acclaimed for their spiritual intensity. >> Claudel, Camille

Claude Lorrain [klohd], originally **Claude Gellée** (1600–82) Landscape painter, born in Champagne, France. He painted about 400 landscapes, including several with biblical or Classical themes, such as 'The Sermon on the Mount' (1656, New York City). He also produced many drawing and etchings.

Claudianus, Claudius [klawdius] (340–410) The last of the great Latin poets, born in Alexandria, Egypt. Several of his works have survived, notably his epic poem *The Rape of Proserpine* (trans title), for which he was famed in the Middle Ages.

Claudius [klawdius], in full **Tiberius Claudius Caesar Augustus Germanicus** (10 BC–AD 54) Roman emperor (41–54), the grandson of the Empress Livia. Kept in the background because of his physical disabilities, he devoted himself to historical studies, and thus survived the in-fighting of the imperial house. Through his public works and reforms, he made a lasting contribution to the government of Rome and the empire, and through the annexation of Britain, Mauretania, and Thrace, a significant extension of its size. He died poisoned, probably by his fourth wife Agrippina. >> Agrippina (the Younger); Livia; Messalina

Claudius, Appius [klohdius], nickname **Caecus** ('the blind') (4th–3rd-c BC) Aristocratic Roman statesman, general, and law-giver. His fame rests chiefly on his reforming censorship (c.312–307 BC) and his public projects, such as the first trunk road, the Appian Way.

Clausewitz, Karl (Philip Gottlieb) von [klowzevits] (1780–1831) General, born in Burg, Germany. His posthumously published *On War* (trans, 1833), advocating a policy of total war, revolutionized military theory.

Clausius, Rudolf (Julius Emanuel) [klowzius] (1822–88) Physicist, born in Köslin, Germany. He worked on optics and electricity, formulated the second law of thermodynamics, and was influential in establishing thermodynamics as a science.

Claussen, Sophus (Niels Christen) [klowsen] (1865–1931) Poet, born in Heletoft, Denmark. Generally regarded as the greatest Symbolist poet of his country, his collected works were published in seven volumes in 1910.

Clavell, James (du Maresq) [klavel] (1924–94) Novelist, film director, and producer, born in Sydney, New South Wales, Australia. He is best known for his series of best-selling novels with an Oriental setting, such as *Shogun* (1975) and *Gai-Jin* (1993). His screen credits include *The Fly* (1958) and *The Great Escape* (1963).

Claverhouse, John Graham of >> **Dundee, Viscount**

Clay, Cassius >> **Ali, Muhammad**

Clay, Cassius Marcellus (1810–1903) Abolitionist, born in Madison Co, KY, the cousin of Henry Clay. The son of a slaveholding planter, he was converted to abolitionism after hearing Garrison speak, founded *The True American* to combat slavery (1845), and became a major-general in the Union army (1862). >> Clay, Henry; Garrison, William Lloyd

Clay, Henry (1777–1852) US statesman and orator, born in Hanover Co, VA. He was active in bringing on the War of 1812 with Britain, served in the US Senate (1831–42), and attempted to hold the Union together in the face of the issue of slavery, earning the title of 'the great pacificator'. >> Clay, Cassius Marcellus

Clay, Lucius (DuBignon) (1897–1978) US soldier, born in Marietta, GA. As a deputy chief-of-staff (1942–4), he oversaw the army's vast production and procurement programmes, and in 1944 commanded the Normandy base and the port of Cherbourg, which supplied the Allied forces.

Clayton, John (fl.c.1650) English scientist. He was the first to discover that gas could be distilled from crude coal and stored, but did not realize the commercial importance of his discovery.

Clayton, John (Middleton) (1796–1856) US statesman, born in Dagsboro, DE. In 1829 he became a US senator, and while secretary of state (1849–50) negotiated the Clayton–Bulwer Treaty with Britain.

Cleanthes [kleeantheez] (c.331–232 BC) Greek Stoic philosopher, born in Assos, Troas. He succeeded Zeno of Citium as head of the Stoa in 262. His own contributions to Stoicism were especially in the areas of theology and cosmology. >> Zeno of Citium

Cleese, John (Marwood) [kleez] (1939–) Comic actor and writer, born in Weston-super-Mare, Avon. He joined *Monty Python's Flying Circus* (1969–74), wrote and starred in the television series *Fawlty Towers* (1975, 1979), and has appeared in several films, such as *A Fish Called Wanda* (1988).

Clegg, Samuel (1781–1861) Inventor, born in Manchester. He worked on improving methods of producing coal gas, and became chief engineer of the Chartered Gas Co, for whom he successfully illuminated an entire district of London by gas in 1814.

Cleland, John [klayland] (1709–89) Novelist, born in London. *Fanny Hill, or the Memoirs of a Woman of Pleasure* (1750), a best-seller in its time, achieved a second success following its revival and prosecution under the Obscene Publications Act in 1963.

Clemenceau, Georges [klemãsoh] (1841–1929) French prime minister (1906–9, 1917–20), born in Mouilleron-en-Pareds, France. In 1876 he became a leader of the extreme left in the Chamber of Deputies. He presided at the Peace Conference in 1919, showing an intransigent hatred of Germany.

Clemens, Samuel Langhorne >> **Twain, Mark**

Clement I, St, known as **Clemens Romanus** or **Clement of Rome** (late 1st-c), feast day 23 November. One of the apostolic Fathers of the Church, reckoned variously as the second or third successor of St Peter at Rome, possibly 88–97 or 92–101. The first of two epistles attributed to him is generally accepted as his. >> **Peter, St**

Clement V, originally **Raymond Bertrand de Got** (c.1260–1314) Pope (1305–14), born in Bordelais, France. As pope, he suppressed the Templars, and removed the seat of the papacy to Avignon (1309), a movement disastrous to Italy.

Clement VII, originally **Giulio de' Medici** (1478–1534) Pope (1523–34), born in Florence, Italy. His indecisiveness, along with his refusal to sanction Henry VIII's divorce from Catherine of Aragon, hastened the Reformation.

Clement of Alexandria, St, Lat **Clemens Alexandrinus** (c.150–c.215), feast day 5 December. Theologian and Father of the early Church, probably born in Athens. He became head of the celebrated Catechetical school in Alexandria, where he related Greek philosophical thought to Christian belief.

Clemente, Bob [klementay], popular name of **Roberto (Walker) Clemente** (1934–1972) Baseball player, born in Carolina, Puerto Rico. He played for the Pittsburgh Pirates (1955–72), making more than 3000 hits and 240 home runs, and led the National League in batting four times.

Clementi, Muzio [klementee] (1752–1832) Composer and pianist, born in Rome. He wrote the *Gradus ad Parnassum* (1817–26), on which subsequent piano methods have been based.

Clementis, Vladimir [klementees] (1902–52) Czech statesman, born in Tesovec, Slovakia. A chief organizer of the 1948 coup, he succeeded Masaryk as foreign minister, but was forced to resign in 1950 as a 'deviationist'. Following a political purge, he was hanged. >> **Masaryk, Jan**

Clements, Sir John Selby (1911–88) Actor and director. In 1946 he married the actress **Kay Hammond** (d.1980), and they became one of Britain's most famous theatrical partnerships.

Cleon [kleeon] (?–422 BC) The first Athenian of rich, bourgeois stock to play a prominent role in 5th-c BC politics. His capture of the Spartans on the island of Sphacteria (425 BC) gave Athens her trump card in the peace negotiations of the late 420s BC.

Cleopatra VII (69–30 BC) Queen of Egypt (51–48 BC, 47–30 BC), the daughter of Ptolemy Auletes. Caesar, to whom she bore a son Caesarion, supported her claim to the throne (47 BC), while Antony, by whom she had three children, restored to her much of the old Ptolemaic empire. Defeated with Antony at Actium (31 BC), she used an asp to commit suicide. >> **Antonius; Caesar**

Clerc, Jacques-Philippe Le >> **Le Clerc, Jacques-Philippe**

Clerk, Sir Dugald [klah(r)k] (1854–1932) Engineer, born in Glasgow, Strathclyde. In 1881 he patented a gas engine working on the two-stroke principle which became known as the *Clerk cycle*.

Clerk Maxwell, James >> **Maxwell, James**

Cleve, Cornelis [klayvuh] (1520–67) Painter, born in Antwerp, Belgium, the son of Joos van Cleve. In 1554 his arrival in England to seek patronage coincided with that of a collection by Titian from Italy, which ousted the

Flemish school from royal favour. The disappointment mentally deranged Cornelis, thereafter known as *Sotte* ('mad') *Cleve*. >> **Cleve, Joos van der Beke**

Cleve, Joos van der Beke (c.1480–1540) Painter, born in Antwerp, Belgium. He is best known for his religious pictures, and is sometimes called 'the Master of the Death of the Virgin' from two triptychs at Munich and Cologne. >> **Cleve, Cornelis**

Cleveland, (Stephen) Grover (1837–1908) US statesman and the 22nd and 24th president (1885–9, 1893–7), born in Caldwell, NJ. In 1895 he caused worldwide excitement by applying the Monroe Doctrine to Britain's dispute with Venezuela.

Cleveland, John (1613–58) Cavalier poet, born in Loughborough, Leicestershire. A popular poet in his day, he was known for his elegies and satires.

Clewlow, Warren (Alexander Morten) (1936–) Businessman, born in KwaZulu Natal, South Africa. Executive chairman of the Barlow Rand Group of Companies, he also became chairman of the State President's Economic Advisory Council and president of the South Africa Foundation.

Cliburn, Van [kliybern], popular name of **Harvey Lavan Cliburn, Jr** (1934–) Pianist, born in Shreveport, LA. The first American to win Moscow's Tchaikovsky Prize (1958), he went on to specialize in the 19th-c standard repertoire. The piano competition he began at Fort Worth, TX (1962) became an international event.

Cliff, Clarice (1899–1972) Ceramic designer, born in Tunstall, Staffordshire. She set up a design studio at Wilkinson's Newport showroom, and by 1929 the Newport pottery was given over entirely to her work, which was marketed under the name 'Bizarre'.

Clifford, John (1836–1923) Clergyman, born in Sawley, Derbyshire. A leading passive resister to the Education Act of 1902, and a strong Nonconformist Liberal, he became first president of the Baptist World Alliance (1905–11).

Clifford, William (Kingdon) (1845–79) Mathematician, born in Exeter, Devon. He wrote on projective and non-Euclidean geometry, and on the philosophy of science, and is especially known for his development of the theory of biquaternions.

Clift, (Edward) Montgomery (1920–66) Film and stage actor, born in Omaha, NE. His performances in *The Search* (1948), *A Place in The Sun* (1951), and *From Here to Eternity* (1953) earned him Oscar nominations.

Cline, Howard Francis [kliyn] (1915–71) Historian, born in Detroit, MI. A pioneer ethnohistorian, the social and ethnic history of Mexico was the subject of two of his major works: *The United States and Mexico* (1953) and *Mexico: Evolution to Revolution* (1962).

Clinton, Bill, popular name of **William Clinton** (1946–) US statesman and 42nd president (1993–), born in Hope, AR. He became Democratic governor of Arkansas (1979–81, 1983–92), and defeated George Bush for the presidency. His wife, **Hillary Rodham Clinton** (1947–), has taken a particular interest in national health care.

Clinton, De Witt [duh wit] (1769–1828) US politician, born in Little Britain, NY. Defeated by Madison in the presidential contest of 1812, he later planned the Erie Canal scheme ('Clinton's ditch'), which he opened in 1825. >> **Madison, James**

Clinton, George (1739–1812) US soldier and politician, born in Little Britain, NY. He served in the American War of Independence (1775–83), and was chosen first Governor of New York (1777–95). He was twice elected vice-president of the USA (1804, 1808). >> **Clinton, James**

Clinton, Sir Henry (c.1738–95) Soldier, born in Newfoundland, Canada. As commander-in-chief he captured Charleston and the entire Southern army (1780), but after the capitulation at Yorktown (1781) he returned to England.

Clinton, James (1736–1812) American soldier, born in Little Britain, NY, the brother of George Clinton. He fought with distinction in the French and Indian War (1755–63) and as a brigadier-general during the War of Independence (1775–83). >> Clinton, George

Clitherow, St Margaret [klit hroh], *née* **Middleton**, feast day 25 March. (c.1556–86) One of the '40 martyrs' of England and Wales, born in York, North Yorkshire. A convert to Catholicism in 1574, she harboured priests in her home, for which she was executed. She was canonized in 1970.

Clive (of Plassey), Robert Clive, Baron (1725–74) Soldier, and administrator in India, born in Styche, Shropshire. In 1755 he was called to avenge the so-called Black Hole of Calcutta, and at Plassey (1757) defeated a large Indian–French force. For three years he was sole ruler of Bengal in all but name. >> Siraj ad Daula

Clodion [klodyō], pseudonym of **Claude Michel** (1738–1814) Sculptor, born in Nancy, France. An acclaimed Rococo sculptor, he specialized in small terracottas and low reliefs of erotic dancing nymphs and satyrs.

Clopinel, Jean >> **Jean de Meung**

Clopton, Sir Hugh (?–1497) Silk merchant and philanthropist, born in Stratford-on-Avon, Warwickshire. A mercer in London, he became sheriff (1486) and mayor (1492), and at Stratford built New Place (c.1483), later the home of Shakespeare. >> Shakespeare, William

Close, Chuck (1940–) Artist, born in Menroe, WA. In 1967–8 he began copying portrait photographs, painstakingly reproducing every detail, and has since continued with this 'Super-Realist' method.

Close, Glenn (1947–) Actress, born in Greenwich, CT. Her theatre work includes *The Singular Life of Albert Nobbs* (1982, Obie) and *The Real Thing* (1984–5, Tony), and her films include *Fatal Attraction* (1987) and *Dangerous Liaisons* (1988).

Clotilde or **Clotilda, St** [klohtilduh] (474–545), feast day 3 June. Queen consort of Clovis I, king of the Franks, and daughter of Chilperic, king of Burgundy. After Clovis's death she lived a life of austerity at the Abbey of St Martin at Tours. >> Clovis

Clouet, François [klooay] (c.1516–1572) Portrait painter, probably born in Tours, France, the son of Jean Clouet. He succeeded his father as court painter to Francis I. His masterpiece is the Louvre portrait of Elizabeth of Austria. >> Clouet, Jean

Clouet, Jean [klooay], also found as **Jehan** or **Janet** (c.1485–1540/41) Portrait painter, probably the son of Flemish painter **Jehan Clouet** (c.1420–c.1480). He became court painter to Francis I, whose portrait in the Louvre is supposed to be by him. >> Clouet, François

Clough, Anne Jemima [kluhf] (1820–92) Educationist, born in Liverpool, Merseyside, the sister of Arthur Hugh Clough. A vigorous proponent of higher education for women, in 1871 she became the first principal of the first hall for women students at Cambridge, later called Newnham College. >> Clough, Arthur Hugh

Clough, Arthur Hugh [kluhf] (1819–61) Poet, born in Liverpool, Merseyside. His best-known poem, beginning 'Say not the struggle nought availeth', was published posthumously in 1862.

Clough, Brian [kluhf] (1935–) Footballer and manager, born in Middlesbrough, Cleveland. As manager, he took Derby County and Nottingham Forest to League championship wins and the latter to two European Cup successes.

Clovis I [klohvis], Ger **Chlodwig** or **Chlodovech** (c.465–511) Merovingian king, who succeeded his father, Childeric (481), as king of the Franks. In 493 he married Clotilde,

and was converted to Christianity. He overthrew the Gallo-Romans, and in 507 defeated Alaric II, but was checked at Arles by Theodoric. >> Alaric II; Clotilde, St; Theodoric

Clowes, William [klohz] (1779–1847) Printer, born in Chichester, West Sussex. In 1803 he started a London printing business carried on by his son, **William** (1807–83), and was the first printer to use steam-driven machines.

Clowes, William [klohz] (1780–1851) Nonconformist, born in Burslem, Staffordshire. In 1805 he was converted to Methodism, and in 1810 co-founded, with Hugh Bourne, the Primitive Methodists. >> Bourne, Hugh

Clune, Frank [kloon], popular name of **Francis Patrick Clune** (1893–1971) Writer of biography, history, and travel, born in Sydney, New South Wales, Australia. He wrote over 60 books, often in collaboration with P R ('Inky') Stephensen, such as *Ben Hall the Bushranger* (1947) and *Wild Colonial Boys* (1948).

Clunies Ross, Sir Ian [klooneez] (1899–1959) Veterinary scientist, born in Bathurst, New South Wales, Australia. In 1949 he became first chairman of the [Australian] Commonwealth Scientific and Industrial Research Organization.

Clurman, Harold (Edgar) [kloorman] (1901–80) Theatre director and critic, born in New York City. He co-founded the Group Theater (1931–40), later working as a director in Hollywood and on Broadway, and as a drama critic.

Cluverius or **Clüver, Phillip** [klooveerius, klüver] (1580–1622) Geographer and antiquarian, born in Gdańsk, Poland (formerly, Danzig of Germany). He wrote *Introduction to Universal Geography* (trans, 1624), and is regarded as the founder of historical geography.

Clyde, Lord >> **Campbell, Sir Colin**

Clynes, Joseph Robert [kliynz] (1869–1949) Trade unionist and British statesman, born in Oldham, Lancashire. He became president (1892) and secretary (1894–1912) of Oldham's Trade Council. Entering parliament (1910), he was Lord Privy Seal in Britain's first Labour cabinet (1924).

Cnut >> **Canute**

Coanda, Henri [kawanda] (1885–1972) Aeronautical engineer, born in Romania. He built the first jet-propelled aeroplane, but the hot exhaust gases set fire to the structure. He investigated this effect, and the entrainment of a free jet alongside a curved surface now bears his name.

Coase, Ronald (Harry) [kohs] (1910–) Economist, born in London. He emigrated to the USA in 1951, where his work led to the development of the economics of property rights and the economics of law. He was awarded the Nobel Prize for Economics in 1991.

Coates, Eric (1886–1957) Composer, born in Hucknall, Nottinghamshire. Among his best-known compositions are the *London Suite* (1933), *The Three Elizabeths* (1944), and a number of popular waltzes and marches.

Coates, Wells Wintemute (1895–1958) Canadian architect, born in Tokyo. A principal figure of the modern movement in architecture, his designs include the BBC studios, the EKCO laboratories, and many other buildings in Great Britain and Canada.

Cobb, Ty(rus Raymond), nickname **the Georgia Peach** (1886–1961) Baseball player, born in Narrows, GA. An outstanding base runner and batter, in a 23-year career with Detroit and Philadelphia he had over 4000 base hits, a record which survived 57 years until broken in 1985.

Cobbe, Frances Power [kob] (1822–1904) Social worker and feminist, born in Newbridge, near Dublin. A strong theist, a supporter of women's rights, and anti-vivisectionist, she was associated with Mary Carpenter in the founding of ragged schools. >> Carpenter, Mary

Cobbett, William (1763–1835) Journalist and reformer, born in Farnham, Surrey. In 1802 he started his *Weekly*

Political Register, which moved from its original Toryism to an uncompromising Radicalism. His works include a *History of the Protestant Reformation* (1824–7) and *Rural Rides* (1830).

Cobbold, Richard (1797–1877) Writer, born in Ipswich, Suffolk. He wrote *Margaret Catchpole* (1845) and other works, and for 50 years was rector of Wortham, near Diss. >> Catchpole

Cobden, Richard (1804–65) Economist and politican, 'the apostle of free trade', born in Heyshott, West Sussex. In 1838 he co-founded the Anti-Corn-Law League, and was its most prominent member, becoming an MP in 1841.

Cobden-Sanderson, Thomas James (1840–1922) Printer and bookbinder, born in Alnwick, Northumberland. He was a leader of the 19th-c revival of artistic typography, in 1900 founding the Doves Press at Hammersmith, London.

Cobham, Lord >> **Oldcastle, John**

Coborn, Charles [kohbaw(r)n], pseudonym of **Colin Whitton McCallum** (1852–1945) Cockney comedian of Scottish descent. On the stage in London's East End (1875), he immortalized the songs 'Two Lovely Black Eyes' (1886) and 'The Man who Broke the Bank at Monte Carlo' (1890).

Coburn, John [kohbern] (1925–) Artist and tapestry designer, born in Ingham, Queensland, Australia. His best-known commissions are the *Curtain of the Sun* and *Curtain of the Moon* for the prosceniums of the new Sydney Opera House.

Coch(e)ba, Simon bar >> **bar Kokhba, Simon**

Cochise [kohchees] (?1812–74) Chiricahua Apache chief, born in present-day Arizona or New Mexico. The main war chief of the Apaches, he surrendered in 1872, after winning assurances from the US government that he and his band could remain in the Chiricahua Mts.

Cochlaeus [koklayus], originally **Johann Dobneck** (1479–1552) Theologian and humanist, born in Wendelstein, Germany. At first sympathetic to Luther, he became his most active critic at many confrontations, including the Diet of Worms (1521). >> **Luther**

Cochran, Sir Charles Blake [kokran] (1872–1951) Theatrical producer, born in Lindfield, West Sussex. His most successful production was *Bless the Bride* (1947), which ran for 886 performances.

Cochran, Jacqueline [kokran] (1910–80) Aviator, born in Pensacola, FL. She was the first woman to fly in the Bendix transcontinental air race in 1935, securing the race record in 1938, and in 1953 was the first woman to fly faster than sound.

Cockcroft, Sir John Douglas (1897–1967) Nuclear physicist, born in Todmorden, West Yorkshire. With Walton he succeeded in disintegrating lithium by proton bombardment in 1932, pioneering the use of particle accelerators, and they shared the Nobel Prize for Physics (1951). >> Walton, E T S

Cocker, Edward (1631–75) English engraver, who also taught penmanship and arithmetic. Reputedly the author of *Cocker's Arithmetic* (1678), which went through 112 editions, it has since been exposed as a forgery made by his editor and publisher.

Cockerell, Charles Robert (1788–1863) British architect, the son of Samuel Pepys Cockerell. His designs include the Taylorian Institute at Oxford, and the Fitzwilliam Museum at Cambridge. >> Cockerell, Samuel Pepys

Cockerell, Sir Christopher (Sydney) (1910–) Engineer, born in Cambridge, Cambridgeshire. Working on hydrodynamics, in the early 1950s he invented the amphibious hovercraft.

Cockerell, Samuel Pepys (1754–1827) British architect. He laid out Brunswick and Mecklenburg Squares in London, and designed the tower of St Anne's, Soho. >> Cockerell, Charles Robert

Cocteau, Jean [koktoh] (1889–1963) Poet, playwright, and film director, born in Maisons-Lafitte, France. His best-known works include (trans titles) the novel *Children of the Game* (1929), the play *Orpheus* (1926), and the film *Beauty and the Beast* (1945).

Cody, Samuel Franklin [kohdee] (1862–1913) Aviator, born in Texas. He came to England in 1896, participated in the construction of the first British dirigible, and built an early aeroplane in 1908.

Cody, William F(rederick) [kohdee], known as **Buffalo Bill** (1846–1917) Showman, born in Scott Co, IA. He received his nickname after killing nearly 5000 buffalo in eight months for a contract to supply workers on the Kansas Pacific Railway with meat. From 1883 he toured with his Wild West Show.

Coe, Kelvin (1946–92) Ballet dancer, born in Melbourne, Victoria, Australia. He joined the newly formed Australian Ballet in 1969, retiring as its principal dancer in 1981.

Coe, Sebastian [koh] (1956–) Athlete, born in London. He broke eight world records, including the mile three times, and at the 1980 Olympics won the gold medal in the 1500 m and the silver in the 800 m, repeating the achievement in 1984. He became a Conservative MP in 1992.

Coetzee, John Michael [kohtzee] (1940–) Writer and critic, born in Cape Town. His novels include *Dusklands* (1974), *In the Heart of the Country* (1977), *Life and Times of Michael K* (1983, Booker), and *Age of Iron* (1990).

Coffin, Henry Sloane (1877–1954) Presbyterian clergyman and educator, born in New York City. An evangelical liberal, he became president of the union seminary (1926–45), promoting open inquiry into theological issues.

Coggan (of Canterbury and of Sissinghurst), (Frederick) Donald Coggan, Baron (1909–) Clergyman, born in London. He was Archbishop of York (1961–74), and Archbishop of Canterbury (1974–80), subsequently becoming a life peer.

Coggeshall, Ralph de [kogshawl] (?–c.1227) Chronicler, a native of Cambridgeshire. Abbot of the Cistercian abbey of Coggeshall, Essex (1207–18), he continued the Latin Chronicle kept there, covering the period 1187–1224.

Cohan, George Michael (Keohane) (1878–1942) Actor, dramatist, and director, born in Providence, RI. He is remembered for his acting roles, and as a writer of such songs as 'Yankee Doodle Dandy', which gave the title of the film made of his life (1942).

Cohan, Robert [kohhan] (1925–) Dancer and choreographer, born in New York City. He danced with the Martha Graham company, becoming co-director in 1966, was artistic director of the London Contemporary Dance Theatre, and founded the London Contemporary Dance School.

Cohen, Hermann (1842–1912) Philosopher, born in Coswig, Germany. Professor of philosophy at Marburg (1876–1912), he founded the Marburg School of neo-Kantianism. His synthesis of Judaism and idealism had a deep influence on early 20th-c Jewish thinkers.

Cohen, Leonard (1934–) Writer, songwriter, and singer, born in Montreal, Quebec, Canada. His first book of poetry was *Let us Compare Mythologies* (1956), and his novels include *Beautiful Losers* (1966). Among his many albums is *Songs of Leonard Cohen* (1967).

Cohen, Seymour (Stanley) (1917–) Biochemist, born in New York City. He did valuable early work in the 1940s using radioactive labelling of bacteriophage, which suggested that DNA plays a key part in heredity.

Cohen, Stanley (1922–) Cell biologist, born in New York City. He discovered the epidermal growth factor from mouse tissue extract, and determined its amino acid sequence and action on cells and wound healing. He shared the Nobel Prize for Physiology or Medicine in 1986. >> Levi-Montalcini

Cohen, Stanley (1935-) >> **Boyer, Herbert**

Cohl, Emile, originally **Emile Courtet** (1857–1938) Cartoonist, and inventor of the animated cartoon film, born in Paris. As comedy film writer/director at the Gaumont Studio, he produced the first frame-by-frame animated cartoon film, *Fantasmagorie* (1908).

Cohn, Ferdinand (Julius) (1828–98) Botanist and bacteriologist, born in Breslau, Germany. He is regarded as the father of bacteriology, the first to account it a separate science. He did important research in plant pathology, and worked with Koch on anthrax. >> Koch, Robert

Cohn, Roy M(arcus) (1927–86) Lawyer, born in New York City. As chief counsel to McCarthy's Communist-hunting subcommittee (1953–4), he became a national figure. Three times acquitted on federal charges of conspiracy, bribery, and fraud, he was disbarred two months before his death. >> McCarthy, Joseph

Cohnheim, Julius Friedrich [kohnhiym] (1839–84) Pathologist, born in Demmin, Poland. He determined the microscopical events of inflammation, and established that tuberculosis was an infectious disease.

Coke, Sir Edward [kook] (1552–1634) Jurist, born in Mileham, Norfolk. As Chief Justice of the King's Bench (1613), he prosecuted for treason Essex, Raleigh, and the Gunpowder conspirators, but after 1606 vindicated national liberties against the royal prerogative. The Petition of Right (1628) was largely his doing.

Coke, Thomas (1747–1814) Methodist clergyman, born in Brecon, Powys. In 1784 he was appointed by John Wesley as the superintendent of the Methodist Church in America, and assumed the title of bishop in 1787. >> Wesley, John

Coke, Thomas William >> **Leicester of Holkham, Thomas, William Coke**

Colbert, Claudette [kolbair], originally **Lily Claudette Chauchoin** (1903-) Film actress, born in Paris. She became a star with *It Happened One Night* (1934, Oscar), followed by several romantic comedy successes, such as *The Palm Beach Story* (1942). Her stage career continued into the 1980s.

Colbert, Jean Baptiste [kolbair] (1619–83) French statesman, born in Reims, France. As the chief financial minister of Louis XIV (1661), he introduced a series of successful reforms, but his successes were undone by wars and court extravagance. >> Louis XIV

Coldstream, Sir William (1908–87) Painter and art teacher, born in Belford, Northumberland. He joined the London Group (1933), and co-founded the Euston Road School (1937). Through his work on the national advisory committee (1958–71), which produced the two *Coldstream Reports*, he helped reshape British art education.

Cole, George (1925-) Actor, born in London. His many films include the *St Trinian's* series, but he is probably best known in the UK as Arthur Daly from the television series, *Minder*, and for his television commercials for a leading building society.

Cole, George Douglas Howard (1889–1958) Economist, historian, and detective-story writer, born in London. Chairman (1939–46, 1948–50) and president (from 1952) of the Fabian Society, he wrote numerous books on socialism. He often wrote in collaboration with his wife, Margaret Isobel Cole.

Cole, Sir Henry, pseudonym **Felix Summerley** (1808–82) Designer, writer, and civil servant, born in Bath, Somerset. He introduced the penny postage system, invented the adhesive stamp, and published the first Christmas card.

Cole, Nat King, originally **Nathaniel Adams Cole**, family name formerly **Coles** (1919–65) Entertainer, born in Montgomery, AL. During the 1930s he became popular as a jazz pianist and singer, his many hit records including 'Route 66', 'Walking My Baby Back Home', and 'Unforgettable'. His daughter, **Natalie Cole** (1950-), is also an entertainer.

Cole, Thomas (1801–48) Painter, born in Bolton, Lancashire. He emigrated to America in 1819, and became founder of the Hudson River school of landscape painters. His best landscapes were American, notably the 'Voyage of Life' series (from 1839).

Coleman, Ornette (1930-) Alto saxophonist, multi-instrumentalist, and composer, born in Fort Worth, TX. Following early recordings with Don Cherry (1936-), he persevered through a discouraging climate for avant-garde jazz, becoming accepted in the 1960s as a major innovator.

Colenso, John William [kolensoh] (1814–83) Clergyman, born in St Austell, Cornwall. He became the first Bishop of Natal in 1853. *The Pentateuch and the Book of Joshua Critically Examined* (1862–79), which cast doubts upon biblical accuracy, was regarded as heretical, and he was deposed in 1869.

Colepeper or **Culpeper, John, Baron** [kuhlpeper] (1600–60) English royalist statesman, a native of Sussex. In 1642 he became Chancellor of the Exchequer, and in 1643 Master of the Rolls, and was an influential counsellor of both Charles I and Charles II. >> Charles I / II (of England)

Coleridge, (David) Hartley (1796–1849) Man of letters, born in Clevedon, Somerset, the eldest son of Samuel Taylor Coleridge. His work includes poetry, biographies, and occasional pieces for *Blackwood's Magazine*. >> Coleridge, Samuel Taylor / Sara

Coleridge, Samuel Taylor (1772–1834) Poet, born in Ottery St Mary, Devon. His friendship with William and Dorothy Wordsworth resulted in a new poetry reacting against Neoclassic artificiality: *Lyrical Ballads* (1798) opens with his 'Rime of the Ancient Mariner'. In 1800 he went to the Lake District, but his career prospects were blighted by his moral collapse, partly due to opium. In 1816 he published 'Christabel' and 'Kubla Khan', both written in his earlier period of inspiration, and went on to write critical and other essays. >> Southey; Wordsworth

Coleridge, Sara (1802–52) Scholar, born in Keswick, Cumbria, the daughter of Samuel Taylor Coleridge. She married her cousin, Henry Nelson Coleridge, in 1829, and helped to edit her father's writings. >> Coleridge, Hartley / Samuel Taylor

Coleridge-Taylor, Samuel (1875–1912) Composer, born in London. He composed a trilogy on the theme of *Hiawatha* (1898–1900), and other popular cantatas and orchestral works.

Colet, John [kolet] (c.1467–1519) Theologian and Tudor humanist, born in London. In 1505 he became dean of St Paul's, where he delivered controversial lectures on the interpretation of Scripture, and founded St Paul's School (1509–12).

Colette, Sidonie Gabrielle [kolet] (1873–1954) Novelist, born in Saint-Sauveur-en-Puisaye, France. Her early books were written in collaboration with her first husband, Henri Gauthier-Villars (pseudonym Willy). Her later novels include the 'Claudine' series (1900–3), *Chéri* (1920), and *Gigi* (1945).

Coligny, Gaspard II de, seigneur de (Lord of) **Châtillon** [koleenyee] (1519–72) Huguenot leader, born in Châtillon-sur-Loing, France. In 1557 he became a Protestant, and commanded the Huguenots during the second and third Wars of Religion. He was one of the first victims in the St Bartholomew's Day massacre in Paris.

Collett, (Jacobine) Camilla, *née* **Wergeland** (1813–95) Novelist, born in Kristiansand, Norway, the sister of

Hendrik Arnold Wergeland. She brought realism to Norwegian fiction in such books as *The Magistrate's Daughter* (trans, 1855) and *In the Long Nights* (trans, 1862). >> Wergeland

Collier, Jeremy (1650–1726) Clergyman, born in Stow cum Quy, Cambridgeshire. He refused to take the oath of allegiance to William III and Mary in 1689, and was consecrated a nonjuring bishop in 1713.

Collings, Jesse (1831–1920) British politician, born in Littleham-cum-Exmouth, Devon. He sat as a Unionist MP (1886–1918), becoming identified with the Agricultural Labourers' Union and measures for promoting allotments and smallholdings.

Collingwood, Cuthbert, Baron (1750–1810) British admiral, born in Newcastle upon Tyne, Tyne and Wear. He fought at Brest (1794), Cape St Vincent (1797), and Trafalgar (1805), where he succeeded Nelson as commander. >> Nelson

Collingwood, R(obin) G(eorge) (1889–1943) Philosopher, historian, and archaeologist, born in Coniston, Cumbria. An authority on the archaeology of Roman Britain, much of his work was concerned with the relationship between history and philosophy.

Collingwood, William (Gershom) (1854–1932) Artist and archaeologist, born in Liverpool, Merseyside. He was private secretary and collaborator to Ruskin, and is best known for his archaeological studies on Viking remains. >> Ruskin

Collins, Joan (Henrietta) (1933–) Actress, born in London. After a film debut in *Lady Godiva Rides Again* (1951), her sultry appeal and headline-catching private life made her an international celebrity, best known for her role in the television soap opera *Dynasty* (1981–9). Her sister is the best-selling novelist, Jackie Collins.

Collins, Michael (1890–1922) Irish politician and Sinn Féin leader, born near Clonakilty, Co Cork. He became an MP (1918–22), and with Arthur Griffith was largely responsible for the treaty with Great Britain in 1921. Regarded as a traitor, he was killed in an ambush. >> Griffith, Arthur

Collins, Michael (1930–) US astronaut, born in Rome. He was one of the members of the Gemini 10 project, and remained in the command module during the successful Apollo 11 Moon-landing expedition.

Collins, (William) Wilkie (1824–89) Novelist, born in London. A master of the mystery story, his best-known works are *The Woman in White* (1860) and *The Moonstone* (1868).

Collins, William (1721–59) Poet, born in Chichester, West Sussex. His fame rests chiefly on his *Odes*. His later poems included 'Ode on the Superstitions of the Highlands' - a work in which, says Lowell, 'the whole Romantic School is foreshadowed'. >> Lowell, Robert

Collins, William (1789–1853) Publisher, born in Eastwood, Strathclyde. He set up business in Glasgow as a bookseller and publisher, specializing in church history and school textbooks.

Collot d'Herbois, Jean Marie [koloh dairbwah] (1751–96) French revolutionary, born in Paris. President of the National Convention, he was a member of the successful plot against Robespierre (1794), but was himself expelled from the Convention and exiled (1795). >> Robespierre

Colm, St >> **Columba, St**

Colman, St (?–676), feast day 18 February/8 August in some parts of Ireland. Irish monk of Iona. In 661 he became Bishop of Lindisfarne, but in 664 withdrew to Iona on the defeat of the Celtic party over the dating of Easter at the Council of Whitby. >> Columba, St

Colman, George, known as **the Elder** (1732–94) Playwright and manager, born in Florence, Italy, the son of

the English envoy. His works include *Polly Honeycombe* (1760) and *The Jealous Wife* (1761). He was manager of Covent Garden Theatre for several years, later acquiring the Haymarket Theatre. >> Colman, George (the Younger)

Colman, George, known as **the Younger** (1762–1836) Theatre manager and playwright, born in London, the son of George Colman. He followed his father as manager of the Haymarket, and wrote many popular comedies, such as *The Heir at Law* (1797) and *John Bull* (1803). >> Colman, George (the Elder)

Colman, Ronald (1891–1958) Film and stage actor, born in Richmond, Surrey. A popular romantic leading man for three decades, his best-known films include *A Tale of Two Cities* (1935), *The Prisoner of Zenda* (1937), and *Random Harvest* (1942).

Colombo, Joe Cesare [kolomboh] (1930–71) Designer, born in Milan, Italy. His special interest in multi-function storage furniture led him to design compact 'core' units containing all the requirements necessary for the living environment.

Colquhoun, Robert [kohoon] (1914–62) Artist, born in Kilmarnock, Strathclyde. His enigmatic, dreamlike figures, such as 'Girl with a Circus Goat', are usually presented in a characteristic colour scheme of reds and browns.

Colt, Samuel (1814–62) Inventor, born in Hartford, CT. In 1835 he took out his first patent for a revolver, which was adopted by the US army, thus founding the fortunes of his company, Colt's Patent Fire-Arms.

Colton, Frank Benjamin (1923–) Chemist and inventor, born in Bialystok, Poland. He emigrated to the USA in 1934, where his pioneering work in steroid chemistry led in 1960 to the development of Enovid, the first oral contraceptive.

Coltrane, John (William) (1926–67) Jazz saxophonist and composer, born in Hamlet, NC. He emerged in the 1950s working with Dizzy Gillespie, Bud Powell, and Miles Davis, then led his own small groups, becoming a controversial and influential avant-garde figure. >> Davis, Miles; Gillespie; Powell, Bud

Colum, Padraic (1881–1972) Poet and playwright, born in Co Longford, Ireland. A leader of the Irish literary revival, he wrote several plays for the Abbey Theatre, and helped to found the *Irish Review* (1911).

Columba, St, also **Columcille** or **Colm** (521–97), feast day 9 June. Missionary and abbot, born in Gartan, Co Donegal, Ireland. He founded monasteries at Derry (546), Durrow (553), and Iona (c.563), from where he and his followers brought Christianity to Scotland.

Columban or **Columbanus, St** (c.543–615), feast day 23 November. Missionary and abbot, 'the younger Columba', born in Leinster, Ireland. About 585 he went to Gaul where he founded several monasteries. His adherence to the Celtic Easter involved him in controversy.

Columbus, Christopher, Ital **Cristoforo Colombo**, Span **Cristóbal Colón** (1451–1506) European discoverer of the New World, born in Genoa, Italy. His plans to reach India by sailing W were supported by Ferdinand and Isabella of Spain. He set sail from Saltes (1492) in the *Santa Maria*, reaching the Bahamas, Cuba, and Hispaniola (Haiti). His second voyage (1493–6) led to the discovery of several Caribbean islands, and on his third voyage (1498–1500) he discovered the South American mainland. His last voyage (1502–4) was along the S side of the Gulf of Mexico. >> Ferdinand (of Castile)

Columcille, St >> **Columba, St**

Colville, Alexander (1920–) Painter, born in Toronto, Ontario, Canada. He has lived and painted in Wolfville, Nova Scotia, since 1971. His subject matter is usually taken from the immediate environment, but is highly representational, always with both beautiful and disturbing elements.

Comaneci, Nadia [komaneech] (1961–) Gymnast, born in Onesti, Moldova. Representing Romania, she was the star of the 1976 Olympic Games when, aged 14, she won gold medals in the beam, vault, and floor disciplines. In 1989 she defected to the USA, and began a career as a model.

Combe, William [koom] (1741–1823) Writer and adventurer, born in Bristol, Avon. He led the life of an adventurer, and was often in debtors' jails, but made his name with his verse satires on popular travel-books, introducing the character of Dr Syntax.

Comenius, John Amos [komeenius], Czech **Komenský, Jan Ámos** (1592–1670) Educational reformer, born in Moravia, Czech Republic. He worked out a new theory of education, and became Bishop of the Moravian Brethren (1632). His *The Visible World in Pictures* (trans, 1658), was the first picture book for children.

Comfort, Alex(ander) (1920–) British physician and writer. His medical work has been devoted to the study of the physical and mental problems of aging. As well as academic books, he has written poems and novels.

Comgall, St (c.516–601), feast day 10 May. Abbot, born in Ulster. He founded the great abbey of Bangor in Co Down (c.558), and is said to have accompanied St Columba on his journey to the N of Scotland. >> Columba

Comines, Philippe de [komeen], also spelled **Commynes** (1445–1511) French statesman and historian, born in the castle of Comines, near Courtrai, France. In 1472 he entered the service of Louis XI of France. His *Mémoires* (1524) are the earliest French example of history as distinguished from chronicle. >> Louis XI

Commodus, Lucius Aurelius [komodus] (161–92) Roman emperor from 180, the son of Marcus Aurelius and Faustina. His reign was one of the worst chapters of Roman imperial despotism, and he was eventually strangled. >> Aurelius

Commynes, Philippe de >> **Comines, Philippe de**

Compton, Arthur (Holly) (1892–1962) Physicist, born in Wooster, OH. He observed and explained the *Compton effect*, the increase in wavelength of X-rays scattered by collisions with electrons, for which he shared the Nobel Prize for Physics in 1927.

Compton, Denis (Charles Scott) (1918–) Cricketer, born in London. He played cricket for England 78 times, scoring 5807 runs, and during his career (1936–57) made 38 942 runs and took 622 wickets.

Compton, Fay (1894–1978) Actress, born in London, the sister of Sir Compton Mackenzie. She won acclaim in *Peter Pan* (1918), and later played many famous parts especially in plays by Barrie. >> Barrie; Mackenzie, Compton

Compton, Henry (1632–1713) Anglican bishop, born in Compton Wynyates, Warwickshire. As Bishop of London (1675), he crowned William of Orange as William III, with his wife Mary. >> William III

Compton, John George Melvin (1926–) St Lucian prime minister (1979, 1982–), born in Canouan, St Vincent and the Grenadines. At independence in 1979 he became St Lucia's first prime minister.

Compton-Burnett, Dame Ivy [bernet] (1884–1969) Novelist, born in Pinner, Greater London. Her novels, set in upper-class Victorian or Edwardian society, include *Pastors and Masters* (1925) and *Mother and Son* (1955, James Tait Black Memorial Prize).

Comrie, Leslie John [komree] (1893–1950) Astronomer, and pioneer in mechanical computation, born in Pukekohe, New Zealand. Regarded as the foremost computer and table-maker of his day, in 1936 he founded the Scientific Computing Service Ltd.

Comstock, Henry (Tompkins Paige) (1820–70) Prospector, born in Trent, Ontario, Canada. He went to Nevada in 1856 and claimed the ground where he found (1859) the silver lode that was given his name.

Comte, Auguste [kõt] (1798–1857) Philosopher and sociologist, the founder of Positivism, born in Montpellier, France. His works on positivist philosophy include *System of Positive Polity* (trans, 4 vols, 1851–4), in which all sciences are regarded as having passed through theological and metaphysical stages into a positive or experiential stage.

Conan Doyle, Arthur >> **Doyle, Arthur Conan**

Conant, James Bryant (1893–1978) Chemist, diplomat, and educator, born in Dorchester, MA. At Harvard he became noted for his work on chlorophyll and haemoglobin. He also chaired the national Defense Research Committee (1941–6), which developed the atomic bomb.

Condamine, Charles Marie de la >> **Lacondamine, Charles Marie de**

Condé, Louis I de Bourbon, Prince de [kõday] (1530–69) Huguenot leader, born in Vendôme, France, the younger brother of **Antony of Bourbon** (1518–61), king of Navarre. He was defeated at Dreux during the first civil war (1562); and in the second war (1567–9) was taken prisoner and shot.

Condé, Louis II de Bourbon, Prince de [kõday], known as **the Great Condé** (1621–86) French military leader, born in Paris. One of Louis XIV's greatest generals, he defeated the Spanish in Franche-Comté (1668) and William of Orange at Seneffe (1674). >> Louis XIV

Conder, Charles Edward (1868–1909) Painter and lithographer, born in London. He worked in Australia and France before returning to London, where he was influenced by the 'Japonais' cult, painting in delicate watercolours on silk, and producing notable fan designs.

Condillac, Etienne Bonnot de [kõdeeyak] (1715–80) Philosopher, born in Grenoble, France. He based all knowledge on the senses, his works including *Essay on the Origin of Human Knowledge* (trans, 1746) and *Treatise on Sensations* (trans, 1754).

Condon, Edward U(hler) (1902–74) Theoretical physicist, born in Alamogordo, NM. Distinguished for his research in atomic spectroscopy, in World War 2 he did notable work on the Manhattan atomic bomb project.

Condorcet, Marie Jean Antoine Nicolas de Caritat, marquis de (Marquess of) [kõdaw(r)say] (1743–94) French statesman, philosopher, and mathematician, born in Ribemont, France. At the Revolution he became president of the Legislative Assembly (1791), but was condemned by the extreme party, captured, and found dead in prison.

Cone, Claribel (1864–1929) and **Etta Cone** (1870–1949) Art collectors and sisters, both born in Jonesboro, TN. Their family moved to Baltimore, MD (c.1870), where the sisters established an artistic salon and collection of antiques, textiles, and paintings, later bequeathed to the Baltimore Museum of Art.

Cone, James Hal (1938–) Chief advocate of black theology in the USA, born in Arkansas. His many writings include *A Black Theology of Liberation* (1970) and the autobiographical *My Soul Looks Back* (1987).

Confucius [konfyooshuhs], Lat name of **Kongfuzi** or **K'ung Fu-tse** (Chin 'Venerated Master Kong') (551–479 BC) Chinese philosopher, born in the state of Lu (modern Shantung). Largely self-educated, in 531 BC he began his career as a teacher. His ideas for social reform made him the idol of the people; but his enemies caused him to leave Lu, and he travelled widely, followed by many disciples. The *Confucian Analects* compiled soon after his death, are a collection of his sayings and doings. His teachings later inspired a cult of veneration, and Confucianism became the state religion of China.

Congreve, William [konggreev] (1670–1729) Playwright and poet, born in Bardsey, West Yorkshire. His plays include the comedies *The Double Dealer* (1693) and *The Way of the World* (1700).

Congreve, Sir William [kong greev] (1772–1828) Artillery officer and scientist, born in London. In 1808 he invented the *Congreve rocket*, first used in the Napoleonic wars.

Conkling, Roscoe (1829–88) US politician and lawyer, born in Albany, NY. A member of the US Senate (1867–81), he gained fame for his florid oratory, and led the powerful New York Republican machine.

Connally, Thomas Terry, known as **Tom Connally** (1877–1963) US politician and lawyer, born near Waco, TX. He served in the US Senate (1929–53), and was an influential internationalist on foreign policy issues, supporting US participation in the UN and NATO.

Connaught, Prince Arthur, Duke of [ko nawt] (1850–1942) British prince and soldier, born in London, the third son of Queen Victoria. His commands included Ireland (1900–4) and the Mediterranean (1907–9). In 1879 he married **Princess Louise Margaret of Prussia** (1860–1917). >> Victoria

Connelly, Marc(us Cook) (1890–1980) Playwright, born in McKeesport, PA. He wrote many plays in collaboration with George S Kaufman, his greatest individual success being *Green Pastures* (1930, Pulitzer). >> Kaufman, George S

Connery, Sean, originally **Thomas Connery** (1930–) Film actor, born in Edinburgh. In 1963 he was cast in *Dr No* as Ian Fleming's secret agent James Bond, a part he played on seven occasions. Later films include *The Untouchables* (1987, Oscar) and *Indiana Jones and the Last Crusade* (1989).

Connolly, Cyril (Vernon) (1903–74) Writer and journalist, born in Coventry, Warwickshire. He wrote regularly for the *Sunday Times*, and was founder/editor of *Horizon* (1939–50). His books include *Enemies of Promise* (1938) and *The Unquiet Grave* (1944).

Connolly, James (1868–1916) Irish political leader, born in Edinburgh. In Ireland he organized the Irish Socialist Republican Party and in the USA helped found the Industrial Workers of the World ('Wobblies'). After taking part in the Easter rebellion (1916) in Dublin, he was executed.

Connolly, Maureen (Catherine), nickname **Little Mo** (1934–69) Tennis player, born in San Diego, CA. She won the Wimbledon singles title (1952–4), the US title (1951–3), the French Open (1953–4), and the Australian title (1953), thus becoming the first woman to win all four major titles in the same year (1953).

Connors, Jimmy, popular name of **James Scott Connors**, nickname **Jimbo** (1952–) Tennis player, born in Belleville, IL. He became Wimbledon champion in 1974 and 1982, and won the US Open in 1974, 1976, 1978, and 1982–3.

Conrad II (c.990–1039) King of Germany from 1024, in 1026 he crossed the Alps, and was anointed Holy Roman Emperor by the pope in 1027.

Conrad III (1093–1152) King of Germany, and the first Hohenstaufen king of the Germans, crowned at Aachen in 1138. When St Bernard of Clairvaux preached a new crusade, he travelled to Palestine with a large army (1148). >> Bernard of Clairvaux

Conrad, Joseph, originally **Józef Teodor Konrad Korzeniowski** (1857–1924) Novelist, born in Berdichev, Ukraine. His books include *The Nigger of the Narcissus* (1897), *Lord Jim* (1900), *Nostromo* (1904), *The Secret Agent* (1907), and *Under Western Eyes* (1911). His fiction has been a favourite subject for film and television adaptation.

Conran, Jasper (1959–) Fashion designer, born in London, the son of Sir Terence Conran. He produced his first collection of easy-to-wear, quality clothes in London in 1978. >> Conran, Terence

Conran, Sir Terence (Orby) (1931–) Designer and businessman, born in Esher, Surrey. He founded and ran the Habitat Company (1971), based on his own success as a furniture designer and the virtues of good design and marketing. >> Conran, Jasper

Conscience, Hendrik (1812–83) Novelist, born in Antwerp, Belgium. His *Phantazy* (1837), a collection of tales, and his most popular romance, *The Lion of Flanders* (trans, 1838), earned him a place as 'the father of the Flemish novel'.

Constable, Archibald (1774–1827) Publisher, born in Carnbee, Fife. He became publisher of the *Edinburgh Review* (1802), and for all the leading writers of the time, notably Walter Scott, but was ruined in the financial crash of 1826. >> Scott, Walter

Constable, John (1776–1837) Landscape painter, born in East Bergholt, Suffolk. Among his best-known works are 'Haywain' (1821) and 'The White Horse' (1819). He is today considered, along with Turner, as the leading painter of the English countryside. >> Turner, J M

Constant (de Rebeque), (Henri) Benjamin [kõstã duh rebek] (1767–1830) French politician and novelist, born in Lausanne, Switzerland. In 1814 he became leader of the Liberal opposition. His best-known work is the novel *Adolphe* (1816), based on his relationship with Mme de Staël. >> Staël

Constantine I (Emperor), known as **the Great**, originally **Flavius Valerius Constantinus** (c.274–337) Roman emperor, born in Naissus, Moesia. He became emperor of the West after his defeat of Maxentius (312), and emperor of the East after his victory over Licinius (324). Believing that his victory in 312 was the work of the Christian God, he became the first emperor to promote Christianity, whence his title 'Great'.

Constantine I (of Greece) (1868–1923) King of Greece (1913–17, 1920–2), born in Athens, the son of George I. During World War 1, his policy of neutrality culminated in virtual civil war, and his abdication. Restored after the War, he abdicated once again (1922) following an internal military revolt. >> George I (of Greece)

Constantine II (of Greece) (1940–) King of Greece (1964–73), born near Athens, who succeeded his father Paul I. He fled to Rome in 1967 after an abortive coup against the military government which had seized power, and was deposed in 1973. >> Paul I

Constantine, Learie (Nicholas) Constantine, Baron (1901–71) West Indian cricketer and statesman, born in Trinidad. In 1928 he became the first West Indian player in England to reach 1000 runs and 100 wickets in one season.

Constantius Chlorus [konstantius klawrus] (c.250–306) Roman emperor, the father of Constantine the Great. He took the title of Caesar in 292, had Britain, Gaul, and Spain as his government, and re-established Roman power in Britain. >> Constantine I

Conte, Lamsana [kontay] (c.1945–) Guinean soldier and president (1984–). On the death of President Seke Toure, he led a bloodless coup and set up a Military Committee for National Recovery, doing much to restore Guinea's international standing.

Converse, Harriet (Arnot) Maxwell (1836–1903) Writer and defender of Indian rights, born in Elmira, NY. She collected Iroquois artifacts for major museums, and successfully defended Native Americans' property rights in several lawsuits.

Conway, Moncure Daniel (1832–1907) Clergyman and abolitionist, born in Stafford Co, VA. A Methodist turned Unitarian preacher, he became a pastor in London (1864–97), and an active abolitionist.

Conwell, Russell (Herman) (1843–1925) Lawyer, minister, and lecturer, born in South Worthington, MA. In 1882 he took charge of the Grace Baptist Church in Philadelphia, and in 1888 the night school he founded under the Church auspices became Temple College.

Conyngham, Barry Ernest (1944–) Composer, lecturer, and performer, born in Sydney, New South Wales, Australia. Much of his varied output is for film or theatre, including the operas *Edward John Eyre* and *Ned*.

Coogan, Jackie, popular name of **John Leslie Coogan** (1914–84) Actor, born in Los Angeles, CA. He featured in *The Kid* (1921) and became Hollywood's first major child star. In later years he became known for his role in the television series *The Addams Family* (1964–6).

Cook, Arthur James (1883–1931) Miners' leader, born in Wookey, Somerset. A coal miner in the Rhondda, he became general secretary of the national union in 1924 and was one of the miners' leaders during the General Strike of 1926.

Cook, Eliza (1818–89) Poet, born in London. She issued volumes of poetry in 1838, 1864, and 1865, and wrote *Eliza Cook's Journal* (1849–54).

Cook, Frederick (Albert) (1865–1940) Explorer and physician, born in Calicoon Depot, NY. He claimed to have reached the North Pole in 1908, ahead of Peary, but an investigative committee discredited his claim. >> Peary

Cook, James (1728–79) Navigator, born in Marton, North Yorkshire. In the *Endeavour*, he carried a Royal Society expedition to Tahiti, circumnavigated New Zealand, and charted parts of Australia. In his second voyage he sailed round Antarctica (1772–5), and discovered several Pacific island groups. His third voyage (1776–9) aimed to find a passage round the N coast of America from the Pacific; but he was forced to turn back, and was killed by natives on Hawaii.

Cook, Peter (Edward) (1937–95) Comedian and actor, born in Torquay, Devon. He became known as one of the performers in *Beyond the Fringe* (1959–64), and for his collaboration with Dudley Moore in the television series *Not Only... But Also* (1965–71). >> Moore, Dudley

Cook, Stanley Arthur (1873–1949) Bible scholar, born in King's Lynn, Norfolk. He wrote on Old Testament history and was joint editor of the *Cambridge Ancient History*.

Cook, Thomas (1808–92) Railway excursion and tourist pioneer, born in Melbourne, Derbyshire. He organized his first railway excursion in 1841, from Leicester to Loughborough, and his travel agency is now a worldwide organization.

Cooke, (Alfred) Alistair (1908–) Journalist and broadcaster, born in Manchester. He settled in the USA in 1937, where he became a commentator on current affairs. His 'Letter from America', first broadcast by the BBC in 1946, is the longest-running solo radio feature programme.

Cooke, Deryck Victor (1919–76) Writer and broadcaster on music, born in Leicester, Leicestershire. A distinguished Mahler scholar, he completed Mahler's Tenth Symphony, premiered in 1964. >> Mahler

Cooke, George >> Maskelyne, John Nevil

Cooke, Morris (Llewellyn) (1872–1960) Mechanical engineer, born in Carlisle, PA. Director of the Department of Public Works of Philadelphia (1911–16), his pamphlet 'Snapping Cords', helped force a reduction in electricity rates to rural users, seen as a landmark in the movement for cheap power.

Cooke, Sir William Fothergill (1806–79) Inventor, born in London. He took up telegraphy and in 1837 became Charles Wheatstone's partner, developing the single needle apparatus in 1845. >> Wheatstone

Cookson, Catherine (Ann) (1906–) Novelist, born in East Jarrow, Tyne and Wear. She published her first book, *Kate Hannigan*, in 1950. Most of her novels are set in the NE of England, several belonging to a series about a single character or family, such as *Tilly Trotter* (1981).

Cookworthy, William (1705–80) Porcelain manufacturer, born in Kingsbridge, Devon. He discovered kaolin near St Austell in 1756, and established a china factory near Plymouth.

Cooley, Denton A(rthur) (1920–) Cardiac surgeon,

born in Houston, TX. With Michael DeBakey and others he pioneered open-heart surgery as well as the surgical treatment of diseases of the arteries. >> DeBakey

Coolidge, (John) Calvin (1872–1933) US statesman and 30th president (1923–29), born in Plymouth, VT. A strong supporter of US business interests, he was triumphantly re-elected by the Republicans in 1924, but refused renomination in 1928 after the stock-market crash which began the Depression.

Coolidge, William D(avid) (1873–1975) Physical chemist, born in Hudson, MA. He is best known as the developer of the modern vacuum X-ray tube.

Coombs, Herbert Cole, nickname **Nugget Coombs** (1906–) Australian public servant, born in Perth, Western Australia. He joined the [Australian] Commonwealth Bank, becoming its governor in 1949, and was later the inaugural governor of the Reserve Bank of Australia (1959–68). He was personal adviser to seven Australian prime ministers.

Coon, Carleton (Stevens) (1904–81) Anthropologist, born in Wakefield, MA. He discovered the remains of Aterian fossil man (N Africa, 1939), Hotu man (Iran, 1951) and Jebel Ighoud man No 2 (Sierra Leone, 1965).

Cooney, Ray(mond) (1932–) Playwright, director, and producer, born in London. His comedies and farces include *One for the Pot* (1961), *Run for Your Wife* (1983), and *Wife Begins at Forty* (1986).

Cooper, Ashley >> Shaftesbury, Anthony Ashley Cooper

Cooper, Sir Astley (1768–1841) Surgeon, born in Brooke, Norfolk. In 1813 he became professor of comparative anatomy in the College of Surgeons, and raised surgery from its primitive state to a science.

Cooper, Gary (Frank) (1901–61) Film actor, born in Helena, MT. He was the archetypal hero of many Westerns, notably in *High Noon* (1952, Oscar), and starred in the Hemingway epics *A Farewell to Arms* (1932) and *For Whom the Bell Tolls* (1943).

Cooper, Dame Gladys (1888–1971) Actress, born in London. On the stage she leapt to fame as Paula in *The Second Mrs Tanqueray* (1922). During her film career, she received Oscar nominations as best supporting actress on three occasions.

Cooper, Henry (1934–) Boxer, born in Bellingham, Kent, the only man to win the Lonsdale Belt outright on three occasions. He won his first British heavyweight title in 1959. His only world title fight was in 1966, losing to Muhammad Ali. After losing to Joe Bugner in 1971, he announced his retirement. >> Ali, Muhammad

Cooper, James Fenimore (1789–1851) Novelist, born in Burlington, NJ. He is best known for his frontier adventure stories such as *The Last of the Mohicans* (1826; filmed 1936, 1992) and *The Pathfinder* (1840).

Cooper, Jilly, née **Sallitt** (1937–) Writer and journalist, born in Yorkshire. A Sunday columnist for many years, her books include general interest works, such as *Angels Rush In* (1990), and novels, such as *Polo* (1991).

Cooper, Leon Neil (1930–) Physicist, born in New York City. His theory of the behaviour of electron pairs (*Cooper pairs*) in certain materials at low temperatures was a major contribution to the theory of superconductivity. He shared the Nobel Prize for Physics in 1972.

Cooper, Peter (1791–1883) Manufacturer, inventor, and philanthropist, born in New York City. In 1830 he built *Tom Thumb*, the first locomotive engine made in America. To provide the working classes with educational opportunities, he established the Cooper Union (1854–9) in New York City.

Cooper, Susie, popular name of **Susan Vera Cooper** (1902–95) Ceramic designer and manufacturer, born in Burslem, Staffordshire. She founded a decorating studio known as Susie Cooper Pottery, and became famous for functional shapes with simple hand-painted patterns.

Cooper, Thomas (1759–1839) Social agitator, scientist, and educator, born in London. In 1794 he emigrated to the USA with Priestley, becoming president of South Carolina College. His libertarianism led him to become a defender of states' rights, and he was one of the first to argue for secession. >> Priestley, Joseph

Cooper, Tommy (1922–84) Comic and magician, born in Caerphilly, Mid Glamorgan. Well known for his trademark headgear of a red fez, he appeared in many television variety shows and his own 1950s series *It's Magic*.

Cooper, Dame Whina (1895–1994) Maori leader, born in Hokianga, New Zealand. Nationally known for her efforts to help her people recover from the problems caused by European settlement, in 1951 she became the founding president of the Maori Women's Welfare League.

Coote, Sir Eyre (1726–83) British soldier, born in Ash Hill, Co Limerick, Ireland. His capture of Pondicherry in 1761 completed the downfall of the French in India, and in 1781 he routed Haidar Ali at Porto Novo. >> Haidar Ali

Cope, Edward Drinker (1840–97) Naturalist and palaeontologist, born in Philadelphia, PA. He was a noted hunter of vertebrate fossils, and contributed materially to the discussion of evolution.

Copeland, William Taylor (1797–1868) China manufacturer, probably born in Stoke-on-Trent, Staffordshire. He became the partner of Spode in 1833, and from 1846 produced Parian (imitation marble) groups and statuettes, and bone china. >> Spode

Coper, Hans [**koh**per] (1920–81) Studio potter, born in Chemnitz, Germany. He came to live in England in 1939, established his own workshop in 1958, and produced thrown vases which were more sculptural than domestic.

Copernicus, Nicolas [ko**per**nikus], Polish **Mikolaj Kopernik** (1473–1543) The founder of modern astronomy, born in Toruń, Poland. His treatise *On the Revolutions of the Celestial Spheres* (trans, completed 1530) had a hostile reception when it was published (1543), as it challenged the ancient teaching of the Earth as the centre of the universe.

Copland, Aaron [**kohp**land] (1900–90) Composer, born in New York City. Among his compositions are those tapping a deep vein of US tradition and folk music, as in the ballets *Billy the Kid* (1938) and *Appalachian Spring* (1944). He also composed film scores, two operas, and three symphonies.

Copleston, Frederick (Charles) [**kohp**lston] (1907–94) Jesuit philosopher, born near Taunton, Somerset. He wrote several books on individual philosophers and movements, as well as *History of Philosophy* (8 vols, 1946–66).

Copley, Sir Godfrey [**kop**lee] (?–1709) Philanthropist, born in Yorkshire. He left a fund in trust to the Royal Society which has been applied since 1736 to the provision of the annual *Copley Medal* for philosophical research.

Copley, John Michael Harold [**kop**lee] (1933–) Theatrical producer, born in Birmingham, West Midlands. In 1960 he joined the Covent Garden Opera Company, becoming resident producer in 1972, and has since produced for opera houses and festivals in many parts of the world.

Copley, John Singleton [**kop**lee] (1738–1815) Portrait and historical painter, born in Boston, MA. In 1774 he left for England, where he was commissioned to paint the king and queen. His paintings include a group of the royal princesses in Buckingham Palace.

Coppard, A(lfred) E(dgar) (1878–1957) Short-story writer and poet, born in Folkestone, Kent. He published *Adam and Eve and Pinch Me* (1921), and became celebrated for his tales of country life and character.

Coppin, Fanny (Marion Jackson) (1837–1913) Educator and missionary, born in Washington, DC. Freed from slavery as a girl, she went on to become principal of the Institute for Colored Youth, Philadelphia (1869–1902), pioneering training for urban blacks.

Coppola, Francis Ford [ko**poh**la] (1939–) Film director and screenwriter, born in Detroit, MI. Among his outstanding productions are *The Godfather* (1972; *Part II*, 1974; *Part III*, 1990) and his controversial study of the Vietnam War, *Apocalypse Now* (1979).

Coram, Thomas [**kaw**ram] (c.1668–1751) Philanthropist, born in Lyme Regis, Dorset. He settled in Taunton, MA (1694–1704), where he promoted settlement schemes in Georgia and Nova Scotia. Back in London (c.1720) he established the Foundling Hospital (1741).

Corbett, James John, nickname **Gentleman Jim** (1866–1933) Heavyweight boxing champion, born in San Francisco, CA. He won the world heavyweight championship in 1892 by knocking out John L Sullivan, and lost it in 1897 to Robert Fitzsimmons. >> Fitzsimmons; Sullivan, John L

Corbett, Ronnie, popular name of **Ronald Balfour Corbett** (1930–) Comedian, born in Edinburgh. His diminutive stature and comic monologues gained him national popularity, known especially for the television series *Sorry!* (1981–8) and *The Two Ronnies* (1971–87), with Ronnie Barker. >> Barker, Ronnie

Corbin, Arthur (Linton) (1874–1967) Legal scholar, born in Linn Co, KS. He taught at the University of Kansas and at Yale, transforming the educational system, and was a national leader in the field of contract law.

Corbin, Margaret, née **Cochran** (1751–c.1800) Revolutionary heroine, born in Franklin Co, PA. Her husband, John Corbin, enlisted in the Revolution, and she accompanied him as carer for the troops. When Corbin was mortally wounded in the Battle of Harlem Heights (1776), she took over his battle station, was wounded, and thus became the first woman pensioner of the USA.

Corbusier, Le >> Le Corbusier

Corday (d'Armont), (Marie) Charlotte [kaw(r)day] (1768–93) Noblewoman, born in St Saturnin, France. Horrified by the acts of the Jacobins, she obtained an audience with the revolutionary leader, Jean Paul Marat, while he was in his bath, and stabbed him. She was guillotined four days later. >> Marat

Cordobés, El [kaw(r)**doh**bez], nickname of **Manuel Benitez Pérez** (c.1936–) Matador, born in Palma del Rio, Spain. The idol of the crowds in the 1960s, his theatrical style and disregard of danger made him the highest paid matador in history.

Corelli, Arcangelo [ko**re**lee] (1653–1713) Composer, born in Fusignano, Italy. His Concerti grossi, and his solo and trio sonatas for violin, mark an epoch in chamber music, and greatly influenced a whole generation of composers.

Corelli, Marie [ko**re**lee], pseudonym of **Mary Mackay** (1855–1924) Novelist, born in London. Her popular romantic melodramas included *A Romance of Two Worlds* (1886), *Barabbas* (1893), and *The Sorrows of Satan* (1895).

Coren, Alan [**ko**ren] (1938–) British writer and journalist. He became editor of *Punch* (1978–87) and *The Listener* (1988–9). His humorous books include *Present Laughter* (1982) and *More Like Old Times* (1990).

Corey, Elias J(ames) [**kaw**ree] (1928–) Molecular chemist, born in Methuen, MA. He is known for the technique of retrosynthetic analysis, used in synthesizing complex pharmaceuticals. He was awarded the Nobel Prize for Chemistry in 1990.

Cori, Carl F(erdinand) (1896–1984) and **Gerty T(heresa) Cori** (1896–1957) [**ko**ree], née **Radnitz** Biochemists, husband and wife, born in Prague. In 1922 they emigrated to the USA, where they researched into glucose–glycogen metabolism and the enzymes of animal tissue, sharing the Nobel Prize for Physiology or Medicine in 1947.

Corinth, Louis [ko̱rint] (1858–1925) Painter, born in Tapiau, Germany. His style became markedly Impressionistic, while later work verged on Expressionism. From 1900 he lived in Berlin, and became president (1915) of the secession movement against the Berlin academic school.

Coriolanus, Gaius or **Gnaeus Marcius** [koriola̱ynus] (5th-c BC) Roman folk hero, so named from his capture of the Volscian town of Corioli. Banished by the Romans for tyrannical behaviour (491 BC), he took refuge with the Volscians, and led them against Rome. After entreaties from his family, he spared the city, and was executed by the Volscians.

Coriolis, Gustave-Gaspard [korio̱hlis] (1792–1843) Mathematician and engineer, born in Paris. *On the Calculation of Mechanical Action* (trans, 1829), aimed to adapt theoretical principles to applied mechanics. He was the first to describe the inertial force now known as the *Coriolis force*.

Corkery, Daniel (1878–1964) Irish cultural leader, born in Cork, Co Cork, Ireland. In 1917 he published a collection of short stories, *A Munster Twilight*, and a novel, *The Threshold of Quiet*. His love of Irish was revealed in *The Fortunes of the Irish Language* (1954).

Corliss, George Henry (1817–88) Engineer and inventor, born in Easton, NY. Of his many improvements to the steam engine the most important were the *Corliss valve*, and his use of springs to assist in closing valves more quickly.

Cormack, Allan Macleod (1924–) Physicist, born in Johannesburg, South Africa. He developed a technique for computer-assisted X-ray imaging (*CAT scanning*) which has proved valuable in diagnostic medicine. He shared the Nobel Prize for Physiology or Medicine in 1979.

Corneille, Guillaume [kaw(r)nay], originally **Cornélis van Beverloo** (1922–) Painter, born in Liège, Belgium. A leading European exponent of action painting, his work includes 'Drawing in Colour' (1955) and 'Summer Flowers' (1958).

Corneille, Pierre [kaw(r)na̱y] (1606–84) Playwright, born in Rouen, France. A master of the alexandrine verse form, his major tragedies include *Le Cid* (1636), *Horace* (1639), and *Polyeucte* (1640). *The Liar* (trans, 1642) entitles him to be called the father of French comedy as well as of French tragedy. >> Corneille, Thomas

Corneille, Thomas [kaw(r)nay] (1625–1709) Playwright, born in Rouen, France, the brother of Pierre Corneille. He was best known for his tragedies, such as *Timocrate* (1656) and *Ariane* (1672), and he also wrote a verse translation of Ovid's *Metamorphoses*. >> Corneille, Pierre

Cornelius, Peter von [kaw(r)ne̱elius] (1783–1867) Painter, born in Düsseldorf, Germany. He influenced the revival of fresco painting in 19th-c Germany, executing large frescoes of Greek mythology in the Glyptothek, and New Testament frescoes in the Ludwigskirche, both in Munich. >> Cornelius, Peter

Cornelius, Peter [kaw(r)ne̱elius] (1824–74) Composer, born in Mainz, Germany, the nephew of Peter von Cornelius. Devoted to the New German school, his works include the comic opera, *The Barber of Baghdad* (trans, 1858), and the grand opera, *Der Cid* (1865). >> Cornelius, Peter von

Cornelius Nepos >> Nepos, Cornelius

Cornell, Ezra [kaw(r)ne̱l] (1807–74) Industrialist and philanthropist, born in Westchester Landing, NY. He founded the Western Union Telegraph in 1855. In 1865, in association with **Andrew Dickson White** (1832–1918), he founded and endowed Cornell University.

Cornell, Joseph [kaw(r)ne̱l] (1903–72) Artist, born in Nyack, NY. He was one of the first exponents of a form of sculpture called 'assemblage', in which unrelated objects are brought together to create new forms.

Cornell, Katharine [kaw(r)ne̱l] (1893–1974) US actress, producer, and manager, born in Berlin. She appeared in many stage productions before embarking on a career as a producer, presenting many Shakespearean and Shavian classics.

Cornforth, Sir John Warcup (1917–) Organic chemist, born in Sydney, New South Wales, Australia. He showed how cholesterol is synthesized in the living cell, and followed this by notable work on the stereochemistry of enzyme-catalyzed reactions, for which he shared the Nobel Prize for Chemistry in 1975.

Cornwallis, Charles Cornwallis, 1st Marquess [kaw(r)nwo̱lis] (1738–1805) British general and statesman, born in London. In the American War of Independence, he defeated Gates at Camden (1780), but was forced to surrender at Yorktown (1781). As Governor-General of India (1786), he defeated Tippoo Sahib, and introduced the series of reforms known as the *Cornwallis Code*. >> Gates; Tippoo Sahib

Cornwell, David John Moore >> Le Carré, John

Cornyshe, William [kaw(r)ni̱sh] (c.1465–1523) Composer at the courts of Henry VII and Henry VIII. He was employed as musician, actor, and producer of entertainments, and in 1509 became master of the Children of the Chapel Royal.

Coronado, Francisco Vázquez de [korona̱ht ho̱h] (1510–54) Conquistador and explorer of Mexico, born in Salamanca, Spain. In 1540 he commanded an expedition which penetrated into what is now the SW of the USA, and discovered the Grand Canyon of Colorado.

Corot, (Jean Baptiste) Camille [koro̱h] (1796–1875) Landscape painter, born in Paris. A member of the Barbizon school, several of his masterpieces, such as 'La Danse des nymphes' (1850), are in the Louvre.

Correggio [kore̱jioh], originally **Antonio Allegri** (c.1494–1534) Renaissance painter, born in Correggio, Italy. In 1518 he began his great series of mythological frescoes for the convent of San Paolo at Parma. His many pictures on religious themes include 'The Adoration of the Shepherds', known as 'The Night' (c.1530).

Correns, Karl (Franz Joseph) Erich (1864–1933) Botanist, born in Munich, Germany. He rediscovered the neglected results reported in Mendel's paper on the principles of heredity, and confirmed them by his research on the garden pea. >> Mendel

Corrigan-Maguire, Mairead (1944–) and **Williams, Betty** (1943–). Roman Catholic women who founded the movement for peace in Northern Ireland known as the 'Peace People' (1976). They shared the Nobel Peace Prize in 1976.

Corso, Gregory (Nunzio) [kaw(r)so̱h] (1930–) Poet, born in New York City. Based in New York City, he was a central member of the Beat poetry movement (1960s), as seen in *The Happy Birthday of Death* (1960).

Corson, Juliet (1841–97) Cookery educator, born in Boston, MA. She became internationally recognized as an expert on dietetics and food education, her many books including *Juliet Corson's New Family Cookbook* (1885).

Cort, Henry (1740–1800) Ironmaster, born in Lancaster, Lancashire. In 1775 he invented the 'puddling' process for converting pig iron into wrought iron, as well as a system of grooved rollers for the production of iron bars.

Cortazar, Julio [kaw(r)taza̱h(r)], pseudonym **Julio Denis** (1914–84) Writer, born in Brussels. He is one of the most widely recognized Spanish-American writers outside the Spanish-speaking world, owing this particularly to the filming of *Rayuela* (1963, Hopscotch) and of a short story, 'Blow-Up' (1968).

Cortés, Hernán [kaw(r)te̱z], also spelled **Cortéz** (1485–1547) The conqueror of Mexico, born in Medellín, Spain.

In 1519 he commanded an expedition against Mexico, founded Vera Cruz, then marched on the Aztec capital, capturing the king, Montezuma. After the Mexicans rose, he was forced to flee, but a siege of the capital led to its fall in 1521. >> Montezuma

Cortona, Pietro (Berrettini) da [kaw(r)tohna] (1596–1669) Painter and architect, born in Cortona, Italy. One of the founders of the Roman High Baroque style in painting, he specialized in highly illusionistic ceilings, such as his 'Allegory of Divine Providence' and 'Barberini Power' (1633–39) in the Palazzo Barberini in Rome.

Cortot, Alfred [kaw(r)toh] (1877–1962) Pianist and conductor, born in Nyon, Switzerland, of French parents. He became known in France as an outstanding player of Beethoven's concertos. In 1905, with Thibaud and Casals, he founded a trio whose chamber music performances won great renown. >> Casals; Thibaud

Corvinus, Matthew >> Matthias I

Corvo, Baron >> Rolfe, Frederick William

Cory, Charles (Barney) [kawree] (1857–1921) Naturalist, born in Boston, MA. He travelled widely in the E USA and the Caribbean, and published his monumental *Birds of the Americas* (4 vols, 1918–19). *Cory's shearwater* was named in his honour.

Coryate, Thomas [kawreeit] (c.1577–1617) Traveller, born in Odcombe, Somerset. In 1608 he set out on a journey on foot throughout Europe, and in 1611 published *Coryat's Crudities*. A further journey to the Middle East and India was published in 1616.

Cosby, Bill [kozbee], popular name of **William Henry Cosby** (1937–) Comedian, born in Philadelphia, PA. His television successes include the series *I Spy* (1965–8), for which he won three Emmy Awards, and his own *The Cosby Show* (1984–92) which consistently topped the ratings. His films include *California Suite* (1978) and *Leonard: Part VI* (1987).

Cosgrave, Liam [kozgrayv] (1920–) Irish prime minister (1973–7) born in Templeogue, Co Dublin, the son of William Cosgrave. He became a member of the Dail (1943–81), and was minister for external affairs (1954–7) before becoming leader of the Fine Gael Party (1965–77). >> Cosgrave, William

Cosgrave, William Thomas [kozgrayv] (1880–1965) First president of the Irish Free State (1922–32), born in Dublin. He was elected a Sinn Féin MP (1918–22), and after his years as president became Leader of the Opposition (1932–44). >> Cosgrave, Liam

Cosimo, Agnolo di >> Bronzino, Il

Cosimo, Piero di >> Piero di Cosimo

Cosimo de' Medici [kozeemoh day maydichee] (1389–1464) Financier, statesman, and philanthropist, born in Florence, Italy. He began the glorious epoch of the Medici family, procuring for Florence security abroad and peace at home, making the city the centre of the new learning. >> Medici

Cosmas [kozmas], known as **Indicopleustes** ('Indian Traveller') (6th-c) A merchant of Alexandria, who travelled widely in Ethiopia and Asia. In monastic retirement he wrote a Greek work on Christian topography to prove the authenticity of the biblical account of the world.

Cosmas and **Damian, Saints** (3rd-c), feast day 26 September (W), 1 July/1 November (E). Arabian twin brothers, said to have been physicians at Aegaea, Cilicia. They were cast into the sea as Christians, rescued by an angel, but then beheaded by Diocletian. They are the patron saints of physicians. >> Diocletian

Cossington-Smith, Grace (1892–1984) Painter, born in Neutral Bay, Sydney, New South Wales, Australia. She was instrumental in introducing Postimpressionism to her country, and her painting, 'The Sock Knitter'(1915), is seen as a key work in the Australian Modernist movement.

Costa, Lucio (1902–) Architect, born in Toulouse, France, of Franco-Brazilian parents. In 1956 his plan for the city of Brasilia was chosen by an international jury, and he is considered the father of modern Brazilian architecture.

Costa, Manuel Pinto da (1937–) First president of the equatorial islands of São Tomé and Príncipe (1975–90), born in Aguada Grande, Venezuela. In 1972 he founded the Movement for the Liberation of São Tomé and Príncipe in Gabon, and persuaded the new government in Lisbon to grant independence.

Costello, Elvis, originally **Declan Patrick McManus** (1955–) Singer and songwriter, born in London. His debut album, *My Aim Is True*, established his reputation. For his second album, *This Year's Model* (1978), he was joined by The Attractions, a three-piece group who worked with him on most of his albums over the next eight years.

Costello, John (Aloysius) (1891–1976) Irish prime minister (1948–51, 1954–7), born in Dublin. One of his first acts as prime minister was to repeal the External Relations Act, which paved the way for the formal change from the State of Eire to the Republic of Ireland.

Costello, Lou >> Abbott and Costello

Coster, Dirk >> Hevesy, George Charles de

Coster, Laurens >> Janszoon, Laurens

Costner, Kevin (1955–) Film actor and director, born in Compton, CA. He established his acting career with *Bull Durham* (1988) and *Field of Dreams* (1989), then directed and starred in *Dances With Wolves* (1990, 7 Oscars). Later films include *JFK* (1991) and *The Bodyguard* (1992).

Cosway, Richard (1742–1821) Miniaturist, born in Tiverton, Devon. He was a fashionable painter of portraits, noted for his use of watercolour on ivory. In 1781 he married the artist **Maria Hadfield** (1759–1838), also a miniaturist.

Cotes, Roger [kohts] (1682–1716) Mathematician, born in Burbage, Leicestershire. He collaborated with Isaac Newton in revising the second edition of Newton's *Principia*, and contributed a preface defending Newton's methodology. >> Newton

Cotman, John Sell (1782–1842) Watercolourist, born in Norwich, Norfolk. A leading member of the Norwich School, his best work shows a masterly arrangement of light and shade, as in 'Greta Bridge' (c.1805).

Cottee, Kay (1954–) Yachting record holder, born in Sydney, New South Wales, Australia. In 1988 she was the first woman to complete a solo, nonstop, unassisted circumnavigation of the world (in 189 days), in her sloop *First Lady*.

Cotton, Charles (1630–87) Writer, born at Beresford Hall, Staffordshire. His works include a burlesque poem, *Scarronides, or the First Book of Virgil Travestie* (1644) and a translation of Montaigne's *Essays* (1685).

Cotton, Sir (Thomas) Henry (1907–87) Golfer, born in Holmes Chapel, Cheshire. He won the British Open Championship (1934, 1937, and 1948), and played in the Ryder Cup against America four times between 1929 and 1953.

Cotton, John (1585–1652) Puritan clergyman, born in Derby, Derbyshire. Cited for his Puritan views before Laud, in 1633 he emigrated to Boston, MA, where he became the head of Congregationalism in the USA. >> Laud

Cotton, Sir Robert Bruce (1571–1631) Antiquary, born in Denton, Northamptonshire. He accumulated books, manuscripts, and coins dispersed by the dissolution of the monasteries. His son, **Sir Thomas Cotton** (1594–1662), greatly increased the library, and his great-grandson, **Sir John Cotton** (1679–1731), bestowed the collection on the nation in 1700.

Coty, François [kohtee] (1874–1934) Industrialist and newspaper proprietor, born in Ajaccio, Corsica. He built up the famous perfumery firm which bears his name, obtained control of *Figaro* in 1924, and founded the *Ami du Peuple* in 1928.

Coty, René [kohtee] (1882–1962) French statesman, the last president of the French Fourth Republic (1953–9), born in Le Havre, France. After the constitutional crisis precipitated by the generals in Algeria (1958), he assisted the return to power of de Gaulle and the birth of the Fifth Republic in 1959. >> de Gaulle

Couch, Arthur Quiller >> **Quiller-Couch, Arthur**

Coué, Emile [kooay] (1857–1926) Pharmacist, hypnotist, and pioneer of 'auto-suggestion', born in Troyes, France. His system became world-famous as *Couéism*, expressed in the famous formula 'Every day, in every way, I am becoming better and better'.

Coughlin, Charles E(dward) [coglin] (1891–1979) Activist Catholic priest, born in Ontario, Canada. Pastor of the Shrine of the Little Flower in Michigan (1926–66), he won a huge radio audience in the 1930s. He later adopted ultraconservative views, and his inflammatory magazine, *Social Justice*, was barred as violating the Federal Espionage Act.

Coulomb, Charles (Augustin de) [koolõ] (1736–1806) Physicist, born in Angoulême, France. He invented the torsion balance for measuring the force of magnetic and electrical attraction. The *coulomb*, the unit of quantity in measuring current electricity, is named after him.

Coulton, George Gordon [koolton] (1858–1947) Historian, born in King's Lynn, Norfolk. His many works include *Life in the Middle Ages* (1928–29) and *Mediaeval Thought* (1939).

Couper, Archibald Scott [kooper] (1831–92) Organic chemist, born in Kirkintilloch, Strathclyde. In 1858 he produced a paper arguing that carbon had a valence of two or four, and that its atoms could self-link to form chains. A delay in presenting the paper resulted in prior publication by others, and credit for the discovery was not given to him until many years later.

Couperin, François [kooperĩ] (1668–1733) Composer, born in Paris. Known mainly as a harpsichord composer, he also produced chamber concertos and church music.

Courant, Richard (1888–1972) Mathematician, born in Lublinitz, Germany. He went to the USA, where he worked in applied analysis, particularly in partial differential equations and the Dirichlet problem. >> Dirichlet

Courbet, Gustave [koorbay] (1819–77) Painter, born in Ornans, France. The founder of Realism, in 1844 he began exhibiting pictures in which everyday scenes were portrayed with complete sincerity and absence of idealism.

Cournand, André F(rédéric) [koornã] (1895–1988) Physician, born in Paris. He emigrated to the USA in 1930, and shared the 1956 Nobel Prize for Physiology or Medicine for developing cardiac catheterization. >> Forssmann; Richards, Dickinson

Courrèges, André [koorezh] (1923–) Fashion designer, born in Pau, France. He opened his own house in Paris in 1961. Famous for stark, futuristic, 'Space Age' designs, he produces ready-to-wear as well as couture clothes.

Court, Margaret (Jean) [kaw(r)t], *née* **Smith** (1942–) Tennis player, born in Albury, New South Wales, Australia. She was the winner of more Grand Slam events (66) than any other player: 10 Wimbledon (including the singles in 1963, 1965, 1970), 22 US, 13 French, and 21 Australian titles.

Courtauld, Samuel [kaw(r)tohld] (1876–1947) British industrialist, a descendant of Samuel Courtauld (1793–1881), the founder of the silk manufacturing company in 1816. He promoted the British rayon and nylon industry, and built the Courtauld Institute of Art in London.

Courteney, Tom [kaw(r)tnee], popular name of **Thomas Daniel Courteney** (1937–) Actor, born in Hull, Humberside. He won acclaim for his stage performance as Norman in the Ayckbourn comedy trilogy, *The Norman Conquests* (1974). His films include *The Loneliness of the Long-Distance Runner* (1962), *Billy Liar* (1963), *Doctor Zhivago* (1965), and *The Dresser* (1983).

Courtneidge, Dame Cicely (Esmerelda) [koortnij] (1883–1980) Actress, born in Sydney, New South Wales, Australia. In London she became widely known in musicals, pantomimes, and revues, including *By-the-Way* (1935), which also starred her husband, **Jack Hulbert** (1892–1978).

Cousin, Jean [koozĩ], known as **Jean Cousin the Elder** (c.1490–c.1560) Engraver, glass-stainer, and painter, born in Soucy, France. He was probably responsible for two stained glass windows in Sens Cathedral, and a picture of a nude woman ('Eva Prima Pandora') in the Louvre. His son, **Jean Cousin (the Younger)** (c.1522–c.1594), was also a versatile artist.

Cousin, Victor [koozĩ] (1792–1867) Philosopher, born in Paris. His eclectic philosophy can be seen in his *Fragments philosophiques* (1826) and *On the True, the Beautiful, and the Good* (1854).

Cousins, Frank [kuhzinz] (1904–86) Trade-union leader, born in Bulwell, Nottinghamshire. In 1955 he became general secretary of the Transport and General Worker's Union. He was minister of technology (1964–6) until he resigned over the prices and incomes policy.

Cousteau, Jacques (Yves) [koostoh] (1910–) Naval officer and underwater explorer, born in Saint-André, France. He invented the aqualung diving apparatus (1943) and a process of underwater television. He has written widely on his subject, and his films include *The Golden Fish* (1960, Oscar).

Cousy, Bob [koozee], popular name of **Robert Joseph Cousy** (1928–) Basketball player, born in New York City. He played with the Boston Celtics (1950–63), then went on to coach with the Cincinatti Royals and the Kansas City-Omaha Kings.

Couthon, Georges [kootõ] (1756–94) French revolutionary, born in Orcet, France. He joined the Committee of Public Safety, crushed the insurrection in Lyon (1793), and supported the Reign of Terror, but was himself executed.

Coutts, Morton (1904–) Brewer, born in Taihape, New Zealand. In 1956 he revolutionized the industry by patenting the continuous fermentation process. In 1992 his Kiwi Lager won the Best Beer in the World international award.

Coutts, Thomas [koots] (1735–1822) Banker, born in Edinburgh. He founded the London banking-house of Coutts & Co with his brother James, on whose death in 1778 he became sole manager. >> Burdett-Coutts

Couve de Murville, (Jacques) Maurice [koov duh mürveel] (1907–) French prime minister (1968–9), born in Reims, France. President de Gaulle appointed him foreign minister (1958–68), finance minister (1968), then premier.

Coverdale, Miles (1488–1568) Bible scholar, born in York, North Yorkshire. His translation of the Bible appeared in 1535 (the first complete one in English), and he then superintended the work which led to the 'Great Bible' (1539). He also edited the work known as 'Cranmer's Bible' (1540).

Coward, Sir Noel (Pierce) (1899–1973) Actor, playwright, and composer, born in London. His many successful plays include *The Vortex* (1924), *Hay Fever* (1925), *Private Lives* (1930), and *Blithe Spirit* (1941), all showing a strong satirical humour. He wrote the music and lyrics for most of his works, and was an accomplished singer.

Cowdrey, (Michael) Colin [**kow**dree] (1932–   ) Cricketer, born in India. He captained Kent, played in 114 Tests for England (23 as captain), and scored 7624 runs, including 22 centuries. He became chairman of the International Cricket Council in 1989. His son, **Chris Cowdrey** (1957–   ), has also captained England.

Cowell, Henry (Dixon) [**kow**el] (1897–1965) Composer, born in Menlo Park, CA. He was noted for his experimental techniques, and his works include two ballets, an unfinished opera, and 20 symphonies. In 1927 he founded *The New Musical Quarterly*.

Cowen, Sir Frederic (Hymen) [**kow**en] (1852–1935) Composer, born in Kingston, Jamaica. In England he became conductor of the Philharmonic (1888–92, 1900–7), and his works include operas, cantatas, oratorios, symphonies, and some 300 songs.

Cowen, Sir Zelman [**kow**en] (1919–   ) Jurist, administrator, and writer, born in St Kilda, Victoria, Australia. Professor of public law at Melbourne University from 1951, he became Governor-General of Australia (1977–82), and Pro-Vice-Chancellor of Oxford (1988–90).

Cowley, Abraham (1618–67) Poet, born in London. His main works were the influential *Pindarique Odes* (1656) and his unfinished epic on King David, *Davideis* (1656).

Cowley, Malcolm (1898–1989) Critic and editor, born in Belsano, PA. His books include *Exile's Return* (1934) and *The Dream of the Golden Mountains* (1980), and he was long associated with *The New Republic* as literary editor (1929–44).

Cowper, William [**koo**per] (1666–1709) Surgeon and anatomist, born in Petersfield, Hampshire. He wrote *The Anatomy of Human Bodies* (1698), and discovered *Cowper's glands*.

Cowper, William [**koo**per] (1731–1800) Poet, born in Berkhamsted, Hertfordshire. He collaborated with the clergyman John Newton to write the *Olney Hymns* (1779). His ballad of John Gilpin (1783) was highly successful, as was his long poem about rural ease, *The Task* (1785).

Cox, (Charles) Brian (1928–   ) British academic. As chairman of the National Curriculum English Working Group (1988–9), his name is most widely known in UK English circles as the author of a report on the teaching of English (the *Cox Report*).

Cox, Brian (1946–   ) British actor, director, and writer. He has played many Shakespearean leading roles, including *Titus Andronicus* (1987) and *King Lear* (1990–1).

Cox, David (1783–1859) Landscape painter, born near Birmingham, West Midlands. He executed about a hundred works in oil, mainly inspired by the scenery of North Wales. His son, **David Cox** (1809–85), was a noted water-colourist.

Cox, Phillip Sutton (1939–   ) Architect, born in Sydney, New South Wales, Australia. His buildings include the Yulara Tourist Resort, Ayers Rock (1983), the Sydney Football Stadium (1988), and the National Maritime Museum, Darling Harbour, Sydney (1990).

Cox, Richard (1500–81) Clergyman and Protestant reformer, born in Whaddon, Buckinghamshire. On the accession of Mary I he was imprisoned, and went into exile in Frankfurt, where he was a bitter opponent of John Knox. Back in England, he became Bishop of Ely (1559–80). >> Knox, John

Cox, William (1764–1837) Pioneer road builder, born in Wimbourne Minster, Dorset. He went to Australia in 1800, and in 1814 was made superintendent of works for a new road over the Blue Mountains, which he completed in just six months.

Coxie, Michiel, also spelled **Coxcie** or **Coxius** (1499–1592) Painter, born in Mechelen, The Netherlands. He introduced the Italian Classical style into Flanders. He painted the frescoes in S Maria dell' Anima at Rome, and was court painter to Philip II of Spain.

Coysevox, Antoine [kwazuhvoks] (1640–1720) Sculptor, born in Lyon, France. He became court sculptor to Louis XIV in 1666, and was responsible for much of the Baroque decoration at the Palace of Versailles.

Cozens, Alexander [**kuh**znz] (?–1786) English watercolour painter, born in St Petersburg, Russia. He came to England in 1746, and in 1785 published a treatise describing his method of using accidental ink-blots as the basis for landscape compositions.

Cozens, John Robert [**kuh**znz] (1752–c.1797) Watercolour landscape painter, born in London, the son of Alexander Cozens. In 1776 he travelled through Switzerland to Rome, painting what he saw on his way. Constable called him 'the greatest genius that ever touched landscape'. >> Constable, John; Cozens, Alexander

Cozzens, James Gould [**kuh**znz] (1903–78) Novelist, born in Chicago, IL. His novels include *Guard of Honour* (1948, Pulitzer) and *By Love Possessed* (1958; filmed 1961).

Crabbe, George (1754–1832) Poet, born in Aldeburgh, Suffolk. His best-known early work is *The Village* (1783). Later narrative poems include *The Parish Register* (1807) and *The Borough* (1810).

Craddock, Charles Egbert, pseudonym of **Mary Noailles Murfree** (1850–1922) Writer, born in Murfreesboro, TN. She wrote short stories, collected as *In the Tennessee Mountains* (1884), and thereafter became a prolific novelist of mountain backwoods life.

Cradock, Fanny, *née* **Phyllis Primrose-Pechey** (1909–94) British writer and television cook. From 1955 she became known for the television programmes presented with her husband, Johnny. She wrote cookery books, children's books, novels, and press columns which were notorious for their social pretension and outspoken opinions.

Crafts, James Mason >> **Friedel, Charles**

Craig, Edward (Henry) Gordon (1872–1966) Stage designer, actor, director, and theorist, born in Stevenage, Hertfordshire. He published the theatre journal, *The Mask* (1908–29) which, together with his scene designs and his books, profoundly influenced modern theatre practice.

Craig, James, 1st Viscount Craigavon (1871–1940) The first prime minister of Northern Ireland (1921–40), born in Belfast. A Unionist MP in the British parliament (1906–21), he became prime minister when the Stormont parliament was established.

Craig, Sir James (Henry) (1748–1812) British soldier, born in Gibraltar. He served with distinction in America, was governor of Cape Colony (1795–7), and later became Governor-General of Canada (1807–11).

Craigie, Sir William Alexander [**kray**gee] (1867–1957) Scholar, born in Dundee, Tayside. He was joint editor of the *New English Dictionary* (1901–33), and also editor of dictionaries on Scots and on American English.

Craik, Kenneth (1914–45) British experimental psychologist. Director of the new Unit for Research in Applied Psychology at Cambridge (1944), he pioneered the school of thought in which the mind is considered as a complex example of an information-processing system.

Cram, Donald (1919–   ) Chemist, born in Chester, VT. He elucidated mechanisms of molecular recognition, working most notably on the properties of crown ether molecules, for which he shared the Nobel Prize for Chemistry in 1987.

Cram, Steve, popular name of **Stephen Cram** (1960–   ) Athlete, born in Gateshead, Tyne and Wear. He won the World Championship gold medal at 1500 m in 1983, and the Commonwealth Games gold medals at 1500 m (1982, 1986) and 800 m (1986). In 1985 he set three world records in 20 days at 1500 m, 1 mi, and 2000 m.

Crampton, Thomas Russell (1816–88) Engineer, born in Broadstairs, Kent. He was a pioneer of locomotive construction, and was responsible for the first successful cross-channel submarine cable, between Dover and Calais, in 1851.

Cranach, Lucas [krahnakh], known as **Lucas Cranach the Elder** (1472–1553) Painter, born in Kronach, Germany, from where he took his name. He was closely associated with the German Reformers, many of whom he painted. A 'Crucifixion' in the Stadkirche, Weimar, is his masterpiece. Of his three sons, all painters, **Lucas Cranach the Younger** (1515–86), painted so like his father that their works are difficult to distinguish.

Crandall, Prudence, married name **Philleo** (1803–90) Educator and abolitionist, born in Hopkinton, RI. Her short-lived attempt to train young black women as teachers in her Canterbury, CN, boarding school (1833–4) provoked the passage of a local 'black law'. She worked for women's rights and temperance throughout her life.

Crane, (Harold) Hart (1899–1932) Poet, born in Garrettsville, OH. His work is contained in *The White Buildings* (1926), a collection on New York life, and *The Bridge* (1930), an epic using Brooklyn Bridge as its focal point.

Crane, Stephen (1871–1900) Writer and war correspondent, born in Newark, NJ. He became known as a novelist through *Maggie: A Girl of the Streets* (1893) and *The Red Badge of Courage* (1895), a vivid story of the Civil War.

Crane, Walter (1845–1915) Painter and illustrator, born in Liverpool, Merseyside. He was a leader with Morris in the Arts and Crafts movement, and became a noted illustrator of children's books. >> Morris, William

Cranko, John [krangkoh] (1927–73) Dancer, choreographer, and director, born in Rustenburg, South Africa. In 1961 he became ballet director of the Stuttgart Ballet. He is known chiefly for his full-length dramatic works, such as *Romeo and Juliet* (1962) and *Onegin* (1965).

Cranmer, Thomas (1489–1556) Archbishop of Canterbury (from 1523), born in Aslacton, Nottinghamshire. He annulled Henry VIII's marriages to Catherine of Aragon and to Anne Boleyn (1536), divorced him from Anne of Cleves (1540), and was largely responsible for the Book of Common Prayer (1549, 1552). On Henry's death, he agreed to the plan to divert the succession from Mary I to Lady Jane Grey (1553), for which he was later arraigned for treason and burned alive. >> Grey, Lady Jane; Henry VIII; Mary I

Crashaw, Richard [krayshaw] (c.1613–49) Religious poet, born in London. He is best known for his volume of Latin poems, *A Book of Sacred Epigrams* (trans, 1634) and *Steps to the Temple* (1646).

Crassus, Lucius Licinius (140–91 BC) Roman orator. In 95 he was elected consul, along with Quintus Scaevola. During their consulship a rigorous law was enacted banishing from Rome all who had not the full rights of citizens, which was one of the chief causes of the Social War (90–88).

Crassus, Marcus Licinius, nickname *Dives* (Lat 'wealthy') (c.115–53 BC) Roman politician. In 70 BC he was made consul with Pompey, and formed the first triumvirate with him and Caesar (60 BC). In 53 BC, as Governor of Syria, he attacked the Parthians, but was killed at the Battle of Carrhae.

Crates of Chalkis [krahteez, kalkis] (fl.335–325 BC) Greek engineer. He carried out notable works for Alexander the Great, including the building of the new city and port of Alexandria in the Nile delta.

Cratinus [kratiynus] (c.519–423 BC) Greek comic poet. Next to Aristophanes, he best represents the Old Attic comedy. Of his 21 comedies, only some fragments are extant. >> Aristophanes

Craven, Dan(iel Hartman), known as **Danie** (1911–93) Rugby union player and administrator, born in Lindley, South Africa. He became chairman of the South African Rugby Board in 1956, and over the next 30 years worked to keep South Africa within the Rugby Union fold.

Crawford, Joan, originally **Lucille Fay Le Sueur** (1904–77) Film actress, born in San Antonio, TX. Her films include *Mildred Pierce* (1945, Oscar) and *Whatever Happened to Baby Jane?* (1962), in which she co-starred with her long-standing rival, Bette Davis. >> Davis, Bette

Crawford, Sir John (Grenfell) (1910–85) Economist and administrator, born in Sydney, New South Wales, Australia. He held various senior positions in agricultural and rural economics, including director of the [Australian] Commonwealth Bureau of Agricultural Economics (1945–50).

Crawford, Michael (1942–) British actor. The 1970s television series *Some Mothers Do 'Ave 'Em*, made him a household name in Britain. He went on to star in such musicals as *Barnum* (1981) and *The Phantom of the Opera* (1986, Tony). His films include *Hello Dolly* (1968) and *The Condorman* (1980).

Crawford, Osbert Guy Stanhope (1886–1957) British archaeologist, born in Bombay, India. He identified the potential of aerial photography in archaeology, producing *Wessex from the Air* (1928), and did much to develop the cartographic recording of archaeology.

Crawford, Thomas (1814–57) Sculptor, born in New York City. His works include the Washington monument at Richmond, and the bronze figure of Liberty surmounting the dome of the capitol at Washington.

Craxi, Bettino [kraksee] (1934–) Italian prime minister (1983–7), born in Milan, Italy. He joined the National Executive (1965), becoming deputy secretary (1970–6), general secretary (1976), and Italy's first socialist prime minister.

Cray, Seymour R (1925–) Computer designer, born in Chippewa Falls, WI. He established himself at the forefront of large-scale computer design, and in 1972 organized Cray Research Inc to develop the most powerful computer systems available.

Crayon, Geoffrey >> **Irving, Washington**

Crazy Horse, Sioux name **Tashunka Witco** (c.1842–77) Oglala Sioux chief, born near the Black Hills, SD. He fought in all the major Sioux actions to protect the Black Hills against white intrusion, defeating Custer's forces at Little Bighorn in 1876. He is regarded as a symbol of Sioux resistance and as their greatest leader. >> Custer, George Armstrong

Creed, Frederick George (1871–1957) Inventor, born in Nova Scotia, Canada. He moved to Glasgow, Scotland, in 1897, and there perfected the *Creed teleprinter*, used in news offices all over the world.

Creeley, Robert (White) (1926–) Writer, born in Arlington, MA. Influenced by the Black Mountain school, he developed a spare, minimalist style evident in *For Love: Poems 1950–60* (1960), *Words* (1965), *Pieces* (1969), and *Hello: A Journal* (1978).

Creevey, Thomas (1768–1838) British politician and diarist, born in Liverpool, Merseyside. He was a Whig MP for Thetford (1802), and is chiefly remembered for the *Creevey Papers*, a journal important as a source of Georgian social history.

Cremer, Sir (William) Randal [kreemer] (1838–1908) Pacifist, born in Fareham, Hampshire. He founded the Workmen's Peace Association, edited the peace journal *Arbitor* from 1889, and was awarded the Nobel Peace Prize in 1903.

Crémieux, Benjamin [kraymyoe] (1888–1944) Writer and critic, born in Narbonne, France. He is known for his works on modern European literature, including *XX siècle* (1924) and for his translation of the plays of Pirandello.

Cremin, Lawrence (Arthur) [cremin] (1925–90) Historian and educator, born in New York City. His major published works include a history of American education (3 vols, 1970–80, Pulitzer) and *Popular Education and its Discontents* (1990).

Crerar, Henry Duncan Graham [kreerer] (1888–1965) Canadian soldier, born in Hamilton, Ontario, Canada. He commanded the 2nd Canadian Division (1942) and the Canadian Corps in Italy (1942–4), and was commander of the Canadian Land Forces in Europe (1944).

Cresson, Edith [kresõ], *née* **Campion** (1934–) French prime minister (1991–2), born in Boulogne-Billancourt, France. She was appointed the first female agriculture minister (1981), and under president Mitterand became France's first woman prime minister. >> Mitterrand

Cretzschmar, Philipp Jakob [krechmah(r)] (1786–1845) Naturalist and physician, born in Sulzbach, Germany. He settled in Frankfurt, where he practised as a doctor and taught zoology. *Cretzschmar's bunting* was named in his honour.

Cribb, Tom (1781–1848) Prizefighter and bare-knuckles champion of the world, born in Bitton, Avon. He twice defeated Jem Belcher for the bare-knuckles championship (1807, 1809), and also defeated the US black pugilist Tom Molineaux (1810, 1811). He retired unbeaten.

Crichton, James [kriytn], known as **the Admirable Crichton** (1560–c.1582) Leading figure of the Scottish Enlightenment, born in Clunie, Tayside. A scholar, poet, linguist, and swordsman on the European mainland, his reputation rests on the account of his exploits by Sir Thomas Urquhart in *The Discoveryie of a Most Exquisite Jewel* (1652). >> Urquhart

Crick, Francis (Harry Compton) (1916–) Biophysicist, born in Northampton, Northamptonshire. In 1953, he and J D Watson constructed a molecular model of the genetic material DNA, and in 1958 he proposed that DNA determines the sequence of amino acids in a polypeptide through a triplet code. He shared the Nobel Prize for Physiology or Medicine in 1962. >> Watson, James; Wilkins, Maurice

Crile, George Washington [kriyl] (1864–1943) Surgeon and physiologist, born in Chili, OH. Founder director of the Cleveland Clinic Foundation (1921–40), he worked on surgical shock, and devised a method ('anoci-association') which made surgical complications easier to control.

Crippen, Hawley Harvey, known as **Dr Crippen** (1862–1910) Physician and murderer, born in Michigan, USA. After poisoning his second wife, he and his mistress attempted to escape to Canada on board the *SS Montrose*, but they were arrested, and he was hanged in London.

Cripps, Sir (Richard) Stafford (1889–1952) British Labour statesman, born in London. Expelled from the Labour Party in 1939 for his 'popular front' opposing Chamberlain's policy of appeasement, he was readmitted in 1945, and appointed President of the Board of Trade. In 1947 he became minister of economic affairs and then Chancellor of the Exchequer, introducing a successful austerity policy. >> Chamberlain, Neville

Crispi, Francesco [kreespee] (1819–1901) Italian prime minister (1887–90, 1893–6), born in Ribera, Sicily. He organized the successful movement of 1859–60, and in the restored Kingdom of Italy he became deputy, president of the chamber, minister, and premier. >> Garibaldi

Crispin, St (?–c.287), feast day 25 October. Christian martyr. According to legend, under the reign of Diocletian he fled from Rome with his brother St Crispinian, and worked as a shoemaker while striving to spread Christianity. The brothers were martyred and are the patron saints of shoemakers. >> Diocletian

Cristofori, Bartolomeo [kristoforee] (1655–1731) Harpsichord-maker, born in Padua, Italy. He is usually credited with the invention of the pianoforte in c.1710.

Critias (c.460–403 BC) Athenian orator and politician, a pupil of Socrates. He became one of the Thirty Tyrants set up by the Spartans after their defeat of Athens (431–404 BC). >> Socrates

Crivelli, Carlo [krivelee] (c.1430–c.1495) Painter of the Venetian school, born in Venice, Italy. His style is a combination of old-fashioned International Gothic opulence with the new Renaissance passion for setting figures in architectural frameworks and against landscapes.

Croce, Benedetto [krohchay] (1866–1952) Italian statesman, philosopher, historian, and critic, born in Pescasseroli, Italy. He founded the review *La Critica* (1903), and made major contributions to idealistic aesthetics. After the fall of Mussolini (1943), he helped to resurrect Liberal institutions in Italy. >> Mussolini

Crocker, Chester A(rthur) (1941–) US statesman, born in New York City. During the Nixon administration, he served on the National Security Council (1970–2). An expert on southern African politics, he joined the Reagan administration (1981–9) as assistant secretary of state for African affairs. >> Nixon; Reagan

Crockett, Davy, popular name of **David Crockett** (1786–1836) Backwoodsman, born in Green Co, TN. He distinguished himself against the Creek Indians in Jackson's campaign of 1814, and died fighting for Texas at the Battle of the Alamo. >> Jackson, Andrew

Crockett, Samuel Rutherford (1860–1914) Writer, born in Little Duchrae, Dumfries and Galloway. He is best known for his sardonic congregational sketches, 24 of which were collected as *The Stickit Minister* (1893).

Crockford, William (1775–1844) British founder of a famous gaming club in London (1827). Previously a fishmonger, he is reputed to have won over £1 million at the game of hazard.

Croesus [kreesuhs] (?–c.546 BC) The last king of Lydia (c.560–546 BC), whose conquests and mines made his wealth proverbial. Cyrus II defeated and imprisoned him (546 BC), but his death is a mystery. >> Cyrus II

Croft, William (1678–1727) Organist and composer, born in Nether Ettington, Warwickshire. In 1708 he became organist of Westminster Abbey and choirmaster of the Chapel Royal. Thirty of his anthems for state ceremonies were printed in 1724.

Croke, Thomas William (1824–1902) Clergyman, born in Ballyclough, Co Cork, Ireland. In 1875 he became Archbishop of Cashel and Emly. A strong nationalist, he backed the Gaelic League and the Land League. Croke Park in Dublin is named after him.

Croker, Richard, known as **Boss Croker** (1841–1922) US politician, born in Co Cork, Ireland. He entered New York City politics in 1862, secured control of the Tammany Hall machine in 1886, and dominated Democratic Party politics for the next 16 years.

Croker, Thomas Crofton (1798–1854) Antiquary and folklorist, born in Cork, Co Cork, Ireland. In 1825 he published his *Fairy Legends and Traditions of the South of Ireland* anonymously, a work which was translated into German by the brothers Grimm (1826). >> Grimm brothers

Crome, John, known as **Old Crome** (1768–1821) Landscape painter, chief of the Norwich School, born in Norwich, Norfolk. He founded the Norwich Society of Artists in 1803. His subjects derived from the scenery of Norfolk, such as 'Poringland Oak' and 'Mousehold Heath'.

Cromer, Evelyn Baring, 1st Earl of [krohmer] (1841–1917) Colonial administrator, born in Cromer, Norfolk. He became British controller-general of Egyptian finance (1879–80), finance minister of India (1880–3), and agent and consul-general in Egypt (1883–1907).

Crompton, Richmal, pseudonym of **Richmal Samuel Lamburn** (1890–1969) Writer of children's books, born in Bury, Greater Manchester. She wrote the first of the

'William' books (*Just William*) in 1922, and had written 40 of them before her death.

Crompton, Rookes Evelyn Bell (1845–1940) Engineer, born near Thirsk, North Yorkshire. An international authority on the distribution of electricity for lighting, he was involved in the establishment of what is now the British Standards Institution.

Crompton, Samuel (1753–1827) Inventor of the spinning-mule, born in Firwood, Greater Manchester. In 1779 he devised a machine which produced yarn of astonishing fineness, and although he was forced to sell his idea to a Bolton manufacturer, he was later awarded a national grant.

Cromwell, Oliver (1599–1658) English soldier and states-man, born in Huntingdon, Cambridgeshire. A convinced Puritan, he sat in both the Short and the Long Parliaments (1640), and when war broke out (1642) he formed his unconquerable Ironsides, combining rigid discipline with strict morality, securing victory at Marston Moor (1644) and Naseby (1645). He brought Charles I to trial, and was one of the signatories of his death warrant (1649). Having established the Commonwealth, he suppressed the Levellers, Ireland (1649–50), and the Scots (1650–1), and established a Protectorate (1653). He was succeeded by his son, Richard, who was forced into French exile in 1659. >> Charles I (of England); Cromwell, Richard

Cromwell, Richard (1626–1712) English statesman, the third son of Oliver Cromwell. In 1658 he succeeded his father as Lord Protector, but fell out with parliament, which he dissolved in 1659. He recalled the Rump Parliament but was forced to abdicate in 1659. >> Cromwell, Oliver

Cromwell, Thomas, Earl of Essex (c.1485–1540) English statesman, born in London, known as 'the hammer of the monks'. He arranged Henry VIII's divorce from Catherine of Aragon, and put into effect the Act of Supremacy (1534) and the dissolution of the monasteries (1536–9). His offices included Chancellor of the Exchequer (1533) and secretary of state (1534), but Henry's aversion to Anne of Cleves, chosen by Cromwell, led to his downfall, and he was beheaded. >> Catherine of Aragon; Henry VIII

Cronenberg, David (1943–) Film director and screen-play writer, born in Toronto, Ontario, Canada. A prolific and acclaimed exponent of the horror film genre, his works include *The Dead Zone* (1983) and *The Fly* (1986), which gave him cult status.

Cronin, A(rchibald) J(oseph) [krohnin] (1896–1981) Novelist, born in Cardross, Strathclyde. His books include *The Citadel* (1937) and *The Keys of the Kingdom* (1942). The tele-vision series *Dr Finlay's Casebook* was based on his stories.

Cronin, James Watson [krohnin] (1931–) Physicist, born in Chicago, IL. In 1964 with Fitch he demonstrated the non-conservation of parity and charge conjugation in certain atomic particle reactions, for which they shared the Nobel Prize for Physics in 1980. >> Fitch, Val

Cronje, Piet [kronyay] (1835–1911) Boer general, born in Colesberg, South Africa. He was a leader in the Boer Wars (1881, 1899–1900), defeated Methuen at Magersfontein, but surrendered at Paardeberg (1900).

Cronkite, Walter (Leland), Jr [krongkiyt] (1916–) Journalist and broadcaster, born in St Joseph, MO. Employed by the United Press (1939–48), he provided vivid eye-witness accounts of the war in Europe. He became a national institution as the anchorman of the *CBS Evening News* (1962–81).

Cronstedt, Axel Fredrik, Baron [kronstet] (1722–65) Metallurgist, born in Turinge, Sweden. He first isolated nickel (1751), made a useful chemical classification of min-erals, and discovered a zeolite (a water-softening silicate).

Crook, George (1829–90) US soldier, born in Ohio. He was

on the Federal side in the Civil War (1861–5), command-ing the army of West Virginia in 1864. In the Indian Wars he captured Cochise (1871), fought in the Sioux War (1876), and fought the Apaches under Geronimo (1882–6). >> Cochise; Geronimo

Crookes, Sir William (1832–1919) Chemist and physicist, born in London. He was an authority on sanitation, dis-covered the metal thallium (1861), and invented the radiometer (1873–6).

Cropsey, Jasper (Francis) (1823–1900) Painter, born in Staten Island, NY. A member of the Hudson River school, his paintings, such as 'Autumn on the Hudson River' (1860), reveal his Romantic approach to nature.

Crosby, Bing, popular name of **Harry Lillis Crosby** (1904–77) Singer and film star, born in Tacoma, WA. His distinctive style of crooning made his recordings of 'White Christmas' and 'Silent Night' the hits of the cen-tury. He starred in many films, notably the *Road* films with Bob Hope and Dorothy Lamour (1914–), *Going My Way* (1944, Oscar), *White Christmas* (1954), and *High Society* (1956). >> Hope, Bob

Crosby, Fanny popular name of **Frances Jane Crosby**, later **Mrs Van Alstyne** (1820–1915) Hymn writer, born in Southeast, NY. Blind from infancy, she composed about 6000 popular hymns, including 'Safe in the Arms of Jesus' and 'Pass Me Not, O Gentle Saviour'.

Crosland, Tony, popular name of **(Charles) Anthony Raven Crosland** (1918–77) British statesman, born in St Leon-ards, East Sussex. A key member of the revisionist wing of the Labour Party, his posts included secretary for educa-tion and science (1965–7), environment secretary (1974–6), and foreign secretary (1976–7).

Cross, Charles (Frederick) (1855–1935) British chemist. With Edward Bevan he invented the modern method of producing artificial silk. >> Bevan, Edward

Crossley, Sir Francis (1817–72) Carpet manufacturer and philanthropist, born in Halifax, West Yorkshire. He was Liberal MP for Halifax (1852–9), and presented to the town a public park (1857), almshouses, and an orphanage.

Crossman, Richard (Howard Stafford) (1907–74) British statesman, born in Cropredy, Oxfordshire. He was minister of housing and local government (1964–6), then secretary of state for social services and head of the Department of Health (1968–70). His diaries of the daily workings of government were published after his death (4 vols, 1975–81), despite attempts to suppress them.

Crothers, Rachel (1878–1958) Playwright, born in Bloom-ington, IL. Her first play, *The Three of Us* (1906), was the first of many successful works about the position of women in contemporary US society.

Crowley, Aleister, originally **Edward Alexander Crowley** (1875–1947) British writer and 'magician'. He became interested in the occult and founded the order known as the Silver Star. He liked to be known as 'the great beast' and 'the wickedest man alive'.

Crowley, Bob, popular name of **Robert Crowley** (1954–) British stage designer. He has worked in several British theatres, including the Bristol Old Vic, the National Theatre, and the Royal Shakespeare Company.

Crowther, Geoffrey Crowther, Baron [krowt her] (1907–72) Economist, born in Claymont, DE. As chairman of the Central Advisory Council for Education (1956–60), he produced the *Crowther Report* (1959), which recom-mended the raising of the school-leaving age to 16.

Crowther, Samuel (Adjai) [krowt her] (c.1809–91) Miss-ionary, born in Ochugu, West Africa. A former slave who was rescued by the British, he became the first African to be ordained by the Church Missionary Society (1842), and was consecrated bishop of the Niger territory in 1864.

Cruden, Alexander [krooden] (1701–70) Scholar and

bookseller, born in Aberdeen, Grampian. He became a bookseller in London, and in 1737 appeared his *Concordance of the Holy Scriptures*.

Cruft, Charles (1852–1939) British showman who organized the first dog show in London in 1886. The annual shows have since become world-famous, and have helped to improve standards of dog-breeding.

Cruickshank, Andrew [krukshangk] (1907–88) Actor, born in Aberdeen, Grampian. He reached the London stage in 1935, and became known worldwide for his portrayal of Dr Cameron in the BBC television series *Dr Finlay's Casebook*.

Cruikshank, George [krookshangk] (1792–1878) Caricaturist and illustrator, born in London. His best-known work includes Grimm's *German Popular Stories* (1824–6) and Dickens's *Oliver Twist* (1837–9).

Cruveilhier, Jean [kru\umvaylyay] (1791–1874) Anatomist, born in Limoges, France. A pioneer of the descriptive method, he was the first to describe multiple sclerosis and progressive muscular atrophy (*Cruveilhier's paralyses*).

Cruyff, Johann [kriyf] (1947–) Footballer, born in Amsterdam. A player for Ajax, in 1974 he captained Holland in the World Cup final (beaten by West Germany). He joined Barcelona as manager in 1988, guiding the Spanish champions to the European Cup in 1992.

Ctesias [tesias] (5th-c BC) Greek historian and physician. He wrote a history of Persia in 23 books, *Persika*, of which only fragments remain.

Ctesibius [tesibius] (2nd-c BC) Alexandrian Greek, the inventor of the force-pump and water organ, and improver of the clepsydra or water-clock. He was the teacher of Hero of Alexandria. >> Hero of Alexandria

Cuauhtémoc [kwowtaymok] (c.1495–1525) The last Aztec ruler, successor to Montezuma. He resisted the Spaniards under Cortés at the siege of Tenochitlán (now Mexico City) in 1521, and was later executed. >> Cortés; Montezuma

Cubitt, Thomas (1788–1855) Builder, born in Buxton, Derbyshire. He revolutionized trade practices in the building industry, and with his brother **Lewis Cubitt** (1799–1883) was responsible for many large London projects, including Belgravia and the E front of Buckingham Palace.

Cubitt, Sir William (1785–1861) Civil engineer, born in Dilham, Norfolk. His constructions include the Bute Docks at Cardiff and the Southeastern Railway. Cubitt Town on the Isle of Dogs is named after him.

Cudworth, Ralph (1617–88) Philosopher and theologian, born in Aller, Somerset. The leader of the 'Cambridge Platonists', his best-known work, *The True Intellectual System of the Universe* (1678), aimed to establish the reality of a supreme divine intelligence against materialism.

Cuellar, Javier Pérez de >> **Pérez de Cuellar, Javier**

Cueva, Juan de la [kwayva] (c.1550–c.1607) Poet and playwright, born in Seville, Spain. He is known especially for his use of new metrical forms and his introduction of historical material into drama.

Cugnot, Nicolas Joseph [koonyoh] (1725–1804) Military engineer, born in Poid, France. He invented a three-wheeled steamdriven artillery carriage c.1770 with a speed of 2–3 mph. Lack of support prevented further development.

Cui, César Antonovich [kwee] (1835–1918) Composer, born in Vilna, Lithuania. His works include the opera *William Ratcliff* (1861), and songs and piano music. He was one of 'The Five' in Russian music.

Cukor, George D(ewey) [kooker] (1899–1983) Film director, born in New York City. His films included *Gaslight* (1944), *A Star is Born* (1954), and *My Fair Lady* (1964, Oscar).

Culbertson, Ely (1891–1955) Contract bridge authority,

born in Romania. He developed contract bridge's first successful bidding system, and established himself as the world's best player in a 1931–2 win.

Cullberg, Birgit Ragnhild (1908–) Dancer, choreographer, and ballet director, born in Nyköping, Sweden. She became resident choreographer of the Royal Swedish Ballet (1952–7), later forming the Cullberg Ballet at the Swedish National Theatre (1967).

Cullen, Countée (Porter) (1903–46) Writer, born in New York City. A leader of the Harlem Renaissance, his first volume of verse was *Color* (1925). He also wrote a novel *One Way to Heaven* (1932), and collaborated with Arna Bontemps (1902–73) in the play *St Louis Woman* (1946).

Cullen, Paul (1803–78) Clergyman, born in Prospect, Co Kildare, Ireland. As Archbishop of Armagh and Primate of Ireland (1850), he helped to found the Catholic University (1854) and Clonliffe College (1859), and was created a cardinal priest in 1866.

Cullen, William (1710–90) Physician, born in Hamilton, Strathclyde. He is largely responsible for the recognition of the important part played by the nervous system in health and disease.

Cullman, Oscar (1902–) Biblical scholar and theologian, born in Strasbourg, France. He was the chief representative in New Testament studies of the 'biblical theology' movement in the 1950s and 1960s, and exponent within the German school of the concept of salvation-history.

Culmann, Karl (1821–81) Engineer, born in Bergzabern, Germany. His principal work was in graphical statics, which he elevated into a major method of structural analysis, introducing the use of force and funicular polygons and the method of sections.

Culpeper, John >> **Colepeper, John**

Culpeper, Nicholas (1616–54) Astrologer, born in London. In 1649 he published an English translation of the College of Physicians' Pharmacopoeia, *A Physical Directory*, and in 1653 appeared *The English Physician Enlarged, or the Herbal*.

Cumberland, Richard (1631–1718) Philosopher and theologian, born in London. Associated with the Cambridge Platonists, his *On the Laws of Nature* (trans, 1672) was written as a direct response to Hobbes, and in some respects anticipated utilitarianism. >> Hobbes

Cumberland, Richard (1732–1811) Writer, born in Cambridge, Cambridgeshire. His plays include *The Brothers* (1769), *The Jew* (1794), and *The Wheel of Fortune* (1795), and he also wrote farces, tragedies, comedies, pamphlets, essays, and novels.

Cumberland, William Augustus, Duke of (1721–65) British general, born in London, the second son of George II. He crushed the Young Pretender's rebellion at Culloden (1746), and by his harsh policies afterwards earned the title of 'Butcher'. >> George II; Stuart, Charles

Cummings, E(dward) E(stlin) (1894–1962) Writer and painter, born in Cambridge, MA. He several successful collections of poetry, starting with *Tulips and Chimneys* (1923), are striking for their unorthodox typography and linguistic style. *Complete Poems* appeared in 1968.

Cunard, Sir Samuel [kyoonah(r)d] (1787–1865) Shipowner, born in Halifax, Nova Scotia, Canada. He emigrated to Britain in 1838, and in 1839 helped to found the British and North American Royal Mail Steam Packet Co, later known as the Cunard Line.

Cunliffe, Barry, popular name of **Barrington Windsor Cunliffe** (1939–) Archaeologist, born in Portsmouth, Hampshire. He became known with excavations at the Roman palace of Fishbourne near Chichester (1961–7), and later worked in Roman Bath and at various sites in Wessex.

Cunningham, Sir Alan Gordon (1887–1983) British soldier, born in Dublin, the brother of Andrew Browne Cunningham. From Kenya in 1941 he struck through Italian Somaliland, and freed Abyssinia and British Somaliland from the Italians. >> Cunningham, Andrew Browne

Cunningham, Allan (1791–1839) Botanist and explorer, born in London. His writings and most of his collections are preserved at Kew, and many indigenous Australian trees now bear his name.

Cunningham (of Hyndhope), Andrew Browne Cunningham, 1st Viscount (1883–1963) British naval commander, the brother of Sir Alan Cunningham. He was admiral commander-in-chief of British naval forces in the Mediterranean (1939–43), and commanded Allied naval forces for the invasion of North Africa (1942) and Italy (1942). >> Cunningham, Alan

Cunningham, Imogen (1883–1976) Photographer, born in Portland, OR. She opened her own portrait studio in Seattle in 1910, working in a personal style of pictorial Romanticism. She also spent a period involved in Group f/64, after meeting Edward Weston in 1932. >> Weston

Cunningham, John (1917–) Military and civil aircraft pilot, born in Croydon, Greater London. He was chief test pilot of the De Havilland Aircraft Company (1946–78) and later chairman of the De Havilland Flying Foundation.

Cunningham, Merce (1919–) Dancer, choreographer, teacher, and director, born in Centralia, WA. He danced with the Martha Graham Company (1939–45), starting his own company in 1952.

Cunninghame Graham, Robert Bontine (1852–1936) Writer and politician, born in London. He became the first president of the Scottish Labour Party (1888), and was elected the first president of the National Party of Scotland (1928), and of the Scottish National Party (1934). He is best known for his essays and short stories.

Cunobelinus >> Cymbeline

Cuomo, Mario [kwohmoh] (1932–) US politician, born in New York City. He became Governor of New York State (1983–94), and was often mentioned as a possible presidential candidate in 1984, 1988, and 1992.

Cupitt, Don (1934–) Anglican clergyman and theologian. His works include *The Nature of Man* (1979), *The Sea of Faith* (1984), accompanying a television series, and *The New Christian Ethics* (1988).

Curie, Marie [kyooree], *née* **Manya Sklodowska** (1867–1934) Physicist, born in Warsaw, who worked in Paris with her French husband **Pierre Curie** (1859–1906) on magnetism and radioactivity, and discovered radium. They shared the 1903 Nobel Prize for Physics with Becquerel for the discovery of radioactivity. Mme Curie isolated polonium and radium in 1910, and was awarded the Nobel Prize for Chemistry in 1911. >> Becquerel; Joliot-Curie

Curlewis, Sir Adrian Herbert [kerloois] (1901–85) Lawyer and surf life-saver, born in Sydney, New South Wales, Australia. A judge of the New South Wales district court (1948–71), he was also president of the Surf Life-Saving Association of Australia (1933–74) and president of the International Council of Surf Life-Saving (1956–73).

Curley, James Michael (1874–1958) US politician, born in Boston, MA. He served in the US House of Representatives as a Democrat (1911–14), and became Mayor of Boston (1914–18, 1922–6, 1930–4, 1945–9). In 1937 he was convicted on bribery charges, and later jailed midterm for influence peddling, until pardoned by President Truman.

Curnonsky [koornôskee], pseudonym of **Maurice Edmond Saillant** (1872–1956) French gourmet and journalist. One of the first to write about 'good food' and where to find it, he published *La France gastronomique* (28 vols, 1921–8) and *Le Trésorier gastronomique de France* (1933).

Curran, John Philpot (1750–1817) Lawyer and orator, born in Newmarket, Co Cork, Ireland. He earned a consid-

erable reputation for his wit and powers of advocacy. Entering the Irish parliament in 1783, he later became Master of the Rolls in Ireland (1806–14).

Curry, John (Anthony) (1949–94) Ice skater, born in Birmingham, West Midlands. He introduced ballet-like movements into the free-skating routine, and won the gold medal for men's figure skating in the winter Olympic Games (1976).

Curry, John (Steuart) (1897–1946) Painter, born in Jefferson Co, KS. 'Tornado Over Kansas' (1933) is an example of his populist subject matter, and 'The Mississipi' (1935) demonstrates his sensitivity to social issues.

Curthose, Robert >> Robert Curthose

Curtice, Harlowe H(erbert) (1893–1962) Automobile industry executive, born in Petrieville, MI. In a 44-year career at General Motors, he became president of the company, known for his single-minded focus on sales, and national advocacy of corporate issues.

Curtin, John (Joseph) (1885–1945) Australian prime minister (1941–5), born in Creswick, Victoria, Australia. He became leader of the Labor Party in 1934, and organized national mobilization during the Japanese war.

Curtis, Charles (Gordon) (1860–1953) Inventor, born in Boston, MA. He is best known for his invention of the *Curtis impulse steam turbine* in 1896.

Curtis, Edward (Sheriff) (1868–1952) Photographer and writer, born in Madison, WI. He devoted much of his career from 1896 to recording North American Indian tribes and their way of life, publishing 20 volumes between 1907 and 1930.

Curtiss, Glenn (Hammond) (1878–1930) Air pioneer and inventor, born in Hammondsport, NY. He achieved the first public one-kilometre flight in the USA (1908), invented the aileron, and flew the first practical seaplane.

Curtius, Ernst (1814–96) Classical archaeologist, born in Lübeck, Germany, the brother of Georg Curtius. His most notable excavations were at Olympia in Greece (1875–80). >> Curtius, Georg

Curtius, Georg (1820–85) Philologist, born in Lübeck, Germany, the brother of Ernst Curtius. One of the greatest of Greek scholars, he was professor of classical philology at Prague (1849), Kiel (1854), and Leipzig (1862–5). >> Curtius, Ernst

Curtiz, Michael, originally **Mihaly Kertész** (1888–1962) Film director, born in Budapest. Working in every film genre, he made some 125 Hollywood films, including *Casablanca* (1943, Oscar).

Curwen, John (1816–80) Music educationist, born in Heckmondwike, West Yorkshire. He devoted himself to promoting the tonic sol-fa musical system, and established a publishing house for music.

Curzon, Sir Clifford (1907–82) Pianist, born in London. He taught at the Royal Academy, then after 1932 devoted himself to concert work, specializing in Mozart and other Viennese classics.

Curzon (of Kedleston), George Nathaniel Curzon, Marquess (1859–1925) British statesman, born in Kedleston Hall, Derbyshire. In 1898 he was made Viceroy of India, where he introduced many reforms, established the North West Frontier Province, and partitioned Bengal. He later became foreign secretary (1919–24).

Cusack, Cyril [kyoosak] (1910–93) Actor, director, and playwright, born in Durban, South Africa. He appeared with the Abbey Theatre, Dublin (1932–45), after which he left to form his own touring company.

Cusack, (Ellen) Dymphna [kyoosak] (1902–81) Writer, born in Wyalong, New South Wales, Australia. Her novels include *Jungfrau* (1936) and *Pioneers on Parade* (1939, written with Miles Franklin), and she also wrote several plays on the theme of disadvantage. >> Franklin, Miles

Cushing, Caleb (1800–79) Lawyer and public official, born in Salisbury, MA. Opposed to slavery and secession, he served as a legal consultant to Lincoln, and under Grant he carried through several notable diplomatic-legal negotiations. >> Grant, Ulysses; Lincoln, Abraham

Cushing, Harvey Williams (1869–1939) Neurosurgeon and physiologist, born in Cleveland, OH. His main research field was the brain and the pituitary gland, describing the symptoms of the pituitary malfunction now called *Cushing's disease*.

Cushing, Peter (1913–94) Actor, born in Kenley, Greater London. He was chiefly known for his long association with the Gothic horror films produced by Hammer Studios, such as *The Curse of Frankenstein* (1956) and *Dracula* (1958), as well as films in which he played Sherlock Holmes.

Cushing, Richard J(ames) (1895–1970) Roman Catholic cardinal, born in Boston, MA. He became archbishop of Boston in 1944, and established many schools and institutions, including the missionary society of St James the Apostle.

Cushman, Charlotte (Saunders) (1816–76) Actress, born in Boston, MA. One of the first major native-born US actresses, she starred at the Walnut Street Theatre in Philadelphia, spent many years in England and Rome, and made a triumphal farewell tour of the USA in 1874–5.

Custer, George Armstrong (1839–76) US soldier, born in New Rumley, OH. He led his 7th US Cavalry to a massive defeat by a combined Sioux–Cheyenne force at the Little Bighorn, MT (25 Jun 1876), with no survivors from his immediate command ('Custer's Last Stand').

Cuthbert, St (c.635–87), feast day 20 March. Missionary, born in Ireland or Northumbria. He became Bishop of Hexham (684) and of Lindisfarne, but soon returned to his hermit cell on the island of Farne.

Cuthbert, Betty, known as **The Golden Girl** (1938–) Sprinter, born in Ermington, New South Wales, Australia. She won gold medals for the 100 m, 200 m, and 4×100 m relay at the Melbourne Olympics in 1956, and won the 400 m at the 1964 Tokyo Olympics.

Cutner, Solomon >> **Solomon** (music)

Cuvier, Georges (Léopold Chrétien Frédéric Dagobert), Baron [küvyay] (1769–1832) Anatomist, born in Montbéliard, France. He originated the natural system of animal classification, and through his studies of animal and fish fossils he established the sciences of palaeontology and comparative anatomy.

Cuyp or **Cuijp, Albert** [kiyp] (1620–91) Painter, born in Dordrecht, The Netherlands. He excelled in the painting of landscapes, often suffused with golden sunlight, such as 'Herdsmen with Cows by a River' (National Gallery, London). His father **Jacob Gerritsz Cuyp** (1594–1651) was primarily a portrait painter.

Cymbeline [simbeleen], also known as **Cunobelinus** (?–c.43) Pro-Roman king of the Catuvellauni, who from his capital at Camulodunum (Colchester) ruled most of SE Britain. Shakespeare's character was based on Holinshed's half-historical Cunobelinus.

Cynewulf [kinewulf] (8th-c) Anglo-Saxon poet, identified by some with Cynewulf, Bishop of Lindisfarne (737–80). Four poems, 'Juliana', 'Christ', 'Elene', and 'The Fates of the Apostles', have his name worked into the text in runes.

Cynthius >> **Giraldi, Giambattista**

Cyprian, St [siprian], originally **Thascius Caecilius Cyprianus** (c.200–58), feast day 16 September. One of the great Fathers of the Church, probably born in Carthage. As Bishop of Carthage (248), his zealous efforts to restore strict discipline forced him to flee, eventually suffering martyrdom under Valerian. >> Valerian

Cypselus [sipselus] (c.655–625 BC) Tyrant of Corinth, one of the earliest in a series of self-made rulers who arose in many Greek cities in the 7th-c and 6th-c BC. He seized power against the Bacchiads, and founded the *Cypselid* dynasty.

Cyrankiewicz, Jozef [sirangkyayvits] (1911–89) Polish prime minister (1947–52, 1954–70), born in Tarnow, Poland. He became secretary-general of the Socialist Party in 1945, and later acted as chairman of the Council of State (1970–2).

Cyrano de Bergerac, Savinien [siranoh duh berzherak] (1619–55) Satirist and playwright, born in Paris. In his youth he fought more than a thousand duels, mostly on account of his extremely large nose. His life was the subject of the play by Edmond Rostand (1897). >> Rostand

Cyril (c.827–69) and **Methodius** (c.825–85), **Saints** , feast day 14 February (W) or 11 May (E). Missionary brothers, born in Thessalonica, Greece. They went to Moravia, where they prepared a Slavonic translation of the Scriptures and the chief liturgical books, and introduced a new, Greek-based alphabet (the *Cyrillic alphabet*).

Cyril of Alexandria, St (376–444), feast day 9 June (E) or 27 June (W). Theologian, one of the Fathers of the Church, born in Alexandria, Egypt. He became Patriarch of Alexandria (412), and relentlessly persecuted Nestorius, whose doctrine was condemned at the Council of Ephesus (431). >> Nestorius

Cyril of Jerusalem, St (c.315–86), feast day 18 March. Theologian, and Bishop of Jerusalem, who took a leading part in the doctrinal controversies concerning Arianism. He spoke for the Orthodox churchmen at the Council of Constantinople (381). >> Arius

Cyrrhestes >> **Andronicus**

Cyrus II [siyrus], known as **the Great** (?–529 BC) The founder of the Achaemenid Persian empire, the son of Cambyses I. As King of Persia (548 BC), he had a policy of religious conciliation, allowing captive nations to return, with their gods, to their native countries.

Cyrus [siyrus], known as **Cyrus the Younger** (424–401 BC) The second son of Darius II of Persia (reigned 423–404 BC). Accused of conspiring against his brother, Artaxerxes II, he was sentenced to death (404 BC), but later restored as satrap of Asia Minor.

Czerny, Karl [chernee] (1791–1857) Pianist and composer, born in Vienna. He studied under Beethoven and Clementi, and his students included Liszt. His piano exercises and studies were widely used. >> Beethoven; Clementi; Liszt.

D

Daché, Lilly [da**shay**] (1892–1989) Fashion designer, born in Béigles, France. In the 1920s she founded the House of Daché in New York City, where her thousands of hat designs became her hallmark.

Dadd, Richard (1819–87) Painter, born in Chatham, Kent. He is best known for the fantastically detailed fairy paintings which made up most of his output after his incarceration in asylums, following a mental breakdown.

Dafydd ap Gruffydd [**da**vith ap **gri**fiith] (?–1283) Prince of Gwynedd in North Wales, the brother of Llywelyn ap Gruffydd. He succeeded his brother in 1282, but was betrayed and executed the following year - the last native prince of Wales.

Dafydd ap Gwilym [**da**viith ap **gwil**im] (c.1320–c.1380) Poet, born probably in Brogynin, Dyfed. He wrote love songs, satirical poems, and nature poems in the complex *cywydd* metre which he perfected, much extending the range of such poetry.

da Gama, Vasco >> Gama, Vasco da

Daguerre, Louis Jacques Mandé [dagair] (1789–1851) Photographic pioneer, born in Cormeilles, France. In Paris from 1826 onwards, and partly in conjunction with Nièpce, he perfected the photographic process named after him. >> Nièpce

Dahl, Roald (1916–90) Writer, born in Llandaff, South Glamorgan, of Norwegian parents. A specialist in short stories of unexpected horror and macabre surprise, his children's books also display a taste for the grotesque, such as *James and the Giant Peach* (1961), *Charlie and the Chocolate Factory* (1964), and *BFG* (1982).

Dahlgren, John (Adolphus Bernard) (1809–70) US naval commander, born in Philadelphia, PA. He did much to advance the science of naval gunnery by founding an ordnance workshop at Washington, where he designed a new type of naval gun (1850).

Dahmer, Jeffrey (1960–94) US convicted murderer. He confessed to 17 killings, committed in the USA over several years, was found guilty in 1992 of 15 of these murders, and sentenced to life imprisonment. He was killed by a fellow prisoner.

Dahrendorf, Ralf (Gustav) Dahrendorf, Baron [**dah**rendaw(r)f] (1929–) Sociologist, born in Hamburg, Germany. He held various academic posts in Germany and the USA, became a member of the European Community Commission (1970–4), then moved to Britain as Director of the London School of Economics (1974–84).

Daiches, David [**day**chiz] (1912–) British literary critic. His many works on English include *Literature and Society* (1938) and *Critical Approaches to Literature* (1956), and he also wrote several books about Scotland, such as *Robert Burns and his World* (1971).

Daimler, Gottlieb (Wilhelm) [**daym**ler] (1834–1900) Engineer, born in Schorndorf, Germany. In 1885 he patented a high-speed internal combustion engine, and in 1889 designed one of the earliest roadworthy motor cars. He founded the Daimler Automobile Co in 1890.

Dakin, Henry Drysdale [**day**kin] (1880–1952) Chemist, born in London. Noted for his research on enzymes and antiseptics, he developed *Dakin's* or the *Carrel–Dakin solution*, widely used for treating wounds in World War 1. >> Carrel

Daladier, Edouard [daladyay] (1884–1970) French prime minister (1933, 1934, 1938–40), born in Carpentras, France. Minister of war in the Popular Front Cabinet, as premier he supported appeasement policies. In 1940 he resigned, became successively war and foreign minister, and on the fall of France was interned until 1945.

Dalai Lama [**da**liy **lah**ma], (Mongolian, 'ocean-like guru'), originally **Tenzin Gyatso** (1935–) Spiritual and temporal head of Tibet, born in Taktser, China, into a peasant family. He was designated the 14th Dalai Lama in 1937. Following Chinese suppression, he was forced into exile in India, where he established a democratically-based alternative government. He was awarded the Nobel Prize for Peace in 1989.

Dalcroze, Emile Jaques >> Jaques-Dalcroze, Emile

Dale, Sir Henry (Hallett) (1875–1968) Physiologist, born in London. He discovered acetylcholine and histamine, and in 1936 shared the Nobel Prize for Physiology or Medicine for work on the chemical transmission of nerve impulses.

Dale, Richard (1756–1826) US naval officer, born in Norfolk Co, VA. He served under John Paul Jones on the *Bonhomme Richard* in the battle with the *Serapis* (1779), and commanded the squadron that blockaded Tripoli (1801–2). >> Jones, John Paul

Dalén, (Nils) Gustav [da**layn**] (1869–1937) Engineer and inventor, born in Stenstorp, Sweden. He invented automatic acetylene lighting for unmanned lighthouses and railway signals, for which he was awarded the Nobel Prize for Physics in 1912.

Daley, Richard J(oseph) (1902–76) Administrator, born in Chicago, IL. He became a senator and state representative for Illinois (1936–46), and was a long-serving Mayor of Chicago (1955–76).

Dalgarno, George [dal**gah(r)**noh] (c.1626–87) Educationist, born in Old Aberdeen, Grampian. He published a book on philosophy using letters of the alphabet for ideas, *Ars signorum, vulgo character universalis* (1661), and a deaf sign language.

Dalglish, Kenny [dal**gleesh**], popular name of **Kenneth Mathieson Dalglish** (1951–) Footballer and manager, born in Glasgow, Strathclyde. He joined Glasgow Celtic in 1967, transferring to Liverpool in 1977, and won 102 caps for Scotland. He later became manager of Liverpool, while still a player.

Dalhousie, James Andrew Broun Ramsay, 1st Marquess of [dal**how**zee] (1812–60) British Governor-General of India (1847–56), born at Dalhousie Castle, Lothian. He annexed Satara (1847) and Punjab (1849), but the annexation of Oudh (1856) caused resentment which fuelled the 1857 rebellion.

Dali, Salvador (Felipe Jacinto) [**dah**lee], Span **Dalí** (1904–89) Artist, born in Figueras, Spain. A principal figure of the Surrealist movement, his study of abnormal psychology and dream symbolism led him to represent 'paranoiac' objects in landscapes remembered from his boyhood. One of his best-known paintings is 'The Persistence of Memory' (known as 'The Limp Watches', 1931).

Dalin, Olof von (1708–63) Writer and historian, born in Vinberg, Sweden. He published *The Swedish Argus* (trans, 1732–4) regarded as the foundation of modern Swedish prose, compiled a monumental history of Sweden (1747–62), and wrote an allegorical masterpiece, *The Story of the Horse* (trans, 1740).

Dallapiccola, Luigi [dala**pee**kohla] (1904–75) Composer, born in Pisino, Italy. His compositions make wide use of 12-note technique, and include songs, a piano concerto, three operas, a ballet, and choral works.

Dallas, George Mifflin (1792–1864) Lawyer and US vice-president (1845–9), born in Philadelphia, PA. Dallas in Texas and in Oregon are both named after him. >> Polk, James K

Dalou, (Aimé) Jules [daloo] (1838–1902) Sculptor, born in Paris. He came to England in 1871, and his realistic modelling influenced many English sculptors of the time. His monument, 'Triumph of the Republic', is at the Place de la Nation, Paris.

Dalton, (Edward) Hugh (John Neale) Dalton, Baron (1887–1962) British statesman, born in Neath, West Glamorgan. He held several ministerial posts, and as Labour Chancellor of the Exchequer (1945–7) he nationalized the Bank of England (1946).

Dalton, John [dawltn] (1766–1844) Chemist, born in Eaglesfield, Cumbria. He first described colour blindness (*Daltonism*) in 1794. His chief physical research was into mixed gases, the force of steam, the elasticity of vapours, and the expansion of gases by heat, his law of partial pressures being also known as *Dalton's law*. In chemistry, his work on atomic theory gave a new basis for all quantitative chemistry.

Daly, (John) Augustin (1838–99) Playwright and manager, born in Plymouth, NC. In New York City he opened his own theatre, Daly's, in 1879, and in 1893 opened the London Daly's. He wrote and adapted nearly 100 plays.

Daly, Mary (1928–) Feminist and theological writer, born in Schenectady, NY. She analyzed the effects of male bias in *The Church and the Second Sex* (1968), and later developed a post-Christian radical feminism in *Beyond God the Father* (1973).

Dam, Carl Peter Henrik (1895–1976) Biochemist, born in Copenhagen. For his discovery of the coagulant agent vitamin K (1934) he shared the Nobel Prize for Physiology or Medicine in 1943.

Damadian, Raymond (Vahan) [damadian] (1936–) Biophysicist and inventor, born in Forest Hills, NY. His invention of the magnetic resonance imaging (MRI) scanner revolutionized the field of diagnostic medicine.

Damasus I, St [damasus] (c.304–384), feast day 11 December. Pope (366–84), possibly of Spanish descent. He opposed Arianism, condemned Apollinaris the Younger at the Council of Constantinople in 381, and commissioned St Jerome's Vulgate Bible. >> Apollinaris; Arius; Jerome, St

D'Amboise, Jacques [dambwahz] (1934–) Ballet dancer and choreographer, born in Dedham, MA. He joined the New York City Ballet in 1949 and for many years performed leading roles in works by Balanchine. In 1977 he formed the National Dance Institute to teach dance in inner-city schools. >> Balanchine

Damian or **Damianus, St** >> **Cosmas and Damian, Saints**

Damiani, Pietro, St [damiahnee], also known as **St Peter Damian** (1007–72), feast day 21 February. Ecclesiastic, born in Ravenna, Italy. He joined the hermitage at Fonte Avellana (1035) and rose to be a cardinal and one of the Doctors of the Church.

Damien, Father Joseph [damyi], originally **Joseph de Veuster** (1840–89) Missionary, born in Tremelo, Belgium. He was renowned for his great work among the lepers of the Hawaiian island of Molokai, where he lived from 1873 until his death from the disease.

Damocles [damokleez] (4th-c BC) Legendary courtier of the elder Dionysius, tyrant of Syracuse (405–367 BC). Damocles was shown the precarious nature of fortune in a singular manner: while seated at a richly-spread table, he looked up to see a keen-edged sword suspended over his head by a single horse-hair.

Damon and Pythias [daymon, pithias], also found as **Phintias** (4th-c BC) Two Pythagoreans of Syracuse, remembered as the models of faithful friendship. Condemned to death by the elder Dionysius, tyrant of Syracuse (405–367 BC), Pythias begged to be allowed home to arrange his affairs, and Damon pledged his own life for his friend's. Pythias returned just in time to save Damon from death. Struck by so noble an example, the tyrant pardoned Pythias.

Dampier, William [dampeer] (1652–1715) Navigator and buccaneer, born in East Coker, Somerset. In 1683 he crossed the Pacific, visiting the Philippines, China, and Australia. He later led voyages to the South Seas, exploring the NW coast of Australia, and naming the *Dampier Archipelago* and *Strait*.

Damrosch, Leopold [damrosh] (1832–85) Conductor and composer, born in Posen, Germany. He was conductor at Breslau (1859–60, 1862–71), before emigrating to New York City. He became conductor at the Metropolitan Opera House, and did much to popularize Wagner in the USA. >> Damrosch, Walter; Wagner, Richard

Damrosch, Walter (Johannes) [damrosh] (1862–1950) Conductor, composer, and educator, born in Breslau, Germany (formerly, Prussia), the son of Leopold Damrosch. He began the Damrosch Opera Company (1895–9), then directed a reorganized New York Symphony Society (1903–27). Through his radio work he introduced generations of children to the world of classical music. >> Damrosch, Leopold

Dana, Charles A(nderson) [dayna] (1819–97) Newspaper editor, born in Hinsdale, NH. He edited the New York *Tribune* (1848–62), and in 1867 purchased the New York *Sun*. With Ripley he edited the *New American Cyclopaedia* (1857–63) and the *American Cyclopaedia* (1873–6). >> Ripley, George

Dana, James D(wight) [dayna] (1813–95) Mineralogist and geologist, born in Utica, NY. He joined the Wilkes expedition (1838–42) to the Antarctic and Pacific. With his father-in-law, **Benjamin Silliman** (1779–1864), he edited the *American Journal of Science* from 1840. >> Wilkes, Charles

Dana, Richard (Henry) [dayna] (1815–82) Writer and lawyer, born in Cambridge, MA. He made a voyage as a common sailor round Cape Horn to California and back, which he described in *Two Years before the Mast* (1840). He later became distinguished in maritime law.

Danby, Lord >> **Leeds, Thomas Osborne**

Dance, George, known as **George Dance the Elder** (1695–1768) Architect, born in London. An exponent of Neoclassicism, he designed the Mansion House (1739) and Newgate Prison (1770–83). His son, **George Dance, the Younger** (1741–1825), was also an architect.

Dandolo, Enrico [dandoloh] (c.1110–1205) Italian statesman, born in Venice, Italy. In 1192 he became Doge of Venice, and in 1202 marched at the head of the Fourth Crusade, establishing the empire of the Latins.

Dandy, Walter (Edward) (1886–1946) Neurosurgeon, born in Sedalia, MO. He did important work on the pathophysiology and surgical treatment of hydrocephalus, and also pioneered spinal surgery.

Dane, Clemence, pseudonym of **Winifred Ashton** (c.1891–1965) Writer, born in London. Her novels include *Regiment of Women* (1917), *Legend* (1919), and *The Flower Girls* (1954). Many of her plays achieved long runs, notably *A Bill of Divorcement* and *Will Shakespeare* (both 1921).

Dane, Nathan (1752–1835) Lawyer and statesman, born in Ipswich, MA. He published *General Abridgement and Digest of American Law* (9 vols, 1823–9), the first comprehensive work on US law.

Dangerfield, Thomas (1650–85) Conspirator, born in Waltham, Essex. In 1679 he conspired against the Presbyterians and was imprisoned. He was convicted of libel, whipped and pilloried at Tyburn, and killed by a bystander.

D'Angers, David >> **David, Pierre Jean**

Dang Xianzu [dang shantsoo], also spelled **Tang Hsien-tsu** (1550–1616) Chinese playwright and minor official. His most famous work, *The Peony Pavilion*, deals with a love of such intensity that it can raise the dead.

Daniel, Arnaut [danyel] (late 12th-c) Provençal poet, born at the Castle of Rebeyrac, Périgord, France. A member of the court of Richard Coeur de Lion, he was esteemed one of the best of the troubadours, particularly for his treatment of the theme of love. >> Richard I

Daniel, Glyn (Edmund) (1914–86) Archaeologist, born in Barry, South Glamorgan. He stimulated popular interest in archaeology through writing, editing, and broadcasting, notably as chairman of the 1950s television panel game, *Animal, Vegetable, Mineral*.

Daniel, Samuel (1562–1619) Poet, born near Taunton, Somerset. His chief work was a poem in eight books, *A History of the Civil Wars between York and Lancaster*. He also wrote sonnets, epistles, masques, and dramas.

Daniell, John Frederic (1790–1845) Chemist and meteorologist, born in London. He invented a hygrometer (1820), a pyrometer (1830), and the *Daniell electric cell* (1836).

Danilova, Alexandra Dionysievna [danilohva] (1904–) Dancer and teacher, born in Peterhof, Russia. She danced as prima ballerina with the Ballet Russe de Monte Carlo (1938–52), and created leading parts in the works of Balanchine and Massine. >> Balanchine; Diaghilev; Massine

Dankworth, John (Philip William) (1927–) Jazz musician, composer, and arranger, born in London. An accomplished saxophonist, and bandleader since 1953, he has also composed works for combined jazz and symphonic ensembles, and film scores. He has recorded many albums with his wife, singer **Cleo Laine** (1927–).

d'Annunzio, Gabriele [danuntseeoh] (1863–1938) Writer, born in Pescara, Italy. His works include several novels influenced by the philosophy of Nietzsche, notably *The Triumph of Death* (trans, 1894); his plays include the tragedy *La gioconda* (1899), which he wrote for Eleonora Duse. >> Duse; Nietzsche

Dante (Alighieri) (1265–1321) Poet, born in Florence, Italy. In 1274, a meeting with **Beatrice** (c.1265–90), possibly the daughter of Florentine aristocrat Folco Portinari, influenced the rest of his life. The *Vita nuova*, which tells of his boyish passion for Beatrice, is probably his earliest work. By far the most celebrated is the *Divina commedia* (Divine Comedy), a vision of hell, purgatory, and heaven which gives an encyclopedic view of the highest culture and knowledge of his age.

Danton, Georges (Jacques) [dãtõ] (1759–94) French revolutionary politician, born in Arcis-sur-Aube, France. He formed the Cordelier's Club (1790), voted for the death of the king (1793), and was a member of the Committee of Public Safety. He tried to abate the severity of his own Revolutionary Tribunal, but lost the leadership to Robespierre, and was guillotined. >> Robespierre

Dantzig, Rudi von (1933–) Dancer, choreographer, and ballet director, born in Amsterdam. He joined the Ballet Recital Group of **Sonia Gaskell** (1904–74), later known as the Netherlands Ballet, and was one of the founding members of Netherlands Dance Theatre.

Da Ponte, Giacomo >> **Bassano, Jacopo da**

Da Ponte, Lorenzo [da pontay], originally **Emanuele Conegliano** (1749–1838) Poet, born in Ceneda, Italy. In Vienna he became poet to the Court Opera, where he wrote the libretti for Mozart's operas *The Marriage of Figaro* (1786), *Don Giovanni* (1787), and *Così fan tutte* (1790). >> Mozart

D'Arblay, Madame >> **Burney, Fanny**

Darby, Abraham (c.1678–1717) Iron-master, born near Dudley, West Midlands. He was the first man to use coke successfully in the smelting of iron (1709). Under his son, **Abraham Darby** (1711–63), his foundry supplied cast-iron cylinders for Newcomen's steam engines, and the first high-pressure steam boiler for Trevithick. >> Newcomen; Trevithick

Darby, Sir (Henry) Clifford (1909–92) Geographer, born in West Glamorgan. A leader in promoting the relationships between geography and other subjects, he was general editor of *The Domesday Geography of England* (7 vols, 1952–77).

Darby, John Nelson (1800–82) Clergyman, born in London. In 1830 he was the principal founder of the Plymouth Brethren, and in 1840 an exclusive sect of it known as *Darbyites*.

Dare, Virginia (1587–?) The first English child born in North America, born in Roanoke, NC. Her parents were Ananias Dare and Elinor White. She disappeared along with the 117 Roanoke colonists in 1588.

Dargomizhsky, Alexander Sergeyevitch [dah(r)gomishskee] (1813–69) Composer, born in Tula, Russia. His setting of Pushkin's *The Stone Guest* anticipated the work of Moussorgsky in its dramatic power and naturalistic treatment. >> Moussorgsky; Pushkin

Darío, Rubén [dareeoh], pseudonym of **Félix Rubén García Sarmiento** (1867–1916) Poet, born in Metapa, Nicaragua. His *Blue* (trans, 1888) and *Profane Hymns* (trans, 1896) gave new vitality to Spanish poetic modernism.

Darius I [dahrius], known as **the Great** (548–486 BC) King of Persia (521–486 BC), one of the greatest of the Achaemenids. He is noteworthy for his administrative reforms, military conquests, and religious toleration. His conquests, especially in the East and Europe (Thrace and Macedonia) consolidated the frontiers of the empire.

Dark, Eleanor, *née* O'Reilly, pseudonym **Patricia O'Rane** or **P O'R** (1901–85) Writer, born in Sydney, New South Wales, Australia. Her novels include the historical trilogy: *The Timeless Land* (1941), *Storm of Time* (1948), and *No Barrier* (1953).

Darlan, (Jean Louis Xavier) François [dah(r)lã] (1881–1942) French politican and naval officer, born in Nérac, France. During the Vichy regime he was admiral of the fleet, vice-premier, foreign minister, and minister for national defence. He was assassinated in Algiers by an anti-Vichy agent.

Darling, Grace (1815–42) Heroine, born in Bamburgh, Northumberland. She lived with her father, **William** (1795–1860), the lighthouse keeper on one of the Farne Islands. In 1838, she braved raging seas in an open rowing boat to rescue the survivors of the stranded *Forfarshire*.

Darling, Jay Norwood, known as **Ding Darling** (1876–1962) Cartoonist, born in Norwood, MI. As a staff cartoonist on the Des Moines *Register* (1906–49) and the New York *Tribune* (1917–49), he won the Pulitzer Prize in 1923 and 1943.

Darlington, William (1782–1863) Botanist, born in Birmingham, PA. The California pitcher plant (*Darlingtonia*) is named after him.

Darnley, Henry Stewart, Lord (1545–67) Nobleman, born at Temple Newsom, Yorkshire, the second husband (in 1565) of Mary, Queen of Scots and father of James I of England. His debauchery and arrogance made him unpopular, and his part in the murder (1566) of the Queen's secretary, David Rizzio, caused his downfall. He became estranged from the Queen, and was killed at Edinburgh. >> James I (of England); Mary, Queen of Scots; Rizzio

Darrow, Charles (1889–1967) The inventor of the board game *Monopoly*, born in the UK. He began producing the game himself, and by 1935 it became so popular that Parker Bros, although originally uninterested, purchased the copyright in exchange for a royalty.

Darrow, Clarence (Seward) (1857–1938) Lawyer, born in Kinsman, OH. Known for his defences of trade union leaders, he also defended in the murder case against Leopold and Loeb (1924), and the trial of John T Scopes (1925) for the teaching of Darwinian evolution in school.

Dart, Raymond (Arthur) (1893–1988) Palaeo-anthropologist, born in Brisbane, Queensland, Australia. His discovery (1924) in a quarry at Taung, near the Kalahari Desert, of *Australopithecus africanus*, substantiated Darwin's view of Africa as the cradle of the human species. >> Darwin, Charles

Dart, Thurston (1921–71) Keyboard player, conductor, and music scholar, born in London. A specialist in early music, he edited several editions of 16th-c and 17th-c English works.

Daru, Pierre Antoine (Noel Mattieu Bruno), comte (Count) [darü] (1767–1829) Military administrator and historian, born in Montpellier, France. He was appointed secretary of the war industry in 1800, and was minister of war from 1811.

Darusmont, Frances >> Wright, Fanny

Darwin, Charles (Robert) (1809–82) Naturalist, born in Shrewsbury, Shropshire, the grandson of Erasmus Darwin. He studied medicine at Edinburgh (1825), then biology at Cambridge (1828). In 1831–6 he was the naturalist on HMS *Beagle*, surveying South American waters. From 1842 he devoted himself to his epoch-making work, *On the Origin of Species by Means of Natural Selection* (1859). He wrote many other works on plants and animals, but is remembered primarily as the leader in the field of evolutionary biology. >> Darwin, Erasmus

Darwin, Erasmus (1731–1802) Physician, born in Elton, Nottinghamshire, the grandfather of Charles Darwin. Known for his freethinking opinions, poetry, large botanical garden, and mechanical inventions, many of his ideas on evolution anticipated later theories. >> Darwin, Charles

Dashkova, Ekaterina Romanovna [dashkohva] (1743–1810) Russian princess and writer, born in St Petersburg. She wrote several plays, and was the first president of the Russian Academy (1783).

Dashwood, Edmée Elizabeth Monica >> Delafield, E M

Dassault, Marcel [dasoh], originally **Marcel Bloch** (1892–1986) Aviation pioneer and industrialist, born in Paris. He founded his own company, building a series of highly successful aircraft in the 1950s, such as the Mystère and Mirage.

Daswanth, also found as **Daswarth** or **Dasvanth** (16th-c) Painter at the court of the emperor Akbar the Great. He became one of the leading artists at the academy established by Akbar for the development of an Indian school of painting. >> Akbar

Daubigny, Charles François [dohbeenyee] (1817–78) Artist, born in Paris. He was a member of the Barbizon School, painting landscapes, especially moonlight and river scenes, such as 'The Banks of the Oise' (1872).

Daubrée, Gabriel Auguste [dohbray] (1814–96) Geologist and mineralogist, born in Metz, France. A pioneer of experimental geology, the mineral *daubreelite* is named after him.

Daudet, Alphonse [dohday] (1840–97) Writer, born in Nîmes, France. His theatrical pieces include *L'Arlésienne*, for which Bizet composed incidental music. Notable are his sketches of Provençal subjects, collected as *Letters from My Mill* (trans, 1869) and *Tartarin de Tarascon* (1872). >> Bizet; Daudet, Léon

Daudet, (Alphonse Marie) Léon [dohday] (1867–1942) Writer and political activist, born in Paris, the son of Alphonse Daudet. He is best remembered for his memoirs and critical works, especially *The Stupid Nineteenth Century* (trans, 1922). >> Daudet, Alphonse

d'Aumale, duc >> Aumale, duc d'

Daumier, Honoré (Victorin) [dohmyay] (1808–79) Painter and caricaturist, born in Marseilles, France. He won contemporary fame for satirical cartoons about government corruption, and at one point was imprisoned for caricaturing the king.

Daurat or **Dorat, Jean** [dohra] (c.1510–1588) Scholar and poet, born in Limoges, France. He superintended the studies of Ronsard, Joachim du Bellay, and others (members of the *Pléiade*), training them for the task of reforming the vernacular and ennobling French literature by imitation of Greek and Latin models. >> Bellay; Ronsard

Dausset, Jean [dohsay] (1916–) Immunologist, born in Toulouse, France. His work in haematology led to 'tissue typing', which has since helped to reduce rejection risks in organ transplant surgery. He shared the Nobel Prize for Physiology or Medicine in 1980.

Davenant or **d'Avenant, Sir William** [davenant] (1606–68) Writer, born in Oxford, Oxfordshire. Rumoured to be Shakespeare's illegitimate son, in 1628 he began writing for the stage, his most successful work being *The Wits* (1636). He became Poet Laureate in 1638.

David (?–c.962 BC) Second king of Israel. According to Jewish tradition he is the author of several of the Psalms, and according to some Christian traditions the ancestor of Jesus. A warrior under King Saul, his successes against the Philistines (including the killing of Goliath) caused the king's jealousy, and he was forced to become an outlaw. After Saul's death, he became king of all Israel, making Jerusalem the centre of his kingdom, and building his palace on its highest hill, Zion (the 'city of David'). He was succeeded by Solomon, his son by Bathsheba. >> Saul; Solomon

David I (c.1085–1153) King of Scots (1124–53), the youngest son of Malcolm Canmore and Queen Margaret. He firmly secured the foundations of the mediaeval Kingdom of Scotland. In 1136 he embarked on wars against Stephen, and from 1141 occupied the whole of N England to the Ribble and the Tees. >> Malcolm III; Margaret of Scotland; Stephen

David II (1324–71) King of Scots (1329–71), the only surviving son of Robert Bruce, born in Dunfermline, Fife. He invaded England, but was defeated and captured at Neville's Cross (1346), and kept prisoner for 11 years. >> Bruce, Robert (1274–1329)

David or **Dewi, St** (?–601), feast day 1 March. Patron saint of Wales, born near St Bride's Bay, Dyfed. He was Bishop of Moni Judeorum, or Menevia (afterwards St David's), and founded many churches in S Wales.

David, Elizabeth, *née* **Gwynne** (1913–92) British writer of cookery books. Her publications include *French Country Cooking* (1951) and *Italian Food* (1954). Her kitchen shop in London (1965–73) became a model for such shops throughout Britain and the USA.

David, Gerard [daveed] (c.1460–1523) Painter, born in Oudewater, The Netherlands. Among his best works are the two altarpiece panels, 'The Judgment of Camlyses' (1498, Bruges).

David, Jacques Louis [dahveed] (1748–1825) Painter, born in Paris. He became known for his paintings of classical themes and historical events, such as 'The Oath of the Horatii' (1784) and 'The Rape of the Sabines' (1799). After the Bourbon restoration, he was banished in 1816 as a regicide.

David, Pierre Jean [daveed], known as **David d'Angers** (1789–1856) Sculptor, born in Angers, France. His most prestigious commission was the pediment of the Pantheon, Paris (1835–7). He was also a prolific sculptor of portrait busts and medallions, many of which are preserved in the Angers museum.

David-Neel, Alexandra (1868–1969) Oriental scholar and traveller, born in Paris. She travelled widely throughout S Asia and the Far East, studying Sanskrit and Tibetan Buddhism, and stayed several years in Tibet (1934–44).

Davidson, Donald (1917–) Philosopher, born in Springfield, MA. An influential analytical philosopher, he made contributions to the philosophy of language, mind, and action.

Davidson, Jo (1883–1952) Sculptor, born in New York City. He is chiefly known for his sculptured portraits, which include Woodrow Wilson (1916) and Gertrude Stein (1920).

Davidson (of Lambeth), Randall Thomas Davidson, Baron (1848–1930) Anglican clergyman, born in Edinburgh. He became Bishop of Winchester (1895) and Archbishop of Canterbury (1903–28).

Davie, Alan (1920–) Painter, born in Grangemouth, Central, Scotland. His early paintings had much in common with US Abstract Expressionism. Since the early 1970s, his work reflects a preoccupation with oriental mysticism.

Davies, Christian, known as **Mother Ross** (1667–1739) Soldier, born in Dublin. She went to Flanders in search of her soldier husband, Richard Welsh, and enlisted as a private under the name of Christopher Welsh. She fought in the Battle of Blenheim (1704), and was reunited with her husband in 1706.

Davies, Clement (Edward) (1884–1962) British politician, leader of the Liberal Party (1945–56), born in Llanfyllin, Powys, Wales. He declined the post of education secretary in Churchill's 1951–5 government, thereby saving the Liberals from being subsumed in the Conservative Party.

Davies, David Davies, Baron (1880–1944) Philanthropist, born in Llandinam, Powys. He was a major benefactor of the University College of Wales, Aberystwyth, and the National Library of Wales, and in 1933 founded the New Commonwealth Society.

Davies, Sir Henry Walford (1869–1941) Composer, organist, and broadcaster, born in Oswestry, Shropshire. Master of the King's Music (1934–41), he was a prolific composer of religious works, and an influential radio educationist.

Davies, Howard (1945–) Stage director, born in Reading, Berkshire. He became an associate director to establish and run the Warehouse, the Royal Shakespeare Company's London studio theatre (1977–82), and a National Theatre associate director in 1988.

Davies, (Edward) Hunter (1936–) Writer, journalist, and broadcaster, born in Renfrew, Strathclyde. He is well known for his 'Father's Day' column in *Punch* (1979–89, televised 1983), and as presenter of the radio programme *Bookshelf* (1983–6). He has also written novels and much non-fiction. >> Forster, Margaret

Davies, Paul (Charles William) (1946–) British physicist and popularizer of science. His many books, such as *God and the New Physics* (1982), reflect his research interests in particle physics and quantum gravity. He was awarded the Templeton Prize in 1995.

Davies, Sir Peter Maxwell (1934–) Composer, born in Manchester. He founded and co-directed the Pierrot Players (1967–70) and was founder/artistic director of The Fires of London (1971–87). A prolific composer, his works include *Taverner* (1972) and three other operas, symphonies, concertos, songs, and chamber music.

Davies, (William) Robertson (1913–95) Writer and critic, born in Thamesville, Ontario, Canada. He is best known for 'The Deptford Trilogy': *Fifth Business* (1970), *The Manticore* (1972), and *World of Wonders* (1975).

Davies, Sarah Emily (1830–1921) Feminist and educational reformer, born in Southampton, Hampshire. A vigorous campaigner for higher education for women, she founded a college for women students at Hitchin (1869),

which was transferred to Cambridge as Girton College (1873).

Davies, Siobhan [shuhvawn], originally **Susan Davies** (1950–) Dancer and choreographer, born in London. She started her own modern dance company in 1981, joined with Ian Spink to found Second Stride, and in 1988 launched the Siobhan Davies Company. >> Spink

Davies, W(illiam) H(enry) (1871–1940) Poet, born in Newport, Gwent. He lived a wandering life to raise enough money to have his poems printed (1905). Once known, he wrote books of poetry, essays, and a well-known prose work, *The Autobiography of a Super-tramp* (1908).

da Vinci, Leonardo >> **Leonardo da Vinci**

Daviot, Gordon >> **Mackintosh, Elizabeth**

Davis, (Daisie) Adelle (1904–74) Nutritionist and writer, born in Lizton, IN. In 1954 she published *Let's Eat Right to Keep Fit*, which emphasised a proper diet as necessary for emotional and physical well-being.

Davis, Arthur Vining (1867–1962) Industrialist and philanthropist, born in Sharon, MA. He became director of the Aluminum Company of America in 1907, and later president and chairman. He gave most of his $400 million estate to the Davis Foundation, supporting educational, scientific, and cultural institutions.

Davis, Bette, popular name of **Ruth Elizabeth Davis** (1908–89) Film actress, born in Lowell, MA. Her leading roles included *Of Human Bondage* (1934), *Dangerous* (1935, Oscar), *Jezebel* (1938, Oscar), *and Whatever Happened to Baby Jane?* (1962).

Davis, Sir Colin (Rex) (1927–) Conductor, born in Weybridge, Surrey. He was chief conductor of the BBC Symphony Orchestra (1967–71), and musical director at Covent Garden (1971–86) where his production of *The Ring* gained him international standing as a Wagner conductor.

Davis, Dwight F(illey) (1879–1945) Public official, born in St Louis, MO. In 1900 he donated an international challenge cup for lawn tennis, competed for annually. The *Davis Cup* signifies the world team championship.

Davis, Fred >> **Davis, Joe**

Davis, Jack (1917–) Writer and actor, born in Perth, Western Australia. A prominent Aboriginal writer, his poetry and plays draw from the traditions of his own people, the Nyoongarah.

Davis, Jefferson (1808–89) US statesman, president of the Confederate States during the Civil War (1861–5), born in Christian Co, KY. In the US Senate he led the extreme States' Rights Party, supported slavery, and was chosen president of the Confederacy. At the close of the Civil War he was imprisoned for two years, and included in the amnesty of 1868.

Davis, Joe, popular name of **Joseph Davis** (1901–78) Billiards and snooker champion, born in Whitwell, Derbyshire. He inaugurated the World Championship in 1927, and won every title between then and 1946, when he retired from world championship play. His brother, **Fred Davis** (1913–), followed the same career, winning the first of his 10 world titles in 1948.

Davis, John (c.1550–1605) Navigator, born in Sandridge, Devon. In 1585–7 he undertook three Arctic voyages in search of a Northwest Passage, in the last of which he reached 73°N, and discovered the Strait later named after him. He discovered the Falkland Is in 1592.

Davis, Judy (1955–) Actress, born in Perth, Western Australia. She came to international attention in *My Brilliant Career* (1979), and her work in *A Passage to India* (1984) and *Husbands and Wives* (1993) brought her Oscar nominations.

Davis, Miles (Dewey) (1926–91) Trumpeter, composer, and bandleader, born in Alton, IL. He became the most admired instrumentalist of the postwar era, from 1948 leading a nonet that introduced the style known as 'cool jazz', as in 'Round About Midnight' (1955) and 'Milestones' (1958).

Davis, Sammy, Jr (1925–90) Singer, actor, and dancer, born in New York City. He starred on Broadway in *Mr Wonderful* (1956) and in *Golden Boy* (1964), and his films include *Porgy and Bess* (1959), *Robin and the Seven Hoods* (1964), and *Taps* (1980).

Davis, Steve (1957–) Snooker player, born in London. He dominated snooker in the 1980s, winning the world championship six times: 1981, 1983–4, and 1987–9.

Davis, Stuart (1894–1964) Painter and graphic artist, born in Philadelphia, PA. The Armory Show in 1913 converted him to avant-garde French art, especially Cubism. His imitation collages such as 'Lucky Strike' (1921) anticipated Pop Art by 35 years.

Davis, William Morris (1850–1934) Geomorphologist, born in Philadelphia, PA. He was responsible for introducing professional geography into the USA, and formulated the cycle of erosion.

Davison, Emily (1872–1913) Suffragette, born in London. A militant member of the Women's Social and Political Union, she died after an incident during the 1913 Derby, when she tried to catch the reins of the king's horse and was trampled underfoot.

Davisson, Clinton J(oseph) [**day**vison] (1881–1958) Physicist, born in Bloomington, IL. In 1927, with Germer, he discovered the diffraction of electrons by crystals, thus confirming Broglie's theory of the wave properties of electrons. In 1937 he shared the Nobel Prize for Physics. >> Broglie, Louis Victor; Germer

Davitt, Michael [**da**vit] (1846–1906) Founder of the Irish Land League, born in Straid, Co Mayo, Ireland. In 1866 he joined the Fenian Movement, was imprisoned (1870–7) for sending guns to Ireland from the USA, and began an anti-landlord crusade which culminated in the Land League (1879).

Davout, Louis Nicolas [davoo] (1770–1823) French soldier, born in Annoux, France. He accompanied Napoleon to the East, and mainly secured the victory at Aboukir (1799). A marshal of the empire (1804), he fought at Austerlitz (1805), Auerstädt (1806), Eckmühl (1809), Wagram (1809), and in the Russian campaign (1812–13).

Davy, Edward (1806–85) Physician and scientist, born in Ottery St Mary, Devon. He invented the electromagnetic repeater, becoming one of the founders of wireless telegraphy.

Davy, Sir Humphry (1778–1829) Chemist, born in Penzance, Cornwall. He found that chemical compounds could be decomposed into their elements using electricity, and in this way discovered potassium, sodium, barium, strontium, calcium, and magnesium. In 1815 he invented the miner's safety lamp.

Dawes, Charles G(ates) (1865–1951) US vice-president (1925–9) and financier, born in Marietta, OH. He headed the Commission which drew up the *Dawes Plan* (1924) for German reparation payments to Europe after World War 1, for which he shared the Nobel Peace Prize in 1925.

Dawes, Sophie, baronne de (Baroness of) **Feuchères** (1790–1840) Adventuress, born in St Helens, Isle of Wight. A servant in London, she became the mistress of the Duc de Bourbon (1756–1830), who arranged her marriage to the Baron de Feuchères (1818) and bequeathed her a fortune. Suspected of the duke's murder (1830), she was not prosecuted due to lack of evidence.

Dawkins, (Clinton) Richard (1941–) British zoologist. His work on animal behaviour and genetics emphasizes that apparently selfish behaviour is designed to ensure survival of the gene, apparently above that of the carrier.

His works include *The Selfish Gene* (1976) and *River Out of Eden* (1995).

Dawson, Charles (1864–1916) Solicitor and antiquarian, born in Sussex. He was the victim (or perpetrator?) of the celebrated 'Piltdown Man' hoax, when cranial fragments found by him at Piltdown (1908–1912) were accepted as the 'Missing Link' in Darwin's theory of evolution. >> Clark, Wilfred; Darwin, Charles

Dawson, George Mercer (1849–1901) Geologist, born in Pictou, Nova Scotia, Canada. He did much pioneer geological work in British Columbia and the Yukon, where Dawson City was named after him.

Dawson, Peter (1882–1961) Bass-baritone, born in Adelaide, South Australia. A prolific recording artist, he was best known for his ballads, many of which were written by Dawson himself, under the name **J P McColl**.

Day, Doris, originally **Doris Kappelhoff** (1924–) Singer and film actress, born in Cincinnati, OH. Her sunny personality made her a star of many musicals, her films including *Calamity Jane* (1953), *The Pajama Game* (1957), and the comedy *Pillow Talk* (1959), which earned her an Oscar nomination.

Day, Dorothy (1897–1980) Writer and radical social reformer, born in New York City. She founded the Catholic Worker Movement, which established 'houses of hospitality' for people hit by the Depression, and helped turn the Catholic Church's attention to peace and justice issues.

Day, Sir (Judson) Graham (1933–) Business executive, born in Halifax, Nova Scotia, Canada. In 1983 he joined British Shipbuilders as chairman and chief executive, later becoming chairman of the Rover Group (1986), Cadbury Schweppes (1989), and Power Gen (1990).

Day, John (1522–84) Printer, born in Dunwich, Suffolk. His most celebrated publication was John Foxe's *Actes and Monuments* (1563), better kown as the *Book of Martyrs*. >> Foxe, John

Day, Sir Robin (1923–) Journalist and broadcaster, born in London. He presented BBC television's *Panorama* (1967–72) and *Question Time* (1979–89), bringing an acerbic freshness to interviewing techniques, and proving a formidable inquisitor of political figures.

Dayan, Moshe [diyan] (1915–81) Israeli general and statesman, born at Deganya, Palestine. He won international acclaim as defence minister in 1967 when his heavily outnumbered forces triumphed over Egypt, Jordan, and Syria in the Six Day War. As foreign minister, he helped to secure the historic peace treaty with Egypt (1977).

Day-Lewis, C(ecil) (1904–72) Poet, born in Ballintubber, Co Kildare, Ireland. During the 1930s he was known as a leading left-wing writer. His *Collected Poems* appeared in 1954, and he became Poet Laureate in 1968. He also wrote detective stories under the pseudonym of **Nicholas Blake**. His son **Daniel Day-Lewis** (1958–) is a well-known film actor.

Deák, Francis [dayak] (1803–76) Hungarian statesman, born in Zala (formerly Söjtör), Hungary. Hailed in 1861 as leader in the Diet, by his efforts Hungary's constitution was restored in 1867 and the dual monarchy of Austria–Hungary established.

Deakin, Alfred (1856–1919) Australian Liberal prime minister (1903–4, 1905–8, 1909–10), born in Melbourne, Victoria, Australia. One of the architects of federation, he established the industrial arbitration system, and advocated the White Australia policy.

Deakin, Arthur (1890–1955) Trade union leader, born in Sutton Coldfield, Warwickshire. In 1945 he became general secretary of the Transport and General Workers Union, and president of the World Federation of Trade Unions.

Dean, Christopher >> **Torvill and Dean**

Dean, Dixie, popular name of **William Ralph Dean** (1907–80) Footballer, born in Birkenhead, Merseyside. He joined Everton in 1925, and scored 349 goals in 399 games. He still holds the scoring record of 60 League goals in one season.

Dean, James (Byron) (1931–55) Film actor, born in Marion, IN. He gained overnight success in the film *East of Eden* (1955), and made only two more films, *Rebel Without a Cause* (1955) and *Giant* (1956), before his early death in a car crash turned him into a cult figure.

Dean, Laura (1945–) Dancer, choreographer, and teacher, born in New York City. She danced in Paul Taylor's company (1965–6), and began choreographing in 1967, forming Laura Dean Dancers and Musicians in 1976. >> Taylor, Paul

Deane, Silas (1737–89) Diplomat and legislator, born in Groton, CT. The first diplomat sent abroad by the united colonies, he was recalled from France following accusations of disloyalty and embezzlement, and although these were never proved (and were dismissed by an enquiry in 1842), his career was ended.

Déat, Marcel [dayah] (1894–1955) French statesman, born in Guerigny, France. Founder of the Socialist Party of France (1933), his pro-Nazi sympathies procured him the post of minister of labour in the Vichy government, and he achieved notoriety by his ruthless deportation of French workers to Germany.

DeBakey, Michael (Ellis) [debaykee] (1908–) Cardiovascular surgeon, born in Lake Charles, LA. At the Baylor University College of Medicine in Houston, TX, he helped to develop a leading centre of cardiovascular surgery.

de Bary, Heinrich Anton [duh baree] (1831–88) Botanist, born in Frankfurt, Germany. He studied the morphology and physiology of the fungi and the Myxomycetae, and is recognized as the founder of modern mycology.

de Basil, Colonel Wassili [duh bazil, vasilee], originally **Vasily Grigorievich Voskresensky** (1881–1951) Ballet impresario, born in Kaunas, Lithuania. In 1932 he and René Blum co-founded the Ballet Russe de Monte Carlo, heir to Diaghilev's Ballets Russes. >> Blum, René; Diaghilev

Debayle, Anastasio / Luis >> Somoza, Anastasio

de Beauvoir, Simone [duh bohvwah(r)] (1908–86) Existentialist writer, born in Paris. Closely associated with Sartre, her works provide existentialism with an essentially feminine sensibility, notably in *The Second Sex* (trans, 1949) and her masterpiece *Les Mandarins* (1954, Prix Goncourt). >> Sartre

de Beer, Sir Gavin (Rylands) [duh beer] (1899–1972) Zoologist, born in London. His work refuted some early theories in embryology, and he went on to contribute to theories of animal evolution, as well as to historical problems such as the origin of the Etruscans.

de Bono, Edward (Francis Charles Publius) [duh bohnoh] (1933–) Psychologist and writer, born in Malta. He is involved with various organizations to promote the skills of thinking which break out of the limitations of the traditional (*lateral thinking*). His books include *The Use of Lateral Thinking* (1967) and *I Am Right, You Are Wrong* (1990).

de Bono, Emilio [duh bohnoh] (1866–1944) Fascist politician and general, born in Cassano d'Adda, Italy. He served in Mussolini's March on Rome (1922), and commanded the Italian forces invading Abyssinia (1935), but voted against Mussolini in the Fascist Supreme Council (1943), and was executed. >> Mussolini

Debray, Regis [duhbray] (1941–) French Marxist theorist. He gained international fame through his association with Che Guevara during the 1960s, was jailed in Bolivia (1967–70), and later advised President Mitterrand

on Third World affairs (1981). His books include *Strategy for Revolution* (1970). >> Guevara; Mitterand

Debrett, John [duhbret] (c.1750–1822) British publisher. He took over a publishing house in London in 1781, and compiled his *Peerage of England, Scotland and Ireland*, which first appeared in 1802.

Debreu, Gerard [debroe] (1921–) Economist, born in Calais, France. For his work on the equilibrium between prices, production, and consumer demand in a free-market economy, he received the Nobel Prize for Economics in 1983.

de Broglie, Louis >> Broglie, Louis Victor, duc de

Debs, Eugene V(ictor) (1855–1926) US politician, born in Terre Haute, IN. In 1893 he became president of the American Railroad Union, helped establish the Socialist Party of America, and stood five times as socialist candidate for president (1900–20).

Deburau, Jean-Gaspard [debüroh], originally **Jan Kaspar Dvorak** (1796–1846) Mime artist, born in Kolín, Czech Republic. He joined the Théâtre des Funambules in Paris (1816), and popularized the character of Pierrot as a pale-faced hero.

Debussy, Claude (Achille) [debüsee] (1862–1918) Composer, born in St Germain-en-Laye, France. His early successes, notably *Prelude to the Afternoon of a Faun* (trans, 1894) and the piano pieces, *Images* and *Préludes*, led to his work being described as 'musical Impressionism', seen also in such orchestral music as *The Sea* (trans, 1905).

Debye, Peter (Joseph Wilhelm) [duhbiy] (1884–1966) Physicist, born in Maastricht, The Netherlands. He worked on molecular structure and X-ray powder photography, and in 1936 was awarded the Nobel Prize for Chemistry.

Decamps, Alexandre Gabriel [duhkã] (1803–60) Painter, born in Paris. A pioneer of the Romantic school, he specialized in Oriental scenes and biblical subjects.

Decatur, Stephen [deekayter] (1779–1820) US naval commander, born in Sinepuxent, MD. In the War of 1812, he led the USS *United States* to victory over HMS *Macedonian* (1812), but surrendered to the British (1815). He was killed in a duel with Barron. >> Barron

Decius [deeshus], in full **Caius Messius Quintus Trajanus Decius** (c.200–251) Roman emperor, born in Lower Pannonia. After being proclaimed emperor against his will, he killed Emperor Philip, warred with the Goths, and persecuted Christians with great severity.

Decroux, Etienne-Marcel [duhkroo] (1898–1991) French actor. He was responsible for the renaissance of mime in the 20th-c by developing and teaching a system of physical expression he termed *mime corporel*.

Dedekind, (Julius Wilhelm) Richard [daydekind] (1831–1916) Mathematician, born in Braunschweig, Germany. He gave one of the first precise definitions of the real number system, worked in number theory, and introduced many concepts which have become fundamental in modern algebra.

de Duve, Christian (René) [duh düv] (1917–) Biochemist, born in Thames Ditton, Surrey. He had a major part in discovering the lysosomes which contain the enzymes within animal and plant cells, and shared the Nobel Prize for Physiology or Medicine in 1974.

Dee, John (1527–1608) Alchemist, geographer, and mathematician, born in London. He travelled widely in Europe, and brought back many astronomical instruments, earning a reputation as a sorcerer.

Deeping, (George) Warwick (1877–1950) Novelist, born in Southend, Essex. His early novels were mainly historical, and he did not gain recognition until the success of *Sorrell and Son* (1925).

Deere, John (1804–86) Inventor and manufacturer, born in Rutland, VT. He designed the first cast steel plough, a major advance that made it substantially easier to farm the heavy soil of the Great Plains.

Defoe, Daniel [de**foh**] (1660-1731) Writer, born in London. Known for his political pamphleteering, he achieved lasting fame with *Robinson Crusoe* (1719-20). His other major works include *A Journal of the Plague Year*, *Moll Flanders* (both 1722), and *Roxana* (1724).

De Forest, Lee [di **fo**rist] (1873-1961) Inventor, born in Council Bluffs, IA. A pioneer of radio, he introduced the grid into the thermionic valve, and invented the Audion and the four-electrode valve.

Degas, (Hilaire Germain) Edgar [**day**gah, duh**gah**] (1834-1917) Artist, born in Paris. He associated with the Impressionists and took part in most of their exhibitions from 1874 to 1886. Among his best-known works are 'Dancer Lacing her Shoe' (c.1878, Paris) and 'Jockeys in the Rain' (1879).

de Gasperi, Alcide >> Gasperi, Alcide de

de Gaulle, Charles (André Joseph Marie) [duh gohl] (1890-1970) French general and first president of the Fifth Republic (1958-69), born in Lille, France. With the fall of France, he fled to England to raise the standard of the 'Free French', and led a liberation force into Paris in 1944. As president he practised a high-handed yet successful foreign policy, repeatedly surviving political crises by the use of the referendum. He developed an independent French nuclear deterrent, granted independence to former colonies, signed a historic reconciliation treaty with West Germany, and blocked Britain's entry into the Common Market.

de Havilland, Sir Geoffrey [duh **h**aviland] (1882-1965) Aircraft designer, born in Haslemere, Surrey. He built his first plane in 1908 and became director of the firm bearing his name, producing such aircraft as the Tiger Moth, Mosquito, and Vampire jet.

Dehmel, Richard [**day**mel] (1863-1920) Poet, born in Brandenburg, Germany. His works include *Woman and World* (trans, 1896) and *Beautiful, Wild World* (trans, 1913).

Dehmelt, Hans G(eorg) [duh**melt**] (1922-) Physicist, born in Goerlitz, Germany. A pioneer in the field of particle physics, he shared the 1989 Nobel Prize for Physics for his work on trapping and separating ions and subatomic particles.

Deighton, Len [**day**tn], popular name of **Leonard Cyril Deighton** (1929-) Thriller writer, born in London. A leading author of spy novels, notable titles are *The Ipcress File* (1962), *Funeral in Berlin* (1964), and the trilogy *Berlin Game* (1984), *Mexico Set* (1985), and *London Match* (1986).

Dekker, Thomas (c.1570-c.1641) Playwright, born in London. His best-known works are the comedy, *The Shoemaker's Holiday* (1600) and *The Honest Whore* (1604; part II, 1630).

de Klerk, F(rederick) W(illem) [duh **klairk**] (1936-) South African president (1989-94), born in Johannesburg, South Africa. He set about the dismantling of apartheid, releasing Nelson Mandela (1990), and signing a new constitutional agreement with him (1993), for which both men were awarded the Nobel Peace Prize. In 1994 he became vice-president in the Mandela administration. >> Mandela

de Kooning, Willem or **William** [duh **koo**ning] (1904-) Painter, born in Rotterdam, The Netherlands. He emigrated to the USA in 1926, and by the 1950s had emerged as a leader of the Abstract Expressionist movement.

Delacroix, (Ferdinand Victor) Eugène [duhla**krwah**] (1798-1863) Painter, born in Charenton, France. A leader of the Romantic movement, his later work left traditional treatment for historical and dramatic scenes, often violent or macabre in subject, such as 'Liberty Guiding the People' (1831).

Delafield, E M, pseudonym of **Edmée Elizabeth Monica**

Dashwood, *née* **de la Pasture** (1890-1943) Novelist, born in Llandogo, Gwent. She was the author of several novels, and a series beginning with *Diary of a Provincial Lady* (1931).

de la Mare, Walter (John) [mair] (1873-1956) Writer, born in Charlton, Kent. Among his best-known works are the prose romance *Henry Brocken* (1904), the poetic collection *The Listeners* (1912), and his fantastic novel *Memoirs of a Midget* (1921).

de la Renta, Oscar (1932-) Fashion designer, born in Santo Domingo, Dominican Republic. In 1965 he started his own company, producing opulent, ornately trimmed clothes, particularly evening dresses, and also day wear and accessories.

de la Roche, Mazo [rosh] (1885-1961) Novelist, born in Newmarket, Ontario, Canada. She wrote *Jalna* (1927), the first of a series of novels about the Whiteoak family. *Whiteoaks* (1929) was dramatized with much success.

Delaroche, (Hippolyte) Paul [duhla**rosh**] (1797-1856) Painter, born in Paris. A master of large historical subject painting, his major work was the series of murals for the Ecole des Beaux-Arts.

de la Rue, Warren [duh la **roo**] (1815-89) Astronomer and physicist, born in Guernsey. He invented the silver chloride battery and researched the discharge of electricity in gases. A pioneer of celestial photography, he invented the photoheliograph.

De La Salle, Jean Baptiste >> La Salle, St Jean Baptiste de

de la Tour, Georges >> La Tour, Georges de

de la Tour, Maurice Quentin >> La Tour, Maurice Quentin de

Delaunay, Robert [duhloh**nay**] (1885-1941) Painter, born in Paris. He was associated with *Der Blaue Reiter* (1911-12), but is chiefly known as the co-founder of Orphism. >> Delaunay, Sonia

Delaunay, Sonia (Terk) [duhloh**nay**], *née* **Stern** (1885-1979) Painter and textile designer, born in Ukraine. In 1910 she married Robert Delaunay, with whom she founded the Orphism movement. In 1918 they designed sets and costumes for Diaghilev, and she became a textile designer of international importance. >> Delauney, Robert; Diaghilev

de la Warr, Thomas West, 12th Baron [waw(r)] (1577-1618) English soldier and colonist. He became the first governor of Virginia in 1610, and the state of Delaware is named after him.

Delbrück, Max [del**brük**] (1906-81) Biophysicist, born in Berlin. He helped to create bacterial and bacteriophage genetics, and to inspire early work in biophysics and molecular biology, sharing the Nobel Prize for Physiology or Medicine in 1969. >> Hershey; Luria, Salvador

Delcassé, Théophile [delka**say**] (1852-1923) French foreign minister (1898-1905, 1914-15), born in Pamiers, France. He promoted the *entente cordiale* with Britain, which was the basis of the Allied coalition in World War 1.

de Leon, Daniel [duh **lee**on] (1852-1914) Radical socialist, born in Curaçao, Netherlands Antilles. He emigrated to the USA in 1874, founding the Socialist Trade and Labor Alliance (1895), and helping to form the Industrial Workers of the World (1905).

Delescluze, (Louis) Charles [duhlay**klüz**] (1809-71) French radical Republican and journalist, born in Dreux, France. His writing was popular, but brought him imprisonment, and transportation. He played a prominent part in the Paris Commune, and died on the last barricade.

Delfont (of Stepney), Bernard >> Grade, Lew

Delibes, (Clément Philibert) Léo [duh**leeb**] (1836-91) Composer, born in St Germain du Val, France. He wrote light operas, of which *Lakmé* had the greatest success, but he is chiefly remembered for the ballet *Coppélia* (1870).

Delille, Jacques [duhleel] (1738–1813) Poet, born near Aigues-Perse, France. Highly regarded by his contemporaries, *The Gardens* (trans, 1782), a didactic poem, was generally accepted as his masterpiece.

de Lisle, Leconte >> **Leconte de Lisle, Charles Marie René**

de Lisle, Rouget >> **Rouget de Lisle, Claude Joseph**

Delius, Frederick [deelius] (1862–1934) Composer, born in Bradford, West Yorkshire, of German–Scandinavian descent. After 1890 he lived almost entirely in France. He wrote six operas, including *A Village Romeo and Juliet* (1901), and a variety of choral and orchestral works, notably *On Hearing the First Cuckoo in Spring* (1912). In 1924 he became paralysed and blind, but with the assistance of Eric Fenby (1906–), his amanuensis from 1928, he continued to compose.

Dell, Floyd (James) (1887–1969) Writer, editor, and social critic, born in Barry, IL. Much involved in the 'Chicago Renaissance', he moved to Greenwich village in 1913, where he edited *Masses* (1914–17), the *Liberator* (1918–24), and *New Masses* (1924–9), and wrote a series of novels.

della Casa, Lisa [dela kahza] (1919–) Soprano, born in Burgdorf, Switzerland. She sang with the Vienna State Opera Company, and was a specialist in the operas of Richard Strauss, singing all three soprano roles in *Der Rosenkavalier*. >> Strauss, Richard

della Robbia, Luca >> **Robbia, Luca della**

Deller, Alfred (George) (1912–79) Countertenor, born in Margate, Kent. He made many recordings of early English songs, and in 1950 formed the *Deller Consort*, devoted to the authentic performance of early music.

De Long, George Washington (1844–81) Arctic explorer, born in New York City. In 1879 he tried to reach the North Pole via the Bering Strait, but was forced to abandon his ship, and travelled 300 mi by sledge and boat to the Siberian coast. Only two of his crew reached safety.

Delorme, Marion [duhlaw(r)m] (1613–50) Courtesan, born in Paris. Her high-born lovers included Richelieu and the Marquis de Cinq-Mars, and her house was a rallying-point for leaders in the Fronde uprising (from 1648). >> Richelieu

Delorme, Philibert [duhlaw(r)m] (c.1510–70) Architect, born in Lyon, France. Royal architect to Henry II (of France), he built the Tuileries for Catherine de' Medici, as well as several chateaux. >> Catherine de' Medici

de Lorris, Guillaume [duh loris] >> **Guillaume de Lorris**

Delors, Jacques [duhlaw(r)] (1925–) French and European statesman, born in Paris. He joined the Socialist Party in 1973, served as minister of economy and finance under Mitterrand (1981–4), and was elected President of the European Commission (1985–95). >> Mitterrand

de los Angeles, Victoria >> **Angeles, Victoria de los**

Delvaux, Paul [delvoh] (1897–1994) Surrealist painter, born in Antheit, Belgium. He produced a series of paintings depicting nude and semi-nude girls in dreamlike settings, such as 'The Call of the Night'.

Demades [demadeez] (c.380–319 BC) Athenian orator and politician. He supported Philip II of Macedon, and after the Battle of Chaeronea (338 BC) secured an honourable peace. He procured the death of Demosthenes, but was himself executed by Cassander. >> Demosthenes (c.383–322 BC); Philip II (of Macedon)

de Man, Paul [man] (1919–83) Cultural theorist, born in Belgium. He emigrated to the USA, where he became a leading exponent of *deconstruction*. His most important essays were published in *Blindness and Insight* (1971) and *Allegories of Reading* (1979).

Demarco, Richard [demah(r)koh] (1930–) Artist, broadcaster, and teacher, born in Edinburgh. A leading promoter of modern art in Scotland, especially at the Edinburgh Festival since 1967, he has presented annual programmes of theatre, music, and dance.

de Mestral, Georges [duh mestral] (1907–90) Swiss engineer. After studying the way burrs attach themselves to clothes, he developed a method of fastening using nylon in 1956 (*Velcro*).

Demetrius (Russian prince) >> **Dmitri**

De Mille, Agnes [duh mil] (1905–93) Dancer, choreographer, and writer, born in New York City, the niece of film director Cecil B De Mille. She became best known for her choreography for musicals such as *Oklahoma!* (1943) and *Carousel* (1945). >> De Mille, Cecil B

De Mille, Cecil B(lount) [duh mil] (1881–1959) Film producer and director, born in Ashfield, MA. He gained a reputation for box-office spectacles with such films as *The Ten Commandments* (1923, remade 1957), *The Plainsman* (1937), and *The Greatest Show on Earth* (1952).

Demirel, Süleyman [demirel] (1924–) Turkish prime minister (1965–71, 1974–7, 1979–80, 1991–3) and president (1993–), born in Islam Kömy, Turkey. A military coup in 1980 brought a ban on political activity, and he was placed in detention until 1983.

de Mita, (Luigi) Ciriaco [duh meeta] (1928–) Italian prime minister (1988–9), born in Fusco, Italy. He held a number of ministerial posts in the 1970s, and in 1982 became secretary-general of the Christian Democratic Party.

Democritus [demokritus] (c.460–370 BC) Greek philosopher, born in Abdera, Thrace. By far the most learned thinker of his time, he is best known for his *atomic system*, derived from Leucippus, and later popularized by Epicurus and Lucretius. >> Epicurus; Leucippus; Lucretius

de Moivre, Abraham [duh mwahvruh] (1667–1754) Mathematician, born in Vitry, France. His chief work is *The Doctrine of Chances* (1718) on probability theory, but he is best remembered for the fundamental formula on complex numbers known as de Moivre's theorem.

De Morgan, Augustus (1806–71) Mathematician, born in Madura, India. He helped to develop the notion of different kinds of algebra, and collaborated with Boole in the development of symbolic logic. >> Boole

de Morgan, William (Frend) (1839–1917) Pre-Raphaelite ceramic artist and novelist, born in London, the son of Augustus de Morgan. He designed tiles and stained glass, established a pottery kiln in Chelsea (1871), and at the age of 65 began writing novels, such as *Joseph Vance* (1906). >> de Morgan, Augustus

Demosthenes [demostheneez] (?–413 BC) Athenian soldier. During the Peloponnesian Wars (431–404 BC) he captured Anacterium (425 BC) but failed to conquer Boeotia. In 413 BC, he was sent to Sicily, but was captured by the Syracusans and killed.

Demosthenes [demostheneez] (c.383–322 BC) The greatest of the Greek orators. He gained prominence in 351 BC with the first of a series of speeches (the 'First Philippic') advocating resistance to Philip of Macedon. Swayed by his oratory, the Athenians did eventually go to war (340 BC), only to be defeated at Chaeronea (338 BC). Put on trial, he vindicated himself in his oratorical masterpiece, *On the Crown*, but was forced to commit suicide after the failure of the Athenian revolt from Macedon. >> Philip II (of Macedon)

Dempsey, Jack, popular name of **William Harrison Dempsey**, nickname **the Manassa Mauler** (1895–1983) World heavyweight champion boxer, born in Manassa, CO. In 1919 he defeated Jess Willard to win the world heavyweight title, which he lost to Gene Tunney in 1926. >> Tunney

Demuth, Charles [demooth] (1883–1935) Painter and book illustrator, born in Lancaster, PA. From 1919 he was a major exponent of 'Precisionism', with its hard outlines and semi-abstract treatment of industrial or urban scenery, as seen in 'My Egypt' (1927).

Dench, Judi, popular name of **Dame Judith Olivia Dench** (1934–) Actress, born in York, North Yorkshire. A member of the Old Vic Company (1957–61), she became a distinguished classical actress. Her films include *A Handful of Dust* (1987) and *Henry V* (1989).

Denck, Hans (c.1495–c.1527) Anabaptist theologian, born in Habach, Germany. From 1524 he preached a doctrine resembling Evangelical Quakerism in various parts of Germany, and became a leader of the Anabaptists in Augsburg.

Deneuve, Cathérine [duh**noev**], originally **Cathérine Dorléac** (1943–) Actress, born in Paris. She became well known through the musical *The Umbrellas of Cherbourg* (trans, 1964), later films including *Repulsion* (1965), *Belle de Jour* (1967), and *The Last Metro* (trans, 1980).

Deng Xiaoping [duhng syowping], or **Teng Hsiao-p'ing** (1902–) Leader of the Chinese Communist Party, born in Sichuan province, China. In 1954 he became secretary-general of the Chinese Communist Party, reacted strongly against the excesses of the Great Leap Forward (1958–9), and was purged by Mao Zedong (1966). Restored to power in 1974, he later took China through a rapid course of pragmatic reforms. >> Mao Zedong

Denham, Dixon [**den**am] (1786–1828) British soldier, and African traveller, born in London. He joined an expedition to discover the source of the Niger, reaching L Chad in 1823. *Denham's bustard* was named after him.

Denham, Sir John [**den**am] (1615–69) Poet, born in Dublin. His best-known works were the tragedy, *The Sophy* (1641), and his descriptive poem, *Cooper's Hill* (1642).

Denikin, Anton Ivanovich [**den**ikin] (1872–1947) Russian soldier, born near Warsaw, Poland. He led the White Army in the S against the Bolsheviks (1918–20), won the Ukraine, but was defeated by the Red Army at Orel (1919).

De Niro, Robert [duh **nee**roh] (1943–) Actor and director, born in New York City. His films include *The Godfather, Part II* (1974, Oscar), *Taxi Driver* (1976), *The Deerhunter* (1978), *Raging Bull* (1980, Oscar), and *The Awakening* (1990). He made his directorial debut with *A Bronx Tale* (1993).

Denis or **Denys, St** [**den**is], Fr [duhnee] (3rd-c), feast day 9 October. Traditional apostle of France, and the first Bishop of Paris, possibly born in Rome. Sent from Rome c.250 to preach the Gospel to the Gauls, he was martyred at Paris under Valerian. >> Valerian

Denis, Julio >> Cortazar, Julio

Denis, Maurice [duhnee] (1870–1943) Artist and art theorist, born in Grandville, France. One of the original group of Symbolist painters, *Les Nabis*, he helped to found the Studios of Sacred Art (1919), devoted to the revival of religious painting.

Denness, Mike [de**nes**], popular name of **Michael Denness** (1940–) Cricketer, born in Bellshill, Strathclyde. He captained England, and in his first-class career made over 25 000 runs and hit four Test centuries.

Denning (of Whitchurch), Alfred Thompson Denning, Baron (1899–) British judge, born in Whitchurch, Hampshire. As Master of the Rolls (1962–82) he was responsible for many often controversial decisions. Among his books are *The Road to Justice* (1955) and *What Next in the Law* (1982).

Dennis, John (1657–1734) Critic and playwright, born in London. A man of fashion, he produced biting criticism to support the Whigs, but his plays were less successful.

Denny-Brown, Derek (Ernest) (1901–81) Neurologist, born in Christchurch, New Zealand. He went to Harvard in 1941, where he researched diseases of the basal ganglia and of the muscles.

Dent, Edward Joseph (1876–1957) Musicologist, born in Yorkshire. He made translations of many libretti, wrote an opera, and published lives of Scarlatti, Busoni, and Handel.

Dent, Joseph (Mallaby) (1849–1926) Publisher, born in Darlington, Durham. In 1888 he founded the publishing house of J M Dent & Sons, which brought out the pocket-sized *Temple Classics* (from 1893) and *Everyman's Library* (from 1904).

Deodoro da Fonseca, Manuel [dayo**doo**roo da fon**say**ka] (1827–92) Brazilian general and president (1889–91), born in Alagoas province, Brazil. He headed the revolt that overthrew Emperor Pedro II, and instituted the republic.

Départdieu, Gérard [daypah(r)dyoe] (1948–) Actor, born in Châteauroux, France. His films include *Danton* (1982), *Jean de Florette* (1986), *Cyrano de Bergerac* (1990), and *Green Card* (1990). He also directed himself in *Le Tartuffe* (1984).

Depew, Chauncey Mitchell [duh**pyoo**] (1834–1928) Lawyer, businessman, and public official, born in Peekskill, NY. He became president of the New York Central Railroad in 1885, served in the US Senate (1899–1911), and became known as an orator and after-dinner wit.

De Priest, Oscar Stanton [duh **preest**] (1871–1951) US politician, born in Florence, AL. A Republican realtor, he became the first black member of the City Council (1915–17), resigning because of alleged mob connections, then fought against Jim Crow laws in the US House of Representatives (1929–35).

de Quincey, Thomas [duh **kwin**see] (1785–1859) Writer, born in Manchester. He met Coleridge, and through him Southey and Wordsworth, and in 1809 went to live near them in Grasmere. His *Confessions of an Opium-Eater* appeared as a serial in 1821. >> Coleridge, Samuel Taylor; Southey; Wordsworth

Derain, André [duhrī] (1880–1954) Artist, born in Chatou, France. Best known for his Fauvist landscape pictures (1904–8), he also designed for the theatre, notably the Diaghilev ballet. >> Diaghilev

Derby, Edward Geoffrey Smith Stanley, 14th Earl of [**dah**(r)bee] (1799–1869) British prime minister (1852, 1858–9, 1866–8), born at Knowsley Hall, Lancashire. He entered parliament as a Whig in 1828, and became chief-secretary for Ireland (1830), and colonial secretary (1833), then joined the Conservatives and became party leader (1846–8). His third administration passed the Reform Bill (1867).

Derby, James Stanley, 7th Earl of [**dah**(r)bee], known as **the Great Earl of Derby** (1606–51) English soldier, born in Knowsley, Merseyside. After the Battle of Worcester in 1651, he helped Charles II to escape, but was himself captured by the Parliamentary forces and beheaded at Bolton. >> Charles II (of England)

Deringer, Henry [**de**rinjer] (1786–1868) Manufacturer of small arms, born in Philadelphia, PA. He supplied rifles to the US army, and in 1852 invented the pocket pistol named after him (later spelled *derringer*).

Dernesch, Helga [**der**nesh] (1939–) Operatic soprano, born in Vienna. Specially noted for her portrayals of Wagner, Strauss, and the modern German repertory, since 1979 she has sung mezzo-soprano roles.

Derrida, Jacques [**de**rida] (1930–) French philosopher-linguist, born in Algeria. His critique of the referentiality of language and the objectivity of structures founded the school of criticism called *deconstruction*. His works include (trans titles) *Of Grammatology* (1967) and *Dissemination* (1972).

Dershowitz, Alan M(orton) [**der**shovitz] (1938–) Lawyer and writer, born in New York City. He became one of the nation's leading defence and appeal lawyers, taking on cases involving issues of civil liberties or constitutional rights. An outspoken critic of the legal system, he wrote *The Best Defense* (1982).

de Ruyter, Michiel Adriaanszoon >> Ruyter, Michiel Adriaanszoon de

Derzhavin, Gavril Romanovich [dairzhavin] (1743–1816) Poet, born in Kazan, Russia. He published much lyric poetry, and is considered one of Russia's greatest poets. He was also secretary of state (1791), imperial treasurer (1800), and minister of justice (1802).

Desaguliers, John Theophilus [dayzagülyay] (1683–1744) Scientist and inventor, born in La Rochelle, France. He proposed a scheme for heating vessels by steam instead of fire, and improved the design of Savery's steam engine. >> Savery

Desai, Anita [desiy], *née* Mazumdar (1937–) Writer, born in Mussoorie, India. Her works include *Clear Light of Day* (1980), *In Custody* (1980), and the children's novel *The Village by the Sea* (1982).

Desai, Morarji (Ranchhodji) [daysiy] (1896–) Indian prime minister (1977–9), born in Gujarat. Deputy prime minister in 1969, he led the Opposition Congress Party, was detained during the state of emergency (1975–7), then appointed leader of the newly-formed Janata Party.

Desalvo, Albert [desalvoh] (?–1973) Convicted US sex offender. After his arrest in 1964 for sex attacks, he confessed to being the Boston Strangler who had murdered 13 women between 1962 and 1964 in Boston, MA. He was found stabbed to death in his cell.

Desani, Govindas (Vishnoodas) [desahnee] (1909–) Novelist, born in Nairobi, Kenya. In Britain from 1926, and a US citizen from 1979, his best-known work is *All About H Hatterr* (1948), which has been resurrected as a modern classic.

Desargues, Girard [dayzah(r)g] (1591–1661) Mathematician, born in Lyon, France. He founded the use of projective methods in geometry, and introduced the notion that parallel lines 'meet at a point at infinity'.

Descartes, René [daykah(r)t], Lat Renatius Cartesius (1596–1650) Rationalist philosopher and mathematician, born in La Haye, France. His task was to refound human knowledge on a basis secure from scepticism, expounded in the *Meditations on First Philosophy* (trans, 1641) - a work which introduced his famous principle that one cannot doubt one's own existence as a thinking being, *cogito ergo sum* ('I think, therefore I am'). He virtually founded coordinate or analytic geometry, and made major contributions to optics.

Deschamps, Eustache [dayshã], known as Morel (c.1345–c.1406) Poet, born in Vertus, France. He composed many lyrics, besides *Le Miroir de mariage*, a long poem satirizing women, and the first treatise on French versification.

de Sica, Vittorio [seeka] (1901–74) Actor and film director, born in Sora, Italy. A romantic star of Italian stage and screen in the 1930s, he became a director in 1940, achieving international success in the neo-Realist style with (trans titles) *Shoeshine* (1946) and *Bicycle Thieves* (1948).

Desiderio da Settignano [dezideryoh da setinyahnoh] (c.1428–61) Sculptor, born in Settignano, Italy. He worked in the early Renaissance style, producing many notable portrait busts of women and children.

Desmarets, Jean, Sieur de (Lord of) Saint-Sorlin [daymaray] (1595–1676) Writer, born in Paris. He wrote many volumes of poetry and critical works, notably *Comparison of the French Language and Poetry with That of Greek and Latin* (1670, trans title).

Desmond, Gerald Fitzgerald, 15th Earl of (c.1538–83) Irish Catholic nobleman. He rebelled (1579–80) against Queen Elizabeth I, sacked Youghal by night, and was proclaimed a traitor. He was later killed in the Kerry Mts.

Desmond, Paul, originally Paul Breitenfeld (1924–77) Jazz alto saxophonist, born in San Francisco, CA. A member of the Dave Brubeck quartet (1951–67), his tune 'Take Five' (1959) is one of the great successes of modern jazz. >> Brubeck

Desmoulins, (Lucie Simplice) Camille (Benoist) [daymoolĩ] (1760–94) French revolutionary and journalist, born in Guise, France. A member of the Cordeliers' Club, he was elected to the National Convention, and voted for the death of the king. He actively attacked the Girondists, but then argued for moderation, and was guillotined.

de Soto, Hernando or Fernando [duh sohtoh] (c.1496–1542) Spanish explorer, born in Jerez de los Caballeros, Spain. In 1539 he entered Florida and crossed the Mississippi (1541), but died of a fever on its banks.

Despard, Charlotte, *née* French (1844–1939) Social reformer, a sister of John French. She was an advocate of women's rights and Irish self-determination. >> French, John

Despenser, Hugh [despenser] (1262–1326) English baron. Chief adviser to Edward I, he was banished in 1321, then recalled by Edward II. After Queen Isabella's landing in England (1326), he was hanged at Bristol. >> Edward II; Isabella of France

Despiau, Charles [despyoh] (1874–1946) Sculptor, born in Mont-de-Marsan, France. Discovered by Rodin, he is noted for his severely Neoclassical portrait busts.

des Prés / Prez, Josquin >> Josquin des Prez

Dessalines, Jean Jacques [desaleen] (c.1758–1806) Emperor of Haiti (1804–6), born a slave probably in Grande Rivière du Nord, Saint Domingue (Haiti). Following the slave insurrection of 1791, he was crowned emperor as Jacques I, but later assassinated. >> Toussaint L'Ouverture

Dessau, Paul [desow] (1894–1979) Composer and conductor, born in Hamburg, Germany. From 1942 he collaborated with Brecht, writing incidental music for *Mother Courage* and other plays. >> Brecht

Deutscher, Isaac [doycher] (1907–67) Marxist historian of Russia, born in Cracow, Poland. His great biography of Trotsky appeared in three volumes: *The Prophet Armed* (1954), *The Prophet Unarmed* (1959), and *The Prophet Outcast* (1963). >> Trotsky

de Valera, Eamon [devalayra] (1882–1975) Irish prime minister (1932–48, 1951–4, 1957–9) and president (1959–73), born in New York City. A commandant in the 1916 rising, he became leader of Sinn Féin (1917–26), was elected president of Dáil Eireann, and in 1926 became leader of Fianna Fáil.

Devant, David >> Maskelyne, John Nevil

Devereux, Robert >> Essex, Robert Devereux, 2nd / 3rd Earl of

Devine, George (Alexander Cassidy) (1910–65) Actor and theatre director, born in Hendon, Greater London. He helped to found the London Theatre Studio (1936–9) and in 1956 became artistic director of the newly formed English Stage Company at the Royal Court Theatre.

Devlin, Bernadette >> McAliskey, Bernadette

Devlin, Joseph (1872–1934) Irish politician, born in Belfast. An Ulster Catholic, he became a Nationalist MP in 1902, and after 1920 was a member of the Stormont parliament at various times.

Devlin (of West Wick), Patrick Arthur Devlin, Baron (1905–92) British judge. He was made a Lord Justice of Appeal in 1960 and a Lord of Appeal in Ordinary in 1961, before retiring in 1964. Among his many publications are *Trial by Jury* (1956) and *The Judge* (1979).

DeVoto, Bernard (Augustine) [devohtoh] (1897–1955) Writer, critic, and historian, born in Ogden, UT. His works include three surveys of the exploration of the American West, and an edition of the journals of Lewis and Clark (1953). >> Clark, William; Lewis, Meriwether

Devoy, John [de**voy**] (1842–1928) Journalist and nationalist, born in Kill, Co Kildare, Ireland. Exiled to the USA, he helped to organize Clan-na-Gael, and to tie the Easter Rising of 1916 to alliance with Germany in World War 1.

Devoy, Susan (Elizabeth Anne) [de**voy**] (1964–) Squash player, born in Rotorua, New Zealand. Ranked first in the world (1984–91), she held the British Open title (1984–90) and was four times World Open champion between 1985 and 1992.

de Vries, Hugo (Marie) [vrees] (1848–1935) Botanist, born in Haarlem, The Netherlands. He carried out research into the nature of mutation in plant-breeding, and his conclusions paralleled those of Mendel, whose work he discovered in 1900. >> Mendel

De Vries, Peter [vrees] (1910–93) Writer, born in Chicago, IL. His comic novels include *The Tunnel of Love* (1954) and *The Mackerel Plaza* (1958). He later wrote a serious novel about a child's terminal illness, *The Blood of the Lamb* (1961).

Dewar, Sir James [**dyoo**er] (1842–1923) Chemist and physicist, born in Kincardine, Fife. In the 1870s he invented the *Dewar flask* (or thermos flask), using it in his studies of low temperatures and gas liquefaction, and with Abel invented cordite. >> Abel, Frederick

de Wet, Christiaan (Rudolf) [wet] (1854–1922) Afrikaner statesman and general, born in Smithfield district, Orange Free State, South Africa. He became conspicuous in the Transvaal War of 1880–1, and in the war of 1899–1902 was the most audacious of all the Boer commanders.

Dewey, George (1837–1917) US naval commander, born in Montpelier, VT. As commander of the US Asiatic squadron (1897–9) he destroyed the Spanish fleet in Manila Bay.

Dewey, John (1859–1952) Philosopher and educator, born in Burlington, VT. A leading exponent of pragmatism, he developed a philosophy of education which stressed development of the person, understanding of the environment, and learning through experience.

Dewey, Melvil (1851–1931) Librarian, born in Adams Centre, NY. He designed the *Dewey system* of book classification by decimals for the Amherst College Library in 1876.

Dewey, Thomas E(dmund) (1902–71) US politician, born in Owosso, MI. He became Governor of New York State (1942, 1946, 1950), and was Republican nominee for president (1944, 1948), when his campaign organization (the *Dewey machine*) made him appear a much stronger candidate than President Truman.

Dewi, St >> **David, St**

de Witt, Jan [wit] (1625–72) Chief minister of the United Provinces of the Netherlands (1653–72), born in Dordrecht, The Netherlands. As leader of the Republican Party, he sought to limit the power of the House of Orange, but after William of Orange was made stadholder (1672) De Witt and his brother, Cornelius, were killed by an infuriated mob. >> William III

De Wolfe, Elsie (1865–1950) US interior designer. Her design for the Trellis Room of the Colony Club (1906) established her reputation.

Dexter, John (1925–90) British stage director. He became an associate of the National Theatre (1963–6), director of the Metropolitan Opera, New York (1974–81), and cofounder of the New Theatre Company (1986).

Dexter, Ted, popular name of **Edward Ralph Dexter** (1935–) Cricketer and sports commentator, born in Milan, Italy. During his career he captained England (1962–5), and scored 4502 runs, including eight Test centuries.

d'Hérelle, Felix [dayrel] (1873–1949) Bacteriologist, born in Montreal, Quebec, Canada. In 1915 he discovered the bacteriophage, a type of virus which infects bacteria, and

this finding later proved to be of great value in molecular biology.

Diaghilev, Sergei Pavlovich [dee**a**gilef] (1872–1929) Ballet impresario, born in Novgorod, Russia. His permanent company was founded in 1911, and triumphantly toured Europe. Many of the great dancers, composers, and painters of his period contributed to the success of his Ballets Russes, and he also encouraged several major choreographers. >> Balanchine; Fokine; Nijinsky; Stravinsky

Diane de France [deean duh frãs] (1538–1619) Duchess of Angoulême, born in Paris, a natural daughter of Henry II of France. She became a favourite of Henry III who gave her the estate of Angoulême. >> Henry II / III (of France)

Diane de Poitiers [deean duh pwatyay] (1499–1566) Mistress of Henry II of France. She won the affections of the boy dauphin, already wedded to Catherine de' Medici. On his accession (1547) Diane enjoyed great influence, and was made Duchess of Valentinois. >> Henry II (of France)

Diaz or **Dias, Bartolomeu** [**dee**az] (c.1450–1500) Navigator and explorer, probably born in Portugal. In 1487 he sailed round the Cape of Good Hope, and discovered Algoa Bay. He also travelled with Vasco da Gama (1497) and with Cabral (1500), but was lost in a storm. >> Cabral; Gama

Díaz, (José de la Cruz) Porfirio [**dee**az] (1830–1915) President of Mexico (1876–80, 1884–1911), born in Oaxaca, Mexico. Defeated in the election of 1875, he seized power, and served as president for 30 years, until the revolution of Madero forced him into exile. >> Madero

Diaz de Vivar, Rodrigo / Ruy >> **Cid, El**

Dibdin, Charles (1745–1814) Composer, writer, and theatre manager, born in Southampton, Hampshire. In 1789 he started his popular series of one-man musical entertainments, writing over 1000 songs, as well as stage works, musical pieces, and novels.

Dibelius, Karl Friedrich Otto [di**bay**lius] (1880–1967) Lutheran clergyman and ecumenical leader, born in Berlin. Bishop of Berlin (1945–61), and President of the World Council of Churches (1954–61), he defended religious freedom in East Berlin and encouraged ecumenism.

Dick, Philip (Kendred) (1928–) Writer of science fiction, born in Chicago, IL. He is known both for his short stories and his novels, such as *Do Androids Dream of Electric Sheep?* (1968) and *Galactic Pot-Healer* (1969).

Dicke, Robert H(enry) (1916–) Physicist, born in St Louis, MO. He deduced in 1964 that a 'big bang' origin of the universe should have left an observable remnant of microwave radiation, and this was later detected. He also proposed that the gravitational constant (G) slowly decreases with time (the *Brans–Dicke theory*, 1961).

Dickens, Charles (John Huffam) (1812–70) Novelist, born in Landport, Hampshire. He joined a London newspaper as a journalist, and in 1836 published his *Sketches by Boz* and *Pickwick Papers*. He wrote several successful novels, often campaigning against the social evils of his time, notably *Oliver Twist* (1837–9), *Nicholas Nickleby* (1838–9), and *The Old Curiosity Shop* (1840–1). Later books include *David Copperfield* (1849–50), *Bleak House* (1852–3), *A Tale of Two Cities* (1859), *Great Expectations* (1860–1), and the unfinished *The Mystery of Edwin Drood* (1870).

Dickey, James (Lafayette) (1923–) Poet and writer, born in Atlanta, GA. *The Stone* (1960) was his first published book of poems. He is also known for his novel *Deliverance* (1970), for which he also wrote the screenplay (1972).

Dickinson, Emily (Elizabeth) (1830–86) Poet, born in Amherst, MA. At the age of 23 she withdrew from all social contacts, and lived a secluded life, writing in secret over 1000 poems. Hardly any of her work was published until after her death.

Dick-Read, Grantly (1890–1959) British gynaecologist. His unorthodox work, *Natural Childbirth* (1933), caused controversy, but later found widespread acceptance.

Dickson, Leonard (Eugene) (1874–1954) Mathematician, born in Independence, IA. He did important work in group theory, finite fields, and linear associative algebras, and his encyclopedic *History of the Theory of Numbers* (1919–23) is the definitive work on the subject.

Dic Penderyn >> Lewis, Richard

Diderot, Denis [deederoh] (1713–84) Writer and philosopher, born in Langres, France. He was chief editor of the *Encyclopédie* (1745–72), a major work of the age of the Enlightenment. A prolific and versatile writer, he published novels, plays, satires, essays, and letters.

Didi [deedee], popular name of **Valdir Pereira** (1928–) Footballer, born in Campos, Brazil. Despite a slightly crippled right leg, he was the strategist of the Brazil side which won the 1958 World Cup. He later managed the Peruvian national side which reached the World Cup quarter-finals (1970).

Didion, Joan (1934–) Writer, born in Sacramento, CA. Originally a magazine journalist, her novels include *Run River* (1963), *A Book of Common Prayer* (1977), and *Democracy* (1984).

Didius Julianus, Marcus [didius juliahnus] (c.135–193) Roman soldier and emperor. He purchased power in 193 by bribing the praetorian guard in a famous 'auction of the empire'. The Senate soon declared for his rival, Lucius Septimius Severus, and he was deposed and murdered. >> Severus, Lucius Septimius

Didot, Firmin [deedoh] (1764–1836) Printer, born in Paris. He revived and developed the stereotyping process, and produced fine editions of many classical, French, and English works.

Didrikson, Babe, nickname of **Mildred Ella Zaharias**, *née* **Didrikson** (1914–56) Golfer and athlete, born in Port Arthur, TX. A great all-round athlete, she won two gold medals at the 1932 Olympics. Excelling also in swimming, tennis, and rifle-shooting, she turned to golf, winning the US Women's Open three times (1948, 1950, 1954).

Diebenkorn, Richard [deebenkaw(r)n] (1922–93) Painter, born in Portland, OR. During the 1950s he developed a style close to Abstract Expressionism; his two major series of paintings focus on Berkeley and Ocean Park.

Diefenbaker, John G(eorge) [deefenbayker] (1895–1979) Canadian prime minister (1957–63), born in Neustadt, Ontario, Canada. Leader of the Progressive Conservatives (1956), he was elected prime minister after 22 years of Liberal rule. His government introduced important agricultural reforms, and extended the federal franchise to Canada's native peoples.

Diels, Otto [deelz] (1876–1954) Chemist, born in Hamburg, Germany. With Alder he demonstrated in 1928 the 'diene synthesis' (*Diels–Alder reaction*), of special importance in the plastics and petrochemicals industry. They shared the Nobel Prize for Chemistry in 1950. >> Alder

Dies, Martin, Jr [diyz] (1900–72) US politician, born in Colorado, TX. He served as a Democrat in the US House of Representatives (1931–45, 1953–9), chairing the notorious Special Committee to Investigate Un-American Activities.

Diesel, Rudolph (Christian Carl) [deezl] (1858–1913) Engineer, born in Paris. He patented a design in 1892 and, subsidized by Krupps, constructed a 'rational heat motor', demonstrating the first compression-ignition engine in 1897.

Dietrich, Marlene [deetrikh], originally **Maria Magdalene von Losch** (1904–92) Film actress, born in Berlin. She became famous in a German film *The Blue Angel* (trans, 1930), and developed a glamorous and sensual film personality in such Hollywood films as *Morocco* (1930) and *Blond Venus* (1932).

Dieudonné, Jean Alexandre [djoedonay] (1906–) Mathematician, born in Lille, France. A founder of the Bourbaki group, his major work is *Eléments d'analyse* (9 vols, 1960–82).

Digby, Sir Kenelm (1603–65) Diplomat, scientist, and writer, born in Gayhurst, Buckinghamshire. During the Civil War he was imprisoned by the parliament (1642–3). After the Restoration, he was chancellor to Queen Henrietta Maria until 1664.

Digges, Leonard (1520–c.1559) English applied mathematician, known for his valuable work in surveying, navigation, and ballistics. His books went through many editions in the 16th-c.

Dilke, Sir Charles Wentworth [dilk] (1843–1911) Radical politician, born in London. He became president of the local government board under Gladstone. In 1885 he married Emilia Frances Pattison, but his involvement in a divorce case led to defeat in 1886.

Dill, Sir John Greer (1881–1944) British soldier, born in Lurgan, Co Armagh. In World War 2 he became Chief of the Imperial General Staff (1940–1), and was head of the British Service Mission in Washington from 1941.

Dillenius, Johann Jacob [dileenius] (1687–1747) Botanist and botanical artist, born in Darmstadt, Germany. From 1734 he was the first Sherardian professor of botany at Oxford. His work was of fundamental importance in the study of mosses.

Dillinger, John (Herbert) [dilinjer] (1903–34) Gangster, born in Indianapolis, IN. He specialized in armed bank robberies, terrorizing Indiana and neighbouring states (1933–4). After escaping from jail, he was shot dead by FBI agents.

Dillon, John (1851–1927) Irish nationalist politician, born in Blackrock, Co Dublin. He became leader of the Anti-Parnellite group (1896–9), and in 1918 led the Irish Nationalist Party, but was defeated in 1919 by de Valera. >> de Valera; Parnell

Dilthey, Wilhelm [diltiy] (1833–1911) Philosopher, born in Biebrich, Germany. Using Hegel as a point of departure, he argued that human knowledge can only be understood as involving the knower's life lived in a historically conditioned culture. His ideas exerted considerable influence on Heidegger. >> Hegel; Heidegger

DiMaggio, Joe [dimajioh], popular name of **Joseph (Paul) DiMaggio**, nicknames **Joltin' Joe** and **the Yankee Clipper** (1914–) Baseball player, born in Martinez, CA. He spent his entire career with the New York Yankees (1936–51), holding the record for hitting safely in 56 consecutive games (1941). His second wife was Marilyn Monroe. >> Monroe, Marilyn

Dimbleby, Jonathan (1944–) Broadcaster, writer, and journalist, born in London, the son of Richard Dimbleby. Well known as a presenter of many television current-affairs documentaries, his controversial 'official' biography of the Prince of Wales appeared in 1994. >> Dimbleby, Richard

Dimbleby, Richard (Frederick) (1913–65) Broadcaster, born in Richmond on Thames, Greater London. He became the BBC's first foreign correspondent and its first war correspondent. In the postwar era he established himself as a magisterial TV anchorman on *Panorama*, and a commentator on major events.

Dimitrov, Georgi Mikhailovich [dimeetrof] (1882–1949) Communist premier (1946–9), born in Pernik, Bulgaria. He helped to form the Bulgarian Communist Party in 1919, led an unsuccessful uprising in 1923, and was forced to flee to the Soviet Union. He returned in 1945 as head of the transitional government.

d'Indy, (Paul Marie Théodore) Vincent [dādee] (1851–1931) Composer, born in Paris. His works include several operas and orchestral pieces, notably *Symphony on a French Mountaineering Song* (trans, 1886).

Dine, Jim [diyn] (1935–) Artist, born in Cincinatti, OH. In 1959 he exhibited his first series of objects as images. One of the foremost US Pop artists, he later turned to more traditional representational painting.

Dinesen, Isak >> **Blixen, Karen**

Ding Ling, also spelled **Ting Ling**, pseudonym of **Jiang Bingzhi** (1904–86) Writer, born in Linli Co, China. She joined the Communist Party (1932), but her outspoken feminism led to her being disciplined, until her novel, *The Sun Shines Over the Sanggan River* (1948), restored her to favour. She was imprisoned (1970–5) during the Cultural Revolution.

Dinkins, David (1927–) US politician, born in Trenton, NJ. A Democrat, his policy of racial harmony was popular, and he was elected New York's first black mayor in 1989, but lost his bid for re-election in 1993.

Dinwiddie, Robert [dinwidee] (1693–1770) Colonial administrator, born in Germiston, Strathclyde. Appointed lieutenant-governor of Virginia (1751–8), he was unable to prevent the French and Indian War (1755–63).

Dio Cassius [diyoh kasius], also found as **Dion Cassius** and **Cassius Dio Cocceianus** (c.150–c.235) Roman senator and prominent man of affairs, from Bithynia in Asia Minor, who wrote a comprehensive history of Rome in Greek. The surviving parts are an invaluable source for historians of the early Roman empire.

Dio Chrysostomus >> **Dion Chrysostom**

Diocletian [diyokleeshn], in full **Gaius Aurelius Valerius Diocletianus** (245–316) Roman emperor (284–305), a Dalmatian of humble birth, born in Diocles, who became the greatest of the soldier emperors of the 3rd-c. In 286 the empire was split in two, with Diocletian retaining the East, and Maximian taking the West. Later, he divided the Empire into four.

Diodorus Siculus [diyohdawrus sikyulus] (1st-c BC) Greek historian, born in Agyrium, Sicily. He travelled in Asia and Europe, collecting the materials for his *Bibliothēkē Historikē*, a history of the world in 40 books, of which some are extant.

Diogenes of Apollonia [diyojeneez, apolohnia] (5th-c BC) Greek philosopher. He continued the pre-Socratic tradition of speculation about the primary constituent of the world, which he identified as air, operating as an active and intelligent life-force.

Diogenes of Sinope [diyojeneez] (c.410–c.320 BC) Cynic philosopher, born in Sinope, Pontus. His unconventional behaviour (eg looking with a lantern in daylight for an honest man) was intended to portray the ideal of a life lived according to nature.

Diogenes Läertius [diyojeneez lairtius] (3rd-c) Greek writer, born in Läerte, Cilicia. He is remembered for his *Lives, Teachings and Sayings of the Great Philosophers*, in 10 books, a compilation of excerpts.

Dion Chrysostom [diyon krisostm], also found as **Dio Chrysostomus** (c.40–c.112) Greek rhetorician and philosopher, born in Prusa, Bithynia. About 80 orations or treatises on politics and philosophy are extant.

Dionne, Cécile, Yvonne, Annette, Emilie, and **Marie** [deeon] (1934–) Quintuplets, born near Callander, Ontario, Canada. They were the first documented set of quintuplets to survive, and became international child celebrities. Emilie died in 1954, and Marie in 1970.

Dionysius Exiguus [diyohnisius eksigyoous], also known as **Dennis the Little** (?–556) Scythian Christian scholar,

abbot of a monastery in Rome. One of the most learned men of his time, he fixed the dating of the Christian era in his *Cyclus Paschalis* (525).

Dionysius of Alexandria, St [diyohnisius], also known as **Dionysius the Great** (c.200–264), feast day 17 November. Greek theologian, born in Alexandria. He succeeded Origen as head of the catechical school in Alexandria in 231, and became Bishop of Alexandria in 247. Only fragments of his writings have survived. >> Origen

Dionysius of Halicarnassus [diyoniysius] (1st-c BC) Greek critic, historian, and rhetorician, from Halicarnassus in Asia Minor, who lived in Rome at the time of Augustus. Much of his writing survives, including about half of his masterpiece, *Early Roman History*.

Dionysius the Areopagite [diyoniysius, ariopagiyt] (1st-c) Greek Church leader, one of the few Athenians converted by the apostle Paul (*Acts* 17.34). Tradition makes him the first Bishop of Athens and a martyr. >> Paul, St

Dionysius the Elder [diyoniysius] (c.431–367 BC) Tyrant of Syracuse (405–367 BC) and ruler of half of Sicily, whose influence extended over most of S Italy. His reign was dominated by intermittent warfare with the Carthaginians. >> Dionysius (the Younger)

Dionysius the Younger [diyoniysius] (c.397–? BC) Tyrant of Syracuse (367–357/6 BC), the son and successor of Dionysius the Elder. Groomed by Plato as a potential philosopher-king, he turned out to be a rake and an oppressor. >> Dionysius the Elder; Plato

Dionysius Thrax [diyoniysius thrayks] (1st–2nd-c) Greek grammarian, a native of Alexandria, who taught at Rhodes and at Rome. His *Technē grammatikē* is the basis of all European works on grammar.

Diophantus [diyofantus] (c.200–299) Greek mathematician, who lived in Alexandria c.275. Of his three known works, only six books of *Arithmetica*, the earliest extant treatise on algebra, have survived. His name was later given to a part of algebra known as *Diophantine analysis*.

Dior, Christian [deeaw(r)] (1905–57) Fashion designer, born in Granville, France. He founded his own Paris house in 1945, and achieved worldwide fame with his long-skirted 'New Look' (1947). Later designs included the 'H' line and the 'A' line.

Dioscorides, Pedanius [diyoskorideez] (fl.1st-c) Greek physician, born in Anazarbus, Cilicia. He wrote *De materia medica*, the standard work on the medical properties of plants and minerals for many centuries.

Diouf, Abdou (1935–) Senegalese president (1981–), born in Louga, Senegal. He became prime minister in 1970, then president, and was also president of the loose Confederation of Senegambia (1982–9).

Dippel, Johann Konrad (1673–1734) Theologian and alchemist, born in Burg Frankenstein, Germany. He invented a panacea known as *Dippel's animal oil*, a distillation of animal bone and offal, and also discovered Prussian blue.

Dirac, Paul A(drien) M(aurice) [dirak] (1902–84) Physicist, born in Bristol, Avon. His main research was in the field of quantum mechanics, in which he applied relativity theory, developed the theory of the spinning electron, and proposed the existence of 'anti-matter'. He shared the Nobel Prize for Physics in 1933.

Dirichlet, Peter Gustav Lejeune [diriklay] (1805–59) Mathematician, born in Düren, Germany. His main work was in number theory, Fourier series, and the boundary value problems in mathematical physics which now carry his name.

Dirks, Rudolph (1877–1968) Strip cartoonist, born in Heinde, Germany. He joined the *New York Journal* where he created the strip, *The Katzenjammer Kids* (1897).

Dirksen, Everett (McKinley) (1896–1969) US politician, born in Pekin, IL. A Republican member of the US House of Representatives (1933–51), he then served in the US Senate (1951–69), supporting the Test Ban Treaty of 1963 and civil rights.

Disney, Walt(er Elias) (1901–66) Artist and film producer, born in Chicago, IL. He set up a small studio producing animated cartoons, his most famous character being Mickey Mouse (1928). His first full-length coloured cartoon film was *Snow White and the Seven Dwarfs* (1937), followed by *Pinocchio* (1940), *Dumbo* (1941), and *Fantasia* (1940). He also produced nature films, such as *The Living Desert* (1953), and films for young people including *Treasure Island* (1950) and *Mary Poppins* (1964). He opened the first Disneyland amusement park in California in 1955.

Disraeli, Benjamin, 1st Earl of Beaconsfield [dizraylee] (1804–81) British prime minister (1868, 1874–80), born in London. As a writer, he is best known for his two political novels, *Coningsby* (1844) and *Sybil* (1846). Chancellor of the Exchequer in Derby's minority governments (1852, 1858–9, 1866–8), he piloted the 1867 Reform Bill through the Commons. During his administration, Britain became half-owner of the Suez Canal (1875), and Queen Victoria became Empress of India (1876). >> Derby, 14th Earl; Gladstone; Peel; Victoria

Dittersdorf, Karl Ditters von (1739–99) Composer and violinist, born in Vienna. The composer of 13 Italian operas, he is chiefly remembered for his contribution to the development of the German comic operatic tradition (*Singspiel*).

Divine, Father >> **Baker, George**

Dix, Dorothea (Lynde) (1802–87) Reformer and nurse, born in Hampden, ME. She investigated the conditions in insane asylums, prisons, and almshouses, and in 1861 became superintendent of women nurses for the federal government.

Dix, Otto (1891–1969) Realist painter, born in Gera-Unternhaus, Germany. He is best known for his etchings and paintings of World War 1 casualties, and of Berlin prostitutes in the decadent post-war period.

Dixon, Jeremiah >> **Mason, Charles**

Djilas, Milovan [jeelas] (1911–95) Yugoslav politician and writer, born in Montenegro. He was imprisoned as a result of his criticism of the Communist system, but released under amnesty in 1966. His books include *The New Class* (1957) and *Conversations with Stalin* (1962).

Dmitri [duhmeetree], also known as **Demetrius** (1583–91) Russian prince, the youngest son of Tsar Ivan the Terrible. He was murdered by the regent Boris Godunov, but c.1603 was impersonated by a Moscow monk, Grigoriy Otrepieff, the 'false Dmitri', who was crowned tsar by the army in 1605 but then killed in a rebellion. >> Godunov, Boris; Ivan IV

Dobbie, Sir William George Sheddon (1879–1964) British soldier, born in Madras, India. He commanded in Malaya (1935–9), and was Governor of Malta (1940–2) during its resolute resistance to German and Italian air attack.

Dobell, Sir William [dohbel] (1899–1970) Portrait painter, born in Newcastle, New South Wales, Australia. His controversial portrait of Joshua Smith won the Archibald Prize in 1944. He left all his estate to establish the art foundation which bears his name.

Döbereiner, Johann Wolfgang [doeberiyner] (1780–1849) Chemist, born in Bug bei Hof, Germany. He is remembered as the inventor of *Döbereiner's lamp*, in which hydrogen, produced in the lamp by the action of sulphuric acid on zinc, burns on contact with a platinum sponge.

Dobrée, Bonamy [dobray] (1891–1974) British literary scholar. Professor of English literature at Leeds (1936–55), he wrote on Restoration comedy (1924) and tragedy (1929), as well as on many individual authors.

Dobrynin, Anataoly Fedorovich [dobreenin] (1919–) Soviet diplomat and statesman, born in Krasnoya Gorka, near Moscow. He became Soviet ambassador to Washington (1962–86) and secretary for foreign affairs (1986–8).

Dobson, Frank (1888–1963) Sculptor, born in London. He was associated with the London Group for many years, and his individual style, with simplified contours and heavy limbs, is shown at its best in his female nudes.

Dobzhansky, Theodosius [dobzhanskee] (1900–75) Geneticist, born in Nemirov, Ukraine. His work gave the experimental evidence which linked Darwinian evolutionary theory with Mendel's laws of heredity, and he applied his ideas to the concept of race in human beings. >> Mendel

Docherty, Tommy [dokertee], popular name of **Thomas Henderson Docherty** (1928–) Footballer and manager, born in Glasgow, Strathclyde. He played 25 times for Scotland, and managed 10 clubs including Aston Villa and Manchester United. He also briefly managed the Scotland side (1971–2).

Doctorow, Edgar (Lawrence) [doktoroh] (1931–) Novelist, born in New York City. His best-known work is *Ragtime* (1975; filmed 1981). Later books include *Loon Lake* (1980) and *The World's Fair* (1985).

Dodd, Charles Harold (1884–1973) Biblical scholar and Congregational pastor, born in Wrexham, Clwyd. He was elected to the Norris–Hulse chair of divinity at Cambridge (1936–49) - the first Nonconformist incumbent for nearly three centuries.

Dodd, Ken(neth) (1929–) Stand-up comedian, singer, and actor, born in Liverpool, Merseyside. His hit songs include 'Tears' and 'Happiness'.

Dodge, Grenville (Mellen) (1831–1916) Soldier and engineer, born in Danvers, MA. As chief engineer of the Union Pacific Railway from 1866, he was responsible for the construction of some of the most famous American railroads.

Dodge, Henry (1782–1867) US politician and pioneer, born in Vincennes, IN. Famous as a frontiersman, he became a member of the US House of Representatives in 1841, and senator for Wisconsin (1848–57).

Dodge, Mary (Elizabeth), née **Mapes** (1831–1905) Writer, born in New York City. Her books for children include *Hans Brinker; or, The Silver Skates* (1865), which became a children's classic.

Dodgson, Charles Lutwidge >> **Carroll, Lewis**

Dodsley, Robert (1704–64) Playwright and publisher, born in Mansfield, Nottinghamshire. He is chiefly remembered for his *Select Collection of Old Plays* (12 vols, 1744–45) and his *Poems by Several Hands* (3 vols, 1748; 6 vols, 1758).

Doe, Samuel (1951–90) Liberian soldier and president (1985–90), born in Tuzin, Grand Gedeh Co, Liberia. He became head of state as chairman of the military Peoples Redemption Council (1981), and was narrowly elected president, but was killed after the outbreak of civil war in 1990.

Doenitz or **Dönitz, Karl** [doenits] (1891–1980) German naval commander, born in Grünau, Germany. He planned the U-boat fleet, and in 1943 became commander-in-chief of the German navy. He was responsible for the final surrender to the Allies, and in 1946 was sentenced to 10 years' imprisonment for war crimes.

Doesburg, Theo van [doozberg], originally **Christian Emil Marie Küpper** (1883–1931) Painter, architect, and writer, born in Utrecht, The Netherlands. With Mondrian he founded the avant-garde magazine *De Stijl* (1917–31), and devoted himself to propagating its new aesthetic ideas. >> Mondrian

Dohnányi, Ernst von [dohnanyee], Hung **Erno** (1877–1960) Composer and pianist, born in Pozsony, Hungary (now Bratislava, Slovak Republic). He is best known for his piano compositions, notably *Variations on a Nursery Song* (1913) for piano and orchestra.

Doisy, Edward (Adelbert) [doyzee] (1893–1987) Biochemist, born in Hume, IL. In collaboration with US embryologist **Edgar Allen** (1892–1943) he conducted research on reproduction and hormones, isolating two forms of the coagulant agent vitamin K. He shared the Nobel Prize for Physiology or Medicine in 1943.

Dolabella, Publius Cornelius [dolabela] (c.70–43 BC) Roman politician and Cicero's profligate son-in-law. On Caesar's murder (44 BC) he usurped the consulate, and was later outlawed. When threatened by capture, he commanded one of his own soldiers to kill him.

Dolci, Danilo [dohlchee] (1925–) Social worker, 'the Gandhi of Sicily', born in Trieste, Italy. He fought poverty in Sicily, building schools and community centres in the poorest areas. Although not a Communist, he was awarded the Lenin Peace Prize in 1956.

Dole, Bob, popular name of **Robert Dole** (1923–) US Republican politician, born in Russell, Kansas. A senator for Kansas, he sought nomination for the presidency in 1980 and 1988, and became majority leader in the Senate following Republican gains in the 1994 elections.

Dolet, Etienne [dolay] (1509–46) Printer and humanist, born in Orléans, France. He set up a printing press in Lyon, producing translations of the classics, as well as of Erasmus and Rabelais. He was found guilty of heresy, and burned in Paris.

Dolin, Anton [dohlin], professional name of **Patrick Healey-Kay** (1904–83) Dancer and choreographer, born in Slinfold, West Sussex. A principal with Diaghilev's Ballet Russes (from 1924), and with the Vic-Wells Ballet (1930s), he co-founded the Markova–Dolin Ballet, and was London Festival Ballet's first artistic director (1960–61). >> Diaghilev; Markova

D'Oliveira, Basil (Lewis) [dolivaira] (1934–) Cricketer, born in Cape Town, South Africa. In England from 1960, he played for England 44 times, and scored five Test centuries. Chosen for the 1968–9 England tour of South Africa, the refusal of the government to admit him (as a Cape Coloured) led to the exclusion of South Africa from international cricket.

Dollfuss, Engelbert [dolfoos] (1892–1934) Austrian chancellor (1932–4), born in Texing, Austria. He suspended parliamentary government, drove the socialists into revolt, and militarily crushed them (1934). An attempted Nazi putsch led to his assassination.

Döllinger, Johann Joseph Ignaz von [doelingger] (1799–1890) Roman Catholic theologian, born in Bamberg, Germany. After the decree of papal infallibility, he issued a letter withholding his submission, and was excommunicated.

Dollo, Louis (Antoine Marie Joseph) [doloh] (1857–1931) Palaeontologist, born in Lille, France. In 1893 he enunciated *Dollo's law* of irreversibility in evolution.

Dollond, John (1706–61) Optician, born in London. He devoted himself with the help of his son **Peter Dollond** (1738–1820) to the invention of an achromatic telescope.

Dolmetsch, (Eugène) Arnold (1858–1940) Musician, born in Le Mans, France. He revived interest in early music and musical instruments, setting up workshops at his home in Haslemere, Surrey. His son **Carl Dolmetsch** (1911–) is also known as an expert in early instruments and as a recorder virtuoso.

Dolomieu, Déodat Guy Gratet de [dolomyoe] (1750–1801) Geologist and mineralogist, born in Dolomieu, France. Renowned for his researches on volcanic rocks, he gave his name to *dolomite*.

Domagk, Gerhard (Johannes Paul) [dohmak] (1895–1964) Biochemist, born in Lagow, Germany. He discovered the chemotherapeutic properties of sulphanilamide. In 1939, on instruction from the German government, he refused the Nobel Prize for Physiology or Medicine.

Domar, Evsey D(avid) [dohmah(r)] (1914–) Economist, born in Lodz, Poland (formerly, Russia). He is the co-inventor of the *Harrod–Domar model* of dynamic equilibrium in economic growth. >> Harrod

Domenichino [domenikeenoh], originally **Domenico Zampieri** (1581–1641) Painter, born in Bologna, Italy. His masterpiece is 'The Last Communion of St Jerome' (1614) in the Vatican.

Domenico Veneziano [domeneekoh venetsiahnoh] (c.1400–61) Italian painter. He is especially known for his altarpiece in the Uffizi at Florence.

Domingo, Placido [dominggoh] (1941–) Tenor, born in Madrid. He first sang in New York City in 1966, and at Covent Garden in 1971. His vocal technique and acting ability have made him one of the world's leading lyric-dramatic tenors, notably in works by Puccini and Verdi.

Dominic, St (c.1170–1221), feast day 8 August. Founder of the Order of Friars Preachers, born in Calaruega, Old Castile. He devoted himself to missionary work, notably among the Albigenses of S France, and he was canonized in 1234.

Domitian [domishn], in full **Titus Flavius Domitianus** (51–96) Roman emperor (81–96), the younger son of Vespasian, and the last of the Flavian emperors. After the revolt of Saturninus (89), he unleashed a reign of terror in Rome which lasted until his own assassination. >> Vespasian

Donaldson (of Lymington), John Francis Donaldson, Baron (1920–) British judge. He became a Lord Justice of Appeal (1979–82), and Master of the Rolls (1982).

Donat, Aelius >> Donatus, Aelius

Donat, Robert [dohnat] (1905–58) Actor, born in Manchester. His many leading film roles include *The Thirty-nine Steps* (1935), *Good-bye, Mr Chips* (1939, Oscar), and *The Winslow Boy* (1948).

Donatello [donateloh], originally **Donato di Betto Bardi** (c.1386–1466) Sculptor, born in Florence, Italy. He may be regarded as the founder of modern sculpture, as the first producer since classical times of statues complete in themselves. Among his works are the marble statues of saints Mark and George for the exterior of Or San Michele, Florence.

Donati, Giambattista [donahtee] (1826–73) Astronomer, born in Pisa, Italy. Director of the observatory at Florence, he discovered the brilliant comet (*Donati's comet*) of 1858.

Donatus, Aelius [donaytus] (c.300–c.399) Latin grammarian and rhetorician, who taught in Rome AD c.360. His treatises on Latin grammar were in the Middle Ages the only textbooks used in schools, so that *Donat* in W Europe came to mean a 'grammar book'.

Donatus Magnus [donaytus magnus] (?–c.355) Bishop of Carthage. He was a leader of the *Donatists*, a 4th-c puritan Christian sect in N Africa, and was later exiled to Gaul (347).

Don Carlos >> Carlos, Don

Dönitz, Karl >> Doenitz, Karl

Donizetti, (Domenico) Gaetano (Maria) [donizetee] (1797–1848) Composer, born in Bergamo, Italy. The work which carried his fame beyond Italy was *Anna Bolena* (1830), and he had several other successes, notably *Lucia di Lammermoor* (1835).

Donkin, Bryan (1768–1855) Engineer and inventor, born in Sandhoe, Northumberland. He co-patented one of the first rotary printing machines (1813), and improved on food-preserving techniques, opening a canning factory in 1812.

Donleavy, J(ames) P(atrick) (1926–) Writer, born in New York City. His first novel, *The Ginger Man* (1955) was hailed as a comic masterpiece, and later works include *A Singular Man* (1963) and *The Onion Eaters* (1971). He has been an Irish citizen since 1967.

Donn-Byrne, Brian Oswald >> Byrne, Donn

Donne, John [duhn] (?1572–1631) Poet, born in London. Originally a Catholic, he joined the established Church, and became dean of St Paul's. His creative years fall into three periods. The first (1590–1601) was a time of passion and cynicism, as seen in his *Elegies* and *Songs and Sonnets*; the second is represented by his *Anniversaries* and funeral poems; and his third includes sonnets and hymns.

Donnelly, Ignatius [donelee] (1831–1901) Politician and writer, born in Philadelphia, PA. He became a radical Republican congressman (1863–9). As a prophet of reform, his most enduring legacy is a novel, *Caesar's Column* (1891), predicting tyranny and oppression.

Donoghue, Steve [donuhyoo], popular name of **Stephen Donoghue** (1884–1945) Jockey, born in Warrington, Cheshire. He won the Derby six times, including a record three consecutive wins (1921–3), and was champion jockey in 10 successive years (1914–23).

Donoso, (Yanez) José [donosoh] (1928–) Novelist, born in Santiago, Chile. In 1962 he received the William Faulkner Foundation Prize for Chile, for his novel *Coronation* (1957).

Donovan, William (Joseph), nickname **Wild Bill Donovan** (1883–1959) US soldier and public official, born in Buffalo, NY. He was head of the US Office of Strategic Services (1942–5), with responsibility for espionage, counter-espionage, and clandestine military operations during World War 2.

Dooley, Mr >> Dunne, Finley Peter

Doolittle, Hilda, pseudonym **H D** (1886–1961) Poet, born in Bethlehem, PA. She lived in London from 1911, and became an exponent of Imagism, her books of poetry including *Sea Garden* (1916) and *Hymen* (1921). In 1913 she married Richard Aldington (divorced, 1937). >> Aldington

Doolittle, James H(arold) (1896–1993) US air force officer, born in Alameda, CA. He commanded the 12th Army Air Force (AAF) in North Africa, the 15th AAF in Italy (1943), and the 8th AAF in Britain for operations in North West Europe (1944).

Doppler, Christian Johann (1803–53) Physicist, born in Salzburg, Austria. He is best known for his explanation of the perceived frequency variation of sound and light waves because of the relative motion of the source and the detector (the *Doppler effect*).

Dora, Sister >> Pattison, Dorothy

Dorat, Jean >> Daurat, Jean

Dorati, Sir Antal [dorahtee] (1906–) Conductor, born in Budapest. Following his US debut (1937), his posts include musical director of the new American Ballet Theater, and senior conductor of the London Royal Philharmonic (1975–9).

Doré, (Paul) Gustave [doray] (1832–83) Painter and book illustrator, born in Strasbourg, France. He illustrated books by Rabelais (1854) and Balzac, notably the latter's *Contes drolatiques* (1865), and editions of Dante, the Bible, Milton, and other works.

Doren, Carl / Mark Van >> Van Doren, Carl / Mark

Doria, Andrea [dawria] (c.1466–1560) Genoese statesman, born in Oneglia, Italy. Commander of the Genoese fleet, after the restoration of imperial power in Genoa (1522) he served Francis I of France, defeated Emperor Charles V, and proclaimed the independence of the republic in 1527. >> Charles V (Emperor); Francis I

Dorn, Friedrich Ernst (1848–1916) Chemist, born in Guttstadt, Germany. He studied at Königsberg, and is known for his discovery of radon.

Dornberger, Walter (Robert) (1895–1980) Rocket engineer, born in Giessen, Germany. He set up an experimental rocket station which successfully fired a 650 lb-thrust motor in 1932. He worked on V-2 rockets in World War 2, and later moved to the USA.

Dornier, Claude [daw(r)nyer] (1884–1969) Aircraft engineer, born in Kempten, Germany. In 1911 he designed the first all-metal plane, and later made seaplanes and flying-boats, including the famous 12-engined Do X (1929).

Dörpfeld, Wilhelm [doepfelt] (1853–1940) Archaeologist, born in Barmen, Germany. The chronology of Troy set out in his *Troja und Ilion* (1902) served to date European prehistory for the first decades of the 20th-c.

Dors, Diana, originally **Diana Fluck** (1931–84) Actress, born in Swindon, Wiltshire. Promoted as a sex symbol, she was cast in various low-budget comedies, achieving more dramatic roles in *Yield to the Night* (1956), *Three Months Gone* (1970), and *The Amazing Mr. Blunden* (1972).

Dorsey, Jimmy >> Dorsey, Tommy

Dorsey, Tommy [daw(r)see], popular name of **Thomas Dorsey** (1905–56) Trombonist and bandleader, born in Shenandoah, PA. His big bands were sometimes co-led by his brother **Jimmy Dorsey** (1904–57, alto saxophone, clarinet). The Dorsey Brothers Orchestra existed from 1932 to 1935, reforming again in 1953 until Tommy's death.

Doshi, Balkrishna Vithaldas [doshee] (1927–) Architect, born in Poona, India. His works include the City Hall, Toronto (1958) and Vidyadhar Nagar New Town, Jaipur.

Dos Passos, John (Roderigo) (1896–1970) Novelist and war correspondent, born in Chicago, IL. His best-known work is the trilogy on US life, *U.S.A.* (1930–6).

Dos Santos, Jose Eduardo (1942–) Angolan president (1979–), born in Luanda. He negotiated a ceasefire in the civil war, achieving a peace agreement in 1991. The war recommenced following accusations of election-rigging in 1992.

Dosso Dossi, originally **Giovanno di Nicolò Lutero** (c.1479–1542) Religious painter, born near Mantua, Italy. He was the leader of the Ferrarese school in the early 16th-c.

Dostoevsky or **Dostoyevsky, Fyodor (Mikhailovich)** [dostoyefskee] (1821–81) Novelist, born in Moscow. Joining revolutionary circles in St Petersburg, he was sent to hard labour in Siberia. In 1859 he returned to St Petersburg, where his major works include (trans titles) *Crime and Punishment* (1866), *The Idiot* (1868–9), and *The Brothers Karamazov* (1879–80).

Dou or **Douw, Gerard** [dow] (1613–75) Painter, born in Leyden, The Netherlands. His 200 works include his own portrait, his wife's, and his celebrated 'Dropsical Woman' (1663).

Douanier, Le >> Rousseau, Henri

Doubleday, Abner (1819–93) US soldier, born in Ballston Spa, NY. In 1908 a commission eager to establish the American origins of baseball credited him with being its inventor, although the claim is now recognized as popular folklore.

Doubleday, Frank (Nelson) (1862–1943) Publisher, born in New York City. He co-founded Doubleday & McClure (1900), established the Country Life Press, and opened a chain of bookshops.

Douglas, Lord Alfred (Bruce) (1870–1945) British poet, the son of the 8th Marquess of Queensberry. He is remembered for his association with Oscar Wilde, to which his father objected, thereby provoking Wilde to bring an abortive libel action. >> Queensberry; Wilde, Oscar

Douglas, David (1798–1834) Botanist, born in Scone, Tayside. In North America he discovered many trees, shrubs, and herbaceous plants which he introduced to Britain. The *Douglas fir* and *Douglas squirrel* were named after him.

Douglas, Donald (Wills) (1892–1981) Aircraft designer and manufacturer, born in New York City. In 1920 he set up his own company in California, and the prototype for the DC series of planes was flown in 1933. His company became part of the McDonnell Douglas Corporation in 1967. >> McDonnell

Douglas, Gawain or **Gavin** (c.1474–1522) Poet and bishop, born in Tantallon Castle, Lothian. His works include a translation of the *Aeneid* (finished c.1513), the first to be published in English.

Douglas, George >> **Brown, George Douglas**

Douglas, Mary, *née* **Tew** (1921–) Social anthropologist, born in Italy. She is especially known for her studies of systems of cultural classification and beliefs about purity and pollution.

Douglas, Stephen A(rnold) (1813–61) US lawyer and statesman, born in Brandon, VT. He became secretary of state in 1840, and judge of the Supreme Court in 1841. Returned to the US Senate in 1847, he was nominated for the presidency in 1860, but was defeated by Lincoln. >> Lincoln, Abraham

Douglas, Tommy, popular name of **Thomas Clement Douglas** (1904–86) Baptist minister and Canadian politician. As premier of Saskatchewan (1944–61), he led the first socialist government elected in Canada, and was later leader of the federal New Democratic Party.

Douglas, William O(rville) (1898–1980) Judge, born in Maine, MN. A supporter of the 'New Deal', he was appointed to the Supreme Court in 1939, and strongly supported civil rights and liberties.

Douglas (of Kirtleside), William Sholto Douglas, Baron (1893–1969) British air force officer. He became head of Fighter Command (1940–2), Middle East Air Command (1943–4), and Coastal Command (1944–5), then commanded the British Air Force of Occupation in Germany (1945–6).

Douglas-Hamilton, Iain (1944–) British zoologist. Following a study of elephants in the wild (1966), his book *Among the Elephants* (1972) became a best seller, and also drew the world's attention to the devasting effect of ivory-poaching.

Douglas-Home, Sir Alec >> **Home of the Hirsel**

Douglas-Home, William [duhglas hyoom] (1912–92) Playwright, born in Edinburgh, the brother of Sir Alec Douglas-Home. He became known for his comedies of upper middle-class and political life, notably *The Chiltern Hundreds* (1947), *The Reluctant Debutante* (1955), and *Her Mother Came Too* (1982). >> Home

Douglass, Andrew (Ellicott) (1867–1962) Astronomer, born in Windsor, VT. He investigated the relationship between sunspots and climate by measuring the annual growth-rings of long-lived Arizona pines and sequoias, and provided a time-sequence for dating purposes.

Douglass, Frederick (c.1817–95) Abolitionist and journalist, born in slavery at Tuckahoe, MD. He escaped in 1838, and in 1841 emerged as a major anti-slavery force. He later obtained his freedom, and became US minister to Haiti.

Douhet, Giulio [dooay] (1869–1930) Italian general, born in Caserta, Italy. He became commander of Italy's first military aviation unit (1912–15), and headed the Italian Army Aviation Service in 1918.

Doulton, Sir Henry [dohltn] (1820–97) Pottery manufacturer, born in London. In 1848 he started works near Dudley, later the largest in the world, and in the 1880s introduced fine porcelain ware, for which the company is better known.

Douw, Gerard >> **Dou, Gerard**

Dove, Arthur (Garfield) (1880–1946) Painter, born in Canadaigua, NY. In 1910 he began a series of abstract paintings, and in the 1920s experimented with collage incorporating mirrors, sand, and metal.

Dow, Gerard >> **Dou, Gerard**

Dow, Henry (Herbert) [dow] (1866–1930) Chemist, inventor, and industrialst, born in Belleville, Ontario, Canada. He invented a simple electrolytic method for extracting bromine from brine, his methods laying the foundation of the electrochemical industry in the USA.

Dowding, Hugh (Caswell Tremenheere) Dowding, Baron (1882–1970) British air chief marshal of World War 2, born in Moffat, Dumfries and Galloway. As commander-in-chief of Fighter Command (1936–40), he organized the air defence of Britain, which resulted in the victorious Battle of Britain (1940).

Dowell, Anthony (1943–) Dancer and director, born in London. He joined the Royal Ballet company in 1961, becoming one of the premier male ballet dancers of the period, and was appointed artistic director there in 1986.

Dowie, John Alexander (1847–1907) Religious leader, born in Edinburgh. In 1888 he emigrated to the USA, where he organized the Christian Catholic Church in Zion (1896), and founded near Chicago the prosperous industrial and banking community called 'Zion City' (1901).

Dowland, John (1563–1626) Composer, lutenist, and songwriter, born possibly in Westminster, London. He produced several collections of music, including *Lachrimae* (1605, Tears), which contains some of the finest instrumental consort music of the period.

Dowling, Stephen (1904–86) Strip cartoonist, born in Liverpool, Merseyside. He teamed with his brother, Frank Dowling, to create newspaper strips, starting with *Tich* (1931) in the *Daily Mirror*, followed by *Ruggles* (1935), and the fantasy super-hero *Garth* (1942).

Downes, Terry (1936–) Boxer, born in London. He was British middleweight champion (1958–9, 1959–62), and held the world championship (1961–2).

Downing, Sir George (1684–1749) Landowner, born in Cambridgeshire. He founded Downing College in Cambridge, which received its charter in 1800.

Dowson, Ernest Christopher (1867–1900) Poet of the 'decadent' school, born in Lee, Greater London. He studied at Oxford, became part of the Rhymers' Club group, and was a friend of Arthur Symons and W B Yeats. >> Symons, Arthur; Yeats, W B

Doyle, Sir Arthur Conan (1859–1930) Writer, born in Edinburgh. His first book, *A Study in Scarlet* (1887), introduced the character of Sherlock Holmes, and the whole apparatus of detection mythology associated with Baker Street, Holmes's fictitious home. He also wrote historical romances, such as *The White Company* (1890).

Doyle, Richard (1824–83) Caricaturist, book illustrator, and watercolour painter, born in London. He became a contributor to *Punch* in 1843, and designed the famous cover that was used from 1849 to 1956.

D'Oyly Carte, Richard [doylee kah(r)t] (1844–1901) Theatrical impresario, born in London. He became a concert agent, and from 1875 produced the first operettas by 'Gilbert and Sullivan'. In 1881 he built the Savoy Theatre in London. >> Gilbert, W S; Sullivan, Arthur

Drabble, Margaret (1939–) Novelist and critic, born in Sheffield, South Yorkshire. Her novels include *A Summer Bird-Cage* (1962), *The Ice Age* (1977), and *Safe as Houses* (1989), and she edited the *Oxford Companion to English Literature* (1985). She married biographer Michael Holroyd in 1982. >> Byatt; Holroyd

Draco [draykoh] (ancient Greece) (7th-c BC) Athenian lawgiver. Archon at Athens in 621 BC, his harsh codification of the law in 621 BC has given us the word 'draconian'.

Drake, Sir Francis (c.1540–96) Elizabethan seaman, born in Crowndale, Devon. In 1577 he set out for the Pacific through the Straits of Magellan in the *Golden Hind*, returning to England via the Cape of Good Hope in 1580. In 1585

he visited the Spanish Indies, bringing home tobacco, potatoes, and the dispirited Virginian colonists. In the week-long battle against the Spanish Armada (1588), his seamanship and courage brought him further distinction.

Draper, Henry (1837-82) Pioneer of astronomical photography, born in Prince Edward Co, VA. An important catalogue of stellar spectra is named after him.

Draper, John William (1811-82) Chemist, born in St Helens, Lanchashire. In 1832 he emigrated to Virginia, and became a pioneer in photography. He made major contributions to the study of the chemical effects of radiant energy.

Draper, Ruth (1884-1956) Monologue performer, born in New York City. Highly successful solo appearances for the US troops in France in 1918, she toured extensively, her repertoire comprising monologues of her own devising.

Drayton, Michael (1563-1631) Poet, born in Hartshill, Warwickshire. His best-known works are *England's Heroical Epistles* (1597), *Poly-Olbion* (1612-22), and the sonnet 'Since there's no help, come let us kiss and part'.

Drazha >> **Mihailović, Dragoljub**

Drebbel, Cornelis (Jacobszoon) (c.1572-1633) Inventor, born in Alkmaar, The Netherlands. He designed a water-supply system for Alkmaar, then moved to England (1604), where his inventions included a rudimentary submarine (1620).

Drees, Willem (1886-1988) Dutch prime minister (1948-58), born in Amsterdam. He became chairman of the Socialist Democratic Workers' Party in 1911, and as minister of social affairs in 1947 introduced the state pension.

Dreiser, Theodore (Herman Albert) [driyzer] (1871-1945) Writer, born in Terre Haute, IN. His first novel, *Sister Carrie* (1900), was criticized for obscenity. He later won acclaim with *Jennie Gerhardt* (1911) and *An American Tragedy* (1925).

Dresser, Christopher (1834-1904) Designer and writer, born in Glasgow, Strathclyde. He designed glass, ceramics, and cast-iron furniture, but his outstanding works were of functional metalwork such as teapots and soup tureens.

Dressler, Marie, originally **Leila Koerber** (1869-1934) Stage and film actress, born in Coburg, Canada. A versatile comic actress, she performed in vaudeville, plays, and musical productions, enjoying great success with the song, 'Heaven will protect the working girl'. Her films include *Min and Bill* (1931, Oscar).

Drew, Richard (1899-1980) US inventor of masking tape. With the backing of his employers, 3M, he developed masking tape by 1925, and Scotch Cellulose Tape by 1930, transforming the fortunes of the previously struggling company.

Dreyer, Carl Theodor [drayer] (1889-1968) Film-maker, born in Copenhagen. He made his debut as a director with *The President* (trans, 1919). Later works included *The Passion of Joan of Arc* (trans, 1928) and *Vampyr* (1932).

Dreyer, John (Louis Emil) [drayer] (1852-1926) Astronomer, born in Copenhagen. He produced the standard catalogue on star clusters, nebulas, and galaxies, the *New General Catalogue* (NGC), which is still in use today.

Dreyfus, Alfred [drayfuhs] (c.1859-1935) French Jewish army officer, born in Mulhouse, France. Falsely charged with delivering defence secrets to the Germans (1893-4), he was transported to Devil's I, French Guiana. After vigorous efforts to prove him innocent, he was re-tried (1899), found guilty, but pardoned, and in 1906 the verdict was reversed.

Dreyfuss, Henry (1904-72) Designer and writer on design, born in New York City. He pioneered research into anthropometry, and his designs include telephones, vac-

uum cleaners, televisions, agricultural machinery, and airliner interiors.

Driesch, Hans (Adolf Eduard) [dreesh] (1867-1941) Zoologist and philosopher, born in Bad Kreuznach, Germany. He did valuable work in embryology and parapsychology, and became an exponent of vitalism.

Drinkwater, John (1882-1937) Poet, playwright, and critic, born in London. His historical dramas include *Abraham Lincoln* (1918) and *Mary Stuart* (1921). In 1923 his first volume of poems appeared, and he also wrote several critical studies.

Drobny, Jaroslav (1921-) Tennis player, and all-round sportsman, born in Prague. In 1948 he was made homeless by the Communist takeover of Czechoslovakia, and competed in tennis first as a stateless player, then for Egypt. He won the Wimbledon singles title in 1954.

Droste-Hülshoff, Annette Elisabeth, Freiin (Baroness) **von** [drostuh hülshohf] (1797-1848) Poet, born near Münster, Germany. Commonly regarded as Germany's greatest woman writer, her poetry is mainly on religious themes and on the Westphalian countryside. Her works were published posthumously in 1851.

Drucker, Peter F(erdinand) (1909-) Management consultant, born in Vienna. He went to the USA in 1937, and became a US citizen. His academic posts included professor of management at the Graduate School of Business, New York University (1950-72).

Drummond, Dugald (1840-1912) Locomotive engineer, born in Ardrossan, Strathclyde. He made his reputation in Scotland in 1876-8 with the 4-4-0 'Abbotsford' class, examples of which were still running in the 1960s.

Drummond, George (1687-1766) Entrepreneur and philanthropist, born in Perthshire. He was the driving force behind the building of the Royal Infirmary (1738) and the Royal Exchange (1760), and the proposal to create a New Town to the N of Princes Street.

Drummond, Henry (1786-1860) Banker, politician, and religious leader, born near Alresford, Hampshire. He became the founder and chief prophet of the Catholic Apostolic (or Irvingite) Church, based on the messianic creed of Edward Irving. >> **Irving, Edward**

Drummond, James Eric, 16th Earl of Perth (1876-1951) British statesman, born in Fulford, North Yorkshire. He was first secretary-general of the League of Nations (1919-32), and ambassador in Rome (1933-9).

Drummond, Thomas (1797-1840) Engineer, born in Edinburgh. In 1820 he joined the ordnance survey, whose work was greatly helped by his improved heliostat and lime-light (the *Drummond light*). He became under-secretary for Ireland in 1835.

Drummond (of Hawthornden), William (1585-1649) Poet, born at Hawthornden, near Edinburgh. He was the first Scottish poet to write in a form of English not from Scotland. His chief collection, *Poems*, appeared in 1616.

Drury, Alfred (1857-1944) Sculptor, born in London. Among his works are 'Edward VII' (1903), 'Sir Joshua Reynolds' (1931), and the 'London Troops' war memorial at the Royal Exchange.

Drusus Germanicus, Nero Claudius [droosus jermanikus], also known as **Drusus Senior** (39-9 BC) Roman soldier, the son of Livia Drusilla, and father of Germanicus Caesar. He campaigned against the Alpine tribes (15 BC), and was engaged chiefly in establishing Roman supremacy in Germany. >> **Germanicus; Livia**

Druten, John van [drootn] (1901-57) Playwright, born in London. He became known with the production of his play *Young Woodley* (1928), and in the USA with *The Voice of the Turtle* (1943).

Dryden, John (1631-1700) Poet, born in Aldwinkle, Northamptonshire. He became Poet Laureate (1668-88) and in 1678 produced his best play, *All for Love*. Called to defend the king's party, he wrote a series of satires, notably *Absalom and Achitophel* (1681). Other works include the didactic poem *Religio laici* (1682) and *The Hind and the Panther* (1687), marking his conversion to Catholicism.

Drygalski, Erich Dagobert von [drigalskee] (1865–1949) Geophysicist and explorer, born in Königsberg, Germany. He headed an expedition in the *Gauss* to the Antarctic (1902–3), where he discovered and named the Gaussberg volcano.

Drysdale, Russell (1912–81) Painter, born in Bognor Regis, West Sussex. His family settled in Melbourne in 1923, and his powerful scenes of the outback were a major contribution to modern art in Australia.

du Barry, Marie Jeanne Gomard de Vaubernier, comtesse (Countess), *née* **Bécu** (c.1743–93) The favourite mistress of Louis XV, born in Vaucouleurs, France. Her influence reigned supreme until the death of Louis in 1774. Later accused of being a counter-revolutionary, she was tried and guillotined. >> Louis XV

Dubček, Alexander [dubchek] (1921–92) Czechoslovakian statesman, born in Uhrovek, Slovak Republic. As first secretary in the Communist Party (1968), his liberalization policy led to the occupation of Czechoslovakia by Soviet forces (1968), and in 1969 he was replaced. In 1989, following a popular uprising, he was elected chairman of the Czechoslovak parliament.

Dubinsky, David, originally **David Dobnievski** (1892–1982) Labour leader, born in Brest-Litovsk, Belarus. He emigrated to the USA in 1911, joined the International Ladies' Garment Workers' Union (ILGWU), and was elected its president (1932–66), making it one one of the most successful unions in America.

Dubois, (Marie) Eugène (François Thomas) [dübwah] (1858–1940) Palaeontologist, born in Eijsden, The Netherlands. In Java during the 1890s, he found the humanoid remains named as *Pithecanthropus erectus* (Java Man), which he claimed to be the 'missing link'.

Dubois, Guillaume [dübwah] (1656–1723) French prime minister (1722), born in Brives-la-Gaillarde, France. He was appointed foreign minister, Archbishop of Cambrai (both in 1720), and a cardinal (1721), before becoming prime minister.

du Bois, Guy Péne [doo bwah] (1884–1958) Painter, born in Brooklyn, NY. He became a member of the Ash Can school of painting, which stressed social realism. His later style developed an elegant and satirical approach, as seen in 'The Opera Box' (1926).

Du Bois, W(illiam) E(dward) B(urghardt) [doo boyz] (1868–1963) Historian, sociologist, and equal rights campaigner, born in Great Barrington, MA. His writings explored the history and lives of African-Americans, and he helped found the National Association for the Advancement of Colored People.

Dubos, René (Jules) [dü boh] (1901–82) Bacteriologist, born in Saint-Brice, France. In the USA from 1924, he discovered tyrothricin (1939), the first commercially produced antibiotic. His books include *So Human an Animal* (1968, Pulitzer).

Dubuffet, Jean [dübüfay] (1901–85) Artist, born in Le Havre, France. He invented the concept of Art Brut, pioneering the use of rubbish to create images, and is regarded as a forerunner of the Pop Art and Dada-like fashions of the 1960s.

du Cange, Charles du Fresne, seigneur (Lord) [dü käzh] (1610–88) Scholar, born in Amiens, France. A prolific writer and editor, he is best known for his glossaries of the Middle Ages (1678, 1688).

Duccio di Buoninsegna [doochioh dee bwoninsenya] (c.1260–c.1320) Painter, founder of the Sienese school, born in Siena, Italy. His masterpiece is the 'Maestà' for the altar of Siena cathedral (1311).

Duce, Il >> **Mussolini, Benito**

Duchamp, Marcel [düshã] (1887–1968) Painter, born in Blainville, France. He was asssociated with Cubism and Futurism, and was a pioneer of Dadaism, shocking his generation with such works as 'Nude Descending a Staircase' (1912, Philadelphia).

Duchamp-Villon, Raymond [düshã veeyõ] (1876–1918) Sculptor, born in Damville, France, the brother of Jacques Villon and half-brother of Marcel Duchamp. He became one of the leading Cubist sculptors in Paris, his most striking work being the bronze 'Horse' (1914). >> Duchamp; Villon, Jacques

Duchenne, Guillaume Benjamin Amand [düshen] (1806–75) Physician, born in Boulogne, France. He became a pioneer in electrophysiology, and was the founder of electrotherapeutics.

Duchesne, André [düshen], Lat **Chesnius** or **Quercetanus** (1584–1640) Historian, born in Ile-Bouchard, France. Known as 'the father of French history', he wrote histories of England, Scotland, and Ireland, of the popes down to Paul V, and of the House of Burgundy.

Duchesne, Père >> **Hébert, Jacques René**

Duclos du Hauron, Louis [dükloh dü ohrõ] (1837–1920) Scientist and inventor, born in Langon, France. *Colour in Photography* (trans, 1869) introduced the principles of additive and subtractive colour reproduction, and in 1891 he proposed the anaglyph method of viewing stereoscopic images.

Duddell, William du Bois (1872–1917) British engineer. He worked on radiotelegraphy, and in 1897 invented an improved version of the oscillograph. The Physical Society instituted the *Duddell Medal* in his honour.

Dudevant, Madame >> **Sand, George**

Dudley, Lord Guildford (?–1554) The fourth son of the Lord Protector John Dudley, Earl of Warwick. His father married him to the unwilling Lady Jane Grey in 1553, then proclaimed her queen. After the accession of Mary I, he and his wife were beheaded. >> Grey, Lady Jane; Mary I; Warwick, John Dudley

Dudley, Sir Robert >> **Leicester, Robert Dudley, Earl of**

Dudley, William (Stuart) (1947–) Stage designer, born in London. He has designed many productions for the Royal Court and the National Theatre (associate designer since 1981).

Dudok, Willem Marinus [doodok] (1884–1974) Architect, born in Amsterdam. He became city architect of Hilversum in 1915, his masterwork being the Hilversum Town Hall (1928–30).

Dufay, Guillaume [düfay] (c.1400–74) Composer, probably born in Cambrai, France. He wrote one of his most famous motets, *Nuper rosarum flores*, for the dedication of the dome of Florence Cathedral (1436). He also wrote Masses and secular songs.

Duffy, Sir Charles Gavan (1816–1903) Irish nationalist, born in Co Monaghan, Ireland. For 12 years he engaged in agitation, being tried for sedition and treason, then emigrated to Australia (1856), where he became prime minister of Victoria in 1871.

Du Fresne, Charles >> **Du Cange, Charles Du Fresne**

Du Fu [doo foo], also spelled **Tu Fu** (712–70) Poet, friend, and admirer of Li Bo. He wrote lyrical poems on friendship and wine, full of social and historical detail. >> Li Bo

Dufy, Raoul [düfee] (1877–1953) Artist and designer, born in Le Havre, France. He produced many fabric designs and engraved book illustrations, and (from 1919) a long series of swift calligraphic sketches of seascapes, regattas, and racecourse scenes.

Dughet, Gaspard [doogay], also called **Gaspard Poussin** and known as **Le Guaspre** (1615–75) Painter, born in Rome. His sister married Nicholas Poussin, and he called himself after his more famous brother-in-law. He specialized in landscapes which combine the classical manner of Poussin and the more lyrical style of Claude Lorrain. >> Claude Lorrain; Poussin

Duhamel, Georges [dooamel] (1884–1966) Novelist, poet, and man of letters, born in Paris. His best-known works are his novel cycles *Salavin* (1920–32) and *The Pasquier Chronicles* (trans, 1933–44).

Duhamel du Monceau, Henri-Louis [dooamel dü mõsoh] (1700–82) Technologist, born in Paris. He proved the distinction between potassium and sodium salts, showed that soda can be made from rock-salt, and improved the making of starch, soap, and brass.

Dühem, Pierre (Maurice Marie) [düem] (1861–1916) Philosopher of science and physicist, born in Paris. His early scientific work was in thermodynamics, and he also made important contributions to the history of science.

Dukakis, Michael [dookakis] (1933–) US politician, born in Boston, MA. He became governor of Massachusetts (1975–9, 1983–91), and in 1988 he was Democratic nominee for the presidency.

Dukas, Paul (Abraham) [dükah] (1865–1935) Composer, born in Paris. His best-known work is the symphonic poem *The Sorcerer's Apprentice* (trans, 1897), and he also wrote orchestral and piano pieces.

Dulbecco, Renato [dulbekoh] (1914–) Molecular biologist, born in Catanzaro, Italy. He used a simple model system to show how certain viruses can transform some cells into a cancerous state, for which he shared the 1975 Nobel Prize for Physiology or Medicine. >> Baltimore, David; Temin

Dulles, Allen W(elsh) [duhles] (1893–1969) Intelligence officer, born in Washington, DC, the brother of John Foster Dulles. He became director of the Central Intelligence Agency in 1953, but was forced to resign when the CIA became the scapegoat for the failed attempt to overthrow Fidel Castro at the Bay of Pigs (1961). >> Castro; Dulles, John Foster

Dulles, John Foster [duhlez] (1888–1959) US Republican secretary of state (1953–9), born in Washington, DC. US delegate to the UN General Assembly, as secretary of state he opened a vigorous diplomacy of personal conferences with statesmen in other countries. Dulles airport, Washington, is named after him. >> Dulles, Alan W

Dulong, Pierre Louis [dülõ] (1785–1838) Chemist, born in Rouen, France. His name is now most linked with the *Dulong–Petit law* (1819), which relates the specific heat capacity of a solid element to its relative atomic mass. >> Petit, Alexis (Thérèse)

Dumas, Alexandre [dümah], known as **Dumas père** ('father') (1802–70) Writer, born in Villers-Cotterêts, France. He began writing plays, then turned to travelogues and historical novels. Among his best-known works are (trans titles) *The Count of Monte Cristo* (1844–55), *The Three Musketeers* (1845), and *The Black Tulip* (1850). >> Dumas, Alexandre (fils)

Dumas, Alexandre [dümah], known as **Dumas fils** ('son') (1824–95) Writer, born in Paris, the illegitimate son of Alexandre Dumas. His novels include *The Lady of the Camellias* (trans, 1848), but he is best-known for his plays, such as *Monsieur Alphonse* (1873). >> Dumas, Alexandre (père)

Dumas, Jean Baptiste André [dümah] (1800–84) Organic chemist, born in Alais, France. His ideas about the relations between organic compounds laid the foundations for Kekulé's later work. >> Kekulé

du Maurier, Dame Daphne [dü mohryay] (1907–89) Novelist, born in London, the grand-daughter of George du Maurier. She wrote several successful period romances and adventure stories, including *Jamaica Inn* (1936),

Rebecca (1938), and *The Flight of the Falcon* (1965). >> du Maurier, George

du Maurier, George (Louis Palmella Busson) [dü mohryay] (1834–96) Artist and illustrator, born in Paris. In 1860 he went to London as a designer and book illustrator, joining the staff of *Punch*. He wrote and illustrated three novels, notably *Trilby* (1894). >> du Maurier, Daphne / Gerald

du Maurier, Sir Gerald [dü mohryay] (1873–1934) Actor-manager, born in London, the younger son of George du Maurier. He became joint manager of Wyndham's Theatre (1910–25), and was manager of the St James's Theatre from 1926 until his death. >> du Maurier, George

Du Mont, Allen B(alcom) [doomont] (1901–65) Electronics engineer, born in New York City. He began the mass production of radio valves, founding his own company in 1931, and in 1937 produced the first fully electronic TV receivers using cathode-ray tubes.

Dumont D'Urville, Jules Sébastien César [dümõ dürveey] (1790–1842) Navigator, born in Condé-sur-Noireau, France. He commanded expeditions to survey the South Pacific (1826–9) and the Antarctic (1837–40), discovering Joinville I and Adélie Land.

Dumouriez, Charles François (du Périer) [dümooryay] (1739–1823) French general, born in Cambrai, France. He defeated the Prussians at Valmy and the Austrians at Jemappes (1792), but lost at Neerwinden (1793). Denounced by the revolutionaries for his monarchist leanings, he then went over to the Austrians.

Dunant, (Jean) Henri [dünã] (1828–1910) Philanthropist, born in Geneva, Switzerland. He inspired the foundation of the International Red Cross, and helped to bring about the conference from which came the Geneva Convention (1864). In 1901 he shared the first Nobel Peace Prize.

Dunbar, William [duhnbah(r)] (1749–1810) Planter and scientist, born near Elgin, Grampian. Moving to the USA in 1773, he built a plantation near Natchez, MI, and undertook explorations of the Quachita and Red R areas.

Dunbar, Paul (Lawrence) [duhnbah(r)] (1872–1906) Poet, born in Dayton, OH, the son of escaped Negro slaves. His many works include *Lyrics of Lowly Life* (1896) and *Complete Poems* (1913).

Dunbar, William [duhnbah(r)] (c.1460–c.1520) Poet, probably born in East Lothian. His poems include *The Thrissil and the Rois, Lament for the Makaris*, and several satires, such as *The Dance of the Sevin Deadly Synnis*.

Duncan I >> **Macbeth**

Duncan, Andrew (1744–1828) Physician, born near St Andrews, Fife. In 1792 he prompted the Royal College of Physicians in Edinburgh to establish a lunatic asylum, which came to fruition in 1807.

Duncan, Isadora, originally **Angela Duncan** (1877–1927) Dancer and choreographer, born in San Francisco, CA. She travelled in Europe, performing her own choreography, and founding schools in several cities. A pioneer of modern dance, she was also known for her unconventional views on women's liberation.

Duncan, Robert (Edward), originally **Edward Howard Duncan**, adopted name **Robert Edward Symmes** (1919–88) Poet, born in Oakland, CA. He became associated with the San Francisco Bay area group of poets, as seen in *The Opening of the Field* (1960).

Duncan-Sandys, Duncan Edwin Sandys, Baron [duhngkn sandz] (1908–87) British statesman and founder of the Civic Trust (1956). His cabinet posts included minister of supply in the Churchill government (1951), minister of housing and local government (1954), minister of defence (1957–9), and secretary of state for commonwealth relations (1960–4).

Dundee, John Graham of Claverhouse, 1st Viscount, known as **Bloody Claverse** or **Bonnie Dundee**

(c.1649–89) Scottish soldier, born of a noble family. He defeated the Covenanters at Bothwell Brig (1679) and raised the standard for James II against William and Mary, but died after his successful battle against Mackay at the Pass of Killiecrankie. >> James II (of England)

Dunér, Nils Christofer [**du**nair] (1839–1914) Astronomer, born in Billeberga, Sweden. He made a study of variable and double stars, was an expert on stellar spectroscopy, and made important observations of the Sun's rotational period.

Dunham, Katherine [**duhn**ham] (1910–) Dancer, choreographer, and teacher, born in Chicago, IL. Her Dunham School of Dance (1945–55) exerted considerable influence on the direction of African-American dance.

Dunhill, Thomas Frederick [**duhn**hil] (1877–1946) Composer and teacher, born in London. He made his name with chamber works, songs, and the light opera *Tantivy Towers* (1931).

Dunlop, Frank (1927–) Stage director and administrator, born in Leeds, West Yorkshire. He became director of Nottingham Playhouse (1961–4) and associate director at the National Theatre (1967–71), founded the Young Vic (1970), and was director of the Edinburgh Festival (1983–91).

Dunlop, Joey, popular name of **(William) Joseph Dunlop** (1952–) Motor-cyclist, born in Ballymoney, Northern Ireland. He won the Isle of Man Senior Tourist Trophy (TT) in 1985 and 1987–8. In 1988 he won the Formula One TT for the sixth successive season, and was Formula One world champion 1982–6.

Dunlop, John Boyd (1840–1921) Inventor, born in Dreghorn, Strathclyde. He invented the pneumatic tyre (c.1887), at first used for bicycles.

Dunlop, Ronald (Ossary) (1894–1973) Painter, born in Dublin. A member of the London Group, he is best known for his palette-knife painting with rich impasto and glowing colour.

Dunn, Douglas (1942–) Dancer and choreographer, born in Palo Alto, CA. With Yvonne Rainer he founded the experimental dance group, Grand Union, and in 1977 founded his own company. >> Rainer

Dunne, Finley Peter (1867–1936) Journalist and humorist, born in Chicago, IL. As **Mr Dooley,** he became widely known from 1900 as the exponent of American-Irish humorous satire on current personages and events.

Dunne, J(ohn) W(illiam) (1875–1949) British inventor and philosopher. He designed the first British military aeroplane (1906–7). His best-selling speculative works include *An Experiment with Time* (1927) and *Nothing Dies* (1940).

Dunning, William A(rchibald) (1857–1922) Historian and educator, born in Plainfield, NJ. His major work was *History of Political Theories* (3 vols, 1916), but his chief significance lies in his direction of doctoral research on US history.

Dunois, Jean d'Orléans, comte (Count) [dünwah], known as **the Bastard of Orléans** (1403–68) French general, born in Paris, the natural son of Louis, Duke of Orléans (1372–1407). He defeated the English at Montargis (1427), defended Orléans until its relief by Joan of Arc (1429), then drove the English out of Paris, Normandy, and Guyenne. >> Joan of Arc

Duns Scotus, Johannes [duhnz skohtus], known as **Doctor Subtilis** (Lat 'the Subtle Doctor') (c.1265–1308) Mediaeval philosopher and theologian, probably born in Maxton, Borders, Scotland. A Franciscan, his works are chiefly commentaries on the Bible, Aristotle, and the *Sentences* of Peter Lombard. His dialectical skill gained him his nickname. >> Lombard, Peter

Dunstable, John [**duhn**stabl] (?–1453) English composer. He wrote motets, Masses, and secular songs, including the three-part 'O rosa bella', and exercised great influence on his continental contemporaries.

Dunstan, St (c.909–88), feast day 19 May. Abbot, born near Glastonbury, Somerset. He became abbot of Glastonbury in 945, making the abbey a centre of religious teaching. In 960 he was appointed Archbishop of Canterbury.

Duparc, (Marie Eugène) Henri (Fouques-) [düpah(r)k] (1848–1933) Composer, born in Paris. He destroyed much of his writing and correspondence, but is remembered for his 15 songs which rank among the world's greatest.

Duplessis, Maurice LeNoblet [düplesee] (1890–1959) Liberal premier and attorney general of Quebec (1936–9, 1944–59). He asserted the authority of the state over the Church, undertook enormous public works projects, and dealt harshly with striking unions and other opposition.

Dupond, Patrick [düpõ] (1959–) Dancer, born in Paris. At the age of 15, he was the youngest dancer ever accepted into the Paris Opera Ballet, and in 1980 reached the rank of *étoile.* In 1988 he became artistic director of Ballet de Nancy.

Du Pont, Pierre Samuel [doo **pont**] (1870–1954) Businessman and management innovator, born in Wilmington, DE. As president (1915–20) of the family gunpowder company, he introduced many new management techniques. He became president of General Motors in 1920.

Dupont, Samuel Francis [doo**pont**] (1803–65) US naval officer, born in Bergen Point, NJ. In the Civil War he captured the ports of South Carolina and Georgia. Unjustly blamed for the failed attack on Charleston (1863), he was relieved of his command.

du Pré, Jacqueline [doo **pray**] (1945–87) Cellist, born in Oxford, Oxfordshire. She quickly established an international reputation, and in 1967 married the pianist Daniel Barenboim, with whom she gave many recitals. Her career as a player ended in 1973, when she developed multiple sclerosis. >> Barenboim

Dupré, Jules [düpray] (1811–89) Landscape painter, born in Nantes, France. He studied in England with Constable, and was a leader of the Barbizon school. >> Constable, John

Dupré, Marcel [düpray] (1886–1971) Organist, born in Rouen, France. Renowned throughout Europe for his organ recitals, he composed many chorales and an organ concerto.

Dupuytren, Guillaume, Baron [düpweetriï] (1777–1835) Surgeon, born in Pierre Buffière, France. He invented many surgical instruments, and devised techniques for several conditions, including *Dupuytren's contracture* (a flexion deformity of the hand).

Duquesne, Abraham, Marquis [düken] (1610–88) French naval officer, born in Dieppe, France. He defeated Ruyter and Tromp several times in 1672–3, and the united fleets of Spain and Holland off Sicily in 1676. >> Ruyter; Tromp

Durand, Asher B(rown) [duh**rand**] (1796–1886) Painter, engraver, and illustrator, born in Jefferson Village, NJ. He became associated with the Hudson River School, painting Romantic and dramatic landscapes. His graphic work strongly influenced the design of US paper currency.

Durand, J(ean) N(icolas) L(ouis) [dürã] (1760–1834) Architect, theorist, and educator, born in Paris. He built little, but greatly influenced contemporary Neoclassical architecture through his *Collection and Comparison of Buildings of All Types* (trans, 1800).

Durante, Francesco [du**ran**tay] (1684–1755) Composer, born in Naples, Italy. Head of the Conservatorio di Santa Maria di Loreto in Naples (1742–5), he wrote a wide variey of church and chamber music.

Durante, Jimmy [du**ran**tee], popular name of **James Francis Durante,** nickname **Schnoz** or **Schnozzle Durante** (1893–1980) Comedian, born in New York City. Known for his large nose (hence his nickname), he was a popular and versatile entertainer on Broadway and radio.

Duras, Marguerite [düra], pseudonym of **Marguerite Donnadieu** (1914–96) Novelist, born in Gia Dinh, Vietnam. She went to France in 1932, and made her reputation with such novels as *The Sea Wall* (trans, 1950). She also wrote the screenplay for *Hiroshima, My Love* (trans, 1959).

Durbin, Deanna, originally **Edna Mae Durbin** (1921–) Entertainer, born in Winnipeg, Manitoba, Canada. Her films include *Three Smart Girls* (1936), *Christmas Holiday* (1944), and *Lady on a Train* (1945).

Dürer, Albrecht [dyoorer], Ger [dürer] (1471–1528) Painter and engraver, born in Nuremberg, Germany. In 1497 he set up his own studio, producing many paintings, then in 1498 published his first great series of designs on wood, the illustrations of the Apocalypse.

Durey, Louis [düree] (1888–1979) Composer, born in Paris. In 1916 he joined the group of young French composers known as *Les Six*, breaking with them in 1921. He is chiefly known for his songs and chamber music.

D'Urfey, Thomas [derfay] (1653–1723) Playwright and songwriter, born in Exeter, Devon. His popular comedies include *The Fond Husband* (1676) and *Sir Burnaby Whig* (1681), and in 1683 he published his *New Collection of Songs and Poems*.

Durham, John George Lambton, Earl of [duhram], known as **Radical Jack** (1792–1840) British statesman, born in London. He was a strong Liberal, his nickname stemming from his reformist views. In the administration of his father-in-law, Lord Grey (1830), he was Lord Privy Seal, and one of the four persons who drew up the Reform Bill. >> Grey, Charles

Durkheim, Emile [derkhiym] (1858–1917) Sociologist, born in Epinal, France. One of the founders of sociology, his works include *The Rules of Sociological Method* (trans, 1894).

Durrell, Gerald (Malcolm) [duhrel] (1925–95) British zoologist, writer, and broadcaster, born in Jamshedpur, India, the brother of Lawrence Durrell. His popular animal stories and reminiscences include *My Family and Other Animals* (1956) and *A Zoo in My Luggage* (1960). He was founder chairman of Wildlife Preservation Trust International in 1972. >> Durrell, Lawrence

Durrell, Lawrence (George) [duhrel] (1912–90) British novelist and poet, born in Darjeeling, India. He is best known for the 'Alexandria Quartet' (1957–60): *Justine*, *Balthazar*, *Mountolive*, and *Clea*. Later novels include *Monsieur* (1974), *Livia* (1978), *Constance* (1982), *Sebastian* (1983), and *Quinx* (1985). >> Durrell, Gerald

Dürrenmatt or **Duerrenmatt, Friedrich** [dürenmat] (1921–90) Writer, born in Konolfingen, Switzerland. His plays include (trans titles) *The Marriage of Mr Mississippi* (1952), *The Physicists* (1962), and *The Appointed Time* (1977). He also wrote novels, short stories, essays, and works for radio.

Duse, Eleonora [doozay] (1859–1924) Actress, born near Venice, Italy. She mainly acted in plays by Ibsen, contemporary French playwrights, and Gabriele d'Annunzio, who was her lover. >> d'Annunzio

Dussek, Jan Ladislav (1760–1812) Composer and pianist, born in Czaslau, Czech Republic. He was popular in London (1788–1800), became instructor to Prince Louis Ferdinand of Prussia (1803–6), and in 1808 entered the service of Talleyrand. >> Talleyrand

Dutrochet, René Joachim Henri [dütrohshay] (1776–1847) Physiologist, born in Néon, France. He was the first to study and to name osmosis.

Duun, Olav [doon] (1876–1939) Novelist, born in Namsdal, Norway. An important representative of new Norwegian writing in *Landsmål* ('national language'), he wrote a major series of saga-like novels, *The People of Juvik* (trans, 6 vols, 1918–23).

Duval, Claude [düval] (1643–70) Highwayman, born in Domfront, France. He came to England at the Restoration

(1660), gaining a popular reputation, especially for his gallantry towards women. He was hanged at Tyburn, London.

Duvalier, François [doovalyay], known as **Papa Doc** (1907–71) Haitian president (1957–71), born in Port-au-Prince. His regime saw the creation of the dreaded civilian militia known as the Tonton Macoute, and the exile of many people. He became life president in 1964, and was succeeded in this post by his son, Jean-Claude. >> Duvalier, Jean-Claude

Duvalier, Jean-Claude [doovalyay], known as **Baby Doc** (1951–) Haitian president (1971–86), born in Port-au-Prince, the son of François ('Papa Doc') Duvalier. At the age of 20 he became president-for-life, ruling through a private army. In 1986 he was deposed in a military coup and went into exile. >> Duvalier, François

Duve, Christian de >> de Duve, Christian

Duveen (of Millbank), Joseph Duveen, Baron (1869–1939) Art dealer, born in Hull, Humberside. He developed a business in the USA specializing in Old Masters, and established significant collections in the USA and Europe.

Du Vigneaud, Vincent [doo veenyoh] (1901–78) Biochemist, born in Chicago, IL. He researched sulphur-containing vitamins, isolated Vitamin H, and deduced the structure of biotin (1942). In 1953 he succeeded in synthesizing oxytocin, for which he was awarded the Nobel Prize for Chemistry in 1955.

Dvořák, Antonín (Leopold) [dvaw(r)zhak] (1841–1904) Composer, born near Prague. His work, known for its colourful Slavonic motifs, includes nine symphonies, much chamber and piano music, and the acclaimed *Stabat mater* (1880).

Dwight, John (c.1637–1703) Potter, born in Oxfordshire. At his pottery in Fulham (1671–98), he patented a 'transparent earthenware' resembling porcelain, thus pioneering the English pottery industry.

Dworkin, Ronald (Myles) (1931–) Legal scholar, born in Wooster, MA. A leading theorist of jurisprudence, his books include *Taking Rights Seriously* (1977) and *A Matter of Principle* (1985).

Dyce, William (1806–64) Historical and religious painter, born in Aberdeen, Grampian. He executed frescoes in several London locations, including the new House of Lords.

Dyck, Anthony van >> van Dyck, Anthony

Dyer, Anson [diyer], originally **Ernest Anson-Dyer** (1876–1962) Animator, born in Brighton, West Sussex. In 1935 he began a series of colour cartoons based on the Stanley Holloway character, *Old Sam*, his biggest popular success. >> Holloway

Dyke, Dick Van >> Van Dyke, Dick

Dylan, Bob [dilan], pseudonym of **Robert Zimmerman** (1941–) Folk-singer and songwriter, born in Duluth, MN. He rose to fame in the 1960s, his lyrics focussing on pacifism, the nuclear bomb, and racial and social injustice, as in 'Blowin' in the Wind' and 'The Times They are a-Changin'. He remains one of the seminal influences on popular songwriting.

Dympna, St [dimpna] (9th, feast day 15 May. Irish princess, said to have been slain by her father at Gheel in Belgium for resistance to his incestuous passion. She is the patron saint of the insane.

Dyson, Sir Frank (Watson) (1868–1939) Astronomer, born in Measham, Leicestershire. He is known for his observations in 1919 which supported Einstein's hypothesis that light could be deflected by a gravitational field, and for his work on the distribution of stars and on solar eclipses.

Dzerzhinsky, Felix Edmundovich [jerzhinskee] (1877–1926) Russian revolutionary, born in Vilna. He fought in the 1905 revolution, and in 1917 became chairman of the secret police and a member of the Bolshevik central committee.

Eadgar >> **Edgar**

Eadmer or **Edmer** (c.1060–c.1128) Monk and historian, born in Canterbury, Kent. His major works were *Historia novorum in Anglia* (6 vols, c.1115) and *Vita Anselmi* (c.1124).

Eads, James B(uchanan) [eedz] (1820–87) Engineer and inventor, born in Lawrenceburg, IN. He built ironclad steamers, invented a diving bell, and constructed the steel triple-arched Eads Bridge (1867–74) across the Mississippi at St Louis.

Eagles, John >> **Eccles, John**

Eakins, Thomas [eekinz] (1844–1916) Painter, born in Philadelphia, PA. His best-known work is the realistic depiction of a surgical operation, 'The Gross Clinic' (1875), which was controversially received on account of its detail.

Ealdhelm, St >> **Aldhelm, St**

Ealdred >> **Aldred**

Eames, Charles [eemz] (1907–78) Designer, born in St Louis, MO. He staged the first ever one-man design show at the New York Museum of Modern Art (1946). He is best known for his furniture, including the celebrated 'Lounge Chair' (1956).

Eardley, Joan [eerdlee] (1921–63) Painter, born in Warnham, West Sussex. She is especially known for her studies of poor children from the Glasgow tenements, and for her Scottish landscapes and seascapes.

Earhart, Amelia [ay(r)hah(r)t] (1897–1937) Aviator, born in Atchison, KS. She was the first woman to fly the Atlantic, as a passenger, and followed this by a solo flight in 1932. In 1937 she set out to fly round the world, but her plane was lost over the Pacific.

Early, Jubal A(nderson) (1816–94) US soldier, born in Franklin County, VA. During the Civil War he commanded a Confederate brigade at Bull Run, and a division at Fredericksburg and Gettysburg (1863), but was relieved of his command after a rout at Waynesboro (1864).

Earp, Wyatt (Berry Stapp) [erp] (1848–1929) Gambler, gunfighter, and lawman, born in Monmouth, IL. During his stay in Tombstone, AZ, he befriended Doc Holliday, who joined with the Earp brothers against the Clanton gang in the famous gunfight at the OK Corral (1881). >> Holliday

East, Sir Alfred (1849–1913) Painter and etcher, born in Kettering, Northamptonshire. He is best known for his landscapes of Japan, and from 1902 he produced a large number of etchings.

East, Michael (c.1580–1648) Composer and organist. His works include church music and madrigals, and he was a contributor to *The Triumphes of Oriana*, dedicated to Elizabeth I in 1603.

Eastlake, Sir Charles Lock (1793–1865) Historical painter, born in Plymouth, Devon. He made his name with two full-length portraits of Napoleon sketched while a prisoner on HMS *Bellerophon* in Portsmouth harbour (1815).

Eastlake, Charles Lock (1836–1906) Architect, designer, and writer, born in Plymouth, Devon, the nephew of the painter Sir Charles Lock Eastlake. His book *Hints on Household Taste in Furniture, Upholstery and Other Details* (1868) gave rise to the *Eastlake style* in the USA. >> Eastlake, Sir Charles Lock

Eastman, George (1854–1932) Inventor and philanthropist, born in Waterville, NY. He produced a successful roll-film (1884), the 'Kodak' box camera (1888), and the transparent celluloid film which made possible the moving-picture industry (1889).

Eastwick, Edward Backhouse (1814–43) Orientalist, born in Warfield, Berkshire. Assistant political secretary in the India Office (1859), he became secretary of the legation in Persia (1860–3), and produced many translations from Persian.

Eastwood, Clint (1930–) Film actor and director, born in San Francisco, CA. He began acting in television Westerns, and rose to international stardom with the 'spaghetti' Western *A Fistful of Dollars* (1964). Later films, several of which he also directed, include *Dirty Harry* (1971), *Bird* (1987), and *Unforgiven* (1992, two Oscars).

Eban, Abba (Solomon) [eeban], originally **Aubrey Solomon** (1915–) Israeli diplomat and statesman, born in Cape Town, South Africa. Israeli ambassador in Washington, DC (1950–9), he later became foreign minister (1966–74).

Ebbinghaus, Hermann [aybinghows] (1850–1909) Experimental psychologist, born in Barmen, Germany. He is best remembered for *On Memory* (trans, 1885) which first applied experimental methods to memory research.

Eberhart, Richard (Ghormley) [ayberhah(r)t] (1904–) Poet and teacher, born in Austin, MN. His books include *Undercliff* (1953) and *Shifts of Being* (1968), and he has also published *Collected Verse Plays* (1962).

Ebert, Friedrich [aybert] (1871–1925) The first president of the German Republic (1919–25), born in Heidelberg, Germany. He became chairman of the Social Democrats (1913), and was a socialist leader in the revolution of 1918.

Eccles or **Eagles, John** (c.1650–1735) Composer, born in London. He composed the music for the coronation of Queen Anne, and published many volumes of theatre music, songs, and masques. A brother, **Henry** (c.1652–1742), achieved success as a violinist in Paris.

Eccles, Sir John (Carew) (1903–) Physiologist, born in Melbourne, Victoria, Australia. A specialist in neurophysiology, he shared the 1963 Nobel Prize for Physiology or Medicine for his work on the functioning of nervous impulses.

Ecevit, Bülent [ejevit] (1925–) Turkish prime minister (1974, 1977, 1978–9), born in Istanbul. He headed a coalition government in 1974, during which he ordered the invasion of Cyprus. After the military coup of 1980, he was imprisoned twice for criticizing the military regime.

Ecgberht / Ecgbryht >> **Egbert**

Echegaray y Eizaguirre, José [aychaygahree ee ayeethageeray] (1832–1916) Spanish statesman, mathematician, and playwright, born in Madrid. He held portfolios in various ministries (1868–74), then won literary fame from his many plays, sharing the 1904 Nobel Prize for Literature. His masterpiece was *The World and his Wife* (trans, 1881).

Eck, Johann Mayer von (1486–1543) Roman Catholic theologian, born in Egg, Switzerland. After his Leipzig disputation with Luther, he wrote on papal authority, and went to Rome in 1520, returning with the bull which declared Luther a heretic. >> Luther

Eckart / Eckehart, Johannes >> **Eckhart, Johannes**

Eckener, Hugo [ekener] (1868–1954) Aeronautical engineer, born in Flensburg, Germany. He piloted the ZR3 on the first Trans-Atlantic airship flight (1924), and commanded the *Graf Zeppelin* on the first airship flight around the world (1929). >> Zeppelin

Eckerman, Johann Peter [ekerman] (1792–1854) Writer, born in Winsen, Germany. He achieved fame with his *Conversations with Goethe* (trans, 3 vols, 1836–48). >> Goethe

Eckert, J(ohn) Presper, Jr (1919–95) Engineer and inventor, born in Philadelphia, PA. He obtained over 85 patents for his electronic inventions, but is best known for his work, with Mauchly, on the Electronic Numerical Integrator And Calculator (ENIAC), one of the first modern computers. >> Mauchly

Eckhart, Johannes [ekhah(r)t], also spelled **Eckart** or **Eckehart**, known as **Meister Eckhart** ('Master Eckhart') (c.1260–c.1327) Theologian, born in Hocheim, Germany. A Dominican, his teaching was a mystic pantheism, influential on later religious mysticism and speculative philosophy. Two years after his death his writings were condemned by Pope John XXII.

Eckstine, Billy [ekstiyn], popular name of **William Clarence Eckstein** (1914–93) Singer, born in Pittsburgh, PA. He formed his own band in 1944, promoting the new bebop style of popular music. Among his hit records was 'That Old Black Magic'.

Eco, Umberto [aykoh] (1929–) Novelist and critic, born in Alessandria, Italy. His intellectual medieval detective story, *The Name of the Rose* (trans, 1981; filmed 1986), achieved instant fame. *Foucault's Pendulum* appeared in 1989.

Eddery, Pat(rick James John) (1952–) Jockey, born in Newbridge, Ireland. A champion jockey (1974–7), he was winner of the Derby (1975, 1982), the Oaks twice, the St Leger, and the Prix de l'Arc de Triomphe (1980, 1985, 1986).

Eddington, Sir Arthur S(tanley) (1882–1944) Astronomer, born in Kendal, Cumbria. In 1919 his observations of star positions during a total solar eclipse gave the first direct confirmation of Einstein's general theory of relativity. He became a renowned popularizer of science, notably in *The Nature of the Physical World* (1928). >> Einstein

Eddy, Mary Baker, married name **Glover** (1821–1910) Founder of the Christian Science Church, born in Bow, NH. In 1866 she received severe injuries after a fall, but read about the palsied man in Matthew's Gospel, and claimed to have risen from her bed similarly healed. She set out her beliefs in *Science and Health with Key to the Scriptures* (1875), and organized the Church of Christ, Scientist, at Boston (1879).

Ede, James Chuter, Baron Chuter-Ede of Epsom [eed] (1882–1965) British statesman, born in Epsom, Surrey. He became home secretary in the 1945 Labour government, and Leader of the House of Commons in 1951. A humanitarian reformer, he was responsible for the Criminal Justice Act of 1948.

Edel, (Joseph) Leon [edl] (1907–) Biographer, born in Pittsburgh, PA. He devoted his scholarly career to Henry James, writing a biography of James (5 vols, 1953–85), and publishing editions of his letters and other writings. >> James, Henry

Edelman, Gerald (Maurice) [aydlman] (1929–) Biochemist, born in New York City. He studied the chemical structure and mode of action of the antibodies which form part of a vertebrate animal's defence against infection, and shared the Nobel Prize for Physiology or Medicine in 1972. >> Mountcastle

Eden, Sir (Robert) Anthony, 1st Earl of Avon [eedn] (1897–1977) British prime minister (1955–7), born at Windlestone Hall, Durham. He became foreign secretary (1935), resigning in 1938 over differences with Chamberlain. Foreign secretary again (1940–5, 1951–5), he succeeded Churchill as prime minister. In 1956 his controversial order to occupy the Suez Canal Zone led to his resignation. >> Chamberlain, Neville; Churchill, Sir Winston

Ederle, Gertrude (Caroline) [ayderlee] (1906–) The first woman to swim the English channel, born in New York City. She won a gold medal at the 1924 Olympic Games as a member of the US 400 m relay team, and on 6 August 1926 swam the Channel in 14 h 31 min.

Edgar or **Eadgar** (943–75) King of Mercia and Northumbria (957) and (from 959) King of all England, the younger son of Edmund I. In c.973 he introduced a uniform currency based on new silver pennies.

Edgar, David (Burman) (1948–) Playwright and teacher, born in Birmingham, West Midlands. His plays include *Saigon Rose* (1976), an eight-hour adaptation of *Nicholas Nickleby* (1980), and *The Shape of the Table* (1990).

Edgar the Ætheling ('Prince') [athuhling] (c.1050–1125) Anglo-Saxon prince, the son of Edward the Ætheling. Though chosen as king after the battle of Hastings, he submitted to William the Conqueror (1066), then rebelled and fled to Scotland (1068). He was reconciled with William in 1074, but later fought against Henry I. >> Edward the Ætheling; William I (of England)

Edger, Kate Millington (1857–1935) New Zealand teacher and suffragist, born in England. In 1877 she became the first woman in the British Empire to earn a BA, and was the founding principal of Nelson College for Girls (1882–93).

Edgerton, Harold E(ugene) [ejerton] (1903–90) Engineer, born in Fremont, NE. A specialist in stroboscopes and high-speed photography, he produced a krypton-xenon gas arc which was employed in photographing the capillaries in the white of the eye without hurting the patient.

Edgeworth, Maria (1767–1849) Writer, born in Blackbourton, Oxfordshire. She is best known for her children's stories and for her novels of Irish life, such as *Castle Rackrent* (1800) and *The Absentee* (1812).

Edinburgh, Prince Philip, Duke of [edinbruh] (1921–) The husband of Queen Elizabeth II of the United Kingdom, born in Corfu, Greece, the son of Prince Andrew of Greece and Princess Alice of Battenberg. He became a naturalized British subject in 1947, when he married the Princess Elizabeth. He is a keen sportsman, yachtsman, qualified airman, and conservationist, and in 1956 began the Duke of Edinburgh Award scheme to foster leisure activities for young people. >> Elizabeth II

Edison, Thomas (Alva) (1847–1931) Inventor and physicist, born in Milan, OH. He held patents for over 1000 inventions, including the printing telegraph (1871), the phonograph (1877), the carbon-filament light bulb (1879), and motion picture equipment. He discovered thermionic emission (1883), which became the basis for the electronic valve.

Edmer >> Eadmer

Edmund I (921–46) King of the English (939–46), the half-brother of Athelstan. He re-established control over the S Danelaw (942) and Northumbria (944) and, until his murder by an exile, ruled a reunited England. >> Athelstan

Edmund II, known as **Edmund Ironside** (c.980–1016) King of the English for a few months in 1016, the son of Ethelred the Unready. He defeated Canute, but was routed at Ashingdon, and agreed to a partition of the country. He died soon after, leaving Canute as sole ruler.

Edmund, St, known as **St Edmund the Martyr** (c.841–70), feast day 20 November. King of East Anglia, the adopted heir of Offa of Mercia. Defeated by the Danes (870), tradition claims that he was shot to death with arrows for his refusal to abjure his Christian faith. In 903 his remains were moved to Bury St Edmunds. >> Offa

Edmund, St, originally **Edmund Rich** (1170–1240), feast day 16 November. Clergyman, born in Abingdon, Oxfordshire. As Archbishop of Canterbury (1234) he became the spokesman of the national party against Henry III, defending Church rights. He was canonized in 1247. >> Henry III (of England)

Edrich, (William) John (1916–86) Cricketer, born in Norfolk. He played in 39 Tests, and with Compton shared a record third-wicket Test partnership of 370 against South Africa at Lord's in 1947. >> Compton, Denis

Edward I (1239–1307) King of England (1272–1307), born in London, the elder son of Henry III and Eleanor of Provence. He married Eleanor of Castile (1254) and later Margaret of France. In the Baron's War (1264–7), he defeated Simon de Montfort at Evesham (1265), then won renown as a crusader to the Holy Land. In two campaigns (1276–7, 1282–3) he annexed N and W Wales, building magnificent castles. His claims to the overlordship of Scotland began the Scottish Wars of Independence, and he died while fighting Robert Bruce. >> Bruce, Robert (1274–1329); Eleanor of Castile; Henry III; Montfort, Simon de

Edward II (1284–1327) King of England from 1307, born in Caernarvon, Wales, the fourth son of Edward I and Eleanor of Castile. In 1308 he married Isabella, the daughter of Philip IV of France. He was decisively defeated at Bannockburn (1314). In conflict with the barons, who sought to rid the country of royal favourites, he was deposed by Isabella and her lover, Roger Mortimer, Earl of March, and imprisoned. He abdicated in favour of his eldest son (1327), and was murdered in Berkeley Castle. >> Edward I / III; Isabella of France

Edward III, known as **Edward of Windsor** (1312–77) King of England from 1327, born in Windsor, Berkshire, the elder son of Edward II and Isabella of France. He married Philippa of Hainault in 1328. By banishing Queen Isabella from court, and executing her lover, Roger Mortimer, Earl of March (c.1287–1330), he began to restore the monarchy's authority. He defeated the Scots at Halidon Hill (1333) and in 1337 revived his hereditary claim to the French crown, thus beginning the Hundred Years' War. He destroyed the French navy at the Sluys (1340), and won a major victory at Crécy (1346). >> Edward II; Edward the Black Prince; Philippa of Hainault

Edward IV (1442–83) King of England (1461–70, 1471–83), born in Rouen, France, the eldest son of Richard, Duke of York. Recognized as king on Henry VI's deposition, and with the support of his cousin, Richard Neville, Earl of Warwick, he decisively defeated the Lancastrians at Towton. He secretly married Elizabeth Woodville in 1464. Warwick forced him into exile (1470), but he returned to England (1471), killed Warwick at Barnet, and destroyed the remaining Lancastrian forces at Tewkesbury. >> Henry VI; Warwick, Richard Neville; Woodville; York, Richard, 3rd Duke of

Edward V (1470–83) King of England (Apr–Jun 1483), born in London, the son of Edward IV and Elizabeth Woodville. He and his younger brother were imprisoned in the Tower by their uncle Richard, Duke of Gloucester, who usurped the throne as Richard III. The two Princes were never heard of again, and were probably murdered on their uncle's orders. >> Edward IV; Richard III

Edward VI (1537–53) King of England (1547–53), born in London, the son of Henry VIII by his third queen, Jane Seymour. During his reign, power was first in the hands of his uncle, the Duke of Somerset, then of John Dudley, Duke of Northumberland. He became a Protestant, and under the Protectors the English Reformation flourished. >> Henry VIII; Seymour, Jane; Somerset, Edward Seymour; Warwick, John Dudley

Edward VII (1841–1910) King of the United Kingdom (1901–10), born in London, the eldest son of Queen Victoria. In 1863 he married Alexandra, daughter of Christian IX of Denmark. They had three sons and three daughters: **Albert Victor** (1864–92), **George** (1865–1936), **Louise** (1867–1931), **Victoria** (1868–1935), **Maud** (1869–1938), and **Alexander** (born and died 1871). As Prince of

Wales, his behaviour led him into several social scandals. >> Alexandra, Queen; Victoria

Edward VIII (1894–1972) King of the United Kingdom (Jan–Dec 1936), born in Richmond, Surrey, the eldest son of George V. He succeeded his father in 1936, but abdicated in the face of opposition to his proposed marriage to Wallis Simpson, a commoner who had been twice divorced. He was given the title of Duke of Windsor, and the marriage took place in France in 1937. >> George V; Windsor, Duchess of

Edward (Antony Richard Louis), Prince (1964–) Prince of the United Kingdom, the third son of Queen Elizabeth II. He joined the Royal Marines in 1986, but left the following year and began a career in the theatre, joining Andrew Lloyd Webber's Really Useful Theatre Company. >> Elizabeth II

Edward the Ætheling (Prince) [at̲huhling] (?–1057) English nobleman, the son of Edmund Ironside, and the nephew of Edward the Confessor. When it became apparent that Edward the Confessor would never have an heir, he was recognized as the proper heir to his throne, but died shortly after returning to England in 1057. >> Edward the Confessor

Edward the Black Prince (1330–76) Prince of England, born in Woodstock, Oxfordshire, the eldest son of Edward III. He was created Prince of Wales in 1343, and fought at Crécy (1346), where he won his popular title from his black armour. His later victories included Poitiers (1356). He had two sons: **Edward** (1356–70) and **Richard**, the future Richard II. >> Edward III; Richard II

Edward the Confessor, St (c.1003–66), feast day 13 October. King of England (1042–66), the elder son of Ethelred the Unready and Emma of Normandy. Although in 1051 he probably recognized Duke William of Normandy (later William I) as his heir, on his deathbed he nominated Harold Godwinson (Harold II) to succeed, the Norman Conquest following soon after. He was canonized in 1161. >> Ethelred II; Harold II; William I (of England)

Edward the Elder (c.870–924) King of Wessex (from 899), the elder son of Alfred the Great. He established himself as the strongest ruler in Britain, annexing the S Danelaw (910–18), and taking control of Mercia (918). >> Alfred

Edward the Martyr, St (c.963–78), feast day 18 March. King of England (975–8). During his reign there was a reaction against the policies supporting monasticism espoused by his father, Edgar. He was murdered by supporters of his stepmother, Elfrida, and canonized in 1001. >> Edgar

Edwardes, Sir Michael (Owen) (1930–) British business executive, born in South Africa. He came to Britain in 1966, and developed a reputation for rescuing ailing companies, including British Leyland.

Edwards, Eli >> McKay, Claude

Edwards, Gareth (Owen) (1949–) Rugby Union player, born in Gwaun-cae-Gurwen, West Glamorgan. He was first capped for Wales while a teenager, became captain before he was 21, and won 63 caps.

Edwards, Sir George (Robert) (1908–) Designer of aircraft, born in Higham's Park, Greater London. He joined Vickers-Armstrong, and designed Viking, Valiant, Viscount, and Vanguard aircraft. He later became chairman of the British Aircraft Corporation.

Edwards, Jonathan (1703–58) Theologian, born in East Windsor, CT. A successful minister for many years, his extreme Calvinistic orthodoxy led to controversy, and he was dismissed in 1750. His works led to the religious revival known as the 'Great Awakening'. >> Edwards, Jonathan (1745–1801)

Edwards, Jonathan (1745–1801) Theologian, born in Northampton, MA, the son of Jonathan Edwards. His works include *A Dissertation concerning Liberty and Necessity* (1797). >> Edwards, Jonathan (1703–58)

Edwards, Robert >> **Steptoe, Patrick**

Edwin, St (584–633), feast day 12 October. King of Northumbria from 616, brought up in North Wales. Under him, Northumbria became united, and he obtained the overlordship of all England, save Kent. He was converted to Christianity (627), fell in battle at Hatfield Chase, and was afterwards canonized.

Egalité, Philippe >> **Orléans, Louis Philippe Joseph**

Egan, Sir John Leopold [eegn] (1939–) Industrial executive, born in Coventry, West Midlands. In 1980 he became chairman and chief executive of the then ailing Jaguar company, and restored the company's high reputation in Britain and abroad.

Egas Moniz, António (Caetano de Abreu Freire) (1874–1955) Neurosurgeon and diplomat, born in Avença, Portugal. The founder of modern psychosurgery, he shared the 1949 Nobel Prize for Physiology or Medicine for the development of prefrontal lobotomy. He was also a member of parliament and foreign minister (1918).

Egbert, in Anglo-Saxon **Ecgberht** or **Ecgbryht** (?–839) King of Wessex (802–39). His successes gave him mastery over S England from Kent to Land's End, and established Wessex as the strongest Anglo-Saxon kingdom.

Egede, Hans [aygeduh], known as **the Apostle of Greenland** (1686–1758) Missionary, born in Norway. In 1721 he founded the first mission in Greenland, and was appointed Bishop of Copenhagen in 1740.

Egerton, Francis, 3rd Duke of Bridgewater [ejuh(r)tn] (1736–1803) British canal builder. He engaged James Brindley to build (1759–61) a canal from Worsley to Manchester, extending it to reach Liverpool (1776), a total distance of 64 km/40 mi. The first canal in England, it became known as the Bridgewater Canal. >> Brindley

Ehrenberg, Christian Gottfried [airenberg] (1795–1876) Naturalist, born in Delitzsch, Germany. His works on microscopic organisms founded a new branch of science, and he discovered that phosphorescence in the sea is caused by living organisms.

Ehrenburg, Ilya Grigoryevich [airenberg] (1891–1967) Writer, born in Kiev, Ukraine. He wrote poetry, short stories, travel books, essays, and several novels, notably *The Fall of Paris* (trans, 1941) and *The Storm* (trans, 1948), both of which won Stalin Prizes.

Ehrenreich, Barbara [airenriyk] (1941–) Sociologist and writer, born in Butte, MT. Known for her outspoken feminist–socialist analyses of contemporary issues, her books include *For Her Own Good* (co-authored, 1978) and *The Worst Years of Our Lives* (1990).

Ehrlich, Paul [airleekh] (1854–1915) Bacteriologist, born in Strzelin, Poland. A pioneer in haematology, immunology, and chemotherapy, he discovered a cure for syphilis, and propounded the side-chain theory in immunology. He shared the Nobel Prize for Physiology or Medicine in 1908.

Ehrlich, Paul Ralph [airlik] (1932–) Entomologist and ecologist, born in Philadelphia, PA. He contributed to field research on Arctic insects and parasitic mites, and performed extensive studies of butterflies. His best-selling book, *The Population Bomb* (1968), advocated the concept of zero population growth.

Eichmann, (Karl) Adolf [iykhman] (1906–62) Nazi war criminal, born in Solingen, Germany. He became a member of the SS in 1932, and organizer of anti-Semitic activities. Captured by US forces in 1945, he escaped from prison, but was traced by Israeli agents, taken to Israel in 1960, and executed. >> Wiesenthal

Eiffel, (Alexandre) Gustave [efel] (1832–1923) Civil engineer, born in Dijon, France. Apart from his most famous project, the *Eiffel Tower*, he also designed the framework of the Statue of Liberty, New York.

Eigen, Manfred [iygen] (1927–) Physical chemist, born in Bochum, Germany. He developed methods for the study of very fast chemical reactions, for which he shared the Nobel Prize for Chemistry in 1967.

Eijkman, Christiaan [iykman] (1858–1930) Physician and pathologist, born in Nijkerk, The Netherlands. His observations of dietary deficiency led to the discovery of vitamins, for which he shared the Nobel Prize for Physiology or Medicine in 1929.

Einem, Gottfried von [iynem] (1917–) Composer, born in Bern. His successful stage works include several ballets and the operas *Danton's Death* (trans, 1947) and *The Visit of the Old Woman* (trans, 1971).

Einstein, Albert (1879–1955) Mathematical physicist, born in Ulm, Germany. He became world famous by his special (1905) and general (1916) theories of relativity, and was awarded the Nobel Prize for Physics in 1921. Director of the Kaiser Wilhelm Physical Institute in Berlin (1914–33), after Hitler's rise to power he left Germany, became a professor at the Institute of Advanced Study in Princeton, and spent the rest of his life attempting by means of his unified field theory (1950) to establish a merger between quantum theory and his general theory of relativity. He was also a champion of pacifism and liberalism.

Einstein, Alfred [iynstiyn] (1880–1952) Musicologist, born in Munich, Germany. He is known for his work on Mozart, especially the revision of Köchel's catalogue. >> Köchel

Einthoven, Willem [aynthohfn] (1860–1927) Dutch physiologist, born in Semarang, Indonesia. He invented the string galvanometer for measuring the electrical rhythms of the heart, and was awarded the Nobel Prize for Physiology or Medicine in 1924.

Eisenhower, Dwight D(avid) [iyznhower], nickname **Ike** (1890–1969) US general and 34th president (1953–61), born in Denison, TX. In 1942 he commanded Allied forces for the amphibious descent on French N Africa, and became Supreme Commander for the 1944 cross-channel invasion of the continental mainland. His popularity swept him to victory in the presidential elections (1952) standing as a Republican, and he was re-elected in 1956.

Eisenstaedt, Alfred [iyznstat] (1898–95) Photojournalist, born in Dirschau, Germany (now Tczew, Poland). He emigrated to the USA in 1935, where he became one of the original photographers working on *Life* (1936–72).

Eisenstein, Sergey (Mikhaylovich) [iyznstiyn] (1898–1948) Film director, born in Riga, Latvia. A major influence on the development of the cinema, his films include *Potemkin* (1925), *Alexander Nevski* (1938), and *Ivan the Terrible* (1945–7).

Eisler, Hanns [iysler] (1898–1962) Composer, born in Leipzig, Germany. A committed Marxist, he wrote political songs, choruses, and theatre music, often in collaboration with Brecht, as well as music for many films and plays. >> Brecht

Eisner, Will, popular name of **William Erwin Eisner** (1917–) Comic-book artist and writer, born in New York City. In 1937 he set up the first 'shop' for mass-producing strips for *Wags*, in which he developed the long-running weekly serial *Hawks of the Seas*.

Ekelöf, (Bengt) Gunnar [ekeloef] (1907–68) Poet, born in Stockholm. Much influenced by the French Symbolists, his works include (trans titles) *Late Arrival on Earth* (1932) and *Guide to the Underworld* (1967).

Ekman, Vagn Walfrid (1874–1954) Oceanographer, born in Stockholm. He designed several instruments for investigating ocean currents, and his name is remembered in the terms *Ekman layer* and *Ekman spiral*.

El Cid >> **Cid, El**

Elder, Sir Thomas (1818–97) Entrepreneur, born in Kirkcaldy, Fife. He emigrated to Adelaide, South Australia, in

1854, and founded one of the world's largest wool-broking firms. It is perpetuated in the international brewing and resources group, Elders IXL.

Eldershaw, Flora M Barnard >> **Barnard, Marjorie Faith**

Eldridge, Roy (David), nickname **Little Jazz** (1911–89) Trumpet player, born in Pittsburgh, PA. A passionate improviser, he was a featured soloist with top bands of the 1930s, such as McKinney's Cotton Pickers and the Teddy Hill and Fletcher Henderson Orchestras. >> Henderson, Fletcher

Eleanor of Aquitaine (c.1122–1204) Queen consort of Louis VII of France (1137–52) and of Henry II of England (1154–89). She was imprisoned (1174–89) for supporting the rebellion of her sons, two of whom became kings as Richard I (in 1189) and John (1199). >> Henry II (of England)

Eleanor of Castile [kasteel] (1246–90) Queen consort of Edward I of England (1254–90), the daughter of Ferdinand III. The *Eleanor Crosses* at Northampton, Geddington, and Waltham Cross are the survivors of the 12 erected by Edward at the halting places of her funeral cortège. >> Edward I

Eleanor of Provence [provãs] (1223–91) Queen consort of Henry III of England (1236–72), the daughter of Raymond Berengar IV, Count of Provence. In the Barons' War of 1264 she raised an army of mercenaries in France to support her husband, but her invasion fleet was wrecked. >> Edward I; Henry III

Eleonora of Arborea [elionawra, ah(r)bawria] (c.1350–1404) Sardinian ruler, regarded as the national heroine of Sardinia. In 1383 she became regent of Arborea for her infant son, Frederick, and in 1395 introduced a humanitarian code of laws. *Eleonora's falcon* is named after her.

Elgar, Sir Edward (1857–1934) Composer, born in Broad Heath, Hereford and Worcester. The *Enigma Variations* (1899) and the oratorio *The Dream of Gerontius* (1900) made him the leading figure of his day in English music. Other works included symphonies, concertos, and incidental music, and in 1924 he became Master of the King's Musick.

Elgin, Thomas Bruce, 7th Earl of Elgin and 11th Earl of Kincardine [elgin] (1766–1841) British diplomat and art connoisseur. He arranged for some of the decorated sculptures on the ruined Parthenon at Athens to be transported to England for safekeeping, and the *Elgin Marbles* are now in the British Museum.

Elia >> **Lamb, Charles**

Eliade, Mirca [elyad] (1907–86) Historian and philosopher of comparative religion, born in Bucharest, Romania. He was a pioneer in the systematic study of world religions.

Elijah [eliyja] (9th-c BC) Hebrew prophet, whose activities are portrayed in four Bible stories (1 *Kings* 17-19, 21; 2 *Kings* 1-2). He opposed the worship of Baal in Israel, and by virtue of his loyalty to God was depicted as ascending directly into heaven.

Eliot, Charles William (1834–1926) Educationist, born in Boston, MA. President of Harvard (1869–1909), his landmark report (1892) on secondary schools led to the standardization of public school curricula and the formation in 1901 of the Board of College Entrance Examinations.

Eliot, George, pseudonym of **Mary Ann Evans** or **Marian Evans** (1819–80) Novelist, born at Arbury Farm, Astley, Warwickshire. She became the centre of a literary circle, one of whose members was G H Lewes, with whom she lived until her death (1878). Her major novels were *Adam Bede* (1859), *The Mill on the Floss* (1860), *Silas Marner* (1861), *Middlemarch* (1871–2), and *Daniel Deronda* (1876). >> Lewes

Eliot, Sir John (1592–1632) English statesman, born in

Port Eliot, Cornwall. In 1628 he helped to force the Petition of Right from Charles I, and after further protests against the king, was sent with others to the Tower, where he died. >> Charles I (of England)

Eliot, John, known as **the Apostle to the Indians** (1604–90) Missionary, born in Widford, Hertfordshire. In 1646 he began to preach to the Indians in Masachusetts, and translated the Bible into their language (1661–3), the first Bible printed in America.

Eliot, Sir Thomas >> **Elyot, Thomas**

Eliot, T(homas) S(tearns) (1888–1965) Poet, critic, and playwright, born in St Louis, MO. The enthusiastic support of Ezra Pound led to his first book of poetry, *Prufrock and Other Observations* (1917), followed by *The Waste Land* (1922) and *The Hollow Men* (1925). Later works include his major poetic achievement, *Four Quartets* (1944), and a series of plays, notably *Murder in the Cathedral* (1935) and *The Cocktail Party* (1950). He was awarded the Nobel Prize for Literature in 1948. >> Pound, Ezra

Elisha [eliysha] (second half of 9th-c BC) Hebrew prophet whose activities are portrayed in 1 *Kings* 19 and 2 *Kings* 2–9,13. He was active in Israel under several kings from Ahab to Jehoash.

Elizabeth I, known as **the Virgin Queen** and later **Good Queen Bess** (1533–1603) Queen of England (1558–1603), the daughter of Henry VIII by his second wife, Anne Boleyn, born in Greenwich, London. She saw her role in Europe as a Protestant sovereign, and it is from this time that the Anglican Church was formally established. Mary, Queen of Scots, was thrown into her power (1568) and imprisoned, causing endless conspiracies among English Catholics. After the most sinister plot was discovered (1586), Elizabeth was reluctantly persuaded to execute Mary (1587), and subsequently persecuted Catholics. Philip of Spain then attacked England with his 'invincible armada' (1588), but was repelled. A strong, cruel, and capricious woman, the 'Virgin Queen' was nevertheless popular with her subjects, becoming later known as 'Good Queen Bess'; and her reign is seen as the period when England assumed the position of a world power. >> Henry VIII; Mary, Queen of Scots; Philip II (of Spain)

Elizabeth II (1926–) Queen of the United Kingdom (1952–) and head of the Commonwealth, born in London, the daughter of George VI. She was proclaimed queen on 6 February 1952, and crowned on 2 June 1953. Her husband was created Duke of Edinburgh, later Prince Philip. They have three sons, Charles, Andrew, and Edward, and a daughter, Anne. >> Anne, Princess; Andrew, Duke of York; Charles, Prince; Edward, Prince; Edinburgh, Duke of; George VI

Elizabeth (of Bohemia) (1596–1662) Queen of Bohemia, the eldest daughter of James I (of England) and Anne of Denmark. She married Frederick V, Elector Palatine, in 1613. Deprived of the Palatinate by Maximilian of Bavaria, the couple then lived in exile in The Hague.

Elizabeth (Queen Mother), originally **Lady Elizabeth Bowes-Lyon** (1900–) Queen-consort of Great Britain, born in St Paul's Walden Bury, Hertfordshire. In 1923 she married the second son of George V. Princess Elizabeth (later Queen Elizabeth II) was born in 1926 and Princess Margaret in 1930. Her husband came to the throne as King George VI in 1936 and after his death (1952), she continued to undertake public duties around the world, becoming a widely loved figure. >> Elizabeth II; George VI; Margaret, Princess

Elizabeth, St (1207–31), feast day 17 November. Hungarian princess, born in Presburg, Hungary. She married Louis IV, Landgrave of Thuringia in 1221. On his death (1227), she was deprived of her regency by her husband's brother, and devoted her life to the service of the poor. She was canonized in 1235.

Elizabeth (of York) >> **Henry VII**

Elizabeth (of Romania) >> **Carmen Sylva**

Elizabeth Petrovna [petrovna] (1709–62) Empress of Russia (1741–62), born in Kolomenskoye, near Moscow, the daughter of Peter the Great and Catherine I. Her animosity towards Frederick the Great led her to take part in the War of the Austrian Succession and in the Seven Years' War.

Elkin, Stanley (Lawrence) (1930–95) Writer and academic, born in New York City. Pre-eminently a novelist, his works include *Boswell* (1964), *The Living End* (1979), and *The Magic Kingdom* (1985).

Elkington, George Richards (1801–65) British inventor and manufacturer. Based in Birmingham from 1832, he introduced electroplating, in association with his cousin, **Henry Elkington** (1810–52).

Ellery, William (1727–1820) US statesman, born in Newport, RI. He sat in the Congress of 1776, and was a signatory of the Declaration of Independence.

Ellet, Charles, known as **the Brunel of America** (1810–62) Civil engineer, born in Penn's Manor, PA. He built the first wire suspension bridges in America, including one over the Schuylkill R at Fairmount (1842) and another over the Ohio R at Wheeling (1849).

Ellicott, Charles John (1819–1905) British clergyman and scholar. A professor of divinity at London and Cambridge, he became Bishop of Gloucester and Bristol (1863–97), and Bishop of Gloucester alone from 1897.

Ellington, Duke, popular name of **Edward Kennedy Ellington** (1899–1974) Composer, arranger, bandleader, and pianist, born in Washington, DC. Among his early successes were 'Black and Tan Fantasy' (1927) and 'Mood Indigo' (1930). His creative peak is generally said to be 1939–42, with such recordings as 'Take the A Train'. Later works included jazz suites, film scores, ballets, and a series of 'sacred concerts' (1968–74) performed in cathedrals around the world.

Elliott, Denholm (1922–92) Actor, born in London. He has won British Film Awards for *Trading Places* (1983), *A Private Function* (1984), and *Defence of the Realm* (1985), and received an Oscar nomination for *A Room with a View* (1986).

Elliott, Herb, popular name of **Herbert James Elliott** (1938–) Athlete, born in Perth, Western Australia. Winner of the gold medal in the 1500 m at the 1960 Olympics in Rome, his time of 3 min 35·6 s for that event was unbeaten for seven years.

Elliott, John Dorman (1941–) Businessman, born in Melbourne, Victoria, Australia. He was a prime mover in the development of Foster's Brewing Group, becoming its managing director (1981), then chairman and chief executive (1985–90).

Ellis, Sir Albert (1869–1951) Businessman, born in Roma, Queensland, Australia. In 1900 he discovered high-grade phosphate rock on the Pacific islands of Nauru and Banaba (Ocean I), and his subsequent career was concerned with the mining of these resources.

Ellis, Alexander John, original surname **Sharpe** (1814–90) British philologist. He advanced the scientific study of phonetics, early English pronunciation, and existing English dialects, as seen in *Early English Pronunciation* (1869–89).

Ellis, (Henry) Havelock (1859–1939) Physician, born in Croydon, Greater London. He compiled his *Studies in the Psychology of Sex* (7 vols, 1897–1928), the first detached treatment of the subject, which was highly controversial at the time.

Ellis, Ruth (1926–55) Convicted murderer, born in Rhyl, Clwyd. She murdered her former lover in London, and was the last woman to be hanged in Britain.

Ellis, William Webb (1805–72) British sportsman. A pupil at Rugby School in 1823, he supposedly inspired the game of rugby by picking up and running with the ball during a game of association football.

Ellison, Ralph (Waldo) (1914–94) Writer, born in Oklahoma City, OK. His major work was the novel *Invisible Man* (1952), a semi-autobiographical account of a young black intellectual's search for identity in the New York City slums.

Ellmann, Richard (1918–87) Biographer and academic, born in Detroit, MI. He is best known for his biographies of Yeats, Wilde, and Joyce.

Ellsworth, Lincoln (1880–1951) Explorer, born in Chicago, IL. He made the first trans-Arctic crossing in the airship *Norge* with Umberto Nobile, and in 1935 the first flight across Antarctica. >> Nobile

Ellsworth, Oliver (1745–1807) Public official and jurist, born in Windsor, CT. A major figure at the Constitutional Convention in 1787, he became Chief Justice of the US Supreme Court (1796–1800).

Elman, Mischa (1891–1967) Violinist, born in Talnoy, Ukraine. In 1911 he settled in New York City, and pursued an international career, especially admired for his treatment of the Romantic repertoire.

Elms, Lauris Margaret (1931–) Opera and Lieder singer, born in Melbourne, Victoria, Australia. She made her debut in 1957 at Covent Garden where she became principal resident artist.

Elsheimer, Adam [els hiymer] (1578–1610) Painter, born in Frankfurt, Germany. Basing his style on Tintoretto and other Italian masters, he excelled in the portrayal of atmosphere and effects of light, influencing the development of German landscape painting. >> Tintoretto

Elster, Julius (1854–1920) German physicist. With the physicist **Hans Friedrich Geitel** (1855–1923), he produced the first photoelectric cell and photometer, and a Tesla transformer. >> Tesla

Elton, Charles Sutherland (1900–91) Ecologist, born in Liverpool, Merseyside. His book *Animal Ecology* (1927) established the basic principles of modern animal ecology.

Eluard, Paul [elwah(r)], pseudonym of **Eugène Grindal** (1895–1952) Poet, born in Saint-Denis, France. One of the founders of the Surrealist movement in literature, his first collection of poetry was *Capital of Sorrow* (trans, 1926).

Elvehjem, Conrad (Arnold) [elvayjem] (1901–62) Biochemist, born in McFarland, WI. In 1937 he showed that nicotinic acid (now known as vitamin B_6) cured two related deficiency diseases, canine blacktongue and human pellagra.

Elvström, Paul [elvstroem] (1928–) Yachtsman, born in Gentofte, Copenhagen. He is the only yachtsman to win four individual Olympic gold medals (in the Firefly class in 1948, and in the Finn class in 1952, 1956, and 1960), the first to win the same event at four consecutive Olympics.

Elyot, Sir Thomas, also spelled **Eliot** (c.1490–1546) Writer and diplomat, born in Wiltshire. His chief work, *The Boke Named the Gouernour* (1531), is the earliest English treatise on moral philosophy.

Elytis, Odysseus [eleetis], pseudonym of **Odysseus Alepoudhelis** (1911–) Poet, born in Heraklion, Crete, Greece. Deeply influenced by the Surrealists, he began publishing verse in the 1930s, his best-known work being *The Axion Esti* (trans, 1959). He was awarded the Nobel Prize for Literature in 1979.

Emanuel or **Manuel I**, known as **the Great** or **the Fortunate** (1469–1521) King of Portugal (1495–1521), born in Alcochete, Portugal. His reign was the Golden Age of Portugal. He prepared the code of laws which bears his name, made his court a centre of art and science, and sponsored the voyages of Vasco da Gama. >> Gama

Emecheta, (Florence Onye) Buchi (1944–) Novelist, born in Lagos, Nigeria. Her novels, graphic in their depiction of man's inhumanity to woman, include *Second-Class Citizen* (1974) and *The Slave Girl* (1977).

Emerson, Ralph Waldo (1803–82) Writer, born in Boston, MA. His works include many poems and essays, notably *The Conduct of Life* (1860), showing him to be a transcendentalist and a bold advocate of spiritual individualism.

Emett, Rowland (1906–90) Cartoonist and designer of eccentric mechanical displays, born in London. He evolved a unique and fantastic style depicting a quaint, Victorian world.

Emin Pasha, originally **Eduard Schnitzer** (1840–92) Doctor and explorer, born in Neisse, Germany. Governor of the Equatorial Province (1878), he studied African languages, wrote many valuable geographical papers, and sent to Europe rich collections of plants and animals.

Emmerich, Anna Katharina [emereekh], known as **the Nun of Dülmen** (1774–1824) Visionary and nun, born near Coesfeld, Germany. She entered the Augustinian order in 1802, and from 1812 bore the stigmata of Christ's passion.

Emmet, Robert (1778–1803) Irish patriot, born in Dublin. He joined the United Irishmen and plotted an insurrection against the English (1803), but it failed, and he was hanged in Dublin.

Empedocles [empedokleez] (c.490–c.430 BC) Greek philosopher and poet, born in Acragas, Sicily. In *On Nature* he introduced the doctrine of four everlasting elements, Earth, Water, Air, and Fire, which became central to Western thought through its adoption by Aristotle. >> Aristotle

Empson, Sir William (1906–84) Poet and critic, born in Howden, Humberside. He wrote several major critical works, notably *Seven Types of Ambiguity* (1930), and his *Collected Poems* were published in 1955.

Encke, Johann Franz [engkuh] (1791–1865) Astronomer, born in Hamburg, Germany. He determined the period of the comet which now bears his name (1819), and accurately calculated the distance from the Earth to the Sun.

Endecott, John [endikot], also spelled **Endicott** (c.1588–1665) Colonist, born in Dorchester, Dorset. In 1628 he landed in America, becoming manager of a plantation near Salem, and local governor there in 1630.

Ender, Kornelia (1958–) Swimmer, born in Bitterfeld, Germany. Representing East Germany, in 1976 she became the first woman to win four gold medals at one Olympic Games: the 100 m and 200 m freestyle, the 100 m butterfly, and the 4 x 100 m medley relay.

Enderby, Samuel (fl.1830–9) Entrepreneur, General Gordon's grandfather, one of a firm of London merchants who fitted out three Antarctic expeditions (1830–9). The name *Enderby Land* was given in 1831 to a tract of Antarctica. >> Gordon, Charles George

Enders, John (Franklin) (1897–1985) Microbiologist, born in West Hartford, CT. He shared the Nobel Prize for Physiology or Medicine in 1954 for the cultivation of polio viruses in human tissue cells, thus making possible the development of a polio vaccine by Salk. >> Robbins, Frederick; Salk; Weller

Endlicher, Stephen (Ladislaus) [endlikher] (1804–49) Botanist, born in Pressburg (now Bratislava, Slovak Republic). He formulated a system of plant classification which was widely used for over half a century.

Endo, Shusaku (1923–) Writer, born in Toyko. Widely regarded as the leading writer in Japan, his books include (trans titles) *Silence* (1966), *Volcano* (1978), and *Stained Glass Elegies* (1984).

Enesco, Georges [eneskoh], originally **Georges Enescu** (1881–1955) Composer, born in Dorohoiu, Romania. His compositions include music in Romanian national style, an opera *Oedipus*, three symphonies, and orchestral and chamber music.

Engels, Friedrich (1820–95) Socialist philosopher, and founder of 'scientific socialism', born in Barmen, Germany. He collaborated with Marx on the *Communist Manifesto* (1848), and spent his later years editing and translating Marx's writings. >> Marx, Karl

Engler, (Gustav Heinrich) Adolf (1844–1930) Botanist, born in Sagan, Germany. Professor and director of the botanical gardens at Berlin (1889–1921), he proposed a major system of plant classification that is still widely used.

Ennin or **Jikaku Daishi** [diyshee] (9th-c AD) Japanese Tendai Buddhist, the abbot of Mt Hiei monastery. He travelled widely in Tang China as a pilgrim and member of an official embassy, keeping an accurate diary which is a major source on Tang China.

Ennius, Quintus [enius] (c.239–169 BC) Latin epic poet and playwright, born in Rudiae, Italy. He introduced the hexameter into Latin; but only fragments of his many writings survive.

Enoch [eenok] Biblical character, the son of Jared, and the father of Methuselah. In the Graeco-Roman era his name became attached to Jewish apocalyptic writings allegedly describing his visions and journeys through the heavens (1, 2, and 3 *Enoch*).

Enright, D(ennis) J(oseph) (1920–) Writer, born in Leamington, Warwickshire. He has written four novels, and much criticism, but is best known for his poetry, as seen in *Collected Poems* (1987).

Ensor, James (Sydney) Ensor, Baron (1860–1949) Painter, born in Ostend, Belgium. He became known for his fantastic images, using masks, skeletons, and other ghostly effects as symbols of the evils of society. His best-known work is 'Entry of Christ into Brussels' (1888).

Enver Pasha (1881–1922) Turkish soldier and politician, born in Istanbul. A leader in the revolution of Young Turks in 1908, he later became minister of war (1914), but fled to Russia after the Turkish surrender in 1918.

Epaminondas [epaminondas] (c.418–362 BC) Theban general and statesman, whose victory at Leuctra (371 BC) broke the military power of Sparta and made Thebes the most powerful state in Greece.

Epée, Charles Michel, Abbé de l' [epay] (1712–89) Educationist, born in Versailles, France. In 1765 he invented a language of signs, and later founded a deaf and dumb institute.

Ephraem Syrus, St [efrayim siyrus], known as **the Harp of the Holy Spirit** (c.306–378), feast day 28 Jan (E), 9 Jun (W). Theologian, born in Nisibis, Syria. A prolific writer, many of his works survive, part of them in Syriac, part in Greek, Latin, and Armenian translations.

Epictetus [epiktaytus] (c.50–c.130) Stoic philosopher, born in Hierapolis. At first a Roman slave, on being freed he devoted himself to philosophy, and is known from the *Enchiridion* collection of maxims dictated to a disciple.

Epicurus [epikyoorus] (c.341–270 BC) Greek philosopher, born in Samos. In 305 BC he established a school of philosophy at Athens, holding that pleasure, in the sense of freedom from pain and anxiety, is the chief good.

Epiphanius, St [epifanius] (c.315–403), feast day 12 May. Bishop of Salamis, (367–403), born in Bezanduca, Palestine. His major work *Panarion* (374–77, Refutation of all Heresies) is a valuable source of the history of theology.

Epstein, Sir Jacob [epstiyn] (1880–1959) Sculptor, born in New York City. Several of his symbolic sculptures, such as 'Ecce homo' (1934), led to accusations of indecency and blasphemy. In the 1950s, 'Christ in Majesty' (in aluminium; Llandaff Cathedral) and 'St Michael and the Devil' (in bronze; Coventry Cathedral) won more immediate acclaim.

Erard, Sébastien [ayrah(r)] (1752–1831) Piano and harp

maker, born in Strasbourg, France. At his Paris workshop he was the inventor of the harp with double pedals, the mechanical harpsichord, and the piano with double escapement.

Erasistratus [erasistratus] (of Ceos) (c.250 BC) Greek physician, born in Ceos. He founded a school of anatomy at Alexandria, and is said to have been the first to trace arteries and veins to the heart.

Erasmus, Desiderius [erazmus], originally **Gerrit Gerritszoon** (1466–1536) Humanist, born in Rotterdam, The Netherlands. His masterpiece, *Colloquia* (1519), is an audacious handling of Church abuses. He also made the first translation of the Greek New Testament into English (1516).

Erastus, Thomas [erastus], originally **Thomas Liebler**, also spelled **Lieber** or **Lüber** (1524–83) Theologian and physician, born in Basel, Switzerland. He was a follower of Zwingli, and opposed Calvin's system of Church government. His name is preserved in *Erastianism*, a doctrine giving the state authority over Church matters. >> Calvin, John; Zwingli

Eratosthenes [eratostheneez] (c.276–c.194 BC) Greek astronomer and scholar, born in Cyrene. He is remembered for the first scientific calculation of the Earth's circumference, which was correct to within 80 km/50 mi.

Ercilla y Zúñiga, Alonso de [ertheelya ee thoonyiga] (1533–c.1595) Poet, born in Madrid. He joined the expedition against the Araucanians in Chile, whose heroism inspired his monumental epic poem, *La Araucana* (1569–89).

Ercker, Lazarus (c.1530–c.1593) Metallurgist, born in Annaberg, Germany. He wrote the first manual of analytical and metallurgical chemistry in 1574.

Erhard, Ludwig [airhah(r)t] (1897–1977) German economist and Christian Democratic chancellor (1963–6), born in Furth, Germany. Chancellor of the Exchequer under Adenauer, he was the pioneer of the West German 'economic miracle' of recovery from wartime devastation. >> Adenauer

Erickson, Arthur Charles (1924–) Architect, born in Vancouver, British Columbia, Canada. His designs include the Simon Fraser University buildings, British Columbia (1963), and the avante-garde Lethbridge University, Alberta (1971).

Ericsson, John (1803–89) Inventor, born in Långbanshyttan, Sweden. Inventor of the first successful screw-propeller (1836), he went to the USA (1839), where he designed the warship *Princeton*, the first steamer with engines and boilers entirely below the water-line.

Erigena, John Scotus [erijena], also known as **John the Scot** (c.810–c.877) Philosopher and theologian, born in Scotia (now Ireland), who stands outside the mainstream of mediaeval thought. His major work, *On the Division of Nature* (trans, c.865), fused Christian and Neoplatonic doctrines, but was later condemned for its pantheistic tendencies.

Erik the Red, originally **Erik Thorvaldsson** (10th-c) Norwegian sailor who explored the Greenland coast and founded the Norse colonies there (985). His son Leif Eriksson landed in 'Vinland', often identified as America (1000).

Erik the Saint (12th-c) Patron saint of Sweden, and king of Sweden from c.1155. He is said to have led a Christian crusade for the conversion of Finland, and to have been murdered in Uppsala by a Danish pretender to his throne.

Erixson, Sven, nickname **X-et** (1899–1970) Artist, born in Tumba, Sweden. His colourful paintings made him much in demand for large-scale public commissions, such as his tapestry *Melodies on the Square* (1937–9) in the Concert Hall, Gothenburg.

Erlanger, Joseph [erlanger] (1874–1965) Physiologist,

born in San Francisco, CA. He shared with Gasser the Nobel Prize for Physiology or Medicine in 1944 for their collaborative work on nerve fibres and nerve impulse transmission. >> Gasser

Ernst, Max(imillian) (1891–1976) Painter, born in Brühl, Germany. In 1919 he founded at Cologne the German Dada group, and later joined the Surrealist movement in Paris, his works including 'Oedipus Rex' (1921) and 'Polish Rider' (1954).

Ershad, Hussain Muhammad [airshad] (1929–) Bangladeshi soldier and president (1983–90). Appointed army chief-of-staff (1978), he led a bloodless military coup in 1982. He was forced to resign in 1990, charged with plundering the nation, and sentenced to 10 years' imprisonment.

Erskine, John (1879–1951) Educator, novelist, and musician, born in New York City. His emphasis on studying the classic texts gave rise to the 'great books' programmes adopted by many educational institutions. His satirical novels include *The Private Life of Helen of Troy* (1925).

Erskine, Thomas Erskine, Baron (1750–1823) Lawyer, born in Edinburgh. Known for his brilliant defences, including the acquittal of Lord George Gordon (1781), he became Lord Chancellor (1806–7). >> Gordon, Lord George

Ervine, St John (Greer) [ervin] (1883–1971) Writer and drama critic, born in Belfast. His plays include *The First Mrs Fraser* (1929) and *Robert's Wife* (1937), and he also wrote novels and biographies.

Erzberger, Matthias [airtsberger] (1875–1921) German statesman, born in Buttenhausen, Germany. Finance minister and vice-premier in 1919, he reformed the tax system and nationalized the German railways. He was assassinated by members of an extremist group.

Esaki, Leo [esahkee], originally **Esaki Reiona** (1925–) Physicist, born in Osaka, Japan. He developed the *Esaki diode* (or tunnel diode), a semiconductor device used in computers and microwave systems, and shared the Nobel Prize for Physics in 1973.

Esarhaddon [eesah(r)hadn] (?–669 BC) King of Assyria (680–669 BC), the son of Sennacherib and father of Assurbanipal. He is best known for his conquest of Egypt (671 BC).

Esau [eesaw] Biblical character, the elder son of Isaac. He was depicted as his father's favourite son, but was deprived of Isaac's blessing and his birthright by his cunning brother Jacob (*Gen* 27). >> Isaac; Jacob

Eschenbach, Wolfram von >> **Wolfram von Eschenbach**

Escoffier, (Georges) Auguste [eskofyay] (c.1847–1935) Chef, born in Villeneuve-Loubet, France. The inventor of *Pêche Melba* and *tournedos Rossini* for the singer and composer respectively, he wrote several books on culinary art. >> Melba; Rossini

Esdras >> **Ezra the Scribe**

Esop >> **Aesop**

Espert, Nuria (1935–) Actress and stage director, born in Spain. She co-founded the Nuria Espert Theatre Company, and appeared as an actress in productions all over the world.

Espronceda (y Delgado), José de [espronthetha] (1808–42) Poet and revolutionary, born in Almendro de los Barros, Spain. Imprisoned several times for revolutionary activities in France and Spain, he wrote Romantic poems in the Byronic manner, and is often called 'the Spanish Lord Byron'. >> Byron, George

Espy, James (Pollard) [espee] (1785–1860) Meteorologist, born in Pennsylvania. He was one of the first to use the telegraph to collect meteorological data, and gave the first correct explanation of cloud formation.

Essex, Robert Devereux, 2nd Earl of (1566–1601)

English soldier and courtier to Elizabeth I, born in Netherwood, Herefordshire. He became a privy councillor (1593) and earl marshal (1597), but alienated the Queen's advisers, and there were constant quarrels with Elizabeth. His six months' lord-lieutenancy of Ireland (1599) proved a failure, and he was imprisoned. He attempted to raise the City of London, was found guilty of high treason, and beheaded. >> Elizabeth I

Essex, Robert Devereux, 3rd Earl of (1591–1646) English parliamentary soldier, born in London, the eldest son of Robert, 2nd Earl of Essex. In 1642 he received the command of the Parliamentary army, but after several military failures he fled abroad. >> Essex, 2nd Earl of

Estes, Richard [esteez] (1932–) Painter, born in Keewane, IL. He is known for his 'Super-Realist' copies of photographs, particularly of New York street-scenes.

Esther (5th-c BC) Biblical queen, a foster-daughter of the Jew, Mordecai. According to the Book of Esther she was chosen by the Persian King Ahasuerus (possibly Xerxes I) as his wife in place of the disgraced Queen Vashti, and brought about the deliverance of her people. >> Mordecai

Estigarribia, José Félix [esteegareebia] (1888–1940) Paraguayan general and war hero, born in Caraguatay, Paraguay. He won fame as a brilliant commander in the Chaco War, on the strength of which he became president (1939–40).

Ethelbert or **Æthelbert** [ethelbert] (c.552–616) King of Kent (560–616). In his reign Kent achieved (c.590) control over England S of the Humber, and Christianity was introduced by St Augustine (597). To him we owe the first written English laws. >> Augustine, St (of Canterbury)

Etheldreda or **Æthelthryth, St** [etheldreeda], also known as **St Audrey** (c.630–679), feast day 23 June. Anglo-Saxon nun. In 673 she founded a double monastery on the Isle of Ely, of which she was appointed abbess.

Ethelflaed or **Æthelflaed** [ethelflad] (?–918) Anglo-Saxon ruler of Mercia, the daughter of Alfred the Great. She married Ethelred, ealdorman of Mercia (c.888), and fought with him against the Danes, winning a decisive victory near Tettenhall (911). >> Alfred

Ethelred I [ethelred], also spelled **Æthelred** (c.830–71) King of Wessex (865–71), the elder brother of Alfred the Great. During his reign, the Danes launched their main invasion of England, but were defeated at Ashdown, Berkshire. >> Alfred

Ethelred II [ethelred], known as **Ethelred the Unready**, also spelled **Æthelred** (c.968–1016) King of England (978–1016), the son of Edgar. He was forced into exile (1013) when Sweyn Forkbeard secured mastery over England. After Sweyn's death (1014), he returned to oppose Canute, but English resistance was broken when his son, Edmund Ironside, rebelled. 'Unready' is a mistranslation of *Unraed*, which means 'ill-advised'. >> Canute; Edgar; Edmund II; Sweyn

Ethelred, St >> Ailred of Rievaulx, St
Ethelred the Unready >> Ethelred II

Etherege, Sir George [etherij] (1635–92) Restoration playwright, probably born in Maidenhead, England. His popular plays, such as *The Comical Revenge; or, Love in a Tub* (1664), introduced the comedy of manners to the English theatre.

Etty, William (1787–1849) Painter, born in York, North Yorkshire. He depicted Classical and historical subjects, and became renowned for his nudes.

Etzioni, Amitai (Werner) [etziohnee] (1929–) Sociologist, born in Cologne, Germany. He emigrated to the USA in 1957, and became an academic, his books including *The Moral Dimension* (1988).

Eucken, Rudolf Christoph [oyken] (1846–1926) Philosopher, born in Aurich, Germany. He propounded a distinctive philosophy of ethical activism, criticized naturalist philosophy, and attacked socialism in *Socialism: an Analysis* (trans, 1920). He was awarded the Nobel Prize for Literature in 1908.

Eucleides of Megara [yookleedeez, megara] (c.435–c.365 BC) Greek philosopher. He founded a school of *Megarians*, associated with various developments in logic. None of their writings have survived.

Euclid [yooklid], Gr **Eucleides** (4th–3rd-c BC) Greek mathematician who taught in Alexandria c.300 BC, and who was probably the founder of its mathematical school. His chief extant work is the 13-volume *Elements*. The approach which obeys his axioms became known as *Euclidean geometry*.

Eudocia [yoodohsha], originally **Athenais** (401–65) Byzantine princess, born in Athens, the wife of the Eastern Roman emperor Theodosius II (ruled 408–50). She was baptized a Christian, and retired to Jerusalem in 443, where she supervised the building of several churches.

Eudoxos of Cnidus [yoodoksus] (c.408 BC–c.353 BC) Greek geometer and astronomer, born in Cnidus, Asia Minor. In geometry he established principles that laid the foundation for Euclid, then applied the subject to the study of the Moon and planets. >> Euclid

Eugene of Savoy, Prince, in full **François Eugène de Savoie Carignan** (1663–1736) Austrian general, born in Paris. Made field marshal in 1693, he defeated the Turks on several occasions, and commanded the imperial army, helping Marlborough at Blenheim (1704), Oudenarde (1708), and Malplaquet (1709). >> Marlborough

Euhemerus [yooheemerus] (fl.300 BC) Greek philosopher and mythographer, probably from Messene, Sicily. The author of *Sacred History*, he was the first to try to link mythical beings and events with historical fact.

Euler, Leonhard [oyler] (1707–83) Mathematician, born in Basel, Switzerland. He was a giant figure in 18th-c mathematics, publishing on every aspect of pure and applied mathematics, physics and astronomy. His treatises on differential and integral calculus and algebra remained standard textbooks for a century, and his notations, such as e and π have been used ever since.

Euler-Chelpin, Hans Karl August Simon von [oyler kelpin] (1873–1964) Biochemist, born in Augsburg, Germany. Director of the Stockholm Biochemical Institute (1929), he shared the Nobel Prize for Chemistry in 1929 for research into enzymes and fermentation.

Eunomius [yoonohmius] (c.335–c.394) Clergyman, born in Cappadocia, Turkey. He was Bishop of Cyzicus c.360, but was deposed for his Arian views. He became the leader of an extreme sect of Arians, known as the *Eunomians*. >> Arius

Euphranor [yoofranaw(r)] (4th-c BC) Greek painter and sculptor from Corinth, famed for his decoration of the Stoa Basileios at Athens.

Euphronios [yoofronios] (c.520–470 BC) Greek potter and vase painter. His name is inscribed on 15 vessels which are some of the finest surviving examples of those painted in the so-called 'red figure' style.

Euripides [yuripideez] (c.480–406 BC) Greek tragic playwright, born in Athens. He wrote about 80 dramas, of which 19 survive, including *Alcestis, Medea, Orestes, Electra, The Bacchae*, and *Iphigenia in Aulis*.

Eusden, Laurence [yoosden] (1688–1730) Poet, born in Spofforth, North Yorkshire. He became poet laureate in 1718, not on merit but by patronage.

Eusebio [yoosaybioh], in full **Eusebio Ferreira da Silva**, nickname **the Black Pearl** (1942–) Footballer, born in Lourenço Marques, Mozambique. He was largely responsible for Portugal's rise in international football in the 1960s, playing for his country 77 times. At club level he played for Benfica, and later became coach there.

Eusebius of Caesarea [yoo**see**bius] (c.264–340) Historian of the early Church, probably born in Palestine. Bishop of Caesarea (c.313), his great work, the *Ecclesiastical History*, is a record of the chief events in the Christian Church until 324.

Eusebius of Nicomedia [yoo**say**bius, nikoh**mee**dia] (?–c.342) Syrian clergyman. He defended Arius at the Council of Nicaea (325), and later led an Arian group known as the *Eusebians*. >> Arius

Eustachio, Bartolommeo [yoo**stak**yoh] (1520–74) Anatomist and pioneer of modern anatomy. He discovered the *Eustachian tube* in the ear and the *Eustachian valve* of the heart.

Euthymides [yoo**thi**mideez] (6th-c–5th-c BC) Greek vase painter of the so-called 'red figure' style. A rival of Euphronios, one of his six surviving signed vessels is inscribed with the words: 'Euphronios never did anything like it'. >> Euphronios

Eutyches [**yoo**tikeez] (c.375–c.454) Monastic superior at Constantinople. He was the founder of *Eutychianism*, holding that, after the incarnation, the human nature became merged in the divine, and that Jesus Christ had therefore but one nature. The view was condemned at the Council of Chalcedon (451).

Euwe, Max (Machgielis) [**ü**vuh] (1901–81) Chess player, born in Watergrafsmeer, The Netherlands. He was the only amateur to win the world championship in the history of chess, by defeating Alekhine (1935–7). >> Alekhine

Evans, Sir Arthur (John) (1851–1941) Archaeologist, born in Nash Mills, Hertfordshire. He excavated the city of Knossos (1899–1935), discovering the remains of the civilization which in 1904 he named *Minoan*.

Evans, Bill, popular name of **William Evans** (1929–80) Jazz pianist, born in Plainfield, NJ. He joined Miles Davis's sextet in 1958, their recordings including the classic 'Kind of Blue' (1959), and from 1960 led a successful trio at the Village Vanguard. >> Davis, Miles

Evans, Caradoc, pseudonym of **David Evans** (1878–1945) Short-story writer and novelist, born in Llanfihangel-ar-Arth, Dyfed. His stories were bitter satires of the Welsh people, and his play *Taffy* (1923) added to his self-defined reputation as 'the best-hated man in Wales'.

Evans, Dame Edith (Mary) (1888–1976) Actress, born in London. She earned a great reputation for her versatility, her most famous role being Lady Bracknell in Wilde's *The Importance of Being Earnest*.

Evans, Frederick Henry (1853–1943) British photographer. He is chiefly known for his architectural photography, especially of the cathedrals of England and France, but he also produced studies of trees and austerely-formed landscapes.

Evans, Gareth (John) (1944–) Australian statesman, born in Melbourne, Victoria, Australia. He was attorney general (1983–4), then served in a range of portfolios, becoming minister for foreign affairs and trade in 1988.

Evans, Sir Geraint (Llewellyn) (1922–92) Baritone, born in Pontypridd, Mid Glamorgan. He soon earned international fame, particularly in comic roles such as Mozart's Leporello, Verdi's Falstaff, and Wagner's Beckmesser.

Evans, Gil, popular name of **Ian Ernest Gilmore Green** (1912–88) Jazz pianist, composer, and arranger, born in Toronto, Ontario, Canada. He was one of the first modern jazz arrangers to use electronics and rock influences successfully in combination with the swing and bebop idioms.

Evans, (Thomas) Godfrey (1920–) Cricketer, born in Finchley, Greater London. First capped as wicket-keeper for England in 1946, he played in 91 Test matches.

Evans, Harold (1928–) Journalist, born in Manchester. He was editor of *The Sunday Times* (1967–83), and a pioneer of investigative journalism.

Evans, Marian / Mary Ann >> **Eliot, George**

Evans, Maurice (1901–89) Stage, cinema, and TV actor, born in Dorchester, Dorset. He made his Broadway debut in *Romeo and Juliet* (1936), then settled in the USA, where he played mainly in classical theatre.

Evans, Merlyn (1910–73) Painter, born in Cardiff. His paintings are largely Surrealist in character, with semi-abstract figures.

Evans, Oliver (1755–1819) Inventor, born in Newport, DE. He invented the first high-pressure steam engine (1790), and his amphibious steam dredging machine (1804) is considered the first US steam land carriage.

Evans, Timothy John >> **Christie, John Reginald Halliday**

Evans, Walker (1903–75) Photographer, born in St Louis, MI. He is known for his collaboration with Agee, documenting the lives of the share-croppers of the Deep South, and published as *Let Us Now Praise Famous Men* (1941). >> Agee

Evans-Pritchard, Sir Edward Evan (1902–73) Social anthropologist, born in Crowborough, East Sussex. He is best known for two books: *Witchcraft, Oracles and Magic among the Azande* (1937) and *The Nuer* (1940), resulting from field studies in the Sudan.

Evarts, William Maxwell (1818–1901) Lawyer and statesman, born in Boston, MA. Defence counsel for President Andrew Johnson in the impeachment proceedings of 1868, he became US attorney general (1868–9), secretary of state (1877–81), and a member of the US Senate (1885–91). >> Johnson, Andrew

Evatt, Elizabeth (Andreas) (1933–) Reformist lawyer, born in Sydney, New South Wales, Australia. She was first Chief Judge of the Family Court of Australia (1976–88), and became president of the Law Reform Commission.

Evatt, Herbert Vere, nickname **Doc Evatt** (1894–1965) Australian statesman and jurist, born in East Maitland, South Australia. As minister of external affairs (1941–9), he developed an independent Australian foreign policy, and represented Australia in Churchill's War Cabinet.

Evelyn, John [evelin, **ee**vlin] (1620–1706) Diarist and writer, born in Wotton, Surrey. He was much at court after the Restoration, and is known for his *Diary*, a detailed sourcebook on life in 17th-c England.

Everdingen, Allart van [**e**verdingen] (1621–75) Landscape painter and etcher, born in Alkmaar, The Netherlands. He is best known for his Scandinavian landscapes, and for the etchings of animals he made to illustrate *Reynard the Fox* by Hendrick van Alcmar.

Everest, Sir George (1790–1866) Military engineer, born in Gwernvale, Powys. He worked on the trigonometrical survey of India (1818–43), being appointed surveyor general in 1830. *Mt Everest* was named after him in 1865.

Everett, Edward (1794–1865) Statesman and scholar, born in Dorchester, MA. An outstanding orator, he was Governor of Massachusetts (1835–9), and briefly secretary of state at the end of 1852.

Evert (Lloyd), Chris(tine Marie) [**e**vert] (1954–) Tennis player, born in Fort Lauderdale, FL. She won Wimbledon titles in 1974, 1976, and 1981, and the US singles title in 1975–80 and 1982.

Evita >> **Perón, Eva**

Evoe >> **Knox, Edmund George Valpy**

Evremond, Saint >> **Saint-Evremond, Charles Marguetel de Saint Denis**

Ewald, Johannes [**i**vahl] (1743–81) Writer, born in Copenhagen. He is best known for his prose tragedy, *Rolf Krage* (1770) and his mythological play *The Death of Baldur* (trans, 1773).

Ewart, James Cossar [**yoo**ert] (1851–1933) Zoologist, born in Penicuik, Lothian. He carried out notable experiments in animal breeding and hybridization.

Ewart, William [yooert] (1798–1869) Politician and reformer, born in Liverpool, Merseyside. As an MP (1828–68) he played a leading part in humanitarian reforms, including the abolition of capital punishment for minor offences.

Ewell, Richard Stoddart [yooel] (1817–72) US soldier, born in Washington, DC. In the Civil War he joined the Confederates (1861), fought at Gettysburg and the Wilderness, and commanded the defences of Richmond.

Ewing, Sir (James) Alfred [yooing] (1855–1935) Engineer and physicist, born in Dundee, Tayside. Professor of mechanism and applied mechanics at Cambridge (1890–1903), he discovered and explained magnetic hysteresis (1890).

Ewing, Juliana (Horatia) [yooing], *née* **Gatty** (1841–85) Writer of children's literature, born in Ecclesfield, South Yorkshire. She suggested to her mother the starting of *Aunt Judy's Magazine* (1866), publishing in it many of her own stories, such as *Jackanapes*.

Ewing, (William) Maurice [yooing] (1906–) Marine geologist, born in Lockney, TX. He pioneered marine seismic techniques, made the first measurements of the thickness of the oceanic crust, and determined the global extent of mid-ocean ridges.

Eworth, Hans (c.1520–after 1573) Flemish painter. He was recorded in the Antwerp Guild in 1540, but was active chiefly in England, being based in London from c.1545 for about 20 years. His surviving paintings are mainly portraits.

Exekias or **Execias** [ekseekias] (c.550–525 BC) Greek potter and vase painter who worked in the so-called 'black figure' style. The most famous of his vessels, on which is inscribed 'Exekias made and decorated me', is in the Vatican Museum.

Eyadema, (Etienne) Gnassingbe [ayadayma] (1937–) Togolese politician and soldier, born in Pya, Togoland. He became army commander-in-chief, leading a bloodless coup to oust President Grunitzky (1967). He founded the Assembly of the Togolese People, and introduced a degree of democracy into the political system.

Eyck, Jan van [iyk] (c.1389–1441) Painter, born near Maastricht, The Netherlands. The greatest Flemish artist of the 15th-c, his most famous work is the altarpiece 'The Adoration of the Holy Lamb' in the Church of St Bavon, Ghent.

Eyre, Edward John [air] (1815–1901) Explorer and colonist, born in Hornsea, Humberside. He emigrated to Australia, and in 1840–1 explored the region between South and Western Australia, discovering *L Eyre*.

Eyre, Richard (Charles Hastings) [air] (1943–) Theatre and television director, born in Barnstaple, Devon. He was artistic director of the Nottingham Playhouse (1973–8), producer of the BBC Television *Play for Today* series (1978–81), and in 1988 was appointed artistic director of the National Theatre, London.

Eysenck, Hans (Jurgen) [iysingk] (1916–) Psychologist, born in Berlin. Much of his work has been psychometric research into the normal variations of human personality and intelligence. He has often held controversial views, particularly with his study of racial differences in intelligence.

Ezekiel [eezeekiel] (early 6th-c BC) Biblical prophet. He wrote a book of Old Testament prophecies which looked forward to a new Jerusalem after the destruction of the old.

Ezra the Scribe [ezra] (5th–4th-c BC) Religious leader who lived in Babylon during the reign of King Ataxerxes (I or II). An Old Testament book bears his name, as well as the apocryphal works of 1 and 2 Esdras.

F

Faber, Frederick William [fayber] (1814–63) Priest and hymn writer, born in Calverley, West Yorkshire. He became a Roman Catholic and founded a lay community of converts (the *Wilfridians*) in 1845.

Fabergé, Peter Carl [faberzhay], originally **Karl Gustavovich Fabergé** (1846–1920) Goldsmith and jeweller, born in St Petersburg, Russia. He is known for the creation of elaborate and fantastic objects, notably the imperial Easter eggs commisioned by Alexander III for his tsarina in 1884.

Fabius, Laurent [fabyoos] (1946–) French socialist prime minister (1984–6), born in Paris. Budget minister (1981) and minister for research and industry (1983), as prime minister he introduced a liberal, 'free-market' economic programme.

Fabius Maximus, Quintus [faybius maksimus], known as **Fabius Cunctator** (Lat 'the delayer') (c.260–203 BC) Roman general, statesman, and hero of the Second Punic War. His refusal to engage Hannibal in set battle earned him his nickname.

Fabre, Ferdinand [fahbruh] (1830–98) Novelist, born in Bédarieux, France. He wrote *L'Abbé Tigrane* (1873) and other stories of rustic life in Cévennes.

Fabriano, Gentile da [fabriahnoh] (c.1370–c.1427) Painter, born in Fabriano, Italy. He painted religious subjects, notably 'The Adoration of the Magi' (1423), but few of his paintings have survived.

Fabricius, David [fabreesyoos] (1564–1617) Astronomer and clergyman, born in Esens, Germany. In 1586 he discovered the first variable star, Mira. His son, **Johannes Fabricius** (1587–1615), discovered the Sun's spots and its revolution.

Fabricius, Hieronymus [fabreetsius], also known as **Girolamo Fabrici** (1537–1619) Anatomist, born in Acquapendente, Italy. He made the first detailed description of the valves of the veins, the placenta, and the larynx.

Fabricius, Johann Christian [fabreetsius] (1745–1808) Entomologist, born in Tøndern, Denmark. One of the founders of entomological taxonomy, his classification of insects was based on the structure of the mouth.

Fabritius, Carel [fabreetsius] (c.1624–54) Painter, born in Beemster, The Netherlands. Vermeer was much influenced by his sensitive experiments in composition and the painting of light, as in the tiny 'View of Delft' (1652). >> Vermeer

Fabry, Marie Paul Auguste Charles [fabree] (1867–1945) Physicist, born in Marseilles, France. Co-inventor of the Fabry–Pérot interferometer with Alfred Pérot, he is also known as the discoverer of the ozone layer in the upper atmosphere.

Fadeyev, Aleksandr Aleksandrovich [fadayef] (1901–56) Novelist, born in Kimry, near Kalinin, Russia. As general secretary of the Soviet Writers' Union (1946–55) he mercilessly exposed any literary 'deviationism', but after becoming a target himself he committed suicide.

Fahd (ibn Abd al-Aziz) (1923–) Ruler of Saudi Arabia (1982–), born in Riyadh. Effectively ruler since the assassination of his older half-brother Faisal in 1975, he became king on the death of his other half-brother, Khaled. >> Faisal (ibn Abd al-Aziz)

Fahrenheit, Gabriel (Daniel) [farenhiyt] (1686–1736) Physicist, born in Gdansk, Poland (formerly Danzig, Germany). He invented the alcohol thermometer in 1709, and a mercury thermometer in 1714.

Faidherbe, Louis Léon César [faydairb] (1818–89) French soldier and scholar, born in Lille, France. Appointed Governor of Senegal in 1854, he greatly extended the frontiers of his province (1858–61), and later carried out anthropological and linguistic studies in N Africa.

Fairbairn, Sir William [fairbairn] (1789–1874) Engineer, born in Kelso, Borders, Scotland. He opened a shipbuilding yard in London, pioneering the use of wrought iron for hulls, and designed the rectangular tubes for Stephenson's bridges over the Menai Strait and at Conway. >> Stephenson, Robert

Fairbank, John K(ing) (1907–91) Historian, born in Huron, SD. Director of the East Asian Research Center (1955–73), his work created the field of modern Chinese history.

Fairbanks, Douglas, (Elton), Snr, originally **Douglas Elton Ulman** (1883–1939) Film actor, born in Denver, CO. He made a speciality of swashbuckling hero parts, as in *The Three Musketeers* (1921), *Robin Hood* (1922), and *The Thief of Baghdad* (1924). >> Fairbanks, Douglas, Jr

Fairbanks, Douglas (Elton), Jr (1909–) Film actor, writer, producer, and businessman, born in New York City, the son of Douglas Fairbanks, Snr. He made Hollywood movies in the style of his father, such as *Sinbad the Sailor* (1947), and later became a diplomat. >> Fairbanks, Douglas, Snr

Fairchild, Sherman (1896–1971) Inventor and businessman, born in Oneonta, NY. He invented an aerial camera for the US War Department (1916), founded an aerial survey company, and became known as 'the father of aerial mapping photography'.

Fairey, Sir (Charles) Richard (1887–1956) Aeronautical engineer and industrialist, born in Hendon, Greater London. He formed Fairey Aviation Co in 1915, producing many different types of aircraft during his 40 years as head of the firm.

Fairfax, John (1804–77) Australian newspaper proprietor, born in England. He went to Sydney in 1838, and in 1841 bought the *Sydney Herald*, changing its name to *The Sydney Morning Herald*.

Fairfax (of Cameron), Thomas Fairfax, 3rd Baron (1612–71) English parliamentary general, born in Denton, North Yorkshire. In the Civil War, he distinguished himself at Marston Moor (1644), and in 1645 commanded the New Model Army, defeating Charles I at Naseby. >> Charles I (of England); Cromwell, Oliver

Fairfield, Cicily Isabel >> **West, Dame Rebecca**

Fairweather, Ian (1891–1974) Painter, born in Bridge of Allan, Central, Scotland. From 1924 he travelled extensively, and in 1952 sailed from Darwin to Indonesia in a home-made raft.

Faisal I [fiyzl], also spelled **Faysal** (1885–1933) King of Iraq (1921–33), born in Ta'if, Iraq, the son of Hussein ibn Ali, king of the Hejaz. He played a major role in the Arab revolt of 1916, and became a leader of Arab nationalism. >> Hussein ibn Ali

Faisal II [fiysl], also spelled **Faysal** (1935–58) King of Iraq (1939–58), born in Baghdad, the great-grandson of Hussein ibn Ali. In February 1958 he concluded with his cousin King Hussein of Jordan a federation of the two countries, but in July he was assassinated during a military coup. >> Hussein

Faisal (ibn Abd al-Aziz) [fiyzl], also spelled **Faysal** (1904–75) King of Saudi Arabia (1964–75), born in Riyadh. He succeeded his half-brother Saud as king, and was assassinated in the royal palace in Riyadh by his nephew Faisal ibn Musaid.

Faithfull, Emily (1835–95) Publisher and feminist, born in Headley, Surrey. In 1860 she founded a printing house with women compositors, and in 1863 started the *Victoria Magazine*, advocating the claims of women to paid employment.

Fajans, Kasimir [fahyans] (1887–1975) Physical chemist, born in Warsaw. His early work was on radioactive elements, but he is now best known for *Fajans' rules*, dealing with the types of bond between atoms in compounds.

Falco, Louis [falkoh] (1942–93) Modern dancer and choreographer, born in New York City. In 1967 he formed his own company, his works being adopted by many of the world's major contemporary dance companies.

Falcone, Giovanni [falkohnay] (1939–92) Judge, born in Palermo, Sicily. In 1978 he was appointed to Palermo, where he began a campaign against the Mafia. He was killed when a bomb exploded under his car.

Falconet, Etienne Maurice [falkohnay] (1716–91) Sculptor, born in Paris. His figures of Venus, bathers, and similar subjects epitomize the Rococo style of the period of Louis XV.

Faldo, Nick [faldoh], popular name of **Nicholas Alexander Faldo** (1959–) Golfer, born in Welwyn Garden City, Hertfordshire. His successes include the Professional Golfing Association championships (1978, 1980, 1981), the British Open Championship (1987, 1990, 1992), and the US Masters (1989, 1990).

Falguière, Jean Alexandre Joseph [falgyair] (1831–1900) Sculptor and painter, born in Toulouse, France. He is celebrated for his portrait statues, such as that of Lafayette in Washington, DC, and several sculptures are in the Luxembourg, Paris.

Falk, Johann Daniel [falk] (1768–1826) Writer and philanthropist, born in Gdańsk, Poland. He founded the 'company of friends in need' for helping destitute children, and established the Falk Institute at Weimar.

Falkender, Marcia Matilda Falkender, Baroness [folkender] (1932–) British political worker. Private and political secretary to Harold Wilson (1956–73), her background influence during the 1964–70 Labour government is chronicled in her book *Inside No. 10* (1972). >> Wilson, Harold

Falkenhayn, Erich (Georg Anton Sebastian) von [falkenhiyn] (1861–1922) German soldier, born near Grudziadz, Poland. He succeeded Moltke as chief of general staff (1914), but was dismissed after the failure of his offensive strategy in 1916. >> Moltke, Helmuth (Karl Bernhard)

Falla, Manuel de [falya] (1876–1946) Composer, born in Cadiz, Spain. His works became famous for their colourful national Spanish idiom, and he is best known for his ballet, *The Three-Cornered Hat* (1919).

Fallon, Martin >> **Higgins, Jack**

Fallopius, Gabriel [falohpius], Ital **Gabriello Fallopio** (1523–62) Anatomist, born in Modena, Italy. He made several discoveries relating to bones and to the organs of reproduction, the *Fallopian tubes* being named after him.

Falwell, Jerry L [fawlwell] (1933–) Religious leader, born in Lynchburg, VA. In 1956, he founded Thomas Road Baptist Church, Lynchburg, which became the basis of an extensive evangelical campaign. He was also responsible for founding The Moral Majority and Liberty University.

Faneuil, Peter [fanl] (1700–43) Merchant and philanthropist, born in New Rochelle, NY. He made a fortune in Boston, MA, where in 1742 he built the Faneuil Hall (known as 'the cradle of American liberty'), presenting it to the town.

Fanfani, Amintore [fanfahnee] (1908–) Italian prime minister (1954, 1958–9, 1960–3, 1982–3), born in Pieve

Santo Stefano, Italy. Nominated a life senator in 1972, he became president of the Italian Senate in 1968–73 and 1976–82.

Fangio, Juan Manuel [fanjioh] (1911–95) Motor-racing driver, born in Balcarce, Argentina. He won 24 Grands Prix, and took the World Championship a record five times (1951, 1954–7).

Fantin-Latour, (Ignace) Henri (Jean Théodore) [fãtī latoor] (1836–1904) Painter, pastellist, and lithographer, born in Grenoble, France. He is best known for his flower studies and portrait groups, such as 'Hommage à Manet' (1870).

Farabi, al- >> **al-Farabi, Abu Nasr**

Faraday, Michael (1791–1867) Chemist, experimental physicist, and natural philosopher, born in Newington Butts, Surrey. His major work is the series of *Experimental Researches on Electricity* (1839–55), in which he reports a wide range of discoveries about the nature of electricity, notably electrolysis, and the relationship between electricity and magnetism.

Farel, Guillaume [farel] (1489–1565) Protestant reformer, born in Gap, France. He became a convert to Protestantism, fled to Switzerland (1524), and was responsible for making Calvin stay in Geneva; but the severity of the ecclesiastical discipline which Calvin imposed caused their expulsion from the city (1538). >> Calvin, John

Farge, John La >> **La Farge, John**

Fargo, William (George) (1818–81) Pioneer expressman, born in Pompey, NY. With Henry Wells he founded Wells, Fargo & Co (1852). Fargo became president of the American Express Co in 1868, and served two terms as Mayor of Buffalo (1862–6). >> Wells, Henry

Farigoule, Louis >> **Romains, Jules**

Farina, Battista [fareena], nickname **Pinin** (1893–1966) Automobile designer, born in Turin, Italy. He established his car bodywork design business in Turin in 1930, producing many classic designs. His son **Sergio Pininfarina** (1926–) took over in 1959.

Farinacci, Roberto [farinahchee] (1892–1945) Italian statesman, born in Isernia, Italy. He became Fascist party secretary (1924–6) and a minister of state (1938). Notorious for his extremism and pro-Nazi tendencies, he was ultimately captured and shot.

Farjeon, Eleanor [fah(r)jn] (1881–1965) Writer, born in London. She wrote fantasies and children's stories, and collaborated with her brother Herbert in *Kings and Queens* (1932). The *Farjeon Award* is for outstanding work in children's books.

Farman, Henri [fah(r)mã] (1874–1958) Pioneer aviator and aircraft manufacturer, born in Paris. In 1912 with his brother **Maurice Farman** (1878–1964), he established a factory to manufacture the *Farman biplane*, and built the first long-distance passenger plane, the *Goliath*, in 1917.

Farnaby, Giles [fah(r)nabee] (c.1560–1640) Composer, probably born in Truro, Cornwall. His works include madrigals and settings of the psalms, but he is best remembered for his keyboard music.

Farnese, Alessandro [fah(r)nayzay] (1545–92) Italian general, born in Rome. As Governor-General of the Spanish Netherlands (1578–92), he captured Antwerp (1585), and compelled Henry IV of France to raise the siege of Paris (1590). >> Henry IV (of France)

Farouk I [farook] (1920–65) Last reigning king of Egypt (1936–52), born in Cairo, the son of Fuad I. Egypt's defeat by Israel (1948) and continuing British occupation led to increasing unrest, and a coup forced his abdication and exile. >> Fuad I

Farquhar, George [fah(r)ker] (c.1677–1707) Playwright, born in Derry, Co Derry. His plays include *Love and a Bottle* (1698), *The Recruiting Officer* (1706), and notably *The Beaux' Stratagem* (1707).

Farragut, David (Glasgow) [faraguht] (1801-70) US naval commander, born near Knoxville, TN. In the Civil War he led the Union forces that captured New Orleans (1862), and took part in the siege and capture of Vicksburg (1863) and Mobile Bay (1864).

Farrakhan, Louis [farakan], originally **Louis Eugene Walcott** (1933-) Black Muslim leader, born in New York City. A convert to the Nation of Islam, he later formed a revitalized movement, Final Call to the Nation of Islam.

Farrar, Frederic William (1831-1903) British clergyman and writer, born in Bombay, India. His theological writings were many, but he is chiefly remembered for the best seller, *Eric, or Little by Little* (1858), one of several school stories.

Farrar, Geraldine (1882-1967) Soprano, born in Melrose, MA. She performed at the Metropolitan in New York City for 16 seasons, and also appeared in silent films, beginning with *Carmen* (1915).

Farrell, James T(homas) (1904-79) Writer of starkly realist novels of American life, born in Chicago, IL. His best-known work is the *Studs Lonigan* trilogy (1932-5; filmed 1960), set in the slums of Chicago.

Farrell, M J >> Keane, Molly

Farrell, Suzanne (1945-) Ballerina, born in Cincinnati, OH. She became a soloist at the New York City Ballet (1963), joined Béjart's Ballet of the 20th Century (1970), and returned to the NYCB in 1975. >> Béjart

Farren-Price, Ronald William (1930-) Pianist, born in Brisbane, Queensland, Australia. Since 1967 he has toured extensively, performed as a soloist with many major orchestras, and recorded widely.

Farrer, William James (1845-1906) Plant breeder, born in Docker, Cumbria. He emigrated to Australia in 1870, where he pioneered scientific wheat-breeding, fostering the growth of the Australian wheat industry.

Farr-Jones, Nick, popular name of **Nicholas Campbell Farr-Jones** (1962-) Rugby union player, born in Sydney, New South Wales, Australia. A fierce cover defender, he was captain of the Australian team (1988-90), and celebrated his 50th Test during the 1991 World Cup.

Farson, James (Negley) (1890-1960) Writer, born in Plainfield, NJ. His varied works include *Sailing Across Europe* (1926), *Bomber's Moon* (1941), and *A Mirror for Narcissus* (1957).

Fasch, Johann Friedrich (1688-1758) Organist and composer, born in Buttelstedt, Germany. He composed numerous works, including church music, orchestral works, and chamber music.

Fassbinder, Rainer Werner [fasbinder] (1946-82) Film director, born in Bad Wöshofen, Germany. His films were largely political criticisms of contemporary Germany, notably *The Bitter Tears of Petra von Kant* (trans, 1972) and *The Marriage of Maria Braun* (trans, 1979).

Fasset, Kaffe [kayf] (1937-) Fashion designer, born in San Francisco, CA. In England from 1964, he formed a design company producing colourful knitting kits, needlepoint, and fabrics.

Fastolf, Sir John (1378-1459) English soldier, born in Caister, Norfolk. He distinguished himself at Agincourt (1415) and at the 'Battle of the Herrings' (1429).

Fateh Singh, Sant [fate sing] (1911-72) Sikh religious leader and campaigner for Sikh rights, born in the Punjab. During the 1950s he agitated for a Punjabi-speaking autonomous state, achieved in 1966.

Fatima (c.605-33) The youngest daughter of the Prophet Mohammed, and wife of the fourth Muslim caliph, Ali; from them descended the *Fatimids*, the dynasty of Shiite caliphs, who ruled over Egypt and N Africa (909-1171), and later over Syria and Palestine. >> Ali; Mohammed

Faulkner or **Falkner, William (Harrison)** [fawkner] (1897-1962) Writer, born in New Albany, MS. His novels

include *The Sound and the Fury* (1929), *As I Lay Dying* (1930), *Absalom, Absalom!* (1936), *Intruder in the Dust* (1948), and *The Reivers* (1962). He was awarded the Nobel Prize for Literature in 1949.

Faure, Edgar (Jean) [fohr], pseudonym of **Edgar Sanday** (1908-88) French writer and prime minister (1952, 1955-6) born in Béziers, France. He was minister of finance and economic affairs in the 1950s, and became president of the National Assembly (1973-8). He wrote several detective novels under his pseudonym.

Fauré, Gabriel (Urbain) [fohray] (1845-1924) Composer, born in Pamiers, France. Though chiefly remembered for his songs, including the evergreen *Après un rêve* (c.1865), he also wrote operas and orchestral pieces, and a much-performed *Requiem* (1887-90).

Favart, Charles Simon [favah(r)] (1710-92) Playwright, born in Paris. He became director (1758) of the Opéra-Comique, and with his wife, **Marie-Justine-Benoiste Duranceray** (1727-71), pioneered a new realism in costume.

Fawcett, Dame Millicent, *née* **Garrett** (1847-1929) Women's rights campaigner, born in Aldeburgh, Suffolk, the sister of Elizabeth Garrett Anderson. She became president of the National Union of Women's Suffrage Societies (1897-1919). >> Anderson, Elizabeth

Fawcett, Percy (Harrison) (1867-1925) Explorer, born in Torquay, Devon. On behalf of the Bolivian government he made several hazardous expeditions in the Mato Grosso area in search of traces of ancient civilizations, and disappeared near the Xingú R in 1925.

Fawkes, Guy (1570-1606) Catholic conspirator, born in York, North Yorkshire. He served in the Spanish army in The Netherlands (1593-1604), came to England at Catesby's invitation, and became a member of the Gunpowder Plot. Caught red-handed, he was tried and hanged. >> Catesby

Fawkner, John Pascoe (1792-1869) Pioneer, born in London. He went to Australia with his father, who had been sentenced to transportation, and established a settlement at the mouth of the Yarra R, the site of the future city of Melbourne.

Faxian [fahshyan], also spelled **Fa-hsien** (AD c.360-c.430) Buddhist pilgrim, explorer, and diarist. He made a momentous journey through Turkestan, India, and SE Asia (399-414), and his *Account of Buddhist Countries* is an important contemporary source.

Faye, Hervé Auguste Etienne (1814-1902) Astronomer, born in Benoît-du-Sault, France. He discovered *Faye's comet* in 1843, and became director of the Paris Observatory in 1878.

Feather, Vic, popular name of **Victor (Grayson Hardie) Feather, Baron Feather (of the City of Bradford)** (1908-76) Trade union leader, born in Gainsborough, Lincolnshire. In 1937 he joined the staff of the Trade Union Council, becoming assistant secretary (1947-60), assistant general secretary (1960-9), and general secretary (1969-73).

Febronius, Justinus >> Hontheim, Johann von

Fechner, Gustav (Theodor) [fekhner] (1801-87) Physicist, philosopher, anthropologist, and psychologist, born in Gross Särchen, Germany. His interest in mind-body relationships led to his book *Elements of Psychophysics* (trans, 1860) which laid the foundations of psychophysics.

Fedden, Sir (Albert Hubert) Roy (1885-1973) Aero-engine designer, born in Bristol, Avon. He established the engine building department of the Bristol Aeroplane Co in 1920, initiating a famous range of piston engines, including the Pegasus and Hercules.

Fehling, Hermann von [fayling] (1812-85) Chemist, born in Lübeck, Germany. Professor of chemistry at Stuttgart, he introduced an important oxidizing agent which bears his name.

Feiffer, Jules [fIyfer] (1929–   ) Cartoonist and writer, born in New York City. He produced many collections during the 1960s, becoming famous for *Feiffer*, a satirical cartoon strip.

Feigenbaum, Mitchell [fIygenbowm] (1945–   ) Mathematician, born in Philadelphia, PA. He developed the mathematics of what is now called Chaos Theory, used in such fields as meteorology, aerodynamics, and ecology.

Feininger, Lyonel (Charles Adrian) [fIyninger] (1871–1956) Painter, born in New York City. After World War 1 he taught at the Bauhaus in Weimar and Dessau, adopted a style reminiscent of Cubism, and helped to found the New Bauhaus in Chicago.

Feld, Eliot (1942–   ) Dancer, choreographer, and artistic director, born in New York City. He joined American Ballet Theatre (1963), founded Eliot Feld Ballet (1974), and started the New Ballet School (1978), offering inner-city children the chance to become dance professionals.

Fell, John (1625–86) Anglican priest, born in Longworth, Oxfordshire. After the Restoration he was made dean of Christ Church, Oxford, and royal chaplain.

Feller, William (1906–70) Mathematician, born in Zagreb, Croatia. In 1939 he emigrated to the USA, where he became best known for his work in probability theory.

Fellini, Federico [feleenee] (1920–93) Film director, born in Rimini, Italy. His films, always from his own scripts, include (trans titles) *The Road* (1954, Oscar), *Nights of Cabiria* (1956, Oscar), *8½* (1963), *Fellini's Roma* (1972), *I Remember* (1973, Oscar), and *The Sweet Life* (1960, Cannes Festival prizewinner).

Fenby, Eric >> Delius, Fredrick

Fénelon, François de Salignac de la Mothe [faynelõ] (1651–1715) Roman Catholic theologian, born in Fénelon, France. His chief work, *The Adventures of Telemachus* (trans, 1699), received the king's censure for its political undertones.

Fenley, Molissa (1954–   ) Dancer and choreographer, born in Las Vegas, NV. Her reputation rests on physically demanding, high-energy solos such as *Eureka* (1982) and *State of Darkness* (1988).

Fenning, Frederick William (1919–88) British nuclear physicist and pioneer of nuclear reactor technology. At Risley he was particularly associated with work on the Advanced Gas-Cooled Reactor (AGR) which led to the operation of the Windscale (now Sellafield) AGR.

Fenton, Roger (1819–69) Photographer, born in Heywood, Lancashire. In 1855 he went to the Crimea as the world's first accredited war-photographer to record the conditions of the campaign.

Ferber, Edna (1887–1968) Writer, born in Kalamazoo, MI. She wrote many novels and short stories, including *So Big* (1924, Pulitzer), but is probably best remembered for *Show Boat* (1926), which inspired the musical of that name.

Ferdinand I (of Bulgaria), in full **Ferdinand Karl Leopold Maria** (1861–1948) King of Bulgaria, born in Vienna. In 1908 he proclaimed Bulgaria independent, and took the title of king. He invaded Serbia in 1915, but his armies were routed, and he abdicated in 1918.

Ferdinand I (of the Two Sicilies) (1751–1825) King of Naples, as Ferdinand IV (1759–99, 1799–1806) and of the Two Sicilies (1816–25), born in Naples, Italy. He joined England and Austria against France (1793), was forced to make a treaty with Napoleon (1801), and took refuge in Sicily (1806). Reinstated by the Congress of Vienna (1815), he then united his two states into the Kingdom of the Two Sicilies. >> Napoleon I

Ferdinand, known as **the Catholic** (1452–1516) King of Castile as Ferdinand V (from 1474), of Aragon and Sicily as Ferdinand II (from 1479), and of Naples as Ferdinand III (from 1503), born in Sos, Aragon, Spain. In 1469 he married Isabella, sister of Henry IV of Castile, and ruled jointly with her until her death (1504). Under him, Spain gained supremacy following the discovery of America, and by 1512 he had become monarch of all Spain. >> Isabella I

Ferdusi >> Firdausi

Ferguson, Adam (1723–1816) Philosopher and historian, born in Logierait, Tayside. A member of the Scottish 'common sense' school of philosophy, his works include *Principles of Moral and Political Science* (1792).

Ferguson, Harry George (1884–1960) Engineer and inventor, born in Hillsborough, Co Down. Over many years he developed the Ferguson farm tractor, which played a large part in the mechanization of British agriculture during and after World War 2.

Ferguson, Patrick (1744–80) British soldier and inventor, born in Pitfour, Grampian. In 1776 he invented a breech-loading rifle, with which he armed a corps of loyalists who helped defeat the Americans at the Battle of Brandywine (1777).

Ferguson, Robert, known as **the Plotter** (c.1637–1714) Conspirator, born near Alford, Grampian. He played a leading part in many treasonable schemes against the last two Stuart kings, and twice had to flee the kingdom.

Ferguson, Sarah >> Andrew, Duke of York

Fergusson, John Duncan (1874–1961) Painter, born in Perthshire. He is best known for his series of World War 1 paintings of naval dockyards, and for his portraits of the female nude.

Ferlinghetti, Lawrence (Monsanto) [ferlinggetee], originally **Lawrence Ferling** (1919–   ) Poet, born in New York City. Regarded as a founder of the Beat poetry movement, as seen in *A Coney Island of the Mind* (1958), he was also a playwright and novelist.

Fermat, Pierre de [fermah] (1601–65) Mathematician, born in Beaumont-de-Lomagne, France. He became a lawyer, then turned to mathematics, making many discoveries in the properties of numbers, probabilities, and geometry. With Descartes, he was one of the two leading mathematicians in the early 17th-c. >> Descartes

Fermi, Enrico [fermee] (1901–54) Nuclear physicist, born in Rome. In 1934 he and his colleagues split a number of nuclei by bombardment with neutrons, for which he was awarded the Nobel Prize for Physics in 1938. In the USA, he constructed the first US nuclear reactor in 1942. >> Teller

Fermor, Patrick (Michael) Leigh (1915–   ) English travel writer. He is best known for two books, *A Time of Gifts* (1977) and *Between the Woods and the Water* (1986), recounting a leisurely walk from Rotterdam to Constantinople.

Fernandel [fernãdel], stage name of **Fernand Joseph Désiré Contandin** (1903–71) Film comedian, born in Marseille, France. He established himself internationally with his moving portrayal of the naive country priest of *The Little World of Don Camillo* (trans, 1953).

Fernandez, Juan [fernandez], Span [fernandeth] (c.1536–1604) Navigator, in the service of Spain. In 1563 he discovered the Pacific island now named after him, and also discovered San Felix and San Ambrosio Is.

Ferrabosco, Alfonso [feraboskoh] (c.1543–88) Composer, born in Bologna, Italy. He came to England before 1562, and was for some time in the service of Queen Elizabeth I. His son, **Alfonso** (1575–1628), served as composer for James I and Charles I.

Ferranti, Sebastian Ziani de [ferantee] (1864–1930) Electrical engineer and inventor, born in Liverpool, Merseyside. He designed a power station at Deptford to supply power to all of London N of the Thames, took out many patents, and founded Ferranti Ltd in 1905.

Ferrar, Nicholas (1592–1637) Anglican clergyman and mystic, born in London. At Little Gidding in Huntingdonshire he founded a small religious community which engaged in constant services and perpetual prayer. It was broken up by the Puritans in 1647.

Ferrari, Enzo [ferahree] (1898–1988) Racing-car designer, born in Modena, Italy. He became a racing driver in 1920, founded the company which bears his name in 1929, and in 1940 began designing his own cars.

Ferraro, Geraldine A(nne) [ferahroh], married name **Zacarro** (1935–   ) US politician, born in Newburgh, NY. She was elected to the US House of Representatives in 1981, and selected in 1984 by Walter Mondale to be the first female vice-presidential candidate of a major party. >> Mondale

Ferrel, William (1817–91) Meteorologist, born in Fulton Co, PA. His name is preserved in the meteorological term *Ferrel cell*, identifying a segment of the wind circulation model of the Earth.

Ferrer, José (Vincente) (1912–92) Actor, director, and producer, born in Santurce, Puerto Rico. The star of many plays and films, he produced and played the leading role in *Cyrano de Bergerac on stage* (1946), and won an Oscar for the film version (1950).

Ferrier, Kathleen (1912–53) Contralto singer, born in Higher Walton, Lancashire. One of her greatest successes was Mahler's *Das Lied von der Erde* (The Song of the Earth) at the first Edinburgh Festival (1947).

Ferris, George (Washington Gale) (1859–96) Engineer, born in Galesburg, IL. His huge revolving observation wheel for the 1892 World's Columbian Exposition in Chicago was the original *Ferris wheel*.

Fessenden, Reginald Aubrey (1866–1932) Radio engineer and inventor, born in East Bolton, Quebec, Canada. He developed the principle of amplitude modulation (AM) and made a broadcast of speech and music in 1906 from Brant Rock, MA, which was heard over 500 mi away.

Fessenden, William Pitt (1806–69) US politician, born in Boscawen, NH. He served in the US House of Representatives as a Whig (1841–3), and was senator for Maine in 1854. He helped to form the Republican Party, and became secretary of the Treasury in 1864.

Festinger, Leon (1919–   ) Psychologist, born in New York City. Working at the New School for Social Research in New York City (from 1968), his work centred on the development of the theory of cognitive dissonance.

Fettes, Sir William [fetiz] (1750–1836) Scottish merchant and philanthropist. He made a fortune from tea and wine, was twice Lord Provost of Edinburgh, and founded Fettes College (1870).

Feuchtwanger, Lion [foykhtvanger] (1884–1958) Writer, born in Munich, Germany. He won a European reputation with the 18th-c historical novel *Jud Süss* (1925), as well as the 14th-c tale *Die hässliche Herzogin* (1923), which as *The Ugly Duchess* (1927) was a great success in Britain.

Feuerbach, Ludwig (Andreas) [foyerbakh] (1804–72) Philosopher, born in Landshut, Germany. His most famous work was *The Essence of Christianity* (trans, 1841), and his naturalistic materialism was a strong influence on Marx. >> Marx, Karl

Feydeau, Georges Léon Jules Marie [faydoh] (1862–1921) Playwright, born in Paris. His name is synonymous with French bedroom farce, the first of almost 40 plays, *Ladies' Tailor* (trans title) appearing in 1886.

Feynman, Richard (Phillips) [fiynman] (1918–88) Physicist, born in New York City. He shared the Nobel Prize for Physics in 1965 for his work on quantum electrodynamics, and is also known for his visual representation of the behaviour of interacting particles (*Feynman diagrams*).

Fiacre, St [feeakruh], also found as **Fiachrach** (?–670) Irish hermit, who founded a monastery on the site of the village of Saint-Fiacre-en-Brie, near Paris. In 1640 Nicholas

Sauvage introduced a carriage-hire service, the carriages coming to be known as *fiacres*.

Fibich, Zdenko (Zdeněk) [feebeekh] (1850–1900) Composer, born in Šěbořic, Czech Republic. He wrote operas, symphonies, and works for solo piano. One of his melodies, *Poéme*, has remained a popular favourite.

Fibonacci, Leonardo [fibonahchee], also known as **Leonardo Pisano** (c.1170–c.1250) Mathematician, born in Pisa, Italy. He popularized the modern decimal system of numerals, and made an advanced contribution to number theory. In the *Fibonacci sequence* of integers, each number is equal to the sum of the preceding two (0,1,1,2,3,5,8...).

Fichte, Johann Gottlieb [fikhtuh] (1762–1814) Philosopher, born in Rammenau, Germany. He modified Kant, substituting for the 'thing-in-itself' as the absolute reality, the more subjective *Ego*, the primitive act of consciousness. His *Addresses to the German Nation* (trans, 1807–8) invoked resistance against Napoleon. >> Kant

Ficino, Marsilio [ficheenoh] (1433–99) Philosopher, born in Figline, Italy. He became head of the Platonic Academy in Florence (1462), translating the works of Plato and his successors into Latin, and trying to reconcile Platonism with Christianity.

Fick, Adolph Eugen (1829–1901) German physiologist, professor at Zürich and Würzburg. A law of diffusion in liquids was named after him, when he discovered that the mass of solute diffusing through unit area per second is proportional to the concentration gradient.

Fick, August (1833–1916) Philologist, born in Petershagen, Germany. He pioneered the comparative study of Indo-European vocabulary with his Indo-Germanic dictionary (1870).

Fiedler, Arthur [feedler] (1894–1979) Conductor, born in Boston, MA. In 1930 he took over the Boston Pops Orchestra, and for almost a half century was the best-known conductor of light classical music in the USA.

Field, Cyrus W(est) (1819–92) Financier, born in Stockbridge, MA. He helped to finance the first telegraph cable across the Atlantic (1866), achieved after several attempts. >> Field, David Dudley

Field, David Dudley (1805–94) Jurist, born in Haddam, CT, the brother of Cyrus W Field. In 1857 he was appointed by New York state to prepare penal, political, and civil codes, and *Field codes* have since been adopted by many states and countries. >> Field, Cyrus W

Field, Eugene (1850–95) Writer, born in St Louis, MO. A columnist with the *Chicago Morning News*, he became known as a humorist and poet with his column 'Sharps and Flats'. He also published several books of children's verse.

Field, John (1782–1837) Composer and pianist, born in Dublin. An infant prodigy, he settled in Russia in 1804, where he wrote mainly for the piano (including seven concertos), and is credited with originating the nocturne.

Field, Joshua >> Maudslay, Henry

Field, Marshall (1834–1906) Merchant, born in Conway, MA. He founded the Chicago department store known from 1881 as Marshall Field & Co, one of the world's largest and most progressive emporia.

Field, Nathan (1587–?1619) Actor and playwright, born in London. He collaborated with Massinger in *The Fatal Dowry* (1632), and wrote two comedies, *A Woman is a Weathercocke* (1612) and *Amends for Ladies* (1618). >> Massinger

Fielding, Henry (1707–54) Writer, born at Sharpham Park, Glastonbury, Somerset. On Richardson's publication of *Pamela* (1740), he wrote his famous parody, *Joseph Andrews* (1742). *The History of Tom Jones, A Foundling* (1749) established his reputation as a founder of the English novel.

Fields, Dame Gracie, originally **Grace Stansfield** (1898–1979) Singer and variety star, born in Rochdale, Lancashire. With her sentimental songs and broad Lancashire humour, she won a unique place in the affections of British audiences, known for her theme tune, 'Sally' (1931).

Fields, W C, originally **William Claude Dukenfield** (1879–1946) Actor, born in Philadelphia, PA. He appeared in the Ziegfeld Follies, and established his comic persona in silent films, but his distinctive voice found its full scope with the coming of sound during the 1930s.

Fiennes, Sir Ranulph (Twisleton-Wykeham-) [fiynz] (1944–) Explorer, born in Windsor, Berkshire. He was the leader of several expeditions, including the Transglobe (1979–82), tracing the Greenwich Meridian across both Poles. With Michael Stroud he completed the first unsupported crossing on foot of the Antarctic in 1993.

Fieschi, Giovanni Luigi, Conte de' (Count of) [fieskee] (c.1522–1547) Italian nobleman, whose family had a feud with that of the admiral, Andrea Doria. During an attempt to overthrow Doria, Fieschi was drowned, and Doria wreaked vengeance on the Fieschi estates. >> Doria

Fieschi, Giuseppe Maria [fieskee] (1790–1836) Conspirator, born in Murato, Corsica. A member of a French republican group, he helped to construct 'an infernal machine' of 25 guns firing simultaneously at King Louis-Philippe in 1835. The king escaped, and Fieschi was executed.

Fiesole, Giovanni da >> **Angelico, Fra**

Figg, James (c.1695–1734) Fencer and pugilist, born in Thame, Oxfordshire. He gave displays of quarterstaff, fencing, and boxing in London, and is regarded as one of the greatest 18th-c sporting figures.

Figueroa, Leonardo de [figeroha] (c.1650–1730) Architect, born in Seville, Spain. He was the designer of several major buildings in Seville, distinctive for their surface complexity.

Filarete, Antonio [filaraytay], originally **Antonio di Pietro Averlino** (c.1400–c.69) Sculptor, architect, and theorist, possibly born in Florence. He is best known for his remarkable *Trattato d'architettura* (1460–64) which includes a scheme for an ideal city built to a symmetrical plan.

Filchner, Wilhelm [filkhner] (1877–1957) Geographer and explorer, born in Munich, Germany. He led expeditions across the Pamirs in C Asia (1900) and to Tibet (1903, 1926, 1934), led the Second German Antarctic Expedition (1911–12), and undertook a magnetic survey of Nepal (1939–40).

Fillmore, Millard (1800–74) US statesman and 13th president (1850–3), born in Summer Hill, NY. Elected to Congress in 1833, he was vice-president to Zachary Taylor in 1848, becoming president on his death.

Finch, Peter, originally **George Frederick Ingle-Finch** (1912–77) Actor, born in London. His films include *The Nun's Story* (1959), *Sunday, Bloody Sunday* (1971), and *Network* (1976), for which he received the first-ever posthumous Oscar.

Fink, Albert (1827–97) Structural engineer, born in Darmstadt, Germany. He emigrated to the USA in 1849, and in 1852 invented the *Fink truss*, used as a support in railway bridges and in roofs.

Finlay, Ian Hamilton (1925–) Poet and artist, born in Nassau and brought up in Scotland. He became widely known as the leading British exponent of concrete poetry in the 1960s.

Finley, James (1762–1828) Civil engineer, born in Pennsylvania. He was one of the first to build a suspension bridge using masonry towers and wrought iron chains, such as that at Newburyport on the Merrimack R in 1810.

Finnbogadóttir, Vigdís [finbohgadoteer] (1930–) President of Iceland (1980–), born in Reykjavík. She is the first woman in world history to be elected head of state.

Finney, Albert (1936–) Actor, born in Salford, Greater Manchester. His performance in *Saturday Night and Sunday Morning* (1960) established him as a star, and he has received Oscar nominations for *Tom Jones* (1963), *Murder on the Orient Express* (1974), *The Dresser* (1983), and *Under the Volcano* (1984).

Finney, Tom (1929–) Footballer, born in Preston, Lancashire. He spent his playing career with Preston North End, and was capped for England 76 times.

Finnian, St (c.495–579), feast day 10 September. Irish clergyman, and chief patron of Ulster. He established a monastery at Moville, after making a pilgrimage to Rome. He should not be confused with **St Finnian of Clonnard** (c.522), who is said to have taught 3000 pupils at the monastery of Clonard.

Finsch, Friedrich Hermann Otto (1839–1917) Naturalist and traveller, born in Silesia. He travelled all over the world, and is best remembered as an expert on parrots. *Finsch's wheatear* was named in his honour.

Finsen, Niels Ryberg (1860–1904) Physician and scientist, born in the Faroe Is, Denmark. He discovered the curative power of different colours of light, and founded phototherapy, receiving the Nobel Prize for Physiology or Medicine in 1903.

Finzi, Gerald Raphael [finzee] (1901–56) Composer, born in London. He wrote orchestral pieces and church music, and is best known for his settings for voice and piano of poems by Hardy, Milton, and Wordsworth.

Fiorelli, Giuseppe [fyorelee] (1823–96) Archaeologist, born in Naples, Italy. He established the meticulous method of studying archaeological sites layer by layer, and founded a training school to teach archaeological technique.

Firbank, (Arthur Annesley) Ronald (1886–1926) Novelist, born in London. His works, known for their witty and inconsequential dialogue, include *Concerning the Eccentricities of Cardinal Pirelli* (1926).

Firdausi or **Ferd(a)usi** [firdowsee], pseudonym of **Abú al-Qásim Mansúr** (940–c.1020) Persian poet, born near Tús, Khorassan. His major work was the epic poem, *Shah Náma* (1010, The Book of Kings), based on actual events from the annals of Persia.

Firestone, Harvey S(amuel) (1868–1938) Industrialist, born in Columbiana, OH. In 1900 he founded the Firestone Tire and Rubber Co, pioneering the pneumatic tyre for the Ford Model T, non-skid treads, and tyres for farm tractors and motor trucks.

First, Ruth (1925–82) Radical opponent of apartheid, born in Johannesburg, South Africa. She worked for various left-wing newspapers and magazines (1946–60), and in 1949 married Joe Slovo, with whom she was charged with treason in 1956. In 1982 she was assassinated by a parcel bomb. >> Slovo

Firth, J(ohn) R(upert) (1890–1960) Linguist, born in Keighley, West Yorkshire. In 1944 he was appointed professor of general linguistics at London University, the first such chair in Great Britain.

Firth, Mark (1819–80) Industrialist and philanthropist, born in Sheffield, South Yorkshire. He established the Norfolk steelworks in 1849, his gifts to Sheffield including almshouses, a park, and the Firth College (1879).

Firth, Sir Raymond (William) (1901–) Social anthropologist, born in Auckland, New Zealand. His major contributions have been in the fields of economic anthropology, social change, and anthropological theory, especially social organization.

Fischer, Bobby, popular name of **Robert (James) Fischer** (1943–) Chess player, born in Chicago, IL. He was world champion in 1972-5, taking the title from Spassky. Ranked as the greatest of all Grand Masters, he resigned his title in 1975, and did not then compete at a major international level until 1992, when he defeated Spassky in a much publicized match. >> Spassky

Fischer, Bram, popular name of **Abram Louis Fischer** (1908-75) Lawyer, born into a prominent Afrikaans family. He defended in the Treason Trial of the 1950s and in the 1964 Rivonia trial. Arrested as a Communist, he was sentenced to life imprisonment in 1966.

Fischer, Carl (1849-1923) Music publisher, born in Buttstadt, Germany. He emigrated to the USA in 1872, opening a music store in New York City which became one of the major US publishers of a wide spectrum of music.

Fischer, Ernst Otto (1918-) Inorganic chemist, born in Munich, Germany. He shared the Nobel Prize for Chemistry in 1973 for explaining how certain metals and organic substances can merge to form organometallic sandwich compounds.

Fischer, Hans (1881-1945) Chemist, born in Höchst, Germany. He studied chlorophylls, showing that they are porphyrins related in structure to haemin, and was awarded the Nobel Prize for Physics in 1930.

Fischer-Dieskau, Dietrich [fisher deeskow] (1925-) Baritone, born in Berlin. One of the foremost interpreters of German *Lieder*, particularly the song-cycles of Schubert, he also appeared in a wide range of operatic roles.

Fischer von Erlach, Johann Bernard [fisher fon airlakh] (1656-1723) Architect, born in Graz, Austria. He moved to Vienna, where he became a leading exponent of the Baroque style, designing the Karlskirche at Vienna and the University church at Salzburg.

Fish, Hamilton (1808-93) Politician, born in New York City. As secretary of state under Grant (1869-77) he signed the Washington Treaty of 1871, and was arbitrator between the USA and Great Britain during the 'Alabama' crisis. >> Grant, Ulysses S

Fishbein, Morris (1889-1976) Physician and writer, born in St Louis, MO. He edited the *Journal of the American Medical Association* (1924-49), campaigned against government involvement in medical practice, and became widely known through his newspaper column and his *Modern Home Medical Adviser* (1935).

Fisher, John, St (1469-1535), feast day 22 June. Clergyman and humanist, born in Beverley, Humberside. In 1527 he pronounced against the divorce of Henry VIII, and was sent with More to the Tower. In 1535 he was made a cardinal, and soon after was beheaded. He was canonized in 1935. >> More, Thomas

Fisher, Alva John (1862-1947) US inventor. In 1910 he patented a washing machine which was marketed as the 'Thor' by the Hurley Machine Co of Chicago, the forerunner of the modern washing machine.

Fisher, Andrew (1862-1928) Australian prime minister (1908-9, 1910-13, 1914-15), born in Crosshouse, Strathclyde. He emigrated to Queensland in 1885, entering the first federal parliament in 1901, and becoming Labor Party leader in 1907.

Fisher, Bud, popular name of **Harry C(onway) Fisher** (1885-1954) Cartoonist, born in Chicago, IL. He brought together his creations of Mutt (1905) and Jeff (1908), drawing the famous *Mutt and Jeff* strip for the *San Francisco Examiner* in 1915.

Fisher, Dorothy Canfield, née **Dorothea Frances Canfield** (1879-1958) Writer, born in Lawrence, KS. Among other contributions to education she popularized the Montessori teaching method in the USA in the 1910s.

Fisher (of Lambeth), Geoffrey Fisher, Baron (1887-1972) Archbishop of Canterbury (1945-61), born in Higham-on-the-Hill, Warwickshire. In 1939 he became Bishop of London, and as archbishop crowned Queen Elizabeth II in Westminster Abbey (1953).

Fisher (of Kilverstone), John Arbuthnot, Baron (1841-1920) British naval commander, born in Ceylon (now Sri Lanka). From 1904, as First Sea Lord, he effected great improvements in the navy, and introduced 'Dreadnought' battleships and 'Invincible' battle cruisers in preparation for war.

Fisher, Sir R(onald) A(ylmer) (1890-1962) Statistician and geneticist, born in East Finchley, Greater London. He studied the genetics of human blood groups, elucidating the Rhesus factor, and developed an analysis of variance which has since become a standard technique.

Fisk, Sir Ernest Thomas (1886-1965) Pioneer of radio, born in Sunbury-on-Thames, Surrey. He founded the Amalgamated Wireless (Australasia) Co, and in 1918 received in Sydney a morse signal from Marconi's transmitter in Britain, the first direct radio signal between the two countries. >> Marconi

Fitch, James Marston (1909-) Architectural preservationist and historian, born in Washington, DC. His early support of 'progressive' urban renewal gave way in the late 1940s to a commitment to historical preservation, as seen in *Architecture and the Aesthetics of Plenty* (1961).

Fitch, John (1743-98) Inventor and pioneer of steampower, born in Windsor, CT. In 1787 he successfully demonstrated a prototype steam boat before building and operating a larger paddle-wheeled ferry between Phildelphia and Burlington, NJ.

Fitch, Val (Logsdon) (1923-) Nuclear physicist, born in Merriman, NE. He did important work in particle physics, sharing the Nobel Prize for Physics in 1980. >> Cronin, James

Fitt, Gerry, popular name of **Gerard, Baron Fitt** (of Bell's Hill) (1926-) Northern Ireland politician, born in Belfast. He founded and led the Social Democratic and Labour Party (1970-9), resigning the leadership to sit as an Independent Socialist. He lost his Westminster seat in 1983 when he received his peerage.

Fittig, Rudolf [fitig] (1835-1910) Scientist, born in Hamburg, Germany. He is best known for his work on organic compounds, in particular their reaction with sodium.

Fitton, Mary (c.1578-1647) English courtier, maid of honour to Elizabeth I. The mistress of William Herbert, Earl of Pembroke, and Sir Richard Leveson, she has been identified by some as the 'dark lady' of Shakespeare's sonnets 127-157. >> Herbert, William

Fitzgerald, Barry, pseudonym of **William Joseph Shields** (1888-1961) Actor, born in Dublin. He went to Hollywood in 1937, where his many films include *Naked City* (1948) and *The Quiet Man* (1952).

Fitzgerald, Lord Edward (1763-98) Irish rebel, born at Carton House, Co Kildare, Ireland. He joined the United Irishmen in 1796, and planned a French invasion of Ireland, but the plot was betrayed, and he died of wounds received in the ensuing scuffle.

Fitzgerald, Edward (1809-83) Scholar and poet, born near Woodbridge, Suffolk. He is best known for his free poetic translation of quatrains from the *Rubáiyát of Omar Khayyám* (1859).

Fitzgerald, Ella (1918-) Jazz singer, born in Newport News, VA. She joined Chick Webb's band and recorded several hits, notably 'A-tisket A-tasket' (1938). Her series of recordings for Verve (1955-9) in multi-volume 'songbooks' are among the treasures of American popular song.

Fitzgerald, F(rancis) Scott (Key) (1896-1940) Novelist, born in St Paul, MN. He captured the spirit of the 1920s jazz era in *The Great Gatsby* (1925). Other novels include *The*

Beautiful and the Damned (1922) and *Tender is the Night* (1934).

Fitzgerald, Garrett (Michael) (1926–) Irish prime minister (1981–2, 1982–7), born in Dublin. In 1969 he was elected a Fine Gael MP, becoming minister for foreign affairs (1973–7) and leader of the Fine Gael Party (1977–87).

Fitzgerald, George Francis (1851–1901) Physicist, born in Dublin. Independently of Lorentz, he concluded that a body becomes shorter as its velocity increases (the *Lorentz–Fitzgerald contraction*), a notion used by Einstein as part of his theory of special relativity.

Fitzgerald, John Francis, nickname **Honey Fitz** (1863–1950) Businessman, born in Boston, MA. A popular Mayor of Boston (1906–8, 1910–14), his administrations were plagued by charges of corruption and political patronage. He was the the grandfather of John, Robert, and Edward Kennedy. >> Kennedy, Edward M / John F / Robert F

Fitz-Gibbon, Bernice Bowles, nickname **Fitz** (1895?–1982) Advertising executive, born in Waunakee, WI. As publicity director at Gimbels, New York City (1940–54), she was one of the highest-paid women in advertising.

Fitzherbert, Mrs Maria Anne, *née* **Smythe** (1756–1857) Wife of George IV, probably born in Brambridge, Hampshire. She secretly married George (then Prince of Wales) in 1785, but the marriage was invalid under the Royal Marriages Act of 1772.

FitzRoy, Sir Charles Augustus (1796–1858) Administrator, born at Shipley Hall, Derbyshire. In 1851 he was commissioned 'Governor-General of All Her Majesty's Australian Possessions', paving the way for the federation of Australian colonies 50 years later.

Fitzroy, Robert (1805–65) Naval officer and meteorologist, born near Bury St Edmunds, Suffolk. In 1831, accompanied by Charles Darwin, he circumnavigated the globe in the *Beagle*. He invented the *Fitzroy barometer*, and instituted the storm warnings that developed into daily weather forecasts. >> Darwin, Charles

Fitzsimmons, Bob, popular name of **Robert Prometheus Fitzsimmons** (1863–1917) Boxer, born in Helston, Cornwall. He went to the USA in 1890, where he won the world middleweight (1891), heavyweight (1897), and light heavyweight championships (1903).

Fitzwilliam, Richard, 7th Viscount Fitzwilliam of Meryon (1745–1816) Irish peer, founder by bequest of the Fitzwilliam Museum in Cambridge. The original building was completed in 1875, and later extended.

Fizeau, Armand Hippolyte Louis [feezoh] (1819–96) Physicist, born in Paris. He was the first to measure the velocity of light by an experiment confined to the Earth's surface (1849), and demonstrated the use of the Doppler principle in determining star velocity in the line of sight.

Flagg, James Montgomery (1877–1960) Illustrator, born in Pelham Manor, NY. He is known for his World War 1 posters, including the 'I Want You' portrait of Uncle Sam, and for his popular images of young women of the time, commonly called 'Flagg Girls'.

Flagstad, Kirsten (1895–1962) Soprano, born in Hamar, Norway. Known especially for her Wagnerian roles, in 1958 she was made director of the Norwegian State Opera.

Flaherty, Robert (Joseph) (1884–1951) Pioneer filmmaker, born in Iron Mountain, MI. He visited Hudson Bay many times to make the silent documentary, *Nanook of the North* (1922). Later films included *Elephant Boy* (1937) and *The Louisiana Story* (1948).

Flaminius, Gaius [flaminius] (?–217 BC) Roman general and statesman, of plebeian origin. Consul in 223 BC, he built a road, the *Flaminian Way*, from Rome to Ariminum (Rimini) in 220 BC, and built the *Circus Flaminius*.

Flamsteed, John (1646–1719) The first Astronomer Royal of England (1675–1719), born in Denby, Derbyshire. In 1676 he instituted reliable observations at Greenwich, near London, providing data from which Newton was later able to verify the gravitational theory. >> Newton

Flanagan, Barry (1941–) Sculptor, born in Prestatyn, Clwyd. His early works were made of cloth or hessian filled with shavings or foam, but he later returned to more traditional materials, as in his bronze 'Leaping Hare' sculptures (1990).

Flanders, Michael (1922–75) Variety performer, born in London. He is best rembered for the revue *At The Drop of a Hat* (1956) and songs, such as the 'Hippopotamus Song', created and performed with Donald Swann. >> Swann

Flaubert, Gustave [flohbair] (1821–80) Writer, born in Rouen, France. His masterpiece, *Madame Bovary* (1857), was condemned as immoral and its author (unsuccessfully) prosecuted. *Three Tales* (trans, 1877) reveals his mastery of the short story.

Flavin, Dan [flayvin] (1933–) Artist, born in New York City. He is known for his 'electric light icons', constructed from fluorescent tubes, sometimes referred to as 'Luminism'.

Flavius Arrianus >> Arrian

Flaxman, John (1755–1826) Sculptor and illustrator, born in York, North Yorkshire. He furnished the Wedgwood house with renowned pottery designs, and also illustrated the *Iliad* and *Odyssey* (1793), and other works.

Fleck, Sir Alexander Fleck, Baron (1889–1968) Industrial chemist, born in Glasgow, Strathclyde. He worked as a physical chemist on radium and on the manufacture of sodium, and became chairman of ICI in 1953.

Flecker, James Elroy (1884–1915) Poet, born in London. His best-known works are the drama *Hassan* (staged, 1922) and *The Golden Journey to Samarkand* (1913).

Fleischer, Max [fliysher] (1883–1972) Cartoonist, inventor, and animated film producer, born in Vienna. In the USA from childhood, he made the first experimental sound-on-film cartoons in the mid-1920s, and went on to produce *Betty Boop Talkartoons* (1930) and *Popeye the Sailor* (1933).

Flémalle, Master of >> Campin, Robert

Fleming, Sir Alexander (1881–1955) Bacteriologist, born near Darvel, Strathclyde. He was the first to use antityphoid vaccines on human beings, pioneered the use of Salvarsan against syphilis, and in 1928 discovered penicillin, for which he shared the Nobel Prize for Physiology or Medicine in 1945. >> Ehrlich, Paul

Fleming, Ian (Lancaster) (1908–64) Writer and journalist, born in London. He achieved worldwide fame as the creator of a series of spy novels, starting with *Casino Royale* (1953), built round the exploits of his amoral hero James Bond.

Fleming, John A(dam) (1877–1956) Geophysicist, born in Cincinnati, OH. He expanded the field of geomagnetism by inventing geomagnetic instruments, designing isomagnetic world charts, and contributing to research in solar and lunar physics.

Fleming, Sir John Ambrose (1849–1945) Physicist, born in Lancaster, Lancashire. He invented the thermionic valve, and was a pioneer in the application of electricity to lighting and heating on a large scale.

Fleming, Peggy (Gale) (1948–) Ice skater, born in San Jose, CA. She won the world championship three times (1966–8), and an Olympic gold medal in 1968 in Mexico City.

Fleming, (Robert) Peter (1907–71) Travel writer and journalist, born in London, the brother of Ian Fleming. His expedition to Central Brazil (1932) in search of Colonel Percy Fawcett resulted in *Brazilian Adventure* (1933), a landmark in travel literature. >> Fawcett, Percy; Fleming, Ian

Fleming, Sir Sandford (1827-1915) Civil engineer and scientist, born in Kirkcaldy, Fife. He went to Canada in 1845, and became chief engineer of the Inter-colonial Railway (1867-76) and of the Canadian Pacific Railway (1872-80).

Fleming, Tom (1929-   ) Actor, director, and poet, born in Edinburgh. In 1965 he was appointed the first director of the Edinburgh Civic Theatre Trust, and founded a new company at the Royal Lyceum Theatre in the city.

Flemming, Walther (1843-1905) Biologist, born in Sachsenberg, Germany. In 1882 he gave the first modern account of cytology, including the process of cell division, which he named *mitosis*.

Fletcher, John (1579-1625) Playwright, born in Rye, East Sussex. He is best known for his collaboration with Beaumont in such works as *Philaster* (1610), *A King and No King* (1611), and *The Maid's Tragedy* (1611). Collaboration with Shakespeare probably resulted in *Two Noble Kinsmen* and *Henry VIII*. >> Beaumont, Francis

Fletcher, John Gould (1886-1950) Writer, born in Little Rock, AR. He followed the Imagists while living in London and Paris (1908-33), but later turned to American subjects. He won the Pulitzer Prize in 1939 for his *Selected Poems*.

Fleury, André-Hercule de [floeree] (1653-1743) French clergyman and statesman, born in Lodève, France. Appointed chief minister (1726), he was made cardinal, and effectively controlled the government of Louis XV until 1743.

Flexner, Abraham (1866-1959) Educational reformer, born in Louisville, KY. His Carnegie Foundation report on medical education in the USA and Canada (1910) sparked a revolution in American medical education.

Flexner, Simon (1863-1946) Microbiologist, born in Louisville, KY. He isolated the dysentery bacillus (1900), developed a serum for cerebrospinal meningitis (1907), and led the team that determined the cause of poliomyelitis.

Flinders, Matthew (1774-1814) Explorer, born in Donington, Lincolnshire. In 1795 he sailed to Australia, where he explored the SE coast, and later (1801-3) circumnavigated the country. The *Flinders River* and *Flinders Range* are named after him.

Flood, Henry (1723-91) Irish statesman. Leader of the Popular Party in the Irish parliament after his election in 1759, he became vice-treasurer of Ireland (1775), but was removed in 1781 as a strong nationalist.

Florence of Worcester (?-1118) Monk and chronicler. He wrote *Chronicon ex chronicis* which supplements and extends the *Chronicon* written by Marianus Scotus, and is a valuable source for Anglo-Saxon history. >> Marianus Scotus

Florey (of Adelaide), Sir Howard Walter Florey, Baron [flawree] (1898-1968) Pathologist, born in Adelaide, South Australia. He became professor of pathology at Oxford (1935-62), where he worked with Chain on penicillin, and shared the Nobel Prize for Physiology or Medicine in 1945. >> Chain

Florio, John [flawrioh], also called **Giovanni Florio** (c.1533-1625) Lexicographer and translator, born in London. His Italian and English dictionary, *A World of Words*, was published in 1598, and his famous translation of Montaigne (1603) has appeared in several modern editions.

Floris, originally **Cornelis de Vriendt** (c.1514-75) Sculptor, ornamentalist, and architect, born in Antwerp, Belgium, the brother of artist **Frans** (1560-70). Most remarkable among his works are the Town Hall, Antwerp (1561-66) and the marble reredos at Tournai Cathedral (1572).

Flory, Paul J(ohn) (1910-85) Chemist, born in Sterling, IL. He worked on commercially successful polymers such as nylon and synthetic rubber, and for his major contributions to the chemistry of polymers he received the Nobel Prize for Chemistry in 1974.

Flotow, Friedrich, Freiherr von (Baron) [flohtoh] (1812-83) Composer, born in Teutendorf, Germany. He made his reputation with *The Wreck of the Medusa* (trans, 1839), *Stradella* (1844), and notably *Martha* (1847).

Fluck, Diana >> Dors, Diana

Fludd, Robert, Lat **Robertus de Fluctibus** (1574-1637) Physician, mystic, and pantheistic theosophist, born in Bearstead, Kent. Influenced by Paracelsus, he recognized three cosmic elements - God (*archetypus*), world (*macrocosmos*), and man (*microcosmos*). >> Paracelsus

Flynn, Elizabeth Gurley (1890-1964) Labour leader and social reformer, born in Concord, NH. She was an organizer for the Industrial Workers of the World, and a founder of the American Civil Liberties Union (1920). In 1936 she joined the Communist Party, and was imprisoned (1955-7) for advocating the overthrow of the US government.

Flynn, Errol (Leslie Thomson) (1909-59) Actor, born in Hobart, Tasmania. *Captain Blood* (1935) established him as a hero of historical adventure stories, seen also in such films as *The Adventures of Robin Hood* (1938) and *The Sea Hawk* (1940). During the 1940s his off-screen reputation for drinking and womanizing became legendary.

Fo, Dario [foh] (1926-   ) Playwright, designer, and actor, born in San Giano, Italy. His populist plays use the comic traditions of farce and slapstick, as well as surreal effects, seen in *Accidental Death of an Anarchist* (trans, 1970) and *Can't Pay, Won't Pay* (trans, 1974).

Foch, Ferdinand [fosh] (1851-1929) French marshal, born in Tarbes, France. He proved himself a great strategist at the Marne (1914), Ypres, and other World War 1 battles, and commanded the Allied Armies in 1918.

Fogerty, Elsie [fohgertee] (1865-1945) Teacher of elocution, born in London. She was founder and director of the Central School of Speech Training and Dramatic Art in London (1906), and a pioneer in the field of speech therapy.

Foix, Gaston [fwah], nickname **the Thunderbolt of Italy** (1489-1512) French soldier, the nephew of Louis XII of France. He twice overthrew the Swiss, at Como and Milan (1511), seized Brescia from the Venetians (1512), and defeated the Spaniards at Ravenna, where he was killed. >> Louis XII

Fokine, Michel [fokeen], originally **Mikhail Mikhaylovich Fokine** (1880-1942) Dancer and choreographer, born in St Petersburg, Russia. He is credited with the creation of modern ballet from the artificial, stylized mode prevalent at the turn of the century.

Fokker, Anthony Herman Gerard (1890-1939) Aircraft engineer, born in Kediri, Java. In 1913 he founded the Fokker aircraft factory at Schwerin, Germany, which made warplanes for the German air force in World War 1.

Foley, John Henry (1818-74) Sculptor, born in Dublin. His statues of public figures include that of Prince Albert for the Albert Memorial in London, and in Dublin those of Burke and Goldsmith at Trinity College.

Folger, Emily Clara, née **Emily Jordan** (1858-1936) Scholar and book collector, born in Ironton, OH. Married in 1885 to Henry Clay Folger, she collaborated with her husband in forming a famous Shakespeare library, later installed in Washington, DC. >> Folger, Henry Clay

Folger, Henry Clay (1857-1930) Lawyer and businessman, born in New York City. His plans to build a Shakespearean library, situated on Capitol Hill, Washington, DC, were realized in 1923, and the building was named after him. >> Folger, Emily Clara

Folkers, Karl August (1906-   ) Biochemist, born in Decatur, IL. His work on antibiotics and vitamins included the first isolation of the anti-pernicious anaemia factor, cyanocobalamin (1948), and the discovery of mevalonic acid.

Follette, Robert M La >> La Follette, Robert M

Fonda, Henry (Jaynes) (1905–82) Actor, born in Grand Island, NE. His performances in *Young Mr Lincoln* (1939) and *The Grapes of Wrath* (1940) established him in the role of the American folk hero. His last major appearance was in *On Golden Pond* (1981, Oscar). >> Fonda, Jane

Fonda, Jane (1937–) Actress, born in New York City, the daughter of Henry Fonda. She married (1965–73) director Roger Vadim, with whom she made *La Ronde* (1964) and *Barbarella* (1968). Later films include *Klute* (1971, Oscar) and *Coming Home* (1978, Oscar). >> Fonda, Henry; Vadim

Fonseca, Manuel Deodoro da >> Deodoro da Fonseca, Manuel

Fontaine, Hippolyte [fōten] (1833–1917) Engineer, born in Dijon, France. He constructed an electric motor and used it in the first transmission of electricity at Vienne (1873).

Fontaine, Jean de La >> La Fontaine, Jean de

Fontaine, Just [fōten] (1933–) Footballer and manager, born in Morocco. He established an enduring record when, playing for France in the final stages of the 1958 World Cup in Sweden, he scored 13 goals.

Fontana, Carlo [fontahna] (1634/8–1714) Architect, born in Bruciato, near Como, Italy. His major works include the fountain in the Piazza di San Pietro, and the tombs of Pope Clement XI, Pope Innocent XII, and Queen Christina of Sweden in St Peter's.

Fontana, Domenico [fontahna] (1543–1607) Architect, born in Melide, Italy. He was papal architect in Rome, employed on the Lateran Palace, the Vatican Library, and St Peter's dome.

Fontana, Lucio [fontahna] (1899–1968) Artist, born in Rosario, Argentina. The inventor of *Spazialismo* (Spatialism), and a pioneer of 'environmental art', he is best known for his bare or monochrome canvases, holed or slashed to create what he called *attese*.

Fontane, Theodor [foontahnuh] (1819–98) Writer, born in Neuruppin, Germany. His works include ballads, such as 'Archibald Douglas', and realistic novels, such as *Before the Storm* (trans, 1878) and *Effi Briest* (1898).

Fontanne, Lynne >> Lunt, Alfred

Fontenelle, Bernard le Bovier, sieur de (Lord of) [fōtuhnel] (1657–1757) Scientist and man of letters, born in Rouen. He won a great literary reputation in Paris, producing idylls, satires, dialogues, critical essays, histories, and tragedies.

Fonteyn, Margot [fontayn], in full **Dame Margot Fonteyn de Arias**, originally **Margaret Hookham** (1919–91) Ballerina, born in Reigate, Surrey. She joined the Sadler's Wells Ballet (later the Royal Ballet) in 1934, and became one of the leading ballerinas of the 20th-c, partnering Nureyev in the 1960s. >> Nureyev

Foot, Sir Dingle (Mackintosh) (1905–78) British politician and lawyer, the brother of Hugh and Michael Foot. He joined the Labour Party in 1956, became MP for Ipswich (1957–70), and was solicitor general (1964–7). >> Foot, Hugh / Michael

Foot, Hugh (Mackintosh), Baron Caradon (1907–90) British administrator, the brother of Dingle and Michael Foot. He held many government administrative posts abroad, and became a UN permanent representative (1964–70). >> Foot, Dingle / Michael

Foot, Michael (Mackintosh) (1913–) British statesman, born in Plymouth, Devon, the brother of Dingle and Hugh Foot. He served as secretary of state for employment (1974–6), and became deputy leader (1976–80) then leader (1980–3) of the Labour Party.

Foote, Andrew (Hull) (1806–63) US naval officer, born in

New Haven, CT. In 1856 he stormed four Chinese forts at Canton, and in the Civil War organized the western flotilla, storming Fort Henry in 1862.

Foote, Arthur (William) (1853–1937) Composer, born in Salem, MA. A noted organist, he wrote church and chamber music, as well as books on harmony and keyboard technique.

Forbes, Bryan (1926–) Actor, script-writer, and director, born in London. He wrote and produced many films, including *The Slipper and the Rose* (1976) and *International Velvet* (1978).

Forbes, Edward (1815–54) Naturalist, born in Douglas, Isle of Man. He advanced several disciplines in natural history, made formative observations in oceanography, and was one of the founders of the science of biogeography.

Forbes, George (1849–1936) Electrical engineer, born in Edinburgh. He invented the carbon brush for dynamos, and also made improvements in the method of measuring the velocity of light (with **James Young**, 1811–83).

Forbes, Malcolm (Stevenson) (1919–90) Publisher, born in New York City. In 1957 he became editor and publisher of *Forbes*, a struggling business magazine, greatly boosting its circulation and profits.

Forbes, (Joan) Rosita (1893–1967) Writer and traveller, born in Swinderby, Lincolnshire. Her travel books include *From Red Sea to Blue Nile* (1928) and *Islands in the Sun* (1950).

Forbes-Robertson, Sir Johnston (1853–1937) Actor, born in London. Actor-manager of the London Lyceum, in 1900 he married **Gertrude Elliot** (1874–1950), a US actress who often partnered him.

Ford, Ford Madox, originally **Ford Hermann Hueffer** (1873–1939) Writer, born in Merton, Surrey. His novels include *The Good Soldier* (1915) and the tetralogy *Parade's End* (1920s), and he founded the *English Review* (1908).

Ford, Gerald R(udolph) (1913–) US Republican statesman and 38th president (1974–6), born in Omaha, NE. Vice-president in 1973, he became president in 1974 when Nixon resigned over the Watergate scandal. The full pardon he granted to Nixon made him unpopular, and he was defeated in the 1976 presidential election by Carter. >> Carter, Jimmy; Nixon

Ford, Harrison (1942–) Actor, born in Chicago, IL. His films include *Star Wars* (1977) and its two sequels, the series of 'Indiana Jones' films, beginning with *Raiders of the Lost Ark* (1981), *Witness* (1985, Oscar nomination), and *The Fugitive* (1993).

Ford, Henry (1863–1947) Automobile engineer and manufacturer, born in Dearborn, MI. He produced his first petrol-driven motor car in 1893, and in 1903 started the Ford Motor Co, pioneering the modern 'assembly line' mass-production techniques for his famous Model T (1908–9).

Ford, John (c.1586–c.1640) Playwright, born in Ilsington, Devon. His plays include *The Lover's Melancholy* (1629) and *'Tis Pity She's a Whore* (1633), and he often collaborated with other Elizabethan playwrights.

Ford, John, originally **Sean Aloysius O'Fearna** (1894–1973) Film director, born in Cape Elizabeth, ME. His portrayal of US pioneering history is seen in *Stagecoach* (1935), *The Informer* (1935, Oscar), and *The Grapes of Wrath* (1940, Oscar). Other films include *How Green Was My Valley* (1941, Oscar) and *The Quiet Man* (1952, Oscar).

Forde, (Cyril) Daryll (1902–73) Anthropologist, born in London. He carried out anthropological fieldwork in Arizona and New Mexico (1928–9), reported in *Habitat, Economy and Society* (1934), and made extensive contributions to the anthropology of Africa.

Forel, Auguste Henri [forel] (1848–1931) Psychiatrist and entomologist, born near Morges, Switzerland. He made notable contributions in the fields of the anatomy of the brain and nerves, hypnotism, and forensic psychiatry.

Foreman, George (1948–) Boxer, born in Marshall, TX. He became the world heavyweight champion in 1973, knocking out Joe Frazier, but lost the title to Muhammad Ali in 1974. He returned to the ring in 1991, losing to Evander Holyfield, then regaining the title in 1994. >> Ali, Muhammad; Frazier

Forest, Lee De >> De Forest, Lee

Forester, C(ecil) S(cott) (1899–1966) Writer, born in Cairo. Known especially for his creation of Horatio Hornblower, he also wrote biographical and travel books.

Forman, Miloš (1932–) Film director, born in Caslav, Czech Republic. His tragi-comedy of insanity, *One Flew Over the Cuckoo's Nest* (1975), won five Oscars, and was followed by films of the stage shows *Hair* (1979), *Ragtime* (1980), and *Amadeus* (1983, Oscar).

Formby, George (1904–61) Entertainer, born in Wigan, Greater Manchester. He appeared in a series of slapstick comedies as a shy young man with an irrepressible grin and ever-ready ukelele to accompany his risqué songs.

Forrest, Edwin (1806–72) Actor, born in Philadelphia, PA. In London in 1845 his Macbeth was hissed by the audience. He retaliated by hissing Macready in Edinburgh, and further antagonism towards Macready in New York City led to a riot which cost 22 lives. >> Macready

Forrest (of Bunbury), John Forrest, Baron (1847–1918) Explorer and politician, born in Bunbury, Western Australia. He led expeditions from Perth to Adelaide along the coast of the Great Australian Bight (1870) and into the interior (1874), and was the first premier of Western Australia (1890–1901).

Forrest, Nathan Bedford (1821–77) US soldier, born in Bedford Co, TN. In the Civil War he joined the Confederate army, then began to operate on his own, using his cavalry as a 'strike force'.

Forrestal, James (1892–1949) US statesman, born in Beacon, NY. He was secretary of the navy (1944–7), then appointed to the newly created post of secretary of defence, resigning in 1949.

Forrester, Jay (Wright) (1918–) Computer engineer, born in Anselmo, NE. At the Massachusetts Institute of Technology (1944–51), he supervised the building of the Whirlwind computer, and devised the first random-access magnetic core store (memory) for an electronic digital computer.

Forssmann, Werner (1904–79) Physician, born in Berlin. He became known for his development of new techniques in heart surgery, including cardiac catheterization, and shared the Nobel Prize for Physiology or Medicine in 1956.

Forster, E(dward) M(organ) (1879–1970) Writer, born in London. His works include *Where Angels Fear to Tread* (1905), *The Longest Journey* (1907), *A Room with a View* (1908), *Howards End* (1910), and his masterpiece, *A Passage to India* (1924).

Förster, Johann Reinhold [foe(r)ster] (1729–98) Naturalist and clergyman, born in Dirschau, Germany. He accompanied Cook as naturalist on his second world voyage (1772–5), making pioneer observations of birds in Antarctica, New Zealand, and the Pacific. *Förster's tern* is named after him. >> Cook, James

Forster, Margaret (1938–) Writer, born in Carlisle, Cumbria. Her works include the biographical *Elizabeth Barrett Browning* (1988), and many novels, such as *Georgy Girl* (1965; filmed 1966) and *The Battle for Christabel* (1991). She married Hunter Davies in 1960. >> Davies, Hunter

Forster, William Edward (1818–86) British statesman, born in Bradpole, Dorset. He entered Parliament as a Liberal MP in 1861, and under Gladstone (1880) became chief secretary for Ireland. >> Gladstone, W E

Forsyth, Bill [faw(r)siyth], popular name of **William David Forsyth** (1947–) Film-maker, born near Glasgow,

Strathclyde. He has made several successful comedies, notably *Gregory's Girl* (1981) and *Local Hero* (1983), as well as productions for television.

Forsyth, Bruce [faw(r)siyth], popular name of **Bruce Joseph Forsyth-Johnson** (1928–) Entertainer, born in Edmonton, Greater London. He is best known as the host of many UK television shows, such as *Sunday Night at the London Palladium* (1958–60) and *The Generation Game* (1971–8, 1992–4).

Forsyth, Frederick [faw(r)siyth] (1938–) Writer of suspense thrillers, born in Ashford, Kent. His reputation rests on three taut thrillers, *The Day of the Jackal* (1971), *The Odessa File* (1972), and *The Dogs of War* (1974).

Forsyth, Gordon Mitchell [faw(r)siyth] (1879–1953) Ceramic designer, born in Fraserburgh, Grampian. His influence as a teacher at the Stoke-on-Trent School of Art was enormous, his pupils including Clarice Cliff and Susie Cooper. >> Cliff; Cooper, Susie

Forsythe, William [faw(r)siyth] (1949–) Dancer, choreographer, and artistic director, born in New York City. His controversial works frequently use spoken text and stage mechanics to enhance the steps, and he is known for his remodelling of ballet vocabulary for contemporary purposes.

Fort, Paul [faw(r)] (1872–1960) Poet, born in Reims, France. He founded the Théâtre des Arts (1890–3) for presenting a wide range of European drama and recitals of symbolist poetry.

Fortas, Abe [faw(r)tas] (1910–82) Jurist, born in Memphis, TN. In 1965 President Johnson appointed him to the US Supreme Court, but in 1969 he was forced to resign (the first man to do so) following a financial enquiry. >> Johnson, Lyndon B

Fosbury, Dick, popular name of **Richard Fosbury** (1947–) Athlete, born in Portland, OR. He pioneered a new technique in high jumping after he won the Olympic gold medal at Mexico City in 1968 with a jump of 2·24 m (7 ft 4 in), using what came to be known as the *Fosbury Flop*.

Foscolo, Ugo [foskoloh] (1778–1827) Writer, born in Zákinthos, Greece. His poems include the *Last Letters of Jacopo Ortis* (trans, 1802) and *Of the Sepulchres* (trans, 1807).

Fosdick, Harry (Emerson) (1878–1969) Minister, born in Buffalo, NY. A pastor of the interdenominational Riverside Church (1926–46), he was a leading modernist in the controversy on fundamentalism in the 1920s.

Foss, Lukas, originally **Lukas Fuchs** (1922–) Composer, born in Berlin. His works include the cantata, *The Prairie* (1941), two symphonies, concertos, chamber music, and operas.

Fosse, Bob, popular name of **Robert Louis Fosse** (1927–87) Choreographer and director, born in Chicago, IL. His choreographic career started with *The Pajama Game* (1954), and went on to include the Broadway success *Sweet Charity* (1966) and the film *Cabaret* (1972).

Foster, Sir Norman (Robert) (1935–) Architect, born in Manchester. A leading exponent of the technological approach to architecture, his buildings include the Third London Airport Terminal (1980) and the Century Tower, Tokyo (1991).

Foster, Stephen (Collins) (1826–64) Songwriter, born in Pittsburgh, PA. He began writing 'minstrel songs', such as 'Oh! Susanna' (1848), 'Old Folks at Home' (1851), and 'Beautiful Dreamer' (1864), which became seminal works of the US tradition.

Foucauld, Charles Eugéne, vicomte de (Viscount of) [fookoh], also known as **Brother Charles of Jesus** (1858–1916) Soldier, explorer, missionary-monk, and mystic, born in Strasbourg, France. He founded the Little Brothers (1933) and Little Sisters (1939) of Jesus, now active worldwide.

Foucault, (Jean Bernard) Léon [fookoh] (1819–68)

Physicist, born in Paris. He determined the velocity of light, and showed that light travels more slowly in water than in air (1850). By means of a freely suspended pendulum, he proved that the Earth rotates (1851).

Foucault, Michel [fookoh] (1926–84) Philosopher, born in Poitiers, France. His work sought to test cultural assumptions in given historical contexts, as seen in (trans titles) *Madness and Civilization* (1961) and *The Order of Things* (1966).

Fouché, Joseph, duc d'Otrante (Duke of Otranto) [fooshay] (1763–1829) French statesman, born in Nantes, France. He was elected to the National Convention in 1792 as a Jacobin, and in 1799 became minister of police, but was banished in 1815.

Foulds, John [fowldz] (1880–1939) Composer, born in Manchester. His major works include *A World Requiem* (1921), a tone poem *April-England* (1926–32), and other chamber, orchestral, vocal, and piano pieces.

Fouqué, Friedrich Heinrich Karl, Baron de la Motte [fookay] (1777–1843) Romantic writer, born in Brandenburg, Germany. He published a long series of romances based on Norse legend and old French poetry, his masterpiece being *Undine* (1811).

Fouquet, Jean [fookay] (c.1420–c.1480) Painter, born in Tours, France. His most notable illuminations are found in the *Antiquities of the Jews* of Josephus and the *Hours of Etienne Chevalier* at Chantilly.

Fouquet, Nicolas, vicomte de (Viscount of) **Melun et de Vaux, Marquis de Belle-Isle** [fookay] (1615–80) French statesman, born in Paris. Mazarin made him superintendent of finance (1653), but he was arrested for embezzlement (1661), and sentenced to life imprisonment.

Fourdrinier, Henry [foordrinier] (1766–1854) British paper-maker and inventor. With his brother **Sealy Fourdrinier** (d.1847) and Bryan Donkin he patented (1806) an improved design of a paper-making machine. >> Donkin

Fourier, (François Marie) Charles [fooryay] (1772–1837) Social theorist, born in Besançon, France. He advocated a reorganization of society into self-sufficient units which would be scientifically planned to offer a maximum of co-operation and self-fulfilment to their members (*Fourierism*).

Fourier, (Jean Baptiste) Joseph, Baron [fooryay] (1768–1830) Mathematician, born in Auxerre, France. While working on the flow of heat he discovered the theorem which now bears his name, that many functions of a single variable can be expanded in a series of sines of multiples of the variable (the *Fourier series*).

Fourneyron, Benoît [foornayrõ] (1802–67) Hydraulic engineer, born in St Etienne, France. In 1832 he patented the general design of his hydraulic turbine installations, and built many of these around the world.

Fournier, Henri-Alban >> **Alain-Fournier, Henri**

Fou Ts'ong [foo tsong] (1934–) Concert pianist, born in Shanghai, China. Acclaimed as an interpreter of Mozart and Chopin, in 1958 he made his base in London, and performed extensively on the international circuit.

Fowke, Francis (1823–65) Engineer and architect, born in Belfast. He planned the Albert Hall in London, produced the original designs for the Victoria and Albert Museum in London, and planned the Royal Scottish Museum in Edinburgh.

Fowler, H(enry) W(atson) (1858–1933) Lexicographer, born in Tonbridge, Kent. In 1903 he began a literary partnership with his brother **F(rank) G(eorge) Fowler** (1871–1918) which led to *The King's English* (1906) and the *Concise Oxford Dictionary* (1911).

Fowler, Sir John (1817–98) Civil engineer, born in Sheffield, South Yorkshire. His projects include the London Metropolitan Railway, Victoria Station, and (with

Baker) the Forth Railway Bridge (1882–90). >> Baker, Benjamin

Fowler, Katherine >> **Philips, Katherine**

Fowler, William A(lfred) (1911–) Astrophysicist, born in Pittsburgh, PA. He worked on the application of nuclear physics to astronomy, and is one of the founders of nucleosynthesis, developed in collaboration with Hoyle and others. He shared the Nobel Prize for Physics in 1983. >> Hoyle, Fred

Fowles, John (Robert) (1926–) Writer, born in Leigh-on-Sea, Essex. His books include *The Magus* (1966), *The French Lieutenant's Woman* (1969; filmed 1981), and *The Ebony Tower* (1974; televised 1984).

Fox, Charles James (1749–1806) British foreign secretary (1782, 1783, 1806), born in London. He became secretary of state after Lord North's downfall, and in 1783 formed a coalition with him, which held office for a short period. >> North, Frederick

Fox, George (1624–91) Founder of the Religious Society of Friends (Quakers), born in Fenny Drayton, Leicestershire. His life is a record of persecutions, imprisonments, and missionary travel to several parts of the world.

Fox, Henry Richard >> **Holland, 3rd Baron**

Foxe, John (1516–87) Preacher and writer, born in Boston, Lincolnshire. He is best known for his *Book of Martyrs* (1563), giving a vivid account of those who suffered in England for the Protestant cause.

Foxe, Richard, also spelled **Fox** (c.1448–1528) Clergyman, born in Ropsley, Lincolnshire. He became bishop successively of Exeter, Bath and Wells, Durham, and Winchester, and in 1517 founded Corpus Christi College, Oxford.

Fox Talbot, William Henry >> **Talbot, William Henry Fox**

Foy, Maximilien Sébastien [fwah] (1775–1825) French soldier, born in Ham, France. Elected to the Chamber of Deputies (1819), he led the Liberal Opposition, and was a constant advocate of constitutional liberty.

Foyt, A(nthony) J(oseph) (1935–) Motor-racing driver, born in Houston, TX. He was one of the most successful drivers in the Indianapolis 500, starting in every race from 1958 to 1990, and winning it four times (1961, 1964, 1967, 1977).

Fra Angelico >> **Angelico, Fra**

Fra Bartolommeo >> **Bartolommeo, Fra**

Fracastoro, Girolamo [frakastawroh] (c.1478–1553) Scholar and physician, born in Verona, Italy. His work *On Contagion and Contagious Diseases* (trans, 1564) contained the first scientifically correct germ theory of disease, predating Pasteur by 300 years. >> Pasteur

Fra Diavolo [frah dyahvoloh] ('Brother Devil'), popular name of **Michele Pezza** (1760–1806) Brigand, born in Itri, Italy. For years he headed a band of desperados in the Calabrian Mts, skilfully evading capture, but was eventually arrested and executed.

Fraenkel-Conrat, Heinz L(udwig) [frengkl konrat] (1910–) Biochemist, born in Breslau, Germany. His work with viruses showed by 1955 that some could be split reversibly into a protein component and a nucleic acid, and that the latter alone was an infective agent.

Fragonard, Jean Honoré [fragonah(r)] (1732–1806) Painter and engraver, born in Grasse, France. He painted genre pictures of contemporary life, landscapes, and the amours of the French court, notably *The Progress of Love* for Madame du Barry.

Frame, Janet Paterson (1924–) Writer, born in Dunedin, New Zealand. Her books include *Scented Gardens for the Blind* (1963), *A State of Siege* (1966), and *an autobiography* (3 vols, 1983–5), filmed as *An Angel at my Table*.

Frampton, Sir George James (1860–1928) Sculptor, born in London. Among his works are 'Peter Pan' in

Kensington Gardens, London, and the Lions at the British Museum.

France, Anatole [frãs], pseudonym of **Jacques Anatole François Thibault** (1844–1924) Writer, born in Paris. He wrote several lively novels, which contrast with his later, satirical works, such as *Penguin Island* (trans, 1908) and *The Gods are Athirst* (trans, 1912). He was awarded the Nobel Prize for Literature in 1921.

France, Celia (1921–) Dancer, born in London. She performed with Ballet Rambert (1937–40) and Sadler's Wells Royal Ballet (1941–50), and founded the National Ballet of Canada in 1951.

Francesca, Piero della >> **Piero della Francesca**

Francesca da Rimini [francheska da reeminee] (?–1285) Daughter of Guido da Polenta, Lord of Ravenna. She was married to Gianciotto the Lame, son of the Lord of Rimini; but she already loved Paolo, Gianciotto's brother. Gianciotto, surprising the lovers together, killed them both. The story is woven into Dante's Inferno. >> Dante

Francesco di Cristofano >> **Franciabigio**

Francesco di Giorgio [francheskoh di jaw(r)jioh], in full **Francesco Maurizio di Giorgio Martini** or **di Martino** (1439–1502) Painter, sculptor, and architect, born in Siena, Italy. Best known as an architect and architectural theorist, as a military engineer he designed the fortifications at Urbino.

Francesco di Paola >> **Francis of Paola, St**

Franchet d'Esperey, Louis Félix Marie François [frãshay desperay] (1856–1942) French soldier, born in Mostaganem, Algeria. He commanded the French Fifth Army in 1914, and later became commander-in-chief of allied armies in Macedonia.

Francheville or **Franqueville, Pierre** [frãshveel] (1548–1616) Sculptor, painter, and architect, born in Cambrai, France. His works include the statues of Jupiter and Janus in the courtyard of the Grimaldi palace, Genoa, and the marble statue of David in the Louvre, Paris.

Francia [franchia], originally **Francesco di Marco di Giacomo Raibolini** (1450–1517) Goldsmith and painter, born in Bologna, Italy. Famed as a craftsman in metal, he designed the first italic type for Aldus Manutius. His sons **Giacomo** (c.1486–1557) and **Giulio** (1487–1543), were also painters. >> Aldus Manutius

Francia, José Gaspar Rodriguez [fransya] (1766–1840) Dictator of Paraguay (from 1814), born near Asunción. He helped to free Paraguay from Spanish rule, and although an unscrupulous despot, the country rapidly improved under his reforms.

Franciabigio [franchabeejoh], also called **Francesco di Cristofano Bigi** (1482–1525) Painter, born in Florence, Italy. He worked with Andrea del Sarto on the Church of the Annunziata and the Chiostro dello Scalzo. >> Sarto

Francis I (1494–1547) King of France (1515–47), born in Cognac, France. His reign was marked by his rivalry with the Emperor Charles V, which led to a series of wars (1521–6, 1528–9, 1536–8, 1542–4). >> Charles V (Emperor)

Francis II (Emperor) (1768–1835) Last Holy Roman Emperor (1792–1806), the first emperor of Austria as Francis I (1804–35), and king of Hungary (1792–1830) and Bohemia (1792–1836), born in Florence, Italy. Defeated several times by Napoleon, he made a short-lived alliance with him, but later joined with Russia and Prussia to win the Battle of Leipzig (1813). >> Marie Louise; Napoleon I

Francis of Assisi, St [aseezee], originally **Giovanni Bernardone** (?1181–1226), feast day 4 October. Founder of the Franciscan Order, born in Assisi, Italy. In 1205 he devoted himself to the care of the poor and the sick, and formed a brotherhood for which he drew up a rule repudiating all property. He was canonized in 1228.

Francis of Paola, St [powla], Ital **Francesco di Paola** (1416–1507), feast day 2 April. Franciscan monk, the

founder of the Minim friars, born in Paola, Italy. He decided on a life of austerity (1431), and became a hermit, his reputation spreading through Italy and France.

Francis of Sales, St [saylz], Fr [sahl] (1567–1622), feast day 24 January. Bishop and writer, born in Sales, France. A distinguished preacher, he became Bishop of Geneva (1602), where he helped to found a congregation of nuns of the Visitation. He was canonized in 1665.

Francis, Dick, popular name of **Richard Stanley Francis** (1920–) Jockey and novelist, born in Surrey. After retiring as a rider in 1957, he began writing popular thrillers with a racing background, such as *Forfeit* (1969), *Whip Hand* (1980), and *Comeback* (1991).

Francis, James (Bicheno) (1815–92) Engineer and inventor, born in South Leigh, Devon. He emigrated to the USA in 1833, where he worked on the design of the turbine that now bears his name, and became known for the *Francis formula* for the flow of water over weirs.

Francis, Sir Philip (1740–1818) Civil servant, born in Dublin. While in Bengal he fought a duel with Warren Hastings and was seriously wounded (1780). He is the probable author of the anonymous political pamphlets known as the 'Junius Letters' (1769–72). >> Hastings, Warren

Francis, Sam (1923–) Abstract painter, born in San Mateo, CA. He began as a medical student, but turned to painting in 1945, and had his first one-man show in Paris in 1955.

Francisco el Viejo >> **Herrera, Francisco**

Francis Ferdinand, Ger **Franz Ferdinand** (1863–1914) Archduke of Austria, the nephew and heir-apparent (from 1896) to the Emperor Francis Joseph. On a visit to Sarajevo, Bosnia, in 1914 he and his wife Sophie were assassinated by Serbian nationalists. Austria then attacked Serbia, precipitating World War 1. >> Francis Joseph; Princip

Francis Joseph I, Ger **Franz Josef I** (1830–1916) Emperor of Austria (1848–1916) and king of Hungary (1867–1916), born near Vienna, the grandson of Emperor Francis I. Defeated by the Prussians in 1866, he established the Dual Monarchy of Austria–Hungary in 1867. His attack on Serbia in 1914 precipitated World War 1.

Francis Xavier, St [zayvier], Span **San Francisco Javier**, known as **the Apostle of the Indies** (1506–52), feast day 3 December. Roman Catholic missionary, born in Navarre, Spain. One of the first seven members of the Jesuit order (1534), he began his missionary work in Goa, India (1542), travelling to the Malay Is (1545) and Japan (1549). He was canonized in 1622.

Franck, César (Auguste) [frãk, sayzah(r)] (1822–90) Composer, born in Liège, Belgium. His reputation rests on a few masterpieces all written after the age of 50, the best known being a string quartet, a symphony, and the *Variations symphoniques* for piano and orchestra.

Franck, James (1882–1964) Physicist, born in Hamburg, Germany. He worked with Gustav Hertz on the laws governing the transfer of energy between molecules, for which they were jointly awarded the Nobel Prize for Physics in 1925. >> Hertz, Gustav

Franco (Bahamonde), Francisco [frangkoh] (1892–1975) Spanish general and dictator (1936–75), born in El Ferrol, Galicia. In 1936 he joined the conspiracy against the Popular Front government, becoming *generalísimo* of the rebel forces. Between 1936 and 1939 he led the Nationalists to victory, and presided over the construction of an authoritarian regime that endured until his death.

Francome, John [frangkuhm] (1952–) Jockey and trainer, born in Swindon, Wiltshire. During 1970–85 he rode a record 1138 winners over fences, and was seven times National Hunt champion jockey (1976, 1979, 1981–5).

Frank, Anne (1929–45) Jewish diarist, born in Frankfurt, Germany. Her family fled to The Netherlands in 1933, and after the Nazi occupation she hid with her family in Amsterdam from 1942 until they were betrayed in 1944. She died in Belsen. The diary she kept during her concealment was published in 1947.

Frank, Hans (1900–46) Nazi politician, born in Karlsruhe, Germany. In 1939 he became Governor-General of Poland, where he conducted a policy of persecution and extermination. He was hanged as a war criminal.

Frank, Ilya Mikhailovich (1908–90) Physicist, born in St Petersburg, Russia. By 1937, working with Cherenkov and Tamm, they were able to explain the 'Cherenkov effect' (dramatically visible in the blue glow in a uranium reactor core containing heavy water). They shared the Nobel Prize for Physics in 1958. >> Cherenkov; Tamm

Frank, Robert (1924–) Photographer and film maker, born in Zürich, Switzerland. He travelled across America to capture images of daily life, publishing *The Americans* in 1959, and was a founder of the New American Cinema Group.

Frankau, Gilbert [frangkow] (1884–1953) Novelist, born in London. His books include *One of Us* (1912), *Men, Maids and Mustard-Pots* (1923), and *World Without End* (1943).

Frankau, Pamela [frangkow], pseudonym **Eliot Naylor** (1908–67) British novelist. Her books include *The Marriage of Harlequin*, *The Willow Cabin* (1949), and *A Wreath for the Enemy* (1954).

Frankenthaler, Helen [frangkentahler] (1928–) Abstract painter, born in New York City. Her technique was to apply very thin paint to unprimed canvas, allowing it to soak in and create atmospheric stains and blots on the surface.

Frankfurter, Felix (1882–1965) Law teacher and judge, born in Vienna. He served as an associate justice of the US Supreme Court (1939–62), and founded the American Civil Liberties Union.

Frankland, Sir Edward (1825–99) Organic chemist, born in Churchtown, Lancashire. He propounded the theory of valency (1852–60), and with Lockyer discovered helium in the Sun's atmosphere in 1868. >> Lockyer

Franklin, Aretha [areetha], nicknames **Lady Soul** and **The Queen of Soul** (1942–) Soul singer and pianist, born in Memphis, TN. Her hit singles include 'Baby, I Love You' and 'Respect', and her albums *Lady Soul* (1968), *Amazing Grace* (1972), and *Aretha* (1986).

Franklin, Benjamin (1706–90) US statesman, writer, and scientist, born in Boston, MA. His research into electricity proved that lightning and electricity are identical. He was actively involved in framing the Declaration of Independence (1776), and played a major part in the Federal Constitutional Convention (1787). In his retirement he wrote an acclaimed autobiography.

Franklin, Frederic (1914–) Dancer, ballet director, and teacher, born in Liverpool, Merseyside. He worked with the Ballets Russes de Monte Carlo (1938–49, 1954–6), his own *Slavenska-Franklin* Ballet (founded 1951), and the National Ballet of Washington (artistic director, 1962–74).

Franklin, Sir John (1786–1847) Arctic explorer, born in Spilsby, Lincolnshire. He commanded an expedition to discover the Northwest Passage, but his ships were hampered by thick ice, and he and his crew died. He is credited with the discovery of the Passage.

Franklin, John Hope (1915–) Historian, born in Rentiesville, OK. He has published several books viewing American history from an African-American standpoint.

Franklin, (Stella Maria Sarah) Miles, pseudonym **Brent of Bin Bin** (1879–1954) Novelist, born in Talbingo, New South Wales, Australia. Her best-known novel, *My Brilliant Career* (1901), was described as 'the very first Australian novel'. The annual *Miles Franklin Awards* are now among Australia's most prestigious literary prizes.

Franklin, Rosalind (Elsie) (1920–58) X-ray crystallographer, born in London. She extended the X-ray diffraction studies by Wilkins on DNA, and obtained photographs which helped Watson and Crick deduce its structure. >> Crick; Watson, James; Wilkins, Maurice

Franqueville, Pierre >> **Francheville, Pierre**

Franz (rulers) >> **Francis**

Frasch, Hermann (1851–1914) Industrial chemist, born in Gailsdorf, Germany. He is best known for the *Frasch process* of extracting sulphur from deep underground deposits by the use of superheated steam.

Fraser, Lady Antonia, *née* **Pakenham** (1932–) British writer. She is best known for her books about important historical figures, such as *Mary Queen of Scots* (1969, James Tait Black Memorial Prize) and *Kings and Queens of England* (1975, 1988). She married Harold Pinter in 1980. >> Pinter

Fraser (of North Cape), Bruce Austin Fraser, Baron (1888–1981) British naval officer, born in Acton, Greater London. He served as chief of staff Mediterranean Fleet (1938–9), and commander-in-chief of the Home Fleet (1943–4), Eastern Fleet (1944), and British Pacific Fleet (1945–6).

Fraser, Dawn (1937–) Swimmer, born in Balmain, near Sydney, New South Wales, Australia. She is the only swimmer to take the same individual title at three consecutive Olympics, winning the 100 m freestyle in 1956, 1960, and 1964. She also won a gold medal in the 4 x 100 m freestyle relay in 1956.

Fraser, (John) Malcolm (1930–) Australian prime minister (1975–83), born in Melbourne, Victoria, Australia. He held various ministerial posts (1966–72), became leader of the Liberal Party (1975), and was prime minister in a Liberal–National coalition.

Fraser, Simon (1776–1862) Fur trader, born in Bennington, VT. In 1805 he was sent to establish the first trading posts in the Rocky Mts, and in 1808 followed the *Fraser R*, named after him, to its mouth. Simon Fraser University, in British Columbia, is also named after him.

Fraunhofer, Joseph von [frownhohfer] (1787–1826) Physicist, born in Straubing, Germany. In 1807 he founded an optical institute at Munich, where he improved prisms and telescopes, enabling him to discover the dark lines in the Sun's spectrum since named after him.

Frayn, Michael (1933–) Writer, born in London. His work includes the novel *The Russian Interpreter* (1966), the comedies *Alphabetical Order* (1975) and *Clouds* (1976), and the script for the film *Clockwise* (1986).

Frazer, Sir James George (1854–1941) Social anthropologist, classicist, and folklorist, born in Glasgow, Strathclyde. His major work was *The Golden Bough* (1890; rewritten in 12 vols, 1911–15).

Frazier, Joe, popular name of **Joseph Frazier** (1944–) Boxer, born in Beaufort, SC. He defeated Jimmy Ellis to become the world heavyweight champion (1970), but lost the title to George Foreman (1973). He retired in 1976, and staged an unsuccessful comeback fight in 1981. >> Foreman

Frederick I (Emperor), known as **Frederick Barbarossa** ('Redbeard') (c.1123–90) Holy Roman Emperor, born of the Hohenstaufen family. His reign was a continuous struggle against unruly vassals at home, the city republics of Lombardy, and the papacy, and he was severely defeated at Legnano (1176). He led the Third Crusade against Saladin (1189). >> Saladin

Frederick II (Emperor) (1194–1250) Holy Roman Emperor (from 1220), King of Sicily (1198) and of Germany (1212), born in Jesi, near Ancona, the last of the Hohenstaufen line. Embarking on the Sixth Crusade (1228), he took possession of Jerusalem, and crowned himself king there.

Frederick II (of Prussia), known as **the Great** (1712–86) King of Prussia (1740–86), the son of Frederick William I, born in Berlin. During the War of the Austrian Succession (1740–8), he seized Silesia, and defeated the Austrians at Mollwitz (1741) and Chotusitz (1742). The second Silesian War (1744–5) left him with further territories which he retained after fighting the Seven Years' War (1756–63), and in 1772 he shared in the first partition of Poland. Under him, Prussia became a leading European power.

Frederick IX (of Denmark) (1899–1972) King of Denmark (1947–72), born near Copenhagen. He married Ingrid, the daughter of King Gustav VI Adolf of Sweden, in 1935, and they had three daughters, Margrethe (later Queen Margrethe II), Benedikte, and Anne-Marie, who married the former King Constantine II of Greece.

Frederick (Augustus), Duke of York (1763–1827) Second son of King George III of Britain. He was unsuccessful as a soldier, and earned the description of the 'grand old Duke of York' in the nursery rhyme, but his reform of the army proved of lasting benefit. >> George III

Frederick William, known as **the Great Elector** (1620–88) Elector of Brandenburg (1640–88), born near Berlin. On his accession, he found the state exhausted by the Thirty Years' War, and began a series of reforms which laid the foundation of future Prussian greatness.

Frederick William III (1770–1840) King of Prussia (1797–1840), the son of Frederick William II (1744–97), born in Potsdam, Germany. In 1806 he declared war against Napoleon, but was defeated at Jena and Auerstadt. He shared in the decisive victory of Leipzig, and recovered his possessions by the Treaty of Vienna (1815). >> Napoleon I

Frederick William IV (1795–1861) King of Prussia (1840–57) born in Cölln, Germany, the son of Frederick William III. He refused the imperial crown offered him in 1849, and in 1857 resigned the administration to his brother, later William I. >> Frederick William III; William I (Emperor)

Fredriksson, Gert (1919–) Swedish canoeist. From 1948–60 he won eight Olympic medals, including six golds, and 13 world titles, all at either kayak singles or pairs.

Freedman, Barnet (1901–58) Painter and lithographer, born in London. A pioneer in the revival of colour lithography, he designed posters, book illustrations, and book covers.

Freeman, Sir Ralph (1880–1950) Civil engineer, born in London. Specializing in the design of steel bridges, he designed Sydney Harbour Bridge, and with his partner Gilbert Roberts the long-span suspension bridges over the estuaries of the Forth, Severn, and Humber rivers. >> Roberts, Gilbert

Freer, Charles Lang (1856–1919) Art collector and businessman, born in Kingston, NY. He became a collector of oriental art, pottery, and paintings, donating his collection to the Smithsonian Institution for the construction of the Freer Gallery (1906).

Frege, (Friedrich Ludwig) Gottlob [frayguh] (1848–1925) Mathematician and logician, born in Wismar, Germany. His *Concept-script* (trans, 1879) outlined the first complete system of symbolic logic, and his philosophical doctrines were set out in *The Foundations of Arithmetic* (trans, 1884).

Frei (Montalva), Eduardo [fray] (1911–82) Chilean president (1964–70), born in Santiago. He became a leader of the Social-Christian Falange Party (1930s), and of the new Christian Democratic Party after 1957.

Freleng, Fritz (Isadore) (1906–) Animated cartoon director and producer, born in Kansas City, KS. He joined Disney, and is best known for Sylvester the lisping cat in *Tweety Pie* (1946, Oscar) and the Mexican mouse, *Speedy Gonzalez* (1955).

Frelinghuysen, Theodorus Jacobus [freelinghiyzn] (1691–1748) Protestant clergyman, born in Lingen, Germany. Sent to America in 1719 as a missionary, he established several churches, and became a leading force in the establishment of the Dutch Reformed faith in the New World.

Frémont, John C(harles) [freemont] (1813–90) Explorer, mapmaker, and politician, born in Savannah, GA. He mapped much of the territory between the Mississippi and the West coast. In 1856 he was the Republican candidate for the presidency, but was defeated by Buchanan. >> Buchanan, James

French, Daniel (Chester) (1850–1931) Sculptor, born in Exeter, NH. His works include 'The Minute Man' (1873–4) in Concorde, MA, and the seated figure of Abraham Lincoln for the Washington Lincoln Memorial (1918–22).

French, John (Denton Pinkstone), Earl of Ypres (1852–1925) British field marshal (1913), born in Ripple, Kent. Chief of the Imperial General Staff (1911–14), he held supreme command of the British Expeditionary Force in France (1914–15), but was criticized for indecision, and resigned.

Freneau, Philip (Morin) [frenoh] (1752–1832) Sailor and poet, born in New York City. He commanded a privateer in the American War of Independence, was captured by the British, and wrote *The British Prison Ship* (1781), and other patriotic poems.

Frescobaldi, Girolamo [freskohbaldee] (1583–1643) Composer, born in Rome. He composed chiefly organ works and madrigals, and from 1608 until his death was organist at St Peter's in Rome.

Fresnel, Augustin Jean [fraynel] (1788–1827) Physicist, born in Broglie, France. He investigated interference fringes in light in 1814, and did much to substantiate the wave theory of light. He also developed a more effective lighthouse lens, the *Fresnel lens*.

Freud, Anna [froyd] (1895–1982) Psychoanalyst, born in Vienna, the daughter of Sigmund Freud. She emigrated with her father to London in 1938, where she became a founder of child psychoanalysis. >> Freud, Sigmund

Freud, Sir Clement (Raphael) [froyd] (1924–) British politician, writer, broadcaster, and caterer. Known for his books about food, and as a long-serving member of the BBC Radio 4 *Just a Minute* team (from 1968), he became a Liberal MP (1972–87).

Freud, Lucian [froyd] (1922–) Painter, born in Berlin, the grandson of Sigmund Freud. In his early years he was one of the neo-Romantic group of English painters, but after the 1950s he developed a realistic style. >> Freud, Sigmund

Freud, Sigmund [froyd] (1856–1939) Founder of psychoanalysis, born in Freiburg, Moravia (now Príbor, Czech Republic). His major work, *The Interpretation of Dreams* (trans, 1900), argued that dreams are disguised manifestations of repressed sexual wishes. In 1902 he was appointed to a professorship in Vienna, out of which grew the Vienna Psychoanalytical Society (1908) and the International Psychoanalytic Association (1910). >> Freud, Anna

Freyberg, Bernard Freyberg, Baron (1889–1963) New Zealand soldier, born in London. In World War 2 he commanded New Zealand forces in the Middle East, Commonwealth forces in Greece and the Sahara, and the New Zealand Corps in Italy.

Freyssinet, Marie Eugène Léon [frayseenay] (1879–1962) Civil engineer, born in Objat, France. He developed pre-stressed concrete, and from 1930 was one of the leading exponents of this virtually new structural material.

Frey-Wyssling, Albert Friedrich [fray visling] (1900–) Botanist, born in Küsnacht, Switzerland. The founder of molecular biology, he did much to establish submicroscopic studies of plant cells by the use of polarization microscopy.

Frick, Ford (Christopher) (1894–1978) Baseball executive, born in Wawaka, IN. A New York sports writer (1922–34) and radio sports broadcaster (1930–4), he became National League president (1934–51) and commissioner (1951–65).

Frick, Henry (Clay) (1849–1919) Industrialist, born in West Overton, PA. He became chairman of the Carnegie Steel Co in 1889, and built up the Frick Collection of fine art, which he bequeathed to New York City.

Frick, Wilhelm (1877–1946) Nazi politician, born in Alsenz, Germany. He participated in Hitler's Munich putsch (1923), led the Nazi faction in the Reichstag, and was minister of the interior from 1933. He was executed for war crimes. >> Hitler

Fricker, Peter (Racine) (1920–90) Composer, born in London. He wrote several symphonies, the oratorio *The Vision of Judgement* (1957–8), and other chamber, choral, and keyboard works.

Fried, Alfred >> **Asser, Tobias**

Friedan, Betty (Naomi) [freedan], *née* **Goldstein** (1921–) Feminist leader and writer, born in Peoria, IL. Best known for her book *The Feminine Mystique* (1963), she was the founder and first president of the National Association for Women in 1966.

Friedel, Charles [freedel] (1832–99) Chemist, born in Strasbourg, France. He collaborated with the US chemist **James Mason Crafts** (1839–1917), developing the *Friedel–Crafts reaction* for the synthesis of benzene homologues.

Friedman, Herbert [freedman] (1916–) Astrophysicist, born in New York City. He pioneered the use of rockets to carry detectors for studying the Sun's X-rays, and also showed (1964) that a non-solar X-ray source coincided with the Crab nebula.

Friedman, Milton [freedman] (1912–) Economist, born in New York City. A leading monetarist, his work includes the permanent income theory of consumption, and the role of money in determining events. He was awarded the Nobel Prize for Economics in 1976.

Friedrich, Carl J(oachim) [freedrikh] (1901–84) Political scientist, born in Leipzig, Germany. A prolific writer on comparative political thought, his analyses of totalitarianism and communism were particularly controversial.

Friedrich, Caspar David [freedrikh] (1774–1840) Painter, born in Greifswald, Germany. His landscapes are vast and desolate expanses in which people, often seen as solitary figures, are depicted as melancholy spectators of Nature's power.

Friel, Brian [freel] (1929–) Playwright, born in Killyclogher, Co Tyrone, Ireland. His many plays include *Philadelphia, Here I Come!* (1964), *Faith Healer* (1979), and *Dancing at Lughnasa* (1990).

Fries, Elias Magnus [frees] (1794–1878) Botanist, born in Femsjö, Sweden. He introduced a classificatory system for fungi which is still valid. The genus *Freesia* is named after him.

Friese-Greene, William [freez green], originally **William Edward Green** (1855–1921) Photographer and inventor, born in Bristol, Avon. In the 1880s he designed a camera to expose a sequence of photographs for projection by lantern slides as a moving image. His first successful picture, using celluloid film, was shown in public in 1890.

Friesz, (Emile) Othon [frees] (1879–1949) Painter, born in Le Havre, France. At first an enthusiastic Impressionist, he was later influenced by Cézanne. >> Cézanne

Frietschie or **Fritchie, Barbara** [fritchee], *née* **Haver** (1766–1862) US heroine, born in Lancaster, PN. According to legend, in 1862, at the age of 95, she boldly displayed the Union flag as Confederate soldiers passed by her

home in Frederick, MD. In tribute to her bravery, she was not harmed, and Whittier immortalized the event in a poem. >> Whittier

Friml, (Charles) Rudolf [friml] (1879–1972) Composer, born in Prague. He settled in the USA in 1906, where he made his name as a composer of light operas, including *Rose Marie* (1924) and *The Vagabond King* (1925).

Frisch, Karl von (1886–1982) Ethologist, born in Vienna. A key figure in the development of ethology, his 40-year study of the honey bee showed that forager bees communicate information in part by use of coded dances. He shared the Nobel Prize for Physiology or Medicine in 1973.

Frisch, Max (Rudolf) (1911–91) Playwright and novelist, born in Zürich, Switzerland. His plays, modern morality pieces, include *Now They Sing Again* (trans, 1945) and *Triptych* (1981), and his novels include *Stiller* (1954) and *Bluebeard* (1983).

Frisch, Otto Robert (1904–79) Physicist, born in Vienna. He and Meitner first described 'nuclear fission' in 1939 to explain Hahn's results with uranium and neutrons. >> Hahn, Otto; Meitner

Frisch, Ragnar (Anton Kittil) (1895–1973) Economist, born in Oslo, Norway. A pioneer of econometrics, he created national economic planning decision models, and shared the first Nobel Prize for Economics in 1969.

Frith, Francis (1822–98) Topographical photographer, born in Chesterfield, Derbyshire. From 1864 he toured throughout Britain and established a nationwide photographic service of local British scenes produced as prints and postcards.

Frith, William Powell (1819–1909) Painter, born in Aldfield, North Yorkshire. He is best known for his huge canvases of Victorian scenes, such as 'Ramsgate Sands' (1854) and 'Derby Day' (1858).

Fritsch, Elizabeth (1940–) Potter, born in Shropshire. Her work uses coiling spires and geometric patterns in coloured slips with a matt texture akin to ivory frescoes. She opened a workshop in London in 1985.

Frobenius, Ferdinand Georg [frohbeenius] (1849–1917) Mathematician, born in Berlin. He founded the theory of group representations, which was later to become essential in quantum mechanics, and a major theme of 20th-c mathematics.

Froberger, Johann Jakob [frohberger] (1616–67) Composer, born in Stuttgart, Germany. Of his many compositions, the best remembered are his suites for harpsichord.

Frobisher, Sir Martin [frohbisher] (c.1535–94) Navigator, born in Altofts, West Yorkshire. He made several attempts to find the Northwest Passage to Cathay (1576–8), reaching Labrador and Hudson Bay. *Frobisher Bay* is named after him.

Fröding, Gustaf [froeding] (1860–1911) Poet, born near Karlstad, Sweden. His use of dialect and folksong rhythm in the portrayal of local characters can be seen in his first collection, *Guitar and Concertina* (trans, 1891).

Froebel, Friedrich (Wilhelm August) [froebl] (1782–1852) Educationist, born in Oberweissbach, Germany. In 1816 he put into practice his educational system whose aim, to help the child's mind grow naturally and spontaneously, he expounded in *The Education of Man* (trans, 1826).

Fröhlich, Alfred >> **Babinski, Joseph**

Froissart, Jean [frwasah(r)] (c.1333–c.1404) Historian and poet, born in Valenciennes, France. His *Chronicles*, covering European history from 1325 to 1400, were heavily influenced by his devotion to chivalric principles.

Froment, Nicolas [fromã] (fl.1450–90) Painter, born in Uzès, France. He was court painter to King René of Anjou, whose portrait is incorporated in his masterpiece, a triptych in the cathedral of Aix-en-Provence.

Fromm, Erich (1900–80) Psychoanalyst and social philosopher, born in Frankfurt, Germany. A neo-Freudian, he is known for his investigations into motivation, as seen in *Escape from Freedom* (1941).

Frontenac, Louis de Buade, comte de (Count of) [frôtenak] (1620–98) French-Canadian statesman, born in St Germain-en-Laye, France. He extended the boundaries of New France down the Mississippi, repulsed the British siege of Quebec, and broke the power of the Iroquois.

Frost, Sir David (Paradine) (1939–) Broadcaster and businessman, born in Tenterden, Kent. He presented the satirical revue, *That Was the Week That Was* (BBC, 1962–3), and hosted many programmes in Britain and America, such as *The Frost Report* (1966–7). A co-founder of London Weekend Television, he was also a co-founder, director, and presenter of Britain's TV-AM (1983).

Frost, John (1784–1877) Chartist leader, born in Newport, Gwent. In 1839 he led an unsuccessful insurrection designed to seize control of Newport. He was sentenced to transportation to Tasmania, but pardoned in 1856.

Frost, Robert (Lee) (1874–1963) Poet, born in San Francisco, CA. His works include *A Boy's Will* (1913), *New Hampshire* (1923, Pulitzer) *Collected Poems* (1930, Pulitzer), and *A Further Range* (1936, Pulitzer). He was regarded as the unofficial laureate of the USA.

Frost, Terry, popular name of **Terence Frost** (1915–) Painter, born in Leamington Spa, Warwickshire. His first abstract paintings date from 1949, and he later became professor of painting at Reading University (1977–81).

Froude, William [frood] (1810–79) Engineer and applied mathematician, born in Dartington, Devon, the brother of James Anthony Froude. His name is preserved in the *Froude dynamometer*, a device for measuring the power output of large engines. >> Froude, James Anthony

Froude, James Anthony [frood] (1818–94) Writer and historian, born in Dartington, Devon. A member of the Oxford Movement, his early novels were controversial, notably *The Nemesis of Faith* (1848). His major work was *History of England* (12 vols, 1856–69). >> Froude, William

Frumentius, St [frumenshius] , (c.300–c.380), feast day 30 November and 18 December. The apostle of Ethiopia, born in Phoenicia. According to the historian Rufinus (345–410), he was accorded the title 'Abuna' (Our Father), still used for the Patriarch of the Ethiopian Orthodox Church.

Fry, Charles Burgess (1872–1956) Sportsman, born in Croydon, Greater London. Best remembered as a cricketer, he played 26 Tests for England. With Bradman he holds the record of six consecutive centuries in first-class cricket. >> Bradman

Fry, Christopher, pseudonym of **Christopher Harris** (1907–) Playwright, born in Bristol, Avon. He wrote a series of major plays in free verse, often with undertones of religion and mysticism, including *A Phoenix Too Frequent* (1946) and *The Lady's Not For Burning* (1949).

Fry, Elizabeth (1780–1845) Quaker prison reformer, born in Norwich, Norfolk. After seeing the terrible conditions for women in Newgate prison, she devoted her life to prison reform at home and abroad.

Fry, Joseph (1728–87) Quaker businessman, born in Sutton Benger, Wiltshire. He founded the well-known chocolate business (later taken over by Cadburys), and from 1764 became known as a typefounder.

Fry, Roger (Eliot) (1866–1934) Art critic, aesthetic philosopher, and painter, born in London. He is mainly remembered for his support of the Postimpressionist movement in England.

Frye, (Herman) Northrop (1912–91) Literary critic and editor, born in Sherbrooke, Quebec, Canada. He achieved international recognition for his literary theories, expounded in his study of William Blake, *Fearful Symmetry* (1947).

Fuad I [fooahd] (1868–1936) King of Egypt (1922–36), the son of Khedive Ismail Pasha, born in Cairo. Sultan of Egypt from 1917, he became king when the British protectorate was ended. >> Farouk I; Ismail Pasha

Fuchs, Klaus (Emil Julius) [fookhs] (1912–88) Physicist and atom spy, born in Rüsselsheim, Germany. From 1943 he worked in the USA on the atom bomb, and in 1946 became head of the theoretical physics division at Harwell, UK. He was imprisoned (1950–59) for disclosing nuclear secrets to the Russians.

Fuchs, Leonhard [fookhs] (1501–66) Physician and botanist, born in Wemding, Germany. He wrote *Historia stirpium* (1542), the first organized and illustrated account of plants. The genus *Fuchsia* was named after him.

Fuchs, Sir Vivian Ernest [fookhs] (1908–) Antarctic explorer and geologist, born in the Isle of Wight, UK. He is best known as the leader of the Commonwealth Trans-Antarctic Expedition (1955–8) which completed the first land crossing of Antarctica.

Fuentes, Carlos [fwentez] (1928–) Novelist and playwright, born in Mexico City. His novel *The Death of Artemio Cruz* (trans, 1962) established him as a major international writer.

Fugard, Athol (Harold Lanigan) [foogah(r)d] (1932–) Playwright, theatre director, and actor, born in Middleburg, Cape Province, South Africa. His plays, set in contemporary South Africa, met with official opposition, notably *Blood Knot* (1960) and *Boesman and Lena* (1969).

Fukui, Kenichi [fookwee] (1918–) Chemist, born in Nara, Japan. He worked on the theory of chemical reactions, and developed the frontier orbital method for predicting the path of pericyclic organic reactions. He shared the Nobel Prize for Chemistry in 1981.

Fulbright, J(ames) William (1905–95) Politician, lawyer, and writer, born in Sumner, MO. A Democrat, he became chairman of the US Senate Committee on Foreign Relations. He is also known for introducing the international exchange programme for scholars (*Fulbright scholarships*).

Fuller, (Richard) Buckminster (1895–1983) Inventor, designer, poet, and philosopher, born in Milton, MA. He developed the Dymaxion ('dynamic and maximum efficiency') House in 1927, and the Dymaxion streamlined, omnidirectional car in 1932. In 1962 he became professor of poetry at Harvard.

Fuller, J(ohn) F(rederick) C(harles) (1878–1966) British general and military thinker, born in Chichester, West Sussex. He planned the breakthrough tank battle of Cambrai in 1917, and proposed the unfulfilled 'Plan 1919', advocating an all-mechanized army.

Fuller, Loie, popular name of **Marie Louise Fuller** (1862–1928) Dancer, choreographer, and producer, born in Fullersburg, IL. In 1891 her exotic solo skirt-dance, using multi-directional coloured lights on yards of swirling silk, created a sensation in Europe.

Fuller, (Sarah) Margaret (1810–50) Writer, feminist, and revolutionary, born in Cambridgeport, MA. A member of Emerson's Transcendentalist circle, her *Woman in the Nineteenth Century* (1845) is the earliest major piece of US feminist writing. >> Emerson

Fuller, Roy (Broadbent) (1912–91) Writer, born in Oldham, Lancashire. His poetic collections include *The Middle of a War* (1942) and *A Lost Season* (1944) prompted by his war-time experiences. His novels include *Second Curtain* (1953) and *Image of a Society* (1956).

Fuller, Thomas (1608–61) Clergyman and antiquary, born in Aldwinkle St Peter's, Northamptonshire. His works were noted for their wittiness, anecdotes, epigrams, and puns. His most famous work, *History of the Worthies of Britain*, was published posthumously (1662).

Fulton, Robert (1765–1815) Engineer, born in Lancaster Co, PA. He is best known for his commercially successful development of the paddle-wheel steamboat which he first demonstrated on the Hudson R in 1807.

Funk, Casimir (1884–1967) Biochemist, born in Warsaw, Poland. He is best known for his work on vitamins, which he identified and named *vitamines* in 1912.

Funk, Walther (1890–1960) Nazi politician, born in Trakehnen, Germany. He played a leading part in planning the economic aspects of the attack on Russia, and in the exploitation of occupied territories.

Furetière, Antoine [fürtyair] (1619–88) Scholar and lexicographer, born in Paris. A writer of comic verse and fables, he compiled a massive *Dictionnaire universel*, eventually published in Rotterdam in 1690.

Furman, Bess (1894–1969) Journalist, born in Danbury, NB. She was a Washington correspondent for the Associated Press in the 1930s, and later reported for the *New York Times* (1943–61).

Furness, Christopher Furness, Baron (1852–1912) Shipowner, born in West Hartlepool, Cleveland. Soon after 1876 he established the Furness Line. He went into partnership with Edward Withy in 1885, which marked the beginning of a huge shipbuilding and engineering business.

Furness, Frank (1839–1912) Architect, born in Philadelphia, PA. His work includes the Pennsylvania Academy of the Fine Arts (1871–6) and the Library (now the *Furness Building*), University of Pennsylvania (1888–91).

Furnivall, Frederick James [fernival] (1825–1910) Philologist, born in Egham, Surrey. He founded the Early English Text Society, and edited the Philological Society's dictionary (from 1861) that became the *Oxford English Dictionary*.

Furphy, Joseph, pseudonym **Tom Collins** (1843–1912) Novelist, born near Melbourne, Victoria, Australia. His reputation rests on one major work, *Such is Life* (1903), which marked a move away from literature's Romantic concept of Australia's pioneering days.

Furth, Harold P(aul) (1930–) Physicist, born in Vienna. A world leader in the fields of plasma physics and controlled thermonuclear fusion, he became widely known for his refutation of the claim that fusion can be achieved at room temperature in a glass of water.

Furtwängler, (Gustav Heinrich Ernst Martin) Wilhelm [foortvengler] (1886–1954) Conductor, born in Berlin. In 1922 he became conductor of the Gewandhaus concerts in Leipzig and of the Berlin Philharmonic, his highly subjective interpretations of the German masters arousing controversy.

Fuseli, Henry [fyoozelee], originally **Johann Heinrich Füssli** (1741–1825) Painter and art critic, born in Zürich, Switzerland. His paintings include 'The Nightmare' (1781) and two series to illustrate the works of Shakespeare and Milton.

Fust, Johann (c. 1400–1466) Printer and goldsmith, born in Mainz, Germany. As payment of a loan, he received Gutenberg's printing plant, with which he started his own business, publishing the Gutenberg Bible in 1465. >> Gutenberg, Johannes

Fysh, Sir (Wilmot) Hudson (1895–1974) Civil aviation pioneer, born in Launceston, Tasmania, Australia. He began the Queensland and Northern Territory Aerial Services Limited in 1920, now known as QUANTAS.

G

Gabelentz, Hans Conon von der [ga belents] (1807–74) Linguist, born in Altenburg, Germany. He is remembered for his great work on the Melanesian languages (1860–73).

Gabelsberger, Franz Xaver [gah belsberger] (1789–1848) Bureaucrat and inventor, born in Munich, Germany. In 1809 he entered the Bavarian civil service, and devised the chief German system of shorthand.

Gabin, Jean [ga bĩ], originally **Jean-Alexis Moncorgé** (1904–76) Actor, born in Paris. A series of dramatic roles brought him international recognition, notably in *Pépé le moko* (1936), *Port of Shadows* (trans, 1938), and *Daybreak* (trans, 1939).

Gabirol, Ibn >> **Avicebrón**

Gable, (William) Clark (1901–60) Actor, born in Cadiz, OH. Growing popularity in tough but sympathetic parts soon labelled him 'the King of Hollywood', reaching its peak with his portrayal of Rhett Butler in *Gone With the Wind* (1939).

Gable, Christopher (1940–) Dancer and choreographer, born in London. In 1986 he became director of the Manchester-based Northern Ballet Theatre.

Gabo, Naum [gah boh], originally **Naum Neemia Pevsner** (1890–1977) Sculptor, born in Bryansk, Russia. In 1920 he helped to form the group of Russian Constructivists, producing many geometrical 'constructions in space'.

Gabor, Dennis [ga baw(r)] (1900–79) Physicist, born in Budapest. He is credited with the invention in 1947 of the technique of holography, and was awarded the Nobel Prize for Physics in 1971.

Gaboriau, Emile [gabawryoh] (c.1835–73) Writer of detective fiction, born in Saujon, France. He leapt to fame with *The Widow Lerouge* (trans, 1866) featuring his detective Lecoq, followed by *Le Dossier 113* (1867), and several others.

Gabriel, Jacques Ange [gabryel] (1698–1782) Architect, born in Paris. He planned a number of additions to Versailles and other palaces, designing the Petit Trianon (1768), and laid out the Place de la Concorde (1753).

Gabrieli, Andrea [gabrielee] (c.1533–86) Composer, born in Venice, Italy. He became organist of St Mark's Church, and wrote Masses and other choral works. Several of his organ pieces foreshadow the fugue. >> Gabrieli, Giovanni

Gabrieli, Giovanni [gabrielee] (c.1555–1612) Composer, born in Venice, Italy, the nephew and pupil of Andrea Gabrieli. He composed choral and instrumental works in which he exploited the acoustics of St Mark's in Venice, as in his well-known *Sonata pian' e forte*. >> Gabrieli, Andrea

Gadamer, Hans-Georg [gah damer] (1900–) Philosopher, born in Marburg, Germany. He is known particularly for his work in hermeneutics, as seen in his major work, *Truth and Method* (trans, 1960).

Gaddafi or **Qaddafi, Colonel Muammar** [ga dafee] (1942–) Libyan political and military leader, born into a nomadic family. He overthrew King Idris in 1969, and became Chairman of the Revolutionary Command Council, encouraging a return to the fundamental principles of Islam. An unpredictable figure, his support of violent revolutionaries in other countries has been a continuing source of international concern.

Gaddi, Agnolo [ga dee] (c.1350–1396) Painter and architect, born in Florence, Italy, the son of Taddeo Gaddi. He painted the frescoes of 'The Discovery of the Cross' in S Croce at Florence, and of the 'Legends of the Holy Girdle' in the cathedral at Prato. >> Gaddi, Taddeo

Gaddi, Gaddo [ga dee] (c.1260–1332) Florentine painter, the founder of the Gaddi family. He worked in mosaic at Rome and Florence. >> Gaddi, Agnolo / Taddeo

Gaddi, Taddeo [ga dee] (c.1300–66) Painter, born in Florence, Italy, the son of Gaddo Gaddi, and best pupil of Giotto. His finest work is seen in the frescoes of 'The Life of the Virgin' in the Baroncelli chapel of S Croce. >> Gaddi, Agnolo / Gaddo; Giotto

Gaddis, William (1922–) Novelist, born in New York City. His experimental novel *The Recognitions* (1955), received a mixed reception. A radical satirist, his other works include *JR* (1976) and *Carpenter's Gothic* (1985).

Gade, Niels (Wilhelm) [ga duh] (1817–90) Composer, born in Copenhagen. He composed eight symphonies, a violin concerto, several choral works, and a number of smaller pieces.

Gadolin, Johan [ga dolin] (1760–1852) Chemist, born in Turku, Finland. A professor of chemistry, he isolated the oxide of the rare element *gadolinium*, named after him.

Gadsden, Christopher (1724–1805) American revolutionary leader, born in Charleston, SC. A member of the first Continental Congress (1774), he became a brigadier-general in the Continental army during the Revolution.

Gadsden, James (1788–1858) US soldier and diplomat, born in Charleston, SC. In 1853 he was appointed US minister to Mexico, and negotiated the purchase (the *Gadsden Purchase*) of part of Arizona and New Mexico for railway construction.

Gagarin, Yuri (Alekseyevich) [ga gah rin] (1934–68) Russian cosmonaut, born in Gagarin (formerly, Gzhatsk), Russia. In 1961 he became the first man to travel in space, completing a circuit of the Earth in the *Vostok* spaceship satellite.

Gage, Thomas (1721–87) British soldier, born in Firle, Sussex. Commander-in-chief of the British forces in America (1763–72), on 18 April 1775 he sent a force to seize arms from the colonists at Concord, and next day the skirmish at Lexington occurred which began the American Revolution.

Gahn, Johan Gottlieb (1745–1818) Chemist and mineralogist, born in Voxna, Sweden. He discovered manganese (1774), and shared the discovery of phosphoric acid in bones with Scheele (1770). The mineral *gahnite* is named after him. >> Scheele

Gainsborough, Thomas [gaynz bruh] (1727–88) Landscape and portrait painter, born in Sudbury, Suffolk. He moved to Bath in 1759, where he established himself with his portrait of Earl Nugent (1760). His best-known paintings include 'The Blue Boy' (c.1770), 'The Harvest Wagon' (1767), and 'The Watering Place' (1777).

Gaiseric or **Genseric** [giy serik] (c.390–477) King of the Vandals and Alans (428–77), who led the Vandals in their invasion of Gaul. He sacked Hippo (430), seized Carthage (439) making it the capital of his new dominions, and sacked Rome (455).

Gaisford, Thomas [gays fuh(r)d] (1780–1855) English Greek scholar. He produced editions of Herodotos, Hephaestion, Stobaeus, and Suidas. The Gaisford Prizes were founded in his memory.

Gaitskell, Hugh (Todd Naylor) (1906–63) British Labour statesman, born in London. He was minister of fuel and power (1947) and of economic affairs (1950), Chancellor of the Exchequer (1950–1), and Leader of the Opposition (1955).

Gaius [gay us] (fl.130–180) Roman jurist, of whom little is known except as author of *Institutes* (trans, c.161), four books of Roman law. They are the only substantial texts of classical Roman law that have survived.

Gajdusek, D(aniel) Carleton (1923–) Virologist, born in Yonkers, NY. He spent much time in Papua New Guinea studying infectious diseases, and shared the Nobel Prize for Physiology or Medicine in 1976 for his work in degenerative neurological disorders.

Gál, Hans (1890–1987) Composer and writer on music, born in Brunn, Austria. His music, in a late Romantic style, included five operas, four symphonies, and many other works.

Galba, Servius Sulpicius (3 BC–AD 69) Roman emperor (68–9). In 68 the Gallic legions rose against Nero, and proclaimed Galba emperor, but he made himself unpopular by favouritism, severity, and avarice, and was assassinated. >> Nero

Galbraith, J(ohn) Kenneth [golbrayth] (1908–) Economist and diplomat, born in Iona Station, Ontario, Canada. He was an advisor to Presidents Kennedy and Johnson, and one of the major intellectual forces in American liberalism. His books include *The Affluent Society* (1958) and *The Age of Uncertainty* (1977, also a TV series).

Galen [gaylen], in full **Claudius Galenus** (c.130–201) Greek physician, born in Pergamum, Mysia. He was a voluminous writer on medical and philosophical subjects, becoming the authority used by later Greek and Roman medical writers.

Galerius [galeerius], in full **Gaius Galerius Valerius Maximus** (c.250–311) Roman emperor (305–11), born near Serdica, Dacia. A Roman soldier of humble origin, he became chief ruler after Diocletians's abdication in 305, and a notorious persecutor of the Christians. >> Diocletian

Galignani, John Anthony [galinyahnee] (1796–1873) Parisian publisher, born in London. Wih his brother **William Galignani** (1798–1882) he greatly improved *Galignani's Messenger*, started in Paris by their father in 1814, and made it a medium for advocating cordiality between England and France.

Galileo [galilayoh], in full **Galileo Galilei** (1564–1642) Astronomer and mathematician, born in Pisa, Italy. He improved the refracting telescope (1610), and was the first to use it for astronomy. His bold advocacy of the Copernican theory brought ecclesiastical censure, and he was forced to retract before the Inquisition. The validity of his work was eventually given official recognition by the Vatican in 1993.

Gall, Franz Joseph [gal] (1758–1828) Anatomist, born in Tiefenbrunn, Germany. As a physician in Vienna (1785), he evolved a theory in which a person's talents and qualities were traced to particular areas of the brain.

Gall, St (c.550–645), feast day 16 October. Irish monk, one of the 12 who followed St Columban to the European mainland in c.585. In 614 he went to live in a cell in Switzerland, around which grew up a great Benedictine abbey and the town of St Gall.

Gallant, Mavis, *née* **Young** (1922–) Writer, born in Montreal, Quebec, Canada. She is known especially for her books of short stories, such as *From the Fifteenth District* (1979), *Home Truths* (1981), and *Overhead in a Balloon* (1985).

Gallatin, (Abraham Alphonse) Albert [galatī] (1761–1849) Financier and statesman, born in Geneva, Switzerland. He was elected to the US House of Representatives (1795), set up the House Committee on Finance (later the Ways and Means Committee), and became secretary of the Treasury (1801–13).

Gallaudet, Thomas (Hopkins) [galuhdet] (1787–1851) Educationist, born in Philadelphia, PA. Interested in the education of the deaf, he learned sign language in Europe, and went on to establish the American Asylum for Deaf-mutes in Hartford, CT (1816).

Gallé, Emile [galay] (1846–1904) Designer and glass maker, born in Nancy, France. His distinctive designs for glass became internationally known after the Paris Exposition (1889).

Galle, Johann Gottfried [gahluh] (1812–1910) Astronomer, born in Pabsthaus, Germany. In 1846, at Berlin Observatory, he discovered the planet Neptune, whose existence had been postulated in the calculations of Leverrier. >> Leverrier

Galli-Curci, Amelita [galee koorchee] (1882–1963) Soprano, born in Milan, Italy. In 1916 she joined the Chicago Opera Company, and from 1919 onwards worked principally at the Metropolitan Opera, New York City.

Galliéni, Joseph Simon [galyaynee] (1849–1916) French soldier, born in St Béat, France. As minister for war, and military governor in Paris from 1914, he saw to the city fortifications, and contributed to the victory of the Marne (1914) by his foresight and planning.

Gallienne, Eva / Richard Le >> **Le Gallienne, Eva / Richard**

Gallienus, Publius Licinius Egnatius [galiaynus] (c.218–68) Roman emperor, colleague (from 253) and successor (from 260) to his father, Valerian. In 268, while besieging one of his rivals in Milan, he was murdered by some of his officers. >> Valerian

Gallitzin, Demetrius Augustine [galitzin], known as **the Apostle of the Alleghenies** (1770–1840) Priest, born in The Hague, The Netherlands. He became a Roman Catholic, and emigrated to the USA in 1792. Sent as a missionary to Cambria County, PA, he founded the town of Loretto (1799).

Gallo, Ernest (1910–) Vintner, born near Modesto, CA. The son of an immigrant Italian grape grower, in 1933 he and his brother **Julio Gallo** (1911–93) took over the family's Modesto vineyards, forming the E and J Gallo Winery.

Gallo, Robert >> **Montagnier, Luc**

Gallup, George (Horace) (1901–84) Public opinion expert, born in Jefferson, IA. In 1935 he founded the American Institute of Public Opinion, and evolved the *Gallup polls* for testing the state of public opinion.

Gallus, Gaius Cornelius [galus] (c.70–26 BC) Poet, born in Forum Julii (now Fréjus) in Gaul. From his four books of elegies upon his mistress 'Lycoris', he is considered the founder of the Roman elegy. Only a few fragments of his work are extant.

Galois, Evariste [galwah] (1811–32) Mathematician, born in Bourg-la-Reine, France. His mathematical reputation rests on fewer than 100 pages of posthumously published work of great originality in group theory.

Galsworthy, John [golzwerthee] (1867–1933) Novelist and playwright, born in Kingston Hill, Surrey. The six novels comprising *The Forsyte Saga* (1906–28) began a new vogue for 'serial' novels. His plays, such as *Strife* (1909) and *The Skin Game* (1920), illustrate his interest in social and ethical problems. He was awarded the Nobel Prize for Literature in 1932.

Galt, Sir Alexander Tilloch [gawlt] (1817–93) Canadian statesman, born in London. He emigrated to Canada in 1835, and entered parliament in 1849, serving as finance minister (1858–62, 1864–6).

Galt, John [gawlt] (1779–1839) Novelist and essayist, born in Irvine, Strathclyde. His novels include *The Ayrshire Legatees* (1820), *The Provost* (1822), and *The Entail* (1823).

Galtieri, Leopoldo (Fortunato) [galtyairee] (1926–) Argentinian soldier and junta president (1981–2), born in Caseras, Buenos Aires. In 1982 he ordered the invasion of the long-disputed Malvinas (Falkland) Is. Their recovery by Britain brought about his downfall, and he was sentenced to 12 years' imprisonment.

Galton, Sir Francis [gawltn] (1822–1911) Scientist and

explorer, born in Birmingham, West Midlands. He is best known for his studies of heredity and intelligence, such as *Hereditary Genius* (1869), which led to the field he called *eugenics*.

Galuppi, Baldassare [galoopee] (1706–85) Light operatic composer, born in the island of Burano, near Venice, Italy. His comic operas were extremely popular, and he also composed sacred and instrumental music.

Galvani, Luigi [galvahnee] (1737–98) Physiologist, born in Bologna, Italy. He is known for his studies of the role of electrical impulses in animal tissue. The *galvanometer* is named after him.

Galway, James [gawlway] (1939–) Flautist, born in Belfast. Since 1975 he has followed a successful solo career, playing on a solid gold flute of remarkable tonal range.

Gama, Vasco da [gahma] (c.1469–1525) Navigator, born in Sines, Alentejo, Portugal. He led the expedition which discovered the route to India round the Cape of Good Hope (1497–9).

Gamage, Albert Walter [gamij] (1855–1930) Merchant, born in Hereford, Hereford and Worcester. He became a draper's apprentice in London, and in 1878 founded the famous store in Holborn which bore his name.

Gamaliel [gamalyel] (?–c.50) Palestinian rabbi, the teacher of St Paul, mentioned in the New Testament (*Acts* 22:3). A prominent Pharisee, he taught 'the law' early in the 1st-c, and encouraged tolerance and peace on all sides. >> Paul, St

Gambetta, Leon (Michel) [gābeta] (1838–82) French Republican prime minister (1881–2), born in Cahors, France. After the surrender of Napoleon III he helped to proclaim the Republic (1870), and was minister of the interior. He led the resistance to MacMahon (1877), and became president of the Chamber (1879).

Gambier, James Gambier, Baron [gambeer] (1756–1833) British naval commander, born in the Bahamas. He served as Lord Commissioner of the Admiralty (1795–1801, 1804–6), and as admiral commanded the British fleet at the bombardment of Copenhagen in 1807.

Gamble, Josias Christopher (1776–1848) Industrialist, born in Enniskillen, Co Fermanagh. He was a founder with **James Muspratt** (1793–1886) of the British chemical industry based at St Helens, near Liverpool.

Gambon, Michael (John) (1940–) Actor, born in Dublin. He joined the Royal Shakespeare Company (1982–3), and has made several television appearances, notably in *The Singing Detective* (1986, BAFTA).

Gamelin, Maurice Gustave [gamlī] (1872–1958) French soldier, born in Paris. Army chief-of-staff and president of the Supreme War Council, his outmoded defensive strategy of 'solid fronts' crumbled under the German *Blitzkrieg* in 1940, and he was replaced and imprisoned (1943–5).

Gamow, George [gamov], originally **Georgy Antonovich Gamov** (1904–68) Physicist, born in Odessa, Ukraine. In 1948 he co-developed the 'big bang' theory of the origin of the universe. In molecular biology he hypothesized that patterns within DNA chains formed a genetic code, a proposal later shown to be correct. >> Alpher; Bethe

Gandar, Laurence (Owen Vine) (1915–) Journalist, born in Durban, South Africa. Editor of *The Rand Daily Mail* in 1957, his challenges to apartheid transformed the newspaper and set new standards in South African journalism.

Gandhi, Indira (Priyadarshini) [gandee] (1917–84) Indian prime minister (1966–77, 1980–4), born in Allahabad, India, the daughter of Nehru. She became president of the Indian Congress Party (1959–60), minister of information (1964), and prime minister after the death of Shastri. She was unable to stem sectarian violence at home, and was assassinated by Sikh extremists. >> Gandhi, Rajiv; Nehru, Jawaharlal; Shastri

Gandhi [gandee], known as **the Mahatma** (Hindi 'of great soul') (1869–1948) Indian nationalist leader, born in Poorbandar, Kathiawar. He studied law in London, and in 1893 went to South Africa, where he spent 20 years opposing discriminatory legislation against Indians. In 1914 he returned to India, where he became leader of the Indian National Congress, advocating a policy of non-violent non-co-operation to achieve independence. In 1930 he led a 320 km/200 mi march to the sea to collect salt in symbolic defiance of the government monopoly. After independence (1947), he tried to stop the Hindu-Muslim conflict in Bengal, a policy which led to his assassination by a Hindu fanatic.

Gandhi, Rajiv [gandee] (1944–91) Indian prime minister (1984–9), born in Bombay, India, the eldest son of Indira Gandhi. After the death of his brother **Sanjay Gandhi** (1946–80) in an air crash, he was elected to his brother's parliamentary seat (1981). He became prime minister following the assassination of Indira Gandhi (1984), but was defeated in the 1989 election. He was assassinated while campaigning for the Congress Party. >> Gandhi, Indira

Gangeśa [ganggesha] (c.1200) Indian philosopher, and founder of the *Navya-nyaya* or new Nyaya school of Hindu philosophy, in Mithila, Bihar. His approach was continued by his son **Vardhamana**. >> Gautama

Ganying, also spelled **Kan-ying** (1st-c AD) Emissary sent by Chinese general Ban Chao from the Caspian to Rome. He traversed Persia and Mesopotamia, but never reached Rome. >> Ban Chao

Gao Gang or **Kao Kang** [gow gahng] (c.1902–55) One of the leaders of the Chinese Communist Party, born in Shensi province, China. A close political ally of Mao Zedong, he became chief party secretary of Manchuria (1949), but was accused of attempting to set up a 'separate kingdom' and apparently committed suicide.

Gaozu [gow tsoo], also spelled **Kao-tsu**, originally **Liu Bang** (247–195 BC) First Han dynasty emperor of China. A bandit leader, he seized the throne from the Qin by conquest in 202 BC, built a new capital at Chang-an (modern Xian), and re-established suzerainty over the S.

Gaozu [gow tsoo], also spelled **Kao-tsu**, originally **Liu Yuane** (c.618–26) First emperor of the Tang dynasty in China (618–907). An official related to the Sui emperors (590–618), he captured Chang-an (Xian) in 617, encouraged by his son Li Shimin (Emperor Taizong), in whose favour he then abdicated. >> Taizong

Garavani, Valentino [garavahnee], known as **Valentino** (1933–) Fashion designer, born in Rome. He opened his own house in Rome in 1959, achieving worldwide recognition with his 1962 show in Florence.

Garbarek, Jan (1947–) Saxophonist and composer, born in Mysen, Norway. He has formed successive small bands which have explored influences from India, South America, and Scandinavian folk roots, often using electronics.

Garbett, Cyril Foster (1875–1955) Anglican clergyman, born in Tongham, Surrey. He became Bishop of Southwark (1919–32), Bishop of Winchester (1932–42), then Archbishop of York, known for his outspoken views on social problems.

Garbo, Greta, originally **Greta Lovisa Gustafsson** (1905–90) Film actress, born in Stockholm. In the USA from 1925, her successes included *Anna Christie* (1930), *Anna Karenina* (1935), *Camille* (1936), and *Ninotchka* (1939).

Garborg, Arne Evenson (1851–1924) Writer, born in Jaeren, Norway. A leader in the movement to establish a new Norwegian literary language, *Nynorsk*, his works include a cycle of lyric poems, *The Hill Innocent* (trans, 1895) and a series of realistic novels, such as *Tired Men* (trans, 1891).

García Perez, Alan [gah(r)seea perez] (1949–) Peruvian

president (1985–90), born in Lima. A member of the moderate left-wing party, he became party secretary-general in 1982, and was the first civilian to win the presidency in democratic elections.

García Gutiérrez, Antonio [gah(r)**thee**a goo**tyair**eth] (1813–84) Playwright, born in Chiclana, Spain. An exponent of 19th-c Romanticism, he is best known for his play *The Troubadour* (trans, 1836), on which Verdi based his opera, *Il trovatore*.

García Lorca, Federico >> **Lorca, Federico García**

García Márquez, Gabriel >> **Márquez, Gabriel García**

García Robles, Alfonso [gah(r)**see**a **rob**lez] (1911–91) Mexican diplomat, born in Zamora, Mexico. He was under-secretary for foreign affairs (1964–71), and instrumental in forming the Treaty of Tlateloco (1967), which aimed to abolish nuclear weapons in Latin America. He shared the Nobel Peace Prize in 1982.

Gardel, Carlos [gah(r)**del**] (1890–1935) Popular singer, born in Toulouse, France. Brought up in Buenos Aires, he made his name as a tango singer and later as a film star.

Garden, Mary (1874–1967) Soprano, born in Aberdeen, Grampian. Her career began in Paris (1900), and in 1910 she began a 20-year association with Chicago Grand Opera.

Gardiner, Samuel Rawson (1829–1902) Historian, born in Ropley, Hampshire. The first instalment of his great *History of England from the Accession of James I to the Restoration* appeared in 1863.

Gardiner, Stephen (c.1483–1555) Clergyman, born in Bury St Edmunds, Suffolk. Bishop of Winchester (1531), he supported the royal supremacy, but opposed doctrinal reformation, and was imprisoned on Edward VI's accession. Released and restored by Mary I in 1553, he became an arch-persecutor of Protestants. >> Mary I

Gardner, Ava (Lavinnia), originally **Lucy Johnson** (1922–90) Film actress, born in Smithfield, NC. Once voted the world's most beautiful woman, she remained a leading lady for two decades, her films including *The Barefoot Contessa* (1954) and *Night of the Iguana* (1964).

Gardner, Erle Stanley (1889–1970) Crime novelist, born in Malden, MA. He is best known as the writer of the 'Perry Mason' books, beginning with *The Case of the Velvet Claws* (1933), which were made into a long-running television series.

Garfield, James A(bram) (1831–81) US Republican statesman and 20th president (Mar–Sep 1881), born in Orange, OH. He identified himself with the cause of civil service reform, irritating many in his own party, and was shot by a disappointed office-seeker.

Garfinkel, Harold [gah(r)**fingkel**] (1917–) Sociologist, born in Newark, NJ. He is the founder of the sociological tradition of ethnomethodology, an approach which focuses on the practical reasoning processes that ordinary people use in order to understand and act within the social world.

Garfunkel, Art >> **Simon, Paul**

Garibaldi, Giuseppe [gari**bawl**dee] (1807–82) Italian patriot, born in Nice, France. At the outbreak of Italy's war of liberation, he sailed from Genoa (1860) with his 'thousand' volunteers and arrived in Sicily, overran much of S Italy, and drove King Francis of Naples from his capital. >> Mazzini

Garioch, Robert [gariokh], pseudonym of **Robert Garioch Sutherland** (1909–81) Poet and translator into Scots, born in Edinburgh. His prose works include *Two Men and a Blanket* (1975), an account of his experience as a prisoner-of-war in World War 2.

Garland, (Hannibal) Hamlin (1860–1940) Writer, born in West Salem, WI. He is best remembered for his 'Middle Border' autobiographical novels, such as *A Daughter of the Middle Border* (1921, Pulitzer).

Garland, Judy, originally **Frances Gumm** (1922–69) Actress and singer, born in Grand Rapids, MN. She became a juvenile film star in *Broadway Melody of 1938*, followed by *The Wizard of Oz* (1939) and *Meet Me in St Louis* (1944), directed by Vincente Minnelli, whom she later married. >> Minnelli, Liza / Vincente

Garner, Errol (Louis) (1923–77) Jazz musician, born in Pittsburg, PA. He was an exhilarating pianist who emerged in 1946 and developed an international following as a concert performer.

Garner, John Nance (1868–1967) US vice-president (1933–41), born near Detroit, TX. During his two terms under Franklin D Roosevelt, he became alarmed at the increase in the executive powers, and unsuccessfully opposed Roosevelt's renomination in 1940. >> Roosevelt, Franklin D

Garnerin, André Jacques [gah(r)neri] (1769–1823) Aeronaut, born in Paris. He gave the first public demonstration of a descent by parachute from a free-flying balloon at Paris in 1797, and with his brother, **Jean Baptiste Olivier** (1766–1849), improved the design of parachutes.

Garnett, David (1892–1981) Novelist, born in Brighton, East Sussex. His books include *Lady into Fox* (1922), *The Grasshoppers Come* (1931), and *Aspects of Love* (1955), which was later adapted as a musical. >> Webber, Andrew Lloyd

Garnett, Tony (1936–) Television and film producer, born in Birmingham, West Midlands. As a producer he enjoyed a long association with director Kenneth Loach on such influential television and film work as *Cathy Come Home* (1966) and *Kes* (1969). >> Loach

Garnier, Francis [gah(r)nyay], originally **Marie Joseph François Garnier** (1839–73) Explorer, born in St Etienne, France. He was second-in-command of the Mekong R Expedition (1866–8) during which he mapped 3100 mi of unknown territory in Cambodia and Yunnan.

Garnier, Robert [gah(r)nyay] (c.1545–90) Poet and playwright, born in La Ferté Bernard, France. His works include eight acclaimed tragedies, notably *Antigone* (1580) and *Les Juives* (1583).

Garnier, Tony [gah(r)nyay], popular name of **Antoine Garnier** (1869–1948) Architect, born in Lyon, France. As architect of Lyon he made a major contribution to the forming of 20th-c architectural and urban planning through his utopian ideal, *Une Cité Industrielle*, exhibited in 1904.

Garofalo, Benvenuto do [garofaloh], also called **Benvenuto Tisi** or **Tisio** (1481–1559) Painter, the last and foremost artist of the Ferrarese school, born in Ferrara, Italy. The church of San Lorenzo, Ferrara, contains his 'Adoration of the Magi'.

Garrett, Elizabeth >> **Anderson, Elizabeth Garrett**

Garrett, João >> **Almeida-Garrett, João**

Garrett, Peter (Robert) (1953–) Popular singer and political activist, born in Sydney, New South Wales, Australia. Since 1977 he has been lead singer with the band Midnight Oil, and in 1989 he became president of the Australian Conservation Foundation.

Garrett, Pat, popular name of **Patrick Floyd Garrett** (1850–1908) Lawman, born in Chambers Co, AL. Sheriff of Lincoln Co, he is remembered for tracking down and killing the escaped murderer, Billy the Kid. >> Bonney

Garrick, David (1717–79) Actor, theatre manager, and playwright, born in Hereford, Hereford and Worcester. In 1741 he won acting fame as Richard III, and for 30 years dominated the English stage. As joint manager of Drury Lane (1747–76) he encouraged innovations in scenery and lighting design.

Garrison, William Lloyd (1805–79) Abolitionist, born in Newburyport, MA. He emerged in 1830 as the foremost anti-slavery voice in the USA, founding both the newspaper *The Liberator* and the American Anti-Slavery Society.

Garrod, Sir Archibald (Edward) (1857–1936) Physician, born in London. His classical study of four inherited human metabolic diseases, described in his *Inborn Errors of Metabolism* (1909), was far ahead of its time.

Garrod, Dorothy (Annie Elizabeth) (1892–1968) Archaeologist, born in London. An expert on the Palaeolithic, she became the first woman to hold a professorial chair at Cambridge in 1939.

Garstin, Sir William Edmund (1849–1925) Engineer, born in India. In Egypt (1885), he was responsible for the construction of the Aswan Dam, reported on the hydrography of the Upper Nile, and initiated the geological survey of Egypt (1896).

Gascoigne, George [gaskoyn] (c.1525–77) Writer and translator, born in Cardington, Bedfordshire. His works include *Certayne Notes of Instruction on Making of Verse* (1575), the first English essay on the subject.

Gascoigne, Paul [gaskoyn], nickname **Gazza** (1967–) Footballer, born in Gateshead, Tyne and Wear. After Tottenham Hotspur signed him in 1988, he established himself as an outstanding player and a flamboyant personality, becoming a member of the England team. His career has since been hindered by leg injuries, but in 1995 he signed for Rangers.

Gaskell, Mrs Elizabeth (Cleghorn), *née* **Stevenson** (1810–65) Writer, born in London. She began to write in middle age, her works including *Mary Barton* (1848), *Wives and Daughters* (1865), and a biography of Charlotte Brontë.

Gasperi, Alcide de [gaspayree] (1881–1954) Italian prime minister (1945–53), born in Trentino, Italy. He headed a succession of coalition cabinets, founded the Christian Democratic Party, and strongly supported a United Europe.

Gass, William H(oward) (1924–) Novelist, born in Fargo, ND. His work includes the novel *Omensetter's Luck* (1966) and his collection of short stories *In the Heart of the Heart of the Country* (1968).

Gassendi, Pierre [gasãdee] (1592–1655) Philosopher and scientist, born in Champtercier, France. A strong advocate of the experimental approach to science, he is best known for his *Objections* (1642) to Descartes' *Meditations*. >> Descartes

Gasser, Herbert (Spencer) (1888–1963) Physiologist, born in Platteville, WI. With Erlanger he made possible the electronic measurement of nerve impulses, and they shared the Nobel Prize for Physiology or Medicine in 1944. >> Erlanger

Gassett, José Ortega y >> **Ortega y Gassett, José**

Gates, Bill, popular name of **William Henry Gates** (1955–) Computer engineer and entrepreneur, born in Seattle, WA. In 1977 he co-founded Microsoft to develop and produce DOS, his basic operating system for computers, adopted in 1981 by IBM.

Gates, Horatio (1728–1806) US general, born in Maldon, Essex. He settled in America, sided with his adoptive country, and in 1777 compelled the surrender of the British at Saratoga. In 1780 he commanded the Army of the South, but was routed by Cornwallis. >> Cornwallis

Gatling, Richard Jordan (1818–1903) Inventor, born in Maney's Neck, NC. He is best remembered for his invention of the rapid-fire *Gatling gun* (1861–2), a crank-operated revolving multibarrel machine gun.

Gatting, Michael William, known as **Mike Gatting** (1957–) Cricketer, born in Kingsbury, Greater London. A forceful batsman, he made his Test debut in 1977, and captained England in 1986–8.

Gatty, Harold (Charles) (1903–57) Aviator and writer, born in Campbell Town, Tasmania, Australia. He flew as navigator on several record-breaking flights (1929–31), published *The Raft Book* (1943) on star navigation, and wrote the best-selling *Nature is your Guide* (1957).

Gatty, Margaret >> **Ewing, Juliana Horatia**

Gaudí (I Cornet), Antonio [gowdee] (1852–1926) Architect, born in Riudoms, Spain. The most famous exponent of Catalan modernism, he is best known for the extravagant and ornate church of the Holy Family in Barcelona (1884–1926).

Gaudier-Brzeska, Henri [gohdyay breska] (1891–1915) Sculptor, born in St Jean de Braye, France. A pioneering modernist who drew upon African tribal art, he developed a highly personal abstract style exemplified in carvings and drawings.

Gaudron, Mary [godron] (1943–) Judge, born in Moree, New South Wales, Australia. In 1974 she became the youngest ever federal judge, and in 1987 was the first woman to be appointed to the High Court of Australia.

Gauguin, (Eugène Henri) Paul [gohgi] (1848–1903) Postimpressionist painter, born in Paris. From 1891 he lived mainly in Tahiti and the Marquesas Is, evolving his own style, *Synthétisme*, reflecting his hatred of civilization and the inspiration he found in primitive peoples.

Gaulle, Charles de >> **de Gaulle, Charles**

Gaumont, Léon Ernest [gohmō], Eng [gohmont] (1864–1946) Cinema inventor, manufacturer, and producer, born in Paris. He was responsible for the first talking pictures, demonstrated at Paris in 1910. He also introduced an early form of coloured cinematography in 1912.

Gaunt, John of >> **John of Gaunt**

Gauss, (Johann) Carl Friedrich [gows] (1777–1855) Mathematician, born in Brunswick, Germany. He wrote the first modern book on number theory, discovered a theory of elliptic and complex functions, and pioneered the application of mathematics to such areas as magnetism and electricity. The unit of magnetic induction has been named after him.

Gautama or **Gotoma** [gohtama] (c.563–c.483 BC) Philosopher, born in Bihar, India. The founder of *Nyaya*, one of the six classical systems of Hindu philosophy, his *Nyaya Sutras* are principally concerned with ways of knowing and of reaching valid logical conclusions.

Gautier, Théophile [gohtyay] (1811–72) Writer and critic, born in Tarbes, France. An extreme Romantic, his works include the novel *Mademoiselle de Maupin* (1835) and the collection *Enamels and Cameos* (trans, 1852).

Gavaskar, Sunil (Manohar) [gavaskah(r)] (1949–) Cricketer, born in Bombay, India. He played 125 Test matches for India, scoring a then record 10 122 runs, and 25 834 runs in first-class cricket at an average of 51·46 per innings.

Gay, John (1685–1732) Writer, born in Barnstaple, Devon. He wrote poems, pamphlets, and in 1727 the first series of his popular satirical *Fables*. His greatest success was the play *The Beggar's Opera* (1728).

Gaye, Marvin (1939–84) Soul singer, born in Washington, DC. The classic 'I Heard It Through the Grapevine' (1968), was a classic Motown recording, later hits including 'What's Going On' (1971).

Gay-Lussac, Joseph Louis [gay luhsak] (1778–1850) Chemist and physicist, born in St Léonard, France. His balloon ascents to 7000 m/23 000 ft (1804) provided the data which led to his major discovery, the law of combining volumes of gases named after him (1808).

Gazza >> **Gascoigne, Paul**

Geber [jayber] (14th-c) Spanish alchemist, who took the name of **Geber** to trade on the reputation of Jabir ibn Hayyan, a celebrated Arabic alchemist. His writings are the clearest exposition of alchemical theory and procedures before the 16th-c.

Geddes, Jenny [gedis] (c.1600–c.1660) Scottish vegetable-seller, traditionally reputed to have started the riots in St Giles' church, Edinburgh, when Laud's prayer book was introduced in 1637. >> Laud

Geddes, Sir Patrick [gedis] (1854–1932) Biologist, sociologist, and pioneer of town planning, born in Perth, Tayside. A disciple of Darwin, he wrote *The Evolution of Sex* (1889), later works on sociology including *Cities in Evolution* (1915). >> Darwin, Charles

Geertgen Tot Sint Jans [geerchen] (c.1460–c.1490) Painter, born in Leyden, The Netherlands. Only about 15 paintings are now attributed to him, mostly fragments of larger altarpieces.

Geertz, Clifford (James) (1923–) Cultural anthropologist, born in San Francisco, CA. His essays, collected in *The Interpretation of Cultures* (1973) and *Local Knowledge* (1983), were particularly influential.

Gehrig, (Henry) Lou(is) [gerig], nickname **the Iron Horse** (1903–41) Baseball player, born in New York City. He played a record 2130 consecutive games for the New York Yankees (1925–39). An outstanding first-baseman, he hit a total 493 home runs.

Geiger, Hans Wilhelm [giyger] (1882–1945) Physicist, born in Neustadt-an-der-Haardt, Germany. He worked under Rutherford at Manchester (1906–12), investigated beta-ray radioactivity, and (with Müller) devised a counter to measure it. >> Müller; Rutherford, Ernest

Geisel, Ernesto [giyzl] (1908–) Brazilian general and president (1974–9), born in Rio Grande do Sul, Brazil. His military presidency was notable for its policy of 'decompression', which led to the restoration of democracy in 1985.

Geisel, Theodor Seuss >> Seuss, Dr

Geissler, Heinrich [giysler] (1814–79) Inventor, born in Igelshieb, Germany. The *Geissler tube*, by which the passage of electricity through rarefied gases can be seen, and the *Geissler mercury pump*, are among his inventions.

Geitel, Hans Friedrich >> Elster, Julius

Gelasius I, St [jelayshius], (?–496), feast day 21 November. Pope (492–6), African by birth. He repressed Pelagianism, renewed the ban against the oriental patriarch, drove out the Manichaeans from Rome, and wrote against the Eutychians and Nestorians. >> Eutyches; Manichaeus; Nestorius; Pelagius

Geldof, Bob [geldof], popular name of **Robert Frederick Xenon Geldof** (1954–) Rock musician and philanthropist, born in Dublin. He formed the successful rock group, the Boomtown Rats (1975–86). Moved by television pictures of famine-stricken Ethiopia, he established the pop charity 'Band Aid' trust in 1984, which raised £8 million for African famine relief through the release of the record 'Do they know it's Christmas?'.

Gelée >> Claude Lorrain

Gelfand, Izrail M(oiseyevich) (1913–) Mathematician, born in Krasnye Okny, Moldova. The leader of an important school of Soviet mathematicians, he has worked mainly in Banach algebras, the representation theory of Lie groups, and in generalized functions. >> Banach; Lie, Sophus

Gell-Mann, Murray [gelman] (1929–) Theoretical physicist, born in New York City. He introduced the concept of *strangeness* into the theory of elemental particles, and proposed the existence of sub-atomic particles, which he named *quarks*. He was awarded the Nobel Prize for Physics in 1969.

Gemayel, Amin [gemiyel] (1942–) Lebanese statesman and president (1982–). He supported his brother, Bashir Gemayel, in the 1975–6 civil war, and succeeded him as president. >> Gemayel, Bashir

Gemayel, Bashir [gemiyel] (1947–82) Lebanese army officer and statesman, the brother of Amin Gamayel. He joined the militia of his father's Phalangist Party, and was an active leader of the Christian militia in the civil war of 1975–6. He was killed in a bomb explosion while still president-elect. >> Gemayel, Amin / Pierre

Gemayel, Sheikh Pierre [gemiyel] (1905–84) Lebanese

politician, a member of the Maronite Christian community of Lebanon, the father of Amin and Bashir Gamayel. He founded the Phalangist Party (1936), and led the Phalangist militia in the 1975–6 civil war. >> Gemayel, Amin / Bashir

Gems, Pam, popular name of **Iris Pamela Gems** (1925–) Playwright, born in England. She is best known for her work with the Royal Shakespeare Company, notably the musical biography of *Piaf*, which moved to the West End and New York City (1980–1).

Geneen, Harold (Sydney) [geneen] (1910–) Accountant and industrialist, born in Bournemouth, Dorset. He became chairman of International Telephone and Telegraph in 1964, and published his views on management in *Managing* (1984).

Genet, Jean [zhuhnay] (1910–86) Writer, born in Paris. His first novel, *Our Lady of the Flowers* (trans, 1944) created a sensation for its portrayal of the criminal world. His plays include *The Maids* (trans, 1947) and *The Screens* (trans, 1961).

Geneviève, St [zhenuhvyev] (c.422–512), feast day 3 January. Patron saint of Paris, born in Nanterre, France. She acquired an extraordinary reputation for sanctity, and in 460 built a church over the tomb of St Denis, where she herself was buried.

Genghis Khan [jengis kahn], also spelled **Jingis** or **Chingis Khan** ('Very Mighty Ruler'), originally **Temujin** (1162/7–1227) Mongol conqueror, born in Temujin on the R Onon. From 1211, in several campaigns, he overran the empire of N China, the Kara-Chitai, Kharezm, and other territories, and by his death the Mongol empire stretched from the Black Sea to the Pacific.

Gennaro, San >> Januarius, St

Gennep, Charles-Arnold Kurr van [genep] (1873–1957) Ethnographer and folklorist, born in Württemberg, Germany, but raised in France. He is chiefly known for *The Rites of Passage* (trans, 1909), a comparative study of rituals marking transitions of social status.

Genscher, Hans-Dietrich [gensher] (1927–) German statesman, born in Reideburg, Germany. In 1974 he became vice-chancellor, foreign minister, and until 1985 was Chairman of the Free Democratic Party.

Genseric >> Gaiseric

Genth, Frederick Augustus (1820–93) Mineralogist, born in Wächtersbach, Germany. He investigated the cobalt-ammonium compounds and discovered 24 new minerals, one of which is named *genthite*.

Gentile, Giovanni [jenteelay] (1875–1944) Philosopher, born in Castelvetrano, Italy. With Croce he became the leading exponent of 20th-c Italian idealism. A philosophical mouthpiece for Mussolini, he was assassinated by an anti-Fascist Communist. >> Croce; Mussolini

Gentile da Fabriano >> Fabriano, Gentile da

Gentileschi, Artemisia [jentileskee] (1597–c.1651) Painter, born in Rome, the daughter of Orazio Gentileschi. Her chief work is 'Judith and Holofernes' in the Uffizi, Florence. >> Gentileschi, Orazio

Gentileschi, Orazio [jentileskee] (1562–1647) Painter, born in Pisa, Italy. The first Italian painter called to England by Charles I, his works include 'The Flight into Egypt' (Louvre) and 'Joseph and Potiphar's Wife' (Hampton Court). >> Gentileschi, Artemisia

Gentz, Friedrich von (1764–1832) German political writer, born in Breslau. Secretary-general of the Congress of Vienna (1814), he was the theorist and practical exponent of 'Balance of Power' in Europe.

Gény, François [zhaynee] (1861–1959) Legal theorist, born in Baccarat, France. He contended that lawyers must supplement the norms derived from the codes, case-law, and doctrine by objective factors, so as to arrive at a decision which takes account of surrounding circumstances.

Geoffrey of Monmouth (c.1100–54) Welsh chronicler, consecrated Bishop of St Asaph in 1152. His *History of the Kings of Britain* (trans) introduced the stories of King Lear and Cymbeline, the prophecies of Merlin, and the legend of Arthur in the form known today.

Geoffroy Saint-Hilaire, Etienne [zhofrwah sĩt eelair] (1772–1844) Zoologist, born in Etampes, France. Professor of zoology in the Museum of Natural History at Paris (1793), he endeavoured to establish the unity of plan in organic structure, and raised teratology to a science.

George I (of Great Britain) (1660–1727) King of Great Britain and Ireland (1714–27), born in Osnabrück, Germany, the great-grandson of James I of England. Elector of Hanover since 1698, he took relatively little part in the government of Britain, living in Hanover as much as possible.

George I (of Greece) (1845–1913) King of Greece (1863–1913), born in Copenhagen, the second son of King Christian IX of Denmark. He was elected king in 1863 by the Greek National Assembly, and in 1867 married the Grand Duchess Olga, niece of Tsar Alexander II of Russia. Involved in the Balkan War (1912–13), he was assassinated at Salonika. >> Constantine I (of Greece)

George II (1683–1760) King of Great Britain and Ireland (1727–60), and Elector of Hanover, born at Herrenhausen, Hanover, the son of George I. In 1705 he married Caroline of Anspach (1683–1737). His reign saw the crushing of Jacobite hopes at Culloden (1746), the foundation of British India after Plassey (1757), and the capture of Quebec (1759). >> George I (of Great Britain)

George II (of Greece) (1890–1947) King of Greece (1922–4, 1935–47), born near Athens. He took the throne after the deposition of his father, Constantine I, he was himself driven out in 1924, and later restored. >> Constantine I (of Greece)

George III (1738–1820) King of Great Britain and Ireland (1760–1820), elector (1760–1815) and king (from 1815) of Hanover, born in London. Eager to govern as well as reign, he caused considerable friction, and with Lord North shared in the blame for the loss of the American colonies. In 1810 he suffered a recurrence of a mental derangement, and the Prince of Wales was made regent. >> George II; North, Frederick

George IV (1762–1830) King of Great Britain and Hanover (1820–30), born in London, the eldest son of George III. In 1795 he married Princess Caroline of Brunswick, whom he tried to divorce when he was king. Her death in 1821 ended a scandal in which the people sympathized with the queen. >> Caroline of Brunswick; Fitzherbert; George III

George V (1865–1936) King of the United Kingdom (1910–36), born in London, the second son of Edward VII. He married Princess Mary of Teck in 1893. His reign saw the Union of South Africa (1910), World War 1, the Irish Free State settlement (1922), and the General Strike (1926). >> Edward VII; Mary of Teck

George VI (1895–1952) King of the United Kingdom (1936–52), born at Sandringham, Norfolk, the second son of George V. He married Lady Elizabeth Bowes-Lyon in 1923, and they had two children: Princess Elizabeth (later Queen Elizabeth II) and Princess Margaret. During World War 2 he set a personal example coping with wartime restrictions, continued to reside in bomb-damaged Buckingham Palace, and visiting all theatres of war. >> Edward VIII; Elizabeth (Queen Mother); George V

George, St , (early 4th-c), feast day 23 April. Patron of chivalry, and guardian saint of England and Portugal. His name was early obscured by fable, such as the story of his fight with a dragon to rescue a maiden.

George, Henry (1839–97) Social reformer and economist, born in Philadelphia, PA. Probably the most influential 19th-c US social analyst, he was renowned for his fervent writing, seen in *Progress and Poverty* (1879).

George, Stefan [gayorguh] (1868–1933) Poet, born in Büdeshein, Germany. His poems show the influence of the French Symbolists. In *The New Reich* (trans, 1928) he advocated a new German culture, not in accord with that of the Nazis, and went into exile.

George-Brown, Baron, originally **George (Alfred) Brown** (1914–85) British statesman, born in London. Deputy Leader of the Labour Party (1960–70), he unsuccessfully contested Wilson for party leadership in 1963. He was secretary of state for economic affairs (1964–6) and foreign secretary (1966–8).

Georgescu-Roegen, Nicholas [zhaw(r)zheskoo roegen] (1906–) Economist, born in Constanza, Romania. His early achievements were based on highly technical mathematical economics, and he later formulated the principles of bioeconomics.

Gephardt, Richard Andrew [gephah(r)t] (1941–) US representative, born in St Louis, MO. He ran for the Democratic nomination as president in 1896, losing to Dukakis, and became house majority leader in 1989. >> Dukakis

Gérard, François (Pascal Simon), Baron [zhayrah(r)] (1770–1837) Painter, born in Rome. His portrait of Isabey the miniaturist (1796) and his 'Cupid and Psyche' (1798) established his reputation. He also painted historical subjects, such as the 'Battle of Austerlitz' (1808).

Gerard, John [jerah(r)d] (1545–1612) Herbalist and barber-surgeon, born in Nantwich, Cheshire. He wrote the first plant catalogue, *The Herball, or General Histoire of Plantes* (1597), containing over 1000 species.

Gerardus Magnus >> Groote, Geert de

Gerber, (Daniel) Frank (1873–1952) Baby-food manufacturer, born in Douglas, MI. In 1901 he helped found the Fremont Canning Co, becoming its president in 1917, and the company began manufacturing baby foods in 1927.

Gerhard, Roberto [gairhah(r)t] (1896–1970) Composer, born in Valls, Spain. He composed ballets, an opera *The Duenna* (1945–7), five symphonies, concertos for violin and piano, chamber music, incidental music, and some electronic music.

Gerhardie, William Alexander [gairhah(r)dee] (1895–1977) Novelist, born of English parents in St Petersburg, Russia. Best known for his novel *The Polyglots* (1925), other works include an autobiography (1931) and a biographical history of *The Romanoffs* (1940).

Gerhardt, Charles (Frédéric) [gairhah(r)t] (1816–56) Chemist, born in Strasbourg, France. Between 1849 and 1855 he wrote on homologous and heterologous series, and on the theory of types with which his name is associated.

Géricault, (Jean Louis André) Théodore [zhayreekoh] (1791–1824) Painter, born in Rouen, France. He painted many unorthodox and realistic scenes, notably 'The Raft of the Medusa' (1819), as well as racing scenes and landscapes.

Gerlach, Walter >> Stern, Otto

German, Sir Edward, originally **Edward German Jones** (1862–1936) Composer, born in Whitchurch, Shropshire. A composer of light opera, his works include *Merrie England* (1902), *Tom Jones* (1907), symphonies, suites, chamber music, and songs.

Germanicus [jermanikus], in full **Gaius Germanicus Caesar** (15 BC–AD 19) The son, father, and brother of Roman emperors (Tiberius, Caligula, and Claudius respectively), and heir apparent himself from AD 14. His suspicious death in Antioch marked a downward turning point in Tiberius's reign. >> Caligula; Claudius; Tiberius

Germanus, St [jermahnus] (c.378–448), feast day 31 July. Bishop of Auxerre. Invited to Britain to combat Pelagianism in 429, under him the Christian Britons won the bloodless 'Alleluia Victory' over the Picts and Saxons at Maes Garmon. >> Pelagius

Germer, Lester (Halbert) [germer] (1896-1971) Physicist, born in Chicago, IL. He worked with Davisson on experiments that demonstrated the diffraction of electrons by crystals (1927), confirming the theories of Louis-Victor de Broglie. >> Broglie, Louis Victor; Davisson

Gérome, Jean Léon [zhayrohm] (1824-1904) Historical genre painter, born in Vesoul, France. A first-rate draughtsman, he achieved distinction as a sculptor and decorative painter of anecdotal and erotic subjects.

Geronimo [jeronimoh], Indian name **Goyathlay** (1829-1909) Chiricahua Apache Indian, born in Mexico. The best known of all Apache leaders, he forcibly resisted the internment of 4000 of his people on a reservation at San Carlos (1874), escaping from white control on several occasions.

Gerry, Elbridge (1744-1814) US vice-president (1813-14), born in Marblehead, MA. As Governor of Massachusetts (1810), he rearranged the electoral districts to advantage the Republican Party, his name giving rise to the term *gerrymander*.

Gershwin, George, originally **Jacob Gershvin** (1898-1937) Composer, born in New York City. In 1924 he began collaborating with his brother Ira as lyricist, producing numerous classic songs, such as 'Lady Be Good' (1924) and 'I Got Rhythm' (1930). He also composed extended concert works, such as *Rhapsody in Blue* (1924). His masterpiece was the jazz-opera *Porgy and Bess* (1935). >> Gershwin, Ira

Gershwin, Ira, originally **Israel Gershvin**, pseudonym **Arthur Francis Gershwin** (1896-1983) Songwriter, born in New York City. In 1924 he began to work with his brother, producing such hits as 'I Got Plenty o' Nothin'' (1935) and 'They Can't Take That Away From Me' (1938). >> Gershwin, George

Gerson, Jean de [zhayrsö], originally **Jean Charlier** (1363-1429) Theologian and mystic, born in Gerson, France. As Chancellor of the University of Paris from 1395, he supported the proposal for ending the Great Schism between Rome and Avignon by the resignation of both the contending pontiffs.

Gerstäcker, Friedrich [gersteker] (1816-72) Writer and traveller, born in Hamburg, Germany. He visited the USA, South America, Polynesia, and Australia, and wrote colourful adventure stories, including *Mississippi River Pirates* (1848).

Gertrude, St , (626-59), feast day 17 March. Frankish religious. The daughter of Pepin the Elder, she became abbess of the monastery at Nivelles, Brabant, on the death of her mother, and after refusing to marry Dagobert I.

Gertrude of Helfta, known as **the Great** (1256-1302) German mystic. She entered the convent of Helfta near Eisleben at the age of five, and when 25 began to have visions which she described in Latin treatises.

Gesell, Arnold (Lucius) [guhzel] (1880-1961) Psychologist, born in Alma, WI, the brother of Gerhard Gesell. He devised standard scales for measuring the progress of infant development, supplementing his writing with extensive use of film. >> Gesell, Gerhard

Gesell, Gerhard (Alden) [guhzel] (1910-93) Jurist, born in Los Angeles, CA, the brother of Arnold Gesell. In 1971 he ruled that the *Washington Post* had a First Amendment right to publish the leaked government documents known as the 'Pentagon Papers', a judgment eventually upheld by the Supreme Court. >> Gesell, Arnold

Gesner, Conrad von (1516-65) Naturalist and physician, born in Zürich, Switzerland. *Bibliotheca universalis* (1545-9) contained the titles of all the books then known in Hebrew, Greek and Latin, and *Historia animalium* (1551-8) attempted to collect all that was then known of every animal.

Gessner, Salomon (1730-88) Pastoral poet, who also painted and engraved landscapes, born in Zürich, Switzerland. His *Death of Abel* (trans, 1758), a type of idyllic heroic prose poem, had the greatest success.

Gesualdo, Don Carlo, Prince of Venosa [jezualdoh] (c.1560-1613) Composer and lutenist, born in Naples, Italy. He wrote many sacred vocal works and published six books of madrigals, remarkable for their homophonic progressions and use of dissonance.

Getty, J(ean) Paul (1892-1976) Oil billionaire and art collector, born in Minneapolis, MN. He entered the oil business in his early twenties, and went on to acquire and control more than 100 companies, becoming one of the world's richest men.

Getz, Stan(ley) (1927-91) Jazz saxophonist, born in Philadelphia, PA. He formed his own groups, developing a distinctive 'cool' sound, and in the 1960s popularized a bossa-nova style.

Geulincx or **Geulingx, Arnold** [goelingks], pseudonym **Philaretus** (1624-69) Philosopher, born in Antwerp, Belgium. A leading exponent of Descartes' philosophy, he is best known for his doctrine of 'Occasionalism'. >> Descartes

Geyl, Pieter [gayl] (1887-1966) Historian and patriot, born in Dordrecht, The Netherlands. During World War 2 he was imprisoned in Buchenwald (1940-1), then interned in The Netherlands until 1944.

Ghazali, Abu Hamid Mohammed al- [gazahlee] (1058-1111) Islamic philosopher, theologian, and jurist, born in Tus, Iran. He abandoned his academic career for the ascetic life of a mendicant *sufi* (mystic), later founding a monastic community at Tus, and writing the monumental *The Revival of the Religious Sciences* (trans title).

Gheorghiu-Dej, Gheorghe [gyaw(r)gyoo dezh] (1901-65) Romanian prime minister (1952-5) and president (1961-5), born in Bîrlad, Romania. In 1944 he became secretary-general of the Romanian Communist Party and minister of communications (1944-6), and was instrumental in establishing a Communist regime.

Ghiberti, Lorenzo [geebairtee] (1378-1455) Goldsmith, bronze-caster, and sculptor, born in Florence, Italy. In 1401 he won the competition to make a pair of bronze gates for the Baptistry of Florence Cathedral, which he completed in 1424.

Ghirlandaio, Domenico [geerlandahyoh], originally **Domenico di Tommaso Bigordi** (1449-94) Painter, born in Florence, Italy. Apprenticed to a metal garland-maker or *ghirlandaio*, his main works were frescoes, notably a series in the choir of Santa Maria Novella, Florence (1490).

Ghose, Aurobindo >> Aurobindo, Sri

Giacometti, Alberto [jiakometee] (1901-66) Sculptor and painter, born in Stampa, Switzerland. He joined the Surrealists in 1930, producing many abstract constructions which culminated in the characteristic 'thin man' bronzes, such as 'Pointing Man' (1947).

Giaever, Ivar [jayver] (1929-) Physicist, born in Bergen, Norway. His research led to a greater understanding of superconductivity, applying results developed by Esaki, and shared the Nobel Prize for Physics in 1973. >> Esaki

Giambologna >> Bologna, Giovanni da

Giannini, Amadeo Peter [jianeenee] (1870-1949) Banker, born in San Jose, CA. In 1904 he co-founded the San Francisco-based Bank of Italy, reorganized in 1928 as the *Bank of America*.

Giap, Vo Nguyen [gyap] (1912-) Vietnamese military leader, born in Quang Binh Province. As vice-premier and defence minister of North Vietnam, he masterminded the military strategy that forced the US forces to leave South Vietnam (1973).

Giauque, William (Francis) [jeeohk] (1895-1982) Chemist, born in Niagara Falls, Ontario, Canada. Most of his work was devoted to studying matter at temperatures very close to absolute zero (-273·15°C), and he was awarded the Nobel Prize for Chemistry in 1949.

Gibb, Sir Alexander (1872–1958) Civil engineer, born near Dundee, Tayside. He worked on the construction of Rosyth naval dockyard (1909–16), and later set up in practice as a consulting engineer.

Gibbon, Edward (1737–94) Historian, born in Putney, Surrey. After a visit to Rome in 1764 he began to plan for his major work, *The History of the Decline and Fall of the Roman Empire* (5 vols, 1776–88).

Gibbon, Lewis Grassic, pseudonym of **James Leslie Mitchell** (1901–35) Writer, born in Auchterless, Grampian. The three novels *Sunset Song* (1932), *Cloud Howe* (1933), and *Grey Granite* (1934), which form the trilogy *A Scots Quair*, appeared under his pseudonym.

Gibbons, Grinling (1648–1721) Sculptor and woodcarver, born in Rotterdam, The Netherlands. He was employed at Chatsworth and other English mansions, which he embellished in typical Baroque style.

Gibbons, James (1834–1921) Roman Catholic clergyman, born in Baltimore, MD. He became archbishop of that city in 1877, a cardinal in 1886, and was largely responsible for the growth of the Roman Catholic Church in the USA.

Gibbons, Orlando (1583–1625) Composer, born in Oxford, Oxfordshire. His compositions include services, anthems, and madrigals (notably *The Silver Swan*), and also hymns, fantasies for viols, and music for virginals.

Gibbons, Stella (Dorothea) (1902–89) Writer, born in London. Her *Cold Comfort Farm* (1932), a light-hearted satire on melodramatic rural novels, has established itself as a classic of parody.

Gibbs, James (1682–1754) Architect, born in Aberdeen, Grampian. His work included the London churches of St Mary-le-Strand (1717) and St Martin-in-the-Fields (1726), and his Palladian ideas influenced the design of many churches of the colonial period in America.

Gibbs, J(osiah) Willard (1839–1903) Mathematician and physicist, born in New Haven, CT. He contributed to the study of thermodynamics; and his most important work, first published as 'On the Equilibrium of Heterogeneous Substances' (1876), established him as a founder of physical chemistry.

Gibbs, William Francis (1886–1967) Naval architect, born in Philadelphia, PA. In partnership with his brother Frederick he designed and built yachts, naval vessels, the 'Liberty Ships' of World War 2, and luxury liners, notably the 53 330 ton *United States*.

Gibbs-Smith, Charles Harvard (1909–81) Aeronautical historian, born in Teddington, Gloucestershire. He wrote the definitive *Aviation - an Historical Survey From its Origins to the End of World War 2* (1960).

Gibson, Sir Alexander Drummond (1926–) Conductor, born in Motherwell, Strathclyde. He became principal conductor and artistic director of the Scottish National Orchestra (1959), and helped to form Scottish Opera (1962).

Gibson, Althea (1927–) Tennis player, born in Silver City, SC. She was the first African-American player to achieve success at the highest levels of the game, winning the French and Italian singles championships in 1956, and the British and US titles in 1957 and 1958.

Gibson, Charles (Dana) (1867–1944) Illustrator and cartoonist, born in Roxbury, MA. In his celebrated 'Gibson Girl' drawings, he created the idealized prototype of the beautiful, well-bred, American woman.

Gibson, Edmund (1669–1748) Church jurist, born in Bampton, Cumbria. He became Bishop of London in 1720, and is best known for his great *Codex of English Church Law* (trans, 1713).

Gibson, Guy (Penrose) (1918–44) British airman. As a

wing-commander in the RAF he led the famous 'dambusters' raid on the Möhne and Eder dams in 1943, an exploit for which he received the VC.

Gibson, James (Jerome) (1904–79) Psychologist, born in McConnelsville, OH. His influential theory of vision viewed perception as the direct detection of invariances in the world, requiring neither inference nor the processing of information.

Gibson, John (1790–1866) Sculptor, born in Gyffin, Gwynedd. He went to Rome in 1817, where he produced his best works, 'Psyche borne by Zephyrs', 'Hylas surprised by Nymphs', and 'Venus with the Turtle'.

Gibson, Josh, nickname **Black Babe Ruth** (1911–47) Baseball player, born in Buena Vista, GA. A legendary hitter, he was barred from major-league baseball because he was an African-American. It is estimated that he hit more than 950 home runs in his career.

Gibson, Richard (1615–90) Painter of miniatures. Only 1·15 m/3 ft 10 in tall, he was a page to Charles I and Henrietta Maria. He later painted several portraits of Cromwell.

Gibson, Robert (1935–) Baseball player, born in Omaha, NE. A noted pitcher with the St Louis Cardinals (from 1959), he was twice named best pitcher in the National League. He set a World Series record of strike-outs against the Detroit Tigers in 1968.

Gide, André (Paul Guillaume) [zheed] (1869–1951) Writer, born in Paris. His best-known works are *Fruits of the Earth* (trans, 1897) and *The Counterfeiters* (trans, 1926), his translations of *Oedipus* and *Hamlet*, and his *Journal*. He received the Nobel Prize for Literature in 1947.

Gideon Greatest of the judges of Israel, the son of Joash. He suppressed Baal-worship, and put an end to the seven years' domination of the Midianites by routing them near Mt Gilboa.

Gielgud, Sir (Arthur) John [geelgud] (1904–) Actor and director, born in London. A leading Shakespearian actor, his many films include *The Prime Minister* (1940), *Arthur* (1970, Oscar), and *Prospero's Books* (1991). The London *Globe* theatre was renamed after him in 1994.

Gielgud, Maina [geelgud] (1945–) Dancer, artistic director, and teacher, born in London, the niece of actor Sir John Gielgud. She danced with Ballet of the 20th Century (1967–71) and the London Festival Ballet (1972–5), and in 1983 became artistic director of the Australian Ballet.
>> Gielgud, John

Gierek, Edward [geerek] (1913–) Polish statesman, born in Porabka, Poland. In 1948 he joined the ruling Polish United Workers' Party, becoming leader in 1970, and embarked on an ambitious industrialization programme which plunged the country heavily into debt. He was forced to resign in 1980.

Gieseking, Walter (Wilhelm) [geezuhking] (1895–1956) Pianist, born of German parents in Lyon, France. After World War 1 he established an international reputation, especially in the works of Debussy and Ravel.

Giffard, Henri [zhifah(r)] (1825–82) Engineer and inventor, born in Paris. In 1852 he built a light 3 hp steam engine, fitted it with a propeller, and succeeded in piloting a coal-gas balloon, steered by a rudder, over a distance of 17 mi, the first powered and controlled flight.

Gifford, William (1756–1826) Editor and critic, born in Ashburton, Devon. Well known for his satirical acerbity, he became the first editor of the *Quarterly Review* (1809–24).

Gigli, Beniamino [jeelyee] (1890–1957) Tenor, born in Recanati, Italy. By 1929 he had won a worldwide reputation as a lyric-dramatic tenor of great vitality, at his best in the works of Verdi and Puccini.

Gilbert, Sir Alfred (1854–1934) Sculptor and goldsmith, born in London. He executed work of remarkable simplicity and grace, including the statue of 'Eros' in Piccadilly Circus, London.

Gilbert, Cass (1859-1934) Architect, born in Zanesville, OH. His designs include the first tower skyscraper, the 60-storey Woolworth Building in New York City (1912), at that time the tallest building in the world.

Gilbert, Grove (Karl) (1843-1918) Geologist, born in Rochester, NY. He was chief geologist of the US geological survey (1889), and formulated many of the laws of geological processes.

Gilbert, Sir Henry >> Lawes, Sir John Bennet

Gilbert, Sir Humphrey (c.1539-83) English navigator, the half-brother of Sir Walter Raleigh. In 1578 he led an unsuccessful colonizing expedition to the New World. In a second attempt (1583) he landed in Newfoundland and established a colony at St John's. >> Raleigh, Walter

Gilbert, Sir John (1817-97) Painter and illustrator, born in London. He is remembered for his illustrations of Shakespeare, Scott, and Cervantes, and for his woodcut illustrations in the *Illustrated London News*.

Gilbert, Walter (1932-) Molecular biologist, born in Boston, MA. He developed an elegant method for finding the sequence of bases in nucleic acids, for which he shared the Nobel Prize for Chemistry in 1980.

Gilbert, William (1544-1603) Physician and physicist, born in Colchester, Essex. He established the magnetic nature of the Earth, and was the first to use the terms *electricity*, *electric force*, and *electric attraction*. The *gilbert* unit of magnetomotive power is named after him.

Gilbert, Sir W(illiam) S(chwenck) (1836-1911) Parodist and librettist, born in London. He wrote much humorous verse under his boyhood nickname 'Bab', collected in 1869 as the *Bab Ballads*, and partnered Arthur Sullivan in writing 14 popular operas, from *Trial by Jury* (1875) to *The Gondoliers* (1889). >> Sullivan, Arthur

Gilbert and George Avant-garde artists: **Gilbert Proesch** (1943-) and **George Passmore** (1944-). They made their name in the late 1960s as performance artists (the 'singing sculptures'), with faces and hands painted gold, holding their poses for hours at a time.

Gilbert of Sempringham, St (c.1083-1189), feast day 4 February. Priest, born in Sempringham, Lincolnshire. He was the founder of the Gilbertine Order (1148), which was dissolved at the Reformation. He was canonized in 1202.

Gilbey, Sir Walter (1831-1914) Wine merchant, born in Bishop's Stortford, Hertfordshire. He was founder of a well-known wine company, a horse-breeder, and an agriculturist.

Gilbreth and Gilbreth **Frank (Bunker) Gilbreth** (1868-1924) and **Lillian (Evelyn) Gilbreth**, *née* **Moller** (1878-1972). Efficiency experts, born in Fairfield, ME, and Oakland, CA, respectively. Together they laid the foundations of modern scientific management, collaborating on several books, and serving as consultants to firms in the USA and abroad.

Gilchrist, Percy Carlyle [**gil**krist] (1851-1935) Metallurgist, born in Lyme Regis, Dorset. He developed, with his cousin **Sydney Gilchrist Thomas** (1850-85), a new process for smelting iron ore, which removed phosphorus-containing impurities (the *Gilchrist-Thomas process*).

Gildas, St (c.493-570), feast day 29 January. Historian and monk, born in Strathclyde. He wrote *The Overthrow and Conquest of Britain* (trans, c.516-47), the only contemporary British version of events from the invasion of the Romans to his own time.

Giles, St, Lat **Aegidius** (?-c.700), feast day 1 September. Athenian hermit. According to legend he went to France and built a hermitage, where he was discovered by a Frankish king who was so impressed with his holiness that he built a monastery on the spot (St Gilles) and made him its abbot. He is the patron of lepers, beggars, and cripples.

Giles, Carl [jiylz] (1916-95) Cartoonist, born in London. Since 1937 he has produced his distinctive and popular humorous drawings, first for *Reynolds News*, then (from 1943) for the *Express* newspapers.

Giles, H(erbert) A(llen) (1845-1935) Scholar and linguist, born in Oxford, Oxfordshire. He succeeded Wade as professor of Chinese at Cambridge (1897-1932), and modified the romanization system of his predecessor in his *Chinese-English Dictionary* (1892). >> Wade, Thomas

Giles, William (Ernest Powell) (1835-97) Explorer, born in Bristol, Avon. He emigrated to Australia in 1850, discovered L Amadeus (1872) and the Gibson Desert (1874), and travelled from Port Augusta to Perth and back (1875-6).

Gill, Sir David (1843-1914) Astronomer, born in Aberdeen, Grampian. He is noted for his measurements of the distances of the Sun and stars from the Earth, and pioneered the use of photography for charting the heavens.

Gill, (Arthur) Eric (Rowton) [gil] (1882-1940) Carver, engraver, and typographer, born in Brighton, East Sussex. His main works include 'Prospero and Ariel' (1931) above the entrance to Broadcasting House, London.

Gillars, Mildred, originally **Mildred Elizabeth Sisk** (1901-88) Axis propagandist, born in Portland, ME. In Berlin during World War 2, she broadcast Nazi propaganda aimed at demoralizing US troops, who nicknamed her 'Axis Sally'. Convicted of treason, she spent 12 years in jail.

Gillespie, Dizzy [gilespee], popular name of **John Birks Gillespie** (1917-93) Jazz trumpeter and composer, born in Cheraw, SC. As a band leader, often with Charlie Parker on saxophone, he developed the music known as *bebop*. His own big band (1946-50) was his masterpiece, affording him scope as both soloist and showman. >> Parker, Charlie

Gillett, Frederick Hunting [jilet] (1851-1935) US politician, born in Westfield, MA. A Republican in the US House of Representatives (1893-1925), he championed the freedman's civil rights and denounced Tammany Hall's election practices.

Gillette, King C(amp) [jilet] (1855-1932) Inventor of the safety razor, born in Fond du Lac, WI. He was a travelling salesman for a hardware company, before founding his razor blade company in 1903.

Gillette, William [jilet] (1855-1937) Actor and playwright, born in Hartford, CT. Known for his portrayal of Sherlock Holmes, his plays include two Civil War dramas, *Held by the Enemy* (1866) and *Secret Service* (1896).

Gilliéron, Jules [zheelyayrõ] (1854-1926) Linguist, born in Neuveville, Switzerland. His dialect atlas, *Atlas linguistiques de la France* (1902-12), provided a model for further studies in linguistic geography.

Gillies, Sir Harold (Delf) [gileez] (1882-1960) Plastic surgeon, born in Dunedin, New Zealand. In 1957 he published *The Principles and Art of Plastic Surgery*, the standard work on this subject.

Gillies, Sir William George [gileez] (1898-1973) Artist, born in Haddington, Lothian. He is known for his finely organized interpretations of Scottish landscape, many in watercolour.

Gillray, James [gilray] (1757-1815) Caricaturist, born in London. He issued about 1500 caricatures of political and social subjects, notably of Napoleon, George III, and leading politicians.

Gilman, Charlotte Anna Perkins, *née* **Perkins**, earlier married name **Stetson** (1860-1935) Feminist and writer, born in Hartford, CT. In 1898 she wrote *Women and Economics*, now recognized as a feminist landmark, and later founded, edited, and wrote for the journal Forerunner.

Gilman, Harold (1878-1919) Artist, born in Rode, Somerset. He became associated with the Camden Town Group (1910), and became the first president of the London Group.

Gilmore, Dame Mary Jane (1865–1962) Poet and writer, born near Goulburn, New South Wales, Australia. She was the editor of the women's columns in the Sydney *Worker* newspaper for 23 years, publishing several books of verse.

Gilmour, John Scott Lennox (1906–86) Botanist, born in London. Director of the Cambridge University Botanic Garden (1951–73), his name has been given to the *Gilmourian* concept of multiple classifications.

Gilpin, Bernard, known as **the Apostle of the North** (1517–83) Clergyman, born in Kentmere Hall, Cumbria. On Elizabeth I's succession (1558) he was appointed rector of Houghton le Spring, from where he made preaching excursions into the remotest parts of N England.

Gilpin, John (1930–) Dancer, born in Southsea, Hampshire. In 1949 he was a principal with Petit's Ballets de Paris, returning to Britain in 1950 to join the London Festival Ballet, where he became artistic director (1962–5). >> Petit, Roland

Gilpin, William (1724–1804) Clergyman, writer, and artist, born in Carlisle, Cumbria. A leader of the 18th-c cult of the picturesque, he wrote works on the scenery of Britain, illustrated by his own engravings. His brother **Sawrey Gilpin** (1733–1807) was a notable animal painter.

Gilruth, Robert (Rowe) (1913–) Aeronautical engineer, born in Nashwauk, MN. In 1958 he was appointed head of the NASA programme which put the first American into Earth orbit in 1962, and the first men on the Moon in 1969.

Gilson, Etienne (Henry) [zheelsö] (1884–1978) Philosopher and historian, born in Paris. Founder of the Pontifical Institute of Mediaeval Studies at Toronto University (1929), he is best known for his works on mediaeval Christian philosophy.

Gil Vicente >> Vicente, Gil

Gimson, Ernest William (1864–1919) Designer, born in Leicester, Leicestershire. He is best known as a furniture designer specializing in untreated native timbers.

Ginckell or **Ginkel, Godert de** [gingkel] (1630–1703) Dutch general, born in Utrecht, The Netherlands. He accompanied William III to England in 1688, and fought at the Battle of the Boyne (1690). As commander-in-chief in Ireland, he defeated the remaining rebels, and was created Earl of Athlone (1692). >> William III

Gingrich, Newt(on Leroy) [ginggrich] (1943–) US politician, born in Harrisburg, PA. Representative for Georgia from 1979, he became Speaker of the House in 1995, proposing to enact a new conservative agenda.

Ginsberg, Allen (1926–) Poet of the 'beat' movement, born in Newark, NJ. *Howl* (1956), his epic poem, launched him as a public speaker against authoritarianism. Other collections include *Kaddish and Other Poems* (1961) and *Reality Sandwiches* (1963).

Gioberti, Vicenzo [jiobairtee] (1801–52) Philosopher and statesman, born in Turin, Italy. He became premier of Sardinia–Piedmont (1848–9), then ambassador to France. His philosophy centred on the concept of being, and is usually described as *ontologism*.

Giolitti, Giovanni [jioleetee] (1842–1928) Italian prime minister (1892–3, 1903–5, 1906–9, 1911–14, 1920–1), born in Mondovi, Italy. He introduced universal suffrage and tried to keep Italy neutral during World War 1.

Giordano, Luca [jiaw(r)dahnoh], known as **Fa Presto** ('Make Haste') (1634–1705) Painter, born in Naples, Italy. He was able to work with extreme rapidity, hence his nickname, and to imitate the great masters.

Giordano, Umberto [jiaw(r)dahnoh] (1867–1948) Operatic composer, born in Foggia, Italy. He is best remembered for *Andrea Chenier* (1896) and *Fedora* (1898).

Giorgio, Francesco di >> Francesco di Giorgio

Giorgione [jiaw(r)jiohnay], also called **Giorgio da Castelfranco**, originally **Giorgio Barbarelli** (c.1478–1510) Painter,

born in Castelfranco, Italy. A great innovator, he created the small, intimate easel picture and a new treatment of figures in landscape, 'the landscape of mood'. His best-known works include 'The Tempest' (c.1505) and 'The Sleeping Venus' (c.1510).

Giotto (di Bondone) [jiotoh] (c.1266–1337) Painter and architect, the founder of the Florentine School of painting, born near Vespignano, Italy. His major work was the fresco cycle, 'The Lives of Christ and the Virgin', in the Arena Chapel, Padua (1305–8).

Giovanni di Paolo [jiohvahnee di powloh], also known as **Giovanni dal Poggio** (c.1403–c.1483) Painter, born in Siena, Italy. He worked in a style which was essentially archaizing, continuing the tradition of Sienese Trecento masters.

Giovanni da Fiesole >> Angelico, Fra

Giovanni di Steffano >> Lanfranco, Giovanni

Gipps, Sir George (1791–1847) Colonial administrator, born in Ringwould, Kent. He became Governor of New South Wales (1838–46), where his policy of selling land by auction showed him to be a farsighted opponent of land monopoly. *Gippsland* in Victoria is named after him.

Giraldi, Giambattista [jiraldee], also called **Cynthius** (1504–73) Writer, born in Ferrara, Italy. He wrote nine plays in imitation of Seneca, and his *Ecatommiti* (1565) is a collection of tales which gave Shakespeare his plots for *Measure for Measure* and *Othello*. >> Seneca (the Younger)

Giraldus Cambrensis [jiraldus kambrensis], also known as **Gerald of Wales** or **Gerald de Barri** (c.1147–1223) Historian and clergyman, born in Manorbier Castle, Dyfed. He wrote *History of the Conquest of Ireland* (trans, c.1189), and in 1188 travelled through Wales to recruit soldiers for the Third Crusade, writing up his observations in the *Itinerary of Wales* (trans, 1191).

Girard, Stephen [jerah(r)d] (1750–1831) Businessman and philanthropist, born near Bordeaux, France. He settled in Philadelphia in 1769, and during the war of 1812 his bank provided most of the finance needed by the US government.

Girardon, François [zhirah(r)dö] (1630–1715) Sculptor, born in Troyes, France. After 1650 he joined the Le Brun group in Paris. He worked on decorative sculpture in Louis XIV's galleries, gardens, and palaces, mostly at Versailles, where he is noted for the fountain figures. >> Le Brun

Giraud, Henri Honoré [zheeroh] (1879–1949) French soldier, born in Paris. In 1940 he commanded in turn the French 7th and 9th armies, suffering capture by the Germans. Escaping in 1942, he commanded the Free French forces in North Africa, and was co-president of the French Committee of National Liberation (1943–4).

Giraudoux, (Hippolyte) Jean [zheerohdoo] (1882–1944) Writer and diplomat, born in Bellac, France. He is chiefly remembered for his plays, mainly fantasies based on Greek myths and biblical lore, such as *Ondine* (1939) and *The Mad Woman of Chaillot* (trans, 1945).

Girtin, Thomas [gertin] (1775–1802) Landscape painter, born in London. His works were among the first to exploit water-colour as a true medium, as distinct from a tint for colouring drawings.

Giscard d'Estaing, Valéry [zheeskah(r) daystï] (1926–) French president (1974–81), born in Koblenz, Germany. He became finance minister (1962–6), and launched his own party, the National Federation of Independent Republicans. Finance minister again in 1969, he defeated Mitterand to become president, and was then beaten by Mitterand in 1981.

Gish, Lillian, originally **Lillian de Guiche** (1893–1993) Actress, born in Springfield, OH. She started in silent films under D W Griffith in 1912, and became the girl heroine in all his classics from *The Birth of a Nation* (1915) to *Orphans of the Storm* (1922).

Gissing, George (Robert) (1857–1903) Novelist, born in Wakefield, West Yorkshire. *Workers in the Dawn* (1880) was the first of over 20 novels largely presenting realistic portraits of poverty and misery. His best-known novel is *New Grub Street* (1891).

Gist, George >> **Sequoia**

Giugiaro, Giorgio [jiujahroh] (1938–) Automobile and industrial designer, born in Cuneo, Italy. His designs for the popular car market include the first Volkswagen 'Golf' (1974), and the Fiat 'Panda' (1980) and 'Uno' (1983).

Giulio Romano [joolioh romahnoh], originally **Giulio Pippi de' Giannuzzi** (c.1499–1546) Painter and architect, born in Rome. He assisted Raphael in the execution of several of his later works, and in 1524 went to Mantua, where he protected the city from floods. >> **Raphael**

Giuseppe del Gesù >> **Guarnieri, Giuseppe**

Givenchy, Hubert James Marcel Taffin de [zhivãshee] (1927–) Fashion designer, born in Beauvais, France. He opened his own house in 1952, producing ready-to-wear clothes under his Nouvelle Boutique label.

Glackens, William (James) (1870–1938) Painter, born in Philadelphia, PA. A member of The Eight, who emphasized Realism and Modernism, his own work - such as 'Nude with Apple' (1910) - tended towards Impressionism.

Gladstone, Herbert John Gladstone, 1st Viscount (1854–1930) British Liberal statesman, born in Dane End, Hertfordshire, the youngest son of W E Gladstone. He became home secretary (1905–10), and was appointed first Governor-General of the Union of South Africa (1910–14). >> **Gladstone, W E**

Gladstone, W(illiam) E(wart) (1809–98) British prime minister (1868–74, 1880–5, 1886, 1892–4), born in Liverpool. He was Chancellor of the Exchequer (1852–5, 1859–66), and in 1867 became leader of the Liberal Party. Frequently in office until 1894, he succeeded in carrying out a scheme of parliamentary reform, but his bills for Irish Home Rule were defeated. >> **Gladstone, Herbert**

Glaisher, James [glaysher] (1809–1903) Meteorologist, born in London. He became chief meteorologist at Greenwich, and made a large number of balloon ascents, once reaching a height of over 11 km/7 mi to study the higher strata of the atmosphere.

Glanvill, Joseph (1636–80) Philosopher and clergyman, born in Plymouth, Devon. He is known for *The Vanity of Dogmatising* (1661), in which he attacked scholastic philosophy, supported experimental science, and appealed for freedom of thought.

Glanvill, Ranulf de (?–1190) Jurist, born in Stratford St Andrew, Suffolk. He is the reputed author of the earliest treatise on English law, the *Treatise on the Laws and Customs of England* (trans, c.1187).

Glanville-Hicks, Peggy (1912–90) Composer, born in Melbourne, Victoria, Australia. Director of Asian Studies at the Australian Music Centre from 1975, she wrote several operas including *Nausicaa* (1961), and much work for theatre and ballet.

Glas, John (1695–73) Clergyman and founder of a small religious sect, born in Auchtermuchty, Fife. Opposed to the concept of a national church, he formed a congregation later known as the *Glassites* or *Sandemanians*, based on simple apostolic practice. Through his son-in-law **Robert Sandeman** (1718–71), his teachings spread to America, where the sect survived until 1890.

Glaser, Donald A(rthur) [glayzer] (1926–) Physicist, born in Cleveland, OH. He developed the 'bubble chamber' for observing the paths of atomic particles, for which he was awarded the Nobel Prize for Physics in 1960.

Glaser, Milton [glayzer] (1929–) Graphic designer and illustrator, born in New York City. A founder of Push Pin Studios (1954–74), in 1974 he became president of his own

graphics/design firm, known for eclectic experiments with graphics, typefaces, and magazine designs.

Glasgow, Ellen (Anderson Gholson) (1873–1945) Novelist, born in Richmond, VA. Her novels include *Barren Ground* (1925), *Vein of Iron* (1935), and *In This Our Life* (1941, Pulitzer).

Glashow, Sheldon (Lee) [glashow] (1932–) Physicist, born in New York City. He was a major contributor to the theory explaining electromagnetic and weak nuclear forces, and to the theory of quantum chromodynamics. He shared the Nobel Prize for Physics in 1979. >> **Salam; Weinberg**

Glaspell, Susan [glaspel] (1882–1948) Writer, born in Davenport, IA. With her husband, **George Carm Cook** (d.1924), she founded the Provincetown Playhouse (1915), which introduced the plays of Eugene O'Neill. Her plays include *Bernice* (1919), *Inheritors* (1921), and *Alison's House* (1931, Pulitzer). >> **O'Neill, Eugene**

Glass, Carter (1858–1946) US politician and newspaper publisher, born in Lynchburg, VA. An active Democrat, he served in the US House of Representatives (1902–18) and was secretary of the Treasury (1918–20).

Glass, Philip (1937–) Composer, born in Baltimore, MD. A proponent of minimalism in music, he attracted public notice with the first of his 12 operas, *Einstein on the Beach* (1976).

Glauber, Johann Rudolph [glowber] (1604–68) Physician, born in Karlstadt, Germany. In 1648 he discovered hydrochloric acid, and was probably the first to produce nitric acid. He also discovered *Glauber's salt* (sodium sulphate).

Glazunov, Alexander (Konstantinovich) [glazunof] (1865–1936) Composer, born in St Petersburg, Russia. Director of the Conservatory at St Petersburg (1906–17), among his compositions are eight symphonies, and works in every branch except opera.

Glemp, Jozef (1929–) Clergyman, born in Inowroclaw, Poland. In 1981 he became Archbishop of Gniezno and Warsaw, Primate of Poland, and a cardinal (1983). He was a prominent figure during Poland's internal political unrest.

Glendower, Owen [glendower], Welsh **Owain Glyndwr** or **Owain ap Gruffudd** (c.1354–1416) Welsh chief, born in Powys. In 1401 he rebelled against Henry IV, proclaimed himself Prince of Wales, established an independent Welsh parliament, and joined the coalition with Harry Percy (1364–1403), who was defeated at the Battle of Shrewsbury (1403). >> **Henry IV (of England)**

Glenn, John H(erschel) (1921–) Astronaut, the first American to orbit the Earth, born in Cambridge, OH. In 1962 he made a three-orbit flight in the Friendship 7 space capsule. A senator since 1975, he sought the Democratic nomination for the presidency in 1984 and 1988.

Gleyre, Charles [glair] (1806–74) Painter, born in Chevilly, Switzerland. He took over Delaroche's teaching school in Paris, where his pupils included Monet, Renoir, and Sisley. Much of his work is at Lausanne. >> **Delaroche; Monet; Renoir, Pierre Auguste; Sisley**

Glidden, Joseph (Farwell) (1813–1906) Inventor, born in Charlestown, NH. He patented an improved type of barbed wire in 1874, but sold his interest in the Barb Fence Co in 1876. By 1880 the factory was turning out 80 million pounds of wire a year.

Glinka, Mikhail (Ivanovich) [glingka] (1804–57) Composer, born in Novospasskoye, Russia. His opera *Russlan and Ludmilla* (1842) pioneered the style of the Russian national school of composers.

Glock, Sir William (1908–) Music critic, born in London. He became chief music critic for *The Observer* (1939–45), editor of the music magazine *The Score* (1949–61), and controller of music at the BBC (1959–72).

Gloucester, Prince Henry, Duke of [gloster] (1900–74) Prince of the United Kingdom, the third son of George V. In 1935 he married Lady Alice Montagu-Douglas-Scott, and they had two children: William (1941–72) and Richard, who succeeded him. >> George V; Gloucester, Richard, Duke of

Gloucester, Humphrey, Duke of [gloster], known as **the Good Duke Humphrey** (1391–1447) Youngest son of Henry IV, and protector during the minority of Henry VI (1422–9). His patronage of literature led to his nickname. >> Henry IV / VI

Gloucester, Prince Richard, Duke of >> **Richard III**

Gloucester, Richard (Alexander Walter George), Duke of [gloster] (1944–) British prince, the younger son of Henry, Duke of Gloucester (the third son of George V). In 1972 he married **Birgitte van Deurs** (1946–); they have one son, **Alexander, Earl of Ulster** (1974–), and two daughters, Lady **Davina Windsor** (1977–) and Lady **Rose Windsor** (1980–). >> Gloucester, Prince Henry

Glubb, Sir John Bagot, known as **Glubb Pasha** (1897–1986) British soldier, born in Preston, Lancashire. In 1930 he went to British-mandated Transjordan, organized the Arab Legion's Desert Patrol, and became Legion Commandant (1939), gaining immense prestige among the Bedouin.

Gluck, Christoph (Willibald) [glook] (1714–87) Composer, born in Erasbach, Bavaria. Known for such works as *Orfeo ed Euridice* (1762) and *Alceste* (1767), in Paris in the late 1770s, support was divided between Gluck's French opera style and the Italian style of Niccolo Piccinni - the *Gluckists* and Piccinnists. Gluck finally won with his *Iphigénie en Tauride* (1779). >> Piccinni

Gluckman, (Herman) Max (1911–75) Social anthropologist, born in Johannesburg, South Africa. He carried out extensive field work among tribes of C and S Africa (1936–44), focusing on their political systems and social cohesion.

Glyn, Elinor, *née* **Sutherland** (1864–1943) Writer, born in Jersey, Channel Is. A writer of romantic novels, she found fame with *Three Weeks* (1907), a book which gained a reputation for being risqué. Her works were glamorized on the Hollywood screen.

Glyndwr, Owen >> **Glendower, Owen**

Gmelin, Leopold [gmayleen] (1788–1853) Chemist, born in Göttingen, Germany. He discovered potassium ferricyanide, known as *Gmelin's salt*, in 1822, and introduced the terms *ester* and *ketone* into organic chemistry. *Gmelin's test* is for the presence of bile pigments.

Gneisenau, August (Wilhelm Anton), Graf (Count) **Neithardt von** [gniyzuhnow] (1760–1831) Prussian general, born in Schildau, Germany. He fought at Jena (1806), helped to reorganize the army after its defeat by Napoleon (1807), and gave distinguished service at Leipzig (1813) and at Waterloo (1815). >> Napoleon I

Göbbels, Joseph >> **Goebbels, Joseph**

Gobbi, Tito (1915–84) Baritone, born in Bassano del Grappa, Italy. He appeared regularly with the Rome Opera from 1938, and made an international reputation, especially in Verdian roles such as Falstaff and Don Carlos.

Gobineau, Joseph Arthur, comte de (Count of) [gobinoh] (1816–82) French diplomat and orientalist, born in Bordeaux, France. He is best known for his *Essay on the Inequality of Human Races* (trans, 4 vols, 1853–5), arguing that racial composition determines the fate of civilization.

Godard, Jean-Luc [gohdah(r)] (1930–) Film director, born in Paris. *Breathless* (trans, 1960) established him as one of the leaders of *Nouvelle Vague* cinema. His prolific output includes *Weekend* (1968), *Detective* (1984), *Hail, Mary* (trans, 1985), and *Nouvelle Vague* (1990).

Goddard, Robert H(utchings) (1882–1945) Physicist and rocketry pioneer, born in Worcester, MA. He elaborated the theory of rocketry, developing the first successful liquid-fuelled rocket, launched in 1926.

Gödel or **Goedel, Kurt** [goedl] (1906–78) Logician and mathematician, born in Brno, Czech Republic. He showed in 1931 that any formal logical system adequate for number theory must contain propositions not provable in that system (*Gödel's proof*).

Godey, Louis Antoine [gohdee] (1804–78) Publisher, born in New York City. He published (1930–77) *Godey's Lady's Book*, the largest circulation magazine of its time.

Godfrey, Bob, popular name of **Robert Godfrey** (1921–) Animated cartoon producer/director, born in New South Wales. Raised in England, he went on to produce cartoons such as *Polygamous Polonius* (1960), bringing a new bawdy humour to British cartoons. His musical cartoon, *Great*, won an Oscar in 1975.

Godfrey of Bouillon [booeeyõ] (c.1061–1100) Duke of Lower Lorraine (1089–95), born in Baisy, Belgium. He became chief leader of the First Crusade, and after the capture of Jerusalem (1099) was proclaimed king, but refused the crown.

Godfrey of Strasburg >> **Gottfried von Strassburg**

Godiva, Lady [godiyva] (11th-c) An English lady and religious benefactress. According to tradition, she rode naked through Coventry in order to obtain the remission of a heavy tax imposed by her husband, Leofric, Earl of Chester, upon the townsfolk (1040).

Godolphin, Sidney Godolphin, 1st Earl of [godolfin] (1645–1712) English statesman, born near Helston, Cornwall. He held various treasury positions under William III and Queen Anne, and his able management of the finances helped Marlborough in the War of the Spanish Succession (1701–13). >> Anne; Marlborough; William III

Godowsky, Leopold [godofskee] (1870–1938) Pianist and composer, born in Soshly, Lithuania. A master of the keyboard, he also wrote over 400 compositions and transcriptions, including *Triakontameron* (1920).

Godoy, Manuel de [gothoy] (1767–1851) Spanish chief minister (1792–1808) under Charles IV, born in Castuera, Spain. He achieved dictatorial power through the favour of the Queen, Maria Luisa. In 1796 he allied with France against England, a disastrous move which contributed to Spain losing her American Empire, and in 1808 he was overthrown and exiled.

Godric, St (c.1069–1170), feast day 21 May. Hermit, born in Norfolk, England. From 1110 he lived as a hermit in a hut at Finchale, on the R Wear near Durham. A priory was later built on the site.

Godunov, Boris (Fyodorovich) [goduhnof] (c.1552–1605) Tsar of Russia (1598–1605). During the reign of the imbecile Tsar Fyodor (1584–98), he virtually ruled the country, becoming tsar himself on Fyodor's death. He later became embroiled in a civil war against a pretender claiming to be Dmitri, the younger son of Ivan IV. >> Dmitri; Ivan IV

Godwin, also spelled **Godwine** (?–1053) Anglo-Saxon nobleman and warrior, the father of Harold Godwinsson. In 1042 he helped to raise Edward the Confessor to the throne, and married him to his daughter Edith. Godwin's son Harold was for a few months Edward's successor. >> Edward the Confessor; Harold II

Godwin, Edward William (1833–86) Architect and designer, born in Bristol, Avon. A central figure in the 'Aesthetic Movement', his furniture designs after 1875 were much influenced by Japanese taste. He also designed textiles and wallpapers.

Godwin, Fay Simmonds (1931–) Photographer, born in Berlin of English parents. She has become best known for her landscapes, including Welsh and Scottish scenes.

Since 1970 she has worked as a freelance photographer, based in London.

Godwin, Francis (1562–1633) Clergyman and writer, born in Hannington, Northamptonshire. He is best known as the author of the first science-fiction romance in English literature, *Man in the Moon or a Voyage Thither, by Domingo Gonsales (1638).*

Godwin, Mary Wollstonecraft >> **Wollstonecraft**

Godwin, William (1756–1836) Political writer and novelist, born in Wisbech, Cambridgeshire. His major work of social philosophy was *An Enquiry Concerning Political Justice* (1793) and his major novel *The Adventures of Caleb Williams* (1794). He married Mary Wollstonecraft in 1797. >> **Wollstonecraft**

Godwin-Austen, Henry Haversham (1834–1923) British soldier and surveyor. He was attached to the trigonometrical survey of India (1856–77). The second highest mountain in the world (also known as K2) was named after him in 1888.

Goebbels or **Göbels, (Paul) Joseph** [goeblz] (1897–1945) Nazi politician, born in Rheydt, Germany. Head of the Ministry of Public Enlightenment and Propaganda (1933), and a bitter anti-Semite, his gift of mob oratory made him a powerful exponent of Nazism. In the Berlin bunker he and his wife committed suicide, after taking the lives of their six children.

Goehr, (Peter) Alexander [ger] (1932–) Composer, born in Berlin. His compositions include the operas *Arden Must Die* (1967) and *Behold the Sun* (1985), as well as concertos, cantatas, and chamber music.

Goeppert-Mayer, Maria [goepert mayer], *née* **Goepert** (1906–72) Physicist, born in Katowice (formerly, Kattowitz), Poland. In 1948 she discovered the 'magic numbers' of subnuclear particles, and from 1950 devised a complete shell theory of nuclear structure. She shared the Nobel Prize for Physics in 1963.

Goerdeler, Karl Friedrich [goe(r)deler] (1884–1945) German politician, born in Pila (formerly, Schneidemühl), Poland. He became one of the leaders of opposition to Hitler, culminating in Stauffenberg's unsuccessful bomb plot of 1944, for which he was executed. >> **Hitler; Stauffenberg**

Goering or **Göring, Hermann (Wilhelm)** [goering] (1893–1946) Nazi politico-military leader, born in Rosenheim, Germany. He joined the Nazi government in 1933, founded the Gestapo, set up the concentration camps, and in 1940 became economic dictator of Germany. Sentenced to death at the Nuremberg War Crimes Trial, he committed suicide. >> **Hitler**

Goes, Hugo van der >> **van der Goes, Hugo**

Goethals, George Washington [gohthalz] (1858–1928) Engineer, born in New York City. He was appointed chief engineer for construction of the Panama Canal (1907–14) and the first civil governor of the Canal Zone (1914–16).

Goethe, Johann Wolfgang von [goetuh] (1749–1832) Poet, dramatist, and scientist, born in Frankfurt, Germany. He captured the spirit of German nationalism with his drama, *Götz von Berlichingen* (1773), following this with his novel *The Sorrows of Young Werther* (trans, 1774). From 1776 he wrote much lyric poetry, inspired by his relationships with a series of women, notably Charlotte von Stein. In his later years he wrote *Wilhelm Meister's Apprentice Years* (trans, 1796), continued as *Wilhelm Meister's Journeyman Years* (1821–9). His masterpiece is a version of *Faust*, published in two parts (1808, 1832). >> **Stein, Charlotte von**

Goffman, Erving (1922–82) Sociologist, born in Alberta, Canada. He is best known for his work on patterns of human communication, and his approach influenced the development of ideas in sociolinguistics.

Gogh, Vincent van >> **van Gogh, Vincent**

Gogol, Nikolai (Vasilievich) [gohgl] (1809–52) Writer, born in Sorochintsi, Ukraine. He became famous through *The Inspector General* (trans, 1836), a satire exposing the corruption and vanity of provincial officials, and a novel, *Dead Souls* (trans, 1842). He also wrote several short stories.

Gold, Thomas (1920–) Astronomer, born in Vienna. He worked with Bondi and Hoyle on the steady-state theory of the origin of the universe (1948), and in 1968 suggested that pulsars are rapidly rotating neutron stars (later confirmed). >> **Bondi; Hoyle, Fred**

Goldberg, Arthur J(oseph) (1908–) Public official, diplomat, and Supreme Court justice, born in Chicago, IL. He was secretary of labour (1961–2), served in the US Supreme Court (1962–5), then resigned at the request of President Johnson in order to replace Adlai Stevenson as the US delegate to the UN (1965–8). >> **Stevenson, Adlai**

Goldberg, Whoopi, originally **Caryn Johnson** (1955–) Film actress, born in New York City. She achieved instant fame with her role in *The Color Purple* (1985), for which she received a Golden Globe Award. Her performance in *Ghost* (1990) won her an Oscar for best supporting actress.

Golding, Louis (1895–1958) Writer, born in Manchester, Greater Manchester. He wrote many books about Jewish life, of which the best known is *Magnolia Street* (1932).

Golding, Sir William (Gerald) (1911–93) Novelist, born near Newquay, Cornwall. His books include *Lord of the Flies* (1954), *Pincher Martin* (1956), the trilogy *Rites of Passage* (1980, Booker), and *Close Quarters* (1987). He was awarded the Nobel Prize for Literature in 1983.

Goldman, Emma, known as **Red Emma** (1869–1940) Anarchist, feminist, and birth control advocate, born in Kaunas, Lithuania. She emigrated to the USA in 1885, and was imprisoned in 1893 for inciting a riot. Imprisoned again during World War 1 she was deported in 1919.

Goldman, Hetty (1881–1972) Archaeologist, born in New York City. She was one of the first female directors of an excavation (at Halae, Greece, 1911–14) and went on to direct numerous other excavations at sites in Greece and Turkey.

Goldmark, Peter (Carl) (1906–77) Engineer and inventor, born in Budapest, Hungary. He developed the first practical colour television system (1940), led the team that invented the long-playing record (1948), and later built a special type of camera for the lunar-orbiting space vehicle.

Goldoni, Carlo [goldohnee] (1707–93) Playwright, born in Venice, Italy. He wrote over 250 comic plays of which the best known are *Mine Hostess* (trans, 1753), *I Rusteghi* (1760), and *Quarrels at Chioggia* (trans, 1762).

Goldschmidt, Berthold [gohldshmit] (1903–) Composer, born in Hamburg, Germany. His first opera was *The Magnificent Cuckold* (trans), premiered in 1932. An expert on Mahler, in 1960 he helped to complete Mahler's unfinished 10th symphony, and conducted its first performance in 1988. >> **Mahler**

Goldschmidt, Hans [gohldshmit], popular name of **Johann Wilhelm Goldschmidt** (1861–1923) Chemist, born in Berlin. He invented the aluminothermic process for the reduction of certain metallic oxides by the use of a highly inflammable mixture of finely divided aluminium powder and the metal oxide.

Goldschmidt, Richard Benedikt [gohldshmit] (1878–1958) Biologist and geneticist, born in Frankfurt am Main, Germany. He was the author of the theory that it is not the qualities of the individual genes, but the chromosome molecules, that are decisive factors in heredity.

Goldschmidt, Victor Moritz [gohldshmit] (1888–1947) Chemist, the founder of geochemistry, born in Zürich, Switzerland. Using X-ray techniques he worked out the crystal structure of over 200 compounds and 75 elements, and in 1929 postulated *Goldschmidt's law* - that the structure of a crystal is determined by the ratio of the numbers of ions, the ratio of their sizes, and polarization properties.

Goldsmith, Oliver (1728–74) Writer, born in Kildare, Ireland. *The Vicar of Wakefield* (1766) secured his reputation as a novelist, 'The Deserted Village' (1770) as a poet, and *She Stoops to Conquer* (1773) as a dramatist.

Goldstein, Eugen [**gohld**stiyn] (1850–1930) Physicist, born in Gleiwitz, Germany. He discovered that cathode rays could produce sharp shadows, and that they were emitted perpendicular to the cathode surface, leading to the development of concave cathodes to produce focused rays.

Goldstein, Joseph (Leonard) [**gohld**stiyn] (1940–) Molecular geneticist, born in Sumter, SC. He carried out research into biomedical genetics, and shared with Michael Brown the 1985 Nobel Prize for Physiology or Medicine for their work in familial hypercholesterolaemia. >> Brown, Michael

Goldthorpe, John Harry (1935–) British sociologist. An authority on the class structure of advanced industrial societies, his studies indicate that equality of opportunity between classes in the UK has not improved since 1945.

Goldwater, Barry M(orris) (1909–) Politician and writer, born in Phoenix, AZ. In 1964 he became the Republican nominee for the presidency, but was defeated by Lyndon Johnson. He returned to the US Senate (1969–87), and was one of the architects of the conservative revival within the Republican Party. >> Johnson, Lyndon B

Goldwyn, Samuel, originally **Samuel Goldfish** (1882–1974) Film producer, born in Warsaw, Poland. He emigrated to the USA and in 1917 founded the Goldwyn Pictures Corporation, and in 1925 Metro-Goldwyn-Mayer, allying himself with United Artists from 1926.

Golgi, Camillo [**gol**jee] (1843–1926) Cell biologist, born in Corteno, Italy. His discovery of the *Golgi bodies* in animal cells opened up a new field of research in physiology. He shared the Nobel Prize for Physiology or Medicine in 1906.

Gollancz, Sir Victor [go**langks**, go**lants**] (1893–1967) Publisher, writer, and philanthropist, born in London. He founded his own publishing firm in 1928, the Left Book Club in 1936, and War on Want in 1951.

Golombek, Harry [go**lombek**] (1911–) Chess master and writer on chess, born in London. Several times British chess champion, he was classed as a master (1948) and a grandmaster (1985), and has published numerous books on chess.

Gomarus, Franciscus, also known as **Francis Gomer** (1563–1641) Calvinist theologian, born in Bruges, Belgium. He became known for his hostility to Arminius, with whom he fiercely debated predestination. At the Synod of Dort (1618) he secured the Arminians' expulsion from the Reformed Church. >> Arminius

Gombrich, Sir Ernst Hans Josef [**gom**brik] (1909–) Art historian, born in Vienna. His books include *The Story of Art* (1950), the influential *Art and Illusion* (1960), and *New Light on Old Masters* (1986).

Gompers, Samuel [**gom**perz] (1850–1924) Labour leader, born in London. He went to the USA in 1863, and in 1886 helped to found the American Federation of Labor, becoming its first president.

Gomułka, Władysław [go**mool**ka] (1905–82) Polish Communist leader, born in Krosno, Poland. Vice-president of the first postwar Polish government (1945–8), his criticism of the Soviet Union led to his imprisonment (1951–4). He returned to power as party first secretary (1956–71).

Gonçalves, Nuno [gon**sal**ves] (fl.1450–72) Portuguese painter. The discovery in 1882 of his only extant work, an

altarpiece for the convent of St Vincent, established him as the founder of the Portuguese school of painting.

Goncharov, Ivan Alexandrovich [gon**cha**rof] (1812–91) Writer, born in Ulyanovsk (formerly, Simbirsk), Russia. His *Oblomov* (1857) is a leading work of Russian Realism.

Goncharova, Natalia Sergeyevna [gon**cha**rova] (1881–1962) Painter and designer, born in Ladyzhino, Russia. Her painting combined the flat colours and primitive forms of Russian folk art with the new influences of Cubism and Fauvism.

Goncourt brothers [gô**koor**] **Edmond de Goncourt** (1822–96) and **Jules de Goncourt** (1830–70) Novelists, born in Nancy and Paris, respectively. They collaborated in several books, such as *Germinie Lacerteux* (1865), and are also remembered for their *Journal*, begun in 1851, a detailed record of French social and literary life.

Góngora y Argote, Luis de [**gon**gora ee ah(r)**goh**tay] (1561–1627) Poet, born in Córdoba, Spain. His later works, consisting mostly of longer poems such as *Solidades* and *Polifemo* (both 1613), are written in an entirely novel style, which his followers designated *Gongorismo*.

Gonne, Maud >> **MacBride, Maud**

Gonzaga, Luigi, St [gon**zah**ga], known as **St Aloysius** (1568–91), feast day 21 June. Jesuit priest, born near Brescia, Italy. In a plague at Rome he devoted himself to the care of the sick, but was himself infected and died. He was canonized in 1726, and is the Italian patron saint of youth.

Gonzales, Pancho [gon**zah**lez], popular name of **Ricardo Alonzo Gonzales** (1928–) Tennis player, born in Los Angeles, CA. His titles include the US singles (1948, 1949), and the doubles at both Wimbledon and France (1949).

González, Felipe [gon**zah**lez] (1942–) Spanish prime minister (1982–96), born in Seville, Spain. He became secretary-general of the Spanish Socialist Workers' Party in 1974, and led it to victory in the 1982 elections, forming the first left-wing administration since 1936.

González, Julio [gon**zah**lez] (1876–1942) Sculptor, born in Barcelona, Spain. His most famous work is 'Montserrat I', a life-size figure of a peasant mother (1936–7), a symbol of popular resistance in the Spanish Civil War.

Gooch, Graham (Alan) (1953–) Cricketer, born in Leytonstone, Greater London. As England captain (1988–93), he led a notable victory over the West Indies in Jamaica (1989). The leading England Test run-scorer, and most-capped player, he announced his retirement in 1995, with 8900 runs scored in 118 Tests.

Goodhart, Arthur (Lehman) (1891–1978) Jurist, born in New York City. He became professor of jurisprudence at Oxford, and edited the *Law Quarterly Review* (1926–75).

Goodman, Benny, popular name of **Benjamin David Goodman**, nickname **the King of Swing** (1909–86) Clarinettist and bandleader, born in Chicago, IL. He formed his own orchestra in New York City (1934), and became one of the best-known leaders of the big-band era, making such recordings as 'Let's Dance' and 'One O'Clock Jump'.

Goodman, Isador (1909–82) Pianist and composer, born in Cape Town, South Africa. He emigrated to Australia in 1930, becoming a renowned exponent of the Romantic repertoire, especially Rachmaninov and Liszt.

Goodrich, Samuel Griswold, pseudonym **Peter Parley** (1793–1860) Publisher, born in Ridgefield, CT. He published some 200 volumes, mostly for the young as 'Peter Parley' books, starting with *The Tales of Peter Parley about America* (1827).

Goodyear, Charles (1800–60) Inventor, born in New Haven, CT. His research led to the invention of vulcanized rubber in 1844, and ultimately to the development of the rubber-manufacturing industry and the production of the tyres named after him.

Goolagong, Yvonne >> **Cawley, Yvonne**

Goossens, Eugène (1845–1906) Conductor, born in Bruges, Belgium. He made his name in comic opera with the Carl Rosa Company in Britain from 1873, and later founded the Goossens Male Voice Choir in Liverpool in 1894. >> Goossens, Eugène (1867–1958)

Goossens, Eugène (1867–1958) Violinist and conductor, born in Bordeaux, France, the son of Eugène Goossens (1845–1906). He played with the Carl Rosa Company under his father (1884–6) and became its principal conductor (1899–1915). His children were also well-known musicians: **Eugène Goossens** became a conductor and composer, **Léon Goossens** an oboist, and **Marie Goossens** (1894–1991) and **Sidonie Goossens** (1899–) both harpists. >> Goossens, Sir Eugène / Léon

Goossens, Sir Eugène (1893–1962) Composer and conductor, born in London, the son of Eugène Goossens (1867–1958). Director of the New South Wales Conservatory (1947–56), he became a major influence on Australian music. His compositions include two operas, a ballet, an oratorio, and two symphonies. >> Beecham; Goossens, Eugène (1867–1958) / Léon

Goossens, Léon (1897–1988) Oboist, born in Liverpool, Merseyside, the son of Eugène Goossens (1867–1958). He held leading posts in most of the major London orchestras, before devoting himself to solo playing and teaching. >> Goossens, Eugene

Gorbachev, Mikhail Sergeyevich [go(r)bachof] (1931–) Soviet statesman, born in Privolnoye, Russia. General secretary of the Central Committee (1985–91), in 1988 he also became chairman of the Presidium of the Supreme Soviet (ie head of state) and in 1990 the first executive president of the USSR. He launched a radical programme of reform (*perestroika*) of the Soviet economic and political system, and a greater degree of civil liberty was allowed under the policy of *glasnost* ('openness' of information). In foreign and defence affairs he pursued detente and nuclear disarmament with the West. He survived an attempted coup in August 1991, but resigned after the break-up of the USSR later that year. >> Yeltsin

Gorboduc [gaw(r)boduk] A legendary King of Britain, first heard about in Geoffrey of Monmouth's *History*. He was the subject of an early Elizabethan tragedy in Senecan style, written by Norton and Sackville (1561). >> Geoffrey of Monmouth

Gorchakov, Prince Alexander Michaelovich [gaw(r)chakof] (1798–1883) Russian statesman, born in Khaapsalu, Estonia, the cousin of Prince Michael Gorchakov. As chancellor of the empire (1863) he was, until the rise of Bismarck, the most powerful minister in Europe. >> Bismarck; Gorchakov, Michael

Gorchakov, Prince Michael [gaw(r)chakof] (1795–1861) Russian soldier, the cousin of Prince Alexander Gorchakov. He was appointed commander-in-chief in the Crimea (1855), was defeated on the Tchernaya, but recovered by his gallant defence of Sebastopol. >> Gorchakov, Alexander Michaelovich

Gordimer, Nadine (1923–) Novelist, born in Springs, South Africa. In novels such as *A Guest of Honour* (1971), *The Conservationist* (1974), and *A Sport of Nature* (1987), she adopts a liberal approach to problems of race and repression. She was awarded the Nobel Prize for Literature in 1991.

Gordon, Adam Lindsay (1833–70) Poet, born in Fayal in the Azores. Recognized as the first poet to write in an Australian style, his best work is collected in *Sea Spray and Smoke Drift* (1867) and *Bush Ballads and Galloping Rhymes* (1870).

Gordon, Charles George (1833–85) British general, born in Woolwich, Greater London. In 1860 he went to China, where he crushed the Taiping Rebellion, for which he

became known as **Chinese Gordon**. Appointed Governor of the Sudan (1877), he was besieged at Khartoum for 10 months by the Mahdi's troops, and killed there two days before a relief force arrived. >> Mohammed Ahmed

Gordon, David (1936–) Choreographer, born in New York City. In 1974 he formed his own Pick-Up Company. Several of his works are in the repertories of major US and British classical and modern dance companies.

Gordon, Dexter (Keith) (1923–89) Jazz musician, born in Los Angeles, CA. He was an influential saxophonist and the leader of his own groups from 1945. He won acclaim for his portrayal of a jazz musician in the 1986 film *Round Midnight*.

Gordon, Lord George (1751–93) Anti-Catholic agitator, born in London. Elected MP in 1774, he formed an association aiming for the repeal of the Catholic Relief Act (1778), and led a protest mob to Parliament, causing a major riot with 500 casualties. He was tried for high treason, but acquitted.

Gordon, Noele (1922–85) Actress, born in London. Her London successes included *Diamond Lil* (1948) and *Brigadoon* (1949–51), and she became a household name in the television soap-opera, *Crossroads* (1964–81).

Gore, Al(bert) (1948–) US vice-president, born in Washington, DC. A Democratic congressman (1977–85) and senator (1985–92), he was elected vice-president to Clinton in 1992. >> Clinton

Gore, Charles (1853–1932) Anglican clergyman and theologian, born in London. He founded the Community of the Resurrection at Pusey House in 1892, and became bishop successively of Worcester (1901–4), Birmingham (1904–11), and Oxford (1911–19).

Gore, Spencer Frederick (1878–1914) Painter, born in Epsom, Surrey. He was a founder member and first president of the Camden Town Group (1911), and a member of the London Group (1913). He painted theatre and music hall subjects, using a quasi-Pointillist technique.

Goren, Charles H(enry) (1901–) Contract bridge expert and writer, born in Philadelphia, PA. As a masterful player, he put his knowledge into print with numerous books, and contributed a daily newspaper column, syndicated in the USA.

Gorges, Sir Ferdinando (c.1566–1647) English colonist, born in Wraxall, Somerset. He founded two Plymouth companies (1606–19, 1620–35) for planting lands in New England, and in 1639 received a charter constituting him proprietor of Maine.

Gorgias [gaw(r)jias] (c.485–c.380 BC) Greek sophist, sceptical philosopher, and rhetorician, born in Leontini, Sicily. He settled in Greece and won fame as a teacher of eloquence.

Göring, Hermann >> **Goering, Hermann**

Goring, Marius [gawring] (1912–) Actor, born in Newport, Isle of Wight. Most of his career has been spent on the stage, often on tour throughout Europe, but he is probably best known as the forensic scientist in the television series *The Expert* (1968–70).

Gorky, Arshile, originally **Vosdanig Manoog Adoian** (1905–48) Painter, born in Khorkom Vari, Turkish Armenia. He emigrated to the USA in 1920, and played a key role in the emergence of the New York school of abstract Expressionists in the 1940s.

Gorky, Maxim, pseudonym of **Alexey Maksimovich Peshkov** (1868–1936) Novelist, born in Nizhni Novgorod (formerly, Gorky), Russia. He produced several Romantic short stories, then social novels and plays, notably the drama *The Lower Depths* (trans, 1902). An autobiographical trilogy (1915–23) contains his best writing.

Gorshkov, Sergey Georgievich [gaw(r)shkof] (1910–88) Soviet admiral, born in Podolsk, Ukraine. He was appointed commander-in-chief of the Soviet navy in 1956, and oversaw a massive naval build-up creating a force capable of challenging the West's by the 1970s.

Gort, John Standish Surtees Prendergast Vereker, 6th Viscount (1886-1946) British soldier, born at Hamsterley Hall, Durham. He became Chief of the Imperial General Staff in 1938, and was commander-in-chief of the British forces overwhelmed in the initial German victories of 1940.

Gorton, Sir John Grey (1911-) Australian prime minister (1968-71), born in Melbourne, Victoria, Australia. He served in the governments of Menzies and Holt before becoming premier. In 1971 he was defeated on a vote of confidence, and resigned in favour of McMahon, becoming deputy leader of his Party. >> Holt; McMahon; Menzies

Gorton, Samuel (1592-1677) Colonist and religious leader, born in Gorton, Greater Manchester. He emigrated to Massachusetts Colony (1637) where, having denied the doctrine of the Trinity and the existence of heaven and hell, he was tried for heresy and banished (1638).

Gossaert, Jan [gosah(r)t] >> **Mabuse, Jan**

Gosse, Sir Edmund William (1845-1928) Critic, essayist, and translator, born in London. His *Studies in the Literature of Northern Europe* (1879), and other critical works, first introduced Ibsen to English-speaking readers. >> Ibsen

Gosse, William Christie (1842-81) Explorer, born in Hoddesdon, Hertfordshire. His family emigrated to Australia in 1850. In 1873 he led an expedition in search of an overland route to Perth, discovering a massive sandstone monolith which he named Ayers Rock. >> Ayers

Gotoma >> **Gautama**

Gottfried von Strassburg or **Godfrey of Strasburg** [gotfreed] (fl.12th-c) German poet. He wrote the masterly German version of the legend of *Tristan and Isolde*, based on the Anglo-Norman poem by Thomas (c.1155).

Gottlieb, Adolph [gotleeb] (1903-74) Painter, born in New York City. He is best known as one the original members of the Abstract Expressionist school of painters.

Gottlieb, Robert (Adams) [gotleeb] (1931-) Publisher and editor, born in New York City. He became editor-in-chief at Simon and Schuster (1955-68) and at Alfred Knopf (1968-87), and was appointed editor of the *New Yorker* in 1987.

Gottschalk, Louis Moreau [gotschawk] (1829-69) Composer, born in New Orleans, LA. He was among the first Americans to feature nationalistic elements in his music, such as the piano piece *Bamboula* (1845).

Gottschalk of Orbais >> **Hincmar**

Gottwald, Klement [gotvald] (1896-1953) Czech prime minister (1946-8) and president (1948-53), born in Dadice, Czech Republic (formerly, Moravia). He became secretary-general of the Communist Party in 1927, and vice-premier in the provisional government of 1945. In 1948 he carried out a Communist coup and became president, establishing a dictatorship.

Götz von Berlichingen [goets fon berlikhingen], known as **Götz of the Iron Hand** (1480-1562) Mercenary knight, born in Jagsthausen, Germany. He lost his hand in the siege of Landshut (1504) and replaced it with one of iron. He also fought in various battles against the Turks (1542) and the French (1544).

Goudsmit, Samuel (Abraham) [gudsmit] (1902-78) Physicist, born in The Hague, The Netherlands. He and his fellow-student **George Uhlenbeck** (1900-) introduced the notion of electron spin in atoms.

Goudy, Frederic William [gowdee] (1865-1947) Type designer and printer, born in Bloomington, IL. He designed many popular typefaces, including two that bear his name (*Goudy Old Style* and *Goudy Modern*).

Gough, Sir Hubert de la Poer [gof] (1870-1963) British soldier, born in Gurteen, Co Waterford, Ireland. His com-

mand of the Fifth Army at the third Ypres campaign impaired his reputation, and he was made a scapegoat for British military failure during the German advance in 1918.

Goujon, Jean [goozhõ] (c.1510-c.68) The foremost French sculptor of the 16th-c, probably born in Normandy, France. His finest work is a set of reliefs for the Fountain of the Innocents (1547-9).

Gould, Benjamin (Apthorp) (1824-1926) Astronomer, born in Boston, MA. He was invited to found and direct the Argentinian National Observatory in 1868. He is best known for his star catalogues of the S hemisphere (1884).

Gould, Bryan (Charles) (1939-) British Labour politician, born in New Zealand. His rise in the Party was rapid, and in 1986 he was elected to the shadow Cabinet, but resigned in 1992 (as a leading 'Eurosceptic') over the Party's policy on Europe.

Gould, Chester (1900-85) Strip cartoonist, born in Pawnee, OK. He submitted a new idea in continuity strips, *Plainclothes Tracy*, to the *New York Daily News*, who rechristened it *Dick Tracy*.

Gould, Glenn (Herbert) [goold] (1932-82) Pianist, born in Toronto, Ontario, Canada. A renowned recording artist, particularly of works by Bach, he was also known for his innovative radio documentaries and television shows.

Gould, Jay, popular name of **Jason Gould** (1836-92) Financier, born in Roxbury, NY. A broker in New York City (1859), he manipulated shares to sieze the presidency of the Erie Railway Co (1868-72). He also tried to corner the gold market, causing the 'Black Friday' stock-market crash of 1869.

Gould, John (1804-81) Ornithologist and publisher, born in Lyme Regis, Dorset. Assisted by his wife Elizabeth (d.1841), he produced 18 monumental books of bird illustrations, including *Birds of Europe* (5 vols, 1832-7) and *Birds of Australia* (7 vols, 1840-8).

Gould, Morton (1913-96) Composer, conductor, and pianist, born in Richmond Hill, NY. His work exploits popular music from both North and South America.

Gould, Nat, popular name of **Nathaniel Gould** (1857-1919) Sporting journalist and novelist, born in Manchester. A newspaper sports columnist in Sydney, Australia, he achieved success with his first novel about the turf, *The Double Event*, and subsequently wrote some 130 thrillers about horse-racing.

Gould, Shane (Elizabeth) (1956-) Swimmer, born in Brisbane, Queensland, Australia. She created Olympic history by being the first and only woman to win three individual gold swimming medals in world record time. She retired in 1973, at the age of 17.

Gould, Stephen Jay (1941-) Palaeontologist, born in New York City. His forceful support for modern views on evolution has been expressed in many articles and books, including *Hen's Teeth and Horses' Toes* (1983).

Gouled Aptidon, Hassan [gooled aptidon] (1916-) President of Djibouti (1977-), born in Djibouti city. He joined the African People's League for Independence (LPAI) in 1967 and became the new country's first president.

Gounod, Charles (François) [goonoh] (1818-93) Composer, born in Paris. His major works include the opera, *The Mock Doctor* (trans, 1858) and his masterpiece, Faust (1859). He also published Masses, hymns, and anthems, and was popular as a songwriter.

Gourment, Rémy de [goormã] (1858-1915) Writer and critic, born in Bazoches-en-Houlme, France. His creative work, in the Symbolist vogue, includes *Very Woman* (trans, 1890) and *A Virgin Heart* (1907).

Gow, Niel (1727-1807) Violinist and songwriter, born in Inver, Tayside. He composed numerous tunes, and from his collection of Strathspey reels and singular skill with the bow, his name is still a household word in Scotland.

Gower, David (Ivon) (1957–) Cricketer, born in Tunbridge Wells, Kent. He was captain of England (1984–6, 1989), and for a time the leading Test run-scorer, with 8231 runs in Test cricket over 117 matches. He retired in 1993.

Gower, John (c.1325–1408) Mediaeval poet, born in Kent, a friend of Chaucer. His best-known work is the long English poem, *Confessio amantis* (c.1383), comprising over 100 stories from various sources on the theme of Christian and courtly love.

Gowers, Sir Ernest (Arthur) (1880–1966) British civil servant, and author of an influential work on English usage. He wrote *Plain Words* (1948) and *ABC of Plain Words* (1951) in an attempt to maintain standards of clear English, especially in official prose.

Gowing, Sir Lawrence Burnett (1918–91) Painter and writer on art, born in London. His Impressionist style was often applied to portraits, such as *Mrs Roberts* (Tate, London). Among his books are studies of Renoir (1947) and Vermeer (1952).

Gowon, Yakubu (1934–) Nigerian soldier and president (1966–75), born in Garam, Nigeria. He led a military takeover in 1966, but could not prevent a costly civil war which lasted until 1970. In 1975 he was ousted in a bloodless coup.

Goya (y Lucientes), Francisco (José) de [gohya] (1746–1828) Artist, born in Fuendetodos, Spain. He became famous for his portraits, and in 1799 was made court painter to Charles IV, which led to 'The Family of Charles IV' (1800).

Goyathlay >> **Geronimo**

Goyen, Jan van [goyen] >> **van Goyen, Jan**

Gozzi, Carlo, conte (Count) [gotzee] (1720–1806) Playwright, born in Venice, Italy. He wrote several satirical poems and plays, defending the traditions of the *commedia dell' arte*. His best-known works include *The Love of the Three Oranges* (trans, 1761) and *Turandot* (1762). His brother, **Gasparo Gozzi** (1713–86) became known for his verse satires.

Gozzoli, Benozzo [gotsohlee], also called **Benozzo di Lese** (1420–97) Painter, born in Florence, Italy. He adorned the Palazzo Medici-Riccardi with scriptural subjects, including his famous 'Journey of the Magi' in which Florentine councillors accompanied by members of the Medici family appear.

Graaf, Reinier de [grahf] (1641–73) Physician and anatomist, born in Schoonhoven, The Netherlands. In 1663 he wrote a famous treatise on the pancreas, and in 1672 discovered the follicles of the ovary (*Graafian follicles*).

Graaff, Robert Van de >> **Van de Graaff, Robert**

Gracchus, Gaius Sempronius [grakus] (c.159–121 BC) Roman statesman, the brother of Tiberius Gracchus. He was elected to the tribuneship (123 BC), renewed his brother's agrarian law, and took other measures to con-trol abuses. He committed suicide after leading a demonstration in support of his reforms, in which many of his followers were slain. >> Gracchus, Tiberius Sempronius

Gracchus, Tiberius Sempronius [grakus] (168–133 BC) Roman statesman, the brother of Gaius Sempronius Gracchus. Elected tribune in 134, he proposed reforms to extend land-ownership among the poor. His measures were strongly disapproved of by wealthy land-owners and he was assassinated. >> Gracchus, Gaius Sempronius

Grace, W(illiam) G(ilbert) (1848–1915) Cricketer, born in Downend, Avon. He twice captained the English team. His career in first-class cricket (1865–1908) as batsman and bowler brought 126 centuries, 54 896 runs, and 2876 wickets.

Grace of Monaco, Princess >> **Kelly, Grace**

Gracián (y Morales), Baltasar [grathyahn] (1601–58) Philosopher and writer, born in Belmonte de Calayatud, Spain. He is best known for his three-part allegorical novel, *The Critic* (1651, 1653, 1657), in which civilization and society are portrayed through the eyes of a savage.

Grade (of Elstree), Lew Grade, Baron, originally **Louis Winogradsky** (1906–) Theatrical impresario, born near Odessa, Ukraine, the eldest of three brothers who were to dominate British show-business for over 40 years. He arrived in Britain in 1912, along with his younger brother **Boris Grade**, who became **Baron Bernard Delfont of Stepney** (1909–94). Bernard entered theatrical management in 1941, and presented the annual Royal Variety Performance (1958–78). Lew headed several large film entertainment and communications companies.

Graebner, (Robert) Fritz [graybner] (1877–1934) Ethnologist, born in Berlin. He is chiefly known for developing the theory of *Kulturkreise* (culture complex), clusters of diffusing cultural traits which he used to explain cultural similarities and differences, as seen in *Method of Ethnology* (trans, 1911).

Graf, Steffi [grahf] (1969–) Tennis player, born in Brühl, Germany. She won all four major titles in 1988, winning the Wimbledon singles title again in 1989, 1991, 1992, 1993, and 1995.

Grafton, Augustus Henry Fitzroy, 3rd Duke of (1735–1811) British prime minister (1768–70). He was secretary of state (1765–6) and First Lord of the Treasury (1766), and undertook the duties of premier during Pitt's illness. >> Pitt, William (the Elder)

Graham, Billy, popular name of **William Franklin Graham, Jr** (1918–) Evangelist, born in Charlotte, NC. A charismatic figure, since the 1950s he has conducted revivalist campaigns in the USA, UK, South America, the former USSR, and W Europe, invariably attracting large audiences.

Graham, Ennis >> **Molesworth, Mary Louisa**

Graham, Sir James Robert George, Bart (1792–1861) British statesman, born in Netherby, Cumbria. Home secretary under Peel (1841), he supported the Corn Law Repeal Bill, and on Peel's death (1850) became leader of the Peelites. >> Peel

Graham, John, of Claverhouse >> **Dundee, Viscount**

Graham, Martha (1894–1991) Dancer, teacher, and choreographer, born in Pittsburgh, PA. She started the Martha Graham School of Contemporary Dance in 1927, and became the most famous exponent of Expressionist modern dance in the USA.

Graham, Otto Everett, Jr, nickname **Automatic Otto** (1921–) Quarterback and coach of American football, born in Waukegan, IL. He played with the Cleveland Browns from 1946, leading them to championship victories in the National Football League (1950, 1954, 1955), and later became head coach of the Washington Redskins (1966–8).

Graham, Thomas (1805–69) Chemist and physcist, born in Glasgow, Strathclyde. One of the founders of physical chemistry, he formulated the law that the diffusion rate of gases is inversely proportional to the square root of their density (*Graham's law*).

Grahame, Kenneth (1859–1932) Writer, born in Edinburgh. He wrote several stories for children, the best known being *The Wind in the Willows* (1908), dramatized in 1930 by A A Milne as *Toad of Toad Hall*. >> Milne, A A

Grahame-White, Claude (1879–1959) Aviator and engineer, born in Bursledon, Hampshire. He founded the first British flying school at Pau, in France (1909), and helped establish London Aerodrome at Hendon (1911).

Grahn, Lucile (1819–1907) Ballerina, born in Copenhagen. A member of the Royal Danish Ballet, she retired from dancing in 1856, and became ballet mistress at the Leipzig State Theatre (1858–61) and the Munich Court Opera (1869–75).

Grainger, Percy (Aldridge), originally **George Percy Grainger** (1882–1961) Composer and pianist, born in Melbourne, Victoria, Australia. He lived in the USA for much of his life, championing the revival of folk music, but was one of the first to compose for electronic instruments.

Gram, Hans Christian Joachim (1853–1938) Bacteriologist, born in Copenhagen. He established in 1884 a microbiological staining method for bacteria, distinguishing the *Gram-positive* from the *Gram-negative*.

Gramme, Zénobe Théophile [gram] (1826–1901) Electrical engineer, born in Jehay-Bodegnée, Belgium. In 1869 he built the first successful direct-current dynamo, and with Fontaine showed that a dynamo could function in reverse as an electric motor (1873). >> Fontaine, Hippolyte

Gramsci, Antonio [gramskee] (1891–1937) Italian political leader and theoretician, born in Ales, Sardinia. He helped to establish the Italian Communist Party (1921), becoming its parliamentary leader (1924). When Mussolini banned the party, he was arrested and sent to prison for life, where he wrote *Letters from Prison* (trans, 1947). >> Mussolini

Granados (y Campiña), Enrique [granahthos] (1867–1916) Composer and pianist, born in Lérida, Spain. A composer of Spanish dances, his *Goyescas* (1911–13) for piano are his most accomplished works.

Granby, John Manners, Marquess of (1721–70) British army officer, whose reputation was made in the Seven Years' War (1756–63) when he led the British cavalry in a major victory over the French at Warburg (1760).

Grand, Sarah, *née* **Frances Elizabeth Clarke** (1854–1943) Novelist, born in Donaghadee, Ireland. Her reputation rests on *The Heavenly Twins* (1893), in which she skilfully handles delicate problems of sexual development, relationships, and disease.

Grandi, Dino, conte di (Count of) **Mordano** (1895–1988) Italian statesman and diplomat, born in Mordano, near Bologna. Mussolini's foreign minister (1929–32), in 1943 he moved the motion in the Fascist Grand Council which brought about Mussolini's resignation, then fled to Portugal. >> Mussolini

Grange, Kenneth Henry (1929–) Industrial designer, born in London. His product designs include food mixers for Kenwood, cameras for Kodak, locomotives for British Rail, and the parking meter for Venner.

Grange, Red, popular name of **Howard Edward Grange**, nickname **the Galloping Ghost** (1903–91) Player and coach of American football, born in Forksville, PA. His achievements as a running back in the 1920s earned him his byname, and he signed for the Chicago Bears in 1925.

Granit, Ragnar Arthur (1900–) Physiologist, born in Helsinki, Finland. He pioneered the study of the neurophysiology of vision by the use of microelectrodes, and shared the Nobel Prize for Physiology or Medicine in 1987.

Grant, Alexander (Marshall) (1925–) Dancer and director, born in Wellington, New Zealand. He spent his dancing career with the Royal Ballet, Covent Garden, and became director of the Royal Ballet's offshoot, Ballet For All (1971–5), and director of the National Ballet of Canada (1976–83).

Grant, Cary, originally **Archibald Leach** (1904–86) Film actor, born in Bristol, Avon. He went to Hollywood in 1928, and gave memorable performances for Hitchcock in *Suspicion* (1941), *Notorious* (1946), *To Catch a Thief* (1955), and *North by North-West* (1959). >> Hitchcock, Alfred

Grant, Duncan (James Corrow) (1885–1978) Painter, born in Rothiemurchus, Highland. Associated with Fry's

Omega Workshops, and then with the London Group, his works were mainly landscapes, portraits, and still-life. >> Fry, Roger

Grant, James Augustus (1827–92) British soldier and explorer, born in Nairn, Highland. He is best known as a colleague of Speke, with whom he explored the sources of the Nile (1860–3), as described in *A Walk Across Africa* (1864). >> Speke

Grant, Ulysses S(impson) (1822–85) US general and 18th president (1869–77), born in Point Pleasant, OH. In the Civil War (1861), he led Union forces to victory, first in the Mississippi Valley, then in the final campaigns in Virginia. Elected president in 1868 and 1872, he presided over the reconstruction of the South. His memoirs (1885–6), have been much acclaimed.

Granville-Barker, Harley (1877–1946) Actor, playwright, and producer, born in London. His plays include *The Voysey Inheritance* (1905), and he wrote a famous series of prefaces to Shakespeare's plays (1927–45).

Grappelli, Stéphane [grapelee] (1908–) Jazz violinist, born in Paris. He and Django Reinhardt were the principal soloists in the Quintet of the Hot Club of France (1934–9), the first European jazz band to exert an influence in the USA. >> Reinhardt, Django

Grass, Günter (Wilhelm) (1927–) Writer, born in Gdansk, Poland (formerly, Danzig, Germany). His political novel *The Tin Drum* (trans, 1959) caused a furore in Germany because of its depiction of the Nazis. Intellectual and experimental, other important books include (trans titles) *Cat and Mouse* (1961) and *The Flounder* (1992).

Grassmann, Hermann (Günther) (1809–77) Mathematician and philologist, born in Stettin, Germany. *The Theory of Linear Extension* (trans, 1844) developed a general calculus for vectors, and he also worked in Indo-European and Germanic philology.

Gratian [grayshian], in full **Flavius Augustus Gratianus** (359–383) Roman emperor (from 375), the son of Valentinian I. On his father's death he became emperor of the West, which he shared with his brother Valentinian II, and appointed Theodosius emperor in the East (378). Overthrown by Magnus Maximus, he was murdered at Lyon. >> Theodosius I; Valentinian I

Gratian [grayshian], also known as **Franciscus Gratianus** (12th-c) Italian jurist and monk of Bologna. He compiled the collection of canon law known as the *Decretum Gratiani* (1139–1150), which remained the first part of the traditional body of canon law in the Roman Catholic Church until 1917.

Grattan, Henry (1746–1820) Irish statesman, born in Dublin. He secured Irish free trade in 1779, and legislative independence in 1782. He was returned for Dublin in 1790, and in 1805 was elected to the House of Commons.

Graun, Karl Heinrich [grown] (1703/4–59) Composer, born near Torgau, Germany. A singer as well as a composer, his works include 32 operas and a 'Passion piece'.

Graveney, Tom [grayvnee], popular name of **Thomas William Graveney** (1927–) Cricketer and television commentator, born in Riding Mill, Northumberland. A batsman, during a patchy Test career he made 11 Test centuries for England and a total 4882 runs.

Graves, Robert James (1796–1853) Physician, born in Dublin. He was an excellent diagnostician, best remembered today for his description of a form of hyperthyroidism (*Graves' disease*).

Graves, Robert (Ranke) (1895–1985) Writer, born in London. His best-known novels are *I, Claudius* and its sequel, *Claudius the God* (both 1934), which were adapted for television in 1976. His *Collected Poems* (1975) draws on more than 20 volumes.

Gray, Asa (1810–88) Botanist, born in Sauquoit, NY. His

main works were the *Flora of North America* (1838–42), which he compiled with John Torrey, and the *Manual of the Botany of the Northern United States* (1848), often known simply as Gray's Manual.

Gray, Elisha (1835–1901) Inventor, born in Barnesville, OH. A manufacturer of telegraphic apparatus, his firm became the Western Electric Co. He claimed the invention of the telephone, but lost the patent rights to Alexander Graham Bell. >> Bell, Alexander Graham

Gray, George Robert (1808–72) Ornithologist and entomologist, born in London. He is best known for his *Genera of Birds* (3 vols, 1844–49). *Gray's grasshopper warbler* is named after him.

Gray, George William (1926–) Chemist, born in Scotland. His research into liquid crystals took on a new importance in the 1960s when electronics companies realized they could be used to form a visual display.

Gray, Harold (Lincoln) (1894–1968) Cartoonist, born in Kankakee, IL. He created his own strip in 1924, called *Little Orphan Annie*. The character was adapted to a hit Broadway musical, *Annie* (1977), and a film based on the musical was released in 1982.

Gray, Milner Connorton (1899–) Graphic designer, born in London. He is best known for his co-ordinated 'corporate identity' schemes for such organizations as Ilford, Austin Reed, ICI, Gilbey, and British Rail.

Gray, Simon (James Holliday) (1936–) Writer and director, born on Hayling Island, Hampshire. His plays include *Wise Child* (1967), *Quartermaine's Terms* (1981), and *An Unnatural Pursuit* (1985).

Gray, Thomas (1716–71) Poet, born in London. His masterpiece is 'Elegy Written in a Country Churchyard' (1751), set at Stoke Poges, Buckinghamshire. He then settled in Cambridge, where he wrote his *Pindaric Odes* (1757).

Graziani, Rodolfo, Marquess of Neghelli [gratsiahnee] (1882–1955) Italian soldier and administrator, born in Filettino, Italy. In World War 2, as Governor of Libya, he attacked Egypt, but was defeated by Wavell (1940–1) and resigned. After the fall of Mussolini he emerged as minister of defence and head of Fascist armed resistance. >> Mussolini; Wavell

Great Elector, The >> **Frederick William**

Greathead, Henry >> **Wouldhave, William**

Greathead, James Henry (1844–96) Civil engineer, born in Grahamstown, South Africa. In order to facilitate the building of tunnels under the Thames in London (1869, 1886), he greatly improved the tunnelling shield designed (1818) by Brunel. >> Brunel, Mark Isambard

Greaves, Jimmy, popular name of **James Greaves** (1940–) English footballer and television commentator, born in London. He scored 357 goals in 517 league matches with Chelsea, Tottenham Hotspur, and West Ham United.

Greco, El [grekoh] (Span 'the Greek'), nickname of **Domenikos Theotokopoulos** (1541–1614) Painter, born in Candia, Crete, Greece. He settled in Toledo, Spain (c.1577), and became a portrait painter whose reputation fluctuated because of the suspicion which greeted his characteristic distortions, such as his elongated, flamelike figures. His most famous painting is probably the 'Burial of Count Orgaz' (1586).

Greeley, Adolphus (Washington) (1844–1935) Arctic explorer, born in Newburyport, MA. In 1881 he led a US Army expedition to Smith Sound to set up a meteorological station, and one of the team travelled to within 396 miles of the Pole, the farthest point reached till then.

Greeley, Andrew M(oran) (1928–) Catholic priest and sociologist, born in Oak Park, IL. He maintained that the Catholic hierarchy was out of touch with priests and laity. Besides sociological and moral studies, he turned out salty popular novels, increasing his reputation as a maverick within the Church.

Greeley, Horace (1811–72) Editor and politician, born in Amherst, NH. He was editor of the weekly *New Yorker* in 1834, and in 1841 founded the daily *New York Tribune*, of which he was the leading editor until his death.

Green, George (1793–1841) Mathematician and physicist, born in Sneinton, Nottinghamshire. In 1828 he published an important essay containing what are now known as *Green's theorem* and *Green's functions*, and introducing the electrical term *potential*.

Green, Henry, pseudonym of **Henry Vincent Yorke** (1905–73) Writer and industrialist, born in Tewkesbury, Gloucestershire. His books include *Blindness* (1926), *Party Going* (1939), *Loving* (1945), and *Doting* (1952).

Green, Julien (Hartridge) (1900–) Writer, born in Paris of American parents. He began a successful series of psychological studies with *Avarice House* (trans, 1925), later works including *Memories of Happy Days* (1942) and *Memories of Evil Days* (1976).

Green, Lucinda, *née* **Prior-Palmer** (1953–) Three-day eventer, born in London. The only person to win the Badminton Horse Trials six times (1973, 1976–7, 1979, 1983–4), she became 1982 world champion on *Regal Realm*, also winning a team gold medal.

Greenaway, Kate, popular name of **Catherine Greenaway** (1846–1901) Artist and book-illustrator, born in London. She became well known in the 1880s for her coloured portrayals of child life, in such works as *The Birthday Book* (1880). The *Greenaway Medal* is awarded annually for the best British children's book artist.

Greenaway, Peter (1942–) Film-maker and painter, born in London. *The Draughtsman's Contract* (1982) won him critical acclaim. His later works explore such preoccupations as sex, death, decay, and gamesmanship, and include *Drowning By Numbers* (1988), *Prospero's Books* (1991), and *The Baby of Macon* (1993).

Greene, (Henry) Graham (1904–91) Writer, born in Berkhamsted, Hertfordshire. In his major novels, central religious issues emerge, especially concerning Catholicism, as in *Brighton Rock* (1938), *The Power and the Glory* (1940), *The End of the Affair* (1951), and *A Burnt-Out Case* (1961). He also wrote plays, film scripts (notably, *The Third Man*, 1950), short stories, and essays. >> Greene, Hugh Carleton

Greene, Sir Hugh Carleton (1910–87) Journalist and television executive, born in Berkhamsted, Hertfordshire, the brother of Graham Greene. He became the BBC's first director of news and current affairs (1958–60) before being chosen as director-general (1960–9). >> Greene, Graham

Greene, Nathanael (1742–86) US general, born in Warwick, RI. In the American Revolution, he took command of the Southern army (1780), and although defeated by Cornwallis (1781), the victory was so costly that he was able to recover South Carolina and Georgia, paving the way to American victory in the South. >> Cornwallis

Greene, Robert (1558–92) Playwright, born in Norwich, Norfolk. His most popular work was the comedy *Friar Bacon and Friar Bungay* (c.1589). He helped to lay the foundations of English drama, and his *Pandosto* (1588) was a source for Shakespeare's *The Winter's Tale*. >> Shakespeare, William

Greenidge, (Cuthbert) Gordon [grenij] (1951–) West Indian cricketer, born in St Peter, Barbados. An opening batsman, he became an English county player with Hampshire. He scored a century on his Test debut, and holds five West Indian Test partnership records.

Greenough, Horatio [greenoh] (1805–52) Sculptor and writer, born in Boston, MA. His principal work is a colossal statue in Classical style of George Washington as Zeus, now in the Smithsonian Institution, Washington, DC.

Greenspan, Alan (1926–) Businessman and financier. He became president of Townsend-Greenspan and Co, New York City (1954–74, 1977–87), and was also a member of the president's economic policy advisory board (1981–7).

Greenway, Francis Howard (1777–1837) Architect, born in Mangotsfield, Avon. He was transported for forgery (1812), and sent to Sydney (1814), where he established himself in practice as an architect, designing most of the early colony's public buildings.

Greenwood, Arthur (1880–1954) British statesman, born in Leeds, West Yorkshire. He became deputy leader of the Labour Party in 1935, served as Lord Privy Seal (1945–47), and did much to shape Labour's social policies.

Greenwood, Joan (1921–1987) Actress, born in London. Her film credits include the Ealing comedies *Whisky Galore* (1948), *Kind Hearts and Coronets* (1949), and *The Man in the White Suit* (1951).

Greenwood, Walter (1903–74) Writer, born in Salford, Greater Manchester. His best-known novel, *Love on the Dole* (1933), was dramatized in 1934 and filmed in 1941.

Greer, Germaine (1939–) Feminist, writer, and lecturer, born in Melbourne, Victoria, Australia. Her controversial book *The Female Eunuch* (1970) portrayed marriage as a legalized form of slavery for women, and attacked the misrepresentation of female sexuality by male-dominated society.

Gregg, John Robert (1867–1948) Publisher, and inventor of a shorthand system, born in Co Monaghan, Ireland. He emigrated to the USA in 1893, where his shorthand system came to be widely used.

Gregg, Sir Norman McAlister (1892–1966) Ophthalmologist, born in Sydney, New South Wales, Australia. His research proved the link between the incidence of German measles in pregnancy and cataracts or blindness in children.

Grégoire, Henri [graygwah(r)] (1750–1831) Clergyman and revolutionary, born near Lunéville, France. He joined the Third Estate Party, and was prominent throughout the revolution, calling for the abolition of the monarchy in 1792.

Gregory, St, known as **the Illuminator** (c.240–332), feast day 30 September. Apostle of Armenia, said to have been a Parthian prince who fled from a Persian invasion, and was brought up a Christian in Cappadocia. Returning to Armenia, he succeeded in converting the king (301), and became Patriarch of Armenia.

Gregory I, St, known as **the Great** (c.540–604), feast day 12 March. Pope (590–604), a Father of the Church, born in Rome. It was here that he saw some Anglo-Saxon youths in the slave market, and was seized with a longing to convert their country to Christianity. He reformed public ritual, and systematized the sacred chants, and was canonized on his death. >> Augustine, St (of Canterbury)

Gregory VII, originally **Hildebrand** (c.1020–85), feast day 25 May. Pope (1073–85), born near Soana, Italy. He worked to change the secularized condition of the Church, which led to conflict with the German Emperor Henry IV, who appointed an antipope (Clement III), and took possession of Rome (1084). He was canonized in 1606.

Gregory XIII, originally **Ugo Buoncompagni** (1502–85) Pope (1572–85), born in Bolgona, Italy. He displayed great zeal for the promotion of education, and in 1582 introduced the calendar named after him.

Gregory, Augustus Charles (1819–1905) Surveyor and explorer, born in Farnsfield, Nottinghamshire. He went to Australia in 1829, and undertook several expeditions to explore the Australian interior.

Gregory, Isabella Augusta, Lady, *née* **Persse** (1852–1932) Playwright, born at Roxborough House, Co Galway, Ireland. An associate of Yeats in the foundation of the Abbey Theatre, Dublin, she wrote several short plays, notably *Spreading the News* (1904) and *The Rising of the Moon* (1907). >> Yeats, W B

Gregory, James (1638–75) Mathematician, born in Drumoak, Grampian. His *The Advance of Optics* (trans, 1663) contained a description of the Gregorian reflecting telescope he had invented in 1661. His work anticipated several discoveries in number theory, including the Taylor expansion.

Gregory of Nazianzus, St [nazianzus] (c.329–90), feast day 2 January (W), 25 or 30 January (E). Bishop and theologian, born in Cappadocia, Asia Minor. He became a close friend of Basil the Great, and was made Bishop of Sasima, but withdrew to a life of religious study at Nazianzus. >> Basil the Great

Gregory of Nyssa, St [nisa] (c.331–95), feast day 9 March. Christian theologian, born in Caesarea, Asia Minor, the brother of Basil the Great. Bishop of Nyssa (c.371), and an outstanding scholarly defender of orthodoxy, he wrote several theological works, sermons, and epistles. >> Basil the Great

Gregory of Tours, St [toor], originally **Georgius Florentinus** (c.538–c.594), feast day 17 November. Frankish historian, born in Arverna (now Clermont). Elected Bishop of Tours (573), his *Historia Francorum* is the chief authority for the history of Gaul in the 6th-c.

Gregory Thaumaturgus [thowmatoorgus] (c.213–c.270) Christian apostle of Roman Asia, born in Neocaesarea in Pontus (now N Turkey). Bishop of Neocaesarea, his *Ekthesis* (Confession of Faith) is an apology for belief in the Trinity, and a forerunner of the Nicene Creed.

Greig, Tony, popular name of **Antony Greig** (1946–) Cricketer, born in Queenstown, South Africa. A good all-rounder, he captained England, scoring 3599 runs, eight centuries, and taking 141 wickets in Test matches. In 1977 he recruited players to join the rival organization, World Series Cricket, and was stripped of the England captaincy. >> Packer, Kerry

Grenfell, Joyce (Irene Phipps) (1910–79) Entertainer, born in London. She appeared in revue until the early 1950s, delivering comic monologues. Her books include her autobiography, *Joyce Grenfell Requests the Pleasure* (1976) and *George, Don't Do That* (1977).

Grenfell, Sir Wilfred (Thomason) (1865–1940) Physician and missionary, born in Parkgate, Cheshire. In 1892 he went to Labrador and founded hospitals, orphanages, and other social services.

Grenville, George (1712–70) British prime minister (1763–5), born in London, the father of William Grenville. In 1762 he became secretary of state and First Lord of the Admiralty. The passing of the American Stamp Act took place during his administration. >> Grenville, William

Grenville, Sir Richard (c.1542–91) English naval commander, a cousin of Sir Walter Raleigh. In 1585 he commanded the seven ships carrying 100 English colonists to Roanoke Island, NC. >> Raleigh, Walter

Grenville, William Wyndham Grenville, 1st Baron (1759–1834) British statesman, the son of George Grenville. He became paymaster-general (1783), home secretary (1790), and foreign secretary (1791), and in 1806–7 formed the coalition 'Government of All the Talents', which abolished the slave trade. >> Grenville, George

Gresham, Sir Thomas [greshm] (1519–79) Financier, born in London. An observation in economics is attributed to him (*Gresham's law*): if there are two coins of equal legal exchange value, and one is suspected to be of lower intrinsic value, the 'bad coin' will tend to drive the other out of circulation, as people will begin to hoard it.

Gresley, Sir (Herbert) Nigel (1876–1941) Locomotive engineer, born in Edinburgh. His A4 class Pacific 4-6-2

'Mallard' achieved a world record speed for a steam locomotive of 126 mph in 1938.

Grétry, André Ernest Modeste [graytree] (1741–1813) Composer, born in Liège, Belgium. He composed over 40 comic operas; among the best known are *Raoul* and *Richard coeur-de-lion*.

Gretzky, Wayne, nickname **the Great One** or **the Great Gretzky** (1961–) Ice-hockey player, born in Brantford, Ontario, Canada. He joined the Edmonton Oilers in 1979, and transferred to the Los Angeles Kings in 1988. He is the National Hockey League's all-time leading scorer.

Greuze, Jean Baptiste [groez] (1725–1805) Genre and portrait painter, born in Tournus, France. His best work is seen in his studies of girls, such as 'The Broken Pitcher' (c.1773).

Greville, Sir Fulke, 1st Baron Brooke (1554–1628) Poet, born at Beauchamp Court, Warwickshire. He wrote several didactic poems, over 100 sonnets, and two tragedies. He was Chancellor of the Exchequer (1614–22).

Grévy, (François Paul) Jules [grayvee] (1807–91) French president (1879–87), born in Mont-sous-Vaudrey, France. In 1871 he became president of the National Assembly, and was re-elected in 1876, 1877, and 1879.

Grew, Nehemiah (1641–1712) Botanist and physician, born in Atherstone, Warwickshire. He is best known as the author of the pioneering *Anatomy of Plants*, where he introduced the idea that the stamen and pistil of flowers correspond to male and female sex organs.

Grey, Dame Beryl, *née* **Groom**, married name **Svenson** (1927–) Ballerina, born in London. The youngest Giselle ever, at the age of 16 she was prima ballerina of the Sadler's Wells Ballet (1942–57), and became artistic director of the London Festival Ballet (1968–79).

Grey, Charles Grey, 2nd Earl (1764–1845) British prime minister (1830–4), born in Fallodon, Northumberland. He secured the passage of the 1832 Reform Bill, and carried the Act for the abolition of slavery in the colonies.

Grey, Sir George (1799–1882) British statesman, born in Gibraltar. He was home secretary (1846), colonial secretary (1854), and again home secretary (1855).

Grey, Sir George (1812–98) British explorer and administrator, born in Lisbon, Portugal. Appointed Governor of South Australia in 1840, he was transferred to New Zealand in 1845, where he succeeded in establishing peace between the warring Maoris and British settlers.

Grey, Henry George Grey, 3rd Earl (1802–94) British statesman, the son of Charles, 2nd Earl Grey. In 1846 he became colonial secretary, where he was in favour of local self-government for the colonies. >> Grey, Charles

Grey, Lady Jane (1537–54) Queen of England for nine days in 1553, the great-granddaughter of Henry VII. In 1553 the Duke of Northumberland aimed to secure the succession by marrying Jane (against her wish) to his fourth son, Lord Guildford Dudley. Three days after Edward's death she was named as his successor, but was forced to abdicate in favour of Mary, and beheaded. >> Dudley, Guildford; Edward VI; Mary Tudor

Grey, Maria Georgina, *née* **Shirreff** (1816–1906) Pioneer of women's education in Britain, the sister of Emily Shirreff. She helped to found the National Union for Promoting the Higher Education of Women (1871), which created the Girls' Public Day School Company (later Trust) in 1872. >> Shirreff

Grey, Zane, pseudonym of **Pearl Grey** (1875–1939) Novelist, born in Zanesville, OH. In 1904 he began to write Westerns, the best known of his 54 books being *Riders of the Purple Sage* (1912).

Grey Eminence >> Joseph, Père

Grieg, Edvard (Hagerup) [greeg] (1843–1907) Composer, born in Bergen, Norway. His works include the incidental music for Ibsen's *Peer Gynt* (1876), the A minor piano concerto, orchestral suites, violin sonatas, and numerous songs and piano pieces.

Grieg, (Johan) Nordahl Brun [greeg] (1902–43) Poet and playwright, born in Bergen, Norway. A committed anti-Fascist, he wrote dramas about national freedom, as in *Our Power and Our Glory* (trans, 1935) and *Defeat* (trans, 1937).

Grien, Hans >> **Baldung, Hans**

Grierson, Sir Herbert John Clifford [greerson] (1866–1960) Critic and scholar, born in Lerwick, Shetland. His books include *Metaphysical Poets* (1921), *Milton and Wordsworth* (1937), and *Essays and Addresses* (1940).

Grierson, John [greerson] (1898–1972) Producer of documentary films, born in Kilmadock, Grampian. He made his name with *Drifters* (1929), and is regarded as the founder of the British documentary movement.

Grieve, Christopher Murray >> **MacDiarmid, Hugh**

Griffes, Charles Tomlinson [grifuhs] (1884–1920) Composer, born in Elmira, NY. Before his early death, he had begun to achieve a highly colourful and personal style in such works as *Pleasure Dome of Kubla Khan* (1920).

Griffin, Bernard (1899–1956) Roman Catholic clergyman, born in Birmingham, West Midlands. He became Archbishop of Westminster in 1943, and was made a cardinal in 1946.

Griffin, Gerald (1803–40) Writer, born in Limerick, Ireland. His novel, *The Collegians*, was published anonymously in 1829.

Griffin, Walter Burley (1736–1937) Architect and town planner, born in Maywood, IL. He designed the new federal capital of Australia, Canberra, and supervised the construction.

Griffith, Arthur (1872–1922) Irish nationalist politician, born in Dublin. In 1905 he founded *Sinn Féin*, editing it until 1915. He became an MP (1918–22), signed the peace treaty with Britain, and was a moderate president of the Dáil Eireann (1922).

Griffith, D(avid) W(ark) (1875–1948) Pioneer film director, born in Floydsfork, KY. He experimented with new techniques in photography and production, and produced two masterpieces, *The Birth of a Nation* (1915) and *Intolerance* (1916).

Griffith, Hugh (Emrys) (1912–80) Actor, born in Anglesey, Gwynedd. A colourful character actor, he won an Oscar for his performance in the motion picture *Ben Hur* (1959).

Griffith, Sir Richard John (1784–1878) Geologist and civil engineer, born in Dublin. As commissioner of valuations after the Irish Valuation Act of 1827 he created *Griffith's valuations* for country rate assessments.

Griffith, Samuel Walker (1845–1920) Judge, born in Merthyr Tydfil, Mid Glamorgan. He emigrated to Australia in 1854, played a major role in drafting the Australian Commonwealth Constitution, and became first Chief Justice of the High Court of Australia (1900–19).

Griffiths, James (1890–1975) British statesman and miners' leader, born in Bettws, Gwent. A leading official in the miners' union in South Wales, he was elected Labour MP for Llanelli (1936–70), and became the first secretary of state for Wales (1964–6).

Griffiths, Trevor (1935–93) Playwright, born in Manchester. His social dramas include *The Party* (1973), *Comedians* (1975), and *Real Dreams* (1987).

Grignard, (François Auguste) Victor [greenyah(r)] (1871–1935) Organic chemist, born in Cherbourg, France. He introduced the use of organo-magnesium compounds (*Grignard reagents*), which form the basis of the most valuable class of organic synthetic reactions, for which he shared the Nobel Prize for Chemistry in 1912.

Grigorovich, Yuri (Nikolayevich) [grigorovich] (1927–)

Dancer, artistic director, teacher, and choreographer, born in Leningrad. He became chief choreographer and artistic director of the Bolshoi Ballet in 1964.

Grigson, Geoffrey (Edward Harvey) (1905-85) Poet, critic, and editor, born in Pelynt, Cornwall. The founder of the influential magazine *New Verse* (1933-9), his works include *Collected Poems, 1924-62* (1963), essays, and anthologies.

Grillparzer, Franz [gril**pah**(r)tzer] (1791-1872) Dramatic poet, born in Vienna. His tragedies include *The Ancestress* (trans, 1817). He also wrote one comedy, as well as lyric poetry and a novel.

Grimald, Nicholas (1519-62) Poet and playwright, born in Cambridgeshire. He contributed 40 poems to Tottel's *Songes and Sonettes* (1557), known as *Tottel's Miscellany*. >> Tottel

Grimké sisters [**grim**kay] Abolitionists and feminists: **Sarah Moore Grimké** (1792-1873) and **Angelina Emily Grimké** (1805-79), born to a major slaveholding family in Charleston, SC. The sisters rejected their family's way of life, and joined the Quakers, becoming prominent figures.

Grimm brothers Folklorists and philologists: **Jacob Ludwig Carl Grimm** (1785-1863) and **Wilhelm Carl Grimm** (1786-1859), both born in Hanau, Germany. They are best known for *Grimm's Fairy Tales* (trans, 3 vols, 1812-22). Jacob's *Germanic Grammar* (trans, 1819, revised 1822-40) is perhaps the greatest philological work of the age; he also formulated *Grimm's law* of sound changes.

Grimmelshausen, Hans Jacob Christoph von [**grim**els-howzen] (c.1622-76) Writer, born in Gelnhausen, Germany. In later life he wrote a series of novels, the best of them on the model of the Spanish picaresque romances, such as the *Simplicissimus* series (1669-72).

Grimond (of Firth), Jo(seph) Grimond, Baron [**grim**uhnd] (1913-93) British politician, born in St Andrews, Fife. Elected leader of the Liberal Party (1956-67), he was largely responsible for the modernizing of Liberalism, and called for a 'realignment of the left' in British politics.

Grimthorpe, Edmund Beckett Denison Grimthorpe, Baron (1816-1905) Lawyer, and authority on architecture and horology, born at Carlton Hall, Nottinghamshire. He helped to design the clock for the tower of the Houses of Parliament, and also for St Paul's Cathedral.

Grinnell, George Bird [gri**nel**] (1849-1938) Naturalist and author, born in Brooklyn, NY. As editor-in-chief (1880-1911) with *Forest and Stream* magazine, he made it the country's leading natural history journal.

Grinnell, Henry (1799-1874) Shipping merchant, born in New Bedford, MA. He financed Arctic expeditions to search for Sir John Franklin in 1850 and 1853-5. *Grinnell Land* is named after him. >> Franklin, John

Gris, Juan [grees], pseudonym of *José Victoriano Gonzàlez* (1887-1927) Painter, born in Madrid. He went to Paris and became one of the most logical and consistent exponents of Synthetic Cubism, seen in *Still Life with Dice* (1922).

Grivas, Georgeios (Theodoros) [**gree**vas] (1898-1974) Greek political leader, born in Trikomo, Cyprus. In 1955 he became head of the underground campaign against British rule in Cyprus (EOKA). In 1971, as leader of EOKA-B, he directed a terrorist campaign for *enosis* (union with Greece) until his death.

Grock, stage name of **Charles Adrien Wettach** (1880-1959) Clown, world-famous for his virtuosity in both circus and theatre, born in Reconvilier, Switzerland. He was particularly known for his clowning with musical instruments, especially using the violin and piano.

Grofé, Ferde [**groh**fay] (1892-1972) Composer, born in New York City. Known for a number of orchestral suites, he also orchestrated *Rhapsody in Blue* for Gershwin. >> Gershwin, George

Grolier (de Servières), Jean, vicomte d' (Viscount of) **Aguisy** [groh**lyay**] (1479-1565) Bibliophile, born in Lyon. He became treasurer-general of France (1547), and built up a magnificent library of 3000 volumes.

Gromyko, Andrei Andreevich [gro**mee**koh] (1909-89) Soviet president (1985-8), born near Minsk, Russia. As longest-serving foreign minister (1957-85), he was responsible for conducting Soviet relations with the West during the Cold War.

Grooms, Red, popular name of **Charles Roger Grooms** (1937-) Sculptor, painter, and performance artist, born in Nashville, TN. He founded Ruckus Productions (1963), a multi-media environmental and performance company, and is known for his lifesize installations and impromptu happenings.

Groot, Huig de >> **Grotius, Hugo**

Groote, Geert de [groht], Lat **Gerardus Magnus** (1340-84) Priest and reformer, born in Deventer, The Netherlands. He founded c.1376 the 'Brethren of Common Life', a teaching order evolved from a centre established to copy manuscripts.

Gropius, Walter (Adolph) [**groh**pius] (1883-1969) Architect, born in Berlin. He was appointed director of the Grand Ducal group of schools of art in Weimar, which he reorganized to form the Bauhaus, moving to Dessau in 1925. When Hitler came to power he went to London (1934-7), and then to the USA.

Gros, Antoine Jean, Baron [groh] (1771-1835) Historical painter, born in Paris. His works, such as 'Charles V and Francis I' (1812) and 'Embarkation of the Duchess of Angoulême' (1815), combine Classicism and Romanticism.

Grose, Francis [grohs] (1731-91) Antiquary, born in Greenford, Greater London. His works include *Antiquities of England and Wales* (1773-87) and *A Classical Dictionary of the Vulgar Tongue* (1785).

Grosman, Tatyana [**grohs**man], *née* **Auguschewitsch** (1904-82) Printmaker, born in Yekaterinburg, Ukraine. She and her husband Maurice Grosman emigrated to New York City (1943), where she founded the Universal Limited Art Editions workshop in East Islip, Long Island (1957).

Gross, Chaim (1904-91) Sculptor and teacher, born in Wolow, Poland. He emigrated to New York City in 1921, and became known for his wood and stone Expressionistic figures, such as 'Strong Woman' (1935).

Gross, Michael [grohs], nickname **the Albatross** (1964-) Swimmer, born in Frankfurt, Germany. In 1981-7 he won a record 13 gold medals at the European Championships. He has won three Olympic gold medals: the 100 m butterfly and 200 m freestyle in 1984, and the 200 m butterfly in 1988.

Grosseteste, Robert [**grohs**test] (c.1175-1253) Scholar, bishop, and Church reformer, born in Stradbroke, Suffolk. Appointed Bishop of Lincoln in 1235, he undertook the reformation of abuses in the Church, which brought him into conflict both locally and with the papacy.

Grossmith, George [**groh**smith] (1847-1912) Comedian and entertainer, born in London. With his brother, **Weedon Grossmith** (1853-1919), he wrote *Diary of a Nobody* in *Punch* (1892). His son, **George Grossmith** (1874-1935) was a well-known musical-comedy actor, songwriter, and theatrical manager.

Grosz, George [grohs] (1893-1959) Artist, born in Berlin. Associated with the Berlin Dadaists (1917-18), he produced a series of bitter, ironic drawings attacking German militarism and the middle classes, and fled to the USA in 1932.

Grosz, Karoly [grohs] (1930-) Hungarian prime minister (1987-8), born in Miskolc, Hungary. He joined the ruling Hungarian Socialist Workers' Party (HSWP) Politburo in 1985, and sought to establish in Hungary a new system of 'socialist pluralism'.

Grotius, Hugo [**groh**shius], also found as **Huig de Groot** (1583–1645) Jurist and theologian, born in Delft, The Netherlands. In 1625 he published his great work on international law, *On the Law of War and Peace* (trans title).

Grotowski, Jerzy [gro**tof**skee] (1933–) Theatre director, teacher, and drama theorist, born in Rzeszów, Poland. His work had a major impact on experimental theatre and actor training in the West during the 1960s and 1970s.

Grouchy, Emmanuel, Marquis de [grooshee] (1766–1847) French Napoleonic soldier, born in Paris. On Napoleon's escape from Elba, he destroyed the Bourbon opposition in the S of France, and helped to rout Blücher at Ligny, but failed to play an effective part at Waterloo due to misleading orders (1815). >> Blücher

Grove, Sir George (1820–1900) Musicologist, born in London. His major work was as editor of the *Dictionary of Music and Musicians* (1878–89).

Grove, Sir William Robert (1811–96) Lawyer and physicist, born in Swansea, West Glamorgan. In 1842 he made the first fuel cell, generating electric current from a chemical reaction using gases, and in 1845 the first filament lamp.

Groves, Sir Charles (1915–92) Conductor, born in London. His various posts included musical director of the Welsh and English National Operas (1961–3 and 1978–9 respectively) and president of the National Youth Orchestra (1977–92).

Grubb, Sir Kenneth (George) (1900–80) Anglican missionary and ecumenist, born in Oxton, Nottinghamshire. He became president of the Church Missionary Society (1944–69), and chairman of the House of Laity in the Church Assembly (1959–70).

Gruen, David >> **Ben-Gurion, David**

Gruenberg, Louis [**groon**berg] (1884–1964) Composer, born near Brest-Litovsk, Belarus. He wrote extensively for orchestra, chamber music combinations, and voices, but is best known for his opera *The Emperor Jones*, based on Eugene O'Neill's play.

Grumman, Leroy (Randle) (1895–1982) Engineer and aircraft pioneer, born in Huntington, NY. He formed his own company, producing a series of navy aircraft during World War 2, jet fighters after the war, and the Lunar Excursion Module for the Apollo flights to the Moon.

Grundtvig, N(ikolai) F(rederik) S(everin) [**grunt**vig] (1783–1872) Theologian and poet, born in Udby, Denmark. His ideas led to the creation of Folk High Schools, and he is also known as the greatest Scandinavian hymn writer.

Gruner, Elioth [**groo**ner] (1882–1939) Painter, born in Gisborne, New Zealand. His best work captures the special quality of the Australian light, and he is regarded as one of Australia's leading landscape artists.

Grünewald, Matthias [grünevalt], originally **Mathis Gothardt** (?1470–1528) Artist, architect, and engineer, probably born in Würzburg, Germany. In 1516 he completed the great Isenheim altarpiece (Colmar Museum).

Guardi, Francesco [**gwah(r)**dee] (1712–93) Painter, born in Venice, Italy. He was noted for his views of Venice, full of sparkling colour, with an Impressionist's eye for effects of light, as in the 'View of the Church and Piazza of San Marco' (National Gallery, London).

Guardia, Fiorello H La >> **La Guardia, Fiorello H**

Guare, John [gwah(r)] (1938–) Playwright, born in New York City. His first success came with *The House of Blue Leaves* (1970). He wrote several plays for Joseph Papp's Public Theater, and had his second major hit with *Six Degrees of Separation* (1990). >> Papp

Guareschi, Giovanni [gwa**res**kee] (1908–68) Writer and

journalist, born in Parma, Italy. He achieved fame with his stories of the village priest, beginning with *The Little World of Don Camillo* (1950).

Guarini, Guarino [gwa**ree**nee], originally **Camillo Guarini** (1642–83) Architect, philosopher, and mathematician, born in Modena, Italy. He designed several churches in Turin, and the Palazzo Carignano (1679), considered his masterpiece. He was responsible for the spread of the Baroque style beyond Italy.

Guarnieri [gwah(r)**nyay**ree], also found as **Giuseppe Guarneri**, known as **Giuseppe del Gesù** (1687–1745) Celebrated violin maker from Cremona, Italy. He was the nephew of **Andrea Guarnieri** (fl.1628–98) who, with his two sons **Giuseppe Guarnieri** (fl.1690–1730) and **Pietro Guarnieri** (fl.1690–1725), also made quality instruments.

Guderian, Heinz (Wilhelm) [gu**der**ian] (1888–1954) German soldier, born in Kulm, Germany. A leading tank expert and exponent of the *Blitzkrieg* theory, he created the panzer armies which overran Poland in 1939 and France in 1940.

Guedella, Philip [gwe**da**la] (1889–1944) Writer, born in London. The most popular historian of his time, his works include *Palmerston* (1926), *The Hundred Days* (1934), and *Middle East* (1944).

Guercino, Il [eel gwer**chee**noh], nickname of **Giovanni Francesco Barbieri** (1591–1666) Painter, born in Cento, Italy. His major work is the ceiling fresco 'Aurora' at the Villa Ludovisi in Rome. After 1642 he became the leading painter of the Bolognese school.

Guericke, Otto von [**gay**rikuh] (1602–86) Physicist, born in Magdeburg, Germany. He improved a water pump so that it would exhaust air from a container, and was able with this air pump to give dramatic demonstrations of pressure reduction (the *Magdeburg hemispheres*).

Guérin, Camille >> **Calmette, Albert**

Guérin, (Georges) Maurice de [gayrĩ] (1810–39) Poet, born in the Château du Cayla, France. He wrote two major poems, *La Bacchante* and *Le Centaure*. A Guérin cult arose after his death, resulting in the publication of everything he had written.

Guérin, Pierre Narcisse, Baron [gayrĩ] (1774–1833) Historical painter, born in Paris. A skilful painter of Classical subjects, but inclined to melodrama, he became director of the French Academy of Painting in Rome (1822–8).

Guesclin, Bertrand du [gayklĩ] (c.1320–80) French knight and military leader during the Hundred Years' War, born in La Motte-Broons, France. On becoming Constable of France (1370) he assumed command of the French armies, reconquering Brittany and most of SW France.

Guest, George >> **Sequoia**

Guevara, Che [gay**vah**ra], popular name of **Ernesto Guevara (de la Serna)** (1928–67) Revolutionary leader, born in Rosario, Argentina. He was prominent in the Cuban revolution (1956–9), and left Cuba in 1965 to become a guerrilla leader in South America. He was captured and executed in Bolivia. >> Castro

Guggenheim, Meyer [**gu**genhiym] (1828–1905) Financier, born in Langnau, Switzerland. He emigrated to the USA in 1848, and formed the Philadelphia Smelting and Refining Co. His seven sons carried on his tradition of business success and philanthropy. >> Guggenheim, Solomon R

Guggenheim, Marguerite [**gu**genhiym], known as **Peggy** (1898–1979) Art collector and patron, born in New York City, the niece of Solomon R Guggenheim. She established art galleries in London, New York City, and Venice, eventually donating her collection to the Solomon R Guggenheim Foundation. She was married to Max Ernst (1941–6). >> Ernst, Max; Guggenheim, Solomon R

Guggenheim, Solomon R(obert) [**gu**genhiym] (1861–

1949) Businessman and art collector, born in Philadelphia, PA, the son of Meyer Guggenheim. He collected Modernist paintings and established the Solomon R Guggenheim Foundation (1937), which later financed the Solomon R Guggenheim Museum, designed in 1959. >> Guggenheim, Meyer / Peggy

Guicciardini, Francesco [gwichiah(r)deenee] (1483–1540) Historian, born in Florence, Italy. He practised as an advocate, but his real field was diplomacy, and he served as a papal governor. His *Storia d'Italia* was an analytical history of Italy from 1494 to 1532.

Guidi, Tommaso >> **Masaccio**

Guido d'Arezzo [gweedoh daretzoh], also known as **Guido Aretino** (c.990–c.1050) Benedictine monk and musical theorist, probably born in Arezzo, Italy. The invention of the musical staff is ascribed to him, and he introduced the system of naming the notes of a scale with syllables.

Guido di Pietro >> **Angelico, Fra**

Guilbert, Yvette [geelbair] (1867–1944) Comedienne of stage and screen, born in Paris. She won fame for her songs and sketches of Parisian life, and after 1890 became known for her revivals of old French ballads.

Guillaume, Charles Edouard [geeohm] (1861–1938) Physicist, born in Fleurier, Switzerland. He discovered a nickel-steel alloy, 'Invar', which does not expand significantly and can therefore be used in precision instruments and standard measures. He was awarded the Nobel Prize for Physics in 1920.

Guillaume de Lorris [geeyohm duh loris] (c.1200–?) Poet, born in France - his surname derives from a village near Orléans. He wrote, before 1260, the first c.4000 lines of the encyclopedic *Roman de la Rose* - an allegory which was widely influential in mediaeval Europe. >> Jean de Meung

Guillaume de Machaut [geeyohm duh mashoh] (c.1300–77) Poet and musician, born possibly in Reims, France. One of the creators of the harmonic art, he wrote a Mass, motets, songs, ballads, and organ music. His poetry greatly influenced Chaucer. >> Chaucer

Guillemin, Roger C(harles) L(ouis) [geelmin] (1924–) Physiologist, born in Dijon, France. He shared the 1977 Nobel Prize for Physiology or Medicine for his work on the isolation of peptide hormones of the hypothalamus.

Guillotin, Joseph Ignace [geeyohti] (1738–1814) Physician and revolutionary, born in Saintes, France. He proposed to the Constituent Assembly, of which he was a deputy, the use of a decapitating instrument as a means of execution. This was adopted in 1791 and named after him (the *guillotine*).

Guimard, Hector Germain [geemah(r)] (1867–1942) Architect, born in Lyon, France. He was the most important Art Nouveau architect active in Paris between 1890 and 1914, best known for the Paris Métro cast-iron entrances of the early 1900s.

Guimerá, Angel [geemayra] (1847–1924) Poet and playwright, born in Santa Cruz, Canary Is. He is regarded as the greatest Catalan dramatist, and a major influence in the movement to revive Catalan literature. His most famous play is *Martha of the Lowlands* (trans, 1896).

Guin, Ursula Le >> **Le Guin, Ursula**

Guinness, Sir Alec (1914–) Actor, born in London. Among his notable films are *Kind Hearts and Coronets* (1949), *The Lavender Hill Mob* (1951), and *The Bridge on the River Kwai* (1958, Oscar). Later roles include Ben Kenobi in the *Star Wars* series, and Smiley in the television version of Le Carré's novels (1979, 1982).

Guinness, Sir Benjamin Lee (1798–1868) Brewer, born in Dublin, the grandson of **Arthur Guinness** (1725–1803), the founder of Guinness's Brewery (1759). Under him the brand of stout became famous, and the business grew into the largest of its kind in the world.

Guiscard, Robert [geeskah(r)] (c.1015–85) Norman adventurer, the son of Tancred de Hauteville. He campaigned with his brothers against the Byzantine Greeks, created a duchy comprising S Italy and Sicily, and defeated Alexius Comnenus at Durazzo (1081). >> Alexius I

Guise, Claude of Lorraine, 1er duc de (1st Duke of) [geez] (1496–1550) French nobleman and soldier, born in the château of Condé-sur-Moselle, France. He defended France against the English (1522), and defeated the army of the Holy Roman Emperor, Charles V, at Neufchâteau. >> Guise, 2e duc; Guise, Mary of Lorraine

Guise, Francis, 2e duc de (2nd Duke of) [geez], known as **le Balafré** ('the Scarred') (1519–63) French soldier and statesman, son of Claude, 1st Duke of Guise. He and his brother, **Cardinal Charles of Guise** (1525–74), shared the chief power in the state during the reign of Francis II (1559–60). He was assassinated while besieging Orléans. >> Guise, 1er duc

Guise, Henri, 3e duc de (3rd Duke of) [geez] (1550–88) French soldier and statesman, the son of Francis, 2nd Duke of Guise, known as **le Balafré** like his father. He fought against the Protestants, and contrived in the massacre on St Bartholomew's Day (1572). Henry III procured his assassination. >> Guise, 2e duc; Henry III (of France)

Guise, Mary of [geez], also known as **Mary of Lorraine** (1515–60) Daughter of Claude of Lorraine, 1st Duke of Guise. In 1538 she married James V of Scotland, at whose death (1542) she was left with a child, Mary, Queen of Scots. >> Guise, 1er duc; James V; Mary, Queen of Scots

Guitry, Sacha [geetree], originally **Alexandre Georges Guitry** (1885–1957) Actor and playwright, born in St Petersburg, Russia, the son of French actor-manager **Lucien Guitry** (1860–1925). He wrote nearly 100 plays, mostly light comedies, and directed several films.

Guizot, François (Pierre Guillaume) [geezoh] (1787–1874) Historian and statesman, born in Nîmes, France. Under Louis XVIII, he was minister of the interior (1830), and of public instruction (1832). He promoted reactionary methods of government, and escaped to London with Louis-Philippe in 1848. >> Louis XVIII; Louis-Philippe

Gulbenkian, Calouste (Sarkis) [gulbengkian] (1869–1955) Financier, industrialist, and diplomat, born in Scutari, Turkey. He entered his father's oil business in 1888, and after a lifetime of deals between Europe, the USA, and the Arab countries, financed an international Gulbenkian Foundation.

Guldberg, Cato Maximilian (1836–1902) Chemist and mathematician, born in Oslo, Norway. With his brother-in-law, **Peter Waage** (1833–1900), he formulated the chemical law of mass action (1864) governing the speed of reaction and the relative concentrations of the reactants.

Gumilev, Nikolay Stepanovich [gumeelyef] (1886–1921) Russian poet, a leader of the Acmeist school which revolted against Symbolism. His exotic and vivid poems include *The Quiver* (1915), *The Pyre*, and *The Pillar of Fire*, which contain his best pieces. His wife was Anna Akhmatova. >> Akhmatova

Gumm, Frances >> **Garland, Judy**

Gundelach, Finn Olav [gundelach] (1925–81) Danish diplomat, born in Vejle, Denmark. He became Denmark's first European commissioner. In 1977 he was made vice-president of the new European Commission, and was given charge of the Common Agricultural Policy.

Gundulf (1024–1108) Norman churchman, and Bishop of Rochester (from 1077). He followed Lanfranc to England, built the Tower of London, rebuilt Rochester cathedral, and founded St Bartholomew's hospital in Chatham. >> Lanfranc

Gunn, Neil (Miller) (1891–1973) Novelist, born in Dunbeath, Highland. His books include *The Silver Darlings* (1941), *Bloodhunt* (1952), and *The Other Landscape* (1954).

Gunn, Thom(son William) (1929–) Poet, born in Gravesend, Kent. His often erotic poems are written in an intriguing variety of regular and free forms. Volumes include *Jack Straw's Castle* (1976) and *The Man With Night Sweats* (1992).

Gunnarsson, Gunnar (1889–1975) Novelist, born in Valthjófsstadur, Iceland. His best-selling book *From the Annals of the House of Borg* (trans, 1912–14), was the first Icelandic work to be turned into a feature film. His masterpiece was the autobiographical novel, *The Church on the Mountain* (trans, 5 vols, 1923–8).

Gunter, Edmund (1581–1626) Mathematician and astronomer, born in Hertfordshire. He invented many measuring instruments that bear his name - *Gunter's chain*, *line*, *scale*, and *quadrant* - and introduced the terms *cosine* and *cotangent* into trigonometry.

Gunther, John (1901–70) Writer and journalist, born in Chicago, IL. He established his reputation with the best-selling *Inside Europe* (1936), following this with several other social and political studies.

Gurevich, Mikhail Iosifovich [gooryayvich] (1893–1976) Aircraft designer, born in Rubanshchina, Russia. He was best known for the fighter aircraft produced by the design bureau he headed with Mikoyan, the MiG (from 'Mikoyan and Gurevich') series. >> Mikoyan

Gurley Brown, Helen (1922–) US writer and editor, born in Arkansas. Her first book, *Sex and the Single Girl* (1962), became a best seller. Made editor of *Cosmopolitan* in 1965, she transformed the struggling magazine into an international journal.

Gurney, Edmund (1847–88) Psychical researcher, born in Hersham, Surrey. He conducted important experimental studies of hypnosis and telepathy, a statistical survey of hallucinations, and wrote the classic *Phantasms of the Living* (with F W H Myers and F Podmore, 1886).

Gurney, Sir Goldsworthy (1793–1875) Inventor, born in Treator, Cornwall. He built a steam-powered carriage, and also improved the lighting and ventilation in the House of Commons.

Gurney, Ivor (1890–1937) Composer and poet, born in Gloucester, Gloucestershire. Gassed and shell-shocked in 1917, he published two volumes of poems from hospital: *Severn and Somme* (1917) and *War's Embers* (1919).

Gustafsson, Greta Lovisa >> **Garbo, Greta**

Gustav I, originally **Gustav Eriksson Vasa** (1496–1560) King of Sweden (1523–60), the founder of the Vasa dynasty, born in Lindholmen, Sweden. He led a peasant rising against the occupying Danes, capturing Stockholm (1523) and driving the enemy from Sweden.

Gustav II Adolf or **Gustavus Adolphus** (1594–1632) King of Sweden (1611–32), born in Stockholm, the son of Charles IX. He recovered his Baltic provinces from Denmark, ended wars with Russia (1617) and Poland (1629), and carried out military and economic reforms. In 1630 he entered the Thirty Years' War, but was killed at Lützen.

Gustav III (1746–92) King of Sweden (1771–92). He reasserted royal power, encouraged agriculture, commerce, and science, and granted religious toleration, but also created a secret police system and introduced censorship. He was shot by a former army officer.

Gustav IV Adolf (1778–1837) King of Sweden (1792–1809), the son of Gustav III. He joined the European coalition against Napoleon in 1805, but his policies provoked a military coup, and he went into exile in 1809.

Gustav V (1858–1950) King of Sweden (1907–50), born in Stockholm. He disliked pomp, and refused a coronation ceremony, thus becoming the first 'uncrowned king' on the Swedish throne.

Gustav VI Adolf (1882–1973) King of Sweden (1950–73), born in Stockholm, the son of Gustav V. He worked to

transform the crown into a democratic monarchy. He was succeeded by his grandson, Carl XVI Gustaf, his eldest son **Gustav Adolf** (1906–47) having been killed in an air-crash. >> Carl XVI Gustaf; Gustav V

Gustavus Adolphus >> **Gustav II Adolf**

Guston, Philip [guhstn] (1913–80) Painter, born in Montreal, Quebec, Canada. His work of the 1950s was in the Abstract Expressionist style, but from the late 1960s he introduced brightly coloured and crudely drawn comic-strip characters into his painting.

Gutenberg, Beno [gootenberg] (1889–1960) Geophysicist, born in Darmstadt, Germany. In 1913 he proposed that data on earthquake shock waves can be interpreted as showing that the Earth's core is liquid, a novel idea now fully accepted. The *Gutenberg discontinuity* is named after him.

Gutenberg, Johannes (Gensfleisch) [gootnberg] (1400–68) Printer, regarded as the inventor of printing from movable type, born in Mainz, Germany. He entered into a partnership with Johann Fust who financed a printing press, but Fust later sued him for repayment of the loan and reclaimed the machinery. His best-known book is the *Gutenberg Bible* (c.1455). >> Fust

Guthlac, St [guthlak] (c.673–714), feast day 11 April. English monk at Repton, Derbyshire in 697, and a hermit at Crowland Abbey in 699, where he lived a life of severe asceticism.

Guthorm or **Guthrum** (?–890) Danish king of East Anglia. He led a major Viking invasion of England in 871 (the 'Great Summer Army'), conquering East Anglia, Northumbria, and Mercia, but was defeated by Alfred at Edington. >> Alfred

Guthrie, Woody, popular name of **Woodrow Wilson Guthrie** (1912–67) Folksinger and songwriter, born in Okemah, OK. He took to the road during the Great Depression, and wrote hundreds of songs, lauding migrant workers, pacifists, and underdogs of all kinds, such as 'So Long, It's Been Good to Know You' and 'This Land is Your Land'.

Guthrie, Sir (William) Tyrone (1900–71) Theatrical director, born in Tunbridge Wells, Kent. He was responsible for many fine productions of Shakespeare during the 1930s, and became administrator of the Old Vic and Sadler's Wells (1939–45), and director of the Old Vic (1950–1).

Guthrie, Thomas Anstey >> **Anstey, F**

Guthrum >> **Guthorm**

Gutiérrez, Gustavo [gootyaires] (1928–) Liberation theologian and priest, born in Lima, Peru. His theology is based on responding to the needs of the poor and oppressed rather than on imposing solutions from the outside, as seen in *A Theology of Liberation* (1971).

Guttuso, Renato [gutoosoh] (1912–87) Artist, born in Palermo, Italy. He was associated with various anti-Fascist groups (1942–5), and much of his work reflects this experience. He later painted dramatic Realist pictures of the lives of Italian peasants.

Guy, Thomas [giy] (c.1644–1724) Philanthropist, born in London. In 1707 he built and furnished three wards of St Thomas' Hospital, and in 1722 founded the hospital in Southwark which bears his name.

Guy de Lusignan [gee, looseenyä] (?–1194) French crusader. He became King of Jerusalem in 1186, but was captured by Saladin (1187). He ceded the throne to Richard I of England in 1192, and in exchange received Cyprus, where his family ruled until 1474. >> Richard I; Saladin

Guy of Arezzo >> **Guido d'Arezzo**

Guyon, Jeanne Marie de la Motte [geeyö], *née* **Bouvier** (1648–1717) Mystic, born in Montargis, France. Widowed at 28, she devoted her life to the poor, and to the cultivation of spiritual perfection. Settling in Paris, she was arrested for heretical opinions, but released by the intervention of Mme de Maintenon. >> Maintenon

Guyot, Arnold Henry [geeyoh] (1807–84) Geographer, born in Boudevilliers, Switzerland. In 1848 he emigrated to the USA, and was in charge of the meteorological department of the Smithsonian Institution. His name is preserved in the term *guyot*, a type of sub-ocean mountain.

Gwyn or **Gwynne, Nell**, popular name of **Eleanor Gwyn** (c.1650–87) Mistress of Charles II, possibly born in London. Originally an orange girl, she established herself as a comedienne at Drury Lane. She had at least one son by the king - Charles Beauclerk, Duke of St Albans. >> Charles II (of England)

Gwynne-Vaughan, Dame Helen Charlotte Isabella [gwin **vawn**], *née* **Fraser** (1879–1967) Botanist and service-woman. In World War 1 she was commandant of the Women's Royal Auxiliary Air Force (1918–19), and in World War 2 was chief controller of the Women's Auxiliary Territorial Service (1939–41).

Gyllenhammar, Pehr Gustaf [gülenhamer] (1935–   ) Industrialist, born in Gothenburg, Sweden. He joined the Volvo Motor Co in 1970, becoming managing director (1971–83), chairman (1983–90), and executive chairman.

Gyp [zhip], pseudonym of **Sibylle-Gabrielle-Marie-Antoinette comtesse de Mirabeau de Martel de Joinvil** (1849–1932) Novelist, born at the château of Koëtsal, Brittany, France. She wrote a series of humorous novels, of which the best known are *Petit Bob* (1882) and *Mariage de Chiffon* (1894).

Haakon VII [hawkon] (1872–1957) King of Norway (1905–57), born in Charlottenlund, Denmark. He became king when Norway voted herself independent of Sweden in 1905, and emerged as the 'people's king'.

Haas, Earle C (1885–1981) US doctor who invented the tampon. A physician in Denver, in 1936 he adapted a surgical cotton plug for use as an intravaginal sanitary towel marketing it under the name Tampax.

Hába, Alois [hahba, aloys] (1893–1973) Composer, born in Vyzovice, Czech Republic. A prolific composer, his works include an opera, *The Mother*, and orchestral, chamber, and piano music.

Haber, Fritz [haber] (1868–1934) Chemist, born in Breslau, Germany. He became known for his invention of the process for making ammonia from the nitrogen in the air. He was awarded the Nobel Prize for Chemistry in 1918.

Habermas, Jürgen [habermas] (1929–) Philosopher and social theorist, born in Düsseldorf, Germany. Director of the Max Planck Institute from 1971, his books include *Knowledge and Human Interests* (trans, 1968) and *Theory of Communicative Action* (trans, 1982).

Habib, Philip C(harles) [habeeb] (1920–92) US diplomat, born in New York City. Under-secretary of state for political affairs (1976–8), he became President Reagan's personal representative to the Middle East (1981–3), where he negotiated for an end to the crisis in Lebanon. >> Reagan

Hácha, Emil [hakha] (1872–1945) Czech president (1938–9), born in Trhové Sviny, Bohemia. He was forced to make over the state to Hitler (1939), and became puppet president of the German protectorate of Bohemia and Moravia (1939–45). >> Hitler

Hackett, Sir John Winthrop (1910–) British soldier and academic. His post-war commands culminated in commander-in-chief, British Army of the Rhine, and of the Northern Army Group in 1966, and he became principal of King's College, London (1968–75).

Hackworth, Timothy (1786–1850) Locomotive engineer, born in Wylam, Northumbria. He built a number of famous engines, including the *Royal George* and the *Sans Pareil*, rival of Stephenson's *Rocket*. >> Stephenson, George

Hadamard, Jacques (Salomon) [adamah(r)] (1865–1963) Mathematician, born in Versailles, France. He worked on complex function theory, differential geometry, and partial differential equations. In 1896 he and Charles Jean de la Vallée Poussin independently proved the definitive form of the prime-number theorem.

Hadas, Moses [hadahs] (1890–1966) Classicist and translator, born in Atlanta, GA. His best-known publications include *History of Greek Literature* (1950) and *History of Latin Literature* (1952).

Hadden, Briton >> Luce, Henry R

Haddon, Alfred Cort (1855–1940) Anthropologist, born in London. He organized the Cambridge Anthropological Expedition to the Torres Straits (1898–9), in which were developed the basic techniques of modern anthropology.

Hadfield, Maria >> Cosway, Richard

Hadfield, Sir Robert Abbot (1858–1940) Metallurgist and industrialist, born in Sheffield, South Yorkshire. He developed manganese steel, an alloy of exceptional durability with many applications in industry.

Hadlee, Sir Richard (John) (1951–) Cricketer, born in Christchurch, New Zealand. New Zealand's best all-round cricketer, he made his Test debut in 1973, scored 3124 Test runs, and 431 Test wickets, before retiring in 1990.

Hadley, John (1682–1744) Mathematician, born in Hertfordshire. He developed improvements to the Gregorian reflecting telescope, making it into an accurate instrument for use in astronomy. He also designed a double-reflecting quadrant which became the basis for the sextant.

Hadley, Patrick (Arthur Sheldon) (1899–1973) Composer, born in Cambridge, Cambridgeshire. Professor of music at Cambridge (1946–62), he wrote his most significant work, the choral symphony *The Hills*, in 1946.

Hadow, Sir William Henry [hadoh] (1859–1937) Scholar, educational administrator, and musicologist, born in Ebrington, Gloucestershire. He was a leading influence in English education at all levels in the 1920s and 1930s, as seen in his report *The Education of the Adolescent* (1926).

Hadrian [haydrian], in full **Publius Aelius Hadrianus** (76–138) Roman emperor (117–38), ward, protégé, and successor of the Emperor Trajan. He spent most of his reign touring the empire, consolidating frontiers, and promoting urban life. In Britain he initiated the building of the wall named after him. >> Trajan

Haeckel, Ernst (Heinrich Philipp August) [haykl] (1834–1919) Naturalist, born in Potsdam, Germany. One of the first to sketch the genealogical tree of animals, he strongly supported Darwin's theories of evolution. >> Darwin, Charles

Hafiz or **Hafez**, pseudonym of **Shams-ed-Din Mohammad** (c.1326–c.1390) Lyrical poet, born in Shiraz, Iran. A member of the mystical sect of Sufi philosophers, his short poems (*ghazals*), all on sensuous subjects, contain an esoteric signification to the initiated.

Hagar [haygah(r)] Biblical character, the maid of Sarah (the wife of Abraham). Due to Sarah's barrenness, Abraham had a son Ishmael by Hagar (*Gen* 16), but Hagar and her son were later expelled into the wilderness by Abraham after Isaac's birth (*Gen* 21). >> Abraham

Hagen, Walter (Charles) [haygn], nickname **the Haig** (1892–1969) Golfer, born in Rochester, NY. At the age of 21 he won the US Open (1914), the first of his 11 major championship titles.

Haggard, Sir H(enry) Rider (1856–1925) Novelist, born at Bradenham Hall, Norfolk. *King Solomon's Mines* (1885) made his work known, and was followed by *She* (1887) and several other stories.

Hahn, Kurt (Matthias Robert Martin) (1886–1974) Educationist, born in Berlin. He founded Gordonstoun School in Grampian (Scotland) in 1934, emphasizing physical rather than intellectual activities in education.

Hahn, Otto (1879–1968) Physical chemist, born in Frankfurt, Germany. With Meitner he discovered the radioactive element protactinium (1917), and in 1938 found the first chemical evidence of nuclear fission products. He was awarded the Nobel Prize for Chemistry in 1944. >> Meitner

Hahnemann, (Christian Friedrich) Samuel [hahnuhman] (1755–1843) Physician and founder of homeopathy, born in Meissen, Germany. He observed that a medicine administered to a healthy person produced similar symptoms to those of the illness it was intended to cure, and developed his law of 'similars', around which he built his system of homeopathy.

Haidar Ali [hiyder alee], also spelled **Hyder Ali** (1722–82) Muslim ruler of Mysore, born in Budikote, India. He waged two wars against the British, in the first of which

(1767–9) he won several gains; but in 1781–2 he was defeated. >> Tippoo Sahib

Haig, Alexander (Meigs) [hayg] (1924–) US army officer and statesman, born in Philadelphia, PA. A full general by 1973, he became White House chief-of-staff during the last days of the Nixon presidency. He served Reagan as secretary of state (1981–2), and sought the Republican nomination for the presidency in 1988. >> Nixon, Richard M; Reagan

Haig (of Bemersyde), Douglas Haig, 1st Earl [hayg] (1861–1928) British field marshal, born in Edinburgh. In 1915 he became commander of the British Expeditionary Force, waging a costly war of attrition, for which he was much criticized.

Haile Selassie I [hiylee selasee], originally **Prince Ras Tafari Makonnen** (1891–1975) Emperor of Ethiopia (1930–6, 1941–74), born near Harer, Ethiopia. He led the revolution in 1916 against Lij Yasu, and became regent and heir to the throne, westernizing the institutions of his country. The disastrous famine of 1973 led to his deposition, but he is still held in reverence by many, notably by Rastafarians.

Hailey, Arthur (1920–) Novelist, born in Luton, Bedfordshire. He became a naturalized Canadian in 1947. He has written many best-selling blockbusters about disasters, several of which have become highly successful films, such as *Airport* (1968) and *Wheels* (1971).

Hailsham, Quintin (McGarel) Hogg, 2nd Viscount [haylsham] (1907–) British statesman, born in London. His many posts included chairman of the Conservative Party (1957–9), minister for science and technology (1959–64), secretary of state for education and science (1964), and Lord Chancellor (1970–4, 1979–87).

Hailwood, Mike, popular name of **Stanley Michael Bailey Hailwood** (1940–81) Motor-cyclist, born in Oxford, Oxfordshire. Between 1961 and 1967 he took nine world titles, and also won a record 14 Isle of Man Tourist Trophy races between 1961 and 1979.

Haitink, Bernard [hiytingk] (1929–) Conductor, born in Amsterdam. He conducted the Amsterdam Concertgebouw Orchestra (from 1961) and the London Philharmonic (1967–79), and was appointed musical director at Glyndebourne in 1977 and at Covent Garden in 1987.

Hakluyt, Richard [hakloot] (c.1552–1616) Geographer, born in Hertfordshire. He wrote widely on exploration, notably his *Principal Navigations, Voyages, and Discoveries of the English Nation* (1598–1600). The *Hakluyt Society* was instituted in 1846.

Halas, George (Stanley) (1895–1983) Founder, owner, and coach with the Chicago Bears American football team, born in Chicago, IL. After more than 40 years of coaching, his record showed 320 wins, 147 defeats, and 30 draws.

Halas, John [halas], original surname **Halasz** (1912–) Animated cartoon producer, born in Budapest. With his wife Joy Batchelor, he formed the Halas–Batchelor animation unit (1940), producing *Animal Farm* (1954), England's first full-length cartoon. >> Batchelor

Halasz, Gyula >> **Brassaï**

Haldane, Elizabeth Sanderson [holdayn] (1862–1937) Writer, born in Edinburgh, the sister of John Scott Haldane and Richard Burdon Haldane. She wrote a life of Descartes (1905) and edited his philosophical works, translated Hegel, and wrote commentaries on George Eliot (1927) and Mrs Gaskell (1930). >> Haldane, John Scott / Richard Burdon

Haldane, J(ohn) B(urdon) S(anderson) [holdayn] (1892–1964) Biologist and geneticist, born in Oxford, Oxfordshire, the son of John Scott Haldane. He became professor of genetics (1933–57) and of biometry (1937–57) at London, then emigrated to India, adopting Indian nationality. >> Haldane, John Scott

Haldane, John Scott [holdayn] (1860–1936) Physiologist, born in Edinburgh. He studied the effects of industrial occupations upon human physiology, especially respiration, and served as director of a mining research laboratory at Birmingham. >> Haldane, Elizabeth Sanderson / Richard Burdon

Haldane (of Cloan), Richard Burdon Haldane, 1st Viscount [holdayn] (1856–1928) Jurist, philosopher, and statesman, born in Edinburgh. He became a Liberal MP in 1885, and is best known for his period as secretary of state for war (1905–12), when he founded the Territorials. >> Haldane, Elizabeth Sanderson / John Scott

Hale, Edward Everett (1822–1909) Unitarian clergyman and writer, born in Roxbury, MA. He is best known for his story 'The Man Without a Country' (1863), which encouraged patriotism during the Civil War. His most popular novels were *In His Name* (1873) and *East and West* (1892).

Hale, George Ellery (1868–1938) Astronomer, born in Chicago, IL. He worked at Mt Wilson and Mt Palomar observatories, which later operated jointly (1948–80) as the Hale Observatories. His research led to the discovery of magnetic fields within sunspots.

Hale, Sir Matthew (1609–76) Judge, born in Alderley, Gloucestershire. In 1671 he became Chief Justice of the King's Bench. His works include a *History of the Common Law* (1713) and a *History of the Pleas of the Crown* (1736).

Hale, Nathan (1755–76) American revolutionary officer, hero, and martyr, born in Coventry, CT. He penetrated the British lines to obtain information, but was captured and hanged.

Hale, Sarah (Josepha), *née* **Buell** (1788–1879) Writer and first female magazine editor, born in Newport, NH. In 1828 she became editor of the *Ladies' Magazine*. Her best-known work was *Woman's Record: or Sketches of All Distinguished Women from 'the Beginning Till AD 1850* (1853–76).

Hales, Stephen (1677–1761) Botanist and chemist, born in Bekesbourne, Kent. His *Vegetable Staticks* (1727) was the foundation of plant physiology.

Halévy, (Jacques François) Fromental (Elié) [alayvee] (1799–1862) Composer, born in Paris. His first successful opera was *Clari* (1828), but he is best known for *La Juive* (1835), which established his reputation.

Halévy, Ludovic [alayvee] (1834–1908) Playwright and novelist, born in Paris. He produced vaudevilles and comedies, and with **Henri Meilhac** (1831–97) wrote libretti for the best-known operettas of Offenbach, and for Bizet's *Carmen.* >> Bizet; Offenbach

Haley, Bill, popular name of **William Haley** (1927–1981) Popular singer and musician, born in Highland Park, MI. With his group 'The Comets' he popularized rock-and-roll in the 1950s. His most famous song was 'Rock Around the Clock' (1955).

Haliburton, Thomas Chandler (1796–1865) Writer and jurist, born in Windsor, Nova Scotia, Canada. He is best known as the creator of 'Sam Slick', originally printed in the Halifax newspaper *Nova Scotian* (1835).

Halifax, Charles Montagu, 1st Earl of (1661–1715) English Whig statesman, born in Horton, Northamptonshire. He established the Bank of England (1694), and as Chancellor of the Exchequer (1694–5) introduced a new coinage. On George I's arrival (1714) he became prime minister.

Halifax, Edward Frederick Lindley Wood, 1st Earl of (2nd creation) (1881–1959) British Conservative statesman, born in Powderham, Devon. He became foreign secretary (1938–40) under Chamberlain, whose 'appeasement' policy he implemented. >> Chamberlain, Neville

Hall, Asaph (1829–1907) Astronomer, born in Goshen, CT. In 1877 he discovered the two satellites of Mars, calculated their orbits, and named them Deimos and Phobos.

Hall, Ben(jamin) (1837–65) Bushranger, born in New South Wales, Australia. He turned to outlawry in a series of audacious exploits, and was killed in a police ambush at the age of 28.

Hall, Charles Francis (1821–71) Arctic explorer, born in Rochester, NH. Interested in the fate of Sir John Franklin he made two expeditions (1860–2, 1864–9), bringing back relics of the Franklin journey. In 1871 he attempted to reach the North Pole, and made 82° 16'N, the northernmost latitude to date. >> Franklin, John

Hall, Charles (Martin) (1863–1914) Chemist, born in Thompson, OH. In 1886 he discovered (independently of Héroult) the electrolyte method of producing aluminium economically, and helped to found the Aluminum Company of America. >> Héroult

Hall, G(ranville) Stanley (1844–1924) Psychologist, born in Ashfield, MA. At Johns Hopkins University (from 1882) he introduced experimental psychology, founded the *American Journal of Psychology* (1887), and influenced the development of educational and child psychology in the USA.

Hall, Sir James (1761–1832) Geologist, born in Dunglass, Lothian. He sought to prove in the laboratory the geological theories of Hutton, and so founded experimental geology, artificially producing many of the igneous rocks of Scotland. >> Hutton, James

Hall, James (1811–98) Geologist and palaeontologist, born in Hingham, MA. He made extensive explorations in the St Lawrence Valley, and was appointed state geologist of New York (1836), producing a classic report, *Geology of New York* (1843).

Hall, Joseph (1574–1656) Clergyman and writer, born in Ashby-de-la-Zouch, Leicestershire. He became Bishop of Exeter (1627–42), and Bishop of Norwich (1642–7), and wrote widely both as a moral philosopher and satirist.

Hall, Marguerite Radclyffe (1880–1943) Writer, born in Bournemouth, Dorset. Her novels include *Adam's Breed* (1926, James Tait Black Memorial Prize) and *The Well of Loneliness* (1928), whose sympathetic approach to female homosexuality caused it to be banned in Britain for many years.

Hall, Marshall (1790–1857) Physician and physiologist, born in Basford, Nottinghamshire. He worked on reflex action of the spinal system (1833–7), and his name is associated with a standard method of restoring suspended respiration.

Hall, Sir Peter (Reginald Frederick) (1930–) Theatre, opera, and film director, born in Bury St Edmunds, Suffolk. He became director of the Royal Shakespeare Company (1960–8), director of Covent Garden Opera (1969–71), and succeeded Olivier as director of the National Theatre (1973–88). >> Olivier

Hall, Rodney (1935–) Writer, arts administrator, and musician, born in Solihull, Warwickshire. He has published widely as a poet, with works such as *Penniless Till Doomsday* (1962) and *Romulus and Remus* (1971), and his novels include *Just Relations* (1982, Miles Franklin Award), and *The Second Bridegroom* (1991).

Hall, Willis >> **Waterhouse, Keith**

Halle, Adam de la [ahl], known as **Adam le Bossu** ('Adam the Hunchback') (c.1250–c.1306) Poet and composer, born in Arras, France. He originated French comic opera with *Le Jeu de Robin et de Marion*, and the partly autobiographical composition *Jeu de la fuellée* (Play of the Greensward).

Hallé, Sir Charles [halay] (1819–95) Pianist and conductor, born in Hagen, Germany. Driven to England by the Revolution of 1848, he settled in Manchester, where in 1858 he founded his famous orchestra.

Halleck, Henry W(ager) (1815–72) US army officer, born in Westernville, NY. He served in the Civil War (1861–5), captured Corinth (1862), and became general-in-chief,

but in 1864 was superseded by General Grant. >> Grant, Ulysses S

Haller, Albrecht von [haler] (1708–77) Biologist, physiologist, and poet, born in Bern. His *Physiological Elements of the Human Body* (trans, 8 vols, 1757) opened the door to modern neurology.

Halley, Edmond [halee, hawlee] (1656–1742) Astronomer and mathematician, born in London. He began a study of planetary orbits, and correctly predicted the return in 1758 of the comet now named after him.

Halliday, M(ichael) A(lexander) K(irkwood) (1925–) Linguist, born in Leeds, West Yorkshire. He is known for his work in linguistics which led to the development of scale-and-category grammar in the 1960s, and then systemic grammar. >> Firth, J R

Hallstrom, Sir Edward John Lees (1886–1970) Pioneer of refrigeration, born in Coonamble, New South Wales, Australia. He designed and manufactured the first popular domestic Australian refrigerator.

Hals, Frans [hals] (c.1580–1666) Portrait and genre painter, probably born in Antwerp, Belgium. Among his best-known works are 'The Laughing Cavalier' (1624) and 'Gypsy Girl' (c.1628–30).

Halsey, William F(rederick), Jr [holzee], known as **Bull Halsey** (1884–1959) US admiral, born in Elizabeth, NJ. In 1944 he commanded the 3rd Fleet in the battles for the Caroline and Philippine Is, and defeated the Japanese navy at the Battle of Leyte Gulf.

Halsted, William (Stewart) (1852–1922) Surgeon, born in New York City. He developed a cocaine injection for local anaesthesia, and devised successful operative techniques for cancer of the breast and inguinal hernia. He also pioneered the use of rubber gloves and sterile conditions in surgery.

Hamada, Shoji [hamada, shohjee] (1894–1978) Japanese potter, widely recognized as one of the great modern potters. He worked primarily in stoneware, using ash or iron glazes producing utilitarian wares in strong, simple shapes brushed with abstract design.

Hamilcar [hamilkah(r)], known as **Hamilcar Barca** ('Lightning') (c.270–228 BC) Carthaginian statesman and general at the time of the First Punic War, the father of Hannibal. He set about founding a new Carthaginian empire in Spain, and between 237 BC and his death had conquered most of the S and E of the peninsula. >> Hannibal

Hamilton, Alexander (1757–1804) US statesman, born in the West Indian island of Nevis. In 1782 he was returned to Congress, and was instrumental in the movement to establish the USA in its present political form. He became secretary to the Treasury (1789–95), and was leader of the Federalist Party until his death. He was killed in a duel with a rival, Aaron Burr. >> Burr

Hamilton, Emma, Lady, *née* **Emily Lyon** (c.1765–1815) Lord Nelson's mistress, probably born in Ness, Cheshire. In 1791 she married Sir William Hamilton, meeting Nelson in 1793. After their deaths she became bankrupt, and in 1814 fled to Calais, where she died. >> Hamilton, Sir William (1730–1803); Nelson

Hamilton, Hamish (1900–88) Publisher, born in Indianapolis, IN. He founded his own firm in 1931, and sold it to Thomson Publications (1965), who later sold it to Viking Penguin.

Hamilton, Iain Ellis (1922–) Composer, born in Glasgow, Strathclyde. He has produced many orchestral and chamber works, as well as operas including *The Royal Hunt of the Sun* and *The Cataline Conspiracy*.

Hamilton, Sir Ian (Standish Monteith) (1853–1947) British soldier, born in Corfu, Greece. He served with distinction in the Boer Wars (1881, 1899–1901), but led the disastrous Gallipoli expedition (1915), and was relieved of his command.

Hamilton, Patrick (1503–28) Protomartyr of the Scottish Reformation, born in the diocese of Glasgow, Strathclyde. He went to Wittenberg in 1527, and wrote a series of theological propositions known as 'Patrick's Places'. Returning to Scotland he was charged with heresy and burned.

Hamilton, Richard (1922–) Pop Art painter, born in London. During the 1950s he devised and participated in several influential exhibitions which introduced the concept of Pop Art, of which he became a leading pioneer.

Hamilton, Thomas (1784–1858) Architect, born in Glasgow, Strathclyde. A leading figure in the international Greek Revival, his designs include the Royal College of Physicians Hall (1844–5), Edinburgh.

Hamilton, Sir William (1730–1803) Diplomat and antiquary, born in Scotland. He was ambassador at Naples (1764–1800), and married Emily Lyon (Emma, Lady Hamilton) in 1791. He wrote on Greek and Roman antiquities. >> Hamilton, Emma

Hamilton, Sir William (1788–1856) Philosopher, born in Glasgow, Strathclyde. His articles on German philosophers introduced Kant to the British public. His main work was published posthumously as *Lectures on Metaphysics and Logic* (1859–60). >> Kant

Hamilton, Sir William Rowan (1805–65) Mathematician, born in Dublin. He introduced quaternions as a new algebraic approach to three-dimensional geometry, and they proved to be the seed of much modern algebra.

Hamlin, Hannibal (1809–91) US vice-president (1861–5), born in Paris Hill, MA. A Democrat in the US Senate (1848–57), he separated from his party over his antislavery opinions, later becoming vice-president under Lincoln. >> Lincoln, Abraham

Hamlyn, Paul (Bertrand), originally **Paul Hamburger** (1926–) British entrepreneur and publisher. He founded Books for Pleasure (1949), Prints for Pleasure (1960), and Records for Pleasure (1961), and later co-founded Sundial Publications with David Frost, and Conran Octopus with Terence Conran (1983). >> Conran, Terence; Frost, David

Hammarskjöld, Dag (Hjalmar Agne Carl) [hamershohld] (1905–61) Swedish statesman, and secretary-general of the UN (1953–61), born in Jönköping, Sweden. At the UN, he helped to set up the Emergency Force in Sinai and Gaza (1956), and worked for conciliation in the Middle East (1957–8). He was awarded the Nobel Peace Prize in 1961.

Hammer, Armand (1899–1990) Businessman, born in New York City. He founded the A Hammer Pencil Co in 1925, operating in New York City, London, and Moscow, and founded Hammer Galleries in New York City (1930).

Hammerstein, Oscar, II [hamerstiyn] (1895–1960) Librettist, born in New York City. With composer Jerome Kern he wrote *Show Boat* (1927), and with Richard Rodgers he wrote *Oklahoma!* (1943, Pulitzer), *South Pacific* (1949, Pulitzer), *The King and I* (1951), and *The Sound of Music* (1959). >> Kern; Rodgers, Richard

Hammett, (Samuel) Dashiell (1894–1961) Crime writer, born in St Mary's Co, MD. He achieved international fame with his 'private eye' novels *The Maltese Falcon* (1930; filmed 1941) and *The Thin Man* (1932), which was also filmed and later made into a television series.

Hammond, Eric (Albert Barratt) (1929–) British trade union leader. He became general secretary of the Electrical, Electronics, Telecommunications and Plumbing Union in 1984, defying Trades Union Congress (TUC) policy by concluding single-union, 'no strike' agreements with employers.

Hammond, Dame Joan (1912–) Soprano, born in Christchurch, New Zealand. She toured widely, and became noted particularly for her Puccini roles.

Hammond, Walter (1903–65) Cricketer, born in Dover, Kent. A bowler and fielder, he scored over 50 000 runs for Gloucestershire, and scored 7249 runs in 85 Tests.

Hammond Innes, Ralph [inis] (1913–) Writer and traveller, born in England. His popular adventure stories include *The Trojan Horse* (1940), *The Lonely Skier* (1947), and *Atlantic Fury* (1962).

Hammurabi [hamurahbee] (18th-c BC) Amorite king of Babylon (c.1792–1750 BC), best known for his Code of Laws, and for his military conquests that made Babylon the greatest power in Mesopotamia.

Hamnett, Katharine (1948–) Fashion designer, born in Gravesend, Kent. She set up her own business in 1979, and draws inspiration for her designs from workwear, and also from social movements, such as the peace movement.

Hampden, John (1594–1643) English parliamentarian and patriot, born in London. In 1634 he became famous for refusing to pay Charles's imposed levy for outfitting the navy, and was one of the five members of parliament whose attempted seizure by Charles (1642) precipitated the Civil War. >> Charles I (of England)

Hampole, Richard Rolle of >> **Rolle of Hampole, Richard**

Hampshire, Susan (1942–) British actress. She won Emmy awards for best actress in the television series *The Forsyte Saga* (1970), *The First Churchills* (1971), and *Vanity Fair* (1973).

Hampson, Frank (1918–85) Strip cartoonist, born in Manchester. In 1950 he designed a Christian comic for boys, which eventually became the *Eagle*, featuring the adventures of 'Dan Dare, Pilot of the Future'.

Hampton, Christopher (James) (1946–) British playwright, born in Fayal, Azores. His finest play is considered to be *Tales From Hollywood* (1982), but his most commercial success has been *Les Liaisons dangereuses* (1985), adapted from the novel by Laclos. >> Laclos

Hampton, Lionel (Leo), nickname **Hamp** (1909–) Jazz musician and bandleader, born in Louisville, KY. He introduced the vibraphone into jazz, playing with Armstrong and with Goodman in the 1930s. He formed a permanent big band in 1940. >> Armstrong, Louis; Goodman, Benny

Hampton, Wade (1812–1902) Hero of the Confederacy, born in Columbia, SC. In the Civil War (1861–5) he raised 'Hampton's Legion', received the command of Lee's cavalry in 1864, and in 1865 served in South Carolina. >> Lee, Robert E

Hamsun, Knut [hamsoon], pseudonym of **Knut Pederson** (1859–1952) Novelist, born in Lom, Norway. His best-known books are *Hunger* (trans, 1890), *Mysteries* (trans, 1892), and his masterpiece, *Growth of the Soil* (trans, 1917). He received the Nobel Prize for Literature in 1920.

Hanbury-Tenison, Robin (Airling) (1936–) Explorer, writer, and broadcaster, brought up in Ireland. He took part in many expeditions, including the British Hovercraft expeditions in Amazonas (1968) and transAfrica (1969). He became a founder member of Survival International, and later its president.

Hancock, John (1737–93) US statesman, born in Braintree, MA. He became president (1775–7) of the Continental Congress, and was the first to sign the Declaration of Independence.

Hancock, Lang(ley) George (1909–92) Australian mining industrialist, born in Perth, Western Australia. He discovered iron ore deposits in several locations, and initiated the growth of Australian extractive industries.

Hancock, Tony, popular name of **Anthony John Hancock** (1924–68) Comedian, born in Birmingham, West Midlands. He achieved national popularity with the radio and TV series *Hancock's Half Hour* (1954–61). A chronic alcoholic, he committed suicide while attempting a comeback on Australian television.

Hancock, Winfield Scott (1824–86) US general, born in Montgomery Co, PA. In 1861 he organized the Army of the Potomac, fought at Gettysburg (1863), and at Wilderness, Spottsylvania, and Cold Harbor in 1864. As the popular Democratic candidate for the presidency in 1880, he was narrowly beaten by Garfield. >> Garfield

Hand, (Billings) Learned (1872–1961) Jurist, born in Albany, NY. A federal judge (1909–61), his judgements extended into all branches of law, influencing the US Supreme Court.

Handel, George Frideric (1685–1759) Composer, born in Halle, Germany. His vast output included over 40 operas, about 20 oratorios, cantatas, sacred music, and orchestral, instrumental, and vocal works. While in London (from 1720), he developed a new form, the English oratorio, which proved to be highly popular. His most memorable work includes *Saul* (1739), *Israel in Egypt* (1739), and *Messiah* (1742).

Handley, Tommy, popular name of **Thomas Reginald Handley** (1892–1949) Comedian, born in Liverpool, Merseyside. In 1939 he achieved nationwide fame through his weekly comedy radio programme *ITMA* (*It's That Man Again*) which helped to boost wartime morale.

Hands, Terry, popular name of **Terence David Hands** (1941–) Stage director, born in Aldershot, Hampshire. He co-founded the Everyman Theatre, Liverpool (1964), then joined the Royal Shakespeare Company (1966), where he became an associate director (1967–77), joint artistic director with Trevor Nunn (1978–86), and sole artistic director. >> Nunn

Handy, Charles (Brian) (1932–) Management educator and writer, born in Dublin. Professor of management development at the London Business School (1972–7), his books include *Understanding Organizations* (1976) and *Inside Organizations* (1990).

Handy, W(illiam) C(hristopher) (1873–1958) Composer, born in Florence, AL. He formed his own publishing company, and was the first to introduce the 'blues' style to printed music, his most famous work being the 'St Louis Blues' (1914).

Hani, Chris [hanee], popular name of **Martin Thembisile Hani** (1942–93) South African political leader, born in Cofimvaba, South Africa. His record as guerrilla leader and his charisma made him the most popular African political figure of his generation. Elected secretary-general of the South African Communist Party (1991), he was shot dead by a white right-winger.

Hanna, Mark, popular name of **Marcus Alonzo Hanna** (1837–1904) Businessman and politician, born in New Lisbon, OH. In favour of McKinley's high protective tariff sponsorship, he financed the successful presidential campaign on his behalf, and later accepted a seat in the US Senate (1897). >> McKinley

Hanna–Barbera [hana bah(r)bera] Animated cartoonists. **William (Denby) Hanna** (1910–), born in Melrose, NM, was one of the first directors at the new MGM animation studio in 1937. He teamed up with **Joseph (Roland) Barbera** (1911–), born in New York City, who had joined MGM as an artist. They created the *Tom and Jerry* cartoons, winning seven Oscars between 1943 and 1952, and such television cartoon series as *The Flintstones*, *Yogi Bear*, and *Huckleberry Hound*.

Hannibal [hanibl] (247–182 BC) Carthaginian general and statesman, the son of Hamilcar Barca. In the Second Punic War (218–202 BC), he completely surprised the Romans by his bold invasion of Italy from the N (with elephants), and inflicted a series of heavy defeats on them. Recalled to Africa (203 BC), he was defeated by Scipio and Zama. >> Scipio Africanus Major

Hanno (fl.5th-c BC) Carthaginian navigator. He undertook a voyage of exploration along the W coast of Africa, and founded Thymaterion (now Kénitra, Morocco).

Hanratty, James [hanratee] (c.1936–62) Convicted murderer, whose case has remained controversial. Picked out by a witness to the murder from an identity parade, he denied the charge and claimed to have alibis, but was found guilty and hanged. Later, people came forward who seemed to confirm his story.

Hansard, Luke (1752–1828) British printer. He and his descendants printed regular parliamentary reports from 1774 to 1889, and in 1943 *Hansard* became the official name for the reports.

Hansom, Joseph Aloysius (1803–82) Inventor and architect, born in York, North Yorkshire. He is best known for his invention of the 'Patent Safety (Hansom) Cab' in 1834.

Hanson, Duane (1925–) Sculptor, born in Alexandria, MN. He specializes in life-size figures, painted realistically and adorned with hats, wristwatches, and other objects.

Hanson, Howard (1896–1981) Composer, born in Wahoo, NE. For many years he was director of the Eastman School of Music in Rochester, NY, and under him the School became an important centre of American musical life.

Hanson, Raymond (1913–76) Composer and teacher, born in Sydney, New South Wales, Australia. His works include the well-known *Trumpet Concerto*, operas, a ballet, a symphony, four concertos, chamber music, and film scores.

Hanson-Dyer, Louise Berta Mosson (1884–1962) Music publisher, born in Melbourne, Victoria, Australia. She helped establish the British Music Society in Melbourne (1921), and in Paris established Editions du Oiseau-Lyre (1927) which set a new standard of music printing.

Han Suyin, originally **Elizabeth Kuanghu Chow** (1917–) Novelist and doctor, born in Beijing. Her many novels include *Destination Chungking* (1942), *A Many-splendoured Thing* (1952; filmed 1955), and *Four Faces* (1963).

Hantzsch, Arthur Rudolf [hanch] (1857–1935) Organic chemist, born in Dresden, Germany. He developed the synthesis of substituted pyridines, investigated the electrical conductivity of organic compounds, and was a pioneer in spectrophotometry.

Harald I Gormsson, nickname **Harald Bluetooth** (c.910–c.985) King of Denmark from c.940, the father of Sweyn Forkbeard. He was the first king to unify all the provinces of Denmark under a single crown. >> Sweyn

Harald I Halfdanarson, nickname **Harald Fairhair** or **Finehair** (c.860–c.940) King of Norway (c.890–c.942), the first ruler to claim sovereignty over all Norway. He gained power with a crushing defeat of his opponents at the naval Battle of Hafursfjord, off Stavanger (c.890).

Harald III Sigurdsson, nickname **Harald Hardrada** ('the Ruthless') (1015–66) King of Norway (from 1045), the half-brother of Olaf II (St Olaf). He invaded England in 1066 to claim the throne after the death of Edward I, but was killed by Harold II at Stamford Bridge. >> Harold II; Olaf II

Harburg, E Y(ip) (1898–1981) Songwriter, born in New York City. His most famous songs include 'April in Paris' (1932) and 'Somewhere Over the Rainbow' (1939), and he also wrote the clown songs for *The Wizard of Oz* (1939).

Harcourt, Sir William (George Granville Venables Vernon) [hah(r)kaw(r)t] (1827–1904) British statesman, born in York, North Yorkshire. He was solicitor general (1873–4), home secretary (1880–5), and Chancellor of the Exchequer (1886, 1892–4).

Harden, Sir Arthur (1865–1940) Chemist, born in Manchester. In 1929 he shared the Nobel Prize for Chemistry for his work on alcoholic fermentation and enzymes.

Hardenberg, Friedrich von >> Novalis

Hardenberg, Karl August, Fürst von (Prince of) (1750–1822) Prussian statesman, born in Essenrode, Germany. In 1810 he was appointed chancellor, and began to complete the reforms begun by Stein. >> Stein, Karl

Hardicanute [hah(r)dikanoot], also spelled **Harthacnut** (c.1018–42) King of Denmark (1035–42), and the last Danish King of England (1040–2), the only son of Canute and Emma of Normandy. His death without children led to the restoration of the Old English royal line in the person of Edward the Confessor. >> Canute; Edward the Confessor

Hardie, (James) Keir (1856–1915) British politician, born near Holytown, Strathclyde. He became the first Labour candidate, entering parliament in 1892, and serving as chairman of the Labour Party (1906–8).

Harding, Stephen, St (c.1060–1134), feast day 16 July. Abbot, born in Sherborne, Dorset. He helped to found the monastery of Cîteaux, S of Dijon, in 1098. Several other abbeys were founded to follow the strict rule he imposed, forming the Cistercian Order.

Harding (of Petherton), John Harding, Baron (1896–1989) British field-marshal, born in South Petherton, Somerset. As Governor-General of Cyprus (1955–7) during the campaign against Britain, he re-organized the security forces to combat terrorism, and banished Archbishop Makarios. >> Makarios

Harding, Warren G(amaliel) (1865–1923) US statesman and 29th president (1921–3), born in Corsica, OH. Emerging as a power in the Republican Party, he won the presidency in 1920, campaigning against US membership of the League of Nations.

Hardinge (of Lahore), Henry Hardinge, 1st Viscount (1785–1856) British soldier and colonial administrator, born in Wrotham, Kent. As Governor-General of India (1844–8), he carried out several reforms, planned a railway system, and commenced construction of the Ganges canal.

Hardouin-Mansart, Jules >> Mansard, Jules

Hardwick, Philip (1792–1870) Architect, born in London. He designed Euston railway station, the hall and library of Lincoln's Inn, Goldsmiths' Hall, and Limerick Cathedral.

Hardwicke, Sir Cedric (Webster) (1893–1964) Actor, born in Lye, Worcestershire. He made his name in Shaw's plays and in *The Barretts of Wimpole Street* (1934). His films include *Things to Come* (1931) and *The Winslow Boy* (1948).

Hardy, Sir Alister (Clavering) (1896–1985) Marine biologist, born in Nottingham, Nottinghamshire. He invented the continuous plankton recorder, which permitted the detailed study of surface life in the oceans.

Hardy, Bert (1913–) Photojournalist, born in London. He was on the staff of *Picture Post* until 1957, except for service as an army photographer from (1942–6), during which he recorded the horrors of the concentration camps.

Hardy, Godfrey (Harold) (1877–1947) Mathematician, born in Cranleigh, Surrey. He worked on analytic number theory, and in applied maths developed independently of **Wilhelm Weinberg** the *Hardy–Weinberg* law fundamental to population genetics.

Hardy, Oliver >> Laurel, Stan

Hardy, Thomas (1840–1928) Novelist and poet, born in Upper Bockhampton, Dorset. His major novels include *The Return of the Native* (1878), *The Mayor of Casterbridge* (1886), *Tess of the D'Urbervilles* (1891), and *Jude the Obscure* (1896). He also wrote moving elegies to his first wife, Emma Gifford (d.1912), and the epic drama *The Dynasts* (1903–8).

Hardy, Sir Thomas (Masterman) (1769–1839) British naval officer, born in Portisham, Dorset. He served Nelson as flag-captain at the Battle of Trafalgar (1805), and became First Sea Lord in 1830. >> Nelson

Hare, David (1947–) Playwright and director, born in London. His politically engaged plays include *Slag* (1970) and *Plenty* (1978). *The Secret Rapture* (1988) won two awards for best play of the year.

Hare, Robertson (1891–1979) Actor, born in London. He built up his reputation as a comedian in the famous 'Aldwych farces', cast invariably in 'henpecked little man' parts in which his ultimate 'debagging' became proverbial.

Hare, William >> Burke, William

Hare, William Henry, nickname **Dusty Hare** (1952–) Rugby union player, born in Newark-on-Trent, Nottinghamshire. When he retired in 1989 he had scored 7337 points, an all-time points-scoring record, and won 23 caps for England.

Harewood, George Henry Hubert Lascelles, 7th Earl of [hah(r)wud] (1923–) Elder son of Princess Mary, and cousin of Queen Elizabeth II, born in Harewood, West Yorkshire. Since the 1950s he has been much involved in the direction of operatic and arts institutions, such as at Covent Garden, Edinburgh, and Leeds.

Hargrave, Lawrence (1850–1915) Aeronautical pioneer, born in Greenwich, Greater London. In Sydney in 1893 he developed the box-kite to produce a wing form used in early aircraft, and in 1894 four tethered kites successfully lifted him 5 m from the ground.

Hargreaves, James (c.1720–78) Inventor, probably born in Blackburn, Lancashire. He invented the spinning jenny in c.1764, but his fellow spinners broke into his house and destroyed his frame (1768).

Harington, Sir Charles Robert (1897–1972) British chemist. He synthesized thyroxine, published *The Thyroid Gland* (1933), and became director of the National Institute of Medical Research (1942–62).

Harington, Sir John (1561–1612) Courtier and writer, born in Kelston, Avon. He is remembered as the metrical translator of Ariosto's *Orlando Furioso* (1591). >> Ariosto

Hariot, Thomas >> Harriot, Thomas

Harlan, John (Marshall) (1833–1911) Jurist, born in Boyle Co, KY. Appointed to the Supreme Court (1877–1911), he is best remembered for defending the Thirteenth and Fourteenth Amendments as upholders of African-American civil rights.

Harland, Sir Edward James (1831–96) British shipbuilder. In 1858 he founded in Belfast the firm which became Harland and Wolff, in whose yard were built many famous Atlantic liners and warships. **Gustav William Wolff** (1834–1913) was his partner from 1860.

Harley, Robert, 1st Earl of Oxford (1661–1724) British statesman, born in London. He was Chancellor of the Exchequer, head of the government, and (1711) Lord High Treasurer. The principal act of his administration was the Treaty of Utrecht (1713).

Harlow, Jean, originally **Harlean Carpentier**, nickname **the Blonde Bombshell** (1911–37) Film star, born in Kansas City, MO. Her films, such as *Hell's Angels* (1930), *Platinum Blonde* (1931), and *Red Dust* (1932), made her the sex symbol of the 1930s.

Harlow, Harry (Frederick) (1905–81) Psychologist, born in Fairfield, IA. He is known for his pioneering methods of research into the behaviour of captive monkeys.

Harmodius [hah(r)mohdius] (?–514 BC) Athenian assassin who, with **Aristogeiton**, in 514 BC killed Hipparchus, the younger brother of the 'tyrant' Hippias. They were later regarded as patriotic martyrs.

Harmsworth, Alfred (Charles William), 1st Viscount Northcliffe (1865–1922) Journalist and newspaper magnate, born near Dublin. In 1896 he revolutionized Fleet Street with his *Daily Mail*, introducing mass circulation journalism to the UK. In 1908, he became proprietor of *The Times*. >> Harmsworth, Harold

Harmsworth, Harold (Sydney), 1st Viscount Roth-ermere (1868-1940) Newspaper magnate, born in London. He founded the Glasgow *Daily Record* and in 1915 the *Sunday Pictorial*. After the death of his brother, Alfred, he acquired control of the *Daily Mail* and *Sunday Dispatch*. >> Harmsworth, Alfred

Harnack, Adolf (Karl Gustav) von (1851-1930) Protestant Church historian and theologian, born in Dorpat, Germany. His major writings include works on the history of dogma, on early Gospel traditions, and on a reconstruction of the essence of Jesus's teachings.

Harnick, Sheldon (1924-) Songwriter, born in Chicago, IL. His greatest success has been *Fiddler on the Roof* (1964), which includes 'Matchmaker, Matchmaker' and 'If I Were a Rich Man'.

Harold I, nickname **Harold Harefoot** (c.1016-40) King of England (1037-40), the younger son of Canute. Canute had intended that Hardicanute should succeed him in both Denmark and England; but in view of Hardicanute's absence in Denmark, Harold was accepted in England. >> Canute; Hardicanute

Harold II (c.1022-66) Last Anglo-Saxon king of England (1066), the second son of Earl Godwin. He defeated his brother Tostig and Harold Hardrada, King of Norway, at Stamford Bridge (Sep 1066), but William of Normandy then invaded England, and defeated him near Hastings (Oct 1066), where he died, shot through the eye with an arrow. >> Godwin; Harold III; William I (of England)

Harold III >> Harald III Sigurdsson

Harper, Edward (1941-) Composer, born in Taunton, Somerset. His works include the opera *Hedda Gabler* (1985), a symphony, concertos, choral works, and other chamber and vocal pieces.

Harper, James (1795-1869) Publisher, born in New York City. Harper & Brothers was established in 1833, and began publishing several periodicals including *Harper's Bazaar* (1867).

Harriman, W(illiam) Averell (1891-1986) US statesman and diplomat, born in New York City. He became ambassador to the USSR (1943) and to Britain (1946), and negotiated the partial nuclear test-ban treaty between the USA and USSR in 1963.

Harriot, Thomas, also spelled **Hariot** (1560-1621) Mathematician and scientist, born in Oxford, Oxfordshire. He studied optics, refraction by prisms, and the formation of rainbows, and developed an effective algebraic notation for the solution of equations.

Harris, Sir Arthur Travers, nickname **Bomber Harris** (1892-1984) British airman, born in Cheltenham, Gloucestershire. As commander-in-chief of Bomber Command in World War 2 (1942-5) he organized mass bomber raids on industrial Germany.

Harris, Barbara (Clementine) (1931-) Social activist, born in Philadelphia, PA. She was ordained a priest in 1980, and made history when she became the first woman to be consecrated an assistant bishop in the Episcopal Church (1989).

Harris, Frank, pseudonym of **James Thomas Harris** (1856-1931) Literary editor and journalist, born in Galway, Co Galway, Ireland. He was editor of the *Evening News* (1882-6), the *Fortnightly Review* (1886-94), and *Saturday Review* (1894-8).

Harris, Howel (1714-73) Clergyman, born in Trefecca, Powys. He became a travelling preacher in Wales, capable of gathering large crowds. Refused ordination, he founded his own community of Calvinistic Methodists at Trefecca.

Harris, Joel Chandler (1848-1908) Humorist and dialect writer, born in Eatonton, GA. His *Uncle Remus* stories about 'Brer Rabbit' and 'Brer Fox', made him internationally famous, known especially for his distinctive use of Southern African-American folklore and dialect.

Harris, Julie, originally **Julia Harris** (1925-) Film, stage, and television actress, born in Michigan. She rose to stardom through her roles in *The Member of the Wedding* (1950) and *The Lark* (1955), and in 1976 successfully performed a one-woman show as Emily Dickinson in *The Belle of Amherst*.

Harris, Paul (1868-1947) Lawyer, born in Racine, WI. He was the founder in 1905 of a club for business and professional men, using the name *Rotary*, which grew into the worldwide organization, Rotary International (including women from 1987).

Harris, Reg(inald Hargreaves) (1920-92) Track cyclist, born in Bury, Lancashire. In 1947 he won the world amateur sprint championship. He turned professional (1948) and was world sprint champion (1949-51, 1954) setting records which stood for 20 years.

Harris, Rolf (1930-) Entertainer and artist, born in Bassendean, Western Australia. He joined the BBC children's department in 1954, and appeared widely on stage and television, known especially for his spontaneous paintings and drawings. Several of his songs have been hit records.

Harris, Rosemary (1930-) British actress. She made her debut in New York City in 1952, performing with many companies on both the English and American stage.

Harris, Roy, popular name of **LeRoy Ellsworth Harris** (1898-1979) Composer, born in Lincoln Co, OK. His music is ruggedly American in character, as in his symphonic overture *When Johnny Comes Marching Home* (1935). He wrote 16 symphonies, the third being the best known.

Harris, Theodore Wilson (1921-) Novelist, born in New Amsterdam, Guyana. One of the pre-eminent Caribbean writers, his masterpiece is *The Guyana Quartet* (1985, a compilation of novels written 1960-3).

Harris, Thomas (Lake) (1823-1906) Spiritualist, born in Fenny Stratford, Buckinghamshire. In America he became a Universalist pastor, and in 1850 set up as a spiritualistic medium, founding the 'Church of the Good Shepherd' (c.1858).

Harrison, Benjamin (1833-1901) US statesman and 23rd president (1889-93), born in North Bend, OH, the grandson of William Henry Harrison. Elected a Republican senator in 1880, in 1888 he defeated Cleveland on the free trade issue, but failed to gain re-election in 1892. >> Cleveland, Stephen Grover; Harrison, William Henry

Harrison, George (1943-) Singer, guitarist, and songwriter, born in Liverpool, Merseyside. He played lead guitar and sang with the Beatles, and developed an interest in Indian music and Eastern religion. His solo albums include *All Things Must Pass* (1970) and *Somewhere in England* (1981).

Harrison, John (1693-1776) Inventor and horologist, born in Foulby, West Yorkshire. By 1726 he had constructed a clock which could correct errors due to variations of climate, and later developed a marine chronometer which determined longitude within two geographical miles.

Harrison, Sir Rex, originally **Reginald Carey Harrison** (1908-90) Actor, born in Houghton, Lancashire. His charming, somewhat blasé style attracted many star comedy parts, such as in *Blithe Spirit* (1945), *The Constant Husband* (1958), and *My Fair Lady* (1964, Oscar).

Harrison, Ross (Granville) (1870-1959) Zoologist, born in Germantown, PA. His observations of animal tissue cultures pioneered modern nerve neurology and physiology, and he also invented methods of tissue grafting which suggested later organ-transplantation techniques.

Harrison, Thomas (1606-60) English Parliamentarian soldier and regicide, born in Newcastle-under-Lyme, Staffordshire. He was a judge at the trial of Charles I, and signed his death warrant (1649). After the Restoration he was executed. >> Charles I (of England)

Harrison, Tony (1937–) Poet, born in Leeds, West Yorkshire. Poems on social conflict ('V', 1985, televised 1987) and the Gulf War ('A Cold Coming', 1991) underline his commitment to public issues, confirmed in *The Gaze of the Gorgon* (1992).

Harrison, William Henry (1773–1841) US soldier, statesman, and ninth president (1841), born in Charles City Co, VA. He became a senator in 1824, and president in 1841, but died of pneumonia a month after his inauguration.

Harrod, Sir (Henry) Roy (Forbes) (1900–78) Economist, born in London. His contributions to economic theory were developed independently of Evsey Domar, leading to the *Harrod–Domar model* of economic development. >> Domar

Hart, Francis Brett >> Harte, Brett

Hart, Gary, originally **Gary Hartpence** (1936–) US politician, born in Ottawa, KS. A 'neo-liberal', he contested the Democrats' presidential nomination in 1980, and almost defeated Mondale. He retired from the Senate in 1986 to concentrate on a bid for the presidency, which failed. >> Mondale

Hart (of South Lanark), Judith (Constance Mary) Hart, Baroness (1924–91) British Labour stateswoman, born in Burnley, Lancashire. She was paymaster-general (1968), and served as minister of overseas development (1969–70, 1974–5, 1977–9).

Hart, Lorenz >> Rodgers, Richard

Hart, Moss (1904–61) Playwright and director, born in New York City. His plays, in collaboration with George S Kaufman, include *Once in a Lifetime* (1929) and *The Man Who Came to Dinner* (1939). >> Kaufman, George

Hart, William S(urrey) (1870–1946) Cowboy hero of silent motion pictures, born in Newburgh, NY. He made his film debut in *The Fugitive* (1913), and went on to enjoy great popularity in Westerns as a defender of justice and the honour of women.

Harte, Bret, pseudonym of **Francis Brett Hart** (1836–1902) Writer, born in Albany, NY. His collection of articles, *The Luck of Roaring Camp* (1870), brought him world fame, and he was contracted to *The Atlantic Monthly* (1871) to write 12 stories a year.

Hartford, George Huntington (1833–1917) Grocery store magnate, born in Augusta, ME. With George F Gilman, he opened a chain of stores which by 1869 was called the Great Atlantic and Pacific Tea Company, or A & P.

Hartley, David (1705–57) Philosopher, physician, and psychologist, born in Armley, West Yorkshire. His *Observations on Man, his Frame, his Duty and his Expectations* (1749) relates psychology closely to physiology. >> Hartley, David (1731–1813)

Hartley, David, known as **the Younger** (1731–1813) Inventor and politician, born in Bath, Avon, the son of the philosopher David Hartley. With Benjamin Franklin, he drafted the Treaty of Paris (1783) that ended the American War of Independence. His major invention was a system of fire-proofing houses. >> Hartley, David (1705–57); Franklin, Benjamin

Hartley, L(eslie) P(oles) (1895–1972) Writer, born near Peterborough, Cambridgeshire. His early short stories, such as *Night Fears* (1924), established his reputation as a master of the macabre. Successful novels include *The Boat* (1950) and *The Go-Between* (1953).

Hartley, Marsden (1877–1943) Painter and writer, one of the pioneers of American modern art, born in Lewiston, ME. Inspired by Kandinsky and Marc, his work became abstract, and he exhibited with the *Blaue Reiter* group. >> Kandinksy; Marc

Hartline, Haldan (Keffer) (1903–83) Physiologist, born in Bloomsburg, PA. He shared the 1967 Nobel Prize for Physiology or Medicine for work on the neurophysiology of vision.

Hartnell, Sir Norman (1901–78) Fashion designer and court dressmaker, born in London. He began his own business in 1923, his work including costumes for leading actresses, wartime 'utility' dresses, and Princess Elizabeth's wedding and coronation gowns.

Hartnett, Sir Laurence John (1898–1986) Automotive engineer, born in Woking, Surrey. He went to Australia in 1934 to take over GM-Holden, the first 'Holden' car appearing in 1946.

Hartree, Douglas Rayner (1897–1958) Mathematician and physicist, born in Cambridge, Cambridgeshire. His work was mainly on the application of computational methods. He invented the method of the self-consistent field in quantum mechanics, the automated control of chemical plants, and an analogue computer, and was involved in the early days of the electronic digital computer.

Hartung, Hans (1904–89) Artist, born in Leipzig, Germany. His later paintings, which have made him one of the most famous French abstract painters, show a free calligraphy allied to that of Chinese brushwork.

Harty, Sir (Herbert) Hamilton (1880–1941) Composer, conductor, and pianist, born in Hillsborough, Lisburn, Co Antrim. His compositions include an *Irish Symphony* and many songs, and he made well-known arrangements of Handel's *Music for the Royal Fireworks* and *Water Music suites*.

Harun al-Raschid [haroon al rasheed] (766–809) Fifth Abbasid caliph, known to posterity especially from the *Arabian Nights*. He was a great patron of the arts, enthusiastic in waging war against the Byzantines, but weakened the empire by trying to divide it among his three sons.

Harvard, John (1607–38) Colonist, born in London. He left his considerable inherited wealth to a new school in New Towne, MA, which was named Harvard College in 1639.

Harvey, David (1935–) Geographer, born in Gillingham, Kent. He was a founder member of the so-called 'positivist' school, his *Explanation in Geography* (1969) being regarded by adherents as the fundamental reference, but he later became one of its major critics.

Harvey, Sir John Martin (1863–1944) Actor-manager, born in Wivenhoe, Essex. At the Lyceum in 1899 he produced *The Only Way*, adapted from *A Tale of Two Cities*, in which he played Sydney Carton, his most successful role.

Harvey, William (1578–1657) Physician, born in Folkestone, Kent. His celebrated treatise, *On the Motion of the Heart and Blood in Animals* (trans, 1628), first described the circulation of the blood.

Harvey-Jones, Sir John (Henry) (1929–) Industrial executive, born in Kent. Chairman of ICI (1982–7), he became well known to the UK general public through the TV series *Troubleshooter* (1990, 1992).

Harwood, Gwen, *née* **Foster** (1920–) Poet, born in Brisbane, Queensland, Australia. She started writing in her late 30s, her books including *Poems* (1963), *The Lion's Bride* (1981), and *Bone Scan* (1990).

Harwood, Sir Henry (1888–1959) British naval commander. He commanded at the Battle of the River Plate, in which the German pocket battleship *Graf Spee* was scuttled (1939), and became commander-in-chief of the Mediterranean fleet in 1942.

Hasdrubal [hazdrubal] (?–221 BC) Carthaginian general, son-in-law of Hamilcar, whom he succeeded as commander in Spain in 229 BC. He peacefully extended the Carthaginian empire in Spain, and founded Cartagena. >> Hamilcar

Hasdrubal [hazdrubal], known as **Hasdrubal Barca** ('Lightning') (?–207 BC) Carthaginian general, the son of Hamilcar and brother of Hannibal. He fought successfully against the Romans (218–208 BC), and in 207 BC marched across the Alps to Italy to aid his brother, but was killed. >> Hamilcar; Hannibal

Hašek, Jaroslav [hashek] (1883–1923) Novelist and short-story writer, born in Prague. He is best known for his novel *The Good Soldier Švejk* (1920–3), a satire on military life and bureaucracy.

Haselrig, Sir Arthur [hayzlrig], also spelled **Hesilrige** (?–1661) English parliamentarian. In 1640 he sat in the Long and Short Parliaments, and was one of the five members whose attempted seizure by Charles I in 1642 precipitated the Civil War. >> Charles I (of England)

Hashman, Judy, popular name of **Judith Hashman**, *née* **Devlin** (1935–) Badminton player, born in Winnipeg, Manitoba, Canada. The winner of the singles title at the All-England Championships a record 10 times (1954, 1957–8, 1960–4, 1966–7), she also won seven doubles titles - six with her sister, **Susan Peard** (1940–).

Hassall, John (1868–1948) Artist and cartoonist, born in Walmer, Kent. The acknowledged pioneer of modern poster design, his railway posters included the popular 'Skegness is so bracing'.

Hassan II (1929–) King of Morocco (1961–), born in Rabat, Morocco. He established a royal dictatorship, but was forced to appoint a coalition 'government of national unity' under a civilian prime minister in 1984.

Hassel, Odd (1897–1981) Physical chemist, born in Oslo, Norway. In 1943, independently of Barton, he developed the basic ideas of chemical conformational analysis, for which he shared the Nobel Prize for Chemistry in 1969. >> Barton, Derek

Hastings, Francis Rawdon-Hastings, 1st Marquess of (1754–1826) British soldier and colonial administrator, born in Dublin. In 1813 he became Governor-General of India, where he defeated the Gurkhas (1814–16), purchased Singapore island (1819), and introduced several reforms. In 1821 he resigned after apparently unfounded charges of corruption had been made against him.

Hastings, Max Macdonald (1945–) British writer, journalist, and broadcaster. He became a journalist for the BBC (1970–3), then worked as a freelance around the world, and became editor of the *Daily Telegraph* in 1990.

Hastings, Thomas (1860–1929) Architect, born in Mineola, NY. With **John Merven Carrére** (1858–1911), he formed a successful New York partnership (1885–1915) that became identified with Beaux-Arts architecture, as in the New York Public Library (1902–11).

Hastings, Warren (1732–1818) British colonial administrator in India, born in Churchill, Oxfordshire. As Governor-General of Bengal (1774), he made the East India Company's power paramount in many parts of India. On his return to England (1784) he was charged with corruption, and after a 7-year trial was acquitted.

Hathaway, Anne >> Shakespeare, William

Hatshepsut [hatshepsoot] (c.1540–c.1481 BC) Queen of Egypt of the XVIIIth dynasty, the daughter of Thutmose I. She was married to Thutmose II, on whose death (1503 BC) she acted as regent for his son, Thuthmose III, then had herself crowned as Pharaoh.

Hattersley, Roy (Sydney George) (1932–) British statesman, born in Sheffield, South Yorkshire. He was secretary of state for prices and consumer protection (1976–9), and later held several Opposition posts, including shadow Chancellor, and deputy leader of the Labour Party (1983–92).

Haughey, Charles (James) [hokhee] (1925–) Irish prime minister (1979–81, 1982, 1987–92), born in Castlebar, Co Mayo. He became a Fianna Fáil MP in 1957, and held posts in justice, agriculture, finance, and health. He was forced to resign in 1992 after allegations of his involvement in a phone-tapping scandal.

Hauptman, Herbert (Aaron) [howptman] (1917–) Mathematical physicist, born in New York City. With Karle he devised new methods for computing molecular structures from X-ray crystal diffraction data, and they shared the Nobel Prize for Chemistry in 1985. >> Karle

Hauptmann, Gerhart (Johann Robert) [howptman] (1862–1946) Writer, born in Obersalzbrunn, Germany. His plays include *Before Dawn* (trans, 1889) and *The Weavers* (trans, 1892). He also wrote several novels and poetry, and was awarded the Nobel Prize for Literature in 1912.

Hauptmann, Bruno Richard >> Lindbergh, Charles A

Hauron, Louis Duclos du >> Duclos du Hauron, Louis

Hausdorff, Felix [howsdaw(r)f] (1868–1942) Mathematician, born in Wroclaw, Poland (formerly Breslau, Germany). He is regarded as the founder of point set topology, and his work on set theory continued that of Cantor and Zermelo. >> Cantor, Georg; Zermelo

Hauser, Gayelord (Helmut Eugene Benjamin Gellert) [howzer] (1895–1984) Popular nutritionist, originally from Germany. He advocated special vegetable diets featuring 'wonder foods', and made a fortune with such best-selling books as *Look Younger, Live Longer* (1950).

Hauser, Kaspar [howzer] (c.1812–33) German foundling, a 'wild boy', found in the market place of Nuremberg in 1828. Though apparently 16 years old, his mind was a blank, and his behaviour childlike. In 1833 he received a wound from which he died, and for which an explanation was never found.

Haussmann, Georges Eugène, Baron [howsman] (1809–91) Financier and town planner, born in Paris. He became prefect of the Seine (1853), improving Paris by widening streets, laying out boulevards and parks, and building bridges.

Hauteclocque, viscomte de >> Le Clerc, Jacques-Philippe

Havel, Vaclav [havl] (1936–) Playwright, president of Czechoslovakia (1989–92), and president of the Czech Republic (1993–), born in Prague. His writing was judged subversive, and he was imprisoned (1979–83), and again in 1989, but released and elected president by direct popular vote following the collapse of communism.

Havelock (Allan), Sir Henry [havlok] (1795–1857) British soldier, born in Sunderland, Tyne and Wear. He led the relief of Cawnpore and Lucknow (1857).

Havergal, William Henry [havergal] (1793–1870) Hymn writer, born in High Wycombe, Buckinghamshire. He composed hymn tunes, chants, and songs, and wrote *History of the Old 100th Tune*.

Havers (of St Edmundsbury), Robert Michael Oldfield Havers, Baron [hayverz] (1923–92) British lawyer and politician. He was solicitor general (1972–4) and attorney general (1979–87), and spent a brief period as Lord Chancellor before his retirement in 1988.

Havilland, Geoffrey de >> de Havilland, Geoffrey

Havlicek, John [havlichek], nickname **Hondo Havlicek** (1940–) Basketball player, born in Lansing, OH. During his career with the Boston Celtics (1963–78) he played in eight National Basketball Association championship teams, and was voted Most Valuable Player in 1974.

Hawes, Harriet (Ann) Boyd (1871–1945) Archaeologist, educator and social activist, born in Boston, MA. She led a team that excavated the Minoan town of Gournia (1901–5), the first woman to head a major archaeological dig. She also worked for women's suffrage, and was a strong advocate of an international body to promote peace.

Hawes, Stephen (?–c.1523) English poet, about whose early life very little is known. His chief work is the allegory, 'The Passetyme of Pleasure' (1509), dedicated to Henry VII.

Haw-Haw, Lord >> Joyce, William

Hawke, Bob, popular name of **Robert (James Lee) Hawke** (1929–) Australian Labor prime minister (1983–91), born in Bordertown, South Australia. A skilled negotiator, who won praise for his handling of industrial disputes, he won a fourth term in 1990, but was defeated in a leadership contest by Keating the following year. >> Keating

Hawke (of Towton), Edward Hawke, Baron (1705–81) British admiral, born in London. His major victory was against the French at Quiberon Bay (1759), which caused the collapse of their invasion plans. He became First Lord of the Admiralty (1766–71).

Hawker, R(obert) S(tephen) (1803–75) Poet, born in Plymouth, Devon. His best-known ballad is 'Song of the Western Men' (1826). Other volumes include *Records of the Western Shore* (1832) and *Cornish Ballads* (1869).

Hawkes, Jacquetta (1910–) British archaeologist and writer. She took part in excavations in Britain, France, and Palestine (1931–40), married J B Priestley in 1953, and with him wrote *Journey Down a Rainbow* (1955). >> Priestley, J B

Hawkesworth, John (c.1715–73) Writer, born possibly in London. In 1752 he started, with Dr Johnson and others, *The Adventurer*, a periodical to which he made the major contribution. >> Johnson, Samuel

Hawking, Stephen (William) (1942–) Theoretical physicist, born in Oxford, Oxfordshire. His work has been concerned with cosmology, dealing with black holes, singularities, and the 'big bang' theory of the origin of the universe. His popular writing includes *A Brief History of Time* (1988). Since the 1960s he has suffered from a neuromotor disease, causing extreme physical disability.

Hawkins, Sir Anthony Hope >> **Hope, Anthony**

Hawkins, Coleman (1901–69; he claimed 1904 as his birth year) Jazz tenor saxophonist, born in St Joseph, MO. He joined Fletcher Henderson's jazz orchestra (1923), popularizing the tenor saxophone, and recorded 'Body and Soul', a jazz landmark. >> Henderson, Fletcher

Hawkins, Erick, popular name of **Frederick Hawkins** (1909–94) Dancer, choreographer, and teacher, born in Colorado. The first man to dance with the Martha Graham company, he married her in 1948 (divorced, 1954), and formed his own company in the mid-1950s. >> Graham, Martha

Hawkins, Sir John >> **Hawkyns, John**

Hawks, Howard (Winchester) (1896–1977) Film director, born in Goshen, IN. He had many successes over some 40 years, in such varied genres as airforce dramas (*The Dawn Patrol*, 1930), crime (*The Big Sleep*, 1946), and Westerns (*Rio Lobo*, 1970).

Hawkshaw, Sir John (1811–91) Civil engineer, born in Leeds, West Yorkshire. His projects include the Manchester and Leeds Railway (1845–50), the Charing Cross station and bridge (1850), and the Amsterdam ship canal (1862).

Hawksmoor, Nicholas (1661–1736) Architect, born in East Drayton, Nottinghamshire. His works include the London churches, St Mary Woolnoth, St George's (Bloomsbury), and Christ Church (Spitalfields).

Hawkyns or **Hawkins, Sir John** (1532–95) English sailor, born in Plymouth, Devon. He became navy treasurer (1573), served against the Armada (1588), and in 1595, with Drake, commanded an expedition to the Spanish Main. >> Drake

Haworth, Sir (Walter) Norman [hah(r)th] (1883–1950) Chemist, born in Chorley, Lancashire. He determined the chemical structure of vitamin C and various carbohydrates, for which he shared the Nobel Prize for Chemistry in 1937.

Hawthorne, Nathaniel (1804–64) Writer, born in Salem, MA. His first major success was the novel *The Scarlet Letter* (1850), still the best-known of his works.

Hay, John (Milton) (1838–1905) US secretary of state (1898–1905) and writer, born in Salem, IN. He wrote poetry, fiction, and a multi-volume biography of Lincoln. As secretary of state, he is best-remembered for the Open Door Policy towards China (1899). >> Lincoln, Abraham

Haydee, Marcia (1939–) Dancer and director, born in Niteroi, Brazil. She joined Stuttgart Ballet in 1961, and in 1976 became artistic director there.

Hayden, Bill, popular name of **William George Hayden** (1933–) Australian statesman, born in Brisbane, Queensland, Australia. He replaced Whitlam as Labor Party leader (1977–83), then served as foreign minister under Hawke (1983–8). In 1989 he became Governor-General of Australia. >> Hawke, Bob; Whitlam

Hayden, Ferdinand (Vandeveer) (1829–87) Geologist, born in Westfield, MA. He became head of the US geological survey, and was influential in securing the establishment of Yellowstone National Park.

Haydn, Franz Joseph [hiydn] (1732–1809) Composer, born in Rohrau, Austria. Among his innovations were the four-movement string quartet and the 'classical' symphony. His prolific output includes 104 symphonies, some 50 concertos, 84 string quartets, 24 stage works, 12 Masses, orchestral divertimenti, keyboard sonatas, and diverse chamber, choral, instrumental, and vocal pieces. >> Haydn, Michael

Haydn, Michael [hiydn] (1737–1806) Composer, born in Rohrau, Austria, the brother of Franz Joseph Haydn. Several of his church pieces and instrumental works are still performed. >> Haydn, Franz Joseph

Hayek, Friedrich A(ugust von) [hiyek] (1899–1992) Economist, born in Vienna. Strongly opposed to Keynesianism, he was often called 'the father of monetarism', and shared the Nobel Prize for Economics in 1974.

Hayem, Georges [ayem] (1841–1920) Physician, born in Paris. He first described the platelets in the blood, and did classic work on the formation and diseases of the red and white blood cells.

Hayes, Helen, originally **Helen Hayes Brown** (1900–93) Actress, born in Washington, DC. Her film appearances include *A Farewell to Arms* (1932), *The Sin of Madelon Claudet* (1931, Oscar), and *Airport* (1970, Oscar). The Helen Hayes Theater in New York City was named after her.

Hayes, Isaac Israel (1832–81) Physician and Arctic explorer, born in Chester Co, PA. Seeking to prove that there were open seas around the North Pole, he led two Arctic expeditions (1860, 1869).

Hayes, Rutherford B(irchard) (1822–93) US statesman and 19th president (1877–81), born in Delaware, OH. Under his presidency, the country recovered commercial prosperity after the Civil War. His policy included reform of the civil service and the conciliation of the Southern states.

Haynes, Elwood (1857–1925) Inventor, born in Portland, IN. He produced in 1893 a one-horsepower, one-cylinder vehicle, the oldest US automobile in existence.

Haynes, John (1934–) Footballer, born in London. He spent his whole career with Fulham, won 56 caps, and captained England 22 times.

Hays, Will(iam Harrison) (1879–1954) Politician and film censor, born in Sullivan, IN. He served as the first president of the Motion Picture Producers and Distributors of America (1922–45), formulating the *Hays Code*, which enforced a rigorous code of morality on American films not superseded until 1966.

Hayter, Stanley William (1901–88) Artist and engraver, born in London. In 1927 he founded a Paris studio where artists of all nationalities could work together, known as Atelier 17. An early member of the Surrealist movement, he was an innovator in printmaking.

Haywood, Eliza, *née* Fowler (c.1693–1756) Novelist, born in

London. She wrote a number of scandalous society novels about real people. Her periodical, *The Female Spectator* (1744–6), was the first to be written by a woman.

Haywood, William D(udley), nickname **Big Bill Haywood** (1869–1928) Political activist, born in Salt Lake City, UT. He became leader of the Industrial Workers of the World (IWW), which lent support to striking industries (1909–13). Arrested on treason charges, he fled to Russia.

Hayworth, Rita, originally **Margarita Carmen Cansino** (1918–87) Film actress, born into a show business family in New York City. She partnered both Fred Astaire and Gene Kelly in musicals of the 1940s, and found her best-known lead in *Gilda* (1946). >> Astaire; Kelly, Gene

Hazlitt, William (1778–1830) Essayist, born in Maidstone, Kent. A master of epigram, invective, and irony, his best-known collections are *Table Talk* (1821) and *The Spirit of the Age* (1825).

Hazzard, Shirley (1931–) Writer, born in Sydney, New South Wales, Australia. Her novel, *The Transit of Venus* (1980), established her as a major contemporary writer.

H D >> Doolittle, Hilda

Head, Bessie (1937–86) Novelist, born in Pietermaritzburg, South Africa. Several of her novels, such as *The Collector of Treasures* (1977) and *Serowe: Village of the Rain Wind* (1981), give literary form to Setswana folk tales and oral tradition.

Head, Sir Henry (1861–1940) Neurologist, born in Stamford Hill, Greater London. He wrote widely on disorders of speech (aphasia) and other neurological disorders, and edited the journal *Brain* (1910–25).

Heal, Sir Ambrose (1872–1959) Furniture designer, born in London. He joined the family firm in 1893, and began designing furniture influenced by the Arts and Crafts Movement.

Healey (of Riddlesden), Denis (Winston) Healey, Baron (1917–) British statesman, born in Eltham, Kent. He was secretary of state for defence (1964–70) and Chancellor of the Exchequer (1974–9). Unsuccessful in the Labour leadership contests of 1976 and 1980, he became deputy leader (1980–3), and in 1983 was appointed shadow foreign minister.

Healy, Timothy Michael (1855–1931) Irish Nationalist leader, born in Bantry, Co Cork, Ireland. In 1890 he headed the revolt against Parnell, and became an Independent Nationalist. He was the first Governor-General of the Irish Free State (1922–8). >> Parnell

Heaney, Seamus (Justin) [**hee**nee, **shay**mus] (1939–) Poet, born on a farm in Co Derry. Early works such as *Death of a Naturalist* (1966) and *Door into the Dark* (1969) established a deep bond between language and the land. Volumes of selected poems appeared in 1980 and 1990.

Hearn, (Patricio) Lafcadio (Tessima Carlos) [hern] (1850–1904) Writer and translator, born on the island of Lefkas, Greece. In 1890 he settled in Japan, and published a series of books that offered the West its first sympathetic view of Japanese culture.

Hearne, Samuel [hern] (1745–92) Explorer of N Canada, born in London. He joined the Hudson's Bay Company, and became the first European to travel overland by canoe and sled to the Arctic Ocean.

Hearns, Thomas [hernz], nicknames **Hit Man** and **Motor City Cobra** (1958–) Boxer, born in Memphis, TN. In 1988 he became the first man to win world titles at four and five different weights, and in 1991 the first to win titles at six different weights.

Hearst, William Randolph (1863–1951) Newspaper publisher, born in San Francisco, CA. His national chain of newspapers and periodicals included the *Chicago Examiner*, *Cosmopolitan*, and *Harper's Bazaar*, and his life inspired the Orson Welles film *Citizen Kane* (1941). >> Hearst, Patty

Hearst, Patty, popular name of **Patricia (Campbell) Hearst**, married name **Shaw** (1954–) Heiress to William Randolph Hearst's empire, born in San Francisco, CA, the daughter of newspaper tycoon Randolph Hearst (d.1993). She was kidnapped in 1974 by the radical Symbionese Liberation Army, joined in their bank robberies, was imprisoned (1976), and later paroled (1979). >> Hearst, William Randolph

Heartfield, John, originally **Helmut Herzfelde** (1891–1968) German photomonteur and painter. Together with Grosz, he was a leading member of the Berlin Dada group, producing satirical collages from pasted, superimposed photographs cut from magazines. >> Grosz, George

Heath, Sir Edward (Richard George), known as **Ted Heath** (1916–) British prime minister (1970–4), born in Broadstairs, Kent. He was minister of labour (1959–60), Lord Privy Seal (1960–3), and Leader of the Opposition (1965–70). He became Father of the House in 1992.

Heathcoat, John (1783–1861) Inventor, born in Duffield, Derbyshire. He designed a machine for making lace (patented in 1809), and set up a factory in Nottingham which was destroyed by the Luddites (1816).

Heathcoat-Amory, Derick >> Amory, Derick Heathcoat

Heaviside, Oliver [**he**veesiyd] (1850–1925) Physicist, born in London. He predicted (independently of Kennelly) the existence of an ionized gaseous layer (the ionosphere) capable of reflecting radio waves, and contributed to theory of electrical communications. >> Kennelly

Hebb, Donald (Olding) (1904–85) Psychologist, born in Chester, Nova Scotia, Canada. He became an influential theorist concerned with the relation between the brain and behaviour, especially in the development of connectionism.

Hebbel, (Christian) Friedrich (1813–63) Playwright, born in Wesselburen, Germany. His favourite settings were of a legendary, historical, or biblical character, as in his masterpiece, the *Nibelungen* trilogy (1862).

Hébert, Jacques René [aybair] (1757–94) French revolutionary extremist, born in Alençon, France. A member of the Revolutionary Council, he played a major part in the September Massacres and the overthrow of the monarchy, but incurred the suspicion of Danton and Robespierre, and was guillotined with his followers. >> Danton; Robespierre

Hecataeus of Miletus [hekat**ee**us, miy**lee**tus] (fl.6th–5th-c BC) Pioneer Greek historian and geographer. He is known for two works, *Genealogies* (or *Histories*) and *Tour of the World*, of which only fragments remain.

Hecht, Ben (1894–1964) Newspaperman, novelist, and playwright, born in New York City. His novel *Fantazius Mallare* (1922) was attacked as obscene. His successful film scripts include *The Scoundrel* (1935), *Spellbound* (1945), and *Notorious* (1946).

Heckel, Erich (1883–1970) Painter, born in Döbeln, Germany. He is best known for his paintings of nudes and landscapes, and as a founder member of the Expressionist school, *Die Brücke*.

Heckel, Johann Adam (c.1812–77) Woodwind instrument maker, born in Germany. He founded his own workshop near Wiesbaden (1831) and improved the structure and key-system of bassoons.

Hecker, Isaac Thomas (1819–88) Roman Catholic priest, born in New York City. Founder of the Paulist Fathers, he greatly extended Catholicism in America, though his tendency to democratize religion created much controversy.

Hedin, Sven Anders [hay**deen**] (1865–1952) Explorer and geographer, born in Stockholm. He made many journeys into uncharted areas, such as the Himalayas (1893–8), the Gobi Desert (1899–1902), and Tibet, of which he made the first detailed map (1908).

Hedley, William (1779–1843) Inventor, born in Newburn, Tyne and Wear. He patented a design for a railway traction engine using smooth wheels on smooth rails. His locomotive, *Puffing Billy*, was the first commercial steam locomotive.

Heemskerck, Maerten van (1498–1574) Portrait and religious painter, born in Heemskerck, The Netherlands. He went to Rome (1532–5) where his surviving sketchbooks supply a vivid account of the ancient monuments of the city as they appeared in the 16th-c.

Heenan, John >> Sayers, Tom

Heenan, John Carmel (1905–75) Roman Catholic cardinal (from 1975), born in Ilford, Essex. He became Archbishop of Liverpool in 1957 and Archbishop of Westminster in 1963, known for his support of ecumenism.

Heezen, Bruce (Charles) (1924–77) Oceanographer, born in Vinton, IA. In 1952 he became the first to show the existence of ocean turbidity currents, and in 1957 (with Ewing) demonstrated that mid-ocean ridges have a central rift. >> Ewing, William

Heffer, Eric (Samuel) (1922–) British politician. A traditional socialist, he distrusted centrist tendencies and had a brief, uncomfortable period as a junior minister (1974–5).

Hefner, Hugh (Marston) (1926–) Editor and publisher of *Playboy* magazine, born in Chicago, IL. He launched *Playboy* in 1953, later extending his empire into real estate, nightclubs (with the 'bunny-girl' hostesses), and sundry products.

Hegel, Georg Wilhelm Friedrich [haygl] (1770–1831) Philosopher, born in Stuttgart, Germany. His major works include (trans titles) *The Phenomenology of the Mind* (1807), *Science of Logic* (1812–16), and *Encyclopedia of the Philosophical Sciences* (1817), in which he set out his tripartite system of logic, philosophy of nature, and mind.

Heidegger, Martin [hiydeger] (1889–1976) Philosopher, born in Messkirch, Germany. In his incomplete main work, *Being and Time* (trans, 1927), he presents an exhaustive ontological classification of 'being', and was a key influence in Sartre's existentialism. >> Sartre

Heifetz, Jascha [hiyfets] (1901–87) Violinist, born in Vilna, Lithuania. A US citizen from 1925, among works commissioned by him from leading composers is Walton's violin concerto. >> Walton, William

Heine, (Christian Johann) Heinrich [hiynuh] (1797–1856) Poet and essayist, born in Düsseldorf, Germany. He established his reputation with *Pictures of Travel* (trans, 4 vols, 1826–7, 1830–1) and *The Book of Songs* (trans, 1827), and after the 1830 revolution, became leader of the cosmopolitan democratic movement.

Heinemann, Gustav [hiynuhman] (1899–1976) West German president (1969–74), born in Schwelm, Germany. A founder of the Christian Democratic Union, he became minister of the interior (1949–50), then joined the Social Democratic Party, and was minister of justice under Kiesinger (1966–9). >> Kiesinger

Heinemann, William [hiynuhman] (1863–1920) Publisher, born in Surbiton, Greater London. He founded his publishing house in London in 1890, and established its reputation with the works of Stevenson, Kipling, H G Wells, and others.

Heinkel, Ernst (Heinrich) [hiyngkel] (1888–1958) Aircraft engineer, born in Grunbach, Germany. He founded the Heinkel-Flugzeugwerke at Warnemünde (1922), making bombers and fighters which achieved fame in World War 2.

Heinz, H(enry) J(ohn) [hiynts] (1844–1919) Food manufacturer, born in Pittsburgh, PA. In 1876 he founded the business which was reorganized in 1888 as H J Heinz Co, and he became its president (1905–19).

Heinze, Sir Bernard Thomas [hiynz] (1894–1982) Conductor and teacher, born in Shepparton, Victoria, Australia. He was conductor of the Melbourne Symphony Orchestra (1933–49), and from 1932 was music adviser to the Australian Broadcasting Corporation.

Heisei >> Akihito

Heisenberg, Werner (Karl) [hiyznberg] (1901–76) Theoretical physicist, born in Würzburg, Germany. He developed a method of expressing quantum mechanics in matrices (1925), and formulated his revolutionary principle of indeterminacy (the *uncertainty principle*) in 1927. He was awarded the Nobel Prize for Physics in 1932.

Held, Al (1928–) Painter, born in New York City. From 1960 he adopted a geometric style, painting complex cube-like structures with heavy impasto paint, turning to acrylic paints in the 1980s.

Helena, St (c.255–c.330), feast day 18 August (W), 21 May (E). Mother of the Emperor Constantine (the Great), born in Bithynia, Asia Minor. The wife of Constantius Chlorus, she early became a Christian. In 326, according to tradition, she founded the basilicas on the Mt of Olives and at Bethlehem. >> Constantine I (Emperor); Constantius Chlorus

Helga, St >> Olga, St

Heliodorus [heliodawrus] (fl.3rd-c) Greek romance writer and Sophist, born in Emesa in Syria. An early Greek novelist, he wrote *Aethiopica*, which narrates in poetic prose the loves of Theagenes and Chariclea.

Heliogabalus [heliohgabalus], divine name of **Caesar Marcus Aurelius Antonius Augustus**, originally **Varius Avitus Bassianus** (204–222) Roman emperor, born in Emesa, Syria. In 218 he was proclaimed emperor by the soldiers. His brief reign was marked by extravagant orgies and intolerant promotion of the god Baal, and he was murdered by the praetorians.

Heller, Joseph (1923–) Novelist, born in New York City. His wartime experience forms the background for his first book, *Catch 22* (1961), which launched him as a successful novelist.

Hellman, Lillian (Florence) (1907–84) Playwright, born in New Orleans, LA. A left-wing activist, she had her first stage success with the controversial *The Children's Hour* (1934), followed by *Days to Come* (1936) and *The Little Foxes* (1939).

Helmholtz, Hermann von (1821–94) Physiologist and physicist, born in Potsdam, Germany. The key figure in the development of science in Germany in the later 19th-c, he studied the eye, ear, and nervous system, and is best known for his statement of the law of the conservation of energy.

Helmont, Jan Baptista van (1579–1644) Chemist, born in Brussels. He invented the term *gas*, and was the first to take the melting-point of ice and the boiling-point of water as standards for temperature.

Helms, Richard (McGarrah) (1913–) Intelligence officer, born in Pennsylvania. He joined the Central Intelligence Agency, and became the organization's director in 1966, but was dismissed by Nixon in 1973. >> Nixon

Héloïse >> Abelard, Peter

Helpmann, Sir Robert (Murray) (1909–86) Dancer, actor, and choreographer, born in Mount Gambier, Victoria, Australia. He was first dancer of the newly founded Sadler's Wells Ballet (1933–50), and became known for his dramatic roles in de Valois' works. >> Valois, Ninette de

Helst, Bartholomaeus van der (1613–70) Painter, born in Haarlem, The Netherlands. He was joint founder in 1653 of the painters' guild of St Luke at Amsterdam, where he flourished as a portrait painter.

Helvétius, Claude-Adrien [elvaysyus] (1715–71) Philosopher, born in Paris. In 1758 he published the controversial *De l'esprit*, advancing the view that sensation is the source of all intellectual activity and that self-interest is the motive force of all human action.

Hemans, Felicia Dorothea [hemanz], *née* **Browne** (1793–1835) Poet, born in Liverpool, Merseyside. She produced books of verse of all kinds, and is perhaps best remembered for the poem 'Casabianca', better known as 'The boy stood on the burning deck'.

Hemingway, Ernest (Miller) (1899–1961) Novelist and short-story writer, born in Oak Park, IL. Obsessed with war, big-game hunting, and bullfighting, his works include *A Farewell to Arms* (1929), *For Whom the Bell Tolls* (1940), and *The Old Man and the Sea* (1952, Pulitzer). He was awarded the Nobel Prize for Literature in 1954.

Hench, Philip (Showalter) (1896–1965) Physician, born in Pittsburgh, PA. In 1948 he discovered with Kendall the use of an adrenal hormone (cortisone) in alleviating the symptoms of rheumatoid arthritis, for which they shared the Nobel Prize for Physiology or Medicine in 1950. >> Kendall, Edward C

Henderson, Fletcher (1897–1952) Pianist, arranger, and jazz bandleader, born in Cuthbert, GA. In 1924 he put together a big band, attracting the finest instrumentalists and arrangers of the time, and setting the standard for the swing era.

Henderson, Mary >> Bridie, James

Hendrix, Jimi, popular name of **James Marshall Hendrix** (1942–70) Rock guitarist, singer, and songwriter, born in Seattle, WA. In London he formed the Jimi Hendrix Experience, and the band's first single, 'Hey Joe', was an immediate success. His raucous blues style influenced heavy metal bands.

Hengist and Horsa Two brothers, leaders of the first Anglo-Saxon settlers in Britain. Bede states that they were invited over by Vortigern, the British king, to fight the Picts in c.450. >> Vortigern

Henie, Sonja [henee] (1912–69) Ice-skater, born in Oslo. After winning the gold medal in figure-skating at the Olympics of 1928, 1932, and 1936, she turned professional and starred in touring ice-shows.

Henle, Friedrich Gustav Jakob [henluh] (1809–85) Anatomist and pathologist, born in Fürth, Germany. A major influence in the development of histology, his *Comprehensive Anatomy* (trans, 1841) was the first systematic treatise of the subject.

Henlein, Konrad [henliyn] (1898–1945) German politician, born near Liberec, Czech Republic. He was the leader in the agitation on the eve of World War 2 leading in 1938 to Germany's seizure of Sudetenland from Czechoslovakia.

Henley, William Ernest (1849–1903) Writer, critic, and editor, born in Gloucester, Gloucestershire. He edited the *Magazine of Art* (1882–6), and published several books of verse, including *In Hospital* (1875), which contains his best-known poem, 'Invictus'.

Hennebique, François [onuhbeek] (1842–1921) Civil engineer, born in Neuville-Saint-Vaast, France. He introduced the use of reinforced concrete for the building industry, progressing to a whole system which he patented in 1892.

Henri (French kings) >> Henry (of France)

Henri, Robert [henree] (1865–1929) Realist painter, born in Cincinnati, OH. He began a movement which became known as the Ashcan school, and later formed the group known as 'The Eight'.

Henrietta Anne, Duchess of Orléans (1644–70) Youngest daughter of Charles I of Great Britain and Henrietta Maria, born in Exeter, Devon. She played an important part in the negotiations of the Secret Treaty of Dover (1670) between Charles and Louis. >> Charles I (of England); Henrietta Maria

Henrietta Maria (1609–69) Queen of Charles I of England,

born in Paris, the youngest child of Henry IV of France. She married Charles in 1625, but her French attendants and Roman Catholic beliefs made her unpopular, and in 1642 she fled to Holland. >> Charles I (of England); Henry IV (of France)

Henry I (of England) (1068–1135) King of England (1100–35) and Duke of Normandy (1106–35), the youngest son of William the Conqueror. During his reign, the Norman Empire attained the height of its power. His only legitimate son, William Adelin, was drowned in 1120, and in 1127 he nominated his daughter Empress Matilda, as his heir for both England and Normandy, but after Henry's death, the crown was seized by Stephen, son of his sister, Adela. >> Matilda; Stephen; William I (of England)

Henry II (of England) (1133–89) King of England (1154–89), born in Le Mans, France, the son of Empress Matilda and Geoffrey of Anjou. He invaded England in 1153, and was recognized as the lawful successor of the usurper, Stephen, founding the Angevin or Plantagenet dynasty of English kings. His reign is chiefly remembered for the conflict with Thomas à Becket, his murder (1170), and the annexation of Ireland (1171). >> Becket; Matilda; Richard I

Henry II (of France) (1519–59) King of France (1547–69), born near Paris, the second son of Francis I. In 1533 he married Catherine de' Medici. As king he formed an alliance with Scotland, and declared war against England, which ended in 1558 with the taking of Calais. >> Catherine de' Medici; Francis I

Henry III (of England) (1207–72) King of England (1216–72), the elder son and successor, at the age of nine, of John. His arbitrary assertion of royal rights led to the rebellion of Simon de Montfort and the barons. He was captured at Lewes (1264), but defeated the rebels at Evesham (1265). >> Edward I; Montfort, Simon de (Earl of Leicester)

Henry III (of France) (1551–89) King of France (1574–89), born in Fontainebleau, the third son of Henry II. His reign was a period of almost incessant civil war between Huguenots and Catholics. The last of the Valois line, he named Henry of Navarre as his successor. >> Henry II / IV (of France)

Henry IV (Emperor) (1050–1106) Holy Roman Emperor (1084–1106). He was crowned King of Germany while still an infant (1053), under the regency of his mother. Twice excommunicated (1076, 1080), he attacked Rome, installed an antipope, and had himself proclaimed emperor.

Henry IV (of England), originally **Henry Bolingbroke** (1366–1413) King of England (1399–1413), the first king of the House of Lancaster, the son of John of Gaunt, who was the fourth son of Edward III. In 1397 he supported Richard II against the Duke of Gloucester, but was banished in 1398. On returning to England, he induced Richard to abdicate in his favour, and defeated Henry Percy (Hotspur) and his followers at Shrewsbury (1403). >> John of Gaunt; Richard II

Henry IV (of France), originally **Henry of Navarre** (1553–1610) The first Bourbon king of France (1589–1610), born in Pau, France. He became leader of the Protestant Party, and after the massacre of St Bartholomew's Day (1572) was spared by professing himself a Catholic. He unified the country, and granted Protestants liberty of conscience. >> Henry III; Marie de Médicis

Henry V (of England) (1387–1422) King of England (1413–22), born in Monmouth, Gwent, the eldest son of Henry IV. In 1415 he invaded France, and won the Battle of Agincourt against great odds. He was recognized as heir to the French throne, and married Charles VI's daughter, Catherine of Valois. >> Catherine of Valois; Henry IV (of England)

Henry VI (of England) (1421–71) King of England (1422–61,

1470-1), born in Windsor, Berkshire, the only child of Henry V and Catherine of Valois. Although crowned King of France in Paris in 1431, he gradually lost England's French conquests. Richard, Duke of York, seized power as Lord Protector in 1454, and defeated the king's army at St Albans (1455), the first battle of the Wars of the Roses, deposing Henry in 1461. Richard Neville, Earl of Warwick, restored him to the throne (Oct 1470), his nominal rule ending when Edward IV returned to London (Apr 1471). After the Yorkist victory at Tewkesbury (May 1471), where his only son was killed, Henry was murdered in the Tower. >> Edward IV; Gloucester, Humphrey, Duke of; Warwick, Earl of; York, 3rd Duke of

Henry VII (of England) (1457-1509) King of England (1485-1509), born at Pembroke Castle, Dyfed, the grandson of Owen Tudor and Catherine of Valois, the widow of Henry V. He founded the Tudor dynasty by defeating Richard III at Bosworth (1485), married Elizabeth of York, and concluded peace with France. >> Catherine of Valois; Richard III

Henry VIII (of England) (1491-1547) King of England (1509-47), born in Greenwich, Greater London, the second son of Henry VII. Soon after his accession he married **Catherine of Aragon**. From 1527 he determined to divorce Catherine, whose children, except for Mary, had died in infancy, and in defiance of Rome was privately married to **Anne Boleyn** (1533). In 1534 it was enacted that his marriage to Catherine was invalid, and that the king was the sole head of the Church of England. In 1536 Catherine died, and Anne Boleyn was executed for infidelity. Henry then married **Jane Seymour**, who died leaving a son, afterwards Edward VI. In 1540 **Anne of Cleves** became his fourth wife, but dislike of her appearance caused him to divorce her speedily. He then married **Catherine Howard** (1540), who was executed on grounds of infidelity (1542). In 1543 his last marriage was to **Catherine Parr**, who survived him. >> Anne of Cleves; Boleyn; Catherine of Aragon; Howard, Catherine; Parr, Catherine; Seymour, Jane

Henry (1594-1612) Prince of Wales, the eldest son of James I (of England) and Anne of Denmark. Notable for the strict morality of his way of life, he became the focus for the hopes of those at court with Puritan sympathies. >> James I (of England)

Henry, Joseph (1797-1878) Physicist, born in Albany, NY. He discovered electrical induction independently of Faraday, and constructed the first electromagnetic motor (1829). The *henry* unit of inductance is named after him. >> Faraday

Henry, O, pseudonym of **William Sydney Porter** (1862-1910) Writer, master of the short story, born in Greensboro, NC. The first of his many volumes was *Cabbages and Kings* (1904), providing a romantic and humorous treatment of everyday life, and noted for their use of coincidence and trick endings.

Henry, Patrick (1736-99) American revolutionary and statesman, born in Studley, VA. Famed for his oratorical skills, he was outspoken in his opposition to British policy towards the colonies, and made the first speech in the Continental Congress (1774).

Henry, William (1774-1836) Chemist, born in Manchester. He formulated the law named after him that the amount of gas absorbed by a liquid varies directly as the pressure of the gas above the liquid, provided no chemical action takes place.

Henry of Blois [blwah] (c.1099-1171) Clergyman, the younger brother of King Stephen. Bishop of Winchester from 1129, and papal legate in England from 1139, he supported Stephen against the Empress Matilda. >> Matilda; Stephen

Henry of Huntingdon (c.1084-1155) English chronicler,

archdeacon of Huntingdon from 1109. He compiled a *Historia Anglorum* down to 1154.

Henry the Fowler (c.876-936) King of Germany as Henry I from 919. The founder of the Saxon dynasty, he brought Swabia and Bavaria into the German confederation, regained Lorraine (925), defeated the Wends (928) and the Hungarians (933), and seized Schleswig (934).

Henry the Lion (1129-95) Duke of Saxony (1142-80) and Bavaria (1156-80), the head of the Guelphs. He retained power through an alliance with Emperor Frederick I Barbarossa, but broke with him in 1176, and was exiled. >> Frederick I

Henry the Navigator (1394-1460) Portuguese prince, the third son of John I, King of Portugal, and Philippa, daughter of John of Gaunt, Duke of Lancaster. He sponsored many exploratory expeditions along the W African coast.

Henryson, Robert [henrison] (c.1425-1508) Scottish mediaeval poet. His works include *The Testament of Cresseid; Robene and Makyne*, the earliest Scottish specimen of pastoral poetry; and a metrical version of 13 *Morall Fabels of Esope*.

Hensen, (Christian Andreas) Viktor (1835-1924) Physiologist, born in Kiel, Germany. He did research work on the anatomy of sense organs (the *Hensen* duct in the ear), and also investigated the production of marine fauna which he named *plankton*.

Henslowe, Philip (c.1550-1616) Theatre manager, born in Lindfield, West Sussex. In 1584 he became owner of the Rose Theatre on the Bankside, London. His business diary (1598-1609) contains invaluable information about the stage of Shakespeare's day.

Henson, Jim, popular name of **James Maury Henson** (1936-90) Puppeteer, born in Greenville, MS. His 'Muppets' achieved nationwide popularity on the children's television workshop, *Sesame Street* (from 1969) and *The Muppet Show* (1976-81), appearing also in a string of films.

Henty, G(eorge) A(lfred) (1832-1902) Writer and journalist, born in Trumpington, Cambridgeshire. He is best known for his 80 historical adventure stories for boys, including *With Clive in India* (1884) and *With Moore at Corunna* (1898).

Henze, Hans Werner [hentsuh] (1926-) Composer, born in Gütersloh, Germany. He was influenced by Schoenberg, exploring beyond the more conventional uses of the 12-tone system. His works include operas, ballets, symphonies, and chamber music.

Hepburn, Audrey, originally **Eda van Heemstra** (1929-93) Actress and film star, born in Brussels, Belgium. She was given the lead in the Broadway production of *Gigi* (1951), and went on to win international acclaim for *Roman Holiday* (1953, Oscar). Other films included *The Nun's Story* (1959), *Breakfast at Tiffany's* (1961), and *My Fair Lady* (1964).

Hepburn, James >> Bothwell, Earl of

Hepburn, Katharine (1909-) Actress, born in Hartford, CT. From 1932 she attained international fame in films, notably in *Morning Glory* (1933), *Guess Who's Coming to Dinner* (1967), *The Lion in Winter* (1968), and *On Golden Pond* (1981), all of which gained her Oscars, and *The African Queen* (1952).

Hepplewhite, George (?-1786) British furniture designer. His simple and elegant designs became famous with the posthumous publication of his *Cabinet-Maker and Upholsterer's Guide* (1788).

Hepworth, Dame (Jocelyn) Barbara (1903-75) Sculptor, born in Wakefield, West Yorkshire. She was one of the foremost nonfigurative sculptors of her time, as seen in her *Contrapuntal Forms* (1951). >> Nicholson, Ben

Heraclitus or **Heracleitos** [herakliytus] (?-460 BC) Greek philosopher, born in Ephesus. He thought that all things are composed of opposites, constantly at strife with one another, and thus in perpetual change. Only fragments of his writings survive.

Heraclius [heraklius] (c.575–641) Byzantine emperor (610–41), born in Cappadocia, the son of the Roman governor of Africa. He overthrew Phocas and became emperor, carrying out far-reaching reforms, and defeating the Persians in a series of campaigns which restored the lost territories (628–33).

Herbart, Johann Friedrich (1776–1841) Philosopher and educational theorist, born in Oldenburg, Germany. His metaphysics posited a multiplicity of 'reals', and led to a psychology which rejected the notions of faculties and innate ideas.

Herbert, Zbigniew [hairbairt, zhbignev] (1924–) Poet, born in Lvov, Poland. His works include (trans titles) *Chords of Light* (1956), *Study of the Object* (1961), and *Report from a Besieged City* (1983).

Herbert, Sir A(lan) P(atrick) (1890–1971) British politician and writer, born in Elstead, Surrey. His series of libretti for comic operas include *Bless the Bride* (1947), and among his novels are *The Secret Battle* (1919) and *The Water Gipsies* (1930).

Herbert (of Cherbury), Edward Herbert, Baron (1583–1648) English soldier, statesman, and philosopher, born in Eyton, Shropshire, the brother of George Herbert. Regarded as the founder of English deism, his main works are *On Truth* (trans, 1624) and *On the Religion of the Gentiles* (1663). >> Herbert, George

Herbert, George (1593–1633) Clergyman and poet, born at Montgomery Castle, Powys. His verse is collected in *The Temple* (1633), and his chief prose work, *A Priest in the Temple*, was published in *Remains* (1652). >> Herbert, Edward

Herbert, Victor (1859–1924) Composer, born in Dublin. His successful comic opera, *Prince Ananias* (1894), was followed by a series of similar works, but he later produced serious operas including *Natoma* (1911).

Herbert, Wally, popular name of **Walter William Herbert** (1934–) Arctic explorer. He led the first surface crossing of the Arctic Ocean (1968–9), and made several attempts to circumnavigate Greenland (1978–82).

Herbert, William, 3rd Earl of Pembroke (1580–1630) English poet. He became Chancellor of Oxford University in 1617, and Pembroke College is named after him. Shakespeare's 'W H', the 'onlie begetter' of the *Sonnets*, has been taken by some to refer to him.

Herder, Johann Gottfried von (1744–1803) Critic and poet, born in Mohrungen, Germany. He wrote on folk-songs, poetry, and mythology, developing a historical method best seen in his masterpiece, *Outlines of a Philosophy on the History of Man* (trans, 1784–91).

Hereward, known as **Hereward the Wake** (?–c.1080) Anglo-Saxon thegn who returned from exile to lead the last organized English resistance against the Norman invaders. He held the Isle of Ely against William the Conqueror (1070–1), and became legendary as an opponent of injustice. >> William I (of England)

Hergé [herzhay], Fr [airzhay], pseudonym of **Georges Rémi** (1907–83) Strip cartoonist, born in Etterbeek, Belgium. He created the *Tin-Tin* strip, using the pseudonym Hergé, a phonetic version of his initials, RG.

Herkomer, Sir Hubert von [herkomer] (1849–1914) Artist and film pioneer, born in Waal, Germany. In 1870 he settled in London, where he was a pioneer producer/director of British silent films, establishing his own studio at Bushey, Hertfordshire.

Herman, Woody, popular name of **Woodrow Charles Herman** (1913–87) Bandleader, alto saxophonist, and clarinettist, born in Milwaukee, WI. He formed the white swing band called the Woodchoppers in 1936, following this with the Herman Orchestra (or 'Herd') in 1944.

Hermandszoon, Jakob >> **Arminius, Jakobus**

Hermannsson, Steingrímur (1928–) Icelandic prime minister (1983–7, 1988–91). In his first term he headed a coalition, after which he became foreign affairs minister under Pálsson, achieving a second term in 1988.

Hermes, Georg [hermes] (1775–1831) Roman Catholic theologian, born in Dreyerwalde, Germany. He sought to combine Catholicism with Kantian philosophy in the *Hermesian method*. His doctrines were condemned by Pope Gregory XVI in 1835. >> Kant

Hero of Alexandria (1st-c AD) Greek mathematician and inventor. He devised many machines, among them the 'aeolipile', the earliest known steam engine. He also devised the formula for expressing the area of a triangle in terms of its sides.

Herod [herod], known as **the Great** (c.73–4 BC) King of Judea (40 BC), the younger son of the Idumaean chieftain, Antipater. An able administrator, he did much to develop the economic potential of his kingdom. His cruelty is reflected in the Gospel account of the Massacre of the Innocents. >> Antipater

Herod Agrippa I [herod agripa] (10 BC–AD 44) King of Judaea (41–4), the grandson of Herod the Great. Reared at the court of the Emperor Augustus, he succeeded to the former kingdom of Herod the Great. He executed St James and imprisoned St Peter. >> Augustus; James, St; Peter, St

Herod Agrippa II [herod agripa] (c.27–c.93) King of Chalcis (49/50–53), ruler of the Ituraean principality (53–c.93), the son of Herod Agrippa I. It was before him that St Paul made his defence and was found innocent. >> Herod Agrippa I; Paul, St

Herod Antipas [herod antipas] (?–AD 39) The son of Herod the Great and ruler (tetrarch) of Galilee and Peraea (4–39), after Herod's death. In the Christian tradition, he looms large as the capricious murderer of John the Baptist. >> Herod; John the Baptist, St

Herodian (?–c.238) Historian, born in Syria. He lived in Rome, and wrote in Greek a history of the Roman emperors dating from 180 to 238.

Herodotos or **Herodotus** [herodotus] (c.485–425 BC) Greek historian, born in Halicarnassus, Asia Minor. He travelled widely in the Middle East, collecting material for his great narrative history, which gave a record of the wars between the Greeks and the Persians.

Hérold, Louis Joseph Ferdinand [ayrold] (1791–1833) Composer, born in Paris. Best remembered for his comic operas, such as *Zampa* (1831), he also wrote several ballets and piano music.

Heron, Patrick (1920–) Painter, writer, and textile designer, born in Leeds, West Yorkshire. He has travelled widely as a lecturer, and has held many one-man exhibitions worldwide.

Herophilus [herofilus] (c.335–c.280 BC) Greek anatomist, founder of the school of anatomy in Alexandria, born in Chalcedon. He was the first to dissect the human body to compare it with that of other animals.

Héroult, Paul Louis Toussaint [ayroo] (1863–1914) Chemist, born in Thury-Harcourt, France. He discovered (independently of Hall) the electrolytic process for the production of aluminium in 1886, and also devised an electric-arc furnace used in steel manufacture. >> Hall, Charles M

Herrera, Francisco [eraya], known as **el Mozo** ('the Younger') (1622–85) Painter, born in Seville, Spain, the son and pupil of Francisco Herrera (the Elder). His best works are a fresco, 'The Ascension', in the Atocha Church in Madrid, and 'St Francis', in Seville Cathedral. >> Herrera, Francisco (the Elder)

Herrera, Francisco [erayra], known as **el Viejo** ('the Elder') (1576–1656) Painter and engraver, born in Seville, Spain. His early works are in a Mannerist style, but later works, such as 'St Basil' (1637, Louvre), show a transition towards naturalism. >> Herrera, Francisco (the Younger)

Herrick, Robert (1591–1674) Poet, born in London. His writing, both secular and religious, is mainly collected in *Hesperides* (1648), and includes such well-known lyrics as 'Cherry ripe'.

Herriman, George (1881–1944) Cartoonist, born in New Orleans, LA. Working for the *New York Journal* (1904), his daily strip, *The Dingbat Family* (1910), featuring the family cat, evolved into *Krazy Kat*, and continued until his death.

Herriot, Edouard [airyoh] (1872–1957) French prime minister (1924–5, 1932), born in Troyes, France. He was minister of transport during World War 1, radical-socialist premier, and later became president of the National Assembly (1947–54).

Herriot, James, pseudonym of **James Alfred Wight** (1916–95) Veterinary surgeon and writer, born in Glasgow, Strathclyde. Beginning in the 1970s, he brought the vet's world to the notice of the public with a number of best-selling books, such as *It Shouldn't Happen to a Vet*. Films and television series made his work widely known, especially the series *All Creatures Great and Small* (1977–80).

Herschel, Caroline Lucretia [hershl] (1750–1848) Astronomer, born in Hanover, Germany, the sister of Sir William Herschel. In 1772 she joined her brother in Bath, Avon, acting as his assistant, and discovered eight comets and several nebulae and star clusters. >> Herschel, William

Herschel, Sir John Frederick William [hershl] (1792–1871) Astronomer, born in Slough, Berkshire, the son of Sir William Herschel. He charted the S hemisphere stars (1834–8), pioneered celestial photography, and carried out research on photo-active chemicals and the wave theory of light. >> Herschel, William

Herschel, Sir William (Frederick) [hershl], originally **Friedrich Wilhelm Herschel** (1738–1822) Astronomer, born in Hanover, Germany. In England he built the largest reflecting telescopes of the day, discovered Uranus in 1781, and greatly added to the knowledge of the Solar System, Milky Way, and nebulae.

Hersey, John (Richard) (1914–93) Writer, born in Tientsin, China. His novel, *A Bell for Adano* (1944, Pulitzer), was acclaimed for his clever fictionalizing of fact, and *Hiroshima* (1946) was the first on-the-spot description of the effects of a nuclear explosion.

Hershey, A(lfred) D(ay) (1908–) Biologist, born in Lansing, MI. An expert on bacteriophages, in the early 1950s he proved that the DNA of these organisms is their genetic information-carrying component. He shared the Nobel Prize for Physiology or Medicine in 1969.

Herskovits, Melville J(ean) [herskovits] (1895–1963) Cultural anthropologist, born in Bellefontaine, OH. An advocate of cultural relativism, he expounded in *Man and His Works* (1948) that all standards of judgment are culture-bound.

Hertz, Gustav (Ludwig) (1887–1975) Physicist, born in Hamburg, Germany, the nephew of Heinrich Hertz. He worked with Franck on experiments that confirmed quantum theory, and they shared the Nobel Prize for Physics in 1925. >> Franck, James; Hertz, Heinrich

Hertz, Heinrich (Rudolf) (1857–1894) Physicist, born in Hamburg, Germany. His main work was on electromagnetic waves (1887), and he was the first to broadcast and receive radio waves. The unit of frequency is named after him.

Hertzog, J(ames) B(arry) M(unnik) [hertzokh] (1866–1942) South African prime minister (1924–39), born in Wellington, Cape Colony, South Africa. He founded the Nationalist Party in 1914, advocating complete independence, but as premier renounced his earlier secessionism.

Hertzsprung, Ejnar [hertshprung] (1873–1967) Astronomer, born in Frederiksberg, Denmark. He showed that for most stars, colour and brightness are related - a relationship which was a major influence on later work on star evolution.

Herzberg, Gerhard [hertsberg] (1904–) Physical chemist, born in Hamburg, Germany. He greatly developed spectroscopic methods for the detailed study of energy levels in atoms and molecules, and for the detection of free radicals. He was awarded the Nobel Prize for Chemistry in 1971.

Herzl, Theodor [hertsl] (1860–1904) Zionist leader, born in Budapest. He was converted to Zionism, and in the pamphlet *The Jewish State* (trans, 1896), called for a world council to discuss the question of a homeland for the Jews. He became the first president of the World Zionist Organization.

Herzog, Werner [hertzog], originally **Werner Stipetic** (1942–) Film director, screenwriter, and producer, born in Sachrang, Germany. He became recognized as a leading member of the New Cinema in Germany with his feature *Aguirre, Wrath of God* (trans, 1973).

Heselrige, Sir Arthur >> **Haselrig, Arthur**

Heseltine, Michael (Ray Dibdin) [heseltiyn] (1933–) British Conservative statesman, born in Swansea, West Glamorgan. He served as secretary of state for the environment (1979–83) and defence secretary (1983–6), later becoming environment secretary (1990–2), President of the Board of Trade (1992–5), and deputy prime minister (1995–).

Heseltine, Philip Arnold >> **Warlock, Peter**

Hesiod [heesiod] (fl.8th-CBC) Poet, born in Ascra, Greece. One of the earliest known Greek poets, his *Works and Days* deals with farming life; *Theogony* teaches the origin of the universe and the history of the gods.

Hess, Germain Henri (1802–50) Chemist, born in Geneva, Switzerland. He formulated *Hess's law* (1840), which states that the net heat evolved or absorbed in any chemical reaction depends only on the initial and final stages.

Hess, Dame Myra (1890–1965) Pianist, born in London. An immediate success on her first public appearance in 1907, during World War 2 she organized the lunchtime concerts in the National Gallery.

Hess, (Walter Richard) Rudolph (1894–1987) German politician, Hitler's deputy as Nazi Party leader, born in Alexandria, Egypt. In 1941, he flew alone to Scotland to plead the cause of a negotiated Anglo-German peace, and was held in Britain until the Nuremberg Trials (1946) when he was sentenced to life imprisonment. He remained in Spandau prison, Berlin, until his death. >> Hitler

Hess, Victor (Francis) (1883–1964) Physicist, born in Waldstein, Austria. He realized during balloon ascents that high-energy radiation in the Earth's atmosphere originated from outer space. For his work on cosmic radiation he shared the Nobel Prize for Physics in 1936.

Hess, Walter Rudolf (1881–1973) Physiologist, born in Frauenfeld, Switzerland. He did important research on the nervous system, and developed methods of stimulating localized areas of the brain by means of needle electrodes. He shared the Nobel Prize for Physiology or Medicine in 1949.

Hesse, Eva [hes] (1936–70) Sculptor, born in Hamburg, Germany. From 1965 she worked in a variety of unusual materials, including rubber, plastic, string, and polythene, producing bizarre objects designed to rest on the floor or against a wall or even be suspended from the ceiling.

Hesse, Hermann [hesuh] (1877–1962) Novelist and poet, born in Calw, Germany. His works include *Rosshalde* (1914), *Siddhartha* (1922), *Steppenwolf* (1927), and *The Glass Bead Game* (trans, 1945). He was awarded the Nobel Prize for Literature in 1946.

Heston, Charlton, originally **John Charles Carter** (1923–) Actor and director, born in Evanston, IL. He is chiefly known for historic or heroic roles in such epics as *The Ten Commandments* (1956), *Ben Hur* (1959, Oscar), and *El Cid* (1961).

Heuss, Theodor [hoys] (1884–1963) First president of the Federal Republic of Germany (1949–59), born in Brackenheim, Germany. In 1946 he became a founder member of the Free Democratic Party, and helped to draft the new federal constitution.

Hevelius, Johannes [heveelius] (1611–87) Astronomer, born in Gdańsk, Poland. He catalogued 1564 stars in *Prodromus Astronomiae* (1690), discovered four comets, and was one of the first to observe the transit of Mercury.

Hevesy, George Charles de [heveshee] (1885–1966) Chemist, born in Budapest, Hungary. In 1923 he discovered, with **Dirk Coster** (1889–1950), the element hafnium. He was awarded the 1943 Nobel Prize for Chemistry for his work on isotopic tracer techniques.

Hewett, Dorothy (1923–) Writer, born in Perth, Western Australia. Her plays are mainly Expressionist works that feature music and poetry, such as *The Chapel Perilous* (1971). Her novels are *Bobbin Up* (1980) and *The Toucher* (1993).

Hewish, Antony (1924–) Radio astronomer, born in Fowey, Cornwall. With his student Susan Jocelyn (Burnell) Bell, he discovered the first radio stars emitting radio signals in regular pulses (pulsars), and shared the Nobel Prize for Physics in 1974. >> Bell Burnell; Ryle, Martin

Hewlett-Packard William Hewlett (1913–) and **David Packard** (1912–) Founders of the Hewlett-Packard electronics and computer equipment company. Their handheld scientific calculator, the HP-35 (1972), was a best seller, and marked the start of personal computing. >> Jobs

Hewson, John (1946–) Australian politician and economist, born in Sydney, New South Wales, Australia. He became shadow minister for finance (1988–9) and shadow treasurer (1989–90), and was elected leader of the Liberal Party in 1990.

Heyden, Jan van der [hayden] (1637–1712) Painter, born in Gorinchem, The Netherlands. He is best known for his highly detailed townscapes of Amsterdam, executed in the 1660s.

Heydrich, Reinhard [hiydrikh], nickname **the Hangman** (1904–42) Nazi politician and deputy-chief of the Gestapo, born in Halle, Germany. He was charged with subduing Hitler's war-occupied countries, which he did by ordering mass executions, and was assassinated. >> Hitler

Heyer, Georgette [hayer] (1902–74) Writer, born in London. Her work includes historical novels, fictional studies of real figures in crisis, such as William I, and comedy detective novels. An authority on the Regency period, she had success with *Regency Buck* (1935).

Heyerdahl, Thor [hiyerdahl] (1914–) Anthropologist, born in Larvik, Norway. In 1947 he proved, by sailing a balsa raft (the *Kon-Tiki*) from Peru to Tuamotu I in the S Pacific, that the Peruvian Indians could have settled in Polynesia. Later journeys include from Morocco to the West Indies in a papyrus boat, *Ra II* (1970).

Heymans, Corneille Jean François [hiymahns] (1892–1968) Physiologist, born in Ghent, Belgium. He discovered the regulatory effect on respiration of certain sensory organs, and how blood pressure and its oxygen content are monitored. He was awarded the Nobel Prize for Physiology or Medicine in 1938.

Heyrovsky, Jaroslav [hiyrofskee] (1890–1967) Chemist, born in Prague. In 1922 he discovered polarography, and continued to develop and improve his discovery and its application. He was awarded the Nobel Prize for Chemistry in 1959.

Heysen, Sir (Wilhelm Ernst) Hans (Franz) [hiysen] (1877–1968) Landscape painter, born in Hamburg, Germany. Primarily a water-colourist, his first important exhibition was in Melbourne, in 1908, and his success grew during the following 20 years.

Heyward, (Edwin) DuBose (1885–1940) Writer, born in Charleston, SC. He dramatized his first novel, *Porgy* (1925), and it was the basis for Gershwin's opera *Porgy and Bess* (1935). >> Gershwin, George

Heywood, John (c.1497–c.1575) Epigrammatist, playwright, and musician, possibly born in London. He was a favourite with Henry VIII and with Mary I, and is best remembered for his collections of proverbs and epigrams. >> Henry VIII; Mary I

Heywood, Thomas (c.1574–1641) Playwright and poet, born in Lincolnshire. By 1633 he had shared in the composition of 220 plays, and written 24 of his own, notably his domestic tragedy, *A Woman Killed with Kindness* (1607).

Hiawatha [hiyawotha], Indian name **Heowenta** (16th-c) Legendary Mohawk leader, born in present-day New York State. It is now generally accepted that he was a real person who was influential in founding the Five Nations League, an alliance of five Iroquois tribes. >> Longfellow

Hibbert, Robert (1770–1849) Merchant and philanthropist, born in Jamaica. He moved to England, and in 1847 founded the Hibbert Trust, whose funds set up the Hibbert Lectures (from 1878) and aided the *Hibbert Journal* (1920–70).

Hick, John (Harwood) (1922–) Theologian and philosopher of religion, born in Scarborough, North Yorkshire. He has questioned the status of Christianity among the world religions in such works as *God and the Universe of Faiths* (1973).

Hickock, Wild Bill >> Calamity Jane

Hicks, Elias (1748–1830) Liberal Quaker preacher, born in Hempstead, Long Island, NY. His successful opposition to the adoption of a set creed in 1817 led to the split of the Quakers into Orthodox and *Hicksite* Friends (1827–8).

Hicks, Sir John Richard (1904–89) Economist, born in Leamington Spa, Warwickshire. He wrote a classic book on the conflict between business-cycle theory and equilibrium theory, *Value and Capital* (1939), and shared the Nobel Prize for Economics in 1972.

Hideyoshi, Toyotomi [hideyoshee] (1536–98) The second of the three great historical unifiers of Japan, sometimes called 'the Napoleon of Japan'. An ordinary soldier who rose to become Nobunaga's foremost general, his law forbade all except samurai to carry swords (1588), and reinforced feudal bonds. >> Nobunaga; Tokugawa

Higden, Ranulph (c.1280–1364) Benedictine monk of St Werburgh's monastery in Chester, Cheshire. He wrote a Latin *Polychronicon*, a general history from the creation to c.1342, which was continued by others to 1377.

Higgins, Alex(ander Gordon), nickname **Hurricane Higgins** (1949–) Snooker player, born in Belfast. He has had a tempestuous career after becoming the youngest world champion in 1972, at age 23. He won the title for a second time in 1982.

Higgins, George (Vincent) (1939–) Novelist, born in Brockton, MA. His acclaimed thrillers include *The Friends of Eddie Coyle* (1972), *Kennedy for the Defence* (1980), and *Outlaws* (1987).

Higgins, Jack, pseudonym of **Harry Patterson** (1929–) Writer, born in Newcastle upon Tyne, Tyne and Wear. He became a best-selling author with the success of *The Eagle Has Landed* (1975; filmed 1976).

Higginson, Thomas Wentworth (Storrow) (1823–1911) Writer and reformer, born in Cambridge, MA. During the Civil War he commanded the first troop of African-American soldiers in the Union army, and out of this experience produced *Army Life in a Black Regiment* (1870).

Highsmith, Patricia (1921–) Writer of detective fiction, born in Fort Worth, TX. Her first novel was *Strangers on a Train* (1949; filmed 1957), but her best novels describe the criminal adventures of her psychotic hero, Tom Ripley, beginning with *The Talented Mr Ripley* (1956).

Hightower, Rosella (1920–) Ballerina and teacher, born in Ardmore, OK. A leading ballerina with the Ballets Russes (1938–46), from 1980 she directed the Opéra Ballet in Paris.

Hijikata, Tatsumi [hijikahta] (1928–86) Performance artist, born in Akita province, Japan. He was a key figure in the Japanese avant-garde of the 1950s and 1960s, and with Kazuo Ohno is credited with the founding of the *butoh* dance-theatre movement.

Hilarion, St (c.291–371), feast day 21 October. Hermit, born in Tabatha, Palestine. He became a Christian and lived as a hermit in the desert between Gaza and Egypt from 306, establishing the first Palestinian monastery in 329.

Hilary (of Poitiers), St (c.315–c.368), feast day 13 January. Clergyman, one of the Doctors of the Church, born of pagan parents in Limonum (Poitiers), France. He was elected Bishop of Poitiers c.350 and became a leading opponent of Arianism. >> Arius

Hilary of Arles, St [ah(r)l] (401–49), feast day 5 May. Clergyman, born probably in N France. He became Bishop of Arles (429), and presided at the synod of Orange (441), whose proceedings involved him in controversy with Pope Leo the Great. >> Leo I

Hilbert, David (1862–1943) Mathematician, born in Königsberg, Germany. He made important contributions to the theory of numbers, the theory of invariants and algebraic geometry, and the application of integral equations to physical problems.

Hilda, St (614–680), feast day 17 November. Abbess, born in Northumbria. In 657 she founded the monastery at Streaneshalch or Whitby, a house for both nuns and monks, which became a great religious centre for the N of England.

Hildebrand, St >> **Gregory VII**

Hildebrand, Adolf [hildebrant] (1847–1921) Sculptor, born in Marburg, Germany. His works include the public monuments to Brahms at Meiningen, Bismarck at Bremen, and Schiller at Nuremberg.

Hildebrandt, Johann Lukas von [hildebrant] (1668–1745) Architect, born in Genoa, Italy. His works include the Mansfield Fondi garden palace (1697–1715), and the less Classical Starhemborg-Schönberg garden palace (1705–6), where his mastery of the relationship between house and garden is clear.

Hildegard of Bingen, St (1098–1199), feast day 17 September. Abbess and mystic, born in Böckelheim, Germany. She experienced visions from childhood, and in c.1147 founded her own convent. Though never formally canonized, she is often listed as a saint.

Hill, Alfred Francis (1870–1960) Composer, born in Melbourne, Victoria, Australia. His work includes 13 symphonies, 10 operas, a *Maori Rhapsody*, five concertos, and much chamber music.

Hill, A(rchibald) V(ivian) (1886–1977) Physiologist, born in Bristol, Avon. He shared the 1922 Nobel Prize for Physiology or Medicine for his research into heat production in muscle contraction.

Hill, Benny, popular name of **Alfred Hawthorne Hill** (1925–92) Comedian, born in Southampton, Hampshire. He gained national popularity with the saucy *Benny Hill Show* (1957–66), and spent over two decades writing and performing in top-rated television specials that were seen around the world.

Hill, David Octavius (1802–70) Photographer and painter, born in Perth, Tayside. In collaboration with Adamson, who had experience of the calotype photographic process, he produced some 1500 pictures considered to be the finest photographic portraits of the 19th-c. >> Adamson, Robert

Hill, Geoffrey (William) (1932–) Poet, born in Bromsgrove, Worcestershire. His works include *For the Unfallen* (1959), *King Log* (1968), *Tenebrae* (1978), and *The Mystery of the Charity of Charles Péguy* (1983).

Hill, (Norman) Graham (1929–75) Motor-racing driver, born in London. He was twice world champion (1962, 1968), and won the Monaco Grand Prix five times (1963–5, 1968–9). His son, **Damon Hill** (1952–), also went into motor-racing, and was runner-up in the world championship in 1994.

Hill, James (Jerome) (1838–1916) Railway magnate, born in Guelph, Ontario, Canada. He took over the St Paul–Pacific line and extended it to link with the Canadian system, later gaining control of the Northern Pacific Railroad.

Hill, J(oseph) Lister (1894–1984) US politician, born in Montgomery, AL. He served as a Democrat in the US House of Representatives (1923–38) and the US Senate (1939–69), and helped shape the Hill–Burton Hospital Act.

Hill, Octavia (1838–1912) Housing reformer and founder of the National Trust, born in London. A leader of the open-space movement, she was a co-founder in 1895 of the National Trust for Places of Historic Interest or Natural Beauty.

Hill, Patty Smith (1868–1946) Educator and composer, born in Anchorage, KY. She initiated curriculum reform, stressing the value of less structured classroom activities and of children's ability to learn through play. Her songs for children include 'Happy Birthday to You'.

Hill, Rowland (1744–1833) Popular preacher, born in Hawkstone Park, Shropshire. Influenced by Methodism, he became an itinerant preacher, and helped to found the Religious Tract Society and the London Missionary Society.

Hill, Sir Rowland (1795–1879) Originator of penny postage, born in Kidderminster, Worcestershire. In his *Post-office Reform* (1837), he advocated a simple rate of postage, to be prepaid by stamps, and in 1840 a uniform penny rate was introduced.

Hillary, Sir Edmund (Percival) (1919–) Mountaineer and explorer, born in Auckland, New Zealand. As a member of Hunt's Everest expedition he attained, with Tenzing Norgay, the summit of Mt Everest in 1953. >> Hunt, John; Tenzing

Hillel [hilel], known as **Hillel Hazaken** (the Elder), or **Hillel Hababli** ('the Babylonian') (1st-c BC–1st-c AD) One of the most respected Jewish teachers of his time, probably born in Babylonia. He founded a school of followers bearing his name, which frequently debated with the contemporary followers of Shammai. >> Shammai

Hiller, Johann Adam (1728–1804) Composer, born in Wendisch-Ossig, Germany. He wrote over 30 comic operas, practically creating this genre in Germany. He was also a noted conductor and teacher.

Hiller, Dame Wendy (1912–) Actress, born in Bramhall, Greater Manchester. One of Britain's leading stage performers, her sporadic film career includes notable performances in *Sons and Lovers* (1960), *A Man for All Seasons* (1966), and *Separate Tables* (1958, Oscar).

Hillery, Patrick (John) (1923–) Irish president (1976–90), born in Miltown Malbay, Co Clare, Ireland. He held various ministerial posts before becoming foreign minister (1969–72), and also served as the EEC commissioner for social affairs (1973–6).

Hilliard, Nicholas (1547–1619) Court goldsmith and miniaturist, born in Exeter, Devon. He founded the English school of miniature painting.

Hillier, James (1915–) Physicist, born in Brantford, Ontario, Canada. He moved to the USA, where he led the group which made the first successful high-resolution electron microscope in 1940.

Hillier, Tristram Paul (1905–) British artist, born in Beijing. Many of his paintings are of ships and beaches, the earlier ones of a Surrealist character.

Hillman, Sidney (1887–1946) Labour leader, born in Zagare, Lithuania. A labour activist in Russia, he emigrated to the USA (1907), leading a split from the United Garment Workers that resulted in the formation of the Amalgamated Clothing Workers of America (1914).

Hilton, Conrad (Nicholson) (1887–1979) Hotelier, born in San Antonio, NM. He formed the Hilton Hotels Corporation in 1946, which became Hilton International in 1948, one of the world's largest hotel organizations.

Hilton, James (1900–54) Novelist, born in Leigh, Lancashire. Many of his successful novels were filmed, notably *Lost Horizon* (1933) and *Goodbye Mr Chips* (1934).

Hilton, Roger (1911–75) Painter, born in Northwood, Greater London. He produced his first abstract paintings in 1950, and won the UNESCO Prize at the Venice Biennale in 1964.

Himmler, Heinrich (1900–45) German Nazi leader and chief of police, born in Munich, Germany. In 1929 he became head of the SS, directed the Gestapo, and initiated the systematic killing of Jews. Captured by the Allies, he committed suicide.

Hinault, Bernard [eenoh] (1954–) Cyclist, born in Yffignac, France. In 1985 he joined Merckx and Anquetil as a five-times winner of the Tour de France. He retired at 32, and became technical adviser to the Tour de France. >> Anquetil; Merckx

Hincmar (c.806–882) Clergyman, born in N France. He is best known for his denunciation of the German theologian **Gottschalk of Orbais** (c.804–c.869) for his predestination doctrines.

Hindemith, Paul [**hin**duhmit] (1895–1963) Composer, born in Hanau, Germany. His works include operas, concertos, and a wide range of instrumental pieces. He also pioneered *Gebrauchsmusik*, pieces written with specific aims, such as for newsreels and community singing.

Hindenburg, Paul (Ludwig Hans Anton von Beneckendorff und) von [**hin**denberg] (1847–1934) German general and president (1925–34), born in Posnan, Poland (formerly, Posen, Prussia). He won victories over the Russians (1914–15), but was forced to direct the German retreat on the Western Front (to the *Hindenburg line*).

Hindley, Myra >> **Brady, Ian**

Hindmarsh, Sir John [**hiynd**mah(r)sh] (c.1782–1860) British naval officer and administrator, probably born in Chatham, Kent. He was appointed the first governor of South Australia.

Hine, Lewis (Wickes) [hiyn] (1874–1940) Photographer, born in Oshkosh, WI. In 1909 he published the first of his many photo stories, such as 'Little Spinner in Carolina Cotton Mill', depicting young children in dangerous work.

Hines, Earl (Kenneth) [hiynz], nickname **Fatha** ('Father') **Hines** (1905–83) Jazz pianist and bandleader, born in Duquesne, PA. He formed his own band in 1928, and his approach to solo improvisation, known as 'trumpet-style piano', was influential.

Hinkler, Bert (Herbert John Louis) (1892–1933) Aviator, born in Bundaberg, Queensland, Australia. In 1928 he created a new England–Australia record, arriving in Darwin, Northern Territory, 16 days after leaving England.

Hinshelwood, Sir Cyril Norman (1897–1967) Chemist, born in London. He did valuable work on the effect of drugs on bacterial cells, and investigated chemical reaction kinetics, for which he shared the Nobel Prize for Chemistry in 1956.

Hinsley, Arthur, Cardinal (1865–1943) Roman Catholic clergyman, born in Carlton, North Yorkshire. Made a cardinal in 1937, he founded in 1940 an ecumenical politico-religious group called the Sword of the Spirit to rally British churchmen against totalitarianism.

Hinton (of Bankside), Christopher Hinton, Baron (1901–83) Nuclear engineer, born in Tisbury, Wiltshire. He constructed the world's first large-scale commercial atomic power station at Calder Hall, Cumbria, opened in 1956.

Hipparchos or **Hipparchus** [hi**pah(r)**kus] (2nd-c BC) Astronomer, born in Nicaea, Rhodes. He discovered the precession of the equinoxes, determined the length of the solar year, estimated the distances of the Sun and Moon from the Earth, and drew up a catalogue of 1080 stars.

Hipper, Franz von (1863–1932) German naval officer. He commanded at the Battles of Dogger Bank (1915) and Jutland (1916), and became commander-in-chief of the German High Seas fleet in 1918.

Hippias of Elis (5th-c BC) Greek Sophist philosopher, a contemporary of Socrates. He was vividly portrayed in Plato's dialogues as a virtuoso performer as teacher, orator, memory man, and polymath. >> Plato; Socrates

Hippius, Zinaida Nikolayevna >> **Merezhkovsky, Dmitry Sergeyevich**

Hippocrates [hi**po**krateez] (c.460–c.377 BC) Physician, known as 'the father of medicine', and associated with the medical profession's *Hippocratic oath*, born on the island of Cos, Greece. The most celebrated physician of antiquity, he gathered together all that was sound in the previous history of medicine.

Hippolytus, St [hi**pol**itus] (170–235), feast day (W) 13 August, (E) 30 January. Christian leader and antipope in Rome. He is generally believed to be the author of a *Refutation of all Heresies* in 10 books, discovered in 1842 in a 14th-c manuscript at Mt Athos.

Hire, Philippe de la [eer] (1640–1718) Engineer, born in Paris. His most notable work is the *Traité de Méchanique* (1695), in which he correctly analyzed the forces acting at various points in an arch, using techniques now known as graphic statics.

Hirohito [hiroh**hee**toh] >> **Showa Tenno**

Hiroshige, Ando [hirohsheegay] (1797–1858) Painter, born in Edo (modern Tokyo). He is celebrated for his impressive landscape colour prints. 'Fifty-three Stages of the Tokaido' had a great influence on Western Impressionist painters.

Hirshhorn, Joseph H(erman) (1899–1981) Financier and art collector, born in Mitvau, Latvia. In New York City from 1907, he became a stockbroker (1916), amassed a fortune, and invested much of his money in art.

His, Wilhelm (1831–1904) Biologist, born in Basel, Switzerland. He invented the microtome (1865, a device to cut very thin slices for microscopic investigation), and discovered that each nerve fibre is linked to a single nerve cell.

Hiss, Alger [aljer] (1904–) US State Department official, born in Baltimore, MD. He reached high office, then stood trial twice (1949, 1950) on a charge of perjury, having denied passing documents to a communist spy ring. He was sentenced to five years' imprisonment, but revelations from Soviet archives in 1992 seem to indicate his innocence.

Hitchcock, Sir Alfred (Joseph) (1899–1980) Film director, born in London. He became a master of suspense, internationally recognized for his intricate plots and novel camera techniques. His films include *The Thirty-Nine Steps* (1935), *The Lady Vanishes* (1938), *Rebecca* (1940, Oscar), *Psycho* (1960), *The Birds* (1963), and *Frenzy* (1972).

Hitchcock, Lambert (1795-1852) Furniture designer, born in Cheshire, CT. In 1818 he established a furniture factory for mass production of Hitchcock chairs, now considered collectors' items.

Hitchens, Ivon (1893-1979) Painter, born in London. His works displayed a strongly expressive feeling for natural forms, especially in the wide, horizontal landscapes which he painted from 1936.

Hitler, Adolf, popular name **der Führer** ('the Leader') (1889-1945) German dictator, born in Braunau, Upper Austria. In 1919 he joined a small political party which in 1920 he renamed as the National Socialist German Workers' Party. While in prison for attempting to overthrow the Bavarian government, he produced his political testament, *Mein Kampf* (1925, My Struggle). Made chancellor in 1933, he suspended the constitution, silenced all opposition, and brought the Nazi Party to power. His domestic policy was one of total Nazification, enforced by the Gestapo, and established concentration camps for political opponents and Jews. His agressive actions in Czechoslovakia and Poland precipitated World War 2 (1939). With his early war successes, he increasingly ignored the advice of military experts, and the tide turned in 1942 after the defeats at El Alamein and Stalingrad. When Germany was invaded, he retired to an air-raid shelter under the Chancellory building in Berlin, where he went through a marriage ceremony with his mistress, Eva Braun. All available evidence suggests that Hitler and his wife committed suicide and had their bodies cremated. >> Braun, Eva

Hittorf, Johann Wilhelm (1824-1914) Physicist, born in Bonn, Germany. He was the first to determine the charge-carrying capacity of ions, which brought greater understanding of electrochemical reactions.

Hjelmslev, Louis (Trolle) [hyelmzlev] (1899-1965) Linguist, born in Copenhagen. He founded the Linguistic Circle of Copenhagen in 1931, and with associates devised a system of linguistic analysis known as glossematics.

Hoad, Lew(is Alan) [hohd] (1934-94) Tennis player, born in Sydney, New South Wales, Australia. With his doubles partner, Ken Rosewall, he won the Wimbledon doubles title before he was 20. He defeated Rosewall in the Wimbledon singles final of 1956, and won again in 1957. >> Rosewall

Hoadley, Silas >> **Thomas, Seth**

Hoagland, Mahlon (Bush) [hohgland] (1921-) Biochemist, born in Boston, MA. In the 1950s he isolated t-RNA (transfer RNA), and went on to show in some detail how cells use it to synthesize proteins from amino acids.

Hoare, Sir Richard (1648-1718) Banker, born in London. In Fleet Street (c.1693) he founded the bank which still bears his name, and was Lord Mayor of London in 1713.

Hoare, Sir Samuel (John Gurney), Viscount Templewood of Chelsea (from 1944) (1880-1959) British statesman, born in London. He was secretary of state for India (1931-5), and foreign secretary (1935), but resigned after criticism of his part in the discussions which led to the abortive Hoare-Laval pact over the Italian invasion of Ethiopia. >> Laval

Hobbema, Meindert [hobema], originally **Meyndert Lubbertsz(oon)** (1638-1709) Landscape painter, probably born in Amsterdam. His masterpiece, 'The Avenue, Middelharnis' (1689) greatly influenced modern landscape artists.

Hobbes, Thomas (1588-1679) Political philosopher, born in Malmesbury, Wiltshire. After being introduced to Euclidean geometry, he thought to extend its method into a comprehensive science of man and society, and wrote several works on government, notably *Leviathan* (1651).

Hobbs, Jack, popular name of **Sir John Berry Hobbs** (1882-1963) Cricketer, born in Cambridge, Cambridgeshire. He played in county cricket for Surrey (1905-34) and for England (1908-30). He made a record number of 197 centuries and 61 167 runs in first-class cricket.

Hobson, Sir Harold (1904-92) Dramatic critic, born in Thorpe Hesley, South Yorkshire. He became drama critic of the *Christian Science Monitor* (1931-74), and of the *Sunday Times* (1947-76), and was a regular member of the radio proramme *The Critics*.

Hobson, Thomas (c.1544-1631) Carrier and inn-keeper of Cambridge, Cambridgeshire. He kept a stable of horses to rent out to students at the university, and required each customer to take the horse nearest the stable door, whatever its quality; hence the expression 'Hobson's choice', meaning no choice at all.

Hoccleve or **Occleve, Thomas** [hokleev] (c.1368-c.1450) Poet, born in London. His chief work is *The Regement of Princes* (1411), but his earlier *The Male Regimen* (trans, 1406) is of value as social history, with its vivid account of night life in Westminster.

Hochhuth, Rolf [hokhhoot] (1931-) Playwright, born in Eschwege, Germany. His play *The Representative* (trans, 1963), focusing on the role of the Pope in World War 2, excited controversy and introduced the fashion for 'documentary drama'.

Ho Chi-Minh [hoh chee min], originally **Nguyen That Thanh** (1892-1969) Vietnamese prime minister (1954-5) and president (1954-69), born in Kim-Lien, North Vietnam. He led the Viet Minh independence movement in 1941, and directed the successful military operations against the French (1946-54), becoming President of North Vietnam.

Hockney, David (1937-) Artist, born in Bradford, West Yorkshire. Associated with the Pop Art movement from his earliest work, he has also worked in printmaking and photography, and designed sets and costumes.

Hoddinott, Alun (1929-) Composer, born in Bargoed, Mid Glamorgan. Artistic director of the Cardiff Festival (1967-89), he is a prolific composer of operas, symphonies, concertos, and a large corpus of choral and chamber works.

Hodges, Johnny (1906-70) Jazz alto and soprano saxophonist, born in Cambridge, MA. He joined Duke Ellington's orchestra (1928-51), then led his own band with moderate success, rejoining in 1955 until his death. >> Ellington, Duke

Hodgkin, Sir Alan (Lloyd) (1914-) Physiologist, born in Banbury, Oxfordshire. With Huxley he researched the passage of impulses in nerve fibres, for which they shared the Nobel Prize for Physiology or Medicine in 1963. >> Eccles, John Carew; Huxley, Andrew

Hodgkin, Dorothy Mary, née **Crowfoot** (1910-94) Chemist, born in Cairo. A crystallographer, she was awarded the Nobel Prize for Chemistry in 1964 for her discoveries, by the use of X-ray techniques, of the structure of certain molecules, including penicillin, vitamin B_{12}, and insulin.

Hodgkin, Howard (1932-) Painter, born in London. His paintings are usually of interiors with people captured at a particular moment in time. In 1985 he won the Turner Prize for contemporary British art.

Hodgkin, Thomas (1798-1866) Physician and pathologist, born in London. He held various posts at Guy's Hospital, London, and described the glandular disease lymphadenoma, which is named after him (*Hodgkin's disease*).

Hodgkins, Frances Mary (1869-1947) Artist, born in Dunedin, New Zealand. Ranked as a leader of contemporary Romanticism, her paintings are characterized by a harmonious use of flat colour.

Hodgkinson, Eaton (1789-1861) Engineer, born in Anderton, Cheshire. He proposed the *Hodgkinson's beam* as the most efficient form of cast-iron beam (1830).

Hodgson, Leonard (1889–1969) Anglican theologian, born in London. His books include *The Doctrine of the Trinity* (1943) and *The Doctrine of the Atonement* (1951).

Hodgson, Ralph (1871–1962) Poet, born in Yorkshire. He is best known for three volumes of poems with the recurring theme of nature and England: *The Last Blackbird* (1907), *Eve* (1913), and *Poems* (1917).

Hodja, Enver >> **Hoxha, Enver**

Hoe, Richard (March) (1812–86) Inventor and industrialist, born in New York City. He developed the first successful rotary press, patented in 1847. An improved model, the *Hoe web perfecting press*, was first used by the *New York Tribune*.

Hofer, Andreas [hohfer] (1767–1810) Tyrolese patriot leader and innkeeper, born in St Leonhard, Austria. In 1808 he successfully led the Tyrolese to expel invaders, but was later executed.

Hoff, Ted, popular name of **Marian Edward Hoff** (1937–) Creator of the microprocessor, born in Rochester, NY. He designed the computer-on-a-chip microprocessor (1968), which came on the market as the Intel 4004 (1971), starting the microcomputer industry.

Hoff, Jacobus Henricus van't (1852–1911) Chemist, a founder of physical chemistry, born in Rotterdam, The Netherlands. He postulated the asymmetrical nature of bonds formed with carbon atoms, was the first to apply thermodynamics to chemical reactions, and discovered that osmotic pressure varies directly with the absolute temperature. He was awarded the first Nobel Prize for Chemistry in 1901. >> Le Bel

Hoffa, Jimmy, popular name of **James R(iddle) Hoffa** (1913–75) Labour leader, born in Brazil, IN. President of the Teamster's Union (1957), he was imprisoned in 1967 for attempted bribery of a federal court jury. Paroled in 1971, he disappeared in 1975, and is thought to have been murdered.

Hoffenberg, Sir Raymond (Bill) (1923–) Physician, born in Port Elizabeth, South Africa. In 1967 he was 'banned' by the South African government, moved to Britain, wrote extensively on endocrinology and metabolism, and became president of the Mental Health Foundation (1989–).

Hoffman, Dustin (1937–) Actor, born in Los Angeles, CA. His first leading film role was *The Graduate* (1967), and this was followed by a number of similar 'anti-hero' roles, such as in *Midnight Cowboy* (1969). He found wider scope in *All The President's Men* (1976), *Kramer v Kramer* (1979, Oscar), and *Rain Man* (1988, Oscar).

Hoffman, Samuel (Kurtz) (1902–) Rocket propulsion engineer, born in Williamsport, PA. From 1949 he led the team developing rocket engines at North American Aviation which powered the Saturn 5 launching vehicle used for the Moon launch in 1969.

Hoffmann, August Heinrich, known as **Hoffman von Fallersleben** (1798–1874) Poet and philologist, born in Fallersleben, Germany. He is best known for his popular and patriotic *Volkslieder*, including the song 'Deutschland, Deutschland über Alles' (1841), which became the German national anthem in 1922.

Hoffmann, E(rnst) T(heodor) W(ilhelm), known as **Amadeus** (1776–1822) Writer, composer, music critic, and caricaturist, born in Königsberg, Germany. His shorter tales, known as 'Hoffman's Strange Stories', were an inspiration for Offenbach's *Tales of Hoffmann*. His musical works include the opera *Undine*. >> Offenbach

Hoffmann, Friedrich (1660–1742) German physician. He introduced various medicines, including *Hoffmann's drops* and *Hoffmann's anodyne*.

Hoffmann, Josef (1870–1956) Architect, born in Pirnitz, Austria. A leader of the Vienna 'Secession' group, he founded in 1903 the *Vienna Workshops* devoted to arts and crafts.

Hoffmann, Leonard Hubert (1934–) Judge, born in Cape Town. In Britain from 1960, he was appointed a judge in the High Court of Justice in 1985, and a Lord Justice of Appeal in 1992.

Hoffmann, Roald (1937–) Chemist, born in Zloczow, Poland. At Harvard he worked with Woodward to develop the *Woodward–Hoffmann rules*, which enable the path of an important class of organic reactions to be predicted. He shared the Nobel Prize for Chemistry in 1981. >> Woodward, R B

Hoffnung, Gerard (1925–1959) Cartoonist and musician, born in Berlin, but raised in England. He was staff cartoonist on the London *Evening News* (1947), and later freelanced for *Punch*. His interest in music led to the Hoffnung Music Festivals at the Royal Festival Hall.

Hofmann, August Wilhelm von (1818–92) Chemist, born in Giessen, Germany. He obtained aniline from coal products, discovered formaldehyde (1867), and devoted much labour to the theory of chemical types. His work was of importance to the aniline-dye industry.

Hofmann, Hans (1880–1966) Painter and art teacher, born in Weissenberg, Germany. In 1930 he emigrated to the USA, settling in New York City, where he opened the Hans Hofmann School of Fine Art, pioneering the use of improvisatory techniques.

Hofmannsthal, Hugo von [hofmanztahl] (1874–1929) Poet and playwright, born in Vienna. His plays include *Electra* (1903), the morality play *Everyman* (trans, 1912), and the comedy *The Difficult Man* (trans, 1921), and he wrote the libretto for *Der Rosenkavalier* (1911).

Hofmeister, Wilhelm (Friedrich Benedikt) [hohfmiyster] (1824–77) Botanist, born in Leipzig, Germany. He did fundamental work on plant embryology, and pioneered the science of comparative plant morphology.

Hofstadter, Richard [hofstater] (1916–70) Historian, born in Buffalo, NY. His popular works on political, social, and intellectual trends in the USA include *The Age of Reform* (1955, Pulitzer) and *Anti-Intellectualism in American Life* (1963, Pulitzer).

Hofstadter, Robert [hofstater] (1915–) Physicist, born in New York City. He studied the atomic structure of protons and neutrons on the large linear accelerator at Stanford, and determined their electromagnetic form factors. He shared the Nobel Prize for Physics in 1961.

Hogan, (William) Ben(jamin) (1912–) Golfer, born in Dublin, TX. In 1948 he became the first man in 26 years to win all three US major titles, and won the US Open four times before retiring in 1970.

Hogan, Paul (1941–) Comedian and actor, born in Lightning Ridge, New South Wales, Australia. He became internationally known for the films *Crocodile Dundee* and *Crocodile Dundee II*, and has since become something of a national folk hero.

Hogarth, William [hohgah(r)th] (1697–1764) Painter and engraver, born in London. His highly detailed engravings of 'modern moral subjects' include 'A Rake's Progress' (1733–5), and his masterpiece, the 'Marriage à la Mode' (1743–5).

Hogben, Lancelot (1895–1975) Physiologist and writer, born in Southsea, Hampshire. His popular books on scientific subjects include *Mathematics for the Million* (1936) and *Science for the Citizen* (1938).

Hogg, Quintin (1845–1903) Philanthropist, born in London. He opened a 'ragged school' for destitute children at Charing Cross, then a Youths' Christian Institute, and in 1882 opened Regent Street Polytechnic to teach various trades.

Hogg, James, known as **the Ettrick Shepherd** (1770–1835) Writer, born near Ettrick, Borders, Scotland. He wrote several works in verse and prose, notably *The Private Memoirs and Confessions of a Justified Sinner* (1824).

Hogg, Quintin >> Hailsham, 2nd Viscount

Hohenheim, Philippus von >> Paracelsus

Hohner, Matthias (1833–1902) German mouth-organ manufacturer. In 1857 he established his firm at Trossingen, Württemberg, to which his five sons added music publishing, the manufacture of instruments, and (in 1931) an accordion school.

Hokusai, Katsushika [hokusiy] (1760–1849) Artist and wood engraver, born in Edo (modern Tokyo). A leader of the *ukiyo-e* school, he is best known for his 'Hundred Views of Mount Fuji' (1835), reproductions of which grace many Western homes today.

Holbein, Hans [holbiyn], known as **the Younger** (1497–1543) Painter, born in Augsburg, Germany, the son of **Hans Holbein the Elder** (c.1460–1524). His works include the celebrated 'Dead Christ' (1521) and the 'Dance of Death' woodcuts (1523–6). In 1526 he went to England where he painted portraits, notably of Henry VIII and his wives.

Holberg, Ludvig, Baron (1684–1754) Poet, playwright, and philosopher, born in Bergen, Norway. His works include the satirical poem *Peder Paars* (1719–20) and the comic romance *Niels Klim's Subterranean Journey* (trans, 1741).

Holbrooke, Josef (Charles) (1878–1958) Composer of chamber music and opera, born in Croydon, Greater London. His works include the symphonic poems *Queen Mab* (1904), *The Bells* (1906), and *Apollo and the Seaman* (1908). His variation of 'Three Blind Mice' formed his most popular composition.

Holden, Sir Edward Wheewall (1896–1978) Pioneer motor manufacturer, born in Adelaide, South Australia. He joined his father's business in the manufacture of car body parts, and by 1929 Holdens was the biggest body builder in the British empire.

Hölderlin, (Johann Christian) Friedrich [hoelderlin] (1770–1843) Poet, born in Lauffen, Germany. His works include Symbolist poetry and the notable philosophical novel, *Hyperion* (1797–9). >> Schiller

Holiday, Billie (Eleanora), originally **Eleanora Fagan**, nickname **Lady Day** (1915–59) Jazz singer, born in Baltimore, MD. In the late 1930s she worked with the big bands of Count Basie and Artie Shaw, singing such memorable ballads as 'Easy Living' (1937) and 'Yesterdays' (1939). >> Basie; Shaw, Artie

Holinshed, Raphael [holinshed] (?–c.1580) English chronicler, born apparently of a Cheshire family. His compilation of *The Chronicles of England, Scotland, and Ireland* (1577) was a major source for many of Shakespeare's plays.

Holkeri, Harri [holkeree] (1937–) Finnish prime minister (1987–91), born in Oripaa, Finland. He joined the centrist National Coalition Party in 1959, later serving as national secretary (1965–71).

Holkham, Leicester of >> Leicester of Holkham, Earl of

Holland, Henry (1746–1806) British architect, pupil and son-in-law of Lancelot ('Capability') Brown. His designs include old Carlton House in London, the original Brighton Pavilion (1786–7), and Brook's Club (1776–8). >> Brown, Lancelot

Holland (of Foxley and of Holland), Henry Richard Vassall Fox, 3rd Baron (1773–1840) British Liberal statesman, born at Winterslow House, Wiltshire. As Lord Privy Seal (1806–7), he worked for reform of the criminal code, attacked the slave trade, and was active in the corn-law struggle.

Holland, John (Philip) (1840–1914) Inventor, born in Liscannor, Co Clare, Ireland. He emigrated to the USA in 1873, where he began designing submarines. In 1898 he successfully launched the *Holland VI*, which was accepted by the US Navy.

Holland, Sir Sidney George (1893–1961) New Zealand prime minister (1949–57), born in Greendale, New Zealand. Entering parliament as a member of the National Party in 1935, he was Leader of the Opposition (1940–9), then premier.

Hollar, Wenzel or **Wenceslaus** (1607–77) Engraver and etcher, born in Prague. His panoramic view of London from Southwark after the Great Fire is one of the most valuable topographical records of the 17th-c.

Hollerith, Herman [holerith] (1860–1929) Inventor, born in Buffalo, NY. Realizing the need for automation in processing mass data, he devised a system based initially on cards with holes punched in them. He established his own company in 1896, which became the International Business Machines Corporation (IBM) in 1924.

Holles (of Ifield), Denzil Holles, Baron [holis] (1599–1680) English statesman, born in Houghton, Nottinghamshire. He entered parliament in 1624, and in 1642 was one of the five members whom Charles I tried to arrest. >> Charles I (of England)

Holley, Robert (William) (1922–93) Biochemist, born in Urbana, IL. He secured the first pure sample of transfer RNA, and by 1965 had determined its structure. He shared the Nobel Prize for Physiology or Medicine in 1968.

Holliday, Doc, popular name of **John Henry Holliday** (1852–87) Gambler and dentist, baptised at Griffin, GA. After training as a dentist, he adopted a life of gambling, drinking, and gunfighting, and in Dodge City was involved in the gunfight at the OK Corral (1882). >> Earp

Hollis, Sir Roger Henry (1905–73) British civil servant. Director general (1956–65) of the British counter-intelligence service MI5, he became publicly known when Peter Wright, in *Spycatcher* (1987), argued that Hollis was a Soviet spy. >> Wright, Peter

Holloway, Stanley (1890–1982) Entertainer, born in London. He was a genial comedy actor in such Ealing film classics as *Passport to Pimlico* (1948) and *The Lavender Hill Mob* (1951), and was perhaps best known for his role of Alfred Dolittle in *My Fair Lady on Broadway* (1956–8; filmed 1964).

Hollows, Fred(erick) Cossom (1929–93) Ophthalmologist, born in Dunedin, New Zealand. He was famed for his work on the prevention and treatment of blinding eye infections among Australian Aborigines, Eritreans, and Vietnamese.

Holly, Buddy, popular name of **Charles Hardin Holley** (1936–59) Rock singer, songwriter, and guitarist, born in Lubbock, TX. With his band, The Crickets, he recorded such hits as 'That'll Be The Day', 'Peggy Sue', and 'Oh Boy'. After his death in a plane crash, he became an important cult figure.

Holm, Hanya, originally **Johanna Kuntze**, *née* **Eckert** (1893–1992) Dancer, choreographer, and teacher, born in Worms, Germany. In 1936 she founded her own studio, becoming especially known for her choreography in Broadway musicals such as *Kiss Me Kate* (1948) and *My Fair Lady* (1956).

Holm, Ian (1931–) Actor, born in Ilford, Greater London. His greatest achievement was at Stratford, when he played Prince Hal, Henry V, and Richard III in *The Wars of The Roses* (1963–4).

Holman, Nat(han) (1896–95) Basketball player and coach, born in New York City. He played for the Original Celtics (1921–8), and was coach at City College of New York (1920–52, 1955–6, 1959–60).

Holmes, Arthur (1890–1965) Geologist, born in Hebburn, Tyne and Wear. He determined the ages of rocks by measuring their radioactive constituents, and supported Wegener's continental drift theory. >> Wegener

Holmes, Larry, nickname **the Easton Assassin** (1949–) Boxer, born in Cuthbert, GA. He beat Ken Norton for the

World Boxing Council heavyweight title in 1978, and held the title until 1985, when he finally lost to Michael Spinks.

Holmes, Oliver Wendell (1809–94) Physician and writer, born in Cambridge, MA. He is best known for his humorous verse and prose, winning national acclaim with *Old Ironsides* (1830) and his 'Breakfast Table' essays. >> Holmes, Oliver Wendell, Jr

Holmes, Oliver Wendell, Jr, nickname **the Great Dissenter** (1841–1935) Judge, born in Boston, MA, the son of writer Oliver Wendell Holmes. As associate justice of the US Supreme Court (1902–32), many of his judgments on common law and equity, as well as his dissent on the interpretation of the 14th amendment, have become famous.

Holmes, William Henry (1846–1933) Archaeologist and museum director, born near Cadiz, OH. He made a major contribution to Mesoamerican archaeology with his illustrated *Archaeological Studies among the Ancient Cities of Mexico* (1895–97).

Holmes a Court, (Michael) Robert Hamilton [hohmz uh kaw(r)t] (1937–90) Entrepreneur, born in South Africa. He established the Bell Group, which in 1984 stunned the business world by bidding for BHP, Australia's largest company. After his death, his widow **Janet Holmes a Court** (1944–   ) became chair of the family company, Heytesbury Holdings.

Holofernes >> Judith

Holroyd, Michael (de Courcy Fraser) (1935–   ) Biographer, born in London. His two-volume life of Lytton Strachey (1967–8), is recognized as a landmark in biographical writing. He married novelist Margaret Drabble in 1982. >> Drabble, Margaret

Holst, Gustav (Theodore) (1874–1934) Composer, born of Swedish origin in Cheltenham, Gloucestershire. His major works include the seven-movement suite *The Planets* (1914–16), *The Hymn of Jesus* (1917), and his orchestral tone poem, *Egdon Heath* (1927).

Holt, Harold (Edward) (1908–67) Australian prime minister (1966–7), born in Sydney, New South Wales, Australia. He joined the United Australia Party (later the Liberal Party of Australia), becoming deputy leader in 1956, and leader when Menzies retired in 1966. >> Menzies

Holtby, Winifred (1898–1935) Writer and feminist, born in Rudston, Humberside. She wrote a number of novels, but is chiefly remembered for *South Riding* (1935).

Holub, Miroslav [holoob] (1933–   ) Poet, born in Plzen, Czech Republic. His collections include (trans titles) *Where the Blood Flows* (1963), *Events* (1971), and *On the Contrary* (1982).

Holyoake, George (Jacob) (1817–1906) Social reformer, born in Birmingham, West Midlands. He lectured on Owen's socialist system, edited the *Reasoner*, and promoted the bill legalizing secular affirmations. >> Owen, Robert

Holyoake, Sir Keith (Jacka) (1904–83) New Zealand prime minister (1957, 1960–72), born near Pahiatua, New Zealand. He became deputy leader of the National Party in 1946, deputy prime minister in 1949, and party leader on the retirement of Holland (1957). >> Holland, Sydney George

Homans, George (Caspar) (1910–89) Sociologist, born in Boston, MA. An authority on the social behaviour of small groups, he posited group behaviour to be the result of individual behaviour.

Home of the Hirsel, Baron [hyoom], formerly **Sir Alec Douglas-Home**, originally **Alexander Frederick Douglas-Home, 14th Earl of Home** (1903–95) British prime minister (1963–4), born in London. He was Commonwealth Relations secretary (1955–60) and foreign secretary (1960–3, 1970–4). After Macmillan's resignation, he astonished

everyone by emerging as premier, renouncing his peerage and fighting a by-election. >> Douglas-Home, William; Macmillan, Harold

Homer, Greek **Homēros** (c.9th-c BC) Greek poet, to whom are attributed the great epics, the *Iliad*, the story of the siege of Troy, and the *Odyssey*, the tale of Odysseus's wanderings. Arguments have long raged over whether his works are in fact by the same hand, or have their origins in the lays of Homer and his followers (*Homeridae*).

Homer, Winslow (1836–1910) Painter, born in Boston, MA. Best known for his maritime scenes, his highly original work is often regarded as a reflection of the American pioneering spirit.

Honda, Soichiro (1906–92) Motor cycle and car manufacturer, born in Iwata Gun, Japan. He began producing motor cycles in 1948, and became president of Honda Corporation in the same year, until 1973.

Hondius, Jodocus, Latin name of **Joost de Hondt** (1563–1612) Flemish cartographer. In addition to his own maps of the world and the hemispheres, he engraved much of John Speed's work. >> Speed

Honecker, Erich [honeker] (1912–94) East German statesman and head-of-state (1976–89), born in Neunkirchen, Germany. He was elected party chief in 1971, and dismissed after the anti-communist revolution. Charges were brought against him, but he was allowed to leave for Chile in 1993 on grounds of illness.

Honegger, Arthur [oneger] (1892–1955) Composer, born in Le Havre, France. He became one of the group of Parisian composers known as *Les Six*, and works include the dramatic oratorio *King David* (1921) and five symphonies.

Honeycombe, (Ronald) Gordon (1936–   ) British playwright and broadcaster, born in Karachi, India. He has written several plays for stage, radio, and television, but is most widely known for his role as a newscaster with ITN (1965–77) and TV-AM (1985–9).

Hongi Hika [honggee heeka] (1772–1828) Maori war leader, born near Kaikohe, New Zealand. In 1820 he visited England and Australia and acquired muskets, then waged war on other Maori tribes.

Hongwu [hong woo], also spelled **Hung-wu**, originally **Zhu Yuanzhang** (1328–98) First emperor of the Chinese Ming dynasty (1368–1644), known posthumously as **Taizu**. He overthrew the Yuan dynasty (1368), established a Ming ('brilliant') dynasty at Nanjing, and took the reign name **Hongwu** ('vast military power').

Honorius, Flavius [onawrius] (384–423) Roman Emperor of the West (393–423), the younger son of Theodosius I. A feeble ruler, he abandoned Britain to the barbarians, and stayed in Ravenna while Alaric and the Goths besieged and sacked Rome (408–10). >> Alaric

Honorius I [onawrius] (?–638) Pope (625–38). In the Monothelite controversy he abstained from condemning the new doctrines, and for so doing was stigmatized as a heretic at the Council of Constantinople (680).

Hontheim, Johann Nikolaus von [honthiym], pseudonym **Justinus Febronius** (1701–90) Theologian and historian, born in Trier, Germany. Bishop of Trier (1848), he is known for an essay (1763) in which he propounded a new system of Church government (*Febronianism*).

Honthorst, Gerrit van [honthaw(r)st] (1590–1656) Painter, born in Utrecht, The Netherlands. He is known for his portraits and candle-lit interiors. His brother **William van Honthorst** (1604–66), was a historical and portrait painter.

Hooch or **Hoogh, Pieter de** [hohkh] (c.1629–c.1684) Painter, born in Rotterdam, The Netherlands. His 'Courtyard of a House in Delft' (1658) and the 'Card Players' are two outstanding examples of the Dutch school of the 17th-c.

Hood, Alexander, 1st Viscount Bridport (1727–1814)

English naval commander, the brother of Samuel, 1st Viscount Hood. He served in the 'Glorious First of June' engagement off Ushant (1794), and later became commander-in-chief of the Channel fleet (1797–1800). >> Hood, Samuel

Hood, John B(ell) (1831–79) US soldier, born in Owingsville, KY. In command at Atlanta (1864), he had to evacuate the city, leaving the road free for Sherman's march to the sea. He pushed northward to Nashville, but was defeated by Thomas. >> Sherman, William Tecumseh; Thomas, George H

Hood, Raymond M(athewson) (1881–1934) Architect, born in Pawtucket, RI. A leading designer of skyscrapers, his designs in New York City include the Daily News Building (1929–30), the Rockefeller Center (1930–40), and the McGraw-Hill Building (1931).

Hood (of Whitley), Samuel Hood, 1st Viscount (1724–1816) British admiral, born in Thorncombe, Dorset. He defeated the French in the West Indies (1782), later directing the occupation of Toulon and the operations in the Gulf of Lyon (1793). >> Hood, Alexander

Hood, Thomas (1799–1845) Poet and humorist, born in London. In his *Whims and Oddities* (1826) he showed his graphic talent in 'picture-puns', of which he seems to have been the inventor.

Hoogh, Pieter de >> **Hooch, Pieter de**

Hook, James (1746–1827) Composer and organist, born in Norwich, Norfolk. He wrote the music for many plays, as well as cantatas, odes, and numerous popular songs, including 'The Lass of Richmond Hill'.

Hook, Sidney (1902–89) Philosopher and educationist, born in New York City. Among his many books are *Towards an Understanding of Karl Marx* (1933) and *Revolution, Reform and Social Justice* (1976).

Hooke, Robert (1635–1703) Chemist and physicist, born in Freshwater, Isle of Wight. He formulated the law governing elasticity (*Hooke's law*), and invented the balance spring for watches. Many of his important observations were published in his *Micrographia* (1665).

Hooker, Joseph, nickname **Fighting Joe** (1814–79) US Union general, born in Hadley, MA. In 1863 he commanded at the Potomac, but was defeated at Chancellorsville. He accompanied Sherman in his invasion of Georgia, and served until the fall of Atlanta in 1864. >> Sherman, William Tecumseh

Hooker, Sir Joseph (Dalton) (1817–1911) Botanist and traveller, born in Halesworth, Suffolk. He went on expeditions to New Zealand, Antarctica, and India, producing his *Himalayan Journals* (1854) and his monumental *Genera plantarum*. >> Hooker, William Jackson

Hooker, Richard (1554–1600) Anglican theologian, born in Heavitree, Devon. He wrote a major work on Church government, *Of the Laws of Ecclesiastical Polity* (8 vols, 1594–1662), which greatly influenced Anglican theology.

Hooker, Sir Stanley George (1907–84) Aero-engine designer, born in the I of Sheppey, Kent. He worked for Rolls-Royce (1938–49), leading them into jet-engine production, then moved to the Bristol Aeroplane Company.

Hooker, Thomas (1586–1647) Nonconformist preacher, born in Markfield, Leicestershire. In 1633 he emigrated to America, and founded the town of Hartford, CT, in 1636.

Hooker, Sir William Jackson (1785–1865) Botanist, born in Norwich, Norfolk. He was the first director of the Royal Botanic Gardens at Kew (1841), which he developed into the leading botanical institute in the world. >> Hooker, Joseph Dalton

Hookham, Margaret >> **Fonteyn, Dame Margot**

Hooks, Benjamin (Lawson) (1925–) Judge, public official, and civil rights reformer, born in Memphis, TN. He gained national recognition as the first African-American to serve on the Federal Communications Com-

mission (1972–7), and served as executive director of the National Association for the Advancement of Colored People (1977–93).

Hooton, Ernest A(lbert) (1887–1954) Physical anthropologist, born in Clemansville, WI. His many popular writings, such as *Apes, Men and Morons* (1937), introduced anthropology to a wide readership.

Hoover, Herbert (Clark) (1874–1964) US statesman and 31st president (1929–33), born in West Branch, IA. His opposition to direct governmental assistance for the unemployed after the world slump of 1929 made him unpopular, and he was beaten by Roosevelt in 1932. The *Hoover Dam* is named after him. >> Roosevelt, Franklin D

Hoover, J(ohn) Edgar (1895–1972) US public servant, born in Washington, DC. He served as FBI director (1924–72), campaigning against city gangster rackets in the inter-war years, and against Communist sympathizers in the post-war period.

Hoover, William (Henry) (1849–1932) Industrialist, born in Ohio. He bought the patent of a light-weight electric cleaning machine and formed the Electric Suction Sweeper Co in 1908. The company was renamed Hoover in 1910.

Hope, A(lec) D(erwent) (1907–) Poet and critic, born in Cooma, New South Wales, Australia. His *Collected Poems* (1972) is one of the major books of Australian verse.

Hope, Anthony, pseudonym of **Sir Anthony Hope Hawkins** (1863–1933) Writer, born in London. He is best known for his 'Ruritanian' romance, *The Prisoner of Zenda* (1894).

Hope, Bob, originally **Leslie Townes Hope** (1903–) Comedian, born in London. In partnership with Bing Crosby and Dorothy Lamour, he appeared in the highly successful *Road to ...* comedies (1940–52), and in many others until the early 1970s. >> Crosby, Bing

Hope, Thomas (1769–1831) Connoisseur and antiquarian, born in Amsterdam of English parents. He settled in London c.1796, and introduced the vogue of Egyptian and Roman decoration in interior design.

Hopf, Heinz (1894–1971) Mathematician, born in Breslau, Germany. A leading topologist, he worked on many aspects of combinatorial topology and, with Alexandrov, wrote the influential *Topologie* (1935). >> Alexandrov

Hopkins, Sir Frederick Gowland (1861–1947) Biochemist, born in Eastbourne, East Sussex. A pioneer in the study of vitamins, he shared the Nobel Prize for Physiology or Medicine in 1929.

Hopkins, Sir Anthony (1937–) Actor, born in Port Talbot, West Glamorgan. His films include *The Elephant Man* (1980), *84 Charing Cross Road* (1987), *The Silence of the Lambs* (1991, Oscar), and *The Remains of the Day* (1994, BAFTA).

Hopkins, Gerard Manley (1844–89) Poet, born in London. He became a Catholic in 1866. An edition of his poems published in 1918 received a mixed reception, largely because of his experiments with 'sprung rhythm'; but a new edition in 1930 was widely acclaimed. His best-known poems include 'The Wreck of the *Deutschland*' and 'The Windhover'.

Hopkins, Harry L(loyd) (1890–1946) US administrator, born in Sioux City, IA. Under Franklin D Roosevelt he headed the 'New Deal' projects (1935–8), became secretary of commerce (1938–40), and supervised the lend-lease programme (1941). >> Roosevelt, Franklin D

Hopkins, John >> **Sternhold, Thomas**

Hopkins, Johns (1795–1873) Businessman and philanthropist, born in Anne Arundel Co, MD. Besides a public park for Baltimore, he endowed an orphanage for African-American children, a free hospital, and Johns Hopkins University.

Hopkins, Samuel (1721–1803) Theologian, born in Waterbury, CT. His *System of Doctrines* (1793) maintains that all virtue consists of disinterested benevolence, and that all sin is selfishness (*Hopkinsianism*).

Hopman, Harry, popular name of **Henry Christian Hopman** (1906–85) Tennis player, born in Sydney, New South Wales, Australia. He specialized in doubles, and is best known for his captaincy of the Australian Davis Cup side.

Hopper, Edward (1882–1967) Painter, born in Nyack, NY. His paintings of ordinary urban scenes, characterized by a pervasive sense of stillness and isolation, had a strong influence on Pop Art and New Realist painters.

Hoppe-Seyler, Ernst Felix (Immanuel) [hopuh ziyler] (1825–95) Physiological chemist, born in Freiburg im Breisgau, Germany. A pioneer in the application of chemical methods to understand physiological processes, he studied haemoglobin, chlorophyll, and the chemistry of putrefaction.

Horace, in full **Quintus Horatius Flaccus** (65–8 BC) Latin poet and satirist, born near Venusia, Italy. His earliest works were chiefly satires and lampoons, and through the influence of Virgil he came under the patronage of Maecenas. The unrivalled lyric poet of his time, his greatest work was the three books of *Odes* (19 BC). >> Maecenas; Virgil

Hordern, Sir Michael (Murray) (1911–95) Actor, born in Berkhamsted, Hertfordshire. A popular actor for 20 years, his major classical roles included King Lear (1960) and Prospero (1978), as well as several modern roles, such as Tom Stoppard's *Jumpers* (1972) and Howard Barker's *Stripwell* (1975).

Hore-Belisha, Leslie Hore-Belisha, Baron [haw(r) belisha] (1893–1957) British statesman and barrister, born in Devonport, Devon. As minister of transport (1934), he inaugurated driving tests for motorists, and introduced *Belisha beacons* to mark pedestrian road crossings. He was also secretary of state for war (1937–40).

Horkheimer, Max [haw(r)khiymer] (1895–1973) Philosopher and social theorist, born in Stuttgart, Germany. Director of the Institute for Social Research (1930–3), he published a series of influential articles, later collected as *Kritische Theorie* (2 vols, 1968).

Hornblower, Jonathan Carter (1753–1815) Engineer, born in Chacewater, Cornwall. He was employed by Boulton and Watt to build one of their engines. Determined to improve Watt's design, he patented (1781) a more efficient engine, but was judged to have infringed Watt's patent and had to abandon further development. >> Boulton; Watt

Hornby, A(lbert) S(idney) (1898–1978) Teacher, grammarian, and lexicographer, born in Chester, Cheshire. He is best known for *A Learner's Dictionary of Current English* (1948).

Hornby, Frank (1863–1936) British inventor of the constructional toy. He devised the perforated strips marketed as *Meccano* from 1907, began production of the model railway, Hornby Trains in 1920, and founded Dinky Toys to make model cars in the 1930s.

Horne, Donald Richmond (1921–) Writer, academic, and arts administrator, born in New South Wales, Australia. His best-known book is *The Lucky Country* (1964), the title of which has become a common Australian expression. A leading member of the Australian Republican Movement, he has written *The Coming Republic* (1992).

Horne, Lena (1917–) Singer and actress, born in Brooklyn, NY. A popular band singer, she went into films, becoming the first African-American to be signed to a long-term contract. She became known for her outspokenness about discrimination.

Horne, Marilyn (Bernice) (1934–) Mezzo-soprano opera singer, born in Bradford, PA. She is noted for her

efforts to revive interest in the lesser-known operas of Rossini and Handel.

Horner, Arthur Lewis (1894–1968) Political activist and trade unionist, born in Merthyr Tydfil, Mid Glamorgan. A founder-member of the British Communist Party, he was elected general secretary of the miners' National Union in 1946.

Horne-Tooke, John >> **Tooke, John Horne**

Horney, Karen, *née* **Danielsen** (1885–1952) Psychoanalyst, born near Hamburg, Germany. During the 1920s she took issue with orthodox Freudianism, particularly in relation to women's psychosexuality, and in the 1930s developed theories about the importance of sociocultural factors in human development. >> Freud, Sigmund

Horniman, Annie E(lizabeth) F(redericka) (1860–1937) Theatre manager and patron, born in London. She sponsored the building of the Abbey Theatre in Dublin (1904) and purchased the Gaiety Theatre in Manchester (1908), putting on many new plays by the 'Manchester School'.

Hornsby, Rogers, nickname **the Rajah** (1896–1963) Baseball player, born in Winters, TX. During his 23-year career as a second baseman (1915–37), mostly with the St Louis Cardinals and Chicago Cubs, he posted a lifetime batting average of ·358, the second highest in major league history.

Hornung, Ernest William (1866–1921) Writer, born in Middlesbrough, Cleveland, the brother-in-law of Arthur Conan Doyle. He was the creator of Raffles the gentleman burglar, hero of *The Amateur Cracksman* (1899) and many other adventure stories. >> Doyle, Arthur Conan

Horowitz, Vladimir [horovits] (1904–89) Pianist, born in Kiev, Ukraine. He toured widely before settling in the USA and becoming a US citizen, but in 1986 he played again in Russia.

Horrocks, Sir Brian (Gwynne) (1895–1985) British general, born in Raniket, India. In 1942 he commanded the 9th Armoured Division and then the 13th and 10th Corps in N Africa, and headed the 30th Corps during the Allied invasion (1944).

Horrocks, Jeremiah (c.1617–41) Astronomer, born in Toxteth, Merseyside. He made the first recorded observation of the transit of Venus (1639), which he had predicted.

Horsa >> **Hengist and Horsa**

Horsely, Sir Victor (Alexander Haden) (1857–1916) Physiologist and surgeon, born in London. He distinguished himself by his work on the localization of brain function and the improvement of operative techniques to allow brain surgery.

Horta, Victor, Baron (1861–1947) Architect, born in Ghent, Belgium. His designs include Maison du Peuple, Brussels (1895–9), a masterpiece in metal, glass, and stone (demolished in 1964). He is considered the originator of Art Nouveau.

Horthy (de Nagybánya), Miklós [haw(r)tee] (1868–1957) Hungarian regent (1920–44), born in Kenderes, Hungary. Minister of war in the counter-revolutionary 'White government' (1919), he opposed Bela Kun's Communist regime, which he suppressed (1920). >> Kun

Hoskins, Bob, popular name of **Robert William Hoskins** (1942–) Actor, born in Bury St Edmunds, Suffolk. He achieved widespread public recognition with the television series *Pennies From Heaven* (1978) and the films *The Long Good Friday* (1980) and *Who Framed Roger Rabbit* (1988).

Hoskins, W(illiam) G(eorge) (1908–92) Historian, born in Exeter. He is best known for his book *The Making of the English Landscape* (1955) and the BBC television series *Landscapes of England* (1976–8).

Hotchkiss, Benjamin (Berkeley) (1826–85) Inventor, born in Watertown, CT. He devised an improved type of cannon shell, the *Hotchkiss revolving-barrel machine gun* (1872), and a magazine rifle (1875).

Hotspur, Harry >> **Glendower, Owen**

Hotter, Hans (1909–) Baritone, born in Offenbach-am-Main, Germany. He sang frequently in Vienna and Bayreuth, one of the leading Wagnerian baritones of his day.

Houdin, (Jean Eugène) Robert [oodĩ] (1805–71) Conjurer, considered the father of modern conjuring, born in Blois, France. He made mechanical toys and automata in Paris, and gave magical soirées at the Palais Royal (1845–55).

Houdini, Harry [hoodeenee], originally **Erich Weiss** (1874–1926) Magician and escape artist, born in Budapest. He gained an international reputation as an escape artist, freeing himself from handcuffs and other devices, often while imprisoned in a box under water or in mid-air.

Houdon, Jean Antoine [oodõ] (1741–1828) Classical sculptor, born in Versailles, France. His works include the colossal figure of 'St Bruno' in Rome, and his busts of Diderot, Voltaire, and Napoleon.

Hounsfield, Sir Godfrey (Newbold) (1919–) Physicist, born in Newark, Nottinghamshire. He developed X-ray computer-assisted tomography (CAT), and shared the Nobel Prize for Physiology or Medicine in 1979.

Houphouët-Boigny, Felix [oofway bwĩnyee] (1905–93) The first president of Côte d'Ivoire (Ivory Coast) (1960–93), born in Yamoussoukro, Côte d'Ivoire. He commenced his seventh term of office in 1990.

House, Edward M(andell) (1858–1938) US diplomat, born in Houston, TX. He represented the USA in many conferences, helped draft terms for peace at the end of the War, and supported the establishment of the League of Nations. >> Wilson, Woodrow

Houseman, John, originally **Jacques Haussman** (1902–89) Stage director, producer, teacher, and actor, born in Bucharest, Romania. He founded (with Orson Welles) the Mercury Theater (1937), and became editor of the Mercury Theater of the Air, producing Welles' famous broadcast adaptation of *The War of the Worlds* (1938). >> Welles, Orson

Housman, A(lfred) E(dward) (1859–1936) Scholar and poet, born near Bromsgrove, Hereford and Worcester, the brother of Laurence Housman. He is best known for *A Shropshire Lad* (1896) and *Last Poems* (1922), but devoted much of his life (1903–30) to an annotated edition of Manilius. >> Housman, Laurence

Housman, Laurence (1865–1959) Writer and playwright, born in Bromsgrove, Hereford and Worcester, the brother of A E Housman. He is best known for his *Little Plays of St Francis* (1922) and his Victorian biographical 'chamber plays'. >> Housman, A E

Houssay, Bernardo Alberto [oosiy] (1887–1971) Physiologist, born in Buenos Aires. He investigated the role of pituitary hormones, and shared the Nobel Prize for Physiology or Medicine in 1947.

Houston, Edwin J(ames) >> **Thomson, Elihu**

Houston, Sam(uel) [hyoostn] (1793–1863) US soldier and statesman, born in Lexington, VA. As commander-in-chief in the Texan War, he defeated the Mexicans on the San Jacinto in 1836, achieving Texan independence, and was then elected president of the republic. Houston, TX, is named after him.

Houstoun, Michael (1952–) Pianist, born in Timaru, New Zealand. A regular performer on the world concert stage, particularly of the works of Beethoven and Rachmaninov, he has worked from New Zealand since 1981.

Howard, Catherine (?–1542) Fifth wife of Henry VIII, a grand-daughter of the 2nd Duke of Norfolk. She was married to the king in 1540, but after Henry learned of Catherine's alleged premarital affairs (1541), she was accused of treason and beheaded.

Howard, Charles, 1st Earl of Nottingham (1536–1624) English Lord High Admiral, a cousin of Elizabeth I, who commanded the English fleet against the Armada (1588). In 1601 he quelled Essex's rising. >> Essex, 2nd Earl of

Howard, Sir Ebenezer (1850–1928) Founder of the garden city movement, born in London. His *Tomorrow* (1898) led to the formation in 1899 of the Garden City Association and to the laying out of Letchworth (1903) and Welwyn Garden City (1919).

Howard, Henry >> **Surrey, Earl of**

Howard, John (1726–90) British prison reformer, born in London. As high sheriff for Bedfordshire, he investigated the condition of prisons, which resulted in two reform acts in 1774. The Howard League for Penal Reform (1866) is named after him.

Howard, John (Winston) (1939–) Australian prime minister (1996–). He became a Liberal MP in 1974, held several ministerial posts in the 1970s, became Leader of the Opposition in 1985, and achieved a landslide victory for the Liberal-Nationalist coalition in March 1996.

Howard, Leslie, originally **Leslie Howard Stainer** (1893–1943) Actor, born in London. During the 1930s his leading films included *The Scarlet Pimpernel* (1935), *Pygmalion* (1938), and *Gone with the Wind* (1939).

Howard, Oliver O(tis) (1830–1909) US soldier, born in Leeds, ME. In 1864 he commanded the Army of Tennessee, and led the right wing of Sherman's army on the march to the sea. >> Sherman, William Tecumseh

Howard, Thomas, 3rd Duke of Norfolk, Earl of Surrey (1473–1554) English statesman, the son of Thomas Howard, 2nd Duke of Norfolk (1443–1524), and brother-in-law of Henry VII. During the reign of Edward VI he was imprisoned for treason, but released on the accession of Mary I in 1553. >> Edward VI; Henry VII

Howard, Trevor (Wallace) (1916–88) Actor, born in Cliftonville, Kent. He sprang to stardom with *Brief Encounter* (1945), followed by *The Third Man* (1949) and *Outcast of the Islands* (1951).

Howe, Elias (1819–67) Inventor, born in Spencer, MA. He constructed the first sewing machine in 1846.

Howe (of Aberavon), (Richard Edward) Geoffrey Howe, Baron (1926–) British statesman, born in Port Talbot, Glamorgan. He was Chancellor of the Exchequer (1979–1983), foreign secretary (1983–9), and deputy prime minister (1989–90), but resigned from the government over European monetary union.

Howe, Joseph (1804–73) Canadian statesman, born in Halifax, Nova Scotia, Canada. Premier of Nova Scotia (1863–1870), after federation he entered the first Canadian government at Ottawa as President of the Council, then as secretary of state.

Howe, Julia Ward, née **Ward** (1819–1910) Feminist, reformer, and writer, born in New York City. A prominent suffragette and abolitionist, she founded the New England Woman Suffrage Association (1868), and also wrote the 'Battle Hymn of the Republic' (1862).

Howe, Richard Howe, 1st Earl (1726–99) British admiral, born in London, the brother of William Howe. He commanded the British fleet (1776) during the American War of Independence. In the French Revolutionary Wars he defeated the French at 'the Glorious First of June' (1794). >> Howe, William

Howe, Samuel (Gridley) (1801–76) Reformer and philanthropist, born in Boston, MA. In Boston he established the Perkins School for the Blind, and became widely known as a campaigner for better education facilities for the mentally ill, the blind, and the deaf.

Howe, William Howe, 5th Viscount (1729–1814) British soldier who commanded the army in North America during the American Revolution, the brother of Richard Howe. His victories included Bunker Hill (1775), the

Brandywine (1777), and the capture of New York City (1776). >> Howe, Richard

Howells, Herbert (1892–1983) Composer, born in Lydney, Gloucestershire. Professor of music at London University (1952–62), he is best known for his choral works, notably the *Hymnus paradisi*.

Howells, John Mead >> Hood, Raymond M

Howells, William Dean (1837–1920) Writer and critic, born in Martin's Ferry, OH. He edited *Atlantic Monthly* (1871–81), and became widely known for his *Easy Chair* column for *Harper's* (1900–20).

Howerd, Frankie, originally **Francis Alex Howard** (1922–92) Comedian and actor, born in London. He appeared regularly on television and in films, his most famous role being that of a Roman slave in the television series *Up Pompeii* (1970–1; film 1971).

Hoxha, Enver, also spelled **Hodja** [hoja] (1908–85) Albanian prime minister (1946–54) and Communist Party secretary (1954–85), born in Gjirokastër, Albania. He founded and led the Albanian Communist Party (1941) in the fight for national independence, deposing King Zog in 1946. >> Zog I

Hoyland, John (1934–) Painter, born in Sheffield, South Yorkshire. In America in 1964 he met 'Colour Field' painters such as Morris Louis, and turned to hard-edge abstraction using broad, freely painted rectangles of rich colour. >> Louis, Morris

Hoyle, Edmond (1672–1769) Writer on card games, called 'the father of whist', who lived in London. His popular *Short Treatise on Whist* (1742) ran into many editions.

Hoyle, Sir Fred(erick) (1915–) Astronomer, mathematician, astrophysicist, and science fiction writer, born in Bingley, West Yorkshire. He is known for his work on the origin of chemical elements, and is a leading proponent of steady-state cosmology, and a believer in an extraterrestrial origin for life on Earth.

Hoyte, (Hugh) Desmond (1929–) Guyanese president (1985–92), born in Georgetown, Guyana. He held a number of ministerial posts before becoming prime minister under Burnham, succeeding him as president. >> Burnham, Forbes

Hrdlička, Aleš [herdlichka] (1869–1943) Physical anthropologist, born in Humpolec, Czech Republic. He was one of the first to argue that North and South American Indians derived from a racial stock that originated in Asia and migrated to the Americas across the Bering Strait.

Hromadka, Josef Luki [hromadka] (1889–1969) Theologian, born in Hodslavice, Czech Republic. Active in the World Council of Churches from its inception, he contributed much to Christian–Marxist dialogue, and received the Lenin Peace Prize in 1958.

Hroswitha [hrohsveeta] (c.932–1002) German poet and Benedictine nun of Gandersheim near Göttingen. She wrote Latin poems and six prose Terentian comedies, and is regarded as the first German woman poet.

Hua Guofeng [hwah gwohfeng], also spelled **Hua Kuo-feng** (1920–) Chinese prime minister (1976–80), born in Jiaocheng, Shanxi province, China. Under him China adopted a more pragmatic domestic and foreign policy, with emphasis on industrial and educational expansion, and closer relations with Western and Third World countries.

Hubbard, Elbert (1856–1915) Writer and craft colonist, born in Bloomington, IL. He established in 1893 the Roycrofters, a craft community in East Aurora, NY, producing mission-style furniture and Art Nouveau household accessories.

Hubbard, L(afayette) Ron(ald) (1911–86) Writer, and founder of the Church of Scientology, born in Tilden, NE. His most famous work, *Dianetics: the Modern Science of Mental Health* (1950) became the basic text of the scientology movement.

Hubble, Edwin (Powell) (1889–1953) Astronomer, born in Marshfield, MO. His work led to the discovery that the universe is expanding, establishing a ratio between the galaxies' speed of movement and their distance (*Hubble's constant*). The *Hubble Space Telescope* is named after him.

Hubel, David (Hunter) (1926–) Neurophysiologist, born in Windsor, Ontario, Canada. With Wiesel he investigated the mechanics of visual perception at the cortical level, and they shared the Nobel Prize for Physiology or Medicine in 1981. >> Wiesel

Hubert, St (656–727), feast day 3rd November. Frankish clergyman, the son of the Duke of Guienne. A convert to Christianity, in 708 he became Bishop of Liège.

Hubert, Walter >> Walter, Hubert

Huch, Ricarda [hookh] (1864–1947) Writer, historian, and feminist, born in Brunswick, Germany. A neo-Romantic, she rejected naturalism, and wrote novels, social and political works, and works on religious themes.

Huddleston, (Ernest Urban) Trevor (1913–) Anglican missionary. He became Bishop of Masasi, Tanzania (1960–8), Bishop Suffragan of Stepney until 1978, then Bishop of Mauritius and Archbishop of the Indian Ocean. After his retirement, he chaired the Anti-Apartheid Movement.

Hudson, George (1800–71) Financier, born near York, North Yorkshire. He invested heavily in the North Midland Railway, made York a major railway centre, and became known as 'the railway king'.

Hudson, Henry (?–1611) English navigator, who explored the NE coast of North America. He sailed in search of a passage across the Pole (1607), later exploring the river, strait, and bay which now bear his name (1609–10).

Hudson, Manley (Ottmer) (1886–1960) Jurist, born in St Peters, MS. He was a member of the Permanent Court of Arbitration at The Hague (1933–45), and a judge of the Permanent Court of International Justice (1936–46).

Hudson, Sir William (1896–1978) Hydro-electric engineer, born in Nelson, New Zealand. He was in charge of the Galloway hydro-electric scheme in Scotland (1931–7), and commissioner of the Snowy Mountains Hydro-Electric Authority Scheme in Australia (1949–67).

Hudson, W(illiam) H(enry) (1841–1922) Writer and naturalist, born near Buenos Aires. He is best known for the account of his rambles in the New Forest in *Hampshire Days* (1903), his romantic novel *Green Mansions* (1904), and the autobiographical *Far Away and Long Ago* (1918).

Huggins, Charles B(renton) (1901–) Surgeon, born in Halifax, Nova Scotia, Canada. He shared the 1966 Nobel Prize for Physiology or Medicine for work on cancer research, notably his discovery of hormonal treatment for cancer of the prostate gland.

Huggins, Sir William (1824–1910) Astronomer, born in London. He invented the stellar spectroscope, which had a major influence on the study of the physical constitution of stars, planets, comets, and nebulae.

Hugh, St (c.1140–1200), feast day 17 November. Clergyman, born in Avalon, France. He was called to England by Henry II to found a Carthusian monastery in Witham, Somerset (1178). He was canonized in 1220. >> Richard I

Hugh Capet >> Capet, Hugo

Hughes, Arthur (1830–1915) Painter, born in London. During the 1850s he produced several of the finest works executed in the style of the Pre-Raphaelite Brotherhood.

Hughes, Charles (Evans) (1862–1948) Jurist and politician, born in Glens Falls, NY. He became secretary of state (1921–5) in the Harding administration, and was appointed Chief Justice (1930–41). >> Harding, Warren

Hughes, David (Edward) (1831–1900) Inventor, born in London. His inventions include a telegraph typewriter (1855) and a carbon microphone (1878), the precursor of modern carbon microphones.

Hughes, Howard (Robard) (1905–76) Businessman, film producer, film director, and aviator, born in Houston, TX. He inherited his father's machine tool company (1923), ventured into films (1926), founded his own aircraft company, and broke several world air speed records (1935–8). He eventually became a recluse.

Hughes, (James Mercer) Langston (1902–67) Poet, short-story writer, and playwright, born in Joplin, MO. A poet of the Harlem Renaissance, his works include the play *The Mulatto* (1935) and his 'Simple Stories', which appeared in the 1950s in comic strips.

Hughes, Richard (Arthur Warren) (1900–76) Writer, born in Weybridge, Surrey. He wrote the first radio drama, *Danger*, for the BBC (1924), and a collection of poems *Confessio juvenis* (1925), but is best known for *A High Wind in Jamaica* (1929).

Hughes, Robert (Studley Forrest) (1938–) Art critic and writer, born in Sydney, New South Wales, Australia. Senior art critic for *Time* magazine (since 1970), his many books include *The Art of Australia* (1966) and *The Shock of the New* (1980).

Hughes, Ted, popular name of **Edward (James) Hughes** (1930–) Poet, born in Mytholmroyd, West Yorkshire. Best known for his distinctive animal poems, his first collections were *The Hawk in the Rain* (1957) and *Lupercal* (1960). He married the US poet Sylvia Plath in 1954, and after her death edited her collected poems (1981). He became poet laureate in 1984. >> Plath

Hughes, Thomas (1822–96) Writer, born in Uffington, Oxfordshire. He was closely associated with the Christian Socialists, but is best remembered as the author of the public school classic, *Tom Brown's Schooldays* (1856). >> Arnold, Thomas

Hughes, William M(orris) (1862–1952) Australian prime minister (1915–23), born in London. He was the major proponent of conscription in World War 1, and as Nationalist prime minister represented Australia at the Versailles conference.

Hugo, Victor (Marie) (1802–85) Writer, born in Besançon, France. The most prolific French writer of the 19th-c, his major works include the novel *The Hunchback of Notre Dame* (trans, 1831), the books of poems *Punishments* (trans, 1853) and *Les Contemplations* (1856), and his panoramic novel of social history, *Les Misérables* (1862).

Hulbert, Jack >> **Courtneidge, Dame Cicely**

Hull, Clark L(eonard) (1884–1952) Psychologist, born in Akron, NY. He developed a rigorous mathematical theory of the learning process that attempted to reduce learned behaviour to a few simple axiomatic principles.

Hull, Cordell (1871–1955) US statesman, born in Overton Co, TN. Secretary of state under Roosevelt (1933–44), he helped to organize the United Nations, for which he received the Nobel Peace Prize in 1944. >> Roosevelt, Franklin D

Hulme, Keri (Ann Ruhi) [hyoom] (1947–) Writer, born in Otautahi, Christchurch, New Zealand. She acquired international renown with her story *The Bone People* (1984, Booker), in which Maori themes figure prominently.

Hulme, T(homas) E(rnest) [hyoom] (1883–1917) Critic, poet, and philosopher, born in Endon, Staffordshire. He became a champion of modern abstract art, the poetic movement known as 'Imagism', and the political writings of Georges Sorel. >> Sorel

Hulst, Hendrik van de >> **van de Hulst, Hendrik**

Hulton, Sir Edward (George Warris) (1906–88) Magazine proprietor and journalist, born in Harrogate, North Yorkshire. He succeeded to his father's newspaper interests, became chairman of Hulton Press Ltd, and was founder of *Picture Post*.

Humboldt, (Friedrich Wilhelm Heinrich) Alexander, Freiherr (Baron) **von** [humbohlt] (1769–1859) Naturalist and geographer, born in Berlin. His major work, *Kosmos* (1845–62), endeavours to provide a comprehensive physical picture of the universe. A major ocean current is named after him.

Humboldt, (Karl) Wilhelm von [humbohlt] (1767–1835) German statesman and philologist, born in Potsdam, Germany. He became a diplomat, and rose to be first minister of public instruction (1808). He was the first to study Basque scientifically.

Hume, (George) Basil, Cardinal [hyoom] (1923–) Roman Catholic Benedictine monk. Abbot of Ampleforth (1963), he was created Archbishop of Westminster and a cardinal in 1976.

Hume, David [hyoom] (1711–76) Philosopher and historian, born in Edinburgh. His masterpiece, *A Treatise of Human Nature* (1739–40), extended the empiricist legacy of Locke and Berkeley. Other works include the popular *Political Discourses* (1752) and his *History of England* (6 vols, 1754–62). >> Berkeley, George; Locke, John

Hume, (Andrew) Hamilton [hyoom] (1797–1873) Explorer, born in Parramatta, New South Wales, Australia. He discovered the Goulburn and Yass plains (1822) and L Bathurst in S New South Wales, and made the first sighting of Mt Kosciusko.

Hume, John [hyoom] (1937–) Northern Ireland politician, born in Londonderry, Co Londonderry. Leader of the Social Democratic Labour Party, in 1993 he and Sinn Féin leader Gerry Adams began a series of talks, the Hume–Adams peace initiative, intended to bring about an end to violence in Northern Ireland. >> Adams, Gerry

Hume, Patrick >> **Baillie, Grizel**

Hummel, Johann (Nepomuk) (1778–1837) Pianist and composer, born in Pressburg, Austria. Best known for his piano and chamber works, he also wrote several ballets and operas, and an influential manual of piano technique (1828).

Humperdinck, Engelbert (1854–1921) Composer, born in Siegburg, Germany. He composed several operas, one of which, *Hänsel und Gretel* (1893), was highly successful.

Humphrey, Doris (1895–1958) Dancer, choreographer, and teacher, born in Oak Park, IL. She formed her own group (1928), and also wrote the key text on modern dance composition, *The Art of Making Dances* (1959).

Humphrey, Duke of Gloucester >> **Gloucester, Humphrey, Duke of**

Humphrey, Hubert H(oratio) (1911–78) US Democratic vice-president (1965–9), born in Wallace, SD. He built up a strong reputation as a liberal, but, as vice-president under Johnson, alienated many of his supporters by defending the policy of continuing the war in Vietnam, and narrowly lost the 1968 election to Nixon. >> Johnson, Lyndon B; Nixon, Richard M

Humphreys, Emyr (Owen) (1919–) Writer, born in Prestatyn, Clwyd. His novels include *Hear and Forgive* (1952, Somerset Maugham Award), *A Toy Epic* (1958, Hawthornden), and *Bonds of Attachment* (1991).

Humphries, (John) Barry (1934–) Comic performer and satirical writer, born in Melbourne, Victoria, Australia. He is best known for his characters Sir Les Patterson and 'housewife megastar' Dame Edna Everage, who have frequently appeared on television and in film.

Hung-wu >> **Hongwu**

Hunt, Geoff(rey) (1947–) Squash rackets player, born in Victoria, Australia. He was the world amateur champion in 1967, 1969, and 1971, and the world Open champion in 1976–7 and 1979–80.

Hunt, Henry, known as **Orator Hunt** (1773–1835) Radical agitator, born in Upavon, Wiltshire. In 1800 he became a staunch radical, and spent his life advocating the repeal of the Corn Laws, and parliamentary reform.

Hunt, James (Simon Wallis) (1947–93) Motor-racing driver and broadcaster, born in London. He joined the McLaren team, and won the World Championship in 1976.

Hunt (of Llanfair Waterdine), (Henry Cecil) John Hunt, Baron (1910–) Mountaineer, born in Marlborough, Wiltshire. In 1953 he led the first successful expedition to Mt Everest, and in 1958 led the British party in the British–Soviet Caucasian expedition. >> Hillary

Hunt, (James Henry) Leigh (1784–1859) Poet and essayist, born in Southgate, Greater London. From 1808 he edited with his brother *The Examiner*, which became a focus of Liberal opinion. His *Autobiography* (1850) is a valuable picture of the times.

Hunt, Richard Morris (1827–95) Architect, born in Brattleboro, VT. In New York City he designed many houses and public buildings, but is best remembered for his luxurious mansions, among them Marble House (1892), Newport, RI.

Hunt, William Henry (1790–1864) Painter, a creator of the English school of watercolour painting, born in London. He chose very simple subjects, such as 'Peaches and Grapes', 'Old Pollard', and 'Wild Flowers'.

Hunt, (William) Holman (1827–1910) Painter, born in London. He helped found the Pre-Raphaelite Brotherhood, his works including 'The Light of the World' (1854) and 'The Finding of Christ in the Temple' (1860).

Hunter, Evan >> McBain, Ed

Hunter, John (1728–93) Physiologist and surgeon, born in Long Calderwood, Strathclyde, the brother of William Hunter. His *Natural History of Human Teeth* (1771–8) revolutionized dentistry, and he is considered to be the founder of scientific surgery. >> Hunter, William

Hunter, William (1718–83) Anatomist and obstetrician, born in Long Calderwood, Strathclyde, the brother of John Hunter. The first professor of anatomy to the Royal Academy (1768), through him obstetrics became a recognized branch of medicine. >> Hunter, John

Huntingdon, Selina Hastings, Countess of, *née* **Shirley** (1707–91) Methodist leader, born in Staunton Harold, Leicestershire. Joining the Methodists in 1739, she made Whitefield her chaplain, and assumed a leadership among his followers, who became known as 'the Countess of Huntingdon's Connexion.' >> Whitefield

Huntington, Collis P(orter) (1821–1900) Railway pioneer, born in Harwinton, CT. He was involved in the construction of the Central Pacific Railway (1869), and of the Southern Pacific (1881), becoming its president. His nephew, **Henry Edwards Huntington** (1850–1927), acquired an immense art collection and library, presented to the nation in 1922.

Huntsman, Benjamin (1704–76) Inventor, born in Barton-upon-Humber, Humberside. He opened a foundry in Sheffield (c.1740) where he developed the crucible (or casting) process which produced a better and more uniform steel.

Hunyady, János [hoonyodi] (c.1387–1456) Hungarian statesman and warrior. His life was one unbroken crusade against the Turks, whom he defeated in several campaigns, notably in the storming of Belgrade (1456).

Hurd, Douglas (Richard) [herd] (1930–) British statesman, born in Marlborough, Wiltshire. He became Northern Ireland secretary (1984), home secretary (1985), and foreign secretary (1989–95)

Hurst, Sir Cecil (James Barrington) (1870–1963) Lawyer, born at Horsham Park, West Sussex. He was a judge of the Permanent Court of International Justice (1929–46), serving as president (1934–6), and in this capacity greatly strengthened the court's prestige and authority.

Hurston, Zora (Neale) (1903–60) Novelist, born in Eatonville, FL. Her works include the novels *Their Eyes Were*

Watching God (1937), *Tell My Horse* (1938), and an autobiography, *Dust Tracks on a Road* (1942).

Hus, John >> Huss, John

Husain, Sadam >> Hussein, Saddam

Husák, Gustáv [hoosak] (1913–91) Czechoslovakian president (1975–89), born in Bratislava, Slovak Republic. After the Soviet invasion of 1968, he replaced Dubček as leader of the Communist Party. He was himself replaced by Havel after the Communist regime was overthrown in 1989. >> Dubček; Havel

Hu Shih [hoo shee] (1891–1962) Liberal scholar and reformer, born in Chiki, Anhwei, China. He led the gradualist New Culture movement from 1919, urging the re-examination of China's culture and increased personal liberty.

Huskisson, William (1770–1830) British statesman, born at Birch Moreton Court, Hereford and Worcester. He served as secretary of the Treasury (1804–9), President of the Board of Trade, treasurer of the navy (1823), and colonial secretary (1827–8).

Huss or **Hus, John** (c.1369–1415) Bohemian religious reformer, born in Husinec, Czech Republic. After writing his main work, *On the Church* (trans, 1413), he was called before a General Council, and burned after refusing to recant. The anger of his followers in Bohemia led to the Hussite Wars.

Hussein (ibn Talal) [husayn] (1935–) King of Jordan since 1952, born in Amman. He steered a middle course in the face of the political upheavals inside and outside his country, favouring the Western powers, and pacifying Arab nationalism. His decision to cut links with the West Bank (1988) prompted the PLO to establish a government in exile.

Hussein, Saddam [husayn], also spelled **Sadam Husain** (1937–) President of Iraq (1979–), born in Takrit. Prominent in the 1968 revolution, he became vice-president of the Revolutionary Command Council in 1969. His attack on Iran (1980) led to a war of attrition which ended in 1988. He invaded Kuwait in 1990, but was forced to withdraw when he was defeated by a coalition of Arab and Western forces in Operation Desert Storm (1991). Iraq has since suffered international isolation and economic sanctions.

Hussein ibn Ali [husayn ibn alee] (1856–1931) King of the Hejaz (1916–24), founder of the modern Arab Hashemite dynasty, the father of Faisal I. After first siding with the Turks and Germans in World War 1, he then supported the Allies. He was forced to abdicate in 1924. >> Faisal I

Husserl, Edmund (Gustav Albrecht) [huserl] (1859–1938) Philosopher, founder of the school of phenomenology, born in Prossnitz, Czech Republic. His chief work was *Logical Investigations* (2 vols, trans, 1900–1), defending the view of philosophy as an *a priori* discipline.

Hussey, Obed (1792–1860) Inventor, born in Exeter, ME. He invented a reaping machine patented in 1833, the year before a very similar machine was patented by McCormick. Hussey eventually lost the competition with McCormick, selling out in 1858. >> McCormick

Huston, John (Marcellus) [hyoostn] (1906–87) Film director, born in Nevada, MO. His films include *The Treasure of the Sierra Madre* (1948, Oscar), *The African Queen* (1951), *Moby Dick* (1956), and the musical, *Annie* (1982).

Hutcheson, Francis (1694–1746) Philosopher, probably born in Drumalig, Co Down. His main work, *A System of Moral Philosophy* (1755), argues that moral distinctions are intuited, rather than arrived at by reasoning.

Hutchinson, Anne, *née* **Marbury** (1591–1643) Religious leader and American pioneer, born in Alford, Lincolnshire. In 1634 she emigrated to Boston, MA, where she acquired territory from the Narragansett Indians of Rhode Island, and set up a democracy (1638). >> Winthrop, John (1588–1649)

Hutchinson, Sir Jonathan (1828–1913) Surgeon, born in Selby, North Yorkshire. He is best known for his lifelong study of syphilis, *Hutchinson's triad* being the three symptoms of congenital syphilis which he first described.

Hutchinson, Sir William Oliphant (1889–1970) Artist, born in Collessie, Fife. He is best known for his portraits and landscapes.

Hutten, Ulrich von (1488–1523) Humanist, born at the castle of Steckelberg, Germany. Crowned poet laureate by Emperor Maximilian I (1517), he took part in the campaign of the Swabian League against Ulrich of Württemberg (1519), and supported Luther. >> Luther

Hutton, James (1726–97) Geologist, born in Edinburgh. The *Huttonian theory*, emphasizing the igneous origin of many rocks, was expounded in *A Theory of the Earth* (1795), which forms the basis of modern geology.

Hutton, Len, popular name of **Sir Leonard Hutton** (1916–90) Cricketer, born in Fulneck, West Yorkshire. Playing for England against Australia at the Oval in 1938, he scored a world record 364 runs. During his first-class career (1934–60) he scored 40 140 runs, including 129 centuries.

Huxley, Aldous (Leonard) (1894–1963) Novelist and essayist, born in Godalming, Surrey, the grandson of T H Huxley. His reputation was made with his satirical novels *Crome Yellow* (1921) and *Antic Hay* (1923). Later novels include *Point Counter Point* (1928) and, his best-known work, *Brave New World* (1932). >> Huxley, Andrew / Julian / T H

Huxley, Sir Andrew Fielding (1917–) Physiologist, born in London, a grandson of T H Huxley, and half-brother of Aldous and Julian Huxley. He helped to provide a physico-chemical explanation for nerve transmission, and outlined a theory of muscular contraction. He shared the Nobel Prize for Physiology or Medicine in 1963. >> Huxley, Aldous / Julian / T H

Huxley, Hugh Esmor (1924–) Molecular biologist, born in Birkenhead, Merseyside. From the 1950s he was the central figure in developing the sliding filament model of muscle contraction.

Huxley, Sir Julian (Sorell) (1887–1975) Biologist, born in London, the grandson of T H Huxley. He applied his scientific knowledge to political and social problems, formulating a pragmatic ethical theory based on the principle of natural selection.

Huxley, T(homas) H(enry) (1825–95) Biologist, born in London. The foremost expounder of Darwinism, he also wrote essays on theology and philosophy from an 'agnostic' viewpoint, a term he introduced. >> Darwin, Charles; Huxley, Aldous / Andrew / Julian

Hu Yaobang [hoo yowbang] (1915–89) Chinese politician, born in Hunan province, China. He became Communist Party leader in 1981, but was dismissed in 1987 for his relaxed handling of a wave of student unrest. Popularly revered as a liberal reformer, his death triggered pro-democracy demonstrations.

Huygens, Christiaan [hoygenz] (1629–95) Physicist and astronomer, born in The Hague, The Netherlands. He discovered the ring and fourth satellite of Saturn (1655), and made the first pendulum clock (1657). In optics he propounded the wave theory of light, and discovered polarization.

Huysmann, Roelof >> **Agricola, Rudolphus**

Huysmans, Joris Karl [hoysmahnz] (1848–1907) Novelist of Dutch origin, born in Paris. His best-known works are (trans titles) *Against the Grain* (1884), a study of aesthetic decadence, and the controversial *Down There* (1891), which dealt with devil-worship.

Huysum, Jan van [hoysum] (1682–1749) Painter, born in Amsterdam. He studied under his father, **Justus** (1659–1716), a landscape painter, and also painted landscapes, but is noted for his exquisite fruit and flower pieces.

Hyacinthe, Père [eeasīt], originally **Charles Loyson** (1827–1912) French preacher. He denounced abuses in the Church, and was excommunicated in 1869, and in 1879 founded a Gallican Catholic Church in Paris.

Hyatt, John Wesley (1837–1920) Inventor, born in Starkey, NY. His discovery of the process to make celluloid laid the foundation for the plastics industry. Other inventions include the *Hyatt roller bearing*.

Hyde, Anne >> **Anne; Clarendon, Earl of; Mary II**

Hyde, Charles Cheney (1873–1952) Jurist, born in Chicago, IL. His major work is *International Law, chiefly as Interpreted and Applied by the United States* (1922).

Hyde, Douglas, Ir **Dubhghlas de Híde** (1860–1949) Writer, philologist, and first president of Eire (1938–45), born in Frenchpark, Co Roscommon, Ireland. Founding president (1893–1915) of the Gaelic League, he wrote *A Literary History of Ireland* (1899), as well as poems, plays, and other works in Irish and English.

Hyder Ali >> **Haidar Ali**

Hyne, Charles (John Cutcliffe Wright) (1865–1944) Traveller and writer, born in Bibury, Gloucestershire. He is best remembered as the creator of the fictional character 'Captain Kettle' in several adventure stories.

Hypatia [hiypateea] (c.375–415) Greek philosopher, who attempted to combine Neoplatonism with Aristotelianism. Associated by many Christians with paganism, she was murdered by a fanatical mob.

Hyperides or **Hypereides** [hiyperiydeez] (390–322 BC) Athenian orator and statesman. He promoted the Lamian War against Macedonia (323–22 BC) after the death of Alexander, but was put to death when the Athenians were defeated.

Hyrcanus I, John [heerkaynus] (2nd-c BC) High priest of Israel, and perhaps also a king subject to Syrian control (c.134–104 BC). He consolidated his own hold over Israel, forcing the Idumeans (residents of S Judea) to adopt Judaism.

Hyrcanus II [heerkaynus] (?–30 BC) Jewish high priest (from 76 BC) and ruler. He warred for power with his younger brother Aristobulus, until Aristobulus died from poisoning (49 BC), and was later captured by one of Aristobulus's sons. On his return to Jerusalem, he was suspected of intriguing against Herod the Great, and killed. >> Herod

Iacocca, Lee [yakocha], popular name of **Lido Anthony Iacocca** (1924–) Businessman, born in Allentown, PA. In 1978 he joined the ailing Chrysler Corporation as president, and steered it back to profitability. He published a best-selling autobiography (with William Kovak), *Iacocca* (1985).

Ibáñez, Vicente Blasco >> Blasco Ibáñez, Vicente

Ibárruri (Gómez), Dolores [eebaruree], known as **la Pasionaria** ('The Passionflower') (1895–1989) Spanish politician and orator, born in Gallarta, Spain. With the outbreak of the Civil War (1936), she became the Republic's most effective propagandist, then president of the Spanish Communist Party in exile, and later (1977) a Communist deputy.

Ibert, Jacques (François Antoine) [eebair] (1890–1962) Composer, born in Paris. His works include seven operas, ballets, cantatas, chamber music, and the orchestral *Divertissement* (1930).

Ibn Battutah (1304–68) Traveller and writer, born in Tangiers, Morocco. He visited all the Muslim countries (1325–54), writing the history of his journey in *Travels* (trans, 1853–8).

Ibn Gabirol >> Avicebrón

Ibn Khaldun [ibn khaldoon] (1332–1406) Philosopher, historian, and politician, born in Tunis. His major work was a monumental history of the Arabs, and his influential *Introduction to History* (trans) outlined a cyclical theory of history.

Ibn Rushd >> Averroës

Ibn Saud, Abdul Aziz [ibn sahood], in full **Ibn Abd al-Rahman al-Saud** (1880–1953) The first king of Saudi Arabia (1932–53), born in Riyadh. He was succeeded by his son, **Saud** (1902–69) in 1953. In 1964 he was peacefully deposed, and his brother Faisal became king. >> Faisal (ibn Abd al-Aziz)

Ibn Sina >> Avicenna

Ibn Zohr >> Avenzoar

Ibrahim >> Abraham

Ibrahim, Abdullah, formerly **Dollar Brand** (1934–) Jazz pianist, born in Cape Town, South Africa. In 1962 he went to work in the USA, and is noted for his jazz interpretations of the melodies and rhythms of his African childhood.

Ibsen, Henrik (Johan) (1828–1906) Playright and poet, born in Skien, Norway. His international reputation began with *Brand* and *Peer Gynt* (1866–7). He regarded his historical drama, *Emperor and Galilean* (trans, 1873) as his masterpiece, but his fame rests more on his social plays, notably *A Doll's House* (trans, 1879) and *Ghosts* (trans, 1881). In his last phase he turned more to Symbolism, as in *The Wild Duck* (trans, 1884), *Rosmersholm* (1886), and *The Master-Builder* (trans, 1892). The realism of *Hedda Gabler* (1890) was a solitary escape from Symbolism.

Ibycus [ibikus] (fl.6th-c BC) Greek poet from Rhegium in Italy. Legend has it that he was slain by robbers near Corinth, and as he was dying he called upon a flock of cranes to avenge him. The cranes then hovered over the theatre at Corinth, causing one of the murderers to exclaim, 'Behold the avengers of Ibycus!', which led to their conviction.

Icahn, Carl [iykn] (1936–) Arbitrageur and options specialist, born in New York City. He has been chairman and chief executive officer of ACF Industries since 1984, and chairman of the airline TWA since 1986.

Ichikawa, Fusaye [ichikahwa] (1893–1981) Japanese politician and feminist. She formed the Women's Suffrage League in Japan (1924), and later became head of the New Japan Women's League, which secured the vote for women in 1945.

Ickes, Harold L(eClaire) [ikeez] (1874–1952) Lawyer and public official, born in Frankstown Township, PA. Prominent in the Progressive Party (1912–16), he changed affiliation, backed Franklin D Roosevelt in 1932, and was appointed interior secretary (1933–46). >> Roosevelt, Franklin D

Ickx, Jacky [iks] (1945–) Motor-racing driver, born in Brussels. He won 34 world sports car championship races, and was world champion in 1982–3 (both Porsche). He won the Le Mans 24-hour race a record six times (1969, 1975, 1976, 1977, 1981–2).

Ictinos or **Ictinus** [iktiynus] (5th-c BC) Greek architect. With Callicrates he designed the Parthenon (447–438 BC). He was also architect of the Temple of the Mysteries at Eleusis and the Temple of Apollo Epicurius at Bassae.

Idriess, Ion Llewellyn [idruhs] (1889–1979) Writer, born in Sydney, New South Wales, Australia. His best-known books are *Flynn of the Inland* (1932), *The Desert Column* (1932), *The Cattle King* (1936), and *Onward Australia* (1944).

Ignatiev, Nikolay Pavlovich, Count [ignatyef] (1832–1908) Russian diplomat, born in St Petersburg. He negotiated the Treaty of Peking (1860) with China, became ambassador at Constantinople (1864), and was responsible for the Treaty of San Stefano after the Russians defeated the Turks in 1878.

Ignatius (of Antioch), St [ignayshus] (c.35–c.107), feast day 17 October. One of the apostolic Fathers of the Church, reputedly a disciple of St John, the second Bishop of Antioch. He died a martyr in Rome.

Ignatius de Loyola, St >> Loyola, Ignatius of, St

Ike >> Eisenhower, Dwight D

Illingworth, Ray(mond) (1932–) Cricketer and broadcaster, born in Pudsey, West Yorkshire. A proficient batsman and spin-bowler, he won 66 Test caps for England (36 as captain), taking 122 wickets and scoring two centuries.

Ilyushin, Sergey Vladimirovich [ilyooshin] (1894–1977) Aircraft designer, born in Dilialevo, Russia. His designs include the Il-4 long-range bomber, which was important in World War 2. Afterwards his passenger aircraft became the basic Soviet carriers.

Imhotep [imhohtep] (fl.27th-c BC) Egyptian physician and adviser to King Zoser (3rd dynasty). Revered as a sage, during the Saite period (500 BC) he was worshipped as the life-giving son of Ptah, god of Memphis.

Immelmann, Max (1890–1916) German airman. He laid the foundation of German fighter tactics in World War 1, and originated the *Immelmann turn* - a half-loop followed by a half-roll. He was killed in action.

Imran Khan, in full **Ahmad Khan Niazi Imran** (1952–) Cricketer, born in Lahore, Pakistan. A fast bowler and astute captain, he inspired Pakistan's rise to prominence in world cricket. After leading Pakistan to the 1992 World Cup, he retired with a Test Match score of 3807 runs and 362 wickets.

Indiana, Robert, originally **Robert Clarke** (1928–) Painter and graphic designer, born in New Castle, IN. He began making hard-edged abstract pictures and stencilled wooden constructions, as part of the early Pop Art movement. His best-known images are based on the letters LOVE.

Indy, Vincent d' >> d'Indy, Vincent

Inge, William (Motter) [inj] (1913–73) Playwright and novelist, born in Independence, KS. His plays include *Come Back, Little Sheba* (1950), *Picnic* (Pulitzer, 1953), and *Bus Stop* (1955).

Inge, William Ralph [ing], known as **the Gloomy Dean** (1860–1954) Clergyman and theologian, born in Crayke, North Yorkshire. He was dean of St Paul's (1911–34), earning his byname from the pessimism displayed in his sermons and newspaper articles.

Ingenhousz, Jan [eenggenhows] (1730–99) Physician and plant physiologist, born in Breda, The Netherlands. He is best known as the discoverer of photosynthesis (1779).

Inglis, Elsie Maud [inggls] (1864–1917) Surgeon and reformer, born in Naini Tal, India. She inaugurated the second medical school for women at Edinburgh (1892), and founded a maternity hospital there, completely staffed by women (1901). She also founded the Scottish Women's Suffragette Federation (1906).

Ingoldsby, Thomas >> Barham, Richard (Harris)

Ingres, Jean Auguste Dominique [ĩgruh] (1780–1867) Painter, the leading exponent of the Classical tradition in France in the 19th-c, born in Montauban, France. He is noted for his nudes, including 'Baigneuse' (1808) and 'La Source' (1807, completed 1856).

Innes, Michael >> Stewart, J I M

Innes, Hammond Ralph >> Hammond Innes, Ralph

Inness, George [inis] (1825–94) Landscape artist, born near Newburgh, NY. Among his best-known paintings are 'Delaware Water Gap' (1861), 'Delaware Valley' (1865), and 'Autumn Oaks' (c.1875).

Innis, Harold Adams (1894–1952) Political economist and pioneer in communication studies. He introduced the staple thesis of economic development, and argued against continentalism in such works as *The Fur Trade in Canada* (1930) and *The Cod Fisheries* (1940).

Innis, (Emile Alfredo) Roy (1934–) Civil rights activist, born in St Croix, US Virgin Isles. He joined the Congress of Racial Equality in 1963, advocating black separatism and community school boards, and became CORE national president in 1968.

Innocent III, originally **Lotario de' Conti di Segni** (1160–1216) Pope (1198–1216), born in Agnagni, Italy. His pontificate is regarded as the high point of the temporal and spiritual supremacy of the Roman see. He excommunicated King John for refusing to recognize Stephen Langton as Archbishop of Canterbury. >> John; Langton

Inönü, Ismet [inoenü], originally **Mustafa Ismet** (1884–1973) Turkish soldier, prime minister (1923–37, 1961–5), and president (1938–50), born in Izmir, Turkey. As the first premier of the new republic, he introduced many political reforms, and was elected president in 1938 on Atatürk's death. >> Atatürk

Ionesco, Eugène [yoneskoh] (1912–94) Playwright, born in Slatina, Romania. After the success of *The Bald Prima Donna* (trans, 1950), he became a prolific writer of one-act plays which came to be seen as typical examples of the Theatre of the Absurd, such as *The Chairs* (trans, 1952) and *Rhinocéros* (1960).

Ipatieff, Vladimir Nikolayevich [eepatyef] (1867–1952) Chemist, born in Moscow. He synthesized isoprene, the basic unit of natural rubber, and made contributions to the catalytic chemistry of unsaturated carbons, of great value to the petrochemical industry.

Iqbal, Sir Mohammed [ikbal] (1875–1938) Poet and philosopher, born in Sialkot, Pakistan. He achieved fame through his mystical and nationalistic poetry. His efforts to establish a separate Muslim state eventually led to the formation of Pakistan.

Ireland, John (Nicholson) (1879–1962) Composer, born in Bowdon, Greater Manchester. He is best known for his picturesque orchestral pieces *The Forgotten Rite* (1913) and

Mai-dun (1921), a piano concerto (1930), and *These Things Shall Be* (1937) for chorus and orchestra.

Ireland, William Henry (1777–1835) Forger of Shakespeare, born in London. He forged an autograph of the poet on a carefully copied old lease, and gradually on many more documents. The material was eventually denounced as false, and he confessed in a public statement (1796).

Irenaeus, St [irenayus] (c.130–c.200), feast day 28 June (W), 23 August (E). One of the Christian Fathers of the Greek Church, probably born near Smyrna. He is chiefly known for his opposition to Gnosticism, and for his attempts to prevent a rupture between Eastern and Western Churches over the computing of Easter.

Irene [ireenee] (752–803) Byzantine empress, the wife of the emperor Leo IV. For her part in the restoration of the use of icons (forbidden in 730) at the Council of Nicaea (787), she was recognized as a saint by the Greek Orthodox Church.

Ireton, Henry [iy(r)tn] (1611–51) English soldier, born in Attenborough, Nottinghamshire. In the English Civil War he served at Edgehill, Naseby, and the siege of Bristol. Cromwell's son-in-law from 1646, he was one of the most implacable enemies of the king. >> Cromwell, Oliver

Irigoyen, Hipólito [irigoyen], also spelled **Yrigoyen** (1852–1933) Argentine president (1916–22, 1928–30), born in Buenos Aires. He became leader of the Radical Civic Union Party in 1896, and the first Radical president of Argentina. He was deposed in 1930 by a military coup.

Ironside, William Edmund Ironside, Baron (1880–1959) British field marshal, born in Ironside, Grampian. Chief of the Imperial General Staff at the outbreak of World War 2, he commanded the home defence forces (1940). The *Ironsides*, fast light-armoured vehicles, were named after him.

Irvine, Andy [ervin], popular name of **Andrew (Robertson) Irvine** (1951–) Rugby union player, born in Edinburgh. He won 51 caps for Scotland, and was the first player in the world to score more than 300 points in international rugby.

Irving, Edward (1792–1834) Church of Scotland clergyman, born in Annan, Dumfries and Galloway. In 1825 he began to announce the imminent second advent of Jesus Christ, and to elaborate his views of the Incarnation. Charged with heresy, he was finally deposed (1833).

Irving, Sir Henry, originally **John Henry Brodribb** (1838–1905) Actor and theatre manager, born in Keinton-Mandeville, Somerset. He gained a reputation as the greatest English actor of his time, and in 1878 began a theatrical partnership with Ellen Terry which lasted until 1902. >> Terry, Ellen

Irving, Washington, pseudonym **Geoffrey Crayon** (1783–1859) Man of letters, born in New York City. Under his pseudonym he wrote *The Sketch Book* (1819–20), a miscellany containing such items as 'Rip Van Winkle' and 'The Legend of Sleepy Hollow'.

Isaac [iyzak] Biblical character, the son of Abraham by Sarah, through whose line of descent God's promises to Abraham were seen to continue. He was nearly sacrificed by Abraham at God's command (*Gen* 22). >> Abraham; Esau; Jacob

Isaacs, Alick (1921–67) Biologist, born in Glasgow, Strathclyde. In 1957, with Swiss virologist Jean Lindenmann, he described a novel protein, *interferon*, a natural antiviral agent.

Isaacs, Jeremy (Israel) (1932–) Television executive, born in Glasgow, Strathclyde. Known for his current affairs series for Granada, BBC, and Thames Television, he also served as the first chief executive of Channel 4 (1981–7).

Isaacs, Rufus Daniel >> Reading, 1st Marquess of

Isaacs, Susan Brierley, *née* **Fairhurst** (1885–1948) Specialist in the education of young children, born in Bromley Cross, Essex. She was a powerful influence on the theory and practice of the education of young children between the wars.

Isabella I (of Castile), also known as **Isabella the Catholic** (1451–1504) Queen of Castile (1474–1504), born in Madrigal de las Altas Torras, Spain, the daughter of John II, King of Castile and León. In 1469 she married Ferdinand V of Aragon, with whom she ruled jointly from 1479. >> Ferdinand the Catholic

Isabella of Angoulême [ãgoolem] (?–1246) Queen of England, the consort of King John, whom she married in 1200. In 1214 she was imprisoned by John at Gloucester, and after his death in 1216 returned to France. Her son became Henry III. >> Henry III (of England); John

Isabella of France (1292–1358) Queen of England, the consort of Edward II, and daughter of Philip IV of France. She married Edward in 1308, but then became the mistress of Roger Mortimer, Earl of March, with whom she overthrew and murdered the king (1327). >> Edward II / III

Isabey, Jean Baptiste [eezabay] (1767–1855) Portrait painter and miniaturist, born in Nancy, France. He painted portraits of revolution notabilities, and afterwards became court painter to Napoleon.

Isaiah [iyziya], Heb **Jeshaiah** (8th-c BC) The first in order of the major Old Testament prophets, the son of Amoz. A citizen of Jerusalem, he began to prophesy c.747 BC. According to tradition, he was martyred.

Isherwood, Christopher (William Bradshaw) (1904–86) Novelist, born in Disley, Cheshire. His best-known novels, such as *Goodbye to Berlin* (1939), were based on the decadence of post-slump, pre-Hitler Berlin, and later inspired *Cabaret* (musical, 1966; filmed, 1972). In collaboration with Auden, he wrote three prose-verse plays with political overtones. >> Auden

Ishmael [ishmayel] Biblical character, the son of Abraham by Hagar, his wife's maid. He was expelled into the desert with his mother after the birth of Isaac, and is considered the ancestor of the Bedouin tribes (the *Ishmaelites*). >> Abraham; Hagar; Isaac

Isidore of Seville, St [izidaw(r), sevil] (c.560–636), feast day 4 April. Ecclesiastic, encyclopedist, and historian, born either in Seville or Carthagena, Spain. Archbishop of Seville in c.600, his episcopate was notable for the Councils at Seville (618 or 619) and Toledo (633). He was canonized in 1598.

Islam, Kazi Nazrul [izlam] (1899–1976) Poet, born in the West Bengali village of Churulia. He rose to fame in the 1920s as a poet and leader of the anti-British movement in India with his poem *The Rebel*. After the partition, he was installed as the national poet in Bangladesh.

Islebius, Magister >> **Agricola, Johann**

Ismail Pasha [ismaeel] (1830–95) Khedive of Egypt, born in Cairo. His massive development programme included the building of the Suez Canal, opened in 1869. He was deposed by the Ottoman sultan, and replaced by his eldest son, Tewfik. >> Tewfik Pasha

Ismay (of Wormington), Hastings Lionel Ismay, Baron, nickname **Pug** (1887–1965) English soldier, born in Naini Tal, India. He was appointed chief-of-staff to Churchill (1940–6), and later became secretary of state for Commonwealth Relations (1951–2) and secretary-general to NATO (1952–7). >> Churchill, Sir Winston

Isocrates [iysokrateez] (436–338 BC) Greek orator and prose writer, born in Athens. He became an influential teacher of oratory (c.390 BC), and presented rhetoric as an essential foundation of education.

Israëls, Jozef [izraelz] (1824–1911) Genre painter, born in Groningen, The Netherlands. He produced scenes from humble everyday life, especially the portrayal of fisher folk.

Issigonis, Alec [iseegohnis], popular name of **Sir Alexander Arnold Constantine Issigonis** (1906–88) Automobile designer, born in Smyrna, Turkey. He is best known as the designer of the Morris Minor (1948–71) and the revolutionary British Motor Corporation Mini, launched in 1959.

Itten, Johannes (1888–1967) Painter and teacher, born in Sudern-Linden, Switzerland. A leading theorist at the Bauhaus (1919–23), he wrote on the theory of colour, and developed the idea of a compulsory 'preliminary course', based on research into natural forms and the laws of basic design.

Itúrbide, Agustín de [eetoorbithay] (1783–1824) Mexican general, born in Morelia, Mexico. He became prominent in the movement for Mexican independence, and made himself emperor as Agustin I (1822–3). Forced to abdicate, he was later executed.

Ivan IV, known as **the Terrible** (1530–84) Grand prince of Moscow (1533–84), born near Moscow, the first to assume the title of 'tsar'. In 1564 the treachery of one of his counsellors caused him to embark on a reign of terror, directed mainly at the feudal aristocracy.

Ivanov, Lev (Ivanovich) [eevahnof] (1834–1901) Choreographer, teacher, and dancer, born in Moscow. He joined the Imperial Ballet in 1852, becoming principal dancer in 1869 and second ballet master under Petipa in 1885. >> Petipa

Ives, Charles E(dward) (1874–1954) Composer, born in Danbury, CT. He composed four symphonies, chamber music (including the well-known 2nd piano sonata, the *Concord Sonata*), and many songs. In 1947 he was awarded the Pulitzer Prize for his third symphony (composed in 1904).

Ives, Frederick (Eugene) (1856–1937) Photographer and inventor, born in Litchfield, CT. He experimented with photography as a means of illustration, and invented (1878) the half-tone process. He later pioneered natural colours for motion pictures (1914).

Iwasaki, Koyota [eewasahkee] (1879–1945) Japanese tycoon. He joined the Mitsubishi Co, founded by his grandfather in the 1870s. President from 1916, he expanded the company into a commercial group, producing most of the ships, aircraft, and equipment used by the Japanese armed forces in the War.

Iwerks, U B, originally **Ubbe Iwwerks** (1901–71) Animated-cartoon director, born in Kansas City, KS. He joined Disney in California to animate *Oswald the Lucky Rabbit* (1924), then animated the first film to star Mickey Mouse, *Plane Crazy* (1928). He won Oscars in 1959 and 1964 for his technical achievements.

Jabir ibn Hayyan >> Geber

Jack the Ripper Unidentified English murderer who, between August and November 1888, murdered and mutilated five prostitutes in the East End of London. The murderer was never discovered, but speculation about the murderer's identity was still continuing in the 1990s.

Jacklin, Tony, popular name of **Anthony Jacklin** (1944–) Golfer, born at Scunthorpe, Humberside. He won the 1969 British Open at Royal Lytham, and in 1970 won the US Open at Hazeltine (the first British winner for 50 years).

Jackson, Andrew, nickname **Old Hickory** (1767–1845) US statesman and seventh president (1829–37), born in Waxhaw, SC. In his presidential campaign he gained the support of the mass of voters - a new development in US politics which came to be called 'Jacksonian democracy'.

Jackson, Glenda (1936–) Actress and politician, born in Birkenhead, Merseyside. She became a leading member of the Royal Shakespeare Company before appearing in films, including *Women in Love* (1969, Oscar) and *A Touch of Class* (1973, Oscar). She became a Labour MP in 1992.

Jackson, Helen (Maria) Hunt, *née* **Fiske** (1830–85) Writer, born in Amherst, MA. A campaigner for American Indian rights, her foremost works were the non-fiction *A Century of Dishonor* (1881) and the novel *Ramona* (1884).

Jackson, (George) Holbrook (1874–1948) Bibliophile and literary historian, born in Liverpool, Merseyside. He helped establish the political and literary *New Age* (1907), and had a life-long devotion to William Morris, as seen in the anthology, *On Art and Socialism* (1947). >> Morris, William

Jackson, Jesse (Louis) (1941–) Clergyman and politician, born in Greenville, NC. A civil rights activist, in 1984 and 1988 he sought the Democratic nomination for the presidency, winning considerable support, and becoming the first African-American to mount a serious candidacy for the office.

Jackson, John, known as **Gentleman Jackson** (1769–1845) Boxer, born in London. He won the English heavyweight boxing championship in 1795, and retired undefeated in 1803 after only three defences of his title.

Jackson, John Hughlings (1835–1911) Neurologist, born in Green Hammerton, North Yorkshire. He investigated unilateral epileptiform seizures, and discovered that certain regions of the brain are associated with certain movements of the limbs.

Jackson, Mahalia (1911–72) Gospel singer, born in New Orleans, LA. Her strong religious background and the influence of contemporary blues music were evident in her singing style. Two notably successful records were 'Move On Up a Little Higher' and 'Silent Night'.

Jackson, Michael (1958–) Pop singer, born in Gary, IN. With his brothers in the pop group The Jacksons, he knew stardom from the age of 11, and sang on four consecutive Number One hits. His first major solo album was *Off The Wall* (1979), and he consolidated his career with *Thriller* (1982) and *HIStory* (1995). He developed a reclusive lifestyle in adulthood, though continuing to tour widely. He married Lisa Marie Presley in 1994.

Jackson, Milt(on) (1923–) Vibraphone player, born in Detroit, MI. He emerged as the most important vibraphone player of the bebop era. In 1952 he was a founding member of the Modern Jazz Quartet, which existed until 1974 and re-formed in the 1980s.

Jackson, Reggie, popular name of **Reginald Martinez**

Jackson, nickname **Mr October** (1946–) Baseball player, born in Wyncote, PA. He joined the Kansas City Athletics (1968–75), establishing himself as a skilled hitter. He then played for the Baltimore Orioles (1976), the New York Yankees, and (1982) the California Angels, retiring after the 1987 season with 563 home runs.

Jackson, Sir Thomas Graham (1835–1924) British architect. His work can be seen at Eton, Harrow, Rugby, the Inner Temple, the Bodleian Library, and the New Examination Schools at Oxford.

Jackson, Thomas Jonathan, nickname **Stonewall Jackson** (1824–63) Confederate general in the American Civil War, born in Clarksburg, WV. He commanded a brigade at Bull Run, where his firm stand gained him his nickname, and gained notable victories at Cedar Run, Manassas, and Harper's Ferry. He was accidentally killed by his own troops.

Jackson, Sir William (Godfrey Fothergill) (1917–) British soldier and historian. He became military historian in the cabinet office (1977–8 and from 1982), and was commander-in-chief at Gibraltar (1978–82).

Jacob Biblical character, the son of Isaac, and patriarch of the nation Israel. He supplanted his elder brother Esau, obtaining his father Isaac's special blessing and thus being seen as the inheritor of God's promises. He fathered 12 sons, to whom Jewish tradition traced the 12 tribes of Israel. >> Esau; Isaac; Joseph; Levi; Rachel

Jacob, François [zhakohb] (1920–) Biochemist, born in Nancy, France. With Lwoff and Monod he conducted research into cell physiology and the structure of genes, for which they were jointly awarded the 1965 Nobel Prize for Physiology or Medicine. >> Lwoff; Monod, Jacques

Jacobi, Carl Gustav Jacob [jakohbee] (1804–51) Mathematician, born in Potsdam, Germany. His book *Fundamenta nova* (1829) was the first definitive study of elliptic functions, which he and Abel had independently discovered. He also made important advances in the study of differential equations, the theory of numbers, and determinants. >> Abel, Niels Henrik

Jacobi, Sir Derek (George) [jakohbee] (1938–) Actor, born in London. He has made several film and television appearances, notably the title role in the television drama serial *I, Claudius* (1977). A member of the Royal Shakespeare Company since 1982, his main work continues to be in the theatre.

Jacobs, David (Lewis) (1926–) British radio and television broadcaster. He has been with BBC radio and television since 1947, presenting shows, panel games, and many light and popular music programmes.

Jacobs, W(illiam) W(ymark) (1863–1943) Short-story writer, born in London. He wrote humorous yarns of seafarers, such as *The Skipper's Wooing* (1897), but his best-known story was the macabre tale, *The Monkey's Paw* (1902).

Jacobsen, Arne [yahkobsen] (1902–71) Architect and designer, born in Copenhagen. A leading exponent of Modernism, his main public buildings were the SAS skyscraper in Copenhagen (1955) and St Catherine's College, Oxford (1964).

Jacobus de Voragine >> Voragine, Jacobus de

Jacopo della Quercia [yakohpoh dela kwairchia] (c.1374–1438) Sculptor, born in Siena, Italy. His greatest works include the city's fountain (the 'Fonte Gaia', executed 1414–19) and the reliefs on the portal of San Petronia, Bologna.

Jacopone da Todi >> **Todi, Jacopone da**

Jacquard, Joseph Marie [zhakah(r)] (1752-1834) Silk-weaver, born in Lyon, France. His invention (1801-8) of the *Jacquard loom* enabled an ordinary workman to produce highly intricate weaving patterns.

Jacque, Charles Emile [zhak] (1813-94) Painter and etcher, born in Paris. A prominent member of the Barbizon school, he is best known for his paintings of sheep and etchings of rural scenes.

Jacques, Hattie [jayks], popular name of **Josephine Edwina Jacques** (1924-80) Comic actress, born in Sandgate, Kent. She frequently played bossy figures of authority, appearing in 14 *Carry On* films, and performing on radio in *ITMA* (1948-50) and *Educating Archie* (1950-4). On television she played opposite Eric Sykes in various long-running series. >> **Sykes**

Jacuzzi, Candido [jakootzee] (1903-86) Inventor, born in Italy. He devised a pump that produced a whirlpool effect in a bath, and when his invention became generally available, this type of bath was known as a *jacuzzi*.

Jagger, Charles Sargeant (1885-1934) Sculptor, born in Yorkshire. He executed mainly mythological and historical subjects. His most famous work is the 'Royal Artillery Memorial' at Hyde Park Corner, London.

Jagger, Mick, popular name of **Michael Phillip Jagger** (1943-) Singer, born in Dartford, Kent. He formed his own rock group, The Rolling Stones, together with Keith Richard, Bill Wyman, Charlie Watts, and Brian Jones. He wrote and sang many of their hit singles including 'The Last Time' (1965) and 'I Can't Get No Satisfaction' (1965).

Jahangir [yahanggeer], originally **Salim** (1569-1627) Mughal emperor of India (1605-27), born in Fatehpur Sikri, India, the son of Akbar the Great. The early part of his reign was peaceful, with growth of trade and flowering of the arts. His later reign was marked by continual rebellions against his rule, mainly on behalf of his sons. >> **Akbar the Great**

Jahn, Frederick Ludwig [yahn] (1778-1852) Physical educationist, born in Lanz, Germany. He became a teacher and began a programme of physical exercise for his students, inventing most of the equipment that is now standard in gymnasia.

Jaimini [jiyminee] (c.200 BC) Indian founder of the *Purva-Mimamsa* school of Hindu philosophy. His *Mimamsa Sutra* emphasizes the need for right action (which presupposes understanding how to acquire valid knowledge) and performing the duties required by the Vedas.

Jakes, Milos [yahkesh, meelosh] (1922-) Czechoslovakian politician, born in České Chalupy, Czech Republic. He became the Communist Party leader in 1987, but was forced to step down in 1989 following a series of pro-democracy rallies.

Jakobson, Roman (Osipovich) [yahkobson] (1896-1982) Linguist, born in Moscow. The founder of the Moscow Linguistic Circle (which generated Russian formalism), he moved in 1920 to Czechoslovakia (starting the Prague Linguistic Circle), and finally in 1941 to the USA.

Jalal ad-Din ar-Rumi [jalal adin aroomee] (1207-73) Persian lyric poet and mystic, born in Balkh, modern Afghanistan. He settled at Iconium (Konya) in 1226 and founded a sect who, after his death, were known in the West as the Whirling Dervishes.

Jamal, Ahmad, originally **Fritz Jones** (1930-) Jazz pianist, born in Pittsburg, PA. In 1952 he became house pianist at the Lounge of the Pershing Hotel in Chicago, and in 1958 a live recording of his trio stayed on the national best-selling lists for 108 weeks, one of the greatest popular successes in jazz history.

James I (of England) (1566-1625) The first Stuart king of England (1603-25), also king of Scots (1567-1625) as James VI, born in Edinburgh, the son of Mary, Queen of Scots. On Elizabeth's death, he ascended the English throne as great-grandson of James IV's English wife, Margaret Tudor. At first well received, his favouritism brought him unpopularity. During his reign the Authorized (or King James) Version of the Bible was published (1611). >> **Anne of Denmark; Margaret Tudor; Mary, Queen of Scots**

James I (of Scotland) (1394-1437) King of Scots (1424-37), born in Dunfermline, Fife, the second son of Robert III. After his elder brother David was murdered (1402), James was captured by the English, and kept a prisoner for 18 years. Once released (1424), he restored order to the country and carried out many reforms, but was murdered by a group of dissidents.

James II (of England) (1633-1701) King of England and Ireland (1685-8), also King of Scotland, as **James VII**, born in London, the second son of Charles I. After he became a convert to Catholicism, several attempts were made to exclude him from the succession. His actions in favour of Catholicism raised general indignation, and William, Prince of Orange, was formally asked to invade. James escaped to France, and made an ineffectual attempt to regain his throne in Ireland, ending in the Battle of the Boyne (1690).

James II (of Scotland) (1430-60) King of Scots (1437-60), the son of James I. Six years old at his father's murder, he assumed control after his marriage to Mary of Gueldres (1449). He became involved in the English struggles between the houses of York and Lancaster, and was killed by the bursting of a cannon. >> **James I** (of Scotland)

James III (1452-88) King of Scots (1460-88), the son of James II. He began to govern from 1469, but was a weak monarch unable to restore strong central government, and he was killed during a rebellion at Sauchieburn. >> **James II** (of Scotland) / **IV**

James IV (1473-1513) King of Scots (1488-1513), the eldest son of James III. In 1503 he married Margaret Tudor, the elder daughter of Henry VII - an alliance which led ultimately to the union of the crowns. He adhered to the French alliance when Henry VIII joined the League against France, and invaded England, but was killed at the Battle of Flodden. >> **Henry VIII; James III; Margaret Tudor**

James V (1512-42) King of Scots (1513-42), the son of James IV. In 1536 he visited France, marrying Magdeleine, the daughter of Francis I (1537), and after her death, Mary of Guise (1538). War with England followed, and he was routed at Solway Moss. >> **Guise, Mary of; James IV; Mary, Queen of Scots**

James, St (the 'brother' of Jesus), also known as **St James the Just** (1st-c), feast day 1 May. One of the 'brothers' of Jesus of Nazareth (*Matt* 13.55), and identified as the foremost leader of the Christian community in Jerusalem. According to Josephus, he was martyred by stoning (c.62). >> **Jesus Christ**

James, St (the son of Alphaeus), also known as **St James the Less** (1st-c), feast day 3 May. One of the 12 apostles. He may be the James whose mother Mary is referred to at the crucifixion of Jesus.

James, St (son of Zebedee), also known as **St James the Great** (1st-c), feast day 25 July. One of Jesus's 12 apostles, often listed with John (his brother) and Peter as part of an inner group closest to Jesus. According to *Acts* 12.2, he was martyred under Herod Agrippa I (c.44). >> **Herod Agrippa; Jesus Christ; John, St**

James, Arthur Lloyd (1884-1943) Phonetician, born in Pentre, Wales. He is chiefly remembered for his *Historical Introduction to French Phonetics* (1929), and for his work with the BBC as adviser in all matters concerning pronunciation.

James, C(yril) L(ionel) R(obert)) (1901-89) Writer and journalist, born in Tunapuna, Trinidad. His most popular book was *Beyond the Boundary* (1963), in which sport and politics are harmoniously and ingeniously conjugated.

James, Clive (Vivian Leopold) (1939–) Writer, satirist, broadcaster, and critic, born in Sydney, New South Wales, Australia. Television critic for *The Observer*, his television programmes include *Saturday Night Clive*, as well as a series of 'documentaries' set in cities around the world.

James (of Rusholme), Eric John Francis James, Baron (1909–92) Educational administrator. He was chairman of the Committee to Inquire into the Training of Teachers (1970–1) which reported in 1972 (*Teacher Education and Training*). The *James Report* recommended a restructuring of the pattern of teacher training.

James, Henry, Snr (1811–82) Religious philosopher, born in Albany, NY. His writings were much influenced by the teachings of Swedenborg, and he also became known as the father of William and Henry James. >> James, Henry / William; Swedenborg, Emanuel

James, Henry (1843–1916) Novelist, born in New York City. His work as a novelist falls into three periods. In the first he is mainly concerned with the impact of American life on older European civilization, as in *Roderick Hudson* (1875), *Portrait of a Lady* (1881), and *The Bostonians* (1886). His second period is devoted to purely English subjects, such as *The Tragic Muse* (1890), *What Maisie Knew* (1897), and *The Awkward Age* (1899). He reverts to Anglo-American attitudes in his last period, which includes his masterpiece, *The Ambassadors* (1903). The acknowledged master of the psychological novel, he was a major influence on 20th-c writing. >> James, Henry, Snr / William

James, Jesse (Woodson) (1847–82) Wild West outlaw, born in Centerville, MO. He and his brother **Frank James** (1843–1915) led many robberies in and around Missouri, before Jesse was murdered by a gang member for a reward. Frank gave himself up, stood trial, and was released.

James, M(ontague) R(hodes) (1862–1936) Scholar and writer, born in Goodnestone, Kent. He wrote on the *Apocrypha*, and the art and literature of the Middle Ages, but is best known as a writer of ghost stories, such as *Ghost Stories of an Antiquary* (1904–11).

James, P D, pseudonym of **Phyllis Dorothy White, Baroness James of Holland Park** (1920–) Detective-story writer, born in Oxford, Oxfordshire. Her novels include *Death of an Expert Witness* (1977) and *Innocent Blood* (1980). The futuristic novel *The Children of Men* (1992) represents a new departure.

James, William (1842–1910) Philosopher and psychologist, born in New York City, the brother of Henry James. His books include *The Principles of Psychology* (1890) and *The Varieties of Religious Experience* (1902). He helped found the American Society for Psychical Research. >> James, Henry, Snr / Henry

Jameson, Sir Leander Starr [jaymsn] (1853–1917) British colonial statesman, born in Edinburgh. He became involved in Rhodes' plan to extend British rule in Africa, and led an attack against the Boers, but was defeated (1896), and sent back to England. He later became premier of Cape Colony (1904–8), and formed the Unionist Party (1910). >> Rhodes, Cecil John

Jameson, (Margaret) Storm [jaymsn] (1891–1986) Writer, born in Whitby, North Yorkshire. Her books include *The Lovely Ship* (1927), *Cloudless May* (1943), and *The White Crow* (1968).

Jamet, Marie [zhamay] (1820–93) French religious, known as Marie Augustine de la Compassion. She was a founder in 1840 of the Little Sisters of the Poor.

Jamison, Judith [jaymisn] (1943–) Dancer, born in Philadelphia, PA. She joined Ailey's American Dance Theater in 1965, becoming one of his top soloists, and starred in the Broadway musical *Sophisticated Ladies* (1981). >> Ailey

Janáček, Leoš [yanachek] (1854–1928) Composer, born in Hukvaldy, Czech Republic. Devoted to the Czech folksong tradition, he wrote several operas, a Mass, instrumental chamber pieces, and song cycles.

Jane, Frederick Thomas (1865–1916) Writer, journalist, and artist, born in Upottery, Devon. He founded and edited *Jane's Fighting Ships* (1898) and *All the World's Aircraft* (1909), the annuals by which his name is still best known.

Janet, Pierre [zhanay] (1859–1947) Psychologist and neurologist, born in Paris. His theory of hysteria, which linked 'dissociation' with a lowering of psychic energy, was described by Freud as the first significant psychological theory. >> Freud, Sigmund

Jannings, Emil, originally **Theodor Friedrich Emil Janenz** (1884–1950) Actor, born in Rorschach, Switzerland. He worked in American films (1926–9), and won the first Oscar for his performances in *The Way of All Flesh* (1928) and *The Last Command* (1928). In Germany he appeared in *The Blue Angel* (1930), his most famous film.

Jansen, Cornelius (Otto) [jansen], Dutch [yahnsen] (1585–1638) Theologian, founder of the reform movement known as Jansenism, born in Acquoi, The Netherlands. His *Augustinus* (4 vols, 1640), sought to prove that the teaching of St Augustine on grace, free will, and predestination was opposed to the teaching of the Jesuit schools. The book was condemned by Pope Urban VIII in 1642, but the controversy raged in France for nearly a century.

Jansky, Karl (Guthe) [yanskee] (1905–50) Radio engineer, born in Norman, OK. His discovery (1932) of radio waves from outer space allowed the development of radio astronomy during the 1950s. The unit of radio emission strength, the *jansky*, is named after him.

Janssen, Cornelis [yahnsen], originally **Cornelius Johnson** (1593–1661) Portrait painter, born in London of Dutch parents. His portraits show the influence of Van Dyck, with whom he worked at the court of Charles I. >> van Dyck

Janssen, Pierre (Jules César) [jansen], Fr [zhänsen] (1824–1907) Astronomer, born in Paris. He greatly advanced spectrum analysis by his observation of the bright line spectrum of the solar atmosphere (1868). A crater on the Moon has been named after him.

Jansson, Tove (Marika) [yansn] (1914–) Writer of children's books, and artist, born in Helsinki. Her books for children, featuring the 'Moomintrolls' and illustrated by herself, have reached an international audience.

Janszoon, Laurens, also called **Laurens Coster** (c.1370–c.1440) Dutch official, sacristan (*Koster*) of the Grote Kerk of Haarlem. He is credited by some with the invention of printing before Gutenberg, and is said to have printed as early as 1430, but no evidence exists to support the claim. >> Gutenberg, Johannes

Januarius, St [janyuahrius], Ital **San Gennaro** (?–c.305), feast day 19 September. Christian martyr, Bishop of Benevento, believed to have been a victim under Diocletian. Two phials kept in Naples cathedral are said to contain his dried blood, believed to liquefy on his feast day, and at other times during the year.

Japheth [jayfeth] Biblical character, one of the sons of Noah who survived the Flood, the brother of Shem and Ham. He is portrayed as the ancestor of peoples in the area of Asia Minor and the Aegean (*Gen* 10). >> Noah

Jaques-Dalcroze, Emile [zhak dalkrohz] (1865–1950) Music teacher and composer, born in Vienna. He originated eurhythmics, a method of expressing the rhythmical aspects of music by physical movement.

Jardine, Douglas (Robert) [jah(r)din] (1900–58) Cricketer, born in Bombay, India. He captained England during the controversial 'bodyline' tour of Australia (1932–3), where he employed Larwood to make the first use of intimidatory bowling in the game. >> Larwood

Jarman, Derek (1942–94) Painter and film maker, born in Northwood, Greater London. His films, often controversial, include *Jubilee* (1977), *Caravaggio* (1985), and *The Last of England* (1987). He also directed pop videos, designed for opera and ballet, and wrote several books.

Jarmusch, Jim [jah(r)mush] (1953–   ) Film scriptwriter and director, born in Akron, OH. He gained critical acclaim with his film *Stranger Than Paradise* (1984). *Down by Law* (1986) and *Mystery Train* (1989) increased his reputation as a maker of offbeat films, noted for their 'European sensibility'.

Jarrell, Randall (1914–65) Poet and critic, born in Nashville, TN. He wrote an early campus novel, *Pictures from an Institution* (1954), and published several volumes of criticism. A dozen volumes feature in his *Complete Poems* (1971).

Jarry, Alfred [zharee] (1873–1907) Writer, born in Laval, France. He wrote short stories, poems, and plays in a Surrealist style, inventing a logic of the absurd which he called *pataphysique*. His satirical play *Ubu-Roi*, written at the age of 15, was later rewritten, and produced in 1896.

Jaruzelski, General Wojciech (Witold) [yaruzelskee] (1923–   ) Polish general, prime minister (1981–5), head of state (1985–90), and president (1989–90), born near Lublin, Poland. His declaration of martial law (1981–2), in an attempt to counteract the increasing influence of the free trade union Solidarity, brought the political situation in Poland to world attention. >> Walesa

Jaspers, Karl (Theodor) [yasperz] (1883–1969) Philosopher, born in Oldenburg, Germany. His many works include *Philosophie* (3 vols, 1932), considered his most important writing. His work was banned by the Nazis, but he stayed in Germany, and was awarded the Goethe Prize in 1947 for his uncompromising stand.

Jastrow, Robert [jastroh] (1925–   ) Physicist and writer, born in New York City. He was involved in the early development of NASA, and his books include *Red Giants and White Dwarfs* (1963) and *Journey to the Stars* (1989).

Jaurès, (Auguste Marie Joseph) Jean [zhohres] (1859–1914) Socialist leader, writer, and orator, born in Castres, France. The main figure in the founding of the French Socialist Party, he was assassinated while advocating reconciliation with Germany.

Javacheff, Christo >> Christo

Javal, Camille >> Bardot, Brigitte

Jawara, Sir Dawda Kairaba [jawahra] (1924–   ) Gambian prime minister (1965–70) and president (1970–   ), born in Barajally, The Gambia. Already premier (1962–5), on full independence he became Gambia's first prime minister, and when the country chose republican status he became its first president.

Jawlensky, Alexey von [yavlenskee] (1864–1941) Painter, born in Kuslovo, Russia. He developed his own brightly-coloured Fauvist style by c.1905, but later came under Cubist influence, and painted simpler, more geometrical arrangements using more subdued colours.

Jay, John (1745–1829) US statesman and jurist, born in New York City. He became secretary for foreign affairs (1784–9), and Chief Justice of the Supreme Court (1789–95). In 1794 he negotiated *Jay's Treaty* with Britain, in an attempt to avoid war.

Jay, Peter (1937–   ) British writer, broadcaster, and businessman. He was presenter of TV-AM (1983) and of *A Week in Politics* (1983–6, Channel 4), and became economics and business editor at the BBC in 1990.

Jayawardene, Junius Richard [jayawah(r)denay] (1906–   ) Sri Lankan prime minister (1977–8) and president (1978–89), born in Colombo. He became vice-presi-

dent of the United National Party, leading it in Opposition, both as deputy leader (1960–5) and leader (1970–7), before gaining in power.

Jean de Meung [zhã duh moë], or **Jean Clopinel** (c.1250–1305) Poet and satirist, born in Meung-sur-Loire, France. His great work is his lengthy continuation (18 000 lines) of the *Roman de la Rose* by Guillaume de Lorris. >> Guillaume de Lorris

Jeanne d'Arc >> Joan of Arc, St

Jeanneret, Charles Edouard >> Le Corbusier

Jeans, Sir James (Hopwood) [jeenz] (1877–1946) Astrophysicist and popularizer of science, born in Ormskirk, Lancashire. He made important contributions to the theory of gases, quantum theory, and stellar evolution, and became widely known for his popular exposition of physical and astronomical theories.

Jefferson, Joseph (1829–1905) Comic actor, born in Philadelphia, PA. In 1858 he created the part of Asa Trenchard in *Our American Cousin*. In 1865 he visited London, and at the Adelphi first played his famous part of Rip Van Winkle.

Jefferson, Thomas (1743–1826) US vice-president (1797–1801) and third president (1801–9), born in Shadwell, VA. He took a prominent part in the first Continental Congress (1774), and drafted the Declaration of Independence. His administration saw the war with Tripoli, the Louisiana Purchase (1803), and the prohibition of the slave trade. >> Adams, John

Jeffreys (of Wem), George Jeffreys, Baron, known as **Judge Jeffreys** (1648–89) Judge, born in Acton, Clwyd. As Chief Justice of the King's Bench (1683), his journey to the West Country to try the followers of Monmouth earned his court the name of 'the Bloody Assizes' for its severity. He was Lord Chancellor (1685–8), but on James's flight was imprisoned in the Tower. >> James II (of England); Monmouth, James

Jeffreys, Sir Harold (1891–1989) Geophysicist, astronomer, and mathematician, born in Fatfield, Tyne and Wear. He investigated the effect of radioactivity on the cooling of the Earth, and postulated that the Earth's core is liquid. He also studied the Solar System, re-calculating the surface temperatures of the outer planets.

Jeffries, James J(ackson), nickname **the Boilermaker** (1875–1953) Boxer, born in Carroll, OH. In 1899 he won the world heavyweight championship by knocking out Bob Fitzsimmons. He retired undefeated in 1905, but in 1910 was knocked out by Jack Johnson in an unsuccessful comeback. >> Fitzsimmons; Johnson, Jack

Jeffries, John (1744–1819) Balloonist and physician, born in Boston, MA. He settled in England and made the first balloon crossing of the English Channel with the French aeronaut Blanchard in 1785. >> Blanchard

Jehu, King of Israel [jeehoo] (9th-c BC) King of Israel (c.842–815 BC). After King Ahab was killed he led a military coup against his son, seized the throne for himself, and founded a dynasty that presided over a decline in the fortunes of Israel. >> Ahab

Jekyll, Gertrude [jeekl] (1843–1932) Horticulturalist and garden designer, born in London. Her designs for more than 300 gardens of Lutyens' buildings had a great influence on promoting colour design in garden planning. >> Lutyens, Edwin Landseer

Jellicoe, John Rushworth Jellicoe, 1st Earl [jelikoh] (1859–1935) British admiral, born in Southampton, Hampshire. Commander-in-chief at the outbreak of World War 1, his main engagement was the Battle of Jutland (1916). He later organized the defences against German submarines.

Jenghiz Khan >> Genghis Khan

Jenkins, David (Edward) (1925–   ) Theologian and clergyman, born in Bromley, Greater London. He was appointed Bishop of Durham (1984–94), amidst controversy over his interpretation of the Virgin Birth and the Resurrection.

Jenkins, Richard Walter >> **Burton, Richard**

Jenkins, Robert (18th-c) English merchant captain, engaged in trading in the West Indies. In 1731 he alleged that his ear had been torn off by a Spanish coastal guard for suspected smuggling. He produced the alleged ear in 1738 in the House of Commons, forcing Walpole into the 'War of Jenkins' Ear' against Spain in 1739. >> Walpole, Robert

Jenkins (of Hillhead), Roy (Harris) Jenkins, Baron (1920–) British statesman, born in Abersychan, Gwent. He served as Chancellor of the Exchequer (1967–70) and home secretary (1965–7, 1974–6), became president of the European Commission (1977–81), then co-founded the Social Democratic Party, becoming its first leader (1981–3). >> Owen, David

Jenkinson, Robert Banks >> **Liverpool, Earl of**

Jenner, Edward (1749–1823) Physician, born in Berkeley, Gloucestershire. Having observed how an infection of the mild disease cowpox prevented later attacks of smallpox, in 1796 he inoculated a child with cowpox, then two months later with smallpox, and the child failed to develop the disease. This led to the widespread use of vaccination.

Jenner, Sir William (1815–98) Physician, born in Chatham, Kent. He established the difference between typhus and typhoid fevers in 1851.

Jennings, Herbert Spencer (1868–1947) Zoologist, the first to study the behaviour of micro-organisms, born in Tonica, IL. He wrote the standard work *Contributions to the Study of the Behavior of the Lower Organisms* (1919).

Jennings, Pat(rick) (1945–) Footballer, born in Newry, Co Down. A goalkeeper, he played for Watford, Tottenham Hotspur, and Arsenal, making 747 League appearances. He is Britain's most capped footballer, playing for Northern Ireland 119 times.

Jennings, Sarah >> **Churchill, Sarah**

Jensen, Georg [yensen] (1866–1935) Silversmith, born in Raadvad, Denmark. He founded his smithy in Copenhagen in 1904, and expanded his business throughout Europe, becoming one of the first to produce high quality, fashionable steel cutlery.

Jensen, (Johannes) Hans (Daniel) [yensen] (1907–73) Physicist, born in Hamburg, Germany. He shared the Nobel Prize for Physics in 1963 for research leading to the development of the shell theory for the structure of the atomic nucleus.

Jensen, Johannes Vilhelm [yensen] (1873–1950) Writer and poet, born in Farsø, Denmark. His best-known work is *The Long Journey* (trans, 1908–22), depicting in a Darwinian perspective the rise of the human race through time. He was awarded the Nobel Prize for Literature in 1944.

Jeremiah [jeruhmiya] (7th-c BC) Old Testament prophet, whose prophecies are recorded in the *Book of Jeremiah*, born near Jerusalem. He is said to have been stoned to death by his fellow Jews for constantly rebuking them for idolatry.

Jerne, Niels K(ai) [yernuh] (1911–94) Immunologist, born in London of Danish parents. For his research into the way the immune system in the body creates antibodies against disease, he shared the Nobel Prize for Physiology or Medicine in 1984.

Jeroboam I [jeroboham] (10th-c BC) First king of the divided kingdom of Israel. After Solomon's death he headed the successful revolt of the N tribes against Rehoboam, and established shrines at Dan and Bethel as rival pilgrimage centres to Jerusalem. >> Solomon

Jerome, St [jerohm], originally **Eusebius Hieronymus** (c.342–420), feast day 30 September. Christian ascetic and scholar, born in Stridon, Croatia. He is chiefly known for making the first translation of the Bible from Hebrew into Latin (the Vulgate).

Jerome, Jerome K(lapka) [jerohm] (1859–1927) Humorous writer, novelist, and playwright, born in Walsall, Staffordshire. He is best known for his novel *Three Men in a Boat* (1889), which became a humorous classic.

Jerome of Prague [jerohm] (c.1365–1416) Religious reformer, born in Prague. A disciple of Wycliffe, he zealously spread his teachings throughout Europe, but was arrested in 1415, and burned at the stake. >> Wycliffe

Jespersen, (Jens) Otto (Harry) [yespersen] (1860–1943) Philologist, born in Randers, Denmark. He wrote several major works on grammar, invented an international language (Novial), and contributed to the development of phonetics and linguistics.

Jesse, Fryn Tennyson [jesee], popular name of **Friniwyd Tennyson Jesse** (1889–1958) British writer and playwright. She is best known for her novels set in Cornwall, such as *The White Riband* (1921), *Moonraker* (1927), and *A Pin to See a Peepshow* (1934).

Jessel, Sir George (1824–83) Judge, born in London. He became solicitor general (1871–3) and Master of the Rolls (1873–83), and made important contributions to legal principle by reshaping older doctrines, especially of equity.

Jessop, William (1745–1814) Civil engineer, born in Devonport, Devon. He was chief engineer on the construction of the Grand Junction Canal, the Surrey Iron Railway (1802), Avon docks at Bristol, and the West India Docks on the Thames.

Jesus Christ (c.6/5 BC–AD c.30/33) The central figure of the Christian faith, whose nature as 'Son of God' and whose redemptive work are fundamental beliefs for adherents of Christianity. 'Christ' became attached to the name 'Jesus' in Christian circles in view of the conviction that he was the Jewish Messiah ('Christ'). Jesus of Nazareth is described as the son of Mary and Joseph, and is credited with a miraculous conception by the Spirit of God. He was born in Bethlehem before the death of Herod the Great (4 BC), but began his ministry in Nazareth. After being baptized by John the Baptist in the Jordan, he gathered a group of 12 apostles, and began his public ministry. The main records of this ministry are the New Testament Gospels, which show him proclaiming the coming of the kingdom of God in the country of Galilee over a 3-year period. He was executed by crucifixion under the order of Pontius Pilate, perhaps because of the unrest Jesus's activities were causing. Accounts of his resurrection from the dead and later events are preserved in the Gospels, Pauline writings, and Acts of the Apostles. >> Joseph, St; John the Baptist, St; Mary (mother of Jesus); Pontius Pilate

Jevons, William Stanley [jevonz] (1835–82) Economist and logician, born in Liverpool, Merseyside. He introduced mathematical methods into economics, and wrote *Theory of Political Economy* (1871), a major work in the development of economic thought.

Jewel, John (1522–71) Clergyman, born in Berrynarbor, Devon. He was appointed Bishop of Salisbury in 1560, and published his famous *Apologia for the English Church* in 1562.

Jewel and Warriss Stage names of **Jimmy Jewel** (1909–95) and **Ben Warriss** (1909–93) Comedy partners, born in Sheffield, South Yorkshire. They achieved national fame as stars on BBC radio's *Up the Pole* (1947) and as cover stars of the weekly children's comic, *Radio Fun*.

Jewett, (Theodora) Sara Orne (1849–1909) Novelist, born in South Berwick, ME. She wrote a series of sketches, *The Country of the Pointed Firs* (1896), as well as romantic novels and stories based on the provincial life of her state, such as *A Country Doctor* (1884).

Jex-Blake, Sophia Louisa (1840–1912) Physician and pioneer of medical education for women, born in Hastings, East Sussex. She studied medicine at Edinburgh University, and was allowed to matriculate in 1869, but the authorities reversed their decision in 1873. She waged a public campaign in London, opened the London School of Medicine for Women (1874), and won her campaign in 1876.

Jezebel (?–c.843 BC) Phoenician princess, the wife of King Ahab of Israel (869–850). After Ahab's death, the usurper Jehu seized power in an army coup, and had her killed. >> Ahab; Jehu

Jhabvala, Ruth [jabvahla], *née* **Prawer** (1927–) Writer, born in Cologne, Germany. Significant novels include *To Whom She Will Marry* (1955), *The Householder* (1960), and *Heat and Dust* (1975, Booker). Among her notable screenplays are *Shakespeare Wallah* (1965) and *A Room with a View* (1986, Oscar).

Jhering, Rudolf von [yayring] (1818–92) Jurist, born in Aurich, Germany. He founded a school of jurisprudence based on teleological principles, and wrote extensively on Roman law and legal history.

Jiang Jieshi [jiang jieshee], or **Chiang Kai-shek** [chang kiy shek] (1887–1975) Revolutionary leader of 20th-c China, the effective head of the Nationalist Republic (1928–49), born in Zhejiang. In 1918 he joined the separatist revolutionary government of Sun Yixian, and in 1925 launched an expedition against the Beijing government, entering Beijing in 1928. During the ensuing decade the Nationalist Party steadily lost support to the Communists, and was eventually defeated by Communist forces. He was forced to retreat to Taiwan (1949), where he headed an emigré regime. >> Jiang Jingguo; Mao Zedong; Sun Yixian

Jiang Jingguo [jiang jinggwoh] , also spelled **Chiang Ching-kuo** (1918–) Taiwanese prime minister (1972–8) and president (1978–87), born in Chekiang Province, China, the son of Jiang Jieshi. In his later years he began a progressive programme of political liberalization. >> Jiang Jieshi; Lee Teng-hui

Jiang Qing [jiang ching], also spelled **Chiang Ch'ing** (1914–91) Chinese politician, born in Zhucheng, Shandong Province, China. She married Mao Zedong (1939), later becoming one of the leaders of the 'Cultural Revolution' (1966–76). After Mao's death she was tried and sentenced to death, though the sentence was later commuted. >> Mao Zedong

Jiang Zemin (1926–) Chinese politician, born in Yangzhou, Jiangsu Province, China. He was elected to the Chinese Communist Party's central committee in 1982, becoming party leader (1989), and chairman of the Central Military Commission (1990).

Jikaku Daishi >> Ennin
Jiménez, Francisco >> Ximénes, Cardinal
Jiménez, Juan Ramón [himayneth] (1881–1958) Lyric poet, born in Moguer, Spain. He made his birthplace famous by his delightful story of the young poet and his donkey, *Platero and I* (trans, 1914), one of the classics of modern Spanish literature. He later emerged as a major poet, and was awarded the Nobel Prize for Literature in 1956.

Jimmu [jimoe] Legendary Japanese emperor, of divine descent (from Izanagi). He supposedly founded the Japanese imperial lineage near modern Kyoto in the Yamato plain.

Jinnah, Muhammad Ali [jina] (1876–1948) Muslim politician and founder of Pakistan, born in Karachi, India (now Pakistan). His advocacy of a separate state for Muslims led to the creation of Pakistan in 1947, and he became its first governor-general.

Joachim, St >> Anne, St
Joachim of Fiore or **Joachim of Floris** [johakim] (c.1135–1202) Mystic, born in Calabria, Italy. In 1177 he became abbot of the Cistercian monastery of Corazzo, and founded the *Ordo Florensis*, a stricter order which was absorbed by the Cistercians in 1505. He is known for his mystical interpretation of history.

Joad, C(yril) E(dwin) M(itchinson) [johd] (1891–1953) Philosopher and broadcaster, born in Durham, Co Durham. He wrote 47 highly personal books, notably *Guide to Philosophy* (1936), and is remembered for his BBC Brains Trust intervention, 'It all depends what you mean by ...'.

Joan of Arc, St, Fr **Jeanne d'Arc**, known as **the Maid of Orléans** (c.1412–31), feast day 30 May. Traditionally recognized patriot and martyr, who halted the English ascendancy in France during the Hundred Years' War, born in Domrémy, France. At the age of 13 she heard saints' voices bidding her rescue France from English domination. She entered Orléans (1429), forced the English to retire, and took the Dauphin to be crowned Charles VII at Reims. Later captured, she stood trial (1431) for heresy and sorcery, and was burned. She was canonized in 1920. >> Charles VII; Dunois

Joan of Navarre, also known as **Joanna of Navarre** (c.1370–1437) Queen consort of Henry IV of England, and stepmother of Henry V. She married the Duke of Brittany (1386), and after his death (1399) married Henry IV (1402). >> Henry IV / V (of England)

Jobs, Steven [jobz] (1955–) Computer inventor and entrepreneur, born in San Francisco, CA. He was cofounder with **Stephen Wozniak** (1950–), of the Apple Computer Co in 1976.

Jochum, Eugen [yokhuhm] (1902–87) Conductor, born in Babenhausen, Germany. He became musical director of the Hamburg Staatsoper and conductor of the Hamburg Philharmonic Orchestra (1934–49), then conducted the Bavarian Radio Symphony Orchestra.

Jodl, Alfred [yohdl] (1890–1946) German general, born in Aachen, Germany. The planning genius of the German High Command and Hitler's chief adviser, he was found guilty of war crimes at Nuremberg (1946), and executed. >> Hitler

Joffre, Joseph Jacques Césaire [zhofruh] (1852–1931) French general, born in Rivesaltes, France. As French chief-of-staff (1914) and commander-in-chief (1915), he carried out a policy of attrition against the German invaders of France.

Joffrey, Robert, originally **Abdullah Jaffa Bey Kahn** (1930–88) Dancer, choreographer, teacher, and ballet director, born in Seattle, WA. In the 1950s he formed the Joffrey Ballet, using rock music and multi-media techniques alongside revivals of contemporary classics.

Johanan ben Zakkai, Rabban [yohhanan ben zakiy] (1st-c) Jewish teacher. He was a leader of the reformulation of Judaism after the fall of Jerusalem in 70 AD.

Johannsen, Wilhelm Ludvig [johhansen] (1857–1927) Botanist and geneticist, born in Copenhagen. His pioneering experiments with princess beans laid the foundation for later developments in the genetics of quantitative characters. The terms *gene*, *phenotype*, and *genotype* are due to him.

Johanson, Donald (Carl) [johhanson] (1943–) Palaeoanthropologist, born in Chicago, IL. His spectacular finds of fossil hominids 3–4 million years old at Hadar in the Afar triangle of Ethiopia (1972–7) generated worldwide interest.

John, also known as **John Lackland** (1167–1216) King of England (1199–1216), born in Oxford, Oxfordshire. He was the youngest son of Henry II. He tried to seize the crown during Richard I's captivity (1193–4), but was forgiven and made successor by Richard, who thus set aside the rights of Arthur, the son of John's elder brother Geoffrey. After Arthur was murdered on John's orders (1203), Philip II of France marched against him and conquered all but a portion of Aquitaine (1204–5). In 1206 John refused to receive Stephen Langton as Archbishop of Canterbury; he was excommunicated (1209), and finally conceded (1213). Demands for constitutional reform by the barons led to the granting of the Magna Carta (1215), and his repudiation of the Charter brought the first Barons' War (1215–17). >> Arthur, Prince; Isabella of Angoulême; Langton, Stephen; Richard I

John, St, also known as **John, son of Zebedee** and **John the Evangelist** (1st-c), feast day 27 December. One of the 12 apostles, the son of Zebedee, and the younger brother of James. He was said to have spent his closing years at Ephesus, after having written the Apocalypse, the Gospel, and the three Epistles which bear his name. >> James, St (son of Zebedee); Jesus Christ

John, St, Chrysostom >> **Chrysostom, St John**

John XXII, originally **Jacques Duèse** (c.1249-1334) Pope (1316–34), born in Cahors, France. He intervened in the contest for the imperial crown between Louis of Bavaria and Frederick of Austria, supporting the latter. In 1327 Louis was crowned emperor at Rome, and deposed him, setting up an anti-pope (1328).

John XXIII, originally **Angelo Giuseppe Roncalli** (1881–1963) Pope (1958-63), born in Sotto il Monte, Italy. He convened the Second Vatican Council to renew the religious life of the Church, with the aim of eventual unity of all Christians.

John, Augustus (Edwin) (1878–1961) Painter, born in Tenby, Dyfed. His favourite themes were gypsies, fishing folk, and naturally regal women, as in 'Lyric Fantasy' (1913); and he painted portraits of several political and artistic contemporary figures.

John, Barry (1945–) Rugby union player, born in Cefneithin, Dyfed. An outside-half, he played 25 times for Wales, scoring a record 90 points, before retiring at the early age of 27.

John, Elton, originally **Reginald Kenneth Dwight** (1947–) Rock singer and pianist, born in Pinner, Greater London. He was one of the top pop stars of the 1970s, known for such songs as 'Rocket Man' (1972) and 'Honky Cat' (1972), and for his clownish garb that included huge glasses, jump suits, and ermine boots.

John, Gwen (1876–1939) Painter, born in Haverfordwest, Dyfed, the elder sister of Augustus John. She went to Paris (1904), where she worked as an artist's model, becoming Rodin's mistress c.1906. >> John, Augustus; Rodin

John, Otto [yohn] (1909–) West German ex-security chief, the defendant in a major postwar treason case. In 1954 he mysteriously disappeared from West Berlin, and later broadcast for the East German Communists. He returned to the West, claiming to have been a drugged kidnap victim, but was imprisoned (1956–8).

John of Austria, Don, Span **Don Juan** (1547–78) Spanish soldier, the illegitimate son of Emperor Charles V, born in Regensburg, Germany. He defeated the Moors in Granada (1570) and the Turks at Lepanto (1571). >> Charles V (Emperor)

John of Beverley, St (?-721), feast day 7 May. Monk, born in Harpham, Humberside. He became Bishop of Hexham (687–705) and Bishop of York (705-17), before retiring to the monastery of Beverley, which he had founded.

John of Capistrano, St [kapistrahnoh], Ital **Giovanni da Capistrano** (1386–1456), feast day 28 March. Monk, born in Capistrano, Italy. A famous Franciscan preacher, in 1451 he was sent to Austria by Pope Nicholas V to counter the teachings of the followers of Huss. He was canonized in 1690. >> Huss

John of Damascus, St, also called **St John Damascene** (c.675–c.749), feast day 4 December. Theologian and hymn writer of the Eastern Church, born in Damascus. He defended the use of images in church worship during the iconoclastic controversy.

John of Gaunt (1340–99) Duke of Lancaster, born in Ghent, Belgium, the fourth son of Edward III. He was highly influential as a peacemaker during the troubled reign of Richard II. On his second wife's death (1394) he married his mistress, Catherine Swynford, by whom he had three sons; from the eldest descended Henry VII. >> Richard II

John of Leyden (1509–36) Anabaptist leader, born in Leyden, The Netherlands. A noted orator, he went to Münster, became head of the Anabaptist movement, and set up a 'kingdom of Zion'.

John of Nepomuk, St (c.1330–93), feast day 16 May. Patron saint of Bohemia, born in Nepomuk, Czech Republic. He became confessor to Sophia, the wife of Wenceslaus IV (ruled 1378–1419). For refusing to betray the confession of the queen, he was tortured and drowned. He was canonized in 1729.

John of Salisbury [sawlzbree] (c.1115–80) Clergyman and scholar, born in Salisbury, Wiltshire. He became Bishop of Chartres (1176) and took part in the third Lateran Council (1179). He was a witness to Thomas à Becket's murder in Canterbury. >> Becket; Henry II (of England)

John of Trevisa (1326–1412) English translator, born in Cornwall. He is known for his translations of Higden, Glanville, and Bartholomaeus Anglicus. >> Higden

John of the Cross, St, originally **Juan de Yepes y Álvarez** (1542–91), feast day 14 December. Christian mystic and poet, the founder with St Teresa of the Discalced Carmelites, born in Fontiveros, Spain. A Carmelite monk, his poems, such as *Spiritual Canticle* (trans), are highly regarded in Spanish mystical literature. He was canonized in 1726. >> Teresa of Avila

John the Baptist, St (1st-c), feast day 24 June. Prophetic figure in the New Testament Gospels, the son of a priest named Zechariah. He baptized Jesus and others at the R Jordan, and was executed by Herod Antipas. >> Herod Antipas; Jesus Christ; Zechariah

John the Scot >> **Erigena, John Scotus**

John Damascene >> **John of Damascus**

John Paul I, originally **Albino Luciani** (1912–78) Pope (Aug–Sep 1978), born in Forno di Canale, Italy. He was the first pope to use a double name (from his two immediate predecessors, John XXIII and Paul VI). He died only 33 days later, the shortest pontificate of modern times.

John Paul II, originally **Karol Jozef Wojtyla** (1920–) Pope (1978–), born in Wadowice, Poland, the first non-Italian pope in 450 years. A champion of economic justice and an outspoken defender of the Church in Communist countries, he has been uncompromising on moral issues.

Johns, Jasper (1930–) Painter, sculptor, and printmaker, born in Augusta, GA. Attracted by the Dadaist ideas of Duchamp, he chose to paint flags, targets, maps, and other pre-existing images in a style deliberately clumsy and banal, and became one of the creators of Pop Art. >> Duchamp

Johns, W(illiam) E(arl) (1893–1968) Writer, author of the 'Biggles' novels, born in Hertford, Hertfordshire. He retired from the Royal Air Force in 1930, and edited *Popular Flying*, where he first wrote his stories featuring Captain James Bigglesworth.

Johns Hopkins >> **Hopkins, Johns**

Johnson, Alexander Bryan (1786-1867) Philosopher, born in Gosport, Hampshire. His philosophical works, such as *The Meaning of Words* (1854), anticipated views familiar to the linguistic philosophers of the 20th-c.

Johnson, Amy (1903–41) Pioneer aviator, born in Hull,

Humberside. She flew solo from England to Australia (1930), to Japan via Siberia (1931), and to Cape Town (1932), making new records in each case.

Johnson, Andrew (1808–75) US statesman and 17th president (1865–9), born in Raleigh, NC. He became vice-president (1865), and president on Lincoln's assassination (1865). A Democrat, his conciliatory policies were opposed by Congress, who wished to keep the Southern states under military government. He vetoed the congressional measures, was impeached, tried, and acquitted. >> Lincoln, Abraham

Johnson, Ben (1961–) Athlete, born in Falmouth, Jamaica. He moved to Canada in 1976, and in the middle 1980s was the world's fastest sprinter, with Carl Lewis. At the 1988 Olympics he set a new world 100-m record, but was stripped of his gold medal for having taken banned substances. >> Lewis, Carl

Johnson, Dame Celia (1908–82) Actress, born in Richmond, Surrey. Well-established on the stage, she had leading roles in the films *In Which We Serve* (1942) and *This Happy Breed* (1944), and is best remembered for her performance in *Brief Encounter* (1945).

Johnson, Clarence Leonard, known as **Kelly Johnson** (1910–90) Aircraft designer, born in Ishpeming, MI. With the Lockheed Corporation from 1933, he was involved in designing over 40 aircraft, including the U-2 high-altitude reconnaissance plane, the F-104 Starfighter, and the P-38 Lightning plane, used during World War 2.

Johnson, Eyvind (1900–76) Writer, born near Boden, Sweden. His four-part *The Story of Olof* (trans, 1934–7) is the finest of the many working-class autobiographical novels written in Sweden in the 1930s. He shared the Nobel Prize for Literature in 1974. >> Martinson

Johnson, Hewlett, nickname **the Red Dean** (1874–1966) Clergyman, born in Macclesfield, Cheshire. Dean of Canterbury (1931–63), in 1938 he visited Russia, and became a champion of Marxist policies, which involved him in continuous controversy in Britain. He received the Stalin Peace Prize in 1951.

Johnson, Howard (Deering) (1896–1972) Business executive, born in Boston, MA. He developed 28 flavours of ice-cream for his Wollaston, MA, drugstore soda fountain, and by 1929 was franchising his name and products.

Johnson, J J, popular name of **James Louis Johnson** (1924–) Jazz trombonist and composer, born in Indianapolis, IN. During the 1940s he became inspired by the bebop movement, and recorded with Charlie Parker. From the 1960s he worked largely as a composer for films and televison. >> Parker, Charlie

Johnson, Jack, popular name of **John Arthur Jackson**, also called **Li'l Arthur** (1878–1946) Boxer, the first African-American world champion (1908–15), born in Galveston, TX. His defeat of Tommy Burns in 1908 provoked violent racial prejudice, and a 'great white hope' was sought to defeat him - former champion James J Jeffries - whom he knocked out in 1910. He lost his title in 1915 to Jess Willard. >> Jeffries, James J

Johnson, James P(rice) (1894–1955) Jazz pianist and composer, born in New Brunswick, NJ. He became the most accomplished player in the post-ragtime 'stride' style. He wrote over 200 songs, as well as several stage shows.

Johnson, James Weldon (1871–1938) Writer and diplomat, born in Jacksonville, FL. He became secretary of the National Association for the Advancement of Colored People (1916–30), and wrote extensively on African-American issues.

Johnson, Lyndon B(aines), also known as **LBJ** (1908–73) US statesman and 36th president (1963–9), born in Stonewall, TX. Vice-president in 1960, he became president after Kennedy's assassination, and was returned to the post in 1964. His administration passed the Civil Rights Act (1964) and the Voting Rights Act (1965), which helped African-Americans, but the escalation of the war in Vietnam led to unpopularity, and he retired in 1969.

Johnson, Magic, popular name of **Earvin Johnson** (1959–) Basketball player, born in Lansing, MI. With the Los Angeles Lakers from 1979, he was a member of NBA championship teams in 1980, 1982, 1985, 1987, and 1988.

Johnson, Martin W(iggo) (1893–1984) Oceanographer, born in Chandler, SD. He made major contributions to biological and military science by investigating invertebrate-produced underwater sounds and acoustic signal reflections.

Johnson, Pamela Hansford (1912–81) Writer, born in London. Best known for the portrayal of her native post-war London, her books include *An Avenue of Stone* (1947), *The Unspeakable Skipton* (1958), *A Bonfire* (1981), and several works of nonfiction. In 1950 she married the novelist C P Snow. >> Snow, C P

Johnson, Philip C(ortelyou) (1906–) Architect and theorist, born in Cleveland, OH. A proponent of the International Style, his designs include the Seagram Building skyscraper, New York City (1945), and the American Telephone and Telegraph building in New York City (1978–84).

Johnson, Richard M(entor) (1780–1850) Vice-president of the USA (1837–41), born near Louisville, KY. He became Democratic vice-president to Van Buren after the elections had not thrown up a majority in the electoral college for any one candidate. >> Van Buren

Johnson, Robert U >> Muir, John

Johnson, Samuel, known as **Dr Johnson** (1709–84) Lexicographer, critic, and poet, born in Lichfield, Staffordshire. From 1747 he worked for eight years on his *Dictionary of the English Language*, started the moralistic periodical, *The Rambler* (1750), and wrote his prose tale *Rasselas* (1759). His reputation as man and conversationalist outweighs his literary reputation. >> Boswell

Johnson, Uwe (1934–84) Writer, born in Pomerania (now part of Poland). His novels, such as *The Third Book about Achim* (trans, 1961) and *Two Views* (trans, 1965) develop the theme of the relation between East and West Germany.

Johnson, Virginia E >> Masters and Johnson

Johnson, Walter (Perry), nickname **the Big Train** (1887–1946) Baseball pitcher, born in Humboldt, KN. During his career with the Washington Senators (1907–27) he won 416 games, the second highest in major league history, and pitched 110 shutouts, a major league record.

Johnson, Sir William (1715–74) Merchant and colonial administrator, born in Co Meath, Ireland. In the Anglo-French Wars he led the Six Iroquois Nations against the French, and in 1760 took part in Amherst's victory over Montreal. >> Amherst, Jeffrey

Johnson, William Eugene, nickname **Pussyfoot** (1862–1945) Reformer and temperance propagandist, born in Coventry, NY. A special officer in the US Indian Service (1908–11), he received his nickname from his methods of raiding gambling saloons in Indian Territory.

Johnson, William H (1901–70) Painter, born in Florence, SC. His work is recognized for its original fusion of such influences as van Gogh and African sculpture, Constructivism and African textiles. >> van Gogh

Johnston, Albert Sidney (1803–62) Confederate general, born in Washington, KY. He commanded a successful surprise attack against Grant at Shiloh (1862), but was later mortally wounded. >> Grant, Ulysses S

Johnston, Brian (Alexander) (1912–94) British broadcaster and commentator. He joined the BBC in 1945, specializing in cricket commentary on radio and TV, and also presented the touring programme *Down Your Way* (1972–87).

Johnston, (William) Denis (1901–84) Playwright, born in Dublin. His major successes were an Expressionistic satire, *The Old Lady Says 'No'* (1929), and *The Moon on the Yellow River* (1931).

Johnston, Edward (1872–1944) Calligrapher, born in Uruguay of Scottish parents. His books, such as *Manuscript and Inscription Letters* (1909), were landmarks in the revival and development of calligraphy.

Johnston, George Henry, pseudonym **Shane Martin** (1912–70) Writer and journalist, born in Melbourne, Victoria, Australia. He is best known for a semi-autobiographical trilogy: *My Brother Jack* (1964), *Clean Straw for Nothing* (1969), and the unfinished *A Cartload of Clay* (1971).

Johnston, Sir Harry Hamilton (1858–1927) Explorer and writer, born in London. He spent much of his life travelling in Africa, and led the Royal Society's botanical expedition to Kilimanjaro (1884).

Johnston, Joseph E(ggleston) (1807–91) Confederate general, born near Farmville, VA. In command of the army of the Shenandoah, after the fall of Vicksburg he was criticised by Jefferson Davis for failing to stem the Union advance, and relieved of his command (1864). >> Davis, Jefferson

Johnstone, William (1897–1981) Painter, born in Denholm, Borders, Scotland. His work in the late 1920s and 1930s shows the influence of Surrealism in its use of rounded semi-abstract images suggestive of dream-like landscapes and human forms.

Joinville, Jean, sieur de (Lord of) [zhwĭveel] (c.1224–1317) Historian, born in Joinville, France. He took part in the Seventh Crusade (1248–54) of Louis IX, was imprisoned with him at Acre, and ransomed. >> Louis IX

Joliot-Curie, (Jean) Frédéric [zholyoh küree], originally **Jean Frédéric Joliot** (1900–58) Physical chemist, born in Paris. In 1925 he became assistant to Marie Curie, and in 1926 married her daughter Irène, with whom he shared the 1935 Nobel Prize for Chemistry. He was awarded the Stalin Peace Prize in 1951. >> Curie; Joliot-Curie, Irène

Joliot-Curie, Irène [zholioh kyooree], *née* **Curie** (1897–1956) Physical chemist, born in Paris, the daughter of Pierre and Marie Curie. In 1934 she and her husband Frédéric succeeded in producing radioactive elements artificially, for which they shared the Nobel Prize for Chemistry in 1935. >> Curie; Joliot-Curie, Frédéric

Jolley, (Monica) Elizabeth (1923–) Writer, born in Birmingham, West Midlands. She settled in Perth, Western Australia, in 1959. Her works include *Mr Scobie's Riddle* (1982, Age Book of the Year Award) and *My Father's Moon* (1989).

Jolson, Al [johlson], originally **Asa Yoelson** (1886–1950) Actor and singer, born in Srednike, Russia. Brought to the USA in 1893, he became known in the 1920s for such sentimental songs as 'Mammy', 'Sonny Boy', and 'Swanee'.

Joly, John [johlee] (1857–1933) Geologist and physicist, born in Holywood, Co Down. He invented a photometer in 1888, and formulated the theory of thermal cycles. With Walter Stevenson he evolved the 'Dublin method' in radiotherapy, and pioneered the radium treatment of cancer.

Jomini, (Antoine) Henri, Baron de [zhomeenee] (1779–1869) French general and writer, born in Payerne, Switzerland. Chief-of-staff to Marshal Ney (1813), he later joined the Russian army as aide-de-camp to Alexander I (1813) and Nicholas I (1826). >> Alexander I (of Russia); Ney; Nicholas I (of Russia)

Jonathan (c.11th-c BC) Biblical character, the son and heir of Saul (the first king of Israel) and loyal friend of David. David succeeded Saul as King of Israel, after Jonathan was killed fighting against the Philistines. >> David; Saul

Jones, Allen (1937–) Painter, sculptor and printmaker, born in Southampton, Hampshire. An early Pop artist, he specialized in slick, fetishistic images taken from pornographic or glossy fashion magazines.

Jones, Bob, popular name of **Robert Reynolds Jones** (1883–1968) Evangelist, born in Dale County, AL. To further his brand of fundamentalism, in 1927 he founded Bob Jones University, which later settled in Greenville, SC (1947), with several thousand students.

Jones, Bobby, popular name of **Robert (Tyre) Jones** (1902–71) Golfer, born in Atlanta, GA. He won the British Open three times (1926–7, 1930) and the US Open four times (1923, 1926, 1929–30).

Jones, Chuck, popular name of **Charles Jones** (1912–) Animated film cartoon director, born in Spokane, WA. His cartoon film characters include Daffy Duck, Wile E Coyote, the Road Runner, and Pepe le Pew (notably *For Scentimental Reasons*, 1951, Oscar). For television he created many specials, including *A Christmas Carol* (1972, Oscar).

Jones, Daniel (1881–1967) Phonetician, born in London. He wrote *An Outline of English Phonetics* (1916) and several other influential textbooks, compiled an *English Pronouncing Dictionary* (1917), and introduced a reference system of 'cardinal vowels' for describing the vowels of real languages.

Jones, David Michael (1895–1974) Poet, born in Kent, UK. His major works are *In Parenthesis* (1937) and *The Anathemata* (1952).

Jones, Edward Burne >> **Burne-Jones, Edward Coley**

Jones, Eli Stanley (1884–1973) Missionary to India, born in Baltimore, MD. In India from 1907, he supported Indian aspirations for independence, and was sensitive to Indian religious traditions.

Jones, (Alfred) Ernest (1879–1958) Psychoanalyst, born in Llwchwy, Glamorgan. A lifelong disciple and friend of Freud, he introduced psychoanalysis to the UK and USA, founding the British Psychoanalytical Society in 1913. >> Freud, Sigmund

Jones, Gwyn (1907–) Scholar and writer, born in Blackwood, Gwent. His work on Norse history and literature includes *A History of the Vikings* (1968); his Welsh studies include a translation of the *Mabinogion* (1948) and *The Oxford Book of Welsh Verse in English* (1977).

Jones, Dame Gwyneth (1936–) Dramatic soprano, born in Pontnewydd, Gwent. She made her Covent Garden debut in 1963, and is internationally renowned as an interpreter of the heroines of Wagner and Strauss operas.

Jones, Sir Harold Spencer (1890–1960) Astronomer, born in London. Astronomer Royal at Greenwich (1933–55), he organized an international project to determine Earth–Sun distance, investigated the Earth's rotation, and introduced a new system of time measurement in astronomy, ephemeris time.

Jones, Henry, pseudonym **Cavendish** (1831–99) Physician and writer, born in London. He wrote manuals on many games, and published *Principles of Whist* (1862), becoming whist editor of *The Field* magazine (1862).

Jones, Henry Arthur (1851–1929) Playwright, born in Grandborough, Buckinghamshire. His first great hit was a melodrama, *The Silver King* (1882), which he followed with more melodramatic successes.

Jones, Inigo (1573–1652) The first of the great English architects, born in London. He introduced the Italian Palladian style into England, where his designs include the Queen's House at Greenwich (1616–35) and the Banqueting House in Whitehall (1619–22).

Jones, Jack, popular name of **James (Larkin) Jones** (1913–93) Trade unionist, born in Liverpool, Merseyside. He was general secretary of the Transport and General Workers Union (1969–78), favouring the decentralization of trade union power to the local branches.

Jones, James (1921–77) Novelist, born in Robinson, IL. His wartime experience led to *From Here to Eternity* (1951, National Book Award). His only further notable work was *The Thin Red Line* (1962).

Jones, Jennifer >> Selznick, David O

Jones, John Paul, originally **John Paul** (1747–92) American naval officer, born in Kirkbean, Dumfries and Galloway. He joined the navy at the outbreak of the War of Independence, and performed a number of daring exploits off the British coast, capturing and sinking several ships.

Jones, Mary Harris, known as **Mother Jones** (1830–1930) US labour agitator, born in Co Cork, Ireland. She devoted herself to the cause of labour, travelling to areas of strife, especially in the coal industry.

Jones, Owen (1809–74) Architect and designer, born in London. He was superintendent of works for the Great Exhibition of 1851 in London, and director of decoration for the Crystal Palace (1852).

Jones, Robert Edmond (1887–1954) Scene designer, born in Milton, NH. His symbolic use of primary colours and light frame construction, a radical departure in 1915 from the prevailing norms of realism, revolutionized stagecraft in the USA.

Jones, Sir William (1746–94) Orientalist, born in London. He devoted himself to Sanskrit, whose resemblance to Latin and Greek he pointed out in 1787, thus motivating the era of comparative philology.

Jongen, Joseph [yongen] (1873–1953) Composer, born in Liège, Belgium. He composed piano, violin, and organ works, the symphonic poem *Lalla Roukh*, an opera, and a ballet.

Jongkind, Johan Barthold [yongkint] (1819–91) Painter, born in Lattrop, The Netherlands. He exhibited with the Barbizon painters, and was an important precursor of Impressionism.

Jonson, Ben(jamin) (1572–1637) Playwright, born in London. His four chief plays are *Volpone* (1606), *The Silent Woman* (1609), *The Alchemist* (1610), and *Bartholomew Fair* (1614), and he also wrote several masques. A major influence on 17th-c poets (known as 'the tribe, or sons, of Ben'), he became poet laureate in 1617.

Jónsson, Asgrímur (1876–1958) Landscape painter, born in Rútsstaða-Suðurkot, Iceland. He was the first artist to portray the Icelandic landscapes in all their variety and colour.

Jónsson, Einar [yohnsn] (1874–1954) Sculptor, born in Galtafell, Iceland. He worked in Denmark and Iceland, and in the USA spent two years making a statue of the first European settler in North America, Thorfinn Karlsefni, for a sculpture park in Philadelphia.

Jónsson, Finnur [yohnsn] (1892–1989) Painter, born in Strýta, Iceland. He held the first exhibition of abstract art in Reykjavík (1925), causing something of a scandal, and thereafter worked in more traditional styles, painting landscapes and scenes from fishing life.

Jooss, Kurt [johs] (1901–79) Dancer, choreographer, and director, born in Wasseralfingen, Germany. Director of the dance department at the Essen Folkwang School (1927), in 1933 in England he formed a new group, Ballets Jooss. His works continue to be mounted by his daughter **Anna Markard** (1931–).

Joplin, Scott (1868–1917) Pianist and composer, born in Texarkana, AR. His 'Maple Leaf Rag' (1899) made ragtime music a national craze, and was the first of his several popular rags.

Jordaens, Jakob [yawdahns] (1593–1678) Painter, born in Antwerp, Belgium. He painted several altarpieces, and became known for his scenes of merry peasant life, such as 'The King Drinks' (1638).

Jordan, Barbara (Charline) (1936–) US politician, born in Houston, TX. She entered Democratic politics in

the Texas Senate (1967–72), continuing in the US House of Representatives (1973–9).

Jordan, (Marie-Ennemond) Camille [zhawdã] (1838–1922) Mathematician, born in Lyon, France. He pioneered group theory, wrote on the theory of linear differential equations, and on the theory of functions, which he applied to the curve which bears his name.

Jordan, Dorothea, *née* **Bland** (1762–1816) Actress, born near Waterford, Ireland. For nearly 30 years she kept her hold on the public, mainly in comic tomboy roles. In 1790 she became involved with the Duke of Clarence, and afterwards with William IV, by whom she had 10 of her 15 children. >> William IV

Jordan, Michael (Jeffrey), nickname **Air Jordan** (1963–) Basketball player, born in New York City. He played with the Chicago Bulls from 1984, holds the record for most points in an NBA play-off game (63), and was a member of the USA Olympic gold medal-winning team in 1984 and 1992.

Jordan, Neil (1950–) Film maker and writer, born in Co Sligo, Ireland. His best-known novels are *The Past* (1980) and *The Dreams of the Beast* (1983). His films include *The Company of Wolves* (1984) and *Mona Lisa* (1986).

Jordanes [jaw(r)dahneez] (fl.6th-c) Gothic monk and historian. His chief work was *On the Origins and Deeds of the Getae* (trans, c.551), important as a contemporary source on both the Goths and the Huns.

Jorn, Asger Oluf [yaw(r)n] (1914–73) Painter, born in Jutland, Denmark. In 1948–50 he founded the 'Cobra' group (Co[penhagen], Br[ussels], A[msterdam]) which aimed to exploit fantastic imagery derived from the unconscious, not directed by reason.

Joseph II (1741–90) Holy Roman Emperor (1765–90), born in Vienna, the son of Francis I and Maria Theresa. An enlightened despot, he was known as 'the revolutionary emperor' for his programme of modernization. >> Maria Theresa

Joseph, St (1st-c BC), feast day 19 March. Husband of the Virgin Mary, a carpenter in Nazareth, who last appears in the Gospel history when Jesus Christ was 12 years old (*Luke* 2.43). >> Jesus Christ; Mary

Joseph Biblical character, the 11th son of Jacob. He is depicted as a favourite son (marked by the gift of a multi-coloured coat), sold into slavery by his jealous brothers, who rises to high office in Pharaoh's court. Eventually he is reconciled with his brothers. >> Jacob

Joseph (of Portsoken), Keith (Sinjohn) Joseph, Baron (1918–94) British statesman, born in London. He was secretary of state for social services (1970–4), industry (1979–81), and education and science (1981–6).

Joseph, Père, known as **l'Eminence grise** ('Grey Eminence'), originally **François Joseph le Clerc du Tremblay** (1577–1638) French diplomat and mystic, born in Paris. He became Cardinal Richelieu's secretary in 1611. His nickname derives from his contact with Richelieu (the 'Red Eminence'), for whom he went on several important diplomatic missions. >> Richelieu

Joseph of Arimathea, St [arimatheea] (1st-c), feast day 17 March (W), 31 July (E). In the New Testament a rich Israelite, a secret disciple of Jesus, and a councillor in Jerusalem. He went to Pontius Pilate and begged the body of Jesus, burying it in his own rock-hewn tomb (*Mark* 15.42–7).

Joséphine de Beauharnais, *née* **Marie Josèphe Rose Tascher de la Pagerie** (1763–1814) First wife of Napoleon Bonaparte, and French empress, born in Trois-Ilets, Martinique. She married Napoleon in 1796, and accompanied him on his Italian campaign. The marriage, being childless, was dissolved in 1809. >> Napoleon I

Josephson, Brian (David) (1940–) Physicist, born in Cardiff. In 1962 he deduced theoretically what is now called the *Josephson effect* at the junction of two superconductors, and for which he shared the Nobel Prize for Physics in 1973.

Josephus, Flavius [johseefus], originally **Joseph ben Matthias** (c.37–?) Jewish historian and soldier, born in Jerusalem. He commanded a Galilean force during the Jewish Revolt against Rome (66), and in Rome produced several writings on Jewish history and religion, including *Antiquities of the Jews* (93).

Joshua, Heb **Yehoshua** In the Old Testament, the son of Nun, of the tribe of Ephraim. Upon Moses' death he was appointed to lead the people into Canaan. The Book of Joshua is a narrative of the conquest and settlement of Canaan. >> Moses

Josiah [johsiya] (7th-c BC) Biblical character, king of Judah (c.639–609 BC). He is credited with destroying pagan cults and attempting to centralize worship in Jerusalem and the Temple.

Josquin des Prez or **Prés** [zhoskĭ day **pray**] (c.1440–1521) Composer, probably born in Condé, France. A master of polyphony, he left a number of valuable Masses, motets, and secular vocal works.

Joubert, Piet (Petrus Jacobus) [zhoobair] (1831–1900) Afrikaaner soldier and statesman, born in Prince Albert, South Africa. Living in the Transvaal from 1840, he negotiated the Pretoria Convention (1881), became vice-president (1883), and opposed Kruger for the presidency over the next 15 years. >> Kruger

Joule, James (Prescott) [jool] (1818–89) Physicist, born in Salford, Greater Manchester. He showed that heat is a form of energy, and established the mechanical equivalent of heat. His name is preserved in the unit of work, the *joule*.

Jourdan, Jean-Baptiste, comte (Count) [zhoordã] (1762–1833) French soldier, born in Limoges, France. He joined the Revolutionary army, fighting against the Austrians (1793–9). Napoleon made him a marshal (1804) and Governor of Naples (1806). He was defeated by Wellington at Vitoria (1813). >> Napoleon I; Wellington

Jouvet, Louis [zhoovay] (1887–1951) Actor and theatre /film director, born in Crozon, France. He became director (1924) of the Comédie des Champs Elysées, and was the first to recognize Giraudoux, whose plays he produced. >> Giraudoux

Jovian [johvian], in full **Flavius Claudius Jovianus** (c.331–64) Roman emperor (363–4), appointed by the army in Mesopotamia on Julian's death in battle. He was forced to make a humiliating peace with Shapur II. >> Julian; Shapur II

Jowett, Benjamin (1817–93) Scholar, born in London. He is best known for his translations of the *Dialogues* of Plato (1871), Thucydides (1881), the *Politics* of Aristotle (1885), and Plato's *Republic* (1894).

Joyce, Eileen Alannah (1912–91) Concert pianist, born in Zeehan, Tasmania, Australia. She is particularly known for her work on film sound-tracks, especially *Brief Encounter*, *The Seventh Veil*, and the film of her childhood, *Wherever She Goes*.

Joyce, James (Augustine Aloysius) (1882–1941) Writer, born in Dublin. His early work includes the short stories, *Dubliners* (1914) and *A Portrait of the Artist as a Young Man* (1914–15). *Ulysses* appeared in Paris in 1922, but was banned in the UK and USA until 1936. *Finnegans Wake* finally emerged in 1939. His work revolutionized the novel form through the abandonment of ordinary plot for 'stream of consciousness', and through his unprecedented exploration of language.

Joyce, William, nickname **Lord Haw Haw** (1906–46) British traitor, born in New York City. Throughout World War 2 he broadcast from Radio Hamburg propaganda against Britain, gaining his nickname from his upper-class drawl. He was captured by the British, tried, and executed in London.

Joyner-Kersee, Jackie, popular name of **Jacqueline Joyner-Kersee** *née* **Joyner** (1962–) Athlete, born in East St Louis, IL. She won the heptathlon silver medal at the 1984 Olympics, and in 1988 won the gold medal in both heptathlon and long jump.

Juan, Don >> **John of Austria**

Juan Carlos I [hwan kah(r)los] (1938–) King of Spain (1975–), born in Rome, the grandson of Spain's last ruling monarch, Alfonso XIII. In 1962 he married **Princess Sophia of Greece** (1938–), and they have three children. Named by Franco as his successor, he presided over Spain's democratization, assuming the role of a constitutional monarch. >> Alfonso XIII; Franco

Juárez, Benito Pablo [hwahres] (1806–72) Mexican national hero and president (1861–72), born in San Pablo Guelatao, Mexico. During the civil war (1857–60), he assumed the presidency, and was elected to that office on the Liberal victory (1861).

Judah [jooda] Old Testament figure, the fourth son of Jacob and Leah. He was the founder of the greatest of the 12 tribes of Israel. >> Jacob

Judas Iscariot [iskaryot] (1st-c) One of the 12 apostles of Jesus. He betrayed Jesus for 30 pieces of silver by helping to arrange for his arrest at Gethsemane by the Jewish authorities (*Mark* 14.43–6). >> Jesus Christ

Judd, Donald (1928–) Minimalist artist, born in Excelsior Springs, MO. He has metal boxes manufactured to his specification, spray-painted one colour, and stood on the floor. He has therefore only 'minimal' contact with his work, which is not 'composed' in any traditional sense.

Jude, St or **Thaddeus** (1st-c), feast day 28 October (W), 19 June or 21 August (E). One of the 12 Apostles, called 'Judas (son) of James' (*Luke* 6.16). He is traditionally thought to have been martyred in Persia with St Simon.

Judith Old Testament Jewish heroine. In the Apocryphal Book of Judith, she is portrayed as a widow who entered the tent of Holofernes, general of Nebuchadnezzar, cut off his head, and so saved her native town of Bethulia.

Judson, Adoniram (1788–1850) Missionary, born in Malden, MA. He went to Burma as a Baptist missionary, was a prisoner during the Anglo-Burmese War (1824–6), and produced a Burmese translation of the Bible (1833).

Jugnauth, Sir Aneerood [jugnawt] (1930–) Mauritian prime minister (1982–). In 1983 his party was reconstituted as the Mauritius Socialist Movement, with a pledge to make the country a republic within the Commonwealth (effective in 1992).

Jugurtha [jugoortha] (c.160–104 BC) King of Numidia (118–105 BC), after whom the *Jugurthine War* (112–104 BC) is named. His surrender to Marius's deputy, Sulla, ended the war, but was the starting point of the feud between Marius and Sulla which plunged Rome into civil war 20 years later. >> Marius, Gaius; Sulla

Juin, Alphonse (Pierre) [zhwĩ] (1888–1967) French soldier, born in Bône, Algeria. He distinguished himself in the Italian campaign, and became chief-of-staff of the National Defence Committee in Liberated France (1944–7).

Julia (39 BC–AD 14) Roman noblewoman, the daughter of Emperor Augustus and Scribonia. Augustus forced her stepson Tiberius to marry her (11 BC), but the marriage was unhappy: she began to lead a promiscuous life and was banished. >> Augustus; Tiberius

Julian, in full **Flavius Claudius Julianus**, known as **Julian the Apostate** (332–63) Roman emperor (361–3), the son of a half-brother of Constantine the Great. He publicly proclaimed himself a pagan, and initiated a vigorous policy of reviving the old pagan cults. >> Shapur II

Julian, Percy (Lavon) (1899–1975) Chemist and inventor, born in Montgomery, AL. In 1935 he synthesized the drug physostigmine, used to treat glaucoma, and later developed cortisone, used in the treatment of arthritis.

Julian or **Juliana of Norwich** (c.1342–1413) English mystic who probably lived in isolation outside St Julian's Church, Norwich. Her work, *Sixteen Revelations of Divine Love*, based on visions she received in 1373, has been a lasting influence on theologians stressing the power of the love of God.

Juliana, in full **Juliana Louise Emma Marie Wilhelmina** (1909–) Queen of The Netherlands (1948–80), born in The Hague. In 1937 she married Prince Bernhard zur Lippe-Biesterfeld; they have four daughters. She became queen on the abdication of her mother, Wilhelmina, and herself abdicated in favour of her eldest daughter, Beatrix. >> Beatrix; Bernhard Leopold; Wilhelmina

Julius II, originally **Giuliano della Rovere** (1443–1513) Pope (1503–13), born in Albizuola, Italy, the nephew of Sixtus IV. He employed Bramante for the design of St Peter's, had Raphael brought to Rome to decorate his private apartments, and commissioned Michelangelo for the frescoes on the ceiling of the Sistine Chapel. >> Bramante; Michelangelo; Raphael; Sixtus IV

Jumblat, Kemal (1919–77) Lebanese socialist statesman and hereditary Druze chieftain, born in the Chouf Mts, Lebanon. He founded the Progressive Socialist Party in 1949, held several cabinet posts (1961–4), and was minister of the interior (1969–70). After his assassination, his son, Walid Jumblat, became leader of the Druze.

Jung, Carl (Gustav) [yung] (1875–1961) Psychiatrist, born in Kesswil, Switzerland. He met Freud in Vienna in 1907, became his leading collaborator, and was president of the International Psychoanalytic Association (1911–14). Increasingly critical of Freud's approach, his *The Psychology of the Unconscious* (trans, 1911–12) caused a break in 1913. He then developed his own theories, which he called 'analytical psychology'. >> Freud, Sigmund

Junkers, Hugo [yungkerz] (1859–1935) Aircraft designer, born in Rheydt, Germany. He established an aircraft factory at Dessau (1910), where he built the first successful all-metal monoplane. His aircraft played an important part in the Luftwaffe during World War 2.

Jussieu, Bernard de [zhüsyoe] (c.1699–1777) Botanist, born in Lyon, France. He adopted a system which became the basis of modern natural botanical classification. His nephew, **Antoine Laurent** (1748–1836), elaborated his uncle's system in *Genera plantarum* (1778–89).

Just, Ernest E(verett) (1883–1941) Cell biologist, born in Charleston, SC. He made pioneering contributions to the cytology and embryology of marine organisms, and in 1925 demonstrated the carcinogenic effects of ultraviolet radiation on cells.

Justin (Martyr), St (c.100–c.165), feast day 1 June. One of the Fathers of the Church, born in Sichem, Samaria. He founded a school of Christian philosophy at Rome, where he wrote two *Apologies* on Christian belief (150–60). He is said to have been martyred at Rome.

Justinian [justinian], in full **Flavius Petrus Sabbatius Justinianus** (c.482–565) Roman emperor (527–65). He presided over the most brilliant period in the history of the late Roman empire. He recovered N Africa, Spain, and Italy, and carried out a major codification of the Roman law. >> Theodora

Justus of Ghent [yustus], originally **Joos van Wassenhove** (c.1435–c.1480) Painter, who became a member of the painters' guild in Antwerp in 1460, and in 1464 was a master in Ghent. His only surviving documented work is *The Institution of the Eucharist* (1472–4).

Juvarra or **Juvara, Filippo** [yuvahra] (1678–1736) Architect, born in Messina, Sicily. Appointed architect to the King of Sicily (1714), he moved to Turin and took charge of its rebuilding and enlargement.

Juvenal, in full **Decimus Junius Juvenalis** (c.55–c.130) Satirist, born in Aquinum, Italy. He is best known for his 16 brilliant satires in verse (c.100–c.127), dealing with life in Roman times under Domitian and his successors. >> Domitian

Kabalevsky, Dmitry (Borisovich) [kabalefskee] (1904–87) Composer and teacher, born in St Petersburg, Russia. His prolific output included four symphonies, operas, concertos, film scores, and much chamber and piano music.

Kádár, János [kahda(r)] (1912–89) Hungarian premier (1956-8, 1961–5) and first secretary (1956–88), born in Kapoly, Hungary. Minister of the interior (1949), when the anti-Soviet uprising broke out in 1956, he was a member of the 'national' government of Imre Nagy, but then formed a puppet government which repressed the uprising. >> Nagy, Imre

Kael, Pauline [kayl] (1919–) Film critic, born in Petaluma, CA. She has been movie critic of the *New Yorker* since 1968, and has published several anthologies of her articles, including *5001 Nights at the Movies* (1982).

Kafka, Franz [kafka] (1883–1924) Novelist, born in Prague, of German Jewish parents. His works include the short story *The Metamorphosis* (trans, 1916), and his posthumously published unfinished novels *The Trial* (trans, 1925), *The Castle* (trans, 1926), and *Amerika* (1927). He has influenced many authors with his vision of society (often called 'Kafkaesque') as a pointless, schizophrenically rational organization, with tortuous bureaucratic and totalitarian procedures.

Kaganovich, Lazar Moiseyevich [kaganohvich] (1893–1991) Russian politician, born near Kiev, Ukraine. In 1928 he became party secretary in Moscow, and during the 1930s played a prominent role in the forced collectivization programme.

Kagawa, Toyohiko [kagahwa] (1888–1960) Social reformer and evangelist, born in Kobe, Japan. He helped to found the Federation of Labour (1918), the Farmer's Union (1921), the Anti-War League (1928), and later led in the women's suffrage movement.

Kagel, Mauricio Raúl [kaygl] (1931–) Composer, born in Buenos Aires. Prominent in the avant-garde movement, he evolved a fantastically complex serial organization of the elements of music, often with a strong visual or theatrical aspect.

Kahanamoku, Duke (Paoa) [kahanamohkoo] (1890–1968) Swimmer and surfer, born in Hawaii. He revolutionized sprint swimming by introducing the flutter kick, and for 20 years was an international freestyle champion, winning Olympic gold medals in 1912 and 1920.

Kahane, Meir [kahayn], originally **Martin Kahane** (1932–90) Zionist, born in New York City. An orthodox rabbi, he founded (1963) the anti-Arab Jewish Defense League, then emigrated to Israel (1971), and founded the extremist Kach Party, banned in 1988. He was assassinated in New York City.

Kahlo, Frida [kahloh] (1907–54) Artist, born in Coyoicoán, Mexico City. Pain and the suffering of women are recurring themes in her Surrealistic and often shocking pictures. She married Diego Rivera in 1928. >> Rivera, Diego

Kahn, Louis I(sadore) (1901–74) Architect, born in Osel, Estonia. He emigrated to the USA in 1905, where he became a pioneer of Functionalist architecture, as in the Richards Medical Research Building, Pennsylvania (1957–61).

Kahn, Otto (Herman) (1867–1934) Financier and art patron, born in Mannheim, Germany. He emigrated to New York City, where he formed Kahn, Loeb & Co, an investment banking firm, in 1897. He was forced to sell his major art works during the Depression.

Kain, Karen [kayn] (1951–) Dancer, born in Hamilton, Ontario, Canada. In 1969 she joined the Canadian National Ballet company, becoming principal dancer in 1970.

Kaiser, Georg [kiyzer] (1878–1945) Playwright, born in Magdeburg, Germany. His plays established him as a leader of the Expressionist movement, such as *From Morn to Midnight* (trans, 1916), *Gas I* (1918), and *Gas II* (1920).

Kaiser, Henry J(ohn) [kiyzer] (1882–1967) Industrialist, born in Sprout Brook, NY. He developed revolutionary methods of assembly in shipbuilding, enabling his ships to be constructed and launched within six days.

Kalashnikov, Mikhail [kalashnikof] (1919–) Russian gun designer. He designed the *Avtomat Kalishnikova*, the AK-47 machine gun, of which over 50 million have been produced.

Kaldor (of Newnham), Nicholas Kaldor, Baron (1908–86) Economist, born in Budapest. He was director of the Research and Planning Division of the Economic Commission for Europe (1947), and later became economic adviser to the Labour Party.

Kalecki, Michal [kaleskee] (1899–1970) Economist and journalist, born in Lodz, Poland. A Marxist, he developed a theory of macroeconomic dynamics, and introduced the new Western methods in economics to the Soviet bloc.

Kalidasa [kalidahsa] (c.5th-c) Indian poet and playwright, best known through his drama *Abhijnana-Sakuntala* (The Recognition of Sakuntala).

Kalinin, Mikhail Ivanovich [kaleenin] (1875–1946) Soviet statesman, born in Tver, Russia. He was the formal head of state after the 1917 Revolution and during the years of Stalin's dictatorship (1919–46).

Kalogeropoulos, Maria >> **Callas, Maria**

Kaltenbrunner, Ernst [kaltenbruner] (1903–46) Nazi leader, born in Ried im Innkreis, Austria. As head of the security police (1943), he sent millions of Jews and political suspects to their deaths in concentration camps. He was condemned by the Nuremberg Tribunal and hanged.

Kamen, Martin (David) (1913–) Biochemist, born in Toronto, Ontario, Canada. He showed that the oxygen formed in plants by photosynthesis is derived from water (and not from CO_2); discovered the carbon isotope $_{14}C$; and contributed to the discovery of messenger-RNA.

Kamenev, Lev Borisovich [kamyaynef], originally **Lev Borisovich Rosenfeld** (1883–1936) Soviet politician, born in Moscow. An active revolutionary from 1901, he was expelled as a Trotskyite in 1927, and shot for conspiring against Stalin.

Kamerlingh Onnes, Heike [kamerling awnes] (1853–1926) Physicist, born in Groningen, The Netherlands. He was the first to produce liquid helium, and worked in low-temperature physics, discovering the phenomenon of superconductivity. He was awarded the Nobel Prize for Physics in 1913.

Kaminski, David Daniel >> **Kaye, Danny**

Kammerer, Paul (1880–1926) Biologist, born in Vienna. He argued that acquired traits could be inherited, and claimed to show this in a series of experiments on toads. When his claims was discredited, he shot himself.

Kamp, Peter Van de >> **Van de Kamp, Peter**

Kandinsky, Wasily [kandinskee] or **Vasily Vasilyevich** (1866–1944) Painter, born in Moscow. In Russia (1914–21) he founded the Russian Academy and in 1922 took charge of the Weimar Bauhaus. He became a naturalized French citizen in 1939, and was a leader of the *Blaue Reiter* group.

Kane, Bob, popular name of **Robert Kane** (1916–) Cartoonist and animator, born in New York City. He created *Batman* for *Detective Comics* in 1939, and later created *Courageous Cat* (1958) and *Cool McCool* (1969) for television.

Kane, Elisha (Kent) (1820–57) Physician and Arctic explorer, born in Philadelphia, PA. He sailed with two expeditions (1850–1, 1853–5) in search of Sir John Franklin, without success. The *Kane Basin* is named after him. >> Franklin, John

Kane, Martin >> O Cadhain, Máirtín

Kangxi [kangshee], also spelled **K'ang-hsi**, originally **Xuanye** (1654–1722) Fifth emperor of the Manchurian Qing dynasty, and the second to rule China. He cultivated the image of an ideal Confucian ruler, stressing traditional morality, and organizing several scholarly activities, such as a 5000-volume encyclopedia (1726). His conquests included Outer Mongolia (1696), Taiwan (1683), and Turkestan (from 1715).

Kang Youwei [kang yooway], also spelled **K'ang Yu-wei** (1858–1927) Philosopher and historian, the leader of the Hundred Days of Reform in China (1898). The movement was ended when the Dowager Empress Ci-Xi executed six of the reformers, and punished all their supporters. >> Ci-Xi

Kanhai, Rohan Babulal [kanhiy] (1935–) Cricketer, born in Berbice, Guyana. One of the West Indies' leading batsmen in the 1960s and 1970s, he played in 79 Tests, scoring 6277 runs and 15 centuries.

Kano, Motonobu (1476–1559) Painter, born in Kyoto, Japan. His most famous works show the decorative treatment of nature, which became standard for the Kano School.

Kant, Immanuel [kant] (1724–1804) Philosopher, born in Königsberg, Germany. His main work, now a philosophical classic, is the *Critique of Pure Reason* (trans, 1781) in which he provided a response to the empiricism of Hume. His views on ethics are set out in the *Foundations of the Metaphysics of Morals* (trans, 1785) and the *Critique of Practical Reason* (trans, 1788), and his views on aesthetics in the *Critique of Judgment* (trans, 1790). >> Hume, David

Kantorovich, Leonid Vitaliyevich [kantorohvich] (1912–86) Economist and mathematician, born in St Petersburg, Russia. He is credited with the development of linear programming, which had been used for optimal economic planning of resources on both the micro and macro level. He shared the Nobel Prize for Economics in 1975.

Kan-ying >> Ganying
Kao Kang >> Gao Gang
Kao-tsu >> Gaozu

Kapila [kapila] (fl.550 BC) Indian founder of the Samkhya school of Hindu philosophy. An almost legendary figure, he is held to be the originator of the philosophical system expounded in the 3rd–5th-c AD commentary of Iśvarakrishna and the *Samkhya Sutra* (AD c.1400).

Kapil Dev, Nihanj (1959–) Cricketer, born in Chandigarh, India. An all-rounder, he led India to victory in the 1983 World Cup, and became the youngest player to perform a Test double of 2000 runs and 200 wickets. In 1994 he broke Hadlee's record by taking 432 wickets in his 130th Test match. >> Hadleee

Kapitza, Pyotr Leonidovich [kapitza] (1894–1984) Physicist, born in Kronstadt, Russia. He is known for his work on high-intensity magnetism, low temperature, and the liquefaction of hydrogen and helium. He shared the Nobel Prize for Physics in 1978.

Kaplan, Viktor (1876–1934) Engineer and inventor, born in Murz, Austria. He patented the turbine with variable pitch blades which now bears his name (1920), widely used in hydro and tidal power schemes throughout the world.

Kaprow, Allen (1927–) Avant-garde artist and theorist, born in Atlantic City, NJ. He promotes 'happenings', involving spectator participation, and welcoming unplanned developments.

Karageorge, Turk **Karadjordje** ('Black George'), also **Czerny George**, nickname of **George Petrović** (1766–1817) Leader of the Serbians in their struggle for independence, born in Viševac, Serbia. He led a revolt against Turkey, and in 1808 was recognized as Prince of Serbia. When Turkey regained control of Serbia in 1813, he was exiled, and on his return was murdered.

Karajan, Herbert von [kara-yan] (1908–89) Conductor, born in Salzburg, Austria. In 1955 he was made principal conductor of the Berlin Philharmonic, with which he was mainly associated until his resignation in 1989.

Karamanlis, Konstantinos [karamanlees], also spelled **Caramanlis** (1907–) Greek prime minister (1955–63, 1974–80) and president (1980–5), born in Próti, Greece. He supervised the restoration of civilian rule after the collapse of the military government in 1979.

Karl (of Sweden) >> Charles (of Sweden)

Karle, Jerome (1918–) Physicist, born in New York City. He specialized in diffraction methods for studying the fine structure of crystalline matter, and shared the Nobel Prize for Chemistry in 1985. >> Hauptman

Karloff, Boris, originally **William Henry Pratt** (1887–1969) Film star, born in London. He went to Hollywood, where he made his name as the monster in *Frankenstein* (1931), and appeared in many other popular horror films.

Karlstadt >> Carlstadt

Karmal, Babrak (1929–) Afghan prime minister (1979–81) and president (1979–86). Deputy leader of the banned People's Democratic Party of Afghanistan, he was forced into exile in E Europe until after the Soviet military invasion (1979), returning as president.

Kármán, Theodore von [kah(r)man] (1881–1963) Physicist and aeronautical engineer, sometimes called 'the father of modern aerodynamics', born in Budapest. He became director of the Guggenheim Aeronautical Laboratories (1930–49) at the California Institute of Technology. Several theories bear his name, such as the *Kármán vortex street* (1911).

Karp, David (1922–) Writer, born in New York City. His novels include *One* (1953), an Orwellian condemnation of totalitarianism, *The Day of the Monkey* (1955), and *Last Believers* (1964).

Karpov, Anatoly Yevgenyevich [kah(r)pof] (1951–) Chess player and world champion (1975–85), born in Zlatoust, Russia. He became world champion by default after Fischer refused to defend his title (1975), and successfully defended his title until losing to Kasparov in a controversial match (1985). He defeated Jan Timman in an official world championship match in 1993. >> Fischer, Bobby; Kasparov

Karrer, Paul [karer] (1889–1971) Chemist, born in Moscow. He was the first to isolate vitamins A and K, and produced synthetically vitamins B_2 and E. He shared the Nobel Prize for Chemistry in 1937.

Karsavina, Tamara (Platonovna) [kah(r)savina] (1885–1978) Ballet dancer, born in St Petersburg, Russia. One of the original members of Diaghilev's Ballets Russes, she moved to London in 1918, and became vice-president of the Royal Academy of Dancing until 1955. >> Diaghilev

Karsh, Yousuf (1908–) Portrait photographer, born in Mardin, Turkey. He emigrated to Canada in 1924, and in 1932 opened his own studio in Ottawa. His wartime studies of Winston Churchill and other national leaders were widely reproduced.

Kasparov, Gary (Kimovich) [kaspahrof] (1963–) Chess player, born in Baku, Azerbaijan. When he beat Karpov for the world title (1985) he became the youngest ever world champion, and is now the highest-ranked active player. He set up the Grandmasters' Association in 1987, and arranged a World Championship match in 1993 when he defeated Nigel Short. >> Karpov; Short

Kassem, Abdul Karim (1914–63) Iraqi soldier and revolutionary, born in Baghdad. He led the coup which resulted in the overthrow of the monarchy and the death of King Faisal II, establishing a left-wing military regime. He was himself killed in a coup. >> Faisal II

Kastler, Alfred (1902–84) Physicist, born in Guebwiller, Germany. He discovered Hertzian resonances in atoms, leading to the development of the maser and laser, and was awarded the Nobel Prize for Physics in 1966.

Kästner, Erich [kestner] (1899–1974) Writer, born in Dresden, Germany. He is best known for his children's books, which include *Emil and the Detectives* (trans, 1928).

Kastrioti, George >> Skanderbeg

Katherine >> Catherine

Katz, Alex (1927–) Painter, born in New York City. From 1959 he began making portraits of his friends in a deliberately gauche, naive style, simplifying forms and using a limited palette.

Katz, Sir Bernard (1911–) Biophysicist, born in Leipzig, Germany. In 1970 he shared the Nobel Prize for Physiology or Medicine for his studies on how transmitter substances are released from nerve terminals.

Kauffmann, (Maria Anna Catharina) Angelica [kowfman] (1741–1807) Painter, born in Chur, Switzerland. A founder member of the Royal Academy (1769), she is best known for her wall paintings for residences designed by Robert Adam. >> Adam, Robert

Kaufman, George S(imon) [kowfman] (1889–1961) Playwright and director, born in Pittsburgh, PA. In collaboration with Hart he wrote *You Can't Take It With You* (1936, Pulitzer) and *The Man Who Came to Dinner* (1939). >> Hart, Moss

Kaufman, Henry [kowfman] (1927–) Economist and banker, born in Wenings, Germany. He moved to the USA in 1937, after a period with the Federal Reserve Bank he joined Salomon Brothers, becoming managing director in 1981.

Kaunda, Kenneth (David) [kaoonda] (1924–) Zambian president (1964–91), born in Lubwa, Zambia. He founded the Zambian African National Congress (1958), and played a leading part in his country's independence negotiations. After a failed military coup in 1990, he agreed to multi-party elections in 1991.

Kaunitz(-Rietberg), Wenzel Anton, Fürst von (Prince of) [kownits reetberg] (1711–94) Austrian chancellor (1793–92), born in Vienna. He instigated the Diplomatic Revolution, and directed Austrian politics for almost 40 years under Maria Theresa and Joseph II. >> Joseph II; Maria Theresa

Kavanagh, Henry Edward [kavana] (1892–1958) Journalist and scriptwriter, born in Auckland, New Zealand. In England from 1914, he wrote scripts for the radio comedy programme *ITMA*, whose anarchic humour influenced much British comedy.

Kavanagh, Patrick (Joseph) [kavana] (1904–67) Poet and writer, born near Inniskeen, Co Monaghan, Ireland. He is best known for his poem of farm life, *The Great Hunger* (1942), and for *Tarry Flynn* (1948), an autobiographical novel.

Kawabata, Yasunari (1899–1972) Writer, born in Osaka, Japan. His novels include *The Dancer of Izu Province* (1925), *Snow Country* (trans, 1935–48), and *The Sound of the Mountain* (trans, 1949–54). He received the Nobel Prize for Literature in 1968.

Kay, John (1704–c.1764) Inventor, born near Bury, Greater Manchester. In 1733 he patented his flying shuttle, but his

house was ransacked by a mob of textile workers, fearful for their livelihood, and he left for France (1753).

Kay, Ulysses (Simpson) (1917–) Composer, born in Tucson, Az. One of the first prominent African-American composers, he wrote mildly Modernist works that won many prizes.

Kaye, Danny, originally **David Daniel Kaminski** (1913–87) Stage, film, and television entertainer, born in New York City. His films include *The Secret Life of Walter Mitty* (1946), *Hans Christian Andersen* (1952), and *The Court Jester* (1956), and he became known for his fundraising activities for UNICEF.

Kaye, Nora, originally **Nora Koreff** (1920–87) Ballerina, born in New York City. She joined American Ballet Theater at its inception in 1939, becoming the leading dramatic ballerina of her day, and co-founded Ballet of Two Worlds with her choreographer-husband **Herbert Ross** (1926–).

Kay-Shuttleworth, Sir James (Phillips), originally **James Phillips Kay** (1804–77) Physician and educationist, born in Rochdale, Greater Manchester. He was instrumental in establishing a system of government school inspection.

Kazan, Elia [kazan], originally **Elia Kazanjoglous** (1909–) Stage and film director, born in Istanbul. With Strasberg, he founded the Actors Studio in 1947. His films include *Gentleman's Agreement* (1948, Oscar), *A Streetcar Named Desire* (1951), *On the Waterfront* (1954, Oscar), and *East of Eden* (1954). >> Strasberg, Lee

Kazantzakis, Nikos [kazanzakis] (1883–1957) Writer, born in Heraklion, Crete, Greece. He is best known for the novel *Zorba the Greek* (trans, 1946; filmed 1964) and the epic autobiographical narrative poem, *The Odyssey, a Modern Sequel* (trans, 1938).

Kean, Edmund (c.1789–1833) Actor, born in London. His first appearance at Drury Lane as Shylock (1814) was followed by a period of great success as a tragic actor, but his reputation was ruined when he was successfully sued for adultery in 1825.

Keane, Molly, professional name of **Mary Nesta Keane**, pseudonym **M J Farrell** (1904–) Writer, born in Co Kildare, Ireland. Her novels include *The Rising Tide* (1937), *Loving Without Tears* (1951), and *Good Behaviour* (1981; televised 1983), which was short-listed for the Booker Prize.

Kearny, Philip [kah(r)nee] (1814–62) Soldier, born in New York City. He served with the French Imperial Guard at the Battles of Magenta and Solferino (1859), and was a commander in the American Civil War. He was killed in action at Chantilly.

Keating, Paul (John) (1944–) Australian prime minister (1991–6), born in Sydney, New South Wales, Australia. As Treasurer (1983–91), he formulated the government's economic policies, and was elected leader by the Labor Party in 1991. He is known as an outspoken republican. >> Hawke, Bob

Keating, Tom (1918–84) Art restorer and celebrated forger of paintings, born in London. A self-confessed 'art imitator', he claimed to have produced some 2000 fakes in 25 years.

Keaton, Buster, popular name of **Joseph Francis Keaton** (1895–1966) Film comedian, born in Piqua, KS. Renowned for his deadpan expression, he starred in and directed such silent classics as *Our Hospitality* (1923), *The Navigator* (1924), and *The General* (1926).

Keats, Ezra Jack (1916–) Illustrator of children's books, born in New York City. His best-known book is *The Snowy Day* (1962), about a small black boy's adventure in the snow.

Keats, John (1795–1821) Poet, born in London. His first book of poems was published in 1817. His poem *Endymion* (1818) was fiercely criticized, but he later produced *Lamia and*

Other Poems (1820), a landmark in English poetry, which contains 'The Eve of St Agnes' and his major odes. *His Letters* (1848) are among the most celebrated in the language

Keble, John [keebl] (1792–1866) Anglican clergyman and poet, born in Fairford, Gloucestershire. His sermon on 'National apostasy' (1833) began the Oxford Movement, encouraging a return to High Church ideals. Keble College, Oxford, was erected in his memory.

Kee, Robert (1919–) British broadcaster and writer. His television work include *Panorama* (1958–62) and *Ireland* (1981) for the BBC, and he co-founded the breakfast programme for TV-AM (1983). His non-fiction books include *Ireland: a History* (1980) and *Trial and Error* (1986).

Keegan, (Joseph) Kevin (1951–) Footballer, born in Armthorpe, South Yorkshire. He has played for various clubs, including Liverpool (1971–7), Hamburg (1977–80), and Newcastle (1982–4). He was a member of the England side (1973–82, captain from 1976), and became manager of Newcastle United in 1992.

Keeler, Christine (1942–) Former model and showgirl, raised in Wraysbury, Berkshire. Her affairs with a Soviet naval attaché and the Conservative cabinet minister, John Profumo, led to Profumo's resignation from politics in 1963. She served a prison sentence for related offences. >> Profumo

Keeler, James (Edward) (1857–1900) Astronomer, born in La Salle, IL. He established the composition of Saturn's rings (as Maxwell had postulated), and carried out important spectroscopic work on nebulae, discovering 120 000 of them. >> Maxwell, James C

Keilin, David (1887–1963) Biochemist, born in Moscow. His ingenious studies of enzymes and animal pigments led to his major discovery, the pigment cytochrome, which occurs in plant and animal cells and has a key role in biochemical oxidation.

Keillor, Garrison [keeler], pseudonym of **Gary Edward Keillor** (1942–) Writer and broadcaster, born in Anoka, MN. In 1974 he first hosted the live radio show, 'A Prairie Home Companion', delivering a weekly monologue set in the fictional mid-western town of Lake Wobegon. His books include the best-selling *Lake Wobegon Days* (1985) and *We Are Still Married* (1989).

Keino, Kip(choge) [kaynoh] (1940–) Athlete, born in Kipsamo, Kenya. At the 1968 Olympics he won the 1500 m, and in 1972 won the gold medal for the 3000 m steeplechase. In 1965 he established new world records for the 3000 m and 5000 m.

Keitel, Wilhelm [kiytl] (1882–1946) German field marshal, born in Helmscherode, Germany. He was made chief of the Supreme Command of the Armed Forces in 1938, and in 1945 was one of the German signatories of surrender in Berlin. He was convicted of war crimes at Nuremberg, and executed.

Keith, Sir Arthur (1866–1955) Physical anthropologist, born in Aberdeen, Grampian. Best known for his work on fossilized humanoid forms, he wrote *Concerning Man's Origin* (1927) and *New Theory of Human Evolution* (1948).

Kekkonen, Urho K(aleva) [kekonen] (1900–86) Prime minister (1950–3, 1954–6) and president of Finland (1956–81), born in Pielavesi, Finland. He encouraged a policy of cautious friendship with the Soviet Union, but his strict neutrality ensured that he retained the confidence of his Scandinavian neighbours. He accepted a Lenin Peace Prize in 1980.

Kekulé von Stradonitz, (Friedrich) August [kaykuhlay fon **shtrad**onits] (1829–1896) Chemist, born in Darmstadt, Germany. He made a major contribution to organic chemistry by developing structural theories, in particular the cyclic structure of benzene.

Keldysh, Mstislav (Vsevoldvich) (1911–78) Mathematician and space programme leader, born in Riga, Latvia.

He was a leading figure in the development of the theory of rocketry and in the emergence of the USSR in space exploration.

Keller, Hans (1919–85) Musicologist, born in Vienna. He emigrated to England in 1938 where he co-founded the magazine *Music Survey*, served on the BBC staff from 1959, and broadcast frequently.

Keller, Helen (Adams) (1880–1968) Writer, born in Tuscumbia, AL. She lost her sight and hearing after an illness at 19 months, but was educated by Anne Sullivan, who taught her to speak, read, and write. >> Sullivan, Anne

Kelley, Florence (1859–1932) Feminist and social reformer, born in Philadelphia, PA. She successfully fought to reduce factory working hours and conditions, was a founder of the National Association for the Advancement of Colored People, and also helped establish the Women's International League for Peace and Freedom (1919).

Kelley, Oliver Hudson (1826–1913) Farmer, born in Boston, MA. In 1867 he co-founded the National Grange of the Patrons of Husbandry, and acted as its secretary. He argued the benefits of the Grange in the agricultural press, and by 1874 there were more than 20 000 Granges.

Kellogg, Frank B(illings) (1856–1937) Jurist and statesman, born in Potsdam, NY. As secretary of state (1925–9), with Briand he drew up the Briand–Kellogg Pact (1928) outlawing war, which became the legal basis for the Nuremberg trials (1945–6). He was awarded the Nobel Peace Prize in 1929. >> Briand

Kellogg, Paul Underwood (1879–1958) Editor and social reformer, born in Kalamazoo, MI. In 1907 he commenced an in-depth study of every aspect of life in Pittsburgh, the first such social survey of a US urban community, published as the *Pittsburgh Survey* (1910–14).

Kellogg, W(illie) K(eith) (1852–1943) Cereal manufacturer and philanthropist, born in Battle Creek, MI. He joined with his brother, **John H(arvey) Kellogg** (1852–1943), to develop a process of toasting wheat and corn into crisp flakes for a breakfast cereal. Their *Corn flakes* revolutionized the breakfast-eating habits of the Western world.

Kelly, Howard (Atwood) (1858–1943) Surgeon and gynaecologist, born in Camden, NJ. He pioneered the use of cocaine anaesthesia, and played an important role in the development of gynaecology as a surgical speciality separate from obstetrics.

Kelly, Ellsworth (1923–) Artist, born in Newburgh, NY. From the late 1950s he made his name as a 'hard-edge' abstract painter, using wide, flat areas of strong colour.

Kelly, Grace (Patricia), married name **Grimaldi, Princess Grace of Monaco** (1929–82) Film actress and princess, born in Philadelphia, PA. Her films included *High Noon* (1952), *Rear Window* (1954), and *The Country Girl* (1954, Oscar). In 1956 she married Prince Rainier III of Monaco, and retired from the screen. She was killed in a car accident. >> Rainier III

Kelly, Gene, popular name of **Eugene Curran Kelly** (1912–96) Dancer and actor, born in Pittsburgh, PA. His stage success in *Pal Joey* (1939) led to a Hollywood debut in *For Me and My Girl* (1942), followed by musicals such as *An American in Paris* (1951) and *Singin' in the Rain* (1952).

Kelly, George A (1905–66) Psychologist, born in Kansas. Best known for his novel approach to the understanding of personality, he devised the repertory grid test, an open-ended method for exploring an individual's 'personal constructs'.

Kelly, Ned, popular name of **Edward Kelly** (1855–80) Outlaw, born in Beveridge, Victoria, Australia. With his brother and two others he formed the Kelly gang. They carried out a series of daring robberies (1878–80) which, coupled with Ned's home-made armour, made them into legendary figures. He was hanged at Melbourne.

Kelly, Petra, originally **Petra Lehmann** (1947–92) Political activist, born in Günzburg, Germany. In 1979 she helped found the Green Party, and was elected to the Bundestag in 1983. She became involved with Gert Bastian, also a Green activist, and her body was found near his in the house they shared.

Kelly, Walt(er Crawford) (1913–73) Animator and strip cartoonist, born in Philadelphia, PA. His most famous comic book characters were Albert Alligator and Pogo Possum of Okefenokee Swamp.

Kelly, William (1811–88) Inventor of the pneumatic process for steelmaking, born in Pittsburgh, PA. He built seven of his 'converters' (1851–6), but the commercial impact of his discovery was much reduced when Bessemer was granted a US patent for the same process. >> Bessemer

Kelsen, Hans (1881–1973) Jurist and legal theorist, born in Prague. He is best known as the creator of the 'pure theory of law' (1934), in which the science of law is required to be exclusively normative and pure, not practical.

Kelvin (of Largs), William Thomson, 1st Baron (1824–1907) Mathematician and physicist, born in Belfast. He carried out fundamental research into thermodynamics, helping to develop the law of the conservation of energy and the absolute temperature scale (now given in kelvin). He also presented the dynamical theory of heat, and developed theorems for the mathematical analysis of electricity and magnetism.

Kemble, Fanny, popular name of **Frances Ann Kemble** (1809–93) Actress, born in London, the niece of John Philip Kemble. For three years she played leading parts in London, then went to America (1832), and later successfully returned to the London stage. >> Kemble, John Philip

Kemble, John Philip (1757–1823) Actor, born in Prescot, Merseyside. The brother of actress Sarah Siddons, he played leading tragic characters at Drury Lane for many years, and became manager of Covent Garden Theatre in 1802. His brother, **Charles** (1775–1854), also an actor, was the father of Fanny Kemble. >> Kemble, Fanny; Siddons

Kemp, Lindsay (1939–) Mime artist, dancer, and director, born on the I of Lewis, Western Isles. He has had his own company in various forms since the early 1960s, and has created his own work in camp, extravagant style.

Kempe, Margery [kemp], *née* **Brunham** (c.1373–c.1440) Writer, the daughter of a mayor of Lynn. Between 1432 and 1436 she dictated her spiritual autobiography, *The Book of Margery Kempe*, valuable as a source of contemporary expression.

Kempe, Rudolf [kempuh] (1910–76) Conductor, born near Dresden, Germany. He appeared frequently at Covent Garden, London, and was principal conductor of the Royal Philharmonic Orchestra (1961–75), then of the BBC Symphony Orchestra until his death.

Kempe, William [kemp] (c.1550–c.1603) Clown, famous in the Elizabethan theatre. A member of the Lord Chamberlain's Company, he left and morris-danced his way to Norwich, publishing an account of his feat in *Nine Daies Wonder* (1600).

Kempis, Thomas à [kempis], originally **Thomas Hemerken** (1379–1471) Religious writer, whose name derives from his birthplace, Kempen, in Germany. An Augustinian monk, his many writings include the influential devotional work *The Imitation of Christ* (c.1415–24).

Kempson, Rachel >> Redgrave, Michael

Kemsley, James Gomer Berry, 1st Viscount (1883–1968) Newspaper proprietor, born in Merthyr Tydfil, Mid Glamorgan. He became chairman of Kemsley Newspapers Ltd in 1937, controlling *The Sunday Times* and other newspapers.

Ken, Thomas (1637–1711) Clergyman, born in Little Berkhampstead, Hertfordshire. Bishop of Bath and Wells (1685), he refused to publish in his diocese the Declaration of Indulgence issued by James II (1688). He was imprisoned, tried for sedition, and acquitted. >> James II (of England)

Kendal, Felicity (1947–) British actress, born in Olton, Warwickshire. She is probably best known for her part in the television series *The Good Life* (1974–8), but much of her work is in the theatre. In 1992 she married Tom Stoppard. >> Stoppard

Kendall, Edward (Calvin) (1886–1972) Chemist, born in South Norwalk, CT. He isolated thyroxin, the active element in the thyroid gland (1915), and adrenal hormones such as cortisone (1935). He shared the Nobel Prize for Physiology or Medicine in 1950. >> Hench

Kendall, Henry W(ay) (1926–) Physicist, born in Boston, MA. He shared the 1990 Nobel Prize for Physics for his experiments confirming the existence of quarks.

Kendrew, Sir John (Cowdery) (1917–) Biochemist, born in Oxford, Oxfordshire. He discovered the structure of the muscle protein myoglobin (1957), and shared the Nobel Prize for Chemistry in 1962. >> Perutz

Keneally, Thomas (Michael) [keneelee] (1935–) Writer, born in Sydney, New South Wales, Australia. His novels are frequently historical, and include *Schindler's Ark* (1982, Booker; filmed as *Schindler's List*, 1993), *Towards Asmara* (1989), and *Flying Hero Class* (1991).

Kennan, George F(rost) (1904–) US diplomat and historian, born in Milwaukee, WI. In 1947 he was appointed director of policy planning, and advocated the policy of 'containment' of the Soviet Union.

Kennaway, James (1928–68) Writer, born in Auchterarder, Tayside. His best-known novel is *Tunes of Glory* (1956), which was made into a successful film of the same name.

Kennedy, Edward M(oore) (1932–) US politician, born in Brookline, MA, the youngest son of Joseph Kennedy. In 1969 he became the youngest-ever majority whip in the US Senate, but his involvement in a car accident at Chappaquidick in which a woman companion (Mary Jo Kopechne) was drowned, dogged his political career, and caused his withdrawal as a presidential candidate in 1979. >> Kennedy, Joseph / John F / Robert F

Kennedy, John F(itzgerald), also known as **JFK** (1917–63) US statesman and 35th president (1961–3), born in Brookline, MA, the son of Joseph P Kennedy. He was the first Catholic, and the youngest person, to be elected president. His 'New Frontier' in social legislation involved a federal desegregation policy in education, and civil rights reform. He displayed firmness and moderation in foreign policy, in 1962 inducing Russia to withdraw its missiles from Cuba, and achieving a partial nuclear test-ban treaty with Russia in 1963. On 22 November, he was assassinated in Dallas, TX. The alleged assassin, Lee Harvey Oswald, was himself shot two days later during a jail transfer. >> Kennedy, Edward M / Jackie / Joseph P / Robert F; Oswald, Lee Harvey

Kennedy, Joseph P(atrick) (1888–1969) Businessman, born in Boston, MA, the father of John F, Robert, and Edward Kennedy. The grandson of an Irish Catholic immigrant, he made a fortune in the 1920s. He had married in 1914 Rose Fitzgerald (d.1995), and they had nine children. The eldest son, **Joseph Patrick** (1915–44), was killed in a flying accident; the others achieved international political fame. >> Fitzgerald, John Francis; Kennedy, Edward M / John F / Robert F

Kennedy, Sir Ludovic (Henry Coverley) (1919–) Broadcaster and writer, born in Edinburgh. His television series include *Your Witness* (1967–70), *Face the Press* (1968–72), *Tonight* (1976–8), and *Did You See?* (1980–8).

Kennedy, Nigel (Paul) (1956–) British violinist. Noted for his unconventional style of dress, and for his remarkable playing ability, his recording of Vivaldi's *Four Seasons* held the No 1 spot in the UK Classical Chart for over a year (1989–90).

Kennedy, Robert F(rancis) (1925–68) US politician, born in Brookline, MA, the third son of Joseph Kennedy. An efficient manager of his brother John F Kennedy's presidential campaign, he was an energetic attorney general (1961–4), notable in his dealings with civil rights problems. After winning the Californian Democratic presidential primary election, he was killed in Los Angeles by Sirhan Sirhan. >> Sirhan

Kennedy, William Joseph (1928–) Novelist and screenwriter, born in Albany, NY. His books include *Ironweed* (1983, Pulitzer), *The Ink Truck* (1969), and *Quinns's Book* (1988).

Kennelly, Arthur E(dwin) [kenelee] (1861–1939) Engineer, born in Bombay, India. He went to the USA in 1887, and in 1902 discovered the ionized layer in the atmosphere, sometimes named after him.

Kenneth I, known as **Kenneth MacAlpin** (?–858) King of the Scots of Dal Riata (from 841) and King of the Picts (from c.843). He combined the territories of both peoples in a united kingdom of Scotia (Scotland N of the Forth–Clyde line).

Kennington, Eric Henri (1888–1960) Painter and sculptor, born in London. He was an official war artist in both world wars, and in the field of sculpture designed many memorials.

Kenny, Elizabeth, known as **Sister Kenny** (1886–1952) Australian nurse. She developed a new technique for treating poliomyelitis by muscle therapy rather than by immobilization with casts and splints

Kensett, John (Frederick) (1816–72) Painter, born in Cheshire, CT. He went to New York City in 1847, and began painting the detailed and luminous landscapes which made him a leader of the Hudson River School, as seen in 'Lake George' (1869).

Kent, Bruce (1929–) Cleric and peace campaigner, born in London. He became increasingly involved in the Campaign for Nuclear Disarmament (CND), becoming its general secretary (1980), vice-chairman (1985), and chairman (1987–90), and resigning his ministry in 1988.

Kent, Edward (George Nicholas Paul Patrick), Duke of (1935–) British prince, the eldest son of George, Duke of Kent. In 1961 he married Katharine Worsley, and they have three children: **George Philip Nicholas, the Earl of St Andrews** (1962–), **Helen Marina Lucy, Lady Helen Windsor** (1964–), and **Nicholas Charles Edward Jonathan, Lord Nicholas Windsor** (1970–). >> Kent, George

Kent, George Edward Alexander Edmund, Duke of (1902–42) Son of King George V and Queen Mary. In 1934 he was created duke, and married **Princess Marina of Greece and Denmark** (1906–68). He was killed on active service. >> George V; Kent, Edward, Duke of / Prince Michael of

Kent, Prince Michael of (1942–) British prince, the younger brother of Edward, Duke of Kent. He married in 1978 Baroness Marie-Christine Von Reibniz, and their children are **Frederick Michael George David Louis, Lord Frederick Windsor** (1979–) and **Gabriella Marina Alexandra Ophelia, Lady Gabriella (Ella) Windsor** (1981–). >> Kent, Edward, Duke of

Kent, Rockwell (1882–1971) Artist, born in Tarrytown, NY. He became a well-known painter and illustrator, and also produced wood engravings, lithographs, and textiles. He received the Lenin Peace Prize in 1967.

Kent, William (1685–1748) Painter, landscape gardener, and architect, born in Bridlington, Humberside. The prin-

cipal exponent of the Palladian style of architecture in England, his buildings include the Horse Guards block in Whitehall, the Royal Mews in Trafalgar Square, and the Treasury Buildings.

Kentigern, St, also known as **St Mungo** (Celtic 'My Friend') (c.518–603), feast day 13 January. Celtic clergyman. According to legend he was the grandson of a British prince, raised by St Serf at Culross, and given by him the name Mungo. He founded a monastery at Cathures (now Glasgow), was consecrated Bishop of Cumbria (543), and founded a monastery in Wales (553).

Kentner, Louis Philip (1905–87) Pianist, born in Karwin, Hungary. An acclaimed interpreter of Chopin and Liszt, he settled in England in 1935, and was a frequent chamber-music partner of his brother-in-law, Yehudi Menuhin. >> Menuhin

Kenton, Stan(ley Newcomb) (1912–79) Pianist, composer, and bandleader, born in Wichita, KS. He first formed his own orchestra in 1941, but is more immediately associated with the big band 'progressive' jazz style of the 1950s.

Kentridge, Sydney (1922–) Lawyer, born in Johannesburg, South Africa. The leading lawyer for the defence in political trials in South Africa, his notable cases include the Treason Trial (1958–61) and the Steve Biko inquest (1977). >> Biko

Kenyatta, Jomo [kenyata], originally **Kamau Ngengi** (c.1889–1978) Kenyan president (1964–78), born in Mitumi, Kenya. Charged with leading the Mau Mau terrorist organization (a charge he denied), he was imprisoned, then exiled. In 1960 he was elected president of the new Kenya African National Union Party, became prime minister in 1963, and president of the new republic in 1964, adopting moderate social and economic policies.

Kenyon, Dame Kathleen (Mary) (1906–78) Archaeologist, born in London. Her major work was the excavation of Jericho to its Stone Age beginnings, revealing it to be the oldest known site that has seen continuous human occupation.

Kenzo, in full **Kenzo Takada** (1940–) Fashion designer, born in Kyoto, Japan. Known for his innovative ideas and use of traditional designs, he creates clothes with both oriental and Western influences, and is a trendsetter in the field of knitwear.

Kepler, Johannes (1571–1630) Astronomer, born in Weilder-Stadt, Germany. He announced his first and second laws of planetary motion in *New Astronomy* (trans, 1609), which formed the groundwork of Newton's discoveries. His third law was promulgated in *Harmonies of the World* (trans, 1619). >> Newton, Isaac

Ker, W(illiam) P(aton) (1855–1923) Scholar, born in Glasgow, Strathclyde. His books include *Epic and Romance* (1897), *The Dark Ages* (1904), and *The Art of Poetry* (1923).

Kérékou, Mathieu Ahmed [kayraykoo] (1933–) Benin soldier and president (1980–91), born in Natitingou, Benin. He led the coup which removed the government (1972), and established a National Council of the Revolution. He was defeated when the first free elections for 30 years were held in 1991.

Kerensky, Alexander Fyodorovich [kerenskee] (1881–1970) Russian socialist, born in Ulyanovsk (formerly Simbirsk). He took a leading part in the 1917 revolution, becoming premier in the provisional government, but was deposed by the Bolsheviks, and fled abroad to France.

Kerguélen-Trémarec, Yves Joseph de [kairgaylen traymarek] (1745–97) French naval officer and aristocrat, born in Quimper, France. On an unsuccessful voyage of exploration seeking Terra Australis, he discovered a group of islands in the South Indian Ocean to which he gave his name (1772).

Kermode, Sir (John) Frank [kermohd] (1919–) Literary critic, born in the Isle of Man. His works include *Romantic Image* (1957), *The Sense of an Ending* (1967), and *Uses of Error* (1991).

Kern, Jerome (David) (1885–1945) Songwriter and composer, born in New York City. He wrote a string of successful Broadway shows, notably *Show Boat* (1928). His songs include 'The Way You Look Tonight' and 'A Fine Romance'.

Kerouac, Jack [kerooak], popular name of **Jean Louis Kerouac** (1922–69) Writer, born in Lowell, MA. He is best known for *On the Road* (1957), a spontaneous work expressing the youthful discontent of the 'beat generation'.

Kerr, Clark [kair] (1911–) Economist and administrator born in Stony Creek, PN. He presided over rapid growth at the University of California (chancellor 1952–8, president 1958–67), coined the term *multiversity*, and wrote the controversial *Uses of the University* (1963).

Kerr, Deborah [kah(r)], popular name of **Deborah Kerr Viertel**, *née* **Deborah Jane Kerr-Trimmer** (1921–) Actress, born in Helensburgh, Strathclyde. Invariably cast in well-bred, lady-like roles, she sensationally strayed from her established image to play an adulterous wife in *From Here to Eternity* (1953). She received a BAFTA Special Award in 1991.

Kerr, John [kair] (1824–1907) Physicist, born in Ardrossan, Strathclyde. He carried out research on light passing through electromagnetic fields, and discovered the effect that is now named after him.

Kerr, Sir John (Robert) [kair] (1914–91) Lawyer and administrator, born in Sydney, New South Wales, Australia. As Governor-General of Australia (1974–7) he made constitutional history in 1975 when he resolved a political impasse by sacking the elected prime minister, Gough Whitlam, and asking leader of the Liberal opposition, Malcolm Fraser, to form a caretaker government and call a general election. >> Fraser, Malcolm; Whitlam

Kertész, André [kertesh] (1894–1985) Photographer, born in Budapest, Hungary. In 1936 he went to the USA, becoming known for his fashion work in New York City in the 1940s and 1950s.

Kesey, Ken (Elton) [keezee] (1935–) Writer, born in La Junta, CO. His best-known work is *One Flew Over the Cuckoo's Nest* (1962). Filmed in 1975, it won five Oscars.

Kesselring, Albert [keslring] (1885–1960) German air commander in World War 2, born in Markstedt, Germany. He led the Luftwaffe attacks on France and Britain, and in 1943 was made commander-in-chief in Italy.

Ketch, Jack, popular name of **John Ketch** (?–1686) English hangman and headsman from about 1663. Notorious for his barbarity and bungling, his name became the popular term for a hangman.

Ketèlbey, Albert William [ketelbee], pseudonym of **Anton Vodorinski** (1875–1959) Composer and conductor, born in Birmingham, West Midlands. His light, colourful and tuneful, orchestral pieces had enormous popularity, and included 'In a Monastery Garden'.

Kettering, Charles F(ranklin) (1876–1958) Inventor, born in Loudonville, OH. He invented the electric starter motor for cars, discovered the cause of 'knocking' in car engines, and invented the refrigerant known as Freonsq.

Kettlewell, Henry (Bernard David) (1907–79) Geneticist and entomologist, born in Howden, Humberside. He showed that the dark coloration developed by the peppered moth in industrial areas had a greater survival value than the original light coloration it had in rural areas, thus demonstrating the effectiveness of natural selection as an evolutionary process.

Key, Ellen (Karolina Sophia) (1849–1926) Reformer and educationist, born in Sundsholm, Sweden. She made her name as a writer with advanced liberal ideas on the feminist movement, child welfare, sex, love, and marriage, in *The Century of the Child* (trans, 1900).

Key, Francis Scott (1779–1843) Lawyer and poet, the writer of the US national anthem, born in Frederick Co, MD. He witnessed the British bombardment of Fort McHenry, Baltimore (1814), and wrote 'The Star-Spangled Banner' (later set to music) about the lone US flag seen flying over the fort as dawn broke.

Keyes (of Zeebrugge and of Dover), Roger John Brownlow Keyes, Baron (1872–1945) British admiral, born in Tundiani Fort, India. He was chief-of-staff Eastern Mediterranean (1915–16), and in 1918 commanded the Dover Patrol, leading the raids on German U-boat bases at Zeebrugge and Ostend (1918).

Keynes (of Tilton), John Maynard Keynes, Baron [kaynz] (1883–1946) Economist, born in Cambridge, Cambridgeshire. In both World Wars he was an adviser to the Treasury. The unemployment crises inspired his two great works, *A Treatise on Money* (1930) and *General Theory of Employment, Interest and Money* (1936).

Keyser, Hendrik de [kiyzer] (1565–1621) Architect and sculptor, born in Utrecht, The Netherlands. Notable works were the tomb of William the Silent in Delft (1614–21), the bronze statue of Erasmus in Rotterdam (1621), and Westerkerk in Amsterdam (1620–38).

Khama, Sir Seretse [kahma] (1921–80) Botswana president (1966–80), born in Serowe, Botswana (formerly, Bechuanaland). He became the first prime minister of Bechuanaland (1965), and the first president of the new republic.

Khan, Jahangir (1963–) Squash rackets player, born in Karachi, Pakistan. He won three world amateur titles (1979, 1983, 1985), a record six World Open titles (1981–5, 1988), and eight consecutive British Open titles (1982–9).

Khan, Mohammad Ayub >> **Ayub Khan, Mohammad**

Khatchaturian, Aram [kachatooryan] (1903–78) Composer, born in Tiflis, Georgia. His compositions include three symphonies, concertos, choral works, and the ballet *Spartacus*.

Khayyám, Omar >> **Omar Khayyám**

Khinchin, Alexander Yakovlevich (1894–1959) Mathematician, born in Kondrovo, Russia. With Kolmogorov he founded the Soviet school of probability theory. He also worked in analysis, number theory, statistical mechanics, and information theory. >> Kolmogorov

Khomeini, Ayatollah Ruhollah [homaynee] (1900–89) Iranian religious and political leader, born in Khomeyn, Iran. A Shiite Muslim opposed to the pro-Western regime of Shah Mohammed Reza Pahlavi, he was exiled in 1964. He returned to Iran amid great popular acclaim in 1979 after the collapse of the Shah's government, and became virtual head of state. Under his leadership, Iran underwent a turbulent 'Islamic Revolution' in which a return was made to the strict observance of Muslim principles and traditions. >> Pahlavi

Khorana, Har Gobind [korahna] (1922–) Molecular biologist, born in Raipur, India. His work on nucleotide synthesis was a major contribution to the elucidation of the genetic code, and in 1970 he synthesized the first artificial gene. He shared the Nobel Prize for Physiology or Medicine in 1968.

Khrushchev, Nikita Sergeyevich [khrushchof, khrushchof] (1894–1971) Soviet statesman, first secretary of the Soviet Communist Party (1953–64), and prime minister (1958–64), born in Kalinovka, Ukraine. He became first secretary on the death of Stalin, and three years later denounced Stalinism. Among the events of his administration were the 1956 Hungarian uprising, and the failed attempt to install missiles in Cuba (1962). He was replaced by Brezhnev and Kosygin, and went into retirement. >> Brezhnev; Kosygin; Stalin

Khwarizmi, al- >> **al-Kwharizmi**

Kidd, Michael (1919–) Dancer, choreographer, and director, born in New York City. He danced with American Ballet Theater (1942–7), and went on to choreograph musicals, including *Guys and Dolls* (1951), *Seven Brides for Seven Brothers* (1954), and *Hello, Dolly!* (1969).

Kidd, William, known as **Captain Kidd** (c.1645–1701) Privateer and pirate, probably born in Greenock, Strathclyde. In 1696 he was commissioned to suppress piracy, and reached Madagascar, but then turned pirate himself. He was eventually arrested and hanged in London.

Kidder, Alfred V(incent) (1885–1963) Archaeologist and pioneer of stratigraphic methods in the USA, born in Marquette, MI. His extensive excavations (1915–29) at Pecos, New Mexico, revolutionized American settlement archaeology, and allowed him to develop a chronological sequence for the cultures of the region.

Kidman, Sir Sidney (1857–1935) Pastoralist, born near Adelaide, South Australia. In 1886 he bought his first grazing station, and went on to control vast areas of land. He made substantial gifts to charities and the government.

Kiefer, Anselm [keefer] (1945–) Avant-garde artist, born in Donaueschingen, Germany. He is known for his 'books' made from photographs or woodcuts, sometimes cut or worked over.

Kienholz, Edward [keenhohlts] (1927–94) Avant-garde artist, born in Fairfield, WA. His 'assemblages' were typically room-size, and incorporated dummies, furniture, bones, rugs, household objects, and quantities of 'blood' arranged to create shockingly violent tableaux.

Kierkegaard, Søren (Aabye) [keerkuhgah(r)d] (1813–55) Philosopher and theologian, a major influence on 20th-c existentialism, born in Copenhagen. Regarded as one of the founders of existentialism, in *Concluding Unscientific Postscript* (trans, 1846), he attacked all philosophical system building.

Kiesinger, Kurt Georg [keesinger] (1904–88) West German Conservative chancellor (1966–9), born in Ebingen, Germany. A supporter of European unity, he formed with Brandt a government combining the Christian Democratic Union and the Social Democrats. >> Brandt, Willy

Kilburn, Tom (1921–) Computer scientist, born in Dewsbury, West Yorkshire. He worked with Frederic Williams to build the world's first operational stored-program computer in 1948, and designed the pioneering ATLAS computer in 1962. >> Williams, Frederick

Kildall, Gary (1942–) US computer software designer. He wrote CP/M (Control Program for Microcomputers) in 1974, the first operating system for general use on microcomputers using the Intel 8080 chip, enabling others to write applications programs.

Killy, Jean-Claude [keelee] (1943–) Alpine skier, born in Val d'Isère, France. He won all three alpine skiing titles at the 1968 Olympics, and was combined world champion in 1966 and 1968.

Kilmuir, David Patrick Maxwell Fyfe, 1st Earl of [kilmyoor] (1900–67) British statesman and jurist, born in Aberdeen, Grampian. He became home secretary and minister for Welsh affairs in the 1951 government, and was appointed Lord Chancellor in 1954.

Kilvert, (Robert) Francis (1840–79) Clergyman and diarist, born near Chippenham, Wiltshire. His *Diary* (1870–9), giving a vivid picture of rural life in the Welsh marches, was discovered in 1937 and published in three volumes (1938–40).

Kimberley, John Wodehouse, 1st Earl of (1826–1902)

British statesman. He was Lord Privy Seal (1868–70), colonial secretary (1870–4, 1880–2), secretary for India (1882–5, 1886), and foreign secretary until 1895. Kimberley in South Africa was named after him.

Kim Il-sung [kim ilsung], originally **Kim Song-ju** (1912–94) North Korean soldier, prime minister (1948–72), and president (1972–), born near Pyongyang, North Korea. He founded the Korean People's Revolutionary Army in 1932, proclaimed the Republic in 1948, and became effective head of state. He established a unique personality cult wedded to an isolationist, Stalinist political-economic system, and named his son, **Kim Jong-Il** (1942–), as his successor.

Kimmel, Husband Edward (1882–1968) Naval officer, born in Henderson, KY. At the time of the surprise attack on Pearl Harbor he was the commander-in-chief of the US fleet. Suspended from command, a presidential board of inquiry found him guilty of dereliction of duty (1942), but a naval court later found no mistakes in his judgment (1944).

Kim Young-Sam (1927–) South Korean president (1993–), born in Pusan, Korea. He helped form the New Korea Democratic Party (1985) and the centrist Reunification Democratic Party (RDP, 1987), merging the RDP with the ruling party to form the new Democratic Liberal Party (1990).

Kincaid, Thomas (Cassin) [kinkayd] (1888–1972) Naval officer, born in Hanover, NH. As naval commander (1943–5) he participated in the New Guinea and Philippines operations, fought the Battle of Leyte Gulf (1944), and landed US troops in Korea in 1945.

Kindi, al- >> **al-Kindi**

King, B B, popular name of **Riley B King** (1925–) Blues singer and guitarist, born in Itta Bena, MI. In 1950 a recording contract led to a string of rhythm-and-blues hits, notable albums including *Live At The Regal* (1965), and *There Must Be a Better World Somewhere* (1981).

King, Billie Jean, *née* **Moffat** (1943–) Tennis player, born in Long Beach, CA. Between 1961 and 1979 she won a record 20 Wimbledon titles, including the singles in 1966–8, 1972–3, and 1975. She also won 13 US titles (including four singles), four French titles (one singles), and two Australian titles (one singles).

King, Cecil (Harmsworth) (1901–87) Newspaper proprietor, born in Totteridge, Hertfordshire, the nephew of the Harmsworth brothers. He became chairman of Daily Mirror Newspapers and Sunday Pictorial Newspapers (1951–63), and chairman of the International Publishing Corporation and Reed Paper Group (1963–8). >> Harmsworth

King, Ernest (Joseph) (1878–1956) US admiral, born in Lorain, OH. In 1941 he became commander-in-chief of the Atlantic Fleet and of the US fleet (1941). As chief of naval operations (1942–5) he masterminded the carrier-based campaign against the Japanese.

King, Francis (Henry) (1923–) Writer, born in Switzerland. His novels include *The Dividing Stream* (1951), *The Needle* (1975), and *The Ant Colony* (1991), and he has also written short stories, poetry and travel books.

King, Jessie Marion (1875–1945) Designer and illustrator, born in Bearsden, Strathclyde. An internationally renowned book illustrator, she also designed jewellery and wallpaper, and was greatly involved with batik and pottery.

King, John (1838–72) Traveller, born in Moy, Co Tyrone. The surviving member of the Burke and Wills expedition (1860), he was the first white man to traverse the Australian continent from S to N and back again. >> Burke, Robert O'Hara; Wills, William John

King, Martin Luther, Jr (1929–68) Clergyman and civil rights campaigner, born in Atlanta, GA. Known for his policy of passive resistance and his acclaimed oratorical skills, his greatest successes came in challenging the segregation laws of the South, and in 1964 he received the Kennedy Peace Prize and the Nobel Peace Prize. He was assassinated in Memphis, TN, by James Earl Ray.

King, W(illiam) L(yon) Mackenzie (1874-1950) Canadian Liberal prime minster (1921-6, 1926-30, 1935-48), born in Kitchener (formerly Berlin), Ontario, Canada. His view that the dominions should be autonomous communities within the British empire resulted in the Statute of Westminster (1931).

King, William Rufus (1786-1853) US statesman, born in Sampson Co, NC. He was senator for Alabama (1820-44), minister to France (1844-6), senator again (1846-53), and just before his death was elected Democratic vice-president of the USA.

Kingman, Sir John (Frank Charles) (1939-) British academic. A mathematician and a university vice-chancellor (Bristol), his name became generally known as chairman of the Committee of Inquiry into the Teaching of the English Language (1987-8), which produced the *Kingman Report*.

Kingsford Smith, Sir Charles Edward (1897-1935) Pioneer aviator, born in Hamilton, Queensland, Australia. With Ulm he completed a record-breaking flight round Australia in 1927. In 1935 he set off on the second leg of an attempt at the England-Australia record, but the plane went missing over the Bay of Bengal. >> Ulm

Kingsley, Ben (1943-) Actor, born in Snainton, North Yorkshire. He is best known for his title role in the film *Gandhi* (1980, Oscar). Other films include *Testimony* (1987), *The Children* (1991), and *Necessary Love* (1991).

Kingsley, Charles (1819-75) Writer, born in Holne, Devon. A 'Christian Socialist', his social novels, such as *Alton Locke* (1850), had great influence at the time. His best-known works are *Westward Ho!* (1855), *Hereward the Wake* (1866), and his children's book, *The Water Babies* (1863).

Kingsley, Mary Henrietta (1862-1900) Traveller and writer, born in London, the niece of Charles Kingsley. She undertook two journeys to West Africa (1893-5), and was the first European to enter some parts of Gabon.

Kingsmill, Hugh (1889-1949) British writer, critic, and anthologist. His anthologies include *Johnson Without Boswell* (1940), and *The Worst of Love* (1931). With Hesketh Pearson he established a genre of conversational literary journeys through such works as *Skye High* (1937). >> Pearson, Hesketh

Kinnock, Neil (Gordon) (1942-) British Labour politician, born in Tredegar, Gwent. Chief Opposition spokesman on education (1979-83), he was elected party leader in 1983, resigning after the 1992 general election. He became a European Commissioner (with responsibility for transport) in 1994.

Kinsey, Alfred (Charles) (1894-1956) Sexologist and zoologist, born in Hoboken, NJ. He is best known for his controversial studies, *Sexual Behavior in the Human Male* (1948, the so-called 'Kinsey Report') and *Sexual Behavior in the Human Female* (1953).

Kinski, Klaus, originally **Nikolaus Gunther Naksznski** (1926-91) Film actor, born in Zoppot, Poland. He became known for his leading roles in the films of Werner Herzog, such as *Aguirre, the Wrath of God* (1972) and *Fitzcarraldo* (1982), and for his role in *Nosferatu, the Vampyre* (1979). His daughter, **Nastassja** (1960-), is also an actor. >> Herzog

Kiphuth, Robert (John Herman) (1890-1967) Physical educator, born in Tonawanda, NY. A highly successful swimming coach, he spent 41 years at Yale, and also coached (1928-48) US Olympic swimming teams.

Kipling, (Joseph) Rudyard (1865-1936) Writer, born of British parents in Bombay, India. His verse collections *Barrack Room Ballads* (1892) and *The Seven Seas* (1896) were highly successful, as were the two *Jungle Books* (1894-5). *Kim* appeared in 1901, and the classic *Just So Stories* in 1902. He was awarded the Nobel Prize for Literature in 1907.

Kipp, Petrus Jacobus (1808-64) Chemist, born in Utrecht, The Netherlands. He invented the apparatus called after him for the continuous and automatic production of gases such as carbon dioxide, hydrogen, and hydrogen sulphide.

Kipping, Frederick (Stanley) (1863-1949) Chemist, born in Manchester. He is now best known as the founder of silicone chemistry, although the technical uses for silicones were developed by others from 1940 onwards.

Kirchhoff, Gustav (Robert) [keerkhhohf] (1824-87) Physicist, born in Königsberg, Germany. He formulated the laws involved in the mathematical analysis of an electrical network (*Kirchhoff's laws*, 1845). He also investigated heat, and with Bunsen developed the technique of spectrum analysis, used in the discovery of caesium and rubidium (1859). >> Bunsen

Kirchner, Ernst Ludwig [keerkhner] (1880-1938) Artist, born in Aschaffenburg, Germany. He became the leading spirit in the formation of *Die Brücke* ('The Bridge', 1905-13), the first group of German Expressionists.

Kirk, Alan G(oodrich) (1888-1963) US naval officer and diplomat, born in Philadelphia, PA. He commanded the amphibious forces in the invasion of Sicily in 1943 and the Western Task Force in the Normandy landing in 1944.

Kirk, Norman Eric (1923-74) New Zealand prime minister (1972-4), born in Waimate, New Zealand. He stressed the need for greater economic co-operation with Australia at a time when Britain's entry into the European Economic Community would restrict the British market for New Zealand produce.

Kirkeby, Per [keerkuhbü] (1939-) Danish painter. For several years he has been a prominent representative of new, experimental Danish painting. He has also published poetry, essays, and novels, and directed documentary films.

Kirkland, Gelsey (1952-) Dancer, born in Bethlehem, PA. She became a principal dancer with the New York City Ballet in 1972, then moved to the American Ballet Theater in 1975, and joined Baryshnikov in one of the decade's most celebrated partnerships. >> Baryshnikov

Kirkpatrick, Jeane (Duane Jordan) (1926-) US stateswoman and academic, born in Duncan, OK. Noted for her anti-Communist defence stance and advocacy of a new Latin-American and Pacific-orientated diplomatic strategy, she was appointed permanent representative to the UN by President Reagan (1981-5).

Kirkwood, Daniel (1814-95) Astronomer and mathematician, born in Harford, MD. He explained the unequal distribution of asteroids in the ring system of Saturn as a result of the influence of Jupiter. These interruptions became known as *Kirkwood gaps*.

Kirov, Sergey Mironovich [kirof] (1886-1934) Russian revolutionary, born in Urzhun, Russia. He played an active part in the October Revolution and Civil War, and in 1934 became a secretary of the Central Committee. He was assassinated at his Leningrad headquarters, possibly at the instigation of Stalin. >> Stalin

Kirstein, Lincoln [kersteen] (1907-) Writer, impresario, and ballet director, born in Rochester, NY. He recognized the talents of Balanchine and took him to the USA to co-found the School of American Ballet in 1934. In 1946 they founded the Ballet Society, and in 1948 became directors of the New York City Ballet. >> Balanchine

Kissinger, Henry (Alfred) [kisinjer] (1923-) US secretary of state (1973-6) and academic, born in Fürth, Germany. He became Nixon's adviser on national security affairs in 1969, was the main American figure in the negotiations to end the Vietnam War (for which he shared the 1973 Nobel Peace Prize), and became secretary of state under Nixon and Ford. His 'shuttle diplomacy' was aimed at bringing about peace between Israel and the Arab states.

Kitaj, R(onald) B(rooks) [kitazh] (1932–) Painter, born in Cleveland, OH. An intellectual Pop artist, his oil paintings and pastels demonstrate a mastery of figure drawing, while his economic use of line and the flattened colour recall Oriental art.

Kitazato, Shibasaburo (1852–1931) Bacteriologist, born in Oguni, Japan. He discovered the bacillus of bubonic plague (1894), isolated the bacilli of symptomatic anthrax, dysentery, and tetanus, and prepared a diphtheria antitoxin.

Kitchener (of Khartoum and of Broome), (Horatio) Herbert Kitchener, 1st Earl (1850–1916) British field marshal, born near Ballylongford, Co Kerry, Ireland. Commander-in-chief in South Africa (1900–2), he brought the Boer War to an end. He then became commander-in-chief in India (1902–9), and secretary for war (1914), when he organized manpower on a vast scale ('Kitchener armies').

Kitt, Eartha (Mae) (c.1928–) Entertainer, singer, and actor, born in North, SC. Her vocal vibrancy, fiery personality, and cat-like singing voice made her a top international cabaret attraction and recording artiste.

Kivi, Aleksis [keevee], pseudonym of **Alexis Stenvall** (1834–72) Playwright and novelist, born in Nurmijärvi, Finland. He wrote penetratingly of Finnish peasant life, notably in *Seven Brothers* (trans, 1870), and is now recognized as one of his country's greatest writers.

Kjarval, Jóhannes (Sveinsson) (1885–1972) Painter, born in Efri-Ey, Iceland. Essentially an eccentric Romantic, he had a powerful sense of historical nationalism, and often featured the 'hidden people' of Icelandic folklore.

Kjeldahl, Johan G(ustav) C(hristoffer) T(horsager) (1849–1900) Danish chemist. He was noted for his analytical methods, and especially for the method of nitrogen determination named after him (1883).

Klammer, Franz (1953–) Alpine skier, born in Mooswald, Austria. He was the Olympic downhill champion in 1976, and the World Cup downhill champion five times (1975–8, 1983).

Klaproth, Martin Heinrich [klaproht] (1743–1817) Chemist, born in Wernigerode, Germany. He did much to develop analytical chemistry, and was able to deduce, but not isolate, the elements zirconium, uranium, strontium, and titanium.

Kléber, Jean Baptiste [klaybair] (1753–1800) French soldier, born in Strasbourg, France. He accompanied Napoleon to Egypt, and won the Battle of Mt Tabor (1799). When Napoleon left Egypt, he entrusted the chief command to Kléber, who destroyed the Turkish army and took Cairo, but then was assassinated. >> Napoleon I

Klee, Paul [klay] (1879–1940) Artist, born in Münchenbuchsee, near Bern, Switzerland. He settled in Munich, became a member of the *Blaue Reiter* group (1911–12), and later taught at the Bauhaus (1920–32). After 1919 he worked in oils, producing small-scale, mainly abstract pictures, as in his 'Twittering Machine' (1922).

Kleiber, Erich [kliyber] (1890–1956) Conductor, born in Vienna. He was director of the Berlin State Opera for 12 years until forced by the Nazis to leave Germany. After the war he was again appointed director of the Berlin State Opera, resigning in 1955.

Klein, Anne (Hannah) [kliyn], originally **Hannah Golofski** (?1921–74) Fashion designer, born in New York City. A

noted leader in designing sophisticated, practical sportswear for young women, she also early recognized a need for blazers, trousers, and separates.

Klein, Calvin (Richard) [kliyn] (1942–) Fashion designer, born in New York City. He set up his own firm in 1968, and became known for the simple but sophisticated style of his clothes, including 'designer jeans'.

Klein, (Christian) Felix [kliyn] (1849–1925) Mathematician, born in Düsseldorf, Germany. He worked chiefly on geometry, including non-Euclidean geometry, and function theory, and also wrote widely on the history of mathematics and the applications of his subject.

Klein, Lawrence (Robert) [kliyn] (1920–) Economist, born in Omaha, NE. He was economic adviser to President Carter (1976–81), and was awarded the 1980 Nobel Prize for Economics for his work on forecasting business fluctuations and portraying economic interrelationships. >> Carter, Jimmy

Klein, Melanie [kliyn] (1882–1960) Austrian child psychoanalyst. A student of Sigmund Freud, she was the first to use the content and style of children's play to understand their mental processes. >> Freud, Sigmund

Kleist, (Bernd) Heinrich (Wilhelm) von [kliyst] (1777–1811) Playwright and poet, born in Frankfurt an der Oder, Germany. His best plays are still popular, notably *Prinz Friedrich von Homburg* (1821) and his finest tale, *Michael Kohlhaas* (1810–11).

Klemperer, Otto (1885–1973) Conductor, born in Breslau, Germany. In his later years, he concentrated mainly on the German classical and Romantic composers, and was particularly known for his interpretation of Beethoven. He also composed six symphonies, a Mass, and Lieder.

Klerk, F W de >> de Klerk, F W

Klimt, Gustav (1862–1918) Painter, born in Vienna. The leading master of the Vienna *Sezession*, his murals for the University of Vienna, painted in a new and shocking Symbolist style, caused great controversy.

Kline, Franz (Joseph) (1910–62) Artist, born in Wilkes-Barre, PA. Throughout the 1940s he worked in a traditional style, painting urban scenery, but after c.1950 he went abstract, using black, irregular shapes on white canvases.

Klinger, Friedrich Maximilian von (1752–1831) Playwright and writer, born in Frankfurt, Germany. The *Sturm-und-Drang* school was named after one of his tragedies, *Der Wirrwarr, oder Sturm und Drang* (1776, Confusion, or Storm and Stress).

Klinger, Max (1857–1920) Painter and sculptor, born in Leipzig, Germany. His pen drawings and etchings were often imbued with macabre realism. Later he turned to painting, and did much work in coloured sculpture.

Klint, Kaare (1888–1954) Architect and furniture designer, born in Copenhagen. He placed great emphasis on the function of furniture, applying ergonomics to his designs, and was one of the initiators of Denmark's prominence in the field of design.

Klippel, Robert Edward (1920–) Sculptor, born in Sydney, New South Wales, Australia. His sculptures are intricate and complex, often made of metal 'found objects' welded together (hence the name 'junk sculpture'), although he does also work with wood, plaster, and bronze.

Kluckhohn, Clyde K(ay) M(aben) (1905–60) Cultural anthropologist, born in Le Mars, IA. His research interest was in the culture of the Navaho Indians, on which he wrote many studies, most notably *Navaho Witchcraft* (1944).

Klug, Sir Aaron [klook] (1926–) Biophysicist, born in Lithuania. He brought together X-ray diffraction methods, electron microscopy, structural modelling, and symmetry arguments to elucidate the structure of viruses. He was awarded the Nobel Prize for Chemistry in 1982.

Kluge, (Hans) Günther von [klooguh] (1882–1944) German soldier, born in Poznan, Poland. In 1944 he became commander-in-chief of the Nazi armies in France confronting the Allied invasion. He committed suicide after being implicated in the plot to kill Hitler. >> Hitler

Kneale, Nigel (1922–) Writer and playwright, born on the Isle of Man. He joined the drama department of the BBC and wrote the serial *The Quatermass Experiment* (1953). His film scripts include *The Abominable Snowman* (1957), and *Halloween III* (1983).

Kneller, Sir Godfrey [kneler], originally **Gottfried Kniller** (1646–1723) Portrait painter, born in Lübeck, Germany. His best-known works are his 48 portraits of the Whig 'Kit-Cat Club' (1700–17), and of nine sovereigns.

Kngwarreye, Emily Kame [nuhwaray] (c.1910–) Artist, born in Alhalkere, Northern Territory, Australia. The pre-eminent artist of the internationally renowned Utopia group of artists, she is known as much for being an Aboriginal artist as a contemporary abstract painter.

Knickerbocker, Harmen Jansen (c.1650–c.1716) Colonist, from Friesland, one of the earliest (1674) settlers of New Amsterdam (New York). A descendant, **Johannes** (1749–1827), was a friend of Washington Irving, who immortalized the name through his *History of New York* by 'Diedrich Knickerbocker' (1809). >> Irving, Washington

Knight, Dame Laura *née* **Johnson** (1877–1970) Artist, born in Long Eaton, Derbyshire. She produced a long series of oil paintings of the ballet, the circus, and gypsy life, in a lively and forceful style.

Knopf, Alfred A (1892–1984) Publisher, born in New York City. He founded a publishing house under his own name which gained a prestigious reputation for the quality and variety of its literature. The company became a subsidiary of Random House in 1966.

Knott, Alan (Philip Eric) (1946–) Cricketer, born in Belvedere, Greater London. A wicket-keeper for Kent, he played in 95 Test matches, making 269 dismissals. He also made 4389 runs, including five centuries.

Knox, Archibald (1864–1933) Designer, born on the Isle of Man. In 1899 he designed silverwork and metalwork for Liberty & Co, and by 1900 was their main designer and the inspiration behind the Celtic revival.

Knox, Edmund George Valpy, pseudonym **Evoe** (1881–1971) Writer and parodist, the brother of Ronald Knox. He became editor of *Punch* (1932–49), contributing articles under his pseudonym. His best work was republished in book form, such as *Parodies Regained*, >> Knox, Ronald

Knox, John (c.1513–72) Protestant reformer, born near Haddington, Lothian. A Catholic priest, he was influenced by Wishart to work for the Lutheran reformation. He became a chaplain to Edward VI, but on Mary's accession (1553) fled to Geneva, where he was much influenced by Calvin. After returning to Scotland he founded the Church of Scotland (1560). >> Calvin; Mary I; Wishart

Knox, Ronald (Arbuthnott) (1888–1957) Theologian and essayist, born in Birmingham, West Midlands. A convert to Catholicism, he wrote an influential translation of the Bible, and several works of apologetics, as well as detective novels. >> Knox, Edmund George Valpy

Knudsen, William S(ignius), originally **Signius Wilhelm Paul Knudsen** (1879–1948) Industrialist and government official, born in Copenhagen. Emigrating to America at 21, he ran assembly-line production for Ford (1913–20), and became President of General Motors (1937–40). >> Ford, Henry

Knussen, (Stuart) Oliver [noosn] (1952–) Composer and conductor, born in Glasgow, Strathclyde. His compositions include symphonies, numerous orchestral, chamber, and vocal works, and operas.

Knut, Sveinsson >> Canute

Koch, Ed(ward Irving) [koch] (1924–) US politician, born in New York City. He was well known as Democratic Mayor of New York City (1978–90), until defeated in 1989 by Dinkins. A colourful and outspoken character, he also found a place in the news media as a TV talk-show host and newspaper columnist. >> Dinkins

Koch, (Heinrich Hermann) Robert [kokh, rohbert] (1843–1910) Bacteriologist, born in Klausthal, Germany. He discovered the tuberculosis bacillus (1882), and the cholera bacillus (1883), and was awarded the Nobel Prize for Physiology or Medicine in 1905. >> Cohn

Köchel, Ludwig Ritter von [koekhel] (1800–77) Musicologist, born in Stein, Austria. He compiled the famous catalogue of Mozart's works, arranging them in chronological order, and giving them the 'K' numbers now commonly used to identify them. >> Mozart

Kodály, Zoltán [kohdiy] (1882–1967) Composer, born in Kecskemét, Hungary. Among his best-known works are his *Háry János* suite (1926) and several choral compositions, especially his *Psalmus Hungaricus* (1923) and *Te Deum* (1936).

Koechlin, Charles (Louis Eugène) [koeshlī] (1867–1950) Composer and writer on music, born in Paris. He excelled in colourful and inventive orchestration in his symphonies, symphonic poems, choral-orchestral works, and film music.

Koechlin, Pat >> **Smythe, Pat**

Koestler, Arthur [kestler] (1905–83) Writer and journalist, born in Budapest. His masterpiece is the political novel, *Darkness at Noon* (1940). His nonfiction books and essays deal with politics, scientific creativity, and parapsychology, notably *The Act of Creation* (1964).

Koetsu, Hon'ami [kohetsoo] (1558–1637) Calligrapher and designer, born in Kyoto, Japan. He became famous for his raku and lacquer ware, but his numerous interests made him one of the most creative figures in the history of Japanese art.

Koffka, Kurt (1886–1941) Psychologist, born in Berlin. He conducted experiments in perception, which led to the founding of the *Gestalt* school of psychology.

Kohl, Helmut (1930–) German chancellor (1982–), born in Ludwigshafen-am-Rhein. He formed a government which adopted a central course between political extremes, and presided over the unification of Germany in 1990.

Köhler, Georges >> **Milstein, César**

Köhler, Wolfgang [koeler] (1887–1967) Psychologist, born in Tallinn, Estonia. He participated in experiments which led to the formation of the school of *Gestalt* psychology.

Kohlrausch, Friedrich Wilhelm Georg [kohlrowsh] (1840–1910) Physicist, born in Rinteln, Germany. He is best known for his research into the properties of electrolytes, determining the transfer velocities of the ions in solution.

Kohr, Leopold (1909–94) Austrian economist and writer. His book *Breakdown of Nations* (1957) advocated a move towards smaller national and industrial groupings at a time most others were proposing larger and larger units.

Kokhba, Simon bar >> **bar Kokhba, Simon**

Kokoschka, Oskar [kokoshka] (1886–1980) Artist and writer, born in Pöchlarn, Austria. He travelled widely, and painted many Expressionist landscapes in Europe.

Kolbe, St Maximilian (Maria) [kolbuh] (1894–1941), feast day 14 August. Franciscan priest, born near Łódź, Poland. He was arrested by the Gestapo in 1941, and imprisoned in Auschwitz, where he gave his life in exchange for one of the condemned prisoners. He was canonized in 1982.

Kolbe, (Adolph Wilhelm) Hermann [kolbuh] (1818–84) Scientist, born near Göttingen, Germany. He did much in the development of organic chemical theory, and was one of the first to synthesize an organic compound from inorganic materials.

Kolchak, Alexander Vasilevich (1874–1920) Russian admiral and leader of counter-revolutionary (White) forces during the Russian Civil War, born in the Crimea. After the 1917 Revolution he established an anti-Bolshevik government in Siberia, and proclaimed himself 'Supreme Ruler' of Russia, but was captured and shot by Red Army forces.

Kolff, Willem (Johan) (1911–) Physician, the developer of the artificial kidney, born in Leyden, The Netherlands. He constructed a rotating drum artificial kidney and treated his first patient with it in 1943.

Kollontai, Alexandra Mikhaylovna [kolontiy], *née* **Domontovitch** (1872–1952) Russian feminist and revolutionary, the world's first female ambassador, born in St Petersburg, Russia. Commissar for public welfare, she agitated for domestic and social reforms. She was minister to Norway (1923–5, 1927–30), Mexico (1926–7), and Sweden (1930–45), becoming ambassador in 1943.

Kollwitz, Käthe [kolvits], *née* **Schmidt** (1867–1945) Artist and sculptor, born in Königsberg, Germany. She chose serious, tragic subjects, with strong social or political content, such as the 'Weaver's Revolt' (1897–8) and 'The Peasants' War' (1902–8).

Kolmogorov, Andrey Nikolayevich [kolmogorof] (1903–87) Mathematician, born in Tambov, Russia. He is particularly remembered for his creation of the axiomatic theory of probability, and for his work with Khinchin on Markov processes. >> Khinchin

Komenský, Ian >> **Comenius, John Amos**

Komorowski, Tadeusz [komorofskee] (1895–1966) Polish soldier, born in Lwów, Poland. As 'General Bór' he led the heroic but unsuccessful Warsaw rising against the occupying Germans in 1944.

Konev, Ivan Stepanovich [konyef] (1897–1973) Soviet military commander, born in Lodeyno, Russia. During World War 2 he commanded several different fronts against the Germans, later becoming commander-in-chief, ground forces (1946–50).

Konigsberg, Allen Stewart >> **Allen, Woody**

Koninck, Philips de (1619–88) Painter, born in Amsterdam. He painted portraits, religious subjects, and scenes of everyday life, but his best paintings were panoramic landscapes with large areas of sky.

Konwicki, Tadeusz [konviskee, tadayush] (1929–) Dissident writer and film-maker, born in Lithuania. In the 1950s, *At the Construction Site* was a much prized novel about the party as an engineer of souls. His films include *Salto* and *The Last Day*.

Kooning, Willem de >> **de Kooning, Willem**

Koopmans, Tjalling C(harles) (1910–85) Economist, born in s'Graveland, The Netherlands. He shared the 1975 Nobel Prize for Economics for his contributions to the theory of optimal allocation of resources.

Köpfel, Wolfgang Fabricius >> **Capito, Wolfgang**

Kopp, Hermann Franz Moritz (1817–92) Chemist, born in Hanau, Germany. His studies of the relationship of physical properties to the chemical structure of compounds formed the basis of modern physical organic chemistry.

Koppel, Herman (1908–) Composer and pianist, born in Copenhagen. His compositions include seven symphonies, four piano concertos, six string quartets, an opera (*Macbeth*, 1970), a ballet, and music for theatre, film, and radio.

Korbut, Olga (1956–) Gymnast, born in Grodno, Belarus. In the 1972 Olympics at Munich she won a gold medal as a member of the winning Soviet team, as well as individual golds in the beam and floor exercises and silver for the parallel bars.

Korda, Sir Alexander, originally **Sándor Laszlo Korda** (1893–1956) Film producer, born in Puszta, Hungary. His films include *The Private Life of Henry VIII* (1932), *The Third Man* (1949), and *Richard III* (1956).

Kornberg, Arthur (1918–) Biochemist, born in New York City. He discovered the DNA enzyme polymerase, for which he shared the 1959 Nobel Prize for Physiology or Medicine. He later became the first to synthesize viral DNA (1967).

Korngold, Erich (Wolfgang) (1897–1957) Composer, born in Brünn, Austria. His finest operas were *Violanta* (1916) and *The Dead City* (trans, 1920). In 1934 he emigrated to Hollywood, where two of his film scores, *Robin Hood* and *Anthony Adverse*, received Oscars.

Kornilov, Lavr Georgyevich [kaw(r)neelof] (1870–1918) Russian soldier, a Cossack born in W Siberia. In 1917 he took command of all troops and marched on St Petersburg, but was imprisoned. He escaped and organized an anti-Bolshevik force, but fell in battle. >> Kerensky

Korolyov, Sergey (Pavlovich) [korolyof], also spelled **Korolev** (1907–66) Aircraft engineer and rocket designer, born in Zhitomir, Ukraine. He directed the Soviet Union's space programme, launching the first artificial satellite (1957), the first manned space flight (1961), the *Vostok* and *Voskhod* manned spacecraft, and the *Cosmos* series of satellites.

Korzybski, Alfred (Habdank Skarbek) [kaw(r)zibskee] (1879–1950) Scholar and philosopher of language, born in Warsaw. He is best known as the originator of a system of linguistic philosophy and expression (*general semantics*), as seen in *Science and Sanity* (1933).

Kościuszko or **Kościusko, Thaddeusz (Andrzej) Bona-wentura** [koshchooshkoh] (1746–1817) Polish general and patriot, born near Slonim, Lithuania. He fought in the American Revolution (1766–84), then returned to Poland, where he became head of the national movement (1794). He defeated the Russians, and established a provisional government, but was defeated at Maciejowice in 1794.

Kosinski, Jerzy (Nikodem) [kosinskee] (1933–91) Novelist, born in Łódź, Poland. His best-known books include *The Painted Bird* (1965), a classic of Holocaust literature, *Being There* (1971), and *Passion Play* (1979).

Kossel, Albrecht (1853–1927) Biochemist, born in Rostock, Germany. He investigated the chemistry of cells and proteins, and the chemical processes in living tissue. He was awarded the Nobel Prize for Physiology or Medicine in 1910. >> Kossel, Walther

Kossel, Walther (1888–1956) German physicist, the son of Albrecht Kossel. He did much research on atomic physics, especially on Röntgen spectra, and was known for his physical theory of chemical valency. >> Kossel, Albrecht

Kossoff, David (1919–) British actor, author, and illustrator. He became known on stage and film for his portrayal of Jewish characters, and for his short stories based on Jewish traditions and culture.

Kossoff, Leon (1926–) Painter, born in London. He paints figures in interiors and city views, in an expressive style using very thick impasto.

Kossuth, Lajos [kosooth, loyosh], also Hung [koshut] (1802–94) Hungarian statesman, a leader of the 1848 Hungarian Revolution, born in Monok, Hungary. He was appointed provisional governor of Hungary (1849), but internal dissensions led to his resignation, and he fled abroad.

Koster, Laurens >> **Janszoon, Laurens**

Kosygin, Alexey Nikolayevich [koseegin] (1904–80) Russian premier (1964–80), born in St Petersburg, Russia. First deputy prime minister (with Mikoyan) from 1960, he succeeded Khrushchev as chairman of the Council of Ministers in 1964, but resigned in 1980 because of ill health. >> Khrushchev; Mikoyan, Anastas Ivanovich

Kotane, Moses [kotahnay] (1905–78) South African politician, born in the Rustenburg district, South Africa. He served as General Secretary of the Communist Party for 40 years. In 1963 he went into exile, and served on the national executive of the African National Congress.

Kotzebue, August (Friedrich Ferdinand) von [kotzebyoo] (1761–1819) Playwright, born in Weimar, Germany. He wrote about 200 poetic dramas, notably *The Stranger* (trans, 1789–90), as well as tales, satires, and historical works. He was assassinated by a radical student. >> Kotzebue, Otto

Kotzebue, Otto [kotzebyoo] (1787–1846) German naval officer and explorer, born in Tallin, Estonia, the son of August von Kotzebue. He led an expedition to the Alaskan coast, tried to find a passage across the Arctic Ocean, and discovered *Kotzebue Sound* (1815–18). >> Kotzebue, August von

Koufax, Sandy [kohfaks], popular name of **Sanford Koufax** (1935–) Baseball player, born in New York City. Famous for his pitching, he played in Los Angeles with the Dodgers, and helped them to a World Series victory in 1963 and 1965.

Koussevitsky, Serge [koosevitskee], originally **Sergei Alexandrovich Koussevitsky** (1874–1951) Conductor, composer, and double-bass player, born in Vishni-Volotchok, Russia. He settled in Boston in 1924, remaining conductor of its symphony orchestra for 25 years.

Kouwenhoven, William Bennett [kohenhohvn] (1886–1975) Electrical engineer, born in New York City. In the 1930s he developed the first practical electrical defibrillator, which has since come into general use for the treatment of heartbeat irregularities.

Kraepelin, Emil [kraypelin] (1856–1926) Psychiatrist, born in Neustrelitz, Germany. He was a pioneer in the psychological study of serious mental diseases (psychoses), and compiled a classification of disorders published in his *Compendium of Psychiatry* (trans, 1883).

Krafft-Ebing, Richard, Freiherr von (Baron) [kraft ebing] (1840–1902) Psychiatrist, born in Mannheim, Germany. Much of his work was on forensic psychiatry and on sexual aberrations. He is best known for *Psychopathia sexualis* (1886).

Kramer, Jack [kraymer], popular name of **John Albert Kramer** (1921–) Tennis player, born in Las Vegas, NV. He turned professional after winning the Wimbledon singles title in 1947. He played a major role in establishing the Association of Tennis Professionals, and was its first director (1972).

Kramer, Dame Leonie (Judith) [kraymer] (1924–) Academic, writer, and administrator, born in Melbourne, Victoria, Australia. She has held posts on a number of influential bodies, and is a prominent member of the group 'Australians for Constitutional Monarchy' founded in 1992.

Krautheimer, Richard [krowthiymer] (1897–) Architectural historian, born in Fuerth, Germany. A specialist in early Christian and mediaeval architecture who later turned to the Baroque period, he was an early exponent of architectural iconography.

Kray brothers Convicted British murderers, twin brothers who ran a criminal Mafia-style operation in the East End of London in the 1960s: **Ronald Kray** (1933–95) and **Reginald Kray** (1933–). They were tried in 1969, and sentenced to life imprisonment of not less than 30 years.

Krebs, Sir Hans (Adolf) (1900–81) Physiologist, born in Hildesheim, Germany. He shared the Nobel Prize for Physiology or Medicine in 1953 for his work on the nature of metabolic processes.

Kreisky, Bruno [kriyskee] (1911–90) Austrian chancellor (1970–83), born in Vienna. In 1970 he became prime minister in a minority Social Democratic government. He

steadily increased his majority in subsequent elections but in 1983, when that majority disappeared, he refused to serve in a coalition and resigned.

Kreisler, Fritz [kriysler] (1875–1962) Violinist, born in Vienna. From 1889 he became one of the most successful violin virtuosos of his day, and composed violin pieces, a string quartet, and an operetta, *Apple Blossoms* (1919), which was a Broadway success.

Kreitman, Esther >> Singer, Esther

Křenek, Ernst [krzhenek] (1900–91) Composer, born in Vienna. He wrote two symphonies, and developed a style which ranged from jazz, as in his opera *Johnny Strikes Up the Band* (trans, 1927), which made his name, to serialism, as in *Karl V* (1930–3).

Kresge, S(ebastian) S(pering) [krezgee] (1867–1966) Merchant and philanthropist, born in Bald Mount, PA. In 1899 he began the S S Kresge Co, which sold nothing over ten cents, and by the mid-1920s had over 300 stores. He founded the Kresge Foundation in 1924.

Kretzer, Marx (1854–1941) Writer, born in Poznan, Poland (formerly, Posen, East Prussia). His books include (trans titles) *The Deceived* (1882), and *Master Timpe* (1888). He has sometimes been called 'the German Zola', on account of his realism.

Kreutzer, Rodolphe [kroytzer] (1766–1831) Violinist, born in Versailles, France. From 1784 until 1810 he was one of the leading concert violinists in Europe. He became friendly with Beethoven, who dedicated a sonata to him.

Kripke, Saul [kripkee] (1940–) Philosopher and logician, born in Bay Shore, NY. He made technical advances in modal logic, whose wider philosophical implications were later explored in such famous papers as 'Naming and Necessity' (1972).

Krishna Menon, V(engalil) K(rishnan) [krishna menon] (1896–1974) Indian politician and diplomat, born in Kozhikode (formerly Calicut), Malabar, India. He was India's first high commissioner in London (1947), and the leader of the Indian delegation to the UN (1952).

Krishnamurti, Jiddu [krishnamoortee] (1895–1986) Theosophist, born in Madras, India. He was educated in England by Annie Besant, who in 1925 proclaimed him the Messiah. Later he rejected this persona, and travelled the world advocating a way of life unconditioned by the narrowness of nationality, race, and religion. >> Besant, Annie

Kristian X (of Denmark) >> Christian X

Kristiansen, Ingrid, *née* **Christensen** (1956–) Athlete, born in Trondheim, Norway. A former cross-country skiing champion, and now an outstanding long-distance runner, she is the only person to hold world best times for the 5000 m, 10 000 m, and marathon, which she achieved in 1985–6.

Kristina (of Sweden) >> Christina

Kroc, Ray (1902–1984) US founder of the McDonald's chain of fast-food restaurants. A milk-shake machine manufacturer in the 1950s, he was impressed by his customers, Mac and Dick McDonald, who sold hamburgers, French fries, and milk-shakes from a stand. He bought the rights to operate similar stands, and by 1959 had opened his 100th store.

Kroeber, A(lfred) L(ouis) [krohber] (1876–1960) Cultural anthropologist, born in Hoboken, NJ. His most influential work, *Anthropology* (1923), helped to establish his subject as a professional academic discipline.

Krogh, (Schack) August (Steenberg) [krawg] (1874–1949) Physiologist, born in Grenå, Denmark. He researched the process of respiration, discovering the motor-regulating mechanism of capillaries. He was awarded the Nobel Prize for Physiology or Medicine in 1920.

Kropotkin, Pyotr Alexeyevich, Knyaz (Prince) [kropotkin] (1842–1921) Revolutionary and geographer, born in Moscow. The son of a prince, in 1871 he renounced his title and devoted himself to a life as a revolutionary. Arrested and imprisoned (1874–6, 1883–6), he then settled in England until the revolution of 1917 took him back to Russia.

Kruger, Paul [krooger], in full **Stephanus Johannes Paulus Kruger**, nickname **Oom** ('Uncle') **Paul** (1825–1904) Afrikaner president of the Transvaal (1883–1902), born in Colesberg, Cape Colony, South Africa. He became leader of the independence movement when Britain annexed Transvaal (1877).

Krupp (von Bohlen und Halbach), Alfried (Alwin Felix) (1906–67) Industrialist, born in Essen, Germany. In 1943 he succeeded to the Krupp empire, and was sentenced to 12 years' imprisonment in 1947 for Nazi activities. Released in 1951, he played a prominent part in the West German 'economic miracle'. >> Krupp, Gustav

Krupp, Bertha >> **Krupp, Gustav**

Krupp, Gustav, originally **Gustav von Bohlen und Halbach** (1870–1950) Industrialist, born in The Hague. A Prussian diplomat who married **Bertha Krupp** (1886–1957), heiress to the Krupp industrial empire, he adopted his wife's surname. During World War 1, his firm manufactured the long-range gun for the shelling of Paris, nicknamed 'Big Bertha'. He later gave financial support to Hitler, and connived in secret rearmament. >> Krupp, Alfried

Krutch, Joseph Wood (1893–1970) Writer, critic, and naturalist, born in Knoxville, TN. He wrote several literary critical studies, and was drama critic for *The Nation* (1924–52).

Kubelík, Rafael (Jeronym) [kubelik] (1914–) Conductor and composer, born in Býchory, Czech Republic. His posts include conductor of the Chicago Symphony Orchestra (1950–3) and the Bavarian Radio Orchestra (1961–79), and he has composed five operas, symphonies, concertos, and other works.

Kubitschek (de Oliveira), Juscelino [kubshek] (1902–76) Brazilian president (1956–61), born in Diamantina, Minas Gerais. His government sponsored rapid economic growth, and the dramatic building of a new capital, Brasília.

Kublai Khan [koobliy kahn] (1214–94) Mongol emperor of China (1279–94), the grandson of Genghis Khan. He established himself at Cambaluc (modern Beijing), and ruled an empire which extended as far as the R Danube. The splendour of his court was legendary. >> Genghis Khan

Kubrick, Stanley [koobrik] (1928–) Screen writer, film producer, and director, born in New York City. His films include *Spartacus* (1960), *Lolita* (1962), *2001: a Space Odyssey* (1965), *A Clockwork Orange* (1971), and *The Shining* (1980).

Kuhn, Richard [koon] (1900–67) Biochemist, born in Vienna. He was noted for his work on the structure and synthesis of vitamins A and B_2, and on carotinoids. He was awarded the 1938 Nobel Prize for Chemistry, received after World War 2.

Kuhn, Thomas (Samuel) [koon] (1922–) Philosopher and historian of science, born in Cincinnati, OH. He is chiefly known through his book, *The Structure of Scientific Revolutions* (1962), which challenged the idea of cumulative, unidirectional scientific progress.

Kuhn, Walt(er Francis) [koon] (1877–1949) Painter, born in New York City. His mature work specialized in portraits of clowns and other circus performers, as seen in 'The Blue Clown' (1931).

Kuiper, Gerard (Peter) [kiyper] (1905–73) Astronomer, born in Harenkarspel, The Netherlands. He pioneered the spectroscopy of planetary atmospheres, and discovered two new satellites: Miranda, the fifth satellite of Uranus; and Nereid, the second satellite of Neptune (1948–9).

Kummer, Ernst Eduard (1810–93) Mathematician, born in Sorau, Germany. In trying to prove Fermat's last theo-

rem, he introduced 'ideal numbers', a fundamental tool of modern algebra. He also developed the *Kummer surface*, the wave surface in four dimensional space. >> Fermat

Kun, Béla (1886–c.1939) Hungarian revolutionary, born in Szilágycseh, Hungary. In 1918 he founded the Hungarian Communist Party, organized a Communist revolution in Budapest, and set up a Soviet republic. His regime was overthrown and he escaped to Russia.

Kundera, Milan [kundaira] (1929–) Novelist, born in Brno, Czech Republic. In 1975 he settled in Paris. His works include *The Unbearable Lightness of Being* (trans, 1984; filmed 1987) and *Immortality* (1991).

Küng, Hans (1928–) Roman Catholic theologian, born in Sursee, Switzerland. His questioning of Catholic doctrine, as in *Justification* (1965), *The Church* (1967), and *Infallible? An Inquiry* (1971), aroused controversy, and the Vatican withdrew his licence to teach as a Catholic theologian in 1979.

Kunitz, Stanley (Jasspon) (1905–) Poet, born in Worcester, MA. His works include *Selected Poems 1928–1958* (1959, Pulitzer) and *The Testing-Tree* (1971).

Kuniyoshi, Yasuo (1893–1953) Painter and graphic artist, born in Okayama, Japan. He emigrated to the USA in 1906. His later work was marked by sinister fantasy, as seen in 'Juggler' (1952).

Kunstler, William M(oses) (1919–95) Lawyer and social activist, born in New York City. In the early 1960s he began to represent the more radical groups opposing the Vietnam war, and mistreatment of African-Americans. His famous cases include the defence of the Cantonsville Nine and the Chicago Seven.

Kupka, František (1871–1957) Painter, born in Opočno, Czech Republic. He settled in France, becoming one of the pioneers of pure abstract painting, a style called Orphism by Apollinaire. >> Apollinaire

Kurath, Gertrude (Prokosch) [koorahht] (1903–92) Musicologist, born in Chicago, IL. She danced and taught professionally as *Tula* (1922–46) before turning to the study of American-Indian dance. In 1962 she founded the Dance Research Center in Ann Arbor, MI.

Kurchatov, Igor (Vasilevich) [koorchatof] (1903–60) Physicist, born in Sim, Russia. He carried out important studies of neutron reactions, and was the leading figure in the building of Russia's first atomic (1949) and thermonuclear (1953) bombs, and the world's first industrial nuclear power plant (1954).

Kuropatkin, Alexey Nikolaievich [kurohpatkin] (1848–1925) Russian soldier, born a noble of Pskov, Russia. He was chief-of-staff in the Turkish war (1877–8), commander-in-chief in Caucasia (1897), minister of war (1898), and commander-in-chief in Manchuria (1904–5). He commanded the Russian armies on the Northern Front in 1916.

Kurosawa, Akira [kurohsahwa] (1910–) Film director, born in Tokyo. He is renowned for his adaptation of the techniques of the Noh theatre to film-making, in such films as *Rashomon* (1950) and *The Seven Samurai* (trans, 1954). Later films include *Kagemusha* (1980) and *Rhapsody in August* (1991).

Kurtzman, Harvey (1924–93) Strip cartoonist and scriptwriter, born in New York City. He became editor of *Frontline Combat* and *Two-Fisted Tales*, and in 1952 created *Mad* as a parody of comic books and characters.

Kusch, Polykarp (1911–93) Physicist, born in Blankenburg, Germany. He shared the 1955 Nobel Prize for Physics for his precise determination of the magnetic moment of the electron.

Kuts, Vladimir Petrovich (1927–75) Athlete and middle-distance runner, born in Aleksino, Ukraine. Former holder of the world record for the 10 000 m and the 5000 m, he won gold medals for these events in the 1956 Olympics.

Kutuzov, Mikhail Ilarionovich, Knyaz (Prince) [kutoozof] (1745–1813) Russian field marshal, born in St Petersburg, Russia. In 1812, as commander-in-chief, he fought Napoleon at Borodino, and later obtained a major victory at Smolensk. >> Napoleon I

Kuznets, Simon (Smith) (1901–85) Economist and statistician, born in Kharkov, Ukraine. His work combined a concern for facts and measurement with original ideas on economic growth and social change, such as the 20-year *Kuznets cycle* of economic growth. He was awarded the Nobel Prize for Economics in 1971.

Kuznetsov, Alexander Vasilievich [kuznetsof] (1929–79) Writer, born in Kiev, Ukraine. He is best known for *Babi Yar* (1966), a novel about the massacre of Ukrainian Jews by the German SS in 1941. He defected to England in 1969, changing his name to **A Anatoli**.

Kyan, John Howard [kiyan] (1774–1850) Inventor, born in Dublin. In 1832 he invented a patent method of preserving wood, known as the *kyanizing* process.

Kyd, Thomas (1558–94) Playwright, born in London. His tragedies early brought him reputation, especially *The Spanish Tragedy* (c.1592), and he has been credited with a share in several plays.

Kylian, Jiri [kilian] (1947–) Dancer and choreographer, born in Prague. He began his choreographic output with Stuttgart Ballet (1970) before moving to the Netherlands Dance Theatre, where he became director in 1978.

Kyprianou, Spyros [kipriahnoo] (1932–) Cypriot president (1978–88), born in Limassol, Cyprus. He was foreign minister (1961–72), and in 1976 founded the Democratic Front. He became president in 1977, but was unsuccessful in finding a peaceful solution to the divisions in Cyprus.

Laar, Pieter van, nickname **i Bamboccio** ('the Cripple') (c.1590–c.1658) Artist, born in Harlem, The Netherlands. Noted for his paintings of country scenes, weddings, wakes, and fairs, he gave his name to the term *bambochades* for genre paintings of bucolic themes.

Labadie, Jean de [labadee] (1610–74) Protestant reformer, born in Bourg, France. He preached a return to primitive Christianity in Holland, and was excommunicated from the Reformed Church in 1670, whereupon he moved his Labadist colony to Germany.

Laban, Rudolf von [laybn] (1879–1958) Dancer, choreographer, dance theorist, and notator, born in Bratislava. In England he established the Art of Movement Studio in 1946, now known as the Laban Centre, and also developed a system of dance notation, *Labanotation*.

Labé, Louise [labay], originally **Louise Charly**, known as **la Belle Cordière** ('the Lovely Ropemaker') (c.1524–66) Poet, born in Parcieux, France. In 1550 she married a wealthy rope manufacturer, which accounts for her nickname, and in 1955 published a book of love sonnets including 'Débat de Folie et d'Amour'.

Labiche, Eugène [labeesh] (1815–88) Playwright, born in Paris. He wrote over 100 comedies, farces, and vaudevilles, including *Frisette* (1846) and *Le Voyage de M. Perrichon* (1860).

La Bruyère, Jean de [brooyair] (1645–96) Writer, born in Paris. His only well-known work, *Characters* (trans, 1688), consists of two parts: a translation of Theophrastus, and a masterpiece of French literature in the form of a collection of maxims, reflections, and character portraits of the time. >> Theophrastus

Lacaille, Nicolas Louis de [lakiy] (1713–62) Astronomer, born in Rumigny, France. He led an expedition to the Cape of Good Hope (1750–54), where he compiled a catalogue of nearly 10 000 southern stars.

Lacépède, Bernard de Laville, comte de (Count of) [laseped] (1756–1825) Naturalist and French politician, born in Agen, France. He published *Natural History of Fish* (5 vols, 1798–1803), and in 1809 became a minister of state.

Lachaise, François d'Aix [lashez] (1624–1709) Jesuit, born at the castle of Aix in Forez, France. Louis XIV selected him as his confessor in 1675, and he retained the post until his death. >> Louis XIV

Lachaise, Gaston [lashez] (1882–1935) Figurative sculptor, born in Paris. He emigrated to Boston in 1906, where he made his name as a portraitist, and also as a sculptor of massively proportioned bronze statues of women, reputedly modelled on his wife, Isabel Nagel.

La Chaussée, Pierre Claude Nivelle de [shohsay] (1692–1754) Playwright, born in Paris. Among his plays are *Stylish Prejudice* (trans, 1735), *Mélanide* (1741), and *Mothers' School* (1744).

Lackland, John >> **John**

Laclos, Pierre (Ambroise François) Choderlos de [lakloh] (1741–1803) Novelist and soldier, born in Amiens, France. His masterpiece, *Les Liaisons dangereuses* (1782, Dangerous Liaisons), a novel in epistolary form, became an immediate sensation for its cynical analysis of personal and sexual relationships. It has been successfully adapted for the theatre and several films.

Lacondamine, Charles Marie de [lakõdameen] (1701–74) Mathematician and scientist, born in Paris. He was sent to Peru (1735–43) to measure a degree of the meridian, explored the Amazon, and brought back curare, as well as information on platinum and India rubber.

Lacoste, Robert [lakost] (1898–1989) French Socialist statesman, born in Azerat, France. In World War 2 he began the first Trade Union Resistance Group, and thereafter held various ministerial posts, including minister for industry and commerce (1946–7, and 1948).

Lacroix, Christian [lakrwah] (1951–) Fashion designer, born in Arles, France. In 1987 he opened the House of Lacroix in Paris, making his name with ornate and frivolous clothes.

Lactantius [laktanshius], in full **Lucius Cae(ci)lius Firmianus Lactantius** (c.240–c.320) Christian apologist, brought up in North Africa. His principal work is his *Divinarum Institutionum libri vii*, a systematic account of Christian attitudes.

Laënnec, René (Théophile Hyacinthe) [laynek] (1781–1826) Physician, born in Quimper, France. He invented the stethoscope, and published the classic *On Mediate Auscultation* (trans, 1819).

Laestadius, Lars Levi [laystadius] (1800–61) Priest and botanist, born in Arjeplog, Sweden. In the early 1840s he underwent a profound spiritual crisis and began the ecstatic revivalist preaching that had great influence among the Lapps. Today there are many *Laestadians* in Finland and Sweden.

La Farge, John (1835–1910) Landscape and ecclesiastical painter, born in New York City. Known for his pre-Impressionist landscapes and flowers, he also produced murals and stained-glass work in churches, notably 'The Ascension' in the Church of the Ascension, New York City.

Lafayette, Marie Joseph (Paul Yves Roch Gilbert Motier), marquis de [lafiyet] (1757–1834) French soldier and politician, born in Chavagniac, France. He fought in America against the British during the War of Independence (1777–9, 1780–2), and in the National Assembly of 1789 presented a draft of a declaration of the Rights of Man. Hated by the Jacobins for his moderation, he defected to Austria, returning to France during the Consulate. He later became a radical leader of the Opposition (1825–30).

La Fayette, Marie Madeleine (Pioche de la Vergne), comtesse de (Countess of) [lafiyet], known as **Madame de La Fayette** (1634–93) Novelist and reformer of French romance-writing, born in Paris. Her masterpiece is *La Princesse de Clèves* (1678), a vivid picture of the court life of her day.

Laffite, Jean [lafeet] (1780?–1825?) Pirate, probably born in France. He was in New Orleans by 1809, where he led a band of smugglers and pirates, but he and his men were pardoned after they manned artillery during the Battle of New Orleans (1815). He reverted to piracy and passed into legend.

La Follette, Robert M(arion) [la folet] (1855–1925) US politician, born in Primrose, WI. A senator from 1905, he became a 'Progressive' candidate for the presidency, but was defeated in 1924.

La Fontaine, Jean de [fonten] (1621–95) Poet, born in Château-Thierry, France. He is best known for the *Fables choisies mises en vers* (12 vols, 1668–94), in translation usually called 'La Fontaine's Fables'.

Lafontaine, Sir Louis Hippolyte >> **Baldwin, Robert**

Lafontaine, Oskar [lafonten], nicknames **Red Oskar** and **Ayatollah of the Saarland** (1943–) West German politician, born in Saarlois, Germany. He was elected as minister-president of the Saarland State Assembly in 1985, and in 1987 was appointed a deputy chairman of the Social Democratic Party's federal organization. His nicknames come from his early reputation for radicalism.

Lagerkvist, Pär (Fabian) [lahgerkvist] (1891–1974) Writer, poet, and playwright, born in Växjö, Sweden. He was awarded the Nobel Prize for Literature (1951) for his novel *Barabbas*. Other works include the novel *The Dwarf* (trans, 1944), and the short-story collection *The Marriage Feast* (1973).

Lagerlöf, Selma (Ottiliana Lovisa) [lahgerloef] (1858–1940) Novelist, born in Mårbacka, Sweden. She sprang to fame with her novel *The Story of Gösta Berling* (trans, 1891), and also wrote the children's classic, *The Wonderful Adventures of Nils* (trans, 1906–7). She was the first woman to receive the Nobel Prize for Literature, in 1909.

Lagrange, Joseph Louis, comte de l'Empire (Count of the Empire) [lagräzh], originally **Giuseppe Luigi Lagrangia** (1736–1813) Mathematician and astronomer, born in Turin, Italy. His major work was *Analytical Mechanics* (trans, 1788). The *Lagrangian point* in astronomy, the *Lagrangian function* in mechanics, and several notions in mathematics are named after him.

La Guardia, Fiorello H(enry) [la gah(r)dia] (1882–1947) US politician and lawyer, born in New York City. He sat in Congress (1917–21, 1923–33) as a Republican, and held three terms of office as Mayor of New York City (1933–45). One of the city's airports is named after him.

La Guma, Alex [la gooma] (1925–85) Novelist, born in Cape Town, South Africa. One of the best-known literary opponents of apartheid, his novels include *A Walk in the Night* (1962), *The Stone Country* (1967), and *Time of the Butcherbird* (1979).

Lahm, Frank (Purdy) (1877–1963) Aviator, born in Mansfield, OH. A pioneer aviator, he trained with Wilbur Wright, and in 1909 became one of the army's first two certified pilots. >> Wright brothers

Lahr, Bert, originally **Irving Lahreim** (1895–1967) Actor, born in New York City. A comedian with a lovably ugly face, and a musical comedy star (1928–64), he also appeared in films (1931–67), notably *The Wizard of Oz* (1939), where he played the Cowardly Lion.

Laine, Cleo >> **Dankworth, John**

Laing, Alexander Gordon [lang] (1793–1826) Explorer, born in Edinburgh. He became the first European to reach the ancient city of Timbuktu (1826), while searching for the source of the R Niger in W Africa. He was murdered by local tribesmen.

Laing, R(onald) D(avid) [lang] (1927–89) Psychiatrist, born in Glasgow, Strathclyde. He is noted for his studies of schizophrenia, and published his revolutionary ideas in *The Divided Self* (1960).

Laird, Macgregor (1808–61) Explorer and merchant, born in Greenock, Strathclyde. Travelling to the lower Niger with Lander's expedition (1832–4), he was the first European to journey up the Benue R. In 1837 he started a transatlantic steamship company. >> Lander, Richard

Laithwaite, Eric Roberts (1921–) Electrical engineer and inventor, born in Atherton, Greater Manchester. His principal research interest was in the linear motor, a means of propulsion using electro-magnetic forces acting along linear tracks.

Lakatos, Imre (1922–74) Philosopher of mathematics and science, born in Debrecen, Hungary. His best-known work is *Proofs and Refutations* (1976), a collection of articles demonstrating the creative and informal nature of real mathematical discovery.

Lake, Simon (1866–1945) Engineer and inventor, born in Pleasantville, NJ. He launched his gasoline-engine-powered *Argonaut*, which became the first submarine to successfully operate in the open sea (1898).

Laker, Jim, popular name of **James Charles Laker** (1922–86) Cricketer and broadcaster, born in Bradford, West Yorkshire. He made test cricket history at Old Trafford in 1956 when he took 19 Australian wickets for 90 runs. During his career (1946–64) he took 1944 wickets.

Laker, Sir Freddie, popular name of **Sir Frederick Alfred Laker** (1922–) Business entrepreneur, born in Kent. In 1966 he headed the successful Laker Airways Ltd, but was severely set back by the failure of the 'Skytrain' project (1982).

Lalande, Joseph Jérôme Le Français de [laläd] (1732–1807) Astronomer, born in Bourg-en-Bresse, France. His chief work is *Traité d'astronomie* (1764), and he also produced the most comprehensive star catalogue of his time (1801).

Lalanne, Maxine [lalan] (1827–86) Etcher and lithographer, born in Bordeaux, France. In 1866 he began a successful collaboration with the 'House of Cadart', who published his treatise on acid engraving.

Lalique, René [laleek] (1860–1945) Jeweller and designer, born in Ay, France. His glass designs, decorated with relief figures, animals, and flowers, were an important contribution to the Art Nouveau and Art Deco movements.

Lalo, (Victor Antoine) Eduard [laloh] (1823–92) Composer, born in Lille, France. His best known musical composition is *Symphonie espagnole* for violin and orchestra.

Lam, Wilfredo (1902–82) Painter, born in Sagua la Grande, Cuba. He fused Latin-American, African, and Oceanic elements with the European modern movement, as in *The Jungle* (1943).

Lamarck, Jean Baptiste (Pierre Antoine) de Monet, Chevalier de [lamah(r)k] (1744–1829) Naturalist and pre-Darwinian evolutionist, born in Bazentin, France. His major works were *Philosophie zoologique* (1809) and *Natural History of Invertebrate Animals* (trans, 1815–22). >> Darwin, Charles

Lamartine, Alphonse (Marie Louis) de [lamah(r)teen] (1790–1869) Poet, statesman, and historian, born in Mâcon, France. His best-known work was his first volume of lyrical poems, *Poetic Meditations* (trans, 1820). He became a member of the provisional government in the 1848 revolution, and acted as minister of foreign affairs.

Lamb, Lady Caroline >> **Melbourne, William Lamb, 2nd Viscount**

Lamb, Charles, pseudonym **Elia** (1775–1834) Essayist, born in London. He achieved success through joint publication with his sister, **Mary** (1764–1847) of *Tales from Shakespeare* (1807). His best-known works are the series of essays under his pseudonym, the *Essays of Elia* (1823–33).

Lamb, Henry (1883–1960) Painter, born in Adelaide, South Australia. He exhibited with the Camden Town Group, and was an official war artist (1940–4). His best-known work is the portrait of Lytton Strachey (1914).

Lamb, William >> **Melbourne, 2nd Viscount**

Lamb, Willis Eugene, Jr (1913–) Physicist, born in Los Angeles, CA. In 1955 he shared the Nobel Prize for Physics for research that led to refinements in the quantum theories of electromagnetic phenomena.

Lambert, Constant (1905–51) Composer, conductor, and critic, born in London. He became conductor of the Sadler's Wells Ballet (1928–47), and was also known as a concert conductor and music critic. His best-known composition is the choral work in jazz idiom, *The Rio Grande* (1927).

Lambert, George Washington Thomas (1873–1930) Painter and sculptor, born in St Petersburg, Russia. As official war artist for Australia (World War I), he later visited Gallipoli to make sketches with C E W Bean, the war historian. >> Bean, C E W

Lambert, Johann Heinrich (1728–77) Mathematician, born in Mülhausen, Germany. He established several theorems in non-Euclidean geometry, and demonstrated that pi (π) is an irrational number (1768). The first to show how to measure scientifically the intensity of light (1760), the unit of light intensity is now named after him.

Lambert, John (1619–84) English general, born in Calton, North Yorkshire. He joined the parliamentary army in the English Civil War, commanding at Marston Moor (1644), but opposed the movement to declare Oliver Cromwell king, and headed the Cabal which overthrew Richard Cromwell in 1659. At the Restoration (1661) he was imprisoned until his death. >> Cromwell, Oliver / Richard

Lambton, John George >> **Durham, Earl of**

Lamennais, Félicité [lamenay], in full **(Hugues-) Félicité (- Robert de) Lamennais** (1782–1854) Priest and writer, born in St-Malo, France. His *Essay on Indifference towards Religion* (1818–24) brought him acclaim, but later works began to combine Roman Catholicism with political liberalism, and were condemned by the pope in 1832.

La Mettrie, Julien Offroy de [la metree] (1709–51) Philosopher and physician, born in St-Malo, France. His *Natural History of the Soul* (trans, 1745) argued that all psychical phenomena were the effects of organic changes in the nervous system - an atheistic view which provoked such hostility that the book was publicly burned.

Lamming, George Eric (1927–) Novelist, born in Carrington Village, Barbados. He moved to England in 1950, where he began to write about his West Indian experiences, notably in *Natives of My Person* (1972).

Lamond, Frederic [lamond], (1868–1948) Pianist and composer, born in Glasgow, Strathclyde. He excelled in playing Beethoven, and among his own compositions are an overture, a symphony, and several piano works.

Lamont, Johann von [lamont] (1805–79) Astronomer, born in Braemar, Grampian. He is noted for discovering that the magnetic field of the Earth fluctuates in a period of over 10 years.

Lamont, Norman [lamont] (1942–) British statesman, born in Lerwick, Shetland Is. He became financial secretary to the Treasury in 1986 and Chancellor of the Exchequer in 1990. Following his replacement in the 1993 Cabinet reshuffle, he launched an attack on John Major's policies. >> Major

L'Amour, Louis (Dearborn) [lamoor], pseudonym **Tex Burns** (1908–88) Novelist, born in Jamestown, ND. His many novels include *Hondo* (1953), *The Quick and the Dead*, and *How the West Was Won* (1963), several of which were made into successful films.

Lampedusa, Giuseppe Tomasi, duca di (Duke of) **Palma** [lampedooza] (1896–1957) Novelist, born in Palermo, Sicily. His only novel, *The Leopard* (trans, 1958) was published posthumously, and has subsequently come to be regarded as a masterpiece.

Lancaster, Burt, popular name of **Stephen Burton Lancaster** (1913–94) Film actor, born in New York City. Cast early on in a succession of tough-guy roles, later notable films include *From Here to Eternity* (1953), *Elmer Gantry* (1960, Oscar), *Birdman of Alcatraz* (1962), and *Local Hero* (1983).

Lancaster, Duke of >> **John of Gaunt**

Lancaster, Joseph (1778–1838) Educator and Quaker, born in London. In 1798 he opened a school in London based on a monitorial system, in which the more able children taught the less able. This led to the founding of the *Lancasterian method*, popular in Europe and North America.

Lancaster, Sir Osbert (1908–86) Cartoonist, writer, and theatrical designer, born in London. He began drawing pocket-sized front-page cartoons for the *Daily Express* in 1939, creating Lady Maudie Littlehampton and friends.

Lanchester, Frederick William (1868–1946) Automobile

and aeronautics pioneer, born in London. He built the first experimental motor car in Britain in 1895, and founded the Lanchester Engine Co in 1899.

Land, Edwin (Herbert) (1909–91) Inventor and physicist, born in Bridgeport, CT. He produced the light-polarizing filter material 'Polaroid' in 1936. His well-known *Land Polaroid camera* (1947) was a self-developing system of instant photography.

Landau, Lev Davidovich [landow], known as **Dev Landau** (1908–68) Physicist, born in Baku, Azerbaijan. He received the Nobel Prize for Physics in 1962 for his work on theories of condensed matter, particularly helium.

Landells, Ebenezer (1808–60) Wood-engraver, born in Newcastle upon Tyne, UK. In 1841 he originated the humorous magazine *Punch*, and contributed wood engravings to both *Punch* and the *Illustrated London News*.

Lander, Harald, originally **Alfred Bernhardt Stevnsborg** (1905–71) Ballet dancer and choreographer, born in Copenhagen. As ballet master (1932–51) of the Royal Danish Ballet School, he was responsible for the enormous success of the company. From 1953 he was ballet master of the Paris Opéra.

Lander, Richard (1804–34) Explorer, born in Truro, Cornwall. In 1825 he accompanied Clapperton to West Africa, publishing an account of the expedition, and in 1830 he and his brother **John** (1807–39) traced the course of the lower Niger. >> Clapperton

Landers, Ann, pseudonym of **Esther Pauline Friedman** (1918–) Journalist, born in Sioux City, IA. In 1955 she inherited her job as a Chicago-based advice columnist from a previous 'Ann Landers', creating an international institution.

Landis, Kenesaw Mountain (1866–1944) Federal judge and baseball commissioner, born in Millville, OH. After the bribery scandal in the World Series of 1919, his autocratic rule as first commissioner of baseball restored the credibility of the game.

Landon, Alf, originally **Alfred Mossman** (1887–1987) Businessman and politician, born in West Middlesex, PA. In 1912 he founded A M Landon & Co to produce oil, and had become a millionaire by 1929. He was Republican Governor of Kansas (1933–7), and lost the 1936 presidential election.

Landor, Walter Savage (1775–1864) Writer, born in Warwick, Warwickshire. He wrote poems, plays, and essays, but his best-known work is the prose dialogue *Imaginary Conversations* (1824–9).

Landowska, Wanda (Louise) [landofska] (1877–1959) Harpsichordist and music teacher, born in Warsaw. A prominent concert pianist in Europe, she also composed and wrote prolifically, her best-known work being *La Musique ancienne* (1908).

Landseer, Sir Edwin (Henry) (1802–73) Artist, born in London. Dogs and deer were his main subjects, often with the Highlands of Scotland as a backdrop, as in 'Monarch of the Glen' (1851). He modelled the four bronze lions at the foot of Nelson's Monument in Trafalgar Square (1867).

Landsteiner, Karl [landstiyner] (1868–1943) Pathologist, born in Vienna. He received the 1930 Nobel Prize for Physiology or Medicine for his discovery of the human ABO blood-group system, and in 1940 he also discovered the Rhesus (Rh) system.

Lane, Sir Allen, originally **Allen Lane Williams** (1902–70) Publisher, born in Bristol, Avon. In 1935 he formed Penguin Books Ltd, where he began by reprinting novels in paper covers, a revolutionary step in the publishing trade.

Lane (of St Ippollitts), Geoffrey Dawson Lane, Baron (1918–) British judge. In 1980 he was appointed Lord Chief Justice of England, in which capacity he proved to be a vigorous leader of the courts.

Lane, Richard James (1800–82) British engraver. An associate engraver of the Royal Academy (1827), he turned to lithography, reproducing works by prominent artists.

Lanfranc [lanfrangk] (c.1005–89) Clergyman, born in Pavia, Italy. A Benedictine monk at Bec, in 1062 William made him prior of St Stephen's Abbey at Caen, and in 1070 Archbishop of Canterbury.

Lanfranco, Giovanni [lanfrangkoh], known as **Giovanni di Steffano** or **il Cavaliere Giovanni Lanfranchi** (1582–1647) Religious painter, born in Parma, Italy. The best of his work can be seen on the dome of San Andrea della Valle in Rome, and in his paintings for the cathedral at Naples, where he worked from 1633 to 1646.

Lang (of Lambeth), (William) Cosmo Gordon Lang, Baron (1864–1945) Anglican clergyman, born in Fyvie, Grampian. He was Archbishop of York (1908), and Archbishop of Canterbury (1928), and became counsellor and friend to George VI.

Lang, Fritz (1890–1976) Film director, born in Vienna. His films include *Dr Mabuse, the Gambler* (trans, 1922), the futuristic *Metropolis* (1926), *Fury* (1936), and *The Big Heat* (1953).

Lang, John Dunmore (1799–1878) Australian politician and clergyman, born in Greenock, Strathclyde. He went to New South Wales in 1823 with a mission to establish Presbyterianism in the new colony.

Langdon, Harry (Philmore) (1884–1944) Comedian, born in Council Bluffs, IA. He appeared in several popular feature films, such as *The Strong Man* (1926) and *Long Pants* (1927), and is remembered for his character as a baby-faced innocent, bemused by the wider world.

Lange, David (Russell) [longee] (1942–) New Zealand prime minister (1984–9), born in Otahuhu, Auckland, New Zealand. Leader of the Labour Party (1983), he became New Zealand's youngest prime minister of the 20th-c.

Lange, Dorothea [lang], originally **Dorothea Nutzhorn** (1895–1965) Photographer, born in Hoboken, NJ. She is best known for her social records of migrant workers, share-croppers, and tenant farmers in the depression years from 1935, notably her study 'Migrant Mother' (1936).

Langer, Susanne K(nauth) [languh] (1895–1985) Philosopher and educator, born in New York City. She published important works in aesthetics, often with reference to language, such as *Problems of Art* (1957) and *Mind: An Essay on Human Feeling* (3 vols, 1967–82).

Langevin, Paul [lãzhvĩ] (1872–1946) French physicist. He was noted for his work on the molecular structure of gases, and for his theory of magnetism. He invented sonar for submarine detection during World War I.

Langland, William, also spelled **Langley** (c.1332–c.1400) Poet, probably born in Ledbury, Herefordshire. He is credited with the authorship of the great mediaeval alliterative poem on the theme of spiritual pilgrimage, *Piers Plowman*.

Langley, John Newport (1852–1925) British physiologist. Professor at Cambridge from 1903, he was noted for his research on the sympathetic nervous system.

Langley, Samuel Pierpont (1834–1906) Astronomer and aeronautical pioneer, born in Roxbury, MA. He invented the bolometer for measuring the Sun's radiant heat, and was the first to build a heavier-than-air flying machine - a steam-powered model aircraft.

Langmuir, Irving [langmyoor] (1881–1957) Physical chemist, born in New York City. He received the Nobel Prize for Chemistry in 1932 for his work on solid and liquid surfaces. His many inventions include the gas-filled tungsten lamp and atomic hydrogen welding.

Langton, Stephen (c.1150–1228) Theologian, probably born in Lincolnshire. He became a cardinal (1206), and

Archbishop of Canterbury (1207), siding warmly with the barons against King John, and his name is the first of the subscribing witnesses of Magna Carta.

Langtry, Lillie, popular name of **Emilie Charlotte Langtry**, *née* **Le Breton**, nickname **the Jersey Lily** (1853–1929) Actress, born in Jersey, Channel Is. One of the most noted beauties of her time, she was the first society woman to appear on stage. She became the mistress of the Prince of Wales, later Edward VII.

Lanier, Sidney [laneer] (1842–81) Poet, born in Macon, GA. He believed in a scientific approach towards poetry-writing, breaking away from traditional metrical techniques, illustrated in such poems as 'Corn' (1875) and 'The Symphony' (1875).

Lankester, Sir Edwin Ray (1847–1929) Zoologist, born in London. He carried out important work in embryology and protozoology, and became president of the Marine Biological Association in 1892.

Lansbury, Angela (Brigid) (1925–) Actress, born in London. Her many films include *Gaslight* (1944) and *The Manchurian Candidate* (1963), both of which received Oscar nominations. She also achieved success in the long-running TV mystery series *Murder She Wrote* (1984–).

Lansbury, George (1859–1940) British politician, born near Lowestoft, Suffolk. Active as a radical, he became a Labour MP in 1910, resigning in 1912 to stand in support of women's suffrage. He founded and edited the *Daily Herald* (1912–22), and was leader of the Labour Party (1931–5).

Lansdowne, Henry Petty-Fitzmaurice, 3rd Marquess of, also known as **Earl of Shelburne** (1780–1863) British statesman. He became Chancellor of the Exchequer, and in 1832 helped to pass the Reform Bill. In 1852 he was requested to form an administration but declined, serving without office in the Aberdeen coalition. >> Aberdeen

Lansing, Robert (1864–1928) US statesman and lawyer, born in Watertown, NY. An authority on international law, he became counsellor for the Department of State in 1914, and was appointed secretary of state in 1915.

Lanston, Tolbert (1844–1913) Inventor, born in Troy, OH. In 1887 he patented the Monotype, a type-forming and composing machine, which revolutionized printing processes.

Lantz, Walter (1900–94) Cartoonist and film animator, born in New Rochelle, NY. He went to Hollywood, where he took over *Oswald the Lucky Rabbit* (1928), and remained with Universal Pictures for over 50 years, creating many characters, notably *Woody Woodpecker*.

Lanza, Mario, originally **Alfredo Arnold Cocozza** (1921–59) Tenor, born in Philadelphia, PA. Discovered while working in the family's grocery business, he went on to Hollywood to appear in several musicals, including his most famous role in *The Great Caruso* (1951).

Lao She [lau shoe], also known as **Shu Ching-chün** (1899–1966) Writer, born in Beijing. His major novel, *Rickshaw Boy* (1937), was filmed in 1984 and serialized on Chinese television.

Lao-tzu >> Laozi

Laozi [lautsee], also spelled **Lao-tzu** or **Lao-tse** ('Old Master') (?6th-c BC) The legendary founder of Chinese Taoism. Taoist tradition attributes their classic text, the *Tao Te Ching* to Laozi, but it was written in the 3rd-c BC. By the 2nd-c AD, Taoists claimed he had lived more than once and had travelled to India, where he became the Buddha.

La Pérouse, Jean François de Galaup, comte de (Count of) [la payrooz] (1741–88) Navigator, born near Albi, France. In 1785 he commanded an expedition of discovery and visited the NW coast of America, explored the NE coasts of Asia, and sailed through *La Pérouse Strait* between Sakhalin and Yezo.

Laplace, Pierre Simon, Marquis de [laplas], also known as **Comte de** (Count of) **Laplace** (1749–1827) Mathematician and astronomer, born in Beaumont-en-Auge, France. His *Celestial Mechanics* (5 vols, trans 1799–1825), is a landmark in applied mathematics. He formulated the fundamental differential equation in physics which now bears his name.

Lapworth, Arthur (1872–1941) Chemist, born in Galashiels, Borders, Scotland. He worked on an electronic theory of organic chemical reactions, and classified reagents by charge type, suggesting the existence of alternating electrical polarity along a chain of atoms.

Lapworth, Charles (1842–1920) Geologist, born in Faringdon, Berkshire. He did important work on the geology of S Scotland and the NW Highlands, wrote on graptolites, and introduced the term *Ordovician*.

Lara, Brian (1969–) Cricketer, born in Trinidad, West Indies. In 1994 he broke several cricketing records, including a world record Test innings of 375 for the West Indies against England.

La Ramée, Marie Louise de >> **Ouida**

Lardner, Dionysius (1793–1859) Scientific writer, born in Dublin. He is best known as the originator and editor of *Lardner's Cabinet Cyclopaedia* (133 vols, 1829–49).

Lardner, Ring(gold Wilmer) (1885–1933) Writer, born in Niles, MI. He wrote prolifically in a variety of forms - as novels, plays, satirical verse (*Bib Ballads*, 1915), and an autobiography, *The Story of a Wonder Man* (1927), but is mainly appreciated for his short stories.

Larionov, Mikhail Fyodorovich [larionof] (1881–1964) Painter and stage designer, born in Tiraspol, Ukraine. With his future wife, Natalia Goncharova, he developed Rayonism (1912–14), a style akin to Italian Futurism. From 1915 they were renowned for their work on ballet designs for Diaghilev. >> Diaghilev; Goncharova

Larivey, Pierre [larivay] (c.1550–1619) Playwright, born in Champagne, France. He introduced Italian-style comedy to the French stage with his licentious *Comédies facétieuses* (2 vols, 1579, 1611).

Larkin, Philip (Arthur) (1922–85) Poet, librarian, and jazz critic, born in Coventry, Warwickshire. *Collected Poems* was published posthumously (1988) and became a best seller, as did his *Letters* (1992). He also edited the *Oxford Book of Twentieth Century English Verse* (1973).

Laroche, Guy [larosh] (1923–89) Fashion designer, born in La Rochelle, France. In 1957 he started his own business, and by 1961 was producing both couture and ready-to-wear clothes, achieving a reputation for skilful cutting.

La Rochefoucauld, François, duc de (Duke of) [la roshfookoh] (1613–80) Classical writer, born in Paris. He was an active member of the opposition to Richelieu, and fought in the Fronde revolts (1648–53). His major works were written while in retirement: *Mémoires* (1664) and the epigrammatic collection commonly known as the *Maximes* (1665, Maxims). >> Richelieu

Larousse, Pierre (Athanase) [laroos] (1817–75) Publisher and lexicographer, born in Toucy, France. He wrote several grammars, dictionaries, and other textbooks, notably his *Great Universal Dictionary of the Nineteenth Century* (15 vols, 1865–76).

Larrieu, Daniel [laryoe] (1957–) Dancer and choreographer, born in Marseilles, France. In 1982 he formed the three-person company, Astrakan. His biggest success was the underwater modern ballet *Waterproof* (1986), performed in swimming pools to video accompaniment.

Larsen, Henning (1925–) Danish architect. His buildings include the University of Trondheim, and the 1100-seat Compton Verney opera house, near Stratford-upon-Avon, Warwickshire.

Larsson, Carl (1853–1919) Artist, born in Stockholm. The series of 26 watercolours entitled *A Home* (1894–9), won

him international renown. He also produced monumental historical paintings and illustrated many books.

Lartigue, Jacques Henri (Charles Auguste) [lah(r)-teeg] (1894–1986) Photographer, born in Curbevoie, France. His work was of everyday subjects, including experiences in World War 1 and the life of the leisured classes of the 1920s. He is noted for his collection, *Diary of a Century* (1970).

Larwood, Harold (1904–95) Cricketer, born in Nuncargate, Nottinghamshire. He played for Nottinghamshire, where he was known for the speed of his opening attack. He bowled 'bodyline' in the 1932–3 tour of Australia, when diplomatic relations between the two countries were imperilled. >> Jardine

La Salle, St Jean Baptist de (1651–1719), feast day 7 April. Educational reformer and philanthropist, born in Reims, France. He co-founded in 1684 the Brothers of the Christian Schools, known as the Christian Brothers. He was canonized in 1900.

La Salle, René Robert Cavelier, sieur de (Lord of) [la sal] (1643–87) Explorer of North America, born in Rouen, France. He settled near Montreal, and descended the Ohio and Mississippi to the sea (1682), claiming Louisiana for France and naming it after Louis XIV. >> Louis XIV

Las Casas, Bartolomé de [las kahsas], known as **the Apostle of the Indians** (1474–1566) Missionary priest, born in Seville, Spain. He sailed in the third voyage of Columbus (1502) to Hispaniola, and travelled to Cuba (1513). Appointed Bishop of Chiapa, his desire to protect the natives brought hostility from the colonists, and he returned to Spain. >> Columbus

Lasdun, Sir Denys (Louis) (1914–) Architect, born in London. His works include the University of East Anglia, Norwich (1962–8) and the National Theatre, London (1965–76).

Lashley, Karl S(pencer) (1890–1958) Psychologist, born in Davis, VA. He made valuable contributions to the study of localization of brain function.

Lasker, Emanuel (1868–1941) Chess player and mathematician, born in Berlinchen, Germany. He won the world chess championship in 1894, retaining it until 1921, when he was defeated by Capablanca. In mathematics he formulated a theorem of vector spaces which is known by his name. >> Capablanca

Lasker, Mary, *née* **Woodward** (1900–) Philanthropist, born in Watertown, WI. In 1942 she and husband **Albert** (1880–1958) founded the Albert and Mary Lasker Foundation, which has influenced and supported medical research and public health initiatives.

Laski, Harold J(oseph) (1893–1950) Political scientist and socialist, born in Manchester. His political philosophy was a modified Marxism which he expounded in many books, including *A Grammar of Politics* (1925) and *The American Presidency* (1940). >> Laski, Marghanita

Laski, Marghanita (1915–88) Writer and critic, born in Manchester, the niece of Harold Laski. Her first novel, *Love on the Supertax*, appeared in 1944, and she published a number of critical works.

Laslett, (Thomas) Peter (Ruffell) (1915–) British historian. He is best known for his book *The World We Have Lost* (1965), and for discovering the lost library of John Locke. >> Locke, John

Lassalle, Ferdinand [lasal] (1825–64) Social Democrat, born in Breslau, Prussia (now Wroclaw, Poland). He took part in the revolution of 1848, and later founded the Universal German Working-Men's Association (the forerunner of the Social Democratic Party) to agitate for universal suffrage.

Lassell, William (1799–1880) Astronomer, born in Bolton, Lancashire. He discovered several planetary satellites, including Triton (1846), Hyperion (1848), Ariel, and Umbriel (both 1851).

Lassus, Orlandus, also known as **Orlando di Lasso**

(c.1532–94) Musician and composer, born in Mons, Belgium. He wrote over 2000 compositions, secular pieces as well as church music, his best-known work being *Psalmi Davidis poenitentiales* (1584).

Latham, Sir John Greig [laytham] (1877–1964) Australian statesman and judge, born in Melbourne, Victoria, Australia. From 1922 he became attorney general of the Commonwealth, Leader of the Opposition, deputy prime minister (1931–4), and Chief Justice of the High Court of Australia (1935–52).

Lathrop, Julia (Clifford) [laythrop] (1858–1932) Social reformer, born in Rockford, IL. She joined Jane Addams's Hull House Settlement in Chicago, and was active in promoting welfare for children and the mentally ill.

Latimer, Hugh (c.1485–1555) Protestant martyr, born in Thurcaston, Leicestershire. Twice during Henry VIII's reign he was sent to the Tower (1539, 1546), and under Mary was committed to jail (1554), found guilty of heresy, and burned at Oxford. >> Mary I

Latimer, Lewis Howard (1848–1928) Inventor and engineer, born in Chelsea, MA. In 1881 he devised a method for making a carbon filament for a light bulb, supervising the installation of electric lights in New York City, Philadelphia, Montreal, and London. >> Edison

La Tour, Georges de (1593–1652) Artist, born in Vic-sur-Seille, France. Only 14 of his paintings have been found, the best known being candle-lit religious scenes such as 'St Jerome' and 'St Joseph' (Louvre).

La Tour, Maurice Quentin de [latoor], also spelled **Latour** (1704–88) Pastellist and portrait painter, born in St Quentin, France. His best works include portraits of Madame de Pompadour, Voltaire, and Rousseau.

Latreille, Pierre André [latray] (1762–1833) Entomologist, born in Brive-la-Gaillarde, France. He is best known for his pioneering work on the classification of crustaceans, arachnids, and insects (1829).

Latrobe, Benjamin (Henry) [latrohb] (1764–1820) Architect and civil engineer, born in Fulneck, West Yorkshire. He emigrated to the USA in 1795, where he introduced the Greek Revival style and was surveyor of public buildings in Washington, DC (1803–17).

Lattimore, Owen (1900–89) Sinologist and defender of civil liberties, born in Washington, DC. He was made political adviser to Jiang Jieshi (1941–2), and became director of Pacific operations in the office of war information. >> Jiang Jieshi

Lattre de Tassigny, Jean (Marie Gabriel) de [latruh duh tasinyee] (1889–1952) French soldier, born in Mouilleron-en-Pareds, France. As commander of the French 1st Army, he took part in the Allied liberation of France (1944–5), signing the German surrender. >> Montgomery, Viscount

Latynina, Larisa Semyonovna [lateenina] (1934–) Gymnast born in Kherson, Ukraine. She competed in three Olympic Games (1956, 1960, 1964), and was the first woman athlete to win nine gold medals.

Laubach, Frank Charles [lowbak] (1884–1970) Missionary and pioneer of adult basic education, born in Benton, PA. Sent to evangelize the Moro tribespeople of the Philippines (1915), he devised a method of combating illiteracy, later used in Southern Asia, India, and Latin America.

Laud, William [lawd] (1573–1645) Clergyman, born in Reading, Berkshire. He became Archbishop of Canterbury in 1633, and worked for uniformity in Church and state. In Scotland, his attempt (1635–7) to anglicize the Church led to the Bishops' Wars. In 1640 the Long Parliament impeached him, and he was executed. >> Strafford

Lauda, Niki [lowda], popular name of **Nikolas Andreas Lauda** (1949–) Motor-racing driver, born in Vienna. He was three times world champion, in 1975, 1977 (both Ferrari), and 1984 (Marlboro–McLaren), despite a horrific crash in 1976. He retired in 1985 after 25 career wins.

Lauder, Estée [lawder], *née* **Mentzer** (c.1910–) Businesswoman, born in New York City. She co-founded Estée Lauder Inc with her husband Joseph Lauder in 1946, and had great success with the fragrance 'Youth Dew' in the 1950s.

Lauder, Sir Harry (MacLennan) [lawder] (1870–1950) Comic singer, born in Edinburgh. He made his name as a singer of Scots songs, many of which he wrote himself, such as 'Roamin' in the Gloamin'.

Lauder, William [lawder] (c.1680–1771) Scottish scholar and charlatan. In 1747 he sought to prove by blatant forgeries that Milton's *Paradise Lost* plagiarized various 17th-c poets writing in Latin. He was exposed in 1750.

Lauderdale, John Maitland, Duke of [lawderdayl] (1616–82) Scottish statesman, born in Lethington, Lothian. A supporter of the Covenanters (1638), he was imprisoned in 1651 for nine years. At the Restoration (1660), he became Scottish secretary of state, and was a member of the Cabal ministry.

Laue, Max (Theordor Felix) von [lowuh] (1879–1960) Physicist, born near Koblenz, Germany. He worked on X-ray diffraction in crystals, leading to the use of X-rays to study the atomic structure of matter, and was awarded the Nobel Prize for Physics in 1914.

Laughton, Charles [lawtn] (1899–1962) Film and stage actor, born in Scarborough, North Yorkshire. Among his memorable films are *The Private Life of Henry VIII* (1932, Oscar), *The Barretts of Wimpole Street* (1934), *Mutiny on the Bounty* (1935), and *The Hunchback of Notre Dame* (1939).

Laurana, Luciano [lowrana] (c.1420–79) Architect, born in Dalmatia. Architect in chief at the Palazzo Ducal of Federico da Montefeltro, he is recognized as one of the leading figures of 15th-c Italian architecture.

Laurel and Hardy Comedians who formed the first Hollywood film comedy team. The 'thin one', **Stan Laurel** (1890–1965), originally **Arthur Stanley Jefferson**, was born in Ulverston, Lancashire, England, and went to the USA in 1910. The 'fat one', **Oliver Hardy** (1892–1957), was born near Atlanta, GA. They came together in 1926 and made many full-length feature films, but their best efforts are generally thought to be their early (1927–31) shorts.

Lauren, Ralph [loren], originally **Ralph Lifschitz** (1939–) Fashion designer, born in New York City. In 1967 he joined Beau Brummel Neckwear and created the Polo range for men. He is famous for his American styles, such as the 'prairie look' and 'frontier fashions'.

Laurence or **Lawrence, St**, also **Laurentius** (d.258), feast day 10 August. Christian martyr, said to have been born in Huesca, Spain. In the persecution of Valerian he was condemned to death, and the Basilica of San Lorenzo, Rome, was later built over his place of burial. >> Valerian

Laurence, (Jean) Margaret, *née* **Wemyss** (1926–87) Novelist, born in Neepawa, Manitoba, Canada. She moved to England in 1962 and wrote her famous Manawaka series including *The Stone Angel* (1964), *The Fire-Dwellers* (1969), and *The Diviners* (1974).

Laurencin, Marie [lorãsi] (1883–1956) Painter, born in Paris. Best known for her portraits of women in misty pastel colours, she also illustrated many books with watercolours and lithographs.

Laurens, Henri [lohrãs] (1885–1954) Sculptor, born in Paris. He was a leading exponent of three-dimensional Cubism, and modelled many works with a marine theme, including 'Bathing Girl' (1947).

Laurent, Auguste [lohrã] (1807–53) Chemist, born in La Folie, France. He propounded the nucleus theory of organic radicals, discovered anthracine, worked on the classification of organic compounds, and gave his name to *Laurent's acid*.

Laurier, Sir Wilfrid [loryay] (1841-1919) Canadian prime minister (1896-1911), born in St Lin, Quebec, Canada. Leader of the Liberal Party (1887-1919), he was the first French-Canadian and Roman Catholic to be prime minister of Canada.

Lauterpacht, Sir Hersch [lowterpakht] (1897-1960) Lawyer, born near Lemberg, Germany. Professor of International Law at Cambridge (1938-55), he acted for Britain in many international disputes, and became a judge of the International Court of Justice (1954-60).

Lautréamont, comte de (Count of) [lohtrayamõ], pseudonym of **Isidore Ducasse** (1846-70) Poet, born in Montevideo, Uruguay. He went to France, where he published the sequence of prose poems *The Songs of Maldoror* (trans, 1868), and became a significant influence on the Surrealists and other Modernist writers.

Laval, Pierre (1883-1945) French prime minister (1931-2, 1935-6), born in Châteldon, France. In the Vichy government he was Pétain's deputy (1940), then his rival, and as prime minister (1942-4) he collaborated with the Germans. After the war he was executed.

Laval, Carl Gustaf Patrik de [laval] (1845-1913) Engineer, scientist, and inventor, born in Blasenborg, Sweden. He invented a centrifugal cream separator in 1878, and made important contributions to the development of the steam turbine (1880-95).

La Vallière, Louise-Françoise de La Baume le Blanc, duchesse de (Duchess of) [la valyair] (1644-1710) Mistress of Louis XIV, born in Tours, France. She became the king's mistress in 1661 and bore him four children. When the Marquise de Montespan superseded her, she was publicly humiliated, then compensated by being made a duchess (1667). >> Louis XIV; Montespan

Laval-Montmorency, François Xavier [laval mõmohrãsee] (1623-1708) Clergyman and missionary, born in Montigny-sur-Avre, France. He became the first Bishop of Quebec (1674-88), and in 1663 founded the seminary of Quebec, which in 1852 was named Laval University after him.

Lavater, Johann Kaspar [lavater] (1741-1801) Physiognomist, theologian, and writer, born in Zürich, Switzerland. He attempted to elevate his subject into a science in *Essays on Physiognomy* (trans, 1775-8).

Laver, James [layver] (1899-1975) Writer and art critic, born in Liverpool, Merseyside. His books include the poetry collection *His Last Sebastian* (1922), critical books on art, such as *French Painting and the 19th century* (1937), and the history of English costume, *Taste and Fashion* (1937).

Laver, Rod(ney George) [layver], nickname **the Rockhampton Rocket** (1938-) Tennis player, born in Rockhampton, Queensland, Australia. The first person to achieve the Grand Slam twice (1962, 1969), he won four singles titles at Wimbledon (1961-2, 1968-9).

Laveran, (Charles Louis) Alphonse [laverã] (1845-1922) Physician and parasitologist, born in Paris. In 1880 he discovered the blood parasite which caused malaria, and was awarded the Nobel Prize for Physiology or Medicine in 1907.

Lavigerie, Charles (Martial Allemand) [lavizheree] (1825-92) Clergyman, born in Bayonne, France. As Primate of Africa (1884) he became well known for his missionary work, and founded the Society of Missionaries of Africa, or White Fathers (1868).

Lavin, Mary (1912-) Writer, born in East Walpole, MA. She is best known for her short stories, her collections including *Tales from Bective Bridge* (1942, James Tait Black Memorial Prize) and *A Family Likeness* (1985).

Lavoisier, Antoine Laurent [lavwazyay] (1743-94) Chemist, born in Paris. In 1788 he showed that air is a mixture of gases which he called *oxygen* and *nitrogen*, and he devised the modern method of naming chemical compounds. His major work is the *Traité élémentaire de chimie* (1789). Although politically a liberal, he was guillotined on a contrived charge of counter-revolutionary activity.

Law, (Andrew) Bonar [boner law] (1858-1923) British prime minister (1922-3), born in New Brunswick, Canada. In 1911 he became Unionist leader, and acted as colonial secretary (1915-16), Chancellor of the Exchequer (1916-18), and Lord Privy Seal (1919), before serving for a short time as premier.

Law, Denis (1940-) Footballer, born in Aberdeen, Grampian. He made his international debut when only 18 years old, and later joined Manchester United, with them winning every major domestic honour.

Lawes, Henry (1596-1662) Composer, born in Dinton, Wiltshire. He set Milton's *Comus* to music, and was highly regarded by Milton, who sang his praises in a sonnet. >> Milton

Lawes, Sir John Bennet (1814-1900) Agriculturist, born in Rothamsted, Hertfordshire. Aided by his partner **Sir (Joseph) Henry Gilbert** (1817-1901), he founded the Rothamsted Experimental Station in 1843, elevating the study of agriculture to scientific levels.

Lawler, Ray(mond Evenor) (1921-) Playwright, producer, and actor, born in Melbourne, Victoria, Australia. He gained an international reputation with his play about the outback, *Summer of the Seventeenth Doll* (1956).

Lawrence, D(avid) H(erbert Richard) (1885-1930) Poet and novelist, born in Eastwood, Nottinghamshire. He achieved fame with *Sons and Lovers* (1913), but was prosecuted for obscenity after publishing *The Rainbow* (1915). Other major novels include *Women in Love* (1921), *The Plumed Serpent* (1926), and *Lady Chatterley's Lover* (1928). He wrote many short stories, short novels, and travel books, and is also known for his letters.

Lawrence, Ernest (Orlando) (1901-58) Physicist, born in Canton, SD. In 1929 he constructed the first cyclotron for the production of artificial radioactivity, and was awarded the Nobel Prize for Physics in 1939.

Lawrence, Geoffrey, 3rd Baron Trevithin and **1st Baron Oaksey** (1880-1971) British lawyer. He became a judge of the High Court of Justice (1932), a Lord Justice of Appeal (1944), and a Lord of Appeal in Ordinary (1947-57). He was president of the International Tribunal for the trial of war criminals at Nuremberg in 1945.

Lawrence, Jacob (1917-) Painter, born in Atlantic City, NJ. A leading African-American artist he is famous for the distinctive flat surfaces of his narrative paintings depicting social problems, as in 'The Migration of the Negro' (1940-1).

Lawrence, James (1781-1813) Naval officer, born in Burlington, NJ. In the Tripolitan War he won a notable victory over the British ship HMS *Peacock* in 1813, but was defeated and mortally wounded in the HMS *Shannon*-USS *Chesapeake* duel the same year.

Lawrence, Marjorie Florence (1908-79) Operatic soprano, born in Deans Marsh, Victoria, Australia. She became a leading Wagnerian soprano at the Metropolitan Opera, New York City (1935-9). In 1941 she contracted poliomyelitis, and subsequently made guest appearances in a wheelchair.

Lawrence, T(homas) E(dward), known as **Lawrence of Arabia** (1888-1935) British soldier and writer, born in Tremadoc, Gwynedd. In 1916 he was appointed British liaison officer to the Arab Revolt, and was present at the taking of Aqaba (1917) and Damascus (1918). His account of the Arab Revolt, *Seven Pillars of Wisdom*, became one of the classics of war literature, and his exploits received so much publicity that he became a legendary figure.

Lawrence, Sir Thomas (1769-1830) Portrait painter, born in Bristol, Avon. His full-length portrait of Queen

Charlotte, painted at the age of 20, is one of his best works.

Lawrence of Arabia >> **Lawrence, T E**

Lawrence, St >> **Laurence, St**

Lawry, Bill [loree], popular name of **William Morris Lawry** (1936–) Cricketer, born in Melbourne, Victoria, Australia. A left-handed batsman and captain, he played 67 times for Australia, scoring 5234 runs, and recording 13 centuries.

Lawson, Henry (1867–1922) Poet, born in Grenfell, New South Wales, Australia, the son of Louisa Lawson. His bush ballads and stories, published by *The Bulletin* from 1888, were immensely popular, and many see him as the national poet. >> Lawson, Louisa

Lawson, Louisa (1848–1920) Suffragist and social reformer, born in Mudgee, New South Wales, Australia. In 1888 she founded *Dawn*, Australia's first feminist journal, which elevated women's affairs and promoted women's suffrage. >> Lawson, Henry

Lawson (of Blaby), Nigel, Baron (1932–) British Conservative statesman, born in London. He served as financial secretary to the Treasury (1979–81), energy secretary (1981-3), and Chancellor of the Exchequer (1983-9).

Lawton, Tommy (1919–) Footballer, born in Bolton, Lancashire. A successful English centre-forward, his most famous days were with Everton and Arsenal. His international record was a remarkable 22 goals in 23 matches.

Laxness, Halldór (Guðjónsson Kiljan) (1902–) Novelist, born in Reykjavík. His major works include *Salka Valka* (1934), a story of Icelandic fishing folk, and the epic *Independent People* (trans, 1934–5). He was awarded the Nobel Prize for Literature in 1955.

Layamon [layamon] (13th-c) Poet and priest, thought to have lived at Areley Kings, Worcestershire. He wrote (c.1200) an alliterative verse chronicle, *Brut*, a mythical history of England after the landing of Brutus.

Layton, Irving Peter, originally **Israel Lazarovitch** (1912–) Poet, born in Romania. His collections include *Here and Now* (1945) and *A Red Carpet for the Sun* (1959).

Lazarsfeld, Paul (Felix) [lahzersfelt] (1901–76) Sociologist, born in Vienna. An influential quantitative methodologist, he also wrote about popular culture in mass communications.

Lazarus, Emma (1849–87) Writer, born in New York City. She is best known for her sonnet, 'The New Colossus' (1883), inscribed in a room in the base of the Statue of Liberty in New York harbour.

LBJ >> **Johnson, Lyndon B**

Leach, Archibald >> **Grant, Cary**

Leach, Bernard (Howell) (1887–1979) Studio potter, born in Hong Kong. With Hamada he established the Leach pottery at St Ives in Cornwall, where he made earthenware and stoneware, and played a crucial role in promoting handmade pottery which could be appreciated as art. >> Hamada

Leach, Sir Edmund (Ronald) (1910–89) Social anthropologist, born in Sidmouth, Devon. His works include *Political Systems of Highland Burma* (1954), *Rethinking Anthropology* (1961), and *Social Anthropology* (1982).

Leach, Johnny, popular name of **John Leach** (1922–) Table tennis player, born in Romford, Essex. He won the world singles title in 1949 and 1951, and represented his country 152 times.

Leacock, Stephen (Butler) (1869–1944) Writer and humorist, born in Swanmore, Hampshire. In Canada from 1875, his popular works include *Literary Lapses* (1910), *Winsome Winnie* (1920), and *The Garden of Folly* (1924).

Leadbelly, nickname of **Huddie Ledbetter** (c.1885–1949) Folk-blues musician, born in Mooringsport, LA. A wandering musician in the US South, his songs highlighted the

plight of African-Americans during the Depression, and several became standards, notably 'Goodnight, Irene'.

Leahy, William (Daniel) [layhee] (1875–1959) US naval officer and public official, born in Hampton, IA. He was chief of naval operations (1937–9), ambassador to Vichy, France (1940–42), and chief-of-staff to Roosevelt (1942–5) and Truman (1945–9). >> Roosevelt, Franklin D

Leakey, L(ouis) S(eymour) B(azett) [leekee] (1903–72) Archaeologist and physical anthropologist, born in Kabete, Kenya. His great discoveries took place in East Africa, where he found remains of *Zinjanthropus* (1959), *Homo habilis* (1964), and *Kenyapithecus africanus* (1967). >> Leakey, Mary / Richard

Leakey, Mary (Douglas) [leekee], *née* **Nicol** (1913–) Archaeologist, born in London. She married L S B Leakey and moved to Kenya, where she undertook archaeological research (1937–42), discovering *Proconsul africanus* (1948) and several other remains with her husband. >> Leakey, L S B / Richard

Leakey, Richard (Erskine Frere) [leekee] (1944–) Palaeoanthropologist, born in Nairobi, the second son of L S B and Mary Leakey. Working with the archaeologist Glynn Isaac on the E shores of L Turkana (1969–75), he discovered crania of *Australopithecus boisei* (1969), *Homo habilis* (1972), and *Homo erectus* (1975).

Lean, Sir David (1908–91) Film director, born in Croydon, Greater London. His films include *Brief Encounter* (1945), *Bridge on the River Kwai* (1957, Oscar), *Lawrence of Arabia* (1962, Oscar), *Dr Zhivago* (1965), and *A Passage to India* (1984).

Lear, Edward (1812–88) Artist and writer, born in London. He is remembered for his illustrated books of travels, and for his books of nonsense verse, illustrated by his own sketches, beginning with *A Book of Nonsense* (1846).

Lear, William P(owell) (1902–78) Inventor and electronic engineer, born in Hannibal, MO. His numerous patents included the first car radio, the first commercial radio compass for aircraft, and an automatic pilot for jet aircraft. In 1962 he founded Lear Jet Corporation.

Leavis, F(rank) R(aymond) [leevis] (1895–1978) Literary critic, born in Cambridge, Cambridgeshire. He edited the journal *Scrutiny* (1932–53), and wrote several major critical works, notably *New Bearings in English Poetry* (1932), *The Great Tradition* (1948), and *The Common Pursuit* (1952). Throughout his work, much of it shared with his wife **Queenie Dorothy Leavis** (1906–91), he stresses the moral value of literary study.

Leavitt, Henrietta Swan (1868–1921) Astronomer, born in Lancaster, MA. Her major work was the discovery of the period–luminosity relationship of Cepheid variable stars (1912), important in establishing the distance scale of the universe.

Le Bel, Joseph Achille [luh bel] (1847–1930) Chemist, born in Pechelbronn, France. In 1874 he published his account of the asymmetric carbon atom, two months after Jacobus van't Hoff's identical but independent work was published. >> Hoff

Lebesgue, Henri (Léon) [luhbeg] (1875–1941) Mathematician, born in Beauvais, France. He developed the theory of measure and integration which bears his name, and applied it to many problems of analysis, in particular to the theory of Fourier series. >> Fourier, Joseph

Leblanc, Nicolas [luhblã] (1742–1806) Chemist and physician, born in Issoudun, France. He devised a simple process for producing sodium carbonate, essential in making glass, soap, and other chemicals (1791).

Lebow, Fred (1932–94) US marathon runner and organizer, born in Romania. He emigrated to the USA in 1951, where he turned the New York Marathon into a major event and the prototype for other city marathons.

Lebrun, Albert [luhbroë] (1871–1950) French statesman,

born in Mercy-le-Haut, France. The last president of the Third Republic, he surrendered his powers to Pétain in 1940, and retired. >> Pétain

Le Brun, Charles [luh broë] (1619–90) Painter and designer, born in Paris. The founder of the French school of painting, he helped to found the Academy of Painting and Sculpture (1648), and was employed by Louis XIV in the decoration of Versailles (1668–83).

Le Carré, John [luh karay], pseudonym of **David John Moore Cornwell** (1931–) Novelist, born in Poole, Dorset. His first published novel, *Call for the Dead* (1961), introduced his 'anti-hero' George Smiley, Other works include *Tinker, Tailor, Soldier, Spy* (1974), *Smiley's People* (1980), and *The Russia House* (1989). Many of his novels have been filmed or televised.

Le Chatelier, Henry >> **Chatelier, Henry le**

Lecky, William Edward Hartpole (1838–1903) Historian, philosopher and politician, born in Newton Park, near Dublin. His works include *The Leaders of Public Opinion in Ireland* (1861), *History of England in the 18th Century* (1878–90), and *The Map of Life* (1899).

Leclanché, Georges [luhklãshay] (1839–82) Chemist, born in Paris. He invented the *Leclanché battery* (1866), now in a slightly modified form known as a *dry-cell battery*.

Le Clerc, Jacques-Philippe [luh klairk], also known as **Philippe-Marie, viscomte de Hauteclocque** or **Jacques-Philippe Leclerc de Hauteclocque** (1902–47) French general, born in Belloy-Saint-Leonard, France. Captured twice during the German invasion, he escaped both times, and joined the Free French forces in England. He commanded the French 2nd Armoured Division in Normandy, and liberated Paris in 1944.

Leconte de Lisle, Charles Marie René [luhkõt duh leel] (1818–94) French poet, born on Réunion. He headed the school called *Parnassiens*, and his works include *Poésies complètes* (1858), and *Poèmes tragiques* (1884).

Lecoq, Jacques [luhkok] (1921–) Mime artist and director, born in Paris. In 1956 he established the Ecole Internationale de Mime et de Théâtre in Paris, and formed his own company in 1959.

Le Corbusier [luh kaw(r)büsyay], pseudonym of **Charles Edouard Jeanneret** (1887–1965) Architect and artist, born in La Chaux-de-Fonds, Switzerland. Settling in Paris in 1917, he met Ozenfant, who introduced him to Purism. His main interest was large urban projects and city-planning, and examples of his work are the *Unité d'habitation* ('Living unit'), Marseille (1945–50) and Chandigarh, the new capital of the Punjab. >> Ozenfant

Ledbetter, Huddie >> **Leadbelly**

Lederberg, Joshua [layderberg] (1925–) Biologist and geneticist, born in Montclair, NJ. With Tatum he demonstrated that bacteria can reproduce by a sexual process, thus founding the science of bacterial genetics. He shared the Nobel Prize for Physiology or Medicine in 1958. >> Beadle; Tatum, Edward L

Lederman, Leon M(ax) [layderman] (1922–) Physicist, born in New York City. He shared the 1988 Nobel Prize for the discovery (1960–2) of a new subatomic particle, the muon neutrino. >> Steinberger

Ledoux, Claude Nicolas [luhdoo] (1736–1806) Architect, born in Dormans-sur-Marne, France. As architect to Louis XVI, his major works include the Château at Louveciennes for Madame du Barry (1771–3) and the Salt-works at Arc-et-Senans (1775–80). >> du Barry

Le Duc Tho [lay duhk toh], originally **Phan Dinh Khai** (1911–90) Vietnamese politician, born in Ninh Province, Vietnam. For his actions as leader of the Vietnamese delegation to the Paris Conference on Indo-China (1968–73), he was awarded the 1973 Nobel Prize for Peace jointly with Kissinger, but declined to accept it. >> Kissinger

Lee, Andrew >> **Auchinloss, Louis Stanton**

Lee, Ann, known as **Mother Ann** (1736–84) Religious mystic, born in Manchester. In 1758 she joined the 'Shaking Quakers', or 'Shakers', who saw in her the second coming of Christ. She emigrated with her followers to the USA in 1774, and in 1776 founded the parent Shaker settlement.

Lee, Charles (1731–82) American revolutionary soldier, born in Dernhall, Cheshire. He went to America in 1773, and fought in the War of Independence. Captured by the British, he was released in an exchange of prisoners in 1778.

Lee, Gypsy Rose, originally **Louise Rose Hovick** (1914–70) Stripper, actress, and writer, born in Seattle, WA. The best-known stripper of the 1930s, she made some films, and wrote two mystery stories, as well as an autobiography that was the basis of the musical, *Gypsy*.

Lee, James (Paris) (1831–1904) Inventor, born in Hawick, Borders, Scotland. He emigrated with his parents to Canada, later settling in Hartford, CT. The *Lee-Enfield* and *Lee-Metford* rifles are based in part on his designs. >> Metford

Lee (of Ashridge), Jennie Lee, Baroness (1904–88) British stateswoman, born in Lochgelly, Fife. A dedicated socialist, she became the youngest elected woman MP (1929–31), and married Aneurin Bevan in 1934. Re-elected to parliament in 1945, as minister for the arts (1967–70), she established the Open University. >> Bevan, Aneurin

Lee, Laurie (1914–) Writer, born in Slad, Gloucestershire. His autobiographical books *Cider With Rosie* (1959), *As I Walked Out One Midsummer Morning* (1969), and *I Can't Stay Long* (1975) are widely acclaimed for their evocation of a rural childhood and of life in the many countries he has visited.

Lee, Ming Cho (1930–) Set designer and water colourist, born in Shanghai, China. From 1958 he made a name for himself with his imaginative sets for productions on and off Broadway, as well as in opera and dance.

Lee, Nathaniel (c.1649–92) English playwright. His best-known play is *The Rival Queens* (1677), and with Dryden he wrote *Oedipus* (1678), and *The Duke of Guise* (1682). >> Dryden

Lee, Robert E(dward) (1807–70) Confederate general, born in Stratford, VA. He was in charge of the defences at Richmond, and defeated Federal forces in the Seven Days' Battles (1862). His strategy in opposing General Pope, his invasion of Maryland and Pennsylvania, and other achievements are central to the history of the Civil War. >> Pope, John

Lee, Spike, popular name of **Shelton Jackson Lee** (1957–) Film-maker, born in Atlanta, GA. *She's Gotta Have It* (1986) established him internationally. Later films, centred around African-American culture, include *School Daze* (1988) and *Mo' Better Blues* (1990).

Lee, Tsung Dao (1926–) Physicist, born in Shanghai, China. With Yang he disproved the parity principle, till then considered a fundamental physical law, and they shared the Nobel Prize for Physics in 1957. >> Yang, Chen Ning

Lee, Vernon, pseudonym of **Violet Paget** (1856–1935) Writer, born in Boulogne, France. She wrote over 30 books, including *Miss Brown* (3 vols, 1884) and a dramatic trilogy, *Satan the Waster* (1920), which gives full rein to her pacifism.

Leech, John (1817–64) Caricaturist, born in London. From 1841 he contributed sketches of middle-class life and political cartoons to *Punch* and the *Illustrated London News* (1856). He illustrated several books, including Dickens's *A Christmas Carol*.

Leeds, Thomas Osborne, Duke of, also known as **Earl of Danby** (1632–1712) English statesman, the son of a Yorkshire baronet. He used his influence to secure the marriage of Princess Mary and William of Orange (1677), and in 1688 signed the invitation to William to seize power from James II. >> William III

Lee Kuan Yew [lee kwan yoo] (1923–   ) Singaporean prime minister (1959–90), born in Singapore City. He remained in power for 31 years, overseeing a successful programme of economic development.

Leese, Sir Oliver (William Hargreaves) (1894–1978) British soldier. In 1942 he commanded an army corps from El Alamein to Sicily, where he succeeded Montgomery as commander of the Eighth Army, and in 1944 commanded an army group in Burma.

Lee Teng-hui [lee teng wee] (1923–   ) Taiwanese president (1988–   ), born in Tamsui, Taiwan. A member of the ruling Kuomintang party, he became vice-president of Taiwan in 1984, and state president on Jiang Jingguo's death. >> Jiang Jingguo

Leeuwenhoek, Antonie van [layvenhook] (1632–1723) Microscopist, born in Delft, The Netherlands. He made a series of discoveries in relation to the circulation of the blood, and was the first to observe bacteria, protozoa, and spermatozoa.

Lefanu, Nicola >> **Maconchy, Elizabeth**

Le Fanu, (Joseph) Sheridan [lefuhnyoo] (1814–73) Writer and journalist, born in Dublin. His best-known novels are *The House by the Churchyard* (1863) and *Uncle Silas* (1864), and he also wrote short stories, mainly of the supernatural.

Lefebvre, Marcel [luhfairbruh] (1905–91) Leader of a 'traditionalist' schismatic group within the Roman Catholic Church, born in Tourcoing, France. In 1970, objecting to the modernized form of the Catholic liturgy, he formed the 'Priestly Cofraternity of Pius X', and was excommunicated in 1988.

Lefrak, Samuel J(ayson) [lefrak] (1918–   ) Real estate developer, born in New York City. He joined his father's Brooklyn construction firm, expanding the Lefrak Organization through major housing, industrial, and commercial developments.

Lefschetz, Solomon [lefshets] (1884–1972) Mathematician, born in Moscow. He emigrated to the USA, where he became the leading topologist of his generation.

Le Gallienne, Eva [luh galyuhn] (1899–1991) Stage actress, born in London, the daughter of Richard Le Gallienne. She founded the Civic Repertory Theater in New York City (1926–32), and later the American Repertory Theater Company. >> Le Gallienne, Richard

Le Gallienne, Richard [luh galyuhn] (1866–1947) Writer, born in Liverpool, the father of Eva Le Gallienne. He published many volumes of prose and verse, including *Quest of the Golden Girl* (1896) and *From a Paris Garret* (1936). >> Le Gallienne, Eva

Legat, Nicolay (1869–1937) Dancer, ballet master, and choreographer, born in St Petersburg, Russia. He was principal dancer with the Maryinsky Theatre for 20 years, and became director there in 1905. In 1923 he moved to the USA to become ballet master of Diaghilev's company, and later established his own school in London. >> Diaghilev

Legendre, Adrien-Marie [luhzhãdr] (1752–1833) Mathematician, born in Paris. He made major contributions to number theory and elliptical functions, but due to the jealousy of his colleague Laplace, he received little recognition for his work. >> Laplace

Léger, Fernand [layzhay] (1881–1955) Painter, born in Argentan, France. He helped to form the Cubist movement, but later developed his own 'aesthetic of the machine' as seen in 'Contrast of Forms' (1913).

Legge, Walter (1906–79) Record producer, born in London. He was a major figure in the European classical record industry, and founder of the Philharmonia Symphony Orchestra.

Legros, Alphonse [luhgroh] (1837–1911) Painter, born in Dijon, France. He produced over 750 etchings, and was noted for his original portraiture, and for his landscape and figure studies.

Le Guin, Ursula [luh gween], *née* **Kroeber** (1929–   ) Science fiction writer, born in Berkeley, CA. Her books include the 'Hain' novels, such as *The Left Hand of Darkness* (1969), and her 'Earth Sea' trilogy: *A Wizard of Earthsea* (1968), *The Tombs of Atuan* (1971), and *The Farthest Shore* (1972).

Lehár, Franz [luhhah(r)] (1870–1948) Composer, born in Komárom, Hungary. He is best known for his operettas, including the internationally acclaimed *The Merry Widow* (1905).

Lehman, Adele Lewisohn [layman] (1882–1965) Philanthropist, art collector, and painter, born in New York City. She married Arthur Lehman in 1901, and became active in the Federation of Jewish Philanthropies, of which he was a founder.

Lehman, Herbert (Henry) [layman] (1878–1963) Banker, politician, and philanthropist, born in New York City. A Democrat in the US Senate (1949–57), he was outspoken in his opposition to McCarthyism and in support of civil rights. >> McCarthy, Joseph R

Lehman, Robert [layman] (1891–1969) Banker and art collector, born in New York City. He joined the family banking business, Lehman Brothers (1919), and became principal partner (1921–64). His art collection was donated to the Metropolitan Museum of Art in 1969.

Lehmann, Beatrix [layman] (1903–79) Actress, born in Bourne End, Buckinghamshire, the sister of John and Rosamond Lehmann. In 1946 she became director-producer of the Arts Council Midland Theatre Company. >> Lehmann, John Frederick / Rosamond

Lehmann, John (Frederick) [layman] (1907–87) Writer and publisher, born in Bourne End, Buckinghamshire. With his sister, Rosamond, he ran John Lehmann Ltd (1946–53), and in 1954 inaugurated the *London Magazine*, which he edited until 1961. >> Lehmann, Beatrix / Rosamond

Lehmann, Lilli [layman] (1848–1929) Soprano, born in Würzburg, Germany. She took part in the first performance of Wagner's *Ring* cycle (1876) at Bayreuth.

Lehmann, Lotte [layman] (1888–1976) Soprano, born in Perleberg, Germany. She was noted particularly for her performances in operas by Richard Strauss, including two premieres. >> Strauss, Richard

Lehmann, Rosamond (Nina) [layman] (1901–90) Novelist, born in Bourne End, Buckinghamshire. Her books include *Dusty Answer* (1927), *The Echoing Grove* (1953), and *A Sea-Grape Tree* (1970). >> Lehmann, Beatrix / John

Leibl, Wilhelm [liybl] (1844–1900) Painter, born in Cologne, Germany. Most of his paintings are genre scenes of Bavaria and the lower Alps, although he painted a number of portraits, notably 'Three Women in a Church' (1878–82).

Leibniz, Gottfried Wilhelm [liybnits] (1646–1716) Philosopher and mathematician, born in Leipzig, Germany. His great influence was primarily as a mathematician, and as a pioneer of modern symbolic logic, but he also wrote on history, law, and political theory, and his philosophy was the foundation of 18th-c Rationalism.

Leicester, Robert Dudley, Earl of [lester], also known as **Baron Denbigh** and **Sir Robert Dudley** (c.1532–88) English nobleman, the favourite and possibly the lover of Elizabeth I. He continued to receive favour in spite of his unpopularity at court and two secret marriages. In 1588 he commanded the forces against the Spanish Armada. >> Elizabeth I

Leicester of Holkham, Thomas William Coke, Earl of [lester, holkam] (1752–1842) Agriculturist, born in

London. One of the first agriculturists of England, people visited his estate from all over the world. Special meetings were held at sheep clipping time (*Coke's Clippings*), the last of which took place in 1821.

Leichhardt, (Friedrich Wilhelm) Ludwig [liykhhah(r)t] (1813–c.48) Naturalist and explorer, born in Trebatsch, Germany. He led an expedition from Brisbane heading NW in 1844. Presumed lost, his arrival back in Sydney in 1846 caused great excitement. On a later expedition (1848), he and his party disappeared without trace.

Leif Eriksson [layv erikson] (fl.1000) Icelandic explorer, the son of Erik the Red, the first European to reach America. In c.1000 he discovered land which he named *Vinland*. >> Erik the Red

Leigh, Mike [lee] (1943–) Playwright and theatre director, born in Salford, Greater Manchester. He has scripted a distinctive genre based on actors' improvizations around given themes, his most successful work having a second life on film, as in *Bleak Moments* (1970), and on television, as in *Abigail's Party* (1977).

Leigh, Vivien [lee], originally **Vivian Hartley** (1913–67) Actress, born in Darjeeling, India. She married Laurence Olivier in 1940 (divorced 1961), and appeared opposite him in many classical plays. She is best-remembered for her performances in the films *Gone With the Wind* (1939, Oscar) and *A Streetcar Named Desire* (1951, Oscar).

Leigh-Mallory, Sir Trafford [lee] (1892–1944) British air force officer, born in Cheshire. He was commander-in-chief of Fighter Command (1942–4), and of Allied expeditionary air forces for the Normandy landings (1944).

Leigh-Pemberton, Robert (Robin) Leigh-Pemberton, Baron [lee **pem**berton] (1927–) Banker, born in Sittingbourne, Kent. A director then chairman (1977–83) of the National Westminster Bank, he became Governor of the Bank of England in 1983.

Leighton (of Stretton), Frederic Leighton, Baron [laytn] (1830–96) Painter, born in Scarborough, North Yorkshire. Several of his paintings became mass best sellers in photogravure reproduction, and he also won distinction as a sculptor.

Leighton, Kenneth [laytn] (1929–88) Composer and pianist, born in Wakefield, West Yorkshire. His works include choral music, piano concertos, three symphonies, organ and chamber music, and an opera, *Columba* (1981).

Leighton, Margaret [laytn] (1922–76) Actress, born in Barnt Green, West Midlands. She worked regularly in London and on Broadway. She won Tony Awards for *Separate Tables* (1956) and *The Night of the Iguana* (1962), and a BAFTA best supporting actress award for *The Go-Between* (1970).

Leighton, Robert [laytn] (1611–84) Clergyman, probably born in London. Soon after the Restoration he was made one of Charles II's new Scottish bishops, and in 1669 he became Archbishop of Glasgow. >> Charles II (of England)

Leino, Eino [leenoh], pseudonym of **Armas Eino Leopold Lönnbohm** (1878–1926) Poet, born in Paltamo, Finland. He developed the *Kalevala* metre into a distinctive style of his own, notably in *Whitsongs* (trans, 1903–16).

Leinsdorf, Erich [liynzdaw(r)f] (1912–93) Conductor, born in Vienna. He came to New York City in 1938 to conduct at the Metropolitan Opera, and was acclaimed especially for his Wagner.

Leiris, Michel [lairees] (1901–90) Writer and anthropologist, born in Paris. Combining anthropology with a career as a literary and art critic, his major works include *Phantom Africa* (trans, 1934).

Leishman, Sir William Boog [leeshman] (1865–1926)

Bacteriologist, born in Glasgow, Strathclyde. He discovered an effective vaccine for inoculation against typhoid, and was also the first to discover the parasite of the disease kala-azar. The bacterium which cause the diseases *leishmaniasis* is named after him.

Lejeune, John A(rcher) [luh**zhoon**] (1867–1942) Marine officer, born in Pointe Coupee Parish, LA. In 1914 he led the marine brigade that assisted in the capture of Vera Cruz, Mexico, and later developed amphibious tactics that were to be applied in the Pacific campaigns of World War 2.

Leland, Charles (Godfrey) [leeland], pseudonym **Hans Breitmann** (1825–1903) Writer, born in Philadelphia, PA. He gained great popularity with his poems in 'Philadelphia German', the famous *Hans Breitmann Ballads* (1871–95).

Leland, John [leeland] (c.1506–52) Antiquary, born in London. In 1533 he became 'king's antiquary', with power to search for records of antiquity throughout England. Most of his papers are in the Bodleian and British Museums, one of his chief works being *The Itinerary*.

Leloir, Luis Federico [luh**wah(r)**] (1906–) Biochemist, born in Paris. He discovered how glycogen, the energy storage material, is synthesized in the body (1957), for which he was awarded the Nobel Prize for Chemistry in 1970.

Lely, Sir Peter [leelee], originally **Pieter van der Faes** (1618–80) Painter, born in Soest, The Netherlands. In 1661 he became court painter to Charles II, and among his best works are the 13 Greenwich portraits, 'Admirals' (1666–7). >> Charles II (of England)

Lemaître, Georges (Henri) [luhmaytruh] (1894–1966) Astrophysicist, born in Charleroi, Belgium. He proposed (1927) the 'big bang' theory of the origin of the universe, later developed by Gamow and others. >> Gamow

LeMay, Curtis (Emerson) [luh**may**] (1906–) Aviator, born in Columbus, OH. In 1944 he commanded the bomber force that carried out long-range attacks on the Japanese home islands, and helped plan the atomic bomb missions of 1945.

Lemmon, Jack, popular name of **John Uhler Lemmon** (1925–) Film and stage actor, born in Boston, MA. *Some Like It Hot* (1959) began a seven-film collaboration with director Billy Wilder. Other films include *Mister Roberts* (1955, Oscar), *Save the Tiger* (1973, Oscar), and *Glengarry Glen Ross* (1992). >> Wilder, Billy

Lemon, Mark (1809–70) Writer and journalist, born in London. In 1841 he helped to establish *Punch*, becoming first joint editor (with Henry Mayhew), then sole editor from 1843. >> Mayhew

Lemonnier, Pierre Charles [luhmonyay] (1715–99) Astronomer, born in Paris. He greatly advanced astronomical measurement in France, and made 12 observations of Uranus before it came to be recognized as a planet.

le Nain, Antoine [luh nã] (c.1588–1648) Painter, born in Laon, France, the brother of **Louis** (c.1593–1648) and **Mathieu** (1607–77), who were also painters. The brothers worked in harmony, painting portraits and scenes of peasant life, signing their work simply 'Le Nain', so any individual attribution is purely speculative.

Lenard, Philipp (Eduard Anton) [laynah(r)t] (1862–1947) Physicist, born in Pressburg, Hungary. His main research concerned the properties of cathode rays, for which he was awarded the Nobel Prize for Physics in 1905.

Lenbach, Franz von [lenbakh] (1836–1904) Portrait painter, born in Schrobenhausen, Germany. One of the finest 19th-c German portraitists, his numerous portraits of Bismarck are particularly famous.

Lenclos, Ninon de [lăkloh], popular name of **Anne de Lenclos** (1620–1705) Courtesan, born in Paris. Her salon attracted the aristocracy as well as leading literary and political figures, and her lovers included the great Condé, and the Duc de La Rochefoucauld. >> Condé, Louis; La Rochefoucauld

Lendl, Ivan [lendl] (1960–) Tennis player, born in Ostrava, Czech Republic. He won the singles title at the US Open (1985–7), French Open (1984, 1986–7), and Australian Open (1989, 1990), and became the Masters champion (1986–7) and the World Championship Tennis champion (1982, 1985).

L'Enfant, Pierre Charles [lãfã] (1754–1825) Architect and city planner, born in Paris. In 1777 he moved to America, in 1791 submitting a plan for the new federal capital in the District of Columbia, which became an influential model of urban planning. >> Washington, George

Leng, Virginia (Helen Antoinette), *née* **Holgate** (1955–) Equestrian rider, born in Malta. She won the World Championship team gold in 1982 and 1986, and the individual title in 1986 on *Priceless*.

Lenglen, Suzanne [lãlã] (1899–1938) Tennis player, born in Compiègne, France. She was the woman champion of France (1920–3, 1925–6), and at Wimbledon won the women's singles and doubles (1919–23, 1925), and the mixed doubles (1920, 1922, 1925). In 1920 she was Olympic champion.

Lenin, Vladimir Ilyich, originally **Vladimir Ilyich Ulyanov** (1870–1924) Marxist revolutionary, born in Ulyanovsk (formerly, Simbirsk), Russia. At a congress in 1903 he caused the split between the Bolshevik and Menshevik factions, and in October 1917 led the Bolshevik revolution, becoming head of the first Soviet government. At the end of the Civil War (1918–21) he introduced the New Economic Policy, which his critics saw as a 'compromise with capitalism' and a retreat from strictly socialist planning. On his death, his body was embalmed and placed in a mausoleum near the Moscow Kremlin.

Lennon, John (1940–80) Pop star, composer, songwriter, and recording artist, born in Liverpool, Merseyside. He was the Beatles rhythm guitarist, keyboard player, and vocalist, and a partner in the Lennon-McCartney song-writing team. He married Japanese artist **Yoko Ono** (1933–) in 1969, and the single recorded under the name of The Plastic Ono Band, 'Give Peace a Chance' (1969), became the 'national anthem' for pacifists. He was shot and killed by a deranged fan. >> McCartney

Leno, Dan [leenoh], originally **George Galvin** (1860–1904) Comedian, born in London. He joined Drury Lane, where he starred for many years in the annual pantomime.

Lenoir, Jean Joseph (Etienne) [luhnwah(r)] (1822–1900) Inventor and engineer, born in Mussy-la-Ville, Belgium. The inventor of the first practical internal combustion engine (c.1859), he later adapted it to run on liquid fuel, and used it to propel a vehicle he built (1860).

Lenormand, Henri René [luhnaw(r)mã] (1882–1951) Playwright, born in Paris. He wrote *The Dream-Eaters* (trans, 1922), a modern equivalent of *Oedipus Rex*, and other plays in which Freud's theories are adapted to dramatic purposes. >> Freud, Sigmund

Le Nôtre, André [luh nohtr] (1613–1700) Landscape architect, born in Paris. His designs include the gardens at Versailles and Fontainebleau, and St James's Park and Kensington Gardens in London.

Lenya, Lotte [laynya], originally **Karoline Wilhelmine Blamauer** (1900–81) Actress and cabaret singer, born in Vienna. In 1926 she married Kurt Weill, and starred in many of his works, notably *The Threepenny Opera* (1928; filmed 1931). >> Weill

Lenz, Heinrich (Friedrich Emil) [lents] (1804–65) Physicist, born in Tartu (formerly Dorpat), Estonia. He was the first to state the law governing induced current (*Lenz's law*), and is also credited with discovering the dependence of electrical resistance on temperature (Joule's law). >> Joule

Leo III, known as **Leo the Isaurian** (c.680–741) Byzantine emperor from 717, born in Syria. He reorganized the army and financial system, and in 726 issued an edict prohibiting the use of images in public worship.

Leo I, St, known as **the Great** (c.390–461), feast day 10 November (W), 18 February (E). Pope (440–61), probably born in Tuscany. One of the most eminent of the Latin Fathers, he summoned the Council of Chalcedon (451), where the intention of his 'Dogmatical Letter', defining the doctrine of the Incarnation, was accepted.

Leo X, originally **Giovanni de' Medici** (1475–1521) Pope (1513–21), born in Florence, Italy. A patron of learning and art, his vast project for the rebuilding of St Peter's, and his permitting the preaching of an indulgence in order to raise funds, provoked Luther's Reformation. >> Luther

Leo XIII, originally **Vincenzo Giocchino Pecci** (1810–1903) Pope (1878–1903), born in Carpineto, Italy. He restored the hierarchy in Scotland, resolved political difficulties with Germany, and in 1888 denounced the Irish Plan of Campaign.

Leo Africanus, originally **Alhassan ibn Mohammed Alwazzan** (c.1485–c.1554) Traveller and geographer, born in Granada, Spain. He wrote *A Geographical Historie of Africa* (trans, 1550), which for some 400 years was the chief source of information about Islam.

Leon, Daniel de >> de Leon, Daniel

León, Juan, Ponce de >> Ponce de León, Juan

Leonard, Elmore (John) (1925–) Thriller writer, born in New Orleans, LA. Regarded as the foremost crime writer in America his books include *Unknown Man No. 89* (1977), *La Brava* (1983), and *Touch* (1987).

Leonard, Sir Graham Douglas (1921–) Clergyman, born in London. He opposed the 1970s Anglican-Methodist unity scheme, and as Bishop of London (1981–91) became the focus of opposition to the ordination of women to the priesthood.

Leonard, 'Sugar' Ray (1956–) US boxer, born in Wilmington, DE. He became WBC world welterweight champion in 1977, and WBA light middleweight champion in 1981. He is the only boxer to have been world champion at five weights.

Leonardo da Vinci [leeonah(r)doh da veenchee] (1452–1519) Painter, sculptor, architect, and engineer, born in Vinci, Rome. In 1482 he settled in Milan, where he painted his 'Last Supper' (1498) on the refectory wall of Santa Maria delle Grazie. In 1500 he entered the service of Cesare Borgia in Florence as architect and engineer, and with Michelangelo decorated the Sala del Consiglio in the Palazzo della Signoria. About 1504 he completed his most celebrated easel picture, 'Mona Lisa' (Louvre). His notebooks contain original remarks on most of the sciences. >> Borgia, Cesare; Michelangelo

Leonardo of Pisa >> Fibonacci, Leonardo

Leoncavallo, Ruggero [leeonkavaloh] (1857–1919) Composer, born in Naples, Italy. His only major success was the opera *I Pagliacci* (1892).

Leoni, Leone [layohnee] (1509–90) Goldsmith, medallist, and sculptor, born in Arezzo, Italy. His portrait medals often depicted well-known artists, such as Michelangelo, and his bronze busts, particularly of Charles V and Philip II, had a significant influence on Spanish sculpture.

Leonidas [leeonidas] (?–480 BC) King of Sparta (c.491–480 BC), and Greek hero. In 480 BC his small command resisted the vast army of Xerxes, King of Persia, at Thermopylae, fighting to the last man.

Leonov, Alexey Arkhipovich [layonof] (1934–) Astronaut, born near Kemerovo, Russia. In 1965 he made the first 'extra-vehicular-activity' (EVA) excursion from the spacecraft Voskhod 2 in orbit round the Earth, 'walking' in space for 10 minutes.

Leontief, Wassily [layontyef, vasilee] (1906–) Economist, born in St Petersburg, Russia. He was awarded the 1973 Nobel Prize for Economics for developing the input-output method of economic analysis.

Leopardi, Giacomo [layohpah(r)dee] (1798–1837) Poet and scholar, born in Recanati, Italy. He was a gifted, handicapped child whose lyric poetry and prose, as collected in *I canti* (1831), reflect a life lived in hopeless despondency and unrequited love.

Leopold I (Emperor) (1640–1705) Holy Roman Emperor (1658–1705), born in Vienna, the second son of Ferdinand III. Committed to the defence of the power of the House of Habsburg, he faced constant threats from the Ottoman Turks and the King of France. There was military conflict over the Rhine frontier (1674–9, 1686–97), and he took the empire into the Grand Alliance (1701).

Leopold I (of Belgium) (1790–1865) First king of Belgium (1831–65), born in Coburg, Germany, the uncle of Queen Victoria. An influential force in European diplomacy In 1816 he married Charlotte, daughter of the future George IV of England, and lived in England after her death in 1817.

Leopold II (of Belgium) (1835–1909) King of Belgium (1865–1909), born in Brussels, the eldest son of Leopold I. He married Maria Henrietta, daughter of the Austrian Archduke Joseph in 1853. Under him Belgium flourished, developing commercially and industrially. >> Leopold I

Leopold III (1901–83) King of Belgium (1934–51), born in Brussels, the son of Albert I. He married Princess Astrid of Sweden in 1926. He ordered the capitulation of his army to the Germans (1940), thus opening the way to Dunkirk. >> Albert I; Baudouin

Leopold, (Rand) Aldo (1887–1948) Conservationist and ecologist, born in Burlington, IA. He wrote *A Sand County Almanac* (1949), the 'bible' of environmental activists of the 1960s and 1970s.

Le Parc, Julio [luh pah(r)k] (1928–) Artist, born in Mendoza, Argentina. He helped found the Groupe de Recherche D'art Visuel, and is remembered for the Op and Kinetic art movements of the 1960s.

Le Pen, Jean-Marie [luh pen] (1928–) French politician. A controversial figure and noted demagogue, he formed the National Front party in 1972 which, with its extreme right-wing policies, emerged as a new 'fifth force' in French politics in the 1986 Assembly elections.

Lepidus, Marcus Aemilius [lepidus] (?–13/12 BC) Roman statesman. Caesar made him dictator of Rome and his colleague in the consulate (46 BC). He became one of the triumvirate with Octavian Augustus and Marcus Antonius. >> Antonius; Caesar

Lepsius, Karl Richard [lepsius] (1810–44) Egyptologist, born in Naumburg, Germany. His *Egyptian Chronology* (trans, 1849) laid the foundation for a scientific treatment of early Egyptian history, and *Egyptian and Ethiopian Monuments* (trans, 1859) remains a masterpiece.

Lermontov, Mikhail Yuryevich [lermontof] (1814–41) Poet and writer, born in Moscow. His best poetry includes 'The Novice' and 'The Demon', and his novel, *A Hero of our Time* (trans, 1840), is a masterpiece of prose writing. He was killed in a duel.

Lerner, Alan J >> Loewe, Frederick

Lesage, Alain René [luhsahzh], also spelled **Le Sage** (1668–1747) Writer, born in Sarzeau, France. He is best known for the novel *The Adventures of Gil Blas of Santillane* (trans, 12 vols, 1715–35). As a playwright, his leading work is *Turcaret* (1708).

Lescot, Pierre [leskoh] (c.1515–78) Architect, born in Paris.

Among his works are the screen of St Germain l'Auxerrois, the Fontaine des Innocents, and the Hôtel de Ligneris. His masterwork was the rebuilding of the Louvre.

LeSieg, Theo >> Seuss, Dr

Leslie, Charles Robert (1794–1859) Painter, born in London. Professor of painting at the Royal Academy (1848–52), his paintings were mostly scenes from famous plays and novels.

Leslie, Sir John (1766–1832) Physicist, born in Largo, Fife. He invented a differential thermometer, a hygrometer, and a photometer, and in 1810 succeeded in creating artificial ice by freezing water under an air pump.

Leslie, Sir Shane (John Randolph) (1885–1971) Writer, born in Glaslough, Co Monaghan, Ireland. He published poems, novels, biographies, memoirs, supernatural short stories, and a much praised analysis of the pre-war generation in *The End of a Chapter* (1916).

L'Esperance, Elise, *née* **Strang** (1878?–1959) Physician, pathologist, and clinic founder, born in Yorktown, NY. Best known for her work in cancer prevention, especially in women, she founded several New York clinics both individually and with her sister, May (the Strang clinics).

Lesseps, Ferdinand (Marie), vicomte de (Viscount of) [leseeps] (1805–94) French diplomat and entrepreneur, born in Versailles, France. In 1854 he began his campaign for the construction of a Suez Canal, finally completed in 1869. A later scheme for a sea-level Panama Canal had to be abandoned.

Lessing, Doris (May), *née* **Tayler** (1919–) Writer, born in Kermanshah, Iran. Brought up in Southern Rhodesia, her first published novel was *The Grass is Singing* (1950), a study of white civilization in Africa. Later works include the five-book sequence *The Children of Violence*, and her best-known novel *The Golden Notebook* (1962).

Lessing, Gotthold Ephraim (1729–81) Playwright and man of letters, born in Kamenz, Germany. *Laokoon* (1766), is a critical treatise defining the limits of poetry and the plastic arts. His *Minna von Barnhelm* (1767) was the first German comedy on the grand scale.

Leszczynski, Stanislaus >> Stanislaus Leszczynski

Lethaby, William Richard (1857–1931) Architect and designer, born in Barnstaple, Devon. He was a founder of the Art Workers' Guild (1884) and the Arts and Crafts Exhibition Society (c.1886).

Letts, Thomas (1803–73) Bookbinder, born in London. John Letts founded the Charles Letts family business in 1796. After his death, Thomas began to manufacture diaries, and by 1839 was producing 28 varieties.

Leucippus [loosipus] (5th-c BC) Philosopher, born in Miletus, Asia Minor. The originator of the atomistic cosmology which Democritus later developed, he is usually credited with two books, *The Great World System* and *On the Mind*. >> Democritus

Leuckart, (Karl Georg Friedrich) Rudolf [loykah(r)t] (1822–98) Zoologist, born in Helmstedt, Germany. A pioneer of parasitology, his work on classification is important, especially his division of the Radiata into Coelenterata and Echinodermata.

Leutze, Emanuel (Gottlieb) [loytzuh] (1816–68) Painter, born in Gmünd, Germany. He emigrated to America in 1825. His historical paintings have been reproduced many times, especially 'Washington Crossing the Delaware' (1851).

Levant, Oscar [levant] (1906–72) Pianist and actor, born in Pittsburgh, PA. As a pianist he became one of the foremost Gershwin interpreters. He also had a career as a screen and radio humorist, his films including *An American in Paris* (1951). >> Gershwin, George

Levassor, Emile >> Panhard, René

Le Vau or **Levau, Louis** [luh voh] (1612–70) Architect, born in Paris. His design of Vaux-le-Vicomte (1657–61), with formal landscape by André Le Nôtre, was an influential milestone in French architecture, leading to his Baroque masterpiece of Versailles (from 1661). >> Le Nôtre

Levene, Phoebus (Aaron Theodor) [luh**veen**], originally **Fishel Aaronovich Lenin** (1869–1940) Biochemist, born in Sagor, Russia. His work, carried out before 1930, established the nature of the sugar component which defines the two types of nucleic acid (RNA and DNA). >> Crick; Watson, James

Lever, Charles (James) [**lee**ver] (1806–72) Writer, born in Dublin. His most popular novel was *Charles O'Malley*, a description of his own college life in Dublin.

Leverhulme (of the Western Isles), William Hesketh Lever, 1st Viscount [**lee**verhyoom], also known as **Baron Leverhulme of Bolton-Le-Moors** (1851–1925) Soapmaker and philanthropist, born in Bolton, Greater Manchester. In 1886, with his brother, James Darcy Lever, he began to develop a small soap works into a national business, founding the model industrial new town of Port Sunlight.

Leverrier, Urbain Jean Joseph [luh**ver**yay] (1811–77) Astronomer, born in St Lô, France. He predicted the existence of an undiscovered planet, and calculated the point in the heavens where, a few days later, Neptune was actually discovered by Galle (1846). >> Galle

Levertov, Denise (1923–) Poet, born in Ilford, Essex. She became a US citizen in 1955, and was appointed poetry editor of *The Nation* in 1961. Her works include *With Eyes at the Back of Our Heads* (1959) and *Footprints* (1972).

Levesque, Rene [luh**vek**] (1922–87) Journalist, and premier (1976–85) of Quebec, Canada. He founded the Parti Québecois, whose main objective became Quebec sovereignty and the creation of a new form of association with Canada.

Levey, Barnett [**lee**vee] (1798–1837) Australian pioneer, born in the East End of London. He arrived in Australia in 1821, the first free Jewish settler to arrive in the new colony. He established one of the first lending libraries in Australia, and built the Theatre Royal in 1833.

Levi [**lee**viy] Biblical character, the third son of Jacob by his wife Leah. It is debated whether his descendants ever formed one of the 12 tribes of Israel descended from Jacob's sons. They seem to have been a kind of priestly class. >> Jacob

Levi, Edward H [**lee**vee] (1911–) Lawyer and university administrator, born in Chicago, IL. A brilliant anti-trust lawyer, he became dean of the University of Chicago Law School (1950–62), university provost (1962–7) and president (1967–75), and served as the US attorney general (1975–7).

Levi, Primo [**lay**vee] (1919–87) Writer and chemist, born in Turin, Italy. His novels are attempts to understand the nature of Nazi barbarity and the variety of responses to it. They include *If this is a Man* (trans, 1947) and its sequel *The Truce* (trans, 1963).

Levi-Civita, Tullio [**lay**vee chi**vee**ta] (1873–1941) Mathematician, born in Padua, Italy. From about 1900 he worked on the absolute differential calculus (or tensor calculus), which became the essential mathematical tool in Einstein's general relativity theory. >> Einstein

Levi-Montalcini, Rita [**lay**vee montal**chee**nee] (1909–) Neurophysiologist, born in Rome. In the USA for several years from 1947, she discovered nerve growth factor, and shared the Nobel Prize for Physiology or Medicine in 1986. >> Cohen, Stanley

Levine, James [luh**viyn**] (1943–) Conductor, born in Cincinnati, OH. In 1976 he became music director of the Metropolitan Opera, building its orchestra into one of the finest in the world.

Lévi-Strauss, Claude [**lay**vee **strows**] (1908–) Social anthropologist, born in Brussels. A major influence on contemporary anthropology, his four-volume study, *Mythologiques* (1964–72), studied the systematic ordering behind codes of expression in different cultures.

Lévy-Bruhl, Lucien [layvee brül] (1857–1939) Philosopher and anthropologist, born in Paris. He developed a theory of primitive mentality, suggesting that the mentality of primitive people was essentially mystical and prelogical, which has little support today. >> Durkheim

Lewald, Fanny [**lay**valt] (1811–89) Writer, born in Königsberg (now Kaliningrad), Germany. She championed women's rights, which were aired in her early novels such as *Clementine* (1842). Later works were family sagas, notably *The Darner Family* (trans, 3 vols, 1887).

Lewes, George Henry [**loo**is] (1817–78) Writer, born in London. His works include *The Spanish Drama* (1846), *Life and Works of Goethe* (1855), and *Problems of Life and Mind* (1874–9). He began a lifelong affair with George Eliot in 1854. >> Eliot, George

Lewis, Alun (1915–44) Writer, born in Cwmaman, Mid-Glamorgan. His works include a volume of short stories about army life, *The Last Inspection* (1942), as well as poems and letters.

Lewis, Sir (William) Arthur (1915–) British economist, born in St Lucia. In 1979 he shared the Nobel Prize for Economics for work on economic development in the Third World.

Lewis, (Frederick) Carl(ton) (1961–) Track and field athlete, born in Birmingham, AL. He won four gold medals at the 1984 Olympic Games, two more in 1988, and an unprecedented third consecutive gold medal in the long jump in 1992. He was awarded the gold medal for the 100 m in 1988 when Ben Johnson was disqualified. >> Johnson, Ben

Lewis, C Day >> **Day-Lewis, C(ecil)**

Lewis, C(live) S(taples) (1898–1963) Academic, writer, and Christian apologist, born in Belfast. His novel *The Screwtape Letters* (1942) is the best known of many works on Christian apologetics. *The Lion, the Witch and the Wardrobe* (1950) was the first in his *Chronicles of Narnia*, a classic children's series.

Lewis, David (1919–) Sailor and writer, born in New Zealand. He has sought to rediscover the traditional sailing methods of the ancient Polynesians, and to vindicate their reputation as master mariners.

Lewis, G(ilbert) N(ewton) (1875–1946) Physical chemist, born in Weymouth, MA. A pioneer in taking ideas from physics and applying them to chemistry, much of his research focused on the arrangement of electrons around atomic nuclei.

Lewis, Hywel (David) (1910–) Religious philosopher, born in Llandudno, Gwynedd. He was founder editor of *Religious Studies* (1965–84), and author of many works, including *Our Experience of God* (1959) and *Freedom and Alienation* (1985).

Lewis, Jerry Lee (1935–) Rock singer, country singer, and pianist, born in Ferriday, LA. His 1957 recordings 'Whole Lotta Shakin'' and 'Great Balls of Fire' became classics of rock, copied by successive generations of musicians.

Lewis, John L(lewellyn) (1880–1969) Labour leader, born in Lucas, IA. He became president of the United Mine Workers' Union (1920–60), and in 1935 formed the Congress of Industrial Organizations, of which he was president until 1940.

Lewis, M(atthew) G(regory), nickname **Monk Lewis** (1775–1818) Novelist, born in London. His best-known work is *The Monk* (1796), a Gothic novel which caught the public's attention and inspired his nickname.

Lewis, Meade, known as **Meade Lux Lewis** (1905–64) Musician, born in Louisville, KY. His recording of 'Honky

Tonk Train Blues' (1929) was belatedly very successful (1936), and he became a leading exponent of the boogie-woogie piano during the late 1930s.

Lewis, Meriwether (1774–1809) Explorer, born in Charlotteville, VA. With William Clark he led an expedition (1804–6) to explore the lands to the W of the Mississippi, the first overland journey across North America to the Pacific Coast.

Lewis, Oscar (1914–70) Anthropologist, born in New York City. His best-selling records of the oral histories of Mexican villagers, Mexican and Puerto Rican slum-dwellers, and the Cuban revolution led to his controversial theory of poverty as a transnational subculture.

Lewis, Richard, known as **Dic Penderyn** (c.1807–31) Folk hero, born near Aberavon, West Glamorgan. Found guilty of wounding a soldier during the Merthyr Tydfil riots of 1831, he was publicly executed. Many were convinced of his innocence, and he became a folk hero in South Wales.

Lewis, Saunders (1893–1958) Playwright, poet, and Welsh nationalist, born in Cheshire. He was co-founder of the Welsh Nationalist Party (later Plaid Cymru) in 1925, and became its president in 1926. He published many essays, plays, poems, novels, and criticism, chiefly in Welsh.

Lewis, (Harry) Sinclair (1885–1951) Novelist, born in Sauk Center, MN. *Main Street* (1920) was the first of a series of best-selling novels satirizing US small-town life. Other works include *Babbitt* (1922) and *Arrowsmith* (1925). He received the 1930 Nobel Prize for Literature.

Lewis, Sir Thomas (1881–1945) Cardiologist and clinical scientist, born in Cardiff. He was the first to master the use of electrocardiograms, establishing the basic parameters which still govern their measurement.

Lewis, (Percy) Wyndham [windam] (1882–1957) Artist, writer, and critic, born on a yacht in the Bay of Fundy, Nova Scotia, Canada. With Pound he founded *Blast* (1914–15), the magazine of the Vorticist school. His books include the satirical novel *The Apes of God* (1930) and the multi-volume *The Human Age* (1955–6). His paintings include works of abstract art, a series of war pictures, and portraits. >> Pound, Ezra

Lewitt, Sol (1928–) Exponent of Conceptual Art, born in Hartford, CT. In the 1970s he made Minimalist 'structures', but was already declaring that the concept was more important than the work, and the planning more than the execution, hence his exhibited wall-drawings were afterwards obliterated.

Ley, Willy [lay] (1906–69) Rocket scientist and writer, born in Berlin. He founded the German Society for Space Travel (1927), made it a centre of rocket research, and helped develop the liquid-fuel rocket. In the USA from 1935, he wrote many science fiction and nonfiction accounts, including the award-winning *The Conquest of Space* (1949).

Leyden, Lucas van >> Lucas van Leyden

Li, Choh Hao [lee] (1913–) Biochemist, born in Canton, China. His main work was on the pituitary hormones: he isolated adrenocorticotrophic hormone (ACTH), establishing its molecular structure (1956), and later had similar success with the growth hormone, somatotropin.

Liang Qichao [leeang cheechow], also spelled **Liang Ch'i-ch'ao** (1873–1929) Chinese reformer. He published the journal *Renovated Citizen*, seeking to reappraise Confucianism in the light of Western liberal democracy. Opposed to Sun Yixian's socialism, he founded (1913) the anti-Guomindang Democratic Party. >> Sun Yixian

Libau or **Libavius, Andreas** [leebow, libayvius] (c.1540–1616) Alchemist, born in Halle, Garmany. His finest work was *Alchemy* (trans, 1606) the first modern chemical textbook, which gives an account of a range of chemical methods and substances, and vigorously attacks the ideas of Paracelsus. >> Paracelsus

Libby, Willard (Frank) (1908–80) Chemist, born in Grand Valley, CO. He received the Nobel Prize for Chemistry in 1960 for his part in the invention of the carbon-14 method of dating.

Liberace [libuhrahchee], also known as **Walter Busterkeys**, originally **Wladziu Valentino Liberace** (1919–87) Entertainer, born in Milwaukee, WI. He developed an act of popular piano classics performed with a lavish sense of showmanship, and his television series, *The Liberace Show* (1952–7), won him an Emmy as Best Male Personality.

Li Bo >> **Li Po**

Lichfield, (Thomas) Patrick (John Anson), 5th Earl of, professional name **Patrick Lichfield** (1939–) British photographer. Successful with many personal royal portraits, he also created the well-known Unipart calendar, and has published many books.

Lichtenstein, Roy [likhtenstiyn] (1923–) Painter, born in New York City. Since the early 1960s he has produced many of the best-known images of American Pop Art, such as the huge 'Whaam' (1963).

Lick, James (1796–1876) Financier and philanthropist, born in Fredericksburg, VA. He made a fortune in real estate investment, and founded the Lick Observatory on Mt Hamilton, CA.

Li Dazhao [lee dajow], also spelled **Li Ta-chao** (1888–1927) One of the founders of the Chinese Communist Party, whose interpretation of Marxism as applied to China had a profound influence on Mao Zedong. He was executed when the Manchurian military leader Chang Tso-lin (1873–1928) raided the Soviet Embassy in Beijing. >> Mao Zedong

Liddell, Eric (Henry) [lidl], nickname **the Flying Scotsman** (1902–45) British athlete and missionary, born in Tientsin, China. In the 1924 Olympics he caused a sensation by winning the gold medal in the 400 m in a world record time of 47·6 s. His story was told in the film *Chariots of Fire* (1981).

Liddell, Henry George [lidl] (1811–98) Scholar and lexicographer, born in Bishop Auckland, Co Durham. His major work was co-editing the *Greek–English Lexicon* (1843). His daughter, Alice, was the little girl for whom Charles Dodgson, his colleague at Christ Church, wrote *Alice in Wonderland*. >> Carroll, Lewis

Liddell Hart, Sir Basil (Henry) [lidl hah(r)t] (1895–1970) Military journalist and theorist, born in Paris. He became military correspondent for the *Daily Telegraph* (1925–35) and *The Times* (1935–9), advocating the principles of modern mobile warfare.

Liddon, Henry Parry (1829–90) Theologian, born in North Stoneham, Hampshire. He strongly opposed the Church Discipline Act of 1874, and was the most able and eloquent exponent of Liberal High Church principles. >> Gladstone, W E

Lidman, Sara (1923–) Writer, born in Missenträsk, Sweden. Her novels include *The Tar Still* (trans, 1952), *Cloudberry Land* (trans, 1955), and *Thy Servant Heareth* (trans, 1977).

Lie, Jonas (Lauritz Idemil) [lee] (1833–1908) Writer, born in Eiker, Norway. His novels include *The Visionary* (trans, 1870) and *Lodsen and his Wife* (trans, 1874), and he also wrote poetry, plays, and fairy-tales.

Lie, (Marius) Sophus [lee] (1842–99) Mathematician, born in Nordfjordeide, Norway. He developed an extensive theory of continuous groups of transformations, now known as *Lie groups*, with important applications in quantum theory.

Lie, Trygve (Halvdan) [lee, trigvuh] (1896–1968) Norwegian statesman and UN secretary-general (1946–52), born in Oslo (formerly, Kristiania). Elected the first secretary-general of the UN, he resigned in 1952 as a result of Soviet opposition to his support of UN intervention in the Korean War.

Lieber, Francis [leeber] (1800–72) Political reformer, editor, and political scientist, born in Berlin. He went to Boston in 1827, and edited a new *Encyclopedia Americana* (13 vols, 1829–33). Known for his ideas on prison reform, he drafted a *Code for the Government of the Armies of the United States* (1863), which was later used as the basis for the Hague Convention.

Liebermann, Max [leeberman] (1847–1935) Painter and etcher, born in Berlin. He painted open-air studies and scenes of humble life which were often sentimental. Later influenced by the French Impressionists, he became the leading painter of that school in Germany.

Liebig, Justus, Freiherr von (Baron) [leebikh] (1803–73) Chemist, born in Darmstadt, Germany. He investigated many aspects of organic, animal, and agricultural chemistry, and developed new techniques for carrying out analyses, such as the distillation equipment known as *Liebig's condenser.*

Liebknecht, Karl [leebknekht] (1871–1919) German barrister and politician. A founder member with Rosa Luxemburg of the German Communist Party in 1918, he led an unsuccessful revolt in Berlin, the 'Spartacus League Revolution' (1919), during which he was killed. >> Luxemburg

Lifar, Serge [lifah(r)] (1905–86) Dancer and choreographer, born in Kiev, Ukraine. In 1923 he joined Diaghilev's company, and became the guiding genius behind the Paris Opéra (1929–58). >> Diaghilev

Ligachev, Yegor Kuzmich [ligachof] (1920–) Soviet politician. He joined the central Party secretariat (1983), served as ideology secretary (1984), and was brought into the Politburo. He initially served as Gorbachev's deputy, but in 1988 was demoted to agriculture secretary. >> Gorbachev

Ligeti, György (Sándor) [ligetee] (1923–) Composer, born in Dicsöszent-Márton, Hungary. He developed an experimental approach to composition, as seen in his large orchestral work *Apparitions* (1958–9), and has also written a choral requiem, a cello concerto, and music for harpsichord, organ, and wind and string ensembles.

Liguori, St Alfonso Maria de' [ligwohree], also known as **St Alphonsus Liguori** (1696–1787), feast day 1 August. Theologian, and founder of the Redemptorists, born in Naples, Italy. With others he founded the order of *Liguorians* or Redemptorists (1732). He was canonized in 1839.

Likert, Rensis [likert] (1903–81) Psychologist and management theorist, born in Cheyenne, WY. His major contributions included the development of a survey methodology that laid the groundwork for probability sampling, the *Likert scale* for measuring attitudes, and a theory of participatory management.

Lilburne, John (c.1614–57) Pamphleteer, probably born in Greenwich, Greater London. In 1638 he imported illegal Puritan literature from Holland, and was imprisoned until 1640. An active agitator for the Levellers, he was repeatedly imprisoned for his pamphlets.

Lilienthal, Otto [leelyentahl] (1849–96) Aeronautical inventor and glider pioneer, born in Anklam, Prussia. He studied bird flight in order to build heavier-than-air flying machines resembling the birdman designs of Leonardo da Vinci. He made many short flights in his gliders, but crashed to his death near Berlin. >> Leonardo da Vinci

Li Lisan [lee leesan] (1900–67) Chinese politician, and effective head of the Communist Party (1928–30), born in Hunan province, China. He enforced what has since become known as the 'Li Lisan line', in which the Party's weak military forces were used in futile attempts to capture cities.

Lillee, Dennis (Keith) (1949–) Cricketer, born in Perth,

Western Australia. A renowned fast bowler, he took 355 wickets in 70 Tests.

Lillehei, Clarence (Walton) [lilhay] (1918–) Thoracic and cardiovascular surgeon, born in Minneapolis, MN. His pioneering work on open-heart surgery began in the early 1950s, before the development of the pump oxygenator made such procedures more reliable.

Lillie, Beatrice (Gladys) (1898–1989) Revue singer, born in Toronto, Ontario, Canada. She became renowned from 1914 in music hall and the new vogue of 'intimate revue'. Her film appearances include *Thoroughly Modern Millie* (1967).

Lilye or **Lily, William** (c.1468–1522) Grammarian, born in Odiham, Hampshire. He was appointed first headmaster of St Paul's School (1512), and wrote *Lily's Grammar*, published as *Eton Latin Grammar* (1758).

Limburg brothers Pol, Jehanequin and **Herman de Limburg** or **Limbourg** (fl. early 15th-c) Three brothers, famous Flemish illuminators or miniaturists, they became Court painters to the Duke of Berry (1411), and produced illustrations for his illuminated manuscript *Les Très riches heures du Duc de Berry*, in the international Gothic style.

Limón, José [limon] (1908–72) Dancer, choreographer, and teacher, born in Culiacan, Mexico. In New York City he formed the José Limón Company in 1946, the first American modern dance company to tour Europe.

Limousin or **Limosin, Léonard** [limoozi] (c.1505–77) Painter in enamel, born in Limoges, France. He became court painter to Francis I from 1930, and was appointed head of the royal factory at Limoges.

Linacre, Thomas (c.1460–1524) Physician and scholar, born in Canterbury, Kent. He was king's physician to Henry VII and Henry VIII, and in 1518 founded the Royal College of Physicians, becoming its first president. >> Henry VII / VIII

Lin Biao or **Lin Piao** [lin byow] (1907–71) A leader of the Chinese Communist Party, born in Hupeh province, China. He became minister of defence in 1959, and heir apparent to Mao Zedong in 1968. After differences with Mao and an abortive coup, he was killed in a plane crash in Mongolia, apparently while fleeing to the USSR.

Lincoln, Abraham (1809–65) US Republican statesman and 16th president (1861–5), born near Hodgenville, KY. He was elected president on a platform of hostility to the expansion of slavery. When the Civil War began (1861), he defined the issue in terms of national integrity, a theme he restated in the Gettysburg Address of 1863, and in the same year proclaimed freedom for all slaves in areas of rebellion. On 14 April 1865 he was shot at Ford's Theatre, Washington, by John Wilkes Booth, and died next morning. >> Booth, John Wilkes

Lincoln, Benjamin (1733–1810) Revolutionary soldier, born in Hingham, MA. In 1780, besieged by Clinton in Charleston, he was forced to surrender with some 7000 troops. He took part in the siege of Yorktown (1781), and later became secretary of war (1781–3). >> Clinton, Henry

Lind, Jenny, originally **Johanna Maria Lind,** known as **the Swedish Nightingale** (1820–87) Soprano, born in Stockholm. She made her debut in Stockholm in 1838, and attained great popularity everywhere, living in England after 1856.

Lind, James (1716–94) Physician, born in Edinburgh. He is remembered for his research into cases of scurvy aboard ship; his recommendation to the Royal Navy to issue citrus fruits and juices to sailors eradicated the disease.

Lindbergh, Charles A(ugustus) [lindberg] (1902–74) Aviator, born in Detroit, MI. In 1927 he made the first non-stop solo transatlantic flight from New York City to Paris in the monoplane *Spirit of St Louis*. In 1932 his infant son was kidnapped and murdered, a sensational crime for which Bruno Richard Hauptmann was executed (1936).

Lindemann, Frederick Alexander >> Cherwell, Viscount

Lindgren, Astrid (1907–) Children's novelist, born in Vimmerby, Sweden. She established her reputation with *Pippi Longstocking* (trans, 1945), later turning to folklore with such titles as *The Brothers Lionheart* (trans, 1973).

Lindley, John (1799–1865) Botanist and horticulturalist, born in Catton, Norfolk. In 1828 he prepared a report on the royal gardens at Kew which saved them from destruction, and this led to the creation of the Royal Botanic Gardens.

Lindrum, Walter (1898–1960) Billiards player, born in Kalgoorlie, Western Australia. He set the current world record break of 4317 while playing Joe Davis in 1932. >> Davis, Joe

Lindsay, Sir David >> Lyndsay, Sir David

Lindsay, (Nicholas) Vachel [linzee] (1879–1931) Poet, born in Springfield, IL. From 1906 he travelled America like a troubadour, reciting his popular ragtime rhymes in return for food and shelter.

Lindwall, Ray(mond Russell) (1921–) Cricketer, born in Sydney, New South Wales, Australia. He took 228 wickets in 61 Tests, and also scored more than 1500 runs, including two Test centuries.

Link, Edwin (Albert) (1904–81) Inventor and aviation executive, born in Huntington, IN. In 1935 he founded Link Aviation Inc, which produced flight simulators and other apparatus, and he also invented equipment for deep-sea exploration.

Linklater, Eric (Robert) (1899–1974) Novelist, born in Dounby, Orkney Is, Scotland. While in the USA (1928–30) he wrote *Poet's Pub* (1929), the first of a series of satirical novels which include *Juan in America* (1931) and *Private Angelo* (1946).

Linley, Viscount >> Margaret, Princess

Linnaeus, Carolus [linayus], Swed **Carl von Linné** (1707–78) Botanist, born in Råshult, Sweden. His *Systema naturae fundamenta botanica* (1735), *Genera plantarum* (1737), and *Species plantarum* (1753), expound his influential system of classification, in which names consist of generic and specific elements, with plants grouped hierarchically into genera, classes, and orders.

Linowitz, Sol Myron [linohvich] (1913–) Lawyer, diplomat, and businessman, born in Trenton, NJ. He co-negotiated the Panama Canal Treaties of 1977, and was personal ambassador for President Carter during the Middle East negotiations (1979–81). >> Carter, Jimmy

Linton, Ralph (1893–1953) Cultural anthropologist, born in Philadelphia, PA. He pioneered the use of the terms *status* and *role* in social science, and influenced the development of the culture-and-personality school of anthropology.

Lin Yü-tang (1895–1976) Writer and philologist, born in Lun-chi, China. He is best known for his novels, essays, and anthologies relating to Chinese wisdom and culture, and as co-author of the official romanization plan for the Chinese alphabet.

Liouville, Joseph [lyooveel] (1809–82) Mathematician, born in St Omer, France. His work in analysis continued the study of algebraic function, and he also studied the theory of differential equations, mathematical physics, and celestial mechanics.

Lipatti, Dinu [lipatee] (1917–50) Pianist and composer, born in Bucharest. He established an international reputation as a pianist, especially in the works of Chopin. His compositions include a *Symphonie concertante* for two pianos and strings, and a concertino for piano and orchestra.

Lipchitz, Jacques [lipshitz], originally **Chaim Jacob**

Lipchitz (1891–1973) Sculptor, born in Druskininkai, Lithuania. In the 1920s he experimented with abstract forms he called 'transparent sculptures', later developing a more dynamic style with bronze figure and animal compositions.

Li Peng [lee peng] (1928–) Chinese prime minister (1987–), born in Chengdu, China. He sought to retain firm control of the economy, favoured improved relations with the Soviet Union, and took a strong line in facing down the student-led, pro-democracy movement.

Lipman, Maureen (Diane) (1946–) Actress and writer, born in Hull, Humberside. She has appeared in a number of West End productions and on television, and is widely known for her award-winning 'You got an Ology?' British Telecom TV commercial. She has written several humorous books, including *How Was It For You?* (1985).

Lipmann, Fritz (Albert) (1899–1986) Biochemist, born in Königsberg, Germany. He isolated and elucidated the molecular structure of co-enzyme A, for which he shared the Nobel Prize for Physiology or Medicine in 1953.

Li Po [lee poh], also found as **Li Bo** and **Li T'ai Po** (c.700–762) Poet, born in Szechwan Province, China. He led a dissipated life at the emperor's court, and wrote colourful verse of wine, women, and nature. He is regarded as the greatest poet of China.

Lippershey, Hans or **Jan** [lipershay], also spelled **Lippersheim** (c.1570–1619) Dutch optician, born in Wesel, Germany. He is one of several spectacle-makers credited with the discovery that the combination of a convex and a concave lens can make distant objects appear nearer. He is believed to be the inventor of the telescope (1608).

Lippi, Filippino [lipee] (c.1458–1504) Painter, born in Florence, Italy, the son of Fra Filippo Lippi. He completed the frescoes in the Brancacci Chapel, Florence, left unfinished by Masaccio (c.1484). 'The Vision of St Bernard' (c.1480–6) is his best-known picture. >> Lippi, Fra Filippo; Masaccio

Lippi, Fra Filippo [lipee], known as **Lippo** (c.1406–69) Religious painter, born in Florence, Italy. His greatest work, on the choir walls of Prato Cathedral, was begun in 1452. His later works, deeply religious, include the series of 'Nativities'. >> Lippi, Filippino

Lippincott, Joshua (Ballinger) (1813–86) Publisher, born in Juliustown, NJ. He had a bookseller's business in Philadelphia (1834–6), then founded his well-known publishing firm, and started *Lippincott's Magazine* in 1868.

Lippmann, Walter (1889–1974) Journalist, born in New York City. Special writer for the *New York Herald Tribune*, his daily columns became internationally famous, and he received the Pulitzer Prize for International Reporting in 1962.

Lippmann, Gabriel (1845–1921) Physicist, born in Hollerich, Luxembourg. He invented a capillary electrometer, and produced the first coloured photograph of the spectrum. He was awarded the Nobel Prize for Physics in 1908.

Lippold, Richard [lipohld] (1915–) Sculptor, born in Milwaukee, WI. He is known for his constructed wire sculptures, as in 'Variation Number 7: Full Moon' (1950).

Lips, Joest >> Lipsius, Justus

Lipscomb, William Nunn, Jr (1919–) Physical chemist, born in Cleveland, OH. He deduced the molecular structures of a curious group of boron compounds by X-ray crystal diffraction analysis in the 1950s, and went on to develop theories for the chemical bonding in these compounds. He was awarded the Nobel Prize for Chemistry in 1976.

Lipsius, Justus [lipsius], also known as **Joest Lips** (1547–1606) Humanist and Classical scholar, born in Issche, Belgium. Noted for his essays in moral and political theory, his writings also include important editions of the Latin prose texts of Tacitus (1574) and Seneca (1605). >> Seneca; Tacitus

Lipton, Seymour (1903-86) Sculptor, born in New York City. During the 1940s he began constructing abstract sculptures from sheet lead, and from the 1950s worked primarily in silver-plated nickel on metal.

Lipton, Sir Thomas Johnstone (1850-1931) Businessman and philanthropist, born in Glasgow, Strathclyde. In 1870 he opened the first of his many prosperous grocery shops, which made him a millionaire by the age of 30.

Li Shih-chen [lee sheechen] (1518-93) Pharmaceutical naturalist and biologist, regarded as 'the father of Chinese herbal medicine'. He compiled the *Pen Tshao Kang Mu* (Great Pharmacopoeia), completed in 1578 and published in 1596.

Lisle, Rouget de >> **Rouget de Lisle**

Lisle, Leconte de >> **Leconte de Lisle**

Lissajous, Jules Antoine [leesazhoo] (1822-80) French physicist. In 1857 he invented the vibration microscope which showed visually the *Lissajous figures* obtained as the resultant of two simple harmonic motions at right angles to one another.

Lissitsky, El(iezer) [lisitskee], also spelled **Lissitzky** (1890-1941) Painter and designer, born in Smolensk, Russia. A leading Constructivist he produced a series of abstract works, called 'Proun' (1919), in which he combined flat rectilinear forms and dramatic architectonic elements.

Lister (of Lyme Regis), Joseph Lister, Baron (1827-1912) Surgeon, born in Upton, Essex, the son of Joseph Jackson Lister. His great work was the introduction (1860) of the use of antiseptic conditions during surgery. >> Lister, Joseph Jackson

Lister, Joseph Jackson (1786-1869) Wine merchant and amateur microscopist, born in London. His method of building lens systems to greatly reduce chromatic and spherical aberrations was used by James Smith in 1826 to develop a much improved microscope. >> Lister, Joseph

Lister, Samuel Cunliffe, 1st Baron Masham (1815-1906) Inventor, born in Bradford, West Yorkshire. He invented a wool-comber in 1845, and made a fortune, at the same time bringing prosperity to Bradford.

Liston, Sonny, popular name of **Charles Liston** (?1917-70) Boxer, born in St Francis Co, AR. He defeated Floyd Patterson to become world heavyweight champion in 1962, but in 1964 lost the title to Cassius Clay (Muhammad Ali). >> Ali, Muhammad; Patterson

Liszt, Franz (1811-86) Composer and pianist, born in Raiding, Hungary. From 1835 to 1839 he lived with the Comtesse d'Agoult, by whom he had three children, and in 1847 met Princess Carolyne zu Sayn-Wittgenstein with whom he lived until his death. A virtuoso pianist who gave concerts throughout Europe, his works include 12 symphonic poems, Masses, two symphonies and a large number of piano pieces.

Li Ta-chao >> **Li Dazhao**

Li Tsang >> **Li Zang**

Little, Malcolm >> **Malcolm X**

Little Richard, popular name of **Richard Wayne Penniman** (1932-) Rock-and-roll singer and pianist, born in Macon, GA. 'Tutti Frutti' (1955) brought him international popularity. Most of his recordings from 1958 to 1964 were of Gospel songs, but in the mid-1960s he made a comeback with 'Whole Lot Of Shaking Goin' On', and other hits.

Littlewood, (Maudie) Joan (1914-) Theatre director, born in London. She pioneered work in left-wing, popular theatre, forming the Theatre Workshop in 1945. After settling at the Theatre Royal Stratford East in 1953, her productions included *Oh! What A Lovely War* (1963).

Littlewood, John (Edensor) (1885-1977) Mathematician, born in Rochester, Kent. With Godfrey Hardy, he wrote papers on summability theory, Tauberian theorems, Fourier

series, analytic number theory, and the Riemann zeta-function. >> Hardy, Godfrey

Littré, (Maximilien) Paul Emile [leetray] (1801-81) Lexicographer and philosopher, born in Paris. A supporter of Comte, he became the leader of the Positivist school in 1857. He published the *Dictionary of the French Language* (trans, 1863-72). >> Comte

Litvinov, Maxim (Maximovich) [litveenof] (1876-1951) Russian politician and diplomat, born in Bialystok, Poland. He became people's commissar for foreign affairs (1930-9), and later served as ambassador to the USA (1941-3).

Liu-Bang >> **Gaozu**

Liu Shaoqi [lyoo showchee], also spelled **Liu Shao-ch'i** (1898-1969) Chinese political leader, born in Ningxiang, Hunan, China. He became Communist Party secretary (1943) and chairman of the People's Republic of China (1958), but during the Cultural Revolution (1966-9) he was denounced and banished.

Liu Sheng [lyoo shang] (?-113 BC) Chinese prince, the brother of Wudi. His tomb, and that of his consort, Princess Don Wan, was opened at Mancheng, Hopei, in 1968, and was found to contain some 2800 objects. >> Wudi

Liu Xin [lyoo sheen], also spelled **Liu Hsin** (1st-c BC-1st-c AD) Astronomer. He antedated Ptolemy's *Almagest* (2nd-c AD) with his astronomical tables, cataloguing 1080 stars in six magnitude categories.

Liu Yuan >> **Gaozu**

Lively, Penelope (Margaret), *née* Greer (1933-) Novelist and children's author, born in Cairo. Her children's books include *The Ghost of Thomas Kempe* (1973) and *The Revenge of Samuel Stokes* (1981). Among her adult novels are *Judgement Day* (1980) and *Moon Tiger* (1987, Booker).

Livermore, Mary Ashton, *née* Rice (1820-1905) Suffragette and reformer, born in Boston, MA. Active in the women's suffrage movement, she was founder-editor of *The Agitator* (1869), which was later merged into the *Woman's Journal*.

Liverpool, Robert Banks Jenkinson, 2nd Earl of (1770-1828) British prime minister (1812-27), born in London. He became foreign secretary (1801-4), home secretary (1804-6, 1807-9), and secretary for war and the colonies (1809-12). As premier, he oversaw the final years of the Napoleonic Wars and the War of 1812-14 with the USA.

Livia Drusilla (58 BC-AD 29) Roman empress, the third wife of the emperor Augustus. The mother of Tiberius by her first husband, Tiberius Claudius Nero, she conspired maliciously to ensure his succession. >> Augustus; Drusus Germanicus; Tiberius

Livingston, M(ilton) Stanley (1905-86) Physicist, born in Brodhead, WI. A leader in atomic particle accelerator design, he developed the first cyclotron with Lawrence in 1931. >> Lawrence, Ernest

Livingstone, David (1813-73) Missionary and traveller, born in Blantyre, Strathclyde. He discovered L Ngami and the Victoria Falls (1852-6), led an expedition to the Zambezi (1858-63), and discovered L Shirwa and L Nyasa. He disappeared while searching for the sources of the Nile, and was found in 1871 by Stanley, sent to look for him by the *New York Herald*. >> Stanley, Henry Morton

Livius >> **Livy**

Livius Andronicus [livius andronikus] (fl.3rd-c BC) Writer and playwright, born in Tarentum, Greece. He translated the *Odyssey* into Latin Saturnian verse, and wrote tragedies, comedies, and hymns after Greek models, but only fragments of his works have survived.

Livy [livee], in full **Titus Livius** (c.59 BC-AD 17) Roman historian, born in Patavium, Italy. His history of Rome, from its foundation to the death of Drusus (9 BC), comprised 142 books, of which 35 have survived.

Li Xiannian [lee shanyan] (1905–92) Chinese statesman, born in Hubei province, China. Inducted into the Politburo in 1956, he fell out of favour during the Cultural Revolution (1966–9). He was rehabilitated as finance minister (1973), and later served as state president under Deng Xiaoping (1983–8). >> Deng Xiaoping

Li Zang [lee tsang], also spelled **Li Tsang** (?–168 BC) Wife of a relatively minor Chinese official of the Han period. Her tomb at Mawangdui, Hunan, was opened in 1972. It contained, besides a well-preserved corpse in a painted lacquer coffin, over 1000 other objects.

Llewellyn, Richard [hlooelin], pseudonym of **Richard Dafydd Vivian Llewellyn Lloyd** (1907–83) Writer, born in St David's, Dyfed. He became a best-selling novelist with *How Green Was My Valley* (1939), a novel about a Welsh mining village.

Llewellyn (Prince of Wales) >> **Llywelyn**

Llosa, Mario Vargas [hohsa] (1936–) Novelist, born in Arequipa, Peru. His first novel *The Time of the Hero* (1926) outraged the Peruvian authorities. Subsequent novels include his masterpiece *Aunt Julia and the Scriptwriter* (1977) and *The War at the End of the World* (1985), and their political impact have led to his being proposed as president of Peru.

Lloyd, Clive (Hubert) (1944–) Cricketer, born in Georgetown, Guyana. A batsman and fielder, he joined Lancashire (1968–86), and played in 110 Test matches for the West Indies (captain 1974–85), scoring 7515 runs and making 19 centuries.

Lloyd, Edward (?–c.1730) English newspaper founder and coffee-house keeper. He owned a coffee house in Lombard St, London (1688–1726) after which is named *Lloyd's*, the London society of underwriters.

Lloyd, George Walter Selwyn (1913–) Composer and conductor, born in St Ives, Cornwall. His third symphony and two operas (*Iernin*, 1935, and *The Serf*, 1938) were well received, and followed by several other symphonies and concertos.

Lloyd, Harold (Clayton) (1893–1971) Film comedian, born in Burchard, NE. He became one of America's most popular daredevil comedians in films such as *High and Dizzy* (1920) and *Safety Last* (1923), and he received an honorary Academy Award in 1952.

Lloyd, Henry Demarest (1847–1903) Journalist and reformer, born in New York City. Dedicated to the exposure of capitalist abuses, his masterpiece, *Wealth Against Commonwealth* (1894), was a searing indictment of the methods by which John D Rockefeller built up Standard Oil. >> Rockefeller, John D

Lloyd, Marie, originally **Matilda Alice Victoria Wood** (1870–1922) Music-hall singer and entertainer, born in London. Among her most famous songs were 'Oh, Mr Porter' and 'My Old Man Said Follow the Van'.

Lloyd, (John) Selwyn >> **Selwyn-Lloyd, Baron**

Lloyd-George (of Dwyfor), David Lloyd-George, 1st Earl (1863–1945) British Liberal prime minister (1916–22), born in Manchester. He was President of the Board of Trade (1905–8), Chancellor of the Exchequer (1908–15), minister of munitions (1915) and secretary for war (1916), and superseded Asquith as coalition prime minister, carrying on a forceful war policy. He negotiated with Sinn Féin, and conceded the Irish Free State (1921) - a measure which brought his downfall. >> Lloyd-George, Gwilym / Megan

Lloyd-George (of Dwyfor), Gwilym, 1st Viscount Tenby of Bulford (1894–1967) British statesman, born in Criccieth, Gwynedd, the second son of David Lloyd-George. He served as parliamentary secretary to the Board of Trade (1939–41), minister of fuel and power (1942–5), minister of food (1951–4), and minister for Welsh affairs (1954–7).

Lloyd-George (of Dwyfor), Lady Megan (1902–66) British politician, born in Criccieth, Gwynedd, the younger daughter of David Lloyd-George. She was elected Liberal MP for Anglesey in 1929, and Independent Liberal between 1931 and 1945. In 1955 she joined the Labour Party. >> Lloyd-George, David / Gwilym

Lloyd-Jones, David Martyn (1899–1981) Preacher and writer, born in Newcastle Emlyn, Dyfed. He preached for 30 years at Westminster Chapel, London, his works including *Studies in the Sermon on the Mount* (2 vols, 1959–60).

Lloyd Webber, Sir Andrew (1948–) Composer, born in London. With Tim Rice he wrote *Joseph and the Amazing Technicolour Dreamcoat* (1968) and the rock opera *Jesus Christ Superstar* (staged 1970). He has since composed the music for many West End hits, including *Evita* (1978), *Cats* (1981), *The Phantom of the Opera* (1986), and *Sunset Boulevard* (1993). His brother **Julian** (1951–) is a cellist.

Llull or **Lull, Ramón** [lul], Eng **Raymond Lully**, known as **the Enlightened Doctor** (c.1235–1315) Theologian and mystic, born in Palma, Majorca. His major work is the *Ars magna* (The Great Art), condemned in 1376 for its attempt to link faith and reason. His followers, known as *Lullists*, combined religious mysticism with alchemy.

Llywelyn ap Gruffydd [hluhwelin ap grifith] (?–1282) Prince of Gwynedd in North Wales, the grandson of Llywelyn ap Iorwerth. In 1258 he proclaimed himself Prince of Wales, and was recognized by the Treaty of Shrewsbury (1265), but Edward I forced him to submit in 1277. In 1282 he rebelled against Edward, but was killed in battle. >> Edward I; Llywelyn ap Iorwerth

Llywelyn ap Iorweth [hluhwelin ap yaw(r)werth], known as **Llywelyn Fawr** ('Llywelyn the Great') (?–1240) Prince of Gwynedd in North Wales. He seized power from his uncle in 1194, and soon had most of N Wales under his control. He extended his kingdom over most of Wales, but by 1223 had to withdraw to the north. >> Llywelyn ap Gruffudd

Loach, Kenneth (1936–) Film-maker, born in Nuneaton, Warwickshire. He made his name in the BBC Wednesday Play series, highlighting social problems such as homelessness in *Cathy Come Home* (1966). Feature films include *Poor Cow* (1967) and *Kes* (1969).

Loane, Sir Marcus Lawrence (1911–) Clergyman, born in Tasmania, Australia. He became Archbishop of Sydney (1966–82), later serving also as Primate of the Anglican Church in Australia.

Lobachevsky, Nikolay Ivanovich [lobachefskee] (1792–1856) Mathematician, born in Nizhni Novgorod, Russia. In the 1820s he developed (independently of Bolyai) a theory of non-Euclidean geometry in which Euclid's parallel postulate did not hold. >> Bolyai; Euclid

L'Obel or **Lobel, Matthias de** [lohbel] (1538–1616) Botanist, born in Lille, France. Botanist and physician to James I of England, he gave his name to the *Lobelia*.

Lochner, Stefan [lokhner] (c.1400–1451) Religious painter, born in Meersburg am Bodensee, Germany. Principal master of the Cologne school, his best-known work is the great triptych, 'Adoration of the Kings', in Cologne Cathedral.

Lock, Tony, popular name of **Graham Anthony Richard Lock** (1929–95) Cricketer, born in Limpsfield, Surrey. A left-arm bowler for Surrey, he played 49 Tests for England and took 174 wickets, taking 10 or more wickets in a match on three occasions.

Locke, Alain (LeRoy) (1886–1954) Educator and writer, born in Philadelphia, PA. A leader of the Harlem Renaissance, his works include *The Negro in America* (1933).

Locke, Bessie (1865–1952) Pioneer of kindergarten education, born in Arlington (formerly West Cambridge), MA. She founded the National Association for the Promotion of Kindergarten Education in 1909, and became chief of the kindergarten division of the US Bureau of Education (1913–19).

Locke, Bobby, popular name of **Arthur D'Arcy Locke** (1917–) Golfer, born in Germiston, South Africa. He won four British Open championships (1949, 1950, 1952, 1957) and between 1947 and 1950 won 11 events on the US tour circuit.

Locke, John (1632–1704) Philosopher, born in Wrington, Somerset. His major work, the *Essay Concerning Human Understanding* (1690), accepted the possibility of rational demonstration of moral principles and the existence of God, but its reliance on the senses was the real starting point of British empiricism.

Locke, Joseph (1805–60) Civil engineer, born in Attercliffe, South Yorkshire. He became articled to George Stephenson in 1823, and went on to build a number of important railways in England, Scotland, and Europe. >> Stephenson, George

Locke, Matthew (c.1630–77) Composer, born in Exeter, Devon. A champion of the 'modern' French style of composition, his works include much incidental music for plays, Latin church music, songs, and chamber works.

Lockhart, John Gibson [lokert] (1794–1854) Biographer, novelist, and critic, born in Wishaw, Strathclyde. His works include lives of Burns (1828) and Napoleon (1829), and his masterpiece, the *Life of Sir Walter Scott* (7 vols, 1837–8). >> Scott, Walter

Lockwood, Belva Ann, *née* **Bennett** (1830–1917) Lawyer and feminist, born in Royalton, NY. She became the first woman to practise before the Supreme Court, and helped to promote the Equal Pay Act for female civil servants (1872).

Lockyer, Sir Joseph Norman (1836–1920) Astronomer, born in Rugby, Warwickshire. He detected and named *helium* in the Sun's chromosphere by daylight (1868), shortly before Ramsay. >> Ramsay, William

Loden, Barbara [lohdn] (1932–80) Actress and film director, born in Marion, NC. Her greatest acting success was in Arthur Miller's *After the Fall* (1964); its director, Elia Kazan, became her (second) husband in 1967. She then began writing and directing her own films, including *Wanda* (1970). >> Kazan, Elia

Lodge, David (John) (1935–) Novelist and critic, born in London. His novels include *Changing Places* (1975), *Small World* (1984; televised 1988), *Nice Work* (1988; televised 1989), and *Paradise News* (1991).

Lodge, George Cabot (1873–1909) Poet, born in Boston, MA, the son of Henry Cabot Lodge. He is known for his sonnets, as in *The Song of the Wave* (1898). >> Lodge, Henry Cabot

Lodge, Henry Cabot (1850–1924) US Republican politician, historian, and biographer, born in Boston, MA. He led the opposition to the Treaty of Versailles in 1919, and prevented the USA joining the League of Nations in 1920. His grandson, **Henry Cabot Lodge Jr**, (1902–85) was US representative at the United Nations (1953–60). >> Lodge, George Cabot

Lodge, Sir Oliver Joseph (1851–1940) Physicist, born in Penkhull, Staffordshire. A pioneer of radio-telegraphy, his early experiments showed that radio-frequency waves could be transmitted along electric wires (1888).

Lodge, Thomas (c.1558–1625) Playwright, romance writer, and poet, probably born in London. His best-known work is the romance, *Rosalynde* (1590), the source of Shakespeare's *As You Like It*.

Loeb, Jacques [loeb] (1859–1924) Biologist, born in Mayen, Germany. He did pioneer work on artificial parthenogenesis, and also carried out research in comparative physiology and psychology.

Loeb, James [lohb] (1867–1933) Banker and scholar, born in New York City. In 1910 he provided funds for the publi-

cation of the famous Loeb Classical Library of Latin and Greek texts with English translations.

Loesser, Frank (Henry) [lerser] (1910–69) Songwriter and composer, born in New York City. He achieved international fame with the music and lyrics for *Guys and Dolls* (1950). Later musicals included *The Most Happy Fella* (1956) and *How to Succeed in Business Without Really Trying* (1961).

Loewe, (Johann) Carl (Gottfried) [loevuh] (1796–1869) Composer, born near Halle, Germany. He is best known for his dramatic ballads, including his setting of Goethe's *Erlkönig*, but also composed operas, oratorios, symphonies, concertos, duets, and works for piano.

Loewe, Frederick [loh] (1904–88) Composer, born in Berlin. He went to the USA in 1924, and worked on a number of Broadway musicals in collaboration with **Alan J Lerner** (1918–86), including *Brigadoon* (1947) and *My Fair Lady* (1956).

Loewi, Otto [loevee] (1873–1961) Pharmacologist, born in Frankfurt, Germany. In 1936 he shared the Nobel Prize for Physiology or Medicine for his work on nerve impulses and their chemical transmission.

Loewy, Raymond (Fernand) [lohee] (1893–1987) Industrial designer, born in Paris. Commissioned to design products and graphics for industrial corporations worldwide, his successes include the design of Lucky Strike cigarette packs, and Apollo and Skylab spacecraft.

Löffler, Friedrich August Johannes [loefler] (1852–1915) Bacteriologist, born in Frankfurt an der Oder, Germany. He first cultured the diphtheria bacillus (1884), discovered the causal organism of glanders and swine erysipelas (1886), and prepared a vaccine against foot-and-mouth disease (1899).

Lofting, Hugh (John) (1886–1947) Children's novelist, born in Maidenhead, Berkshire. He created the immensely successful 'Dr Dolittle' books from letters he wrote to his children from the front lines in World War 1.

Logan, James (1674–1751) Colonial statesman and scholar, born in Lurgan, Co Armagh. He became William Penn's secretary, arrived in Pennsylvania in 1699, and was chief justice of the colony's Supreme Court (1731–9). >> Penn

Logan, James, originally **Tahgajute** [tagajoot] (?1723–80) American Indian leader, (probably named for the Quaker, James Logan), born in Sunbury (formerly Shamokin), PA. He was a friend of the white settlers until his family were killed in 1774. Dedicating himself to revenge, he attacked white settlements, and aided the British during the revolution.

Logan, John A(lexander) (1826–86) US soldier and politician, born in Jackson County, IL. He raised an Illinois regiment in the Civil War, and retired at its close as major-general. Returned to Congress as a Republican in 1866, he was repeatedly chosen as a senator.

Lo Guangzhong [loe gwangjong], also spelled **Lo Kuanchung** (1330–1400) Writer, born in Hangzhou, China. He is associated with two of the four great Ming-period novels. *The Romance of the Three Kingdoms* (published 1522) and *The Water Margin*, translated by Pearl Buck as *All Men Are Brothers* (1933). >> Buck

Loisy, Alfred Firmin [lwazee] (1857–1940) Theologian, born in Ambrières, France. His controversial books included *The Gospel and the Church* (trans, 1902), and for later works of the same kind he was excommunicated in 1908.

Lomax, Alan (1915–) Ethnomusicologist, born in Austin, TX. Devoting his life to the study of folk and blues music, he discovered blues singer Leadbelly, and in 1938 interviewed Jelly Roll Morton, obtaining an oral record of early jazz. >> Leadbelly; Morton, Jelly Roll

Lombard, Carole, originally **Jane Alice Peters** (1908–42) Actress, born in Fort Wayne, IN. She revealed a comic flair in the film *Twentieth Century* (1934), and made the perfect heroine of screwball comedies such as *My Man Godfrey* (1936). She married Clark Gable in 1939. >> Gable, Clark

Lombard, Peter, known as **Magister Sententiarum** ('Master of Sentences') (c.1100–60) Theologian, born near Novara, Italy. He was styled 'Master of Sentences', because of his collection of sentences from Augustine and others on points of Christian doctrine. His work became the standard textbook of Catholic theology until the Reformation.

Lombardi, Vince(nt Thomas) [lombah(r)dee] (1913–70) Coach of American football, born in New York City. His best work was with the Green Bay Packers from Michigan (1959–69), winning five league titles and taking them to two Super Bowls (1967–8).

Lombardo, Pietro [lombah(r)doh] (c.1435–1515) Sculptor and architect, born in Carona, Italy. He headed the major sculpture workshop of the day, and was responsible for both the architecture and sculptural decoration of Santa Maria dei Miracoli (1481–9) in Venice.

Lombroso, Cesare [lombrohsoh] (1836–1909) Founder of the science of criminology, born in Verona, Italy. Professor of forensic medicine (1876), psychiatry (1896), and criminal anthropology (1906) at Turin, his theory (now discredited) postulated the existence of a criminal type distinguishable from a normal person.

Lomonosov, Mikhail Vasilyevich [lomonohsof] (1711–65) Scientist and linguistic reformer, born in Denisovka, Russia. His writings include works on rhetoric, grammar, and Russian history, and he systematized Russian grammar and orthography.

London, Fritz (Wolfgang) (1900–54) Physicist, born in Breslau, Germany. He devised the quantum theory of the chemical bond with Walter Heitler (1927), and in 1930 calculated the non-polar component of forces between molecules, now called *Van de Waals* or *London forces*.

London, Heinz (1907–70) Physicist, born in Bonn, Germany. With his brother Fritz he fled to England (1933), where they worked on conductivity, giving the *London equations* (1935). Briefly interned in 1940, he was released to work on the development of the atomic bomb. >> London, Fritz

London, Jack, pseudonym of **John Griffith Chaney** (1876–1916) Novelist, born in San Francisco, CA. His books include *The Call of the Wild* (1903), the political novel *The Iron Heel* (1907), and several autobiographical tales, notably *John Barleycorn* (1913).

Lonergan, Bernard (Joseph Francis) (1904–85) Jesuit theologian and philosopher, born in Buckingham, Quebec, Canada. The findings of his massive and seminal studies are summarized in *Philosophy of God, and Theology* (1973) and *Understanding and Being* (1980).

Long, Earl K(emp) (1895–1960) US politician, born near Winnfield, LA, the brother of Huey Long. He was Governor of Louisiana (1939–40, 1948–52, 1956–60), but suffered from paranoid schizophrenia, and was at his wife's request placed in a mental hospital in 1959. >> Long, Huey

Long, George Washington De >> De Long, George Washington

Long, Huey (Pierce), nickname **Kingfish** (1893–1935) US politician, born in Winnfield, LA. As Governor of Louisiana (1928–31) and a US senator (1930–5), he enjoyed virtually total control of his state until his assassination by Carl Weiss. >> Long, Earl K

Long, Richard (1945–) 'Land artist', born in Bristol, Avon. He takes country walks, which he considers works of art in themselves, sometimes marking a place with a simple 'sculpture', such as a circle of stones, and afterwards exhibits photographs, maps, and texts. He won the 1989 Turner Prize.

Longchamp, William de [longshā] (d.1197) English clergyman and statesman. He was a lowly-born favourite of Richard I, who in 1189–90 made him chancellor, Bishop of Ely, and joint justiciar of England. >> Richard I

Longfellow, Henry Wadsworth (1807–82) Poet, born in Portland, ME. He published many works, notably *Ballads and Other Poems* (1841), including 'The Wreck of the Hesperus'. His most popular work was 'Hiawatha' (1855), and in 1863 appeared *Tales of a Wayside Inn*, which included the famous 'Paul Revere's Ride'.

Longhi, Pietro [longgee], originally **Pietro Falca** (1702–85) Painter, born in Venice, Italy. He excelled in small-scale satirical pictures of Venetian life. His son **Alessandro** (1733–1813) was also a painter, and some of his portraits are now attributed to his father.

Longinus, Dionysius [lonjiynus] (c.213–73) Greek Neoplatonic rhetorician and philosopher. He is the supposed author of the treatise on excellence in literature, *On the Sublime*, which influenced many Neoclassical writers.

Longman, Thomas (1699–1755) Publisher, born in Bristol, Avon. He bought a bookselling business in Paternoster Row, London, in 1724, and was the founder of the British publishing house that still bears his name.

Longstreet, James (1821–1904) US soldier, born in Edgefield District, SC. He fought in both Battles of Bull Run (1861, 1862) and at Gettysburg (1863), and surrendered with Lee at Appomattox Courthouse in 1865.

Longuett-Higgins, (Hugh) Christopher [longgee higinz] (1923–) Theoretical chemist and neurophysicist, born in Lenham, Kent. He made contributions to theories of chemical bonding from the 1940s, and later worked on language acquisition, music perception, and speech analysis.

Longus (fl.3rd-c) Greek writer, the author of the Greek prose romance *Daphnis and Chloë*. The first pastoral romance known, it is the most popular of the Greek erotic romances.

Lönnrot, Elias [loenrot] (1802–84) Philologist and folklorist, born in Sammatti, Finland. His major achievement was the epic poem of ancient life in the far north, the *Kalevala* (1835, 1849).

Lonsdale, Hugh Cecil Lowther, 5th Earl of (1857–1944) English sportsman. As president of the National Sporting Club he founded and presented the *Lonsdale belts* for boxing in 1909.

Lonsdale, Dame Kathleen, *née* **Yardley** (1903–71) Crystallographer, born in Newbridge, Co Kildare, Ireland. From the 1920s she applied X-ray crystal diffraction to determine chemical structures, and in 1945 became the first female Fellow of the Royal Society.

Loon, Hendrik Willem van >> van Loon, Hendrik Willem

Loos, Adolf [loos] (1870–1933) Architect and writer on design, born in Brno, Czech Republic. A major architect of the 'Modern Movement', he held the view that ornament is decadent, and argued against modern civilized design. His work includes the Villa Karma, Clarens, Switzerland (1904–6).

Lope de Vega >> Vega, Lope de

Lopez, Nancy [lohpez] (1957–) Golfer, born in Torrance, CA. She won the Ladies' Professional Golf Association (LPGA) championship in 1978, and was voted LPGA player of the year four times (1978–9, 1985, 1988).

Lopukhov, Fyodor [lopookof] (1886–1973) Dancer, choreographer, and teacher, born in St Petersburg, Russia. A choreographer from 1916, he set the foundation of Neoclassical and modern dance in Russia, and was artistic director of the Kirov, Maly Theatre, and Bolshoi Ballet companies.

Lorant, Stefan (1901–) Pioneer photo-journalist, born

in Budapest. In Britain he founded *Weekly Illustrated* (1934) and *Picture Post* (1938). He moved to the USA in 1940, his photographic books including *Sieg Heil: an Illustrated History of Germany from Bismarck to Hitler* (1974).

Lorca, Federico García [**law(r)**ka, gah(r)**see**a] (1899–1936) Poet, born in Fuente Vaqueros, Spain. His best-known works are *Songs* (trans, 1927) and *The Gypsy Ballads* (trans, 1928, 1935). Prose plays include the trilogy *Blood Wedding* (trans, 1933), *Yerma* (1934), and *The House of Bernarda Alba* (trans, 1936). He was assassinated in the Spanish Civil War.

Lord, Thomas (1755–1832) Sportsman, born in Thirsk, North Yorkshire. He founded Lord's Cricket Ground in London, first opening a cricket ground in Dorset Square in London (1787), which became the home of the Marylebone Cricket Club (MCC).

Loren, Sophia [**lor**en], originally **Sofia Scicolone** (1934–) Actress and filmstar, born in Rome. Under contract to film producer **Carlo Ponti** (1910–), later her husband, she won an Oscar for *Two Women* (trans, 1961). Other films include *The Millionairess* (1961) and *Marriage Italian Style* (1964).

Lorente de No, Rafael [**lor**entay] (1902–) Neurophysiologist, born in Zaraguza, Spain. His research covered a wide range of problems, including the co-ordination of eye movements and the functional anatomy of neurone networks.

Lorentz, Hendrik Antoon [**loh**rents] (1853–1928) Physicist, born in Arnhem, The Netherlands. In 1902 he shared with Zeeman the Nobel Prize for Physics for his theory of electromagnetic radiation. Their work led to Einstein's theory of special relativity. >> Einstein; Zeeman

Lorenz, Edward N(orton) [**lo**rens] (1917–) Meteorologist, born in West Hartford, CT. He was the first to describe what is known as 'deterministic chaos' as a shaper of weather, and was the originator of the term 'the butterfly effect'.

Lorenz, Konrad (Zacharias) [**loh**rents] (1903–89) Zoologist, born in Vienna. The founder of ethology, his studies led to a deeper understanding of behaviour patterns in animals, notably imprinting in young birds, and he shared the Nobel Prize for Physiology or Medicine in 1973. His books, such as *On Aggression* (1963) and *King Solomon's Ring* (1949) enjoyed wide popularity.

Lorenzetti, Ambrogio [lor**en**zetee] (c.1280–c.1348) Painter, born in Siena, Italy. He is best known for his allegorical frescoes in the Palazzo Pubblico at Siena, symbolizing the effects of good and bad government.

Lorenzetti, Pietro [lor**en**zetee] (c.1280–c.1348) Painter from Siena, Italy. He worked at Arezzo (the polyptych in S Maria della Pieve) and Assisi, where he painted dramatic frescoes of 'The Passion' in the Lower Church of S Francis.

Lorenzo [lor**en**zoh], known as **il Monaco** ('the Monk'), originally **Piero di Giovanni** (c.1370–c.1425) Painter, born in Siena, Italy. A monk in the Camaldolite monastery of S Maria degli Angeli, Florence, his great altarpiece, 'The Coronation of the Virgin' (1414) was painted for the high altar there.

Lorenzo de' Medici [lor**en**zoh day **may**deechee], known as **the Magnificent** (1449–92) Florentine ruler, born in Florence, Italy, the grandson of Cosimo de' Medici. He was an able if autocratic ruler, who made Florence the leading state in Italy. >> Cosimo de' Medici

Lorjou, Bernard [law(r)zhoo] (1908–) Painter, born in Blois, France. He was the founder of the L'Homme Témoin group in 1949. Among a number of large satirical paintings is his 'Atomic Age' (1951).

Lorrain, Claude >> Claude Lorrain

Lorre, Peter [**lo**ree], originally **László Löwenstein** (1904–64) Actor, born in Rosenberg, Hungary. He was succesfully cast in many sinister film parts, including *Crime and Punishment* (1935) and *Casablanca* (1942), and also played the Japanese detective in the *Mr Moto* films.

Lorris, Guillaume de >> Guillaume de Lorris

Losey, Joseph (Walton) [**loh**see] (1909–84) Film director, born in La Crosse, WI. His films include *The Servant* (1963), *Modesty Blaise* (1966), *Accident* (1967), and *The Go-Between*, which won the Cannes Film Festival in 1971.

Lothrop, Harriet Mulford, *née* **Stone**, pseudonym **Margaret Sidney** (1844–1924) Writer, born in New Haven, CT. She is remembered, among many other works, for the *Five Little Peppers and How They Grew* (1881) series for children.

Loti, Pierre >> Viaud, Louis Marie Julien

Lotto, Lorenzo (c.1480–1556) Religious painter, born in Venice, Italy. He worked in several cities, becoming known for his altarpieces and portraits.

Lotze, Rudolf Hermann [**lots**uh] (1817–81) Philosopher, born in Bautzen, Germany. He helped to found the science of physiological psychology, but is best known for his religious philosophy, Theistic Idealism, expounded in *Mikrokosmos* (3 vols, 1856–8).

Loudon, John Claudius [**low**dn] (1783–1843) Horticultural writer and architect, born in Cambuslang, Strathclyde. A major influence in London landscape and domestic architecture, his major work was *Arboretum et fruticetum Brittanicum* (8 vols, 1838).

Louganis, Greg(ory) [**loo**ganis] (1960–) Diver, born in El Cajon, CA. He was Olympic champion (1984, 1988), platform world champion (1978, 1982, 1986), and springboard champion (1982, 1986).

Louis I, known as **the Pious** (778–840) King of Aquitaine (781–814) and emperor of the Western empire (814–40), the son of Charlemagne. His reign was marked by reforms of the Church and for the raids of the Norsemen in the NW of the empire. >> Charlemagne

Louis IX, St (1214–70), feast day 25 August. King of France (1226–70), born in Poissy, near Paris, the son of Louis VIII. He led the Seventh Crusade (1248), but was defeated in Egypt. In 1270 he embarked on a new Crusade, and died of plague at Tunis. He was canonized in 1297.

Louis XI (1423–83) King of France (1461–83), born in Bourges, France. During his reign he broke the power of the nobility, and by 1483 had succeeded in uniting most of France under one crown, laying the foundations for absolute monarchy in France. >> Charles VII

Louis XII (1462–1515) King of France (1498–1515), born in Blois, France, the son of Charles, duc d'Orléans. He foiled the Emperor Maximilian's dynastic designs on Brittany, but paid the price when his forces were driven from Italy (1512), and was then defeated by an Anglo–Imperial alliance at Guinegate (1513). To guarantee peace, Louis married Mary Tudor, the sister of Henry VIII (1515). >> Anne of Brittany; Mary Tudor; Maximilian I

Louis XIII (1601–43) King of France (1610–43), born in Fontainebleau, France, the eldest son of Henry IV and Marie de Médicis. He succeeded to the throne on the assassination of his father (1610), and married Anne of Austria in 1615. In 1617 he took over the reins of government, but by 1624 was entirely dependent upon Richelieu, his chief minister. His later years saw French military victories in the Thirty Years' War. >> Anne of Austria; Marie de Médicis; Richelieu

Louis XIV, known as **le Roi soleil** ('the Sun King') (1638–1715) King of France (1643–1715), born in St Germain-en-Laye, the son of Louis XIII. In 1660 he married Maria Theresa, elder daughter of Philip IV of Spain, through whom he was later to claim the Spanish succession for his second grandson. His obsession with France's greatness led him into aggressive foreign policies, his major political rivals being the Austrian Habsburgs, particularly Leopold I. His attempt to create a Franco–Spanish Bourbon bloc led to the War of the Spanish Succession (1701–13), and there was also conflict with the Jansenists, the Huguenots, and the papacy. His long reign nonetheless marked the cultural ascendancy of France within Europe, symbolized by the Palace of Versailles. >> Leopold I (Emperor); Loius XIII

Louis XV, known as **Louis le Bien-Aimé** ('Louis the Well-Beloved') (1710–74) King of France (1715–74), born in Versailles, France, the great-grandson of Louis XIV. His reign coincided with the great age of Rococo decorative art (the 'Louis XV style'). Until he came of age (1723) he was guided by the Regent, Philippe d'Orléans, and then by the Duc de Bourbon. In 1726 Bourbon was replaced by Fleury, who skilfully steered the French state until his death (1744). Thereafter Louis allowed the government to drift into the hands of ministerial factions, while indulging in secret diplomatic activity through his own network of agents - a system which brought confusion to French foreign policy. France was drawn into wars which culminated in the loss of the French colonies in America and India (1763). >> du Barry; Fleury

Louis XVI (1754–93) King of France (1774–93), born in Versailles, France, the grandson of Louis XV. He was married in 1770 to the Archduchess Marie Antoinette, daughter of the Habsburg Empress Maria Theresa, to strengthen the Franco–Austrian alliance. He failed to give consistent support to ministers who tried to reform the outmoded financial and social structures of the country and was forced in 1789 to summon the States General. He resisted demands from the National Assembly for sweeping reforms, and was brought with his family from Versailles to Paris as hostages to the revolutionary movement. Their attempted flight to Varennes (1791) branded them as traitors. The monarchy was abolished, he was tried for conspiracy, and guillotined in Paris. >> Marie Antoinette

Louis (Charles) XVII (1785–95) Titular King of France (1793–5), born in Versailles, France, the second son of Louis XVI and heir to the throne (from 1789). After the execution of his father (1793) he remained in the Temple prison in Paris until his death. The secrecy surrounding his last months led to rumours of his escape, and produced several claimants to his title.

Louis XVIII, originally **Louis Stanislas Xavier, comte de** (Count of) **Provence** (1755–1824) King of France (in name from 1795 and in fact from 1814), born in Versailles, France, the younger brother of Louis XVI. He fled from Paris in 1791, finally taking refuge in England, becoming the focal point for the Royalist cause. >> Charles X; Napoleon I

Louis, Joe [loois], popular name of **Joseph Louis Barrow**, nickname **the Brown Bomber** (1914–81) Boxer, born in Lafayette, AL. He beat Braddock for the world heavyweight title in 1937, and held the title for a record 12 years, making a record 25 defences. >> Braddock, James J; Marciano

Louis, Morris, originally **Morris Bernstein** (1912–62) Painter, born in Baltimore, MD. His later work shows an individual use of colour, and he came to be associated with the New York school of Abstract Expressionism.

Louis Napoleon >> Napoleon III

Louis-Philippe [fileep], known as **the Citizen King** (1773–1850) King of the French (1830–48), born in Paris, the eldest son of Philippe Egalité. At the Revolution he entered the National Guard, renounced his title to demonstrate his progressive sympathies, then lived in exile (1793–1814). After the revolution (1830) he was given the title of King of the French. Political corruption and economic depression caused discontent, and he abdicated at the onset of the 1848 revolution. >> Orléans, Louis Philippe Joseph, Duc d'

Loutherbourg, Philip James de [lootherboorg] (1740–1812) Stage designer and illustrator, born in Fulda, Germany. Hired by Garrick as artistic adviser at the Drury Lane theatre, London (1771–81), his innovations in scene design and stage lighting laid the foundations for the development of the picture-frame concept in stagecraft. >> Garrick

L'Ouverture, Toussaint >> **Toussaint L'Ouverture**

Louvois, François Michel le Tellier, marquis de [loovwah] (1641–91) French secretary of state for war under Louis XIV, born in Paris. He was recognized as a brilliant administrator and the king's most influential minister in the years 1683–91. >> Louis XIV

Louÿs, Pierre [lwee], pseudonym of **Pierre Louis** (1870–1925) Poet and novelist, born in Ghent, Belgium. His lyrics, based on the Greek form which he so much admired, are masterpieces of style. His novels include *Aphrodite* (1896) and *Woman and Puppet* (trans, 1898).

Lovecraft, H(oward) P(hillips) (1890–1937) Science fiction writer and poet, born in Providence, RI. His cult following derives from the 60 or so horrific 'Cthulhu Mythos' stories. His novellas include *The Case of Charles Dexter Ward* (1928) and *At the Mountains of Madness* (1931).

Lovejoy, Arthur O(ncken) (1873–1963) Philosopher, born in Berlin. His method of detailed 'philosophical semantics', investigating the history of key terms and concepts, is best exemplified in *The Great Chain of Being: a Study of the History of an Idea* (1936).

Lovelace, Augusta Ada King, Countess of, *née* **Byron** (1815–52) Writer, mathematician, and socialite, the daughter of Lord Byron. She owes much of her fame to her friendship with Babbage, the computer pioneer. In 1983 the high-level universal computer programming language, ADA, was named in her honour. >> Babbage; Byron, George

Lovelace, Richard (1618–57) English Cavalier poet. In 1642 he wrote 'To Althea, from Prison' ('Stone walls do not a prison make...'), and in 1649 published his best-known work, *Lucasta*. >> Charles I (of England)

Lovell, Sir (Alfred Charles) Bernard (1913–) Astronomer, born in Oldland Common, Gloucestershire. Director of the Nuffield Radio Astronomy Laboratories at Jodrell Bank, he is distinguished for his pioneering work in radio telescope design, space research, and the physics of radio sources.

Lovell, James A(rthur) (1928–) Astronaut, born in Cleveland, OH. He was crew member of several historic flights: Gemini 7 (1965), Gemini 12 (1966), Apollo 8 (1968), and commanded the unsuccessful Apollo 13 Moon mission (1970).

Lovelock, Jack, popular name of **John Edward Lovelock** (1910–49) Athlete, born in Temuka, New Zealand. In 1932 he set a British record for the mile, in 1933 a world record for that distance, and at the Olympics in 1936 a world record of 3 min 47·8 s for the 1500 m.

Lovelock, James (Ephraim) (1919–) British scientist. He is best known as the originator of the 'Gaia hypothesis', a controversial ecological idea that considers the Earth as a single living entity, in his book *Gaia* (1979).

Low, Sir David (Alexander Cecil) (1891–1963) Political cartoonist, born in Dunedin, New Zealand. He joined the *Evening Standard* in 1927, for which he drew some of his most successful cartoons, notably the character 'Colonel Blimp', whose name has been incorporated into the language.

Lowe, Arthur (1914–82) Actor, born in Hayfield, Derbyshire. It was television that brought him his greatest popularity, first as Mr Swindley in *Coronation Street* (1960–5), then as the bumbling Captain Mainwaring in *Dad's Army* (1968–77).

Lowell, A(bbott) Lawrence (1856–1943) Lawyer and educator, born in Boston, MA, the brother of Amy and Percival Lowell. While president of Harvard (1909–33), he doubled enrolment and trebled the faculty. >> Lowell, Amy / Percival

Lowell, Amy (1874–1925) Imagist poet, born in Brookline, MA, the sister of Percival and A Lawrence Lowell. She produced volumes of free verse which she named 'unrhymed cadence' and 'polyphonic prose', as in *Sword Blades and Poppy Seed* (1914). >> Lowell, A Lawrence / Percival

Lowell, Francis Cabot (1775–1817) Textile manufacturer, born in Newburyport, MA. He started the Boston Manufacturing Co (1813) in Waltham, MA, the first mill to combine all the operations of making finished cloth from raw cotton. Lowell, MA was named after him.

Lowell, James Russell (1819–91) Poet, essayist, and diplomat, born in Cambridge, MA. He worked on what was to become *The Biglow Papers* (1848), a poem denouncing the pro-slavery party and the government, the second series of which appeared in 1867.

Lowell, Percival (1855–1916) Astronomer, born in Boston, MA, the brother of Amy and A Lawrence Lowell. He is best known for his observations of Mars, and for his prediction of the existence of the planet Pluto (discovered in 1930). >> Lowell, A Lawrence / Amy; Tombaugh

Lowell, Robert (Traill Spence), Jr (1917–77) Poet, born in Boston, MA. His first collection was the autobiographical *Land of Unlikeness* (1944), followed by *Lord Weary's Castle* (1946, Pulitzer). Other confessional volumes include *Life Studies* (1959) and *The Dolphin* (1973).

Lower, Richard (1631–91) Physician and physiologist, born in Tremeer, Cornwall. His *Treatise on the Heart* (trans, 1669) was a major work on pulmonary and cardiovascular anatomy and physiology. >> Hooke

Lowie, Robert Harry [lohee] (1883–1957) Cultural anthropologist, born in Vienna. He made several ethnographic studies of North American Indian societies, publishing *Social Life of the Crow Indians* (1912) and *The Crow Indians* (1935).

Lowry, L(aurence) S(tephen) [lowree] (1887–1976) Artist, born in Manchester. From 1939 he produced many pictures of the Lancashire industrial scene, mainly in brilliant whites and greys, peopled with scurrying sticklike men and women.

Lowry, (Clarence) Malcolm [lowree] (1909–57) Novelist, born in New Brighton, Merseyside. His reputation is based on *Under the Volcano* (1947), a novel set in Mexico, where he lived in 1936–7.

Lowry, Thomas Martin >> Brønsted, Johannes

Lowth, Robert [lowth] (1710–87) Clergyman and scholar, born in Winchester, Hampshire. He was one of the first to treat the Bible poetry as literature in its own right. His highly prescriptive English grammar strongly influenced English language teaching in British schools.

Lowther, Hugh Cecil >> Lonsdale, 5th Earl of

Loyola, Ignatius of, St [loyohla], originally Iñigo López de Recalde (1491 or 1495–1556), feast day 31 July. Theologian and founder of the Jesuits, born in his ancestral castle of Loyola in the Basque province Guipúzcao. He founded with six associates the Society of Jesus in 1584, and wrote the influential *Spiritual Exercises*. He was canonized in 1622. >> Francis Xavier, St

Loyson, Charles >> Hyacinthe, Père

Lü, Empress [lü] (?–180 BC) Consort of the first Han dynasty Chinese emperor, Gaozu, and dowager empress after his death (195 BC). She tried to ensure her own family's succession, but after her death all were murdered. >> Gaozu; Wendi

Lubbers, Ruud (Franz Marie) (1939–) Dutch prime minister (1982–). He led a Christian Democratic Appeal coalition, which continued as the main party in a new coalition formed after the 1989 elections.

Lubbock, Percy (1879–1965) Critic and biographer, born in London. Among his writings are *The Craft of Fiction* (1920), *Earlham* (1922), a book of personal childhood memories, and studies of Pepys (1909) and Edith Wharton (1947).

Lubetkin, Berthold [lubetkin] (1901–90) Architect, born in Tbilisi. His major works include the Penguin Pool at London Zoo (1933), and Highpoint in Hampstead (1935), a block of high-rise flats.

Lubin, David [loobin] (1849–1919) Agriculturalist, born in Klodowa, Poland (formerly Russia). His family settled in New York City in 1855. For 12 years he sought a sovereign state to support an International Institute of Agriculture; in 1910 Italy agreed, and the Institute's treaty was ratified by 46 nations.

Lubitsch, Ernst [loobich] (1892–1947) Film director, born in Berlin. He went to Hollywood and became an acknowledged master of light, sophisticated sex comedics graced with 'the Lubitsch touch' of elegance, including *Forbidden Paradise* (1924) and *Heaven Can Wait* (1943).

Lübke, Heinrich [lübkuh] (1894–1972) President of the German Federal Republic (1959–69), born in Westphalia, Germany. He helped to found the Christian Democratic Party, and was minister of food, agriculture, and forestry (1953–9).

Luca da Cortona >> Signorelli, Luca

Lucan [lookn], in full **Marcus Annaeus Lucanus** (39–65) Roman poet, born in Córdoba, Spain. In 62 he published the first three books of his epic *Pharsalia* on the civil war between Pompey and Caesar. After Nero forbade him to write poetry, he joined a conspiracy against him, but was betrayed and committed suicide. >> Nero

Lucan, George Charles Bingham, Earl of [lookn] (1800–88) British soldier, born in London. Commander of cavalry in the Crimean War (1853–6), he passed on the disastrous order for the Charge of the Light Brigade at Balaclava (1854).

Lucan, Richard John Bingham, 7th Earl of [lookn], known as **Lord Lucan** (1934–) British aristocrat, and alleged murderer. He disappeared in 1974, after police found the body of the Lucan family's nanny. Speculation about his whereabouts continues to this day.

Lucaris or **Lukaris, Cyril** [lukahris] (1572–1638) Orthodox theologian, born in Candia, Crete, Greece. He negotiated with the Calvinists of England and Holland with a view to union and the reform of the Greek Church.

Lucas, Colin Anderson (1906–) Architect, born in London. In 1930 he designed a house in Bourne End, Buckinghamshire, the first English example of the domestic use of monolithic reinforced concrete.

Lucas, Edward Verrall (1868–1938) Essayist and biographer, born in Eltham, Kent. He compiled anthologies, and wrote novels, books of travel, a biography of Lamb (1905), and many volumes of light essays.

Lucas, F(rank) L(awrence) (1894–1967) Critic and poet, born in Hipperholme, West Yorkshire. His scholarly works of criticism include *Seneca and Elizabethan Tragedy* (1922) and *Eight Victorian Poets* (1930). He also wrote poetry, plays, novels, and popular translations of Greek drama and poetry.

Lucas, Victoria >> Plath, Sylvia

Lucas van Leyden [laydn], or **Lucas Jacobsz** (1494–1533) Painter and engraver, born in Leyden, The Netherlands. His paintings include the triptych 'The Last Judgement' (1526) and 'Blind Man of Jericho Healed by Christ' (1531). He is believed to have been the first to etch on copper rather than iron.

Luce, Clare Boothe, née *Boothe* (1903–87) Playwright, editor, and public figure, born in New York City. She was editor of *Vanity Fair* (1930–4), and wrote several Broadway successes including *Kiss the Boys Goodbye* (1938). A major influence in the Republican Party, she was US ambassador to Italy (1953–7). >> Luce, Henry R

Luce, Henry R(obinson) (1898–1967) Magazine publisher and editor, born in Shandong, China. He co-founded the news magazine *Time* (1923), later founding magazines *Fortune* (1929), and *Life* (1936). He married Clare Boothe in 1935. >> **Luce, Clare Boothe**

Lucian [looshan] (c.117–c.180) Rhetorician, born in Samosata, Syria. He devoted himself to philosophy, and produced a new form of literature - humorous dialogue. His satires include *Dialogues of the Gods* and *Dialogues of the Dead.*

Luciano, Lucky [loosiahnoh], popular name of **Charles Luciano**, originally **Salvatore Lucania** (1897–1962) Gangster, born in Lercara Friddi, Sicily, Italy. He moved to New York City in 1906, where he became the chief of organized crime. Although imprisoned (1936), he set up the Crime Syndicate of Mafia families, and in 1946 was deported to Italy.

Lucilius, Gaius [loosilius] (c.180–102 BC) Satirist, born in Suessa Aurunca, Italy. He wrote 30 books of *Satires*, of which only fragments remain.

Lucretia [lookreesha] (6th-c BC) Roman heroine, the wife of Lucius Tarquinius Collatinus who, according to legend, was raped by Sextus, the son of Tarquinius Superbus. She incited her father and husband to take an oath of vengeance against the Tarquins, then committed suicide. >> **Brutus, Lucius Junius**

Lucretius [lookreeshus], in full **Titus Lucretius Carus** (1st-c BC) Roman poet and philosopher. His major work is the six-volume hexameter poem *On the Nature of Things* (trans title) in which he tried to popularize the philosophical theories of Democritus and Epicurus on the origin of the universe. >> **Democritus; Epicurus**

Lucullus, Lucius Licinius [lookulus] (c.110–57 BC) Roman politican and general, famous for his victories over Mithridates VI, and also for his enormous wealth, luxurious lifestyle, and patronage of the arts.

Lucy, St (?–303), feast day 13 December. Christian martyr, the patron saint of virgins and of the blind. According to legend, she was a virgin denounced as a Christian by a rejected suitor, and martyred under Diocletian at Syracuse. >> **Diocletian**

Lucy, Sir Thomas (1532–1600) Squire, member of parliament, and justice of the peace, born near Stratford-on-Avon, Warwickshire. He may have been caricatured as Shakespeare's Justice Shallow in *The Merry Wives of Windsor*. >> **Shakespeare, William**

Ludd, Ned (fl.1779) Farm labourer from Leicestershire. Legend has it that he destroyed some stocking frames c.1782, and it is from him that the *Luddite* rioters (1812–18) took their name.

Lüdendorff, Erich von [lüdendaw(r)f] (1865–1937) General, born near Poznan, Poland. He became chief-of-staff under Hindenburg, defeated the Russians at Tannenberg (1914), and conducted the 1918 offensives on the Western Front. He became a Nazi, but from 1925 led a minority party of his own. >> **Hindenburg; Hitler**

Ludlow, Edmund (c.1617–92) English politician, born in Maiden Bradley, Wiltshire. He urged the restoration of the Rump Parliament, was nominated to the Committee of Safety, and strove in vain to reunite the Republicans. After the Restoration he escaped to Switzerland.

Ludmila, St [ludmila] (c.860–921), feast day 16 September. Patron saint of Bohemia, born near Melník, Bohemia. She married the first Christian Czech prince, Borivoj, and pioneered the establishment of Christianity. She was murdered by her heathen daughter-in-law, Drahomira, the mother of Wenceslaus. >> **Wenceslaus**

Ludwig II [ludveekh], nickname **Mad King Ludwig** (1845–86) King of Bavaria (1864–86), born in Munich, the son of Maximilian II. Siding with Prussia (1870–1) against France, he took Bavaria into the new German Reich. A German patriot of Romantic disposition, he devoted himself to patronage of Wagner and his music

Ludwig, Carl F(riedrich) W(ilhelm) [ludveekh] (1816–

95) Physiologist, born in Witzenhausen, Germany. He did pioneer research on glandular secretions, and his invention of the mercurial blood-gas pump revealed the role of oxygen and other gases in the bloodstream.

Ludwig, Emil [ludveekh], pseudonym of **Emil Ludwig Cohn** (1881–1948) Writer, born in Breslau, Germany. He was popular as a biographer, emphasizing the personality of his subjects, including (English translations) *Napoleon* (1927), *Bismarck* (1927), and the controversial biography of Christ, *The Son of Man* (1928).

Lugard (of Abinger), Frederick John Dealtry, Baron (1858–1945) British soldier and colonial administrator, born in Fort St George, Madras, India. He was responsible for Uganda becoming a British protectorate (1894), and was high commissioner for N Nigeria (1900–7). He became governor-general (1914–19) on the amalgamation of the two protectorates.

Lugosi, Bela [lugohsee], popular name of **Bela Ferenc Denzso Blasko** (1884–1956) Actor, born in Lugos, Romania (formerly Hungary). He enjoyed his greatest success on Broadway as *Dracula* (1927), a role he repeated on film in 1931, and found himself typecast in low-budget horror films.

Lukács, Georg or **György** [lookach] (1885–1971) Marxist philosopher and critic, born in Budapest. He was a major figure in the Marxist theory of literature and Socialist Realism, especially through his work on the novel, as in *The Theory of the Novel* (1916, trans 1971).

Lukaris, Cyril >> **Lucaris, Cyril**

Luke, St (1st-c), feast day 18 October. New Testament evangelist, a Gentile Christian, perhaps 'the beloved physician' and companion of St Paul (*Col* 4.14). He is first named as author of the third Gospel in the 2nd-c, and tradition has ascribed to him both that work and the Acts of the Apostles. >> **Paul, St**

Lull, Ramón >> **Llull, Ramón**

Lully, Jean Baptiste [loolee], originally **Giovanni Battista Lulli** (1632–87) Composer, born in Florence, Italy. He composed many operas in which he made the ballet an essential part, and also wrote church music, dance music, and pastorals.

Lully, Raymond >> **Llull, Ramón**

Lumet, Sidney [loomet] (1924–   ) Film director, born in Philadelphia, PA. His films include *Twelve Angry Men* (1957), *The Pawnbroker* (1965), *Murder on the Orient Express* (1974), *Network* (1976), and *Q & A* (1991).

Lumière brothers [lümyair] **Auguste (Marie Louis) Lumière** (1862–1954) and **Louis (Jean) Lumière** (1864–1948) Chemists, born in Besançon, France. In 1893 they developed a cine camera, the *cinématographe*, and showed the first motion pictures using film projection in 1895.

Lumumba, Patrice (Hemery) [lumumba] (1925–61) Congolese prime minister (1960), born in Katako Kombé, Congo. The first premier of the new republic, he was deposed after four months, and assassinated, becoming a national hero.

Lunceford, Jimmie, popular name of **James Melvin Lunceford** (1902–47) Jazz dance-band leader, born in Fulton, MO. He began a career as a professional bandleader in 1929, and enjoyed success during the 1930s and early 1940s.

Lunn, Sir Arnold (Henry Moore) (1888–1974) British alpine ski pioneer and Roman Catholic apologist, born in Madras, India, the brother of Hugh Kingsmill. He is remembered for his debates about Catholicism, first as a Methodist, then as a Catholic. He founded the Ski Club of Great Britain and the Alpine Ski Club, and gained Olympic recognition for the modern Alpine slalom race and downhill races. >> **Kingsmill**

Lunt, Alfred (1892–1977) and **Fontanne, Lynne** originally **Lillie Louise Fontanne** (1887-1983) Acting partnership, born in Milwaukee, WI, and Woodford, Essex, respectively. They were married in 1922, and from 1924 became a popular husband-and-wife team, known especially for their performances in Noel Coward's plays. Broadway's Lunt–Fontanne Theatre (1958) was named in their honour. >> Coward

Lupino, Ida [lupeenoh] (1914/18–95) Actress and director, born in London, the daughter of popular comedian **Stanley Lupino** (1893–1942). She moved to Hollywood in 1933, and made several films for Warner Brothers, notably *High Sierra* (1941), *Ladies in Retirement* (1941), and *The Hard Way* (1942).

Lupus >> Wulfstan

Luria, Alexander Romanovich [looria] (1902–77) Psychologist, born in Kazan, Russia. One of the founders of neuropsychology, his books include *The Man with a Shattered World* (trans, 1972) and *The Working Brain* (trans, 1973).

Luria, Salvador (Edward) [looria] (1912–91) Biologist, born in Turin, Italy. In the USA he worked with Delbrück and Hershey on the role of DNA in the viruses that infect bacteria, sharing with them the Nobel Prize for Physiology or Medicine in 1969. >> Delbrück; Hershey

Lusignan, Guy of >> Guy de Lusignan

Luther, Martin (1483–1546) Religious reformer, born in Eisleben, Germany. During a visit to Rome (1510–11), he was angered by the sale of indulgences. In 1517 he drew up 95 theses on indulgences, which he nailed on the church door at Wittenberg, and publicly burned the papal bull issued against him. He was summoned to appear before the Diet at Worms, and was put under the ban of the Empire. The drawing up of his views in the Augsburg Confession marks the culmination of the German Reformation (1530). His translation of the Bible became a landmark of German literature.

Luthuli or **Lutuli, Albert (John Mvumbi)** [lutoolee] (c.1899–1967) Resistance leader, born in Zimbabwe (formerly Rhodesia). He became president-general of the African National Congress (1952–60), and dedicated himself to a campaign of nonviolent resistance, for which he was awarded the Nobel Peace Prize in 1960.

Lutoslawski, Witold [lootohslavskee] (1913–94) Composer and conductor, born in Warsaw. His many works include *Symphonic Variations* (1938), *a cello concerto* (1970), and *a piano concerto* (1988).

Lutuli, Albert John >> Luthuli, Albert John

Lutyens, Sir Edwin Landseer [lutyenz] (1869–1944) Architect, born in London. His best-known projects are the Cenotaph, Whitehall (1919–20), and the laying out of New Delhi, India (1912–30). >> Jekyll; Lutyens, Elizabeth

Lutyens, (Agnes) Elizabeth [lutyenz] (1906–83) Composer, born in London. The daughter of Sir Edwin Lutyens, she was one of the first British composers to adopt the 12-tone technique, notably with the *Chamber Concerto No 1* (1939). >> Lutyens, Edwin

Luwum, Janani (1922–77) Anglican clergyman and archbishop, born in East Acholi, Uganda. As Archbishop of Uganda (1974), he spoke out fearlessly on behalf of victims of Amin's reign of terror, and was assassinated. >> Amin

Luxembourg, François Henri de Montmorency-Bouteville, duc de [lüksåboor] (1628–95) French soldier, born in Paris. In 1667 he served in Franche-Comté, successfully invading Holland in 1672. He stormed Valenciennes, commanded in Flanders in 1690, and defeated the Allies at Fleurus in 1690.

Luxemburg, Rosa (1871–1919) Revolutionary, born in Russian Poland. With the German politician Karl Liebknecht she formed the Spartacus League, which later became the German Communist Party. She was murdered during the Spartacus revolt in Berlin. >> Liebknecht

Lu Xun [loo shün], also spelled **Lu-hsün** or **Lu-hsin** (1881–1936) Writer, born in Shaoxing, China. His short story, 'Diary of a Madman' (1918), was an immediate success, as was his book *The True Story of Ah Q* (1921). A revolutionary hero, he was posthumously adopted by the Chinese Communists as an exemplar of Socialist Realism.

Lvov, Prince Georgy Yevgenyevich [lvof] (1861–1925) Russian statesman and social reformer, born in Popovka, Russia. He briefly became head of the provisional government in the revolution of 1917. He was arrested by the Bolsheviks, but escaped to Paris. >> Kerensky

Lwoff, André (Michael) [lwof] (1902–94) Biochemist, born in Ainay-le-Chateau, France. He researched the genetics of bacterial viruses and demonstrated the process of lysogeny, with implications for cancer research. He shared the Nobel Prize for Physiology or Medicine in 1965.

Lyautey, Louis Hubert Gonzalve [lyohtay] (1854–1934) French soldier and colonial administrator, born in Nancy, France. His most brilliant work was done in Morocco, where he was resident commissary-general (1912–16, 1917–25); he was also French minister of war (1916–17).

Lycurgus [likoorgus] (c.7th-c BC) Traditional, possibly legendary, law-giver of Sparta. He is said to have instigated the Spartan ideals of harsh military discipline.

Lycurgus [likoorgus] (c.390–c.325 BC) Athenian orator and statesman. Only one complete speech, *Against Leocrates*, and a fragment of his orations have survived.

Lydgate, John [lidgayt] (c.1370–c.1451) Monk and poet, born in Lidgate, Suffolk. A court poet, his longer moralistic works include the *Troy Book*, the *Siege of Thebes*, and the *Fall of Princes*.

Lydiard, Arthur Leslie (1917–) Athletics coach and author, born in Auckland, New Zealand. He achieved fame as the coach of many successful middle-distance runners, using a method which emphasized building up strength through distance running before developing speed.

Lyell, Sir Charles [liyl] (1797–1875) Geologist, born in Kinnordy, Tayside. His *Principles of Geology* (3 vols, 1830–3) was highly influential in shaping modern understanding of the processes operating on the Earth's surface.

Lyle, Sandy [liyl], popular name of **Alexander Walter Barr Lyle** (1958–) Golfer, born in Shrewsbury, Shropshire. His successes include the European Open (1979), the French Open (1981), the British Open (1985), and the US Masters Championship (1988).

Lyly, John [lilee] (c.1554–1606) Writer, born in the Weald of Kent. He is remembered for the style of his writing, as seen in his two-part prose romance *Euphues* (1578, 1580), which gave rise to the term *euphuism* for artificial and extremely elegant language.

Lynch, Benny (1913–46) Boxer, born in Glasgow, Strathclyde. In 1935 he won the National Boxing Association/International Boxing Union version of the world flyweight title.

Lynch, David (1946–) Film director, born in Missoula, MT. His film, *Eraserhead* (1977), gained him recognition and a reputation for the bizarre. This was followed by *The Elephant Man* (1980) and *Blue Velvet* (1986), but he is probably best known for the cult television series *Twin Peaks*, which he co-wrote.

Lynch, Edmund C >> Merrill, Charles E

Lynch, Jack, popular name of **John Lynch** (1917–) Irish lawyer and prime minister (1966–73, 1977–9), born in Cork, Co Cork, Ireland. Leader of Fianna F il, his ministerial posts included education (1957–9), industry and commerce (1959–65), and finance (1965–6). He was a strong supporter of the Catholic minority in Ulster.

Lynd, Robert (Staughton) (1892–1970) and **Helen Lynd**, *née* **Merrell** (1894–1982) Sociology authors, born in

New Albany, IN, and La Grange, IL, respectively. Married in 1921, they conducted a sociological study of Muncie, IN, on which they based two successful books about *Middletown* (1929, 1937).

Lyndsay or **Lindsay, Sir David** [lindzee] (c.1486–1555) Poet, born probably near Cupar, Fife. For two centuries he was the poet of the Scottish people. His most remarkable work was *The Satyre of the Thrie Estaitis*, a dramatic work first performed in 1540.

Lynen, Feodor (Felix Konrad) [leenen] (1911–79) Biochemist, born in Munich, Germany. For his work in lipid biochemistry on the formation of the cholesterol molecule, and discovering the biochemistry of the vitamin biotin, he shared the Nobel Prize for Physiology or Medicine in 1964.

Lyon, John (?–1592) Middlesex land-owner, regarded as the founder of the great public school of Harrow. In 1572 he obtained a royal charter from Elizabeth I for the pre-Reformation school at Harrow, which he supported with endowments to guarantee its continuation.

Lyon, John (1962–) Boxer, born in St Helens, Merseyside. He is the only man to win eight Amateur Boxing Association titles – the light-flyweight title in 1981–4, and the flyweight title in 1986–9.

Lyons, Sir John (1932–) Linguist, born in Manchester. A specialist in semantics and linguistic theory, his major publications include *Semantics* (2 vols, 1977) and *Language, Meaning and Context* (1980).

Lyons, Sir Joseph (1848–1917) Businessman, born in London. He joined with three friends to establish a teashop in Piccadilly, and became head of one of the largest catering businesses in Britain - J Lyons and Co.

Lyons, Joseph Aloysius (1879–1939) Australian prime minister (1932–9), born in Stanley, Tasmania, Australia. In 1931 he founded and led an Opposition party, the United Australian Party, and as prime minister saw the country's economic recovery after the Depression.

Lyot, Bernard (Ferdinand) [lyoh] (1897–1952) Astronomer, born in Paris. In 1930 he invented the coronagraph, a device which allows the Sun's corona to be observed without a total solar eclipse.

Lysander [lisander] (?–395 BC) Greek political leader and naval commander. He commanded the Spartan fleet which defeated the Athenians at Aegospotami (405 BC),

and in 404 BC took Athens, thus ending the Peloponnesian War.

Lysenko, Trofim Denisovich [lisengkoh] (1898–1976) Geneticist and agronomist, born in Karlovka, Ukraine. As director of the Institute of Genetics of the Soviet Academy of Sciences (1940–65), he declared the accepted Mendelian theory erroneous, and ruthlessly silenced any Soviet geneticists who opposed him. He was dismissed in 1965. >> Mendel

Lysias [lisias] (c.445–c.380 BC) Greek orator, the son of a rich Syracusan. He first used his eloquence in 'Against Eratosthenes' to prosecute the tyrant chiefly to blame for the murder of his brother, Polemarchus.

Lysimachus [lisimakus] (c.355–281 BC) Macedonian general of Alexander the Great. He became King of Thrace, to which he later added NW Asia Minor and Macedonia. He was defeated and killed at Koroupedion by Seleucus. >> Alexander the Great; Seleucus

Lysippos or **Lysippus of Sicyon** [lisipus] (4th-c BC) Greek sculptor. He is said to have made more than 1500 bronzes and introduced a new naturalism. He also made several portrait busts of Alexander the Great.

Lyttelton, Oliver >> Chandos, 1st Viscount

Lyttelton, Humphrey [litltuhn] (1921–) Jazz trumpeter and bandleader, born in Windsor, Berkshire. He formed a band in 1948, and became the leading figure in the British revival of traditional jazz. His group expanded to an octet, and presented a range of more modern jazz styles.

Lytton (of Knebworth), Edward George Earle Bulwer-Lytton, Baron [litn] (1803–73) Writer and statesman, born in London. His vast output includes the novel *The Last Days of Pompeii* (1834), the play *Money* (1840), and the epic poem 'King Arthur' (1848–9). He became colonial secretary in 1858–9.

Lytton, (Edward) Robert Bulwer-Lytton, 1st Earl of, pseudonym **Owen Meredith** (1831–91) Poet and statesman, born in London. His works include novels, poems, and translations from Serbian. He held diplomatic posts all over Europe before succeeding his father as second Lord Lytton in 1873.

Lyubimov, Yuri [lyubeemof] (1917–) Russian theatre director. He joined the Vakhtangov Theatre Company in Moscow after World War 2, and was appointed director of the Taganka Theatre, Moscow in 1964.

Ma, Yo-Yo (1955–) Cellist, born in Paris. He is noted for his warmth of playing, superlative technique, a repertoire stretching from Bach to the moderns, and an energetic stage presence.

Maazel, Lorin (Varencove) [mahzel] (1930–) Conductor, born to American parents in Neuilly, France. He directed the Deutsche Oper, Berlin (1965–71), the Cleveland Orchestra (1972–82), and the Vienna Staatsoper (1982–4), and in 1986 became conductor of the Pittsburgh Symphony Orchestra.

Mabillon, Jean [mabeeyõ] (1632–1707) Scholar and historian, born near Reims, France. Considered the founder of Latin palaeography, he edited St Bernard's works (1667) and wrote a history of his order (9 vols, 1668–1702).

Mabo, Eddie Koiki [mahboh] (1940–92) Traditional leader of the Meriam people of Murray I in Torres Strait, Australia. In 1982 he began legal proceedings against the Queensland government, seeking recognition of their traditional ownership of the island and its seas. In 1992 the High Court of Australia held that Australian common law recognizes a form of native title, making it a landmark case.

Mabuse, Jan [mabüz], originally **Jan Gossaert** or **Jenni Gossart** (c.1478–c.1532) Painter, born in Maubeuge, France. He was the first artist to introduce the Italian High Renaissance style to Holland, and his works in that genre include 'Hercules and Deianeira' (1517).

McAdam, John Loudon (1756–1836) Inventor of macadamized roads, born in Ayr, Strathclyde. Appointed surveyor to the Bristol Turnpike Trust (1816), he re-made the roads there with crushed stone bound with gravel. His *macadam surfaces* were adopted in many other countries.

McAliskey, Bernadette (Josephine) [muhkaliskee], *née* **Devlin** (1947–) Northern Ireland political activist, brought up in Dungannon, Co Tyrone. She was elected as an Independent Unity candidate (1969–74), and in 1975 co-founded the Irish Republican Socialist Party.

McAnally, Ray(mond) [makanalee] (1926–89) Actor, born in Buncrana, Co Donegal, Ireland. A member of Dublin's Abbey Theatre from 1947, he won BAFTA awards for his roles in *The Mission* (1986), *A Perfect Spy* (1988), and *A Very British Coup* (1989).

MacArthur, Douglas (1880–1964) US general, born in Little Rock, AR. In 1941 he became commanding general of the US armed forces in the Far East, and from Australia directed the recapture of the SW Pacific (1942–5), formally accepting the Japanese surrender. In 1950 he led the UN forces in the Korean War.

Macarthur, Elizabeth , *née* **Veale** (1766–1850) Australian pioneer, born in Bridgerule, Devon. In 1788 she married John Macarthur and emigrated to New South Wales, where she introduced merino sheep, establishing the Australian wool industry. >> Macarthur, John

Macarthur, John (1767–1834) Pioneer and wool merchant, born in Stoke Damerel, Devonshire. In 1789 he emigrated to Australia, where he became leader of the settlers in New South Wales, and later made a fortune in the wool trade. >> Macarthur, Elizabeth

Macarthur, Robert (Helmer) (1930–72) Ecologist, born in Toronto, Ontario, Canada. His early work on birds led him to devise methods for quantifying ecological factors, and he categorized animals, in terms of their development, into two main types.

Macaulay, Dame (Emilie) Rose (1881–1958) Writer, born in Rugby, Warwickshire. She won a considerable reputation as a social satirist, with such novels as *Dangerous Ages* (1921). Her best-known novel is *The Towers of Trebizond* (1956).

Macaulay (of Rothley), Thomas Babington Macaulay, Baron [muhkawlee] (1800–59) Essayist and historian, born in Rothley Temple, Leicestershire. He established his powers as an orator in the Reform Bill debates, and became secretary of war (1839–41). He wrote the popular *Lays of Ancient Rome* (1842) and the *History of England from the Accession of James II* (1848–61), the fifth volume unfinished.

McAuley, Catherine [muhkawlee] (1787–1841) Founder of a religious order, born in Dublin. She founded the Roman Catholic House of Mercy, an institution for educating the poor, later founding the Sisters of Mercy.

McBain, Ed, pseudonym of **Evan Hunter**, originally **Salvatore A Lambino** (1926–) Novelist, born in New York City. Renowned for his '87th Precinct' thrillers, he is best known for *The Blackboard Jungle* (1954), acclaimed for its realism and topicality.

McBean, Angus (Rowland) (1904–90) Stage photographer, born in Newbridge, Monmouth, Gwent. Noted for his individual approach to portraiture, he used elaborate settings, photographic montage, collage, and double-exposure to achieve a Surrealistic interpretation of character.

Macbeth (c.1005–57) King of Scots (1040–57), the legend of whose life was the basis of Shakespeare's play. The provincial ruler of Moray, he became king after slaying Duncan I in battle near Elgin. He was killed by Duncan's son, Malcolm Canmore. >> Malcolm III

Macbeth, Ann (1875–1948) Embroideress, born in Little Bolton, Greater Manchester. Influential in advocating new methods of teaching embroidery, she wrote an instruction manual, *Educational Needlecraft*.

McBey, James [muhkbay] (1883–1959) Artist and etcher, born in Newburgh, Grampian. Well known as a master of British etching, he was also a war artist in France, Egypt, and Palestine during World War 1.

MacBride, Maud, *née* **Gonne** (1865–1953) Irish nationalist and actress, born in Aldershot, Surrey. Active for the cause of Irish independence, she was one of the founders of Sinn Féin. She married Major John MacBride, who was executed as a rebel in 1916. Their son **Sean** (1904–) was foreign minister of the Irish Republic (1948–51), and was awarded the Nobel Peace Prize in 1974.

McBride, Willie John, popular name of **William John McBride** (1940–) Rugby union player, born in Toomebridge, Co Antrim. He was with Ballymena from 1962, won a total of 63 caps, and played in 17 Tests on five British Lions tours.

MacBryde, Robert [muhkbriyd] (1913–66) Painter, born in Ayr, Strathclyde. He painted brilliantly-coloured Cubist lifes and, later, brooding Expressionist figures.

MacCaig, Norman (Alexander) [muhkayg] (1910–96) Poet, born in Edinburgh. The leading Scottish poet of his generation writing in English, he produced several collections of quick, imagistic, and philosophic poems, his *Collected Poems* being published in 1985.

McCarthy, Eugene J(oseph) (1916–) US politician, born in Watkins, MN. He became nationally known when he challenged President Johnson in the race for the Democratic presidential nomination (1968). He was eventually defeated by Robert Kennedy. >> Johnson, Lyndon B; Kennedy, Robert F

McCarthy, Joseph R(aymond) (1909–57) US Republican

politician, born in Grand Chute, WI. He achieved fame for his unsubstantiated accusations, in the early 1950s, that 250 Communists had infiltrated the State Department, and in 1953 became chairman of the powerful Permanent Subcommittee on Investigations. The kind of anti-Communist witchhunt he instigated became known as *McCarthyism*, and he was formally condemned by the US Senate.

McCarthy, Mary (Therese) (1912–89) Writer and critic, born in Seattle, WA. Her novels include *The Company She Keeps* (1942) and *The Group* (1963), and she also wrote critical works, travel books, and an autobiography, *Memories of a Catholic Girlhood* (1957).

McCartney, Paul [muhkah(r)tnee] (1942–) Pop star and composer, born in Liverpool, Merseyside. The Beatles' bass guitarist, vocalist, and member of the Lennon–McCartney songwriting team, he made his debut as a soloist with the album *McCartney* (1970), heralding the break-up of the group. In 1971 he formed the band Wings with his wife, **Linda** (1942– , née **Eastman**). 'Mull of Kintyre' (1977) became the biggest selling UK single (2·5 million). With Carl Davis he wrote the *Liverpool Oratorio* (1991). >> Lennon

McCay, Winsor (Zezic) [muhkay], pseudonym **Silas** (1867–1934) Cartoonist and film animator, born in Spring Lake, MI. He drew under his pseudonym, but used his own name for the successful *Little Nemo in Slumberland* (1905). His films include *The Sinking of the Lusitania* (1918), the first dramatic/documentary cartoon.

McClellan, George B(rinton) (1826–85) US Union general in the American Civil War, born in Philadelphia, PA. His Peninsular Campaign in Virginia ended disastrously at Richmond (1862), and though he forced Lee to retreat at Antietam, he failed to follow up his advantage, and was recalled. >> Lee, Robert E

McClintock, Barbara (1902–92) Geneticist and biologist, born in Hartford, CT. She discovered a new class of mutant genes in corn, concluding that the function of some genes is to control other genes, and that they can move on the chromosome to do this. In 1983 she received the first unshared Nobel Prize for Physiology or Medicine to be awarded to a woman.

McCloy, John (Jay) (1895–1989) Lawyer and government official, born in Philadelphia, PA. President of the World Bank (1947–9) and US High Commissioner of Germany (1949–50), he provided loans and oversaw Germany's return to statehood.

McClung, Nellie (Letitia), née **Mooney** (1873–1951) Suffragist, writer, and public speaker, born in Chatsworth, Ontario, Canada. Prominent in the Women's Christian Temperance Union and the suffrage movement, she was elected to the Alberta Legislative Assembly (1921–6).

McClure, Sir Robert (John le Mesurier) [muhkloor] (1807–73) Explorer, born in Wexford, Co Wexford, Ireland. He commanded a ship in Franklin's 1850 Artic expedition that penetrated E to the coast of Banks Land, where he was icebound for nearly two years. Rescued by another ship which had travelled from the W, he thus became the first person to complete the Northwest Passage. >> Franklin, John

MacColl, Dugald Sutherland (1859–1948) Painter and art historian, born in Glasgow, Strathclyde. As keeper of the London Tate Gallery (1906–11) and of the Wallace Collection (1911–24), he instituted many reforms and improvements.

MacColl, Ewan, pseudonym of **James Miller** (1915–89) Folk-singer, composer, and writer, born in Salford, Lancashire. A pioneer of the British folk-music revival, his series of Radio Ballads, begun in 1957, combining contemporary social comment with traditional musical forms, was highly influential.

McCollum, Elmer (Verner) [muhkoluhm] (1879–1967) Biochemist, born in Fort Scott, KS. In 1913 he showed that more than one vitamin was necessary for normal animal growth, classifying these as vitamins A (fat-soluble) and B (water-soluble), and in 1920 added the rickets-preventative factor, D.

McCormack, John (Francis) (1884–1945) Tenor, born in Athlone, near Dublin. He was engaged by Covent Garden opera for the 1905–6 season, appearing also in oratorio and as a *Lieder* singer. He later turned to popular sentimental songs.

McCormack, Mark (Hume) (1930–) Sports agent, promoter, and lawyer, born in Chicago, IL. He founded the International Management Group (IMG) in 1962, handling the sponsorship deals and promotion of sports stars and other personalities.

McCormick, Cyrus (Hall) (1809–84) Inventor of the reaper, born in Rockbridge Co, VA. He produced a successful model in 1831, and manufactured over 6 million machines during his lifetime. In 1902 his company became the International Harvester Co, with his son **Cyrus Hall, Jr** (1859–1936) as first president.

McCracken, Esther (Helen), née **Armstrong** (1902–71) Playwright and actress, born in Newcastle upon Tyne, Tyne and Wear. *Quiet Wedding* (1938) made her reputation as a writer of domestic comedy. Other successes were *Quiet Weekend* (1941) and *No Medals* (1944).

McCracken, James (1927–88) Tenor, born in Gary, IN. One of the Metropolitan Opera's leading tenors in the 1960s, he was internationally acclaimed, particularly for his Otello.

MacCready, Paul (Beattie) [muhkreedee] (1925–) Aeronautical engineer and inventor, born in New Haven, CT. He was the designer of the ultra-light aircraft *Gossamer Condor*, which in 1977 made the first man-powered flight over a one-mile course.

McCubbin, Frederick (1855–1917) Landscape painter, born in Melbourne, Victoria, Australia. With other painters he established the first of the artist camps which became the Heidelberg school of Australian painting.

McCullers, (Lula) Carson, née **Smith** (1917–67) Writer, born in Columbus, GA. Her work reflects the sadness of lonely people, as in her first book, *The Heart Is a Lonely Hunter* (1940). Later works include *The Ballad of the Sad Café* (1951).

McCullough, Colleen [muhkuhluh] (1937–) Novelist, born in Wellington, New South Wales, Australia. Her books include the best-selling *The Thorn Birds* (1977), *A Creed for the Third Millennium* (1985), and *The Grass Crown* (1991).

MacDiarmid, Hugh [muhkdermid], pseudonym of **Christopher Murray Grieve** (1892–1978) Poet, born in Langholm, Dumfries and Galloway. He established himself as the leader of a vigorous Scottish Renaissance with *A Drunk Man Looks at the Thistle* (1926). He was a founder member of the Scottish Nationalist Party, and an active Communist.

MacDonagh, Donagh [muhkdona] (1912–68) Playwright, born in Dublin, the son of Thomas MacDonagh. He co-edited *The Oxford Book of Irish Verse* (1958), and was an acclaimed broadcaster. >> MacDonagh, Thomas

MacDonagh, Thomas [muhkdona] (1878–1916) Poet, critic, and nationalist, born in Cloughjordan, Co Tipperary, Ireland. An outstanding critic of English literature, he took part in the Irish Volunteers, was belatedly involved in the Easter Rising of 1916, and was executed. >> MacDonagh, Donagh

MacDonald, Dwight (1906–82) Writer and film critic, born in New York City. A social and political commentator, he wrote regularly for *Partisan Review*, *New Yorker*, and *Esquire*.

MacDonald, Elaine (1943–) Dancer, born in Tadcaster, North Yorkshire. She joined Western Ballet Theatre in 1964, and moved with the company to Glasgow when it became Scottish Ballet in the late 1960s, becoming artistic controller 1988–9.

Macdonald, Flora (1722–90) Scottish heroine, born in South Uist, Western Isles. After the rebellion of 1745, she conducted the Young Pretender, Charles Edward Stuart, disguised as 'Betty Burke', to safety in Skye. She was imprisoned in the Tower of London, but released in 1747. >> Stuart, Charles

MacDonald, Jeanette (1907–65) Soprano, born in Philadelphia, PA. She was best known for roles opposite Nelson Eddy (1901 67) in film operettas such as *Naughty Marietta* (1935) and *Rose Marie* (1936).

Macdonald, Sir John A(lexander) (1815–91) Canadian prime minister (1857–8, 1864, 1867–73, 1878–91), born in Glasgow, Strathclyde. His family emigrated in 1820, and he became leader of the Conservative Party. He was instrumental in bringing about the confederation of Canada, and in 1867 formed the first government of the new Dominion.

MacDonald, (James) Ramsay (1866–1937) British prime minister (1924, 1929–31, 1931–5), born in Lossiemouth, Grampian. In 1894 he joined the Independent Labour Party, becoming its leader (1911–14, 1922–31), and was prime minister and foreign secretary of the first British Labour government.

MacDonald, (John) Ross, pseudonym **Kenneth Millar** (1915–83) Thriller writer, born in Los Gatos, CA. His books include *The Moving Target* (1949), *The Galton Case* (1959), and *The Blue Hammer* (1976). Many of his novels have been filmed.

McDonald-Wright, Stanton >> **Russell, Morgan**

McDonnell, James S(mith) (1899–1980) Aircraft manufacturer, and pioneer in space technology, born in Denver, CO. He set up his own company in 1928, producing successful military and naval aircraft. In 1967 the company merged to become the McDonnell Douglas Corporation. >> Douglas, Donald

McDougall, William [muhk**doo**gl] (1871–1938) Psychologist, born in Chadderton, Lancashire. Influential in establishing experimental and physiological psychology, he wrote the well-known *Introduction to Social Psychology* (1908).

MacDowell, Edward (Alexander) (1860–1908) Composer and pianist, born in New York City. He composed extensively for orchestra, voices, and piano, and is best remembered for some of his small-scale piano pieces, such as *Woodland Sketches* and *Sea Pieces*.

McEnroe, John (Patrick) [**ma**kenroh] (1959–) Tennis player, born in Wiesbaden, Germany. He won four US Open singles titles (1979–81, 1984) and three Wimbledon singles titles (1981, 1983-4). His skill as a player was often overshadowed by his outbursts on court which led to professional censure on several occasions.

MacEwen, Sir William [muh**kyoo**an] (1848–1924) Neurosurgeon, born in Glasgow, Strathclyde. He extended Lister's antiseptic surgical techniques, and pioneered operations on the brain for tumours, abscesses, and trauma. >> Lister, Joseph

McGee, Thomas D'Arcy (1825–68) Writer and politician, born in Carlingford, Co Louth, Ireland. He took Canadian citizenship, became an MP in 1858, and was minister of agriculture (1864–8). He was assassinated while opposing a threatened Fenian invasion of Canada.

McGill, Donald, pseudonym of **Fraser Gould** (1875–1962) Comic postcard artist, born in London. He became famous for his outsize women in bathing costumes, paddling alongside weedy henpecked husbands, and for the double meanings in his captions.

McGill, James (1744–1813) Entrepreneur and philanthropist, born in Glasgow, Strathclyde. He emigrated to Canada in the 1770s, and made a fortune in the NW fur trade. McGill University, Montreal, is named after him.

MacGill, Patrick (1890–1963) Navvy, novelist, and poet, born in the Glenties, Co Donegal, Ireland. He published his semi-autobiographical novel *Children of the Dead End* (1914), and this was followed by many other successful books.

MacGill-Eain, Somhairle >> **Maclean, Sorley**

MacGillivray, James Pittendrigh [muh**gil**ivray] (1856–1938) Sculptor and poet, born in Inverurie, Grampian. His major sculptures include the huge statue of Robert Burns in Irvine, and the Knox statue in St Giles's Cathedral, Edinburgh.

McGonagall, William [muh**gon**agl] (1830–1902) Scottish doggerel poet and novelist, the son of an immigrant Irish weaver. His best-known poem is 'The Tay Bridge Disaster' (1880). He travelled in C Scotland, giving readings and selling his poetry in broadsheets, and was lionized by the legal and student fraternity.

McGovern, George S(tanley) [muh**guh**vern] (1922–) US politician, born in Avon, SD. He sought the Democratic presidential nomination in 1968, and opposed Nixon in 1972, but was defeated. He tried again for the nomination in 1984, but withdrew. >> Nixon

McGrath, John (Peter) (1935–) Playwright and theatre director, born in Birkenhead, Merseyside. He founded the 7:84 Theatre Company in 1971, and was artistic director until 1988. His many popular political plays include *Swings and Roundabouts* (1981) and *The Wicked Old Man* (1992).

McGraw, John (Joseph), nickname **the Little Napoleon** (1873–1934) Baseball player manager, born in Truxton, NY. His playing career (1891–1906) was spent mostly with the Baltimore Orioles. He went on to manage the New York Giants (1902–32), winning ten league pennants and three world championships.

Macgregor, Douglas (1906–64) US industrial psychologist. His highly regarded book, *The Human Side of Enterprise* (1960), discussed two contrasting theories of motivation at work.

McGregor, Sir Ian (Kinloch) (1912–) Business executive, born in Kinlochleven, Highland. He became chairman of the British Steel Corporation in 1980, and chairman of the National Coal Board in 1983. Both industries required drastic cutbacks to survive, which he carried out despite strong trade union opposition.

MacGregor, Robert >> **Rob Roy**

McGuffey, William (Holmes) [muh**guh**fee] (1800–73) Educator, born near Claysville, PA. He compiled the famous *McGuffey Readers*, six elementary schoolbooks (1836–57) that became standard texts for generations of 19th-c US children.

Mach, Ernst [mahk] (1838–1916) Physicist and philosopher, born in Turas, Austria. He carried out experimental work in aeronautical design and projectiles, and his name has been given to a unit of velocity (*Mach number*) and to the angle of a shock wave to the direction of motion (*Mach angle*).

Machado, (y Ruiz) Antonio [ma**shaht**hoh] (1875–1939) Poet and playwright, born in Seville, Spain. He wrote lyrics characterized by a nostalgic melancholy, among them *Campos de Castilla* (1912). With his brother **Manuel** (1874-1947) he also wrote several plays.

Machaut, Guillaume de >> **Guillaume de Machaut**

Machel, Samora Moïsés [ma**shel**] (1933–86) Guerrilla Leader against Portuguese rule in Mozambique and first president (1975–86). Although a Marxist, he established warm relations with Western governments, and attempted an accommodation with the South African regime. >> Chissano

Machiavelli, Niccolò (di Bernardo dei) [makiavelee] (1469–1527) Italian political theorist, born in Florence, Italy. His masterpiece is *The Prince* (trans, 1532), whose main theme is that all means may be used to maintain authority, and that the worst acts of the ruler are justified by the treachery of the governed. It was condemned by the pope.

MacIndoe, Sir Archibald [muhkindoh] (1900–60) Plastic surgeon, born in Dunedin, New Zealand. In England during World War 2, he became known for his work on the faces and limbs of severely injured airmen.

Macintosh, Charles (1766–1843) Manufacturing chemist, born in Glasgow, Strathclyde. He developed in 1823 a method of waterproofing cloth, which resulted in the manufacture of the raincoat, or *macintosh*.

McIntyre, Sir Donald (Conroy) (1934–) Opera singer, born in Auckland, New Zealand. A bass baritone, he established himself as one of the world's leading Wagnerian singers.

Mack, Connie, originally **Cornelius Alexander McGillicuddy** (1862–1956) Baseball player and manager, born in East Brookfield, MA. He began his managerial career at Pittsburgh (1894–6), and moved on to Philadelphia (1901–51), winning World Championships in 1910–11, 1913, and 1929–30.

McKay, Claude [muhkiy], originally **Festus Claudius McKay**, pseudonym **Eli Edwards** (1889–1948) Writer, born in Sunny Ville, Jamaica. He went to New York City, where he influenced the 'Harlem Renaissance'. In addition to his major work, *Harlem Shadows* (1922), he wrote novels, short stories, and the sociological study, *Harlem: Negro Metropolis* (1940).

Mackay, Fulton [muhkiy] (1922–87) Actor, born in Paisley, Strathclyde. A prolific performer on stage, televison, and in films, he is probably best remembered for playing the role of Mr Mackay, the officious prison warder, in the 1970s television series, *Porridge*.

McKay, Heather [muhkiy], *née* **Blundell** (1941–) Squash player, born in Queanbeyan, New South Wales, Australia. She won the British Open in 16 successive years (1962–77), 14 Australian titles (1960–73), and was World Champion in 1976 and 1979.

Mackay (of Clashfern), James Peter Hymers Mackay, Baron [muhkiy] (1927–) Jurist, born in the village of Scourie, Highland. As Lord Chancellor (from 1987), he proposed several radical reforms of the legal profession.

Macke, August [mahkuh] (1887–1914) Painter, born in Meschede, Germany. Profoundly influenced by Matisse, he founded the *Blaue Reiter* group together with Marc. He was killed in action in France. >> Marc; Matisse

McKellen, Sir Ian (Murray) [muhkelen] (1939–) Actor, born in Burnley, Lancashire. He co-founded the Actors' Company in 1972, and played many memorable parts for the Royal Shakespeare Company (1974–8).

McKenna, Siobhan [muhkena, shuhvawn], originally **Siobhan Giollamhuire Nic Cionnaith** (1923–86) Actress, born in Belfast. Her major roles include Pegeen Mike in *The Playboy of the Western World* (1951) and *Saint Joan* (1954).

Mackenzie, Sir Alexander (c.1755–1820) Explorer and fur-trader, born in Stornoway, Western Isles. He discovered the Mackenzie R (1789), and became the first European to cross the Rockies to the Pacific (1792–3).

Mackenzie, Sir (Edward Montague) Compton (1883–1972) Writer, born in West Hartlepool, Co Durham. His many novels include *Sinister Street* (1913–14) and *Whisky Galore* (1947).

Mackenzie, Henry (1745–1831) Writer, born in Edinburgh. His novel *The Man of Feeling* (1771), was followed by more than 100 other novels, plays, and biographies, notably on Burns.

McKenzie, Julia (1941–) Actress and singer. An outstanding interpreter of Sondheim, her musical appearances include *Maggie May* (1965), *Guys and Dolls* (1982), and *Into the Woods* (1990). She has also appeared in many plays, notably by Alan Ayckbourn. >> Sondheim

Mackenzie, William Lyon (1795–1861) Canadian politician, born in Dundee, Tayside. In Canada from 1820, he published a declaration of Canadian independence (1837), and headed a band of insurgents, but was forced to flee to the USA. He returned to Canada in 1849, and became an MP (1850–8).

Mackenzie King, William Lyon >> **King, William Lyon Mackenzie**

Mackenzie Stuart (of Dean), Alexander John Mackenzie Stuart, Baron (1924–) Judge, born in Aberdeen, Grampian. He was the first British judge appointed to the Court of Justice of the European Communities (1972–88, president 1984–8).

Mackerras, Sir (Alan) Charles (MacLaurin) [muhkeras] (1925–) Conductor, born in Schenectady, NY. He was musical director of the Sadler's Wells Opera, the BBC Symphony Orchestra, Sydney Symphony Orchestra, and Welsh National Opera.

Mckillop, Mary Helen [muhkilop], known as **Mother Mary of the Cross** (1842–1909) Religious, born in Fitzroy, Queensland, Australia. With Father Tenison-Woods she founded in 1866 the Society of the Sisters of St Joseph of the Sacred Heart. Her beatification was approved in 1993.

McKim, Charles Follen (1847–1909) Architect, born in Isabella Furnace, PA. He designed over a thousand buildings, including the Boston Public Library (1887–95) and the Pierpont Morgan Library (1902–7), New York City.

Mackinder, Sir Halford John [muhkinder] (1861–1947) Geographer and politician, born in Gainsborough, Lincolnshire. He held numerous senior university appointments, became an MP (1910–22), and was British high commissioner for South Russia (1919–20).

McKinley, William (1843–1901) US statesman and 25th president (1897–1901), born in Niles, OH. His name was identified with the high protective tariff carried in the *McKinley Bill* of 1890. His first term as president saw the war with Spain (1898), with the conquest of Cuba and the Philippines. He was shot by an anarchist.

MacKinnon, Catharine (1946–) Legal scholar, born in Minneapolis, MN. She published a landmark study, *Sexual Harassment of Working Women: a Case of Sex Discrimination* (1979). She has also urged that pornography be recognized as another form of sex discrimination, and pioneered the approach to law from the perspective of women's experience of sex inequality.

MacKinnon, Donald MacKenzie (1913–94) Philosopher of religion, born in Oban, Strathclyde. He explored the relations between theology, metaphysics, and moral philosophy, championing realism over idealism.

Mackintosh, Charles Rennie (1868–1928) Architect, designer, and painter, born in Glasgow, Strathclyde. He became a leader of the 'Glasgow Style', a movement related to Art Nouveau, his designs including detailed interiors, textiles, furniture, and metalwork.

Mackintosh, Elizabeth Daviot, pseudonyms **Josephine Tey** and **Gordon Daviot** (1896–1952) Novelist and playwright, born in Inverness, Highland. As Gordon Daviot she wrote the historical drama *Richard of Bordeaux* (1932); as Josephine Tey she wrote many popular detective novels, including *The Franchise Affair* (1949).

Mackintosh, Sir Cameron (Anthony) (1946–) British impresario. He financed Lloyd Webber's *Cats*, and later produced such musicals as *Little Shop of Horrors* (1983), *Les Misérables* (1985), *Phantom of the Opera* (1986), and *Miss Saigon* (1989).

Mackmurdo, Arthur Heygate (1851–1942) Architect

and designer, born in London. A member of the Arts and Crafts movement, in 1882 he co-founded the Century Guild, a group which designed for all aspects of interiors. >> Morris, William; Ruskin

McKnight Kauffer, Edward [kowfer] (1890–1954) Poster designer, illustrator, and artist, born in the USA. He moved to England in 1914, became a commercial artist, and designed posters for the Underground Railway Co, London Transport Board, Shell-Mex, BP, and many others.

MacLaine, Shirley, stage name of **Shirley Maclean Beaty** (1934–) Actress, born in Richmond, VA. Her films include *Irma La Douce* (1963), *Sweet Charity* (1969), *Terms of Endearment* (1983, Oscar), and *Postcards from the Edge* (1990). >> Beatty, Warren

McLaughlin, John [muhglokhlin] (1942–) Electric guitarist and composer, born in Doncaster, South Yorkshire. In 1969 he played with Miles Davis, and from 1971 led the Mahavishnu Orchestra, starting a movement of jazz and rock fusion with Indian rhythms. >> Davis, Miles

Maclaurin, Colin [muhklorin] (1698–1746) Mathematician, born in Kilmodan, Strathclyde. His best-known work, *Treatise on Fluxions* (1742) gave a systematic account of Newton's approach to the calculus. >> Newton, Isaac

Maclean, Alistair [muhklayn] (1922–87) Writer, born in Glasgow, Strathclyde. His first novel *HMS Ulysses* (1955) became an immediate best-seller. Later books included *The Guns of Navarone* (1957) and *Where Eagles Dare* (1967). Many of his books were made into films.

Maclean, Donald (Duart) [muhklayn] (1913–83) British traitor, born in London. He joined the diplomatic service in 1934, and from 1944 was recruited by Soviet intelligence as an agent. In 1951 he disappeared with Burgess, reappearing in Russia in 1956. >> Burgess, Guy

Maclean, Sorley [muhklayn], Gaelic **Somhairle MacGill-Eain** (1911–) Gaelic poet, born on the I of Raasay, off Skye, Highland. His works include *Seventeen Poems for Sixpence* (1940), *Poems to Eimhir* (trans, 1943), and his major collection, *Spring Tide and Neap Tide* (trans, 1977).

Maclehose, Agnes [maklhohz], née **Craig** (1759–1841) Scots literary figure, the daughter of an Edinburgh surgeon. She met Robert Burns in 1787, and subsequently carried on the well-known correspondence with him under the name of Clarinda. >> Burns, Robert

Macleish, Archibald [muhkleesh] (1892–1982) Poet, born in Glencoe, IL. His first volumes of poetry appeared in 1917, and he won Pulitzer Prizes for *Conquistador* (1932), *Collected Poems 1917–52* (1953), and his social drama in modern verse, *J B* (1959).

MacLennan, (John) Hugh (1907–90) Novelist and essayist, born in Nova Scotia, Canada. He won the Governor-General's Award three times for fiction - *Two Solitudes* (1945), *The Precipice* (1948), and *The Watch that Ends the Night* (1959) - and twice for non-fiction, with *Cross Country* and *Thirty and Three*.

McLennan, Sir John (Cunningham) (1867–1935) Physicist, born in Ingersoll, Ontario, Canada. He carried out leading research in radioactivity, spectroscopy, and low-temperature physics, and investigated the use of radium to treat cancer.

Maclennan, Robert (Adam Ross) (1936–) British politician, born in Glasgow, Strathclyde. A founder member of the Social Democratic Party, he became a leading member of the Social and Liberal Democrats.

MacLeod (of Fuinary), George (Fielden) MacLeod, Baron [muhklowd] (1895–1991) Clergyman, born in Glasgow, Strathclyde. He founded the Iona Community, and as moderator of the General Assembly (1957–8) supported the controversial scheme to introduce bishops into the kirk.

Macleod, Iain (Norman) [muhklowd] (1913–70) British

Conservative statesman, born in Skipton, North Yorkshire. He became minister of health (1952–5), minister of labour (1955–9), secretary of state for the Colonies (1959–61), and chairman of the Conservative Party (1961–3). He was appointed Chancellor of the Exchequer (1970), but died suddenly a month later.

Macleod, J(ohn) J(ames) R(ickard) [muhklowd] (1876–1935) Physiologist, born in Cluny, Tayside. In 1922 he discovered insulin with Banting and Best, and shared the Nobel Prize for Physiology or Medicine in 1923. >> Banting; Best, Charles

Mac Liammóir, Micheál [muhkleeamer] (1899–1978) Actor, painter, and writer, born in Cork, Co Cork, Ireland. He wrote fiction, plays, and memoirs in Irish and in English, and in the 1960s his one-man shows brought him an international reputation.

Maclise, Daniel [muhkleez] (1806–70) Painter, born in Cork, Co Cork, Ireland. He is noted for the frescoes in the Royal Gallery of the House of Lords: 'The Meeting of Wellington and Blücher' (1861) and 'The Death of Nelson' (1864).

McLuhan, (Herbert) Marshall [muhklooan] (1911–80) Writer, born in Edmonton, Alberta, Canada. His controversial views on the effect of the communication media are propounded in *The Gutenberg Galaxy* (1962), *Understanding Media* (1964), and *The Medium is the Message* (with Q Fiore, 1967).

Maclure, William [muhkloor] (1763–1840) Geologist, born in Ayr, Strathclyde. His *Observations on the Geology of the United States* (1817) gives the first full account of its subject.

Macmahon, Marie Edme Patrice Maurice de, duc de (Duke of) **Magenta** [makmahon] (1808–93) Marshal and second president of the Third Republic (1873–9), born in Sully, France. He suppressed the Commune (1871), and succeeded Thiers as president. Failing to assume dictatorial powers, he resigned in 1879, thus ensuring the supremacy of parliament. >> Thiers

McMahon, Sir William [muhkmahn] (1908–88) Australian prime minister (1971–2), born in Sydney, New South Wales, Australia. He became premier when Gorton lost a vote of confidence in 1971. The following year the Liberals lost the election, but he continued to lead his party until 1977. >> Gorton, John Grey

MacMaster, John (Bach) (1852–1932) Social historian, born in New York City. His chief work was *A History of the People of the United States from the Revolution to the Civil War* (8 vols, 1883–1913).

Macmillan, Daniel (1813–57) and **Alexander Macmillan** (1818–96) Booksellers and publishers, brothers, born in Strathclyde. In 1843 they opened a bookshop in London, and by 1893 had become a limited company, with Daniel's son, **Frederick** (1851–1936), as chairman. >> Macmillan, Harold

McMillan, Edwin (Mattison) (1907–91) Physical chemist, born in Redondo Beach, CA. He shared with Seaborg the 1951 Nobel Prize for Chemistry for his part in the discovery of the transuranic elements. >> Seaborg

Macmillan, (Maurice) Harold, 1st Earl of Stockton (1894–1986) British prime minister (1957–63), born in London, the grandson of Daniel MacMillan. He was minister of housing (1951–4), minister of defence (1954–5), foreign secretary (1955), and Chancellor of the Exchequer (1955–7). He gained unexpected popularity with his infectious enthusiasm, effective domestic policy ('most of our people have never had it so good'), and resolute foreign policy. >> Macmillan, Daniel

Macmillan, Sir Kenneth (1929–92) Ballet dancer, choreographer, and ballet company director, born in Dunfermline, Fife. He became artistic director of the Royal Ballet in 1970, and its principal choreographer in 1977.

Macmillan, Kirkpatrick (1813–78) Blacksmith, born near

Thornhill, Dumfries and Galloway. In 1839 he made the world's first pedal cycle, with wooden frame and iron-tyred wheels.

McMillan, Margaret (1860–1931) Educational reformer, born in New York City, and brought up near Inverness. In 1902 she joined her sister **Rachel** (1859–1917) in London, where they opened the first school clinic (1908) and the first open-air nursery school (1914).

Macnaghten, Edward, Lord [muhk**naw**tn] (1830–1913) Judge, born in London. He became an MP in 1880, declined the home secretaryship and a judgeship, and was then appointed direct from the bar in 1887 to be a Lord of Appeal in Ordinary.

McNaghten or **M'Naghten, Daniel** [muhk**naw**tn] (fl. 19th-c) British murderer. He was tried in 1843 for the murder of Edward Drummond, private secretary to Sir Robert Peel. His sanity came into question, and whether he knew the nature of his act. As a result arose the *McNaghten Rules*, on the criminal responsibility of the insane.

McNamara, Frank (1917–57) US businessman and innovator. He launched the Diners Club Card in 1950, gaining 42 000 members in the first year, and initiating the credit card industry.

Macnamara, Dame (Annie) Jean (1899–1968) Physician, born in Beechworth, Victoria, Australia. With Burnet she found that there was more than one strain of the polio virus, a discovery which led to the development of the Salk vaccine. >> Burnet; Salk

McNamara, Robert S(trange) (1916–) US Democratic politician and businessman, born in San Francisco, CA. In 1961 he joined the Kennedy administration as secretary of defense, and was much involved in the Vietnam War. He resigned to become president of the World Bank (1968–81). >> Kennedy, John F

McNaught, William [muhk**nawt**] (1813–81) Engineer and inventor, born in Paisley, Strathclyde. He manufactured steam-engine components, and in 1845 created a 'compound engine', the process of which was called *McNaughting*.

MacNeice, Louis [muhk**nees**] (1907–63) Poet, born in Belfast. He became closely associated with the new British left-wing poets of the 1930s, especially Auden, with whom he wrote *Letters from Iceland* (1937). Other volumes include *Collected Poems* (1949), and several verse plays for radio.

McNeile, Herman Cyril >> **Sapper**

MacNeill, John or **Eoin** (1867–1945) Historian and nationalist, born in Glenarm, Co Antrim, Northern Ireland. He helped to organize the new Sinn Féin Party, becoming MP for Derry, but after the revision of Irish partition in the Catholics' favour he resigned.

Maconchy, Dame Elizabeth [muhk**ong**kee] (1907–) Composer, born in Broxbourne, Hertfordshire. Among her best-known compositions are her *Symphony* (1953) and the overture *Proud Thames* (1953). She married writer William Richard LeFanu in 1930; their daughter, **Nicola LeFanu** (1947–), is also a composer.

Macphail, Agnes [muhk**fayl**],*née* **Campbell** (1890–1954) Suffragette and politician, Canada's first woman MP, born in Grey Co, Ontario, Canada. She was a leader of the Co-operative Commonwealth Federation of Canada, and represented Canada in the Assembly of the League of Nations.

McPherson, Aimée Semple, *née* **Kennedy** (1890–1944) Pentecostal evangelist and healer, born near Ingersoll, Ontario, Canada. In 1918 she founded the Foursquare Gospel Movement in Los Angeles, and for nearly two decades conducted a flamboyant preaching and healing ministry.

Macpherson, James (1736–96) Poet, born in Ruthven, Highland. In 1762 he published poetry which he claimed was related to the legendary hero Fingal as told by his son,

Ossian; acclaimed at first, it transpired that most of the material was his own invention.

Macquarie, Lachlan [muhk**kwo**ree] (1761–1824) Soldier and colonial administrator, born on the I of Ulva, Strathclyde. Governor of New South Wales from 1810, he gave his name to the Lachlan and Macquarie rivers, and to Macquarie I.

Macquarrie, John [muhk**kwo**ree] (1919–) Theologian and philosopher of religion, born in Renfrew, Strathclyde. The influence of Bultmann and Tillich may be traced in *An Existentialist Theology* (1955) and *Principles of Christian Theology* (1966). >> Bultmann; Tillich

McQueen, (Terence) Steve(n) (1930–80) Film actor, born in Slater, MO. He became the archetypal 1960s cinema hero/rebel with his performances in *The Great Escape* (1963), *The Cincinnati Kid* (1965), and *Bullitt* (1968). He was married (1973–8) to actress **Ali McGraw** (1938–).

Macrae, (John) Duncan [muhk**ray**] (1905–67) British actor. He made his first London appearance in 1945, and his performances ranged from Ibsen and Shakespeare to pantomime, television, and film, but he became known especially as a Scottish actor.

Macready, William Charles [muhk**kree**dee] (1793–1873) Actor, born in London. He was the leading English actor of his day, notable for his Shakespearian roles. He became manager of Covent Garden in 1837, and of Drury Lane in 1841.

Macrobius, Ambrosius Theodosius [ma**kroh**bius] (5th-c) Roman writer and Neoplatonist philosopher, probably born in Africa. He wrote a commentary on Cicero's *Somnium Scipionis*, and a series of historical, mythological, and critical dialogues.

MacSwiney, Terence [muhk**swee**nee] (1879–1920) Irish nationalist, born in Cork, Co Cork, Ireland. He helped form the Irish Volunteers (1913), and was elected a Sinn Féin MP (1918). He died in Brixton prison after a 74-day hunger strike which aroused worldwide sympathy.

McTaggart, David (1932–) Canadian conservationist. On behalf of Greenpeace, a Vancouver-based conservation group, he took an active part in their campaigns, and formed Greenpeace International (1979) as an alliance of national groups.

McWhirter, Norris (Dewar) (1925–) British publisher, writer, journalist, and broadcaster. With his twin brother **Ross McWhirter** (1925–75), they compiled the first edition of *The Guinness Book of Records* (1954). Norris was editor (1954–86), and is director of Guinness Publications. Ross was assassinated by IRA terrorists.

Madariaga (y Rojo), Salvador de [mat**haria**hga] (1886–1978) Writer, scholar, and diplomat, born in La Coruña, Spain. An opponent of the Franco regime, he went into exile (1936–76), and wrote many historical works, especially on Spain and Spanish-America.

Maderna, Bruno [ma**dair**na] (1920–73) Composer and conductor, born in Venice, Italy. In 1955 he began experimenting in electronic music, founding with Berio the Studio di Fonologia Musicale of Italian Radio. >> Berio

Maderna or **Maderno, Carlo** [ma**dair**na] (1556–1629) Architect, born in Bissone, Italy. The leading exponent of the early Baroque in Rome, in 1603 he was appointed architect to St Peter's, where he lengthened the nave and added a massive facade (1606–12).

Madero, Francisco (Indalécio) [mat**hay**roh] (1873–1913) Revolutionary and president of Mexico (1911–13), born in Parras, Mexico. He faced a succession of revolts, and in 1913 was murdered following a military coup led by General Victoriano Huerta.

Madhva [mahdva] (14th-c) Kanarese Brahmin philosopher, born near Mangalore, S India. He promoted *dvaita* or dualistic *Vedanta*, allowing for the separate existence of the Divine, human souls, and matter.

Madison, Dolly, *née* **Payne Todd** (1768–1849) US first lady, born in New Garden, NC. She married James Madison in 1794, and became a popular first lady. She was later granted a lifelong seat on the floor of the US House of Representatives. >> Madison, James

Madison, James (1751–1836) US statesman and fourth president (1809–17), born in Port Conway, VA. He played a major role in the Constitutional Convention of 1787, becoming known as 'the father of the Constitution'. Secretary of state under Jefferson, and president for two terms, his administration saw the Napoleonic Wars and the War of 1812. >> Jefferson, Thomas; Madison, Dolly

Madoc [**ma**dog] (12th-c) Legendary Welsh prince, long believed by his countrymen to have discovered America in 1170. The story, in Hakluyt's *Voyages* (1582), was proved baseless in the 19th-c. >> Hakluyt

Madonna, in full **Madonna Louise Ciccone** (1958–) Pop singer, born in Rochester, MI. Her albums include *Madonna* (1983), *Like A Virgin* (1984), and *Erotica* (1992), and she has also acted in films, including *Desperately Seeking Susan* (1985). Her raunchy stage appearances were being reinforced in several media in the early 1990s, including photography (*Sex*, 1992).

Maecenas, Gaius (Cilnius) [miy**see**nas] (?–8 BC) Roman politician of ancient Etruscan lineage. Together with Agrippa he played a key role in the rise to power of Octavian/Augustus, and his establishment of the empire after 31 BC. >> Augustus

Maes, Nicholas [mays] (1634–93) Painter, born in Dordrecht, The Netherlands. He specialized in small genre subjects, especially kitchen scenes and old women praying.

Maeterlinck, Maurice (Polydore Marie Bernard) [**may**terlingk], also known as **comte** (Count) **Maeterlinck** (1862–1949) Playwright, born in Ghent, Belgium. A disciple of the Symbolist movement, his masterpiece was the prose-play *Pelléas et Mélisande* (1892), and he was awarded the Nobel Prize for Literature in 1911.

Magdalene, St Mary >> Mary Magdalene, St

Magellan, Ferdinand [ma**jel**an] (c.1480–1521) Navigator, born in Sabrosa or Porto, Portugal. He sailed in 1519 around the foot of South America to reach the ocean which he named the Pacific (1520). He was killed in the Philippines, but his ships completed the first circumnavigation of the world. The *Strait of Magellan* is named after him.

Magendie, François [mazhãdee] (1783–1855) Physiologist and physician, born in Bordeaux, France. His research demonstrated the functional differences in the spinal nerves, and the effects of drugs on the body.

Maginot, André (Louis René) [**ma**zhinoh] (1877–1932) French statesman, born in Paris. As minister of war (1922–4, 1926–31), he began the system of frontier fortifications facing Germany which was named the *Maginot Line*.

Magnani, Anna [man**yah**nee] (1908–73) Actress, born in Alexandria, Egypt. She achieved recognition in *Rome, Open City* (trans, 1945) and *The Rose Tattoo* (1955, Oscar). Much of her later work was for the Italian stage and television.

Magnus, Heinrich Gustav (1802–70) German physicist. In 1853 he described the *Magnus effect* - the sideways force experienced by a spinning ball which is responsible for the swerving of golf or tennis balls when hit with a slice.

Magnusson, Magnus (1929–) Writer and broadcaster, born in Edinburgh of Icelandic parents. He is chiefly known as a radio and television presenter, most famously in the annual series of *Mastermind*. His books include *Vikings!* (1980) and *Treasures of Scotland* (1981).

Magoun, Horace (Winchell) (1907–) Neuroscientist, born in Philadelphia, PA. He did important work on many neurological and psychopharmacological topics, and was one of the leaders in the new field of neuroscience.

Magritte, René (François Ghislain) [ma**greet**] (1898–

1967) Surrealist painter, born in Lessines, Belgium. A leading member of the Belgian Surrealist group (1924), his major paintings include 'The Wind and the Song' (1928–9) and 'The Human Condition' (1934, 1935). He was an early innovator of the Pop Art of the 1960s.

Mahan, Alfred Thayer [ma**han**] (1840–1914) Naval officer and writer, born in West Point, NY. His many books, such as *The Influence of Sea Power upon History: 1660–1783* (1890), were influential in Britain, the USA, and Germany.

Mahathir bin Mohamad [ma**ha**teer] (1925–) Malaysian prime minister, (1979–), born in Alur Setar, Malaysia. He became United Malays' National Organisation (UMNO) leader, and as premier launched a new economic policy, emulating Japanese industrialization.

Mahdi >> Mohammed Ahmed

Mahfouz, Naguib [ma**fooz**] (1911–) Novelist, born in Cairo. The *Children of Gebelawi* (1961), which portrays average Egyptians living the lives of Cain and Abel, Moses, Jesus, and Mohammed, was banned in most of the Arab world. He was awarded the Nobel Prize for Literature in 1988.

Mahler, Gustav (1860–1911) Composer, born in Kalist, Czech Republic (formerly Bohemia). His mature works consist entirely of songs and nine large-scale symphonies (with a 10th left unfinished) the best known being the song-symphony *The Song of the Earth* (trans, 1908–9).

Mahmud of Ghazna [mah**mood**] (971–1030) Muslim Afghan conqueror of India. The son of Sebuktigin, ruler of Ghazna (modern Afghanistan), he succeeded to the throne in 997. He invaded India many times and created an empire that included Punjab and much of Persia.

Mahomet >> Mohammed

Mahon, Derek [mahn] (1941–) Poet, born in Belfast. Drawn to squalid landscapes and desperate situations, his works include *Twelve Poems* (1965), *The Hunt by Night* (1982), and *A Kensington Notebook* (1984).

Mahony, Francis Sylvester [ma**hoh**nee], pseudonym **Father Prout** (1804–66) Priest, journalist, and humorous writer, born in Cork, Co Cork, Ireland. He is remembered as author of the poems 'The Bells of Shandon' and 'The Lady of Lee'.

Mahy, Margaret [**may**hee] (1936–) Children's author, born in Whangarei, New Zealand. Since 1986, with *The Trickster*, the settings of her stories have increasingly had a New Zealand flavour. She has twice won the Carnegie Award for children's literature.

Mailer, Norman [**may**ler] (1923–) Writer, born in Long Branch, NJ. His best-known novels are *The Naked and the Dead* (1948), a panoramic World War 2 novel, and *American Dream* (1964). Identified with many of the US liberal protest movements, his political studies include *The Armies of the Night* (1968, Pulitzer).

Maillart, Ella Kini [mayah(r)] (1903–) Travel writer, born in Geneva, Switzerland. She worked and journeyed in Iran and Afghanistan, and was one of the first travellers into Nepal when it opened in 1949, producing *The Land of the Sherpas* (1955).

Maillart, Robert [mayah(r)] (1872–1940) Civil engineer, born in Bern, Switzerland. His designs in the Swiss Alps include the bridge over the Inn at Zuoz (1901) and the spectacular curving Schwandbach Bridge at Schwarzenburg (1933).

Maillet, Antonine [mayay] (1929–) Novelist, born in Buctouche, New Brunswick, Canada. Her novels are rooted in the geography, history, and people of Acadia, such as *La Sagouine* (1971) and *Pelagie-La-Charrette* (1979, Goncourt).

Maillol, Aristide (Joseph Bonaventure) [ma**yol**] (1861–1944) Sculptor, born in Banyuls-sur-Mer, France. He is particularly known for his representation of the nude female figure in a style of simplicity and classical serenity, such as 'Mediterranean' (c.1901).

Maiman, Theodore H(arold) [**miy**man] (1927–) Physicist, born in Los Angeles, CA. He improved the design of the maser, and by 1960 devised the first working laser, which gave coherent visible light.

Maimonides, Moses [miymonideez], originally **Moses ben Maimon** (1138–1204) Philosopher, born in Córdoba, Spain. A major influence on Jewish thought, he wrote an important commentary on the Mishna, and a philosophical work, the *Guide of the Perplexed* (trans, 1190).

Mainbocher [maynboshay], originally **Main Rousseau Bocher** (c.1890–1976) Fashion designer, born in Chicago, IL. He started a couture house in Paris in 1930, one of his creations being the wedding dress designed for the Duchess of Windsor (1937). >> Windsor, Wallis Warfield

Maintenon, Françoise d'Aubigné, Marquise de (Marchioness of) [mītenõ], (1635–1719) Second wife of Louis XIV of France, born in Niort, France. She married the poet Paul Scarron in 1652, but when left an impoverished widow she took charge of the king's two sons by her friend Mme de Montespan, and became the king's mistress. After the queen's death (1683), Louis married her secretly. >> Louis XIV; Montespan; Scarron

Mairet, Ethel [mairet] (1872–1952) English weaver. She established 'Gospels', a workshop based at Ditchling, East Sussex, which became a creative centre for many weavers from all over the world.

Maitland (of Lethington), William (c.1528–73) Scottish statesman, probably born in Lethington, Lothian. He represented Mary, Queen of Scots, at the court of Elizabeth, but made her his enemy by his connivance at Rizzio's murder in 1566. He died in prison at Leith. >> Mary, Queen of Scots; Rizzio

Major, John (1943–) British prime minister (1990–), born in London. He became an MP in 1976, and rose to become Treasury chief secretary in 1987. In 1989 he became foreign secretary, and soon after returned to the Treasury as Chancellor. He won the leadership contest following Mrs Thatcher's resignation, and became prime minister in 1990. >> Thatcher

Makarios III [makaryos], originally **Mihail Khristodoulou Mouskos** (1913–77) Archbishop of the Orthodox Church of Cyprus, and president of Cyprus (1960–74, 1974–7), born in Ano Panciyia, Cyprus. He reorganized the *enosis* (union) movement, was arrested in 1956, but returned in 1959 to become chief Greek-Cypriot Minister in the new Greek–Turkish provisional government.

Makarova, Nataliya (Romanovna) [makahrova] (1940–) Ballerina, born in St Petersburg, Russia. A ballerina with the Kirov Ballet, she defected to the West, joined the American Ballet Theatre in New York City, and became a guest dancer with the Royal Ballet, Covent Garden.

Makeba, Miriam [makayba] (1932–) Singer, born in Johannesburg, South Africa. She settled in the USA, where she became the first African performer to gain an international following, becoming best known for her recordings of 'click' songs from S Africa.

Malachy, St [malakhee], originally **Máel Máedoc úa Morgair** (c.1094–1148), feast day 3 November. Monk and reformer, born in Armagh, Co Armagh. In 1139 he journeyed to Rome, visiting St Bernard at Clairvaux, and introduced the Cistercian Order into Ireland on his return in 1142. In 1190 he became the first Irishman to be canonized.

Malamud, Bernard [malamuhd] (1914–86) Novelist and short-story writer, born in New York City. His novels reflect his keen interest in Jewish-American life, and include *The Natural* (1952), *The Fixer* (1966, Pulitzer), and *Dublin's Lives* (1979).

Malan, Daniel (François) [malan] (1874–1959) South African prime minister (1948–54), born in Riebeek West, South Africa. In 1939 he founded with Herzog the Reunited (Afrikaans *Herenigde*) National Party, and in 1948 introduced the apartheid policy. >> Hertzog

Malatesta, Enrico [malatesta] (1853–1932) Anarchist, born in Campania, Italy. He organized anarchist revolutionary groups in Europe, was imprisoned many times, sentenced to death on three occasions, and spent more than half his adult life in exile.

Malcolm III, nickname **Malcolm Canmore** ('Big Head') (c.1031–93) King of Scots (1058–93), the son of Duncan I. He conquered S Scotland, but did not become king until he had defeated Macbeth (1057). His second wife was the English Princess Margaret, and he launched five invasions of England between 1061 and his death. >> Macbeth; Margaret (of Scotland)

Malcolm, George (John) (1917–) Harpsichordist and conductor, born in London. He was Master of the Music at Westminster Cathedral (1947–59), then earned a wide reputation as a harpsichord soloist.

Malcolm X, originally **Malcolm Little** (1925–65) African-American nationalist leader, born in Omaha, NE. A convert to the Black Muslims, he pressed for black separatism and the use of violence in self-defence. In 1964 his views changed, and he founded the Organization of Afro-American Unity. A factional feud led to his assassination in Harlem.

Malebranche, Nicolas [malbrāsh] (1638–1715) Philosopher, born in Paris. His major work is *Search after Truth* (trans, 1674), which explains all causal interaction between mind and body by a theory of divine intervention known as *occasionalism*. >> Descartes

Malenkov, Georgiy Maksimilianovich [malyenkof] (1902–88) Soviet prime minister (1953–5), born in Orenburg, Russia. He joined the Communist Party in 1920 and was involved in the collectivization of agriculture and the purges of the 1930s under Stalin, succeeding him in 1953.

Malesherbes, Chrétien (Guillaume de Lamoignon) de [malzairb] (1721–94) French statesman, born in Paris. At Louis XVI's accession (1774) he became secretary of state for the royal household, instituting prison and legal reforms. Despite his reforming zeal, he was mistrusted as an aristocrat during the Revolution, and was guillotined.

Malevich, Kazimir (Severinovich) [malayevich] (1878–1935) Painter and designer, born in Kiev, Ukraine. He pioneered pure abstraction, founding the Suprematist movement. He claimed to have painted the first totally abstract picture, a black square on a white background, as early as 1913.

Malherbe, François de [malairb] (1555–1628) Poet, born in Caen, France. He produced odes, songs, epigrams, epistles, translations, and criticisms, and founded the literary tradition of classicism.

Malik, Jacob Alexandrovich (1906–80) Soviet politician, born in the Ukraine. He became Soviet spokesman at the UN (1948–53), ambassador to Britain (1953–60), deputy foreign minister (1960–8), and again ambassador to the UN (1968–76).

Malina, Judith >> Beck, Julian

Malinovsky, Rodion Yakovlevich [malinofskee] (1898–1967) Soviet soldier and statesman, born in Odessa, Ukraine. He led the Russian advance on Budapest and into Austria (1944–5), took a leading part in the Manchurian campaign, and later became minister of defence (1957–67).

Malinowski, Bronislaw (Kasper) [malinofskee] (1884–1942) Anthropologist, born in Kraków, Poland. He was the pioneer of 'participant observation' as a method of fieldwork (notably in the Trobriand Is), and a major proponent of functionalism in anthropology.

Mallarmé, Stéphane [malah(r)may] (1842–98) Symbolist poet, born in Paris. A leader of the Symbolist school, his works include *Hérodiade* (1864), and *L'Après-midi d'un faune* (1865), which inspired Debussy's prelude.

Malle, Louis [mal] (1932–95) Film director, born in

Thumeries, France. His films include *The Lovers* (trans, 1958), *Calcutta* (1969), *Goodbye, Children* (trans, 1987), and *Damage* (1993).

Mallowan, Sir Max (Edgar Lucien) [malohan] (1904–78) Archaeologist, born in London. He excavated in the Near East, principally at Nimrud, with striking results described in detail in *Nimrud and its Remains* (1970). He married Agatha Christie in 1930. >> Christie, Agatha

Malmesbury, William of >> **William of Malmesbury**

Malone, Edmund (1741–1812) Scholar, and editor of Shakespeare, born in Dublin. He devoted himself to literary work in London, and his 11-volume edition of Shakespeare (1790) was warmly received. >> Shakespeare, William

Malory, Sir Thomas (? 1471) English writer, known for his work, *Le Morte d'Arthur* (The Death of Arthur). From Caxton's preface, we are told that Malory was a knight, and that he finished his work in the ninth year of the reign of Edward IV (1469–70). >> Caxton

Malouf, David [maloof] (1934–) Novelist, born in Brisbane, Queensland, Australia. His books include *An Imaginary Life* (1978), *The Great World* (1991, Miles Franklin Award), and *Remembering Babylon* (1993).

Malpighi, Marcello [malpeegee] (1628–94) Anatomist, born near Bologna, Italy. The founder of microscopic anatomy, he described the major types of plant and animal structures, and did investigative work, notably on silkworms and the embryology of chicks.

Malraux, André (Georges) [malroh] (1901–76) French statesman and novelist, born in Paris. Minister of information (1945–6) and of cultural affairs (1960–9), he is known for his novels, notably *Man's Fate* (trans, 1937, Goncourt) and *Man's Hope* (trans, 1937).

Malthus, Thomas Robert (1766–1834) Economist, born near Dorking, Surrey. He is chiefly known for the *Essay on the Principle of Population* (1798) which argued that the population has a natural tendency to increase faster than the means of subsistence, and that efforts should be made to cut the birth rate, either by self-restraint or birth control.

Malus, Etienne Louis [malüs] (1775–1812) Physicist, born in Paris. A military engineer in Napoleon's army (1796–1801), he carried out research in optics and discovered the polarization of light by reflection.

Mamet, David (Alan) [mamet] (1947–) Playwright and film director, born in Chicago, IL. His works include the play *American Buffalo* (1976), the screenplay *The Postman Always Rings Twice* (1981), the film (as director) *Homicide* (1991), and the novel *The Village* (1994). He received the Pulitzer Prize for Drama in 1984.

Man, Paul de >> **de Man, Paul**

Manasseh [manasuh] Biblical king of Judah, the eldest son of Joseph, who was adopted and blessed by Jacob. He was the ancestor of one of the 12 tribes of Israel, who later became the Jewish people. >> Jacob

Manasseh [manasuh] (7th-c BC) Biblical king of Judah (696–642 BC), the son of Hezekiah. He earned an evil name for idolatry until taken captive by the Assyrians in Babylon, when he repented. *The Prayer of Manasseh* is apocryphal.

Manasseh ben Israel [manasuh] (1604–57) Scholar, born in Lisbon. He was chief rabbi in Holland where he set up the country's first printing press (1626). He later went to England (1655–7), securing from Cromwell the readmission of the Jews. >> Cromwell, Oliver

Manchester, Edward Montagu, 2nd Earl of (1602–71) Parliamentary soldier, born in London. He defeated the royalists at Newbury, but was deprived of his command (1645). He opposed the trial of the king, protested against the Commonwealth, and was made Lord Chamberlain at the Restoration (1660). >> Charles I (of England)

Manchester, William (1922–) Novelist, foreign correspondent, and contemporary historian, born in Attleboro,

MA. His major work is *The Death of the President* (1967), written at the request of the Kennedy family. >> Kennedy, John F

Mandela, Nelson (Rolihlahla) [mandela] (1918–) South African president (1994–), born in Transkei, South Africa. He joined the African National Congress in 1944, directed a campaign of defiance against the South African government, and in 1964 was sentenced to life imprisonment. Released in 1990, he was elected president of the African National Congress (1991), and was closely involved in the negotiations with President de Klerk which led to the first all-race elections in April 1994. In 1993 he shared the Nobel Prize for Peace with de Klerk for their work towards dismantling apartheid. >> de Klerk; Mandela, Winnie

Mandela, Winnie [mandela], popular name of **Nomzano Zaniewe Winnifred Mandela** (1934–) Wife of Nelson Mandela, born in Bizana, South Africa. She married Mandela in 1958 (separated, 1992), and was frequently banned, detained, and jailed. She took an increasingly active role in the African National Congress (ANC), until convicted on charges of kidnapping and assault. She continued to operate as a militant figure, making a political comeback in late 1993. She was given a ministerial role in the 1994 government, but dismissed in 1995. >> Mandela, Nelson

Mandelbrot, Benoit (1924–) Mathematician, born in Warsaw. His book *The Fractal Geometry of Nature* (1982) was important in demonstrating the potential application of fractals to natural phenomena.

Mandelstam, Osip [manduhlstam] (1891–1938) Poet, born in Warsaw. His early poems led to arrest (1934) by the Soviet authorities, and his death was reported from Siberia. His collected works were published in three volumes (1964–71), and his wife, **Nadezhda** (1899–1980), wrote their story in *Hope Against Hope* (1970).

Mandeville, Bernard [mandevil] (1670–1733) Physician and satirist, born in Dort, The Netherlands. He is known as the author of a short work in doggerel verse originally entitled *The Grumbling Hive* (1705), and finally *The Fable of the Bees* (1723).

Mandeville, Geoffrey de, 1st Earl of Essex [mandevil] (?–1144) English baron. He became constable of the Tower c.1130, and proved a traitor alternately to King Stephen and Empress Matilda. He was besieged by Stephen, and killed. >> Matilda; Stephen

Mandeville, Jehan de or **Sir John** [mandevil] (14th-c) The name assigned to the compiler of a famous book of travels (*The Voyage and Travels of Sir John Mandeville, Knight*), published apparently in 1366, and soon translated from the French into many languages.

Manen, Hans van (1932–) Ballet dancer and choreographer, born in Nieuwer, The Netherlands. He became one of the founding members of Netherlands Dance Theatre, and its artistic director. In 1973 he joined the Dutch National Ballet as choreographer and ballet master.

Manet, Edouard [manay] (1832–83) Painter, born in Paris. His 'Déjeuner sur l'herbe' (1863, Luncheon on the Grass) was rejected by the Salon, which remained hostile to him. He helped to form the group out of which the Impressionist movement arose.

Manetho [manethoh] (fl.c.300 BC) Egyptian historian. He was high-priest of Heliopolis, and wrote in Greek a history of the 30 dynasties from mythical times to 323 BC.

Mangan, James Clarence (1803–49) Poet, born in Dublin. He published English versions of Irish poems in *The Poets and Poetry of Munster* (1849), notably 'My Dark Rosaleen', 'The Nameless One', and 'The Woman of Three Cows'.

Mangeshkar, Lata [mangeshkah(r)] (1928–) Indian singer. In 1948 she was engaged to provide the singing voice of actresses in Indian musical films, and had made over 30 000 recordings for more than 2000 films by the time she retired in 1984.

Manichaeus or **Mani** [mani**kee**us, **mah**nee], known as **the Apostle of Light** (c.215–276) Religious leader, born in Ecbatana, Persia. He was the founder of *Manichaeism*, a dualistic religion which offered salvation through the acquisition of special knowledge of spiritual truth. He was crucified by his Zoroastrian enemies.

Mankowitz, (Cyril) Wolf [**mang**kohvits] (1924–) Writer, born in London. His fiction includes the novel *A Kid for Two Farthings* (1953), the play *The Bespoke Overcoat* (1954), the films *The Millionairess* (1960), and *Casino Royale* (1967), and the musicals *Expresso Bongo* (1958–9) and *Pickwick* (1963).

Manley, Delariviere, often called, incorrectly, **Mary** (1663–1724) Writer, born in Jersey. She wrote plays, and chronicles disguised as fiction, especially the anti-Whig *The New Atalantis* (1709), and in 1711 succeeded Swift as editor of *The Examiner*. >> Swift, Jonathan

Manley, Michael (Norman) (1923–) Jamaican prime minister (1972–80, 1989–92), born in Kingston, Jamaica. He embarked on a radical, socialist programme, cooling relations with the USA.

Mann, Heinrich (1871–1950) Novelist, born in Lübeck, Germany, the brother of Thomas Mann. He is best known for the macabre novel, *Professor Unrat* (1904), translated and filmed as *The Blue Angel* (1932). >> Mann, Thomas

Mann, Horace (1796–1859) Educationist, born in Franklin, MA. As secretary of the board of education (1837–48), he reorganized public-school teaching, and was responsible for setting up the first normal school in the USA (1839).

Mann, Thomas (1875–1955) Novelist, born in Lübeck, Germany. His works include *Buddenbrooks* (1901), *Death in Venice* (trans, 1913; filmed, 1971), *The Magic Mountain* (trans, 1924), and his greatest work, a modern version of the mediaeval legend, *Doktor Faustus* (1947). He was awarded the Nobel Prize for Literature in 1929. >> Mann, Heinrich

Mannerheim, Carl Gustav (Emil), vapaaherra (Baron) [**man**erhiym] (1867–1951) Finnish soldier and president (1944–6), born in Villnäs, Finland. Commander-in-chief against the Russians in the Winter War of 1939–40, he continued to command the Finnish forces until 1944, when he became president of the Finnish Republic.

Manners, John >> **Granby, Marquess of**

Mannheim, Karl [**man**hiym] (1893–1947) Sociologist, born in Budapest. In England from 1933, he became known primarily for his contribution to the sociology of knowledge, of which he was one of the founders.

Manning, Henry Edward, Cardinal (1808–92) Roman Catholic clergyman, born in Totteridge, Hertfordshire. At the Council of 1870, he was a zealous supporter of the infallibility dogma, and a leader of the Ultramontanes.

Manning, Olivia (1911–80) Novelist, born in Portsmouth, Hampshire. Her experiences abroad during World War 2 led to the 'Balkan Trilogy' (1960–5) and 'Levant Trilogy' (1978–80), which form a single narrative entitled *Fortunes of War*.

Mannion, Wilfred (1918–) Footballer, born in Yorkshire. His career was spent with Middlesbrough and Hull City, and he was an integral part of the great English national side of the late 1940s.

Mannix, Daniel (1864–1963) Roman Catholic clergyman, born at Ráth Luirc, Co Cork, Ireland. He went to Melbourne, Australia in 1913, succeeding as archbishop in 1917.

Mannyng, Robert, also known as **Robert of Brunne** (?–c.1338) Chronicler and poet, born in Bourne, Lincolnshire. His chief work is the poem *Handlynge Synne* (c.1303), a landmark in the transition from early to later Middle English.

Mansard or **Mansart, François** [mäsah(r)] (1598–1666)

Architect, born in Paris. He brought a simplified adaptation of the Baroque style into use in France. His first major work, the N wing of the Château de Blois, featured the double-angled high-pitched roof which now bears his name. >> Mansard, Jules Hardouin

Mansard or **Mansart, Jules Hardouin** [mäsah(r)] (1645–1708) Architect, born in Paris, the great-nephew and possibly pupil of François Mansard. He extended Le Vau's garden facade at Versailles (1678), built the domed chapel of the Invalides (1680–91), and laid out the Place Vendôme in Paris (1698). >> Mansard, François

Mansbridge, Albert (1876–1952) Adult educator, born in Gloucester, Gloucestershire. He was instrumental in the formation of the Workers' Educational Association, of which he become general secretary (1905), and the National Central Library (1916).

Mansell, Nigel [**man**sl] (1954–) Motor-racing driver, born in Birmingham, West Midlands. In 1992 he retired from Formula 1 racing after winning the driver's championship with eight wins, and joined the Haas-Newman Indy car racing team in the USA, becoming champion in 1993. He briefly returned to Formula 1 in 1995, driving for McLaren.

Mansfield, Katherine, pseudonym of **Kathleen Mansfield Murry**, *née* **Beauchamp** (1888–1923) Short-story writer, born in Wellington, New Zealand. In 1918 she married writer John Middleton Murry. Her chief works are *Prelude* (1917), *Bliss, and Other Stories* (1920), and *The Garden Party, and Other Stories* (1922), but she is also known for her revealing *Journal* (1927) and *Letters* (1928). >> Murry

Mansfield (of Caen Wood), William Murray, 1st Earl of (1705–93) Judge, born in Scone, Tayside. In 1756 he became Chief Justice of the King's Bench. He made important contributions to international law, but his opinions were unpopular, and during the Gordon riots of 1780 his house was burned.

Manship, Paul (Howard) (1885–1966) Sculptor, born in St Paul, MN. He became renowned for his bronze figurative sculptures, which drew heavily on Roman and Greek sources, such as the gilded 'Prometheus Fountain' (1934) for the Rockefeller Center, New York City.

Manson, Charles (1934–) Cult leader, born in Cincinnati, OH. He set up a commune, and in 1969 members of his cult conducted a series of murders in California, including that of actress **Sharon Tate** (1943–69). He was spared the death penalty due to a Supreme Court ruling against capital punishment. >> Polanski

Manson, Sir Patrick, nickname **Mosquito Manson** (1844–1922) Doctor, born in Old Meldrum, Grampian. His pioneer work with Ross showed that the mosquito was host to the malaria parasite (1877). >> Ross, Ronald

Manstein, (Fritz) Erich von [**man**shtiyn] (1887–1973) German field marshal, born in Berlin. In World War 2 he became chief-of-staff to Rundstedt in the Polish campaign, and in France was the architect of Hitler's *Blitzkrieg*. >> Rundstedt

Mansur, al- [man**soor**], in full **Abua Jafar Abd Allah al-Mansur ibn Muhammad** (c.710–75) Second caliph of the Abbasid dynasty. He defeated several revolts, established a firm government dominated by the Abbasid family, and founded a new capital for the empire, Baghdad (762).

Mantegna, Andrea [man**ten**ya] (c.1431–1506) Painter, born in Vicenza, Italy. His most important works were nine tempera pictures of 'The Triumph of Caesar' (1482–92), and his decoration of the ceiling of the Camera degli Sposi in Mantua.

Mantle, Mickey (Charles) (1931–95) Baseball player, born in Spavinaw, OK. A great centrefielder, he was a member of the renowned New York Yankees team of the 1950s and 1960s, and in 1956 won a rare Triple Crown in batting, home runs, and runs batted in.

Manucci, Aldo >> **Aldus Manutius**

Manuel I >> **Emanuel I**

Manuel, Nikolaus (1484–1530) Painter, poet, and reformer, born in Bern. He produced biblical and mythological pictures in the Renaissance style, often showing a tendency towards the macabre.

Manuzio, Aldo >> **Aldus Manutius**

Manzoni, Alessandro [mantsohnee] (1785–1873) Novelist and poet, born in Milan, Italy. The work which gave him European fame is his historical novel, *The Betrothed* (trans, 1825–7), one of the most notable works of fiction in Italian literature.

Manzú, Giacomo [manzoo] (1908–91) Sculptor, born in Bergamo, Italy. He revived Classical techniques of relief sculpture in bronze, such as the doors of St Peter's in Rome (1950).

Mao Dun [mow dun], also spelled **Mao Tun**, pseudonym of **Shen Yen-ping** (1896–1981) Writer, born in Ch'ing-chen, China. In 1930 he helped to organize the League of Left-Wing Writers, and his major works include a best-selling novel, *Midnight* (trans, 1932). He was China's first minister of culture (1949–65).

Mao Zedong [mow dzuhdoong], also spelled **Mao Tse-tung** (1893–1976) Leader of the Chinese communist revolution, born in Hunan province, the son of a farmer. He took a leading part in the May Fourth Movement, then became a Marxist and a founding member of the Chinese Communist Party (1921). After the break with the Nationalists (1927), he evolved the guerrilla tactics of the 'people's war', and led the Communist forces on the Long March to Shanxi (1924). He ousted the regime of Jiang Jieshi from the Chinese mainland, and proclaimed the new People's Republic of China (1949). In 1958 he launched his Great Leap Forward in rural and agricultural development, and in 1965 the Cultural Revolution. After his death, a strong reaction set in against the excessive collectivism which had emerged, but his anti-Stalinist emphasis on rural industry and on local initiative was retained. >> Jiang Jeshi

Maradona, Diego [maradona] (1960–) Footballer, born in Lanus, Argentina. He captained Argentina to their second World Cup in 1986, only for his career to founder amid accusations of drug-taking. He returned to the World Cup side as captain in 1994, but was again suspended following a drug test.

Marat, Jean Paul [mara] (1743–93) French revolutionary politician, born in Boudry, Switzerland. Elected to the National Convention, he became a leader of the Mountain, and advocated radical reforms. He was fatally stabbed in his bath by a Girondin supporter, Charlotte Corday; thereafter he was hailed as a martyr. >> Corday

Maratti, Carlo [marahtee] (1625–1713) Painter, born in Camerano, Italy. A leader of the 17th-c Baroque school, he produced many altarpieces, and also became a noted portraitist.

Marc, Franz (1880–1916) Artist, born in Munich, Germany. With Kandinsky he founded *Der Blaue Reiter* in Munich in 1911. Most of his paintings were of animals, such as 'Tower of the Blue Horses' (1911). >> Kandinsky

Marcantonio [mah(r)kantohnioh], in full **Marcantonio Raimondi** (1480–1534) Engraver, born in Bologna, Italy. He moved to Rome in 1510 and became an engraver of other artists' works, especially those of Raphael and Michelangelo. >> Michelangelo; Raphael

Marceau, Marcel [mah(r)soh] (1923–) Mime artist, born in Strasbourg, France. In 1948 he founded the Compagnie de Mime Marcel Marceau, developing the art of mime, and becoming himself the leading exponent known especially for his white-faced character, Bip.

Marcel, Gabriel (Honoré) [mah(r)sel] (1889–1973) Existentialist philosopher and playwright, born in Paris.

He became known as a 'Christian existentialist', partly to contrast his views with those of Sartre. >> Sartre

Marcello, Benedetto [mah(r)cheloh] (1686–1739) Composer, born in Venice, Italy. He is noted for *Estro poetico armonico* (1724–7), an eight-volume collection of settings for 50 of the Psalms of David, the oratorio *The Four Seasons* (1731), and keyboard and instrumental sonatas.

March, Francis (Andrew) (1825–1911) Philologist, born in Millbury, MA. The founder of comparative Anglo-Saxon linguistics, his publications included the monumental *Comparative Grammar of the Anglo-Saxon Language* (1870).

Marchais, Georges (René Louis) [mah(r)she] (1920–) Political leader, born in La Hoguette, France. He became general-secretary of the French Communist Party in 1972, leading the Party to join with the Socialist Party, but the union was severed in 1977.

Marchand, Jean Baptiste [mah(r)shã] (1863–1934) Soldier and explorer, born in Thoissey, France. He explored the Niger, W Sudan, and Ivory Coast, and caused a Franco-British crisis in 1898 by hoisting the tricolor at Fashoda on the White Nile.

Marciano, Rocky [mah(r)siahnoh], originally **Rocco Francis Marchegiano**, nickname **the Rock from Brockton** (1923–69) Heavyweight boxing champion, born in Brockton, MA. He made his name when he defeated the former world champion, Joe Louis, in 1951. When he retired in 1956 he was the only undefeated world heavyweight champion. >> Louis, Joe

Marcion [mah(r)shuhn] (c.100–c.165) Christian Gnostic believer. In c.140 he went to Rome, where he founded the *Marcionites* in 144. He was expelled from the Church as a heretic, but his Gnostic sect flourished during the 2nd-c.

Marconi, Guglielmo [mah(r)kohnee] (1874–1937) Physicist and inventor, born in Bologna, Italy. In 1899 he erected a wireless station at La Spezia, and formed the Marconi Telegraph Co in London. In 1898 he transmitted signals across the English Channel, and in 1901 across the Atlantic. He shared the Nobel Prize for Physics in 1909. >> Popov

Marco Polo >> **Polo, Marco**

Marcos, Ferdinand (Edralin) [mah(r)kos] (1917–89) Philippines president (1965–86), born in Ilocos Norte, Philippines. His regime was marked by repression and political murders (notably the assassination of Benigno Aquino in 1983), and he was overthrown by a popular front led by Corazon Aquino. He went into exile in Hawaii, where his wife **Imelda** (1930–) was convicted of corruption in 1993. >> Aquino

Marcus Aurelius Antoninus >> **Aurelius**

Marcus Aurelius Antoninus (188–217) >> **Caracalla**

Marcuse, Herbert [mah(r)koozuh] (1898–1979) Marxist philosopher, born in Berlin. An influential figure in the Frankfurt School, he later taught in the USA, his books including *Eros and Civilization* (1955) and *One Dimensional Man* (1964), condemning the 'repressive tolerance' of modern industrial society.

Marden, Brice (1938–) Painter, born in Bronxville, NY. From 1968 he became known for his two- and three-panel canvases, each of contrasting monochromatic colour.

Mare, Walter de la >> **de la Mare, Walter**

Marenzio, Luca [marenzioh] (1553–99) Composer, born near Brescia, Republic of Venice (modern Italy). A prolific writer of madrigals, he was in service with Cardinal Luigi d'Este of Rome (1578–86), and later became a musician at the papal court.

Marey, Etienne Jules [maray] (1830–1903) Physiologist, born in Beaune, France. He pioneered scientific cinematography with his studies of animal movement (1887–1900), and succeeded in reducing exposure time to c. 1/25 000 of a second to photograph the flight of insects.

Margaret (of Scotland), St (c.1046–93), feast day 16

November or 19 June. Scottish queen, born in Hungary, sister of Edgar the Ætheling. She married Malcolm Canmore, and did much to assimilate the old Celtic Church to the rest of Christendom. She was canonized in 1250. >> Edgar the Ætheling; Malcolm III

Margaret (Rose), Princess (1930–) British princess, born at Glamis Castle, Scotland, the second daughter of George VI. In 1960 she married Antony Armstrong-Jones (divorced, 1978), who was created Viscount Linley and Earl of Snowdon in 1961. The former title devolved upon their son, **David Albert Charles** (1961–), who married Serena Alleyne Stanhope in 1993. They also have a daughter, **Sarah Frances Elizabeth** (1964–), who married Daniel Chatto in 1994. >> Elizabeth II; George VI; Snowdon

Margaret of Angoulême [ăgoolem], also known as **Margaret of Navarre** (1492–1549) Queen of Navarre, born in Angoulême, France, the sister of Francis I of France. She married first the Duke of Alençon (d.1525), then Henry d'Albret (titular king of Navarre). Interested in Renaissance learning, her court was the most intellectual in Europe. She wrote poems, dramas, and the celebrated *Heptaméron* (published 1558–9), a collection of stories on the theme of love. >> Francis I

Margaret of Anjou [āzhoo] (1430–82) Queen consort of Henry VI of England, probably born in Pont-à-Mousson, France. She married Henry in 1445, and owing to his mental weakness she was in effect sovereign. In the Wars of the Roses, she was defeated at Tewkesbury (1471), and imprisoned for four years in the Tower. >> Henry VI (of England)

Margaret of Navarre >> **Margaret of Angoulême**

Margareta or **Margaret** (1353–1412) Queen of Denmark (1375), Norway (1380), and Sweden (1388), born in Søborg, Denmark. She had her infant cousin, Eric of Pomerania, crowned king of the three kingdoms at Kalmar in 1397, but remained the real ruler of Scandinavia until her death.

Margaret Tudor (1489–1541) Queen of Scotland, born in London, the eldest daughter of Henry VII. She became the wife of James IV of Scotland (1503), and the mother of James V, for whom she acted as regent.

Marggraf, Andreas Sigismund [mah(r)graf] (1709–82) Chemist, born in Berlin. He is noted particularly for the discovery of sugar in sugar-beet (1747), and so prepared the way for the sugar-beet industry.

Margrethe II [mah(r)gretuh] (1940–) Queen of Denmark (1972–), born in Copenhagen, the daughter of Frederick IX. In 1967 she married a French diplomat, now Prince Henrik of Denmark. Their children are the heir apparent, **Frederik André Henrik Christian** (1968–) and **Joachim Holger Waldemar Christian** (1969–).

Marguerite d'Angoulême >> **Margaret of Angoulême**

Maria de' Medici >> **Marie de Médicis**

Marianus Scotus [mariahnus skohtus] (1028–c.1083) Chronicler, born in Ireland. He entered a Benedictine monastery at Cologne (1052–8), and became a recluse. He wrote *Chronicon Universale*, the story of the world from the Creation to 1082.

Maria Theresa (1717–80) Archduchess of Austria, and Queen of Hungary and Bohemia (1740–80), born in Vienna, the daughter of Emperor Charles VI. In 1740 she succeeded to the Habsburg lands, her claim leading to the War of the Austrian Succession. In 1745 her husband was elected Holy Roman Emperor. Military conflict was renewed in the Seven Years' War, and in 1763 she was forced to recognize the status quo of 1756. >> Joseph II

Marie, Pierre (1853–1940) Neurologist, born in Paris. Professor of neurology at the University of Paris (1907–25), he is noted for his contribution to the modern science of endocrinology.

Marie Antoinette (Josèphe Jeanne) (1755–93) Queen of France, born in Vienna, the daughter of Maria Theresa and Francis I. She married Louis XVI (1770), and exerted a growing influence over him, arousing criticism for her extravagance and opposition to reform. In 1791 she and Louis tried to escape to Austria, but were caught and imprisoned in Paris. After the king's execution, she was later guillotined.

Marie de France (12th-c) Poet, born in Normandy, France. She spent much of her life in England, where she wrote several verse narratives based on Celtic stories.

Marie de Médicis [maydeesees], Ital **Maria de' Medici** [maydichee] (1573–1642) Queen consort of Henry IV of France, born in Florence, Italy, the daughter of Francesco de' Medici, Grand Duke of Tuscany. She married Henry in 1600, and acted as regent for her son, later Louis XIII, but her capricious behaviour led to her confinement when Louis assumed power in 1617. Further intrigues led to her exile in 1630. >> Henry IV (of France); Louis XIII

Marie Louise (1791–1847) Empress of France, born in Vienna, the daughter of the Holy Roman Emperor, Francis II. She married Napoleon in 1810 (after his divorce from Joséphine), and in 1811 bore him a son, who became Napoleon II. >> Francis II; Napoleon I / II

Marin, John [marin] (1870–1953) Artist, born in Rutherford, NY. Well known for his water-colours and etchings in an extremely individual style, his later works were adapted from Cubist concepts.

Marin, Maguy [marī] (1951–) Dancer and choreographer, born in Toulouse, France. She joined Béjart's Ballet of the 20th Century in the mid-1970s, and in 1978 founded her own troupe. >> Béjart

Marina, Princess >> **Kent, George, Duke of**

Marinetti, Filippo (Tommaso) Emilio [marinetee] (1876–1944) Italian writer, born in Alexandria, Egypt. He published the original Futurist manifesto in *Figaro* in 1909. In his writings he glorified war, the machine age, speed and 'dynamism', and condemned all traditional forms of literature and art. >> Nevinson; Severini

Marini, Marino [mareenee] (1901–80) Sculptor and painter, born in Pistoia, Italy. His work, mainly in bronze, was figurative, his best-known theme being the horse and rider. He was also a noted portraitist.

Marino, Dan [mareenoh] (1961–) Player of American football, born in Pittsburgh, PA. A quarterback with the Miami Dolphins, in the 1984 season he gained 5084 yards passing, to create a National Football League record.

Mario, Giovanni Matteo (1810–83) Tenor, born in Cagliari, Italy. After a successful debut in 1838, there followed a series of operatic triumphs in Paris, London, St Petersburg, and America. He married the singer **Giulia Grisi** (1811–69).

Marion, Francis (c.1732–95) US soldier, born in Berkeley Co, SC. He commanded the remaining resistance in South Carolina after the colonials' loss at Camden, and used guerrilla tactics to strike at British and Loyalist forces.

Mariotte, Edme (1620–84) Physicist and priest, born in Dijon, France. In his *Discours de la nature de l'air* (1676) he independently stated Boyle's law of 1662, long known in France as Mariotte's law. >> Boyle, Robert

Marisol, (Escobar) [marisol] (1930–) Sculptor, painter, and graphic artist, born in Paris. She is known for her witty satirical carvings and assemblages in wood, plaster, paint, and other materials, such as 'Woman and Dog' (1964).

Maritain, Jacques [mareetī] (1882–1973) Philosopher and diplomat, born in Paris. He converted to Catholicism in 1906. His main works include (trans titles) *The Degree of Knowledge* (1932) and *Moral Philosophy* (1960), but he is best known outside France for his many writings on art, politics, and history.

Marius, Gaius (c.157–86 BC) Roman general and politician, born in Arpinum. Famous for his victories over Jugurtha (105 BC), the Teutones (102 BC), and the Cimbri (101 BC), his army reforms made a great impact on the state. His final years were dominated by his rivalry with Sulla. >> Sulla

Marius, Simon (1573-1624) Astronomer, born in Gunzenhausen, Germany. In 1609 he claimed to have discovered the four satellites of Jupiter independently of Galileo, and named them Io, Europa, Ganymede, and Callisto. >> Galileo

Marivaux, Pierre (Carlet de Chamblain de) [mareevoh] (1688-1763) Playwright and novelist, born in Paris. He wrote several comedies, notably *The Game of Love and Chance* (trans, 1730). His best-known novel, *The Life of Murianne* (trans, 1731-41), displays an affected style dubbed Marivaudage.

Mark, St, also called **John Mark** (fl.1st-c), feast day 25 April. Christian disciple. He is described in the New Testament as 'John whose surname was Mark' (*Acts* 12.12, 25), and a helper of the apostles Barnabas and Paul during their first missionary journey. He is often considered the Mark who is accredited in 2nd-c traditions with the writing of the second Gospel.

Mark Antony >> Antonius, Marcus

Markard, Anna >> Jooss, Kurt

Markievicz, Constance (Georgine), Countess [mah(r)-kyayvich], *née* Gore-Booth (1868-1927) Irish nationalist, born in London. She married the Polish Count Casimir Markievicz, fought in the Easter Rising (1916), and was sentenced to death but reprieved. Elected the first British woman MP in 1918, she did not take her seat, but was a member of the Dáil from 1923.

Markov, Andrey Andreyevich [mah(r)kof] (1856-1922) Mathematician, born in Ryazan, Russia. His name is best known for the concept of the *Markov chain*, a series of events in which the probability of a given event occurring depends only on the immediately previous event.

Markova, Dame Alicia [mah(r)kohva], originally **Lilian Alicia Marks** (1910-) Prima ballerina, born in London. She danced with Ballets Russes in 1924, and in Britain formed a partnership with Anton Dolin which led to the establishment of the Markova-Dolin Company in 1935. >> Dolin

Marks (of Broughton), Simon Marks, Baron (1888-1964) Businessman, born in Leeds, West Yorkshire. In 1907 he inherited the 60 penny bazaars which his father Michael Marks, with Thomas Spencer, had built up from 1884. In collaboration with Israel Seiff, he developed Marks and Spencer into a major retail chain.

Marlborough, John Churchill, 1st Duke of [mah(r)l-bruh] (1650-1722) English general, born in Ashe, Devon. In 1678 he married Sarah Jennings, a friend of Princess Anne, through whom he obtained advancement. He commanded the British forces in the War of the Spanish Succession, winning several great victories, including Blenheim (1704) and Ramillies (1706), for which he was rewarded with Blenheim Palace and a dukedom. Forced by political interests to align himself with the Whig war party (1708), his influence waned with theirs after 1710. >> Anne; Churchill, Sarah

Marley, Bob, popular name of **Robert Nesta Marley** (1945-81) Singer, guitarist, and composer of reggae music, born near Kingston, Jamaica. A Rastafarian, in 1965 he formed the vocal trio, The Wailers, who popularized reggae during the 1970s. His most famous songs include 'No Woman, No Cry' and 'I Shot the Sheriff'.

Marlowe, Christopher (1564-93) Playwright, born in Canterbury, Kent. His *Tamburlaine the Great* (c.1587) shows his discovery of the strength and variety of blank verse, and this was followed by *The Jew of Malta* (c.1590), *The Tragical History of Dr Faustus* (c.1592), and *Edward II* (c.1592). He was fatally stabbed in a tavern brawl.

Marot, Clément [maroh] (c.1497-1544) Poet, born in Cahors, France. One of the celebrated poets of the French Renaissance, his work included elegies, epistles, rondeaux, ballads, sonnets, madrigals, epigrams, and nonsense verses.

Marquand, J(ohn) P(hillips) [mah(r)kwond] (1893-1960) Novelist, born in Wilmingon, DE. He is best known for a series of novels which gently satirized affluent middle-class American life, including *The Late George Apley* (1937) and *Point of No Return* (1949).

Marquet, (Pierre) Albert [mah(r)kay] (1875-1947) Artist, born in Bordeaux, France. One of the original Fauves, he became primarily an Impressionist landscape painter, producing many pictures of Le Havre, Algiers, and the Seine, such as his 'Pont neuf'.

Marquette, Jacques [mah(r)ket] (1637-75) Jesuit missionary and explorer, born in Laon, France. Sent in 1666 to North America, he brought Christianity to the Ottawa Indians around L Superior, and went on the expedition which discovered and explored the Mississippi (1673).

Márquez, Gabriel García [mah(r)kez] (1928-) Novelist, born in Aracataca, Colombia. A journalist in Europe (1950-65), he published his first novel in 1955. His best-known work is *One Hundred Years of Solitude* (trans, 1967). *Love in a Time of Cholera* (trans title) appeared in 1985. He received the Nobel Prize for Literature in 1982.

Márquez, Felipe González >> González, Felipe Márquez

Marquis, Don(ald Robert Perry) [mah(r)kwis] (1878-1937) Novelist, playwright, and poet, born in Walnut, IL. A literary journalist in New York City, writing for *The Sun*, he achieved fame as a comic writer in his column 'The Sun Dial' with the popular *archy and mehitabel* (1927).

Marriner, Sir Neville (1924-) Conductor, born in Lincoln, Lincolnshire. He held posts with the Los Angeles Chamber Orchestra (1968-77), the Minnesota Orchestra (1979-86), and the Stuttgart Radio Symphony Orchestra (1984-9), and became founder-director of the Academy of St Martin-in-the-Fields chamber ensemble (1956).

Marrison, Warren (1896-1980) US electrical engineer. He investigated the use of quartz crystals in long-distance telephone and radio transmissions (c.1923), and in 1929 produced the first quartz-controlled electric clock.

Marryat, Frederick (1792-1848) Naval officer and novelist, born in London. He wrote novels based on his experiences of sea life, notably *Peter Simple* (1833) and *Mr Midshipman Easy* (1836). His best-known work is the children's story *The Children of the New Forest* (1847).

Marsalis, Wynton [mah(r)sahlis] (1961-) Trumpeter and composer, born in New Orleans, LA. After many engagements as a classical virtuoso, he was recruited in 1980 to Blakey's Jazz Messengers, and left in 1982 to lead the first of a succession of small groups. >> Blakey

Marsden, Samuel (1764-1838) Clergyman, magistrate, and farmer, born in Farsley, West Yorkshire. In New South Wales from 1794, he became a pioneer breeder of sheep for wool production, and in 1807 took the first commercial consignment of Australian wool to England.

Marsh, James (1789-1846) British chemist. An expert on poisons, he invented the standard test for arsenic, which has been given his name.

Marsh, Dame Ngaio (Edith) [niyoh] (1899-1982) Detective-story writer, born in Christchurch, New Zealand. Her series of novels and short stories, featuring Superintendent Roderick Alleyn of Scotland Yard, include *Vintage Murder* (1937), *Opening Night* (1951), and *Black as He's Painted* (1974).

Marsh, O(thniel) C(harles) (1831-99) Palaeontologist, born in Lockport, NY. His classification of extinct vertebrates helped confirm Darwinian theories of evolution. He described 80 new species of dinosaurs, the reptilian origin of birds, the evolution of the horse, and the presence of early primates in North America. >> Darwin, Charles

Marsh, Reginald (1898–1954) US painter, born in Paris. Known for his water colours and egg tempera paintings of contemporary urban life, he combined the Baroque with a Realistic style, as seen in 'The Bowery' (1930) and 'Negroes on Rockaway Beach' (1934).

Marshal, William, 1st Earl of Pembroke (and Strigul) (c.1146–1219) Knight, and regent of England (1216–19), a nephew of the Earl of Salisbury. He supported Henry II against Richard I, and went on a crusade to the Holy Land. After King John's death in 1216, he was appointed regent for the nine-year-old Henry III. >> Henry II / III (of England)

Marshall, George C(atlett) (1880–1959) US soldier and statesman, born in Uniontown, PA. He became secretary of state (1947–9), and originated the *Marshall Aid* plan for the post-war reconstruction of Europe. He was awarded the Nobel Peace Prize in 1953.

Marshall, John (1755–1835) Jurist, born in Germantown, VA. He became Chief Justice of the USA (1801–35), during which time he dominated the Supreme Court, and established the US doctrine of judicial review.

Marshall, Sir John Hubert (1876–1958) Archaeologist and administrator, born in Chester, Cheshire. His excavations at Mohenjo-daro and Harappa in the Indus Valley in the 1920s revealed for the first time the antiquity of Indian civilization.

Marshall, Paule (1929–) Writer, born in New York City. Her first novel, *Brown Girl, Brownstones* (1959), is regarded as a classic of African-American literature.

Marshall, Peter (1902–49) Presbyterian clergyman, born in Coatbridge, Strathclyde. In 1937 he was appointed to the historic New York Avenue Presbyterian Church in Washington, DC, and in 1948 became chaplain to the US Senate.

Marshall, Thurgood (1908–93) Judge, born in Baltimore, MD. As an attorney he won a historic victory in the case of *Brown v. Board of Education of Topeka* (1954) which declared that racial segregation in public schools was unconstitutional. He became the first African-American member of the Supreme Court (1967–91).

Marsilius of Padua [mah(r)silius] (c.1275–c.1342) Political theorist and philosopher, born in Padua, Italy. In 1324 he completed *Defensor pacis*, a political treatise which argued against the temporal power of clergy and pope, and was excommunicated.

Marston, John (1576–1634) Playwright and satirist, born in Wardington, Oxfordshire. His plays include *The Malcontent* (1604) and *Eastward Ho!* (1605), a satirical comedy written in conjunction with Chapman and Jonson. >> Chapman, George; Jonson

Martel, Charles >> **Charles Martel**

Martel, Sir Giffard Le Quesne [mah(r)tel] (1889–1958) British soldier. In 1925 he was responsible for the construction of the first one-man tank, and in 1940 commanded the Royal Armoured Corps.

Martel de Janville, comtesse de >> **Gyp**

Marten, Henry or **Harry** (1602–80) Parliamentary judge and regicide, born in Oxford, Oxfordshire. He fought in the parliamentary army, sat on Charles I's trial, and signed his death warrant. After the Restoration he was imprisoned. >> Charles I (of England)

Martens, Conrad (1801–78) Landscape painter, born in London. In 1833 he was appointed a topographer on Darwin's voyage from Rio de Janeiro to Valparaiso. He arrived in Sydney in 1835, and produced a set of lithographs, 'Sketches of Sydney' (1850–1). >> Darwin, Charles

Martens, Wilfried (1936–) Belgian prime minister (1979–81, 1981–92). He was president of the Dutch-speaking Social Christian Party (1972–9), when he became

prime minister at the head of a coalition, eventually heading six coalition governments.

Martial, in full **Marcus Valerius Martialis** (c.40–c.104) Latin poet and epigrammatist, born in Spain. He went to Rome in 64, and is remembered for his 12 books of epigrams, mainly satirical comments on contemporary events and society.

Martin, St (c.316–c.400), feast day 11 (W) or 12 November (E). Patron saint of France, born in Sabaria, Pannonia. He founded the first monastery near Poitiers (c.360), became famous for his sanctity, and was made Bishop of Tours (c.372).

Martin, Agnes (1912–) Painter, born in Maklin, Saskatchewan, Canada. During the 1940s she started to paint in a style called 'biomorphic abstraction', in 1959 producing the repetitive abstract grids of vertical and horizontal lines which have preoccupied her ever since.

Martin, A(rcher) J(ohn) P(orter) (1910–) Biochemist, born in London. His work on nutrition led him to the study of protein structure, and the development of partition chromatography to separate and analyze proteins, for which he shared the Nobel Prize for Chemistry in 1952. >> Synge

Martin, Frank [mah(r)tī] (1890–1974) Composer and pianist, born in Geneva, Switzerland. His works include the oratorios *Golgotha* and *In terra pax*, a Mass, and the cantata *Le Vin herbé*.

Martin, Glenn L(uther) (1886–1955) Aircraft manufacturer, born in Macksburg, IA. The production of the MB-1 bomber at his factory at Cleveland in 1918 established him as a leading military aircraft manufacturer.

Martin, (Basil) Kingsley (1897–1969) Journalist, born in London. As editor of the *New Statesman and Nation* (1932–62), he transformed it into a strongly self-assured weekly journal of socialist opinion.

Martin, Paul [mah(r)tī] (1864–1942) Photographer, born in Herbenville, France. He used a concealed camera to record working people in the streets of London and on holiday at the seaside (1888–98), and his records have since been much used to represent late-Victorian everyday life.

Martin, Pierre Emile [mah(r)tī] (1824–1915) Metallurgist, born in Bourges, France. He devised an improved method of producing high-quality steel in an open-hearth furnace using the heat-regeneration process introduced by Siemens. >> Siemens, William

Martin, Richard (1754–1834) Lawyer and humanitarian, born in Dublin. As MP for Galway (1801–26), he sponsored a bill in 1822 to make the cruel treatment of cattle illegal. His efforts led to the formation of the Royal Society for the Prevention of Cruelty to Animals.

Martin, Violet Florence, pseudonym **Martin Ross** (1862–1915) Writer, born in Co Galway, Ireland. She is known chiefly for a series of novels written in collaboration with her cousin Edith Somerville, such as *An Irish Cousin* (1889). >> Somerville, Edith

Martin de Porres, St [pohres] (1579–1639), feast day 3 November. South American saint, who spent his entire life in the Dominican Order in Lima, Peru, ministering to the sick and poor. Canonized in 1962, he is the patron saint of social justice.

Martin du Gard, Roger [mah(r)tī dü gah(r)] (1881–1958) Novelist, born in Neuilly, France. He is best known for his eight-novel series, *Les Thibault* (1922–40), dealing with family life during the first decades of the present century. He was awarded the Nobel Prize for Literature in 1937.

Martineau, Harriet [mah(r)tinoh] (1802–76) Writer, born in Norwich, Norfolk. A successful social, economic, and historical writer, her works include *Illustrations of Political Economy* (25 vols, 1832–4) and *Poor Laws and Paupers Illustrated* (1833–4).

Martinet, Jean [mah(r)teenay] (?–1672) French army officer. He won renown as a military engineer and tactician, and became notorious for his stringent and brutal forms of discipline, which led to the common use of the word *martinet*.

Martínez Ruiz, José >> Azorín

Martínez Sierra, Gregorio [mah(r)teeneth syayra] (1881–1947) Novelist and playwright, born in Madrid. His masterpiece is the play *The Cradle Song* (trans, 1911), which was also popular in Britain and America. Much of his writing was done in collaboration with his wife **María** (1874–1974).

Martini, Simone [mah(r)teenee] (c.1284–1344) Painter, born in Siena, Italy. He was the most important artist of the 14th-c Sienese school, notable for his grace of line and exquisite colour, as in 'Annunciation' (Uffizi).

Martins, Peter (1946–) Ballet dancer, born in Copenhagen. A former dancer with the New York City Ballet, he later shared the directorship of the company with Jerome Robbins. >> Robbins, Jerome

Martinson, Harry (Edmund) (1904–78) Poet and novelist, born in Jäshög, Sweden. His works include the autobiographical novels *Flowering Nettle* (trans, 1935) and *The Way Out* (trans, 1936), and the poetic space epic *Aniara* (1956). He shared the Nobel Prize for Literature in 1974.

Martinů, Bohuslav [mah(r)tinoo] (1890–1959) Composer, born in Polička, Czech Republic. His work ranges from 18th-c orchestral works to modern programme pieces evoked by unusual stimuli such as football or aeroplanes. His operas include the miniature *Comedy on a Bridge*.

Marty, Martin (Emil) (1928–) Religious historian and scholar, born in West Point, NE. Among his many books are *A Short History of Christianity* (1959) and *Protestantism in the United States* (1985).

Marvell, Andrew [mah(r)vl] (1621–78) Poet, born in Winestead, Humberside. He is remembered for his pastoral and garden poems, notably 'To His Coy Mistress' and 'Upon Appleton House' (c.1652–3), but he was also a pamphleteer and satirist.

Marx, Karl (Heinrich) (1818–83) Founder of modern international communism, born in Trier, Germany, the son of a Jewish lawyer. With Engels as his closest collaborator, he reorganized the Communist League, and in 1848 finalized the *Communist Manifesto*, which attacked the state as the instrument of oppression, and religion and culture as ideologies of the capitalist class. In 1849 he settled in London, where he wrote the first volume of his major work, *Das Kapital* (1867), and was a leading figure in the First International from 1864 until its demise in 1872. >> Engels

Marx Brothers Family of film comedians, born in New York City, comprising **Julius** (1895–1977), or **Groucho**; **Leonard** (1891–1961), or **Chico**; **Arthur** (1893–1961), or **Harpo**; and **Herbert** (1901–79), or **Zeppo**. Another brother, **Milton** (?1897–1977), known as **Gummo**, left the act early on. Their main reputation was made in a series of films, such as *Animal Crackers* and *Monkey Business* (both 1932). The team broke up in 1949.

Mary (mother of Jesus), also known as **Our Lady** or **the Blessed Virgin Mary** (?–c.63) Mother of Jesus Christ. In the New Testament she is most prominent in the stories of Jesus's birth (Matthew and Luke), and only occasionally appears in Jesus's ministry. She remained in Jerusalem during the early years of the Church, and tradition places her tomb there. The belief that her body was taken up into heaven is celebrated in the festival of the Assumption, defined as Roman Catholic dogma in 1950. Her Immaculate Conception has been a dogma since 1854. Belief in the apparitions of the Virgin at Lourdes, Fatima, and in several other places attracts many thousands of pilgrims each year. >> Jesus Christ; Joseph, St

Mary I, Tudor (1516–58) Queen of England and Ireland (1553–8), born in Greenwich, Greater London, the daughter of Henry VIII by his first wife, Catherine of Aragon. A Catholic, on her accession she repealed anti-Catholic legislation, and aimed to cement a union with Philip II of Spain. These aspirations provoked Wyatt's rebellion, followed by the execution of Jane Grey and the imprisonment of Mary's half-sister, Elizabeth. >> Grey, Lady Jane; Henry VIII; Philip II (of Spain)

Mary II (1662–94) Queen of Britain and Ireland from 1689, born in London, the daughter of the Duke of York (later James II) and his first wife, **Anne Hyde** (1638–71). She was married in 1677 to her cousin, William, Stadtholder of the United Netherlands. When James II fled to France, she was proclaimed queen, sharing the throne with her husband (later William III). >> James II (of England); William III

Mary, Queen of Scots (1542–87) Queen of Scotland (1542–67) and Queen Consort of France (1559–60), born at Linlithgow Palace, Lothian, the daughter of James V of Scotland by his second wife, Mary of Guise. In 1565 she married her cousin, Lord Darnley, but was soon alienated from him. The murder of her secretary by Darnley and a group of Protestant nobles (1566) confirmed her insecurity, and the birth of a son (the future James VI) failed to bring a reconciliation. Darnley was mysteriously killed in 1567, the chief suspect being the Earl of Bothwell, who underwent a mock trial and was acquitted. Mary's involvement is unclear, but she consented to marry Bothwell. The Protestant nobles rose against her and she was compelled to abdicate. Placing herself under the protection of Queen Elizabeth, her presence in England gave rise to countless plots, and after the Babington conspiracy (1586) she was executed. >> Babington; Bothwell; Darnley; Elizabeth I; Rizzio

Mary of Modena, *née* **Maria Beatrice d'Este** (1658–1718) Queen of Britain and Ireland (1685–88), the second wife of James II. In 1688 she gave birth to James Francis Edward Stuart (the future 'Old Pretender'), and escaped to France when William of Orange landed in England (1688). >> James II (of England); Stuart, James; William III

Mary of Teck, in full **Victoria Mary Augusta Louise Olga Pauline Claudine Agnes** (1867–1953) Queen-consort of Great Britain, the wife of George V, born in London, the daughter of Francis, Duke of Teck. She married the king when Duke of York in 1893. After the abdication of her eldest son, Edward VIII, she strengthened the popular appeal of the monarchy throughout the reign of her second son, George VI. >> Edward VIII; George V / VI

Mary Magdalene, St [magdalen] (1st-c), feast day 22 July. Disciple of Jesus. *Magdalene* possibly means 'of Magdala', in Galilee. *Luke* 8.2 reports that Jesus exorcised seven evil spirits from her; thereafter she appears only in the narratives of Jesus's passion and resurrection. >> Jesus Christ

Mary Tudor (1495/6–1533) Royal princess, the daughter of Henry VII. She married Louis XII of France in 1514, and following his death in 1515 secretly married Charles Brandon, Duke of Suffolk. One of their daughters became the mother of Lady Jane Grey. >> Grey, Lady Jane; Henry VII; Louis XII

Masaccio [masachio], originally **Tommaso de Giovanni di Simone Guidi** (1401–28) Painter and pioneer of the Renaissance, born in Castel San Giovanni di Altura, Duchy of Milan. He brought about a revolution in the dramatic representation of biblical events, his greatest work being the fresco cycle in the Brancacci Chapel of the Church of S Maria del Carmine in Florence (1424–7).

Masaryk, Jan (Garrigue) [masarik] (1886–1948) Diplomat and statesman, born in Prague, the son of Tomáš Masaryk. In 1941 he was appointed foreign minister of the Czechoslovak government in exile, becoming a popular broadcaster to his home country during the war. >> Masaryk, Tomáš

Masaryk, Tomáš (Garrigue) [masarik] (1850–1937) Founder-president of the Czechoslovakian Republic (1918–35), born in Hodonin, Czech Republic. In 1914 he escaped to London, where he organized the Czech independence movement.

Mascagni, Pietro [maskanyee] (1863–1945) Composer, born in Livorno, Italy. In 1890 he produced the very successful one-act opera, *Cavalleria rusticana*.

Mascall, Eric Lionel (1905–) Anglo-Catholic theologian and writer. His books *He Who Is* (1943) and *Existence and Analogy* (1949) have acquired the character of textbooks on natural theology.

Masefield, John (1878–1967) Poet and novelist, born in Ledbury, Herefordshire. His best-known poetical work is *Salt Water Ballads* (1902), and he also wrote novels, plays, and works for children, such as *The Box of Delights* (1935). He became poet laureate in 1930.

Masham, Lady Abigail, *née* **Hill** (?–1734) Queen Anne's confidante, the cousin of Sarah Churchill, Duchess of Marlborough. She gradually turned the queen against the Marlboroughs, and in 1710 superseded her cousin as the power behind the throne. >> Anne; Churchill, Sarah

Masire, Quett (Ketumile Joni) (1925–) President of Botswana (1980–). A founder member of the Botswana Democratic Party (1962), he became vice-president at independence (1966), then president, continuing a policy of non-alignment.

Maskelyne, John Nevil [maskelin] (1839–1917) Magician, born in Cheltenham, Gloucestershire. In 1865 he joined forces with **George Cooke** (d.1904) and they appeared together in London for 31 years. He later had **David Devant** (1868–1941) as his partner.

Maskelyne, Nevil [maskelin] (1732–1811) Astronomer, born in London. He became Astronomer Royal, improved methods and instruments of observation, invented the prismatic micrometer, and in 1774 measured the Earth's density.

Maslow, Abraham (Harold) (1908–70) Psychologist, born in Brooklyn, NY. Regarded as the founder of humanistic psychology, his *Motivation and Personality* (1954) introduced such concepts as the need hierarchy, self-actualization, and peak experience.

Masolino (da Panicale) [masohleenoh], originally **Tommaso di Cristoforo Fini** (1383–c.1447) Painter, born in Panicale, Romagna. His greatest work is the fresco cycle in the Baptistery and Collegiata of Castiglione d'Olona near Como (1430s), discovered only in 1843.

Mason, A(lfred) E(dward) W(oodley) (1865–1948) Novelist, born in London. With *At the Villa Rose* (1910) he started writing detective novels, and introduced his ingenious Inspector Hanaud. Several of his books have been filmed.

Mason, Charles (1730–87) Astronomer, known for the 'Mason-Dixon Line' in the USA. With the English surveyor **Jeremiah Dixon** (d.1777), from 1763 to 1767 they were engaged to survey the boundary between Maryland and Pennsylvania.

Mason, Daniel (Gregory) (1873–1953) Composer, born in Brookline, MA. A leading exponent of Neoclassical composition in the USA, he composed three symphonies and much chamber music.

Mason, James (1909–84) Actor, born in Huddersfield, West Yorkshire. He was nominated for an Oscar for *A Star Is Born* (1954), *Georgy Girl* (1966), and *The Verdict* (1982), and was also acclaimed for *Lolita* (1962) and *The Shooting Party* (1984).

Massaddiq, Mohammed >> **Mosaddeq, Mohammed**

Masséna, André [masayna] (1758–1817) French general, born in Nice, France. He distinguished himself in Napoleon's Italian campaign (1796–7), and defeated the Russians at Zürich (1799). Forced to retreat in the Iberian Peninsula, he was relieved of his command (1810). >> Napoleon I

Massenet, Jules (Emile Frédéric) [masenay] (1842–1912) Composer, born in Montaud, France. He made his name with the comic opera *Don César de Bazan* (1872) and his opera *Manon* (1884). Other works include oratorios, orchestral suites, music for piano, and songs.

Massey, Raymond (Hart) (1896–1983) Actor, born in Toronto, Ontario, Canada, the brother of Vincent Massey. He is best known for his long-running television role as 'Dr Gillespie' in the *Dr Kildare* series during the 1960s.

Massey, (Charles) Vincent (1887–1967) Canadian statesman, diplomat, and governor-general, born in Toronto, Ontario, Canada, the brother of Raymond Massey. He became Canada's first minister in Washington (1926–30), high commissioner to Britain (1935–46), and Governor-General of Canada (1952–9). >> Massey, Raymond

Massey, William Ferguson (1856–1925) New Zealand prime minister (1912–25), born in Limavady, Co Londonderry. He emigrated to New Zealand in 1870, became Conservative Leader of the Opposition (1894–1912), and as prime minister led the coalition during World War 1.

Massine, Léonide [maseen], originally **Leonid Fyodorovich Miassin** (1896–1979) Ballet dancer and choreographer, born in Moscow. He was principal dancer in Diaghilev's Ballets Russes, and went on to choreograph such acclaimed works as *Parade* (1917) and *La Boutique fantasque* (1919). >> Diaghilev

Massinger, Philip (1583–1640) Playwright, born near Salisbury, Wiltshire. Much of his work after 1613 is in collaboration with others, especially Fletcher. *A New Way to Pay Old Debts* (1633) is his best-known satirical comedy. >> Fletcher, John

Massys or **Matsys, Quentin** [masees] (c.1466–c.1530) Painter, born in Louvain, Belgium. In 1491 he joined the painters' Guild of St Luke in Antwerp, painting religious and genre pictures. His many portraits include Erasmus.

Massys or **Matsys, Jan** [masiys, matsiys] (1509–75) Painter, born probably in Louvain, Belgium, the son of Quentin Massys. An imitator of his father, he worked in Antwerp, becoming Master of the Guild in 1531. His brother, **Cornelius** (1513–79), was also a painter. >> Massys, Quentin

Masters, Edgar Lee (1869–1950) Poet and novelist, born in Garnett, KS. His most memorable work is the *Spoon River Anthology* (1915), a book of epitaphs in free verse in the form of monologues about a small town community.

Masters and Johnson Human sexuality researchers and authors: **William H(owell) Masters** (1915–) and **Virginia E(shelman) Johnson** (1925–), born in Cleveland, OH, and Springfield, MO, respectively. In 1964 they established the Reproductive Biology Research Foundation, and published the best-selling *Human Sexual Response* (1966). They married in 1971 and divorced in 1991.

Mastroianni, Marcello [mastroyahnee] (1924–) Actor, born in Fontana Liri, Italy. Fellini's *La dolce vita* (1959, The Sweet Life) established him as an international star. He also received Oscar nominations for (trans titles) *Divorce, Italian Style* (1962), *A Special Day* (1977), and *Dark Eyes* (1987).

Mata Hari [mahta hahree], (Malay 'sun'), pseudonym of **Margaretha Geertruide MacLeod**, *née* **Zelle** (1876–1917) Spy, born in Leeuwarden, The Netherlands. She became a dancer in France (1905), had many lovers - several in high military and governmental positions - and, found guilty of espionage for the Germans, was shot in Paris.

Mather, Cotton [mather] (1663–1728) Colonial minister and writer, born in Boston, MA, the son of Increase Mather. He reported on American botany, and was one of the earliest New England historians. His reputation suffered after his involvement in the Salem witchcraft trials (1692). >> Mather, Increase

Mather, Increase [mather] (1639–1723) Congregational minister and writer, born in Dorchester, MA. His works include *Remarkable Providences* (1684) and a *History of the War with the Indians* (1676), and he became president of Harvard (1681–1701). >> Mather, Cotton

Mathewson, Christy, popular name of **Christopher Mathewson** (1880–1925) Baseball player, born in Factoryville, PA. A right-handed pitcher, he played 17 seasons (1900–16) for the New York Giants, and shares the record of 373 wins. >> Alexander, Grover

Mathieu, Georges [matyoe] (1921–) Painter, born in Boulogne, France. He developed a form of lyric, nongeometrical abstraction, in close sympathy with the American neo-Expressionists.

Matilda, also called **Maud** (1102–67) English princess, born in London, the only daughter of Henry I. She married Geoffrey Plantagenet of Anjou (1128), by whom she had a son, the future Henry II of England. When Henry I died (1135), his nephew Stephen of Blois seized the throne, and in 1139 Matilda invaded England from Anjou, capturing Stephen. He regained control and in 1148 she left for Normandy. >> Henry I / II (of England); Stephen

Matisse, Henri (Emile Benoît) [matees] (1869–1954) Painter, born in Le Cateau, France. From 1904 he was the leader of the Fauves, his most characteristic paintings displaying a bold use of brilliant areas of primary colour, organized within a rhythmic two-dimensional design.

Matsys, Jan >> Massys, Jan

Matsys, Quentin >> Massys, Quentin

Matteotti, Giacomo [matiotee] (1885–1924) Italian politician, born in Fratta Polesine, Italy. He organized the United Socialist Party (1921), and was an outspoken opponent of Mussolini's Fascists (1922–4). His protests against Fascist election outrages led to his murder in 1924. >> Mussolini

Matthew, St (1st-c), feast day 21 September (W) or 16 November (E). One of the 12 apostles in the New Testament, identified with Levi (in *Mark* 2.14 and *Luke* 5.27). According to tradition he was the author of the first Gospel, a missionary to the Hebrews, and a martyr. >> Jesus Christ

Matthew Corvinus >> Matthias I

Matthew Paris (c.1200–59) Chronicler and Benedictine monk. His *Chronica majora* is the fullest available account of events in England between 1236 and 1259, and he is especially famous for his maps and drawings.

Matthews, (James) Brander (1852–1929) Writer, born in New Orleans, LA. During his career he worked as an editor, essayist, drama critic, and novelist, these works being the foundation of the Brander Matthews Dramatic Museum at Columbia University.

Matthews, Sir Stanley (1915–) Footballer, born in Hanley, Staffordshire. He began his career with Stoke City (1931), before transferring to Blackpool (1947). He played for England 54 times, was twice Footballer of the Year (1948, 1963), and won the first European Footballer of the Year Award (1956).

Matthias I, known as **Matthew Corvinus**, Hung **Mátyás Corvin** (c.1443–90) King of Hungary (1458–90), born in Koloszvár, Hungary, the second son of János Hunyady. He drove back the Turks, and greatly extended his territory, capturing and a large part of Austria (1485). He encouraged industry, promoted industry, and reformed the justice system. >> Hunyady

Matthias, Bernard (Teo) (1918–) Physicist, born in Frankfurt, Germany. In his search for new superconducting materials, he discovered that alloys of metals with five or seven valence electrons were the most effective.

Matthias, William (James) (1934–92) Composer, born in Whitland, Dyfed. His works include an opera, *The Servants* (1980), three symphonies, several concertos, much chamber, choral, and church music, and an anthem for the wedding of the Prince and Princess of Wales (1981).

Matthiessen, Peter [mathesen] (1927–) Novelist, travel writer, naturalist, and explorer, born in New York City. He wrote novels and a number of ecological and natural history studies, notably *The Snow Leopard* (1978, National Book Award).

Matzeliger, Jan Earnst [matzeliger] (1852–89) Inventor, born in Dutch Guiana. He emigrated to the USA (c.1872), where he invented a shoe-making machine (1891) and shoe-nailing machine (1896) which revolutionized the shoe industry.

Mauchly, John W(illiam) [mawklee] (1907–80) Physicist and inventor, born in Cincinnati, OH. He joined Eckert (1943) in the development of the ENIAC, EDVAC, and UNIVAC systems, helping to launch the computer revolution. >> Eckert

Maud, Empress >> Matilda

Maudling, Reginald (1917–79) British Conservative statesman, born in London. His senior posts were President of the Board of Trade (1959–61), Chancellor of the Exchequer (1962–4), deputy leader of the Opposition (1964), and home secretary (1972–4), resigning when implicated in the bankruptcy proceedings of architect John Poulson.

Maudslay, Henry [mawdzlee] (1771–1831) Engineer and inventor, born in Woolwich, Kent. He invented various types of machinery, including a screw-cutting lathe, and with **Joshua Field** (1757–1863) began producing marine engines.

Maudsley, Henry [mawdzlee] (1835–1918) Psychiatrist, born in Giggleswick, North Yorkshire. Professor of medical jurisprudence at University College (1869–79), the Maudsley Hospital, Denmark Hill, London, is named after him.

Mauger, Ivan (Gerald) [mawger] (1939–) Speedway rider, born in Christchurch, New Zealand. He won the world individual title a record six times (1968–70, 1972, 1977, 1979). He also won two pairs world titles, four team titles, and two world long-track titles.

Maugham, W(illiam) Somerset [mawm] (1874–1965) Novelist, playwright, and short-story writer, born in Paris. His works include the novel *Of Human Bondage* (1915), and the plays *The Moon and Sixpence* (1919) and *Cakes and Ale* (1930). Best known for his short stories, *The Complete Short Stories* (3 vols) was published in 1951.

Maundeville / Maundevylle, Sir John >> Mandeville, Sir John

Maupassant, (Henry René Albert) Guy de [mohpasã] (1850–93) Novelist and short-story writer, probably born at the Château de Miromesnil, Dieppe, France. He wrote some 300 short stories and several novels, including *A Woman's Life* (trans, 1883), and the autobiographical *Bel-Ami* (1885).

Maupertuis, Pierre Louis Moreau de [mohpertwee] (1698–1759) Mathematician, born in St Malo, France. He is best known for his 'principle of least action' in mechanics, in explaining the paths of moving bodies.

Mauriac, François [mohriak] (1885–1970) Novelist, born in Bordeaux, France. Regarded as the leading French Catholic novelist of the 20th-c, his novels include *The Kiss to the Leper* (trans, 1922) and *Viper's Tangle* (1932). He was awarded the Nobel Prize for Literature in 1952.

Maurice, (John) Frederick Denison (1805–72) Theologian and writer, born in Normanston, Suffolk. With Hughes and Kingsley he founded the Christian Socialism movement, and was the founder and first principal of the Working Man's College (1854). >> Kingsley, Charles; Hughes, Thomas

Maurice, Prinz van Oranje, Graaf van Nassau (Prince of Orange, Count of Nassau) (1567–1625) Stadholder of the United Provinces of the Netherlands, born in Dilenburg, the son of William the Silent. He became captain-general of the armies of the United Provinces during their War of Independence from Spain. He checked the Spanish advance, and by his steady offensive (1590–1606) liberated the N provinces. >> William I (of the Netherlands)

Maurier, du >> du Maurier

Maurin, Peter >> Day, Dorothy

Maurois, André [mohrwah], pseudonym of **Emile Herzog** (1885–1967) Writer and biographer, born in Elbeuf, France. His many biographies include studies of Shelley (1923), Disraeli (1927), Voltaire (1935), and Proust (1949).

Mauroy, Pierre [mohrwah] (1928–) French prime minister (1981–4). He was prominent in the creation of a new French Socialist Party in 1971, and a close ally of Mitterrand, acting as his spokesman during the socialists' successful election campaign. >> Mitterrand

Maurras, Charles [mohra] (1868–1952) Journalist, born in Martigues, France. He was an avant-garde journalist and aggressive critic of the government, who supported the Vichy government in 1940, and was sentenced to life imprisonment in 1945.

Maury, Matthew (Fontaine) [mawree] (1806–73) Naval officer and hydrographer, born in Spotsylvania, VA. He wrote *Physical Geography of the Sea* (1856), and works on the Gulf Stream, ocean currents, and Great Circle sailing.

Mauser, (Peter) Paul von [mowzer] (1838–1914) Fire-arm inventor, born in Oberndorf, Germany. With his brother **Wilhelm** (1834–82) he improved the needle-gun and the breech-loading cannon, and produced the *Mauser magazine-rifle* in 1897.

Mausolus >> Artemisia II

Mauss, Marcel [mohs] (1872–1950) Sociologist and anthropologist, born in Epinal, France. His masterpiece was *Essay on the Gift* (trans, 1925) in which he demonstrated the importance of gift exchange in primitive social organization.

Mauve, Anton [mowvuh] (1838–88) Painter, born in Zaandam, The Netherlands. Regarded as one of the greatest landscapists of his time, from 1878 he lived in Laren, where he founded the Dutch Barbizon school.

Mavor, Osborne Henry >> Bridie, James

Maw, (John) Nicholas (1935–) Composer, born in Grantham, Lincolnshire. His works include the operas *One Man Show* (1964) and *The Rising of the Moon* (1970), two string quartets, and many orchestral works.

Mawson, Sir Douglas (1882–1958) Explorer and geologist, born in Shipley, West Yorkshire. He joined Shackleton's Antarctic expedition (1907), and with T W E David discovered the South Magnetic Pole. He led further Antarctic expeditions in 1911–14 and 1929–31. >> Shackleton

Max, Adolphe (1869–1939) Belgian statesman, born in Brussels. In 1914 he bravely defended the rights of the Belgian population against the invading German troops, and was imprisoned. After the War, he became a minister of state.

Maxim, Sir Hiram (Stevens) (1840–1916) Inventor and engineer, born in Sangerville, ME. From 1867 he took out patents for a wide range of inventions, including electric lamps and gas equipment, but is best known for the *Maxim machine-gun* (1883).

Maximilian, Ferdinand Joseph (1832–67) Emperor of Mexico (1864–7), born in Vienna, the younger brother of Emperor Francis Joseph. In 1863 he accepted the offer of the crown of Mexico, supported by France; but when Napoleon III withdrew his troops, he refused to abdicate, and was executed. >> Francis Joseph; Napoleon III

Maximilian I (1459–1519) Holy Roman Emperor (1493–1519), born as Archduke of Austria in Weiner Neustadt, Austria, the eldest son of Emperor Frederick III and Eleanor of Portugal. He inherited the Habsburg territories, and pursued an ambitious foreign policy, involved in conflict with the Flemish, the Swiss, the German princes, and especially the Valois kings of France. >> Charles V (Emperor); Louis XII

Max-Müller, Friedrich >> Müller, Max

Maxwell, James C(lerk) (1831–79) Physicist, born in Edinburgh. In 1873 he published his great *Treatise on Electricity and Magnetism*, which gives a mathematical treatment to Faraday's theory of electrical and magnetic forces. His greatest work was his theory of electromagnetic radiation, which established him as the leading theoretical physicist of the century. >> Faraday

Maxwell, (Ian) Robert, originally **Ludvik Hoch** (1923–91) Publisher and politician, born in Slatinske Dòly, Czech Republic. He founded the Pergamon Press, became a Labour MP (1964–70), and chairman of the Mirror group of newspapers in 1984, but was forced to float the company on the London stock market in 1991. Following his death at sea, it transpired that he had secretly siphoned large sums of money from two of his companies and from employee pension funds. The subsequent investigations were continuing in 1995.

Maxwell Davies, Sir Peter >> Davies, Sir Peter Maxwell

May, Peter (Barker Howard) (1929–94) Cricketer and administrator, born in Reading, Berkshire. He played in 66 Tests for England (41 as captain), scoring 4537 runs, and in all first-class matches scored 27 592 runs, including 85 centuries. He later became chairman of the England Cricket Selection Committee (1982–8).

May, Phil(ip William) (1864–1903) Caricaturist, born in Wortley, West Yorkshire. In 1890 he established himself with contributions to *Punch* (staff member from 1896). He excelled in depicting East London types, and brought a new simplicity of line to popular cartooning.

May, Sir Robert (1936–) Australian scientist. He is one of a growing number of scientists who have contributed to chaos theory, his work having applications in ecology and public health.

Mayakovsky, Vladimir (Vladimirovich) [miyakofskee] (1893–1930) Poet and playwright, born in Bagdadi, Georgia. Regarded as the leader of the Futurist school, during the Russian Revolution (1917) he emerged as the propaganda mouthpiece of the Bolsheviks.

Maybach, Wilhelm [maybakh] (1846–1929) Inventor and car manufacturer, born in Heilbronn, Germany. He joined Daimler (1882), introducing the float-feed carburettor (1893), and improvements in timing, gearing, and steering. In 1909 he set up his own works, where he produced luxury Maybach cars (1922–39). >> Daimler

Mayer, Louis B(urt) [mayer], originally **Eliezer Mayer** (1885–1957) Film mogul, born in Minsk, Belarus. In 1907 he emigrated to the USA, joining Goldwyn to form the Metro–Goldwyn–Mayer film company (1924). He was instrumental in the creation of Hollywood as a dream factory and the establishment of the star system. >> Goldwyn

Mayhew, Henry (1812–87) Writer, born in London. His best-known work is the classic social survey, *London Labour and the London Poor* (4 vols, 1851–62). In 1841, with Mark Lemon, he founded the humorous magazine, *Punch*. >> Lemon

Mayo, Charles Horace [mayoh] (1865–1939) Surgeon, born in Rochester, MN. In 1905 he helped his brother, William James Mayo, to organize the Mayo Clinic in Rochester, which their father had founded. >> Mayo, William James

Mayo, Henry Thomas [mayoh] (1856–1937) US naval officer, born in Burlington, VT. He commanded the Atlantic Fleet (1916–19), and was in charge of all naval forces in Atlantic and European waters during World War 1.

Mayo, Katherine [mayoh] (1868–1940) Journalist, born in Ridgeway, PA. She is remembered for her books exposing social evils, especially *Isles of Fear* (1925) and *Mother India* (1927).

Mayo, William James [**may**oh] (1861–1939) Surgeon, born in Le Sueur, MN. He established the Mayo Clinic with his brother Charles Horace at St Mary's Hospital, Rochester, MN, and in 1915 set up the Mayo Foundation for Medical Education and Research. >> Mayo, Charles Horace

Mayr, Ernst (Walter) [**may**er] (1904–) Zoologist, born in Kempten, Germany. He is best known for his neo-Darwinian views on evolution, as developed in such books as *Animal Species and Evolution* (1963). >> Darwin, Charles

Mays, Willie (Howard), nickname **the Say Hey Kid** (1931–) Baseball player, born in Westfield, AL. He played for the New York (1951–7) and San Francisco (1958–72) Giants, and the New York Mets (1972–3). A fielder, batter, and baserunner, only he and Aaron have performed the baseball double of more than 3000 hits and 600 home runs. >> Aaron, Hank

Mazarin, Jules [mazarī], known as **Cardinal Mazarin**, originally **Giulio Raimondo Mazzarino** (1602–61) Neopolitan cleric, diplomat, and statesman, born in Pescine, Italy. He entered the service of Louis XIII (1639), and through Richelieu was elevated to cardinal, succeeding him as first minister (1642). Blamed by many for the Frondes, he twice fled the kingdom. He concluded the Peace of Westphalia (1648) and negotiated the Treaty of the Pyrenees (1659), ending the prolonged Franco-Spanish conflict. >> Richelieu

Mazzini, Giuseppe [mat**see**nee] (1805–72) Patriot and republican, born in Genoa, Italy. He founded the Young Italy Association (1833), and in 1848 was involved in the Lombard revolt. In 1859–60 he worked strenuously but vainly to make the new Italy a republic. >> Garibaldi

Mbeki, Thabo (Mvuyelwa) [**mbe**kee] (1942–) Leading member of the African National Congress (ANC), born in Idutywa, South Africa. After the ANC was unbanned in 1990, he played a major role in the negotiations for a new political dispensation, and was made first deputy president in the new administration (1994).

Mbiti, John Samuel [**mbi**tee] (1931–) Theologian, born in Kenya. He became director of the World Council of Churches Ecumenical Institute in Switzerland (1972–80). His books include *African Religions and Philosophy* (1969).

Mboya, Tom [**mbo**ya], popular name of **Thomas Joseph Mboya** (1930–69) Kenyan statesman and nationalist leader, born in Kilima Mbogo, Kenya. In 1960 he was general secretary of the Kenya African National Union, and became minister of labour (1962–3), of justice (1963–4), and of economic development and planning (1964–9). He was assassinated in 1969.

Mead, George Herbert (1863–1931) Social psychologist, born in South Hadley, MA. His work gave rise to Symbolic Interactionism, a social science approach concerned with the meanings that people give to the world, and how these are worked out through interpersonal interaction.

Mead, Margaret (1901–78) Anthropologist, born in Philadelphia, PA. She carried out field studies in the Pacific, writing academic and popular books, such as *Coming of Age in Samoa* (1928), and later became a media personality well known for her views on educational and social issues.

Meade, James Edward (1907–) Economist, born in Swanage, Dorset. His principal contributions have been in the area of international trade, including *The Theory of International Economic Policy* (2 vols, 1951–5). He shared the Nobel Prize for Economics in 1977.

Meade, George G(ordon) (1815–72) US army officer, born in Cadiz, Spain. In the American Civil War (1861–5) he distinguished himself at Antietam and Fredericksburg

(1862), and in 1863 commanded the Army of the Potomac, defeating Lee at Gettysburg. >> Lee, Robert E

Meade, Richard (John Hannay) (1938–) Equestrian rider, born in Chepstow, Gwent. Among his successes are three Olympic gold medals - the Three-day Event team golds in 1968 and 1972, and the individual title in 1972.

Meads, Colin (Earl), nickname **Pine Tree** (1936–) Rugby union player, born in Cambridge, New Zealand. A lock forward, he wore the All Black jersey in 133 representative matches, including a national record 55 in Test matches between 1957 and 1971.

Meale, Richard Graham (1932–) Composer, conductor, and teacher, born in Sydney, New South Wales, Australia. His first opera *Voss* (1982), with a libretto by Malouf, is part of the Australian Opera's repertoire. His second opera, *Mer de Glace*, was premiered in 1991. >> Malouf

Meany, George [**mee**nee] (1894–1980) Labour leader, born in New York City. Elected secretary-treasurer of the American Federation of Labor (AFL) in 1939, he became its president (1952), and president of the combined organization, AFL-CIO (1955–80).

Mechnikov or **Metchnikoff, Ilya** [**mech**nikof] (1845–1916) Biologist, born in Ivanovka, Ukraine. He shared the 1908 Nobel Prize for Physiology or Medicine for his work on immunology, in which he discovered the cells (*phagocytes*) which devour infective organisms. >> Pasteur

Medawar, Sir Peter (Brian) [**me**dawah(r)] (1915–87) Zoologist, born in Rio de Janeiro, Brazil. He pioneered experiments in the prevention of rejection in transplant operations, and in 1960 shared the Nobel Prize for Physiology or Medicine for research on immunological tolerance in relation to skin and organ grafting.

Medici >> **Catherine de'/ Cosimo de'/ Lorenzo de' Medici; Clement I; Leo X; Pius IV; Marie de Médecis**

Medina-Sidonia, Alonso Pérez de Guzmán, duque de (Duke of) [me**dee**na si**doh**nia] (1550–1619) Commander of the Spanish Armada, and captain-general of Andalusia, born in Sanlúcar, Spain. He was thwarted by the action of the English fleet, and by adverse weather conditions. >> Drake

Medlicott, William Norton (1900–87) Diplomatic historian, born in London. He was known especially for his studies of the Bismarck period in international relations, and of British diplomacy in the 20th-c.

Mee, Arthur (1875–1943) Journalist, editor, and writer, born in Stapleford, Nottinghamshire. He was most widely known for his *Children's Encyclopaedia* (1908) and *Children's Newspaper*.

Mee, Margaret (Ursula) (1909–88) British botanical artist and traveller. Having settled in Brazil, she travelled extensively in Amazonia, collecting new species and painting many others. The Margaret Mee Amazon trust was set up in 1988 to draw attention to the area's ecological crisis.

Meegeren, Han van >> **van Meegeren, Han**
Meer, Simon van der >> **van der Meer, Simon**
Megasthenes [megas**thee**neez] (c.350–c.290 BC) Greek historian. He was ambassador (306–298 BC) at the Indian court of Chandragupta, where he gathered materials for *Indica*, from which Arrian and Strabo borrowed. >> Arrian; Chandragupta; Strabo

Mège Mouriés, Hippolyte [mezh moor**ies**] (1817–80) Chemist and inventor, born in Draguignan, France. He patented margarine in its original form (1869), but it was not until F Boudet patented a process for emulsifying it with skimmed milk and water (1872) that it became a commercial success.

Mehemet Ali >> **Mohammed Ali**
Mehta, Ved (Parkash) [**may**ta] (1934–) Writer, born in Lahore, India. Blind from the age of eight, he went to the USA when he was 15, and had a distinguished career as a

journalist, contributing chiefly to *The New Yorker*. His *Continents of Exile* is an acclaimed series of autobiographical books (1972–89).

Mehta, Zubin [**may**ta] (1936–) Conductor, born in Bombay, India. His posts include conductor and musical director of the Los Angeles Philharmonic (1962–78) and the New York Philharmonic (1978–91), and he is now the musical director of the Israel Philharmonic Orchestra.

Meighen, Arthur [**mee**uhn] (1874–1960) Canadian prime minister (1920, 1921, 1926), born in Anderson, Ontario, Canada. He was solicitor general (1913), secretary of state (1917), and minister of the interior (1917), and became leader of the Conservatives in 1920.

Meigs, Montgomery C(unningham) [megz] (1816–92) Engineer, born in Augusta, GA. He supervised the construction of several important buildings and public works in Washington, DC, notably The Old Pension Building (1883).

Meiji Tenno >> **Mutsuhito**

Meikle, Andrew [**mee**kl] (1719–1811) Millwright and inventor, born in Houston Mill, Lothian. His most significant invention was a drum threshing machine which could be worked by wind, water, horse, or (some years later) steam power.

Meilhac, Henri >> **Halévy, Ludovic**

Meillet, Antoine [mayay] (1866–1936) Philologist, born in Moulins, France. A great authority on Indo-European languages, his works encompass Old Slavonic, Greek, Armenian, Old Persian, comparative Indo-European grammar, and linguistic theory.

Meinhof, Ulrike (Marie) [**miyn**hof] (1934–76) Terrorist, born in Oldenburg, Germany. She joined Andreas Bader in heading an underground urban guerrilla organization which conducted terrorist attacks against post-war West Germany. She was imprisoned (1974), and committed suicide. >> Baader, Andreas

Meir, Golda [may**eer**], originally **Goldie Myerson**, *née* **Mabovitch** (1898–1978) Israeli prime minister (1969–74), born in Kiev, Ukraine. She was minister of labour (1949–56) and foreign minister (1956–66). Her efforts for peace in the Middle East were halted by the fourth Arab–Israeli War (1973), and she was forced to resign.

Mei Sheng [may sheng] (?–140 BC) Chinese poet. He is often credited with the introduction of the five-character line, and for this reason is sometimes called 'the father of modern Chinese poetry'.

Meissonier, (Jean Louis) Ernest [maysonyay] (1815–91) Painter, born in Lyon, France. His works were largely of military and historical scenes, including several of the Napoleonic era.

Meitner, Lise [**miyt**ner] (1878–1968) Physicist, born in Vienna. In 1917 she shared with Hahn the discovery of the radioactive element protactinium, and became known for her work on nuclear physics. With her nephew, Otto Frisch, she developed the idea of nuclear fission in 1938. >> Frisch, Otto; Hahn, Otto

Mela, Pomponius [**mee**la] (fl.43) Latin geographer, born in Tingentera, Spain. He was the author of *De situ orbis* (3 vols, A Description of the World), largely borrowing from Greek sources.

Melanchthon, Philipp [me**langk**thon], originally **Philipp Schwartzerd** (1497–1560) Protestant reformer, born in Bretten, Germany. His *Loci communes* (1512) is the first great Protestant work on dogmatic theology, and he also composed the Augsburg Confession (1530).

Melba, Dame Nellie, professional name of **Helen Armstrong**, *née* **Mitchell** (1861–1931) Prima donna, born in Melbourne, Victoria, Australia. She appeared at Covent Garden in 1888, and the purity of her coloratura soprano voice won her worldwide fame. 'Peach Melba' and 'Melba toast' were named after her.

Melbourne, William Lamb, 2nd Viscount (1779–1848) British Whig prime minister (1834, 1835–41), born in London. He became home secretary (1830–4), and formed a close relationship with the young Queen Victoria. Defeated in the election of 1841, he resigned. His wife wrote novels as **Lady Caroline Lamb** (1785–1828).

Melchett, Baron >> **Mond, Alfred Moritz**

Melchior, Lauritz (Lebrecht Hommel) (1890–1973) Tenor, born in Copenhagen. One of the foremost Wagnerian singers of the century, he sang at Bayreuth (1924–31) and regularly at the New York Metropolitan (1926–50).

Meleager [meli**ayj**er] (fl.80 BC) Greek poet and epigrammatist, from Gadara, Syria. He wrote 128 short elegiac poems, and many epigrams, contained in his anthology *Stephanos* (Garland).

Méliès, Georges [maylyes] (1861–1938) Illusionist and film maker, born in Paris. He made his name in Paris as a stage magician, and in 1895 was a pioneer in trick cinematography to present magical effects.

Melissus [me**lis**uhs] (5th-c BC) Greek philosopher and statesman. His book *On Nature*, elaborated Parmenides' views on the properties of reality. >> Parmenides

Mellanby, Kenneth (1908–93) Entomologist and environmentalist, born in Barrhead, Strathclyde. In 1961 he founded and directed the Nature Conservancy's experimental station at Monks Wood, Huntingdon, where he led research into the effects of pesticides on the environment.

Mellitus of Canterbury, St [**mel**itus] (?–624), feast day 24 April. Christian leader, born in Rome. In 601 Pope Gregory I sent him to England to convert Saxon places of pagan worship into Christian churches. He became the first Bishop of London (c.604) and the third Archbishop of Canterbury (619–624). >> Gregory I

Mellon, Andrew W(illiam) (1855–1937) Financier, philanthropist, and statesman, born in Pittsburgh, PA. He made a reputation for himself as an industrial magnate, and endowed the National Gallery of Art in Washington, DC. As secretary of the Treasury (1921–32), he controversially reduced taxation of the wealthy. >> Mellon, Paul

Mellon, Paul (1907–) Art collector and philanthropist, born in Pittsburgh, PA, the son of Andrew Mellon. As chairman of two foundations set up to dispense the family fortune, he made generous gifts to several universities.

Melville, Andrew (1545–c.1622) Presbyterian religious reformer, born in Baldovie, Tayside. He succeeded John Knox in trying to preserve the independence of the Church from state control, heading a deputation to remonstrate with King James I (1606). >> Knox, John

Melville, Herman (1819–91) Novelist, born in New York City. His masterpiece, *Moby-Dick* (1851), became a classic among sea stories. After 1857, he wrote only some poetry, leaving his long story *Billy Budd, Foretopman* in manuscript.

Memlinc or **Memling, Hans** [**mem**ling] (c.1435–1494) Religious painter, born in Seligenstadt, Germany. His works include the triptych of the 'Madonna Enthroned' at Chatsworth (1468). He was also an original and creative portrait painter.

Menaechmus [me**nek**mus] (4th-c BC) Greek mathematician. A tutor to Alexander the Great, he was the first to investigate conics as sections of a cone. >> Alexander the Great

Menander [me**nan**der] (c.343–291 BC) Greek comic playwright, born in Athens. Only a few fragments of his work were known until 1906, and in 1957 the complete text of the comedy *Dyskolos* ('The Bad-Tempered Man') was found in Geneva.

Menander (1894–1958) >> **Morgan, Charles Langbridge**

Menchik-Stevenson, Vera (Francevna), *née* **Menchik**

(1906–44) Chess player, born in Moscow. She held the world title from 1927 (the first female champion) to 1944.

Mencius [**men**shius], Latin name **Meng-tzu** (Master Meng) (c.371–c.289 BC) Philosopher and sage, born in Shantung, China. He founded a school modelled on that of Confucius, and travelled China for 20 years searching for a ruler to implement Confucian ideals. After his death his disciples collected his sayings and published them as the *Book of Meng-tzu*.

Mencken, H(enry) L(ouis) (1880–1956) Philologist, editor, and satirist, born in Baltimore, MD. His major work was *The American Language* (1918), and in 1924 he founded the *American Mercury*, editing it until 1933.

Mendel, Gregor (Johann) (1822–84) Biologist and botanist, born in Heinzendorf, Austria. Abbot of the Augustinian monastery in Brno (1868), he researched the inheritance characters in plants, and his experiments led to the formulation of his laws governing the nature of inheritance, which became the basis of modern genetics.

Mendeleyev, Dmitri Ivanovich [mende**lay**ef] (1834–1907) Chemist, born in Tobolsk, Russia. He devised the periodic classification (or table) of chemical elements, predicting the existence of several elements which were later discovered. Element No 101 (*mendelevium*) is named after him.

Mendelsohn, Erich [**men**dlsuhn] (1887–1953) Architect, born in Allenstein, Germany. He designed the Einstein Tower in Potsdam (1919–21), and became noted for his use of modern materials (particularly expanses of glass) and construction methods. Other works include the Hebrew University at Jerusalem.

Mendelssohn, Moses [**men**delsuhn] (1729–86) Philosopher, literary critic, and biblical scholar, born in Dessau, Germany. His works reflect his commitment both to Judaism and rationalism, notably *Phädon* (1767) and *Jerusalem* (1783). >> Mendelssohn, Felix

Mendelssohn(-Bartholdy), (Jakob Ludwig) Felix [**men**dlsuhn] (1809–47) Composer, born in Hamburg, Germany, the grandson of Moses Mendelssohn. Among his early successes was the *Midsummer Night's Dream* overture (1826). A tour of Scotland inspired him with the *Hebrides* overture and the *Scottish Symphony*, and other major works include his oratorios *St Paul* (1836) and *Elijah* (1846).

Menderes, Adnan [**men**derez] (1899–1961) Turkish prime minister (1950–60), born near Aydin, Turkey. In 1945 he became leader of the new Democratic Party, and was made prime minister when it came to power. He was deposed in an army coup, and hanged.

Mendes, Chico [**men**dez] (1944–88) Brazilian rubber tapper who organized resistance to the wholesale exploitation of the Amazon. He formed an alliance between the tappers and the Amazonian Indians to fight against the deforesters, but was assassinated.

Mendès-France, Pierre [mendez **frã**s] (1907–82) French prime minister (1954–5), born in Paris. He became minister for national economy in 1945, and a prominent member of the Radical Party. He ended the war in Indo-China, but his government was defeated on its N African policy.

Menem, Carlos (Saul) [**men**em] (1935–) Argentinian prime minister (1989–), born in Anillaco, Argentina. He was elected president of the Justice Party in 1963, and in 1989 defeated the Radical Union Party candidate for the presidency.

Mengele, Josef [**men**ggele] (1911–79) Doctor, born in Günzburg, Germany. Appointed doctor at Auschwitz, he became known as 'the Angel of Death'. After the war he escaped, and assumed a false identity in Brazil until his death.

Mengistu, Haile Mariam [**men**ggistoo] (1937–) Ethiopian soldier and president (1987–91), born in the Harar

region, Ethiopia. He joined the 1974 coup which removed Emperor Haile Selassie, and in 1987 established one-party civilian rule under the Marxist–Leninist Workers Party. In 1991, when rebel groups closed in, he fled the country. >> Haile Selassie

Mengs, Anton Raphael (1728–79) Painter, born in Aussig, Germany. He settled in Rome, and under Winckelmann's influence became the most famous of the early Neoclassical painters. >> Winckelmann

Mengzi / Meng-tzu >> **Mencius**

Menken, Adah Isaacs (1835–1868) Actress, born near New Orleans, LA. She appeared throughout the USA in *Mazeppa* (1861), almost naked, and bound to a wild horse on stage, which brought her considerable notoriety. She became the idol of literary men, and was involved in many scandalous alliances.

Mennin, Peter (1923–83) Composer, born in Erie, PA. He established himself as a composer of large-scale works, composing nine symphonies, including *The Cycle* - a choral work to his own text.

Menno Simons (1496–1561) Anabaptist leader, born in Witmarsum, The Netherlands. He organized Anabaptist groups in N Europe that were persecuted by Catholics and Protestants alike. The evangelical *Mennonite* sect was named after him.

Menon, Krishna >> **Krishna Menon**

Menotti, Gian Carlo [me**not**ee] (1911–) Composer, born in Cadegliano, Italy. He achieved international fame with a series of operas, notably *Amelia Goes to the Ball* (1937), *The Consul* (1950, Pulitzer), *The Saint of Bleecker Street* (1954, Pulitzer), and the television opera *Amahl and the Night Visitors* (1951).

Menuhin, Yehudi Menuhin, Baron [**men**yooin] (1916–) Violinist, born in New York City. A child prodigy, he went on to international renown, especially for his interpretation of Bartók and Elgar. In 1962 he founded a school for musically gifted children near London.

Menzel, Donald (Howard) (1901–76) Astrophysicist, born in Florence, CO. Director of the Harvard College Observatory (1954–66), he did valuable work on planetary atmospheres and on the composition of the Sun.

Menzies, Sir Robert Gordon [**men**zees] (1894–1978) Australian lawyer and prime minister (1939–41, 1949–66), born in Jeparit, Victoria, Australia. He was Commonwealth attorney general (1935–9). In 1949 he headed a coalition government, maintaining political links with Britain and cultivating a close economic and military alliance with the USA.

Mercator, Gerardus [mer**kay**ter], originally **Gerhard Kremer** or **Cremer** (1512–94) Mathematician, geographer, and map-maker, born in Rupelmonde, Belgium. He is best known for introducing the map projection (1569) which bears his name, and in 1585 was the first to use the word *atlas* to describe a book of maps.

Mercé, Antonia >> **Argentina, La**

Mercer, Cecil William >> **Yates, Dornford**

Mercer, David (1928–80) Playwright, born in Wakefield, West Yorkshire. His stage plays include *Ride a Cock Horse* (1965) and *Cousin Vladimir* (1978). He has also written screenplays, such as *Morgan* (1965), and many plays for television.

Mercer, Joe, popular name of **Joseph Mercer** (1914–90) Footballer and manager, born in Ellesmere Port, Cheshire. He played for Everton (from 1932), transferring to Arsenal in 1946, and went on to manage Aston Villa and Manchester City.

Mercer, John (1791–1866) Dye chemist, born near Blackburn, Lancashire. He is chiefly known for his invention of *mercerization* - a process by which cotton is given a silky lustre resembling silk.

Mercer, Johnny, popular name of **John H Mercer** (1909–76) Singer and composer, born in Savannah, GA. He won

Oscars for several of his lyrics, including 'Days of Wine and Roses' (1961) and 'Moon River' (1962), and contributed to many musicals and films.

Merck, George W(ilhelm Emanuel) (1894–1957) Chemicals executive, born in New York City. In 1915 he joined Merck & Co, the family chemical firm, becoming its president (1925–50), and shifting its focus to pharmaceuticals.

Merckx, Eddy [merks], nickname **the Cannibal** (1945–) Racing cyclist, born in Woluwe St Pierre, Belgium. He won the Tour de France a record-equalling five times (1969–72, 1974), the Tour of Italy five times, and all the major classics.

Mercouri, Melina [merkooree], originally **Anna Amalia Mercouri** (1923–94) Film actress, born in Athens. She found international fame in 1960 in *Never on Sunday*. Always politically involved, she was exiled from Greece (1967–74), elected to parliament in 1977, and became minister of culture from 1981.

Mercury, Freddie, originally **Frederick Bulsara** (1946–91) British pop star, born in Zanzibar. He formed the heavy metal group Queen in 1971, known for its combination of flamboyant musical technique and visual impact, as seen in 'Bohemian Rhapsody' (1975).

Meredith, George (1828–1909) Writer, born in Portsmouth, Hampshire. His novels include *The Ordeal of Richard Feverel* (1859), *The Egoist* (1879), and *Diana of the Crossways* (1885). His main poetic work is *Modern Love* (1862).

Meredith, Owen >> Lytton, Edward Robert Bulwer

Merezhkovsky, Dmitry Sergeyevich [merezhofskee] (1865–1941) Writer, born in St Petersburg, Russia. He is best known for the historical trilogy, *Christ and Antichrist* (trans, 1896–1905), and for books on Tolstoy, Ibsen, and Gogol. He opposed the Revolution in 1917, and fled to Paris with his wife, **Zinaida Nikolayevna Hippius** (1870–1945), also a writer.

Mergenthaler, Ottmar [mergentahler] (1854–99) Inventor of the Linotype machine, born in Hachtel, Germany. He emigrated to the USA in 1872, and developed the famous typesetting machine in 1886.

Mérimée, Prosper [mayreemay] (1803–70) Writer, born in Paris. Among his novels are *Colomba* (1840), *Carmen* (1845, popularized by Bizet's opera), and *The Blue Room* (trans, 1872). He also wrote plays, and the famous *Letters to an Unknown Girl* (trans, 1873).

Merleau-Ponty, Maurice [mairloh pōtee] (1908–61) Philosopher, born in Rochefort-sur-mer, France. His two main works investigating the nature of consciousness, are *The Structure of Behaviour* (trans, 1942) and *Phenomenology of Perception* (trans, 1945).

Merovius or **Merovius** [merohvius] (5th-c) Frankish ruler, the father of Childeric I (died c.481) and grandfather of Clovis I. The *Merovingian* dynasty is traditionally held to have taken its name from him. >> Clovis I

Merriam, Clinton Hart (1855–1942) Naturalist, zoologist, and early conservationist, born in New York City. Head of the US Bureau of Biological Survey (1885–1910), his chief work was *Life Zones and Crop Zones of the United States* (1898).

Merrick, Joseph >> Treves, Frederick

Merrifield, (Robert) Bruce (1921–) Organic chemist, born in Fort Worth, TX. He devised (1959–62) the 'solid phase' method for synthesizing peptides and proteins from amino acids, for which he received the Nobel Prize for Chemistry in 1984.

Merrill, Charles E(dward) (1885–1956) Investment banker, born in Green Cove Springs, FL. With Edmund C Lynch he started the investment banking firm of Merrill Lynch, introducing stocks and bonds to America's growing middle-class.

Merrill, Frank (Dow) (1903–55) US soldier, born in Hopkinton, MA. He was assigned to raise the volunteer

unit, known as *Merrill's marauders*, which fought in the Burma jungle behind the Japanese lines (1943–4).

Merrill, Robert (1917–) Baritone, born in New York City. He joined the Metropolitan Opera in 1945, remaining a favourite there for 30 years.

Merriman, Brian (1747–1805) Irish Gaelic poet, born in Ennistymon, Co Clare, Ireland. He wrote the epic *The Midnight Court* (trans, c.1786), which was banned in all English translations after Irish independence.

Mersenne, Marin [mairsen] (1588–1648) Mathematician and scientist, born in Oize, France. A pioneer in the theory of prime numbers, he also experimented with the pendulum and found the law relating its length and period of oscillation.

Merton, Robert K(ing) (1910–) Sociologist, born in Philadelphia, PA. The founder of the sociology of science, his main works include *Social Theory and Social Structure* (1949) and *The Sociology of Science* (1973).

Merton, Thomas (1915–68) Catholic monk and writer, born in Prades, France. In 1941 he joined the Trappist order at Our Lady of Gethsemane Abbey, Kentucky. His best-selling autobiography, *The Seven Storey Mountain* (1946), brought him international fame.

Merton, Walter de (?–1277) Clergyman, probably born in Surrey. In 1264 he founded Merton College, Oxford, the prototype of the collegiate system in English universities.

Merwin, W(illiam) S(tanley) (1927–) Poet, born in New York City. He is known for his plays, prose parables, translations, and Surrealist poetry, as in the poetic collection *Opening the Hand* (1983).

Meselson, Matthew (Stanley) (1930–) Molecular biologist, born in Denver, CO. In 1957, with **Franklin Stahl** (1929–), he carried out experiments which developed Watson and Crick's ideas on the way the double helix of the DNA molecule carries genetic information. >> Crick; Watson, James

Mesmer, Franz Anton [mezmer] (1734–1815) Physician, born near Constance, Austria. In c.1772 he took up the idea that there exists a power which he called 'animal magnetism'. This led to the founding of *mesmerism*, precurser of hypnotism in modern psychotherapy.

Messager, André (Charles Prosper) [mesazhay] (1853–1929) Composer and conductor, born in Montluçon, France. Artistic director of Covent Garden Theatre, London (1901–7), and of the Opéra Comique, Paris (1898–1903, 1919–20), he wrote operettas, piano pieces, and several ballets, notably *The Two Pigeons* (trans, 1886).

Messalina, Valeria [mesaleena] (c.22–c.48) Third wife of the emperor Claudius, whom she married at the age of 14. She instigated a reign of terror, but her end came when Claudius was told that she had married secretly and was plotting against him. >> Claudius

Messerer, Asaf (1903–) Ballet dancer, teacher and choreographer, born in Vilnius. A versatile principal at the Bolshoi ballet, he retired from dancing in 1954 to concentrate on teaching, for which he is best known.

Messerschmitt, Willy [mesershmit], popular name of **Wilhelm Messerschmitt** (1898–1978) Aircraft engineer and designer, born in Frankfurt, Germany. During World War 2 he supplied the Luftwaffe with its foremost types of combat aircraft, and in 1944 produced the Me262 jet fighter.

Messiaen, Olivier (Eugène Prosper Charles) [mesiã] (1908–92) Composer and organist, born in Avignon, France. His music was motivated by religious mysticism, and he is best known for *Twenty Looks at the Infant Jesus* (trans, 1944) and the *Turangalila symphony*.

Messier, Charles [mesyay] (1730–1817) Astronomer, born in Badonviller, France. He is mainly remembered for the *Messier Catalogue* (1784), containing 103 star clusters, nebulae, and galaxies.

Messmer, Otto (1894–1985) Animator, born in New Jersey. In 1920 he created *Feline Follies*, making Felix the Cat the first cartoon film star to win international fame.

Mestral, Georges de >> de Mestral, Georges

Meštrović, Ivan [**mesh**trohvich] (1883–1962) Sculptor, born in Vrpolje, Slavonia, Croatia. He designed the national temple at Kosovo (1907–12) and the colossal *Monument to the Unknown Soldier* in Belgrade (1934).

Metastasio, Pietro [metastahzioh], originally **Pietro Armando Dominico Trapassi** (1698–1782) Poet, born in Rome. He gained his reputation by his masque *The Garden of Hesperides* (1722), and wrote the libretti for 27 operas, including Mozart's *Clemenza di Tito*.

Metaxas, Ioannis [m**ct**aksas] (1871–1941) General and dictator of Greece (1936–41), born in Ithaka. As premier he established a Fascist dictatorship, and led the resistance to the Italian invasion of Greece in 1940.

Metcalf, John, known as **Blind Jack of Knaresborough** (1717–1810) British engineer. Although blind from age six, he became an outstanding athlete and horseman. He set up a stagecoach between York and Knaresborough, and from 1765 constructed 185 mi of road, and many bridges.

Metchnikoff, Ilya >> Mechnikov, Ilya

Metford, William Ellis (1824–99) Engineer and inventor, born in Taunton, Devon. He designed a breech-loading rifle (1871), which was adapted by the American James Lee as the Lee-Metford rifle. >> Lee, James

Methodius, St >> Cyril, St

Methuen, Sir Algernon (Methuen Marshall) [methooen], originally **Stedman** (1856–1924) Publisher, born in London. A teacher of classics and French, in 1889 he began publishing as a sideline to market his own textbooks, later producing Kipling, Belloc, Conrad, and other major authors.

Metternich, Klemens (Wenzel Nepomuk Lothar), Fürst von (Prince of) [**me**ternikh] (1773–1859) Austrian statesman, born in Coblenz, Germany. In 1809 he became foreign minister, and negotiated the marriage between Napoleon and Marie Louise. He took a prominent part in the Congress of Vienna, and between 1815 and 1848 was the most powerful influence for conservatism in Europe. >> Marie Louise; Napoleon I

Mettrie, Julien de la >> La Mettrie, Julien Offroy de

Meung, Jean de >> Jean de Meung

Meyer, Adolf [**mi**yer] (1866–1950) Psychiatrist, born in Niederweningen, Switzerland. He sought to integrate psychiatry and medicine, seeing mental disorder as the consequence of unsuccessful adjustment patterns.

Meyer, (Julius) Lothar [**mi**yer] (1830–95) Chemist, born in Varel, Germany. He discovered the periodic law independently of Mendeleyev in 1869, and showed that atomic volumes were functions of atomic weights. >> Mendeleyev

Meyer, Viktor [**mi**yer] (1848–97) Chemist, born in Berlin. Professor at Zürich, Göttingen, and Heidelberg, he discovered and investigated thiophene and the oximes.

Meyerbeer, Giacomo [**mi**yerbayer], originally **Jakob Liebmann Meyer Beer** (1791–1864) Operatic composer, born in Berlin. His works include the highly successful *Robert le Diable* (1831) and *Huguenots* (1836).

Meyerhof, Otto Fritz [**mi**yerhohf] (1884–1951) Physiologist, born in Hanover, Germany. He shared the 1922 Nobel Prize for Physiology or Medicine for his work on the metabolism of muscles.

Meyerhold, Vsevolod Emilievich [**mi**yerhohld] (1874–c.1940) Actor and director, born in Penza, Russia. He was appointed director of the new Studio on Povarskaya Street in 1905, later becoming director of the Theatre of the Revolution (1922–4) and of the Meyerhold Theatre (1923–38).

Meynell, Alice (Christiana Gertrude), *née* **Thompson** (1847–1922) Essayist and poet, born in London. Her volumes of essays include *The Colour of Life* (1896) and *Hearts of Controversy* (1917), and her poetic collections began with *Preludes* (1875).

Meyrink, Gustav [**mi**yringk] (1868–1932) Writer, born in Vienna. He wrote satirical novels with a strong element of the fantastic and grotesque, such as *Der Golem* (1915) and *Walpurgisnacht* (1917).

Mialert, Adèle >> Michelet, Jules

Miaskovsky, Nikolay Yakovlevich [miyas**kof**skee] (1881–1950) Composer, born near Warsaw. Among his works are 27 symphonies, orchestral pieces, concertos for violin and cello, string quartets, songs, and piano sonatas.

Micah [**mi**yka], also known as **Micheas** (735–665 BC) One of the 12 so-called 'minor' prophets of the Hebrew Bible, a native of Moresheth Gath in SW Judah. He is known for predicting the punishment of Samaria and Jerusalem because of the sins of their people.

Michael VIII Palaeologus [paylee**o**logus] (c.1224–1282) Byzantine emperor (1261–82), born in Nicaea into the Greek nobility. His army took Constantinople in 1261, thus re-establishing the Byzantine Empire.

Michael (of Romania) (1921–   ) King of Romania (1927–30, 1940–7), born in Sinaia, Romania, the son of Carol II. He succeeded to the throne on the death of his grandfather, his father having renounced his own claims in 1925. In 1930 he was supplanted by his father but was again made king in 1940 when the Germans gained control of Romania. Forced in 1945 to accept a Communist government, he was compelled to abdicate (1947), and went into exile. >> Carol II

Michaelis, Leonor [mee**kay**lis] (1875–1949) Biochemist, born in Berlin. He made early deductions on enzyme action, and is especially known for the *Michaelis–Menten equation* on enzyme-catalysed reactions.

Michael Romanov [**roh**manof] (1596–1645) Tsar of Russia (1613–45), the great-nephew of Ivan IV. He was the founder of the Romanov dynasty that ruled Russia until the revolution of 1917. >> Ivan IV

Micheas >> Micah

Michel, Claude >> Clodion

Michelangeli, Arturo Benedetti [meekel**an**jelee] (1920–) Pianist, born in Brescia, Italy. He acquired a legendary reputation as a virtuoso in the post-war years, and became highly regarded as a teacher.

Michelangelo [miykl**an**jeloh], in full **Michelangelo di Lodovico Buonarroti Simoni** (1475–1564) Sculptor, painter, and poet, born in Caprese, Italy. In Florence he sculpted the marble 'David', and the 'Pietà' in the cathedral. In 1503 Julius II summoned him to Rome, where he was commissioned to design the pope's tomb, and decorated the ceiling of the Sistine Chapel with paintings (1508–12). In 1538 he was appointed architect of St Peter's, to which he devoted himself until his death.

Michelangelo Merisi >> Caravaggio

Michelet, Jules [meeshlay] (1798–1874) Historian, born in Paris. The greatest of his many historical works is his monumental *Histoire de France* (24 vols, 1833–67).

Michelin, André [**mi**chelin], Fr [meesh**lī**] (1853–1931) Tyre manufacturer, born in Paris. He and his younger brother **Edouard** (1859–1940) established the Michelin tyre company in 1888, and were the first to use demountable pneumatic tyres on motor cars.

Michell, John (1724–93) Geologist, born in Nottinghamshire. He described a method of magnetization, founded the science of seismology, and is credited with the invention of the torsion balance.

Michelozzi (di Bartolommeo) [meeke**lot**see] (1396–1472) Architect and sculptor, born in Florence, Italy. He was court architect to Cosimo de' Medici, with whom he was in exile at Venice. One of his finest works is the Ricardi Palace in Florence. >> Cosimo de' Medici

Michelson, A(lbert) A(braham) [mikelsn] (1852–1931) Physicist, born in Strelno, Germany. He is chiefly remembered for the *Michelson–Morley* experiment (1887) to determine ether drift, the negative result of which set Einstein on the road to the theory of relativity. He was the first US scientist to receive a Nobel Prize (1907). >> Einstein, Albert; Morley, Edward Williams

Michie, Donald [michee] (1923–   ) Specialist in artificial intelligence, born in Rangoon, Burma. In *The Creative Computer* (1984) and *On Machine Intelligence* (1974) he argues that computer systems are able to generate new knowledge.

Michurin, Ivan Vladimirovich [michoorin] (1855–1935) Horticulturist, born near Dolgoye, Russia. At his private orchard he developed many new varieties of fruit and berries, and his theory of cross-breeding became state doctrine, amid much controversy.

Mickiewicz, Adam (Bernard) [mitskyayvich] (1798–1855) The national poet of Poland, born near Novogrodek, Lithuania. His masterpiece is the epic *Thaddeus* (trans, 1834). In 1853 he organized the Polish legion in Italy.

Micklewhite, Maurice >> Caine, Michael

Middleton, Thomas (c.1570–1627) Playwright, probably born in London. His stage masterpieces include *Women Beware Women* (c.1621) and *The Changeling* (1622, with William Rowley), and he also collaborated with Dekker and other playwrights. >> Dekker; Rowley, William

Midgley, Thomas, Jr (1889–1944) Engineer and inventor, born in Beaver Falls, PA. He worked on the problem of 'knocking' in petrol engines, and by 1921 found tetraethyl lead to be effective as an additive to petrol.

Midler, Bette [bet] (1945–   ) Comedienne and actress, born in Honolulu, HI. She developed a popular nightclub act with outrageously bawdy comic routines, and in 1974 received a Tony Award for a record-breaking Broadway show. Her films include *The Rose* (1979), for which she had an Oscar nomination, and *Scenes from a Mall* (1991).

Mielziner, Jo [meelzeener] (1901–1976) US set and theatre designer, born in Paris. He designed the sets for over 400 Broadway plays, and was the designer of the Washington Square Theatre and the Vivian Beaumont Theatre at Lincoln Center (with Saarinen). >> Saarinen, Eero

Mies van der Rohe, Ludwig [mees van duh rohuh], also spelled **Miës**, originally **Ludwig Mies** (1886–1969) Architect and designer, born in Aachen, Germany. Among his major works are the Seagram Building in New York City (1956–8) and the Public Library in Washington, DC (1967). He also designed tubular-steel furniture, particularly the 'Barcelona chair'.

Mihailović, Dragoljub [mihiylohvich], nickname **Drazha** (1893–1946) Serbian soldier, born in Ivanjica, Serbia. In 1941 when Germany occupied Yugoslavia, he organized resistance, forming groups (Chetniks) to wage guerrilla warfare. He allied himself with the Germans, then with the Italians, and was executed by the Tito government for collaboration.

Mikan, George (Lawrence) [miykn] (1924–   ) Basketball player, born in Joliet, IL. He played with Minneapolis in the National Basketball Association (1948–56), winning the championship five times, and led the NBA in points-scoring three times.

Mikoyan, Anastas Ivanovich [mikoyan] (1895–1978) Politician, born in Sanain, Armenia. He supported Stalin against Trotsky, and in 1926 became minister of trade, doing much to improve Soviet standards of living, and introducing several ideas from the West. >> Mikoyan, Artem Ivanovich; Stalin; Trotsky

Mikoyan, Artem Ivanovich [mikoyan] (1905–70) Air-

craft designer, born in Sanain, Armenia, the brother of Anastas Ivanovich Mikoyan. He was best known for the MiG fighter aircraft produced by the design bureau he headed with Gurevich. >> Gurevich; Mikoyan, Anastas Ivanovich

Miles, Bernard (James) Miles, Baron (1907–91) Actor and stage director, born in Uxbridge, Greater London. In 1959 he founded the Mermaid Theatre, financed by public subscription, built at Puddle Dock, Blackfriars, London.

Miles, Nelson (Appleton) (1839–1925) US soldier, born in Westminster, MA. He fought the Indians on the W frontier (1869–91), capturing Chief Joseph (1877) and Geronimo (1866), but his reputation never recovered from allowing the massacre at Wounded Knee (1890). >> Geronimo

Milgram, Stanley (1933–84) Psychologist, born in New York City. He became concerned to understand how apparently ordinary people in Nazi Germany had committed the atrocities of the Holocaust. The results of his study were published in *Obedience to Authority: an Experimental View* (1974).

Milhaud, Darius [meeoh] (1892–1974) Composer, born in Aix-en-Provence, France. He was for a while a member of *Les Six*. His ballets include the jazz ballet *The Creation of the World* (trans, 1923), and he composed several operas, music for plays, symphonies, and orchestral, choral, and chamber works.

Milken, Michael (Robert) (1946–   ) Investment entrepreneur, born in California. Using high-risk, high-yield bonds to finance corporate takeovers, he was condemned for inventing 'junk bonds'. In 1989 he admitted to fraud and racketeering charges, and was imprisoned until 1993.

Mill, James (1773–1836) Philosopher, historian, and economist, born in Northwater Bridge, Tayside, the father of John Stuart Mill. His works include *Analysis of the Phenomenon of the Human Mind* (1829), providing a psychological basis for utilitarianism, and History of British India (1817–18). >> Bentham, Jeremy; Mill, John Stuart

Mill, John Stuart (1806–73) Empiricist philosopher and social reformer, born in London, the son of James Mill. Leader of the Benthamite utilitarian movement, he helped form the Utilitarian Society. His major works include *A System of Logic* (1843), the essay *On Liberty* (1859), and *Utilitarianism* (1863). >> Bentham, Jeremy; Mill, James

Millais, Sir John Everett [milay] (1829–96) Painter, born in Southampton, Hampshire. A founder member of the Pre-Raphaelite Brotherhood, his works include the controversial 'Christ in the House of His Parents' (1850). Later works included portraits, landscapes, and woodcut illustrations for magazines.

Millar, Kenneth >> MacDonald, Ross

Millay, Edna St Vincent [milay] (1892–1950) Poet, born in Rockland, ME. Her works include *The Harp Weaver and Other Poems* (1923, Pulitzer), three verse plays, and the libretto for the American opera, *The King's Henchman* (1927).

Mille, De >> De Mille

Miller, Arthur (1915–   ) Playwright, born in New York City. His major works include *All My Sons* (1947), *Death of a Salesman* (1949, Pulitzer), and *The Crucible* (1953). His brief marriage to Marilyn Monroe (divorced 1961), and alleged early Communist sympathies, brought him considerable publicity. >> Monroe, Marilyn

Miller, (Alton) Glenn (1904–44) Trombonist and bandleader, born in Clarinda, IA. He achieved a distinctive sound with a saxophone–clarinet combination, his many successes including 'Moonlight Serenade' (his theme song), 'Little Brown Jug', and 'In the Mood' (1939). He joined the US Air Force in 1942, and took his orchestra to

Europe, but he was killed while travelling in a small aircraft lost without trace over the English Channel.

Miller, Henry (Valentine) (1891–1980) Writer, born in New York City. His early books *Tropic of Cancer* (1934) and *Tropic of Capricorn* (1938), much of which is autobiographical and explicitly sexual, were not published in Britain and the USA until the early 1960s. Later work includes the series *Sexus* (1945), *Plexus* (1949), and *Nexus* (1960).

Miller, Joaquin, pseudonym of **Cincinnatus Hiner Miller** (1837–1913) Poet, born in Liberty, IN. he settled in California from 1877 as a fruit-grower. His best-known poem is 'Columbus', and other works include *Songs of the Sierras* (1871) and *The Danites in the Sierras* (1881).

Miller, Jonathan (Wolfe) (1934–) Actor and director, born in London, He qualified as a doctor, and his career has combined medical research with contributions to stage and television. He was part of the *Beyond the Fringe* team (1961–4), and has directed for several theatres, including the National Theatre, English National Opera, and the Old Vic.

Miller, Keith (Ross) (1919–) Cricketer, born in Melbourne, Victoria, Australia. A leading all-rounder, during his career he scored 2598 runs in 55 Test matches for Australia, including seven centuries, and took 170 wickets.

Miller, Stanley Lloyd (1930–) Chemist, born in Oakland, CA. His most familiar work concerns the possible origin of life on Earth. He passed electric discharges through a mixture of those gases which probably formed the early planetary atmosphere, and analysis showed the presence of organic substances.

Miller, William (1781–1849) Religious leader, born in Pittsfield, MA. Believing that the Second Coming of Christ was imminent in 1843 or 1844, he founded the religious sect of Second Adventists or *Millerites*. His followers organized the Seventh Day Adventist Church in 1863. >> White, Ellen Gould

Milles, Carl (Wilhelm Emil) [milz], original surname **Andersson** (1875–1955) Sculptor, born in Uppsala, Sweden. His works include the Sten Sture monument near Uppsala (1925), the Gustav I Vasa statue, and after settling in the USA, 1931, the *Wedding of the Rivers* (1940) in St Louis, MO.

Millet, Jean François [meeay] (1814–75) Painter, born in Gruchy, France. He settled in Barbizon, painting the rustic life of France, as seen in 'Sower' (1850), 'Peasants Grafting' (1855), and 'The Gleaners' (1857). He also produced charcoal drawings of high quality.

Milligan, Spike, popular name of **Terence Alan Milligan** (1918–) Humorist, born in Ahmadnagar, India. He became known as co-writer and performer in BBC radio's *The Goon Show* (1951–9). His irrepressible sense of the ridiculous has been a major influence on British humour, and he has published a variety of children's books, poetry, and comic novels.

Millikan, Robert (Andrews) (1868–1953) Physicist, born in Morrison, IL. He determined the charge on the electron, for which he was awarded the Nobel Prize for Physics in 1923, and did important work on cosmic rays, showing them to come from space.

Mills, Charles Wright (1916–62) Sociologist, born in Waco, TX. Strongly critical of mainstream US sociology, he was something of an outcast from academic life, but his writings attracted a large popular audience, and he had an important influence on the American New Left.

Mills, Sir John (Lewis Ernest Watts) (1908–) Actor and director, born in Felixstowe, Suffolk. His early films include *Scott of the Antarctic* (1948) and *The Colditz Story* (1954), and for two generations he represented the figure of a fundamentally decent and reliable Englishman. Among his later films is *Ryan's Daughter* (1978, Oscar). He

is the father of actresses **Juliet** (1941–) and **Hayley** (1946–).

Mills, Martin >> **Boyd, Martin**

Mills, Wilbur (Daigh) (1909–92) US politician, born in Kensett, AR. A Democratic member of the US House of Representatives (1939–77), he chaired the powerful Committee on Ways and Means (1957–73).

Milne, A(lan) A(lexander) (1882–1956) Writer, born in London. In 1924 he achieved world fame with his book of children's verse, *When We Were Very Young*, written for his son, Christopher Robin, who was immortalized with his toy bear Winnie-the-Pooh in such children's classics as *Winnie-the-Pooh* (1926).

Milne, David Brown (1882–1953) Artist and writer, born in Ontario, Canada. His oils and watercolours were much influenced by Impressionism, especially Monet; but his drypoints, made by a method he invented, are often thought to be his finest work. >> Monet

Milne, Edward Arthur (1896–1950) Astrophysicist, born in Hull, Humberside. He made notable contributions to the study of cosmic dynamics, and estimated the age of the universe to be c.2 thousand million years.

Milner, Alfred Milner, 1st Viscount (1854–1925) British statesman, born in Bonn, Germany. As Governor of Cape Colony (1897–1901) he negotiated with Kruger at Bloemfontein (1899), giving an ultimatum which led to the second Boer War. He later became secretary for war (1918–19) and colonial secretary (1919–21).

Milner, Brenda Atkinson, *née* **Langford** (1918–) British psychologist. A specialist in neuropsychology, much of her research into brain function has had particular application to the surgical treatment of temporal-lobe epilepsy.

Milnes, Richard Monckton, 1st Baron Houghton (1809–85) Politician and man of letters, born in London. He championed oppressed nationalities, liberty of conscience, fugitive slaves, and the rights of women, and carried a bill for establishing reformatories (1846).

Milo of Croton [miyloh, meeloh] (6th-c BC) Legendary Greek wrestler from the Greek colony of Croton in S Italy. He won the wrestling contest at five successive Olympic Games, and swept the board at all other festivals.

Milosz, Czeslaw [meewosh, chezhwof] (1911–) Poet and man of letters, born in Szetejnie, Lithuania. He was a founder of the catastrophist school of Polish poetry. His books include (trans titles) *Hymn of the Pearl* (1981) and *Hymn of the Earth* (1986). In the USA from 1960, he was awarded the Nobel Prize for Literature in 1980.

Milstein, César [milstiyn] (1927–) Molecular biologist, born in Bahía Blanca, Argentina. He worked on antibody research, and in 1975 developed monoclonal antibodies with **Georges Köhler** (1946–), for which they shared the Nobel Prize for Physiology or Medicine in 1984.

Milstein, Nathan (Mironovich) [milstiyn] (1904–92) Violinist, born in Odessa, Ukraine. He left Russia in 1925, gave recitals in Paris, and made his US debut in 1929.

Miltiades, the Younger [miltiyadeez] (c.550–489 BC) Athenian general and statesman. He masterminded the Greek victory against the Persians at Marathon (490).

Milton, John (1608–74) Poet, born in London. His early works include *L'Allegro* and *Il Penseroso* (1632), *Comus* (1633), and *Lycidas* (1637). During the Civil War he chiefly wrote political pamphlets. Blind from 1652, after the Restoration he devoted himself wholly to poetry: his epic sacred masterpiece, *Paradise Lost* (completed in 1665), *Paradise Regained*, and *Samson Agonistes* (both 1671).

Mindszenty, József, Cardinal [mindsentee], (1892–1975) Roman Catholic clergyman, born in Mindszent, Hungary. Primate of Hungary (1945) and cardinal (1946), he became internationally known in 1948 when he was charged with treason by the Communist government. He was granted asylum in the US legation at Budapest (1956–71), then went to Rome.

Mingus, Charlie [**ming**guhs], popular name of **Charles Mingus** (1922–79) Jazz bassist, composer, and bandleader, born in Nogales, AZ. During the 1940s he worked with big bands, and from 1953 led groups called the 'Jazz Workshop', which experimented with atonality and other devices of European symphonic music.

Minkowski, Hermann [ming**kof**skee] (1864–1909) Mathematician, born near Kaunas, Lithuania. He discovered a new branch of number theory, the geometry of numbers, and gave a precise mathematical description of space-time as it appears in Einstein's relativity theory. >> Einstein

Minnelli, Liza (May) [mi**nel**ee] (1946–) Singer and actress, born in Los Angeles, CA, the daughter of Vincente Minnelli and Judy Garland. A versatile performer, she is best known for her role in *Cabaret* (1972, Oscar), and later appeared with Dudley Moore in the *Arthur* films. >> Garland, Judy; Minnelli, Vincente; Moore, Dudley

Minnelli, Vincente [mi**nel**ee] (1910–86) Film director, born in Chicago, IL, the husband of Judy Garland. An outstanding director of film musicals of lavish visual style, his best-known works include *The Clock* (1945), *Kismet* (1955), and *Gigi* (1958, Oscar). >> Garland, Judy; Minnelli, Liza

Minogue, Kylie [mi**nohg**] (1968–) Singer and actress, born in Melbourne, Victoria, Australia. She achieved fame for her role in the television soap opera *Neighbours*. In 1987 she began a successful recording career.

Minot, George (Richards) [**miy**nuht] (1885–1950) Physician, born in Boston, MA. His experiments with Murphy into the treatment of pernicious anaemia led to the preparation of vitamin B_{12}. He shared the Nobel Prize for Physiology or Medicine in 1934. >> Murphy, William P; Whipple, George H

Minter, Alan (1951–) Boxer, born in Crawley, Surrey. He held the European middleweight title (1977, 1978–9) and the British crown (1975–7, 1977–8), becoming world champion in 1980.

Mintoff, Dom(inic) (1916–) Maltese prime minister (1955–8, 1971–84), born in Cospicua, Malta. His demands for independence led to the suspension of Malta's constitution in 1959. He resigned in 1958 to lead the Malta Liberation Movement, and in his second term followed a policy of moving away from British influence.

Minton, (Francis) John (1917–57) Artist, born in Cambridge, Cambridgeshire. He was noted as a book illustrator and brilliant watercolourist, and also as a designer of textiles and wallpaper.

Minton, Thomas (1765–1836) Pottery and china manufacturer, born in Shrewsbury, Shropshire. In 1793 he built a pottery works at Stoke, producing fine bone china, much of it tableware decorated with finely painted flowers and fruit.

Minton, Yvonne (Fay) (1938–) Mezzo-soprano, born in Sydney, New South Wales, Australia. Since 1964 she has been resident artist at the Royal Opera House, Covent Garden, noted for her Wagnerian roles.

Mirabeau, Honoré Gabriel Riqueti, comte de (Count of) [meera**boh**] (1749–91) Revolutionary politican and orator, born in Bignon, France. Known for his political essays, for which he was imprisoned (1777), he was elected to the Estates General. His political acumen made him a force in the National Assembly, while his audacity and eloquence endeared him to the people. Elected president of the Assembly in 1791, he died soon afterwards. >> Louis XVI

Mirabilis, Doctor >> **Bacon, Roger**

Mirandola, Pico della >> **Pico della Mirandola**

Miró, Joán [mee**roh**, hwan] (1893–1983) Artist, born in Barcelona, Spain. In 1920 he settled in Paris and became a founder of Surrealism. His paintings are predominantly abstract, and his humorous fantasy makes play with a restricted range of pure colours and dancing shapes, as in 'Catalan Landscape' (1923–4).

Mirza Ali Mohammed >> **Bab-ed-Din**

Mirza Huseyn Ali >> **Baha-Allah**

Mirza Muhammad >> **Siraj ud Daula**

Mises, Richard von [**mee**zes] (1883–1953) Mathematician and philosopher, born in Lember, Austria. An authority in aerodynamics and hydrodynamics, he set out in *Probability, Statistics and Truth* (trans, 1928) a controversial frequency theory of probability.

Mishima, Yukio, pseudonym of **Hiraoka Kimitake** (1925–70) Writer, born in Tokyo. His great tetralogy, *Sea of Fertility* (1965–70), with a central theme of reincarnation, spanned Japanese life and events in the 20th-c. Passionately interested in the chivalrous traditions of imperial Japan, he founded the Shield Society in 1968, and in 1970 committed ritual suicide in protest against modern Japanese decadence.

Missoni, Tai Otavio [mi**soh**nee] (1921–) Knitwear designer, born in Yugoslavia. In 1953 he founded the Missoni company in Milan with his wife, Rosita, producing innovative knitwear notable for its distinctive colours and patterns.

Mistinguett [meesti**get**], originally **Jeanne Marie Bourgeois** (1875–1956) Dancer, singer, and actress, born in Enghien-les-Bains, France. She became the most popular French music-hall artiste of the first three decades of the century.

Mistral, Frédéric [mee**stral**] (1830–1914) Poet, born in Maillane, France. A founder of the Provençal renaissance movement (the *Félibrige* school), he is best known for his long narrative poems, such as *Miréio* (1859) and *Calendau* (1861). He was awarded the Nobel Prize for Literature in 1904.

Mistral, Gabriela [mee**stral**], pseudonym of **Lucila Godoy de Alcayaga** (1889–1957) Poet, diplomat, and teacher, born in Vicuña, Chile. She combined her writing with a career as a diplomat and cultural minister. Her works include 'Sonnets of Death' (trans, 1914) and *Desolation* (trans, 1922). She was awarded the Nobel Prize for Literature in 1945.

Mita, Ciriaco de >> **de Mita, Ciriaco**

Mitchell, Arthur (1934–) Dancer, choreographer, and director, born in New York City. The first African-American principal dancer to join the New York City Ballet, he founded the Dance Theater of Harlem (1971) to develop opportunities for fellow black dancers.

Mitchell, Billy, popular name of **William Mitchell** (1879–1936) Aviation pioneer, born in Nice, France. Commander of the US air forces in World War 1, he foresaw the importance of air power in warfare, but his outspoken criticism of those who did not share his convictions led to his resignation.

Mitchell, James Fitz Allan (1931–) Prime minister of St Vincent and the Grenadines (1972–4, 1984–). He headed the People's Political Party, and in 1975 founded the New Democratic Party.

Mitchell, James Leslie >> **Gibbon, Lewis Grassic**

Mitchell, Joan (1926–) Painter, born in Chicago, IL. One of the early Abstract Expressionists, in 1959 she moved to France, where her work seemed to echo French Impressionism, as in 'No Birds' (1987–8) and 'Wind' (1990).

Mitchell, John (Newton) (1913–88) Lawyer and US cabinet member, born in Detroit, MI. Nixon's 1968 campaign manager and attorney general (1969–73), he used illegal surveillance methods, was convicted in the Watergate investigation, and imprisoned (1977–9). >> Nixon

Mitchell, Joni, *née* **Roberta Joan Anderson** (1943–) Singer and songwriter, born in McLeod, Alberta, Canada.

She moved to the USA in the mid-1960s, and in 1968 recorded her first album. Many of her songs, notably 'Both Sides Now' (1971), have been recorded by other singers.

Mitchell, Lucy, *née* **Sprague** (1878–1967) Educationist, born in Chicago, IL. With her cousin, Elizabeth Sprague Coolidge, she co-founded the Bureau of Educational Experiments (1916), and directed it until 1956. She also co-founded (1931) the Co-operative School for Teachers.

Mitchell, Margaret (1900–49) Novelist, born in Atlanta, GA. Her only novel, *Gone with the Wind* (1936, Pulitzer), was made into an Oscar-winning-film (1939).

Mitchell, Sir Peter (Chalmers) (1864–1945) Zoologist and journalist, born in Dunfermline, Fife. He was responsible for improvements at London Zoo, including the Mappin terraces, Whipsnade, and the Aquarium.

Mitchell, Peter (Dennis) (1920–92) Biochemist, born in Mitcham, Surrey. In the 1960s he proposed an entirely novel theory of the way energy is generated at the molecular level in biochemical cells. He was awarded the Nobel Prize for Chemistry in 1978.

Mitchell, R(eginald) J(oseph) (1895–1937) Aircraft designer, born in Talke, Staffordshire. He designed seaplanes that won many of the Schneider trophy races (1922–31) and from them evolved the Spitfire.

Mitchell, S(ilas) Weir (1829–1914) Physician and writer, born in Philadelphia, PA. He specialized in nervous diseases, and pioneered the application of psychology to medicine. He wrote psychological and historical novels and poems, and his medical texts included the best-selling *Fat and Blood* (1877).

Mitchell, Sir Thomas Livingstone (1792–1855) Explorer, born in Craigend, Strathclyde. In four expeditions (1831, 1835, 1836, 1845–7) he did much to explore eastern and tropical Australia, especially the Murray, Glenelg, and Barcoo rivers.

Mitchell, Warren (1926–) Actor, born in London. He is best known for playing the character of Alf Garnett in the television series *Till Death Us Do Part* (1966–78), and later productions.

Mitchison, Naomi (Mary Margaret), *née* **Haldane** (1897–) Writer, born in Edinburgh. Known especially for her evocations of ancient civilizations, her novels include *The Conquered* (1923), *Black Sparta* (1928), and *Corn King and Spring Queen* (1931).

Mitchum, Robert (1917–) Film actor, born in Bridgeport, CT. A leading man particularly associated with the post-war thriller, his films include *Night of the Hunter* (1955), *The Sundowners* (1960), *Farewell My Lovely* (1975), and *Mr North* (1988).

Mitford, Jessica (Lucy) (1917–) Writer, the sister of Diana, Nancy, and Unity Mitford. Her books include *The American Way of Death* (1963), *The Trial of Dr Spock* (1970), and *The Making of a Muckraker* (1979). >> Mitford, Diana / Nancy / Unity

Mitford, Mary Russell (1787–1855) Essayist and playwright, born in Alresford, Hampshire. Her gift was for charming sketches of country manners, scenery, and character, which were collected as *Our Village* (5 vols, 1824–32).

Mitford, Nancy (Freeman) (1904–73) Writer, born in London, the sister of Diana, Jessica, and Unity Mitford. She established a reputation with such witty novels as *Pursuit of Love* (1945) and *Love in a Cold Climate* (1949), and edited *Noblesse Oblige* (1956). >> Mitford, Diana / Jessica / Unity

Mitford, Unity (Valkyrie) (1914–48) Socialite, the daughter of the 2nd Baron Redesdale, and sister of Diana, Jessica, and Nancy Mitford. She was notorious for her associations with Hitler and other leading Nazis in Germany, but returned to Britain in 1940. >> Mitford, Diana / Jessica / Nancy

Mithridates VI (Eupator) [mithridahteez], also spelled **Mithradates**, known as **the Great** (?–63 BC) King of Pontus (c.115–63 BC), a Hellenized ruler in the Black Sea area, whose attempts to expand his empire led to the Mithridatic Wars with Rome (88–66 BC). He was finally defeated by Pompey (66 BC), and later took his own life. >> Pompey the Great

Mitropoulos, Dimitri [mitropulos] (1896–1960) Conductor, born in Athens. He conducted the Minneapolis Symphony Orchestra (1937–49), later becoming principal conductor of the New York Philharmonic (1951–7), and is known also as a pianist and composer.

Mitterrand, François (Maurice Marie) [meetuhrã] (1916–96) French president (1981–95), born in Jarnac, France. He held several ministerial posts (1947–58), became a stubborn opponent of de Gaulle, and was appointed secretary of the Socialist Party in 1971. As president he embarked on a programme of nationalization and job creation in an attempt to combat stagnation and unemployment. >> de Gaulle

Miyake, Issey [meeyahkay] (1938–) Fashion designer, born in Hiroshima, Japan. His distinctive style combines Eastern and Western influences. Loose fitting, but with dramatic outline, his clothes achieve richness by varied textures, weaves, and patterns.

Mnouchkine, Arianne [nushkeen] (1938–) French stage director and playwright. In 1963 she founded the Théâtre du Soleil as a theatre co-operative; *1789*, first produced in 1970, is one of the company's best-known works.

Moberg, (Carl Artur) Vilhelm [mohberg] (1898–1973) Writer, born in Algutsboda, Sweden. His best-known work is the series of novels that deal with the 19th-c mass migration of Swedes to the USA, including *The Emigrants* (trans, 1949) and *Last Letter to Sweden* (trans, 1959).

Möbius, August Ferdinand [moebius] (1790–1868) Mathematician, born in Schulpforta, Germany. He is chiefly known for the discovery of the *Möbius strip* and the *Möbius net*, important in projective geometry.

Mobutu, Sese Seko [mobootoo], originally **Joseph Désiré Mobutu** (1930–) Zairean president (1965–), born in Lisala, Zaire (formerly, Belgian Congo). He took command of the Congolese army in 1960, and came to power in a military coup the same year.

Modigliani, Amedeo [mohdeelyahnee] (1884–1920) Painter and sculptor, born in Livorna, Italy. In 1918, in Paris, his first one-man show included some very frank nudes, and the exhibition was closed for indecency. He obtained recognition only after his death.

Modigliani, Franco [mohdeelyahnee] (1918–) US economist, born in Rome. He was awarded the 1985 Nobel Prize for Economics for his work on personal saving and corporate finance.

Moe, Jörgen >> Asbjörnsen, Peter Christian

Moeran, Ernest John [mooran] (1894–1950) Composer, born in Middlesex. His works include the orchestral *Rhapsody* (1924), many songs, a symphony, and concertos for violin, piano, and cello.

Moffatt, James (1870–1944) Theologian and scholar, born in Glasgow, Strathclyde. His most famous work is the translation of the Bible into modern English: his New Testament was published in 1913, and his Old Testament in 1924.

Mohammad Reza Pahlavi >> Pahlavi, Mohammad Reza

Mohammed or **Mahomet** (Western forms of Arabic **Muhammad**) (c.570–c.632) Founder of Islam, born in Mecca, the son of Abdallah, a poor merchant. When he was 40, Gabriel appeared to him on Mt Hira, near Mecca, and commanded him in the name of God to preach the true religion. Four years later he was told to come forward publicly as a preacher, expounding the Koran, which had been revealed to him by God. When the Meccans rose against him, he sought refuge at Medina in 622 (the date of the Mohammedan Era, the *Hegira*), and engaged in war against the enemies of Islam. In 630 he took Mecca, where he was recognized as chief and prophet, and thus secured the new religion in Arabia. In 632 he undertook his last pilgrimage to Mecca, and there fixed the ceremonies of the pilgrimage (*Hajj*). He fell ill after his return, and died at the house of the favourite of his nine wives, Aïshah. >> Aïshah; Ali; Fatima; Uthman

Mohammed II or **Mehmet II**, known as **the Conqueror** (1432-81) Sultan of Turkey (1451-81), and founder of the Ottoman empire, born in Adrianople. He took Constantinople in 1453, renaming it Istanbul, thus extinguishing the Byzantine empire. He also annexed most of Serbia, all of Greece, and most of the Aegean Is.

Mohammed Ahmed, known as **the Mahdi** (1844-85) African political leader, born in Dongola, Sudan. A rebel against Egyptian rule in E Sudan, he annihilated an Egyptian army under **William Hicks** ('Hicks Pasha', 1830-83), and in 1885 took Khartoum. >> Gordon, Charles George

Mohammed Ali or **Mehemet Ali** (c.1769-1849) Governor and later viceroy of Egypt (1805-49). He was the founder of the Egyptian royal family which endured until the 1953 revolution, extending Egypt's influence over the Sudan, the Hejaz, and Greater Syria, through the generalship of his adopted son **Ibrahim Pasha** (1789-1848).

Moholy-Nagy, László [mohhoy nodj] (1895-1946) Artist and photographer, born in Bácsborsód, Hungary. He worked with Dada and Constructionist groups in Vienna and Berlin (1919-23), joined the Bauhaus (1925), and headed the New Bauhaus school in Chicago (1937).

Mohorovičić, Andrija [mohhorohvuhchich] (1857-1936) Geophysicist, born in Volosko, Croatia. He deduced that the Earth's crust must overlay a denser mantle, and calculated the depth of this transition (the *Moho discontinuity*) to be about 30 km.

Mohs, Friedrich [mohz] (1773-1839) Mineralogist, born in Gernrode, Germany. The *Mohs scale* for measuring mineral hardness, introduced in 1812, is still in use.

Moi, Daniel Arap [moy] (1924-) Kenyan president (1978-), born in the Rift Valley Province, Kenya. He was vice-president under Kenyatta (1967), and succeeded him as president. >> Kenyatta

Moiseiwitsch, Benno [moyzayvich] (1890-1963) Pianist, born in Odessa, Ukraine. He first appeared in Britain in 1908, and won rapid recognition as an exponent of the music of the Romantic composers.

Moiseyev, Igor Alexandrovich [moysayef] (1906-) Dancer, choreographer, and ballet director, born in Kiev, Ukraine. He joined the Bolshoi Ballet in 1924, remaining as soloist and choreographer until 1939. In 1937 he formed a professional folk dance company, and in 1967 founded the State Ensemble of Classical Ballet.

Moissan, (Ferdinand Frédéric) Henri [mwasã] (1852-1907) Chemist, born in Paris. He was awarded the Nobel Prize for Chemistry in 1906 for his work in isolating the element fluorine, and for the development of the electric furnace.

Moivre, Abraham de >> **de Moivre, Abraham**

Mokanna (Arabic 'the Veiled One'), nickname of **Hakim ben Atta** (?-778) Arab prophet, the founder of a sect in the Persian province of Khorasan. Setting himself up as a reincarnation of God, he seized several fortified places, but the caliph Almahdi defeated him and he committed suicide (778).

Molesworth, Mary Louisa, née **Stewart**, pseudonym **Ennis Graham** (1839-1921) British writer, born in Rotterdam, The Netherlands. She is best known as a writer of

children's stories, such as *The Cuckoo Clock* (1877), *The Carved Lions* (1895), and *Peterkin* (1902).

Molière [molyair], pseudonym of **Jean Baptiste Poquelin** (1622-73) Playwright, born in Paris. His major achievements include *The Affected Young Ladies* (trans, 1659), *The School for Wives* (trans, 1622), *Tartuffe* (1664), *The Misanthropist* (trans, 1666), and *Le Bourgeois Gentilhomme* (1670). One of the greatest French dramatists, many of his plays have been translated for performances in English theatres, giving him a considerable reputation abroad.

Molina, Luis de [mohleena] (1535-1600) Jesuit theologian, born in Cuenca, Spain. In *The Harmony of Free Will with Gifts of Grace* (trans, 1588), he argues that predestination to eternal happiness or punishment is consequent on God's foreknowledge of the free determination of human will (later known as *Molinism*).

Molina, Mario >> **Rowland, F Sherwood**

Molina, Tirso de >> **Tirso de Molina**

Mollet, Guy (Alcide) [molay] (1905-75) French prime minister (1956-7), born in Flers-de-l'Orne, France. He survived the international crisis over the Anglo-French intervention in Suez, but fell from office after only 15 months. >> Eden

Mollison, James (1931-) Arts administrator, born in Melbourne, Victoria, Australia. Responsible for much of the work in the Australian National Gallery, he is known for his promotion of contemporary Australian artists and Aboriginal art.

Mollison, James (Allan) (1905-59) Aviator, born in Glasgow, Strathclyde. He won fame for his record flight, Australia-England (1931) in 8 days 19 hours and 28 minutes. In 1932 he married Amy Johnson (divorced, 1938). >> Johnson, Amy

Molnár, Ferenc [mohlnah(r), ferents] (1878-1952) Writer, born in Budapest. He is best known for his novel *The Paul Street Boys* (1907), and for his plays *The Devil* (1907), *Liliom* (1909), and *The Good Fairy* (1930).

Molotov, Vyacheslav Mikhailovich [molotof], originally **Vyacheslav Mikhailovich Skriabin** (1890-1986) Russian prime minister (1930-41), born in Kukaida, Russia. He served as foreign minister (1939-49, 1953-6), emerging as the uncompromising champion of world Sovietism; his *nyet* ('no') at meetings of the UN became a byword, and fostered the Cold War.

Moltke, Helmuth (Karl Bernhard), Graf von (Count of) [moltkuh] (1800-91) Field marshal, born in Parchim, Germany (formerly, Prussia). His reorganization of the Prussian army led to success in the wars with Denmark (1863-4), Austria (1866), and France (1870-1). >> Moltke, Helmuth (Johannes Ludwig)

Moltke, Helmuth (Johannes Ludwig) von [moltkuh] (1848-1916) German soldier, born in Gersdorff, Germany, the nephew of Helmuth von Moltke. He rose to be chief of the general staff (1906), but in World War 1, after losing control of his armies at the Battle of the Marne (1914), he was superseded by Falkenhayn. >> Falkenhayn; Moltke, Helmuth (Karl Bernhard)

Moltmann, Jürgen (1926-) Theologian, born in Hamburg, Germany. His support of a theology of hope marked a reaction against the individualistic existential approach of Bultmann, and a revival in Protestant theology of concern for the social nature of Christian faith in the modern world. >> Bultmann

Molyneux, Edward (Henry) [molinyoo] (1891-1974) Fashion designer, born in London. He opened his own couture house in Paris in 1919, becoming famous for the elegant simplicity of his tailored suits with pleated skirts, and for his evening wear.

Mommsen, (Christian Matthias) Theodor (1817-1903) Historian, born in Garding, Germany. His greatest works are (trans titles), *History of Rome* (3 vols, 1854-5) and

The Roman Provinces (1885) in which he applied the new historical method of critical examination of sources. He was awarded the Nobel Prize for Literature in 1902.

Momoh, Joseph Saidu (1937–) Sierra Leonese soldier and president (1985–92), born in Binkolo, Sierra Leone. He disassociated himself from the policies of his predecessor, pledging to fight corruption and improve the economy, but was ousted in a military coup. >> Stevens, Siaka

Mompesson, William (1639–1709) Rector of Eyam, Derbyshire, where in 1665–6 the plague carried off 267 of his 350 parishioners. He persuaded his people to confine themselves entirely to the parish, and the disease was not spread.

Monash, Sir John (1865–1931) Australian soldier, born in Melbourne, Victoria, Australia. He commanded the 4th Australian Brigade at Gallipoli (1914–15), the 3rd Australian Division in France (1916), and the Australian Corps as lieutenant-general (1918).

Monboddo, James Burnett, Lord [mon**bod**oh] (1714–99) Judge and pioneer anthropologist, born in Monboddo, Grampian. His theory of human affinity with monkeys anticipated Darwin and the modern science of anthropology. >> Darwin, Charles

Monceau, Henri-Louis Duhamel du >> **Duhamel du Monceau, Henri-Louis**

Monck, George >> **Monk, George**

Monckton, Lionel (1861–1924) Composer, born in London. He contributed songs to many of the shows of **George Edwardes** (1852–1915) in London, and composed musical comedies, notably *The Quaker Girl* and *The Country Girl.*

Monckton (of Brenchley), Walter Turner Monckton, 1st Viscount (1891–1965) Lawyer and statesman, born in Plaxtol, Kent. He became attorney general to the Prince of Wales, and was adviser to him (as Edward VIII) in the abdication crisis of 1936. He served as Conservative minister of labour (1951–5), minister of defence (1955–6), and paymaster-general (1956–7). >> Edward VIII

Monczer, Thomas >> **Müntzer, Thomas**

Mond, Alfred Moritz, Baron Melchett (1868–1930) Industrialist and Liberal statesman, born in Farnsworth, Cheshire, the son of Ludwig Mond. He became the first commissioner of works (1916–21) and minister of health (1922). In 1926 he helped to form ICI, and became chairman. >> Mond, Ludwig

Mond, Ludwig (1839–1909) Chemist and industrialist, born in Kassel, Germany. Settling in England (1864), he perfected a sulphur recovery process, founded an alkaliworks (1873), and made discoveries in nickel manufacture. >> Mond, Alfred Moritz

Mondale, Walter F(rederick) (1928–) US Democratic vice-president (1977–81), born in Ceylon, MN. He served under President Carter, but was defeated with him in their bid for re-election in 1980. In 1984 he was the Democratic presidential nominee, but lost to Reagan. >> Carter, Jimmy; Reagan

Mondrian, Piet [**mon**drian], originally **Pieter Cornelis Mondriaan** (1872–1944) Artist, born in Amersfoort, The Netherlands. One of the founders of the *De Stijl* movement, he moved to Paris in 1909, his work becoming increasingly abstract. He is considered the leader of Neoplasticism.

Monet, Claude [monay] (1840–1926) Painter, born in Paris. He exhibited at the first Impressionist Exhibition in 1874, where his painting 'Impression: Sunrise' (1872) gave the name to the movement. Among his best known works are several series of paintings of subjects under different aspects of light, such as 'Haystacks' (1890–1).

Monge, Gaspard, comte de (Count of) **Péluse** [mõzh] (1746–1818) Mathematician and physicist, born in Beaune, France. In his *Leçons de géométrie descriptive* (1795),

he stated his principles regarding the general application of geometry to the arts of construction (descriptive geometry).

Monier-Williams, Sir Monier, originally **Monier Williams** (1819–99) Sanskrit scholar, born in Bombay, India. Professor of Sanskrit at Oxford (1860), he helped establish the Indian Institute (1896).

Moniz, António Egas >> **Egas Moniz, António**

Monk or **Monck, George, 1st Duke of Albemarle** (1608–70) General, born in Great Potheridge, Devon. He joined the Commonwealth cause and served successfully in Ireland, Scotland, and the first Dutch War (1652–4). Fearing a return to Civil War, he was instrumental in bringing about the restoration of Charles II. >> Charles II (of England)

Monk, Maria (c.1817–50) Impostor, born in Quebec, Canada. She pretended in 1835 to have escaped from cruel treatment in a nunnery at Montreal, and published *Awful Disclosures by Maria Monk* (1836) and *Further Disclosures* (1837), before being exposed as a fake.

Monk, Meredith (1943–) Dancer, choreographer, and musician, born in Lima, Peru. She developed her own multimedia events in unconventional venues, and in 1968 formed her own company, The House.

Monk, Thelonious (Sphere) (1917–82) Jazz pianist and composer, born in Rocky Mount, NC. Although credited with helping to create the jazz style of the 1940s, his angular, idiosyncratic melodies stood apart from the main currents of the day. His compositions include 'Round Midnight' (1947) and 'Criss Cross' (1951).

Monmouth, James Scott, Duke of (1649–85) Illegitimate son of Charles II of England, born in Rotterdam, The Netherlands. He had great popular support, and as a Protestant became a focus of opposition to James II. In 1685 he asserted his right to the crown, but was defeated at Sedgemoor, and executed. >> Charles II (of England); James II (of England)

Monnet, Jean [monay] (1888–1979) French statesman, born in Cognac, France. A distinguished economist and expert in financial affairs, he became in 1947 commissioner-general of the 'Plan de modernisation et d'équipement de la France' (the *Monnet plan*).

Monod, André Théodore [monoh] (1902–) Naturalist and explorer, born in Rouen, France. He made extensive botanical and geological studies of remote regions of the Sahara, and made a memorable trans-Saharan crossing of 560 mi by camel from Mauritania to Mali.

Monod, Jacques (Lucien) [monoh] (1910–76) Biochemist, born in Paris. With Jacob he discovered genes that regulate other genes (*operons*), and shared the Nobel Prize for Physiology or Medicine in 1965. >> Jacob, François; Lwoff

Monroe, Harriet (1860–1936) Poet and critic, born in Chicago, IL. She wrote the 'Columbian Ode' for the Chicago World's Columbian Exposition (1892), and in 1912 founded the magazine *Poetry.*

Monroe, James (1758–1831) US statesman and fifth president (1817–25), born in Westmoreland Co, VA. He recognized the Spanish American republics, and in 1823 promulgated the *Monroe Doctrine*, embodying the principle 'that the American continents ... are henceforth not to be considered as subjects for future colonization by any European power'.

Monroe, Marilyn, stage name of **Norma Jean Mortenson** or **Baker** (1926–62) Film star, born in Los Angeles, CA. She starred as a 'dumb blonde' in such films as *How to Marry a Millionaire* (1953), and went on to win acclaim in *Bus Stop* (1956) and *The Misfits* (1961), written for her by her third husband, Arthur Miller (divorced 1961). >> DiMaggio; Miller, Arthur

Monsarrat, Nicholas (John Turney) [**mon**sarat] (1910–

79) Novelist, born in Liverpool, Merseyside. During World War 2 he served in the navy, and out of his experiences emerged his best-selling novel, *The Cruel Sea* (1951; filmed 1953).

Mont, Allen B Du >> **Du Mont, Allen B**

Montagna, Bartolomeo [montanya] (c.1450–1523) Painter, born in Brescia, Italy. He founded a school of painting at Vicenza, and is best known for the altarpiece in S Michele at Vicenza (1499).

Montagnier, Luc [mōtanyay] (1932–) French virologist, co-discoverer of the virus which causes AIDS. In 1983, working in Paris, and independently of US virologist **Robert Gallo** (1937–), he discovered the virus now known as HIV (Human Immune-deficiency Virus).

Montagu >> **Halifax, Charles; Manchester, Edward; Sandwich, Edward / John**

Montagu, (Montague Francis) Ashley [montagyoo] (1905–) Anthropologist, born in London. Throughout his work on human biosocial evolution, he has argued strongly against the view that cultural phenomena are genetically determined, and is best known as the author of UNESCO's 'Statement on Race' (1950).

Montagu, Elizabeth [montagyoo], *née* **Robinson** (1720–1800) Writer and society leader, born in York, North Yorkshire. She established a social and literary salon in Mayfair, London. The female members became known as 'Bluestockings', from the way several of them dressed. >> Montagu, Mary Wortley

Montagu, George [montagyoo] (1753–1815) Naturalist and British soldier, born at Lackham House, Wiltshire. His chief work is *Ornithological Dictionary; or Alphabetical Synopsis of British Birds* (2 vols, 1802).

Montagu, Lady Mary Wortley [montagyoo], *née* **Pierrepont** (1689–1762) Writer, born in London. A poet and essayist as well as a feminist and a beauty, she gained a brilliant reputation among literary figures. While in Constantinople, she wrote her entertaining *Letters* describing Eastern life.

Montaigne, Michel (Eyquem) de [mōten] (1533–92) Essayist and courtier, born at Château de Montaigne, Périgord, France. He is remembered for his *Essais* (1572–80, 1588) on the new ideas and personalities of the time, which introduced a new literary genre.

Montale, Eugenio [montahlay] (1896–1981) Poet, born in Genoa, Italy. The leading poet of the modern Italian 'Hermetic' school, his works include *Cuttlefish Bones* (trans, 1925), *The Occasions* (trans, 1939), and *Xenia* (1966). He was awarded the Nobel Prize for Literature in 1975.

Montalembert, Charles (Forbes René), comte de (Count of) [mōalãbair] (1810–70) French historian and politician, born in London. His greatest work was *Monks of the West* (trans, 7 vols, 1860–77).

Montana, Joe [montana], popular name of **Joseph C Montana, Jr** (1956–) Player of American football, born in Monongahela, PA. He led the San Francisco 49ers to victories in four Super Bowls during the 1980s, and was named the National Football League's most valuable player in 1989.

Montand, Yves [mōtã, eev], originally **Ivo Livi** (1921–91) Actor-singer, born in Monsummano Alto, Italy. His films include *The Wages of Fear* (trans, 1953), *Z* (1968), and *The Confession* (trans, 1970). He married Simone Signoret in 1951. >> Signoret

Montcalm (de Saint Véran), Louis Joseph de Montcalm-Grozon, marquis de [mōkalm] (1712–59) French general, born in Condiac, France. In 1758 he defended Ticonderoga, and proceeded to the defence of Quebec, where he died in the battle on the Plains of Abraham. >> Wolfe, James

Montefiore, Sir Moses (Haim) [montefyohray] (1784–1885) Philanthropist, born in Livorno, Italy. From 1829 he was prominent in the struggle for Jewish equality, and made seven journeys to Palestine in the interests of his oppressed co-religionists in Europe.

Montesi, Wilma [montayzee] (1932–53) Fashion model, the daughter of a Roman carpenter. The finding of her body in 1953 led to prolonged but unresolved investigations involving sensational allegations of drug and sex orgies in Roman society, and exposed corruption in high public places.

Montespan, Françoise Athenaïs de Rochechouart, marquise de (Marchioness of) [mōtespã] (1641–1707) Mistress of Louis XIV, born in Tonnay-Charente, France. Lady-in-waiting to Queen Maria Theresa, she became the king's mistress (c.1667), and after her own marriage was annulled (1674), was given official recognition of her position. She bore the king seven children, who were legitimized (1673). >> Louis XIV; Maintenon

Montesquieu, Charles Louis de Secondat, Baron de la Brède et de [mōteskyoe] (1689–1755) Philosopher and jurist, born at Château La Brède near Bordeaux, France. His best-known work is the comparative study of legal and political issues, *The Spirit of Laws* (trans, 1748), which was a major influence on 18th-c Europe.

Montessori, Maria [montesawree] (1870–1952) Doctor and educationist, born in Rome. She opened her first 'children's house' in 1907, developing a system of education based on freedom of movement, the provision of considerable choice for pupils, and the use of specially designed activities and equipment.

Monteux, Pierre [mōtoe] (1875–1964) Conductor, born in Paris. He conducted Diaghilev's Ballets Russes in Paris (1911–14, 1917), founded the Orchestre Symphonique de Paris, and from 1960 until his death was principal conductor of the London Symphony Orchestra.

Monteverdi, Claudio [montayvairdee] (1567–1643) Composer, born in Cremona, Italy. His works include eight books of madrigals (1587–1638), two operas, and the *Mass* and *Vespers of the Blessed Virgin* (1610), which contained tone colours and harmonies well in advance of their time.

Montez, Lola [montez], originally **Marie Dolores Eliza Rosanna Gilbert** (1818–61) Dancer, born in Limerick, Ireland. An outstanding beauty, she trained to be a Spanish dancer. In Munich (1846) she met King Ludwig I of Bavaria, with whom she had a scandalous affair that greatly boosted her career.

Montezuma II [montezooma] (1466–1520) The last Aztec emperor (1502–20). A distinguished warrior and legislator, he died during the Spanish conquest of Cortés. >> Cortés

Montfaucon, Bernard de [mōfohsō] (1655–1741) Scholar and monk, born in Soulage, France, the founder of the science of palaeography. His *Greek Palaeography* (trans, 1708) was the first work to be based on a study of manuscript handwriting.

Montfort, Simon de (c.1160–1218) Norman crusader, born in Toulouse, France. He took part in the 4th Crusade (1202–4), and also undertook a crusade against the Albingenses in 1208. He was killed at the siege of Toulouse.

Montfort, Simon de, Earl of Leicester (c.1208–1265) English statesman and soldier, born in Montfort, France. In 1238 he married Henry III's youngest sister, Eleanor. He led the barons against the king, defeated him at Lewes (1264), and became virtual ruler of England; but the barons grew dissatisfied with his rule, and he was killed at the Battle of Evesham.

Montgolfier brothers [mōgolfyay] Aeronautical inventors: **Joseph Michel Montgolfier** (1740–1810) and **Jacques Etienne Montgolfier** (1745–99) brothers, born in Annonay, France. They constructed a balloon which in 1783 achieved a flight of 9 km/5½mi, the world's first manned flight.

Montgomery (of Alamein), Bernard Law Montgomery, 1st Viscount (1887–1976) British field marshal, born in London. He commanded the 8th Army in N Africa, defeated Rommel at El Alamein (1942), played a key role in the invasion of Sicily and Italy (1943), and was appointed commander-in-chief, ground forces, for the Allied invasion of Normandy (1944). In 1945, the German forces surrendered to him at Lünenberg Heath.

Montgomery, L(ucy) M(aud) (1874–1942) Novelist, raised in Cavendish, Prince Edward Island, Canada. Her first book was the highly successful *Anne of Green Gables* (1908), after which she published several sequels.

Montherlant, Henri (Marie Joseph Millon) de [mõtairlã] (1896–1972) Novelist and playwright, born in Paris. His major work is a four-novel cycle, beginning with *Les jeunes filles* and *Pitié pour les femmes* (1936, published together as *Pity for Women*).

Montholon, Charles Tristan, marquis de [mõtolõ] (1783–1853) French soldier and diplomat, born in Paris. He accompanied Napoleon to St Helena, and published memoirs dictated by him (8 vols, 1822–5). He was imprisoned (1840–8) for helping Louis Napoleon's attempted seizure of power. >> Napoleon I / III

Monti, Eugenio [montee] (1928–) Bobsleigh driver, born in Dobbiaco, Italy. The winner of a record six Olympic bobsleighing medals, he won golds in the two- and four-man events at the 1968 Games, after winning the silver in both events in 1956, and the bronze in 1964.

Montini, Giovanni Battista >> Paul VI

Montpensier, Anne Marie Louise d'Orléans, duchesse de (Duchess of) [mõpãsyay], known as **la Grande Mademoiselle** (1627–93) Niece of Louis XIII, born in Paris. She supported her father, the Duke of Orléans, and Condé in the revolt of the Fronde (1651–2), where she commanded an army that occupied Orléans and later the Bastille. >> Condé, Louis II de Bourbon

Montrose, James Graham, 1st Marquess of (1612–50) Scottish soldier and royalist. He served in the Covenanter army in 1640, but transferred his allegiance to Charles I, and led the Royalist army to victory at Tippermuir (1644). After the Royalist defeat at Naseby (1645) he fled to Europe, but was later taken prisoner and hanged.

Moodie, Susanna, née **Strickland** (1803–85) Writer, born in Bungay, Suffolk. She moved to Canada in 1832. Her best-known work concerns her life in Cobourg, Ontario, *Roughing It in the Bush: or, Life in Canada* (1852), and she also wrote novels, poems, memoirs, and stories for children.

Moody, Dwight L(yman) (1837–99) Evangelist, born in Northfield, MA. In 1856 he went to Chicago to engage in missionary work, and founded the Moody Church. In 1870 he was joined by **Ira David Sankey** (1840–1908), who accompanied his preaching with singing.

Moon, William (1818–94) Inventor, born in Kent. Totally blind from 1840, in 1845 he invented a system of embossed type based on Roman capitals (*Moon type*), easier to learn than Braille for those who have become blind late in life. >> Braille

Mooney, Edward (Francis) (1882–1958) Roman Catholic clergyman, born in Mt Savage, MD. A major spokesman on social issues, he became Archbishop of Detroit in 1937 and was made a cardinal in 1946.

Moorcroft, William (1872–1945) Potter, born in Staffordshire. In 1913 he set up his own firm in Burslem, producing a range of white-bodied ceramics decorated with stylized flowers and leaves, known as 'Florian Ware'.

Moore, Archie, originally **Archibald Lee Wright**, nickname **the Mongoose** (1913/16–) Boxer, born in Benoit, MI. His actual date of birth is uncertain but he is still the oldest man to hold a world title. He was 39 (or 36) when he beat Joey Maxim for the light-heavyweight title in 1952. >> Ali, Muhammad

Moore, Bernard (1850–1935) Potter, born in Staffordshire. He started his own business (1905–15), and was particularly interested in glazes, producing a series of rouge flambés, turquoise, sang-de-boeuf, crystalline, and aventurine glazes as well as fine lustres.

Moore, Bobby, popular name of **Robert Frederick Chelsea Moore** (1941–93) Footballer, born in London. In a long career with West Ham United (1958–74) and Fulham (1974–7), he was capped a record 108 times, 90 of them as captain. He led the victorious England side in the 1966 World Cup.

Moore, Brian (1921–) Writer, born in Belfast. His works include the novels *The Lonely Passion of Judith Hearne* (1955; filmed 1987), *The Doctor's Wife* (1976), and *Black Robe* (1985), and the play *Lies of Silence* (1990; filmed 1991).

Moore, Clement (Clarke) (1779–1863) Educator, Hebraist, and poet, born in New York City. He is known especially for a poem written for his children, 'A Visit From St. Nicholas' (1822), later known as 'The Night Before Christmas'.

Moore, Dudley (Stuart John) (1935–) Actor, comedian, and musician, born in London. One of the *Beyond the Fringe* team (1960–64), he joined Peter Cook for the TV series *Not Only... but also* (1964–70). His films include *10* (1979), *Arthur* (1981) and *Santa Claus - The Movie* (1985). An accomplished musician, he has performed with his own jazz trio, and composed for several films and plays. >> Cook, Peter

Moore, Edward (1712–57) Playwright, born in Abingdon, Berkshire. The comedy *Gil Blas* (1751) and the tragedy *The Gamester* (1753) are his best-known plays.

Moore, Francis (1657–c.1715) Astrologer, born in Bridgnorth, Shropshire. In 1700 he published *Vox Stellarum* (Voices of the Stars), which later became known as *Old Moore's Almanac*.

Moore, George (Augustus) (1852–1933) Writer, born in Ballyglass, Co Mayo, Ireland. A novelist of the Realist school, he introduced this type of fiction into England, notably with *Esther Waters* (1894). Later works include *The Brook Kerith* (1916) and *Héloïse and Abelard* (1921).

Moore, G(eorge) E(dward) (1873–1958) Philosopher, born in London. His major ethical work was *Principia Ethica* (1903), in which he argued against the naturalistic fallacy. A leading influence on the Bloomsbury group, he also edited the journal *Mind* (1921–47).

Moore, Gerald (1899–1987) Pianoforte accompanist, born in Watford, Hertfordshire. He established himself as an outstanding accompanist of the world's leading singers and instrumentalists.

Moore, Henry (Spencer) (1898–1986) Sculptor, born in Castleford, West Yorkshire. His style is based on the organic forms and undulations found in landscape and natural rocks, and influenced by primitive African and Mexican art. Major collections can be seen at the Henry Moore Sculpture Center, Toronto, The Tate Gallery, London, and at his home in Much Hadham, Hertfordshire.

Moore, Sir (John) Jeremy (1928–) British soldier. In 1982, he successfully commanded the British land forces during the recapture of the Falkland Is from Argentina.

Moore, Sir John (1761–1809) British soldier, born in Glasgow, Strathclyde. He commanded the English army in Spain (1808–9), where he was forced to retreat to Coruña. There he defeated a French attack, but was mortally wounded (as recounted in the poem by Wolfe). >> Wolfe, Charles

Moore, Marianne (Craig) (1887–1972) Poet, born in St Louis, MO. Associated with the Greenwich Village group, Idiosyncratic, her *Complete Poems* appeared in 1968.

Moore, Mary Tyler (1936–) Actress, born in New York City. *The Dick Van Dyke Show* (1961–6) highlighted her talent for domestic comedy, and launched her career on

Broadway and in the cinema, returning to television with *The Mary Tyler Moore Show* (1970–7, three Emmys). >> Van Dyke, Dick

Moore, Patrick (Alfred Caldwell) (1923–) British amateur astronomer, writer, broadcaster, and musician. He is best known as the enthusiastic and knowledgeable presenter of the long-running BBC television programme *The Sky at Night* (1957–).

Moore, Roger (George) (1927–) Film star, born in London. On television he won stardom as the hero of such series as *Ivanhoe* (1958), and *The Saint* (1962–9), and brought a lightweight insouciance to the role of James Bond in seven films between *Live and Let Die* (1973) and *A View to a Kill* (1985).

Moore, Stanford (1913–82) Biochemist, born in Chicago, IL. In the 1950s, with Stein, he devised a general method for identifying the number of amino acids in protein molecules, developing an automated way of analyzing the structure of RNA on a small sample. They shared the Nobel Prize for Chemistry in 1972. >> Stein, William

Moore, Thomas (1779–1852) Poet, born in Dublin. His best-known work, *Irish Melodies* (1807–34), included such memorable poems as 'The Last Rose of Summer'. Other works include his narrative poem *Lalla Rookh* (1817), and an edition of Byron's letters and journals (1830). >> Byron, George

Moorer, Thomas H(inman) (1912–) US naval officer, born in Mount Willing, AL. He was commander of the Atlantic Fleet (1965–7), chief of naval operations (1967–70), and chairman of the joint chiefs-of-staff (1970–4).

Moores, Sir John (1896–1993) Businessman, born in Eccles, Greater Manchester. He founded Littlewoods football pools in 1923, established a mail-order business in Britain (1932), and opened the first store in the Littlewoods chain in 1937.

Moors Murderers >> Brady, Ian

Mor, Anthonis >> More, Sir Anthony

Morandi, Giorgio [mo**ran**dee] (1890–1964) Painter, born in Bologna, Italy. He concentrated on landscapes, portraits, and above all still-life, painting arrangements of everyday objects on a tabletop in subdued tones, and with a simplicity of form.

Morant, Harry Harbord [mo**rant**], originally **Edwin Henry Murrant**, nickname **Breaker Morant** (1865–1902) Adventurer and poet, born probably in Bridgwater, Somerset. He went to N Queensland in 1883, married Daisy May O'Dwyer (later Daisy Bates), and earned a living as a rider and horse-breaker. In 1899 he went to fight in the Boer Wars, and after the murder by the Boers of a friend, he and a companion were executed for their retaliation against the surrendering Boers. >> Bates, Daisy May

Morata, Olympia [mo**rah**ta] (1526–55) Italian humanist scholar and poet. She wrote numerous Latin and Greek poems, a treatise on Cicero, dialogues, and letters.

Moravia, Alberto [mo**ray**via], pseudonym of **Alberto Pincherle** (1907–90) Novelist and short-story writer, born in Rome. His novels include (trans titles) *The Time of Indifference* (1929), *Disobedience* (1948), and *Time of Desecration* (1978).

Moray, James Stuart, Earl of [**muh**ree] (1531–70) Regent of Scotland (1567–70), the illegitimate son of James V of Scotland, and half-brother of Mary, Queen of Scots. He acted as Mary's chief adviser (1560), but opposed her marriage to Darnley. He became regent for Mary's baby son (James VI), defeated her army at Langside (1568), but was killed by one of Mary's supporters. >> Darnley; Mary, Queen of Scots

Mordecai [**maw(r)**dekiy] (c.5th-c BC) Biblical hero. He is described in the Book of Esther as a Jew in exile in Persia,

who gained the favour of King Xerxes, and used his influence to protect Jews from an edict issued against them. The event is commemorated by the annual Jewish feast of Purim. >> Xerxes I

Mordkin, Mikhail (1880–1944) Ballet dancer, teacher, and director, born in Moscow. He appeared in Diaghilev's 1909 Paris season, and in 1912 joined the Bolshoi, becoming director in 1917. After the Revolution he settled in the USA and was a pioneer of American ballet. >> Diaghilev

More, Sir Anthony [moor], originally **Anthonis Mor**, also known as **Antonio Moro** (c.1519–75) Portrait painter, born in Utrecht, The Netherlands. In 1553 he visited England, where he painted Queen Mary I for her bridegroom, Philip II of Spain.

More, Hannah [moor] (1745–1833) Playwright and religious writer, born in Fishponds, Avon. She wrote two tragedies, *Percy* (1777) and *The Fatal Secret* (1779), and her moral tracts for the poor, *Village Politics by Will Chip* (1793), led to the founding of the Religious Tracts Society.

More, Henry [moor] (1614–87) Philosopher and theologian, born in Grantham, Lincolnshire. A leading figure in the 'Cambridge Platonists', his main works include *Philosophical Poems* (1647) and *Divine Dialogues* (1668).

More, Sir Thomas [moor], also **St Thomas More** (1478–1535), feast day 22 June. English statesman and scholar, born in London. On the fall of Wolsey (1529), he became Lord Chancellor, but resigned in 1532 following his opposition to Henry's break with Rome. On refusing to recognize Henry as head of the English Church, he was beheaded. A leading humanist scholar, as revealed in his Latin *Utopia* (1516), he was canonized in 1935. >> Henry VIII; Wolsey

Moreau, Gustave [mo**roh**] (1826–98) Painter, born in Paris. An eccentric Symbolist, he painted colourful but usually rather sinister scenes from ancient mythology and the Bible, as in 'Salome' (1876).

Moreau, Jeanne [mo**roh**] (1928–) Actress and director, born in Paris. Her major film roles include *Jules et Jim* (1961), *Diary of a Chambermaid* (trans, 1964), *Viva Maria* (1965), and *The Bride Wore Black* (trans, 1967).

Moreau, (Jean) Victor (Marie) [mo**roh**] (1763–1813) French general in the Napoleonic Wars, born in Morlaix, France. He assisted Napoleon in the coup of 18th Brumaire, and gained victories over the Austrians in 1800, but Napoleon accused him of sharing in the royalist plot against him, and he was banished. >> Napoleon I

Morecambe, Eric, originally **Eric Bartholomew** (1926–84) Comedian, born in Morecambe, Lancashire. He teamed up in 1943 with fellow entertainer, **Ernie Wise** (originally **Ernest Wiseman**) (1925–), and as **Morecambe and Wise**, they became the leading British comedy double-act known especially for their shows on television.

Morel >> Deschamps, Eustache

Morelli, Giovanni [mo**relee**] (1816–91) Art critic, born in Verona, Italy. His criticism concentrated on attribution, which he claimed to have reduced to scientific principles - the *Morellian method*. He was also instrumental in the passing of an act, later named after him, which gave state protection to important works of art.

Moresby, John [maw(r)zbee] (1830–1922) Naval commander and explorer, born in Allerton, Somerset. He conducted exploration and survey work in New Guinea, where he discovered the fine natural harbour now fronted by Port Moresby, which was named after him.

Morey, Samuel [**maw**ree] (1762–1843) Inventor, born in Hebron, CT. After 1790, he built a series of paddle-wheel steamboats, but none were commercially successful. His American Water Burner (1817–18) was a precursor of the water-gas process widely used half a century later.

Morgagni, Giovanni Battista [maw(r)**gan**yee] (1682–1771) Physician, born in Forlì, Italy. He correlated pathological lesions with symptoms in over 700 cases, and is traditionally considered to be the founder of the science of pathological anatomy.

Morgan, Agnes Fay, originally **Jane Agnes Fay** (1884–1968) Biochemist and nutritionist, born in Peoria, IL. She focused on the analysis of nutrients in foods, the stability of vitamins and proteins during food processing, and the physiological effects of vitamin deficiencies, discovering the role of pantothenic acid in adrenal function and pigmentation.

Morgan, Augustus De >> **De Morgan, Augustus**

Morgan, Charles (Langbridge), pseudonym **Menander** (1894–1958) Writer, born in Bromley, Kent. He was principal drama critic for *The Times* (1926–39), and wrote two series of critical essays. His novels include *Portrait in a Mirror* (1929, Femina Vie Heureuse Prize), *The Fountain* (1932, Hawthornden), and *The Voyage* (1940, James Tait Black Memorial Prize).

Morgan, Sir Henry (c.1635–88) Buccaneer, born in Llanrumney, South Glamorgan. Kidnapped as a child, he joined the buccaneers, leading many raids against the Spanish and Dutch in the West Indies and Central America. He later became Deputy Governor of Jamaica.

Morgan, John Hunt (1825–64) Confederate guerrilla leader, born in Huntsville, AL. He led the *Morgan raiders* in a series of raids on Union supply lines, and was killed in action.

Morgan, J(ohn) P(ierpont) (1837–1913) Banker, financier, and art collector, born in Hartford, CT. The son of the financier **John Spencer Morgan** (1813–90), he built his father's firm into the most powerful private banking house in the USA.

Morgan, Thomas Hunt (1866–1945) Geneticist and biologist, born in Lexington, KY. Following experiments with the *Drosophila* fruit fly, he established a chromosome theory of heredity involving genes for specific tasks aligned on chromosomes, which earned him the Nobel Prize for Physiology or Medicine in 1933.

Morgan, William de >> **de Morgan, William**

Morganwg, Iolo >> **Williams, Edward**

Morison, James (1816–93) Clergyman, born in Bathgate, Lothian. Suspended by the United Secession Church in 1841 for preaching universal atonement, in 1843 he co-founded the Evangelical Union of Congregational churches.

Morison, Stanley (1889–1967) Typographer and scholar, born in Wanstead, Essex. On the staff of *The Times* from 1929, he designed the Times New Roman type, introduced in 1932.

Morisot, Berthe (Marie Pauline) [morisoh] (1841–95) Painter and printmaker, born in Bourges, France, the grand-daughter of Fragonard. The leading female exponent of Impressionism, she painted chiefly women and children. >> Fragonard

Morita, Akio [moreeta] (1921–) Manufacturer, born in Nagoya, Japan. With Masaru Ibuka he founded the electronics firm which since 1958 has been known as Sony.

Morley, Christopher (Darlington) (1890–1957) Novelist and essayist, born in Haverford, PA. His varied works include *Parnassus on Wheels* (1917), *Swiss Family Manhattan* (1932), and *The Ironing Board* (1949).

Morley, Edward Williams (1838–1923) Chemist and physicist, born in Newark, NJ. His early research was on the oxygen content of air, and he worked with Michelson in their famous experiments to detect the 'ether-drift' (1887). >> Michelson

Morley, John Morley, 1st Viscount (1838–1923) Journalist, biographer, and statesman, born in Blackburn, Lancashire. He edited the *Fortnightly Review* (1867–82) and the *Pall Mall Gazette* (1880–3), and wrote biographies of Voltaire (1872), Gladstone (4 vols, 1903), and others. He served as Irish secretary (1886, 1892–5).

Morley, Robert (1908–92) Actor and writer, born in Semley,

Wiltshire. In his film career, from 1938, he played many individual character parts, including the title role in *The Trials of Oscar Wilde* (1960). He was well known for his edited collections, such as *Robert Morley's Book of Bricks* (1979).

Morley, Thomas (1557/8–1602) Composer, born in Norwich, Norfolk. He is best known for *A Plaine and Easie Introduction to Practicall Musicke* (1597), and for his volumes of madrigals and canzonets, which include such evergreens as 'It was a lover and his lass'.

Morny, Charles Auguste Louis Joseph, duc de (Duke of) [maw(r)nee] (1811–65) Nobleman, born in Paris, believed to be the half-brother of Napoleon III. After 1848 he supported Louis Napoleon, took a leading part in the coup, and became minister of the interior. >> Napoleon III

Moro, Aldo [moroh] (1916–1978) Italian prime minister (1963–4, 1964–6, 1966–8, 1974–6, 1976), born in Maglie, Italy. Leader of the Christian Democrats (1976), Red Brigade left-wing terrorists kidnapped him in Rome in 1978 and murdered him.

Moro, Antonio >> **More, Sir Anthony**

Moroni, Giovanni Battista [morohnee] (1525–78) Artist, born in Albino, Italy. His work was almost always confined to portraiture, making him unique among the artists of the Italian Renaissance.

Morphy, Paul (Charles) (1837–84) Chess player, born in New Orleans, LA. During his meteoric chess career (1857–9), he won the US championship and beat the strongest masters in Europe, becoming unofficial world champion.

Morris, Arthur (Robert) (1922–) Cricketer, born in Sydney, New South Wales, Australia. An opening batsman for Australia, he was capped 46 times, and his 3533 Test runs included 12 centuries.

Morris, Desmond (John) (1928–) British zoologist and writer. His study of human behaviour in *The Naked Ape* (1967) became a best seller, and was followed by many television programmes on animal and social behaviour. Later books include *The Human Zoo* (1969), *Manwatching* (1977), and *The Soccer Tribe* (1981).

Morris, George Pope (1802–64) Journalist and poet, born in Philadelphia, PA. In 1823 he founded the *New York Mirror* and became its editor (1824–42). He published many poems, including the celebrated 'Woodman, Spare that Tree'.

Morris, Gouverneur (1752–1816) US statesman, born in Morrisania, NY. In 1791 he went to England as Washington's agent, acted as US minister to France, and later became a member of the US Senate (1800–3). >> Washington, George

Morris, Sir Lewis (1833–1907) Poet and lawyer, born in Carmarthen, Dyfed. His main literary works were *Songs of Two Worlds* (3 vols, 1872–5) and *The Epic of Hades* (1876), drawing largely on incidents in Welsh history and mythology.

Morris, Mark (1956–) Dancer and choreographer, born in Seattle, WA. He made an informal New York City debut with his company in 1980, and in 1988 the Mark Morris Dance Group began a permanent residency at Theâtre de le Monnaie in Brussels.

Morris, Robert (1734–1806) Financier and statesman, born in Liverpool, Merseyside. He organized the finance for Washington's military supplies, and in 1782 founded the Bank of North America. A member of the Continental Congress (1775–8), he was a signatory of the Declaration of Independence. >> Washington, George

Morris, Robert L(yle) (1942–) Psychologist, born in Canonsburg, PA. In 1985 he was appointed the first Koestler professor of parapsychology at the University of Edinburgh. >> Koestler

Morris, William (1834–96) Craftsman, poet, and political activist, born in Walthamstow, Greater London. Associated with the Pre-Raphaelite Brotherhood, in 1861 he founded the firm of Morris, Marshall, Faulkner & Co, which revolutionized the art of house decoration and furniture in England, and in 1890 he founded the Kelmscott Press. He also organized the Socialist League.

Morris-Jones, Sir John, originally **John Jones** (1864–1929) Scholar, poet, and teacher, born in Llandrygarn, Gwynedd. His devotion to Welsh language and literature helped restore classical standards to Welsh poetry.

Morrison, Arthur (1863–1945) Novelist and short-story writer, born in London. His realistic novels of London slum life include *A Child of the Jago* (1896), which is believed to have accelerated changes in British housing legislation.

Morrison (of Lambeth), Herbert Stanley Morrison, Baron (1888–1965) British Labour statesman, born in London. He was minister of transport (1929–31), minister of supply (1940), and home secretary (1940–5), and became a powerful postwar figure, acting as deputy prime minister (1945–51). >> Churchill, Sir Winston

Morrison, Marion Michael >> **Wayne, John**

Morrison, Richard James >> **Zadkiel**

Morrison, Toni, *née* **Chloe Anthony Wofford** (1931–) Novelist, born in Lorain, OH. Her novels include *The Bluest Eye* (1970), *Song of Solomon* (1977), *Tar Baby* (1981), and *Beloved* (1988, Pulitzer). She received the Nobel Prize for Literature in 1993.

Morse, Samuel F(inley) B(reese) (1791–1872) Inventor and artist, born in Charlestown, MA. He developed the magnetic telegraph (1832–5), which along with the Morse code (1838) brought him honours and rewards after the opening of the first telegraph line between Washington and Baltimore (1844).

Morshead, Sir Leslie James [**moorz**hed] (1889–1959) Australian military commander, born in Ballarat, Victoria, Australia. He led the 9th Division at Tobruk (1941) and at the Battles of El Alamein, and in 1945 commanded the Australian and USA task force in Borneo.

Mort, Thomas Sutcliffe (1816–78) Businessman, born in Bolton, Lancashire. He went to Sydney in 1838, and engaged in shipbuilding, farming, and refrigeration, building a freezing-plant at Darling Harbour (1875).

Mortara, Edgar [maw(r)**tah**ra] (1852–1940) Italian religious, born into a Jewish family, and the unwitting principal in the celebrated 'Mortara' case. In 1858 he was carried off from his parents by the Archbishop of Bologna, on the grounds that he had been secretly baptized as an infant. Discovered in Rome in 1870, he became an Augustinian monk.

Mortensen, Erik (1926–) Danish fashion designer. In 1948 he joined the Balmain fashion house in Paris, becoming the artistic director in 1960, and manager in 1982. >> Balmain

Mortenson, Norma Jean >> **Monroe, Marilyn**

Mortimer, John (Clifford) (1923–) Playwright, novelist, and barrister, born in London. He came to public prominence as a dramatist with his one-act play *The Dock Brief* (1957), and his television screenplays include *I, Claudius* (1976) and *Brideshead Revisited* (1981). His novels featuring the disreputable barrister, Horace Rumpole, were adapted for television as Rumpole of the Bailey.

Mortimer, Roger, Earl of March >> **Edward II / III**

Morton, H(enry) V(ollam) (1892–1979) Travel writer, born in Birmingham, West Midlands. He devoted himself to informal books on travel, becoming known for his many 'In Search of ...' titles.

Morton, James Douglas, 4th Earl of (c.1516–81) Regent of Scotland (1572–8) for James VI. He was made Lord High Chancellor by Mary Stuart (1563), but was involved in the murders of Rizzio (1566) and Darnley (1567), and helped to overthrow the queen. His high-handed treatment of

the nobles and clergy caused his downfall (1581), and he was executed. >> Darnley; James I (of England); Mary, Queen of Scots; Rizzio

Morton, Jelly Roll, popular name of **Ferdinand Joseph La Menthe Morton** (1885–1941) Jazz pianist, composer, and bandleader, born in Gulfport, LA. His unaccompanied piano solos made best sellers of such tunes as 'King Porter Stomp' and 'Jelly Roll Blues', and he made powerful orchestral arrangements for his band, The Red Hot Peppers.

Morton, John (c.1420–1500) Statesman and cardinal, probably born in Milborne St Andrew, Dorset. After the accession of Henry VII he was made Archbishop of Canterbury (1486), Chancellor (1487), and a cardinal (1493). >> Henry VII

Morton, John Cameron (Andrieu Bingham Michael), pseudonym **Beachcomber** (1893–1979) British writer and journalist. From 1924 to 1975 he contributed a regular humorous column, 'By the Way', to the *Daily Express* under his pseudonym.

Morton, Levi (Parsons) (1824–1920) Banker and US vice-president (1889–93) under Harrison, born in Shoreham, VT. In 1863 he founded banking-houses in New York City and London, was returned to Congress as a Republican (1878–80). >> Harrison, Benjamin

Morton, William (Thomas Green) (1819–68) Dental surgeon, born in Charlton, MA. He was the first to administer ether as an anaesthetic in 1846.

Mosaddeq, Mohammed [**mo**sadek], also spelled **Massaddiq** or **Mossadegh** (1880–1967) Iranian president (1951–3), born in Tehran. His government was overthrown by a royalist uprising, and he was imprisoned. Released in 1956, he remained under house arrest for the rest of his life.

Mosby, John Singleton (1833–1916) US soldier and lawyer, born in Edgemont, VA. He joined the Confederate forces in Virginia, leading hit-and-run raids against scattered outposts of the Federals.

Mosconi, Willie [mos**koh**nee], popular name of **William Joseph Mosconi** (1913–93) Pocket billiards player, born in Philadelphia, PA. He took the first of many world titles in 1941, and wrote *Willie Mosconi on Pocket Billiards* (1959).

Moseley, Harry [**mohz**lee], popular name of **Henry Gwyn Jeffreys Moseley** (1887–1915) Physicist, born in Weymouth, Dorset. He worked on radioactivity, determining by means of X-ray spectra the atomic numbers of the elements (*Moseley's law*), the basis of 20th-c atomic and nuclear physics.

Moser-Pröll, Annemarie [**moh**zer **proel**], *née* **Pröll** (1953–) Alpine skier, born in Kleinarl, Austria. She won a women's record 62 World Cup races (1970–9), her achievements including Olympic downhill champion (1980), world combined champion (1972, 1978), and world downhill champion (1974, 1978, 1980).

Moses [**moh**ziz] (c.13th-c BC) Major character of Israelite history, portrayed in the Book of Exodus as the leader of the deliverance of Hebrew slaves from Egypt and the recipient of the divine revelation at Mt Sinai. Stories about his early life depict his escape from death as an infant, his upbringing in the Egyptian court, and his prediction of a series of miraculous plagues to persuade the Pharaoh to release the Hebrews. Traditions then describe Moses' leadership of the Israelites during their 40 years of wilderness wanderings. >> Aaron

Moses, Sir Charles Joseph Alfred (1900–88) Broadcaster and administrator, born in Bolton, Lancashire. He emigrated to Australia in 1922, and rose to be general manager of the Australian Broadcasting Company (1935–65).

Moses, Ed(win Corley) (1955–) Hurdler, born in

Dayton, OH. He was the World Cup gold medal winner at the 400 m hurdles (1977, 1979, 1981), world champion (1983), and Olympic champion (1976, 1984).

Moses, Grandma, popular name of **Anna Mary Robertson Moses** (1860–1961) Artist, born in Greenwich, NY. She began to paint childhood country scenes at about the age of 75, such as 'Catching the Thanksgiving Turkey', achieving great popular success throughout the USA.

Moses, Robert (1888–1981) US public official, born in New Haven, CT. Chief-of-staff of the New York State reconstruction committee (1919), and commissioner of the City Parks (1934), he is thought to be responsible for much of the modern appearance of New York City.

Moses Ben Maimon >> Maimonides

Moshoeshoe [moshweshwe], also spelled **Mshweshwe** (c.1796–1870) African statesman, the founder of the modern state of Lesotho, born in N Basutoland. Through a blend of warfare and diplomacy, he created and defended a kingdom in the face of pressure from the Boer republic of the Orange Free State.

Moshoeshoe II [moshweshwe], originally **Constantine Bereng Seeiso** (1938–96) King of Lesotho (1966–90, 1994–6). Installed as Paramount Chief of the Basotho people (1960), he was proclaimed king when Lesotho became independent in 1966, but was forced to abdicate (1990–4) following a military coup in 1986.

Mosley, Sir Oswald (Ernald) [mohzlee] (1896–1980) Politician, born in London. He became leader of the British Union of Fascists, remembered for its anti-Semitic violence and its support for Hitler. Detained under the Defence Regulations during World War 2, in 1948 he founded another racialist party, the Union Movement.

Moss, Stirling (1929–) Motor-racing driver, born in London. He won many major races in the 1950s, but never a world title, though he was runner-up twice.

Mossadegh, Mohammed >> Mosaddeq, Mohammed

Mössbauer, Rudolph (Ludwig) [mocsbower] (1929–) Physicist, born in Munich, Germany. He discovered the recoil-free adsorption and subsequent re-emission of gamma rays by matter - the *Mössbauer effect*, for which he shared the Nobel Prize for Physics in 1961.

Most, Johann Joseph (1846–1906) Anarchist, born in Augsburg, Germany. Emigrating to America in 1882, he became the leader of an extreme faction of US anarchists, and composed the declaration which became the manifesto of Communist anarchism in America.

Mostel, Zero [mostel], originally **Samuel Joel Mostel** (1915–77) Actor, singer, and artist, born in New York City. He established a successful theatre career, particularly in comedy roles, appearing in the musicals *A Funny Thing Happened on the Way to the Forum* (1962) and *Fiddler on the Roof* (1964).

Mother Ann >> Lee, Ann

Motherwell, Robert (Burns) (1915–91) Artist, born in Aberdeen, WA. He wrote on the theory of modern art, and helped found the Abstract Expressionist group in New York City in the 1940s. He married Helen Frankenthaler in 1955. >> Frankenthaler

Mott, John R(aleigh) (1865–1955) Religious leader and social worker, born in Livingston Manor, NY. He became world known by his work for the Young Men's Christian Association (1915–31), the Student Volunteer Movement (1888–1920), and the World Missionary Council (1941–2), and shared the Nobel Peace Prize in 1946.

Mott, Lucretia, *née* **Coffin** (1793–1880) Feminist and reformer, born in Nantucket, MA. She married fellow-teacher James Mott in 1811, and together they campaigned against slavery. With Elizabeth Stanton she organized the first Woman's Rights Convention in 1848. >> Stanton, Elizabeth

Mott, Sir Nevill F(rancis) (1905–) Physicist, born in

Leeds, West Yorkshire. He shared the 1977 Nobel Prize for Physics for his independent work on the electronic properties of disordered materials. >> Anderson, Philip W; Van Vleck

Mottelson, Ben R(oy) (1926–) Physicist, born in Chicago, IL. He worked with Aage Bohr on the problem of combining the two models of the atomic nuclei. They secured experimental evidence in support of Rainwater's collective model of the atomic nucleus, and all three shared the Nobel Prize for Physics in 1975. >> Bohr, Aage; Rainwater

Mottram, R(alph) H(ale) (1883–1971) Novelist, born in Norwich, Norfolk. He became known with *Spanish Farm* (1924) and its sequels, *Sixty-Four, Ninety-Four* (1925) and *The Crime at Vanderlynden* (1926).

Moule, Charles (Francis Digby) (1908–) British biblical scholar, born in Hanchow, China. His many books include *The Holy Spirit* (1978) and *Essays in New Testament Interpretation* (1982).

Moulins, Master of [moolĩ] (c.1460–c.1529) The name given to an unknown French artist whose principal work was the triptych in Moulins Cathedral of the 'Virgin and Child'. Some authorities identify him as Jean Perreal or Jean de Paris, court painter to Charles VIII.

Mountbatten, Edwina (Cynthia Annette) Mountbatten, Countess of, *née* **Ashley** (1901–60) Wife of Louis, Earl Mountbatten of Burma, whom she married in 1922. She rendered distinguished service during the London blitz (1940–2) to the Red Cross and St John Ambulance Brigade, becoming its superintendent-in-chief in 1942. >> Mountbatten (of Burma)

Mountbatten, Prince Louis Alexander, 1st Marquess of Milford Haven, originally **Prince Louis of Battenberg** (1854–1921) British naval commander, born in Graz, Austria, the son of Prince Alexander of Hesse. He became a British subject, serving in the Mediterranean fleet and as director of naval intelligence. In 1917 he changed the family name from Battenberg to Mountbatten. >> Mountbatten (of Burma)

Mountbatten (of Burma), Louis (Francis Albert Victor Nicholas) Mountbatten, 1st Earl (1900–79) British admiral and statesman, born in Windsor, Berkshire, the younger son of Prince Louis of Battenberg and Princess Victoria of Hesse, the granddaughter of Queen Victoria. He became chief of Combined Operations Command (1942), and played a key role in preparations for D-Day. In 1943 he was appointed supreme commander in SE Asia, where he defeated the Japanese offensive into India (1944), and worked with Slim to reconquer Burma (1945). He received the Japanese surrender at Singapore, and in 1947 became last Viceroy of India prior to independence. He was assassinated by Irish terrorists. >> Mountbatten, Louis / Edwina; Slim

Mountbatten, Prince Philip >> Edinburgh, Duke of

Mountcastle, Vernon (Benjamin) (1918–) Neurophysiologist, born in Shelbyville, KY. His research has been concerned with neural mechanisms in sensation and perception, and his book (with G M Edelman) *The Mindful Brain* (1978) has been influential. >> Edelman

Mountevans, Edward (Ratcliffe Garth Russell) Evans, Baron (1881–1957) British naval commander. In World War 1 he fought at Jutland, and scored an outstanding victory over four German destroyers. In 1929 he was appointed rear-admiral commanding the Royal Australian Navy, and served in World War 2 as London Regional Commissioner.

Mountford, Charles Pearcy (1890–1976) Ethnologist, writer, and film director, born in Hallett, South Australia. He led several expeditions into C Australia (1939–60), wrote a series of books about the Aborigines and their culture, and went on to direct feature films on Aboriginal life.

Mountjoy, Charles Blount, Lord >> **Blount, Charles**

Moussorgsky, Modest (Petrovich) [musaw(r)gskee], also spelled **Mussorgsky** or **Musorgsky** (1839–81) Composer, born in Karevo, Russia. His chief works are the opera *Boris Godunov* (1874) and the piano suite *Pictures from an Exhibition* (1874). Rimsky-Korsakov arranged or completed many of his unfinished works. >> Rimsky-Korsakov

Mowatt, Marina / Zenouska >> **Alexandra, Princess**

Moynihan (of Leeds), Berkeley George Andrew Moynihan, Baron (1865–1936) Surgeon, born in Malta. Working in England, he promoted scientific surgery, as seen in *Abdominal Operations* (1905), and formed the Moynihan Chirurgical Club.

Moynihan, Daniel P(atrick) (1927–) Academic and politician, born in Tulsa, OK. He served under Johnson and Nixon, acquiring notoriety as the author of *The Negro Family: the Case for National Action* (1965), and became a Democratic senator in 1976.

Moynihan, Rodrigo (1910–) British painter. Most of his works are of an Impressionist nature, with soft tones, such as his portrait of 'Princess Elizabeth', but he later changed to non-figurative painting.

Mozart, Wolfgang Amadeus [mohtsah(r)t] (1756–91) Composer, born in Salzburg, Austria. A child prodigy, he toured Europe as a pianist when he was six. After some years in Salzburg he settled in Vienna. After his operas *The Marriage of Figaro* (1786) and *Don Giovanni* (1787), he was appointed court composer to Joseph II. Other major operas include *Così fan tutte* (1790) and *The Magic Flute* (1791). He wrote over 600 compositions (indexed by Köchel), including 41 symphonies, a Requiem Mass, and many concertos, string quartets, and sonatas. >> Köchel

Mphahlele, Es'kia [mpahlaylay], popular name of **Ezekiel Mphahlele** (1919–) Writer, born in Pretoria, South Africa. His ghetto childhood bulks large in his autobiographical works *Down Second Avenue* (1959) and *Afrika My Music* (1984). His criticism includes *The African Image* (1962), a pioneering analysis of African literature in its political context.

Mtshali, Oswald Mbuyiseni [mchahlee] (1940–) Poet, born in Vryheid, South Africa. He was one of the wave of 'township poets' whose angry verse in the 1970s broke a decade of black creative silence, seen in *Sounds of a Cowhide Drum* (1971).

Muawiyah I [mwawiya] (c.602–680) First Umayyad caliph (661–80). With the help of Amr ibn al-As he gained control of Egypt, and after the assassination of Ali (661) took over the caliphate, thus founding the Umayyad dynasty. >> Ali; Amr ibn al-As

Mubarak, (Mohammed) Hosni (Said) [mubarak] (1928–) Egyptian president (1981–), born in al-Minufiyah, Egypt. Vice-president under Sadat (1975), as president he continued the same policies, including firm treatment of Muslim extremists, and the peace process with Israel. >> Sadat

Mueller, Erwin (Wilhelm) [müler] (1911–77) Physicist, born in Berlin. In 1936 he invented the field-emission microscope, and in 1951 the field-ion microscope, which gave the first photographs affording a direct view of atoms and some heat-stable molecules.

Mueller, Sir Ferdinand (Jakob Heinrich) von, Baron [müler] (1825–96) Explorer and botanist, born in Rostock, Germany. He emigrated to Australia in 1847, was appointed government botanist for the state of Victoria (1853), and built up a valuable collection of native flora.

Mueller, George E [muhler] (1918–) US engineer. He was in charge of the NASA manned space flight and Moon programme (1963–9), and responsible for the successful landings on the Moon.

Mugabe, Robert (Gabriel) [mugahbay] (1924–) Zimbabwean prime minister (1980–) and president (1987–), born in Kutama, Zimbabwe. In 1963 he co-founded the Zimbabwe African National Union (ZANU), and joined with Nkomo in 1976 to form the Patriotic Front. Formerly a pragmatic Marxist, intending to turn Zimbabwe into a one-party state, multi-party elections were held in 1990, and references to 'Marxism-Leninism' were dropped from the 1991 constitution. >> Nkomo

Muggeridge, Malcolm (1903–90) Journalist and sage, born in London. He was editor of *Punch* (1953–7), and appeared in several television series, such as *Let Me Speak* (1964–5). In 1982 he became a Roman Catholic, and wrote *Chronicle of Wasted Time*.

Muggleton, Lodowick (1609–98) Sectarian, born in London. With his cousin, **John Reeve** (1608–58), he presented himself as the messenger of a new divine dispensation in 1652, and founded the sect of *Muggletonians*.

Muhammad >> **Mohammed**

Muhammad, Elijah, originally **Elijah Poole** (1897–1975) Religious movement leader, born near Sandersville, GA. He fell in with the Nation of Islam movement, and in 1934 proclaimed himself the 'Messenger of Allah'. He made a national movement out of the Black Muslims, arguing for separation of the races. >> Farrakhan; Malcolm X

Muhlenberg, Frederick Augustus (Conrad) [myoolenberg] (1750–1801) US politician and clergyman, born in Trappe, PA. He was appointed to the Continental Congress, became a Federalist member of the House (1789–97), and served as speaker during the first three Congresses.

Muir, Edwin [myoor] (1887–1959) Poet and critic, born in Deerness, Orkney Is. In 1919 he married the novelist **Willa Anderson** (1890–1970), with whom he collaborated in notable translations of Kafka and others. His poems appeared in eight slim volumes, notably *The Voyage* (1946) and *The Labyrinth* (1949).

Muir, Frank [myoor] (1920–) Writer and broadcaster, born in London. He joined Denis Norden to become one of the best-known teams of comedy script-writers (1947–64), contributing to many shows on radio and television. >> Norden, Denis

Muir, Jean (Elizabeth) [myoor] (1933–95) Fashion designer, born in London. In 1966 she established her own company, Jean Muir, designing clothes noted for classic shapes, softness, and fluidity.

Muir, John [myoor] (1838–1914) Naturalist and conservationist, born in Dunbar, Lothian. With **Robert U Johnson** (1853–1937) he campaigned for a national park in California, and in 1890 Congress approved a bill creating the Yosemite National Park. The John Muir Trust to acquire wild land in Britain was established in 1984.

Muirhead, (Litellus) Russell (1896–1976) British editor and traveller. In 1930 he became editor of the 'Blue Guides' to Europe, and also edited the Penguin guides to England and Wales (1938–49).

Mujibur Rahman >> **Rahman, Mujibur**

Mulcaster, Richard [muhlkaster] (c.1530–1611) Educationist, probably born in Cumbria. In 1582 he published his famous *The First Part of the Elementairie*, which included a list of 7000 words in his proposed reformed spellings.

Muldoon, Sir Robert (David) [muhldoon] (1921–92) New Zealand prime minister (1975–84), born in Auckland, New Zealand. He served as minister of finance, and then as deputy prime minister. From 1974 he became Leader of the Opposition, and led the National Party to victory in the 1975 elections.

Müller, Hermann (Joseph) [müler] (1890–1967) Geneticist, born in New York City. He was awarded the 1946 Nobel prize for Physiology or Medicine for his discovery of the use of X-rays to induce genetic mutations.

Müller, Johannes >> **Regiomontanus**

Müller, Karl (Alexander) [müler] (1927–) Physicist,

born in Basel, Switzerland. In 1986 he and Bednorz demonstrated that some mixed-phase oxides would superconduct above 30 K, and by 1987 related materials were found to show the effect up to 90 K. They shared the Nobel Prize for Physics in 1987. >> Bednorz, Georg

Müller, (Friedrich) Max [müler] (1823–1900) Philologist and orientalist, born in Dessau, Germany. He prepared an edition of the *Rigveda* (1849–74), edited the *Sacred Books of the East* (51 vols, 1879–1910), and was an influential comparative philologist at Oxford.

Müller, Paul Hermann [müler] (1899–1965) Chemist, born in Olten, Switzerland. In 1939 he synthesized DDT and demonstrated its insecticidal properties. He received the Nobel Prize for Physiology or Medicine in 1948.

Mulligan, Gerry, popular name of **Gerald Joseph Mulligan** (1927–96) Jazz musician, born in New York City. A technically accomplished musician, he experimented to produce a distinctive sound which proved popular and commercially successful. His motion pictures include *Jazz on a Summer's Day* (1958).

Mulliken, Robert (Sanderson) (1896–1986) Chemist and physicist, born in Newburyport, MA. He was awarded the Nobel Prize for Chemistry in 1966 for his work on chemical bonds and the electronic structure of molecules.

Mulready, William [muhlreedee] (1786–1863) Painter, born in Ennis, Co Clare, Ireland. He specialized in genre paintings, becoming best known for his rural scenes such as 'Interior of an English Cottage' (1828).

Mulroney, (Martin) Brian (1939–) Canadian prime minister (1984–93), born in Baie Comeau, Quebec, Canada. Leader of the Progressive Conservative Party, he won a landslide election victory in 1984. His office was marked by controversy over French-speaking Quebec, and he was forced to resign.

Mumford, Lewis (1895–1990) Sociologist and writer, born in Flushing, NY. He wrote on architecture and urbanization in such works as *The Story of Utopias* (1922) and *The City in History* (1961), stressing the unhappy effects of technology on society.

Munch, Edvard [mungk] (1863–1944) Painter, born in Löten, Norway. He was obsessed by subjects such as death and love, which he illustrated in an Expressionist Symbolic style, using bright colours and a tortuously curved design, as in 'The Scream' (1893).

Münchhausen, (Karl Friedrich Hieronymus), Freiherr von (Baron) [munchhowzen] (1720–97) Soldier, born in Bodenwerder, Germany. Proverbial as the narrator of ridiculously exaggerated exploits, he served in Russian campaigns against the Turks. A collection of stories attributed to him was produced in 1785 by **Rudolf Erich Raspe** (1737–94).

Mungo, St >> Kentigern, St

Munk, Kaj (Harald Leininger) (1898–1944) Playwright, priest, and patriot, born in Maribo, Denmark. He wrote heroic and religious plays that led the Danish dramatic revival in the 1930s. His sermons attracted many to the Resistance, and he was killed by the Nazis in 1944.

Munnings, Sir Alfred (1878–1959) Painter, born in Suffolk. A specialist in the painting of horses and sporting pictures, he was also well known for his forthright criticism of modern art.

Munro, Alice [muhnroh] (1931–) Writer, born in Wingham, Ontario, Canada. Her novel *Lives of Girls and Women* appeared in 1971, and her short-story collections include *Dance of the Happy Shades* (1968) and *The Progress of Love* (1987).

Munro, H(ector) H(ugh) [muhnroh], pseudonym **Saki** (1870–1916) Writer, born in Akyab, Myanmar (formerly, Burma). He is best known for his humorous and macabre short stories, as collected in *Reginald* (1904) and *Beasts and Superbeasts* (1914).

Munthe, Axel (Martin Fredrik) [muntuh] (1857–1949) Physician and writer, born in Oskarshamn, Sweden. He became Swedish court physician, then retired to Capri, where he wrote his best-selling autobiography, *The Story of San Michele* (1929).

Müntzer, Thomas [müntser], also spelled **Münzer** or **Monczer** (c.1489–1525) Religious reformer, born in Stolberg, Germany. In 1525 he was elected pastor of the Anabaptists at Mülhausen, where his communistic ideas aroused the whole country. He joined the Peasants' Revolt (1524–5), and was executed.

Muqaddasi [mukadasee] (945–88) Arab geographer, and pioneer of fieldwork, born in Jerusalem. He described Muslim lands in a geographical compendium published in 985.

Murasaki, Shikibu [murasahkee] (978–c.1031) Lady of the court, and writer, born in Kyoto, Japan. She wrote the world's earliest surviving long novel, also considered the greatest Japanese literary work, *Genji Monogatari* or *The Tale of Genji*.

Murat, Joachim [mürah] (1767–1815) French marshal and king of Naples (1808–15), born in La Bastide-Fortunière, France. He married Napoleon's sister, Caroline, and was proclaimed King of the Two Sicilies. He concluded a treaty with the Austrians, but on Napoleon's return from Elba he recommenced war against them, and was captured and executed. >> Bonaparte, Caroline; Napoleon I

Murchison, Sir Roderick Impey (1792–1871) Geologist, born in Tarradale, Highland. Struck by the resemblance between the Ural Mts and Australian chains, he predicted the discovery of gold in Australia (1844). *Murchison Falls* (Uganda) and *Murchison R* (Australia) are named after him.

Murdoch, Dame (Jean) Iris (1919–) Novelist and philosopher, born in Dublin. Her many novels include *Under the Net* (1954), *The Bell* (1958), and *The Sea, The Sea* (1978, Booker). She has also written plays, philosophical works, and critical studies.

Murdoch, (Keith) Rupert (1931–) Media proprietor, born in Melbourne, Victoria, Australia. He built a substantial newspaper and magazine publishing empire, including the *News of the World*, *The Sun*, *The Times*, and the *New York Post*. He also has major business interests in other media industries.

Murdock, George P(eter) (1897–1985) Cultural anthropologist, born in Meriden, CT. He initiated the cross-cultural survey as an instrument of anthropological generalization. His best-known work is *Social Structure* (1949), in which he focused on family and kinship organization.

Murdock, William (1754–1839) Engineer, and pioneer of coal gas for lighting, born in Old Cumnock, Strathclyde. His distillation of coal gas began at Redruth in 1792, when he illuminated his own home with it. >> Boulton

Murfree, Mary Noailles >> Craddock, Charles Egbert

Murger, (Louis) Henri [mürzhay] (1822–61) Writer, born in Paris. His novel *Scènes de la vie de Bohème* (1845), was the basis of Puccini's opera *La Bohème*, and he also wrote a great deal of poetry. >> Puccini

Murillo, Bartolomé Esteban [mooreelyoh] (1618–82) Painter, born in Seville, Spain. His pictures naturally fall into two groups: scenes from low society, mostly executed early in his life, and religious works, notably of the Immaculate Conception or the Assumption of the Virgin.

Murnau, F W [moornow], pseudonym of **Friedrich Wilhelm Plumpe** (1888–1931) Film director, born in Bielefeld, Germany. His expressive use of light and shade heightened the menace in such macabre works as *Janus-Faced* (trans, 1920) and *Nosferatu* (1922). *Sunrise* (1927) won three of the first-ever Oscars.

Murphy, Eddie, popular name of **Edward Reagan Murphy** (1961–) Comic actor, born in New York City. His films include *Trading Places* (1983), *Beverly Hills Cop* (1984; sequel, 1987), *Coming to America* (1988), and *Big Baby* (1991). He made his directorial debut with *Harlem Nights* (1989).

Murphy, Graeme (1951–) Ballet dancer, choreographer, and ballet director, born in Melbourne, Victoria, Australia. As director of the Sydney Dance Company (1976), he created dances which feature a sexy, eclectic range of subjects and styles, all rooted in the classical idiom, such as *Poppy* (1978).

Murphy, Thomas Bernard (1935–) Playwright, born in Tuam, Co Galway, Ireland. His major works include *The Sanctuary Lamp* (1975), *The Blue Macushla* (1980), and *The Gigli Concert* (1983).

Murphy, William P(arry) (1892–1987) Haematologist, born in Stoughton, WI. In conjunction with Minot, he shared the 1934 Nobel Prize for Physiology or Medicine for devising dietary liver and liver extract therapy for patients with pernicious anaemia. >> Minot, George

Murrant, Harry >> **Morant, Harry**

Murray, (George) Gilbert (Aimé) (1866–1957) Classical scholar and writer, born in Sydney, New South Wales, Australia. The leading Greek scholar of his time, he worked as a Classical historian and as a translator of Greek plays, including *Medea* and *Electra*.

Murray, Sir James (Augustus Henry) (1837–1915) Philologist and lexicographer, born in Denholm, Borders, Scotland. His life's work was the editing of the *New English Dictionary* (later the *Oxford English Dictionary*), begun in 1879, completing about half the work himself.

Murray, Joseph E(dward) (1919–) Surgeon, born in Milford, MA. He performed the first human kidney transplant between identical twins in 1954, and the first transplant from an unrelated donor in 1962. He shared the Nobel Prize for Physiology or Medicine in 1990.

Murray, Keith (Bay Pearce) (1892–1991) Architect and designer, born in Auckland, New Zealand. He began designing glass in England in the 1930s, moving to silver and then to ceramics, principally for Wedgwood.

Murray, Len, popular name of **Baron Lionel Murray of Telford** (1922–) Trade union leader, born in Hadley, Shropshire. He became general secretary of the Trades Union Congress (1973–84), and played a major role in the 'social contract' partnership between the TUC and the Labour governments of the 1970s.

Murray, Les(lie Allen) (1938–) Poet, born in Nabiac, New South Wales, Australia. His poetry is revered for its evocation of rural life, as seen in *The Ilex Tree* (1965) and *Dog Fox Field* (1990).

Murray, Lindley (1745–1826) Grammarian, born in Swatara Creek, PA. His *English Grammar* (1795) was for long the standard text, and was followed by *English Exercises* and the *English Reader*.

Murray, Matthew (1765–1826) Inventor and mechanical engineer, born near Newcastle upon Tyne, Tyne and Wear. He founded an engineering works in 1795, manufacturing textile machinery and steam engines, and made improvements to Watt's steam engine. >> Watt, James

Murray, William Staite (1881–1962) British potter. He taught pottery first as a fine art medium, attributing to it the same importance as is usually given to painting and sculpture.

Murrow, Ed(ward Egbert) R(oscoe) (1908–65) Journalist and broadcaster, born in Greensboro, NC. Joining CBS in 1935, he became a compassionate conveyor of the wartime spirit in Britain. In postwar America he produced and presented hard-hitting current affairs programmes.

Murry, John Middleton (1889–1957) Writer and critic, born in London. His poetry, essays, and criticism had a strong influence on the young intellectuals of the 1920s.

Major works include critical studies of *D H Lawrence* (1931) and *Swift* (1954). He was the husband of Katherine Mansfield. >> Mansfield, Katherine

Musaeus [moozeeus] (5th–6th-c) Greek poet. He is chiefly known for preserving the legend of Hero and Leander in the poem of the same name.

Museveni, Yoweri Kaguta [moosevaynee] (1945–) Soldier and president of Uganda (1986–). He became head of the Front for National Salvation against Idi Amin (1971–9), and was responsible for the reconstruction of the country after its civil war.

Musgrave, Thea (1928–) Composer, born in Edinburgh. Her music includes the dramatic choral work *The Five Ages of Man* (1963), the ballet, *Beauty and the Beast* (1968), and the chamber opera *The Voice of Ariadne* (1972–3).

Mushet, David (1772–1847) Iron-master, born in Dalkeith, Lothian. He discovered black band ironstone, patented a process for making cast steel from wrought iron, and discovered the beneficial effects of adding manganese to iron and steel. >> Mushet, Robert Forester

Mushet, Robert Forester (1811–91) Metallurgist, born in Coleford, Gloucestershire, the son of David Mushet. His discovery, patented in 1856, of the beneficial effects of adding ferro-manganese to blown steel, enabled the Bessemer steel-making process to become a commercial success. >> Bessemer; Mushet, David

Musial, Stan(ley Frank) [myoozial], nickname **Stan the Man** (1920–) Baseball player, born in Donora, PA. He spent his entire career with the St Louis Cardinals (1941–62), topping the National League's batting list seven times (1943–57), and retiring with a then National League record of 3630 hits.

Musil, Robert (Elder von) [moosil] (1880–1942) Novelist, born in Klagenfurt, Austria. His unfinished masterpiece, *The Man Without Qualities* (1930–42, trans 1969), depicting a society on the brink of an abyss, is widely acknowledged as one of the great novels of the century.

Muskie, Edmund S(ixtus) (1914–) US lawyer and statesman, born in Rumford, ME. Secretary of state under Carter, he was Democratic candidate for the vice-presidency in 1968. >> Carter, Jimmy

Musorgski, Modest >> **Moussorgsky, Modest**

Muspratt, James >> **Gamble, Josias Christopher**

Musset, (Louis Charles) Alfred de [müsay] (1810–57) Poet and playwright, born in Paris. In 1833 he met George Sand, and their love affair, according to his autobiographical poem *The Confession of a Child of the Age* (trans, 1835), coloured much of his work after that date. >> Sand

Mussolini, Benito (Amilcare Andrea), known as **il Duce** ('the Leader') (1883–1945) Prime minister of Italy (1922–43) and dictator, born in Predappio, Romagna. In 1919 he helped found the *Fasci di Combattimento* as a revolutionary force, his success symbolized by the March on Rome (1922). His rule saw the introduction of a totalitarian system, and the formation of the Axis with Germany. His declaration of war on Britain and France was followed by defeat in Africa and the Balkans, and after the Allied invasion of Sicily (1943) he was overthrown and arrested (1943). Rescued by German paratroopers, he was placed in charge of the puppet Italian Social Republic, but in 1945 was captured by the Italian Resistance and shot.

Mussorgsky, Modest >> **Moussorgsky, Modest**

Mutsuhito [mutsuheetoh]], **Meiji Tenno** (1852–1912) Emperor of Japan (1867–1912) who became the symbol of Japan's modernization, born in Kyoto, Japan. His long reign saw the rapid political and military westernization of Japan.

Muybridge, Eadweard [moybrij], originally **Edward James Muggeridge** (1830–1904) Photographer and inventor, born in Kingston-on-Thames, Surrey. He emigrated to California in 1852, and became chief photographer to the

US government. In 1880 he devised the zoopraxiscope to show his picture sequences of movements, achieving a rudimentary kind of cinematography in his Zoopraxographical Hall in Chicago (1893), hailed as the world's first motion picture theatre.

Muzorewa, Abel (Tendekayi) [muzoraywa] (1925–) Zimbabwean politician and clergyman, born in Umtali, South Africa. In 1971 he became president of the African National Council, and later prime minister of 'Zimbabwe Rhodesia' (1979). After independence his party was defeated by the Patriotic Front of Mugabe and Nkomo. >> Mugabe; Nkomo

Mwinyi, (Ndugu) Ali Hassan [mweenyee] (1925–) Tanzanian president (1985–), born in Zanzibar. He held a variety of ministerial and ambassadorial posts until, in 1985, he succeeded Nyerere as president of the new republic. >> Nyerere

Myers, F(rederic) W(illiam) H(enry) (1843–1901) Poet and essayist, born in Keswick, Cumbria. A founder of the Society for Psychical Research (1882), he wrote *Human Personality and its Survival of Bodily Death* (1903).

Myles na Gopaleen >> **O'Brien, Flann**

Mylonas, George [miylohnas] (1898–1988) Archaeologist, born in Smyrna, Greece. His main excavation was at the Outer Grave Circle at Mycenae, where he also built a new museum.

Myrdal, Alva [merdal], *née* **Reimer** (1902–86) Sociologist, Swedish stateswoman, and peace reformer, born in Uppsala, Sweden. She acted as Swedish representative on the UN Disarmament Committee (1962–73), and was prominent in the international peace movement, sharing the Nobel Peace Prize in 1982. She was married to Gunnar Myrdal. >> Myrdal, Gunnar

Myrdal, (Karl) Gunnar [merdal] (1898–1987) Economist, Swedish statesman, and international civil servant, born in Gustafs Dalecarlia, Sweden. He was awarded the Nobel Prize for Economics in 1974, principally for his work on the critical application of economic theory to Third World countries. >> Myrdal, Alva

Myron [miyron] (fl.c.480–440 BC) Sculptor, born in Eleutherae, Greece. He worked in bronze, and is best known for his studies of athletes in action, such as the celebrated 'Discobolos' and 'Marsyas'.

N

Nabokov, Vladimir [nabohkof] (1899–1977) Writer, born in St Petersburg, Russia. He emigrated to the USA where he published many short stories and novels, including the controversial *Lolita* (1958; filmed 1962), *Pale Fire* (1962), and a lyrical autobiography *Speak Memory* (1967). Among 20th-c novelists he is highly regarded for his linguistic versatility and intellectual range.

Nadar [nadah(r)], pseudonym of **Gaspard Félix Tournachon** (1820–1910) Writer, artist, and photographer, born in Paris. In 1853 he opened a photographic studio where he produced natural studies of literary and artistic contemporaries, in 1886 presenting the first 'photo-interview'.

Nadel, S(iegfried) F(rederick) [nahdl] (1903–56) Social anthropologist, born in Vienna. Known for his fieldwork in Africa in the 1930s, his major theoretical works include *The Foundations of Social Anthropology* (1951) and *The Theory of Social Structure* (1957).

Nadelman, Elie [naydlman] (1882–1946) Sculptor, born in Warsaw. His early work reveals a simplification close to Cubism. In 1914 he moved to the USA, where he produced painted figure sculptures in wood, and from the 1930s worked in ceramics.

Nader, Ralph [nayder] (1934–) Lawyer and consumer activist, born in Winsted, CT. His best-seller about the automobile industry, *Unsafe at Any Speed* (1965), led to the passage of improved car safety regulations in 1966.

Nadir Shah, Mohammed (c.1880–1933) King of Afghanistan (1929–33). After a period in exile, he seized the throne, and embarked on a programme of economic and social reforms which alienated the Muslim clergy. He was assassinated, and succeeded by his son, Mohammed Zahir Shah. >> Zahir Shah

Naevius, Gnaeus [neevius] (c.264–c.194 BC) Poet and playwright, probably born in Campania. He satirized the Roman nobles in his plays, and was compelled to leave Rome. Fragments of an epic on the Punic War are extant.

Nagano, Osami [nagahnoh] (1880–1947) Admiral of the Japanese navy, born in Kochi, Japan. As chief of naval general staff (1941–4) he planned and ordered the attack on Pearl Harbor in 1941. He died while on trial for war crimes.

Nagarjuna [nagah(r)juna] (c.150–c.250) Indian Buddhist monk-philosopher. He was the founder of the Madhyamika or Middle Path school of Buddhism.

Nagel, Ernest [naygl] (1901–85) Philosopher of science, born in Nové Město, Czech Republic. His best-known works are *An Introduction to Logic and Scientific Method* (1934, with M R Cohen), *Logic without Metaphysics* (1957), and *The Structure of Science* (1961).

Nagle, Kelvin [naygl] (1920–) Golfer, born in Sydney, New South Wales, Australia. He won the Australian Open in 1959 and the British Open in 1960. A formidable player into his 50s, he took the World Senior title in 1971.

Naguib, Mohammed [nageeb] (1901–84) Egyptian general and president (1952–4), born in Khartoum. In 1952 he carried out a coup in Cairo which banished Farouk I, took office as prime minister, abolished the monarchy, and became president. He was deposed in 1954 and succeeded by Nasser. >> Farouk I; Nasser

Nagy, Imre [noj, imray] (1895–1958) Hungarian prime minister (1953–5), born in Kaposvar, Hungary. He introduced milder political control, but when Soviet forces began to put down the 1956 revolution, he was displaced by the Soviet puppet, János Kádár, and executed. >> Kádár

Nahum [nayhuhm] (7th-c BC) Old Testament minor proph-

et. An Israelite or Judaean, he prophesied the destruction of Nineveh by the Medes in 612 BC.

Nahyan, Zayed ibn Sultan al-Shaykh [nayahn] (?1918–) President of the United Arab Emirates (1971–), raised as a desert nomad. He was governor of Abu Dhabi, one of the Trucial States, and when the States became the United Arab Emirates (1971) he was elected president of its Supreme Council.

Naidoo, Jay (Jayaseelan) [niydoo] (1954–) South African labour leader, born in Durban, South Africa. In 1985 he was elected general-secretary of the newly founded Congress of South African Trade Unions, and from 1990 was active in the negotiations for a new political dispensation in South Africa.

Naidu, Sarojini [niydoo], née **Chattopadhyay** (1879–1949) Feminist, poet, and activist, born in Hyderabad, India. She published three volumes of lyric verse, *The Golden Threshold* (1905), *The Bird of Time* (1912), and *The Broken Wing* (1915), and was the first Indian woman to be president of the Indian National Congress (1925).

Nain, Antoine le >> **le Nain, Antoine**

Naipaul, Sir V(idiadhar) S(urajprasad) [niypawl] (1932–) Novelist, born in Chaguanas, Trinidad. He became known with *A House for Mr Biswas* (1961), a satire spanning three Trinidadian generations. Other works include *In a Free State* (1971, Booker) and *A Bend in the River* (1979), and he has also written several travel books.

Naismith, James A [naysmith] (1861–1939) Physical educationist, born in Almonte, Ontario, Canada. He originated the game of basketball in 1891, which acquired the status of an Olympic sport in 1936.

Najibullah, Mohammad [najibula] (1947–) Afghan Communist leader and president (1987–92), born in Kabul. He promulgated a non-Marxist constitution enshrining a multi-party system, and a dominant position for Islam, but his regime collapsed after the withdrawal of Soviet military forces (1989) and opposition from Mujaheddin guerrillas.

Nakasone, Yasuhiro [nakasohnay] (1918–) Japanese prime minister (1982–7), born in Takasaki, Japan. He supported the renewal of the US-Japan Security Treaty, and maintained close relations with President Reagan. >> Reagan

Namath, Joe, popular name of **Joseph William Namath**, nickname **Broadway Joe** (1943–) Player of American football, born in Beaver Falls, PA. He joined the New York Jets in 1965, and became a leading quarterback. His lifestyle outside football attracted much publicity, hence his nickname.

Namatjira, Albert [namatjeera] (1902–59) Artist, born in Hermannsberg Lutheran mission, near Alice Springs, Northern Territory, Australia. A member of the Aranda Aboriginal people, he achieved fame for his European-influenced watercolour landscapes.

Namier, Sir Lewis (Bernstein) [naymyer], originally **Ludwik Bernstein Niemirowski** (1888–1960) Historian, born near Warsaw. Professor of modern history at Manchester (1931–52), he created a school of history in which the emphasis was on the detailed analysis of events and institutions, particularly parliamentary elections.

Nanak [nanak], known as **Guru Nanak** (1469–1539) Religious leader, the founder of Sikhism, born near Lahore, India. A Hindu by birth and belief, he travelled to Hindu and Muslim centres in search of spiritual truth. His doctrine, set out later in the *Adi-Granth*, sought a fusion of Brahmanism and Islam.

Nana Sahib [**na**na **sah**eeb], originally **Brahmin Dundhu Panth** (c.1820–c.59) Prominent rebel of the Indian Mutiny. At the outbreak of the Indian Mutiny (1857), he became the leader of the Sepoys in Cawnpore, and organized the massacre of the British residents.

Nanni, di Banco (c.1380–1421) Sculptor, one of the most important artists of the early Renaissance, born in Florence, Italy. His chief later work was the relief of the 'Assumption of the Virgin' above the Porta della Mandorla, Florence Cathedral (1414–21).

Nansen, Fridtjof [**frit**yof] (1861–1930) Explorer, born near Oslo, Norway. He planned to reach the North Pole by letting his ship get frozen into the ice N of Siberia and drift towards Greenland. He reached 84°4', and continued on foot, achieving 86°14', the highest latitude then attained (1895). In 1922 he was awarded the Nobel Peace Prize for Russian relief work.

Naomi [**nay**ohmee] >> **Ruth**

Napier, Sir Charles [**nayp**yer] (1786–1860) British naval commander, born near Falkirk, Central, Scotland. He commanded the Baltic Fleet in the Crimean War (1854), but refused to attack Kronstadt and was recalled in disgrace. He later sat in parliament, and worked to reform the naval administration.

Napier, Sir Charles James [**nayp**yer] (1782–1853) British soldier, the conqueror of Sind (now part of Pakistan), born in London. In 1841 he was sent to India to command in the war with Sind, and at the Battle of Meeanee (1843) broke the power of the amirs.

Napier, John [**nayp**yer] (1550–1617) Mathematician, born at Merchiston Castle, Edinburgh. He invented logarithms and also devised a calculating machine, using a set of rods called *Napier's bones*.

Napier (of Magdala), Robert (Cornelius) Napier, 1st Baron [**nayp**yer] (1810–90) British field marshal, born in Colombo, Sri Lanka (formerly Ceylon). He distinguished himself at the siege of Lucknow (1857), later becoming commander-in-chief in India (1870).

Napoleon I, Fr **Napoléon Bonaparte**, Ital **Napoleone Buonaparte** (1769–1821) French general and emperor (1804–15), born in Ajaccio, Corsica. He commanded the artillery at the siege of Toulon (1793), and in 1796 married Joséphine, widow of the Vicomte de Beauharnais. In the Revolutionary Wars he made gains in Italy, but his fleet was destroyed at the Battle of the Nile (1799). After the *coup d'état* of 18th Brumaire (1799) he assumed dictatorial power as First Consul, routing the Austrians at Marengo (1800), and consolidated French domination by the Peace of Amiens (1802). He assumed the title of emperor in 1804. War with England was renewed, and extended to Russia and Austria. Forced by England's naval supremacy at Trafalgar (1805) to abandon the notion of invasion, he defeated Austria, Russia, and Prussia (1805–7), becoming the arbiter of Europe. He sent armies into Portugal and Spain, which resulted in the unsuccessful Peninsular War (1808–14). In 1809 he divorced the childless Joséphine, and married Marie Louise of Austria, a son being born in 1811. He invaded Russia, but was forced to retreat (1812), and abdicated after defeat at Leipzig. He regained power for a time (the Hundred Days), but after defeat at Waterloo (1815), he again abdicated, and was banished to St Helena. >> Bonaparte, Jérôme / Joseph / Louis; Joséphine

Napoleon II, in full **François Charles Joseph Bonaparte** (1811–32) Son of Napoleon I by the Archduchess Marie Louise, born in Paris. Styled King of Rome at his birth, after his father's abdication he was brought up in Austria, though allowed no active political role. >> Marie Louise; Napoleon I

Napoleon III, until 1852 **Louis Napoleon**, originally **Charles Louis Napoleon Bonaparte** (1808–73) President of the Second French Republic (1850–2) and emperor of the French (1852–70), born in Paris, the third son of Louis Bonaparte and Hortense Beauharnais. He made abortive attempts on the French throne (1836, 1840) and was imprisoned, but after the 1848 Revolution was elected president, and assumed the title of emperor. He declared war on Prussia in 1870, but was defeated and went into exile. >> Bonaparte, Louis; Napoleon II

Narayan, R(asipuram) K(irshnaswamy) [na**ri**yan] (1906–) Writer, born in Madras, India. One of the most highly acclaimed Indian writers of his generation, his novels include *Swami and Friends* (1935), *Mr Sampath* (1949), *The Guide* (1958), and *The World of Nagaraj* (1990), and he has also published stories, travel books, books for children, and essays.

Narses [**nah(r)**seez] (c.478–573) Persian statesman and general, born in Armenia. Serving under Emperor Justinian, he defeated the Ostrogoths, took possession of Rome, and extinguished Gothic power in Italy. >> Justinian

Nash, John (1752–1835) Architect, born in London. He designed Regent's Park (1811–25) and Marble Arch, laid out Trafalgar Square and St James's Park, and recreated Buckingham Palace from old Buckingham House.

Nash, (Frederic) Ogden (1902–71) Humorous writer, born in Rye, NY. His subject-matter was the everyday life of middle-class America, which he described in a witty and acute manner taking outrageous rhyming liberties with the English language, frequently published in the *New Yorker*. His collections include *Hard Lines* (1931).

Nash, Paul (1899–1946) Painter, born in London. A renowned landscape painter, he was also a war artist (in both World Wars), producing such works as 'Battle of Britain' and 'Totes Meer' (1940–1).

Nash, Richard, nickname **Beau Nash** (1674–1762) Dandy, born in Swansea, West Glamorgan. In 1704 he became master of ceremonies at Bath, conducting the entertainments with great splendour, and transforming Bath into a leading fashionable centre.

Nash, Sir Walter (1882–1968) New Zealand prime minister (1957–60), born in Kidderminster, Worcester. Serving on the national executive of the New Zealand Labour Party (1919–60), he encouraged a moderate reform programme.

Nashe or **Nash, Thomas** (1567–1601) Playwright and satirist, born in Lowestoft, Suffolk. A master of the vituperative pamphlet, he attacked the Puritans in the play *Pierce Penilesse* (1592), and wrote several satirical works, such as the masque, *Summer's Last Will and Testament* (1592).

Nasier, Alcofribas >> **Rabelais, François**

Nasmyth, James [**nay**smith] (1808–90) Engineer, born in Edinburgh. He devised and patented a steam hammer to assist with forging work (1842), and it became a major tool in the Industrial Revolution.

Nasser, Gamal Abdel (1918–70) Egyptian prime minister (1954–6) and president (1956–70), born in Alexandria. Dissatisfied with the corruption of the Farouk regime, he was involved in the military coup of 1952. He nationalized the Suez Canal, which prompted Britain and France to seek his forcible overthrow, and created a federation with Syria as the United Arab Republic (1958–61). He resigned after the six-day Arab–Israeli War (1967), but was persuaded to stay on, and died in office. >> Farouk I

Nast, Condé (Montrose) (1873–1942) Publisher, born in New York City. After transforming *Vogue* into America's premier fashion magazine, he acquired several other high-class magazines including *Vanity Fair* and *House and Garden*.

Nast, Thomas (1840–1902) Cartoonist, born in Landau, Germany. In the USA from childhood, he joined *Harper's Weekly* (1861–6), where he defined the genre of the political cartoon.

Nathan, Isaac [**nay**than] (1790–1864) Composer and music teacher, born in Canterbury, Kent. He moved to Australia in 1841, where he wrote *Australia the Wide and Free* (1842) and the first opera to be composed and performed in Australia, *Don John of Austria* (1847).

Nathanael [na**than**ial], (Heb 'God has given') (fl.1st-c) New Testament character, who appears only in *John* (1.45–51). He is said to have been brought to Jesus by Philip, and is one of the first to confess Jesus as 'Son of God, King of Israel'. >> Jesus Christ; Philip, St

Nathans, Daniel [**nay**thanz] (1928–) Microbiologist, born in Wilmington, DE. He pioneered research on the use of restriction enzymes which had been isolated by Hamilton Smith to fragment DNA molecules, and they shared the Nobel Prize for Physiology or Medicine in 1978. >> Smith, Hamilton

Nation, Carry (Amelia), *née* **Moore** (1846–1911) Temperance agitator, born in Garrard Co, KY. A large, powerful woman, she went on hymn-singing, saloon-smashing expeditions with a hatchet in many US cities, attacking what she considered to be illegal drinking places.

Natta, Giulio (1903–79) Chemist, born in Imperia, Italy. He carried out research on polymers which led to important commercial developments in plastics and other industrial chemicals, and he shared the Nobel Prize for Chemistry in 1963. >> Ziegler

Nattier, Jean Marc [natyay] (1685–1766) Artist, born in Paris. He painted historical pictures and portraits, such as Peter the Great and Catherine II of Russia, and developed the fashionable stereotyped style of court portraiture, now labelled *le portrait Nattier*, for the court of Louis XV.

Nauman, Bruce (1941–) Sculptor, born in Fort Wayne, IN. In the 1960s he became a leading exponent of Conceptual Art, using neon lights and holograms in addition to producing minimalist sculptures from more conventional materials.

Navier, Claude (Louis Marie Henri) [navyay] (1785–1836) Civil engineer, born in Dijon, France. He is mostly remembered for the *Navier–Stokes equation* (with George Stokes) describing the mechanics of a viscous fluid, relating changes in the velocity of the fluid to the pressure and viscous forces acting on it. >> Stokes

Navratilova, Martina [navrati**lohv**a] (1956–) Tennis player, born in Prague. The winner of a record nine singles titles at Wimbledon (1978–9, 1982–7, 1990), she won 167 singles titles (including 18 Grand Slam events) and 165 doubles titles with her partner Pam Shriver, becoming the most prolific winner in women's tennis.

Naylor, Eliot >> Frankau, Pamela

Nazianzus, Gregory of >> Gregory of Nazianzus

Nazimova, Alla [na**zim**ohva], originally **Alla Leventon** (1879–1945) Actress, born in Yalta, Ukraine. A highly popular dramatic actress, she specialized in the plays of Ibsen, Turgenev, Chekhov, and O'Neill. Her films included *Camille* and *A Doll's House*.

Nazor, Vladimir [na**saw**(r)] (1876–1949) Croatian poet, born in Postire on the island of Brač. His works include *Slav Legends* (1900), *Lirika* (1910), and *Carmen Vitae*.

Nazrul Islam, Kazi >> Islam, Kazi Nazrul

Neagle, Dame Anna, originally **Marjorie Robertson** (1904–86) Actress, born in London. She starred in several historical film dramas, such as *Victoria, the Great* (1937), *Odette* (1950), and *The Lady With the Lamp* (1951), and was also known for her role in musicals.

Neale, John Mason (1818–66) Hymnologist, born in London. Among his best-known pieces are 'Jerusalem the golden' and 'O happy band of pilgrims'.

Nearchus [neeah(r)kus] (4th-c BC) Macedonian general, originally from Crete. In 329 he joined Alexander the Great and took part in the Indian campaigns. >> Alexander the Great

Nebuchadnezzar II [nebookad**ne**zer], also spelled **Nebuchadrezzar** (c.630–562 BC) King of Babylon (605–562 BC). During his 43-year reign he rebuilt Babylon as a supreme nation, and in 597 captured Jerusalem, later deporting the Jews to Babylonia (586 BC).

Necker, Jacques (1732–1804) French statesman, born in Geneva, Switzerland. As director-general of finances, he attempted reforms, but was dismissed (1781). Recalled in 1788, he summoned the States General, but his proposals for change aroused royal opposition, and he was again dismissed.

Nedreaas, Torborg [**ned**rias] (1906–) Novelist, born in Bergen, Norway. Her books highlight social life and class struggle in Norwegian urban society, notably (trans titles) *Music from a Blue Well* (1960) and *At the Next New Moon* (1971).

Needham, Joseph [**need**am] (1900–95) Historian of science, born in London. His interest in the Chinese tradition of science, technology, and medicine, led to his major work, the multi-volume series *Science and Civilisation in China* (from 1956).

Néel, Louis Eugène Félix [nayel] (1904–) Physicist, born in Lyon, France. His research on magnetism in solids, led to the development of 'memories' in computers. He shared the Nobel Prize for Physics in 1970.

Neer, Aernout or **Aert van der** (1603/4–77) Painter, born in Amsterdam. He specialized in moonlit canal and river scenes. Two of his sons became artists: **Eglon** (1634–1703) and **Jan** (1638–65).

Nefertiti [nefer**tee**tee] (14th-c BC) Egyptian queen, the consort of Akhenaton, by whom she had six children. She is immortalized in the beautiful sculptured head found at Amarna in 1912. >> Akhenaton

Negus, Arthur (George) [**nay**guhs] (1903–85) Broadcaster and antiques expert, born in Reading, Berkshire. A regular panel member on the television series *Going for a Song* (1966–76), he became a popular broadcaster in such series as *The Antiques Roadshow* (1982–3).

Nehemiah [nehe**miy**a] (5th-c BC) Old Testament prophet. He was cupbearer to Artaxerxes I, who in 444 BC made him Governor of Judaea. He had the walls of Jerusalem rebuilt, and carried out many reforms. >> Artaxerxes I

Nehru, Jawaharlal [**nair**oo], known as **Pandit** ('Teacher') **Nehru** (1889–1964) India's first prime minister (1947–64), born in Allahabad, India, the son of Motilal Nehru. He introduced industrialization, reorganized the states on a linguistic basis, and brought the dispute with Pakistan over Kashmir to a peaceful solution. >> Nehru, Motilal

Nehru, Motilal [**nair**oo] (1861–1931) Nationalist leader of India, lawyer, and journalist, born in Delhi, the father of Jawaharlal Nehru. He became a follower of Gandhi (1919), founded the *Independent* of Allahabad, and became the first president of the reconstructed Indian National Congress. >> Gandhi; Nehru, Jawaharlal

Neill, A(lexander) S(utherland) (1883–1973) Educationist and writer, born in Kingsmuir, Fife. The most radical of British progressive schoolmasters, he founded the experimental Summerhill School in Leiston, Suffolk, in 1927.

Neill, Sam, originally **Nigel Neill** (1948–) Actor, born in Northern Ireland. He has starred in many Australian and international films, including *The Hunt for Red October* (1990) and *The Piano* (1993).

Neilson, Donald, originally **Donald Nappey** (1936–) Convicted murderer and kidnapper, born near Bradford, West Yorkshire. Because of the black hood he wore as a disguise, he became known as 'the Black Panther'. He received life sentences for four murders committed in 1974.

Neiman, LeRoy [**nee**man, **lee**roy] (1927–) Illustrator, born in St. Paul, MN. He specialized as a sports artist, and in 1972 was named the official artist for the Olympic Games.

Neisser, Ulric (Richard Gustav) [**niy**ser] (1928–) Psychologist, born in Kiel, Germany. The modern growth of cognitive psychology was greatly boosted by the publication of his book *Cognitive Psychology* (1967).

Nelson, (John) Byron, Jr (1912–) Golfer, born in Fort Worth, TX. He won the US Open (1939), the US Masters (1937, 1942), and a record 18 tournaments on the US Professional Golfers Association (PGA) tour in 1945.

Nelson, George (1907–86) Designer, architect, and writer, born in Hartford, CT. Influenced by the 'Modern Movement', his best known design work is his range of wall storage furniture (1946) for the manufacturer Herman Miller, whose design policy he directed.

Nelson, Horatio (1758–1805) British admiral, born in Burnham Thorpe, Norfolk. In 1794 while commanding a naval brigade he lost the sight of his right eye, and later had his right arm amputated. In 1798 he followed the French fleet to Egypt, destroying it at Aboukir Bay. On his return to Naples, he fell in love with Emma, Lady Hamilton, and began a liaison with her which lasted until his death. In 1805 he gained his greatest victory, against the combined French and Spanish fleet at Trafalgar, but was mortally wounded on his flagship, HMS *Victory*. >> Hamilton, Emma

Nelson, Thomas (1780–1861) Publisher, born in Edinburgh. He founded his publishing company in 1798. His son **William** (1816–87) joined the business in 1835, and did much to improve the city of Edinburgh. Another son, **Thomas** (1822–92), is credited with the invention of a rotary press (1850).

Nemerov, Howard (Stanley) [nemerof] (1920–91) Poet, born in New York City. Named poet laureate by the Library of Congress (1988), he is known for his literary prose works and blank verse, as in *Collected Poems* (1977).

Nemirovich-Danchenko, Vladimir (Ivanovich) [nemirohvich danchengkoh] (1858–1943) Theatre director, writer, and teacher, born in Ozurgety, Russia. Co-founder with Stanislavsky of the Moscow Art Theatre, he became sole director in 1938. >> Stanislavsky

Nenni, Pietro [nenee] (1891–1980) Italian statesman, born in Faenza, Italy. In 1963 he became deputy prime minister in the coalition government with Social Democrats and Socialists, uniting the two groups as the United Socialist Party (1966–8). He was later foreign minister in a new coalition (1968–9).

Nennius (fl.769) Writer, from Wales. He is reputedly the author of the early Latin compilation known as the *Historia Britonum*, giving a mythical version of early British history.

Neot, St [neeot] (?–877), feast day 31 July. Anglo-Saxon monk. According to mediaeval legends, he was a monk of Glastonbury who became a hermit. His relics are thought to have been taken to St Neots in Cambridgeshire.

Nepomuk, St John of >> **John of Nepomuk, St**

Nepos, Cornelius [neepos] (c.99–25 BC) Roman historian, a native of Pavia or Hostilia. He wrote a lost universal history in three books (*Chronica*), and a series of *Lives of Famous Men*, of which only 25 survive.

Neri, St Philip [nairee] (1515–95), feast day 26 May. Mystic, born in Florence, Italy. In 1551 he became a priest, and gathered around him a following of disciples which became the Congregation of the Oratory (1564). He was canonized in 1622.

Nernst, Walther Hermann (1864–1941) Physical chemist, born in Briesen, Germany. He proposed the heat theorem (the third law of thermodynamics) in 1906, and the atom chain-reaction theory in photochemistry. He was awarded the Nobel Prize for Chemistry in 1920.

Nero [neeroh], in full **Nero Claudius Caesar**, originally **Lucius Domitius Ahenobarbus** (37–68) Emperor of Rome (54–68), the son of Gnaeus Domitius Ahenobarbus and the younger Agrippina, daughter of Germanicus. His mother engineered his adoption by the Emperor Claudius, her fourth husband. After her murder (59), Nero neglected affairs of state, corrup-

tion set in, and he was blamed for the Great Fire of Rome (64). He was toppled from power by the army, and forced to commit suicide. >> Agrippina (the Younger); Claudius

Neruda, Pablo (Neftali Reyes) [nerootha] (1904–73) Poet and diplomat, born in Parral, Chile. He made his name with *Twenty Love Poems and a Song of Despair* (trans, 1924). Other works include *Residence on Earth* (trans, 1925–31) and *General Song* (trans, 1950). He was awarded the Nobel Prize for Literature in 1971.

Nerva, Marcus Cocceius [nairva] (c.32–98) Emperor of Rome (96–98), elected by the Senate after the assassination of Domitianus. One of the 'five good emperors', he rejected terrorism and introduced liberal reforms.

Nervi, Pier Luigi [nairvee] (1891–1979) Architect and engineer, born in Sondrio, Italy. His designs include the two Olympic stadiums in Rome (1960) and San Francisco cathedral (1970).

Nesbit, E(dith), maiden name and pseudonym of **Mrs Hubert Bland** (1858–1924) Writer, born in London. She is best remembered for her children's stories, notably *The Railway Children* (1906; filmed 1970), but she also wrote novels and ghost stories.

Nesselrode, Karl (Robert) Vasilyevich, Graf (Count) [neselrohduh] (1780–1862) Russian statesman, born in Lisbon, the son of the Russian ambassador. He became foreign minister (1822), and dominated Russian foreign policy for 30 years, his Balkan policy contributing to the outbreak of the Crimean War (1853).

Nestorius [nestawrius] (?–c.451) Ecclesiastic, a native of Germanicia in N Syria. Eminent for his zeal, ascetic life, and eloquence, he was selected as patriarch of Constantinople (428). He defended the idea that the Virgin Mary could not be truly called the Mother of God, and was deposed in 431.

Netaji >> **Bose, Subhas Chandra**

Neumann, St John (Nepomucene) [noyman] (1811–60), feast day 5 January. Catholic prelate and saint, born in Prachatice, Czech Republic (formerly Bohemia). As Bishop of Philadelphia (from 1852), he was well known as a preacher, retreat master, and champion of the poor. He was canonized in 1977.

Neumann, (Johann) Balthasar [noyman] (1687–1753) Architect, born in Eger, Germany. Many outstanding examples of the Baroque style were designed by him, notably the Würzburg Palace and Schloss Bruchsal.

Neumann, John Von [noyman] >> **Von Neumann, John**

Neumeier, John [noymayer] (1942–) Ballet dancer, choreographer, and artistic director, born in Milwaukee, WI. Leader of the Hamburg Ballet (since 1973), he is known for his acrobatically expressive contemporary ballets.

Neurath, Konstantin, Freiherr von (Baron) [noyraht] (1873–1956) German statesman, born in Klein-Glattbach, Germany. He was Hitler's foreign minister (1933–8), and the Reich protector of Bohemia and Moravia (1939–43). At the Nuremberg trial he was imprisoned for war crimes, but released in 1954. >> Hitler

Neurath, Otto [noyraht] (1882–1945) Philosopher and social theorist, born in Vienna. A member of the influential 'Vienna Circle' of logical positivists, he was particularly associated with 'physicalism', which aimed to establish an entirely materialist foundation of knowledge. He also wrote on sociology, education, and social policy.

Nevelson, Louise, née **Berliawsky** (1899–1988) Sculptor and printmaker, born in Kiev. Her family settled in the USA in 1905. She is best known for her 'environmental' sculptures - abstract, wooden, box-like shapes stacked up to form walls and painted white or gold.

Neville, Richard >> **Warwick, Richard Neville, Earl of**

Nevinson, Christopher (Richard Wynne) (1889–1946)

Artist, born in London. A leader of the pre-1914 avant garde, he joined Marinetti as co-signatory of the Futurist Manifesto (1914). He later moved away from Futurism to paint, in a poetic manner, New York, Paris, and the English landscape. >> Marinetti

Newbery, John (1713-67) Publisher and bookseller, born in Berkshire. He was the first to publish books specifically for children, and since 1922 the Newbery Medal has been awarded annually for the best American children's book.

Newbigin, James Edward Lesslie [nyoobigin] (1909-) Missionary and theologian, born in Northumberland. He went to Madras as a Church of Scotland missionary (1936), and became Bishop of Madurai and Ramnad (1947-59) and Bishop of Madras (1965-74), in the Church of S India.

Newbolt, Sir Henry (John) (1862-1938) Poet, born in Bilston, Staffordshire. He is best known for his sea songs - *Admirals All* (1897), which include 'Drake's Drum', *The Island Race* (1898), and *Songs of the Sea*.

Newby, Eric (1919-) Travel writer, born in London. His various adventures are described in such books as *The Last Grain Race* (1956), *A Short Walk in the Hindu Kush* (1958), and *Slowly Down the Ganges* (1966).

Newcastle, Duke of >> **Cavendish, William; Pelham, Thomas**

Newcomb, Simon [nyookuhm] (1835-1909) Astronomer and mathematician, born in Wallace, Nova Scotia, Canada. His major contribution was the calculation of all the known positions and motions of the bodies of the Solar System and the major celestial reference objects.

Newcombe, John (1944-) Tennis player, born in Sydney, New South Wales, Australia. He won the Wimbledon singles title in 1967, 1970, and 1971, and with Tony Roache won the doubles competition in 1965 and 1968-70.

Newcomen, Thomas [nyookuhmen] (1663-1729) Inventor, born in Dartmouth, Devon. By 1698 he had invented the atmospheric steam engine, and from 1712 this device was being used for pumping water out of mines.

Newdigate, Sir Roger [nyoodigayt] (1719-1806) Antiquary, born in Arbury, Warwickshire. He built up a famous collection of antiquities, and endowed the *Newdigate Prize* for English verse at Oxford.

Ne Win, U [nay win], also known as **Shu Maung** (1911-) Prime minister of Burma (1958-60, 1962-74). In 1962, after a military coup, he ruled as chairman of the revolutionary council, becoming state president in 1974. In 1981 he became chairman of the ruling Burma Socialist Programme Party, but was forced to step down in 1988.

Newlands, John (Alexander Reina) (1837-98) Chemist, born in London. He was the first to arrange the elements in order of atomic number and to see the connection between every eighth. This 'law of octaves' led to the idea of a periodic law.

Newman, Barnett (1905-70) Painter, born in New York City. An Abstract Impressionist, he developed a simple, single-image style and became a founder of the 'Subject of the Artist' school (1948). His work includes a series of 14 paintings, 'Stations of the Cross'.

Newman, Ernest (1868-1959) Music critic, born in Liverpool, Merseyside. Successively music critic of the *Manchester Guardian*, the *Birmingham Post*, and *The Sunday Times* (from 1920), he is best known for his studies of Wagner. >> Wagner, Richard

Newman, Francis William (1805-97) Scholar, born in London. In religion he took a position directly opposite that of his brother (John Henry Newman), being eager for a religion including whatever is best in all the historical religions. *Phases of Faith* (1853) is his best-known work.

Newman, John Henry, Cardinal (1801-90) Theologian,

born in London into a Calvinist family. A vigorous member of the Oxford Movement, he composed a number of its tracts. A convert to Catholicism (1845), he joined the Oratorians, published a spiritual autobiography, *Apology for His Life* (trans, 1864), and was made a cardinal (1879). >> Newman, Francis William

Newman, Nanette (1939-) British actress and writer. In 1959 she married Bryan Forbes, and appeared in a number of his films including *The L-Shaped Room* (1962) and *The Stepford Wives* (1974). Her popular books include *God Bless Love* (1972). >> Forbes, Bryan

Newman, Paul (Leonard) (1925-) Film actor and director, born in Cleveland, OH. His many films include *Cool Hand Luke* (1967), *Butch Cassidy and the Sundance Kid* (1969), *The Sting* (1973), and *The Color of Money* (1986, Oscar). >> Woodward, Joanne

Newnes, Sir George (1851-1910) Publisher and politician, born in Matlock, Derbyshire. He founded the *Westminster Gazette* (1873), *Tit-Bits* (1881), the *Strand Magazine* (1891), and *Country Life* (1897), and also became an MP (1885-95).

Newton, Isaac (1642-1727) Physicist and mathematician, born in Woolsthorpe, Lincolnshire. In 1665-6 the fall of an apple is said to have suggested the train of thought that led to the law of gravitation. He studied the nature of light, and devised the first reflecting telescope. His *Mathematical Principles of Natural Philosophy* (trans, 1687) established him as the greatest of all physical scientists. He was involved in many controversies, notably with Leibniz over the question of priority in the discovery of calculus. >> Leibniz

Nexø, Martin Andersen [neksoe] (1869-1954) Novelist, born in Copenhagen. His major works are *Pelle the Conqueror* (trans, 1915-17) and *Ditte, Daughter of Man* (trans, 1920-2).

Ney, Michel, duc d' (Duke of) **Elchingen** [nay] (1769-1815) French marshal, born in Saarlouis, France. He commanded the third corps of the Grand Army in the Russian campaign (1813), and received the title of Prince of Moskowa. He accepted the Bourbon restoration, but deserted to Napoleon and led the centre at Waterloo. Condemned for high treason, he was shot. >> Napoleon I

Ngata, Sir Apirana Turupa Nohopari [nggahta] (1874-1950) New Zealand statesman and Maori scholar, born in Te Araroa, New Zealand. A cabinet minister (1928-36), he worked for the economic development of Maori land and for a revival of interest in Maori culture.

Ngugi wa Thiong'o [ngoogee wa tyonggoh], formerly **James Ngugi** (1938-) Writer, born in Limuru, Kenya. His novel *Weep Not, Child* (1964) was the first novel in English by an East African, but in the 1970s he made a political statement by choosing Kikuyu as the medium for his fiction. His play *Ngaahika Ndeenda* (I will Marry When I Want) led to his year-long detention without trial (1978), and he has lived in exile since 1982.

Nguyen Van Linh [ngooyen van lin] (1914-) Vietnamese politician. Under his leadership of the Communist Party of Vietnam (1986-91), there was notable economic liberalization, and he undertook a phased withdrawal of Vietnamese troops from Cambodia and Laos.

Niarchos, Stavros (Spyros) [nyah(r)kos] (1909-) Shipowner, born in Athens. He became controller of one of the largest independent fleets in the world, pioneering the construction of supertankers, in competition with his brother-in-law Aristotle Onassis. >> Onassis

Niccola Pisano >> **Pisano, Nicola**

Nicholas I (1796-1855) Tsar of Russia (1825-55), born near St Petersburg, Russia, the third son of Paul I. An absolute despot, he engaged in wars with Persia and Turkey, suppressed a rising in Poland, and attempted to Russianize all the inhabitants of the empire. >> Alexander II (of Russia)

Nicholas II (1868–1918) The last tsar of Russia (1895–1917), born near St Petersburg, Russia, the son of Alexander III. He took command of the Russian armies against the Central Powers in 1915. Forced to abdicate at the Revolution, he was shot with his family at Yekaterinburg. >> Alexander III (of Russia); Alexandra Feodorovna; Anastasia

Nicholas, St (4th-c), feast day 6 December. Bishop of Myra, Lucia, and patron saint of Russia. His identification with Father Christmas began in Europe, and spread to America, where the name was altered to *Santa Claus*.

Nicholas I, St, known as **the Great** (c.820–867), feast day 13 November. Pope (858–67), born in Rome. He tried to depose Photius as Patriarch of Constantinople, leading to the Photian schism. >> Photius

Nicholas, Grand-Duke, Russ **Nikolay Nikolayevich** (1856–1929) Russian army officer, born in St Petersburg, Russia, the nephew of Alexander II. In World War 1 he was Russian commander-in-chief against Germany and Austria, and commander-in-chief in the Caucasus (1915–17). >> Alexander II (of Russia)

Nicholas or **Nicolaus of Cusa** [kyooza] (1401–64) Cardinal and philospher, born in Cusa, Germany. As papal legate he visited Constantinople to promote the union of the Eastern and Western Churches. A Renaissance scientist, he wrote on astronomy, mathematics, philosophy, and biology.

Nicholls, Sir Douglas (Ralph) (1906–88) Aboriginal clergyman, activist, and administrator, born near Echuca, Victoria, Australia. As pastor, he established an Aborigines' mission at Fitzroy in 1943, and worked actively for Aboriginal advancement.

Nichols, Mike, originally **Michael Igor Peschkowsky** (1931–   ) Film and theatre director, born in Berlin. A US citizen from 1944, he has received seven Tony Awards for his theatre work, which includes *The Odd Couple* (1965) and *The Real Thing* (1984). He also directed the hit musical, *Annie* (1977), and his films include *The Graduate* (1967, Oscar) and *Catch 22* (1970).

Nicholson, Ben (1894–1982) Artist, born in Denham, Buckinghamshire, the son of Sir William Nicholson. A leading abstract artist, he produced a number of purely geometrical paintings and reliefs, although he generally used conventional still-life objects as his starting point. His second wife was Barbara Hepworth. >> Hepworth

Nicholson, Jack (1937–   ) Film actor, born in Neptune, NJ. His major films include *One Flew Over the Cuckoo's Nest* (1975, Oscar), *The Shining* (1980), *Terms of Endearment* (1983, Oscar), *The Witches of Eastwick* (1987), and *Batman* (1989).

Nicholson, Seth Barnes (1891–1963) Astronomer, born in Springfield, IL. He is remembered for his discovery of the 9th, 10th, 11th, and 12th satellites of Jupiter.

Nicholson, William (1753–1815) Chemist, born in London. He helped to construct the first voltaic pile in England, thus discovering that water could be dissociated by electricity (1800).

Nicholson, Sir William Newzam Prior, pseudonym **W Beggarstaff** (1872–1949) Artist, born in Newark, Nottinghamshire, the father of Ben Nicholson. He is chiefly remembered for the posters produced with his brother-in-law, **James Pryde** (1866–1941) under their joint-pseudonym of J and W Beggarstaff. >> Nicholson, Ben

Nicias [nisias] (?–413 BC) Wealthy politician and general, from Athens, prominent during the Peloponnesian War. Appointed commander in Sicily (416 BC), his incompetence contributed to the total destruction of the Athenian forces, and his own death at the hands of the Syracusans.

Nicklaus, Jack (William) [niklows] (1940–   ) Golfer, born in Columbus, OH. His tournament wins include the British Open (1966, 1970, 1978), the US Open (1962, 1967,

1972, 1980), the US Professional Golfers Association a record-equalling five times (1963, 1971, 1973, 1975, 1980), and the US Masters a record six times (1963, 1965–6, 1972, 1975, 1986).

Nicol, William (1768–1851) Geologist and physicist, born in Edinburgh. In 1828 he invented the *Nicol prism*, which proved invaluable in the investigation of polarized light.

Nicolai, (Carl) Otto (Ehrenfried) [nikoliy] (1810–49) Composer, born in Königsberg, Germany. Conductor of the Berlin Opera (1847), his opera *The Merry Wives of Windsor* was produced just before he died.

Nicolaus of Cusa >> **Nicholas of Cusa**

Nicolle, Charles (Jules Henri) [neekol] (1866–1936) Physician and bacteriologist, born in Rouen, France. He discovered that the body louse is a transmitter of typhus fever, and was awarded the Nobel Prize for Physiology or Medicine in 1928.

Nicolson, Sir Harold (George) (1886–1968) British diplomat, writer, and critic, born in Teheran, where his father was British chargé d'affaires. He had a distinguished career as a diplomat (1909–29), then turned to writing, producing several biographies, and books on history, politics, and manners. He married Vita Sackville-West in 1913. >> Sackville-West

Nicot, Jean [neekoh] (1530–1600) Diplomat and scholar, born in Nîmes, France. In 1561 he introduced into France from Portugal the tobacco plant, called after him *Nicotiana*. The word *nicotine* derives from his name.

Nidetch, Jean [niydich] (1923–   ) Entrepreneur who founded Weight Watchers, born in Brooklyn, NY. She began a diet, and to help her maintain her weight-loss she formed a mutual support group with several overweight friends, out of which grew Weight Watchers International.

Niebuhr, H(elmut) Richard [neeboor] (1894–1962) Protestant theologian, born in Wright City, MO, the brother of Reinhold Niebuhr. His classic study, *The Meaning of Revelation* (1941), was followed by several books advocating critical reflection on the relation between faith and moral action and on the quest for a Christian transformation of society. >> Niebuhr, Reinhold

Niebuhr, Reinhold [neeboor] (1892–1971) Theologian, born in Wright City, MO, the brother of Richard Niebuhr. An advocate of Christian Realism, he was a political activist with the Socialists and then the Democratic Party, his works including *The Irony of American History* (1952). >> Niebuhr, H Richard

Nielsen, A(rthur) C(harles) [neelsen] (1897–1980) Businessman and market-researcher, born in Chicago, IL. He founded the A C Nielsen Co in 1923, establishing a national television rating service (1950) popularly known as the *Nielsen Ratings*.

Nielsen, Carl (August) [neelsen] (1865–1931) Composer, born in Nørre-Lyndelse, Denmark. His work includes six symphonies, concertos, choral and chamber music, the operas *Saul and David* (1902) and *Masquerade* (1906), and a huge organ work, *Commotio* (1931).

Niemeyer, Oscar [neemiyer] (1907–   ) Architect, born in Rio de Janeiro, Brazil. He co-ordinated the development of Brasilia, his major works including the President's Palace, Law Courts and Cathedrals in the capital.

Niemöller, (Friedrich Gustav Emil) Martin [neemoeler] (1892–1984) Lutheran pastor, born in Lippstadt, Germany. He publicly opposed the Nazi regime, and was placed in concentration camps (1937–45). Released in 1945, he was responsible for the 'Declaration of Guilt' by the German Churches for not opposing Hitler more strenuously. >> Hitler

Niépce, (Joseph) Nicéphore [nyeps] (1765–1833) Chemist, born in Chalon-sur-Saône, France. He succeeded in producing a permanent photographic image on metal (1826), said to be the world's first.

Nietzsche, Friedrich (Wilhelm) [neechuh] (1844–1900) Philosopher and critic, born in Röcken, Germany. His major work, *Thus Spake Zarathustra* (trans, 1883–5), develops the idea of the 'overman'. Much of his esoteric doctrine appealed to the Nazis, and he was a major influence on existentialism.

Nieuwland, Julius (Arthur) [nyooland] (1878–1936) Chemist, born in Hansbeke, Belgium. His research led to the production of the first commercially successful synthetic rubber, neoprene, in 1932.

Nightingale, Florence, known as **the Lady of the Lamp** (1820–1910) Hospital reformer, born in Florence, Italy. She led a party of 38 nurses to organize a nursing department at Scutari, where she soon had 10 000 wounded under her care. She later formed an institution for the training of nurses, in London.

Nijinska, Bronislava [nizhinska] (1891–1972) Ballet dancer and choreographer, born in Minsk, Belarus, the sister of Vaslav Nijinsky. She danced with the Diaghilev company in Paris and London (1909–14), and in 1921 joined Diaghilev as principal choreographer. After 1938 she worked mainly in the USA.

Nijinsky, Vaslav [nizhinskee] (1890–1950) Ballet dancer, born in Kiev, Ukraine, brother of Bronislava Nijinska. As the leading dancer in Diaghilev's Ballets Russes, he became phenomenally successful. His choreograpic work included *The Rite of Spring* (trans, 1913), regarded as outrageous at the time. >> Diaghilev; Nijinska

Nikodim, Boris Georgyevich Rotov [nikohdeem] (1928–78) Orthodox clergyman, metropolitan of Leningrad, born in Frolovo, Russia. In 1960 he became head of foreign relations of the Russian Church, which he led into the World Council of Churches amid great acclaim in 1961.

Nikolais, Alwin (1912–93) Choreographer, born in Southington, CT. In New York City he founded his own modern dance company, the Nikolais Dance Theater, in 1951.

Nikolayevich, Nikolai, Grand Duke >> **Nicholas, Grand Duke**

Niland, D'Arcy (Francis) [niyland] (1919–67) Writer, born in Glen Innes, New South Wales, Australia. In 1955 he achieved international fame with his novel *The Shiralee*. He also wrote radio and television plays, and numerous short stories. He married Ruth Park in 1942. >> Park, Ruth

Niles, Daniel (Thambyrajah) (1908–70) Ecumenical leader and evangelist, born near Jaffna, Sri Lanka. He became president of the World Council of Churches (1968), and chaired the East Asian Christian Conference.

Nilsen, Dennis (1948–) British convicted murderer. He admitted the murder and mutilation of between 12 and 16 young men in England between 1978 and 1983, and was sentenced to life imprisonment.

Nilsson, (Märta) Birgit (1922–) Operatic soprano, born in Karup, Sweden. The leading Wagnerian soprano of the period, she sang with the Stockholm Royal Opera (1947–51) and at Bayreuth Festivals (1953–70). >> Wagner, Richard

Nilsson, Lennart (1922–) Photographer, born in Sweden. He is best known for his microbiological and medical photography, notably his pictures of the human fetus in the womb from conception to birth.

Nimitz, Chester W(illiam) [nimits] (1885–1966) US admiral, born in Fredericksburg, TX. He commanded the US Pacific fleet (1941–5), contributing to the defeat of Japan, and signed the Japanese surrender documents for the USA (1945).

Nin, Anaïs [neen, anaees] (1903–77) Writer, born in Neuilly, France. Her early work includes novels and short stories, but her reputation as an artist and seminal figure in the new feminism of the 1970s rests on her sexually explicit *Journals* (1966–83).

Ninagawa, Yukio (1935–) Stage director, born in Japan. Well known in Japanese avant-garde theatre, in 1985 he created a sensation at the Edinburgh Festival with his Samurai-influenced production of *Macbeth*, and he won the Olivier Award for director of the year in 1987.

Ninian, St, also called **Ringan** (fl.390), feast day 16 September. Missionary, and the earliest-known Christian leader in Scotland. He selected Wigtownshire for the site of a monastery and church, called Candida Casa, which was built c.400.

Nipkow, Paul [nipkof] (1860–1940) Engineer and inventor, born in Lauenburg, Germany. A television pioneer, he invented in 1884 the *Nipkow disc*, a mechanical scanning device.

Nirenberg, Marshall (Warren) (1927–) Biochemist, born in New York City. For his work towards deciphering the genetic code, he shared the Nobel Prize for Physiology or Medicine in 1968. >> Khorana

Niro, Robert De >> **De Niro, Robert**

Nivelle, Robert [neevel] (1857–1924) French soldier, born in Tulle, France. He commanded the army of Verdun, and was made commander-in-chief (1916–17). When his Aisne offensive failed, he was superseded by Pétain. >> Pétain

Niven, Frederick John (1878–1944) Novelist, born in Valparaiso, Chile. His major work was a trilogy on Canadian settlement: *The Flying Years*, *Mine Inheritance*, and *The Transplanted* (1935–44).

Niven, David, popular name of **James David Graham Nevins** (1909–83) Actor, born in Kirriemuir, Tayside. He became established in urbane romantic roles with an English style, his films including *Around the World in 80 Days* (1956), *Separate Tables* (1958, Oscar), *The Guns of Navarone* (1961), and *55 Days at Peking* (1963).

Nixon, Richard M(ilhous) (1913–94) US Republican statesman and 37th president (1969–74), born in Yorba Linda, CA. He lost the 1960 election to Kennedy, but won in 1968, and was re-elected in 1972. He resigned in 1974 under the threat of impeachment, after several leading members of his government had been found guilty of involvement in the Watergate affair, but was given a full pardon by President Ford. >> Ford, Gerald R; Kennedy, John F

Nizer, Louis [niyzer] (1902–94) Lawyer and writer, born in London. He formed the law firm Phillips, Nizer, Benjamin & Krim in 1926, and remained with it throughout his career, becoming an authority on contracts, copyright, and plagiarism law.

Nkomo, Joshua (Mqabuko Nyongolo) [nkohmoh] (1917–) Zimbabwean statesman, born in Semokwe, Zimbabwe. President of the Zimbabwe African People's Union (ZAPU), in 1976 he formed the Popular Front with Mugabe to press for black majority rule in an independent Zimbabwe, and was given a Cabinet post in the Mugabe government (1980–2). >> Mugabe

Nkrumah, Kwame [nkrooma] (1909–72) Ghanaian prime minister (1957–60) and president (1960–6), born in Nkroful, Ghana. He was a significant leader both of the movement against white domination and of Pan-African feeling. Economic reforms led to the formation of a one-party state in 1964, and his regime was overthrown by a military coup.

Noah [nohuh] Biblical character, depicted as the son of Lamech. He is described as a 'righteous man' who was given divine instruction to build an ark in which he, his immediate family, and a selection of animals were saved from a widespread flood over the Earth (*Gen* 6–9). >> Shem

Nobel, Alfred Bernhard [nohbel] (1833–96) Chemist and industrialist, born in Stockholm. In 1866 he discovered how to make a safe and manageable form of nitroglycerin he called *dynamite*, and also invented smokeless gunpowder and (1875) gelignite. He left much of his fortune to endow annual prizes for physics, chemistry, physiology or medicine, literature, and peace.

Nobile, Umberto [nohbilay] (1885–1978) Aviator, born in Lauro, Italy. He flew across the North Pole in the *Norge* airship in 1926, but in 1928 was wrecked in the *Italia* when returning from the Pole.

Nobili, Leopoldo [nohbilee] (1784–1835) Physicist, born in Italy. He invented the thermopile used in measuring radiant heat, and the astatic galvanometer.

Noble, Adrian (Keith) (1950–   ) British stage director. He joined the Royal Shakespeare Company in 1980 as a resident director, becoming artistic director in 1991.

Nobunaga, Oda [nobunahga] (1534–82) The first of the three great historical unifiers of Japan, born into a noble family near Nagoya. He occupied the old capital, Kyoto, in 1568, destroying the power of the Buddhist Church, and favouring Christianity. >> Hideyoshi; Tokugawa

Noddack, Ida Eva (1896–   ) Chemist, born in Germany. Working with her husband, **Walter Karl Friedrich** (1893–1960), she discovered the elements masurium and rhenium in 1925.

Noel-Baker (of the City of Derby), Philip (John) Noel-Baker, Baron (1889–1982) British Labour statesman, born in London. He became secretary of state for air (1946–7) and of commonwealth relations (1947–50), and minister of fuel and power (1950–1). A life-long campaigner for peace through multilateral disarmament, he was awarded the Nobel Peace Prize in 1959.

Noether, (Amalie) Emmy [noeter] (1882–1935) Mathematician, born in Erlangen, Germany. She emigrated to the USA in 1933. One of the leading figures in the development of abstract algebra, the theory of *Noetherian rings* has been an important subject of later research.

Noguchi, Hideyo [nogoochee] (1876–1928) Bacteriologist, born in Inawashiro, Japan. He made important discoveries in the cause and treatment of syphilis, and also of yellow fever.

Noguchi, Isamu [nogoochee] (1904–88) Sculptor, born in Los Angeles, CA. From the mid-1940s he gained worldwide commissions for large-scale public sculptures, such as the fountain for the Detroit Civic Center Plaza (1975).

Noke, Charles John (1858–1941) Ceramic specialist, born in Worcester, Hereford and Worcester. In 1914 he became art director at Doulton's in Burslem, where he experimented with reproducing red glazes from the Sung, Ming, and early Ching dynasties.

Nolan, Sir Sidney (Robert) (1917–92) Painter, born in Melbourne, Victoria, Australia. He remains best known for his Australian paintings, including the 'Ned Kelly' series (begun in 1946) and an 'explorer' series, but he also designed operatic productions and illustrated books.

Noland, Kenneth (1924–   ) Painter, born in Asheville, NC. He developed his own kind of hard-edge minimalist abstract painting in the late 1950s, using circles, ovals, chevrons, and (after c.1966) horizontal stripes.

Nolde, Emil [nolduh], pseudonym of **Emil Hansen** (1867–1956) Artist and printmaker, born in Nolde, Germany. A leading Expressionist painter, he produced his own powerful 'blood and soil' style of distorted forms in violent religious pictures such as 'The Life of Christ' (1911–12).

Nollekens, Joseph [nolekenz] (1737–1823) Neoclassical sculptor, born in London. He executed likenesses of most of his famous contemporaries, including Garrick, Sterne, Goldsmith, Johnson, Fox, Pitt, and George III.

Nollet, Jean Antoine (1700–70) Abbé and physicist, born in France. He discovered osmosis (1748), invented an electroscope, and made an improved Leyden jar.

Nono, Luigi [nohnoh] (1924–90) Composer, born in Venice. A leading composer of electronic, aleatory, and serial music, *The Suspended Song* (trans, 1956) brought him to international notice.

Noonuccal, Oodgeroo [nunuhkl, ujuhroo], originally **Kath(leen Jean Mary) Walker** (1920–93) Poet and Aboriginal rights activist, born in Brisbane, Queensland, Australia. She was the first Aboriginal writer to be published in English, with her collection of poems *We Are Going* (1964).

Nordal, Sigurður (Johannesson) (1886–1974) Scholar, born in Vatnsdalur, Iceland. His *Icelandic Culture I* (trans, 1942) had a profound impact, and he founded the *Islenzk Fornrit* series of literary editions of the sagas.

Norden, Carl (Lucas) (1880–1965) Mechanical engineer, born in Semarang, Java. In 1911 he developed the first gyrostabilizing equipment for US ships, and became known for his contributions to military hardware.

Norden, Denis (1922–   ) British script-writer and broadcaster. With Frank Muir he formed a comedy script-writing duo (1947–64), contributing to many shows, such as *Take It From Here* (1947–58). He is well known as the television presenter of *It'll Be Alright on the Night* (1977–90). >> Muir, Frank

Nordenskjöld, Nils (Adolf Erik), Baron [naw(r)denshoel] (1832–1901) Arctic navigator, born in Helsinki. He accomplished the navigation of the Northeast Passage from the Atlantic to the Pacific along the N coast of Asia (1878–79). >> Nordenskjöld, Otto

Nordenskjöld, (Nils) Otto (Gustaf) [naw(r)denshoel] (1869–1928) Explorer and geologist, born in Småland, Sweden, the nephew of Nils Nordenskjöld. In 1901 he led a Swedish party to the Antarctic Peninsula area; the ship was crushed by ice, but they were rescued. >> Nordenskjöld, Nils

Nörgård, Per [noe(r)gaw(r)d] (1932–   ) Composer, born in Denmark. He composed operas, symphonies, ballet and chamber music, and the music for the Oscar-winning Danish film *Babette's Feast* (1987).

Noriega, Manuel (Antonio) [noriayga] (1939–   ) Soldier and politician, born in Panama City. He became the ruling force behind the Panamanian presidents (1983–9). Alleging his involvement in drug trafficking, the US authorities ordered his arrest and invaded Panama (1989). Found guilty in 1992, he was sentenced to 40 years imprisonment.

Norman, Greg(ory John), nickname **the Great White Shark** (1955–   ) Golfer, born in Mount Isa, Queensland, Australia. He won the Australian Open (1980, 1985, 1987), the British Open (1986, 1993), and the World Match Play Championship (1986).

Norman, Jessye (1945–   ) Soprano, born in Augusta, GA. She made her operatic debut in *Tannhäuser* at Berlin (1969), and in *Aïda* at both La Scala and Covent Garden in 1972.

Norris, George W(illiam) (1861–1944) US politician, born in Sandusky, OH. He sponsored the Norris–La Guardia Anti-injunction Act (1932), and broke with his Party on the issue of public ownership of water power. The Tennessee Valley Authority's first dam was named in his honour. >> La Guardia

Norris, Kathleen, *née* **Thompson** (1880–1966) Novelist, born in San Francisco, CA. Her works include *Mother* (1911), *Certain People of Importance* (1922), and *Over at the Crowleys* (1946).

Norrish, Ronald (George Wreyford) (1897–1978) Chemist, born in Cambridge, Cambridgeshire. He collaborated with Porter to develop flash photolysis and kinetic spectroscopy for the investigation of very fast reactions, and they shared the Nobel Prize for Chemistry in 1967. >> Porter, George

North, Frederick, 8th Baron North (1732–92) British prime minister (1770–82), born in London. He was widely criticized both for failing to avert the Declaration of Independence by the North American colonies (1776) and for failing to defeat them in the subsequent war (1776–83).

North, John Dudley (1893–1968) Applied mathematician, aircraft engineer, and designer, born in London. His aircraft included the Grahame-White Popular, Type XIII, the Bobolink, Phoenix, and Defiant.

North, Marianne (1830–90) British flower painter. She travelled widely, painting colourful, exotic flowers, and gave her collection to Kew Gardens, where they can be seen in a gallery (opened in 1882) which bears her name.

North, Oliver (1943–) US soldier, born in San Antonio, TX. Appointed a deputy-director of the National Security Council (1981), he played a key role in a series of controversial military and security actions. Implicated in the Irangate scandal, he was forced to resign in 1986.

North, Robert (1945–) Ballet dancer and choreographer, born in Charleston, SC. A founding member of London Contemporary Dance Theatre, he spent 12 years as dancer and choreographer there before becoming artistic director of Ballet Rambert (1981–6).

North, Sir Thomas (?1535–?1601) Translator, born in London. He is known for his translation of Plutarch's *Lives of the Noble Grecians and Romans* in 1579, which Shakespeare used in many of his plays. >> Plutarch; Shakespeare, William

Northcliffe, Lord >> Harmsworth, Alfred Charles William

Northcote, (Thomas) James (1746–1831) Painter, born in Plymouth, Devon. He painted portraits and historical pictures, among them the well-known 'Princes in the Tower' and 'Prince Arthur and Hubert'.

Northrop, John Howard (1891–1987) Biochemist, born in Yonkers, NY. He discovered the fermentation process for the manufacture of acetone, and successfully crystallized the enzyme pepsin showing it to be a protein (1930). He shared the Nobel Prize for Chemistry in 1946.

Northrop, John K(nudsen) (1895–1981) Aircraft designer and manufacturer, born in Newark, NJ. He became president and director of engineering of Northrop Aircraft Inc (1939–52). His company built military planes such as the F-89 Scorpion jet and fighter.

Northumberland, Duke of >> Warwick, John Dudley

Norton, Caroline (Elizabeth Sarah), *née* **Sheridan** (1808–77) Writer and reformer, born in London, the grand-daughter of Richard Brinsley Sheridan. In 1827 she married **George Chapple Norton** (1800–75), and had three sons. In 1836 she separated from her husband who obtained custody of the children, and tried to obtain the profit from her books. Her protests led to improvements in the legal status of women.

Norton, Charles (Eliot) (1828–1908) Editor, writer, and teacher, born in Cambridge, MA. He helped found *The Nation* (1865) and pioneered the teaching of art history at Harvard (1873–97).

Norton, Mary (1903–92) Children's novelist, born in Leighton Buzzard, Bedfordshire. She is best known for the series of books beginning with *The Borrowers* (1952, Carnegie Medal), about a family of tiny people who live under the floorboards.

Norton, Thomas (1532–84) Lawyer and poet, born in London. With Sackville he wrote the tragedy *Gorboduc*, performed before Elizabeth I in 1562. >> Sackville

Norway, Nevil Shute >> Shute, Nevil

Nossal, Sir Gustav (Joseph Victor) (1931–) Immunologist, born in Bad Ischl, Austria. His discovery of the 'one cell–one antibody' rule is crucial to modern work in immunology.

Nostradamus [nostra**dah**mus], Latin name of **Michel de Notredame** (1503–66) Physician and astrologer, born in St Rémy, France. His *Centuries* of enigmatic predictions in rhymed quatrains (two collections, 1555–8) brought him fame, and continue to be referred to today.

Nott, Sir John (William Frederick) (1932–) British statesman and merchant banker, born in Bideford, Devon. He became trade secretary (1979–81) and defence secretary (1981–3), his period of office including the Falklands War.

Novák, Vitezslav [**noh**vak] (1870–1949) Composer, born in Kamenitz, Czech Republic. His many compositions, which include operas and ballets, show the influence of his native folk melody.

Novalis [noh**va**lis], pseudonym of **Friedrich Leopold von Hardenberg** (1772–1801) Romantic writer, born in Oberwiederstedt, Germany. A poet and novelist, sometimes called the 'prophet of Romanticism', his poetic works include *Sacred Songs* (trans, 1799) and *Hymns to the Night* (trans, 1800).

Novatian [noh**vay**shn] (3rd-c) Theologian and anti-pope, born in Rome. In 251 a controversy arose about the status of those who fell away during the persecution under Decius. Novatian was chosen bishop in opposition to Pope Cornelius, and was excommunicated in 251.

Novello, Ivor [no**vel**oh], originally **David Ivor Davies** (1893–1951) Actor, composer, songwriter, and playwright, born in Cardiff. His most characteristic works were his 'Ruritanian' musical plays such as *Glamorous Night* (1935), *The Dancing Years* (1939), and *King's Rhapsody* (1949).

Novello, Vincent [no**vel**oh] (1781–1861) Organist, composer, and music publisher, born in London. His publication of two volumes of sacred music (1811), began the publishing house of Novello & Co.

Noverre, Jean-Georges [no**vair**] (1727–1810) Dancer, choreographer, and ballet master, born in Paris. He became ballet master at the Paris Opéra Comique (1754), the royal court theatre of Württemberg (now the Stuttgart Ballet, 1760–6), and the Paris Opéra (1776–9).

Novotný, Antonin [**no**votnee] (1904–75) Czech president (1957–68), born near Prague. He became first secretary of the Czechoslovak Communist Party, and virtual dictator in 1953. His state planning policy brought an economic recession (1961) and he was forced to resign. >> Dubček

Noyes, Alfred [noyz] (1880–1958) Poet, born in Wolverhampton, Staffordshire. His most successful work deals with the sea and the Elizabethan tradition, notably the epic *Drake* (1908).

Noyes, Eliot [noyz] (1910–77) Designer and architect, born in Boston, MA. He established his own practice in 1947, and worked as a consultant for major companies, notably IBM.

Nu, U [noo] ('uncle'), originally **Thakin Nu** (1907–95) Burmese prime minister (1948–56, 1957–8, 1960–2), born in Wakema, Myanmar (formerly, Burma). The first prime minister of the independent Burmese Republic, he was overthrown by a military coup in 1962, and imprisoned, but released in 1966.

Nuffield, William Richard Morris, 1st Viscount (1877–1963) Motor magnate and philanthropist, born in Worcester, Hereford and Worcester. The first British manufacturer to develop the mass production of cheap cars (Morris), he used part of his fortune to establish the Nuffield Foundation for medical, scientific, and social research (1943).

Nujoma, Sam Daniel [nu**joh**ma] (1929–) Namibian nationalist leader, and first president of independent Namibia (1990–), born in Ongandjern, Namibia. He founded the South-West Africa People's Organization (SWAPO), and led the armed struggle against South Africa from 1966.

Numa Pompilius [nyooma pompilius] (c.700 BC) The second of Rome's early kings, ruling (according to tradition) from 715 to 673 BC. A peaceful ruler, he was credited with organizing the religious life of the community.

Nunn, Trevor (Robert) (1940–   ) Stage director, born in Ipswich, Suffolk. His directorship of the Royal Shakespeare Company (1968–87) saw the opening of two new theatres in Stratford: The Other Place (1974) and The Swan (1986). He has also directed the musicals *Cats* (1981), *Starlight Express* (1984), and *Aspects of Love* (1989). >> Webber, Andrew Lloyd

Nureyev, Rudolf (Hametovich) [noorayef] (1938–93) Ballet dancer, born in Irkutsk, Russia. While touring with the Kirov Ballet in 1961, he obtained political asylum in Paris. He made his debut at Covent Garden with the Royal Ballet in 1962, and formed a famous partnership with Fonteyn. He was ballet director of the Paris Opéra (1983–9) and principal choreographer (1989–92). >> Fonteyn

Nurmi, Paavo (Johannes) [noormee] (1897–1973) Athlete, born in Turku, Finland. He won nine gold medals at three Olympic Games (1920–8), and set 22 world records at distances ranging from 1500 m to 10 000 m.

Nuvolari, Tazio [noovohlahree] (1892–1953) Italian motor-racing driver. He joined the Alfa Romeo team in 1930, and scored many wins, including the German Grand Prix in 1935.

Nyerere, Julius (Kambarage) [nyerairay] (1922–   ) Tanzanian president (1962–85), born in Butiama, Tanzania (formerly, Tanganyika). He was premier when Tanganyika was granted internal self-government (1961), and in 1964 negotiated the union of Tanganyika and Zanzibar as Tanzania.

Oakeshott, Michael Joseph (1901–90) Philosopher and political theorist, born in Harpenden, Hertfordshire. His main philosophical work was *Experience and its Modes* (1933), written broadly from within the English idealist tradition.

Oakley, Annie, popular name of **Phoebe Anne Oakley Moses** (1860–1926) Rodeo star and sharp-shooter, born in Darke Co, OH. She formed a trick-shooting act with her husband, Frank E Butler, and from 1885 they toured with the Buffalo Bill Wild West Show.

Oaksey, Baron >> Lawrence, Geoffrey

Oates, Joyce Carol (1938–) Writer, born in Lockport, NY. Her works include the novels *With Shuddering Fall* (1964) and *Them* (1969, National Book Award), and the short-story collection *The Wheel of Love* (1970).

Oates, Lawrence (Edward Grace) (1880–1912) Explorer, born in London. In 1910 he joined Scott's Antarctic Expedition, and was one of the party of five to reach the South Pole in 1912. Lamed by severe frostbite, and convinced that his condition would fatally handicap his companions' prospect of survival, he walked out into the blizzard, sacrificing his life. >> Scott, R F

Oates, Titus (1649–1705) Conspirator, born in Oakham, Leicestershire. In 1677 he publicized a fictitious 'Popish Plot' to murder Charles II and restore Catholicism. Many innocent people were executed for complicity in it, but two years later he was found guilty of perjury, and imprisoned until the 1688 Revolution.

Oatley, Sir Charles (1904–) Electronic engineer and inventor, born in Frome, Somerset. From 1948 his research led to the development of the scanning electron microscope.

Obadiah [ohba**di**ya], also called **Abdias** One of the 12 'minor' prophets of the Old Testament. He prophesies the fall of Edom in retribution for taking sides against Jerusalem, predicting judgment on the nations and the restoration of Israel.

Obel, Matthias de l' >> L'Obel, Matthias de

Oberth, Hermann (Julius) [**oh**bairt] (1894–1990) Astrophysicist, born in Sibiu, Hungary. In World War 2 he worked at the experimental rocket centre at Peenemünde, and later assisted Wernher von Braun in developing space rockets in the USA (1955–61). >> von Braun

Obote, (Apollo) Milton [o**boh**tay] (1924–) Ugandan prime minister (1962–71) and president (1967–71, 1981–5), born in Lango, Uganda. Deposed by Amin in 1971, he became president again after Amin's removal, but was ousted in a coup in 1985, and granted political asylum in Zambia. >> Amin

O'Brien, (Donal) Conor (Dermod David Donat) Cruise (1917–) Historian, critic, and Irish statesman, born in Dublin. His best-known work is *To Katanga and Back* (1962), an autobiographical narrative of the Congo crisis of 1961. An MP from 1969, he became minister for posts and telegraphs (1973–7).

O'Brien, Edna (1932–) Writer, born in Tuamgraney, Co Clare, Ireland. Her novels include *The Country Girls* (1960) and *August Is a Wicked Month* (1965). The best of several collections of short-stories appear in *The Fanatic Heart* (1985).

O'Brien, Flann, pseudonym of **Brian O'Nolan**, also known as **Myles na Gopaleen** (1911–66) Writer and journalist, born in Strabane, Co Tyrone. He contributed a satirical column to the *Irish Times* for some 20 years under his Irish pseudonym. His major novel was *At Swim-Two-Birds* (1939).

O'Brien, Jeremiah (1744–1818) Revolutionary hero, born in Kittery, ME. He captured HMS *Margaretta* in what was counted as the first naval battle of the Revolution.

O'Brien, Kate (1897–1974) Writer, born in Limerick, Co Limerick, Ireland. Her plays include *Without My Cloak* (1931), *The Land of Spices* (1941), and *As Music and Splendour* (1958).

O'Brien, (Michael) Vincent (1917–) Horse trainer, born in Churchtown, Co Cork, Ireland. One of his best years was 1977, when his horse, *The Minstrel*, won the Derby, the Irish Derby, the King George VI Stakes, and the Queen Elizabeth Stakes.

O'Brien, William (1852–1928) Journalist and nationalist, born in Mallow, Co Cork, Ireland. A Nationalist MP (1883–95, 1900–18), he founded the United Irish League (1898) and the All-for-Ireland League (1910).

O'Brien, William Smith (1803–64) Irish nationalist, born in Dromoland, Co Clare, Ireland. In 1848 he urged the formation of a National Guard and a national rebellion; he was arrested and served five years in Tasmania.

O'Bryan, William (1778–1868) Nonconformist clergyman, born in Gunwen, Cornwall. He quarrelled with the Methodists, and in 1815 founded a new Methodist communion, the (Arminian) Bible Christians, or *Bryanites*.

O'Byrne, Dermot >> Bax, Sir Arnold

O Cadhain, Máirtín [oh **kayn, mah(r)**tin], Eng **Martin Kane** (1906–70) Gaelic novelist, born in Galway, Ireland. His masterpiece was *Cré na Cille* (1949), a ruthless social analysis of rural community ill-feeling. He also wrote short stories and was an official translator of Irish parliamentary debates.

O'Casey, Sean, originally **John Casey** (1880–1964) Playwright, born in Dublin. His early plays, such as *The Shadow of a Gunman* (1923) and *Juno and the Paycock* (1924), were written for the Abbey Theatre. Later works, more experimental and impressionistic, include *Cockadoodle Dandy* (1949) and *The Bishop's Bonfire* (1955). He was awarded the Hawthornden Prize in 1926.

Occam, William >> William of Ockham

Occleve, Thomas >> Hoccleve, Thomas

Ochino, Bernardino [oh**kee**noh] (1487–1564) Protestant reformer, born in Siena, Italy. Vicar-general of the Capuchins (1538), he was summoned to Rome to answer for evangelical tendencies (1542), and fled to Calvin in Geneva. >> Calvin, John

Ochoa, Severo [oh**choh**a] (1905–93) Biochemist, born in Luarca, Spain. For his work on the biological synthesis of nucleic activities, he shared the Nobel Prize for Physiology or Medicine in 1959.

Ockeghem, Jean d' >> Okeghem, Jean d'

Ockham, William of >> William of Ockham

O'Connell, Daniel, known as **the Liberator** (1775–1847) Irish Catholic political leader, born near Cahirciveen, Co Kerry, Ireland. His election as MP for Co Clare precipitated a crisis in Wellington's government, which eventually granted Catholic Emancipation (1829), enabling him to take his seat in the Commons. >> Wellington

O'Connor, (Mary) Flannery (1925–64) Writer, born in Savannah, GA. Best known for her short stories, her collections include *A Good Man Is Hard To Find, and Other Stories* (1955) and *Everything That Rises Must Converge* (1965). She also wrote two novels.

O'Connor, Frank, pseudonym of **Michael O'Donovan** (1903–66) Writer, in Cork, Co Cork, Ireland. His volumes of short stories include *Guests of the Nation* (1931) and *Crab*

Apple Jelly (1944), and he also wrote critical studies, novels, and plays.

O'Connor, Sandra Day, *née* **Day** (1930–) Jurist, born in El Paso, TX. She became the first female justice of the US Supreme Court in 1981.

Octavia (c.69 BC–11 BC) Sister of the emperor Augustus, distinguished for her beauty and virtue. On the death of her first husband, Marcellus, in 40 BC she married Mark Antony, but in 32 BC Antony divorced her and forsook her for Cleopatra. >> Antonius; Augustus

Octavian >> **Augustus**

Odets, Clifford [ohdets] (1906–63) Playwright and actor, born in Philadelphia, PA. A leading playwright in the 1930s, his works include *Waiting for Lefty* (1935) and *Golden Boy* (1937). His film scripts include *None but the Lonely Heart* (1944), which he also directed.

Odling, William (1829–1921) Chemist, born in London. He classified the silicates, and put forward suggestions with regard to atomic weights which made O =16 instead of 8.

Odo [ohdoh] (c.1036–97) Anglo-Norman clergyman, Bishop of Bayeux, and half-brother of William I. He was regent for William during his absences in Normandy, but left England after rebelling against William II. >> William I / II (of England)

Odoacer [ohdohayser], also found as **Odovacar** (?–493) Germanic warrior who destroyed the W Roman empire, and became the first barbarian king of Italy (476–93). He was challenged and overthrown by the Ostrogothic King Theodoric (489–93). >> Theodoric

O'Donnell, Peadar or **Peter** (1893–1986) Revolutionary and writer, born in Meenmore, Co Donegal, Ireland. An IRA leader, he opposed the 1921 Anglo-Irish Treaty, was captured in Civil War fighting, and escaped after a 41-day hunger-strike. He edited *The Bell* (1946–54), and wrote the novel *Islanders* (1927).

O'Donovan, Michael >> **O'Connor, Frank**

Odovacar >> **Odoacer**

O'Duffy, Eimar Ultan (1893–1935) Satirical playwright and novelist, born in Dublin. His works, reflecting the new Irish revolutionary cultural nationalism, include the play *The Phoenix on the Roof* (1915) and the novel *The Wasted Island* (1919).

Oecolampadius, John [eekohlampadius], Latinized Greek form of **Johannes Hüssgen**, **Huszgen** or **Hausschein** (1482–1531) Clergyman and scholar, born in Weinsberg, Germany. He became a preacher at Basel (1515), where Erasmus employed him on his Greek New Testament, and entered a monastery; but left under Luther's influence to become a reformer at Basel in 1522. >> Erasmus; Luther

Oehlenschläger, Adam Gottlob [oelenshlayger] (1779–1850) Writer, born in Vesterbro, Denmark. Leader of the Danish Romantic movement, his fame rests mainly on his 24 tragedies, beginning with *Hakon Jarl* (1807).

Oersted, Hans Christian [oe(r)sted] (1777–1851) Physicist, born in Rudkøbing, Denmark. In 1820 he discovered the magnetic effect of an electric current. The unit of magnetic field strength is named after him.

Oerter, Al(fred) [erter] (1936–) Athlete and discus-thrower, born in Astoria, NY. He won four consecutive gold medals for the discus (1956, 1960, 1964, 1968), breaking the Olympic record each time.

O'Faolain, Sean [ohfaylen], pseudonym of **Sean Whelan** (1900–) Writer, born in Dublin. His works include the novel *A Nest of Simple Folk* (1933), an edition of translations from Gaelic – *The Silver Branch* (1938) – and many biographies.

Offa (?–796) King of Mercia (757–96). He was the greatest Anglo-Saxon ruler in the 8th-c, treated as an equal by Charlemagne. He was responsible for constructing Offa's Dyke, stretching for 70 mi along the Welsh border.

Offenbach, Jacques [ofenbahkh], originally **Jacob Eberst** (1819–80) Composer, born in Cologne, Germany. He composed many light, lively operettas, such as *Orpheus in the Underworld* (trans, 1858). He also produced one grand opera, *The Tales of Hoffmann*, which was not produced until 1881. >> Hoffman, E T W

O'Flaherty, Liam (1897–1984) Writer, born on Inishmore in the Aran Is, Co Galway, Ireland. A leading figure of the Irish Renaissance, his novels include *Thy Neighbour's Wife* (1923) and *The Informer* (1926, James Tait Black Memorial Prize), and he has also published collections of short stories.

Ogden, C(harles) K(ay) (1889–1957) Linguistic reformer, born in Fleetwood, Lancashire. In the 1920s he conceived the idea of 'Basic English', a simplified system of English as an international language with a restricted vocabulary of 850 words. >> Richards, I A

Ogdon, John (Andrew Howard) (1937–89) Pianist, born in Mansfield Woodhouse, Nottinghamshire. He also composed, his works including a piano concerto. Illness forced him to give up playing for several years.

Ogilby, John [ohgilbee] (1600–76) Topographer, printer, and map-maker, born in Edinburgh. His chief publications were engravings of maps and atlases, including Africa (1670), America (1671), and Asia (1673), and a road atlas of Britain (1675), unfinished at his death.

Ogilvie, St John (1579/80–1615), feast day 10 March. Jesuit priest and martyr, born in Banff, Grampian. He was hanged for his defence of the spiritual supremacy of the pope, and finally canonized in 1976, the only officially recognized martyr in post-Reformation Scotland.

Ogilvie, Angus / James >> **Alexandra, Princess**

Ogilvie Thompson, Julian (1934–) Businessman, born in Cape Town, South Africa. In 1990 he became chairman of Anglo American Corporation of SA, South Africa's largest corporation.

Oglethorpe, James Edward (1696–1785) Army officer, born in London. He founded the colony of Georgia (1732), and fought against the Spanish in Florida (1740). He was tried and acquitted after the 1745 Jacobite Rising for failing to overtake Prince Charles Stuart's army. >> Stuart, Charles

O'Gorman, Juan (1905–82) Architect, born in Mexico City. His masterpieces include the library of the National University of Mexico in Mexico City (1952) and his own house (now demolished) which was part-cave and harmonized with the volcanic rocks surrounding it.

O'Hara, John (Henry) (1905–70) Writer, born in Pottsville, PA. His best-known works - *Butterfield 8* (1935) and *Pal Joey* (1940) - became film and stage successes. His short-story collections include *The Doctor's Son* (1935) and *Waiting for Winter* (1967).

O'Hara, Frank, popular name of **Francis Russell O'Hara** (1926–66) Poet and art critic, born in Baltimore, MD. He wrote plays and art criticism, and is noted for his Surrealist poetry, as in *Selected Poems* (1973).

O'Higgins, Bernardo, known as **the Liberator of Chile** (1778–1842) Revolutionary, born in Chillán, Chile. He played a great part in the Chilean revolt of 1810–17, and became first president of the republic in 1817, but was deposed in 1823.

Ohlin, Bertil (Gotthard) (1899–1979) Economist and politician, born in Klippan, Sweden. He is best known for the Heckscher–Ohlin theorem on the dynamics of trade, for which he shared the Nobel Prize for Economics in 1977.

Ohm, Georg Simon (1787–1854) Physicist, born in Erlangen, Bavaria. *Ohm's law* was published in 1827 as a result of his research in electricity, and the measure of resistance is now called the *ohm*.

Ohno, Kazuo >> **Hijikata, Tatsumi**

Oistrakh, David (Fyodorovitch) [oystrak] (1908–74) Violinist, born in Odessa, Ukraine. He made concert tours in Europe and America, and was awarded the Stalin Prize in 1945 and the Lenin Prize in 1960.

O'Keeffe, Georgia (1887–1986) Painter, born in Sun Prairie, WI. As early as 1915 she pioneered abstract art in the USA (eg 'Blue and Green Music', 1919), but later moved towards a more figurative style, painting flowers and architectural subjects frequently with a Surrealist flavour, and with New Mexico settings (where she lived after 1949). She married Alfred Stieglitz in 1924. >> Stieglitz

Okeghem [okegem] or **Ockeghem, Jean d'** (c.1430–c.1495) Composer, probably born in Termonde, Belgium. Renowned as a teacher, he played an important part in the stylistic development of church music. His works include 14 Masses, motets, and songs.

O'Kelly, Sean T(homas), Gaelic **Seán Tómas O Ceallaigh** (1882–1966) Irish president (1945–59), born in Dublin. Elected to the first Dáil in 1918, his early posts include minister for local government (1932–9) and for finance and education (1939–45).

Olaf I Tryggvason (c.965–c.1000) King of Norway (995–c.1000), the great-grandson of Harald I. Converted to Christianity, he seized the Norwegian throne (995), and tried to convert Norway to Christianity by force, but was overwhelmed at the Battle of Svold (1000). >> Harald I Halfdanarson

Olaf II Haraldsson, also called **St Olaf** (c.995–1030), feast day 29 July. King of Norway (1014–30), the half-brother of Harald III (Hardrada). A convert to Christianity, in 1014 he seized the throne and tried to complete the conversion of Norway. He was killed at the Battle of Stiklestad (1030), and is regarded as the patron saint of Norway. >> Harald III Sigurdsson; Olaf I Tryggvason

Olaf III Haraldsson (?–1093) King of Norway (1067–93), the son of Harald III (Hardrada). His long reign was marked by unbroken peace and prosperity in Norway. >> Harald III Sigurdsson

Olav V [ohlaf] (1903–91) King of Norway (1957–91), born near Sandringham, Norfolk, the son of Haakon VII and Maud, daughter of Edward VII of Britain. In 1929 he married **Princess Martha of Sweden** (1901–54), and had two daughters and a son, **Harald** (1937–), who succeeded as Harald V in 1991.

Olbers, (Heinrich) Wilhelm (Matthäus) (1758–1840) Physician and astronomer, born in Arbergen, Germany. He calculated the orbit of the comet of 1779 and discovered the minor planets Pallas (1802) and Vesta (1807).

Olcott, Henry Steel (1832–1907) Theosophist, born in Orange, NJ. Founder president of the Theosophical Society in 1875, he travelled to India and Ceylon with Annie Besant (1879–84). >> Besant, Annie

Oldcastle, Sir John, nickname **Good Lord Cobham** (c.1378–1417) Lollard leader, born in Herefordshire. Convicted on charges of heresy (1413), he escaped and conspired with other Lollards to capture Henry V and take control of London, but was executed. >> Henry V

Oldenbarneveldt, Jan van >> Barneveldt, Jan van Olden

Oldenburg, Claes (Thure) (1929–) Sculptor, born in Stockholm. He moved to New York City in 1956, where he became involved in the development of Pop Art. In 1963 he introduced soft sculptures of normally hard objects such as light switches, for which he became best known.

Oldfield, (Berna Eli) Barney (1878–1946) Motor-racing driver, born in Wauseon, OH. A colourful showman who specialized in short 'match' races on dirt tracks, he also established a land speed record in 1910 for a one-mile distance at over 131 mph.

Oldfield, Bruce (1950–) Fashion designer, born in London. He showed his first collection in London in 1975. He designs evening dresses for royalty and film-stars, as well as ready-to-wear clothes.

Oldham, Richard Dixon [ohldam] (1858–1936) Geologist and seismologist, born in Dublin. In 1906 he established from seismographic records the existence of the Earth's core.

Ole Luk-Oie >> Swinton, Ernest Dunlop

Olga, St, also called **St Helga** (c.890–969), feast day 11 July. Russian saint, the wife of prince Igor of Kiev. Baptized at Constantinople (c.957), she returned to Russia where her labours to bring Christianity were continued by her grandson, St Vladimir I. >> Vladimir I

Oliphant, Margaret, née **Wilson** (1828–97) Novelist, born in Wallyford, Lothian. Her novels include *Mrs Margaret Maitland* (1849) and *The Chronicles of Carlingford*, a series of novels dealing with Scottish life. She also wrote histories and biographies.

Oliphant, Sir Mark, in full **Marcus Laurence Elwin Oliphant** (1901–) Nuclear physicist, born in Adelaide, South Australia. He worked on the atomic bomb project at Los Alamos (1943–5), but later strongly argued against the US monopoly of atomic secrets, and designed a proton-synchrotron for the Australian government.

Olivares, Gaspar de Guzman y Pimental, conde-duque de (Count-Duke of) [olivahrez] (1587–1645) Spanish favourite and chief minister (1623–43) of Philip IV, born in Rome. He took Spain into renewed conflict with the United Provinces and challenged France in the Thirty Years' War (1635–48). After the Spanish fleet was destroyed at the Battle of the Downs (1639), he was dismissed, and went into exile.

Oliver, King, popular name of **Joseph Oliver** (1885–1938) Cornettist, composer, and bandleader, born in Abend, LA. He moved to Chicago, where in 1922 he formed his Creole Jazz Band, several of his compositions, such as 'Dr Jazz', becoming part of the standard traditional repertoire.

Olivetti, Adriano [olivetee] (1901–60) Manufacturer, born in Ivrea, Italy. After a period in the USA, he successfully transformed the manufacturing methods of the typewriter firm founded by his father **Camillo Olivetti** (1868–1943).

Olivier (of Brighton), Laurence (Kerr) Olivier, Baron (1907–89) Actor, producer, and director, born in Dorking, Surrey. He played all the great male Shakespearean roles, while his versatility was underlined by his virtuoso display in *The Entertainer* (1957). His films include *Henry V*, *Hamlet*, and *Richard III*. In 1940 he married actress Vivien Leigh (divorced 1960), and in 1961 actress Joan Plowright. He became first director of the National Theatre (1963–73), and after 1974 appeared chiefly in films and on television, notably in *Brideshead Revisited* (1982) and *King Lear* (1983). >> Leigh, Vivien; Plowright

Olmsted, Frederick (Law) (1822–1903) Landscape architect, born in Hartford, CT. He was architect-in-chief of the improvement scheme for Central Park, New York City, and later designed other public park schemes, including the campus at Berkeley, CA.

Olsen, Ken(neth) (1926–) US computer designer and engineer. He helped to build Whirlwind, the first 'real-time' computer (1951), and later formed his own company, DEC, to manufacture mini-computers (1964).

Olson, Harry (Ferdinand) (1901–82) Radio engineer and inventor, born in Mount Pleasant, IA. In the 1940s he carried out tests which established the standards for high-fidelity sound reproduction, then in 1955 developed the first electronic music synthesizer.

Olympias (c.375–316 BC) Wife of Philip II of Macedon, and mother of Alexander the Great. After Alexander died (323 BC), she had his half-brother and successor killed, and made Alexander's posthumous son, Alexander IV, king. She was murdered by relatives of those she had put to death.

Omar or **Umar** [ohmah(r)] (c.581–644) The second caliph

(634–4), the father of one of Mohammed's wives, who succeeded Abu-Bakr. He built up an empire comprising Persia, Syria, and all North Africa, and was assassinated by a slave. >> Abu-Bakr; Mohammed

Omar Khayyám [kaɣam], also spelled **Umar Khayyám** (c.1050–c.1122) Poet, mathematician, and astronomer, born in Nishapur, Persia. He was known to the Western world as a mathematician, until in 1859 Edward Fitz-Gerald published a translation of his *Rubáiyát* ('Quatrains') - though little or nothing of this may actually be by Omar.

Onassis, Aristotle (Socrates) [ohnasis] (1906–75) Millionaire shipowner, born in Smyrna, Turkey. He built up one of the world's largest independent fleets, and was a pioneer in the construction of super-tankers. In 1968 he married Jacqueline Kennedy. >> Onassis, Jacqueline Kennedy

Onassis, Jacqueline Kennedy, *née* **Jacqueline Lee Bouvier**, popularly known as **Jackie Kennedy** (1929–94) US first lady (1961–3), born in Southampton, NY. She married John F Kennedy in 1953, and her stoic behaviour after Kennedy's death enhanced her standing with the public. In 1968 she married the Greek millionaire shipping magnate, Aristotle Onassis. >> Kennedy, John F; Onassis, Aristotle

Ondaatje, Michael [ondiykee] (1943–) Poet, novelist, and editor, born in Colombo, Sri Lanka. He moved to Canada in 1962. His works include *The Collected Works of Billy the Kid* (1970, Governor General's Award), and the novel *The English Patient* (1992, Booker).

O'Neill, Hugh, 3rd Baron of Dungannon, 2nd Earl of Tyrone (1540–1616) Irish rebel leader who petitioned Spain for help in expelling the English from Ireland. He defeated the English at Yellow Ford on Blackwater (1598), but was later defeated by Blount (1601–2), and fled abroad. >> Blount

O'Neill, Eugene (Gladstone) (1888–1953) Playwright, born in New York City. His works *Beyond the Horizon* (1920), *Anna Christie* (1922), *Strange Interlude* (1928), and *Long Day's Journey Into Night* (1956), all gained Pulitzer Prizes. Other classics include *Desire Under The Elms* (1924), *Mourning Becomes Electra* (1931), and *The Iceman Cometh* (1946). He was awarded the Nobel Prize for Literature in 1936.

O'Neill, Jonjo, popular name of **John Joseph O'Neill** (1952–) National Hunt jockey, born in Castletown-roche, Co Cork, Ireland. He twice became champion jockey (1977–8, 1979–80), riding 148 winners in one season.

O'Neill (of the Maine), Terence (Marne) O'Neill, Baron (1914–90) Northern Ireland prime minister (1963–9), born in Co Antrim. He was minister for home affairs (1956) and of finance (1956–63). After the 1969 general election, dissension in the Unionist Party increased and he resigned.

O'Neill, Tip, popular name of **Thomas Phillip O'Neill, Jr** (1912–94) US politician, born in Cambridge, MA. A member of the US House of Representatives (1953–1987), he became majority leader in 1973 and was elected speaker in 1977.

Ong, Walter (Jackson) (1912–) Catholic scholar and educator, born in Kansas City, MO. A Jesuit priest, he won esteem for his wide ranging studies in Renaissance literature, modern poetry, and criticism, as in *The Presence of the Word* (1967).

Onions, C(harles) T(albut) (1873–1965) Scholar and lexicographer, born in Edgbaston, West Midlands. He revised and completed the *Shorter Oxford English Dictionary* (1933) and led the team which produced the *Oxford Dictionary of English Etymology* (1966).

Onnes, Heike Kamerlingh [ohnes] >> **Kamerlingh Onnes, Heike**

Ono, Yoko >> **Lennon, John**

O'Nolan Brian >> **O'Brien, Flann**

Onsager, Lars [onsager] (1903–76) Physical chemist, born in Oslo (formerly, Christiania), Norway. His researches in solution chemistry and in chemical thermodynamics led to his receiving the Nobel Prize for Chemistry in 1968.

Oort, Jan Hendrik [aw(r)t] (1900–92) Astronomer, born in Franeker, The Netherlands. In 1950 he suggested the existence of a sphere of incipient cometary material surrounding the Solar System, proposing that comets detached themselves from this *Oort cloud*, and went into orbits about the Sun.

Oosting, Henry J(ohn) [oosting] (1903–68) Botanist, born in Holland, MI. He was an authority on the plant ecology of E USA, including Maine forest birches and the effects of salt spray on the vegetation of the North Carolina coastal dunes.

Opel, Fritz von [ohpel] (1899–1971) Automotive industrialist, born in Rüsselsheim, Germany. The world's first rocket-propelled car was the Opel-Rak 1 (1928), followed by the Opel-Rak 2, which he himself test-drove.

Ophuls or **Opüls, Max** [opüls], originally **Max Oppenheimer** (1902–57) Film director, born in Saarbrücken, Germany. His greatest successes made in France, include *La Ronde* (1950, The Round) and *Lola Montez* (1955).

Opie, John [ohpee] (1716–1807) Portraitist and historical painter, born in St Agnes, Cornwall. He became renowned as a portraitist of contemporary figures, and also painted historical pictures, such as 'The Murder of Rizzio' (1787).

Opie, Peter (Mason) (1918–82) and **Opie, Iona (Margaret Balfour)** (1923–) *née* **Archibald** [ohpee] British children's literature specialists, folklorists and anthologists. They married in 1943, and published *The Oxford Book of Nursery Rhymes* in 1951.

Opitz (von Boberfeld), Martin (1597–1639) Poet, born in Bunzlau, Germany. His scholarly and stilted style influenced German poetry for 200 years, and introduced Renaissance poetic thinking into Germany.

Oppenheim, E(dward) Phillips [openhiym] (1866–1946) Novelist, born in London. He became known for his popular espionage novels, his books including *Kingdom of the Blind* (1917), *The Great Impersonation* (1920), and *Envoy Extraordinary* (1937).

Oppenheimer, Sir Ernest [openhiymer] (1880–1957) Mining magnate, politician, and philanthropist, born in Friedberg, Germany. He went to Kimberley in 1902, and became a leader of the diamond industry, forming with John Pierpoint Morgan Jr the Anglo-American Corporation of South Africa in 1917. >> Morgan, John Pierpoint; Oppenheimer, Harry

Oppenheimer, Harry (Frederick) [openhiymer] (1908–) Industrialist, born in Kimberley, South Africa, the son of Sir Ernest Oppenheimer. He succeeded his father as chairman of the Anglo-American Corporation of South Africa (1957–83). >> Oppenheimer, Ernest

Oppenheimer, J(ulius) Robert [openhiymer] (1904–67) Nuclear physicist, born in New York City. He became director of the atom bomb project at Los Alamos (1943–5). Opposing the hydrogen bomb project, in 1953 he was suspended from secret nuclear research as a security risk, but was awarded the Enrico Fermi prize in 1963.

Opüls, Max >> **Ophüls, Max**

O'Rane, Patricia >> **Dark, Eleanor**

Orange, Princes of >> **William I** (of The Netherlands); **William III**

Orbison, Roy (1936–88) Country-pop singer and songwriter, born in Vernon, TX. His hit records include 'Only The Lonely' (1960), 'Cryin'' (1961), and 'Oh, Pretty Woman' (1964), and tributes to his music have continued long after his death.

Orcagna [aw(r)kanya], originally **Andrea de Cione** (c.1308–c.1368) Painter, sculptor, and architect, born in

Florence, Italy. His greatest paintings are frescoes, an altarpiece in Santa Maria Nobella, and the 'Coronation of the Virgin' (National Gallery, London).

Orchardson, Sir William Quiller (1832-1910) Painter, born in Edinburgh. Notable among his historical paintings is his scene of Napoleon on board the *Bellerophon* (1880).

Orczy, Emma, Baroness [awtsee, awksee] (1865-1947) Writer, born in Tarna-Eörs, Hungary. *The Scarlet Pimpernel* (1905) was followed by many popular adventure romances.

Orellana, Francisco de [orelyahna] (c.1490-c.1546) Explorer, born in Trujillo, Spain. He went to Peru with Francisco Pizarro, crossed the Andes in 1541, and descended the Amazon R (to which he gave the present-day name) to its mouth. >> Pizarro, Francesco

Orff, Carl (1895-1982) Composer, born in Munich, Germany. He is best known for his operatic setting of a 13th-c poem, *Carmina Burana* (1937).

Orfila, Mathieu (Joseph Bonaventure) [aw(r)feela] (1787-1853) Chemist, founder of toxicology, born in Mahon, Minorca. His celebrated work was *Treatise on General Toxicology* (trans, 1813).

Orford, Earl of >> **Walpole, Horace / Robert**

O Riain, Liam P >> **Ryan, William Patrick**

Origen [orijen] (c.185-c.254) Christian biblical scholar and theologian of Alexandria, Egypt, who became head of the catechetical school in Alexandria. His views on the unity of God and speculations about the salvation of the devil were condemned by Church Councils in the 5th-6th-c.

Orlando di Lasso >> **Lassus, Orlandus**

Orléans, Charles, duc d' (Duke of) [aw(r)layä] (1391-1465) French soldier, nobleman, and poet, born in Paris. In 1406 he married his cousin Isabella, the widow of Richard II of England. He commanded at Agincourt (1415), was taken prisoner, and lived in England for 25 years.

Orléans, Jean d' >> **Dunois, Jean d'Orléans**

Orléans, Louis Philippe Joseph, duc d' (Duke of) [aw(r)layä], known as **Philippe Egalité** ('equality') (1747-93) Bourbon prince, born in Saint-Cloud, France, the cousin of Louis XVI and father of Louis Philippe. At the Revolution he supported the Third Estate, and in 1792 renounced his title of nobility for his popular name. He was himself arrested after the defection of his eldest son to the Austrians (1793), and guillotined. >> Louis XVI; Louis-Philippe

Orm (fl.c.1200) Monk and spelling reformer, probably born in Lincolnshire. He invented an idiosyncratic orthography in which he wrote the *Ormulum*, a series of homilies in verse on the Gospel history.

Ormandy, Eugene [aw(r)mandee], originally **Jenõ Ormandy** (1899-1985) Conductor, born in Budapest. His chief posts were with the Minneapolis Symphony Orchestra (1931-35) and the Philadelphia Orchestra (1936-80).

Ormond, John (1923-90) Poet and film-maker, born in Dunvant, West Glamorgan. He joined BBC Wales in 1957 as a director/producer of documentary films, including studies of Welsh painters and writers, and also established a reputation as an Anglo-Welsh poet.

Ornstein, Leo (1895-) Composer, born in Kremenchug, Ukraine. In the USA from 1906, he composed much music that placed him among the avant garde, greatly influencing younger American composers.

Orosius, Paulus [orohzius] (5th-c) Priest and historian, probably born in Braga, Spain. He wrote the first Christian history of the world, *Historiarum adversus Paganos*, from the Creation to 417.

Orozco, José Clemente [oroskoh] (1883-1949) Painter, born in Ciudad Guzmán, Mexico. One of the greatest mural painters of the 20th-c, he decorated many public buildings in Mexico and the USA, his powerful Realistic style verging on caricature.

Orr, Bobby, popular name of **Robert Gordon Orr** (1948-) Ice hockey player, born in Parry Sound, Ontario, Canada. The highest goal-scorer ever in North American National League hockey, he played mainly with the Boston Bruins, moving to the Chicago Black Hawks in 1976 (and retiring through injury in 1979).

Orr, John Boyd >> **Boyd Orr, John**

Orsini, Felice [aw(r)seenee] (1819-58) Revolutionary, born in Meldola, Italy. In Paris in 1857 he made an unsuccessful attempt to assassinate Napoleon III by throwing a bomb under his carriage, and was arrested and executed. >> Napoleon III

Örsted, Niels-Henning [oe(r)sted] (1946-) Jazz double-bass player, born in Denmark. He has played with many famous jazz performers, and in 1977 was voted the 'World's Best Bass Player' by *Melody Maker* magazine.

Ortega (Saavedra), Daniel [aw(r)tayga] (1945-) Nicaraguan guerrilla leader and president (1984-90), born in La Libertad, Nicaragua. He joined the Sandinista National Liberation Front (1963), becoming its national director (1966), and played a major part in the overthrow of Somoza (1979). >> Somoza

Ortega y Gasset, José [aw(r)tayga ee gaset] (1883-1955) Philosopher and existentialist humanist, born in Madrid. His critical writings on modern authors made him an influential figure, and his *The Revolt of the Masses* (trans, 1930) foreshadowed the Civil War.

Ortelius [aw(r)teelius], Lat name of **Abraham Ortels** (1527-98) Cartographer and engraver, born in Antwerp, Belgium. His *Epitome of the Theatre of the World* (trans, 1570) was the first great atlas.

Orton, Joe, popular name of **John Kingsley Orton** (1933-67) Playwright and actor, born in Leicester, Leicestershire. He pioneered a style of black farce in such plays as *What the Butler Saw* (1969), *Entertaining Mr Sloane* (1964), and *Loot* (1966). He was murdered by his male lover.

Orwell, George, pseudonym of **Eric Arthur Blair** (1903-50) Novelist and essayist, born in Motihari, Bengal, India. He developed his own brand of socialism in *The Road to Wigan Pier* (1937) and many essays. He is best known for his satire of totalitarian ideology in *Animal Farm* (1945), and for the prophetic study of political tyranny, *1984* (1949).

Ory, Kid, popular name of **Edward Ory** (1886-1973) Trombonist and composer, born in Laplace, LA. During the 1920s he made numerous records, and is remembered for his composition, 'Muskrat Ramble' (1926).

O'Ryan, W P >> **Ryan, William Patrick**

Osborn, Henry Fairfield (1857-1935) Zoologist and palaeontologist, born in Fairfield, CT. He is best known for his work at the American Museum of Natural History in New York City, where he used innovative and popular instructional techniques.

Osborne, John (James) (1929-94) Playwright, film producer, and actor, born in London. His play *Look Back in Anger* (1956; filmed 1958), established him as the first of the 'Angry Young Men'. Other works include *The Entertainer* (1957; filmed 1959) and *Inadmissible Evidence* (1964; filmed 1965).

Osborne, Thomas >> **Leeds, Duke of**

Osbourne, Lloyd (1868-1947) Writer, born in San Francisco, CA, the stepson of Robert Louis Stevenson. He collaborated with Stevenson on several books, including *The Wrong Box* (1889), *The Wrecker* (1892), and *The Ebb Tide* (1894). >> Stevenson, Robert Louis

Osceola [oskeeohla], also known as **Powell** (c.1800-38) Seminole Indian leader, born in Georgia. He led the opposition to remove the Seminole from their Florida homeland, but was seized and imprisoned.

O'Shane, Pat(ricia) June (1941-) Magistrate, born in

Mossman, Queensland, Australia. In 1978 she became the first person of Aboriginal descent to be called to the bar. A magistrate in the local courts of New South Wales from 1986, she has made a number of progressive decisions concerning women and Aboriginal people.

Osman >> **Uthman**

Osman I (1258–1324) Founder of the Ottoman Turkish empire, born in Bithynia. He founded a small Turkish state in Asia Minor called *Osmanli* (Ottoman), and gradually subdued a great part of Asia Minor.

Osmund, St (?–1099), feast day 4 December. Norman clergyman, nephew and chaplain to William I. He became Chancellor of England (1072) and helped to compile the *Domesday Book*. >> William I (of England)

Ossietzky, Carl von [osyetskee] (1888–1938) Pacifist and writer, born in Hamburg, Germany. Editor of the *Weltbühne*, which exposed German military leaders' secret rearmament activities, he was sent to Papenburg concentration camp (1933). He was awarded the Nobel Peace Prize in 1935.

Ostade, Adriaen van [ostahduh] (1610–85) Painter and engraver, born in Haarlem, The Netherlands. His subjects are taken mostly from everyday life, such as markets and village greens. His brother **Isaak** (1621–49) excelled at winter scenes and landscapes.

Ostwald, (Friedrich) Wilhelm (1853–1932) Chemist, born in Riga, Latvia. He discovered the dilution law which bears his name, and was awarded the 1909 Nobel Prize for Chemistry for his work on catalytic reactions.

Oswald, St (c.605–642), feast day 5 August. Anglo-Saxon king of Northumbria (633–41), the son of Ethelfrith of Benicia. He established Christianity in Northumbria with St Aidan's help, and fell in battle with the pagan King Penda. >> Aidan; Penda

Oswald, Lee Harvey (1939–1963) Alleged killer of President John F Kennedy, born in New Orleans, LA. The day after President Kennedy's assassination (22 November 1963) he was charged with his murder, but before he could come to trial, he was shot by nightclub owner Jack Ruby. >> Kennedy, John F; Ruby

Otake, Eiko (1952–   ) and **Otake, Koma** (1948–   ) [ohtahkay] Dance-theatre artists from Japan, now resident in New York City. They joined *butoh* master Hijikata's company in Toyko, and developed a partnership in which they perform and choreograph only their own work. >> Hijikata

Otho, Marcus Salvius [othoh] (32–69) Roman emperor for three months (69). He joined Galba in his revolt against Nero (68), but when he was not proclaimed Galba's successor, he rose against the new emperor, who was slain. Otho then became emperor, but was defeated by Aulus Vitellius, and committed suicide. >> Galba; Nero; Vitellius

Otis, Elisha (Graves) [ohtis] (1811–61) Inventor, born in Halifax, VT. He designed and installed the first elevator to incorporate an automatic brake (1852), thus paving the way for the development of the skyscraper.

Otis, James [ohtis] (1725–83) US politician, born in West Barnstable, MA. In 1761, elected to the Massachusetts Assembly, he was prominent in resisting the revenue acts. His fame chiefly rests on *The Rights of the Colonies Asserted* (1764).

O'Toole, Peter (Seamus) (1932–   ) Actor, born in Connemara, Co Galway, Ireland. His performance in *Lawrence of Arabia* (1962) made him an international film star. Nominated seven times for an Oscar, his other films include *The Lion in Winter* (1968) and *The Last Emperor* (1987).

Ott, Mel, popular name of **Melvin Thomas Ott** (1909–58) Baseball player, born in Gretna, LA. He was a player and later manager with the New York Giants in the National League for 22 years (1926–48), playing 2732 games and hitting 511 home runs.

Otto I, known as **the Great** (912–73) King of the Germans (from 936) and Holy Roman Emperor (from 962). He maintained almost supreme power in Italy, and encouraged Christian missions to Scandinavian and Slavonic lands. >> Adelaide, St

Otto, Nikolaus (August) (1832–91) Engineer, born near Schlangenbad, Germany. In 1876 he built the first internal combustion engine that operated on a four-stroke cycle, now generally known as the *Otto cycle*.

Otto, Rudolf (1869–1937) Protestant theologian and philosopher, born in Peine, Germany. In *The Idea of the Holy* (trans, 1917) he describes religious experience as inspiring both awe and a promise of exaltation and bliss.

Otway, Thomas (1652–85) Playwright, born in Trotton, West Sussex. His best-known works are the tragedies *The Orphan* (1680) and his masterpiece *Venice Preserved, or a Plot Discovered* (1682).

Oud, Jacobus Johannes Pieter [owd] (1890–1963) Architect, born in Purmerend, The Netherlands. He collaborated in launching the review *De Stijl*, and became a pioneer of the modern architectural style based on simplified forms and pure planes.

Oughtred, William [awtred] (1575–1660) Mathematician, born in Eton, Buckinghamshire. He wrote *Clavis mathematica* (1631), a textbook on arithmetic and algebra, and in c.1633 invented the slide rule.

Ouida [weeda], pseudonym of **Marie Louise de la Ramée** (1839–1908) Novelist, born in Bury St Edmunds, Suffolk. Her first novel was *Held in Bondage* (1863), followed by *Strathmore* (1865), and she was soon established as a bestselling writer of hot-house romances.

Ouimet, Francis (1893–1967) Golfer, born in Brookline, MA. He recorded the first major success in US golfing history when he won the US Open of 1913, breaking British supremacy of top-level events.

Our Lady >> **Mary**

Overbeck, Johann Friedrich (1789–1869) Painter, born in Lübeck, Germany. He led the group of German artists known as the Nazarenes, or Lucas Brotherhood, which went to Rome in 1810. He painted mainly religious and historical subjects, notably the 'Rose Miracle of St Francis' (1829).

Ovett, Steve [ohvet], popular name of **Steven Michael James Ovett** (1955–   ) Athlete, born in Brighton, East Sussex. Gold medallist in the 800 m at the 1980 Olympics, he also won a bronze in the 1500 m. He broke the world record at 1500 m (three times), one mile (twice), and two miles.

Ovid [ovid], in full **Publius Ovidius Naso** (43 BC–AD 17) Latin poet, born in Sulmo, Italy. His major works are the three-book *Ars amatoria* (Art of Love) and the 15-book *Metamorphoses* (Transformations), one of the most influential works from antiquity.

Owain Glyndwr >> **Glendower, Owen**

Owen (of the City of Plymouth), David (Anthony Llewellyn), Baron (1938–   ) British Labour statesman, born in Plymouth, Devon. He was secretary for health (1974–6) and foreign secretary (1977–9), and one of the 'Gang of Four' who formed the Social Democratic Party (SDP) in 1981, becoming leader in 1983. Retiring from parliament in 1992, he became, with Cyrus Vance, a UN peace envoy in former Yugoslavia (1992–3). >> Vance

Owen, Robert (1771–1858) Social and educational reformer, born in Newtown, Powys. In 1800 he became manager and part owner of the New Lanark cotton mills, Strathclyde, where he set up a social welfare programme, and established a 'model community'. >> Owen, Robert Dale

Owen, Robert Dale (1801–77) Social reformer, born in Glasgow, Strathclyde. In 1825 he accompanied his father to America to help set up the New Harmony colony in Indiana. He became a noted abolitionist of slavery. >> Owen, Robert

Owen, Wilfred (1893–1918) Poet, born near Oswestry, Shropshire. His poems, expressing a horror of the cruelty and waste of war, were first collected in 1920 by Sassoon. He was killed in action a week before the armistice. >> Sassoon

Owen Glendower >> **Glendower, Owen**

Owens, Jesse (James Cleveland) (1913–80) Athlete, born in Danville, AL. Within 45 min on 25 May 1935 at Ann Arbor, MI, he set five world records (100 yd, long jump, 220 yd, 220 yd hurdles, and 200 m hurdles).

Oxenstierna or **Oxenstern, Axel Gustafsson, Greve** (Count) [**oks**ensherna, **oks**enstern] (1583–1654) Swedish statesman, born near Uppsala, Sweden. From 1612 he served as chancellor, and during most of the minority of Queen Christina was effective ruler of the country (1636–44). >> Christina

Oxford, Earl of >> **Asquith, Herbert Henry**

Oz, Amos (1939–) Novelist, born in Jerusalem, Israel. His novels describe the tensions of life in modern Israel, and include (trans titles) *Elsewhere, Perhaps* (1966), *In the Land of Israel* (1982), and *Don't Call it Night* (1995).

Özal, Turgut [**oe**zal] (1927–93) Turkish president (1989–93), born in Malatya, Turkey. He founded the Islamic, right-of-centre Motherland Party in 1983, and in 1989 became Turkey's first civilian president for 30 years.

Ozawa, Seiji [**ozah**wa] (1935–) Conductor, born in Hoten, China. He conducted the Toronto and San Francisco Symphonies, before beginning in 1973 his long tenure as conductor of the Boston Symphony.

Ozenfant, Amédée [ohzãfã] (1886–1966) Artist, born in St Quentin, France. He published a manifesto of Purism with Le Corbusier in 1919. His still-lifes based on this theory reduce vases and jugs to a static counterpoint of two-dimensional shapes. >> Le Corbusier

Ozick, Cynthia (1928–) Writer, born in New York City. Her fiction explores the dilemmas of being Jewish in a Christian world, as in her first novel *Trust* (1966) and her short stories, such as *The Pagan Rabbi and Other Stories* (1971).

Ozu, Yasujiro [ohzoo] (1903–63) Film director, born in Tokyo. In the 1930s he conceived the *shomin-geki* genre of films, dealing with lower middle-class family life, as seen in (trans titles) *Late Spring* (1949) and *Good Morning!* (1959).

Paasikivi, Juo Kusti [pahsikivee] (1870–1956) Finnish prime minister (1918, 1944–6) and president (1946–56), born in Tampere, Finland. He took part in all Finnish–Soviet negotiations, sought to avoid war in 1939, and conducted the armistice negotiations.

Pabst, G(eorg) W(ilhelm) (1895–1967) Film director, born in Raudnitz, Czech Republic (formerly, Germany). His darkly realistic style was acclaimed in *The Love of Jeanne Ney* (trans, 1927), the pacifist *Westfront 1918* (1930), and *Comradeship* (trans, 1931).

Pachelbel, Johann [pakhelbel] (c.1653–1706) Composer and organist, born in Nuremberg, Germany. His works profoundly influenced J S Bach. His best-known composition is the Canon in D Major. >> Bach, J S

Pacher, Michael [pahkher] (c.1435–98) Painter and woodcarver, born in the Tyrol, Austria. His masterpiece was the high altar for the Church of St Wolfgang on the Abersee (1481).

Pachomius, St [pakohmius] (4th-c), feast day 9 May. Founder of communal monasticism, from Egypt. He founded (AD c.318) the first monastery on the island of Tabenna on the Nile, with its properly regulated communal life and rule.

Pacino, Al(berto) [pacheenoh] (1940–) Film actor, born in New York City. His films include *The Godfather* (1972, 1974, 1990), *Serpico* (1973), *Sea of Love* (1989), and *Scent of a Woman* (1992, Oscar).

Packer, Sir (Douglas) Frank (Hewson) (1906–74) Newspaper proprietor, born in Sydney, New South Wales, Australia. He founded the magazine *Australian Women's Weekly* (1933), the success of which led to the formation of the Australian Consolidated Press group. >> Packer, Kerry

Packer, Kerry (Francis Bullmore) (1937–) Media proprietor, born in Sydney, New South Wales, Australia, the son of Frank Packer. In the 1977–8 season his creation of 'World Series Cricket', contracting leading Test cricketers for a knock-out series of one-day matches and 'Super-Tests', led to disputes with national cricket bodies and many legal battles. >> Packer, Frank

Paderewski, Ignacy (Jan) [paduhrefskee] (1860–1941) Pianist, composer, and patriot, born in Kurylowka, Poland. A virtuoso pianist, he became director of Warsaw Conservatory in 1909. He was elected president of Poland's provisional parliament in 1940.

Padilla, Juan de [padeelya] (c.1490–1521) Spanish revolutionary leader, born in Toledo, Spain. He was commandant of Saragossa under Charles V, headed an insurrection against the intolerable taxation, and was executed.

Páez, José Antonio [paez] (1790–1873) Venezuelan general and president (1831–5, 1839–43, 1861–3), born in Aragua, Venezuela. He commanded forces of *llaneros* ('cowboys') in the war of independence as principal lieutenant of Simón Bolívar, and became president after the break-up of Gran Colombia. >> Bolívar

Paganini, Niccolo [paganeenee] (1782–1840) Violin virtuoso, born in Genoa, Italy. He revolutionized violin technique, his innovations including the use of stopped harmonics. His compositions include the celebrated *24 Capricci* (1820).

Page, Sir Frederick Handley (1885–1962) Pioneer aircraft designer and engineer, born in Cheltenham, Gloucestershire. In 1909 he founded the firm of aeronautical engineers which bears his name. His Hampden and Halifax bombers were used in World War 2.

Paget, Sir James [pajet] (1814–99) Physician and pathologist, born in Yarmouth, Isle of Wight. He discovered the cause of trichinosis, and described the breast cancer known as *Paget's disease*, and the bone disease *osteitis deformans*, known as *Paget's disease of the bone*.

Paget, Violet >> Lee, Vernon

Pahlavi, Mohammad Reza [pahlavee] (1919–80) Shah of Persia (1941–79), born in Tehran, Iran, who succeeded on the abdication of his father, Reza Shah. His reign was marked by social reforms, but protest at western-style 'decadence' grew among the religious fundamentalists, and he was forced to leave Iran in 1979. >> Khomeini; Soraya

Paige, Elaine (1951–) Actress and singer, born in London. Her performances in *Jesus Christ Superstar* (1972) and *Billy* (1974) established her as a musical actress. Later musicals include *Evita* (1978) and *Cats* (1981).

Paige, Satchel, popular name of **Leroy Robert Paige** (1906?–82) Baseball player, born in Mobile, AL. One of the first African-Americans to make a breakthrough into the major leagues, he joined the Cleveland Indians, helping them to win the 1948 World Series.

Paine, Thomas (1737–1809) Revolutionary philosopher and writer, born in Thetford, Norfolk. In 1774 he went to Philadelphia, where his pamphlet *Common Sense* (1776) argued for complete independence. In 1787 he returned to England and wrote *The Rights of Man* (1791–2) in support of the French Revolution.

Paisley, Bob [payzlee], popular name of **Robert Paisley** (1919–96) Football manager, born in Hetton-le-Hole, Durham. It was during his spell as manager of Liverpool (1974–83) that the club became the most successful in England.

Paisley, Rev Ian (Richard Kyle) [payzlee] (1926–) Militant Protestant clergyman and politician, born in Armagh, Co Armagh. He founded the Protestant Unionist Party, and became the Democratic Unionist MP for North Antrim. A rousing orator, he is strongly pro-British, fiercely opposed to the IRA, Roman Catholicism, and the unification of Ireland.

Palach, Jan [palakh] (1948–69) Czech philosophy student. As a protest against the invasion of Czechoslovakia by Warsaw Pact forces (1968), he burnt himself to death in Wenceslas Square, Prague. Huge popular demonstrations marking the 20th anniversary of his death were held in Prague in 1989.

Palade, George E(mil) [palad] (1912–) Cell biologist, born in Iasi, Romania. In 1956 he discovered the small organelles within cells (ribosomes) in which RNA synthesizes protein, and shared the Nobel Prize for Physiology or Medicine in 1974. >> Claude, Albert

Palestrina, Giovanni Pierluigi da [palestreena] (c.1525–94) Composer, born in Palestrina, Italy. The most distinguished composer of the Renaissance, he composed over 100 Masses, motets, hymns, and other church pieces.

Paley, William (1743–1805) Theologian, born in Peterborough, Northamptonshire. In 1802 he published his most popular work, *Natural Theology, or Evidences of the Existence and Attributes of the Deity*.

Palgrave, Francis Turner [palgrayv] (1824–97) Poet and critic, born in Great Yarmouth, Norfolk. He edited the *Golden Treasury of Songs and Lyrical Poems* (1861), better known as 'Palgrave's Golden Treasury'.

Palin, Michael Edward [paylin] (1943–) Script-writer and actor, born in Sheffield, Yorkshire. He joined the BBC

TV team in *Monty Python's Flying Circus* (1969–74), co-wrote and acted in the Monty Python films, won a BAFTA Award for his role in *A Fish Called Wanda* (1988), and presented a popular series of travel documentaries for the BBC.

Palissy, Bernard [paleesee] (c.1510–90) Potter, born in Agen, France. He devised new techniques for glazing earthenware, depicting in high-relief plants and animals coloured to represent nature.

Palladio, Andrea [paladioh], originally **Andrea di Pietro della Gondola** (1508–80) Architect, born in Vicenza, Italy. He developed the *Palladian* style, modelled on the ancient Roman, of which a notable example is the Villa Rotonda (1550–1).

Pallas, Peter Simon (1741–1811) Naturalist, born in Berlin. He wrote a series of works on the regions he had visited, *Journey Through Various Provinces of the Russian Empire* (trans, 1771–6). Several birds are named after him.

Palma, Jacopo [palma], also called **Palma Vecchio** ('Old Palma') (c.1480–1528) Painter of the Venetian School, born in Serinalta, Italy. He is remembered for the ample blonde women who appear in many of his works, notably 'Three Sisters'.

Palme, (Sven) Olof [palmuh] (1927–86) Swedish prime minister (1969–76, 1982–6), born in Stockholm. Leader of the Social Democratic Labour Party, he carried out major constitutional reforms, but was defeated over taxation proposals. He headed a minority government in 1982, and was re-elected in 1985, but was then assassinated.

Palmer, Arnold (Daniel) (1929–) Golfer, born in Latrobe, PA. He won the British Open (1961–2), the US Open (1960), and the US Masters (1958, 1960, 1962, 1964).

Palmer, Daniel (David) (1845–1913) Osteopath and founder of chiropractic, born in Toronto, Ontario, Canada. He settled at Davenport, IA, where he founded the Palmer School of Chiropractic in 1898.

Palmer, Geoffrey (Winston Russell) (1942–) New Zealand prime minister (1989–90), born in Nelson, New Zealand. A Labour politician, he proved an unpopular leader, and was forced by his party to resign just before the 1990 general election.

Palmer, Nettie, popular name of **Janet Gertrude Palmer Higgins** (1885–1964) Writer and critic, born in Bendigo, Victoria, Australia. Her works include volumes of poetry and literary criticism, and she was a vigorous promoter of Australian writing.

Palmer, Samuel (1805–81) Landscape painter and etcher, born in London. He produced chiefly watercolours in a mystical and imaginative style, as in 'Repose of the Holy Family' (1824).

Palmer, Vance (1885–1959) Writer and critic, born in Bundaberg, Queensland, Australia. A leading member of the Pioneer Players theatre group, he was best known as a novelist, publishing a number of outback novels including *The Passage* (1930). >> Palmer, Nettie

Palmerston (of Palmerston), Henry John Temple, 3rd Viscount (1784–1865) British Liberal prime minister (1855-8, 1859–65), born in Broadlands, Hampshire. He became a Tory MP in 1807, served as secretary of war (1809–28), joined the Whigs (1830), and was three times foreign secretary (1830–4, 1835–41, 1846–51). His robust defences of what he considered to be British interests abroad secured him the name of 'Firebrand Palmerston'.

Panaetius [paneeshus] (c.185–c.110 BC) Stoic philosopher, from Rhodes. Head of the Stoa in Athens (129 BC), he was an important figure in the popularization of Stoicism in Rome.

Pancras, St (?–304), feast day 12 May. Christian martyr, the son of a heathen noble of Phrygia. He was baptized in Rome, but immediately afterwards was slain in the Diocletian persecutions while only a young boy. >> Diocletian

Pander, Christian Heinrich (1794–1865) Anatomist, the father of embryology, born in Riga, Latvia. With Baer he did valuable research on chick development in the egg, with particular regard to the embryonic layers now called by his name. >> Baer

Pandit, Vijaya Lakshmi, *née* **Swarup Kumari Nehru** (1900–90) Indian diplomat, born in Allahabad, India, the sister of Nehru. In 1953 she became the first woman president of the UN General Assembly, and was Indian High Commissioner in London (1954–61). >> Nehru, Jawaharlal

Pandulf, Cardinal (?–1226) Papal legate, born in Rome. He was the commissioner sent by Innocent III to King John of England after his excommunication to receive his submission (1213), and exercised great authority during the minority of Henry III (1299–1321). >> Henry III (of England); John

Paneth, Friedrich Adolf [panet] (1887–1958) Chemist, born in Vienna. With Hevesy he developed the concept of radioactive tracers (1912–13), and from the 1920s used them to establish the age of rocks and meteorites by their helium content. >> Hevesy

Panhard, René [panah(r)] (1841–1908) Engineer and inventor, a pioneer of the motor industry, born in Paris. With Emile Levassor (1843–97) he was the first to mount an internal combustion engine on a chassis (1891).

Panini [pahninee] (5th–7th-c BC) Grammarian, born in India. He wrote the *Astadhyayi* (Eight Lectures), a grammar of Sanskrit which formed the basis of all later Sanskrit grammars.

Panizzi, Sir Anthony [paneetsee], originally **Antonio Genesio Maria Panizzi** (1797–1879) Bibliographer, born in Brescello, Italy. Chief librarian (1856–66) of the British Museum, he undertook a new catalogue, and designed the famous Reading Room.

Pankhurst, Emmeline, *née* **Goulden** (1857–1928) Suffragette, born in Manchester. She founded the Women's Franchise League (1889), and in 1903, with her daughter **Christabel Harriette** (1880–1958), the Women's Social and Political Union. From 1905 she actively fought for women's suffrage, on several occasions being arrested and going on hunger strike.

Panofsky, Erwin [panofskee] (1892–1968) Art historian, born in Hanover, Germany. He is best known for developing the iconological approach to art - a method of interpreting works of art by analyzing the symbolism, history, and other non-aesthetic aspects of the subject matter.

Panov, Valeri [panof] (1938–) Ballet dancer, born in Vitebsk, Belarus. He became known internationally when refused emigration papers by the Soviet authorities, who eventually allowed him to resettle in Israel in 1974.

Paola, St Francis of >> **Francis of Paola, St**

Paolozzi, Eduardo (Luigi) [powlotsee] (1924–) Sculptor and printmaker, born in Edinburgh. His mature sculptures in bronze and steel often resemble stylized robotic figures, such as 'Medea' (1964).

Papa Doc >> **Duvalier, François**

Papandreou, Andreas (Georgios) [papandrayoo] (1919–) Greek Socialist prime minister (1981–9), born in Chios, Greece, the son of Georgios Papandreou. Exiled after the military coup in 1967, he returned in 1974, and founded the Pan-Hellenic Liberation Movement. >> Papandreou, Georgios

Papandreou, Georgios [papandrayoo] (1888–1968) Greek Republican prime minister (1944–5, 1963, 1964–5), born in Kaléntizi, Greece. In 1944 he headed a coalition government, and in 1961 founded the Centre Union Party. >> Papandreou, Andreas

Papanek, Victor [papanek] (1925–) Designer, teacher, and writer, born in Vienna. In developing countries he has specialized in design appropriate to local materials and technology, and is best known for *Design for the Real World* (1971).

Papanicolaou, George (Nicholas) [papanikolow] (1883–1962) Physiologist and microscopist, born in Kimi, Greece. He pioneered the techniques, now called *Papanicolaou's stain*, or the *pap smear*, of routine examination for the early detection of cervical and other forms of cancer.

Papen, Franz von [papen] (1879–1969) German politician, born in Werl, Germany. He was Hindenburg's chancellor (1932) and Hitler's vice-chancellor (1933–4). Taken prisoner in 1945, he was acquitted at the Nuremberg Trials. >> Hindenburg; Hitler

Papin, Denis [papĩ] (1647–c.1712) Physicist, born in Blois, France. He invented the steam digester (1679), forerunner of the domestic pressure cooker, and in c.1690 made a working model of an atmospheric condensing steam engine.

Papineau, Louis Joseph [papeenoh] (1786–1871) French-Canadian leader, born in Montreal, Quebec, Canada. Speaker of the House of Assembly for Lower Canada (1815–37), he opposed the union with Upper Canada.

Papp, Joe, originally **Joseph Papirofsky** (1921–91) Stage director and producer, born in New York City. He formed a workshop which became the New York Shakespeare Festival (1960), and in 1967 founded the off-Broadway Public Theater.

Paracelsus [paraselsus], originally **Philippus Aureolus Theophrastus Bombastus von Hohenheim** (1493–1541) Alchemist and physician, born in Einsiedeln, Switzerland. He travelled widely, acquiring great fame as a medical practitioner (1526), and was the first to argue that small doses of what makes people ill can also cure them.

Parbo, Sir Arvi Hillar [pah(r)boh] (1926–) Industrialist, born in Tallinn, Estonia. He emigrated to Australia (1949), joined the Western Mining Corporation, becoming chairman (1974–91), and leading its expansion into gold.

Parc, Julio Le >> **Le Parc, Julio**

Pardo Bazán, Emilia, condesa de (Countess of) [pah(r)tho bathahn] (1852–1921) Writer, born in La Coruña, Spain. An ardent feminist, her best-known works include the novels (trans titles) *The Son of a Bondswoman* (1886) and *Mother Nature* (1887), and she also wrote plays, short stories, and literary criticism.

Paré, Ambroise [paray] (c.1510–1590) Surgeon, born in Bourg-Hersent, France. He improved the treatment of gunshot wounds, and introduced several other new surgical techniques.

Parer, Damien [parer] (1912–44) News photographer, born in Malvern, Victoria, Australia. In 1940 he became an official war cameraman, filmed the action at the siege of Tobruk, but was killed while filming the US landing at Peleliu, Caroline Is.

Pareto, Vilfredo [paraytoh] (1848–1923) Economist and sociologist, born in Paris. He wrote influential textbooks on political economy, in which he demonstrated a mathematical approach. In sociology, his *The Mind and Society* (trans, 1916) anticipated some of the principles of Fascism.

Paris, Matthew >> **Matthew Paris**

Park, Maud May, *née* **Wood** (1871–1955) Suffrage leader, born in Boston, MA. She co-founded the College Equal Suffrage League (from 1901), helped to bring about the 19th Amendment (1920), securing the vote for women, and was the first president of the League of Women Voters (1920–4). >> Paul, Alice

Park, Mungo (1771–1806) Explorer of Africa, born in Fowlshiels, Borders, Scotland. In 1795–6 he made a journey along the Niger R, recounted in *Travels in the Interior of Africa* (1799), and was drowned during a later expedition.

Park, Robert E(zra) (1864–1944) Sociologist, born in Harveyville, PA. In Chicago (1913–33) he played a formative part in the founding of urban sociology, pioneering the use of participant observation, and made important contributions to the study of race relations.

Park, Ruth (c.1923–) Writer, born in Auckland, New Zealand. She went to Australia in 1942 and married the author D'Arcy Niland. Her novels include the trilogy *The Harp in the South* (1947), *Poor Man's Orange* (1949), and *Missus* (1986). Other works include the *Muddle-Headed Wombat* series of children's books. >> Niland

Parker, Bonnie >> **Bonnie and Clyde**

Parker, Charlie, popular name of **Charles (Christopher) Parker**, nickname **Bird** or **Yardbird** (1920–55) Jazz saxophonist, born in Kansas City, KS. In New York City, he joined Gillespie, Monk, and others in expanding the harmonic basis for jazz, and developing the new music called 'bebop'. >> Gillespie; Monk, Thelonious

Parker, Dorothy, *née* **Rothschild** (1893–1967) Writer, born in West End, NJ. She became drama critic of *Vanity Fair* (1917–20), and contributed to *The New Yorker* (1927–33). Noted for her satirical humour, her poetry collections include the best-selling *Enough Rope* (1926).

Parker, Matthew (1504–75) The second Protestant Archbishop of Canterbury, born in Norwich, Norfolk. Appointed by Elizabeth I in 1559, he was in charge of the formulation of the Thirty-nine Articles (1562).

Parker, Robert LeRoy >> **Cassidy, Butch**

Parkes, Alexander (1813–90) Chemist and inventor, born in Birmingham, West Midlands. He was noted for his inventions in electroplating, and invented xylonite (a form of celluloid), first patented in 1855.

Parkes, Sir Henry (1815–96) Australian statesman, born in Stoneleigh, Warwickshire. He emigrated to New South Wales in 1839, became a well-known journalist in Sydney, and from 1872 was five times premier of New South Wales.

Parkinson, Cecil (Edward) (1932–) British statesman, born in Carnforth, Lancashire. He became Conservative Party national chairman (1981–3), and secretary of state for trade and industry (1983), but resigned from both posts following a scandal. He returned as secretary of state for energy (1987–9) and as transport secretary (1989–90).

Parkinson, C(yril) Northcote (1909–93) Political scientist, born in Barnard Castle, Durham. He wrote many works on historical, political, and economic subjects, but achieved wider renown by his serio-comic tilt at bureaucratic malpractices in *Parkinson's Law: the Pursuit of Progress* (1957).

Parkinson, James (1755–1824) British physician. In 1817 he gave the first description of paralysis agitans, or *Parkinson's disease*.

Parkinson, Michael (1935–) British journalist and broadcaster. He has produced and presented several television programmes, and is best known as the host of his own chat show *Parkinson* (BBC, 1971–82).

Parkinson, Norman, originally **Ronald William Parkinson Smith** (1913–90) Photographer, born in London. He opened his own studio in 1934, and became one of Britain's favourite portrait and fashion artists, with his work widely used in quality magazines.

Parley, Peter >> **Goodrich, Samuel Griswold**

Parmenides [pah(r)menideez] (c.515–c.445 BC) The most influential of the Presocratic philosophers, a native of the Greek settlement of Elea in S Italy, and founder of the Eleatic school. He is the first philosopher to insist on a distinction between the world of appearances and reality.

Parmigianino [pah(r)mijianeenoh], also called **Parmigiano**, originally **Girolamo Francesco Maria Mazzola** (1503–40) Painter of the Lombard school, born in Parma,

Italy. At Bologna he painted his famous Madonna altarpiece for the nuns of St Margaret.

Parnell, Charles Stewart [pah(r)**nel**] (1846–91) Irish politician, born in Avondale, Co Wicklow, Ireland. In 1879 he became president of the Irish National Land League, and in 1886 allied with the Liberals in support of Gladstone's Home Rule Bill. He remained an influential figure until 1890, when a divorce scandal forced his retirement. >> Gladstone, W E

Parr, Catherine (1512–48) Sixth wife of Henry VIII, the daughter of Sir Thomas Parr of Kendal. She married Henry in 1543, and persuaded him to restore the succession to his daughters, Mary I and Elizabeth. >> Henry VIII; Seymour, Thomas

Parr, Thomas, known as **Old Parr** (?1483–1635) Centenarian, born, according to tradition, in 1483. He was a Shropshire farm-servant, and by his 152nd year his fame had reached London. He went to see Charles I at court, where he was treated so royally that he died.

Parra, Violeta [**pa**ra] (1917–67) Internationally celebrated Chilean folklorist, songwriter, and singer, born in San Carlos, Chile. Her work inspired the New Chilean Song movement of the later 1960s.

Parrhasios or **Parrhasius** [pah(r)**has**ius] (c.5th-c) Painter, born in Ephesus, Ionia. He worked in Athens and, according to tradition, was the greatest painter of ancient Greece. His works are mostly of mythological groups.

Parrish, (Frederick) Maxfield (1870–1966) Illustrator and painter, born in Philadelphia, PA. He became known for his skilled and highly decorative illustrations, book-covers, murals, and best-selling colour prints, such as 'Daybreak' (1920).

Parry, Sir (Charles) Hubert (Hastings) (1848–1918) Composer, born in Bournemouth, Dorset. He composed three oratorios, an opera, five symphonies, and many other works, but is best known for his unison chorus, 'Jerusalem' (1916).

Parry, Joseph (1841–1903) Musician, born in Merthyr Tydfil, Mid Glamorgan. He composed oratorios, operas, and songs, and became one of the leading hymn-writers in the Welsh tradition.

Parry, Sir William Edward (1790–1855) Arctic navigator, born in Bath, Avon. He took command in five expeditions to the Arctic regions (1818–27) which reached further N than anyone had done before.

Parsons, Sir Charles (Algernon) (1854–1931) Engineer, born in London. In 1884 he developed the high-speed steam turbine, and in 1897 built the first turbine-driven steamship, the *Turbinia*.

Parsons, Robert (1546–1610) Jesuit, born in Nether Stowey, Somerset. With Campion he masterminded a secret Jesuit mission in England (1580), and in 1588 was sent to Spain to establish seminaries for English priests. >> Campion, Edmund

Parsons, Talcott [**tawl**cot] (1902–79) Sociologist, born in Colorado Springs, CO. He developed a functionalist analysis of social systems through his principal publications, *The Structure of Social Action* (1939) and *The Social System* (1951).

Partridge, Eric (Honeywood) (1894–1979) Lexicographer, born in Waimata Alley, New Zealand. He is best known for his specialized studies of etymology, slang, and usage, his works including the pioneering *Dictionary of Slang and Unconventional English* (1937).

Pascal, Blaise [pas**kal**] (1623–62) Mathematician, physicist, theologian, and man-of-letters, born in Clermont-Ferrand, France. He invented a calculating machine (1647), the barometer, the hydraulic press, and the syringe. He defended Jansenism against the Jesuits (1656–7), and fragments jotted down for a case book of Christian truth were later published as the *Pensées* (1669, Thoughts).

Pashukanis, Evgeny Bronislavitch (1894–c.1937) Legal philosopher, born in Russia. An influential Marxist writer, widely known outside Russia, his approach made him unpopular with Stalin, and he disappeared in 1937. >> Stalin

Pasionaria, la >> **Ibárruri, Dolores**

Pasmore, (Edwin John) Victor (1908–) Artist, born in Chelsham, Surrey. One of the founders of the London 'Euston Road School' (1937), he began to paint in a highly abstract style, his works including *Inland Sea* (1950).

Pasolini, Pier Paolo [pasoh**lee**nee] (1922–75) Film director and writer, born in Bologna, Italy. He became known for controversial, bawdy film adaptations, such as *The Gospel According to St Matthew* (trans, 1964), *The Decameron* (trans, 1971), and *The Canterbury Tales* (1973).

Passfield, Baron >> **Webb, Sidney James**

Passmore, John (1914–) Philosopher, born in Manly, New South Wales, Australia. Regarded as a principal exponent of the 'Andersonian' school, his publications include the classic *A Hundred Years of Philosophy* (1957). >> Anderson, John (1893–1962)

Passmore, George >> **Gilbert and George**

Passy, Paul (Edouard) (1859–1940) Philologist and phonetician, born in Versailles, France. He was one of the founders of the Phonetic Teachers' Association (which became the International Phonetic Association) in 1886.

Pasternak, Boris (Leonidovich) [**pas**ternak] (1890–1960) Writer and translator, born in Moscow. His first novel, *Dr Zhivago*, was banned in the Soviet Union, but became an international success after its publication in Italy in 1957. Expelled by the Soviet Writers' Union, he was compelled to refuse the 1958 Nobel Prize for Literature.

Pasteur, Louis [pas**ter**] (1822–95) Chemist and microbiologist, born in Dôle, France. He established that putrefaction and fermentation were caused by micro-organisms, and in 1881 showed that sheep and cows 'vaccinated' with the attenuated bacilli of anthrax received protection against the disease.

Patanjali [patan**jalee**] (?2nd-c BC) A pseudonym attributed to the author (or authors) of the *Yoga* system of Hindu philosophy. The *Yoga Sutra*, extant versions dating from the 3rd-c AD, expounds the moral and physical disciplines necessary for attaining absolute freedom of the self.

Pataudi, Iftikhar Ali, Nawab of [pa**tow**dee] (1910–52) Cricketer, born in Bhopal, India. He played with Worcestershire, was first capped by England on the controversial 'bodyline' tour of Australia (1932–3), and made seven Test centuries before ill health forced his retirement. >> Jardine; Pataudi, Mansur Ali

Pataudi, Mansur Ali, Nawab of [pa**tow**dee] (1941–) Cricketer, born in Bhopal, India, the son of Iftikhar Ali Pataudi. Despite the loss of an eye in a car crash, he captained the Indian Test team, made 2793 runs in his Test career, and scored six centuries. >> Pataudi, Iftikhar Ali

Patenier, Joachim (de) [patenyay], also spelled **Patinir** or **Patinier** (c.1485–1524) Painter, probably born in Bouvignes, Belgium. Recorded as a member of the Antwerp painters' guild (1515), he was arguably the first Western artist to paint scenes in which the natural world clearly dominates the religious narrative.

Pater, Walter (Horatio) [**pay**ter] (1839–94) Critic and essayist, born in London. He became known with his *Studies in the History of the Renaissance* (1873), and exercised considerable influence on the aesthetic movements of his time.

Paterson, A(ndrew) B(arton), nickname **Banjo Paterson** (1864–1941) Journalist and poet, born near Orange, New South Wales, Australia. He wrote several books of light verse, including *The Animals Noah Forgot* (1933), but is best known as the author of 'Waltzing Matilda', which became Australia's national song.

Paterson, William (1658-1719) Financier, born in Tinwald, Dumfries and Galloway. After making a fortune by commerce in London, he founded the Bank of England, and was one of its first directors (1694).

Pathé, Charles [pathay], Fr [patay] (1863-1957) Film pioneer, born in Paris. In 1896 he founded Société Pathé Frères with his brothers Emile, Théophile, and Jacques, and by 1912 it had become one of the largest film production organizations in the world.

Patinier / Patinir, Joachim >> Patenier, Joachim

Patmore, Coventry (Kersey Dighton) (1823-96) Poet, born in Woodford, Essex. Associated with the Pre-Raphaelite Brotherhood, his major work, *The Angel in the House* (1854-62), was followed by his conversion to Catholicism, and he then wrote mainly on mystical or religious themes.

Paton, Alan (Stewart) [paytn] (1903-88) Writer and educator, born in Pietermaritzburg, South Africa. From his concern with the racial problem in South Africa sprang several novels, notably *Cry, the Beloved Country* (1948), *Too Late the Phalarope* (1953), and *Ah, but Your Land is Beautiful* (1981).

Patou, Jean [patoo] (1880-1936) Fashion designer, born in Normandy, France. He opened as a couturier in 1919, becoming noted for his designs for sports stars, actresses, and society ladies, and for his perfume, 'Joy'.

Patrick, St (c.385-461), feast day 17 March. Apostle of Ireland, born (perhaps) in South Wales. Ordained a bishop at 45, he became a missionary to Ireland (432), fixed his see at Armagh (432), and was probably buried there.

Patten, Chris(topher Francis) (1944–) British statesman, born in London. He became secretary of state for the environment (1989) and Conservative party chairman (1991). Credited with master-minding the Tory victory in the 1992 election, he lost his own seat and was appointed Governor of Hong Kong.

Patterson, Floyd (1935–) Boxer, born in Waco, TX. Having knocked out Moore in 1956 to take the heavyweight title, he lost to Ingemar Johansson in 1959, but defeated him in 1960, thereby becoming the first heavyweight champion to regain his title. He finally lost to Liston in 1962. >> Moore, Archie; Liston

Patterson, Harry >> Higgins, Jack

Patti, Adelina (1843-1919) Singer, born in Madrid. She is best remembered for her comedy roles, notably in Rossini's *The Barber of Seville*.

Pattison, Dorothy (Wyndlow) (1832-78) British philanthropist and nurse. As **Sister Dora** she became a nurse at Walsall, and in 1877 was appointed head of the municipal epidemic hospital at Walsall (mainly for smallpox).

Patton, George S(mith) (1885-1945) US general, born in San Gabriel, CA. He played a key role in the Allied invasion of French N Africa (1942), led the US 7th Army in its assault on Sicily (1943), commanded the 3rd Army in the invasion of France, and contained the German counter-offensive in the Ardennes (1944).

Paul (1754-1801) Tsar of Russia (1796-1801), born in St Petersburg, Russia, the second son of Peter III and Catherine II. He declared for the Second Coalition Allies against France (1798), and sent an army into Italy, but later allied with Napoleon. An unpopular ruler, his own officers conspired to compel him to abdicate, and he was killed. >> Catherine II; Napoleon I

Paul I (of Greece) (1901-64) King of the Hellenes (1947-64), born in Athens. His reign covered the latter half of the Greek Civil War (1946-9) and its difficult aftermath. During the early 1960s his personal role became the source of bitter political controversy.

Paul, St, originally **Saul of Tarsus** (?10-65/7 AD), feast day 29 June. Apostle to the Gentiles and theologian of the early Christian Church, born of Jewish parents at Tarsus, Cilicia. A persecutor of Christians, on his way to Damascus (c.34-35) he was converted by a vision of Christ. He carried out many missionary journeys in regions of the E Mediterranean, such as Galicia, Corinth, and Ephesus. He is said to have been executed by Nero in Rome. Thirteen New Testament letters are traditionally attributed to him. >> Jesus Christ; Nero

Paul III, originally **Alessandro Farnese** (1468-1549) Pope (1534-49), born in Canino, Italy. The first of the popes of the Counter-Reformation, he issued the bull of excommunication and deposition against Henry VIII (1538), and summoned the Council of Trent (1545). >> Henry VIII

Paul VI, originally **Giovanni Battista Montini** (1897-1978) Pope (1963-78), born in Concesio, Italy. He became known for his liberal views and support of social reform, travelled more widely than any previous pope, and initiated important advances in the move towards Christian unity.

Paul, Alice (1885-1977) Feminist and social reformer, born in Moorestown, NJ. She devoted her career to fighting for equal rights for women, in particular for the 19th Amendment, and in 1928 founded the World Party for Equal Rights for Women. >> Park, Maud May

Paul, Charles Kegan (1828-1902) Writer and publisher, born in White Laekington, Somerset. He took over a publishing firm in 1877 which became C Kegan Paul & Co, publishing contemporary authors, translations, and works on religion.

Paul, Jean >> Richter, Johann Paul Friedrich

Paul, Les, originally **Lester Polfus** (1915–) Musician, and inventor of the solid-body electric guitar (the 'Gibson Les Paul'), born in Waukesha, WI. Well known as a jazz guitarist, his design was produced by the Gibson Guitar Co in 1947.

Paul, Lewis (?-1759) Inventor, son of a Huguenot refugee in England. He invented the first power roller-spinning machine in conjunction with John Wyatt (1700-66), which was a commercial failure, but the idea was later used by Arkwright. >> Arkwright

Paul, Oom Uncle >> Kruger, Paul

Paul, Vincent de >> Vincent de Paul

Paula, St Francesco di >> Francis of Paola, St

Paulding, James (Kirke) (1778-1860) Writer, born in Putnam Co, NY. With Washington Irving he founded the periodical *Salmagundi* (1807-8). His best-known work was *Westward Ho!* (1832). >> Irving, Washington

Pauli, Wolfgang [powlee] (1900-58) Theoretical physicist, born in Vienna. In 1924 he formulated the 'exclusion principle' in atomic physics, and in 1931 postulated the existence of an electrically neutral particle (the neutrino). He was awarded the Nobel Prize for Physics in 1945.

Pauling, Linus (Carl) [pawling] (1901-94) Chemist, born in Portland, OR. He applied quantum theory to chemistry, and was awarded the Nobel Prize for Chemistry in 1954 for his contributions to the theory of valency. He became a controversial figure from 1955 as the leading scientific critic of US nuclear deterrent policy. Awarded the Nobel Peace Prize in 1962, he was the first person to receive two full Nobel Prizes.

Paulinus [pawliynus] (?-644) Roman Catholic missionary. Sent to England with St Augustine in 601, he became the first Archbishop of York in 633. >> Augustine, St

Paulinus of Nola, St [pawliynus], in full **Pontius Meropius Anicius Paulinus** (353-431), feast day 22 June. Bishop and writer, born in Bordeaux, France. Consecrated Bishop of Nola in c.409, he is remembered for his *Carmina* and for his epistles.

Paulus, Friedrich [powlus] (1890-1957) German soldier and tank specialist, born in Breitenau, Germany. As commander of the 6th Army he led the attack on Stalingrad

(1942), but was trapped there by a Russian counter-attack. Totally cut off, he held out for three months before capitulating. >> Zhukhov

Pausanias [pawsaynias] (5th-c BC) Greek soldier and regent of Sparta, the nephew of Leonidas. Capturing the Cyprian cities and Byzantium, he had aspirations to become ruler of all Greece, but he was betrayed and forced to flee. >> Leonidas

Pausanias [pawsaynias] (2nd-c) Geographer and historian, probably born in Lydia, Greece. He travelled widely, and composed an *Itinerary* of Greece, describing the country and the monuments of art.

Pavarotti, Luciano [pavarotee] (1935–) Tenor, born in Modena, Italy. He won the international competition at the Teatro Reggio Emilia in 1961, and made his operatic debut the same year. He made his US debut in 1968, and is internationally known as a concert performer.

Pavlov, Ivan Petrovich [pavlov] (1849–1936) Physiologist, born in Ryazan, Russia. From 1902 he studied what later became known as *Pavlovian conditioning* in animals. A major influence on the development of behaviourism in psychology, he was awarded the Nobel Prize for Physiology or Medicine in 1904.

Pavlova, Anna [pavlova] (1881–1931) Ballerina, born in St Petersburg. She became particularly known for her role in Fokine's *The Dying Swan* (1907), and after a period with Diaghilev's Ballets Russes, she began touring Europe with her own company (1909). >> Diaghilev; Fokine

Paxton, Sir Joseph (1801–65) Gardener and architect, born near Woburn, Bedfordshire. He designed a revolutionary building of prefabricated sections of cast-iron and glass for the Great Exhibition of 1851 (nicknamed 'the Crystal Palace'), which he re-erected in Sydenham in 1854. It was destroyed by fire in 1936.

Paxton, Steve (1939–) Experimental dancer and choreographer, born in Tucson, AZ. A founding member of the experimental Grand Union, in 1972 he invented the dance form known as *contact improvization*.

Payton, Walter (1954–) Player of American football, born in Columbia, MS. In his career with the Chicago Bears (1975–88), he rushed for 16 726 yards, a National Football League record, and his score of 125 touchdowns (1975–87) is second only to that of Jim Brown. >> Brown, Jim

Paz, Octavio (1914–) Poet, born in Mexico City. A prolific writer, his best-known works include *Collected Poems* (1957–87), in Spanish and English, and the prose *One Earth, Four or Five Worlds* (trans, 1984). He received the Nobel Prize for Literature in 1990.

Paz Estenssoro, Victor [pahs estensawroh] (1907–) Bolivian revolutionary and president (1952–6, 1960–4, 1985–9), born in Tarija, Bolivia. In 1942 he founded the National Revolutionary Movement, and was exiled during 1946–52.

Peabody, George (1795–1869) Merchant, financier, and philanthropist, born in Peabody, MA. He fitted out Kane's Arctic expedition to search for Franklin, and endowed the Peabody Institutes in Baltimore and Peabody, and the Peabody Museums at Yale and Harvard.

Peacock, Andrew Sharp (1939–) Australian Liberal statesman, born in Melbourne, Victoria, Australia. He was foreign minister (1975–80) and minister for industrial relations (1980–1), and leader of the Opposition (1989–90).

Peacock, Thomas Love (1785–1866) Writer, born in Weymouth, Dorset. His conversational satirical romances include *Headlong Hall* (1816), *Melincourt* (1817), and *Nightmare Abbey* (1818).

Peake, Mervyn (Laurence) (1911–68) Writer and artist, born in Kuling, China, where his father was a missionary. He is best known for his Gothic fantasy trilogy of novels,

Titus Groan (1946), *Gormenghast* (1950), and *Titus Alone* (1959), and for the novel *Mr Pye* (1953), which was televised.

Peale, Charles Willson (1741–1827) Painter, born in Queen Annes Co, MD. His Portrait Gallery of the Heroes of the Revolution (1782) was the first art gallery in America.

Peale, Norman Vincent (1898–1993) Pastor and writer, born in Bowersville, OH. A Methodist Episcopal minister in 1922, he worked at Marble Collegiate Reformed Church, New York City (1932–84), and wrote the best seller, *The Power of Positive Thinking* (1952).

Peano, Giuseppe [payahnoh] (1858–1932) Mathematician, born in Cuneo, Italy. Known for his work on mathematical logic, the symbolism he invented was the basis of that used by Russell and Whitehead in *Principia mathematica*. >> Russell, Bertrand; Whitehead, Alfred North

Pearce, Richard William (1877–1953) Inventor and pioneer aviator, born in Waitohi, New Zealand. In 1903, at Waitohi, he flew for a distance of possibly 137 m/150 yd, the most successful powered take-off before that of the Wright brothers. >> Wright brothers

Peard, Susan >> Hashman, Judy

Pearlstein, Philip [perlstiyn] (1924–) Painter, born in Pittsburgh, PA. His detailed studies of the male and female nude emphasize the impersonal aspect of the subject, often omitting the head of his model to concentrate on an unidealized representation of the naked body.

Pears, Sir Peter (Neville Luard) [peerz] (1910–86) Tenor, born in Farnham, Surrey. He joined Benjamin Britten in the English Opera Group, and was co-founder with him of the Aldeburgh Festival (1948). >> Britten

Pearse, Patrick (or **Pádraic**) **Henry** [peers] (1879–1916) Writer and nationalist, born in Dublin. In the 1916 Easter Rising he commanded the insurgents, was proclaimed president of the provisional government, and was later court-martialled and shot.

Pearson, Sir Cyril (Arthur) (1866–1921) Newspaper and periodical proprietor, born in Wookey, Somerset. He produced *Pearson's Weekly* (1890), and founded the *Daily Express* (1900) and other newpapers.

Pearson, Gerald (Leondus) (1905–) Physicist, born in Minneapolis, MN. He led the team that developed the first practical solar battery in 1954.

Pearson, Hesketh (1887–1964) Biographer, born in Hawford, Hereford and Worcester. His popular and racy biographies include *Gilbert and Sullivan* (1935), *Oscar Wilde* (1946), *Dizzy* (Disraeli, 1951), and *Charles II* (1960).

Pearson, Karl (1857–1936) Mathematician and scientist, born in London. A founder of modern statistical theory, his work established statistics as a subject in its own right.

Pearson, Lester B(owles) (1897–1972) Canadian prime minister (1963–8), born in Newtonbrook, Ontario, Canada. Minister of external affairs (1948–57), his efforts to resolve the Suez Crisis were rewarded with the Nobel Peace Prize in 1957. >> Nasser

Peary, Robert (Edwin) [peeree] (1856–1920) Naval commander and explorer, born in Cresson Springs, PA. He made eight Arctic voyages to Greenland, and on 6 April 1909 reached the North Pole. >> Cook, Frederick

Pease, Francis (Gladheim) (1881–1938) Astronomer, born in Cambridge, MA. At the Mount Wilson Observatory, Pasadena (1908–13), he designed the 100 in telescope and the 50 ft interferometer telescope.

Pechstein, Max [pekhshtiyn] (1881–1955) Painter and print-maker, born in Zwickau, Germany. He joined the avant-garde *Die Brücke* group in 1906, and from 1908 helped found the rival *Neue Sezession* in Berlin, developing a colourful style indebted to Matisse and the Fauvists. >> Matisse

Peck, (Eldred) Gregory (1916–) Film star, born in La Jolla, CA. Among his best-known films are *Spellbound*

(1945), *The Gunfighter* (1950), *The Omen* (1976), and *To Kill a Mockingbird* (1962, Oscar).

Peckinpah, Sam [pekinpah] (1925–84) Film director, born in Fresno, CA. He portrayed a harshly realistic view of the lawless US West, accentuating the inherent violence, as in *Major Dundee* (1965) and *The Wild Bunch* (1969).

Pecock, Reginald [peekok] (c.1395–c.1460) Theologian and writer, born in Laugharne, Dyfed. He became Bishop of Chichester (1450–58), but in 1457 was denounced for making reason paramount to the authority of the old doctors, and deprived of his office.

Pedersen, Holger [paydersn] (1867–1953) Linguist, born in Gelballe, Denmark. He is chiefly remembered for his work in the field of comparative Celtic grammar.

Pederson, Charles J (1904–89) Chemist, born in Fusan, Korea. He developed the compounds called *Crown ethers* in the 1960s, initiating a field known as *host–guest chemistry*, and shared the Nobel Prize for Chemistry in 1987.

Pedro I (1798–1834) Emperor of Brazil (1822–31), born in Lisbon, the second son of John VI of Portugal (reigned 1816–26). A liberal in outlook, he declared for Brazilian independence in 1822, but was forced to abdicate, and withdrew to Portugal.

Peel, Sir Robert (1788–1850) British prime minister (1834–5, 1841–6), born near Bury, Lancashire. As home secretary (1822–7, 1828–30), he carried through the Catholic Emancipation Act and reorganized the London police force (who became known as *Peelers* or *Bobbies*). As prime minister, his decision to repeal the Corn Laws (1846) split his party and brought his resignation.

Peele, George (c.1558–96) Elizabethan playwright, born in London. His best-known works are *The Arraignment of Paris* (1584), *Edward I* (1593), and *The Old Wives' Tale* (1595).

Péguy, Charles Pierre [paygee] (1873–1914) Poet and publisher, born in Orléans, France. A fervent socialist, his bookshop became a centre for political agitation.

Pei, I(eoh) M(eng) [pay] (1917–) Architect, born in Canton, China. In the USA from 1935, his principal projects include Mile High Center, Denver, the 60-storey John Hancock Tower, Boston, and the glass pyramids at the Louvre, Paris.

Pei, Mario (Andrew) [pay] (1901–1978) Linguist, born in Rome. He became known for his popularizations of language study, such as *The Story of English* (1952) and *Dictionary of Linguistics* (1954).

Peierls, Sir Rudolph (Ernest) [piylz] (1907–) Physicist, born in Berlin. He applied quantum theory to solids and to magnetic effects, then turned to nuclear physics, working on the atomic bomb (the Manhattan project) throughout World War 2.

Peirce, Charles Sanders [peers] (1839–1914) Philosopher, logician, and mathematician, born in Cambridge, MA. A pioneer in the development of modern, formal logic and the logic of relations, he is best known as the founder of pragmatism, and his theory of meaning helped establish the field of semiotics.

Peisistratos >> Pisistratus

Pelagius [pelayjius] (c.360–c.420) British or Irish monk, who settled in Rome c.400. His view that salvation can be achieved by the exercise of human powers (*Pelagianism*) was condemned by Church Councils in 416 and 418, and he was excommunicated.

Pelé [pelay], popular name of **Edson Arantes do Nascimento** (1940–) Footballer, widely held to be the best player in the game's history, born in Três Corações, Brazil. His first-class career was spent at Santos (1955–74) and the New York Cosmos (1975–7), and he played in Brazil's winning World Cup team in 1958, 1962, and 1970. Regarded as a national hero in Brazil, he was appointed a sports minister in 1994.

Pelham, Henry [pelam] (1696–1754) British statesman

and prime minister (1743–54), born in London, the younger brother of Thomas Pelham. He was active in suppressing the Jacobite Rising of 1715 and became secretary for war in 1724. >> Pelham, Thomas

Pelham (-Holles), Thomas, 1st Duke of Newcastle [pelam] (1693–1768) British prime minister (1754–6, 1757–62), the brother of Henry Pelham. A Whig and a supporter of Walpole, he became secretary of state (1724–54), and was extremely influential during the reigns of George I and II. >> Pelham, Henry

Pell, John (1610–85) Mathematician and clergyman, born in Southwick, Sussex. He is remembered chiefly for the equation named after him, and for introducing the division sign ('÷') into England.

Pelletier, Pierre Joseph [peltyay] (1788–1842) Chemist, born in Paris. With Caventou he discovered strychnine, quinine, brucine, and other alkaloids, and was responsible for the naming of chlorophyll. >> Caventou

Pelopidas [pelopidas] (c.410–364 BC) Theban general and statesman. With Epaminondas, he established the short-lived Theban hegemony over Greece in the 360s BC. Prominent in the Theban victory over Sparta at Leuctra (371 BC), he was later killed in battle. >> Epaminondas

Peltier, Jean Charles Athanase [peltyay] (1785–1845) Physicist, born in Ham, France. He discovered the thermoelectric reduction of temperature now known as the *Peltier effect*.

Pelton, Lester (Allen) (1829–1918) Inventor and engineer, born in Vermillion, OH. He devised a type of waterwheel used to drive mining machinery, and was granted a patent in 1880. *Pelton wheels* are now in use world-wide for high-head hydro power generation.

Pemberton, Sir Max (1863–1950) Writer, born in Birmingham, West Midlands. He wrote reviews, plays, and a series of historical romances, such as *Impregnable City* (1895) and *The Mad King Dies* (1928).

Pembroke, Earl of >> Marshal, William

Pen, Jean-Marie Le >> Le Pen, Jean-Marie

Penck, Albrecht (1858–1945) Geographer and geologist, born in Leipzig, Germany. He wrote the classic *Morphology of the Earth's Surface* (1894) and is believed to have introduced the term *geomorphology*.

Penda (c.575–655) King of Mercia (c.632–55). He established mastery over the English Midlands, and was frequently at war with the kings of Northumbria, killing Edwin and Oswald, but was himself slain by Oswald's successor, Oswiu. >> Edwin; Oswald

Penderecki, Krzysztof [pendreskee] (1933–) Composer, born in Debica, Poland. A leading composer of the Polish avant garde, his works include *Threnody for the Victims of Hiroshima* (1960), operas, and a St Luke Passion.

Penfield, Wilder Graves (1891–1976) Neurosurgeon, born in Spokane, WA. He is best known for his experimental work on the exposed brains of living human beings, which pioneered understanding of the causes of brain disease symptoms such as epilepsy.

Peniakoff, Vladimir [penyakof], nickname **Popski** (1897–1951) British soldier, born in Belgium. In 1942, with the sanction of the army, he formed his own force, 'Popski's Private Army', which carried out spectacular raids behind the German lines.

Penn, William (1644–1718) Quaker reformer and colonialist, born in London. In 1681 he obtained a grant of land in North America, which he called Pennsylvania in honour of his father, Admiral Sir William Penn (1621–70). He sailed in 1682, and governed the colony for two years.

Penney, J(ames) C(ash) (1875–1971) Retailer and philanthropist, born in Hamilton, MO. He opened his own store in Wyoming in 1904, and by 1971 J C Penney's was the second largest non-food retailer in the USA.

Penney, William (George) Penney, Baron (1909–91)

Physicist, born in Gibraltar. He became well known for his research work on nuclear weapons in the UK, and was director of the Atomic Weapons Research Establishment at Aldermaston (1953–9).

Penniman, Richard Wayne >> **Little Richard**

Pennington, Mary Engle (1872–1952) Chemist, born in Nashville, TN. Her pioneering work in methods of preserving dairy products, particularly by refrigeration, led to several practical innovations including refrigerated railroad cars.

Pennington, Michael (Vivian Fyfe) (1943–) British actor. A leading Shakespearean actor, in 1986 he co-founded and became co-artistic director, with Bogdanov, of the English Shakespeare Company. >> Bogdanov

Penrose, Sir Roland (Algernon) (1900–84) Painter, connoisseur, and art collector, born in London. In 1936 he organized the International Surrealist Exhibition in London, and in 1947 founded the Institute of Contemporary Arts. >> Picasso

Penzias, Arno (Allan) [**pen**zias] (1933–) Astrophysicist, born in Munich, Germany. In 1964, with colleague Robert Wilson, he discovered cosmic microwave background radiation, providing strong evidence for the 'big bang' theory for the origin of the universe. They shared the Nobel Prize for Physics in 1978. >> Wilson, Robert Woodrow

Pepin III, known as **Pepin the Short** (c.714–68) King of the Franks (751–68), the father of Charlemagne. He was the founder of the Frankish dynasty of the Carolingians. >> Charlemagne

Peploe, Samuel John (1871–1935) Artist, born in Edinburgh. After a visit to Paris, he remodelled his style in accordance with Fauve colouring and Cézannesque analysis of form. >> Cézanne

Pepusch, Johann Christoph [pe**poosh**] (1667–1752) Composer and musical theorist, born in Berlin. Best known as the arranger of the music for John Gay's The Beggar's Opera, he was a prolific composer of music for the theatre and Church, as well as of instrumental works. >> Gay

Pepys, Samuel [peeps] (1633–1703) Diarist and naval administrator, born in London. His celebrated diary, from 1 January 1660 to 31 May 1669, is both a personal record and a vivid picture of contemporary life. Written in cipher, it was not decoded until 1825.

Perahia, Murray [puh**riy**a] (1947–) Pianist, born in New York City. An international soloist, he is especially admired for his Mozart performances.

Perceval, John de Burgh (1923–) Ceramic artist and painter, born in Bruce Rock, Western Australia. After being exhibited in Melbourne, some of his paintings were reproduced in the avant-garde periodical, Angry Penguins.

Perceval, Spencer (1762–1812) British prime minister (1809–12), born in London. He was solicitor general (1801), attorney general (1802), and Chancellor of the Exchequer (1807). He was assassinated in the lobby of the House of Commons.

Percy, Thomas (1729–1811) Antiquarian, poet, and bishop, born in Bridgnorth, Shropshire. His fame rests on his Reliques of Ancient English Poetry (1765), largely compiled from a 17th-c manuscript of mediaeval ballads found in a house in Shropshire, and much 'restored' by him.

Percy, Walker (1916–90) Novelist, born in Birmingham, AL. His novels include The Moviegoer (1961, National Book Award), The Second Coming (1980), and The Thanatos Syndrome (1987).

Perdiccas [per**dik**as] (c.365–321 BC) Macedonian general, the second-in-command to Alexander the Great. He became virtually regent of the empire after Alexander's death, but was soon murdered by mutineers from his own army. >> Alexander the Great

Perdue, Frank(lin Parsons) (1920–) Food executive, born in Salisbury, MD. He joined his father's chicken farm in Salisbury in 1939, transforming Perdue Farms into one of the country's largest poultry processors.

Peregrinus (de Maricourt), Petrus [pere**griy**nus], also called **Peter of Maricourt** or **Peter the Pilgrim** (13th-c) Scientist and soldier, born in Picardy, France. He was the first to mark the ends of a round natural magnet and call them poles, and also invented a compass with a graduated scale.

Pereira, Valdir >> **Didi**

Perelman, S(ydney) J(oseph) (1904–79) Humorous writer, born in New York City. His writing is known for its linguistic dexterity and ingenuity - at its best in Crazy Like a Fox (1944) and Westward Ha! or, Around the World in 80 Clichés (1948).

Peres, Shimon [**pe**rez], originally **Shimon Perski** (1923–) Israeli Labour prime minister (1984–6), born in Wolozyn, Poland. He entered into a unique power-sharing agreement with the leader of the Consolidation Party, Yitzhak Shamir, becoming prime minister for two years, when Shamir took over. >> Rabin; Shamir

Pérez de Ayala, Ramón [**pe**reth, a**yah**la] (1881–1962) Writer and critic, born in Oviedo, Spain. His poetry includes The Peace of the Path (trans, 1904), and among his novels is the philosophical Belarmino y Apolonio (1921).

Pérez de Cuellar, Javier [**pe**rez duh **kway**ah(r)] (1920–) Peruvian diplomat, born in Lima. As secretary-general of the UN (1982–91) he played a prominent role in trying to secure a peaceful solution to the Falklands crisis, a ceasefire in the Iran–Iraq War, and the release of the Iranian hostages.

Pérez Galdós, Benito [**pe**rez gal**dos**] (1843–1920) Writer, born in Las Palmas, Canary Is, Spain. Regarded as Spain's greatest novelist after Cervantes, his 46 short Episodios nacionales (National Episodes) give a vivid picture of 19th-c Spain. Many of his plays are based on his novels. >> Cervantes

Pergolesi, Giovanni Battista [pergo**lay**zee] (1710–36) Composer, born in Jesi, Italy. His comic intermezzo La serva padrona (1732) influenced the development of opera buffa. He wrote much church music, notably his great Stabat Mater.

Peri, Jacopo [**pay**ree] (1561–1633) Composer, born in Rome. The leading composer in a group whose aim was to restore the true principles of Greek tragic declamation, he wrote Dafne (1597–89) and Euridice (1600), which have been historically accepted as the first genuine operas.

Periander [peri**an**der] (c.625–585 BC) Tyrant of Corinth, successor to his father, Cypselus. He extended Corinth's power and position in the Greek world, and cultivated links with foreign rulers. >> Cypselus

Pericles [**peri**kleez] (c.495–429 BC) General and statesman, a member of the aristocratic Alcmaeonid family, who presided over the 'Golden Age' of Athens, and virtually its uncrowned king (443–429 BC). His unremitting hostility to Sparta brought about the Peloponnesian War (431–404 BC).

Perkin, Sir William Henry (1838–1907) Chemist, born in London. In 1856 he made the discovery of a mauve substance with dyeing properties, which led to the foundation of the aniline dye industry.

Perkins, Anthony (1932–92) Actor, born in New York City. He is best known for his role as the maniacal Norman Bates in Hitchcock's Psycho (1960), with its three sequels (1983, 1986, 1990). >> Hitchcock

Perkins, Charles (Nelson) (1936–) Bureaucrat and activist, born in Australia of Arunta and European descent. A leader of the Aboriginal movement in the 1960s, his 'freedom rides' brought injustice to Aboriginal people to public attention.

Perkins, Francis (1882–1965) Social reformer and politician, born in Boston, MA. For 30 years she played a significant role in introducing women's issues into Democratic Party policy, and was US secretary of labor (1933–45).

Perkins, Jacob (1766–1849) Mechanical engineer and inventor, born in Newburyport, MA. He made counterfeiting more difficult by replacing copper plates with steel plates in the engraving process, thus enabling much more complicated patterns to be used for bank-notes.

Perkins, Maxwell (Evarts) (1884–1947) Editor and publisher, born in New York City. He joined Scribner's as an editor in 1914, and showed a genius for recognizing talent, publishing early works by F Scott Fitzgerald, Thomas Wolfe, Ernest Hemingway, and others.

Perlman, Itzhak (1945–) Violinist, born in Tel Aviv, the son of Polish immigrants. He made his debut at Carnegie Hall in 1963. A noted chamber music player, he has recorded almost all the standard violin works.

Permeke, Constant [permaykuh] (1886–1951) Painter and sculptor, born in Antwerp, Belgium. Leader of the modern Belgian Expressionist school, after 1936 he concentrated mainly on the sculpture of nudes and torsos.

Perón, (Maria) Eva (Duarte de) [peron], known as **Evita** (1919–52) The second wife of Argentinian President Juan Perón, born in Los Toldos, Argentina. An actress before her marriage in 1945, she became a powerful political influence and the mainstay of the Perón government. *Evita* (1979) was based on her life. >> Perón, Juan

Perón, Isabelita [peron], popular name of **Maria Estela Perón** *née* **Martínez Cartas** (1931–) President of Argentina (1974–6), born in La Rioja Province, Argentina. The third wife of Juan Perón (1961), she became vice-president under him in 1973. She took over the presidency at his death, but after a military coup she was imprisoned (1976–81), later settling in Madrid. >> Perón, Juan

Perón, Juan (Domingo) [peron] (1895–1974) Argentinian soldier and president (1946–55, 1973–4), born in Lobos, Buenos Aires. He took a leading part in the army coup of 1943, and gained widespread support through his social reforms. He was deposed and exiled in 1955, but returned to win an overwhelming electoral victory in 1973. >> Peron, Eva / Isabelita

Perosi, Lorenzo [perohsee] (1872–1956) Priest and composer, born in Tortona, Italy. His works include the oratorios *The Resurrection of Lazarus* and *The Passion of Christ*.

Perot, (Henry) Ross [peroh] (1930–) Businessman and politician, born in Texarkana, TX. He founded the Electronic Data Systems Corporation in 1962, and was its chairman and chief executive (1982–6). He became internationally known when he stood as an independent candidate in the 1992 US presidential election.

Pérouse, comte de la >> **La Pérouse, comte de**

Perrault, Charles [peroh] (1628–1703) Writer, born in Paris. He is best known for his *Tales of Mother Goose* (trans, 1697), which included 'The Sleeping Beauty' and 'Red Riding Hood'.

Perrin, Jean (Baptiste) [perī] (1870–1942) Physicist, born in Lille, France. For his research in molecular physics and radioactivity, and his discovery of the equilibrium of sedimentation, he was awarded the Nobel Prize for Physics in 1926.

Perronet, Jean Rodolphe [peronay] (1708–94) Civil engineer, born in Suresnes, France. His outstanding masonry arch bridges include the Pont de Neuilly and the Pont de la Concorde in Paris.

Perry, (Mary) Antoinette (1888–1946) Actress and director, born in Denver, CO. She had a long career on the stage, founding the American Theatre Wing (1941), and the annual 'Tony' Awards of the New York theatre are named after her.

Perry, Fred(erick John) (1909–95) Lawn tennis and table tennis player, born in Stockport, Cheshire. He won the world table tennis title in 1929, the lawn tennis singles title at Wimbledon in 1934–6, and was the first man to win all four major titles.

Perry, Matthew Galbraith (1794–1858) US naval officer, born in South Kingston, RI, the brother of Oliver Hazard Perry. He commanded the first US steam warship (USS *Fulton*), the Africa Squadron (1843–6), and the Home Squadron during the last phase of the Mexican War (1847–8). >> Perry, Oliver Hazard

Perry, Oliver Hazard (1785–1819) US naval officer, born in South Kingston, RI. During the War of 1812, he led the US Fleet against the British fleet, defeating a British squadron on L Erie. >> Perry, Matthew Galbraith

Perse, Saint-John >> **Saint-John Perse**

Pershing, John J(oseph), nickname **Black Jack** (1860–1948) US general, born in Laclede, MO. In 1917 he was made commander-in-chief of the US Expeditionary Force in Europe, and later became chief-of-staff of the US army (1921–4).

Persius, in full **Aulus Persius Flaccus** (34–62) Satirist, born of a distinguished equestrian family in Volaterrae, Etruria. At his death he left only six satires, published after his death.

Perthes, Jacques Boucher de >> **Boucher de Perthes, Jacques**

Perugino [perujeenoh] (Ital 'the Perugian'), originally **Pietro di Cristoforo Vannucci** (c.1450–1523) Painter, born in Città della Pieve, Umbria. He established himself in Perugia, and painted several frescoes in the Sistine Chapel, Rome, notably 'Christ Giving the Keys to Peter' (1481–2).

Perutz, Max (Ferdinand) [peruhts] (1914–) Scientist, born in Vienna. He worked on the molecular structure of haemoglobin, using the technique of X-ray diffraction, and shared the Nobel Prize for Chemistry in 1962. >> Kendrew

Peruzzi, Baldassare (Tommaso) [perutsee] (1481–1536) Architect, probably born in Siena. In 1503 he went to Rome, where he designed the Villa Farnesina and the Ossoli Palace, and painted frescoes in the Church of S Maria della Pace (1516).

Pestalozzi, Johann Heinrich [pestalotsee] (1746–1827) Educationist, born in Zürich, Switzerland. He wrote *How Gertrude Educates her Children* (trans, 1801), the recognized exposition of the Pestalozzian method, in which the process of education is seen as a gradual unfolding of the children's innate facilities. Pestalozzi International Children's Villages were established in Switzerland (1946) and Surrey, UK (1958).

Pétain, (Henri) Philippe (Omer) [paytĩ] (1856–1951) French soldier and statesman, born in Cauchy-à-la-Tour, France. He became a national hero for his defence of Verdun (1916). When France collapsed in 1940, he negotiated the armistice with Germany and Italy, and became chief-of-state at Vichy. After the liberation, he was tried for treason, and given life imprisonment.

Peter I, known as **the Great** (1672–1725) Tsar of Russia (1682–1721) and emperor (1721–5), born in Moscow. He embarked on a series of sweeping military, domestic, and ecclesiastical reforms. His defeat of Sweden in the Great Northern War established Russia as a major European power and gained a maritime exit on the Baltic coast, where he founded his new capital, St Petersburg. >> Alexis; Catherine I; Sophia Alexeyevna

Peter I (of Serbia) (1844–1921) King of Serbia (from 1903), born in Belgrade, the son of Prince Alexander Karadjordjević. He accompanied his army into exile in Greece in 1916, but returned in 1918, and was proclaimed titular king of the Serbs, Croats, and Slovenes until his death. >> Alexander I (of Yugoslavia)

Peter II (1923–70) King of Yugoslavia (1934–45), born in Belgrade, the son of Alexander I. He assumed sovereignty in 1941, but the German attack on Yugoslavia forced him into exile, and he lost his throne when Yugoslavia became a republic in 1945. >> Alexander I (of Yugoslavia)

Peter, St, originally **Simon** or **Simeon bar Jona** ('son of Jona') (1st-c), feast day 29 June. One of the 12 apostles of Jesus, a fisherman living in Capernaum, who was renamed by Jesus as **Cephas** or Peter (meaning 'rock') in view of his leadership among the disciples. Immediately after Jesus's ascension, Peter appears as the leader of the Christian community in Jerusalem. Tradition says that he was executed in Rome, and he is regarded by the Roman Catholic Church as the first Bishop of Rome. Two New Testament letters bear his name. >> Jesus Christ

Peter the Hermit (c.1050–c.1115) Monk, a preacher of the first Crusade, born in Amiens, France. He led the second army, which reached Asia Minor, but was defeated by the Turks at Nicaea. He then accompanied the fifth army in 1096, which reached Jerusalem.

Peter the Pilgrim >> **Peregrinus, Petrus**

Peter Damian, St >> **Damiani, Pietro**

Peter Lombard >> **Lombard, Peter**

Peters, Mary (Elizabeth) (1939–) Athlete, born in Halewood, Lancashire. She won the gold medal in the pentathlon in the 1972 Olympics, setting a new world record, and was also the Commonwealth champion twice, winning the shot as well in the 1970 Games.

Peterson, Oscar (Emmanuel) (1925–) Jazz pianist and composer, born in Montreal, Quebec, Canada. In 1949 he became an international star when he joined a concert tour called 'Jazz at the Philharmonic' in New York, known for his extraordinary keyboard facility.

Peterson, Roger Tory (1908–) Ornithologist, born in Jamestown, NY. His field guides, such as the best-selling *Field Guide to the Birds* (1934), and other works helped build popular awareness of wildlife conservation and environmental protection.

Petipa, Marius [peteepa] (1818–1910) Ballet-master and choreographer, credited with the development of Russian classical ballet, born in Marseille, France. He went to St Petersburg in 1847 to join the Imperial Theatre, becoming ballet master in 1869.

Petit, Alexis (Thérèse) [puhtee] (1791–1820) Physicist, born in Vesoul, France. He enunciated with Dulong the *law of Dulong and Petit*, that for all elements the product of the specific heat and the atomic weight is the same. >> Dulong

Petit, Roland [puhtee] (1924–) Choreographer and dancer, born in Paris. In 1948 he founded Ballets de Paris de Roland Petit, which toured widely in Europe and the USA. He later founded the Ballet de Marseille (1972), and became its director.

Petitot, Jean [puhteetoh] (1607–91) Painter of enamel miniatures, born in Geneva, Switzerland. His works included many portaits of King Louis XIV, most based on larger paintings done by other artists.

Petőfi, Sandor [petoefee] >> **Arany, János**

Pétomane, Le >> **Pujol, Joseph**

Petrarch [petrah(r)k], in full **Francesco Petrarca** (1304–74) Poet and scholar, born in Arezzo, Italy. In 1327 at Avignon he first saw Laura (possibly Laure de Noves), who inspired him with a passion which has become proverbial for its constancy and purity, seen in the series of love poems the *Canzoniere*. Crowned poet laureate at Rome in 1341, he was the earliest of the great Renaissance humanists and wrote widely on the classics.

Petrie, Sir (William Matthew) Flinders [peetree] (1853–1942) Archaeologist and Egyptologist, born in Charlton, Kent. He surveyed Stonehenge (1874–7), but

turned entirely to Egyptology from 1881, surveying the pyramids and temples of Giza and excavating the mounds of Tanis and Naucratis.

Petronio, Stephen [petrohnioh] (1956–) Dancer and choreographer, born in Nutley, NJ. He joined the modern dance experimental company of Trisha Brown (1979–86), then headed his own troupe. >> Brown, Trisha

Petronius Arbiter [petrohnius ah(r)bitair] (1st-c) Latin writer, supposedly the Gaius Petronius whom Tacitus called *arbiter elegantiae* (arbiter of taste), and possible author of *Satyricon*, a satirical romance in prose. >> Tacitus

Petrosian, Tigran V(artanovich) [petrohzian] (1929–84) Chess player, born in Tbilisi, Georgia (formerly, USSR). He won the world title from Botvinnik in 1963, and made one successful defence before losing it to Spassky in 1969. >> Botvinnik; Spassky

Petrovitch, Alexey >> **Alexis**

Petrov-Vodkin, Kuzma Sergeyevich [petrof vodkin] (1878–1939) Painter, born in Khvalynsk, Russia. His importance rests mainly on his influence as a teacher of the first generation of Soviet painters at the Leningrad Art Academy.

Pettit, Bob, popular name of **Robert F Lee Pettit** (1932–) Basketball player, born in Baton Rouge, LA. He joined the Milwaukee (later the St Louis) Hawks in the National Basketball Association (NBA) in 1954, and throughout his career averaged 26·4 points per game.

Petty, Sir William (1623–87) Economist, born in Romsey, Hampshire. He was appointed surveyor-general of Ireland by Charles II, his chief economic work being *Treatise on Taxes* (1662).

Pétursson, Hallgrímur [payterson] (1614–74) Devotional poet, pastor, and hymn-writer, born in Hólar, Iceland. His masterpiece, *Passion Hymns* (trans, 1666), is a cycle of 50 meditations on the Crucifixion.

Peuerbach, Georg von >> **Purbach, Georg von**

Pevsner, Antoine (1886–1962) Constructivist sculptor and painter, born in Oryol, Russia. In Moscow he helped to form the Suprematist group, but in 1920 broke away and issued the *Realist Manifesto* with his brother, ultimately causing their exile from Russia. >> Gabo

Pevsner, Sir Nikolaus (Bernhard Leon) (1902–83) Art historian, born in Leipzig, Germany. An authority on English architecture, his best-known works are *An Outline of European Architecture* (1942) and the Penguin series *The Buildings of England* (50 vols, 1951–74).

Pfitzner, Hans (Erich) (1869–1949) Composer, born in Moscow. He wrote *Palestrina* (1917) and other operas, as well as choral, orchestral, and chamber music.

Phaedrus or **Phaeder** [feedrus, feeder] (1st-c) The translator of Aesop's fables into Latin verse, born a slave in Macedonia. He went to Italy, where he was the freedman of Emperor Augustus, and published five books of fables, many his own invention. >> Aesop

Phalaris [falaris] (?–554 BC) Tyrant of Acragas (modern Agrigento) in Sicily, notorious for his cruelty. On his overthrow, he suffered the same fate as his former victims: he was roasted alive in a bronze bull.

Pheidippides [fiydipideez] (5th-c BC) Long-distance runner from Greece. Sent to Sparta to ask for aid against the Persians before the Battle of Marathon in 490 BC, he is reputed to have covered 150 mi in two days.

Phidias [fiydias] (5th-c BC) The greatest sculptor of Greece, born in Athens. He constructed the Propylaea and the Parthenon, carving the gold and ivory 'Athena' there and the 'Zeus' at Olympia.

Philaretus >> **Geulincx, Arnold**

Philby, Kim, popular name of **Harold Adrian Russell Philby** (1912–88) Double agent, born in Ambala, India. Already recruited as a Soviet agent, he was employed by the British Secret Intelligence Service (1944–6) as head of anti-Communist counter-espionage. In 1963 he disappeared to Russia, where he was granted citizenship.

Philidor, François André, originally **François André Danican** (1726–95) Composer of operas, and chess master, born in Dreux, France. From a prominent musical family, he wrote 21 operas, but then turned to chess, publishing the first book laying down the strategic principles of the game.

Philip II (of France), known as **Philip Augustus** (1165–1223) King of France (1179–1223), born in Paris, the son of Louis VII. His reign formed a key period in the development of the mediaeval kingdom of France. He embarked on the Third Crusade in 1190, but returned the next year to attack the continental lands of the Angevin kings of England.

Philip II (of Macedon) (382–336 BC) King of Macedon (359–336 BC), the father of Alexander the Great. He created a powerful unified state at home (359–353 BC), then made himself master of the whole of independent Greece with his decisive victory at Chaeronea (338 BC). >> Alexander the Great; Olympias

Philip II (of Spain) (1527–98) King of Spain (1556–98) and Portugal (as Philip I, 1580–98), born in Valladolid, Spain. He married Mary I (1554), becoming joint sovereign of England, and after Mary's death (1558), having inherited the Habsburg possessions, married Elizabeth of France to seal the end of Valois–Habsburg conflict. He was the champion of the Counter-Reformation, and although his armada was later destroyed (1588), he defeated the Ottomans at Lepanto (1571) and conquered Portugal (1580). >> Charles V (Emperor); Mary I; William I (of the Netherlands)

Philip III, known as **Philip the Good** (1396–1467) Duke of Burgundy (1419–67), born in Dijon, France, the grandson of Philip the Bold. He at first recognized Henry V of England as heir to the French crown, but concluded a separate peace with the French in 1435.

Philip V (1683–1746) First Bourbon king of Spain (1700–46), born in Versailles, France, the grandson of Louis XIV and Maria Theresa. He gained the throne at the Peace of Utrecht (1713), but lost the Spanish Netherlands and Italian lands.

Philip VI (1293–1350) First Valois king of France (1328–50). His right to the throne was denied by Edward III of England, which led to the Hundred Years' War with England, and he was defeated at Crécy (1346).

Philip, St (1st-c, feast day 3 May (W) or 14 November (E). One of the disciples of Jesus, listed among the 12 (in *Acts* 1). He is prominent in John's Gospel, and traditions suggest he was martyred on a cross.

Philip (?–1676) American-Indian chief (Indian name, Metacomet), the son of Massoit, chief of the Wampanoag Indians of Massachusetts. He led a confederation of tribes against the European settlers (1675–6), but was shot on the battlefield by one of his own braves.

Philip, Prince >> Edinburgh, Duke of

Philip Neri, St >> Neri, St Philip

Philippa of Hainault [enoh] (c.1314–1369) Queen consort of England, who married her second cousin Edward III at York in 1327. She is said to have roused the English troops before the defeat of the Scots at the Battle of Neville's Cross in 1346. >> Edward III

Philips, Anton (1874–1951) Dutch businessman. In 1921 he took over the light-bulb manufacturing business founded by his brother, began mass production of one of the first radio sets, and built the company into a major supplier of electrical domestic equipment.

Philips, Katherine, also known by her maiden name **Katherine Fowler** (1631–64) Poet, born in London. The first English woman poet to have her work published, she organized a salon for the discussion of poetry and religion.

Philipson, Sir Robin, popular name of **Sir Robert James Philipson** (1916–92) Painter, born in Broughton-in-Furness, Cumbria. He handled paint freely and colours boldly, but always retained a precise figurative element in his work.

Phillip, Arthur (1738–1814) Admiral, founder and first governor of New South Wales, born in London. He was appointed commander of the 'First Fleet' carrying convicts to Australia, and founded a penal colony settlement at Sydney in 1788.

Phillips, David (Graham) (1867–1911) Writer, born in Madison, IN. He wrote powerfully in favour of the emancipation of women, notably in his novels *The Plum Tree* (1905) and *Susan Lennox: Her Fall and Rise* (1917).

Phillips, John Bertram (1906–82) Bible translator, writer, and broadcaster, born in London. His best sellers include *Your God is Too Small* (1952) and *A Man Called Jesus* (1959).

Phillips, Mark (Antony Peter), Captain (1948–) Former husband of Princess Anne (1973–92), and a noted horseman. A regular member of the British equestrian team (1970–6), he won the team event gold medal at the Munich Olympic Games in 1972. >> Anne (Elizabeth Alice Louise)

Phillips, Peter / Zara >> Anne (Elizabeth Alice Louise), Princess

Phillpotts, Eden (1862–1960) British writer, born in Mount Aboo, India. His many novels about Dartmoor include *Children in the Mist* (1898), *The Secret Woman* (1905), and *Widecombe Fair* (1913).

Philo [fiyloh] (2nd-c) Byzantine scientist. He wrote a treatise on military engineering, and was probably the first to record the contraction of air in a globe over water when a candle is burnt in it.

Philo Judaeus [fiyloh judayus] (c.20 BC–c.AD 40) Hellenistic Jewish philosopher, born in Alexandria. His work brought together Greek philosophy and the Hebrew Scriptures.

Philostratus, Flavius [filostratus] (c.170–245) Greek sophist. He wrote an idealized life of Apollonius of Tyana, *Lives of the Sophists*, and the amatory *Epistles*.

Phintias >> Damon and Pythias

Phipps, Sir William (1651–95) Colonial governor, born in Pemmaquid, ME. In 1690 he captured Port Royal (now Annapolis) in Nova Scotia, but failed in 1691 in a naval attack upon Quebec. Governor of Massachusetts in 1692, he was involved in the Salem witchcraft trials.

Phiz >> Browne, Hablot Knight

Phocion [fohshion] (c.402–318 BC) Athenian soldier. Virtual ruler in Athens from 318 BC, he vainly endeavoured to prevent the Athenians from going to war with Antipater. He was put to death on a charge of treason.

Phomvihane, Kaysone (1920–92) Laotian prime minister (1975–91), born in Savannakhet province, Laos. General-secretary of the Lao People's Revolutionary Party, he began with a radical socialist programme, but changed to one of economic and political liberalization.

Photius [fohtius] (c.820–91), feast day 6 February (E). Patriarch of Constantinople (858–67, 877–86), born in Constantinople (Istanbul). On the deposition of Ignatius from the patriarchate, he was hurriedly installed in his place, but a Council at Rome declared Photius's election invalid and he was exiled in 886. >> Nicholas I

Phryne [friynee] (4th-c BC) Greek courtesan of antiquity, who reputedly was Praxiteles' model for his statue of Aphrodite. Accused of profaning the Eleusinian Mysteries, she was successfully defended by the orator Hyperides. >> Hyperides; Praxiteles

Piaf, Edith [peeaf], popular name of **Edith Giovanna Gassion** (1915–63) Singer, born in Paris. Known as *Piaf*, from the Parisian slang for 'sparrow', she became legendary for her nostalgic songs, such as 'Non, je ne regrette rien'.

Piaget, Jean [pyahzhay] (1896–1980) Psychologist, born in Neuchâtel, Switzerland. He is best known for his research on the development of cognitive functions in children, in such pioneering studies as *The Origins of Intelligence in Children* (trans, 1948).

Piatigorsky, Gregor [pyatigaw(r)skee] (1903–76) Cellist, born in Dnepropetrovsk, Ukraine. He embarked on an international solo career in 1928, and became a US citizen in 1942.

Piazzi, Giuseppe [pyatsee] (1746–1826) Astronomer, born in Ponte di Valtellina, Italy. He set up an observatory at Palermo in 1789, published a catalogue of the stars (1803, 1814), and discovered and named the first minor planet, Ceres.

Picabia, Francis [pikahbia] (1879–1953) Painter, born in Paris. One of the most anarchistic of modern artists, his anti-art productions, often portraying senseless machinery, include 'Parade Amoureuse' (1917) and cover designs for the American anti-art magazine *291*.

Picard, (Charles) Emile [peekah(r)] (1856–1941) Mathematician, born in Paris. He was especially noted for his work in complex analysis, and on integral and differential equations.

Picard, Jean [peekah(r)] (1620–82) Astronomer, born in La Flèche, France. He made the first accurate measurement of a degree of a meridian, and thus arrived at an estimate of the radius of the Earth.

Picasso, Pablo [pikasoh] (1881–1973) Artist, born in M laga, Spain. The dominant figure of early 20th-c art, his 'blue period' (1902–4), a series of striking studies of the poor, gave way to the life-affirming 'pink period' (1904–6), full of the incidents of circus life. He then turned to brown, and began to work in sculpture. His break with tradition came with 'Les Demoiselles d'Avignon' (1906–7), the first exemplar of analytical Cubism, a movement which he developed with Braque (1909–14). His major creation is 'Guernica' (1937). >> Braque

Piccard, Auguste (Antoine) [peekah(r)] (1884–1962) Physicist, born in Basel, Switzerland, the twin brother of Jean Piccard. In 1932 he ascended in a balloon 16 940 m/55 563 ft into the stratosphere, and in 1948 explored the ocean depths off West Africa in a bathyscaphe of his own design. >> Piccard, Jean

Piccard, Jean (Felix) [peekah(r)] (1884–1963) Chemist, born in Basel, Switzerland, the twin brother of Auguste Piccard. In 1934 he designed and ascended in a balloon from Dearborn, Detroit, to a height of 11 mi, collecting valuable data concerning cosmic rays. >> Piccard, Auguste

Piccaver, Alfred (1884–1958) Tenor, born in Long Sutton, Somerset. He was the leading tenor at Vienna (1910–37), singing Beethoven, Wagner, Verdi, and Puccini roles.

Piccinni, Niccola [peecheenee] (1728–1800) Composer, born in Bari, Italy. He wrote over 100 operas as well as oratorios and church music. In 1766 he was summoned to Paris, and became the representative of the musical party opposed to Gluck.

Pick, Frank (1878–1941) Administrator and design patron, born in Spalding, Lincolnshire. As vice-chairman of the London passenger transport board (1933–40), he transformed London Transport into a unified modern system.

Pickering, Edward Charles (1846–1919) Astronomer, born in Boston, MA, the brother of William Henry Pickering. His work was concerned with stellar photometry and classification of star spectra, and he invented the meridian photometer. >> Pickering, William Henry

Pickering, Sir George (1904–80) Clinician who pioneered the study of blood pressure, born in Whalton, Northumberland. He studied the mechanism of pain in peptic ulcer, and the physiological causes and epidemiology of high blood pressure in human populations.

Pickering, William Henry (1858–1938) Astronomer, born in Boston, MA. In 1919 he discovered Phoebe, the ninth satellite of Saturn, and in 1919 predicted the existence of a ninth planet in the Solar System (Pluto, discovered in 1930). >> Pickering, Edward Charles

Pickett, George Edward (1825–75) US soldier, born in Richmond, VA. A Confederate in the Civil War, at Gettysburg he led one last desperate charge across an open field (*Pickett's charge*).

Pickford, Mary, originally **Gladys Mary Smith** (1893–1979) Actress, born in Toronto, Ontario, Canada. Her beauty and charm won her the title of 'The World's Sweetheart', her many films including *Rebecca of Sunnybrook Farm* (1917) and *Poor Little Rich Girl* (1917). Her second husband was Douglas Fairbanks, Snr. >> Fairbanks, Douglas, Snr

Pico della Mirandola, Giovanni, Comte (Count) [peekoh, mirandola] (1463–94) Renaissance philosopher, born in Mirandola, Italy. He wrote Latin epistles and elegies, a series of Italian sonnets, and a major study of free will.

Pieck, Wilhelm [peek] (1876–1960) East German president (1949–60), born near Berlin. He helped found the Spartacus League (1915) and the German Communist Party (1918), leading the unsuccessful 'Spartacus uprising' in Berlin in 1919. In 1946 he founded the Socialist Unity Party.

Pierce, Franklin (1804–69) US statesman and 14th president (1853–7), born in Hillsborough, NH. As president he tried unsuccessfully to bridge the widening chasm between the South and the North.

Pierce, John Robinson (1910–) Electrical engineer, born in Des Moines, IA. In the 1950s he saw the possibilities of satellite communication, taking a leading part in the development work that resulted in the launch of *Echo* (1960) and *Telstar* (1962).

Piero della Francesca [pyayroh, franchayska] (c.1420–92) Painter, born in Borgo San Sepolcro, Italy. His major work is a series of frescoes illustrating 'The Legend of the True Cross' (1452–66) in the choir of S Francesco at Arezzo.

Piero di Cosimo [pyairoh di kohzimoh], originally **Piero di Lorenzo** (c.1462–c.1521) Painter, born in Florence, Italy. Among his best-known works are 'The Death of Procris' (c.1500) and 'The Rescue of Andromeda' (c.1515).

Pierre, Abbé [pyair], originally **Henri Antoine Grouès** (1912–) Priest, born in Lyon, France. Committed to helping the homeless of Paris, he formed his band of Companions of Emmaus, providing shelter for hundreds of families.

Pigalle, Jean Baptiste [peegal] (1714–85) Sculptor, born in Paris. His works include a statue of Voltaire, and the tomb of Marshal Maurice de Saxe in Strasbourg.

Piggott, Lester (Keith) (1935–) Flat racing jockey, born in Wantage, Berkshire. He rode 4349 winners in Britain (1948–85), and was champion jockey 11 times. After retiring he became a trainer but was imprisoned (1987–8) for tax offences. He later resumed his career as a jockey.

Pike, Kenneth (Lee) (1912–) Linguist and anthropologist, born in Woodstock, CT. He developed the system of linguistic analysis known as *tagmemics*. Among his many books are *Language in Relation to a Unified Theory of the Structure of Human Behavior* (1954–60).

Pike, Zebulon (Montgomery) (1779–1813) US army officer and explorer, born in Lamberton, NJ. Sent to explore the area around the Arkansas and Red Rivers, his party encountered a mountain peak in the Rocky Mountains, Colorado, later named *Pike's Peak*.

Pilate, Pontius [ponshus], Lat **Pontius Pilatus** (1st-c) Roman prefect of Judaea, appointed by Tiberius in c.26. His fame rests entirely on his role in the story of Jesus of Nazareth, permitting his execution at the prompting of the Jewish authorities. >> Jesus Christ

Pilbeam, David Roger (1940–) Physical anthropologist, born in Brighton, East Sussex. A leading student of human and primate evolution, his many publications include *Evolution of Man* (1970) and *The Ascent of Man* (1972).

Pile, Sir Frederick Alfred (1884–1976) British soldier. In World War 1 he won the DSO and the MC, and throughout World War 2 commanded Britain's anti-aircraft defences.

Pilger, John (Richard) [piljer] (1939–) Journalist and documentary film-maker, born in Sydney, New South Wales, Australia. He has twice won the British Journalist of the Year award and is a winner of the UNESCO Peace Prize. His film *Year Zero* (1979) exposed the atrocities of Pol Pot to the world. >> Pol Pot

Pilkington, Sir Alastair, originally **Lionel Alexander Bethune Pilkington** (1920–) Glass manufacturer, born in Newbury, Berkshire. He joined the family firm of glassmakers, and in 1952 conceived a new technique for manufacturing plate glass.

Pillsbury, Charles Alfred (1842–99) Flour miller, born in Warner, NH. In 1869 he bought into a flour mill, acquired new milling technology, and organized C A Pillsbury & Co in 1872.

Pilnyak, Boris, pseudonym **Boris Andreyevich Vogau** (1894–?1937) Writer, born in Mozhaisk, Russia. He wrote novels and short stories, including (trans titles) *The Naked Year* (1922) and *The Volga Flows Down to the Caspian Sea* (1930). An anti-Communist, he disappeared in 1937.

Pilon, Germain [peelô] (1537–90) Sculptor, born in Paris. He is known for 'The Three Graces', and the statues at the tomb of Henry II and Catherine de' Medici at St Denis.

Piłsudski, Józef (Klemens) [pilsudskee] (1867–1935) Polish marshal and first president (1918–22), born near Vilna, Poland. He became leader of the Polish Socialist Party in 1892, and declared Poland's independence in 1918. He returned to power in 1926 by means of a military coup, and established a dictatorship.

Pinchback, Pinckney (Benton Stewart) (1837–1921) US politician and Union army officer, born in Macon, GA. The son of a white planter and a slave mother, he was freed by his father. After the Civil War, he played a leading role in Louisiana politics (1865–77).

Pinchbeck, Christopher (c.1670–1732) Clockmaker and toymaker, from London. He invented the gold-coloured alloy of copper and zinc for making imitation gold watches, which has since been given his name.

Pinckney, Charles (Cotesworth) (1746–1825) US statesman, born in Charleston, SC. A member of the Constitutional Convention (1787), he was twice Federalist candidate for the presidency (1804, 1808). >> Pinckney, Thomas

Pinckney, Thomas (1750–1828) US diplomat and soldier, born in Charleston, SC, the brother of Charles Pinckney. He negotiated the San Lorenzo or *Pinckney Treaty* with Spain, which established rights on the Mississippi R (1795). >> Pinckney, Charles

Pincus, Gregory (Goodwin) (1903–67) Physiologist, born in Woodbine, NJ. His research found that some of the new synthetic hormones controlled fertility effectively, and led to the development of the contraceptive pill.

Pindar (c.522–c.440 BC) The chief lyric poet of Greece, born near Thebes. He became famous as a composer of odes for people in all parts of the Greek world. Only his *Epinikia* (Triumphal Odes) have survived entire.

Pindling, Sir Lynden O(scar) (1930–) Bahamian prime minister (1973–92), born in the Bahamas. Leader of the Progressive Liberal Party, he became prime minister in 1969, leading his country to full independence within the Commonwealth in 1973.

Pinero, Sir Arthur (Wing) [pinairoh] (1855–1934) Playwright, born in London. He wrote several farces, but is best known for his social dramas, notably *The Second Mrs Tanqueray* (1893).

Pinin Farina >> **Farina, Battista**

Pinkerton, Allan (1819–84) Detective, born in Glasgow, Strathclyde. In 1850 he founded the Pinkerton National Detective Agency, and headed a Federal intelligence network during the Civil War.

Pinkham, Lydia (Estes) [pingkham] (1819-83) Manufacturer, born in Lynn, MA. She began selling a herbal remedy called 'Mrs Lydia E Pinkham's Vegetable Compound' which, for some 50 years, was one of the most popular patent medicines in America.

Pinochet (Ugarte), Augusto [peenohshay] (1915–) Chilean dictator (1973–90), born in Valparaíso, Chile. He led the military coup ousting the Allende government in 1973, and in 1980 enacted a constitution giving himself an eight-year presidential term (1981–9). >> Allende, Salvador

Pinter, Harold (1930–) Playwright and director, born in London. His plays include *The Birthday Party* (1958), *The Caretaker* (1960; filmed 1963), *The Homecoming* (1965), and *Moonlight* (1993). His screenplays include *The Servant* (1962) and *The Go-Between* (1969). His work is highly regarded for the way it uses the unspoken meaning behind inconsequential everyday talk to induce an atmosphere of menace. >> Fraser, Antonia

Pinturicchio [pintureekyoh], originally **Bernardino di Betto Vagio** (1454–1513) Painter, born in Perugia, Italy. He painted frescoes in several churches and the Vatican Library, and assisted Perugino on the frescoes in the Sistine Chapel at Rome. >> Perugino

Pinza, Ezio, originally **Fortunio Pinza** (1892–1957) Bass singer, born in Rome. A favourite at the Metropolitan Opera, New York City (1926–48), he later appeared in Broadway shows and films, including *South Pacific*.

Pinzón, Vicente Yáñez [peenthon] (c.1460–c.1524) Discoverer of Brazil, born in Palos, Spain. In 1500 he landed near Pernambuco on the Brazil coast, which he followed N to the Orinoco.

Piombo, Sebastiano del [pyomboh] ('of the Seal'), originally **Sebastiano del Luciani** (1485–1547) Painter, born in Venice, Italy. He went to Rome in c.1510, where he worked in conjunction with Michelangelo. His masterpiece was 'The Raising of Lazarus' (1519).

Piozzi, Hester Lynch [pyotsee], previously **Harriet Lynch Thrale** née **Salusbury** (1741–1821) Writer, born near Pwllheli, Gwynedd. Dr Samuel Johnson conceived an extraordinary affection for her, and lived in her house at Streatham Place for over 16 years. >> Johnson, Samuel

Piper, Charles V(ancouver) (1867–1926) Agronomist, born in Victoria, British Columbia, Canada. Working for the US Department of Agriculture (1903–26), he introduced new varieties of drought-resistant grass which became vitally important for American hay crops.

Piper, John (1903–92) Artist, born in Epsom, Surrey. He is known for his pictures of war damage, and for his topographical works, notably the watercolours of Windsor Castle commissioned by the Queen (1941–2).

Piper, Otto (1891–) Theologian, born in Lichte, Germany. He advocated a 'biblical realism' which neither took Scripture literally nor ignored its teaching, but sought to be true to the writers' intentions.

Piper, Watty >> **Bragg, Mabel Caroline**

Piper, William (Thomas) (1881–1970) Aircraft manufacturer, born in Knapps Creek, NY. In 1931 he began producing small affordable planes, 'Cubs', for ordinary people, developing the Piper Aircraft Corporation.

Pippi, Giulio >> **Giulio Romano**

Piquet, Nelson [peekay], originally **Nelson Souto Maior** (1952–) Motor-racing driver, born in Rio de Janeiro, Brazil. He was world champion in 1981, 1983 (both

Brabham), and 1987 (Williams). He won 23 grand prix between 1978 and a serious accident in 1991.

Pirandello, Luigi [pirandeloh] (1867–1936) Writer, born in Girgenti, Sicily, Italy. After writing novels and short stories, he became a leading exponent of contemporary drama, as seen in (trans titles) *Six Characters in Search of an Author* (1921) and *Henry IV* (1922). He was awarded the Nobel Prize for Literature in 1934.

Piranesi, Giambattista [piranayzee], or **Giovanni Battista** (1720–78) Architect and copper-engraver of Roman antiquities, born in Mestre, Italy. He went to Rome in 1740, where he developed his own printing techniques, producing many etchings of the city.

Pire, Dominique (Georges) [peer] (1910–69) Dominican priest, born in Dinant, Belgium. He received the 1958 Nobel Prize for Peace for his scheme of 'European villages' for elderly refugees and destitute children.

Pirenne, Henri [peeren] (1862–1935) Historian of Belgium and mediaeval Europe, born in Verviers, Belgium. His chief works are (trans titles) *Economic and Social History of Mediaeval Europe* (1936) and *History of Belgium* (7 vols, 1900–32).

Pirie, (Douglas Alastair) Gordon (1931–91) Athlete, born in Leeds, West Yorkshire. A middle-distance runner, at various times he held the world records for 3000 m and 5000 m.

Pirie, Norman Wingate (1907–) British biochemist. In 1936 he isolated and crystallized the tobacco mosaic virus, an important step in the understanding of DNA and RNA. >> Stanley, Wendell

Pisanello, Antonio [peesaneloh], originally **Antonio Pisano** (c.1395–1455) Court painter, born in Pisa, Italy. The foremost draughtsman of his day, his drawings became models for later Renaissance artists. His most famous picture is 'The Vision of Saint Eustace'.

Pisano, Andrea [peesahnoh], also known as **Andrea da Pontedera** (c.1270–1349) Sculptor, born in Pontedera, Italy. In 1337 he became chief artist in the cathedral at Florence, and later worked on reliefs and statues in the cathedral at Orvieto (1347).

Pisano, Giovanni [peesahnoh] (c.1250–c.1320) Sculptor and architect, born in Pisa, Italy, the son of Nicola Pisano. The greatest sculptor of his day in the Italian Gothic tradition, he worked with his father on the pulpit in Siena, the fountain in Perugia, and the facade of Siena Cathedral (1284–6).

Pisano, Nicola [peesahnoh] (c.1225–78/84) Sculptor, architect, and engineer, probably born in Apulia, Italy. He worked on the pulpit in the Baptistery in Pisa (1260), the pulpit for the cathedral at Siena, and on the Fontana Maggiore in Perugia. >> Pisano, Giovanni

Piscator, Erwin [piskahter] (1893–1966) Theatre director, born in Ulm, Germany. He was the first to use the term *epic theatre* to describe a theatre composed of short, episodic plays with political ambitions, and pioneered staging techniques using films and mechanical devices.

Pisistratus [piysistratus], also spelled **Peisistratos** (c.600–527 BC) Tyrant of Athens (561–c.556 BC, 546–527 BC). A noted patron of the arts, he was succeeded by his sons Hippias and Hipparchus, the so-called *Pisistratidae*, but the dynasty was overthrown in 510 BC.

Pissarro, Camille [peesaroh] (1830–1903) Impressionist artist, born in St Thomas, Danish West Indies. The leader of the original Impressionists, most of his works depicted the countryside around Paris, such as 'Boulevard Montmartre' (1897). >> Pissarro, Lucien

Pissarro, Lucien [peesaroh] (1863–1944) Painter, designer, wood-engraver, and printer, the son of Camille Pissarro. He went to England in 1890, where he founded the Eragny press (1894), designed types, and painted landscapes in the Divisionist manner. >> Pissarro, Camille

Piston, Walter (Hamor) (1894–1976) Composer, born in Rockland, ME. His compositions are in a modern, Neoclassical style that includes elements from jazz and popular music.

Pitcairn, Robert (c.1745–1770) British sailor. A midshipman on board the *Swallow* in 1767, he was the first to sight the island now named after him. >> Christian, Fletcher

Pitman, Benjamin (1822–1910) Educationist and pioneer of shorthand in the USA, born in Trowbridge, Wiltshire, the brother of Sir Isaac Pitman. In 1852 he went to the USA to teach his shorthand system there, and established the Phonographic Institute in Cincinnati (1853). >> Pitman, Isaac

Pitman, Sir Isaac (1813–97) Educationist, and inventor of a shorthand system, born in Trowbridge, Wiltshire. In Bath he established a Phonetic Institute for teaching shorthand (1839–43), and brought out the *Phonetic Journal* (1842). >> Pitman, Benjamin

Pitot, Henri [peetoh] (1695–1771) Hydraulic and civil engineer, born in Aramon, France. In 1730 he invented the device now known as the *Pitot tube*, by means of which the relative velocity of a fluid past the orifice of the tube may be measured.

Pitt, Thomas (1653–1726) Merchant, born in Blandford St Mary, Dorset. A wealthy East India merchant, he bought the *Pitt diamond*, which he sold in 1717 to the French regent to become one of the state jewels of France. William Pitt, the Elder, was his grandson. >> Pitt, William, Earl of Chatham

Pitt, William, 1st Earl of Chatham, also known as **Pitt the Elder** (1708–78) British statesman and virtual premier (1756–61, 1766–8), born in London. He led the young 'Patriot' Whigs, and in 1756 became secretary of state. The king's enmity led him to resign in 1757, but public demand caused his recall, though he was again compelled to resign when his Cabinet refused to declare war with Spain (1761). >> Pitt, Thomas / William (the Younger)

Pitt, William, also known as **Pitt the Younger** (1759–1806) British prime minister (1783–1801, 1804–6), born in Hayes, Kent, the second son of the Earl of Chatham (William Pitt, the Elder). In his first ministry he carried through important reforms, negotiated coalitions against France (1793, 1798), and proposed a legislative union with Ireland (1800). He resigned rather than contest George III's hostility to Catholic emancipation. >> Pitt, William, Earl of Chatham

Pittacus of Mytilene [mituhleenee] (650–570 BC) Statesman from ancient Greece, one of the Seven Wise Men of Greece. His experience, according to the ancients, was embodied in 'know thine opportunity' and other aphorisms.

Pitter, Ruth (1897–1992) Poet, born in Ilford, Essex. Her volumes include *First and Second Poems* (1927), *A Mad Lady's Garland* (1934), and *End of Drought* (1975). She won the Hawthornden Prize in 1936.

Pitt-Rivers, Augustus (Henry Lane-Fox) (1827–1900) British soldier and archaeologist, born at Hope Hall, Yorkshire. He inherited Wiltshire estates, rich in Romano-British and Saxon remains, and developed a new scientific approach to excavation which became a model for later workers.

Pius IV, originally **Giovanni Angelo Medici** (1499–1565) Pope (1559–65), born in Milan, Italy. He brought to a close the deliberations of the Council of Trent, and issued the Creed of Pius IV (the Tridentine Creed) in 1564.

Pius V, St, originally **Michele Ghislieri** (1504–72), feast day 30 April. Pope (1566–72), born near Alessandria, Italy. He implemented the decrees of the Council of Trent (1545–63), excommunicated Elizabeth I (1570), and organized the expedition against the Turks (1571). He was canonized in 1712.

Pius VI, originally **Giovanni Angelo Braschi** (1717–99) Pope (1775–99), born in Cesena, Italy. During his reign, Napoleon attacked Italy, took possession of several provinces, and expelled him from Rome. >> Napoleon I

Pius VII, originally **Gregorio Barnaba Chiaramonti** (1742–1823) Pope (1800–23), born in Cesena, Italy. In 1809 the French annexed the Papal States, and he was removed to France, but papal territory was restored by the Congress of Vienna (1814). >> Napoleon I

Pius IX, known as **Pio Nono**, originally **Giovanni Maria Mastai-Ferretti** (1792–1878) Pope (1846–78), born in Senigallia, Italy. He decreed the dogma of the Immaculate Conception in 1854, and called the Vatican Council (1869–79), which proclaimed papal infallibility.

Pius X, St, originally **Giuseppe Sarto**, feast day 21 August. (1835–1914) Pope (1903–14), born in Riese, Italy. He condemned theological modernism and revolutionary movements, championed social reforms, reformed the liturgy, and re-codified canon law. He was canonized in 1954.

Pius XI, originally **Ambrogio Damiano Achille Ratti** (1857–1939) Pope (1922–39), born in Desio, Italy. He signed the Lateran Treaty (1929), which brought into existence the Vatican State.

Pius XII, originally **Eugenio Maria Guiseppe Giovanni Pacelli** (1876–1958) Pope (1939–58), born in Rome. Under his leadership during World War 2 he did much to help prisoners of war and refugees, but there has been continuing controversy over his attitude to the treatment of the Jews in Nazi Germany.

Pivot, Bernard [peevoh] (1935–) French literary critic and broadcaster. He became famous as the host of the French television programme *Apostrophes* (1975–90), and the organizer of *Les championnats d'orthographe* spelling contests.

Pizarro, Francisco [peethahroh] (c.1478–1541) Conquistador, born in Trujillo, Spain. In 1526 he and Almagro sailed for Peru, and in 1531 began the conquest of the Incas. In 1537, conflict with Almagro led to the latter's execution, and in revenge Almagro's followers assassinated Pizarro. >> Almagro; Pizarro, Gonzalo

Pizarro, Gonzalo [peethahroh] (c.1506–48) Spanish conquistador, born in Trujillo, Spain, the half-brother of Francisco Pizarro. He accompanied him in the conquest of Peru (1531–3), and was declared governor there. He defeated a force sent against him, but his soldiers deserted him, and he was executed. >> Pizarro, Francisco

Pizzetti, Ildebrando [pitsetee] (1880–1968) Composer, born in Parma, Italy. He won a particular reputation for opera with *Fedra* (1912) and *Debora e Jaele* (1923).

Pizzey, Erin Patria Margaret >> **Shapiro, Erin Patria Margaret**

Plaatje, Sol(omon Tshekisho) [pliykee] (1879–1932) Writer and South African political figure, born in Boshof, South Africa. He is remembered for his graphic *Native Life in South Africa* (1916), and as a founder member of the African National Congress, becoming its first secretary-general.

Planchon, Roger [plãshõ] (1931–) Theatre director, playwright, and actor, born in the Ardèche, France. His theatre company was the recipient of the title, subsidy, and touring obligations of the Théâtre National Populaire in 1972.

Planck, Max (Karl Ernst Ludwig) (1858–1947) Theoretical physicist, born in Kiel, Germany. His work on the law of thermodynamics and black body radiation led him to abandon classical Newtonian principles and introduce the quantum theory (1900), for which he was awarded the Nobel Prize for Physics in 1918.

Planté, Gaston [plãtay] (1834–89) Physicist, born in Orthy, France. His experiments, begun in 1859, led to the production of a battery which could store electrical energy.

Plantin, Christophe [plãtĩ] (c.1520–89) Printer, and publisher of the Antwerp Polyglot Bible, born in St Avertin, France. His *Biblia Polyglotta* (1569–73), Latin, Hebrew and Dutch Bibles, and editions of the classics are all famous.

Plantinga, Alvin (1932–) Philosopher of religion, born in Ann Arbor, MI. His works include *God, Freedom and Evil* (1974) and *Does God have a Nature?* (1980).

Plaskett, John Stanley (1865–1941) Astronomer, born in Woodstock, Ontario, Canada. In 1918 the Dominion astrophysical observatory was built at Victoria to house the 72 in reflector telescope which he had designed. He discovered the largest known star, which was named after him.

Plateau, Joseph Antoine Ferdinand [platoh] (1801–83) Physicist, born in Brussels. He was the discoverer of the tiny second drop, named after him, which always follows the main drop of a liquid falling from a surface.

Plater, Alan (Frederick) [playter] (1935–) Playwright, born in Jarrow-on-Tyne, Tyne and Wear. Known for his work for such television series as *Softly Softly* (1966–76), his plays for televison include *Close the Coalhouse Door* (1968) and his film screenplays *It Shouldn't Happen to a Vet* (1974). Notable novels are *The Beiderbecke Affair* (1985) and *The Beiderbecke Tapes* (1986), based on his television series.

Plath, Sylvia (1932–63) Poet, born in Boston, MA. She married Ted Hughes in 1957, and he edited her collected poems in 1981. Her only novel, *The Bell Jar* (1963), was published under the pseudonym **Victoria Lucas** just before her suicide in London. >> Hughes, Ted; Sexton, Ann

Platière, Jean Marie Roland de la >> **Roland de la Platière, Jean Marie**

Plato (c.428–347 BC) Greek philosopher, probably born in Athens of an aristocratic family. He became a disciple of Socrates, and before 368 BC founded an Academy at Athens. His writings, which consist of 35 philosophical dialogues (eg *Laches, Republic, Sophist*) and a series of letters, have had a pervasive and incalculable influence on almost every period and tradition, rivalled only by that of his greatest pupil, Aristotle. >> Aristotle; Socrates

Plautus, Titus Maccius [plawtus] (c.250–184 BC) Comic playwright, born in Sarsina, Italy. About 130 plays have been attributed to him, but many are thought to be the work of earlier playwrights which he revised.

Player, Gary (Jim) (1935–) Golfer, born in Johannesburg, South Africa. His successes include the British Open (1959, 1968, 1974), the US Open (1965), the US PGA title (1962, 1972), and the US Masters (1961, 1974, 1978).

Playfair, John (1748–1819) Mathematician and geologist, born in Benvie, Tayside. He wrote an important textbook on geometry, and also investigated glaciation and the formation of river valleys. >> Playfair, William Henry

Playfair, William Henry (1789–1857) Architect, born in London, the nephew of John Playfair. He designed many of Edinburgh's most prominent buildings, including the National Gallery of Scotland and the Royal Scottish Academy. >> Playfair, John

Playford, Sir Thomas (1896–1981) Australian politician, born at Norton Summit, South Australia. He served as premier of South Australia (1933–65).

Pleasence, Sir Donald [plezuhns] (1919–95) Actor, born in Worksop, Nottinghamshire. On the stage he scored a huge success as the malevolent tramp, Davies, in Harold Pinter's *The Caretaker* (1960), and went on to appear in many films, often as a villain, such as *Dr Crippen* (1962) and *Cul-de-Sac* (1966).

Plekhanov, Georgiy Valentinovich [plekahnof] (1856–1918) Marxist philosopher, historian, and journalist, born in Gundalovka, Russia. In 1883 he founded the first Russian Marxist group in Geneva, and was a major intellectual influence on the young Lenin. >> Lenin

Plessner, Helmuth (1892–) Philosopher and social theorist, born in Wiesbaden, Germany. He helped found the new discipline of 'philosophical anthropology', as expounded in such works as *The Unity of the Senses* (trans, 1923).

Pleydell-Bouverie, Katherine [**play**dl **boo**veree] (1895–1985) British potter. In 1946 she established an oil-fired kiln in Kilmington Manor near Warminster, where her output consisted of a series of unique small works often decorated with vertical ribbing.

Plimsoll, Samuel (1824–98) Social reformer, known as 'the sailors' friend', born in Bristol, Avon. Concerned about the unseaworthiness of ships, he promoted the Merchant Shipping Act (1876), and the *Plimsoll line* on the side of a ship was named after him.

Pliny (the Elder), in full **Gaius Plinius Secundus** (23–79) Roman scholar, born in Novum Comum (now Como), Gaul. His only work to survive was an encyclopedia, the *Natural History* (trans, 37 vols, 77). >> Pliny (the Younger)

Pliny (the Younger), in full **Gaius Plinius Caecilius Secundus** (c.62–c.114) Roman writer and administrator, born in Novum Comum (now Como), Gaul, the nephew and adopted son of Pliny the Elder. The master of epistolary style, his many letters provide an insight into the life of the upper class in the 1st-c. >> Pliny (the Elder)

Plisetskaya, Maya (Mikhaylovna) [pli**set**skiya] (1925–) Ballerina, born in Moscow, the niece of Asaf Messerer. She joined the Bolshoi company as principal in 1943, and became celebrated for her classical roles, representing the epitome of the Bolshoi style. >> Messerer

Plomer, William (Charles Franklyn) [**pluh**mer] (1903–73) Writer, born in Pietersburg, South Africa. His works include the novels *Turbott Wolfe* (1926) and *Ali the Lion* (1936), the short story collection *I Speak of Africa* (1928), and *Collected Poems* (1960).

Plotinus [plo**ty**nus] (c.205–70) Philosopher, the founder of Neoplatonism, probably born in Lycopolis, Egypt. His 54 works were edited by his pupil, Porphyry, who arranged them in six groups of nine books, or *Enneads*. >> Porphyry

Plowden, Bridget Hortia, Lady, *née* **Richmond** (1907–) British educationist. The first woman to chair the Central Advisory Council for Education (1963–6), she is known for her government report, *Children and their Primary Schools* (1967).

Plowright, Joan (Anne) (1929–) Actress, born in Brigg, Lincolnshire. Her stage performances include *The Entertainer* (1957) and *Roots* (1959), and her films *The Dressmaker* (1988) and *Avalon* (1991). She married Laurence Olivier in 1961. >> Olivier

Plücker, Julius [**plü**ker] (1801–68) Mathematician and physicist, born in Eberfeld, Germany. He investigated diamagnetism, originated the idea of spectrum analysis, and in 1859 discovered cathode rays.

Plume, Thomas (1630–1704) Theologian, born in Maldon, Essex. He endowed an observatory and the Plumian chair of astronomy and experimental philosophy at Cambridge, and bequeathed his extensive library to the town of Maldon, where it still exists intact.

Plumer, Herbert Charles Onslow (1857–1932) British soldier and colonial administrator. He commanded the 2nd Army of the British Expeditionary Force (1915–18), notably at Messines, and was commander of the Italian Expeditionary Force (1917–18).

Plutarch [**ploo**tah(r)k], Gr **Ploutarchos** (c.46–c.120) Historian, biographer, and philosopher, born in Chaeronea, Boeotia, Greece. His extant writings comprise essays and historical works, notably *Parallel Lives*. North's translation of his work into English (1579) was the source of Shakespeare's Roman plays. >> North, Thomas

Pocahontas [pohka**hon**tas], personal name **Matoaka** (1595–1617) American-Indian princess, born near James-

town, VA, the daughter of Powhatan. She helped maintain peace between the colonists and Indians, and saved the life of English adventurer John Smith. In 1613 she married John Rolfe (1585–1622), and in 1616 went with him to England. >> Powhatan

Podgorniy, Nikolay Victorovich [podgaw(r)nee] (1903–) Soviet party official, born in Karlovka, Ukraine. He held various senior posts (1950–65), and after the dismissal of Khrushchev (1964) became chairman of the Presidium (1968–77). >> Khrushchev

Poe, Edgar Allan (1809–49) Poet and story writer, born in Boston, MA. He became known for his weird and fantastic stories, notably *Tales of the Grotesque and Arabesque* (1840) and 'The Murders in the Rue Morgue' (1841), the first detective story.

Poelzig, Hans [**poel**tsikh] (1869–1936) Expressionist architect, born in Berlin. His works include the remodelling of the Grosses Schauspielhaus, Berlin (1919).

Poggio (Bracciolini), Giovanni Francesco [**po**jioh] (1380–1459) Florentine humanist, born in Terranuova, Italy. His writings include letters, moral essays, invectives, and the *Liber facetiarum*, a collection of humorous stories.

Pohl, Frederik (1919–) Science-fiction writer, born in New York City. In 1938 he became a founder-member of a group of left-wing science fiction writers known as the Futurists. His books include *The Space Merchants* (1953) and *Gladiator-at-Law* (1955).

Poincaré, (Jules) Henri [pwi**karay**] (1854–1912) Mathematician, born in Nancy, France, the cousin of Raymond Poincaré. He created the theory of automorphic functions, and in a famous paper of 1889 originated the theory of chaos. Many of the basic ideas in modern topology, triangulation, and homology are due to him. >> Poincaré, Raymond

Poincaré, Raymond (Nicolas Landry) [pwi**karay**] (1860–1934) French prime minister (1912–13, 1922–4, 1926–9) and president (1913–20), born in Bar-le-Duc, France. He also held ministerial posts in public instruction, foreign affairs, and finance.

Poindexter, John (Marlan) [**poyn**dekster] (1936–) US naval officer and statesman, born in Washington, IN. He became National Security Adviser in 1985, but resigned in the aftermath of the 'Irangate' scandal. He was convicted in 1990 by a Federal court on charges including conspiracy.

Poiré, Emmanuel >> **Caran d'Ache**

Poiret, Paul [pwaray] (1879–1944) Fashion designer, born in Paris. In 1904 he set up on his own, his designs producing a softer, more natural outline to women's clothes. He gained fame for his 'hobble' skirt.

Poisson, Siméon Denis [pwasõ] (1781–1840) Mathematician, born in Pithiviers, France. He is known for his research into celestial mechanics, electromagnetism, and also probability, where he established the law governing the distribution of rare and randomly occurring events (the *Poisson distribution*).

Poitier, Sidney [**pwa**tyay] (1924–) Actor and director, born in Miami, FL. His films include *Lilies of the Field* (1963, Oscar), *In the Heat of the Night* (1967) and *Guess Who's Coming to Dinner* (1967). He has also directed a number of lowbrow comedies, such as *Stir Crazy* (1980) and *Ghost Dad* (1990).

Polano, Fra / Pietro Soave >> **Sarpi, Pietro**

Polanski, Roman [po**lan**skee] (1933–) Polish filmmaker, born in Paris. His films include *Rosemary's Baby* (1968), *Tess* (1979), and *Frantic* (1988). His second wife, actress Sharon Tate (1943–69), was a victim in the Manson killings. >> Manson, Charles

Polanyi, Michael [po**lan**yee] (1891–1976) Physical chemist and social philosopher, born in Budapest. He did notable work on reaction kinetics and crystal structure, and wrote much on the freedom of scientific thought, philosophy of science, and social science.

Polding, John Bede [pohlding] (1794–1877) First Roman Catholic bishop of Australia, born in Liverpool, Merseyside. He went to Sydney in 1835, and as Archbishop of Sydney and Metropolitan of Australia (1842–75) oversaw the growth of the Catholic Church there.

Pole, Reginald, Cardinal (1500–58) Roman Catholic archbishop, born in Stourton Castle, Staffordshire. After opposing Henry VIII on divorce, he left for Italy, where he was made a cardinal (1536). In the reign of Mary I, he returned to England (1554) as papal legate, and became Archbishop of Canterbury. >> Henry VIII; Mary I

Poliakoff, Stephen [polyakof] (1952–) Playwright and film director, born in London. A run of plays including *Hitting Town* and *City Sugar* (both 1975) established his reputation. Later works include *Breaking the Silence* (1984) and *Playing with Trains* (1989).

Polignac, Auguste Jules Armand Marie, prince de [poleenyak] (1780–1847) French statesman, born in Versailles, France. In 1829 he headed the last Bourbon ministry, which promulgated the St Cloud Ordinances that cost Charles X his throne (1830). >> Charles X

Politian [polishan], originally **Angelo Ambrogini** (1454–94) Humanist, scholar, and poet, born in Montepulciano, Italy. Among his works are Latin translations of a long series of Greek authors, an edition of the *Pandects* of Justinian, and *Orfeo* (1480), the first secular drama in Italian.

Polk, James K(nox) (1795–1849) US statesman and 11th president (1845–9), born in Mecklenburg Co, NC. During his presidency, Texas was admitted to the Union (1845), and after the Mexican War (1846–7) the USA acquired California and New Mexico. >> Polk, Leonidas

Polk, Leonidas (1806–64) US soldier and Episcopalian bishop, born in Raleigh, NC, a cousin of James K Polk. In the Civil War he forced Grant to retire at Belmont (1861), fought at Shiloh and Corinth, and conducted the retreat from Kentucky. >> Grant, Ulysses S; Polk, James K

Pollaiuolo, Antonio [poliywoloh] (c.1432–98) Goldsmith, medallist, metal-caster, and painter, born in Florence, Italy. One of the first painters to study anatomy and apply it to his art, he was skilled in suggesting movement. His brother **Piero** (1443–96) was associated with him in his work.

Pollard, Albert Frederick (1869–1948) Historian, born in Ryde, Isle of Wight. Among his many historical works are lives of Henry VIII (1902) and Thomas Cranmer (1904), and *Factors in American History* (1925).

Pollard, Alfred William (1859–1944) Scholar and bibliographer, born in London. An authority on Chaucer and Shakespeare, his work included *A Chaucer Primer* (1893) and *Shakespeare's Fight with the Pirates* (1917).

Pollio, Gaius Asinius [polioh] (76 BC–AD 4) Roman orator, poet, and soldier. His orations, tragedies, and history of the civil wars have perished save for a few fragments.

Pollitt, Harry (1890–1960) Communist politician, born in Droylesden, Lancashire. He became secretary of the Communist Party of Great Britain (1929–56), then its chairman.

Pollock, (Paul) Jackson (1912–56) Artist, born in Cody, WY. The first exponent of Action Painting in America, his art developed from Surrealism to abstract art and the first drip paintings of 1947.

Polo, Marco (1254–1324) Merchant and traveller, born in Venice, Italy. He accompanied his father and uncle on a visit to Kublai Khan in China (1271–5), where he became an envoy in his service. Returning home in 1295, he compiled *The Travels of Marco Polo* (trans), commonly believed to have given Europe the first eye-witness account of Chinese civilization. >> Kublai Khan

Pol Pot [pol pot], also called **Saloth Sar** (1926–) Cambodian prime minister (1976–9), born in Kompong Thom Province, Cambodia. He became leader of the Khmer Rouge guerrillas, set up a totalitarian regime which caused the death, imprisonment, or exile of millions. Overthrown when the Vietnamese invaded Cambodia, he withdrew to the mountains to lead the Khmer Rouge forces.

Polybius [polibius] (c.200–c.120 BC) Greek politician, diplomat, and historian, from Megalopolis in the Peloponnese, who wrote of the rise of Rome to world power status (264–146 BC). Only five of the original 40 books survive.

Polycarp, St (c.69–c.155), feast day 23 February. Greek bishop of Smyrna who bridges the little-known period between the age of his master, the apostle John, and that of his own disciple, Irenaeus. His only extant writing is the *Epistle to the Philippians*. >> Irenaeus; John, St

Polyclitus or **Polycleitos** [polikliytus] (5th-c BC) Greek sculptor from Samos. Known for his statues of athletes, one of his greatest works is the bronze *Doryphorus* ('Spear Bearer').

Polycrates [polikrateez] (6th-c BC) Tyrant of Samos (540–522 BC). He turned Samos into a major naval power, and made her the cultural centre of the E Aegean.

Polygnotos or **Polygnotus** [polignohtus] (5th-c BC) Greek painter, born on the I of Thasos. Innovative in giving life and character to painting, his monumental wall paintings were in Athens, Delphi, and Plataea.

Pombal, Sebastião (José) de Carvalho (e Mello), marquês de (Marquess of) [pobal] (1699–1782) Portuguese chief minister (1756–77), born near Coimbra, Portugal. He opposed Church influence, reorganized the army, and improved agriculture, commerce, and finance.

Pompadour, Jeanne Antoinette Poisson, marquise de (Marchioness of) [pompadoor], known as **Madame de Pompadour** (1721–64) Mistress of Louis XV, born in Paris. A woman of remarkable grace, beauty, and wit, she assumed the entire control of public affairs, and for 20 years swayed state policy, appointing her own favourites. She was a lavish patroness of architecture, the arts, and literature. >> Louis XV

Pompey [pompee], in full **Gnaeus Pompeius Magnus**, known as **Pompey the Great** (106–48 BC) Roman politician and general of the late Republic. His victories include those over the Marians (83–82 BC), Spartacus (71 BC), and Mithridates VI (66 BC). He was defeated by Caesar at Pharsalus (48 BC), and later assassinated. >> Caesar, Julius; Mithridates VI; Spartacus

Pompidou, Georges (Jean Raymond) [pompeedoo] (1911–74) French prime minister (1962, 1962–6, 1966–7, 1967–8) and president (1969–74), born in Montboudif, France. He helped to draft the constitution for the Fifth Republic (1959), negotiated a settlement in Algeria (1961), and played a key role in resolving the political crisis of 1968.

Ponce de León, Juan [ponthay thay layon] (1460–1521) Explorer, born in San Servas, Spain. A member of Columbus's second expedition (1493), he explored Puerto Rico (1510) and was the first European to discover Florida (1513). >> Columbus

Poniatoff, Alexander [ponyatof] (1892–1980) US electronics engineer and inventor, born in Russia. He emigrated to the USA in the 1920s, founded the Ampex Co, making sound recording equipment, and built the first video recorder in 1956.

Poniatowski, Stanislaw >> **Stanislaw II Poniatowski**

Pons, Lily (Alice Joséphine) [ponz] (1898–1976) Soprano, born in Draguignan, France. A dramatic coloratura, she excelled in opera, achieving international success, especially when at the New York Metropolitan (1931–61).

Ponselle, Rosa [ponsel], originally **Rosa Ponzillo** (1897–1981) Soprano, born in Meridan, CT. She sang in leading French and Italian grand opera roles at the New York Metropolitan (1918–37), and also appeared at Covent Garden (1929–31).

Ponsonby, Sarah >> **Butler, Lady Eleanor**

Pont, Pierre Samuel Du >> **Du Pont, Pierre Samuel**

Pontecorvo, Guido [pontaykaw(r)voh] (1907–93) Geneticist, born in Pisa, Italy. He co-discovered the parasexual cycle in fungi (1950), which allows genetic analysis of asexual fungi, and soon afterwards proposed that the gene is the unit of function in genetics.

Pontedera, Andrea da >> **Pisano, Andrea**

Ponti, Carlo >> **Loren, Sophia**

Pontiac [pontiak] (c.1720–69) Chief of the Ottawa Indians from 1755. In 1763 he organized a multi-tribal rising against the English garrisons (*Pontiac's War* or *Conspiracy*, 1763–4), and for five months besieged Detroit, but concluded a peace treaty in 1766. >> Putnam, Israel

Pontius Pilatus >> **Pilate, Pontius**

Pontormo, Jacopo da [pontaw(r)moh], originally **Jacopo Carrucci** (1494–1557) Painter, born in Pontormo, Italy. His masterpiece is 'The Deposition' (c.1525), a chapel altarpiece in Santa Felicità, Florence.

Pontryagin, Lev Semyonovich [pontryahgin] (1908–88) Mathematician, born in Moscow. He was a leading Russian topologist, and his book, *Topological Groups* (trans 1939), remains a standard work.

Pope, Alexander (1688–1744) Poet, born in London. He became well known as a satirical poet and a master of the heroic couplet, notably in *The Rape of the Lock* (1712–14). Other major works include *The Dunciad* (1728, continued 1742), the *Epistle to Doctor Arbuthnot* (1735), the philosophical *Essay on Man* (1733–4), and a series of satires imitating the epistles of *Horace* (1733–8).

Pope, John (1822–92) US soldier, born in Louisville, KY. In the Civil War (1861–5) he commanded the Army of the Mississippi (1862) and then that of Virginia, but was defeated at the second Battle of Bull Run (1862).

Pope, Sir William Jackson (1870–1939) Chemist, born in London. He demonstrated that in an optically active compound the asymmetric centres could be due to elements other than carbon, and that compounds containing no asymmetric atoms could still be optically active.

Pope-Hennessy, Sir John (1913–) Art historian, born in London. A leading authority on Italian Renaissance art, his books include studies of Sienese painting and a series of authoritative volumes on Italian sculpture.

Popielusko, Jerzy [popyewuskoh], popular name of **Alfons Popielusko** (1947–84) Priest, born in Okopy, Poland. His sermons at 'Masses for the Country' held in St Stanislaw Kostka Church were widely acclaimed. He was kidnapped and murdered by the secret police.

Popov, Alexander Stepanovich [popof] (1859–1905) Physicist, born in Turinskiye Rudniki, Russia. Independently of Marconi, he is acclaimed in Russia as the inventor of wireless telegraphy (1896). >> Marconi

Popova, Liubov Sergeyevna [popohva], née **Eding** (1889–1924) Painter and stage designer, born near Moscow. In 1923 she designed textiles for the First State Textile Print Factory, Moscow, notable for their exploration of abstract colour values.

Popper, Sir Karl (Raimund) (1902–94) Philosopher, born in Vienna. Associated with the 'Vienna Circle' of philosophers, his major work on scientific methodology was *The Logic of Scientific Discovery* (trans, 1934). Later books include *The Open Society and its Enemies* (1945), a polemic directed against totalitarian systems.

Popski >> **Peniakoff, Vladimir**

Poquelin, Jean Baptiste >> **Molière**

Porphyry [paw(r)fuhree] (c.233–304) Neoplatonist philosopher, born in Tyre or Batanea. His works include a celebrated treatise against the Christians, of which only fragments remain, and the *Isagoge*, a commentary on Aristotle, widely used in the Middle Ages.

Porres, St Martín de >> **Martín de Porres, St**

Porsche, Ferdinand [paw(r)shuh] (1875–1951) Auto-mobile designer, born in Hafersdorf, Germany. In 1934 he produced a revolutionary type of cheap car with the engine in the rear, to which the Nazis gave the name *Volkswagen* ('people's car'). The Porsche sports car was introduced in 1950.

Porsenna, Lars [paw(r)sena] (6th-c BC) Etruscan ruler of Clusium. According to tradition he laid siege to Rome after the overthrow in 510 BC of Tarquinius Superbus, but was prevented from capturing the city by the heroism of Horatius Cocles. >> Tarquinius Superbus

Porta, Baccio della >> **Bartolommeo, Fra**

Porta, Giacomo della (c.1541–1604) Architect, the most important of the late 16th-c, born in Rome. He is best known for the cupola of St Peter's and his work on the Palazzo Farnese.

Portal (of Hungerford), Charles Frederick Algernon Portal, 1st Viscount (1893–1971) Chief of British air staff during World War 2, born in Hungerford, Berkshire. He became director of organization at the Air Ministry (1937–8), commander-in-chief of Bomber Command (1940), and chief of air staff (1940–6).

Porter, Cole (1892–1964) Composer, born in Peru, IN. He composed lyrics and music for many stage successes, such as *Kiss Me Kate* (1948) and *Can-Can* (1953). His songs include 'Night and Day' (1932) and 'Begin the Beguine' (1935).

Porter, David Dixon (1813–91) US naval officer, born in Chester, PA. In the Civil War, he led the attack on the New Orleans forts (1862), and with the Mississippi squadron he passed the Vicksburg batteries, and bombarded the city.

Porter, Eleanor, née **Hodgman** (1868–1920) Novelist, born in Littleton, NH. Her best known book is *Pollyanna* (1913), followed by a sequel *Pollyanna Grows Up* (1915).

Porter, Eric (Richard) (1928–95) Actor, born in London. He appeared with the Royal Shakespeare Company and the National Theatre, and made several film and television appearances, notably as Soames Forsyte in the BBC television series, *The Forsyte Saga*.

Porter, Sir George (1920–) Physical chemist, born in Stainforth, North Yorkshire. He studied very fast reactions in gases, using a combination of electronic and spectroscopic techniques, and shared the Nobel Prize for Chemistry in 1967. >> Norrish

Porter, Jane (1776–1850) Novelist, born in Durham, Co Durham. She wrote popular historical romances, such as *Thaddeus of Warsaw* (1803) and *The Scottish Chiefs* (1810).

Porter, Katherine Anne (1890–1980) Short-story writer and novelist, born in Indian Creek, TX. Her works include a long allegorical novel, *The Ship of Fools* (1962), and *The Collected Stories of Katherine Anne Porter* (1965, Pulitzer).

Porter, Michael (c.1947–) Management theorist, born in Ann Arbor, MI. He wrote *Competitive Analysis* (1980), and in 1983 founded Monitor, a strategic consulting firm.

Porter, Peter (Neville Frederick) (1929–) Poet, born in Brisbane, Queensland, Australia. He settled in England in 1951, and his *Collected Poems* appeared in 1983.

Porter, Rodney Robert (1917–85) Biochemist, born in Liverpool, Merseyside. His work helped to link the biochemistry of antibodies with immunology, and he shared the Nobel Prize for Physiology or Medicine in 1972. >> Edelman

Porter, William S >> **Henry, O**

Portillo, Michael (1953–) British Conservative Statesman. He became minister for transport (1988–90) and the environment (1990–2), chief secretary for the teasury (1992–4), secretary of state for employment (1994–5), and secretary of state for defence (1995–).

Posidonius or **Poseidonius** [posidohnius], (c.135–c.51 BC) Greek Stoic philosopher, scientist, and polymath, born in Apamea, Syria. He made important contributions to the development of Stoic doctrines.

Post, Emily, *née* **Price** (1872–1960) Authority on etiquette, born in Baltimore, MD. In her classic *Etiquette - The Blue Book of Social Usage* (1922), and her syndicated etiquette column and radio show, she defined good manners for millions of Americans.

Post, Laurens van der >> van der Post, Laurens

Post, Wiley (1900–35) Pioneer aviator, born in Grand Saline, TX. In 1931, with Gatty as navigator, he flew around the world in a record time of 8 days, 15 hr, 51 min. In 1933 he made the first solo flight round the world, taking 7 days, 18 hr, 49 min. >> Gatty, Harold

Potemkin, Grigoriy Alexandrovich [potyomkin] (1739–91) Russian field marshal, born near Smolensk, Russia. He became the intimate favourite of Catherine II, heavily influencing Russian foreign policy, and distinguished himself in the Russo–Turkish Wars (1768–74, 1787–92). >> Catherine II

Pott, Percivall (1714–88) Surgeon, born in London. In 1765 he described a compound leg fracture suffered by himself, still called *Pott's fracture*, and gave a clinical account of tuberculosis of the spine called *Pott's disease*.

Potter, (Helen) Beatrix (1866–1943) Writer of children's books, born in London. She illustrated her books herself, creating such popular characters as *Peter Rabbit* (1900) and *Benjamin Bunny* (1904).

Potter, Dennis (Christopher George) (1935–94) Playwright, born in the Forest of Dean, Gloucestershire. His plays for television, often technically innovative and controversial, include *Vote, Vote, Vote for Nigel Barton* (1965), *Blue Remembered Hills* (1979, BAFTA), *The Singing Detective* (1986), and *Lipstick on Your Collar* (1993).

Potter, Paul (1625–54) Painter and etcher, born in Enkhuizen, The Netherlands. His best pictures are small pastoral scenes with animal figures, but he also painted large pictures, notably the life-size 'Young Bull' (1647).

Potter, Philip (1921–) Ecumenical leader, born in Roseau, Dominica. He was appointed director of World Mission and Evangelism (1967–72), then became general secretary (1972–84) of the World Council of Churches.

Potter, Stephen Meredith (1900–69) British writer and radio producer. He is best known for a series of humorous books on the art of demoralizing the opposition, beginning with *The Theory and Practice of Gamesmanship; or the Art of Winning Games Without Actually Cheating* (1947).

Poujade, Pierre [poozhad] (1920–) Political leader, born in St Céré, France. In 1954 he organized his *Poujadist* movement (a union for the defence of tradesmen and artisans) as a protest against the French tax system.

Poulenc, Francis [poolāk] (1899–1963) Composer, born in Paris. A member of *Les Six*, he was prominent in the reaction against Impressionism. His works include much chamber music and the ballet *Les Biches*, but he is best known for his many songs, such as *Fêtes galantes* (1943).

Poulsen, Valdemar (1869–1942) Electrical engineer, born in Copenhagen. He invented the telegraphone, forerunner of magnetic tape recorders (1898).

Pound, (Alfred) Dudley Pickman Rogers (1877–1943) British naval commander. He commanded the battleship *Colossus* at the Battle of Jutland (1916), and became commander-in-chief of the Mediterranean fleet (1936–9), then Admiral of the Fleet and First Sea Lord. >> Jellicoe

Pound, Ezra (Loomis) (1885–1972) Poet and critic, born in Hailey, ID. He was an experimental poet, whom T S Eliot regarded as the motivating force behind modern poetry. His main work is *The Cantos*, a loosely knit series of poems published in many instalments (1930–59). >> Eliot, T S

Pound, Roscoe (1870–1964) Jurist and botanist, born in Lincoln, NE. His legal writings include *Jurisprudence* (5 vols, 1959), and he was largely responsible for the botanical survey of Nebraska.

Pounds, John (1766–1839) Shoemaker, born in Portsmouth. He became an unpaid teacher of poor children, and is regarded as the founder of what came to be called 'ragged schools' in England and Scotland.

Poussin, Charles de la Vallée >> Hadamard, Jacques

Poussin, Gaspard >> Dughet, Gaspard

Poussin, Nicolas [poosī] (1594–1665) Painter, born near Les Andelys, France. The greatest master of French Classicism, his masterpieces include two sets of the 'Seven Sacraments'.

Powderly, Terence V(incent) (1849–1924) Labour leader, born in Carbondale, PA. He joined the secret oathbound Knights of Labor in 1874, becoming grand master workman (1879), then general master workman (1883–93).

Powell, Adam Clayton, Jr (1908–72) US politician and minister, born in New Haven, CT. He served as a Democrat in the US House of Representatives (1945–69), where he fought to outlaw Jim Crow laws, and became chairman of the House Committee on Education and Labor (1960–7).

Powell, Anthony (Dymoke) (1905–) Novelist, born in London. His series of novels called *A Dance to the Music of Time* (12 vols, 1951–75) covered 50 years of British upper middle-class life and attitudes. Later books include the memoirs *To Keep the Ball Rolling* (4 Vols, 1976–82) and *The Fisher King* (1986).

Powell, Baden >> Baden-Powell, Robert

Powell, Bud, popular name of **Earl Powell** (1924–66) Jazz pianist, born in New York City. He became involved with the modern jazz movement in the 1940s, and was the most influential jazz pianist of his time.

Powell, Cecil (Frank) (1903–69) Physicist, born in Tonbridge, Kent. He is best known for his work on the photography of nuclear processes, for which he was awarded the Nobel Prize for Physics in 1950.

Powell, Colin (Luther) (1937–) US army general, born in New York City. He was appointed head of the National Security Council (1987–9) and chairman of the joint chiefs-of-staff (1989–), the first African-American officer to receive this distinction. He had overall responsibility for the US military operation against Iraq in 1990–1.

Powell, (John) Enoch (1912–) British statesman, born in Birmingham, West Midlands. He became a Conservative minister of health (1960–3), and was dismissed from the shadow cabinet in 1968 for his outspoken attitude on racial integration. He was later elected an Ulster Unionist MP (1974–87).

Powell, Michael (1905–90) Film director, scriptwriter, and producer, born in Bekesbourne, Kent. With Emeric Pressburger (1902–88) he formed The Archers Company in 1942, and made a series of unusual and original features, such as *Black Narcissus* (1947) and *The Tales of Hoffman* (1951).

Powhatan [powhatan] (?–1618) American Indian chief of the confederacy of Tidewater tribes of New England. He maintained an uneasy peace with white settlers in Virginia. >> Pocahontas

Powys, John Cowper [powis] (1872–1964) Writer and critic, born in Shirley, Derbyshire. He is best known for his novels on the West Country and historical themes, such as *A Glastonbury Romance* (1932) and *Owen Glendower* (1940). >> Powys, Llewelyn / T F

Powys, Llewelyn [powis] (1884–1939) Essayist and novelist, born in Dorchester, Dorset. His works include *Ebony and Ivory* (1922) and *Apples be Ripe* (1930). >> Powys, John Cowper / T F

Powys, T(heodore) F(rancis) [powis] (1875–1953) Novelist and short-story writer, born in Dorchester, Dorset, the brother of John and Llewelyn Powys. His best-known novel is *Mr Weston's Good Wine* (1927). >> Powys, John Cowper / Llewelyn

Poynings, Sir Edward (1459–1521) English soldier and diplomat, probably born in London. He is best remembered for *Poyning's laws*, subjecting the Irish Parliament to the control of the English king and privy council.

Poynter, Sir Edward John (1836–1919) Painter, born in Paris. Among his works are 'The Ides of March' (1883) and a portrait of Lillie Langtry.

Praagh, Peggy van >> **van Praagh, Peggy**

Prandtl, Ludwig [prantl] (1875–1953) Physicist, born in Freising, Germany. A pioneer of aerodynamics, he made outstanding contributions to boundary layer theory, airship profiles, supersonic flow, wing theory, and turbulence.

Prasad, Rajendra [prasad] (1884–1963) Indian president (1950–62), born in Zeradei, India. He was president of the Indian National Congress several times between 1934 and 1948, and first president of the Republic in 1950.

Pratt, William Henry >> **Karloff, Boris**

Praxiteles [praksiteleez] (4th-c BC) Sculptor from Athens, considered one of the greatest of Greek sculptors. His works have almost all perished, though his 'Hermes Carrying the Boy Dionysus' was found at Olympia in 1877.

Pré, Jacqueline du >> **du Pré, Jacqueline**

Preece, Sir William Henry (1834–1913) Electrical engineer, born in Bryn Helen, Gwynedd. A pioneer of wireless telegraphy and telephony, he introduced the first telephones to Great Britain.

Pregl, Fritz [praygl] (1869–1930) Chemist, born in Laibach, Austria. He was specially noted for developing microchemical methods of analysis, for which he was awarded the Nobel Prize for Physics in 1923.

Prelog, Vladimir (1906–   ) Organic chemist, born in Sarajevo, Bosnia and Herzegovina. For his work in organic chemistry, and especially stereochemistry, he shared the Nobel Prize for Chemistry in 1975.

Premadasa, Ranasinghe (1924–93) Prime minister (1978–89) and president (1989–93) of Sri Lanka, born in North Colombo, Sri Lanka. He implemented a popular poverty alleviation programme, but as president faced mounting civil unrest. He was assassinated in a suicide bomb attack.

Preminger, Otto [preminjer] (1906–86) Film director and producer, born in Vienna. He emigrated to the USA in 1935, and after some years of directing on Broadway, made *Laura* (1944), a *film noir*, often considered his best film. Later films included *Porgy and Bess* (1959) and *Exodus* (1960).

Prendergast, Maurice (Brazil) (1859–1924) Painter, born in St John's, Newfoundland, Canada. He experimented with style, but his work always had an Impressionistic vitality, as in 'Central Park' (1900).

Prés, Josquin >> **Josquin, des Prez**

Prescott, John (Leslie) (1938–   ) British politician, born in Prestatyn, Clwyd. In the shadow Cabinet he has been spokesman for employment, energy, and transport, and became deputy leader of the party in 1994.

Presley, Elvis (Aaron) (1935–77) Rock singer, born in Tupelo, MS. He made 45 records that sold in millions, including 'Heartbreak Hotel' (1956), 'Hound Dog', 'Love Me Tender', and 'Jailhouse Rock'. His Hollywood films such as *Loving You* (1957), *King Creole* (1958), and *GI Blues* (1960) became enormous moneymakers. Graceland, his Memphis mansion, is now a souvenir shrine.

Press, Frank (1924–   ) Seismologist and government science advisor, born in New York City. He identified the 'free oscillations' of the Earth - the persistent global vibrations arising from earthquakes and other geological disturbances.

Pressburger, Emeric >> **Powell, Michael**

Preston, Margaret Rose (1875–1963) Artist and teacher, born in Port Adelaide, South Australia. An active champion of Aboriginal painting, its influence is evident in her still-lifes of Australian flowers, and her wood and linocut engravings.

Pretender, Old / Young >> **Stuart, Prince James / Charles**

Pretorius, Andries (Wilhelmus Jacobus) [pretawrius] (1799–1853) Afrikaner leader, born in Graaff-Reinet, South Africa (then Cape Colony). He joined the Great Trek of 1835 into Natal, where he was chosen commandant-general, and later trekked across the Vaal. Pretoria was named after him. >> Pretorius, Marthinus

Pretorius, Marthinus (Wessel) [pretawrius] (1819–1901) Afrikaner soldier and statesman, born in Graaff-Reinet, South Africa, the son of Andries Pretorius. He succeeded his father as commandant-general (1853), and became president of the South African Republic (1857–71), and of the Orange Free State (1859–63). >> Pretorius, Andries

Prévert, Jacques [prayvair] (1900–77) Poet, born in Neuilly-sur-Seine, France. His collections include (trans titles) *Words* (1946) and *Things and Others* (1972). He also wrote the screenplay for the celebrated film, *The Children of Paradise* (trans, 1946).

Previn, André (George) [previn] (1929–   ) Conductor, composer, and pianist, born in Berlin. A notable jazz pianist, he became musical director of symphony orchestras at Houston, London, Pittsburgh, and Los Angeles, then composer laureate of the London Symphony Orchestra (1991). He has written musicals, film scores, and orchestral works, and done much to bring classical music to the attention of a wide public.

Prévost, (Antoine François), l'Abbé [prayvoh] (1697–1763) Novelist, born in Hesdin, France. He is best known for *Manon Lescaut* (1731), originally published as the final part of a seven-volume novel.

Prévost, Eugène Marcel [prayvoh] (1862–1941) Novelist, born in Paris. Many of his novels and plays have been translated, including *Cousin Laura* and *Léa*.

Prey, Hermann (1929–   ) Baritone, born in Berlin. He sang at the Hamburg Opera (1953–60), Bayreuth (1956), and the New York Metropolitan (1960), excelling in the Mozart repertoire.

Price, Vincent (Leonard) (1911–93) Actor and writer, born in St Louis, MO. Achieving his first major success with *The Fall of the House of Usher* (1960), he went on to star in a series of acclaimed Gothic horror movies, such as *The Pit and the Pendulum* (1961) and *The Abominable Dr Phibes* (1971).

Price, George (Cadel) (1919–   ) Prime minister of Belize (1981–4, 1989–   ). In 1950 he founded the People's United Party (PUP), and led his country to full independence in 1981.

Price, H(enry) H(abberley) (1899–1985) Philosopher, born in Neath, West Glamorgan. His major work was *Perception* (1932), in which he argued against causal theories of perception.

Price, (Mary Violet) Leontyne (1927–   ) Soprano, born in Laurel, MS. A notable Bess (1952–4) in Gershwin's *Porgy and Bess*, she was the first black opera singer on television, in *Tosca* for NBC (1955).

Price, Richard (1723–91) Moral philosopher and unitarian minister, born in Tynton, Glamorgan. His *Observations on Reversionary Payments* (1771) helped to establish a scientific system for life-insurance and pensions.

Prichard, Katharine Susannah (1883–1969) Writer, born in Levuka, Fiji. Her work includes the Australian goldfields trilogy: *The Roaring Nineties* (1946), *Golden Miles* (1948), and *Winged Seeds* (1950).

Pride, Sir Thomas (?–1658) English parliamentarian during the Civil War, born (possibly) near Glastonbury, Somerset. When the House of Commons indicated it might effect a settlement with Charles I, he was appointed by the army (1648) to expel its Presbyterian Royalist members (*Pride's Purge*). >> Charles I (of England)

Priest, Oscar Stanton De >> **De Priest, Oscar Stanton**

Priestley, J(ohn) B(oynton) (1894–1984) Writer, born in Bradford, West Yorkshire. His humorous novels include *The Good Companions* (1929). He established his reputation as a playwright with *Dangerous Corner* (1932), *Time and the Conways* (1937), and other plays on space-time themes. He married the archaeologist Jacquetta Hawkes in 1953. >> Hawkes

Priestley, Joseph (1733–1804) Chemist and clergyman, born in Fieldhead, Cumbria. He is best known for his research into the chemistry of gases, and for his discovery of oxygen. His controversial views on religion and political theory (he was a supporter of the French Revolution) forced him in 1794 to move to America.

Prigogine, Ilya [prigogeenay] (1917–) Physical chemist, born in Moscow. For his contributions to nonequilibrium thermodynamics he was awarded the Nobel Prize for Chemistry in 1977.

Primo de Rivera (y Orbaneja), Miguel [preemoh the rivera] (1870–1930) Spanish general, born in Jerez de la Frontera, Spain. In 1923 he led a military coup, beginning a dictatorship which lasted until 1930. His son, **José Antonio Primo de Rivera** (1903–36), founded the Spanish Fascist Party (*Falange Española*) in 1933, and was executed by the Republicans in 1936.

Primus, Pearl [preemus] (1919–94) Dancer, anthropologist, and teacher, born in Trinidad. She formed her own dance group in 1944, choreographed on Broadway, and became director of the Art Center of Black African Culture in Nigeria.

Prince, Hal, popular name of **Harold Smith Prince** (1928–) Stage director and producer, born in New York City. His Broadway musicals included *The Pajama Game* (1954), *West Side Story* (1957), and *Cabaret* (1968), and he also directed *Evita* (1978) and *The Phantom of the Opera* (1986).

Prince, stage name of **Prince Roger Nelson** (1958–) Pop-singer and composer, born in Minneapolis, MN. Named after the Prince Roger Trio, a jazz band in which his father was a pianist, international success followed the release of *1999* (1982), the film and album *Purple Rain* (1984), and *Batman* (1989).

Princip, Gavrilo [printsip] (1894–1918) Nationalist and revolutionary, born in Obljaj, Bosnia. In 1914, he took part in the assassination of Archduke Francis Ferdinand of Austria and his wife Sophie on a visit to Sarajevo. >> Francis Ferdinand

Pringle, Mia (Lilly) Kellmer (1920–83) Educational psychologist, born in Vienna. Her many publications, such as *Psychological Approaches to Child Abuse* (1980), have greatly influenced parent–child relationships.

Printemps, Yvonne [prīta] (1894–77) Actress, born in Ermont, France. She appeared in revue and musical comedy until 1916, when she began to work with Sacha Guitry, whom she married. She later managed the Théâtre de la Michodière, with her second husband, the actor Pierre Fresnay (1897–1973). >> Guitry

Prior, Matthew (1664–1721) Diplomat and poet, born in Wimborne, Dorset. He is best known for his light occasional verse collected as *Poems on Several Occasions* (1709).

Priscian [prishian], Lat **Priscianus** (6th-c) Latin grammarian, born in Caesarea. His works include the 18-volume *Institutiones grammaticae* (Grammatical Foundations).

Priscillian [prisilian] (c.340–385) Christian bishop, born in Trier, Gaul. He was excommunicated for heresy by a synod at Saragossa in 380, and ultimately executed. The

Priscillian doctrine contained Gnostic and Manichaean elements, and was based on dualism.

Pritchett, Sir V(ictor) S(awdon) (1900–) Writer and critic, born in Ipswich, Suffolk. He became known for his critical works, such as *The Living Novel* (1946), short stories, travel books, and autobiography.

Proclus [prohklus] (c.412–85) Greek Neoplatonist philosopher, born in Constantinople. The last head of Plato's Academy, his approach combined the Roman, Syrian and Alexandrian schools of thought in Greek philosophy into one theological metaphysic.

Procop(ius) >> **Prokop**

Procopius [prokohpius] (c.499–565) Byzantine historian, born in Caesarea (now in Israel). His principal works are histories of the Persian, Vandal, and Gothic wars, and an attack on the court of Justinian. >> Justinian

Procter, Mike, popular name of **Michael John Procter** (1946–) Cricketer, born in Durban, South Africa. He joined Gloucestershire, and in first-class cricket scored 48 centuries. His Test career was restricted by the sporting ban imposed on South Africa.

Proesch, Gilbert >> **Gilbert and George**

Profumo, John (Dennis) [profyoomoh] (1915–) British Conservative statesman. He became minister for foreign affairs (1959–60) and secretary of state for war (1960–3), but resigned after deceiving the House of Commons about the nature of his relationship with Christine Keeler, who at the time was also involved with a Russian diplomat. >> Keeler, Christine

Prokhorov, Alexander Mikhailovich [prokorof] (1916–) Physicist, born in Atherton, Queensland, Australia. In Moscow he worked on the principles of lasers with Nikolai Basov, and they shared the Nobel Prize for Physics in 1964.

Prokofiev, Sergey Sergeyevitch [prohkofief] (1891–1953) Composer, born in Sontsovka, Ukraine. His vast range of works include seven symphonies, nine concertos, ballets, operas, suites, cantatas, sonatas, songs, and his most popular work, *Peter and the Wolf* (1936).

Prokop or **Procop(ius)** [prohkop, prokohpius], known as **the Bald** or **the Great** (c.1380–1434) Bohemian Hussite leader, a follower of Žiška, and on his death, the leader of the Taborites. He repeatedly defeated German armies, but fell in battle in Lipany, Hungary.

Prony, Gaspard François Clair Marie Riche, baron de [prohnee] (1755–1839) Civil engineer, born in Chamelet, France. He is most noted for the equations he developed dealing with the flow of water, and for the *Prony brake* (1821) which measures the power of an engine under test.

Propertius, Sextus [propershius] (c.48–c.15 BC) Latin elegiac poet, probably born in Asisium (Assisi), Italy. The central figure of his inspiration was his mistress, to whom he devoted the first of his four surviving books, *Cynthia*.

Prost, Alain [prost], nickname **the Professor** (1955–) Motor-racing driver, born in St Chamond, France. He won the world title in 1985–6 (both for McLaren–Porsche), was runner-up in 1983–4 and 1988, and won again in 1989 (for Maclaren–Honda) and 1993, when he announced his retirement.

Protagoras [prohtagoras] (c.490–421 BC) The earliest self-proclaimed Greek Sophist, born in Abdera, Greece. He taught a system of practical wisdom based on the doctrine that 'man is the measure of all things'.

Proudhon, Pierre Joseph [proodō] (1809–65) Socialist and political theorist, born in Besançon, France. His greatest work was *System of Economic Contradictions* (trans, 1846). During the 1848 Revolution, the violence of his utterances brought him three years' imprisonment.

Proust, Joseph Louis [proost] (1754–1826) Chemist, born in Angers, France. He developed the law of constant proportion for a chemical compound, known as *Proust's law*, over which he was in a controversy with Berthollet. >> Berthollet

Proust, Marcel [proost] (1871–1922) Novelist, born in Auteuil, France. In 1912 he produced the first part of his 13-volume masterpiece, *A la recherche du temps perdu* (trans Remembrance of Things Past). His massive novel, exploring the power of the memory and the unconscious, as well as the nature of writing itself, has been profoundly influential.

Prout, Father >> **Mahony, Francis Sylvester**

Prout, Samuel [prowt] (1783–1852) Watercolour painter, born in Plymouth, Devon. He was famed for his picturesque views of buildings and streets.

Prout, William [prowt] (1785–1850) Chemist and physiologist, born in Horton, Gloucestershire. He discovered the presence of hydrochloric acid in the stomach, and also hypothesized (1815) that the relative atomic masses of all elements are whole number multiples of that of hydrogen.

Prudentius [prudenshius], in full **Aurelius Clemens Prudentius** (348–c.410) Christian poet, born in Caesaraugusta, Spain. His religious poetry includes *Cathemerinon liber*, a series of 12 hymns, and *Hamartigeneia*, on the origin of evil.

Prudhomme, Paul [prooduhm] (1940–   ) Chef, born in Opelousas, LA. In 1979, he and his wife, K Hinrichs Prudhomme, opened K-Paul's Louisiana Kitchen in New Orleans, which became widely known for its traditional cajun and creole cooking. He has since written several popular cookbooks, and often appears on television.

Prud'hon, Pierre Paul [prüdõ] (1758–1823) Painter, born in Cluny, France. Patronized by the empresses of Napoleon, he was made court painter, and among his best work is a portrait of Joséphine. >> Napoleon I

Pryde, James >> **Nicholson, William Newzam Prior**

Prynne, William [prin] (1600–69) Puritan pamphleteer, born in Swanswick, Somerset. In 1633 appeared his *Histrio-Mastix: the Players Scourge*, which contained an apparent attack on the queen, for which he was imprisoned. Released in 1640, he prosecuted Laud (1644), and after Cromwell's death returned to parliament as a Royalist.

Prys-Jones, Arthur Glyn [prees] (1888–1987) Poet, born in Denbigh, Clwyd. He edited the first anthology of Anglo-Welsh poetry, *Welsh Poets* (1917), and his own volumes include *Poems of Wales* (1923) and *Valedictory Verses* (1978).

Przhevalski, Nikolay Mikhailovich [pshuhvalskee] (1839–88) Traveller, born near Smolensk, Russia. From 1867 he made important journeys in Mongolia, Turkestan, and Tibet, during which he amassed a valuable collection of plants and animals, including the wild horse which now bears his name.

Ptolemy I Soter ('Saviour') [tolemee] (c.366–c.283 BC) Macedonian general in the army of Alexander the Great, and ruler of Egypt after Alexander's death (323 BC). In 304 BC he adopted the royal title, and thus founded the Ptolemaic dynasty. >> Ptolemy II

Ptolemy [tolemee], in full **Claudius Ptolemaeus** [tolemayus] (fl.127–145) Greek astronomer and geographer, who worked in the great library in Alexandria. His book known as *Almagest* ('the greatest') is the most important compendium of astronomy produced until the 16th-c, its Earth-centred universe becoming known as the *Ptolemaic system*. >> Copernicus

Ptolemy II Philadelphus [tolemee] (308–246 BC) King of Egypt (283–246 BC, the son and successor of Ptolemy I, Soter. Under him the power of Egypt attained its greatest height. >> Ptolemy I

Pucci, Emilio, marchese (Marquess) **di Barsento** [poochee] (1914–92) Fashion designer, born in Naples, Italy. He opened his couture house in 1950, becoming famous for his use of bold patterns and brilliant colour.

Puccini, Giacomo (Antonio Domenico Michele Secondo Maria) [pucheenee] (1858–1924) Operatic composer, born in Lucca, Italy. His first great success was *Manon Lescaut* (1893), but this was eclipsed by *La Bohème* (1896), *Tosca* (1900), *Madame Butterfly* (1904), and the unfinished *Turandot*.

Pucelle, Jean [püsel] (c.1300–c.1355) French painter. He ran an important workshop in Paris from the 1320s onwards, specializing in illuminated manuscripts, such as the 'Hours of Jeanne d'Evreux'.

Pudovkin, Vsevoled (Illarianovich) [pudofkin] (1893–1953) Film director and writer, born in Penza, Russia. His silent classics include *The End of St Petersburg* (trans, 1927) and *Storm Over Asia* (trans, 1928).

Puffendorf, Samuel, Freiherr (Baron) **von**, also spelled **Pufendorf** (1632–94) Jurist and historian, born in Dorfchemnitz, Germany. His major works include *Of the Law of Nature and Nations* (trans, 1672), and he also published a history of Sweden.

Pugachev, Yemelyan Ivanovich [pugachef], also spelled **Pugachov** (1726–75) Russian Cossack, pretender to the Russian throne, born in Zimoveyskaya-na-Donu, Russia. Proclaiming himself to be Peter III, Catherine's murdered husband, he led a mass rebellion against Catherine II (1773-5), and was executed. >> Catherine II

Pugachov >> **Pugachev**

Puget, Pierre [püzhay] (1620–94) Sculptor, painter, and architect, born in Marseilles, France. His painting can be seen on the ceilings of the Berberini Palace in Rome and the Pitti Palace in Florence.

Pugh, Clifton Ernest (1924–90) Artist, born in Richmond, Victoria, Australia. His paintings divide into two genres: his love of native Australian wildlife, reflected in his 'bush' paintings, and his portraits of academics and politicians.

Pugin, Augustus (Welby Northmore) [pyoojin] (1812–52) Architect, born in London. He worked with Barry designing a large part of the decoration and sculpture for the new Houses of Parliament (begun 1840), and did much to revive Gothic architecture in England. >> Barry, Charles

Pujol, Joseph [püzhol], known as **le Pétomane** (the manic farter) (1857–1945) Music-hall entertainer, born in Marseilles, France. His fame was based on his phenomenal capacity for farting, by drawing in air through his rectum and expelling it.

Pulaski, Kazimierz [pulaskee] (1748–79) Nobleman and soldier, born in Winiary, Poland. In 1777 he went to America, organized *Pulaski's legion*, entered Charleston (1779), and held it until it was relieved.

Pulitzer, Joseph [poolitser] (1847–1911) Newspaper proprietor, born in Makó, Hungary. In 1864 he emigrated to the USA, made his fortune in newspapers, and established annual Pulitzer Prizes in the fields of literature, drama, history, music, and journalism.

Pullman, George (Mortimer) (1831–97) Inventor and businessman, born in Brocton, NY. He designed the Pullman railroad sleeping-car (1865), and later introduced dining-cars (1868).

Pupin, Michael (Idvorsky) [pyoopeen] (1858–1935) Physicist and inventor, born in Idvor, Hungary. He devised the *Pupin inductance coil*, which made long-distance telephony practical, and wrote an autobiography, *From Immigrant to Inventor* (1923, Pulitzer).

Purbach or **Peuerbach, Georg von** [poorbakh] (1423–61) Astronomer and mathematician, born in Austria. He is thought to have been the first to introduce sines into trigonometry.

Purcell, E(dward) M(ills) [persel] (1912–   ) Physicist, born in Taylorville, IL. He was the first to detect the interstellar microwave radiation predicted by van der Hulst.

For his work on the magnetic moments of atomic particles, he shared the Nobel Prize for Physics in 1952. >> van der Hulst

Purcell, Henry [per**sel**] (1659–95) Composer, born in London. Best known for his vocal and choral works, he also wrote much incidental state music and an opera, *Dido and Aeneas* (1689). Of his many songs, 'Nymphs and Shepherds' is well known.

Purchas, Samuel (1577–1626) Compiler of travel books, born in Thaxted, Essex. His great works were *Purchas his Pilgrimage, or Relations of the World in all Ages* (1613) and *Hakluytus Posthumus, or Purchas his Pilgrimes* (1625), based on the papers of Hakluyt. >> Hakluyt

Purdy, James (1923–) Writer, born in Ohio. His first collection of short stories was *Color of Darkness* (1957), and his novels include a trilogy, *Sleepers in Moon-Crowned Valleys* (1970–81).

Purkinje, Johannes (Evangelista) [**poor**kinyay] (1787–1869) Histologist and physiologist, born in Libochovice, Czech Republic. He discovered a number of new and important microscopic anatomical structures, some of which are named after him.

Pusey, E(dward) B(ouverie) [**pyoo**zee] (1800–82) Theologian, born in Pusey, Berkshire. He joined the Oxford Movement (1833), contributing several tracts, notably those on baptism and the Eucharist, and later became leader of the Movement. >> Newman, John Henry

Pushkin, Alexander Sergeyevich [**push**kin] (1799–1837) Poet, born in Moscow. Hailed in Russia as its greatest poet, his first success was the romantic poem 'Ruslan and Lyudmila' (1820), followed by the verse novel *Eugene Onegin* (1828) and the historical tragedy *Boris Godunov* (1831).

Puskas, Ferenc [**pus**kas, **fe**rents] (1927–) Footballer, born in Budapest. A member of the great Hungarian side of the early 1950s, he later signed for Real Madrid, and as a coach took the Greek side Panathinaikos to the European Cup final.

Putnam, Frederic Ward (1839–1915) Archaeologist and ethnographer, born in Salem, MA. Pioneering the study of the archaeological remains of native Americans, he led field expeditions to the American southwest, Mexico, and South America.

Putnam, George Palmer (1814–72) Publisher, born in Brunswick, ME. He founded a book-publishing business in 1848, and began *Putnam's Monthly Magazine* (1853).

Putnam, Hilary (1926–) Philosopher, born in Chicago, IL. He argues strongly for a conception of philosophy that makes it essential to a responsible view of the real world and our place in it, as seen in *Reason, Truth and History* (1982).

Putnam, Israel (1718–90) American revolutionary soldier, born in Danvers, MA. Given command of the forces of Connecticut (1775), then of New York, he was defeated by Howe (1776) at Brooklyn Heights. >> Howe, William

Putnam, Rufus (1738–1824) American revolutionary soldier, born in Sutton, MA. In 1789 he was appointed a judge of the Supreme Court of the Northwest Territory, and later became surveyor-general of the United States (1793–1803).

Puttnam, David (Terence) (1941–) Film-maker, born in London. His films include *Bugsy Malone* (1976), *Chariots of Fire* (1981, four Oscars), *The Killing Fields* (1984), and *The Mission* (1986).

Puvis de Chavannes, Pierre (Cécile) [püvee duh sha**van**] (1824–98) Painter, born in Lyon, France. He is best known for his murals on public buildings, including the life of St Geneviève in the Panthéon, Paris.

Puyi, Pu Yi, or **P'u-i** [pooyee], personal name of the

Xuantong Emperor (1906–67) Last emperor of China (1908–12) and the first of Manchukuo (1934–5), born in Beijing. Known in the West as **Henry Puyi**, in 1932 he was called by the Japanese to be provincial dictator of Manchukuo, under the name of **Kangde**. The story of his life was made into a successful film *The Last Emperor* (1988).

Puzo, Mario [**poo**zoh] (1920–) Novelist, born in New York City. He is best known for his epic best-selling mafia story *The Godfather* (1969; filmed 1972).

Pye, John David (1932–) Zoologist, born in Mansfield, Nottinghamshire. His principal research has been into the use of ultrasound by animals, particularly the echolocation used by bats.

Pyke, Magnus (1908–92) Food scientist and broadcaster, born in London. He hosted the television science series *Don't Ask Me* (1974–80), and wrote a number of popular scientific books, including *Butter-side Up* (1976).

Pyle, Ernie, popular name of **Ernest Taylor Pyle** (1900–45) Journalist, born near Dana, IN. During World War 2 he accompanied Allied forces in the invasions of North Africa, Italy, and Normandy, his reports earning him a Pulitzer Prize. He was killed during the US landing on Okinawa.

Pym, Barbara (Mary Crampton) (1913–80) Novelist, born in Oswestry, Shropshire. She is best known for her series of satirical novels on English middle-class society, including *Excellent Woman* (1952) and *Quartet in Autumn* (1977).

Pym (of Sandy), Francis (Leslie) Pym, Baron [pim] (1922–) British Conservative statesman. He was defence secretary (1979–81), and foreign secretary during the Falklands Crisis of 1982.

Pym, John [pim] (1584–1643) English politician, born in Brymore, Somerset. He took a leading part in the impeachment of Strafford (1641), helped to draw up the Grand Remonstrance, and was one of the five members whom Charles I singled out by name (1642). >> Strafford

Pynchon, Thomas [**pin**chon] (1937–) Novelist, born in Glen Cove, NY. An experimentalist, esoteric and elusive, his novels include *V* (1963), *The Crying of Lot 49* (1966), *Gravity's Rainbow* (1973), and *Vineland* (1992), all displaying a preoccupation with codes, quests, and coincidences.

Pynson, Richard [**pin**son] (?–1530) Printer, born in Normandy, France. In 1497 his edition of the Latin poet Terence appeared, the first classic to be printed in London, and he became printer to Henry VIII (1508).

Pyrrho [**pi**roh] (c.360–c.270 BC) Philosopher, born in Elis, Greece. He taught that we can know nothing of the nature of things, but that the best attitude of mind is suspense of judgment, which brings with it calmness of mind. *Pyrrhonism* is often regarded as the foundation of scepticism.

Pyrrhus [**pi**rus] (c.318–272 BC) King of Epirus (modern Albania) (307–303 BC, 297–272 BC), whose aim was to revive the empire of his second cousin, Alexander the Great. Though he won two battles (280–279 BC), his losses were so great that they gave rise to the phrase *Pyrrhic victory*.

Pythagoras [piy**thag**oras] (6th-c BC) Philosopher and mathematician, born in Samos, Greece. He settled at Crotona, S Italy (c.530 BC) and founded a moral and religious school. The famous geometrical theorem attributed to him was probably developed later by members of the Pythagorean school.

Pytheas [**pith**ias] (4th-c BC) Mariner, born in Massilia (Marseille), Gaul. He sailed past Spain, Gaul, and the E coast of Britain (c.330 BC), and reached the island of 'Thule' (possibly Iceland).

Pythias (of Syracuse) >> **Damon and Pythias**

Qaboos bin Said [kaboos] (1940–) Sultan of Oman (1970–), born in Muscat, Oman, the son of Said bin Taimar of the ruling dynasty of the Albusaid family. In 1970 he overthrew his father in a bloodless coup, and pursued more liberal and expansionist policies.

Qaddafi, Muammar >> **Gaddafi, Muammar**

Qianlong [chyan lung], also spelled **Ch'ien-Lung** (1711–99) Seventh emperor of the Manchurian Qing (Ch'ing) dynasty (1735–96), and the fourth to rule China. He annexed E Turkestan, conquered Burma (1769) and Nepal (1790–1), and suppressed revolt in Taiwan. His policies provoked a rebellion, and he abdicated.

Qin Shihuangdi [chin shihwangdee], also spelled **Ch'in Shih Huang-ti** (259–210 BC) First true emperor of China, who forcibly unified much of modern China following the decline of the Zhou dynasty. He was buried in a starry mausoleum with 6000 life-size terracotta guards, excavated since 1974.

Quant, Mary [kwont] (1934–) Fashion designer, born in London. The geometric simplicity of her designs, especially the mini-skirt, and the originality of her colours, became an essential feature of the new young Chelsea look in the 1960s.

Quantrill, William (Clarke) [kwontril] (1837–65) Guerrilla chief and soldier, born in Canal Dover, OH. When the Civil War broke out, he formed a group of irregulars, known as *Quantrill's Raiders*, that robbed mail coaches and attacked Union communities. He was killed by Federal troops.

Quantz, Johann Joachim (1697–1773) Flautist and composer, born near Göttingen, Germany. He composed some 300 concertos for one or two flutes as well as a vast quantity of other music for this instrument.

Quarles, Francis [kwaw(r)lz] (1592–1644) Religious poet, born near Romford, Essex. His best-known work is *Emblems* (1635) (a series of symbolic pictures with verse commentary), and a prose book of aphorisms, *Enchyridion* (1640).

Quarton, Enguerrand [kah(r)tõ], also found as **Charonton** or **Charrenton** (15th-c) Gothic religious painter, born in Laon, France. His style united French and Italian influences, and some have attributed to him the most famous of 15th-c French paintings, the 'Pietà' of Villeneuve-lès-Avignon.

Quasimodo, Salvatore [kwazeemohdoh] (1901–68) Poet, born in Syracuse, Sicily. His early work was Symbolist in character, as in *And Suddenly It's Evening* (trans, 1942), and he became a leader of the 'hermetic' poets.

Quayle, Sir Anthony [kwayl] (1913–89) Actor and director, born in Ainsdale, Lancashire. He joined the Shakespeare Memorial Theatre Company as actor and theatre director (1948–56), and helped create the Royal Shakespeare Company (1960). His major films include *Lawrence of Arabia* (1962).

Quayle, (James) Dan(forth) [kwayl] (1947–) US vice-president (1989–93), born in Indianapolis, IN. He became a member of the Congress (1977–81) and US Senate (1981–8), and was elected with Bush in 1988. >> Bush, George

Queen, Ellery Pseudonym of two writers of crime fiction, **Frederick Dannay** (1905–82) and his cousin **Manfred B Lee** (1905–71), both born in New York City. They wrote many popular books, using Ellery Queen both as pseudonym and as the name of their detective.

Queensberry, Sir John Sholto Douglas, 8th Marquess of (1844–1900) British aristocrat, a patron of boxing, who supervised the formulation in 1867 of new rules to govern that sport, since known as the *Queensberry Rules*. In 1895 he was tried and acquitted for publishing a defamatory libel on Oscar Wilde. >> Wilde, Oscar

Queneau, Raymond [kenoh] (1903–76) Writer, born in Le Havre, France. The best of his poetry is contained in *Les Ziaux* (1943) and *If You Suppose* (trans, 1952). His novels include *Zazie in the Metro* (trans, 1959; filmed 1960).

Quennell, Sir Peter (Courtney) [kwenel] (1905–93) Biographer, born in Bickley, Greater London. His studies include those of Byron (1935, 1941), Ruskin (1949), Shakespeare (1963), and Pope (1968).

Quercetanus >> **Duchesne, André**

Quercia, Jacopo della >> **Jacopo della Quercia**

Quesada, Elwood (Richard) [kesahda] (1904–) Aviator, born in Washington, DC. As head of the 9th Tactical Air Command, he directed thousands of sorties in preparation for the Allied landings in Normandy in 1944.

Quesada, Gonzalo Jiménez de [kaysahtha] (c.1497–1579) Conquistador, born in Córdoba or Granada, Spain. In 1536 he headed an expedition in South America, establishing New Granada, and its chief town, Santa Fé de Bogotá.

Quesnay, François [kenay] (1694–1774) Physician and economist, born in Méry, France. Known for his essays in political economy, he became a leader of the *Economistes*, also called the Physiocratic School.

Quesnel, Pasquier [kenel] (1634–1719) Jansenist theologian, born in Paris. In 1662 he became director of the Paris Oratory, but he refused to condemn Jansenism, and was forced to flee to Brussels (1684).

Quevedo y Villegas, Francisco Gómez de [kevaythoh ee veelyaygas] (1580–1645) Spanish writer, born in Madrid. One of the most prolific Spanish poets, his greatest work remains the picaresque novel, *The Life of a Scoundrel* (trans, 1626).

Quezon, Manuel (Luis) [kayson] (1878–1944) First Philippine president (1935–44), born in Baler, Philippines. The new capital of the Philippines on the island of Luzon is named after him.

Quiller-Couch, Sir Arthur [kwiler kooch], pseudonym **Q** (1863–1944) Man of letters, born in Bodmin, Cornwall. He edited *The Oxford Book of English Verse* (1900), published several volumes of essays and criticism, and also wrote poems, short stories, and several humorous novels.

Quilter, Roger (1877–1953) Composer, born in Brighton, East Sussex. Best known for his songs, he also wrote the *Children's Overture*, based on nursery tunes, and operas.

Quincey, Thomas de >> **de Quincey, Thomas**

Quincy, Josiah (1772–1864) US statesman, born in Boston, MA. A leading member of the Federal Party, he was elected to Congress (1804) and distinguished himself as an orator.

Quine, Willard Van Orman [kwiyn] (1908–) Philosopher and logician, born in Akron, OH. Much influenced by the Vienna Circle and the empiricist tradition, his books include *Mathematical Logic* (1940) and *Word and Object* (1960).

Quinet, Edgar [keenay] (1803–75) Poet, historian, and politician, born in Bourg-en-Bresse, France. His reputation was established with the epic poem *Ahasvérus* (1833), and his historical works include *The Religious Revolution in the 19th-c* (trans, 1857).

Quintana, Manuel José [keentahna] (1772–1857) Poet

and advocate, born in Madrid. He wrote the classic *Lives of Famous Spaniards* (1807-34), tragedies, and poetry, the best of which are his patriotic odes. He was crowned national poet by Isabella in 1855. >> Isabella II

Quintero, Serafin Alvarez and **Joaquin Alvarez** >> **Alvarez Quintero, Serafin**

Quintilian [kwintilian], in full **Marcus Fabius Quintilianus** (c.35-c.100) Roman rhetorician, born in Calagurris, Spain. His reputation rests on his great work, *Institutio Oratoria* (Education of an Orator), a complete system of rhetoric in 12 books.

Quirk, (Charles) Randolph, Baron (1920-) Grammarian and writer on the English language, born in the Isle of Man. Major grammars in which he was involved are *A Grammar of Contemporary English* (1972) and *A Comprehensive Grammar of the English Language* (1985).

Quisling, Vidkun (Abraham Lauritz Jonsson) [kwizling] (1887-1945) Diplomat and fascist leader, born in Fyresdal, Norway. In 1933 he founded the National Party in imitation of the German National Socialist Party, and became puppet prime minister in occupied Norway. He was executed in 1945.

Raab, Julius (1891–1964) Austrian chancellor (1953–61), born in St Pölten, Austria. He was federal minister of trade and transport (1938) and in 1945 became one of the founders of the People's Party.

RAB >> Butler, R A, Baron

Rabban Sauma [raban sowma] (c.1225–c.1300) The first Chinese known to have visited Europe, born in Beijing. Sent by the Mongol court via Baghdad and Trebizond to establish an anti-Arab alliance with Europe, he kept a famous record of his travels.

Rabelais, François [rabelay], pseudonym (an anagram of his name) **Alcofribas Nasier** (?1494–?1553) Satirist, physician, and humanist, born in or near Chinon, France. He is remembered for a sequence of books beginning with the comic and satirical *Pantagruel* (1532) and *Gargantua* (1534), published under his pseudonym, condemned by the Church for their unorthodox ideas and mockery of religious practices.

Rabi, Isidor (Isaac) [rahbee] (1898–1988) Physicist, born in Rymanow, Austria. An authority on nuclear physics and quantum mechanics, in 1944 he was awarded the Nobel Prize for Physics for his precision work on neutrons.

Rabin, Itzhak [rabeen] (1922–95) Israeli soldier and prime minister (1974–7, 1992–5), born in Jerusalem. He was made chief-of-staff in 1964, heading the armed forces during the Six-Day War (1967). He became Labour Party leader and also served as defence minister (1984–90). He was assassinated by a right-wing Israeli law student.

Rabinowitz, Solomon J >> Aleichem, Sholem

Rabuka, Sitiveni [rabooka] (1948–93) Fijian soldier and prime minister (1992–3), born near Suva, Fiji. After the 1987 elections, he staged a coup and set up his own provisional government. When prime minister Mara was reinstated, he retained control of the security forces and internal affairs.

Rachel Biblical character, the daughter of Laban and wife of Jacob, and the mother of Joseph and Benjamin. According to *Genesis* 29, Jacob worked 14 years to earn Rachel as his wife. >> Jacob; Joseph

Rachman, Peter [rakman] (1919–62) Property developer and landlord, born in Poland. He came to Britain in 1946, and began to acquire property in London, letting rooms at exorbitant rents to people whom no-one else would house (*Rachmanism*).

Rachmaninov, Sergey Vasilyevich [rakhmaninof], also spelled **Rachmaninoff** and **Rakhmaninov** (1873–1943) Composer and pianist, born in Nizhni Novgorod, Russia. He is best known for his piano music, which includes four concertos, the *Prelude in C Sharp Minor*, and his last major work, the *Rhapsody on a Theme of Paganini* (1934) for piano and orchestra.

Racine, Jean (Baptiste) [raseen] (1639–99) Dramatic poet, born in La Ferté-Milon, France. Widely regarded as the master of tragic pathos, his major verse tragedies include *Andromaque* (1667), *Phèdre* (1677), and *Bérénice* (1679).

Rackham, Arthur [rakam] (1867–1939) Artist, born in London. A water-colourist and book illustrator, he was well known for his typically Romantic and grotesque pictures in books of fairy tales, such as *Peter Pan* (1906).

Radcliffe, Ann, *née* **Ward** (1764–1823) Novelist, born in London. Her Gothic novels included *The Romance of the Forest* (1791), *The Mysteries of Udolpho* (1794), and *The Italian* (1797).

Radcliffe, Cyril John, Viscount (1899–1978) British lawyer. He was director-general of the ministry of information (1941–5), became a Lord of Appeal in Ordinary (1949), and was chairman of many commissions and committees.

Radcliffe, John (1650–1714) Physician, born in Wakefield, West Yorkshire. He attended William III and Queen Mary, and bequeathed the bulk of his property to form the Radcliffe Library, Infirmary, and Observatory at Oxford.

Radcliffe-Brown, A(lfred) R(eginald) (1881–1955) Social anthropologist, born in Birmingham, West Midlands. One of the principal architects of modern social anthropology, his chief concern was to emulate the methods of natural science.

Radde, Gustav Ferdinand Richard [rahduh] (1831–1903) Naturalist, ornithologist, and explorer, born in Gdańsk, Poland (formerly, Danzig, Germany). He travelled widely in the Caucasus and nearby regions. *Radde's warbler* and *Radde's accentor* are named after him.

Radek, Karl Bernhardovich [rahdek], originally **Karl Sobelsohn** (1885–?1939) Russian revolutionary and politician, born in Lwow, Ukraine. A leading member of the Communist International, he lost standing with his growing distrust of extremist tactics. He was charged as a Trotsky supporter, and in 1937 was a victim of one of Stalin's show trials.

Radetzky, Joseph, Graf (Count) **von** [radetskee] (1766–1858) Military reformer, born in Trebnitz, Czech Republic (formerly, Bohemia). In 1848 he was driven out of Milan, but held Verona and Mantua, then forced Venice to surrender, and until 1857 again ruled the Lombardo-Venetian territories.

Radford, Arthur (William) (1896–1973) US naval officer, born in Chicago, IL. He became vice-chief of naval operations (1948–9), commander of the Pacific Fleet (1949–53), and chairman of the joint chiefs-of-staff (1953–7).

Radhakrishnan, Sir Sarvepalli [rahdakrishnan] (1888–1975) Indian philosopher and president (1962–7), born in Tiruttani, Madras, India. A member of the Indian Assembly in 1947, he became vice-president of India (1952–62), then president.

Radiguet, Raymond [radeegay] (1903–23) Novelist and poet, born in Saint-Maur, France. He is best known for his masterpieces *The Devil in the Flesh* (trans, 1923) and *Count Orgel Opens the Ball* (trans, 1924).

Radzinowicz, Sir Leon [rajinovich] (1906–) Criminologist, born in Poland. He wrote a major *History of English Criminal Law* (5 vols, 1948), and edited many works on criminal science.

Rae, John [ray] (1813–93) Arctic traveller, born near Stromness, Orkney Is. In 1848 he accompanied Sir John Richardson in search of Franklin's lost expedition, and on another journey (1853–4) met the Eskimos who gave definite news of its fate. >> Franklin, John; Richardson, John

Raeburn, Sir Henry [raybern] (1756–1823) Portrait painter, born near Edinburgh. He painted the leading members of Edinburgh society in a typically bold, strongly shadowed style.

Raeder, Erich [rayder] (1876–1960) German grand admiral, born in Wandsbek, Germany. In 1928 he was made commander-in-chief of the navy, and encouraged the building of submarines and warships. At the Nuremberg Trials (1946) he was sentenced to life imprisonment but released in 1955.

Raemaekers, Louis [rahmakerz] (1869–1956) Political cartoonist and artist, born in Roermond, The Netherlands. He joined the *Telegraaf* in 1909, and attained worldwide fame by 1915 with his striking anti-German war cartoons.

Raffaello Sanzio >> **Raphael**

Raffles, Sir (Thomas) Stamford (1781–1826) Colonial adminstrator, born at sea, off Port Morant, Jamaica. As Lieutenant-Governor of Bengkulu (1818–23) he established a settlement at Singapore. A famous Singapore hotel carries his name.

Rafsanjani, Ali Akbar Hashemi [rafsanjahnee] (1934–) Iranian president (1989–), born in Rafsanjan, Iran. After the 1979 revolution, he helped to found the ruling Islamic Republican Party, and in 1980 was chosen as Speaker of the Majlis (Lower House). >> Khomeini

Ragaz, Leonhard (1862–1945) Reformed pastor and social activist, born in Canton-Graubünden, Switzerland. In World War 1 he denounced violence as an evil solution, later rejecting Fascism, Nazism, and Communism, and established an educational centre for working people.

Raglan (of Raglan), Lord Fitzroy James Henry Somerset, Baron (1788–1855) British general, born at Badminton, Gloucestershire, the son of the Duke of Beaufort. In 1854 he led an ill-prepared force against the Russians in the Crimea, where his ambiguous order led to the Charge of the Light Brigade (1854) at Balaclava.

Rahere (?–1144) Clergyman of Frankish descent. He was the founder of St Bartholomew's Hospital in London, begun in 1123.

Rahman, Shaikh Mujibur [rahman] (1920–75) First prime minister (1972–5) and president (1975) of Bangladesh, born in Tongipara, Bangladesh (formerly East Bengal). In 1970 he launched a non-co-operation campaign which escalated into civil war and the creation of Bangladesh; but after becoming president he was killed in a military coup.

Rahner, Karl (1904–84) Roman Catholic theologian, born in Freiburg, Germany. His multi-volume *Theological Investigations* combines the philosophy of existentialism with the tradition of Aquinas.

Raibolini, Francesco >> **Francia**

Raikes, Robert [rayks] (1735–1811) Philanthropist and pioneer of the Sunday-School movement, born in Gloucester, Gloucestershire. His pity for the misery and ignorance of many children in his native city led him to start the Sunday School movement in 1780.

Raimondi, Marcantonio >> **Marcantonio**

Raimu [remü], stage name of **Jules Auguste César Muraire** (1883–1946) Actor, born in Toulon, France. He appeared throughout the 1920s in revues, operettas, and comedies before creating the character of César in *Marius* (1929), which he repeated on film in 1931.

Rainer, Yvonne (1934–) Experimental dancer, choreographer, and film-maker, born in San Francisco, CA. A major influence on post-modern dance, she became involved with the radical Judson Dance Theater, for which she was the most prolific choreographer.

Rainier III [raynyay], in full **Rainier Louis Henri Maxence Bertrand de Grimaldi** (1923–) Prince of Monaco (1949–), born in Monaco. In 1956 he married film actress Grace Kelly. They had two daughters, **Caroline Louise Marguerite** (1957–) and **Stephanie Marie Elisabeth** (1965–), and a son, **Albert Alexandre Louis Pierre** (1958–). >> Kelly, Grace

Rainwater, (Leo) James (1917–) Physicist, born in Council, ID. He unified two theoretical models of the atomic nucleus, and shared the Nobel Prize for Physics in 1975. >> Bohr, Aage; Mottelson

Rainy, Robert (1826–1906) Theologian, born in Glasgow, Strathclyde. He organized the union of the Free and United Presbyterian Churches in 1900 as the United Free Church of Scotland, and became the first moderator of its General Assembly.

Raitz, Vladimir Gavrilovich [riyts] (1922–) British travel consultant and entrepreneur. He set up Horizon Holidays, and initiated the package holiday industry.

Raja Ram Mohan Rai >> **Rammohun Roy**

Rakhmaninov, Sergei >> **Rachmaninov, Sergei**

Raleigh, Sir Walter [rawlee, ralee], also spelled **Ralegh** (1552–1618) Courtier, navigator, and writer, born in Hayes Barton, Devon. He became prime favourite of Elizabeth I, and in 1584 sent the first of three expeditions to America, but later lost influence at court. When his enemies turned James I against him, he was imprisoned (1603–16), and after a failed expedition to the Orinoco in search of a gold-mine, he was executed. >> Elizabeth I

Raleigh, Sir Walter (Alexander) [rawlee, ralee] (1861–1922) Scholar, critic, and essayist, born in London. Among his writings are *The English Novel* (1891), *Milton* (1900), *Wordsworth* (1903), and *Shakespeare* (1907).

Ralph de Coggeshall >> **Coggeshall, Ralph de**

Ramadhin, Sonny [ramadin] (1930–) Cricketer, born in Trinidad. With Valentine he formed a devastating spin attack in the West Indies Test sides of the 1950s. In 43 Tests he took 188 wickets. >> Valentine, Alfred

Ramakrishna [ramakrishna], originally **Gadadhar Chatterjee** (1836–86) Hindu religious teacher, born in Hooghly, Bengal, India. He formed his own religious order, which taught that all religions were different paths to the same goal. His most noteworthy disciple was Vivekananda. >> Vivekananda

Raman, Sir Chandrasekhara (Venkata) [rahman] (1888–1970) Physicist, born in Trichinopoly, India. In 1930 he was awarded the Nobel Prize for Physics for his discoveries relating to the scattering of light (the *Raman effect*).

Ramana Maharishi [ramahna maharishee] (1879–1950) Philosopher, born in Madurai, India. A life-long hermit at the holy mountain of Arunachala, his philosophy of seeking self-knowledge became known to Westerners through his *Collected Works* (1969) and other anthologies.

Ramanuja [ramahnuja] (traditionally c.1017–1137) Hindu theologian and philosopher, born in Sriperumbudur, Tamil Nadu, India. He organized temple worship, and provided the intellectual basis for the practice of *bhakti*, or devotional worship.

Ramanujan, Srinivasa [ramahnujan] (1887–1920) Mathematician, born in Erode, India. He worked on elliptic integrals, partitions, and analytic number theory, and was the first Indian to be elected a Fellow of the Royal Society.

Ramaphosa, Cyril (Matamela) [ramapohza] (1952–) South African politician and trade unionist, born in Johannesburg, South Africa. In 1982 he was elected as the first general-secretary of the National Union of Mineworkers, and in 1991 became secretary-general of the African National Congress.

Ramazzini, Bernardino [ramatseenee] (1633–1714) Physician, born in Capri, Italy. His major work, *Diseases of Workers* (trans, 1700), was the first systematic treatise on occupational diseases.

Rambert, Dame Marie [rombair], originally **Cyvia Rambam** (1888–1982) Ballet dancer and teacher, born in Warsaw. She settled in London in 1918, and in 1935 formed the Ballet Rambert, remaining closely associated with it through its change to a modern dance company in the 1960s.

Rambouillet, Catherine de Vivonne, marquise de (Marchioness of) [rābweeyay] (1588–1665) French noblewoman, born in Rome, the daughter of Jean de Vivonne, marquis de Pisani. For 50 years she gathered together in the Hôtel de Rambouillet the talent and wit of France drawn from both the nobility and the literary world.

Rameau, Jean Philippe [ramoh] (1683–1764) Composer, born in Dijon, France. He wrote many operas, notably

Hippolyte et Aricie (1733) and *Castor et Pollux* (1737), as well as ballets, harpsichord pieces, and vocal music, and an influential treatise on harmony (1722).

Ramée, de la >> Ouida; Ramus, Petrus

Rameses or **Ramses II** [ram̱zeez], known as **the Great** (13th-c BC) King of Egypt (1304–1237 BC), whose long and prosperous reign marks the last great peak of Egyptian power. His many monuments include the great sandstone temples at Abu Simbel.

Rammohun Roy or **Raja Ram Mohan Rai** (1774–1833) Religious reformer, born in Bengal. In 1828 he began the Brahmo Samaj Association, and in 1830 the Emperor of Delhi bestowed on him the title of raja.

Ramón y Cajal, Santiago [ram̱on ee kaẖal] (1852–1934) Physician and histologist, born in Petilla de Aragón, Spain. He was specially noted for his work on the brain and nerves, isolating the neuron and discovering how impulses are transmitted to brain cells. He shared the Nobel Prize for Physiology or Medicine in 1906.

Ramphal, Sir Shridath Surrendranath [ram̱fal], known as **Sonny Ramphal** (1928–　) Guyanese lawyer and diplomat, born in Guyana. He became Guyana's foreign minister and attorney general (1972), then justice minister (1973), becoming internationally known as secretary-general of the Commonwealth (1975–89).

Rams, Dieter (1932–　) Product designer, born in Wiesbaden, Germany. Best known as the chief designer for Braun AG (since 1955), his food mixers, record players, radios, shavers, and other products are all examples of rational and unadorned modern design.

Ramsay, Allan (c.1685–1758) Poet, born in Leadhills, Strathclyde. His works include the pastoral comedy, *The Gentle Shepherd* (1725), and an edited collection of Scots poetry, *The Evergreen* (1724).

Ramsay, Allan (1713–84) Artist, born in Edinburgh, the son of the poet Allan Ramsay. Well known for his portraits of women, in 1767 he was appointed portrait painter to George III. >> Ramsay, Allan (c.1685–1758)

Ramsay, Sir Bertram (Home) (1883–1945) Naval officer, born in London. He directed the Dunkirk evacuation of Allied troops in 1940, commanded the British naval forces for the Allied invasion of Sicily (1943), and in 1944 was Allied naval commander-in-chief for the Normandy landings.

Ramsay, James Andrew Broun >> Dalhousie, Marquess of

Ramsay, Sir William (1852–1916) Chemist, born in Glasgow, Strathclyde. In conjunction with Rayleigh he discovered argon in 1894. Later he identified helium, neon, krypton, and xenon, and was awarded the Nobel Prize for Chemistry in 1904. >> Rayleigh, John

Ramsey, Norman F(oster), Jr (1915–　) Physicist, born in Washington, DC. His research led to the development of the caesium atomic clock (1960), and he shared the Nobel Prize for Physics in 1989.

Ramsey, Sir Alf(red) (1922–　) Footballer and manager, born in Dagenham, Essex. He played with Southampton and Tottenham Hotspur, managed Ipswich Town, and as manager of England (1963–74) saw his team win the World Cup in 1966.

Ramsey, Frank (Plumpton) (1903–30) Philosopher and mathematician, born in Cambridge, Cambridgeshire. In his short life he made outstanding contributions to philosophy, logic, mathematics, and economics.

Ramsey, Ian (Thomas) (1915–72) Anglican bishop, and philosopher of religion, born in Kearsley, Lancashire. His philosophical works include *Models and Mystery* (1964) and *Models for Divine Activity* (1973).

Ramsey (of Canterbury), (Arthur) Michael Ramsey, Baron (1904–88) Archbishop of Canterbury (1961–74), born in Cambridge, Cambridgeshire. He worked for Church unity, making a historic visit to Pope Paul VI in the Vatican in 1966. >> Paul VI

Ram Singh [rahm sing] (1816–85) Sikh philosopher and reformer, born in Bhaini, India. He formed a sect to rejuvenate Sikhism, and built up a *khalsa*, or private army, prophesying that British rule would be broken.

Ramus, Petrus [ram̱ü], Lat name of **Pierre de la Ramée** (1515–72) Humanist, born in Cuts, France. His attempts to reform the science of logic excited much hostility, and his *Dialectic* (1543) was suppressed. He was killed in the massacre of St Bartholomew.

Ramuz, Charles Ferdinand [ram̱üz] (1878–1947) Writer, born in Cully, Switzerland. His books include (trans titles) *The Little Village* (1903), *The Triumph of Death* (1922), and *Beauty on Earth* (1927).

Rancé, Armand Jean Le Bouthillier de [rãsay] (1626–1700) Abbot, founder of the Trappists, born in Paris. He became abbot of the Cistercian abbey of La Trappe in 1662, establishing a religious order whose principles were perpetual prayer and austere self-denial.

Rand, Ayn (1905–82) Writer and philosopher, born in St Petersburg, Russia. She became a US citizen in 1931. Her novels include *Atlas Shrugged* (1957), the bible of her 'objectivism'. This philosophy, promoted in such books as *The Virtue of Selfishness* (1965), glorified self-assertion and competition.

Randall, James Ryder (1839–1908) Poet, born in Baltimore, MD. His lyrics, which in the Civil War (1861–5) gave powerful aid to the Southern cause, include 'Maryland, My Maryland', 'Stonewall Jackson', and 'There's Life in the Old Land Yet'.

Randall, John (1905–84) British physicist. With Harry Boot (1917–83), he invented in 1940 the cavity magnetron to generate radio waves of very short wavelength, essential for radar. Their device is now also used in microwave cookers.

Randolph, A(sa) Philip (1889–1979) Labour leader and civil rights activist, born in Crescent City, FL. He founded the first successful African-American trade union (1925) and the Negro American Labor Council (1960), and directed the civil rights march on Washington (1963).

Randolph, Edmund (Jennings) (1753–1813) US statesman, born in Williamsburg, VA. He became attorney general (1789) and secretary of state (1794), but an accusation of bribery forced his resignation (1795).

Randolph, John, known as **John Randolph of Roanoke** (1773–1833) US politician, born in Prince George Co, VA. As Democratic leader of the US House of Representatives, he opposed the War of 1812 and the Missouri Compromise and Nullification.

Randolph, Sir Thomas (?–1332) Soldier and statesman, the nephew of King Robert I of Scotland. He recaptured Edinburgh Castle from the English (1314), reinvaded England (1320, 1327), and was guardian of the kingdom after the death of Bruce (1329). >> Bruce, Robert

Randolph, Thomas (1605–35) Writer, born in Newnham-cum-Badby, Northamptonshire. He left a number of fanciful poems, and six plays, including *Aristippus, or the Jovial Philosopher* (c.1626).

Ranjit Singh [raṉjit sing], known as **the Lion of the Punjab** (1780–1839) Sikh ruler, born in Budrukhan, India. Succeeding his father as ruler of Lahore, he fought to unite all the Sikh provinces, and became the most powerful ruler in India.

Ranjitsinhji, Prince [raṉjitsinjee] (1872–1933) Indian nobleman and cricketer, born in Sarodar, India. He became a leading batsman for Sussex and England, and from 1906 did much to modernize and improve conditions in his home state, Nawanagar.

Rank (of Sutton Scotney), J(oseph) Arthur Rank, Baron (1888–1972) Film magnate, born in Hull, Humberside. He became chairman of many film companies, including Gaumont-British and Cinema-Television, and did much to promote the British film industry.

Ranke, Leopold von [rangkuh] (1795–1886) Historian, born in Wiehe, Germany. A prolific writer on many aspects of European history, his major work was *History of the Popes in the 16th and 17th Centuries* (trans, 1834–7).

Rankin, Dame Annabelle (Jane Mary) (1908–86) Australian stateswoman, born in Brisbane, Queensland, Australia. She became the first Australian woman of ministerial rank, holding the housing portfolio (1966–71).

Rankin, Jeannette (1880–1973) Feminist and pacifist, born near Missoula, MT. The first female member of Congress, entering US House of Representatives as a Republican (1917–19, 1941–3), she was instrumental in the first bill granting married women independent citizenship.

Rankine, William (John Macquorn) [rangkin] (1820–72) Engineer and scientist, born in Edinburgh. His works on the steam engine, machinery, shipbuilding, and applied mechanics became standard textbooks.

Ransom, John Crowe (1888–1974) Poet and critic, born in Pulaski, TN. His work includes *Poems About God* (1919), and the critical books *God Without Thunder* (1930) and *The New Criticism* (1941).

Ransome, Arthur (Mitchell) (1884–1967) Writer, born in Leeds, West Yorkshire. He wrote critical works and travel books before making his name with books for young readers, notably *Swallows and Amazons* (1931).

Rantzen, Esther (Louise) (1940–) Television presenter and producer, born in Berkhamsted, Hertfordshire. She is best known as the producer and presenter of BBC television's *That's Life* (1973–94), and for many documentary programmes. She also founded the charity 'Childline'.

Raoult, François Marie [rahoo] (1830–1901) Chemist, born in Fournes, France. He discovered the law (named after him) which relates the vapour pressure of a solution to the number of molecules of solute dissolved in it.

Raphael [rafael], in full **Raffaello Sanzio** (1483–1520) Painter, born in Urbino, Italy. In 1508 he went to Rome, where he produced his greatest works, including the frescoes in the papal apartments of the Vatican, and the cartoons for the tapestries of the Sistine Chapel. In 1514 he succeeded Bramante as architect of St Peter's. >> Bramante

Rapp, George (1770–1847) Religious leader, born in Württemberg, Germany. He became leader of a separatist group who emigrated to W Pennsylvania and Indiana, where they established communities of Harmonites (or *Rappites*).

Rask, Rasmus (Kristian) (1787–1832) Founder of historical comparative linguistics, born in Braendekilde, Denmark. His *Essay on the Origin of the Ancient Scandinavian or Icelandic Tongue* (1818) opened up the science of comparative philology.

Rasmussen, Knud (Johan Victor) [razmusen] (1879–1933) Explorer and ethnologist, born in Jacobshavn, Greenland. From 1902 he directed several expeditions in Greenland, and in 1921–4 crossed by dog-sledge from Greenland to the Bering Strait.

Rasp, Charles (1846–1907) Prospector, born in Stuttgart, Germany. He emigrated to Australia in 1869, discovered silver, and formed the Broken Hill Proprietary Company (now known as BHP Ltd).

Raspe, Rudolf Erich >> **Münchhausen, Baron von**

Rasputin, Grigoriy [raspyootin] (?1871–1916) Peasant and self-styled religious 'elder', born in Pokrovskoye, Russia. He gained the confidence of the emperor (Nicholas II) and empress by his ability to control through hypnosis the bleeding of the haemophiliac heir to the throne, Alexey. His political influence led to his murder by a group of aristocrats. >> Nicholas II

Ras Tafari Makonnen, Prince >> **Haile Selassie I**

Rastrick, John (Urpeth) (1780–1856) Civil and mechanical engineer, born in Morpeth, Northumberland. His greatest achievement was the London & Brighton railway, opened in 1841.

Ratcliffe, Derek (1929–) British conservationist. His main work is the *Nature Conservation Review* (1977), cataloguing the prime examples of habitat in the British Is in need of protection.

Rathbone, Eleanor (Florence) (1872–1946) Feminist and social reformer, born in Liverpool, Merseyside. She was a leader in the constitutional movement for female suffrage, and worked vigorously in the housing campaign between the wars.

Rathbone, Harold Stewart (1858–1929) British painter, designer, and poet. He founded the Della Robbia Pottery with the sculptor, Conrad Dressler, in Birkenhead (1893), producing a wide range of architectural and domestic earthenware.

Rathenau, Walther [rahtenow] (1867–1922) Industrialist and statesman, born in Berlin. As minister of reconstruction (1921) and foreign minister (1922) he dealt with reparations, but his attempts to negotiate an agreement made him unpopular in nationalist circles, and he was murdered. >> Behrens

Rathke, Martin H(einrich) [rahtkuh] (1793–1860) Biologist, born in Danzig, Germany. In 1829 he discovered gill-slits and gill-arches in embryo birds and mammals.

Ratsiraka, Didier (1936–) President of Madagascar (1975–93), born in Vatomandry, Madagascar. In 1976 he formed the Advance Guard of the Malagasy Revolution, which became the nucleus of a one-party state, but ethnic discontent led to his defeat in the 1993 elections.

Rattigan, Sir Terence (Mervyn) (1911–77) Playwright, born in London. His plays include *French Without Tears* (1936), *The Winslow Boy* (1946), *The Browning Version* (1948), and *Ross* (1960).

Rattle, Sir Simon (Denis) (1955–) Conductor, born in Liverpool, Merseyside. Since 1980 he has been principal conductor of the City of Birmingham Symphony Orchestra, and from 1981 principal guest conductor of the Los Angeles Philharmonic.

Rau, Johannes [row] (1931–) West German politician, born in Wuppertal, Germany. He became minister-president of the Social Democratic Party in 1978, and its (unsuccessful) chancellor-candidate for the 1987 Bundestag election.

Rauschenberg, Robert [rowshenberg] (1925–) Avant-garde artist, born in Port Arthur, TX. His collages and 'combines' incorporate a variety of rubbish (rusty metal, old tyres, fragments of clothing, etc) splashed with paint.

Ravel, Maurice [ravel] (1875–1937) Composer, born in Ciboure, France. His works include *Pavane for a Dead Princess* (trans, 1899), *Rapsodie espagnole* (1908), the 'choreographic poem' *La Valse* (1920), and *Boléro* (1928), intended as a miniature ballet.

Raven, Simon (Arthur Noël) (1927–) Writer, born in Leicester, Leicestershire. His most notable work is his series of novels *Alms for Oblivion* (1964–76). Television dramatizations of well-known works include *The Way We Live Now* (1969) and *The Pallisers* (1974).

Ravilious, Eric William (1903–42) Artist, designer, and illustrator, born in London. A designer for J Wedgwood & Sons, his patterns included the travel series, coronation mugs, and Christmas tableware.

Ravitch, Diane, *née* **Silvers** (1938–) Educator and historian, born in Houston, TX. She helped define the neo-Conservative agenda for school reform in such works as *The Troubled Crusade* (1983) and *What Do Our Seventeen-Year Olds Know?* (co-authored, 1987).

Rawlings, Jerry J(ohn) (1947–) Ghanaian leader (1979,

1981–   ) and president (1992–   ), born in Accra. He led a coup in 1979, and again in 1981, but in 1992 announced a return to multi-party elections, and was elected president.

Rawlings, Marjorie, *née* **Kinnan** (1896–1953) Writer, born in Washington, DC. Her first novel for young readers, *The Yearling* (1938), won the Pulitzer Prize.

Rawlinson, Sir Henry Creswicke (1810–95) Diplomat and Assyriologist, born in Chadlington, Oxfordshire. He was British minister in Persia (1859–60), a member of the Council of India (1858–9, 1868–95), and wrote books on cuneiform inscriptions, the Russian question, and the history of Assyria. >> Rawlinson, Henry Seymour

Rawlinson, Henry Seymour Rawlinson, Baron (1864–1925) British soldier, the eldest son of Sir Henry Creswicke Rawlinson. He commanded the 4th Army at the Somme (1916), and broke the Hindenburg line near Amiens (1918). >> Rawlinson, Henry Creswicke

Rawls, John (1921–   ) Philosopher, born in Baltimore, MD. His best-known work is *A Theory of Justice* (1971), reviving an interest in social contract theory, rights, and liberalism.

Rawsthorne, Alan (1905–71) Composer, born in Haslingden, Lancashire. His wide-ranging works include three symphonies, eight concertos, choral and chamber music, and several film scores.

Ray, James Earl >> **King, Martin Luther**

Ray, John (1627–1705) Naturalist, born in Black Notley, Essex. His classification of plants, with its emphasis on the species as the basic unit, was the foundation of modern taxonomy, as seen in *Historia Plantarum* (3 vols, 1686–1704).

Ray, Man, originally **Emanuel Rudnitsky** (1890–1976) Painter, photographer, and film-maker, born in Philadelphia, PA. He co-founded the New York Dadaist movement, experimented with new techniques in painting and photography, and during the 1930s produced *rayographs* (photographic images made without a camera).

Ray, Satyajit [riy] (1921–92) Film director, born in Calcutta, India. His first film, *Pather Panchali* (1954, On the Road), was a major success at Cannes. Later films include *The Unvanquished* (trans, 1956), and *The World of Apu* (trans, 1959), and he became India's leading film-maker.

Rayburn, Sam(uel Taliaferro) (1882–1961) US politician, born in Roane Co, TN. He rose to prominence in the US House of Representatives (1913–61) on the Committee on Interstate and Foreign Commerce, and became speaker of the House (1940–61).

Rayleigh, John William Strutt, 3rd Baron [raylee] (1842–1919) Physicist, born near Maldon, Essex. He studied the wave theory of light (*Rayleigh scattering*), and with Ramsay discovered argon (1894). He was awarded the Nobel Prize for Physics in 1904. >> Ramsay, William; Rayleigh, 4th Baron

Rayleigh, Robert John Strutt, 4th Baron [raylee] (1875–1947) Physicist, born at Terling Place, Essex, the son of Lord Rayleigh. He was noted for his work on rock radioactivity.

Raymond, Alex(ander Gillespie) (1905–56) Strip cartoonist, born in New Rochelle, NY. His popular adventure strips included *Jungle Jim*, the science-fiction hero *Flash Gordon* (both 1934), and *Rip Kirby* (1946).

Rayner, Claire (Berenice), pseudonyms **Ruth Martin, Sheila Brandon, Ann Lynton** (1931–   ) British writer, broadcaster, and agony aunt. A trained nurse, she contributed an advice column to national newspapers (1973–91), has regularly appeared on radio and television to advise on family problems, and is also known as a novelist.

Razi >> **Rhazes**

Razin, Stepan Timofeyevich [razeen], known as **Stenka Razin** (c.1630–71) Russian Cossack and folk-hero. He led a Cossack and peasant revolt (1670–1) directed against the boyars and landowning nobility, but was executed.

Read, Sir Herbert (1893–1968) Poet and art critic, born near Kirkby Moorside, North Yorkshire. He became known as a writer on aesthetics in such works as *The Meaning of Art* (1931). His *Collected Poems* were published in 1946.

Reade, Charles (1814–84) Writer, born in Ipsden House, Oxfordshire. His masterpiece was his long historical novel of the 15th-c, *The Cloister and the Hearth* (1861).

Reading, Rufus Daniel Isaacs, 1st Marquess of [reding] (1860–1935) Jurist and statesman, born in London. He was appointed solicitor general (1910) and attorney general, a member of the Cabinet (1912), Lord Chief Justice (1913), and Viceroy of India (1921–6).

Reagan, Ronald (Wilson) [raygn] (1911–   ) US Republican statesman and 40th president (1981–9), born in Tampico, IL. He went to Hollywood in 1937 and made over 50 films. In 1980 he defeated Carter in the presidential election and won a second term in 1984, defeating Mondale. He introduced a major programme of economic reform, took a strong anti-communist stand, introduced the Strategic Defence Initiative, and reached a major arms-reduction accord with Gorbachev. >> Carter, Jimmy; Gorbachev; Mondale

Réard, Louis [rayah(r)] (1897–1984) French designer. He designed the modern two-piece swimsuit, which he named after the nuclear test site in the Pacific, Bikini Atoll (1946).

Reardon, Ray(mond) [reerdn] (1932–   ) Snooker player, born in Tredegar, Gwent. The first of the great snooker players of the modern era, he was world professional champion six times (1970, 1973–6, 1978).

Réaumur, René Antoine Ferchault de [rayohmür] (1683–1757) Polymath, born in La Rochelle, France. His studies included metallurgy, glassmaking, and entomology. His thermometer (with spirit instead of mercury) has 80 degrees between the freezing and boiling points.

Reber, Grote [rayber] (1911–   ) Radio astronomer, born in Wheaton, IL. He built the first radio telescope, 31 ft in diameter, in his own back yard (1937), and for several years was the only radio astronomer in the world.

Récamier, (Jeanne Françoise) Julie (Adélaide) [ruhkamyay], *née* **Bernard** (1777–1849) Hostess, born in Lyon, France. Her salon became a fashionable meeting place, especially for former Royalists and those opposed to Napoleon. >> Napoleon I

Recorde, Robert [rekaw(r)d] (c.1510–58) Mathematician, born in Tenby, Dyfed. He wrote the first English textbooks on elementary arithmetic and algebra, which became the standard works in Elizabethan England.

Redding, Otis (1941–67) Soul singer, born in Dawson, GA. An appearance at the Monterey pop festival in 1967 secured his popularity, but he died in a plane crash the same year. Several of his songs, such as 'Try a Little Tenderness' and 'Mr Pitiful' (1965), are now regarded as classics.

Redfield, Robert (1897–1958) Cultural anthropologist, born in Chicago, IL. A leading theorist in the study of peasant societies, especially of Central America, he introduced the concept of the 'folk–urban continuum'.

Redford, (Charles) Robert (1937–   ) Actor and director, born in Santa Barbara, CA. His films include *Butch Cassidy and the Sundance Kid* (1969), *The Sting* (1973), *All the President's Men* (1976), and *Out of Africa* (1985). He gained an Oscar for his direction of *Ordinary People* (1980).

Redgrave, Sir Michael (Scudamore) (1908–85) Actor, born in Bristol, Avon. His notable stage performances included Richard II (1951), Prospero (1952), and Uncle Vanya (1962), and his film career began with *The Lady Vanishes* (1938). He married the actress **Rachel Kempson** (1910–   ) in 1935, and their three children are all actors; **Vanessa, Corin** (1939–   ), and **Lynn** (1944–   ). >> Redgrave, Vanessa

Redgrave, Richard (1804–88) Subject painter, born in London. With his brother **Samuel** (1802–76) he wrote *A Century of English Painters* (1866) and other works.

Redgrave, Vanessa (1937–) Actress, born in London, the daughter of Michael Redgrave. Her films include *Julia* (1977, Oscar), *The Bostonians* (1983), and *Howard's End* (1992). She is also well known for her active support of left-wing causes. >> Redgrave, Michael

Redi, Francesco [raydee] (1626–97) Physician and poet, born in Arezzo, Italy. He wrote on animal parasites, and proved that maggots cannot form spontaneously on meat which has been covered. As a poet, his chief work is *Bacchus in Tuscany* (trans, 1685).

Redman, Don(ald Matthew) (1900–64) Saxophonist, arranger, and bandleader, born in Piedmont, WV. In the mid-1920s he created a distinctive style for the Fletcher Henderson Orchestra, his swing-style orchestration influencing many jazz composers. >> Henderson, Fletcher

Redmond, John (Edward) (1856–1918) Irish politician, born in Dublin. A champion of Home Rule, he became chairman of the Nationalist Party (1900), but declined a seat in Asquith's coalition ministry (1915).

Redon, Odilon [ruhdõ] (1840–1916) Artist, born in Bordeaux, France. Usually regarded as a pioneer Surrealist, because of his use of dream images, he also made charcoal drawings, lithographs, and (after 1900) intensely coloured pastels of flowers and portraits.

Redpath, Anne (1895–1965) Painter, born in Galashiels, Borders, Scotland. One of the most important modern Scottish artists, her works show great richness of colour and vigorous technique.

Redpath, Jean (1937–) Folk-singer, born in Edinburgh. In 1961 she emigrated to the USA, where she became noted as an interpreter of traditional Scots ballads and the songs of Burns. >> Burns, Robert

Reed, Sir Carol (1906–76) Film director, born in London. His major films include *Kipps* (1941), *The Fallen Idol* (1948), and *Oliver!* (1968, Oscar), but is best known for *The Third Man* (1949).

Reed, Lou, originally **Louis Firbank** (1944–) Rock singer, guitarist, and songwriter, born in Long Island, NY. His 1973 album, *Transformer*, included 'Walk On The Wild Side', and later albums have included *Street Hassle* (1978) and *New Sensations* (1984).

Reed, (Robert) Oliver (1938–) Film actor, born in London, the nephew of Sir Carol Reed. He became known through his role as Bill Sykes in Carol Reed's musical, *Oliver!* (1968). His many films include *Women in Love* (1969), *The Devils* (1971), *Three Musketeers* (1974), and *Treasure Island* (1990).

Reed, Talbot Baines (1852–93) Writer of books for boys, born in London. His school stories included *The Fifth Form at St Dominic's* (1881), *The Master of the Shell* (1887), and *Cockhouse at Fellsgarth* (1891).

Reed, Walter (1851–1902) Army surgeon, born in Belroi, VA. In 1900 he proved that the transmission of yellow fever was by mosquitoes, and his research led to the eventual eradication of this disease from Cuba.

Rees, Lloyd Frederick (1895–1988) Artist, born in Yeronga, Queensland, Australia. His early drawings, meticulous in draughtsmanship and Romantic in style, were etched or lithographed, and he later turned to oils.

Rees-Mogg (of Hinton Blewitt), William Rees-Mogg, Baron (1928–) Journalist, born in Bristol, Avon. He became editor of *The Times* (1967–81), and in 1988 was appointed to head the Broadcasting Standards Council.

Reeve, Clara (1729–1807) Novelist, born in Ipswich, Suffolk. She is best known for *The Champion of Virtue, a Gothic Story* (1777), renamed *The Old English Baron*, avowedly an imitation of Walpole's The Castle of Otranto. >> Walpole, Horace

Reeve, John >> **Muggleton, Lodowick**

Reeves, Sir Paul Alfred (1932–) Clergyman, born in Wellington, New Zealand. He was Primate and Archbishop of New Zealand (1980–5) before becoming Governor-General of New Zealand (1985–90), the first Maori to hold those positions.

Regan, Donald (Thomas) [reegn] (1918–) US politician, born in Cambridge, MA. Appointed Treasury secretary in 1981, he became White House chief-of-staff in 1985, but was forced to resign in 1987 following criticism of his role in the 'Irangate Affair' (1985–6).

Regener, Erich [raygener] (1881–1955) German physicist. He is known for his pioneering work on cosmic rays, and for his research on the stratosphere.

Reger, Max [rayger], popular name of **Johann Baptist Joseph Maximilian Reger** (1873–1916) Composer, born in Brand, Germany. He wrote organ music, piano concertos, choral works, and songs.

Regiomontanus [rejiohmontaynus], Lat name of **Johannes Müller** (1436–76) Mathematician and astronomer, born in Königsberg (Lat *Mons Regius*, hence his pseudonym), Germany. He established the study of algebra and trigonometry in Germany.

Régnier, Henri (François Joseph) de [raynyay] (1864–1936) Symbolist writer, born in Honfleur, France. His poetical works include *Tomorrows* (trans, 1885) and *The Winged Sandal* (trans, 1906), and his novels *Fear of Love* (trans, 1907) and *The Sinner* (trans, 1912).

Regulus, Marcus Atilius [regyulus] (3rd-c BC) Roman general and statesman of the First Punic War, whose heroic death at the hands of the Carthaginians earned him legendary status.

Regulus or **Rule, St** (4th-c) According to legend, a monk of Constantinople or Bishop of Patras, who in 347 came to Muckross or Kilrimont (St Andrews), bringing relics of St Andrew from the East.

Rehnquist, William H(ubbs) [renkwist] (1924–) Jurist, born in Milwaukee, WI. Appointed Chief Justice of the Supreme Court in 1986, he later framed a series of conservative rulings on abortion, affirmative action, and capital punishment.

Reich, Steve [riykh] (1936–) Composer, born in New York City. Strongly influenced by Stravinsky, jazz, African and Balinese music, and his training in drumming, he uses a variety of vocal and instrumental timbres, including taped and electronic effects.

Reich, Wilhelm [riykh] (1897–1957) Psychoanalyst and cult figure, born in Dobrzcynica, Austria. He developed a theory in which neuroses resulted from repressed feelings or sexual energy. He emigrated to the USA in 1939, established the 'Orgone' Institute, and died in gaol after being prosecuted for promoting a fraudulent treatment.

Reicha, Antonín [riykha] (1770–1836) Composer, teacher, and music theorist, born in Prague. His use of counterpoint and instrumental sonority was highly original, as seen in his 36 *Fugues* and 24 quintets for woodwind.

Reichenbach, Georg (Friedrich) von [riykhenbakh] (1772–1826) Engineer, instrument-maker, and inventor, born in Durlach, Germany. In 1804 he established a firm in Munich for the manufacture of high quality precision instruments used by astronomers and surveyors.

Reichenbach, Hans [riykhenbakh] (1891–1953) Philosopher of science, born in Hamburg, Germany. An early associate of the Vienna School of logical positivists, he made important contributions to probability theory, and wrote widely on logic and the philosophical bases of science.

Reichenbach, Karl, Freiherr (Baron) **von** [riykhenbakh] (1788–1869) Natural philosopher and industrialist, born in Stuttgart, Germany. He discovered paraffin (1830) and creosote (1833), and after studying animal magnetism claimed to have found a new force (*Od*), intermediate between electricity, magnetism, heat, and light.

Reichstein, Tadeusz [riykhshtiyn] (1897–) Chemist, born in Włocławek, Poland. For his research on the adrenal hormones, he shared the Nobel Prize for Physiology or Medicine in 1950.

Reid, Beryl (1920–) Comedienne and actress, born in Hereford, Hereford and Worcester. Her films include *The Killing of Sister George* (1968) and *Entertaining Mr Sloane* (1969), and she received a British Academy Award for her role in *Smiley's People* (1982).

Reid, Sir Bob, popular name of **Sir Robert Paul Reid** (1934–) Industrial executive, born in Scotland. His appointments include chairman and chief executive of Shell UK (1985), chairman of the British Institute of Management (1988), and chairman of the British Railways Board (1990).

Reid, Sir George (Houstoun) (1845–1918) Australian prime minister (1904–5), born in Johnstone, Strathclyde. In Australia from 1852, he became premier of New South Wales (1894–9) and Leader of the Opposition in the House of Representatives (1901).

Reid, John (Richard) (1928–) Cricketer, born in Auckland, New Zealand. Six of his 39 first-class centuries were made in Tests, for which he was selected 58 times.

Reid, (Thomas) Mayne, Captain (1818–83) Writer of boys' stories, born in Ballyroney, Co Down. His popular novels included *The Maroon* (1862), *The Headless Horseman* (1866), and *The Castaways* (1870).

Reid, Thomas (1710–96) Philosopher, born in Strachan, Grampian. The leader of the 'Scottish' school, which rejected the scepticism of David Hume, his main publications include *Essays on the Intellectual Powers of Man* (1785).

Reik, Theodor [riyk] (1888–1969) Psychoanalyst, born in Vienna. A protégé of Sigmund Freud, in 1938 he emigrated to the USA, and in 1946 established the National Psychological Association for Psychoanalysis. >> Freud, Sigmund

Reiner, Fritz [riyner] (1888–1963) Conductor, born in Budapest. After several seasons with the Metropolitan Opera in New York City, he conducted the Chicago Symphony Orchestra (1953–62).

Reinhardt, Ad(olf Frederick) [riyn]hah(r)t] (1913–67) Painter and critic, born in Buffalo, NY. He joined the American Abstract Artists, an avant-garde association which promoted hard-edge abstraction, and later became influential with the Minimal artists of the 1960s.

Reinhardt, Django [riyn]hah(r)t], popular name of **Jean Baptiste Reinhardt** (1910–53) Jazz guitarist, born in Liverchies, Belgium. He played in the Quintet of the Hot Club of France with Stephane Grappelli (1934–9), and became the first European jazz musician to influence the music. >> Grappelli

Reinhardt, Max [riyn]hah(r)t], originally **Max Goldmann** (1873–1943) Theatre director, born in Baden, Germany. Known for his 1905 production of *A Midsummer Night's Dream*, he was a master in theatre art and technique, often mounting spectacular, large-scale productions.

Reischauer, Edwin O(ldfather) [riyshower] (1910–90) US diplomat and scholar, born in Tokyo, Japan. He collaborated with John K Fairbank on two classic textbooks, *East Asia: the Great Tradition* (1960) and *East Asia: the Modern Transformation* (1965). He became ambassador to Japan (1961–6). >> Fairbank

Reisner, George (Andrew) [riyzner] (1867–1942) Egyptologist, born in Indianapolis, IN. His outstanding discovery (1925) was the tomb of Queen Hetepheres, mother of Cheops, the only major find of jewellery and furniture surviving from the Old Kingdom. >> Cheops

Reith (of Stonehaven), John (Charles Walsham) Reith, Baron [reeth] (1889–1971) British statesman and engineer, born in Stonehaven, Grampian. He became the first general manager of the BBC (1922) and its director-general (1927–38), and was minister of works and buildings (1940–2).

Reitz, Dana [riyts] (1948–) Dancer and choreographer, born in New York City. Best known as a soloist, she made a notable contribution to Wilson and Glass's opera, *Einstein on the Beach* (1976). >> Glass, Philip; Wilson, Robert

Reizenstein, Franz [riyzenshtiyn] (1911–68) Composer and pianist, born in Nuremberg, Germany. Among his compositions are cello, piano, and violin concertos, the cantata *Voices by Night*, two radio operas, and chamber and piano music.

Remak, Robert (1815–65) Physician and pioneer in electrotherapy, born in Posen, Germany. He discovered the *fibres of Remak* (1830) and the nerve cells in the heart now called *Remak's ganglia* (1844).

Remarque, Erich Maria [ruhmah(r)k] (1898–1970) Novelist, born in Osnabrück, Germany. He is best known for his war novel, *All Quiet on the Western Front* (1929; filmed 1930).

Rembrandt (Harmenszoon van Rijn) [rembrant] (1606–69) Painter, born in Leyden, The Netherlands. He settled in Amsterdam (1631), where he ran a large studio and took numerous pupils. 'The Anatomy Lesson of Dr Nicolaes Tulp' (1632) assured his reputation as a portrait painter, and his masterpiece was 'The Night Watch' (1642). His preserved works number over 650 oil paintings, 2000 drawings and studies, and 300 etchings.

Rémi, Georges >> **Hergé**

Remington, Frederic (Sackrider) (1861–1909) Painter, sculptor, and illustrator, born in Canton, NY. A painter of the American West, he recorded the Indian Wars of 1890–91, and wrote and illustrated several books that recounted his adventures.

Remington, Philo (1816–89) Inventor, born in Litchfield, NY, the son of the inventor, Eliphalet Remington (1793–1861). As president of his father's small-arms company from 1860, he perfected the Remington breech-loading rifle.

Remizov, Alexey Mikhaylovich [remizof] (1877–1957) Writer, born in Moscow. His main works are the novels (trans titles) *The Pond, The Clock, Fifth Pestilence*, and *Sisters of the Cross*, as well as several legends, plays, and short stories.

Remy, St [ruhmee], Latin **St Remigius** (c.437–533), feast day October 1. Bishop of Reims. He is traditionally said to have converted Clovis I, King of the Franks, to Christianity. >> Clovis I

Renan, (Joseph) Ernest [ruhnã] (1823–92) Philosopher and historian, born in Tréguier, France. His controversial *The Life of Jesus* (trans, 1863) was the first of a series on the origins of Christianity.

Renaud, Madeleine >> **Barrault, Louis**

Renaudot, Théophraste [ruhnohdoh] (1586–1653) Physician and journalist, founder of the first French newspaper, born in Loudoun, France. Appointed commissary general for the poor, he started an information agency for them, and in 1631 founded the *Gazette de France*.

Renault, Louis [renoh] (1877–1944) Automobile manufacturer, born in Paris. With his brothers he built a series of small cars and formed the Société Renault Frères (1898).

Rendell, Ruth [rendl], pseudonym of **Ruth Barbara Grasemann**, occasional pseudonym **Barbara Vine** (1930–) Detective-story writer, born in London. Several of her detective stories feature Chief Inspector Wexford, such as *Shake Hands Forever* (1975) and she has also written mystery thrillers, including *A Judgement in Stone* (1977). Many of her stories have been filmed or televised, notably in *The Ruth Rendell Mysteries*.

René, France-Albert [ruhnay] (1935–) Seychelles president (1977–). In 1977 he staged a coup, and created a one-party state. He has followed a non-nuclear policy of non-alignment, and resisted several attempts to remove him.

Renfrew (of Kaimsthorn), (Andrew) Colin Renfrew, Baron (1937–) Archaeologist, born in Stockton-on-Tees, Durham. Widely known for pioneering archaeological programmes on BBC television, notably in the *Chronicle* series, his books include *The Emergence of Civilization* (1972) and *The Cycladic Spirit* (1991).

Reni, Guido [raynee] (1575–1642) Baroque painter, born near Bologna, Italy. The fresco painted for the Borghese garden house in Rome, 'Aurora and the Hours' (1613–14), is usually regarded as his masterpiece.

Rennenkampf, Pavel Karlovich von (1853–1918) Russian cavalry officer, of Baltic German origins. In command of the 1st Army, he defeated the German 8th Army at Insterburg and Gumbinnen (1914), but was decisively defeated at Tannenberg a few days later.

Renner, Karl (1870–1950) Austrian chancellor (1918–20, 1945) and president (1945–50), born in Unter-Tannowitz, Austria. He was the first chancellor of the Austrian Republic, and the first president of the new republic.

Rennie, John (1761–1821) Civil engineer, born at Phantassie, Lothian. He constructed several bridges, including the old Southwark and Waterloo Bridges over the R Thames, and designed London Bridge, London docks, and several other ports.

Renoir, Jean [renwah(r)] (1894–1979) Film director, born in Paris, the son of Pierre Auguste Renoir. His major films include *The Great Illusion* (trans, 1937), *The Rules of the Game* (trans, 1939), and *Lunch on the Grass* (trans, 1959). >> Renoir, Pierre Auguste

Renoir, Pierre Auguste [ruhnwah] (1841–1919) Impressionist artist, born in Limoges, France. His picture of sunlight filtering through leaves - *Le Moulin de la Galette* (1876, Louvre) - epitomizes his colourful, happy art.

Renshaw, Willie, popular name of **William (Charles) Renshaw** (1861–1904) Tennis player, the first great tennis champion, born in Cheltenham, Gloucestershire. He was Wimbledon singles champion in 1881–6 and 1899, and won the All-England doubles title in 1884–6 and 1888–9.

Rensselaer, Stephen Van >> Van Rensselaer, Stephen

Renta, Oscar de la >> de la Renta, Oscar

Repin, Ilya Yefimovich [repeen] (1844–1930) Painter, born in Chuguyev, Ukraine. He was the major representative of naturalism in Russia during the second half of the 19th-c, and he also painted portraits of famous contemporaries, such as Tolstoy (1887).

Repton, Humphrey (1752–1818) Landscape designer, born in Bury St Edmunds, Suffolk. He completed the change from formal gardens of the early 18th-c to the 'picturesque', his designs including Sheringham Hall, Norfolk.

Reshevsky, Samuel (Herman) [reshefskee] (1911–92) Chess player, born in Ozorkow, Poland. Seven times the US champion, his world-title hopes were stalled by World War 2, then by Soviet-dominated candidates' matches.

Resnais, Alain [ruhnay] (1922–) Film director, born in Vannes, France. His major films were *Hiroshima mon amour* (1959) and the controversial *Last Year at Marienbad* (trans, 1961).

Resolutus, Doctor >> Baconthorpe, John

Respighi, Ottorino [respeegee] (1879–1936) Composer, born in Bologna, Italy. His works include nine operas, the symphonic poems *Fountains of Rome* (trans, 1916) and *Pines of Rome* (trans, 1924), and the ballet *La Boutique fantasque* (1919).

Restif, Nicolas Edme [resteef], known as **Restif de la Bretonne** (1734–1806) Writer, born in Sacy, France. His many novels, such as *The Perverted Peasant* (trans, 1776), give a vividly truthful picture of 18th-c French life, and make him a forerunner of Realism.

Retz (Jean François Paul de Gondi), Cardinal de (1614–79) Clergyman, born in Montmirail, France. He plotted against Mazarin, and exploited the Parlementary Fronde (1648) to further his own interests and the power of the Church. His *Mémoires* is a classic of 17th-c French literature. >> Mazarin

Retz, Gilles de Laval, Baron de, also spelled **Rais** or **Raiz** (1404–40) Breton nobleman, born in Champtocé, France. For over 10 years he is alleged to have indulged in satanism and the most infamous orgies. He was executed after being condemned for heresy.

Reuter, Paul Julius, Freiherr (Baron) **von** [royter], originally **Israel Beer Josaphat** (1816–99) Founder of the first news agency, born in Kassel, Germany. He developed the idea of a telegraphic news service, and in 1851 moved his headquarters to London.

Reuther, Walter (Philip) [royter] (1907–70) Trade-union leader, born in Wheeling, WV. He rose to become president of the American Auto Workers' Union, eventually the largest trade union in the world.

Revans, Reginald William (1907–) Management consultant, born in London. As director of education in the coal industry (1945–50), he pioneered 'action learning', founding the Action Learning Trust in 1977.

Revelle, Roger [revel] (1909–) Oceanographer and sociologist, born in Seattle, WA. As a result of his geophysical studies of the Pacific Ocean, he contributed to the theory of sea-floor spreading.

Revels, Hiram R(hoades) (1822–1901) Clergyman and educator, born in Fayetteville, NC. He was the first African-American citizen to be elected to the US Senate (1870–1).

Revere, Paul [reveer] (1735–1818) US patriot, born in Boston, MA. On 18 April 1775, the night before Lexington and Concord, he started out for Concord, where arms were secreted. He was turned back by a British patrol, and his mission was completed by Dr Samuel Prescott (1751–?77), but it was Revere whom Longfellow immortalized for the 'midnight ride'. >> Longfellow

Revie, Don [revee] (1927–89) Footballer and manager, born near Middlesbrough, Cleveland. He played for Manchester City, became player-manager of Leeds United (1961), and took over as England team manager (1974–77).

Revson, Charles (Haskell) (1906–75) Business executive, born in Boston, MA. He co-founded the cosmetics firm Revlon Inc in 1932, becoming its president (1932–62) and chairman (1962–75).

Reyes, Alfonso [rayes] (1889–1959) Literary scholar, poet, and diplomat, born in Monterrey, Mexico. He produced both academic and creative works including (trans titles) *Vision of Anáhuac* (1917) and *Sundial* (1926).

Reynaud, Paul [raynoh] (1878–1966) French prime minister (1940), born in Barcelonnette, France. He resigned rather than agree to an armistice with Germany, and was imprisoned by the Germans for the duration of the War.

Reynolds, Albert (1933–) Irish prime minister (1992–4), born in Roosky, Co Roscommon, Ireland. In 1993 his party (Fianna Fáil) lost its majority, forcing the formation of a coalition with the Labour Party, and after losing its support he had to resign.

Reynolds, Sir Joshua [renuhldz] (1723–92) Portrait painter, born in Plympton, Devon. He left over 2000 works, including such notable paintings as 'Dr Samuel Johnson' (c.1756) and 'Sarah Siddons as the Tragic Muse' (1784).

Reynolds, Osborne [renuhldz] (1842–1912) Engineer, born in Belfast. Best known for his work in hydrodynamics and hydraulics, he greatly improved centrifugal pumps. The *Reynolds number*, a dimensionless ratio characterizing the dynamic state of a fluid, takes its name from him.

Rhazes or **Razi** [ray̆zeez, ray̆zee], in full **Abu Bakr Muhammad ibn Zakariya ar-Razi** (10th-c) Physician and alchemist, who lived in Baghdad. He wrote an immense encyclopedia which had considerable influence on medical science in the Middle Ages.

Rhee, Syngman (1875–1965) President of South Korea (1948–60), born near Kaesong, Korea. After the unsuccessful rising of 1919, he became president of the exiled Korean Provisional Government, and was the first elected president of South Korea.

Rheticus [retikus], originally **Georg Joachim von Lauchen** (1514–76) Astronomer and mathematician, born in Feldkirch, Austria. He is noted for his trigonometrical tables and for the first account of the Copernican theory. >> Copernicus

Rhine, J(oseph) B(anks) (1895–1980) Psychologist, the pioneer of parapsychology, born in Juniáta, PA. His experiments involving packs of specially designed cards attempted to establish the phenomena of extrasensory perception and telepathy on a statistical basis.

Rhodes, Cecil (John) (1853–1902) British colonial statesman, born in Bishop's Stortford, Hertfordshire. He secured the charter for the British South Africa Company (1889), whose territory was later named after him as Rhodesia. Prime minister of Cape Colony (1890–6), he was a conspicuous figure during the Boer War (1899–1902), when he organized the defences of Kimberley.

Rhodes, Wilfred (1877–1973) Cricketer, born in Kirkheaton, West Yorkshire. He played for Yorkshire and England, and during his career (1898–1930) took a world record 4187 wickets and scored 39 722 runs. He performed the 'double' of 1000 runs and 100 wickets 16 times.

Rhodes, Zandra (1940–) Fashion designer, born in Chatham, Kent. She showed her first collection in 1969, and is noted for her distinctive, exotic designs in floating chiffons and silks.

Rhondda (of Llanwern), David Alfred Thomas, 1st Viscount [rontha] (1856–1918) Coal mine owner, financier, and politician, born in Ysgyborwen, Glamorgan. He served as minister of food (1917–18), introducing war-time food rationing.

Rhys, Jean [rees], pseudonym of **Gwen Williams** (1894–1979) Writer, born in Roseau, Dominica. Her best-known novel is *Wide Sargasso Sea* (1966), a 'prequel' to Charlotte Bronte's *Jane Eyre*. She also wrote short stories and an autobiography.

Rhys, Ernest (Percival) [rees] (1859–1946) Editor and writer, born in London. He is best-remembered as editor of the Everyman Library of Classics, the first volume appearing in 1906.

Ribalta, Francisco [reebalta] (1565–1628) Painter, born in Castellón de la Plana, Spain. He was the first Spanish *tenebroso* - a painter who emphasizes darkness rather than light. His works include 'The Last Supper' and 'Christ Embracing St Bernard' (Prado, Madrid).

Ribbentrop, Joachim von [ribentrop] (1893–1946) German statesman, born in Wesel, Germany. He was responsible for the Anglo-German naval pact (1935), and became foreign minister (1938–45). Captured in 1945, he was executed at Nuremberg.

Ribera, José or **Jusepe de** [reevera], known as **Lo Spagnoletto** ('the Little Spaniard') (1588–1656) Painter and etcher, born in Játiva, Spain. He is noted for the often gruesome realism with which he treated religious and mythological subjects, such as the martyrdom of the saints.

Ricardo, David [rikah(r)doh] (1772–1823) Political economist, born in London. His reputation chiefly rests on *Principles of Political Economy and Taxation* (1817), and he made important contributions to the labour theory of value, the theory of rents, and the theory of comparative advantage.

Ricardo, Sir Harry (Ralph) [rikah(r)doh] (1885–1974) Mechanical engineer, born in London. He designed and built several small petrol engines, and recognized the importance of the type of fuel in avoiding detonation or 'knocking'.

Ricci, Marco [reechee] (1676–1730) Painter, born in Belluno, Italy. He was a pupil of his uncle, Sebastiano Ricci. He came to England in 1708, working mostly on the design of stage scenery for the opera. >> Ricci, Sebastiano

Ricci, Matteo [reechee] (1552–1610) Founder of the Jesuit missions in China, born in Macerata, Italy. He went to China in 1583, and met with great success as a missionary and Chinese scholar.

Ricci, Sebastiano [reechee] (1659–1734) Painter, born in Belluno, Italy. One of the leading decorative painters of his day, in 1712 he travelled to England with his nephew Marco Ricci. >> Ricci, Marco

Riccio, David >> **Rizzio, David**

Rice, Elmer, originally **Elmer Reizenstein** (1892–1967) Playwright, born in New York City. His best-known work is *The Adding Machine* (1923), an Expressionist play about the dehumanization of people.

Rice, (Henry) Grantland (1880–1954) Sportswriter, born in Murfreesboro, TN. He joined the *New York Tribune* (later the *Herald Tribune*) (1911–30), after which he wrote a widely syndicated column, 'The Sportlight'.

Rice, (Edmund) Ignatius (1762–1844) Philanthropist and religious founder, born near Callan, Co Kilkenny, Ireland. In 1808 he took religious vows, and founded the order now known as the Christian Brothers, becoming its superior-general.

Rice, Tim, popular name of **Sir Timothy Miles Bindon Rice** (1944–) Lyricist, writer, and broadcaster, born in Buckinghamshire. He is best known for writing the lyrics for *Joseph and the Amazing Technicolour Dreamcoat* (1968), *Jesus Christ Superstar* (1971), and *Evita* (1978). >> Lloyd Webber

Rice-Davies, Mandy, popular name of **Marilyn Rice-Davies** (1944–) Model, born in Wales. She became a showgirl in London where she befriended Christine Keeler, and achieved notoriety in relation to the Profumo affair. >> Keeler, Christine; Profumo

Rich, Adrienne (Cecile) (1929–) Poet, born in Baltimore, MD. She became known for her highly personal poetry, as in *Diving into the Wreck: Poems 1971–2* (1973).

Rich, Barbara >> **Riding, Laura**

Rich, Edmund >> **Edmund, St**

Richard I, known as **Richard Coeur de Lion** or **Richard the Lionheart** (1157–99) King of England (1189–99), born in Oxford, Oxfordshire, the third son of Henry II and Eleanor of Aquitaine. His reign was largely spent crusading and defending the Angevin lands in France. He was mortally wounded while besieging the castle of Châlus, Aquitaine. >> Henry II (of England)

Richard II (1367–1400) King of England (1377–99), born in Bordeaux, France, the younger son of Edward the Black Prince. His reign was dominated by a series of power struggles which led to the execution or banishment of several lords, including Henry Bolingbroke (later Henry IV). Bolingbroke invaded England unopposed, and Richard was deposed, dying in Pontefract Castle. >> Edward the Black Prince; Henry IV (of England)

Richard III (1452–85) King of England (1483–5), born in Fotheringhay Castle, Northamptonshire, the youngest son of Richard, Duke of York. He was created Duke of Gloucester (1461), and after the death of Edward IV, had himself crowned king. He was killed fighting Henry Tudor (later Henry VII) at Bosworth Field. >> Edward IV / V; Henry VII

Richard, Cliff, popular name of **Sir Harry Roger Webb** (1940–) Pop-singer, born in Lucknow, India. He formed his own band in 1958, and with The Shadows was hailed as Britain's answer to American rock, his hits including 'Living Doll' (1959). He also made a series of family musical films, such as *The Young Ones* (1961) and *Summer Holiday* (1962).

Richard, Joseph Henri Maurice, nickname **Rocket** (1921–) Ice hockey player, born in Montreal, Quebec, Canada. He joined the Montreal Canadians in 1942, and retired in 1960 with a National Hockey League tally of 544 goals, a record at the time.

Richards, Alun (1929–) Writer, born in Pontypridd, Mid Glamorgan. His works include the novels *A Woman of Experience* (1969) and *Barque Whisper* (1979), short stories, and the television adaptation of *The Onedin Line*.

Richards, Ceri (1903–71) Artist, born in Dunvant, West Glamorgan. Influenced by the Surrealists, he joined the London Group in 1937, also becoming known for his opera sets, stained-glass windows, and vestments.

Richards, Dickinson (Woodruff) (1895–1973) Physician, born in Orange, NJ. With Cournand he developed the technique of cardiac catheterization introduced by Forssmann, and they shared the Nobel Prize for Physiology or Medicine in 1956. >> Cournand; Forssmann

Richards, Ellen Henrietta, née **Swallow** (1842–1911) Chemist, sanitation engineer, and educator, born in Dunstable, MA. The first woman admitted to the Massachusetts Institute of Technology, she became a leader in the movement to educate women in the sciences.

Richards, Frank, pseudonym of **Charles (Harold St John) Hamilton** (1875–1961) Children's writer, born in London. He wrote for boys' papers, creating 'Billy Bunter' and 'Greyfriars School' for *The Magnet*.

Richards, Sir Gordon (1904–86) Jockey and trainer, born in Oakengates, Shropshire. Between 1921 and 1954 he rode a record 4870 winners in Britain, and was champion jockey a record 26 times (1925–53).

Richards, I(vor) A(rmstrong) (1893–1979) Literary critic and scholar, born in Sandbach, Cheshire. He pioneered the detailed critical study of literary texts in the 20th-c, his books including *Principles of Literary Criticism* (1924).

Richards, Theodore (William) (1868–1928) Chemist, born in Germantown, PA. He is best known for his work on atomic weights, which indicated the existence of isotopes. He was awarded the Nobel Prize for Chemistry in 1914.

Richards, Viv, popular name of **Isaac Vivian Alexander Richards** (1952–) Cricket player, born in Antigua. He captained the West Indies (1985–91), and scored 8540 runs in 121 Test matches, including 24 centuries.

Richardson, Dorothy M(iller) (1873–1957) Novelist, born in Abingdon, Berkshire. Her first novel, *Pointed Roofs* (1915), was the first of her well-known 12-volume sequence entitled *Pilgrimage*, culminating with *Clear Horizon* (1935) and *Dimple Hill* (1938).

Richardson, Elliot (Lee) (1920–) Lawyer and cabinet member, born in Boston, MA. He served as secretary of health, education, and welfare (1970–3), secretary of defense (1973), US attorney general (1973), and secretary of commerce (1976–7).

Richardson, Henry Handel, pseudonym of **Ethel Florence Lindesay Robertson**, née **Richardson** (1870–1946) Novelist, born in Melbourne, Victoria, Australia. She attained distinction with the third part of her trilogy which was published as *The Fortunes of Richard Mahony* (1929).

Richardson, Henry Hobson (1838–86) Architect, born in Priestley Plantation, LA. He initiated the Romanesque revival in the USA, designing a number of churches, notably Trinity Church, Boston (1872–7).

Richardson, Sir John (1787–1865) Naturalist and explorer, born in Dumfries, Dumfries and Galloway. He served in several Arctic expeditions, and made major contributions to the knowledge of ichthyology of the Indo-Pacific region.

Richardson, Sir Owen Willans (1879–1959) Physicist, born in Dewsbury, West Yorkshire. For his work on thermionics, he was awarded the Nobel Prize for Physics in 1928.

Richardson, Sir Ralph (David) (1902–83) Actor, born in Cheltenham, Gloucestershire. His association with the Old Vic Company began in 1930, and he led its postwar revival. His films include *Anna Karenina* (1948), *A Doll's House* (1973), and *Invitation to the Wedding* (1983).

Richardson, Samuel (1689–1761) Novelist, born in Mackworth, Derbyshire. In using the epistolary method, as in *Pamela* (1740) and *Clarissa* (1748), he helped to develop the dramatic scope of the novel, then little regarded as a literary form.

Richardson, Tony, popular name of **Cecil Antonio Richardson** (1928–91) Stage and film director, born in Shipley, West Yorkshire. He co-founded Woodfall Film Productions Ltd (1958), notable films including *Saturday Night and Sunday Morning* (1960), *A Taste of Honey* (1961), and *Tom Jones* (1963, Oscar).

Richelieu, Armand Jean du Plessis, Cardinal, duc de (Duke of) [reesh]lyoe] (1585–1642) French statesman, born in Richelieu, France. As chief minister (1624–42) he was the effective ruler of France. His principal achievement was to check Habsburg power, ultimately by sending armies into the Spanish Netherlands, Alsace, Lorraine, and Roussillon.

Richepin, Jean [reeshpī] (1849–1926) Writer, born in Médéa, Algeria. His works of poetry include (trans titles) *Song of the Poor* (1876), *Caresses* (1877), *Blasphemies* (1884), and *The Sea* (1886).

Richler, Mordecai (1931–) Writer, born in Montreal, Quebec, Canada. His best-known novel is *The Apprenticeship of Duddy Kravitz* (1959), although *St Urbain's Horseman* (1971) is a more ambitious work.

Richter, Burton (1931–) Particle physicist, born in New York City. He led a team which discovered the J/psi hadron independently of Ting, for which he shared the Nobel Prize for Physics in 1976. >> Ting

Richter, Charles (Francis) (1900–85) Seismologist, born near Hamilton, OH. With Gutenberg he devised the scale of earthquake strength which now bears his name (1927–35). >> Gutenberg, Beno

Richter, Hans (1843–1916) Conductor, born in Raab, Hungary. He was conductor of the Hallé Orchestra (1897–1911) and an authority on the music of Wagner, with whom he was closely associated in the Bayreuth festivals. >> Wagner, Richard

Richter, Johann Paul (Friedrich), pseudonym **Jean Paul** (1763–1825) Novelist and humorist, born in Wunsiedel, Germany. His wide-ranging works included such romances as *Hesperus* (1795) and the four-volume *Titan* (1800–3).

Richter, Sviatoslav (Teofilovich) (1915–) Pianist, born in Zhitomir, Ukraine. He won the Stalin Prize in 1949, and has been associated with the music festivals at Aldeburgh and Spoleto.

Richthofen, Manfred, Freiherr (Baron) **von**, nickname **the Red Baron** (1882–1918) German airman, born in Breslau, Germany. During World War 1 his Squadron became commonly known as 'Richthofen's Flying Circus' because of their decorated, scarlet aircraft.

Rickenbacker, Eddie, popular name of **Edward Vernon Rickenbacker** (1890–1973) Aviator and World War 1 ace, born in Columbus, OH. In four months of combat flying he scored 26 victories, and received the Congressional

Medal of Honor. He later formed the Rickenbacker Motor Co (1921), and became chairman of Eastern Air Lines in 1959.

Rickert, Heinrich (1863–1936) Philosopher, born in Danzig, Germany. He founded with Wilhelm Windelband (1848–1915) the Baden school of neo-Kantianism. He argued for a *Kulturwissenschaft* ('science of culture'), his views greatly influencing Weber. >> Weber, Max

Rickey, Branch (Wesley) (1881–1965) Baseball manager and administrator, born in Stockdale, OH. He became manager of the St Louis Cardinals (1919), and introduced the 'farm system' whereby major league clubs linked up with lower-grade clubs to develop their own young players.

Rickover, Hyman G(eorge) (1900–86) Naval engineering officer, born in Makov, Ukraine. He led the team that successfully adapted nuclear reactors as a means of ship propulsion, the first such vessel being the US submarine *Nautilus* (1954).

Ricoeur, Paul [reekoe(r)] (1913–) Philosopher, born in Valence, France. An influential figure in French and Anglo-American philosophy, his works include *Philosophy of the Will* (trans, 3 vols, 1950–60) and *The Living Metaphor* (trans, 1975).

Riddell, William Renwick (1852–1945) Judge and legal historian. Judge of the Supreme Court of Canada from 1917, he made notable contributions to Canadian legal history.

Ride, Sally (Kristen) (1951–) Astronaut, the first US woman in space, born in Los Angeles, CA. She became a mission specialist on space-shuttle flight crews, and served on a six-day flight of the orbiter *Challenger* in 1983.

Rideal, Sir Eric Keightley [riydl] (1890–1974) British chemist. He studied colloids and catalysis, and devised the *Rideal–Walker test* for the germicidal power of a disinfectant.

Ridgeway, John (1938–) British oarsman and explorer. In 1966 he rowed the Atlantic in 92 days from the USA to Eire with Chay Blyth. He then sailed the Atlantic single-handed to South America, and led an expedition that followed the R Amazon from source to sea. >> Blyth, Chay

Ridgway, Matthew B(unker) (1895–1993) US soldier, born in Fort Monroe, VA. He commanded the 82nd Airborne Division in Sicily (1943) and Normandy (1944), the 18th Airborne Corps in the North West Europe campaign (1944–5), and the US 8th Army in UN operations in Korea (1950).

Ridgway, Robert (1850–1929) Ornithologist, born in Mount Carmel, IL. His books included *A History of North American Birds* (1874–84) and *The Birds of Middle and North America* (8 vols, 1901–19).

Riding, Laura, *née* **Reichenthal**, pseudonyms **Barbara Rich** and **Madeleine Vara** (1901–91) Writer, critic, and polemicist, born in New York City. Her *Collected Poems* appeared in 1938. Other critical and literary works include *Contemporaries and Snobs* (1918) and *Experts are Puzzled* (1930).

Ridley, Nicholas (c.1500–1555) Protestant martyr, born near Haltwhistle, Northumberland. An ardent reformer, he became Bishop of London (1550), and helped Cranmer prepare the Thirty-nine Articles. On the death of Edward VI he espoused the cause of Lady Jane Grey, and was executed. >> Cranmer, Thomas; Grey, Jane

Ridley (of Liddesdale), Nicholas Ridley, Baron (1929–93) British Conservative statesman, born in Newcastle upon Tyne, Tyne and Wear. He was secretary of state for transport (1983–6), environment (1986–9), and trade and industry (1989–90).

Ridolfo, Roberto di [ridolfoh], also known as **Roberto Ridolfi** (1531–1612) Florentine conspirator, born in Florence, Italy. In 1570 he organized a Roman Catholic plot to marry Mary, Queen of Scots, to Thomas Howard,

4th Duke of Norfolk, and overthrow Elizabeth I. The plot was discovered but Ridolfo was safely abroad at the time. >> Elizabeth I; Mary, Queen of Scots

Rie, Dame Lucie [ree] (1902–95) Studio potter, born in Vienna. In 1938 she moved to England, producing ceramic jewellery and buttons, and later stoneware, tinglazed earthenware, and porcelain pots.

Riefenstahl, Leni [reefenshtahl], popular name of **Berta Helene Amalie Riefenstahl** (1902–) Film-maker, born in Berlin. Her films include *Triumph of the Will* (trans, 1935), a compelling record of a Nazi rally at Nuremberg, and *Olympia* (1938), an epic documentary of the Berlin Olympic Games.

Riegger, Wallingford [reeger] (1885–1961) Composer, born in Albany, GA. His works received little attention until the performance of his third symphony in 1948, after which he was increasingly recognized, writing extensively for orchestra and for chamber music combinations.

Riel, Louis [ree-el] (1844–85) Canadian political leader, born in Red River Settlement, Rupert's Land, Canada. Leader of the Métis, he headed the Red River Rebellion in 1869–70, and became president of the provisional government. After a second uprising (1885), he was executed.

Riemann, (Georg Friedrich) Bernhard [reeman] (1826–66) Mathematician, born in Breselenz, Germany. His early work was on the theory of functions, but he is best remembered for his development of non-Euclidian geometry.

Riemerschmid, Richard [reemershmit] (1868–1957) Architect and designer, born in Munich, Germany. A major figure in the development of 20th-c German design, his output included furniture and interiors, glass and ceramics, cutlery, light-fittings, and graphics.

Rienzi, Cola di [rienzee], also spelled **Rienzo** (1313–54) Italian patriot, born in Rome. In 1347 he incited the citizens to rise against the rule of the nobles, and was briefly successful, but was later killed in a reaction against him.

Riesener, Jean Henri [reezener] (1734–1806) Cabinet-maker, born in Gladbeck, Münster. A master of marquetry and ebony work, he became the best known cabinet-maker in France, completing the famous 'king's desk' for Louis XV.

Riesman, David [reezman] (1909–) Sociologist, born in Philadelphia, PA. His most notable work is the co-authored study of the urban middle class, *The Lonely Crowd* (1950).

Riesz, Frigyes [rees] (1880–1956) Mathematician, born in Györ, Hungary. He worked in functional analysis, integral equations, and subharmonic functions, and developed a new approach to the Lebesgue integral. >> Lebesgue

Rietveld, Gerrit Thomas [reetfelt] (1888–1964) Architect and furniture designer, born in Utrecht, The Netherlands. His work includes the Schröder House in Utrecht (1924) and the Van Gogh Museum, Amsterdam.

Rieu, Emile Victor [ryoe] (1887–1972) Editor and translator, born in London. A classical scholar, his own version of the *Odyssey* (1946) became the cornerstone of the new Penguin Classics, of which he became editor.

Rifkind, Malcolm (Leslie) (1946–) British Conservative statesman. He became secretary of state for Scotland (1986–90), transport (1990–2), and defence (1992–5), and foreign secretary (1995–).

Riley, Bridget (1931–) Artist, born in London. A leading practitioner of Op Art, as seen in 'Fall' (1963), she was the first English painter to win the major painting prize at the Venice Biennale (1968).

Riley, James Whitcomb, known as **the Hoosier poet** (1849–1916) Poet, born in Greenfield, IN. He published several volumes of homely dialect poems, and is well known for his poems about children, including 'Little Orfant Annie'.

Riley, Terry (1935–) Composer, born in Colfax, CA. His compositions include *In C* (1964), *Reed Streams* (1966), and *A Rainbow in Curved Air* (1968).

Rilke, Rainer Maria [rilkuh] (1875–1926) Lyric poet, born in Prague. His major works include the three-part poem cycle, *The Book of Hours* (trans, 1905), which shows the deep influence of Russian Pietism.

Rimbaud, (Jean Nicolas) Arthur [ri boh] (1854–91) Poet, born in Charleville, France. His works include *The Drunken Boat* (trans, 1871) and *Les Illuminations* (1872), a series of prose and verse poems, which show him to be a precursor of Symbolism.

Rimet, Jules [reemay] (1873–1956) French football administrator. He promoted the Fédération Internationale de Football Association (FIFA), of which he was president (1921–56), and founded the World Cup competition (1930), his name being added to the title in 1946.

Rimini, Francesca da >> **Francesca da Rimini**

Rimsky-Korsakov, Nikolai (Andreyevich) [rimskee kaw(r)sakof] (1844–1908) Composer, born in Tikhvin, Russia. He produced three great orchestral masterpieces, *Capriccio Espagnol*, *Easter Festival*, and *Scheherazade* (1887–8), after which he chiefly wrote operas, such as *The Golden Cockerel* (1907).

Ringan, St >> **Ninian, St**

Ripley, George (1802–80) Social reformer and literary critic, born in Greenfield, MA. He joined in the Transcendental movement, founded *The Dial* (1840), became literary critic for the *New York Tribune* (1849–80), and founded *Harper's New Monthly Magazine* (1850).

Ripley, Robert, originally **LeRoy Ripley** (1893–1949) Illustrator, cartoonist, and writer, born in Santa Rosa, CA. He moved to New York City to work for the *Globe* (1913), and in 1918 began his *Believe It or Not!* cartoons of oddities.

Rippon (of Hexham), (Aubrey) Geoffrey (Frederick) Rippon, Baron (1924–) British Conservative statesman. A committed European, he led the UK delegation to the Council of Europe and the Western European Union (1967–70).

Ritchie, Anne Isabella Lady (1837–1919) Writer, born in London. The daughter of Thackeray, she contributed valuable personal reminiscences to an 1898–9 edition of his works. >> **Thackeray**

Ritchie-Calder, Peter, Baron >> **Calder, (Peter) Ritchie**

Rits, Jacob (August) (1849–1914) Journalist and social critic, born in Ribe, Denmark. His horrifying description of immigrant poverty in New York City in 1890, *How the Other Half Lives*, was the first use of photographic evidence in social reportage.

Ritter, Carl (1779–1859) Geographer, born in Quedlinburg, Germany. He laid the foundations of modern scientific geography, his most important work, *Earth Science* (trans, 1817), stressing the relation between people and their natural environment.

Rivera, Diego [rivayra] (1886–1957) Painter, born in Guanajuato, Mexico. In 1921 he began a series of huge murals in public buildings depicting the life and history of the Mexican people, notably a series in the presidential palace in Mexico City.

Rivero, Miguel Primo de >> **Primo de Rivera, Miguel**

Rivers, Augustus Pitt- >> **Pitt-Rivers, Augustus**

Rivers, Joan, professional name of **Joan Alexandra Molinsky** (1933–) Comedienne and writer, born in Larchmont, NY. She became the regular guest host of *The Tonight Show* (1983–6), and hosted *The Late Show* (1986–7) and *Hollywood Squares* (from 1987). She has also worked as a film director and recording artist.

Rivers, Larry, originally **Larry Grossberg** (1923–) Painter and sculptor, born in New York City. An Abstract Expressionist as well as a predecessor of Pop Art, he is known for ironic historical works, such as 'Washington Crossing the Delaware' (1953), and realistic paintings such as 'Double Portrait of Birdie' (1955).

Rivers, W(illiam) H(alse) R(ivers) (1864–1922) Anthropologist and medical psychologist, born near Chatham, Kent. He took part in the Cambridge University expedition to the Torres Straits (1898–9), and subsequently worked among the Todas of India and in Melanesia, publishing the well-known *The Todas* (1906).

Rix, Sir Brian (Norman Roger) (1924–) Actor and manager, born in Cottingham, Humberside. He established a reputation for farce at the Whitehall Theatre with such productions as *Reluctant Heroes* (1950), *Dry Rot* (1954), and *Simple Spymen* (1958). He later left the stage for charity work with the mentally handicapped.

Rizzio, David [ritsioh], also spelled **Riccio** (?1533–1566) Courtier and musician, born in Pancalieri, Italy. He entered the service of Mary, Queen of Scots (1561), and was made her French secretary (1564). He negotiated her marriage with Darnley (1565), who became jealous of his influence, and plotted his death with a group of nobles. >> **Darnley; Mary, Queen of Scots**

Roach, Hal, popular name of **Harald Eugene Roach** (1892–92) Film-maker, born in Elmira, NY. After producing many short silent comedies, he went on to make a wide range of sound feature films, such as *Way Out West* (1937) and *One Million BC* (1940).

Roach, Max (1924–) Jazz drummer, bandleader, and composer, born in New Land, NC. He played with many of the pioneers of 'bop' and modern jazz, including Dizzy Gillespie, Charlie Parker, and Miles Davis. >> **Davis, Miles; Gillespie, Dizzy; Parker, Charlie**

Robards, Jason [rohbah(r)dz], known as **Robards Jr** (1922–) Actor, born in Chicago, IL. Primarily known as a stage actor, in 1956 he won critical acclaim for his performances in Eugene O'Neill's *The Iceman Cometh* and *Long Day's Journey into Night*. He was married to the actress Lauren Bacall (1961–9). >> **Bacall**

Robbe-Grillet, Alain [rob greeyay] (1922–) Novelist, born in Brest, France. After his first novel, *The Erasers* (trans, 1953), he emerged as the leader of the *nouveau roman* group. His film scenarios include *Last Year at Marienbad* (trans, 1961).

Robbia, Luca della (c.1400–82) Sculptor, born in Florence, Italy. He executed 10 panels for the cathedral there (1431–40), and a bronze door for the sacristy with 10 panels of figures in relief (1448–67). He established a business producing glazed terracottas which was carried on by his nephew **Andrea della Robbia** (1435–1525) and Andrea's son **Giovanni della Robbia** (1469–c.1529).

Robbins, Frederick (Chapman) (1916–) Physiologist and paediatrician, born in Auburn, AL. He helped devise techniques for cultivating the poliomyelitis virus, and shared the Nobel Prize for Physiology or Medicine in 1954. >> **Enders; Weller**

Robbins, Harold (1916–) Writer, born in New York City. His string of earthy best sellers includes *Never Love a Stranger* (1948), *A Stone for Danny Fisher* (1952), and *The Carpetbaggers* (1961).

Robbins, Jerome (1918–) Dancer and choreographer, born in New York City. He became director of New York City Ballet (1949–59), and joint ballet master (from 1983). He collaborated with Bernstein in *West Side Story* (1957), and won two Oscars in the 1961 Hollywood version. >> **Bernstein, Leonard**

Robbins (of Clare Market), Lionel Charles Robbins, Baron (1898–1984) Economist and educationist, born in Sipson, Greater London. He chaired the *Robbins Committee* on the expansion of higher education in the UK (1961–4).

Robens (of Woldingham), Alfred Robens, Baron (1910–) Trade unionist and industrialist, born in Manchester. He became a Labour MP (1945–60), was briefly minister of labour and national service (1951), and became chairman of the National Coal Board (1961–71).

Robert I >> **Bruce, Robert**

Robert II (1316–90) King of Scots (1371–90), the son of Walter, hereditary steward of Scotland. He acted as sole regent during the exile and captivity of David II, and on David's death founded the Stuart royal dynasty. >> David II

Robert of Brunne >> **Mannyng, Robert**

Robert Bellarmine, St >> **Bellarmine, St Robert**

Robert Curthose (c.1054–1134) Duke of Normandy, the eldest son of William I, the Conqueror. He took part in the First Crusade (1096–1101), and in his absence the English throne was seized by his younger brother Henry I. He was captured at Tinchebray, and spent the rest of his life a prisoner. >> Henry I (of England); William I / II (of England)

Roberti, Ercole (Grandi d'Antonio) de' [robairtee, airkolay] (c.1450–1496) Painter, born in Ferrara, Italy. His work is less austere than that of his contemporaries of the Ferrarese school, as seen in his 'Madonna and Child with Saints' (1480).

Roberts, Sir Charles G(eorge) D(ouglas) (1860–1943) Writer and naturalist, born in Douglas, New Brunswick, Canada. His books include *Orion and Other Poems* (1880) and the nature study *Eyes of the Wilderness* (1933).

Roberts (of Kandahar, Pretoria, and Waterford), Frederick Sleigh Roberts, 1st Earl (1832–1914) British field marshal, born in Cawnpore, India. He became commander-in-chief in India (1885–93), then supreme commander in South Africa during the Boer War, relieving Kimberley (1900).

Roberts, Sir Gilbert (1899–1978) Civil engineer, born in London. In 1949 he joined Freeman, Fox & Partners, and was put in charge of the design of the Forth, Severn, and Humber bridges. >> Freeman

Roberts, Kate (1891–1985) Writer, born in Rhosgadfan, Gwynedd. Regarded as the most distinguished prose writer in Welsh this century, among her novels are (trans titles) *Feet in Chains* (1936) and *The Living Sleep* (1956).

Roberts, (Granville) Oral (1918–) Evangelist and faith healer, born in Ada, OK. Flamboyant and enterprising, he is known for his weekly national TV programme, a radio station, and a mass circulation monthly magazine.

Roberts, Richard (1789–1864) Inventor, born in Carreghova, Mid Glamorgan. His firm of Sharp, Roberts and Co manufactured a spinning mule as well as railway locomotives, beginning with the *Experiment* for the Liverpool & Manchester Railway in 1833.

Roberts, Sir Stephen Henry (1901–71) Historian, born in Maldon, Victoria, Australia. His works include *History of Modern Europe* (1933) and *The House that Hitler Built* (1937).

Roberts, Tom (1856–1931) Painter, born in Dorchester, Dorset. His best work, which deals with pioneering life in the bush, was produced in Australia in the late 1880s and 1890s.

Roberts, William Patrick (1895–1980) Artist, born in London. He was associated with the London group, and in both World Wars was an official war artist.

Roberts-Austen, Sir William (Chandler) (1843–1902) Metallurgist, born in London. A pioneer of alloy research, he demonstrated the possibility of diffusion occurring between a sheet of gold and a block of lead.

Robertson, Ethel Florence Lindesay >> **Richardson, Henry Handel**

Robertson, Jeannie (1908–75) Folk singer, born in Aberdeen, Grampian. Her huge repertoire of classic traditional ballads and other songs exerted a profound influence on the folk-music revival.

Robertson, Sir William Robert (1860–1933) British soldier, born in Welbourn, Lincolnshire. In World War 1 he rose to become Chief of the Imperial General Staff (1915–18).

Robeson, Paul (Bustill) [rohbsn] (1898–1976) Singer and actor, born in Princeton, NJ. Success as an African-American actor was matched by popularity as a singer, and he appeared in works ranging from *Show Boat* to *Othello*.

Robespierre, Maximilien François Marie Isidore de [rohbspyair] (1758–94) French revolutionary leader, born in Arras. A prominent member of the Jacobins, he emerged in the National Assembly as a popular radical, became a member of the Committee of Public Safety (1793), and for three months dominated the country, introducing the Reign of Terror and the cult of the Supreme Being. His ruthlessness led to his fall from power, and he was guillotined.

Robey, Sir George [rohbee], originally **George Edward Wade** (1869–1954) Comedian, born in Herne Hill, Kent. He made a name for himself in musical shows, and became famous for his bowler hat, black coat, hooked stick, and thickly painted eyebrows.

Robin Hood Legendary 13th-c outlaw who lived in Sherwood Forest in the N Midlands, England. Known for his archery, he protected the poor, and outwitted wealthy and unscrupulous officials, notably the Sheriff of Nottingham.

Robins, Benjamin (1707–51) Mathematician and pioneer of gunnery, born in Bath, Avon. He invented the ballistic pendulum, which allowed the measurement of muzzle velocities, and laid the groundwork for modern field-artillery.

Robinson, Arthur Howard (1915–) Geographer, born in Montreal, Quebec, Canada. He is known for his major cartographic textbooks, notably *Elements of Cartography*.

Robinson, Bill 'Bojangles', originally **Luther Robinson**, nickname **the King of Tapology** (1878–1949) Tap dancer, born in Richmond, VA. A star of the movie *Stormy Weather* (1943), he is credited with originating the routine of tapping up and down stairs.

Robinson, Brooks (Calbert), Jr (1937–) Baseball player, born in Little Rock, AR. Recognized as the greatest third baseman to date, he won the Golden Glove in that position for 15 consecutive years from 1960.

Robinson, Edwin Arlington (1869–1935) Poet, born in Head Tide, ME. He was three times a Pulitzer prizewinner, for his *Collected Poems* (1922), *The Man Who Died Twice* (1924), and *Tristram* (1927).

Robinson, Edward (1749–1863) Biblical scholar, born in Southington, CT. He established himself as the father of biblical geography with his *Biblical Researches in Palestine and Adjacent Countries* (1841).

Robinson, Edward G, originally **Emanuel Goldenberg** (1893–1973) Film actor, born in Bucharest, Romania. He became famous with his portrayal of a vicious gangster in *Little Caesar* (1930), and went on to play hoodlums in such films as *Key Largo* (1948), and strong character parts as in *Double Indemnity* (1944).

Robinson, (William) Heath (1872–1944) Artist, cartoonist, and book illustrator, born in London. His fame rests mainly on his humorous drawings satirizing the machine age, displaying 'Heath Robinson' contraptions of absurd and complicated design but with highly practical and simple aims.

Robinson, Henry Crabb (1775–1867) Journalist and diarist, born in Bury St Edmunds, Suffolk. He joined *The Times* in 1807 and covered the Peninsular War as a war correspondent, the first of his kind (1808–9).

Robinson, Henry Peach (1830–1901) Photographer, born in Ludlow, Shropshire. He opened a studio at Leamington Spa (1857), and moved to 'high art photography', creating literary and narrative genre scenes using costumed models and painted settings.

Robinson, Joan V(iolet), *née* **Maurice** (1903–83) Economist, born in Camberley, Surrey. She was a leader of the Cambridge school, which developed macro-economic theories of growth and distribution, based on the work of Keynes. >> Keynes

Robinson, Jackie, popular name of **Jack Roosevelt Robinson** (1919–72) The first African-American player to play major league baseball, born in Cairo, GA. A star infielder and outfielder for the Brooklyn Dodgers (1947–56), he led them to six National League pennants and one World Series, in 1955.

Robinson, John (c.1576–1625) Clergyman, born in Sturton-le-Steeple, Nottinghamshire. He established a Church in Leyden in 1609, and in 1620 saw part of his congregation set sail for Plymouth, where they joined the *Mayflower*.

Robinson, John (Arthur Thomas) (1919–83) Anglican clergyman and theologian, born in Canterbury, Kent. In 1963 he published his controversial best-seller *Honest to God*, which he described as an attempt to explain the Christian faith to modern society.

Robinson, (Esmé Stuart) Lennox (1886–1958) Writer and director, born in Douglas, Co Cork, Ireland. His first play, *The Clancy Game*, was produced in 1908 at the Abbey Theatre, Dublin, where he later became director (1923–56). His volumes of Irish verse included Golden Treasury (1925).

Robinson, Mary, *née* **Bourke** (1944–) Irish president (1990–), born in Ballina, Co Mayo, Ireland. She left the Labour Party in protest against the Anglo-Irish Agreement (1985), and against all the odds defeated Brian Lenihan of the Fianna Fáil Party to take office as Ireland's first female president.

Robinson, (Arthur Napoleon) Raymond (1926–) Prime minister of Trinidad and Tobago (1986–91). In 1984 he helped form a left-of-centre coalition which became the National Alliance for Reconstruction, sweeping to power in the 1986 general election.

Robinson, Sir Robert (1886–1975) Chemist, born near Chesterfield, Derbyshire. He is particularly noted for his work on plant pigments, alkaloids, and other natural products, and on the development of penicillin. He was awarded the Nobel Prize for Chemistry in 1947.

Robinson, Sugar Ray, originally **Walker Smith** (1920–89) Professional boxer, born in Detroit, MI. He held the world welterweight title (1946–51) and the world middleweight title (1950–1), and was never knocked out in 201 contests.

Robinson, William (1838–1935) Gardener and horticultural writer, born in Co Down, Ireland. An exponent of natural rather than formal gardens, his many books include *The English Flower Garden* (1883).

Rob Roy (Gaelic 'Red Robert'), nickname of **Robert MacGregor** or **Campbell** (1671–1734) Highland outlaw, born in Buchanan, Central, Scotland. He began a life of brigandining after his lands were seized (1712), and was eventually captured and imprisoned in London, but pardoned in 1727. His life was romanticized in the novel by Sir Walter Scott. >> Scott, Walter

Robson, Dame Flora (McKenzie) (1902–84) Actress, born in South Shields, Durham. She gained fame in historical roles in plays and films, such as Queen Elizabeth in *Fire over England* (1931) and Thérèse Raquin in *Guilty* (1944).

Rocard, Michel [rokah(r)] (1930–) French prime minister (1988–91), born near Paris. A Social Democrat, he served as minister of planning and regional development (1981–3) and of agriculture (1983–5). He was appointed prime minister by Mitterrand, but regarded as too moderate, and replaced. >> Mitterrand

Roche, Mazo de la >> de la Roche, Mazo

Rochefoucauld, François de La >> La Rochefoucauld, François

Rochester, John Wilmot, 2nd Earl of (1647–80) Courtier and poet, born in Ditchley, Oxfordshire. A patron of the arts, he wrote poems, letters, satires, and bacchanalian and amatory songs and verses.

Rockefeller, David [rokuhfeler] (1915–) Banker and philanthropist, born in New York City, the brother of Nelson Rockefeller. He joined Chase National Bank (now Chase Manhattan), rising to be chief executive officer (1969–80). >> Rockefeller, John D, Jr / Nelson A

Rockefeller, John D(avison) [rokuhfeler] (1839–1937) Industrialist and philanthropist, born in Richford, NY. In 1875 he founded with his brother William Rockefeller (1841–1922) the Standard Oil Company, securing control of the US oil trade, and in 1913 established the Rockefeller Foundation. >> Rockefeller, John D, Jr

Rockefeller, John D(avison), Jr [rokuhfeler] (1874–1960) Philanthropist, born in Cleveland, OH, the son of John D Rockefeller. He built the Rockefeller Center in New York City (1939). >> Rockefeller, John D

Rockefeller, Laurance (Spelman) [rokuhfeler] (1910–) Business executive and conservationist, born in New York City, the son of John D Rockefeller, Jr. He managed several family enterprises, and oversaw the donation of 33 000 acres of Rockefeller land to the Grand Teton National Park. >> Rockefeller, John D

Rockefeller, Nelson A(ldrich) [rokuhfeler] (1908–79) US vice-president (1974–7), born in Bar Harbor, ME, the third son of John D Rockefeller, Jr. He sought the Republican presidential nomination in 1960, 1964, and 1968, and was elected vice-president under Ford. >> Ford, Gerald R; Rockefeller, David / John D, Jr

Rockingham, Charles Watson Wentworth, 2nd Marquess of (1730–82) British prime minister (1765–6, 1782). He repealed the Stamp Act, affecting the American colonies, and opposed Britain's war against the colonists.

Rockne, Knute (Kenneth) [roknee] (1888–1931) Coach of American football, born in Voss, Norway. He dominated American college football, markedly changing the emphasis from sheer physical brawn to pace, elusiveness, and ball handling.

Rockwell, George Lincoln (1918–67) Political extremist, born in Bloomington, IL. The founder of the American Nazi Party (1958), he called for the extermination of Jews and the deportation of all blacks, and was assassinated by a disaffected former party member.

Rockwell, Norman (Percevel) (1894–1978) Illustrator, born in New York City. He illustrated major periodicals, such as *Collier's*, *Life*, *Look*, and *The Saturday Evening Post* (1916–63), as well as literary classics, advertisements, and calendars.

Rodbertus, Johann Karl [rodbertus] (1805–75) Economist and politician, born in Greifswald, Germany. The founder of scientific socialism, he held that the socialistic ideal would come gradually according to the natural laws of change and progress.

Rodchenko, Alexander Mikhailovich [rodchengkoh] (1891–1956) Painter, designer, and photographer, born in St Petersburg, Russia. His most original works were his abstract spatial constructions and his documentary photographs of the new Communist society.

Roddenberry, Gene, popular name of **Eugene Wesley Roddenberry** (1921–91) Writer, and film and television producer, born in El Paso, TX. He is best known as the creator and producer of the science-fiction series *Star Trek*.

Roddick, Anita (Lucia) (1943–) Retail entrepreneur, born in Brighton, East Sussex. In 1976 she opened her first shop selling beauty products made from natural products, not tested on animals, and supplied in refillable containers.

Rodgers, Richard (1902–79) Composer, born in New York City. With the lyricist **Lorenz Hart** (1895–1942) he had many successful songs, such as 'The Lady Is a Tramp' and 'My Funny Valentine'. He later collaborated in a series of hit musicals with Oscar Hammerstein II, notably *Oklahoma!* (1943, Pulitzer), *South Pacific* (1949, Pulitzer), *The King and I* (1951), and *The Sound of Music* (1959). >> Hammerstein

Rodgers, Bill, popular name of **William Thomas Rogers** (1928–) British statesman, born in Liverpool, Merseyside. He became a Labour MP in 1962, and served as transport secretary (1976–9). In 1981 he helped form the Social Democratic Party, and was its vice-president (1982–7).

Rodin, (René François) Auguste [rohdī] (1840–1917) Sculptor, born in Paris. His greatest work was 'La Porte de l'enfer' (The Gate of Hell) for the Musée des Arts Décoratifs in 1880, on which he worked for some 30 years. Among his other works is 'The Thinker' (trans, 1904), in front of the Panthéon in Paris.

Rodney, George Brydges Rodney, Baron (1718–92) British naval commander, born in London. Appointed commander-in-chief on the Leeward Is station (1761), he captured Martinique, St Lucia, and Grenada (1762), and won several victories against the French and Spanish.

Rodrigo, Joaquín [rodreegoh] (1902–) Composer, born in Sagunto, Spain. He is best known for his compositions for guitar, such as *Concierto de Aranjuez* (1940).

Rodzinski, Artur [rodzinskee] (1892–1958) Conductor, born in Spalato, Dalmatia. He became conductor of the Los Angeles Philharmonic (1929–33), Cleveland (1933–43), New York Philharmonic (1943–7), and Chicago Symphony (1947–8) orchestras.

Roe, Sir (Edwin) Alliot Verdon (1877–1958) Aircraft manufacturer, born near Manchester. With his brother Humphrey Verdon Roe (1878–1949), he formed A V Roe & Co in 1910, producing the famous AVRO 504 bomber/trainer type. He later formed Saunders-Roe, building flying boats.

Roebling, John Augustus [rohbling] (1806–69) Civil engineer, born in Mühlhausen, Germany. He emigrated to the USA in 1831, where he proposed the use of wire ropes in bridge building, as in the railway suspension bridge at Niagara Falls (1851–5, replaced 1897).

Roebuck, Alvah >> Sears, R W

Roehm, Ernst >> Röhm, Ernst

Roentgen, Wilhelm Konrad von >> Röntgen, Wilhelm Konrad von

Roethke, Theodore (Huebner) [retkuh] (1908–63) Poet, born in Saginaw, MI. He became known with *The Waking* (1953, Pulitzer), and *Collected Poems* appeared posthumously in 1968.

Roger of Wendover (?–1236) Chronicler, and Benedictine monk at the monastery of St Albans. He revised and extended the abbey chronicle from the Creation to the year 1235.

Roger of Taizé, Brother, originally **Roger Louis Schutz-Marsauche** (1915–) Founder of the Taizé Community, born in Provence, France. In 1940 he founded in Taizé a community devoted to reconciliation and peace in Church and society.

Rogers, Carl R(ansom) (1902–87) Psychotherapist, born in Oak Park, IL. His book *Client-centered Therapy* (1951) pioneered open therapy sessions and encounter groups in which patients talk out their problems under the supervision of a passive therapist.

Rogers, Claude (1907–79) Artist, born in London. He co-founded the Euston Road School in 1937, and was president of the London Group (1952–65).

Rogers, Ginger, originally **Virginia Katherine McMath** (1911–95) Film actress, born in Independence, MO. She first danced with Fred Astaire in *Flying Down to Rio* (1933), going on to make nine other films with him. She won an Oscar for best actress in *Kitty Foyle* (1940). >> Astaire

Rogers, John (c.1500–55) Protestant reformer, born in Aston, Staffordshire. He helped to prepare a revised translation of the Bible, pseudonymously called 'Thomas Matthew's Bible' (1537). Following Mary's accession, he was burned as a heretic. >> Mary I

Rogers, Randolph (1825–92) Sculptor, born in Waterloo, NY. He is best known for his 'Columbus Doors' of the Capitol in Washington, DC, and the heroic figure of 'Michigan' on the Detroit monument.

Rogers, Richard (1933–) British architect, born in Florence, Italy. A founder member of Team 4 with Norman Foster, he was concerned with advanced technology in architecture. His controversial works include the Pompidou Centre, Paris (1971–9) and Lloyds of London (1979–85). >> Foster, Norman

Rogers, Will(iam Penn Adair) (1879–1935) Humorous actor and folk-hero, born in Oolagah, OK. In his frequent radio broadcasts he came to personify the common man offering simple sagacity to the great and powerful, and gained huge popularity with films such as *State Fair* (1933).

Rogers, William Pierce (1913–) US Republican politician, born in Norfolk, NY. In his capacity as attorney general (1957), he played a leading role in drafting the Civil Rights Act of 1957, and later became secretary of state under Nixon (1969–73). >> Nixon

Roget, Peter Mark [rozhay] (1779–1869) Physician and scholar, born in London. He is best known for his *Thesaurus of English Words and Phrases* (1852), which he wrote after his retirement from medical practice.

Rogier van der Weyden >> Weyden, Rogier van der

Rohde, Ruth [rohd], née **Bryan** (1885–1954) Diplomat and feminist, born in Jacksonville, IL. In 1928 she ran for Congress, and won a victory on feminist grounds, resulting in an amendment to the Cable Act. She was appointed US minister to Denmark (1933–6), the first US diplomatic post ever held by a woman.

Rohe, Ludwig Mies van der >> Mies van der Rohe, Ludwig

Rohlfs, (Friedrich) Gerhard (1831–96) Explorer, born in Vegesack, Germany. He crossed Africa from the Mediterranean to the Gulf of Guinea (1865–6), the first known European to do so.

Röhm, Ernst [roem], also spelled **Roehm** (1887–1934) Nazi leader, born in Munich, Germany. He organized and commanded the stormtroopers ('Brownshirts' and 'Blackshirts'), but in 1934 his plans to increase the power of this force led to his execution on Hitler's orders.

Rohmer, Sax, pseudonym of **Arthur Sarsfield Ward** (c.1883–1959) Writer of mystery stories, born in Birmingham, West Midlands. He found literary fame with his oriental, criminal genius villain, Fu Manchu, featured in such spine-chilling tales as *The Yellow Claw* (1915).

Roh Tae-Woo [roh tay woo] (1932–) South Korean president (1988–92), born in Sinyong, Kyongsang, South Korea. Elected chairman of the ruling Democratic Justice Party (1985), his political reforms helped restore democracy to the country.

Rokitansky, Karl, Freiherr (Baron) **von** [rokitanskee] (1804–78) Pathologist, born in Königgrätz, Austria. One of the founders of modern pathological anatomy, he established the New Vienna School as an internationally known medical centre.

Rokossovsky, Konstantin [rokosofskee] (1896–1968) Soviet military commander, born in Velikiye Lukie, Russia. He played a leading part in the Battle of Stalingrad (1943), recaptured Orel and Warsaw, and led the Russian race for Berlin.

Roland [rolã] (?–778) Semi-legendary French knight, hero of the *Chanson de Roland* (11th-c, Song of Roland). He is said to have been the nephew of Charlemagne, and the ideal of a Christian knight. >> Charlemagne

Roland de la Platière, Jean Marie [platyair] (1734–93) Industrial scientist, born in Thizy, France. In 1791 he went to Paris, and briefly became minister of the interior (1792). As a Girondist he fell foul of Robespierre, and committed suicide.

Rolf, Dr Ida (1896–1979) Physician who developed a system of deep massage known as *rolfing*, designed to remedy defective posture. Patients may be up to half an inch taller if they persevere to the end of the course.

Rolfe, Frederick William (Serafino Austin Lewis Mary), pseudonym **Baron Corvo** (1860–1913) Novelist and essayist, born in London. A convert to Roman Catholicism, his rejection from the novitiate for the Roman priesthood prompted his most famous work, *Hadrian the Seventh* (1904).

Rolfe, John >> **Pocahontas**

Rolland, Romain [rolã] (1866–1944) Writer, born in Clamecy, France. His works include biographies, the novel *Jean-Christophe* (10 vols, 1904–12), several plays, music criticism, and much political writing. He received the Nobel Prize for Literature in 1915.

Rolle, Richard of Hampole [rohl] (c.1290–1349) Hermit, mystic, and poet, born in Thornton, West Yorkshire. At 19 he became a hermit, first at Dalton and then at Hampole, near Doncaster. He wrote lyrics, meditations, and religious works in Latin and English.

Rollins, Sonny, popular name of **Theodore Walter Rollins** (1930–) Jazz saxophonist and composer, born in New York City. From the mid-1950s he emerged as an important voice in the 'hard bop' movement, and became a powerful improviser on tenor and soprano saxophones.

Rollo, originally **Hrolf** (c.860–c.932) Viking leader. He secured from Charles III of France in 911 a large district on condition that he was baptized and became Charles's vassal - the nucleus of the Duchy of Normandy.

Rolls, C(harles) S(tewart) (1877–1910) Motorist and aeronaut, born in London. From 1895 he experimented with the earliest motor cars, forming a partnership with Henry Royce in 1906 for their production.

Romains, Jules [romĩ], pseudonym of **Louis Farigoule** (1885–1972) Writer, born in Saint-Julien-Chapteuil, France. His poems *The Unanimous Life* (trans, 1908) brought about the Unanimist school, devoted to a belief in universal brotherhood and group consciousness. His best-known works are the comedy *Dr Knock*, or the *Triumph of Medicine* (trans, 1923) and the cycle of novels, *Men of Good Will* (27 vols, 1932–46).

Romano, Giulio >> **Giulio Romano**

Romanova, Grand Duchess Anastasia Nikolaievna >> **Anastasia**

Romanus, Clemens >> **Clement I, St**

Romberg, Sigmund (1887–1951) Composer of operettas, born in Nagykanizsa, Hungary. He settled in the USA in 1909. His most famous works include *The Student Prince* (1924) and *The Desert Song* (1926).

Romer, Alfred Sherwood (1894–1973) Palaeontologist, born in White Plains, NY. He traced the evolution of fishes to terrestrial vertebrates, as recorded in his book *The Vertebrate Story* (1959).

Rømer, Ole (Christensen) [roemer] (1644–1710) Astronomer, born in Århus, Denmark. In 1675 he made the first determination of the velocity of light.

Romero (y Galdames), Oscar (Arnulfo) [rohmairoh] (1917–80) Roman Catholic clergyman, born in Ciudad Barrios, Salvador. An outspoken critic of the government, he was shot down during Mass a year after he was nominated for the Nobel Peace Prize.

Romilly, Sir Samuel (1757–1818) Lawyer and law reformer, born in London. He worked to reduce the severity of English criminal law, notably to end capital punishment for minor felonies, and also took part in anti-slavery agitation.

Rommel, Erwin (Johannes Eugen) (1891–1944) German field marshal, born in Heidenheim, Germany. He led a Panzer division during the 1940 invasion of France, then commanded the Afrika Korps, where he achieved major successes, but was eventually driven into retreat. He condoned the plot against Hitler's life, and after its discovery committed suicide.

Romney, George [romnee, ruhmnee] (1734–1802) Painter, born in Dalton-in-Furness, Lancashire. He moved to London in 1762, where his reputation as a portrait painter rivalled that of Reynolds, producing many pictures of Lady Hamilton. >> Reynolds, Joshua

Romney, George (Wilcken) (1907–) US politician and businessman, born in Chihuahua, Mexico, the son of missionaries. A front runner for the Republican presidential nomination (1968), he became secretary of housing and urban development (1969–73).

Romulus Augustulus [romyulus awguhstyulus] >> **Augustulus**

Ronald, Sir Landon, originally **Landon Russell** (1873–1938) Conductor, composer, and pianist, born in London. He conducted the New Symphony Orchestra, and wrote many songs, including 'Down in the Forest Something Stirred'.

Ronay, Egon [ronay, eegon] (1920–) Gastronome and writer, born in Hungary. He emigrated to England (1946), opened his own restaurant in London (1952–5), and founded the annual *Egon Ronay's Guide to Hotels and Restaurants* (1956).

Roncalli, Angelo Giuseppe >> **John XXIII**

Ronsard, Pierre de [rõsah(r)] (1524–85) Renaissance poet, born in La Possonnière, France. A leader of the *Pléiade* group, his early works include *Odes* (1550) and *Amours* (1552).

Röntgen, Wilhelm Konrad von [roentguhn], also spelled **Roentgen** (1845–1923) Physicist, born in Lennep, Germany. In 1895 he discovered the electromagnetic rays which he called *X-rays*, and received the first Nobel Prize for Physics in 1901.

Roon, Albrecht (Theodor Emil), Graf (Count) **von** (1803–79) Prussian army officer, born near Kolberg, Poland. He became war minister (1859–73) and reorganized the army, making possible the Prussian victories in the Wars of the 1860s and 1870s.

Roosevelt, (Anna) Eleanor [rohzuhvelt, roozvelt] (1884–1962) Diplomat and humanitarian, born in New York City, the wife of Franklin D Roosevelt, whom she married in 1905. An independent activist, she had a strong part in shaping her husband's New Deal administration, and was later much involved with the UN.

Roosevelt, Franklin D(elano) [rohzuhvelt, roozvelt], nickname **FDR** (1882–1945) US Democratic statesman and 32nd president (1933–45), born in Hyde Park, NY. He met the economic crisis with his *New Deal* for national recovery (1933), and became the only president to be re-elected three times. He strove in vain to ward off war, and was brought in by Japan's action at Pearl Harbor (1941). He met with Churchill and Stalin at Teheran (1943) and Yalta (1945). >> Roosevelt, Eleanor

Roosevelt, Theodore [rohzuhvelt, roozvelt], known as **Teddy Roosevelt** (1858–1919) US statesman and 26th president (1901–9), born in New York City. Elected Republican vice-president in 1900, he became president after the assassination of McKinley. An 'expansionist', he insisted on a strong navy, and introduced a *Square Deal* policy for social reform. >> McKinley

Root, Elihu (1845–1937) Jurist and statesman, born in Clinton, NY. He became US secretary of war (1899–1904)

and secretary of state (1905-9), and was awarded the Nobel Prize for Peace in 1912 for his promotion of international arbitration.

Roper, Elmo (Burns), Jr (1900-71) Public opinion analyst, born in Hebron, NE. He founded his own New York firm (1934), pioneering modern polling techniques, and published *Fortune's* public opinion surveys (1935-50).

Rorem, Ned (1923-) Composer and writer, born in Richmond, IN. His musical works include three symphonies, six operas, concertos, and ballets, as well as theatrical, choral, and chamber music.

Rorschach, Hermann [raw(r)shahkh] (1884-1922) Psychiatrist and neurologist, born in Zürich, Switzerland. He devised a diagnostic procedure for mental disorders based upon the patient's interpretation of a series of standardized ink blots (the *Rorschach test*).

Rorty, Richard (McKay) (1931-) Philosopher, born in New York City. His controversial *Philosophy and the Mirror of Nature* (1979) attacked the foundationalist, metaphysical aspirations of traditional philosophy.

Rosa, Carl (August Nicolas) [rohza], original surname **Rose** (1842-89) Impresario and violinist, born in Hamburg. In 1873 he founded the Carl Rosa Opera Company, giving a great impulse to opera sung in English, and also to operas by English composers.

Rosa, Salvator [rohza] (1615-73) Painter, born near Naples, Italy. He owes his reputation mainly to his landscapes of wild and savage scenes.

Roscellinus, Johannes [roseliynus] (c.1050-c.1120) Scholar, probably born in Compiègne, France. Considered to be the founder of Nominalism, his most famous pupil was Abelard. In 1092 the Council of Soissons condemned his teaching. >> Abelard

Roscius [roshius], in full **Quintus Roscius Gallus** (c.134-62 BC) Roman comic actor, a slave by birth. He became the greatest comic actor in Rome, and was freed from slavery by the dictator, Sulla. >> Sulla

Rose, Billy, professional name of **William Samuel Rosenberg** (1899-1966) Composer of popular music, born in New York City. A prolific song writer during the 1920s, his many hits included 'Me and My Shadow' and 'Without a Song'.

Rose, Sir John (1820-88) Canadian diplomat, born in Turriff, Grampian. He emigrated to Canada in 1836, and played a critical part in adjusting British-American relations after the American Civil War.

Rose, Lionel (Edmund) (1948-) Bantamweight boxer, born in Warragul, Victoria, Australia. He won the world championship (1968-9), becoming the first Aborigine to hold a world title.

Rose, (Iain) Murray (1939-) Swimmer, born in Birmingham, West Midlands. At the 1956 Melbourne Olympics he became the youngest-ever triple gold medallist in swimming, with wins in the 400 m and 1500 m freestyle and the relay team.

Rose, Pete(r Edward) (1942-) Baseball player and manager, born in Cincinnati, OH. In his career (1963-86), spent mainly with the Cincinnati Reds, he had a record 4256 base hits.

Rose, William (Cumming) (1887-1984) Biochemist, born in Greenville, SC. From the 1930s he studied mammalian nutrition, and showed that only eight amino acids are essential in the adult human diet.

Rosebery, Archibald Philip Primrose, 5th Earl of (1847-1929) British Liberal prime minister (1894-5), born in London. He became foreign secretary (1886, 1892-4) under Gladstone, whom he succeeded as premier. >> Gladstone, W E

Rosecrans, William S(tarke) [rohzkrans] (1819-98) US soldier and politician, born in Kingston, OH. During the Civil War (1861-5) he commanded the Army of the

Mississippi, winning victories at Iuka and Stone River (1862-3), and later became a member of the US House of Representatives (1881-5).

Rose-Innes, Sir James [inis] (1855-1942) Judge, born in Uitenkage, South Africa. He became judge president (later Chief Justice) of the Supreme Court of the Transvaal (1902-10), judge of appeal (1910-14), and Chief Justice of the Union of South Africa (1914-27).

Rosenbach, A(braham) S(imon) W(olf) [rohzenbak] (1876-1952) Book dealer and collector, born in Philadelphia, PA. He helped assemble the volumes at the core of such institutions as the Huntington Library and the Folger Shakespeare Library.

Rosenberg, Alfred [rohzenberg] (1893-1946) German politician, born in Reval, Estonia. In *The Myth of the 20th Century* (1930) he expounded extreme Nazi doctrines later put into practice in E Europe, for which crime he was hanged at Nuremberg in 1946.

Rosenberg [rohzenberg] Alleged spies: **Julius Rosenberg** (1918-53) and **Ethel Rosenberg** (1915-53), husband and wife, both born in New York City. They joined the Communist Party, and became part of a transatlantic spy ring, and were the first US civilians to be executed for espionage.

Rosenfeld, Lev Borisovich >> **Kamenev, Lev Borisovich**

Rosenquist, James (Albert) (1933-) Painter, born in Grand Falls, ND. He began as an abstract painter, but c.1960 took to Pop Art and painted enlarged bits and pieces of unrelated everyday objects.

Rosenthal, Jack (Morris) [rohzentahl] (1931-) Playwright, born in Manchester. His television plays include *The Evacuees* (1975), *Barmitzvah Boy* (1976), *The Knowledge* (1979), and *Sleeping Sickness* (1991), and he also writes for film and stage. In 1973 he married Maureen Lipman. >> Lipman

Rosenzweig, Franz [rohzentsviyk] (1886-1929) Jewish theologian, born in Kassel, Germany. He reacted against German Idealism, and expounded an existential approach, as seen in his major work, *The Star of Redemption* (trans, 1921).

Rosewall, Ken(neth Ronald) (1934-) Tennis player, born in Sydney, New South Wales, Australia. The best player never to have won the Wimbledon singles title, although playing in three finals, he won the British, US, French, and Australian doubles titles (with Hoad) in 1956. >> Hoad

Rosmini(-Serbati), Antonio [rozmeenee] (1797-1855) Theologian and philosopher, born in Rovereto, Austria. He founded the Institute of the Fathers of Charity in 1828, and later became an adviser to Pope Pius IX (1848), but several of his works were prohibited in 1849 by the Congregation of the Index.

Rosny [rohnee] Pseudonym of the brothers **Joseph Henri Boëx** (1856-1940) and **Séraphin Justin François Boëx** (1859-1948), French novelists, born in Brussels. Their vast output of naturalistic social novels includes *L'Immolation* (1887) and *L'Impérieuse Bonté* (1905). They wrote separately after 1908.

Ross, Herbert >> **Kaye, Nora**

Ross, Harold (Wallace) (1892-1951) Newspaper editor, born in Aspen, CO. In 1917 he enlisted in the Railway Engineer Corps of the US army, becoming editor of *Stars and Stripes*, and in 1925 was founder-editor of the *New Yorker*.

Ross, Sir James Clark (1800-62) Polar explorer, born in London. He discovered the north magnetic pole in 1831, then commanded an expedition to the Antarctic seas (1839-43), where the *Ross Barrier*, *Sea*, and *Island* are named after him. >> Ross, John

Ross, Sir John (1777-1856) British naval officer and Arctic explorer, born at Balsaroch, Dumfries and Galloway. In 1829-33 he led an expedition with Sir Felix Booth (1775-1850) in search of the Northwest passage, but his ship was crushed in the ice, and the party had to be rescued by whalers. >> Ross, James Clark

Ross, Martin >> **Martin, Violet Florence**

Ross, Sir Ronald (1857-1932) Physician, born in Almora, India. He received the Nobel Prize for Physiology or Medicine in 1902 for his discovery of the malaria parasite and later work on the natural history of the disease.

Rossby, Carl-Gustav (Arvid) (1898-1957) Meteorologist, born in Stockholm. In 1940 he demonstrated the large-scale undulatory disturbances (*Rossby waves*) in the flow of the westerly winds in the upper atmosphere, and is credited with the discovery of the jet stream.

Rossellini, Roberto [roseleenee] (1906-77) Film director, born in Rome. His film *Rome, Open City* (trans, 1945) was made with hidden cameras in a style which came to be known as 'neo-Realism'. Later films include (trans titles) *Paisan* (1946) and *General della Rovere* (1959).

Rossellino, Antonio [roseleenoh] (1427-79) Renaissance sculptor, born in Florence, Italy, the youngest brother and pupil of Bernardo Rossellino. He is best known for his portrait busts and for his sculptural reliefs of the Madonna and Child. >> Rossellino, Bernardo

Rossellino, Bernardo [roseleenoh] (1409-64) Architect and sculptor, born in Florence, Italy, the brother and teacher of Antonio Rossellino. His most complete architectural work is the palace and cathedral of Pienza, and his sculptural masterpiece is the tomb of Leonardo Bruni (1450) in S Croce, Florence. >> Rossellino, Antonio

Rossetti, Christina (Georgina) [rozetee] (1830-94) Poet, born in London, the daughter of Gabriele Rossetti. A devout Anglican, and influenced by the Oxford Movement, she wrote mainly religious poetry, such as *Goblin Market and Other Poems* (1862). >> Rossetti, Gabriele

Rossetti, Dante Gabriel [rozetee] (1828-82) Poet and painter, born in London, the elder son of Gabriele Rossetti. A founder of the Pre-Raphaelite Brotherhood (c.1850), his early painting was on religious themes, such as 'The Annunciation' (1850). *Ballads and Sonnets* (1881) contains some of his best poetry. >> Rossetti, Gabriele

Rossetti, Gabriele [rozetee] (1783-1854) Poet, scholar, and revolutionary, born in Vasto, Italy. He is best known as the father of four exceptionally talented children, three of whom have entries in this volume; the fourth was **Maria Francesca** (1827-76). >> Rossetti, Christina / Dante Gabriel / William Michael

Rossetti, William Michael [rozetee] (1829-1919) Art critic and man of letters, born in London, the younger son of Gabriele Rossetti. He wrote biographies of Shelley and Keats, and published editions of Coleridge, Milton, Blake, and Whitman. >> Rossetti, Gabriele

Rossi, Bruno (1905-) Physicist, born in Venice, Italy. He studied cosmic rays, showing them to be positively charged particles, and helped to develop X-ray astronomy.

Rossi, Giovanni Battista de (1822-94) Archaeologist, born in Rome. He is known for his research on the Christian catacombs of St Callistus in Rome, and has been called 'the founder of Christian archaeology'.

Rossini, Gioacchino (Antonio) [roseenee] (1792-1868) Composer, born in Pesaro, Italy. Among his early successes were *Tancredi* (1813) and *The Italian Girl in Algiers* (trans, 1813), and in 1816 he produced his masterpiece, *The Barber of Seville*. Also known for his *Stabat Mater* (1841) and the *Petite messe solennelle* (1863), his overtures have continued to be highly popular items in concert programmes.

Rossiter, Leonard (1926-84) Actor, born in Liverpool, Merseyside. He is best remembered for his appearances in the television series' *Rising Damp* (1974-8) and *The Fall and Rise of Reginald Perrin* (1976-80).

Rosso, Fiorentino, originally **Giovanni Battista de Jacopo di Gasparre** (1495-1540) Painter, born in Florence, Italy. A leading exponent of the Mannerist style, and founder of the Fontainebleau school, his most famous work is 'The Deposition' (1521).

Rostand, Edmond [rostã] (1868-1918) Writer, born in Marseille, France. He achieved international fame with his play, *Cyrano de Bergerac* (1897), the story of the gifted nobleman who felt no-one could love him because of his enormous nose.

Rostow, Walt (Whitman) (1916-) Economist, born in New York City. Best known for his theory that societies pass through five stages of economic growth, his publications include *The World Economy: History and Prospect* (1978).

Rostropovich, Mstislav Leopoldovich [rostropohvich] (1927-) Cellist and composer, born in Baku, Azerbaijan (formerly, USSR). In 1975, while in the USA, he decided not to return to the USSR, and became musical director and conductor of the National Symphony Orchestra, Washington, DC (1977-94). His wife is the soprano, Galina Vishnevskaya (1926-).

Roth, Henry (1906-) Novelist, born in Tymenica, Austria-Hungary. He moved to New York City in 1907. His only novel is *Call It Sleep* (1934), a classic treatment of Jewish immigrant life and childhood.

Roth, Joseph (1894-1939) Writer and critic, born in Brod, Slovenia (formerly, Brody, Austria-Hungary). His novels include (trans titles) *Radetzky March* (1932), *The Capuchin Tomb* (1938), and the posthumously published *The Silent Prophet* (1966).

Roth, Philip (Milton) (1933-) Novelist, born in Newark, NJ. His books include *Letting Go* (1962), *Portnoy's Complaint* (1969), *My Life as a Man* (1974), and the trilogy *Zuckerman Bound* (1989). He is married to Claire Bloom. >> Bloom, Claire

Rothacker, Erich [rotaker] (1888-1965) Philosopher, born in Pforzheim, Germany. A leading exponent of philosophical anthropology, his main works include *Problems of Cultural Anthropology* (trans, 1948).

Rotheim, Erik [rothiym] (1898-1938) Norwegian inventor. He filed the first patent for an aerosol-type dispenser in 1926.

Rothenstein, Sir John (Knewstub Maurice) [rothenstiyn] (1901-92) Art historian, born in London, the son of Sir William Rothenstein. He became director and keeper of the Tate Gallery (1938-64), his many works on art including *Modern English Painters* (1952-73). >> Rothenstein, William

Rothenstein, Sir William [rothenstiyn] (1872-1945) Artist, born in Bradford, West Yorkshire. He won fame as a portrait painter, and was an official war artist in both world wars. >> Rothenstein, John

Rothermere, Viscount >> **Harmsworth, Harold Sydney**

Rothko, Mark, originally **Marcus Rothkovitch** (1903-70) Painter, born in Dvinsk, Russia. His family emigrated to the USA in 1913. During the 1940s he was influenced by Surrealism, but by the early 1950s had evolved his own meditative form of Abstract Expressionism.

Rothschild, Meyer (Amschel), Eng [rothschiyld], Ger [rohtshilt] (1743-1812) Financier, the founder of a banking dynasty, born in Frankfurt, Germany. He began as a moneylender, and became the financial adviser of the Landgrave of Hesse. His five sons continued the firm, opening branches in other countries.

Rothschild, Nathaniel Mayer Victor Rothschild, 3rd Baron (1910-90) Administrator, born in London. He was chairman of the Agricultural Research Council (1948-58) and research director/co-ordinator of Shell UK.

Rothwell, Evelyn >> **Barbirolli, John**

Rouault, Georges (Henri) [roo-oh] (1871-1958) Painter

and engraver, born in Paris. Apprenticed to a stained-glass designer in 1885, he retained the art's glowing colours, outlined with black, in his paintings of clowns, prostitutes, and biblical characters.

Roubillac, Louis François [roobeeyak], also spelled **Roubiliac** (1702–1762) Sculptor, born in Lyon, France. His statue of Handel for Vauxhall Gardens (1738) first made him popular, and he completed statues of Newton, Shakespeare and others.

Rouget de Lisle, Claude Joseph [roozhay duh **leel**] (1760–1836) French army officer, born in Lons-le-Saunier, France. He wrote and composed the *Marseillaise* (1792), which became known in Paris during the French Revolution.

Roughead, William (1870–1952) Criminologist, from Edinburgh. In 1906 the *Trial of Dr Pritchard* was the first of his 10 volumes in the 'Notable British Trials' series.

Rous, (Francis) Peyton [rows] (1879–1970) Pathologist, born in Baltimore, MD. The *Rous chicken sarcoma*, which he discovered in 1911, remains the best-known example of a cancer produced by a virus. He shared the Nobel Prize for Physiology or Medicine in 1966.

Rousseau, Henri Julien Félix [roosoh], known as **le Douanier** ('the Customs Officer') (1844–1910) Primitive painter, born in Laval, France. He produced painstaking portraits, exotic imaginary landscapes, and dreams, such as 'Sleeping Gypsy' (1897).

Rousseau, Jean Jacques [roosoh] (1712–78) Political philosopher, educationist, and essayist, born in Geneva, Switzerland. His works include *Discourse on the Origin and Foundations of Inequality Amongst Men* (trans, 1755), his masterpiece, *The Social Contract* (trans, 1762), which was a great influence on French revolutionary thought, and his major work on education, *Emile*.

Rousseau, (Pierre Etienne) Théodore [roosoh] (1812–67) Landscape painter, born in Paris. During the 1840s he settled at Barbizon, where he worked with other painters, becoming leader of the Barbizon school.

Roussel, Albert (Charles Paul Marie) [roosel] (1869–1937) Composer, born in Tourcoing, France. His works include ballets, notably *The Spider's Feast* (trans, 1912) and *Bacchus and Ariane* (1931), four symphonies, and numerous choral and orchestral works.

Roussel, Ker Xavier [roosel] (1867–1944) Artist, born in Lorry-les-Metz, France. A member of *Les Nabis*, he is best known for his classical subjects portrayed in typical French landscapes, using the Impressionist palette.

Rout, Ettie Annie [rowt] (1877–1936) Journalist and social reformer, born in Hobart, Australia. During World War 1 she became famous for her campaign to control venereal disease among New Zealand troops in Europe, and later turned her attention to the sexual education of women.

Routledge, George [rowtlij] (1812–88) Publisher, born in Brampton, Cumbria. He went to London in 1833, and started up as a bookseller (1836) and publisher (1843).

Roux, (Pierre Paul) Emile [roo] (1853–1933) Bacteriologist, born in Confolens, France. Assistant to Pasteur, in 1894 he helped to discover diphtheria antitoxin, and also worked on rabies and anthrax. >> Pasteur

Roux, Wilhelm [roo] (1850–1924) Anatomist and physiologist, born in Jena, Germany. He was one of the first to do extensive practical and theoretical work on experimental embryology.

Rowan, Carl (Thomas) (1925–) Journalist, born in Ravenscroft, TN. A prizewinning reporter for the *Minneapolis Tribune* (1950–61), he later became a nationally syndicated columnist, radio commentator, and panelist on television public affairs programmes.

Rowbotham, Sheila [rohbotham] (1943–) Social historian and feminist, born in Leeds, West Yorkshire. An active socialist, her most important historical works include *Women, Resistance and Revolution* (1972).

Rowe, Nicholas [roh] (1674–1718) Poet and playwright, born in Little Barford, Bedfordshire. His plays include *Tamerlane* (1702), *The Fair Penitent* (1703), and *Jane Shore* (1714), and in 1715 he was appointed poet laureate.

Rowland, Tiny, originally **Rowland W Furhop** (1917–) Financier, born in India. He joined Lonrho (London and Rhodesian Mining and Land Company) in 1961, and became chief executive and managing director, stepping down in 1994.

Rowland, F Sherwood (1927–) US scientist. In 1974, with his Mexican colleague Mario Molina (1943–), he predicted the destruction of ozone in the Earth's atmosphere as a by-product of using CFCs (confirmed in 1985).

Rowland, Henry Augustus (1848–1901) Physicist, born in Honesdale, PA. He invented the concave diffraction grating used in spectroscopy, and discovered the magnetic effect of a moving electric charge.

Rowlandson, Thomas (1756–1827) Caricaturist, born in London. Some of his best-known works are his illustrations to the 'Dr Syntax' series (1812–21) and 'The English Dance of Death' (1815–16).

Rowley, Thomas [rohlee] >> **Chatterton, Thomas**

Rowley, William (c.1585–c.1642) Actor and playwright, born in London. He collaborated on many plays, but four are extant under his own name, including *All's Lost by Lust* (c.1620) and *A Match at Midnight* (1633).

Rowling, Sir Wallace Edward, known as **Bill Rowling** (1927–) New Zealand prime minister (1974–5), born in Motueka, New Zealand. He was finance minister in the Labour administration of Kirk, and succeeded him briefly as prime minister. >> Kirk, John

Rowntree, B(enjamin) Seebohm (1871–1954) Manufacturer and philanthropist, born in York, North Yorkshire, the son of Joseph Rowntree. Chairman of the family chocolate firm (1925–41), he introduced enlightened schemes of worker-participation, and devoted his life to the study of social problems and welfare. >> Rowntree, Joseph

Rowntree, Joseph (1836–1925) Quaker industrialist and reformer, born in York, North Yorkshire, the son of Joseph Rowntree. With his brother, Henry Isaac (d.1883), he became a partner in a cocoa manufacturing firm in York in 1869. >> Rowntree, B Seebohm

Rowse, A(lfred) L(eslie) [rows] (1903–) Historian, born in St Austell, Cornwall. His many works on English history include *Tudor Cornwall* (1941), *The Use of History* (1946), and *The England of Elizabeth* (1950).

Roy, Rammohun >> **Rammohun Roy**

Royal, The Princess >> **Anne, Princess**

Royce, Sir (Frederick) Henry (1863–1933) Engineer, born in Alwalton, Cambridgeshire. In 1884 he founded the firm of Royce Ltd in Manchester, made his first car in 1904, and with C S Rolls founded Rolls-Royce, Ltd in 1906.

Royce, Josiah (1855–1916) Philosopher, born in Grass Valley, CA. Much influenced by Hegel, he developed a philosophy of Idealism, emphasizing the importance of the individual in such works as *Religious Aspects of Philosophy* (1885). >> Hegel

Royden, Agnes Maud (1876–1956) Social worker and preacher, born in Liverpool, Merseyside. Prominent in the women's suffrage movement, her publications include *Woman and the Sovereign State* and *Modern Sex Ideals*.

Rozanov, Vasily Vasilyevich [rozahnof] (1856–1919) Writer, thinker, and critic, born in Vetluga, Russia. Much of his work is highly introspective, his literary reputation being based on two books of fragments and essays, *Solitaria* (1912) and *Fallen Leaves* (trans, 1913, 1915).

Rózsa, Miklós (Nicholas) [rowsha] (1907–95) Composer, born in Budapest. He settled in Hollywood in 1939, and began to write film scores, receiving Oscars for *Spellbound* (1945), *A Double Life* (1947), and *Ben Hur* (1959).

Rubbia, Carlo (1934–) Physicist, born in Gorizia, Italy. He shared the Nobel Prize for Physics in 1984 for work leading to the discovery of the W and Z sub-atomic particles. >> van der Meer

Rubbra, Edmund (1901–86) Composer, born in Northampton, Northamptonshire. He wrote 11 symphonies, chamber, choral and orchestral music, songs, and solo instrumental works.

Rubens, (Peter Paul) [roobenz] (1577–1640) Painter, born in Siegen, Germany. His major works include a triptych 'The Descent from the Cross' (1611–14) in Antwerp Cathedral, 21 large subjects on the life and regency of Marie de Médicis of France, and many works painted while on diplomatic missions in Spain and England, such as 'Peace and War' (National Gallery, London). >> Marie de Médicis

Rubik, Ernö [roobik] (1944–) Architect, born in Budapest. He is the creator of *Rubik's cube* (1974), which became a world craze in the late 1970s.

Rubinstein, Anton (Grigoryevich) [roobinstiyn] (1829–94) Pianist and composer, born in Vykhvatinets, Russia. Director of the St Petersburg Conservatory (1862–7), his compositions include operas, oratorios, and piano concertos. His brother **Nikolay** (1835–81) founded Moscow Conservatory.

Rubinstein, Artur [roobinstiyn] (1887–1982) Pianist, born in Lódź, Poland. He became a US citizen in 1946, where he performed with enormous success, making over 200 recordings.

Rubinstein, Helena [roobinstiyn] (1870–1965) Beautician and business executive, born in Cracow, Poland. She moved in the 1890s to Australia, where she opened the country's first beauty salon, in Melbourne (1902), and in 1915 launched an international business empire from New York City.

Rublyov or **Rublev, Andrey** [rublyof] (c.1360–c.1430) Painter, born in Russia. Generally regarded as the greatest of Russian icon painters, he is traditionally believed to have produced his most famous work, the icon of the Old Testament Trinity, in Troitsky-Sergieva.

Ruby, Jack L, originally **Jacob Rubenstein** (1911–67) Assassin, born in Chicago, IL. Two days after the assassination of President John F Kennedy, he shot and killed Lee Harvey Oswald, the alleged assassin of the president. He was sentenced to death in 1964, but died while awaiting a second trial. >> Kennedy, John F; Oswald, Lee Harvey

Rudbeck, Olof (1630–1702) Anatomist, botanist, writer, and architect, born in Sweden. He discovered the lymphatic system (1652) simultanilously with the Danish physician Thomas Bartholin (1616–80). The botanical genus *Rudbeckia* is named after him.

Rudkin, Margaret, née **Fogarty** (1897–1967) Businesswoman, born in New York City. In 1937 she began a mail-order business selling Pepperidge Farm Bread, producing a special bread for asthmatics and other patients.

Rudolf I (1218–91) German king (1273–91), born in Schloss Limburg, Germany. He was the founder of the Habsburg sovereign and imperial dynasty.

Rudolph, Wilma (Glodean) (1940–94) Sprinter, born in St Bethlehem, TN. At the Rome Olympics in 1960 she won the 100 m, 200 m, and sprint relay events, making her the first US woman to win three gold medals for track and field events.

Rue, Warren de la >> **de la Rue, Warren**

Ruether, Rosemary Radford [roother] (1936–) Theologian, born in Minneapolis, MN. Her books analyze the effects of male bias in official Church theology, and seek to affirm the feminine dimension of religion and the importance of women's experience.

Ruggles, Carl (1876–1971) Composer, born in Marion, MA. A radical modern writer, he destroyed many of his early works, but the best known and longest of those which survive is the 17-minute orchestral *Sun-treader* (1926–31).

Ruggles-Brise, Sir Evelyn (John) (1857–1935) Prison reformer, born in Finchingfield, Essex. He visited the USA (1897) to study the reformatory system, and on his return brought together a group of young prisoners at Borstal, Kent, where he implemented 'Borstal detention'.

Ruïsdael, Jacob van >> **Ruysdael, Jacob van**

Ruiz, José Martínez >> **Azorín**

Rukeyser, Muriel [rookiyzer] (1913–80) Writer, born in New York City. She became a social activist and feminist poet, as seen in her collected poems (1979), and also wrote plays, screenplays, and children's books.

Rule, St >> **Regulus, St**

Rumford, Count >> **Thompson, Benjamin**

Ruml, Beardsley [ruhml] (1894–1960) Public official, born in Cedar Rapids, IA. He devised the federal tax witholding system (1943), and was instrumental in establishing the International Monetary Fund (1944).

Rummell, Joseph (Francis) (1876–1964) Roman Catholic clergyman, born in Baden, Germany. Archbishop of New Orleans (1935–62), he became best known for his stand in the 1950s against racial segregation in school.

Rumsey, James (1743–92) Engineer and inventor, born in Cecil Co, MD. His early steamboat, propelled by the ejection of water from the stern, was exhibited on the Potomac in 1787.

Runcie (of Cuddesdon), Robert (Alexander Kennedy) Runcie, Baron [ruhnsee] (1921–) Archbishop of Canterbury (1980–91), born in Crosby, Lancashire. His period as archbishop was marked by a papal visit to Canterbury, ongoing controversies over homosexuality and women in the Church, and the Lambeth Conference of 1987.

Runciman, Lord Walter Runciman, 1st Viscount (1870–1949) British statesman. He is remembered for his mission to Czechoslovakia in 1938 to persuade the government to make concessions to Nazi Germany as part of Britain's 'appeasement strategy'. >> Chamberlain, Neville

Runcorn, (Stanley) Keith (1922–) Geophysicist, born in Southport, Lancashire. He is best known for his studies of terrestrial magnetism, by which he helped to confirm the theory of continental drift.

Rundstedt, (Karl Rudolf) Gerd von [rundshtet] (1875–1953) German field marshal, born in Aschersleben, Germany. In 1939 he directed the attacks on Poland and France, and directed the Ardennes offensive in 1944.

Runeberg, Johan Ludvig [roonuhberg] (1804–77) Finnish poet, writing in Swedish, born in Jakobstad, Finland. Known for his epic poems, his major work is the verse romance based on Scandinavian legend, *King Fjala* (1844).

Runyon, (Alfred) Damon (1884–1946) Writer and journalist, born in Manhattan, KS. Best known for his short stories about underworld New York life, his collection *Guys and Dolls* (1932) was adapted for a musical revue (1950) and film (1955).

Rupert, Prince, also known as **Rupert of the Rhine** (1619–82) Royalist commander in the English Civil War, born in Prague, the third son of Elizabeth, the daughter of James I of England. A notable cavalry leader, he won several victories, but was defeated at Marston Moor (1644), and banished by Parliament.

Rupert, Anthony Edward (1916–) Financier, patron of the arts, and leading conservationist, born in Graff-Reiner, South Africa. He is the founder and retired chairman of the Rembrandt Group of Companies, and the doyen of Afrikaans language business.

Rüppell, (Wilhelm Peter) Eduard (Simon) [rüpel] (1794–1884) Zoologist and explorer, born in Frankfurt, Germany. He went on major expeditions to the Sudan (1821–7) and Ethiopia (1830–4). *Rüppell's warbler* is named after him.

Rush, Benjamin (1745–1813) Physician and politician, born in Byberry, PA. One of the first to argue that mental disorders could be treated as well as could physical ones, he wrote a famous treatise on psychiatry (1812).

Rush, Ian (1961–) Footballer, born in St Asaph, Clwyd. He joined Liverpool in 1981, scoring 110 goals in 182 league matches, then played for Juventus (1986–8) before returning to Liverpool. He has been a regular member of the Welsh international team since 1980.

Rush, Richard (1780–1859) Lawyer, public official, and diplomat, born in Philadelphia, PA, the son of Benjamin Rush. He became US attorney general (1814), interim secretary-of-state (1817), and minister to Great Britain (1817–25). >> Rush, Benjamin

Rushdie, (Ahmad) Salman (1947–) Writer, born in Bombay, India, of Muslim parents. He became widely known after his second novel, *Midnight's Children* (1981, Booker). *The Satanic Verses* (1988) caused worldwide controversy for its secular treatment of Islam, and he was forced to go into hiding because of a sentence of death passed on him by Ayatollah Khomeini of Iran. >> Khomeini

Rusk, (David) Dean (1909–94) US statesman, born in Cherokee Co, GA. He was secretary of state (1961–9), playing a major role in handling the Cuban crisis of 1962.

Rusk, Howard A(rchibald) (1903–89) Physician and writer, born in Brookfield, MO. At New York University in 1946 he started the world's first comprehensive rehabilitation programme.

Ruska, Ernst (1906–88) Physicist, born in Heidelberg, Germany. For his development of the electron microscope, he was awarded the Nobel Prize for Physics in 1986.

Ruskin, John (1819–1900) Writer and art critic, born in London. His major works include *Modern Painters* (1843–60), *The Seven Lamps of Architecture* (1848), and *The Stones of Venice* (1851–3).

Russell, Anna, originally **Claudia Anna Russell-Brown** (1911–) Singer and musical satirist, born in London. After her debut as a concert comedienne in New York City (1948), she took her show to many cities throughout the world.

Russell, Bertrand (Arthur William) Russell, 3rd Earl (1872–1970) Philosopher and mathematician, born in Trelleck, Gwent. His major works were *Principles of Mathematics* (1903) and (with A N Whitehead) *Principia mathematica* (1910–13). Later works included *An Enquiry into Meaning and Truth* (1940) and *Human Knowledge* (1948). After 1949 he became a champion of nuclear disarmament. The single most important influence on 20th-c analytic philosophy, he was awarded the Nobel Prize for Literature in 1950.

Russell, Bill, popular name of **William Felton Russell** (1934–) Basketball player, born in Monroe, LA. He played with the Boston Celtics (1956–69), winning 11 NBA championships in 13 seasons.

Russell, Charles Taze, nickname **Pastor Russell** (1852–1916) Religious leader, born in Pittsburgh, PA. He dedicated his life to founding a millenarian movement, the international Bible Students' Association (1872) in Pittsburgh, which was the forerunner of the Jehovah's Witnesses.

Russell, Sir Edward John (1872–1965) Agriculturist, born in Frampton-on-Severn, Gloucestershire. He published his classic *Soil Conditions and Plant Growth* in 1912.

Russell, Francis, 4th Earl of Bedford (1593–1641) English nobleman, the son of William, Baron Russell. With the help of Inigo Jones he developed Covent Garden and built the mansion of Woburn. >> Jones, Inigo; Russell, Baron

Russell, Frederick Stratten (1897–1984) Marine biologist, born in Dorset. Director of the Plymouth Laboratory, he is best known for his work on medusae and plankton.

Russell, George William, pseudonym **Æ** (1867–1935) Poet and mystic, born in Lurgan, Co Armagh. His first book, *Homeward: Songs by the Way* (1894), made him a recognized figure in the Irish literary renaissance. His best-known book is *The Candle of Vision* (1918).

Russell, Sir (Sydney) Gordon (1892–1980) Furniture designer, born in London. In 1923 he started a furniture-making business in Worcestershire, and with his brother Dick (1903–81), Gordon Russell Ltd went on to produce some of the finest modern furniture of the 1930s.

Russell, Henry Norris (1877–1957) Astronomer, born in Oyster Bay, NY. Independently of Hertzsprung, he discovered the relationship between stellar absolute magnitude and spectral type, and represented the results in the Hertzsprung–Russell diagram (1913). >> Hertzsprung

Russell, Jack, popular name of **John Russell** (1795–1883) Clergyman, born in Dartmouth, Devon. He developed the West Country smooth-haired, short-legged terrier, since named after him.

Russell, John, 1st Earl of Bedford (c.1486–1555) English courtier. He became a gentleman usher to Henry VIII, and later held many court appointments. He led the mission to Spain in 1554 which escorted Philip home to marry Mary I. >> Henry VIII; Mary I

Russell (of Kingston Russell), John Russell, 1st Earl, known as **Lord John Russell** (1792–1878) British Whig-Liberal prime minister (1846–52, 1865–6), born in London. He first became prime minister after the Conservative Party split over the repeal of the Corn Laws (1846), and also served as foreign secretary (1852–5, 1859), though forced to retire over alleged incompetence during the Crimean War.

Russell, John Robert, 13th Duke of Bedford (1917–) British nobleman. He became well known for his successful efforts to keep Woburn Abbey for the family, running it commercially with popular amenities.

Russell, John Scott (1808–82) Engineer and naval architect, born near Glasgow, Strathclyde. He helped design many ships, including the *Great Eastern* (1856) and HMS *Warrior* (1860), the first ironclad battleship.

Russell, Ken, popular name of **Henry Kenneth Alfred Russell** (1927–) Film director, born in Southampton, Hampshire. After several experimental studies for BBC television (eg Debussy, Isadora Duncan), he began to make feature films, including *Women in Love* (1969), *The Devils* (1971), and *Lady Chatterley's Lover* (1993).

Russell, Morgan (1886–1953) Painter, born in New York City. In 1912 he and the US painter Stanton McDonald-Wright (1890–1973) developed the theory of Synchromist colour, in which colour was given precedence over descriptive form.

Russell, Pee Wee, popular name of **Charles Ellsworth Russell** (1906–69) Jazz clarinet player, born in Maple Wood, MO. Associated with the Chicago-based Dixielanders of the 1920s, he was part of the Eddie Condon (1905–73) troupe for nearly two decades, and in the 1960s he was discovered again by a younger audience.

Russell, William, Lord (1639–83) English Whig politician. A leading member of the movement to exclude James II from the succession, he was arrested for participation in the Rye House Plot (1683), and beheaded.

Russell, Sir William Howard (1821–1907) War correspondent and writer, born near Tallaght, Co Dublin, Ireland. From the Crimea (1854–5) he wrote despatches (collected 1856) which opened the eyes of the British to the sufferings of the soldiers, and went on to cover other major events of the period, such as the Indian Mutiny and the American Civil War.

Russell (of Thornhaugh), William Russell, Baron (c.1558–1613) English statesman. His experience of lowland drainage methods while Governor of Flushing (1587–8) led him to initiate reclamation work in the Cambridgeshire fens (the 'Bedford level').

Russell, Willy, popular name of **William Martin Russell** (1947–) Playwright, born in Whiston, Lancashire. Known for his cheerful but sharp portrayal of Liverpudlian life, his best-known plays include *Educating Rita* (1979), *Blood Brothers* (1983), and *Shirley Valentine* (1986).

Rust, Mathias (1968–) German aviator. He achieved worldwide fame in 1987 when he landed his light aircraft in Red Square, Moscow, having been undetected on a flight from Finland.

Rustin, Bayard (1910–87) Civil rights activist, born in West Chester, PA. In 1955 he joined the Southern Christian Leadership Conference as Martin Luther King's special assistant, serving as the co-ordinator for the March on Washington in 1963. >> King, Martin Luther

Rutebeuf [rütuhboef] (c.1245–c.1285) French poet, whose name may have been a pseudonym. His works include the semi-liturgical drama, *Miracle de Théophile* (c.1260, a prototype of the Faust story), and humorous verse stories (*faibliaux*).

Ruth Biblical character described in the Book of Ruth as a woman from Moab who, after the death of her husband, refused to abandon her widowed mother-in-law Naomi. Naomi arranged Ruth's marriage to Boaz, and their son was said to be the grandfather of David. >> David

Ruth, Babe, popular name of **George Herman Ruth**, nicknames **the Babe, the Bambino, the Sultan of Swat** (1895–1948) Baseball player, born in Baltimore, MD. He joined the New York Yankees in 1920, and when he retired in 1935 had hit 714 home runs, a figure not bettered until 1974.

Rutherford (of Nelson), Ernest Rutherford, 1st Baron (1871–1937) Physicist, born near Nelson, New Zealand. With Soddy he proposed that radioactivity results from the disintegration of atoms (1903), and later he developed the modern conception of the atom, receiving the Nobel Prize for Chemistry in 1908. >> Soddy

Rutherford, Dame Margaret (1892–1972) Theatre and film actress, born in London. She gained fame as a character actress and comedienne, and played Agatha Christie's 'Miss Marple' in a series of films from 1962. She won an Oscar for her role in *The VIPs* in 1964.

Ruthven, William, 1st Earl of Gowrie (c.1541–84) Scottish nobleman. Involved in the murder of Rizzio (1566), he was custodian of Mary, Queen of Scots, during her captivity (1567–8). In 1582 he kidnapped the boy king, James VI, and was ordered to leave the country, but was beheaded for conspiring to take Stirling Castle. >> James I (of England); Mary, Queen of Scots; Rizzio

Ruysdael, Jacob van [roysdahl], also spelled **Ruisdael** (c.1628–82) Landscape painter, born in Haarlem, The Netherlands. His best works are country landscapes, and he also excelled in cloud effects, particularly in his seascapes.

Ruyter, Michiel Adriaanszoon de [royter] (1607–76) Dutch naval commander, born in Flushing, The Netherlands. He defeated the English in the 'Four Days' Battle' off Dunkirk (1666), destroying much of the English fleet at Medway (1667).

Ružička, Leopold (Stephen) (1887–1976) Chemist, born in Vukovar, Croatia. He was the first to synthesize sex hormones, for which he shared the Nobel Prize for Chemistry in 1939.

Ryan, Desmond (1893–1964) Socialist and historian, born in London, the son of William Patrick Ryan. His novels include *Invisible Army* (1932) and *St Eustace and the Albatross* (1934). >> Ryan, William Patrick

Ryan, Elizabeth (1892–1979) Tennis player, born in Anaheim, CA. She won 19 Wimbledon titles (12 doubles and seven mixed doubles), a record which stood from 1934 until 1979, when it was surpassed by Billie Jean King. >> King, Billie Jean

Ryan, (Lynn) Nolan (1947–) Baseball player, born in Refugio, TX. One of the fastest pitchers ever seen in major league baseball, he played with the New York Mets, the California Angels, the Houston Astros, and the Texas Rangers, retiring in 1993 with a record 5714 strikeouts.

Ryan, William Patrick, also known as **Liam P O Riain** and **W P O'Ryan** (1867–1942) Journalist and historian, born in Templemore, Co Tipperary, Ireland. His books include *The Irish Literary Revival* (1894) and *The Irish Labour Movement* (1919). >> Ryan, Desmond

Rydberg, Johannes Robert [rüdberg] (1854–1919) Physicist, born in Halmstad, Sweden. Best known for his theoretical studies of spectral series, he developed a formula for spectral lines, incorporating the *Rydberg constant*.

Ryder, Samuel (1859–1936) Businessman, born in Cheshire. In 1927 he donated the *Ryder Cup*, the trophy of the international golf match known by the same name, played by professional teams of British (now European) and American golfers.

Ryder (of Warsaw and Cavendish), Sue Ryder, Baroness (1923–) Philanthropist, born in Leeds, West Yorkshire. She established the Sue Ryder Foundation in 1953, now comprising some 80 centres worldwide, offering residential care for the sick and disabled. The Ryder–Cheshire Foundation links her work with that of her husband. >> Cheshire

Rykov, Alexey Ivanovich [reekof] (1881–1938) Russian revolutionary and politician, born in Saratov, Russia. He helped organize the October Revolution in Petrograd and was appointed People's Commissar for Internal Affairs. In 1928 he opposed Stalin's economic policies, and was shot.

Rylands, John (1801–88) Textile manufacturer and merchant, born in St Helens, Merseyside. In 1899 his widow established the John Rylands Library in Manchester.

Ryle, Gilbert (1900–76) Philosopher, born in Brighton, East Sussex. He is best known for his book *The Concept of Mind* (1949), which argued against the mind/body dualism ('the ghost in the machine') proposed by Descartes. >> Descartes; Ryle, Martin

Ryle, Sir Martin (1918–84) Radio astronomer, born in Brighton, East Sussex, the nephew of Gilbert Ryle. His development of interferometers enabled him to survey the most distant radio sources, and his work paved the way for renewed interest in the 'big bang' theory. He shared the Nobel Prize for Physics in 1974. >> Hewish; Ryle, Gilbert

Rymer, Thomas (1641–1713) Critic and historian, born in Northallerton, North Yorkshire. He is chiefly remembered as the compiler of the collection of historical materials known as the *Foedera* (20 vols, 1704–35).

Rysbrack, John Michael [riysbrak] (c.1694–1770) Sculptor, born in Antwerp, Belgium. Among his works are the monument to Newton in Westminster Abbey (1731) and statues of William III, Queen Anne, and George II.

Ryun, Jim [riyuhn], popular name of **James Ryun** (1947–) Athlete, born in Wichita, KS. In 1966 he set a world record time of 3 min 51·3 s for the mile, and the next year established a world record in the 1500 m of 3 min 33·1 s.

Ryzhkov, Nikolay Ivanovich [rushkof] (1929–) Soviet prime minister (1985–90), born in the Urals, Russia. Head of the Uralmash engineering conglomerate, he became chairman of the Council of Ministers in 1985, but suffered a heart attack and was replaced.

Saadi >> Sadi

Saarinen, Eero (1910–61) Architect and furniture designer, born in Kirkkonummi, Finland, the son of Eliel Saarinen. His designs for Expressionist modern buildings include the Trans-World Airlines Kennedy Terminal, New York City (1956–62). >> Eames; Saarinen, Eliel

Saarinen, (Gottlieb) Eliel (1873–1950) Architect, born in Rantasalmi, Finland. The leading architect in his native country, he designed the Helsinki railway station (1904–14), and in 1923 emigrated to the USA, where he designed many churches. >> Saarinen, Eero

Saatchi & Saatchi [sahchee] Advertisers: **Charles Saatchi** (1943–) and **Maurice Saatchi** (1946–), both born in Iraq. They moved to England in 1947, set up an advertising agency in 1970, and became famous for their election campaign for the Conservative Party in 1978.

Sabatier, Paul [sabatyay] (1854–1941) Chemist, born in Carcassonne, France. He did notable work in catalysis, and shared the Nobel Prize for Chemistry in 1912.

Sabatini, Rafael [sabateenee] (1875–1950) Writer, born in Jesi, Italy. His many historical romances include *The Sea Hawk* (1915), *Scaramouche* (1921), and *Captain Blood* (1922).

Sabin, A(lbert) B(ruce) [saybin] (1906–93) Microbiologist, born in Białystok, Poland. He is best known for his research into a live virus as a polio vaccine, which gives longer-lasting immunity than the Salk vaccine, and may be given orally.

Sabine, Sir Edward [sabin] (1788–1883) Physicist, astronomer, and explorer, born in Dublin. From his work on terrestrial magnetism, he discovered a relationship between sunspots and magnetic disturbances on Earth.

Sabine, Wallace Clement (Ware) [sabin] (1868–1919) Physicist, the founder of architectural acoustics, born in Richwood, OH. He devised the *Sabine law* (1898), that the product of the reverberation time multiplied by the total absorptivity of the room is proportional to the volume of the room.

Sacchi, Andrea [sachee] (1599–1661) Painter, born in Netturo, near Rome. His works include 'The Vision of St Romuald' (1640), 'Miracle of Saint Gregory' (1625–7), and religious works in many Roman churches.

Sacco and Vanzetti [sakoh, vanzetee] **Nicola Sacco** (1891–1927) and **Bartolomeo Vanzetti** (1888–1927), born in Italy. Found guilty of a payroll murder and robbery in Massachusetts in 1920, they were executed in spite of conflicting evidence. Both had been anarchists, and the suspicion that this had provoked injustice aroused an international outcry.

Sacher-Masoch, Leopold von [zahkher mahzokh] (1836–95) Lawyer and writer, born in Lemberg, Austria. He wrote many short stories and novels, and the term *masochism* was coined for the form of eroticism he describes in his later works.

Sacheverell, Henry [sasheverel] (c.1674–1724) Political preacher, born in Marlborough, Wiltshire. In 1709 a strong attack in a sermon on the Whig minister, Godolphin, caused his impeachment and suspension for three years. >> Godolphin

Sacheverell, William [sasheverel] (1638–91) English politician, sometimes called the 'First Whig'. He became one of the leaders of the anti-Court party, instrumental in framing the Test Act, which overthrew Charles II's Cabal ministry. >> Charles II (of England)

Sachs, Hans [zahkhs] (1494–1576) Writer and composer, born in Nuremberg, Germany. He headed the Meister-singers of Nuremberg in 1554, and in that role was idealized in Wagner's opera. >> Wagner

Sachs, (Ferdinand Gustav) Julius von (1832–97) Botanist, born in Breslau, Germany. He conducted important experiments on the influence of light and heat upon plants, and on the organic activities of vegetable growth, and published the influential *Textbook of Botany* (trans, 1875).

Sachs, Nelly (Leonie) [zahkhs] (1891–1970) Poet and playwright, born in Berlin. Her best-known play is *Eli: a Mystery Play of the Sufferings of Israel* (trans, 1951), and she shared the Nobel Prize for Literature in 1966.

Sackville, Thomas, 1st Earl of Dorset (1536–1608) English statesman and poet, born in Buckhurst, Sussex. He collaborated with Thomas Norton (1532–84) in the tragedy *Gorboduc* (1561), the first English play in blank verse.

Sackville-West, Vita, popular name of **Victoria Mary Sackville-West** (1892–1962) Poet and novelist, born at Knole, Kent. Her best-known novels are *The Edwardians* (1930) and *All Passion Spent* (1931). In 1913 she married Harold Nicolson, and her friendship with Virginia Woolf occasioned the latter's *Orlando* (1928). >> Nicolson; Woolf, Virginia

Sadat, (Mohammed) Anwar el- [sadat] (1918–81) Egyptian president (1970–81), born in the Tala district. He sought settlement of the conflict with Israel, meeting the Israeli premier in Jerusalem (1977) and at Camp David, USA (1978), in which year he and Begin were jointly awarded the Nobel Peace Prize. He was assassinated by extremists. >> Begin

Saddam Hussein >> Hussein, Saddam

Sade, Marquis de [sahd], popular name of **Donatien Alphonse François, comte** (Count) **de Sade** (1740–1814) Writer, born in Paris. Condemned to death for his cruelty and sexual perversions (1772), he escaped, but was later imprisoned in the Bastille (1784–90), where he wrote *The 120 Days of Sodom* (trans, c.1784).

Sadi or **Saadi,** assumed name of **Sheikh Muslih Addin** (c.1184–?1292) Poet, born in Iran. His most celebrated writings are a series of moral and religious works (trans titles): *Rose Garden, Orchard Garden,* and *Book of Instructions.*

Sadler, Sir Michael Ernest (1861–1943) Pioneer of secondary education, born in Barnsley, South Yorkshire. In 1895 he joined the government Education Department as Director of Special Inquiries and Reports, forming a powerful research bureau that came to be internationally known.

Sadler, Michael Thomas (1780–1835) Factory reformer, born in Snelston, Derbyshire. A leader of the factory reform movement, he promoted the Factory Act of 1833, which reduced the working-hours in textile mills for children and young people.

Saenredam, Pieter Jansz(oon) [sanredam] (1597–1665) Painter, born in Assendelft, The Netherlands. Unlike earlier architectural paintings, his works are precisely drawn images of known churches, such as 'View in the Nieuwe Kerk at Haarlem' (1652).

Sagan, Carl (Edward) [saygn] (1934–) Astronomer and writer, born in New York City. He has worked on the physics and chemistry of planetary atmospheres and surfaces, and investigated the origin of life on Earth and the possibility of extraterrestrial life. His popular books include *Cosmic Connection* (1973).

Sagan, Françoise [sagã], pseudonym of **Françoise Quoirez**

(1935–) Novelist, born in Paris. At 18 she wrote the best-selling *Bonjour tristesse* (1954, Good Morning, Sadness) followed by *A Certain Smile* (trans, 1956).

Saha, Meghnad (1894–1956) Astrophysicist, born near Dacca, India. He worked on the thermal ionization that occurs in the extremely hot atmosphere of stars, and in 1920 demonstrated that elements in stars are ionized in proportion to their temperature (*Saha's equation*).

Sahlins, Marshall David (1930–) Cultural anthropologist, born in Chicago, IL. He has made major contributions in the field of Oceanic ethnography, cultural evolution, economic anthropology, and the analysis of symbolism.

Said, Edward W(adi) [saeed] (1935–) Writer and political commentator, born in Jerusalem, Israel. He is one of the major Palestinian spokesmen in the debate on the future of the Middle East.

Sailer, Toni (Anton) [ziyler] (1935–) Alpine skier, born in Kitzbühel, Austria. In 1956, he became the first man to win all three Olympic skiing titles (downhill, slalom, giant slalom), and was the world combined champion in 1956 and 1958.

Sainsbury (of Drury Lane), Alan John Sainsbury, Baron [saynzbree] (1902–) Retailer, born in London. In 1921 he joined the family grocery business, founded by his grandparents. He became chairman (1956–67), and since then has been joint president of J Sainsbury plc with his younger brother, Sir Robert Sainsbury (1906–).

Saint-Denis, Michel (Jacques Duchesne) [sï duhnee] (1897–1971) Theatre director, actor, and teacher, born in Beauvais, France. He settled in England, founding with George Devine the London Theatre Studio (1936), and later worked with the Old Vic and the Royal Shakespeare Company. >> Devine

Saint Denis, Ruth, originally **Ruth Dennis** (1879–1968) Dancer, director, choreographer, and teacher, born in Somerville, NJ. With Ted Shawn, whom she married in 1914, she founded the Denishawn school and company (1915), and became known for her exotic, colourful, Eastern dances. >> Shawn

Sainte-Beuve, Charles Augustin [sït boev] (1804–69) Literary critic, born in Boulogne, France. He produced several volumes of poetry, critical articles, books of 'portraits' of literary contemporaries, and a novel, *Volupté* (1835).

Sainte-Claire Deville, Henri Etienne [sït klair duhveel] (1818–81) Chemist, born in St Thomas, West Indies. His interest in high temperature reactions led to the discovery of reversible changes in relative molecular mass with temperature (*dissociations*).

Saint-Evremond, Charles Marguetel de Saint Denis, seigneur de (Lord of) [sït ayvruhmõ] (1610–1703) Writer, born in St Denis le Gast, France. Known throughout W Europe for his wit, his works include the satire, *La Comédie des académistes* (1644).

Saint-Exupéry, Antoine (Marie Roger) de [sït egzü-payree] (1900–44) Airman and writer, born in Lyon, France. His philosophy of 'heroic action' is found in such novels as *Night Flight* (trans, 1931), but he is best known for his popular children's fable for adults, *The Little Prince* (trans, 1943).

Saint-Gaudens, Augustus [saynt gawdnz] (1848–1907) Sculptor, born in Dublin. His major works include Lincoln in Lincoln Park, Chicago, and the Mrs Henry Adams Memorial in Rock Creek Cemetery, Washington, DC.

Saint John, Henry >> Bolingbroke, 1st Viscount

Saint-John Perse, pseudonym of **Marie René Auguste Alexis Saint-Léger Léger** (1887–1975) Poet and diplomat, born in St Léger des Feuilles, Guadeloupe. His works include the long poem *Anabase* (1924), *Exile* (1942), *Amers* (1957), and *Chroniques* (1960). He was awarded the Nobel Prize for Literature in 1960.

Saint Joseph, John Kenneth Sinclair (1912–94) Aerial photographer and archaeologist, born in Hereford and Worcester. He helped to develop the first university department able to provide an aerial photography service, and established a valuable photographic archive.

Saint-Just, Louis (Antoine Léon Florelle) de [sï zhüst] (1767–94) French revolutionary, born in Decize, France. He was elected to the National Convention (1792), joined the Committee of Public Safety (1793), and was made president of the Convention (1794). He was a devoted follower of Robespierre, with whom he was guillotined. >> Robespierre

Saint Laurent, Louis (Stephen) [sï lohrã] (1882–1973) Canadian Liberal prime minister (1948–57), born in Compton, Quebec, Canada. He was also minister of justice and attorney general (1941–6) and minister of external affairs (1946–8).

Saint-Laurent, Yves (Henri Donat Mathieu) [sï lohrã] (1936–) Fashion designer, born in Oran, Algeria. In 1962 he opened his own house, and launched the first of his 160 Rive Gauche boutiques in 1966, selling ready-to-wear clothes.

Saint-Léger, Alexis >> Saint-John Perse

Saint Leger, Barry [selinjer, saynt lejer] (1737–89) British army colonel. He is best known as the founder of the Classic horse race at Doncaster, South Yorkshire, first run in 1776 and named after him in 1778.

Saint-Léon, (Charles Victor) Arthur [sï layõ] (1821–71) Dancer, choreographer, and violinist, born in Paris. He was ballet master with the St Petersburg Imperial Theatre (1859–69) and Paris Opéra (1863–70).

Saint Martin, Alexis >> Beaumont, William

Saint-Saëns, (Charles) Camille [sï sãs] (1835–1921) Composer and music critic, born in Paris. His many works include five symphonies, 13 operas, notably *Samson et Dalila* (1877), the popular *Carnival of the Animals* (trans, 1886), and concertos for piano, violin, and cello.

Saintsbury, George Edward Bateman [sayntsbree] (1845–1933) Literary critic and scholar, born in Southampton, Hampshire. One of the most active critics of the day, his works include *The Peace of the Augustans* (1916) and *A History of the French Novel* (1917–19).

Saint-Simon, Claude Henri de Rouvroy, comte de (Count of) [sï seemõ] (1760–1825) Social reformer, the founder of French socialism, born in Paris. His writing was a reaction against the savagery of the revolutionary period, and proclaimed a brotherhood of man in which science and technology would become a new spiritual authority.

Saint-Simon, Louis de Rouvroy, duc de (Duke of) [sï seemõ] (1675–1755) Writer, born in Paris. He joined the court of Louis XIV, and from the 1690s kept a journal, published as his *Mémoires* (1752).

Saint Vincent, John Jervis, Earl (1735–1823) British naval commander, born in Stone, Staffordshire. In 1797, during preparations for the invasion of England by French, Dutch, and Spanish fleets, he intercepted them off Cape St Vincent and totally defeated them.

Sakharov, Andrey [sakarof] (1921–89) Physicist, born in Moscow. He had a critical role in developing the Soviet hydrogen bomb, but from 1958 openly opposed nuclear weapon tests, supported human rights, and in 1975 was awarded the Nobel Peace Prize. Exiled in 1980 as a leading dissident, he was released in 1986. >> Bonner

Saki >> Munro, Hector Hugh

Saladin [saladin], in full **Salah ed-din Yussuf ibn Ayub** (1137–93) Sultan of Egypt and Syria, born in Tekrit, Mesopotamia. He defeated the crusaders in 1187, recapturing almost all their fortified places in Syria, but a further crusade captured Acre in 1191, and he was defeated.

Salam, Abdus (1926–) Theoretical physicist, born in

Jhang Maghhiana, Pakistan. In 1979 he shared the Nobel Prize for Physics for his role in work explaining both the weak nuclear force and electromagnetic interactions between elementary particles. >> Glashow; Weinberg

Salazar, António de Oliviera [salazah(r)] (1889–1970) Portuguese dictator (1932–68), born near Coimbra, Portugal. He introduced a new, authoritarian regime, the *Estado Novo* ('New State'). He was also minister of war (1936–44) and of foreign affairs (1936–47) during the Spanish Civil War.

Salchow, (Karl Emil Julius) Ulrich [salkoh] (1877–1949) Swedish figure skater, born in Copenhagen. The first man to win an Olympic gold medal for this sport (1908), he was a record 10 times world champion (1901–5, 1906–11). He originated a type of jump since named after him.

Saleh, Ali Abdullah [sale] (1942–) North Yemeni soldier and president (1978–90), and president of the Republic of Yemen (1990–). Under his leadership, the war with South Yemen was ended, and the two countries agreed to eventual re-union.

Sales, Francis of >> **Francis of Sales**

Salieri, Antonio [salyayree] (1750–1825) Composer, born in Verona, Italy. He settled in Vienna, becoming court composer (1774), and wrote over 40 operas, an oratorio, and Masses. He was a famous rival of Mozart. >> Mozart

Salinger, J(erome) D(avid) [salinjer] (1919–) Novelist and short-story writer, born in New York City. His fame rests on *The Catcher in the Rye* (1951), his only and enduringly popular novel.

Salisbury, Marquess of [sawlzbree] >> **Cecil, Robert**

Salisbury, Sir Edward James [sawlzbree] (1886–1978) Botanist, born in Harpenden, Hertfordshire. Director of the Royal Botanic Gardens, Kew (1943–56), his books include *The Reproductive Capacity of Plants* (1942).

Salisbury, John of >> **John of Salisbury**

Salk, Jonas E(dward) [sawlk] (1914–95) Virologist, born in New York City. In 1953–4 he discovered the first vaccine against poliomyelitis. >> Enders; Sabin

Salle, Jean Baptiste de La >> **La Salle, St Jean Baptiste de**

Sallé, Marie [salay] (1707–56) Dancer, born in Paris. She first performed with the Paris Opéra in 1727, and was a pioneer of dance without masks or elaborate hairstyles.

Sallinen, Aulis (1935–) Composer, born in Salmi, Finland. His works include four operas, six symphonies, chamber music, concertos, songs, and choral music.

Sallust, in full **Gaius Sallustius Crispus** (86–34 BC) Historian and Roman politician, born in Amiternum, Samnium. His major works are the histories of two wars: the *Bellum Catalinae* (43–42 BC) and the *Bellum Jugurthinum* (41–40 BC).

Salome [salohmee] (1st-c) The traditional name of the daughter of Herodias. She danced before Herod Antipas (*Mark* 6.17–28), and as a reward was given the head of John the Baptist. >> Herod Antipas; John the Baptist, St

Salote Tupou III [salohtay] (1900–65) Queen of Tonga, who succeeded her father, King George Tupou II, in 1918. She is remembered in Britain for her colourful and engaging presence during her visit for the coronation of Elizabeth II in 1953. >> Taufa'ahau Tupou IV

Saloth Sar >> **Pol Pot**

Salt, Sir Titus (1803–76) Manufacturer and benefactor, born in Morley, West Yorkshire. He started wool-spinning in 1834, and was the first to manufacture alpaca fabrics in England.

Salten, Felix [sawltn], pseudonym of **Siegmund Salzmann** (1869–1945) Novelist and essayist, born in Budapest. He is known especially for his animal stories, particularly *Bambi* (1929), which was filmed by Disney.

Salvator Rosa >> **Rosa, Salvator**

Salvi, Niccolò or **Nicola** (1697–1751) Sculptor, born in Rome. He is noted for his late Roman Baroque master-

piece, the Trevi Fountain, Rome, which was completed in 1762, after his death.

Salviati, Cecchino [salviahtee, kecheenoh], originally **Francesco de' Rossi** (1510–63) Painter, born in Florence, Italy. One of the major Italian Mannerist painters, his work is characterized by strong colour, complex figure arrangements, and spatial ambiguity, as seen in his frescoes in the Palazzo Vecchio, Florence (1544–8).

Samson (c.11th-c BC?) Biblical character, a legendary hero of the tribe of Dan. When Delilah cut his hair, breaking his Nazirite vow, he lost his great strength, and was held by the Philistines until his hair grew back and he pulled down their temple upon them (*Jud* 13–16).

Samsonov, Alexander [samsonof] (1859–1914) Russian soldier. He commanded the army which invaded East Prussia in 1914. He was decisively defeated at Tannenburg, and committed suicide.

Samudragupta [samudragupta] (?–c.380) North Indian emperor with a reputation as a warrior, poet, and musician. He epitomized the ideal king of the golden age of Hindu history.

Samuel (Heb probably 'name of God') (11th-c BC) Biblical character, the last of the judges and first of the prophets. He presided over Saul's election as the first king of Israel, but anointed David as Saul's successor, rather than Saul's own son, Jonathan. >> David; Saul

Samuel (of Mt Carmel and Toxteth), Herbert Louis Samuel, 1st Viscount (1870–1963) Liberal statesman and philosophical writer, born in Liverpool, Merseyside. He became postmaster-general (1910, 1915) and home secretary (1916, 1931–2).

Samuelson, Paul (Anthony) (1915–) Economist and journalist, born in Gary, IN. His classic publication, *Foundations of Economic Analysis* (1947), is a treatise on economic theory, for which he was awarded the Nobel Prize for Economics in 1970.

Samuelsson, Bengt Ingemar (1934–) Biochemist, born in Halmstad, Sweden. He shared the Nobel Prize for Physiology or Medicine in 1982 for discoveries concerning prostaglandins and related substances. >> Bergström

Sanchez, Francisco (c.1550–1623) Physician and philosopher, probably from Braga in Portugal. His main work is a study of philosophical scepticism, *That Nothing is Known* (trans, 1581).

Sanctorius [sangktawrius], Latin name of **Santorio Santorio** (1561–1636) Physician, born in Capodistria, Italy. He invented the clinical thermometer and other instruments, but is best known for his investigations into the fluctuations of the body's weight under different conditions.

Sand, George [sã, zhaw(r)zh], pseudonym of **Armandine Aurore Lucile Dudevant**, *née* **Dupin** (1804–76) Writer, born in Paris. She wrote over 100 books, the most successful being those describing rustic life, such as *François le champi* (1848). Her autobiographical works and letters include accounts of her notorious affairs with de Musset and Chopin. >> Chopin, Frédéric; Musset

Sandage, Allan Rex (1926–) Astronomer, born in Iowa City, IA. In 1960 he made the first optical identification of a quasar.

Sanday, Edgar >> **Faure, Edgar**

Sandburg, Carl (1878–1967) Poet, born in Galesburg, IL. He won a Pulitzer Prize in 1950 for his *Complete Poems*, and also in 1940 for a popular two-part biography on Abraham Lincoln.

Sandby, Paul (1725–1809) Painter, born in Nottingham, Nottinghamshire, the brother of Thomas Sandby. His watercolours, outlined with the pen and only finished with colour, take the purely monochrome drawing of the watercolour school one step forward. >> Sandby, Thomas

Sandby, Thomas (1721–98) Artist and architect, the brother of Paul Sandby. He built Lincoln's Inn Fields

(1776), and was joint architect of His Majesty's Works (1777). >> Sandby, Paul

Sandeman, Robert >> **Glas, John**

Sander, August (1876–1964) Photographer, born in Herdorf, Germany. In 1929 he published *Faces of Our Times*, the first part of a documentary study, but his social realism was discouraged by the Nazi Ministry of Culture in 1934.

Sandino, Augusto César [san**dee**noh] (1895–1934) Nicaraguan revolutionary, born in Niquinohome, Nicaragua. He led guerrilla resistance to USA occupation forces after 1926, and was murdered. The Nicaraguan revolutionaries of 1979 (*Sandinistas*) took him as their principal hero.

Sands, Bobby, popular name of **Robert Sands** (1954–81) Irish revolutionary, born in Belfast. Sentenced in 1977 to 14 years imprisonment after an IRA bombing attack in Northern Ireland, he went on hunger-strike at Long Kesh prison, and died after 66 days.

Sandwich, Edward Montagu, 1st Earl of (1625–72) British admiral, born in Barnwell, Northamptonshire. As ambassador to Spain (1666–9), he helped to negotiate Charles II's marriage, and escorted Catherine of Braganza to England. >> Catherine of Braganza; Charles II (of England)

Sandwich, John Montagu, 4th Earl of (1718–92) British politician, remembered as the inventor of *sandwiches*, which he devised in order to eat while playing around the clock at a gaming-table. He was First Lord of the Admiralty (1748–51, 1771–82).

Sandys, Duncan >> **Duncan-Sandys**

Sandys, George [sandz] (1578–1664) Colonist and traveller, born near York, North Yorkshire. In America he acted as treasurer of the colony of Virginia (1621–31), and made an important verse translation of Ovid's *Metamorphoses* (1626), upon which his reputation largely rests.

Sangallo, Antonio (Giamberti) da [sang**gah**loh], known as **the Younger** (1483–1546) Architect and engineer, born in Florence, Italy. He was the foremost architect of the High Renaissance in Rome, his masterpiece being the Palazzo Farnese, Rome (1534–46).

Sanger, Frederick (1918–) Biochemist, born in Rendcombe, Gloucestershire. He revealed the full sequence of the 51 amino acids in insulin, for which he was awarded the Nobel Prize for Chemistry in 1958. He then devised methods to elucidate the molecular structure of the nucleic acids, and received a second Nobel Prize for Chemistry in 1980 - the first to receive two such awards.

Sanger, Margaret (Louise), *née* **Higgins** (1883–1966) Social reformer and founder of the birth control movement, born in Corning, NY. She started the first US birth-control clinic in New York City in 1916, and founded the American Birth Control League in 1921.

Sanguinetti Cairolo, Julio María [sanggwi**nee**tee] (1936–) Uruguayan president (1984–90). A member of the long-established, progressive Colorado Party, he headed the ministries of labour and industry, and of education and culture, before becoming president in 1984.

Sankara [sangk**a**ra, shangk**a**ra] (?700–?750) Hindu philosopher and theologian, born in Kalati, Kerala. He is the most famous exponent of *Advaita* (the Vedanta school of Hindu philosophy), and the source of the main currents of modern Hindu thought.

Sankey, Ira David >> **Moody, Dwight L**

San Martín, José de [san mah(r)**teen**] (1778–1850) South American patriot, born in Yapeyú, Argentina. He played a major role in winning independence from Spain for Argentina, Chile, and Peru (1817–22).

Sanmichele, Michele [sanmi**kel**ee] (1484–1559) Architect and military engineer, born in San Michele, Italy. Noted for his treatment of military fortifications, his most important works include the Porta Nuova (1533–40) and the Porta S Zeno (1541).

Sansovino [sanso**vee**noh], originally **Andrea Contucci** (1460–1529) Religious sculptor, born in Monte Sansovino, Italy. His surviving work includes the identical tombs of Cardinal Ascanio Sforza and Girolamo Basso della Rovere, at S Maria del Popolo in Rome (1509). >> Sansovino, Jacopo

Sansovino, Jacopo [sanso**vee**noh], originally **Jacopo Tatti** (1486–1570) Sculptor and architect, born in Florence, Italy. He was responsible for bringing the High Renaissance style of his native Florence to Venice, where his notable buildings include the Library of St Mark's (1540s). >> Sansovino

Santa Anna, Antonio López de (1797–1876) Mexican soldier, president (1833–6, 1846–7, 1853–5), and dictator (1839, 1841–5), born in Jalapa, Mexico. Following the Texas revolt (1836), he defeated Texan forces at the Alamo, but was routed at San Jacinto R. He was recalled from exile in 1846 to be president during the war with the USA.

Santamaria, Bartholomew Augustine [santam**aree**a] (1915–) Political writer, born in West Brunswick, Victoria, Australia. He was a leading force against Communist influence in Australia, and in the establishment of the Democratic Labor Party.

Santander, Francisco de Paula [santan**dair**] (1792–1840) Colombian statesman, born in Rosario de Cúcuta, New Granada (modern Colombia). He acted as vice-president of Grancolombia (1821–7) during Bolívar's campaigns, and was president of New Granada (1832–7). >> Bolívar

Santayana, George [santa**yah**na], originally **Jorge Augustín Nicolás Ruiz de Santayana** (1863–1952) Philosopher, poet, and novelist, born in Madrid. He became known as a philosopher and stylist in such works as *The Life of Reason* (5 vols, 1905–6), *Realms of Being* (4 vols, 1927–40), and his novel *The Last Puritan* (1935).

Santos-Dumont, Alberto [**san**tos doo**mont**] (1873–1932) Aviation pioneer, born in Santos Dumont (formerly, Palmyra), Brazil. He experimented with heavier-than-air machines, and achieved the first officially observed powered flight in Europe in 1906.

Sapir, Edward [sa**peer**] (1884–1939) Linguist and anthropologist, born in Lauenburg, Germany. One of the founders of ethnolinguistics, he is best known for his work on the languages of the North American Indians, and for his view (developed by his pupil, Whorf) that language determines the way its speakers perceive the world (the *Sapir–Whorf hypothesis*). >> Whorf

Sapor II >> **Shapur II**

Sapper, pseudonym of **Herman Cyril McNeile** (1888–1937) Novelist, born in Bodmin, Cornwall. He achieved fame as the creator of 'Bulldog' Drummond, the aggressively patriotic hero of a series of thrillers, such as *The Final Count* (1926).

Sappho [**sa**foh] (c.610–c.580 BC) Greek poet, born in Lesbos. The most celebrated female poet of antiquity, only two of her odes are extant in full.

Sarah or **Sarai** (Heb 'princess') Biblical character, the wife and half-sister of Abraham, who is portrayed (*Gen* 12–23) as having accompanied him from Ur to Canaan. Long barren, she is said to have eventually given birth to Isaac in her old age. >> Abraham; Isaac

Sarasate (y Navascué), Pablo (Martín Melitón) [sara**sah**tay] (1844–1908) Violinist and composer, born in Pamplona, Spain. One of the greatest violinists of his day, many prominent composers wrote pieces for him.

Sardanapalus [sah(r)da**nap**alus] (7th-c BC) Legendary Assyrian king, notorious for his effeminacy and sensual lifestyle. He probably represents an amalgam of at least three Assyrian rulers, one of them being Assurbanipal. >> Assurbanipal

Sardou, Victorien [sah(r)doo] (1831–1908) Playwright, born in Paris. His plays include *A Scrap of Paper* (trans, 1860), *La Tosca* (1887), on which Puccini's opera is based, and over 60 others, many written for Sarah Bernhardt. >> Bernhardt

Sargent, John Singer [sah(r)jnt] (1856–1925) Painter, born in Florence, Italy. Most of his work was done in England, where he became the most fashionable portait painter of his age, but he also worked on decorative paintings for public buildings in the USA.

Sargent, Sir (Harold) Malcolm (Watts) [sah(r)jnt] (1895–1967) Conductor, born in Ashford, Kent. He conducted the Royal Choral Society from 1928, the Liverpool Philharmonic Orchestra (1942–8), and the BBC Symphony Orchestra (1950–7), and from 1948 was the popular leader of the London Promenade Concerts.

Sargeson, Frank [sah(r)jeson], pseudonym of **Norris Frank Davey** (1902–83) Writer, born in Hamilton, Waikato, New Zealand. He made his name with his collections of short stories, such as *Conversations with My Uncle* (1936) and *A Man and His Wife* (1940), later writing novels, including *The Hangover* (1967).

Sarich, Ralph [sarich] (c.1939–) Inventor, born in Perth, Western Australia. In 1972 he developed a working model of an orbital two-stroke reciprocating piston engine, which was developed under licence by Ford and General Motors in the USA.

Sarney (Costa), Jose (1930–) Brazilian soldier and president (1985–90), born in Maranhao state, Brazil. In 1985 he became deputy to Neves, the country's first civilian leader for 21 years, taking up the presidency on Neves' death.

Sarnoff, David (1891–1971) US entrepreneur, born in Minsk, Russia. Working for Marconi, he was the radio operator who picked up the *Titanic*'s distress calls in 1912. He later became general manager of the Radio Corporation of America (1921), set up the NBC radio network, and established the first US television service (1939).

Saroyan, William [saroyan] (1908–81) Writer, born in Fresno, CA. His first volume of short stories, *The Daring Young Man on the Flying Trapeze* (1934), was a great success, and followed by several novels and plays. He was awarded (but declined) the Pulitzer Prize for his play *The Time of Your Life* (1939).

Sarpi, Pietro [sah(r)pee], pseudonym **Pietro Soave Polano**, also known as **Fra Paolo** (1552–1623) Historian, theologian, and patriot, born in Venice, Italy. He was the champion of Venice in the dispute with Pope Paul V (reigned 1605–21) over the immunity of clergy from the jurisdiction of civil tribunals.

Sarrail, Maurice Paul Emmanuel [sariy] (1856–1929) French soldier, born in Carcassonne, France. He led the 3rd Army at the Battle of the Marne (1914), and commanded (1915–17) the Allied forces in the East (Salonica), where he deposed Constantine I of Greece. >> Constantine I (of Greece)

Sarraute, Nathalie [saroht], *née* **Nathalie Ilyanova Tcherniak** (1902–) Writer, born in Ivanova, Russia. The leading theorist of the *nouveau roman* ('new novel'), her books include *Portrait of a Man Unknown* (trans, 1947) and *The Golden Fruits* (trans, 1963).

Sarsfield, Patrick (?–1693) Soldier, born in Lucan, Co Dublin, Ireland. He drove the English out of Sligo, and was present at the Boyne (1690) and Aughrim (1691).

Sarto, Andrea del [sah(r)toh], originally **Andrea d'Agnolo** or **Andrea Vannucchi** (1486–1531) Painter, born in Florence, Italy, the son of a tailor (It *sarto* 'tailor'). He was engaged by the Servites to paint a series of frescoes for their Church of the Annunciation (1509–14).

Sarton, George (Alfred Leon) (1884–1956) Historian of science, born in Ghent, Belgium. The dominant figure of his subject, he founded its principal journal, *Isis*, in 1912, and *Osiris* in 1936. His *Introduction to the History of Science* (3 vols, 1927–48) had reached the 14th-c by the time of his death.

Sartre, Jean-Paul [sahtr] (1905–80) Existentialist philosopher and writer, born in Paris. His novels include the trilogy, *The Roads to Freedom* (1945–9), and he also wrote many plays, such as *Huis clos* (1944, trans In Camera/No Exit). His philosophy is presented in *Being and Nothingness* (trans, 1943). In 1964 he was awarded (but declined) the Nobel Prize for Literature. In the later 1960s he became heavily involved in opposition to US policies in Vietnam.

Sassau-Nguesso, Denis [sasoh ngwesoh] (1943–) Congolese soldier and president (1979–92). He strengthened the Congo's relationship with France and the USA in preference to maintaining its traditional ties with the USSR.

Sassetta, originally **Stefano do Giovanni** (?–c.1450) Painter, probably born in Siena, Italy. His finest work was the altarpiece of St Francis (1437–44), painted for S Francesco, Borgo San Sepolcro, but now dispersed.

Sassoon, Siegfried (Lorraine) [sasoon] (1886–1967) Poet and novelist, born in Brenchley, Kent. His hatred of war was fiercely expressed in his *Counterattack* (1918) and *Satirical Poems* (1926).

Satie, Erik (Alfred Leslie) [satee] (1866–1925) Composer, born in Honfleur, France. He wrote ballets, lyric dramas, and whimsical pieces which were in violent revolt against musical orthodoxy.

Saud, Ibn >> **Ibn Saud**

Sauer, Carl O(rtwin) [sower] (1889–1975) Geographer, born in Warrenton, MO. He researched the historical geography of Latin America and the relationships between human societies and plants.

Saul [sawl] (11th-c BC) Biblical character, the first king to be elected by the Israelites. He became jealous of David, his son-in-law, feuded with the priestly class, and fell in battle with the Philistines. >> David

Saunders, Dame Cicely (Mary Strode) (1918–) Founder of the modern hospice movement, born in London. She became founder (1967), medical director (1967–85), and chairman (from 1985) of St Christopher's Hospice, Sydenham.

Saussure, Ferdinand de [sohsür] (1857–1913) Linguist, the founder of modern linguistics, born in Geneva, Switzerland. The work by which he is best known, the *Course in General Linguistics* (trans, 1916), inspired a great deal of later semiology and structuralism.

Saussure, Horace Bénédict de [sohsür] (1740–99) Physicist and geologist, born in Geneva, Switzerland. A pioneer in the study of mineralogy, botany, geology, and meteorology, his observations are recorded in *Travels in the Alps* (trans, 1779–96).

Savage, Michael Joseph (1872–1940) New Zealand prime minister (1935–40), born in Benalla, Victoria, Australia. He emigrated to New Zealand in 1907. As prime minister of the first Labour government, he presided over a notable set of social reforms, and died in office.

Savage, Richard (c.1697–1743) English poet and satirist. His work includes *The Convocation* (1717) and the notable poem 'The Wanderer' (1729).

Savarin, Anthelme Brillat >> **Brillat-Savarin, Anthelme**

Savart, Félix [savah(r)] (1791–1841) Physician and physicist, born in Mézières, France. He invented *Savart's wheel* for measuring tonal vibrations, the *Savart quartz plate* for studying the polarization of light, and with Biot discovered the law (named after them) governing the relationship of a magnetic field around a conductor to the current producing it. >> Biot

Savery, Thomas (c.1650–1715) Engineer, born in Shilstone, Devon. He developed and patented a device for pumping water out of mines (1698), the first practical steam engine.

Savi, Paolo (1798–1871) Naturalist and zoologist, born in Pisa, Italy. His great work, *Ornitologia Italiana*, was published posthumously (1873–6). *Savi's warbler* is named after him.

Savigny, Friedrich Karl von [saveenyee] (1779–1861) Jurist, born in Frankfurt, Germany. Leader of the historical school of jurists, he contended that law evolved from the spirit of a people and was not made for them.

Savile, Sir Henry [savil] (1549–1622) Scholar and courtier, born in Bradley, West Yorkshire. He helped to found the Bodleian Library, and founded the Savilian chairs of mathematics and astronomy at Oxford (1619). >> Bodley

Savile, Jimmy [savil], popular name of **Sir James Wilson Vincent Saville** (1926–) Television and radio personality, born in Leeds, West Yorkshire. He achieved fame with regular appearances on *Top of the Pops* (from 1963) and as host of *Jim'll Fix It* (from 1975).

Savimbi, Jonas [savimbee] (1934–) Angolan soldier and politician. He has been leader of the Union for the Total Independence of Angola (UNITA) since its formation in 1966, much involved in civil war.

Savonarola, Girolamo [savonarohla] (1452–98) Religious and political reformer, born in Ferrara, Italy. A Dominican, his preaching began to point towards a political revolution as the means of restoring religion and morality. He was excommunicated for heresy and burned.

Savundra, Emil, originally **Michael Marion Emil Anacletus Savundranayagam** (1923–76) Convicted swindler, born in Sri Lanka. He gave himself the title 'Doctor', and perpetrated huge financial swindles in Costa Rica, Goa, Ghana, China, and Britain.

Sawchuk, Terry, popular name of **Terrance (Gordon) Sawchuck** (1929–70) Ice hockey player, born in Winnipeg, Manitoba, Canada. One of the game's greatest goaltenders (1950–70), he played with the Detroit Red Wings, Boston Bruins, Toronto Maple Leafs, Los Angeles Kings, and New York Rangers. His 103 shutouts are a National Hockey League record.

Sax, Antoine Joseph, also known as **Adolphe Sax** (1814–94) Musician and inventor, born in Dinant, France. With his father he invented (patented 1845) a valved brass wind-instrument he called the sax-horn, also the saxophone, the saxtromba, and the sax-tuba.

Saxe, (Hermann) Maurice, comte de (Count of), usually called **Marshal de Saxe** (1696–1750) Marshal of France, born in Goslar, Germany, the illegitimate son of Augustus II, King of Poland. In the War of the Austrian Succession (1740–8) he invaded Bohemia, taking Prague by storm, and later commanded in Flanders, winning victories at Fontenoy (1745), Raucoux (1746), and Lauffeld (1747). >> Augustus II

Saxe-Coburg-Gotha, Alfred Ernest Albert, Prince of [saks kohberg gotha] (1844–1900) Second son of Queen Victoria, born at Windsor Castle, Berkshire. In 1874 he married the Russian Grand Duchess Marie Alexandrovna (1853–1920), and in 1893 succeeded his uncle as reigning Duke of Saxe-Coburg-Gotha. >> Victoria

Saxo Grammaticus (Lat 'the Scholar') (c.1140–1206) Danish chronicler, born in Zealand, Denmark. He wrote the partly legendary *Gesta Danorum*, a Latin history of the Danes, in 16 books.

Saxton, Christopher, (c.1544–c.1611) Surveyor and cartographer, probably born in Sowood, West Yorkshire. His atlas of all the counties of England and Wales (1579) was the first national atlas of any country.

Say, J(ean) B(aptiste) [say] (1767–1832) Political economist, born in Lyon, France. He is best remembered for *Say's law*, which expounds the idea of supply creating its own demand, and the automatic adjustment of under- or over-production.

Say, Thomas (1787–1834) Naturalist and entomologist, born in Philadelphia, PA. His works include *American Entomology* (1824–8) and *American Conchology* (1830–4).

Sayce, Archibald H(enry) (1845–1933) Philologist, born in Gloucester, Gloucestershire. He wrote on biblical criticism and Assyriology, including an *Assyrian Grammar* (1872) and *Principles of Comparative Philology* (1874–75).

Sayers, Dorothy L(eigh) (1893–1957) Writer, born in Oxford, Oxfordshire. She became a celebrated writer of detective stories, introducing her hero Lord Peter Wimsey in *Clouds of Witness* (1926), and later earned a reputation as a leading Christian apologist with her plays, radio broadcasts, and essays.

Sayers, Gale (1943–) Player of American football, born in Wichita, KS. He achieved many records as running back with the Chicago Bears (1965–72), and later became a coach.

Sayers, James (1912–) British physicist. In 1949 he was given a government award for his work on the cavity magnetron valve, of great importance in the development of radar.

Sayers, Peig [peg] (1873–1958) Gaelic story-teller, born in Dunquin, Co Kerry, Ireland. Her traditional narratives are recorded in *Peig* (1935) and *An Old Woman's Reflections* (1939, trans 1962).

Sayers, Tom, known as **the Little Wonder** and **the Napoleon of the Prize Ring** (1826–65) Boxer, born in London. He became English heavyweight champion in 1857, and throughout his career he lost only one fight.

Scales, Prunella (Margaret Rumney) (1945–) Actress, born in Abinger, Surrey. She has made numerous appearances in the West End, becoming widely known for her television roles in the comedy series *Fawlty Towers* (1975, 1978) and *After Henry* (1988, 1990). >> Cleese

Scaliger, Joseph Justus [skalijer] (1540–1609) Scholar, born in Agen, France, the son of Julius Caesar Scaliger. A classical linguist and historian, he is best known for his *Opus de emendatione temporum* (1583), a study of earlier methods of calculating time. >> Scaliger, Julius Caesar

Scaliger, Julius Caesar [skalijer], originally **Benedetto Bordone** (1484–1558) Humanist scholar, born in Riva, Italy. He wrote learned works on grammar, philosophy, botany, zoology, and literary criticism, notably *Poetice* (1561).

Scarfe, Gerald (1936–) Cartoonist, born in London. His cartoons, based on extreme distortion in the tradition of Gillray, have appeared in several periodicals and newspapers, notably *The Sunday Times*. >> Gillray

Scargill, Arthur (1938–) Trade unionist, born in Leeds, West Yorkshire. He became president of the National Union of Mineworkers in 1982, and is primarily known for his strong, socialist defence of British miners, especially during the miners' strike of 1984–5.

Scarlatti, (Pietro) Alessandro (Gaspare) [skah(r)latee] (1660–1725) Composer, born in Palermo, Sicily. He reputedly wrote over 100 operas (of which 40 survive complete), 10 Masses, c.700 cantatas, and oratorios, motets, and madrigals. >> Scarlatti, Domenico

Scarlatti, (Giuseppe) Domenico [skah(r)latee] (1685–1757) Composer, born in Naples, Italy, the son of Alessandro Scarlatti. He was a skilled harpsichordist, and is mainly remembered for the 555 sonatas written for this instrument. >> Scarlatti, Alessandro

Scarron, Paul [skarõ] (1610–60) Writer, born in Paris. He wrote many sonnets, madrigals, songs, and epistles, as well as a realistic novel, *The Comic Novel* (trans, 1651–7). In 1652 he married Françoise d'Aubigné (later, Madame de Maintenon). >> Maintenon

Scarry, Richard (McClure) (1919–94) Illustrator and writer of children's books, born in Boston, MA. His many titles include *What Do People Do All Day?* (1968) and *Hop Aboard, Here We Go!* (1972).

Schacht, (Horace Greely) Hjalmar [shahkht] (1877–1970) Financier, born in Tinglev, Germany. He was minister of economics (1934–7), but in 1939 was dismissed from his bank office for disagreeing with Hitler over rearmament expenditure, and interned by the Nazis.

Schaefer, Vincent (Joseph) [shayfer] (1906–93) Physicist, born in Schenectady, NY. He worked on the problem of icing on aeroplane wings, which led him in 1946 to demonstrate for the first time the possibility of inducing rainfall by seeding clouds with dry ice.

Schall (von Bell), (Johann) Adam [shahl] (1591–1666) Jesuit missionary and astronomer, born in Cologne, Germany. He went to China in 1622, where he was appointed to translate astronomical books and reform the Chinese calendar.

Schally, Andrew Victor [shalee] (1926–) Biochemist, born in Wilno, Poland. He discovered and synthesized the hormones that control the pituitary gland, for which he shared the Nobel Prize for Physiology or Medicine in 1977.

Scharnhorst, Gerhard Johann David von [shah(r)n-haw(r)st] (1755–1813) Prussian general, born in Bordenau, Germany. He worked with Gneisenau to reform the Prussian army after its defeat by Napoleon, and was fatally wounded fighting the French at Lützen. >> Gneisenau; Napoleon I

Scharwenka, Xaver [shah(r)vengka] (1850–1924) Pianist and composer, born near Posen, Germany. In 1881 he started a music school in Berlin, and spent the years 1891–98 in New York City directing the Scharwenka Music School.

Schaudinn, Fritz (Richard) [showdin] (1871–1906) Zoologist and microbiologist, born in Röseningken, Germany. He demonstrated the amoebic nature of tropical dysentery, and discovered the spirochaete *Treponema Pallidum* which causes syphilis (1905).

Schaufuss, Peter [showfus] (1949–) Ballet dancer and director, born in Copenhagen. He danced for various companies in London, New York, and Canada, then became artistic director of the London Festival Ballet (1984), and director of ballet at the Deutsche Oper, Berlin (1990).

Schawlow, Arthur (Leonard) [showloh] (1921–) Physicist, born in Mount Vernon, NY. With his brother-in-law, Charles Townes, he devised the laser, and shared the Nobel Prize for Physics in 1981 for his work in spectroscopy. >> Bloembergen; Maiman; Townes

Scheel, Walter [shayl] (1919–) West German president (1974–9), born in Solingen, Germany. He was also minister for economic co-operation (1961–6) and foreign minister (1969–74).

Scheele, Carl Wilhelm [sheeluh] (1742–86) Chemist, born in Stralsund, Germany. Among his major discoveries were oxygen (1772), which he called 'fire air', chlorine (1774), glycerine, and hydrogen sulphide, as well as several types of acid.

Scheer, Reinhard [sheer] (1863–1928) German naval commander, born in Obernkirchen, Germany. He commanded the 2nd Battle Squadron of the German High Seas fleet at the outset of World War 1, and was commander-in-chief at the indecisive Battle of Jutland (1916).

Scheidemann, Philipp [shiyduhman] (1865–1939) Social Democratic politician, born in Kassel, Germany. He became minister of finance and colonies in the provisional government of 1918, and was the first chancellor of the republic in 1919.

Scheler, Max [shayler] (1874–1928) Philosopher and social theorist, born in Munich. He developed a distinctive version of phenomenology which he set out in his major work, *Formalism in Ethics and the Material Value Ethics* (trans, 1921).

Schelling, Friedrich (Wilhelm Joseph) von [sheling] (1775–1854) Philosopher, born in Leonberg, Germany. His early work culminated in his *System of Transcendental Idealism* (trans, 1800), an important influence on Romanticism.

Schepisi, Fred [skepsee] (1939–) Film director, born in Melbourne, Victoria, Australia. In the USA his films include *Barbarosa* (1982), *The Iceman* (1984), *A Cry in the Dark* (1988), and *The Russia House* (1991).

Schiaparelli, Elsa [skyaparelee] (1896–1973) Fashion designer, born in Rome. Her designs were inventive and sensational, and she was noted for her use of colour, including 'shocking pink', and her original use of traditional fabrics.

Schiaparelli, Giovanni (Virginio) [skyaparelee] (1835–1910) Astronomer, born in Savigliano, Italy. He discovered the asteroid Hesperia, and termed vague linear features on Mars as 'canals' (1877).

Schiele, Egon [sheeluh] (1890–1918) Painter, born in Tulln, Austria. He developed a powerful form of Expressionism in which figures, often naked and emaciated, fill the canvas with awkward, anguished gestures.

Schillebeeckx, Edward (Cornelis Florentius Alfons) [skilebeeks] (1914–) Theologian, born in Antwerp, Belgium. He has attracted Vatican investigations for questioning received interpretations of doctrine and Church order, as in *The Church with a Human Face* (1985). >> Küng

Schiller, (Johann Christoph) Friedrich (von) [shiler] (1759–1805) Historian, playwright, and poet, born in Marbach, Germany. He began to write *Sturm und Drang* ('storm and stress') verse and plays. His poem *An die Freude* (Ode to Joy) was later set to music by Beethoven in his Choral Symphony). During his last decade he wrote the dramatic trilogy, *Wallenstein* (1796–9), *Maria Stuart* (1800), and *Wilhelm Tell* (1804).

Schimper, Andreas (Franz Wilhelm) [shimper] (1856–1901) German botanist, born in Strasbourg, France. Noted as a plant geographer, he divided the continents into floral regions, and in 1880 established that starch is a source of stored energy for plants.

Schinkel, Karl Friedrich [shingkl] (1781–1841) Architect, born in Neuruppin, Germany. He designed a wide range of buildings, in Classical style, and introduced new streets and squares in Berlin.

Schirach, Baldur von [sheerakh] (1907–74) Nazi politician, born in Berlin. He founded and organized the Hitler Youth (1933), of which he was leader until 1940. At Nuremberg he was found guilty of the mass deportation of Jews, and sentenced to 20 years' imprisonment.

Schlegel, August Wilhelm von [shlaygl] (1767–1845) Poet and critic, born in Hanover, Germany. A leading figure of the Romantic movement, he is famous for his translations of Shakespeare and other authors, and for founding Sanskrit studies in Germany. >> Schlegel, Karl Wilhelm Friedrich von

Schlegel, Karl Wilhelm Friedrich von [shlaygl] (1772–1829) Writer and critic, born in Hanover, Germany, the brother of August von Schlegel. He wrote widely on comparative literature and philology, his works inspiring the early German Romantic movement. >> Schlegel, August Wilhelm von

Schleicher, August [shliykher] (1821–68) Philologist, born in Meiningen, Germany. His major work is *A Compendium of the Comparative Grammar of the Indo-European, Sanskrit, Greek and Latin Languages* (trans, 1861–2).

Schleicher, Kurt von [shliykher] (1882–1934) German soldier and politician, born in Brandenburg, Germany. He succeeded von Papen as chancellor, but his failure to obtain dictatorial control provided Hitler with an opportunity to seize power in 1933, and he was murdered. >> Hitler; Papen

Schleiermacher, Friedrich (Ernst Daniel) [shliyermahkher] (1768–1834) Theologian and philosopher, born in Breslau, Germany. He was a leader of the movement which led to the union in 1817 of the Lutheran and Reformed Churches in Prussia, and is generally held to be the founder of modern Protestant theology.

Schlemmer, Oskar [shlemer] (1888–1943) Painter, sculptor, designer, dancer, and theorist, born in Stuttgart, Germany. He developed his notions of theatre as a mix of colour, light, form, space, and motion, using puppet-like human figures as the centrepiece ('architectonic dances').

Schlesinger, Arthur M(eier) [shlezinjer] (1888–1965) Historian, born in Xenia, OH. His most important work is *New Viewpoints in American History* (1922), in which he emphasized social and cultural history, and he later wrote *History of American Life* (13 vols, 1928–43). >> Schlesinger, Arthur M, Jr

Schlesinger, Arthur M(eier), Jr [shlezinjer] (1917–) Historian, born in Columbus, OH. Special assistant to President Kennedy (1961–3), his publications include *The Age of Jackson* (1945) and *A Thousand Days: John F Kennedy in the White House* (1965), both Pulitzer prizewinners. >> Kennedy, John F; Schlesinger, Arthur M

Schlesinger, John [shlezinjer] (1926–) Film director, born in London. His many films include *A Kind of Loving* (1962), *Billy Liar* (1963), *Midnight Cowboy* (1969, Oscar), *Marathon Man* (1976), and *Honky Tonk Freeway* (1980).

Schlick, Moritz [shlik] (1882–1936) Philosopher, born in Berlin. One of the leaders of the Vienna Circle of logical positivists, he was also an early exponent of Einstein's relativity theories. >> Einstein

Schlieffen, Alfred, Graf von (Count of) [shleefn] (1833–1913) Prussian field marshal, born in Berlin. As chief of general staff (1891–1905), he advocated the plan, which bears his name (1895), on which German tactics were unsuccessfully based in World War 1.

Schliemann, Heinrich [shleeman] (1822–90) Archaeologist, born in Neubukow, Germany. He hoped to find the site of the Homeric poems by excavating the tell at Hisarlik in Asia Minor, the traditional site of Troy, and from 1871 discovered nine superimposed city sites.

Schlüter, Poul (Holmskov) [shlüter] (1929–) Danish prime minister (1982–). His centre-right coalition survived the 1987 and 1990 elections, after which he reconstituted the coalition with Liberal support.

Schmelzer, Johann Heinrich [shmeltser] (1623–80) Composer, born in Scheibbs, Austria. The first to adapt the tunes of the Viennese street musicians and Tyrolean peasants to the more sophisticated instrumental styles of the court, he is often regarded as the true father of the Viennese waltz.

Schmidt, Bernhard Voldemar [shmit] (1879–1935) Astronomer, born in Naissaar, Estonia. In 1929 he devised a new mirror system for reflecting telescopes which overcame previous problems of aberration of the image, and which is now widely used in astronomy.

Schmidt, Franz [shmit] (1874–1939) Composer, born in Pressburg, Austria. His works include four symphonies, an oratorio, two operas, two piano concertos for the left-hand alone, and chamber and organ music.

Schmidt, Helmut (Heinrich Waldemar) [shmit] (1918–) West German chancellor (1974–82), born in Hamburg, Germany. He was minister of defence (1969–72) and of finance (1972–4), and succeeded Brandt as chancellor, describing his aim as the 'political unification of Europe in partnership with the United States'. >> Brandt, Willy

Schmidt, Maarten [shmit] (1929–) Astronomer, born in Groningen, The Netherlands. He studied the spectrum of quasars, discovering their massive red shifts, and that the number of quasars increases with distance from Earth, thus providing evidence for the 'big bang' theory.

Schmidt, Wilhelm [shmit] (1868–1954) Ethnologist, born in Hörde, Germany. He sought to develop and refine Graebner's system of *Kulturkreise* or trait clusters, proposing a theory of devolution to counter that of cultural evolution. >> Graebner

Schmidt-Rottluff, Karl [shmit rotluhf] (1884–1976) Painter and print-maker, born in Rottluff, Germany. A founder member of the avant-garde group, *Die Brücke* (1905), he developed a harsh, angular style exemplified in such woodcuts as 'Woman with Hat' (1905).

Schnabel, Artur [shnahbl] (1882–1951) Pianist and composer, born in Lipnik, Austria. An authoritative player of a small range of German classics, notably Beethoven, Mozart, and Schubert, he also wrote chamber music and piano works.

Schnittke, Alfred [shnitkuh] (1934–) Composer, born near Saratov, Russia. His compositions, known for their eclectic style, include four symphonies, concertos, ballets, film scores, and chamber, vocal, choral, and piano works.

Schnitzer, Eduard >> Emin Pasha

Schnitzler, Arthur [shnitsler] (1862–1931) Playwright and novelist, born in Vienna. His highly psychological, often strongly erotic works include his one-act play cycles *Anatol* (1893) and *Reigen* (1900; filmed as *La Ronde*, 1950).

Schoenberg, Arnold [shoenberg], also spelled **Schönberg** (1874–1951) Composer, born in Vienna. His *Chamber Symphony* caused a riot at its first performance in 1907 through its abandonment of the traditional concept of tonality, and he became known for his concept of '12-note' or 'serial' music, used in most of his later works.

Schoenheimer, Rudolf [shoenhiymer] (1898–1941) Biochemist, born in Berlin. He used two new isotopes to trace biochemical pathways, and the methods he pioneered have since been used with a variety of isotopic tracers in a range of biochemical studies.

Schöffer, Peter [shoefer] (c.1425–1502) Printer, born in Gernsheim, Germany. He took over the Gutenberg printing works, and with his father-in-law, Johann Fust, completed the Gutenberg Bible (1456) and issued the *Mainz Psalter* (1457). >> Fust; Gutenberg, Johannes

Scholes, Percy Alfred [skohlz] (1877–1958) Musicologist, born in Leeds, West Yorkshire. He became the first music adviser to the BBC, and edited *The Oxford Companion to Music* (1938).

Scholl, William (1882–1968) US physician and businessman. He patented an arch support and founded his manufacturing company (1904), bringing a scientific basis to shoe fitting.

Schomberg, Frederick Hermann, Duke of [shomberg] (1615–90) Soldier of fortune, born in Heidelberg, Germany. During the Thirty Years War he fought for the Dutch (1634–7), then with the French (1652–4) and the Portuguese (1660–8), and under William of Orange in the English expedition (1688), serving as commander-in-chief in Ireland. >> William III

Schomburgk, Sir Robert Hermann [shomboork] (1804–65) Explorer and surveyor, born in Freyburg am der Unstrut, Germany. Sent to explore British Guiana (1835), he drew the *Schomburgk line* marking its boundary (1841–3).

Schönberg, Arnold >> Schoenberg, Arnold

Schongauer or **Schön, Martin** [shongower, shoen] (1450–91) Painter and engraver, born in Colmar, France. His famous 'Madonna of the Rose Garden' altarpiece (1473, Colmar, S Martin) is regarded as one of the best early representations of the Virgin.

Schoolcraft, Henry Rowe (1793-1864) Ethnologist, born in Albany Co, NY. His main work is *Information Respecting the Indian Tribes of the US* (6 vols, 1851-7).

Schopenhauer, Arthur [shohpenhower] (1788-1860) Philosopher, born in Gdańsk, Poland. His chief work, *The World as Will and Idea* (trans, 1819) emphasizes the central role of human will as the creative factor in understanding. A collection of his writings, published as *Parerga und Paralipomena* (1851), influenced existentialism and other philosophical movements.

Schouten, Willem Corneliszoon [showten] (c.1580-1625) Navigator, born in Hoorn, The Netherlands. He was the first European to traverse Drake Passage (1615), and to discover Cape Horn (1616), named after his birthplace.

Schreiber, Lady Charlotte Elizabeth [shriyber], née **Bertie** (1812-95) Scholar and collector, born in Uffington, Lincolnshire. She is best known for her part in translating and editing the Welsh stories, *The Mabinogion* (1838-49).

Schreiner, Olive (Emilie Albertina) [shriyner], pseudonym **Ralph Iron** (1855-1920) Writer, born in Wittebergen, South Africa. *The Story of an African Farm* (1883) was the first sustained, imaginative work in English to come from Africa.

Schrieffer, John (Robert) [shreefer] (1931-   ) Physicist, born in Oak Park, IL. Collaboration with Bardeen and Cooper led to the BCS (Bardeen-Cooper-Schrieffer) theory of superconductivity, for which they shared the Nobel Prize for Physics in 1972. >> Bardeen; Cooper, Leon

Schrödinger, Erwin [shroedinger] (1887-1961) Physicist, born in Vienna. He originated the study of the wave behaviour of matter within quantum mechanics with his celebrated wave equation (1926), and shared the Nobel Prize for Physics in 1933.

Schubert, Franz (Peter) [shoobert] (1797-1828) Composer, born in Vienna. His major works include the Trout Piano Quintet (1819), the C major symphony (1825), and the B minor symphony (1822), known as the 'Unfinished'. He is particularly remembered as the greatest exponent of German songs (*Lieder*), which number c.600.

Schultz, Theodore (William) [shults] (1902-   ) Economist, born in Arlington, SD. He shared the Nobel Prize for Economics in 1979 for his work stressing the importance of the human factor in agriculture.

Schultze, Max (Johann Sigismund) [shultzuh] (1825-74) Zoologist, born in Freiburg, Germany. His best-known work is on unicellular organisms, and in 1861 he argued that cells in general contain a nucleus and protoplasm as 'the basis of life'.

Schulz, Charles (Monroe) [shults] (1922-   ) Strip cartoonist, born in Minneapolis, MN. In 1950 his sample strip about children was taken up by United Features and titled *Peanuts*, since adapted for television and stage.

Schumacher, E F [shoomaker] (1911-77) German economist. He served as economic adviser to the British Control Commission in Germany (1946-50), and with the National Coal Board (1950-70).

Schumacher, Kurt (Ernst Karl) [shoomakher] (1895-1953) German statesman, born in Kulm, Germany. In 1946 he became chairman of the Social Democratic Party and of the parliamentary group of the Bundestag.

Schuman, Robert [shooman] (1886-1963) French prime minister (1947-8), born in Luxembourg. As foreign minister (1948-52) he proposed the *Schuman plan* (1950) for pooling the coal and steel resources of West Europe, which came to fruition in the European Coal and Steel Community.

Schuman, William (Howard) [shooman] (1910-92) Composer, born in New York City. In 1943 he received the first Pulitzer Prize to be awarded to a composer. His works include 10 symphonies, concertos for piano and violin, and several ballets, as well as choral and orchestral works.

Schumann, Clara (Josephine) [shooman], née **Wieck** (1819-96) Pianist and composer, born in Leipzig, Germany. Her compositions include chamber music, songs, and many piano works, including a concerto. She married Robert Schumann in 1840. >> Schumann, Robert

Schumann, Elisabeth [shooman] (1885-1952) Operatic soprano and *Lieder* singer, born in Merseburg, Germany. In 1919 she was engaged by Richard Strauss for the Vienna State Opera, and later specialized in *Lieder*. >> Strauss, Richard

Schumann, Robert (Alexander) [shooman] (1810-56) Composer, born in Zwickau, Germany. He produced a large number of compositions for piano, then married Clara Wieck, and under her influence began to write orchestral works, notably his A minor piano concerto (1845) and four symphonies. He also wrote chamber music and a large number of songs (*Lieder*). >> Schumann, Clara

Schumann-Heink, Ernestine [shooman hiyngk], née **Rossler** (1861-1936) Contralto, born near Prague. Having come to fame in Europe, especially for her Wagnerian roles, she made her US debut in Chicago in 1898, singing regularly with the Metropolitan Opera until 1932.

Schurz, Carl [shoorts] (1829-1906) Journalist and political reformer, born in Liblar, Germany. He arrived in the USA in 1852, and became a journalist, senator (1869-75), and secretary of the interior (1877-81).

Schuschnigg, Kurt von [shushnik] (1897-1977) Austrian chancellor (1934-8), born in Riva, Italy (formerly Austria-Hungary). He was elected a Christian Socialist Deputy (1927), and became minister of justice (1932) and of education (1933). His attempt to prevent Hitler occupying Austria led to his imprisonment until 1945.

Schuster, Sir Arthur [shuster] (1851-1934) Physicist, born in Frankfurt, Germany. He carried out important pioneer work in spectroscopy and terrestrial magnetism. The *Schuster-Smith magnetometer* is the standard instrument for measuring the Earth's magnetic force.

Schütz, Heinrich [shüts], Lat **Heinricus Sagittarius** (1585-1672) Composer, born in Köstritz, Germany. Regarded as the founder of the Baroque school of German music, his compositions include church music, psalms, motets, passions, a German requiem, and the first German opera, *Dafne* (1627).

Schutz, Alfred [shuts] (1899-1959) Social philosopher, born in Vienna. He reacted against the positivism and behaviourism of the Vienna Circle, producing *The Phenomenology of the Social World* (trans, 1932).

Schuyler, Philip John [skiyler] (1733-1804) US soldier and politician, born in Albany, NY. He was a member of Congress (1777-81), and became state senator (1780-97), US senator (1789-91, 1797-8), and surveyor-general of New York (from 1782).

Schwann, Theodor [shvahn] (1810-82) Physiologist, born in Neuss, Germany. He discovered the enzyme pepsin, demonstrated the role of micro-organisms in putrefaction, and extended the cell theory from plants to animal tissues, thus founding modern histology.

Schwartz, Delmore [shvaw(r)ts] (1913-66) Writer and critic, born in New York City. He became known with his first book of stories and poems, *In Dreams Begin Responsibilities* (1938). His collection of short stories, *The World is a Wedding* (1948), deals with the problems of Jewish life in America.

Schwarz, Harvey (Fisher) [shvaw(r)ts] (1905-88) Electrical engineer, born in Edwardsville, IL. During World War 2, working for Decca, he helped to develop a prototype radio-navigation system that was put into operation for the first time during the D-Day landings in 1944.

Schwarzenberg, Karl Philipp, Fürst zu (Prince of) [shvah(r)tsenberg] (1771–1820) Austrian soldier and diplomat, born in Vienna. He conducted the negotiations for the marriage between Napoleon and Marie Louise of Austria (1810), and commanded the allied armies which won the Battles of Dresden and Leipzig (1813). >> Marie Louise; Napoleon I

Schwarzkopf, (Olga Maria) Elisabeth (Friederike) [shvah(r)tskopf] (1915–) Soprano, born in Janotschin, Poland. She sang in the Vienna State Opera (1944–8) and at Covent Garden (1949–52). She first specialized in coloratura roles, and later appeared more as a lyric soprano, especially in recitals of *Lieder*.

Schwarzkopf, H Norman [shvah(r)tskopf], nickname **Stormin' Norman** (1934–) US general, born in Trenton, NJ. In 'Operation Desert Storm' (1991), he commanded the Allied forces that liberated Kuwait from the Iraqi occupation led by Saddam Hussein. >> Hussein, Saddam

Schwarzschild, Karl [shvah(r)tsshild] (1873–1916) Theoretical astrophysicist, born in Frankfurt, Germany. He computed exact solutions of Einstein's field equations in general relativity, which led to modern research on black holes. The *Schwarzschild radius* is the critical radius at which an object becomes a black hole if collapsed or compressed indefinitely.

Schweitzer, Albert [shviytser] (1875–1965) Medical missionary, theologian, musician, and philosopher, born in Kaysersberg, Germany. In 1896 he made his famous decision that he would live for science and art until he was 30, then devote his life to serving humanity. True to his vow, despite his international reputation in music and theology, he began to study medicine in 1905, and after qualifying (1913) set up a hospital to fight leprosy and sleeping sickness at Lambaréné, French Equatorial Africa, where he remained for the rest of his life. He was awarded the Nobel Peace Prize in 1952.

Schwenkfeld (von Ossig), Kaspar [shvengkfelt] (1489–1561) Writer and preacher, born in Ossig, Germany. His doctrines resembled those of the Quakers, and brought him banishment and persecution, but he gained many followers, some of whom went to Pennsylvania (in the 1730s), where they formed the *Schwenkfelder Church*.

Schwimmer, Rosika [shvimer] (1877–1948) Feminist and pacifist, born in Budapest. She became vice-president of the Women's International League for Peace and Freedom. In 1920 she emigrated to the USA, where she continued to campaign for pacifism.

Schwinger, Julian (Seymour) [shwingger] (1918–94) Physicist, born in New York City. He shared the Nobel Prize for Physics in 1965 for his independent work on quantum electrodynamics.

Schwitters, Kurt [shviterz] (1887–1948) Artist, born in Hanover, Germany. He joined the Dadaists, and developed 'Merz', a form of collage using such everyday detritus as broken glass, tram tickets, and scraps of paper.

Sciascia, Leonardo [shiashia] (1921–89) Novelist, born in Racalmuto, Sicily. His novels, which take Sicily as a focus, include (trans titles) *Salt in the Wound* (1956), *The Council of Egypt* (1963), and *To Each His Own* (1968).

Scicolone, Sofia >> **Loren, Sophia**

Scipio Africanus [skipioh], in full **Publius Cornelius Scipio Africanus**, also called **Scipio Africanus Major** (236–c.183 BC) Innovative Roman general of the Second Punic War. His victory at Ilipa (206 BC) forced the Carthaginians out of Spain, and his defeat of Hannibal at Zama (202 BC) broke the power of Carthage altogether. >> Hannibal

Scipio Aemilianus [skipioh aymiliahnus], in full **Scipio Aemilianus Publius Cornelius**, also called **Scipio Africanus Minor** (185–129 BC) Roman statesman, general, and orator, the adopted grandson of Scipio Africanus Major. He is famous primarily for the sack of Carthage in the Third Punic War (146 BC), the destruction of Numantia (133 BC), and his patronage of the arts. >> Scipio Africanus

Scofield, (David) Paul [skohfeeld] (1922–) Actor, born in Hurstpierpoint, West Sussex. In the 1940s he began to distinguish himself in Shakespearian roles, and later starred in *King Lear* (1962), *Othello* (1980), and as Sir Thomas More in *A Man For All Seasons* (1960; filmed 1966).

Scopas [skohpas] (c.4th-c BC) Sculptor, from the Greek island of Paros. He is traditionally believed to have worked on the Temple of Athena Alea at Tegea, the temple of Artemis at Ephesus, and the Mausoleum at Halicarnassus.

Scorel, Jan van [skorel] (1495–1562) Painter, architect, and engineer, born in Schoorel, The Netherlands. He established the style of the Italian Renaissance in Holland, and became noted for his portraiture.

Scoresby, William (1789–1857) Arctic explorer, born near Whitby, North Yorkshire. He wrote *The Arctic Regions* (1820), the first scientific accounts of the Arctic seas and lands, and in 1822 surveyed the E coast of Greenland.

Scorsese, Martin [skaw(r)sayzee] (1942–) Film director, writer, and producer, born in Flushing, Long Island, NY. His many films include *Taxi Driver* (1976), *Raging Bull* (1980), the controversial *The Last Temptation of Christ* (1988), and *The Age of Innocence* (1993).

Scott, Alexander (c.1525–c.1584) Lyrical poet from Scotland. Regarded as one of the last of the *makaris* (poets of the 14th-c who used the old Scottish metrical forms), he wrote 35 short poems, which appear in the Bannatyne Manuscript (1568).

Scott, C(harles) P(restwich) (1846–1932) Newspaper editor, born in Bath, Somerset. He bought *The Manchester Guardian* in 1905 (known as *The Guardian* since 1959), and as editor raised it to be a rival of *The Times*.

Scott, Cyril Meir (1879–1970) Composer, born in Oxton, Cheshire. Best known for his piano pieces and songs, other compositions include an opera, three symphonies, piano, violin, and cello concertos, and many choral and orchestral works.

Scott, Dunkinfield Henry (1854–1934) Botanist, born in London, the son of George Gilbert Scott. He collaborated with **William Crawford Williamson** (1816–95) in a number of notable studies of fossil plants, and established in 1904 the class Pteridospermeae. >> Scott, George Gilbert

Scott, Francis George (1880–1958) Composer, born in Hawick, Borders, Scotland. His *Scottish Lyrics* (5 vols, 1921–39) comprise original settings of songs by Dunbar, Burns, and other poets. Primarily a song composer, he also wrote several orchestral works.

Scott, Sir George Gilbert (1811–78) Architect, born in Gawcott, Buckinghamshire. He became the leading practical architect of the British Gothic revival, as seen in the Albert Memorial (1862–3), St Pancras Station and Hotel in London (1865), and Glasgow University (1865).

Scott, Sir Giles Gilbert (1880–1960) Architect, born in London, the grandson of George Gilbert Scott. His designs include the Anglican cathedral in Liverpool (begun 1904), the new Bodleian Library at Oxford (1936–46), and the new Waterloo Bridge (1939–45). >> Scott, George Gilbert

Scott, Mackay Hugh Baillie (1865–1945) Architect and designer, born in Kent. He designed the decoration for the palace of the Grand Duke of Hesse at Darmstadt. His furniture is simple, solid, bold, and generally decorated with a degree of Art Nouveau ornamentation.

Scott, Michael (1907–83) British missionary and political activist. He served in various missions in South Africa (1943–50), where he exposed atrocities, defended the Basutos against wrongful arrest, and brought the case of the dispossessed Herero tribe before the UN.

Scott, Paul (Mark) (1920–78) Novelist, born in London.

His reputation is based on four novels collectively known as *The Raj Quartet* (1966–74), which detailed the British withdrawal from India. The quartet was adapted for the Granada television series *The Jewel in the Crown* (1982).

Scott, Sir Percy Moreton (1853–1924) British naval commander and gunnery expert, born in London. He became gunnery adviser to the Royal Navy, and commanded the anti-aircraft defences of London (1915–18), his methods and inventions transforming naval gunnery.

Scott, Sir Peter (Markham) (1909–89) Artist, ornithologist, and broadcaster, born in London, the son of Robert Falcon Scott. He began to exhibit his paintings of bird scenes in 1933, and led several ornithological expeditions in the 1950s. His writing and television programmes helped to popularize natural history. >> Scott, R F

Scott, R(obert) F(alcon) (1868–1912) Antarctic explorer, born in Devonport, Devon. In 1910 he led an expedition to the South Pole (17 Jan 1912), only to discover that the Norwegian expedition under Amundsen had beaten them by a month. All members of his party died. >> Amundsen; Scott, Peter

Scott, Ronnie (1927–) Jazz saxophonist and night club owner, born in London. In 1959 he opened a club in the Soho district of London, and it quickly became an international jazz centre.

Scott, Sheila, originally **Sheila Christine Hopkins** (1927–88) Aviator, born in Worcester, Hereford and Worcester. In 1966 she broke the around-the-world record with the longest solo flight of 49 910 km/31 014 mi.

Scott, Sir Walter (1771–1832) Novelist and poet, born in Edinburgh. His ballads, such as *The Border Minstrelsy* (1802), made him the most popular author of the day. His historical novels fall into three groups: those set in the background of Scottish history, from *Waverley* (1814) to *A Legend of Montrose* (1819); a group which takes up themes from the Middle Ages and Reformation times, from *Ivanhoe* (1819) to *The Talisman* (1825); and his remaining books, from *Woodstock* (1826) until his death.

Scott, William (1913–89) Painter, born in Greenock, Strathclyde. His preferred subject was still-life, painted in a simplified, nearly abstract way.

Scott, Winfield (1786–1866) US soldier, born in Petersburg, VA. He became chief commander of the army in 1841, put Santa Anna to flight, and entered the Mexican capital in triumph (1847). >> Santa Anna

Scott, Dred (c.1795–c.1858) Slave, born in Southampton Co, VA. He made legal and constitutional history in the *Dred Scott Case* (1848–57), which sought to obtain his freedom on the ground that his master took him from Missouri (a slave state) to Illinois (a free state). The Supreme Court ruled against him, but the decision served to increase anti-slavery agitation in the North.

Scotus >> Duns Scotus; Erigena

Scriabin, Alexander Nikolayevich [skryahbyin] (1872–1915) Composer and pianist, born in Moscow. His compositions include three symphonies, two tone poems, and 10 sonatas.

Scribe, (Augustin) Eugène [skreeb] (1791–1861) Playwright, born in Paris. His best-known plays are *The Glass of Water* (trans, 1840), *Adrienne Lecouvreur* (1848), and *Battle of the Ladies* (trans, 1851). He also wrote novels and composed the libretti for 60 operas.

Scriblerus >> Arbuthnot, John

Scribner, Charles, originally **Charles Scrivener** (1821–71) Publisher, born in New York City. In 1846 he co-founded the publishing firm which became Charles Scribner's Sons from 1878. He also founded *Scribner's Monthly* (1870–81), which later became *Scribner's Magazine* (1887–1939).

Scrutton, Sir Thomas Edward (1856–1934) Legal textwriter and judge, born in London. *The Contract of Affreigt-*

ment as Expressed in Charter-parties and Bills of Lading (1886) has become a standard text. He was a judge of the Court of Appeal (1916–34).

Scudéry, Madeleine de [skoodayree] (1607–1701) Novelist, born in Le Havre, France. Her best-known work is *Artamène, ou le Grand Cyrus* (10 vols, 1649–59), written with her brother, followed by *Clélie* (10 vols, 1654–60).

Sculthorpe, Peter Joshua (1929–) Composer, born in Launceston, Tasmania, Australia. His major works include the operas *Rites of Passage* (1974) and *Quiros* (1982), and *Child of Australia* (1987), written for Australia's bicentennial celebrations.

Seaborg, Glenn T(heodore) (1912–) Nuclear chemist, born in Ishpeming, MI. He produced the elements berkelium and californium in 1950, and shared the Nobel Prize for Chemistry in 1951. The 106th element was named seaborgium in his honour in 1994. >> McMillan, Edwin

Seabury, Samuel (1729–96) Clergyman, born in Groton, CT. He was elected the first Episcopal Bishop of Connecticut and Rhode Island in 1785.

Seaga, Edward (Philip George) (1930–) Jamaican Labour prime minister (1980–9), born in the USA. He became Leader of the Opposition in 1974, and in 1980 had a resounding win over the People's National Party.

Seagram, Joseph Emm (1848–1919) Canadian distiller and turfman. He was founder of the world's largest producer and marketer of distilled spirits and wines, and owner and breeder of an unprecedented 15 Queen's/King's Plate horse-race winners.

Searle, Humphrey [serl] (1915–82) Composer, born in Oxford, Oxfordshire. An exponent of the '12-note system', his compositions include five symphonies, two piano concertos, and three operas.

Searle, John [serl] (1932–) Philosopher, born in Denver, CO. He has expounded a distinctive approach to the study of language and mind, and is also known for his work on the theory of speech acts.

Searle, Ronald (William Fordham) [serl] (1920–) Artist, born in Cambridge, Cambridgeshire. He became widely known as the creator of the macabre schoolgirls of 'St Trinian's'.

Sears, R(ichard) W(arren) (1863–1914) Founder of a mail-order jewellery business, born in Stewartville, MN. He founded the R W Sears Watch Co in 1886, and went into partnership with Alvah Roebuck, establishing Sears, Roebuck & Co.

Seastrom, Victor >> Sjöström, Victor

Seaver, Tom, popular name of **George Thomas Seaver**, nickname **Tom Terrific** (1944–) Baseball pitcher, born in Fresno, CA. His 20-year career (1967–86) was spent primarily with the New York Mets and Cincinnati Reds, winning 311 games and the Cy Young Award three times (1969, 1973, 1975).

Sebastian, St (?–288), feast day 20 January. Roman martyr, a native of Narbonne. He was a captain of the praetorian guard, and secretly a Christian. When his belief was discovered, Diocletian ordered his death. >> Diocletian

Sebastiano del Piombo [pyomboh] >> Piombo, Sebastiano del

Sebuktigin >> Mahmud of Ghazna

Secchi, Pietro Angelo [sekee] (1818–78) Astronomer, born in Reggio nell'Emilia, Italy. Director of the observatory in Rome, he originated the classification of stars by spectrum analysis.

Secombe, Sir Harry (Donald) [seekm] (1921–) Comedian, singer, and media personality, born in Swansea, West Glamorgan. A member of BBC radio's *The Goons* (1951–9), he has starred on stage in *Pickwick* (1963) and on film in *Oliver!* (1968), recorded several albums as a professional singer, and presented television series.

Seddon, Richard John, nickname **King Dick** (1845–1906)

New Zealand prime minister (1893–1906), born in Eccleston, Lancashire. He led a Liberal Party government remembered for its social legislation, such as the introduction of old-age pensions.

Sedges, John >> **Buck, Pearl S**

Sedgman, Frank (1927–) Tennis player, born in Mont Albert, Victoria, Australia. In 1951 he defeated Drobny to win the Wimbledon singles final. >> **Drobny**

Sedgwick, Adam (1785–1873) Geologist, born in Dent, Cumbria. In 1835 he calculated the stratigraphic succession of fossil-bearing rocks in North Wales, naming the oldest of them the *Cambrian period*.

Seebeck, Thomas Johann (1770–1831) Physicist, born in Tallin, Estonia. He discovered the thermoelectric effect, now much used in thermocouples for temperature measurement.

Seefried, Irmgard [**zay**freet] (1919–88) Soprano, born in Köngetried, Germany. She became famous for her performances with Vienna State Opera, especially in the operas of Mozart and Richard Strauss.

Seeger, Pete(r) (1919–) Folk-singer and songwriter, born in New York City. In 1940 he started the 'protest' movement in contemporary folk-music. With his group, the Weavers, his best-known songs include 'Where Have All the Flowers Gone?', 'If I Had a Hammer', and 'Little Boxes'.

Seferiades, George [sefer**yah**deez], also called **Giorgios** or **George Seferis** (1900–71) Poet and diplomat, born in Izmir (formerly, Smyrna), Turkey. His lyrical poetry was collected in *The Turning Point* (1931), *Mythistorema* (1935), and other books, and in 1963 he was awarded the Nobel Prize for Literature.

Segal, George [**see**gl] (1924–) Sculptor, born in New York City. He is best known for his life-sized plaster figures, cast from life and usually unpainted, such as 'Girl in a Doorway' (1969).

Segar, Elzie (Crisler) [**see**ger] (1894–1938) Strip cartoonist, born in Chester, IL. In 1919 he began a strip about Olive Oyl and her brother Castor, and in 1929 introduced Popeye the Sailor, who became internationally popular.

Seghers, Hercules [**say**gerz] (c.1589–c.1635) Painter, born in Haarlem, The Netherlands. He produced some of the most romantic mountain landscapes of the 17th-c, but fewer than 15 pictures survive.

Segonzac, André Dunoyer de [suh**gō**zak] (1884–1974) Painter and engraver, born in Boussy-Saint-Antoine, France. He produced many delicate watercolour landscapes, etchings, and illustrations.

Segovia, Andrés [se**goh**via] (1894–1987) Guitarist, born in Linares, Spain. He evolved a revolutionary guitar technique permitting the performance of a wide range of music, and many modern composers wrote works for him.

Segrave, Sir Henry (O'Neal de Hane) [**see**grayv] (1896–1930) Motor-racing driver, born in Baltimore, MD. He helped to design the Sunbeam car, in which he broke the land speed record at 203·9 mph, raising this to 231 mph in 1929. He was killed on L Windermere, after setting a new world water speed record of 98·76 mph.

Segrè, Emilio (Gino) [**se**gray] (1905–89) Physicist, born in Tivoli, Italy. He helped to develop the atomic bomb at Los Alamos, and shared the Nobel Prize for Physics in 1959 for the discovery of the antiproton (1955). >> **Chamberlain, Owen**

Séguin, Marc [say**gī**], known as **the Elder** (1786–1875) Mechanical and civil engineer, born in Annonay, France. He invented the multi-tubular (fire-tube) boiler, which he patented in 1827, and which was used by Stephenson in his *Rocket* locomotive. >> **Stephenson, George**

Segundo, Juan Luis [se**goon**doh] (1925–) Jesuit liberation theologian, born in Montevideo. His major exposition of liberation theology is *Jesus of Nazareth Yesterday and Today* (5 vols, 1984–8).

Seiber, Mátyás [**shiy**ber] (1905–60) Composer, born in Budapest. He gained only belated recognition, his works including chamber music, piano pieces, and songs.

Seidler, Harry [**siyd**ler] (1923–) Architect, born in Vienna. Responsible for much of the Sydney skyline, his work includes the award-winning Australia Square tower and Grosvenor Place.

Seifert, Jaroslav [**siy**fert] (1901–86) Poet, born in Prague. National poet of Czechoslovakia, his major works include (trans titles) *The Carrier Pigeon* (1929), *Put out the Lights* (1938), and *A Helmet of Earth* (1945). He was awarded the Nobel Prize for Literature in 1984.

Sejanus [se**jay**nus] (?–31) Prefect of the Praetorian Guard (14–31). He was all-powerful at Rome after Emperor Tiberius's retirement to Capri (26), but when his ambitions were made known to Tiberius, he met a sudden fall from grace. >> **Tiberius**

Selcraig, Alexander >> **Selkirk, Alexander**

Selden, John (1584–1654) Historian and antiquary, born in Salvington, West Sussex. In 1628 he helped to draw up the Petition of Rights, for which he was imprisoned until 1634. His best-known book, *Table Talk*, was published posthumously (1689).

Seles, Monica [**sel**esh] (1973–) Tennis player, born in Novi Sad, Yugoslavia. In 1990 she became the youngest woman to win a 'Grand Slam' singles title this century (the French Championship at 16 years 169 days). In 1993 she was unable to play after an incident on court in which she was stabbed by a deranged onlooker.

Seleucus I Nicator ('Conqueror') [si**loo**kus, niy**kay**ter] (c.358–281 BC) Macedonian general of Alexander the Great, and founder of the Seleucid dynasty. He rose to become ruler of an empire which stretched from Asia Minor to India.

Selfridge, Harry Gordon (c.1864–1947) Businessman, born in Ripon, WI. While visiting London in 1906, he bought a site in Oxford St, and built upon it the large store which now bears his name (opened 1909).

Seligman, C(harles) G(abriel) (1873–1940) Anthropologist, born in London. Known for such works as *The Veddas* (Ceylon) (1911), co-authored with his wife, he pioneered the application of a psychoanalytic approach to anthropology.

Selkirk, Alexander, also spelled **Selcraig** (1676–1721) Sailor whose story suggested that of Defoe's *Robinson Crusoe*, born in Largo, Fife. He joined the South Sea buccaneers, and at his own request was put ashore on Juan Fernández I, off the coast of Chile (1704). He lived there alone until 1709, when he was discovered and brought back to Britain.

Sellars, Peter (1958–) Stage director, born in Pittsburgh, PA. Director of the Boston Shakespeare Company (1983–4), and of the American National Theater in Washington, DC (1984–6), he is known for his innovative operatic productions.

Sellers, Peter (1925–80) Actor and comedian, born in Southsea, Hampshire. His meeting with Spike Milligan heralded *The Goon Show* (1951–9), which revolutionized British radio comedy. His films include *I'm All Right Jack* (1959), *Only Two Can Play* (1962), and *Being There* (1980), and his popularity was unrivalled as Inspector Clouseau in the series of films that began with *The Pink Panther* (1963). >> **Milligan**

Sellin, Thorsten (Johan) (1896–) Educator and criminologist, born in Ornskoldsvik, Sweden. He emigrated to America in 1915, advised the census Bureau on criminal statistics (1931–46), and became president of the International Penal and Penitentiary Foundation (1965–71).

Selous, Frederick Courtenay [suh**loos**] (1815–1917) Explorer and big-game hunter, born in London. He spent many years exploring and hunting in the country between the Transvaal and the Congo basin. The *Selous National Park* in Tanzania is named after him.

Selwyn, George Augustus [**sel**win] (1809–78) Anglican churchman, born in London. In 1841 he was consecrated the first (and only) Bishop of New Zealand and Melanesia, and was largely responsible for the organization of the Church of New Zealand.

Selwyn-Lloyd, (John) Selwyn (Brooke) Lloyd, Baron [**sel**win **loyd**] (1904–78) British Conservative statesman, born in Liverpool, Merseyside. He served as minister of state (1951), supply (1954–5), and defence (1955), as foreign secretary (1955–60), and as Chancellor of the Exchequer (1960–2).

Selye, Hans (Hugo Bruno) [**say**lee] (1907–82) Physician, born in Vienna. He was best known for his 'stress-general adaptation syndrome', an attempt to link stress and anxiety and their biochemical and physiological consequences to many modern human disorders.

Selznick, David O(liver) (1902–65) Cinema mogul, born in Pittsburgh, OH. In 1936 he formed his own company, producing *A Star Is Born* (1937) and his greatest achievement, *Gone With the Wind* (1939, Oscar). Among the stars he created was Jennifer Jones (1919–), to whom he was married from 1949.

Semenov, Nikolay Nikolayevich [sem**yo**nof] (1896–1986) Physical chemist, born in Saratov, Russia. He carried out important research on the kinetics of gas reactions, for which he shared the Nobel Prize for Chemistry in 1956, the first Soviet citizen to receive a Nobel Prize.

Semiramis [se**mi**ramis] (9th-c BC) Semi-legendary Queen of Assyria. She founded many cities, including Nineveh and Babylon.

Semmelweiss, Ignaz Philipp [**zem**elviys] (1818–65) Physician, born in Buda, Hungary. He dramatically reduced the high mortality rate of women suffering 'childbed' or puerperal fever, by instructing medical students to wash their hands in a chlorinated lime after visiting each patient. >> Lister, Joseph

Semmes, Raphael [semz] (1809–77) Confederate naval officer, born in Charles Co, MD. Early in the Civil War he commanded the *Alabama*, with which he captured 82 vessels.

Sen, Amartya Kumar (1933–) Economist, born in India. He is noted for his work on the nature of poverty and famine.

Senanayake, Don Stephen [sena**niy**kee] (1884–1952) First prime minister of Sri Lanka (1947–52), born in Colombo. He also held the post (pre-independence) of minister of agriculture, and later served as minister of defence and external affairs.

Sendak, Maurice (Bernard) (1928–) Illustrator and writer of children's books, born in New York City. *Where the Wild Things Are* (1963) made him internationally famous, followed by *In The Night Kitchen* (1970).

Senebier, Jean [senebyay] (1742–1809) Botanist and pastor, born in Geneva, Switzerland. In 1782 he first demonstrated the basic principle of photosynthesis, which he published in *Physiologie végétale* (1800).

Seneca, Lucius Annaeus [**sen**eka], known as **the Elder** (c.55 BC–c.AD 40) Roman rhetorician, born in Córdoba, Spain. Besides a history of Rome, now lost, he wrote several works on oratory. >> Seneca (the Younger)

Seneca, Lucius Annaeus [**sen**eka], known as **Seneca the Younger** (c.5 BC–AD 65) Roman philosopher, statesman, and writer, born in Córdoba, Spain, the son of Seneca (the Elder). He was tutor to Nero, but his high moral aims incurred the emperor's displeasure. Drawn into conspir-

acy, he was condemned, and committed suicide. >> Nero; Seneca (the Elder)

Senefelder, Aloys [**zay**nefelder, **a**lohis]] (1771–1834) Inventor, born in Prague. He accidentally discovered the technique of lithography by using a grease pencil on limestone (1796), and later trained others in the process.

Senghor, Léopold Sédar [sä**gaw(r)**] (1906–) Senegalese president (1960–80), born in Joal, Senegal. He became deputy for Senegal in the French National Assembly (1948–58), and president following his country's independence.

Senna, Ayrton, in full **Ayrton Senna da Silva** (1960–94) Motor racing driver, born in São Paulo, Brazil. He had 41 Grand Prix victories (second only to Alain Prost), and was World Formula One champion (1988, 1990, 1991). He was killed during the 1994 San Marino Grand Prix.

Sennacherib [se**nak**erib] (8th–7th-c BC) King of Assyria (704–681 BC), the grandfather of Assurbanipal. His fame rests mainly on his conquest of Babylon (689 BC) and his rebuilding of Nineveh. >> Assurbanipal

Sennett, Mack, originally **Michael** or **Mikall Sinnott** (1880–1960) Film director, producer, and actor, born in Richmond, Quebec, Canada. He made hundreds of shorts, establishing a tradition of knockabout slapstick under the name of Keystone Komics (1912) and the Sennett Bathing Beauties (1920).

Senusrit >> **Sesostris**

Sequoia or **Sequoyah** [se**kwoy**a], also known as **George Gist** or **Guest** (c.1770–1843) Cherokee Indian Leader, born in Taskigi, NC. Probably the son of Nathaniel Gist, a British trader, and a Cherokee mother, he was a major figure behind the decision of the Cherokee to adopt as much as possible of the white culture, while retaining their own identity.

Serao, Matilde [say**row**] (1856–1927) Novelist and newspaper editor, born in Patras, Greece. Her many novels of Neapolitan life include *A Girl's Romance* (trans, 1886), and in 1904 she founded the daily newspaper *Il Giorno*.

Seraphicus, Doctor >> **Bonaventure, St**

Sergeyev-Tsensky, Sergey [ser**gay**ef **tsen**skee] (1875–1958) Novelist, born in Tambov province, Russia. His major work was the 10-volume novel sequence, *Transfiguration* (trans, 1914–40, Stalin Prize).

Serkin, Peter (1947–) Pianist, born in New York City, the son of Rudolf Serkin. He concentrated on contemporary music, co-founding the new-music quartet, Tashi, and later performing the whole range of piano repertoire. >> Serkin, Rudolf

Serkin, Rudolf (1903–91) Pianist, born in Eger, Austria. He settled in the USA in 1939, and founded the Marlboro School of Music (1949) and the Marlboro Music Festival (1950). >> Serkin, Peter

Serling, Rod (1924–75) Television script-writer, born in Syracuse, NY. He won the first of six Emmy Awards for *Patterns* (1955), and created, wrote, and hosted the popular anthology series *The Twilight Zone* (1959–64) and *Night Gallery* (1970–3).

Serlio, Sebastiano [**sair**lioh] (1475–1554) Architect and painter, born in Bologna, Italy. He wrote an influential treatise on Italian architecture, *Regole generali di architettura* (1537–51).

Serote, Mongane Wally [se**roh**tay] (1944–) Writer, born in Sophiatown, South Africa. He became one of the 'township poets' of the 1970s, whose angry verse broke a decade of African creative silence. In 1981 he published a novel, *To Every Birth Its Blood*.

Serra, Junipero [hoo**nee**peroh] (1713–84) Missionary, born in Petra, Majorca. He founded nine missions in present-day California, and was beatified by the Roman Catholic Church in 1988.

Serra, Richard (1939–) Sculptor, born in San Francisco,

CA. In the late 1960s he began manufacturing austere minimalist works from sheet steel, iron, and lead, and became a controversial but highly influential artist.

Serre, Jean-Pierre [sair] (1926–) Mathematician, born in Bages, France. He has carried out research in homotopy theory, algebraic geometry, class field theory, group theory, and number theory, and in 1954 was awarded the Fields Medal.

Sertorius, Quintus [sertawrius] (123–72 BC) Roman soldier, born in Nursia. In 80 BC he headed a successful rising of natives and Roman exiles against Rome, holding out against Sulla's commanders for eight years until assassinated by his chief lieutenant. >> Sulla

Servan-Schreiber, Jean-Jacques [sairvä shriybair] (1924–) French politician and journalist, born in Paris. President of the Radical Party (1971–5, 1977–9), he was elected to the National Assembly (1970), served as minister of reforms, and co-founded the Reform Movement (1972).

Servetus, Michael [servaytus] (1511–53) Theologian and physician, born in Tudela, Spain. His theological writings denied the Trinity and the divinity of Christ, and he was burnt at Geneva for heresy. While studying medicine he discovered the pulmonary circulation of the blood.

Service, Robert W(illiam) (1874–1958) Poet, born in Preston, Lancashire. He emigrated to Canada in 1894. Known as 'the Canadian Kipling', he wrote popular ballads, such as 'Rhymes of a Rolling Stone' (1912) and 'The Shooting of Dan McGrew'.

Sesostris [sesostris], also known as **Senusrit** According to Greek legend, an Egyptian monarch who extended his dominion to India. He was possibly Sesostris I (c.1980–1935 BC), II (c.1906–1887 BC), and III (c.1887–1849 BC) compounded into one heroic figure.

Sesshu, Toyo [seshoo] (1420–1506) Painter and priest, born in Akahama, Japan. His knowledge of Zen Buddhism and communion with nature allowed him to renew the traditional lyricism of Japanese landscapes, and he came to be the greatest Japanese painter of his time.

Sessions, Roger (Huntingdon) (1896–1985) Composer, born in New York City. His compositions include eight symphonies, a violin concerto, piano and chamber music, two operas, and a Concerto for Orchestra (1981, Pulitzer).

Seton, St Elizabeth Ann [seetn], née **Bayley** (1774–1821), feast day 4 January. The first native-born saint of the USA, born in New York City. She founded the USA's first religious order, the Sisters of Charity, in 1809 and was canonized in 1975.

Seton, Ernest Thompson [seetn], originally **Ernest Evan Thompson** (1860–1946) Naturalist, writer, and illustrator, born in South Shields, Durham. He emigrated to Canada in 1866, wrote and illustrated a series of books about birds and animals, notably *Wild Animals I Have Known* (1898), and founded the Boy Scouts of America (1910).

Seurat, Georges (Pierre) [soerah] (1859–91) Artist, born in Paris. His works, such as 'Une Baignade' (A Bather, 1883–4), painted in a Divisionist style, show the marrying of an Impressionist palette to Classical composition.

Seuss, Dr, pseudonym of **Theodor Seuss Geisel**, other pseudonyms **Theo LeSieg** and **Rosetta Stone** (1904–91) Writer and illustrator of children's books, born in Springfield, MA. His famous series of 'Beginner Books' in reading started with *The Cat in the Hat* (1957).

Severin, (Giles) Timothy (1940–) British historian, traveller, and writer. He has recreated many voyages following the routes of early explorers, using vessels reconstructed to the original specifications.

Severini, Gino [severeenee] (1883–1966) Artist, born in Cortona, Italy. He signed the first Futurist manifesto in 1910, but after 1914 reverted to a more representational style, particularly in Swiss and Italian churches.

Severus, Lucius Septimius [severus] (c.146–211) Roman emperor (193–211), the founder of the Severan dynasty (193–235). Declared emperor by the army, he proved to be an able administrator, effecting many reforms.

Sévigné, Madame de [sayveenyay], née **Marie de Rabutin-Chantal** (1626–96) Writer, born in Paris. A member of French court society, she began a series of detailed letters published posthumously in 1725, covering 25 years of the inner history of her time.

Seward, Sir Albert Charles [sooerd] (1863–1941) Palaeobotanist, born in Lancaster, Lancashire. He is best known for his work on *English Wealden Flora* (1894–95), *Jurassic Flora* (1900–3), and a panoramic survey, *Plant Life Through the Ages* (1931).

Seward, Anna [sooerd], known as **the Swan of Lichfield** (1747–1809) Poet, born in Eyam, Derbyshire. Her best known work is the poetic novel *Louisa* (1784), which was popular for its sentiment.

Seward, William H(enry) [sooerd] (1801–72) US statesman, born in Florida, NY. As secretary of state (1861–9), he negotiated the purchase of Alaska from Russia (1867) and in the 'Trent affair' during the Civil War advised that the Confederate envoys should be given up to England.

Sewell, Anna [syooel] (1820–78) Novelist, born in Great Yarmouth, Norfolk. She wrote *Black Beauty* (1877; filmed 1946, 1971), the story of a horse, written as a plea for the more humane treatment of animals.

Sexton, Ann, née **Harvey** (1928–74) Poet, born in Newton, MA. A confessional poet, *To Bedlam and Part Way Back* (1962) was her first collection of poetry. Her *Complete Poems* were published in 1981.

Sexton, Thomas (1848–1932) Irish nationalist politician, born in Ballygannon, Co Waterford, Ireland. He controlled the leading Home Rule daily newspaper, the *Freeman's Journal* (1892–1912).

Sextus Empiricus [empirikus] (c.early 3rd-c) Greek philosopher and physician, active at Alexandria and Athens. He is the main source of information for the Sceptical school of philosophy.

Seymour, Edward >> Somerset, Duke of

Seymour, Jane [seemoor] (c.1509–37) Third queen of Henry VIII, the mother of Edward VI. Lady-in-waiting to Henry's first two wives, she married him 11 days after the execution of Anne Boleyn. She died soon after the birth of her son. >> Edward VI; Henry VIII

Seymour, Lynn [seemoor] (1939–) Ballet dancer, born in Wainwright, Alberta, Canada. Best known for her passionate interpretations of the choreography of MacMillan and Ashton, she became artistic director of the Bavarian State Opera (1978–81). >> Ashton, Frederick; MacMillan, Kenneth

Seymour (of Sudeley), Thomas Seymour, Baron [seemoor] (c.1508–1549) English soldier and statesman, the brother-in-law of Henry VIII through marriage to Jane Seymour. In 1547 he married Catherine Parr, widow of Henry VIII. After her death (1548) he tried to marry Princess Elizabeth, and was executed for treason. >> Seymour, Jane; Somerset, Edward Seymour

Seymour, William >> Stuart, Arabella

Seyss-Inquart, Arthur [siys ingkwah(r)t] (1892–1946) Nazi leader, born in Stannern, Austria-Hungary. Chancellor of Austria during the *Anschluss* (1938), he was appointed commissioner for The Netherlands (1940), where he ruthlessly recruited slave labour. He was executed for war crimes.

Sforza, Ludovico [sfaw(r)tsa], known as **the Moor** (1451–1508) Ruler of Naples, born in Vigevano, Italy. He made an alliance with Lorenzo de' Medici of Florence and, under his rule, Milan became the most glittering court in Europe. >> Lorenzo de' Medici

Sgambati, Giovanni [sgambahtee] (1841–1914) Composer and pianist, born in Rome. His compositions include two symphonies, a requiem Mass, chamber music, and piano music.

Shackleton, Sir Ernest Henry (1874–1922) Explorer, born in Kilkea, Co Kildare, Ireland. He nearly reached the South Pole in his own expedition of 1909, and in 1915 his ship *Endurance* was crushed in the ice, forcing him to make a perilous journey to bring relief.

Shadwell, Thomas (c.1642–92) Playwright, born in Brandon, Norfolk. He found success with his satirical comedy, *The Sullen Lovers* (1668), and such later 'comedies of manners' as *Epsom-Wells* (1672). He became Poet Laureate in 1689.

Shaffer, Peter (Levin) (1926–) Playwright, born in Liverpool, Merseyside. His plays include *Five Finger Exercise* (1958–60), *The Private Ear* (1962; filmed 1966), and *The Public Eye* (1962; filmed 1972). Other notable works include *Equus* (1973–4; filmed 1977) and *Amadeus* (1979; filmed 1984, Oscar).

Shaftesbury, Anthony Ashley Cooper, 1st Earl of [shahftsbree] (1621–83) English statesman, born in Wimborne St Giles, Dorset. A member of the Short Parliament (1640), he was made one of Cromwell's Council of State, but from 1655 was in Opposition. At the Restoration he became Chancellor of the Exchequer (1661–72), a member of the Cabal (1667), and Lord Chancellor (1672–3).

Shaftesbury, Anthony Ashley Cooper, 3rd Earl of [shahftsbree] (1671–1713) Philosopher, born in London, the grandson of the 1st Earl of Shaftesbury. One of the leading English deists, he is best known for his essays, collected as *Characteristics of Men, Manners, Opinions, Times* (1711).

Shaftesbury, Anthony Ashley Cooper, 7th Earl of [shahftsbree] (1801–85) Factory reformer and philanthropist, born in London. He became the main spokesman of the factory reform movement, and piloted successive factory acts (1847, 1859) through parliament.

Shagall, Marc >> Chagall, Marc

Shah Jahan [jahahn] (1592–1666) Mughal emperor of India (1628–58), born in Lahore, Pakistan. A ruthless but able ruler, the magnificence of his court was unequalled. His buildings included the Taj Mahal, the tomb of his third wife, Mumtaz Mahal (1592–1631).

Shahn, Ben(jamin) (1898–1969) Painter, born in Kaunas, Lithuania. His 23 satirical gouache paintings on the trial of the Italian anarchists Sacco and Vanzetti (1932), and the 15 paintings of Tom Mooney, the labour leader (1933), earned him the title of 'the American Hogarth'.

Shaka [shahka] (c.1788–1828) African ruler, born near Melmoth, KwaZulu Natal, South Africa. He was a successful military ruler, who intensified the centralization of Zulu power, and set about the incorporation of neighbouring peoples.

Shakespeare, John (c.1530–1601) Glover and wool dealer, born in Snitterfield, near Stratford, Warwickshire, the father of William Shakespeare. In 1568 he was made bailiff (mayor) of Stratford and a justice of the peace.

Shakespeare, William (1564–1616) Playwright and poet, born in Stratford-upon-Avon, Warwickshire, the son of John Shakespeare and Mary Arden. He married Anne Hathaway in 1582, who bore him a daughter, Susanna, in 1583, and twins Hamnet and Judith in 1585. He moved to London, possibly in 1591, and became an actor. His sonnets, known by 1598, fall into two groups: 1 to 126 are addressed to a fair young man, and 127 to 154 to a 'dark lady' who holds both the young man and the poet in thrall. The first evidence of his association with the stage is in 1594, when he was acting with the Lord Chamberlain's company of players. When the company built the Globe Theatre S of the Thames (1597), he became a

partner. He later returned to Stratford (c.1610), living as a country gentleman at his house, New Place. The first collected works, the First Folio, appeared in 1623. It is conventional to group the plays into early, middle, and late periods, and to distinguish comedies (eg *A Midsummer Night's Dream*, 1595; *As You Like It*, 1599; *Twelfth Night*, 1600–2), tragedies (eg *Hamlet*, 1600–1; *Othello*, 1605–6; *King Lear*, 1605–6; *Macbeth*, 1605–6), and histories (eg *Richard II*, 1595; *Henry IV, I* and *II*, 1596–7; *Henry V*, 1599), recognizing other groups that do not fall neatly into these categories, such as the Greek and Roman plays (eg *Julius Caesar*, 1599) and the late comedies (eg *The Tempest*, 1613). The authorship of some plays (eg *Titus Andronicus*) is still a matter of controversy. >> Shakespeare, John

Shaliapin, Fedor Ivanovich [shalya**peen**] >> **Chaliapin, Fedor Ivanovich**

Shamir, Yitzhak [sha**meer**], originally **Yitzhak Jazernicki** (1915–) Zionist leader and prime minister of Israel (1983–4, 1986–92), born in Ruzinoy, Poland. He was foreign minister (1980–3), before taking over the leadership of the right-wing Likud Party.

Shammai [sha**miy**] (c.1st-c BC–AD 1st-c) Jewish scholar and Pharisaic leader, apparently a native of Jerusalem. The head of a famous school of Torah scholars, his interpretation of the Law was often in conflict with the equally famous school led by Hillel. >> Hillel

Shankar, Ravi [**shang**kah(r)] (1920–) Sitarist, born in Benares, India. Widely regarded as India's most important musician, he set up schools of Indian music, founded the National Orchestra of India, and in the mid-1950s became the first Indian instrumentalist to undertake an international tour.

Shankly, Bill, popular name of **William Shankly** (1913–81) Footballer and manager, born in Scotland. He won an FA Cup Medal with Preston North End, and five Scotland caps, and became manager of Liverpool (1959–74).

Shannon, Claude E(lwood) (1916–) Mathematician and pioneer of communication theory, born in Gaylord, MI. He worked at the Bell Telephone Laboratories (1941–72) in the area of information theory, and wrote *The Mathematical Theory of Communication* (1949) with Warren Weaver.

Shapiro, Erin Patria Margaret, formerly **Pizzey**, *née* **Carney** (1939–) British writer and campaigner for women's rights. She founded the first Shelter for Battered Wives and their children in London in 1971, and wrote *Scream Quietly or the Neighbours Will Hear*.

Shapiro, Karl (Jay) [sha**peer**oh] (1913–) Writer, born in Baltimore, MD. He is noted for his mastery of poetic forms, as seen in *Collected Poems 1940–77* (1978), and has also written literary criticism and a novel.

Shapley, Harlow (1885–1972) Astrophysicist, born in Nashville, MO. He demonstrated that the Milky Way is much larger than had been supposed, and that the Solar System is located on the Galaxy's edge, not at its centre.

Shapur or **Sapor II** [sha**poor**], known as **the Great** (309–79) King of Persia (309–79). Under him the Sassanian empire reached its zenith. He successfully challenged Roman control of the Middle East, and established Persian control over Armenia.

Sharp, Cecil (James) (1859–1924) Collector of folk songs and dances, born in London. He published several collections of British and US folk material, and in 1911 founded the Folk-Dance Society.

Sharp, Sir Percival (1867–1953) British educationist. As secretary of the Association of Education Committees (1933–44), he played a prominent part in the development of English education in the first half of this century.

Shastri, Lal (Bahadur) [**shas**tree] (1904–66) Indian prime minister (1964–6), born in Mughalsarai, Uttar Pradesh, India. He became minister of transport (1957), commerce

(1958), and home affairs (1960), and succeeded Nehru as premier. >> Nehru, Jawaharlal

Shaw, Anna Howard (1847–1919) Suffragist, born in Newcastle upon Tyne, Tyne and Wear. She emigrated to the USA in 1851, and in 1880 became the first woman to be ordained as a Methodist preacher. She was president of the National American Woman Suffrage Association (1904–15).

Shaw, Artie, originally **Arthur Arshawsky** (1910–) Clarinet player and bandleader, born in New York City. He became internationally known after recording 'Begin the Beguine' (1938), and rivalled Goodman as a clarinet soloist. >> Goodman

Shaw, George Bernard (1856–1950) Playwright, essayist, and pamphleteer, born in Dublin. In 1882 he turned to socialism, joined the committee of the Fabian Society, and became known as a journalist. Among his major plays are *Arms and the Man* (1894), *The Devil's Disciple* (1897), *Man and Superman* (1905), *Major Barbara* (1905), *The Doctor's Dilemma* (1906), *Pygmalion* (1913), and *Saint Joan* (1923). He was awarded the Nobel Prize for Literature in 1935.

Shaw, Henry Wheeler >> Billings, Josh

Shaw, Martin Fallus (1876–1958) Composer, born in London. He is best known for his songs, and as co-editor of national songbooks with his brother, Geoffrey Turton (1879–1943).

Shaw, Sir (William) Napier (1854–1945) Meteorologist, born in Birmingham, West Midlands. He introduced the use of the millibar as a unit of atmospheric pressure, and helped to establish the 'polar front' theory of cyclones.

Shaw, (Richard) Norman (1831–1912) Architect, born in Edinburgh. In London he was a leader of the trend away from Victorian style back to traditional Georgian design, as in New Scotland Yard (1888) and the Piccadilly Hotel (1905).

Shaw, Percy (1890–1976) British inventor. He devised the idea of self-cleaning, reflective road studs ('cat's eyes'), and set up a factory to manufacture them.

Shawcross (of Friston), Hartley William Shawcross, Baron (1902–) Jurist, born in Giessen, Germany. He established an international legal reputation as chief British prosecutor at the Nuremberg Trials (1945–6).

Shaw, Geoffrey Turton >> Shaw, Martin Fallus

Shawn, Ted, popular name of **Edwin Myers Shawn** (1891–1972) Dancer and director, born in Kansas City, MO. In 1914 he met and married Ruth Saint Denis, and in 1915 they founded *Denishawn*, which branched out across America with a wide-ranging curriculum. When the couple separated in 1931, he founded his own group. >> Saint Denis

Shays, Daniel (1747–1825) US soldier, probably born in Hopkinton, MA. In 1786 he led an unsuccessful insurrection by the farmers in W Massachusetts against the US government, protesting against heavy taxation and mortgages.

Shcharansky, Natan [sharanskee], originally **Anatoly Borisovich Shcharansky** (1948–) Soviet dissident, born in Donetsk, Ukraine. A mathematician, in 1977 he was sentenced to 13 years in a labour colony for allegedly spying on behalf of the CIA. Released in 1986, he moved to Israel.

Shearer, Moira, originally **Moira Shearer King** (1926–) Ballerina and actress, born in Dunfermline, Fife. She danced in both classical and modern ballets, but is especially remembered for her role in the film *The Red Shoes* (1948).

Sheba, Queen of [sheeba] (c.10th-c BC) Monarch mentioned in the Bible (1 *Kings* 10), perhaps from SW Arabia (modern Yemen). She is said to have journeyed to Jerusalem to test the wisdom of Solomon and to exchange gifts. >> Solomon

Sheeler, Charles (1883–1965) Painter and photographer, born in Philadelphia, PA. He was acclaimed for his photographic record of the building of the Ford Motor installation at River Rouge, MI (1927), and later came to regard photography as a basis for his abstract-realistic paintings and graphic work.

Sheen, Fulton (John) (1895–1979) Roman Catholic clergyman and broadcaster, born in El Paso, IL. He became known internationally as a broadcaster on the 'Catholic Hour' (1930–52) and with the TV programme 'Life is Worth Living' (1952–65).

Shelburne, Earl of >> Lansdowne, Marquess of

Shelburne, William Petty Fitzmaurice, 2nd Earl of (1737–1805) British prime minister (1782–3), born in Dublin. He was President of the Board of Trade (1763) and secretary of state (1766), and became premier on the death of Rockingham. >> Rockingham, Marquess of

Sheldon, Gilbert (1598–1677) English clergyman. In 1663 he became Archbishop of Canterbury, and built the Sheldonian Theatre at Oxford in 1669.

Shelley, Mary (Wollstonecraft), *née* **Godwin** (1797–1851) Writer, born in London, the daughter of William Godwin and Mary Wollstonecraft. She eloped with Shelley in 1814, and married him two years later. She wrote several novels, notably *Frankenstein, or the Modern Prometheus* (1818). >> Godwin, William; Shelley, Percy Bysshe; Wollstonecraft

Shelley, Percy Bysshe [bish] (1792–1822) Poet, born at Field Place, near Horsham, West Sussex. From 1818 he lived in Italy, where he wrote the bulk of his poetry, including odes, lyrics, and the verse drama *Prometheus Unbound* (1818–19). >> Shelley, Mary

Shelton, Ian (1958–) Canadian astronomer. He recognized and identified a celestial phenomenon now known as Supernova Shelton 1987A - an exploding star located 170 000 light years from Earth.

Shem Biblical character, the eldest son of Noah, the brother of Ham and Japeth. His descendants are listed (in *Gen* 10), and he is depicted as the legendary father of 'Semitic' peoples, including the Hebrews. >> Noah

Shen Kua [shen kwah] (1031–95) Administrator, engineer, and scientist, born in Qiantang, China. His book *Brush Talks from Dream Brook* (trans title), is an important source of information on early science and technology.

Shenstone, William (1714–63) Poet, born in Leasowes, Shropshire. In 1737 he published his best-known poem, 'The Schoolmistress', written in imitation of Spenser. >> Spenser

Shepard, Alan B(artlett) (1923–) Astronaut, the first American in space, born in East Derry, NH. His sub-orbital flight in a Mercury space capsule 'Freedom 7' took place on 5 May 1961, and lasted 15 min. In 1971 he commanded the Apollo 14 lunar mission.

Shepard, Ernest (Howard) (1879–1976) Artist and cartoonist, born in London. He made his name with his illustrations for children's books such as A A Milne's *Winnie the Pooh* (1926) and Kenneth Grahame's *The Wind in the Willows* (1931).

Shepard, Sam, popular name of **Samuel Shepard Rogers** (1943–) Playwright and actor, born in Fort Sheridan, IL. His works include *The Tooth of Crime* (1972), *Killer's Head* (1975), and *Buried Child* (1978, Pulitzer), and the screenplay *Paris, Texas* (1984).

Sheppard, David (Stuart) (1929–) Anglican clergyman and cricketer, born in Reigate, Surrey. A former Sussex (1953) and England (1954) cricket captain, he became Bishop of Liverpool in 1975, where his profound social concern made a lasting impact on the city. >> Worlock

Sheppard, Dick, popular name of **Hugh Richard Lawrie Sheppard** (1880–1937) Anglican clergyman and pacifist, born in Windsor, Berkshire. A popular preacher with distinctly modern views, he was a pioneer of religious broadcasting and in 1936 founded the Peace Pledge Union.

Sheppard, Jack, popular name of **John Sheppard** (1702–24) Thief, born in London. The subject of numerous ballads and popular plays, he was imprisoned and escaped four times, but was eventually hanged.

Sheppard, Kate, popular name of **Catherine Wilson Sheppard** (1848–1934) Suffragist, born in Liverpool, Merseyside. She emigrated to New Zealand in 1869, led a nation-wide campaign for the enfranchisement of women, and in 1893 New Zealand became the first country in the world to give women the vote.

Sher, Antony [shair] (1949–) Actor and writer, born in Cape Town, South Africa. He joined the Royal Shakespeare Company in 1982, and became known for his innovative creations of Shakespearian characters.

Sherard, Robert Harborough, originally **Robert Harborough Kennedy** (1861–1943) Biographer of Oscar Wilde. He befriended Wilde in 1883 and, although deeply shocked by the Wilde scandal, wrote several works in his favour. >> Wilde, Oscar

Sheraton, Thomas (1751–1806) Cabinet maker, born in Stockton-on-Tees, Durham. He wrote a *Cabinetmaker and Upholsterer's Drawing Book* (1794), and produced a range of Neoclassical designs which had a wide influence on contemporary taste in furniture.

Sherbrooke (of Sherbrooke), Robert Lowe, Viscount (1811–92) Liberal politician, born in Bingham, Nottinghamshire. He is best remembered for his defeat of the Reform Bill of 1866, which caused the fall of the Liberal Government. He was Chancellor of the Exchequer under Gladstone, and in 1873 became home secretary. >> Gladstone, W E

Shere Ali [shair ahlee] (1825–79) Amir of Afghanistan (1853–79). His refusal to receive a British mission (1878) led to the second Anglo-Afghan war (1878–80).

Sheridan, Philip H(enry) (1831–88) US general, born in Albany, NY. In 1864 he was given command of the Army of the Shenandoah, defeating General Lee, and was active in the final battle which led to Lee's surrender. >> Lee, Robert E

Sheridan, Richard Brinsley (Butler) (1751–1816) Playwright, born in Dublin. His highly successful comedy of manners, *The Rivals* (1775), was followed by several other comedies and farces, notably *The School for Scandal* (1777).

Sheriff, Lawrence (?–1567) Philanthropist, born in Rugby, Warwickshire. He founded Rugby School (1567), which became the model public (fee-paying) school for boys for many generations afterwards.

Sherman, Roger (1721–93) US statesman, born in Newton, MA. A signatory of the Declaration of Independence, as a delegate to the Convention of 1787 he took a prominent part in the debates on the Constitution.

Sherman, William Tecumseh (1820–91) US general in the Union army, born in Lancaster, OH. His most famous campaign was in 1864, when he captured Atlanta, and commenced his famous 'March to the Sea' which divided the Confederate forces.

Sherriff, R(obert) C(edric) (1896–1975) Playwright and scriptwriter, born in Hampton Wick, Surrey. Drawing on his wartime experiences, he wrote *Journey's End* (1929), which became an immediate success in London. His film scripts include *Goodbye Mr Chips* (1939) and *The Dambusters* (1955).

Sherrin, Ned, popular name of **Edward George Sherrin** (1931–) Producer, director, and writer, born in Low Ham, Somerset. He became known through producing and directing the BBC satirical revue, *That Was The Week That Was* (1962–3), and has since written or produced several works for stage and screen, and became a popular media panellist.

Sherrington, Sir Charles Scott (1857–1952) Physiologist, born in London. His research on the nervous system constituted a landmark in modern physiology, and he shared the Nobel Prize for Physiology or Medicine in 1932.

Sherwood, Robert E(mmet) (1896–1955) Writer, born in New Rochelle, NY. He was awarded four Pulitzer Prizes, the first three for drama - *Idiot's Delight*, (1936), *Abe Lincoln in Illinois* (1939), and *There Shall be No Night* (1941) - and the last for his biographical *Roosevelt and Hopkins* (1949).

Shevardnadze, Eduard Amvrosiyevich [shevernadze] (1928–) Georgian head of state (1992–) and former Soviet statesman, born in Mamati, Georgia. A member of the USSR Politburo, in 1985 he was appointed foreign minister, but resigned in 1990, expressing concern over some of Gorbachev's decisions. He was then elected Chairman of the State Council of Georgia. >> Gorbachev

Shih Huangdi >> Qin Shihuangdi

Shillibeer, George (1797–1866) Omnibus pioneer, born in London. From 1829 he ran the first London omnibus coach service from the City to Paddington.

Shilton, Peter (1949–) Footballer, born in Leicester, Leicestershire. He played for Leicester City, Stoke City, Nottingham Forest, Southampton, and Derby County, and became the first England goalkeeper to gain over 100 caps.

Shinwell, Emmanuel Shinwell, Baron, popularly known as **Manny Shinwell** (1884–1986) British statesman, born in London. In the postwar Labour government he was minister of fuel and power, secretary of state for war (1947), and minister of defence (1950–1). In his later years he mellowed into a back-bench 'elder statesman'.

Shipton, Eric (Earle) (1907–77) British mountaineer. Between 1933 and 1951 he either led or was a member of five expeditions to Mt Everest, and helped pave the way for the successful Hunt–Hillary expedition of 1953.

Shipton, Mother, popular name of **Ursula Southiel** (1488–c.1560) Witch, born near Knaresborough, North Yorkshire. A book in 1684 tells how she was carried off by the devil, and bore him an imp. Her 'prophecies' were edited in 1797.

Shirer, William L(awrence) (1904–93) Journalist, broadcaster, and historian, born in Chicago, IL. He joined CBS in 1937, broadcast on the momentous events in Europe from both sides until 1940, and wrote a monumental history, *The Rise and Fall of the Third Reich* (1960).

Shirley, James (1596–1666) Playwright, born in London. His works include the comedies *The Witty Fair One* (1628) and *The Lady of Pleasure* (1635), and the tragedies *The Traitor* (1631) and *The Cardinal* (1641).

Shirreff, Emily Anne Eliza (1814–97) British pioneer of women's education. With her sister, Maria Georgina Grey, she wrote *Thoughts on Self-Culture, Addressed to Women* (1850). She also founded the National Union for the Higher Education of Women (1872). >> Grey, Maria Georgina

Shockley, William B(radford) (1910–89) Physicist, born in London. In 1947 he helped devise the point-contact transistor, then devised the junction transistor, which heralded a revolution in radio, TV, and computer circuitry. He shared the Nobel Prize for Physics in 1956. >> Bardeen; Brattain

Shoemaker, Willie, popular name of **William Lee Shoemaker**, nickname **the Shoe** (1931–) Jockey and trainer, born in Fabens, TX. He won more races than any other jockey - nearly 9000 winners between 1949 and his retirement in 1989.

Shoenberg, Isaac (1880–1963) British electrical engineer, born in Russia. He joined Electrical and Musical Industries (EMI) in 1931, and initiated the development of electronic television which led to the BBC's high definition service (1936). >> Baird

Sholes, Christopher Latham [shohlz] (1819–1890) Inventor, born near Mooresburg, PA. His best-known invention is the typewriter, which he patented in 1868, and sold to the Remington Arms Co, who then marketed the first Remington Typewriter.

Sholokhov, Mikhail Alexandrovich [sholokhof] (1905–84) Novelist, born near Veshenskaya, Russia. Best known for his novel tetralogy *And Quietly Flows the Don* (trans, 1928–40), he received the Nobel Prize for Literature in 1965.

Shore, Jane (?–c.1527) Mistress of Edward IV, born in London. She became Edward's mistress (1470–83), but after his death a liaison with William, Lord Hastings, alienated her from Richard III, who forced her to do public penance. >> Edward IV; Richard III

Shore, Peter (David) (1924–) British Labour statesman. He served as secretary of state for economic affairs (1967–9), trade (1974–6), and the environment (1976–9), and became shadow Leader of the House of Commons (1983–7).

Short, Nigel (1965–) Chess player, born in Atherton, Lancashire. In 1984 he became the UK's youngest ever grandmaster, and in 1993 was the first UK grandmaster to qualify for a World Championship match, but was defeated by Kasparov. >> Kasparov

Short, Sir Frank (1857–1945) Artist, born in Stourbridge, West Midlands. He became a master of all the engraving processes, and president of the Royal Society of Painter Etchers (1910–39).

Shorter, Frank (1947–) US marathon runner, born in Munich, Germany. He won the 1972 Olympic title in only his sixth marathon, his success helping to inspire the running and jogging boom in the USA.

Shorter, Wayne (1933–) Jazz saxophonist, born in Newark, NJ. He played with the Art Blakey Jazz Messengers (1959–63) and Miles Davis (1964–70), then co-founded the quintet Weather Report, which performed from 1971 until the mid-1980s. >> Blakey; Davis, Miles

Shorthouse, Joseph Henry (1834–1903 Novelist, born in Birmingham, West Midlands. A Quaker who converted to the Church of England, his works include the philosophical romance *John Inglesant* (1881) and *Sir Percival* (1886).

Shostakovich, Dmitri Dmitriyevich [shostakohvich] (1906–75) Composer, born in St Petersburg, Russia. At first highly successful, his operas and ballets were for a time criticized for a failure to observe 'Soviet realism'. He wrote 15 symphonies, violin, piano, and cello concertos, chamber music, and choral works.

Shotoku Taishi [shotohkoo tiyshee] (574–622) Japanese Yamato period ruler. A member of the Soga ruling clan, he was regent to Empress Suiko (c.592–628). His patronage of Buddhism aided its ascendancy from c.600.

Showa Tenno ('Emperor') Hirohito [shoha tenoh hirohheetoh] (1901–89) Emperor of Japan (1926–89), the 124th in direct lineage, born in Tokyo. His reign was marked by wars against China (1931–2, 1937–45) and the USA and Britain (1941–5). In 1946 he renounced his legendary divinity to become a democratic constitutional monarch.

Shrapnel, Henry (1761–1842) British artillery officer. In c.1793 he invented the *shrapnel shell*, an anti-personnel device which exploded while in flight, scattering lethal lead shot.

Shu Ching-Chün >> Lao She

Shultz, George P(ratt) (1920–) US statesman, born in New York City. He became labour secretary under Nixon (1969–74), and later under Reagan served as secretary of state (1982–9). >> Nixon; Reagan

Shumway, Norman (Edward) (1923–) Cardiac surgeon, born in Kalamazoo, MI. He did much of the early experimental work in cardiovascular surgery before heart transplants were attempted in human beings, and performed the first adult heart transplant in the USA in 1968.

Shuster, Joseph, >> Siegel and Shuster

Shute, Nevil, pseudonym of **Nevil Shute Norway** (1899–1960) Writer, born in London. After World War 2 he emigrated to Australia, which became the setting for most of his later books, notably *A Town Like Alice* (1949) and *On the Beach* (1957).

Sibelius, Jean (Julius Christian) [sibaylius] (1865–1957) Composer, born in Tavastehus, Finland. A passionate nationalist, he wrote a series of symphonic poems, notably *Finlandia* (1899), as well as seven symphonies and a violin concerto.

Sibley, Dame Antoinette (1939–) Dancer, born in Bromley, Kent. A dancer of great sensuality and beauty, her partnership with Anthony Dowell led them to be dubbed 'the Golden Pair'. >> Dowell

Sica, Vittorio de >> de Sica, Vittorio

Sickert, Walter (Richard) (1860–1942) Artist, born in Munich, Germany. The Camden Town Group (later the London Group) was formed under his leadership (c.1910), and he became a major influence on later English painters.

Sickingen, Franz von (1481–1523) Knight, born in Ebernburg, Germany. A champion of the poorer classes, he became a prominent leader of the early Reformation in Germany.

Siddons, Sarah, née **Kemble** (1755–1831) Actress, born in Brecon, Powys. A member of the theatre company run by her father, Roger Kemble, she became the unquestioned queen of the stage, unmatched as a tragic actress. She married her fellow actor, William Siddons (1744–1808), in 1773.

Sidgwick, Henry (1838–1900) Philosopher, born in Skipton, North Yorkshire. His best-known work, *Methods of Ethics* (1874), develops the utilitarian theories of John Stuart Mill. >> Mill, John Stuart

Sidgwick, Nevil Vincent (1873–1952) Chemist, born in Oxford, Oxfordshire. He is known for his work on molecular structure and his formulation of a theory of valency.

Sidmouth (of Sidmouth), Henry Addington, 1st Viscount [sidmuhth] (1757–1844) British prime minister (1801–4), born in London. His Tory administration negotiated the Peace of Amiens (1802), and he later became home secretary under Liverpool (1812–21). >> Liverpool, Earl of

Sidney, Algernon (1622–83) English politician, born at Penshurst, Kent. An extreme Republican, he fought in the English Civil War, and in 1645 entered parliament. In 1683 he was implicated on flimsy evidence in the Rye House Plot, and beheaded.

Sidney, Margaret >> Lothrop, Harriet Mulford

Sidney, Sir Philip (1554–86) Poet, born at Penshurst, Kent. His literary work, written in 1578–82 but published posthumously, includes the unfinished pastoral romance, *Arcadia*, the *Defence of Poesie*, and a sonnet cycle, *Astrophel and Stella*.

Siebold, Karl Theodor Ernst von [zeebolt] (1804–85) Zoologist, born in Würzburg, Germany, the brother of Philipp Franz von Siebold. He carried out research on invertebrates, and made significant contributions to parasitology. >> Siebold, Philip von

Siebold, Philipp Franz von [zeebolt] (1796–1866) Physician and botanist, born in Würzburg, Germany. He was largely responsible for the introduction of Western medicine into Japan, and Japanese plants into European gardens. >> Siebold, Karl von

Sieff (of Brimpton), Israel Moses Sieff, Baron [seef] (1889–1972) Commercial executive, born in Manchester. With Simon Marks he developed Marks and Spencer, and became joint managing director of the company (1926–67). >> Marks, Simon

Siegbahn, Kai (Manne Börje) [seegbahn] (1918–) Physicist, born in Lund, Sweden, the son of Manne Siegbahn. He devised the technique of ESCA (electron spectroscopy for chemical analysis), and also worked on ultraviolet photoelectron spectroscopy. He shared the Nobel Prize for Physics in 1981. >> Siegbahn, Manne

Siegbahn, (Karl) Manne (Georg) [seegbahn] (1886–1978) Physicist, born in Örebro, Sweden. He discovered the M series in X-ray spectroscopy, for which he was awarded the Nobel Prize for Physics in 1924. >> Siegbahn, Kai

Siegel and Shuster [seegl, shuster] **Jerry Siegel** (1914–96), born in Cleveland, OH, and **Joseph Shuster** (1914–92), born in Toronto, Ontario, Canada. Strip cartoonists, they created *Superman* for Action Comics in 1938.

Siegen, Ludwig von [zeegen] (1609–c.1675) Painter, engraver, and inventor, born in Utrecht, The Netherlands. In 1642 he invented the mezzotint process, but only a handful of his prints are in existence.

Sielmann, Heinz [zeelman] (1917–) Naturalist and nature film photographer, born in Königsberg, Germany. He evolved techniques enabling him to film the inside of animal lairs and birds' nests, which revolutionized the study of animal behaviour.

Siemens, (Ernst) Werner von [zeemens] (1816–92) Electrical engineer, born in Lenthe, Germany, the brother of William (Wilhelm) Siemens. He developed the telegraphic system in Prussia, devised several forms of galvanometer, and determined the electrical resistance of different substances.

Siemens, Sir (Charles) William [zeemens], originally **Karl Wilhelm Siemens** (1823–83) Electrical engineer, born in Lenthe, Germany, the brother of Werner von Siemens. From 1858, as managing partner of the London branch of Siemens & Halske, he was responsible for the development of the first telegraph cable from Britain to America. >> Siemens, Werner von

Sienkiewicz, Henryk (Adam Alexander Pius) [shengkyayvich] (1846–1916) Novelist, born in Wola Okrzejska, Poland. His major work was a war trilogy about 17th-c Poland, beginning with *With Fire and Sword* (trans, 1884), but his most widely known book is *Quo Vadis?* (1896). He received the Nobel Prize for Literature in 1905.

Sierpinski, Wacław [serpinskee] (1882–1969) Mathematician, born in Warsaw. The leader of the Polish school of set theorists and topologists, he worked on set theory, topology, number theory, and logic.

Sierra, Gregorio Martínez >> **Martínez Sierra, Gregorio**

Sieyès, Emmanuel Joseph, comte de (Count of) [syayes], also known as **Abbé Sieyès** (1748–1836) French political theorist and clergyman, born in Fréjus, France. He became a member of the National Convention, the Committee of Public Safety (1795), and the Directory, helped organize the revolution of 18th Brumaire (1799), and was a member of the Consulate. He was exiled in 1815.

Sigismund (1368–1437) Holy Roman Emperor (1433–7), probably born in Nuremberg, Germany, the son of Charles IV. He became King of Hungary (1387), Germany (1411), and Bohemia (1419), but his succession in Bohemia was opposed by the Hussites. >> Huss

Signac, Paul [seenyak] (1863–1935) Artist, born in Paris. With Seurat he developed Divisionism (but using mosaic-like patches of pure colour rather than Seurat's pointillist dots), mainly in seascapes. >> Seurat

Signorelli, Luca [seenyawrelee], also known as **Luca da Cortona** (c.1441–1523) Painter, born in Cortona, Italy. The cathedral at Orvieto contains his greatest work, the frescoes of 'The Preaching of Anti-Christ' and 'The Last Judgment' (1500–4).

Signoret, Simone [seenyawray], originally **Simone Kaminker** (1921–85) Actress, born in Wiesbaden, Germany, raised in Paris. Her films include *La Ronde* (1950), *Room at the Top* (1959, Oscar), and *Ship of Fools* (1965). She was married to actor Yves Montand from 1951. >> Montand

Sigurdsson, Jón [seegoordson] (1811–79) Scholar and statesman, born in Hrafnseyri, Iceland. He led the movement to secure political autonomy and freedom of trade from Denmark, helped restore the ancient Althing (parliament), and became its speaker.

Sigurjónsson, Jóhann [seegoorjohnson] (1880–1919) Playwright and poet, born in Laxamýri, Iceland. The first Icelandic writer in modern times to achieve international recognition, his major play was *Eyvind of the Mountains* (trans, 1911).

Sihanouk, Prince Norodom [seeanook] (1922–) Cambodian leader, born in Phnom Penh. He was King of Cambodia (1941–55), chief of state (1960–70, and of the Khmer Republic 1975–6), prime minister on several occasions between 1952 and 1968, president of the government in exile (1970–5, 1982–91), president (1991–3), and once again king (1993–). His return to Cambodia in 1991 followed the peace treaty ending 13 years of civil war.

Sikorski, Władysław (Eugeniusz) [sikaw(r)skee] (1881–1943) Polish general and prime minister (1922–3), born in Galicia. In World War 2 he commanded the Free Polish forces, and from 1940 was premier of the Polish government in exile in London.

Sikorsky, Igor (Ivan) [sikaw(r)skee] (1889–1972) Aeronautical engineer, born in Kiev, Ukraine. He built and flew the first four-engined aeroplane in 1913, and in the USA developed the first successful helicopter, the VS-300 (1939).

Silas >> **McCay, Winsor**

Silhouette, Etienne de (1709–67) French statesman. Minister of finance in 1759, his hobby was the cutting out of paper profile portraits, which came to be called *silhouettes*.

Silius Italicus [silius italikus], in full **Tiberius Catius Asconius Silius Italicus** (c.25–101) Roman poet and politician. He wrote the longest surviving Latin poem, *Punica*, an epic in 17 books on the 2nd Punic War (218–201 BC).

Sillanpää, Frans Eemil [silanpah] (1888–1964) Novelist, born in Hämeenkyrö, Finland. His major works were *Meek Heritage* (trans, 1919) and *Fallen Asleep When Young* (trans, 1931). He was awarded the Nobel Prize for Literature in 1939.

Silliman, Benjamin >> **Dana, James D**

Sillitoe, Alan [silitoh] (1928–) Writer, born in Nottingham, Nottinghamshire. His best-known novels include *Saturday Night and Sunday Morning* (1958) and *The Loneliness of the Long Distance Runner* (1959; filmed 1962), and he has also written poetry and children's books.

Sills, Beverley, stage name of **Belle Miriam Silverman** (1929–) Operatic soprano, born in New York City. A gifted coloratura, she performed throughout the USA and Europe, retiring in 1979 to become general director of New York City Opera.

Silone, Ignazio [silohnay], pseudonym of **Secondo Tranquilli** (1900–78) Novelist, born in Aquilo, Italy. His books include *Fontamara* (1933), *Bread and wine* (trans, 1937), and *The Seed Beneath the Snow* (trans, 1941).

Silvers, Phil, popular name of **Philip Silver** (1912–85) Comic actor, born in New York City. The television series *The Phil Silvers Show* (1955–9) earned him three Emmy Awards and established him irrevocably as Sergeant Bilko.

Silvia, originally **Silvia Renate Sommerlath** (1943–) Queen of Sweden (1976–), born in Heidelberg, Germany. In 1971 she was appointed chief hostess in the

Organization Committee for the Olympic Games in Munich (1972), where she met Carl Gustaf, then heir to the Swedish throne. >> Carl XVI Gustaf

Sim, Alastair (1900–76) Actor, born in Edinburgh. His many films include *Scrooge* (1951), *An Inspector Calls* (1954), and *The Belles of St Trinians* (1954).

Sima Guang [seema gwang], also spelled **Ssu-ma Kuang** (1019–86) Chinese statesman-historian. His *Comprehensive Mirror for Aid in Government* (1066–84) gives complete dynastic coverage of Chinese history 403 BC–AD 959. >> Zhu Xi

Simak, Clifford (Donald) (1904–88) Science fiction writer, born in Milville, WI. His major work was the story sequence *The City* (1952), a chronicle in which dogs and robots take over a world abandoned by people.

Sima Qian [seema chyan] or **Ssu-ma Ch'ien** (c.145–c.87 BC) Historian, born in Lung-men, China. He is chiefly remembered for the *Shih Chi*, the first history of China compiled as dynastic histories.

Simenon, Georges (Joseph Christian) [seemenõ] (1903–89) Crime novelist, born in Liège, Belgium. He revolutionized detective fiction with his tough, morbidly psychological Inspector Maigret series, beginning in 1933.

Simeon, Charles (1759–1836) Evangelical clergyman, born in Reading, Berkshire. A renowned preacher, he led the evangelical revival in the Church of England, and helped form the Church Missionary Society (1797).

Simeon Stylites, St [stiyliyteez] (387–459), feast day 5 January (W), 1 September (E). The earliest of the Christian ascetic 'pillar' saints. In c.420 he established himself on top of a pillar c.20 m/70 ft high at Telanessa, near Antioch, where he spent the rest of his life preaching. His imitators were known as *stylites*.

Simmel, Georg (1858–1918) Sociologist and philosopher, born in Berlin. Instrumental in establishing sociology as a social science, he also wrote extensively on philosophy.

Simmonds, Kennedy A(lphonse) (1936–) Prime minister of St Kitts and Nevis (1983–). In 1965 he founded the People's Action Movement, and in 1980 formed a coalition government with the Nevis Reformation Party.

Simms, William Gilmore (1806–70) Writer, born in Charleston, CA. Best known for his historical novels, notably *The Yemassee* (1835), he also published short stories, poetry, biographies, and criticism.

Simnel, Lambert (c.1475–c.1535) Pretender to the throne, the son of a joiner. He bore a resemblance to Edward IV, and was set up in Ireland (1487) as his son, then as the Duke of Clarence's son, Edward, Earl of Warwick (1475–99). Crowned in Dublin as Edward VI, he landed in Lancashire, but was defeated. >> Clarence; Edward IV / V

Simon, Claude (Eugène Henri) [seemõ] (1913–) Novelist, born in Tananarive, Madagascar. His novels include (trans titles) *The Wind* (1957), *The Grass* (1958), and part of a four-volume cycle *The Flanders Road* (1960). He received the Nobel Prize for Literature in 1985.

Simon, Sir Francis (Eugen) (1893–1956) Physicist, born in Berlin. At the Clarendon Laboratory, Oxford, he verified experimentally the third law of thermodynamics, and under his influence Oxford became a centre for low-temperature physics.

Simon, Herbert (Alexander) (1916–) Economist, born in Milwaukee, WI. He wrote a pioneering economics study, *Administrative Behavior* (1947), and was awarded the Nobel Prize for Economics in 1978.

Simon (of Stackpole Elidor), John (Allsebrook) Simon, 1st Viscount (1873–1954) British statesman and lawyer, born in Manchester. He was attorney general (1913–15) and home secretary (1915–16), formed the Liberal National Party, and became foreign secretary (1931–5), home secretary (1935–7), Chancellor of the Exchequer (1937–40), and Lord Chancellor (1940–5).

Simon, (Marvin) Neil (1927–) Playwright, born in New York City. His shows include *Barefoot in the Park* (1963), *California Suite* (1976), *Biloxi Blues* (1985, Tony), and *Lost in Yonkers* (1991, Pulitzer, Tony).

Simon, Paul (1941–) Singer, songwriter, and guitarist, born in Newark, NJ. He teamed up with **Art Garfunkel** (1941–) at the age of 15, achieving major successes with 'The Sound Of Silence' (1965) and the album *Bridge Over Troubled Water* (1970). In 1970 Garfunkel quit the duo for films, appearing in *Catch 22* (1970) and *Carnal Knowledge* (1971), and also made solo recordings. Simon's solo career, using Third-World choirs and percussionists, led to one of the most successful albums of the 1980s, *Graceland* (1986).

Simone, Nina, stage name of **Eunice Waymon** (1933–) Jazz singer, pianist, and songwriter, born in Tryon, NC. Her early hits included 'I Loves You, Porgy' and 'My Baby Just Cares for Me' (1958), and she became known for her protest songs in the 1960s.

Simonides of Ceos [siymonideez, seeos] (c.556–c.468 BC) Poet, born in Iulis on the island of Ceos. When Persia invaded Greece he celebrated the heroes and the battles in elegies, epigrams, odes, and dirges.

Simon Magus [maygus], Eng **Simon the Magician** (1st-c) Practitioner of magic arts, who appears in Samaria c.37. His offer to buy the gift of the Holy Ghost was condemned by Peter (*Acts* 8), and the term *simony* derives from his name.

Simonov, Konstantin Mikhailovich [seemonof] (1915– 79) Russian writer and journalist. His chief works are a historical poem about Alexander Nevski, poems of World War 2, the novel *Days and Nights*, and the play *The Russians*. He was awarded the Stalin Prize three times.

Simpson, Sir George (c.1787–1860) Explorer and administrator, born in Lochbroom, Highland. In 1828 he made an overland journey around the world. *Simpson's Falls* and *Cape George Simpson* are named after him.

Simpson, Sir George (Clarke) (1878–1965) Meteorologist, born in Derby, Derbyshire. He was Scott's meteorologist on the Antarctic expedition (1910), and investigated the causes of lightning. >> Scott, R F

Simpson, George Gaylord (1902–84) Palaeontologist, born in Chicago, IL. He was a central figure in the fusion of genetics and palaeontology to form modern Darwinism.

Simpson, Sir James Young (1811–70) Obstetrician, born in Bathgate, Lothian. He introduced chloroform as an anaesthetic, and was the first to use it as such in labour.

Simpson, O(renthal) J(ames) (1947–) Player of American football, born in San Francisco, CA. He joined the Buffalo Bills in 1968, leading the League as top rusher four times (1972–6). In 1994 he was arrested on a charge of murder, his court case achieving unprecedented media publicity in 1995. He was acquitted later that year.

Simpson, Robert (Wilfred Levick) (1921–) Composer and writer, born in Leamington, Warwickshire. His works include 11 symphonies, 14 string quartets, concertos for piano and flute, and a great deal of chamber music.

Simpson, Thomas (1710–61) Mathematician, born in Nuneaton, Warwickshire. He published a long series of works (1737–57) on algebra, trigonometry, chance, and other topics.

Simpson, Thomas (1938–67) Cyclist, born in Easington, Durham. In 1962 he became the first Briton ever to wear the leader's yellow jersey in the Tour de France, but died during the 1967 race.

Simpson, Wallis Warfield >> Windsor, Duchess of

Sims, William (Sowden) (1858–1936) US naval officer, born in Port Hope, Ontario, Canada. In World War 1 he was commander of US Naval Forces in Europe, devising a convoy system to protect merchant shipping.

Sinatra, Frank, popular name of **Francis Albert Sinatra**

(1915–) Singer and actor, born in Hoboken, NJ. His films include *From Here to Eternity* (1953, Oscar), *High Society* (1956), and *The Manchurian Candidate* (1962), and he produced his masterworks in a series of recordings (1956–65), especially the albums *Songs for Swinging Lovers*, *Come Fly With Me*, and *That's Life*.

Sinclair, Sir Clive (Marles) (1940–) British electronic engineer and inventor. He launched a company in 1962 which successfully marketed calculators, miniature television sets, and personal computers, and later developed a small three-wheeled 'personal transport' vehicle, the C5.

Sinclair, Sir Keith (1922–93) Historian and author, born in Auckland, New Zealand. He established New Zealand history as an object of scholarly study in its own right.

Sinclair, Upton (Beall) (1878–1968) Novelist and social reformer, born in Baltimore, MD. He exposed meat-packing conditions in Chicago in his novel *The Jungle* (1906). Later works include an 11-volume series about 'Lanny Budd', starting with *World's End* (1940) and including *Dragon's Teeth* (1942, Pulitzer).

Sinden, Donald (Alfred) (1923–) Actor, born in Plymouth, Devon. Known for his theatre work, he gave acclaimed performances in the classics. His films include *The Cruel Sea* and *Doctor in the House*, and his television series *Two's Company*, *Our Man From St Mark's*, and *Never the Twain*.

Singer, Esther, married name **Kreitman** (1892–) Yiddish novelist, born in Radzymin, Poland, the sister of Isaac Bashevis and Israel Joshua Singer. Her *Der sheydim tants* (1936), was later translated as *Deborah* (1946). >> Singer, Isaac Bashevis / I J

Singer, Isaac Bashevis (1904–91) Yiddish writer, born in Radzymin, Poland. He emigrated to the USA in 1935. His novels include *The Family Moskat* (1950), *The Manor* (1967), *The Estate* (1970), and *Enemies: a Love Story* (1972). He was awarded the Nobel Prize for Literature in 1978.

Singer, Isaac (Merritt) (1811–75) Inventor and manufacturer of sewing machines, born in Pittstown, NY. At Boston in 1852 he devised an improved single-thread, chain-stitch sewing machine. >> Howe, Elias

Singer, I(srael) J(oshua) (1893–1944) Yiddish writer, born in Bilgorai, Poland, the brother of Isaac Bashevis and Esther Singer. His novels have been widely translated, and include *The Brothers Ashkenazi* (1936), *The River Breaks Up* (1938), and *East of Eden* (1939). >> Singer, Esther / Isaac Bashevis

Singh, V(ishwanath) P(ratap) (1931–) Indian prime minister (1989–90), born in Allahabad, India. He served as minister of commerce (1976–7), finance (1984–6), and defence (1986–7), and became head of the Vanseta Dal coalition.

Siqueiros, David Alfaro [sikayros] (1896–1974) Mural painter, born in Chihuahua, Mexico. One of the principal figures in 20th-c Mexican mural painting, he was notable for his experiments with modern synthetic materials.

Siraj-ud-Daula [siraj ud dowla], originally **Mirza Muhammad** (c.1732–57) Ruler of Bengal under the nominal suzerainty of the Mughal Empire. He forced the British to surrender at Calcutta, but was defeated at Plassey (1857), and executed. >> Clive

Sirhan, (Bishara) Sirhan [sirhahn] (c.1943–) Assassin of Senator Robert Kennedy, born in Palestine. He shot Kennedy for his pro-Israeli views, during the lead-up to the presidential nomination in 1968, and was sentenced to life imprisonment.

Sisley, Alfred [seeslay] (1839–99) Impressionist painter and etcher, born in Paris. He painted landscapes almost exclusively, particularly in the valleys of the Seine, Loire, and Thames.

Sithole, Reverend Ndabaningi [sitohlay] (1920–) Zimbabwean politician and clergyman, born in Nya-

mandhlovu, Zimbabwe (formerly, Rhodesia). President of the Zimbabwe African National Union in 1963, he joined Mugabe in his struggle against Nkomo, and later moved into a close political alliance with Muzorewa. >> Mugabe; Muzorewa; Nkomo

Sitsky, Larry (1934–) Composer, pianist, and teacher, born in Tientsin, China. A prolific writer in many genres, his major compositions include *The Fall of the House of Usher* (1965) and the opera *Lenz* (1970).

Sitter, Willem de (1872–1934) Astronomer, born in Sneek, The Netherlands. He computed the size of the universe as 2000 million light years in radius, containing about 80 000 million galaxies.

Sitting Bull, Sioux name **Tatanka Iyotake** (1834–90) Warrior and chief of the Dakota Sioux, born near Grand River, SD. He was a leader in the Sioux War (1876–7), and led the defeat of Custer and his men at the Little Big Horn (1876). >> Custer

Sitwell, Dame Edith (1887–1964) Poet, born in Scarborough, North Yorkshire, the sister of Osbert and Sacheverell Sitwell. Her experimental poetry was controversially received with *Façade* (1922); her later works, such as *The Outcasts* (1962), reflect a deeper religious symbolism. >> Sitwell, Osbert / Sacheverell

Sitwell, Sir Osbert (1892–1969) Writer, born in London, the brother of Edith and Sacheverell Sitwell. He gained notoriety with his satirical novel *Before the Bombardment* (1927), but is best known for his five-volume autobiographical series, beginning with *Left Hand: Right Hand* (1944). >> Sitwell, Edith / Sacheverell

Sitwell, Sir Sacheverell [sasheverell] (1897–1988) Poet and art critic, born in Scarborough, North Yorkshire, the brother of Edith and Osbert Sitwell. His many volumes of poetry cover a period of over 30 years, from *The People's Palace* (1918) to *An Indian Summer* (1982).

Sivaji [sivahjee] (c.1627–80) Founder of the Maratha Kingdom in W India, born at Shivner, Poona. Enthroned as an independent ruler in 1674, he became renowned as a military leader, social reformer, and advocate of religious tolerance.

Sixtus IV, originally **Francesco della Rovere** (1414–84) Pope (1471–84), a former Franciscan preacher, born in Cella Ligure, Italy. He fostered learning, and built the *Sistine Chapel* and the *Sistine bridge*.

Sjöström, Victor [sjoestroem], also known as **Victor Seastrom** (1879–1960) Film actor and director, born in Silbodal, Sweden. His ability to adapt classic Swedish writers to the screen gave Swedish cinema popular appeal. His best-known Hollywood films were *The Scarlet Letter* (1926) and *The Wind* (1928).

Skalkottas, Nikos or **Nikolaus** [skalkotas] (1904–49) Composer, born in Khalkis, Greece. His works, dating mostly from the period 1935–45, show a complex use of serial techniques, and exploit Greek and Balkan folk elements.

Skallagrímsson, Egill (c.910–990) Poet and warrior, born in Iceland. In 960 he lost two young sons, and composed the greatest lament in Old Icelandic poetry, *Sonatorrek* (On the Loss of Sons). He is the hero of *Egils saga*.

Skanderbeg [skanderbek], nickname of **George Castriota** or **Kastrioti** (1405–68) Albanian patriot, the son of a prince of Emathia. In 1443 he drove the Turks from Albania, and for 20 years maintained Albanian independence.

Skeat, W(alter) W(illiam) (1835–1912) Philologist, born in London. Founder of the Dialect Society (1873), his main works include the *Etymological English Dictionary* (1879–82) and *Chaucer* (6 vols, 1894–5).

Skelton, John (c.1460–1529) Satirical poet, born in Norfolk. He wrote satirical vernacular poetry, such as *The Bowge of Courte* (c.1499) and *Colyn Cloute* (1522).

Skelton, Red, popular name of **Richard Bernard Skelton**

(1913–) Entertainer, born in Vincennes, IN. A variety performer of stage, radio, television, and films, he is remembered for the NBC television programme *The Red Skelton Show* (1951–71).

Skinner, B(urrhus) F(rederic) (1904–90) Psychologist, born in Susquehanna, PA. A leading behaviourist, he was a proponent of operant conditioning, and the inventor of the *Skinner box* for facilitiating experimental observations. His main scientific works include *The Behavior of Organisms* (1938) and *Verbal Behavior* (1957).

Skinner, James (1778–1841) Soldier of Eurasian origin in the Indian army. He formed *Skinner's Horse*, one of the most famous regiments in India, and later settled in Delhi.

Skobtsova, Maria [skobtsohva] (1891–1945) Russian Orthodox nun, born in Riga, Latvia. Unconventional and radical, she worked among society's cast-offs, and was sent to Ravensbrück concentration camp in 1943, where she was killed.

Skorzeny, Otto [skaw(r)tsaynee] (1908–75) Austrian soldier, born in Vienna. He was noted for his commando-style operations in World War 2, freeing Mussolini from internment (1943), and abducting Horthy (1944), but failing to capture Tito. >> Horthy; Mussolini; Tito

Skram, (Bertha) Amalie, *née* Alver (1846/7–1905) Novelist, born in Bergen, Norway. Her tetralogy, *People of Hellemyr* (trans, 1887–90), is a Norwegian classic of Naturalism, outlining the emotional deterioration of a family over four generations.

Skriabin, Alexander >> Scriabin, Alexander

Skum, Nils Nilsson [skoom] (1872–1951) Artist of the Sami (Lapp) people. Born into a nomadic family of reindeer hunters, his paintings form one of the first comprehensive studies of traditional Sami life.

Slade, Felix (1790–1868) Antiquary and art collector, born in Halsteads, Yorkshire. He bequeathed his engravings and Venetian glass to the British Museum, and founded the Slade School of Art, London.

Slater, Samuel (1768–1835) Mechanical engineer, born in Belper, Derbyshire. In the USA from 1789, he became a partner in the firm of Almy, Brown & Slater, whose prosperity laid the foundation for the US cotton textile industry.

Sleep, Wayne (1948–) Dancer and choreographer, born in Plymouth, Devon. In 1980 he formed his own touring group, Dash, and later adapted *The Hot Shoe Show* (1983–4) into a fast-paced, live revue.

Slessor, Sir John (Cotesworth) (1897–1979) British air-marshal, born in Rhanikhet, India. In World War 2 he was commander-in-chief of Coastal Command (1943) and of the Mediterranean theatre (1944–5).

Slessor, Kenneth (Adolf) (1901–71) Writer and journalist, born in Orange, New South Wales, Australia. His best-known poem is 'Beach Burial', a tribute to Australian troops who fought during World War 2, and he also co-edited *The Penguin Book of Australian Verse* (1958).

Slessor, Mary (1848–1915) Presbyterian missionary, born in Aberdeen, Grampian. She spent many years working as a teacher for the United Presbyterian Church, in Calabar, Nigeria, from 1876.

Slevogt, Max [slayfohkht] (1868–1932) Impressionist painter and engraver, born in Landshut, Germany. His works comprise murals of historical scenes, landscapes, and portraits.

Slim (of Yarralumia and of Bishopston), William (Joseph) Slim, 1st Viscount (1891–1970) British field marshal, born in Bristol, Avon. In World War 2, his greatest achievement was to lead his reorganized forces, the famous 14th 'Forgotten Army', to victory over the Japanese in Burma.

Slipher, Vesto Melvin (1875–1969) Astronomer, born in Mulberry, IN. In 1912 he determined the periods of rota-

tion of Uranus, Jupiter, Saturn, Venus, and Mars, and later discovered the general recession of galaxies (outside the Local Group) from our own galaxy.

Sloan, Alfred P(ritchard), Jr (1875–1966) Industrialist and philanthropist, born in New Haven, CT. He became president (1924) of General Motors, founded the Alfred P Sloan Foundation (1937), and established the Sloan-Kettering Institute for Cancer Research (1945).

Sloan, John (French) (1871–1951) Artist, born in Lock Haven, PA. A member of 'The Eight', he produced a series of intimate warm-hearted etchings based on New York City life, which gave rise to the name 'Ashcan school'.

Sloane, Sir Hans (1660–1753) Physician, born in Killy-leagh, Co Down. His museum and library of 50 000 volumes and 3560 manuscripts formed the nucleus of the British Museum.

Slocum, Joshua [slohkm] (1844–c.1910) Mariner, the first man to sail round the world single-handed, born in Wilmot Township, Nova Scotia, Canada. In 1895 he set out from Boston on the sloop *Spray*, arriving back at Newport in 1898.

Slovo, Joe [slohvoh] (1926–95) South African political leader, born in Lithuania. He held high office in both the Communist Party and the African National Congress, and played a major role in the negotiations for a new dispensation. In 1994 he was appointed minister for housing in Mandela's first cabinet. >> First; Mandela, Nelson

Sluter, Claus or **Claes** [slooter] (c.1350–c.1405) Sculptor, probably born in Haarlem, The Netherlands. His chief works are the porch sculptures of the Carthusian house of Champmol near Dijon, and the tomb of Philip the Bold.

Smeaton, Bruce (James) (1938–) Composer for film and television, born in Brighton, Victoria, Australia. His work for major feature films has won many awards, such as *Picnic at Hanging Rock* (1975). Other works include a cello concerto, music for brass, chamber music, and a ballet.

Smeaton, John (1724–94) Civil engineer, born in Austhorpe, West Yorkshire. He became known with a design for the third Eddystone lighthouse (1756–9), using dovetailed blocks of stone.

Smellie, William (1740–95) Editor, printer, and antiquary, born in Edinburgh. In 1765 he set up a printing business and, with Andrew Bell (1726–1809) and Colin MacFar-quhar (?1745–?93), produced the first edition of the *Encyclopaedia Britannica* (1768–71).

Smetana, Bedřich [smetana] (1824–84) Composer, born in Litomyšl, Czech Republic. His compositions, intensely national in character, include nine operas, notably *The Bartered Bride* (trans, 1866), and many chamber and orchestral works, including the series of symphonic poems *My Country* (trans, 1874–9).

Smiles, Samuel (1812–1904) Writer and social reformer, born in Haddington, Lothian, Scotland. His main work was a guide to self-improvement, *Self-Help* (1859), with its short lives of great men and the admonition 'Do thou likewise'.

Smirke, Sir Robert (1781–1867) British architect, the son of Robert Smirke (1752–1845), painter and book-illustrator. The British Museum (1823–47) was his best known work, completed by his brother, Sydney (1799–1877).

Smith, Adam (1723–90) Economist and philosopher, born in Kirkcaldy, Fife. In 1776 he published *An Inquiry into the Nature and Causes of the Wealth of Nations*, the first major work of political economy.

Smith, Alfred E(manuel), also called **Al Smith** (1873–1944) US politician, born in New York City. The first Roman Catholic to run for the presidency, he was beaten by Hoover in the 1928 election. >> Hoover, Herbert

Smith, Bessie, nickname **Empress of the Blues** (c.1898–1937) Blues singer, born in Chattanooga, TN. Considered one of the outstanding African-American artistes of her day, she made a series of classic blues recordings throughout the 1920s, and starred in the 1929 film, *St Louis Blues*.

Smith, David R(oland) (1906–65) Sculptor, born in Decatur, IN. His first welded-steel sculptures date from 1932. During the 1930s he assimilated avant-garde European styles, later producing nonrepresentational works such as the 'Zig' series (1960).

Smith, Dodie, pseudonym **C I. Anthony** (1896–1990) Playwright, novelist, and theatre producer, born in Whitefield, Greater Manchester. Among her best known works are the play *Dear Octopus* (1938) and the children's book *The Hundred and One Dalmatians* (1956; filmed 1961).

Smith, Florence Margaret >> Smith, Stevie

Smith, George (1824–1901) Publisher, born in London. He joined his father's firm of Smith & Elder in 1838, and became head in 1846, founding the *Cornhill Magazine* (1860) and the *Pall Mall Gazette* (1865), and publishing the *Dictionary of National Biography* (63 vols, 1885–1900).

Smith, Gerrit (1797–1874) Reformer and philanthropist, born in Utica, NY. He financed John Brown's anti-slavery crusades, and was a leader in the organization of the anti-slavery Liberal Party. >> Brown, John

Smith, Hamilton (Othanel) (1931–) Molecular biologist, born in New York City. In the 1970s he obtained enzymes from bacteria which would split genes to give genetically active fragments ('restriction enzymes'), and shared the Nobel Prize for Physiology or Medicine in 1978. >> Arber, Werner; Nathans

Smith, (Robert) Harvey (1938–) Show-jumper, born in Bingley, Yorkshire. He won the British championships and the British Grand Prix on several occasions, and represented Britain in the 1968 and 1972 Olympic Games.

Smith, Henry Edward >> Smith, William Henry

Smith, Henry (John Stephen) (1826–83) Mathematician, born in Dublin. The greatest authority of his day on the theory of numbers, he also wrote on elliptic functions and modern geometry.

Smith, Horace >> Wesson, Daniel Baird

Smith, Ian (Douglas) (1919–) Rhodesian prime minister (1964–79), born in Selukwe, Zimbabwe (formerly, Rhodesia). He unilaterally declared independence (1965), which led to severe economic sanctions. After formal independence (1980), he continued to be a vigorous opponent of the one-party state.

Smith, James (microscopist) >> **Lister, Joseph Jackson**

Smith, Jedediah (Strong) (1799–1831) Fur trader and explorer, born in Jericho, NY. He explored the Central Rockies and Columbia R areas (1823–30), and became the first white man to reach California overland across the Sierra Nevada Mts and Great Basin to the Pacific.

Smith, John (1580–1631) Adventurer, born in Willoughby, Lincolnshire. He joined an expedition to colonize Virginia (1607), where his energy in dealing with the Indians led to his being elected president of the colony (1608–9).

Smith, John (1938–94) British politician, born in Dalmally, Strathclyde. He became shadow Chancellor of the Exchequer (1988) and Labour leader (1992). His unexpected death caused an unusually strong sense of national loss.

Smith, John Stafford (1750–1836) Composer, and musical scholar, born in Gloucester, Gloucestershire. He wrote vocal music, and the tune of 'The Star-spangled Banner'.

Smith, Joseph (1805–44) Religious leader, born in Sharon, VT. He received his first 'call' as a prophet in 1820, and in 1827 the *Book of Mormon* was delivered into his hands. He established the new 'Church of the Latter-day Saints', and founded Nauvoo, IL (1840), becoming mayor, but was imprisoned for conspiracy, and killed by a mob. >> Young, Brigham

Smith, Keith >> Smith, Ross

Smith, Logan Pearsall (1865–1946) Writer, born in Millville, NJ. He is best remembered for his essays, collected in *All Trivia* (1933) and *Reperusals and Re-collections* (1936), and his short stories.

Smith, Maggie, popular name of **Dame Margaret Natalie Smith** (1934–) Actress, born in Ilford, Essex. Her films include *The Prime of Miss Jean Brodie* (1969, Oscar) and *California Suite* (1978, Oscar), and she received BAFTA Awards for her roles in *A Private Function* (1984), *A Room With a View* (1986), and *The Lonely Passion of Judith Hearne* (1987).

Smith, Maria Ann (c.1801–70) Orchardist, born in Australia. In the 1860s she experimented with a hardy French crab-apple from the cooler climate of Tasmania, from which she developed the *Granny Smith* apple.

Smith, Sir Matthew Arnold Bracy (1879–1959) Artist, born in Halifax, West Yorkshire. In 1915 he exhibited with the London Group, and later painted much in Provence.

Smith, Rodney, known as **Gypsy Smith** (1860–1947) Evangelist, born of nomadic gypsy parents near Epping Forest, Essex. He joined William Booth as one of the first officers in the newly formed Salvation Army, after 1882 evangelizing for the Free Church. >> Booth, William

Smith, Sir Ross Macpherson (1892–1922) Aviator, born in Semaphore, South Australia. In 1919 he and his brother, Keith (1890–1955), flew from London to Darwin in 28 days in a Vickers Vimy bi-plane.

Smith, Sophia (1796–1870) Philanthropist, born in Hartfield, MA. Inheriting a fortune, she willed this money to be used to found a women's college; Smith College, Northampton, MA, was opened in 1875.

Smith, Stevie, pseudonym of **Florence Margaret Smith** (1902–71) Writer and novelist, born in Hull, Humberside. She gained a reputation as an eccentrically humorous poet on serious themes, illustrated by 'Not Waving but Drowning' (1957).

Smith, Sydney (1771–1845) Clergyman, essayist, and wit, born in Woodford, Essex. Well known as a preacher, his writings include several collections of articles, letters, and pamphlets on a wide variety of themes.

Smith, Sir Sydney Alfred (1883–1969) Forensic medical expert, born in Roxburgh, New Zealand. As professor of forensic medicine at Edinburgh (1928–53), he played a major part in the medical and ballistic aspects of crime detection. >> Smith, Sydney Goodsir

Smith, Sydney Goodsir (1915–75) Poet, born in Wellington, New Zealand, the son of Sydney Alfred Smith. He moved to Edinburgh in 1928, and became known as a Lallans poet with such works as *Skail Wind* (1941) and *So Late into the Night* (1952). >> Smith, Sydney Alfred

Smith, Theobald (1859–1934) Microbiologist and immunologist, born in Albany, NY. He worked on human and bovine tuberculosis, improved the range of vaccines, and established techniques for the bacteriological examination of water, milk, and sewage.

Smith, Tommie (1944–) Sprinter, born in Clarksville, TN. He set world records for both the 220 yd and the 200 m in 1966, and in the 1968 Olympics won the gold medal in the 200 m in a world record time of 19·8 s.

Smith, William (1769–1839) Civil engineer, born in Churchill, Oxfordshire. His epoch-making Geological Map of England (1815) was followed by 21 coloured maps of the geology of the English counties (1819–24).

Smith, Sir William (1854–1914) Businessman, and founder of the Boys' Brigade, born near Thurso, Highland, Scotland. He began his movement for 'the advancement of Christ's Kingdom among Boys' in 1883.

Smith, W(illiam) Eugene (1918–78) Photojournalist, born in Wichita, KS. A photographer with *Life* (1939–41)

and a war correspondent (1942-54), his photo essays focused on life in small villages in many parts of the world.

Smith, William Henry (1792-1865) British newsagent. He entered his father's newsagent's business in the Strand, London (1812), and aided by his brother, Henry Edward, expanded it into the largest in Britain. >> Smith, W(illiam) H(enry)

Smith, W(illiam) H(enry) (1825-91) Newsagent, bookseller and statesman, born in London, the son of William Henry Smith. In 1849 he secured the privilege of selling books and newspapers at railway stations. He later became secretary for war (1885) and Leader of the House of Commons. >> Smith, William Henry

Smithson, James Louis Macie (1765-1829) Chemist, born in Paris. In 1826 he endowed his inherited fortune for the founding of the Smithsonian Institution in Washington, DC (opened 1855).

Smithson, Robert (1938-73) Land artist, born in Passaic, NJ. From c.1966 he began to exhibit his 'non-sites' - maps of sites he had visited, together with samples of rocks and soil, such as the 'Spiral Jetty on the Great Salt Lake, Utah' (1970).

Smollett, Tobias (George) (1721-71) Novelist, born in Cardross, Strathclyde. He achieved success with his picaresque novels *The Adventures of Roderick Random* (1748) and *The Adventures of Peregrine Pickle* (1751), and his masterpiece, *Humphry Clinker* (1771).

Smuts, Jan (Christiaan) (1870-1950) South African general and prime minister (1919-24, 1939-48), born in Malmesbury, Cape Colony, South Africa. He was a significant figure at Versailles, instrumental in the founding of the League of Nations. His coalition with the Nationalists in 1934 produced the United Party.

Smyslov, Vasily Vasiliyevich [smislof] (1921-) Chess player, and world champion (1957-58), born in Moscow. He beat Botvinnik to become world champion in 1957, but lost the title in the 1958 re-match. >> Botvinnik

Smyth, Dame Ethel Mary (1858-1944) Composer and suffragette, born in London. Her works include a Mass in D Minor, symphonies, choral works, and operas. She composed the battle-song of the Women's Social and Political Union, 'The March of the Women' (1911).

Smythe, Francis Sydney (1900-49) Mountaineer, born in Maidstone, Kent. He took part in three Everest expeditions (1933, 1936, 1938), and as a member of the Swiss Kanchenjunga expedition became the first to climb the Himalayan peak Kamet in 1931.

Smythe, Pat(ricia), married name **Koechlin** (1928-96) Show jumper, born in Switzerland. She won the European championship four times on *Flanagan* (1957, 1961-3), and in 1956 was the first woman to ride in the Olympic Games.

Smythe, Reg(inald Smith) (1917-) Strip cartoonist, born in Hartlepool, Cleveland. He created *Andy Capp* for the *Daily Mirror* in 1958, the first British strip to be syndicated worldwide.

Smythson, Robert (c.1535-1614) English architect. Trained as a mason, his masterpiece was Wollaton Hall, Nottingham (1580-8), a mock mediaeval castle, which introduced a new vertical plan into contemporary building.

Snagge, John (Derrick Mordaunt) (1904-) British broadcaster, whose voice came to represent the traditional values of the BBC. He provided the commentary on the Oxford and Cambridge Boat Race for many years (1931-80).

Snead, Sam(uel Jackson), nickname **Slammin' Sammy** (1912-) Golfer, born in Hot Springs, VA. He won the British Open (1946), the US PGA Championship (1942, 1949, 1951), and the US Masters (1949, 1952, 1954).

Snell, George (Davis) (1903-) Immunologist, born in

Bradford, MA. His experiments in immunology did much to make future organ transplants possible, and he shared the Nobel Prize for Physiology or Medicine in 1980.

Snell, Peter (1938-) Athlete, born in Opunake, Taranaki, New Zealand. He won the Olympic 800 m in 1960, and went on to win golds in both the 800 m and 1500 m in 1964.

Snell, Willebrod van Roijen, Lat **Snellius** (1580-1626) Mathematician, born in The Netherlands. He discovered the law of refraction known as *Snell's law*.

Snorri Sturluson >> Sturluson, Snorri

Snow, C(harles) P(ercy) Snow, Baron (1905-80) Novelist and physicist, born in Leicester, Leicestershire. He is known for a cycle of successful novels portraying English life from 1920 onwards, beginning with *Strangers and Brothers* (1940), and for his controversial lecture, *The Two Cultures and the Scientific Revolution* (1959). He married the novelist Pamela Hansford Johnson in 1950. >> Johnson, Pamela Hansford

Snow, John (1813-58) Anaesthetist and epidemiologist, born in York, North Yorkshire. He did pioneering experimental work on ether and chloroform, and devised apparatus to administer anaesthetics.

Snowdon, Antony Armstrong-Jones, 1st Earl of (1930-) Photographer and designer, born in London. He designed the Aviary of the London Zoo in 1965, and later presented the conditions of the handicapped, both in photographic studies and in television documentaries. He married Princess Margaret in 1960 (divorced 1978).

Snyder, Gary (Sherman) (1930-) Poet, born in San Francisco, CA. Associated with the Beat poets, his writing also displays his interest in Asian religious practices and literary traditions, as in *Turtle Island* (1975, Pulitzer).

Snyders, Frans (1579-1657) Painter, born in Antwerp, Belgium. He specialized in still-life and animals, and is well known for his hunting scenes.

Soames (of Fletching), (Arthur) Christopher (John) Soames, Baron (1920-87) British Conservative statesman. He served as secretary of state for war (1958-60) and agriculture minister (1960-64).

Soane, Sir John (1753-1837) Architect, born in Goring, Oxfordshire. His designs include the Bank of England (1792-1833, now rebuilt), and Dulwich College Art Gallery (1811-14).

Soares, Mario (Alberto Nobre Lopez) [swahresh] (1924-) Portuguese prime minister (1976-8, 1983-5) and president (1986-), born in Lisbon. In 1968 he was deported by Salazar, then returned to co-found the Social Democratic Party, becoming Portugal's first civilian president for 60 years. >> Salazar

Sobers, Garry [sohberz], popular name of **Sir Garfield St Aubrun Sobers** (1936-) Cricketer, born in Barbados. A great West Indian all-rounder, he is the only man to score 8000 Test runs and take 200 wickets. During his career (1953-74) he scored 28 315 runs in first-class cricket and took 1043 wickets.

Sobukwe, Robert Mangaliso [sohbookway] (1924-78) African nationalist leader, born in Graaff-Reinet, South Africa. He was the co-founder and first president of the Pan African Congress, and was jailed in 1960, detained under legislation (nicknamed the 'Sobukwe clause') used only against him.

Socinus, Faustus [sosiynus], Ital **Fausto Paulo Sozini** (1539-1604) Protestant reformer, born in Siena, Italy. He developed the anti-Trinitarian doctrines of his uncle, Laelius Socinus, founding the *Socinian* sect. >> Socinus, Laelius

Socinus, Laelius [sosiynus], Ital **Lelio (Francesco Maria) Sozini** (1525-62) Protestant reformer, born in Siena, Italy. He trained as a lawyer at Padua, then turned to biblical studies, developing anti-Trinitarian views later known as *Socinianism*. >> Socinus, Faustus

Socrates [sok**rateez**] (469–399 BC) Greek philosopher, born in Athens. His personality and his doctrines were immortalized in Plato's dialogues. He devoted his last 30 years to convincing the Athenians that their opinions about moral matters could not bear the weight of critical scrutiny. He was tried on charges of impiety and corruption of the youth by defenders of a restored democracy in Athens, found guilty, and put to death. >> Plato

Soddy, Frederick (1877–1956) Radiochemist, born in Eastbourne, East Sussex. In 1913 he discovered forms of the same element with identical chemical qualities but different atomic weights (*isotopes*), for which he received the Nobel Prize for Chemistry in 1921.

Söderberg, Hjalmar (Erik Fredrik) [soederberg] (1849–1941) Writer, born in Stockholm. He wrote collections of witty short stories, novels, such as *Aberrations* (trans, 1985) and *Doktor Glas* (1905), and plays, such as *Gertrud* (1905).

Söderblom, Nathan [soederblom] (1866–1931) Lutheran archbishop, born in Trönö, Sweden. Primate of the Swedish Lutheran Church and a leader in the ecumenical movement, he was awarded the Nobel Peace Prize in 1930.

Södergran, Edith (Irene) [soedergran] (1892–1923) Expressionist poet, born in St Petersburg, Russia. Regarded as the originator of the Swedish-Finnish Modernist movement, her best-known work is *The Non-Existent Country*, published posthumously in 1925.

Söderström, Elisabeth Anna [soederstroem] (1927–) Soprano, born in Sweden. She appeared at Glyndebourne in 1957, the Metropolitan Opera Company in 1959, and Covent Garden in 1960, and subsequently sang in all the leading international opera houses.

Sodoma, Il, ('The Sodomite'), originally **Giovanni Antonio Bazzi** (1477–1549) Religious and historical painter, born in Vercelli, Duchy of Savoy. Called to the Vatican in 1508, he began to paint the fresco of 'The Marriage of Alexander and Roxane' in the Villa Farnesina.

Soeharto >> Suharto

Soekarno, Achmad >> Sukarno, Achmad

Sokolow, Anna [sokoloh] (1912–) Dancer, choreographer, and teacher, born in Hartford, CT. One of Martha Graham's original dancers (1930–9), she began choreographing from 1934, and founded the first modern dance company in Mexico, La Paloma Azul, in 1939. >> Graham, Martha

Solario, Antonio [solahrioh], nickname **lo Zingaro** ('the Gypsy') (c.1382–1455) Painter, born in Civita, in the Abruzzi, Italy. He painted frescoes in the Benedictine monastery at Naples.

Solomon (Hebrew Bible) (10th-c BC) King of Israel, the second son of David and Bathsheba. His outwardly splendid reign (1 *Kings* 1–11) saw the expansion of the kingdom and the building of the great Temple in Jerusalem. Credited with great wisdom, his name was attached to several biblical and extra-canonical writings. >> David

Solomon (music), professional name of **Solomon Cutner** (1902–88) Pianist, born in London. He won a high reputation as a performer of the works of Beethoven, Brahms, and some of the modern composers.

Solon [sohlon] (7th–6th-c BC) Athenian statesman, lawgiver, and poet. As chief archon, he enacted many economic, constitutional, and legal reforms, and paved the way for the development of democracy at Athens.

Solovyev, Vladimir Sergeyevich [solevyof] (1853–1900) Philosopher, theologian, and poet, born in Moscow. He proposed a universal Christianity which would unite the Catholic and Orthodox churches, and attempted a synthesis of religious philosophy with science.

Solow, Robert (Merton) [soloh] (1924–) Economist, born in New York City. He was awarded the 1987 Nobel Prize for Economics for his 'study of the factors which permit production growth and increased welfare'.

Solti, Sir Georg [sholtee] (1912–) Conductor, born in Budapest. He became director at the Munich Staatsoper (1946–1952), Frankfurt (1952–61), and Covent Garden, London (1961–71), later conducting the Chicago Symphony Orchestra (1969–91) and the London Philharmonic (1979–83).

Solvay, Ernest (1838–1922) Industrial chemist, born in Rebecq-Rognon, Belgium. In 1863 he solved the problems of large-scale commercial production of sodium carbonate used in the manufacture of glass and soap.

Solzhenitsyn, Alexander Isayevich [solzhenitsin] (1918–) Writer, born in Kislovodsk, Russia. *One Day in the Life of Ivan Denisovich* (trans, 1962) was acclaimed both in the USSR and the West, but his denunciation of Soviet censorship led to the banning of *Cancer Ward* (trans, 1968) and *The First Circle* (trans, 1968). He was awarded the Nobel Prize for Literature in 1970 (received in 1974). His later books include *The Gulag Archipelago* (trans, 1973–8), for which he was exiled (1974), returning to Russia in 1994.

Somers, Sir George [suhmerz] (1554–1610) English colonist, a founder of the South Virginia Company. In 1610 he was commander of a fleet of settlers shipwrecked on the Bermudas (originally known as the *Somers Is*), and claimed the islands for the British crown.

Somers (of Evesham), John Somers, Baron [suhmerz] (1651–1716) English statesman, born in Worcester, Hereford and Worcester. He helped to draft the Declaration of Rights (1689), and later held several posts under William III, culminating as Lord Chancellor (1697). >> William III

Somerset, Edward >> Worcester, Marquess of

Somerset, Edward Seymour, Duke of, known as **Protector Somerset** (c.1506–52) English soldier and statesman, the brother of Jane Seymour, and Protector of England during the minority of Edward VI. In 1549 he had his younger brother, Thomas Seymour, beheaded for attempting to marry the future Queen Elizabeth, and was himself executed for over-ambition. >> Edward VI; Seymour, Jane / Thomas

Somervell, Sir Arthur (1863–1937) Composer, born in Windermere, Cumbria. He is known for the cantata *The Forsaken Merman*, a symphony, children's operettas, and for a collection of English folksongs.

Somerville, Edith (Anna Oenone), published under the name **Somerville and Ross** (1858–1949) Novelist, born in Corfu, and raised in Co Cork, Ireland. With her cousin, Violet Florence Martin (pseudonym, Martin Ross), she began a literary partnership, their works including *An Irish Cousin* (1889) and *In Mr Knox's Country* (1915). >> Martin, Violet Florence

Somerville, Sir James (Fownes) (1882–1949) British naval commander. He was vice-admiral in the Mediterranean (1940–1), then became commander-in-chief of the British fleet in the Indian Ocean.

Somerville, Mary, née **Fairfax** (1780–1872) Scientific writer, born in Jedburgh, Borders, Scotland. In 1831 she published *The Mechanism of the Heavens*, an account for the general reader of Pierre Simon Laplace's *Mécanique céleste*. >> Laplace

Sommerfeld, Arnold (Johannes Wilhelm) [zomerfelt] (1868–1951) Physicist, born in Königsberg, Germany. He is best known for his work on the Bohr atomic model, and for the notion of elliptical rather than circular electron orbits. >> Bohr, Aage

Somoza (García), Anastasio [somohza] (1896–1956) Nicaraguan dictator, born in San Marcos, Nicaragua. He gained power in the early 1930s and, after his assassination, his sons **Luis Somoza Debayle** (1923–67) and **Anastasio Somoza Debayle** (1925–80) continued dynastic control until the 1979 revolution.

Sondheim, Stephen (Joshua) [sondhiym] (1930–)

Composer and lyricist, born in New York City. Lyricist for *West Side Story* (1957), his own musicals include *A Funny Thing Happened on the Way to the Forum* (1962), *Sweeney Todd* (1979), and *Sunday in the Park with George* (1984, Pulitzer).

Song Ziwen [sung tseewen], also spelled **Sung Tsu-wen** or **Soong Tse-ven**, abbreviated as **Soong, T V** (1894–1971) Chinese diplomat and financier, born in Shanghai, China. Closely associated with the Nationalist Party, he served as finance minister, foreign minister, and premier of the Guomindang government (1931–49).

Sonnino, (Girogio) Sidney, barone (Baron) [soneenoh] (1847–1922) Prime minister of the Kingdom of Italy (1906, 1909–10), born in Pisa, Italy. He was unable to conciliate parliament, and as foreign minister (1914–20) denounced the Triple Alliance and brought Italy into the European War (1915).

Son of Sam >> Berkowitz, David

Sontag, Susan [sontag] (1933–) Critic, born in New York City. Though she has written novels and stories, she is best known for her innovative essays, for which she has been dubbed a 'new intellectual'.

Soong, Mayling / Tse-ven >> Song, Ziwen

Soper, Donald (Oliver) Soper, Baron [sohper] (1903–) Methodist minister, born in London. Widely known for his open-air speaking on London's Tower Hill, he has written many books on Christianity and social questions, particularly from the pacifist angle.

Sophia of Greece >> Juan Carlos I

Sophia Alexeyevna [sohfeea aleksayevna] (1657–1704) Regent of Russia (1682–9), born in Moscow, the daughter of Tsar Alexey I Mihailovitch. She opposed the accession of her half-brother, Peter, supporting instead her mentally weak brother, Ivan. The brothers were proclaimed joint tsars, with Sophia as regent, but she became the *de facto* ruler until removed from power. >> Peter I (of Russia)

Sophocles [sofokleez] (c.496–406 BC) Greek tragic playwright, born in Colonus Hippius. He wrote 123 plays, of which only seven survive: *Ajax, Electra, Women of Trachis, Philoctetes*, and his three major plays *Oedipus Rex, Oedipus at Colonus*, and *Antigone*.

Sophonisba [sofohnizba] (?–c.204 BC) Noblewoman, the daughter of a Carthaginian general. Although betrothed to the Numidian prince Masinissa, she was forced to marry his rival, Syphax. In 203 Syphax was defeated by a Roman army led by Masinissa, who captured Sophonisba and married her. The Romans objected, and Masinissa poisoned her to prevent her being sent as a captive to Rome.

Sopwith, Sir Thomas (Octave Murdoch) (1888–1989) Aircraft designer and sportsman, born in London. He founded the Sopwith Aviation Co in 1912, building many of the aircraft used in World War 1, such as the Sopwith Camel.

Sorabji, Kaikhosru Shapurji [sorabjee], originally **Leon Dudley Sorabji** (1892/5–1988) Composer, pianist, and polemical essayist, born in Chingford, Essex. His compositions include piano music, concertos, organ works, choral music, and songs.

Soraya [soriya], in full **Princess Soraya Esfandiari Bakhtiari** (1932–) Ex-queen of Persia, born in Isfahan, Iran. She became Queen of Persia on her marriage to Muhammad Reza Shah Pahlavi (1951, dissolved in 1958). >> Pahlavi

Sorbon, Robert de [saw(r)bõ] (1201–74) Theologian, born in Sorbon, France. He founded the Maison de Sorbonne in 1259, a theological college for the poor, which has since become a prestigious college of the University of Paris.

Sorby, Henry Clifton (1826–1908) Geologist and metallurgist, born in Woodbourne, South Yorkshire. He was the first to study rocks in thin sections under the microscope (1849), and adapted the technique to study metals.

Sorel, Georges (1847–1922) Social philosopher, born in Cherbourg, France. His best-known work is *Reflections on Violence* (trans, 1908), in which he argued that socialism would be achieved only by confrontation and revolution.

Sörensen, Sören (Peter Lauritz) [soerensen] (1868–1939) Danish biochemist. He did pioneer work on hydrogen-ion concentration, and in 1909 invented the pH scale for measuring acidity.

Sorokin, Pitirim A(lexandrovich) [sorohkin] (1889–1968) Sociologist, born in Turia, Russia. He specialized in the study of the social structure of rural communities. Banished by the Soviet government in 1922, he became professor at Harvard (1930–64).

Sorolla y Bastida, Joaquin [sorolya ee basteetha] (1863–1923) Painter, born in Valencia, Spain. He was one of the leading Spanish Impressionists, known especially for his sunlight effects, as in 'Swimmers' and 'Beaching the Boat' (Metropolitan, New York City).

Sorsa, (Taisto) Kalevi [1930–] Finnish prime minister (1972–5, 1977–9, 1982–7), born in Keuruu, Finland. He also served as foreign minister (1972, 1975–6), and was deputy prime minister of the coalition in 1987.

Sosigenes of Alexandria [sosijeneez] (1st-c BC) Astronomer and mathematician who advised Julius Caesar on calendar reform. He recommended a year of 365·25 days, and inserted an extra 67 days into the year 46 BC to bring the months back in register with the seasons. >> Caesar, Julius

Sotatsu >> Koetsu, Hon'ami

Sotheby, John [suhthebee] (1740–1807) Auctioneer and antiquarian. In 1780 he became a director of the first sale room in Britain exclusively for books, manuscripts, and prints.

Soto, Hernando / Fernando de >> de Soto, Hernando

Sottsass, Ettore, Jr (1917–) Architect and designer, born in Innsbruck, Austria. He moved to Milan, and became involved in the reconstruction of N Italian towns. He also designed typewriters and office equipment for Olivetti.

Soufflot, Jacques Germain [soofloh] (1713–80) Architect, born in Irancy, France. The leading French exponent of Neoclassicism, he designed the Panthéon and the Ecole de Droit in Paris, the Hôtel Dien in Lyon, and the Cathedral in Rennes.

Soult, Nicolas Jean de Dieu [soolt] (1769–1851) French marshal, born in Saint-Amans-La-Bastide, France. He led the French armies in the Peninsular War (1808–14), and was Napoleon's chief-of-staff at Waterloo. Exiled until 1819, he later presided over three ministries of Louis Philippe (1832–4, 1839–4, 1840–7). >> Louis Philippe; Napoleon I

Souphanouvong, Prince [soofanoovong] (1909–95) Laotian president (1975–87), born in Luang Prabang, Laos. He founded the Lao Independence Front to fight French rule, and when his country became a socialist republic (1975) he was given the honorific post of state president.

Sousa, John Philip [sooza] (1854–1932) Composer and bandmaster, born in Washington, DC. He composed more than 100 popular marches, including 'The Stars and Stripes Forever' (1896), and also invented the *sousaphone*.

Soustelle, Jacques (-Emile) [soostel] (1912–90) French politician and anthropologist, born in Montpellier, France. Leader of the Gaullist group (1956–8), he was instrumental in the return to power of General de Gaulle, but later broke with him over the question of Algerian independence. >> de Gaulle

Soutar, William [sooter] (1898–1943) Poet, born in Perth, Tayside. His volumes of verse in Scots include *Seeds in the Wind* (1933) and *Riddles in Scots* (1937), and he also wrote the autobiographical *Diaries of a Dying Man* (1954).

South, Robert (1634–1716) High Church theologian, born

in London. Public orator of Oxford (1660), his vigorous sermons, full of mockery of the Puritans, delighted the restored Royalists.

Southampton, Henry Wriothesley, 3rd Earl of [rothslee] (1573–1624) Courtier, born in Cowdray, Sussex. He was known as a patron of poets, notably of Shakespeare, who dedicated to him both *Venus and Adonis* (1593) and *The Rape of Lucrece* (1594).

Southcott, Joanna (c.1750–1814) Religious fanatic, born in Dorset. In c.1792 she declared herself to be the woman (predicted in *Rev* 12) who would give birth to the second Prince of Peace. She obtained a great following, but died soon after the predicted date of the birth.

Southerne, Thomas [suhthern] (1660–1746) Playwright, born in Oxmantown, Dublin. His two most successful works were tragedies based on novels by Aphra Behn: *The Fatal Marriage* (1694) and *Oroonoko* (1696).

Southey, Robert [suhthee] (1774–1843) Writer, born in Bristol, Avon. Although made poet laureate in 1813, his prose became more widely known than his poetry, and included a life of Nelson, a naval history, and his letters.

Southwell, Robert (1561–95) Poet and martyr, born in Horsham, Norfolk. Ordained as a Jesuit, in 1586 he began aiding persecuted Catholics, but was betrayed and executed; he was beatified in 1929. He is known for his devotional lyrics and for several prose treatises and epistles.

Soutine, Chaim [sooteen, khiym] (1893–1943) Artist, born in Smilovich, Belarus. A leading Expressionist painter, he became known for his paintings of carcases, and for his series of 'Choirboys' (1927).

Sowerby, Leo (1895–1968) Composer and organist, born in Grand Rapids, MI. His music, which includes symphonies, concertos, and choral works, employs a traditional European style often evocative of American scenes.

Soyinka, Wole [soyingka, wolayi], popular name of **Akinwande Oluwole Soyinka** (1934–) Writer, born near Abeokuta, Nigeria. His writing is deeply concerned with the tension between old and new in modern Africa, and his first novel, *The Interpreters* (1965), was called the first really modern African novel. He was awarded the Nobel Prize for Literature in 1986.

Spaak, Paul Henri (1899–1972) Belgian Socialist prime minister (1938–9, 1946, 1947–9), born in Schaerbeek, Belgium. He was also foreign minister (1954–7, 1961–8), in which role he became one of the founding fathers of the EEC, and secretary-general of NATO (1957–61).

Spaatz, Carl, nickname **Tooey Spaatz** (1891–1974) Aviator, born in Boyertown, PA. He became chief of the Strategic Air Force, Europe, in 1944. After the end of the European war he commanded the air force in the Pacific, directing the atomic bombing of Japanese cities (1945).

Spagnoletto, Lo >> **Ribera, Jusepe de**

Spahn, Warren (Edward) (1921–) Baseball player, born in Buffalo, NY. He played for the Boston Braves (1942–52), then moved with the team to Milwaukee (1953–64), and holds the record for games won by a left-handed pitcher (363).

Spallanzani, Lazaro [spalantsahnee] (1729–99) Physiologist, born in Modena, Italy. His work centred on regeneration and reproduction in a wide range of animals, and he was the first to use artificial insemination on small animals, and on a dog.

Spark, Dame Muriel (Sarah) (1918–) Writer, born in Edinburgh. She is best known for her novels, notably *Memento Mori* (1959), *The Ballad of Peckham Rye* (1960), *The Prime of Miss Jean Brodie* (1961; filmed 1969), and *The Mandelbaum Gate* (1965, James Tait Black Memorial Prize).

Spartacus [spah(r)takus] (?–71 BC) Thracian-born slave and gladiator at Capua, who led the most serious slave uprising in the history of Rome (73–71 BC). He inflicted numer-

ous defeats on the Roman armies sent against him, until defeated and killed by Crassus. >> Crassus

Spassky, Boris Vasilyevich (1937–) Chess player, born in Leningrad, Russia. He gained the world championship against Petrosian in 1969, and lost it to Fischer in Reykjavík in 1972. Fischer again defeated Spassky in a rematch in 1992. >> Fischer, Bobby; Petrosian

Speaight, Robert William [spayt] (1904–76) British writer and actor. He performed most of the major Shakespearean roles for the Old Vic Company from 1930, and also wrote biographies and works on drama.

Speaker, Tris(tram E), nickname **the Grey Eagle** (1888–1958) Baseball player, born in Hubbard, TX. During his 22-year career (1907–28), mostly with the Boston Red Sox and Cleveland Indians, he was considered the greatest defensive center fielder in the game's history.

Spearman, Charles Edward (1863–1945) British psychologist, born in London. He was a pioneer of the statistical technique of factor analysis, and played a considerable role in the early development of intelligence testing.

Spedding, Frank (Harold) (1902–84) Inorganic chemist, born in Hamilton, Ontario, Canada. He devised a method for purifying uranium metal in quantity, and *Spedding's eggs* formed the core of Fermi's first atomic pile, set up in Chicago in 1942. >> Fermi

Spee, Maximilian (Johannes Maria Hubert), Graf von (Count of) [shpay] (1861–1914) German naval commander, born in Copenhagen. In 1914 he commanded a commerce-raiding force in the Pacific, sinking the British warships *Good Hope* and *Monmouth*. The same year his ships were sunk by a British squadron.

Speed, John (1552–1629) Antiquary and cartographer, born in Cheshire. He published his 54 *Maps of England and Wales* in 1608–10.

Speer, Albert [shpeer] (1905–81) Architect and Nazi government official, born in Mannheim, Germany. He was minister of armaments in 1942, but openly opposed Hitler in the final months of the war. Tried at Nuremberg, he was imprisoned for 20 years in Spandau, Berlin.

Speidel, Hans [shpiydl] (1897–) German soldier, born in Württemberg, Germany. As Rommel's chief-of-staff during the Allied invasion of Europe (1944), he was imprisoned after the anti-Hitler bomb plot.

Speight, Johnny [spayt] (1920–) Comic writer, born in London. He made his mark on television with the creation of Alf Garnett in *Till Death Do Us Part* (1964–74), and also wrote the series *In Sickness and In Health* (1985) and *The Nineteenth Hole* (1989).

Speke, John Hanning (1827–64) Explorer, born in Bideford, Devon. He and Burton discovered L Tanganyika (1858), then Speke travelled on alone, finding the lake he named Victoria. His claims to have discovered the source of the Nile were doubted, so a second expedition set out (1860–3). He died before he was able to defend his discovery. >> Burton, Richard (Francis)

Spelling, Aaron (1928–) Television producer, born in Dallas, TX. His successful productions include *Starsky and Hutch*, *Charlie's Angels*, *Cagney and Lacey*, *Hart to Hart*, and *Dynasty*.

Spellman, Francis (Joseph) (1889–1967) Roman Catholic clergyman, born in Whitman, MA. Archbishop of New York (1939), and a cardinal (1946), his writings include a best-selling novel, *The Foundling* (1951).

Spemann, Hans [shpayman] (1869–1941) Embryologist, born in Stuttgart, Germany. He worked on embryonic development, discovering the function of certain tissues, and received the Nobel Prize for Physiology or Medicine in 1935.

Spence, Sir Basil (Urwin) (1907–76) Architect, born in Bombay, India. He emerged as the leading postwar British architect, with his fresh approach to new university buildings, the pavilion for the Festival of Britain (1951), and the new Coventry Cathedral (1951).

Spence, Catherine Helen (1825–1910) Writer and feminist, born near Melrose, Borders, Scotland. In Australia from 1839, *Clare Morrison* (1854) was the first novel of Australian life written by a woman. She became involved with social problems, and in 1897 was Australia's first woman political candidate.

Spence, (James) Lewis Thomas Chalmers (1874–1955) Writer, born in Dundee, Tayside. Some of his poetry is collected in *The Phoenix* (1924) and *Weirds and Vanities* (1927). An authority on folklore and mythology, he wrote many books on the subject.

Spencer, Sir (Walter) Baldwin (1860–1929) Anthropologist and biologist, born in Stretford, Lancashire. In 1894 he went to C Australia where, with Francis James Gillen, he began a collaborative study of the local Aboriginal tribes.

Spencer, Lady Diana (Frances), The Princess of Wales (1961–) Estranged wife of Charles, Prince of Wales, born at Sandringham, Norfolk, the youngest daughter of the 8th Earl Spencer. She married the Prince of Wales in 1981 (separated 1992). They have two sons, **Prince William (Arthur Philip Louis)** (1982–) and **Prince Henry (Charles Albert David)** (1984–). Seriously interested in social concerns, she became a popular public figure in her own right.

Spencer, Herbert (1820–1903) Evolutionary philosopher, born in Derby, Derbyshire. His main work is *System of Synthetic Philosophy* (9 vols, 1862–93), and was a leading advocate of 'Social Darwinism'.

Spencer, Sir Stanley (1891–1959) Artist, born in Cookham, Berkshire. His main works interpret the Bible in terms of everyday life, such as 'Resurrection: Port Glasgow' (1950).

Spencer-Churchill, Baroness >> Churchill, Sir Winston

Spender, Sir Stephen (Harold) (1909–95) Poet and critic, born in London. One of the group of modern poets with Auden and Day-Lewis in the 1930s, his *Collected Poems, 1928–85* were published in 1985. >> Auden; Day-Lewis

Spengler, Oswald [shpenggler] (1880–1936) Philosopher of history, born in Blankenburg, Germany. His *The Decline of the West* (2 vols, trans, 1918–22), argues that all cultures are subject to the same cycle of growth and decay in accordance with predetermined 'historical destiny'.

Spens, Sir Will(iam) (1882–1962) Educational administrator, born in Glasgow, Strathclyde. He produced the report on *Secondary Education (Grammar Schools and Technical High Schools)* (1938), which recommended the raising of the school-leaving age to 15.

Spenser, Edmund (?1552–99) Poet, born in London. His first original work was a sequence of pastoral poems, *The Shepheards Calendar* (1579). His major work, *The Faerie Queene*, used a nine-line verse pattern which later came to be called the *Spenserian stanza*.

Speransky, Mikhail Mikhaylovich, Graf (Count) [speranskee] (1772–1839) Russian statesman and reformer, born in Cherkutino, Russia. In 1809 he produced a plan for the restructure of Russian government on the Napoleonic model, but was dismissed when Napoleon invaded Russia (1812).

Speranza >> Wilde, Jane Francesca

Sperry, Elmer Ambrose (1860–1930) Inventor and electrical engineer, born in Cortland, NY. His chief inventions were the gyroscopic compass (1911) and stabilizers for ships and aeroplanes.

Sperry, Roger (Wolcott) (1913–94) Neuroscientist, born in Hartford, CT. In the 1950s and 1960s he pioneered surgical and experimental behavioural investigations. He shared the Nobel Prize for Physiology or Medicine in 1981.

Speusippus [spyoosipus] (?–339/338 BC) Philosopher, who lived in Athens. He was Plato's nephew, and succeeded him as head of the Academy in 348. He produced a large corpus of writings, but only one fragment of this work, on Pythagorean numbers, survives.

Speyr, Adrienne von >> Balthasar, Hans Urs von

Spielberg, Steven [speelberg] (1947–) Film director, born in Cincinnati, OH. His highly successful films include *Jaws* (1975), *Close Encounters of the Third Kind* (1977), *ET, The Extra-Terrestrial* (1982), *Indiana Jones and the Temple of Doom* (1984), *The Color Purple* (1986), *Who Framed Roger Rabbit?* (1988), *Jurassic Park* (1993), and *Schindler's List* (1993, 2 Oscars, 2 BAFTAs).

Spies-Kjaer, Janni [spiys kyair] (1962–) Danish businesswoman. In 1983 she married Simon Spies, the founder of Spies Travel, and became the owner of Scandinavia's largest group of tour operators, the Spies Concern and the Tjaereborg Concern.

Spillane, Mickey [spilayn], pseudonym of **Frank Morrison Spillane** (1918–) Detective fiction writer, born in New York City. During the 1940s and 1950s, he wrote a series of novels featuring detective Mike Hammer. *Kiss Me Deadly* (1952) is a typical example of his work, in its representation of sadism, cheap sex, and casual violence.

Spilsbury, Sir Bernard (Henry) (1877–1947) Pathologist, born in Leamington Hastings, Warwickshire. He specialized in the new science of forensic pathology, and made his name at the trial of Crippen (1910). >> Crippen

Spinello Aretino [spineloh areteenoh], originally **Spinello di Luca Spinelli** (c.1346–1410) Painter, born in Arezzo, Italy. His principal frescoes were done for San Miniato, in Florence, for the *campo santo* of Pisa, and for the municipal buildings of Siena.

Spink, Ian (1947–) Dancer, choreographer, and director, born in Melbourne, Victoria, Australia. He moved to England in 1977, where he co-founded Second Stride in 1982, becoming artistic director in 1987.

Spinola, Ambrogio di Filippo, marqués de (Marquess of) **Los Balbases** [spinohla] (1569–1630) Soldier in Spanish service, born in Genoa, Italy. Early in the Thirty Years' War (1618–48) he was in Germany, subduing the Lower Palatinate, but he was recalled to Holland to fight Maurice of Nassau at Breda.

Spinoza, Baruch or **Benedictus de** [spinohza] (1632–77) Philosopher and theologian, born in Amsterdam. Regarded as one of the great Rationalist thinkers of the 18th-c, his major works include the *Tractatus theologico-politicus* (1670) and *Ethica* (published posthumously, 1677).

Spitteler, Carl (Friedrich Georg) [shpiteler] (1845–1924) Writer, born in Liestal, Switzerland. *The Olympic Spring* (trans, 1900–5) is his great mythological epic, for which he was awarded the Nobel Prize for Literature in 1919.

Spitz, Mark (Andrew) (1950–) Swimmer, born in Modesto, CA. His outstanding achievement came at the Munich Olympic Games (1972), when he became the first athlete to win seven gold medals at one Games.

Spitzer, Lyman, Jr (1914–) Astrophysicist, born in Toledo, OH. His interest in energy generation in stars led to his early attempt to achieve controlled thermonuclear fusion, for which he devised a method of containing a plasma in a magnetic field.

Spock, Benjamin (McLane), popular name **Dr Spock** (1903–) Paediatrician, born in New Haven, CT. *The Common Sense Book of Baby and Child Care* (1946) made his name a household word, and sold more than 30 million copies.

Spode, Josiah [spohd] (1755–1827) Potter, born in Stoke-on-Trent, Staffordshire. He inherited the pottery founded c.1770 by his father, Josiah Spode (1733–97), making it renowned for transfer-printed earthenware, stoneware, and superbly decorated bone-china.

Spoerli, Heinz [sper lee] (1941–) Dancer, choreographer, and ballet director, born in Basel, Switzerland. A dancer with Basel Ballet (1960–3), he became director there in 1973, developing it into one of the best of Europe's smaller dance ensembles.

Spofforth, Frederick Robert, nickname **the Demon** (1853–1926) Cricketer, born in Sydney, New South Wales, Australia. In 1878 he took 11 wickets for 20 runs against the MCC, and during 1884 took 218 wickets in first-class cricket. He was reputed to be the greatest bowler of his time.

Spohr, Louis [shpohr], originally **Ludwig Spohr** (1784–1859) Composer, violinist, and conductor, born in Brunswick, Germany. He is remembered chiefly as a composer for the violin, for which he wrote 17 concertos, but he also composed nine symphonies, 11 operas, and other choral and chamber works.

Spontini, Gasparo (Luigi Pacifico) [spon tee nee] (1774–1851) Composer, born in Maiolati, Italy. His major work is the opera *The Vestal Virgin* (trans, 1807).

Spooner, William Archibald (1844–1930) Anglican clergyman and educationist, warden (1903–24) of New College, Oxford. His name is associated with a nervous tendency to transpose initial letters or half-syllables in speech, the *spoonerism* (eg 'a half-warmed fish' for 'a half-formed wish').

Spottiswoode, William (1825–83) Mathematician, physicist, and publisher, born in London. He did original work in polarization of light and electrical discharge in rarefied gases, and wrote a mathematical treatise on determinants.

Sprague, Frank (Julian) (1857–1934) Electrical engineer and inventor, born in Milford, CT. He set up the Sprague Electric Railway and Motor Co, and developed a new type of motor for trams (1887). >> Edison

Spring, Howard (1889–1965) Novelist, born in Cardiff. His works include the best-selling *Oh Absalom* (1938), renamed *My Son, My Son, Fame is the Spur* (1940), and *Time and the Hour* (1957).

Springsteen, Bruce (1949–) Rock singer and guitarist, born in Freehold, NJ. In 1976, he released a hit in 'Born to Run', and by the mid-1980s had become the world's most popular white rock star. His albums include *The River* (1980), *Born in the USA* (1985), and *Tunnel of Love* (1987).

Spruance, Raymond (Ames) (1885–1969) US naval officer, born in Baltimore, MD. He played an important part in the planning and execution of massive amphibious operations, notably as commander of the 5th Fleet (1944–5).

Spurgeon, C(harles) H(addon) (1834–92) Baptist preacher, born in Kelvedon, Essex. In 1854 he became pastor of the New Park Street Chapel, London, where he drew such a large congregation that the Metropolitan Tabernacle, seating 6000, was erected for him (1859–61).

Spurr, Josiah (Edward) (1870–1950) Geologist, born in Gloucester, MA. As a result of his work, the age of the Tertiary period has been estimated at 45 to 60 million years. His explorations in Alaska (1896, 1898) were commemorated by the naming of *Mt Spurr*.

Squarcione, Francesco [skwah(r)choh nay] (1397–c.1468) Painter, and founder of the Paduan school, born in Padua, Italy. His extant works include a Madonna in the Staatliche Museen Preußischer Kulturbesitz, Berlin, and panels and frescoes for the Church of S Francesco in Padua.

Squier, E(phraim) G(eorge) [skwiy er] (1821–88) Archaeologist, born in Bethlehem, NH. He surveyed the native American burial mounds and earthworks, publishing the results in *Ancient Monuments of the Mississippi Valley* (1848).

Squire, Sir J(ohn) C(ollings) (1882–1958) Writer, and journalist, born in Plymouth, Devon. He became literary editor of the *New Statesman* (1913) and founder editor of the *London Mercury* (1919–34). His work included light verse and parody, as in *Steps to Parnassus* (1913), criticisms, and short stories.

Ssu-ma Ch'ien >> **Sima Qian**

Staal, Marguerite Jeanne, baronne de (Baroness), *née* **Cordier**, pseudonym **Marguerite Delaunay** (1684–1750) Writer of memoirs, born in Paris. Her *Mémoires* (1755) describe the world of the regency, and her *Complete Works* appeared in 1821.

Stabler, Harold (1872–1945) Designer and craftsman, born at Levens, Cumbria. With his wife, Phoebe Stabler, he designed and produced ceramic figures and groups, decorative and architectural details, enamels, and jewellery.

Stacpoole, Henry de Vere (1863–1951) Physician and writer, born in Dun Laoghaire, Co Dublin, Ireland. His many popular novels include *The Blue Lagoon* (1909), *The Pearl Fishers* (1915), and *Green Coral* (1935).

Staël, Madame de [stahl], popular name of **Anne Louise Germaine Necker, Baroness of Staël-Holstein** (1766–1817) Writer, born in Paris, the daughter of Jacques Necker. Both before and after the French Revolution, her *salon* was a centre of political discussion. She became known with her *Letters* (trans, 1788), her romantic novel, *Corinne* (1807), and her major work, *On Germany* (trans, 1813). >> Necker

Staël, Nicolas de [stahl] (1914–55) Painter, born in St Petersburg, Russia. His early abstract paintings made inspired use of rectangular patches of colour. Later pictures were more representational and in subdued colours.

Stafford, Jean (1915–79) Writer, born in Covina, CA. Her works include novels, such as *Boston Adventure* (1944), children's books, and her major achievement, *Collected Stories* (1969, Pulitzer).

Stafford-Clark, Max (1941–) Theatre director, born in Cambridge, Cambridgeshire. He was director of the Traverse Theatre Workshop Company (1970–4), and in 1981 became artistic director of the English Stage Company at the Royal Court Theatre, London.

Stagnelius, Erik Johan [stag nee lius] (1793–1823) Romantic poet, born on the island of Öland, Sweden. His works include (trans titles) the epic *Vladimir the Great* (1817), plays such as *The Martyrs* (1821), and lyric poetry, much of it found in *Lilies in Sharon* (1821).

Stahl, Franklin >> **Meselson, Matthew**

Stahl, Georg Ernst [shtahl] (1660–1734) Physician and chemist, born in Ansbach, Germany. He expounded the phlogiston theory of combustion, and believed that animism played a part in the phenomenon of living organisms.

Ståhlberg, Kaarlo Juho [stawl berg] (1865–1952) Lawyer and first president of Finland (1919–25), born in Suomussalmi, Finland. A member of the Finnish Diet (1908–17), he drafted the Finnish constitution of 1919.

Stainer, Sir John (1840–1901) Composer, born in London. He served as organist at St Paul's (1872–88), founded the Musical Association (1874), and wrote cantatas and church music, notably *The Crucifixion* (1887).

Stakhanov, Alexey Grigorievich [sta kahn of] (1906–77) Coalminer, and legendary worker, from Sergo (renamed Stakhanov in 1978), Ukraine. In 1935 he started an incentive scheme for exceptional output and efficiency by individual steel workers, coalminers, and others. Such prize workers were called *Stakhanovites*.

Stalin, Joseph (1879–1953) Marxist revolutionary and virtual dictator of the Soviet Union (1928–53), born in Gori, Georgia. As a leading Bolshevik he played an active role in the October Revolution, and in 1922 became general secretary of the Party Central Committee. In 1928 he launched the campaign for the collectivization of agriculture during which millions of peasants perished, and in 1934-8 inaugurated a massive purge of the party, government, armed forces, and intelligentsia. He took part in the conferences of Teheran, Yalta, and Potsdam which resulted in Soviet control over the liberated countries of postwar E and C Europe, his foreign policies contributing to the Cold War between the Soviet Union and the West. He was posthumously denounced by Khrushchev (1956), and under Gorbachev 'Stalinism' was officially condemned. >> Gorbachev; Khrushchev

Stamitz, Carl (Philipp) [shtamits] (1745-1801) Composer and violinist, born in Mannheim, Germany. He wrote 80 symphonies, and concertos for violin, viola, cello, flute, oboe, clarinet, and harpsichord.

Stamitz, Johann (Wenzel Anton) [shtamits] (1717-57) Violinist and composer, born in Havlíčkův Brod, Czech Republic. His works include 74 symphonies, several concertos, chamber music, and a Mass.

Stamp, Sir (Lawrence) Dudley (1898-1966) Geographer, born in London. He founded and worked on the British Land Utilization Survey until after World War 2, and was adviser to the government on many land-related topics.

Stamp (of Shortlands), Josiah Charles Stamp, Baron (1880-1941) Economist, born in London. An expert on taxation, in 1939 he was made economic adviser to the government.

Standish, Myles (c.1584-1656) Colonist, probably born in Ormskirk, Lancashire. He sailed with the *Mayflower* in 1620, and became military head of the first American settlement at Plymouth, MA, and treasurer of the colony (1644-9).

Stanford, Sir Charles (Villiers) (1852-1924) Composer, born in Dublin. He wrote several major choral works, six operas, seven symphonies, and a great deal of chamber music, songs, and English Church music.

Stanford, (Amasa) Leland (1824-93) Railway magnate, born in Watervliet, NY. In 1856 he became president of the Central Pacific Co, and superintended the construction of the line. He founded Leland Stanford Junior University (now Stanford University) in 1891.

Stanhope, Charles Stanhope, 3rd Earl (1753-1816) British politician and scientist, born in London. He broke with Pitt over the French Revolution, and advocated peace with Napoleon. His inventions include a microscope lens that bears his name, two calculating machines, and the first hand-operated iron printing press. >> Pitt, William (the Younger)

Stanhope, Lady Hester Lucy (1776-1839) British traveller, the eldest daughter of Charles, 3rd Earl Stanhope. She left England in 1810, and settled on Mt Lebanon, where she became a figurehead of the mountain community. >> Stanhope, Charles

Stanhope, James Stanhope, 1st Earl [stanuhp] (1675-1721) British soldier and statesman, born in Paris. He commanded in Spain during the War of the Spanish Succession (1701-13), was secretary of state for foreign affairs under George I, and became his chief minister (1717). >> George I

Stanhope, Philip Dormer >> **Chesterfield, 4th Earl of**

Stanier, Sir William Arthur (1876-1965) Mechanical engineer, born in Swindon, Wiltshire. He brought out many successful locomotive designs, including in 1937 the 4-6-2 'Coronation' class.

Stanislavsky [stanislavskee], originally **Konstantin Sergeyevich Alexeyev** (1863-1938) Actor, theatre director, and teacher, born in Moscow. In 1898 he helped to found the Moscow Arts Theatre, where his teaching on acting remains the basis of much Western actor-training and practice.

Stanisław I Leszczyński [stanislav leshinskee] (1677-1766) King of Poland (1704-9, 1733-5), born in Lwow, Ukraine. After his election in 1704, he was driven out by Peter the Great. Re-elected in 1733, he lost the War of the Polish Succession, and formally abdicated. >> Peter I (of Russia)

Stanisław II Poniatowski [stanislav, ponyatofskee] (1732-98) Last king of Poland (1764-95), born in Wolczyn, Poland. Unable to stop the partitions of Poland (1772, 1793, 1795), he abdicated.

Stanley, Edward Geoffrey Smith >> **Derby, 14th Earl of**

Stanley, Sir Henry Morton, originally **John Rowlands** (1841-1904) Explorer and journalist, born in Denbigh, Clwyd. In 1867 he joined the *New York Herald*, and in 1869 was instructed to 'find Livingstone' in Africa, eventually doing so at Ujiji (1871). He later traced the Congo to the sea, and founded the Congo Free State. >> Livingstone

Stanley, John (1713-86) Composer, born in London. His works include the oratorios *Zimri* and *The Fall of Egypt*, cantatas, organ voluntaries, concerti grossi, and instrumental sonatas.

Stanley, Wendell (Meredith) (1904-71) Biochemist, born in Ridgeville, IN. He isolated and crystallized the tobacco mosaic virus, and worked on sterols and stereoisomerism. He shared the Nobel Prize for Chemistry in 1946. >> Pirie, Norman Wingate

Stanley, William (1858-1916) Electrical engineer, born in New York City. He invented the transformer (1885), and developed a long-range transmission system for alternating current.

Stansfield, Grace >> **Fields, Dame Gracie**

Stansgate (of Stansgate), William Wedgwood Benn, 1st Viscount (1877-1960) British Labour statesman. He served as secretary for India (1929-31) and secretary for air (1945-6). >> Benn, Anthony Wedgwood

Stanton, Edwin (McMasters) (1814-69) Lawyer and public official, born in Steubenville, OH. He served as attorney general (1860-1) and secretary of war (1862-68), and was appointed to the Supreme Court in 1869, but died before joining the Court.

Stanton, Elizabeth, née **Cady** (1815-1902) Social reformer and women's suffrage leader, born in Johnstown, NY. In 1848 she helped to organize the first women's rights convention, and with Susan B Anthony founded the National Woman Suffrage Movement in 1869. >> Anthony, Susan B; Mott, Lucretia

Stanwyck, Barbara, originally **Ruby Stevens** (1907-90) Actress, born in New York City. Best remembered for her portrayal of pioneering women in such Westerns as *Annie Oakley* (1935) and *Union Pacific* (1939), she received a special Academy Award in 1982.

Stapleton, Maureen (1925-) Actress, born in New York City. A major interpreter of the plays of Tennessee Williams, she won acclaim for her roles in *The Rose Tattoo* (1951), *Orpheus Descending* (1957), *The Glass Menagerie* (1965), and other plays.

Stapleton, Ruth, née **Carter** (1929-83) Evangelist and faith healer, born in Plains, GA, the younger sister of President Carter. She carried out a ministry which stressed the necessity for inner healing. >> Carter, Jimmy

Stark, Harold (Raynsford) (1880-1972) US naval officer, born in Wilkes-Barre, PA. As chief of naval operations (1939-42), he was relieved after Pearl Harbor (1942), and became commander of US Naval Forces Europe (1942-3).

Stark, Dame Freya (Madeline) (1893-1993) Writer and traveller, born in Paris. Her writings include *The Southern Gates of Arabia* (1938), *Dust in the Lion's Paw* (1961), and *The Journey's Echo* (1963).

Stark, Johannes [shtah(r)k] (1874-1957) Physicist, born in Schickenhof, Germany. In 1913 he discovered the effect, named after him, concerning the splitting of spectrum lines by subjecting the light source to a strong electrostatic field. He was awarded the Nobel Prize for Physics in 1919.

Stark, John (1782–1822) American Revolutionary soldier, born in Londonderry, NH. In the American War of Independence (1775–83) he served at Bunker Hill (1775) and won a victory at Bennington (1777).

Starkie, Enid Mary (1897–1970) Critic of French literature, born in Killiney, Co Dublin, Ireland. She played a major part in establishing the poetic reputation of Rimbaud (1938), and published two major volumes on Flaubert (1967, 1971).

Starley, James (1830–81) Inventor, born in Albourne, West Sussex. He invented the 'Coventry' tricycle, and the 'Ariel' geared bicycle (1871), which became a standard bicycle design.

Starling, Ernest Henry (1866–1927) Physiologist, born in London. He introduced the term *hormones* for the internal secretions of the ductless glands and, with Sir William Bayliss, discovered the intestinal hormone *secretin* (1902). >> Bayliss

Starr, (Myra) Belle, *née* **Shirley** (1848–89) Bandit queen, born at or near Carthage, MO. Said to be 'the leader of a band of horse thieves', she was convicted once in 1883 by 'Hanging Judge' Parker. Shot down by an unknown assassin, she was immortalized in popular literature.

Stassen, Harold (Edward) (1907–   ) US state governor, born in Dakota City, MN. Governor of Minnesota (1939–43), and highly regarded as a liberal Republican, he lost the 1948 presidential nomination to Thomas Dewey. >> Dewey, Thomas

Statham, (John) Brian [stay**th**m] (1930–   ) Cricketer, born in Gorton, Greater Manchester. A fast bowler, he took 252 Test wickets for England in 70 appearances, and 2260 in his first-class career.

Statius [stayshius], in full **Publius Papinius Statius** (c.45–96) Epic and lyric poet, born in Naples, Italy. His major work was the *Thebaïd*, an epic in 12 books on the struggle between the brothers Eteocles and Polynices of Thebes.

Statler, Ellsworth (Milton) (1863–1928) Hotel owner, born in Somerset Co, PA. He built the Statler Hotel in 1904 and established the Statler chain.

Staudinger, Hermann [**shtow**dinger] (1881–1965) Chemist, born in Worms, Germany. He was awarded the Nobel Prize for Chemistry in 1953 for his research in macro-molecular chemistry, which contributed to the development of plastics.

Stauffenberg, Claus, Graf von (Count of) [**shtow**fnberg] (1907–44) German soldier, born in Jettingen, Germany. A colonel on the German general staff in 1944, he placed the bomb in the unsuccessful attempt to assassinate Hitler at Rastenburg (20 Jul 1944). He was shot next day. >> Hitler

Stavisky, (Serge) Alexandre [sta**vis**kee] (?1886–1934) Swindler, born in Kiev, Ukraine. He settled in Paris in 1900, where he floated a series of fraudulent companies. When the affair was discovered (1933), it revealed widespread corruption in high places, and precipitated the fall (1934) of the prime minister, Camille Chautemps.

Stead, Christina Ellen (1902–83) Novelist, born in Sydney, New South Wales, Australia. Her best-known work is *The Man Who Loved Children* (1940, revised 1965), and she also became known for her short stories.

Stebbins, George (Ledyard) (1906–   ) Botanist, born in Lawrence, NY. He was the first to apply modern ideas of evolution to botany, as expounded in his *Variation and Evolution in Plants* (1950).

Steel, Sir David (Martin Scott) (1938–   ) British Liberal politician, born in Kirkcaldy, Fife. He became Liberal leader (1976–88), and in 1981 led the party into an alliance with the Social Democratic Party, the parties successfully merging in 1987–8.

Steele, Sir Richard (1672–1729) Essayist, playwright, and politician, born in Dublin. He is best known for the satirical, political, and moral essays which formed much of the content of the *Tatler* (1709–11), which he founded, and the *Spectator* (1711–12), which he co-founded with Addison. >> Addison, Joseph

Steele, Tommy, originally **Thomas Hicks** (1936–   ) Actor, singer, and director, born in London. He achieved fame as a pop singer in the 1950s and in musicals during the 1960s, notably in *Half a Sixpence* (1963–4). His films include *The Tommy Steele Story* and *Finian's Rainbow*.

Steen, Jan (Havickszoon) [stayn] (1626–79) Painter, born in Leyden, The Netherlands. His best works were genre pictures depicting the everyday life of ordinary folk, as in 'The Music Lesson' (National Gallery, London).

Steensen, Niels >> **Steno, Nicolaus**

Steenstrup, Johannes Iapetus Smith (1813–97) Zoologist, born in Vang, Norway. He identified the animal remains from Ertebolle settlements and shell mounds (1851), making the earliest contribution to the discipline of archaeozoology.

Steer, Philip Wilson (1860–1942) Painter, born in Birkenhead, Merseyside. A founder of the New English Art Club, he excelled as a figure painter, as shown in 'Self-Portrait, The Music Room' (Tate, London).

Stefan, Josef (1835–93) Physicist, born in St Peter, Austria. From his research on thermal radiation, begun in 1879, he found a law describing radiant heat loss from a hot surface (*Stefan's law*), important for later developments in quantum theory. >> Planck

Stefánsson, Jón (1881–1962) Landscape painter, born in Sauðárkrókur, Iceland. One of the founders of modern art in Iceland, he painted landscapes on a grand scale, exploiting colour with great luminosity.

Stefánsson, Vilhjalmur (1879–1962) Arctic explorer, born of immigrant Icelandic parents in Arnes, Manitoba, Canada. He led the Canadian Arctic Expedition which mapped the Beaufort Sea (1913–18), and his popular books include *My Life with the Eskimo* (1913).

Steffens, (Joseph) Lincoln (1866–1936) Journalist, born in San Francisco, CA. He became managing editor of *McClure's Magazine* (1902–6), and produced a highly successful series on city corruption, later republished as *The Shame of the Cities* (1904).

Steichen, Edward (Jean) [**stiy**khn] (1879–1973) Photographer, born in Luxembourg. In 1902 he helped Stieglitz found the American Photo-Secession Group, and achieved success in the 1920s with his 'New Realism' fashion and portrait photography. >> Stieglitz

Stein, Sir (Mark) Aurel [stiyn] (1862–1943) Archaeologist and explorer, born in Budapest. He led expeditions tracing the ancient caravan routes between China and the West (1900–30), and discovered the Cave of a Thousand Buddhas near Tan Huang.

Stein, Charlotte von [shtiyn] *née* **von Schardt** (1742–1827) Writer, born in Eisenach, Germany. In 1775 she met Goethe, who fell in love with her, and she became the inspiration for many of his works. Her own works include dramas such as *Rino* (1776) and *Dido* (1792). >> Goethe

Stein, Edith [stiyn], Ger [shtiyn], also known as **Teresa Benedicta of the Cross** (1891–1942) Carmelite nun, born in Breslau, Germany. She converted to Roman Catholicism (1922), and entered the Carmelite Convent at Cologne (1934), but was sent to Auschwitz, where she was executed. The Edith Stein Guild for converts was founded in the USA (1955).

Stein, Gertrude [stiyn] (1874–1946) Writer, born in Allegheny, PA. Her main works include *Three Lives* (1908),

Tender Buttons (1914), and *The Autobiography of Alice B Toklas* (1933). Her Paris home became a salon for artists and writers between the two World Wars.

Stein, Jock [steen], popular name of **John Stein** (1922-85) Footballer and manager, born in Burnbank, Strathclyde. He managed Glasgow Celtic (1965-78) and later the Scotland national side, taking them to the World Cup Finals in 1982 and 1986.

Stein, (Heinrich Friedrich) Karl, Freiherr (Baron) **vom** [shtiyn] (1757-1831) Prussian statesman, born in Nassau, Germany. As chief minister (1807-8), he carried out important reforms in the army, economy, and both national and local government.

Stein, Peter [shtiyn] (1937-) Theatre director, born in Berlin. In 1967 he became a leading avant-garde director in Germany, and in 1970 was made responsible for a series of collective creations at the Berlin Schaubuhne.

Stein, William H(oward) [stiyn] (1911-80) Biochemist, born in New York City. With Moore he developed a method for finding the number of amino acid residues in a protein molecule, and they shared the Nobel Prize for Chemistry in 1972. >> Moore, Stanford

Steinbeck, John (Ernst) [stiynbek] (1902-68) Novelist, born in Salinas, CA. His best-known work is *The Grapes of Wrath* (1939, Pulitzer; filmed 1940), and other major works include *Of Mice and Men* (1937) and *East of Eden* (1952). He was awarded the Nobel Prize for Literature in 1962.

Steinberg, Saul [stiynberg] (1914-) Graphic artist, born in Ramnicul-Sarat, Rumania. He settled in New York, and became an influential observer and satirist of modern culture, as seen in 'Manassas, Virginia: Main Street' (1978).

Steinberger, Jack [stiynberger] (1921-) Physicist, born in Bad Kissigen, Germany. He shared the Nobel Prize for Physics in 1988 for work creating an accelerated beam of neutrinos (1960-2) and for the subsequent discovery that neutrinos exist in two types. >> Lederman

Steinem, Gloria [stiynem] (1934-) Feminist and writer, born in Toledo, OH. In the 1960s she emerged as a leading figure in the women's movement. A co-founder of Women's Action Alliance in 1970, she also helped set up *Ms* magazine.

Steiner, George [stiyner] (1929-) Critic and scholar, born in Paris. A leading exponent of comparative literature, his publications include *The Death of Tragedy* (1961), *After Babel* (1975), and *Antigones* (1984).

Steiner, Jakob [shtiyner] (1796-1863) Mathematician, born in Utzenstorf, Switzerland. He founded and became the classical authority on modern synthetic (projective) geometry.

Steiner, Max(imilian Raoul Walter) [stiyner] (1888-1971) Composer, born in Vienna. He wrote scores for such enduring screen classics as *Gone With the Wind* (1939) and *Casablanca* (1942), and won Oscars for *The Informer* (1935), *Now Voyager* (1942), and *Since You Went Away* (1945).

Steiner, Rudolph [shtiyner] (1861-1925) Social philosopher, the founder of anthroposophy, born in Kraljevec, Croatia. In 1912 he established his first 'school of spiritual science', or *Goetheanum*, in Dornach, Switzerland. The Rudolf Steiner Schools, and others, arose from his ideas, focusing on the development of the whole personality of the child.

Steinitz, William [stiynits], originally **Wilhelm Steinitz** (1836-1900) Chess player, born in Prague. In 1886 he beat Zukertort in the first official championship of the world, and retained his title three times before losing it in 1894 to Lasker. >> Lasker, Emanuel

Steinmetz, Charles (Proteus) [stiynmets], originally **Karl August Rudolph Steinmetz** (1865-1923) Electrical engineer, born in Breslau, Germany. He formulated a law for magnetic hysteresis, developed a simple notation for calculating alternating current circuits, and introduced lightning arresters for high-power transmission lines.

Steinway, Henry (Engelhard) [stiynway], originally **Heinrich Engelhardt Steinweg** (1797-1871) Piano-maker, born in Wolfshagen, Germany. In 1850 he moved his piano factory from Brunswick to the USA, where he introduced many innovations into the instrument, such as a cast-iron frame.

Stella, Frank (Philip) (1936-) Painter, born in Malden, MA. His earliest Minimal paintings date from 1959. Using house-painters' techniques to avoid any trace of 'artistic' brushwork, he creates a totally impersonal effect.

Stella, Joseph, originally **Guiseppe Stella** (1877-1946) Painter, born in Muro Lucano, Italy. He emigrated to New York City in 1896, and from 1913 painted the first American Futurist pictures, and interpretations of New York scenery, such as 'Brooklyn Bridge' (c.1919).

Steller, Georg Wilhelm [steler], originally **Georg Wilhelm Stöhler** (1709-46) Naturalist and explorer, born in Windsheim, Germany. He joined Bering's Kamchatka expedition (1737-44). *Steller's sea-cow* (now extinct), *sea lion*, *jay*, and *eider* are all named after him. >> Bering

Stendhal [stendahl], pseudonym of **Marie-Henri Beyle** (1783-1842) Writer, born in Grenoble, France. He is best known for his novels, notably *Scarlet and Black* (trans, 1831) and *The Charterhouse of Parma* (trans, 1839), but also wrote biographies, critical works on music, art, and literature, and a famous *Journal* (1888).

Stengel, Casey, popular name of **Charles Dillon Stengel** (1889-1975) Baseball player and manager, born in Kansas City, MO. As a player (1912-31), he was an outfielder mainly with the Brooklyn Dodgers. From 1932, as manager, he led the New York Yankees to seven World Series wins between 1949 and 1960, then managed the New York Mets (1962-5).

Stenmark, Ingemar (1956-) Skier, born in Tärnaby, Sweden. Overall champion three times (1976-8), he won 15 slalom/giant slalom titles and five world titles.

Steno, Nicolaus [steenoh], Lat name of **Niels Steensen** (1638-86) Anatomist and geologist, born in Copenhagen. He discovered the duct of the parotid gland and explained the function of the ovaries. He was also the first to explain the structure of the Earth's crust.

Stephen (c.1090-1154) Last Norman king of England (1135-54), and son of Stephen, Count of Blois, and Adela, daughter of William the Conqueror. He had sworn to accept Henry I's daughter, Matilda, as queen, but seized the English crown on Henry's death. After 18 years of virtually continuous warfare, he was forced in 1153 to accept Matilda's son, the future Henry II, as his successor. >> Adela; Henry of Blois; Matilda

Stephen I, St (c.975-1038), feast day 16 August. The first king of Hungary (997-1038). He received from the pope the title of 'Apostolic King' and, according to tradition, St Stephen's Crown, now a Hungarian national treasure. He was canonized in 1083.

Stephen, St (1st-c AD), feast day 26 December. The first Christian martyr, (*Acts* 6-7). Charged by the Jewish authorities for speaking against the Temple and the Law, he was tried by the Sanhedrin, and stoned to death by the crowds in Jerusalem.

Stephen, Sir Leslie (1832-1904) Scholar and critic, born in London. *The History of English Thought in the Eighteenth Century* (1876) is generally regarded as his most important work. Vanessa Bell and Virginia Woolf were among his children. >> Bell, Vanessa; Woolf, Virginia

Stephen, Sir Ninian (Martin) (1923-) Judge, born in England. Appointed Governor-General of Australia (1982-9), he then became Australia's first ambassador for the environment (1989-91).

Stephens, Alexander H(amilton) (1812–83) US politician, born in Wilkes Co, GA. He sat in Congress (1843–59), defended the Kansas–Nebraska Act (1854), and became Confederate vice-president (1861). He sat in Congress again (1874–83), and was elected Governor of Georgia (1882).

Stephens, James (1825–1901) Irish nationalist, born in Kilkenny, Co Kilkenny, Ireland. In 1853 he founded and led the Irish Republican Brotherhood (Fenians), started the *Irish People* newspaper (1863) to urge armed rebellion, and was arrested (1865), but escaped to the USA.

Stephens, James (1880–1950) Writer, born in Dublin. He began as a poet, then became known with *The Crock of Gold* (1912), a prose fantasy. Later works include *Songs from the Clay* (1914) and *Reincarnation* (1917).

Stephens, John Lloyd (1805–52) Archaeologist and traveller, born in Shrewsbury, NJ. With Frederick Catherwood (1799–1856) he explored Mesoamerica (1839–42), their work founding the field of Mayan archaeology.

Stephens, Meic [miyk] (1938–) Poet and editor, born in Treforest, Mid Glamorgan. He founded *Poetry Wales* in 1965, and compiled *The Oxford Companion to the Literature of Wales*.

Stephenson, George (1781–1848) Railway engineer, born in Wylam, Northumberland. His most famous engine, the *Rocket*, running at 58 km/36 mi an hour, was built in 1829. He was an engineer for several railway companies. >> Stephenson, Robert

Stephenson, Robert (1803–59) Civil engineer, born in Willington Quay, Northumberland, the son of George Stephenson. His designs include the Britannia Bridge over the Menai Straits in N Wales (1850), and bridges at Conwy, Montreal, and elsewhere. >> Stephenson, George

Stephenson, Sir William, known as **Intrepid** (1896–1989) Secret intelligence chief, born in Point Douglas, near Winnipeg, Canada. In 1940 he was appointed British intelligence chief in North and South America. The novelist Ian Fleming, a member of his wartime staff, is said to have adopted him as a model for the character 'M' in the James Bond books. >> Fleming, Ian

Stepinac, Aloysius, Cardinal [stepinak] (1898–1960) Roman Catholic clergyman, born in Krasić, Croatia. Primate of Hungary, he was imprisoned (1946–51) for alleged wartime collaboration, then kept under house arrest.

Stepnyak ('son of the Steppe'), nickname of **Sergius Mikhailovich** (1852–95) Russian revolutionary. He wrote studies of the Nihilist movement, and was believed to be the assassin of General Mesentzieff, head of the St Petersburg police (1878).

Steptoe, Patrick (Christopher) (1913–88) Gynaecologist and reproduction biologist, born in Witney, Oxfordshire. From 1968, with Robert Edwards (1925–), he worked on the problem of *in vitro* fertilization of human embryos, which was successful a decade later.

Stern, Daniel >> **Agoult, Marie de Flavigny, comtesse d'**

Stern, Isaac [shtern] (1920–) Violinist, born in Kremenets, Belarus (formerly, USSR). He became well known in the 1940s, establishing a reputation as one of the world's greatest violinists.

Stern, Otto [shtern] (1888–1969) Physicist, born in Sohrau, Germany. In 1920 he carried out an experiment with Walter Gerlach (1889–1979), demonstrating that some atomic nuclei have a magnetic moment, which provided major evidence in favour of quantum theory. He was awarded the Nobel Prize for Physics in 1943.

Sternberg, Josef von [shternberg], originally **Jonas Stern** (1894–1969) Film director, born in Vienna. He went to Germany to make his most famous film, *The Blue Angel* (trans, 1930), starring Marlene Dietrich, and went on to make several Hollywood features. >> Dietrich

Sterne, Laurence (1713–68) Novelist, born in Clonmel, Co Tipperary, Ireland. In 1759 he wrote the first two volumes of his comic novel *The Life and Opinions of Tristram Shandy*, other volumes appearing between 1761 and 1767.

Sternhold, Thomas (1500–49) Psalmist, born near Blakeney, Gloucestershire, or in Hampshire. With John Hopkins (d.1570) he wrote the English version of psalms formerly attached to the Prayer Book.

Steuben, Frederick William (Augustus) Freiherr (Baron) **von** [stooben], Ger [shtoyben] (1730–94) Soldier in the American Revolutionary army, born in Magdeburg, Germany. In 1777 he went to America, where he carried out reforms in the army, commanded in Virginia (1780), and took part in the siege of Yorktown.

Stevens, Alfred (1818–75) Painter, sculptor, and designer, born in Blandford, Dorset. He is especially known for the Wellington monument in St Paul's Cathedral, and the lions at the British Museum.

Stevens, Bernard (1916–83) Composer, born in London. His works include the *Symphony of Liberation* (1946), an opera *The Shadow of the Glen* (1978–9), concertos for piano, violin, and cello, and other chamber, choral, and instrumental pieces.

Stevens, George (1904–75) Film director, born in Oakland, CA. He won Oscars for *A Place in the Sun* (1951) and *Giant* (1956).

Stevens, John (Cox) (1749–1838) Engineer and inventor, born in New York City. He experimented with steamboat design, producing *Juliana* (1811), the world's first steam-powered ferry. In 1825 he operated the first steam locomotive in the USA. >> Stevens, Robert Livingston

Stevens, Robert Livingston (1787–1856) Engineer and inventor, born in Hoboken, NJ, the son of John Stevens. He assisted his father in the design and construction of steamboats, becoming an important figure in naval design.

Stevens, Siaka (Probin) [shahka] (1905–88) Sierra Leone prime minister (1967) and president (1971–85), born in Tolubu, Sierra Leone. The country's first president under its new constitution, he ruled a one-party state until his retirement at 80.

Stevens, S(tanley) S(mith) (1906–73) Experimental psychologist, born in Ogden, UT. He made important contributions to our understanding of the sense of hearing. His major reference work is *The Handbook of Experimental Psychology* (1951).

Stevens, Thaddeus (1792–1868) US politician, born in Danville, VT. A member of the US House of Representatives (1849–53, 1859–68), he emerged as the leader of the 'Radical Republicans'. He led the move to impeach Johnson, and died soon after Johnson's acquittal. >> Johnson, Andrew

Stevens, Wallace (1879–1955) Poet, born in Reading, PA. His *Collected Poems* appeared in 1954, and he is now regarded as a major if idiosyncratic poet in the Symbolist tradition.

Stevenson, Adlai (Ewing) [adliy] (1900–65) US politician and lawyer, born in Los Angeles, CA. He helped to found the UN (1946), stood twice against Eisenhower as presidential candidate (1952, 1956), and became the US delegate to the UN (1961–5). >> Eisenhower

Stevenson, Robert Louis (Balfour) (1850–94) Writer, born in Edinburgh. His romantic fiction included *Treasure Island* (1883), *Kidnapped* (1886), *The Strange Case of Dr Jekyll and Mr Hyde* (1886), *The Master of Ballantrae* (1889), and the unfinished *Weir of Hermiston* (1896), considered his masterpiece.

Stevenson, Ronald (1928–) Composer, pianist, and writer on music, born in Blackburn, Lancashire. He champions music as a world language, and his compositions include the 80-minute *Passacaglia on DSCH* for piano, concertos for piano and violin, choral works, and songs from many cultural backgrounds.

Stevenson, William (?-1575) English scholar. He probably wrote the earliest surviving English comedy, *Gammer Gurton's Needle* (1553), sometimes attributed to John Still or John Bridges.

Stevin, Simon [steviyn] (1548-1620) Mathematician and engineer, born in Bruges, Belgium. He was responsible for introducing the use of decimals, which were soon generally adopted. He also invented a system of sluices to be used for defence by flooding certain areas.

Steward, Julian H(aynes) (1902-72) Cultural anthropologist, born in Washington, DC. He was concerned with cultures as adaptive systems geared to specific environments, and advocated a multilinear approach to cultural evolution. He edited the major *Handbook of the South American Indians* (1946-59).

Stewart, Dugald (1753-1828) Philosopher, born in Edinburgh. Much influenced by Reid's 'common sense' philosophy, he became the leader of the Scottish school. His major work is *Elements of the Philosophy of the Human Mind* (3 vols, 1792, 1814, 1827). >> Reid, Thomas

Stewart, Jackie, popular name of **John (Young) Stewart** (1939–) Motor-racing driver, born in Milton, Strathclyde. He won 27 world championship races between 1965 and 1973, and was world champion in 1969, 1971, and 1973.

Stewart, James (Maitland) (1908–) Film star, born in Indiana, PA. His early films include *The Philadelphia Story* (1940, Oscar) and *It's a Wonderful Life* (1946). He made a series of outstanding Westerns (1950-5) and two successes for Hitchcock, *Rear Window* (1954) and *Vertigo* (1958).

Stewart, J(ohn) I(nnes) M(ackintosh), pseudonym **Michael Innes** (1906-94) Critic, and writer of detective fiction, born in Edinburgh. His work as Michael Innes includes *The Secret Vanguard* (1940), *A Private View* (1952), and *A Family Affair*.

Stewart, (Robert) Michael (Maitland) Stewart, Baron (1906-90) Politician, born in London. He served as Labour foreign secretary (1968), and later headed the British delegation to the European Parliament (1975-77).

Stewart, Arabella / Charles / James >> **Stuart, Arabella / Charles / James**

Stewart, Douglas (Alexander) (1913-85) Poet and playwright, born in Eltham, Taranaki, New Zealand. His major contributions to Australian literature include biographies, two collections of bush ballads (1955-7), and *Modern Australian Verse* (1964).

Steyn, Johan [stayn] (1932–) Judge, born in Stellenbosch, South Africa. He settled in Britain in 1973, and was appointed a Lord Justice of Appeal in 1992.

Stickley, Gustav (1858-1942) Furniture designer, born in Osceola, PA. He formed the Gustav Stickley Co, which became (1900) the Craftsman Workshops. His simple, sturdy oak designs became known as the much copied 'Mission Furniture'.

Stieglitz, Alfred [steeglits] (1864-1946) Photographer, born in Hoboken, NJ. He founded the American Photo-Secession Group with Steichen in 1902, influencing the development of creative photography through his magazine *Camera Work* (1903-17) and his gallery of modern art in New York City. >> Steichen

Stiernhielm, Georg [steernhyelm] (1598-1672) Poet, born in Vika, Sweden. Court poet of Queen Christina, he wrote much lyric poetry, as well as a didactic allegorical poem, *Hercules* (1647).

Stigand [steegand] (?-1072) English clergyman. He became Archbishop of Canterbury in 1052. On the death of Harold II, he supported Edgar Ætheling, and was deprived of his offices by William I.

Stigler, George J(oseph) (1911-91) Economist, born in Renton, WA. He was awarded the Nobel Prize for Economics in 1982 for his work on market forces and regulatory legislation.

Stilicho, Flavius [stilikoh] (?-408) Roman general, virtual ruler of the W Roman empire (395-408) under the feeble Emperor Honorius. His greatest achievements were his victories over Alaric and the Visigoths in N Italy at Pollentia (402) and Verona (403). >> Alaric I; Honorius

Still, Clyfford (1904-80) Painter and printmaker, born in Grandin, ND. By c.1940 he had arrived at his personal style, rejecting European ideas, and employing the currently fashionable organic forms of Biomorphism.

Still, William Grant (1895-1978) Composer, born in Woodville, MS. Known especially for his 'Afro-American Symphony' (1931), his other works include five operas, three ballets, chamber and choral music, and orchestral pieces.

Stiller, Mauritz (1883-1928) Film director, born in Helsinki. He adapted the novels of Selma Lagerlöf (1858-1940), notably *Sir Arne's Treasure* (trans, 1919), which won him international acclaim. His Hollywood films include *Hotel Imperial* (1927) and *The Street of Sin* (1927).

Stilwell, Joseph W(arren), nickname **Vinegar Joe** (1883-1946) US general, born in Palatka, FL. In 1942 he commanded US forces in China, Burma, and India. Recalled after a dispute with Jiang Jieshi in 1944, he commanded the US 10th Army in the Pacific until the end of the War. >> Jiang Jieshi

Stimson, Henry L(ewis) (1867-1930) US statesman, born in New York City. He became secretary of war (1911-13) and secretary of state (1929-33), and served again as secretary of war (1940-5), influencing Truman to use the atomic bomb against Japan. >> Truman

Stirling, James, known as **Stirling the Venetian** (1692-1770) Mathematician, born in Garden, Central, Scotland. In *Methodus differentialis* (1730), he made important advances in the theory of infinite series and finite differences, and gave an approximate formula for the factorial function named after him. He also published a work on the techniques of Venetian glass-making.

Stirling, Patrick (1820-95) Mechanical engineer, born in Kilmarnock, Strathclyde. He is best-known for his 8-ft diameter locomotive driving wheel 4-2-2 'Stirling Single' (1870).

Stirling, Robert (1790-1878) Clergyman and inventor, born in Perth, Tayside. He patented a hot-air engine operating on what became known as the *Stirling cycle*, in which the working fluid (air) is heated externally.

Stockhausen, Karlheinz [stokhowzn] (1928–) Composer, born in Mödrath, Germany. He joined the *musique concrète* group in Paris, and experimented with compositions based on electronic sounds. He has written orchestral, choral, and instrumental works, some combining electronic and normal sonorities.

Stockton, Frank Richard, popular name of **Francis Richard Stockton** (1834-1902) Humorist and engraver, born in Philadelphia, PA. He is best known for the collection of children's stories, *The Lady or the Tiger* (1884).

Stoker, Bram, popular name of **Abraham Stoker** (1847-1912) Writer, born in Dublin. He is chiefly remembered for the classic horror tale *Dracula* (1897); other novels include *The Mystery of the Sea* (1902) and *The Lady of the Shroud* (1909).

Stokes, Sir George Gabriel (1819-1903) Physicist and mathematician, born in Skreen, Co Sligo, Ireland. He first used spectroscopy as a means of determining the chemical compositions of the Sun and stars, and formulated *Stokes' law* for the force opposing a small sphere in its passage through a viscous fluid.

Stokowski, Leopold (Antonin Stanislaw Boleslawawicz) [stokofskee] (1882-1977) Conductor, born in London. He conducted the Philadelphia Symphony

Orchestra (1912–36), the New York Philharmonic (1946–50), and the Houston Symphony Orchestra (1955–60), and in 1962 founded the American Symphony Orchestra in New York City.

Stolypin, Peter Arkadyevich [sto**lip**in] (1862–1911) Russian prime minister (1906–11), born in Dresden, Germany. As governor of Saratov province (1903–6), he helped suppress the revolutionary upheavals of 1905. In 1907 he suspended the second Duma, and arbitrarily limited the franchise. He was assassinated in Kiev.

Stommel, Henry M(elson) (1920–) Oceanographer, born in Wilmington, DE. He developed the first theory of the Gulf Stream, and made major contributions to studies of cumulus clouds, oceanic salinity and thermal gradients, and plankton distribution.

Stone, Barton W(arren) (1772–1844) Presbyterian clergyman, born in Charles Co, MD. He preached at Cane Ridge Church, Paris, KY, which became the centre of the Great Revival (1801–3), and co-founded the Disciples of Christ.

Stone, Edward Durell (1902–78) Architect, born in Fayetteville, AR. His many public buildings include the US Embassy in New Delhi, India, and the John F Kennedy Center for the Performing Arts in Washington, DC.

Stone, Harlan (Fiske) (1872–1946) Lawyer and judge, born in Chesterfield, NH. Appointed Chief Justice of the US Supreme Court (1941), he upheld the view that in matters of constitutionality, except where questions of individual liberty were involved, courts should defer to legislatures.

Stone, Irving, originally **Irving Tennenbaum** (1903–89) Writer, born in San Francisco, CA. He is sometimes credited with creating the non-fiction novel, such as *Lust for Life* (1934), based on the life of Van Gogh, and *The Agony and the Ecstasy* (1961), based on Michelangelo.

Stone, I(sidor) F(einstein) (1907–89) Radical journalist, born in Philadelphia, PA. He joined the liberal reformist *New York Post* (1933–8) and its ally, the *New York Nation* (1938–46), later founding the influential *I F Stone's Weekly* (1953–71).

Stone, Lucy (1818–93) Feminist, born in West Brookfield, MA. She called the first national Women's Rights Convention at Worcester, MA, in 1850, and later helped to form the American *Women's Journal*.

Stone, Sir (John) Richard (Nicholas) (1913–91) Economist, born in London. He was awarded the 1984 Nobel Prize for Economics for his development of the complex models on which worldwide standardized national income reports are based.

Stone, Rosetta >> Seuss, Dr

Stonehouse, John (Thompson) (1925–88) British Labour politician, born in Southampton, Hampshire. He served as minister of technology (1967–8) and minister of posts and telecommunications (1968–70). Problems in his financial affairs led him to fake his death by supposed drowning (1974), but he was later identified and imprisoned.

Stoney, George Johnstone (1826–1911) Irish physicist. He calculated an approximate value for the charge of an electron (1874), a term he himself introduced.

Stopes, Marie (Charlotte Carmichael) [st**ohps**] (1880–1958) Pioneer advocate of birth control, suffragette, and palaeontologist, born in Edinburgh. Her book *Married Love* (1918) caused a storm of controversy, and she founded the first birth control clinic, in London (1921).

Stoppard, Miriam, *née* **Stern** (1937–) British physician, writer, and broadcaster. She is well known for her television series, especially *Miriam Stoppard's Health and Beauty Show* (1988–), and has written books on health matters. She married Tom Stoppard in 1972 (divorced, 1991). >> Stoppard, Tom

Stoppard, Tom, originally **Tom Straussler** (1937–) Playwright, born in Zlín, Czech Republic. He made his name in 1967 with *Rosencrantz and Guildenstern are Dead*. Other plays include *Jumpers* (1972), *Travesties* (1974), *The Real Thing* (1982, Tony), and *Arcadia* (1993). >> Stoppard, Miriam

Storey, David (Malcolm) (1933–) Writer, born in Wakefield, West Yorkshire. His novels include *This Sporting Life* (1960) and *Saville* (1976, Booker), and among his plays are *The Changing Room* (1972) and *Life Class* (1974).

Störmer, Fredrik (Carl Mülertz) [sto**e(r)**mer] (1874–1957) Mathematician and geophysicist, born in Skien, Norway. He carried out research on auroral phenomena, making important contributions to the understanding of their formation.

Storni, Alfonsina (1892–1938) Feminist and poet, born in Sala Capriasca, Switzerland. Her books include (trans titles) *The Inquietude of the Rosebush* (1916) and *The Sweet Injury* (1918).

Storrier, Timothy Austin (1949–) Figurative and landscape artist, born in Sydney, New South Wales, Australia. His delicate greys, pinks, and blues unite the harsh desert environment with symbolic or domestic *trompe l'oeil* objects in a blending of Classical and Romantic styles.

Story, Joseph (1779–1845) Jurist, born in Marblehead, MA. He became a justice of the Supreme Court (1811–45) and his many works, notably *Equity Jurisprudence* (1835–6), were a great influence on the development of US law.

Stoss or **Stozz, Veit** [shtohs] (c.1447–1533) Woodcarver and sculptor, born in Nuremberg, Germany. He worked mainly in Kraków (1477–96), where he carved the high altar of the Marjacki Church.

Stothard, Thomas (1755–1834) Painter and engraver, born in London. He is best known for his painting 'The Canterbury Pilgrims', and for his book illustrations in such classic works as *Robinson Crusoe* and *The Pilgrim's Progress*.

Stott, John Robert Walmsley (1921–) Anglican clergyman and writer, born in London. A leading spokesman for Anglican Evangelicals, he was director of the London Institute for Contemporary Christianity (1982–6) and later became its president.

Stout, Rex (Todhunter) (1886–1975) Detective-story writer, born in Noblesville, IN. His great creation was Nero Wolfe, the phenomenally fat private eye who solved numerous mysteries, beginning with *Fer-de-Lance* (1934).

Stow, John (1525–1605) Chronicler, born in London. His chief works are the *Summary of English Chronicles* (1565) and the noted *Survey of London and Westminster* (1598).

Stowe, Harriet (Elizabeth) Beecher [stoh], *née* **Beecher** (1811–96) Novelist, born in Litchfield, CT. She became famous with her first novel, *Uncle Tom's Cabin* (1852), which immediately focused anti-slavery sentiment in the North.

Stozz, Veit >> Stoss, Veit

Strabo [**stray**boh] (Gr 'squint-eyed') (c.64 BC–c.AD 23) Geographer and historian, born in Amaseia, Pontus. Only a few fragments remain of his 47-volume *Historical Studies*, but his *Geographica* in 17 books has survived almost complete.

Strachan, Douglas [strakhn] (1875–1950) Artist, born in Aberdeen, Grampian. His stained-glass work includes the window group which Britain contributed to the Palace of Peace at The Hague, and the windows for the shrine of the Scottish National War Memorial.

Strachey, (Evelyn) John (St Loe) [**stray**chee] (1901–63) British Labour statesman, born in Guildford, Surrey. His controversial period as minister of food (1946–50) included the food crisis (1947) and unpopular prolongation of rationing. He was secretary of state for war (1950–1) during the Korean hostilities.

Strachey, (Giles) Lytton [straychee] (1880-1932) Biographer, born in London. A member of the Bloomsbury group of writers and artists, he created a literary bombshell with his *Eminent Victorians* (1918), an impertinent challenge to the self-assured studies previously typical of this genre.

Stradella, Alessandro [stradela] (1642-82) Composer, born in Monfestino, Italy. One of the finest composers of chamber music, he wrote more than 200 cantatas, notably the *Christmas Cantata*.

Stradivari or **Stradivarius, Antonio** [stradivahrius] (c.1644-1737) Violin maker, born in Cremona, Italy. He perfected the Cremona type of violin, and is thought to have made over a thousand violins, violas, and violoncellos between 1666 and his death; about 650 of these still exist.

Strafford, Thomas Wentworth, 1st Earl of (1593-1641) English statesman, born in London. In 1639 he became the king's principal adviser, but his suppression of the rebellion in Scotland failed, and he was impeached by the Long Parliament. Despite a famous defence at Westminster, he was executed. >> Charles I (of England)

Strand, Paul (1890-1976) Photographer, born in New York City. From 1935 he produced socially significant documentary films, and after 1942 concentrated on still photography for his records of life in many parts of the world.

Strasberg, Lee, originally **Israel Strassberg** (1901-82) Actor, director, and teacher, born in Budzanow, Austria. He emigrated to the USA in 1909, and in 1931 was involved in the formation of the Group Theater, evolving an influential teaching technique known as 'method acting'.

Strasburger, Eduard Adolf [shtrasberger] (1844-1912) Botanist, born in Warsaw, Poland. In *Cell Formation and Cell Division* (trans, 1876), he laid down the basic principles of cytology, the study of cells.

Stratemeyer, Edward L [stratemiyer], pseudonyms include **Arthur M Winfield, Horatio Alger, Jr, Captain Ralph Bonehill, Nick Carter** (1862-1930) Writer, born in Elizabeth, NJ. He founded the Stratemeyer Literary Syndicate in New York City (1906), which produced numerous books under some 60 pseudonyms, such as the 'Hardy Boys' series (by Franklin W Dixon). The syndicate was later directed by his daughter, **Harriet S Adams** (?1893-1982), who had created the 'Nancy Drew' series (as Carolyn Keene).

Stratford (de Redcliffe), Stratford Canning, Viscount (1786-1880) Diplomat, born in London, a cousin of George Canning. As ambassador in Constantinople periodically between 1825 and 1851, he influenced Turkish policy, but was unsuccessful in his attempts to prevent the outbreak of the Crimean War (1854-6). >> Canning

Strathcona (of Mount Royal and of Glencoe), Donald Alexander Smith, Baron [strathkohna] (1820-1914) Canadian businessman and statesman, born in Forres, Grampian. He entered Canadian politics in 1870 as a Conservative, but withdrew during the Pacific Scandal (1873), returning to parliament in 1887.

Strato or **Straton of Lampsacus** [straytoh, strayton] (?-c.270 BC) Greek philosopher, the third head of the Peripatetic School. His writings are lost, but he seems to have worked mainly to revise Aristotle's physical doctrines. >> Aristotle; Theophrastus

Stratton, Charles (Sherwood), nickname **General Tom Thumb** (1838-83) Midget showman, born in Bridgeport, CT. He measured only 63 cm/25 in until his teens, eventually reaching 101 cm/40 in. Barnum displayed him in his museum, from the age of five, and in 1863 his marriage to Lavinia Warren (1841-1919), also a midget, was widely publicized. >> Barnum

Straus, Oscar [shtrows] (1870-1954) Composer, born in Vienna. He is best known for his many operettas and comic operas, such as *Waltz Dream* (1907) and *The Chocolate Soldier* (1908).

Strauss, David Friedrich [shtrows] (1808-74) Theologian, born in Ludwigsburg, Germany. His major works include the controversial *Leben Jesu* (1835-6, trans, 1846) and *Die christliche Glaubenslehre* (1840-1), a review of Christian dogma.

Strauss, Franz Josef [shtrows] (1915-88) German statesman, born in Munich. He became leader of the Christian Social Union (1961), and was successively minister for nuclear energy (1955-6), defence (1956-62), and finance (1966-9). From 1978 he was state premier of Bavaria, and wielded great influence in Kohl's coalition government. >> Kohl

Strauss, Johann [strows], known as **the Elder** (1804-49) Violinist, conductor, and composer, born in Vienna. He founded with Josef Lanner (1801-43) the Viennese Waltz tradition. He composed several marches, notably the *Radetzky March* (1848), and many waltzes. >> Strauss, Johann (the Younger)

Strauss, Johann [strows], known as **the Younger** (1825-99) Violinist, conductor, and composer, born in Vienna, the eldest son of Johann Strauss (the Elder). He wrote over 400 waltzes, notably *The Blue Danube* (trans, 1867) and *Tales from the Vienna Woods* (trans, 1868). Other works include the operetta *Die Fledermaus* (1874, The Bat), and a favourite concert piece, *Perpetuum Mobile*. >> Strauss, Johann (the Elder)

Strauss, Richard [strows] (1864-1949) Composer, born in Munich, Germany. He is best known for his symphonic poems, such as *Till Eulenspiegel's Merry Pranks* (trans, 1894-5), and his operas, notably *Der Rosenkavalier* (1911). He also wrote concertos, songs, and several small-scale orchestral works.

Stravinsky, Igor (Fyodorovich) [stravinskee] (1882-1971) Composer, born near St Petersburg, Russia. He became famous with his music for the Diaghilev ballets *The Firebird* (1910), *Petrushka* (1911), and *The Rite of Spring* (1913). He later devoted himself to Neoclassicism, as in the opera-oratorio *Oedipus Rex* (1927) and the choral *Symphony of Psalms* (1930). >> Diaghilev

Strawson, Sir Peter (Frederick) (1919-) Philosopher, born in London. His early work dealt with the links between logic and language, later integrating this with metaphysical studies of the structure of human thought, as in *The Bounds of Sense* (1966).

Strayhorn, Billy, popular name of **William Strayhorn** (1915-67) Jazz musician, born in Dayton, OH. He composed 'Lush Life', 'Take the 'A' Train', and many works associated with Duke Ellington, for whom he was a staff arranger, lyricist, and key collaborator from 1938. >> Ellington

Streep, Meryl (Louise) (1949-) Actress, born in Summit, NJ. Her films include *Kramer vs. Kramer* (1979, Oscar), *The French Lieutenant's Woman* (1981), *Sophie's Choice* (1982, Oscar), *Out of Africa* (1985), and *Postcards From the Edge* (1990).

Street, George Edmund (1824-81) Architect, born in Woodford, Essex. He restored Christ Church in Dublin, and designed neo-Gothic buildings, including the London Law Courts and many churches.

Street, Jessie (Mary Grey), Lady (1889-1970) Feminist and writer, born in Ranchi province, Chota Nagpur, India. In 1929 she was the founding president of the United Associations of Women. Her husband, **Sir Kenneth Whistler Street** (1890-1972), was Lieutenant-Governor and Chief Justice of New South Wales, as was her son, **Sir Laurence Whistler Street** (1926-).

Streeton, Sir Arthur Ernest (1867-1943) Landscape

painter, born in Mount Duneera, Victoria, Australia. He helped establish the 'Heidelberg school' of painting, and his works include 'Still Glides the Stream' (c.1890).

Strehler, Giorgio [strayler] (1921–   ) Theatre director, born in Trieste, Italy. A pioneer and figurehead in post-World War 2 theatre, he became artistic director of Milan's Piccolo Teatro in 1947, and a leading force in the Theatre de l'Europe.

Streicher, Julius [shtriykher] (1885–1946) Nazi journalist and politician born in Fleinhausen, Germany. Associated with Hitler in the early days of Nazism, he became a ruthless persecutor of the Jews, and was hanged at Nuremberg as a war criminal.

Streisand, Barbra [striysand], originally **Barbara Joan Streisand** (1942–   ) Singer, actress, and director, born in New York City. She played the lead in the Broadway show *Funny Girl* (1964), which she repeated in the 1968 film version to win an Oscar. Later films included *Hello Dolly* (1969), *A Star Is Born* (1976), and *Yentl* (1983). Her 1965 television special, *My Name is Barbra*, won five Emmy Awards.

Stresemann, Gustav [shtrayzeman] (1878–1929) German statesman, born in Berlin. He was briefly (1923) chancellor of the new German (Weimar) Republic, then minister of foreign affairs (1923–9), securing the entry of Germany into the League of Nations (1926). He shared the Nobel Peace Prize in 1926.

Stretton, Hugh (1924–   ) Writer and academic, born in Melbourne, Victoria, Australia. An important social theorist with a strong concern for social justice, he was one of the first people to look at the problems of urban Australia.

Streuvels, Stijn [stroevels], pseudonym of **Frank Lateur** (1871–1969) Writer, born in Heule, Belgium. His works in lyrical prose style illustrate peasant life in Flanders, and are considered masterpieces of Flemish literature. They include *Old Jan* (trans, 1902) and *The Flax Field* (trans, 1907).

Strijdom, Johannes Gerhardus [striydom], also spelled **Strydom** (1893–1958) South African prime minister (1954–8), born in Willowmore, South Africa. Leader of the extremists in the National Party, his two main political ends were the setting up of an Afrikaner Republic outside the Commonwealth, and the policy of apartheid, which he helped introduce.

Strindberg, (Johan) August (1849–1912) Playwright, born in Stockholm. He first achieved fame with the novel *The Red Room* (trans, 1879). His plays *The Father* (trans, 1887) and *Miss Julie* (trans, 1888) brought him to the forefront as the exponent of naturalistic drama; later plays were more symbolic in form and religious in theme.

Stroessner, Alfredo [stresner] (1912–   ) Paraguayan dictator, born in Encarnación, Paraguay. He became president in 1954, but was forced to stand down after a coup in 1989.

Stroheim, Erich (Oswald) von [strohhiym] (1886–1957) Film director and actor, born in Vienna. His first success as film director was with *Blind Husbands* (1919), followed by the classic film *Greed* (1923). Later he returned to film acting, often playing the roles of German officers.

Strong, Leonard (Alfred George) (1896–1958) Writer, born in Plymouth, Devon. He established a reputation as a lyric poet with *Dublin Days* (1921) and *The Lowery Road* (1923). Other works include novels, such as *Deliverance* (1955), and a collection of short stories, *Travellers* (1945).

Strong, Sir Roy (Colin) (1935–   ) Art historian and museum director, born in London. He became director of the National Portrait Gallery, London, in 1967, and was later director of the Victoria and Albert Museum (1974–87).

Stroud, William (1860–1938) Physicist and inventor, born in Bristol, Avon. He began a long association with Archibald Barr (1889–1913), with whom he invented

naval range-finders. They founded Barr Stroud Ltd in 1931, producing scientific instruments.

Strube, Sidney (1891–1956) Cartoonist, born in London. He was a staff cartoonist with the *Daily Express* (1910–46), creating the character of 'Little Man', symbolic of the average *Express reader*.

Struther, Jan, pseudonym of **Joyce Anstruther Placzek**, *née* **Anstruther** (1901–53) Writer, born in London. Her most successful creation was 'Mrs Miniver', whose activities, first narrated in articles in *The Times*, became the subject of one of the most popular films of World War 2.

Struve, Friedrich Georg Wilhelm [shtroovuh] (1793–1864) Astronomer, the first of four generations of eminent astronomers, born in Altona, Germany. He founded the study of double stars, published a catalogue (1837) of over 3000 binary stars, and carried out one of the first determinations of stellar distance. >> Struve, Otto / Peter

Struve, Otto [shtroovuh] (1897–1963) Astronomer, the great-grandson of Friedrich Struve, born in Kharkov, Ukraine. He is best known for his work in stellar spectroscopy, and for establishing the presence of hydrogen and other elements in inter-stellar space (1938). >> Struve, Friedrich / Peter

Struve, Peter Bergardovich [shtroovuh] (1870–1940) Political economist, born in Perm, Russia, the grandson of Friedrich Struve. A leading Marxist, he wrote a critical account of Russia's economic development (1894), which Lenin attacked for its 'revisionism'. >> Struve, Friedrich

Strydom, Johannes Gerhardus >> **Strijdom, Johannes Gerhardus**

Stuart, Arabella, also spelled **Stewart** (1575–1615) English noblewoman. She was second in succession to the English throne after her first cousin, King James VI of Scotland, and when he became James I of England (1603) he had her imprisoned. After her release she secretly married William Seymour (1588–1660), for which they were imprisoned.

Stuart or **Stewart, Prince Charles Edward (Louis Philip Casimir)**, known as **the Young Pretender** and **Bonnie Prince Charlie** (1720–88) Claimant to the British crown, born in Rome, Italy, the son of James Francis Edward Stuart. In 1745, he landed at Eriskay in the Hebrides and raised his father's standard. The clansmen flocked to him, Edinburgh surrendered, and he kept court at Holyrood. Victorious at Prestonpans, he invaded England, but was routed at Culloden (1746). With the help of Flora Macdonald he escaped to the Continent. >> Macdonald, Flora; Stuart, James

Stuart, Gilbert (Charles) (1755–1828) Painter, born in North Kingstown, RI. In 1775 he went to London, where he became a fashionable portrait painter. He returned to America (1792), where his portraits included those of Washington, Jefferson, and Madison.

Stuart or **Stewart, Prince James (Francis Edward)**, also known as **the Old Pretender** (1688–1766) Claimant to the British throne, born in London, the only son of James II of England and his second wife, Mary of Modena. In 1715 he landed at Peterhead during the Jacobite rising, but left Scotland some weeks later, thereafter living mainly in Rome. >> James II (of England); Mary of Modena; Stuart, Charles

Stuart, Jeb, popular name of **James Ewell Brown Stuart** (1833–64) Confederate soldier, born in Patrick Co, VA. The Confederacy's best-known cavalry commander, he fought at the first Battle of Bull Run (1861), and in 1862 led 1200 troopers in a famous ride around McClellan's army. He was mortally wounded at Yellow Tavern.

Stuart, John McDouall (1815–66) Explorer, born in Dysart, Fife. He accompanied Sturt's Australian expedition (1844–6), and in 1860 crossed Australia from south to north. *Mt Stuart* is named after him. >> Sturt

Stubbs, George (1724–1806) Anatomist, painter, and engraver, born in Liverpool, Merseyside. He excelled in painting horses, and in 1766 published his monumental *Anatomy of the Horse*, illustrated by his own engravings.

Stubbs, William (1825–1901) Clergyman and historian, born in Knaresborough, North Yorkshire. His many works include the monumental *Constitutional History of England*, down to 1485 (3 vols, 1874–8), which put the study of English constitutional origins on a firm basis.

Studdy, George Edward (1878–1948) Cartoonist, born in Devon, the creator of Bonzo the Dog. In 1924 he produced the first fully-animated cartoon film series made in England (*Bonzo*, 26 films), and also drew a *Bonzo* strip for *Titbits* (1926).

Studebaker, Clement [**stood**bayker] (1831–1901) Manufacturer of horse-drawn vehicles and automobiles, born in Pinetown, PA. Together with two brothers he founded the Studebaker Brothers Manufacturing Co (1868), forming the Studebaker Corporation in 1911.

Sturdee, Sir Frederick (Charles Doveton) (1859–1925) British naval commander. He commanded HMS *Invincible* in the action which wiped out the German squadron under von Spee off the Falkland Is in 1914. >> Spee

Sturge, Joseph (1794–1859) Quaker philanthropist and reformer, born in Elberton, Gloucestershire. He became a prominent campaigner against slavery and the Corn Laws, and campaigned for the extension of adult suffrage, and Chartism.

Sturgeon, William (1783–1850) Electrical engineer, born in Whittington, Lancashire. He built the first practical electromagnet (1825), invented the commutator for electric motors (1832), and made the first moving-coil galvanometer (1836).

Sturges, Preston, originally **Edmund Preston Biden** (1898–1959) Film-maker and scriptwriter, born in Chicago, IL. His enduring hits include *The Lady Eve* (1941) and *Sullivan's Travels* (1942), and he received an Oscar for the script of *The Great McGinty* (1940).

Sturluson, Snorri [**stur**luson] (1179–1241) Icelandic poet and historian. His main works were the *Prose Edda* and *Heimskringla* (The Circle of the World), a series of sagas of the Norwegian kings down to 1177.

Sturm, (Jacques) Charles François [stürm] (1803–55) Mathematician, born in Geneva, Switzerland. He discovered the theorem named after him concerning the location of the roots of a polynomial equation, and did important work on linear differential equations.

Sturm, Johannes [shtoorm] (1507–89) Educationist, born in Schleiden, Germany. Appointed rector of a new *Gymnasium* in Strasbourg, his new curriculum was adopted by other Protestant countries, including Britain, and became a model for secondary schools.

Sturt, Charles (1795–1869) Explorer, born in Bengal, India. In Australia he led three expeditions (1828–45), discovering the Darling (1828) and the lower Murray Rivers (1830).

Sturtevant, Alfred (Henry) [**ster**tevant] (1891–1970) Geneticist, born in Jacksonville, IL. While working on fruit fly genetics, he had the idea of chromosome mapping, and went on to develop a range of related ideas, fundamental to modern genetic analysis.

Stuyvesant, Peter [**sti**yvesant] (1592–1672) Dutch administrator, born in Scherpenzeel, The Netherlands. From 1646 he directed the New Netherland colony, and did much for the commercial prosperity of New Amsterdam until his reluctant surrender to the English in 1664.

Stylites, Simeon >> Simeon Stylites, St

Styne, Jule (1905–94) Songwriter, born in London. His melodies for films and Broadway musicals include 'Diamonds are a Girl's Best Friend' (1949), 'Three Coins in the Fountain' (1954, Oscar), and 'People' (1964).

Styron, William (1925–) Novelist, born in Newport News, VA. His books include *Lie Down in Darkness* (1951), *The Confessions of Nat Turner* (1967), and *Sophie's Choice* (1979).

Suárez, Francisco [**swah**reth], known as **Doctor Eximus** ('Exceptional Doctor') (1548–1617) Philosopher and theologian, born in Granada, Spain. His *Disputationes metaphysicae* (1597) was highly influential in the 17th-c and 18th-c, and he also wrote important studies in political theory.

Subbotin, Mikhail Fedorovich (1893–1966) Astronomer and mathematician, born in Ostrolenka, Poland. He is best known for his work on celestial mechanics and theoretical astronomy.

Subtilis, Doctor >> Duns Scotus, Johannes

Suchet, Louis Gabriel, duc (Duke) **d'Albufera da Valencia** [süshay] (1770–1826) French general, born in Lyon, France. He played a major role in Napoleon's successful crossing of the Alps (1800), defeated the British (1809–10), and conquered Valencia (1812). >> Napoleon I

Suckling, Sir John (1609–42) Poet and playwright, born in Whitton, Middlesex. His plays, such as *Aglaura* (1637) are austere, but his highly acclaimed lyrics were published in *Fragmenta aurea* (1646).

Sucksdorff, Arne (1917–) Film director, born in Stockholm. After a series of prominent nature films, his first major feature was *The Great Adventure* (trans, 1953), filmed on a farm, using no professional actors.

Sucre, Antonio José de [**soo**kray] (1793–1830) South American soldier–patriot, born in Cumaná, Venezuela. He was Bolívar's lieutenant, defeated the Spaniards at Ayacucho (1824), and became the first president of Bolivia (1826–8), but was assassinated.

Sue, Eugène [sü], pseudonym of **Marie Joseph Sue** (1804–57) Novelist, born in Paris. He wrote a vast number of Byronic novels, such as *The Mysteries of Paris* (trans, 1843), which was a major influence on Hugo. >> Hugo

Suess, Eduard [züs] (1831–1914) Geologist, born in London. His theory that there had once been a great supercontinent made up of the present southern continents led to modern theories of continental drift.

Suetonius [swe**toh**nius], in full **Gaius Suetonius Tranquillus** (75–160) Roman biographer and antiquarian. His best-known work is *De vita Caesarum* (The Lives of the [First Twelve] Caesars).

Suger [süzhay] (1081–1151) Churchman, and abbot of St Denis from 1122, born near Paris. He rebuilt the church of St Denis in the Gothic style, the first of its kind. He was one of the regents during Louis VII's absence on the second crusade.

Suharto [soo**hah(r)**toh] (1921–) Indonesian soldier and president (1968–), born in Kemusu, Java. Following a threat of civil war (1965–66), he assumed executive power in 1967, ordering the mass arrest and internment of alleged Communists. >> Sukarno

Suk, Joseph [sook] (1875–1935) Composer and violinist, born in Křechaovice, Czech Republic. His works include *Fantaisie* (1903) for violin, the symphonic poem *Prague*, and the symphony *Asrael* (1905).

Sukarno or **Soekarno, Achmed** [su**kah(r)**noh] (1902–70) First president of Indonesia (1945–66), born in Surabaya, Java. He formed the Indonesia National Party in 1927, and became president when Indonesia was granted independence in 1945. After a takeover by the army, his powers gradually devolved onto General Suharto. >> Suharto

Sukuna, Ratu Sir Josefa Lalabalavu Vanaaliali [su**koo**na] (1888–1958) Fijian leader. He joined the Colonial service in Fiji, and was appointed District Commissioner (1932), adviser on Fijian Affairs (1943), and Speaker of the Legislative Council (1956).

Sulaiman or **Suleyman I** [süla**yman**], known as **the Magnificent** (1494–1566) Ottoman Sultan (1520–66). He conquered Belgrade, Budapest, Rhodes, Tabriz, Baghdad, Aden, and Algiers, and his fleets dominated the Mediterranean. He was also known for his system of laws, and as a great patron of arts and architecture.

Sulla, Lucius Cornelius, nickname **Felix** ('Lucky') (138–78 BC) Ruthless and enigmatic Roman politician of the late Republic, whose bitter feud with Marius twice plunged Rome into civil war in the 80s BC. Appointed 'Dictator' in 82 BC, he enacted a number of measures to boost the authority of the Senate. >> Marius, Gaius

Sullivan, Anne, originally **Joanna Mansfield Sullivan** (1866–1936) The teacher of Helen Keller, born in Feeding Hills, MA. She remained Keller's life-long companion, while establishing her own reputation as an author, lecturer, and advocate for the deaf. >> Keller, Helen

Sullivan, Sir Arthur (Seymour) (1842–1900) Composer, born in London. From 1871 he became known for his collaboration with W S Gilbert in their series of comic operas, and also composed a grand opera, *Ivanhoe* (1891), cantatas, ballads, a *Te Deum*, and hymn tunes. >> Gilbert, W S

Sullivan, Ed(ward Vincent) (1902–74) Newspaper columnist and broadcaster, born in New York City. He gained national popularity as the host of the television variety show *Toast of the Town*, later renamed *The Ed Sullivan Show* (1948–71).

Sullivan, Jim, popular name of **James Sullivan** (1903–77) Rugby league player, born in Cardiff. He joined Wigan rugby league club in 1921, where he kicked a world record 2859 goals, and became player-coach of Wigan (1932–46).

Sullivan, John (1740–95) US soldier and political leader, born in Somersworth, NH. He served at the siege of Boston (1775–6) and Staten Island (1977), and in 1779 fought against the Six Nations.

Sullivan, John L(awrence) (1858–1918) Boxer, born in Roxbury, MA. He won the world heavyweight boxing championship as a bareknuckle fighter in 1882, but lost it under the Queensberry rules in 1892 to Corbett. >> Corbett, James John

Sullivan, Louis (Henry) (1856–1924) Architect, born in Boston, MA. He is known for his experimental, functional skeleton constructions of skyscrapers and office blocks, particularly the Stock Exchange, Chicago.

Sully, Maximilien de Béthune, duc de (Duke of) [sülee] (1560–1641) French Huguenot soldier, financier, and statesman, born in Rosny, France. Instrumental in arranging Henry of Navarre's marriage to Marie de Médicis (1600), he became the king's trusted counsellor, and restored the economy after the civil wars. >> Henry IV (of France); Marie de Médicis

Sully, Thomas (1783–1872) Painter, born in Horncastle, Lincolnshire. He emigrated to Charleston, SC (1792), where from 1807 he became known for his portraits.

Sully-Prudhomme [sülee prüdom], pseudonym of **René François Armand Prudhomme** (1839–1907) Poet, born in Paris. A leader of the Parnassian movement, which tried to restore elegance and control to poetry in reaction against Romanticism, he received the first Nobel Prize for Literature in 1901.

Summerley, Felix >> Cole, Sir Henry

Summers, Anne (Fairhurst) (1945–) Academic, journalist, and bureaucrat, born in Deniliquin, New South Wales, Australia. Her book *Damned Whores and God's Police* (1975) was a ground-breaking study of the role of women in Australian history. She became editor of *Ms* (1987–92) and adviser on women's affairs to Paul Keating (1992), then editor of the *Sydney Morning Herald*. >> Keating, Paul

Summers, (Alphonsus Joseph-Mary Augustus) Montague (1880–1948) British priest and man of letters. His chief works are two major reference books on witchcraft, *The History of Witchcraft and Demonology* (1926) and *The Geography of Witchcraft* (1927).

Summerskill, Edith Summerskill, Baroness (1901–80) Doctor and politician, born in London. As a Labour MP (1938–55), she fought for women's welfare on all issues, often provoking great hostility. She became under-secretary to the ministry of food (1949), and chairman of the Labour Party (1954–5).

Sumner, Charles (1811–74) US statesman, born in Boston, MA. In 1851 he was elected senator from Massachusetts, standing alone as the uncompromising opponent of slavery.

Sumner, James (Batcheller) (1887–1955) Biochemist, born in Canton, MA. He was the first to crystallize an enzyme (1926), proving it to be a protein, for which he shared the Nobel Prize for Chemistry in 1946.

Sumter, Thomas (1734–1832) Revolutionary soldier and US political leader, born near Charlottesville, VA. He opposed the British in South Carolina, and gained a victory at Blackstock Hill (1780).

Sundance Kid, popular name of **Harry Longabaugh** or **Langbaugh** (1870–1909?) Outlaw, born in Phoenixville, PA. He teamed up with Butch Cassidy, and drifted throughout North and South America robbing banks, trains, and mines. It is generally held that he was fatally shot by a cavalry unit in Bolivia.

Sung Tsu-wen >> Song Ziwen

Sun Yixian [sun yeeshan], or **Sun Yat-sen**, originally **Sun Wen** (1866–1925) Founder of China's Nationalist Party, born in Xiangshan, Guangdong, China. He helped to organize risings in S China, but after the 1911 Wuhan rising voluntarily handed over the office to Yuan Shikai. Civil war ensued (1913), and he set up a separate government at Guangzhou (Canton). He was widely accepted as the true leader of the nation. >> Yuan Shikai

Supervielle, Jules [süpervyel] (1884–1960) Writer, born in Montevideo. He wrote in French, producing many volumes of poems, notably *Poems of Unhappy France* (trans, 1939–41). He also wrote novels and plays, and the libretto for the opera *Bolivar* (1950).

Suppé, Franz von [soopay] (1819–95) Composer, born in Split, Croatia. His works include operettas, songs and Masses, and his *Light Cavalry* and *Poet and Peasant* overtures are still firm favourites.

Surrey, Henry Howard, Earl of (c.1517–47) Courtier and poet, born in Hunsdon, Hertfordshire. He is remembered for his love poetry, influenced by the Italian tradition, in which he pioneered the use of blank verse and the Elizabethan sonnet form.

Surtees, John (1934–) Motor-racing driver and motorcyclist, born in Westerham, Kent, the only man to win world titles on both two and four wheels. He won the 350 cc motorcycling world title (1958–60) and the 500 cc title (1956, 1958–60), then won the motor-racing world title (1964).

Surtees, Robert (1779–1834) Antiquary and topographer, born in Durham, Co Durham. He is best known for his *History of the County of Durham* (1816–23).

Surtees, Robert Smith (1803–64) Journalist and novelist, born in The Riding, Northumberland. He started the *New Sporting Magazine* (1831), and introduced John Jorrocks, a sporting Cockney. His other great character, Soapy Sponge, appears in *Mr Sponge's Sporting Tour* (1853).

Susann, Jacqueline (c.1926–74) Popular novelist, born in Philadelphia, PA. Her novels include the best-selling *Valley of the Dolls* (1968) and *The Love Machine* (1969).

Suslov, Mikhail Andreyevich [suslof] (1902–82) Soviet politician, born in Shakhovskoye, Russia. He opposed Khrushchev's 'de-Stalinization' measures, economic reforms, and foreign policy, and was instrumental in unseating him in 1964. >> Khrushchev

Sutcliffe, Bert (1923–) Cricketer, born in Auckland, New Zealand. He played 42 Tests for New Zealand and made 2727 runs, scoring five centuries.

Sutcliffe, Frank Meadow (1853–1941) Portrait photographer, born near Whitby, North Yorkshire. His studies of the vanishing world of English farmhands and fisher-folk brought him many awards between 1881 and 1905.

Sutcliffe, Peter, known as **the Yorkshire Ripper** (1946–) Convicted murderer, born in Bingley, West Yorkshire. He murdered 13 women over five years in N England and the Midlands. Arrested in 1981, he was sentenced to life imprisonment.

Sutherland, Graham (Vivian) (1903–80) Artist, born in London. He was an official war artist (1941–5), and later produced several memorable portraits, including 'Sir Winston Churchill' (1955). His large tapestry, 'Christ in Majesty', was hung in the new Coventry Cathedral in 1962.

Sutherland, Dame Joan (1926–) Operatic soprano, born in Sydney, New South Wales, Australia. She made her debut at Sydney in 1947, came to London in 1951, and joined the Royal Opera, becoming resident soprano at Covent Garden. In 1954 she married the conductor Richard Bonynge (1930–).

Sutherland, Margaret Ada (1897–1984) Composer, born in Adelaide, South Australia. Her works include a violin concerto (1954), and the opera, *The Young Kabbarli* (1965), based on the life of Daisy Bates. She has also written much chamber music and a number of song cycles. >> Bates, Daisy

Sutter, John Augustus (1803–80) California colonist, born in Kandern, Germany. He went to the USA in 1834, obtained large land grants from the Mexican authorities, and set up a colony on the American R near present-day Sacramento.

Sutter, Joseph P (1921–) Aircraft designer, born in Seattle, WA. He worked for Boeing, becoming head of the aerodynamics unit for the 707 family of jet-airliners, and chief engineer for the development of the 747.

Suttner, Bertha, Freifrau (Baroness) **von**, *née* **Kinsky** (1843–1914) Writer and pacifist, born in Prague. In 1876 she married a fellow novelist, Baron Arthur von Suttner (1850–1902), and founded in 1891 an Austrian Society of Friends of Peace. She received the Nobel Prize for Peace in 1905.

Su Tung-p'o, pseudonym of **Su Shih** (1036–1101) Poet, essayist, calligrapher, and public official, born in Meishan, Szechwan, China. One of the most prominent men of his time, he excelled in all fields of literature, and epitomized the cultural ideal of 11th-c Chinese humanism.

Suvorov, Alexander Vasilyevich [suvorof] (1729–1800) Russian soldier, born in Moscow. He fought in the Seven Years' War (1756–63), the Russo-Polish War (1768–72), the war against the Turks (1787–92), and the French Revolutionary Wars (1799). >> Masséna

Suzman, Helen, *née* **Gavronsky** (1917–) South African politician, born in Germiston, Transvaal, South Africa. She gained the respect of the black community and, for years the sole MP of the Progressive Party, proved to be a fierce opponent of apartheid.

Suzman, Janet (1939–) Actress, born in Johannesburg, South Africa. Her notable roles include *Antony and Cleopatra* (1972) and *Hedda Gabler* (1976–7), and in 1987 she directed *Othello* in Johannesburg, defying apartheid by casting a black actor in the title role.

Suzuki, Shinichi [suzookee] (1898–) Music teacher, born in Nagoya, Japan. His mass instruction methods of teaching young children to play the violin have been adopted in many countries, and adapted to other instruments.

Suzuki, Zenko [suzookee] (1911–) Japanese prime minister (1980–2), born in Yamada, Japan. He became Liberal Democratic Party president, but factional strife within the party, and opposition to his defence policy, led to his resignation.

Svedberg, Theodor [svayberg] (1884–1971) Physical chemist, born in Fleräng, Sweden. In 1924 he devised his ultracentrifuge, using it to develop methods for separating proteins. He was awarded the Nobel Prize for Chemistry in 1926.

Svein I / II >> Sweyn I / II

Sveinsson, Asmundur [svenson] (1893–1982) Sculptor, born in Iceland. His work was both figurative and abstract, and drew for inspiration on traditional Icelandic Saga material and folk-tales.

Svensson, Jon Stefán (1857–1944) Writer and clergyman, born in Möðruvellir, Iceland. His series of children's books about a boy called Nonni, growing up in the N of Iceland, made him a best-selling author.

Sverrir Sigurdsson [svayreer seegoordson] (c.1150–1202) King of Norway from 1184, born in the Faeroe Is. He emerged from obscurity in 1179 to lay claim to the throne from Magnus V Erlingssonz (reigned 1162–84), whom he finally defeated and killed in 1184.

Svevo, Italo [zvayvoh], pseudonym of **Ettore Schmitz** (1861–1928) Novelist, born in Trieste, Italy. He had a considerable success with *The Confessions of Zeno* (trans, 1923), a psychological study of inner conflicts.

Svoboda, Ludvík [svoboda] (1895–1979) Czech soldier and president (1968–75), born in Hroznatín, Czech Republic. In 1948 he joined the Communist Party, was minister of defence until 1950, and in 1968 succeeded Novotný as president. >> Novotný

Swainson, William (1789–1855) Naturalist and bird illustrator, born in Hoylake, Cheshire. His works included *Zoological Illustration* (3 vols, 1820–23). *Swainson's thrush* is named after him.

Swami Vivekananda >> Vivekananda

Swammerdam, Jan [svamerdam] (1637–80) Naturalist, born in Amsterdam. He devised a classification which laid the foundations of entomology. He first observed red blood corpuscles (1658), and discovered the valves in the lymph vessels and the glands in the Amphibia, named after him.

Swan, Sir Joseph (Wilson) (1828–1914) Physicist and chemist, born in Sunderland, Tyne and Wear. He patented the carbon process for photographic printing (1864), and invented an electric lamp (1860), the dry plate (1871), and bromide paper (1879).

Swann, Donald (1923–94) Composer and lyricist, born in Llanelli, Dyfed. His long collaboration with Michael Flanders began in 1956, when he wrote the music for *At the Drop of a Hat*, followed by *At the Drop of Another Hat* (1965). >> Flanders

Swanson, Gloria [swonsn], originally **Gloria May Josephine Svensson** (1897–1983) Actress, born in Chicago, IL. She played leading roles in silent films, and survived the arrival of sound, receiving Oscar nominations for *Sadie Thompson* (1928) and *The Trespasser* (1929). Her film career dwindled despite a sensational comeback in *Sunset Boulevard* (1950).

Swedenborg, Emmanuel [sweednbaw(r)g], originally **Emmanuel Swedberg** (1688–1772) Mystic and scientist, born in Stockholm. His monumental *Philosophical and Logical Works* (trans, 1734), was a mixture of metallurgy and metaphysical speculation on creation. He expounded his doctrines in such works as *The New Jerusalem* (1758), and in 1787 his followers (known as Swedenborgians) formed the Church of the New Jerusalem.

Sweelinck, Jan Pieterszoon [swaylingk] (1562–1621) Composer, organist, and harpsichordist, born in Amsterdam. He composed mainly church music and organ works, developed the fugue, and founded the distinctive North German school.

Sweet, Henry (1845–1912) Philologist, born in London. His works include Old and Middle English texts, primers, and dictionaries, and a historical English grammar.

Swettenham, Sir Frank (Athelstane) [swetenam] (1850-1946) Colonial administrator in Malaya, born in Belper, Derbyshire. He was governor and commander-in-chief of the Straits Settlement (1901-4), and became an authority on Malay language and history.

Sweyn or **Svein** [svayn], known as **Forkbeard** (?-1014) King of Denmark (c.985-1014) and England (1013-14), the son of Harold Blue-tooth, and the father of Canute. He first attacked England in 994, and during his final campaign in 1013 established mastery over the whole country. >> Canute

Sweyn or **Svein II**, also known as **Sweyn Estridsen** (c.1020-74) King of Denmark from 1047, the son of Ulf, a regent of Denmark, and Estrid, sister of Canute the Great. Harald III Sigurdsson laid claim to Denmark as well, and began a long war of attrition against him, but at the peace of 1064 Harald accepted his right to the Danish throne. >> Harald III Sigurdsson

Swift, Gustavus Franklin (1839-1903) Meat packer, born near Sandwich, MA. He revolutionized the meat-packing industry in 1877, and in 1885 established Swift & Co, pioneering the use of waste products to make glue, oleomargarine, soap, and fertilizer.

Swift, Jonathan (1667-1745) Clergyman and satirist, born in Dublin. He attacked religious dissension in *A Tale of a Tub* (1704), and produced a wide range of political and religious essays and pamphlets. His world-famous satire, *Gulliver's Travels*, appeared in 1726. >> Temple, William

Swinburne, Algernon Charles (1837-1909) Poet and critic, born in London. He achieved success with his play *Atalanta in Calydon* (1865), and the first of his series of *Poems and Ballads* (1865). Later works include several critical studies of major authors.

Swinburne, Sir James (1858-1958) British scientist. He was a pioneer in the plastics industry, and the founder of Bakelite Ltd.

Swinhoe, Robert (1836-77) Naturalist and consular official, born in Calcutta, India. British consul in Formosa (1861-6), Amoy (1866-9), and Ningpo (1871-5), he compiled the first checklist of Chinese birds (1871). *Swinhoe's pheasant, petrel,* and *snipe* are all named after him.

Swinton, Alan Archibald Campbell (1863-1930) Electrical engineer and inventor, born in Edinburgh. He was one of the first to explore the medical applications of radiography (1896), and in 1908 outlined the principles of an electronic system of television.

Swinton, Sir Ernest Dunlop, pseudonym **Ole Luk-Oie** (1868-1951) British soldier, writer, and inventor, born in Bangalore, India. Under his pseudonym he wrote *The Green Curve* (1909), *A Year Ago* (1916), and several translations. He was one of the originators of the tank.

Swithin or **Swithun, St** (?-862), feast day 15 July. English saint and divine. In 852 he was made Bishop of Winchester, where he died. When in 971 the monks exhumed his body to bury it in the rebuilt cathedral, the removal (on 15 July) is said to have been delayed by violent rains.

Sydenham, Thomas [sidenam], known as **the English Hippocrates** (1624-89) Physician, born in Wynford Eagle, Dorset. He described the symptoms of several diseases, and gave his name to the mild convulsions of children (*Sydenham's chorea*) and to the medicinal use of liquid opium (*Sydenham's laudanum*). >> Hippocrates

Sydney, Algernon >> **Sidney, Algernon**

Sydow, Max von [sidoh], originally **Carl Adolf von Sydow** (1929-) Actor, born in Lund, Sweden. In 1949 he began a long professional association with Ingmar Bergman, appearing in such films as *The Seventh Seal* (1957) and *Through a Glass Darkly* (1961). Hollywood films include *The Exorcist* (1973) and *Awakenings* (1991). >> Bergman, Ingmar

Sykes, Eric (1923-) Comedy writer and performer, born in Oldham, Lancashire. The creator of his own BBC series

(1959-65, 1972-80), he has also appeared in films, such as *One Way Pendulum* (1964) and *Shalako* (1968). >> Jacques

Sylvester, James Joseph (1814-97) Mathematician, born in London. He made important contributions to the theory of invariants and to number theory.

Sylvius, Franciscus [silvius], Latin name of **Franz de la Boë** (1614-72) Physician, born in Hanau, Germany. He founded the iatrochemical school of medicine, which was paramount in the rational application of science to medicine. His discoveries include the *Sylvian fissure* of the brain (1641).

Symington, Stuart [siymingtn] (1901-88) US senator, born in Amherst, MA. He was first secretary of the air force during the first Truman administration, and became US senator for Missouri (1952-75). >> Truman

Symington, William [simington] (1763-1831) Engineer and inventor, born in Leadhills, Strathclyde. In 1802 he completed at Grangemouth the *Charlotte Dundas*, one of the first practical steamboats ever built.

Symmes, Robert Edward >> **Duncan, Robert**

Symonds, Henry Herbert [simonz] (1885-1958) British educationist and classical scholar. He was instrumental in opening the first Youth Hostels in Britain (1931).

Symonds, John Addington [simonz] (1840-93) Writer and critic, born in Bristol, Avon. His major work was *Renaissance in Italy* (7 vols, 1875-86), and he also wrote travel books, biographies, translations, and poetry.

Symons, A(lphonse) J(ames) A(lbert) [simonz] (1900-41) Bibliographer and biographer, born in London. His *The Quest for Corvo* (1934), the biography of Frederick Rolfe, is regarded as a modern masterpiece. >> Rolfe, Frederick William

Symons, Arthur (William) [simonz] (1865-1945) Critic and poet, born in Milford Haven, Dyfed. He did much to familiarize the British with the literature of France and Italy, and published the influential *The Symbolist Movement in Literature* (1899).

Symons, George James [simonz] (1838-1900) Meteorologist, born in London. He founded the British Rainfall Organization for collecting rainfall data with the co-operation of the general public, increasing the number of reporting stations in Britain from 168 to over 3500.

Synge, J(ohn) M(illington) [sing] (1871-1909) Playwright, born near Dublin. He settled among the people of the Aran Is, who provided the material for his plays, notably *Riders to the Sea* (1904) and *The Playboy of the Western World* (1907), and became a major influence on Irish playwrights.

Synge, R(ichard) L(aurence) M(illington) [sing] (1914-94) Biochemist, born in Chester, Cheshire. With Martin he devised the chromatographic methods that revolutionized analytical chemistry, and they shared the Nobel Prize for Chemistry in 1952. >> Martin, A J P

Szasz, Thomas (Stephen) [shash] (1920-) Psychiatrist, born in Budapest. He is known for his view that all disease must be physical, and that consequently the idea of 'mental disease' is a myth.

Szell, George [sel] (1897-1970) Conductor and pianist, born in Budapest. He conducted many of the world's major orchestras, and from 1946 was musical director and conductor of the Symphony Orchestra in Cleveland, OH.

Szent-Györgyi, Albert von Nagyrapolt [sent dyoordyee] (1893-1986) Biochemist, born in Budapest. He was awarded the Nobel Prize for Physiology or Medicine in 1937 for his work on the function of organic compounds (especially vitamin C) within cells.

Szeryng, Henryk [shering] (1918-88) Violinist, born in Warsaw. He wrote several violin and chamber music works, and taught internationally. He took Mexican citizenship in 1946, and was Mexican cultural ambassador from 1960.

Szewinska, Irena [shevinska], *née* **Kirszenstein** (1946–   )
Athlete, born in St Petersburg, Russia. She set world
records at 100 m and 200 m in 1965, won three gold
medals at the European Championships in 1966, took the
Olympic 200 m title in 1968 in world record time, and in
1976 won the Olympic 400 m in a new world record
(49·28 sec).

Szilard, Leo [zilah(r)d] (1898–1964) Physicist, born in Budapest. He was a central figure in the Manhattan Project,
and after the War became a strong proponent of the
peaceful uses of atomic energy.

Szymanowski, Karol [shimanofskee] (1882–1937) Composer, born in Tymoszowska, Ukraine. His works include the
operas *Hagith* (1913) and *King Roger* (trans, 1918–24), incidental music, symphonies, concertos, chamber music,
piano music, and many songs.

T

Tabari, al- [tabahree], in full **Abu Jafar Mohammed Ben Jarir al-Tabari** (839–923) Historian, born in Amol, Persia. He wrote a major commentary on the Koran, and a history of the world from creation until the early 10th-c.

Tabarley, Eric (1931–) French yachtsman. He was twice winner of the single-handed trans-Atlantic race - in 1964 in *Pen Duick II*, and in 1976 in *Pen Duick VI*.

Tacitus [tasitus], in full **Publius** or **Gaius Cornelius Tacitus** (c.55–120) Roman historian. His major works are *Historiae* (12 vols, Histories), of which only the first four books survive whole, and the *Annales* (Annals), of possibly 18 books, of which only eight are complete.

Taddeo di Bartoli [tadayoh di bah(r)tohlee] (c.1362–c.1422) Painter of the Sienese school. 'Descent of the Holy Ghost' in the Church of San Agostino at Perugia is his masterpiece. Other work includes the frescoes of Paradise and Hell in Pisa Cathedral.

Tadema, Sir Lawrence Alma >> **Alma-Tadema, Sir Lawrence**

Taft, Robert A(lphonso) (1889–1953) US politician, born in Cincinnati, OH, the son of William Howard Taft. He co-sponsored the Taft–Hartley Act (1947) directed against the power of the trade unions and the 'closed shop'. He failed three times (1940, 1948, 1952) to secure the Republican nomination for the presidency. >> **Taft, William Howard**

Taft, William Howard (1857–1930) US statesman and 27th president (1909–13), born in Cincinnati, OH. He secured an agreement with Canada which meant relatively free trade, and later served as Chief Justice of the USA (1921–30).

Tagore, Rabindranath [tagaw(r)] (1861–1941) Writer and philosopher, born in Calcutta, India. He is best known for his poetic works, notably *Song Offering* (trans, 1912) and his short stories, such as *A Bunch of Stories* (trans, 1912). He received the Nobel Prize for Literature in 1913.

Tahgahjute >> **Logan, James**

Taillefer [tiyfair] (?–1066) Norman minstrel. He sang war songs at the Battle of Hastings, in which he was killed. He is shown in the Bayeux tapestry.

Tailleferre, Germaine [tiyfair] (1892–1983) Pianist and composer, born in Park-St-Maur, France. One of *Les Six*, her works include chamber music, a ballet, a piano concerto, and songs.

Taine, Hippolyte (Adolphe) [ten] (1828–93) Critic, historian, and positivist philosopher, born in Vouziers, France. His greatest work, *The Origins of Contemporary France* (trans, 1875–94), constituted a strong attack on the men and the motives of the Revolution.

Tairov, Alexander Yakovlevich [taeerof], originally **Alexander Kornblit** (1885–1950) Theatre director and actor, born in Rovno, Ukraine. He founded the Moscow Chamber Theatre in 1914, pioneering a 'synthetic theatre' of abstract balletic movement which aspired to the emotional precision of music.

Tait, Peter Guthrie (1831–1901) Mathematician, born in Dalkeith, Lothian. A major influence in the development of mathematical physics, he wrote on quaternions, thermodynamics, and the kinetic theory of gases.

Tait, Thomas Smith (1882–1952) British architect. His designs include the *Daily Telegraph* office in London (1927) and St Andrew's House in Edinburgh (1934).

Tait, William (1792–1864) Publisher, born in Scotland. He was the founder of *Tait's Edinburgh Magazine* (1832–64), a literary and radical political monthly.

Tait, Archibald Campbell (1811–82) Anglican clergyman, born in Edinburgh. He entered the Church of England in 1836, and was an opponent of the Oxford Movement. In 1869 he was appointed Archbishop of Canterbury. >> Newman, John Henry

Taizong [tiytsung], also spelled **T'ai-tsung** (600–49) Second emperor of the Tang dynasty in China (627–50). He seized the crown after assassinating two brothers and their families, and forcing his father's abdication. His reign saw the zenith of Tang power.

Taizu [tiysoo], also spelled **T'ai-tsu**, originally **Zhao Kuangyin** (928–76) First emperor of the Song (Sung) dynasty in China (960–76), born into a Beijing military family. He reunified China after the post-Tang disintegration.

Takamine, Jokichi [takameenay] (1854–1922) Biochemist, born in Takaoka, Japan. In 1901 he isolated crystalline adrenaline (epinephrine) from the suprarenal gland, the first hormone to be isolated in pure form from a natural source.

Takei, Kei [takay] (1939–) Post-modern dancer and choreographer, born in Tokyo. In 1969 she formed her own company, Moving Earth, and began her major work, *Light*.

Takeshita, Noboru [takeshita] (1924–) Japanese prime minister (1987–9), born in Kakeyamachi, Japan. A member of the Liberal Democratic Party, he also served as minister of finance (1982–6). His administration was undermined by a share-dealing scandal.

Tal, Mikhail Nekhemyevich (1936–92) Chess player, born in Riga, Latvia. In 1960 he defeated Botvinnik to become the youngest grandmaster to hold the world title until then, but was forced to retire through illness in 1961. >> Botvinnik

Talbot, William Henry Fox (1800–77) Pioneer of photography, born in Melbury Abbas, Dorset. In 1838 he succeeded in making photographic prints on silver chloride paper, which he termed 'photogenic drawing', and later developed the Calotype process.

Talese, Gay [talayzee] (1932–) Journalist, born in Ocean City, NJ. His best-selling nonfiction 'novels' include *The Kingdom and the Power* (1969), about the *New York Times*, and *Honor Thy Father* (1971), about the Mafia.

Taliesin [talyesin] (6th-c) Welsh bard, possibly mythical, known only from a collection of poems, *The Book of Taliesin*, written in the late 13th-c.

Tallchief, Maria, originally **Betty Marie Tallchief** (1925–) Ballet dancer, teacher, and artistic director, born in Fairfax, OK. One of the Ballet Russe de Monte Carlo's four native American stars in the early 1940s, she married Balanchine, and performed with the New York City Ballet until 1965. >> Balanchine

Talleyrand (-Périgord), Charles Maurice de [talayrã] (1754–1838) French statesman, born in Paris. As foreign minister under the Directory (1797–1807), he helped to consolidate Napoleon's position; but, alarmed by Napoleon's ambitions, he resigned in 1807. He became foreign minister under Louis XVIII, and was Louis Philippe's chief adviser at the July Revolution. >> Louis Philippe; Napoleon I

Tallien, Jean Lambert [talyĩ] (1767–1820) French revolutionary politician, born in Paris. As president of the Convention (1794), he was denounced by Robespierre, but conspired with Barras and Fouché to bring about Robespierre's downfall. >> Barras; Fouché; Robespierre

Tallis, Thomas (c.1505–85) English musician. One of the greatest contrapuntists of the English School, he wrote much church music, including a motet in 40 parts, *Spem in alium.*

Talmadge, Eugene [**tal**maj] (1884–1946) US governor, born in Forsyth, GA. Governor of Georgia (1933–7, 1941–3), he and Huey Long led Southern opposition to President Roosevelt. >> Long, Huey; Roosevelt, Franklin D

Tamayo, Rufino [ta**mah**yoh] (1899–) Painter, born in Oaxaca, Mexico. His style combines pre-Columbian art with the art of modern Europe. Among his works are 'The Birth of Nationality' and 'Mexico Today' (1952–3) for the Palace of Fine Arts in Mexico City.

Tambo, Oliver (1917–93) South African politician, born in Bizana, South Africa. He became deputy president of the African National Congress (1958), acting president (1967), and president (1977). >> Mandela, Nelson

Tamburlaine; Tamerlane >> Timur

Tamm, Igor Yevgenyevich (1895–1971) Physicist, born in Vladivostock, Russia. He shared the 1958 Nobel Prize for Physics for his work explaining the Cherenkov effect. >> Cherenkov

Tanaka, Kakuei [ta**naka**] (1918–93) Japanese prime minister (1972–4), born in Kariwa Niigata Prefecture, Japan. He also served as minister of finance (1962–4), secretary-general (1965, 1968), and minister of international trade and industry (1971–2). In 1976 he was found guilty of corruption.

Tancred [**tang**kred] (c.1076–1112) Norman crusader, the grandson of Robert Guiscard. He distinguished himself in the First Crusade, and was given the principality of Tiberias (1099). >> Guiscard

Tandy, Jessica (1909–94) Stage and film actress, born in London. She went to the USA in 1930, and played in the original production of *A Streetcar Named Desire* (1947). She married Hume Cronyn (1911–), often appearing with him on stage. Her films include *Driving Miss Daisy* (1989, Oscar).

Taney, Roger Brooke [**taw**nee] (1777–1864) Jurist, born in Calvert Co, MD. Appointed Chief Justice in 1836, his most famous decision was in the Dred Scott case, when he ruled that no negro could claim state citizenship for legal purposes. >> Scott, Dred

Taneyev, Sergey (Ivanovich) [tan**yay**of] (1856–1915) Composer and pianist, born in Vladimir, Russia. He wrote a variety of music, including six symphonies and two cantatas, and was a proponent of counterpoint.

Tange, Kenzo [**tang**gay] (1913–) Architect, born in Imabari, Japan. His works include the Hiroshima Peace Centre (1949–55), the National Gymnasium for the 1964 Olympic Games, and the theme pavilion for the 1970 Osaka Exposition.

Tang Hsien-tsu >> Dang Xianzu

Tanguy, Yves [**tā**gee] (1900–55) Artist, born in Paris. All his pictures are at the same time Surrealist and nonfigurative, being peopled with numerous small objects or organisms, whose meaning and identity are unknown.

T'ang Yin (1470–1523) Painter and poet, born in Su-chou, Kiangsu, China. He painted in a popular and decorative style for the burghers of Souchou: portraits, pretty women, and erotica.

Tanizaki, Junichiro [ta**ni**zakee] (1886–1965) Novelist, born in Tokyo. He became known in the West only after the translation in 1957 of his long novel *The Makioka Sisters* (trans, 1943–8), a notable example of descriptive realism.

Tannenbaum, Frank [**tan**enbowm] (1893–1969) Historian, born in Brod, Galicia, Austria-Hungary. He emigrated to the USA in 1905. His most famous book, *Slave and Citizen* (1947), was a pioneering work on the historiography of American slavery.

Tansley, Sir Arthur George (1871–1955) Botanist, born in London. A pioneer British ecologist, he published *Practical Plant Ecology* (1923) and *The British Isles and their Vegetation* (1939).

Tantia Topi, originally **Ramchandra Panduranga** (c.1819–59) Leader of the Indian Mutiny (1857), a rebel from Gwalior. He was Nana Sahib's lieutenant in the Mutiny, and took part in the massacre of the British at Cawnpore (1857). He was captured in 1859, and executed. >> Nana Sahib

Tao Qian [tow chyan], also found as **T'ao Ch'ien** or **Tao Yuanming** (369–427) Poet, born near Nanchang, China. His poems describe the hardship of cottage-life, but he also wrote many on wine, notably 'Fifth Poem on Drinking'. He is also known for his short stories.

Tapiès, Antonio [ta**pyes**] (1923–) Painter, born in Barcelona, Spain. He was a founder member of the *Dau al Set* ('Seven on the Die') group of avant-garde artists and writers. From 1955 he produced 'matter' paintings, using objects such as a desk instead of a canvas, as in 'Desk with Straw'.

Tarbell, Ida M(inerva) (1857–1944) Reform journalist, born in Erie Co, PA. She campaigned against corruption and big business interests, and her history, *The Nationalizing of Business* (1936), became a standard work.

Tarkenton, Fran(cis Asbury) (1940–) Player of American football, born in Richmond, VA. He joined the Minnesota Vikings (1961), was traded to the New York Giants (1967), then rejoined the Vikings (1972). He gained 47 003 yds passing, a National Football League record.

Tarkington, (Newton) Booth (1869–1946) Writer, born in Indianapolis, IN. His novels include *Monsieur Beaucaire* (1900), the *Growth* trilogy (1927), which includes *The Magnificent Ambersons* (1918, Pulitzer), and *Alice Adams* (1921, Pulitzer).

Tarkovsky, Andrey [tah(r)**kof**skee] (1932–86) Film-maker, born in Moscow. His films include *Ivan's Childhood* (trans, 1962), *Solaris* (1972), and *The Sacrifice* (trans, 1986).

Tarleton, Sir Banastre (1754–1833) British soldier, born in Liverpool, Merseyside. Serving in the American War of Independence (1775–83), he was victorious at Waxham Creek (1780), and defeated Gates at Camden, but was beaten at Cowpens. >> Gates, Horatio

Tarquinius Priscus, Lucius [tah(r)**kwin**ius **pris**kus] (c.7th–8th-c BC) Traditionally the fifth king of Rome (616–578 BC). Guardian to the sons of King Ancus Marcius, he assumed the throne on the king's death, but the sons eventually had him murdered. He is said to have instigated the Roman Games.

Tarquinius Superbus, Lucius [tah(r)**kwin**ius soo**per**bus] (6th-c BC) Tyrannical king of Rome, possibly of Etruscan extraction, whose overthrow (510 BC) marked the end of monarchy at Rome, and the beginning of the Republic.

Tarski, Alfred (1902–83) Logician and mathematician, born in Warsaw, Poland. He made contributions to many branches of pure mathematics, but is most remembered for his definition of 'truth' in formal logical languages.

Tartini, Giuseppe [tah(r)**tee**nee] (1692–1770) Violinist and composer, born in Pirano, Italy. Perhaps one of the greatest violinists of all time, he was also an eminent composer. His best-known work is the *Devil's Trill* (c.1735).

Tasman, Abel Janszoon [**taz**mn] (1603–c.1659) Navigator, born near Groningen, The Netherlands. In 1642 he discovered the area he named Van Diemen's Land (now Tasmania) and New Zealand, followed by Tonga and Fiji (1643).

Tassie, James (1735–99) Modeller and gem engraver, born in Pollokshaws, Strathclyde. In London from 1766, he made reproductions of famous gems, cameo portraits of his eminent contemporaries, and the plaster reproductions of the Portland Vase.

Tassigny, Jean de Lattre de >> Lattre de Tassigny, Jean de

Tasso, Torquato (1544–95) Poet, born in Sorrento, Italy. His epic masterpiece on the capture of Jerusalem during the first crusade, *Gerusalemme Liberata* (1581, Jerusalem Liberated), was later rewritten, in response to criticisms, as *Gerusalemme Conquistata* (1593).

Tate, (John Orley) Allen (1899-1979) Critic and poet, born in Winchester, KY. He became known primarily as a proponent of the New Criticism. In 1928 he contributed several poems to *Fugitives: an Anthology of Verse*, among them 'Ode to the Confederate Dead', one of his most famous pieces.

Tate, Sir Henry (1819-99) Sugar magnate, art patron, and philanthropist, born in Chorley, Lancashire. He patented a method for cutting sugar cubes (1872) and attained great wealth as a Liverpool sugar refiner. He founded The Tate Gallery.

Tate, Nahum [**nay**uhm] (1652-1715) Poet and playwright, born in Dublin. He is known for his 'improved' versions of Shakespeare's tragedies, substituting happy endings to suit the popular taste, and in collaboration with Nicholas Brady (1659-1726) compiled a metrical version of the psalms. He became poet laureate in 1692.

Tate, Sharon >> Manson, Charles; Polanski, Roman

Tati, Jacques [tatee], popular name of **Jacques Tatischeff** (1908-82) Actor and film producer, born in Pecq, France. He made his reputation as the greatest film comedian of the postwar period, notably in *Mr Hulot's Holiday* (trans, 1953) and *My Uncle* (trans, 1958).

Tatian [**tay**shn] (2nd-c) Christian thinker, from Syria. He established an ascetic religious community of Encratites, which fostered a heretical combination of Christianity and Stoicism.

Tatlin, Vladimir (1885-1953) Painter and designer, born in Moscow. He founded Russian Constructivism, a movement at first approved by the Soviet authorities, and was commissioned to design the 'Monument to the Third International' which, had it been built, would have been 1300 ft tall.

Tattersall, Richard (1724-95) Auctioneer, born in Hurstwood, Lancashire. In 1776 he set up auction rooms at Hyde Park Corner, which became a celebrated mart of thoroughbred horses and a great racing centre.

Tattnal, Josiah (1795-1871) US naval officer, born near Savannah, GA. While serving in the US navy (1812-61) he compromised US neutrality by assisting a British squadron in its attack on a Chinese fort (1859), and later served as a Confederate naval officer (1861-5).

Tatum, Art(hur) [**tay**tm] (1910-56) Jazz pianist, born in Toledo, OH. He became the first supreme keyboard jazz virtuoso, known for his technique, drive, and improvisational powers.

Tatum, Edward L(awrie) [**tay**tm] (1909-75) Biochemist, born in Boulder, CO. With Beadle he demonstrated the role of genes in biochemical processes, and with Lederberg showed that bacteria reproduce by a sexual process, thus founding the science of bacterial genetics. He shared with them the Nobel Prize for Physiology or Medicine in 1958. >> Beadle; Lederberg

Taube, Henry [towb] (1915-) Inorganic chemist, born in Saskatchewan, Canada. He devised new methods for the study of electron transfer reactions in inorganic chemistry, and was awarded the Nobel Prize for Chemistry in 1989.

Tauber, Richard [**tow**ber] (1892-1948) Tenor, born in Linz, Austria. He established himself as one of Germany's leading tenors, particularly in Mozartian opera, after 1925 increasingly appearing in light opera.

Taufa'ahau [**tow**fa-ahow], also known as **King George Tupou** (1797-1893) Tongan nation builder, born of an aristocratic lineage in Ha'apai. He modernized administration, and founded the hereditary monarchy which continues to rule the country.

Taufa'ahau Tupou IV [towfa-a**how too**poh] (1918-) King of

Tonga, the eldest son of Queen Salote Tupou III. On succeeding to the throne on his mother's death in 1965, he shared power with his brother, Prince Fatafehi Tu'ipelehake, who became prime minister. >> Salote Tupou III

Taussig, Helen (Brooke) [**tow**sig] (1898-1986) Paediatrician, born in Cambridge, MA. Her work on the pathophysiology of congenital heart disease was done partly in association with Alfred Blalock, and between them they pioneered the 'blue baby' operations. >> Blalock

Tavener, John (Kenneth) (1944-) Composer, born in London. His music is predominantly religious, and includes the cantata *The Whale* (1966) and a sacred opera *Therese* (1979).

Tawfiq Pasha >> Tewfik Pasha

Tawney, Richard Henry (1880-1962) Economic historian, born in Calcutta. His works include *The Acquisitive Society* (1926) and *Religion and the Rise of Capitalism* (1926).

Taylor, A(lan) J(ohn) P(ercivale) (1906-90) Historian, born in Lancashire. His major work was *The Struggle for Mastery in Europe, 1848-1918* (1954). He aroused passionate hostility with his revisionist *The Origins of the Second World War* (1961).

Taylor, Brook (1685-1731) Mathematician, born in Edmonton, Greater London. His *Methods of Incrementation* (trans, 1715), containing his theorem on power series expansions, was later recognized as the basic principle of differential calculus.

Taylor, Cecil (Percival) (1933-) Avant-garde pianist and composer, born in New York City. In 1956 he made his first important quartet recordings, which diverged sharply from established approaches to jazz.

Taylor, Elizabeth, *née* **Coles** (1912-75) Novelist, born in Reading, Berkshire. Her novels include *At Mrs Lippincote's* (1946), *A Wreath of Roses* (1950), and *The Wedding Group* (1968).

Taylor, Elizabeth (Rosemond) (1932-) Film star, born in London. Her early films include *Cat on a Hot Tin Roof* (1958) and *Butterfield 8* (1960, Oscar). *Cleopatra* (1962) provided the background to her well-publicized romance with Richard Burton, her co-star in several films, including *Who's Afraid of Virginia Woolf?* (1966, Oscar). She has been married eight times, twice to Burton. >> Burton, Richard

Taylor, Frederick W(inslow) (1856-1915) Engineer, born in Philadelphia, PA. He introduced time-and-motion study as an aid to efficient management, and developed the notion of 'scientific management'.

Taylor, Sir Geoffrey Ingram (1886-1975) Physicist and applied mathematician, born in London. He applied his studies on turbulent motion in fluids to such domains as oceanography and aerodynamics, and in 1934 proposed the important idea of 'dislocation' in crystals.

Taylor, Lady Helen >> Kent, Edward, Duke of

Taylor, Jeremy (1613-67) Theologian, probably born in Cambridge, Cambridgeshire. During the Civil War he is said to have accompanied the Royal Army as chaplain, and was taken prisoner at Cardigan Castle (1645).

Taylor, John Henry (1871-1963) Golfer, born in Northam, Devon. He was the first Englishman to win the British Open championship (1894, 1895, 1900, 1909, 1913), and was a founder and first president of the British Professional Golfer's Association.

Taylor, Maxwell D(avenport) (1901-87) US soldier, born in Keystesville, MO. In World War 2 he commanded the 101st Airborne Division, and was the first general to land in Normandy on D-Day. He later commanded the US Eighth Army in the Korean War (1953-5).

Taylor, Sir Patrick Gordon (1896-1966) Pioneer aviator, born in Mosman, New South Wales, Australia. He was awarded the George Cross for his bravery in dealing with a mechanical crisis during a pioneering flight over the Tasman Sea with Kingford Smith (1935). >> Kingsford Smith

Taylor, Paul (Belville) (1930–) Modern-dance choreographer, born in Pittsburgh, PA. He began choreographing in 1956, and developed a highly original and witty style, often using classical music to contemporary effect.

Taylor, Peter Hillsman (1917–) Short-story writer, born in Trenton, TN. His stories on urban middle-class life in the southern states of America include 'The Scoutmaster', 'The Old Forest', and 'The Death of a Kinsman'.

Taylor, Zachary (1784–1850) US general and 12th president (1849–50), born in Montebello, VA. A hero of the Mexican War (1846–8), the main issue of his presidency was the status of the new territories and the extension of slavery there.

Tchaikovsky or **Tschaikovsky, Piotr Ilyich** [chiykofs-kee] (1840–93) Composer, born in Kamsko-Votkinsk, Russia. Among his greatest works are the ballets *Swan Lake* (1876–7), *The Sleeping Beauty* (1890), and *The Nutcracker* (1892), the last three of his six symphonies, two piano concertos, and several tone poems, notably *Romeo and Juliet* and *Capriccio Italien*.

Tcherepnin, Nikolay (Nikolayevich) [cherepneen] (1873–1945) Composer, born in St Petersburg, Russia. He worked with Diaghilev (1908–14), conducting ballet and opera throughout Europe. His works include operas, ballets, symphonies, other orchestral music, piano pieces, and nationalist songs. >> Diaghilev

Teagarden, Jack, popular name of **Weldon John Teagarden** (1905–64) Jazz trombonist and singer, born in Vernon, TX. A featured soloist in Paul Whiteman's orchestra (1933–8), he led his own orchestra (1939–46), then joined Armstrong's All Stars (1947–51). >> Armstrong, Louis

Teague, Walter (Dorwin) [teeg] (1883–1960) Designer, born in Decatur, IN. He established his own industrial design consultancy in 1926, creating a corporate identity for such clients as Kodak, Ford, and Texaco.

Teasdale, Sara, *née* **Sarah Trevor** (1884–1933) Poet, born in St Louis, MO. Her books include *Love Songs* (1917) and *Strange Victory* (1933).

Tebaldi, Renata [tebaldee] (1922–) Operatic soprano, born in Pesaro, Italy. She has sung in many opera houses, including La Scala, Milan (1946–54), and the Metropolitan Opera, New York City (1955).

Tebbit (of Chingford), Norman (Beresford) Tebbit, Baron (1931–) British Conservative statesman, born in Enfield, Greater London. He was employment secretary (1981–3), secretary for trade and industry (1983–5), and party chairman (1985–7).

Tecumseh [tekumsuh] (c.1768–1813) Indian chief of the Shawnees, born in Old Piqua, OH. He joined his brother in a rising against the whites, suppressed at Tippecanoe (1811), and commanded the Indian allies in the War of 1812.

Tedder (of Glenguin), Arthur William Tedder, Baron (1890–1967) British marshal of the Royal Air Force, born in Glenguin, Central, Scotland. He commanded in the Mediterranean theatre (1943) and became deputy supreme commander of the Allied Expeditionary Force under Eisenhower (1943–5). >> Eisenhower

Teilhard de Chardin, Pierre [tayah duh shah(r)dĩ] (1881–1955) Geologist, palaeontologist, Jesuit priest, and philosopher, born in Sarcenat, France. His unorthodox ideas led to a Church ban on his teaching and publishing. His major work, *The Phenomenon of Man* (1938–40) was posthumously published.

Tekakwitha, Blessed Kateri [tekakwitha] (1656–80) American Indian Catholic convert, born in Ossernenon, in Mohawk territory (now Auriesville, NY). To escape con-

tinuing persecution she fled to a Christian Indian village near Montreal, where she became noted for her religious fervour. She was beatified in 1980.

Te Kanawa, Dame Kiri [tay kahnawa] (1944–) Operatic soprano, born in Gisborne, New Zealand. She made her debut with the Royal Opera Company in 1970, and has since taken a wide range of leading roles, in 1981 singing at the wedding of the Prince and Princess of Wales.

Teleki, Pál, Gróf (Count) [telekee] (1879–1941) Hungarian prime minister (1920–1, 1939–41), born in Budapest. He also served as foreign minister (1919) and minister of education (1938).

Telemann, Georg Philipp [tayleman] (1681–1767) Composer, born in Magdeburg, Germany. His many works include church music, 46 passions, over 40 operas, oratorios, many songs, and a large body of instrumental music.

Telford, Thomas (1757–1834) Engineer, born near Langholm, Dumfries and Galloway. His many projects include the Ellesmere (1793–1805) and Caledonian (1803–23) canals, and the road from London to Holyhead, with the Menai Suspension Bridge (1825).

Tell, Wilhelm, Eng **William Tell** (13th–14th-c) Legendary Swiss patriot. According to tradition, he was compelled by a tyrannical Austrian governor to shoot an apple off his own son's head with a crossbow at a distance of 80 paces. Later, Tell slew the tyrant, initiating the movement which secured the independence of Switzerland.

Teller, Edward (1908–) Physicist, born in Budapest. He contributed profoundly to the modern explanation of solar energy, anticipating the theory behind thermonuclear explosions, and was a member of the team under Fermi that produced the first nuclear chain reaction (1941). >> Fermi

Téllez, Gabriel >> Tirso de Molina

Temin, Howard (Martin) [teemin] (1934–94) Virologist, born in Philadelphia, PA. For his work on the way viruses can make normal cells malignant, he shared the Nobel Prize for Physiology or Medicine in 1975.

Temminck, Coenraad Jacob (1778–1858) Ornithologist, born in Amsterdam. His best-known work is the *Manual of Ornithology* (1815). *Temminck's stint, cat,* and *horned lark* are named after him.

Temple, Frederick (1821–1902) Archbishop of Canterbury, born in Levkás, Greece. In 1897 he became Archbishop of Canterbury, and was responsible, with Archbishop Maclagen of York, for the 'Lambeth Opinions' (1889), which attempted to solve some controversies over ritual.

Temple, Shirley, married name **Black** (1928–) Child film star, born in Santa Monica, CA. She became a world favourite in such films as *Curly Top* (1935) and *Dimples* (1936), and received an honorary Academy Award in 1934. Retiring from the screen, she entered Republican politics, her posts including ambassador to Ghana (1974–6) and Czechoslovakia (1989–93).

Temple, Sir William (1628–99) Diplomat and essayist, born in London. He negotiated the Triple Alliance (1668) against France, and in 1677 helped to bring about the marriage of the Prince of Orange to the Princess Mary. His essay style was a major influence on Swift, who was his secretary. >> Swift, Jonathan; William III

Temple, William (1881–1944) Anglican clergyman, born in Exeter, Devon. Archbishop of Canterbury (1942–4), he was an outspoken advocate of social reform, a leader in the reform of Church structures, and a noted ecumenist.

Templer, Sir Gerald (1898–1979) British soldier. In World War 2 he was commander of the 6th Armoured Division, later becoming Chief of the Imperial General Staff (1955–8) and commander-in-chief in Malaya (1952–4).

Templeton, Sir John Marks (1912–) Businessman and philanthropist, born in Winchester, TN. In 1972 he established the Templeton Prize for Progress in Religion.

Templewood, Viscount >> Hoare, Sir Samuel

Teng Hsiao-p'ing >> Deng Xiaoping

Teniers, David [teneerz], known as **the Elder** (1582–1649) Baroque genre painter, born in Antwerp, Belgium. He became a master in the Antwerp guild (1606), and an art dealer in the 1630s. Some paintings by his son were formerly attributed to him.

Teniers, David [teneerz], known as **the Younger** (1610–90) Painter, born in Antwerp, Belgium. He is best known for his scenes of peasant life, such as 'Peasants Playing Music' and 'Village Fete' (1646).

Tenniel, Sir John [teneel] (1820–1914) Artist, born in London. He became known as a book illustrator, notably in his work for *Alice's Adventures in Wonderland* (1865) and *Through the Looking-glass* (1872).

Tennyson, Alfred Tennyson, Baron [tenison], known as **Alfred, Lord Tennyson** (1809–92) Poet, born in Somersby, Lincolnshire. His major works include 'The Lady of Shalott' and 'The Lotus-eaters' (1842), 'In Memoriam' (1850), and a series of poems on the Arthurian theme, *Idylls of the King* (1859–85). He became poet laureate in 1850.

Tenzing Norgay, known as **Sherpa Tenzing** (1914–86) Mountaineer, born in Tsa-chu, Nepal. In 1953 he succeeded in reaching the Everest summit with Hillary, for which he was awarded the George Medal. >> Hillary

Tenzin Gyatso >> Dalai Lama

Te Puea, Princess Herangi [tay pooa] (1883–1952) Maori leader, born in Waikato, New Zealand. By 1930 she had built the Maori nationalist movement, Kingitanga, into a major instrument for the social and cultural rehabilitation of the Maori.

Terborch or **Terburg, Gerard** [terbaw(r)kh] (1617–81) Painter, born in Zwolle, The Netherlands. He produced genre pictures and fashionable portraits, but is best known for his painting of 'The Peace of Munster' (1648).

Terbrugghen, Hendrik [tairbrookhen] (c.1588–1629) Painter, born in Deventer, The Netherlands. He excelled in chiaroscuro effects and in the faithful representation of facial details and drapery, as in his 'Jacob and Laban' (1627).

Terburg, Gerard >> Terborch, Gerard

Terence, in full **Publius Terentius Afer** (c.190–159 BC) Latin comic poet, born in Carthage, N Africa. His surviving six comedies are Greek in origin and scene, directly based on Menander. >> Menander

Teresa of Ávila, St (1515–82), feast day 15 October. Saint and mystic, born in Ávila, Spain. Famous for her ascetic religious exercises and sanctity, in 1562 she re-established the ancient Carmelite rule, with additional observances. She was canonized in 1622.

Teresa (of Calcutta), Mother, originally **Agnes Gonxha Bojaxhiu** (1910–   ) Christian missionary in India, born in Skopje, Yugoslavia (formerly, Albania). Her sisterhood, the Missionaries of Charity, was founded in 1950, and in 1957 she began work with lepers, and in many disaster areas of the world. She was awarded the Nobel Peace Prize in 1979.

Tereshkova, Valentina [tereshkova] (1937–   ) Cosmonaut, the first woman to fly in space, born in Maslennikovo, Russia. She was solo crew member of the three-day Vostok 6 flight launched on 16 June 1963.

Terkel, Studs, popular name of **Louis Terkel** (1912–   ) Writer and oral historian, born in New York City. He travelled worldwide conducting interviews with the famous and the anonymous. His publications include *The Good War: an Oral History of World War Two* (1984, Pulitzer).

Terman, Fred(erick Emmons) (1900–82) Electrical engineer, born in English, IN. He set up the Stanford Industrial Park (1951), which eventually became the centre of the electronics industry, earning the area the name of Silicon Valley.

Terman, Lewis M(adison) (1877–1956) Psychologist and pioneer of intelligence tests, born in Johnson Co, IN. He introduced Terman Group Intelligence Tests into the US army in 1920, and pioneered the use of the term *IQ* (Intelligence Quotient) in 1916.

Terry, Eli (1772–1852) Inventor and clock manufacturer, born in East Windsor, CT. In 1800 he established the USA's first clock factory in Plymouth, CT. >> Thomas, Seth

Terry, Dame (Alice) Ellen (1847–1928) Actress, born in Coventry, West Midlands, a member of a large family of actors. She established herself as the leading Shakespearean actress in London, dominating the English and US theatre (1878–1902) in partnership with Irving. >> Irving, Henry

Tertullian [tertulian], in full **Quintus Septimus Florens Tertullianus** (c.160–220) Christian theologian, born in Carthage. A leader of the Montanist sect (c.207), he was the first to produce major Christian works in Latin.

Terzaghi, Karl (Anton von) [tairtsagee] (1883–1963) Civil engineer, born in Prague. He established the subject of soil mechanics as an independent scientific discipline.

Tesla, Nikola [tesla] (1856–1943) Physicist and electrical engineer, born in Smiljan, Croatia. His inventions included improved dynamos, transformers, electric bulbs, and the high-frequency coil which now bears his name. The unit of magnetic induction is named after him.

Tessin, Carl Gustaf, Greve (Count) [teseen] (1695–1770) Swedish writer and court official, born in Stockholm, the son of Nicodemus Tessin (the Younger). He was elected leader of the Nobility Estate when the Hats gained a majority in 1738, and bore heavy responsibility for the unsuccessful war against Russia in 1741.

Tessin [teseen], Nicodemus known as **the Elder** (1615–81) Architect, born in Stralsund, Germany. His major works include Kalmar Cathedral (started 1660) and the palace of Drottningholm on Mälaren, completed by his son. >> Tessin, Carl Gustaf / Nicodemus (the Younger)

Tessin [teseen], Nicodemus known as **the Younger** (1654–1728) Architect, from Stockholm, the son of Nicodemus Tessin (the Elder). His greatest achievement was the Royal Palace, Stockholm, with an Italian style facade and French interior design. >> Tessin, Carl Gustaf / Nicodemus (the Elder)

Tetley, Glen (1926–   ) Ballet dancer and choreographer, born in Cleveland, OH. He made his name as a choreographer in Europe with the Stuttgart Ballet (1973–5), and later became artistic director for the National Ballet of Canada.

Tetrazzini, Luisa [tetratseenee] (1871–1940) Coloratura soprano, born in Florence, Italy. Appearing mostly in Italian opera of the older school, one of her most notable successes was in *Lucia di Lammermoor*.

Tetzel, Johann (c.1465–1519) Monk, born in Pirna, Germany. In 1516 he was appointed to preach an indulgence in favour of contributors to the building fund of St Peter's in Rome. This he did with great ostentation, thereby provoking the Wittenberg theses of Luther. >> Luther

Tewfik or **Tawfiq Pasha, Mohammed** [tyoofik] (1852–92) Khedive of Egypt (from 1879), born in Cairo, the eldest son of Ismail Pasha. His reign saw Arabi's insurrection (1882), British intervention, and the war with the Mahdi (1884–5). >> Abbas Hilmi Pasha; Ahmed Arabi; Ismail Pasha; Mohammed Ahmed

Te Whiti-O-Rongomai [tay feetee oh ronggomiy] (1830–1907) Maori prophet, born in Taranaki, New Zealand. He actively opposed the occupation of Maori land by European settlers, but efforts were crushed when government soldiers invaded his village in 1880.

Tey, Josephine >> Mackintosh, Elizabeth

Thackeray, William Makepeace (1811–63) Novelist,

born in Calcutta, India. His major novels are *Vanity Fair* (1847-8), *Pendennis* (1848), *Henry Esmond* (1852), and *The Newcomes* (1853-5). In 1860 he became the first editor of *The Cornhill Magazine*, where much of his later work appeared.

Thais [thayis] (4th-c BC) Athenian courtesan, famous for her wit and beauty. According to legend, she was the mistress of Alexander the Great, whom she induced to burn down Persepolis.

Thalben-Ball, Sir George Thomas (1896-1987) Organist and composer, born in Sydney, New South Wales, Australia. From the early 1920s his name was synonymous with the Temple Church, both in radio broadcasts and on HMV records, and he also appeared regularly in the Henry Wood promenade concerts. >> Wood, Henry

Thales [thayleez] (c.620-c.555 BC) Greek natural philosopher, traditionally regarded as the first philosopher, born in Miletus. None of his writings survive.

Thant, U [oo tant] (1909-74) Burmese diplomat, born in Pantanaw, Myanmar (formerly, Burma). As secretary-general of the UN (1962-71), he played a major diplomatic role during the Cuban crisis (1962), and mobilized a UN peace-keeping force in Cyprus (1964).

Tharp, Twyla (1942-) Dancer, choreographer, and director, born in Portland, IN. She has choreographed and danced with her own group, and made new work for other ballet and modern dance companies.

Tharpe, Sister Rosetta, *née* Nubin (1915-73) Gospel musician, born in Cotton Plant, AR. Beginning in 1944, she developed a huge following in the burgeoning Gospel market.

Thatcher (of Kesteven), Margaret (Hilda) Thatcher, Baroness, *née* Roberts (1925-) British Conservative prime minister (1979-90), born in Grantham, Lincolnshire. She was minister of education (1970-4), and in (1975) became the first woman party leader in British politics. Her government instituted the privatization of nationalized industries and national utilities, tried to institute a market in state-provided health care and education, and reduced the role of local government as a provider of services. She resigned in 1990, following her opposition to full economic union with Europe, having become the longest serving premier of the 20th-c.

Thayendanegea >> Brant, Joseph

Theaetetus [theeaytetus] (c.414-c.369 BC) Greek mathematician. He was an associate of Plato at the Academy, whose work was later used by Euclid in Books X and XIII of the *Elements*. Plato named after him the dialogue *Theaetetus*. >> Euclid; Plato

Theiler, Max [tiyler] (1899-1972) Bacteriologist, born in Pretoria. He was awarded the Nobel Prize for Physiology or Medicine in 1951 for his research on yellow fever, for which he discovered the vaccine 17-D in 1939.

Themistocles [themistokleez] (c.523-c.458 BC) Athenian general. He made possible the great naval victory at Salamis (480 BC), and laid the foundations of the Athenian maritime empire. >> Aristides

Thenard, Louis Jacques [tenah(r)] (1777-1857) Chemist, born in La Louptière, France. He discovered sodium and potassium peroxides, the pigment *Thenard's blue* (used for colouring porcelain), and proved that caustic soda and potash contain hydrogen.

Theobald (c.1090-1161) Archbishop of Canterbury, born near Bec, France. In 1138 he was appointed Archbishop of Canterbury. He crowned King Stephen, but after the king's death refused to regard Stephen's son as his successor, and eventually crowned Henry II (1154). >> Henry II (of England); Stephen

Theocritus [theeokritus] (c.310-250 BC) Greek pastoral poet, probably born in Syracuse. His short poems dealing with pastoral subjects, and representing a single scene, came to be called 'idylls'.

Theoderic >> Theodoric

Theodora (c.500-47) Byzantine empress (527-47). She became the mistress, then wife, of Justinian, and played a major role throughout his reign. >> Justinian

Theodorakis, Mikis [thayodorahkees] (1925-) Composer, born in Khios, Greece. His prolific musical output includes oratorios, ballets, song cycles, and music for film scores, the best known being *Zorba the Greek* (1965).

Theodore, called **King of Corsica**, also known as **Baron von Neuhoff** (1686-1756) Adventurer, born in Metz, Germany. In 1736 he led a Corsican rising against the Genoese, and was elected king, but after leaving to procure foreign aid, his attempts to return were frustrated.

Theodore of Mopsuestia (c.350-428) Christian theologian, born in Antioch. The teacher of Nestorius, his views on the Incarnation were condemned by the fifth ecumenical council in 553. >> Nestorius

Theodoret (of Cyrrhus) [theeodoret] (c.393-c.458) Theologian, born in Antioch, Syria. Deeply involved in the Nestorian and Eutychian controversies, his works consist of commentaries, histories of the Church, orations, and letters.

Theodoric or **Theoderic** [theeodorik], known as **the Great** (?-526) King of the Ostrogoths (471-526). He invaded Italy in 489, defeating the barbarian ruler, Odoacer, and securing for Italy a period of tranquillity and prosperity. >> Odoacer

Theodoric I (?-451) King of the Visigoths (418-51), the son of Alaric I. Alternately an ally and an enemy of Rome, in 421-2 he joined the Vandals to attack the Roman troops, but in 451 helped the Romans drive back the Huns under Attila. >> Alaric I; Attila

Theodoric II (?-466) King of the Visigoths (453-466). In 456 he broke the friendship with Rome and besieged Arles, but was forced by Emperor Majorian to make peace. He was murdered by his brother Euric, who succeeded him.

Theodorus of Samos [theeodorus], also spelled **Theodoros** (6th-c BC) Greek sculptor. He is said to have developed sculptural hollow-casting for large figures in bronze, and invented several kinds of tools for use in casting.

Theodosius I [theeodohshus], known as **the Great** (c.346-95) Roman emperor of the East (379-95). His title comes from his vigorous championship of orthodox Christianity.

Theophilus [theeofilus] (?-180) One of the Fathers of the Christian Church, from Syria. Bishop of Antioch (169-177), he wrote an important Apology for Christianity (c.180).

Theophilus, St [theeofilus] (?-412), feast day 15 October. Patriarch of Alexandria (from 385). He destroyed the pagan temple of Serapis, and drove out the Originist monks of Nitria.

Theophrastus [theeohfrastus] (c.372-286 BC) Greek philosopher, born in Eresus, Lesbos. He became head of the Peripatetic school after Aristotle's death. >> Aristotle

Theorell, (Axel) Hugo Theodor [tayorel] (1903-82) Biochemist, born in Linköping, Sweden. He was awarded the 1955 Nobel Prize for Physiology or Medicine for his work on oxidation enzymes.

Theotokopoulos, Domenikos >> Greco, El

Theresa, St >> Teresa of Ávila, St

Theresa of Lisieux, St [leesyoe], originally **(Marie Françoise) Thérèse Martin**, also known as **the Little Flower** and **St Theresa of the Child Jesus** (1873-97), feast day 1 October. Saint, born in Alençon, France. She entered the Carmelite convent of Lisieux in Normandy at the age of 15, where she remained until her death from tuberculosis nine years later. Her account of her life was published posthumously as *Story of a Soul* (trans, 1898). She was canonized in 1925.

Theroux, Paul (Edward) [theroo] (1941-) Novelist and

travel writer, born in Medford, MA. His novels include *Saint Jack* (1973; filmed 1979), *Picture Palace* (1978, Whitbread Award), and *The Mosquito Coast* (1981, James Tait Black Memorial Prize; filmed 1987). His rail journeys are recounted in such books as *The Great Railway Bazaar* (1975).

Thesiger, Wilfred Patrick [**the**sijer] (1910–   ) Explorer of Arabia, born in Addis Ababa. He explored the Empty Quarter of S Arabia and the borderlands of Oman (1945–50), which he described in *Arabian Sands* (1959).

Thespis (6th-c BC) Poet from Icaria. According to Aristotle, he was the first to use single actors to deliver speeches in stage work, as well as the traditional chorus.

Thibaud, Jacques [teeboh] (1880–1953) Violinist, born in Bordeaux, France. He was renowned for his interpretations of Mozart, Beethoven, and Debussy.

Thibault, Jacques >> France, Anatole

Thielicke, Helmut [**tee**likuh] (1908–86) Lutheran theologian and preacher, born in Barmen, Germany. In 1944 he contributed to a draft declaration on Church–State relations for a revolutionary government to follow a successful plot against Hitler. >> Hitler

Thiers, (Louis) Adolphe [tyair] (1797–1877) French historian and first president of the Third Republic (1871–3), born in Marseille, France. He was chief of the executive power in the provisional government, and suppressed the Paris Commune. His major literary work was *History of the Consulate and the Empire* (20 vols, trans, 1845–62).

Thirkell, Angela Margaret [**ther**kl] (1890–1961) Novelist, born in London, a cousin of Rudyard Kipling. She wrote more than 30 novels dealing with the descendants of characters from Trollope's Barsetshire novels, including *Northbridge Rectory* (1941). >> Kipling; Trollope

Thistlewood, Arthur (1770–1820) Conspirator, born in Tupholme, Lincolnshire. In 1820 he planned the Cato Street Conspiracy to murder Castlereagh and other ministers who were dining at the Earl of Harrowby's house. The conspirators were intercepted, and he was hanged. >> Castlereagh

Thom, Alexander [tom] (1894–1985) British engineer and archaeo-astronomer, born in Scotland. From 1934 he was engaged on a detailed study of stone circles, and published two major works: *Megalithic Sites in Britain* (1967) and *Megalithic Lunar Observatories* (1971).

Thom, René Frédéric [tom] (1923–   ) Mathematician, born in Montbéliard, France. He is best known for his book *Structure and morphogenetic stability* (trans, 1972), which introduced the controversial 'catastrophe theory'.

Thomas, St (1st-c AD), feast day 21 December. A disciple of Jesus Christ. He is most prominent in John's Gospel, where he is also called **Didymus** ('the Twin'), and portrayed as doubting the resurrection until he touches the wounds of the risen Christ (*John* 20). He is the patron saint of Portugal. >> Jesus Christ

Thomas, (Charles Louis) Ambroise [tohmah] (1811–96) Composer, born in Metz, France. He wrote many light operas for the Opéra Comique and the Grand Opéra, of which *Mignon* (1866) is the best known.

Thomas, Brandon (1849–1914) Actor and playwright, born in Liverpool, Merseyside. He wrote a number of successful light plays, notably *Charley's Aunt* (1892).

Thomas, Clarence (1948–   ) Jurist, born in Savannah, GA. Named to the Supreme Court in 1992, his Senate confirmation hearings attracted publicity due to allegations of sexual misconduct brought by a former female colleague.

Thomas, Dylan (Marlais) (1914–53) Poet, born in Swansea, West Glamorgan. He established himself with the publication of *Eighteen Poems* in 1934. His *Collected Poems* appeared in 1953, and he then produced his best-known work, the radio 'play for voices', *Under Milk Wood* (1954).

Thomas, (Philip) Edward, pseudonym **Edward Eastaway** (1878–1917) Poet and critic, born in London. He wrote most of his work during active service between 1915 and his death in action, just before the publication of *Poems* (1917), under his pseudonym.

Thomas, E(dward) Donnall (1920–   ) Surgeon and oncologist, born in Mart, TX. He began his pioneering studies of bone marrow transplants for treatment of human leukaemia in the 1950s, and performed the first successful brother–sister transplant in 1970. He shared the Nobel Prize for Physiology or Medicine in 1990.

Thomas, Sir George (Alan) (1881–1972) Badminton player, born in Istanbul. He won a record 21 All-England titles between 1903 and 1928, including the singles four times (1920–3). In 1939 he presented the *Thomas Cup* to be contested by national teams.

Thomas, George H(enry) (1816–70) US soldier, born in Southampton Co, VA. In the Civil War (1861–5) he joined the Federal army, saved the Battle of Stones River, defended Chickamauga (1863), and captured Mission Ridge (1863).

Thomas, Hugh Owen (1833–91) Orthopaedic surgeon, born in Anglesey, Gwynedd. He pioneered orthopaedic surgery, constructing many appliances which are still used, notably *Thomas' splints* for the hip and the knee.

Thomas, Margaret Haig, Viscountess Rhondda (1883–1958) Feminist and publisher, born in London. She became a suffragette, and in 1920 founded *Time and Tide*, a weekly journal of politics and literature, mainly publishing work that was boycotted elsewhere.

Thomas, Martha Carey (1857–1935) Feminist and educationist, born in Baltimore, MD. She established summer schools for women working in industry (1921), campaigned for women's right to vote, and wrote *The Higher Education of Women* (1900).

Thomas, Michael Tilson (1944–   ) Conductor, born in Hollywood, CA. He has guest-conducted widely, and in 1988 became conductor of the London Symphony Orchestra.

Thomas, Norman (Mattoon) (1884–1968) Socialist leader, born in Marion, OH. He was co-director of the League for Industrial Democracy (1922–37), and in 1926 became leader of the Socialist Party of America.

Thomas, R(onald) S(tuart) (1913–   ) Poet, born in Cardiff. A rector in the Church of Wales (1942–78), his collections include *Selected Poems, 1946–68* (1973) and *Counterpoint* (1990).

Thomas, Seth (1785–1859) Clock maker, born in Wolcott, CT. He began his own factory in 1812, then bought the rights to Eli Terry's popular shelf clock, developing a highly successful business in Plymouth, CT. >> Terry, Eli

Thomas, Sydney Gilchrist >> Gilchrist, Percy Carlyle

Thomas, (Christian Friedrich) Theodore (1835–1905) Conductor, born in Essen, Germany. In 1877 he became conductor of the New York Philharmonic, and in 1891 of the Chicago Orchestra.

Thomas à Becket >> Becket, Thomas à

Thomas à Kempis >> Kempis, Thomas à

Thomas of Hereford, St >> Cantelupe, St Thomas de

Thomas Aquinas >> Aquinas, St Thomas

Thompson, Sir Benjamin, Graf (Count) **von Rumford**, known as **Count Rumford** (1753–1814) Administrator and scientist, born in Woburn, MA. In 1784 he entered the service of Bavaria, where he carried out military, social, and economic reforms. An amateur scientist, he first showed the relation between heat and work, a concept fundamental to modern physics.

Thompson, Daley, popular name of **Francis Morgan Thompson** (1958–   ) Athlete, born in London. An outstanding decathlete, he was world champion (1983), European champion (1982, 1986), and Olympic champion (1980, 1984).

Thompson, Sir D'Arcy (Wentworth) (1860–1948) Zoologist and classical scholar, born in Edinburgh. His major work is the influential *On Growth and Form* (1917).

Thompson, David (1770–1857) Fur trader and explorer, born in London. In Canada he mapped the Saskatchewan, Hayes, Nelson, Churchill, and Colombia rivers, and later mapped W Canada.

Thompson, Emma (1959–   ) Actress, born in London. In 1989 she appeared in the film of *Henry V*, directed by Kenneth Branagh, whom she married the same year. Her other films include *Howards End* (1992, Oscar), *Remains of the Day* (1993), and *In the Name of the Father* (1994). >> Branagh

Thompson, Flora (June), *née* **Timms** (1876–1947) Writer, born in Juniper Hill, Oxfordshire. In her 60s she published the semi-autobiographical trilogy combined as *Lark Rise to Candleford* (1945).

Thompson, Francis (1859–1907) Poet, born in Preston, Lancashire. His later work was mainly religious in theme, including the well-known 'The Hound of Heaven'.

Thompson, Hunter (Stockton) (1939–   ) Journalist and writer, born in Louisville, KY. An adherent of the 'new journalism', he was the first reporter to infiltrate the Hell's Angels.

Thompson, J(ames) Walter (1847–1928) Advertising executive, born in Pittsfield, MA. In 1878 he bought William Carlton's New York advertising agency, and his success in advertising in magazines made national product campaigns possible.

Thompson, John T(alafierro) (1860–1940) US soldier and inventor, born in Newport, KY. In 1918 he originated the Thompson submachine gun, which came to be known as the *Tommy gun*.

Thompson, Randall (1899–1984) Composer, born in New York City. His works include symphonies, an oratorio, two operas, a variety of chamber, piano, orchestral, and theatre music, and sacred vocal music.

Thomsen, Christian Jörgensen (1788–1865) Archaeologist, born in Copenhagen. He is credited with developing the three-part system of prehistory, named as the Stone, Bronze, and Iron Ages, described in *A Guide to Northern Antiquities* (trans, 1836).

Thomson, Sir C(harles) Wyville (1830–82) Marine biologist and oceanographer, born in Linlithgow, Lothian. Famous for his deep-sea research, described in *The Depths of the Oceans* (1872), he was appointed scientific head of the *Challenger* round-the-world expedition (1872–6).

Thomson, D(avid) C(ouper) (1861–1954) Newspaper proprietor, born in Dundee, Tayside. At age 23 he took charge of a Dundee newspaper concern, whose publications included the *Sunday Post* and the popular children's comics, *Beano* and *Dandy*.

Thomson, Elihu (1853–1937) Electrical engineer and inventor, born in Manchester, UK. In the USA, his 700 patented electrical inventions were developed in co-operation with Edwin J(ames) Houston (1847–1914). In 1892 their company merged with Thomas Edison's company to form the General Electric Company. >> Edison

Thomson, Sir George (Paget) (1892–1975) Physicist, born in Cambridge, Cambridgeshire, the son of Sir Joseph Thomson. He shared the Nobel Prize for Physics in 1937 for his discovery of electron diffraction by crystals. >> Thomson, J J

Thomson, James (1700–48) Poet, born in Ednam, Borders, Scotland. He is best known for his four-part work, *The Seasons* (1730), the first major nature poem in English; his ode 'Rule, Britannia' (1740); and the Spenserian allegory, *The Castle of Indolence* (1748).

Thomson, James, pseudonym **Bysshe Vanolis** or **BV** (1834–82) Poet, born in Port Glasgow, Strathclyde. His best-known work is 'The City of Dreadful Night' (1874).

Thomson, Joseph (1858–95) Explorer, born in Penpont, Dumfries and Galloway. He joined the Royal Geographical Society African Expedition (1878–9), and was the first European to reach L Nyasa (Malawi) from the N.

Thomson, Sir J(oseph) J(ohn) (1856–1940) Physicist, born in Cheetham Hill, Greater Manchester. He showed in 1897 that cathode rays were rapidly-moving particles, and deduced that these 'corpuscles' (electrons) must be nearly 2000 times smaller in mass than the lightest known atomic particle, the hydrogen ion. He received the Nobel Prize for Physics in 1906.

Thomson (of Fleet), Kenneth (Roy) Thomson, 2nd Baron (1923–   ) Businessman and financier, born in Toronto, Ontario, Canada, the son of Roy Thompson. In 1979 he bought the Hudson's Bay Co, and in 1980 the FP publications newspaper chain. >> Thomson, Roy

Thomson, Peter (1929–   ) Golfer, born in Melbourne, Victoria, Australia. He won the British Open three times in succession (1954–6), and on two later occasions.

Thomson (of Fleet), Roy (Herbert) Thomson, Baron (1894–1976) Newspaper and television magnate, born in Toronto, Ontario, Canada. He settled in Edinburgh on acquiring his first British paper, *The Scotsman* (1952), bought the Kemsley newspapers in 1959 (including *The Sunday Times*), and in 1966 took over *The Times*. >> Thomson, Kenneth

Thomson, Tom, popular name of **Thomas John Thomson** (1877–1917) Painter, born in Claremont, Ontario, Canada. He worked frequently in Algonquin Park, Ontario, producing many sketches and some larger canvases, such as 'The West Wind' (1917).

Thomson, Virgil (1896–1989) Composer and critic, born in Kansas City, KS. Best known for his operas with libretti by Gertrude Stein, *Four Saints in Three Acts* (1934) and *The Mother of Us All* (1947), he also wrote symphonies, ballets, and choral, chamber, and film music. >> Stein, Gertrude

Thomson, Sir William >> **Kelvin, Baron**

Thonet, Michael (1796–1871) Manufacturer of bentwood furniture, born in Boppard, Germany. In 1856 he had perfected his technique, and mass-produced cafe chairs, rocking chairs, and hatstands.

Thorarensen, Bjarni Vigfusson [thaw(r)ah(r)nsn] (1786–1841) Romantic poet and jurist, born in Brautarholt, Iceland. As a lyric poet he celebrated Icelandic nature and nationalism, his 'Eldgamla Isafold' (Ancient Iceland) being seen as an unofficial national anthem.

Thorburn, Archibald (1860–1935) Bird artist, born in Lasswade, Lothian. He painted most of the plates of the monumental *Coloured Figures of the Birds of the British Isles* (1885–97).

Thoreau, Henry (David) [thoroh] (1817–62) Essayist and poet, born in Concord, MA. In c.1839 he began the walks and studies of nature which became his major occupation, recorded in a daily journal. His writings include the classic *Walden, or Life in the Woods* (1854).

Thorfinn, nickname **Thorfinn Karlsefni** ('Man-Material') (fl.1002–7) Norse explorer. In c.1000 he led an expedition of would-be colonists from Greenland, which sailed along the NE coasts of North America and attempted to found a colony in an area called *Vínland*, somewhere near Newfoundland.

Thorkelin [thaw(r)kelin], pseudonym of **Grímur Jónsson** (1752–1829) Scholar and antiquary, from Iceland. He was the first editor of the Anglo-Saxon epic *Beowulf*, and published his transcript in 1815.

Thorndike, Edward L(ee) (1874–1949) Psychologist, born in Williamsburg, MA. As a result of studying animal intelligence, he formulated his famous 'law of effect', which states that a given behaviour is learned by trial-and-error, and is more likely to occur if its consequences are satisfying.

Thorndike, Dame (Agnes) Sybil (1882–1976) Actress, born in Gainsborough, Lincolnshire. In 1924 she played the title role in the first English performance of Shaw's *Saint Joan*, and during World War 2 was a notable member of the Old Vic Company. She married Lewis Casson in 1908. >> Casson, Lewis

Thorneycroft (of Dunston), (George Edward) Peter Thorneycroft, Baron (1909–94) British Conservative statesman, born in Dunstan, Staffordshire. He served as President of the Board of Trade (1951–7), Chancellor of the Exchequer (1957–8), minister of aviation (1960–2), and secretary of state for defence (1962–4).

Thornhill, Sir James (1675–1734) Baroque painter, born in Melcombe Regis, Dorset. He executed paintings for the dome of St Paul's, Blenheim, Hampton Court, and Greenwich Hospital.

Thoroddsen, Jón [thorodsn], originally **Jón Thóróarson** (1818–68) Novelist and poet, born in Reykhólar, Iceland. Regarded as the father of the modern Icelandic novel, he wrote *Boy and Girl* (trans, 1850), and an unfinished sequel, *Man and Woman* (trans, 1876), published posthumously.

Thorpe, Sir (Thomas) Edward (1845–1925) Chemist, physicist, and historian of science, born near Manchester. He wrote on the history of chemistry, and his *Dictionary of Applied Chemistry* (1893) was a long-used standard work.

Thorpe, (John) Jeremy (1929–) British politician, born in London. Elected leader of the Liberal Party in 1967, he was forced to resign in 1976 following allegations of a homosexual relationship. In 1979 he was acquitted of charges of conspiracy and incitement to murder.

Thorpe, Jim, popular name of **James Francis Thorpe** (1888–1953) Athlete, born in Prague, OK. In the 1912 Olympic Games at Stockholm he won both the pentathlon and decathlon, but was disqualified (his titles being posthumously restored). He played professional baseball (1913–19) with the New York Giants, Cincinnati Reds, and Boston Braves.

Thorpe Davie, Cedric (1913–83) Composer, born in London. His works include the *Dirge for Cuthullin* (1935) for chorus and orchestra, Symphony in C (1945), and music for Guthrie's production of *Ane Satyre of the Thrie Estaitis* (1948). >> Guthrie, Tyrone

Thothmes (Thutmose) I / II >> Hatshepsut

Thothmes III >> Thutmose III

Thrale, Mrs >> Piozzi, Hester Lynch

Thrasybulus [thrasiboolus] (?–388 BC) Athenian general. A strenuous supporter of the democracy, in 411 BC he helped to overthrow the Four Hundred, and was responsible for the recall of Alcibiades. >> Alcibiades

Throckmorton, Francis (1554–84) English conspirator. His plot to overthrow Queen Elizabeth I in 1583 and restore papal authority was uncovered, and he was executed. >> Elizabeth I

Thucydides [thyoosidideez] (c.460–c.400 BC) Athenian aristocratic historian of the Peloponnesian War. Although accurate in his narrative of events, he was critical of the democratic system and its leaders.

Thumb, General Tom >> Stratton, Charles

Thurber, James (Grover) (1894–1961) Writer and cartoonist, born in Columbus, OH. His popular drawings first appeared in *Is Sex Necessary?* (1929), and his short stories include *The Secret Life of Walter Mitty*.

Thurmond, J(ames) Strom (1902–) US politician, born in Edgefield, SC. Originally appointed a Democrat to the US Senate (1954), he switched to the Republican Party (1964) and became a prominent force in the emergence of a conservative Republican Party in the South.

Thurston, Robert Henry (1839–1903) Mechanical engineer and educator, born in Providence, RI. At the newly-formed Stevens Institute of Technology, Hoboken, NJ, he drew up a four-year course in mechanical engineering that included training students on actual research.

Thurstone, L(ouis) L(eon) (1887–1955) Psychologist, born in Chicago, IL. His academic work was devoted to the theory and practice of intelligence testing and to the development of statistical techniques.

Thutmose I / II >> Hatshepsut

Thutmose III [thutmohsuh], also **Thothmes** or **Tuthmosis** (?–1450 BC) Egyptian pharoah (c.1504–1450 BC). He established Egyptian control over Syria and Nubia, built the temple of Amon at Karnak, and erected many obelisks, including 'Cleopatra's Needle'.

Tiberius [tiybeerius], in full **Tiberius Julius Caesar Augustus** (42 BC–AD 37) Roman emperor (14–37), the son of Livia, and stepson and successor of the Emperor Augustus. The suspicious death of his heir Germanicus (19), followed by the excesses of his chief henchman, Sejanus, and the reign of terror that followed Sejanus's downfall (d.31), made him widely hated. >> Sejanus

Tibullus, Albius [tibulus] (c.54–19 BC) Latin poet, considered by Quintilian to be the greatest elegaic writer. He is known for his books of love poetry, but several works under his name are probably by other authors.

Tidy, Bill, popular name of **William Edward Tidy** (1933–) Cartoonist and broadcaster, born in Liverpool, Merseyside. He created the cartoon strips *The Cloggies* and *The Fosdyke Saga*, which he adapted for radio.

Tieck, (Johann) Ludwig [teek] (1773–1853) Critic and writer of the Romantic school, born in Berlin. He is best known for his critical writings, which include a series of Shakespearian essays (1823–9).

Tiepolo, Giovanni Battista [tyaypoloh] (1696–1770) Artist, born in Venice, Italy. The last of the great Venetian painters, he became renowned as a decorator of buildings throughout Europe, such as the ceiling paintings of the Würzburg and Madrid palaces.

Tiffany, Charles (Lewis) (1812–1902) Goldsmith and jeweller, founder of Tiffany & Co, born in Killingly, CT. He began dealing in fancy goods in New York City in 1837, and by 1883 was one of the largest manufacturers of silverware in the USA. >> Tiffany, Louis

Tiffany, Louis (Comfort) (1848–1933) Glassmaker and interior decorator, born in New York City, the son of Charles Lewis Tiffany. Best known as a leader of the Art Nouveau movement for his work in glass, he also produced furniture, fabrics, wallpaper, and *Tiffany lamps*.

Tikhonov, Nikolay Alexandrovich [tikhonof] (1905–) Soviet prime minister (1980–5), born in Kharkov, Ukraine. His period as state premier was characterized by progressive economic stagnation.

Tilden, Bill, popular name of **William Tatem Tilden** (1893–1953) Tennis player, born in Philadelphia, PA. He was Wimbledon singles champion three times (1920, 1921, 1930) and doubles champion in 1927. He was also six times US singles champion, and four times doubles champion in the 1920s.

Tilden, Samuel Jones (1814–86) Lawyer and public official, born in New Lebanon, NY. After taking a leading role in breaking up Boss Tweed's rings, he was elected Governor of New York (1875–7). He ran for president as a Democrat (1876), but lost the disputed election to Hayes. >> Tweed; Hayes, Rutherford B

Tilden, Sir William Augustus (1842–1926) Chemist, born in London. He made possible the manufacture of artificial rubber by his synthetic preparation of isoprene.

Tillett, Ben(jamin) (1860–1943) Trade union leader, born in Bristol, Avon. He achieved prominence as leader of the great dockers' strike (1889), and of the transport workers' strike in London (1911).

Tilley, Vesta, stage name of **Matilda Alice, Lady de Frece**, *née* **Powles** (1864–1952) Music-hall entertainer, born in

Worcester, Hereford and Worcester. A celebrated male impersonator, her many popular songs included 'Burlington Bertie' and 'Following in Father's Footsteps'.

Tillich, Paul (Johannes) [tilikh] (1886–1965) Protestant theologian and philosopher, born in Starzeddel, Germany. A Lutheran pastor, in 1933 he settled in the USA, where his main scholarly work was *Systematic Theology* (3 vols, 1951–63).

Tilly, Johann Tserclaes, Graf (Count) **von** (1559–1632) Flemish soldier, born in Tilly, Belgium. He commanded the forces of the Catholic League in the Thirty Years' War, gaining decisive victories at the White Mountain and Prague (1620), but was routed at Breitenfeld (1631). >> Gustav II Adolf

Tilman, Harold William (1898–?1978) Mountaineer, explorer, and sailor, born in Wallasey, Merseyside. He made the first ascents of Midget Peak, Mt Kenya (1930), and Nanda Devi (1936), was a member of the 1935 Everest expedition, and led the 1938 attempt.

Timoleon [timohlion] (?–c.337 BC) Greek statesman, and general of Corinth. He manoeuvred Dionysius into abdication and fought the Carthaginians, defeating them at the Crimessus in 341. >> Dionysius (the Younger)

Timon [tiymon], nickname **the Misanthrope of Athens** (5th-c BC) Nobleman from Athens, a contemporary of Socrates. Shakespeare's play *Timon of Athens* is based on his story as told in Painter's *Palace of Pleasure*. >> Socrates

Timoshenko, Semyon Konstantinovich [timoh-shengkoh] (1895–1970) Russian general, born in Furmanka, Ukraine. In 1940 he smashed Finnish resistance during the Russo-Finnish War, then commanded in the Ukraine, but failed to stop the German advance (1942).

Timur [timoor], known as **Timur Lenk** (Turk 'Timur the Lame'), English **Tamerlane** or **Tamburlaine** (1336–1405) Tatar conqueror, born near Samarkand, Uzbekistan. In 1369 he ascended the throne of Samarkand, and subdued nearly all Persia, Georgia, and the Tatar empire. He defeated the Turks at Angora (1402), taking Bayezit prisoner. >> Bayezit I

Tinbergen, Jan [tinbergen] (1903–94) Dutch economist, born in The Hague, the brother of Nikolaas Tinbergen. His major contribution was the econometric modelling of cyclical movements in socio-economic growth, and he shared the first Nobel Prize for Economics in 1969. >> Tinbergen, Nikolaas

Tinbergen, Nikolaas [tinbergen] (1907–88) Ethologist, born in The Hague, the brother of Jan Tinbergen. His major concern was with the patterns of animal behaviour in nature, showing that many are stereotyped, and he shared the Nobel Prize for Physiology or Medicine in 1973. >> Tinbergen, Jan

Tindale, William >> **Tyndale, William**

Ting, Samuel C(hao) C(hung) (1936–) Physicist, born in Ann Arbor, MI. He conducted an experiment in which protons were directed onto a beryllium target; a long-lived product particle was observed in 1974, and later named the J/psi particle. He shared the Nobel Prize for Physics with Richter in 1976. >> Richter, Burton

Ting Ling >> **Ding Ling**

Tinguely, Jean [tilee] (1925–) Sculptor, born in Fribourg, Switzerland. A pioneer of Kinetic Art, from 1953 he exhibited his 'meta-mechanical' moving metal constructions, and from c.1960 began programming them to destroy themselves ('auto-destructive art').

Tino di Camaino [teenoh dee kamiynoh] (c.1285–1337) Sculptor, born in Siena, Italy. He was master of works at Pisa Cathedral, and later worked in Siena, Florence, and Naples.

Tinsley, Pauline (1928–) Dramatic soprano, born in Wigan, Greater Manchester. She excelled as a singing

actress in many diverse roles, performing throughout USA and Europe.

Tintoretto [tintoretoh], originally **Jacopo Robusti** (1518–94) Venetian painter, probably born in Venice, Italy, the son of a dyer (Ital *tintore*). His most spectacular works are sacred murals, notably the canvases decorating the Church and Scuola of S Rocco. Other major works include 'The Last Supper' (1547) and the 'Paradiso' (1588).

Tiomkin, Dimitri [tyomkin] (1894–1980) Composer, born in Russia. In 1930 he began writing theme music for Hollywood films, earning Oscars for the background music to *High Noon* (1952), *The High and the Mighty* (1954), and *The Old Man and the Sea* (1958).

Tippett, Sir Michael (Kemp) (1905–) Composer, born in London. His works include the oratorio, *A Child of our Time* (1941), the operas *The Midsummer Marriage* (1952) and *King Priam* (1961), four symphonies, a piano concerto, and string quartets.

Tippoo Sultán [tipoo], also known as **Tippoo Sahib** (1749–99) Sultan of Mysore (1782–99), born in Devanhalli, India, the son of Haidar Ali. He continued his father's policy of opposing British rule, but was defeated by Cornwallis, and had to cede half his kingdom. >> Cornwallis; Haidar Ali

Tiro, Marcus Tullius [tiyroh] (fl.1st-c) Freedman of Rome who invented the *Tironian* system of shorthand. He was the author of a lost *Life of Cicero* and editor of some of Cicero's letters. >> Cicero

Tirpitz, Alfred (Friedrich) von [teerpits] (1849–1930) German admiral, born in Kostrzyn, Poland (formerly Küstrin, Prussia). As secretary of state for the imperial navy (1897–1916), he raised a fleet to challenge British supremacy of the seas, and acted as its commander (1914–16).

Tirso de Molina [teersoh, moleena], pseudonym of **Gabriel Téllez** (c.1571–1648) Playwright, born in Madrid. He wrote many comedies and religious plays, but is best known for his treatment of the Don Juan legend in *The Seducer of Seville* (trans, 1635).

Tischendorf, (Lobegott Friedrich) Konstantin von [tishendaw(r)f] (1815–74) Biblical scholar, born in Lengenfeld, Germany. His lifetime's work, journeying in search of New Testament manuscripts, resulted in the discovery of the 4th-c Sinaitic Codex.

Tiselius, Arne (Wilhelm Kaurin) [tisaylius] (1902–71) Chemist, born in Stockholm. He investigated serum proteins by electrophoretic analysis, and in chromatography evolved new methods for the analysis of colourless substances. He was awarded the Nobel Prize for Chemistry in 1948.

Tissot, James Joseph Jacques [teesoh] (1836–1902) Painter, born in Nantes, France. He painted highly accomplished scenes of Victorian life in London, and produced a series of the life of Christ in water-colour.

Titian [tishan], Ital **Tiziano Vecellio** (c.1490–1576) Venetian painter, born in Pieve di Cadore, Italy. For the Duke of Ferrara he painted three great mythological subjects, 'The Feast of Venus' (c.1515–18), 'Bacchanal' (c.1518), and 'Bacchus and Ariadne' (c.1523). Later works include 'Ecce Homo' (1543) and 'Christ Crowned with Thorns' (c.1570).

Tito [teetoh], known as **Marshal Tito**, originally **Josip Broz** (1892–1980) Yugoslav statesman and president (1953–80), born in Kumrovec, Croatia. In 1941 he organized partisan forces against the Axis conquerors, and after the war became the country's first Communist prime minister (1945), then president (1953). He broke with Stalin and the Cominform in 1948, developing Yugoslavia's independent style of Communism (*Titoism*).

Titterton, Sir Ernest (William) (1916–90) Nuclear physicist, born in Tamworth, Staffordshire. A member of the British mission to the USA for the development of the atomic bomb (1943), he was involved with the first atomic test in 1945.

Titus [tiytus], in full **Titus Flavius Vespasianus** (39–81) Roman emperor (79–81), the elder son of Vespasian. Popular with the Romans, he is execrated in Jewish tradition for his destruction of Jerusalem (70) and suppression of the Jewish Revolt. >> Vespasian

Titus, St [tiytus] (1st-c), feast day 6 February (W), 23 August (E). In the New Testament, a Gentile companion of the apostle Paul. Ecclesiastical tradition makes him the first Bishop of Crete.

Tizard, Dame Catherine Anne [tizah(r)d] (1931–) New Zealand politician and public administrator, born in Auckland, New Zealand. In 1990 she became Governor-General of New Zealand, the first woman to hold the position.

Tobey, Mark [tohbee] (1890–1976) Artist, born in Centerville, WI. The influence of Chinese calligraphy is reflected in his later work, usually white on a dark background, as exemplified by his cityscapes of the 1930s.

Tobias, Phillip Vallentine [tobiyas] (1925–) Anatomist and physical anthropologist, born in Durban, South Africa. A leading authority on human biological evolution, his many works include *The Meaning of Race* (1972) and *Hominid Evolution: Past, Present and Future* (1985).

Tobin, James [tohbin] (1918–) Economist, born in Champaign, IL. In 1981 he was awarded the Nobel Prize for Economics, primarily for his 'portfolio selection theory' of investment.

Tocqueville, Alexis (Charles Henri Maurice Clérel) de [tokveel] (1805–59) Historian and political scientist, born in Verneuil, France. After a period in the USA he published his political study, *Democracy in America* (trans, 1835), which gave him a European reputation.

Todd (of Trumpington) Todd, Alexander Robertus, Baron (1907–) Chemist, born in Glasgow, Strathclyde. He was awarded the Nobel Prize for Chemistry in 1957 for his research on vitamins B^{-1} and E.

Todd, Sir (Reginald Stephen) Garfield (1908–) Rhodesian missionary and prime minister (1953–8), born in Otago, New Zealand. A Church of Christ minister, he went to Southern Rhodesia (now Zimbabwe), and was superintendent of the Dadaya Mission (1934–53). He was detained by the Smith regime for supporting the Zimbabwe nationalist movement (1972–6). >> Smith, Ian

Todd, Mark James (1956–) Show jumper, born in Cambridge, New Zealand. He won the gold medal in the individual Three Day Event at the Olympics in 1984 and 1988.

Todd, Mike, popular name of **Michael Todd**, originally **Avrom Hirsch Goldbogen** (1909–58) Showman, born in Minneapolis, MN. He sponsored the TODD-AO wide-screen process with his film *Around the World in Eighty Days* (1956, Oscar). He married Elizabeth Taylor in 1957, but was killed in an aircrash the next year. >> Taylor, Elizabeth

Todd, Richard B >> **Bowman, William**

Todd, Ron(ald) (1927–) Trade union leader, born in London. A skilled negotiator, he rose steadily from shop steward to be general-secretary (1985–92) of the Transport and General Workers' Union.

Todi, Jacopone da [tohdee, jakopohnay] (c.1230–1306) Religious poet, born in Todi, Italy. To him is ascribed the authorship of the *Stabat Mater* and other Latin hymns, and he wrote *laudi spirituali* ('spiritual praises'), important in the development of Italian drama.

Todt, Fritz [toht] (1891–1942) Engineer, born in Pforzheim, Germany. As Hitler's inspector of German roads (1933) he oversaw the construction of the autobahns, and his organization constructed the Siegfried Line (1937). >> Hitler

Togo, Heihachiro, Koshaku (Marquess) [tohgoh] (1847–1934) Japanese admiral, born in Kagoshima, Japan. He

served against China (1894), and as commander during the war with Russia (1904–5) defeated the Russian fleet at Tsushima (1905).

Tojo, Hideki [tohjoh] (1885–1948) Japanese general and prime minister (1941–4), born in Tokyo. During World War 2 he was minister of war (1940–1) and premier. He was hanged as a war criminal.

Tokugawa, Ieyasu [tokugahwa] (1542–1616) The third of the three great historical unifiers of Japan, born in Okazaki, Japan. He founded the Tokugawa shogunate (1603–1868), instituting centralized control of Japanese life. >> Hideyoshi; Nobunaga

Toland, John [tohland] (1670–1722) Religious writer, born near Londonderry, Co Londonderry. A convert to Protestantism, and a controversial pamphleteer, his major works debate the comparative evidence for the canonical and apocryphal Scriptures.

Tolkien, J(ohn) R(onald) R(euel) [tolkeen] (1892–1973) Philologist and writer, born in Bloemfontein, South Africa. His interest in language and saga led to his books about a fantasy world in which the beings have their own language and mythology, notably *The Hobbit* (1937), *The Lord of the Rings* (3 vols, 1954–5), and *The Silmarillion* (1977).

Tolley, Howard Ross (1889–1958) Agricultural economist, born in Howard Co, IN. When the Bureau of Agricultural Economics opened (1923), he helped to develop a research programme for analyzing farm problems, and was also involved in implementing the 'New Deal' farm programme.

Tolly, Prince Barclay de >> **Barclay de Tolly, Knaz**

Tolman, Edward C(hace) (1886–1959) Psychologist, born in West Newton, MA. His *Purposive Behavior in Animals and Men* (1932) postulated purpose ('goals') as well as spatial representations ('cognitive maps') in the minds of animals, to fully explain their behaviour.

Tolstoy, Count Leo Nikolayevich (1828–1910) Russian writer, moralist, and mystic, born at Yasnaya Polyana, Russia. He became known for his short stories, then wrote his epic *War and Peace* (1865–9), followed by *Anna Karenina* (1875–7). After a spiritual crisis he made over his fortune to his wife and lived poorly as a peasant under her roof. His doctrines founded a sect, and Yasnaya Polyana became a place of pilgrimage.

Tolton, Augustine (1854–97) Catholic priest, born in Ralls, MO. He was the first Catholic priest whose parents were both African-Americans, being ordained in 1886.

Tomasi di Lampedusa, Giuseppe >> **Lampedusa, Giuseppe Tomasi di**

Tombaugh, Clyde W(illiam) [tombow] (1906–) Astronomer, born in Streator, IL. He discovered the planet Pluto in 1930, and galactic star clusters.

Tomkins, Thomas (1572–1656) Composer and organist, born in St David's, Dyfed. His compositions include a vast amount of church music, madrigals, part songs, and instrumental works.

Tomlinson, H(enry) M(ajor) (1873–1958) Writer, born in London. He wrote travel books, such as *The Sea and the Jungle* (1912), and a novel, *Gallions Reach* (1927).

Tomonaga, Shin'ichiro [tomonahga] (1906–79) Scientist, born in Kyoto, Japan. He shared the Nobel Prize for Physics in 1965 for his work which resolved the inconsistencies of the theory of quantum electrodynamics.

Tompion, Thomas (c.1639–1713) Clockmaker, born in Northill, Bedfordshire. He became Master of the London Clockmakers' Company in 1703, made one of the first English watches equipped with a balance spring (1675), and patented the cylinder escapement (1695).

Tone, (Theobald) Wolfe (1763–98) Irish nationalist, born in Dublin. He helped to organize the United Irishmen, and had to flee to the USA and to France (1795). He twice induced France to invade Ireland, but was captured and committed suicide.

Tonks, Henry (1862–1937) Artist, born in Solihull, West Midlands. He joined the New English Art Club, and was associated with Sickert and Steer. >> Sickert; Steer

Tonti, Lorenzo [**ton**tee] (1620–90) Financier, born in Naples, Italy. He proposed the *tontine* or latest-survivor system of life insurance.

Tonypandy (of Rhondda), (Thomas) George Thomas, 1st Viscount [toni**pan**dee] (1909–   ) British Labour statesman, born in S Wales. He served as secretary of state for Wales (1968–70), but is chiefly remembered as a popular Speaker of the House of Commons (1976–83).

Tooke, John Horne [tuk], originally **John Horne** (1736–1812) Radical politician, born in London. In 1771 he formed the Constitutional Society, supporting the American colonists and parliamentary reform. *The Diversions of Purley* (1786) was written while in prison for supporting the American cause.

Topelius, Zacharias [to**peel**ius] (1818–98) Novelist and scholar, born in Kuddnäs, Finland. He is regarded as the father of the Finnish historical novel, with stories of life in the 17th-c and 18th-c published as *The Surgeon's Stories* (trans, 1851–60).

Topolski, Feliks [to**pol**skee] (1907–89) Painter, draughtsman, and illustrator, born in Poland. He went to England in 1935, and was an official war artist (1940–45). His lively drawings depicting everyday life include *Topolski's Chronicle* (1953–79, 1982–9).

Torquemada, Tomás de [taw(r)kay**mah**tha] (1420–98) First inquisitor-general of Spain, born in Valladolid, Spain. As grand inquisitor from 1483, he displayed great cruelty, and was responsible for an estimated 2000 burnings.

Torrance, Thomas (Forsyth) (1913–   ) British theologian, born of missionary parents in Chengtu, China. He holds that theology should respond to the reality it encounters, both in relation to science and in the quest for an acceptable ecumenical theology.

Torrens, Sir Robert Richard (1814–84) Legal reformer, born in Co Cork, Ireland. As registrar general of South Australia (1852), he sponsored the Real Property Act of 1857 which introduced the *Torrens system*, whereby title to land was secured by registration.

Torrey, John (1796–1873) Botanist, born in New York City. He prepared *A Flora of North America* (1838–43), and also collected over 40 000 plant species. The genus *Torreya* in the yew family is named after him.

Torricelli, Evangelista [tori**che**lee] (1608–47) Physicist and mathematician, born in Faenza, Italy. He discovered the effect of atmospheric pressure on water in a suction pump, and gave the first description of a barometer, or *Torricellian tube*.

Torrigiano, Pietro [tori**jiah**noh] (1472–1528) Sculptor, born in Florence, Italy. He introduced Italian Renaissance art to England, and created the tombs of Margaret Beaufort in Westminster Abbey, and of her son Henry VII and his queen.

Torrington, Viscount >> Byng, George

Tortelier, Paul [taw(r)**tel**yay] (1914–90) Cellist, born in Paris. He achieved worldwide recognition as a leading soloist. His son **Yan Pascal Tortelier** (1947–   ) is a violinist and his daughter **Maria de la Pau Tortelier** (1950–   ) is a pianist.

Torvill and Dean Figure skaters **Jayne Torvill** (1957–   ) and **Christopher Dean** (1958–   ), both from Nottingham, Nottinghamshire. World ice dance champions (1981–4), and Olympic champions (1984), they then turned professional, but returned to international competition in 1993–4, winning the gold medal in the 1994 European Championships and a bronze in the 1994 Winter Olympics.

Toscanini, Arturo [toska**nee**nee] (1867–1957) Conductor, born in Parma, Italy. He conducted at La Scala, Milan (1898–1908), the Metropolitan Opera House, New York (1908–15), and the New York Philharmonic (1926–36). He also brought into being the Orchestra of the National Broadcasting Corporation of America (1937–53).

Tottel, Richard (?–1594) Printer, based in London. From his shop in Fleet St, he compiled an anthology of contemporary Elizabethan poetry, *Songes and Sonettes* (1557), which came to be known as *Tottel's Miscellany*.

Toulouse-Lautrec (-Monfa), Henri (Marie Raymond) de [too**looz** loh**trek**] (1864–1901) Painter and lithographer, born in Albi, France. Physically frail, at the age of 14 he broke both his legs, which then ceased to grow. He is best known for his paintings of Montmartre society, as in 'The Bar' (1898) and 'At the Moulin Rouge' (1892), but he also depicted fashionable society and produced several portraits.

Tour, Georges / Maurice Quentin de La >> La Tour, Georges de / Maurice Quentin de

Tournefort, Joseph Pitton de [toorn**faw**(r)] (1656–1708) Physician and botanist, born in Aix-en-Provence, France. Professor at the Jardin des Plantes in Paris (1688–1708), his definitions of the genera of plants were of fundamental importance to Linnaeus. >> Linnaeus

Tourneur, Cyril [**ter**ner] (c.1575–1626) English playwright. He is best known for his two plays, *The Revenger's Tragedy* (1607, sometimes assigned to Webster or Middleton), and *The Atheist's Tragedy* (1611). >> Middleton; Webster, John

Tournier, Paul [toorn**yay**] (1898–1986) Physician and writer on the integration of psychology and Christianity, born in Geneva, Switzerland. *The Meaning of Persons* (1957) and *The Strong and the Weak* (1963) were among his best-selling books.

Tourville, Anne Hilarion de Contentin, comte de (Count of) [toor**veel**] (1642–1701) Naval commander, born in Château Tourville, Manche, France. He became commander-in-chief of the Mediterranean fleet during the War of the Grand Alliance, and defeated the Anglo-Dutch fleet off Beachy Head (1690).

Toussaint, Pierre [too**sī**] (1766–1853) Philanthropist, born in Santo Domingo. Brought to New York City as a slave in 1787, he was freed in 1807, became highly successful in business, and gave much of his money to charities.

Toussaint l'Ouverture [toosī loover**tür**], originally **François Dominique Toussaint** (1746–1803) Revolutionary leader, born a slave in Haiti (formerly, St Domingue). In 1791 he joined the insurgents, and by 1797 was effective ruler of the former colony. After Napoleon sent an expedition to restore slavery, he was arrested, and died in a French prison. >> Napoleon I

Tovey, Sir Donald Francis [**toh**vee] (1875–1940) Pianist, composer, and writer on music, born in Eton, Berkshire. His fame rests largely on his writings, notably *Companion to the Art of Fugue* (1931) and *Essays on Musical Analysis* (1935–9).

Tovey, John Cronyn Tovey, Baron [**toh**vee] (1885–1971) British naval commander. As commander-in-chief of the Home Fleet (1941–3), he was responsible for the operations leading to the sinking of the German battleship *Bismarck*.

Tower, John (1925–   ) US politician, born in Houston, TX. The first Republican to be elected senator for Texas (1961), he became chairman of the Armed Services Committee (1981–83), and chaired the *Tower Commission* (1986–7).

Towne, Francis (c.1739–1816) Painter, probably born in London. As a landscapist he was little known until the 20th-c, when his gift for painting simple but graphic watercolours was recognized.

Townes, Charles (Hard) (1915–   ) Physicist, born in Greenville, SC. He shared the Nobel Prize for Physics in

1964 for his work on the development of the maser, and later the laser. >> Basov; Prokhorov

Townsend, Sir John (Sealy Edward) (1868–1957) Physicist, born in Galway, Co Galway, Ireland. He contributed to the theory of ionization of gases by collision, and calculated in 1897 the charge on a single gaseous ion.

Townshend (of Rainham), Charles Townshend, 2nd Viscount [townzend], known as **Turnip Townshend** (1674–1738) British statesman, born in Raynham, Norfolk. Made secretary of state by George I (1714–16, 1721–30), he became a leading figure in the Whig ministry. He acquired his nickname for his proposal to use turnips in crop rotation.

Townshend, Charles [townzend] (1725–67) British statesman, the grandson of Charles, 2nd Viscount Townshend. As Chancellor of the Exchequer (1766), he imposed high taxes on necessities in the American colonies, especially on tea (the *Townshend Acts*, 1767) - a policy which ultimately provoked the American War of Independence (1775–83). >> Townshend, 2nd Viscount

Toynbee, Arnold [toynbee] (1852–83) Economic historian and social reformer, born in London. He is best known as the coiner of the phrase and author of *The Industrial Revolution in England* (1884). Toynbee Hall in London was founded in his memory in 1885. >> Toynbee, Arnold (Joseph)

Toynbee, Arnold (Joseph) [toynbee] (1889–1975) Historian, born in London, the nephew of Arnold Toynbee. His major work was the multi-volume *Study of History* (1933–61). >> Toynbee, Arnold

Toyoda, Kiichiro [toyohda] (1894–1952) Japanese car designer and manufacturer. He set up a car manufacturing business in 1934, changing the company name to Toyota in 1936.

Tracey, Stan(ley William) (1926–) Jazz pianist, bandleader, and composer, born in London. He has led a succession of bands, from quartets to 16-piece orchestras, and written jazz suites such as *Under Milk Wood* (1965) and *Genesis* (1987).

Tracy, David (1939–) Theologian, born in Yonkers, NY. He has explored the problems of theological communication in modern pluralistic society in such works as *Blessed Rage for Order* (1975) and *Plurality and Ambiguity* (1986).

Tracy, Spencer (Bonadventure) (1900–67) Film actor, born in Milwaukee, WI. He received Oscars for *Captains Courageous* (1937) and *Boys' Town* (1938). He co-starred with Katharine Hepburn in nine films, including *Guess Who's Coming to Dinner* (1967). >> Hepburn, Katharine

Tradescant, John [tradiskant] (1570–c.1638) Naturalist, gardener, and traveller, probably born in Suffolk. He established the first museum open to the public, the Musaeum Tradescantianum, in London. A genus of plants (*Tradescantia*) is named after him. >> Tradescant, John (1608–62)

Tradescant, John [tradiskant] (1608–62) Gardener, born in Meopham, Kent. He bequeathed the Musaeum Tradescantianum in London to Elias Ashmole (1617–92), and it became the basis for the Ashmolean Museum in Oxford. >> Tradescant, John (1570–c.1638)

Traherne, Thomas [trahern] (1637–74) Mystical writer, born in Hereford, Hereford and Worcester. The manuscripts of his *Poetical Works* (1903) and *Centuries of Meditations* (1908) were discovered on a London street bookstall in 1896.

Trajan [trayjn], in full **Marcus Ulpius Trajanus** (c.53–117) Roman emperor (98–117), selected as successor by the aged Nerva for his military skills. He was the first emperor after Augustus to expand the Roman empire significantly, and in Rome built a new forum, library, and aqueduct. >> Nerva

Tranströmer, Tomas [transtroemer] (1931–) Poet and psychologist, born in Stockholm. A leading poet of the post-war era, his works include *Selected Poems* (1974) and *Collected Poems* (1987).

Trapassi, Pietro >> **Metastasio, Pietro**

Traubel, Helen [trowbl] (1899–1972) Soprano, born in St Louis, MO. She was the leading Wagnerian soprano at the New York Metropolitan between 1941 and 1953.

Traven, B [trayvn], pseudonym of **Benick Traven Torsvan** (?1882/90–1969) Writer, who claimed he was born in Chicago, IL, but was probably originally called **Otto Frege**, born in Zwiebodzin, Poland. He wrote *The Treasure of the Sierra Madre* (trans, 1935), on which the celebrated film by John Huston is based.

Travers, Ben(jamin) (1886–1980) Playwright, born in London. He became famous for the farces which played in the Aldwych Theatre, London, continuously from 1922 until 1933, but he was still writing in his nineties.

Travers, Morris William (1872–1961) Chemist, born in London. He discovered, with Ramsay, the inert gases krypton, xenon, and neon (1894–1908), and investigated the phenomena of low temperatures. >> Ramsay, William

Travers, P(amela) L(yndon) (1906–) Writer of children's stories, born in Queensland, Australia. She came to England at 19. Her first novel, *Mary Poppins* (1934; filmed, 1964), became an international success.

Traylor, Bill (1854–1947) Folk artist and plantation worker, born a slave in Alabama. He worked on a plantation until his early 80s, then began drawing the world around him in a bold, primitive, but original way.

Tredgold, Thomas (1788–1829) Engineer and cabinetmaker, born in Brandon, Durham. His *Elementary Principles of Carpentry* (1820) was the first serious manual on the subject.

Tree, Sir Herbert (Draper) Beerbohm (1853–1917) Actor-manager, born in London, the half-brother of Max Beerbohm. He built His Majesty's Theatre (1897), and in 1904 he founded the Royal Academy of Dramatic Art. >> Beerbohm

Treece, Henry (1911/12–66) Writer, born in Wednesbury, West Midlands. Notable works include collections of verse, such as *The Exiles* (1952), the novel *The Bronze Sword* (1965), and the historical novel *The Eagles Have Flown* (1954).

Trelawny, Edward John [trelawnee] (1792–1881) Writer and adventurer, born in London. A great favourite in London society and an incurable Romantic, he wrote *Records of Shelley, Byron and the Author* (1878).

Tremblay, Michel [träblay] (1942–) Playwright, born in Montreal, Quebec, Canada. His works include (trans titles) *The Train* (1959), *The Sisters-in-law* (1968), and *The Real World* (1987).

Trench, Richard Chenevix [shenevee] (1807–86) Anglican clergyman, philologist, and poet, born in Dublin. He became Archbishop of Dublin (1864–84). He popularized the scientific study of words, and published several volumes of poetry (1835–46).

Trenchard (of Wolfeton), Hugh Montague Trenchard, 1st Viscount (1873–1956) British marshal of the Royal Air Force, born in Taunton, Somerset. He commanded the Royal Flying Corps in World War 1, helped to establish the RAF (1918), and became the first chief of air staff (1918–29).

Trent, Baron >> **Boot, Jesse**

Treurnicht, Andries Petrus [troyernikht] (1921–93) South African politician, born in Piketberg, South Africa. He became Transvaal provincial National Party leader (1978), held posts under P W Botha, then resigned to form the new, right-wing Conservative Party (1982). >> Botha, P W

Trevelyan, G(eorge) M(acaulay) [trevelyan] (1876–1962) Historian, born in Welcombe, Warwickshire, the son of Sir George Trevelyan. Best known as a pioneer social historian, his *English Social History* (1944) was a companion volume to his *History of England* (1926). >> Trevelyan, George Otto

Trevelyan, Sir George Otto [trevelyan] (1838–1928) British Liberal statesman, born in Leicestershire. He served as chief secretary for Ireland (1882–4) and secretary for Scotland (1886, 1892–5), and wrote a famous biography of his uncle, Macaulay (1876). >> Macaulay, Thomas; Trevelyan, G M

Treves, Sir Frederick [treevz] (1853–1923) Surgeon, born in Dorchester, Dorset. He was a founder of the British Red Cross Society. He found Joseph Merrick (1862–90), the 'Elephant Man', at a freak show, and brought him to the London Hospital in 1886.

Trevino, Lee (Buck) [treveenoh], nickname **Supermex** (1939–) Golfer, born in Dallas, TX. He won his first US Open in 1968, and in 1971 established a golfing record by winning three Open championships (US, Canadian, British) in the same year.

Trevisa, John of >> **John of Trevisa**

Trevithick, Richard [trevithik] (1771–1833) Engineer and inventor, born in Illogan, Cornwall. He invented (1796–1801) a steam carriage, which ran between Camborne and Tuckingmill, and which in 1803 was run from Leather Lane to Paddington by Oxford St.

Trevor, William, pseudonym of **William Trevor Cox** (1928–) Writer, born in Mitchelstown, Co Cork, Ireland. His acclaimed collections of short-stories include *The Day We Got Drunk on Cake* (1969) and *The News from Ireland* (1986).

Trevor-Roper, Hugh Redwald, Baron Dacre of Glanton (1914–) Historian, born in Glanton, Northumberland. *The Last Days of Hitler* (1947) won international fame for its vivid reconstruction of occupied Germany. Other works include *The Rise of Christian Europe* (1965) and *The Philby Affair* (1968).

Trilling, Lionel (1905–75) Literary critic, born in New York City. He wrote studies on Matthew Arnold (1939), E M Forster (1948), and Sigmund Freud (1962), as well as many books of critical essays.

Trinder, Tommy, popular name of **Thomas Edward Trinder** (1909–89) Comedian and actor, born in London. He made his name in the Band Waggon show at the London Palladium (1939), and went on to become a national favourite with his catch-phrase 'you lucky people'.

Trintignant, Jean-Louis [trīteenyā] (1930–) Actor, born in Pont-St Esprit, France. His films include (trans titles) *And God Created Woman* (1956), *A Man and a Woman* (1966), and *The Conformist* (1970).

Trippe, Juan T(erry) (1899–1981) Airline founder, born in Seabright, NJ. In 1927 he founded Pan American Airways, which offered the first scheduled round-the-world air service in 1947.

Tristram, Henry Baker (1822–1906) Clergyman, naturalist, and traveller, born in Eglingham, Northumberland. He made the first ornithological surveys of Palestine, and *Tristram's warbler* and *serin* are named after him.

Trog, Walter, pseudonym of **Ernest Fawkes** (1924–) Cartoonist and musician, born in Ontario, Canada. He joined the *Daily Mail* (1945), creating *Rufus* (later *Flook*), a daily strip for children (1949), and later took up political cartooning in the *Spectator* and other magazines.

Trollope, Anthony [troluhp] (1815–82) Novelist, born in London. His novels in the Barsetshire series include *The Warden* (1855), *Barchester Towers* (1857), and *Framley Parsonage* (1861). Later novels include *Phineas Finn* (1869) and *The Way We Live Now* (1875).

Tromp, Cornelis (Maartenszoon) (1629–91) Naval commander, born in Amsterdam, the son of Maarten Tromp. He shared the glory of de Ruyter's Four Days' Battle (1666) off Dunkirk, and was appointed Lieutenant-Governor of the United Provinces (1676). >> Ruyter; Tromp, Maarten

Tromp, Maarten (Harpertszoon) (1598–1653) Dutch Admiral, born in Briel, The Netherlands. In 1639 he defeated a superior Spanish fleet off Gravelines, and won the Battle of the Downs. His encounter with Blake in 1652 started the first Anglo-Dutch War, where he was killed. >> Tromp, Cornelis

Trotsky, Leon, pseudonym of **Lev Davidovich Bronstein** (1879–1940) Russian Jewish revolutionary, born in Yanovka, Ukraine. He joined the Bolsheviks and played a major role in the October Revolution. In the Civil War he was Commissar for War, and created the Red Army. After Lenin's death (1924) he was ousted from the Party by Stalin, expelled from the Soviet Union (1929), and assassinated in Mexico City. >> Lenin; Stalin

Troyes, Chrétien de >> **Chrétien de Troyes**

Troyon, Constant [trwahyō] (1810–65) Painter, born in Sèvres, France. A member of the Barbizon Group, he specialized in landscapes, and particularly in animals.

Trubetzkoy, Nikolay Sergeyevich [troobetskoy] (1890–1938) Linguist, born in Moscow. Noted for his major contribution to the Prague school of linguistics, he wrote its most important work on phonology, *Principles of Phonology* (trans, 1939).

Trübner, Nicholas (1817–88) Publisher, born in Heidelberg, Germany. He started a London business in 1852, publishing oriental texts as well as works for the Early English Text Society.

Trudeau, Pierre (Elliott) [troodoh] (1919–) Canadian Liberal prime minister (1968–79, 1980–4), born in Montreal, Quebec, Canada. His terms of office saw the October Crisis (1970) in Quebec, the introduction of the Official Languages Act, federalist victory during the Quebec Referendum (1980), and the introduction of Canada's constitution (1982).

Trueblood, (David) Elton (1900–94) Quaker scholar, born in Pleasantville, IA. He was appointed chief of religious information at the US Information Agency (1954).

Trueman, Freddy, popular name of **Frederick Sewards Trueman** (1931–) Cricketer and broadcaster, born in Stainton, South Yorkshire. A Yorkshire fast bowler (1949–68), he played in 67 Tests for England between 1952 and 1965, and took a record 307 wickets.

Truffaut, François [troofoh] (1932–84) Film critic and director, born in Paris. His first feature, *The 400 Blows* (trans, 1959) effectively launched the French 'Nouvelle Vague' movement. Later films include *Shoot the Pianist* (1960), *Jules et Jim* (1962), *Fahrenheit 451* (1966), and *Day for Night* (trans, 1972, Oscar).

Truman, Harry S (1884–1972) US Democratic statesman and 33rd president (1945–53), born in Lamar, MO. His decisions included the dropping of two atom bombs on Japan and the sending of US troops to South Korea. He promoted the policy of giving military and economic aid to countries threatened by Communist interference (the *Truman Doctrine*), and at home introduced a *Fair Deal* of economic reform.

Trumbull, John (1750–1831) Lawyer and poet, born in Watertown, CT. He wrote a satire on British blunders in the American War of Independence, *M'Fingal* (1775–82), in imitation of Samuel Butler's *Hudibras*. >> Butler, Samuel

Trumbull, John (1756–1843) Historical painter, born in Lebanon, CT. His works include a series of celebrated war paintings, portraits of Washington, and four large historical pictures for the Rotunda of the Capitol in Washington, DC (1817).

Trump, Donald (John) (1946–) Real estate developer, born in New York City. He took over the Trump Organization, greatly expanded its holdings, and built the grandiose Trump Tower, New York City (1982). A high-profile celebrity of the 1980s, he suffered a spectacular crash into near-bankruptcy in 1990.

Trumpler, Robert (Julius) (1886–1956) Astronomer, born in Zürich, Switzerland. In 1922, by observing a solar eclipse, he was able to confirm Einstein's theory of relativity. He also made extensive studies of star clusters and galaxies. >> Einstein

Truth, Sojourner, originally **Isabella Van Wagener** (c.1797–1883) Evangelist, abolitionist, and feminist, born a slave in Ulster County, NY. She was appointed counsellor to the freedmen of Washington by Lincoln, and continued to promote black civil rights until her retirement in 1875. >> Lincoln

Truxtun, Thomas (1753–1822) US naval officer and merchant captain, born near Hempstead, NY. During the undeclared war with France, he captured the French *Insurgente* (1799) and defeated *La Vengeance* in a five-hour battle (1800).

Tsai-t'ien >> **Zai Tian**

Ts'ao Hsüeh-ch'in >> **Cao Xuequin**

Tschaikovsky, Piotr Ilyich >> **Tchaikovsky, Piotr Ilyich**

Tseng Kuo-fan >> **Zeng Guofan**

Tshombe, Moise(-Kapenda) [chombee] (1919–69) Congolese statesman, born in Musumba, Zaire. When his party won a majority in Katanga's Provincial Assembly, he became president of the province and declared Katanga independent. The UN sent troops into Katanga, but he escaped and was later made premier of the united Congo (Kinshasa) Republic (1964–5).

Tsiolkovsky, Konstantin Eduardovich [tseeolkofskee] (1857–1935) Russian physicist and rocketry pioneer, born in Izhevsk, Russia. In 1881 he independently developed the kinetic theory of gases, and from 1911 developed the basic theory of rocketry and multi-stage rocket technology (1929). >> Maxwell, James C

Tswett or **Tsvett, Mikhail Semenovich** [tsvet] (1872–1919) Botanist, born in Asti, Italy. He devised a percolation method of separating plant pigments in 1906, thus making the first chromatographic analysis.

Tuan, Yi-Fu [twahn] (1930–) Geographer, born in Tients'in, China. One of the newer generation of geographers concerned with broader philosophical issues, his books include *Morality and Imagination: Paradoxes of Progress* (1989).

Tubman, Harriet (1820–1913) Abolitionist, born in Dorchester Co, MD. She escaped from slavery in Maryland (1849) and went north via the 'Underground Railway', a network of secret safe-houses. She returned to the South frequently to escort escaping slaves through this route.

Tucker, Albert Lee (1914–) Painter, born in Melbourne, Victoria, Australia. He is known as a pioneer of Surrealism in Australia, and for his paintings of harsh Australian landscape as well as for his self-portraits.

Tucker, Sophie, originally **Sophie Abuza** (1884–1966) Singer, born in Russia. In the USA she established a successful stage career in burlesque, vaudeville, and nightclubs, and is remembered for her theme song 'Some of These Days'.

Tuckwell, Barry Emmanuel (1931–) Conductor and instrumentalist, born in Melbourne, Victoria, Australia. A horn soloist, he conducted many international orchestras, and became conductor of the Maryland Symphony Orchestra in 1982.

Tudor, Antony (1908–87) Dancer and choreographer, born in London. He formed the London Ballet (1938–40), then moved to New York's Ballet Theatre (now American Ballet Theatre), and became director of the Metropolitian Opera Ballet School.

Tudor, Owen >> **Catherine of Valois**

Tu Fu >> **Du Fu**

Tuke, Samuel [tyook] (1784–1857) Psychiatric reformer, born in York, North Yorkshire, the grandson of William Tuke. He acquired an interest in the York Retreat, and

wrote a classic account of the 'moral therapy' approach employed there. His son, **Daniel Hack Tuke** (1827–95), became a leading psychiatrist. >> Tuke, William

Tuke, William (1732–1822) Quaker philanthropist. He founded a home for the mentally sick (the York Retreat) in 1796, the first of its kind in England. He also pioneered new methods of treatment and care of the insane. >> Tuke, Samuel

Tukhachevsky, Mikhail Nikolayevich [tookachefskee] (1893–1937) Russian soldier and politician, born near Slednevo, Russia. He commanded Bolshevik forces against the Poles, White Russians, and Kulaks (1920–1), later becoming chief of armaments (1931), renowned for his work on tactical doctrine. He was executed during Stalin's purge.

Tull, Jethro (1674–1741) Agriculturist, born in Basildon, Berkshire. He introduced several new farming methods, including the invention of a seed drill which planted seeds in rows (1701).

Tully >> **Cicero**

Tulsidas [tulseedas] (c.1543–1623) Devotional poet, born in E India. His best-known work is *Ramacaritamanas* (The Holy Lake of Rama's Deeds), a popular Eastern Hindi version of the *Ramayana* epic, which he began in 1574.

Tunney, Gene, popular name of **James Joseph Tunney**, nickname **the Fighting Marine** (1897–1978) Boxer and world heavyweight champion, born in New York City. He joined the US marines and won the world light-heavyweight championship, then took the world heavyweight crown from Dempsey in 1926. >> Dempsey

Tunnicliffe, Charles Frederick (1901–79) Bird artist, born in Langley, Cheshire. He provided innumerable illustrations for the Royal Society for the Protection of Birds, and published six books of his own, including *Bird Portraiture* (1945).

Tunström, Göron [tunstroem] (1937–) Writer, born in Sunne, Sweden. His most popular works are *The Christmas Oratorio* (trans, 1982) and *The Thief* (trans, 1986), and he has also published poems, plays, and travel books.

Tupolev, Andrey Nikolayevich [toopolef] (1888–1972) Aircraft designer, born in Moscow. From 1922 he produced over 100 types of aircraft, including the first Soviet civil jet, the Tu-104 (1955) and in 1968 completed the first test flight of a supersonic passenger aircraft, the Tu-144.

Tura, Cosmè [toora] (c.1430–1495) Painter, born in Ferrara, Italy. The founder and leader of the Ferrarese school, his metallic, tortured forms and unusual colours can be seen in his 'Pietà'(c.1472) and 'St Jerome' (National Gallery, London).

Turenne, Henri de la Tour d'Auvergne, vicomte de (Viscount of) [türen] (1611–75) French marshal, born in Sedan, France. In the Thirty Years' War he fought with distinction for the armies of the Protestant alliance. In the Franco-Spanish war he conquered much of the Spanish Netherlands winning the Battle of the Dunes (1658), and won fame for his campaigns in the United Provinces during the Dutch War (1672–5).

Turgenev, Ivan (Sergeyevich) [toorgyaynyef] (1818–83) Writer, born in Orel province, Russia. best known for his novel, *Fathers and Sons* (1862), he also wrote poetry, plays, short stories, and tales of the supernatural.

Turgot, Anne Robert Jacques [toorgoh] (1727–81) French statesman and economist, born in Paris. Appointed comptroller-general of finance by Louis XVI (1774), he embarked on a comprehensive scheme of national economic reform, but opposition to his Six Edicts led to his overthrow (1776).

Turina, Joaquín [tooreena] (1882–1949) Composer and pianist, born in Seville, Spain. He wrote four operas, orchestral and chamber works, and piano pieces, the best of which combine strong Andalusian colour and idiom with traditional forms.

Turing, Alan (Mathison) [**toor**ing] (1912–54) Mathematician, born in London. He provided a precise mathematical characterization of computability, and introduced the theoretical notion of an idealized computer (since called a *Turing machine*), laying the foundation for the field of artificial intelligence.

Turnbull, Colin Macmillan (1924–94) Anthropologist, born in Harrow, Greater London. His many books on social change and relationships in Africa included *The Forest People* (1961) and *The Human Cycle* (1983).

Turnbull, Malcolm Bligh (1954–) Merchant banker, lawyer, and republican, born in Sydney, New South Wales, Australia. He became known for successfully defending Peter Wright in the *Spycatcher* trial. He was appointed chairman of the Republic Advisory Committee in 1993. >> Wright, Peter

Turnbull, William (1922–) Artist, born in Dundee, Tayside. His sculptures are typically upright forms of roughly human height, standing directly on the floor, since the 1960s purely abstract, geometrical shapes.

Turner, Ethel Sibyl (1872–1958) Novelist and children's writer, born in Doncaster, South Yorkshire. She moved to Australia at the age of nine. Her first book, *Seven Little Australians* (1894) is now a classic of Australian literature.

Turner, Frederick Jackson (1861–1932) Historian, born in Portage, WI. His works include *The Significance of Sections in American History* (1932, Pulitzer).

Turner, John Napier (1929–) Canadian Liberal statesman and prime minister (1984), born in Richmond, Surrey. He became attorney general and finance minister, and succeeded Trudeau when he retired as prime minister, but then lost the general election. >> Trudeau ,

Turner, J(oseph) M(allord) W(illiam) (1775–1851) Landscape artist and watercolourist, born in London. His best-known works include 'The Fighting Téméraire' (1839) and 'Rain, Steam and Speed' (1844). His art foreshadowed Impressionism, and was championed by Ruskin. >> Ruskin

Turner, Nat (1800–31) Slave leader, born in Southampton Co, VA. The son of an African native, he mounted the only sustained slave revolt in US history (1831), but was captured and hanged.

Turner, Ted (1938–) US television news vendor. He built up the 'Superstation' WTBS, and in 1980 founded Cable News Network to provide 24-hour news coverage.

Turner, Victor Witter (1920–83) Social anthropologist, born in Glasgow, Strathclyde. He carried out fieldwork among the Ndembu of Zambia (1950–4), which resulted in the classic monograph *Schism and Continuity in an African Society* (1957).

Turner, Walter (James Redfern) (1889–1946) Writer, born in Melbourne, Victoria, Australia. His works include the poetic collection *The Dark Fire* (1918), the novel *The Aesthetes* (1927), and studies of Beethoven, Mozart, and Wagner.

Turner, William (c.1508–68) Clergyman, physician, and naturalist, born in Morpeth, Northumberland. The author of the first original English works on plants, including *Names of Herbes* (1548) and *A New Herball* (1551–68), he named many plants.

Turpin, Dick, popular name of **Richard Turpin** (1706–39) Robber, born in Hempstead, Essex. He was hanged at York for murder. His legendary ride from London to York was probably actually carried out by 'Swift John Nevison' (1639–84).

Turpin, Randolph (1925–66) Middleweight boxer, born in Leamington Spa, Warwickshire. British champion (1950–4) and European champion (1951–4), he defeated Robinson in 1951 to become world champion, but lost the re-match later that year. >> Robinson, Sugar Ray

Tussaud, Marie [tuh**sawd**], Fr [tüsoh], *née* **Grosholtz** (1761–1850) Modeller in wax, born in Strasbourg, France. She toured Britain with her life-size portrait waxworks, and in 1835 set up a permanent exhibition in London.

Tutankhamen or **Tut'ankhamun** [tootan**kah**men, tootang-ka**moon**] (14th-c BC) Egyptian pharaoh of the 18th dynasty (1361–1352 BC), the son-in-law of Akhenaton. He is famous only for his magnificent tomb at Thebes, discovered intact in 1922. >> Akhenaton; Carnarvon; Carter, Howard

Tuthmosis >> Thutmose

Tutin, Dorothy [**tyoo**tin] (1931–) Actress, born in London. She has played many leading roles in classical and modern plays, including Queen Victoria in *Portrait of a Queen* (1965), and her films include *Savage Messiah* (1972) and *The Shooting Party* (1984).

Tutu, Desmond (Mpilo) (1931–) Anglican clergyman, born in Klerksdorp, South Africa. He became Bishop of Lesotho (1977) and Johannesburg (1984), and Archbishop of Cape Town (1986). A fierce critic of the apartheid system, he was awarded the Nobel Peace Prize in 1984.

Tutuola, Amos [tut**woh**la] (1920–) Novelist, born in Abeokuta, Nigeria. He is celebrated in the West for *The Palm-Wine Drinkard* (1952), a transcription in pidgin English prose of an oral tale of his own invention.

Twain, Mark, pseudonym of **Samuel Langhorne Clemens** (1835–1910) Writer, born in Florida, MO. *The Innocents Abroad* (1869) established his reputation as a humorist. His two masterpieces, *Tom Sawyer* (1876) and *Huckleberry Finn* (1884), drawn from his own boyhood experiences, are firmly established among the world's classics.

Tweed, William Marcy, nickname **Boss Tweed** (1823–78) Politician and criminal, born in New York City. In 1870 he became commissioner of public works for the city and, as head of the 'Tweed Ring', controlled its finances. He was convicted, and died in jail.

Tweedsmuir, Baron >> Buchan, John

Twiggy, professional name of **Lesley Lawson**, *née* **Hornby** (1949–) Fashion model, actress, and singer, born in London. She became a modelling superstar at the age of 17, and was a symbol of the 'swinging sixties' in London's Carnaby Street. Her films include *The Boy Friend* (1971) and *The Blues Brothers* (1981).

Twining, Nathan F(arragut) [**twiy**ning] (1897–) Aviator, born in Monroe, WI. He commanded in the Southwest Pacific (1942) and in the Mediterranean (1944), and was chairman of the joint chiefs-of-staff (1957–60).

Twombly, Cy (1928–) Painter, born in Lexington, VA. His gestural or 'doodle' technique derives from a Surrealist belief in the expressive power of automatic writing to tap the unconscious.

Twomey, Patrick Joseph [**too**mee] (1892–1963) Philanthropist, born in Wellington, New Zealand. He devoted his life to fund-raising for the treatment of lepers and other sufferers from tropical diseases in the SW Pacific.

Tworkov, Jack (1900–82) Painter, born in Biala, Poland. He emigrated to the US in 1913, where he became a leading exponent of the Abstract Expressionist movement.

Twort, Frederick William (1877–1950) Bacteriologist, born in Camberley, Surrey. In 1915 he discovered the bacteriophage, a virus that attacks certain bacteria.

Tyana >> Apollonius of Tyana

Tycho Brahe >> Brahe, Tycho

Tye, Christopher (c.1500–1573) Composer and organist, an innovator of English cathedral music, probably born in London. His surviving work includes two Latin Masses, 14 English anthems, instrumental music, and psalm settings.

Tyler, Anne (1941–) Writer, born in Minneapolis, MN. Her novels include *If Morning Ever Comes* (1965), *The Accidental Tourist* (1985), and *Breathing Lessons* (1989, Pulitzer).

Tyler, John (1790–1862) US statesman and 10th president (1841–5), born in Charles City Co, VA. He became president on the death of Harrison, only a month after his inauguration. His administration was marked by the annexation of Texas. >> Harrison, William Henry

Tyler, Wat (?–1381) English leader of the Peasants' Revolt (1381). The rebels of Kent chose him as captain, and marched to London, where the Mayor, William Walworth (d.1385), had him beheaded.

Tylor, Sir Edward Burnet (1832–1917) Anthropologist, born in London. His monumental *Primitive Culture* (2 vols, 1871), sought to show that human culture is governed by definite laws of evolutionary development.

Tynan, Katharine [tiynan] (1861–1931) Writer, born in Dublin. She wrote volumes of tender, gentle verse, and many novels and autobiographical works, including *Oh! What a Plague is Love* (1896) and *Memoires* (1924).

Tynan, Kenneth [tiynan] (1927–80) Theatre critic, born in Birmingham, West Midlands. He was drama critic for *The Observer* (1954–63), became literary manager of the National Theatre (1963–9), and wrote the controversial revue *Oh! Calcutta* (1969).

Tyndale or **Tindale, William** [tindayl] (?–1536) Translator of the Bible, probably born in Slymbridge, Gloucestershire. In Cologne (1525) he completed his translation of the English New Testament, then moved to Antwerp (1531), where he worked on an Old Testament translation, but was accused of heresy, and executed. His work was a major influence on the Authorised Version of the Bible (1611).

Tyndall, John [tindl] (1820–93) Physicist, born in Leighlin Bridge, Co Carlow, Ireland. He is known for his research on heat radiation, the acoustic properties of the atmosphere, and the blue colour of the sky.

Tyson, Mike, popular name of **Michael (Gerald) Tyson** (1966–) Boxer, born in New York City. He beat Trevor Berbick (1952–) for the World Boxing Council world heavyweight title in 1986, and added the World Boxing Association title in 1987, when he beat James Smith (1954–). Later that year he became the first undisputed champion since 1978, when he beat Tony Tucker (1958–). He lost the title in 1990, and in 1992 was jailed following a trial for rape (released, 1995).

Tyson, Frank (Holmes), nickname **Typhoon Tyson** (1930–) Cricketer, born in Farnworth, Lancashire. A fast bowler, of his 17 Tests only four were played in England, and he is best remembered for his performance in the Australian tour of 1954–5.

Tytler, James, known as **Balloon Tytler** (c.1747–1804) Journalist and balloonist, born in Fearn, Highland. After many ill-fated literary ventures, he became editor of the second edition of the *Encyclopaedia Britannica* (1776–84).

Tz'u-hsi >> **Ci-xi**

U

Uccello, Paolo [oocheloh], originally **Paolo di Dono** (1397–1475) Painter, born in Pratovecchio, Italy. He applied the principles of perspective to his paintings, as seen in 'The Flood' (1447–8, Florence), his use of foreshortening giving a sternly realistic effect.

Udall, Nicholas [yoodal] (1504–56) Playwright, born in Southampton, Hampshire. He is chiefly remembered as the author of the first significant comedy in English, *Ralph Roister Doister* (c.1563).

Udall, Stewart (Lee) [yoodahl] (1920–) US public official and conservationist, born in St John, AZ. As secretary of the interior (1961–9), he curbed abuses in the sale and exploitation of public lands, and reformed the Bureau of Indian Affairs.

Udet, Ernst [oodet] (1896–1941) German airman, born in Frankfurt, Germany. He was a leading air ace in World War 1, and from 1935 worked in the German air ministry. Having fallen foul of the Gestapo, he committed suicide by crashing his aircraft.

Udine, Giovanni da [oodinay] (1487–1564) Painter, decorative artist, and architect, born in Udine, Italy. He specialized in a style of decoration called 'grotesque', influenced by the graceful ornamental schemes being discovered in the excavations of ancient Rome.

Uemura, Naomi [waymoora] (1942–84) Explorer and mountaineer, born in Tajima region, Japan. After solo ascents of Mont Blanc, Kilimanjaro, Aconcagua, and Mt McKinley, he reached the summit of Everest in 1970, the first person to reach the highest peak on five continents.

Uhland, (Johannn) Ludwig [oolant] (1787–1862) Lyric poet, the leader of the Swabian School, born in Tübingen, Germany. His collection of poems (1815) contained many popular ballads reflecting his interest in folklore and mediaeval studies.

Uhle, Max [ooluh] (1856–1944) German archaeologist. His pioneering work in Peru and Bolivia (1892–1912) revolutionized the archaeology of South America.

Uhlenbeck, George >> Goudsmit, Samuel

Ulanova, Galina Sergeyevna [oolahnova] (1910–) Ballerina, born in St Petersburg, Russia. The leading ballerina of the Soviet Union, four times a Stalin Prize winner, she became ballet mistress at the Kirov in 1962.

Ulbricht, Walter (Ernst Karl) [ulbrikht] (1893–1973) East German statesman, born in Leipzig, Germany. He became deputy premier of the German Democratic Republic (1945) and general secretary of the Communist Party (1950), and was largely responsible for the 'sovietization' of East Germany. He built the Berlin wall in 1961.

Ulfilas or **Wulfila** [ulfilas, wulfila] (c.311–83) Gothic translator of the Bible. Consecrated a missionary bishop, he devised the Gothic alphabet, and carried out the first translation of the Bible into a Germanic language.

Ulianov, Vladimir Ilyich >> Lenin, Vladimir Ilyich

Ullman, Tracey (1959–) Actress and singer, born in Slough, Berkshire. She became known as an impressionist in the comedy television show *Three of a Kind*. The Tracey Ullman Show won an Emmy Award in 1990.

Ullmann, Liv (Johanne) (1939–) Actress, born in Tokyo. Her films with Bergman include *Cries and Whispers* (trans, 1972), *Face to Face* (trans, 1975), and *Autumn Sonata* (trans, 1978), and she also makes regular theatre appearances. >> Bergman, Ingmar

Ulm, Charles (Thomas Philippe) (1898–1934) Pioneer aviator, born in Melbourne, Victoria, Australia. He carried the first airmail between Australia, New Zealand, and New Guinea (1934).

Ulster, Alexander, Earl of >> Gloucester, Richard, Duke of

Ulugh Beg [ooloog bayg] (1394–1449) Ruler of the Timurid empire (1447–9), grandson of Tamerlane. He founded an observatory at Samarkand, compiled astronomical tables, and corrected errors made by Ptolemy of Alexandria. >> Ptolemy; Tamerlane

Ulyanov, Vladimir Ilyich >> Lenin, Vladimir Ilyich

Umar >> Omar

Umar Khayyám >> Omar Khayyám

Umberto II [umbairtoh] (1904–83) Last king of Italy (1946), born in Racconigi, Italy. He succeeded to the throne after the abdication of his father, Victor Emmanuel III, but himself abdicated a month later, and in 1947 he and his descendants were banished from Italy. >> Victor Emmanuel III

Unamuno (y Jugo), Miguel de [oonamoonoh] (1864–1936) Philosopher and writer, born in Bilbao, Spain. His main philosophical work is *The Tragic Sense of Life in Men and Peoples* (trans, 1913). He also wrote historical studies, essays, travel books, and poetry.

Underhill, Evelyn (1875–1941) Anglican mystical poet and writer, born in Wolverhampton, West Midlands. Her *Mysticism* (1911) became a standard work, and she also wrote volumes of verse, and four novels.

Underwood, Derek (Leslie) (1945–) Cricketer, born in Bromley, Kent. A slow left-arm bowler, he took 296 wickets in 86 Tests for England.

Underwood, Oscar (Wilder) (1862–1929) US politician, born in Louisville, KY. He served as a Democrat in the US House of Representatives (1897–1915), and in the US Senate (1915–27) masterminded wartime appropriations.

Undset, Sigrid [oonset] (1882–1949) Novelist, born in Kalundborg, Denmark. Her major novels were *Kristin Lavransdatter* (1920–2), a 14th-c trilogy, followed by a series *Olav Audunssön* (4 vols, 1925–7). She was awarded the Nobel Prize for Literature in 1928.

Ungaretti, Giuseppe [unggaretee] (1888–1970) Poet, born in Alexandria, Egypt. His poems, characterized by symbolism, compressed imagery, and modern verse structure, became the foundation of the *hermetic* movement.

Ungaro, Emanuel (Maffeolti) [unggaroh] (1933–) Fashion designer, born in Aix-en-Provence, France, of Italian parents. In 1965 he opened his own house, and in 1968 produced his first ready-to-wear lines.

Unitas, Johnny [yoonitas], popular name of **John Constantine Unitas** (1933–) Player of American football, born in Pittsburgh, PA. A quarter-back, he joined the Baltimore Colts in 1956, and led them to a championship victory against the New York Giants in 1958.

Universalis, Doctor >> Albertus Magnus, St

Unruh, Fritz von [oonroo] (1885–1970) Writer, born in Koblenz, Germany. An ardent pacifist, the ideal of a new humanity underlies all his Expressionist works, particularly the novel *Way of Sacrifice* (trans, 1916).

Unser, Al (1939–) Motor-racing driver, born in Albuquerque, NM. He won the Indianapolis 500 four times (1970–1, 1978, 1987), beating his brother, **Bobby** (1934–), who won the race in 1968, 1975, and 1981. His son, **Al Unser, Jr** (1962–), has also become a champion auto racer.

Unwin, Sir Stanley (1884–1968) British publisher. He became chairman of the firm of George Allen and Unwin, founded in 1914, and president of the International Publishers Association (1936–8, 1946–54).

Updike, John (Hoyer) (1932–) Writer, born in Shillington, PA. His novels, exploring human relationships in contemporary US society, include *Rabbit is Rich* (1981, Pulitzer), *The Witches of Eastwick* (1984; filmed 1987), and *Rabbit at Rest* (1990, Pulitzer).

Upham, Charles Hazlitt [uhpam] (1908–) New Zealand soldier, born in Christchurch, New Zealand. For valour in Crete (1941) and N Africa (1942) during World War 2, he became the only combatant soldier ever awarded the Victoria Cross and Bar.

Upjohn, Richard (1802–78) Architect, born in Shaftesbury, Dorset. In the USA from 1829, his first and best-known major building was Trinity Church, New York City (1839–46), introducing the Gothic Revival style.

Urbain, Georges [ürbĩ] (1872–1938) Chemist, born in Paris. He discovered the rare earth lutecium (1907) and the law of optimum phosphorescence of binary systems.

Ure Smith, Sydney George [yoor] (1887–1949) Artist, editor, and publisher, born in London. In Australia from childhood, he published the seminal journal *Art in Australia* (1916–39), founded his own publishing house (1939), and was active in promoting the contemporary arts.

Urey, Harold C(layton) [yooree] (1893–1981) Chemist, born in Walkerton, IN. In 1932 he isolated heavy water and discovered deuterium, for which he received the Nobel Prize for Chemistry in 1934. His work on lunar and planetary formation laid the scientific foundation for the space age exploration of the Solar System.

Urfé, Honoré d' [ürfay] (1568–1625) Writer, born in Marseille, France. His pastoral romance, *Astrée* (1610–27), is regarded as the first French novel.

Uris, Leon (Marcus) [yooris] (1924–) Novelist, born in Baltimore, MD. *Exodus* (1958) is his best-known book, depicting the early years of struggle to defend the state of Israel.

Urquhart, Sir Thomas [erkert] (c.1611–60) Writer, born in Cromarty, Highland. In 1653 he issued the first two books of *The Works of Mr Francis Rabelais*, a brilliant translation and an English classic.

Ursula, St (fl.4th-c), feast day 21 October. Legendary saint and martyr, said to have been killed by Huns in Cologne. She became the patron saint of many educational institutes, particularly the teaching order of the Ursulines.

Ussher or **Usher, James** (1581–1656) Bishop and biblical scholar, born in Dublin. His major work was the *Annals of the Old and New Testament* (1650–4), which gave a long-accepted chronology of Scripture, and fixed the Creation at 4004 BC.

Ustinov, Sir Peter (Alexander) [yustinof] (1921–) Actor and playwright, born in London. A prolific playwright, his works include *The Love of Four Colonels* (1951), *Romanoff and Juliet* (1956), and *Overheard* (1981). He has acted in over 50 films, and in recent years has established a reputation as a raconteur.

Utamaro, (Kitagawa) [ootamahroh], originally **Kitagawa Nebsuyoshi** (1753–1806) Painter and engraver, born in Tokyo. Trained in Edo (modern Tokyo), he came to specialize in portraits of court ladies, and carried the technique of the *ukiyo-e* to its highest artistic level.

Uthman or **Osman** (?–656) Third caliph to rule after the death of Mohammed. Elected in succession to Omar in 644, he established a commission of scholars, who collected the revelations of Mohammed to produce the definitive version of the Qur'an. >> Mohammed; Omar

Utrillo, Maurice [ootreeloh] (1883–1955) Painter, born in Paris, the illegitimate son of Suzanne Valadon. A prolific artist, he produced picture-postcard views of the streets of Paris, particularly old Montmartre. >> Valadon

Uttley, Alison (1884–1976) Writer, born at Castle Top Farm, near Cromford, Derbyshire. She wrote a series of books for children, featuring much-loved characters such as 'Little Grey Rabbit' and 'Sam Pig'.

Utzon, Jørn (1918–) Architect, born in Copenhagen. He is best known for the design of Sydney Opera House, other buildings including the Kuwait House of Parliament and Bagsüaerd Church (Copenhagen).

Vadim, Roger [va**dim**], originally **Roger Vadim Plemiannikov** (1928–) Film director, born in Paris. *And God Created Woman* (trans, 1956), starring his wife Brigitte Bardot paved the way for further sex-symbol presentations of his later wives, Annette Stroyberg in *Dangerous Liaisons* (trans, 1959), Jane Fonda in *Barbarella* (1968), and his lover, Catherine Deneuve, in *Vice and Virtue* (trans, 1962). >> Bardot; Fonda, Jane; Deneuve

Vakhtangov, Evgeny Bagrationovich [vakh**tang**of] (1883–1923) Theatre director, actor, and teacher, born in Vladikavkaz, Armenia. He made a synthesis of Stanislavsky's and Meyerhold's methods, stressing the expressiveness of the actor and the concept of 'fantastic realism'. >> Meyerhold; Stanislavsky

Valachi, Joseph (Michael) [va**lah**chee] (1904–71) Gangster, born in New York City. A member of a mob family, he was convicted of drugs offences and turned informer, the first syndicate member ever to reveal the inner workings of the Mafia (1962).

Valadon, Suzanne [valadõ] (1869–1938) French painter, the mother of Utrillo. She excelled in her realistic treatment of nudes, portraits, and figure studies, her work having some affinity with that of Degas. >> Degas; Utrillo

Valdemar I (of Denmark) >> **Absalon**

Valdes, Peter >> **Waldo, Peter**

Valdivia, Pedro de [val**div**ia] (c.1498–1559) Spanish soldier, born near La Serena, Spain. He commanded Pizarro's expedition to Chile (1540), and founded Santiago (1541) and other cities, including Concepción (1550) and Valdivia (1552). >> Pizarro, Francisco

Valens >> **Valentinian I**

Valentine, St (?–c.269), feast 14 February. Roman priest and Christian martyr, said to have been executed during the persecution under Claudius II, the Goth; but claims have been made for another St Valentine, supposedly Bishop of Turni, taken to Rome for martyrdom. The custom of sending lover's greetings on 14 February has no connection with either saint.

Valentine, Alf(red Lewis) (1930–) Cricketer, born in Kingston, Jamaica. A spin bowler of genius, especially in partnership with Ramadhin, in 36 Tests he took 139 wickets. >> Ramadhin

Valentinian I, in full **Flavius Valentinianus** (321–375) Roman emperor (364–75), born in Pannonia (C Europe), the son of an army officer. On the death of the Emperor Jovian he was chosen as his successor (364). He resigned the East to his brother **Valens** (ruled 364–78), and himself governed the West, successfully defending it against Germanic invasions. >> Gratian

Valentino [valen**tee**noh] >> **Garavani, Valentino**

Valentino, Rudolph [valen**tee**noh] (1895–1926) Film actor, born in Castellaneta, Italy. His performances in *The Sheikh* (1921), *Blood and Sand* (1922), and other silent film dramas made him the leading 'screen lover' of the 1920s.

Valera, Eamon de >> **de Valera, Eamon**

Valerian, Publius Licinius [va**leer**ian] (?–260) Roman emperor (253–60). He was proclaimed emperor after the murder of Gallus (253), and appointed his son Gallienus as co-ruler. Marching against the Persians, he was seized by Shapur I (ruled 242–72), and died in captivity. >> Gallienus

Valéry, (Ambroise) Paul (Toussaint Jules) [valay**ree**] (1871–1945) Poet and critic, born in Sète, France. After writing a great deal of poetry he relapsed into a 20 years' silence, taken up with mathematics and philosophical speculations, later published as *Cahiers* (29 vols, 1957–60). He emerged with a new Symbolist poetic technique in *The Young Fate* (trans, 1917).

Valette, Jean Parisot de la (1494–1568) French knight, born in Toulouse, France. He became grand master of the Knights of St John of Jerusalem (Hospitallers) in 1557, successfully defended Malta (1565) against the Turks, and founded the city of Valetta.

Valla, Lorenzo (1407–57) Humanist and critic, born in Rome. He greatly advanced New Testament criticism by his comparison of the Vulgate with the Greek original.

Vallière, Louise Françoise de La Baume le Blanc >> **La Vallière, duchesse de**

Vallisnieri, Antonio [valis**nyay**ree] (1631–1730) Naturalist, born in Modena, Italy. He studied the reproductive systems of insects, and wrote on the ostrich (1712) and the chameleon (1715). The waterweed *Vallisneria spiralis* is named after him.

Vallotton, Felix [valohtõ] (1865–1925) Painter, born in Lausanne, Switzerland. He was a member of the *Nabis*, and one of the principal collaborators in *Le Revue Blanche* (1894–1901). His most notable works were wood engravings, which brought him immediate success.

Valois, Dame Ninette de [**val**wah], originally **Edris Stannus** (1898–) Dancer, born in Blessington, Co Wicklow, Ireland. In 1931 she founded the Sadler's Wells Ballet (now the Royal Ballet), continuing as its artistic director until 1963, and is regarded as the pioneer of British ballet.

Valour, Count of >> **Visconti, Gian Galeazzo**

Vámbéry, Arminius [**vam**bayree], originally **Armín Vámbéry** (1832–1913) Traveller and philologist, born in Duna-Szerdahely, Hungary. He published works on Altaic languages, the ethnography of the Turks, the origin of the Magyars, and many other oriental subjects.

van Aken, Jerome >> **Bosch, Hieronymus**

Van Allen, James (Alfred) (1914–) Physicist and pioneer in space physics, born in Mt Pleasant, IA. Using data from satellite observations, he showed the existence of two zones of radiation around the Earth (the *Van Allen radiation belts*).

Vanbrugh, Sir John [**van**bruh] (1664–1726) Playwright and Baroque architect, born in London. He scored a success with his comedies *The Relapse* (1696) and *The Provok'd Wife* (1697). As architect, he designed Castle Howard, Yorkshire (1699–1726) and Blenheim Palace (1705–20).

Van Buren, Martin (1782–1862) US statesman and eighth president (1837–41), born in Kinderhook, NY. In 1824 he was a founder member of the Democratic Party. Arriving in office during the financial panic of 1837, his measure introducing a treasury independent of private banks led to his defeat in 1840.

Vance, Cyrus (Roberts) (1917–) Lawyer and statesman, born in Clarksburg, WV. He served as secretary of state under Carter, resigning in 1980 over the Iran hostage crisis. He also worked with Lord Owen for the UN Security Council during the Yugoslavian conflict, drawing up the unsuccessful Vance–Owen peace initiative (1992–3). >> Carter, Jimmy; Owen, David

Vancouver, George (1757–98) Navigator and explorer, born in King's Lynn, Norfolk. He sailed with James Cook on his second and third voyages, and is best known for his extensive survey of the Pacific coast of North America (1791–4). >> Cook, James

Van de Graaff, Robert (Jemison) (1901–67) Physicist,

born in Tuscaloosa, AL. He devised an improved type of electrostatic generator (later called the *Van de Graaff generator*), and developed this into the *Van de Graaff accelerator*, which became a major tool of nuclear physicists.

van de Hulst, Hendrik Christofell (1918–) Pioneer of radio astronomy, born in Utrecht, The Netherlands. In 1944 he predicted theoretically that interstellar hydrogen would be detectable by radio techniques (eventually detected in 1951).

Van de Kamp, Peter (1901–) Astronomer, born in Kampen, The Netherlands. His best-known work began in the 1960s with his deduction that some stars, other than the Sun, possess planets.

Vandenberg, Arthur H(endrick) (1884–1951) US Republican politician, born in Grand Rapids, MI. An isolationist before World War 2, he strongly supported the formation of the UN, and was delegate to the UN Assembly from 1946.

Vanderbilt, Harold S(tirling) (1884–1970) Industrialist, born in Oakdale, NY. He developed the current scoring system for contract bridge in 1925, invented the first unified bidding system, and presented the Vanderbilt Cup.

Vanderbilt, Cornelius (1794–1877) Financier, born on Staten I, NY. A steamship owner in New York City, he later became a railroad financier. He endowed Vanderbilt University at Nashville, TN.

Vanderbilt, Gloria, in full **Gloria Morgan Vanderbilt-Cooper** (1924–) Artist and socialite, born in New York City. She achieved notoriety for her four marriages, but considerable respect for her work as a painter, stage and film actress, author, and designer of housewares and fashion.

van der Goes, Hugo [khoos] (c.1440–82) Painter, probably born in Ghent, Belgium. Among his notable works is the Portinari Altarpiece containing 'The Adoration of the Shepherds' (c.1475) for the S Maria Nuova Hospital in Florence.

van der Meer, Simon (1925–) Physicist and engineer, born in The Hague. He shared the Nobel Prize for Physics in 1984 for work on the CERN project which led to the discovery of the short-lived subatomic W and Z particles. >> Rubbia

van der Post, Sir Laurens (Jan) [post] (1906–) Writer and philosopher, born in Philippolis, South Africa. He is best known for his books in the mixed genre of travel, anthropology, and metaphysical speculation, such as *Venture to the Interior* (1951) and *The Lost World of the Kalahari* (1958).

van der Rohe, Ludwig Mies >> **Mies van der Rohe, Ludwig**

van der Waals, Johannes Diderik [vahlz] (1837–1923) Physicist, born in Leyden, The Netherlands. He extended the classical 'ideal' gas laws (of Boyle and Charles) to describe real gases, deriving the *van der Waals equation of state* (1873). He also investigated the weak attractive forces (*van der Waals forces*) between molecules, and was awarded the Nobel Prize for Physics in 1910. >> Boyle, Robert; Charles, Jacques

van der Weyden, Rogier >> **Weyden, Rogier van der**

van Diemen, Anthony >> **Tasman, Abel Janszoon**

Van Doren, Carl (Clinton) (1885–1950) Critic and biographer, born in Hope, IL, the brother of Mark Van Doren. He edited the *Cambridge History of American Literature* (1917–21), and his biographies include Benjamin Franklin (1938, Pulitzer). >> Van Doren, Mark

Van Doren, Mark (Albert) (1894–1972) Poet and critic, born in Hope, IL, the brother of Carl Van Doren. His volumes of poetry include *Collected Poems* (1939, Pulitzer), and he edited the *Oxford Book of American Prose*. >> Van Doren, Carl

van Dyck, Sir Anthony [diyk] (1599–1641) Painter, one of

the great masters of portraiture, born in Antwerp, Belgium. In 1632 he went to London, where he was made painter-in-ordinary to Charles I, and produced thoroughly romantic pictures of the Stuart monarchy.

Van Dyke, Dick (1925–) Popular entertainer, born in West Plains, MO. His television series, *The Dick Van Dyke Show* (1961–6), was highly popular, and won him Emmys in 1962, 1964, and 1965. His film career includes *Mary Poppins* (1964), *Chitty, Chitty, Bang, Bang* (1968), and *Dick Tracy* (1990).

Vane, Sir Henry (1613–62) English statesman, born in Hadlow, Kent. He supported the parliamentary cause in the Civil War, and during the Commonwealth became one of the Council of State (1649–53). At the Restoration, he was imprisoned and executed.

Vane, Sir John (Robert) (1927–) Biochemist, born in Tardebigg, Worcestershire. He researched the chemistry of prostaglandins, discovering a type that inhibits blood clots, and shared the Nobel Prize for Physiology or Medicine in 1982.

van Gogh, Vincent (Willem) [hokh], Br Eng [gof], US Eng [goh] (1853–90) Painter, born in Groot-Zundert, The Netherlands. His first masterpiece was 'The Potato Eaters' (1885), a domestic scene of peasant poverty. At Arles, the Provençal landscape gave him many of his best subjects, such as 'Sunflowers' (1888) and 'The Bridge' (1888). One of the pioneers of Expressionism, he used colour primarily for its emotive appeal, and profoundly influenced 20th-c art.

van Goyen, Jan (1596–1656) Painter, born in Leyden, The Netherlands. He was a pioneer of realistic 'tonal' landscape, emphasizing the movement of light and shadow across wide plains and rivers under huge cloudy skies.

van Heemskerck, Martin >> **van Veen, Otto**

van Leyden, Lucas >> **Lucas van Leyden**

Vanloo, Charles André (1705–65) Painter, born in Nice, France, the brother of Jean Baptiste Vanloo. He settled as a portrait painter in Paris, becoming chief painter to Louis XV. >> Vanloo, Jean Baptiste

Vanloo, Jean Baptiste (1684–1745) Painter, born in Aix-en-Provence, France, the brother of Charles André Vanloo. A fashionable portrait painter in Paris, in 1737 he visited England, and painted the Prince and Princess of Wales and Sir Robert Walpole. >> Vanloo, Charles André

Van Loon, Hendrik Willem (1882–1944) Popular historian, born in Rotterdam, The Netherlands. He emigrated to the USA in 1903, where he published the best-selling illustrated *Story of Mankind* (1922) and other popular histories.

van Meegeren, Han or **Henricus** [may geren] (1889–1947) Artist and forger, born in Deventer, The Netherlands. Accused in 1945 of selling art treasures to the Germans, he confessed to having forged the pictures, and was imprisoned (1947).

Vannucci, Pietro >> **Perugino**

Vanolis, Bysshe >> **Thomson, James** (1834–82)

van Praagh, Peggy [prahg], popular name of **Dame Margaret van Praagh** (1910–90) Ballet dancer, teacher, and producer, born in London. She joined Sadler's Wells Ballet as dancer and teacher, became assistant director at Sadler's Wells Theatre Ballet (1941–56), and later was the founding artistic director for the Australian Ballet (1962–79).

Van Rensselaer, Stephen [ren seler] (1765–1839) US soldier and politician, born in New York City. In the War of 1812 he held command on the N frontier, and captured Queenston Heights. A member of the US House of Representatives (1822–9), he founded the Rensselaer Technical Institute (1826).

Vansittart (of Denham), Robert Gilbert Vansittart, Baron [van sitah(r)t] (1881–1957) British diplomat, born in Farnham, Surrey. In 1930 he became permanent under-secretary for foreign affairs, known as the uncompromising, blunt-speaking opponent of Nazism.

van't Hoff, Jacobus Henricus >> **Hoff, Jacobus Henricus van't**

van Veen, Otto (c.1556–1634) Painter, born in Leyden, The Netherlands. He settled in Antwerp, where Rubens was his pupil. The name *van Veen* is also sometimes given to the Haarlem painter, **Martin van Heemskerck** (1498–1574). >> Rubens

Van Vleck, John H(asbrouck) (1899–1980) Physicist, born in Middletown, CT. His classical treatise, *The Theory of Electric and Magnetic Susceptibilities* (1932), was followed by work in magnetic resonance and the development of computer memory systems. He shared the Nobel Prize for Physics in 1977. >> Anderson, Philip W; Mott, Nevill F

Vanzetti, Bartolomeo >> **Sacco and Vanzetti**

Vara, Madeleine >> **Riding, Laura**

Varah, (Edward) Chad [vara] (1911–) Anglican clergyman, born in Barton-on-Humber, Humberside. He set up the Samaritans, a free telephone counselling service available 24 hours a day to support those feeling suicidal.

Vardon, Harry (1870–1937) Golfer, born in Grouville, Jersey. He won the British Open championship six times (1896, 1898, 1899, 1903, 1911, 1914) and the US Open (1900). His overlapping grip is still known as the *Vardon grip*.

Varèse, Edgar [varez] (1885–1965) Composer, born in Paris. His work is almost entirely orchestral, abstract in nature, and often using unconventional percussion instruments.

Vargas, Getúlio (Dornelles) [vah(r)gas] (1883–1954) President of Brazil (1930–45, 1951–4), born in São Borja, Brazil. His government did much to unify Brazil, but from 1937 he governed as a mild dictator, and in the face of mounting opposition, he committed suicide.

Varley, John (1778–1842) Painter in watercolours, born in London. A founder member of the Watercolour Society, he was also interested in astrology and wrote on perspective. His brothers **Cornelius** (1781–1873) and **William Fleetwood** (1785–1856) were also water-colourists.

Varmus, Harold E(lliot) >> **Bishop, J Michael**

Varro, Marcus Terentius (116–27 BC) Roman scholar and writer, born in Reate. He wrote over 600 works, but only his work on agriculture and part of his book on Latin survive.

Varro, Publius Terentius (c.82–37 BC) Roman poet, called **Atacinus** from his birth in the valley of the Atax in Narbonensian Gaul. He wrote satires and erotic elegies, and an epic poem on Caesar's Gallic wars.

Varus, Publius Quintilius (? BC–AD 9) Roman general and consul (13 BC). In AD 9 he was sent to command in Germany, where he led three legions into a trap set by Arminius, and killed himself after his troops were routed. >> Arminius

Vasarely, Viktor [vazaraylee] (1908–) Painter, born in Pecs, Hungary. His particular kind of geometrical-abstract painting, which he began to practise c.1947, pioneered the visually disturbing effects that were later called Op Art.

Vasari, Giorgio [vazahree] (1511–74) Art historian, architect, and painter, born in Arezzo, Italy. Known for his design of the Uffizi in Florence, his fame chiefly rests on *The Lives of the Most Eminent Italian Architects, Painters, and Sculptors* (trans, 1550).

Vasco da Gama >> **Gama, Vasco da**

Vassilou, Georgios Vassos [vasiloo] (1931–) Cypriot president (1988–93), born in Famagusta, Cyprus. He worked consistently but without success towards the reunification of the island.

Vau, Louis Le >> **Le Vau, Louis**

Vauban, Sebastien le Prestre de [vohbã] (1633–1707) French soldier and military engineer, born in Saint Léger,

France. He brought about a revolution in siege warfare and fortification, surrounding the kingdom with a cordon of fortresses (1667–88).

Vaucanson, Jacques de [vohkãsõ] (1709–82) Engineer and inventor, born in Grenoble, France. Appointed an inspector of silk factories (1741), he succeeded in making the first fully automatic loom (1745), controlled through a system of perforated cards.

Vauclain, Samuel (Matthews) (1856–1940) Engineer and inventor, born in Port Richmond, PA. He joined the Baldwin Locomotive Works in Philadelphia (1883), where he became a world authority on locomotive design.

Vaugelas, Claude Favre, seigneur de (Lord of) [vohzhlah] (1585–1650) Grammarian, born in Meximieux, France. His *Remarks on the French Language* (trans, 1647) helped to standardize the language.

Vaughan, Henry [vawn] (1622–95) Religious poet, born in Newton-by-Usk, Gwent. His best-known works are the pious meditations *Silex scintillans* (1650) and the prose devotions *The Mount of Olives* (1652).

Vaughan, Herbert (Alfred), Cardinal [vawn] (1832–1903) Roman Catholic cardinal, born in Gloucester, Gloucestershire. He became cardinal in 1893, and was responsible for the building of Westminster Cathedral.

Vaughan, Sarah (Lois) [vawn] (1924–90) Jazz singer and pianist, born in Newark, NJ. Internationally acclaimed for her vibrato, range, and expression, her most notable hits include 'It's Magic' and 'I Cried for You'.

Vaughan Williams, Ralph [vawn] (1872–1958) Composer, born in Down Ampney, Gloucestershire. He developed a national style of music deriving from English choral tradition. His works include nine symphonies, the ballet *Job* (1930), the opera *The Pilgrim's Progress* (1948–9), and numerous choral works, songs, and hymns. His scores for the stage and for films include *The Wasps* (1909).

Vauquelin, Nicolas Louis [vohklĩ] (1763–1829) Analytical chemist, born in St André d'Hébertot, France. In 1798 he discovered chromium and its compounds, later beryllium compounds, and was the first to isolate an amino acid, asparagine, which he obtained from asparagus.

Vaux, Calvert [voh] (1824–95) Landscape designer and architect, born in London. A pioneer in the public parks movement, he joined Olmstead (1857–72), and together they produced the winning design for New York City's Central Park. >> Olmstead

Vavilov, Nikolay Ivanovich [vavilof] (1887–1943) Plant geneticist, born in Moscow. In 1930 he was appointed to direct Soviet agricultural research, and established 400 institutes and a collection of 26 000 varieties of wheat. Denounced by Lysenko, he is thought to have died in a Siberian camp. >> Lysenko

Veblen, Thorstein (Bunde) [veblen] (1857–1929) Economist and social scientist, born in Manitowoc Co, WI. In his best-known work, *The Theory of the Leisure Class* (1899), he applied an evolutionary approach to the study of economics.

Vecellio, Tiziano >> **Titian**

Vedder, Elihu (1836–1923) Painter and illustrator, born in New York City. Among his major works are 'Minerva' and other murals in the Library of Congress, Washington, DC, and his illustrations for the *Rubáiyát of Omar Khayyám* (1884).

Veeck, Bill, popular name of **William Louis Veeck Jr** (1914–86) Baseball executive, born in Chicago, IL, the son of William Veeck who owned the Chicago Cubs (1919–33). He became the owner of the Cleveland Indians (1947–9), St Louis Browns (1951–3), and Chicago White Sox (1959–61, 1976–80).

Veen, Otto van >> **van Veen, Otto**

Vega (Carpio), Lope (Félix) de [vayga] (1562–1635) Playwright and poet, born in Madrid. He first made his mark as a ballad writer, and after 1588 produced a wide range of historical and contemporary dramas – about 2000 plays and dramatic pieces, of which over 400 still survive.

Veil, Simone (-Annie) [vayl], *née* **Jacob** (1927–) Administrator and public official, born in Nice, France. She served as minister of health (1974–9), became a campaigner for women's rights, and was elected the first president of the European Parliament (1979–82).

Velázquez, Diego (Rodriguez de Silva) [vay**las**keth] (1599–1660) Painter, born in Seville, Spain. He is best known for his three late masterpieces, 'The Maids of Honour' (trans, 1655), 'The Tapestry Weavers' (c.1657), and 'Venus and Cupid', known as 'The Rokeby Venus' (c.1658).

Velázquez de Cuéllar, Diego [vay**las**keth, **kway**ah(r)] (1465–1524) Spanish conquistador and colonialist, born in Cuéllar, Spain. He accompanied Columbus to Hispaniola in 1494, and in 1511 conquered Cuba, becoming governor (1511–24) and founding Havana.

Velde, Henry (Clemens) van de [**vel**duh] (1863–1957) Architect, designer, and teacher, one of the originators of the Art Nouveau style, born in Antwerp. He was a director of the Weimar School of Arts and Crafts from which the Bauhaus sprang.

Velde, Willem van de [**vel**duh], known as **the Elder** (c.1611–93) Painter of maritime scenes, born in Leyden, The Netherlands. In 1657 he went to England, and painted large pictures of sea battles for Charles II and James II. >> Velde, Willem van de (the Younger)

Velde, Willem van de [**vel**duh], known as **the Younger** (1633–1707) Painter, son of Willem van de Velde, born in Leyden, The Netherlands. Like his father, he was almost exclusively a marine painter, and worked with him in England for Charles II. >> Velde, Willem van de (the Elder)

Vendler, Helen (Hennessy) (1933–) Literary critic and educator, born in Boston, MA. Through her numerous reviews for the *New Yorker* (1978) and the *New York Review of Books*, she exerted a powerful influence over contemporary poets.

Vendôme, Louis Joseph, duc de (Duke of) [vā**dohm**] (1654–1712) French general, born in Paris, the great-grandson of Henry IV. He commanded in Italy and Flanders during the War of the Spanish Succession (1701–14), was victorious at Cassano (1705) and Calcinato (1706), but was defeated at Oudenarde (1708).

Vening Meinesz, Felix Andries [**miyn**es] (1887–1966) Geophysicist, born in The Hague. He devised a gravity measuring instrument for use on unstable platforms, and modified it for use in submarines to enable gravity surveys of the ocean floor.

Venizelos, Eleutherios (Kyriakos) [vaynee**zay**los] (1864–1936) Greek prime minister (1910–15, 1917–20, 1924, 1928–32, 1933), born in Mourniés, Crete, Greece. He promoted the Balkan League against Turkey (1912) and Bulgaria (1913), and so extended the Greek kingdom. His opposition to King Constantine I led to the king's abdication in 1917. >> Constantine I (of Greece)

Venn, John (1759–1813) Anglican clergyman, born in London. He became a prominent member of the Clapham sect, and founded the Church Missionary Society (1799).

Venn, John (1834–1923) Mathematician, born in Hull, Humberside. He developed Boole's symbolic logic, and is best known for *Venn diagrams*, pictorially representing the relations between sets. >> Boole

Ventris, Michael (George Francis) (1922–1956) Linguist, born in Wheathampstead, Hertfordshire. He investigated Minoan scripts found on tablets excavated at palace sites in Crete (Linear B), and in 1952 announced that the language was early Greek.

Venturi, Giovanni Battista [ven**toor**ee] (1746–1822) Physicist, born near Reggio, Italy. He is remembered for his discovery of the *Venturi effect*, the decrease in the pressure of a fluid in a pipe where the diameter has been reduced by a gradual taper.

Venturi, Robert [ven**toor**ee] (1925–) Architect and writer, born in Philadelphia, PA. He spearheaded the reaction against Modernism by embracing historical and popular architectural styles. His buildings include the Sainsbury Wing of the National Gallery, London (1991).

Verdaguer, Mosen Jacinto [**vair**t̲hagair] (1845–1902) Poet, born in Catalonia, Spain. He wrote the epic poems *L'Atlántida* and *Lo canigó*, and on the first of these Manuel de Falla based his choral work *Atlántida*. >> Falla

Verdi, Giuseppe (Fortunino Francesco) [**vair**dee] (1813–1901) Composer, born in Le Roncole, Italy. The leading operatic composer of the day, his major successes include *Nabucco* (1842), *Rigoletto* (1851), *Il trovatore* (1853), *La traviata* (1853), and *Aida* (1871). Later works include the *Requiem* (1874), *Otello* (1887), and *Falstaff* (1893).

Verdross, Alfred (1890–1980) Austrian jurist. A judge of the European Court of Human Rights (1958–77), he was also president of the Institute of International Law.

Verdy, Violette [vairdee], originally **Nelly Guillerm** (1933–) Dancer and ballet director, born in Pont-L'Abbé-Lambour, France. She joined Petit's Ballets de Paris (1950), the New York City Ballet (1958–77), and other companies, then became artistic director of Paris Opéra Ballet (1977–80). >> Petit, Roland

Vérendrye, Pierre Gaultier de Varennes, sieur de (Lord of) **la** [vayrādree] (1685–1749) Explorer, born in Three Rivers, Quebec, Canada. He and his three sons travelled over much of unexplored Canada, establishing a chain of trading posts (1731–8) and discovering L Winnipeg.

Vereshchagin, Vasili [vyeresh**chah**gyin] (1842–1904) Painter of battles, born in Cherepovets, Russia. He travelled widely as a war correspondent, and portrayed what he saw in gruesomely realistic pictures.

Verga, Giovanni [**vair**ga] (1840–1922) Writer, born in Catania, Sicily, Italy. A member of the Italian *verismo* ('realist') school of novelists, he wrote many violent short stories describing the miserable life of Sicilian peasantry, including *Life in the Fields* (trans, 1880).

Vergil >> Virgil

Vergil, Polydore [**ver**jil], Ital **Polidoro Vergilio** (1470–1555) Writer of a history of England, born in Urbino, Italy. He is best known for his great *Twenty-six Books of English History* (trans title) which in 1582 became required reading in English schools.

Vergniaud, Pierre Victurnien [vairnyoh] (1753–93) French politician, born in Limoges, France. He was sent to the National Assembly (1791), where he became spokesman for the Girondins. After clashing with the Montagnards, he was guillotined.

Verhaeren, Emile [ver**hah**ren] (1855–1916) Poet, born in St Armand lez-Pueres, Belgium. Among his most notable works are *La Multiple Splendeur* (1906) and the five-part *Tout la Flandre* (1904). He also wrote short stories and verse plays.

Verlaine, Paul (Marie) [verlen] (1844–96) Poet, born in Metz, France. He mixed with the leading Parnassian writers, and achieved success with his second book of poetry, *Fêtes galantes* (1869). Later works include *Songs Without Words* (trans, 1874), *Les Poètes maudits* (1884), short stories, and sacred and profane verse.

Vermeer, Jan [ver**mayr**] (1632–75) Painter, born in Delft, The Netherlands. He painted small detailed domestic interiors, notable for their use of perspective and treatment of the various tones of daylight, such as 'Woman Reading a Letter' (c.1662).

Verne, Jules (1828–1905) Writer, born in Nantes, France.

He developed a new vein in fiction, anticipating the possibilities of science, as seen in (trans titles) *Journey to the Centre of the Earth* (1864), *Twenty Thousand Leagues under the Sea* (1870), and *Around the World in Eighty Days* (1873).

Vernet, Carle [vairnay], pseudonym of **Antoine Charles Horace Vernet** (1758–1836) Historical and animal painter, born in Bordeaux, France, the son of Claude Vernet. He painted battle scenes such as 'Marengo' (1804), and sporting scenes, such as 'The Race' (Louvre). >> Vernet, Claude / Horace

Vernet, Claude (Joseph) [vairnay] (1714–89) Landscape and marine painter, born in Avignon, France, the father of Carle Vernet. His paintings of France's 16 chief seaports are now in the Louvre.

Vernet, (Emile Jean) Horace (1789–1863) Painter of battles, born in Paris, the son of Carle Vernet. Renowned for his military and sporting scenes, he decorated the vast Constantine room at Versailles with battle scenes, including 'Napoleon at Friedland'. >> Vernet, Carle / Claude

Vernier, Pierre [vairnyay] (c.1580–1637) Scientific instrument-maker, born in Ornans, France. In 1631 he invented the measuring caliper which now bears his name.

Vernon, Edward, nickname **Old Grog** (1684–1757) British admiral. In 1739, during the War of Jenkins' Ear, his capture of Portobello made him a national hero. He was nicknamed 'Old Grog', from his grogram coat, and in 1740 ordered the dilution of navy rum with water, the mixture being thereafter known as 'grog'. >> Jenkins, Robert

Vernon, Robert (1774–1849) British breeder of horses. He was a founder of the Jockey Club, and established horse-training at Newmarket.

Veronese, Paolo [vayro**nay**zay], originally **Paolo Caliari** (c.1528–88) Venetian decorative painter, born in Verona, Italy. His major paintings include 'The Marriage Feast at Cana' (1562–3), 'The Adoration of the Magi' (1573), and 'Feast in the House of the Levi' (1573).

Veronica, St (1st-c), feast day 12 July. Woman of Jerusalem who, according to tradition, met Jesus Christ during his Passion, and offered him her veil to wipe sweat from his brow, with the result that the divine features were miraculously imprinted upon the cloth.

Verrazzano, Giovanni da [vera**zah**noh], also spelled **Verrazano** (1485–1528) Navigator and explorer, born in Tuscany, Italy. The first European to sight New York and Narragansett Bays, the *Verrazano Narrows* at the mouth of New York harbour are named after him.

Verres, Gaius [**ve**res] (c.115–43 BC) Roman official. He became praetor by bribery in 74 BC, and Governor of Sicily (73–70 BC). Summoned before a senatorial court in Rome, Cicero amassed such strong incriminating evidence that Verres fled before the trial. >> Cicero

Verrio, Antonio [ve**rioh**] (c.1640–1707) Decorative painter, born in Lecce, Italy. He was brought to London by Charles II to decorate Windsor Castle, and by William III to decorate Hampton Court.

Verrocchio, Andrea del [ve**rohk**ioh], originally **Andrea del Cione** (c.1435–88) Sculptor, painter, and goldsmith, born in Florence, Italy. He is best known for his equestrian statue of Colleoni at Venice.

Verulam, Baron >> **Bacon, Francis** (1561–1626)

Verwoerd, Hendrik (French) [fer**voort**] (1901–66) South African prime minister (1958–66), born in Amsterdam, The Netherlands. His administration was marked by the policy of apartheid, and the establishment of South Africa as a Republic (1962). He was assassinated in Cape Town.

Very, Edward Wilson [**vee**ree] (1847–1910) US ordnance expert and inventor. In 1877 he invented chemical flares (*Very lights*) for signalling at night.

Very, Jones [**vair**ee] (1813–80) Poet, born in Salem, MA. A Transcendentalist poet, he published *Essays and Poems* (1839).

Vesalius, Andreas [ve**zay**lius], Lat name of **Andries van Wesel** (1514–64) Anatomist, born in Brussels. His major work was *The Seven Books on the Structure of the Human Body* (trans, 1543), which greatly advanced the science of anatomy with its detailed descriptions and drawings.

Vespasian [ves**pay**zhn], in full **Titus Flavius Vespasianus** (9–79) Roman emperor (69–79), the founder of the Flavian dynasty (69–96). He ended the civil wars that had been raging since Nero's overthrow, and put the state on a sound financial footing.

Vespucci, Amerigo [ves**poo**chee] (1454–1512) Explorer, born in Florence, Italy. He promoted a voyage to the New World in the track of Columbus. His name was given to America through an inaccurate account of his travels, in which he is said to have discovered the mainland in 1497. >> Columbus

Vestris, Auguste, originally **Marie Jean Augustin Vestris** (1760–1842) Ballet dancer and teacher, born in Paris. He made his debut at the age of 12, going on to join the Paris Opera, and becoming the most celebrated dancer in Europe. >> Vestris, Madame

Vestris, Madame, popular name of **Lucia Elizabeth Vestris** or **Mathews**, *née* **Bartolozzi** (1797–1856) Actress, born in London. At 16 she married the dancer Armand Vestris (1787–1825), the son of Auguste Vestris, but they soon separated. She appeared at Drury Lane in 1820, and later managed Covent Garden and the Lyceum. >> Vestris, Auguste

Vian, Boris [veeã] (1920–59) Writer, born in Ville d'Avray, France. A tragi-comic writer, he won a cult following for such novels as *Froth on the Daydream* (trans, 1947) and *Heartsnatcher* (trans, 1953).

Vian, Sir Philip [**vi**yan] (1894–1968) British naval commander. He played a leading role in the destruction of the German battleship *Bismarck* (1941), and commanded in the Mediterranean fleet, skilfully handling convoy operations for the relief of Malta (1941–2).

Vianney, Jean-Baptiste-Marie, St [vee**a**nee], known as **the Curé d'Ars** (1786–1859), feast day 4 August. Roman Catholic clergyman, born in Dardilly, France. He became priest of Ars in 1818, gaining renown as a holy confessor, gifted with supernatural powers. He was canonized as the patron saint of parish priests in 1925.

Viaud, Louis Marie Julien [vee**oh**], pseudonym **Pierre Loti** (1850–1923) Writer and French naval officer, born in Rochefort, France. His best-known novel is *Fisherman of Iceland* (trans, 1886).

Vicente, Gil [vee**sen**tay] (c.1470–c.1537) Portuguese playwright and poet. He wrote on religious, national, and social themes, as well as farces, and pastoral and romantic plays, all with great lyricism and a predominantly comical spirit.

Vicky, pseudonym of **Victor Weisz** (1913–66) Political cartoonist, born in Berlin. He emigrated to Britain in 1935, and established himself as the leading left-wing political cartoonist of the period.

Vico, Giambattista [**vee**koh] (1668–1744) Historical philosopher, born in Naples, Italy. In his *New Science* (trans, 1725) he attempted to systematize the humanities into a single human science in a cyclical theory of the growth and decline of societies.

Victor Emmanuel II (1820–78) First king of Italy (1861–78), born in Turin, Italy. He fought on the side of Prussia in the Austro-Prussian War (1866), and after the fall of the French empire (1870) entered and annexed Rome.

Victor Emmanuel III (1869–1947) King of Italy (1900–46), born in Naples, Italy. He initially ruled as a constitutional monarch, but defied parliamentary majorities by bringing Italy into World War 1 in 1915, and in 1922 by offering Mussolini the premiership. He abdicated in 1946. >> Umberto II

Victoria, in full **Alexandrina Victoria** (1819–1901) Queen of Great Britain (1837–1901) and (from 1876) Empress of India, born in London, the only child of George III's fourth son, Edward, and Victoria Maria Louisa of Saxe-Coburg. Taught by Lord Melbourne, her first prime minister, she had a clear grasp of constitutional principles. In 1840 she married Prince Albert, and had four sons and five daughters. Strongly influenced by her husband, after his death (1861) she went into lengthy seclusion, but with her recognition as Empress of India, and the celebratory golden (1887) and diamond (1897) jubilees, she increased the prestige of the monarchy. >> Albert, Prince; Edward VII; Melbourne, Viscount

Victoria, Tomás Luis de, Ital **Vittoria, Tommaso Ludovico da** (c.1548–1611) Composer, born in Ávila, Spain. He wrote only religious music, his 180 works including several books of motets and over 20 Masses.

Vidal, Gore (Eugene Luther, Jr) [vidal] (1925–) Writer, born in West Point, NY. His novels include several satirical comedies, such as *Myra Breckenridge* (1968) and *Duluth* (1983), and the historical trilogy, *Burr* (1973), *1876* (1976), and *Lincoln* (1984). He has also written short stories, plays, film scripts, essays, reviews, and a volume of memoirs.

Vidal de La Blache, Paul [vidal duh la blash] (1845–1918) Geographer, born in Pézenas, France. The founder of modern French geography, he advocated a regional geography based on the intensive study of small physically defined regions, and the interrelations of people with their environment.

Vidor, King (Wallis) [veedaw(r)] (1894–1982) Film director, born in Galveston, TX. His many films include *The Big Parade* (1925), *The Crowd* (1928), and *Our Daily Bread* (1934). He also directed Westerns, melodramas, and historical epics such as *Solomon and Sheba* (1959).

Vieira, António [vyayra] (1608–97) Missionary, born in Lisbon. He went to Brazil in 1614, where he joined the Jesuit order (1623), and preached widely for the freedom of the Indians and slaves.

Vieira, João Bernardo [vyayra] (1939–) President of Guinea-Bissau (1984–), born in Bissau. After independence (1974), he served in the government of Luiz Cabral, but in 1980 led the coup which deposed him, becoming head of state and then executive president.

Viélé-Griffin, Francis [veelay grifi], pseudonym of **Egbert Ludovicus Viele** (1864–1937) Symbolist poet, born in Norfolk, VA. He settled in France, and became a leading exponent of free verse, which he practised in such books as *April's Harvest* (trans, 1886) and *Poèmes et poésies* (1895).

Vigée-Lebrun, (Marie Louise) Elisabeth [veezhay luhbroë], *née* **Vigée** (1755–1842) Painter, born in Paris. Her portrait of Marie Antoinette (1779, Versailles) led to a lasting friendship with the queen, and she painted numerous portraits of the royal family.

Vigneaud, Vincent Du >> Du Vincent, Vigneaud

Vignola, Giacomo (Barozzi) da [veenyohla] (1507–73) Architect, born in Vignola, Italy. The leading Mannerist architect of his day in Rome, his designs include the Villa di Papa Giulio and the Palazzo Farnese in Piacenza.

Vigny, Alfred Victor, comte de (Count) [veenyee] (1797–1863) Romantic writer, born in Loches, France. His best-known works include the historical novel *Cinq-Mars* (1826), a volume of exhortatory tales *Stello* (1832), and the Romantic drama *Chatterton* (1835).

Villa, Pancho [veeyah], also known as **Francisco Villa**, originally **Doroteo Arango** (1878–1923) Mexican revolutionary, born in Hacienda de Río Grande, Mexico. Together with Venustiano Carranza (1859–1920), he led a successful revolt against the regime of Victoriano Huerta (1914), but the two leaders became rivals, and Villa was forced to flee and was later assassinated.

Villa-Lobos, Heitor [veela lohbush] (1887–1959) Composer and conductor, born in Rio de Janeiro, Brazil. His many compositions include 12 symphonies, as well as operas, large-scale symphonic poems, concerti, ballets, and the nine suites *Bachianas Brasileiras* (1930–45).

Villars, Claude Louis Hector, duc de (Duke of) [veelah(r)] (1653–1734) French marshal under Louis XIV, born in Moulins, France. In the War of the Spanish Succession (1701–14) he inflicted heavy losses on Marlborough at Malplaquet (1709), and defeated the British and Dutch at Denain (1712). >> Marlborough

Villas-Boas Brothers A family of brothers - **Orlando Villas-Boas** (1916–), **Claudio Villas-Boas** (1918–), and **Leonardo Villas-Boas** (1920–61) - who have devoted their lives to the care and welfare of the Amerindians living around the Xingu R, Matto Grosso, Brazil.

Villehardouin, Geoffroi de [veelah(r)dwi] (c.1160– c.1213) French mediaeval chronicler, born near Bar-sur-Aube, France. He took part in the Fourth Crusade, and his *Histoire de l'empire de Constantinople'* described the events from 1198 to 1207, including the capture of Constantinople (1204).

Villella, Edward [vilela] (1936–) Dancer, born in New York City. He joined New York City Ballet (1957), becoming known for his speed and high leaps. He later became artistic director of the Eglevsky Ballet Company (1979–84).

Villemin, Jean Antoine [veelmi] (1827–92) Physician, born in Vosges, France. He discovered that tuberculosis is a contagious disease (1865), but his results were ignored at the time. He also discovered that certain bacteria could attack other bacteria, for which he created the term *antibiotic*.

Villeneuve, Pierre (Charles Jean Baptiste Sylvestre) de [veelnoev] (1763–1806) French admiral, born in Valensole, France. In 1805 he was in charge of the French fleet at Trafalgar, where he was taken prisoner. Released in 1806, he committed suicide during his return to Paris to face Napoleon. >> Napoleon I

Villiers >> Buckingham; Clarendon, 4th Earl of

Villiers, Charles Pelham (1802–98) British statesman and corn-law reformer, a younger brother of George, 4th Earl of Clarendon. He moved a resolution against the corn laws each year from 1838 until they were repealed in 1846. >> Clarendon, 4th Earl of

Villiers de L'Isle Adam, comte (Count) **(Philippe) Auguste (Mathias)** [veelyay duh leel adä] (1840–89) Writer, born in St-Brieuc, France. A pioneer of the Symbolist movement, he wrote much poetry, but is best known for his short stories, such as *Cruel Tales* (trans, 1883), and novels, such as *Isis* (1862). His plays include his masterpiece, *Axel* (1885).

Villon, François [veeyõ], pseudonym of **François de Montcorbier** (1431–?) Poet, born in Paris. His works include 'Le Lais' (The Legacy, also known as 'Le Petit Testament'), and his long poetic sequence, 'Le Grand Testament' (1461).

Villon, Jacques [veeyõ], pseudonym of **Gaston Duchamp** (1875–1963) Painter, born in Damville, France, the brother of Marcel Duchamp and Raymond Duchamp-Villon. He took up Cubism c.1911, and exhibited with others working in that new style. >> Duchamp; Duchamp-Villon

Vincent, St (?–304), feast day 22 January. Protomartyr, born in Zaragoza, Spain. Under Diocletian's persecution of Christianity, he was imprisoned and tortured to death at Valencia. >> Diocletian

Vincent de Beauvais [visä duh bohvay], Lat **Vincentius Bellovacensis** (c.1190–c.1264) French Dominican priest and encyclopedist. He compiled the *Speculum majus* (Great Mirror) on natural, doctrinal, and historical subjects.

Vincent de Paul, St (c.1580–1660), feast day 27 September. Priest and philanthropist, born in Pouy, France. In 1625 he founded the Congregation of Priests of the Missions (or *Lazarists*, from their priory of St Lazare) and in 1634 the Sisterhood of Charity. He was canonized in 1737.

Vinci, Leonardo da >> **Leonardo da Vinci**

Vine, Barbara >> **Rendell, Ruth**

Viner, Charles [**viy**ner] (1678–1756) Legal scholar, born in Salisbury, Wiltshire. He produced a massive *Abridgment* of the law of England in 23 volumes (1741–56).

Vinson, Carl (1883–1981) US politician, born in Milledgeville, GA. He served in the US House of Representatives (1914–65), and as chairman of the Committee on Naval Affairs (1933–47) prepared the Navy for World War 2.

Vio, Thomas de >> **Cajetan**

Viollet-le-Duc, Eugène (Emmanuel) [**vyoh**lay luh **dük**] (1814–79) Architect and archaeologist, born in Paris. He directed restoration of Ste Chapelle, Paris (1840), the cathedrals of Notre Dame, Amiens, and Laon, and the Château de Pierrefonds.

Virchow, Rudolf (Carl) [**veer**khoh] (1821–1902) Physician and anthropologist, born in Schivelbein, Germany. He established the importance of cellular pathology (1858), and was largely responsible for the growth of anthropology in Germany.

Virgil or **Vergil**, in full **Publius Vergilius Maro** (70–19 BC) Latin poet, born in Andes, Italy. His works include the *Eclogues* (37 BC) and the *Georgics*, or *Art of Husbandry* (36–29 BC), and for the rest of his life he worked on the *Aeneid*.

Virgil, Polydore >> **Vergil, Polydore**

Virgin Mary >> **Mary**

Virtanen, Artturi Ilmari [**veer**tanen] (1895–1973) Biochemist, born in Helsinki. He studied nutrition and the development of food resources, for which he was awarded the Nobel Prize for Chemistry in 1945.

Visconti, Gian Galeazzo [vis**kon**tee], known as **Count of Valour** (1351–1402) Milanese statesman, born in Milan. He controlled the N half of Italy, bringing many independent cities into one state, and arranging marriage alliances.

Visconti, Luchino [vis**kon**tee] (1906–76) Stage and film director, born in Milan, Italy. His first film, *Obsession* (trans, 1942) took Italy by storm, with its strict realism and concern with social problems. Later films included (trans titles) *The Leopard* (1963) and *Death in Venice* (1971).

Visser 't Hooft, Willem Adolf [tohft] (1900–85) Clergyman and ecumenist, born in Haarlem, The Netherlands. He served as general-secretary of what later became the World Council of Churches (1938–66).

Vitellius, Aulus [vi**tel**ius] (15–69) Roman emperor, a successor of Nero. Proclaimed emperor (69), he defeated Otho at Bedriacum, but was defeated by his rival Vespasian, and murdered. >> Otho; Vespasian

Vitruvius [vi**troo**vius], in full **Marcus Vitruvius Pollio** (1st-c AD) Roman architect and military engineer. He wrote the 10-volume *De architectura* (On Architecture), the only extant Roman treatise on this subject.

Vittoria, Tommasso Ludovica da >> **Victoria, Tomás Luis de**

Vittorini, Elio [vito**ree**nee] (1908–66) Novelist, critic, and translator, born in Syracuse, Sicily, Italy. He was Italy's most influential writer of his time, known for the help he gave to younger writers. *Conversations in Sicily* (trans, 1941) is his masterpiece.

Vittorino da Feltre [vito**ree**noh da **fel**tray], originally **Vittorino dei Ramboldini** (c.1378–1446) Educationist, born at Feltre, Italy. In Mantua he founded a school for both rich and poor children (1425), in which he devised new methods of instruction, integrating the development of mind and body through the study of the Classics and Christianity.

Vitus, St [**viy**tus] (4th-c), feast day 15 June. Christian martyr, said to have been the son of a Sicilian pagan. He suffered martyrdom under Diocletian. He is invoked

against sudden death, hydrophobia, epilepsy, and chorea (*St Vitus' dance*), and is also the patron of comedians and actors. >> Diocletian

Vivaldi, Antonio (Lucio) [vi**val**dee] (1678–1741) Violinist and composer, born in Venice, Italy. The 12 concertos of *L'Estro Armonico* (1712) gave him a European reputation, and *The Four Seasons* (trans, 1725), an early example of programme music proved highly popular. He also wrote many operas, sacred music, and over 450 concertos.

Vivarini, Alvise [viva**ree**nee], also called **Luigi Vivarini** (c.1446–c.1505) Painter, born in Venice, Italy, the son of Antonio Vivarini. His works include portrait busts and altarpieces, especially a 'Madonna and Six Saints' (1480) in the Academy, Venice. >> Vivarini, Antonio / Bartolommeo

Vivarini, Antonio [viva**ree**nee] (c.1415–c.1480) Painter, the founder of the Vivarini studio, born in Venice, Italy. His paintings often depict Madonnas and saints. >> Vivarini, Alvise / Bartolommeo

Vivarini, Bartolommeo [viva**ree**nee] (c.1432–c.1499) Painter, born in Venice, Italy, the brother of Antonio Vivarini. Among his works are several altarpieces in churches of Venice. >> Vivarini, Antonio / Alvise

Vivekananda [vivay**kan**anda], also known as **Swami Vivekananda**, originally **Narendranath Datta** or **Dutt** (1862–1902) Hindu philosopher, born in Calcutta, India. He met Ramakrishna and became his leading disciple, attempting to combine Indian spirituality with Western materialism, and was the main force behind the Vedanta movement in the West. >> Ramakrishna

Vivés, Juan Luis [vee**vays**], Lat **Ludovicus Vives** (1492–1540) Philospher and humanist, born in Valencia, Spain. His writings include *Against the Pseudo-Dialecticians* (trans, 1570) and several other works on educational theory and practice.

Viviani, René [vivy**ah**nee] (1862–1925) French prime minister (1914–15), born in Sidi-bel-Abbés, Algeria. Appointed just before the outbreak of World War 1, he resigned after being attacked for a shortage of munitions, then became minister of justice (1915).

Vivin, Louis [vee**vi**] (1861–1936) Primitive painter, born in Hadol, France. He painted meticulously detailed still-lifes and views of Paris and its parks.

Vladimir I, St, in full **Vladimis Svyatoslavich**, known as **the Great** (956–1015), feast day 15 July. First Christian sovereign of Russia (980–1015), the son of Svyatoslav, Grand Prince of Kiev (d.972). He accepted Christianity and ordered the conversion of his subjects, punishing those who resisted.

Vlaminck, Maurice de [vla**mik**] (1876–1958) Artist, born in Paris. By 1905 he was one of the leaders of the Fauves, using typically brilliant colour, then painted more Realist landscapes, and later developed a more sombre Expressionism.

Vleck, John Van >> **Van Vleck, John H**

Vodorinski, Anton >> **Ketèlbey, Albert William**

Voelcker, Augustus [**foel**ker] (1822–84) Agricultural chemist and writer, born in Frankfurt, Germany. His work on farm feeding-stuffs, soils, and artificial manures greatly advanced agricultural chemistry.

Vogel, Hans-Jochen [**foh**gl] (1926–) German politician. A former minister of housing and town planning (1972–4) and minister of justice (1974–81), he replaced Brandt as Social Democratic Party chairman in 1987. >> Brandt, Willy

Vogel, Sir Julius [**voh**gl] (1835–99) New Zealand prime minister (1873–5, 1876), born in London. He is best known for the large-scale public works he initiated with the help of loans arranged with the British government.

Vogel, Vladimir [**voh**gl] (1896–1984) Composer, born in Moscow. He composed orchestral works, chamber music, and secular oratorios.

Volcker, Paul A [**vol**ker] (1927–) Economist, born in Cape May, NJ. He served as the chairman of the Federal Reserve Board (1979–87), then became professor of international economics at Princeton University.

Volstead, Andrew J [**vol**sted] (1860–1947) US politician, born in Goodhue Co, MN. He is best known for the Prohibition Act of 1919, named after him, which forbade the manufacture and sale of intoxicant liquors, in force until 1933.

Volta, Alessandro (Giuseppe Antonio Anastasio) [**vol**ta] (1745–1827) Physicist, born in Como, Italy. He experimented on current electricity, and developed the first electric battery (1800). His name is given to the unit of electric potential, the volt.

Voltaire [vol**tair**], pseudonym of **François Marie Arouet** (1694–1778) Writer, the embodiment of the 18th-c Enlightenment, born in Paris. His works include the tragedy *Oedipe*, poetry, historical and scientific treatises, his *Lettres philosophiques* (1734), and the satirical short story, *Candide* (1759). From 1762 he produced a range of anti-religious writings and the *Dictionnaire philosophique* (1764).

Volterra, Vito [vol**ter**a] (1860–1940) Mathematician, born in Ancona, Italy. He developed a general theory of functionals which strongly influenced modern calculus and analytical methods.

von Braun, Wernher >> **Braun, Wernher von**

Vondel, Joost van den (1587–1679) Writer, born in Cologne, Germany. He began writing satirical verse, then turned to Sophoclean drama and produced *Lucifer* (1654) and *Jephtha* (1659), greatly influencing the 17th-century German poetical revival. >> Sophocles

von Euler, Ulf (Svante) [**oy**ler] (1905–83) Physiologist, born in Stockholm, Sweden. He found the first prostaglandin in 1935, and in 1970 shared the Nobel Prize for Physiology or Medicine for his isolation and identification of noradrenaline (norepinephrine).

von Klitzing, Klaus (1943–) Physicist, born in Schroda/Posen, Germany. In 1977 he presented a paper on two-dimensional electronic behaviour in which the quantum Hall effect was clearly seen. He was awarded the Nobel Prize for Physics in 1985.

Vonnegut, Bernard [**von**eguht] (1914–) Physicist, born in Indianapolis, IA. In 1947 he improved a method for artificially inducing rainfall by using silver iodide as a cloud-seeding agent.

Vonnegut, Kurt, Jr [**von**eguht] (1922–) Novelist, born in Indianapolis, IN. His novels are satirical fantasies, usually cast in the form of science fiction, as in *Player Piano* (1952), *Cat's Cradle* (1963), and *Slaughterhouse Five* (1969).

Von Neumann, John [**noy**man], originally **Johann von Neumann** (1903–57) Mathematician, born in Budapest. He wrote a major work on quantum mechanics (1932), which led him to a new axiomatic foundation for set theory. His work on high-speed calculations for H-bomb development contributed to the development of computers, and he also introduced game theory (1944).

Von Stade, Frederica [**stah**duh] (1945–) Mezzo-soprano, born in Somerville, NJ. She made her Metropolitan Opera debut in 1970, her celebrated roles including Cherubino and Mélisande.

von Sydow, Max >> **Sydow, Max von**

von Wright, Georg Henrik (1916–) Philosopher and logician, born in Helsinki. Associated with the Vienna Circle, his works include *The Logical Problem of Induction* (1941) and *Freedom and Determination* (1980).

Voragine, Jacobus de [vo**ra**jinay] (c.1230–1298) Clergyman and hagiologist, born in Viareggio, Italy. He became Archbishop of Genoa in 1292, and wrote the *Golden Legend*, a famous collection of lives of the saints.

Voronoff, Serge [**vo**ronof] (1866–1951) Physiologist, born in Voronezh, Ukraine. He specialized in grafting animal glands into the human body, experimented with testicle transplants as a means to rejuvenation, and wrote on his theory connecting gland secretions with senility.

Voroshilov, Kliment Yefremovich [voro**shee**lof] (1881–1969) Soviet marshal and president (1953–60), born near Dniepropetrovsk, Ukraine. He played a military rather than a political role in the 1917 Revolution, and as commissar for defence (1925–40) was responsible for the modernization of the Red Army. He became head of state after Stalin's death. >> Stalin

Vorster, John [**faw**(r)ster], originally **Balthazar Johannes Vorster** (1915–83) South African prime minister (1966–78) and president (1978–9), born in Jamestown, South Africa. He was minister of justice under Verwoerd (1961), whom he succeeded, maintaining the policy of apartheid. >> Verwoerd

Vortigern [**vaw**(r)tijern] (fl.425–50) Semi-legendary British king. According to Bede, he recruited Germanic mercenaries led by Hengist and Horsa to help fight off the Picts after the final withdrawal of the Roman administration from Britain (409). >> Hengist and Horsa

Vos, Cornelis de (1585–1651) Flemish painter. Working in Antwerp, he chiefly painted portraits and religious and mythological pieces. His brother **Paul** (1590–1678) painted animals and hunting scenes.

Voss, Johann Heinrich (1751–1826) Poet and philologist, born in Sommersdorf, Germany. He is best known for his translations of the *Odyssey* (1781) and *Iliad* (1793).

Vouet, Simon [**voo**ay] (1590–1649) Painter, born in Paris. His religious and allegorical paintings and decorations in the Baroque style became very popular.

Vought, Chance (Milton) [vawt] (1890–1930) Aircraft designer and manufacturer, born in New York City. He formed his own firm in 1917, and among his famous designs were the Vought–Wright Model V military biplane (1916) and the FU-1 single-seat high-altitude supercharged fighter (1925).

Voysey, Charles (Francis Annesley) [**voy**zee] (1857–1941) Architect and designer, born in London. His designs for traditional country houses were influenced by the Arts and Crafts Movement, and he was also an important designer of wallpaper, textiles, furniture, and metalwork. >> Morris, William

Voznesensky, Andrey Andreyevich [vozhne**shen**skee] (1933–) Poet, born in Moscow. His best-known volume (trans titles) *Antiworlds* appeared in 1964, and *Temptation* in 1979.

Vranitzky, Franz [vra**nit**skee] (1937–) Austrian chancellor (1986–). After holding senior appointments in the banking world, he became minister of finance (1984) and federal chancellor.

Vriendt, Cornelis de >> **Floris**

Vries, Hugo / Peter de >> **de Vries, Hugo / Peter**

Vuillard, (Jean) Edouard [vwee**yah**(r)] (1868–1940) Painter and printmaker, born in Cuiseaux, France. One of the later Impressionists, a member of *Les Nabis*, he executed mainly flower pieces and simple interiors, and is also known for his textiles, wallpapers, and decorative work in public buildings.

Vygotsky, Lev Semenovich [vi**got**skee] (1896–1934) Psychologist, born in Orsha, Belarus. His writings, such as *Thought and Language* (1934–62) and *Mind in Society* (1978), have had a major influence on Soviet and (since the 1960s) Western psychology, particularly on specialists in child development.

Vyshinsky, Andrey Yanuaryevich [vi**shin**skee] (1883–1954) Russian jurist and politician, born in Odessa, Ukraine. He was the public prosecutor at the state trials (1936–8) which removed Stalin's rivals, and later became foreign minister (1949–53). >> Stalin

Waage, Peter >> Guldberg, Cato Maximilian
Waals, Johannes Diderik van der >> van der Waals, Johannes Diderik
Wace, Robert [ways] (12th-c) Anglo-Norman poet, born in Jersey, Channel Is. His works include a Norman-French version of Geoffrey of Monmouth's *Historia regum Britanniae* entitled the *Roman de Brut* (1155), and the *Roman de Rou* (1160–74), an epic of the Dukes of Normandy. >> Geoffrey of Monmouth
Waddington, C(onrad) H(al) (1905–75) Embryologist and geneticist, born in Evesham, Worcestershire. He introduced important concepts into evolutionary theory, and helped to popularize science in such general books as *The Ethical Animal* (1960).
Waddington (of Read), David Charles Waddington, Baron (1929–) British statesman. After a number of junior posts, he became home secretary (1989–90), and was appointed Lord Privy Seal and Leader of the House of Lords (1990–2).
Wade, George (1673–1748) English soldier, probably born in Westmeath, Ireland. In the Scottish highlands he constructed (1726–37) a system of metalled military roads, with 40 stone (*Wade*) bridges. During the Jacobite Rising of 1745 he commanded George II's forces in England. >> Stuart, Charles
Wade, Sir Thomas (Francis) (1818–95) English diplomat and scholar, born in London. His system of romanization for Chinese was later modified by his successor at Cambridge, Herbert Giles, and is now referred to as the *Wade–Giles* system. >> Giles, H A
Wade, (Sarah) Virginia (1945–) Tennis player, born in Bournemouth, Dorset. Her successes include the Wimbledon singles title (1977), the US Open title (1968), and the French championship (1972).
Wadsworth, Edward (1889–1949) Artist, born in Yorkshire. He was associated with the London Group, and is known for his still-lifes and seascapes with marine objects.
Waerden, van der, Bartel Leendert [**vair**den] (1903–) Mathematician, born in Amsterdam, The Netherlands. He worked in algebra, algebraic geometry, and mathematical physics, and produced a classic textbook, *Modern Algebra* (1931).
Wagenfeld, Wilhelm [**vahg**enfelt] (1900–) Designer of glassware and ceramics, born in Bremen, Germany. Faithful to the principles of the Bauhaus, his designs are simple, unadorned, and functional.
Wagley, Charles (Walter) (1913–91) Social anthropologist, born in Clarksville, TX. He worked in the 1930s among the descendants of the Maya in Guatemala, and in the 1940s was among the first Americans to work in the South American lowlands, notably in Brazil.
Wagner, Honus [**wag**ner], properly **John Peter Wagner**, nickname **the Flying Dutchman** (1874–1955) Baseball player, born in Carnegie, PA. An all-round player, his career (1897–1917) was spent mostly with the Pittsburgh Pirates (as coach, 1933–51). He holds the National League record for the most consecutive seasons batting ·300 or more (17).
Wagner, Otto [**vahg**ner] (1841–1918) Architect and teacher, born in Penzing, Austria. The founder of the Vienna School, he became an important advocate of purely functional architecture.
Wagner, (Wilhelm) Richard [**vahg**ner] (1813–83) Composer, born in Leipzig, Germany. His *Rienzi* (1842) was a

great success, but his next operas, including *Tannhäuser* (1845), were failures. He then began to write *The Rhinegold* (trans, 1853), *The Valkyries* (trans, 1856), *Siegfried* (1857), *The Mastersingers* (trans, 1867), and *Twilight of the Gods* (trans, 1874), opening the Bayreuth theatre in 1876 with a performance of the whole *Ring* cycle. >> Wagner, Siegfried / Wieland
Wagner, Robert (John) [**wag**ner] (1930–) Film and television actor, born in Detroit, MI. His greatest popularity has been in television series, such as *It Takes A Thief* (1965–9), *Switch* (1975–7), and *Hart to Hart* (1979–84), in which he co-starred with his wife, Natalie Wood (1938–81).
Wagner, Siegfried [**vahg**ner] (1869–1930) Musician, born near Lucerne, Switzerland, the son of Richard Wagner. He became a conductor and composer of operas and other music, and was director of the Bayreuth Festspielhaus from 1909. >> Wagner, Richard
Wagner, Wieland [**vahg**ner] (1917–66) Opera house director, born in Bayreuth, Germany, the son of Siegfried Wagner. He took over the directorship of the Festspielhaus after World War 2, and revolutionized the production of the operas. >> Wagner, Siegfried
Wagner-Jauregg, Julius [**vahg**ner **yow**rek], originally **Julius Wagner, Ritter** (Knight) **von Jauregg** (1857–1940) Neurologist and psychiatrist, born in Wels, Austria. He was awarded the Nobel Prize for Physiology or Medicine in 1927 for his discovery (1917) of a treatment for general paralysis by infection with malaria, the forerunner of shock therapy.
Wagoner, Dan (1932–) Modern dancer and choreographer, born in Springfield, WV. After dancing with several companies, he formed Dan Wagoner and Dancers in 1969, and in 1988 was appointed artistic director of the London Contemporary Dance Company.
Wain, John (Barrington) [wayn] (1925–94) Writer and critic, born in Stoke-on-Trent, Staffordshire. His novels include *Hurry on Down* (1953), *The Contenders* (1958), and *Young Shoulders* (1982, Whitbread), and he also wrote poetry (*Poems, 1949–79*), plays, and several books of literary criticism.
Wainwright, Jonathan M(ayhew) (1883–1953) US general, born in Walla-Walla, WA. In 1942 he commanded the epic retreat in the Bataan peninsula during the Philippines campaign, and was taken prisoner by the Japanese.
Waismann, Friedrich [**viys**man] (1896–1959) Philosopher, born in Vienna. A prominent member of the Vienna Circle, his works include *The Principles of Linguistic Philosophy* (1965).
Waite, Terry [wayt], popular name of **Terence (Hardy) Waite** (1939–) Consultant, born in Bollington, Cheshire. As the Archbishop of Canterbury's special envoy, he was involved in negotiations to secure the release of hostages held in the Middle East, and was himself kidnapped in Beirut (1987–91).
Waitz, Georg [viyts] (1813–86) Historian, born in Flensburg, Germany. Founder of the Göttingen historical school, his major work was *German Constitutional History* (trans, 1844–78).
Waitz, Grete [viyts], *née* **Andersen** (1953–) Athlete, born in Oslo. World marathon champion (1983) and the Olympic silver medallist (1984), she four times set world best times for the marathon.
Wajda, Andrzej [**viy**da] (1926–) Film director, born in Suwalki, Poland. He is best known outside Poland for *Man*

of Marble (trans, 1977), dealing with the Stalinist era, and *Man of Iron* (trans, 1981).

Wakefield, Edward Gibbon (1796–1862) Originator of subsidized emigration from Britain, born in London. He proposed (1929) the sale of small units of crown land in the colonies to subsidize colonization by the poor from Britain (later called *Wakefield settlements*).

Wakeley, Thomas (1795–1862) Surgeon, born in Membury, Devon. He was the founder and first editor of *The Lancet* (1823).

Waksman, Selman (Abraham) [waksman] (1888–1973) Biochemist, born in Priluka, Ukraine. His research into antibiotics led to his discovery of streptomycin (1943), for which he was awarded the Nobel Prize for Physiology or Medicine in 1952.

Walburga, Walpurga, or **Walpurgis, St >> Walpurga**

Walcott, Clyde [wolkot] (1926–) Cricketer, born in Bridgetown, Barbados. A leading West Indian batsman of the 1950s, he was capped 44 times, scoring 3798 runs, and 15 of his 40 centuries were obtained in Tests.

Walcott, Derek [wolkot] (1930–) Poet and playwright, born in St Lucia, West Indies. He founded the Trinidad Theatre Workshop in 1959. His works include *Collected Poems 1948–84* (1986) and the epic *Omeros* (1990), and he was awarded the Nobel Prize for Literature in 1992.

Wald, George [wawld] (1906–) Biochemist, born in New York City. In 1933 he discovered the presence of vitamin A in the retina, and later showed that rhodopsin has a molecule composed of a protein fragment linked to a structure derived from vitamin A. He shared the Nobel Prize for Physiology or Medicine in 1967.

Wald, Lillian D [wawld] (1867–1940) Public health nurse and settlement leader, born in Cincinnati, OH. She is best known as a founder of public health nursing and related services through the establishment in 1895 of the Nurses' Settlement in New York City.

Waldheim, Kurt [valthiym] (1918–) Austrian president (1986–92), born near Vienna. He was foreign minister (1968–70) and UN secretary-general (1972–81). His presidential candidature was controversial because of claims that he had been involved in wartime atrocities, but he denied the allegations.

Waldo or **Valdes, Peter** [woldoh, valdes] (fl.1175) Religious leader, born in Lyon, France. He took up a life of poverty and preaching (c.1170), gathered a group of followers, known as *Waldensians*, and sought papal approval, but was excommunicated (1184).

Waldock, Sir Claud (Humphrey Meredith) [wawldok] (1904–81) British jurist, born in Colombo, Sri Lanka. He became president of the European Commission on Human Rights (1955–61), judge of the European Court of Human Rights (1966–74), and judge of the International Court of Justice (1973–81), president 1979–81).

Waldorf, William >> Astor, William Waldorf, 1st / 2nd Viscounts

Waldseemüller, Martin [valtsaymüler] (c.1470–c.1521) Cartographer, born in Radolfzell, Germany. He used an account of the travels of Amerigo Vespucci to publish in 1507 the map and globe on which he named the New World *America* in Vespucci's honour. >> Vespucci

Waldstein, Albrecht >> Wallenstein, Albrecht

Waldteufel, (Charles) Emil [valttoyfel] (1837–1915) Composer, born in Strasbourg, France. A prolific composer of dance music, several of his waltzes, notably the *Skaters Waltz* and *Estudiantina*, remain popular.

Wales, Prince of >> Charles, Prince of Wales

Wales, Prince Harry (Henry) / William of >> Charles, Prince of Wales

Wałesa, Lech [vawensa] (1943–) Polish president (1990–5), born in Popowo, Poland. A Gdańsk shipyard worker, he became leader of the independent trade union,

Solidarity, which openly challenged the Polish government. He was detained (1981–2), and awarded the Nobel Peace Prize in 1983. He continued to be prominent in Polish politics, and gained a landslide victory in the 1990 election but was defeated by Alexander Kwasniewski in 1995.

Walewska, Maria (Countess) [valefska], *née* **Laczynska** (1786–1817) Mistress of Napoleon Bonaparte, born in Brodno, Poland. She met Napoleon in Poland in 1806, and bore him a son, who became Count Walewski. >> Napoleon I; Walewski

Walewski, Alexandre Florian Joseph Colonna, Count [walefskee] (1810–68) French diplomat, born in Walewice, Poland, the illegitimate son of Napoleon and Maria, Countess Walewska. Under Napoleon III his appointments included foreign minister (1855–60) and minister of state (1860–3). >> Napoleon III; Walewska

Walker, Sir Alan (1911–) Methodist clergyman and social activist, born in Sydney, New South Wales, Australia. He was superintendent of the Waverley Methodist Mission (1944–54) and of the influential Sydney Central Methodist Mission (1958–78).

Walker, Alice (Malsenior) (1944–) Writer, born in Eatonville, GA. She is best known for her novels, notably *The Color Purple* (1982, Pulitzer), later made into a successful film. She has also written volumes of poetry, short stories, and essays.

Walker, George (1618–90) Irish clergyman and governor, born in Northern Ireland. In 1688 he raised a regiment to help garrison Londonderry for its successful resistance to the 105-day siege by James II's forces (1689), and became joint governor.

Walker, John (1732–1807) Dictionary-maker, born in Colney Hatch, UK. His works include a *Rhyming Dictionary* (1775) and a *Critical Pronouncing Dictionary* (1791).

Walker, John (c.1781–1859) Inventor, born in Stockton-on-Tees, Cleveland. In 1827 he made the first friction matches, called by him 'Congreves', later named *lucifers*, and eventually *matches*.

Walker, Kath >> Noonuccal, Oodgeroo

Walker, Peter (Edward) (1932–) British Conservative statesman, born in London. He was agriculture secretary (1979–83), energy secretary (1983–7), and secretary of state for Wales (1987–90).

Walker, William (1824–60) Adventurer and revolutionary, born in Nashville, TN. He invaded Nicaragua (1855), took Granada, and was elected president (1856–7). Twice expelled from Nicaragua, he entered Honduras (1860), but was captured and shot.

Wall, Max (Wall George Lorimer) (1908–90) Actor and comedian, born in London. He built a reputation as one of the finest British comics of his time in music hall and radio performances with a laconic comedy routine.

Wallace, Alfred Russel (1823–1913) Naturalist, born in Usk, Gwent. He contributed greatly to the scientific foundations of zoogeography, including his proposal for the evolutionary distinction between the fauna of Australia and Asia ('Wallace's line').

Wallace, DeWitt (1889–1981) Publisher, born in St Paul, MN. In 1922 he launched the *Reader's Digest* as a mail-order magazine with 1500 subscribers.

Wallace, (Richard Horatio) Edgar (1875–1932) Writer, born in London. He wrote over 170 novels and plays, and is best remembered for his crime novels, such as *The Clue of the Twisted Candle*.

Wallace, George (Corley) (1919–) US state governor, born in Clio, AL. He became Alabama's governor (1963–7), proclaiming 'segregation forever'. In 1972, while campaigning for the Democratic presidential nomination, he was shot and paralysed, but still served three more terms as governor (1971–9, 1983–7).

Wallace, Henry A(gard) (1888–1965) Agriculturist and

statesman, born in Adair Co, IA, the son of Henry Cantwell Wallace. He was nominated vice-president to Franklin D Roosevelt, whose 'New Deal' policy he supported. >> Roosevelt, Franklin D; Wallace, Henry Cantwell

Wallace, Henry Cantwell (1866–1924) Journalist and US politician, born in Rock Island, IL. As secretary of agriculture (1921–4), he instituted the bureau of agricultural economics. >> Wallace, Henry A

Wallace, Lew(is) (1827–1905) Writer and soldier, born in Brookville, IN. He served in the Federal army in the American Civil War (1861–5), and became Governor of New Mexico (1878–81). His books include the successful religious novel *Ben Hur* (1880; filmed 1927, 1959).

Wallace, Sir Richard (1818–90) Art collector, born in London, the illegitimate son of Viscount Beauchamp and Agnes Jackson, *née* Wallace. He helped his father build up the large collection of paintings and *objets d'art* which now comprise the *Wallace Collection*.

Wallace, Sir William (c.1270–1305) Scottish knight and champion of Scots independence, probably born in Elderslie, Strathclyde. He routed the English army at Stirling (1297), and took control of the government of Scotland as 'Guardian', but was defeated at Falkirk (1298), and executed.

Wallace, William (1860–1940) Composer, born in Greenock, Strathclyde. He was the first British composer to experiment with symphonic poems, and also wrote a symphony and songs.

Wallenberg, Raoul (1912–?47) Swedish businessman and diplomat, born in Stockholm. When Hitler began deporting Hungarian Jews, he was sent to Hungary with the aid of the US and Swedish governments to rescue as many Jews as he could, saving up to 100 000. In 1945 he was taken to Soviet headquarters and never returned; rumours of his fate continue to circulate.

Wallenstein or **Waldstein, Albrecht (Wenzel Eusebius), Herzog von** (Duke of) [**wo**lenstiyn], Ger [**val**enshtiyn] (1583–1634) Bohemian general, born in Heřmanice, Czech Republic. During the Thirty Years' War he became commander of the Imperial armies and won a series of victories (1625–9), but was defeated at Lützen (1632), and soon after was assassinated.

Waller, Augustus (Volney) (1816–70) Physiologist, born near Faversham, Kent. He discovered the *Wallerian* degeneration of nerve fibres, and the related method of tracing nerve fibres.

Waller, Edmund (1606–87) Poet, born in Coleshill, Buckinghamshire. In 1643 he plunged into a conspiracy (*Waller's plot*) against parliament, was arrested, and banished, but returned to England in 1651. His collected poems were published in 1645.

Waller, Fats, popular name of **Thomas Wright Waller** (1904–43) Jazz pianist, organist, singer, and songwriter, born in New York City. He played in the stride tradition, and wrote such hits as 'Ain't Misbehavin'' (1929) and 'Keeping Out of Mischief Now' (1932).

Waller, Sir William (c.1598–1688) English soldier, born in Knole, Kent. He suggested reforms on which the New Model Army was to be based, but resigned command in 1645, and was later imprisoned for Royalist sympathies (1648–51).

Walling, William English (1877–1936) Labour reformer, born in Louisville, KY. He co-founded the National Women's Trade Union League (1903) and the National Association for the Advancement of Colored People (1908).

Wallis, Sir Barnes (Neville) (1887–1979) Aeronautical engineer and inventor, born in Ripley, Derbyshire. He designed the R100 airship, the Wellington Bomber, the 'bouncing bombs' which destroyed the Mohne and Eder dams, and in the 1950s the first swing-wing aircraft.

Wallis, John (1616–1703) Mathematician, born in Ashford, Kent. *The Arithmetic of Infinitesimals* (trans, 1655) stimulated Newton's work on calculus and the binomial theorem. He also wrote on proportion, mechanics, grammar, logic, theology, and the teaching of the deaf. >> Newton, Isaac

Wallis, Samuel (1728–95) English explorer and naval officer. He circumnavigated the globe (1766–68) and was the first European to discover Tahiti (1767). The *Wallis Is* were named after him.

Walpole, Horace (or **Horatio**), **4th Earl of Orford** (1717–97) Writer, born in London, the youngest son of Sir Robert Walpole. He initiated a vogue for Gothic romances with *The Castle of Otranto* (1764), although his literary reputation rests chiefly upon his letters.

Walpole, Sir Hugh (Seymour) (1884–1941) Writer, born in Auckland, New Zealand. His many novels include *The Secret City* (1919) and the family saga, *The Herries Chronicle* (4 vols, 1930–3).

Walpole, Sir Robert, 1st Earl of Orford (1676–1745) Chief minister (1721–42) of George I and George II, born in Houghton, Norfolk. George I made him a privy councillor and (1715) Chancellor of the Exchequer. He was Chancellor again in 1721 and widely recognized as 'prime minister'- a title (unknown to the Constitution) which he hotly repudiated. >> George I / II (of Great Britain)

Walpurga, Walburga, or **Walpurgis, St** [val**poor**ga] (c.710–c.777), feast day 25 February. Missionary, born in Wessex, England. She joined St Boniface on his mission to Germany, and became Abbess of Heidenheim, where she died. Her relics were transferred (c.870) to Eichstätt. >> Boniface

Walschaerts, Egide [val**s**herts] (1820–1901) Mechanical engineer, born in Malines, Belgium. He invented a type of valve gear (1844) and several other improvements for use in steam engines.

Walsingham, Sir Francis [**wol**singam] (c.1530–90) English secretary of state to Elizabeth I (1573–90), born in Chislehurst, Kent. A strong opponent of the Catholics, he developed a complex system of espionage at home and abroad, enabling him to reveal several plots against the Queen. >> Babington; Mary, Queen of Scots; Throckmorton

Walsingham, Thomas [**wol**singam] (?–c.1422) English chronicler and monk. He was associated chiefly with St Albans abbey, and compiled *Historia Anglicana, 1272–1422* and other works.

Walter, Bruno [**val**ter], originally **Bruno Walter Schlesinger** (1876–1962) Conductor, born in Berlin. He was in charge of the Munich Opera (1913–22), and from 1919 was chief conductor of the Berlin Philharmonic. He later settled in the USA, where he became chief conductor of the New York Philharmonic (1951).

Walter, Hubert (c.1140–1205) English clergyman and statesman, who accompanied Richard I on the Third Crusade (1190–3). He was appointed Archbishop of Canterbury in 1193, and justiciar of England (1193–8). On John's accession (1199), he became chancellor. >> John; Richard I

Walter, John (1739–1812) Printer and newspaper publisher, born in London. In 1785 he founded *The Daily Universal Register* newspaper, which in 1788 was renamed *The Times*. >> Walter, John (1818–94)

Walter, John (1818–94) Newspaper proprietor, born in London, the grandson of John Walter. He took over *The Times* in 1847, and in 1866 introduced the cylindrical *Walter press*. >> Walter, John (1739–1812)

Walter, Lucy, known as **Mrs Barlow** (c.1630–58) Mistress of Charles II, born near Haverfordwest, Dyfed. They met in 1644 when he was fleeing England during the Civil War, and she bore him a son, James, Duke of Monmouth. >> Charles II (of England); Monmouth

Walters, Julie (1950–   ) Actress, born in Birmingham, West Midlands. Her films include *Educating Rita* (1983, BAFTA), *Car Trouble* (1986), and *Killing Dad* (1989). She partnered Victoria Wood in the television series *Wood and Walters* (from 1981). >> Wood, Victoria

Walther von der Vogelweide [valter fon der **foh**glviy-duh] (c.1170–1230) German lyric poet. He wrote political, religious, and didactic poems, and a wide range of love poems.

Walton, E(rnest) T(homas) S(inton) (1903–95) Nuclear physicist, born in Dungarvan, Co Waterford, Ireland. With Cockcroft he built the first successful particle accelerator, with which they disintegrated lithium by proton bombardment (1931), the first artificial nuclear reaction using nonradioactive substances. He shared the Nobel Prize for Physics in 1951. >> Cockcroft

Walton, Izaak (1593–1683) Writer, born in Stafford, Staffordshire. Best known for his treatise on fishing and country life, *The Compleat Angler* (1653), he also wrote several biographies.

Walton, Sir William (Turner) (1902–83) Composer, born in Oldham, Lancashire. He became known through his instrumental setting of poems by Edith Sitwell, *Façade* (1923). Other works include two symphonies, concertos for violin, viola, and cello, the biblical cantata *Belshazzar's Feast* (1931), and the opera *Troilus and Cressida* (1954).

Wanamaker, Sam [**won**amayker] (1919–93) Actor and director, born in Chicago, IL. He became known for his acting and directing on stage (notably in Shakespearean productions) and in films and television. In 1970 he founded the Globe Theatre Trust in London.

Wand, John William Charles (1885–1977) Anglican clergyman and scholar, born in Grantham, Lincolnshire. He became Bishop of Bath and Wells (1943–5) and Bishop of London (1945–55), and wrote many books on Christianity and Church history.

Wang, An (1920–89) Physicist and business executive, born in Shanghai, China. A computer specialist, he invented the magnetic core memory, and founded Wang Laboratories in Boston, MA (1951). He introduced a desktop computer in 1956, the forerunner of Wang electronic desk calculators.

Wang Anshi, also spelled **Wang An-shih** (1021–86) Chinese reformer, born in Kiangsi Province, China. He was the chief councillor to Song Emperor Shenzong (ruled 1068–85).

Wanger, Walter [**wayn**jer], originally **Walter Feuchtwanger** (1894–1968) Film producer, born in San Francisco, CA. Among his major films were *Stagecoach* (1939) and *Joan of Arc* (1948).

Wang Jingwei [wang jingway] (1883–1944) Associate of Sun Yixian, born in Guangzhou (Canton), China. In 1932 he became titular head of the Nationalist Party, and after the outbreak of war with Japan, became head of a puppet regime ruling the occupied areas. >> Sun Yixian

Wang Mang (ruled 8–23 AD) Chinese minister-regent, who usurped the throne and established the Xin (Hsin) or 'New' dynasty. In AD 11 his 300 000-strong army attacked the Huns and annexed their land.

Wang Meng (1934–   ) Writer, born in Beijing. He is known for his novels, such as (trans titles) *Long Live Youth* (1953), and short stories, such as *A Night in the City* (1980).

Wang Wei [way] (699–759) Poet and painter of the T'ang dynasty, born in Ch'i-hsien, China. He is best known as one of the first to paint landscapes, which he executed in ink monochrome, and as the founder of the Southern school of painter-poets.

Wang Yangming, also found as **Wang Shouren** or **Wang Shou-jen** (1472–1529) Philosopher, civil administrator, and general, born in Yu-yao, China. His belief in the essential goodness of all, and in the human spirit as central to

the universe, influenced many later Japanese thinkers and writers.

Wankel, Felix [vangkl] (1902–   ) Mechanical engineer, the designer of a rotary engine, born in Luhran, Germany. He developed an alternative configuration to the conventional piston-and-cylinder internal combustion engine, producing a successful prototype in 1956.

Warbeck, Perkin (c.1474–99) Pretender to the English throne, born in Tournai, Belgium. In 1492 he professed to be Richard, Duke of York, the younger of Edward's two sons who were murdered in the Tower. He made an ineffectual landing in Kent (1495), then landed in Cornwall (1497), but was executed. >> Edward IV

Warburg, Otto (Heinrich) [**vah**(r)boork] (1883–1970) Biochemist, born in Freiburg Baden, Germany. Much of his work was on cellular respiration, for which he devised the *Warburg manometer* to measure oxygen uptake of living tissue. He was awarded the Nobel Prize for Physiology or Medicine in 1931.

Warburton, Peter Egerton (1813–89) Australian soldier and explorer, born in Cheshire. In 1873 he became the first to cross Australia from the S coast to C Australia via Alice Springs, and across to the De Grey R on the W coast.

Ward, Artemus >> Browne, Charles Farrar

Ward, Arthur Sarsfield >> Rohmer, Sax

Ward, Dame Barbara (Mary), Baroness Jackson of Lodsworth (1914–81) Journalist, economist, and conservationist, born in York, North Yorkshire. A popular writer on politics, economics, and ecology, her books include *Spaceship Earth* (1966) and *Only One Earth* (1972).

Ward, James (1843–1925) Psychologist and philosopher, born in Hull, Humberside. He was professor of mental philosophy and logic at Cambridge (1897–1925), his major work being *Psychological Principles* (1918).

Ward, Sir Joseph (George) (1856–1930) New Zealand prime minister (1906–12, 1928–30), born in Melbourne, Victoria, Australia. Noted for his social welfare measures, he created the world's first ministry of public health (1901) and the National Provident Fund (1910), and made provision for widows' pensions (1911).

Ward, Judith (Minna) (1949–   ) Victim of a miscarriage of justice. She was convicted and jailed for life in 1974 for an IRA bombing, but her conviction was quashed in 1992.

Ward, Sir Leslie, pseudonym **Spy** (1851–1922) Caricaturist and portrait painter, born in London. He became the regular caricaturist for *Vanity Fair* (1873–1909), picturing a wide selection of notable persons.

Ward, Mary (1585–1645) English religious reformer. She set up a society modelled on the Jesuits to provide education for women (1609), her institute later becoming the model for modern Catholic Women's Institutes.

Ward, Mary Augusta, known as **Mrs Humphry Ward** (1851–1920) Novelist, born in Hobart, Tasmania, Australia, a niece of Matthew Arnold. In London from 1881, her best-selling spiritual romance, *Robert Elsmere*, inspired the foundation of a settlement for the London poor in Tavistock Square (1897). >> Arnold, Matthew

Warfield, William (1920–   ) Baritone, born in Helena, AR. In 1950 he began a celebrated international career as a recitalist, including the lead in productions of *Porgy and Bess*.

Warhol, Andy [**waw**(r)hohl], originally **Andrew Warhola** (1927–87) Artist and film-maker, born in Pittsburgh, PA. He was a pioneer in 1961 of Pop Art, with his brightly-coloured exact reproductions of familiar everyday objects such as the famous soup-can label. His films include the 3-hour silent observation of a sleeping man, *Sleep* (1963). In the 1960s he also turned to music, founding a rock revue called The Exploding Plastic Inevitable (1966–7).

Warlock, Peter, pseudonym of **Philip Arnold Heseltine** (1894–1930) Musicologist and composer, born in London.

His works include the song cycle *The Curlew* (1920–2), the orchestral suite *Capriol* (1926), many songs, often in the Elizabethan manner, and choral works.

Warmerdam, Cornelius, nickname **Dutch Warmerdam** (1915–) Pole-vaulter, born in Long Beach, CA. Seven times the world record holder, in 1941 he was the first man to reach 15 ft (4·57 m), and in 1941 his vault of 4·78 m (1943) was not beaten for over 14 years.

Warming, Johannes (Eugenius Bülow) [vah(r)ming] (1841–1924) Botanist, a founder of plant ecology, born in Manø, Denmark. He is noted for his research on the relationships of living plants with their environment.

Warner, Glenn (Scobey), known as **Pop Warner** (1871–1954) Coach of American football, born in Springville, NY. His most successful tenures were at Carlisle Indian School (1899–1903, 1907–14), the University of Pittsburgh (1915–23), and Stanford University (1924–32), achieving a then record of 312 victories.

Warner, Jack, originally **Jack Leonard Eichelbaum** (1892–1978) Film mogul, born in London, Ontario, Canada. In partnership with his older brothers **Harry** (1881–1958), **Albert** (1884–1967), and **Sam** (1887–1927), he set up studios in 1923. The Warners were the first to introduce sound into their films, and had great success with *The Jazz Singer* (1927). Jack's later productions included *My Fair Lady* (1964) and *Camelot* (1967).

Warner, Rex (Ernest) (1905–86) Writer, Greek scholar, and translator, born in Birmingham, West Midlands. He is best known for his historical novels, such as *The Young Caesar* (1958), and for his novels, such as *Goose Chase* (1937).

Warner, Sylvia Townsend (1893–1978) Writer, born in Harrow, Greater London. Notable novels are *Lolly Willowes* (1926) and *Summer Will Show* (1936), and she also wrote volumes of poetry, essays, and short stories.

Warner, William Lloyd (1898–1970) Anthropologist, born in Redlands, CA. He is noted for his studies of Australian Aboriginal social and kinship organization, and for pioneering the field of urban anthropology.

Warnock (of Weeke), (Helen) Mary Warnock, Baroness, *née* **Wilson** (1924–) British philosopher and educationist. She has chaired several important committees of inquiry: special education (1974–8), animal experiments (1979–85), human fertilization (1982–4), higher education (1984), and teaching quality (1990).

Warr, Baron de la >> de la Warr, Baron

Warren, Sir Charles (1840–1927) British soldier and archaeologist, born in Bangor, Gwynedd. He is chiefly remembered for his archaeological exploration of Palestine, especially Jerusalem.

Warren, Earl (1891–1974) US politician and judge, born in Los Angeles, CA. Appointed chief justice of the US Supreme Court (1953–69), his notably liberal decisions included the ending of segregation in schools in *Brown v. Board of Education of Topeka* (1954). He also headed the Commission which investigated the assassination of President John F Kennedy (1963–4). >> Kennedy, J F K

Warren, Lavinia >> Stratton, Charles

Warren, Mercy Otis, *née* **Otis** (1728–1814) Historian and poet, born in Barnstable, MA, the sister of James Otis. In addition to her poetry, plays, and letters, her historical works included *Observations on the New Constitution* (1788). >> Otis, James

Warren, Robert Penn (1905–89) Writer, born in Guthrie, KY. Recipient of two Pulitzer Prizes (for fiction in 1947, for poetry in 1958), he established an international reputation with his political novel, *All the King's Men* (1943, Pulitzer; filmed 1949).

Warriss, Ben >> Jewel and Warriss

Warton, Thomas (1728–90) Poet laureate and critic, born in Basingstoke, Hampshire. Best remembered for his *History of English Poetry* (1774–81), he became poet laureate in 1785.

Warwick, John Dudley, Earl of, Duke of Northumberland [worik] (1502–53) English soldier and statesman. He was appointed joint regent for Edward VI and High Chamberlain of England (1547). He married his fourth son, Lord Guildford Dudley, to Lady Jane Grey, and proclaimed her queen on Edward's death, but was executed for treason on the accession of Mary I. >> Grey, Lady Jane

Warwick, John Rich, 2nd Earl of [worik] (1587–1658) English colonial administrator. In 1628 he obtained the patent of the Massachusetts Bay colony, and in 1635 founded the settlement of Saybrook, CT.

Warwick, Richard Neville, Earl [worik], also known as **Warwick the Kingmaker** (1428–71) English soldier and politician, who exercised great power during the Wars of the Roses. He championed the Yorkist cause, captured Henry VI, and had his cousin, Edward of York, proclaimed king as Edward IV (1461). When Edward tried to assert his independence, Warwick joined the Lancastrians, and restored Henry VI to the throne (1470). He was killed by Edward IV at Barnet. >> Edward IV; Henry VI

Washburn, Sherwood (Larned) (1911–) Biological anthropologist, born in Cambridge, MA. A leading authority on primate and human evolution, he stressed the importance of field studies of primate behaviour for modelling the behaviour of extinct hominid forms.

Washington, George (1732–99) Commander of American forces and first president of the USA, born in Bridges Creek, VA. He represented Virginia in the first (1774) and second (1775) Continental Congresses, and was given command of the American forces. He inflicted notable defeats on the enemy at Trenton and Princeton (1777), then suffered defeats at Brandywine and Germantown, but held his army together through the winter of 1777–8 at Valley Forge, and forced the surrender of Cornwallis at Yorktown in 1781. In 1787 he became president, eventually joining the Federalist Party.

Washington, Booker T(aliaferro) (1856–1915) Educationist, born a slave in Franklin Co, VA. In 1881 he was appointed principal of the newly-opened Tuskegee Institute, Alabama, and built it up into a major centre of black education.

Wasserman, August Paul von [vaserman] (1866–1925) Bacteriologist, born in Bamberg, Germany. He discovered a blood-serum test for syphilis in 1906 (the *Wasserman reaction*).

Watanabe, Kazan [watanahbay, kazan], originally **Jozei Watanabe** (1793–1841) Scholar and painter, born in Edo (now Tokyo). He is noted for his pioneering efforts to integrate Western perspective into Japanese art.

Waterhouse, Alfred (1830–1905) Architect, born in Liverpool, Merseyside. He designed the romanesque Natural History Museum in London (1873–81), and many educational buildings, and from his great use of red bricks came the name *redbrick university*.

Waterhouse, Keith (Spencer) (1929–) Writer, born in Hunslet, West Yorkshire. His novel *Billy Liar* (1959) became a best-seller, and was adapted for stage (1960) and screen (1963). He is especially known for his partnership with Willis Hall (1929–), with whom he wrote several plays, screenplays, and revues.

Waters, Ethel (1900–77) Stage actress and singer, born in Chester, PA. An eloquent performer, she is remembered for her role in *The Member of the Wedding* (1950).

Waters, Muddy, stage name of **McKinley Morganfield** (1915–83) Blues singer, composer, and guitarist, born in Rolling Fork, MI. His band had a profound influence on the white rhythm-and-blues artists of the mid-1960s.

Watkins, Dudley Dexter (1907–67) Strip cartoonist and illustrator, born in Manchester. He created *Oor Wullie* and

The Broons strips for the *Sunday Post* (1936), then *Desperate Dan* for the *Dandy* (1937), and many more.

Watkins, Vernon (Phillips) (1906–67) Poet, born in Maesteg, Mid Glamorgan. He published eight collections of verse during his lifetime, including *Ballad of Mari Lwyd* (1941) and *Affinities* (1962).

Watson, James (Dewey) (1928–) Geneticist, born in Chicago, IL. With Crick and Wilkins he helped to discover the molecular structure of DNA, sharing with them the Nobel Prize for Physiology or Medicine in 1962. >> Crick; Wilkins, Maurice

Watson, John B(roadus) (1878–1958) Psychologist, born in Greenville, SC. He became known for his behaviourist approach, which he later applied to human behaviour.

Watson, Thomas (c.1557–92) Lyric poet, born in London. He excelled in English 'sonnets', as seen in *The Tears of Fancie* (1593), and also translated classics into Latin and English.

Watson, Tom, popular name of **Thomas (Sturges) Watson** (1949–) Golfer, born in Kansas City, MO. He has won the British Open five times (1975, 1977, 1980, 1982–3), the US Open (1982), and the US Masters (1977, 1981).

Watson, Sir William (1715–87) Scientist, born in London. He was the first to investigate the passage of electricity through a rarefied gas, and did much to introduce the Linnaean system of botanical classification to Britain.

Watson-Watt, Sir Robert Alexander (1892–1973) Physicist, born in Brechin, Tayside. His work on locating aircraft led to the development of radar.

Watt, James (1736–1819) Inventor, born in Greenock, Strathclyde. He studied steam as a motive force, went into partnership with Boulton, and manufactured a new engine at Birmingham (1774). Several other inventions followed, including the design of a steam locomotive (1784). The term *horse-power* was first used by him, and the SI unit of power is named after him. >> Boulton

Watteau, (Jean) Antoine [vatoh] (1684–1721) Rococo painter, born in Valenciennes, France. His best-known works include 'Embarkation for the island of Cythera' (trans, 1717) and 'Fêtes galantes' (Scenes of Gallantry) – quasi-pastoral idylls in court dress which became fashionable in high society.

Watts, André (1946–) Pianist, born in Nuremberg, Germany. After his first world tour in 1967, he became an international favourite, primarily noted for his 19th-c repertoire.

Watts, George Frederick (1817–1904) Painter, born in London. He became known for his penetrating portraits of notabilities, 150 of which he presented to the National Portrait Gallery in 1904.

Watts, Isaac (1674–1748) Nonconformist hymnwriter, born in Southampton, Hampshire. His hymns include 'When I Survey the Wondrous Cross' and 'O God, Our Help in Ages Past'.

Waugh, Alec [waw], popular name of **Alexander Raban Waugh** (1898–1981) Novelist and travel writer, born in London, the brother of Evelyn Waugh. His novels include *Loom of Youth* (1917), and notable among his travel books is *Island in the Sun* (1975). >> Waugh, Evelyn

Waugh, (Alexander) Auberon [waw] (1939–) Journalist and novelist, the eldest son of Evelyn Waugh, born in Dulverton, Somerset. His work has appeared in such journals as the *New Statesman* and the *Spectator*, and he became editor of the *Literary Review* in 1986. >> Waugh, Evelyn

Waugh, Evelyn (Arthur St John) [waw] (1903–66) Writer, born in London. His social satirical novels include *Decline and Fall* (1928), *Vile Bodies* (1930), and *Scoop* (1938). Later books include *Brideshead Revisited* (1945) and the 'sword of honour' trilogy: *Men at Arms* (1952), *Officers and Gentlemen* (1955), and *Unconditional Surrender* (1961). >> Waugh, Alec / Auberon

Wavell, Archibald Percival Wavell, 1st Earl [wayvl] (1883–1950) British field marshal, born in Winchester, Hampshire. In 1939 he was given the Middle East Command, defeated the Italians in N Africa, but failed against Rommel, and in 1941 was transferred to India, where he became viceroy (1943). >> Rommel

Waverley, John Anderson, 1st Viscount (1882–1958) British administrator and politician, born in Eskbank, Lothian. He was home secretary and minister of home security (1939–40, the *Anderson air-raid shelter* being named after him), and became Chancellor of the Exchequer in 1943.

Wayne, Anthony, known as **Mad Anthony** (1745–96) Revolutionary soldier, born in Easttown, PA. He commanded at Ticonderoga until 1777, when he joined Washington in New Jersey. He fought at Brandywine (1777), led the attack at Germantown, carried Stony Point, and saved Lafayette in Virginia (1781). >> Lafayette; Washington, George

Wayne, John, originally **Marion Michael Morrison**, nickname **the Duke** (1907–79) Film actor, born in Winterset, IA. He achieved stardom as the Ringo Kid in *Stagecoach* (1939), and went on to make over 80 films, many in the Western genre, such as *She Wore a Yellow Ribbon* (1949), *The Man who Shot Liberty Vallance* (1962), and *True Grit* (1969, Oscar).

Waynflete, William of >> **William of Waynflete**

Weaver, Sigourney (1949–) Film actress, born in New York City. She became well known through her role as astronaut Ripley in the film *Aliens* (1979). Later films include *Ghostbusters* (1984) and the two *Aliens* sequels.

Webb, Sir Aston (1849–1930) Architect, born in London. He designed the E facade of Buckingham Palace, the Admiralty Arch, Imperial College of Science, and many other London buildings.

Webb, Beatrice >> **Webb, Sidney James**

Webb, Harry Roger >> **Richard, Cliff**

Webb, James E(dwin) (1906–92) US official and NASA administrator, born in Tally Ho, NC. He was chosen in 1961 to create in NASA an agency capable of successfully undertaking the Apollo Project.

Webb, Mary (Gladys), *née* **Meredith** (1881–1927) Novelist, born in Keighton, Shropshire. Her early novels met with little success, but *Precious Bane* (1924) became a best seller.

Webb, Matthew (1848–83) Swimmer, the first man to swim the English Channel, born in Dawley, Shropshire. In 1875 he swam from Dover to Calais in 21 hrs 45 mins.

Webb, Philip (1831–1915) Architect and designer, born in Oxford, Oxfordshire. He met William Morris, with whom he founded Morris, Marshall, Faulkner & Co (1861) and the Society for the Protection of Ancient Buildings (1877). >> Morris, William

Webb British social reformers, historians, and economists: **Sidney James Webb** (1859–1947) and **(Martha) Beatrice Webb**, *née* **Potter** (1858–1943), born in London, and Standish, Gloucestershire, respectively. Married in 1892, he joined the Fabian Society, and she became involved with social problems, publishing their classic *History of Trade Unionism* (1894), *English Local Government* (9 vols, 1906–29), and other works. Sidney later served as President of the Board of Trade (1924) and dominions and colonial secretary (1929–30).

Weber, Carl (Maria Friedrich) von [vayber] (1786–1826) Composer and pianist, born in Eutin, Germany. The founder of German Romantic opera, as seen in *Euryanthe* (1823) and *Oberon* (1826), he also wrote orchestral works, as well as piano, chamber, and church music, and many songs.

Weber, Ernst (Heinrich) [vayber] (1795–1878) Physiologist, born in Wittenberg, Germany, the brother of Wilhelm Weber. He devised a method of determining the sensitivity of the skin, and his findings were expressed mathematically by Fechner (the *Weber–Fechner Law of the Increase of Stimuli*). >> Fechner; Weber, Wilhelm

Weber, Max [vayber] (1864–1920) Sociologist and economist, born in Erfurt, Germany. His best known work is *The Protestant Ethic and the Spirit of Capitalism* (trans, 1904), a major influence on sociological theory.

Weber, Max [vayber] (1881–1961) Painter, born in Bialystok, Poland. He emigrated to the USA, where he became one of the pioneer Abstractionist painters, later abandoning this form for a distorted naturalism.

Weber, Wilhelm (Eduard) [vayber] (1804–91) Scientist, born in Wittenberg, Germany, the brother of Ernst Weber. He invented the electrodynamometer, was the first to apply the mirror and scale method of reading deflections, and with his brother wrote a notable treatise on waves. >> Weber, Ernst

Webern, Anton (Friedrich Ernst von) [vaybern] (1883–1945) Composer, born in Vienna. One of Schoenberg's first musical disciples, he made wide use of 12-tone techniques. His works include a symphony, cantatas, several short orchestral pieces, chamber music, a concerto for nine instruments, and songs.

Webster, Daniel (1782–1852) US orator, lawyer, and statesman, born in Salisbury, NH. He is best remembered for the *Webster–Ashburton Treaty* (1842) between Britain and the USA, which established the present-day boundaries between NE USA and Canada.

Webster, John (c.1580–c.1625) English playwright. He collaborated with several other writers, especially Thomas Dekker, but is best known for his two tragedies, *The White Devil* (1612) and *The Duchess of Malfi* (1623). >> Dekker

Webster, Noah (1758–1843) Lexicographer, born in Hartford, CT. He achieved fame with the first part (later known as 'Webster's Spelling Book') of *A Grammatical Institute of the English Language* (1783). His *American Dictionary of the English Language* (2 vols, 1828) was a major influence on US dictionary practice.

Webster, Tom, popular name of **Gilbert Thomas Webster** (1890–1962) Sports cartoonist and animator, born in Bilston, West Midlands. He joined the *Daily Mail* in 1919, introducing such sporting characters as Tishy the Racehorse.

Wechsler, David [weksler] (1896–1981) Psychologist, born in Lespedi, Romania. Chief psychologist at Bellevue Psychiatric Hospital (1932–67), NY, he developed the Wechsler–Bellevue Intelligence Scale (1939), devised for testing adult intelligence, and later adapted for children.

Weddell, James [wedl] (1787–1834) Navigator, explorer, and seal hunter, born in Ostend, Belgium. In a third voyage to Antarctica (1822–3), he penetrated to the point 74°15 S by 34°17 W in that part of Antarctica which was later given his name (*Weddell Sea*).

Wedderburn, Joseph (Henry Maclagan) (1882–1948) Mathematician, born in Forfar, Tayside. His work on algebra includes two fundamental theorems known by his name, one on the classification of semi-simple algebras, the other on finite division rings.

Wedekind, Frank [vaydekint] (1864–1918) Playwright, born in Hanover, Germany. He is best known for his unconventional tragedies, in which he anticipated the Theatre of the Absurd, such as *Earth Spirit* (trans, 1895) and *Pandora's Box* (trans, 1903).

Wedgwood, Dame Cicely (Veronica) (1910–) Historian, born in Stocksfield, Northumberland. A specialist in 17th-c history, her biographies include *Oliver Cromwell* (1939) and *William the Silent* (1944, James Tait Black Memorial Prize).

Wedgwood, Josiah (1730–95) Potter, born in Burslem, Staffordshire. In 1759 he opened a factory at Burslem, and a later one near Hanley, which he called 'Etruria'.

Inspired by antique models, he invented unglazed black basalt ware and blue jasper ware with raised designs in white.

Weelkes, Thomas (c.1575–1623) Madrigal composer, probably born in Elsted, Surrey. Nearly 100 of his madrigals have survived, as well as some instrumental music and fragments of his sacred music.

Weems, Mason Locke, known as **Parson Weems** (1759–1825) Clergyman, bookseller, and writer, born in Ann Arundel Co, MD. He was well-known for his uplifting sermons, moral tracts, and fictionalized biographies, notably his best-selling life of Washington. >> Washington, George

Weenix, Jan [vayniks] (1640–1719) Painter, born in Amsterdam. He was known for hunting scenes, animal subjects, and still-life paintings featuring dead gamebirds, hares, and other creatures.

Wegener, Alfred (Lothar) [vaygener] (1880–1930) Explorer and geophysicist, born in Berlin. He is the originator of the theory of continental drift (*Wegener's hypothesis*).

Weidenreich, Franz [viydnriykh] (1873–1948) Anatomist and anthropologist, born in Edenkoben, Germany. His studies of hominid fossil remains led him to an orthogenetic view of human evolution which he summarized in *Apes, Giants and Man* (1946).

Weidman, Charles (Edward), Jr [wiydman] (1901–75) Modern dancer, choreographer, and teacher, born in Lincoln, NE. In partnership with Doris Humphrey, he formed the Humphrey–Weidman school (1928–45), developing his work as a choreographer of comic and satirical works. In 1945 he founded his own school and company. >> Humphrey, Doris

Weierstrass, Karl (Theodor Wilhelm) [viyershtrahs] (1815–97) Mathematician, born in Ostenfelde, Germany. He became famous for his lectures, in which he gave a systematic account of analysis with previously unknown rigour.

Weigel, Helene [viygl] (1900–71) Actress-manager, born in Austria. She married Bertolt Brecht in 1929, and became a leading exponent of his work, taking control of the Berliner Ensemble after Brecht's death in 1956. >> Brecht

Weil, André [vayl] (1906–) Mathematician, born in Paris, the brother of Simone Weil. A founder of the Bourbaki group, he worked in number theory, algebraic geometry, and group theory. >> Weil, Simone

Weil, Simone [vayl] (1909–43) Philosophical writer and mystic, born in Paris. She taught philosophy, interspersing this with periods of manual labour to experience the working-class life, and developed a deep mystical feeling for the Catholic faith, as seen in *Waiting for God* (trans, 1950). >> Weil, André

Weill, Kurt [viyl] (1900–50) Composer, born in Dessau, Germany. He collaborated with Brecht in *The Threepenny Opera* (trans, 1928), its best-known song, 'Mack the Knife', becoming an international classic. >> Brecht; Lenya

Weinberg, Steven [wiynberg] (1933–) Nuclear physicist, born in New York City. In 1967 he produced a gauge theory that correctly predicted both electromagnetic and weak nuclear forces related to elementary particles. He shared the Nobel Prize for Physics in 1979. >> Glashow; Salam

Weinberg, Wilhelm >> Hardy, Godfrey Harold

Weinberger, Caspar (Willard) [wiynberger] (1917–) US statesman, born in San Francisco, CA. He became secretary of defense after Reagan's election victory in 1980, and developed such high-profile projects as the strategic defence initiative.

Weinberger, Jaromir [viynberger] (1896–1967) Composer, born in Prague. He wrote theatre music, orchestral works, and four operas, the most famous of which is *Schvanda the Bagpiper* (trans, 1927).

Weingartner, (Paul) Felix, Edler (Lord) **von Munzberg** [viyngah(r)tner] (1863–1942) Conductor and composer, born in Zara, Austria. His works include operas, symphonies, and his famous pamphlet *On Conducting* (trans, 1895).

Weinstock (of Bowden), Arnold, Baron [wiynstok] (1924–) Industrial executive, born in London. He was involved in property development, the radio industry, and other concerns, and became managing director of the General Electric Co in 1963.

Weir, Peter (Lindsay) (1944–) Film director, born in Sydney, New South Wales, Australia. He came to the forefront of the Australian film industry with *Picnic at Hanging Rock* (1975) and *Gallipoli* (1980). In America his films include *Dead Poets Society* (1989) and *Green Card* (1990).

Weismann, August (Friedrich Leopold) [viysman] (1834–1914) Biologist, born in Frankfurt, Germany. He is best known for his theory of *germ plasm* (1886), now recognized as a forerunner of the DNA theory.

Weiss, Peter (Ulrich) [viys] (1916–82) Playwright, filmmaker, and novelist, born in Nowawes, Germany. He became famous with his first play, usually called *Marat/Sade* (1964). He also wrote the autobiographical novels *Leave Taking* (1961) and *Vanishing Point* (1962).

Weissmuller, Johnny [wiyzmuhler], popular name of **(Peter) John** (originally **Jonas**) **Weissmuller** (1904–84) Swimmer and film-star, born in Freidorf, Romania. He won the 100 m freestyle at the 1924 and 1928 Olympics, and the 400 m in 1928. His name is widely known for his starring role in 12 Tarzan films between 1932 and 1948.

Weisz, Victor >> **Vicky**

Weizmann, Chaim (Azriel) [viytsman, khiym] (1874–1952) President of Israel (1949–52), born near Pinsk, Belarus. He helped to secure the Balfour Declaration (1917), was president of the Zionist Organization (1920–30, 1935–46), and played a major role in the establishment of the state of Israel (1948).

Weizsäcker, Richard Freiherr, Freiherr (Baron) **von** [viytseker] (1920–) President of Germany (1990–), and president of the former Federal Republic of Germany (1984–90), born in Stuttgart, Germany. He signed the treaty re-uniting East and West Germany in 1990.

Welch, Raquel, originally **Raquel Tejada** (1940–) Actress, born in Chicago, IL. She was launched as a sex symbol after her scantily clad appearance in *One Million Years BC* (1966). For her role in *The Three Musketeers* (1973) she received a Best Actress Golden Globe Award.

Welch, Robert (1929–) Silversmith and product designer, born in Hereford, Hereford and Worcester. He is best known as the designer of the stainless steel ware produced under the name 'Old Hall'.

Welensky, Sir Roy [welenskee] (1907–91) Rhodesian statesman, born in Harare, Zimbabwe (formerly, Southern Rhodesia). From 1956 to its break-up in 1963 he was prime minister of the Federation of Rhodesia and Nyasaland.

Welland, Colin (Williams) (1934–) Actor and playwright, born in Liverpool, Merseyside. In 1970, 1973, and 1974 he was voted best TV playwright in Britain, his work including *Roll on Four O'Clock* (1970) and *Kisses at Fifty* (1973). His screenplays include *Chariots of Fire* (1981).

Wellcome, Henry (1853–1936) British pharmaceutical manufacturer, born in the USA. He came to Britain and became sole owner of a pharmaceutical business in 1895, in his will setting up the Wellcome Trust for medical research.

Weller, Thomas H(uckle) (1915–) Physiologist, born in Ann Arbor, MI. With Enders and Robbins he devised techniques which made possible the development of a polio vaccine, for which they shared the Nobel Prize for Physiology or Medicine in 1954. >> Enders, John; Robbins, Frederick

Welles, Gideon (1802–78) US statesman and journalist, born in Glastonbury, CT. Opposed to slavery, he helped organize the new Republican Party, and was appointed secretary of the navy (1861–9).

Welles, (George) Orson (1915–85) Director, producer, writer, and actor, born in Kenosha, WI. In 1941 he wrote, produced, directed, and acted in *Citizen Kane*, a landmark in cinema. He played a variety of memorable stage and film roles, most notably that of Harry Lime in *The Third Man* (1949).

Wellesley, Arthur >> **Wellington, Duke of**

Wellesley (of Norragh), Richard (Colley) Wellesley, 1st Marquess (1760–1842) British administrator, born in Dangan, Co Meath, Ireland, the brother of Arthur Wellesley. While he was governor-general of India (1797–1805), British rule in India became supreme. He later became foreign minister (1809) and Lord-Lieutenant of Ireland (1821, 1833). >> Wellington, Duke of

Wellesz, Egon (Joseph) [veles] (1885–1974) Composer and musicologist, born in Vienna. His works include six operas, nine symphonies, and much choral and chamber music.

Wellhausen, Julius [velhowzn] (1844–1918) Biblical scholar, born in Hameln, Germany. He is best known for his investigations into Old Testament history and source criticism of the Pentateuch.

Wellington, Arthur Wellesley, 1st Duke of (1769–1852) British general and prime minister (1828–30), born in Dublin, Ireland, the brother of Richard Wellesley. In the Peninsular War he drove the French out of Portugal and Spain, gaining victories at Talavera (1809), Salamanca (1812), and Toulouse (1814), then routed the French at Waterloo (1815). His period as prime minister weakened the Tory Party, which split over the question of Catholic emancipation. >> Napoleon I; Wellesley, Richard

Wells, Henry (1805–78) Pioneer expressman, born in Thetford, VT. He joined with William Fargo and Daniel Dunning to found Wells & Co (1844), the first express company to operate W of Buffalo, NY. It later merged to become Wells, Fargo & Co (1852). >> Fargo

Wells, H(erbert) G(eorge) (1866–1946) Writer, born in Bromley, Kent. He achieved fame with scientific fantasies such as *The Time Machine* (1895) and *War of the Worlds* (1898), and a range of comic social novels, notably *Kipps* (1905) and *The History of Mr Polly* (1910). A member of the Fabian Society, he also wrote several socio-political works.

Wells, John (Campbell) (1936–) British actor, playwright, humorist, and director. Known for his satirical contributions to *Private Eye* and on radio and television, his plays include *Mrs Wilson's Diary* (1968) and *Anyone for Denis* (1981), in which he played the title role.

Welsh, Christopher >> **Davies, Christian**

Welty, Eudora (1909–) Writer, born in Jackson, MS. She published several collections of short stories, and five novels, mostly drawn from Mississippi life, including *The Optimist's Daughter* (1972, Pulitzer).

Wenceslaus or **Wenceslas, St** [wenseslas], known as **Good King Wenceslas** (c.903–35), feast day 28 September. Duke and patron of Bohemia, born in Stochov, Czech Republic. He encouraged Christianity in Bohemia, and was murdered by his brother, Boleslaw. He became patron saint of Bohemia and Czechoslovakia. >> Ludmila

Wenders, Wim [venderz] (1945–) Film director, born in Düsseldorf, Germany. He has won several awards at Cannes, including Best Director for *Wings of Desire* (1987).

Wendi [wendee], also spelled **Wen-ti** (ruled 179–157 BC) Han dynasty Chinese emperor and Confucian scholar, the son of Gaozu. He consolidated his father's achievements, and initiated the system of written civil service examinations (165 BC). >> Gaozu

Wendi [wendee], also spelled **Wen-ti** (541–604) First emperor (590–604) of the Chinese Sui dynasty. He conquered S China and secured the submission of Annam. He was murdered by his son and successor, Yang Guang (Yangdi). >> Yangdi

Wenner-Gren, Axel Leonard [wener gren] (1881–1961) Swedish financier and industrialist. He founded Electrolux in 1919, and undertook large-scale projects abroad. He donated vast sums for scientific research to institutions in Stockholm and New York City.

Wentworth, Charles Watson >> **Rockingham, Marquess of**

Wentworth, Thomas >> **Strafford, 1st Earl of**

Wentworth, W(illiam) C(harles) (1790–1872) Australian politician and landowner, born on Norfolk I, New South Wales, Australia. A staunch protagonist of self-government for Australia, he made this the policy of his newspaper, *The Australian* (1824).

Wenzel, Hanni [ventsl] (1956–) Alpine skier, born in Staubirnen, Germany. At the 1980 Olympics she won the gold medal in the slalom and giant slalom, and the silver in the downhill. Her total of four Olympic medals (including a bronze in 1976) is a record for any skier.

Werfel, Franz [verfel] (1890–1945) Writer, born in Prague. He wrote Expressionist poems and plays, but is best known for his novels, notably the epic *The Forty Days of Musa Dagh* (trans, 1933) and the story of the Lourdes visionary, *The Song of Bernadette* (trans, 1941).

Wergeland, Henrik Arnold [vergeland] (1808–45) Writer and patriot, born in Kristiansand, Norway. He is best known for his poetry, notably his Creation epic, *Creation, Humanity, and Desire* (trans, 1830). He became Norway's national poet.

Werner, Abraham Gottlob [verner] (1750–1817) Geologist, born in Wehrau, Germany. He was one of the first to frame a classification of rocks, and gave his name to the *Wernerian* or Neptunian theory of deposition, which he advocated in controversy with Hutton. >> Hutton, James

Wernicke, Carl [vernikuh] (1848–1905) Neurologist, born in Tarnowitz, Germany. He studied brain damage leading to loss of comprehension in aphasia, and deduced the part of the brain chiefly involved (*Wernicke's area*).

Wertheimer, Max [vairthymer] (1880–1943) Psychologist and philosopher, born in Prague. In 1912 with Koffka and Köhler he conducted experiments in perception which led to the founding of the Gestalt school of psychology. >> Husserl; Koffka; Köhler

Wesker, Arnold (1932–) Playwright, born in London. His plays include the Kahn family trilogy, *Chicken Soup with Barley, Roots*, and *I'm Talking about Jerusalem* (1958–60), *The Kitchen* (1959), and *Chips with Everything* (1962).

Wesley, Charles (1707–88) Hymn-writer and evangelist, born in Epworth, Lincolnshire, the brother of John Wesley. After an evangelical conversion in 1738, he wrote over 5500 hymns, including the well-known 'Hark, the Herald Angels Sing' and 'Love Divine, All Loves Excelling'. >> Wesley, John / Samuel

Wesley, John (1703–91) Evangelist and founder of Methodism, born in Epworth, Lincolnshire. In 1738, at a meeting in London, he experienced an assurance of salvation which led him to preach, but his zeal alarmed the parish clergy, who closed their pulpits against him. This drove him into the open air at Bristol (1739), where he founded the first Methodist chapel. His many writings included collections of hymns, sermons and journals, and a magazine. >> Wesley, Charles; Whitefield

Wesley, Samuel (1766–1837) Organist and composer, born in Bristol, Avon, the son of Charles Wesley. A famous organist of his day, his works include motets and anthems, including *In exitu Israel*. >> Wesley, Charles

Wessel, Horst [vesel] (1907–30) Martyr of the Nazi Party, born in Bielefeld, Germany. A member of the Storm Troopers, he was killed in his home, possibly by Communists. Nazi propogandists had the song 'Horst Wessel Lied' adopted as their anthem, and made a martyr of him.

Wesselmann, Tom (1931–) Painter, born in Cincinnati, OH. Most of his paintings depict overtly erotic female nudes in contemporary American environments, forming a series known as 'The Great American Nude'.

Wesson, Daniel Baird (1825–1906) Gunsmith, born in Worcester, MA. With Horace Smith (1808–93) he devised a new type of repeating mechanism for small-arms (1854), and founded the firm of Smith & Wesson.

West, Anthony >> **West, Rebecca**

West, Benjamin (1738–1820) Painter, born in Springfield, PA. He settled in London in 1763. The representation of modern instead of classical costume in his best-known picture, 'The Death of General Wolfe' (c.1771), was an innovation in English historical painting.

West, Jerry (Alan) (1938–) Basketball player, born in Cabin Creek, WV. He played for the Los Angeles Lakers (1960–74), and went on to coach and manage the club.

West, Mae (1893–1980) Actress, born in New York City. Throughout the 1930s a series of racy comedies exploited her voluptuousness, although under much pressure from censorship.

West, Morris (Langlo) (1916–) Novelist, born in Melbourne, Victoria, Australia. His books, often of a religious or moral nature, include *Children of the Sun* (1955), *The Devil's Advocate* (1959; filmed 1977), *The Tower of Babel* (1968), and *Lazarus* (1990).

West, Nathanael, pseudonym of **Nathan Wallenstein Weinstein** (1903–40) Novelist, born in New York City. He wrote four short fantasy novels, of which the best known are *Miss Lonelyhearts* (1933) and *The Day of the Locust* (1939).

West, Dame Rebecca, pseudonym of **Cicily Isabel Andrews**, *née* **Fairfield** (1892–1983) Novelist and critic, born in London. She is best known for her studies arising out of the Nuremberg war trials: *The Meaning of Treason* (1947) and *A Train of Powder* (1955). Her novels include *The Thinking Reed* (1936) and *The Birds Fall Down* (1966). Her long association with H G Wells produced a son, the critic and author Anthony West (1914–). >> Wells, H G

West, Timothy (Lancaster) (1934–) British actor and director. A member of the Royal Shakespeare and other companies, his television appearances include *Churchill and the Generals* (1979), and his films *Cry Freedom* (1986). He married Prunella Scales in 1963. >> Scales

Westbrook, Mike, popular name of **Michael John David Westbrook** (1936–) Jazz composer, bandleader, and pianist, born in High Wycombe, Buckinghamshire. He wrote extended pieces specifically for his own ensembles, ranging from trios to big bands, often in partnership with his wife, Kate (tenor horn, piccolo, voice).

Westermarck, Edward (Alexander) [vestermah(r)k] (1862–1939) Social philosopher, born in Helsinki. His *History of Human Marriage* (3 vols, 1922) was an attack on the theory of primitive promiscuity.

Westinghouse, George (1846–1914) Engineer, born in Central Bridge, NY. He was a pioneer in the use of alternating current for distributing electric power, and founded the Westinghouse Electrical Co in 1886.

Westmoreland, William C(hilds) (1914–) US soldier, born in Spartanburg Co, SC. In 1964 he became commander of US forces in Vietnam, but his 'search and destroy' strategy proved unsuccessful, and he was recalled to the USA to serve as army chief-of-staff.

Weston, Edward (1886–1958) Photographer, born in Highland Park, IL. He became recognized as a Modernist, emphasizing sharp images and precise definition in landscapes, portraits, and still-life.

Wet, Christian de >> **de Wet, Christian**

Wettach, Charles Adrien >> **Grock**

Weyden, Rogier van der [vīydn] (c.1400–64) Religious painter, born in Tournai, Belgium. He executed many portraits and altarpieces, notably 'The Descent from the Cross' (c.1435–40) and the 'Last Judgment' altarpiece (c.1450).

Weygand, Maxime [vaygã] (1867–1965) French soldier, born in Brussels. He served as chief-of-staff of the French army (1931–5), but in 1940 failed to stem the German advance, and was imprisoned by the Germans.

Weyl, Hermann [viyl] (1885–1955) Mathematician, born in Elmshorn, Germany. He made important contributions to the mathematical foundations of relativity and quantum mechanics, and to the philosophy of mathematics.

Wharton, Edith (Newbold), *née* **Jones** (c.1861–1937) Novelist and short-story writer, born in New York City. She is best known for her novels, which include *The House of Mirth* (1905), *Ethan Frome* (1911), and *The Age of Innocence* (1920, Pulitzer).

Wheatley, Denis (Yates) (1897–1977) Novelist, born in London. He produced a popular mix of satanism and historical fiction, as in *The Devil Rides Out* (1935), *The Scarlet Impostor* (1942), and *The Sultan's Daughter* (1963).

Wheatley, Phillis (c.1753–85) Poet, born in Senegal. She started writing poetry in English at the age of 13, and later published *Poems on Various Subjects, Religious and Moral* (1783).

Wheaton, Henry (1785–1848) US statesman and jurist, born in Providence, RI. He was chargé d'affaires at Copenhagen (1827–35), and minister at Berlin (1835–46), and wrote *Elements of International Law* (1836).

Wheatstone, Sir Charles (1802–75) Physicist, born in Gloucester, Gloucestershire. His inventions include a sound magnifier, for which he introduced the term *microphone*. Wheatstone's bridge, a device for the comparison of electrical resistances, was brought to notice (though not invented) by him.

Wheeler, Sir Charles (1892–1974) Sculptor, born in Codsall, Staffordshire. He is noted for his portrait sculpture and for his decorative sculptures on monuments and buildings.

Wheeler, John Archibald (1911–) Theoretical physicist, born in Jacksonville, FL. He worked with Bohr on the paper 'The Mechanism of Nuclear Fission' (1939), and helped develop the hydrogen bomb project. Later he worked with Feynman on the search for a unified field theory. >> Bohr, Niels; Feynman

Wheeler, Sir (Robert Eric) Mortimer (1890–1976) Archaeologist, born in Glasgow, Strathclyde. He carried out notable excavations in Britain and in India, and was well known for spirited popular accounts of his subject, in books and on television.

Wheeler, William (Almon) (1819–1887) US politician and businessman, born in Malone, NY. He was elected vice-president under Hayes (1877–81), but displayed little enthusiasm for the office. >> Hayes, Rutherford B

Wheldon, Sir Huw (1916–86) Broadcaster, from Wales. He joined the BBC in 1952, and was responsible for the seminal arts programme *Monitor* (1957–64). He became controller of television programmes (1965), and the BBC's managing director (1968–75).

Whewell, William [waywel] (1794–1866) Scholar, born in Lancaster, Lancashire. His works include *History of the Inductive Sciences* (1837), *Elements of Morality* (1855), and several translations.

Whichcote, Benjamin (1609–83) Philosopher and theologian, born in Stoke, Shropshire. He became Provost of King's College, Cambridge (1644–60), and is regarded as the spiritual founder of the 'Cambridge Platonists'.

Whicker, Alan (Donald) [wiker] (1925–) British broadcaster and journalist, born in Cairo. He joined the BBC (1957–68), worked on the *Tonight* programme (1957–65), and began his *Whicker's World* documentary series in 1958.

Whipple, Fred (Lawrence) (1906–) Astronomer, born in Red Oak, IA. Known for his work on the Solar System, in 1950 he suggested that comets are composed of ice and dust, and later work has confirmed this 'dirty snowball' model.

Whipple, George H(oyt) (1878–1976) Pathologist, born in Ashland, NH. He shared the Nobel Prize for Physiology or Medicine in 1934 for the discovery of liver therapy against pernicious anaemia. >> Minot; Murphy, William

Whistler, James (Abbott) McNeill (1834–1903) Artist, born in Lowell, MA. He is best known for his evening scenes ('nocturnes'), such as 'Old Battersea Bridge' (c.1872–5), and for the famous portrait of his mother (1871–2).

Whistler, Rex (John) (1905–44) British artist. He excelled in the rendering of 18th-c life, ornament, and architecture, particularly in book illustration, murals, and designs for the theatre and ballet.

Whitaker, Joseph (1820–95) Bookseller and publisher, born in London. In 1868 he started *Whitaker's Almanac*, now a publishing institution.

Whitbread, Samuel (1758–1815) British politician, the son of the founder of the famous brewing firm, Samuel Whitbread (1720–96). He became Leader of the Opposition under Pitt. >> Pitt, William (the Younger)

White, Ellen Gould, *née* **Harmon** (1827–1915) Seventh-day Adventist leader, born in Gorham, ME. A convert to Adventism in 1842, her book *Steps to Christ* sold over 20 million copies.

White, E(lwyn) B(rooks) (1899–1985) Writer, born in Mount Vernon, NY. Associated with the *New Yorker* from 1925, he also wrote three best-selling novels for children, *Stuart Little* (1945), *Charlotte's Web* (1952), and *The Trumpet of the Swan* (1970).

White, Gilbert (1720–93) Clergyman and naturalist, born in Selborne, Hampshire. *The Natural History and Antiquities of Selborne* (1789) has become an English classic.

White, John (fl.1585–93) Painter, cartographer, and colonial governor, born in England. In 1585 he was sent to Roanoke I (now in North Carolina) as artist and mapmaker, and went as governor on the second expedition (1587).

White, Leslie A(lvin) (1900–75) Cultural anthropologist, born in Salida, CO. He is best known for his theory of cultural evolution, propounded in *The Science of Culture* (1949) and *The Evolution of Culture* (1959).

White, Minor (1908–76) Photographer, born in Minneapolis, MN. Director of the photographic department in the California School of Fine Art (1947–52), he founded and edited the periodicals *Aperture* (1952) and *Image* (1953–7). >> Stieglitz; Weston

White, Patrick (Victor Martindale) (1912–90) Writer, born in London of Australian parents. His several novels include *Happy Valley* (1939) and *Voss* (1957). He also wrote short stories and plays, achieving international success with *The Tree of Man* (1954). He received the Nobel Prize for Literature in 1973.

White, Paul (Dudley) (1886–1973) Cardiologist, born in Roxburg, MA. His major textbook, *Heart Disease* (1931), secured his international reputation.

White, Pearl (Fay) (1889–1938) Film-actress, born in Green Ridge, MO. As the heroine of long-running serials, such as *The Perils of Pauline* (1914), she made a reputation as the exponent of the 'cliff-hanger' serial.

White, Stanford (1853–1906) Architect, born in New York City. A partner (1879–1906) in McKim, Mead & White, he was a prolific designer of furniture, interiors, and jewellery.

White, T(erence) H(anbury) (1906–64) Novelist, born in Bombay, India. Apart from the largely autobiographical *The Goshawk* (1951), his best work was in the form of legend and fantasy, notably his sequence of novels about King Arthur, beginning with *The Sword in the Stone* (1937).

White, William Allen (1868–1944) Editor and writer, born in Emporia, KS. He became proprietor and editor of the internationally-known Emporia *Daily* and *Weekly Gazette* in 1895, and also wrote short stories and a novel. He received a Pulitzer Prize for his editorials in 1923.

Whitefield, George [whitfeeld] (1714–70) Methodist evangelist, born in Gloucester, Gloucestershire. Associated with the Wesleys, he founded no distinct sect, but had many adherents in Wales and Scotland, who formed the Calvinistic Methodists. He played an important role in the Great Awakening in the USA. >> Wesley, Charles / John

Whitehead, A(lfred) N(orth) (1861–1947) Mathematician and Idealist philosopher, born in Ramsgate, Kent. He collaborated with Russell in writing the *Principia mathematica* (1910–13). Other more popular works include *Adventures of Ideas* (1933) and *Modes of Thought* (1938). >> Russell, Bertrand

Whitehead, William (1715–85) Poet and playwright, born in Cambridge, Cambridgeshire. He wrote tragedies, such as *The Roman Father* (1750), and a comedy, *School for Lovers* (1762). In 1757 he was appointed poet laureate.

Whitelaw, Billie (1932–) Actress, born in Coventry, West Midlands. A noted interpreter of Beckett, her performances include *Play* (1964), *Not I* (1973), and *Footfalls* (1976). Her films include *Frenzy*, *The Omen*, and *The Krays*. >> Beckett, Samuel

Whitelaw, William (Stephen Ian) Whitelaw, 1st Viscount, popularly known as **Willie Whitelaw** (1918–) British Conservative statesman, born in Nairn, Highland. He served as secretary of state for Northern Ireland (1972–3) and for employment (1973–4), home secretary (1979–83), and Leader of the House of Lords.

Whiteley, Brett [wiytlee] (1939–92) Artist, born in Sydney, New South Wales, Australia. He is known for his series of paintings of the English murderer, John Christie, his sensuous representations of the female form, and his paintings of Sydney harbour.

Whiteman, Paul (1890–1967) Jazz bandleader, born in Denver, CO. Known in his early days as 'the King of Jazz', he was the most popular bandleader of the 1920s and early 1930s, before the swing era.

Whitfield, June (Rosemary), stage name of **Mrs T J Aitchison** (1925–) Comic actress, born in London. She is known for her radio role as Eth Glum in *Take It From Here* (1953–60), a long television association with Terry Scott (1927–94) in the series *Terry and June* (1979–87), and appearances in films, such as *Carry on Nurse* (1959).

Whitgift, John (c.1530–1604) Anglican clergyman, born in Grimsby, Lincolnshire. He became Archbishop of Canterbury (1583) and a privy councillor (1586), vindicating the Anglican position against the Puritans.

Whiting, John (Robert) (1917–63) Playwright, born in Salisbury, Wiltshire. His best-known work was *The Devils* (1961), a dramatization of Huxley's *The Devils of Loudon*.

Whitlam, (Edward) Gough [gof] (1916–) Australian Labor prime minister (1972–5), born in Melbourne, Victoria, Australia. He was dismissed by the governor-general after the Opposition blocked his money bills in the upper house of the Senate - the first time the crown had so acted against an elected prime minister.

Whitley, John Henry (1866–1935) Politician, born in Halifax, West Yorkshire. He also presided over the committee that proposed (1917) industrial councils for joint consultation between employers and employees, since named *Whitley Councils*.

Whitman, Walt(er) (1819–92) Poet, born in Long Island, NY. An outstanding proponent of free verse, his major poetic work was *Leaves of Grass* (1855), which grew in successive editions to over 400 pages.

Whitney, Eli (1765–1825) Inventor, born in Westborough, MA. He invented a cotton-gin (patented 1793) for separating cotton fibre from the seeds, and developed a new system for the mass-production of firearms.

Whitney, Gertrude Vanderbilt (1875–1942) Sculptor and art patron, born in New York City. She established the Whitney Museum of American Art in New York City (1930), and is also known for her architectural sculptures, as in 'Titanic Memorial' (1931).

Whitney, Josiah Dwight (1819–96) Geologist, born in Northampton, MA, the brother of William Dwight Whitney. In 1864 he led an expedition which discovered the highest mountain in the USA (outside of Alaska) - Mt *Whitney*, in S California. >> Whitney, William Dwight

Whitney, William Dwight (1827–94) Philologist, born in Northampton, MA, the brother of Josiah Dwight Whitney. He edited numerous Sanskrit texts, and was editor of the 1864 edition of *Webster's Dictionary*. >> Whitney, Josiah Dwight

Whittaker, Robert H(arding) (1920–80) Botanist and ecologist, born in Wichita, KS. He made major contributions to ecological niche theory in his classifications of plant communities.

Whittier, John Greenleaf (1807–92) Quaker poet and abolitionist, born near Haverhill, MA. He is best known for a collection of poems and stories, *Legends of New England* (1831).

Whittington, Dick, popular name of **Richard Whittington** (c.1358–1423) English merchant, supposed to have been the youngest son of Sir William Whittington of Pauntley in Gloucestershire. He set out at 13 to find work in London, where he became Lord Mayor (1397–9, 1406–7, 1419–20).

Whittle, Sir Frank (1907–) Aviator and inventor of the British jet engine, born in Coventry, West Midlands. He developed a turbo-jet engine which successfully powered an aircraft flight in 1941.

Whitworth, Sir Joseph (1803–87) Engineer and machine-tool manufacturer, born in Stockport, Greater Manchester. He established standard screw threads and the equipment for forming and gauging them, and developed a method of casting ductile steel.

Whitworth, Kathy, popular name of **Kathrynne Ann Whitworth** (1939–) Golfer, born in Monahans, TX. The most successful woman golfer to date, she won the US Ladies Professional Golf Association Championship four times (1967, 1971, 1975, 1982).

Whorf, Benjamin Lee (1897–1941) Linguist, born in Winthrop, MA. He developed Sapir's insights into the influence of language on people's perception of the world into what became known as the *Sapir-Whorf hypothesis*. >> Sapir

Whymper, Edward (1840–1911) Mountaineer and wood-engraver, born in London. During 1860–9 he conquered several hitherto unscaled peaks of the Alps, including the Matterhorn (1865).

Whyte, William H(ollingsworth) Jr (1917–) Urban sociologist and writer, born in West Chester, PA. *The Organization Man* (1956) identified a new type of modern person – someone whose life is shaped according to the requirements of organizational employers.

Wicliffe, John >> Wycliffe, John

Widgery, John Passmore Widgery, Baron (1911–81) Judge, born in South Molton, Devon. As Lord Chief Justice of England (1971–80), he was responsible for overseeing a restructuring of the English courts.

Widor, Charles Marie (Jean Albert) [weedaw(r)] (1844–1937) Composer, born in Lyon, France. He composed 10 symphonies for the organ, as well as a ballet, chamber music, and other orchestral works.

Wieck, Clara >> **Schumann, Clara Josephine**

Wieland, Christoph Martin [veelant] (1733–1813) Writer, born near Biberach, Germany. He made the first German translation of Shakespeare (1762–6), and wrote a number of popular romances, notably *Agathon* (1766–7). His best-known work is the heroic poem 'Oberon' (1780).

Wien, Wilhelm (Carl Werner Otto Fritz Franz) [veen] (1864–1928) Physicist, born in Gaffken, Germany. By 1896 he had developed *Wien's formula* describing the distribution of energy in a radiation spectrum as a function of wavelength and temperature. He was awarded the Nobel Prize for Physics in 1911.

Wiener, Norbert [weener] (1894–1964) Mathematical logician, born in Columbia, MO. His study of the handling of information by electronic devices, based on the feedback principle, encouraged comparison between these and human mental processes in *Cybernetics* (1948) and other works.

Wiertz, Anton Joseph [veerts] (1806–65) Painter, born in Dinant, Belgium. From c.1848–50 he began to paint speculative and mystical pieces, dreams, visions, and the products of a morbid imagination.

Wiesel, Torsten N(ils) [veezel] (1924–) Neurobiologist, born in Uppsala, Sweden. He performed pioneering research on the visual cortex of the brain, and with Hubel shared the Nobel Prize for Physiology or Medicine in 1981 for their discovery of how the brain interprets the messages it receives from the eyes. >> Hubel

Wiesenthal, Simon [veezntahl] (1908–) Austrian Jewish survivor of the Nazi concentration camps, born in Buczacz, Poland. He tracked down and prosecuted former Nazis who had organized the persecution of the Jews during World War 2, notably Eichmann in 1961. >> Eichmann

Wiggin, Kate Douglas, née **Smith** (1856–1923) Novelist and kindergarten educator, born in Philadelphia, PA. She led the kindergarten movement in the USA, but is best remembered for her children's novels, notably *Rebecca of Sunnybrook Farm* (1903).

Wigglesworth, Sir Vincent (Brian) (1899–1994) Entomologist, born in Kirkham, Lancashire. He investigated the role of hormones in the growth of insects, and carried out detailed studies on the function of body-parts, often involving organ transplantation.

Wigman, Mary, originally **Marie Wiegmann** (1886–1973) Dancer, choreographer, and teacher, born in Hanover, Germany. She opened a school in Dresden in 1920, creating solo and group dances which typified German Expressionist dancing.

Wigmore, John Henry (1863–1943) Jurist, born in San Francisco, CA. His major work was *Treatise on the Anglo-American System of Evidence in Trials at Common Law* (10 vols, 1904–5), usually called *Wigmore on Evidence*.

Wigner, Eugene (Paul) [wigner] (1902–95) Physicist, born in Budapest. He is known for his contributions to the theory of nuclear physics, including the law of conservation of parity, and his theory of neutron absorption (1936) was used in building nuclear reactors. He shared the Nobel Prize for Physics in 1963.

Wilberforce, Samuel (1805–73) Anglican clergyman, born in London, the third son of William Wilberforce. Bishop of Winchester (1869), he initiated the modernization of the language of the King James Bible. >> Wilberforce, William

Wilberforce, William (1759–1833) British politician, evangelist, and philanthropist, born in Hull, Humberside. In 1788 he began the movement which resulted in the abolition of the slave trade in the British West Indies in 1807. >> Wilberforce, Samuel

Wilbur, Richard (Purdy) (1921–) Poet, born in New York City. He won acclaim for his translations as well as for his own lyrical poetry, as in *New and Collected Poems* (1988), and was named poet laureate of the USA in 1987.

Wilbye, John (1574–1638) Madrigal composer, born in Diss, Norfolk. He is known for only 66 madrigals, but these are renowned for his careful setting of literary texts, and for several translations of Italian poems.

Wilcox, Ella, née **Wheeler** (1850–1919) Writer and journalist, born in Johnstown Center, WI. Her many volumes of verse include *Drops of Water* (1872) and *Poems of Passion* (1883).

Wilde, Jane Francesca, Lady née **Elgee**, pseudonym **Speranza** (1826–96) Writer and journalist, born in Dublin, the wife of Sir William Wilde and mother of Oscar Wilde. An ardent nationalist, she contributed poetry and prose to the *Nation* from 1845 under her pseudonym. Her works on folklore include *Ancient Legends of Ireland* (1887). >> Wilde, Oscar / William

Wilde, Oscar (Fingal O'Flahertie Wills) (1854–1900) Writer, born in Dublin. Celebrated for his wit and flamboyant manner, he became a leading member of the 'art for art's sake' movement. His early work included his *Poems* (1881), the novel *The Picture of Dorian Gray* (1891), and several comic plays, notably *Lady Windermere's Fan* (1892) and *The Importance of being Earnest* (1895). *The Ballad of Reading Gaol* (1898) and *De profundis* (1905) reveal the effect of two years' hard labour for homosexual practices. >> Wilde, William

Wilde, Sir William (Robert Wills) (1815–76) Physician, born in Castlerea, Co Roscommon, Ireland, the father of Oscar Wilde. He wrote on ocular and aural surgery, invented an ophthalmoscope, and founded St Mark's Ophthalmic Hospital. >> Wilde, Jane Francesca / Oscar

Wilder, Billy, originally **Samuel Wilder** (1906–) Filmmaker, born in Sucha, Austria. His films include *Double Indemnity* (1944), *The Lost Weekend* (1945, Oscar), *Stalag 17* (1953), *Sunset Boulevard* (1955), and *The Apartment* (1960, Oscar).

Wilder, Laura, née **Ingalls** (1867–1957) Children's writer, born in Pepin, WI. When she was in her 60s she began to write down her childhood memories of the American West. Her books were popularized as the *Little House on the Prairie* television series in the 1970s.

Wilder, Thornton (Niven) (1897–1975) Writer, born in Madison, WI. His novels include *The Bridge of San Luis Rey* (1927, Pulitzer) and *The Ides of March* (1948). The plays *Our Town* (1938) and *The Skin of Our Teeth* (1942) both won Pulitzer Prizes.

Wilenski, Reginald Howard [wilenskee] (1887–1975) Art critic and art historian, born in London. His analysis of the aims and achievements of modern artists, *The Modern Movement in Art* (1927), has had considerable influence.

Wiley, Harvey Washington (1844–1930) Food chemist, born near Kent, IN. His main interest was in improving purity and reducing food adulteration, and his efforts led to the Pure Food and Drug Act of 1906.

Wilfrid or **Wilfrith, St** (634–709), feast day 12 October. Monk and bishop, born in Northumbria. As Bishop of York (c.665), he was involved in controversy over the organization of the Church in Britain, and was the first churchman to appeal to Rome to settle the issue.

Wilhelm I / II >> **William I / II** (of Germany)

Wilhelmina (Helena Pauline Maria) [wiluhmeena] (1880–1962) Queen of The Netherlands (1890–1948), born in The Hague. During World War 2 she was compelled to seek refuge in Britain, from where she encouraged Dutch resistance. In 1948 she abdicated in favour of her daughter Juliana. >> Juliana

Wilkes, Charles (1798–1877) US naval officer, born in New York City. During the Civil War he intercepted the British mail-steamer *Trent* off Cuba, and took off two Confederate commissioners accredited to France, thereby creating a risk of war with Britain (1861).

Wilkes, John (1727–97) British politician and journalist, born in London. He became an MP (1757), and attacked the ministry in his weekly journal, *North Briton* (1762–3), for which he was expelled from the house. Re-elected several times, and repeatedly expelled, he came to be seen as an upholder of press freedom.

Wilkes, Maurice (Vincent) (1913–) Computer scientist, born in Dudley, West Midlands. He became known for his pioneering work with the EDSAC (Electronic Delay Storage Automatic Calculator), the first stored-program computer (1949).

Wilkie, Sir David (1785–1841) Painter, born in Cults, Fife. His fame mainly rests on his genre painting, but he also painted portraits, and in his later years sought to emulate the richness of colouring of the old masters, choosing more elevated subjects.

Wilkins, Sir George (Hubert) (1888–1958) Polar explorer and pioneer aviator, born at Mt Bryan East, South Australia. He flew from England to Australia (1919), explored the Antarctic with Shackleton (1921–2), and made a pioneer flight from Alaska to Spitsbergen over polar ice (1928). >> Shackleton

Wilkins, John (1614–72) Anglican clergyman, born in Fawsley, Northamptonshire. He joined a group which met to further interest in science, and which became the Royal Society (1662), acting as its first secretary.

Wilkins, Maurice (Hugh Frederick) (1916–) Biophysicist, born in Pongaroa, New Zealand. His X-ray diffraction studies of DNA helped Crick and Watson determine its structure, and he shared with them the Nobel Prize for Physiology or Medicine in 1962. >> Crick; Watson, James

Wilkins, Roy (1910–81) Journalist and civil rights leader, born in St Louis, MO. In 1931 he held posts with the National Association for the Advancement of Colored People, becoming editor of the organization's newspaper, *Crisis* (1934–49).

Wilkinson, Ellen Cicely (1891–1947) Feminist and stateswoman, born in Manchester. An active campaigner for women's suffrage, she became a Labour MP in 1924, and served as minister of education (1945), the first woman to hold such an appointment.

Wilkinson, Sir Geoffrey (1921–) Inorganic chemist, born in Todmorden, West Yorkshire. In 1952 he showed that ferrocene has a molecule with an iron atom sandwiched between two carbon rings; since then, thousands of such *metallocenes* have been made and studied. He shared the Nobel Prize for Chemistry in 1973.

Wilkinson, John (1728–1808) Iron-master, born in Clifton, Cumbria. His chief invention (1774) was a cannon-boring machine, which he used to bore more accurate cylinders for steam engines.

Willaert, Adrian [wilah(r)t] (c.1490–1562) Composer, probably born in Bruges, Belgium. He composed works in many of the contemporary genres of sacred music, as well as secular chansons and madrigals.

Willard, Emma, *née* **Hart** (1787–1870) Pioneer of higher education for women, born in Berlin, CT. As founder of the Troy (NY) Female Seminary in 1821 (now the Emma Willard School), she was instrumental in the emergence of higher-level co-education.

Willard, Frances (Elizabeth Caroline) (1839–98) Temperance campaigner, born in Churchville, NY. She became secretary of the Women's Christian Temperance Union in 1874, and helped to found the International Council of Women.

William I (of England), known as **the Conqueror** (c.1028–1087) Duke of Normandy (1035–87) and the first

Norman king of England (1066–87), the illegitimate son of Duke Robert of Normandy. When Harold Godwinson took the throne as Harold II, William invaded with the support of the papacy, defeated and killed Harold at the Battle of Hastings, and was crowned king in 1066. By the time of the Domesday Book (1086), the leaders of Anglo-Saxon society S of the Tees had been almost entirely replaced by a new ruling class closely tied to William by feudal bonds. >> Edward the Confessor; Harold II; Henry I (of England)

William I (of Germany), Ger **Wilhelm** (1797–1888) King of Prussia (1861–88) and first German emperor (1871–88), born in Berlin, the second son of Frederick William III. He placed Bismarck at the head of the ministry, and was victorious against Denmark (1864), Austria (1866), and France (1871). >> Bismarck; Frederick William III

William I (of the Netherlands), **Prince of Orange**, known as **William the Silent** (1533–84) First of the hereditary stadholders of the United Provinces of the Netherlands (1572–84), born in Dillenburg, The Netherlands. In 1568 he took up arms against Spain, and became stadholder of the Northern provinces, united in the Union of Utrecht (1579). He was assassinated by a Spanish agent. >> Henry II (of France)

William II (of England), known as **William Rufus** (c.1056–1100) King of England (1087–1100), the second surviving son of William the Conqueror. His main goal was the recovery of Normandy from his elder brother Robert Curthose. He also led expeditions to Wales (1095, 1097), and came to exercise a controlling influence over Scottish affairs. He was killed by an arrow while hunting in the New Forest. >> Robert Curthose; William I (of England)

William II (of Germany), Ger **Wilhelm**, known as **Kaiser Wilhelm** (1859–1941) German Emperor and King of Prussia (1888–1918), born in Potsdam, Germany, the eldest son of Frederick III and Victoria, daughter of Britain's Queen Victoria. He dismissed Bismarck (1890), and began a long period of personal rule, displaying a bellicose attitude in international affairs. During World War 1 he became a figurehead, and later abdicated. >> Bismarck

William III (of Great Britain), known as **William of Orange** (1650–1702) Stadholder of the United Provinces (1672–1702) and King of Great Britain (1689–1702), born in The Hague, the son of William II of Orange by Mary, the eldest daughter of Charles I of England. In 1677 he married his cousin, Mary. Invited to redress the grievances of the country, he landed at Torbay in 1688, and forced James II to flee, defeating his supporters at Dunkeld (1689) and the Boyne (1690). >> Anne; James II (of England); Mary II

William IV, known as **the Sailor King** (1765–1837) King of Great Britain and Ireland, and King of Hanover (1830–7), born in London, the third son of George III. He was the last monarch to use his powers to dismiss a ministry with a parliamentary majority when he sacked Melbourne in 1834. >> George III; Melbourne, Viscount

William of Auvergne [ohvairn], also called **William of Paris** (c.1180–1249) Philosopher and theologian, born in Aurillac, France. His chief work is the monumental *The Divine Teaching* (trans, 1223–40), in which he integrated classical Greek and Arabic philosophy with Christian theology.

William of Auxerre [ohsair] (c.1150–1231) Theologian and philosopher, born in Auxerre, France. His *Golden Compendium on the Four Books of Sentences* (trans title) is a commentary on early and mediaeval Christian thought.

William of Malmesbury [mahmzbree] (c.1090–c.1143) English chronicler and Benedictine monk, the librarian of Malmesbury Abbey, Wiltshire. His main works include *Gesta regum anglorum*, a general history of England from the coming of the Anglo-Saxons.

William of Ockham or **Occam** [okam] (c.1285–c.1349) Scholastic philosopher, born in Ockham, Surrey. He is especially known for his use of the principle of parsimony (*Ockham's razor*): 'Do not multiply entities beyond necessity'.

William of Tyre (c.1130–86) Chronicler and clergyman, born in Palestine of French parents. Archbishop of Tyre (1175), his main work, *History of Deeds in Foreign Parts* (trans title), deals with the history of Palestine from 614 to 1184.

William of Waynflete (c.1395–1486) English statesman and clergyman. As a Lancastrian he played an important role as adviser to Henry VI in the Wars of the Roses, and was Lord Chancellor (1456–60). >> Henry VI

William of Wykeham or **Wickham** [wikam] (1324–1404) English statesman and clergyman, born in Wickham, Hampshire. He was appointed Bishop of Winchester (1367), and was twice Chancellor of England (1367–71, 1389–91).

Williams, Bernard (Arthur Owen) (1929–) English philosopher. His notable works in moral philosophy include *Morality: an Introduction to Ethics* (1972), and he chaired the Committee on Obscenity and Film Censorship which produced the *Williams Report* (1979). He was married (1955–74) to Shirley Williams. >> Williams, Shirley

Williams, Betty >> **Corrigan-Maguire, Mairead**

Williams, (George) Emlyn (1905–87) Playwright and actor, born in Mostyn, Clwyd. He achieved success as a playwright with *A Murder Has Been Arranged* (1930) and *Night Must Fall* (1935), featured in several films, and gave widely acclaimed readings from Dickens and Dylan Thomas.

Williams, Edward, known as **Iolo Morganwg** (1747–1826) Poet and antiquary, born in Llancarfan, South Glamorgan. He wrote poetry in Welsh and English, and also published poems and cultural material purportedly from earlier periods, which were in fact his own work.

Williams, Fred(erick Ronald Williams) (1927–82) Painter and etcher, born in Richmond, Victoria, Australia. A significant painter of the Australian landscape, he gained an international reputation with his 1977 exhibition *Landscapes of a Continent* in New York City.

Williams, Sir Frederic (Calland) (1911–77) Electrical engineer, born in Manchester. He is best known for his development of the *Williams tube*, the first successful electrostatic random access memory for the digital computer.

Williams, Sir George (1821–1905) Social reformer, born in Dulverton, Somerset. In 1844 he founded the Young Men's Christian Assocation (YMCA).

Williams, Hank, popular name of **Hiram King Williams** (1923–53) Singer and guitarist, born in Georgiana, AL. His many hit records include 'Lovesick Blues' (1949) and 'Hey, Good Lookin''. His son, **Hank Williams Jr** (1949–), continues as a successful country singer and songwriter.

Williams, John (1796–1839) Missionary, born in London. Joining the London Missionary Society, he worked in the S Pacific, and wrote *Narrative of Missionary Enterprises in the South Seas* (1837).

Williams, John (Christopher) (1942–) Guitarist, born in Melbourne, Victoria, Australia. Several modern composers have written works for him. In England from 1952, he founded a jazz and popular music group known as Sky (1979–84), and later formed the contemporary music group Attacca.

Williams, J(ohn) P(eter) R(hys) (1949–) Rugby union player and physician, born in Bridgend, Mid Glamorgan. He played rugby for London Welsh and Bridgend, as well as for Wales (captain, 1978) and the British Lions. He is the most capped Welshman, with 55 appearances.

Williams, Kenneth (1926–87) Actor and comedian, born in London. He starred in the radio series *Round the Horne* and was later a regular on *Just a Minute*. He also appeared in several of the *Carry On* series of comedy films, his affected style of speech making him instantly recognizable.

Williams, Mary Lou (1910–81) Jazz pianist, arranger, and composer, born in Atlanta, GA. Her outstanding qualities as an arranger brought her work from Ellington, Goodman, and others. >> Ellington; Goodman, Benny

Williams, Raymond (1921–88) Social historian, critic, and novelist, born in Pandy, Gwent. His *Culture and Society* (1958) established his reputation as a cultural historian. Active in New Left intellectual movements, he was increasingly identified with Welsh nationalism in his novels, such as *The Fight for Manod* (1979).

Williams, Robley Cook (1908–) Biophysicist, born in Santa Rosa, CA. From the 1940s he was concerned with electron microscopy, and with Wyckoff devised a metal-shadowing technique that could be used for sensitive biological materials such as viruses. >> Wyckoff

Williams, Roger (c.1604–83) Colonist, born in London. An extreme Puritan, he emigrated to New England in 1630, founded the city of Providence (1636), and became first president of Rhode Island (1654–8).

Williams, Shirley (Vivien Teresa Brittain) Williams, Baroness, *née* **Catlin** (1930–) British stateswoman, born in London. She was Labour secretary of state for prices and consumer protection (1974–6) and for education and science (1976–9). She became a co-founder of the Social Democratic Party in 1981, its first elected MP (1981–3), and its president (1982–7). >> Brittain; Williams, Bernard

Williams, Ted, popular name of **Theodore Samuel Williams** (1918–) Baseball player, born in San Diego, CA. An outstanding hitter, he played with the Boston Red Sox (1939–60), and was twice named Most Valuable Player.

Williams, Tennessee, pseudonym of **Thomas Lanier Williams** (1911–83) Playwright, born in Columbus, MS. His plays, mainly set in the Deep South, include *A Streetcar Named Desire* (1947, Pulitzer), *Cat on a Hot Tin Roof* (1955, Pulitzer), *Suddenly Last Summer* (1958), and *Night of the Iguana* (1961). He also wrote short stories, essays, poetry, and two novels.

Williams, William Carlos (1883–1963) Writer, born in Rutherford, NJ. Especially known for his 'personal epic' poem, *Paterson* (5 vols, 1946–58), he also wrote plays, essays, and a trilogy of novels. He was awarded a posthumous Pulitzer Prize for *Pictures from Brueghel, and Other Poems* (1962).

Williamson, David Keith (1942–) Playwright, born in Melbourne, Victoria, Australia. His plays include *Don's Party* (1971), *The Club* (1977), and *Brilliant Lies* (1993), and he also wrote the scripts for the films *Gallipoli* (1981) and *Phar Lap* (1983).

Williamson, Henry (1895–1977) Writer, born in Bedfordshire. He is best known for his classic nature stories, such as *Tarka the Otter* (1927).

Williamson, James Cassius (1845–1913) Theatrical producer, born in Mercer, PA. He settled in Australia in 1879, where he co-founded the theatrical organization popularly known as 'The Firm', which was to dominate Australian theatre until 1976.

Williamson, Malcolm (Benjamin Graham Christopher) (1931–) Composer, born in Sydney, New South Wales, Australia. His compositions include the operas *Our Man in Havana* (1963) and *The Red Sea* (1972), as well as a wide variety of orchestral, vocal, choral, and other works.

Williamson, William Crawford >> **Scott, Dunkinfield Henry**

Willibald [wilibawld] (700–86), feast day 11 July. Clergyman and missionary, born in Wessex, England, the brother of St Walburga. He was sent to Germany to assist St Boniface, who made him the first Bishop of Eichstätt. >> Boniface; Walburga

Willibrord, St [wilibraw(r)d] (c.658–739), feast day 7 November. Anglo-Saxon missionary, born in Northumbria. In c.690 he was sent as missionary to Friesland, where he became Archbishop of the Frisians (695).

Willis, Norman (David) (1933–) Trade union leader, born in Ashford, Greater London. He was appointed assistant general-secretary of the Trades Union Congress (1974), and later became general-secretary (1984–93).

Willis, Thomas (1621–75) Physician, one of the founders of the Royal Society (1662), born in Great Bedwyn, Wiltshire. He was a pioneer in the study of the anatomy of the brain, and discovered the *circle of Willis*.

Willkie, Wendell (1892–1944) Businessman and US presidential candidate, born in Elwood, IN. He was recruited as the Republican candidate against Roosevelt in 1940. His 1943 book, *One World*, was a best-seller. >> Roosevelt, Franklin D

Wills, Helen (Newington), married names **Moody** and **Roark** (1905–) Tennis player, born in Berkeley, CA. She won the Wimbledon singles title eight times in nine attempts (1927–30, 1932–3, 1935, 1938), and in all won 31 Grand Slam events.

Wills, William John (1834–61) Explorer, born in Devon. He accompanied Burke's ill-fated expedition to the N of Australia, on which he died of starvation. >> Burke, Robert O'Hara

Willstätter, Richard [vilshteter] (1872–1942) Organic chemist, born in Karlsruhe, Germany. He did notable work on natural product chemistry, especially on plant pigments, for which he was awarded the Nobel Prize for Chemistry in 1915.

Willumsen, Jens Ferdinand (1863–1958) Painter and sculptor, born in Copenhagen. His best-known painting is 'After the Storm' (1905), and as a sculptor his masterpiece is the 'Great Relief'.

Wilmot, John >> **Rochester, 2nd Earl of**

Wilson, Alexander (1766–1813) Ornithologist, born in Paisley, Strathclyde. He emigrated to the USA in 1794, and completed the first seven volumes of the illustrated *American Ornithology* (1808–14). *Wilson's storm-petrel* and *phalarope* were named after him.

Wilson, Sir Angus (Frank Johnstone) (1913–91) Writer, born in Bexhill, East Sussex. His works include the short stories *The Wrong Set* (1949), the novels *Anglo-Saxon Attitudes* (1956) and *The Old Men at the Zoo* (1961), and the play *The Mulberry Bush* (1955).

Wilson, August (1945–) Playwright, born in Pittsburgh, PA. His plays *Fences* (1987) and *The Piano Lesson* (1988), both won Pulitzer Prizes.

Wilson, Charles Edward, known as **Electric Charlie** (1886–1972) Businessman, born in New York City. He ended a 51-year career with General Electric as its president (1940–50).

Wilson, Charles E(rwin), known as **Engine Charlie** (1890–1961) Businessman and US statesman, born in Minerva, OH. He was vice-president of General Motors (1928–41), then president (1941–52). As Eisenhower's outspoken secretary of defence (1953–7), he angered the military with severe cuts in the defence budget.

Wilson, C(harles) T(homson) R(ees) (1869–1959) Physicist, born in Glencorse, Lothian. His major achievement was to devise the *Wilson cloud chamber* method for observing the track of alpha particles and electrons. He shared the Nobel Prize for Physics in 1927.

Wilson, Colin (Henry) (1931–) Novelist and writer on philosophy, sociology, and the occult, born in Leicester, Leicestershire. His books include *The Outsider* (1956), *The Mind Parasites* (1966), and *Poltergeist!* (1981). His psychic interests brought him status as a cult figure in the 1980s.

Wilson, Edmund (1895–1972) Literary and social critic, born in Red Bank, NJ. He was a prolific and wide-ranging author, producing several studies on aesthetic, social, and political themes, as well as verse, plays, travel books, and historical works.

Wilson, Edmund (Beecher) (1856–1939) Zoologist, born in Geneva, IL. He contributed greatly to cytology and embryology, and wrote *The Cell in Development and Inheritance* (1925).

Wilson, Edward A(drian) (1872–1912) Physician, naturalist, and explorer, born in Cheltenham, Gloucestershire. In 1910 he accompanied Scott's expedition to the Antarctic as chief of scientific staff, and died with the others on the return journey. >> Scott, R F

Wilson, Edward (Osborne) (1929–) Biologist, born in Birmingham, AL. His book *Sociobiology: the New Synthesis* (1975), virtually founded the subject of sociobiology, and he also wrote *On Human Nature* (1978, Pulitzer).

Wilson (of Rievaulx), (James) Harold Wilson, Baron (1916–95) British prime minister (1964–70, 1974–6), born in Huddersfield, West Yorkshire. He was President of the Board of Trade (1947–51), and in 1963 succeeded Gaitskell as Leader of the Labour Party. His economic plans were badly affected by a balance of payments crisis, leading to severe restrictive measures. Following his third general election victory, he resigned as Labour leader in 1976.

Wilson, Henry, originally **Jeremiah Jones Colbath** (1812–75) US politician and abolitionist, born in Farmington, NH. He represented Massachusetts in the US Senate (1855–73), and became Grant's second-term vice-president, but died in office. >> Grant, Ulysses S

Wilson, Sir Henry Hughes (1864–1922) British field marshal, born in Edgeworthstown, Ireland. He entered World War 1 as director of military operations (1914), and later became Chief of the Imperial General Staff (1918–22).

Wilson (of Libya and of Stowlangtoft), Henry Maitland Wilson, Baron (1881–1964) British field marshal, born in London. He led the initial British advance in Libya (1940–1) and the unsuccessful Greek campaign (1941), and became commander-in-chief Middle East (1943) and supreme allied commander in the Mediterranean theatre (1944).

Wilson, J(ohn) Dover (1881–1969) Shakespearean scholar, born in Mortlake, Surrey. He was editor of the New Shakespeare series (1919–66), and his works include *Life in Shakespeare's England* (1911).

Wilson, James (1742–98) Political ideologist, born in Carskerdo, Fife. He emigrated to Philadelphia in 1765, and was a delegate to the Constitutional Congress (1787), playing a major role in formulating the US Constitution.

Wilson, John Burgess >> **Burgess, Anthony**

Wilson, Kemmons (1913–) US hotelier. He devised the Holiday Inn motel, opening the first one in Memphis in 1952.

Wilson, Kenneth (Geddes) (1936–) Theoretical physicist, born in Waltham, MA. He applied mathematical methods to the understanding of the magnetic properties of atoms, and later used similar methods in the study of phase transitions between liquids and gases, and in alloys. He was awarded the Nobel Prize for Physics in 1982.

Wilson, Lanford (1937–) Playwright, born in Lebanon, MO. His works include *The Hotel Baltimore* (1972), *The Fifth of July* (1978), and *Tally's Folly* (1979, Pulitzer).

Wilson, Peter (1913–84) British auctioneer. In 1958 he became chairman of Sotheby's, and introduced new techniques, such as selling by satellite link simultaneously in New York City and London.

Wilson, Richard (1714–82) Landscape painter, born in Penygroes, Powys. He began as a portrait painter, but after a visit to Italy (1752–6) turned to landscapes.

Wilson, Robert (1941–) Theatre, director and designer, born in Waco, TX. In contrast with traditional theatre, he mixes a combination of movement, contemporary music, and exciting imagery, often in very long performances, as in *The CIVIL WarS* (begun in 1984).

Wilson, Robert Woodrow (1936-) Physicist, born in Houston, TX. With Penzias he detected in 1964 an unusual radio noise background which was discovered to be residual radiation, supporting the 'big bang' theory of creation. They shared the Nobel Prize for Physics in 1978. >> Penzias

Wilson, Roy(ston Warner Wilson) (1900-65) Strip cartoonist, born in Kettering, Northamptonshire. He worked from 1930 on *Steve and Stumpy* (for *Butterfly*) and other strips, notably *George the Jolly Gee-Gee* (for *Radio Fun*, 1938).

Wilson, Teddy, popular name of **Theodore Shaw Wilson** (1912-86) Pianist, bandleader, and arranger, born in Austin, TX. He was one of the most influential stylists of the swing era of the late 1930s.

Wilson, William Griffith, known as **Bill W** (1895-1951) US founder of Alcoholics Anonymous. An excessive drinker on the verge of ruin, following a religious experience (1934), he successfully counselled a fellow-sufferer, Robert Holbrook Smith (1879-1950, known as 'Dr Bob S'), and instituted the well-known self-help group.

Wilson, (Thomas) Woodrow (1856-1924) US Democratic statesman and 28th president (1913-21), born in Staunton, VA. His administration saw the prohibition and women's suffrage amendments to the constitution, America's participation in World War 1, his peace plan proposals (the *Fourteen Points*), and his championship of the League of Nations. He won the Nobel Peace Prize in 1919.

Wilton, Marie >> Bancroft, Squire

Winant, John [wiynant] (1889-1947) US politician and government official, born in New York City. Although a Republican, he was recognized as sympathetic to labour, and in 1935 was appointed to the International Labor Organization in Geneva, becoming its director in 1939.

Winchester, Oliver (Fisher) (1810-80) Gun manufacturer, born in Boston, MA. He owned the Winchester Repeating Arms Co (1867), patenting a design for a repeating rifle (1860) which was the forerunner of the famous *Winchester rifle*.

Winchilsea, Anne Finch, Countess of, *née* **Kingsmill** (1661-1721) Poet, born in Sidmonton, Hampshire. Her works include a Pindaric ode, 'The Spleen' (1701), and *Miscellany Poems* (1713).

Winckelmann, Johann (Joachim) [vingkelmann] (1717-68) Archaeologist and art historian, born in Stendal, Germany. His works include the pioneering study, *History of the Art of Antiquity* (trans, 1764).

Windelband, Wilhelm >> Rickert, Heinrich

Windsor, Duke of >> Edward VIII

Windsor, Lady Davina >> Gloucester, Richard, Duke of

Windsor, Prince Edward >> Edward, Prince

Windsor, Lord Frederick >> Kent, Prince Michael of

Windsor, Lady Gabriella >> Kent, Prince Michael of

Windsor, George Philip Nicholas >> Kent, Edward, Duke of

Windsor, Lady Helen >> Kent, Edward, Duke of

Windsor, Princess Margaret >> Margaret, Princess

Windsor, Lord Nicholas >> Kent, Edward, Duke of

Windsor, Lady Rose >> Gloucester, Richard, Duke of

Windsor, (Bessie) Wallis, Duchess of, *née* **Warfield**, previous married names **Spencer** and **Simpson** (1896-1986) Wife of Edward VIII, born in Blue Ridge Summit, PA. Well-known in London society, she met Edward, the Prince of Wales, who made clear his intention to marry her, and was forced to abdicate. They married in 1937, subsequently living abroad. >> Edward VIII

Wingate, Orde (Charles) (1903-44) British general, born in Naini Tal, India. In Burma (1942) he organized the Chindits - specially trained jungle-fighters drawn from British, Ghurka, and Burmese forces.

Winifred, St (7th-c), feast day 3 November. Legendary Welsh saint, a noble British maiden, beheaded by Prince Caradog for repelling his unholy proposals. The legend relates that her head rolled down a hill, and where it stopped a spring gushed forth – famous still as a place of pilgrimage, Holywell in Clwyd.

Winkelried, Arnold von [vingkelreed] (?-1386) Swiss patriot, knight of Unterwalden. At the Battle of Sempach (1386), when the Swiss failed to break the line of Austrian spears, he is said to have grasped as many pikes as he could reach, buried them in his bosom and bore them into the earth. His comrades rushed into the breach, and gained a decisive victory.

Winkler, Hans-Günther [vingkler] (1926-) Show jumper, born in Wuppertal-Barmen, Germany. He is the only man to have won five Olympic gold medals at show jumping: the team golds in 1956, 1960, 1964, and 1972, and the individual title on *Halla* in 1956.

Winner, Michael (Robert) (1935-) Film producer and director, born in London. He has written the screenplay for many of his films, which include *The Big Sleep* (1977), *Death Wish* (and its sequels), and *Bullseye!* (1990).

Winslow, Edward (1595-1655) Colonist, one of the Pilgrim Fathers, born in Droitwich, Worcestershire. He sailed in the *Mayflower* in 1620, and from 1624 was assistant governor or governor of the Plymouth colony.

Wint, Peter de (1784-1849) Water-colourist, born in Stone, Staffordshire. His fame rests on his watercolour illustrations of English landscape, architecture, and country life, such as 'The Hay Harvest' and 'Richmond Hill'.

Winterhalter, Franz Xaver [vinterhalter] (1806-73) Painter, born in Menzenschwand, Germany. In 1834 he went to Paris, where he became the fashionable artist of his day, painting many royal figures.

Winters, (Arthur) Yvor (1900-68) Critic and poet, born in Chicago, IL. He is remembered as an irascible anti-Expressionist critic, his books including *In Defence of Reason* (1947), *The Function of Criticism* (1957), and *Collected Poems* (1952).

Winthrop, John (1588-1649) Colonist, born in Edwardstone, Suffolk, UK. He was appointed governor of Massachusetts colony in 1629, and was a major influence in forming the political institutions of the Northern states of America. >> Winthrop, John (1606-76)

Winthrop, John (1606-76) Colonist, born in Groton, Suffolk, the son of John Winthrop. In 1635 he went to Connecticut, and was elected governor there. >> Winthrop, John (1588-1649) / (1639-1707)

Winthrop, John (1639-1707) Soldier and colonial administrator, born in Ipswich, MA, the son of John Winthrop. He settled in Connecticut in 1663, and was governor of the colony from 1698. >> Winthrop, John (1606-76)

Wirén, Dag Ivar [viren] (1905-86) Swedish composer. His large output includes five symphonies, five string quartets, a variety of large-scale orchestral works, and film and theatre music. His most popular work is the *Serenade for Strings* (1937).

Wirth, Philip Peter Jacob [werth] (1864-1937) Circus proprietor, born in Victoria, Australia. His father and his three brothers formed their own circus troupe (1878), and after a world tour established permanent bases in Sydney and Melbourne.

Wisdom, (Arthur) John (Terence Dibben) (1904-93) British philosopher. Profoundly influenced by Wittgenstein, his chief works include *Other Minds* (1952) and *Paradox and Discovery* (1965). >> Wittgenstein

Wisdom, Norman (1918-) Comedian, born in London. He made his stage debut in 1946, and appeared in variety throughout Britain as an inadequate but well-meaning character in ill-fitting clothes.

Wise, Ernie >> Morecambe, Eric

Wiseman, Nicholas (Patrick Stephen), Cardinal (1802–65) Roman Catholic clergyman, born in Seville, Spain, of Irish parents. His appointment as the first Archbishop of Westminster and a cardinal (1850) led to the passing of the Ecclesiastical Titles Assumption Act.

Wishart, George [wishert] (c.1513–46) Reformer and martyr, born in Pitarrow, Grampian. He preached the Lutheran doctrine in several towns, and was arrested and burned at St Andrews. One of his converts was John Knox. >> Knox, John

Wister, Owen (1860–1938) Writer, born in Philadelphia, PA. He won fame with his innovative novel of cowboy life in Wyoming, *The Virginian* (1902). His other major work was *Roosevelt: The Story of a Friendship, 1880–1919* (1930).

Witherspoon, John (1723–94) Clergyman, born in Gifford, Lothian. In 1768 he emigrated to America. A representative of New Jersey to the Continental Congress (1776–82), he was the only clergyman to sign the American Declaration of Independence (1776).

Witt, Jan de >> **de Witt, Jan**

Witt, Katerina [vit] (1965–) Figure skater, born in Karl-Marx-Stadt, Germany. She was world champion (1984–5, 1987–8) and Olympic champion (1984, 1988).

Wittgenstein, Ludwig (Josef Johann) [witgenstiyn], Ger [vitgenshtiyn] (1889–1951) Philosopher, born in Vienna. He produced major works on the philosophy of language, notably *Tractatus logico-philosophicus* (1921) and *Philosophical Investigations* (trans, 1953), in which he studies the 'language games' whereby language is given its meaning in actual use.

Wittig, Georg [vitik] (1897–1987) Organic chemist, born in Berlin. He developed a technique (1953) for the synthesis of natural substances, allowing the economical industrial production of Vitamin A and prostaglandins. He shared the Nobel Prize for Chemistry in 1979.

Wittkower, Rudolf [witkuhver] (1901–71) Architectural historian, born in Berlin. His major scholarly contributions include *Architectural Principles in the Age of Humanism* (1949) and his distinction between Mannerism and Baroque architecture.

Witz, Konrad [vits] (c.1400–c.1445) Painter, born in Rottweil, Germany. The only signed and dated painting of his which survives is 'Christ Walking on the Water' (1444, Geneva), remarkable because it is set on L Geneva - the earliest known recognizable landscape in European art.

Wodehouse, Sir P(elham) G(renville) [wudhows] (1881–1975) Writer, born in Guildford, Surrey. A prolific writer, he produced a succession of over 100 novels, as well as many short stories, sketches, librettos, and lyrics. His best-known works fall within his 'country house' period, involving the creation of Bertie Wooster and Jeeves, as in *Quick Service* (1940) and *The Mating Season* (1949).

Wogan, Terry [wohgn], popular name of **Michael Terence Wogan** (1938–) Broadcaster and writer, born in Limerick, Ireland. His television shows include *Blankety Blank* (1977–81), the annual Eurovision Song Contests, and an early evening chat-show (1982–92), but he is also well known for his radio series.

Wöhler, Friedrich [voeler] (1800–82) Chemist, born near Frankfurt, Germany. He isolated aluminium (1827) and beryllium (1828), and discovered calcium carbide. His synthesis of urea from ammonium cyanate (1828) was the first synthesis of an organic compound from an inorganic substance.

Wojtyła, Karol Jozef >> **John Paul II**

Wolf, Hugo (Philipp Jakob) [volf] (1860–1903) Composer, born in Windischgraz, Austria. From 1888 he composed c.300 songs, settings of poems by Goethe and others, the opera *Der Corregidor* (1895), and other works.

Wolf, Max(imilian Franz Joseph Cornelius) (1863–1932) Astronomer, born in Heidelberg, Germany. He invented the photographic method of discovering asteroids, and with Barnard was the first to appreciate 'dark' nebulae in the sky. >> Barnard, Edward

Wolfe, Charles (1791–1823) Poet, born in Dublin. He is remembered for his poem 'The Burial of Sir John Moore' (1817).

Wolfe, James (1727–1759) British soldier, born in Westerham, Kent. Sent to Canada during the Seven Years' War (1756–63), in 1758 he commanded in the famous capture of Quebec (1759), where he was killed. >> Montcalm

Wolfe, Thomas (Clayton) (1900–38) Writer, born in Asheville, NC. He achieved success with his first novel, *Look Homeward, Angel* (1929). Some of his best work is to be found in the stories in *From Death to Morning* (1935).

Wolfe, Tom, popular name of **Thomas Kennerley Wolfe** (1931–) Journalist, pop-critic, and novelist, born in Richmond, VA. A proponent of New Journalism, his books include *The Electric Kool-Aid Acid Test* (1968) and the best selling novel, *The Bonfire of the Vanities* (1988).

Wolfe-Barry, John >> **Barry, Charles**

Wolfenden, John (Frederick) Wolfenden, Baron [wulfenden] (1906–1985) Educationist, born in Halifax, West Yorkshire. He was best known for his government investigation of homosexuality and prostitution (the *Wolfenden Report*, 1957).

Wolff, Christian, Freiherr (Baron) **von** [volf] (1679–1754) Philosopher, mathematician, and scientist, born in Breslau, Germany. He is best known for popularizing the philosophy of Leibniz, and he is usually regarded as the German spokesman of the Enlightenment in the 18th-c. >> Leibniz

Wolff, Gustav William >> **Harland, Edward James**

Wolf-Ferrari, Ermanno [volf ferahree] (1876–1948) Composer, born in Venice, Italy. His best-known works are *The School for Fathers* (trans, 1906) and *Susanna's Secret* (trans, 1909). He also composed choral and chamber works, and music for organ and piano.

Wölfflin, Heinrich [voelflin] (1864–1945) Art historian, born in Winterthur, Switzerland. A founder of modern art history, he pioneered the 'scientific' method of formal analysis, as in *Principles of Art History* (1915).

Wolfit, Sir Donald [wulfit] (1902–68) Actor-manager, born in Newark, Nottinghamshire. He formed his own company in 1937, and became known for his Shakespeare performances, also appearing in several films.

Wolfram von Eschenbach [volfram fon eshenbakh] (c.1170–c.1220) Poet, born near Anspach, Germany. He is best known for his epic *Parzival* (c.1200–10), which introduced the theme of the Holy Grail into German literature.

Wolfson, Sir Isaac (1897–1991) Businessman and philanthropist, born in Glasgow, Strathclyde. In 1955 he set up the Wolfson Foundation for the advancement of health, education, and youth activities in the UK and the Commonwealth.

Wollaston, William Hyde (1766–1828) Chemist, born in East Dereham, Norfolk. He developed a method, now basic to powder metallurgy, of making malleable platinum.

Wollstonecraft, Mary [wulstonkraft], married name **Godwin** (1759–97) Feminist, born in London. In 1792 she wrote *Vindication of the Rights of Woman*, advocating equality of the sexes. After an earlier marriage to Gilbert Imlay (1754–1828), she married William Godwin in 1797, and died soon after giving birth to a daughter, Mary (later, Mary Shelley). >> Godwin, William; Shelley, Mary

Wolpe, Joseph [volpay] (1915–) Psychiatrist, born in Johannesburg, South Africa. He was co-author of *Behavioural Therapy Techniques* (1966), with which he founded the field of behavioural therapy, widely used in the treatment of neurotic disorders.

Wolseley, Garnet (Joseph) Wolseley, 1st Viscount

[**wul**zlee] (1833–1913) British field marshal, born in Golden Bridge, Co Dublin, Ireland. He served in campaigns in many parts of the world, and led the attempted rescue of Gordon at Khartoum. As army commander-in-chief (1895–1901), he mobilized forces for the Boer War (1899–1902). >> Gordon

Wolsey, Thomas, Cardinal [**wul**zee] (c.1475–1530) English cardinal and statesman, born in Ipswich, Suffolk. Under Henry VIII, he became Archbishop of York (1514) and a cardinal (1515). Made Lord Chancellor (1515–29), he was Henry VIII's leading adviser. When he failed to persuade the pope to grant Henry's divorce, he was arrested, and died while travelling to London. >> Henry VIII

Wonder, Stevie, originally **Steveland Judkins** (1951–) Soul singer, songwriter, and instrumentalist, born in Saginaw, MI. Blind from birth, he played the harmonica, drums, keyboards, and guitar from an early age, and was signed to Motown Records in 1961. His albums include *Songs In The Key Of Life* (1976) and *Hotter Than July* (1980).

Wood, Ellen, *née* **Price**, known as **Mrs Henry Wood** (1814–87) Writer, born in Worcester, Hereford and Worcester. She wrote a series of melodramatic novels, of which *East Lynne* (1861) was particularly successful.

Wood, Sir Henry (Joseph) (1869–1944) Conductor, born in London. In 1895 he helped to found the Promenade Concerts which he conducted annually until his death. He also composed operettas and an oratorio.

Wood, Haydn (1882–1959) Composer and violinist, born in Slaithwaite, West Yorkshire. He wrote prolifically for orchestra, brass band, chamber music groups, and voices. His best known ballet is 'Roses of Picardy'.

Wood, John, known as **the Elder**, or **Wood of Bath** (c.1704–54) Architect, born in Yorkshire, UK. He was responsible for many of the best-known streets and buildings of Bath, such as the North and South Parades and Prior Park. His son **John (the Younger)** (1728–82) designed the Royal Crescent and the Assembly Rooms.

Wood, Natalie >> Wagner, Robert

Wood, Robert (Williams) (1868–1955) Physicist, born in Concord, MA. He carried out research on optics, atomic and molecular radiation, and sound waves, and was the first (in 1897) to observe electric-field emission.

Wood, Victoria (1953–) Comedienne, born in Prestwich, Lancashire. The creator of all her own sketches, songs, and stand-up routines, her television career includes *Wood and Walters* (1981–2) and *An Audience With Victoria Wood* (1988, BAFTA). >> Walters

Woodcock, George (1904–79) Trade union leader, born in Bamber Bridge, Lancashire. He joined the Trades Union Congress, becoming assistant general secretary (1947–60) and general secretary (1960–9).

Wooden, John (Robert) (1910–) Basketball coach, born in Martinsville, IN. He was head basketball coach at the University of California, Los Angeles (1948–75), and named Coach of the Year six times between 1964 and 1973.

Woodhull, Victoria, *née* **Claflin** (1838–1927) Reformer, born in Homer, OH. With her sister, Tennessee Claflin (1846–1923), she became involved with a socialist group called Pantarchy, won support from the women's suffrage movement, and became the first woman nominated for the presidency (1872).

Woodruff, Robert (1890–1985) US businessman. His father bought control of Coca-Cola in 1919, and he became president of the company in 1923.

Woodson, Carter G(odwin) (1875–1950) Historian and educator, born in New Canton, VA. He devoted his life to promoting black education, and created a public climate for what later developed as African-American studies.

Woodsworth, James Shaver (1874–1942) Reformer and political leader, born in Islington, Ontario, Canada. He

was elected as a Manitoba Independent Labour Party MP in 1921, and was founder and first chairman of the Commonwealth Co-operative Federation (1932).

Woodville, Elizabeth (1437–92) Queen consort of Edward IV of England. She married Edward IV in 1464, and was crowned in 1465. In 1483 her sons, Edward V and Richard, Duke of York, were murdered (the 'Princes in the Tower'). Her eldest daughter, Elizabeth of York (1465–1503), married Henry VII in 1486. >> Edward IV / V; Henry VII

Woodward, Bob >> Bernstein, Carl

Woodward, Joanne (1930–) Film actress, born in Thomasville, GA. Her films include *The Three Faces of Eve* (1957, Oscar) and *Rachel Rachel* (1968). She is married to Paul Newman. >> Newman, Paul

Woodward, R(obert) B(urns) (1917–79) Organic chemist, born in Boston, MA. Best known for his work on organic synthesis, including his synthesis of chlorophyll (1961), he was awarded the Nobel Prize for Chemistry in 1965.

Woodward, Roger Robert (1944–) Concert pianist, born in Sydney, New South Wales, Australia. Noted for his playing of Chopin and Beethoven, he has appeared with many international orchestras and conductors.

Wooldridge, Sydney William (1900–63) Geographer, born in London. He played a leading role in the establishment of geomorphology within British geography.

Woolf, Arthur (1766–1837) Mechanical engineer, born in Camborne, Cornwall. After the expiry of Watt's patent in 1800, he patented a compound engine and boiler (1803), and later worked on perfecting the high-pressure engines of Trevithick. >> Trevithick; Watt, James

Woolf, Leonard (Sidney) (1880–1969) Publisher and writer, born in London. With his wife, Virginia Woolf, he founded the Hogarth Press (1917), and they became the centre of the Bloomsbury Group. His major work was a five-volume autobiography (1960–69). >> Woolf, Virginia

Woolf, (Adeline) Virginia, *née* **Stephen** (1882–1941) Novelist, born in London. A leading member of the Bloomsbury Group, she made a major contribution to the development of the novel, in such works as *Mrs Dalloway* (1925), *To the Lighthouse* (1927), and *The Waves* (1931), noted for their impressionistic style. She is also known for her *Diary* (5 vols, 1977–84) and *Letters* (6 vols, 1975–80). >> Woolf, Leonard

Woolley, Frank (1887–1978) Cricketer, born in Tonbridge, Kent. An all-rounder, he played 64 Test matches for England, scoring 3283 Test runs and recording five centuries.

Woolley, Sir (Charles) Leonard (1880–1960) Archaeologist, born in London. He directed the important excavations (1922–34) at Ur in Mesopotamia, revealing in 1926 spectacular discoveries of gold and lapis lazuli in the royal tombs. He wrote several popular accounts of his work, notably *Digging Up the Past* (1930).

Woolman, John (1720–72) Quaker preacher and reformer, born in Rancocas, NJ. A prolific writer, he is best remembered for his *Journal* (1774), a major work on spiritual life.

Woolton, Frederick James Marquis, Baron (1883–1964) Politician and businessman, born in Liverpool, Merseyside. He made his name at the ministry of food (1940), and in 1946 became chairman of the Conservative Party.

Woolworth, Frank W(infield) (1852–1919) Merchant, born in Rodman, NY. In 1879 he opened a store in Utica, NY, for 5-cent goods only; this failed, but a second store, in Lancaster, PA, selling also 10-cent goods, was successful. He then built a chain of similar stores, setting up the F W Woolworth Co in 1905.

Wootton (of Abinger), Barbara Frances Wootton,

Baroness (1897–1988) Social scientist, born in Cambridge, Cambridgeshire. She is best known for her *Testament for Social Science* (1950), in which she attempted to assimilate the social to the natural sciences.

Worcester, Edward Somerset, 2nd Marquess of [**wus**ter] (1601–67) English aristocrat, probably born in London. In 1645 he was sent to Ireland to raise troops for the king, but his mission failed and he was briefly imprisoned. >> Charles I (of England)

Worcester, Joseph (Emerson) [**wus**ter] (1784–1865) Lexicographer, born in Bedford, NH. His major work was the *Dictionary of the English Language* (1860), but he was also long involved in legal battles over his unauthorized abridgement of Webster's dictionary in 1829 (the 'Dictionary War').

Worde, Wynkyn de [werd] (?–?1535) Printer, born in The Netherlands or in Alsace. A pupil of Caxton, in 1491 he succeeded to his stock-in-trade, making great improvements in printing and typecutting.

Wordsworth, Dorothy (1771–1855) Writer, born in Cockermouth, Cumbria, the sister of William Wordsworth. Her *Alfoxden Journal* (1798) and *Grasmere Journals* (1800–3) show a keen sensibility and acute observation of nature. >> Wordsworth, William

Wordsworth, William (1770–1850) Poet, born in Cockermouth, Cumbria. *Lyrical Ballads* (1798), written with Coleridge, was the first manifesto of the new Romantic poetry. He settled at Dove Cottage, Grasmere, married Mary Hutchinson in 1802, and wrote much of his best work, including his poetic autobiography, *The Prelude* (1805, published in 1850). He became poet laureate in 1843. >> Coleridge, Samuel Taylor; Wordsworth, Dorothy

Wordsworth, William Brocklesby (1908–88) Composer, born in London. His works include symphonies, a piano concerto, songs, and chamber music.

Worlock, Derek (John Harford) (1920–96) Roman Catholic clergyman. Appointed Archbishop of Liverpool in 1976, he developed a close working relationship with the Anglican Bishop of Liverpool, speaking out with him on matters of social concern. >> Sheppard, David

Wörner, Manfred [**vaw(r)**ner] (1934–94) German politician, born in Stuttgart, Germany. Appointed defence minister in 1982, he oversaw the controversial deployment of US nuclear missiles in West Germany. He became secretary-general of NATO in 1988.

Worrall, Denis John (1935–) South African politician, born in Benoni, South Africa. He established the Independent Party, which in 1989 merged with other white Opposition parties to form the reformist Democratic Party.

Worrell, Sir Frank (Mortimer Magilinne) (1924–67) Cricketer, the first black West Indian Test captain, born in Bridgetown, Barbados. In 51 Test matches he made nine centuries, and was a useful pace bowler.

Worth, Charles Frederick (1825–95) Costumier, born in Bourn, Lincolnshire. He went to Paris in 1845 and established a ladies' tailors in 1858. He introduced the bustle, and became known for his elegant crinolined gowns.

Worth, Irene (1916–) Actress, born in Nebraska. She has won awards for several theatre roles, including *Tiny Alice* (1965), *Sweet Bird of Youth* (1975), and *Lost in Yonkers, NY* (1991).

Wortley Montagu, Lady Mary >> Montagu, Lady Mary Wortley

Wotton, Sir Henry (1568–1639) English diplomat, traveller, scholar, and poet, born in Boughton Malherbe, Kent. His tracts and letters were collected as *Reliquiae Wottonianae* (1651).

Wouk, Herman [wohk] (1915–) Novelist, born in New York City. His books include the classic war novel, *The Caine Mutiny* (1951, Pulitzer), and the two-volume historical novel, *The Winds of War* (1971) and *War and Remembrance* (1975).

Wouldhave, William (1751–1821) Lifeboat inventor, born in North Shields, Durham. Both he and Henry Greathead (1757–1816) designed a local lifeboat but neither was approved. Greathead later presented a new model incorporating Wouldhave's features (1790), and claiming the title of lifeboat inventor.

Wouwerman, Philips [**vow**verman], also found as **Wouwermans** (c.1619–68) Painter of battle and hunting scenes, born in Haarlem, The Netherlands. His pictures are mostly small landscapes, with several figures in energetic action. He had two brothers, also painters, **Peter Wouwerman** (1623–82) and **Jan Wouwerman** (1629–66), who chose similar subjects.

Wozniack, Stephen >> Jobs, Steven

Wrangel, Ferdinand Petrovich, Baron von [**vrang**gl] (1794–1870) Explorer, born in Pskov, Russia. The reported island in the Arctic Ocean he nearly reached in 1821 was sighted in 1849, and named after him in 1867.

Wrangel, Pyotr Nikolayevich, Baron [**vrang**gl] (1878–1928) Russian army officer, born in Aleksandrovsk, Lithuania. In the Civil War, he commanded in the Ukraine, and in 1920 became commander-in-chief of the White Russian forces in the South.

Wren, Sir Christopher (1632–1723) Architect, born in East Knoyle, Wiltshire. In 1669 he designed the new St Paul's and many other public buildings in London, such as the Greenwich Observatory and Kensington Palace.

Wren, P(ercival) C(hristopher) (1885–1941) Writer, born in Devon. He joined the French Foreign Legion, and this provided him with the background of several novels of adventure, notably *Beau Geste* (1924).

Wright, Benjamin (1770–1842) Civil engineer, born in Wethersfield, CT. His projects include the Erie Canal (1817–25), the original St Lawrence Ship Canal and the Chesapeake and Ohio Canal (1825–31), and the New York and Erie Railroad.

Wright, Billy, popular name of **William Ambrose Wright** (1924–94) Footballer, born in Wolverhampton, West Midlands. A player for Wolverhampton Wanderers, he was the first player to win more than 100 caps for England (105, 90 as captain).

Wright, Sir (Almroth) Edward (1861–1947) Bacteriologist, born in Middleton Tyas, North Yorkshire. He developed an anti-typhoid vaccine used successfully during the Boer War and in World War 1.

Wright, Fanny, popular name of **Frances Wright**, married name **Frances Darusmont** (1795–1852) Reformer and abolitionist, born in Dundee, Tayside. She emigrated to the USA in 1818, published with Owen a socialist journal, *Free Enquirer*, and campaigned vigorously against religion and for the emancipation of women. >> Owen, Robert Dale

Wright, Frank Lloyd (1867–1959) Architect, born in Richland Center, WI. He became known for his low-built, prairie-style residences, but soon launched out into more controversial designs, planning houses in conformity with the natural features of the land. Among his larger works is the Guggenheim Museum of Art in New York City.

Wright, Georg von >> von Wright, Georg Henrik

Wright, Joseph, known as **Wright of Derby** (1734–97) Genre and portrait painter, born in Derby, Derbyshire. He is best known for his industrial scenes such as 'The Air Pump' (1768), and his treatment of artificial light.

Wright, Joseph (1855–1930) Philologist, born in Bradford, West Yorkshire. He became professor of comparative philology at Oxford, editor of the *Dialect Dictionary*, and author of many philological works.

Wright, Judith (Arundel) (1915–) Poet, born near

Armidale, New South Wales, Australia. In *The Moving Image* (1946), she was one of the first white writers to recognize Aboriginal claims. Her *Collected Poems* appeared in 1971.

Wright, Peter (1916–95) British intelligence officer, born in Chesterfield, Derbyshire. He joined MI5 (counter-intelligence) (1955–76) and in his autobiography, *Spycatcher* (1987), alleged that Sir Roger Hollis, the former director-general of MI5, had been a Soviet double-agent. Attempts to suppress the book's publication for 'security reasons' were eventually unsuccessful.

Wright, Richard (1908–60) Writer, short-story writer, and critic, born on a plantation in Mississippi. Among the first African-Americans to write about their ill-treatment by whites, he is best known for his autobiographical novel, *Black Boy* (1945).

Wright, Sewall (1889–1988) Geneticist, born in Melrose, MA. A founder of population genetics, he is best remembered for his concept of genetic drift, termed the *Sewall Wright effect*.

Wright brothers Aviation pioneers: **Orville Wright** (1871–1948), born in Dayton, OH, and **Wilbur Wright** (1867–1912), born near Millville, IN. They were the first to fly in a powered heavier-than-air machine (17 Dec 1903), at Kitty Hawk, NC.

Wrigley, William, Jr [**rig**lee] (1861–1932) Chewing-gum manufacturer, born in Philadelphia, PA. He successfully marketed the famous spearmint flavour (1899) and established the William Wrigley Jr Co.

Wriothesley, Henry >> **Southampton, 3rd Earl of**

Wu, Empress, in full **Wu Zhao** (?625–?706) Empress of China, the only woman ever to rule China in her own name. A concubine of Emperor Taizong, she married his son, Emperor Gaozong. After his death (683) she first ruled through her own sons, then seized the title *emperor* in 690 with the dynastic name Zhou. She was forced to abdicate in 705. >> Lü; Taizong; Xuanzong

Wu, Chien-Shiung (1912–) Physicist, born in Shanghai, China. Her research was in particle physics, notably her confirmation that some physical processes (such as beta-particle emission) are not identical in a mirror-image system.

Wu Chengen [woo chengen], also spelled **Wu Ch'eng-en** (1505–82) Writer, born in Huai-an, Kiangsu Province, China. He fused popular oral traditions into *Journey to the West*, one of four great Ming period novels, and known in the West in its English translation *Monkey*. >> Xuanzang

Wudi [woo dee], also spelled **Wu-ti** (141–86 BC) Han dynasty emperor of China. He annexed S China, conquered Korea, Tonkin, and the SW, and invaded the Hun territories, setting a precedent for later Han triumphs.

Wulfila >> **Ulfilas**

Wulfstan, St (c.1009–95), feast day 19 January. Clergyman, born in Long Itchington, Warwickshire. Appointed Bishop of Worcester (1062), he helped to compile the *Domesday Book*. He was canonized in 1203.

Wulfstan, also known as **Lupus** (?–1023) Anglo-Saxon clergyman and writer. Archbishop of York from 1002, and also Bishop of Worcester (1003–16), he wrote homilies in the vernacular, including the celebrated address *Sermon of Wolf to the English* (trans, 1014).

Wunderlich, Carl August [**vun**derlikh] (1815–77) Physician, born in Sulz-on-Neckar, Germany. He was the first to introduce temperature charts into hospitals, contending that fever is a symptom and not a disease.

Wundt, Wilhelm (Max) [vunt] (1832–1920) Physiologist and psychologist, born in Neckarau, Germany. An experimental psychologist, he wrote on the nerves and the senses, and the relations between physiology and psychology.

Wuornos, Aileen [**waw(r)**nos] (1956–) US convicted murderer. Dubbed the world's first female serial killer, she was convicted in the USA in 1992 of the murder of seven men between 1989 and 1991, and sentenced to die in the electric chair.

Wu Peifu [woo payfoo], also spelled **Wu P'ei-fu** (1874–1939) Major figure in the warlord struggles of China (1916–27), born in Shandong province, China. When Duan Qirui sought to reunite China by force, Wu refused his orders, but was defeated in battle near Tientsin.

Wurlitzer, Rudolph [**wer**litser] (1831–1914) Musical instrument maker, born in Schöneck, Germany. In the USA from 1853, he formed the Rudolph Wurlitzer Co (1890), and served as president (1890–1912).

Wu-ti >> **Wudi**

Wyatt, James (1746–1813) Architect, born in Burton Constable, Staffordshire. His best-known work is the Gothic revival Fonthill Abbey (1796–1807), which largely collapsed in the 1820s.

Wyatt, Sir Thomas, known as **the Elder** (1503–42) Poet and courtier, born in Allington, Kent. In 1557 his poems, published in *Tottel's Miscellany*, helped introduce the Italian sonnet and other forms into English literature.

Wyatt, Sir Thomas, known as **the Younger** (?1520–54) English soldier, son of Sir Thomas Wyatt. In 1554, with Lady Jane Grey's father, he led the Kentish men to Southwark. Failing to capture Ludgate, he was taken prisoner and executed. >> Grey, Lady Jane; Wyatt, Thomas (the Elder)

Wycherley, William [**wich**erlee] (c.1640–1716) Playwright, born in Clive, Shropshire. He wrote several satirical comedies, notably *The Country Wife* (1675) and *The Plain Dealer* (1677), both based on plays by Molière. >> Molière

Wyckoff, Ralph (Walter Greystone) [**wik**off] (1897–) Biophysicist, born in Geneva, NY. In 1944 with Robley Cook Williams he developed the metal shadowing method for imaging viruses in the electron microscope. >> Williams, Robley Cook

Wycliffe or **Wicliffe, John** [**wik**lif], also spelled **Wyclif, Wycliff** (c.1330–84) Religious reformer, born near Richmond, Yorkshire. He attacked the Church hierarchy, priestly power, and the doctrine of transubstantiation, and issued the first English translation of the Bible. His opinions were condemned, and he was forced to retire. His followers were known as *Lollards*.

Wyeth, Andrew (Newell) (1917–) Painter, born in Chadds Ford, PA. His soberly realistic pictures typically represent poor people or rustics in landscapes from the traditional 'American scene', as in 'Christina's World' (1948).

Wykeham, William of >> **William of Wykeham**

Wyler, William [**wiy**ler] (1902–81) Film director, born in Mulhouse, France (formerly, Germany). He received Oscars for *Mrs Miniver* (1942), *The Best Years of Our Lives* (1946), and *Ben Hur* (1959).

Wylie, Elinor, *née* **Elinor Morton Hoyt** (1885–1928) Writer, born in Somerville, NJ. She is best known for her delicate poetry, as in *Angels and Earthly Creatures* (1929), but she also wrote critical essays, reviews, and four comic fantasy novels. In 1923 she married William Rose Benét. >> Benét, William Rose

Wyndham, Sir Charles [**wind**am] (1837–1919) Actor-manager, born in Liverpool, Merseyside. He made his London debut in 1866, and in 1899 opened Wyndham's Theatre.

Wyndham, John [**wind**am], pseudonym of **John Wyndham Parkes Lucas Beynon Harris** (1903–69) Science-fiction writer, born in Knowle, Warwickshire. His novels include *The Day of the Triffids* (1951), *The Kraken Wakes* (1953), and *The Midwich Cuckoos* (1957), as well as collections of short stories.

Wynfrith, St >> **Boniface, St**

Wynkyn de Worde >> **Worde, Wynkyn de**

Wyss, Johann Rudolf [vees] (1781–1830) Writer, born in Bern. He is best known for his completion and editing of *The Swiss Family Robinson* (trans, 1812–13), written by his father, **Johann David Wyss** (1743–1818).

Wyszyński, Stefan, Cardinal [vishinskee] (1901–81) Roman Catholic clergyman, born in Zuzela, Poland. He became Archbishop of Warsaw and Gniezno (1948), and a cardinal (1952). Following his indictment of the Communist campaign against the Church, he was imprisoned (1953–6).

Xavier, Francis, St >> **Francis Xavier, St**

Xenakis, Iannis [zenahkees] (1922–   ) Composer, born in Braila, Romania. He developed a highly complex style which incorporated mathematical concepts of chance and probability (so-called *stochastic music*), as well as electronic techniques.

Xenocrates [zenokratees] (c.395–314 BC) Greek philosopher and scientist, born in Chalcedon on the Bosphorus. In 339 BC he became head of the Academy which Plato had founded, writing prolifically on natural science, astronomy, and philosophy, but only fragments survive.

Xenophanes [zenofaneez] (c.570–c.480 BC) Greek philosopher, born in Colophon, Ionia. He attacked traditional Greek conceptions of the gods, arguing against anthropomorphism and polytheism.

Xenophon [zenofon] (c.435–354 BC) Greek historian, essayist, and soldier, born in Attica. In 401 BC he served with an army of Greek mercenaries under Persian Prince Cyrus, and led them successfully back to the Black Sea. This heroic feat formed the basis of his major work, *Anabasis Kyrou* (The Expedition of Cyrus).

Xerxes I [zerkseez] (c.519–465 BC) Achaemenid king of Persia (485–465 BC), the son of Darius I. He is remembered in the West mainly for the failure of his forces against the Greeks in the Second Persian War at Salamis, Plataea, and Mycale. >> Darius I

Ximénes (de Cisneros) Francisco Jiménez, Cardinal [heemeneth] (1436–1517) Clergyman and statesman, born in Torrelaguna, Spain. Created a cardinal in 1507, on the death of Ferdinand (1516) he was appointed regent during the minority of the later Charles V. >> Ferdinand the Catholic

Xuanzang [shwantsang], also spelled **Hsüan-tsang** (600–664) Buddhist pilgrim, explorer, and diarist, born in Chenlu, China. He made an epic journey to India (629–45), publishing an account which is a major source on 7th-c Asia. >> Faxian

Xuanzong [shwantsong], also spelled **Hsüan-tsung** (685–761) Chinese Tang emperor (ruled 712–55). Of royal lineage, he eliminated the usurper Wu's family in 710, and seized the crown. >> Wu

Yacoub, Magdi (Habib) [yakoob] (1935–) Physician, born in Cairo. Based in Britain since 1969, he is one of the leading developers of the techniques of heart and heart–lung transplantation.

Yadin, Yigael [yadeen], originally **Yigael Sukenik** (1917–84) Archaeologist and military leader, born in Jerusalem. He led major archaeological expeditions in Israel, including the Dead Sea Caves (1960–1) and Masada (1963–5), and is noted for his work on the Dead Sea Scrolls.

Yale, Elihu (1649–1721) Colonial administrator and benefactor, born in Boston, MA. He donated money to the collegiate school established (1701) at Saybrook, CT, which later moved to New Haven, and in 1887 became Yale University.

Yale, Linus (1821–68) Lock manufacturer, and inventor of the Yale lock, born in Salisbury, NY. He set up business as a locksmith and invented various types, including the small cylinder locks by which his name is known.

Yalow, Rosalyn S(ussman) [yaloh] (1921–) Medical physicist, born in New York City. She developed radioimmunoassay, a technique for measuring minute concentrations of active biological substances, and shared the Nobel Prize for Physiology or Medicine in 1977.

Yamagata, Prince Aritomo [yamagahta] (1838–1922) Japanese general and premier (1890–1, 1898–1900), born in Hagi, Japan. As war minister (1873) and chief-of-staff (1878), he instituted major army reforms which led to Japan's defeat of China (1895) and Russia (1905).

Yamamoto, Isoroku [yamamohtoh] (1884–1943) Japanese naval officer, born in Nagaoka, Japan. Commander-in-chief of the combined fleet (1939–43), he planned and directed the attack on Pearl Harbor (1941). His forces were defeated at the Battle of Midway (1942).

Yamamoto, Yohji [yamamohtoh] (1943–) Fashion designer, born in Tokyo. He started his own company in Tokyo in 1972, designing loose, functional clothes for men and women, featuring a great deal of black, which conceal rather than emphasize the body.

Yamani, Ahmed Zaki, Sheikh [yamahnee] (1930–) Saudi Arabian politician. Minister of petroleum and mineral resources (1962–86), he was an important and 'moderate' member of the Organization of Petroleum-Exporting Countries (OPEC).

Yamashita, Tomoyuki [yamashita] (1885–1946) Japanese soldier, born in Kochi, Japan. In 1942 he commanded the forces which overran Singapore, then took over the Philippines campaign. He was tried for war crimes, and hanged.

Yamashita, Yashiro [yamashita] (1957–) Judo fighter, born in Kyushu, Japan. He won the Olympic open class gold medal (1984), and four world titles: 1979, 1981, 1983 (over 95 kg class), and 1981 (open class).

Yang, Chen Ning, known as **Frank Yang** (1922–) Physicist, born in Hofei, China. He specialized in particle physics, and with Lee disproved the established physical principle known as the *parity law*, for which they shared the Nobel Prize for Physics in 1957. >> Lee, Tsung-Dao

Yangdi [yangdee], also spelled **Yang-ti** (569–618) Second Chinese Sui dynasty emperor (604–18). As Yang Guang he murdered his father, Wendi. He conquered Taiwan (610), established colonies on the W trade routes, and built the Grand Canal (610). The expense of his reign provoked insurrection and he was killed. >> Wendi

Yang Shangkun (1907–) President of the People's

Republic of China (1988–93), born in Tongnan, Sichuan, China. A trusted supporter of Deng Xiaoping, it was his army troops who carried out the massacre of pro-democracy students in Tiananmen Square, Beijing (1989). >> Deng Xiaoping

Yanofsky, Charles [yanofskee] (1925–) Geneticist, born in New York City. Working on gene mutations, he used microbiological methods to prove that the sequence of bases in the genetic material DNA acts by determining the order of the amino acids which make up proteins, including the enzymes which control biochemical processes.

Yashin, Lev (1929–90) Footballer, born in Moscow. He played for Moscow Dynamo (1949–71) and for his country (1954–71), taking part in three World Cup tournaments.

Yates, Dornford, pseudonym of **Cecil William Mercer** (1885–1960) Novelist, born in London. He achieved popularity with an entertaining series of fanciful escapist adventure fiction, such as *Berry and Co* (1921).

Yeager, Chuck [yayger], popular name of **Charles E(lwood) Yeager** (1923–) The first pilot to break the sound barrier, born in Myra, WV. In 1947 he flew the Bell X-1 rocket research aircraft to a level speed of more than 670 mph.

Yeats, Jack B [yayts], popular name of **John Butler Yeats** (1870–1957) Painter, born in London, the brother of W B Yeats. He is best known for his colourful, freely painted pictures of Irish daily life and Celtic mythology, produced after 1915. >> Yeats, William Butler

Yeats, W(illiam) B(utler) [yayts] (1865–1939) Poet and playwright, born near Dublin. *The Wanderings of Oisin* (1888), a long narrative poem, established his reputation. His most popular plays were *The Countess Cathleen* (1892), *The Land of Heart's Desire* (1894), and *Cathleen ni Houlihan* (1903), and many of his best-known poems appeared in *The Tower* (1928), *The Winding Stair* (1929), and *A Full Moon in March* (1935). He received the Nobel Prize for Literature in 1923.

Yeltsin, Boris (Nikolayevich) (1931–) Russian president (1990–), and prime minister of the Russian Federation, born in Yekaterinburg (formerly, Sverdlovsk), Ukraine. He was appointed Moscow party chief (1985), but after criticizing party conservatives for sabotaging *perestroika*, he was downgraded to a lowly administrative post (1987). He returned to public attention in 1989 as a member of the new Congress of USSR People's Deputies, and was elected president of the Russian Federation. His political standing increased when he led the protestors who defeated the Gorbachev coup (1991), and following the break-up of the Soviet Union he remained in power as president. >> Gorbachev

Yentob, Alan (1947–) British broadcaster. He joined the BBC (1968), edited *Arena* (1978–85), became head of BBC-TV music and arts (1985), and was appointed controller of BBC2 television (1988).

Yerkes, Charles (Tyson) [yerkeez] (1837–1905) Financier, born in Philadelphia, PA. He headed the consortium that built Chicago's street railways, but in 1899 was forced to sell out in Chicago after allegations of political chicanery.

Yersin, Alexandre Emile John [yairsi] (1863–1943) Bacteriologist, born in Aubonne, Switzerland. In 1894, at the same time as Kitasato, he discovered the plague bacillus, now called *Yersinia* in his honour, and developed a serum against it. >> Kitasato

Yesenin, Sergey [yesaynin] (1895–1925) Poet, born in Yesenino (formerly, Konstantino), Russia. He gained literary success with his first volume *Mourning for the Dead* (trans, 1916), and his suicide prompted a wave of imitative suicides in Russia.

Yevtushenko, Yevegeny (Alexandrovich) [ye tu**sheng**-koh] (1933–   ) Poet, born in Zima, Russia. His early poetry, such as *The Third Snow* (1955), made him a spokesman for the young post-Stalin generation. Major poems include *Zima Junction* (trans, 1956) and *Babi Yar* (1962). His first major stage piece, *Under the Skin of the Statue of Liberty*, was a huge success in 1972.

Yezhov, Nikolai [ye**zhof**] (1895–1939?) Soviet secret police chief, born in St Petersburg, Russia. As head of the NKVD (1936), he staged the show-trials (1937–8) that removed many of Stalin's potential rivals. He disappeared soon after and is presumed to have been killed. >> Stalin

Yonai, Mitsumasa [yoniy] (1880–1940) Japanese naval officer and prime minster (1940), born in Iwate Prefecture, Japan. He was also commander of the imperial fleet (1936–7), and navy minister (1937–9, 1944–5).

Yonge, Charlotte M(ary) [yung] (1823–1901) Novelist, born in Otterbourne, Hampshire. She achieved great popular success with *The Heir of Redclyffe* (1853).

Yongle or **Yung-lo** [yonglay], originally **Zhu Di** (1360–1424) Third emperor (1403–24) of the Chinese Ming dynasty (1368–1644), born in Nanking, China, the fourth son of Hongwu. He seized the crown from his nephew, moved the capital to Beijing (1421), and conquered the Mongols.

York, Alvin (Cullum) (1887–1964) US soldier and popular hero, born in Pall Mall, TN. While in France during World War 1, he led a small detachment against a German machine-gun emplacement, killing 25 of the enemy, and inducing 132 to surrender.

York, Prince Andrew, Duke of >> **Andrew, Prince**
York, Princess Beatrice of >> **Andrew, Prince**
York, Princess Eugenie of >> **Andrew, Prince**
York, Michael, stage name of **Michael York-Johnson** (1942–   ) Actor, born in Fulmer, Buckinghamshire. His films include *Cabaret* (1971) and *The Joker* (1988), and his television appearances *Jesus of Nazareth* (1976) and *The Night of the Fox* (1990).

York, Richard, 3rd Duke of (1411–60) English nobleman, the father of Edward IV, Richard III, and George, Duke of Clarence. He loyally served the weak-minded Henry VI, and in 1460 was promised the succession, but was killed in a rising by Lancastrian forces. >> Clarence; Edward IV; Henry VI; Richard III

Yorkshire Ripper, The >> **Sutcliffe, Peter**
Yoshida, Shigeru [yo**shee**da] (1878–1967) Japanese prime minister (1946–7, 1948–54), born in Tokyo. He became foreign minister (1945), and formed the government which inaugurated the new constitution in 1946.

Young, Andrew (Jackson), Jr (1932–   ) Civil rights activist and politician born in New Orleans, LA. He joined the Southern Christian Leadership Conference (1960), and came to be a close associate of Martin Luther King. Elected as a Democrat to the US House of Representatives (1973–7), he was the first African-American to represent Georgia in Congress since 1871. >> King, Martin Luther

Young, Arthur (1741–1820) Agricultural and travel writer, born in London. In his writings he helped to elevate agriculture to a science, founding and editing the monthly *Annals of Agriculture* (1784).

Young, Brigham (1801–77) Mormon leader, born in Whitingham, VT. Converted in 1832, he became president of the Church upon the death of Joseph Smith in 1844. He led the Mormons to Utah (1847), where they founded Salt Lake City. >> Smith, Joseph

Young, Chic, pseudonym of **Murat Bernard Young** (1901–73) Strip cartoonist, born in Chicago, IL. He was the creator of the popular *Blondie* (1930), King Features most widely syndicated strip.

Young, Cy, popular name of **Denton True Young** (1867–1955) Baseball pitcher, born in Gilmore, OH. During his career (1890–1911) he threw 749 complete games and won 511 games, both records.

Young (of Graffham), David (Ivor), Baron (1932–   ) British statesman and businessman. He became secretary of state for employment (1985–7) and trade and industry (1987–9).

Young, Edward (1683–1765) Poet, born in Upham, Hampshire. His best-known work is 'The Complaint, or, Night-Thoughts on Life, Death and Immortality' (1742–6).

Young, Francis Brett (1884–1954) Novelist, born in Halesowen, Worcestershire. His novels include *Portrait of Clare* (1927, James Tait Black Memorial Prize), *A Man about the House* (1942), and *Portrait of a Village* (1951).

Young, George Malcolm (1882–1959) Historical essayist, born in Greenhithe, Kent. His works include a life of Gibbon (1932), and he also edited *Early Victorian England* (2 vols, 1934).

Young, Jimmy, professional name of **Leslie Ronald Young** British broadcaster and singer. He topped the charts with 'Unchained Melody' and 'The Man From Laramie' (1955), becoming the first British singer to have two consecutive No 1 hits. Since 1967 he has presented the *Jimmy Young* BBC radio show.

Young, Lester (Willis), nickname **Prez** (1909–59) Tenor saxophonist, born in Woodville, MS. He worked with a succession of bands in the mid-west, before joining the newly-formed Count Basie Orchestra in 1934.

Young (of Dartington), Michael Young, Baron (1915–   ) British educationalist. He played a leading role in the development of 'distance learning' in the Third World and, via the National Extension College, within Britain.

Young, Neil (Percival) (1945–   ) Singer, songwriter, and guitarist, born in Toronto, Ontario, Canada. Much influenced by Bob Dylan, he has released over 20 albums, including *Harvest* (1972), *Reactor* (1981), and *Freedom* (1989). >> Dylan, Bob

Young, Thomas (1773–1829) Physicist, physician, and egyptologist, born in Milverton, Somerset. His *Lectures* (1807) established the wave theory of light, and he also made a fundamental contribution to the deciphering of the Rosetta Stone.

Young, Whitney M(oore), Jr (1921–71) Social reformer, born in Lincoln Ridge, KY. Author of *To Be Equal* (1964) and *Beyond Racism* (1969), he worked to improve African-Americans' conditions in the community.

Younger, (Thomas) Cole(man) (1844–1916) Bandit, born in Jackson Co, MO. He joined with Jesse James and formed the James–Younger band, which included Cole's two brothers, James and Robert. They were captured during a bank raid and imprisoned. >> James, Jesse

Younghusband, Sir Francis Edward (1863–1942) British soldier and explorer, born in Murree, India. He explored Manchuria in 1886, and in 1902 went on the expedition which opened up Tibet to the Western world.

Yourcenar, Marguerite [yer**senah**(r)], pseudonym of **Marguerite de Crayencour** (1903–87) Novelist and poet, born in Brussels. Her novels, many of them historical reconstructions, include *Memoirs of Hadrian* (trans, 1951) and *The Abyss* (trans, 1968).

Ypres, Earl of >> **French, John**
Yrigoyen, Hipólito [eerigoh**zhen**] >> **Irigoyen, Hipólito**
Yuan Shikai [yüan sheekiy], also spelled **Yuan Shih-k'ai** (1859–1916) Chinese soldier and first president of China (1912–16), born in Xiancheng, Henan, China. In power after the Wuhan uprising (1911), he lost support by procuring the murder of the parliamentary leader of the Nationalists, accepting Japan's Twenty-One Demands of 1915, and proclaiming himself emperor (1915).

Yukawa, Hideki [yukahwa] (1907–81) Physicist, born in Tokyo. He predicted (1935) the existence of the meson, developed a theory of strong nuclear forces, and for his work on quantum theory and nuclear physics was awarded the Nobel Prize for Physics in 1949.

Yung-lo >> Yongle

Yunupingu, Mandawuy [yunupinggoo, mandawoy] (1956–) Singer, born in Yirrkala, Northern Territory, Australia. In 1986 he established the group *Yothu Yindi* which has achieved wide success in terms of sales, critical acclaim, and its political message.

Zabaleta, Nicanor [thabalayta] (1907–93) Harpist, born in San Sebastian, Spain. He was influential in popularizing the harp's solo repertory, and several composers wrote works for him.

Zaccaria, St Antonio Maria [zakahria] (1502–39), feast day 5 July. Italian religious. He founded the Barnabite preaching order (1530) and the Angelicals of St Paul order for women (1535), and was canonized in 1897.

Zacharias, St (?–752), feast day 15 March. Pope (741–52), born in San Severino, Italy, of Greek parents. He is best known in the East for his translation into Greek of the *Dialogues* of Pope Gregory the Great. >> Gregory I

Zadkiel [zadkeel], pseudonym of **Richard James Morrison** (1794–1874) English astrologer. He started a best selling astrological almanac in 1831, *Zadkiel's Almanac*.

Zadkine, Ossip [zadkeen] (1890–1967) Sculptor, born in Smolensk, Russia. His individual Cubist style made effective use of the play of light on concave surfaces, as in 'The Three Musicians' (1926) and the war memorial in Rotterdam, 'The Destroyed City' (1952).

Zaharias, Babe >> Didrikson, Babe

Zaharoff, Sir Basil [zaharof], originally **Basileios Zacharias** (1849–1936) Armaments magnate and financier, born in Anatolia, Turkey. He amassed a fortune from arms sales (1880–1900) and was knighted by the British in 1918 for his services to the Allies in World War 1.

Zahir Shah, King Mohammed [zaheer shah] (1914–) King of Afghanistan (1933–73), born in Kabul. He succeeded to the throne after the assassination of his father, Nadir Shah (c.1880–1933), and he became a constitutional monarch in 1964. He was overthrown in a republican coup led by his cousin, General Daud Khan.

Zai Tian [dziy tyen], also spelled **Tsai-t'ien**, reign title **Guang Xu** (1871–1908) Ninth emperor of the Qing dynasty (1875–1908), who remained largely under the control of the Empress Dowager Ci-Xi. In 1898 he issued a series of reforming edicts, but his attempts to gain power led to a coup. >> Ci-Xi

Zakharov, Rostislav [zakhahrof] (1907–84) Dancer, choreographer, ballet director, and teacher, born in Astrakhan, Russia. He joined both the Kharkov and Kirov Ballets, and from 1936 until the mid-50s was associated with the Bolshoi Ballet.

Zamenhof, L(azarus) L(udwig) [zamenof], pseudonym **Doktoro Esperanto** (1859–1917) Oculist and philologist, born in Białystok, Poland. An advocate of an international language to promote world peace, he invented Esperanto ('one who hopes').

Zamyatin, Yevgeny Ivanovich [zamyatin], also spelled **Zamiatin** (1884–1937) Writer, born in Lebedyan, Russia. In 1921 he was a founder member of the Modernist group, the Serapion Brothers. His novel *We* (trans, 1920), a fantasy set in the 26th-c AD, prophesied Stalinism, and led to the banning of his works.

Zangwill, Israel (1864–1926) Writer, born in London. A leading Zionist, he was widely known for his novels on Jewish themes, such as *Children of the Ghetto* (1892) and *Ghetto Tragedies* (1893).

Zanuck, Darryl F(rancis) [zanuhk] (1902–79) Film producer, born in Wahoo, NE. He co-founded Twentieth-Century Pictures (later Twentieth-Century Fox) in 1933. Among his many successful films are *The Jazz Singer* (1927), *The Longest Day* (1962), and *The Sound of Music* (1965).

Zapata, Emiliano [sapahta] (1879–1919) Mexican revolutionary, born in Anencuilio, Mexico. Along with Pancho Villa, he fought the Carranza government, and was eventually lured to his death at the Chinameca hacienda. >> Villa

Zappa, Frank, popular name of **Francis Vincent Zappa** (1940–93) Avant-garde rock musician and composer, born in Baltimore, MD. He led the the satirical 'underground' band The Mothers of Invention, his albums including *Freak-Out!* (1966) and *We're Only in it for the Money* (1967).

Zarathustra >> Zoroaster

Zaslavskaya, Tatyana Ivanova [zaslavskaya] (1927–) Economist and sociologist, born in Kiev, Ukraine. Her 'Novosibirsk Memorandum' (1983), a criticism of the Soviet economic system, contributed to the policy change in Russia in the late 1980s.

Zatopek, Emil [zatopek] (1922–) Athlete and middle-distance runner, born in Kopřivnice, Czech Republic. He won the gold medal for the 10 000 m at the 1948 Olympics, subsequently breaking 13 world records. In the 1952 Olympics he retained his gold medal and also won the 5000 m and the marathon.

Zeckendorf, William (1905–76) Real estate developer, born in Paris, IL. He joined Webb & Knapp, New York City, of which he became sole owner in 1949.

Zeeman, Erik Christopher (1925–) British mathematician. His early work developing topology and catastrophe theory produced many applications to physics, social sciences, and economics.

Zeeman, Pieter (1865–1943) Physicist, born in Zonnemaire, The Netherlands. He discovered the *Zeeman effect*: when a ray of light from a source placed in a magnetic field is examined spectroscopically, the spectral line splits into several components. This discovery confirmed Lorentz's theory of electromagnetic radiation, and they shared the Nobel Prize for Physics in 1902. >> Lorentz

Zeffirelli, Franco [zefirelee] (1923–) Stage, opera, and film director, born in Florence, Italy. His films include *The Taming of the Shrew* (1966) and *Romeo and Juliet* (1968), the television *Jesus of Nazareth* (1977), and film versions of the operas *La traviata* (1983) and *Otello* (1986).

Zeiss, Carl [tsiys] (1816–88) Optician and industrialist, born in Weimar, Germany. In 1846 he established at Jena the factory which became noted for the production of lenses, microscopes, and other optical instruments.

Zemlinsky, Alexander von [zemlinskee] (1871–1942) Composer and conductor, born in Vienna. His compositions, in post-Romantic style, include operas, orchestral works, chamber music, choral works, and songs.

Zeng Guofan [dzeng gwohfan], also spelled **Tseng Kuo-fan** (1811–72) Provincial administrator, born in Hsianghsiang, Hunan Province, China. He supported improvements in technical and linguistic education, and the development of industries such as munitions and shipbuilding.

Zenobia [zenohbia] (3rd-c) Queen of Palmyra (in modern Syria). Her husband became Governor of the East in AD 264. After his murder (c.267) she conquered Egypt (269), and overran much of E Asia Minor (270), but was defeated by Emperor Aurelian. >> Aurelian

Zeno of Citium [zeenoh, sishium] (c.336–c.265 BC) Philosopher, the founder of Stoicism, born in Citium, Cyprus. He went to Athens c.315 BC, where he opened his own school at the *Stoa poikile* ('painted colonnade'), from which the name of his philosophy derives.

Zeno of Elea [zeenoh, eelia] (c.490–c.420 BC) Greek philosopher and mathematician, a native of Elea, Italy. He became known for a series of paradoxes (such as 'Achilles and the Tortoise'), many of which denied the possibility of spatial division or motion.

Zephaniah [zefaniya] (7th-c BC) Old Testament prophet of the time of King Josiah of Judah. His account of a coming Day of Wrath inspired the mediaeval Latin hymn *Dies irae*.

Zeppelin, Ferdinand (Adolf August Heinrich), Graf von (Count of) (1838–1917) German army officer, born in Konstanz, Germany. In 1897–1900 he constructed his first airship, setting up a factory at Friedrichshafen.

Zermelo, Ernst Friedrich Ferdinand [tsairmeloh] (1871–1953) Mathematician, born in Berlin. He gave the first axiomatic description of set theory (1908), and also first revealed the importance of the axiom of choice, when he proved that any set could be well-ordered, a key result in many mathematical applications of set theory.

Zernike, Frits [zairnikuh] (1888–1966) Physicist, born in Amsterdam. He developed the phase-contrast microscope (1938), which allows the study of internal cell structure without the use of stains that kill the cell. He was awarded the Nobel Prize for Physics in 1953.

Zetkin, Clara, *née* **Eissner** (1857–1933) Communist leader, born in Wiederau, Germany. In 1917 she was one of the founders of the radical Independent Social Democratic Party (the Spartacus League), and became a founder of the German Communist Party (1919).

Zeuss, Johann Kaspar [tsoys] (1806–56) Philologist, born in Vogtendorf, Germany. The founder of Celtic philology, his *Grammatica celtica* (1853) is one of the great philological achievements of the century.

Zeuxis [zyooksis] (5th-c BC) Painter, born in Heraclea, Greece. He excelled in the representation of natural objects, such as bunches of grapes.

Zhang Guotao [jang gwohtow], also spelled **Chang Kuo-t'ao** (1897–1979) Founding member of the Chinese Communist Party, born in Jiangxi, China. He opposed the elevation of Mao Zedong, but his army was destroyed and he defected to the Nationalists in 1938. >> Mao Zedong

Zhang Heng [jang heng], also spelled **Chang Heng** (78–139) Chinese scientist. He invented the seismograph (132), calculated the value of π, understood the Earth was spherical, and worked out that the Moon revolved around the Earth.

Zhang Qian [jang chyan], also spelled **Chang Ch'ien** (2nd-c BC) Chinese military officer, sent westwards (138–125 BC) by Emperor Wudi to ally with Bactria to protect the Silk Road against the Huns. His report comprises the major source for contemporary C Asia. >> Wudi

Zhao Ziyang [jow zeeyang] (1918–) Chinese prime minster (1980–9), born in Henan, China. He oversaw a radical new 'market socialist' and 'open door' economic programme, and in 1987 became Communist Party general-secretary, but was dismissed for alleged liberalism towards student demonstrations.

Zheng He [zheng hay], also spelled **Cheng Ho** (1371–1433) Chinese admiral. He led seven major voyages (1405–33) to E Africa, Arabia, the Indian Ocean and SE Asia - the earliest extensive naval expeditions in world history.

Zhivkov, Todor [zhivkof] (1911–) Bulgarian prime minister (1962–71) and president (1971–89), born in Botevgrad, Bulgaria. His conservative policies led to mounting economic problems in the 1980s. He was ousted in 1989, found guilty of corruption and other charges, and sentenced to seven years imprisonment in 1992.

Zhou Enlai [joh enliy], also spelled **Chou En-lai** (1898–1975) One of the leaders of the Communist Party of China, and prime minister of the Chinese People's Republic from its inception in 1949 until his death. He vastly increased China's international influence, and during the Cultural Revolution worked to preserve national unity against the forces of anarchy.

Zhuangzi [jwangtsee], also spelled **Chuang-tzu** (369–286 BC) Chinese Taoist philosopher, and minor official in S China. His *Zhuangzi*, of which 33 chapters survive, first mentioned the concepts of Laozi, and elaborated ideas on the *Tao* ('Way'). >> Laozi

Zhu Da [joo dah], also spelled **Chu-ta**, originally **Pa Ta Shan Jen** (c.1625–1705) Painter, and Buddhist monk, born in Nan-ch'ang, China. The individualism of his ink paintings of flowers, birds, fish, and landscapes appealed to the Japanese, and his style has become synonymous with Zen painting in Japan.

Zhu De [joo de], also spelled **Chu-teh** (1886–1976) One of the founders of the Chinese Red Army, born in Sichuan, China. He joined with Mao Zedong to found the Jiangxi Soviet, and in 1934 led the Red Army in the Long March. >> Mao Zedong

Zhukov, Giorgiy Konstantinovich [zhookof] (1896–1974) Soviet marshal, born in Strelkovka, Russia. He became army chief-of-staff in 1941, lifted the siege of Moscow, and in 1944–5 captured Warsaw, conquered Berlin, and accepted the German surrender.

Zhu Xi [joo shee], also spelled **Chu-hsi** (1130–1200) Philosopher, classical commentator, scientific thinker, and historian, born in Yu-hsi, Fukien Province, China. His *Collected Works* systematized previous Confucian thought and established a creed for the perfection of state and society.

Zia ul-Haq, Muhammad [zeea ul hak] (1924–88) Pakistani general and president (1978–88), born near Jullundhur, Punjab, India. He led a bloodless coup in 1977, imposed martial law, and introduced an Islamic code of law. Despite international protest, he sanctioned the hanging of Bhutto in 1979. >> Bhutto, Zulfikar Ali

Ziaur Rahman [zeeaoor ramahn] (1935–81) Bangladeshi soldier and president (1977–81). Appointed chief of army staff after the assassination of Mujibur Rahman (1975), he became the dominant figure within the military, but was eventually assassinated in Dhaka. His wife, Khaleda Zia, became prime minister in 1991. >> Rahman, Mujibur

Ziegfeld, Florenz [zeegfeld] (1869–1932) Theatre manager, born in Chicago, IL. His *Follies of 1907* was the first of an annual series that continued until 1931, and made his name synonymous with extravagant theatrical production.

Ziegler, Karl [zeegler] (1898–1973) Chemist, born in Helsa, Germany. With Natta he was awarded the Nobel Prize for Chemistry in 1963 for his research into long-chain polymers leading to new developments in industrial materials, such as polypropylene. >> Natta

Zimbalist, Efrem (1889–1985) Violinist and composer, born in Rostov, Russia. He became director of the Curtis Institute of Music in Philadelphia (1941–68), and composed for both violin and orchestra.

Zimmerman, Robert >> **Dylan, Bob**

Zimmermann, Arthur [tsimerman] (1864–1940) Politician, born in Marggrabowa, Germany. As foreign secretary (1916–17), he sent the famous *Zimmermann telegram* (1917) to the German minister in Mexico with the terms of an alliance between Mexico and Germany. Intercepted and decoded, it brought the hesitant US government into the war against Germany.

Zinder, Norton (David) (1928–) Geneticist, born in New York City. He discovered bacterial transduction, which led to new knowledge of the location and behaviour of bacterial genes.

Zinnemann, Fred [zinuhman] (1907–) Film director, born in Vienna. A recurrent theme in his films is the conflict of conscience of reluctant heroes, as explored in *High Noon* (1952), *From Here to Eternity* (1953, Oscar), and *A Man For All Seasons* (1966, Oscar).

Zinoviev, Grigoriy Yevseyevich [zinovyef], originally **Grigoriy Yevseyevich Radomyslskiy** (1883–1936) Russian

Jewish revolutionary, born in Kherson province, Ukraine. He was executed following the first of Stalin's Great Purge trials in Moscow. The *Zinoviev letter*, urging British Communists to incite revolution in Britain, contributed to the downfall of the Labour government in 1924.

Zinsser, Hans (1878–1940) Bacteriologist and immunologist, born in New York City. He is best known for clarifying the rickettsial disease typhus, differentiating epidemic and endemic forms (the endemic form is still called *Brill–Zinsser's disease*).

Zinzendorf, Nicolaus Ludwig, Graf von (Count of) [**tsin**tsendaw(r)f] (1700–60) Religious leader, born in Dresden, Germany. He invited the persecuted Moravians to his estates, and there founded for them the colony of *Herrnhut* ('the Lord's keeping'). He later became Bishop of the Moravian Brethren.

Ziolkovsky, Konstantin Eduardovitch [zyol**kof**skee] (1857–1935) Engineer, born in Ijevsk, Russia. His outstanding work on the fundamental physics and engineering of space vehicles was recognized by the Soviet authorities, and all his works were translated into English by NASA in 1965.

Ziska, John [**zhish**ka] or **Žižka, Jan** (c.1370–1424) Bohemian Hussite leader, born in Trocznov, Czech Republic. He was chosen leader of the popular party, captured Prague (1421), and erected the fortress of Tabor, his party coming to be called Taborites. His successes compelled Emperor Sigismund to offer the Hussites religious liberty. >> Huss; Sigismund

Zoffany, John or **Johann** [**tsof**anee] (1734–1810) Portrait painter, born in Frankfurt (am Main), Germany. His speciality was the conversation piece.

Zog I [zohg], originally **Ahmed Bey Zogu** (1895–1961) Albanian prime minister (1922–4), president (1925–8), and king (1928–39), born in Burgajet, Albania. After Albania was overrun by the Italians (1939), he fled to Britain, and abdicated in 1946.

Zola, Emile [**zoh**la] (1840–1902) Novelist, born in Paris. After his major novel, *Thérèse Raquin* (1867), he began the long series called *Les Rougon-Macquart*, which contains such acclaimed studies as *Nana* (1880), *Germinal* (1885), and *The Beast in Man* (trans, 1890).

Zorach, William [**zaw**rakh] (1887–1966) Sculptor and painter, born in Eurburick-Kovno, Lithuania. Based in New York, he focused on sculpture (1922), carving directly in stone and wood, as in 'Floating Figure' (1922).

Zorn, Anders (Leonhard) (1860–1920) Etcher, sculptor, and painter, born in Mora, Sweden. He achieved European fame as an etcher, known for his series of nudes, and for his portraits.

Zoroaster [zoro**has**ter], Greek form of **Zarathustra** (6th-c BC) Iranian prophet and founder of the ancient Parsee religion which bears his name. He appears as a historical person only in the earliest portion of the Avesta.

Zorrilla y Moral, José [tho**ree**lya ee mo**ral**] (1817–93) Poet, born in Valladolid, Spain. He wrote many plays based on national legend, notably *Don Juan Tenorio* (1844), performed annually on All Saints' Day in Spanish-speaking countries.

Zsigmondy, Richard (Adolf) [**zhig**mondee] (1865–1929) Chemist, born in Vienna. A pioneer of colloid chemistry, in 1903 he introduced the ultramicroscope, and was awarded the Nobel Prize for Chemistry in 1925.

Zuccarelli, Francesco [tsuka**ray**lee] (1702–88) Painter, born in Pitigliano, Italy. His pastoral landscapes painted

in a soft Rococo style were very popular, especially in England.

Zuccari or **Zuccaro, Taddeo** [tsu**kah**ree] (1529–66) Painter, born in Vado, Italy. He executed several frescoes and easel pieces. His brother **Federigo Zuccari** (c.1543–1609) painted portraits and frescoes, and together they were leaders of the Roman late Mannerist school.

Zuckerman, Pinchas (1948–) Violinist, born in Tel Aviv, Israel. From 1967 he pursued a solo career, and later conducted the St Paul Chamber Orchestra (1980).

Zuckerman (of Burnham Thorpe), Solly Zuckerman, Baron (1904–93) Zoologist, born in Cape Town, South Africa. He carried out extensive research into primates, publishing such classic works as *The Social Life of Monkeys and Apes* (1932).

Zuckmayer, Carl [**tsuk**mayer] (1896–1977) Playwright, born in Nackenheim, Germany. His best-known plays are *The Captain of Köpenick* (trans, 1931) and *The Devil's General* (trans, 1946). He also wrote essays, novels, and film scripts.

Zukofsky, Louis [zu**kof**skee] (1904–78) Poet, born in New York City. A leading experimentalist after Pound, his works include *An Objectivist Anthology* (1932) and *All: the Collected Short Poems* (1965, 1967).

Zuloaga, Ignacio [thulo**hah**ga] (1870–1945) Painter, born in Eibar, Spain. A reviver of the national tradition in Spanish painting, he painted bullfighters, gipsies, beggars, and other themes of Spanish life.

Zurbarán, Francisco de [thoorba**ran**] (1598–1664) Religious painter, born in Fuente de Cantos, Spain. He spent most of his life at Seville, where his best-known work, an altarpiece, is to be found. His main subjects were monastic and historical, and he came to be called 'the Spanish Caravaggio'. >> Caravaggio

Zuse, Konrad [**tsoo**zuh] (1910–95) Computer pioneer, born in Berlin. He built a number of prototype calculating machines, the most historic of which was the Z3, the first operational general-purpose program-controlled calculator.

Zweig, Arnold [tsviyk] (1887–1968) Writer, born in Glogua, Germany. He is best known for his pacifist novel, *The Case of Sergeant Grischa* (trans, 1928).

Zweig, Stefan [tsviyk] (1881–1942) Writer, born in Vienna. He became known as a poet and translator, then as a biographer, short-story writer, and novelist, his major work being a set of historical portraits, *The Tide of Fortune* (trans, 1928).

Zwicky, Fritz [**zvik**ee] (1898–1974) Physicist, born in Varna, Bulgaria. He researched extensively into galaxies and interstellar matter, and produced the standard catalogue on compact galaxies. In 1934 he predicted the existence of neutron stars and black holes.

Zwingli, Huldrych or **Ulrich** [**tsving**glee], Lat **Ulricus Zuinglius** (1484–1531) Protestant reformer, born in Wildhaus, Switzerland. He espoused the Reformed doctrines, obtaining the support of the civil authorities, but in 1524 split with Luther over the question of the Eucharist. >> Luther

Zworykin, Vladimir (Kosma) [**tsvo**rikin] (1889–1982) Physicist, born in Murom, Russia. In 1923–4 he patented an all-electronic television system using a scanned camera-tube (the *iconoscope*), in 1929 demonstrated a cathode-ray display (the *kinescope*), and in later years contributed to the development of colour television and the electron microscope.

	DATE DUE		